Schroeder's
ANTIQUES
Price Guide

cb

COLLECTOR BOOKS
A Division of Schroeder Publishing Co., Inc.

Identification & Values of Over 50,000 Antiques & Collectibles

COLLECTOR BOOKS
P.O. Box 3009
Paducah, Kentucky 42002-3009

www.collectorbooks.com

The current values in this book should be used only as a guide. They are not
intended to set prices, which vary from one section of the country to another.
Auction prices as well as dealer prices vary greatly and are affected by condition
as well as demand. Neither the editors nor the publisher assumes responsibility
for any losses that might be incurred as a result of consulting this guide.

Searching for a Publisher?

We are always looking for people knowledgeable within their fields. If you
feel that there is a real need for a book on your collectible subject and
have a large comprehensive collection, contact Collector Books.

Proudly printed and bound in the
United States of America

Introduction

We have received many positive comments concerning the color photos in *Schroeder's*. We have continued with this smart look with this edition. Beth Summers has continued to express her great artistic talents by designing another beautiful cover. Of course the information inside is what we are most proud of.

As *Schroeder's* editors and staff, we continue to compile the most useful, comprehensive, and accurate background and pricing information possible. We continue to enlarge our advisory board, which over the years has doubled its original size, with more than 400 advisors currently taking part in the production of our book. We appreciate their assistance very much. It is their special expertise and experience in their specific fields that enables us to offer with confidence what we feel are useful, accurate evaluations that provide a sound understanding of the dealings in the marketplace today. Correspondence with so large an advisory panel adds months of extra work to an already monumental task, but we feel that to a very large extent this is the foundation that makes *Schroeder's* the success it has become today. Encompassing nearly 500 categories, many of which you will not find in other price guides, we carefully edit and revise categories each year to bring the latest information to publication. Our sources are greatly varied. We use auction results, dealer lists, and (of course) the Internet. We consult with national collectors' clubs, recognized authorities (including other Collector Book authors), researchers, and appraisers. We have by far the largest Advisory Board of any similar publication on the market. With the addition of new advisors each year, nearly all of our categories are covered by an expert who goes over our computer print-outs each year, checking each listing line by line, deleting those listings that are somewhat vague or misleading. Many of these advisors often send background information and photos. In sharing their knowledge with us, we are able to pass it on and share it with you. We appreciate their assistance very much. In this way we can offer with confidence what we believe to be useful and accurate evaluations that provide a sound understanding of the dealings in the marketplace today.

Our Directory, which you will find in the back of the book, lists each contributor by state or country. These are people who have allowed us to photograph various antiques and collectibles from their show or mall booths, sent us pricing information, or in some way have contributed to this year's book. If you happen to be traveling, consult the Directory for shops along your way. Don't forget that we also lists clubs who have worked with us as well as auction houses who have agreed to permit us to use the lovely colored photographs from their catalogs.

Our Advisory Board lists only names and partial addresses, so check the Directory for addresses and telephone numbers should you want to correspond with one of our experts. We list an international Advisory Board; so remember, when you do contact them, *always* enclose a self-addressed, stamped envelope (SASE) when inquiring within the United States. Thousands of people buy our guide, and hundreds contact our advisors. The only agreement we have with our advisors is that they edit their categories. They are in no way obligated to answer mail. Many of these people are very busy, spending much time on the road. Time at home is always precious, and they may not be open to contacts. There's no doubt that the reason behind the success of our book is their assistance. We regret seeing them becoming more and more burdened by phone and mail inquiries. We have lost some of our good advisors for this reason, and when we do, the book suffers and consequently, so do our readers. Many of our listed reference sources report that they constantly receive long distance calls (at all hours) that are really valuation requests. If they are registered appraisers, they make their living at providing such information and expect a fee for their service and expertise.

Since *Schroeder's* cannot provide all available information on antiques and collectibles, there are other sources available that you may want to pursue. The local library is always a good place to start. Check their section on reference books. I'm sure you will find many Collector Books books there. Museums are public facilities that are willing and able help you establish the origin and possibly even the value of your particular treasure. A more recent source of information includes the world of e-commerce, where many websites provide pertinent, up-to-date information. Another alternative is the yellow pages of your phone book. Other cities' phone books are available from either your library or from the telephone company office. The Antique Dealers heading in the yellow pages is a good place to start. Look for qualified appraisers (this may be mentioned in their advertisement). Always remember that a dealer buying your merchandise will set a price low enough that he will be able to make a reasonable profit when the item is sold. Once you decide to contact one of these appraisers, unless you intend to see them directly, you'll need to take photographs. Don't send photos that are under- or over-exposed, out of focus, or shot against a background that detracts from important details you want to emphasize. It is almost impossible for them to give you a value judgement on items they've not seen when your photos are of poor quality. Shoot the front, top, and the bottom; describe any marks and numbers (or send a pencil rubbing); explain how and when you acquired the article; and give accurate measurements and any further background information that may be helpful.

The section of the Directory titled Auction Houses includes auctions houses whose catalogs have been used for pricing information. Nearly all have appraisal experts on staff. If the item you're attempting to research is of the caliber of items they deal with, they can offer extremely accurate evaluations. Be sure to send them only professional-quality photographs and expect to pay a fee. Let the auction house know if you expect to consign your item. You will be under no obligation to do so, especially if you disagree with the value they suggest.

We have tried to used simple logic in the organization of this book. With nearly 500 categories included, topics are listed alphabetically, using either manufacturer or type of product. Sometimes listings may fall in several sections of the book. For example furniture may be listed under several major headings by specific manufacturers or types. Please consult the index. It is as complete as we know how to make it, with many cross-references. It will save you much time. We are constantly doing research on background information and have devoted more space to sharing it with our readers than any other publication of this type. The positive feedback from this tells us that we are on the right track. In order to provide this information, we have a single-line format, wherein we describe the items to the fullest extent possible by using several common-sense abbreviations; they will be easy to read and understand if you will first take the time to quickly scan through them.

The Editors

Editorial Staff

Senior Editor
Sharon Huxford

Editors
Loretta Suiters and Donna Newnum

Research and Editorial Staff
Kimberly Vincent

Layout
Terri Hunter, Heather Warren

Scanning
Donna Ballard

Cover Design
Beth Summers

On the Cover

Front: Armchair, American Rococo, rosewood, Rosalie pattern, mid-nineteenth century, 42½", $5,100.00; Comport, Flower Garden with Butterflies, U.S. Glass, 4¾" $85.00; Dog figurines, Mortens Studio, 3¼ to 4½", $60.00 to $65.00; Candy container, large angel, bisque head and rabbit fur robe, spun glass wings, rare, $4,125.00; Necklace, Navajo, squash blossom with naja, ca 1970s, $1,200.00; Vase, RumRill, #420, 9½" $75.00; Bit, Crockett & Renalde, $95.00; Cider pitcher, Pickard, Arabian pattern, 8", $1,600.00; Rug, hooked wool and cotton, ornate background, mounted on wood frame, 31½x62½", $4,410.00.

Back: Vase, Steuben Glass, Aurene with caramel and white vines at shoulder, 6½", $3,100.00.

Listing of Standard Abbreviations

The following is a list of abbreviations that have been used throughout this book in order to provide you with the most detailed descriptions possible in the limited space available. No periods are used after initials or abbreviations. When two dimensions are given, height is noted first. If only one dimension is listed, it will be height, except in the case of bowls, dishes, plates, or platters, when it will be diameter. The standard two-letter state abbreviations apply.

For glassware, if no color is noted, the glass is clear. Hyphenated colors, for example blue-green, olive-amber, etc., describe a single color tone; colors divided by a slash mark indicate two or more colors, i.e. blue/white. Biscuit jars, teapots, sugar bowls, and butter dishes are assumed to be 'with cover.' Condition is extremely important in determining market value. Common sense suggests that art pottery, china, and glassware values would be given for examples in pristine, mint condition, while suggested prices for utility wares such as Redware, Mocha, and Blue and White Stoneware, for example, reflect the probability that since such items were subjected to everyday use in the home they may show minor wear (which is acceptable) but no notable damage. Values for other categories reflect the best average condition in which the particular collectible is apt to be offered for sale without the dealer feeling it necessary to mention wear or damage. A basic rule of thumb is that an item listed as VG (very good) will bring 40% to 60% of its mint price — a first-hand, personal evaluation will enable you to make the final judgement; EX (excellent) is a condition midway between mint and very good, and values would correspond.

AD	after dinner	Fed	Federal	o/l	overlay
Am	American	fr	frame, framed	o/w	otherwise
appl	applied	Fr	French	Pat	patented
att	attributed to	ft, ftd	foot, feet, footed	pc	piece
bbl	barrel	G	good	ped	pedestal
bk	back	gr	green	pk	pink
bl	blue	grad	graduated	pnt	paint
blk	black	grpt	grain painted	porc	porcelain
brd	board	H	high, height	prof	professional
brn	brown	Hplwht	Hepplewhite	QA	Queen Anne
bulb	bulbous	hdl, hdld	handle, handled	re	regarding
bsk	bisque	HP	hand painted	rfn	refinished
b3m	blown 3-mold	illus	illustration, illustrated by	rnd	round
C	century	imp	impressed	rpl	replaced
c	copyright	ind	individual	rpr	repaired
ca	circa	int	interior	rpt	repainted
cb	cardboard	Invt T'print	Inverted Thumbprint	rstr	restored
Chpndl	Chippendale	irid	iridescent	rtcl	reticulated
CI	cast iron	jtd	jointed	rvpt	reverse painted
compo	composition	L	length, long	s&p	salt and pepper
cr/sug	creamer and sugar	lav	lavender	sgn	signed
c/s	cup and saucer	ldgl	leaded glass	SP	silverplated
cvd	carved	litho	lithograph	sq	square
cvg	carving	lt	light	std	standard
dbl	double	M	mint	str	straight
dc	die cut	mahog	mahogany	sz	size
decor	decoration	mc	multicolor	trn	turned, turning
demi	demitasse	MIB	mint in box	turq	turquoise
dk	dark	MIG	Made in Germany	uphl	upholstered
dmn	diamond	MIP	mint in package	VG	very good
Dmn Quilt	Diamond Quilted	mk	mark	Vict	Victorian
drw	drawer	MOC	mint on card	vnr	veneer
dtd	dated	MOP	mother-of-pearl	W	width
dvtl	dovetail	mt, mtd	mount, mounted	wht	white
emb	embossed, embossing	NE	New England	w/	with
embr	embroidered	NM	near mint	w/o	without
Emp	Empire	NRFB	never removed from box	X, Xd	cross, crossed
eng	engraved, engraving	NP	nickel plated	x	times (i.e. 4x)
EPNS	electroplated nickel silver	opal	opalescent	yel	yellow
EX	excellent	orig	original	(+)	has been reproduced

A B C Plates

Children's china featuring the alphabet as part of the design has been made since the late eighteenth century up to the present day. The earliest creamware items, plates, and mugs were often decorated with embossed or printed letters and prim, moralistic verses or illustrations and were made in Staffordshire, England. In later years they were made by American potters as well, and varied pictures of animals, events, famous people, and childhood activities became popular design themes. All were decorated by the transfer method, and many had colors brushed on for added interest.

Be sure to inspect these plates carefully for damage, since condition is a key price-assessing factor, and aside from obvious chips and hairlines, even wear can substantially reduce their values. Another problem for collectors is the fact that there are current reproductions of glass and tin plates, particularly the glass plate referred to as Emma (child's face in center) and a tin plate showing children with hoops. These plates are so common as to be worthless as collectibles. Our advisor for this category is Dr. Joan George; she is listed in the Directory under New Jersey.

Ceramic

A, Apple, Ape, Air, mc transfer, unmk, 7"............................ 185.00
Aesop's Fable, man & boy carrying donkey, bl transfer, unmk, 7" ...135.00
Birds of Paradise, mc transfer, Edge Malkin & Co, 6"................... 150.00
Boy w/instrument eats bread by fence, brn transfer, unmk, 7½" ... 120.00
Boys playing marbles, mc transfer, unmk, 5½" 165.00
Cats (3) pulling tablecloth, brn transfer, unmk, 7¼"................... 175.00
Child on chair w/puppet, blk transfer, unmk, 6" 125.00
Children w/rabbit, red transfer, unmk, 7½" 125.00
David & Goliath, blk transfer, HC Edmiston, 6" 145.00
Dog, The; mc transfer, unmk, 7¼".. 165.00
Dove, mc transfer at left, printed ABCs right, RD No 154, 6½" .. 145.00
Federal Generals, mc transfer, unmk, 7"..................................... 350.00
Flowers That Never Fade, Cheerfulness, blk transfer, Meakin, 5¾" ...235.00
Franklin's Proverbs, Employ Time Well..., mc transfer, unmk, 7½" 165.00
Franklin's Proverbs, Plough Deep..., blk transfer, unmk, Germany, 7" .. 110.00
Girls (2) w/flowers, mc transfer, unmk, 7"................................... 140.00
Guardian, dog & sleeping boy, mc transfer, Elsmore & Foster, 7"....185.00
Hunter's (2) w/dogs (2), brn transfer, CA & Sons, 6½"................ 125.00
Kittens (3) taking bath, mc transfer, unmk, 8" 165.00
Lovers in interior scene, mc transfer, emb rim, unmk, 5¾" 140.00
Man w/Alpine horn & dog, monochrome, unmk, 6".................... 140.00
Nursery Tales, Whittington & His Cat, RD No 75,500, 8" 275.00
Oriental Hotel, red transfer, unmk, 5½"..................................... 135.00
Queen Victoria, coronation portrait, from $800 to...............1,200.00
Spelling Bee, children in scene, mc transfer, unmk, 5¾" 175.00
Tiger, mc transfer in sq, BP Co, 6½".. 275.00
Timely Rescue, tiger scene, blk transfer, CA & Sons, 6½ " 135.00
Tulip & the Butterfly..., mc transfer, Meakin, 6" 165.00
Walk, The; figure on horse, mc transfer, unmk, 7"....................... 145.00

Glass

ABCs, numerals, clock face, unmk, 7", from $50 to 60.00
Christmas Eve, unmk, 6".. 150.00
Ducks, deep yel, unmk, 6", from $60 to.. 70.00
Emma (child's face), vaseline, bl or orange, unmk, 8" (+)............. 30.00
Fan center, scalloped rim, unmk, 6", from $65 to 75.00
President Garfield, smooth rim, 6"... 150.00
Rooster, smooth rim, unmk, 6", from $65 to 75.00
Sancho Panza & Dapple center, unmk, 6", from $50 to 60.00

Tin

Victoria and Albert, 4¼", $175.00. (Photo courtesy Irene and Ralph Lindsay)

ABCs emb in center sq, unmk, 8", from $80 to 100.00
General Tom Thumb, full-length portrait, mc enamel, unmk, 3", up to..300.00
Girl & boy w/hoop, unmk, 3" (+) 125.00
Her Majesty Queen Victoria, emb rim, unmk, 8", from $300 to... 400.00
Hi Diddle Diddle..., unmk, 8¾", from $80 to 100.00
Liberty, emb rim, unmk, 5½", from $110 to 150.00
Mary Had a Little Lamb, unmk, 7¾", from $130 to 160.00
Simple Simon, Tudor Plate Oneida Community, 6", from $65 to .. 95.00
Who Killed Cock Robin?, unmk, 7¾" 115.00

Abingdon

From 1934 until 1950, the Abingdon Pottery Co. of Abingdon, Illinois, made a line of art pottery with a white vitrified body decorated with various types of glazes in many lovely colors. Novelties, cookie jars, utility ware, and lamps were made in addition to several lines of simple yet striking art ware. Fern Leaf, introduced in 1937, featured molded vertical feathering. La Fleur, in 1939, consisted of flowerpots and flower-arranger bowls with rows of vertical ribbing. Classic, 1939 – 1940, was a line of vases, many with evidence of Chinese influence. Several marks were used, most of which employed the company name. In 1950 the company reverted to the manufacture of sanitary ware that had been their mainstay before the art ware division was formed.

Highly decorated examples and those with black, bronze, or red glaze usually command at least 25% higher prices.

For further information we recommend *Abingdon Pottery Artware 1934 – 1950, Stepchild of the Great Depression*, by Joe Paradis (Schiffer).

#102, vase, Beta, 10"... 32.00
#116, vase, Classic, 10".. 32.50
#125, bowl, Classic, 6½x11"... 45.00
#151, flowerpot, La Fleur, 5".. 15.00
#155, bowl, La Fleur, 10".. 10.00
#166, vase, Floral, 10".. 60.00
#170, vase, Classic, 7".. 27.50
#200, pitcher, ice lip, 2-qt.. 100.00
#256, lamp base, sq std, 22½".. 90.00
#306, bookends, Sea Gull, 6".. 135.00
#311, bowl, flower; 6½"... 30.00
#316, ashtray, Trojan, 3½x5" 50.00
#321, bookends, Russian, 6½"... 285.00
#327, vase, Modern #2, 6"... 60.00
#338, bowl, sq, w/lid, 4¾".. 55.00
#348, box, cigarette; Trix, 3¾x4¾"... 40.00
#359, flowerpot, Mart, 3½"... 15.00
#366, flowerpot, Egg & Dart, 5¼"... 15.00
#376F, wall mask, Female, 7½"... 175.00
#380, vase, Rhythm, 7¾" 40.00

#387, plate, salad; Daisy, 7½"..15.00
#395, ashtray, 3x8"..45.99
#401, tea tile, Coolie, 5x5"..75.00
#407, bowl, Rose, 6"..50.00
#416, figurine, Peacock, 7".......................................45.00
#425, bowl, Fern Leaf, 10½".....................................95.00
#444D, bookend, Dolphin, 5¾", ea...........................55.00
#454, bowl, Asters, 6½"..55.00
#467, vase, Wreath, 8"..65.00
#496D, vase, Hollyhock, 7"......................................40.00
#510, ashtray, Donkey, 5½".....................................135.00
#521, vase, Bali, 9"...80.00
#527, bowl, Hibiscus, 10"...28.00
#533, bowl, Shell, 12" L...20.00
#539, urn, Regency, 7"..20.00
#551, ashtray, 8-sided, 7"...20.00
#566, vase, scalloped, 9"...20.00
#572, figurine, Pelican, 5"...35.00
#577, vase, pillow form, 7"...16.00
#601D, wall pocket, Butterfly, 8½"...........................95.00
#604D, vase, Tulip, 6"...60.00
#613, vase, floor; Grecian Pitcher, 15"....................135.00
#644, bowl, Ripple, 6"...20.00
#656, planter, sq, 3½"..10.00
#666D, jam set, 4-pc...75.00
#676D, wall vase, book form, 6½"..............................85.00
#792, bowl, oval, low, 10½" L...................................12.50
Cookie jar, #471, Old Lady, decor, minimum value.....250.00
Cookie jar, #495, Fat Boy..250.00

Cookie jar, #561, Little Ol' Lady (Black face), from $300.00 to $375.00. (Photo courtesy Ermagene Westfall)

Cookie jar, #588, Hippo, decor, 1942......................250.00
Cookie jar, #588, Money Bag......................................65.00
Cookie jar, #602, Hobby Horse..................................185.00
Cookie jar, #611, Jack-in-the-Box.............................275.00
Cookie jar, #622, Miss Muffet....................................205.00
Cookie jar, #651, Choo Choo (Locomotive)..............145.00
Cookie jar, #653, Clock, 1949.....................................90.00
Cookie jar, #663, Humpty Dumpty, decor..................200.00
Cookie jar, #665, Wigwam...200.00
Cookie jar, #674, Pumpkin, 1949, minimum value......300.00
Cookie jar, #677, Daisy, 1949......................................45.00
Cookie jar, #678, Windmill, from $200 to.................225.00
Cookie jar, #693, Little Girl, from $60 to..................75.00
Cookie jar, #694, Bo Peep..235.00
Cookie jar, #695, Mother Goose.................................295.00
Cookie jar, #696, Three Bears, from $90 to...............100.00

Adams, Matthew

In the 1950s a trading post in Alaska contacted Sascha Brastoff to design a line of porcelain with scenes of Eskimos, Alaskan motifs, and animals indigenous to that area. These items were to be sold in Alaska to the tourist trade.

Brastoff selected Matthew Adams, born in April 1915, to design the Alaska series. Pieces from the line he produced have the Sascha B mark on the front; some have a pattern number on the reverse. They did not have the rooster backstamp. (See the Sascha Brastoff category for information on this mark.)

After the Alaska series was introduced and proved to be successful, Matthew Adams left the employment of Sascha Brastoff (working three years there in all) and opened his own studio. Pieces made in his studio are signed Matthew Adams in script and may have the word Alaska on the front. Mr. Adams's studio is now located in Los Angeles, but at this time, due to his age, he has ceased production.

Our advisor for this category is Marty Webster; his is listed in the Directory under Michigan. He welcomes new information on this subject.

Ashtray, Eskimo face, hollow star shape, 13".................45.00
Ashtray, Eskimo family, 8½".....................................20.00
Ashtray, hooded; Walrus on blk, 5½".......................65.00
Ashtray, Walrus on gr, boomerang shape, 6x11"........65.00
Bowl, console; Glacier on bl, 12x20"........................165.00
Bowl, Grizzly Bear on brn, free-form, 6½"................45.00
Bowl, Igloo & Dog, boat shape, #138, 9½"................50.00
Bowl, Ram on gr, free-form, 7"..................................45.00
Bowl, Seal, oval, 9"..50.00
Bowl, Walrus, yel, w/lid, 7".......................................75.00
Bowl, Walrus on blk, free-form, #104, 6½" L............50.00
Box, Seal, wht, 2¼x6"..50.00
Charger, Eskimo w/Harpoon, 16".............................135.00
Cigarette lighter, Cabin on Stilts, 5x5".....................50.00
Coffeepot, Ram on gr, 11½", +6 4½" mugs................180.00
Cookie jar, Cabin, elliptical shape, #023, 7x5"..........100.00
Creamer, Polar Bear on blk, 4¾"...............................30.00
Creamer & sugar bowl, Eskimo Child, #144 & #144a....65.00
Dish, Eskimo Child, #099, 2¼x7½" dia....................45.00
Dish, Log Cabin, w/lid, #145, 4x7½x5"....................20.00
Ginger jar, Seal on brn/wht, #095, 6½".....................55.00
Jar, Eskimo Lady on brn, w/lid, 7½"..........................50.00
Jar, Polar Bear on gr, w/lid, 7½"................................65.00
Lamp, Eskimo w/Sled, 22"...100.00
Pitcher, Eskimo, 13"...90.00
Pitcher, Grizzly Bear, 11", +6 4" tumblers................200.00
Plate, Eskimo Girl, #162, 7½"...................................50.00
Plate, Seal on Ice, 12"..60.00
Platter, Polar Bears (2) on ice, 12x10"......................75.00
Shakers, Eskimo Child on gray, pr.............................30.00
Tankard, Eskimo Man on brn, 19", +6 mugs.............250.00
Teapot, Walrus on ice bl, 6½"....................................75.00
Tile, Mountains & Glacier on blk, 10x8½"................75.00
Tile, Walrus on bl, 10x8½"...75.00
Tumbler, Cabin..20.00
Vase, Glacier on gray, #143, 5½"...............................50.00
Vase, Iceberg on gray, 7"..50.00
Vase, Polar Bear on gr, 10"...100.00
Vase, Sea Lion & Seaweed, oval, #128, 8"..................95.00
Vase, Seal & Glacier on brn, free-form, #911, 11"......105.00

Advertising

The advertising world has always been a fiercely competitive field. In an effort to present their product to the customer, every imaginable gimmick was put into play. Colorful and artfully decorated signs and posters, thermometers, tape measures, fans, hand mirrors, and attractive tin containers (all with catchy slogans, familiar logos, and often-bogus claims) are only a few of the many examples of early advertising memorabilia that are of interest to today's collectors.

Porcelain signs were made as early as 1890 and are highly prized for their artistic portrayal of life as it was then . . . often allowing amusing insights into the tastes, humor, and way of life of a bygone era. As a general rule, older signs are made from a heavier gauge metal. Those with three or more fired-on colors are especially desirable.

Tin containers were used to package consumer goods ranging from crackers and coffee to tobacco and talcum. After 1880 can companies began to decorate their containers by the method of lithography. Though colors were still subdued, intricate designs were used to attract the eye of the consumer. False labeling and unfounded claims were curtailed by the Pure Food and Drug Administration in 1906, and the name of the manufacturer as well as the brand name of the product had to be printed on the label. By 1910 color was rampant with more than a dozen hues printed on the tin or on paper labels. The tins themselves were often designed with a second use in mind, such as canisters, lunch boxes, even toy trains. As a general rule, tobacco-related tins are the most desirable, though personal preference may direct the interest of the collector to peanut butter pails with illustrations of children or talcum tins with irresistible babies or beautiful ladies. Coffee tins are popular, as are those made to contain a particularly successful or well-known product.

Perhaps the most visual of the early advertising gimmicks were the character logos, the Fairbank Company's Gold Dust Twins, the goose trademark of the Red Goose Shoe Company, Nabisco's ZuZu Clown and Uneeda Kid, the Campbell Kids, the RCA dog Nipper, and Mr. Peanut, to name only a few. Many early examples of these bring high prices on the market today.

Our listings are alphabetized by product name or, in lieu of that information, by word content or other pertinent description. Items are evaluated according to condition as stated in each line description. Remember that condition greatly affects value (especially true for tin items). For instance, a sign in excellent or mint condition may bring twice as much as the same one in only very good condition, sometimes even more. On today's market, items in good to very good condition are slow to sell, unless they are extremely rare. Mint (or near-mint) examples are high.

We have several advertising advisors; see specific subheadings. For further information we recommend *Hake's Price Guide to Character Toys, 3rd Edition,* by Ted Hake; and *Antique & Contemporary Advertising Memorabilia, Collectible Soda Pop Memorabilia,* and *Value Guide to Gas Station Memorabilia,* all by B.J. Summers. *Garage Sale and Flea Market Annual* is another good reference. All of these books are available at your local bookstore or from Collector Books. See also Advertising Dolls; Advertising Cards; Automobilia; Coca-Cola; Banks; Calendars; Cookbooks; Paperweights; Posters; Sewing Items; Thermometers.

Key:
cb — cardboard	ps — porcelain sign
cl — celluloid	sf — self-framed
dc — die-cut	tc — tin container
fs — flange sign	tm — trademark
gs — glass sign	ts — tin sign

Ace High Thyme, tc, biplane over water, gold lid, 3", EX+ 550.00
Alka-Seltzer, pharmacy dispenser, cylindrical, ped, bl/wht, 15", EX...500.00
Allen's Root Beer Extract, paper sign, girl/3 cherubs, fr, 22x15", NM... 2,900.00
American Biscuit Co, stereo viewer, tin litho, w/cards, EXIB 450.00
American Blend, pocket tc, vertical, 4½", EX 725.00
American Harrow/Manure Spreader, match holder, tin litho, 5x3", EX+.675.00
American Mills Blend Coffee, tc, rnd w/sm rnd lid, red, 1-lb, VG+...550.00
Andes Stoves & Ranges, ts, curved, wht/gold on dk bl, 20x20", VG+ ...475.00
Apache Trail, cigar tin, 5¢, Indian scout on horse, bl, 6x6x4", EX+ 1,540.00

Arbuckle's Ariosa Coffee, paper sign, promoting US states cards, 28", EX...1,550.00
Artie the Best Cigar, ts, sf standup, graphics on red, 10x6½", EX+...1,250.00
Ath-Lo-Pho-Ros Searles Remedy..., trifold display, cb, 19x23", EX+..550.00
August Flower/German Syrup, match holder, dc cb, Blk man on wall, EX+...1,250.00
Aunt Jemima, trolley sign, cb, Perfect Pancakes Everytime!, 12x22", EX...275.00
Aunt Jemima Pancake Flour, dc cb display/game, AJ's head, 4", EX ..475.00
Aunt Jemima's Sugar Butter, pail, bail hdl, red, 1 ½-lb, EX+........750.00
Ayer's Cathartic Pills, sign, dc cb, Blk Dr w/2 kids, 1880s, 13", EX+...600.00
Babbit's Cleanser, pot scraper, tin litho, 5¢ can, 3x3½", EX 160.00
Babe Ruth Underwear, baseball bat, wood, mini, 13⅞", EX 150.00
Bagdad Smoking Tobacco, tc, man in fez, 3½x3¾x1", VG+ 50.00
Baker's Chocolate, display urn, tin litho, chocolate girl, 24", EX+ ...4,100.00
Baker's Chocolate, ts, sf, cb bk, chocolate girl in oval, 9x6", EX.......1,150.00
Bar Keeper's Friend, cl pocket mirror, draped nude, 2" dia, EX ... 950.00
Bartholomy Beers/Ales/Porter, tip tray, girl on winged wheel, 4", EX ...275.00
Bauer Wild West Whiskey, sign, cb, 3 gambling on blanket, 21x28", EX.. 1,450.00
Bayle Peanut Butter, pail, tin litho scouting scenes, 2¼x2¾", EX .. 90.00
Beaver Coal, statuette, beaver, bronze-pnt compo, 5x3¼", EX.......50.00
Bee Hive Overalls, pocket mirror, girl in overalls, oval, 3", EX....200.00

Beech-Nut Chewing Tobacco, slant-front store bin, 5½x10x8", NM, $400.00. (Photo courtesy Buffalo Bay Auction)

Beef Peptoids, tc, rnd w/slip lid, factory on gr, 4", EX+ 120.00
Best Pal, candy box, cb, child & dog, 1930s, 2¾x9½x8⅝", EX....... 50.00
Betsy Ross 5¢ Cigar, ts, sf oval portrait on woodgrain, 25x20", M .. 4,900.00
Beverwyck Lager, tray, The Invitation, lady w/glass, 13" dia, EX.....350.00
Bevo The Beverage 10¢, ts, cb bk, bottle/mascot, beveled, 6x9", EX+ ...300.00
Bill Dugan Cigars, cb sign, man's portrait, 24¼x20¼" in fr, EX.... 160.00
Birely's Tomato Cocktail, rvpt sign in metal fr, easel bk, 10x7", EX..80.00
Black Cat Enamel Stove Polish, paper sign, metal strips, 16x11", EX+..625.00
Blackwell's Durham Smoking Tobacco, board game, complete, EX+ ...625.00
Blanke's World's Fair Coffee, tc, red w/gold litho, 1-lb, 12", VG+ ..625.00
Blue Bird Marshmallows, tc, birds, pry lid, 4½x4⅜", EX...............160.00
Bond Bread, ps, ...The Home-Like Loaf, blk on yel, 14x19", EX+ ..150.00
Borden's (Malted Milk), tip tray, girl in center, 4½" dia, EX 400.00
Borden's Ice Cream, ts, Elsie in daisy on bl, 24x44", NM 210.00
Borden's Malted Milk, tip tray, tin litho, serving maid, 4½", EX.. 140.00
Brater's Asthma Powder, tc, man's portrait, Am Can Co, 1⅝x3x2", EX... 50.00
Brewer's Union No 5, tip tray, 15th Anniversary, 4" dia, NM+ ...675.00
Bromo Seltzer, dispenser, cobalt bl glass, w/ad header, 24", EX 400.00
Brotherhood Tobacco, cb sign, train engine/men, fr, 30x21", EX.. 925.00
Buckeye Fences, pocket mirror, cl, 4-season girls, 2" dia, EX...............475.00
Budweiser, paper sign, Budweiser girl in long red dress, fr, 38", EX+.... 1,200.00
Bull Durham, sign, dc cb hanger w/2 Blk kids in a swing, 11x9", EX+....1,550.00
Bunny Bread, ps, dc bunny's head, bl/yel/wht, 3-D, 1968, 37x26", EX ...395.00
Burma-Shave, ts, In This World of Toil & Sin..., wht on red, 2x6", EX+..875.00

Buster Brown

Buster Brown was the creation of cartoonist Richard Felton Outcault; his comic strip first appeared in the *New York Herald* on May 4, 1902. Since then Buster and his dog Tige (short for Tiger) have adorned sundry commercial products but are probably best known as the trademark for the Brown Shoe Company established early in this century. Today hundreds of Buster Brown premiums, store articles, and advertising items bring substantial prices from many serious collectors.

Balloon blower, molded fiberglass head, 1960s, EX.......................300.00
Bank, molded plastic, BB & Tige busts atop ball, 1960s, 4" dia, EX..35.00
Cigar box, BB Cigars, wood w/paper labels, 9x9x3", EX...............375.00
Clicker, tin, head image of BB & Tige, VG 20.00
Comic book, Happy Days, Cupples & Leon, 1910s, 19" W, EX ...235.00
Match holder, tin, BB Bread, mc graphics, 7", EX+..................1,800.00
Pennant, BB Guaranteed Hosiery, BB & Tige on red, 29", EX.....200.00
Pin-back button, cl, BB Bread, Long Co, 1½" dia, EX...................40.00
Pocket mirror, cl, BB & Tige, JB Carroll, 2¼" dia, EX+...............150.00
Pocket mirror, cl, BB & Tige, 1¾" dia, EX 110.00
Pocket mirror, cl, BB Shoes, BB & Tige, Bastian Bros, 1¼", EX+ ...250.00
Rug, BB & Tige, used in shoe stores, 54" dia, EX...........................315.00
Sign, BB Apples, cb hanger, Buster/Tige, fr, 14x14", VG+........2,100.00
Sign, emb CI, BB Shoes for Boys & Girls, BB & Tige, 18" dia, EX...11,200.00
Sign, neon, BB Shoes, BB & Tige, 55x54", EX..........................1,400.00
Sign, plastic & metal light-up, BB & Tige, 6x15", VG................200.00
Spice box, cb, BB & Tige in reserve on red, 5⅜x3⅛" dia, EX.......220.00
Trade card, Memphis Bread, BB & Tige on train track, 3½x5½", EX..300.00

Calumet Baking Powder, ts, curved/emb, 25¢ a Pound, yel, 23x17", EX+...2,100.00
Campbell's Soups, pocket mirror, cl, 10¢ can, 2¾x1¼", EX..........130.00
Canada Dry Spur, flanged ts, 2-sided, 4-color, 1940s, 14x15", EX ...215.00
Capital Coffee, store bin, red-stained wood w/blk stenciling, 33", VG+..650.00
Carborundum Pocket Hone, display, tin standup, slots for hones, EX+ ..1,250.00
Carey's GESS Liniment for Horses, ts, emb, blk on yel, 6½x14", VG.....825.00
Carter's Overalls, ps, tm train, wht/red on bl, 6x15", NM 2,900.00
Castle Hall Twins Cigars, cb sign, stork w/twins, 10x12", NM.......40.00
Cat's Paw Cushion Rubber Heels, paper sign, blk cat/man, 42x30", EX ..900.00
CD Kenny, tip tray, America's Pride, red/wht/bl rim, 4" dia, EX ..300.00
Check Cigars, tc, rnd w/slip lid, Good As Gold, 50¢, 5", EX+.....300.00
Cheon Tea, tip tray, For Iced Tea Use.../geisha girl, 4½" dia, NM ...140.00
Cherry Blush, ts, cb bk, beveled, graphics on blk, 6x9", EX 750.00
Chesterfield Cigarettes, paper sign, 1927 New Year, 10x21", EX...250.00
Chocolate Cigarettes, cb sign, Victorian children, 8¾x8½", EX ..250.00
Chocolate Cigars, cb sign, boy w/cigar, dmn shape, 6¼x6¼", EX ..1,450.00
Chocolate-Crush, ts, emb, Drink..., wht/blk on yel, 1920s, 14x20", EX+..175.00
Cleanzum Antiseptic Hand Cleaner, sample tin, Oilzum kid, 1½" dia...725.00
Coats & Co Gin, ashtray, porc, 5¼" dia, EX 180.00
Colgate Cashmere Bouquet, dc cb sign, easel-bk, toiletries, 7x10", NM...180.00
Columbia Brewing, tip tray, lady/eagle, 4¼", EX............................625.00
Columbian Extra Pale Bottle Beer, ts, emb, bottle on lt gr, 18x14", EX..220.00
Columbus Buggy Co, paper sign, ostrich-drawn buggy, fr, 24x36", VG+..2,590.00
Comfort Talc, tc, children on front, nurse on bk, 4¼x1⅜x1", EX ...130.00
Continental Brewing Co, ts, soldier, ornate gold fr, 28x20", VG+ ..675.00
Continental Cubes Tobacco, cl pocket mirror, Whitehead & Hoag, 3", EX...175.00
Coronoa Athlete Pineapple Chewing Gum, pocket tc, flat, 1x3¼", EX+....70.00
Court House Typewriter Ribbon, tc, bl on wht, 2⅛" dia, EX........500.00
Covered Wagon Syrup, tc, wagon shape, 5-lb, very scarce, EX+ ...1,050.00
Cream of Wheat, paper sign, tm chef & boy w/hot bowl, fr, 41x30", EX+...825.00
Crescent Club Tobacco, tc, Turkish girls, hinged lid, 3x4½x2", EX ...120.00
Cresco Biscuits, sign, dc cb, 2 Blk kids w/gun & dog at fence, 10", EX ...325.00
Cuban Seal 5¢ Cigar, gambling change receiver, glass/tin, 7" dia, NM...950.00
Cutter, Waitt & Bond Little Lord Fauntleroy, metal/wood base, rnd, VG...700.00
Dan Patch, match safe, U-shaped, Compliments of...on bk, 2", VG+...525.00
Dandro Solvent, tin on cb sign, hand w/bottle, 9x13", EX.............80.00
DB Cough Drops, sign, emb dc cb, girl leaning on sign, 9x7", EX+ ...150.00
Deer Run Whiskey, ts, sf, stag graphic, Shonk litho, 12" dia, EX+ ...500.00
DeLaval Cream Separators, broom holder, tin litho, 3½", VG.....120.00
DeLaval Cream Separators, match holder, dc tin, 6¼x4x1", EX+...210.00

DeLaval Cream Separators, tip tray, lady w/separator, 4¼", EX+.....110.00
Dentyne Gum, display, dc tin litho, tm girl at top, 7", EX+ 300.00

Diamond Dyes, cabinet, tin litho, rare blue background, 30", EX+, $3,100.00. (Photo courtesy Bertoia Auctions)

Diamond Dyes, tin cabinet insert, fairies/vignettes, 10¢, 24x18", VG ..460.00
Diamond Match Co, match safe, tin litho, fisherman in rain, 2", EX+ ..200.00
Domino Sugar, cb sign, early product packs, ca 1910, 14x10½", EX ..150.00
Dr Caldwell's Syrup Pepsin, door push, porc, mc on yel, 6½x4", EX..230.00
Dr Caldwell's Syrup Pepsin, door push, porc, yel/blk, 6x4", EX+ .. 425.00
Dr Caldwell Syrup Pepsin, sign, dc cb standup, Dr figure, 14x6", M ..450.00
Dr Daniels' Veterinary Medicines, cabinet, wood w/tin insert, 29", EX ..3,920.00
Dr Daniels' Veterinary Remedies, paper sign, Snowbound, fr, 15x20", EX...575.00
Dr Haile's Ole Injun System Tonic, paper sign, yel/wht/bl, 14x20", EX..130.00
Dr Hobbs Kidney Pills, tc, gr asparagus designs on lid, ½x3x2", EX . 110.00

Dr. Pepper

A young pharmacist, Charles C. Alderton, was hired by W.B. Morrison, owner of Morrison's Old Corner Drug Store in Waco, Texas, around 1884. Alderton, an observant sort, noticed that the drugstore's patrons could never quite make up their minds as to which flavor of extract to order. He concocted a formula that combined many flavors, and Dr. Pepper was born. The name was chosen by Morrison in honor of a beautiful young girl with whom he had once been in love. The girl's father, a Virginia doctor by the name of Pepper, had discouraged the relationship due to their youth, but Morrison had never forgotten her. On December 1, 1885, a U.S. patent was issued to the creators of Dr. Pepper. See also Soda Fountain Collectibles.

Ashtray, clear glass w/chevron logo in center, EX.......................... 35.00
Bottle, plastic blow-up, Dr Pepper in script, 27", EX 25.00
Bottle carrier, cb, 6-pack, 16-oz bottles, 1950s, EX....................... 15.00
Clock, compo w/glass front, electric, Telechron, 14" dia, EX.......275.00
Clock, octagonal Deco style, red 10/2/4 clock #s, 16x23", VG...1,350.00
Fan, cb w/wooden hdl, Earl Morgan art of pretty girl, EX.............. 75.00
Menu board, tin chalkboard, bottle/clock/grid logo on yel, 23x17", VG..200.00
Pencil/opener, cl bullet form, logo on hdl, 1930s-40s, 4½", G........ 75.00
Sign, cb, Join Me!, girl in car, 1940s, 32x40", NM 500.00
Sign, cl on tin standup, Thank You Call Again, 8x11", VG 425.00
Sign, flange; tin, dc 10-2-4 bottle on light burst/red sign, EX.......725.00
Sign, flange; tin, 2-sided, bottle cap, 1959, 18x22", EX.............1,000.00
Sign, porc, Drink...Good for Life, red/wht/gr, 11x27", G.............. 125.00
Sign, porc, sf, Drink..., red & wht, 9x24", G.................................. 65.00
Sign, porc, triangular, wht letters on red, 18x23", EX................... 875.00
Thermometer, dial, aluminum w/glass front, Hot or Cold, 12" dia, VG....110.00
Thermometer, metal, 10-2-4 on lg bottle, 26", G 130.00
Thermometer, tin, Frosty Cold beside scale, 24x10", G............... 100.00
Thermometer, tin, Hot or Cold, red & wht, 26x7", NM.............. 150.00

Dr Pierce's Family Medicines, display, dc cb trifold, 27x32", EX+...575.00
Drummer Coffee, tc, rnd, slip lid, yel/wht, 1-lb, EX+ 375.00

DTF Cigars, Currier/Ives Prints, Darktown Rescue/Saved, 1890s, EX, pr.. 300.00
Dukes Cameo Cigarettes, chair, wood foldup w/tin insert, VG+.. 400.00
Dunwoody's Facial Soap Powder, container, cylindrical, cb/tin, 5", EX+ . 400.00
Durham Cigars, clock, bull figural w/clock in side, 1885, 10x13x3", EX... 1,400.00
Dutch Boy Red Seal White Lead, sign, dc cb hanger, boy in swing, 26". 4,300.00
E Bement/Sons Steel King Spring Tooth Harrows, paper sign, fr, 27", EX ... 500.00
E Robinson's Sons Pilsener Bottled Beer, tray, boating, 12" dia, EX ... 615.00
Eatsum Peanut Butter, pail, tin litho of child & dog, VG.............. 40.00
Economy Whiskey, gs, rvpt, wood fr, 32x44", EX 4,200.00
Edgworth Tobacco, tc, bl woven-look bkground, 4½x3x⅞", EX...... 210.00
Edison Mazda Lamps, sign, dc cb standup, girl w/bulb atop box, 28", M .. 525.00
Edison Phonograph, paper sign, Sent to Bed Too Early, fr, 37x28", EX+.. 11,600.00
Efficiency Gas Oil, can, yel label, hdl & spout, ½-gal, EX+.......... 900.00
Eisenlohr's Cinco Cigars, ps, red/yel/blk, 12x36", EX 120.00
Elfenbrau Beer, cb sign, elves/fairies partying, 13x21", EX 625.00
Empire Axle Grease, pail, bail hdl, wht on bl, 1-lb, VG+ 300.00
Empire Cream Separator, cl pocket mirror, girl in bonnet, 2¾" L, EX .. 220.00
Empire Mills Coffee, tc, St Nick/reindeer/etc, Ginna Litho, 8¾", EX... 675.00
Esquire Boot Polish, display box, holds 12 29¢ tins, 6½x9x3", EX . 40.00
Ever-Ready Safety Razors, clock sign, emb tin litho, 18x12", EX+..... 775.00
Eye-Fix, tip tray, cherub doctoring woman's eye, HD Beach, 4" dia, EX+ . 500.00
Faultless Wonder Nipples, store jar, lg baby bottle w/nipple, NM .. 7,400.00
FE Dawley Dairy, cheese container, ceramic, 4x3⅝", EX.............. 140.00
Fehr's Malt Tonic, sf ts, topless lady w/product/cherubs, 19x23", VG.. 900.00
Forest & Stream Tobacco, pocket tc, vertical, red w/gold lid, 4", EX+.. 450.00
Foss & Deering Co's Pure Mustard, pail, bail hdl, ¼-lb, EX+ 575.00
Franco-American Soups, paper sign, chef, early 1900s, fr, 35x22", EX+ . 1,850.00
Friends' Oats, bowl, china, girl holding box, 1¼x5⅜", EX............ 230.00
Frog in Your Throat Cough Drops, display, dc cb, frog/banjo on box, EX.. 4,100.00
Frog in Your Throat for Coughs & Colds, sign, dc cb, 2 girls, fr, EX+ ... 425.00
Full Dress Pipe & Cigarette Tobacco, pocket tc, vertical, 4", EX+ ... 575.00
FW Cough Drops, store tc, sq w/sm rnd top, yel, 8x5x5", NM+.. 2,300.00
Gail & Ax Navy Tobacco, paper sign, tm sailor on yel, fr, 41x21", EX ... 1,400.00
Galaxy Java Blend Roasted Coffee, pail, bl milk can shape, 2-lb, EX+ ... 1,050.00
Garland Stoves & Ranges, whiskbroom holder, tin litho, 5", EX+........ 325.00
Garrett's XXXX Baker Rye, cl pocket mirror, draped nude, 2¾" L, EX . 700.00
General Arthur Cigars, match safe, hinged lid, blk on gold, 1x2", EX+ . 130.00
Geo Washington Cut Plug, sign, dc cb oval hanger, 2-sided, 11x8", NM.. 200.00
German America Brewing Co, tray, 2 bottles, blk rim, 13x13", EX ... 390.00
Gettelman Milwaukee Beer, compo sign, deer scene, mc, 17x11", EX... 100.00
Gillette safety Razor, cl pocket mirror, baby shaving, 2¼" dia, EX .. 160.00
Gillis Lunch Pail Coffee, pail, red, bail hdl, 1-lb, EX+ 1,200.00
Gillis Tea, tc, red, rnd w/sm rnd lid, 6", EX+ 450.00
Gladiator Blend Fancy Roasted Coffee, store bin, tin litho, 22", EX+.. 1,250.00
Glory Cocoanut Oil Soap, glass jar w/hinged metal lid, 11", EX.. 500.00
Gobblers Cigars, tc, rnd, slip lid, 5", EX+ 425.00
Goebel Beer, tip tray, Dutch scene w/man & beer, 4½", EX 40.00
Gold Dust Tobacco, pocket tc, vertical, metallic gold, 4½", EX+..4,500.00
Gold Dust Twins Powder, tc w/cb sides, Free Sample, 2¾x2", EX+ .. 150.00
Golden West Coffee, tc, cowgirl drinking from cup on red, 3-lb, EX+ . 250.00
Golden West Coffee, tc, cowgirl on red, keywind, 3½x5", EX 140.00
Gollam's Ice Cream, menu board, cb & glass in fr, 21", EX 195.00
Good Year Akron Bicycle Tires, paper sign, 2 men/bikes, fr, 21x13", EX . 500.00
Gotfried Krueger Brewing Co, tip tray, tankard, 4½" dia, NM 335.00
Granulated 54, sign, easel/hanger, The Secret of Contentment, 8x9", EX .. 300.00
Great Western Ins Co, pocket calendar, cl, 3¾x2½", EX............. 130.00
Gypsy Boy, tc, Cream of Tartar, gypsy boy, 2x2¼x1½", VG........... 70.00
Hamm's Beer, motion sign, waterfall/canoe scene, roof, 20x34", NM. 840.00
Harding Cream Co, dc ps, milk-can shape, blk on orange, 27x15", EX+ .. 2,500.00
Harmony Slice Cut...Tobacco, dc cb display, man's head/pipe, 10", EX.. 140.00
Harrison Paint, ps, 2-sided flange, bl & wht, 17x17", VG 110.00
Heinz Dill Pickles, store jar, glass w/paper label, knob lid, 14", EX..... 475.00
Heinz Preserved Strawberries, crock, paper label, bail hdl, 6", EX+ ... 775.00
Heinz's Tomato Preserves, crock, stoneware w/paper label, bail, 8", EX.. 900.00

Heller's Fancy Pastry Baking Powder, tc, sq w/sm rnd lid, 10-lb, 11".. 190.00
Heptol Splits, tip tray, cowboy/bucking bronco, dtd 1904, 4" dia, EX+.. 2,000.00
Hi-Plane Tobacco, pocket tc, airplane on red, 4⅜x3x⅞", EX....... 220.00
High Art Coffee, tc, mtn/palms/workers, 3⅞x5⅛" dia, EX 130.00
Hills Bros Tea & Coffee, ps, curved, tm man, red, wht/blk rim, 18", EX.. 2,800.00
Hindoo Smoking Tobacco, tc, Eastern man smoking, 3⅝x3½x2", VG.. 350.00

Hires

Charles E. Hires, a drugstore owner in Philadelphia, became interested in natural teas. He began experimenting with roots and herbs and soon developed his own special formula. Hires introduced his product to his own patrons and began selling concentrated syrup to other soda fountains and grocery stores. Samples of his 'root beer' were offered for the public's approval at the 1876 Philadelphia Centennial. Today's collectors are often able to date their advertising items by observing the Hires boy on the logo. From 1891 to 1906, he wore a dress. From 1906 until 1914, he was shown in a bathrobe; and from 1915 until 1926, he was depicted in a dinner jacket. The apostrophe may or may not appear in the Hires name; this seems to have no bearing on dating an item. See also Soda Fountain Collectibles.

Baseball scorekeeper, Shoot 'Em a Hires/Josh Slinger, cl, 3", M............. 350.00
Clock, Drink Hires..., red/wht/bl, orig glass lens, 15" dia, EX....... 185.00
Dispenser, hourglass shape, w/spigot & pump, 13", EX............. 1,550.00
Dispenser, wooden keg w/metal strips, ftd, 31x21" dia, EX............ 500.00
Display, pressed tin, Made at Home..., 18½", EX 110.00
Festoon, girl in shuttered window/R-J logo/flowers, 5-pc, 1930s, EX.. 1,500.00
Mug, ceramic, cylindrical, Hires boy w/frothy mug, 5", NM+ 200.00
Mug, ceramic, hourglass shape, Hires boy, #3095, 4", NM 200.00
Sign, cb dc standup, kid holding early bottle, 5x3½", EX............. 230.00
Sign, dc cb, Say, Drink Hires, Hires boy, 1905-15, 15", VG+....... 400.00

Sign, embossed cardboard, Hires Rootbeer, package and centennial bottle, 1890s, 7x11", NM, $1,900.00. (Photo courtesy Craig Stifter)

Sign, paper, Josh Slinger, glue strip for window, 1914, 13x17", EX... 375.00
Sign, paper, Thirsts Gently Suffocated..., Josh w/mug, 1914, 7x11" EX.. 400.00
Sign, porc, red/wht/bl/blk, 11x28", VG... 180.00
Sign, tin, dc oval, Drink Hires/bottle, wht/bl stripes, 20x29", EX ... 175.00
Sign, tin, emb, R-J bull's-eye hanger, 14½" dia, EX 85.00
Sign, tin, oval tray type w/2 girls drink from straws, 20x24", EX.. 165.00
Sign, tin, R-J logo on disk, lt bl border, 12" dia, NM+ 75.00
Sign, tin, Say/Drink.../So Refreshing, oval portrait on wht, 14", EX.. 2,800.00
Sign, tin behind glass, girl w/glass, in oak fr, 21½" H, G.............. 135.00
Sign, tin litho, Hires... w/Real Root Juices, 4-color, 7x12", NM 75.00
Syrup bottle, rvpt label, metal lid, 12", EX.................................. 225.00
Thermometer, bottle die-cut, 29", EX 70.00
Thermometer, tin bottle form, bl dot logo, 18", EX...................... 125.00
Thermometer, tin bottle form, Since 1879 label, 29", NM........... 275.00

Tray, Hires boy pointing, blk w/gold rim, 12" dia, VG+ 600.00
Tray, Josh Slinger soda fountain jerk illustration, 1915, 13", G.... 285.00
Tray, owl & parrot images, 12" dia, EX+ 5,100.00
Watch fob, emb metal, Josh Slinger, 1⅝x1½", EX 110.00

Hoadley's Tolu Chewing Gum, display box, tin litho, yel, 1x2x¾", EX.... 825.00
Hoffman's Polish, match safe, cl/metal, nude/can images, 3", EX.. 575.00
Home Brand Oats, cb box w/paper label, mansion reserve, 3-lb, EX.. 50.00
Home Oil Co Grease, tc, racecar on orange, pry lid, 4⅝x3⅜", EX...170.00
Home Run Cigarettes, pack, ball players, dtd 1921, sealed, 2⅞", EX..130.00
Honey Moon Smoking Tobacco, trolley sign, cb, couple/canoe, 22" L, EX..725.00
Hood's Ice Cream, menu board, rvpt glass & wood, 24", EX 120.00
Howdy, ts, boy w/bottle, orange/blk/wht, 9x19", EX+ 240.00
Hummer Spices, tc, hummingbird label, 3", EX+ 800.00
Hunter Ale, display, rider on horse jumping fence, spelter, 14", EX ...360.00
Hunter Baltimore Rye, match safe, cl/metal, 3x1½", EX+............. 325.00
Huyler's Chocolates, cl pocket mirror, brunette, 1903, 3x2", EX . 120.00
Ideal White Soap, easel-bk dc sign, tabby cat, Cosack, 12x8½", EX ..180.00
Imperial Sugar, butter pail, tin litho, tree & cow, 3⅛x3½", VG 40.00
Invincible Lamp Oil, can, Ginna litho on yel, w/nozzle & hdl, 9", EX+..600.00
Iroquois Beer, bottle receiver, cast-metal chief, 6x6x4½", EX 190.00

The J. Leisy Brewing Co., Cleveland. U.S.A., serving tray, factory scene, slight paint loss, 17x14", $1,540.00. (Photo courtesy Randy Inman Auctions Inc.)

Java & Mocha Coffee, tc, sq w/sm rnd slip lid, gr/red/gold, 6", EX+. 450.00
Jefferson Union Glass Fuses, display, tin, hangs on wall, 10x8x4", EX+ . 325.00
Jersey-Creme, sign/tray, tc, Victorian lady, 12" dia, EX+ 375.00
Jewett's Indian Girl Rolled Oats, box, cb cylinder, 3-lb 7-oz, EX+ ... 875.00
JH Cutter Whiskey, tray, sailing ship in sunrise, 16½x13½", EX....1,200.00
Johnson Robbins & Co Premium Seeds, display box, wood, 1897, 25" L, EX..2,400.00
Kiewel Standard Beer, tin-on-cb sign, girl w/flowers, 1908, 17x14", NM.2,400.00
Kik Soda, bottle carrier, wood, 6-pack, stamped logo, 11x9", EX.. 140.00
King Arthur Flour, pocket mirror, king/horse, Bastian Bros, 2¼", EX ..80.00
King George Cross Cut, pocket tc, vertical, 4", EX 350.00
King Midas Flour, string holder, ts w/cutout for string, 20x15", EX+..2,400.00
Kis-Me Gum, ts, cb bk, The Popular Favorite/smiling girl, 8x6", EX 450.00
Klondike-Cough Nuggets 5¢, cb sign, girl bursting thru sign, 7x10", EX...825.00
Lactated Food for Infants & Invalids, cb sign, string-hung, 8x14", EX ...100.00
Lakeside Grape Juice, tray, bottle/grape cluster, 13½" dia, EX+ ... 350.00
Lavine Soap, paper roll-down sign, lady cleaning, fr, 1890, 29x13", EX.800.00
Leafmint Chewing Gum, display box, cb, bl/wht, w/20 orig packs, EX ..325.00
Lee Union-Alls, ps, 2 workers flank lettering, 11x30", EX 1,790.00
Liberty Beer, tip tray, Indian maiden in center, gr, 4" dia, NM..... 300.00
Lictonic, ts, emb, vet advertising, red/yel on blk, 9x20", EX+...... 425.00
Lime Kiln Club, paper sign, club meeting scene, fr, 1890s, 31x37", EX..875.00
Little Polly Brooms, broom holder, tin litho w/mc logo, 6", EX+ .. 110.00

Log Cabin Syrup

Log Cabin Syrup tins have been made since the 1890s in variations of design that can be attributed to specific years of production. Until about 1914, they were made with paper labels. These are quite rare and

highly prized by today's collectors. Tins with colored lithographed designs were made after 1914. When General Foods purchased the Towle Company in 1927, the letters 'GF' were added.

A cartoon series, illustrated with a mother flipping pancakes in the cabin window and various children and animals declaring their appreciation of the syrup in voice balloons, was introduced in the 1930s. A Frontier Village series followed in the late 1940s. A schoolhouse, jail, trading post, doctor's office, blacksmith shop, inn, and private homes were also available.

Bank, glass cabin form, rnd metal lid w/slot, 5", NM..................... 35.00
Chef's hat, wht cotton w/logo on band 15.00
Opener, CI, emb lettering, 5¼x1¼", EX.. 40.00
Pitcher, glass w/fired-on red Log Cabin in rectangle, 2-spout, 2¼". 12.00
Puzzle game, cb dc cabin, instructions on bk, 2½"x3", EX............ 240.00
Spoon, SP, emb cabin finial, 4½", EX 25.00
Syrup pitcher, glass w/wht plastic lid w/emb logo, 7½" 15.00
Syrup tin, Blacksmith, 2-lb, EX 100.00
Syrup tin, boy in doorway, 1918, 4½x4½x3¼", EX, from $135 to.. 225.00
Syrup tin, cabin w/red 'tacked-on' Log Cabin Syrup sign, Gen Foods, 4". 40.00
Syrup tin, family activity at cabin, no lid, 4½x4½x2¾", EX 65.00
Syrup tin, Frontier Jail, 12-oz, EX.. 165.00
Syrup tin, Log Cabin Express, on wheels, 6x5½", EX 480.00

Long Tom Tobacco, pack, paper label on cloth, tall man, 4¾", EX .. 230.00
Lovell & Covel...Candies, pail, tin litho, rabbit/rhyme, 3x3", EX+ ...100.00
Lucky Strike Roll Cut Tobacco, pocket tc, vertical, wht, 4", EX+ ..525.00
Lutted's Cough Drops, jar, clear glass/frosted name, ftd, 12", EX ...1,250.00
Lutted's Fine Candies, tc, hinged lid, winter scenes, 4x6x2", NM...500.00
Magnet Cream Separators, ts, factory scene, 13½x20", VG 400.00
Maillard's Vanilla Chocolate/Breakfast Cocoa, ts, cherub, 22x16", EX...2,100.00
Malted Grape-Nuts, jar, clear w/metal knob lid, paper labels, 8", EX.. 700.00
Mammy Favorite Brand Coffee, pail, bail hdl, dk orange, 4-lb, EX 230.00
Mammy Favorite Brand Coffee/CD Kenny Co, pail, orange, 4-lb, 11", EX+..425.00
May Queen, pocket tin, flat, curved corners, blk on yel, 2x4", VG+... 275.00
Mayo's Plug Smoking Cock O' the Walk, ps, tm rooster on wht, 13x7", EX...1,750.00
Mayo Tobacco, sign, dc cb portrait of lady w/curly hair, 14x10", EX+ ..275.00
McFadden's Select Ground Spices, ts, hanger, girl in oval, 19x13", EX+...625.00
Mecca Cigarettes, cb sign, Earl Christy girl, dtd 1912, fr, 20x11", EX...500.00
Mellor & Rittenhouse Lozenges, store tin, gold w/glass insert, 8", EX+....650.00
Mission of California Orange, ts, early bottle, 24x24", EX........... 150.00
Mo-Jo Chewing Gum, tray, tin litho, Chicle, 16x12½" 110.00
Mount Vernon Evaporated Milk, tip tray, product, tin litho, 4¼", EX.. 120.00

Moxie

The Moxie Company was organized in 1884 by George Archer of Boston, Massachusetts. It was at first touted as a 'nerve food' to improve the appetite, promote restful sleep, and in general to make one 'feel better'! Emphasis was soon shifted, however, to the good taste of the brew, and extensive advertising campaigns rivaling those of such giant competitors as Coca-Cola and Hires resulted in successful marketing through the 1930s. Today the term moxie has become synonymous with courage and audacity, traits displayed by the company who dared compete with such well-established rivals.

Blackboard, sf, 28", VG 135.00
Cooler, bottle shape, bk doors, United Indurated Fibre, 1886, 35", EX...1,665.00
Drinking glass, str sides, frosted logo, NM+ 165.00
Fan, cb, girl w/bow in hair, bk: canoe scene, 12x10", EX.............. 180.00
Fan, cb, lady w/pocket mirror gazes at man's image, 8x7", EX 65.00
Fan, cb, Muriel Ostriche on top half, Moxie man below, 12x10", EX... 150.00

Match holder, tin litho bottle shape, 7", VG+.............................240.00
Sign, tin, dc image of soda jerk's head, 7x5", EX+.......................525.00
Sign, tin, Try Our Soda Syrups, lists flavors, ornate border, 19", G..665.00
Sign, tin, Victorian girl w/glass, 1910, 6" dia, VG.......................800.00
Sign, ts, dc image of Frank Archer above Drink Moxie sign, 6x6", EX+..1,450.00
Sign, 2-sided, pnt steel, Drink Moxie ea side, 9x18"......................230.00
Tip tray, tin litho, blond w/glass, gray rim, 6", EX.......................135.00
Tip tray, tin litho, lady among lav flowers, 6", VG......................200.00
Tip tray, tin litho, lady w/glass, I Just Love..., 1907, 6", EX..........230.00
Tip tray, tin litho, lady w/glass, woodgrain rim, 1930s, 6", VG.....185.00

Munsing Wear, door push, blk on wht, 7x3", EX+.......................300.00
Musselman's Boot Jack Tobacco, bootjack, emb CI, EX..............200.00
Nat'l Cash Register, paperweight, register form, bronze, 2¾", EX....250.00
Nature's Remedy Laxative, ps, gr sf, 17½x23½", NM................1,100.00
Nebo (Cigarettes), clock, wood cigarette shape w/man's face, 40" H, VG...8,050.00
Nestles, display case, glass/wood, labels in glass, 5x10x7½", EX...275.00
Neuweiler's Beer, sign, 2-sided, octagonal, neon rim, 50x50", EX..3,900.00
Neverslips Horse Shoes, sign, 2-sided dc cb, horse head/shoe, 12", EX+..450.00
New Tungsten (Cigars), store tc, 2 For 15¢, sq/slip lid, 6x4", EX+....220.00
Noaker Ice Cream Co, tray, boy/girl eating ice cream, 13" dia, EX..700.00
None-Such, coffee grinder, tin litho w/wooden base, 10", VG+..475.00
North Star Tobacco, tc, goddess/star, hinged lid, 3¾", EX...........275.00
Oak Motor Oil, ps, tree logo on red, wht rim, 1920s, 17x36", EX..1,800.00
Occident Flour, tin-on-cb sign, 2 domes w/wheat kernels, 9x14", EX...375.00
OFC Bourbon, ts, elk scene, 36x24" in factory fr (43x32"), NM....3,100.00
Ohio No 18 ...5 Horse Electric Motor, pocket mirror, 1¾" dia, EX....650.00

Old Crow

Old Crow Whiskey items have become popular with collectors primarily because of the dapper crow dressed in a tuxedo and top hat that was used by the company for promotional purposes during the 1940s through the 1960s. However, there is a vast variety of Old Crow collectibles, some of which carry only the whiskey's name. In the 1970s ceramic decanters shaped like chess pieces were available; these carried nothing more than a paper label and a presentation box to identify them. In 1985, the 150th anniversary of Old Crow, the realistic crow that had been extensively used prior to 1950 re-emerged.

Very little Old Crow memorabilia has been issued since National Distillers Products Corporation, the parent company since 1933, was purchased by Jim Beam Brands in 1987. No reproductions have surfaced, although a few fantasies have been found where the character crow was borrowed for private use. Note that with the increased popularity of Old Crow memorabilia, many items have surfaced, especially the more common ones, thus their values have decreased.

Ashtray, Bakelite, 3½" dia, NM...25.00
Bank, wooden bbl, 1985, 6", EX...15.00
Decanter, figural, orange vest, Royal Doulton, 12½", MIB, $100 to...125.00
Dice, I Buy, You Buy, crow on 1 side, ½" set of 2, M.......................45.00
Dice cup, Bakelite, blk w/yel lettering, felt-lined, NM.................100.00
Figure, plastic, Advertising Novelty & Sign Co, 32", EX.............200.00
Label, paper, gold w/Hermitage Distillery bbls, ca 1903, 4x4+", NM...25.00
Money clip, chromed metal, emb disk w/crow on 2" clip, EX........35.00
Pocketknife, pearlized hdls, 2 blades, NM.................................20.00
Shot glass, Old Crow name & image in blk, M..............................20.00
Thermometer, rnd dial, 1950s, 9x13", EX.................................150.00

Old Gold Cigarettes, gs, Love at First Light!, R Armstrong, 8x14", EX..800.00

Old Manse Canadian Maple Syrup, pocket mirror, cl, 2" dia, EX....350.00
Old Rip Smoking Tobacco, tc, sq w/slip lid, blk on red, 5", EX+...1,600.00
Orange-Crush, bottle topper, dc cb, girl in early swimsuit, 11", EX..450.00
Orange-Crush, clock, wood/glass, Ward's Orange-Crush Time, 32", VG..225.00
Orange-Crush, display, cb standup, 3-D, Crushy, new brn bottle, VG..225.00
Orange-Crush, sign, dc cb, Exhilarating, girl/beach/bottle, 22x32", EX...600.00
Orange-Crush, ts, sf, red/wht/yel/blk, 2x16", EX...........................110.00
Orange-Julep, tray, beach girl under umbrella, 13x11", EX..........225.00
Ox-Heart Coca, ps, We Sell..., wht/red on bl, 7x20", EX..........1,200.00
Ox-Heart Dutch Process Cocoa, door push, porc, wht on bl, 7x4", NM..1,750.00
Paul Jones Rye Whiskey, sign, sf, wood, milkmaid w/2 cows, 20x14", EX+...650.00
Pearl Lustre Dyes, display cabinet, wood w/tin insert, 1890s, 22", EX+...1,350.00
Pedro Cut Plug Smoking Tobacco, tc, rnd w/sm rnd lid, orange, 6", EX..550.00
Pedro Smoking Tobacco, lunch box, bail hdl, red on yel, 8" L, NM..300.00
Pepper's Ginger Ale, cl-over-cb sign, yel/blk, 4½x6½", NM...........80.00
Pepsi, door push, enamel & metal, adjusts to fit door, 5x30"+, NM...130.00

Pepsi-Cola

Pepsi-Cola was first served in the early 1890s to customers of Caleb D. Bradham, a young pharmacist who touted his concoction to be medicinal as well as delicious. It was first called 'Brad's Drink' but was renamed Pepsi-Cola in 1898. Various logos have been registered over the years. The familiar oval was first used in the early 1940s. At about the same time, the two 'dots' (indicated in our listings by '=') between the words Pepsi and Cola became one, though more recent items may carry the double-dot logo as well, especially when they're designed to be reminiscent of the old ones. The bottle cap logo came along in 1943 and with variations was used through the early 1960s. See also Soda Fountain Collectibles.

Bottle, clear glass, pnt P=C label, 12-oz, EX.................................45.00
Bottle carrier, metal, 6-pack, 8x8x5", VG.....................................50.00
Bottle carrier, wood, 6-pack, triangular w/cut-out hdl, 1930s, EX+..150.00
Bottle opener, cast brass w/emb name, EX patina, 5¼"....................48.00
Can, metal, cap on side, diagonal stripes, Seattle WA, 1950s, EX....65.00
Carrier, pnt wood w/zinc trim, 6-bottle, ca 1935, 11x8½x6", NM.120.00
Clock, dbl bubble, 1950s, EX...875.00
Clock, lights up, Say Pepsi Please, sq, 1960s, 13", EX+................365.00
Clock, neon, metal/plastic, P-C logo, battery-op, 15" dia, EX........85.00
Coaster, P=C label in center, 1940s, 4", VG....................................8.00

Display, die-cut Pepsi cop, easel back, ca 1930s – 1940s, EX+, $375.00. (Photo courtesy Gary Metz)

Sign, cb, hostess & festive table, metal fr, 29" L, G.......................90.00
Sign, metal, bottle cap w/neon lettering, 31", EX........................670.00
Sign, metal, emb bottle, More Bounce..., 1950s, 48x18", EX.......525.00
Sign, metal/glass/cb/mirror, Enjoy...Now/cap, 1950s, sq, 10", EX..500.00
Sign, paper, Bigger & Better, bottle at left, 6x19½", NM............275.00
Sign, paper sign, 1940s lady in bl boa w/bottle, fr, 20x15", NM...725.00
Sign, porc, Enjoy a Pepsi/bottle cap, 12x29", VG.......................225.00
Sign, tin, dc bottle w/P=C label, 1930s, 45x12", EX....................625.00

Sign, tin, early bottle/5¢, slight fading, 49x16", VG.....................600.00
Sign, tin, emb, Drink P=C Delicious Delightful, red border, 4x10", NM ..600.00
String holder, Join the Swing..., P=C logo, 1940s, 16x12", EX 650.00
Syrup can, heavy steel, red stencil on wht, ca 1930?, 17x14" dia, EX...85.00
Thermometer, dial type, metal w/glass cover, 20½" dia, EX 175.00
Thermometer, tin, Any Weather's..., red/wht/bl, 26x8" 135.00
Thermometer, tin, Pepsi Please, 1969, 28", NM 175.00
Thermometer, tin, yel w/emb bottle cap, 27", EX.....................150.00
Tray, Enjoy P=C/Hits the Spot, 10x14", NM..............................100.00
Tray, 3 children w/songbook & new 1940 jingle, 1940s, 14x10½", VG.. 60.00

Peter Schuyler 10¢ Cigar, sign, metal, blk & wht, wood fr, 35x35", EX+.1,500.00
Physicians Beef Peptoids, sample tc, Sommers Bros litho, EX+ ... 130.00
Pickaninny Brand Peanut Butter, pail, bail hdl, yel, 1-lb, EX+ 600.00
Pickininy Jelly Beans, display box, wood w/paper labels, 18x20x13", EX.400.00
Piedmont Cigarettes, paper sign, elegant lady's portrait, fr, 26", EX+.875.00
Pilsener Brewing Co, tip tray, bottle/frothy glass, 4" dia, EX 280.00
Pioneer Brand Evaporated Milk, sign, 2-sided cb can hanger, 8", EX.. 300.00
Piper Heidsieck Chewing Tobacco 10¢, paper sign, yel/gr, fr, 16" L, EX.200.00

Planters Peanuts

The Planters Peanut Co. was founded in 1906. Mr. Peanut, the dashing peanut man with top hat, spats, monocle, and cane, has represented Planters since 1916. He took on his modern-day appearance after the company was purchased by Standard Brands in November 1960. He remains perhaps the most highly recognized logo of any company in the world. Mr. Peanut has promoted the company's products by appearing in ads; on product packaging; on or as store displays, novelties, and premiums; and even in character at promotional events (thanks to a special Mr. Peanut costume).

Among the favorite items of collectors today are the glass display jars which were sent to retailers nationwide to stimulate 'point-of-sale' trade. They come in a variety of shapes and styles. The first, distributed in the early 1920s, was a large universal candy jar (round covered bowl on a pedestal) with only a narrow paper label affixed at the neck to identify it as 'Planters.' In 1924 an octagonal jar was produced, all eight sides embossed, with Mr. Peanut on the narrow corner panels. On a second octagonal jar, only seven sides were embossed, leaving one of the large panels blank to accommodate a paper label.

In late 1929 a fishbowl jar was introduced, and in 1932 a beautiful jar with a blown-out peanut on each of the four corners was issued. The football shape was also made in the 1930s, as were the square jar, the large barrel jar, and the hexagonal jar with yellow fired-on designs alternating on each of the six sides. All of these early jars had glass lids which after 1930 had peanut finials.

In 1937 jars with lithographed tin lids were introduced. The first of these was the slant-front streamline jar, which is also found with screened yellow lettering. Next was a squat version, the clipper jar, then the upright rectangular 1940 leap year jar, and last, another upright rectangular jar with a screened, fired-on design similar to the red, white, and blue design on the cellophane 5¢ bags of peanuts of the period. This last jar was issued again after WWII with a plain red tin lid.

In 1959 Planters first used a stock Anchor Hocking one-gallon round jar with a 'customer-special' decoration in red. As the design was not plainly evident when the jar was full, the decoration was modified with a white under-panel. The two jars we've just described are perhaps the rarest of them all due to their limited production. After Standard Brands purchased Planters, they changed the red-on-white panel to show their more modern Mr. Peanut and in 1963 introduced this most plentiful, thus very common, Planters jar. In 1966 the last counter display jar was distributed: the Anchor Hocking jar with a fired-on large four-color

design such as that which appeared on peanut bags of the period. Prior to this, a plain jar with a transfer decal in an almost identical but smaller design was used.

Some Planters jars have been reproduced: the octagonal jar (with only seven of the sides embossed), a small version of the barrel jar, and the four peanut corner jar. Some of the first were made in clear glass with 'Made in Italy' embossed on the bottom, but most have been made in Asia, many in various colors of glass (a dead giveaway) as well as clear, and carrying only small paper stickers, easily removed, identifying the country of origin. At least two reproductions of the Anchor Hocking jar with a four-color design have been made, one circa 1978, the other in 1989. Both, using the stock jar, are difficult to detect, but there are small differences between them and the original that will enable you to make an accurate identification. With the exception of several of the earliest and the Anchor Hocking, all authentic Planters jars have 'Made in USA' embossed on the bottom, and all, without exception, are clear glass. Unfortunately, several paper labels have also been reproduced, no doubt due to the fact that an original label or decal will greatly increase the value of an original jar. Jar prices continue to remain stable in today's market.

In the late 1920s, the first premiums were introduced in the form of story and paint books. Late in the 1930s, the tin nut set (which was still available into the 1960s) was distributed. A wood jointed doll was available from Planters Peanuts stores at that time. Many post-WWII items were made of plastic: banks, salt and pepper shakers, cups, cookie cutters, small cars and trucks, charms, whistles, various pens and mechanical pencils, and almost any other item imaginable. Since 1981 the company, as a division of Nabisco (NGH) has continued to distribute a wide variety of novelties. In late 2000 NGH was sold to Philip Morris Cos. and Nabisco was combined with its Kraft Foods unit. With the increased popularity of Mr. Peanut memorabilia, more items surface, and the value of common items decrease.

Note that there are many unauthorized Planters/Mr. Peanut items. Although several are reproductions or 'copycats,' most are fantasies and fakes. Our advisor for this category is Anthony Scola; he is listed in the Directory under Pennsylvania.

Ashtray, ceramic, MrP (gr pants) by peanut dish, 1930s, 4x3", EX .. 325.00
Blotter, cb, early 5¢ pack, peanut shape, 1940s, 3½x7", EX............ 50.00
Box, shipping; heavy cb, Jumbo Block candy bars, 14¼x12¾x12", EX... 140.00
Candy wrapper, Planters Old Fashion Pnut Candy, orange, 1-lb, VG+.... 1,950.00
Display, cb standup, shelf w/MrP on ad header, holds cans, 1930s, VG+ . 1,750.00
Display, dc cb seated lady w/box, sits on edge of shelf, 1938, 25", EX...... 800.00
Display rack, tin, Planters Peanut Specialties, Z-shaped, 5x14x8", EX+... 1,650.00
Display shelf, dc tin litho, MrP/...Best Peanut Bars 5¢, 12" L, EX........ 1,200.00
Funnel, aluminum, Planters Peanut Oil, 1930s, 4¾x6", EX 40.00
Jar, Fishbowl, octagon knob lid, no label, 1929, 12½", EX 50.00
Jar, Four Peanut Corner, peanut finial lid, 1932, 14", EX (+)....... 225.00
Jar, Hexagon, yel screened design, peanut finial lid, 7", EX............ 75.00
Jar, Octagon, emb, octagonal knob lid, 1924, 12", EX................. 250.00

Jar, slanted, original labels on each side, 1937, 10x8x5", M, $2,225.00. (Photo courtesy Wm. Morford Auctions)

Jar & jar holder, dc tin w/MrP flanking sign, gold-trimmed sq jar, EX+ ..2,500.00
Punchboard, MrP & product tin at top, unused, 6¼x8", NM........ 50.00

Scale, Mr P figure, cast aluminum, Hamilton Scale Co, 45", VG.. 10,350.00
Sign, emb tin litho w/Mr Peanut, lt rust/pitting, 9¾x23⅜", VG ..575.00
Thermometer, plastic key, 1940s, 8⅜x2¾", NMIB........................ 825.00
Tin, Mother's Brand (pre MrP), pry lid, rare, 5-lb, EX+ 8,200.00
Trolley sign, cb, butler w/tray, Delicious w/Cocktails!.., 25" L, NM ...425.00
Trolley sign, cb, MrP & Cocktail Peanuts tc w/Lent theme, 1930s, VG..550.00
Trolley sign, Webster Dictionary Only 10¢..., 1930s, 11x21", NM.....725.00
Vendor, MrP on front panel, metal litho, 28½x12⅝x10", EX....... 190.00

Plow Boy Chewing & Smoking, cloth sign, tm image, fr, 16", EX...525.00
Plowman Cigars, paper-on-canvas sign, farm scene, 1880s, 16x34", VG+...725.00
Poker Club Mixture, tc, sq corners, royal flush card hand, 3x5x2", EX...750.00
Polar Bear Coffee, tc w/polar bear paper label, 1-lb, 5¾x4⅛", VG ..300.00
Polar Bear Tobacco, ps, Chew..., wht on dk bl, 5x8½", NM 500.00
Police Foot Powder, tc, tm image of police officer, 5", EX+ 1,200.00
Pop Bicycles, paper sign, Victorian ladies conversing, fr, 29x20", EX+ ...525.00
Pratts Food for Horses & Cattle, paper sign, horse breeds, fr, 24x31" 925.00
Premium Mills Cloves, tin, sq w/slip lid, St Bernard, 3½", EX+ ... 425.00
Puritan Crushed Plug Mixture, pocket tc, man's portrait, 4½", EX+ ... 300.00
Queen Dairy 5¢ Chilled Churned Buttermilk, porc churn dispenser, NM..5,200.00

RCA Victor

Nipper, the RCA Victor trademark, was the creation of Francis Barraud, an English artist. His pet's intense fascination with the music of the phonograph seemed to him a worthy subject for his canvas. Although he failed to find a publishing house who would buy his work, the Gramophone Co. in England saw its potential and adopted Nipper to advertise their product. The painting was later acquired and trademarked in the United States by the Victor Talking Machine Co., which was purchased by RCA in 1929. The trademark is owned today by EMI in England and by General Electric in the U.S. Nipper's image appeared on packages, accessories, ads, brochures, and in three-dimensional form. You may find a life-size statue of him, but all are not old. They have been manufactured for the owner throughout RCA history and are marketed currently by licensees, BMG Inc. and Thomson Consumer Electronics (dba RCA). Except for the years between 1968 and 1976, Nipper has seen active duty, and with his image spruced up only a bit for the present day, the ageless symbol for RCA still listens intently to 'His Master's Voice.' Many of the items have been reproduced in recent years. Exercise care before you buy. The true Nipper collectible is one which has been authorized by either Victor or RCA Victor as an advertising aid. This includes items used in showrooms, billboards, window dressings, and customer give-aways. The showroom items included three-dimensional Nippers first in papier-mache, later in spun rubber, and finally in plastic. Some were made in chalk. Throughout the years these items were manufactured largely by one company, Old King Cole, but often were marketed through others who added their names to the product. The key to collecting Nipper is to look for those items which were authorized and to overlook those items that were copied or made without permission of the copyright/trademark owner. Some of the newer but unauthorized items, however, are quite good and have become collectible notwithstanding their lack of authenticity.

The recent phenomenon of Internet auctions has played havoc with prices paid for Victor and RCA Victor collectibles. Often prices paid for online sales bear little resemblance to the true value of the item. Reproductions are often sold as old on the Internet and bring prices accordingly. Auction prices, more often than not, are inflated over sales made through traditional sales outlets. The Internet has exacerbated the situation by focusing a very large number of buyers and sellers through the narrow portal of a modem. The prices here are intended to reflect what one might expect to pay through traditional sales.

Items marked (+) are often reproduced and care should be taken to ascertain age or provenance. Our advisor for RCA Victor is Roger R. Scott; he is listed in the Directory under Oklahoma.

Bank, Nipper figure, flocking over metal, 6", EX+ 125.00
Clock, light-up, PAM, EX 400.00
Figure, Nipper, ceramic, on plaque (Visco), VG/EX.................... 100.00
Figure, Nipper, chalkware, 4", EX... 45.00
Figure, Nipper, clear glass, Fenton... 50.00
Figure, Nipper, papier-mache, orig decal, 14", VG 500.00
Figure, Nipper, papier-mache, 11", VG/EX............................... 200.00
Figure, Nipper, papier-mache, 18"... 300.00
Figure, Nipper, papier-mache, 36", VG/EX............................... 600.00
Figure, Nipper, papier-mache (Old King Cole), 42", VG/EX 1,000.00
Figure, Nipper, rubber or plastic, 11", VG/EX........................... 100.00
Figure, Nipper, rubber or plastic, 18", VG/EX........................... 150.00

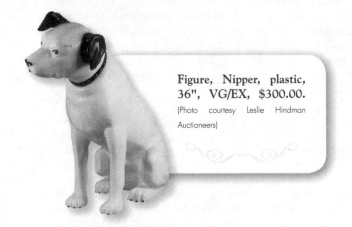

Figure, Nipper, plastic, 36", VG/EX, $300.00.
(Photo courtesy Leslie Hindman Auctioneers)

Radiotron Man, blk coat, yel legs, red boots, Parrish design, 15", EX....900.00
Shakers, dog & phonograph, plastic, pr, M 45.00
Shakers, Lenox, dog, pr... 50.00
Stick pin, cl, VG/EX.. 150.00
Watch fob, EX.. 30.00

Red Goose Shoes

Realizing that his last name was difficult to pronounce, Herman Giesecke, a shoe company owner resolved to give the public a modified, shortened version that would be better suited to the business world. The results suggested the use of the goose trademark with the last two letters, 'ke,' represented by the key that this early goose held in his mouth. Upon observing an employee casually coloring in the goose trademark with a red pencil, Giesecke saw new advertising potential and renamed the company Red Goose Shoes. Although the company has changed hands down through the years, the Red Goose emblem has remained. Collectors of this desirable fowl increase in number yearly, as do prices. Beware of reproductions; new chalkware figures are prevalent.

Bank, CI, goose figural, red pnt, 4", EX... 195.00
Display, chalkware goose, orig pnt, 11½", EX................................. 40.00
Display/dispenser, papier-mache goose lays eggs, 1930s, 26x22x12", EX..175.00
Pencil box, tin litho, paper insert inside, 2⅜x7¾x¾", EX............. 120.00
Sign, neon goose on wht oval, 1930s-40s, 24x12", NM+ 1,900.00
Sign, tin, ...For Boys & Girls, yel/red, 13x19", EX....................... 125.00
Sign, tin flange, goose on yel, 16x9¾", EX.................................. 165.00

Red Man Tobacco, paper sign, shows 1952 baseball cards, 16x11", EX..130.00
Red Raven, tip tray, Pittsburg Exposition, red/blk, 4½" dia, EX+. 150.00

Red Ribbon Beer, tray, tin, bear scene, pre-prohibition, 13x13", EX... 525.00
Red Rock Ginger Ale, gs, paper bk, chain border, cowgirl, 10", EX+.. 400.00
Reddy Kilowatt, display doll, stuffed cloth w/light-up nose, 17", EX... 450.00
Remmington, dc cb sign, boy shooting .22, fr, 10x15" (actual), EX+.. 650.00
Richard Hudnut Perfumer/Rouge, rvpt glass case w/8 holes, blk/gold, EX. 165.00
Rising Sun Stove Polish, cb dc sign, Black lady/stove, 10x8", EX. 575.00
Robert H Graupers Brewery, tray, brewery building, 12" dia, EX.. 725.00
Robinson Crusoe Salted Peanuts, tc, rnd w/pry lid, 10-lb, EX+ ... 900.00
Rockford Watch, match holder, dc tin litho, red, 5x2½", VG+ ... 775.00

Roly Poly

The Roly Poly tobacco tins were patented on November 5, 1912, by Washington Tuttle and produced by Tindeco of Baltimore, Maryland. There were six characters in all: Satisfied Customer, Storekeeper, Mammy, Dutchman, Singing Waiter, and Inspector. Four brands of tobacco were packaged in selected characters; some tins carry a printed tobacco box on the back to identify their contents. Mayo and Dixie Queen Tobacco were packed in all six; Red Indian and U.S. Marine Tobacco in only Mammy, Singing Waiter, and Storekeeper. Of the set, the Inspector is considered the rarest and in near-mint condition may fetch more than $1,000.00 on today's market.

Butler, Mayo, G... 275.00
Dutchman, red neckscarf, wht belt, Mayo, VG 300.00

Mammy, Mayo, EX, from $600.00 to $700.00. (Photo courtesy Morphy Auctions)

Satisfied Customer, man w/pipe, tooth on watch chain, Mayo, EX.. 420.00
Singing Waiter, song sheet in hands, Mayo, VG 420.00
Storekeeper, bald man, smoking pipe, Mayo, G.......................... 300.00

Rose of Kansas Coffee, tc, pry lid, gr, 1-lb, EX 3,200.00
Runkel's Breakfast Cocoa, cl pocket mirror, lady w/product, 2¾", EX... 375.00
Schlitz, ps, tm globe shape, bl & wht, 13", EX+ 700.00
Scottie Cigars, tc, sq, slip lid, red, dog portrait, holds 50, 5", EX . 275.00
Seal of Minnesota Coffee, tc, rnd w/knob lid, farm scene, 1-lb, EX+.. 3,700.00
Seal of North Carolina Plug Cut, tc, rnd w/sm rnd slip lid, 6", EX+ ..230.00
Sensation 5¢ Cigars, tc, tm girl, gold trim, rnd, 50¢, 5", EX+ 800.00

Seven-Up

The Howdy Company of St. Louis, Missouri, was founded in 1920 by Charles L. Grigg. His first creation was an orange drink called Howdy. In the late 1920s Howdy's popularity began to wane, so in 1929 Grigg invented a lemon-lime soda called Seven-Up as an alternative to colas. Grigg's Seven-Up became a widely accepted favorite. Our advisor for this category is Craig Stifter; he is listed in the Directory under Illinios. See also Soda Fountain Collectibles.

Clock, light-up, wood w/plastic front, You Like It..., sq, 15", G+. 100.00

Clock, neon, metal/plastic, battery-op, 15" dia, NM 75.00
Cooler, metal w/emb logo, swing hdls, drain plug, 1950s, EX......... 50.00
Sign, cb dc, dbl-sided, bottle on gr, 9x5½", NM 50.00
Sign, cb stand-up, We Serve Nothing Better, 1930s, 10x14", VG+ ..25.00
Sign, cb stand-up, You Stand-By, man w/bottle, 18", EX+ 300.00
Sign, light-up, plastic, 2-sided, revolves, 1940s, 30x20x8", NM... 375.00
Sign, tin, First Against Thirst, Canada, 1960s, 20x28", VG.......... 40.00
Thermometer, dial type, 7-Up Likes You, 10" dia, NM, from $225 to ..275.00
Thermometer, metal, 7-Up in wht dots/red logo on blk, 20", EX... 85.00

Shasta Coffee, tc, key-wind lid, yel, 2-lb, 7", EX+ 625.00
Sherwin Williams, ps, dc Cover the Earth logo, emb, 36x18", EX ..840.00
Shinola Shoe Polish, shoe horn, tin litho, Shonk, 1907, 4¾", VG+.. 40.00
Slade's Pure Spices, display box, wood w/color graphics, 14x19x12", VG. 175.00
Slippery Elm Lozenges, tc, sq w/slip lid, gold, 5-lb, 8", EX+ 300.00
Smith Bros Cough Drops, display, tin, 3-sided, slant top, 10", EX...325.00
Spear Head Tobacco, cb sign, Palmer Cox Brownies/balloon, 14x14", EX..650.00
Spencerian/Steel Pens/Are the Best, 3-way sign, tin litho, 4x18", EX ..950.00
Spic & Span Polish for All Metals, canister, cb w/metal lid, 5", EX......140.00
Splendid Varnish, display shelf, 3-step, wood w/tin header, 15" W, EX+ ... 575.00
Squadron Leader Tobacco, pocket tc, biplane scene, 3x4¼x1", EX 150.00
Squire's Kettle Rendered Pure Leaf Lard..., dc cb standup, pig on box..475.00
Squirrel Peanut Butter, pail, yel, bail hdl, 1-lb, EX+..................... 325.00
Stag Tobacco, postcard, vinyl record built in, stag image, unused, EX ...50.00
Star Brand Shoes, toy racing car, dc tin litho, 8x4x1", M...........3,900.00
Star Cough Drops, tin, gr, 'Jimmie' dog graphics, slip lid, 7", EX+.. 1,500.00
Star Soap, fan pull sign, dc cb, 2 kids in swing, 9x6", EX+ 545.00
Stickney & Poor Spice Co, wood w/mustard can in center, fr, 33x25", EX.... 1,000.00
Stransky Steel Ware, tray, wht/bl, The Wear That Wears, 24" oval, EX+. 450.00
Success Manure Spreader, tip tray, Kemp & Burpee Mfg Co, 3½x5", NM..525.00
Sunlight Flour, paper sign, rnd logo/lettering on wht, 28x20", EX+.... 200.00
Surbrug's Golden Sceptre (Tobacco), sample tc, sq, slip lid, yel, EX+. 200.00
Swan Pencil Co, lg display pencil w/swan logo, yel, 32x2" dia, EX+... 625.00
Sweet Burley (Light) Tobacco, store tc, rnd w/sq lid, yel, 11", EX+ ...200.00
Sweet Carporal Cigarettes, cb sign, lady's portrait, fr, 12x9", EX+ ..200.00
Sweet Girl Peanut Butter, pail, pry lid, bail hdl, 16-oz, VG 390.00
Sweet Mist Chewing Tobacco, store tc, rnd, sq lid, red/yel, 11", EX ..300.00
Sweet-Orr Overalls, pc, men pulling on jeans, 8x29¾", EX 160.00
Taka-Kola, tip tray, girl on clock face, 4" dia, EX......................... 335.00
Tavern Coffee, tc, slip lid, orange, 1-lb, 6", EX+.........................3,200.00
Terre Haute Brewing, cl pocket mirror, lady w/lg bottle, 2⅛", EX ...575.00
Texaco Gasoline/Motor Oil, star logo, 1930s, 42" dia, EX......... 1,345.00
Texaco Roofing...Compound, tin pail, farm/factory scenes, 10-lb, EX ...50.00
Texaco Sky Chief Gasoline, ps, red/wht/gr/blk, 1953, 18x12", EX ..500.00
Thurber & Co Tea, tc, rnd w/sm rnd lid, gr, Ginna, 1-lb, 9", EX+ ..575.00
Tiger Chewing Tobacco, store tc, sq w/sm slip lid, red, 11", EX+ 180.00
Tivoli White Ribbon (Beer), ts, emb, wht on blk, 14x19", EX+ .. 300.00
Totem 5¢ Cigar, sign, dc cb hanger, totem scene, 6" dia, EX......... 625.00
Toy Tal Co, container, compo figural bear atop tin base, 5½", EX...200.00
Turkey Brand Coffee, tc, pry lid, gr w/red & wht graphics, 3-lb, EX+ . 925.00
Turkey Roasted Coffee, tc, paper label, sm screw lid, 3-lb, 11", EX+... 675.00
Union Leader Tobacco, cb box, pack shown ea side, 12x9x7½", EX... 150.00
Union Made (Cigars), sign, wood, 3 men at counter, 15x21", EX+ 400.00
US Tires, cb fan, early motorists, 9⅝x8", EX................................. 120.00
Van Heusen Shirts, sign, multimedia, 3-D cameo on red, fr, 37x24", EX... 110.00
Vanity Self-Rising Flour, cl pocket mirror, peacock, 2¾", EX+ 230.00
Velvet Candy, tip tray, See/Hear/Speak No Evil monkeys, 4" dia, EX ..225.00
Veteran Brand Spice, tc, Civil War officer, 3x2⅜x1¼", EX 120.00
Vicar Pear Smoking Tobacco/Gail & Ax, ts, pear, 13" diagonal, EX... 650.00
Vulcan Plows, match holder, dc tin w/blacksmith, 8x3", NM ...1,200.00
Vulcanol, banner, cloth, Better Than Stove Polish/dog, yel, 34", EX ... 140.00
Walla Walla Pepsin Chewing Gum, store jar, emb glass, Indian, 13", EX....625.00

Walter Baker & Co Breakfast Cocoa, ts, tm girl, fr, 23x17", EX .. 1,550.00
War Eagle Cigars, tc, eagle on dk brn, 5¼x3½", EX 325.00
Ward's Cake, display case, tin litho, 1920s, 21x17x13", EX+ 1,650.00
Waterman's Ideal Ink, step display shelf, tin, pouring ink graphics, M.. 2,400.00
Western Farms, ts, cb bk, beveled, Milk That Is Milk, 4x13", EX+ .. 400.00
Whip Ready Rolled Tobacco, canister, emb tin octagon, 5½", EX+ . 230.00
Whistle, sf cb sign, smiling girl, 1950s, 20x14", NM 50.00
White Manor Tobacco, pocket tc, plantation house, 3x3½x1", EX ... 130.00
White Rock Water, ts, hanger, octagonal w/rolled corners, 14", EX+ ... 1,500.00
Whiz Metal Polish, sample tc, paper label, sm rnd screw lid, 2", EX+ . 350.00
Wilbur's Cocoa, paper sign, child's profile/phrase, fr, 14x24", NM .. 600.00
Wilburt Razors, tc, red & blk, 1¾x2½x1⅜", EX 475.00
William's Khush-Amadi Talc, tc, mc fairy graphics, gold top, 5", EX+ ... 925.00
Winner Cut Plug, lunch box, bail hdl, 8" L, EX+ 425.00
Woodbury & Latham Coffee, tin, red, tall sq w/sm rnd lid, 1-lb, EX+ .. 350.00

Wrigley's Gum, die-cut card-board standup, 32x21", VG, $1,150.00. (Photo courtesy Randy Inman Auctions)

Wrigley's Gum, display shelf, tin w/cb dummy gum inserts, 6x17x4", EX+ .. 475.00
Wrigley's Gum, sign, dc cb standup, Wrigley kid w/lg pack, 13x11", EX 800.00
Wrigley's Gum, tray, Happy To Serve You/Wrigley elves, 13x11", EX .. 335.00
Y-B Havana Cigars, litho plate, brunette lady, Shonk, 10", EX+ ... 575.00
Yellow Cab Cigars, ts, traffic cop & taxi cab, 6⅝x19⅞", EX 625.00
Yorkshire Farm Peanut Butter, pail, press lid, bail hdl, gr, 14-oz, EX... 525.00
Yucatan Gum, tin display box w/oval window, 6x6½x5", EX+ 350.00
Yuengling's Lager, Ale & Porter, tray, girl in plumed hat, rnd, EX .. 1,345.00
Yueta Chewing Gum, display box, cb w/paper labels, 5x8x1", EX+ .. 70.00
Zeno Gum, display cabinet, wood w/slanted glass front, 18", EX+ .. 775.00
5A Horse Blankets, puzzle, cb litho, EX in partial 3½x3¼" box 40.00

Advertising Cards

Advertising trade cards enjoyed great popularity during the last quarter of the nineteenth century when the chromolithography printing process was refined and put into common use. The purpose of the trade card was to acquaint the public with a business, product, service, or event. Most trade cards range in size from 2" x 3" to 4" x 6"; however, many are found in both smaller and larger sizes.

There are two classifications of trade cards: 'private design' and 'stock.' Private design cards were used by a single company or individual; the images on the cards were designed for only that company. Stock cards were generics that any individual or company could purchase from a printer's inventory. These cards usually had a blank space on the front for the company to overprint with their own name and product information.

Four categories of particular interest to collectors are:

Mechanical — a card which achieves movement through the use of a pull tab, fold-out side, or movable part.

Hold-to-light — a card that reveals its design only when viewed before a strong light.

Die-cut — a card in the form of something like a box, a piece of clothing, etc.

Metamorphic — a card that by folding down a flap shows a transformed image, such as a white beard turning black after use of a product.

For a more thorough study of the subject, we recommend *Reflections 1* and *Reflections 2* by Kit Barry; his address can be found in the Directory under Vermont. Values are given for cards in near-mint condition.

Alaska Down Bustle, woman, bustle in front of mirror 20.00
Armour's Extract of Beef, girl in bl dress w/serving tray 8.00
Ayer's Cherry Pectoral, girl under tree watching 2 birds 6.00
Ayer's Pills, soldier on wht horse w/banner in battle 6.00
Babbit Soap, boy & girl playing w/jester doll & dog 6.00
Babbitt Soap, girl & boy winning soap box boat race 10.00
Barlow's Vienna pudding, waiter tripping over dog 12.00
Buckeye Lawn Mower, boy on tree limb reading to birds 12.00
Burdock Bitters, girl holding bottle & cat 8.00
Clark's ONT Thread, baby w/spool rattle 6.00
Clark's ONT Thread, boy sailor on ship raising flag 6.00
Clark's ONT Thread, girl sewing rip on boy's pants 6.00
Colburn's Mustard, man by fireplace serving meat platter 9.00
Davies Clother, woman berating boy, gr tones & blk 9.00
Estey Organ, woman playing string instrument, all bl 12.00
Hood's Olive Ointment, girl & boy w/top in hand 8.00
Horsford's Acid Phosphate, wht cap w/red bow & baby 7.00
Household Sewing Machine Co, 2 women, tennis racquet 8.00
Hoyt's German Cologne, girl w/flower basket & 2 birds 12.00
J&P Coats Thread, old woman & boy w/thread box 6.00
Jayne's Expectorant, milkmaid w/2 cows in field 6.00
Lavine Soap, die-cut painter's palette w/owl 6.00
Metropolitan Life Insurance Co, woman lifting dress 8.00
Murray & Lanman Florida Water, girl w/dog at fountain 9.00
Muzzy Starch, boy throwing snowballs 8.00
New Home Sewing Machine, brother & sister on beach 7.00
Niagara Starch, girl in purple & brn w/hand muff 6.00
Niagara Starch, girl putting flowers in boy's hat 6.00
Niagara Starch, girl w/doll reading 6.00
Parker's Ginger Tonic, woman in bonnet, left arm raised 7.00
Pearline Soap, crying child w/4 geese stealing cracker 7.00
Prudential Insurance, boy in cap holding puppy 9.00
Ridge's food, girl w/rattle & baby in crib, blk & wht 8.00
Singer Sewing Maching Co, image of Campanini (singer) 9.00
Soapine, sailor on ship's mast, waving banner 5.00
Solar Tip Shoes, 2 girls & 2 boys w/hoop & ball 8.00
St Charles Evaporated milk, jury scene w/children 18.00
Tarrant's Seltzer Aperient, baby in straw basket 6.00
Tenexine Glue, man on post, Sticking to My Post 12.00
Thomas Electric Oil Medicine, woman in hat facing right 6.00
Thurbers' Preserves & Jellies, 7 children raiding cupboard 16.00
Vienna mold for cakes, chef w/cakes, blk & wht 16.00
Wheeler & Wilson Sewing Machine, woman, parrot & girl 7.00
Willimantic Thread, 2 girls in spool pony cart 8.00
Wilson's Beef, dancing sailor w/product, fiddle player 12.00

Agata

Agata is New England peachblow (the factory called it 'Wild Rose') with an applied metallic stain which produces gold tracery and dark blue mottling. The stain is subject to wear, and the amount of remaining stain greatly affects the value. It is especially valuable (and rare) on satin-finish items when found on peachblow of intense color. Caution! Be sure to use only gentle cleaning methods.

Currently rare types of art glass have been realizing erratic prices at auction; until they stabilize, we can only suggest an average range of values. In the listings that follow, examples are glossy unless noted otherwise. A condition rating of 'EX' indicates that the stain shows a moderate amount of wear. To evaluate an item with very worn stain, deduct from 60% to 75% from these prices.

Bowl, sauce; G color & mottling	350.00
Celery, EX stain, 6⅜"	800.00
Cruet, alabaster stopper & hdl, EX color & stain, 6"	1,300.00
Pitcher, sq mouth, reed hdl, EX mottle & stain, 7"	5,465.00
Shaker, pillar form, EX color & stain, 4", ea	2,070.00
Toothpick holder, crimped top, 2½"	425.00
Toothpick holder, cylindrical w/sq mouth, 2¼"	400.00
Toothpick holder, tricorner, EX mottling, 2⅜", from $525 to	625.00
Tumbler, lemonade; w/hdl, EX stain, 5"	1,750.00
Vase, lily; EX gold & stain, intense color, 6¾"	1,250.00
Vase, lily; in Cattail & Reed Tufts fr, 11"	1,500.00
Vase, lily; 3-fold rim, EX color & stain, 12"	975.00
Vase, much gold tracery, petal top, thin walls, 4½"	800.00
Vase, satin (rare), 3-fold rim, emb ring at neck, dk stain, 3¾"	1,750.00
Vase, 4-sided body w/lg rnd depressions, flared/crimped rim, 4½"	1,400.00

Agate Ware

Clays of various natural or artificially dyed colors combined to produce agate ware, a procedure similar to the methods used by Niloak in potting their Mission Ware. It was made by many Staffordshire potteries from about 1740 until about 1825.

Cheese dish, Copeland and Garrett, 1840s, 11¾" tall, $1,920.00. (Photo courtesy Skinner Inc. Auctioneers & Appraisers of Antiques & Fine Art)

Canister, tea; brn/cream/rust w/gr band, silver lid/neck, 5"	1,400.00
Cup & saucer, bls & brns, 2⅜", 4½"	1,995.00
Jardiniere, pearlware, brn tones/off-wht rim, Wedgwood, 3¾x5", EX	480.00
Sauceboat, 2-spout, Whieldon style, missing pc of rim, 7" L	1,600.00
Tankard, buff/iron red, 8-sided, 1760, 7"	7,650.00
Teapot, brn/bl, shell form, foo lion finial, serpent hdl, 5"	7,650.00
Teapot, brn/buff/rust w/gr trim, globular, early, 4½"	4,115.00
Teapot, scalloped shell form, griffin finial, 5", EX	3,000.00
Vase, gilt laurel hdls w/mask heads, w/lid, Wedgwood & Bentley, 12"	2,700.00
Vase, mc speckles, porphyry type, Ralph Wood, 9¼"	700.00
Vase, mc w/gilt-to-cream bird-form hdls & swags, Neale, w/lid, 13"	1,000.00
Vase, mc w/portrait/florets, gilt/cream hdls, bl plinth, 9"	700.00

Akro Agate

The Akro Agate Company operated in Clarksburg, West Virginia, from 1914 until 1951. In addition to their famous marbles, they also produced children's dishes and a general line consisting of vases, planters, and flowerpots in the garden line. They made ashtrays, bathroom fixtures, lamps, powder jars, bells, baskets, and candlesticks as well. Akro made a number of novelty items which were distributed in 5 & 10¢ stores such as Woolworth. Though many pieces are not marked, you will find some that bear their distinctive logo: a crow flying through the letter 'A' holding an Aggie in its beak and one in each claw. Some novelty items may instead carry one of these trademarks: 'J.V. Co., Inc.,' 'Braun & Corwin,' 'N.Y.C. Vogue Merc Co. U.S.A.,' 'Hamilton Match Co.,' and 'Mexicali Pickwick Cosmetic Corp.'

Color is a very important worth-assessing factor. Some pieces may be common in one color but rare in others. Occasionally an item will have exceptionally good colors, and this would make it more valuable than an example with only average color. When buying either marbles or juvenile tea sets in original boxes, be sure the box contains its original contents.

Note: Recently unearthed original written information has discounted the generally accepted attribution of the Chiquita and J.P. patterns to the Akro company, proving instead that they were made by the Alley Agate Company.

Due to the influence of eBay and other online auctions, the prices of children's dishes have fallen considerably over the past few years, with only the rare boxed sets retaining their higher values.

For more information we recommend *The Complete Line of the Akro Agate Co.* by our advisors, Roger and Claudia Hardy (available from the authors); they are listed in the Directory under West Virginia. Our advisor for miscellaneous Akro Agate is Albert Morin, who is listed in the Directory under Massachusetts. See also Marbles.

Concentric Rib

Creamer, lt bl, 1⁵⁄₁₆"	16.00
Cup, purple, 1⁵⁄₁₆"	60.00
Pitcher, dk or med bl, 3¼"	32.00
Plate, dk gr, 3¼"	3.00
Saucer, wht, 2¾"	3.00
Sugar bowl, pk or dk ivory, 1⁵⁄₁₆"	20.00
Teapot, orange, 2⅜"	48.00
Teapot lid, pk or dk ivory, 2⁵⁄₁₆"	12.00
Tumbler, wht, 2"	6.00

Concentric Ring

Creamer, ivory or wht, 1⅜"	16.00
Creamer, royal bl, 1⁹⁄₁₆"	32.00
Cup, bl & wht marbleized, 1⁹⁄₁₆", from $90 to	100.00
Cup, purple, 1⅜"	60.00
Pitcher, bl transparent, 2⅞"	60.00
Plate, apple or dk gr, 3⁵⁄₁₆"	3.00
Plate, apple or dk gr, 4¼"	20.00
Sugar bowl, bl transparent, 1⁹⁄₁₆"	60.00
Sugar bowl, med or royal bl, 1⅜"	16.00
Teapot, med or royal bl, 2⅜"	50.00
Teapot lid, bl & wht marbleized, 2¹¹⁄₁₆"	20.00
Tumbler, bl transparent, 2"	26.00

Interior Panel

Cereal, dk gr, 16 panels, 3⅜"	24.00
Creamer, canary yel, 18 panels, 1⁵⁄₁₆"	55.00
Creamer, pk, 16 panels, 1½"	35.00
Creamer, royal bl, 18 panels, 1⁵⁄₁₆"	34.00
Cup, orange, 16 panels, 1½"	24.00
Plate, canary yel, 18 panels, 3⁵⁄₁₆"	16.00
Plate, dk gr (lustre), 16 panels, 4¼"	16.00
Plate, pk (lustre), 18 panels, 3⁵⁄₁₆"	12.00

Saucer, royal bl, 16 panels, 3¼" 12.00
Sugar bowl, gr & wht marbleized, 18 panels, 1⁵⁄₁₆" ... 32.00
Teapot, royal bl, 16 panels, 2¾" 65.00
Teapot, topaz transparent, 18 panels, 2½" 34.00
Teapot lid, ivory, 16 panels, 2¹¹⁄₁₆" 20.00
Tumbler, gr transparent 15.00

Miss America

Boxed set, red onyx, 8-pc (serves 4) 700.00
Boxed set, wht, 11-pc 632.00
Creamer, red transparent, 1⁹⁄₁₆" 160.00
Cup, wht, 1⁹⁄₁₆" 38.00
Plate, gr transparent, 4½" 40.00
Plate, red onyx, 4½" 60.00
Saucer, wht w/decal, 3⅝" 23.00
Sugar bowl, wht w/decal, 1⁹⁄₁₆" 60.00
Sugar bowl lid, wht, 2⅝" 40.00
Teapot, gr transparent, 2½" 100.00

Octagonal

Cereal, wht or ivory, 3⅜" 15.00
Creamer, canary yel, closed hdl, 1½" 20.00
Creamer, pale bl, open hdl, 1¼" 24.00
Cup, med or dk bl, 1½" 12.00
Cup, orange, open hdl, 1¼" 32.00
Pitcher, med or dk bl, open hdl, 2¾" 34.00
Saucer, canary yel, 2¾" 10.00
Saucer, pk, 3⅜" 8.00

Set, 21-piece, mixed solid colors, service for four plus teapot with lid, pitcher, creamer, and sugar bowl, large, MIB, $450.00. (Photo courtesy Roger and Claudia Hardy)

Sugar bowl, wht or ivory, closed hdls, 1½" 16.00
Teapot, orange, closed hdl, 3⅝" 60.00
Teapot, pale bl, open hdl, 3⅜" 32.00
Tumbler, canary yel, 2" 16.00

Raised Daisy

Creamer, dk ivory, 1⁵⁄₁₆" 100.00
Cup, dk gr, 1⁵⁄₁₆" 32.00
Pitcher/teapot, Daisy, dk turq or dk bl, 2⅜" 34.00
Saucer, lt or dk yel, 2½" 12.00
Sugar bowl, dk turq or dk bl, 1⁵⁄₁₆" 85.00
Teapot, dk turq or dk bl, w/lid, 2½" 60.00
Tumbler, Daisy, dk ivory, 2" 30.00
Tumbler, plain, dk turq or dk bl, 2" 85.00

Stacked Disk

Creamer, pk or dk ivory, 1⁵⁄₁₆" 20.00

Cup, dk gr, 1⁵⁄₁₆" 6.00
Pitcher, med or dk bl, 2⅞" 68.00
Sugar bowl, dk gr, 1⁵⁄₁₆" 12.00
Teapot, wht, 2⅜" 16.00
Tumbler, canary yel, 2" 8.00

Stacked Disk and Interior Panel

Cereal, dk gr, 3⅜" 40.00
Creamer, gr transparent, 1⅜" 40.00
Cup, orange, 1⁹⁄₁₆" 32.00
Pitcher, bl transparent, 2⅞" 60.00
Sugar bowl, bl or wht marbleized, 1⅜" 70.00
Teapot, med or royal bl, 2⅜" 100.00
Tumbler, ivory or wht, 2" 85.00

Stippled Band

Creamer, gr transparent, 1¼" 68.00
Pitcher, gr transparent, 2⅞" 32.00
Saucer, topaz transparent, 3¼" 6.00
Sugar bowl, gr transparent, 1½" 40.00
Teapot lid, azure bl transparent, 2⅝" 140.00
Tumbler, azure bl transparent, 2⅛" 160.00
Tumbler, topaz transparent, 1¾" 12.00

Miscellaneous

Ashtray, orange & wht, from $75 to 90.00
Basket, #328, hdls, from $40 to 45.00
Bowl, blk or marbleized, ftd 600.00
Candlestick, Short Ribbed, mk 800.00
Creamer, pk 350.00
Finger bowl 200.00
Jar, cold cream; blk 55.00
Jar, powder; #323, marbleized 40.00
Jar, powder; #323, solid colors or crystal 100.00
Jar, powder; #760 Type II, solid colors, from $45 to 50.00
Jar, powder; Ribbed, bl transparent 90.00
Jardiniere, solid colors, bell shape, from $65 to 85.00
Mug, shaving; blk, Vivaudou 45.00
Pin tray, crystal 100.00
Pitcher, lg 1,500.00
Planter, #650, blk 500.00
Puff box, Colonial lady, amber 1,500.00
Puff box, Scottie dog, dk gr 400.00
Sawtooth jar, orange or yel, from $300 to 450.00
Sugar bowl, marbleized, lg 500.00
Sugar bowl, pk 200.00
Tumbler 65.00

Alexandrite

Alexandrite is a type of art glass introduced around the turn of the century by Thomas Webb and Sons of England. It is recognized by its characteristic shading, pale yellow to rose and blue at the edge of the item. Although other companies (Moser, for example) produced glass they called Alexandrite, only examples made by Webb possess all the described characteristics and command premium prices. Amount and intensity of blue determines value. Our prices are for items with good average intensity, unless otherwise noted.

Bowl, slightly ruffled edge, shallow, 5" 400.00

Compote, Honeycomb, petal rim, wide amber ft, 5½" dia........2,070.00
Cordial, bl rim to amber bowl, stem & ft, lt ribbing, 3"................635.00
Finger bowl, Honeycomb, ruffled, +5¾" underplate..................2,130.00
Finger bowl, wide cupped pie-crust ruffle rim, 5".....................1,095.00
Hat, deep bl rim shading to amber at bottom, ground pontil, 2¾"...1,265.00
Vase, cylindrical w/ruffled top, 2½"..1,095.00
Vase, Dmn Quilt, bulbous w/ruffled rim, 3"..............................1,095.00

Almanacs

The earliest evidence indicates that almanacs were used as long ago as ancient Egypt. Throughout the Dark Ages they were circulated in great volume and were referred to by more people than any other book except the Bible. *The Old Farmer's Almanac* first appeared in 1793 and has been issued annually since that time. Usually more of a pamphlet than a book (only a few have hard covers), the almanac provided planting and harvesting information to farmers, weather forecasts for seamen, medical advice, household hints, mathematical tutoring, postal rates, railroad schedules, weights and measures, 'receipts,' and jokes. Before 1800 the information was unscientific and based entirely on astrology and folklore. The first almanac in America was printed in 1639 by William Pierce Mariner; it contained data of this nature. One of the best-known editions, Ben Franklin's *Poor Richard's Almanac,* was introduced in 1732 and continued to be printed for 25 years.

By the nineteenth century, merchants saw the advertising potential in a publication so widely distributed, and the advertising almanac evolved. These were distributed free of charge by drugstores and mercantiles and were usually somewhat lacking in information, containing simply a calendar, a few jokes, and a variety of ads for quick remedies and quack cures.

Today their concept and informative, often amusing, text make almanacs popular collectibles that may usually be had at reasonable prices. Because they were printed in such large numbers and often saved from year to year, their prices are still low. Most fall within a range of $4.00 to $15.00. Very common examples may be virtually worthless; those printed before 1860 are especially collectible. Quite rare and highly prized are the Kate Greenaway 'Almanacks,' printed in London from 1883 to 1897. These are illustrated with her drawings of children, one for each calendar month. See also Kate Greenaway.

1915, Barker's Illustrated Almanac, EX, $25.00. (Photo courtesy Frank Daniels)

1755, Rider's, unusual red & wht print, 80+ pg, pocket sz, EX.......55.00
1785, Bickerstaff Astonomical Diary, 22-pg, 6¼x3½", G................90.00
1798, Thomas Almanack, string bound, 4x6", VG........................58.00
1808, New York & Vermont Almanac, string bound, 30-pg, 4½x7", VG....25.00
1809, Farmer's Almanack, Robert B Thomas, 1st ed, 24-pg, VG...38.00
1812, Farmer's Calendar, A Beers, softcover, 16-pg, EX................30.00
1866, Magnetic Almanac, D Ransom & Co, softcover, 36-pg, EX....31.00

1873, National Elgin Watch Co, illustrated, EX............................31.00
1901, Almanack, Joseph Whitaker, hardcover, leather spine, 776-pg, VG....25.00
1905, Rational Almanac, bl cloth w/gold gilt, 474-pg, 4x9½", EX...30.00
1907, Wilson's Monarch Almanac, red cover, 64-pg, 9¼x6¼", EX..30.00
1909, Eagle Almanac, red hardcover, 600+ pg, 6x9", EX..............30.00
1915, British Journal Photographic Almanac, 1066-pg, 7¼x5", EX..25.00
1915, Watkins Almanac, Home Doctor..., color cover, 96-pg, EX.27.00
1917, World Almanac & Encyclopedia, color cover, 944-pg, VG..31.00
1929, Peter Rabbit's Almanac, c F Warn 1928, 1st ed, VG..........245.00
1930, Swamp-Root Almanac, Dr Kilmer & Co, color cover, 36-pg, EX..25.00
1968, Jim Garrison's Investigation, 1st ed, softcover, 29-pg, EX.....65.00

Aluminum

Aluminum, though being the most abundant metal in the earth's crust, always occurs in combination with other elements. Before a practical method for its refinement was developed in the late nineteenth century, articles made of aluminum were very expensive. After the process for commercial smelting was perfected in 1916, it became profitable to adapt the ductile, nontarnishing material to many uses.

By the late '30s, novelties, trays, pitchers, and many other tableware items were being produced. They were often handcrafted with elaborate decoration. Russel Wright designed a line of lovely pieces such as lamps, vases, and desk accessories that are becoming very collectible. Many who crafted the ware marked it with their company logo, and these signed pieces are attracting the most interest. Wendell August Forge (Grove City, PA) is a mark to watch for; this firm was the first to produce hammered aluminum (it is still made there today), and some of their examples are particularly nice. Upwardly mobile market values reflect their popularity with today's collectors. In general, 'spun' aluminum is from the '30s or early '40s, and 'hammered' aluminum is from the '30s to the '60s.

An excellent reference is *Hammered Aluminum, Hand Wrought Collectibles,* by our advisor, Dannie Woodard; she is listed in the Directory under Texas.

Basket, hammered, divided glass insert, rectangular, 3x7x5"..........25.00
Bowl, anodized purple w/grape clusters, West Bend, 3x14"............17.50
Bowl, cereal; anodized, Bascal, 2x5¼", set of 4.............................25.00
Butter dish, bamboo on lid, Everlast BB55, 7½" L.........................16.00
Cake cover, wooden hdl, 5¾x10", +clear glass 11¼" plate.............20.00
Candy dish, decor base & lid, red Bakelite finial, 4½" dia..............10.00
Canister set, spun body w/gold anodized lids, blk knobs, Italy, 5 for...15.00
Coasters, anodized, oak leaves, West Bend, set of 4........................16.00
Cocktail shaker, anodized gr & gold, 9¾".....................................20.00
Coffee/tea set, wooden hdls, Picquot Ware, 2 coffee+1 teapot, +cr/sug.70.00
Condiments, 2 glass dishes w/aluminum lids & plastic spoons on tray...25.00
Cup, collapsible; star on lid, 2¾x2⅝"..18.00
Ice bucket, hinged, use hdl to open/close, EE65-01, 12½".............25.00
Ice bucket, knight's helmet form, Japan, 11½x13x7½".................85.00
Jars/shakers, pk anodized w/glass tops, RCA Whirlpool, 8 on rack...32.00
Lazy Suzan, 3 plastic Melmac inserts, West Bend, 20" dia, NM.....35.00
Leaf nappy, curled form w/vein details, Buenilum, 6x6½"+hdl......16.00
Nappy, pine cone, scalloped, coiled hdl..10.00
Nut server, hammered, tools in center, ring hdls, 14"....................25.00
Pitcher, champagne anodized w/blk plastic Deco hdl, Regal Ware, 8".28.00
Pitcher, cylindrical, tubular twisted hdl, Buenilum, 8x4¼"............20.00
Pitcher, gold anodized, ice lip, Color Craft, 7½"...........................22.00
Pitcher, pk anodized, cylindrical, Color Craft, 4¾x2½"..................15.00
Plate, birds at birdhouse, Wendell August Forge, 4½".....................20.00
Relish tray, glass insert, fruit on lid, shaped hdl, Cromwell............25.00
Shakers, blk plastic lids, on 4-leg wht plastic stand, 3-pc set..........12.00
Silent butler, hinged lid, Everlast, #552......................................35.00
Tidbit, 2-tier, hammered, Everlast EM6, plastic finial, 8x8"..........25.00

Tidbit, 3-tier, anodized w/C-hdl, base: 11" dia 55.00
Tidbit, 3-tier, top tray w/3 shallow compartments, 16x12" 25.00
Tray, berries & pears at rim w/pie-crust edge, Everlast, 15½" 25.00
Tray, bread; tulips, ornate hdls, Rodney Kent #404, 14x8" 20.00
Tray, floral, twisted hdls, Cromwell, 18x12½" 25.00
Tray, floral sprigs & buds, 8½" 3-part glass insert, 14" dia 15.00
Tray, grapes & trailing vines, hdls, Everlast #468, 16x12" 30.00
Tray, ivy & roses on hammered ground, hdls, Everlast, 15¾x9½" .. 20.00
Tray, roses, 3-compartment, Continental #737, 11¾x6" 17.50
Tray, sailboats (5), pierced hdls, Wendell August Forge, 18x12" 55.00
Tray, tulips on hammered ground, hdls, Rodney Kent, 10x14" 50.00
Water set, anodized, Color Craft, 7½" pitcher+8 5" tumblers+carrier....80.00

AMACO, American Art Clay Co.

AMACO is the logo of the American Art Clay Co. Inc., founded in Indianapolis, Indiana, in 1919, by Ted O. Philpot. They produced a line of art pottery from 1931 through 1938. The company is still in business but now produces only supplies, implements, and tools for the ceramic trade.

Values for AMACO have risen sharply, especially those for figurals, items with Art Deco styling, and pieces with uncommon shapes. Our advisors for this category are Suzanne Perrault and David Rago; they are listed in the Directory under New Jersey.

Bust, woman w/head trn, 3 long curls at nape, wht gloss, #158, 8" 100.00
Sculpture, woman's head, hair pulled bk, ivory gloss, 7" 390.00
Sculpture, woman's head, long hair w/flipped ends, bl gloss, label, 7" ...390.00
Vase, bl mottle, incurvate rim, 4" 40.00
Vase, stylized trees, bl on red, sgn EA, #31, 7", EX 150.00

Amberina

Amberina, one of the earliest types of art glass, was developed in 1883 by Joseph Locke of the New England Glass Company. The trademark was registered by W.L. Libbey, who often signed his name in script within the pontil.

Amberina was made by adding gold powder to the batch, which produced glass in the basic amber hue. Part of the item, usually the top, was simply reheated to develop the characteristic deep red or fuchsia shading. Early amberina was mold-blown, but cut and pressed amberina was also produced. The rarest type is plated amberina, made by New England for a short time after 1886. It has been estimated that less than 2,000 pieces were ever produced. Other companies, among them Hobbs and Brockunier, Mt. Washington Glass Company, and Sowerby's Ellison Glassworks of England, made their own versions, being careful to change the name of their product to avoid infringing on Libbey's patent. Prices realized at auction seem to be erratic, to say the least, and dealers appear to be 'testing the waters' with prices that start out very high only to be reduced later if the item does not sell at the original asking price. Lots of amberina glassware is of a more recent vintage — look for evidence of an early production, since the later wares are worth much less than glassware that can be attributed to the older makers. Generic amberina with hand-painted flowers will bring lower prices as well. Our values are taken from auction results and dealer lists, omitting the extremely high and low ends of the range.

Bottle, scent; optic ribs, ftd baluster w/4-fold rim, Libbey, 8" 1,500.00
Celery vase, Dmn Quilt, scalloped rim, 6½" 285.00
Celery vase, internal Dmn Quilt, scalloped rim, NE, 6" 460.00
Creamer & sugar bowl, Invt T'print, sq mouth, amber reed hdls, 4½" .. 750.00
Cruet, Invt T'print, onion body/short neck, faceted amber stopper, 6" ...230.00

Finger bowl, ruffled/scalloped, NE, 5" 200.00
Lamp, ovoid ruffled shade; rtcl metal base mk Pat Aug 4 1896, 23" .1,000.00
Pitcher, Coin Spot, bulbous, sq mouth, amber hdl, Hobbs Brockunier, 8" ...230.00
Pitcher, Dmn Optic 10-lobe cylindrical body, sq mouth, clear hdl, 10" ..285.00
Pitcher, Dmn Quilt, melon rib, clear reed hdl, 8" 145.00
Pitcher, Hobnail, rnd w/sq mouth, Hobbs Brockunier, 8" 400.00
Pitcher, Lincoln Drape, amber reed hdl, Phoenix 7" 175.00
Pitcher, optic ribs, amber hdl, 7¾" 145.00
Pitcher, optic ribs, pk flowers/gold tracery, amber hdl, 10" 435.00
Pitcher, tankard; Invt T'print, reed hdl, 8", NM 230.00
Shakers, bl floral, 5", pr; in rtcl Aurora SP caddy w/appl leaves ... 400.00
Spoon holder, Invt T'print insert; Aurora 2-hdl/ftd SP fr w/floral, 6" .. 4,250.00
Vase, bud; optic ribs, #3008, Libbey, 9" 725.00
Vase, diagonal swirls, amber rigaree rim, trumpet neck, Harrach, 10" ...175.00
Vase, Dmn Quilt, raspberry prunts/rigaree bands, pinched sides, NE, 8" ..1,840.00
Vase, Dmn Quilt, U-form w/3-fold rim, 3 reeded ft, NE, 6" 635.00
Vase, lily; optic ribs, ruffled rim, Libbey, 10½" 400.00
Vase, lily; 3-fold rim, ftd 8" 165.00
Vase, swans in relief, rectangular w/4 upright scallops, NE, 5" 1,200.00
Vase, swirled, amber rigaree/hdls, urn form, Harrach, 12½" 250.00
Vase, T'print & Coinspot patterns, amber rigaree collar, 3" 450.00

Plated Amberina

Bride's basket, 5-lobe rim, 8"; in James W Tufts fr w/rtcl hdls/ft 10,000.00
Celery vase, EX color, 6" 7,000.00
Cruet, amber hdl, faceted stopper, 7", from $4,600 to 5,200.00

Finger bowl, 12-crimp rim, fuchsia with rare green tint to ribs, 2¾x5¼", $6,750.00.

(Photo courtesy Early Auction Co.)

Pitcher, tankard; w/label, 8½" 28,000.00
Punch cup, amber loop hdl, 2½" 2,585.00
Syrup pitcher, mfg flaw, SP flip lid, 6"; on James W Tufts tray....2,000.00
Tumbler, EX color, 3¾" 2,200.00
Tumbler, lemonade; appl hdl, 5" 3,500.00
Vase, lily; in James W Tufts holder w/3-D eagle on rock, 12"....1,850.00
Vase, 4 pinched sides, tightly ruffled/flared 4-lobe rim, 4" 27,600.00

American Indian Art

That time when the American Indian was free to practice the crafts and culture that was his heritage has always held a fascination for many. They were a people who appreciated beauty of design and colorful decoration in their furnishings and clothing; and because instruction in their crafts was a routine part of their rearing, they were well accomplished. Several tribes developed areas in which they excelled. The Navajo were weavers and silversmiths, the Zuni, lapidaries. Examples of their craftsmanship are very valuable. Today even the work of contemporary Indian artists — weavers, silversmiths, carvers, and others — is highly collectible. Unless otherwise noted, values are for items with no obvious damage or excessive wear (EX/NM). For a more thorough study we recommend *Arrowheads and Projectile Points; Indian Artifacts of the Midwest Books I through V; Indian Trade Relics; Paleo-Indian Artifacts; Ornamental Indian Artifacts; Antler, Bone and Shell Artifacts; Rare and Unusual Indian Artifacts;* and *Indian Artifacts: The Best of the Midwest*, all by Lar Hothem (Collector Books).

Key:
bw — beadwork   p-h — prehistoric
COA — Certificate of Authenticity   s-s — sinew sewn
dmn — diamond

Apparel and Accessories

Before the white traders brought the Indian women cloth from which to sew their garments and beads to use for decorating them, clothing was made from skins sewn together with sinew, usually made of animal tendon. Porcupine quills were dyed bright colors and woven into bags and armbands and used to decorate clothing and moccasins. Examples of early quillwork are scarce today and highly collectible.

Early in the nineteenth century, beads were being transported via pony pack trains. These 'pony' beads were irregular shapes of opaque glass imported from Venice. Nearly always blue or white, they were twice as large as the later 'seed' beads. By 1870 translucent beads in many sizes and colors had been made available, and Indian beadwork had become commercialized. Each tribe developed its own distinctive methods and preferred decorations, making it possible for collectors today to determine the origin of many items. Soon after the turn of the century, the craft of beadworking began to diminish.

Belt, loom bw, mtd on leather, studs down sides, 1940s, 46x4" 125.00
Belt, Plateau, floral bw on hide, 1940s-50s, 3½x34" 110.00
Dress, Jicarilla Apache child's, hide w/bw front/bk, 1960s-70s, 40" .. 225.00
Dress, regular & tube bw on tanned hide, fringe, 1940s-50s, 43" ... 250.00
Dress, S Plains, hide w/bw/tin cone drips/yel ochre, 1950s, 32" ... 225.00
Gauntlets, Kutenai, full floral bw, 1950s, 15½x7" 175.00
Hat, Iroquois, geometric & floral bw allover, 1890-1900s, 3x10x6" ... 525.00
Kilt, Hopi, cotton w/wool embr, 1930s, 19x44" 225.00
Leggings, Cheyenne, lazy stitch bw/gr ochre/fringe, 1900s, 35" .. 1,300.00
Leggings, Cheyenne woman's, bw on hide, 1920s, 16x7" 350.00
Leggings, Plains, bw strips on rainbow bl stroud, 1920s, 25x12" .. 150.00
Leggings, Plains, floral bw on bl stroud, 1900s, 25x18", VG 325.00
Leggings, S Plains, tanned leather w/ochre-dyed fringe, 1900s, 32" . 850.00
Moccasins, Apache, full bw uppers, 1920s, 10" 1,300.00
Moccasins, Apache, high-top yel ochred hide w/hard soles, 1940s, 10" . 175.00
Moccasins, Cheyenne, tan w/toe bw, parfleche soles, 1900-10, 10" 450.00
Moccasins, Plains, hide w/bw, s-s, hard soles, 1940s, 11x4" 325.00
Moccasins, Plateau, high-top, floral w/bw on hide, 1940s, 12x9". 165.00
Moccasins, S Cheyenne, full bw upper & tongues, hard soles, 1930s, 9".. 200.00
Moccasins, S Plains, full bw uppers, parfleche soles, 1890s-1900s, 9".750.00
Skirt & blouse, Apache, hide w/bw/tin cones, 1950s.................... 500.00

Bags and Cases

The Indians used bags for many purposes, and most display excellent form and workmanship. Of the types listed below, many collectors consider the pipe bag to be the most desirable form. Pipe bags were long, narrow, leather and bead or quillwork creations made to hold tobacco in a compartment at the bottom and the pipe, with the bowl removed from the stem, in the top. Long buckskin fringe was used as trim and complemented the quilled and beaded design to make the bag a masterpiece of Indian art.

Apache, dice type, bw front & bk, beaded fringe, 1930s, 8½x5½" ..200.00
Great Lakes, bw front & bk, beaded fringe, 1900s, 8x6"............... 325.00
Muscalero Apache, pouch, overal bw, tin cones on hide, 1920s, 6" dia.. 500.00
Plains, bow case, hide w/s-s wrapped hdl, 1920s, 34", w/45" long bow.... 750.00
Sioux, awl case, bw on hide w/horsehair & tin cone drops, 1900s, 16"... 425.00
Sioux, pipe, tab style w/bw, hide is dirty, 1920s, 19x6" 350.00

Baskets

In the following listings, examples are coil built unless noted otherwise.

Apache, burden, band design, hide fringe, cloth bottom, 1940s, 11x16" .300.00
Apache, burden, hide & tin cone decor, 1940s, 9x11" 125.00
Apache, tray, eagle & stick figures, 1940s, 2x10½" 275.00
Apache, tray, 3-color star design, 1920s, 15" dia.......................... 550.00
Chickasaw, box, plaited weave, oblong, 1920s-30s, 9x21x13"...... 125.00
Hopi, bowl, 3rd Mesa wicker, loop hdls, 1930s, 5x8" 150.00
Hopi, plaque, 2nd Mesa, geometrics, 1950-60s, 14"................... 150.00
Hopi, tray, 3rd Mesa wicker, eagle design, 1920s-30s, 15" 200.00
Jicarilla, cylinder, 3-color geometrics, fading, 1920-30s, 14x11" .. 125.00
Klamath, bowl, dbl-band design, 1920s, 5x8" 250.00
Klikitat, burden, faded gr geometrics/gr humans, 1920s, 11x11x9" 250.00
Maidu, bowl, geometrics, rim stitch loss, 1930s, 2¾x4" 525.00
Mission, bowl, variegated juncos/mud-dyed design, 3½x7½x5".... 450.00
Mono, bowl, dbl-band design, 1910-20s, 5½x12½"...................... 750.00
Mowhawk, purse, blk ash splint, sweet grass hdl, 1960s, 9½x4½".. 100.00
Navajo, bowl, wedding pattern, 1950s, 2½x13" 95.00
Nootka/Maka, hat, whale & bird design, w/straps, 1930s, 7x13".. 500.00
Panamint, bowl, mc stair steps, rim ticking, sm losses, 1910-20s, 3x5" ... 400.00
Papago, olla, rattlesnake & bug, 1970s, 3½x4" 250.00
Papago, tray, 3-color friendship/man-in-maze, M Chico, 1960s, 2x16" ..275.00
Pima, bowl, geometrics, minor stitch loss, 1920s-30s, 4½x11½" .. 475.00
Pima, bowl, star design, minor stitch loss, 1920s, 2x7" 325.00
Pima, olla, geometrics/coyote tracks, 1910s-20s, 7½x5", VG 150.00
Pitt River, bowl, star/stylized butterfly, 1940s-50s, 3½x6"............ 300.00
Pitt River, bowl, twine weave, serrated design, 1910s-20s, 6x8".... 750.00
Quiver, Klamath, serrated bands, 18x9" 1,200.00
Salish, cone, burden type, missing loops on rim, 1930s, 12x12"....400.00
Tillamook, bottle, dog & human, woven over wine bottle, 1890s, 9"... 1,300.00
Tlingit, cylinder, woven cedar, band design, 1900s, 10x9½", EX . 325.00

Tlingit, twined basket with stair-step design, ca 1920, 9x10", $1,600.00.
(Photo courtesy Allard Auctions Inc.)

Tulare, bowl, mc geometrics, 1920s-30s, 2½x8" 425.00
Tulare, tray, gambling, mc bands, gap stitch, 1900s, 18½", +dice. 900.00
W Apache, tray, eagle/star/coyote tracks, 1950s, 2½x12" 400.00
Yavapai Apache, tray, star & stick figures, V Valonte, 1980s, 2x12" ..625.00
Yokuts, bowl, mc stylized butterflies, 1910-20s, 4x6" 700.00

Blades and Points

Relics of this type usually display characteristics of a general area, time period, or a particular location. With study, those made by the Plains Indians are easily discerned from those of the west coast. Because modern man has imitated the art of the Indian by reproducing these artifacts through modern means, use caution before investing your money in 'too good to be authentic' specimens. For a more thorough study we recommend *Arrowheads and Projectile Points*, *Paleo-Indian Artifacts*, and *Indian Artifacts of the Midwest, Books I* through *V*, by Lar Hothem.

Adena pre-form, gray flint, early Woodland, IN/IL, 4½x22⅞" 200.00
Clovis, mc chert, early Paleo, IA, 2¼x1" 400.00
Clovis, red-brn Carter Co flint, thin, early Paleo, KY, 2¹/₁₆x⅞"......1,000.00
Dalton Lanceolate, sugar quartzite, late Paleo, MO, 4⅝x1¾"....... 700.00

Etley, Burlington chert, ca 1500 BC, OH, 5" 325.00
Hardin, barbed, Burlington chert, early Archaic, 3¼" 300.00
Hopewell, hornstone, mid-Woodland, OH, 4½x1¾" 1,500.00
Pine Tree, greatly resharpened, early Archaic, KY, 2x1" 100.00
Stemmed, gray flint, EX chipping, Archaic, 2¼x½" 100.00
Stemmed, pale flint or chert, late Archaic, KY, 2½x1¼" 100.00
Thebes, IN gr flint, resharpened, early Archaic, IN, 3¼x1⅞"....... 450.00
Thebes, patinated gray/tan Upper Mercer, early Archaic, OH, 2⅞"...250.00
Turkeytail, red ochre/Wyandotte flint, early Woodland, 4x1½" ... 325.00

Ceremonial Items

Arm bands, N Plains, full bw, quill wrapped/cone drops, 1890s, 2x11"... 350.00
Dance club, Plains, wood w/yel ochre/bw medicine charm, 1900s, 27" .. 400.00
Dance drum, Kiowa, pnt heads (1 split), 1940s, 9x18" 200.00
Dance kilt, Hopi, cotton/wool w/embr & ribbon, 1967, 23x44" .. 200.00
Dance kilt, Pueblo, pnt serpents on red hide/cone drops, 1950s, 33x47" .. 200.00
Dance mask, NW Coast, thinly cvd cedar, 1970s, 10x8x5" 325.00
Dance outfit, hide w/deer tails/cones, top/skirt/belt/scarf, 1950s .. 350.00
Dance outfit, Mescalero Apache, bw skirt/top w/fringe/cones, 1950s.. 650.00
Dance rattle, NW Coast, Man of See cvd in cedar, R Hunt, 1970s, 10x4"..325.00
Dance shirt, Apache, yel ochred hide w/studs/beads/cones, 1950s ..400.00
Dance yoke, Sioux, floral bw on navy bl, 1930s, 15x17" 275.00
Drum, Plains, pnt hide over old cheese container, 1920s, 2x13".. 350.00
Gan mask, Apache, pine slats w/butterflies, rpl face cover, 1950s, 42".. 650.00
Headdress, Sioux, feathers/ermine tail drops, bw headband, 1950s, 34"..1,400.00
Mask, Iroquois, hand-woven corn husks, 1930s, 12x9x2"............. 250.00
Roach, Plains, porcupine hair w/horsehair trim, felt base, 1900s, 12" ... 875.00

Dolls

Cheyenne, bw on commercial hide outfit, yarn hair, 1940s, 13½"... 160.00
Hopi, Kachina, Buffalo Dancer, Yowytewa, 1980s, 13" 150.00
Hopi, Kachina, Cicada, EX details, Grover, 1970s, 16" 130.00
Hopi, Kachina, Eagle Dancer, Less David, 1970s, 20" 100.00
Hopi, Kachina, Hemis, Pattucio, 1970s-80s, 22½" 250.00
Hopi, Kachina, Piggyback Mudhead Dancer w/drum, 1950s, 15"....425.00
Hopi, Kachina, pnt cottonwood root, lg tabletta, early/mid-1900s, 21" .. 650.00
Hopi, Kachina, White Bear, 1-pc, H Sehongda, 1970s-80s, 12"... 425.00
Plains, bw on hide, horsehair braids, cloth leggings, 1920s-30s, 13"...450.00

Ute, beaded hide and cloth female doll, beaded moccasins, plaited horsehair, ca 1900, 21", $550.00. (Photo courtesy Jackson's International Auctioneers & Appraisers of Fine Art & Antiques)

Domestics

Blanket, Navajo, Moki style, indigo bl stripes, 1870s-80s, 74x48", VG .. 550.00
Cradleboard, Apache, yucca slat/visor/yel canvas cover, 1920s, 40" 500.00
Cradleboard, Chippewa, bw velvet wraps, attached amulet, 1950s, 32".950.00

Cradleboard, Paiute, sun visor, yarn design, hide cover, 1930s, 39".........400.00
Cradleboard, Paiute, wicker sun visor/floral bw, 1950s, doll sz, 11"..........100.00
Cradleboard, Paiute, wicker sun visor/loom bw/hide cover, 1960s, 17" ..135.00
Cradleboard, Sioux, buffalo hide w/bw, quills/feathers/bells, 1870s 3,750.00
Picture frame, Plains, loom bw, cloth bk, native photo, 1920s, 7x6".......125.00

Jewelry and Adornments

As early as 500 A.D., Indians in the southwest drilled turquoise nuggets and strung them on cords made of sinew or braided hair. The Spanish introduced them to coral, and it became a popular item of jewelry; abalone and clam shells were favored by the Coastal Indians. Not until the last half of the nineteenth century did the Indians learn to work with silver. Each tribe developed its own distinctive style and preferred design, which until about 1920 made it possible to determine tribal origin with some degree of accuracy. Since that time, because of modern means of communication and travel, motifs have become less distinct.

Quality Indian silver jewelry may be antique or contemporary. Age, though certainly to be considered, is not as important a factor as fine workmanship and good stones. Pre-1910 silver will show evidence of hammer marks, and designs are usually simple. Beads have sometimes been shaped from coins. Stones tend to be small; when silver wire was used, it is usually square. To insure your investment, choose a reputable dealer.

Belt, Navajo, 7 2½x2" silver conchos, fancy buckle, 1930s, 29"... 400.00
Bracelet, Navajo, floral design w/dome centers, 1940s, 1" W 85.00
Bracelet, Navajo, silver cuff w/bump outs/Xd arrows/etc, 1930s, ¾" W ..150.00
Bracelet, Navajo, silver cuff w/oval turq stone, 1950s, 1½" W 100.00
Bracelet, NW Coast, silver w/cvd eagle/X-hatching, 1960s,½" W ..150.00
Bracelet, Zuni, silver w/2 rows of 24 sq natural turq, 1940s,½" W ... 150.00
Bracelet, Zuni, silver w/90 sq inlaid turq stones, 1950s, 1" W 275.00
Brooch, Navajo, silver bow shape w/natural turq, hand cut, 3½x2" ...160.00
Buckle, Apache, brass w/metal studs, Haozous, 1970s, 4" dia....... 325.00
Buckle, Navajo, sand-cast silver w/turq in center, 1960s, 2½x3½" ..200.00
Necklace, Pueblo, natural turq beads/nuggets, 1930s-40s, 24" 350.00
Necklace, Pueblo, 3 strands natural turq & shell heshi, 1940s, 27".. 125.00
Necklace, Pueblo, 3 strands of coral/silver beads, 1950s, 22" 100.00
Necklace, Pueblo, 5 strands of tube coral beads/turq, 1960s, 28"... 700.00
Necklace, Pueblo, 92 natural turq stones spaced w/shells, 1950s, 24" ... 225.00
Necklace, Santo Domingo, 10 strands of jet/shell heshi, 1970s, 27" ..375.00
Pendant, sand-cast silver w/kachina face design, 1970s, 2½" 50.00
Squash blossom, Bisbee turq set in silver, bow style, 1960s, 23" ... 500.00
Watchband, Navajo, silver w/appl thunderbird, stamped decor, ¾" W..75.00

Pipes

Pipe bowls were usually carved from soft stone, such as catlinite or red pipestone, an argilaceous sedimentary rock composed mainly of hardened clay. Steatite was also used. Some ceremonial pipes were simply styled, while others were intricately designed naturalistic figurals, sometimes in bird or frog forms called effigies. Their stems, made of wood and often covered with leather, were sometimes nearly a yard in length.

Bird effigy, blk steatite, Woodland, sm rstr, 1¾x3⅞" 1,800.00
Elbow type, close-grained limestone, Mississippian, KY, 2¼x3⅛"....850.00
Frog effigy, Niagara limestone, Mississippian, 1¾x2½" 3,600.00
Hopewell, platform type, grit-tempered pottery, Woodland, 3½" L.. 1,000.00
Micmac type, close-grained gray stone, late Mississippian, 2½x2"...500.00
Plains, lead inlaid T bowl, wood stem w/bw/lead/cone drops, 1930s, 28"... 575.00
Sioux, pipestone T-bowl, cvd wood stem, 1930s-40s, 32x3" 200.00
Tomahawk type, pewter head, tin cone drops on hdl, 1890s, 18x7½" .. 1,400.00
Tomahawk type, pipestone, eng floral, 1920s, 5½x15½" 450.00
Tubular, fine-grained sandstone, late Archaic, KY, 2½x4½" 1,000.00

Tubular, steatite, nearly drilled, late Archaic, 3⅛" 375.00
Vase type, red-brn claystone, polished, Mississippian, 1½x1½" 500.00

Pottery

Indian pottery is nearly always decorated in such a manner as to indicate the tribe that produced it or the pueblo in which it was made. For instance, the designs of Cochiti potters were usually scattered forms from nature or sacred symbols. The Zuni preferred an ornate repetitive decoration of a closer configuration. They often used stylized deer and bird forms, sometimes in dimensional applications.

Acoma, bowl, blk on wht, Kokopell player, MZ Cino, 1950s, 2½x3" ... 225.00
Casas Grandes, effigy, 3-color fish, hanging holes, p-h, 5x9x7" 800.00
Casas Grandes, jar, red & blk geometrics, fading, p-h, 6½x7" 550.00
Cochiti, basket, blk on cream, geometrics, rpr hdl, 1930s, 7x6".. 125.00
Cochiti, jar, rain cloud & mc birds, sm cracks, 1930s, 10x12"... 1,000.00
Hopi, tile, 3-color stylized bird, 1930s-40s, 6½x4½" 200.00
Mimbres, seed jar, blk on wht, rstr, ca 1200 AD, 4x5½" 550.00
Papago, effigy jar, human face w/blk highlights, 1940s, 6½x7" 375.00
Santa Clara, blkware, serpents, S Chavarria, 1970s, 4½x5" 125.00
Santa Clara, vase, blkware, feathers/geometrics, Verlarde, 1980s, 7"... 130.00
Santo Domingo, dough bowl, blk on cream, 1930s, 6½x11", EX . 300.00
Santo Domingo, vase, mc abstracts, 1930s, 11x6½" 240.00
Zia, jar, mc bird & deer, H Gachupin, 1970s-80s, 9½x10" 600.00

Pottery, San Ildefonso

The pottery of the San Ildefonso pueblo is especially sought after by collectors today. Under the leadership of Maria Martinez and her husband Julian, experiments began about 1918 which led to the development of the 'black-on-black' design achieved through exacting methods of firing the ware. They discovered that by smothering the fire at a specified temperature, the carbon in the smoke that ensued caused the pottery to blacken. Maria signed her work (often 'Marie') from the late teens to the 1960s; she died in 1980. Today examples with her signature may bring prices in the $500.00 to $4,500.00 range.

Bowl, blkware, cvd abstract, Juanite, 1940s-50s, 4½x7", EX 325.00
Bowl, blkware, feathers, Lucy Martinez, 1980s, 4x5½" 140.00
Bowl, blkware, geometrics, Alice Martinez, 1970s-80s, 3x4"........ 125.00
Bowl, blkware, geometrics, Blue Corn, scratches, 1960s, 1½x3" .. 250.00
Bowl, mc geometrics, Blue Corn, 1960s-70s, 2x3" 250.00
Bowl, red on cream matt, geometrics, A&J Vigil, 1974, 4x8½", EX...200.00
Figurine, turtle, blkware, sgraffito w/turq eyes, Tafoya, 1975, 5"...250.00

Jar, blackware, Carlos Dunlop (deceased), 1979, 12x10", $1,600.00. (Photo courtesy Allard Auctions Inc.)

Jar, blkware, checkerboard, Marie, 1930s, 4¼x4½" 1,000.00
Jar, blkware, cvd geometrics, Rose, 1960s, 6x6" 400.00
Jar, blkware, feathers, Blue Corn, 1970s, 3¼x7"........................... 1,000.00
Jar, blkware, feathers, Marie & Popovi, ca 1962, 3x4".................. 500.00
Jar, blkware, polished, Maria Poveka, 1970s, 3½x4" 825.00
Jar, blkware, serpents, Marie, w/booklet about her works, 5¼x8" .. 1,300.00

Vase, blkware, feathers, Albert & Josephine Vigil, 1975, 5½" 325.00
Vase, blkware, feathers, Santana & Adam, 1960s, 4½x4½"........... 450.00
Vase, blkware, wide geometric band, bulbous, Marie & Julian, 4½x5" ... 1,680.00
Vase, mc feathers, Blue Corn, 1960s-70s, 5½x5" 875.00
Vase, tan matt w/red feathers, Blue Corn, 1960s-70s, 5x5" 700.00

Rugs, Navajo

Crystal, pictorial/stars/arrows/bugs, natural, 1930s, 72x49" 900.00
Dmns overall, red w/tan/cream/brn accents, 1930, 68x48"........... 900.00
Ganado, dmns on red field, 1950s, 47x35" 625.00
Geometric, elongated 6-sided medallion, red/cream/blk/gray, 75x48", VG...840.00
Geometric rows, yel/brn/oatmeal, 1940, 60x31", VG 1,080.00
Klagetoh-type runner, stylized bug center, 1940s, 46x18", VG+ .. 350.00
Red Mesa, positive pattern, 1940s-50s, 56x32" 800.00
Two Grey Hills, geometrics, brn/tan/cream, 1950s, edge wear, 68x49" ...725.00
Xs in center w/geometric medallion ea end, red+3 color, 1930, 51x32" .840.00
Zigzag lines, red alternating w/cream w/blk detail, 1925, 62x40", VG 780.00
3rd Phase chief's, traditional block 9-spot, 1950s, 50x47"............ 625.00

Shaped Stone Artifacts

Bannerstone, butterfly type, banded slate, Archaic, 4¾x3½" 1,700.00
Bannerstone, crescent type, slate, cleanly drilled, Archaic, 4¼" W....750.00
Bannerstone, elongated ball type, banded slate, Archaic, 1½" 500.00
Bannerstone, winged, banded slate, Archaic, IN, 6x2⅝".........2,500.00
Discoidal, biscuit type, diorite, Mississippian, 3x1" 400.00
Discoidal, semi-bbl, conglomerate, ½" cups ea face, Woodland, 3x2".. 650.00
Gorget, banded slate, crisp lines, Woodland, IN, 4½x1¼"............. 500.00
Gorget, reel shaped, banded slate, Hopewell of Middle Woodland, 3¼"..750.00
Pendant, anchor type, banded slate, Woodland, 3¾x1¾", $600 to .. 1,200.00
Pendant, bell form, banded slate, centered hold, OH, 3¾" 400.00
Pendant, keyhole type, banded slate, EX patina, Woodland, 4⅝" ...450.00
Plummet, brn hardstone w/polish, grooved top, Archaic, 2⅛x1" 250.00

Tools

Adz, dk brn hardstone, ¾-groove, Archaic type, IN, 7".............. 1,800.00
Adz, speckled deck stone, Woodland, OH, 5⅝"............................. 275.00
Awl, split animal bone, TN, up to 4¼", from $12 to....................... 15.00
Awl, trigger; deer ulna, much used, IL, from $25 to......................... 30.00
Ax, Keokuk ½-groove, lt brn hardstone, Archaic, IA, 5⅞" 350.00
Ax, ¾-groove, gr-gray hardstone, some polish, late Archaic, 4x2½" 475.00
Ax, full groove, brn hardstone, Archaic, OH, 6½x4" 425.00
Ax, full groove, hematite, well formed, some polish, MO, 5½".... 375.00
Celt, gr & blk mottled hardstone, polished, OH, 3⅝" 250.00
Celt, incised lines on face, bl-gr hardstone, IL, 3¼" 100.00
Drill, Dalton, wht flint, serrated edges, late Paleo, 3⅝x1" 400.00
Drill, Harrison County flint, Woodland, 3¾x¾".......................... 200.00
Fishhook, cvd deer bone, grooved at shaft top, 1⅜"....................... 125.00
Hoe, Mill Creek chert, flared, silica polish, IL, 7x5¼" 300.00
Knife, crescent form, Prairie du Chein chert, Paleo, WI, 5¾x2" .. 750.00
Spade, Mill Creek chert, Mississippian, IL, 10" 250.00

American Painted Porcelain

The American china-painting movement can be traced back to an extracurricular class attended by art students at the McMicken School of Design in Cincinnati. These students, who were the wives and daughters of the city's financial elite, managed to successfully paint numerous porcelains for display in the Woman's Pavilion of the 1876 United States Centennial Exposition held in Philadelphia — an amazing feat considering the high technical skill required for proficiency, as well as the length of time and multiple firings necessary to finish the ware. From then until 1917 when the United States entered World War I, china painting was a profession as well as a popular amateur pursuit for many people, particularly women. In fact, over 25,000 people were involved in this art form at the turn of the last century.

Collectors and antique dealers have discovered American hand-painted porcelain, and they have become aware of its history, beauty, and potential value. For more information on this subject, *Antique Trader's Comprehensive Guide to American Painted Porcelain*, and *Painted Porcelain Jewelry and Buttons: Collector's Identification & Value Guide* by Dorothy Kamm are the culmination of a decade of research; we recommend them highly for further study.

Though American pieces are of high quality and commensurate with their European counterparts, they are much less costly today. Generally, you will pay as little as $20.00 for a 6" plate and less than $75.00 for many other items. Values are based on aesthetic appeal, quality of the workmanship, size, rarity of the piece and of the subject matter, and condition. Age is the least important factor, because most American painted porcelains are not dated. (Factory backstamps are helpful in establishing the approximate time period an item was decorated, but they aren't totally reliable.)

Bar pin, brass-plated bezel, 1½" W, from $25 to	55.00
Bowl, 4¾", from $50 to	75.00
Brooch, gold-plated bezel, 1½" dia, from $35 to	55.00
Cake plate, from $35 to	75.00
Celery tray, from $35 to	75.00
Cup & saucer	45.00
Cup & saucer, bouillon; from $35 to	55.00
Gravy boat, from $55 to	75.00
Mug, from $40 to	75.00
Pin tray, from $30 to	50.00
Plate, 6", from $10 to	35.00
Plate, 8", from $45 to	75.00
Salt cellar, from $20 to	40.00
Scarf pin, medallion, brass-plated bezel & shank, 1¼", from $35 to	65.00
Shakers, pr, from $25 to	40.00
Shirtwaist button, 1" dia, from $20 to	40.00

Amphora

The Amphora Porcelain Works in the Teplitz-Turn area of Bohemia produced Art Nouveau-styled vases and figurines during the latter part of the 1800s through the first few decades of the twentieth century. They marked their wares with various stamps, some incorporating the name and location of the pottery with a crown or a shield. Because Bohemia was part of the Austro-Hungarian empire prior to WWI, some examples are marked Austria; items marked with the Czechoslovakia designation were made after the war.

Teplitz was a town where most of the Austrian pottery was made. There are four major contributors to this pottery. One was Amphora, also known as RStK (Reissner, Stellmacher & Kessel). This company was the originator of the Amphora line. Edward Stellmacher, who was a founding member, went out on his own, working from 1905 until 1910. During this same time, Ernst Wahliss often used Amphora molds for his wares. He did similar work and was associated with the Amphora line. Turn Teplitz was never a pottery line. It was a stamp used to signify the towns where the wares were made. There were four lines: Amphora, Paul Dachsel, Edward Stellmacher, and Ernst Wahliss. More information can be found by referring to *Monsters and Maidens*, *Amphora Pottery of the Art Nouveau Era*, by Byron Vreeland, and *The House of Amphora* by Richard L. Scott. All decoration described in the listings that follow is hand painted unless otherwise indicated.

Our advisor for this category is John Cobabe; he is listed in the Directory under California.

Amphora

Figurine, Arab man on camel, mc w/gold, earthenware, 1900s, 18"	585.00
Pitcher, lg 3-D iris as rim, pastel lustres, #55/3683, sgn, 19x7", EX	3,000.00

Vase, birds, jeweled background, two old repairs, 13", $14,400.00.
(Photo courtesy Morphy Auctions)

Vase, dk gr irid, 4 integral hdls on organic form, Reissner, 9⅛"	600.00
Vase, gilt fruited vines on sage gr, crown mk, early 20th C, 8"	120.00
Vase, gnarled tree branch, setting sun beyond, wide teardrop form, 6"	525.00
Vase, lg appl yel roses/red & gr foliage, #8000/5-8, 11", NM	635.00
Vase, lobster wraps entire shoulder, multi-tone gr, rstr, 14"	1,700.00
Vase, wht flower heads w/jewel centers at shoulder, spider webs, 11"	2,000.00
Vases, lizards/flowers, branch hdls, RStK, ca 1900, 16", pr	900.00

Dachsel, Paul

Vase, artichoke form w/faux jewels, #103/10, 6"	1,925.00
Vase, birch trees/clouds repeated all around, #094, 8½"	860.00
Vase, irises & foliage w/gold, 4-hdl, 9¼x8½"	480.00
Vase, mushrooms among birch trees, rtcl rim, #1107/6, 13½"	2,400.00
Vase, stylized pine tree w/appl red pine cones, yel/gr, 6"	1,140.00
Vase, trees emb in soft gr matt, ink stamp, #1072/10, 7¾"	2,640.00

Stellmacher, Edward

Bust, lady w/down-trn eyes, bl bodice, #539/12, 15x17x8½"	1,080.00
Bust of woman, hair pulled bk, sq neckline, bl/ivory, #539-12, 15x17"	1,050.00
Creamer, sylized fish w/in alternate blocks, #2124, 3½"	210.00
Figure, maid w/flower on shoulder, gown forms bowl, 27"	4,000.00
Figure, maid w/lg leaf ea side, maid in water below, 21"	8,050.00
Head of lady in surround of lg curled/trn-bk leaves, tan, 13", VG	4,200.00
Humidor, modeled as a pod with 4 'stem' ft, brn mottle, 7"	175.00
Vase, Bedouin on horsebk, mc on blk, 2 sets of hdls, 10½"	150.00
Vase, leaves, 2-color w/gold on tan, gold hdls fork at shoulder, 8"	17.50
Vase, lg frog/newspaper, br/red/bl/wht on dk ground, #2063/23, 3½"	100.00
Vase, organic spade-shaped panels/riveting, hdls, 15"	1,440.00

Wahliss, Ernst

Vase, appl/molded floral, rtcl top, integral hdls, #5698/2710, 12"	780.00
Vase, floral & architectural decor, Secessionist style, #9627, 11"	660.00
Vase, Pergamon, floral on wht porc, #5660/2444 11, ca 1900, 11"	1,450.00
Vase, sculpted/applied mythological figures, gr lustre, hdls, 9¾"	425.00
Vase, stylized lotus pads w/gold, 4-hdl Secessionist style, 9⅝"	3,360.00

Animal Dishes With Covers

Covered animal dishes have been produced for nearly two centuries and are as varied as their manufacturers. They were made in many types of glass (slag, colored, clear, and milk glass) as well as china and pottery. On bases of nests and baskets, you will find animals and birds of every sort. The most common was the hen.

Some of the smaller versions made by McKee, Indiana Tumbler and Goblet Company, and Westmoreland Specialty Glass of Pittsburgh, Pennsylvania, were sold to food-processing companies who filled them with prepared mustard, baking powder, etc. Occasionally one will be found with the paper label identifying the product and processing company still intact.

Many of the glass versions produced during the latter part of the nineteenth century have been recently reproduced. In the 1960s, the Kemple Glass Company made the rooster, fox, lion, cat, lamb, hen, horse, turkey, duck, dove, and rabbit on split-ribbed or basketweave bases. They were made in amethyst, blue, amber, and milk glass, as well as a variegated slag. Kanawha, L.G. Wright, and Imperial made several as well. It is sometimes necessary to compare items in question to verified examples of older glass in order to recognize reproductions. Reproduction continues today.

For more information, we recommend *Glass Hen on Nest Covered Dishes* by Shirley Smith and *Collector's Encyclopedia of Milk Glass* by Betty and Bill Newbound. In the listings below, when only one dimension is given, it is the greater one, usually length. See also Greentown and other specific companies. For information on modern Westmoreland issues, we recommend *The Garage Sale and Flea Market Annual* (Collector Books).

Boar's Head, milk glass, Atterbury, May 29 1888 on lid/base, 9½" L ..2,000.00
Bull Head, purple slag, molded eyes, LG Wright, 4¼x3¾" 60.00
Bulldog, amber mist, rhinestone eyes, Westmoreland, 3½" 35.00
Camel, Recumbent; gr mist, Westmoreland, 1979, 6" 125.00
Cat, lacy base, blk carnival, Westmoreland, 5x8" 175.00
Chick on Egg Pile, lacy base, milk glass, ftd, Atterbury, 1889, 6x7" ...200.00
Chick on Egg Pile, wht carnival, Westmoreland, 1979, 6¼" (+)..185.00
Chicken Server, milk glass & gr, Fenton #5189-MG, 1953-54, $325 to ..350.00
Chicks Emerging From Eggs, milk glass, 2-hdl, Westmoreland, 4⅛" dia... 100.00
Crawfish, milk glass, 3-hdl, Westmoreland, 4x7" 250.00
Deer on Fallen Trees, milk glass w/some opal, Flaccus, 6½" L 240.00
Dog, Recumbent; rib base, milk glass, Westmoreland, 5½" 75.00
Duck, Atterbury; milk glass w/red glass eye, Atterbury, 1887, 11" L...260.00
Duck, rimmed base, bl mist, Westmoreland, 8x6"........................... 85.00
Eagle w/Spread Wing, on basket, chocolate, Westmoreland, 1982, 8x6" ..250.00
Elephant, Walking; pk, Indiana, 1980s, 4" 75.00
Fish, Entwined; milk glass w/ruby eyes, Atterbury, Pat 1889, 6" dia...250.00
Fox, lacy base, purple marble, oval, Westmoreland, 1978, 7½" L. 200.00
Frog, pk, eyes/upper bk on lid, Co-Operative Flint, 1927, 5½" L . 275.00
Hen, American; milk glass, title on base, Puerto Rico..., 6⅛" 75.00
Hen, lg lacy base, milk glass w/glass eye, Atterbury, 7½x6x3¾" ... 275.00
Hen on Basket, milk glass, Fenton #5183-MI, 1953-47, from $75 to...85.00
Hen on Nest, bl marble, Fenton #5186-MB, 1971-73, sm, from $45 to...55.00
Hen on Nest, bl w/milk glass head, Westmoreland, 1979, 7½x6" (+)..95.00
Hen on Nest, carnival, Fenton #5182-CN, 1970-74, lg, from $65 to...75.00
Hen on Nest, coral w/HP, Westmoreland, 1982, 7½x6" (+)......... 100.00

Hen on nest, diamond basketweave base, blue, Greentown, $300.00.

(Photo courtesy Everett Grist)

Horse, split-rib base, milk glass, McKee, from $250 to 265.00
Lamb, fence base, milk glass w/gold, Westmoreland, 5½" L 125.00
Lamb, Woolly; Bo Peep base, milk glass, Flaccus, 6" L, from $275 to.295.00
Lion, basketweave base, antique bl opaque, Westmoreland, 5½x4" ...175.00
Lion, basketweave base, antique bl opaque, Westmoreland, 8x6" ...175.00
Lion on Fence, milk glass, Westmoreland, 5½x3¾"...................... 110.00
Lovebirds, brn marble, Westmoreland, 1980, 6½x5¼" 150.00
Lovebirds, ruby, Westmoreland, 1978, 6½x5¼" 135.00
Rabbit on Egg, bl opaque, ftd, Vallerysthal, 5x5¼" 225.00
Rabbit on Picket Fence, Antique Blue, Westmoreland, 1982, 5½" (+)..100.00
Robin on Nest, milk glass, Portieux-Vallerysthal, solid head, 6" ..175.00
Rooster, basket base, milk glass w/red comb, Westmoreland, 6x7½" .. 90.00
Swan, Block; basket base, milk glass, Challinor Taylor, 7" L 300.00
Swan, Open Neck; milk glass, Vallerysthal, 5x5½" (+) 120.00
Swan, Raised-Wing; milk glass w/red eyes, Atterbury, 5x10" 250.00
Turkey, amber, head lid, Cambridge, 1940-50, 7¼x4¾" 650.00
Turkey, Rubigold, legs folded/sitting, Imperial #4393, 1970s, 5" L ...75.00
Turtle, milk glass, 2-hdl, Westmoreland, 4¼x7¼" 200.00
Turtle, Snapping; milk glass, LG Wright, 9¾" L 300.00
Turtle Bonbon Dish, gr, Fenton, 1929, 9" L 400.00

Appliances, Electric

Antique electric appliances represent a diverse field and are always being sought after by collectors. There were over 100 different companies manufacturing electric appliances in the first half of the twentieth century; some were making over 10 different models under several different names at any given time in all fields: coffeepots, toasters, waffle irons, etc., while others were making only one or two models for extended periods of time. Today collectors and decorators alike are seeking those items to add to a collection or to use as accent pieces in a period kitchen. Refer to *Toasters and Small Kitchen Appliances* published by L-W Book Sales for more information.

Always check the cord before use and make sure the appliance is in good condition, free of rust and pitting. Unless noted otherwise, our values are for appliances in excellent condition. Prices may vary around the country.

Blender, Marvelmatic, all chrome, Bakelite hdls, 13", NM 60.00
Blender, Waring, blk Bakelite top, rocket Art Deco style, 16", NM...220.00
Blender, Waring, glass jar, pk base/lid, #PB-5, 1950s 70.00
Bun warmer, Mirro #3508, aluminum w/wood knob/hdl, 8x10", VG ..35.00
Bun warmer, West Bend, winter wheat on yel, 3-pc, MIB............. 35.00
Can opener, Hoover, chrome legs, w/knife sharpener, 7½", NM 15.00
Can opener, Waring, avocado enamel, 1960s-70s, MIB 40.00
Coffee urn, Fire-King #435, glass cap, eng, ornate hdls, ftd, 15" 53.00
Coffeepot, GE, chrome w/blk hdl, 10-cup.................................... 170.00
Egg cooker, Oster #581, 4-pc, brn plastic w/amber top, 1960s-70s ...24.00
Egg cooker, Sunbeam, chrome/Teflon, 4-pc, 1967, NMIB w/papers..30.00
Fan, ceiling; Victor Zephyr, blk enamel, 4-blade, 14" 780.00
Fan, Emerson #21666, brass cage & 6 blades, blk base 185.00
Fan, window; GE #F13W12, turq enamel, 3-blade, 20"............... 250.00
Grill/waffle iron, Sunbeam #CG-1, chrome w/blk hdl, 11x11" 90.00
Heater, Arvin #5130, turq enamel, 1950s-60s, 12" 45.00
Heater, Wesix RCS-11/4, chrome, Art Deco shape, 1930s............. 32.00
Kettle, Bulpitt & Sons #4A 7842, copper, 1921 .... 120.00
Kettle, GE #AIK52 243, chrome, 1950s-60s 25.00
Mixer, GE, wht, 8-speed, 3 beaters, w/bowls 45.00
Mixer, hand; Dormeyer, wht, w/attachments, NMIB w/papers....... 30.00
Mixer, Naxon, gr glass bowl, 1 beater, bail hdl, 1920s, 6½" 25.00
Mixer, Sunbeam, Harvest Gold, w/attachments/bowls, 1975, 13".. 35.00
Percolator, Farberware, chrome, blk hdl, base & knob, 8-cup 37.00
Percolator, Kenmore #307-67323, chrome, blk hdl, 1970s............. 35.00

Percolator, Manning-Bowman #1551504, chrome Deco style, 9" dia..... **32.00**
Percolator, Proctor-Silex #P003H, Harvest Gold, 1974, 10-cup, MIB.... **45.00**
Percolator, West Bend Fiesta Perk, orange enamel, 1960s, 5-cup, MIB. **35.00**
Popcorn popper, Dominion #1702, metal w/blk hdl/lid, +accessories, MIB ..**84.00**
Popcorn popper, Grants #WTG-90092, red w/blk ft, glass lid, 3-qt, MIB.....**60.00**
Popcorn popper, Mirro #M-9235-45, yel enamel w/blk ft & hdl, 4-qt **76.00**
Popcorn popper, West Bend, orange enamel w/blk hdl, plastic lid, 4-qt... **50.00**
Roaster, Proctor Electric Co #122, wht enamel w/aluminum lid, 1940s, M...**25.00**
Roaster on stand, GE, red & wht enamel, 1950s, 39x22x15" **125.00**
Rotisserie/broiler, Black Angus King Sz #S-7RT, M w/booklet..... **100.00**
Skillet, Corning #P-12-ES, Cornflower pattern, sq, w/lid, 10" **65.00**
Skillet, Farberware #310-A, stainless steel, w/blk ft & hdl, 12" dia ...**35.00**
Skillet, Presto Jumbo, blk w/pk enamel lid, 1979, 15x10", MIB..... **50.00**
Skillet, Toastmaster, stainless steel w/chrome lid, sq, 12" **46.00**
Slow cooker, West Bend, beige w/brn stripes, brn glass lid, 4-qt, M ..**46.00**
Toaster oven, GE #A11T93B, gold enamel/blk/chrome **100.00**
Toaster oven, GE #T-93, wht enamel/blk/chrome, M w/tag **160.00**
Vacuum, Electrolux Model R, wht canister, w/accessories............. **225.00**
Vacuum, Singer #S3, cream & gr, 20' cord, 1948, 45", NM **325.00**
Vacuum, Streamline Air Flow #VC6702, bl/chrome canister, 1950s, MIB...**235.00**
Waffle iron, Vitantonio #180, chrome w/blk hdls/ft, 6" dia **130.00**
Waffle iron, Westinghouse Electric #CNC-4, chrome, Art Deco, 13" dia...**125.00**

Arequipa

Following the example of the Marblehead sanatorium and pottery, the director of the Arequipa sanatorium turned to the craft of pottery as a curative occupation for his patients. In 1911 Dr. Philip K. Brown asked Frederick Hurten Rhead and his wife Agnes to move to Fairfax, California, to organize such a department. Rhead had by then an impressive resume, having worked at Vance/Avon, Weller, Roseville, Jervis, and University City. The Rheads' stay at Arequipa would be short-lived, and by 1913 they were replaced by Albert Solon, another artist from a renowned pottery family. That same year, the pottery was incorporated as a separate entity from the sanatorium and would greatly expand in the following few years. It distinguished itself with two medals at the Pan-Pacific Exposition in 1915. A third Englishman, Frederick H. Wilde, replaced Solon in 1916 and remained at the helm of the pottery until its closing in 1918.

The finest pieces produced at Arequipa were done during the Rhead years, decorated in squeezebag or slip-trail. Others were embossed with floral patterns and covered in single-color glazes. Early vases are marked with a hand-painted Arequipa in blue on applied white glaze or incised in the clay. Our advisors for this category are Suzanne Perrault and David Rago; they are listed in the Directory under New Jersey.

Vase, orange trees in squeeze-bag and enamel, hand-painted mark (Rhead period), 8½x4", $18,000.00. (Photo courtesy David Rago)

Bowl, appl shell to ea side of incurvate rim, bl/gray crystalline, 9" ...780.00
Jardiniere, acanthus leaves molded at rim, bl/gray matt, 4½x9"... **1,800.00**
Vase, butterflies, bl-gray, bulbous, 5½x6"....................................**1,200.00**

Vase, floral cvg, charcoal & gr crystalline, rnd, 6" W **1,925.00**
Vase, floral wreath emb at shoulder on ivory to pk, hairlines, 5x7" ..**2,000.00**
Vase, foliage cvgs, gr & turq, baluster, 13½x6¼" **3,600.00**
Vase, fruit branches emb, lt bl on mottled indigo, rstr, 6x3¼"...**6,600.00**
Vase, leaves, HP brn on gray, 3½x3"...**1,200.00**
Vase, semi-sheer bl/gray over red clay, shouldered/ribbed, 6x4".. **1,800.00**
Vase, slip-trailed wreaths, brn/gr on dk gr, 1912, 2½x5½" **2,500.00**
Vase, squeeze-bag design at neck, purple matt, 1913, 7½x4" **8,400.00**
Vase, squeeze-bag design in yel on gr, 8x4" **9,000.00**

Argy-Rousseau, G.

Gabriel Argy-Rousseau produced both fine art glass and quality commercial ware in Paris, France, in 1918. He favored Art Nouveau as well as Art Deco and in the '20s produced a line of vases in the Egyptian manner, made popular by the discovery of King Tut's tomb. One of the most important types of glass he made was pate-de-verre. Most of his work is signed. Items listed below are pate-de-verre unless noted otherwise.

Atomizer, poppy band near base of pear shape, orange/brn/ivory, 6" ..**3,680.00**
Bowl, modeled as a stylized poppy head, mottled rose on clear ft, 4"..**2,040.00**
Box, Papyrus, floral, red/dk bl on amethyst, rnd, 3" H **4,000.00**
Brooch, roses in bl vase on frosted ground, oval, 2½" **575.00**
Frame, flowerheads, red w/bl centers on wht, wht inner fr, 4x4¾"..**3,275.00**
Lamp, grotesque masks in zigzag-band panels, egg shape on ftd base, 6"..**8,400.00**
Lamp, 3 peonies/pc-work panels, red/dk brn, tall bullet-nose shade, 7"..**8,400.00**
Lamp, 5-section floral fan shape on sgn ft; 2-tier metal base, 9x8" ..**10,925.00**
Nightlight, roses, red/gr on purple to maize mottle, vase form, 8"..**4,680.00**
Paperweight, moths atop sq, gr/purple on lime gr w/brn, 2x2¾" .. **2,185.00**
Pendant, leaves, amethyst/rose, 10k gold fr, 3" dia......................**2,900.00**
Pendant, lg winged insect, blk/red/amber, on amber ribbed oval, 2½".. **1,020.00**
Pendant, rose w/gr accents on 2¼" disk, strung on silk w/tassel... **1,555.00**
Pendant, wht flower head w/yel stamens on clear, on cord, 2¼" L..**1,150.00**
Vase, curling leafy fronds, yel/brn/amber on mottled frost, 7" ...**5,400.00**
Vase, dancing nudes, brn/amethyst, cylinder w/flared top, 6" ..**12,075.00**
Vase, Libations: women w/water jugs on shoulders in sq reserves, 12"..**14,950.00**
Vase, mums on long stems, wine/red/orange/yel on purple mottle, 6" ..**11,000.00**
Vase, snail-like hdls at rim, zigzag panels down sides, 6"............**4,920.00**
Vase, wolves, wine/blk on lav, snow-effect rim & bottom, 9½x6" ...**44,850.00**

Art Glass Baskets

Popular novelty and gift items during the Victorian era, these one-of-a-kind works of art were produced in just about any type of art glass in use at that time. They were never marked. Many were not true production pieces but 'whimsies' made by glassworkers to relieve the tedium of the long work day. Some were made as special gifts. The more decorative and imaginative the design, the more valuable the basket. For more information we recommend *The Collector's Encyclopedia of American Art Glass* by John A. Shuman, III (Collector Books).

Note: Prices on art glass baskets have softened due to the influence of the Internet which has made them much more accessible.

Amber, fanned/pleated rim, raised on 5 tab ft, 10" 80.00
Amethyst to amber at base, sides flow together into long hdl, 8x7" ..90.00
Cafe-au-lait w/gilt foliage & enamel blossoms, wht int, 8½" 125.00
Clear, brilliant cuttings/intaglio florals, waisted, high hdl, 18".....235.00
Clear, etched leaf band, opposing arched sides, rectangular, 12" 50.00
Cranberry, invt hat shape, ribs in bowl, clear hdl, 9x9" 95.00
Cranberry bowl w/opal scrolled leaf-shape rim, pointed gr hdl, 9x7" .. 180.00
Cranberry opal w/opal int, vaseline leaf ft & twist hdl, 7x7"........ 115.00
Cranberry overshot; SP Reed & Barton Egyptian-style fr, ftd, 9" dia .. 450.00

Custard to red to dk red at ruffled/crimped rim, vaseline hdl, 7x9"...... 195.00
Custard w/HP floral, gilt-metal hdl, rim & ft, 6x7½" 160.00
Peachblow, sq w/pleated/ruffled rim, clear thorn hdl, 5½x7" 180.00
Peppermint swirl, emb swirls in body, rim w/both sm & lg crimps, 7" ... 180.00

Pink mother-of-pearl with bright green interior, Mt. Washington, 9x11", $570.00.
(Photo courtesy Jackson's International Auctioneers & Appraisers of Fine Art & Antiques)

Pull-up, red w/wht & yel stripes, crystal hdl/ft, Northwood, 12x12" ... 900.00
Red, band of emb overlapping circles, sqd wicker hdl, 8x10" 120.00
Spangle, wht w/bright bl int w/mica, ruffled/flared, twist hdl, 6x5" ..75.00
Spatter, mc in pk, wht int, 8-pinch rim, clear invt V hdl, 5".......... 80.00
Spatter, orange/yel/red, wht int, upright ruffled rim, thorn hdl, 7" ... 125.00
Spatter, pk/wht, ruffled rim, clear sqd thorn hdl, 6½x5" 95.00
Spatter, tortoise coloring, ruffled star-shape rim, twist hdl, 6x5".... 60.00
Vaseline opal stripes w/appl bl flower, leaf & stem, twist hdl, 7x4"...115.00
Vaseline w/lt bl tightly ruffled wide flared rim, vaseline hdl, 9x10" 325.00
Wht satin to bl, ruffled/scalloped rim w/tiny petal-like edge, 8x12" ...100.00
Wht w/purple ruffle, arch hdl & disk ft, cone shape, 11x10"........ 120.00
Wht w/yel int, down-trn notched rim, frosted ribbed twist hdl, 7"...65.00
Yel w/emb ribs & pinwheels, rose int, clear twist hdl, 10" 275.00
Yel w/emb swirl ribs, orange trn-down ruffle, clear thorn hdl, 8x6" ... 180.00

Arts and Crafts

The Arts and Crafts movement began in England during the last quarter of the nineteenth century, and its influence was soon felt in this country. Among its proponents in America were Elbert Hubbard (see Roycroft) and Gustav Stickley (see Stickley). They rebelled against the mechanized mass production of the Industrial Revolution and against the cumulative influence of hundreds of years of man's changing taste. They subscribed to a theory of purification of style: that designs be geared strictly to necessity. At the same time they sought to elevate these basic ideals to the level of accepted 'art.' Simplicity was their virtue; to their critics it was a fault.

The type of furniture they promoted was squarely built, usually of heavy oak, and so simple was its appearance that as a result many began to copy the style which became known as 'Mission.' Soon factories had geared production toward making cheap copies of their designs. In 1915 Stickley's own operation failed, a victim of changing styles and tastes. Hubbard lost his life that same year on the ill-fated *Lusitania*. By the end of the decade the style had lost its popularity.

Metalware was produced by numerous crafts people, from experts such as Dirk van Erp and Albert Berry to unknown novices. Metal items or hardware should not be scrubbed or scoured; to do so could remove or damage the rich, dark patina typical of this period. Collectors have become increasingly fussy, rejecting outright pieces with damage or alteration to their original condition (such as refinishing, patina loss, repairs, and replacements). As is true for other categories of antiques and collectibles, premium prices have been paid for objects in mint original and untouched condition. Our advisor for this category is Bruce Austin;

he is listed in the Directory under New York. See also Heintz; Jewelry; Limbert; Roycroft; Silver; Stickley; van Erp; specific manufacturers.

Note: When no condition is noted within the description lines, assume that values are given for examples in excellent condition. That is, metal items retain their original patina and wooden items are still in their original finish. Values for examples in conditions other than excellent will be indicated in the descriptions with appropriate condition codes.

Key: h/cp — hammered copper

Armchair, wing-bk w/cvd medieval figures on wings, oak & leather, 39" ..825.00
Bookcase, Paine, 2 12-pane doors w/sq copper knobs, rfn, 45x48", VG ..2,400.00
Bookcase, 2 glazed doors, 3 int shelves adjust, #529, 56x43x12", EX .. 1,000.00
Bookcase, 3 6-pane doors, gallery top, cast hdw, 44x55x12" 4,200.00
Bookcase, 3-door, ea w/2 sm panes over 2, arched apron, 56x64x14", VG ..3,500.00
Bookends, Albert Berry, h/cp w/ship design, scalloped top, 5½x4" 400.00
Bowl, Arthur Stone, silver, lobed, rnd ft, sgn T, 25 troy oz........1,000.00
Bowl, Cellini, sterling, ftd oval w/4 deep lobes, floral mts, 3x11". 350.00
Bowl, ET Hurley, bronze w/sculpted turtles inside, #26, 8"........5,500.00
Bowl, h/cp, rolled incurvate rim, unmk, 13½" 350.00
Bowl, Kalo, silver, flared/lobed/ftd, #38S, 4½x7" 900.00
Bowl vase, Jarvie, h/cp, 3" H 900.00
Box, Chas Rohlfs, ornate cvg, cedar int, sgn/1901, 6x15x9" ...12,000.00
Box, wood w/cut-out copper o/l & jewels, leather under cutouts, 6x3"...335.00
Cabinet, Lakeside Craft, slag glass panel in door, sides flare, 34x12" 900.00
Candelabrum, Jarvie, brass, 2 riveted coils w/tapered cups, 11", VG ..4,800.00
Candlesticks, Benedict, silvered metal/copper, #1927, 6", pr 250.00
Candlesticks, C Fridell, sterling, hammered, 4 tapered sides, 7", pr..1,400.00
Candlesticks, Jarvie, Alpha, bronze, removable bobeche, 11", pr...1,800.00
Candlesticks, Jarvie, brass, pencil stems, thimble cups, 14", pr...1,000.00
Candlesticks, Jarvie, Omicron, brass, 2-arm, 10½x8", ea.............. 840.00
Candlesticks, Kalo, silver gilt, elongated teardrop stems, 12", pr...5,100.00
Chair, billiards; Heywood-Wakefield, 5-slat bk, plank seat, rfn, 45"...1,950.00
Chair, corner; even arms, 2 diagonal slats ea side, new rush seat, 30".1,920.00
Chair, Cortland, 3-slat bk/sides, rpl cushion, cleaned, unmk, 36" ...360.00
Chair, hall; 2 thin+1 wide bk slat (w/cloverleaf), shoe ft, 53x17x17" ... 8,400.00
Chair, hall: oak w/oval bk over 3 slats, Macintosh influenced, 48".....600.00
Chair, office; swivel base, oak w/rpl tacked-on leather seat/bk, 37" .. 750.00
China cabinet, Lifetime, 2 doors w/3 mullions over rectangles, 55x46"..3,000.00
China cabinet, trapezoidal, 2 8-pane doors, overhang top, 61x41", VG ..3,600.00
Chocolate pot, KF Leinonen, swollen form w/ebony hdl, 10" 560.00
Clock, grandfather; Colonial Furniture Co, corbels at top, 85"..6,000.00
Compote, Goldsmiths & Silversmiths, hammered silver, 5-'claw' base, 6" ..900.00
Compote, Joseph Heinrichs, hammered silver, petal rim/column std, 14". 750.00
Desk, drop front; Brooks, mullioned door ea side, lower shelf, 50x62".. 1,400.00
Desk, oak, slant top over drw, 2-post sides, bk stretcher, 30" W ... 300.00
Fire fender, copper w/appl trinity knots, probably English, 4½x53".. 585.00
Frame, Chas Rohlfs, dtd 1901, 4" W w/Indian chief lithograph, 24x26"..1,800.00
Frame, wood w/HP floral, hinged, shaped top/bracket base, 9x7½" ..200.00
Garden stool, mahog w/press-cvd foliage in 8 side panels, 18x13" ..660.00
Hall seat, McHugh, crown mold above X detail, arms w/3 slats, 66x28"..1,080.00
Humidor, ldgl geometrics, brass lid/bottom, 8¼", VG.................... 60.00
Lamp, Chas Eaton (att), h/cp, 17" 6-panel mica shade; sq flaring std ... 2,000.00
Lamp, h/cp fr shade w/4 mica (rpl) panels; h/cp squat/orb base, 8x10"....2,400.00
Lamp, Revere, 4-panel slag glass shade; flaring 4-sided base, 24x22" 1,800.00
Lamp base, ET Hurley, bronze upright sea horses w/verdigris, 24x7" 4,200.00
Magazine stand, Lakeside, inv't V crest rail/sides w/sq cutouts, 47"...1,200.00
Mirror, cvd mahog w/vines & leaves, oval, 33" L......................1,320.00
Mirror, h/cp, raised rectangular base w/2 uprights, adjusts, 12x14"...420.00
Mirror, 2-post sides center glass, wrought-iron hooks, 38x24"...... 395.00
Pipe rack, h/cp w/raised designs, shaped sides, unmk, 9½x13½"...200.00
Pitcher, Kalo, hammered sterling, 6-panel, M monogram, 8x7" ..4,200.00
Pitcher, Kalo, silver, lt hammering, ovoid w/flared spout, 6" 765.00
Rug, leaves/flowers, rose/navy/olive, Wm Morris style, 110x96"....1,200.00

Rug, oak leaf repeats, brn/rose/olive on tan, Wm Morris style, 135x55"...960.00
Rug, oatmeal w/blk Greek key border, mc geometrics, 84x51".....540.00
Rug, overall floral on cinnabar, navy foliate border, 140x86".......960.00
Rug, poppy/scrolling vines, wool, Wm Morris style, 210x140"..1,200.00
Rug, pumpkins/flowers, vine border, Wm Morris style, 118x163"..2,040.00
Rug, stylized tulips, bl/red, Wm Morris style, 70x40"....................660.00
Salver, Wm Connell, hammered silver, holly berry rim, 8½" dia..650.00
Sconce, Jarvie, brass disk mts, pencil stems w/tulip cups, 13x6", pr..3,000.00
Settee, Lifetime, 5 wide bk slats, open drop arms, 64" L, VG....1,800.00
Settle, Liberty (att), thin rail over 9 bk slats, 3 ea side, rfn, 67"..1,560.00
Sideboard, Lifetime, mirrored bksplash/2 sm drw over 1 long+doors, 49"..1,200.00
Spratling, fruit bowl, incised bands, 3 curved/beaded hdls, 10"..5,760.00
Stool, oak, rnded corners, wide apron, X-stretcher, 21x12x12"....120.00
Table, Chas Rohlfs, floriform cvd top, rtcl legs, unmk, 26x26", VG...5,000.00
Table, console; Lifetime Puritan Line, 6 legs/long corbels, 31x67x22"..8,000.00
Table, dining; Lifetime, Puritan Line, 48" dia top, 5-leg, 2 9" leaves..1,100.00
Table, dining; 45" dia top, sq ped base w/4 sqd ft, G.....................660.00
Table, gaming; Lifetime, canted corner top w/metal ashtrays, sm rpr..230.00
Table, Harden, low 5-slat sides flank lower shelf, 26x18x18"....2,300.00
Table, library; Lifetime #909, 1 drw, thru-tenons, 44" L, VG.......720.00
Table, library; Shop-of-the-Crafters, cutouts/corners canted, rfn, 51"...1,440.00
Table, library; 3-drw, overhang top, rpl hdw/rfn, 30x90x36", EX.960.00
Table, octagonal 19" brass top, 4-post base w/inlay & ball ft, Austria...1,680.00
Vase, Jarvie, h/cp, tapering sides, cleaning/verdigris spot, 11x5".......1,680.00
Woodblock print, pr of swans in park pond, sgn/#d, 9x9", +mat & fr.660.00
Woodblock print, sea gulls, Frances Gearhart, 9x7", +new mat/fr....1,020.00
Woodblock print, 3 girls on bridge/raining, sgn/1908, sight: 10x15"..1,200.00

Austrian Glass

Many examples of fine art glass were produced in Austria during the times of Loetz and Moser that cannot be attributed to any glasshouse in particular, though much of it bears striking similarities to the products of both artists.

Vase, deep amethyst with irridescent lines, 10", NM, $180.00.
(Photo courtesy David. Rago Auctions)

Candlestick, clear w/ornate rtcl silver mts & bobeche, Schee, 5"...360.00
Compote, floral/scrolls, bl/blk/gr/orange on clear, 3¼x6½"...........150.00
Compote, purple w/oil spots, dk bl irid int; SP metal std/ft, 8x9".450.00
Inkwell, metallic w/bl threading, Kralik Glass Works, 2½"..........325.00
Inkwell, purple w/random threading, flat/conical, 5¼" dia...........450.00
Tankard, gr w/checkerboard threading, copper top/lid/hdl, 11x9"..1,200.00
Trophy cup, bl cornucopia w/enamel; gilt metal griffin, stag, ftd, 19"..3,000.00
Vase, amethyst w/purple/bl irid oil spots, long neck, bun base, 13...150.00
Vase, appl red/gr threading, 3-sided w/3 pull-down free-form hdls, 9"...540.00
Vase, bl irid w/allover pock mks & dents at shoulder, 7"..............480.00
Vase, bl oilspots, trumpet form w/bulbous rim, 12"......................275.00
Vase, bl/copper mottle on clear irid, rtcl copper o/l, 6"................350.00
Vase, deep purple w/random threads, ruffled rim, att Palme-Koenig, 7"...540.00
Vase, emerald gr; in rtcl pewter mt w/crest & crown hallmark, 8x4¾"...720.00
Vase, gold irid w/gr spiral appl to columnar neck, 6"..................85.00

Vase, gr w/purple highlights & oil spots, ogee sides w/wide neck, 7"..210.00
Vase, gr/purple w/allover zigzag pulled bands, flared/ruffled, 14"...240.00
Vase, orange w/clear striations & mottle, ftd V-form, Ikora, 9"......95.00
Vase, red w/bl irid & pulled decor, cupped top w/4-lobe rim, 11½"..165.00
Vase, silver o/l floral sgn Black Starr & Frost on bl irid, 5"........1,115.00
Vase, threading, maroon on semi-opaque irid, folded rim, Koenig, 4"...300.00
Vase, yel to purple cased w/amber & pk oil spots, sq rim, 8".....2,280.00

Austrian Ware

From the late 1800s until the beginning of WWI, several companies were located in the area known at the turn of the century as Bohemia. They produced hard-paste porcelain dinnerware and decorative items primarily for the American trade. Today examples bearing the marks of these firms are usually referred to by collectors as Austrian ware, indicating simply the country of their origin. Of those various companies, these marks are best known: M.Z. Austria; Victoria, Carlsbad, Austria (Schmidt and Company); and O. & E.G. (Royal) Austria. Of these three companies, Victoria, Carlsbad, Austria, is the most highly valued.

Though most of the decorations were transfer designs which were sometimes signed by the original artist, pieces marked Royal Austria were often hand painted and so indicated alongside the backstamp.

Collectors should note that in our listings transfer decorations showing 'signatures' (sgn), such as 'Wagner,' 'Kauffmann,' 'LeBrun,' etc., were not actually painted by those artists but were merely based on their original paintings. Our advisor for this category is Mary Frank Gaston; she is listed in the Directory under Texas.

Charger, Cupid aiming at 3 ladies, gold/maroon border, 1890s, 15".2,000.00
Figurine, seated nude, head & arms resting on knees, gr mottle, 9".....360.00
Plaque, Desdemona & Iago, sgn CRH, 1873, late 19th C, 11x8½", EX...265.00
Vase, Echo (classical maiden) reserve, Wagner, maroon/gold, 1890s, 9"..550.00
Vase, irid gr w/bl/purple/gold, swirled 4-sided mold, Heliosine, 7"..450.00
Vases, wht w/mc fruit at hdls, Weiner Kunst, ca 1928, 10", pr.....235.00

Autographs

Autographs can be as simple as signatures on cards or album pages, signed photos, signed documents or letters, but they can also be signed balls, bats, T-shirts, books, and a variety of other items.

Simple signatures are the most common form and thus are usually of lesser value than signed photos, letters, or anything else. But as with any type of collectible, the condition of the autograph is paramount to value. If the signature is in pencil, value drops automatically by one-half or more. If the item signed is torn, creased, stained, laminated or is a menu, bus ticket, magazine page, or something unusual, many collectors will avoid buying these because they are less desirable than a nice dark ink signature on an undamaged card or autograph album page.

When pricing signed photos, many variables come into play. Size is important (all things being equal, the larger the photo, the more it's worth), as is condition (wrinkles, tape stains, tears, or fading will all have a negative impact). If the signature is signed over a dark area, making it difficult to see, the photo's value can drop by 90%. Finally, the age of the signed photo will cause the value to increase or decrease. Generally speaking, if the photo is signed when the celebrity was young and not well known, it will be worth more than those signed in later years. For example, the photos signed by Shirley Temple as a child are worth hundreds of dollars, whereas her adult-signed photos can be purchased for as little as $20.00.

The savvy autograph buyer or antique/collectibles dealer needs to know that since the 1950s, many U.S. Presidents, politicians, and astronauts commonly used (and still do) a machine known as the 'autopen,' a mechanical device that 'signs' photos and letters for fans requesting an autograph through the mail. The tip-off to an auto-penned signature is that each one will be identical.

Autopens aren't so common with movie and television stars, however. If you were to write to a famous entertainer asking for a signed photo, the chances are extremely high you'll either receive a photo signed by a secretary or one bearing a 'machine-imprinted' signature which will appear as real ink on the photo.

Yes, there are authentic and valuable autographs out there, but make sure you are buying from a reputable autograph dealer or from a seller who has convincing evidence that what his offering is genuine. The Internet is full of autograph auction sites that sell forgeries, so always beware of a deal with a price that's too good to be true — you might be getting conned!

Most reputable autograph dealers belong to one of several autograph organizations: the UACC (The Universal Autograph Collectors Club) or The Manuscript Society. If you buy from a dealer, make sure the autograph has a lifetime guarantee of authenticity. If you buy from a private party, then as the old saying goes, '...let the buyer beware!' Our advisor for autographs is Tim Anderson; he listed in the Directory under Utah.

Key:
ALS — handwritten letter
ANS — handwritten note signed
AQS — autographed quotation signed
COA — certificate of authenticity
DS — document signed
ins — inscription
ISP — inscribed signed photo
LH — Letterhead
LS — signed letter, typed or written by someone else
sig — signature
SP — signed photo

Adams, John; autographed letter endorsement dated 1787 requesting payment to a London merchant, matted and framed, sight: 4½x7", $2,300.00. (Photo courtesy James D. Julia Inc.)

Armstrong, Neil; SP, mc print, Apollo 11 crew, 8x10" 750.00
Bailey, Pearl; SP, blk & wht, 1970s, 8x10" 58.00
Bernstein, Leonard; SP, color, bl ink, 4¼x3", COA 145.00
Burns, George; ISP, blk & wht, bold red ink, 8x10" 55.00
Carol, Marine; ISP, blk & wht, COA 45.00
Carol, Sue; SP postcard, blk & wht, bl ink, 1920s, COA 60.00
Carpenter, Richard; ISP, blk & wht, 1995, 8x10" 95.00
Chaffee, Roger; mc print of astronaut in bl suit & tie, 8x10" 660.00
Chaliapin, Feodor Ivanovich; sig on album pg, bold fountain ink...145.00
Churchill, Winston; ALS, varied subjects, 4 pgs, 1905, 5x8" 4,000.00
Cooper, Gary; sig on album pg, VG.. 145.00
Crawford, Joan; LS, personal stationery, 1975 .... 75.00
Eysler, Edmund; ISP postcard, dedication w/cord, 1948, 4x6", COA...62.00
Field, Robert; ALS, varied subjects, 2 pgs, 1800, 8x9½" 115.00
Ford, Gerald; SP, color, 1974, 7x10", COA.................................... 185.00
Garbo, Greta; SP, blk & wht, 5x7" 4,500.00
Garcia, Jerry; SP, color, 8x10".. 134.00
Geronimo, pencil sig on card..6,000.00
Hancock, John; ALS, written to General Assembly, Feb 10 1783, 8x9½" ..4,250.00
Hepburn, Katherine; sig on short typed note, 1987, 6x8"............. 195.00
Hoover, Herbert; bold sig on Waldorf-Astoria stationery, 1956 ... 125.00

Hope, Bob; sig on card w/name & 8/3/67 at top, 3x5".................... 59.00
Ives, Burl; sig on card w/name & 10/16/64 at top, 3x5"................. 38.00
Jenner, Alexander; SP, blk & wht, 1969, 4x6" 68.00
Lallemand, Charles; ALS, orders wood for warships, 1825, 8x10" ..130.00
Lancaster, Burt; SP, blk & wht, 1984, 5x7" 130.00
Lee, Robert E; ALS, 1 pg, 1870 ....4,575.00
Leslie, Joan; ISP, blk & wht, 1941, 4x6", COA 35.00
Loren, Sophia; SP, early postcard, bl ink, 4x5½", COA.................. 65.00
Mantle, Mickey; sig on pk album pg... 225.00
March, Hal; ISP, blk & wht, 1950s, 8x10" 44.00
Matthau, Walter; ISP, blk & wht, 4x5", COA 70.00
McCartney, Paul; SP, blk & wht, 1964...................................... 760.00
Monroe, Marilyn; sig on album pg, red ink, 3x5".....................1,200.00
Niesen, Gertrude; ISP, sepia, 1930s, 5x7"...................................... 39.00
Nixon, Richard; ins & bold sig inside Six Crises book, 1st ed, 1962 ... 395.00
O'Hara, Maureen; ISP, blk & wht, 4x6", COA 115.00
Page, Ruth; ISP, sepia, early in career, 7½x9"............................... 59.00
Polk, James K; sig on postal frank, as president.........................2,500.00
Presley, Elvis; SP, blk & wht, 1961, 8x10"................................. 900.00
Reagan, Ronald; ALS, on RWR letterhead, 1 pg, 1950, 7x10½"..660.00
Romero, Ceasar; ISP, blk & wht, 7½x9½".................................... 59.00
Scott, Fred; SP, blk & wht, 1988, 8x10" 44.00
Seberg, Jean; SP, blk & wht, 3½x5½"... 132.00
Shaw, Robert; ISP, sepia, 4x6" 123.00
Sinatra, Frank; SP, mc, bold bl sig, 8x10"................................. 400.00
Skelton, Red; bold sig on card w/name & 8/18/64 at top, 3x5"...... 39.00
Smith, Joseph; DS, 1840...1,850.00
Temple, Shirley; SP, sepia, rare sig Shirley Temple Agar, 1940s, 8x10"...295.00
Tracy, Spencer; SP, blk & wht, bold sig, 4x6", COA 425.00
Truman, Harry; ALS on White House stationery, 1951, 6¼x9¼" .. 1,700.00
Twitty, Conway; bl sig on pk album pg, 1960.............................. 44.00
Wayne, John; True Grit program card w/sig, 7x10".................... 515.00
Werner, Hans; ISP, blk & wht, 1950s, 4x6", COA 85.00
Woods, Tiger; sig on Bush Field Aviation Services paper............. 127.00
Wray, Fay; SP, blk & wht, bold sig, 4x6", COA 68.00

Automobilia

While some automobilia buffs are primarily concerned with restoring vintage cars, others concentrate on only one area of collecting. For instance, hood ornaments were often quite spectacular. Made of chrome or nickel plate on brass or bronze, they were designed to represent the 'winged maiden' Victory, flying bats, sleek greyhounds, soaring eagles, and a host of other creatures. Today they often bring prices in the $75.00 to $200.00 range. R. Lalique glass ornaments go much higher!

Horns, radios, clocks, gear shift knobs, and key chains with company emblems are other areas of interest. Generally, items pertaining to the classics of the '30s are most in demand. Paper advertising material, manuals, and catalogs in excellent condition are also collectible.

License plate collectors search for the early porcelain-on-cast-iron examples. First year plates (e.g., Massachusetts, 1903; Wisconsin, 1905; Indiana, 1913) are especially valuable. The last of the states to issue regulation plates were South Carolina and Texas in 1917, and Florida in 1918. While many northeastern states had registered hundreds of thousands of vehicles by the 1920s making these plates relatively common, those from the southern and western states of that period are considered rare. Naturally, condition is important. While a pair in mint condition might sell for as much as $100.00 to $125.00, a pair with chipped or otherwise damaged porcelain may sometimes be had for as little as $25.00 to $30.00. Unless noted otherwise our values are for examples in excellent or better condition. Our advisor for this category is Leonard Needham; he is listed in the Directory under California. See also Gas Globes and Panels.

Ad, Oldsmobile 98 Convertible, 1953 Summer Classic, 12½x9½", G...13.00
Ad, 1960 Studebaker Lark Convertible, 1959, 8¼x11" 11.00
Brochure, New Chevrolet 1946, 14-pg, 8x10" 28.00
Card, ownership: Hudson Terraplene Coupe, 1936, 2¼x3½", VG ..55.00
Catalog, Edsel Master Parts, 1958-60, 931-pg 235.00
Catalog, Reading Standard Motorcycles, illustrated, 1916, 12-pg, 10x7" ..130.00
Clock, dash; LaSalle, Jaeger Watch Co NY, 1928 .... 100.00
Clock, dash; Pierce Arrow, jeweled on front, Borg Corp, 1930s... 110.00
Clock, Packard, tabletop, neon w/aluminum housing, 21" dia ..1,100.00
Comic book, Chevrolet, Once a Champion, 1963 .... 30.00
Emblem, Hupmobile w/in H, faded enameling, 2" dia.................. 35.00
Emblem, Oldsmobile Hydra-Matic Drive, enamel on chrome, 15" L, VG ..30.00
Emblem, Oldsmobile 88 Rocket, chrome 35.00
Emblem, trunk; Camaro by Chevrolet, w/mts, ca 1968-69, unused...30.00
Game, Test Driver at the Chrysler Corp, board game, 1956, EXIB ..35.00
Gauge, oil pressure; LaSalle, 1928, unused........................ 75.00
Gauge, tire; Buick models 28-58 pressures listed on front, +pouch ..55.00
Gauge, tire; Hupmobile, rpl dial, orig NP 55.00
Grill pc, Studebaker Bullet Nose, 1950, VG...................... 165.00
Grille, Packard, chrome, 1946-47, unused 175.00
Hood ornament, Buick Special, airliner style, 1956, 14" L 88.00
Hood ornament, Chrysler Imperial, eagle w/in circle, early 1960s . 25.00
Hood ornament, Deco lady w/flowing hair, chrome, 1930s, 3½x9½".. 125.00
Hood ornament, DeSoto, goddess w/wings, needs rechromed, VG..... 215.00
Hood ornament, Dodge, ram on base, 1936, 5½x4¾" 150.00
Hood ornament, Dodge, ram's head for truck, early 1980s 45.00
Hood ornament, Pierce Arrow, nude man, chromed, Franklin Mint, 1987 ..95.00
Hood ornament, Studebaker, goose, NP, 1932-34, lt pitting, VG....165.00
Horn, Model T Ford (script), rpt blk finish, 9½x4½"dia+bracket....145.00
Hubcap, H (Hupmobile) emb on brass, screw-on type, ca 1920s, single ..20.00
Hubcap, Pierce Arrow V8, 1935, single, VG 50.00
Hubcaps, Cadillac, 1962, set of 4 .... 70.00
Hubcaps, Chrysler Imperial, 1959, set of 4...................... 100.00
Hubcaps, Hudson, chrome w/red enameled triangle, pr 35.00
Hubcaps, Mercury, for 15" wheels, 1956, pr 110.00
Hubcaps, Mercury V8, 1940s, pr 35.00
Hubcaps, Oldsmobile, red enamel on chrome, 1935, 9", set of 4.... 40.00
Hubcaps, Oldsmobile, shield emblem on chrome, 1950s, 10½", pr ..30.00
Hubcaps, Packard, enamel on chrome, 1952, unused, pr............. 160.00
Hubcaps, Studebaker Air Flow, 1959-64, set of 4 .... 350.00
License plate topper, Pierced Arrow, emb brass w/blk enamel........ 65.00
License plate topper, Woco Pep, emb die-cut tin, 5½x9½".......... 70.00
Manual, owner's; Buick, 1948, 32-pg, VG.......................... 45.00
Manual, owner's; Cadillac, 1965.................................... 18.00
Manual, owner's; Packard Six, brn cover, 1939, VG.................. 18.00
Manual, owner's; Studebaker Big Six, 1926, 62-pg, EX 27.50
Medallion, Chevrolet, bl & wht enamel on porc, 4¼" L 24.00
Mirror, side; Buick, 1950s, 6½x5"................................. 37.50
Mirror, sun visor; Buick, 1950s-60s, 3½x10" 45.00
Motometer, Pierce Arrow radiator cap/temperature gauge, M in G- box ..325.00
Paperweight, Studebaker, clear glass, emb banner/tire in center 90.00
Pennant, Dort, red, Own a Dort You Will Like It, 1915-1924, 5½x2" ...88.00
Pennant, Ford dealership printing on felt, ca 1915, 16" 375.00
Pin, Studebaker Master Mechanic, emb metal, ½" dia 210.00
Pocket mirror, Chevrolet, celluloid, 1920s Maine dealership, 2x3"....230.00
Postcard, 16 HP Decauville w/Fred Terry & J Neilson photo, 1906, VG ..9.00
Promotional car, Buick 1956 hardtop, bl, AMT 60.00
Promotional car, Cadillac Coupe de Ville, Johan, 1964, MIB........ 60.00
Promotional car, Cadillac Eldorado, olive gr, Johan, 1968 .... 165.00
Promotional car, Chevrolet Camaro SS, bright orange, 1969 .... 90.00
Promotional car, Chrysler New Yorker, Johan, 1958 .... 65.00
Promotional car, Dodge Royal Lancer 1955 hardtop, AMT........... 75.00
Promotional car, Edsel, bl & wht, friction drive, 1958 .... 75.00
Promotional car, Ford Fairlane 300, Hubley, 1960s, VG 100.00

Promotional car, Ford Thunderbird convertible, AMT, 1960s 125.00
Promotional car, Mercury Monterey convertible, silver & wht, 1961..70.00
Promotional car, Mercury sedan, dk red, AMT, 1962, VG 165.00
Promotional truck, Chevrolet Pickup, friction drive, 1959, 3x8", MIB..95.00
Radiator cap, Ford Model A, flying quail, chrome, 4", VG 100.00
Radiator emblem, Hudson Motor Car Co, mc enamel on triangle, 1920s. 18.00
Seat covers, 1957 Chevrolet convertible, clear plastic, 1980s, MIB.......50.00
Sign, Authorized Studebaker Service, 2-sided, red/wht/yel, 42" dia.2,520.00
Sign, dealer's; 1955 Studebaker President V-8 4-door sedan, 19x24" 90.00

Sign, MoPar Parts, double-sided tin with flange, 24" wide, EX, $250.00. (Photo courtesy Dunbar Gallery)

Specimeter, Ford Special (Model T), Stewart Warner.................. 135.00
Spotlight, chrome, Lorraine Controllable, 1930s, complete......... 145.00
Step plate, rumble-seat rear-foot; LaSalle, 1937-38 .... 60.00
Thermometer, Cadillac, Weld It, NP, 3" dia 130.00
Tire pump, 3-cylinder hand type, Acorn Stevens NY, 1920s-30s, VG...65.00
Tool box, Model T Ford running board type, Yale lock, 10x24x12".... 135.00
Wrench, adjustable; Pierce Arrow, brass, Billings & Spencer, VG...35.00

Autumn Leaf

In 1933 the Hall China Company designed a line of dinnerware for the Jewel Tea Company, who offered it to their customers as premiums. Although you may hear the ware referred to as 'Jewel Tea,' it was officially named 'Autumn Leaf' in the 1940s. In addition to the dinnerware, frosted Libbey glass tumblers, stemware, and a melmac service with the orange and gold bittersweet pod were available over the years, as were tablecloths, plastic covers for bowls and mixers, and metal items such as cake safes, hot pads, coasters, wastebaskets, and canisters. Even shelf paper and playing cards were made to coordinate. In 1958 the International Silver Company designed silver-plated flatware in a pattern called 'Autumn' which was to be used with dishes in the Autumn Leaf pattern. A year later, a line of stainless flatware was introduced. These accessory lines are prized by collectors today.

One of the most fascinating aspects of collecting the Autumn Leaf pattern has been the wonderful discoveries of previously unlisted pieces. Among these items are two different bud-ray lid one-pound butter dishes; most recently a one-pound butter dish in the 'Zephyr' or 'Bingo' style; a miniature set of the 'Casper' salt and pepper shakers; coffee, tea, and sugar canisters; a pair of candlesticks; an experimental condiment jar; and a covered candy dish. All of these china pieces are attributed to the Hall China Company. Other unusual items have turned up in the accessory lines as well and include a Libbey frosted tumbler in a pilsner shape, a wooden serving bowl, and an apron made from the oilcloth (plastic) material that was used in the 1950s tablecloth. These latter items appear to be professionally done, and we can only speculate as to their origin. Collectors believe that the Hall items were sample pieces that were never meant to be distributed.

Hall discontinued the Autumn Leaf line in 1978. At that time the date was added to the backstamp to mark ware still in stock in the Hall warehouse. A special promotion by Jewel saw the reintroduction of basic dinnerware and serving pieces with the 1978 backstamp. These pieces have made their way into many collections. Additionally, in 1979 Jewel released a line of enamel-clad cookware and a Vellux blanket made by Martex which were decorated with the Autumn Leaf pattern. They continued to offer these items for a few years only, then all distribution of Autumn Leaf items was discontinued.

It should be noted that the Hall China Company has produced several limited edition items for the National Autumn Leaf Collectors Club (NALCC): a New York-style teapot (1984); an Edgewater vase (1987, different than the original shape); candlesticks (1988); a Philadelphia-style teapot, creamer, and sugar set (1990); a tea-for-two set and a Solo tea set (1991); a donut jug; and a large oval casserole. Later came the small ball jug, one-cup French teapot, and a set of four chocolate mugs. Other special items over the past few years made for them by Hall China include a sugar packet holder, a chamberstick, and an oyster cocktail. Additional items are scheduled for production. All of these are plainly marked as having been made for the NALCC and are appropriately dated. A few other pieces have been made by Hall as limited editions for China Specialties, but these are easily identified: the Airflow teapot and the Norris refrigerator pitcher (neither of which was previously decorated with the Autumn Leaf decal), a square-handled beverage mug, and the new-style Irish mug. A production problem with the square-handled mugs halted their production. Additional items available now are a covered onion soup, tall bud vase, china kitchen memo board, canisters, and egg drop-style salt and pepper shakers with a mustard pot. They have also issued a deck of playing cards and Libbey tumblers. See *Garage Sale & Flea Market Annual* (Collector Books) for suggested values for club pieces. Our advisor for this category is Gwynneth Harrison; she is listed in the Directory under California. For more information we recommend *Collector's Encyclopedia of Hall China, Third Edition*, by Margaret and Kenn Whitmyer.

Baker, French, 2-pt 175.00
Baker, oval, Fort Pitt, 12-oz ind 225.00
Baker/souffle, 4½" 80.00
Bean pot, 2-hdl, 2¼-qt 250.00
Book, Mary Dunbar Cookbook 30.00
Bowl, cream soup; hdls 40.00
Bowl, flat soup; 8½", from $16 to 20.00
Bowl, refrigerator; metal w/plastic lids, 3 for 275.00
Bowl, Royal Glas-bake, set of 4, from $400 to 500.00
Bowl, soup; Melmac 20.00
Bowl, vegetable; divided, oval 125.00
Bowl cover set, plastic, 8-pc, 7 assorted covers in pouch 100.00
Butter dish, ¼-lb, sq top, rare 2,000.00

Butter dish, quarter-pound, wings top, from $1,500.00 to $2,000.00.

Butter dish, 1-lb, ruffled top, regular 500.00
Calendar, 1920s-30s, from $100 to 200.00
Candy dish, metal base, from $500 to 600.00
Canister, brn & gold, wht plastic lid 30.00
Canisters, metal, rnd, w/copper-tone lids, set of 4, from $600 to ... 1,200.00
Case, carrying; Jewel salesman, from $150 to 300.00
Casserole, Heatflow, Dunbar, clear, w/lid, rnd, 1½-qt, from $50 to ... 75.00

Catalog, Jewel, hardback, from $20 to 50.00
Cleanser can, from $750 to 1,500.00
Clock, electric 550.00
Clock, salesman's award 250.00
Coffee dispenser, from $200 to 400.00
Coffeepot, Jewel's Best, 30-cup 600.00
Cookie jar, Big Ear, Zeisel, from $250 to 350.00
Creamer & sugar bowl, Nautilus 125.00
Creamer & sugar bowl, Rayed, 1930s style 80.00
Custard cup, Heatflow clear glass, Mary Dunbar, from $40 to 60.00
Dripper, metal, for 8- or 9-cup coffeepot 35.00
Flatware, SP, ea 35.00
Flatware, stainless steel, ea, from $25 to 30.00
Flatware, stainless steel, serving pc, ea from $90 to 130.00
Fondue set, complete, from $200 to 300.00
Fry pan, Mary Dunbar, top stove-ware glass 175.00
Hurricane lamps, Douglas, w/metal base, pr, minimum value 500.00
Jug, utility; Rayed, 2½-pt, 6" 25.00
Loaf pan, Mary Dunbar, from $90 to 125.00
Mug, conic 65.00
Pickle fork, Jewel Tea 40.00
Pie plate, Heatflow, clear glass, Mary Dunbar, from $45 to 60.00
Plate, salad; Melmac, 7" 20.00
Plate, 10" 18.00
Platter, oval, 11½", from $20 to 28.00
Pressure cooker, Mary Dunbar, metal 225.00
Saucepan, metal, w/lid, 2-qt 100.00
Shakers, range, hdl, pr, from $20 to 45.00
Shelf liner, 108" roll 50.00
Syrup pitcher, club pc, 1995 .... 95.00
Tablecloth, cotton sailcloth w/gold stripe, 54x72" 140.00
Tablecloth, muslin, 56x81" 300.00
Tablecloth, plastic 150.00
Teapot, Newport, dtd 1978, from $200 to 250.00
Teapot, Solo, club pc, 1,400 made, 1991 .... 100.00
Tidbit tray, 3-tier 100.00
Towel, tea; cotton, 16x33" 60.00
Tumbler, Libbey, gold frost etched, flat or ftd, 15-oz, ea 65.00
Vase, bud; regular decal, 6" 350.00
Vase, Edgewater, club pc, 626 made, 1987 .... 550.00
Warmer, oval, from $150 to 225.00

Aviation

Aviation buffs are interested in any phase of flying, from early developments with gliders, balloons, airships, and flying machines to more modern innovations. Books, catalogs, photos, patents, lithographs, ad cards, and posters are among the paper ephemera they treasure alongside models of unlikely flying contraptions, propellers and rudders, insignia and equipment from WWI and WWII, and memorabilia from the flights of the Wright Brothers, Lindbergh, Earhart, and the Zeppelins. See also Militaria. Our advisor for this category is John R. Joiner; he is listed in the Directory under Georgia.

Altimeter, aneroid #1576, Th Usteri-Reinacher, brass, w/vernier, 2" .. 415.00
Badge, hat; Pan Am pilot's, golden globe, 5th issue, ca 1979-91 .... 55.00
Badge, Pan Am Deputy Sheriff, eng Indian scene on silver, 2½" . 365.00
Badge, TWA pilot's, world logo, gold filled w/red enamel, 1950s . 165.00
Bank, United Airlines, plastic Menehune (Hawaiian male) figure, 9" ... 265.00
Blanket, Braniff Airlines, bl/aqua/purple wool, Girard, 1966, 58x42" .. 45.00
Blanket, Pan Am & globe logo on bl polyester, 60x37" 50.00
Brochure, American Airlines, stewardess career info, 1960s 95.00
Brochure, Continental Airlines, aircraft fleet, ca 1973, 30 mc pgs. 45.00

Cigarette lighter, Pan Am logo, plays Pan Am jingle, Prince, NMIB ..60.00
Coffee/tea set, American Airlines, stainless steel, 3-pc+tray..........95.00
Cup & saucer, American Airlines, AA logo w/gold, Wessco, set of 12.. 5.00
Hat, Eastern Airlines pilot's, w/cap badge, ca 1970s 80.00
Hat, Eastern Airlines stewardess', w/wings pin, w/1966 certificate ... 100.00
Hat, TWA pilot's, w/Indian head hat badge, 1930s, EX 400.00
Head phones, Pan Am, turq-bl ear pcs, lt rust on hinges................70.00
Headset, David Clark Model H10-13.4...200.00
Jacket, Pan Am Cargo Services, bl w/breast patch, red quilted lining... 115.00
Log book, Pan Am Stewardess Air Log, 1950s, w/passport.............60.00
Luggage label, Deco couple & Black porter, ca 1930, 3x3"..............55.00
Manual, Eastern Airlines, Lockheed Constellation plane, 1950 .. 115.00
Model, Delta Airlines Boeing 747, Inflight 200, 13¾", MIB 180.00
Model, Douglas DC-8F, shiny metal, K&B Allyn Co, 1950s, 10" wingspan...275.00
Model, Pan Am Boeing B-377 Stratocruiser, plastic, 1950s, 11" wingspan ..85.00
Model, TWA Boeing 707, metal w/ashtray base, Riff #5226, 1957, 10½"....365.00
Model, TWA Tri-Star L-1011, pnt mahog, 17½" wingspan, on base.. 95.00
Pen & pencil set, American Airlines (AA red/bl), sterling/cobalt, MIB.. 90.00
Pendant, Pan Am 1927-1991, globe center, yel gold, 1¾"..............90.00
Pin, TWA 25 Years Service, propeller, single dmn in center..........80.00
Propeller, Gardner, mahog w/copper-edged tips & edges, 8' L, VG..940.00
Tie tack, Eastern Airlines, Hat in the Ring, 10k gold/2 sm dmns.. 215.00
Timetable, E African Airways, 1975, 63-pg 55.00
Timetable, Northwest Airlines, showing Boeing 720B jet, 1961.... 35.00
Timetable, Pan Am Airways System, DC-3 Clipper photos, 1937, NM.. 75.00
Travel bag, Japan Airlines, JAL logo on red, zipper/strap, 14x12x5".. 85.00
Travel bag, Pan Am, bl & wht cloth, zipper/strap, 15" L................60.00
Travel bag, Swiss Air, bl cloth, zipper/strap, 1960s, 15x11x5" 60.00
Uniform, Eastern Airlines stewardess', bl/wht, w/purse, 1960s, 6-pc ..315.00
Wing, Pan Am stewardess', 10k gold w/bl enameling.................200.00
Wings, Air Atlanta Airlines pilot's, blk/gold, ca 1985-87, 3" 35.00
Wings, cap; Piedmont Airline pilot's, screw-bk, 1974-89, 3"........230.00
Wings, Intercontinental Airways pilot's, pin-bk, 1970s, 3¼" 110.00
Wings, TWA pilot's, Indian head center, 1930s-40s, 3⅜"............385.00
Wings, TWA stewardess', red/wht enamel, gold-tone metal, 1960s, 2¼" ..180.00

Baccarat

The Baccarat Glass company was founded in 1765 near Luneville, France, and continues to this day to produce quality crystal tableware, vases, perfume bottles, and figurines. The firm became famous for the high-quality millefiori and caned paperweights produced there from 1845 until about 1860. Examples of these range from $300.00 to as much as several thousand. Since 1953 they have resumed the production of paperweights on a limited edition basis. Our advisors for this category are Randall Monsen and Rod Baer; their address is listed in the Directory under Virginia. See also Bottles, Commercial Perfume; Paperweights.

Vase, cameo-cut flower on cobalt, 7¼", EX, $325.00.

(Photo courtesy Cincinnati Art Galleries)

Bowl, cameo, translucent leaves, red/gr on gr martele, w/gilt, 10"...310.00
Candelabrum, 2-light, swirl-form base, prisms, 13x9½"...............350.00
Champagne, Vence, 4¼", 12 for 135.00
Decanter, fluted sides, spherical w/stick neck, stopper, 12½"........180.00
Decanter, slender neck ovoid body, flat stopper, 9½x5½" 60.00
Decanter, sloped shoulders, sq sides, w/stopper, 7⅞" 150.00
Figurine, alligator, 17" L 500.00
Figurine, duck, frosted, 3½" 50.00
Figurine, eagle resting on boulder, 10x4x4½", from $185 to.........215.00
Figurine, frog, 2¾x4⅞"...100.00
Figurine, giraffe, recumbent, amber frost, Vanderveen, 4⅝x9" 495.00
Figurine, horse head, windswept mane, Prigot, 7½x13½"...........600.00
Figurine, Lioness Awakening, reclining/yawning, 9½" 7,000.00
Figurine, nautilus shell, frosted ribs, 4½x6" 400.00
Figurine, owl, 4⅛"..50.00
Figurine, panther reclining, 10½" 480.00
Figurine, parrot resting on boulder, #62/125, 6¾x3x9" 175.00
Figurine, porcupine, 2¾"...150.00
Figurine, rabbit w/head turned, 3" 70.00
Figurine, squirrel w/tail up, 4½x2½x¾"..................................130.00
Figurine, stallion rearing, blk, 12" 340.00
Ice bucket, emb ribs, SP hdl, 5½x5⅝".....................................200.00
Jar, scrolling foliage & trellis, ruby & gold on squat bombe form, 6" ..1,500.00
Mirror, crystal & bronze, ped ft, ca 1830, att, 28½" 1,000.00
Placecard holders, upright shell form, 2", 8 for 210.00
Plate, graduated teardrop-shaped petals, 9¾" 150.00
Sculpture, flame, Clausen, 13"...750.00
Sculpture, ice crystal, 7½x6"...50.00
Stem, cordial, Carcassone, 3¼x1½"...15.00
Stem, goblet, Piccadilly, 8 for 395.00
Stem, sherbet/champagne, Lucullus, 1950s-60s, 5".......................65.00
Stem, wine, Lucullus, 5¾" 75.00
Tumbler, highball; Harmonie, 12-oz, 5½", 6 for 350.00
Vase, cameo floral spray, pastels on red to frost, 12½"...............1,200.00
Vase, classical figures HP on opaline, ftd, 1870s, 36x11¾", pr.17,500.00
Vase, gold decor, bronze mts at rim & ft, ca 1880, 12¾x5"...........550.00
Vase, shell-form body, ftd, 8¼x4"..125.00
Vase, swirls on globular form, 7¼x5½"....................................110.00

Badges

The breast badge came into general usage in this country about 1840. Since most are not marked and styles have changed very little to the present day, they are often difficult to date. The most reliable clue is the pin and catch. One of the earliest types, used primarily before the turn of the century, involved a 't-pin' and a 'shell' catch. In a second style, the pin was hinged with a small square of sheet metal, and the clasp was cylindrical. From the late 1800s until about 1940, the pin and clasp were made from one continuous piece of thin metal wire. The same type, with the addition of a flat back plate, was used a little later. There are exceptions to these findings, and other types of clasps were also used. Hallmarks and inscriptions may also help pinpoint an approximate age.

Badges have been made from a variety of materials, usually brass or nickel silver; but even solid silver and gold were used for special orders. They are found in many basic shapes and variations — stars with five to seven points, shields, disks, ovals, and octagonals being most often encountered. Of prime importance to collectors, however, is that the title and/or location appear on the badge. Those with designations of positions no longer existing (City Constable, for example) and names of early western states and towns are most valuable.

Badges are among the most commonly reproduced (and faked) types of antiques on the market. At any flea market, 10 fakes can be found for every authentic example. Genuine law badges start at $30.00 to $40.00

for recent examples (1950 – 1970); earlier pieces (1910 – 1930) usually bring $50.00 to $90.00. Pre-1900 badges often sell for more than $100.00. Authentic gold badges are usually priced at a minimum of scrap value (karat, weight, spot price for gold); fine gold badges from before 1900 can sell for $400.00 to $800.00, and a few will bring even more. A fire badge is usually valued at about half the price of a law badge from the same era and material. Our values have been gleaned from Internet auctions and are actual selling prices.

Chicago Police, 6-point star w/red enamel, Meyer & Wenth, early 1900s...500.00
City Marshall Police, 6-point star, nickel, early 1900s, 2½" 165.00

DeLaval Special Police, nickel plated, rare, VG, $275.00.

Deputy Sheriff, 5-point star in shield, nickel, hallmk, 1900s, 2" ..160.00
Deputy Sheriff Baltimore MD, eagle top, gold plate, Hahn, 1920s.....155.00
Deputy Sheriff Franklin Co OH, eagle on shield, gold plate, 1890s...160.00
Deputy Sheriff Nueces Co (TX), 5-point star, Sterling mk, 1½" ..115.00
Deputy Sheriff Ramsey Co MN, 6-point star, nickel, 1910s........... 70.00
Deputy Sheriff, star in circle, brass, Pannier Bro, 1900s, 2½" 110.00
Deputy Sheriff Wyandotte Co, 5-point star in shield, 1900s, 3¾" ...165.00
Deputy Yolo Co Sheriff, 5-point star in circle, 1¾" 195.00
Director of Public Safety Toledo OH, gold metal, 1910, 2½" 850.00
Special Deputy Pierce Co WA, nickel, ca 1930s-40s.....................125.00
Special Deputy Sheriff, nickel, CD Reese...NY, early 1900s.........135.00
Special Deputy Sheriff New Haven CT, shield, nickel, 2½" 60.00
Special Officer (Gothic letters), 6-point star, nickel, 1900s, 2½" .. 115.00
Stock Yards Protection Police, 5-point star, chrome plate, 1938, 3"...315.00
Wm J Burns Internat'l Detective, eagle on shield, hallmk, 2x1½" ..315.00

Banks

In general, bank values are established on the auction block and sales between collectors and dealers, and the driving force that determines the final price is condition. The spread between the price of a bank in excellent condition and the identical model in only good condition continues to widen. In order to be a seasoned collector in the pursuit of wise investments, one must learn to carefully determine overall condition by assessing the amount and strength (depth) of the paint, and by checking for breaks, repairs, and replaced parts; all bear heavily on value. Paint and casting variations are other considerations the collector should become familiar with.

Banks continue to maintain their value. Mechanicals often bring astronomical prices, making it imperative that collectors understand the market. Let's take a look at the price variations possible on an Uncle Sam mechanical bank. If you find one with considerable paint missing but with some good color showing, the price would be around $1,000.00. If it has repairs or restoration, the value could drop to somewhere near $800.00 or less. Still another example with two-thirds of its original paint and no repairs would probably bring $1,800.00. If it had only minor nicks, it could go as high as $3,500.00. Should you find one in 95% paint with

no repairs, $5,000.00 or more would not be out of line. After considering all of these factors, remember: the final price is always determined by what a willing buyer and seller agree on for a specific bank.

Mechanical banks are the 'creme de la creme' in the arena of cast-iron toy collecting. They are among the most outstanding products of the Industrial Revolution and are recognized as some of the most successful of the mass-produced products of the nineteenth century. The earliest mechanicals were made of wood or lead. In 1869 John Hall introduced Hall's Excelsior, made of cast iron. It was an immediate success. J. & E. Stevens produced the bank for Hall and as a result soon began to make their own designs. Several companies followed suit, most of which were already in the hardware business. They used newly developed iron-casting techniques to produce these novelty savings devices for the emerging toy market. The social mores and customs of the times, political attitudes, racial and ethnic biases, the excitement of the circus, and humorous everyday events all served as inspiration for the creation of hundreds of banks. Designers made the most of simple mechanics to produce models with captivating actions that served not only to amuse but promote the concept of thrift to the children. The quality and detail of the castings were truly remarkable. The majority of collectible banks were made from 1870 to 1910; however, they continued to be manufactured until the onset of WWII. J. & E. Stevens, Shepard Hardware, and Kyser and Rex were some of the most prolific manufacturers of mechanicals. They made still banks as well.

Still banks are widely collected. Various materials were used in their construction, and each material represents a subfield in still bank collections. No one knows exactly how many different banks were made, but upwards of 3,000 have been identified in the various books published on the subject. Cast-iron examples still dominate the market, but lead banks from Europe are growing in value. Tin and early pottery banks are drawing more interest as well. American pottery banks which were primarily collected by Americana collectors are becoming more important in the still bank field.

To increase your knowledge of banks, attend shows and auctions. Direct contact with collectors and knowledgeable dealers is a very good way to develop a feel for prices and quality. It will also help you in gaining the ability to judge condition, and you'll learn to recognize the more desirable banks as well.

Both mechanical and still banks have been reproduced. One way to detect a reproduction is by measuring. The dimensions of a reproduced bank will always be fractionally smaller, since the original bank was cast from a pattern while the reproduction was made from a casting of the original bank. As both values and interest continue to increase, it becomes even more important to educate ourselves to the fullest extent possible. We recommend these books for your library: *The Bank Book* by Norman, *The Dictionary of Still Banks* by Long and Pitman, *The Penny Bank Book* by Moore, *Penny Banks Around the World* by Don Duer, *Registering Banks* by Robert L. McCumber, and *Penny Lane* by Davidson, which is considered the most complete reference available. It contains a cross-reference listing of numbers from all other publications on mechanical banks.

All banks are assumed to be complete and original unless noted otherwise in the description. A number of banks are commonly found with a particular repair. When this repair is reflected in our pricing, it will be so indicated. When traps (typically key lock, as in Uncle Sam) are an integral part of the body of the bank, lack of such results in a severe reduction in the value of the bank. When the trap is underneath the bank (typically a twist trap, as in Eagle and Eaglets), reduction in value is minimal.

To most accurately represent current market values, we have used condition codes in our listings that correspond with guidelines developed by today's bank collectors.

During the past year the demand for mechanical banks has been quite strong with greater emphasis on better-condition banks — the better examples bringing higher prices exponentially against lesser condition mechanical banks, even for the more common examples. Still banks also have maintained their value with higher values and greater demand leaning towards rarity and condition, although cast iron painted building banks still seem to be the most sought after by collectors.

Our advisor for mechanical and still banks is Clive Devenish, who is listed in the Directory under California.

NM — 98% paint	VG — 80% paint
PR (pristine) — 95% paint	G — 70% paint
EX — 90% paint	

Key:

AL — aluminum	NP — nickel-plated
CI — cast iron	RM — Robert McCumber Book:
M — Andy Moore Book:	*Registering Banks*
The Penny Bank Book	SM — sheet metal
N — Bill Norman Book:	WM — white metal
The Bank Book	

Book of Knowledge

Book of Knowledge Banks were produced by John Wright (Pennsylvania) from circa 1950 until 1975. Of the 30 models they made during those years, a few continued to be made in very limited numbers until the late 1980s; these they referred to as the 'Medallion' series. (Today the Medallion banks command the same prices as the earlier Book of Knowledge series.) Each bank was a handcrafted, hand-painted duplicate of an original as was found in the collection of The Book of Knowledge, the first children's encyclopedia in this country. Because the antique banks are often priced out of the range of many of today's collectors, these banks are being sought out as affordable substitutes for their very expensive counterparts. It should also be noted that China has reproduced banks with the Book of Knowledge inscription on them. These copies are flooding the market, causing authentic Book of Knowledge banks to decline in value. Buyers should take extra caution when investing in Book of Knowledge banks and purchase them through a reputable dealer who offers a satisfaction guarantee as well as a guarantee that the bank is authentic. Our advisor for Book of Knowledge banks is Dan Iannotti; he is listed in the Directory under Michigan.

The Magician, MIB, $175.00. (Photo courtesy Dan Iannotti)

Always Did 'Spise a Mule, Boy on Bench, M	175.00
Artillery Bank, NM	150.00
Boy on Trapeze, M	250.00
Butting Buffalo, M	135.00
Cat & Mouse, NM	150.00
Cow (Kicking), NM	195.00
Creedmore Bank, M	195.00
Dentist Bank, EX	125.00
Eagle & Eaglets, M	195.00
Humpty Dumpty, M	150.00

Indian & Bear, M	195.00
Jonah & the Whale, M	150.00
Leap Frog, NM	175.00
Organ Bank (Boy & Girl), NM	150.00
Owl (Turns Head), NM	150.00
Paddy & Pig, NM	175.00
Punch & Judy, NM	150.00
Teddy & the Bear, NM	135.00
Uncle Remus, M	150.00
US & Spain, M	150.00
William Tell, M	195.00

Mechanical

Afghanistan, N-1020, CI, VG	3,200.00
Always Did 'Spise a Mule (Bench), N-2940, CI, PR	3,800.00
Artillery (Union), N-1060, CI, G	1,100.00
Bad Accident, N-1150, CI, EX	3,800.00
Bear (slot in chest), N-1220, CI, VG	2,200.00
Bismark Bank, N-1280, CI, VG	5,500.00
Boys Stealing Watermelons, N-1380, CI, VG	2,200.00
Bread Winners Bank, N-1390, CI, PR	30,000.00
Bulldog (coin on nose), N-1430, CI, G	1,100.00
Butting Goat, N-1580, CI, EX	950.00
Calamity Bank, N-1630, CI, VG	9,500.00
Chief Big Moon, N-1740, CI, EX	3,500.00
Clever Dick, N-1840, tin, EX	2,000.00
Clown & Dog, N-1850, tin, EX	2,000.00
Clown Bust, N-1880, CI, VG	6,000.00
Clown on Globe, James Capron, NM	450.00
Confectionery, N-1970, CI, PR	20,000.00
Cowboy w/Tray, N-1990, tin, PR	1,800.00
Eagle & Eaglets, N-2230, CI, PR	2,500.00
Fowler, N-2480, CI, EX	18,000.00
Giant Standing, N-2610, CI, PR	20,000.00
Girl in Victorian Chair, N-2630, CI, VG	2,500.00
Girl Skipping Rope, N-2680, CI, EX	35,000.00
Guessing Bank, N-2680, CI, VG	3,800.00
Hall's Liliput, N-2740, CI, EX	1,600.00
Hen & Chick (wht hen), N-2790, CI, VG	3,800.00
Horse Race, N-2890, CI, G	5,500.00
Humpty Dumpty, N-2900, CI, VG	2,800.00
Lighthouse Bank, N-3620, CI, PR	5,500.00
Lion & Monkeys, James Capron, NM	550.00
Lion & 2 Monkeys, N-3650, CI, EX	3,500.00
Lion Hunter, N-3660, CI, PR	14,000.00
Lucky Wheel Money Box, N-3710, CI, PR	700.00
Magic Bank, James Capron, M	450.00
Magician, N-3760, CI, EX	4,500.00
Milking Cow, N-3870, CI, fence rpr, overpnt	5,000.00
Monkey & Coconut, N-3940, CI, VG	2,200.00
Monkey Bank, N-3960, CI, VG	400.00
Organ Bank (mini), N-4340, CI, VG	1,400.00
Owl, slot in book, N-4360, CI, VG	500.00
Picture Gallery, N-4560, CI, G	12,000.00
Pig in a High Chair, N-4570, PR	1,600.00
Presto (Building), N-4650, CI, EX	650.00
Punch & Judy, N-4740, CI, VG	3,000.00
Rabbit in Cabbage, N-4790, CI, VG	1,100.00
Rooster, N-4920, CI, EX	1,200.00
Speaking Dog, N-5170, CI, VG	1,500.00
Stump Speaker, N-5370, CI, EX	3,800.00
Tammany, N-5420, CI, PR	1,800.00
Tank & Cannon, N-5440, CI, EX	750.00

Trick Dog (6-part base), N-5620, CI, VG 2,200.00
Uncle Remus, N-5730, CI, VG 6,800.00
Uncle Sam, N-5740, CI, rpl trap, VG 2,500.00
Unites States Bank (safe), N-5790, CI, G 800.00
Wireless Bank, N-5980, wood, VG 300.00
World's Fair Bank, N-6040, CI, EX 1,000.00
Zoo Bank, N-6070, CI, EX 2,200.00

Registering

Beehive, NPCI, window on side, detailed, H&H, 1891, 5⅜", EX ...200.00
Captain Marvel's Magic Dime Saver (pocket), tin, RM-223, EX 275.00
Chein Mercury Dime (pocket), tin, RM-227, EX 60.00
Clock Face, 2 hands registering dollars & cents, ornate CI, VG ...1,450.00
Clown & Monkey Daily Dime (pocket), tin, RM-224, EX 60.00
Coin Registering Bank, mid-Eastern building, Kayser & Rex, 1890s, EX 7,750.00
Columbian Recording Bank, NPCI, RM-24, EX 250.00
Dime a Day Thrifty Elf (pocket), tin, RM-229, EX 100.00
Donald Duck Bank (cash register), tin, RM-97, EX 225.00
Dopey Dime Register (pocket), tin, RM-218, EX 180.00
Gem Registering, w/orig paper label, J&E Stevens, ca 1893, NM ..3,000.00
George Washington Bank, tin, RM-67, EX 150.00
Imperial 3 Coin Bank, bronze, RM-16, EX 400.00
Jackie Robinson (pocket), tin, RM-234 ....500.00
Keep 'Em Sailing Dime Register (pocket), tin, RM-220, EX 440.00
Little Orphan Annie (pocket), tin, RM-213, EX 225.00
National Recording Bank, dime register, CI, Pat Apr 7, 1891, ...265.00
Penny Register Bank (pail), CI, RM-22, EX 225.00
Popeye Daily Quarter, tin litho, USA, 4½", EX 150.00
Prince Valiant (pocket), tin, RM-231, EX 125.00
Prudential Registering Savings Bank (25¢), NPCI, RM-17, EX ..400.00
Superman Dime Register (pocket), tin, RM-216, EX 125.00
Time Clock, NPCI, Ives, Blakeslee & Williams, ca 1893, EX ...2,750.00
Trunk Savings Bank, NPCI, RM-35, EX 200.00
Uncle Sams Nickel Register Bank, sheet steel cash register, RM-79, EX... 125.00
United Nations Register (pocket), tin, RM-236, EX 60.00
Woven Basket Dime Bank, CI, RM-28, EX 200.00

Still

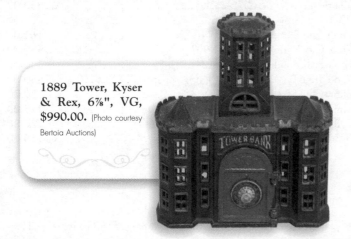

1889 Tower, Kyser & Rex, 6⅞", VG, $990.00. (Photo courtesy Bertoia Auctions)

Airplane Spirit of St Louis, M-1423, steel, EX 600.00
Amherst Buffalo, M-556, CI, 5¼", EX 525.00
Andy Gump, M-217, CI, EX 1,500.00
Arcade Steamboat, M-1460, CI, 2⅜" H, EX 500.00
Baby in Cradle, M-51, NPCI, EX 2,200.00
Baby in Egg (Black), M-261, lead, 7¼", EX 495.00
Baseball on 3 Bats, M-1608, CI, EX 1,500.00
Baseball Player, M-19, CI, 5¾", NM 1,125.00

Battleship Maine, M-1439, CI, 6", EX 4,950.00
Battleship Oregon, M-1439, CI, EX 3,800.00
Bear Stealing Pig, M-693, CI, rpl screw, 5½", G 600.00
Beehive Bank, M-683, CI, EX 225.00
Begging Rabbit, M-566, CI, 5⅛", EX 250.00
Billiken Bank, M-74, CI, EX 85.00
Billy Bounce (Give Billy a Penny), M-15, CI, 4¾", VG 385.00
Bird on Stump (Songbird), M-664, CI, EX 400.00
Boston Bull Terrier, M-421, CI, 5¼", EX 220.00
Boy Scout, M-45, CI, EX 150.00
Buffalo, M-560, CI w/gold pnt, 3⅛", EX 145.00
Bugs Bunny (Barrel), M-270, WM, EX 175.00
Building w/Eagle Finial, M-1134, CI, 9¾", EX 935.00
Bulldog (seated), M-396, CI, 3⅞", NM 440.00
Buster Brown & Tige, M-241, CI, gold & red pnt, 5½", VG 175.00
Buster Brown & Tige, M-242 variant, CI, 5½", NM 935.00
Cadet, M-8, CI, crack at slot, 5¾", VG 165.00
Camel (Oriental), M-769, CI, EX 1,800.00
Camel (Oriental), M-769, CI, 3¾", G 360.00
Camel (Sm), M-768, CI, 4¾", EX 250.00
Campbell Kids, M-163, CI, gold pnt, 3¾", EX 330.00
Cat on Tub, M-358, CI, gold pnt, 4⅛", EX 175.00
Cat on Tub, M-358, CI, 4⅛", EX 195.00
Cat w/a Bowtie, M-350, CI, EX 175.00
Cat w/Ball, M-352, CI, EX 225.00
Charlie McCarthy on Trunk, M-207, compo, 5¼", M 475.00
City Bank w/Chimney, M-1101, CI, old rpt, 6¾" 1,595.00
Clock 'Time Is Money,' M-1555, CI, EX 350.00
Clown, M-211, CI, EX 125.00
Colonial House, M-992, CI, 4", EX 140.00
Columbia Bank, M-1070, CI, 5¾", EX 615.00
Columbia Tower, M-1118, CI, rpl turn pin, 6⅞", VG 745.00
Crystal Bank, M-926, CI & glass, EX 70.00
Cupola, M-1146, CI, 4⅛", EX 375.00
Deer (Lg), M-737, CI, EX 200.00
Deer (Sm), M-736, CI, EX 100.00
Dime Bank, M-1183, CI, 4¾", EX 140.00
Dog (Cutie), M-414, CI, EX 250.00
Dog (Scottie standing), M-435, CI, 3¾", VG 155.00
Dog (Scottie), M-419, CI, EX 275.00
Dog (Spaniel), M-418, CI, EX 225.00
Dog on Tub, M-359, CI, 4 1/16", EX 195.00
Dog w/Pack (Lg), M-437, CI, EX 200.00
Dog w/Pack (Sm), M-439, EX 100.00
Dolphin, M-33, CI, gold pnt, 4½", EX 880.00
Double Decker Bus, M-1490, CI, bl pnt, 2¼", NM 1,130.00
Duck, M-624, CI, 4¾", EX 330.00
Dutch Boy, M-180, CI, EX 150.00
Dutch Girl w/Flowers, M-181, CI, 5¼", EX 120.00
Elephant on Wheels, M-446, CI, 4⅛", EX 365.00
Elmer at Barrel, M-306, WM, EX 150.00
Eureka Trust & Savings Safe, CI, 5¾", EX 470.00
Every Copper Helps, M-71, CI, EX 900.00
Feed My Sheep (lamb), M-596, lead, gold pnt, 2¾", VG 155.00
Fidelity Trust Vault, M-903, CI, EX 650.00
Fido on a Pillow, M-443, CI, 7⅜", EX 385.00
Flat Iron Building, M-1159, CI, 8¼", EX 2,640.00
Flat Iron Building, M-1160, CI, no trap, 5¾", EX 410.00
Forlorn Dog, M-408, WM, 4¾", G 85.00
Fortune Ship, M-1457, CI, 4⅛", NM 1,760.00
Foxy Grandpa, M-320, CI, 5½", G 215.00
Gas Pump, M-1485, CI, EX 250.00
General Butler, M-54, CI, 6½", EX 3,960.00
General Grant, M-115 variant, CI, Harper, 5⅝", EX 3,740.00

Give Me a Penny, M-166, CI, EX.............................. 300.00
Globe on Arc, M-789, CI, red pnt, 5¼", EX............. 420.00
Globe on Arc, M-789, CI, 5¼", G............................ 140.00
Golliwog, M-85, CI, 6¼", EX.................................. 550.00
Goose (Red Goose Shoes), M-628, CI, EX................ 175.00
Grizzly Bear, M-703, lead, pnt worn in bk, 2¾"....... 110.00
Hansel & Gretel, M-1016, tin, 2¼", EX.................... 140.00
Hen on Nest, M-546, CI, EX............................... 1,600.00
High Rise, M-1217, CI w/japanning, 5½", EX........... 330.00
High Rise, M-1219, CI, 4⅝", EX............................. 430.00
Home Savings, M-1126, CI, 5⅞", EX....................... 320.00
Horse on Tub (decorated), M-509, CI, 5¼", VG....... 170.00
Horse Prancing, M-517, CI, EX.............................. 85.00
Horse Tally Ho, M-535, CI, EX............................... 275.00
Horseshoe 'Good Luck,' M-508, CI, EX................... 300.00
Horseshoe Wire Mesh, M-524, CI/tin, G- Arcade label, 3¼", VG... 110.00
Independence Hall Tower, M-1205, CI, 9½", EX..... 2,850.00
Indian w/Tomahawk, M-228, CI, EX....................... 400.00
Iron Master's Cabin, M-1027, CI, 4¼", EX............ 3,630.00
Jimmy Durante, M-259, WM, 6¾", EX..................... 220.00
Junior Cash Register, M-930, NPCI, EX.................. 200.00
Key, M-1616, CI, EX... 800.00
King Midas, M-13, CI, EX................................... 1,200.00
Labrador Retriever, M-412, CI, 4½", EX.................. 295.00
Lamb, M-595, CI, EX... 150.00
Liberty Bell (Harper), M-780, CI, EX..................... 300.00
Lindy Bank, M-124, AL, 6½", EX............................ 200.00
Lion, M-765, CI, sm, 4", EX.................................. 110.00
Lion (Sm, tail right), M-755, CI, 4", EX................... 85.00
Lion on Tub, M-747, CI, 4⅛", EX........................... 165.00
Litchfield Cathedral, M-968, CI, 6⅝", EX............... 495.00
Main Street Trolley (no people), M-1469, CI, gold pnt, 3", EX... 330.00
Maine (sm battleship), M-1440, CI, 4⅝", EX........... 440.00
Mammy w/Hands on Hips, M-176, CI, 5¼", EX........ 165.00
Man on Bale of Cotton, M-37, CI, 4⅞", EX........... 3,960.00
Mary & Lamb, M-164, CI, 4¾", VG......................... 770.00
Mascot Bank, M-3, CI, EX.................................. 2,200.00
Metropolitan Safe, CI, 5⅞", NM.......................... 2,420.00
Mickey Mouse Post Office, tin, cylindrical, 6", NM... 155.00
Middy, M-36, CI, w/clapper, 5¼", G....................... 150.00
Model T (2nd version), M-1483, CI, 4", NM.......... 1,155.00
Mule 'I Made St Louis Famous,' M-489, CI, Harper, 4¾", EX... 2,145.00
Mulligan, M-177, CI, 5¾", EX................................ 175.00
Newfoundland (dog), M-440, CI, 3⅝", EX............... 330.00
Ocean Liner, M-1444, lead, 2¾" H, VG................... 155.00
Oregon (Battleship), M-1452, CI, rpl turn pin, VG... 440.00
Owl on Stump, M-598, CI, EX................................ 225.00
Pass Round the Hat (Derby), M-1381, CI, 1⅝", EX... 220.00
Pearl Street Building, M-1096, worn gold overpnt, 4¼"... 420.00
Pelican, M-679, CI, EX...................................... 1,400.00
Pet Safe, M-866, CI, 4½", EX................................ 250.00
Pig 'I Made Chicago Famous,' M-629, CI, Harper, 2⅛", EX... 245.00
Pig 'I Made Chicago Famous,' M-631, CI, EX.......... 175.00
Pig (standing), M-478, CI, 3", EX.......................... 265.00
Policeman, M-182, CI, Arcade, 5½", EX................ 1,200.00
Polish Rooster, M-541, CI, 5½", EX..................... 1,375.00
Porky Pig, M-264, CI, 6", EX+.............................. 440.00
Porky Pig (Barrel), M-265, WM, EX....................... 150.00
Possum, M-561, CI, EX... 400.00
Potato Bank, M-1663, CI, EX................................ 900.00
Professor Pug Frog, M-311, CI, 3¼", EX................. 365.00
Puppo, M-416, CI, 4⅞", VG.................................. 170.00
Quilted Lion, M-758, CI, 3¾", EX.......................... 330.00
Rabbit Begging, M-566, CI, EX.............................. 150.00

Radio (Crosley), M-819, CI, 5⅛", EX...................... 745.00
Radio (Sm Crosley), M-820, CI, EX........................ 175.00
Reindeer, M-376, CI, 6¼", NM.............................. 310.00
Retriever w/a Pack, M-436, CI, 4¹¹⁄₁₆", EX............. 165.00
Rhino, M-721, CI, EX... 400.00
Roller Safe, M-880, CI, 3¹¹⁄₁₆", EX........................ 250.00
Roof Bank Building, M-1122, CI, 5¼", G................. 330.00
Rumplestiltskin, M-27, CI, 6", VG......................... 220.00
Sailor, M-27, CI, 5¼", G.. 95.00
Sailor, M-28, CI, 5½", G....................................... 140.00
Santa Claus, Ive's, M-56, CI, 7¼", EX.................... 770.00
Santa Claus w/Tree, M-61, CI, EX......................... 900.00
Save & Smile, M-1641, CI, 4¼", EX........................ 415.00
Scotties (6 in basket), M-427, WM, 4½", EX............. 85.00
Seated Rabbit, M-368, CI, 3⅝", EX........................ 165.00
Sharecropper, M-173, CI, 5½", EX......................... 305.00
Shell Out, M-1622, CI, EX.................................... 500.00
Skyscraper, M-1239, CI, 4⅜", EX.......................... 150.00
Skyscraper (6 posts), M-1241, CI, 6½", EX............. 330.00
Squirrel w/Nut, M-660, CI, 4⅛", VG...................... 515.00
State Bank, M-1078, CI, w/key, 8", NM................ 1,485.00
State Bank, M-1083, CI, 4⅛", EX........................... 275.00
State Bank, M-1085, CI, 3", EX.............................. 330.00
Statue of Liberty (Lg), M-1166, CI, EX................... 850.00
Statue of Liberty (Sm), M-1164, CI, EX.................. 150.00
Tank, M-1436, lead, 3", VG................................... 800.00
Tank Bank USA 1918 (Sm), M-1437, CI, 2⅜", EX..... 250.00
Teddy Roosevelt, M-120, CI, EX............................ 350.00
Tower Bank, M-1208, CI, 9¼", EX.......................... 440.00
Transvaal Money Box, M-1, CI, recast pipe, 6¼", VG... 3,500.00
Trust Bank, The; M-154, CI, 7¼", EX.................... 4,950.00
Turkey (Lg), M-585, CI, 4¼", EX............................ 495.00
Turkey (Sm), M-587, CI, 3⅜", EX.......................... 165.00
Two Kids (Goats), M-594, CI, EX........................... 900.00
Two-Faced Black Boy (sm), M-84, CI, 3⅛", EX........ 220.00
Two-Faced Devil, M-31, CI, 4¼", EX...................... 770.00
US Army/Navy Safe, electroplated CI, 6⅛", EX...... 1,320.00
USA Mail Mailbox w/Eagle, M-851, CI, 4⅛", EX........ 85.00
USA Mail w/Eagle, M-850, CI, EX.......................... 135.00
Villa Bank, M-1179, CI, EX................................... 850.00
Watch Me Grow, M-279 variant, tin, 5¾", EX............ 75.00
White City Barrel #1, M-908, NP, EX..................... 165.00
White City Barrel on Cart, M-907, CI, 4", EX.......... 580.00
Woolworth Building (Lg), M-1041, CI, 7⅞", EX........ 330.00
World Time Bank, M-1539, CI, orig paper, 4⅛", EX... 550.00
Yellow Cab, M-1493, CI, 4¼", VG........................ 1,320.00
Young Negro, M-170, CI, 4½", EX.......................... 275.00
1890 Tower Bank, M-1198, CI, 6⅞", EX................ 1,320.00
1893 World's Fair Administration Building, M-1072, CI, 6", EX... 715.00

Barbershop Collectibles

Even for the stranger in town, the local barbershop was easy to find, its location vividly marked with the traditional red and white striped barber pole that for centuries identified such establishments. As far back as the twelfth century, the barber has had a place in recorded history. At one time he not only groomed the beards and cut the hair of his gentlemen clients but was known as the 'blood-letter' as well, hence the red stripe for blood and the white for the bandages. Many early barbers even pulled teeth! Later, laws were enacted that divided the practices of barbering and surgery.

The Victorian barbershop reflected the charm of that era with fancy barber chairs upholstered in rich wine-colored velvet; rows of bottles made from colored art glass held hair tonics and shaving lotion. Back-bars of richly carved oak with beveled mirrors lined the wall behind the barber's station. During the late nineteenth century, the barber pole with a blue stripe added to the standard red and white as a patriotic gesture came into vogue.

Today the barbershop has all but disappeared from the American scene, replaced by modern unisex salons. Collectors search for the barber poles, the fancy chairs, and the tonic bottles of an era gone but not forgotten. Our advisor for this category is Robert Doyle; he is listed in the Directory under New York. See also Bottles; Razors; Shaving Mugs.

Barber's bowl, faience, birds/leaves/berries, rnd w/cutout, 10", VG .. 230.00
Blade bank, Listerine, porc elephant 25.00
Bottle, Pauline Hair Oil, orig label, Gibson...Dallas TX 22.50
Brush/duster, wooden soldier hdl, mc pnt 18.00
Chair, horse head at front of chair, porc & nickel, 45", EX, $1,700 to .. 1,800.00
Chair, porc/leather/nickel, lt rust/sm tears, 50" 250.00
Chair, rstr blk leather, porc arms, Koken, 53", EX 175.00
Chair, wrought iron w/wooden seat, child's, 42", EX 300.00
Chair attachment, horse's head, solid cast aluminum, 19", EX 155.00
Heater, hot water; CI, Hoffman 45, early 1900s, 30x18" dia 125.00
Jar, disinfectant; Barbicide, wht pyro on clear glass, chrome lid 20.00
Machine, Campbell Hot Lather, shiny chrome, 115 volts, 1950s?, EX... 145.00
Pole, acorn top pnt bl over red/wht pnt spirals, wall mt, 37x7", G ... 690.00
Pole, pine w/red/wht/bl rpt, trn accents, splits, 34¼" 285.00
Pole, red/wht/bl, new cylinder, Koch #8500, runs well, EX 350.00
Pole, self-standing, top half lights up & turns, metal/porc/glass, 73"...1,100.00
Pole, trn wood w/crazed mc pnt over gesso undercoat, VT, 31x8".. 2,250.00
Sign, Barber Shop between 2 poles pnt on tin, 2-sided, 21x32" ... 265.00
Sign, Masonite, barber pole depicted, Yorkcraft, 1960s, 33x7"..... 100.00
Sign, Member Assoc Master Barbers of Am, tin on cb, 6⅛x15", VG... 75.00
Steamer, towel; copper, ball top, Laria & Co...NY, 36x15" dia 275.00
Sterilizer, towel; NP, cylinder on stand, Chisholm Co NY, 64x20" .. 325.00
Stone, blade sharpening; Koken Moor, ½x3⅞x2", NM 50.00
Strop, brn leather, Genuine Shell #356 Lakeside, EX 30.00

Barometers

Barometers are instruments designed to measure the weight or pressure of the atmosphere in order to anticipate approaching weather changes. They have a glorious history. Some of the foremost thinkers of the seventeenth century developed the mercury barometer, as the discovery of the natural laws of the universe progressed. Working in 1644 from experiments by Galileo, Evangelista Torrecelli used a glass tube and a jar of mercury to create a vacuum and therefore prove that air has weight. Four years later, Rene Descartes added a paper scale to the top of Torrecelli's mercury tube and created the basic barometer. Blaise Pascal, working with Descartes, used it to determine the heights of mountains; only later was the correlation between changes in air pressure and changes in the weather observed and the term 'weather-glass' applied. Robert Boyle introduced it to England, and Robert Hook modified the form and designed the wheel barometer.

The most common type of barometer is the wheel or banjo, followed by the stick type. Modifications of the plain stick are the marine gimballed type and the laboratory, Kew, or Fortin type. Another style is the Admiral Fitzroy of which there are 12 or more variations. The above all have mercury contained either in glass tubing or wood box cisterns.

The aneroid is a variety of barometer that works on atmospheric pressure changes. These come in all sizes ranging from 1" in diameter to 12" or larger. They may be in metal or wood cases. There is also a barograph which records on a graph that rotates around a drum powered by a seven-day clock mechanism. Pocket barometers (altimeters) vary in sizes from 1" in diameter up to 6". One final type of barometer is the

symphisometer, a modification of the stick barometer; these were used for a limited time as they were not as accurate as the conventional marine barometer. Our advisor for this category is Bob Elsner; he is listed in the Directory under Florida. Prices are subject to condition of wood, tube, etc.; number of functions; and whether or not they are signed.

American Stick Barometers

Chas Wilder, Peterboro, NH 1,250.00
DE Lent, Rochester, NY 1,250.00
EO Spooner, Storm King, Boston, MA 1,450.00
FD McKay Jr, Elmira, MA 3,100.00
Simmons & Sons, Fulton, NY 1,250.00

English Barometers

Note: The 10" mahogany wheel listed below is marked 'Royal Exchange London Optician to King George IV Prince of Wales.' It may be referenced in Goodison, page 85.

Admiral Fitzory, various kinds, ea from $500 to 3,000.00
Fortin type (Kew or Laboratory), metal on brd w/milk glass, $750 to ... 950.00
Marine gimballed, sgn Walker, London 4,000.00

P. Brambano, Evesham, inlaid mahogany, two dials, 39", $1,530.00.
(Photo courtesy Garth's Auctions Inc.)

Right angle, sgn John Whitehurst, ca 1790 .... 15,000.00
Stick, mahog bowfront w/urn-shaped cistern, S Mason, Dublin, 1824-30... 5,000.00
Stick, rosewood, sgn L Casella, London 1,650.00
Stick, rosewood w/ivory scale, sgn Adie, dbl vernier, ca 1840... 3,200.00
Symphisometer, sgn Adie 3,950.00
Wheel, 6", sgn Stanley, Peterborough 1,500.00
Wheel, 8", sgn F Molten, Norwich 1,450.00
Wheel, 10", mahog, J Smith Royal Exchange...Optican...Prince of Wales.. 1,950.00
Wheel, 10", MOP, sgn Spelizini, London 1,950.00

Other Types

Aneroid, 4-6" dia in brass case w/half-rnd thermometer, $150 to.... 250.00
Mahog barograph (recording type), sgn Negretti & Zambra 950.00
Pocket barometer (altimeter), w/case, from $200 to 300.00

Barware

Back in the '30s when social soirees were very elegant affairs thanks to the influence of Hollywood in all its glamour and mystique, cocktails were often served up in shakers styled as miniature airplanes, zeppelins, skyscrapers, ladies' legs, penguins, roosters, bowling pins, etc. Some were by top designers such as Norman Bel Geddes and Russel Wright. They were made of silver plate, glass, and chrome, often trimmed with colorful Bakelite handles. Today these are hot collectibles, and even the more common Deco-styled chrome cylinders are often priced at $25.00 and up. Ice buckets, trays, and other bar accessories are also included in this area of collecting.

For further information we recommend *Vintage Bar Ware Identification & Value Guide* by Stephen Visakay, our advisor for this category; he is listed in the Directory under New Jersey. See also Bottle Openers.

Bar towel, cloth w/mc printed bar motif 18.00
Cigarette dispenser, brass & Bakelite bartender, Art Metal, 8" 550.00
Cocktail dish, bar scene w/drink names, 1930s, 8" 90.00

Cocktail set, chromed metal with wooden handles, Farberware, ca 1935, tray: 18x12", from $900.00 to $1,200.00.

(Photo courtesy David Rago Auctions)

Cocktail set, hammered aluminum, shaker/4 cups/rnd tray, TKE, 1930s ... 175.00
Decanter tag, Brandy, SP 1¾x2⅜" rectangle on chain 30.00
Ice bowl w/tongs, chrome, R Wright/Chase, 1930s-40s, 7" dia, $35 to ... 65.00
Ice bucket, chrome w/caramel Catalin hdls, 6" dia, from $250 to ... 350.00
Ice bucket, chrome w/porc lining, Bakelite trim, Keystone Ware, 11" ... 75.00
Ice bucket, ebony w/SP stars/lid, SP liner, Wm Spratling, 1950s .. 950.00
Ice chopper, cobalt glass w/silk-screened recipes, 1930s, 11½" 65.00
Martini picks, swirled Bakelite bar w/shaped picks (6), EX 225.00
Napkin, rooster bartender on wht, Fabres 10.00
Napkins, orange & brn linen, tuxedoed man & shaker, set of 8 ... 130.00
Pitcher, brass thermos type w/rattan-woven hdl, Maxwell Phillip, 11" ... 150.00
Pitcher, martini; glass, clear w/brn plasic-wrapped hdl, w/stick, 13" ... 45.00
Shaker, aluminum, anodized bl, cylindrical, 11¼" 75.00
Shaker, aluminum skyscraper, Lurell Guild, Kensington, 13½x3⅜" ... 165.00
Shaker, chrome, skyscraper, blk, enamel cap & base, 12¼" 60.00
Shaker, glass, glass top, orange w/yel spatter, 1930s, 7" 85.00
Shaker, glass, gr w/chrome lid, Catalin finial, Cambridge, 13" 275.00
Shaker, NP, hammered, Bernard Rice & Sons, 1920s, 13¾" 75.00
Shaker, NP, hammered & plain, Expressware NY Stamping Co, 17½" .. 300.00
Shaker, ruby glass w/silver deer o/l, 54-oz, +6 ftd ruby cocktails ... 250.00
Shaker, silver, dragon pursues sacred pearl, China, ca 1890 .... 750.00
Shaker, silver, penguin form, Napier, D101559, 1936, 13" 1,150.00
Shaker, SP, bell shape, Dunhill, 11" 90.00
Shaker, SP, rooster, hammered, tail as hdl, Wallace Bros, 1928, 15" ... 1,500.00
Shaker, wooden bbl form w/metal insert, chrome top, 9½" 75.00
Shot set, 6 glasses in chrome fr, Farberware, 1935, 5x6" dia 85.00
Soda siphon, chrome w/enameled top, Bel Geddes, mk, Pat, 10" 160.00

Stopper, horse head, Heisey, 13½", from $350 to 450.00
Traveling bar, brass/chrome, red stripes, 8-pc, Germany, 1928, 14" .. 250.00
Tray, metal, Here's How, flappers w/drinks, J Held Jr art, 12x17", NM .. 100.00
Tumbler rack w/4 tumblers, gyroscope, 20x4½" dia rings 125.00
Tumblers, pinup girl decal on clear, 4¾", 6 for 70.00

Basalt

Basalt is a type of unglazed black pottery developed by Josiah Wedgwood and copied by many other companies during the late eighteenth and early nineteenth centuries. It is also called 'Egyptian Black.' See also Wedgwood.

Bust, Tsar Alexander, inscr medallion, Wood & Caldwell, 11¼" ..1,055.00
Font, Cathedral of Wincht, paneled sq sides, Copeland, 1870s, 5⅜" .. 1,175.00
Vase, classic figures, rosso antico on blk, hdls, 19th C, 10½" 2,115.00
Vase, drapery swags emb, engine-trn neck/socle, Wedgwood/Bentley, 9" .. 1,525.00
Vase, Hercules medallions/florets, uptrn scroll hdls, 1790s, 9" .. 1,000.00
Vase, portrait & florets, acanthus leaf border, w/lid, 1800s, 11" ... 995.00

Baskets

Basketweaving is a craft as old as ancient history. Baskets have been used to harvest crops, for domestic chores, and to contain the catch of fishermen. Materials at hand were utilized, and baskets from a specific region are often distinguishable simply by analyzing the natural fibers used in their construction. Early Indian baskets were made of corn husks or woven grasses. Willow splint, straw, rope, and paper were also used. Until the invention of the veneering machine in the late 1800s, splint was made by water-soaking a split log until the fibers were softened and flexible. Long strips were pulled out by hand and, while still wet and pliable, woven into baskets in either a crosshatch or hexagonal weave.

Most handcrafted baskets on the market today were made between 1860 and the early 1900s. Factory baskets with a thick, wide splint cut by machine are of little interest to collectors. The more popular baskets are those designed for a specific purpose, rather than the more commonly found utility baskets that had multiple uses. Among the most costly forms are the Nantucket Lighthouse baskets, which were basically copied from those made there for centuries by aboriginal Indians. They were designed in the style of whale-oil barrels and named for the South Shoal Nantucket Lightship where many were made during the last half of the nineteenth century. Cheese baskets (used to separate curds from whey), herb-gathering baskets, and finely woven Shaker miniatures are other highly-prized examples of the basketweaver's art.

In the listings that follow, assume that each has a center bentwood handle (unless handles of another type are noted) that is not included in the height. Unless another type of material is indicated, assume that each is made of splint. Prices are subjective and hinge on several factors: construction, age, color, and general appearance. Baskets rated very good (VG) will have minor losses and damage.

Bee skep, rye, tall haystack shape, scarce, 17¼" 400.00
Buttocks, copper rivets w/emb stars, sqd, 8¾x16½" 460.00
Buttocks, 12-rib w/woven twigs, dmn to ends of hdl, 6x10x12" 90.00
Buttocks, 18-rib, splint hdl, 6x16x12" 115.00
Buttocks, 24-rib, tight weave, natural finish, mini, 2½" 285.00
Buttocks, 60-rib, well woven, EX color, 5x12¼" 895.00
Gathering, orig dk surface, kicked-up base, 14x12½", EX 350.00
Gathering, 2-hdl, 8x14" 290.00
Half-buttocks, bl-gr tinted bands, 7½x8¼", EX 100.00
Half-buttocks, old dk red pnt, minor damage, 4x8½" 200.00
Mini, tight weave, checks on center band, 2⅝" 400.00

Mini, 18 melon ribs, varnished, 3" 175.00
Nantucket, disk base, hdl held by brass tabs, 3½x6½", VG 635.00
Nantucket, purse, hinged hdl, ivory knobs/pin closure, 20th C, 7x11x7".. 200.00
Nantucket, rattan, rnd maple base, swing hdl, losses, ca 1900, 6x14" ... 765.00
Nantucket, swing hdl, 1940s, 9" dia 660.00
Nantucket, wooden disk, hdl held by brass tabs, tight weave, 4x10"... 1,265.00
Octagonal, red/gr lines bordering red dmns, w/lid, 4x6" 90.00
Produce, raised bottom, 2 hdls, ca 1900, 13x23¼" 175.00
Rectangular, checkered red/gr rpt, wire hinged lid, dbl hdls, 7x13x10" .. 350.00
Rectangular, gr rpt over red, 5½x12½x8" 320.00
Rectangular, wide splint, 9½x11" 125.00
Rectangular, wrapped rim, EX color, 7x19x14" 165.00
Rnd, bl rpt over brn, batten ft & X-pc, 2 bentwood rim hdls, 13x22"... 575.00
Rnd, gr bands, looped decor on natural brn patina, w/lid, late, 13"... 60.00
Rnd, gr pnt, swing hdl, 8x12", VG 520.00
Rnd, natural/bl/red pnt splints, att ME, 9x15", VG 175.00
Rnd, red pnt, swing hdl, 8x12", EX 750.00
Rnd w/domed base, bl rim/base bands, hdls, spiral weave, 1800s, 7x17"... 2,700.00
Rnd w/domed base, brn pnt, swing hdl, 19th C, 11⅛" 415.00
Rnd w/domed base, sliding dome lid, 19th C, 7¼x14¼" 175.00
Rnd w/domed base, swing hdl, NY, 19th C, 7¼" 440.00
Rnd w/sq base, appl cvd runners, copper tacks, 12x12" 235.00
Rnd w/sq base, gray-bl pnt, 19th C, 5¼" 1,295.00
Rnd w/sq base, swing hdl, NY, 19th C, 10⅜" 350.00
Rnd w/sq base, swing hdl, 3 thin reinforcing runners, NY, 10"..... 385.00
Strawberry, wooden base, staves w/wire/tin bands, 2 hdls, 3x6x4"... 325.00
Utility, coiled rye straw, bowl w/flaring sides, PA, 6x18" 60.00

Batchelder

Ernest A. Batchelder was a leading exponent of the Arts and Crafts movement in the United States. His influential book, *Design in Theory and Practice*, was originally published in 1910. He is best known, however, for his artistic tiles which he first produced in Pasadena, California, from 1909 to 1916. In 1916 the business was relocated to Los Angeles where it continued until 1932, closing because of the Depression.

In 1938 Batchelder resumed production in Pasadena under the name of 'Kinneola Kiln.' Output of the new pottery consisted of delicately cast bowls and vases in an Oriental style. This business closed in 1951. Tiles carry a die-stamped mark; vases and bowls are hand incised. For more information we recommend *Collector's Encyclopedia of California Pottery, Second Edition*, by Jack Chipman (Collector Books) and *American Art Tiles*, in four volumes by Norman Karlson (Schiffer, 2005). Our advisors for this category are Suzanne Perrault and David Rago; they are listed in the Directory under New Jersey.

Fountain, two children playing flutes, rabbits at their feet, birds in trees, F565, 31x19x12", $6,800.00. (Photo courtesy David Rago Auctions)

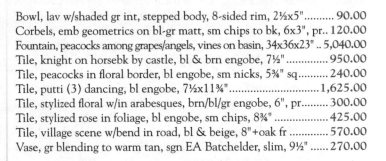

Bowl, lav w/shaded gr int, stepped body, 8-sided rim, 2½x5".......... 90.00
Corbels, emb geometrics on bl-gr matt, sm chips to bk, 6x3", pr.. 120.00
Fountain, peacocks among grapes/angels, vines on basin, 34x36x23" .. 5,040.00
Tile, knight on horsebk by castle, bl & brn engobe, 7½" 950.00
Tile, peacocks in floral border, bl engobe, sm nicks, 5¾" sq.......... 240.00
Tile, putti (3) dancing, bl engobe, 7½x11¾" 1,625.00
Tile, stylized floral w/in arabesques, brn/bl/gr engobe, 6", pr........ 300.00
Tile, stylized rose in foliage, bl engobe, sm chips, 8¾" 425.00
Tile, village scene w/bend in road, bl & beige, 8"+oak fr 570.00
Vase, gr blending to warm tan, sgn EA Batchelder, slim, 9½" 270.00

Battersea

Battersea is a term that refers to enameling on copper or other metal. Though originally produced at Battersea, England, in the mid-eighteenth century, the craft was later practiced throughout the Staffordshire district. Boxes are the most common examples. Some are figurals, and many bear an inscription. Unless a condition is noted in the description, values are given for examples with only minimal damage, which is normal. Please note that items with printed Bilston labels are new. Our advisor for this category is John Harrigan; he is listed in the Directory under Minnesota.

Bottle, scent; bl floral panels on wht areas w/red scallops, 2", G .. 200.00
Box, fishing scene reserve on wht w/sm flowers, Bilston, 3" L, G .. 175.00
Box, Love the Giver/flowers, brass mt, mirrored lid, ¾x1½x1"..... 350.00
Box, May the Enemies of Liberty Feel the Evils..., 1775, ⅝x⅞" dia .. 1,500.00
Box, naval scene, officer's portraits, Xd anchors, 1⅝x3¾x2⅝"... 1,000.00
Box, pastoral scene, brn on cream, lav base, oval, 19th C, ¾x1½" .. 200.00
Box, peach form & color, stem finial, 2x1½" dia.................... 2,500.00
Box, purple & gr stripes, Thank You on metal hinged lid, 1⅛x2¼"... 50.00
Box, scenic reserve on pk w/gilt highlights, dome top, 3½".......... 900.00
Box, 2 ships engaging for battle, officer portrait w/in, sgn, 3½" L .. 1,140.00
Candlesticks, paneled floral w/gold on turq, 1750s, 10¾", pr ... 3,000.00
Tiebacks, Commodore Truton bust, beaded brass surround, 2", pr.... 1,650.00

Bauer

The Bauer Pottery Company is one of the best known of the California pottery companies, noted for both its artware and its dinnerware. In the past 10 years, Bauer has become particularly collectible, and prices have risen accordingly. The pottery actually started in Kentucky in 1885. It moved to Los Angeles in 1910 where it remained in operation until 1962. The company produced several successful dinnerware lines, including La Linda, Monterey, and Brusche Al Fresco. Most popular, and most significant, was the Ringware line introduced in 1932 which preceded Fiesta as a popular solid-color everyday dinnerware. The earliest pieces are unmarked, although to collectors they are unmistakable, partly due to their distinctive glazes which have an almost primitive charm due to their drips, misses, and color variations.

Another dinnerware line favored by collectors is Speckleware, its name derived from the 1950s-era speckled glaze Bauer used on various products, including vases, flowerpots, kitchenware items, and dinnerware. Though not as popular as Ringware, Speckleware holds its value and is usually available at much lower prices than Ring. Keep an eye out for other flowerpots and mixing bowls as well.

Artware by Bauer is not so easy to find now, but it is worth seeking out because of its high values. So-called oil jars sell for upwards of $1,500.00, and Rebekah vases routinely fetch $400.00 or more. Matt Carlton is one of the most desirable designers of handmade ware.

After WWII a flood of foreign imports and loss of key employees drastically curtailed their sales, and the pottery began a steady decline that ended in failure in 1962. Prices listed below reflect the California market. For more information we recommend *Collector's Encyclopedia of California Pottery, Second Edition,* by Jack Chipman (Collector Books).

In the lines of Ring and Plain ware, pricing depends to some extent on color. Low-end colors include light brown, Chinese Yellow, orange-red, Jade Green, red-brown, olive green, light blue, turquoise, and gray; the high-end colors are Delph Blue, ivory, dusty burgundy, cobalt, chartreuse, papaya, and burgundy. In Monterey, Monterey Blue, burgundy, and white are high-end colors; all others are considerably less. Black is highly collectible in all of these lines; to evaluate black, add at least 100% to an item's value in any other color. An in-depth study of colors may be found in the book referenced above.

Brusche Al Fresco and Contempo

Bowl, divided vegetable; brn, 9½" L	30.00
Bowl, fruit; chartreuse, str sides, 5"	10.00
Casserole, French; Dubonnet, 2-qt	100.00
Creamer, jumbo; olive gr	20.00
Cup, burgundy	10.00
Plate, dinner; gray, 10"	15.00
Platter, lime, 10¼"	20.00
Tumbler, brn, 8-oz	15.00

Gloss Pastel Kitchenware (aka GPK)

Bowl, batter; yel, 2-qt	65.00
Bowl, mixing; pk, #30	35.00
Pitcher, ivory, 1-qt	35.00
Ramekin, lt bl	10.00
Teapot, Aladdin, pk, 8-cup, minimum value	250.00

La Linda

Bowl, cereal	25.00
Chop plate, yel	75.00
Creamer, 2 styles, ea	15.00

Creamer, old style, $15.00. (Photo courtesy Jack Chipman)

Cup, gray	12.50
Gravy boat	25.00
Plate, bread & butter; gr, 6"	10.00
Saucer, gr	5.00
Shakers, pr	25.00

Monterey

Bowl, fruit; horizontal rings, 3-ftd, 9", from $100 to	150.00
Bowl, fruit; 6", from $20 to	30.00
Bowl, serving; blk, very rare, minimum value	300.00
Candleholders, pr from $100 to	150.00
Plate, dinner; 10½", from $40 to	60.00
Relish plate, 10", from $75 to	100.00
Teapot, old style, 6-cup, from $100 to	150.00

Monterey Modern and Related Kitchenware

Bowl, batter; yel	50.00
Bowl, soup; blk, 5¼", minimum value	50.00
Bowl, soup; colors other than blk, 5¼", from $15 to	20.00
Bowl, vegetable; chartreuse, oval, 9"	40.00
Casserole, brn, copper-plated metal fr, 1-qt	45.00
Creamer, burgundy	20.00
Cup, pk	12.00
Mug, colors other than blk, 10-oz, from $30 to	35.00
Mug, no hdl, burgundy, 8-oz	20.00

Ring Ware

Bowl, batter; 1-qt, from $300 to	450.00
Bowl, mixing; cobalt, dbl ring, #09	250.00
Bowl, punch; chartreuse, ftd, 14"	1,200.00
Coffee server, Jade Green, orig lid, 8-cup	140.00
Coffeepot, dripolator, minimum value	1,500.00
Custard cup, orange-red	45.00
Egg cup, ftd, 3¼", from $300 to	450.00
Honey jar, 1- or 2-bee lid, complete, minimum value	3,000.00
Pitcher, beer; minimum value	1,000.00
Pitcher, 1½-pt, from $55 to	80.00
Shaker, Dusty Burgundy, squat, ea	50.00
Shaker, Jade Green, squat, ea	25.00
Sugar bowl, flat lid, early, from $250 to	375.00
Teacup, Chinese Yellow	60.00

Speckled Kitchenware

Bowl, mixing; pk, #36, sm	20.00
Bowl, salad; yel, low, 7"	30.00
Buffet server, brn	45.00
Casserole, pk, brass-plated metal fr, 2½-qt	75.00
Pitcher, pk, 1-pt	30.00
Pitcher, yel, Brusche style, 1-pt	25.00

Miscellaneous

Art pottery, bowl, Half Pumpkin, speckled yel, Tracy Irwin, 10¼"	85.00
Art pottery, vase, Ring, red-brn, sm, 6⅜"	85.00
Cal-Art, flowerpot, Swirl, olive gr, 6"	55.00
Cal-Art, flowerpot, Swirl, speckled pk, #7	60.00
Cal-Art, flowerpot, Swirl, wht matt, 3"	25.00
Florist ware, flowerpot saucer, gr, 7⅜"	40.00
Florist ware, jardiniere/flowerpot, speckled pk, #9	65.00
Florist ware, Spanish pot, speckled gr, 4"	20.00

Beer Cans

In the early 1930s one of America's largest can-manufacturing companies approached an east coast brewery with a novel concept — beer in cans. The brewery decided to take a chance on the idea, and in January, 1935, the beer can was born.

The 'church key' style can opener was invented at the same time, and early flat top cans actually had instructions on how to use it to open a can. Canned beer soared in popularity, and breweries scrambled to meet the canning challenge. Since many companies did not have a machine to fill a flat-top can, the cone top was invented. Brewery executives believed its shape would be more acceptable to consumers used to buying bottled beer, and it easily passed through existing bottling machinery. The more compact flat-top can dominated sales, and by the 1950s cone tops were obsolete.

About values: Condition is critical when determining the value of a beer can. Like any collectible, value drops in direct proportion to condition, and off-grade cans are often worth no more than one-half of retail value.

Key: instr — opening instructions   IRTP — International Revenue Tax Paid

ABC Beer, cone top, World's Gold Medal 1929-30, Aztec Brewing, CA, EX..325.00
Blatz, 1955 Christmas special, pk, Blatz Brewing, Milwaukee WI, EX.. 425.00

Beverwyck Irish Brand Cream Ale, cone top, Continental Can Co. Inc., Beverywyck Breweries Inc., Albany, New York, rust and soiling, 7¾", $45.00.

Brownie, flat top, Monarch Brewing Co, Los Angeles CA, EX.... 615.00
Brucks Jubilee, cone top, Bruckman Brewing, Cincinnati OH, qt, EX... 315.00
Fox, flat top, steel, Peter Fox Brewing, IRTP, EX 815.00
Griesedieck Bros, flat top, pilsner glass/Xmas series, EX 295.00
Jacob Ruppert Ale, flat copper top, gr woodgrain, IRTP, NM 245.00
Lion Ale, flat top, Lion Brewery, NY NY, IRTP/instr, EX............. 315.00
Martin's Beer, cone top, Selah WA, EX 850.00
Milwaukee Valley Beer, West Bend Lithia Co, West Bend WI, EX ...340.00
Namar Premium Beer, cone top, Philadelphia PA, EX 335.00
Regal Amber Ale, flat top, Regal Amber Brewing Co, G............. 400.00
Reingold Extra Dry, flat top, Miss Reingold 1957, NY NY, EX 295.00
Ruppert Dark Beer, flat top, Jacob Ruppert, NY NY, NM 375.00
Silver Fox, cone top, Fox Deluxe Brewing Co, Marion IN, qt, EX... 530.00
Tudor Bock Beer, flat top, Metropolis Brewery, Trenton NJ, 1950s, NM... 245.00
Utica Club, West End Brewing Co, cone top w/cap, 1930s, 1-qt, VG.. 550.00
Valley Brew, cone top, El Dorado Brewing, Stockton CA, EX..... 300.00
Waldorf Sampson Ale, flat top, Forest City Brewery, Cleveland OH, EX....465.00
Wilshire Club Ale, flat top, San Francisco Brewing Corp, VG 235.00

Bellaire, Marc

Marc Bellaire, originally Donald Edmund Fleischman, was born in Toledo, Ohio, in 1925. He studied at the Toledo Museum of Art under Ernest Spring while employed as a designer for the Libbey Glass Company. During World War II while serving in the Navy, he traveled extensively throughout the Pacific, resulting in his enriched sense of design and color.

Marc settled in California in the 1950s where his work attracted the attention of national buyers and agencies who persuaded him to create ceramic lines of his own, employing hand-decorating techniques throughout. He built a studio in Culver City, and there he produced high-quality ceramics, often decorated with ultramodern figures or geometric patterns and executed with a distinctive flair. His most famous line was Mardi Gras, decorated with slim dancers in spattered and striped colors of black, blue, pink, and white. Other major patterns were Jamaica, Balinese, Beachcomber, Friendly Island, Cave Painting, Hawaiian, Bird Isle, Oriental, Jungle Dancer, and Kashmir. Kashmir usually has the name Ingle on the front and Bellaire on the reverse.

It is to be noted that Marc was employed by Sascha Brastoff during the 1950s. Many believe that he was hired for his creative imagination and style.

During the period from 1951 to 1956, Marc was named one of the top 10 artware designers by *Giftwares Magazine*. After 1956 he taught and lectured on art, design, and ceramic decorating techniques from coast to coast. Many of his pieces were one of a kind, commissioned throughout the United States.

During the 1970s he set up a studio in Marin County, California, and eventually moved to Palm Springs where he opened his final studio/gallery. There he produced large pieces with a Southwestern style. Mr. Bellaire died in 1994. Our advisor for this category is Marty Webster; he is listed in the Directory under Michigan.

Ashtray, Balinese Dancers, 14" 60.00
Ashtray, Beachcomber, free-form, 13½" 65.00
Ashtray, Bird Isle, blk birds on cream, 8" 55.00
Ashtray, Clown, mc on cream, 7" 65.00
Ashtray, Jamaica Musicians on brn, 10x14" 85.00
Ashtray, Mardi Gras, figures on blk, rolled rim, 9" 100.00
Ashtray, Mardi Gras, figures on blk, 14x14" 125.00
Ashtray, Mardi Gras, figures on blk, 4x8½" 35.00
Ashtray, Still Life, matt fruits & leaves, 10x15" 80.00
Bowl, Beachcomber, low teardrop shape, 12" L 100.00
Bowl, Cave Painting, 5x15x13" 70.00
Bowl, Cortillian, lady w/bl bird, 13x9" 100.00
Bowl, Fruit - Three Pears, yel & gr 35.00
Bowl, Jungle Dancer, 5½x11½" 150.00
Box, African Figures on lid, 6" 85.00
Box, Geisha Girls (3), wht & gray, 6" 35.00
Box, Jamaican Man w/guitar, free-form, 6x7" 150.00
Box, Jamaican Musicians, 2x11x6" 60.00
Box, Mardi Gras, 10" dia 75.00
Candlestick, Jamaica Man, 10½", ea 125.00
Charger, Fisherman w/net, 16" 150.00
Charger, Polynesian King & Queen, 15" 200.00
Charger, stylized bird on branch, 15" 165.00
Coaster, Mardi Gras, 4½" dia 15.00
Compote, Cave Painting, 4-ftd, 6x12" 100.00
Compote, Cortillian, 4-ftd, 8x17" 200.00
Cookie jar, Stick People, wood lid, 10" 150.00
Dish, African Dancer, free-form, 5½x11½" 65.00
Dish, Balinese Dancer, 8x10" 55.00
Dish, Mardi Gras, divided, 10x9½" 100.00
Dish, Zulu Dancer, free-form, 16" 90.00
Ewer, Mardi Gras, figures on blk, hdl, 18" 400.00
Figurine, Bali Dancer w/fancy headdress, 24"........................1,200.00
Figurine, bird w/long neck, 17" 250.00
Figurine, buffalo, brn & cream, 10x10" 90.00
Figurine, bull, 9" 145.00
Figurine, horse, gray/gr/brn, 8x7½" 140.00
Figurine, Jamaica Man playing bongo, 8½" 135.00
Figurine, Mardi Gras, lady seated, 5½" 150.00
Figurine, Mardi Gras, man reclining, very slim, 18" 500.00
Figurine, Mardi Gras, man standing, very slim, 24" 700.00
Figurine, Mardi Gras, man standing, 11½" 235.00
Figurine, Polynesian, man standing, 12" 500.00
Lamp, Mardi Gras, long-neck vase on wood base, 28" 450.00
Pitcher, Sea Gull, 4½" 50.00
Platter, Friendly Island, 10" 135.00
Platter, Hawaiian figures (3) on orange, 13x7" 55.00
Platter, Mardi Gras, figures on blk, 18x12"................................ 250.00
Platter, Polynesian Dancer, egg shaped, 15x11" 150.00
Platter, underwater design in sea gr, 16" 100.00
Switch plate, dancer on blk, B-26, 4¾x3" 150.00
Tray, Beachcomber, low teardrop shape, 12" L........................... 75.00
Tray, Black Man dancing, triangular, 8½x17" 75.00

Tray, Hawaiian Figures, peach & blk, 14x10"	145.00
Tray, Jungle Dancer, figure on blk/gr, 12" dia	145.00
Vase, Balinese Women, hourglass shape, 8"	100.00
Vase, Black Cats, houglass shape, 8"	100.00
Vase, Indian on Horseback, mk Bellaire 89, 10"	150.00
Vase, Mardi Gras, figures on blk, 18"	250.00
Vase, Mardi Gras, houglass shape on 3 ft, 11"	125.00
Vase, Polynesian Woman, 9"	100.00
Vase, Rooster, bottle form, 13"	115.00
Vase, Stick People, irregular beak-like opening, 12"	250.00

Belleek, American

From 1883 until 1930, several American potteries located in New Jersey and Ohio manufactured a type of china similar to the famous Irish Belleek soft-paste porcelain. The American manufacturers identified their porcelain by using 'Belleek' or 'Beleek' in their marks. American Belleek is considered the highest achievement of the American porcelain industry. Production centered around artistic cabinet pieces and luxury tablewares. Many examples emulated Irish shapes and decor with marine themes and other naturalistic styles. While all are highly collectible, some companies' products are rarer than others. The best-known manufacturers are Ott and Brewer, Willets, The Ceramic Art Company (CAC), and Lenox. You will find more detailed information in those specific categories. Our advisor for this category is Mary Frank Gaston; she is listed in the Directory under Texas.

Key: AAC — American Art China   CAP — Columbian Art Pottery

Teapot, dragon shape, gold-paste leaf designs, 7½x9", $1,000.00.
(Photo courtesy Mary Frank Gaston)

Cream soup & liner, pheasants & fruit w/gold, Gordon Belleek, 8 for	185.00
Cup & saucer, floral, bl & orange, mk Coxon Belleek	200.00
Cup & saucer, morning glories, Morgan	175.00
Hatpin holder, silver Art Deco decor, obelisk shape, mk, 7"	200.00
Mug, monk playing violin, CAP, 5", from $35 to	150.00
Plate, mixed floral, bright mc on wht w/gold rim, Coxon, 5¾"	115.00
Salt cellar, sponged gold on scalloped rim & base, AAC, 2½"	125.00
Stein, currants & leaves, red & gr on brn, 5"	250.00

Belleek, Irish

Belleek is a very thin translucent porcelain that takes its name from the village in Ireland where it originated in 1859. The glaze is a creamy ivory color with a pearl-like lustre. The tablewares, baskets, figurines, and vases that have always been made there are being crafted yet today. Shamrock, Tridacna, Echinus, and Thorn are but a few of the many patterns of tableware which have been made during some periods of the pottery's history. Throughout the years, their most popular pattern has been Shamrock.

It is possible to date an example to within 20 to 30 years of crafting by the mark. Pieces with an early stamp often bring prices nearly triple that of a similar but current item. With some variation, the marks have

always incorporated the Irish wolfhound, Celtic round tower, harp, and shamrocks. The first three marks (usually in black) were used from 1863 to 1946. A series of green marks identified the pottery's offerings from 1946 until the seventh mark (in gold/brown) was introduced in 1980 (it was discontinued in 1992). The eighth mark was blue and closely resembled the gold mark. It was used from 1993 to 1996. The ninth, tenth, and eleventh marks went back to the simplicity of the first mark with only the registry mark ® to distinguish them from the original. The ninth mark, which was used from 1997 to 1999, was blue. A special black version of that mark was introduced for the year 2000 and a Millennium 2000 banner was added. The tenth or Millennium mark was retired at the end of 2000, and the current green mark was introduced as the eleventh mark. Belleek Collector's International Society limited edition pieces are designated with a special mark in red. In the listings below, numbers designated with the prefix 'D' relate to the book *Belleek, The Complete Collector's Guide and Illustrated Reference, Second Edition*, by Richard K. Degenhardt (published by Wallace-Homestead Book Company, One Chilton Way, Radnor, PA 19098-0230). The numbers designated with the prefix 'B' are current production numbers used by the pottery. Our advisor for this category is Liz Stillwell; she is listed in the Directory under California.

Key:

A — plain (glazed only)	I — 1863 – 1890
B — cob lustre	II — 1891 – 1926
C — hand tinted	III — 1926 – 1946
D — hand painted	IV — 1946 –1955
E — hand-painted shamrocks	V — 1955 – 1965
F — hand gilted	VI — 1965 – 3/31/1980
G — hand tinted and gilted	VII — 4/1/1980 – 1992
H — hand-painted shamrocks and gilted	VIII — 1/4/1993 – 1996
J — mother-of-pearl	IX — 1997 – 1999
K — hand painted and gilted	X — 2000 only
L — bisque and plain	XI — 2001 – current
M — decalcomania	
N — special hand-painted decoration	
T — transfer design	

Further information concerning Periods of Crafting (Baskets):
1 — 1865 – 1890, BELLEEK (three-strand)
2 — 1865 – 1890, BELLEEK CO. FERMANAGH (three-strand)
3 — 1891 – 1920, BELLEEK CO. FERMANAGH IRELAND (three-strand)
4 — 1921 – 1954, BELLEEK CO. FERMANAGH IRELAND (four-strand)
5 — 1955 – 1979, BELLEEK® CO. FERMANAGH IRELAND (four-strand)
6 — 1980 – 1985, BELLEEK® IRELAND (four-strand)
7 — 1985 – 1989, BELLEEK® IRELAND 'ID NUMBER' (four-strand)
8 – 12 — 1990 to present (Refer to *Belleek, The Complete Collector's Guide and Illustrated Reference, 2nd Edition*, Chapter 5)

Aberdeen Tea Ware Tea & Saucer, D489-II, B	575.00
Artichoke Tea Ware Teapot, D710-I, F	800.00
Bamboo Teapot, D516-I, A, sm	800.00
Basket Compote, D30-I, A	950.00
Bird's Nest Basket, D123-II, J	700.00
Bust of Queen of the Hops, D1130-III, L&B, 11½"	4,000.00
Celtic Design Tea Ware Coffee & Saucer, D1428 & 1430-III, K	300.00
Cherub Font, D1110-III, A, lg	350.00
Chinese Tea Ware Teapot, D484-I, K	1,500.00
Cleary Mug, D218-II, B, 2½"	150.00
Diamond Biscuit Jar, D600-IV, D	400.00

Earthenware Soup Plate, D888-II, T, 10" 195.00
Echinus Tea Ware Dejeuner Set, D650-II, C 4,500.00
Egyptian Napkin Ring, D1551-I, F.. 600.00
Flowered Crate, D268-II, J... 475.00
Forget-Me-Not Box, D111-II, A, 2" 650.00
Gospel Plates (4), D1811-VI, D1813-VII, D1815-VII, D1817-VII, M&F..650.00
Grass Tea Ware Teapot, D733-II, D, med 650.00
Harp w/Applied Shamrocks, D1640-II, K 550.00
Irish Harp, D77-V, E, sm... 280.00
Irish Squirrel Wall Bracket, D1803-I, A 4,750.00
Ivy Sugar & Cream, D237-I & D238-I, B, lg 325.00
Ivy Tea Ware Bread Plate, D1410-III, B..................................... 325.00
Killarney Candlestick, D1982-VII, D, ea 85.00
Lily Tea Ware Tea & Saucer & Side Plate, D536-II & D542II, G...450.00
Milk Maid Lithophane, B2436-XI, L&B, 9¼x11⅛"...................... 175.00
Neptune Tea Ware Kettle, D431-VII, B, lg 275.00
Nickel Flowerpot, D209-III, B... 275.00
Oak Flowerpot, ftd, D46-II, J..2,700.00
Pierced Spill, Flowered, D49-III, A, lg 350.00
Prince Arthur Vase, D73-II, J 800.00
Rope Handle Mug, D215-II, B 250.00
Shamrock Flowerpot, D98-II, H, 8" 850.00
Shamrock Mug, D216-II, E... 150.00
Shamrock Tea Ware Kettle, D386-II, E, lg 600.00
Shamrock Ware TV Set, D2017-VII, E.. 110.00
Single Henshall's Spill, Flowered, D61-IV, B 135.00
Table Centre, D56-IV, D..1,200.00
Thorn Tea Ware Bread Plate, D767-II, K, 9" 1,200.00
Tridacna Tea Ware Covered Muffin Dish, D479-II, A................. 425.00
Tridacna Tea Ware Milk Jug, D480-V, B....................................... 95.00
Victoria Tea Ware Tea & Saucer, D593-II, G 550.00
Wall Plaque, Praise Ye the Lord, Earthenware, D1807-1, D......... 800.00

Bells

Some areas of interest represented in the study of bells are history, religion, and geography. Since Biblical times, bells have announced morning church services, vespers, deaths, christenings, school hours, fires, and community events. Countries have used them en masse to peal out the good news of Christmas, New Year's, and the endings of World Wars I and II. They've been rung in times of great sorrow, such as the death of Abraham Lincoln.

For further information, we recommend *World of Bells* by Dorothy Malone Anthony (a series of 10 books). All have over 200 colored pictures covering many bell categories. See also Nodders; Schoolhouse Collectibles.

Brass, acorn dinger, hotel type, 4½x3"................................. 120.00
CI, dbl-sided upright hotel type w/twister knob, 6x3½" 190.00
CI, lady in hooped skirt, mc pnt, 3¾" 170.00
CI, turtle figural, press head or tail, hotel type, 3½x5½x2" 350.00
Lutz type, blown, pk w/wht & pk swirls on stem & bell, 10", EX ... 86.00
NP CI, knight in armor figural, hotel type, GES #103, 7x4½x2", EX+ .. 160.00
Sleigh, 51 on 14' strap ranging in sz from 1" to 3" dia 225.00
SP, hotel twist style, dtd 1887, 3x3¾" dia, EX.............................. 60.00
SP, 3 ladies' faces, hotel twist type, Meriden, ca 1887, 4" dia 160.00

Bennett, John

Bringing with him the knowledge and experience he had gained at the Doulton (Lambeth) Pottery in England, John Bennett opened a studio in New York City around 1877, where he continued his methods of decorating faience under the glaze. Early wares utilized imported English biscuit, though subsequently local clays (both white and cream-colored) were also used. His first kiln was on Lexington Avenue; he built another on East 24th Street. Pieces are usually signed 'J. Bennett, N.Y.,' often with the street address and date. Later examples may be marked 'West Orange, N.J.,' where he retired. The pottery was in operation approximately six years in New York. Pieces signed with other initials are usually worth less. Our advisor for this category is Robert Tuggle; he is listed in the Directory under New York.

Jar, dogwood and roses on black, J. Bennett, New York, 1881, $64,625.00. (Photo courtesy David Rago Auctions)

Vase, floral, red/gr on turq, bottle shape, sgn/E 24 NY/CR, 11x5" .. 5,100.00
Vase, florals/leaves, pk/gr on dk bl mottle, bulbous w/stick neck, 10" .. 5,585.00
Vase, monkey, pilgrim flask, ftd/hdls, 1896/Albion, 7x6½"........ 1,920.00
Vase, mums, wht/amber on dk ground, red clay, EX color, sgn/dtd, 11x7"....3,600.00
Vase, squirrels/pine bough, pillow form, 1895/AHB/Albion, 8x8½" ..3,400.00

Bennington

Although the term has become a generic one for the mottled brown ware produced there, Bennington is not a type of pottery, but rather a town in Vermont where two important potteries were located. The Norton Company, founded in 1793, produced mainly redware and salt-glazed stoneware; only during a brief partnership with Fenton (1845 – 1847) was any Rockingham attempted. The Norton Company endured until 1894, operated by succeeding generations of the Norton family. Fenton organized his own pottery in 1847. There he manufactured not only redware and stoneware, but more artistic types as well — graniteware, scroddled ware, flint enamel, a fine parian, and vast amounts of their famous Rockingham. Though from an aesthetic standpoint his work rated highly among the country's finest ceramic achievements, he was economically unsuccessful. His pottery closed in 1858.

It is estimated that only one in five Fenton pieces were marked; and although it has become a common practice to link any fine piece of Rockingham to this area, careful study is vital in order to be able to distinguish Bennington's from the similar wares of many other American and Staffordshire potteries. Although the practice was without the permission of the proprietor, it was nevertheless a common occurrence for a potter to take his molds with him when moving from one pottery to the next, so particularly well-received designs were often reproduced at several locations. Of eight known Fenton marks, four are variations of the '1849' impressed stamp: 'Lyman Fenton Co., Fenton's Enamel Patented 1849, Bennington, Vermont.' These are generally found on examples of Rockingham and flint enamel. A raised, rectangular scroll with 'Fenton's Works, Bennington, Vermont,' was used on early examples of porcelain. From 1852 to 1858, the company operated under the title of the United States Pottery Company. Three marks — the ribbon mark with the initials USP, the oval with a scrollwork border and the name in full, and the plain oval with the name in full — were used during that period.

Among the more sought-after examples are the bird and animal figurines, novelty pitchers, figural bottles, and all of the more finely modeled items. Recumbent deer, cows, standing lions with one forepaw on a ball, and opposing pairs of poodles with baskets in their mouths and 'coleslaw' fur were made in Rockingham, flint enamel, and occasionally in parian. Numbers in the listings below refer to the book *Bennington Pottery and Porcelain* by Barret. Our advisors for Bennington (except for parian and stoneware) are Barbara and Charles Adams; they are listed in the Directory under Massachusetts.

Key: c/s — cobalt on salt glaze

Book flask, Bennington Suffering, flint enamel, 10¾" 5,000.00
Bottle, Coachman, flint enamel, tassels on cloak, rprs, 10¾" 900.00
Bottle, Coachman, Rockingham, 10¼" 1,100.00
Box, toiletry; flint enamel, 8-sided, sm rpr, 7¾" 795.00
Candlestick, flint enamel, 6⅛", ea...675.00
Candlestick, flint enamel, 9½", ea...675.00
Coffee urn, flint enamel, paneled form on ped ft, 20½", EX 5,000.00
Coffeepot, flint enamel, paneled, domed lid, flakes/rpr, 12" 3,000.00
Cuspidor, flint enamel, sm flake, 4x8½" 150.00
Cuspidor, flint enamel, Type A, 3¾x8" 145.00
Cuspidor, Rockingham, imp mk, 1849-58, 9¾" 375.00

Figurine, lion, flint enamel, facing right with tongue up, 1849 mark, 9x11", NM, $18,400.00. (Photo courtesy Garth's Auctions Inc.)

Figurine, lion, flint enamel, Lyman Fenton..., 1848, 9x11", NM ..10,000.00
Figurine, poodle w/basket, Rockingham w/coleslaw fur, 9x11", pr....9,000.00
Flowerpot, cattails emb on dk brn, saucer base, flakes, 10x11" 145.00
Frame, flint enamel, scalloped edge, flakes, 10¾x9⅝" 2,070.00
Frame, Rockingham, oval, flakes, 8¾x9¾" w/4¼x3½" opening 900.00
Pie plate, flint enamel, lt wear, 11" 175.00
Pitcher, alternate ribs, flint enamel, faint mk, 10⅛" 900.00
Pitcher, floral sprays in panels, Rockingham, Norton & Fenton, 9"...950.00
Pitcher, tulips & hearts, brn/cream/gr flint enamel, 1849 mk, 12", VG..900.00
Pitcher, tulips & hearts, flint enamel w/gr & bl, rpr hdl, 11"........450.00
Spill holder, buck & doe on base, flint enamel, rprs, 9x11x11", pr...1,150.00
Teapot, flint enamel, appl hdl, mini, 5½", NM 1,800.00
Toby pitcher, seated figure, grapevine hdl, Rockingham, 6" 675.00
Vase, tulip; flint enamel w/dk gr & bl on raised ribs, flakes, 9" 925.00
Washbowl & pitcher, scalloped ribs, flint enamel, 12¼", 5x15" .. 2,750.00

Stoneware

Churn, #6/floral cornucopia, c/s, J Norton, ca 1861, 19", EX 8,250.00
Cream pot, #2/flower, c/s, Norton & Fenton, 1840s, stain/lines, 7½"..440.00
Cream pot, #4/lg floral spray, c/s, J&E Norton, ca 1855, crack, 14"..360.00
Crock, #1/flower, c/s, J&E Norton, ca 1855, sm stain, 9"..............470.00
Crock, #2/bird on plume, c/s, E&LP Norton, 1880s, stain/chip, 11"..700.00
Crock, #2/chicken pecking corn, c/s, unsgn Norton, ca 1865, 9½"....3,300.00
Crock, #2/flower (triple), c/s, Norton & Fenton, 1840s, 10½" 475.00
Crock, #3/flower, Benny Blue, c/s, E&LP Norton, 1880s, prof rstr, 13" ..525.00
Crock, #3/flower (triple), c/s, Norton & Fenton, crack, 1840s, 12"..165.00

Crock, #4/flower, c/s, E&LP Norton, ca 1880, separation, 11"..... 275.00
Crock, #5/deer/house/trees, c/s, J&E Norton, line, ca 1855, 13"...23,650.00
Crock, cake; #1½/thistle flower, c/s, J&E Norton, line, ca 1855, 7"..635.00
Jar, #2/flower (triple), c/s, Norton & Fenton, ca 1845, lines, 11". 165.00
Jug, #1½/bird on plume, c/s, E&LP Norton, lines, 1880s, 12" 360.00
Jug, #1½/plume, c/s, E Norton & Co, ca 1886, flaw, 11½"............180.00
Jug, #2 & accents, c/s, L Norton & Son, stain, ca 1835, 13½" 360.00
Jug, #2/flower, c/s, J&E Norton, ca 1855, tight line, 13½"............330.00
Jug, #2/flower, c/s, Julius Norton, hairlines/flakes, 14"...............175.00
Jug, #2/flower & leaf, c/s, J&E Norton, ca 1855, 13½" 1,375.00
Jug, #2/peacock (lg), c/s, J&E Norton, ca 1855, 4"....................4,950.00
Jug, #2/rabbit running, c/s, Norton & Fenton, spider, 1840s, 13½" ..1,150.00
Jug, #3/flower, c/s, E&LP Norton, ca 1880, separation, 16" 275.00
Jug, #4/flower, c/s, E&LP Norton, ca 1880, stain/chip, 17"...........415.00
Jug, bird on branch, c/s, J&E Bennington, lt wear, ca 1855, 11" ..715.00
Jug, bird on twig, c/s, J&E Norton, stain, ca 1855, 11½" 385.00
Pitcher, Albany slip, J Norton & Co, ca 1861, flaw, 11½" 90.00

Beswick

In the early 1890s, James Wright Beswick operated a pottery in Longston, England, where he produced fine dinnerware as well as ornamental ceramics. Today's collectors are most interested in the figurines made since 1936 by a later generation Beswick firm, John Beswick, Ltd. They specialize in reproducing accurately detailed bone-china models of authentic breeds of animals. Their Fireside Series includes dogs, cats, elephants, horses, the Huntsman, and an Indian figure, which measure up to 14" in height. The Connoisseur line is modeled after the likenesses of famous racing horses. Beatrix Potter's characters and some of Walt Disney's are charmingly recreated and appeal to children and adults alike. Other items, such as character Tobys, have also been produced. The Beswick name is stamped on each piece. The firm was absorbed by the Doulton group in 1973.

Alice in Wonderland, Dodo, 1st version, 4" 385.00
Alice in Wonderland, Frog Footman, 1970s 485.00
American Indian chief on piebald horse, #1391, 8½", from $650 to..750.00
Animaland, Ginger Nutt, #1152, 1949-55, 4" 185.00
Beatrix Potter, Christmas Stocking, BP6A 295.00
Beatrix Potter, Duchess w/Pie, BP3B, 3¾" 370.00
Beatrix Potter, Flopsy, Mopsy & Cottontail, P4161 ....1,050.00
Beatrix Potter, Head Gardener, BP11A 295.00
Beatrix Potter, Mr Todd, BP4 ....285.00
Beatrix Potter, Ribby, gold circle mk, 1951-54, 3¼" 425.00
Beatrix Potter, Samuel Whiskers, gold circle mk, BP1, 1948-54..350.00
Beatrix Potter, Sir Isaac Newton, BP3A 600.00
Beatrix Potter, Tommy Brock, sm eye patch (1974 only), BP3A...1,100.00
Bird, Evening Grosbeak, #2190, 4"..355.00
Bird, Fantail Pigeon, #1614, 1959-69, 5" 625.00
Bird, Gouldian Finch, #1178, 4x4½"..325.00
Bird, Mandarin Duck, #1519-1, 4½" L...285.00
Butterfly, Purple Emperor, #1487, 1957-63..................................650.00
Cat, Colin Melbourn, #1435, 5x4½"...500.00
Cockerel, Leghorn, #1892 ....315.00
Cow, Charolais cow & calf, #3075A & #1827B on base 400.00
Cow, Dairy Shorthorn, brn & wht, Gredington, #1510, 4¾" 835.00
Cow, Friesian bull, #1439A, 1985-89...285.00
Cow, Gwersylt Lord Oxford 74th, shorthorn dairy bull, #1504 ....925.00
Cow, Hereford cow & calf on wooden plinth, #A2267/2669, 1981-89..500.00
Cow, Limousin bull, brn, #2463A 525.00
Cow, Sabrina's Sir Richmond 14th, guernsey bull, #1451 ....365.00
Disney's Peter Pan, Smee, #1302, 4¼"...450.00
Dog, Ivanola Gold Digger, poodle, #2108, 5¾"............................600.00
Dog, Old English Sheepdog, w/Dulux tin, 1990, rare 665.00

Fish, Atlantic Salmon, #1233......................................350.00
Hog, Wessex Saddleback Boar, #1512, 1957-69............................615.00
Horse, Boy on a Pony, palomino, #1500..............................415.00
Horse, Cardigan Bay, #2340, 1st version w/bk leg free from base .. 755.00
Horse, Girl's Pony, piebald, Gredington, #1483, 5" 1,100.00
Horse, Hollydell Dixie, Shetland pony, #BCC95 ....395.00
Horse, huntsman's, chestnut, #1484, 1958-67, 6¾" 615.00
Horse, Shire mare, rocking-horse gray, Gredington, 1940-62....1,200.00
Horse, stylized, 2-colored, Colin Melbourne, #1411, 8½" 1,550.00
Horse, Welsh Cob, chestnut, Gredington, #1793, 1962-75, 7½"...1,400.00
Horse, Welsh Cob stallion, blk w/wht socks, #A270 ....415.00
Horse, Welsh mountain pony, #A247, 8x9"............................375.00
Huntswoman, on gray horse, #1730, 1960-95, 8¼", from $600 to...685.00
Huntswoman Jumping Fence, #982, 10x10½", from $575 to 650.00
Kitty MacBride, A Good Read, #2529, 2½"..................................155.00
Kitty MacBride, Guilty Sweethearts, #2566, 1976-83, 2¼" 70.00
Kitty MacBride, Just Good Friends, #2533, 1973-83, 3"................55.00
Kitty MacBride, Racegoer, #2528, 1975-83, 3½" 55.00
Kitty MacBride, Snack, #2531, 1975-83, 3"...................................65.00

Bicycle Collectibles

Bicycles and related ephemera and memorabilia have been collected since the end of the nineteenth century, but for the last 20 years, they have been regarded as bonafide collectibles. Today they are prized not only for their charm and appearance, but for historical impact as well. Many wonderful items are now being offered through live and Internet auctions, rare book sites, etc.

Hobby horse/draisienne bicycles were handmade between circa 1818 and 1821. If found today, one of these would almost certainly be 'as found.' (Be suspect of any that look to be restored or are brightly painted; it would be very doubtful that it was authentic.)

Bicycle collectors are generally split as specializing in pre- and post-1920. Those specializing in pre-1920 might want only items from the hobby horse era (1816 – 1821), velocipede and manumotive era (1830 – 1872), high-wheel and hard-tired safety era (1873 – 1890), or the pneumatic safety era (post 1890). With the introduction of the pneumatic tire, the field was impacted both socially and technically. From this point, collector interest relates to social, sport, fashion, manufacturing, urbanization, financial, and technical history. Post 1920 collectors tend to be drawn to Art Deco and Aerodynamic design, which forge prices. Many seek not only cycles but signage, prints and posters, watches, medals, photographs, porcelains, toys, and various other types of ephemera and memorabilia. Some prefer to specialize in items relating to military cycling, certain factories, racing, country of origin, type of bike, etc. All radiate from a common interest.

The bicycle has played an important role in the rapid developement of the twentieth century and onwards, impacting the airplane, motorcycle, and automobile, also the manufacture of drawn tubing, differentials, and spoked wheels. It has affected advertising, urbanization, women's lib, and the vote. There are still many treasures to be discovered.

Barnes White Flyer Tandem, rstr, from $1,200 to 1,500.00
Colson Firestone Cruiser, girl's, snap-in tank/fender light, 1930s, G-....200.00
Columbia Model 40, boy's, 1890s, rstr..650.00
Elgin Bluebird, boys', 1936, VG, from $8,000 to 12,000.00
Evinrude Imperial Steam Flow, boy's, 1937, EX, from $9,500 to ...1,400.00
Hawthorn Zep, boy's, 1938, rstr, EX, from $2,900 to 3,625.00
Huffy Am Thunderbird, boy's, 1960s, G, from $75 to 100.00
Indian, boy's, 1937, complete w/saddlebags, VG orig................1,300.00
JC Higgins Murray, boy's, 1948, rstr, from $150 to.......................200.00
Monarch Firestone Pilot, boy's, chrome headlight/rear rack, 1941, VG.400.00
Monarch Silver King Racer, boy's, 1935, rstr, from $1,000 to ...1,500.00

Murray Fire Cat, boy's, 1977, VG..250.00
Roadmaster Luxury Liner, girl's, 26", EX, from $500 to 700.00
Schwinn Aero-Cycle, boy's, 1936, rstr, EX 3,150.00
Schwinn Auto Cycle Super Deluxe, boy's, 1941, rstr, EX..........3,100.00
Schwinn Black Phantom, boy's, balloon tires, 1950s, rstr, $1,000 to..1,500.00
Schwinn Gray Ghost Sting Ray, boy's, 5-speed, 1971, rstr, 54" 650.00
Schwinn Sting Ray Tornado, boy's, 1970s, NM, from $150 to 250.00
Shelby Airflo, boy's, 1938, rstr, EX, from $3,300 to 4,625.00

Streamlined pressed steel tricycle with headlight, restored, $450.00. (Photo courtesy Morphy Auctions)

Swiss Army, boy's, 1941, VG, from $700 to 1,000.00
Western Flyer Buzz Bike 2+1, boy's, 1960-70, G...........................475.00

Big Little Books

The first Big Little Book was published in 1933 and copyrighted in 1932 by the Whitman Publishing Company of Racine, Wisconsin. Its hero was Dick Tracy. The concept was so well accepted that others soon followed Whitman's example; and though the 'Big Little Book' phrase became a trademark of the Whitman Company, the formats of his competitors (Saalfield, Goldsmith, Van Wiseman, Lynn, and World Syndicate) were exact copies. Today's Big Little Book buffs collect them all.

These hand-sized sagas of adventure were illustrated with full-page cartoons on the right-hand page and the story narration on the left. Colorful cardboard covers contained hundreds of pages, usually totaling over an inch in thickness. Big Little Books originally sold for 10¢ at the dime store; as late as the mid-1950s when the popularity of comic books caused sales to decline, signaling an end to production, their price had risen to a mere 20¢. Their appeal was directed toward the pre-teens who bought, traded, and hoarded Big Little Books. Because so many were stored in attics and closets, many have survived. Among the super heroes are G-Men, Flash Gordon, Tarzan, the Lone Ranger, and Red Ryder; in a lighter vein, you'll find such lovable characters as Blondie and Dagwood, Mickey Mouse, Little Orphan Annie, and Felix the Cat.

In the early to mid-'30s, Whitman published several Big Little Books as advertising premiums for the Coco Malt Company, who packed them in boxes of their cereal. These are highly prized by today's collectors, as are Disney stories and super-hero adventures.

Note: At the present time, the market for these books is fairly stable — values for common examples are actually dropping. Only the rare, character-related titles are increasing somewhat.

Adventure of Krazy Kat & Ignatz Mouse in Koko Land, VG 100.00
Adventures of Huckleberry Finn, Whitman, #1422, NM............... 40.00
Alley Oop & Dinny in the Jungles of Moo, 1938, EX+................. 45.00
Bambi, #1469, 1942, NM 40.00
Billy the Kid, Whitman #773, 1935, EX 35.00
Blondie & Baby Dumpling, 1937, NM.. 40.00
Bonanza, Bubble Gum Kid, Whitman #2002, 1967, EX................ 12.00
Buck Rogers & The Planetoid Plot, 1936, VG 85.00
Buck Rogers in City of Floating Globes, Cocomalt premium, EX....150.00

Convoy Patrol, Whitman #1446, NM 20.00
Cowboy Malloy, 1940, EX 20.00
Dan Dunn on the Trail of Wu Fang, 1938, EX 65.00
Dick Tracy & the Stolen Bonds, 1934, EX 65.00
Dick Tracy & Tiger Lily Gang, Whitman #1460, 1949, VG 35.00
Donald Duck & Ghost Morgan's Treasure, 1946, VG 55.00
Donald Duck in Volcano Valley, Whitman #1457, 1949, NM 95.00
Eddie Cantor in an Hour With You, 1934, EX+ 65.00
Ellery Queen the Master Detective, Whitman #1472, 1942, NM .. 60.00
Flash Gordon & the Ape Men of Mor, 1942, VG 75.00
Freckles & the Lost Diamond Mine, Whitman #1164, EX 35.00
Gang Busters Smash Through, 1942, EX+ 50.00
Ghost Avenger, 1943, VG 18.00
Houdini's Big Little Book of Magic, Whitman #715, 1927, EX 50.00
It Happened One Night, 1935, EX+ 80.00
Jack London's Call of the Wild, 1935, EX+ 50.00
Junior G-Men, 1937, EX 30.00
Ken Maynard in Gun Justice, 1934, VG 40.00
Last of the Mohicans, 1936, VG 30.00
Li'l Abner in New York, Whitman #1198, 1936, EX 60.00
Little Orphan Annie & the Gooneyville Mystery, 1947, EX 50.00
Mickey Mouse & the Magic Carpet, 1935, VG 150.00
Mickey Mouse & the Sacred Jewel, 1936, EX 80.00
Moon Mullins & Kayo, 1933, EX+ 50.00
Mutt & Jeff, Whitman #1113, NM 75.00
Nancy & Sluggo, 1946, EX+ 45.00
Once Upon a Time, 1933, EX+ 60.00
Popeye & Queen Olive Oyl, Whitman #1458, EX+ 40.00
Porky Pig & Petunia, 1942, EX+ 60.00
Prairie Bill & the Covered Wagon, 1934, EX 50.00
Radio Patrol Outwitting the Gang Chief, 1939, EX 25.00
Roy Rogers & the Dwarf-Cattle Ranch, 1947, VG 25.00
Shadow & the Ghost Makers, 1942, VG 100.00
Smilin' Jack & Stratosphere Ascent, Whitman #1152, 1937, EX .. 35.00
Story of Skippy, 1934, premium, EX 100.00
Tarzan & the Golden Lion, Whitman #1448, NM 75.00

Tarzan and the Tarzan Twins With Jad-Bal-Ja the Golden Lion, EX, $50.00. (Photo courtesy Morphy Auctions)

Tim McCoy in the Prescot Kid, 1935, EX+ 75.00
Union Pacific, 1939, EX+ 50.00
World of Monsters, 1935, EX+ 60.00

Bing and Grondahl

In 1853 brothers M.H. and J.H. Bing formed a partnership with Frederick Vilhelm Grondahl in Copenhagen, Denmark. Their early wares were porcelain plaques and figurines designed by the noted sculptor Thorvaldsen of Denmark. Dinnerware production began in 1863, and by 1889 their underglaze color 'Copenhagen Blue' had earned them worldwide acclaim. They are perhaps most famous today for their Christmas plates, the first of which was made in 1895. See also Limited Edition Plates.

Note: Prices for all figurines are auction values plus buyer's premium.

Blue Traditional, bowl, rimmed soup; 8⅜", from $40 to 50.00
Blue Traditional, chop plate, 12" 125.00
Blue Traditional, cup & saucer, flat, #108 .... 50.00
Blue Traditional, gravy boat 50.00
Blue Traditional, leaf dish, 10", from $35 to 45.00
Blue Traditional, plate, bread & butter; 6", from $15 to 18.00
Blue Traditional, plate, dinner; 10½" 70.00
Blue Traditional, sugar bowl, w/lid 70.00
Christmas Rose, coffeepot 115.00
Christmas Rose, cup & saucer 20.00
Christmas Rose, egg cup, 2½" 18.00
Christmas Rose, plate, dinner; 9½" 50.00
Christmas Rose, plate, luncheon; 8" 24.00
Christmas Rose, tureen, w/lid, from $300 to 325.00
Christmas Rose, vase, 8½" 115.00
Figurine, ape, upright, gazing upward, #2053, 1930, 14½" 700.00
Figurine, bison, sgn KN, #7054, 1980 ltd ed, 19" L, from $900 to .. 1,050.00
Figurine, Borzoi, #2115, ca 1940, 8¼" 325.00
Figurine, boy & girl reading, #1567, 4¼x4½" 50.00
Figurine, boy & girl stand bk-to-bk, #2372, 7⅞" 100.00
Figurine, bull, S Madsen, #2121, 1930, 14" L, from $475 to 550.00
Figurine, cat lying on side, gray w/blk stripes, #2236, 1915, 7" L ... 470.00
Figurine, doe & nursing fawn, Moller, #1971, 1921, 6" 475.00
Figurine, elephant kneeling, trunk up, #1502, ca 1950, 10¾" 225.00
Figurine, farmer w/pig, #2263, ca 1955, 8¼" 225.00
Figurine, farmer w/2 workhorses, #2119, ca 1935, 9½" 500.00
Figurine, fox, #1719, 1950, 12" L 235.00
Figurine, girl buckling shoe, #2317, 4" 100.00
Figurine, girl seated, holding flowers, #2298, 6¼" 75.00
Figurine, girl w/kitten in basket, #2249, 4x4½" 60.00
Figurine, grebe & chicks, #2439, ca 1984, 11" L 225.00
Figurine, greyhound, brn & wht, #2076, 9½x11½" 180.00
Figurine, guillemot, JP Dahl-Jensen, #1632, 1920, 7" 385.00
Figurine, Japanese Chin, S Madsen, #2114, 1950s, 6¾" L 300.00
Figurine, lady w/chickens, Locher, #2220, ca 1955, 9" 400.00
Figurine, lady w/3 geese, #2254, ca 1955, 9¼" 175.00
Figurine, lion (male) on rock, L Jensen, #2057, 1955, 7¾" 385.00
Figurine, lioness & cub, L Jensen, #2268, 1930, 12½" L 530.00
Figurine, Little Match Girl, #2012, ca 1935, 3½" 200.00
Figurine, llama, #1791, 1910, 5" 175.00
Figurine, Love Refused, boy & girl together, #1614, 4¼x4½" 45.00
Figurine, monkey, seated, #1646, 1940, 6¾" 235.00
Figurine, monkey scratching chin, #2045, 1935, 4" 300.00
Figurine, monkey studies turtle in left hand, Dahl-Jensen, #1510, 5" .. 175.00
Figurine, nude male w/pitcher holds bowl for eagle, wht, 8½x10" ... 600.00
Figurine, Old Fisherman, #2370, 8⅛" 125.00
Figurine, orangutan pr cuddling, K Kyhn, #1454/721, 1925, 3½" 525.00
Figurine, Oriental man w/gold crown seated, 2nd man behind, #8049, 9" ... 150.00
Figurine, Padding About, barefoot boy, #1757, 8" 60.00
Figurine, panther raised on front legs, L Jensen, #1797, 1930, 7½" .. 500.00
Figurine, penguin on rock, #2059, ca 1950, 18" 1,200.00
Figurine, polar bear crouching, #1857, 8½x14" 250.00
Figurine, snail, #1536, 4" L 550.00
Figurine, tiger, Laurits Jensen, #2056, 1975, 9½" 825.00
Figurine, tiger & cub, mother grooms young, #1948, 1930, 11" L .. 1,050.00
Paperweight, nude child on rectangular base, #1649, 1950s, 4½" 235.00
Seagull, bowl, rimmed soup; 8½" 25.00
Seagull, bowl, vegetable; oval, 8¾" 85.00
Seagull, cake plate, hdls, 10½" 55.00
Seagull, coffeepot 100.00

Seagull, creamer, 3½", from $30 to 35.00
Seagull, cup & saucer, flat, 2½" 30.00
Seagull, egg cup, ftd 45.00
Seagull, jardiniere, #699, 7" 50.00
Seagull, mustard pot, 3⅛" 85.00
Seagull, pitcher, 16-oz, 5¼", from $75 to.................................. 90.00
Seagull, plate, dinner; 9½".. 50.00
Seagull, plate, open lace rim, 8½" 42.00
Seagull, plate, salad; crescent shape 40.00
Seagull, plate, salad; 7½" 25.00
Seagull, plate, triangular, 9x9½" 42.00
Seagull, shakers, 3", pr from $45 to 55.00
Seagull, vase, bud; 2¾".. 27.50
Seagull, vase, 5½"... 30.00
Seagull, vase, 8½".. 115.00
Tray, nude boy seated on seashell, 8½" L................................ 70.00
Tray, 2 wht mice, Dahl-Jensen, #1562, 1955, 3" 200.00
Vase, boats in harbor, gray on bl to cream, bulbous, late 20th C, 12".. 300.00
Vase, floral on soft gray-bl, #3925/112, ca 1910, 6"............... 300.00
Vase, mahog mottle, bulbous top w/sm opening, A Jorgensen, 24½".. 2,000.00
Vase, rose crystalline, slender neck, 7⅞" 500.00
Vase, stylized floral, att T Madsen, #1008/57, ca 1900, 7" 600.00

Binoculars

There are several types of binoculars, and the terminology used to refer to them is not consistent or precise. Generally, 'field glasses' refer to simple Galilean optics, where the lens next to the eye (the ocular) is concave and dished away from the eye. By looking through the large lens (the objective), it is easy to see that the light goes straight through the two lenses. These are lower power, have a very small field of view, and do not work nearly as well as prism binoculars. In a smaller size, they are opera glasses, and their price increases if they are covered with mother-of-pearl (fairly common but very attractive), abalone shell (more colorful), ivory (quite scarce), or other exotic materials. Field glasses are not valuable unless very unusual or by the best makers, such as Zeiss or Leitz. Prism binoculars have the objective lens offset from the eyepiece and give a much better view. This is the standard binocular form, called Porro prisms, and dates from around 1900. Another type of prism binocular is the roof prism, which at first resembles the straight-through field glasses, with two simple cylinders or cones, here containing very small prisms. These can be distinguished by the high quality views they give and by a thin diagonal line that can be seen when looking backwards through the objective. In general, German binoculars are the most desirable, followed by American, English, and finally French, which can be of good quality but are very common unless of unusual configuration. Japanese optics of WWII or before are often of very high quality. 'Made in Occupied Japan' binoculars are very common, but collectors prize those by Nippon Kogaku (Nikon). Some binoculars are center focus (CF), with one central wheel that focuses both sides at once. These are much easier to use but more difficult to seal against dirt and moisture. Individual focus (IF) binoculars are adjusted by rotating each eyepiece and tend to be cleaner inside in older optics. Each type is preferred by different collectors. Very large binoculars are always of great interest. All binoculars are numbered according to their magnifying power and the diameter of the objective in millimeters. Optics of 6 x 30 magnify six times and have 30 millimeter objectives.

Prisms are easily knocked out of alignment, requiring an expensive and difficult repair. If severe, this misalignment is immediately noticeable on use by the double-image scene. Minor damage can be seen by focusing on a small object and slowly moving the binoculars away from the eye, which will cause the images to appear to separate. Overall cleanliness should be checked by looking backwards (through the objective) at a light or the sky, when any film or dirt on the lenses or prisms can eas-ily be seen. Pristine binoculars are worth far more than when dirty or misaligned, and broken or cracked optics lower the value far more. Cases help keep binoculars clean but do not add materially to the value.

As of 2007, any significant changes in value are due to Internet sales. Some of the prices listed here are lower than would be reached at an online auction. Revisions of these values would be inappropriate at this point for these reasons: First, values are fluctuating wildly on the Internet; 'auction fever' is extreme. Second, some common instruments can fetch a high price at an Internet sale, and it is clear that the price will not be supported as more of them are placed at auction. In fact, an over-looked collectible like the binocular will be subject to a great increase in supply as they are retrieved from closets in response to the values people see at an online auction. Third, sellers who have access to these Internet auctions can use them for price guides if they wish, but the values in this listing have to reflect what can be obtained at an average large antique show. The following listings assume a very good overall condition, with generally clean and aligned optics. Our advisor for this category is Jack Kelly; he is listed in the Directory under Washington.

Field Glasses

Fernglas 08, German WWI, 6x39, military gr, many makers.......... 50.00
Folding, modern, hinged flat case, oculars outside 10.00
Folding or telescoping, no bbls, old.. 125.00
Ivory covered, various sm szs & makers....................................... 200.00
LeMaire, bl leather/brass, various szs, other Fr same 25.00
Metal, emb hunting scene, various sm szs & makers...................... 45.00
Pearl covered, various sm szs & makers.. 90.00
Porc covered, delicate HP, various sm szs & makers..................... 200.00
US Naval Gun Factory Optical Shop 6x30 .... 75.00
Zeiss 'Galan' 2.5x34, modern design look, early 1920s................. 170.00

Prism Binoculars (Porro)

Barr & Stroud, 7x50, Porro II prisms, IF, WWII 120.00
Bausch & Lomb, 6x30, IF, WWI, Signal Corps 50.00
Bausch & Lomb, 7x50, IF, WWII, other makers same.................. 140.00
Bausch & Lomb Zephyr, 7x35 & other, CF.................................. 160.00
Bausch & Lomb/Zeiss, 8x17, CF, Pat 1897................................. 140.00
Crown Optical, 6x30, IF, WWI, filters 50.00
France, various makers & szs, if not unusual 30.00
German WWII 10x80, eyepcs at 45 degrees 500.00
German WWII 6x30, 3-letter code for various makers.................. 60.00
Goertz Trieder Binocle, various szs, unusual adjustment.............. 110.00
Huet, Paris 7x22, other sm szs, unusual shapes........................... 80.00
Leitz 6x30 Dienstglas, IF, good optics.. 75.00
Leitz 8x30 Binuxit, CF, outstanding optics................................. 150.00
M19, US military 7x50, ca 1980 .... 180.00
Nikon 9x35, 7x35, CF, 1950s-70s.. 140.00
Nippon Kogaku, 7x50, IF, Made in Occupied Japan 150.00
Ross Stepnada, 7x30, CF, wide angle, 1930s 250.00
Ross 6x30, standard British WWI issue.. 50.00
Sard, 6x42, IF, very wide angle, WWII 900.00
Toko (Tokyo Opt Co) 7x50, IF, Made in Occupied Japan.............. 45.00
Universal Camera 6x30, IF, WWII, other makers same.................. 50.00
US Naval Gun Factory Optical Shop 6x30, IF, filters, WWI 70.00
US Naval Gun Factory Optical 10x45, IF, WWI............................ 200.00
US Navy, 20x120, various makers, WWII & later.................... 2,200.00
Warner & Swasey (important maker) 8x20, CF, 1902................. 200.00
Wollensak 6x30, ca 1940... 50.00
Zeiss Deltrintem 8x30, CF, 1930s.. 95.00
Zeiss DF 95, 6x18, sq shoulder, very early 160.00
Zeiss Starmorbi 12/24/42x60, turret eyepcs, 1920s 2,500.00
Zeiss Teleater 3x13, CF, bl leather.. 120.00

Zeiss 15x60, CF or IF, various models... 700.00
Zeiss 8x40 Delactis, CF or IF, 1930s 230.00

Roof Prism Binoculars

Hensoldt Dialyt, various szs, 1930s-80s 140.00
Hensoldt Universal Dialyt, 6x26, 3.5x26, 1920s........................... 120.00
Leitz Trinovid, 7x42 & other, CF, 1960s-80s, EX........................ 500.00
Zeiss Dialyt, 8x30, CF, 1960s 400.00

Birdcages

Birdcages can be found in various architectural styles and in a range of materials such as wood, wicker, brass, and gilt metal with ormolu mounts. Those that once belonged to the wealthy are sometimes inlaid with silver or jewels. In the 1800s, it became fashionable to keep birds, and some of the most beautiful examples of cages found today date back to that era. Musical cages that contained automated bird figures became popular; today these command prices of several thousand dollars. In the latter 1800s, wicker styles came into vogue. Collectors still appreciate their graceful lines and find they adapt easily to modern homes.

Mahog cathedral style w/central dome, 4 porticos, waste drw, 83x27".. 4,000.00
Metal, allover twist/scroll wirework, dome top, Fr style, 20x15" .. 150.00
Metal, red 'tile' roof, 3 arches over wire, elk head over door, 15x15" .. 230.00
Pine, cvd/pnt cottage w/stoop & fence, thick trn laminated stand, 66" ..7,200.00
Pnt iron, cage hangs from J-form stand w/inset scrolls, 58" 190.00
Wirework (brass), cage in open 'o' top, ornate base, on stand, 66"... 275.00
Wirework (silver), chased band, 2 songbirds w/in, Continental, 13" .. 840.00
Wirework cylinder w/sphere top & bulbous bottom on ornate stand, 72" ...235.00
Wirework house w/peaked roof & silo ea side, pnt tole details, 31x30" ..300.00
Wirework pagoda, tole-pnt frieze & top, scrolled iron base, 78", VG.. 1,020.00
Wirework tall dome w/metal finial, Fr, 1800s, 41x19" dia 275.00

Wirework, two-tower top with turned finials, metal bottom, painted base, 34x28x9", $700.00. (Photo courtesy Neal Auction Company, Auctioneers & Appraisers of Fine Art)

Wood, elaborate 3-dome Vict house on table, wht/gilt pnt, 78x27x27"...600.00
Wood & wire, acorn finial, dome top on sq base, 19x15x15" 80.00
Wood & wire, bowfront 2-tier house w/gilt pcs, 18x19x12" 325.00
Wood fr w/wire, dbl-pagoda top, acorn finials, red pnt, 41x24x12" ..265.00

Bisque

Bisque is a term referring to unglazed earthenware or porcelain that has been fired only once. During the Victorian era, bisque figurines became very popular. Most were highly decorated in pastels and gilt and demonstrated a fine degree of workmanship in the quality of their modeling. Few were marked. See also Heubach; Nodders; Dolls; Piano Babies.

Bust, maid looking left, necklace/floral dress, gr anchor mk, 24", EX .. 540.00
Bust, shy young girl in floral dress, hat, pastels/gilt, 17" 210.00
Bust, young maid in hat, scarf about neck, mc, on socle, 1870, 24"..2,350.00
Group, boy & girl, he in knickers, she holds/reaches into cone, 18" ... 325.00
Group, pr w/arms about ea other hold hands of child, rstr, 26" 780.00
Madonna, on ornate scrollwork base, palms reaching outward, 31"....210.00
Male in feathered hat, wide gold necklace, gr anchor mk, 27", VG.... 390.00
Nude child carries amphora/bends bk for support, wht, Moreau, 15"..325.00
Pr, boy & girl in peach/gold/wht winter attire, he w/snowballs, 12" 390.00
Pr, elaborate attire, both w/hats, she presenting her hand, 36", EX ..1,440.00
Pr, he w/knife sheath, she w/braids, hand Xd over heart, 19", EX ...150.00
Pr, he w/mandolin, she w/tambourine held to forehead, 18", NM...210.00
Pr, mother & father, ea w/child on shoulder, floral attire, 20", EX...360.00
Putti w/basket of grapes on ea side sits on stump, wht, 8x10"....... 180.00
Rooster, standing, bright colors, German, 8¾x7½", EX................ 210.00
Vase, standing child in hat w/basket behind, hdl at his waist, 6" .. 35.00
Young girl, 1 hand holding flowers, 1 behind her bk, rstr hands, 14"....80.00

Black Americana

Black memorabilia is without a doubt a field that encompasses the most widely exploited ethnic group in our history. But within this field there are many levels of interest: arts and achievements such as folk music and literature, caricatures in advertising, souvenirs, toys, fine art, and legitimate research into the days of their enslavement and enduring struggle for equality. The list is endless.

In the listings below are some with a derogatory connotation. Thankfully, these are from a bygone era and represent the mores of a culture that existed nearly a century ago. They are included only to convey the fact that they are a part of this growing area of collecting interest. Black Americana catalogs featuring a wide variety of items for sale are available; see the Directory under Clubs, Newsletters, and Catalogs for more information. Our advisor for this category is Judy Posner; she is listed in the Directory under Florida. See also Cookie Jars; Postcards; Posters; Salt Shakers; Sheet Music.

Ashtray, boy standing w/cigar, head nods, Made in Austria, 1920-30s..255.00
Bank, dbl head, bronze, orig patina, 1910, 2½x2½x3", EX 350.00
Bell, girl praying figural, porc, Japan, 1950s, 3¾" 35.00
Book, His Eye Is on the Sparrow, Ethel Waters, 1951, 278-pgs, EX ..35.00
Book, Little Colored Boy & Other Stories, Abingdon Press, late 1800s..125.00
Book, Railroad to Freedom, Hildegard Hoyt Swift, 2nd ed, 1960 .. 25.00
Book, Restaurant Family Funbook, premium, 1978, 12-pg, EX 29.00
Book, SNCCERS..., poetry, Bob Washington, 1968, 44-pg, EX..... 55.00
Book, Story Book of Games, book 1, Kellogg's, 1931, 8x9¾" 59.00
Book, Uncle Tom's Cabin, Stowe/Jackson, children's 1st ed, 1853, G..395.00
Bowl, porringer; mk BABY, china, int scene w/children in 1930s garb .. 35.00
Box, Sambo Cherub gift, full color on gold foil, 1930s, 4¼x5¾".... 25.00
Card, greeting; Can't You Take a Hint?, Volland, 1940s, 5x4"..........7.00
Card, Missed Yo' Birthday, man behind 8-ball, 1950s, 6x5" 18.00
Catalog, Loeser Toy, promo for Federick Loeser & Co, 1920s, 12-pg, EX ..65.00
Cigarette holder & match strike, sleepy man's head w/earrings, 2½" ..299.00
Decanter, butler figure, head as stopper, holding jug, pottery, 7½"...145.00
Doll, Mammy, cloth w/HP features, bandana scarf, clothes, 1940s, 18"..165.00
Figurine, baby sitting on wht bedpan, porc, 3¼x 3¼" 45.00
Figurine, boy sitting w/watermelon on 3 lg seashells, 3x6¼x3¼" ... 55.00
Figurine, child w/umbrella, chalkware, 1950s, hook on bk, 9" 38.00
Figurine, native w/spear, chenille, wooden base, Japan, 1950s, 3¾" ..15.00
Flour sack, So-Easy, Flour Mills of America..., 4 singing chefs, rare...45.00
Handkerchief, scene in ea corner, pk & sage gr on wht, 1900s, 10x9".65.00
Label, fruit crate; Victor Fruit Growers, baby in center, 4x13" 20.00
Letter opener, alligator w/boy head (top of pencil) in mouth, 5½"... 100.00
Match book, M&M Cafeterias, waiters w/trays on cover 18.00

Match holder, 2 boys by cotton bale, metal w/dk bronze finish, 2½" .. 150.00
Measuring spoons, ceramic Mammy w/4 red plastic spoons, 6½x4½" .. 95.00
Muffler, Sambo's Restaurant, knit, 54"+fringe, EX 35.00
Mug, Sambo's Restaurant, pottery, USA, 1970s, 3¼" 24.00
Newspaper, Le Petit Journal, lynching photos, 1900s, 8-oz 195.00
Noisemaker, minstrel, tin litho, US Metal Toy Mfg, 5⅜x3" 22.00
Planter, girl eating watermelon, vivid shiny pnt, 1940-50s, 4½x4" ... 51.00
Playbill, Hobo-Band & Idaho Play Boys, blackfaced minstrels, 12x8" ... 50.00
Postcard, Christmas Greetings..., Raphael Tuck & Sons 38.00
Postcard, Happy New Year, couple kiss under umbrella, sgn Pippo .. 22.00
Postcard, Our Motor, series 9427, Tuck's, sgn H Dix Stanford, 1907.... 22.00
Postcard, Thanksgiving Greetings, emb w/gold, vivid colors, 1911 ... 35.00
Postcard, The Love Drop, ladies w/women making a potion, 1910 ... 25.00
Puppets, doll; couple, celluloid heads w/wood shoes, jtd, 1930s, pr .. 225.00
Recipe box, plastic, Aunt Jemima on front, 3½x5x3¾", EX 125.00
Record, Blue Tail Fly, 78 rpm, banjo player picture sleeve, 1953 ... 30.00
Record, Brave Little Sambo, 1950, 78 rpm, in picture sleeve, EX.. 55.00
Record, Porgy & Bess, C Spivak, 1940s, 2 78 rpm records in album, EX.. 35.00
Score card, Robert's Golliwog Hit the Jack, giveaway, 4½x5" 10.00
Shakers, Mammy & Chef, ceramic, yel pnt w/red accents, 4½" ... 165.00
Shakers, Mammy w/gr or red skirt, Luzianne, plastic, F&F, 5¼", pr .. 125.00
Shakers, Mammy w/red skirt, Luzianne Coffee, plastic, F&F, pr, $100 to. 125.00
Sheet music, Hear Dem Bells, couple singing to steeple, 1880s 32.00
Sheet music, Ladies Man Dapper-Dan From Dixie Land, 1921 ...... 15.00
Sheet music, Lazy Darkey Song, Ben D Allen, Deco cover w/gold, 1940 .. 35.00
Soap dispenser, ceramic Mammy, red dress w/wht apron, 8¾" 95.00
Stein, stereotype man & lady emb, Coburg logo, mini, 3" 25.00
String holder, Mammy, hole above hands, Made in Japan, 1920-30s, 7" ... 125.00
Tablecloth, Mammy w/family, vivid border w/flowers, 1940s, 50" sq.. 110.00
Towel, Mammy w/cake & spoon embr on wht, 1950s, 24x15" 55.00
Towel, woman in kitchen, vivid colors, Startex label, 16x30" 45.00
Wall plaque, girl w/red bow, chalkware, 2 hooks in front, 6" 35.00
Wall pocket, lady's head, metal coil necklace, Horton, 1950s 35.00

Black Cats

Made in Japan during the '50s, these novelty cats may be found bearing the labels of several different importers, all with their own particular characteristics. The best known and most collectible of these cats are from the Shafford line. Even when unmarked, they are easily identified by their red bows, green eyes, and white whiskers, eyeliners, and eyebrows. Relco/Royal Sealy cats are tall and slender, and their bow ties are gold with red dots. Wales is a wonderful line with yellow eyes and gold detailing; Enesco cats have blue eyes, and there are other lines as well. When evaluating your black cats, be sure to inspect their paint and judge them accordingly. Fifty percent paint should relate to 50% of our suggested values, which are given for cats in mint (or nearly mint) paint. Our advisor for this category is Peggy Way; she is listed in the Directory (Clubs) under International Cat Collector's Club.

Ashtray, flat face, Shafford, hard-to-find sz, 3¾" 30.00
Ashtray, flat face, Shafford, 4¾", from $18 to 25.00
Ashtray, head shape, not Shafford, several variants, ea from $15 to.. 20.00
Ashtray, head shape, Shafford, 3", from $20 to 30.00
Bank, seated, coin slot in top of head, Shafford, from $125 to 150.00
Bank, upright, Shafford features, mk Tommy, 2-part, minimum value.. 100.00
Cigarette lighter, Shafford, 5½", from $175 to 200.00
Cigarette lighter, sm cat stands on book by table lamp 30.00
Condiment set, upright, yel eyes, 2 bottles/pr shakers in wire fr..... 95.00
Condiment set, 2 joined heads, J&M bows, spoons, Shafford, 4", $125 to... 135.00
Cookie jar, head form, Shafford 75.00
Cookie jar, head w/fierce look, yel eyes, brn-blk glaze, red clay, lg... 150.00
Creamer, Shafford, 5½", from $20 to 30.00
Creamer, upraised left paw is spout, yel eyes, gold trim, 6½x6" 25.00
Creamer & sugar bowl, head lids are shakers, yel eyes, 5⅜" 50.00
Cruets, upright, she w/V eyes, he w/O eyes, Shafford, pr from $65 to .. 75.00
Decanter, long cat w/red fish in mouth as stopper 65.00
Decanter, upright cat holds bottle w/cork stopper, Shafford, $50 to... 65.00
Decanter set, upright, yel eyes, 6 plain wines 35.00
Demitasse pot, tail hdl, bow finial, Shafford, 7½", from $100 to .. 150.00
Egg cup, cat face on bowl, ped ft, Shafford, from $25 to 35.00
Grease jar, sm head, Shafford, from $125 to 150.00
Ice bucket, cylinder w/emb yel-eyed cat, 2 szs, ea 75.00
Measuring cups, 4 szs on wood wall rack w/pnt cat face, Shafford, rare... 450.00
Mug, cat's head above rim, Shafford, 3½", from $25 to 30.00
Mug, Shafford, hard to find, 4", from $50 to 75.00
Paperweight, head on stepped chrome base, open mouth, yel eyes, rare... 75.00
Pincushion, cushion on bk, tongue measure 25.00
Pitcher, milk; upright, Shafford, 6" or 6½", ea from $130 to 150.00
Pitcher, squatting cat, pour through mouth, rare, 4½" 75.00
Pitcher, squatting cat, pour through mouth, Shafford, rare, 5" 90.00
Pitcher, squatting cat, pour through mouth, Shafford, very rare, 5½ ... 250.00
Planter, upright, Shafford, from $25 to 35.00
Planter, 2 cats in overturned top hat, 4½x3½x3¾" 125.00
Pot holder caddy, 'teapot' cat, 3 hooks, Shafford, minimum value .. 150.00

Salad set, six pieces, wooden rack, Royal Sealy, from $500.00 to $650.00. (Photo courtesy Peggy Way)

Shaker, long & crouching (shaker ea end), Shafford, 10", from $30 to... 50.00
Shakers, range; upright, Shafford, 5", pr 65.00
Shakers, rnd-bodied 'teapot' cats, Shafford, pr from $60 to 75.00
Shakers, upright, Shafford, 3¾" (or slightly smaller), pr, $22 to..... 28.00
Spice set, triangular, 3 rnd tiers (8 in all) in wood fr, Shafford..... 750.00
Spice set, 4 cat shakers hook onto wireware cat-face rack, Shafford... 600.00
Spice set, 6 pcs in wood fr, Shafford, from $75 to 150.00
Spice set, 6 pcs in wood fr, yel eyes, Wales, from $60 to 75.00
Spice set, 9 pcs in wood fr, yel eyes, Wales, from $75 to 100.00
Store plaque, Orig Black Cats...Shafford, blk w/red letters & cat, EX... 800.00
Sugar bowl, Shafford, from $20 to 30.00
Teapot, ball-shaped body, head lid, Shafford, 4-4½" 35.00
Teapot, ball-shaped body, head lid, Shafford, 6½" 45.00
Teapot, cat face w/dbl spout, Shafford, scarce, 5", from $150 to... 250.00
Teapot, upright, lift-off head, Shafford, rare, 8", minimum value. 200.00
Utensil rack, flat-bk cat w/3 slots for utensils, cat only, Shafford ... 75.00
Utensil: strainer, dipper or funnel, wood hdls, Shafford, ea 150.00
Wall pocket, 'teapot' cat, Shafford, minimum value 150.00

Black Glass

Black glass is a type of colored glass that when held to strong light usually appears deep purple, though since each glasshouse had its own formula, tones may vary. It was sometimes etched or given a satin finish;

and occasionally it was decorated with silver, gold, enamel, coralene, or any of these in combination. The decoration was done either by the glasshouse or by firms that specialized in decorating glassware. Crystal, jade, colored glass, or milk glass was sometimes used with the black as an accent. Black glass has been made by many companies since the seventeenth century. Contemporary glasshouses produced black glass during the Depression, seldom signing their product. It is still being made today.

To learn more about the subject, we recommend *A Collector's Guide to Black Glass, Books I* and *II*, written by our advisor, Marlena Toohey; she is listed in the Directory under Colorado. Look for her newly updated value guide. See also Tiffin, L.E. Smith, and other specific manufacturers.

Ashtray, Club/Dmn/Spade/Heart, Imperial, 1981, 3½" ea, 4 for 40.00
Ashtray, silver o/l, Cambridge, 1930s, 5" dia.................................. 22.00
Bowl, console; Autumn, McKee, 1934, 12x5½" 60.00
Bowl, console; HP floral w/gold, Diamond Glassware, 1925-32, 10".. 45.00
Bowl, console; HP Maytime decor, Imperial, #320, 1930s, 5x10½"..49.50
Bowl, rose; ftd, Tiffin, #8098, 1924-34, 7¼x5" 52.00
Bowl, violet; New Martinsville, 3¾" 10.00
Candlesticks, HP flowers & gilt edges on satin, Westmoreland, 3"..40.00
Candy dish, divided, in chrome basket, ca 1920-30s, 8½" 35.00
Champagne, milk glass, w/blk stem, Fostoria, 8-oz 38.50
Cigarette box, w/intaglio dog on lid, Cambridge, #607, 1920s-30s ..62.50
Compote, #1533, crimped, dolphin hdls & silver decor, ca 1930s, 6"... 145.00
Decanter, pewter stopper & decor, ca 1930s, 9½" 95.00
Doorknob, unknown maker, 1920s-30s, 2½"................................. 20.00
Figurine, boy praying, Fenton label, #5100, 1970s, 3¾" 33.00
Figurine, kitten on pillow, Boyd, 1978-83 .... 18.00
Flower bowl, Lotus, unmk Westmoreland, 2-pc, 1970s, 2½x7" 35.00
Flower frog, unknown maker, 1930-40s, 3" 12.50
Mirror, vanity; Boyd, 1991, 8⅛" 22.00
Plate, Forget-Me-Not border, Mary Gregory decor, Westmoreland, 8"..75.00
Platter, octagonal, w/silver decor, Cambridge, 1920s-40s, 10¼" 71.50
Rose bowl, HP decor, Fenton logo & label, #2759, 1995, 3½" 35.50
Shakers, bird, Boyd, 1978-83, 3", pr... 38.50
Shakers, horizontal ribs, Hazel Atlas, ca 1930s, 3½", pr 45.00
Shakers, milk & blk glass, Fenton, #3602BW, 1962-65, 3⅛", pr 44.00
Toothpick holder, elephant head, Boyd, 2¼x4¼" 22.00
Vase, Diadem, Fostoria, #2430, 1929-33, 8"................................. 45.00
Vase, fan, Fenton, #847, 1932, 6" 73.50
Wine, Farberware, Cambridge, #3400, 1940s, 2-oz........................ 22.00

Blown Glass

Blown glass is rather difficult to date; eighteenth and nineteenth century examples vary little as to technique or style. It ranges from the primitive to the sophisticated, but the metallic content of very early glass caused tiny imperfections that are obvious upon examination, and these are often indicative of age.

In America, Stiegel introduced the English technique of using a patterned, part-size mold, a practice which was generally followed by many glasshouses after the Revolution. From 1820 to about 1850, glass was blown into full-size three-part molds. In the listings below, glass is assumed clear unless color is mentioned. See also Bottles and specific manufacturers. Our advisor for this category is Mark Vuono; he is listed in the Directory under Connecticut. See also Bottles; Lamps, Whale Oil, Burning Fluid.

Bowl, aquamarine, on short std & rnd ft, NY, 6x6" 1,200.00
Bowl, med cobalt, 20 left-swirl ribs, ftd, Pittsburgh, 4x4¼" 450.00
Bowl, med yel olive, rolled rim, pontil scar, 1830-60, 4¾x10⅝".. 1,600.00

Bowl, yel olive, rolled rim, pontil scar, 2¼x5¾" 1,000.00
Cane whimsey, clear w/red & bl swirls, 50".................................. 150.00
Canister, clear w/2 cobalt rings at base, cobalt lid, 11x5" dia 435.00
Creamer, aquamarine, rigaree on hdl, flared mouth, ball lid, 7⅜".. 700.00
Creamer, cobalt, sheared rim, solid hdl, Pittsburgh area, 3½" 375.00
Creamer, cobalt, 12-dmn, ornate hdl, pontil scar, 3⅝" 2,400.00
Creamer, cobalt, 20-rib, flared rim/spout, solid hdl, ftd, 4¼" 400.00
Creamer, Lockport Blue, bulbous body, solid hdl, NM, 5x3½" 650.00
Cruet, sapphire bl, 25 vertical ribs, Pittsburgh area, 1700-30, 4½" ...1,000.00
Decanter, dk amethyst, vertical ribs at base, 2-pc mold, 5¼"........ 750.00
Decanter, sunburst stopper, 3 rings to neck, bulbous, open pontil, 11".. 150.00
Demijohn, olive gr, 22x12".. 385.00
Dish, lt amethyst, faint 15-Dmn Quilt, folded rim, ftd, 2½x4"..... 350.00
Flask, lt to med gr, globular, 24 vertical ribs, 1780-1820, 5⅛" 750.00
Flip, tulip in flowerpot eng, pot stones/blisters, 8⅜x6¾".............. 460.00
Gazing ball, dk olive gr, rough pontil, att NE, early 1800s, 2⅝" ... 525.00
Goblet, ruby w/eng presentation, clear stem/ft, ca 1874, 12¾"..1,500.00
Goblets, cranberry w/band of leaves, dots, tendrils, 1850s, 6", 8 for ...370.00
Jar, aquamarine, sheared/tooled mouth, pontil scar, Am, 6x5"...... 550.00
Jar, dk yel olive, sloping collared mouth, pontil scar, NE, 8½" 850.00
Jar, golden amber w/reddish tone, cylindrical, pontil, 10x6½" 1,300.00
Jar, yel amber, sheared mouth w/rim, pontil, burst bubble, NE, 7"...850.00
Pan, aqua-bl, folded rim, att Lockport, blisters, 4⅜" 465.00
Pan, golden amber, 16-rib, folded rim, 5¼" 2,750.00
Pan, pale gr, flared sides, folded rim, blisters, 2⅛x6" 460.00
Pitcher, amethystine w/lav tone, sheared rim, att Mantua, 2¾" ... 900.00
Pitcher, emerald gr, urn form w/loop hdl, rnd base w/pontil, 11x7".. 415.00
Pitcher, Lily Pad, aquamarine, bulbous, solid hdl, NY, 6½" 2,100.00
Rolling pin, amber, NH, early 19th C, 13¼" 200.00
Rolling pin, clear w/red & bl spots, plaster cased, knob hdls, 16"....220.00
Rolling pin, dk sapphire bl, knob hdls, 1850s, 12" 100.00
Salt cellar, bl aquamarine soda-lime glass, knop stem, 1850s, 2⅛".. 2,425.00
Salt cellar, yel olive, ogee bowl, short stem, flared ft, 1820-50, 3"... 1,700.00
Snuff jar, bright gr, rectangular w/chamfered corners, 4½" 600.00
Sugar bowl, dk cobalt, Dmn Quilt, appl ft, conical finial, 6½x4"...2,750.00
Top hat, golden amber, 2" 175.00
Tumbler, cobalt w/12 vertical ribs, cylindrical, pontil, 3¾" 2,750.00
Tumbler, gray w/topaz tone, 12 vertical ribs, 1800-30, 3½" 450.00

Vase, applied cobalt rim and globular base with ring, Pittsburgh, 9½", $2,185.00. (Photo courtesy Garth's Auctions Inc.)

Blown Three-Mold Glass

A popular collectible in the 1920s, 1930s, and 1940s, blown three-mold glass has again gained the attention of many. Produced from approximately 1815 to 1840 in various New York, New England, and Midwestern glasshouses, it was a cheaper alternative to the expensive imported Irish cut glass.

Distinguishing features of blown three-mold glass are the three distinct mold marks and the concave-convex appearance of the glass. For every indentation on the inner surface of the ware, there will be a corresponding protuberance on the outside. Blown three-mold glass is most often clear with the exception of inkwells and a few known decanters. Any colored three-mold glass commands a premium price.

The numbers in the listings that follow refer to the book *American Glass* by George and Helen McKearin. Our advisor for this category is Mark Vuono; he is listed in the Directory under Connecticut.

Creamer, GIII-24, dk cobalt, tooled rim, appl hdl, rayed base, 4" ... **2,200.00**
Creamer, milky med gr (nearly opaque), solid hdl, smooth base, 5" ... **300.00**
Decanter, GI-8, Brandy (wine), vertical ribs, slim bbl form, pr . **2,100.00**
Decanter, GII-43, bulbous w/3 neck rings, tooled mouth, rpl stopper . **700.00**
Decanter, GIII-16, med olive gr, plain lip, rayed base, Keene, 7¼" ... **770.00**
Decanter, GV-16, bulbous, tooled mouth, period stopper, qt **700.00**
Hat, GII-13, swirled rib, concave base, rough pontil, 1825-40, 2" ... **125.00**
Inkwell, GII-16, dk yel olive gr, plain base, early 19th C, 1½" **125.00**
Inkwell, GIII-29, med olive amber, plain base, pontil, Keene, 1½" .. **185.00**
Salt cellar, GII-21, 16-dmn, dk amethyst, flared mouth, Keene, 1⅞".. **10,000.00**
Tumbler, GII-13, plain base, rough pontil, NE, 1820-40, 2⅝x2¼" .. **300.00**

Blue and White Stoneware

'Salt glaze' (slang term) or molded stoneware was most commonly produced in a blue and white coloration, much of which was also decorated with numerous 'in-mold' designs (some 150 plus patterns). It was made by practically every American pottery from the turn of the century until the mid-1930s. Crocks, pitchers, wash sets, rolling pins, and other household wares are only a few of the items that may be found in this type of 'country' pottery, now one of today's popular collectibles.

Logan, Brush-McCoy, Uhl Co., and Burley Winter were among those who produced it, but very few pieces were ever signed. Research and the availability of some manufacturers' sales catalogs has enabled collectors to attribute certain pattern lines to some companies. Naturally condition must be a prime consideration, especially if one is buying for resale; pieces with good, strong color and fully molded patterns bring premium prices. Be mindful that very good reproductions are on the market and are often misrepresented as the real thing. Normal wear and signs of age are to be expected, since this was utility ware and received heavy use in busy households.

In the listings that follow, crocks, salts, and butter holders are assumed to be without lids unless noted otherwise. Items are in near-mint condition unless noted otherwise. Though common pieces seem to have softened to some degree, scarce items and those in outstanding mint condition are stronger than ever. Nationwide Internet sales such as eBay have stabilized and standardized prices that once fluctuated from region to region. They have also helped to determine what is really rare and what isn't. See also specific manufacturers. Our advisor for this category is Steve Stone; he is listed in the Directory under Colorado. For information on the Blue & White Pottery Club, see the Clubs, Newsletters, and Catalogs section of the Directory or visit their website at: www.blue andwhitepottery.org.

Bowl, Apricot, common **80.00**
Bowl, milk; Flying Bird shoulder, w/matching lid, 3¾x9½" **1,200.00**
Bowl, Wildflower (stenciled), 4½x8" **179.00**
Bowl (milk crock), Apricot, w/hdl **225.00**
Butter crock, Apricot, appl wood & wire hdl, w/lid, 4x7" **275.00**
Butter crock, Butterfly, w/lid & bail, 6½" **225.00**
Butter crock, Daisy & Waffle, 4x8" **175.00**
Butter crock, Eagle, w/lid & bail, M.......................... **1,000.00**

Butter crock, Peacock, w/lid, 6x6"........................... **600.00**
Canister, Basketweave, Cloves, w/lid, 4½"................... **200.00**
Canister, Basketweave, Crackers, w/lid...................... **740.00**
Canister, Basketweave, Pepper, w/lid, 4½".................. **200.00**
Canister, Basketweave, Raisins.............................. **479.00**
Canister set, Basketweave, 9-pc............................. **5,000.00**
Chamberpot, Peacock, att Brush-McCoy, 9¾"................. **1,250.00**
Chamberpot, Wildflower & Fishscale, w/lid **400.00**
Coffeepot, Bull's Eye, rim chips, 9¾x3¾" (base)............ **5,200.00**
Coffeepot, Swirl, w/lid & metal base plate.................. **900.00**
Cooler, water; Blue Band, w/lid............................. **250.00**
Cooler, water; Polar Bear, Ice Water, w/lid, hairlines, 6-gal, 15¼"... **900.00**
Cuspidor, Flower Panels & Arches, 7x7½".................... **225.00**
Grease jar, Flying Bird, w/lid, 4x4½" **1,000.00**
Jardiniere pedestal, Tulip pattern **183.00**
Mug, Basketweave & Flower, 5x3"............................ **150.00**
Mug, Dainty Fruit, 5x3".................................... **800.00**
Mug, plain... **65.00**

Mug, Windy City, Robinson Clay Product Co., 5½", $100.00.

Pitcher, Acorns, stenciled, 8x6½" **175.00**
Pitcher, Barrel, +6 mugs.................................... **395.00**
Pitcher, Bluebird, 9x7"..................................... **450.00**
Pitcher, Cattails, stenciled design, bulbous, 7"............ **225.00**
Pitcher, Cherry Band, w/advertising, 8¼" **1,600.00**
Pitcher, Columns & Arches, 8¾x5".......................... **425.00**
Pitcher, Dutch Boy & Girl by Windmill, 9"................... **200.00**
Pitcher, Flying Bird, 9".................................... **625.00**
Pitcher, Girl & Dog, regular bl, 9"......................... **800.00**
Pitcher, Grape w/Rickrack, common, any sz **250.00**
Pitcher, Grazing Cows, 6½" (scarce sz)..................... **500.00**
Pitcher, Indian Good Luck (Swastika), 8½".................. **200.00**
Pitcher, Leaping Deer, 8½".................................. **375.00**
Pitcher, Leaping Deer in 1 oval, Swan in other (mfg error), 8" .. **2,424.00**
Pitcher, Lincoln, allover deep bl, 7x5".................... **500.00**
Pitcher, Lovebird, arc bands, deep color, 8½", EX.......... **500.00**
Pitcher, Lovebird, pale color, 8½"......................... **300.00**
Pitcher, Peacock, scarce................................... **1,700.00**
Pitcher, Poinsettia, common, 6½".......................... **250.00**
Pitcher, Shield, prof rpr, 8".............................. **200.00**
Pitcher, Swan, sponged, extremely rare, 8½" **1,548.00**
Pitcher, Wild Rose, sponged bands, 9" **500.00**
Pitcher, Windmills, common, 7¼", EX....................... **175.00**
Roaster, Wildflower, domed lid, 8½x12".................... **225.00**
Rolling pin, Colonial pattern, M........................... **1,000.00**
Rolling pin, Swirl, orig wooden hdls, 13".................. **1,500.00**
Rolling pin, Wildflower, advertising on 2 sides............ **1,100.00**
Salt crock, Butterfly, w/lid............................... **350.00**
Salt crock, Peacock, w/lid................................. **1,000.00**
Soap dish, Indian in War Bonnet (beware, highly reproduced) ... **250.00**
Toothbrush holder, Bow Tie, stenciled flower **50.00**
Washboard, sponged... **400.00**
Water bottle, Diffused Blue Swirl, stopper w/cork, 10x5½".......... **800.00**

Blue Ridge

Blue Ridge dinnerware was produced by Southern Potteries of Erwin, Tennessee, from the late 1930s until 1956 in 12 basic styles and 2,000 different patterns, all of which were hand decorated under the glaze. Vivid colors lit up floral arrangements of seemingly endless variation, fruit of every sort from simple clusters to lush assortments, barnyard fowl, peasant figures, and unpretentious textured patterns. Although it is these dinnerware lines for which they are best known, collectors prize the artist-signed plates from the '40s and the limited line of character jugs made during the '50s most highly. Examples of the French Peasant pattern are valued at double the prices listed below; very simple patterns will bring 25% to 50% less.

Our advisors, Betty and Bill Newbound, have compiled four lovely books, *Blue Ridge Dinnerware, Revised Third Edition*; *The Collector's Encyclopedia of Blue Ridge, Volumes I and II*; and *Best of Blue Ridge*, all with beautiful color illustrations. They are listed in the Directory under North Carolina. For information concerning the National Blue Ridge Newsletter, see the Clubs, Newsletters, and Catalogs section of the Directory.

Ashtray, ind. 20.00
Baking dish, plain, 8x13" 25.00
Basket, aluminum edge, 10" 25.00
Batter jug, w/lid 75.00
Bonbon, flat shell, china 75.00

Bonbon, Verna, from $75.00 to $90.00. (Pattern has bearing on values.)

Bowl, cereal/soup; Premium, 6" 20.00
Bowl, mixing; med 25.00
Bowl, vegetable; oval, 9" 30.00
Bowl, vegetable; w/lid 65.00
Box, cigarette; sq 90.00
Box, Mallard Duck 700.00
Box, Rose Step, pearlized 100.00
Box, Sherman Lily 900.00
Breakfast set 500.00
Butterdish, Woodcrest 45.00
Carafe, w/lid 125.00
Celery, Skyline 40.00
Child's plate 125.00
Chocolate pot 225.00
Coffeepot, ovoid 175.00
Creamer, demitasse, china 95.00
Creamer, regular 18.00
Cup & saucer, artist-sgn 425.00
Cup & saucer, regular 20.00
Demitasse pot, earthenware 175.00
Dessert cup 14.00
Egg cup, Premium 60.00

Gravy boat 30.00
Lazy Susan, side pcs. 75.00
Pitcher, Alice, earthenware, 6¼" 200.00
Pitcher, Antique, 3½" 175.00
Pitcher, Rebecca 225.00
Pitcher, Sally, china 250.00
Pitcher, Spiral, china, 4¼" 220.00
Plate, advertising, lg 325.00
Plate, artist-signed, Turkey Gobbler 750.00
Plate, Christmas Doorway 95.00
Plate, dinner; Premium, 10½" 40.00
Plate, divided, heavy 45.00
Plate, 6" 10.00
Plate, Still Life, 8½" 30.00
Platter, 15" 55.00
Ramekin, w/lid, 7½" 45.00
Relish, deep shell, china 75.00
Relish, Mod Leaf, china 80.00
Shakers, Apple, 1¾", pr 45.00
Shakers, Blossom Top, pr 85.00
Spoon, salad; china 50.00
Sugar bowl, ped ft, china 65.00
Teapot, Charm House 350.00
Teapot, Mini Ball, china 250.00
Teapot, rope hdl 130.00
Tidbit, 3-tier 55.00
Toast, Premium, w/lid 250.00
Tray, cake; Maple Leaf, china 75.00
Tray, chocolate 500.00
Vase, boot, 8" 95.00
Vase w/hdls, china 100.00

Blue Willow

Blue Willow, inspired no doubt by the numerous patterns of the blue and white Nanking imports, has been popular since the late eighteenth century and has been made in as many variations as there were manufacturers. English transfer wares by such notable firms as Allerton and Ridgway are the most sought after and the most expensive. Japanese potters have been producing Willow-patterned dinnerware since the late 1800s, and American manufacturers have followed suit. Although blue is the color most commonly used, mauve and black lines have also been made. For further study we recommend the book *Gaston's Blue Willow*, with full-color photos and current prices, by Mary Frank Gaston, our advisor for this category; she is listed in the Directory under Texas. In the listings, if no manufacturer is noted, the ware is unmarked. See also Buffalo.

Ashtray, fish figural, Japan, 1970s, 5", from $30 to 35.00
Ashtray, Japan, sq, 7½", from $45 to 55.00
Baking dish, Two Temples II, line border, Hall China, 3x8" 30.00
Bank, kitten figural, unmk Japan, 9¼" L, from $325 to 375.00
Bank, 3 stacked pigs, Japan, 7" 75.00
Basket, aluminum edge, 7", from $25 to 30.00
Biscuit jar, SP lid & bail, unmk English, 7", from $250 to 275.00
Bonbon, divided, center hdl, from $85 to 95.00
Bonbon, flat shell, from $55 to 65.00
Bone dish, kidney shape, Bourne & Leigh, 6¼", from $45 to 55.00
Bowl, chestnut; rtcl sides, unmk English, early 1800s, from $1,000 to .. 1,200.00
Bowl, divided vegetable; smooth edge, Allerton & Sons, 7¼" 165.00
Bowl, Maestricht, 2¾x9⅞" 120.00
Bowl, ped ft, John Tams Ltd, 5x9½", from $150 to 175.00
Bowl, rice; Puntney & Co, 1930s, from $30 to 45.00
Bowl, soup/cereal; scalloped, flow bl, Doulton, 1883-90 .... 130.00

Bowl, vegetable; int pattern, w/lid, Grimwades...Hanley..., 1900s ... 185.00
Bowl, vegetable; Japan, w/lid, from $100 to 125.00
Bowl, vegetable; oval, Alfred Meakin, from $100 to 120.00
Bowl, vegetable; oval, Japan 35.00
Bowl, vegetable; ped ft, John Tams Ltd, post-1930, from $150 to ... 175.00
Bowl, vegetable; scalloped, Allerton, 1890-1912, 8" 110.00
Bowl, vegetable; sq, Ridgways, w/lid, 1912-27 mk, 10" 250.00
Bowl, vegetable; variant center pattern, pictorial border, 10" 25.00
Bowl, vegetable; Wood's Ware, 10" 40.00
Bowl & pitcher, Wedgwood 1,200.00
Box, dresser; porc, unmk English, ca 1880s, 2x4", from $175 to ... 200.00
Butter dish, Royal China, ¼-lb 45.00
Butter dish, w/drainer, Ridgways, 1927 & after, from $300 to 350.00
Butter pat, Ridgways, 1912-27 mk, 3¾", 4 for 60.00
Cake stand, Traditional pattern, unmk English, 4x10½" 325.00
Canisters, sq, tin, unmk, set of 4, from $400 to 500.00
Chamber pot, flow bl, Doulton, 1891-1902, from $350 to 400.00
Cheese dish, sq plate w/canted corners, sq lid, Wiltshaw & Robinson ... 250.00
Child's feeding dish, divided, from $150 to 175.00
Coffeepot, Booths, gold trim, Real Old Willow, 8½" 210.00
Coffeepot, ovoid, from $150 to 175.00
Creamer, demi; china, from $75 to 85.00
Creamer & sugar bowl, w/lid, Steventon & Sons, 3", 4", from $70 to ... 80.00
Cup, chili; Japan, 3½x4" 50.00
Cup, chili; w/liner plate, Japan 75.00
Cup & saucer, jumbo; from $75 to 100.00
Cup & saucer, Meakin for Nieman-Marcus, 1970s 30.00
Cuspidor, rnd, Doulton, 1891-1902, 7½", from $350 to 450.00
Egg cup, dbl, 4¼" 30.00
Egg cup, single, flat base, unmk English, from $20 to 30.00
Gravy boat, Homer Laughlin, from $20 to 25.00
Gravy boat, Wood & Sons, ca 1971, from $55 to 65.00
Gravy boat & tray, scalloped, Allerton & Sons, 1929-42, 4x8", 9" .. 195.00
Horseradish dish, Doulton, 5½" 65.00
Jug, milk; Homer Laughlin, from $125 to 150.00
Knife rest, Traditional border, unmk English, late 1800s, 4", $125 to .. 150.00
Lamp, kerosene; ceramic shade, Japan, 11½", from $125 to 150.00
Leaf dish, unmk English, 6" 175.00
Match safe, Shenango, from $75 to 85.00
Muffin bowl, w/lid, illegible English mk, from $175 to 225.00
Mustard pot, bbl shape, 2½", from $65 to 75.00
Pepper pot/muffineer, unmk English, 3½", from $250 to 275.00
Pie plate, Royal China, 10" 30.00
Pitcher, milk; tankard form, Allerton, 7", EX 125.00
Pitcher, scalloped, Allerton & Sons, 1929-42, 6", from $150 to .. 175.00
Pitcher, Traditional center, Wedgwood, 11¼" 150.00
Plate, dinner; Imperial, 9¾" 27.00
Plate, dinner; Liner & Carter, 9½" 24.00
Plate, grill; Booth's center pattern, Bowknot border, 10¾" 35.00
Plate, grill; Made in Poland, 10", from $25 to 35.00
Plate, salad; red, Jackson China Restaurant Ware 8.00
Plate, scalloped rim, Wedgwood & Co, post-1891, 8", from $45 to .. 55.00
Plate, smooth rim, Samuel Radford, 1928-38, 8", from $25 to 35.00
Plate, sq, gold trim, HM Williamson & Sons, ca 1928-41, 6½" 45.00
Platter, Allerton, 16x12" 275.00
Platter, on base, rtcl inner border, J&R Riley, 1802-28, 10" 550.00
Platter, rectangular, smooth edge, WM&S Edge, 1841-47, 14x11¼" .. 325.00
Platter, scalloped, Allerton & Sons, 1929-42, 11x9", from $175 to .. 225.00
Platter, Traditional center, 1912-27, 15½x12½" 225.00
Punch bowl, ped ft, hdls, Josiah Wedgwood, post-1891, 6x9" .. 1,300.00
Relish, divided; lug hdls, Adderly, 1929-47, 8" 130.00
Relish, mitten; scalloped/ribbed, unmk English, 19th C, from $120 to .. 140.00
Relish, sq, Doulton, in nickel silver fr mk Beresford EPNS, 1891-1902 .. 285.00
Relish tray, Booth's center pattern, Bowknot border, Wood & Sons, 9" ... 30.00

Salt box, unmk Japan, wall mt, wood lid, 5" 110.00
Shakers, jug form, Japan, 3", pr from $40 to 50.00
Shakers, Royal China, pr 25.00
Spoon rest, dbl rests, Japan, 9", from $40 to 50.00
Sugar bowl, w/lid, Japan 15.00
Tankard, pewter lid, Burleigh, scroll/flower border, English, 7" 350.00
Tea set, Japan, stacking 2-cup pot+cr/sug, from $150 to 175.00
Teapot, Allerton, 6", NM 225.00
Teapot, gold finial & trim, Sadler & Sons, ca 1947, 2-cup, $70 to . 80.00
Teapot, musical base, unmk Japan, from $130 to 150.00
Teapot, Two Temples II, butterfly border, Malkin mk: MIE, 3½" .. 125.00
Teapot, Well's shape, Homer Laughlin, from $80 to 100.00

Teapot and trivet, Burgess & Leigh mark, pot: 5x10", $250.00; trivet: 7½" diameter, $140.00. (Photo courtesy Mary Frank Gaston)

Trivet, unmk English, 5½", from $75 to 100.00
Tumbler, ceramic, Japan, 3½", from $30 to 35.00
Tumbler, juice; glass, Jeannette, 3½" 12.00
Tureen, soup; Traditional center, Ridgways, 1912-27 mk, 7¾x11" . 45.00
Vase, pillow or canteen shape, Mintons, ca 1873, 7", from $375 to ... 425.00
Washbowl & pitcher, flow bl, Doulton, ca 1891-1902, from $1,800 to ... 2,000.00

Bluebird China

The earliest examples of the pudgy little bluebird in the apple blossoms decal appear in the late 1890s. The craze apparently peaked during the early to mid-1920s and had all but died out by 1930. More than 50 manufacturers, most of whom were located in East Liverpool, Ohio, produced bluebird dinnerware. There are variations on the decal, and several are now accepted as 'bluebird china.' The larger china companies like Homer Laughlin and KT&K experimented with them all. One of the variations depicts larger, more slender bluebirds in flight. The latter variety was made by Knowles, Taylor, Knowles, W.S. George (Derwood), French Co., Sterling Colonial, and Pope Gosser. The dinnerware was never expensive, and shapes varied from one manufacturer to another. Today, the line produced by Homer Laughlin is valued most highly; Besides the companies we've already mentioned producers of Bluebird China include Limoges China of Sebring, Ohio; Salem; Taylor Smith Taylor; and there are others. Our advisor for this category is Kenna Rosen, author of a new book on this subject (Schiffer); she is listed in the Directory under Texas.

Bone dish, Empress, Homer Laughlin 125.00
Bowl, berry; Cleveland, ind 20.00
Bowl, gravy; Hopewell China, w/saucer 100.00
Bowl, oatmeal; Newell pattern, Homer Laughlin 50.00
Bowl, soup; PMC Co, 8" 30.00
Bowl, vegetable; Cleveland, 9¾" 50.00
Butter dish, Salem China 150.00
Butter dish, sq, Carrollton, 6¼" 100.00
Calendar plate, 1921 advertising pc, DE McNicol 50.00
Canister set, rnd, unmk, 6½x5", 6 for 300.00
Casserole, Homer Laughlin Empress, w/lid, 8½" dia 150.00
Casserole, Pope Gosser, w/lid, 10½x10½" 100.00
Casserole, Taylor Smith & Taylor, w/lid, 11x7½" 150.00

Casserole, Vodrey China, early 1900s, w/lid, 12x6" 100.00
Chocolate cup, ftd, no mk, 3½" 85.00
Chocolate pot, Knowles Taylor & Knowles 200.00
Creamer, no mk, 4¼" 25.00
Creamer & sugar bowl, HR Wyllie, w/lid 125.00
Creamer & sugar bowl, TA McNichol, w/lid 75.00
Cup & saucer, Owen China, St Louis 40.00
Custard cup, KT&K, 3½" 35.00
Egg cup, Buffalo China, very rare, 2½" 75.00
Mug, baby's, Cleveland China 100.00
Mug, coffee; unmk, 3½" 60.00
Pitcher, water; Buffalo Pottery, 7" 100.00
Pitcher, water; Cable, Homer Laughlin 200.00
Pitcher, water; DE McNicol 150.00
Pitcher, water; Empress, Homer Laughlin 250.00
Pitcher, water; National China 200.00
Plate, baby's, ELP Co China, 7½x7½" 150.00
Plate, Knowles Taylor Knowles, 9¾" 40.00
Plate, Steubenville, 9" 40.00
Platter, Edwin M Knowles, 14½x11" 60.00
Platter, Hopewell China, 13x10" 60.00
Platter, souvenir; gold leaves & stenciled initials, dtd 1923, 6" 65.00
Platter, Thompson Glenwood, 13x10" 50.00
Platter, West End Pottery Co, 15½x11" 60.00
Platter, 10 bluebirds, gold trim at rim, DE McNichol, 15¼x11¼" ...100.00
Shakers, Art Deco styling, tall, unmk, extremely rare, pr 250.00
Shaving mug, The Potters Co-Op 65.00
Sugar bowl, Illinois China Co, w/lid, 7x6" 50.00
Syrup, Homer Laughlin, 6½" 175.00
Tea set, child's, CPCo, 21-pc 400.00
Tea set, child's, Summit China Co 1,025.00
Teapot, ELP Co, 8½x8½" 250.00
Teapot, Homer Laughlin, from $750 to 1,200.00
Teapot, West Virginia Pottery Co, sm 150.00

Boch Freres

Founded in the early 1840s in La Louviere, Boch Freres Keramis became the foremost producer of art pottery in Belgium. Though primarily they served a localized market, in 1844 they earned worldwide recognition for some of their sculptural works on display at the International Exposition in Paris.

In 1907 Charles Catteau of France was appointed head of the art department. Before that time, the firm had concentrated on developing glazes and perfecting elegant forms. The style they pursued was traditional, favoring the re-creation of established eighteenth-century ceramics. Catteau brought with him to Boch Freres the New Wave (or Art Nouveau) influence in form and decoration. His designs won him international acclaim at the Exhibition d'Art Decoratif in Paris in 1925, and it is for his work that Boch Freres is so highly regarded today. He occasionally signed his work as well as that of others who under his direct supervision carried out his preconceived designs. He was associated with the company until 1950 and lived the remainder of his life in Nice, France, where he died in 1966. The Boch Freres Keramis factory continues to operate today, producing bathroom fixtures and other utilitarian wares. A variety of marks have been used, most incorporating some combination of 'Boch Freres,' 'Keramis,' 'BFK,' or 'Ch Catteau.' A shield topped by a crown and flanked by a 'B' and an 'F' was used as well.

Bowl, bird of paradise/flower int, rstr to ft, 5x14" 1,900.00
Box, floral on wht crackle, petals on lid, ormolu, La Louviere, 4x6" ..175.00
Box, floral-on-blk stripes alternate w/gr, La Louviere, 3x4½" 300.00
Charger, horse-drawn sleigh w/riders, Delft style, 15" 125.00

Charger, lady holds borozi by collar, red/gr/brn mottle, Keramis, 14" ..11,700.00
Stein, seated robed man in Gothic arch, brn/tan pottery, 8", EX .. 165.00
Tile, heraldic eagles, dk bl/yel/brn/gr, cuerda seca, 8" 60.00
Vase, antelopes on ivory crackle, ovoid, Catteau, #D943, ca 1925, 10" ..1,175.00
Vase, Deco elements on Persian Blue, front/bk w/8 facets, 10x8" .. 900.00
Vase, exotic birds/flowers, matt glaze, Keramis #907/D 1130, 11½" .. 960.00
Vase, floral, mc on blk & yel stripes, brass rim, #D681, 10¾x5" ... 350.00
Vase, floral & snake-like coils on wht, bulbous, #738A, 9½x6¼" .. 275.00
Vase, floral on copper lustre, floral neck band, 8¾" 400.00
Vase, flying birds (repeated), blk/bl/gold on wht, Catteau, #894, 9x8" 2,700.00
Vase, panels w/3 sqs alternate w/panels w/stripes, crackle, #675, 7" 500.00

Vase, penguins above geometric border, D1104, ca. 1930, 15", $9,400.00.
(Photo courtesy Skinner Inc. Auctioneers & Appraisers of Antiques & Fine Art)

Vase, polar bears/mtns, blk/gr mottle on wht, Keramis #1060, 8½" ... 16,000.00
Vase, yel neck band w/vivid floral, upright 'stems' on wht, 8x6" .. 240.00

Boehm

Boehm sculptures were the creation of Edward Marshall Boehm, a ceramic artist who coupled his love of the art with his love of nature to produce figurines of birds, animals, and flowers in lovely background settings accurate to the smallest detail. Sculptures of historical figures and those representing the fine arts were also made and along with many of the bird figurines, have established secondary-market values many times their original prices. His first pieces were made in the very early 1950s in Trenton, New Jersey, under the name of Osso Ceramics. Mr. Boehm died in 1969, and the firm has since been managed by his wife. Today known as Edward Marshall Boehm, Inc., the private family-held corporation produces not only porcelain sculptures but collector plates as well. Both limited and non-limited editions of their works have been issued. Examples are marked with various backstamps, all of which have incorporated the Boehm name since 1951. 'Osso Ceramics' in upper case lettering was used in 1950 and 1951. Our advisor for this category is Leon Reimert; he is listed in the Directory under Pennsylvania.

American Redstarts, #447V, 11½" 325.00
Arctic Tern, #78, 19x22" 750.00
Baby Koala, #400-36, 1976, 8½" 325.00
Bengel tiger cub, #200-21, 6½x12x5" 175.00
Bobolink on corn stalk, #475, 14¾" 400.00
Chick, yel, #1011, 1976, 3½" 120.00
Chickadee (chick) on pine branch, #461Y, 1962-72, 3¼" 150.00
Chipmunk, #514-01, 3½" 150.00
Eagle of Freedom II, 1975 ltd ed, 15" 1,800.00
Goddess Selket, gold pnt, ltd ed, 16¾" 550.00
Goldfinches, #457R, 11½x4¾" 950.00
Helen Boehm Camellia, #88, 1978, 3x7" 200.00
Hooded Merganser (male) on hollow log w/fish in beak, #4966, 10¾" ..700.00
Hummingbird w/columbine, #199, 1⅛" 150.00
Lesser Prairie Chickens, #464G, 10½", NM 150.00

Mockingbird, butterfly in mouth, #439, 11½"....150.00
Mute Swan beside cattails, #68, 19⅝"....750.00
Orchard Oriole on flowering branch, ltd ed, 11¼x12"....550.00
Osprey in flight along cattails, 26"....1,100.00
Panda seated, #40237, 5x4x3"....65.00
Parakeet on orchid, #40517, 11½"....650.00
Puffin (chick), #RPC-514-01, ca 1973, 5"....150.00
Roadrunner, #135, 8½x18x13", from $400 to....500.00
Robin beside nest, #149, 9x10"....350.00
Robin beside yel daffodil, #472, 15"....750.00
Rufus Hummingbirds among lg yel flower, #487, 14¾"....1,400.00
Screech Owl, wings wide, #85, 14x21½"....600.00
Sister Angel, narrow sleeves, wht bsk, #613-02, ca 1955, 5"....200.00

Towhee on stump with fungus and mushrooms, limited edition, #741E, 7½", $650.00. (Photo courtesy Cincinnati Art Galleries)

Trumpeter Swan, #112, 14½x18½"....425.00
Tufted Titmice, #482P, 13"....425.00
Woodcock, #413R, 10"....325.00
Young & Spirited, 2 young Am Bald Eagles, 1976, 9½x11x7"....375.00
Young Am Bald Eagle, #498, mid-20th C, 10"....300.00
40th Anniversary Rose, #F274, 1989, 5"....100.00

Bohemian Glass

The term 'Bohemian glass' has come to refer to a type of glass developed in Bohemia in the late sixteenth century at the Imperial Court of Rudolf II, the Hapsburg Emperor. The popular artistic pursuit of the day was stone carving, and it naturally followed to transfer familiar procedures to the glassmaking industry. During the next century, a formula was discovered that produced a glass with a fine crystal appearance which lent itself well to deep, intricate engraving, and the art was further advanced.

Although many other kinds of art glass were made there, we are using the term 'Bohemian glass' to indicate glass overlaid or stained with color through which a design is cut or etched. (Unless otherwise described, the items in the listing that follows are of this type.) Red or yellow on clear glass is common, but other colors may also be found. Another type of Bohemian glass involves cutting through and exposing two layers of color in patterns that are often very intricate. Items such as these are sometimes further decorated with enamel and/or gilt work.

Beaker, red, hunting dogs & birds, ca 1980, 6"....150.00
Bowl, cranberry, scallops & geometrics, 10"....100.00
Bowl, red, gilt/enamel scrolls, scalloped, ftd, 20th C, 8" dia....75.00
Decanter, red, grapes & leaves in dmns, silver mts, 12x5"....175.00
Decanter, red, stag/scrolls/castle, slim neck, 20th C, 10½"....75.00
Decanters, amber, optic pattern, slim neck, ca 1900, 15½", pr....275.00
Pitcher, red, deer running on 1 side only, 7½"....150.00
Pokal, amber, floral, w/lid, 20th C, 7½"....90.00
Pokal, amber, scenes w/German names, w/lid, 19th C, 10½"....450.00
Pokal, red, deer/landscape, scalloped ft, w/lid, early 20th C, 14"....350.00
Tumbler, red, European buildings & flowers, ca 1900, 4¾"....100.00
Vase, amber, floral/deer/castle, slim neck, ca 1900, 14"....100.00
Vase, uranium glass, enamel/gilt bouquets, ca 1850, 10"....450.00

Bookends

Though a few were produced before 1880, bookends became a necessary library accessory and a popular commodity after the printing industry was revolutionized by Mergenthaler's invention, the linotype. Books became abundantly available at such affordable prices that almost every home suddenly had need for bookends. They were carved from wood; cast in iron, bronze, or brass; or cut from stone. Chalkware and glass were used as well. Today's collectors may find such designs as ships, animals, flowers, and children. Patriotic themes, art reproductions, and those with Art Nouveau and Art Deco styling provide a basis for a diverse and interesting collection.

Currently, figural cast-iron pieces are in demand, especially examples with good original polychrome paint. This has driven the value of painted cast-iron bookends up considerably.

For further information we recommend *Collector's Encyclopedia of Bookends* by Louis Kuritzky and Charles De Costa. Mr. Kuritzky is our advisor for this category; he is listed in the Directory under Florida. See also Arts and Crafts, Bradley and Hubbard.

Angelfish, gray metal on polished stone base, JB Hirsch, ca 1930, 6"....120.00
Athens, CI, Bradley & Hubbard, ca 1925, 4½"....90.00
Aztec archer, CI, ca 1925, 7½"....150.00
Boy w/frog, bronze-clad, Armor Bronze, S Morani, 1914, 7½"....250.00
Buddha, resin, ca 1960, 6"....35.00
Castle Lichtenstein, CI, Bradley & Hubbard, ca 1925, 5"....150.00
Chinese students, gray metal, Ronson, #16138, 5¼"....95.00
Cottage scene emb w/in fr, CI, Bradley & Hubbard, 5⅜x4⅛"....450.00
Dante, CI, Bradley & Hubbard, ca 1925, 5½"....175.00
Donkey, gray metal, Ronson, 1932, paper tag, 6"....225.00
Doric temple facade, cast metal, Bradley & Hubbard, 3½x5", VG....80.00
Egyptian face, bronze, Genuine Solid Bronze, ca 1935, 3½"....175.00
Elephant, gray metal, Jennings Bros, ca 1925, 5½"....175.00
Feather, SP over bronze, 7½"....450.00
Flying duck, bronze-clad, Pompeian Bronze, ca 1925, 9¼"....250.00
General Grant, CI, ca 1925, 7¼"....100.00
Globe, bronze, Marion Bronze, ca 1950, 8"....150.00
Goose Children Hummeloids, porc, ca 1990, 6"....35.00
Greyhound, gray metal on marble base, ca 1925, 7½"....375.00
Hindu dancer, gray metal w/celluloid, marble base, Hirsch, 1925, 9"....395.00
Horse & pup, gray metal, Frankart Inc Pat Appl, 1930, 6"....150.00
Ibex couple, CI, Hubley, #417, ca 1925, 5"....175.00
Indian archer, gray metal, ca 1922, 7¾"....475.00
Indian lancer, hollow-cast bronze on marble base, ca 1930, 8½"....495.00
Jockey at fence, aluminum, Kentucky Tavern Creations, ca 1947, 6½"....175.00
Kiwi bird, gray metal on bronze base, Judd, ca 1923, 5¼"....295.00
Lincoln's cabin, CI, Bradley & Hubbard, ca 1925, 5"....75.00
Linden Hall insignia, gray metal, ca 1960, 3"....25.00
Lion, glass, Cambridge, ca 1940, 6"....200.00
Love Always, scroll above flowers, wood, 1935, 4-leaf clover mk, 7"....75.00
Lyre, glass, Fostoria, 1943, 7"....150.00
Maid-servant, chalk on polished stone base, JB Hirsch, ca 1932, 6"....50.00
Man in chair, CI, Bradley & Hubbard, 5¼"....550.00
Marlin, Art Deco, chrome & bronze, ca 1935, 3¼"....225.00
Mermaid, Art Deco, chrome & brass, ca 1940, 6¾"....165.00
Nude dancer w/sash, CI, ca 1925, 6"....195.00
Owl, bronze-clad, Pompeian Bronze, ca 1925, mk PB, 4½"....125.00
Ox wagon, CI, 1931, mk 1849, 3"....65.00
Peter Pan, bronze-clad, Marion Bronze, ca 1965, 7½"....175.00

Polar bear, CI, Hubley, ca 1925, 3½" 150.00
Ralph Waldo Emerson, bronze-clad, Galvano Bronze, ca 1925, 7½" .. 135.00
Ram, gray metal, ca 1935, 5½" 60.00
Roses, bl leather w/gold trim, ca 1930, 5" 40.00
Scottie dog, glass, Cambridge, ca 1940, 6½" 125.00

Scotties at the Fence, cast iron, #430, 5", EX, $250.00. (Photo courtesy Morphy Auctions)

Swans, gray metal on polished stone base, JB Hirsch, ca 1928, 7" ...175.00
Temple of Saturn, CI, Bradley & Hubbard, ca 1925, 5½" 110.00
Three kittens, CI, Bradley & hubbard, 4⅝" 350.00
Train, gray metal, ca 1924, 5¼" 95.00
Victorian couple, CI, Judd, #9662, ca 1925, 6" 85.00
Vines, brass, expandable, ca 1930, 5" 150.00
Who Is It?, girl w/hands over boy's eyes, bronze-clad, Galvno, ca 1925 .. 195.00
Windmill, bronze, ca 1930, 6¾" 150.00
Young lady, plated wht metal, 7", from $80 to 100.00
Zion Park, sandstone on wood, ca 1968, 8" 75.00

Bootjacks and Bootscrapers

Bootjacks were made from metal or wood. Some were fancy figural shapes, others strictly business! Their purpose was to facilitate the otherwise awkward process of removing one's boots. Bootscrapers were handy gadgets that provided an effective way to clean the soles of mud and such. Our advisor for this category is Louis Picek; he is listed in the Directory under Iowa.

Bootjacks

Aluminum, bull's head, Ricardo, worn pnt 55.00
Am Bull Dog, pistol shape, CI, blk pnt, 8" 90.00
Brass, sunflower, Musselman's Plug advertising 150.00
CI, Baroque scrollwork set in marble block, 14" 95.00
CI, Boss emb on shaft, lacy, 15" L 135.00
CI, cat silhouette, blk pnt, 10½x10" 295.00
CI, cricket, Harvester Bros & Co, Reading PA, 11x4¾" 110.00
CI, Labrador retriever, 3x10x4¾" 15.00
CI, moose, 11x8" 15.00
CI, Naughty Nellie, nude lady on bk, great old pnt, 9½", M 2,705.00
CI & wood, lever action, EX 150.00
Wood w/brass hinges, unfolds, att military, 19th C, 10¼x2" 1,200.00

Bootscrapers

CI, Black man sits above base, rust/soiling, 13x10", EX 225.00
CI, Black shoeshine boy atop, oval base, 13", VG 140.00
CI, cat w/long tail sticking up, 10x15" 35.00
CI, dachshund, no pnt, tail forms ring, 10½x7½x7" 185.00
CI, duck, full body, 14½" L 350.00
CI, eagle relief & classical lady in oval, Portland Foundry 300.00
CI, horseshoe mtd on rimmed base, 9x11x9" 2,500.00
CI, pan base w/flared rim & emb decor, pitting, 17x13x16" 195.00

CI, quatrefoil base, 5½x10½x11" 625.00
Wrought iron, ram's-horn scrolls, marble block 150.00
Wrought iron, scrolled finial (detailed), 21x24" 500.00

Borsato, Antonio

Borsato was a remarkable artist/sculptor who produced some of the most intricately modeled and executed figurines ever made. He was born in Italy and at an early age enjoyed modeling wildlife from clay he dug from the river banks near his home. At age 11, he became an apprentice of Guido Cacciapuotti of Milan, who helped him develop his skills. During the late '20s and '30s, he continued to concentrate on wildlife studies. Because of his resistance to the fascist government, he was interred at Sardinia from 1940 until the end of the war, after which he returned to Milan where he focused his attention on religious subjects. He entered the export market in 1948 and began to design pieces featuring children and more romantic themes. By the 1960s his work had become very popular in this country. His talent for creating lifelike figures has seldom been rivaled. He contributed much of his success to the fact that each of his figures, though built from the same molded pieces, had its own personality, due the unique way he would tilt a head or position an arm. All had eyelashes, fingernails, and defined musculature; and each piece was painted by hand with antiquated colors and signed 'A. Borsato.' He made over 600 different models, with some of his groups requiring more than 160 components and several months of work to reach completion. Various pieces were made in two mediums, gres and porcelain, with porcelain being double the cost of gres. Borsato died in 1982. Today, some of his work is displayed in the Vatican Museum as well private collections.

Boulevardier, man seated on rustic bench, 6¼x5½" 1,350.00
Canine Casualty, man applies first aid to dog, 9x9" 2,560.00
Child's Prayer, child on lady's lap w/hands folded, 8x6x9½" 1,925.00
Cobbler's Dilemma, man & boy at bench, 10½x7½x8½" 2,900.00
Columbine, lady in costume from comedy opera, 6⅛" 475.00
Cowboy w/Guitar, man seated on saddle w/instrument, 6¼" 500.00
Elders' Delight, aged couple w/basket of snails, 11x8" 3,240.00
Expresso Vendors, 2 men & 1 woman at coffee stand, 8x11x7½" ... 2,450.00
Farmer's Twilight, man offers produce to lady, 7x10" 3,475.00
Good Hunting, barefoot hunter w/dog, complete w/rifle strap, 6¾x9" ... 875.00
Grandma's Well, lady/child/goose at well, 10x12" 5,125.00
Lady in fine fashion stands w/arms akimbo, bustle skirt, 8½" 485.00
Man w/pipe, head of old man smoking pipe w/eyes closed, 7½" ... 250.00
Mother & Child, mother wrapping baby in blanket, 6½x6" 650.00
Nomads, 2 figures w/loaded pack horse & sheep on rocky base, 13x22" ..11,240.00
Psyche & Eros, classical couple on base, 7¾x8" 1,575.00
Round-Up, 3 rearing horses on base, 13¾" 5,800.00
Sailor & Old Lady, aged couple seated on rocks, 7¾x7" 775.00
Serenity, lady seated by sm tree w/birds, butterfly on finger, 9½" ...3,000.00
Spring Song, 2 birds on branch, 6" 485.00
Titian Madonna, Madonna embracing Christ Child 1,025.00

Bossons Artware

The late William Henry Bossons founded Bossons in 1946. When he died in 1951, his son, W. Ray Bossons took charge and in 1958 designed the first 'Character Wall Masks.' Jane Bossons Roberts, Ray's daughter, directed operations from 1994 until the company's closing in December 1996. Today, unauthorized paintings and fraudulent moldings are circulating throughout secondary markets worldwide, especially on the Internet. Illegal copies of all types of Bossons are being distributed from Pakistan. These include character masks of Caspian Woman, Gilded Winston Churchill and Wheatcroft; Wildlife that include Squirrels, Raccoons, and Chipmunks; and Dogs of Distinction. Know your supplier/dealer and make certain they are well informed.

The last Character Masks (heads) were released in 1995 and 1996. Currently they are commanding unusually high prices when new and in original condition. These final editions, pictured in full color on the last mini-folder leaflet from Bossons entitled 'Autumn 1996 Collection,' included the Cook, a Series B wall mask that was never released into regular production (contrary to rumors that 500 were made, the actual number is closer to five) and more than a dozen Bossons.

As with all collectibles, original, unused copyright names, markings, and condition are critical worth-assessing factors. Mint in the box examples can command several hundred dollars (see final listing). Literature by Bossons such as large descriptive, colored brochures and the miniature folders that they published nearly every year is also collectible.

Ken Potts was the head mold maker and factory foreman. The principle sculptors/modelers of Bossons were (in chronological order): Fred Wright (FW), Alice Brindley (AB), and Ray Bossons (WRB), who oversaw all Bossons creations and made sure that they met the company's highest standards.

Bossons articles in previous editions of *Schroeder's Antiques Price Guide* contain many important details on Bossons; reviewing past issues will disclose many fluctuations in prices over the years. With many exceptions (see final listing), the very earliest editions (from 1957 to 1959) sell for the highest prices. Popular Bossons from the mid-1960s to early 1990 may be found in great numbers and can often be purchased for under $100.00. However, with only a few facial blemishes, even plentiful Bossons are not worth more than $10.00 to $20.00. Caspian Woman (1958 – 1959) with no veil covering the face in original condition with untarnished gold and silver decorations, smooth unblemished face and eyes and multicolored headdress can sell for as much as $1,900.00. In the same condition, the Caspian Woman (1958 – 1959) with a veil covering most of the face may sell for as much as $2,500.00. Examples purchased at very low prices may have been repainted and/or sustained structural damage — or (in the case of the woman without the veil) they could be illegal copies. Wheatcroft is another Bossons falling into this category. Beware! (Detailed pictures of fakes of Wheatcroft are included on our advisor's website at www.bossons.us.)

Buyers and sellers should seek advice from authorities in the field before investing in 'rare' Bossons. Following is a picture of a Caspian Woman without the veil in new condition. Also shown is a common but popular Bossons depicting an Old Timer with Western cowhand hat and corncob pipe (1977 – March 1992). It was from the Americans Collection and was created by Mrs. Alice Brindley, who served as resident modeler and art director at Bossons from 1977 to 1995. (The mold was destroyed in March 1992, as were Bretonne Lady, Rumanian, Sardinian, Cheyenne, and Pancho.) As with most, the copyright date and the name for Old Timer is incised under the collar. Alice Brindley's initials (AB) appear at the rear edge of the right collar. The back is silver and has a recessed hook. Some early Bossons also have the recessed hook, but for a period of about 20 years, the hook was not recessed and is called exterior or protruding hook. The hooks are a very easy way to recognize an authentic Bossons.

No matter when they were produced or released, each Bossons carries the same copyright date, so that date has no effect on value. Though it has changed slightly over the years, this is how the incision appears on the back: 'Bossons CongletonEnglandWorld Copyright.'

Our advisor, Donald M. Hardisty is a recognized authority in the field of Bossons. He has been recommended by Bossons since 1984. Don has given many demonstrations/lectures for various collector organizations and meetings, spends countless hours advising buyers and sellers via phone and on the Internet, offers official appraisals for dealers and insurance claimants, and has published numerous articles on this subject. He is listed in the Directory under New Mexico. For more information you may link to www.donsbossons.com.

Our values are for items that are in new condition and in their original boxes. (When dates are given they are release dates, not copyright dates.)

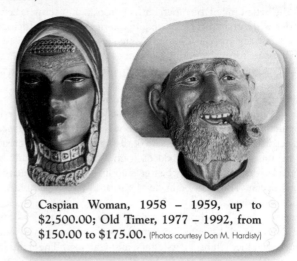

Caspian Woman, 1958 – 1959, up to $2,500.00; Old Timer, 1977 – 1992, from $150.00 to $175.00. (Photos courtesy Don M. Hardisty)

Abduhl, from $85 to	125.00
Aruj Barbarossa, 1994-96, from $225 to	275.00
Blackbeard, 1993-96, from $150 to	175.00
Boatman, from $85 to	125.00
Bossons Santa Claus, from $175 to	200.00
Captain Pierre Le Grand, from $185 to	245.00
Carnival Annie, 1961-63, from $600 to	900.00
Carnival Joe, 1961-63, from $500 to	900.00
Cheyenne w/red coat, 1970-92, from $185 to	215.00
Churchill, 1988 for IBCS, must have gold name tag on bk, from $200 to	250.00
Clipper Captain, from $165 to	185.00
Coolie, 1964-70, from $150 to	165.00
Cossack, from $185 to	225.00
Dickens Characters, 1964-96, from $85 to	145.00
Evzon, from $185 to	275.00
Fly-Fisherman, from $175 to	200.00
Geisha, 1963-65, from $750 to	900.00
Golfer, from $150 to	185.00
Harry Wheatcroft, 1970-72 (see intro for more info), $900 to	1,250.00
Highwayman, from $250 to	400.00
Indian Chief, 1961-64, from $350 to	500.00
Jolly Tar, from $150 to	175.00
Karim, 1967-69, from $145 to	165.00
King Henry VIII, 1986-94, from $225 to	275.00
Kurd, 1964-96, from $45 to	65.00
Lifeboatman, 1966-96, from $85 to	145.00
Mikado, from $650 to	800.00
Nigerian Woman, 1961-62, from $800 to	1,100.00
Nuvolari, 1996, from $185 to	250.00
Paddy, blk hair, 1959, from $165 to	185.00
Paddy, issue for IBCS, must have sgn certificate, from $200 to	250.00
Paddy, 1969, from $85 to	125.00
Parson, from $145 to	165.00
Persian, from $45 to	85.00
Pony Girl, 1969-70, from $450 to	600.00
Rawhide, from $125 to	145.00
Rob Roy, 1995-96, from $175 to	200.00
Shepherd, 1995-96, from $150 to	175.00
Sinbad, from $250 to	325.00
Smuggler, from $45 to	65.00
Squire, from $165 to	175.00
Syrian, 1960-96, from $85 to	125.00
Tecumpseh, 1962-96, from $165 to	185.00

Bottle Openers

At the beginning of the nineteenth century, manufacturers began to seal bottles with a metal cap that required a new type of bottle opener. Now the screw cap and the flip top have made bottle openers nearly obsolete. There are many variations, some in combination with other tools. Many openers were used as means of advertising a product. Various materials were used, including silver and brass.

A figural bottle opener is defined as a figure designed for the sole purpose of lifting a bottle cap. The actual opener must be an integral part of the figure itself. A base-plate opener is one where the lifter is a separate metal piece attached to the underside of the figure. The major producers of iron figurals were Wilton Products, John Wright Inc., Gadzik Sales, and L & L Favors. Openers may be free-standing and three-dimensional, wall hung or flat. They can be made of cast iron (often painted), brass, bronze, or aluminum.

Those seeking additional information are encouraged to contact FBOC (Figural Bottle Opener Collectors), whose address can be found in the Directory under Clubs, Newsletters, and Catalogs. The items below are all in excellent original condition unless noted otherwise.

Alligator w/head up, CI, mc pnt, John Wright, 2½x5⅛" 250.00
Bear head, CI, brn-tone pnt, wall mt, John Wright, 3¾x3⅛", VG ..200.00
Billy goat, CI, mc pnt, John Wright, 2¾x2¾" 85.00
Black caddy, NP CI, mc pnt, Pat #86,603, 1932, 5¾x1⅞" 840.00
Boy winking, CI, mc pnt, wall mt, Wilton, rare, 3¾x3⅝", VG .. 2,000.00
Canadian goose, CI, mc pnt, Wilton, 1¾x3⅝", G 140.00
Canvasback duck, CI, mc pnt, 1¾x2⅞" 195.00
Cathy Coed, CI, mc pnt, Pledge Dance '57, I&I Favors, rare, 4½"... 1,000.00
Cockatoo, CI, mc pnt, John Wright, 3¼x2⅞" 225.00
Cowboy (drunk) by cactus, CI, mc pnt, John Wright, 3¾x2⅝".... 165.00
Cowboy in chaps (bow-legged), CI, mc pnt, Wilton, 4½x2¾", NM .. 450.00
Cowboy w/guitar, CI, mc pnt, John Wright, 4¾x3⅛" 165.00
Dinky Dan, CI, mc pnt, Initiatory Formal '53, rare, 3⅞x2⅛" 500.00
Elephant walking, trunk up, pnt CI, Wilton, 2½x3¼", EX 50.00
Fish w/tail up, CI, mc pnt, John Wright, 1⁵⁄₁₆x4⅝" 165.00
Foundry man pouring hot lead, CI, mc pnt, John Wright, 3⅛x2⅝" ...140.00
Freddie Frosh, CI, mc pnt, Pledge Formal '65, rare, 4x2" 400.00

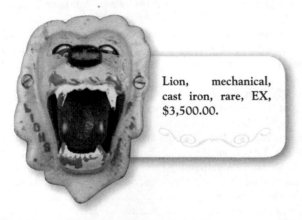

Lion, mechanical, cast iron, rare, EX, $3,500.00.

Monkey, CI, brn & gr, John Wright, 2⅝x2⅝", VG 500.00
Palm tree, CI, mc pnt, John Wright, 4¼x2¼" 195.00
Parrot, CI, mc pnt, Wilton, 3¼x3¼", NM 170.00
Parrot on perch, CI, mc pnt, 4⅝x3¼" 615.00
Pelican w/head up, beak open, CI, mc pnt, Wilton, 3⅝x3¾", VG ..390.00
Pheasant, CI, mc pnt, John Wright, 2¼x3⅞" 335.00
Sammy Samoa, CI, mc pnt, I&I Favors, 4⅝x2", VG 400.00
Sawfish, CI, mc pnt, Wilton Products, 2x5¾" 670.00
Seagull, CI, mc pnt, John Wright, 3¼x2¾" 195.00
Squirrel (gray), CI, mc pnt, John Wright, 2x2⅞" 225.00

Toucan, open mouth, CI, mc pnt, John Wright, 3⅜x2⅞", NM 140.00
Trout fish, CI, mc pnt, Wilton, 3⅝x4⅞" 280.00

Bottles and Flasks

As far back as the first century B.C., the Romans preferred blown glass containers for their pills and potions. American business firms preferred glass bottles in which to package their commercial products and used them extensively from the late eighteenth century on. Bitters bottles contained 'medicine' (actually herb-flavored alcohol). Because of a heavy tax imposed on the sale of liquor in seventeenth-century England by King George, who hoped to curtail alcohol abuse among his subjects, bottlers simply added 'curative' herbs to their brew and thus avoided taxation. Since gin was taxed in America as well, the practice continued in this country. Scores of brands were sold; among the most popular were Dr. H.S. Flint & Co. Quaker Bitters, Dr. Kaufman's Anti-Cholera Bitters, and Dr. J. Hostetter's Stomach Bitters. Most bitters bottles were made in shades of amber, brown, and aquamarine. Clear glass was used to a lesser extent, as were green tones. Blue, amethyst, red-brown, and milk glass examples are rare. Color is a strong factor when pricing bottles.

Perfume or scent bottles were produced by companies all over Europe from the late sixteenth century on. Perfume making became such a prolific trade that as a result beautifully decorated bottles were fashionable. In America they were produced in great quantities by Stiegel in 1770 and by Boston and Sandwich in the early nineteenth century. Cologne bottles were first made in about 1830 and toilet-water bottles in the 1880s. Rene Lalique produced fine scent bottles from as early as the turn of the century. The first were one-of-a-kind creations done in the cire perdue method. He later designed bottles for the Coty Perfume Company with a different style for each Coty fragrance. (See Lalique.)

Spirit flasks from the nineteenth century were blown in specially designed molds with varied motifs including political subjects, railroad trains, and symbolic devices. The most commonly used colors were amber, dark brown, and green.

Pitkin flasks were the creation of the Pitkin Glass Works which operated in East Manchester, Connecticut, from 1783 to 1830. However, other glasshouses in New England and the Midwest copied the Pitkin flask style. All are known as Pitkins.

From the twentieth century, early pop and beer bottles are very collectible as is nearly every extinct commercial container. Dairy bottles are also desirable; look for round bottles in good condition with both city and state as well as a nice graphic relating to the farm or the dairy.

Bottles may be dated by the methods used in their production. For instance, a rough pontil indicates a date before 1845. After the bottle was blown, a pontil rod was attached to the bottom, a glob of molten glass acting as the 'glue.' This allowed the glassblower to continue to manipulate the extremely hot bottle until it was finished. From about 1845 until approximately 1860, the molten glass 'glue' was omitted. The rod was simply heated to a temperature high enough to cause it to afix itself to the bottle. When the rod was snapped off, a metallic residue was left on the base of the bottle; this is called an 'iron pontil.' (The presence of a pontil scar thus indicates early manufacture and increases the value of a bottle.) A seam that reaches from base to lip marks a machine-made bottle from after 1903, while an applied or hand-finished lip points to an early mold-blown bottle. The Industrial Revolution saw keen competition between manufacturers, and as a result, scores of patents were issued. Many concentrated on various types of closures; the crown bottle cap, for instance, was patented in 1892. If a manufacturer's name is present, consulting a book on marks may help you date your bottle. For more information we recommend *Bottle Pricing Guide*, *3rd Edition*, by Hugh Cleveland.

Among our advisors for this category are Madeleine France (see the Directory under Florida), Mark Vuono (Connecticut), Monsen and Baer (Virginia), and Robert Doyle (New York). Values suggested below reflect hammer prices (plus buyer's premium) of bottles that were sold through cataloged auctions. See also Advertising, various companies; Blown Glass; Blown Three-Mold Glass; California Perfume Company; Czechoslovakia; De Vilbiss; Fire Fighting; Lalique; Steuben; Zanesville Glass.

Key:

am — applied mouth	GW — Glass Works
bbl — barrel	ip — iron pontil
bt — blob top	op — open pontil
b3m — blown 3-mold	ps — pontil scar
cm — collared mouth	rm — rolled mouth
fl — filigree	sb — smooth base
fm — flared mouth	sl — sloping
gm — ground mouth	sm — sheared mouth
gp — graphite pontil	tm — tooled mouth
grd — ground pontil	

Barber Bottles

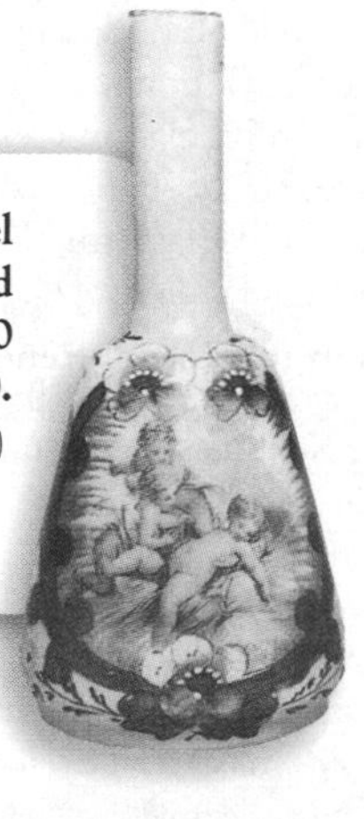

Milk glass with enamel cherubs on blue and yellow ground, ca 1890 – 1925, 7¾", $350.00.
(Photo courtesy Glass-Works Auctions)

Amethyst, Mary Gregory, boy among flowers, 8" 230.00
Amethyst, Vegederma & lady in wht enamel, long neck, ps, 7⅞" ... 300.00
Bl, geometric cuttings, gold trim (worn), 6¼x4" 60.00
Bl opal, Hobnail, ground/p, 7¼x4½" 160.00
Bl opal w/seaweed, 7" 225.00
Bl w/HP dots, ps, sm, 8" 120.00
Clear, Koken's Quinine Tonic, label under glass, 7¾" 230.00
Cobalt, Mary Gregory, tennis girl, slim neck, 8½" 270.00
Cranberry opal, Coin Dot, ca 1940s, 8½" 200.00
Cranberry w/wht opal ferns, corseted bell form, 7⅜" 600.00
Wht opal w/seaweed, sq body, Rose Water label, 9½" 225.00

Bitters Bottles

AM Binneger Old Kentucky Bourbon..., amber, bbl, 1848, 9½" .. 325.00
Brown's Celebrated Indian..., yel olive, queen, Pat 1868, 12¼" ... 9,000.00
Dr CW Roback's Stomach..., yel olive, sl cm, sb, bbl, 1860-80, 9¼" .. 1,500.00
Dr Fisch's...Pat 1866, yel olive, sb, fish, 11⅝" 2,750.00
Dr Harter's Wild Cherry, amber, full label & contents, 8" 125.00
Dr Tompkin's Vegetable..., lt gr, lg rough/p, seed bubbles 6,000.00
Drake's Plantation...Pat 1860, D-106, yel w/olive tone, 6-log, 9¾" .. 700.00
Drake's Plantation...Pat 1862, D-106, citron, cabin, 9¾", NM ... 3,000.00
Gentiana Root & Herb..., bluish aqua, sb, cm, haze, 10" 200.00
Greeley's Bourbon, G-101, med olive gr, sb, bbl, prof rpr, 9⅜" 350.00
Hall's/EE Hall New Haven...1842, golden yel amber, sb, bbl, 9¼" ... 130.00
Kelly's Old Cabin..., med to dk golden amber, 2-story cabin, 9⅛" ... 275.00

Black Glass Bottles

Many early European and American bottles are deep, dark green, or amber in color. Collectors refer to such coloring as black glass. Before held to light, the glass is so dark it appears to be black.

Horse Hoof onion, med yel olive amber, sm w/appl string lip, 8⅜" .. 165.00
Mallet, med yel olive gr, sm w/appl lip, ps, 1750-70, 7¼x4⅜" 325.00
Mallet, yel olive, sm w/string rim, ps, ca 1700-40, haze, 4½" 1,100.00
Onion, dk olive gr, am, dullness/wear, chip, ca 1725-35, 5⅞x4½" ... 450.00
Onion, emerald gr, ps, sm w/appl string lip, scuffs, 1720-50, 5⅝" ... 90.00
Onion, med olive gr, am, ps, 1730-40, lt wear, 7x5¼" 350.00
Pancake onion, dk olive gr, am, stain, ca 1690-1715, 5x6⅜" 1,000.00
Seal: IC HOffman, med olive gr, ps, dbl cm, cylinder, 8⅜" 3,325.00
Seal: JW Boott, sl cm w/ring, ps, 1800-20, 7⅝x3⅜" 1,000.00
Seal: WR/1752, yel amber, mallet form, sm, ps, chip, 7⅝x4⅛" .. 2,750.00

Blown Glass Bottles and Flasks

Chestnut flask, bl aqua, 18 right-swirl ribs, to right, ps, 6¾" 100.00
Chestnut flask, lt bl aqua, 20 left-swirl ribs, ps, sm, 5⅝" 110.00
Chestnut flask, med cobalt w/purple tone, 22 broken ribs, ps, tm, 5" .. 375.00
Flattened triangular form, yel gr, Pillar molded, 8-rib, ps, 5¾" .. 3,750.00
Globular, amber, 24 right-swirl ribs, ps, rm, potstone, 8½" 120.00
Globular, aquamarine, 12-dmn, sm, ps, 1800-40, 5¾" 130.00
Globular, bl aqua, 24 right-swirl ribs, ps, rm, 8⅛" 325.00
Globular, bl aqua, 25 vertical ribs, op, rm, good emb, 8⅞" 160.00
Globular, brilliant amethyst, 20-dmn, sm, ps, att Midwest, 6⅜" ... 550.00
Globular, golden amber, tooled outward rm, ps, Midwest, mini, 3¼" .. 1,200.00
Globular, lt yel amber, 24 right-swirl ribs, ps, Midwest, 5⅛" 1,100.00
Globular, med amber, 24 right-swirl ribs, ps, rm, 8⅛" 650.00
Globular, yel amber, no ribs, ps, rm, 8¼" 375.00
Globular, yel amber w/hint of olive, 24 vertical ribs, ps, 7¾" 800.00
Pitkin flask, amethyst, 18 right-swirl ribs, ps, NJ, 1920-30, 6x4" .. 160.00
Pitkin flask, forest gr w/olive amber top, 24 right-swirl ribs, 6¼" ... 1,900.00
Pitkin flask, lt yel olive, 36 left-swirl ribs, ps, 5⅜" 750.00
Pitkin flask, lt yel olive, 38 vertical/33 right-swirled ribs, 4½" .. 1,100.00
Pitkin flask, med yel olive, 32 right-swirl ribs, sm, ps, 6¼" 650.00
Pitkin flask, yel olive, right-swirl ribs, sm, ps, 6½x5½" 2,500.00
Pitkin flask, yel olive, 36 left-swirl ribs, sm, ps, Midwest, 6" 1,500.00
Pitkin flask, yel olive, 36 right-swirl ribs, sm, ps, 4⅞" 850.00
Teardrop, golden amber, 10-rib, sm, ps, Midwest, 6⅝" 650.00

Cologne, Perfume, and Toilet Water Bottles

Bulbous w/long neck, lt amethyst w/16 left-swirl ribs, fm, ps, 5¼" .. 1,000.00
Bulbous w/long neck, sapphire bl, 16-rib, w/stopper, 5", EX 550.00
Corseted, 8-sided, cobalt, fm, ps, Sandwich, 5¾" 1,300.00
Corseted, 8-sided, cobalt, inward rm, ps, Sandwich, 6x2¼" 850.00
Corseted, 8-sided, electric bl opal, gm, metal lid, Sandwich, 2⅜" ... 475.00
Flared body, sapphire bl w/20 vertical ribs, rm, ps, 1820-40, 6" .. 1,100.00
Flattened ovoid, cobalt w/ribbed shoulder/waist, center band, 2⅛" .. 275.00
Flattened ovoid tapering to base, canary yel, Sandwich, 3" 1,500.00
Horseshoe, silver & agate w/foliate scrolls, agate cap, 2¼" 700.00
Ovoid, teal gr w/pigeon blood striations, emb ribs, ps, 2⅞" 500.00
Rectangular, powder bl, bulbous neck, fm, ps, 1830-60, 5" 950.00
Rectangular, yel olive, floral urns on 3 panels, sl cm, ps, NY, 7¼" .. 5,500.00
Shield w/sunburst, cobalt, sm, ps, Am, 1820-50, 2⅝" 200.00
Tapered cylinder w/plain & beaded flutes, cobalt, Sandwich, 10x3" .. 2,100.00
Tapered cylinder w/plain & beaded flutes, emerald gr, Sandwich, 10" .. 2,200.00
Teardrop, custard w/etched flowers w/bronze tone, SP cap, 3⅞" ... 115.00
12-sided, deep teal, outward tm, sb, Sandwich, 1860-80, 11" 750.00
12-sided, dk amethyst, flared tm, sb, Sandwich, 6⅞" 1,100.00
12-sided, dk amethyst, slim, tm, sb, Sandwich, 1860-80, 7½" 375.00

12-sided, emerald gr (rare), tm, sb, Sandwich, 7¼".....................1,300.00
12-sided, sapphire bl, rm, ps, partial label, burst bubble, 4⅝" 275.00
12-sided, sapphire bl w/lower magenta swirls, ps, Sandwich, 11⅛"...1,100.00
12-sided, teal bl, tm, sb, eagle label, Sandwich, 11x1½" 550.00

Commercial Perfume Bottles

One of the most popular and growing areas of perfume bottle collecting is what are called 'commercial' perfume bottles. They are called commercial because they were sold with perfume in them — in a sense one pays for the perfume and the bottle is free. Collectors especially value bottles that retain their original label and box, called a perfume presentation. If the bottle is unopened, so much the better. Rare fragrances and those from the 1920s are highly prized. 'Tis a sweet, sweet hobby. Our advisors are Randy Monsen and Rod Baer; they are listed in the Directory under Virginia.

Bichara, Chypre, clear w/gold, paneled, wigged man's-head dauber, 6"...1,000.00
Corday, Femme du Jour, blk w/gilt letters, Baccarat, 4", +box...1,200.00
D'orsay, Belle de Jour, clear w/'eng' Lucite disk dauber, 6½".........600.00
Elizabeth Arden, Cyclamen, wht fan w/spire dauber, Baccarat, 6", MIB..5,000.00
Elizabeth Arden, My Love, clear, plume dauber, 3", +box w/Lucite front..425.00

Hattie Carnegie, Hypnotic, gold enamel over clear glass, empty, 4", in excellent original box, $575.00. (Photo courtesy Monsen and Baer)

Lancome, Fetes de L'Hiver, label w/lady in arch shape, 9½".........800.00
Lanvin, My Sin, gold w/blk resist figures, artichoke dauber, 2" 425.00
Lentheric, Ambre-Mousse, clear w/gr o/l, lady on whale, Baccarat, 5" .450.00
Marcel Guerlain, Caravelle, blk ship form w/gilt detail, 1927, 5".......3,500.00
Richard Hudnut, Fadette, clearw/emb vines, seated maid dauber, 4".1,700.00
Rigaud, Pres de Vous, 'stained glass' enameling to body & dauber, 6"...600.00
Rosine, Chez Poiret, clear hemispherical body w/gr dauber, 2½"...400.00
Schiaparelli, Succes Fou, gr-pnt leaf w/gilt, 2½", +heart box 1,100.00
Vigny, Golliwog, clear/blk w/enamel details, sealed, 4¾", MIB....900.00

Dairy Bottles

Arlington Diary, Bangor MI, rnd qt 115.00
Bergjan's Dairy, St Louis MO emb, rnd pt..75.00
Blais Dairy, Lewiston ME, red pyro, Baby Face, rnd qt 80.00
Blue Ribbon Dairy, Noblesville IN, red pyro, sq qt.......................100.00
Cherry Valley Dairy, red pyro, Baby Face, Pat #98609, rnd qt......115.00
Crown Dairy, Chelsea MA, orange pyro, rnd qt 85.00
Dairy Distributers..., Milwaukee WI, 2-color pyro, rnd qt 120.00
Davis Dairy, Anderson IN, red pyro, rnd qt 100.00
DD Lunsford Dairy, Minden LA, red pyro, rnd qt.........................135.00
Elsie Says Buy War Bonds, brn/red pyro, squat rnd qt...................115.00
Fairview Jersey Farm, Jackson MI, orange pyro, 1944, tall rnd qt... 75.00
Farmers Cooperative Dairy, Winston-Salem NC, gr pyro, tall rnd qt...75.00
Flat Creek Dairy, Corryton TN emb, rnd qt....................................125.00
Gagnon's Dairy, Fort Kent ME, blk pyro, rnd qt 110.00
Hefner Dairy, Lima OH, red pyro, tall rnd pyro.............................75.00

Kolb Dairy, Lena IL, red pyro, rnd qt...95.00
Kruft Jersey Dairy, Phoenix AZ, 2-color pyro, rnd qt...................110.00
Maple City Dairy, Monmouth IL, Keep 'em Flying..., red pyro, rnd qt ...100.00
Maple Lawn Dairy WV emb, rnd qt..150.00
McDonald Flint Dairy, red pyro, rnd ½-pt......................................105.00
Milk & Sunshine... St Augustine FL, red pyro, rnd qt.....................75.00
Niehoff Dairy, Eureka MO emb, rnd qt..132.00
Otto's Suburban Dairy, red pyro, cream top, rnd qt 85.00
Purity Dairy, blk pyro, Baby Face, rnd pnt.....................................110.00
Rose Tree Dairy Inc, Mt Vernon IN, red pyro, rnd qt....................145.00
Sand Hill Dairy, Cary NC emb, rnd pt..110.00
Sunlight Dairy, Oshkosh WI, cream top, qt....................................150.00
Sunset View, Waterbury VT, gr & yel pyro, rnd qt 110.00
Thomas Brothers, Raleigh NC emb, rnd pt 85.00
Valentine Dairy, Ventura CA, red pyro, tall rnd ½-gal.................110.00
Village Dairy, Toledo OH, brn/orange pyro, rnd qt.......................110.00
Village Farm Dairy, Toledo OH emb, rnd qt..................................100.00
Welwyn Garden City's Dairy emb, 1930s, ½-pt...............................100.00

Figural Bottles

Barrel, Greeley's Bourbon, grayish strawberry puce, cm, sb, 9⅛" ..550.00
Barrel, Greeley's Bourbon Bitters, bright yel gr, sq cm, sb, 9", NM ...1,700.00
Bear (seated, upright), bright gr, fm, ps, Am, 1840-60, 4" 750.00
Bell, golden amber, Proclaim Liberty..., zinc lid, sb, 5⅛" 450.00
Black waiter, clear frost, sb, frosted blk head, 13" 170.00
Bricked column, milk glass, tm, sb, Sandwich, 1860-80, 7¾".......475.00
Bunker Hill monument, fiery opal, sb, paper label, Sandwich, 9⅛"..850.00
Clam, clear, Pat Apld For, sb, 3½"..70.00
Clam, cobalt, gm w/metal cap, sb, 1880-1900, 5¼" 550.00
Clam, whiskey nip, med amber, metal screw-on cap, 5¼" 70.00
Fruit basket, clear, ps, tm, rare, 5⅝"..275.00
Globe on metal stand, clear, gm, Pat Applied For label, MIB 230.00
Grant's Tomb, milk glass, Grant metal cap, sb, gm, 10"................700.00
Ham, amber, orig metal screw-on cap, 7" 70.00
Hessian soldier seated, clear, sb, tm, 5" 90.00
Indian maiden, Brown's Celebrated Indian Herb Bitters, yel amber, 12" ...700.00
James Garfield bust, clear w/orig wood base/gold pnt, EX label, 7¼"...325.00
Joan of Arc praying at stake, clear, ps, tm, 14"..............................110.00
Liberty Bell, E Hoyt & Co...1776-1926, clear bell, sb, 2½" 80.00
Man's head, League Bouquet, milk glass, sb, 3"..............................750.00
Man seated, By Jingo Trade Mark, clear, sb, tm, 5¼"....................100.00
Monument, bright bl gr, tooled fm, sb, Sandwich, 8⅛"..................750.00
Octopus draped over coin dtd 1901, milk glass, gm, sb, 4⅜" 475.00
Oil derrick, Genuine Crude Oil Hair... label, clear, sb, 6⅜".........375.00
Pig, clear, appl features, stain, 11⅛" L 140.00
Plane, Spirit of St Louis, cobalt w/metal parts, gold trim, 13" 350.00
Poincare Depose, milk glass bonbon jar, tin lid, 13½" 425.00
Pouch w/drawstring, yel gr, sb, sm, screw-on cap missing, 2¾" 90.00
Revolver, electric bl w/metal cap, sb, Am, 1890-1900, 8⅛" 275.00
Roasted turkey, clear, sb, screw-on cap, 4¾" L 60.00
Soldier, clear, ps, am, rare, 9⅞"..70.00
Statue of Liberty, metal on milk glass ped, sb, 17½" 375.00
Tommy Dodd sitting on chamber pot, clear, CF Knapp Phila on sb, 4⅝"..170.00
Uncle Tom Log, clear, sb, tm, 3¾"..90.00
Yellow Kid, Say Ain't I Hot Stuff, milk wht opal, sb, 5¼".........1,000.00
2-story building, cobalt, sq cm, sb, Am, 1860-80, 4¾"...............1,100.00

Flasks

Baltimore Monument/Corn for the World, GVI-4, Prussian Blue, sb, qt..1,300.00
Baltimore Monument/Corn for World, GVI-4, golden amber, dbl cm, sb, qt...950.00
Baltimore/Anchor, GXIII-53, yel olive, sm, ps, sm chip, pt........1,200.00
Dove/Sheaf of Rye w/Rake & Scythe, yel olive, sm, ps, ½-pt.......600.00

Eagle/Louisville KY GW, GII-33, root beer amber, tm, sb, ½-pt... 425.00
Eagle/Starburst, GII-7, lt bl gr, sm, ps, haze/stain, pt 4,250.00
Eagle/Sunburst, GII-7, dk amber, sm, ps, Pittsburgh area, pt ... 26,000.00
Flag w/13 Stars/Granite GW..., GX-027, yel amber, sm, ps, rpr, pt ... 1,100.00
For Pike's Peak Prospector/Eagle, GXI-8, dk aqua, sl cm, sb, qt ... 550.00
Hunter/Fisherman, GXIII-4, apricot, sl cm, ip, 1845-60, qt 375.00
Lafayette/D Clinton, GI-80, yel amber w/olive tone, sm, ps, pt, EX... 550.00
Lafayette/Liberty Pole & Cap, GI-85, aquamarine, sm, ps, pt ... 7,500.00
Masonic/Eagle, GIV-32, golden amber w/reddish tone, sm, ps, pt ... 800.00
Masonic/Eagle, GIV-7a, bright med gr w/yel tone, sm, ps, Keene, pt, EX .. 650.00
Pantaloon Eagle/Cornucopia, GII-75, olive amber, sm, ps, Marlboro, pt... 7,000.00
Pitkin, bright med gr, 16-rib, sm, ps, Midwest or NJ, 5½".......... 1,000.00
Ravenna GW, GXV-17, yel apple gr, cm w/ring, sb, OH, 1860-64, pt .. 750.00
Scroll, GIX-30 variant, aqua, fleur-de-lis only, sm, ps, 2-qt 600.00
Summer/Winter, GX-19, dk amber (blk), dbl cm, sb, 1860-70, qt ... 1,000.00
Sunburst, GVIII-1, bright gr w/bluish tone, sm, ps, flake, pt 950.00
Sunburst, GVIII-3, yel olive, sm, ps, 1815-30, pt........................ 1,100.00
Sunburst, GVIII-7, bright yel olive, sm, ps, pt 3,500.00
Sunburst, GVIII-9, yel olive, rm, ps, Keene, 1820-30, ½-pt 750.00
Sunburst, GVIII-16, lt yel olive, sm, ps, 1815-30, ½-pt 750.00
Sunburst, GVIII-18, yel olive, sm, ps, 1815-30, ½-pt.................... 950.00
Traveler's Companion/Ravenna Glass Co, GXIV-3, golden amber, ip, pt ... 750.00
Urn, GIII-16, bright yel gr, sm, ip, burst bubble, pt 650.00
Washington/Sheaf of Wheat, GI-59, cobalt, sm, ps, flakes, ½-pt... 13,000.00
Washington/Taylor, GI-37, yel gr w/amber streaks, dbl cm, qt 750.00
Washington/Taylor, GI-39, bl gr, sm, ps, lt haze, qt 400.00
Will You Take.../Will a (duck) Swim?, GXIII-29a, aquamarine, ½-pt... 500.00

Food Bottles and Jars

Fruit, forest gr, petaled shoulder, am, ip, flake, 1-qt 1,900.00
Maple Sap & Boiled Cider Vinegar, cobalt, fluted shoulder, 11½" .. 750.00
Pickle, EHVB NY, lt bl gr, hexagonal w/cathedral arches, rm, 12" ... 1,000.00
Pickle, golden amber, sq cm, b3m, NH, 1860-70, 8⅜x3½"........... 375.00
Pickle, golden amber, 6-sided w/simple arches, fm, sb, 13" 1,500.00
Pickle, gr aqua, cathedral arches, rm, ip, 1845-60, 11½" 500.00
Pickle, med bl gr, 6-sided w/cathedral arches, rm, sb, 12⅞" 2,750.00
Pickle, Skilton Foote & Co's Bunker Hill, olive yel, lighthouse, 11" .. 950.00
Pickle, Wells & Miller/NY, bright yel gr, rm, ps, 1840-60, 6¼" .. 1,100.00
Pickle, Wells Miller & Provost, bl gr, sq cm, ip, chip, 11¾" 375.00
Pickle, WM Underwood, bl gr, 8-lobe, 16 shoulder flutes, 11½" .. 800.00
Pickle, Wm Underwood & Co Boston, lt to med gr, 7-panel, ps, 11¼" .. 1,900.00

Ink Bottles

Cone, C-23, med emerald gr, op, rm, 2½" 650.00
Cone, C-27, Drape, med sapphire bl, op, am, 2⅛" 2,400.00
Cone, Drape, aqua, op, am, 2¾" 1,500.00
Cone, Drape, bright bl gr, rm, ps, 1840-60, 2⅜"........................ 1,000.00
Cone, Drape, deep sapphire bl, dbl cm, ps, 1840-60, 2⅝x2⅛" ... 2,750.00
Cone, sapphire bl, outward rm, ps, 2¼" 700.00
Cone/umbrella, yel olive, 16-sided, sm, ps, 1840-60, 2¼x2¼" 550.00
Cylinder w/16 vertical lobes, dk olive amber, disk mouth, 1⅝x2⅝" ... 9,500.00
Dome, clear w/red/wht swirl stripes, pewter closure, Sandwich, 2¾" .. 1,800.00
Geometric, GII-2, olive gr, ps, tm, 1⅞" 150.00
Geometric, GII-15, dk yel olive amber, ps, tm, 1¾"....................... 210.00
Geometric, GII-15, med sapphire bl, op, disk tm, 1¾" 12,000.00
Geometric, GII-18B, blk, ps, disk tm, roughness, 1⅞" 650.00
Geometric, GII-29, dk olive amber, ps, tm, 1½" 160.00
Igloo, J&IEM, C-628, bright yel, sb, tm, 1¾"................................... 800.00
Igloo, lt pk puce w/vertical ribs, sb, 1870-90, 2x2" 450.00
Igloo, pk puce w/vertical ribs, gm, sb, 1870-90, 2x2" 950.00
Master, Hover Phila, med bl gr, sl dbl cm, tooled spout, op, 9⅜" ... 800.00
Snail, C-1293, clear, sb, gm, 1⅝" 190.00
Teakettle, C-1257, med pk amethyst, 8-panel, sb, 2" 325.00
Teakettle, C-1272, dk cobalt, dbl font, 8-sided, sb, 3⅝" 8,000.00
Teakettle, C-1294, aqua, 8-sided, sb, sm, 1½" 80.00
Teakettle/bbl, blk pnt w/gold staves, brass collar, sb, 2¼" 500.00
Teakettle/bbl, med amethyst, gm, brass collar/lid, sb, 2½" 850.00
Teakettle/bbl, sapphire bl, gm, brass collar/cap, sb, 2¼", EX......... 275.00
Teakettle/beehive, med purple amethyst, loose brass band, 2⅜"... 850.00
Turtle, C-1288, clear, st, sm, bruise, 1⅞" 220.00
Umbrella, C-137, med bl gr, 8-sided, op, rm, 3⅛"......................... 550.00
Umbrella, C-143, med bl gr, 8-sided, op, rm, 2½"......................... 130.00
Umbrella, JW Seaton Louisville, med bl gr, 10-sided, op, 10⅛" .. 1,600.00
Umbrella, midnight bl, 8-sided, rm, ps, 2¼"................................ 1,000.00
12-sided, Harrison's Columbian, C-760, dk bl aqua, flake, 5¾" 100.00

Medicine Bottles

Alexanders Silameau, sapphire bl, bell form, sq cm, ps, stain, 6¼" ... 750.00
Dodge Brothers Melanine..., plum amethyst, rectangular, cm, sb, 7½" ... 375.00
Dr CW Roback's Scandanavian..., lt bl gr, sq cm, ip, 1845-60, 7¾" . 900.00
Dr RC Flower's Scientific..., yel, dbl cm, NM label, 9", +box....... 375.00
Febrifuge Wine (label), aquamarine, cylindrical hock form, 13" .. 300.00
Jennison's Pile & Worm Compound..., aquamarine, 12-sided, rm, 4½" ... 600.00
Lynch's Celebrated Dyspectic Cordial, med forest gr, sl cm, ip, 7½" ... 8,500.00
Potter's Catholicon..., gr aqua, vertical panels, ps, 7⅝" 2,000.00
SP Hullihen's Tooth Wash, aquamarine, 2-pc mold, rm, ps, 6½" .. 160.00
Vaughn's Vegetable Lithontriptic..., dk gr aquamarine, sq w/panels, 8" .. 600.00

Mineral Water, Beer, and Soda Bottles

Carter & Wilson Manuf's Boston, med bl gr, sl cm, ip, ½-pt, 6¾" .. 1,200.00
Eagle, bl-gr w/eagle in slug plate, heavy cm, ip, 1845-60, ½-pt, 7" .. 375.00
Franklin Spring/Mineral water, lt to med yel olive, cylindrical, pt ... 900.00
Gardner & Landon Sharon..., forest gr, cylindrical, cm, qt 3,250.00
GW Weston & Co...NY, yel olive, sl cm w/ring, ps, pt................. 325.00
I Sutton & Co Covington KY, cobalt, 12-sided, heavy cm, sb, 8¼" ... 750.00
Lynch & Clarke NY, olive amber, sl cm, ps, 1823-33, qt........... 1,400.00

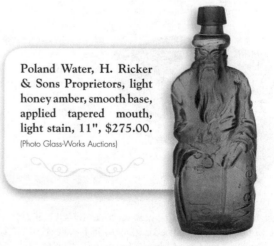

Poland Water, H. Ricker & Sons Proprietors, light honey amber, smooth base, applied tapered mouth, light stain, 11", $275.00.
(Photo Glass-Works Auctions)

Richfield Sulpher Water..., dk bl gr, sl cm w/ring, sb, pt 2,750.00
Saratoga High Rock Spring 1767..., bl emerald gr, sl cm, sb, qt.. 4,000.00
Washington Spring Co/Washington, emerald gr, sl cm, sb, pt... 1,400.00

Poison Bottles

Coffin shape, golden amber, tm, sb, Mercury Oxycanie Poison label, 5". 1,000.00
FA Thompson & Co Detroit, amber coffin, 1900s, from $500 to.. 550.00
Lattice & Dmn, dk cobalt, sb, tm, orig Poison stopper, 7⅛" 150.00
Owl Drug, owl emb on dk cobalt, needs cleaned, 3¼"................. 115.00

Poison, dk cobalt coffin, Crystal on sb, tm, NM label, 3¼" 3,750.00
Poison emb on cobalt, ribbed sq body, ERS&S on cobalt stopper, 5¼" ..250.00
Skull, cobalt, X-bone base, Poison on forehead, Pat Appl For, 4", G..780.00
Sq hobnails on teal gr, tm, ps, sliver chip, 7" 145.00
Yapoo, Poisonous...Ammonia, cobalt, emb hobnails, 6¼" 175.00

Spirits Bottles

AM Bininger & Co...NY, shaded yel amber, tm, sb, cannon bbl, 12¼" ..1,300.00
Callahan's Old Cabin..., yel amber, cabin w/arched windows, 9" .. 11,000.00
Casper's...Made by Honest NC People, cobalt, sl cm, sb, 12"....... 600.00
City Bottling Works...Ohio EHE, med cobalt, sb, bt, wire bale, 10" ..1,800.00
G Andrae Port Huron Mich, cobalt, C&Co on sb, sl cm, 12"....... 950.00
H Ingermann's XXX Ale, med amber, G&Co Lim on sb, sl cm, 9"..150.00
Mist of Morning..., rootbeer amber, bbl, sb, dbl cm, potstone, 10" ...240.00
Mist of Morning/SM Barnett..., amber w/olive tone, sb, bbl, 10" ..350.00
Pure Malt Whiskey Bourbon Co..., golden amber, sl cm, sb, 8½" ..550.00
Renault & Co Cognac 1805 WHY, yel olive, sl cm, sb, 3-pc mold, 11"..2,000.00
Seal: Class of 1846..., yel olive, sl cm, Dyottville, flake, NM 450.00
Seal: EIJ, yel olive, sl cm w/ring, lg ip, Dyottville, qt................. 1,800.00
Seal: F&Co NY, yel amber, invt cone form, dbl cm, ps, 1840-60, 16" ..3,500.00
Seal: P&V, aquamarine, b3m, sl cm w/ring, sb, qt, 11¼x3" 2,000.00
Seal: T Goddard & Co 233 Dock..., yel gr, sl cm, sb, 11" 2,100.00
SS Smith Jr & Co..., med golden amber, modified cabin, sb, 9¾" .. 1,300.00
Wm H Daly Sole...NY, yel gr, bell form w/sq cm, ps, 1840-60, 9"..2,500.00
Wormser Bros San Francisco, golden yel amber, bbl, sb, am, 9½"...1,600.00

Boxes

Boxes have been used by civilized man since ancient Egypt and Rome. Down through the centuries, specifically designed containers have been made from every conceivable material. Precious metals, papier-mache, Battersea, Oriental lacquer, and wood have held riches from the treasuries of kings, snuff for the fashionable set of the last century, China tea, and countless other commodities. In the following descriptions, when only one dimension is given, it is length. See also Toleware; specific manufacturers.

Pennsylvania Dutch German folk art decor by Weber, minor wear, 5x5x10", $14,000.00.

(Photo courtesy Garth's Auctions Inc.)

Bible, oak slant front w/blk pnt, rose-head nails, dtd 1667, 11x26x15" 550.00
Bible, pine w/sponged pnt/floral decor, sq nails, att PA, 11x17x14" ...1,550.00
Bible, red-pnt pine, dvtl, wire hinges, 1820s, VT, 10x26x13" 470.00
Bible, walnut/pine/poplar, rose-head nails, hinged lid, rprs, 8x18x15" ..550.00
Bible, wht pine, cotter-pin hinged molded-edge top, dvtl, 1700s, 19" L....575.00
Bride's, bentwood w/floral bands on sides, decoupage lid, 7x19x12" 600.00
Bride's, bentwood w/laced seams, lady/German text on lid, 8x18x12"..575.00
Bride's, colonial couple/flowers/German text, bl/wht pnt, 18" L, VG ...575.00
Candle, pine w/red pnt, sq nails/iron straps, 2-lobe crest, 9x16", VG.. 1,495.00
Candle, poplar w/tulips & stripes on red, PA, 1834, 7x10x6" ..8,900.00
Candle, reddish finish, sliding top, rectangular, early, 12" L........ 200.00
Hanging, reddish finish, slant open front w/triangle bk, 14x12x6"....800.00
Knife, birch, canted sides, dvtl corners, 2-compartment, 6x14x10" ...375.00

Knife, mahog, dvtl w/beveled edge lift lid, heart cutout, 9x15x11"....550.00
Knife, mahog Geo III w/inlay, serpentine front, 14¾x9x12" 150.00
Knife, mahog vnr, crotch mahog top & front, inlaid compass, 12x7", VG ..290.00
Knife, mahog vnr, slant lid, 3 ball & claw ft, 14x9x8", VG.......... 460.00
Knife, mahog w/inlay Geo IV, bowfront, fluted pilasters, 13x9x8" ..735.00
Pantry, bentwood, swallowtail fingers, copper tacks, varnish, 3x9x6" ...230.00
Pantry, red finish remnants, swing hdl, str tacked seam, w/lid, 6x8"......800.00
Pear shape, treenware w/realistic coloring, sm trn stem, 4½" 185.00
Pipe, blk-pnt (over salmon) cedar, shaped tall bk/dvtl drw, 1820s, 24"..530.00
Pipe, walnut/chestnut, old dry red pnt, dvtl drw, scalloped, 20x7x6" .8,350.00
Slide-lid, bird's-eye maple w/pnt rural vignettes, ca 1830s, 3x11x9"..2,415.00
Slide-lid, grpt pine w/sq nails, 8x14x7¾" 175.00
Spice, dvtl pine w/heart cut-out crest, 2-drw, PA or NE, 16x15x9"....5,175.00
Wig, Fr decor: Orientals/scene, ogee base w/flowers, red int, 12" L ..180.00
Writing, mahog Regency, rectangular w/brass inlay, 6x18x10½"....450.00
Writing, mahog w/brass mts, calamander wood compartments, Wm IV, 19" ...615.00
Writing, mahog w/brass mts, compartments/hidden drws, 1930, 14" L ..340.00
Writing, papier-mache w/MOP inlay & gilt, slant front, 1850, 16" L... 1,175.00
Writing, Regency rosewood, brass bound, 1820s, 12" L................ 400.00

Bradley and Hubbard

The Bradley and Hubbard Mfg. Company was a firm which produced metal accessories for the home. They operated from about 1860 until the early part of this century, and their products reflected both the Arts and Crafts and Art Nouveau influence. Their logo was a device with a triangular arrangement of the company name containing a smaller triangle and an Aladdin lamp. Our advisor is Bruce Austin; he is listed in the Directory under New York. See also Bookends; Doorstops.

Lamps

Angle, dbl; clear globes, milk glass shades, blk rpt, 35x22" 350.00
Desk, 4-sided slag shade w/Greek key border; 2 inkwells in base, 15x9"...800.00
Hanging, 14" opaque shade w/HP flowers; similar font, 40" 400.00
Oil, lantern form, dragon hdl, ribbed shade, 19½" to top of chimney ...500.00
Parlor, 19" cranberry shade, brass insert, griffins mt, 36" 2,700.00
Table, 13" 6-panel shade w/o/l (simple); fluted std, 20" 700.00
Table, 14" rvpt 6-panel Deco shade; dbl-sgn metal base, 22" 600.00
Table, 15" red on cream/caramel shade w/o/l (floral); #261 std 450.00
Table, 16" gr/ruby #216 shade w/o/l (feathers); simple std............650.00
Table, 16" ldgl floral-band shade; squat sgn std, 21"...................1,400.00
Table, 16" rvpt 6-panel shade; bronzed #302B std, 21" 1,400.00
Table, 16" slag shade w/o/l (foliage); squat urn base w/3 sockets, 21" ..800.00
Table, 16" 8-panel shade w/o/l (palms); gilt metal std, 22½", VG ...800.00
Table, 17" caramel slag 6-panel shade w/o/l (floral), mk std, 23"..750.00
Table, 18" ldgl shade w/flower border; flaring vasiform base, 24" ...2,400.00
Table, 19" slag glass 4-panel shade w/o/l (floral), slim std, 24" 600.00
Table, 20" rvpt 6-panel floral shade; emb acanthus std, 25" 2,200.00
Table, 20" slag 6-panel shade w/o/l (leaves), foliate CI std, 25"... 1,550.00
Table, 3 brass hemispherical shades w/jewels on 3-stem base, 22½" ...2,000.00

Miscellaneous

Andirons, lion-head medallions atop, brn patina, 23x12".........2,520.00
Ashtray, rabbit figural, pnt CI..350.00
Candlesticks, chrome socket/copper capital/brass std, sq base, 9", pr...150.00
Clock, John Bull, man figural, blinking eyes, 1857, 14¼", NM .1,100.00
Desk set, laurel swags/scrolls/rayed medallions on gilt metal, 7-pc ..400.00
Doorstop, cat seated on base (detailed), CI, 7⅜x4⅞", NM...........500.00
Fire tools, hammered copper, shovel/broom/tongs/poker, w/stand...800.00
Inkstand, elk being chased by hounds, brass-plated CI, 2 wells, 5x9"..100.00
Letter holder, 2 hounds chase stag, brass, mid-20th C, 6½x9x5".. 100.00

Match holder, Scottie dog at side, pnt metal, 4¼" 100.00
Pipe stand, CI base w/metal tray top, 10", +match holder & ashtray .. 100.00
Plaque, lady w/flowers in relief, mc pnt on metal, #1810, NM+ ... 300.00

Brass

Brass is an alloy consisting essentially of copper and zinc in variable proportions. It is a medium that has been used for both utilitarian items and objects of artistic merit. Today, with the inflated price of copper and the popular use of plastics, almost anything made of brass is collectible, though right now, at least, there is little interest in items made after 1950. Our advisor, Mary Frank Gaston, has compiled a lovely book, *Antique Brass and Copper*, with full-color photos. Mrs. Gaston is listed in the Directory under Texas. See also Candlesticks.

Ash can, lion mask hdls, domed lid w/orb-shaped finial, 19x13" ... 315.00
Ashtray, lady w/skirt up at side, erotic, 6x4" 35.00
Box, tobacco; eng scrolls/florals, canted corners, 1800, 5¾" L 290.00
Brazier, pierced, 32x30" dia 1,495.00
Bucket, wrought-iron swing hdl, 8½x13" 98.00
Kettle stand, pierced shelf, cabriole front legs, wrought-iron base ... 150.00
Saucepan, iron rattail hdl, 5x10½" dia 285.00
Skimmer, 21" 200.00
Stand, music; lyre-shaped rest, 40", EX 40.00
Stand, studded/chased, shield w/eagles & lion, Ottoman Empire, 46x28" ... 585.00
Standish, sander/ink/cup w/candle socket on base, 5x9¾", VG ... 920.00
Sundial, chased w/Roman numerals around sun face, 8" 285.00
Tiebacks, cast rosettes & acanthus leaves w/berries, 3¾", 4 for 315.00
Umbrella stand, inside tray removes, 7-lb, 18½" 125.00
Wall sconce, emb bird & landscape, 2-light, English, 19x15" 650.00

Brastoff, Sascha

The son of immigrant parents, Sascha Brastoff was encouraged to develop his artistic talents to the fullest, encouragement that was well taken, as his achievements aptly attest. Though at various times he was a dancer, sculptor, Hollywood costume designer, jeweler, and painter, it is his ceramics that are today becoming highly regarded collectibles.

Sascha began his career in the United States in the late 1940s. In a beautiful studio built for him by his friend and mentor, Winthrop Rockefeller, he designed innovative wares that even then were among the most expensive on the market. All designing was done personally by Brastoff; he also supervised the staff which at the height of production numbered approximately 150. Wares signed with his full signature (not merely backstamped 'Sascha Brastoff') were personally crafted by him and are valued much more highly than those signed 'Sascha B.,' indicating work done under his supervision. Until his death in 1993, he continued his work in Los Angeles, in his latter years producing 'Sascha Holograms,' which were distributed by the Hummelwerk Company.

Though the resin animals signed 'Sascha B.' were neither made nor designed by Brastoff, collectors of these pieces value them highly. After he left the factory in the 1960s, the company retained the use of the name to be used on reissues of earlier pieces or merchandise purchased at trade shows.

In the listings that follow, items are ceramic and signed 'Sascha B.' unless 'full signature' or another medium is indicated. For further information we recommend *Collector's Encyclopedia of California Pottery, Second Edition*, by Jack Chipman, available from Collector Books or your local bookstore.

Base, bl/wht/blk bands on wht crackle, irregular rim, 13½x4" 165.00
Bowl, console; horizontal stripes on cream, tall ft, #061, 9¼x9" 55.00

Bowl, Hawaiian Dancer, 4½x13" 140.00
Bowl, Surf Ballet, pk & gold, 3-ftd, 2½x5¾" 40.00
Chalice, gold w/decor, mk #080, 6x5" 115.00
Charger, grapes, enamel on copper, 11¾", NM, from $110 to 130.00
Charger, Star Steed, 15¼" 155.00
Chip & dip set, mosaic fish on free-form, center hdl 185.00

Figurine, bird, amber resin, 6", $185.00.

Figurine, cat, amber resin, 10x3½" 285.00
Figurine, elephant, wht w/HP decor, 7½x9" 400.00
Figurine, mermaid holding fish over head, HP mc w/gold, 12x8¼" .. 215.00
Figurine, owl, gr resin, 14" 335.00
Figurine, pelican, gr resin, 10½" 285.00
Figurine, seal, bl resin, 4x9" 250.00
Figurine, whale, bl resin, 4x10" 250.00
Jar, Jewel Bird ea side, 11x7" 125.00
Jug, stylized floral, orange on brn, bulbous, tall spout, 10" 100.00
Lighter, Star Steed on bl, 5" 65.00
Planter, 2 contemporary figures in relief on steel gray, 5x6¾" 100.00
Plate, fish figural, dk gr w/mc, 8" 50.00
Plate, tree design etched in gold, Limited Edition, 1978, 5x6½" .. 110.00
Platter, fish figural, 11½" 125.00
Vase, horizontal gr & gold bands on tan, #082, 8¼" 35.00
Vase, horizontal mc bands w/gold, leaf band, teardrop shape, 10" .. 95.00
Vase, Mosaic Mayan mask design, #M66, 6" 90.00
Vase, purple/wht/metallic, triangular free-form, 5½x7½" 50.00
Vase, stylized floral on creamy wht, irregular rim, 13½x4" 175.00

Brayton Laguna

A few short years after Durlin Brayton married Ellen Webster Grieve, his small pottery, which he had opened in 1927, became highly successful. Extensive lines were created and all of them flourished. Hand-turned pieces were done in the early years; today these are the most difficult to find. Durlin Brayton hand incised ashtrays, vases, and dinnerware (plates in assorted sizes, pitchers, cups and saucers, and creamers and sugar bowls). These early items were marked 'Laguna Pottery,' incised on unglazed bases.

Brayton's childrens' series is highly collected today as is the Walt Disney line. Also popular are the Circus line, Calasia (art pottery decorated with stylized feathers and circles), Webton ware, the Blackamoor series, and the Gay Nineties line. Each seemed to prove more profitable than the lines before it. Both white and pink clays were utilized in production. At its peak, the pottery employed more than 150 people. After World War II when imports began to flood the market, Brayton Laguna was one of the companies that managed to hold their own. By 1968, however, it was necessary to cease production.

For more information on this as well as many other potteries in the state, we recommend *Collector's Encyclopedia of California Pottery* and *California Pottery Scrapbook*, both by Jack Chipman; he is listed in the Directory under California.

Biscuit jar, Coachman, made for Disney, 1938, rare, minimum value... 2,600.00
Bowl, wht & yel flowers w/gr leaves on brn, 3x9" 32.00
Box, pk/beige, molded fern-like fronds, oval w/knob on lid, 5½" ... 15.00
Bud vase, little girl stands/holds doll, tree behind, ST-20, 9", NM...45.00
Candleholders, Blackamoor, seated w/legs crossed, 4¾", pr.......... 140.00
Chamberstick, orange, tri-cornered rim, w/hdl, early, 3¼" 165.00
Cookie jar, Brayton Maid, blk stamp, 12½", minimum value 2,000.00
Cookie jar, Dutch Lady, arms Xd, appl flowers on apron, crazing, EX ... 145.00
Cookie jar, Gingham Dog, 8½x7½x5¾" 120.00
Cookie jar, Granny, #40-85, from $400 to 450.00
Cookie jar, Matilda, from $350 to 400.00
Figure vase, Sally, girl in bl dress w/wht apron, 7" 35.00
Figurine, Black dice player.. 55.00
Figurine, cat (stylized), brn bsk w/wht crackle eyes, 15½" 50.00
Figurine, cats, stylized, wht, 4½x5½", pr....................................... 45.00
Figurine, cow, purple flambe, 5¾x9" 100.00
Figurine, fawn, brn w/wht spots, Disney, 6"................................. 80.00
Figurine, Figaro, playing, 3⅜" 100.00
Figurine, horse, lt brn w/dk patch on ea side, 3x4" 45.00
Figurine, Inger, 7" 50.00
Figurine, lady in gr dress w/wolfhound on ea side, 11" 60.00
Figurine, lady in lav dress, basket in 1 hand, 8½" 65.00
Figurine, Olga, 7⅛" 50.00
Figurine, panther, snarling, jewelled collar, 20" L, from $175 to ..225.00
Figurine, pirate, playing fiddle, mc, 5½" 50.00
Figurine, queen (Alice in Wonderland), 6¾" 180.00
Figurine, Sambo, bl overalls w/yel hat, 7¾" 140.00
Figurine, stylized bird, blk w/wht trim, twisted neck, #H49, 9½".....140.00
Figurine, Victorian couple, in nightclothes, 3rd in series of 4, 9" 150.00
Figurine, Victorian couple, man seated, 1st in series of 4 .... 110.00
Figurine, walrus (Alice in Wonderland), unmk, 7"...................... 110.00
Figurine, 3 men at bar w/spittoon, Gay 90s, 9x6¾x5" 85.00
Figurines, Hillbilly Shotgun Wedding, Preacher/Ma/Pa/Bride/Groom/Jr ..400.00
Figurines, piano, musician & lady, 5¼x6", 8", 3-pc set 375.00
Pitcher, turq, handmade, mk Durlin, 3½" 60.00
Planter, peasant woman w/baskets... 50.00
Plate, bl, handmade, 9¾" 70.00
Plate, maroon, handmade, 10¾" 110.00
Plate, yel matt, handmade, 11" 75.00
Shakers, Black Chef & Mammy, 6½" pr... 185.00
Shakers, cat & dog, seated, dog: plaid, cat: flowers on wht, pr 40.00
Shakers, rooster & hen, mc, 5¼", 3½", pr 45.00
Sugar bowl, wht & yel flowers w/gr leaves on brn, 4x4½".............. 25.00
Teapot, wht & yel flowers w/gr leaves on blk, 6½" 45.00
Vase, blended grs, fan form w/hand-crimped rim, D Brayton, early, 6" ...750.00
Wall pocket, bowl-shaped w/floral decor, Webton-Ware, 3½x6".... 35.00

Bread Plates and Trays

Bread plates and trays have been produced not only in many types of glass but in metal and pottery as well. Those considered most collectible were made during the last quarter of the nineteenth century from pressed glass with well-detailed embossed designs, many of them portraying a particularly significant historical event. A great number of these plates were sold at the 1876 Philadelphia Centennial Exposition by various glass manufacturers who exhibited their wares on the grounds. Among the themes depicted are the Declaration of Independence, the Constitution, McKinley's memorial 'It Is God's Way,' Remembrance of Three Presidents, the Purchase of Alaska, and various presidential campaigns, to mention only a few.

'L' numbers correspond with a reference book by Lindsey. Our advisor for this category is Darlene Yohe; she is listed in the Directory under Arkansas.

Actress, HMS Pinafore, oval, La Belle, 1880s, 11¼" 100.00
Banner Baking Powder, shield center, 11"..................................... 85.00
Bunker Hill, L-44, 13½x9" 75.00
Canadian, amber, rnd 45.00
Classic, Logan 250.00
Constitution w/eagle... 60.00
Cupid & Venus 45.00
Diana the Huntress, tab hdls, hexagonal, 11x7" 175.00
Egyptian, Cleopatra center, 13" L.. 95.00
GAR.. 265.00
Garfield Drape.. 80.00
Gladstone, 9" 45.00
Goddess of Hunt, rectangular, hdls.. 110.00
Grant Maple Leaf, Let Us Have Peace, gr...................................... 160.00
Heroes of Bunker Hill... 95.00
It Is Pleasant To Labor, grapes & leaf center, 12¾" dia 55.00
Last Supper.. 40.00
McCormick's Reaper.. 160.00
Minerva.. 75.00
National, shield shape, rare 85.00
Panelled Fishbone 35.00
Preparedness, L-481.. 300.00
Ruth the Gleaner, Gillinder 145.00
Sheraton.. 45.00
Sheridan Memorial 40.00
Spill, Lincoln Drape.. 60.00
Statuette, Ruth the Gleaner, frosted, 1876 Phila Expo, Gillinder ...175.00
US Grant, Patriot & Soldier, sq, 11".. 85.00
Washington, First War/First Peace, L-27, 12x8½" 100.00
Washington Centennial, frosted center 145.00
101, farm implement center 65.00

Bretby

Bretby art pottery was made by Tooth & Co., at Woodville, near Burton-on-Trent, Derbyshire, from as early in 1884 until well into the twentieth century. Marks containing the 'Made in England' designation indicate twentieth century examples.

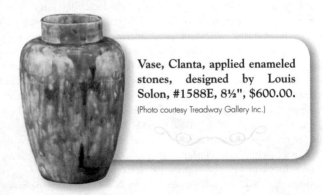

Vase, Clanta, applied enameled stones, designed by Louis Solon, #1588E, 8½", $600.00.

(Photo courtesy Treadway Gallery Inc.)

Bookends, lions on box w/ball, lime gr.. 70.00
Figurine, Barn Owl, wht w/brn wash, #1317, ca 1890, 12"........... 625.00
Jug, bl-gr drip over red, red rope-twist hdl, #113, 7" 100.00
Vase, hammered bronze look, 3 tear-shaped cabochons, 3-hdl, 9"...100.00

Bride's Baskets and Bowls

Victorian brides were showered with gifts, as brides have always been; one of the most popular gift items was the bride's basket. Art glass inserts from both European and American glasshouses, some in lovely transparent hues with dainty enameled florals, others of Peachblow, Vasa Murrhina, satin or cased glass, were cradled in complementary silverplated holders. While many of these holders were simply engraved or delicately embossed, others (such as those from Pairpoint and Wilcox) were wonderfully ornate, often with figurals of cherubs or animals or birds. The bride's basket was no longer in fashion after the turn of the century.

Watch for 'marriages' of bowls and frames. To warrant the best price, the two pieces should be the original pairing. If you can't be certain of this, at least check to see that the bowl fits snugly into the frame. Beware of later-made bowls (such as Fenton's) in Victorian holders and new frames being produced in Taiwan. In the listings that follow, if no frame is described, the price is for a bowl only.

Apricot cased w/floral, swirl ribs, pinched sides/rim, 9½" 225.00
Bl Herringbone MOP, appl crimped ribbon edge; Reed & Barton fr, 11".. 1,500.00
Bl to wht tricon w/wht int; SP fr, 12x12" 175.00
Cranberry Invt T'print w/HP decor; rstr SP Pairpoint fr w/berries, 9".. 1,500.00
Cranberry irid w/gr oil spots & gold floral, deep ruffles, 12" W 365.00
Cream w/variegated pk/wht int, Dmn Quilt, ruffled/lobed; SP fr, 11"... 230.00
Custard w/HP decor; rstr Meriden Silverplate #01532 fr, 7"......... 850.00
Gold satin w/birds & floral, clear ruffle, 13"; mk fr 495.00
Opal w/spaced floral, gently ruffled rim; Pairpoint fr #4732, 9x9" ...350.00
Peach to vaseline opal, Rib Optic; Adelphi SP fr, 10¾" 950.00
Pk cased, ruffled/fluted rim, HP floral; Aurora SP fr, 11x10¼"...... 240.00
Pk Dmn Quilt w/floral, 2-lobe crimp rim; Pairpoint ft, 14x15" .. 2,500.00
Pk Herringbone MOP w/floral & gilt, bl int, crimped rim stations, 10"..1,035.00

Pink mother-of-pearl Diamond Quilt with enamel florals; chased frame marked Webster, 12x10", $500.00. (Photo courtesy Early Auction Co.)

Pk satin w/gold branch, Webb; SP base w/2 lions, 11½" H........2,450.00
Pk to wht, ruffled rim, HP floral; unmk SP fr, ca 1870, 11½x13"..335.00
Red w/gold scrolls, lobed/crimped; Reed & Barton fr: 2 lg cherubs, 14" ...900.00
Rose cased in wht; SP Knickerbocker fr w/ornate hdl, 13½x12" ..480.00
Teapot, bird/scenes on cream, appl spout, 5¼x4½" 275.00
Wht opal w/rose pk int, Dmn Quilt; gold-wash metal fr, 13x12" .. 300.00

Bristol Glass

Bristol is a type of semi-opaque opaline glass whose name was derived from the area in England where it was first produced. Similar glass was made in France, Germany, and Italy. In this country, it was made by the New England Glass Company and to a lesser extent by its contemporaries. During the eighteenth and nineteenth centuries, Bristol glass was imported in large amounts and sold cheaply, thereby contributing to the demise of the earlier glasshouses here in America. It is very difficult to distinguish the English Bristol from other opaline types. Style, design, and decoration serve as clues to its origin; but often only those well versed in the field can spot these subtle variations.

Vase, bud; wht, gold foliage, 12", pr 75.00
Vase, lt bl, allover floral/scrolls, EX art, U300-3, ftd, 8½".............275.00

Vase, med bl w/gold floral, rnd w/ruffled trumpet tops, 8", pr 125.00
Vase, pk, bird/florals, ftd teardrop shape, 14" 85.00
Vase, pk, waist-up profile of maid in gold-scrolled wht reserve, 14"....450.00
Vase, wht, bird on floral branches, 2 moon shapes behind, 8½", pr 135.00
Vase, wht, boy (& girl) in outdoor scene, ftd, 12½", pr 120.00
Vase, wht, parrot/foliage, bright mc, gold trim, 16½", pr 300.00
Vase, wht, portrait reserve w/in floral-scroll fr, ftd, 10½" 75.00
Vase, wht, stork/lg flowers, ovoid w/cupped neck, 12x6" 60.00

British Royalty Commemoratives

Royalty commemoratives have been issued for royal events since Edward VI's 1547 coronation through modern-day occasions, so it's possible to start collecting at any period of history. Many collectors begin with Queen Victoria's reign, collecting examples for each succeeding monarch and continuing through modern events.

Some collectors identify with a particular royal personage and limit their collecting to that era, ie., Queen Elizabeth's life and reign. Other collectors look to the future, expanding their collection to include the heir apparents Prince Charles and his first-born son, Prince William.

Royalty commemorative collecting is often further refined around a particular type of collectible. Nearly any item with room for a portrait and a description has been manufactured as a souvenir. Thus royalty commemoratives are available in glass, ceramic, metal, fabric, plastic, and paper. This wide variety of material lends itself to any pocketbook. The range covers expensive limited edition ceramics to inexpensive souvenir key chains, puzzles, matchbooks, etc.

Many recent royalty headline events have been commemorated in a variety of souvenirs. Buying some of these modern commemoratives at the moderate issue prices could be a good investment. After all, today's events are tomorrow's history.

For further study we recommend *British Royal Commemoratives* by our advisor for this category, Audrey Zeder; she is listed in the Directory under Washington.

Key:
ann — anniversary	jub — jubilee
C/D — Charles and Diana	mem — memorial
chr — christening	Pr — prince
cor — coronation	Prs — princess
ILN — Illustrated London News	QM — queen mother
inscr — inscription, inscribed	wed — wedding

Beaker, Edward VII 1902 King's Dinner, gr, Doulton................... 150.00
Beaker, Victoria '87 jub, enamel mc portrait/decor, gold bands, 4"... 190.00
Book, Victoria 1897, Queen's Resolve, some wear......................... 65.00
Booklet, C/D wed, Royal Wedding Official Souvenir, 11x8"........... 30.00
Bookmark, Elizabeth II cor, mc portrait/decor on woven silk......... 25.00
Bottle, scent; C/D wed, mc portrait, ceramic 45.00
Bottle, Victoria cor, brn crown, beige decor Imperial Pottery 750.00
Bowl, George VI cor, mc portrait/decor, scalloped rim, 5½".......... 45.00
Child's toy dish, Victoria 1858, chidren w/cart, Prattware, 4¼" ... 295.00
Coin, Wm IV 1830, 4 pence, silver groat.................................... 45.00
Compact, Geo V jub, mc portrait, cor robes, hinged, 2¼"............. 80.00
Cup & saucer, Edward VII cor, portrait/decor on turq.................. 165.00
Doll, C/D wed, vinyl, Goldberger, 12", MIB 195.00
Doll, Prs Diana, vinyl, gr satin dress, Peggy Nisbet, 8" 250.00
Egg cup, Geo VI cor, shaded portrait, gold rim, ftd......................... 35.00
Ephemera, Geo III 1761, 8-pg Act of Parliment 75.00
Framed picture, Elizabeth II jub, needlepoint textile, 15x10" 60.00
Glass, Victoria 1887 jub dish, amber w/emb portrait/decor, 10"... 165.00
ILN Record No, George V Cor, rnd cover/gold decor, 16½x11½" ...175.00
Jewelry, Elizabeth II pin, mc portrait on MOP, 2⅝" 45.00

Jewelry, Geo VI stickpin, cut-out profile, brass 20.00
Jug, George III, emb portrait, Westerwald, late 18th C 425.00
Magazine, Daily Mail, Prs Diana mem, 9-6-97............................. 30.00
Magazine, Elizabeth II cor, ILN, cor week, dbl number, 1953 ...... 35.00
Magazine, Geo V jub, ILN, May 4, 1935................................. 35.00
Magazine, Sphere, Prs Margaret wed, 5-14-60 .... 35.00
Medal, C/D wed, emb portrait, bronze, Tower Mint, MIB.............. 50.00
Medal, Geo III 1761 cor, emb cor scene, 1⅝" 195.00
Medal, Victoria cor, profile & cor scene, pierced, 2".................... 160.00
Medallion, Pr of Wales Open 1887 Jub Exhibit, bronze, 1¾" 125.00
Miniature, Elizabeth II cor, book, gold metal, w/photos, 1x1"........ 35.00
Miniature, QM 80s plate, mc portrait, purple headdress, 2¼" 30.00
Mug, Edward VII, king's profile, Art Deco decor & shape.............. 45.00
Mug, Edward VII cor bl & gr portrait, bbl shape, CTM 165.00
Mug, Geo V cor, mc portrait in robes, presentation pc.................. 150.00
Mug, Geo VI cor, mc Coat of Arms, lion hdl, Paragon, 3"........... 75.00
Mug, Prs Diana '95 Argentina vis, mc decor, Chown, LE 50........ 125.00
New Testament, Geo VI cor, red cover w/silver seal...................... 55.00
Newpaper, Gleason's Pictorial 1862, royal coverage inside 20.00
Newspaper, Illustrated Mail 1902, Edward VI cor.......................... 45.00
Novelty, Geo VI crumb pan, emb portrait/decor on brass 75.00
Novelty, George V toasting fork, emb portait on brass, 19 ½ 75.00
Picture, Elizabeth II jub needlepoint, in wooden fr, 15x13" 60.00
Pin-bk, Edward VII cor, mc figure on bl w/copper lustre, 6" 360.00

Pitcher, inscribed 'Peace (King Edward VII) Maker Born Nov. 9th, 1841 – Died May 6, 1910,' unmarked, 8", from $300.00 to $400.00. (Photo courtesy Mary Frank Gaston)

Pitcher, Victoria 1840 wed, mc figure on bl w/copper lustre, 6" ... 360.00
Pitcher, Victoria 1897 jub, Queen/Prince Edward, Balmoral, 4" .. 270.00
Plate, C/D wed, mc portrait, emb design on rim, 9½" 65.00
Plate, Edward VII cor, mc portrait, emb/scalloped rim, 8½" 165.00
Plate, Edward VIII '37, mc portrait in cor robe, Royal Winston, 9" ..90.00
Plate, Prs Margaret 1930 birth, bird design, Paragon, 7"............... 120.00
Plate, Victoria 1887, brn portrait, mc relief, 8½" 195.00
Playing cards, Edward VII cor, mc portrait/decor, full deck 95.00
Postcard, C/D wed, mc portrait, line of descent, 32x23" 35.00
Postcard, Edward VII mem, blk/wht inscr, blk border, Rotary 25.00
Postcard, Queen Alexandra on yacht, blk/wht, ca 1905, used........ 15.00
Print, Marriage Prs Louise/Marquis of Lorne, 1871, blk & wht 20.00
Program, Elizabeth II cor, Church of England Services, 16-pg 20.00
Ribbon, Victoria mem, blk w/gold inscr, attached pin-bk, 5" 135.00
Spoon, Edward VII 1900s w/Fr President, hallmk......................... 80.00
Spoon, Victoria 1897, emb portrait/design, Sterling hallmk 150.00
Tea caddy, Elizabeth II cor, emb inscr, copper/brass, Purity Tips..... 75.00
Teapot, Elizabeth II '02 jub, head shape, gold crown, 8"................. 95.00
Teapot, Victoria 1887 jub, blk w/gold enameling, 2-cup 325.00
Textile, tea towel, C/D wed, mc portrait, Irish linen 35.00
Tin, C/D wed, royal bl w/4 mc portraits, 5½" 40.00
Tin, Geo V 1910, mc portrait w/generals, 4x3"............................. 95.00
Tin, Pr of Wales 1930, mc portrait/decor, hinged, Throne's, 4x2½" ..65.00
Tin, Pr Wales '33 Morley vis, mc portrait/decor, hinged................. 85.00
Tray, Victoria 1897 jub, 4 generations, mc, 12" 250.00

Broadmoor

In October of 1933, the Broadmoor Art Pottery was formed and space rented at 217 East Pikes Peak Avenue, Colorado Springs, Colorado. Most of the pottery they produced would not be considered elaborate, and only a handful was decorated. Many pieces were signed by P.H. Genter, J.B. Hunt, Eric Hellman, and Cecil Jones. It is reported that this plant closed in 1936, and Genter moved his operations to Denver.

Broadmoor pottery is marked in several ways: a Greek or Egyptian-type label depicting two potters (one at the wheel and one at a tile-pressing machine) and the word Broadmoor; an ink-stamped 'Broadmoor Pottery, Colorado Springs (or Denver), Colorado'; and an incised version of the latter.

The bottoms of all pieces are always white and can be either glazed or unglazed. Glaze colors are turquoise, green, yellow, cobalt blue, light blue, white, pink, pink with blue, maroon red, black, and copper lustre. Both matt and high gloss finishes were used.

The company produced many advertising tiles, novelty items, coasters, ashtrays, and vases for local establishments around Denver and as far away as Wyoming. An Indian head was incised into many of the advertising items, which also often bear a company or a product name. A series of small animals (horses, dogs, elephants, lambs, squirrels, a toucan bird, and a hippo), each about 2" high, are easily recognized by the style of their modeling and glaze treatments, though all are unmarked.

Ashtray, bl w/wht puppy in center, 5⅜" dia............................... 50.00
Bust of lady, 1 shoulder raised, looking upward, turq gloss, 5½" ... 420.00
Paperweight, scarab, ivory semimatt, ink stamp/paper label, 4" ... 110.00
Vase, burgundy gloss, rim-to-hip hdls, 1937-40, 6¾" 35.00
Vase, gunmetal blk, baluster, JB Hunt, 7" 275.00
Vase, orange-red, incurvate rim, PH Genter, 4½x5½" 35.00

Broadsides

Websters defines a broadside as simply a large sheet of paper printed on one side. During the 1880s, they were the most practical means of mass communication. By the middle of the century, they had become elaborate and lengthy with information, illustrations, portraits, and fancy border designs. Those printed on coated stock are usually worth more.

Many old broadsides are worth very little; some of the more interesting examples are listed here. Look for unusual content, those that relate to political campaigns, the military, or those with cross-over interest in such topics as Black Americana, the circus, theatre, or fashions of the day.

$25,000 Reward for Information...Kidnapers (sic) Lindbergh baby, 17" L....485.00
$500 Reward, for murderer in CA, 1895, 14x9½".......................... 200.00
Animated Moving Picture Exhibition, Sears & Roebuck, ca 1900, 28x21" ...325.00
Anti-John Fremont, Keystone Club in Suffield, 1856, 18½x12" .. 500.00
Anti-Slavery Meetings!, Letterpress, OH, 1850, 15x11" 1,100.00
Duke of Wellington's Funeral Official Programme, 1852, 18x11" ...425.00
Exhibition of Franklin Philomathean Society, ca 1845, 16x7¼".. 150.00
Negro Woman's Lamentation, lady w/Bible vignette, 1840s, 8x10"...500.00
President Harrison & Cabinet, portraits, Friedenwald, 24x18" 250.00
Ship Wreck of Francis Mary, detailed account, newsprint, 1826, VG...750.00
Single & Dbl Hand Alphabet, 2 portrait vignettes, 1840s, 19x24" 275.00
To Arms! State of Georgia, state militia, 1862, 7x7½" 4,500.00
Treatise on Prevention...of Diseases..., Philadelphia, 1796, 17x7" .. 3,000.00
Veterans to the Front!, Philadelphia Mayor's Office, 1865, 19x13", VG..800.00
White Hall Fire Works Exhibit, July 4, 1866, 7¾x5" 50.00

Bronzes

Thomas Ball, George Bessell, and Leonard Volk were some of the earliest American sculptors who produced figures in bronze for home decor during the 1840s. Pieces of historical significance were the most popular, but by the 1880s a more fanciful type of artwork took hold. Some of the fine sculptors of the day were Daniel Chester French, Augustus St. Gaudens, and John Quincy Adams Ward. Bronzes reached the height of their popularity at the turn of the century. The American West was portrayed to its fullest by Remington, Russell, James Frazier, Hermon Mac-Neil, and Solon Borglum. Animals of every species were modeled by A.P. Proctor, Paul Bartlett, and Albert Laellele, to name but a few.

The Art Nouveau and Art Deco movements influenced the medium during the '20s, evidenced by the works of Allen Clark, Harriet Frismuth, E.F. Sanford, and Bessie P. Vonnoh.

Be aware that recasts abound. While often aesthetically satisfactory, they are not original and should be priced accordingly. In much the same manner as prints are evaluated, the original castings made under the direction of the artist are the most valuable. Later castings from the original mold are worth less. A recast is not made from the original mold. Instead, a rubber-like substance is applied to the bronze, peeled away, and filled with wax. Then, using the same 'lost wax' procedure as the artist uses on completion of his original wax model, a clay-like substance is formed around the wax figure and the whole fired to vitrify the clay. The wax, of course, melts away, hence the term 'lost wax.' Recast bronzes lose detail and are somewhat smaller than the original due to the shrinkage of the clay mold. Values in the listings that follow are prices realized at auction.

Asian, elephant w/ivory tusks, 1880s, 8¾" 325.00
Austrian, bear w/open mouth, EX detail, Geschutzt, 4x7" 660.00
Austrian, cat/mouse & shoe, Geschutzt, 3¼" L.............................635.00
Austrian, lady in fur coat, hands in muff, opens to find her nude, 8"...980.00
Austrian, lamp: Oriental dome w/drapery, man w/lute on rug, Gesh, 15"..8,050.00
Austrian, pheasant hen, crouching w/tail extended, mc, 3½" L...315.00
Badin, JV; elephant on ovoid base, Goldscheider seal, 10" L 3,525.00
Barye, AL; lioness standing, Barbedienne Foundeur, 8x11" 6,600.00
Barye, Antoine-Louis; stag walking, detailed, Susse Freres, 11x12"..3,300.00
Belvedere, Apollo (after); classical male figure on ovoid base, 5¾" 325.00
Bergman, Middle Eastern merchant w/maid, cloak opens, Vienna, 5"....2,468.00
Blum, Charles; The Carver, man at work, brn patina, 11x9x9" ...290.00
Cain, Auguste N; pheasant w/6 chicks, sm lizard in its beak, 23" L....825.00
Calandrelli, nude w/drape, surprised expression, 1891, 15" 675.00
Charron, Amedee; fairy w/book, rouge marble ped, 19th C, 16½" ...2,950.00
Chemin, JV; dog w/raised ft, 4x6½" L..575.00
Chiparus, female dancer on tiptoes, hands clasped above head, 15" ..690.00
Chiparus, Friends Forever, Deco maid w/2 whippets, ivory/enamel, 25"..26,450.00
Chiparus, Solo, dancer in studded outfit on 1 leg, marble base, 26" ..920.00
Christophe, F; lion walking, dk gr patina, 11" 17,665.00
Clara, Juan; Pulling the Cat's Tail, 8x6x3"....................................635.00
Colinet, CL JR; dancing nude, parrot on ea arm, marble ped, 11" ..920.00
Colinet, CL JR; nude dancer on 1 ft, rnd marble base, 18" 1,900.00
Coustou, Chevaux de Marly, men w/rearing horses, facing pr, 23x21"....2,350.00
Dallin, E; Appeal to the Great Spirits, chief on horsebk, 9x9x6" ...2,500.00
Detrier, Pierre; lady at column w/birds, 18"................................1,800.00
Deva, A; recumbent hound, Continental, 1980s, 5¾"..................325.00
Dubucand, Alfred; Hunting in Sahara, Arab/camel/greyhounds, 31" L...14,100.00
Erte, Summer Breeze, pnt surface, ltd ed, 1987, 23¾"................1,525.00
Erte, 2 ladies in long gowns w/mc patina, marble base, 1989, 17x20"...5,750.00
Fayral, dancer, arms out, holding skirt in ea hand, gilt, Tiffany, 16"..2,300.00
Fr, urns, rococo style, bird on shoulder, marble base, 13", pr 1,300.00
Frishmuth, Harriet; Speed, Deco nude w/bk-swept wings on orb, SP, 5"..4,600.00
Giambologna, after; Mercury on stepped base w/putti frieze, 26" ..1,350.00
Gregoire, Jean-Louis; La Charite, woman w/purse & book, 28" ..4,935.00

Gregoire, L; child on draped ped caresses mom's face, Suisse, 22x16" 2,300.00
Houdon, Jean-Antoine (after); Country Girl, harvest figure, 1875, 18" ...1,645.00
Jenkins, F Lynn; nude mother/child, she w/dove on her hand, 1914, 11"..1,295.00
Jffland, cherub on tiptoes w/lute, stone ped, 9¾" 1,725.00
Larrous, A; Beton woman at the harvest, w/basket of grapes, 15"...2,350.00
Lorenzl, nude lady standing on 1 leg, rnd marble ped, 15¼" 1,880.00
Marchal, A; bacchantes (2) dancing/putto w/horn, gilt, 1882, 30"..8,800.00
Marque, Albert; nude child wiping away tears w/drapery, 25"...2,585.00
McKnight, RJ; Apollo crouched on bks of 2 lg horses, 1929, 12x12" ..2,200.00
Mene, PJ; 2 playfull whippets w/ball, 6x5x8" 1,265.00
Michelangelo (after); Lorenzo de Medici, Suisse Freres, 1880s, 8½" ..500.00
Moigniez, Jules; Fighting Cock, on grassy base, 5½x4" 520.00
Moreau, A; vase, insects/flowers emb, lg 3-D child on shoulder, 12"..2,875.00
Moxian, nude by tree w/flowing drape supports seashell above, 20"..2,300.00
Muller, H; lady w/lg bucket of water, 17½"+wooden base 975.00
Neandross, S; cougar standing, brn patina, sgn/1894, 5x11" 575.00
Pallenberg, JF; male deer stands by feeding doe, slat base, 6½" L.350.00
Powell, Ace; seated Indian w/knife belt & pot, on sq wood block, 7".1,150.00
Salvatore, Victor D; bust of lady, dtd 1922, 4" 445.00
Siccardi, G; plaque: girl w/beach ball, wood base, bronze: 5" dia .115.00
Tereszcuzuk, P; boy & girl jesters w/ivory faces, gr marble base, 6".......1,495.00
Unmk, Deco lady rests 1 knee on marble column, bird on right arm, 21"....1,210.00
Unmk, Diana the Huntress, seated, dog beside, Continental, 10x12" ..440.00
Unmk, figural jardiniere, fluted basin w/putto & goat support, 41", pr...3,000.00
Unmk, figure of dying Gaul, rouge marble base, 19th C, 12x19x10" .1,995.00
Unmk, fountain, Greek temple top w/cherubs, 4 3-D maids at base, 92" ..8,000.00
Unmk, sleepy hound, Continental, early 20th C, 6" L.................400.00
Valton, Charles; mtn lion struck w/2 arrows, med brn patina, 26" L.2,000.00
Van der Straten, Geo; Acting Coy, bust of girl, 1900, 8"..............415.00
Vienna, Arabian leading camel, pnt, Bergman, 2"........................325.00
Vienna, hound standing, blk/wht spots, 1900, 3"..........................120.00
Vienna, lizard, bright gr skin, early 20th C, 4¾" L........................60.00
Vienna, Moorish child in teal robe & striped scarf seated, 3".......700.00
Vienna, pen wipe, exotic fighting bird, pnt, 1880s, 4¾".................700.00
Vienna, pheasant, male w/colorful plumage, 1½x3" 120.00
Vienna, pug dog standing/wearing bl 3-bell collar, 1880s, 1½".....150.00
Vienna, setter sanding, long-haired tail, pnt, Bergman, 2¾" 265.00
Vienna, terrier standing, gray coat, Bergman, 3½"........................385.00
Villanit, E; La Sibylle, bust of maid w/decorated headband, 14"..2,100.00

Vonnoh, Bessie Potter; Cinderella, $20,160.00. (Photo courtesy Jackson's International Auctioneers & Appraisers of Fine Art & Antiques)

Brouwer

Theophilis A. Brouwer operated a one-man studio on Middle Lane in East Hampton, Long Island, from 1894 until 1903, when he relocated to West Hampton. He threw rather thin vessels of light, porous white clay which he fired at a relatively low temperature. He then glazed them and fired them in an open-flame kiln, where he manipulated them with a technique he later patented as 'flame painting.' This resulted in lustered glazes, mostly in the orange and amber family, with organic, free-form patterns. Because of the type of clay he used and the low firing, the wares are brittle and often found with damage. This deficiency has kept them undervalued in the art pottery market.

Brouwrer turned to sculpture around 1911. His pottery often carries the 'whalebone' mark, M-shaped for the Middle Lane Pottery, and reminiscent of the genuine whalebones Brouwer purportedly found on his property. Other pieces are marked 'Flame' or 'Brouwer.' Our advisors for this category are Suzanne Perrault and David Rago; they are listed in the Directory under New Jersey.

Vase, flame-painted lustred gold and amber, M under whalebone mark, 6½x6", $1,900.00. (Photo courtesy David Rago Auctions)

Vase, gold & amber lustre, rnd w/4-scallop rim, 5x6", NM 1,680.00
Vase, gold & amber lustre, shouldered, 6½x6" 1,900.00
Vase, orange/gold/purple, mk Flame, 7½x4½" 2,400.00
Vase, yel & orange lustre w/brn drips, drilled, 12" 3,500.00
Vase, yel/gr/beige mottle, squat, 3x4½" 540.00
Vessel, Aladdin lamp w/lotus leaf (stem hdl), gold/brn, 3½x6½" ... 2,800.00

Brownies by Palmer Cox

Created by Palmer Cox in 1883, the Brownies charmed children through the pages of books and magazines, as dolls, on their dinnerware, in advertising material, and on souvenirs. Each had his own personality, among them The Dude, The Cadet, The Policeman, and The Chairman. They represented many nations; one national character was Uncle Sam. But the oversized, triangular face with the startled expression, the protruding tummy, and the spindle legs were characteristics of them all. They were inspired by the Scottish legends related to Cox as a child by his parents, who were of English descent. His introduction of the Brownies to the world was accomplished by a poem called *The Brownies Ride*. Books followed in rapid succession, 13 in the series, all written as well as illustrated by Palmer Cox.

By the late 1890s, the Brownies were active in advertising. They promoted such products as games, coffee, toys, patent medicines, and rubber boots. 'Greenies' were the Brownies' first cousins, created by Cox to charm and to woo through the pages of the advertising almanacs of the G.G. Green Company of New Jersey. The Kodak Brownie camera became so popular and sold in such volume that the term became synonymous with this type of camera. (However, it was not endorsed by Cox. George Eastman named the camera but avoided royalty payment to Palmer Cox by doing his own version of them.)

Since the late 1970s a biography on Palmer Cox has been written, a major rock band had their concert T-shirts adorned with his Brownies, and a reproduction of the Uncle Sam candlestick is known to exist. Because of the resurging interest in Cox's Brownies, beware of other possible reproductions. Our advisors for this category are Don and Anne Kier; they are listed in the Directory under Ohio.

Ad, Brownie Rubber Stamps & the Greatest Show on Earth, 10x7", EX.. 15.00

Book, A Fox Grows Old, 1946, EX 12.00
Book, Another Brownie Book, NY, 1890, 1st ed, w/dust jacket, VG .. 250.00
Book, Brownie Clown of Brownie Town, 1908 .... 170.00
Book, Brownies & Other Stories, 1918, EX 40.00
Book, Brownies & Prince Florimel, Century, 1918, VG 70.00
Book, Brownies at Home, w/dust jacket, 1942, VG 35.00
Book, Funny Stories About Funny People, 1905, EX 35.00
Book, The Brownies, Their Book, 1897, EX 185.00
Bottle, soda; emb Brownies, M 30.00
Calendar, Brownies, color litho, 1898, EX 225.00
Cigar box, wood w/Our Brownies emb inner lid label, EX+ 145.00
Comic book, The Brownies, Dell Four-Color, #398, 1952, VG 20.00
Creamer, Scottsman head, majolica, 3¼" 125.00
Cup & saucer, demi; comical action Brownies, Ceramic Art Co ... 95.00
Figure, Chinaman, papier-mache head, 9", EX 450.00
Humidor, Policeman (Bobby) head, majolica, 6" 350.00
Magazine page, Ladies' Home Journal, Cox illus, ca 1890 .... 15.00
Match holder, Brownie on striker, majolica 235.00
Needle book, Brownies, 1892 World's Fair, rare 75.00
Paper doll, Indian Brownie, Lion Coffee, EX 35.00
Pencil box, rolling-pin shape, 15 Brownies in boat 70.00
Pitcher, china, Brownies playing golf on tan, 6" 150.00
Plate, porc, mk La Francaise, 7" 75.00
Print, Brownies fishing, matted, 1895, 13½x15½" 55.00
Rubber stamp, set of 12, NM 120.00
Sheet music, Dance of the Brownies 35.00
Sign, If You Like Chocolate Soda Drink Brownie, MCA Co, 59x21", G....230.00
Sign, orange crate; serving & drinking juice, Brownies Brand, 11x10"..35.00
Table set, brass, emb Brownies, 6", in orig box 95.00
Trade card, Estey Organ Co, playing instruments, 3x5" 18.00
Tray, china, 2 fencing Brownies, self hdls, 6¼x4½" 150.00

Brush-McCoy, Brush

George Brush began his career in the pottery industry in 1901 working for the J.B. Owens Pottery Co. in Zanesville, Ohio. He left the company in 1907 to go into business for himself, only to have fire completely destroy his pottery less than one year after it was founded. In 1909 he became associated with J.W. McCoy, who had operated a pottery of his own in Roseville, Ohio, since 1899. The two men formed the Brush-McCoy Pottery in 1911, locating their headquarters in Zanesville. After the merger, the company expanded and produced not only staple commercial wares but also fine artware. Lines of the highest quality such as Navarre, Venetian, Oriental, and Sylvan were equal to that of their larger competitors. Because very little of the ware was marked, it is often mistaken for Weller, Roseville, or Peters and Reed.

In 1918 after a fire in Zanesville had destroyed the manufacturing portion of that plant, all production was contained in their Roseville (Ohio) plant #2. A stoneware type of clay was used there, and as a result the artware lines of Jewel, Zuniart, King Tut, Florastone, Jetwood, Krakle-Kraft, and Panelart are so distinctive that they are more easily recognizable. Examples of these lines are unique and very beautiful, also quite rare and highly prized!

After McCoy died, the family withdrew their interests, and in 1925 the name of the firm was changed to The Brush Pottery. The era of hand-decorated art pottery production had passed for the most part, having been almost completely replaced by commercial lines. The Brush-Barnett family retained their interest in the pottery until 1981 when it was purchased by the Dearborn Company.

For more information we recommend *The Collector's Encyclopedia of Brush-McCoy Pottery* by Sharon and Bob Huxford; and *Sanford's Guide to Brush-McCoy Pottery*, Books I and II, written by Martha and Steve Sanford, our advisors for this category, and edited by David P. Sanford. They are listed in the Directory under California.

Of all the wares bearing the later Brush script mark, their figural cookie jars are the most collectible, and several have been reproduced. Information on Brush cookie jars (as well as confusing reproductions) can be found in *The Ultimate Collector's Encyclopedia of Cookie Jars* by Joyce and Fred Roerig; they are listed in the Directory under South Carolina. Beware! Cookie jars marked Brush-McCoy are not authentic.

Cookie Jars

Antique Touring Car, from $850 to	1,000.00
Boy w/Balloons, minimum value	800.00
Chick in Nest, #W38 (+), from $275 to	375.00
Cinderella Pumpkin, #W32	200.00
Circus Horse, gr (+), from $700 to	750.00
Clown, yel pants, #W22	200.00
Clown Bust, #W49, from $200 to	250.00
Cookie House, #W31, from $60 to	75.00
Covered Wagon, dog finial, #W30, (+), from $400 to	450.00
Cow w/Cat on Bk, brn, #W10 (+), from $100 to	125.00
Cow w/Cat on Bk, purple, minimum value (+)	900.00
Davy Crockett, no gold, mk USA (+), from $225 to	250.00
Dog & Basket, from $250 to	275.00
Donkey Cart, ears down, gray, #W33, from $300 to	400.00
Donkey Cart, ears up, #W33	700.00
Elephant w/Ice Cream Cone, #W18 (+)	450.00
Elephant w/Monkey on Bk	450.00
Fish, #W52 (+), from $400 to	450.00
Formal Pig, gold trim, #W7 Brush USA (+), from $350 to	400.00
Formal Pig, no gold, gr hat & coat (+), from $225 to	275.00
Gas Lamp, #K1, from $45 to	65.00
Granny, pk apron, bl dots on skirt, #W19, from $200 to	250.00
Granny, plain skirt, from $250 to	275.00
Happy Bunny, wht, #W25, from $150 to	175.00
Hen on Basket, unmk, from $75 to	100.00
Hillbilly Frog, from $3,000 to	3,500.00

Humpty Dumpty With Beanie and Bow Tie, rare gold trim, from $400.00 to $500.00. (Watch for reproductions.)

(Photo courtesy Joyce and Fred Roerig)

Humpty Dumpty, w/peaked hat & shoes, #W29	200.00
Laughing Hippo, #W27 (+), from $650 to	750.00
Little Angel (+), from $650 to	700.00
Little Boy Blue, gold trim, #K25, sm, from $650 to	750.00
Little Boy Blue, no gold, #K24 Brush USA, lg (+), from $600 to	650.00
Little Girl, #017 (+), from $450 to	500.00
Little Red Riding Hood, gold trim, mk, lg, (+) minimum value	800.00
Little Red Riding Hood, no gold, #K24 USA, sm, from $425 to	475.00
Night Owl, #W40, from $65 to	95.00
Old Clock, #W20, from $75 to	100.00

Old Shoe, #W23 (+), from $65 to	85.00
Panda, #W21 (+), from $175 to	200.00
Peter, Peter Pumpkin Eater, #W24, from $200 to	250.00
Peter Pan, gold trim, lg (+), from $725 to	775.00
Peter Pan, no gold, sm, from $425 to	475.00
Puppy Police, #W8 (+), from $450 to	500.00
Raggedy Ann, #W16, from $400 to	450.00
Sitting Pig, #W37 (+) from $325 to	375.00
Smiling Bear, #W46 (+), from $225 to	275.00
Squirrel on Log, #W26, from $60 to	80.00
Squirrel w/Top Hat, blk coat & hat, #W15, from $225 to	300.00
Squirrel w/Top Hat, gr coat, from $200 to	225.00
Stylized Owl, from $250 to	300.00
Stylized Siamese, #W41, from $375 to	425.00
Teddy Bear, ft apart, from $175 to	225.00
Teddy Bear, ft together, #014 USA, from $125 to	175.00
Treasure Chest, #W28, from $100 to	125.00

Miscellaneous

Bookends, Venetian, Indian chief, Ivotint, 1929, 5x5½"	300.00
Bowl, Moss Green, #01, 6", from $20 to	30.00
Butter crock, Corn, w/lid, #60, from $300 to	350.00
Candlestick, Vogue, blk geometrics on wht, 12", ea	325.00
Casserole, Grape Ware, w/lid, #178, 1913, from $150 to	200.00
Clock, Flapper, Onyx (gr), #336, 1926, 4½", from $75 to	150.00
Decanter, Onyx (bl), 7", from $100 to	150.00
Flower arranger, Princess Art Line, #560, 5½-6½", ea $30 to	40.00
Garden ornament, squirrel, #482, 8x8", from $100 to	125.00
Garden ornament, turtle, gr or brn, #487D, 6½", from $75 to	100.00
Hanging pot, #168, 1962, 8", from $24 to	40.00
Jardiniere, Egyptian, bl, 1923, 5½"	200.00
Jardiniere, Fancy Blended, #202, 1910, 10½", from $150 to	175.00
Jardiniere, Modern Kolorkraft, #260, 1929, 10", from $125 to	175.00
Jardiniere, Woodland, #2230, 7", +7½" ped, from $300 to	400.00
Jewelry caddy, mermaid	150.00
Jug, Decorated Ivory, #131, 1915, 2-qt, from $150 to	175.00
Lamp base, Kolorkraft, 1920s, 10½", from $125 to	175.00
Ornament, birdbath; wht, 2 frogs (standing/sitting), 7½"	200.00
Pitcher, Nurock, #351, 1916, 5-pt, 8½", from $165 to	200.00
Pitcher, Peacock, Bristol glaze, #351, from $900 to	1,500.00
Planter, penguin, #332A, from $30 to	40.00
Radio bug, 1927, 9½x3", from $500 to	950.00
Umbrella stand, Liberty, #73, 1912, from $600 to	800.00
Urn, Onyx (gr), #699, 11½", from $125 to	175.00
Vase, Bronze Line, palette mk USA 720, 8", from $2,500 to	40.00
Vase, Cleo, #042, 11¾", from $750 to	900.00
Vase, Onyx (brn), shouldered, 4"	45.00
Vase, Vestal, #729, 10½", from $250 to	300.00
Wall plaques, African Masks, mk USA, 10½", pr	300.00

Buffalo Pottery

The founding of the Buffalo Pottery in Buffalo, New York, in 1901, was a direct result of the success achieved by John Larkin through his innovative methods of marketing 'Sweet Home Soap.' Choosing to omit 'middle-man' profits, Larkin preferred to deal directly with the consumer and offered premiums as an enticement for sales. The pottery soon proved a success in its own right and began producing advertising and commemorative items for other companies, as well as commercial tableware. In 1905 they introduced their Blue Willow line after extensive experimentation resulted in the development of the first successful underglaze cobalt achieved by an American company. Between 1905 and 1909, a line of pitchers and jugs were hand decorated in historical, literary, floral, and outdoor themes. Twenty-nine styles are known to have been made.

Their most famous line was Deldare Ware, the bulk of which was made from 1908 to 1909. It was hand decorated after illustrations by Cecil Aldin. Views of English life were portrayed in detail through unusual use of color against the natural olive green cast of the body. Today the 'Fallowfield Hunt' scenes are more difficult to locate than 'Scenes of Village Life in Ye Olden Days.' A Deldare calendar plate was made in 1910. These are very rare and are highly valued by collectors. The line was revived in 1923 and dropped again in 1925. Every piece was marked 'Made at Ye Buffalo Pottery, Deldare Ware Underglaze.' Most are dated, though date has no bearing on the value. Emerald Deldare, made on the same olive body and on standard Deldare Ware shapes, featured historical scenes and Art Nouveau decorations. Most pieces are found with a 1911 date stamp. Production was very limited due to the intricate, time-consuming detail. Needless to say, it is very rare and extremely desirable.

Abino Ware, most of which was made in 1912, also used standard Deldare shapes, but its colors were earthy and the decorations more delicately applied. Sailboats, windmills, and country scenes were favored motifs. These designs were achieved by overpainting transfer prints and were often signed by the artist. The ware is marked 'Abino' in hand-printed block letters. Production was limited; and as a result, examples of this line are scarce today.

Commercial or institutional ware was another of Buffalo Pottery's crowning achievements. In 1917 vitrified china production began, and the firm produced for accounts worldwide. After 1956 all of their wares bore the name Buffalo China. In the early 1980s, the Oneida Company purchased Buffalo China and continued production of commercial and institutional ware. However, in 2004, Oneida divested itself of Buffalo china.

All items listed below are in near-mint to mint condition unless otherwise noted. Our advisor for this category is Lila Shrader; she is listed in the Directory under California. See also Bluebird China.

Key:
BC — Buffalo China
BC-Oneida — Buffalo China
    after 1983
BM — bottom mark
BS — bottom stamp

SL — side logo
SM — side mark
TL — top logo
TM — top mark

Abino

Tankard, signed C. Harris 1912, 7x6", $550.00. (Photo courtesy Smith & Jones Inc.)

Cup & saucer, nautical theme w/sailboats, sgn Harris 420.00
Plaque, sunset theme, shepherd, sheep, stream, sgn Stuart, 12"... 1,600.00
Plate, harbor scene w/sailboats/windmill, Stuart, 9¾", $250 to 485.00
Teapot, nautical theme, sgn Harris, no lid, 2-cup, 3½" 475.00
Tray, harbor scene, village/sailboats/windmill, Stuart, 13x10½" .. 1,500.00
Vase, sailboat on high seas at sunset, 6¾" 825.00
Vase, tall-masted ship, colorful clouded sky, corseted, 12" 1,450.00

Commercial China

All items listed below are of the heavy 'restaurant' weight china.

Advertising, cowboy hat for Buffalo China, TM, TL, 5½" dia 50.00
Ashtray, SCECo, blk on ivory, 3 rests, TM, 1920s, 4½" dia............ 45.00
Ashtray, Sea Cave, Multifleure Lamelle, 3 rests, TM, 4½" dia 65.00
Ashtray w/match holder center, Finers, blk script on ivory, TM, 6" dia.. 40.00
Ashtray/matchbox holder, Pat's Cafe...8100 S Hoover, TM, 6" dia..80.00
Bowl, natural wood HP grain effect, 1940s, 7½" 110.00
Butter pat, Blue Willow, 3" dia, from $6 to 12.00
Butter pat, cactus & tipsy rabbit, mc, TM, 1930s, 3¼" 55.00
Butter pat, ICC w/Xd golf club & tennis rackets, TM, 1920s, 3" ... 88.00
Butter pat, Plymouth pattern, gr on wht, 1925, 3"........................... 10.00
Butter pat, US Forest Service, gr on wht, TL, 1932, 3" 70.00
Chop plate, Morgan's Red Coach Tavern, hunt scene, TM, 11½" ..140.00
Compote, seaside scene border, waves splashing, ped ft, 2½x8" 50.00
Creamer, Connor Dairy Lunch, gr 4-leaf clovers, hdl, SL, 3½" 45.00
Creamer, Hotel Terminal/San Pedro, red & bl stripes, hdl, TM, ind, 3"...88.00
Creamer, Paso Del Norte, El Paso TX, hdl, SL, 4" 35.00
Creamer, Standard Oil & logo, no hdl, SM, 2¾" 245.00
Cup & saucer, Biltmore Hotel, Los Angeles, BM 45.00
Cup & saucer, demitasse; Hotel Metropole, SM & TM 22.00
Cup & saucer, demitasse; Multifleure, 1930s.................................. 78.00
Cup & saucer, demitasse; US Forestry, SL, TL, 1920s, 2½" 110.00
Cup & saucer, Lester's Diner/Open 24 Hours, cup: SL/saucer unmk....26.00
Egg cup, dbl; Hotel Metropole, SL, 3" 50.00
Mug, Arroyo Seco/#101, SM, 3¾".. 55.00
Mug, Tahoe Tavern, Rouge Ware, SM, 3¾" 75.00
Mug, World's Fair, Trylon & Perisphere, SL, 1939, 3½" 210.00
Pitcher, railroad-theme border, scrolled florals, bulbous, 5½" 28.00
Pitcher & bowl, Art Deco, Arrowhead Lodge, Arrowhead Springs, 1920s...375.00
Plate, Ahwahnee Hotel (for Yosemite Nat'l Park), BM, 1928, 9½" ..78.00
Plate, Country Garden, bl, gr or red, 10½", from $10 to................. 25.00
Plate, gr stripe on wht, BC-Oneida, 9½", from $5 to 10.00
Plate, Sea Cave Restaurant, Multifleure Lamelle, 8" 62.00
Plate, US Forest Service, TM, 1920s, 9½" 100.00
Platter, Hotel Atlantic, anchor & key TL, 1920s, 6½x4¼" 30.00
Platter, Long-Bell, TM, 1920s, 12½x8½", from $85 to 170.00
Platter, Mandalay, 9½x6½", from $9 to 18.00
Shakers, Roycroft, BM, 1928, 2¾", pr 490.00
Shaving mug, Wildroot, detachable metal hdl, SM, dbl sz, 3¾"...... 145.00
Spittoon, dk gr trim on ivory, Buffalo Pottery in script, 7½" dia 95.00
Toothpick holder, pk/peach, conch shell shape, 1930s, 2".............. 35.00
Vase/toothbrush holder, Art Deco, Arrowhead Lodge, BM, 1920s, 3"...75.00

Deldare

Ashtray/match holder, untitled Village Life scene, sgn EB, 3¼" .. 510.00
Ashtray/matchbox holder, Emerald Ware, sgn MGB.................1,850.00
Ashtray/matchbox holder, Scenes of Village Life Ye Olden Days, H Ford...410.00
Bowl, apple sauce/fruit; Fallowfield Hunt, Breaking Cover, 5½" ..225.00
Bowl, cereal; Ye Olden Days, 5½"...165.00
Bowl, Fallowfield Hunt Breaking Cover, A Lang, 9" 435.00
Bowl, nut; Ye Lion Inn, unsgn, 3¼x8" 490.00
Bowl, punch; untitled Fallowfield Hunt scenes, 9x14½" 5,350.00
Bowl, Ye Village Tavern, sgn G Beatty, 9"......................................250.00
Candleholder, shield-bk; untitled Village Scene, hdl, HB, 7" ...1,150.00
Candlesticks, Village Scene, drilled for wiring, 8½", pr................590.00
Chamberstick, untitled Village scene, sgn EB, w/finger ring, 5½" ...525.00
Chocolate pot, Ye Village Street, H Ford, 10" 1,350.00
Creamer & sugar bowl, Fallowfield scene, Breaking Cover, w/lid.. 395.00
Creamer & sugar bowl, Scenes of Village Life, Ye Olden Days, w/lid.285.00
Cup & saucer, bouillon; Fallowfield Hunt, both sgn O Sauter, hdls ...760.00
Desk set, Emerald Ware, 4x9" tray+2 2" ink pots (no lids)........2,400.00
Hair receiver, Ye Village scene, 1" factory hole in lid, 4¾" dia.....465.00
Humidor, There Was an Old Sailor, Emerald Ware, sgn CB, 8" .. 1,200.00
Humidor, Ye Lion Inn, 8-sided 7"..385.00

Mug, Emerald Ware, Dr Syntax Again Fills His Glass..., 4½" 300.00
Mug, Fallowfield Hunt, At Three Pigeons, Ditmars, 3½" 440.00
Mug, Fallowfield Hunt, 4¼" 325.00
Pitcher, Dr Syntax Stopt by Highwaymen, H Robin, 8-sided, 6" .. 900.00
Pitcher, Fallowfield Hunt, Breaking Cover, 8-sided, unsgn, 10" ... 600.00
Pitcher, tankard, Fallowfield Hunt, The Hunt Supper, 12½".....1,225.00
Pitcher, tankard, Village Scene, Great Controversy, 1909, 12½"...1,025.00
Pitcher, tankard, Ye Olde English Village, unusual wht int, 6½" ...1,050.00
Plaque, Fallowfield Hunt, Breakfast at Three Pigeons, N Sheehan, 12".970.00
Plaque, Ye Lion Inn, P Holland, pierced for hanging, 12½" 485.00
Plate, cake; Ye Village Gossips, W Foster, open fancy hdls, 10½"....380.00
Plate, calandar; 1910, 9½" 1,460.00
Plate, Fallowfield Hunt, Breaking Cover, M Bron, 10" 290.00
Plate, Fallowfield Hunt, The Death, unsgn, 8½" 185.00
Plate, Fallowfield Hunt, The Start, sgn MHF, 9¼" 190.00
Plate, Mr Pickwick Addresses the Club, L Anna, 7½" 485.00
Plate, soup; Fallowfield Hunt, Breaking Cover, E Dowman, 9" 325.00
Powder dish, Ye Village Street, M Harison, w/lid, 5" 435.00
Relish dish, Fallowfield Hunt, The Dash, A Lang, 6½x12" 575.00
Sugar bowl, untitled Village Scene, 6-sided, 3½" 360.00
Tile, Dr Syntax Sketching Lake, Emerald Ware, J Gerhardt, 6½" dia...975.00
Tile, Dr Syntax Taking Possession of...Living, Emerald Ware, Robin, 6" ...690.00
Tile, Fallowfield Hunt, untitled rider & horse, Ed J Mars, 6" dia..300.00
Tiles, Village scenes, 6 4" tiles fr in sm Mission-style tabletop ..2,250.00
Toothpick holder, untitled Village Scene, 2¼" 250.00
Tray, calling card; Fallowfield Hunt, O Sauter, tab hdls, 7½" dia.. 395.00
Tray, Dr Syntax Mistakes a..., Emerald Ware, M Gerhardt, 10x13¾" ... 1,450.00
Tray, dresser; Dancing Ye Minuet, W Foster, 9x12", from $280 to...390.00
Tray, pin; Art Nouveau border, AH intertwined in center, 3½x6½" ..540.00
Tray, pin; Ye Olden Days, sgn GHS, 3½x6½" 210.00
Vase, untitled Village Scene, fashionable people, sgn BS, 8" 1,350.00
Vase, Ye Village Parson/Ye Village Schoolmaster, sgn EB, 8½"...1,120.00

Miscellaneous

Berry set, mc roses & vines, 8½" serving bowl+6 5" ind 98.00
Bone dish, Blue Willow, 3½x6½", from $35 to............................... 88.00
Bowl, berry; Queen, tiny pk roses, emb rim, 9¼" 26.00
Bowl, rim soup; dbl pk rose border/gr leaves/gold border, 9"....... 42.00
Bowl, vegetable; Bangor, rust & bl flowers w/gr scrolls, 8½" 55.00
Butter dish, Bluebird, domed lid w/knob & perforated ice ring, 7½"..165.00
Butter pat, Blue Willow, 1916, 3½" dia, from $12 to 34.00
Butter pat, Bonrea, ornate scrolled teal-gr border, gold trim, 3¼" .. 12.00
Butter pat, Geranium in rich cobalt, 3¼"..................................... 125.00
Butter pat, Masonic emblem TM, 1925, 3¼" 18.00
Butter pat, Pink Rose sprays w/rich gold, 3"................................. 19.00
Butter pat, Princess, gr floral border w/gold, 3¼" 20.00
Butter pat, Vienna, dk bl on ivory w/gold, 3", from $10 to............. 35.00
Butter pat, Wild Rose, sponged gold border, 3", from $8 to............ 22.00
Butter tub, Bluebird, vertical tab hdls, perforated icer insert, 4" 55.00
Canisters, Cinnamon, Nutmeg & Pepper, bl & wht floral, 3¼", 3 pcs...88.00
Canisters, Coffee, Tea, Rice, Flour, Sugar, bl/wht floral, 7", 5 pcs.. 165.00
Chamber pot, Chrysanthemum, w/lid, 7½"................................... 118.00
Chamber set, roses, pitcher+bowl+soap dish+chamber pot/lid+shaving mug..325.00
Chamber slop jar, pk tint w/gold trim, scroll hdls, w/lid, 12"........ 135.00
Chocolate pot, floral on sprayed gr ground w/gold, 11½" 135.00
Creamer, Roosevelt bears, w/hdl, child's ind, 2½"......................... 345.00
Cup & saucer, demitasse; Blue Willow.. 32.00
Cup & saucer, Wild Rose, sponged gold border, from $11 to.......... 35.00
Egg cup, dbl; Blue Willow, 3½".. 65.00
Egg cup set, Blue Willow, 4 1¾" cups on 4¾" indented stand....... 255.00
Feeding dish, Campbell Kids-like, Grace Drayton, ABC rim, 8" ... 90.00
Feeding dish, Campbell Kids-like, Grace Drayton, 7½"................. 65.00
Feeding dish, warm water; Bluebird, in metal fr, orig cap, 8" 145.00

Game set, 11x15" deer platter+6x9½" varied wild game plates.... 245.00
Gravy boat, Gaudy Willow, cobalt/rust/gr HP, no liner, 3½x6" 200.00
Gravy boat w/attached liner, Bluebird, hdl, 3¼x5¾" 118.00
Jug, Gaudy Willow, mc w/rich gold, flat lid w/recessed hdl, 6" 365.00
Jug, Iris, bl transfer on wht, flat lid w/recessed hdl, 6"................... 92.00
Jug, John Paul Jones, bl & wht, 1907, 9½", from $300 to 365.00
Jug, Mason, teal gr, classic scenes at collar, fruit & flowers, 8½"... 425.00
Jug, Rip Van Winkle, mc, 1906, 6" 345.00
Jug, Robin Hood, HP, mc, 8¼", from $325 to 525.00
Jug, Whaling City, souvenir of New Bedford, MA, 6" 485.00
Matchbox holder, Blue Willow (for penny matchbox), 2¾x5½" dia .. 135.00
Mug, Bing & Nathan Complete...Furnishings, SM, Buffalo NY, 4½" ..55.00
Mug, Celebration, Meditation, Vacation, etc, 4½", from $50 to 125.00
Mug, children at play decal on yel ware-type body, hdl, child sz, 4"..20.00
Mug, Fallowfield scene on Olde Ivory (not Deldare), 4½" 138.00
Pitcher, Chrysanthemum, bl transfer on wht, Cairo shape, 11" ... 155.00
Pitcher, Gaudy Willow, cobalt/rust/gr HP w/gold, 6¼" 475.00
Pitcher, Geranium, cobalt w/mc HP/gold trim, cylindrical, 7½" ..228.00

Pitcher, Glorianna, standing Glorianna on reverse, light crazing 9", $460.00. (Photo courtesy Smith & Jones Inc.)

Pitcher, Gunner, teal gr w/rich gold, bulbous, 7" 315.00
Pitcher, Roosevelt Bears, mc, 8"..1,800.00
Plate, Bangor, cobalt/dk red/gold on ivory, 10½" 35.00
Plate, Blue Willow, 10", from $20 to.. 45.00
Plate, Bluebird, 7¼", from $18 to... 45.00
Plate, Bonrea, gr w/gold scalloped edge, 8", from $12 to 32.00
Plate, calendar; 1911, Bing & Nathan, Buffalo NY, some fading, 7¼"..55.00
Plate, Christmas, 1955, scene: Christmas Carol by Dickens, 9½" .. 55.00
Plate, commemorative; Erie Tribe of Improved..., teal gr, 7½" 112.00
Plate, commemorative; Washington's Home at Mt Vernon, mc, 7½" 90.00
Plate, commemorative; Woman's Christian Temperance..., cobalt, 9" ...195.00
Plate, Gaudy Willow, cobalt/rust/gr w/gold, HP, 1909, 9½" 165.00
Plate, historical; White House, Washington, cobalt, 10" 60.00
Plate, historical; White House, Washington, teal gr, 10" 30.00
Plate, Roosevelt Bears, Western Teddy+Teddy G center+10 bears, 10"...395.00
Plate, Wanamaker Dept Store, 1861 Jubilee 1911, BM, 4½".......... 26.00
Platter, Blue Willow, 12x9½"... 88.00
Platter, Blue Willow w/gold, 16x12"... 225.00
Platter, Wild Rose w/sponged gold, 12x9½" 75.00
Relish dish, Blue Willow, shell form, 1909, 4x7" 65.00
Sauceboat, Blue Willow, attached liner, hdls, 4½x7½" 150.00
Tea set, Baby Bunting, pot+cr/sug w/lid+4 plates, child sz 140.00
Teapot, Argyle, w/orig infuser, bl on wht vitreous, mk 85.00
Teapot, Japan, cobalt on ivory, hdl, squarish, 5¼" 335.00
Vase, Geranium, cobalt, rose-bowl style, 3¾" 260.00
Vase, pk & yel rose sprays w/gold, flared rim, 8½" 95.00

Burley-Winter

Located in Crooksville, Ohio, this family venture had its roots in a company started in 1872 by William Newton Burley and Wilson Winter. From 1885 it operated under the name of Burley, Winter and Brown, reverting back to Burley & Winter after Mr. Brown left the company in 1892. They merged with the Keystone Pottery about 1900 (its founders were brothers Z.W. Burley and S.V. Burley), and merged again in 1912 with the John G. Burley Pottery. This company was dissolved in the early 1930s. A variety of marks were used.

Jardiniere, rust & gr mottle w/geometrics at shoulder, 8x10½"	120.00
Mug, old sailor emb on brn gloss, 4⅝"	40.00
Vase, gr & pk mottle, hdls at waist, unmk, 12¼"	450.00
Vase, lion-head medallions on purple/rose mottle, hdls, 21x17"	450.00
Vase, medallion emb on orange & gr matt, rim-to-hip hdls, 17½"	700.00
Vase, nudes emb on pk & gray matt, sm nicks, 17"	200.00
Vase, pk & gr mottle, hdls, unmk, 12¼"	525.00
Vase, pk & gr mottled, shouldered, flared rim, #201-K, 12¼"	200.00
Vase, purple & bl semimatt, wide shoulder, 12"	180.00

Burmese

Burmese glass was patented in 1885 by the Mount Washington Glass Co. It is typically shaded from canary yellow to a rosy salmon color. The yellow is produced by the addition of uranium oxide to the mix. The salmon color comes from the addition of gold salts and is achieved by reheating the object (partially) in the furnace. It is thus called 'heat sensitive' glass. Thomas Webb of England was licensed to produce Burmese and often added more gold, giving an almost fuchsia tinge to the salmon in some cases. They called their glass 'Queen's Burmese,' and this is sometimes etched on the base of the object. This is not to be confused with Mount Washington's 'Queen's Design,' which refers to the design painted on the object. Both companies added decoration to many pieces. Mount Washington-Pairpoint produced some Burmese in the late 1920s and Gundersen and Bryden in the '50s and '70s, but the color and shapes are different. Our advisors for this category are Dolli and Wilfred Cohen; they are listed in the Directory under California. In the listings that follow, examples are assumed to have the satin finish unless noted 'shiny.' See also Lamps, Fairy.

Syrup pitcher, enamel flowers, repousse rim and lid, 6", $4,600.00.
(Photo courtesy Jackson's International Auctioneers & Appraisers of Fine Art & Antiques)

Biscuit jar, Webb, florals, 8½" to top of hdl	650.00
Bottle, scent; butterfly/floral branch, rnd w/silver lid, 5½"	920.00
Bottle, scent; melon ribs, cupped rim on long neck, ribbed stopper, 7"	800.00
Bottle, scent; Webb, gilt leaves/berries, spherical, 4"	900.00
Bowl, Mt WA, appl feather, bk: appl 2-branch floral, 4-fold neck, 7"	3,450.00
Bowl, Mt WA, wht daises on gr leafy stems, squat/ftd, 7" L	425.00
Bowl, spider mums, 4-fold pleated rim, mfg flaw, 10½" dia	1,435.00
Creamer, Mt WA, conical, tight ruffled rim, 5"	250.00

Creamer, Mt WA, shiny, ewer form, 5½"	345.00
Cruet, Mt WA, shiny, ribbed squat body & stopper, 7"	865.00
Marmalade, Mt WA, pine needles/cones, SP mts, ovoid, 6"	490.00
Pitcher, Mt WA, elongated slim form w/ped ft, 11"	575.00
Pitcher, Mt WA, lg oval shape w/sqd hdl, 6½x8"	550.00
Pitcher, Mt WA, rose/Thos Hood poem, wide ovoid, sqd hdl, 5½x7½"	6,900.00
Rose bowl, Gundersen, 3½" H	140.00
Rose bowl, Webb, acorns/leaves, squatty w/6-sided rim, 3x4"	345.00
Rose bowl, Webb, berries/leaves, Queen's mk, 2x3"	288.00
Rose jar, Mt WA, ivy/Dickens quote, ovoid w/sqd hdls, sm lid, 7x6"	8,920.00
Salt cellar, Webb, oak branch, ovoid w/ruffled rim, 1⅜"	1,250.00
Shade, Mt WA, shiny, ruffled rim, jack-in-pulpit form, 5"	150.00
Toothpick holder, Mt WA, Dmn Quilt, bulbous w/sq mouth, 2¾"	180.00
Toothpick holder, Mt WA, floral, paneled w/4 sm ft, 2¼"	520.00
Toothpick holder, shiny, hat form w/bl threading at collar, 2"	285.00
Toothpick holder, shiny, tightly fluted rim, rigaree below, 2½x3"	635.00
Tumbler, Mt WA, rose buds, 3¾"	750.00
Vase, bud; Mt WA, slim/elongated, 7"	300.00
Vase, delicate floral/wht dots, dbl-bulb shape, long neck, 6½"	700.00
Vase, jack-in-pulpit; Mt WA, slim w/tightly ruffled flared rim, 9"	230.00
Vase, lily; Mt WA, 10"	230.00
Vase, lily; Mt WA, 3-fold rim, 15"	345.00
Vase, lily; Pairpoint, wht flowers inside 4-fold rim, 1991, 9"	200.00
Vase, lily; Webb, roses/flowers, 7"	200.00
Vase, Mt WA, daisies on random vines, spherical w/stick neck, 12"	1,125.00
Vase, Mt WA, Dmn Quilt, shouldered w/4-lobe rim, appl ft, pontil, 6"	460.00
Vase, Mt WA, egg shape w/3-fold rim, 3 reeded ft, raspberry pontil, 7"	325.00
Vase, Mt WA, Egyptian ftd urn w/2 above-rim hdls, 7½"	345.00
Vase, Mt WA, floral, cup rim, stick neck, wide squatty bottom, 8"	1,150.00
Vase, Mt WA, floral, diagonal ribs, free-form 4-pointed rim, 3x4"	430.00
Vase, Mt WA, floral (pointillism style), flared w/elongated neck, 10"	2,400.00
Vase, Mt WA, Hawthorne, bulbous w/stick neck, 10"	575.00
Vase, Mt WA, Japanese dragons/stylized flowers, stick neck, 10"	1,700.00
Vase, Mt WA, needlepoint-lined floral, stick neck w/sm hdls, 13"	920.00
Vase, Mt WA, prunus sprays, wht beadwork at rim, bottle form, 12"	920.00
Vase, Mt WA, rose encircling Hood poem, elongated teardrop, 12"	2,585.00
Vase, Mt WA, shiny, flattened Hobnail, rigaree below scalloped rim, 4"	800.00
Vase, Mt WA, storks fly above pyramids, w/gold, 11x5¾"	10,925.00
Vase, Mt WA, violets, wht beadwork at 4-lobe rim, lg hdls, 4½"	1,200.00
Vase, Mt WA, wht seeds on autumn branches, ovoid w/3-fold rim, 3½"	575.00
Vase, Mt WA, yel/orange flowers w/gr stems, stick neck, 20½"	1,150.00
Vase, Webb, acorns/oak leaves, star-shaped everted rim, Queen's mk, 7"	690.00
Vase, Webb, berries on gr leaves, bulbous w/scalloped rim, 3¼"	375.00
Vase, Webb, bird/3 red roses, bk: butterfly, bulbous, Queen's mk, 8"	920.00
Vase, Webb, crimped/ruffled, 2½"	75.00
Vase, Webb, floral, bulbous w/long can neck & low hdls, 5"	520.00
Vase, Webb, floral, ring collar/raspberry prunt, +3-leg metal fr, 5"	400.00
Vase, Webb, mc prunus, rnd w/stick neck, disk ft, 7½"	600.00
Vase, Webb, oak leaves/acorns, squatty w/flared point-crimped rim, 4"	1,380.00
Vase, Webb, oak leaves/berries, ruffled rim on long cone neck, 3½"	400.00
Vase, Webb, pine cones/needles, melon ribs, cupped top, 4½"	325.00

Butter Molds and Stamps

The art of decorating butter began in Europe during the reign of Charles II. This practice was continued in America by the farmer's wife who sold her homemade butter at the weekly market to earn extra money during hard times. A mold or stamp with a special design, hand carved either by her husband or a local craftsman, not only made her product more attractive but also helped identify it as hers. The pattern became the trademark of Mrs. Smith, and all who saw it knew that this was her butter. It was usually the rule that no two farms used the same mold within a certain area, thus the many variations and patterns available to the collector today. The most valuable are those which have animals, birds, or odd shapes. The most sought-after motifs are the eagle, cow, fish, and rooster. These works of early folk art are quickly disappearing from the market.

Molds

Acorns (2) & leaves divided by twisted rope, 6x4½" 135.00
Anchor, rectangular, 5x4" 195.00
Anchor, rope border, tight hairline, 1860s, 3½" 150.00
Birds in nests, worm holes, 2-pc, screw eyes ea end, 1⅝x11¾" 130.00
Cow, stylized, rope-twist border, dk patina, 4⅞" 220.00
Cow (dbl), dvtl corners, 1800s, 6x3" w/7" plunger 350.00
Cow standing at fence, rope-twist border scrubbed, 4¼" 225.00
Fish (3 lg, 2 sm) swimming, notched border, 1840s, 3" 1,000.00
Flower (stylized), cvd border, rectangular, 19th C, 2½x8x4¾" 235.00
Flowers/cow/farming couple, 5-part, hinged, canted sides, 20½" .. 330.00
Flowers/star/house/deer, 5-part, hinged, canted sides, 7½x7½" 175.00
Goat lying in grass w/fence beyond, detailed, 1880s, 2⅛" 100.00
Hearts (4) in 2 different designs, EX cvg, lollipop, 4" 225.00
Horse in grassy spot below tree, dbl-lined border, 2⅛" 225.00
Maple leaf, detailed, notched border, ca 1880, 3½" 100.00
Olive branch, scrubbed, 4⅞" 100.00
Pomegranate, case mk Patd Apr 17, 1886, 3¾" 135.00
Rooster crowing & standing on branches, chips, 1960s, 4⅝" 150.00
Sheaves of wheat (2), dvtl corners, 5x6¼x4"+hdl 150.00
Sheep in grass, branch over bk, hairlines, 1860s, 3⅛" 225.00
Strawberry, scrubbed, 1¾" 200.00
Sunflower, single line border, ca 186, 4⅜" 200.00
Swan, wings out, EX details, mini, 1¾" 330.00
War bonnet w/feathers, vine border, hdl, cracked/edge damage, 2" .. 110.00

Stamps

Acorn, detailed, lightly scrubbed, 1-pc hdl, 4" 400.00
Am eagle w/shield in talons, shallow cvg, rfn, 1-pc hdl, 2⅝" 230.00
Am eagles (facing) w/shields & arrows, EX patina, 1-pc hdl, 3½" ... 285.00
Basket of mixed flowers, worm holes/scrubbed, 3½" 285.00
Beaver w/rope-twist border, EX patina, 3¼" 110.00
Bird w/long legs & short beak, threaded hdl, scratch, 3¾" 250.00
Bud & leaves, coggled rim, rpr crack, lollipop, 7½x3¾" 250.00
Chip cvgs w/central flower, EX patina/lt scrubbing, elongated, 12" ... 80.00
Compass star & hearts, scrubbed, 1-pc hdl, 4¼" 490.00
Cow, EX details, threaded hdl, 4⅛" 880.00
Cow named Doll, 1-pc hdl, scrubbed, 3⅛" 255.00

Cow under a tree, grass at his feet, turned handle, 4½" diameter, $270.00.
(Photo courtesy Jackson's International Auctioneers & Appraisers of Fine Art & Antiques)

Cow's head, rfn, 3" 110.00
Daisy, soft natural finish, 3¾" dia 55.00
Deer & sunburst w/X-hatching, scrubbed, hdl missing, 4" 575.00
Eagle & star, deeply cvd, 2-pc hdl, rfn/splits, 4¼" 345.00
Eagle on laurel branch (lg image), coggled rim, 1-pc hdl, 4½" 580.00
Eagle w/star & laurel branch, 1-pc hdl, 4½" 345.00
Fish swimming among water plants, 1-pc hdl, scrubbed, 3" 700.00

Flower basket (EX/complex), 2-pc hdl w/damage, 3½" 880.00
Heart w/in circles, scrubbed, rpl hdl, 4¼" 125.00
Hen w/EX details, long threaded hdl, scrubbed, chip, 4" 575.00
Leaves around circumference, scrubbed, 3x2½" 110.00
Longhorn cow at gate in grass, 2 lg leaves over bk, 1860s, 4⅝" 175.00
Partridge, delicate cvg, threaded hdl, 4⅛" 800.00
Peafowl in grass under tree, dbl-line notched border, 1880s, 2" 75.00
Pheasant, crisp cvg, old rfn, rpl hdl, 4⅜" 285.00
Pomegranate w/coggled rim, 1-pc cvd hdl, cracked/scrubbed, 4½" .. 195.00
Ram w/curled horns, scalloped border, unusual hdl, rfn, 3½" 350.00
Rooster amid circles, folky syle, 1-pc hdl, scrubbed, 4⅜" 175.00
Rose, EX detail, 1-pc hdl, scrubbed, age cracks, 3¾" 330.00
Semicircle w/X-hatched heart & leaves, scrubbed, inset hdl, 3½" ... 260.00
Songbird on 3 leaves, 1-pc hdl, scrubbed, 3¾" 175.00
Star flower w/ridged edges, lollipop hdl, 9½x4" 660.00
Strawberry, simple cvg, scrubbed, 3¼" 110.00
Tree & sm flowers, 1-pc hdl, scrubbed, 4" 150.0

Buttonhooks

The earliest known written reference to buttonhooks (shoe hooks, glove hooks, or collar buttoners) is dated 1611. They became a necessary implement in the 1850s when tight-fitting high-button shoes became fashionable. Later in the nineteenth century, ladies' button gloves and men's button-on collars and cuffs dictated specific types of buttoners, some with a closed wire loop instead of a hook end. Both shoes and gloves used as many as 24 buttons each. Usage began to wane in the late 1920s following a fashion change to low-cut laced shoes and the invention of the zipper. There was a brief resurgence of use following the 1948 movie 'High Button Shoes.' For a simple, needed utilitarian device, buttonhook handles were made from a surprising variety of materials: natural wood, bone, ivory, agate, and mother-of-pearl to plain steel, celluloid, aluminum, iron, lead and pewter, artistic copper, brass, silver, gold, and many other materials in lengths that varied from under 2" to over 20". Many designs folded or retracted, and buttonhooks were often combined with shoehorns and other useful implements. Stamped steel buttonhooks often came free with the purchase of shoes, gloves, or collars. Material, design, workmanship, condition, and relative scarcity are the primary market value factors. Prices range from $1.00 to over $500.00, with most being in the $10.00 to $100.00 range. Buttonhooks are fairly easy to find, and they are interesting to display.

See the Buttonhook Society listing in the Directory under Clubs, Newsletters, and Catalogs.

Buttonhook/penknife, ivory side plates, man's 50.00
Collar buttoner, stamped steel, advertising, closed end, 3" 20.00
Glove hook, gold-plated, retractable, 3" 90.00
Glove hook, loop end, agate hdl, 2½" 60.00
Shoe hook, colored celluloid hdl, 8" 15.00
Shoe hook, lathe-trn hardwood hdl, dk finish, 8" 15.00
Shoe hook, SP w/blade, repousse hdl, Pat Jan 5 1892, 5" 40.00
Shoe hook, stamped steel, advertising, 5" 8.00
Shoe hook, sterling, floral & geometrics, 8" 55.00
Shoe hook, sterling, Nouveau lady's face, 6½" 75.00
Shoe hook, sterling, W w/arrow, hammered Florentine decor, mk. 55.00
Shoe hook/shoehorn, combination, steel & celluloid, 9" 35.00

Bybee

The Bybee Pottery was founded in 1845 in the small town of Bybee, Kentucky, by the Cornelison family. Their earliest wares were primarily stoneware churns and jars. Today the work is carried on by sixth-generation Cornelison potters who still use the same facilities and production methods to make a more diversified line of pottery. From a fine white clay mined only a few miles from the potting shed itself, the shop produces vases, jugs, dinnerware, and banks in a variety of colors, some of which are shipped to the larger cities to be sold in department stores and specialty shops. The bulk of their wares, however, is sold to the thousands of tourists who are attracted to the pottery each year.

Jar, orange (uranium oxide) on stoneware, 3-hdl, 17½" 450.00
Mug, gr crystalline, sgn Cornelison, 3½" 25.00
Vase, cattails emb on purple to bl matt, slim w/flaring rim, 11" ... 180.00

Cabat

From its inception in New York City around 1940, through various types of clays, designs, and glazes, the Rose Cabat 'Feelie' evolved into present forms and glazes in the late 1950s, after a relocation to Arizona. Rose was aided and encouraged through the years by her late husband Erni. Their small 'weed pots' are readily recognizable by their light weight, tiny necks, and soft glazes. Pieces are marked with a hand-incised 'Cabat' on the bottom.

Vase, butterscotch w/brn drips/spatters, onion form, #384, 3¼x2" ..400.00
Vase, gr w/purple-bl, #841/47, 2¾" 385.00
Vase, ivory w/olive gr & yel, #841/28, 2⅝" 335.00
Vase, lilac over spring gr, plum form, #840, 3¾" 515.00
Vase, multi-gr on charcoal, shouldered, #34/481, 2¾x2¼" 380.00
Vase, ochre/wht/chartreuse w/gr drips, lower emb bands, 7⅜x3½" . 2,200.00
Vase, pumpkin w/brn streaks & speckles, 5x2¾" 650.00
Vase, shaded yel, globular, #d, 3x2¼" 300.00
Vase, toffee & ivory w/brn speckles over lt gr, #841, 3¼" 480.00
Vase, turq w/olive gr, 3⅞" 850.00

Calendar Plates

Calendar plates were advertising giveaways most popular from about 1906 until the late 1920s. They were decorated with colorful underglaze decals of lovely ladies, flowers, animals, birds and, of course, the 12 months of the year of their issue. During the 1950s they came into vogue again but never to the extent they were originally. Those with exceptional detailing or those with scenes of a particular activity are most desirable, so are any from before 1906.

1895, months in center w/floral & swirl border, 8" 270.00
1905, floral (bl) center, months along rim, 10" 70.00
1907, 4 ladies in vintage clothing, Pownall Hardware, 10" 105.00
1908, lg red rose w/leaves, MC Kittle, Bell Vernon PA, 9" 40.00
1909, autumn mountain scene, Sterling China, 9¼" 50.00
1909, dog's face in center, Evergreen Supply Co, 9½" 70.00
1909, Jack Russell terrier's portrait, gold trim, 9¼" 60.00
1909, rope encircles months, bl rim, 9¼" 25.00
1909, tabby cat, Comp AE Palmer, Dresden China, 8⅜" 45.00
1909, William Jennings Bryan sepia-tone portrait, 9¼" 90.00
1910, angels (2) ringing in the New Year, 8½" 55.00
1910, holly berries on 3 sides w/Hauri Bros Grocery ad, 7¼" 45.00
1910, lady center w/seasonal flowers between ea group of 3 months, 9" . 55.00
1910, magnolias w/holly leaves & berries, Am China Co, 8½" 50.00
1910, months on pgs of open book, gr ivy & forget-me-nots, 6¾" . 40.00
1910, winter church scene & summer lakeside home, months in 3 groups ... 48.00
1911, deer scene, wildlife & months at rim, 8½" 80.00
1911, Niagara Falls scene, gold trim, 9¼" 65.00
1911, sea & shoreline w/sm boat on beach, 7⅝" 50.00
1911-12, dbl-year, pk ribbons & roses, 8½", from $65 to 75.00
1912, Lincoln, Garfield & McKinley, Am flag, 9¼" 70.00
1913, lady & cherub at creek's bank w/lady & man reflection 50.00
1914, deer at stream, 7" 35.00
1914, mallards in flight, 9⅛" 35.00
1914, Washington Capitol, gold scalloped rim, 9⅛" 65.00
1916, trapper in canoe, 9¼" 35.00
1918, American flag, Theodore Goodman Furniture/Carpets..., 8"..45.00
1920, The Great War, 8¼" 40.00
1922, hunting dogs & game, 9¼" 45.00
1924, Happy New Year, antique auto, months grouped to 1 side, EX.100.00
1963, God Bless This House...1963, brn on wht, Royal Staffordshire, 9". 30.00
1973, Bountiful Butterfly theme, Wedgwood 55.00

Calendars

Calendars are collected for their colorful prints, often attributed to a well-recognized artist of the period. Advertising calendars from the turn of the century often have a double appeal when representing a company whose tins, signs, store displays, etc., are also collectible. Our advisor for this category is Robert Doyle; he is listed in the Directory under New York. See also Parrish, Maxfield; Railroadiana; Winchester.

1893, S Allen's Sons, military man & horse, full pad, 16x11", EX. 90.00
1895, Nordeck 10¢ Cigars, die-cut, blond lady, full pad, 11x8½", EX.130.00
1896, Norton Bros Cans..., folding pocket type, 3½", EX+ 375.00
1900, Hood's Sarsaparilla, 2 Victorian girls die-cut, EX 50.00
1904, Marlin Repeating Rifles & Shot Guns, cb w/sm blk pad, 6", EX. 925.00

1905, DeLaval Cream Separator, full date pad, NM, $1,100.00.

1907, Harrington & Richardson Arms, figure on showshoes, 27x14", NM..3,100.00
1910, Western Dressed Beef, wood fr, complete, vertical, NM..... 615.00
1921, Lane Lumber, Off to Market..., farm scene, 22x18", EX 140.00
1930, Peters Cartridge Co, mountain lion/hunter, fr, 35", complete, M.. 1,050.00
1931, Western Champion Ammunition, Bird Scents, 28x15", EX .750.00
1933, Hercules Powder, men w/dogs, Wyeth, December only, 30x13", VG.245.00
1933, Rett Bros...Taxidermists, Scouting for Game, Russeau, 22x14", VG..70.00
1937, Hercules Powder, Autumn Fields, Wileur, partial pad, 30x13", EX.. 80.00
1947, Harrington & Richardson Arms, 6 game-bird images, 24x18", EX.. 80.00

California Faience

California Faience was founded in 1913 as 'The Tile Shop' by Chauncey R. Thomas in Berkeley, California. He was joined by William V. Bragdon in 1915 who became sole owner in 1938. The product line was apparently always marked 'California Faience,' which became the company's legal name in 1924. Production was reduced after 1933, but the firm stayed in business as a studio and factory until it closed in 1959. Products consisted of hand-pressed tiles and slip-cast vases, bowls, flower frogs, and occasional figures. They are notable for high production quality and aesthetic simplicity. Items produced before 1934 were of dark brown or reddish brown clay. After that, tan clay was used. Later production consisted mainly of figurines made by local artists. The firm made many of the tiles used at Hearst Castle, San Simeon, California. From 1928 to 1930 a line marked 'California Porcelain' was produced in white porcelain at West Coast Porcelain Manufacturers in Millbrae.

The multicolored art tiles are especially popular with collectors. Generally speaking, matt glazes were in use mostly before 1921 and are rare. Prices continue to be depressed, especially for glossy glaze and low bowls. A few rare tiles and matt pieces have brought strong prices. Collectors are quite fussy about condition; impared pieces sell for very low prices. Almost all known pieces are marked. Unmarked pieces in a pale creamy clay were made from cast-off West Coast Porcelain molds by Potlatch pottery in Seattle, Washington, from 1934 to 1941. Unmarked tiles are presently being made from original molds by Deer Creek Pottery, Grass Valley, California (deercreekpottery.com). They can be distinguished from the old tiles as they are thinner and in each case there is a repetition of the raised design on the back. Our advisor for this category is Dr. Kirby William Brown; he is listed in the Directory under California. Dr. Brown is currently researching a book on this topic and welcomes input from collectors.

Bowl, bl (shaded) gloss, globular, 3x6" 50.00
Bowl, bl (shaded) gloss, wide, flared, 5x11½" 150.00
Bowl, blk matt, incurvate rim, broad ped, 10½" 165.00
Bowl, dk bl/turq gloss, flat w/wavy cuenca rim, 2x9" 50.00
Bowl, raspberry/turq gloss, 2x8½" 140.00
Bowl, rose/turq gloss, incurvate rim, wide mouth, low, 5½" 190.00
Bowl, turq gloss, squat, tapered, 3x5" 60.00
Bowl, variegated pale bl gloss, lobed, 3x6" 180.00
Candlesticks, bl (shaded) gloss, 4½x4¼", pr 80.00
Figurine, peasant girl & babe, sgn Stevick, mc gloss, 11" 375.00
Flower frog, boat shape, turq gloss, 1½x6x3" 70.00
Flower frog, rnd w/3 crabs, turq gloss, 2x5" 165.00
Flower frog, turq gloss, 2½" dia 15.00
Flower frog, 2 ducks side by side, turq gloss, 6x5½" 50.00
Humidor, blk gloss, porc, 6x6½" 375.00
Lamp, wave pattern, creme matt, porc, squat, tapered, 7" 1,025.00
Plate, saz leaf & 2 flowers, mc gloss, sgn CRT, 9¼" 825.00

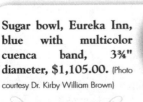

Sugar bowl, Eureka Inn, blue with multicolor cuenca band, 3¾" diameter, $1,105.00. (Photo courtesy Dr. Kirby William Brown)

Sugar bowl, Hotel Petaluma, yel gloss w/mc band, 4½" W 900.00
Tea bowl, turq gloss, 2x4½" 40.00
Tile, cypress tree by ocean, mc matt, 5½x5½" pr (in copper) 3,675.00
Tile, dolphin, mc matt, 2x5" 350.00
Tile, fleur-de-lis, wht/dk bl gloss, 4x4½" 150.00
Tile, long-horned goat, yel/dk bl gloss, 6x6" 500.00
Tile, ship on waves, mc gloss, 5½x5½" (in fr) 710.00

Tile, sq flower, mc gloss, 6x6" 300.00
Tile, stylized tulip, mc gloss, 5x5" 225.00
Tile, 6-petal flower, bl/wht gloss, 4x4" 160.00
Trivet, flower basket, mc gloss, 5½" dia 390.00
Trivet, peacock, mc gloss, 5½" dia 320.00
Trivet, saz leaf & flowers, mc gloss, hexagonal, 6¼" 210.00
Vase, bl (shaded) gloss, ovoid w/raised rim, 8½" 190.00
Vase, dk bl gloss, cylindrical, ribbed, 5" 260.00
Vase, dk bl matt, cylindrical, for brushes, 6" 315.00
Vase, dk bl matt, incised panels & buds, volcano form, 3¼" 1,680.00
Vase, gr matt, squat apple w/raised rim, 2½" 570.00
Vase, gr microcrystalline matt, flask shape, 11" 345.00
Vase, incised lovebirds & tree, oxblood gloss, ovoid, 7" 790.00
Vase, maroon gloss, ovoid, 5" 85.00
Vase, pale yel, porc, globular w/flared lip 60.00
Vase, plum gloss, Pueblo Indian form, 5" 105.00
Vase, rose-pk gloss, porc, ovoid, 6" 200.00
Vase, tan matt, cvd Art Deco leaves, porc, ovoid, 6" 340.00
Vase, turq gloss, narrow trumpet, 7" 120.00
Vase, turq gloss, sgn Shibuya, club shape, 10" 340.00
Vase, turq gloss, volcano form, 4" 95.00
Vase, yel gloss, volcano form, 4" 120.00

California Perfume Company

D.H. McConnell, Sr., founded the California Perfume Company (C.P. Company; C.P.C.) in 1886 in New York City. He had previously been a salesman for a book company, which he later purchased. His door-to-door sales usually involved the lady of the house, to whom he presented a complimentary bottle of inexpensive perfume. Upon determining his perfume to be more popular than his books, he decided that the manufacture of perfume might be more lucrative. He bottled toiletries under the name 'California Perfume Company' and a line of household products called 'Perfection.' In 1928 the name 'Avon' appeared on the label, and in 1939 the C.P.C. name was entirely removed from the product. The success of the company is attributed to the door-to-door sales approach and 'money back' guarantee offered by his first 'Depot Agent,' Mrs. P.F.E. Albee, known today as the 'Avon Lady.'

The company's containers are quite collectible today, especially the older, hard-to-find items. Advanced collectors seek 'go with' items labeled Goetting & Co., New York; Goetting's; or Savoi Et Cie, Paris. Such examples date from 1871 to 1896. The Goetting Company was purchased by D.H. McConnell; Savoi Et Cie was a line which they imported to sell through department stores. Also of special interest are packaging and advertising with the Ambrosia or Hinze Ambrosia Company label. This was a subsidiary company whose objective seems to have been to produce a line of face creams, etc., for sale through drugstores and other such commercial outlets. They operated in New York from about 1875 until 1954. Because very little is known about these companies and since only a few examples of their product containers and advertising material have been found, market values for such items have not yet been established. Other items sought by the collector include products marked Gertrude Recordon, Marvel Electric Silver Cleaner, Easy Day Automatic Clothes Washer, pre-1915 catalogs, California Perfume Company 1909 through 1914 calendars, and 1926 Calopad Sanitary Napkins.

There are hundreds of local Avon Collector Clubs throughout the world that also have C.P.C. collectors in their membership. If you are interested in joining, locating, or starting a new club, contact the National Association of Avon Collectors, Inc., listed in the Directory under Clubs, Newsletters, and Catalogs. Those wanting a National Newsletter Club or price guides may contact Avon Times, listed in the same section. Inquiries concerning California Perfume Company items and the companies or items mentioned in the previous paragraphs should be directed toward our advisor, Dick Pardini, whose address is given under California. (Please send a large SASE and be sure to request clearly the information you are seeking; not interested in Avons, 'Perfection' marked C.P.C.'s, or Anniversary Keepsakes.) For more information we recommend *Bud Hastin's Avon Collector's Encyclopedia.*

Note: Our values are for items in mint condition. A very rare item or one in super mint condition might go for 10% more. Damage, wear, missing parts, etc., must be considered; items judged to be in only good to very good condition should be priced at up to 50% of listed values, with fair to good at 25% and excellent at 75%. Parts (labels, stoppers, caps, etc.) might be evaluated at 10% of these prices.

Mission Garden Perfume, clear and frosted glass bottle with gold label shaped as a California mission, empty, ca 1922 – 1925, in original box, $450.00. (Photo courtesy Monsen & Baer)

Narcissus Perfume, 1925, 1-oz, M	120.00
Narcissus Perfume, 1929-30, mc box, 1-oz, MIB	165.00
Natoma Rose Perfume, 1914-15, glass bottle/stopper, ½-oz, M	165.00
Natoma Rose Talcum Powder, tin container, 1911, 3 ½-oz, MIB	257.50
Olive Oil, glass bottle, 1915, 8-oz, rare, M	93.00
Perfume Sample Set, 1923, MIB	175.00
Powder Sachet, bottle, ca 1915, M	48.00
Powder Sachets, 1890s, M	90.00
Powder tin, 2 nude babies play w/giant rose ea side, 1912, M	110.00
Radiant Nail Powder, tin container, 1923, M	25.00
Rose Pomade, jar, milk glass, 1914, M	55.00
Shampoo Cream, milk glass, 1908, 4-oz, M	75.00
Sweet Sixteen Face Powder, paper container, 1918, M	91.00
Tooth Tablet, aluminum lid, clear on milk wht bottom, 1920s, M	50.00
Tooth Wash, emb bottle w/label, 1915, M	105.00
Trailing Arbutus Face Powder, paper container, 1925, MIB	40.00
Trailing Arbutus Talcum, tin container, 1920, 1-lb, M	70.00
Verna Talc, mc container, 1928, 4-oz, MIB	95.00
Vernafleur Face Powder, tin container, 1925, M	20.00
Vernafleur Perfume, 1923, 1-oz, MIB	140.00
Violet Almond Meal, tin container, 1923, 4-oz, M	50.00
Witch Hazel Cream, 1904, 2-oz tube, MIB	53.00

Calling Cards, Cases, and Receivers

The practice of announcing one's arrival with a calling card borne by the maid to the mistress of the house was a social grace of the Victorian era. Different messages (condolences, a personal visit, or a good-bye) were related by turning down one corner or another. The custom was forgotten by WWI. Fashionable ladies and gents carried their personally engraved cards in elaborate cases made of such materials as embossed silver, mother-of-pearl with intricate inlay, tortoise shell, and ivory. Card receivers held cards left by visitors who called while the mistress was out or 'not receiving.' Calling cards with fringe, die-cut flaps that cover the name, or an unusual decoration are worth about $3.00 to $4.00, while plain cards usually sell for around $1.00.

Cases

Ivory w/cvd floral border & initials, China, 1880s, 4½x3"	750.00
Silver, bright-cut scrolls/presentation, J Deacon & Sons	180.00
Silver, cartouch w/eng/emb eagle/flowers, mk B, 3½x2½"	235.00
Tortoiseshell w/MOP inlay flowers, 4½x3"	500.00
Wood, Oriental scenic cvgs, 4⅜x2¾"	120.00

Receivers

Bronze w/emb scrolls & flowers, 1880s, 2⅜x18x14¼"	360.00
Cast metal bat w/wings outstretched, brn enamel, Europe, 5½"	385.00
Champleve & HP porc w/courting scene, 1900, 11½x6½"	950.00
Silver, standing Nouveau maid centers lobed tray, WMFB, 8½x14"	865.00
SP, etched glass vase w/butterfly ea side, 12½"	850.00
SP, figural bird on leaf by etched glass vase, SH&M #116	650.00
SP, Nouveau lady reclines by pond w/lilies/lily pads, WMF #9610, 10" L	210.00
SP (rstr) w/etched glass vase, 10½x12½"L	85.00
SP Greenaway girls w/dog, Derby #3537, rstr, 7¼"	550.00

Camark

The Camden Art and Tile Company (commonly known as Camark) of Camden, Arkansas, was organized in the fall of 1926 by Samuel J. 'Jack' Carnes. Using clays from Arkansas, John Lessell, who had been hired as art director by Carnes, produced the initial lustre and iridescent Lessell wares for Camark ('CAM'den, 'ARK'ansas) before his death in December 1926. Before the plant opened in the Spring of 1927, Carnes brought John's wife, Jeanne, and stepdaughter, Billie, to oversee the art department's manufacture of Le-Camark. Production by the Lessell family included variations of J.B. Owens' Soudanese and Opalesce and Weller's Marengo and Lamar. Camark's version of Marengo was called Old English. They also made wares identical to Weller's LaSa. Pieces made by John Lessell back in Ohio were signed 'Lessell,' while those made by Jeanne and Billie in Arkansas during 1927 were signed 'Le-Camark.' By 1928 Camark's production centered on traditional glazes. Drip glazes similar to Muncie Pottery were produced, in particular the green drip over pink. In the 1930s commercial castware with simple glossy and matt finishes became the primary focus and would continue so until Camark closed in the early 1960s. Between the 1960s and 1980s the company operated mainly as a retail store selling existing inventory, but some limited production occurred. In 1986 the company was purchased by the Ashcraft family of Camden, but no pottery has yet been made at the factory.

Our advisor for this category is Tony Freyaldenhoven; he is listed in the Directory under Arkansas.

Basket, ivory scratch ware, bl/gr int, hdl, unmk, 9"	60.00
Basket, Rose-Green Overflow, decor hdl, ftd, unmk, 6¾"	120.00
Bowl, bl/wht stipple, ftd, unmk, 3½x9¾"	250.00
Bowl, cream mottle, scalloped edge, ftd, unmk, 9½x4¾"	180.00
Bowl, ivory scratch ware, bl/gr int, 4-scallop rim, unmk, 9x4x9"	80.00
Bowl, Rose Pink, HP tulip, scalloped edge, hdls, ftd, unmk, 13¾"	250.00
Candlestick, bl/wht stipple, Arkansas stamp, 1¼", ea	50.00
Charger, flowers, Lechner, Arkansas sticker, 13¼"	400.00
Dealer sign, Gun Metal, unmk, 6"	300.00
Figurine, dog, wht w/blk spots, ears & tail (up), umk, 10"	300.00
Figurine, horse, Delphinium Blue, Arkansas sticker, 10x8"	100.00
Flower vase, Green-White Overflow, Arkansas stamp, 5¼"	160.00
Flower vase, Orange-Green Overflow, unmk, 4¾"	140.00
Ginger jar, flower, gold on blk, Arkansas stamp, LeCamark, 8½"	700.00
Humidor, bl/wht stipple, Arkansas stamp	16.00
Lamp base, ivory crackle w/emb flower, hdls, ftd, unmk, 8½"	500.00
Pitcher, brn stipple, Brown Arkansas sticker, 10¾"	250.00

Planter, Frosted Green, ruffled rim, Arkansas sticker, 4½" 60.00
Planter, gray/bl mottle, ruffled rim, unmk, 4¾" 100.00
Sign, Camark Pottery on Arkansas state shape, melon gr, 6⅜" 360.00
Vase, bl/gold, Deco style, high hdls, ftd, unmk, 13½" 60.00
Vase, Burgundy, emb flower, integral hdls, ftd, USA #571, 7½" 45.00
Vase, cream mottle, unmk, 5½" 70.00
Vase, Emerald Green, integral hdls, USA Camark N #40, 14" 80.00
Vase, gr & bl matt, Arkansas stamp, 16½" 1,600.00
Vase, gr crackled matt w/gold, bulbous, gold Arkansas sticker, 10" .900.00
Vase, gray/bl mottle, flared, ftd, #345, 14" 300.00
Vase, gray/bl mottle, sq Deco syle, unmk, 9¼" 275.00
Vase, Mirror Black, shouldered, 1st block letter, 4½" 60.00
Vase, Old English Ivory, shouldered, Camark, 8½" 700.00
Vase, Oxford w/silver lustre, LeCamark, 8½" 1,000.00
Vase, Pastel Blue-Green Overflow, 1st block letter, 7½" 140.00
Vase, Purple-Green Overflow, integral hdls, Deco syle, unmk, 7½"..300.00
Vase, Rose-Green Overflow, shouldered, unmk, 2¾" 50.00
Vase, yel, Nouveau floral, hdl, #800-R, bl/gold Arkansas sticker, 14".225.00

Cambridge Art Pottery

The Cambridge Art Pottery (not to be confused with the Cambridge Art Tile Works of Covington, Kentucky) was founded in 1901 in Cambridge, Ohio. Charles Upjohn, formerly from the Weller Pottery, was hired as designer and modeler. Cambridge would be known mostly for three artware lines: Terrhea, their variation of Rookwood's Standard Glaze line, underglaze painted with polychrome slips and covered in an amber overglaze; Oakwood, a flambe glaze mix of autumnal colors; and Acorn, a smooth and satiny matt green finish in the Arts and Crafts style. They also produced a commercially successful utilitarian line, Guernsey, named after the county for which Cambridge was the seat. After 1908 only the Guernsey line remained, so in 1909 the pottery name was changed to Guernsey Earthenware. Cambridge pieces are usually stamped with a CAP mark ('AP' within a larger 'C') with the name of the line above or below. Our advisor for this category is Suzanne Perrault; she is listed in the Directory under New Jersey.

Vase, clover blossom on standard glaze, 6", $200.00. (Photo courtesy Treadway Gallery Inc.)

Tankard, Terrhea, Indian in full headdress, #212, 1902-10, 14½" ... 3,500.00
Vase, Terrhea, floral, #974, 12⅝" 200.00
Vase, Terrhea, floral, sgn MW, squat, 3x5½" 60.00
Vase, Terrhea, mums, CAP logo, #226, 15⅛" 275.00

Cambridge Glass

The Cambridge Glass Company began operations in 1901 in Cambridge, Ohio. Primarily they made crystal dinnerware and well-designed accessory pieces until the 1920s when they introduced the concept of color that was to become so popular on the American dinnerware mar-

ket. Always maintaining high standards of quality and elegance, they produced many lines that became bestsellers; through the '20s and '30s they were recognized as the largest manufacturer of this type of glassware in the world.

Of the various marks the company used, the 'C in triangle' is the most familiar. Production stopped in 1958. For a more thorough study of the subject, we recommend *Colors in Cambridge Glass* by the National Cambridge Collectors, Inc.; their address may be found in the Directory under Clubs. *Glass Animals, Second Edition,* by Dick and Pat Spencer is a wonderful source for an in-depth view of that particular aspect of glass collecting. They are listed in the Directory under Illinois. See also Carnival Glass; Glass Animals.

Achilles, crystal, bowl, bonbon; #3900/130, hdls, ftd, 7½" 50.00
Achilles, crystal, compote, #3121, blown, 5⅜" 75.00
Achilles, crystal, cordial, #3121, 1-oz.................................... 75.00
Achilles, crystal, cup, demitasse; #3400/69 .... 65.00
Achilles, crystal, plate, luncheon; #3900/22, 8½" 16.00
Achilles, crystal, saucer, demitasse; #3400/69 .... 20.00
Achilles, crystal, tumbler, water; #3121, ftd, 10-oz.................... 40.00
Achilles, crystal, vase, #278, ftd, 11" 225.00
Adonis, crystal, candlestick, #627, ea................................... 35.00
Adonis, crystal, ice pail #1402/52...................................... 135.00
Adonis, crystal, sugar bowl, #3900/41 .... 25.00
Adonis, crystal, urn, #3500/41, w/lid, 10" 395.00
Candlelight, crystal, butter dish, #3400/52, 5" 325.00
Candlelight, crystal, cocktail, #3114, 3-oz 40.00
Candlelight, crystal, cocktail shaker, #P101, 36-oz.................... 245.00
Candlelight, crystal, cruet, #3900/100, w/stopper, 6-oz 175.00
Candlelight, crystal, cup, #3900/17...................................... 33.00
Candlelight, crystal, decanter, #1321, ftd, 28-oz....................... 265.00
Candlelight, crystal, nut cup, #3400/71, 4-ftd, 3" 70.00
Candlelight, crystal, plate, dinner; #3900/24, 10½"...................... 95.00
Candlelight, crystal, tumbler, juice; #3776, 5-oz....................... 30.00
Candlelight, crystal, vase, #279, ftd, 13" 195.00
Candlelight, crystal, vase, #6004, ftd, 6" 100.00
Caprice, bl or pk, ashtray, #216, 5".................................... 22.00
Caprice, bl or pk, bowl, fruit; #18, 5" 75.00
Caprice, bl or pk, bowl, salad; #84, 15" 175.00
Caprice, bl or pk, compote, #136, tall, 7"............................. 100.00
Caprice, bl or pk, ice bucket, #201 .... 175.00
Caprice, bl or pk, tumbler, juice; #310, flat, 5-oz 75.00
Caprice, bl or pk, vase, #254, blown, 6" 200.00
Caprice, bl or pk, wine, #6, 3-oz...................................... 100.00
Caprice, crystal, bowl, #82, shallow/cupped, 4-ftd, 13½".............. 50.00
Caprice, crystal, bowl, jelly; #151, hdls, 5"........................... 15.00
Caprice, crystal, cocktail, #301, blown, 3-oz........................... 22.00
Caprice, crystal, decanter, #187, w/stopper, 35-oz..................... 195.00
Caprice, crystal, pitcher, #179, ball shape, 32-oz..................... 135.00
Caprice, crystal, shakers, #96, flat, pr 35.00
Caprice, crystal, tumbler, tea; #300, ftd, 12-oz........................ 20.00
Caprice, crystal, vase, #344, crimped top, 4½" 175.00
Chantilly, crystal, bowl, bonbon; ftd, hdls, 7" 25.00
Chantilly, crystal, bowl, flared, 4-ftd, 12" 55.00
Chantilly, crystal, butter dish, ¼-lb 325.00
Chantilly, crystal, cordial, #3600, 1-oz 50.00
Chantilly, crystal, creamer.. 18.00
Chantilly, crystal, hat, sm 225.00
Chantilly, crystal, oil cruet, w/stopper, w/hdl, 6-oz 135.00
Chantilly, crystal, plate, cake; tab hdls, 13½" 65.00
Chantilly, crystal, plate, salad; 8" 12.50
Chantilly, crystal, saucer, #3900/17....................................4.00
Chantilly, crystal, sugar bowl.. 18.00
Chantilly, crystal, tumbler, water; #3775, ftd, 10-oz 20.00

Chantilly, crystal, vase, keyhole base, 12" 110.00
Chantilly, crystal, wine, #3775, 2½-oz 32.00
Cleo, bl, bowl, cranberry; 3½" 70.00
Cleo, bl, bowl, vegetable; oval, Decagon, 9½" 145.00
Cleo, bl, candy box 295.00
Cleo, bl, creamer, #867, ftd 40.00
Cleo, bl, pitcher, #955, w/lid, 62-oz 550.00
Cleo, bl, platter, 12" 195.00
Cleo, bl, tumbler, #3077, ftd, 5-oz 60.00
Cleo, pk, gr, yel or amber, basket, Decagon, hdls, uptrn sides, 7" ... 30.00
Cleo, pk, gr, yel or amber, bowl, celery; #1083, oval, 11" 75.00
Cleo, pk, gr, yel or amber, cocktail, #3077, 2½-oz 35.00
Cleo, pk, gr, yel or amber, salt dip, 1½" 95.00
Cleo, pk, gr, yel or amber, syrup pitcher, glass lid 250.00
Cleo, pk, gr, yel or amber, vase, 9½" 155.00
Daffodil, crystal, basket, #55, low ft, hdls, 6" 40.00
Daffodil, crystal, brandy, #1937, ¾-oz 80.00
Daffodil, crystal, cordial, #3779, 1-oz 100.00
Daffodil, crystal, creamer, #254 .... 25.00
Daffodil, crystal, cup, #11770 .... 25.00
Daffodil, crystal, oil cruet, #293, 6-oz 145.00
Daffodil, crystal, plate, bonbon; #3400/1181, hdls, 6" 22.50
Daffodil, crystal, plate, cake; #1495, 11½" 80.00
Daffodil, crystal, shakers, #360, squat, pr 65.00
Daffodil, crystal, sherbet, tall, #1937, 6-oz 22.00
Daffodil, crystal, sherry, #1937, 2-oz 70.00
Daffodil, crystal, tumbler, #1937, ftd, 10-oz 28.00
Daffodil, crystal, tumbler, iced tea; #3779, ftd, 12-oz 40.00
Daffodil, crystal, wine, #3779, 2½-oz 60.00
Decagon, bl, bowl, almond; #611, ind, 2½" 50.00
Decagon, bl, bowl, bouillon; #866, w/liner 35.00
Decagon, bl, creamer, #979, ftd 20.00
Decagon, bl, mayonnaise, #983, w/liner & ladle 65.00
Decagon, bl, plate, grill; #1200, 10" 50.00
Decagon, bl, tray, pickle; #1082, 9" 40.00
Decagon, bl, tumbler, #3077, ftd, 8-oz 22.00
Decagon, pastel colors, bowl, cereal; #1011, belled, 6" 20.00
Decagon, pastel colors, cordial, #3077, 1-oz 40.00
Decagon, pastel colors, cup, #865 .... 6.00
Decagon, pastel colors, ice pail, #851 .... 45.00
Decagon, pastel colors, plate, dinner; 9½" 40.00
Decagon, pastel colors, plate, salad; #597, 8½" 14.00
Decagon, pastel colors, tray, celery; #1083, 11" 30.00
Diane, crystal, basket, ftd, hdls, 6" 35.00
Diane, crystal, cabinet flask 295.00
Diane, crystal, claret, #1066, 4½-oz 50.00
Diane, crystal, cocktail shaker, glass top 250.00
Diane, crystal, cup 20.00
Diane, crystal, decanter, ftd, lg 225.00
Diane, crystal, ice bucket, w/chrome hdl 120.00
Diane, crystal, oyster cocktail, #1066, 5-oz 25.00
Diane, crystal, pitcher, ball shape 225.00
Diane, crystal, plate, salad; 8" 14.00
Diane, crystal, plate, torte; 14" 60.00
Diane, crystal, sugar bowl, #3400, scroll hdl 22.00
Diane, crystal, tumbler, juice; #3106, ftd, 5-oz 22.00
Diane, crystal, vase, flower, 13" 165.00
Elaine, crystal, basket, hdls, uptrn sides, 6" 30.00
Elaine, crystal, bowl, tab hdls, 11" 95.00
Elaine, crystal, candy box, rnd 125.00
Elaine, crystal, compote, 5½" 45.00
Elaine, crystal, decanter, lg, ftd 235.00
Elaine, crystal, goblet, #1402 .... 40.00
Elaine, crystal, hat, 9" 395.00

Elaine, crystal, parfait, #3121, low stem, 5-oz 40.00
Elaine, crystal, pitcher, #3900/115, 78-oz 250.00
Elaine, crystal, plate, service; 4-ftd, 12" 60.00
Elaine, crystal, shakers, ftd, pr 45.00
Elaine, crystal, sherbet, low, #1402 .... 20.00
Elaine, crystal, tumbler, tea; #3121, ftd, 12-oz 40.00
Elaine, crystal, tumbler, water; #1402, ftd, 9-oz 25.00
Elaine, crystal, vase, cornucopia, #3900/575, 10" 195.00
Elaine, crystal, vase, ftd, 6" 75.00
Gloria, crystal, bowl, cereal; sq, 6" 35.00
Gloria, crystal, compote, tall, 7" 45.00
Gloria, crystal, goblet, #3115, 9-oz 28.00
Gloria, crystal, oil cruet, w/stopper, tall, ftd, w/hdl & stopper 110.00
Gloria, crystal, plate, dinner; sq 65.00
Gloria, crystal, plate, tea; #3400/60, 7½" 14.00
Gloria, crystal, saucer, AD; rnd 12.00
Gloria, crystal, tray, sandwich; center hdl, 11" 35.00
Gloria, crystal, vase, 11" 125.00
Gloria, gr, pk or yel, bowl, cranberry; 3½" 75.00
Gloria, gr, pk or yel, candy box, 4-ftd, tab hdl 225.00
Gloria, gr, pk or yel, creamer, tall, ftd 35.00
Gloria, gr, pk or yel, pitcher, ball shape, 80-oz 495.00
Gloria, gr, pk or yel, plate, bread & butter; 6" 15.00
Gloria, gr, pk or yel, plate, salad; sq 20.00
Gloria, gr, pk or yel, saucer, sq 6.00
Gloria, gr, pk or yel, tumbler, #3130, ftd, 12-oz 50.00
Gloria, gr, pk or yel, vase, #1308, 6" 85.00
Imperial Hunt Scene, colors, bowl, 8" 95.00
Imperial Hunt Scene, colors, humidor 595.00
Imperial Hunt Scene, colors, plate, #554, 7" 22.50
Imperial Hunt Scene, colors, sugar bowl, #842, flat, w/lid 150.00
Imperial Hunt Scene, colors, tumbler, #3085, ftd, 2½-oz 65.00
Imperial Hunt Scene, crystal, bowl, cereal; 6" 20.00
Imperial Hunt Scene, crystal, creamer, flat 15.00
Imperial Hunt Scene, crystal, cup, #933/481 .... 50.00
Imperial Hunt Scene, crystal, mayonnaise, w/liner 40.00
Imperial Hunt Scene, crystal, plate, #810, 9½" 20.00
Imperial Hunt Scene, crystal, tumbler, #3085, flat, 5-oz 20.00
Marjorie, crystal, bottle, oil & vinegar; 6-oz 350.00
Marjorie, crystal, cafe parfait, #7606, 5½-oz 45.00
Marjorie, crystal, compote, #4004, 5" 70.00
Marjorie, crystal, creme de menthe, #7606 .... 100.00
Marjorie, crystal, decanter, #7606, 28-oz 400.00
Marjorie, crystal, jug, #104, 30-oz 265.00
Marjorie, crystal, saucer 30.00
Marjorie, crystal, tumbler, #3750, ftd, 10-oz 25.00
Marjorie, crystal, tumbler, #8858, 5-oz 15.00
Marjorie, crystal, tumbler, whiskey; #7606, 1½-oz 25.00
Mt Vernon, amber or crystal, ashtray, #68, 4" 12.00
Mt Vernon, amber or crystal, bowl, fruit; #6, 5¼" 10.00
Mt Vernon, amber or crystal, cake stand, #150, ftd, 10½" 35.00
Mt Vernon, amber or crystal, celery; #98, 11" 17.50
Mt Vernon, amber or crystal, coaster, #70, ribbed, 3" 5.00
Mt Vernon, amber or crystal, creamer, #8, ftd 10.00
Mt Vernon, amber or crystal, cup, #7 .... 6.00
Mt Vernon, amber or crystal, ice bucket, #92, w/tongs 40.00
Mt Vernon, amber or crystal, oyster cocktail, #41, 4-oz 9.00
Mt Vernon, amber or crystal, pitcher, #13, 66-oz 95.00
Mt Vernon, amber or crystal, plate, bread & butter; #19, 6⅜" 4.00
Mt Vernon, amber or crystal, plate, salad; #5, 8½" 7.00
Mt Vernon, amber or crystal, shakers, #28, pr 22.50
Mt Vernon, amber or crystal, vase, #58, 7" 30.00
No 520 Byzantine, Peach Blo, amber or gr, bowl, cream soup 25.00
No 520 Byzantine, Peach Blo, amber or gr, bowl, fruit; #928, 5¼" 22.50

No 520 Byzantine, Peach Blo, amber or gr, cup, #933 .... 18.00
No 520 Byzantine, Peach Blo, amber or gr, plate, grill; 10" 35.00
No 520 Byzantine, Peach Blo, amber or gr, plate, luncheon; 8" 18.00
No 520 Byzantine, Peach Blo, amber or gr, sherbet, #3060, high, 6-oz . 22.50
No 520 Byzantine, Peach Blo, amber or gr, sugar bowl, #138 .... 20.00
No 520 Byzantine, Peach Blo, amber or gr, tumbler, #3060, ftd, 10-oz. 25.00
No 703 Florentine, gr, claret, #3060, 4½-oz 27.50
No 703 Florentine, gr, creamer, #138 .... 15.00
No 703 Florentine, gr, platter, #901, oval, 12½" 75.00
No 703 Florentine, gr, saucer, #494 ....3.00
No 703 Florentine, gr, tumbler, juice; #3060, 5-oz 12.00
No 704 Windows Border, colors, bowl, cereal; 6" 25.00
No 704 Windows Border, colors, bowl, soup; 8½" 33.00
No 704 Windows Border, colors, butter dish, #920 .... 125.00
No 704 Windows Border, colors, cafe parfait, #3075, 5½-oz........... 35.00
No 704 Windows Border, colors, cheese plate, #468 .... 35.00
No 704 Windows Border, colors, cup, demitasse; #925 .... 35.00
No 704 Windows Border, colors, ice bucket, #957, w/bail, tall 125.00
No 704 Windows Border, colors, parfait, #3060, 5-oz 35.00
No 704 Windows Border, colors, plate, service; 10½" 75.00
No 704 Windows Border, colors, plate, 8½" 20.00
No 704 Windows Border, colors, tray, celery; #652, 11" 45.00
No 704 Windows Border, colors, tumbler, #3060, ftd, 12-oz 25.00
No 704 Windows Border, colors, tumbler, whiskey; #3075, 2-oz.... 30.00
Nude stem, ashtray, Pistachio, #3011 .... 350.00
Nude stem, bud vase, royal bl, #3011/26 .... 750.00
Nude stem, candlestick, Crown Tuscan, #3011, 9", ea 150.00
Nude stem, candy box, Carmen w/satin stem, #3011/28 ....2,000.00
Nude stem, cigarette box, Crown Tuscan, blk enamel trim, #3011 . 1,250.00
Nude stem, cocktail, Pistachio, #3011, 3-oz................................ 275.00
Nude stem, compote, amber, #3011/27, 5⅜" W 350.00
Nude stem, cordial, royal bl, #3011/14, 1-oz 450.00
Nude stem, goblet, banquet; royal bl, #3011/1 .... 400.00
Nude stem, sauterne, royal bl, #3011/8, 4½-oz 400.00
Portia, crystal, basket, 7" 350.00
Portia, crystal, brandy, #3121, low ft, 1-oz................................. 60.00

Portia, crystal, candleholder, double; $45.00.

Portia, crystal, candlestick, #3400/646, keyhole shape, 5", ea 35.00
Portia, crystal, cigarette holder, urn shape 60.00
Portia, crystal, cup, sq, ftd 25.00
Portia, crystal, ice bucket, w/chrome hdl 125.00
Portia, crystal, mayonnaise, #3400/11, w/liner & ladle.................. 60.00
Portia, crystal, pitcher, #3400/100, 76-oz 195.00
Portia, crystal, plate, bread & butter; 6½" 7.50
Portia, crystal, puff box, ball shape, w/lid, 3½".......................... 225.00
Portia, crystal, tray, sandwich; hdls, 11" 40.00
Portia, crystal, tumbler, #3400/38, 12-oz 30.00
Portia, crystal, tumbler, tea; #3121, ftd, 12-oz 28.00
Portia, crystal, vase, ftd, 8"... 100.00
Portia, crystal, vase, ped ft, 11" 110.00
Portia, crystal, wine, #3130, 2½-oz 38.00

Rosalie, amber or crystal, bowl, cream soup 20.00
Rosalie, amber or crystal, cup 25.00
Rosalie, amber or crystal, platter, 12" 95.00
Rosalie, amber or crystal, sugar bowl, #867, ftd.......................... 13.00
Rosalie, amber or crystal, vase, ftd, 6½" 60.00
Rosalie, bl, pk or gr, bottle, French dressing.............................. 125.00
Rosalie, bl, pk or gr, cocktail, #3077, 3½-oz 20.00
Rosalie, bl, pk or gr, plate, salad; 7½" 15.00
Rosalie, bl, pk or gr, sugar shaker 325.00
Rosalie, bl, pk or gr, vase, 6" 90.00
Rose Point, crystal, ashtray, #721, sq, 2½" 35.00
Rose Point, crystal, bell, dinner; #3121..................................... 150.00
Rose Point, crystal, bowl, fruit; #3400/56, 5¼" 80.00
Rose Point, crystal, brandy, #3121, 1-oz 135.00
Rose Point, crystal, butter dish, #506, rnd 210.00
Rose Point, crystal, cocktail shaker, #3400/157, metal top........... 210.00
Rose Point, crystal, decanter, #1380, sq, 26-oz........................... 695.00
Rose Point, crystal, ice bucket, #1402/52 .... 210.00
Rose Point, crystal, marmalade, #147, 8-oz 195.00
Rose Point, crystal, pitcher, #3900/118, 32-oz 400.00
Rose Point, crystal, plate, salad; #3900/22, 8" 20.00
Rose Point, crystal, plate, torte; #3500/38, 13" 185.00
Rose Point, crystal, shakers, #1468, egg shape, pr 135.00
Rose Point, crystal, sherry, #3106, 2-oz 65.00
Rose Point, crystal, tray, sandwich; #3400/10, center hdl, 11" 145.00
Rose Point, crystal, tumbler, #3500, ftd, 2½-oz 75.00
Rose Point, crystal, tumbler, cordial; #3400/1341, 1-oz 125.00
Rose Point, crystal, urn, #3500/41, w/lid, 10" 695.00
Rose Point, crystal, vase, #1309, 5"... 125.00
Rose Point, crystal, vase, #629, sweet pea 395.00
Tally Ho, amber or crystal, creamer, ftd...................................... 12.50
Tally Ho, amber or crystal, plate, sandwich; hdls, 11½" 35.00
Tally Ho, Carmen or Royal, ashtray, 4" 22.50
Tally Ho, Carmen or Royal, bowl, punch; ftd, 13" 350.00
Tally Ho, Forest Green, candlestick, 6", ea 40.00
Tally Ho, Forest Green, sugar bowl, ftd 20.00
Valencia, crystal, ashtray, #3500/126, rnd, 4" 15.00
Valencia, crystal, ashtray, #3500/16, sq, 3¼" 12.00
Valencia, crystal, bowl, #1402/88, 11" 55.00
Valencia, crystal, claret, #3500, 4½-oz 40.00
Valencia, crystal, cup, #3500/1 .... 20.00
Valencia, crystal, honey dish, #3500/139, w/lid 195.00
Valencia, crystal, plate, #3500/67, 12" 40.00
Valencia, crystal, plate, breakfast; #3500/5, 8½" 12.00
Valencia, crystal, saucer, #3500/1 ....3.00
Valencia, crystal, shakers, #3400/18, pr 65.00
Valencia, crystal, sherbet, #1402, tall 18.00
Valencia, crystal, tumbler, #3500, ftd, 10-oz 22.00
Wildflower, crystal, basket, #3400/1182, hdls, ftd, 6"................... 35.00
Wildflower, crystal, cocktail shaker, #3400/175 .... 165.00
Wildflower, crystal, compote, #3500/148, 6" 40.00
Wildflower, crystal, hat, #1704, 5" 295.00
Wildflower, crystal, pitcher, Doulton, #3400/141 .... 395.00
Wildflower, crystal, plate, dinner; #3900/24, 10½" 95.00
Wildflower, crystal, shakers, #3900/1177, pr 50.00
Wildflower, crystal, tray, creamer & sugar; #3900/37 .... 15.00
Wildflower, crystal, vase, bud; 10" 110.00

Cameo

The technique of glass carving was perfected 2,000 years ago in ancient Rome and Greece. The most famous ancient example of cameo glass is the Portland Vase, made in Rome around 100 A.D. After glassblowing was developed, glassmakers devised a method of casing several layers of colored glass together, often with a light color over a darker base, to enhance the design. Skilled carvers meticulously worked the fragile glass to produce incredibly detailed classic scenes. In the eighteenth and nineteenth centuries, Oriental and Near-Eastern artisans used the technique more extensively. European glassmakers revived the art during the last quarter of the nineteenth century. In France, Galle and Daum produced some of the finest examples of modern times, using as many as five layers of glass to develop their designs, usually scenics or subjects from nature. Hand carving was supplemented by the use of a copper engraving wheel, and acid was used to cut away the layers more quickly.

In England, Thomas Webb and Sons used modern machinery and technology to eliminate many of the problems that plagued early glass carvers. One of Webb's best-known carvers, George Woodall, is credited with producing over 400 pieces. Woodall was trained in the art by John Northwood, famous for reproducing the Portland Vase in 1876. Cameo glass became very popular during the late 1800s, resulting in a market that demanded more than could be produced, due to the tedious procedures involved. In an effort to produce greater volume, less elaborate pieces with simple floral or geometric designs were made, often entirely acid etched with little or no hand carving. While very little cameo glass was made in this country, a few pieces were produced by James Gillinder, Tiffany, and the Libbey Glass Company. Though some continued to be made on a limited scale into the 1900s (and until about 1920 in France), for the most part, inferior products caused a marked reduction in its manufacture by the turn of the century. Beware of new 'French' cameo glass from Romania and Taiwan. Some of it is very good and may be signed with 'old' signatures. Know your dealer! Our advisor for this category is Don Williams; he is listed in the Directory under Missouri. See also specific manufactures.

English

Bottle, lay-down; floral branch, wht on red, Tiffany lid, 6" 2,500.00
Bottle, lay-down; floral/bk: butterfly, wht/citron, emb silver cap, 4".. 1,150.00
Bottle, scent; floral, wht on amber-yel, squat/bulbous, silver top, 4".. 1,265.00
Salt cellar, acanthus leaf-shoulder border, wht on bl, silver rim, 2" . 750.00
Sweetmeat, floral vine, wht on bl, low bowl form, SP mts, 5½" W . 1,600.00

Vase, apple branches, white on red, factory-polished rim, 9", $1,700.00. (Photo courtesy Cincinnati Art Galleries)

Vase, blackberry vines, wht on purple, ftd/shouldered, 10" 3,450.00
Vase, floral, wht on citron, bottle shape, 5x3" 775.00
Vase, floral, wht on pk satin, shouldered, 9" 1,725.00
Vase, floral, wht on red, squat bottle form, 2¾x3½" 1,900.00
Vase, floral branch, bk: butterflies, red/wht on bl, shouldered, 9" ... 5,200.00
Vase, floral branch, bl on opal, squatty, 3¾" 635.00
Vase, floral/lg leaves, wht on Prussian bl, teardrop w/long neck, 11".. 1,800.00
Vase, fuchsia, wht on Rose du Barry, shouldered, 4¾" 800.00
Vase, irises/poppies etc, wht on lt turq, shouldered, 9", pr 3,450.00
Vase, leafy branch, bl/wht on citron, bulbous w/can neck, 3½" 800.00
Vase, morning-glory stem, wht on Prussian Blue, ovoid, 5½" 400.00

Vase, petunias, wht on turq, bowl shape w/3 leaf-cvd O-shape ft, 4".6,000.00
Vase, trumpet flower vine, wht on bl, lip/ft w/wht trim, 3¾" 800.00

French

Atomizer, berried branches, amethyst on wht, Raspiller, 7" 750.00
Bowl, Deco flowers, wht/amethyst on orange mottle, Degue, 14"....690.00
Box, roses, royal bl on lime gr, oval, J Michel, 2½" L.................... 460.00
Plaque, medieval castle ruins by river valley, J Gruber, 9x16"+fr. 1,750.00
Vase, Deco floral, orange to dk bl bun ft on wht frost, 20x11" .. 1,035.00
Vase, floral, cut/pnt on clear, stick neck, Cristallerie HT, 6" 460.00
Vase, floral stalk, orange/gr on creamy yel, flared rim, bun ft, 16"..1,140.00
Vase, flowers/leaves on front, red/amber to yel, Desire Christian, 8" .2,590.00
Vase, iris, cut/pnt on lime/wine, martele areas, Burgun-Schverer, 9". 10,925.00
Vase, iris, gr/lt pk on yel, slim, Crois Mare, 11" 635.00
Vase, leaves/flowers, blk amethyst to red on frost, Degue, 10x8".. 920.00
Vase, lg floral, orange/gr on amber, silver o/l at rim & ft, 4x3½".. 4,370.00
Vase, Songs of Hellas (Greek), W Crane, 3 hdls, Burgun-Schverer, 8" .12,000.00
Vase, trees/bridge/mtns, gr/red on citron, slim, Arsall, 8" 520.00
Vase, trees/island/distant castle, brn on yel, bulbous, J Michel, 8" . 865.00

Camphor Glass

The term 'camphor glass' refers to a type of acid-finished lustreless glassware, so named for its resemblance to gum camphor.

Box, trinket; rvpt dog's head medallion, enameled hinges, 3¼" L. 225.00
Vase, poppies emb, repousse brass rim & ft, 9x8" 125.00
Vase, storks emb, 4-sided w/upright scallops, NE Glass, 4½" 275.00

Canary Ware

Canary ware was produced from the late 1700s until about the mid-nineteenth century in the Staffordshire district of England. It was potted of yellow clay and the overglaze was yellow as well. More often than not, copper or silver lustre trim was added. Decorations were usually black-printed transfers, though occasionally hand-painted polychrome designs were also used.

Bowl, primitive floral band, ftd, early 19th C, 6½" 135.00
Jar, wide band: blk/wht Fr Watteau-style people scenic, w/lid, 12", pr.. 1,800.00
Mug, child's; Dr Franklin's Maxims transfer, 2⅜", VG.................. 450.00
Mug, child's; eagle/Lafayette/Washington, blk transfer, rpr, 2½" .. 655.00
Mug, child's; simple floral/leaf, gr/bl/brn, copper lustre rim, EX ... 240.00
Mug, lady & putti in garden, rust transfer, 19th C, 2⅛x2¼" 350.00
Pitcher, gaudy floral, mask spout, emb grapevines, mc w/brn bands, 5".. 900.00
Pitcher, Greek key neck band, grapevines on body, bulbous, 5¾" . 240.00
Pitcher, reserve w/2 children under tree, bk: man/dog, 4¾" 420.00
Pitcher, transfer band w/LaFayette, bk: Gen Cornwallis, 3¾", EX...570.00
Plate, gaudy floral center/rim, overglaze enamels, Pratt, 8¼"........ 660.00
Plate, roses, red/gr leaves w/brn rim, strong colors, 8¾", NM 1,320.00
Teabowl & saucer, roses, red/gr w/brn rim, strong colors, NM......660.00
Teabowl & saucer, scenic transfer: man in rowboat, Sewell, ca 1780.210.00
Vase, gaudy floral, 5 necks on fan form, ftd, 1800s, 7½x8½"......8,400.00

Candleholders

The earliest type of candlestick, called a pricket, was constructed with a sharp point on which the candle was impaled. The socket type, first used in the sixteenth century, consisted of the socket and a short stem with a wide drip pan and base. These were made from sheets of silver or other metal; not until late in the seventeenth century were candlesticks made by casting. By the 1700s, styles began to vary from the traditional fluted column or baluster form and became more elaborate. A Rococo style with scrolls, shellwork, and naturalistic leaves and flowers came into vogue that afforded the individual silversmith the opportunity to exhibit his skill and artistry. The last half of the eighteenth century brought a return to fluted columns with neoclassic motifs. Because they were made of thin sheet silver, weighted bases were used to add stability. The Rococo styles of the Regency period were heavily encrusted with applied figures and flowers. Candelabra with six to nine branches became popular. By the Victorian era when lamps came into general use, there was less innovation and more adaptation of the earlier styles. For more information, we recommend *Glass Candlesticks of the Depression Era, Vol. 1* and *2* by Gene and Cathy Florence and *The Glass Candlestick Book, Vol. 1* through *3* by Tom Felt and Elaine and Rich Stoer (Collector Books). Unless noted 'pair,' values are for single candleholders. See also Silver; Tinware; specific manufacturers.

Brass, chamberstick w/scissor & cone snuffers, sq base, 5x7x5".... 200.00
Brass, domed base w/6 lg/6 sm scallops, side pushup, 7½", pr ... 1,265.00
Brass, gilt/pnt swags, domed leafy base, Emp style, 1850s, 11", pr..2,465.00
Brass, hollow baluster stem on sq base w/gallery rim, 5¼x5¼" 285.00
Brass, hollow knobbed column, sq base w/4 ft, 6½" 200.00
Brass, open spiral sticks, threaded posts, rnd bases, 12", pr 230.00
Brass, scalloped base, hollow stem w/pushup, 8½" 375.00
Brass pricket, Gothic revival, bl/wht enamel/turq-studded finials, 20"..555.00
Bronze, Gothic style w/hexagonal drip pan, arched base, 34", pr ..1,400.00
Bronze dore, Fr Emp, core cast/seamed, removable bobeches, 10", pr.1,050.00
Bronze dore, pricket, elaborate std, busts at base, paw ft, 34", pr . 2,760.00
Bronze dore, putto rests on oval base, scroll brackets, 13", pr....... 470.00
Bronze dore/lapis lazuli, 3-arm, ornate castings, 13x9", pr.........4,400.00
Candelabra, alabaster w/gilt bronze mts, rose branches/cups, 12", pr..150.00
Candelabra, bronze w/gilt, Napoleon III, 6-arm, scrolls/swags, 28", pr..2,350.00
Candelabra, SP, 7-arm, std w/3 scroll supports, Fr, 1880s, 32x20", pr.4,200.00
Gilt gesso, trn post on tringular base w/3 cvd ft, early, 31", G...... 100.00

Gilt metal, Art Nouveau, five-candle, probably German or Austrian, #89, 19x14", $2,880.00. (Photo courtesy David Rago Auctions)

Giltwood w/cream enamel, Italian classical style, 38", pr..........1,500.00
Glass, amber, twist stem, Cambridge, from $25 to 30.00
Glass, amethyst w/silver o/l, trumpet shape, Diamond, 9x4⅜" 45.00
Glass, burgundy, Fostoria #4113, 1936-44, 5⅝x3¼", from $40 to... 50.00
Glass, crystal, Chaucer (No 1504 Line), Paden City, 6½x4⅞" 30.00
Glass, emerald, 3-light, Cambridge #824, 4⅜x9⅛x3¾" 35.00
Glass, Florentine No 2, gr, Hazel-Atlas, 2½x4¼", from $25 to 30.00
Glass, Heirloom candle-vase, yel opal, Fostoria #2730/319, 6" 200.00
Glass, Loop & Pillar, crystal, US Glass #15077, 6x3½", from $60 to . 75.00
Glass, Moongleam, swan hdls, Heisey #133, 1929-36, 6½" 325.00
Glass, Willow, gr, 2-light, Indiana, 5½x4¾x2¾", from $20 to 30.00
Maple, trn columnar std on sq base, pewter cup, 1800s, 32"........ 235.00
Pewter, Queen Ann, oval base, early, 4½x4", pr 175.00

Pewter, rnd base w/trumpet shaft, Reed & Barton I, 9" 230.00
Silver, shaped ovals w/floral vines, Silver City, 1900, 10", pr 175.00
SP, Corinthian columns w/stepped bases, Sheffield style, 12", pr . 320.00
Tin, rnd column on cone-shape weighted base, pushup, 1820s, 10", pr. 865.00
Tin hogscraper, brass wedding ring above pushup stamped Fisher, 7".525.00
Tin hogscraper w/seamed brass wedding band, Shaw's Birm on pushup, 7".430.00
Wood w/dk gr & gilt over gesso, acanthus leaves, 14", VG, pr..1,700.00
Wrought iron, spiral, twisted iron strip adjusts height, wood base, 8"..235.00

Candlewick

Candlewick crystal was made by the Imperial Glass Corporation, a division of Lenox Inc., Bellaire, Ohio. It was introduced in 1936, and though never marked except for paper labels, it is easily recognized by the beaded crystal rims, stems, and handles inspired by the tufted needlework called candlewicking, practiced by our pioneer women. During its production, more than 741 items were designed and produced. In September 1982 when Imperial closed its doors, 34 pieces were still being made.

Identification numbers and mold numbers used by the company help collectors recognize the various styles and shapes. Most of the pieces are from the #400 series, though other series numbers were also used. Stemware was made in eight styles — five from the #400 series made from 1941 to 1962, one from #3400 series made in 1937, another from #3800 series made in 1941, and the eighth style from the #4000 series made in 1947. In the listings that follow, some #400 items lack the mold number because that information was not found in the company files.

A few pieces have been made in color or with a gold wash. At least two lines, Valley Lily and Floral, utilized Candlewick with floral patterns cut into the crystal. These are scarce today. Other rare items include gifts such as the desk calendar made by the company for its employees and customers; the dresser set comprised of a mirror, clock, puff jar, and cologne; and the chip and dip set.

Ashtray, heart shape, #400/173, 5½" 12.00
Ashtray, oblong, #400/134/1, 4½" 6.00
Ashtray, sq, #400/652, 4½" 35.00
Basket, #400/40/0, 6½" 37.50
Bottle, bitters; w/tube, #400/117, 4-oz.. 75.00
Bowl, cottage cheese; #400/85, 6" 25.00
Bowl, cream soup; #400/50, 5" 45.00
Bowl, mint; hdl, #400/51F, 6" 23.00
Bowl, oval, flared, #400/131B, 14"...295.00
Bowl, sq, #400/232, 6" 125.00
Butter dish, rnd, #400/144, 5½" 35.00
Cake stand, high ft, #400/103D, 11" 75.00
Candleholder, heart shape, #400/40HC, 5" 110.00
Candleholder, mushroom, #400/86 .... 40.00
Candy box, sq, w/rnd lid, #400/245, 6½"......................................350.00
Champagne/sherbet, #3800, 6-oz 28.00
Cocktail, #400/190, 4-oz 20.00
Compote, fruit; crimped, ftd, #40/103C, 10".................................225.00
Compote, 4-bead stem, #400/45, 5½" 30.00
Condiment set, 4-pc, #400/1769 .... 80.00
Cruet, w/stopper, #400/70, 4-oz 55.00
Cup, punch; #400/211 ....8.00
Decanter, cordial; w/stopper, #400/82/2, 15-oz.............................495.00
Ladle, marmalade; 3-bead stem, #400/130 .... 12.00
Ladle, punch; #400/259 .... 30.00
Lamp shade 85.00
Mustard jar, w/spoon, #400/156 .... 40.00
Oil bottle, bead base, #400/166, 6-oz 75.00
Oil bottle, bulbous bottom, #400/275, 6-oz................................... 65.00
Oyster cocktail, #3400, 4-oz 16.00

Parfait, #3400, 6-oz 60.00
Pitcher, beaded ft, #400/18, 80-oz 265.00
Pitcher, Manhattan; #400/18, 40-oz 250.00
Pitcher, plain, #400/416, 20-oz 40.00
Plate, #400/34, 4½" 8.00
Plate, birthday cake; 72 holes for candles, #400/160, 14" 550.00
Plate, bread & butter; #400/1D, 6" 8.00
Plate, cracker; #400/145, 13½" 40.00
Plate, oval, #400/124, 12½" 90.00
Plate, salad; #400/5D, 8½" 12.00
Plate, salad; oval, #400/38, 9" 45.00
Plate, service; #400/13D, 12" 35.00
Plate, torte; #400/17D, 14" 50.00
Plate, triangular, #400/266, 7½" 100.00

Relish, five-part, five-handle, #400/56, 10½", $75.00. (Photo courtesy Gene and Cathy Florence)

Relish, oval, #400/256, 10½" 30.00
Salt spoon, #400/616, 3" 11.00
Saucer, AD; #400/77AD 5.00
Shakers, #400/167, pr 16.00
Shakers, bulbous, chrome top, beaded ft, #400/96, pr 18.00
Sherbet, #400/190, 6-oz 15.00
Sugar bowl, plain ft, #400/31 .... 7.00
Tea, #4000, 12-oz 35.00
Tidbit set, 3-pc, #400/18TB 225.00
Tray, #400/113E, hdl, 14" 95.00
Tray, condiment; #400/148, 5¼x9¼" 48.00
Tray, wafer; hdl extends to center of dish, #400/51T, 6" 25.00
Tumbler, #3800, 12-oz 35.00
Tumbler, old-fashioned; #400/18, 7-oz 70.00
Tumbler, parfait; #400/18, 7-oz 85.00
Tumbler, tea; #400/19, 14-oz 22.00
Vase, bud; beaded ft, #400/28C, 8½" 110.00
Vase, ivy bowl, #400/74J, 7" 165.00
Vase, mini bud; beaded ft, #400/107, 5¾" 65.00
Vase, rose bowl, #400/142K, 7" 300.00

Candy Containers

Figural glass candy containers were first created in 1876 when ingenious candy manufacturers began to use them to package their products. Two of the first containers, the Liberty Bell and Independence Hall, were distributed for our country's centennial celebration. Children found these toys appealing, and an industry was launched that lasted into the mid-1960s.

Figural candy containers include animals, comic characters, guns, telephones, transportation vehicles, household appliances, and many other intriguing designs. The oldest (those made prior to 1920) were usually hand painted and often contained extra metal parts in addition to the metal strip or screw closures. During the 1950s these metal parts were replaced with plastic, a practice that continued until candy con-

tainers met their demise in the 1960s. While predominately clear, they are found in nearly all colors of glass including milk glass, green, amber, pink, emerald, cobalt, ruby flashed, and light blue. Usually the color was intentional, but leftover glass was used as well and resulted in unplanned colors. Various examples are found in light or ice blue, and new finds are always being discovered. Production of the glass portion of candy containers was centered around the western Pennsylvania city of Jeannette. Major producers include Westmoreland Glass, West Bros., Victory Glass, J.H. Millstein, J.C. Crosetti, L.E. Smith, Jack Stough, and T.H. Stough. While 90% of all glass candies were made in the Jeannette area, other companies such as Eagle Glass, Play Toy, and Geo. Borgfeldt Co. have a few to their credit as well.

Buyer beware! Many candy containers have been reproduced. Some, including the Camera and the Rabbit Pushing Wheelbarrow, come already painted from distributors. Others may have a slick or oily feel to the touch. The following list may also alert you to possible reproductions:

Amber Pistol, L #144 (first sold full in the 1970s, not listed in E&A)

Auto, D&P #173/E&A #33/L #377

Auto, D&P #163/E&A #60/L #356

Black and White Taxi, D&P #182/L #353 (silk-screened metal roofs are being reproduced. They are different from originals in that the white section is more silvery in color than the original cream. These closures are put on original bases and often priced for hundreds of dollars. If the top is not original, the value of these candy containers is reduced by 80%.)

Camera, D&P #419/E&A #121/L #238 (original says 'Pat Apld For' on bottom, reproduction says 'B. Shakman' or is ground off)

Carpet Sweeper, D&P 296/E&A #133/L #243 (currently being sold with no metal parts)

Carpet Sweeper, E&A #132/L #242 (currently being sold with no metal parts)

Charlie Chaplin, D&P 195/E&A #137/L #83 (original has 'Geo. Borgfeldt' on base; reproduction comes in pink and blue)

Chicken on Nest, D&P #10/E&A #149/L #12

Display Case, D&P #422/E&A #177/L #246 (original should be painted silver and brown)

Dog, D&P #21/E&A #180/L #24 (clear and cobalt)

Drum Mug, D&P #431/E&A #543/L #255

Happifats on Drum, D&P #199/E&A #208/L #89 (no notches on repro for closure to hook into)

Fire Engine, D&P 258/E&A #213/L #386 (repros in green and blue glass)

Independence Hall, D&P #130/E&A #342/L #76 (original is rectangular; repro has offset base with red felt-lined closure)

Jackie Coogan, D&P #202/E&A #345/L #90 (marked inside 'B')

Kewpie, D&P #204/E&A #349/L #91 (must have Geo. Borgfeldt on base to be original)

Mailbox, D&P #216/E&A #521/L #254 (repro marked Taiwan)

Mantel Clock, D&P #483/E&A #162/L #114 (originally in ruby flashed, milk glass, clear and frosted only)

Mule and Waterwagon, D&P #51/E&A #539/L #38 (original marked Jeannette, PA)

Naked Child, E&A 546/L #94

Owl, D&P #52/E&A #566/L #37, (original in clear only, often painted; repro found in clear, blue, green, and pink with a higher threaded base and less detail)

Peter Rabbit, D&P #60/E&A #618/L #55

Piano, D&P #460/E&A #577/L #289 (original in only clear and milk glass, both painted)

Rabbit Pushing Wheelbarrow, D&P #72/E&A #601/L #47 (eggs are speckled on the repro; solid on the original)

Rocking Horse, D&P #46/E&A #651/L #58 (original in clear only, repro marked 'Rocky')

Safe, D&P #311/E&A #661/L #268 (original in clear, ruby flashed, and milk glass only)

Santa, D&P 284/E&A #674/L #103 (original has plastic head; repro [1970s] is all glass and opens at bottom)

Santa's Boot, D&P #273/E&A #111/L #233

Scottie Dog, D&P #35/E&A #184/L #17 (repro has a ice-like color and is often slick and oily)

Station Wagon, D&P #178/E&A #56/L #378

Stough Rabbit, D&P #53/E&A #617/L #54

Uncle Sam's Hat, D&P #428/E&A #303/L #168

Wagon, U.S. Express D&P #530 (glass is being reproduced without any metal parts).

Others are possible. If in doubt, do not buy without a guarantee from the dealer and return privilege in writing. Also note that other reproductions are possible.

Our advisor for glass containers is Jeff Bradfield; he is listed in the Directory under Virginia. You may contact him with questions, if you will include an SASE. See Clubs, Newsletters, and Catalogs for the address of the Candy Container Collectors of America. A bimonthly newsletter offers insight into new finds, reproductions, updates, and articles from over four hundred collectors and members, including authors of books on candy containers. Dues are $25.00 yearly. The club holds an annual convention in June in Lancaster, Pennsylvania, for collectors of candy containers.

'L' numbers used in this guide refer to a standard reference series, *An Album of Candy Containers, Vol. I and II*, by Jennie Long. 'E&A' numbers correlate with *The Compleat American Glass Candy Containers Handbook* by Eikelberner and Agadjanian, revised by Adele Bowden. 'D&P' numbers refer to *The Collector's Guide to Candy Containers* by Doug Dezso and Leon and Rose Poirier (out of print).

Airplane, P-38 Lightning; Victory Glass, D&P 82/E&A 12/L 326 .... 225.00
Airplane, Red Plastic Wing; Musical Toy on cap, D&P 83/E&A 3 .. 55.00
Baseball Player on Base, gold w/pnt accents, D&P 191/E&A 78 . 700.00
Betty Lou Toy Town Dairy, cb carrier, D&P 107/E&A 529.......... 450.00
Binoculars, Victor, brass-plated tin fr & box, D&P 98/E&A 560/L 624... 600.00
Blimp, heavy glass, D&P 88 .... 200.00
Boat, Queen Mary; heavy glass, emb, D&P 103 .... 300.00
Boat, Uruguay; anchor ea side of bow, D&P 105 .... 250.00
Bottle, Dairy Sweets; w/metal fr, D&P 108/E&A 532/L 501 .... 150.00
Bottle, Seltzer; w/hdl & spout, D&P 112 .... 500.00
Bureau, slide-on closure, real mirror, D&P 294/E&A 112/L 125 . 200.00
Bus, Greyhound w/Luggage Rack; Victory Glass, D&P 151/E&A 113/L 342. 300.00
Bus, NY - San Francisco; D&P 154/E&A 118-2/L 346 .... 600.00

**Bus, screw-on closure, D&P 153, 7",
from $300.00 to $400.00.** (Photo courtesy Doug
Dezso and Leon and Rose Poirier)

Bus, Victory Lines Special, G pnt, D&P 146/E&A 115/L 347 .... 75.00
Camel, Shriner's; clear or amber glass, sitting, D&P 4.................... 35.00
Candlestick w/Hdls, ruby flashed, gold trim, D&P 321/E&A 119. 300.00
Cannon, US Defense Field Gun; tin bbl, D&P 387/E&A 128/L 142. 350.00
Cannon, 2-Wheel Mount #2; cobalt, D&P 385/E&A 124/L 536 ...650.00
Cannon on Truck, no mk, D&P 382/E&A 126 .... 2,500.00

Car, Boyd; various colors, D&P 159 .... 25.00
Car, Lg Flat Top Hearse; tassels side/front, G pnt, D&P 166/E&A 59.. 600.00
Car, Miniature Streamlined; D&P 173/E&A 33/L 377 (+)............. 25.00
Car, Sedan w/12 Vents; mk VG Co, 90% pnt, D&P 177/E&A 36.. 125.00
Car, Station Wagon; JH Millstein, D&P 178/E&A 56/L 378 (+).. 40.00
Carpet Sweeper, Baby; wire hdl, D&P 295/E&A 132/L 242 (+).. 475.00
Carpet Sweeper, Dolly; twisted wire hdl, D&P 296/E&A 133 ..... 475.00
Cash Register, 4 rows of keys, D&P 420/E&A 135/L 244............. 450.00
Cheery Cholly Clown, cb suit/shoes, compo head, D&P 194/L 530..300.00
Chick, Baby Standing; G yel pnt, D&P 7/E&A 145 .... 150.00
Chicken on Sagging Basket, D&P 14/E&A 148/L 8 .... 75.00
Clock, Betty Barker Time Teacher; D&P 478................................ 150.00
Clock, Mantel; stippled w/scrollwork, D&P 482/E&A 164/L 116 . 200.00
Coach, Angeline - No Couplers; all orig, D&P 519/E&A 168 .... 525.00
Coal Car - w/Couplers; all orig, D&P 522/E&A 171..................... 450.00
Die, glass box w/1 to 6 pips on faces, D&P 421/E&A 175-1/L 268..25.00
Dirigible, Mu-Mu; Bakelite closure, D&P 90.............................. 150.00
Dog, Bulldog on Rnd Base, Victory Glass, D&P 18/E&A 189/L 15.. 60.00
Dog, Hot Doggie; bl, HE Widmer, D&P 23/E&A 320/L 14 .... 1,100.00
Dog, Little Doggie in the Window; Stough, D&P 30/E&A 178/L 483 .. 30.00
Dog, Mutt; sm stippled glass hat, tooled fur, D&P 32/E&A 194 .... 85.00
Dog by Barrel, LE Smith, D&P 19/E&A 190/L 13 .... 250.00
Drum Bank, HP milk glass, cannon etc, +closure, D&P 289/E&A 195/L 279. 475.00
Elephant, Genteel; dressed/standing, D&P 42/E&A 207/L 33..... 350.00
Elephant, GOP, orig pnt, D&P 43/E&A 206/L 31........................ 250.00
Felix by Barrel, D&P 200/E&A 211 .... 625.00
Fire Engine, Lg Boiler; D&P 255/E&A 221 .... 125.00
Fire Engine, Three Dot USA; D&P 260/E&A 220/L 380............. 100.00
Flapper, paper face glued inside, D&P 203/E&A 227 .... 65.00
Flat Iron, snap-on bottom, D&P 306/E&A 344/L 249 .... 625.00
Flossie Fischer's Chair, seat slides open, D&P 300/E&A 232/L 128...700.00
Gas Pump, 23c To-Day; D&P 439/E&A 240/L 316 .... 375.00
Gun, Beaded Border Grip; D&P 390/E&A 246 .... 20.00
Gun, Kolt; dmn-emb grip, D&P 393/E&A 285 .... 125.00
Gun, Sm Revolver; grip w/dmn emb, D&P 398/E&A 253 .... 30.00
Gun, Stough's 1939 Pat Pending, D&P 400/E&A 249 .... 25.00
Harmonica, Sweetone; harp shape, 13-note, D&P 447 .... 175.00
Helicopter, attached rotor, Stough, D&P 91/E&A 306/L 329...... 300.00
Horn, Stough's 1953; 3 valve buttons, D&P 453/E&A 310/L 283 . 40.00
Horn, 3-Valve; gilt valves, D&P 455/E&A 312/L 281 .... 175.00
House w/Chimney, front dormer, D&P 129/E&A 324/L 75 .... 250.00
Irish Hat, shamrock on front, D&P 426/E&A 302/L 167.......... 3,000.00
Jack O'Lantern, Slant Eyes; orig pnt, D&P 265/E&A 349 .... 225.00
Kettle, Wee Soup; on tripod fr, complete, D&P 308/E&A 356...... 75.00
Kettle on 3 Feet, horizontal ribs/orig closure, D&P 307/E&A 355/L 251.45.00
Lamp, Kerosene w/Swizzle Stick; D&P 333 .... 75.00
Lamp, Metal Shade; Stough, D&P 335/L 464................................ 50.00
Lamp, Monkey; yel plastic shade, D&P 338/E&A 533................. 525.00
Lamppost, glass globe/pewter stand, D&P 341/L 553 .... 90.00
Lantern, Dec 20 '04-Medium; shaker top, D&P 351/E&A 407/L 173. 30.00
Lantern, Stough's No 81; tin shade/base, D&P 366/E&A 447....... 35.00
Lantern, 16-hole; D&P 376/E&A 444/L 190................................ 35.00
Lantern on Stand, shaker closure, ruby stain, D&P 358/L 571 ...... 50.00
Lanterns, Twins on Anchor; hang on metal fr, D&P 370/E&A 385/L 186 .25.00
Liberty Bell w/Hanger, gr glass, D&P 95/E&A 85/L 229 .... 45.00
Locomotive, Curved Line 888; D&P 490/E&A 483....................... 35.00
Locomotive, Dbl Window w/Rear Screw Cap; D&P 525 .... 200.00
Locomotive, Mapother's; D&P 499/E&A 494................................ 325.00
Locomotive, Stough's Musical Toy; D&P 506/E&A 476................ 40.00
Luggage, Trunk w/Rnd Top; milk glass, D&P 378/E&A 789........ 135.00
Milk Bottle, German, wire closure at neck, D&P 111 .... 100.00
Mug, Child's; false bottom/base holds candy, D&P 432/E&A 541/L 256. 325.00
Mug, Kiddies' Drinking; Millstein, D&P 433/E&A 540/L 258 ...... 25.00
Mug, Victory Glass Co; flat-top hdl w/curl at base, D&P 434/E&A 542..15.00

Nurser, Plain; rubber nipple, D&P 123/E&A 549.......................... 30.00
Nurser, Waisted; Crosetti, D&P 125/E&A 548/L 71 .... 25.00
Owl, sitting on base, D&P 52/E&A 566/L 37 (+) 200.00
Parlor Car, arched windows, D&P 516/E&A 169 .... 325.00
Pencil, Baby Jumbo; holds real pencil, D&P 218/E&A 567/L 263. 95.00
Pencil, Kiddies Candy; w/box, D&P 217 .... 50.00
Phonograph w/Glass Horn, gold pnt trim, D&P 458/E&A 576/L 286 (+).450.00
Pipe, Germany, cork closure, D&P 437/E&A 585 .... 60.00
Play Packs, Toy Assortment, Christmas; D&P 469 .... 125.00
Pumpkin-Head Mounted Policeman, no pnt, D&P 269............1,000.00
Pumpkin-Head Mounted Policeman, w/pnt, D&P 269 ....1,800.00
Pumpkin-Head Witch, holds broom, NM pnt, D&P 272/E&A 594..900.00
Rabbit w/Aluminum Ears, mk Germany/Ges Gesch, D&P 63/L 487 .600.00
Racer, Stutz Bear Cat; 10-rib radiator, D&P 474/E&A 639 ......1,500.00
Stop & Go, metal post/blades, D&P 441/E&A 706/L 317 .... 525.00
Telephone, Redlich's Bell/Crank; wood receiver, D&P 238/E&A 752/L 294...350.00
Uncle Sam by Barrel, slot in closure, 95% pnt, D&P 215/E&A 801/L 112..700.00
Watch, Eagle; w/eagle fob, D&P 486/E&A 823/L 122 .... 450.00

Miscellaneous

These types of candy containers are generally figural. Many are holiday related. Small sizes are common; larger sizes are in greater demand. Because of eBay's influence, prices have dropped and remain soft. Our prices reflect this trend. Our advisor for this category is Jenny Tarrant; she is listed in the Directory under Missouri. See also Christmas; Easter; Halloween.

Key: pm — papier-mache

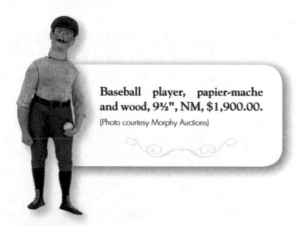

Baseball player, papier-mache and wood, 9½", NM, $1,900.00.

(Photo courtesy Morphy Auctions)

Baseball player, compo, w/wood bat, early, 7½", EX...................... 780.00
Bulldog, compo, cream w/orange hat Germany, 4", VG 130.00
Cat, pm w/gesso, mc pnt, glass eyes, red ribbon, rpt 6" 225.00
Cat, seated, pm w/gesso, worn flocking, glass eyes, rpt 4" 200.00
Cat in shoe, compo & gesso w/mc pnt, rpr, 4" 175.00
Doll, bsk open dome head, crepe-paper/cb cylinder body, Germany, 6".120.00
Dove, compo w/gray pnt, pk-pnt metal fr, orange glass eyes, 4½x8".100.00
Elephant, pm, porc tusks, Germany, ca 1885-1920, 6" 155.00
English Bobby, pm, EX pnt, Pat No 28063, 12" 160.00
George Washington, compo, stands on rnd box w/silk flag, Germany, 5"..150.00
George Washington bust, compo, bottom plug, 2-3" 75.00
George Washington bust, compo, bottom plug, 4-6" 150.00
George Washington w/tree stump, compo, Germany, 3-4" 150.00
George Washington w/tree stump, compo, Germany, 5-7".............225.00
Hen, compo w/metal fr, yel/red/brn pnt, lt ft wear, 4½x4¾" 75.00
Horse, pm, head removes, 4½", VG 155.00
Pig, pm, gr w/HP features, Made in Germany, 5¼x5½x3" 90.00
Pig, pm, sleeping, pk flocking, 5⅝" 90.00
Pigeon, comp w/metal fr, gray/wht/irid purple, 4½x6" 75.00
Rooster, compo, w/metal fr, yel/red/brn pnt, lt ft wear, 4½x4¾" 95.00

Rooster, pm, red/wht/blk pnt, metal legs, glass eyes, 9¼"............. 250.00
St Patrick's Day, Irishman bust, compo, w/plug, Germany, 3-4" 75.00
St Patrick's Day, Irishman bust, compo, w/plug, Germany, 5-6" ...125.00
St Patrick's Day, Irishman on candy box, compo, Germany, 3½".155.00
St Patrick's Day, pig, flocked gr, wood legs, plug in tummy, 3-5" 95.00
St Patrick's Day, potato, compo, Germany, 3-4" 50.00
Stag, compo w/metal rack, brn flock, yel glass eyes, Germany, 5", VG .275.00
Stork w/baby, spun cotton & paper, lifts legs, Germany, 1930s, 6½" .95.00
Turkey, compo w/metal ft, head removes, Germany, 3½" 65.00
Turkey, compo w/metal ft, head removes, Germany, 5" 100.00
Turkey, compo w/metal ft, head removes, Germany, 8" 300.00
Turkey, compo w/metal ft, head removes, Germany, 10" 375.00
Turkey, compo w/metal ft, head removes, Germany, 12" 425.00
Watermelon w/face, molded cb w/celluloid body, Austria, 4¼".... 125.00

Canes

Fancy canes and walking sticks were once the mark of a gentleman. Hand-carved examples are collected and admired as folk art from the past. The glass canes that never could have been practical are unique whimseys of the glassblower's profession. Gadget and container sticks, which were produced in a wide variety, are highly desirable. Character, political, and novelty types are also sought after as are those with handles made of precious metals.

Our values reflect actual prices realized at auction. For more information we recommend *American Folk Art Canes, Personal Sculpture,* by George H. Meyer, Sandringham Press, 100 West Long Lake Rd., Suite 100, Bloomfield Hills, MI 48304. Other possible references are *Canes in the United States* by Catherine Dike and *Canes From the 17th – 20th Century* by Jeffrey Snyder. For information concerning the Cane Collectors Club, see the Directory under Clubs, Newsletters, and Catalogs.

Alligator (4") atop L-shape hdl, cvd ivory, EX detail, gold collar.. 345.00
Conifer wood hdl contains 13x15" US flag w/39 stars, ca 1889 ...800.00
Gilt silver Masonic folding ball hdl opens to form cross, ca 1890..6,000.00
Glass whimsey, mc spiral, knob hdl, hollow blown, silver tip, 45". 180.00
Ivory Baden Powell hdl, sterling/gilt collar, malacca shaft, dtd 1931..1,000.00
Ivory bonneted child hdl, brass collar, rosewood shaft, 1890s 550.00
Ivory dragon hdl w/jtd jaw, silver collar, malacca shaft, 1900s ..3,300.00
Ivory full skeleton hdl, silver collar, partridgewood shaft, ca 1885..1,100.00
Ivory Geo II head hdl, silver collar, ebony shaft, 1890s.............1,100.00
Ivory hound hdl w/brn glass eyes, silver collar, blk shaft, 1900s ...850.00
Ivory man & tortoise hdl, silver collar, hardwood shaft, 1880s .1,400.00
Ivory Prince Albert hdl, silver collar, rosewood shaft, 1850s........900.00
Ivory skull w/jtd jaw & eyes that trn, hardwood shaft, 1890s 2,750.00
Ivory umbrella-like hdl, baleen separators, whalebone shaft, 1870s .2,500.00
Ivory 2-bunny hdl, glass eyes, silver collar, ebony shaft, ca 1871..650.00
Ivory/wood pug in doghouse automaton hdl, hardwood shaft, 1890s .900.00
Porc dog hdl w/pointed end, mc, gilt collar, ebony shaft, 1880s .5,250.00
Quartz hdl, amethyst w/silver collar, ebony shaft/horn ferrule, 1900s.. 550.00
Rino horn (all), pistol grip hdl, thorn shaft w/silver band, 1870s.. 900.00
Rock crystal hdl w/jewels/pearls, silver collar, horn ferrule, 1900s.1,400.00
Silver & champleve mushroom hdl w/dmns, hardwood shaft, Russia, 1900s..3,000.00
Silver elephant w/ivory tusks crook hdl, malacca shaft, 1890s ..1,500.00
Silver emb knob hdl, rfn malacca shaft w/silver eyelets, 1770s .2,000.00
Tortoiseshell w/gold crown inlay hdl, gold collar, blk shaft, 1890s ...700.00
Vermeil silver/bl enamel perfume bottle hdl, ebony shaft, 1900s...1,700.00
Vertebrae, horn knop top/tip, graduated, 35", VG........................115.00
Walnut knob hdl, silver hdl, narwhal tusk shaft, ca 1860..........3,750.00
Wood, crocodile hdl w/jtd jaw, ivory teeth, hardwood shaft, 1900s..1,350.00
Wood, cvd spiraling rattlesnake/bull/horse/etc, missing cap.........575.00
Wood, cvd wood w/decoupage prints, varnish, JCS 1935..............115.00
Wood, monkey bellhop hdl w/mechanical tongue, hardwood shaft, 1920s..800.00

Canton

Canton is a blue and white porcelain that was first exported in the 1790s by clipper ships from China to the United States. Importation continued into the 1920s. Canton became very popular along the East Coast where the major ports were located. Its popularity was due to several factors: it was readily available, inexpensive, and (due to the fact that it came in many different forms) appealing to homeowners.

The porcelain's blue and white color and simple motif (teahouse, trees, bridge, and a rain-cloud border) have made it a favorite of people who collect early American furniture and accessories. Buyers of Canton should shop at large outdoor shows and up-scale antique shows. Collections are regularly sold at auction and many examples may be found on eBay. However, be aware of reproductions and fantasy pieces being sold on eBay by sellers in Hong Kong and Shanghai. Collectors usually prefer a rich, deep tone rather than a lighter blue. Cracks, large chips, and major repairs will substantially affect values. Prices of Canton have escalated sharply over the last 20 years, and rare forms are highly sought after by advanced collectors. Our advisor for this category is Hobart D. Van Deusen; he is listed in the Directory under Connecticut.

Bowl, salad; cut corners, 4½x9½" 900.00
Bowl, soup; 10" 65.00
Bowl, vegetable; oval, pine-cone finial, 19th C, 4½x11" 300.00
Bowl, vegetable; rectangular w/cut corners, nut finial, 10" 600.00
Bowl, 6 lobes, late 19th C, 3⅛" H, EX 500.00
Charger, bottom w/bamboo leaf decor, 15" dia, NM 400.00
Plate, bread & butter; 5¾", set of 8 .... 115.00
Plate, salad; 7", set of 8 .... 325.00

Platter, canted corners, 13", $285.00. (Photo courtesy Jackson's International Auctioneers & Appraisers of Fine Art & Antiques)

Platter, 17¼x14¼" 700.00
Shrimp dish, 19th C, 10⅜" 300.00
Teapot, C strap hdl, str flaring sides, slightly domed lid, rpr, 7x9" . 270.00

Capodimonte

The relief style, highly colored and defined porcelain pieces in this listing are commonly called and identified in our current marketplace as Capodimonte. It was King Ferdinand IV, son of King Charles, who opened a factory in Naples in 1771 and began to use the mark of the blue crown N (BCN). When the factory closed in 1834, the Ginori family at Doccia near Florence, Italy, acquired what was left of the factory and continued using its mark. The factory operated until 1896 when it was then combined with Societa Ceramica Richard of Milan which continues today to manufacture fine porcelain pieces marked with a crest and wreaths under a blue crown with R. Capodimonte.

Boxes and steins are highly sought after as they are cross collectibles. Figurines, figure groupings, flowery vases, urns, and the like are also very collectible, but most items on the market today are of recent manufacture. In the past several years, Europeans have been attending U.S. an-

tique shows and auctions in order to purchase Capodimonte items to take back home, since many pieces were destroyed during the two world wars. This has driven up prices of the older ware. Our advisor for this category is James Highfield; he is listed in the Directory under Indiana.

Box, cherubs cavorting on hillside, BCN France, 4½x3½x2½" 66.00
Box, cherubs on wine bbl, BCN, 5x4x3¼" 265.00
Box, couple w/dog on lid, gilt int, Meissen, BCN, 3¼x1¾x1½" ... 245.00
Casket, nudes/angels/cherubs, BCN, 11x8x5" 400.00
Charger, Caesar Chariot Down Appian Way, 13" dia, NM 200.00
Charger, Roman orgy scene among ruins, BCN, 12" 225.00
Cigarette case, cherubs dancing, BCN, 4" 225.00
Cup & saucer, wine harvest scene(s), twig hdl, BCN, set of 6 ..... 200.00
Ewer, Pan hdl, cherub on goat below spout, 12½", NM 375.00
Ewer, representing earth & sea, sq base, BCN, 17", pr 1,800.00
Figurine, monkey band trumpet player, BCN, 4⅜" 85.00
Jardiniere, 7 cherubs, 4 rams' head hdls, BCN, 10½x10¾" dia 412.00
Pedestal & urn, nude & partially draped figures, BCN, 16" 2,900.00
Plates, cherubs on rim, floral int, BCN, 10⅛", set of 6 .... 240.00
Stein, Bacchus Wine Festival, monkey finial, camel hdl, BCN, 9" .290.00
Tureen platter, floral center, cherubs surround, BCN, 13½" dia ... 142.00
Urn, cherubs/ram heads/birds/flowers, fluted w/crown lid, BCN, 17½".385.00
Urn, mythological Pan-face hdls, BCN, 15½", pr 515.00
Urns, continuous putto Bacchanal scene, BCN, 16¼", pr 750.00
Vase, cherubs representing 4 seasons, BCN, 5¾" 60.00
Wine mug, drunken Bacchus, grapevine hdl, BCN, 3¾x3¾" dia ... 76.00

Carlton

Carlton Ware was the product of Wiltshaw and Robinson, who operated in the Staffordshire district of England from about 1890. During the 1920s, they produced ornamental ware with enameled and gilded decorations such as flowers and birds, often on a black background. From 1935 until about 1961, in an effort to thwart the theft of their designs by Japanese potters, Carlton adapted the 'Registerd Australian Design' mark, taking advantage of the South East Asia Treaty Organization which prohibited such piracy. In 1958 the firm was renamed Carlton Ware Ltd. Their trademark was a crown over a circular stamp with 'W & R, Stoke on Trent,' surrounding a swallow. 'Carlton Ware' was sometimes added by hand.

Biscuit barrel, Carnation, Wiltshaw & Robinson, ca 1906, 6¼" .. 365.00
Bowl, Apple Blossom, #1665/2, 10¼x7" 60.00
Bowl, Buttercup, 2¼x10x6¼" 68.00
Bowl, Convolvulus on lt bl, 2-compartment, 13" L 25.00
Bowl, fruit; Butterfly (inside & out) on cobalt lustre, 4x9¼" 265.00
Bowl, Gumnut on gr, triangular, 8¼" 50.00
Bowl, Hazelnut, brn & cream, script Australian mk, 2x9½" 32.00
Bowl, Moonlight & Cameo on orange lustre, 1894-1927, 4x14x8" .1,250.00
Bowl, New Flies on Fairy Lustre, ca 1894-1927, 11" 3,500.00
Bowl, Paradise Bird & Tree on pearl mottle, 1925-70, 7x13½x5½" .1,400.00
Bowl, serving; Morning Glory, irregular shape, 9x5¾" 20.00
Bowl, Thistle, blossom form, 4¾" L 20.00
Bowl, Water Lily, Australian script mk, 8x5½" 60.00
Box, Butterfly on gr lustre, pearl lustre int, 2½x5x4" 400.00
Butter pat, Foxglove, 1930s 16.00
Butter/jam dish, Forget-Me-not, 4½x4¼" 40.00
Coffee set, crocodile-form pot, cr & sug, Cooper blk mk, 3-pc 150.00
Coffee set, Sketching Bird on rouge, pot+cr/sug+4 c/s 525.00
Coffeepot, Parisienne on Rouge Royale, Rouge Royale mk, 7" 100.00
Compote, Foxglove, ftd, 4x11" 165.00
Creamer & sugar bowl, Primrose on lt gr 20.00
Cruet, Walking, pk shoes, 4¾" 60.00

Cruet set, mushroom form mustard+shakers+in invt mushroom stand .95.00
Cup, Walking, brn or gr shoes 60.00
Cup, Walking, I Am 21, pk hearts.. 45.00
Cup & saucer, demitasse; Noir Royale w/gold............................... 65.00
Egg cup, Prince Charles, wht, for L&F, 1986 .... 95.00
Egg cup, Walking, Hawaiian decor, yel shoes................................. 80.00
Egg cup, Walking, long legs, yel shoes... 60.00
Ginger jar, Barge, Crown mk, 10" 850.00
Ginger jar, Spider's Web on Rouge Royale, ca 1940, 11x7".......2,000.00
Jam dish, Apple Blossom on gr, 4¾" 20.00
Jam pot, Foxglove on lt gr, w/lid, 4x3¼" 36.00
Jam pot, pineapple form, #3064, 1971-72, w/lid.......................... 35.00
Jam pot, strawberry form, 1968-78, w/lid 60.00
Jar, temple; Barge on cobalt, w/lid, 8" 235.00
Jar, temple; Mikado on bl w/gold, w/lid, 12" 265.00
Jug, Apple Blossom, tree trunk hdl, Australian script mk, 10½" .. 465.00
Jug, Clematis on beige mottle, 7x7⅛" 395.00
Jug, Fruit Basket, bright gr, script Registered mk, 3½" 40.00
Jug, Petunia on blush, bl Crown mk, 6¼" 225.00
Leaf dish, brn & beige halves, ca 1950s, 14x4½" 20.00
Leaf dish, wht w/gold trim, 13½" 12.50
Leaf dish, Wild Rose, script Australian mk, 6" 40.00
Money box, bug-eyed snail, ca 1969.. 40.00
Mug, man hanging from scaffold, verse about drinking, 3¾" 40.00
Napkin ring/serviette holder, lady in pk crinoline, 3¾" 175.00
Nut dish, Currant, w/spoon 100.00
Pen stand, butterfly & flowers on red mottle w/gold, 6¾" W 435.00
Plate, escargot; Gourmet line, wht snail shape, 7⅜" L 20.00
Plate, Foxglove, Australian script mk, #1994/6, 7¼x6½" 60.00
Salt shakers, pear & lemon on yel banana base, 1960s, 3-pc set 50.00
Sauceboat & saucer, tomato on lettuce leaf 45.00
Sauceboat & saucer, Wild Rose 60.00
Shakers, chess pcs, blk & wht, pr on blk & wht tray, 3-pc set 50.00
Tea set, Foxglove on gr, 1930s, 4¾" pot+cr/sug............................ 265.00
Teapot, Apple Blossom on cream, ca 1940s, 5" 70.00
Teapot, Denim, torsos in jeans, wicker hdl, 1978 .... 50.00
Teapot, Walking, legs crossed 130.00
Toast rack, Apple Blossom on lt gr, 5-bar, 2½x4½" 125.00
Toast rack, cat & mouse figural, blk Cooper mk, 3½" 60.00
Toast rack, Poppies, 3-bar 185.00
Tray, Flowers & Basket, gr rope-twist hdl, 1¼x11½x7" 50.00
Tray, Magnolia on lt gr, 3-compartment, 13x10" 50.00
Vase, Garden Wall on lt bl, hdls, 2½" 55.00
Vase, Mandarin Tree, cylinder w/flared rim, 6x5" 500.00
Vase, Mikado on bl lustre, flared rim, W&R mk, ca 1894-1927, 6x3½". 300.00
Vase, Pagoda on cobalt, shouldered, 10" 275.00
Vase, Persian on bl lustre, baluster, ca 1894-1927, 11" 2,500.00
Vase, posy; Devil's Copse on turq, ca 1930, 3½x8¼".................. 1,125.00
Vase, Rabbits at Dusk on orange & blk lustre, hdls, 10⅛x9¾" 685.00
Vase, temple; Floral Comets, w/lid, #3387, 1930s, 6¾" 565.00
Vase, Tutankhamen on bl, flared rim, ftd, ca 1904-1927, 7¾" ...2,500.00
Vase, willows/prunus trees, gilt/mc on red flambe, turq int, 1900s,10" ..585.00

Carnival Collectibles

Carnival items from the early part of this century represent the lighter side of an America that was alternately prospering and sophisticated or devastated by war and domestic conflict. But whatever the country's condition, the carnival's thrilling rides and shooting galleries were a sure way of letting it all go by — at least for an evening.

In the shooting gallery target listings below, items are rated for availability from 1, commonly found, to 10, rarely found (these numbers appear just before the size), and all are made of cast iron. Our advisors for

shooting gallery targets are Richard and Valerie Tucker; their address is listed in the Directory under Texas.

Chalkware Figures

Abe Lincoln bust, 1940-50, 12".. 55.00
Alice the Goon, from Popeye cartoon, 1930-40, 6"...................... 95.00
Apache Babe, unmk, ca 1936, 15".. 65.00

Beach Bather, unmarked, ca 1940 – 1950, 7½", $60.00. (Photo courtesy Tom Morris)

Bell Hop, mk, ca 1946, 13".. 85.00
Betty Boop, Fleischer Studios, 1930-40, 14½" 395.00
Boy & dog, mk Pals, 1935-45, 10x9"... 35.00
Bulldog sitting, 1925-35, 10¼" 65.00
Call Me Papa, 1935-45, 14"... 15.00
Cat & goldfish bowl (clear glass), 1930-40, 9½" 47.05
Clara Belle (cow) sitting, wearing bonnet, Disney, 1945-50, 11¾" ..65.00
Colonial lady standing w/dog, 1935-45, 11¼" 17.00
Dead End Kid, ca 1935-45, rare, 15" 165.00
Dog sitting upright w/flower, 1935-45, 10¾" 30.00
Donald Duck, 1934-50, 14" 70.00
Dopey standing w/hands on tummy, 1937-50, 13" 100.00
Girl reading, bust, 1910-25, 12x8½" 65.00
Good Time Willie, mk 7/1939, 9" 70.00
Horse, sad face, 1945-50, 5".. 20.00
Indian chief on horseback, 1930-1950, 11", from $50 to............... 60.00
Indian chief standing w/arms crossed, 1930-45, 19" 45.00
Lady in evening dress, 1935-45, 3½" 75.00
Little Sheba, orig feathers, HP, 1920s, 13" 165.00
Lone Ranger, 16".. 85.00
Mexican taking siesta, ashtray, mk 1936, 6½"............................. 45.00
Monkey sitting upright scratching head, bank, 1940-50, 12¼" 47.50
Navy WAVE, mk Remember Pearl Harbor, 1944, 13" 65.00
Nude bust, lamp, Art Deco style, 1930-40, 8½" 135.00
Oriental lady, bust, 1930-40, 5½".. 65.00
Pinocchio standing w/arms down to side, 1940-50, 11½" 95.00
Pirate girl, 1930s, 14¼" 95.00
Porky Pig standing, wearing top hat, 1940-50, 11" 70.00
Sailor at ease holding rifle, 1935-45, 13½" 120.00
Shirley Temple, 1935-45, 14½" 245.00
Uncle Sam rolling up his sleeve, 1935-45, 15"............................. 125.00
Wimpy eating hamburger (You Bring the Ducks), mk 1929, 13" . 175.00
Young girl holding fan, 1925-35, 11".. 55.00

Shooting Gallery Targets

Battleship, worn wht pnt, Mangels, 5, 6¼x11⅜", from $200 to.... 300.00
Birds (8) on bar, worn pnt, Mangels, 9, 3½x41½", from $700 to.. 800.00
Bull's-eye w/pop-up duck, old pnt, Quackenbush, 7, 12" dia, $500 to...600.00
Clown, worn red/wht/pnt, Mangels, 9, 19x19½"+movable arms, min. 1,000.00
Clown standing, bull's-eye, mc pnt, Evans or Hoffman, 10, 12" min .1,000.00
Dog running, worn wht pnt, Smith or Evans, 6, 6x11", from $100 to. 200.00

Duck, detailed feathers, old pnt, Parker, 8, 3¾x5½", $100 to 200.00
Duck, detailed feathers, worn pnt, Evans, 4, 5½x8½", $100 to..... 200.00
Eagle w/wings wide, mc pnt, Smith or Evans, 6, 14¾", $650 to ... 750.00
Elephant, wht pnt, flakes, 9½" 250.00
Greyhound, bull's-eye, old patina, Parker, 8, 26" W, min 1,000.00
Indian chief, worn mc pnt, Hoffmann or Smith, 10, 20x15", min.. 1,000.00
Lion running, old wht pnt, 12½" L 220.00
Monkey standing, worn pnt, 10, 9¾x8½", from $300 to 400.00
Mountain goat leaping, worn wht pnt, 8¾" 150.00
Owl, bull's-eye, wht traces, Evans, 6, 10¾x5⅛", from $400 to...... 500.00
Pipe, old patina, Smith, 1, 5¾x1¾", value less than 50.00
Rabbit running, bull's-eye, old patina, Parker, 8, 12x25x1", min...1,000.00
Rabbit standing, worn pnt, Smith or Mueller, 8, 18x10", from $900 to ..1,000.00
Reindeer (elk), wht pnt (worn/rusty), 7, 10x9", from $300 to...4,000.00
Saber-tooth tiger, old patina, Mangels, 7, 7¾x13", from $300 to . 400.00
Soldier w/rifle, pnt traces/old patina, Mueller, 5, 9x5", from $100 to .200.00
Squirrel running, old patina, Smith, 4, 5⅛x9¼", from $100 to 200.00
Stag running, worn blk pnt, hooves missing, 9½" 220.00
Star spinner, dbl, worn mc pnt, Mangels, 6, 8x2¾", from $200 to. 300.00
Swan, worn pnt, Mueller, 7, 5¾x5", from $100 to 200.00

Carnival Glass

Carnival glass is pressed glass that has been coated with a sodium solution and fired to give it an exterior lustre. First made in America in 1905, it was produced until the late 1920s and had great popularity in the average American household, for unlike the costly art glass produced by Tiffany, carnival glass could be mass produced at a small cost. Colors most found are marigold, green, blue, and purple; but others exist in lesser quantities and include white, clear, red, aqua opalescent, peach opalescent, ice blue, ice green, amber, lavender, and smoke.

Companies mainly responsible for its production in America include the Fenton Art Glass Company, Williamstown, West Virginia; the Northwood Glass Company, Wheeling, West Virginia; the Imperial Glass Company, Bellaire, Ohio; the Millersburg Glass Company, Millersburg, Ohio; and the Dugan Glass Company (Diamond Glass), Indiana, Pennsylvania. In addition to these major manufacturers, lesser producers included the U.S. Glass Company, the Cambridge Glass Company, the Westmoreland Glass Company, and the McKee Glass Company.

Carnival glass has been highly collectible since the 1950s and has been reproduced for the last 25 years. Several national and state collectors' organizations exist, and many fine books are available on old carnival glass, including *Standard Encyclopedia of Carnival Glass*, *Standard Companion to Carnival Glass*, and *Standard Companion to Non-American Carnival Glass*, all by Mike Carwile.

Acorn Burrs (Northwood), pitcher, green, $800.00.
(Photo courtesy Bill Edwards and Mike Carwile)

A Dozen Roses (Imperial), bowl, gr, ftd, scarce, 8-10" 800.00
A-Q, perfume, amethyst, rare, 4".. 150.00
Acorn Burrs (Northwood), butter dish, amethyst........................ 300.00
Anemone (Northwood), pitcher, marigold 225.00

Apple Tree (Fenton), pitcher, marigold, vase whimsey, rare 7,500.00
Asters, bowl, bl 100.00
Aurora Pearls, bowl, bl w/decor, 2 szs, ea.................................... 750.00
Australian Daisy (Jain), tumbler, marigold, very scarce............... 175.00
Australian Diamond (Crystal), sugar bowl, marigold 70.00
Autumn Acorns (Fenton), bowl, amethyst, 8½".............................. 95.00
Aztec (Mckee), pitcher, marigold, rare.....................................1,300.00
Baby's Bouquet, child's plate, marigold, scarce........................... 115.00
Balloons (Imperial), cake plate, marigold, ... 85.00
Bamboo Bird, jar, marigold, complete 800.00
Banded Diamonds (Crystal), flower set, amethyst, 2-pc 195.00
Banded Moon & Stars Variant (Jain), tumbler, marigold,........... 275.00
Banded Rose, vase, marigold, sm 175.00
Basket (Northwood), opal, either shape, ftd 465.00
Basket Variant (Northwood), basket, gr, smooth hdl, scarce........ 575.00
Beaded Basket (Dugan), basket, bl, flared 350.00
Beaded Cable (Northwood), candy dish, wht............................... 200.00
Beaded Shell (Dugan), pitcher, amethyst.................................... 650.00
Beaded Stars (Fenton), plate, marigold, 9" 110.00
Beetle Ashtray (Argentina), bl, 1 sz, rare.................................... 500.00
Bells & Beads (Dugan), gravy boat, peach opal, handled............. 140.00
Berry Basket, marigold, one sz 50.00
Big Basketweave (Dugan), vase, peach opal, squat, 4-7" 300.00
Bird Galaxy, vase, gr, 10¼" 4,200.00
Blackberry, Miniture (Fenton), compote, gr, sm......................... 200.00
Blackberry (Fenton), basket, gr, hat shaped w/open edge............. 165.00
Blackberry Spray (Fenton), compote, bl 50.00
Blossomtime (Northwood), compote, amethyst 325.00
Boggy Bayou (Fenton), vase, marigold, 12-15" 60.00
Bouquet (Fenton), pitcher, bl... 485.00
Brocaded Acorns (Fostoria), cake tray, ice bl, center hdl 200.00
Brocaded Daisies (Fostoria), vase, ice gr 275.00
Brocaded Roses (Fostoria), bowl, ice gr, ftd, lg............................. 210.00
Bull's Eye & Diamonds, mug, marigold 150.00
Butterflies (Fenton), bonbon, gr... 75.00
Butterflies & Bells (Crystal), compote, marigold 220.00
Buttermilk, Plain (Fenton), compote, gr... 70.00
Cameo Pendant, cameo, amethyst 250.00
Canary Tree (Jain), tumbler, marigold 235.00
Cane & Panels, tumbler, marigold 250.00
Cannonball Variant, pitcher, wht.. 400.00
Captive Rose (Fenton), plate, bl, 9"..87,500.00
Caroline (Dugan), banana bowl, peach opal.................................. 125.00
Cathedral Arches, punch bowl, marigold, 1-pc 400.00
Chain & Star (Fostoria), butter dish, marigold...........................1,500.00
Chatham (US Glass), candlesticks, marigold, pr 90.00
Cherokee, tumbler, bl 65.00
Cherries & Little Flowers (Fenton), pitcher, amethyst................. 265.00
Cherry (Millersburg), milk pitcher, bl, rare................................7,000.00
Cherry & Cable (Northwood), bowl, marigold, scarce, 9" 110.00
Cherry Smash (CherryBerry) (US Glass), bowl, marigold, 8" 55.00
Chesterfield (Imperial), champagne, marigold, 5½" 35.00
Circled Rose, plate, marigold, 7" 95.00
Classic Arts, powder jar, marigold.. 400.00
Colonial Tulip (Northwood), compote, gr, rayed int...................... 80.00
Columbine (Fenton), tumbler, marigold 30.00
Concave Diamonds (Northwood), pickle castor, marigold, complete .. 750.00
Coral (Fenton), bowl, bl, 9" 500.00
Cornflowers, bowl, marigold, ftd... 125.00
Coronation (English), vase, marigold, Victoria Crown design, 5"...250.00
Cosmos & Cane (US Glass), rose bowl, amethyst, lg..............1,200.00
Country Kitchen (Millersburg), creamer or spooner, amethyst.... 350.00
Crackle (Imperial), punch bowl & base, marigold......................... 55.00
Creole, rose bowl, marigold 750.00

Curved Star/Cathedral, bowl, marigold, 10" 50.00
Cut Flowers (Jenkins), vase, marigold, 10" 125.00
Czechoslavakian, liquor set, marigold, complete 350.00
Daisy & Cane (Brockwitz), bowl, marigold, oval, 12" 90.00
Daisy & Plume (Northwood), rose bowl, wht, 3-ftd 750.00
Daisy Block (English), rowboat, amethyst, scarce 325.00
Dandelion (Northwood), pitcher, ice gr 30,000.00
DeVilbliss, atomizer, marigold, complete 100.00
Diamond & Daisy Cut Variant (Jenkins), punch bowl w/base, marigold .. 625.00
Diamond Checkerboard, cracker jar, marigold 85.00
Diamond Cut (Crystal), compote, marigold 75
Diamond Lace (Imperial), bowl, gr, 10-11" 250.00
Diamond Rain, tumbler, marigold, scarce 150.00
Diamond Thumbprint, oil lamp, marigold, mini, 6½" 250.00
Diamond Wedge, tumbler, marigold 125.00
Double Diamonds (Inwald), cologne, marigold 90.00
Double Star (Cambridge), bowl, gr, rare, 9" 400.00
Drapery (Northwood), candy dish, ice gr 225.00
Dugan's Flute, vase, marigold, 7-13" 45.00
Dutch Mill, ashtray, marigold 65.00
Eleckra, sugar bowl, marigold 65.00
Elks (Millersburg), bowl, amethyst, rare 2,500.00
Emu (Crystal), bowl, marigold, rare, 10" 900.00
Enameled Freesia, pitcher, bl 190.00
Enameled Panel, goblet, marigold 190.00
Encrusted Vine, tumbler, marigold 25.00
Estate (Westmoreland), bud vase, marigold 50.00
Etched Deco (Trudy), nappy, marigold, hdl 40.00
Exotic Lustre, lemonade tumbler, marigold, scarce 50.00
Fans, cracker jar, marigold, metal lid 175.00
Fashion (Imperial), bride's basket, marigold 125.00
Fenton's #643, plate, ice gr, 7" 40.00
Fenton's Flowers (Fenton), nut bowl, bl 500.00
Fentonia (Fenton), fruit bowl, bl, 10" 100.00
Field Thistle (US Glass), bowl, ice bl, 6-10" 250.00
File (Imperial & English), compote, amethyst 50.00
Fine Cut & Star, banana boat, marigold, 5" 150.00
Fine Rib (Dugan), vase, peach opal, 8-15" 125.00
Fish Bowl, bowl, marigold, very scarce, 7½" 375.00
Five Petals, bowl, amethyst, rare 60.00
Flashing Stars, tumbler, bl, rare 275.00
Floating Hen, candy dish, marigold, ftd, w/lid 400.00
Floral & Wheat (Dugan), bonbon, wht, stemmed 125.00
Floral Sunburst (Sweden), vase, bl, flared top 100.00
Flowers & Spades (Dugan), bowl, peach opal, scarce, 5" 65.00
Flute (Northwood), bowl, amethyst, 9" 55.00
Folding Fan (Dugan), compote, peach opal 125.00
Four Flowers (Dugan), plate, amethyst, 9-10½" 2,500.00

Four-Seven-Four (Imperial), pitcher, green, $500.00. (Photo courtesy Bill Edwards and Mike Carwile)

French Grape, bowl, marigold, 4" 180.00
Fruit Band, decanter, bl 350.00

Ganador (Papini), pitcher, marigold 350.00
Garden Path (Dugan), bowl, ice cream; wht, scarce, 10" 1,000.00
Gem Dandy, butter churn, marigold 500.00
Georgia Belle (Dugan), compote, peach opal, ftd 140.00
God & Home (Dugan), tumbler, bl, rare 175.00
Golden Honeycomb, sugar bowl, marigold 40.00
Good Luck (Northwood), bowl, peach opal, 8½" 3,000.00
Grace, bowl, bl 225.00
Grape & Cable (Fenton), bowl, gr, flat, 7-8" 80.00
Grape & Cable (Northwood), dresser tray, gr 300.00
Grape & Cable Banded (Northwood), bowl, orange; bl 650.00
Grape & Cable Variant (Northwood), bowl, aqua opal, 6-8" 2,000.00
Grape & Cable w/Thumbprint (Northwood), shot glass, marigold .115.00
Grape Arbor (Northwood), tumbler, ice gr 325.00
Grape Wreath (Millersburg), bowl, ice cream; gr, 10" 300.00
Grecian Daisy, pitcher, marigold, scarce 400.00
Ground Cherries, pitcher, bl 125.00
Handled Tumbler, amethyst, 1 sz 125.00
Hatpins (Various Makers), bee on flower, amethyst 600.00
Hattie (Imperial), rose bowl, amethyst 3,000.00
Hawaiian Moon, pitcher, marigold 200.00
Heart & Trees (Fenton), bowl, gr, 8¼" 700.00
Heart & Vine Variant (Fenton), plate, bl, scarce, 9" 1,000.00
Hearts & Flowers (Northwood), bowl, wht, ruffled, 8½" 300.00
Heavy Grape (Imperial), plate, wht, 11" 450.00
Heavy Vine, shot glass, marigold 80.00
Heisey Colonial, dresser tray, marigold 100.00
Heisey Flute, punch cup, marigold 35.00
Hickman, caster set, marigold, 4-pc 325.00
Hobnail (Millersburg), spittoon, gr, scarce 1,800.00
Hobstar (Imperial), cookie jar, gr 100.00
Hobstar & Feather (Millersburg), punch cup, bl, scarce 1,300.00
Hobstar & Shield (European), pitcher, marigold 325.00
Hobstar Band, sugar bowl, marigold, w/lid 115.00
Hobstar Reversed (English), rose bowl, amethyst 95.00
Holly (Fenton), goblet, red 750.00
Holly Sprig (Millersburg), bonbon, amethyst 75.00
Homestead, shade, marigold 65.00
Hoops, rose bowl, marigold, low, 6½" 75.00
Hourglass, vase, bud; marigold 45.00
Iceburg (Czech), bowl, ice bl 95.00
Imperial #499, bowl, sherbet; gr 30.00
Imperial Grape, basket, bl, hdl 225.00
Imperial Jewels, hat shape, red 225.00
Indian Key (India), tumbler, marigold 135.00
Interior Swirl, spittoon, peach opal 140.00
Inverted Feather (Cambridge), cracker jar, amethyst 750.00
Inverted Strawberry (Cambridge), butter dish, amethyst 1,100.00
Jack-in-the-Pulpit (Dugan), vase, peach opal 125.00
Jewel Box, inkwell, gr 200.00
Jewel's (Dugan), candlesticks, red, pr 275.00
Jeweled Heart (Dugan), bowl, wht, 10" 250.00
Kittens (Fenton), cup, bl, scarce 400.00
Kokomo (English), rose bowl, marigold, ftd 75.00
Lake Shore Honey, honey jar, marigold 200.00
Late Strawberry, tumbler, marigold 75.00
Lattice & Daisy (Dugan), pitcher, bl 1,500.00
Laurel, shade, marigold 40.00
Laurel Band, pitcher, marigold 95.00
Leaf Chain (Fenton), bowl, ice gr, 7-9" 2,600.00
Leaf Tiers (Fenton), butter dish, marigold, ftd 175.00
Lightning Flower (Northwood), bowl, marigold, rare, 5" 100.00
Lion (Fenton), bowl, bl, scarce, 7" 300.00
Little Stars (Millersburg), bowl, bl, scarce, 7-7½" 3,000.00

Long Buttress, toothpick, marigold 200.00
Long Leaf (Dugan), bowl, peach opal, ftd 175.00
Lovebirds, bottle, marigold, w/stopper 575.00
Lustre, tumbler, marigold 45.00
Lustre Rose (Imperial), bowl, fruit; amethyst, ftd, 11-12" 750.00
Magnolia Rib (Fenton), butter dish, marigold 125.00
Manhattan (US Glass), decanter, marigold 250.00
Maple Leaf (Dugan), bowl, bl, stemmed, 9" 100.00
Marilyn (Millersburg), tumbler, gr, rare 350.00
McKee's Squiggy, vase, gr 125.00
Memphis (Northwood), bowl, fruit; ice gr, w/base 6,000.00
Millersburg Four Pillars, vase, gr, star base, rare 350.00
Minnesota (US Glass), mug, marigold 100.00
Moller (EDA), bowl, bl 325.00
Moonprint (Brockwitz), pitcher, marigold, squat, scarce 225.00
My Lady, powder jar, marigold 125.00
Napoli (Italy), decanter, marigold 75.00
Nesting Swan (Millersburg), bowl, gr, sq, rare 1,500.00
Niagara Falls (Jeannette), pitcher, marigold 50.00
Nippon (Scandanavian), basket, marigold, hdl 65.00
Northern Star (Fenton), card tray, marigold, 6" 40.00
Northwood #657, candlesticks, bl, pr 135.00
Notches, plate, marigold, 8" 50.00
O' Hara (Loop), pitcher, marigold 120.00
Octagon (Imperial), cordial, marigold 250.00
Octagon (Imperial), pitcher, milk; amethyst, scarce 350.00
Old Fashion, tray w/6 tumblers, marigold 150.00
Omera (Imperial), bowl, marigold, 10" 45.00
Omnibus, pitcher whimsey, gr, no spout 1,200.00
Open Flower (Dugan), bowl, peach opal, flat or ftd, 7" 85.00
Optic (Imperial), bowl, amethyst, 9" 75.00
Orange Peel (Westmoreland), punch bowl w/base, amethyst 250.00
Orange Tree (Fenton), bowl, orange; gr, lg, ftd 1,000.00
Orange Tree (Fenton), goblet, marigold, lg 100.00
Orchid, tumbler, wht 65.00
Palm Beach (US Glass), pitcher, wht, scarce 600.00
Paneled Dandelion (Fenton), candle-lamp whimsey, rare 3,200.00
Paneled Prism, jam jar, marigold, w/lid 55.00
Pansy (Imperial), pickle dish, bl, oval 275.00
Parlor, ashtray, bl 95.00
Passion Flower, vase, marigold 125.00
Peach (Northwood), bowl, wht, 9" 150.00
Peacock (Millersburg), bowl, gr, 9" 550.00
Peacock & Urn (Northwood), bowl, ice cream; marigold, 6" 125.00
Peacock Tail (Fenton), plate, bl, 9" 600.00
Pearly Dots (Westmoreland), compote, peach opal 150.00
Persian Garden (Dugan), bowl, berry; peach opal, 10" 350.00
Persian Medallion (Fenton), punch bowl w/base, bl 800.00
Petals & Prisms (English), bowl, fruit; marigold, 2-pc 90.00
Pine Cone (Fenton), plate, amethyst, 7½" 550.00
Pineapple (English), bowl, marigold, 4" 40.00
Plain Jane (Imperial), basket, ice gr 200.00
Pony (Dugan), bowl, marigold, 8½" 90.00
Poppy Show (Imperial), lamp whimsey, amethyst 1,400.00
Premium Swirl (Imperial), candlesticks, marigold, pr 50.00
Primrose & Ribbon, lightshade, marigold 90.00
Prism & Daisy Band (Imperial), bowl, marigold, 8" 25.00
Provence, tumbler, marigold 150.00
Quilted Rose (EDA), bowl, marigold 150.00
Radiance, mustard jar, marigold, w/lid 175.00
Rainbow (Northwood), compote, amethyst 65.00
Ranger (Imperial), sherbet, marigold, ftd 55.00
Raspberry (Northwood), gravy boat, bl, ftd 300.00
Regal Cane, goblet, marigold 200.00

Rekord (EDA), bowl, bl, scarce 225.00
Ribbed Swirl, pitcher, gr 225.00
Riihimaki, tumbler, bl 225.00
Rising Sun (US Glass), sugar bowl, marigold 95.00
River Glass, celery vase, marigold 85.00
Rococo (Imperial), bowl, marigold, ftd, 5" 40.00
Rosalind (Millersburg), bowl, marigold, scarce, 10" 200.00
Rose Garden (Sweden & Germany), vase, bl, sm, scarce 1,500.00
Rosetime, vase, marigold, 7½" 100.00
Royal Garland (Jain), tumbler, marigold 200.00
Royalty (Imperial), fruit bowl w/stand, marigold 100.00
Sailboat (Fenton), compote, bl 195.00
Scales (Westmoreland), plate, amethyst, 9" 100.00
Scroll Embossed (Imperial), compote, bl, sm 750.00
Shasta Daisy, pitcher, marigold 250.00
Shell & Jewel (Westmoreland), sugar bowl, wht, w/lid 90.00
Singing Birds (Northwood), mug, ice bl 435.00
Ski-Star (Dugan), banana bowl, amethyst 175.00
Smooth Rays (Imperial), champagne, marigold 40.00
Spice Grater (India), pitcher, marigold 350.00
Spiral (Imperial), candlesticks, gr, pr 195.00
Springtime (Northwood), bowl, amethyst, 9" 200.00
Star & File (Imperial), tumbler, iced tea; marigold 70.00
Star Medallion (Imperial), pickle dish, marigold 40.00
Starburst (Finland), spittoon, bl 900.00
Stippled Petals (Dugan), basket, peach opal, hdl 170.00
Stippled Salt Cup, marigold 45.00
Stork & Rushes (Dugan), pitcher, bl 500.00
Strawberry Wreath (Millersburg), bowl, amethyst, sq, 9" 400.00

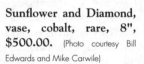

Sunflower and Diamond, vase, cobalt, rare, 8", $500.00. (Photo courtesy Bill Edwards and Mike Carwile)

Swirl (Imperial), candlestick, ea 35.00
Swirl Variant, vase, peach opal, 6½" 200.00
Ten Mums (Fenton), bowl, amethyst, flat, 8-10" 275.00
Thread & Cane (Crystal), salver, marigold 100.00
Three Fruits (Northwood), bowl, ice gr, stippled, 9" 2,600.00
Tiny Bubbles, vase, gr, 8½" 225.00
Tree Bark (Imperial), console bowl, marigold 35.00
Tree of Life, perfume, marigold, w/lid 35.00
Triplets (Dugan), bowl, peach opal, 6-8" 75.00
Two Flowers (Fenton), bowl, gr, ftd, 8-10" 250.00
Unshod, pitcher, marigold 85.00
US #310 (US Glass), mayonnaise set, ice gr 95.00
Vineyard (Dugan), tumbler, wht 250.00
Vintage (Fenton), bowl, red, 10" 5,000.00
Vintage Banded (Dugan), pitcher, amethyst 550.00
Violet, basket, bl 95.00
Waffle Block (Imperial), basket, marigold, 10" 50.00
Wagon Wheel, candy dish, marigold, enameled 45.00
Western Thistle Variant, vase, marigold 250.00

Whirling Leaves (Millersburg), bowl, gr, tricornered, 10" 475.00
Wickerwork (English), bowl, amethyst, w/base 400.00
Wide Panel (Imperial), underplate, marigold, 14-15" 85.00
Wide Panel Variant (Northwood), pitcher, marigold, tankard..... 300.00
Wild Fern (Australian), compote, amethyst 275.00
Windmill (Imperial), pitcher, marigold.. 170.00
Wishbone (Northwood), bowl, ice gr, ftd, 7-9"........................ 1,500.00
Wreathed Cherry (Dugan), pitcher, amethyst 550.00
Zig Zag (Millersburg), bowl, gr, rnd or ruffled, 9½" 450.00
Zip Zip (English), flower frog holder, marigold 60.00
Zipper Variant, bowl, marigold, oval, 10" 60.00
Zippered Heart (Imperial), bowl, amethyst, 5" 65.00
Zippered Loop (Imperial), lamp, marigold, lg, rare, 10" 450.00
474 (Imperial), punch bowl & base, gr... 700.00
49er, pin box, marigold 60.00

Carousel Figures

For generations of Americans, visions of carousel horses revolving majestically around lively band organs rekindle wonderful childhood experiences. These nostalgic memories are the legacy of the creative talent from a dozen carving shops that created America's carousel art. Skilled craftsmen brought their trade from Europe where American carvers took the carousel animal from a folk art creation to a true art form. The golden age of carousel art lasted from 1880 to 1929.

There are two basic types of American carousels. The largest and most impressive is the 'park style' carousel built for permanent installation in major amusement centers. These were created in Philadelphia by Gustav and William Dentzel, Muller Brothers, and E. Joy Morris who became the Philadelphia Toboggan Company in 1902. A more flamboyant group of carousel animals was carved in Coney Island, New York, by Charles Looff, Marcus Illions, Charles Carmel, and Stein & Goldstein's Artistic Carousel Company. These park-style carousels were typically three, four, and even five rows with 45 to 68 animals on a platform. Collectors often pay a premium for the carvings by these men. The outside row animals are larger and more ornate and command higher prices. The horses on the inside rows are smaller, less decorated, and of lesser value.

The most popular style of carousel art is the 'country fair style.' These carousels were portable affairs created for mobility. The horses are smaller and less ornate with leg and head positions that allow for stacking and easy loading. These were built primarily for North Tonawanda, New York, near Niagara Falls, by Armitage Herschell Company, Herschell Spillman Company, Spillman Engineering Company, and Allen Herschell. Charles W. Parker was also well known for his portable merry-go-rounds. He was based in Leavenworth, Kansas. Parker and Herschell Spillman both created a few large park-style carousels as well, but they are better known for their portable models.

Horses are by far the most common figure found, but there are two dozen other animals that were created for the carousel platform. Carousel animals, unlike most other antiques, are oftentimes worth more in a restored condition. Figures found with original factory paint are extraordinarily rare and bring premium amounts. Typically, carousel horses are found in garish, poorly applied 'park paint' and are often missing legs or ears. Carousel horses are hollow. They were glued up from several blocks for greater strength and lighter weight. Bass and poplar woods were used extensively.

If you have an antique carousel animal you would like to have identified, send a clear photograph and description along with a LSASE to our advisor, William Manns, who is listed in the Directory under New Mexico. Mr. Manns is the author of *Painted Ponies*, containing many full-color photographs, guides, charts, and directories for the collector.

Key:
IR — inside row   OR — outside row
MR — middle row   PTC — Philadelphia Toboggan Company

Coney Island-Style Horses

Carmel, IR jumper, unrstr...4,800.00
Carmel, MR jumper, unrstr...7,900.00
Carmel, OR jumper w/cherub, rstr 17,000.00
Illions, IR jumper, rstr..5,200.00
Illions, MR stander, rstr..9,200.00
Looff, IR jumper unrstr...3,200.00
Looff, OR jumper, unrstr...14,000.00
Stein & Goldstein, IR jumper, unrstr..4,700.00
Stein & Goldstein, MR jumper, rstr..8,000.00
Stein & Goldstein, OR stander w/bells, unrstr 18,000.00

European Horses

Anderson, English, unrstr...3,500.00
Bayol, French, unrstr...2,500.00
Heyn, German, unrstr..3,200.00
Hubner, Belgian, unrstr...2,000.00
Savage, English, unrstr...2,500.00

Menagerie Animals (Non-Horses)

Dentzel, bear, unrstr..20,000.00
Dentzel, cat, unrstr..22,000.00
Dentzel, deer, unrstr..16,000.00
Dentzel, lion, unrstr...35,000.00
Dentzel, pig, unrstr..9,500.00

Dentzel, pig with acorn and green leaves on one side, pole and base missing, 30x50", $11,500.00. (Photo courtesy Skinner Inc. Auctioneers & Appraisers of Fine Art)

E Joy Morris, deer, unrstr 10,000.00
Herschell Spillman, cat, unrstr...11,000.00
Herschell Spillman, chicken, portable, unrstr..............................5,500.00
Herschell Spillman, dog, portable, unrstr....................................6,500.00
Herschell Spillman, frog, unrstr...18,000.00
Looff, camel, unrstr...10,000.00
Looff, goat, rstr..13,500.00
Muller, tiger, rstr 32,000.00

Philadelphia-Style Horses

Dentzel, IR 'topknot' jumper, unrstr..5,500.00
Dentzel, MR jumper, unrstr 7,800.00
Dentzel, OR stander, female cvg on shoulder, rstr 20,000.00
Dentzel, prancer, rstr...8,000.00
Morris, IR prancer, rstr..4,500.00
Morris, MR stander, unrstr...7,000.00
Morris, OR stander, rstr..17,000.00

Muller, IR jumper, rstr 5,000.00
Muller, MR jumper, rstr 7,500.00
Muller, OR stander, rstr 23,000.00
Muller, OR stander w/military trappings 27,000.00
PTC, chariot (bench-like seat), rstr 7,500.00
PTC, IR jumper, rstr 4,000.00
PTC, MR jumper, rstr 8,500.00
PTC, OR stander, armored, rstr.............................30,000.00
PTC, OR stander, unrstr...19,000.00

Portable Carousel Horses

Allan Herschell, all aluminum, ca 1950...........................500.00
Allan Herschell, half & half, wood & aluminum head..............1,300.00
Allan Herschell, IR Indian pony, unrstr........................2,200.00
Allan Herschell, OR, rstr 3,200.00
Allan Herschell, OR Trojan-style jumper 3,500.00
Armitage Herschell, track-machine jumper.....................2,800.00
Dare, jumper, unrstr..3,000.00
Herschell Spillman, chariot (bench-like seat) 3,800.00
Herschell Spillman, IR jumper, unrstr..........................2,400.00
Herschell Spillman, MR jumper, unrstr.........................2,900.00
Herschell Spillman, OR, eagle decor............................4,500.00
Herschell Spillman, OR, park machine 10,000.00
Parker, MR jumper, unrstr.......................................4,200.00
Parker, OR jumper, park machine, unrstr....................6,500.00
Parker, OR jumper, rstr 5,800.00

Carpet Balls

Carpet balls are glazed china spheres decorated with intersecting lines or other simple designs that were used for indoor games in the British Isles during the early 1800s. Mint condition examples are rare.

Bl intersecting lines on wht, 3¼", EX............................ 40.00
Blk dots w/wht jagged outlines on blk, 4¼", EX.............. 45.00
Blk lines form plaid pattern on wht, 3½", NM.................150.00
Blk thistle & crown, thick overglaze (rare/possibly glass), 3¼", NM.65.00
Brn dots w/wht jagged outlines on brn, 3¼", NM............. 65.00
Four red bull's eyes on wht equator, red rings around ea pole, 3", NM..135.00
Gr & blk lines intersect at right angles, 3", NM..............120.00
Gr crown & thistle design on wht, allover pattern, 3⅛", M.........150.00
Gr/red sponging on wht, 3¼", M 135.00
Mc allover spatter, 3¼", NM 65.00
Mochaware wht/blk/brn swirls, rare, 2⅝", M.................360.00

Pennsylvania Dutch four-petal flower, red and green on white, 2⅞", NM, $500.00. (Photo courtesy Robert S. Block/The AuctionBlocks)

Purple bands & lines intersect at right angles on wht, 3¼", NM..100.00
Red crown & thistle design on wht, 3¼", M................... 90.00
Salmon lines intersect on wht, wider salmon band at equator, 3", EX+ .210.00
Solid wht, 3¼", M.. 48.00
Transfer-printed to mimic stone marble on wht, 2½", NM............. 45.00
Wht starbursts w/red dot centers on red, 3", M.................75.00

Cartoon Art

Collectors of cartoon art are interested in many forms of original art — animation cels, sports, political or editorial cartoons, syndicated comic strip panels, and caricature. To produce even a short animated cartoon strip, hundreds of original drawings are required, each showing the characters in slightly advancing positions. Called 'cels' because those made prior to the 1950s were made from a celluloid material, collectors often pay hundreds of dollars for a frame from a favorite movie. Prices of Disney cels with backgrounds vary widely. Background paintings, model sheets, storyboards, and preliminary sketches are also collectible — so are comic book drawings executed in India ink and signed by the artist. Daily 'funnies' originals, especially the earlier ones portraying super heroes, and Sunday comic strips, the early as well as the later ones, are collected. Cartoon art has become recognized and valued as a novel yet valid form of contemporary art. In the listings below all cels are untrimmed and full size unless noted otherwise.

Cel, Bugs Bunny & Daffy Duck in desert, Warner Bros, '80s, 13x16".225.00
Cel, Bugs Bunny & Elmer Fudd (Lumberjack Rabbit), 1950s, 8x10".1,200.00
Cel, Bugs Bunny as emcee, Warner Bros, 1980s, 9¼x11½" 175.00
Cel, Bugs Bunny in dressing gown, Warner Bros, 1970s, 9x11¾".225.00
Cel, Copper (Fox & Hound), Disney, 1981, 7x8½" 150.00
Cel, Daffy Duck & Porky Pig in space scene, Warner Bros, 1987, 9x12".350.00
Cel, Donald Duck, color image, 1950s, 6x3"....................................50.00
Cel, Donald Duck in auto, pastel chalk/pencil, ca 1940, 6x8" 200.00
Cel, Donald Duck w/gun (Donald Gets Drafted), Courvoisier, 1942, 8x8".1,100.00
Cel, dragon breathing fire (Sleeping Beauty), 1959, 11x30" ...12,000.00
Cel, Jiminy Cricket w/umbrella, 1950s, 7¼x3" 225.00
Cel, Madame Medusa (Rescuers), Disney, 1977, 8½x12" 75.00
Cel, Marvin the Martian & Bugs Bunny, Warner Bros, 1988 ltd ed, 12x10" ..500.00
Cel, Mickey & broom (Fantasia), Courvoisier ground, 1940, 9x12".11,000.00
Cel, Nana as nursemaid (Peter Pan), 1953, 6x8" 450.00
Cel, Pistol Pete (2-Gun Goofy), Disney, 1952, 5x5" (trimmed)..... 75.00
Cel, Princess Tiger Lily dancing (Peter Pan), 1953, 6x4" 300.00
Cel, Ralf Wolf, HP background, Warner Bros, 1960s, 9x12"........900.00
Cel, Sgt Tibbs (cat, 101 Dalmatians), Disney, 1961, 4x7" 650.00
Cel, Siamese cats (2 from Lady & Tramp), Disney, 1955, 8x6".1,300.00
Cel, Simba & Nala (Lion King), detailed ground, ltd ed, 11x13" .450.00
Cel, Snow White & 7 dwarfs, Off to Bed, ltd ed, 7x14¾" 1,100.00
Cel, Sylvester & Pepe Le Pew, hand-colored ground, 1954, 9x12" .1,300.00
Cel, tea party scene (Alice in Wonderland), gouache, 1951, 9x12".5,500.00
Cel, Toby & Basil (Great Mouse Detective), figures only, Disney, 1986 ..250.00
Cel, Willie the Giant w/grapes (Mickey's Christmas Carol), '83, 12x16"..150.00
Cel, Wyle E Coyote in desert scene, Warner Bros, 9x12"..............650.00
Concept art, Cinderella on stairs, M Blair, Disney, 1950, 6x9" .3,250.00
Concept art, fauns/unicorns/etc, chalk pastels, 1940, 9x12"......1,200.00
Concept art, John & monkey (Peter Pan), Hall, Disney, 1953, 8x11" .3,250.00
Concept art, landscape, So Dear to My Heart, M Blair, 1948, 10x12" .4,000.00
Concept art, landscape from Song of the South, Disney, 1946, 6x8".3,500.00
Concept art, Paul Bunyan logging, Disney, tempera, 1958, 6x8"...3,250.00
Concept art, Peter Pan looks at portrait, Disney, 1953, 6x8" 4,000.00
Concept art, Prince leaping crevasse (Sleeping Beauty), tempera, 6x15".7,000.00
Drawing, Aunt Jemima (broken toy), mc pencils, Disney, 1935, 6x5".50.00
Drawing, Charley McCarthy, blk/red/gr/pencil, Disney, 1938, 7x4".450.00
Drawing, chorus line (Mother Goose Goes Hollywood), Disney, 1938, 6x7".100.00
Drawing, Cinderella upper torso, blk & red pencil, 1950, 5x4"....100.00
Drawing, Dandy Jim Crow (Dumbo), blk pencil, red notations, 1941, 5x4"...100.00
Drawing, Donald & Goofy in canoe (Moose Hunters), 1937, 6x11".400.00
Drawing, Donald Duck on donkey at RR track, mc, 1940, 6x8" ..250.00
Drawing, Donald singing (Donald's Dream Voice), blk pencil, 1948, 6x4"..25.00
Drawing, Dumbo w/feather, blk pencil, lg image, 1941 ....550.00
Drawing, evil creature (Fantasia), blk pencil, 1940, 8½x11".......600.00

Drawing, Gepetto's shelves (Pinocchio), blk pencil, 1940, 11x15" .. 300.00
Drawing, Mickey (Brave Little Tailor), mc pencils, 1937, 3x4" ... 300.00
Drawing, Mickey & elephant, blk pencil, Disney, 1936, 3½x7½" 250.00
Drawing, Mickey & Minnie (Touchdown Mickey), pencil, 1932, 10x7".. 850.00
Drawing, Mickey & Pluto (Society Dog Show), blk pencil, 1939, 10x12"..450.00
Drawing, Mickey Mouse (Society Dog Show), blk pencil, 1930s. 250.00
Drawing, Mickey Mouse policeman (Dognappers), blk pencil, 1934, 8x5".200.00
Drawing, Mickey Mouse w/shotgun (Mickey's Parrot), 1938 .... 225.00
Drawing, Mickey/Goofy/Donald w/roadster, mc pencils, 1935, 5x7" .1,000.00
Drawing, Mr Mag, blk/red/gr pencil, sm image, 12x15¾" 25.00
Drawing, Pete w/machine Gun (Mail Pilot), Disney, 1933, 5x9" . 450.00
Drawing, Pinocchio, pencil w/color details, Disney, 1940 .... 1,100.00
Drawing, Pinocchio swinging ft, blk pencil, Disney, 1940............ 700.00
Drawing, Scrooge McDuck in money bath, blk/mc pencils, 9¾x12" .1,400.00
Drawing, Stromboli & Pinocchio, blk pencil, 1940, 8¾x11" 1,100.00
Drawing, Timothy Mouse (Dumbo), blk pencil, 1941 .... 250.00
Model sheet, Elmer Elephant, various members of cast, 1936, 14x14" . 100.00
Model sheet, Little Lulu in 15 poses, blk pencil, 1943, 13x18" 250.00
Model sheet, Moose Hunters, Goofy & Donald in disguise, 1937, 10x12" ..25.00
Presentation art, Brer Rabbit & Brer Fox, watercolor, 1946, 5x7"...750.00
Presentation art, Katzenjammer Kids (Hans & Fritz), 1928, 4x5½" . 300.00
Sericel, Dudley Do-Right/Nel/Snidley Whiplash, 1961, 9½x12" . 400.00
Sericel, Scar w/cub Simba, limited ed, 5x11½" 50.00
Sericel, Simba w/mane of leaves (Lion King/Main Event), 7½x8¼" .50.00
Sunday page, Flash Gordon, pen & ink, 1935, 29x18" 41,000.00

Cast Iron

In the mid-1800s, the cast-iron industry was raging in the United States. It was recognized as a medium extremely adaptable for uses ranging from ornamental architectural filigree to actual building construction. It could be cast from a mold into any conceivable design that could be reproduced over and over at a relatively small cost. It could be painted to give an entirely versatile appearance. Furniture with openwork designs of grapevines and leaves and intricate lacy scrollwork was cast for gardens as well as inside use. Figural doorstops of every sort, bootjacks, trivets, and a host of other useful and decorative items were made before the 'ferromania' had run its course. For more information, we recommend *Antique Iron*, by Kathryn McNerney (Collector Books). See also Kitchen, Cast-Iron Bakers and Kettles; and other specific categories.

Garden planter, rusted patina, large, $1,585.00. (Photo courtesy Jackson's International Auctioneers & Appraisers of Fine Art & Antiques)

Architectural ornament, eagle w/wings spread on orb, 18x47" .1,295.00
Architectural ornament, star finial w/arches/scrolls/etc below, 37" .235.00
Bench, allover grape leaves & vines, J McLean, 30x47" L 2,000.00
Bench, allover rococo scrolls, serpentine legs, lady's portrait, 44" L..2,115.00
Bench, Am Gothic, Brown & Owen, 1860, 45" L, +pr armchairs . 8,800.00
Bench, scalloped bk, scrolled seat/arms, old wht rpt, 36x48x17" . 975.00
Bench, scrolling bamboo seat supports, 1800s, 31" L.................1,175.00
Candleholder, flower form, mc pnt, LVL Patg 12-2-04,⅞x5¾", ea.. 85.00
Cemetery gate, weeping willow/lambs, name above/1955, rpr, 42x28".920.00
Chair, Am rococo, lyre bk/floral garlands, scrolled arms, 32", 4 for ..1,645.00
Figure, colt, mc pnt, Hubley #150, 4", NM 140.00
Figure, crocodile, mouth open/stalking, 88" L 6,150.00
Figure, geese, 20", pr 380.00
Figure, Geo Washington w/scroll, mc pnt, Design Pat Aug 26 1843, 47" . 18,115.00
Figure, greyhounds, old patina/lt pitting, att Robert Wood, 21x50", pr...8,000.00
Figure, rabbit, 11x11", pr 350.00
Figure, rooster, Fr, 35x21x11", pr.. 700.00
Finial, pineapple, wht pnt, 20th C, 18x6", pr 265.00
Finial, pineapple top, gray pnt w/chips, 21½" 285.00
Fireplace, Ionic columns w/acanthus designs, Diamond Flue, 37x36x36" . 315.00
Gate, scrolled/foliate castings, 1800s, 17x35" 180.00
Grate, circles/semicircles in rows, old gold pnt, 22x13"................ 85.00
Hitching post, jockey, right arm extended, mc, 1800s, 24", VG ..240.00
Hitching post, jockey w/hand extended, worn mc pnt, 47x16".... 750.00
Hitching post finial, bridled horse w/acanthus-leaf base, rpt, 13". 200.00
Jardiniere, floral panels, loose ring hdls/ftd, oval, 1800s, 35" L, pr.3,290.00
Kettle, sugar; flared rim, LA, 27x72" 6,400.00
Kettle, sugar; 1800s, 20x35" 2,000.00
Kettle, 3-legged/hdld, A Baldwin & Co, No 2½, w/lid, 11" 650.00
Lawn sprinkler, frog on ball, mc pnt, NUYDA mk, 10⅛x7".......1,900.00
Lawn sprinkler, frog w/spread legs, realistic pnt, 8⅝x14" 2,500.00
Lawn sprinkler, mallard duck, old rpt, B&H mk, VG 2,250.00
Lawn sprinkler, mermaid on fluted base, mc pnt, rare, 14¼x7¼"..10,000.00
Mirror, rtcl oval, hoop-skirted lady ea side, flag at base, 21"...1,680.00
Paperweight, Black Sambo smoking cigar, mc pnt, Hubley, 3x1⅜", EX .335.00
Paperweight, Charles Lindbergh, mc pnt, 3⅞x1⅝", VG 115.00
Paperweight, lion, yel w/brn mane, Hubley, 3x3¼", NM.............. 395.00
Pencil holder, Dutch girl figural, mc pnt, Wilton, 2¾", EX 150.00
Pencil holder, Peter Rabbit figural, mc pnt, Wilton, 2⅝" 280.00
Place card holder, elephant figural, mc pnt, Hubley #449, NM.... 395.00
Place card holder, swan, mc pnt, Hubley #449, NM 195.00
Pot, indigo; flared lip, 2 knob hdls, cast w/center seam, 15x26" .1,175.00
Pot, 3-ftd, w/lid mk A Baldwon...New Orleans, 19th C, 5¼x9"... 250.00
Settee, fern-pattern bk, lion-head terminals, wht pnt, 30" H....2,500.00
Table, 30" dia top w/branch legs, pnt, 33" 800.00
Tiebacks, zinnias, yel & gr pnt, sgn LVA, 2½x3⅛", pr, NM 195.00
Urn, emb cherubs in garden pursuits, sq foliate base, 48x32", pr . 2,800.00
Urn, scrolled bowl, narrow neck, sq plinth, Dayton OH, 19th C, 29x21".265.00
Urn, swallows/geometrics/flowers, cast in 3 pcs, old gr rpt, 34" 300.00
Whist counter, game counting device, 1880s, 1½x3" dia, EX....... 110.00

Castor Sets

Castor sets became popular during the early years of the eighteenth century and continued to be used through the late Victorian era. Their purpose was to hold various condiments for table use. The most common type was a circular arrangement with a center handle on a revolving pedestal base that held three, four, five, or six bottles. A few were equipped with a bell for calling the servant. Frames were made of silverplate, glass, or pewter. Though most bottles were of pressed glass, some of the designs were cut, and on rare occasion, colored glass with enameled decorations was used as well. To maintain authenticity and value, castor sets should have matching bottles. Prices listed below are for those with matching bottles and in frames with plating that is in excellent condition (unless noted otherwise). Note: Watch for new frames and bottles in clear, cranberry, cobalt, and vaseline Inverted Thumbprint as well as reproductions of Czechoslovakian cut glass bottles. These have recently been appearing on the market. Our advisor for this category is Barbara Aaronson; she is listed in the Directory under California.

3-bottle, Daisy & Button; SP fr w/toothpick holder finial............ 275.00
3-bottle, Gothic Arch, orig stoppers; pewter fr............................ 115.00
5-bottle, clear; rstr Meriden B #157 fr w/cherub atop hdl............ 525.00
5-bottle, clear/sq; rstr #2165 fr revolves.. 650.00
5-bottle, cut facets/etched leaves; SP fr, 17½".............................. 100.00
5-bottle, etched amberina, cut amberina stoppers; gilt fr, EX.... 2,200.00
5-bottle, etched floral w/cutting, much decor; Meriden ft............ 450.00
5-bottle, sq; SP #2165 fr revolves.. 650.00
5-bottle, vaseline glass; Meriden #827 fr, 13¾"............................ 850.00

Six-bottle, Daisy and Button, one cruet damaged, mismatched tops, 15½", $300.00. (Photo courtesy Jackson's International Auctioneers & Appraisers of Fine Art & Antiques)

6-bottle, Daisy & Button; ornate rstr Wilcox fr revolves.............. 375.00
6-bottle, mold-blown castors w/ribbed acorn stoppers, Sandwich, 8".. 585.00
6-bottle, pressed; 18" Simpson-Hall-Miller fr w/EX SP................ 550.00
6-bottle+bud vase, pressed glass; rstr SP #2114 fr revolves........... 750.00
7-bottle, cut crystal, w/stoppers; lg ped-ft Gleason fr w/doors, EX . 2,500.00
7-bottle, cut crystal; gadrooned/shell-border Geo III SP fr........... 495.00

Catalina Island

Catalina Island pottery was made on the island of the same name, which is about 26 miles off the coast of Los Angeles. The pottery was started in 1927 at Pebble Beach, by Wm. Wrigley, Jr., who was instrumental in developing and using the native clays. Its principal products were brick and tile to be used for construction on the island. Garden pieces were first produced, then vases, bookends, lamps, ashtrays, novelty items, and finally dinnerware. The ware became very popular and was soon being shipped to the mainland as well.

Some of the pottery was hand thrown; some was made in molds. Most pieces are marked Catalina Island or Catalina with a printed incised stamp or handwritten with a pointed tool. Cast items were sometimes marked in the mold, a few have an ink stamp, and a paper label was also used. The most favored colors in tableware and accessories are 1) black (rare), 2) Seafoam and Monterey Brown (uncommon), 3) matt blue and green, 4) Toyon Red (orange), 5) other brights, and 6) pastels with a matt finish.

The color of the clay can help to identify approximately when a piece was made: 1927 to 1932, brown to red (Island) clay (very popular with collectors, tends to increase values); 1931 to 1932, an experimental period with various colors; 1932 to 1937, mainly white clay, though tan to brown clays were also used on occasion.

Items marked Catalina Pottery are listed in Gladding McBean. For further information we recommend *Catalina Island Pottery Collectors Guide* by Steven and Aisha Hoefs, and *Collector's Encyclopedia of California Pottery, Second Edition*, and *California Pottery Scrapbook*, both by Jack Chipman (Collector Books). Our advisor for this category is Steven Hoefs; he is listed in the Directory under Georgia.

Ashtray, cowboy hat form, yel.. 275.00
Ashtray, fish shape, wht w/blk features, 6⅞x5"............................ 195.00
Ashtray/match holder, bl, Mexican man taking a siesta, 3½x6x7"..475.00
Bowl, bl, #710, 3½x13"... 75.00
Bowl, gray, patterned rim, #721, 14".. 110.00
Bowl, serving; oval... 125.00
Bowl, wht, fluted to rim, 3x8".. 75.00
Candelabrum, 3 leaf-form holders, turq, 2½x11", ea..................... 325.00
Candlestick, cactus flask form, Descanso Green, 6¼", ea............. 900.00
Candlestick, gr, flared base, 3¼", ea... 75.00
Candlesticks, pearly wht, 3¼", pr... 225.00
Candlesticks, satin bl, 4¼", pr.. 70.00
Carafe, bl, bulbous bottom w/triangular top, wooden hdl, 8½".... 265.00
Casserole, bl, single serving, w/lid.. 425.00
Casserole, w/lid, lg.. 275.00
Coaster, bl or gr, #501, 4" dia.. 60.00
Coffee server, gr w/metal hdl, 10½"... 500.00
Coffeepot, Deco-style, Catalina Blue, 4½x11", +cr/sug............ 1,400.00
Creamer & sugar bowl, gr, Art Deco style, w/lid, creamer mk #63..145.00
Cup, demitasse; 2⅝".. 35.00
Cup & saucer, yel, red clay, sq hdl... 45.00
Figurine, cat, bl, 4½".. 600.00
Pitcher, beverage; Mandarin Manchu Yellow, 7½"....................... 375.00
Plaque, stagecoach w/2 drivers, mk Graham #745-65B, 12½"... 1,200.00
Plate, Serenade, HP by FM Graham, 12½", from $800 to......... 1,200.00
Plate, Submarine Garden, mc scene w/gr border, 12½"............ 1,500.00
Plate, Swordfish, red, 14", from $1,200 to................................. 1,600.00
Platter, med gr, 16" dia... 175.00
Table top, 6-tile, parrots on branch, mc, 17x21x16", from $5,000 to.6,000.00
Teapot, bl, Art Deco style, #65, 4½x7⅜"..................................... 790.00
Tumbler, turq, honeycomb design at base..................................... 100.00
Tumbler, wht clay, 4".. 50.00
Vase, gourd shape w/hdls, 9"... 425.00
Vase, Toyon Red, red clay, 7½x5½".. 355.00
Vase, yel w/emb birds in tree, cylindrical, 11", from $900 to..... 1,200.00
Wall pocket, basketweave, 9½"... 525.00

Catalogs

Catalogs are not only intriguing to collect on their own merit, but for the collector with a specific interest, they are often the only remaining source of background information available, and as such they offer a wealth of otherwise unrecorded data. The mail-order industry can be traced as far back as the mid-1800s. Even before Aaron Montgomery Ward began his career in 1872, Laacke and Joys of Wisconsin and the Orvis Company of Vermont, both dealers in sporting goods, had been well established for many years. The E.C. Allen Company sold household necessities and novelties by mail on a broad scale in the 1870s. By the end of the Civil War, sewing machines, garden seed, musical instruments, even medicine, were available from catalogs. In the 1880s Macy's of New York issued a 127-page catalog; Sears and Spiegel followed suit in about 1890. Craft and art supply catalogs were first available about 1880 and covered such varied fields as china painting, stenciling, wood burning, brass embossing, hair weaving, and shellcraft. Today some collectors confine their interests not only to craft catalogs in general but often to just one subject. There are several factors besides rarity which make a catalog valuable: age, condition, profuse illustrations, how collectible the field is that it deals with, the amount of color used in its printing, its size (format and number of pages), and whether it is a manufacturer's catalog verses a jobber's catalog (the former being the most desirable).

AG Spalding & Bros, Spring/Summer sports, 1906, 128 pgs, G... 120.00
Aluminum Goods MFG Co, kitchen products, 1956, 20 pgs, VG+. 12.00

American Printing Equipment, 1968, 264 pgs, VG+.......................32.00
Bankers Wholesale Drug Co, pharmaceuticals, 1926, 36 pgs, VG .10.00
Bonwit Teller, women's clothing & accessories, 1981, 54 pgs, VG+ .14.00
Buffalo Scale Co, ca 1923, 8 pgs, G..26.00
Coats & Clark, knitting supplies, ca 1940, 35 pgs, VG 56.00
Cortland Wagon Co, bicycles, 1897, 16 pgs, G.........................40.00
DeMoulin Bros & Co, burlesque/props/costumes, 1924, 200-pg, 6x9", EX .80.00
Dennison MFG Co, arts & crafts, 1922, 32 pgs, VG 12.00
Detective Publishing Co, law enforcement supplies, ca 1914, 8 pgs, VG.93.00
Dierks Lumber & Coal Co, architecture, 1946, 40 pgs, VG+.........15.00
Divison Street Fair, jewelry, ca 1907, 19 pgs, G+......................22.00
E Keller Co, boilers, 1900, 28 pgs, G.......................................32.00
Eclipse Buggy Co, 1914, 15 pgs, VG 84.00
Excelsior Stove & MFG Co, 1912, 8 pgs, G+............................10.00
Federal Telephone MFG Co, radio, 1924, 12 pgs, G...................23.00
Fireside Furnishings, fireplace accessories, 1929, 24 pgs, VG+.......46.00
Forestry Suppliers Inc, camping, 1960, 168 pgs, G+..................32.00
Franklin Railway Supply, early 1900, 16 pgs, G.........................12.00
Gorham MFG Co, kitchenware, 1950, 2 pgs, VG+.....................12.00
Grisswold, Palmer & Co, clothing, 1893, G+.............................88.00
Harley-Davidson, 1976, 6 pgs, VG+...19.00
Herter's Inc, hunting supplies, 1957, 216 pgs, VG....................34.00
International Shoe Co, 1932, 112 pgs, G+................................56.00
Iroquois Door Co, door products, 1915, 207 pgs, VG+.................165.00
Isaac A Sheppard & Co, stoves, 1905, 9 pgs, VG 17.00
JC Penney, 1991, 543 pgs, M..23.00
JM&N MS Browning Co, guns, 1942, 62 pgs, G+......................42.00
Joliet Manufacturing Co, farming, 1918, 32 pgs, G 41.00
Kem-Tone, paint, 1944, 8 pgs, G...7.00
Lane Bryant, women's clothing, 1959, 98 pgs, G 19.00
Liberty Display Fireworks, 1973, 44 pgs, VG+...........................28.00
Marv Koep's, fishing, 1974, 108 pgs, G+.................................24.00
Michael-Leonard Co, seeds, 64 pgs, G..7.00
Murray's Athletic Equipment, sporting equipment, 1949, 32 pgs, G.18.00
National Auto Stores, toys, 1950s, 66 pgs, G+..........................44.00
NE Grocer & Tradesman, 1909, 48 pgs, G+...............................18.00
O'Neill-Adams Co, furniture, ca 1920, 40 pgs, VG....................22.00
OshKosh, luggage, 1947, 36 pgs, VG+.....................................12.00
Peck & Hills, furniture, 1942, 224 pgs, VG..............................65.00
Pittsburgh Steel Co, fencing, 1923, 23 pgs, G..........................25.00
Poole Silver Co Inc, kitchenware, ca 1929, 44 pgs, VG 48.00
Reach, Wright & Ditson, Fall/Winter sports, 1933, 72 pgs, G 33.00
Robert M Green & Sons, soda supplies, 1896, 16 pgs, VG...........190.00
Roderick Payne Inc, outdoor decorations, 1928, 16 pgs, VG 23.00
Samuel Kirk & Son, silverware, 1931, 64 pgs, G.......................84.00
Scott Stamp & Coin Co, 1893, 210 pgs, G................................27.00
Sears Roebuck & Co, 1929, 66 pgs, G 19.00
Studebaker Motors, automobiles, 1936, 8 pgs, G+.....................16.00
Trenton Potteries Co, plumbing, 1925, 32 pgs, VG...................34.00
Triumph Corporation, motorcycles, ca 1957, 4 pgs, G 24.00
Unadilla Silo Co, outdoor decorations, 1928, 32 pgs, VG..........36.00
Underwood Corporation, typewriters, 1956, 13 pgs, VG...............9.00
William Owen, gloves, 1920s, 12 pgs, G...................................15.00
WM Boekel & Co, surgical supplies, 1922, 200 pgs, VG+ 110.00
Woodworkers Tool Works, 1929, 258 pgs, VG..........................42.00
Yale & Towne MFG Co, locks, 1929, 517 pgs, VG.....................180.00
Yost Manufacturing Co, bicycles, 1897, 24 pgs, G+..................70.00

Caughley Ware

The Caughley Coalport Porcelain Manufactory operated from about 1775 until 1799 in Caughley, near Salop, Shropshire, in England. The owner was Thomas Turner, who gained his potting experience from his association with the Worcester Pottery Company. The wares he manufactured in Caughley are referred to as 'Salopian.' He is most famous for his blue-printed earthenwares, particularly the Blue Willow pattern, designed for him by Thomas Minton. For a more detailed history, see Coalport.

Asparagus server, pleasure boat, bl transfer, mk S, ca 1780...........300.00
Bowl, Willow Nankin, bl transfer, hdls, +pierced liner, unmk, 12" L.935.00
Cup & saucer, floral reserve, chain device at rim, bl on wht, mk S/C.450.00
Cup & saucer, floral sprigs, floral chain w/in 2 pk borders w/gilt ..265.00
Dish, Chantilly Sprigs, bl-line rim, heart shape, S mk, 10½" 480.00
Dish, Conversation, pagoda/lush trees, bl transfer, shell shape, 8" .295.00
Dish, Weir pattern, bl transfer, heart w/shaped rim, 10½" 450.00
Mustard pot, fence pattern/floral, bl transfer, flower finial............575.00
Pitcher, fenced garden, bl transfer, gilt bands, 4½" 195.00
Pitcher, Fisherman, cabbage mold, mask spout, bl transfer, 8½", EX ...525.00
Plate, Tower, pagoda/boats, bl transfer, 1700s, 7½" 240.00
Platter, Carnation, florals/insects, scalloped rim, unmk/#6, 19" L .360.00
Sauceboat, relief floral/cell pattern, bl transfer, ftd, 7½" L............295.00
Teapot, gilt guilloche band: shoulder/lid, ribbed bbl form, 6½", EX..270.00
Vase, flower/fruit group on wht, gilt band of ovals at shoulder, 5" ...865.00

Cauldon

Formerly Brown-Westhead, Moore & Co., Cauldon Ltd. was a Staffordshire pottery that operated under that name from 1905 until 1920, producing dinnerware that was most often transfer decorated. The company operated under the title Cauldon Potteries Ltd. from 1920 until 1962.

Bowl, continuous rose band, wht/gilt shell/leaf ft, sgn Pope, 10"....85.00
Bowl, salad; Bittersweet, Imari coloring, #X2500, MIE, from $80 to..100.00
Cup & saucer, roses on wht, bl/gold reserves, gold hdl, 10 for......135.00
Egg cup, Blue Onion pattern, 2¼"..35.00
Pitcher, Abraham Lincoln reserve, bl on wht, 1891, 8½"..........1,560.00
Plate, blk w/tan devices, Tiffany Co/Brown Westhead Moore, 10", 18 for..1,800.00
Plate, floral/leaf on tan, Tiffany repro of 1805 ware, 11", 6 for 200.00
Plate, lt gr w/gold scrolls & grapevines in center, King's, 8 for 360.00
Plate, portrait of lady, sgn Maurice, mk Chateau Des Tulieries, 10" .200.00
Plate, red/gold border, floral center, Mappin's Ltd, 11", 12 for......720.00
Plate, red/gold wide border w/bl flowering branches, dinner sz, 12 for ..2,280.00
Plate, wht, scalloped w/lg gr-lined leaves, floral center, 9", 12 for .300.00
Plate, wide gold bands border blk band in rim, wht center, 11", 12 for...420.00
Plate, wide yel border w/gilt devices, sm wht center, 10", 12 for..450.00

Plates, gold devices on yellow, first half of twentieth century, 10", 12 for $450.00. (Photo courtesy Skinner Inc. Auctioneers & Appraisers of Antiques & Fine Art)

Platter, vining border, turkey in center, bl on wht, 1890s, 20" L..275.00
Spittoon, bldgs/etc, gr on wht semiporc, 1800s, 6x8" 60.00
Vase, flowers HP on tan by F Rhead, Royal Cauldon, 7", pr.........150.00

Celluloid

In 1869 John Wesley Hyatt invented plastic in an attempt to devise a material that could be used to replicate the look of ivory. Eventually it became a substitute not only for ivory (which was protected by game preservation laws), but for tortoiseshell as well, especially in the manufacture of combs. Many others filed patents to improve, decorate, and widen its uses. Today, the term celluloid is used to encompass all types of early plastic.

Lithographed works of famous artists were often added to the lids of celluloid boxes and the covers of photograph albums; other items had embossed patterns. (In the listings that follow, assume the decoration is lithographed unless noted 'in relief.')

Collectors should be critical of condition; avoid items that are cracked and peeling.

Atomizer, tan marbled w/gold pnt, Deco style, rpl bulb, 5x2¾" 65.00
Autograph album, girl's face in red flower, ca 1900, 6⅛x4" 55.00
Box, lady reserve/roses on pk, gr floral border, slide drw, 9x18x10" .315.00
Box, lady w/birds, flower borders, intact felt liner, 4x14x7" 85.00
Box, mc mums on bl, hinged lid, brass hasp, 11¾" 40.00
Box, Victorian girl in landscape, hinged lid, 3¼x7½x6" 85.00
Hand mirror, cherubs in garden in wood fr, brass hdl, 18x6" 45.00
Hand mirror, gr w/pebbled texture, 6 flaring lines on bk, 10½" 40.00
Powder dish, orange, w/orange pelican-hdld puff w/fine feathers, Deco.. 120.00
Vanity set, monograms on ivory, 5 brushes+2 mirrors+jar+tools+6 pcs.. 90.00

Ceramic Art Company

Johnathan Coxon, Sr., and Walter Scott Lenox established the Ceramic Art Company in 1889 in Trenton, New Jersey, where they introduced fine belleek porcelain. Both were experienced in its production, having previously worked for Ott and Brewer. They hired artists to hand paint their wares with portraits, scenes, and lovely florals. Today artist-signed examples bring the highest prices. Several marks were used, three of which contain the 'CAC' monogram. A green wreath surrounding the company name in full was used on special-order wares, but these are not often encountered. Coxon eventually left the company, and it was later reorganized under the Lenox name. Lenox beleek items are included in this listing. Our advisor for this category is Mary Frank Gaston; she is listed in the Directory under Texas.

Vase, peonies, professional decoration, 18", $500.00.
(Photo courtesy Mary Frank Gaston)

Bell, tulip form, silver decor on wht, unmk................................... 150.00
Bowl, gold florals, pastel sponging, ruffled, 2x4½".......................... 135.00
Bowl, Nouveau lady w/flowing hair profile on lid, FM Brooks, 7½"....310.00

Buttonhook, mc floral w/gold, factory decor, umk, 7¾" 285.00
Creamer, gold floral, hdl & trim, mk 3¾" 135.00
Cup, chocolate; bl beading & gold on ivory, ped ft......................... 90.00
Cup, demitasse; gold-paste floral, ring hdl, 2" 100.00
Cup, line of bl enameled dots w/gold bands, ped ft......................... 55.00
Finger bowl; gold leaves & flowers on gr, scalloped rim................. 130.00
Humidor, lilies, red-orange on orange, ca 1897, 6x5½" 350.00
Inkwell, mums (non-factory) w/gold on wht, sq, CAC mk, 4½" .. 200.00
Jug, Rye, brn & gr w/silver o/l, palette mk 200.00
Loving cup, commemorative w/initials, much gold, 8x6" 225.00
Loving cup, roses on gr, 3 pk hdls w/gold, EX art, purple mk, 8" .. 350.00
Loving cup, 3 roses, 3-hdl, amateur artist, 1889-1906, 7¼x3¾" ... 150.00
Mug, gr hops, artist sgn, palette mk, 4¾" 75.00
Mug, strawberries, emb hdl & base, palette mk, 6" 95.00
Pitcher, cider; apples & leaves on purple apricot, 1894-1906, 6" .550.00
Pitcher, cider; roses (lg/mc), angular hdl w/emb dots, 5½" 495.00
Pitcher, strawberries & leaves w/gold, sgn Lenox, 6" 400.00
Pitcher, tankard; grapes & vines, cylindrical, palette mk, 14"...... 725.00
Pitcher, tankard; pines & full moon on dk gr, gr mk...................... 265.00
Salt cellar, scalloped rim, palette mk.. 25.00
Stein, monks eating in cellar, copper/sterling lid, mk, ½-liter 600.00
Vase, chrysanthemums, bulbous, sgn, 7½" 725.00
Vase, irises, WH Morley, gold-hdld urn form, CAC mk, 13¼x8"..3,750.00
Vase, mc roses, G Morley, shouldered, CAC mk, 14¾x9" 1,300.00
Vase, wht gloss, cherub hdls, waisted neck, flared rim, CAC mk, 12"...200.00

Ceramic Arts Studio, Madison, Wisconsin

Although most figural ceramic firms of the 1940s and 1950s were located on the West Coast, one of the most popular had its base of operations in Madison, Wisconsin. Ceramic Arts Studio was founded in 1940 as a collaboration between entrepreneur Reuben Sand and potter Lawrence Rabbitt. Early ware consisted of hand-thrown pots by Rabbitt, but CAS came into its own with the 1941 arrival of Betty Harrington. A self-taught artist, Harrington served as the studio's principal designer until it closed in 1955. Her imagination and skill quickly brought Ceramic Arts Studio to the forefront of firms specializing in decorative ceramics. During its peak production period in the late 1940s, CAS turned out more than 500,000 figurines annually.

Harrington's themes were wide-ranging, from ethnic and theatrical subjects, to fantasy characters, animals, and even figural representations of such abstractions as fire and water. While the majority of the studio's designs were by Harrington, CAS also released a limited line of realistic and modernistic animal figures designed by 'Rebus' (Ulle Cohen). In addition to traditional figurines, the studio responded to market demand with such innovations as salt-and-pepper pairs, head vases, banks, bells, shelf sitters, and candleholders. Metal display shelves for CAS pieces were produced by Jon-San Creations, a nearby Reuben Sand operation. Most Jon-San designs were by Ceramic Art Studio's head decorator Zona Liberace, stepmother of the famed pianist.

Betty Harrington carved her own master molds, so the finished products are remarkably similar to her initial sketches. CAS figurines are prized for their vivid colors, characteristic high-gloss glaze, lifelike poses, detailed decoration, and skill of execution. Unlike many ceramics of the period, CAS pieces today show little evidence of crazing.

Most Ceramic Arts Studio pieces are marked, although in pairs only one piece may have a marking. While there are variants, including early paper stickers, one common base stamp reads 'Ceramic Arts Studio, Madison, Wis.' (The initials 'BH' which appear on many pieces do not indicate that the piece was personally decorated by Betty Harrington. This is simply a designer indicator.)

In the absence of a base stamp, a sure indicator of a CAS piece is the decorator 'color marking' found at the drain hole on the base. Each studio decorator had a separate color code for identification purposes, and almost any authentic CAS piece will display these tick marks.

Following the Madison Studio's closing in 1955, Reuben Sand briefly moved his base of operations to Japan. While perhaps a dozen master molds from Madison were also utilized in Japan, most of the Japanese designs were original ones and do not correlate to those produced in Madison. Additionally, about 20 master molds and copyrights were sold to Mahana Imports, which created its own CAS variations, and a number of molds and copyrights were sold to Coventry Ware for a line of home hobbyware. Pieces produced by these companies have their own individual stampings or labels. While these may incorporate the Ceramic Arts Studio name, the vastly different stylings and skill of execution are readily apparent to even the most casual observer, easily differentiating them from authentic Madison products. When the CAS building was demolished in 1959, all remaining molds were destroyed. Betty Harrington's artistic career continued after the studio's demise; and her later works, including a series of nudes and abstract figurals, are especially prized by collectors. Mrs. Harrington died in 1997. Her last assignment, the limited-edition *M'amselle* series, was commissioned for the Ceramic Arts Studio Collectors Association Convention in 1996.

Our advisors for this category are BA Wellman (his address can be found under Massachusetts) and Donald-Brian Johnson (Nebraska). Both encourage collectors to e-mail them with any new information concerning company history and/or production. Mr. Johnson, in association with Timothy J. Holthaus and James E. Petzold, is the co-author of *Ceramic Arts Studio: The Legacy of Betty Harrington* (Schiffer). See also Clubs, Newsletters, and Catalogs.

Bank, Skunky, 4", from $260 to 280.00
Bank, Tony the Barber (blade bank), 4¾", from $75 to 100.00
Candleholders, Triad Girls, left & right, 7", center, 5", from $250 to.340.00

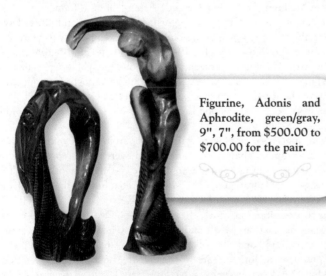

Figurine, Adonis and Aphrodite, green/gray, 9", 7", from $500.00 to $700.00 for the pair.

Figurine, Alice & March Hare (White Rabbit), 4½", 6", pr, $350 to.. 450.00
Figurine, All Children's Orchestra, 5" boys/4½"girls, 5-pc, $700 to.. 800.00
Figurine, Annie (baby elephant) & Benny, 3¼", 3¾", pr, $115 to ..160.00
Figurine, Bear Mother & Cub, realistic, 3¼", 2¼", pr, $320 to..... 380.00
Figurine, Bird of Paradise, A&B, 3", pr from $360 to 440.00
Figurine, Blythe & Pensive, 6½", 6", pr from $300 to................... 350.00
Figurine, Bride & Groom, 4¾", 5", pr from $250 to...................... 300.00
Figurine, Butch & Billy (boxer dogs), snugglers, 3", pr from $120 to .160.00
Figurine, Chinese Girl w/umbrella, very rare, 5½", from $400 to. 500.00
Figurine, Dachshund, 3½" L, from $85 to 100.00
Figurine, Dawn, sandstone, 6½", from $175 to 200.00
Figurine, Donkey Mother & Young Donkey, 3¼", 3", pr from $320 to.380.00
Figurine, Duck Mother & Duckling, 3¼", 2¼", pr from $80 to 125.00
Figurine, Fifi/Fufu poodles, stand/crouch, 3", 2½", pr, $180 to...... 240.00

Figurine, Frisky & Balky Colts, 3¾", pr from $200 to 250.00
Figurine, Giraffes, 5½", 4", pr from $150 to.............................. 200.00
Figurine, Gypsy Man & Woman, 6½", 7", pr from $80 to 100.00
Figurine, Harem Trio, Sultan & 2 harem girls, from $320 to 395.00
Figurine, Isaac & Rebekah, 10", pr from $140 to 200.00
Figurine, King's Flutist & Lutist Jesters, 11½", 12", pr, $250 to ... 350.00
Figurine, Leopards A&B, fighting, 3½", 6¼" L, pr from $180 to .. 250.00
Figurine, Lion & Lioness, 7¼", 5½" L, pr from $340 to 380.00
Figurine, Little Miss Muffet #1, 4½", from $50 to 75.00
Figurine, Love Trio, Lover Boy, Willing & Bashful Girls, 3-pc, $300 to .375.00
Figurine, Mermaid Trio, 4" mother, 3" & 2½" babies, 3-pc, $475 to...550.00
Figurine, Minnehaha & Hiawatha, 6½", 4½", pr from $480 to 540.00
Figurine, Modern Doe & Fawn, 3¾", 2", pr from $175 to............. 225.00
Figurine, Modern Fox, sandstone, 6½" L, from $120 to............... 150.00
Figurine, Mother Horse & Spring Colt, 4¼", 3½", pr from $425 to.. 475.00
Figurine, Musical Trio, Accordion & Harmonica Boys/Banjo Girl, $420 to...480.00
Figurine, Our Lady of Fatima, 9", from $260 to 285.00
Figurine, Peek-a-Boo Pixie, 2½", from $40 to 50.00
Figurine, Peter Pan & Wendy, 5¼", pr from $220 to 270.00
Figurine, Petrov & Petrushka, 5½", 5", pr from $120 to 150.00
Figurine, Pied Piper Set, piper+running boy+praying girl, $380 to .. 465.00
Figurine, Rhumba Man & Woman, 7¼", 7", pr from $80 to....... 120.00
Figurine, Saucy Squirrel w/Jacket, 2¼", from $175 to 200.00
Figurine, Seal Mother on Rock & Pup, 5", pr from $950 to 1,100.00
Figurine, Smi-Li & Mo-Pi, chubby man & woman, 6", pr from $50 to..80.00
Figurine, St Agnes w/Lamb, 6", from $260 to 285.00
Figurine, Tembo Elephant & Tembino Baby, 6½", 2½", pr, $345 to ...415.00
Figurine, Tom Cat standing, 5", from $75 to 95.00
Figurine, tortoise w/wht hat crawling, 2½" L, from $150 to 175.00
Figurine, Water Man & Woman, 11½", pr from $350 to 400.00
Figurine, Wing-Sang & Lu-Tang, 6", pr from $90 to 110.00
Figurine, Winter Willie, 4", from $90 to 120.00
Figurine, Zulu Man & Woman #1, 5½", 7", pr from $1,100 to ..1,400.00
Figurine, 4 Seasons Children, Spring Sue/etc, 3½-5", 4-pc, $490 to...610.00
Head vase, Becky, 5¼", from $100 to 125.00
Head vase, Manchu & Lotus, head vase plaques, 8½", pr from $400 to .450.00
Head vase, Mei-Ling, 5", from $150 to....................................... 175.00
Lamp, Fire Man (on base), very scarce, Moss Mfg, 19½", from $350 to..375.00
Miniature, Adam & Eve Autumn Pitcher, 3", from $40 to 50.00
Miniature, Aladdin's Lamp Server, 2" L, from $65 to 85.00
Mug, Barbershop Quartet (1949), 3½", from $650 to 750.00
Pitcher, Pine Cone, mini, 3¾", from $65 to 85.00
Planter, Lorelei on Shell, 6", from $250 to................................. 300.00
Plaque, Attitude & Arabesque, 9½", 9¼", pr from $70 to 100.00
Plaque, Comedy & Tragedy masks, 5¼", pr from $180 to 220.00
Plaque, Dutch Boy & Girl, 8½", 8", pr form $120 to 150.00
Plaque, Goosey Gander, scarce, 4½", from $140 to..................... 160.00
Plaque, Greg & Grace, 9½", 9", pr from $50 to........................... 70.00
Plaque, Hamlet & Ophelia, 8", pr from $360 to 440.00
Plaque, Jack Be Nimble, 5", from $400 to 450.00
Shakers, bear & cub, snuggle, 4¼", 2¼", pr from $40 to 60.00
Shakers, Blackamoors, 4¾", pr from $140 to.............................. 160.00
Shakers, Calico Cat & Gingham Dog, 3", 2¾", pr from $90 to.... 100.00
Shakers, Chihuahua & Doghouse, snugglers, 1½", 2" L, pr, $120 to ..160.00
Shakers, Children in Chairs, boy & girl+2 chairs, from $240 to..320.00
Shakers, Covered Wagon & Ox, 3" L, pr from $100 to 135.00
Shakers, Fish Up on Tail, 4", from $40 to 70.00
Shakers, Monkey Mother & Baby, snugglers, 4", 2½", pr, $40 to ... 60.00
Shakers, Native Boy & Crocodile, 3", 4½" L, pr from $200 to..... 240.00
Shakers, Paul Bunyan & Evergreen, 4½", 2½", pr from $200 to... 250.00
Shakers, Sambo & Tiger, 3½", 5" L, pr from $500 to.................. 575.00
Shakers, Santa Claus & Evergreen, 2¼", 2½", pr from $325 to 375.00
Shakers, Wee Scotch Boy & Girl, 3¼", 3", pr from $70 to........... 80.00
Shelf sitter, collie mother, 5", from $75 to 100.00

Shelf sitter, Little Jack Horner #1, 4½", from $50 to 75.00
Shelf sitter, Maurice & Michelle, 7", pr from $130 to 150.00
Shelf sitter, Wally, ball up, 4½", from $220 to............................ 250.00
Shelf sitters, Canaries, sleeping/singing, 5", pr from $300 to........ 350.00
Shelf sitters, Dutch Boy & girl, 4½", pr from $50 to 70.00
Shelf sitters, Young Love Couple (kissing boy & girl), 4½", $90 to .. 100.00
Teapot, appl swan, mini, 3", from $60 to............................... 75.00
Vase, Bamboo, 6", from $55 to 75.00
Vase, Flying Duck, rnd, 2½", from $75 to.............................. 85.00

Metal Accessories

Arched Window for religious figure, 6½", from $125 to 150.00
Artist palette w/shelves, left & right, 12" W, pr from $200 to...... 250.00
Circle Bench w/Crescent Planter, 8¾" dia, from $200 to 245.00
Corner Spider Web for Miss Muffet, flat bk, 4", from $175 to...... 225.00
Diamond shape, 15x13", from $45 to 55.00
Garden shelf for Mary Contrary, 4x12", from $100 to 120.00
Ladder for Jack, rare, 13", from $125 to............................. 150.00
Musical score, flat bk, 14x12", from $85 to 100.00
Parakeet Cage, 13", from $125 to 150.00
Rainbow Arch w/Shelf, blk, 13½x19", from $100 to 120.00
Sofa for Maurice & Michelle, 7½" L, from $250 to 275.00
Stairway to the Stars, 18½", from $100 to........................... 120.00
Star for Angel, flat bk, 9¾", from $65 to 75.00
Triple Ring, left or right, w/shelf, 15", from $110 to 130.00

Chalkware

Chalkware was popular from 1860 until 1890. It was made from gypsum or plaster of Paris formed in a mold and then hand painted in oils or watercolors. Items such as animals and birds, figures, banks, toys, and religious ornaments modeled after more expensive Staffordshire wares were often sold door to door. Their origin is attributed to Italian immigrants. Today regarded as a form of folk art, nineteenth-century American pieces bring prices in the hundreds of dollars. Carnival chalkware from this century is also collectible, especially figures that are personality related. For those, see Carnival Collectibles.

Cat seated, good form, bright yel pnt, 6⅝" 515.00
Dove on cherry branch base w/unpunched coin slot, rpr/rpt, 11", pr .175.00
Dove on stump, mc, worn beak, 10" 230.00
Ewe reclining w/lamb, rpr ears/flakes, 6½x9" 400.00
Garniture, fruit basket, worn orig pnt, edge flakes, 11" 285.00
Garniture, fruit/foliage on ped base, strong colors, wear, 11" 545.00
Garniture, mc fruit & leaves on wht plinth, PA, 19th C, 13¾" ... 2,935.00
Garniture, yel fruit & orange foliage on ped base, lt wear, 10½" .. 550.00
Lovebirds, facing pr on oval base, pnt traces, 9½" 400.00
Parrot, red & blk pnt, lt wear/flake, 8" 400.00
Poodle standing, brn rpt on ears, lt wear, 7½" 285.00
Ram, EX color & form, 7¾".. 1,725.00
Rooster, pronounced tail feathers, mc pnt, 7¼", EX 200.00
Rooster, red & gr feathers, rprs/sm rpt, 6½"......................... 60.00

Champleve

Champleve, enameling on brass or other metal, differs from cloisonne in that the design is depressed or incised into the metal, rather than being built in with wire dividers as in the cloisonne procedure. The cells, or depressions, are filled in with color, and the piece is then fired.

Casket, gilt brass and multicolor enamels, French, nineteenth century, 7x6x4", $3,000.00. (Photo courtesy Jackson's International Auctioneers & Appraisers of Fine Art & Antiques)

Desk set, mc inkwell on gr marble base, 4x13x8" 325.00
Urn, lady in garden w/Cupid, sgn, gilt mts, 8¾" 480.00
Vase, long neck, ped ft on sq base, stone center (body), 5½" 150.00

Chase Brass & Copper Company

Chase introduced this logo in 1928. The company was incorporated in 1876 as the Waterbury Manufacturing Company and was located in Waterbury, Connecticut. This location remained Chase's principal fabrication plant, and it was here that the 'Specialties' were made.

In 1900 the company chose the name Chase Companies Inc., in honor of their founder, Augustus Sabin Chase. The name encompassed Chase's many factories. Only the New York City sales division was called Chase Brass and Copper Co., but from 1936 on, that name was used exclusively.

In 1930 the sales division invited people to visit their new Specialties Sales Showroom in New York City 'where an interesting assortment of decorative and utilitarian pieces in brass and copper in a variety of designs and treatments are offered for your consideration.' Like several other large companies, Chase hired well-known designers such as Walter Von Nessen, Lurelle Guild, the Gerths, Russel Wright, and Dr. A Reimann. Harry Laylon, an in-house designer, created much of the new line.

From 1930 to 1942 Chase offered lamps, smoking accessories, and housewares similar to those Americans were seeing on the Hollywood screen — generally at prices the average person could afford.

Besides chromium, Chase manufactured many products in a variety of finishes, some even in silver plate. Many objects were of polished or satin-finished brass and/or copper; other pieces were chromium plated.

After World War II Chase no longer made the Specialties line. It had represented only a tiny fraction of this huge company's production. Instead they concentrated on a variety of fabricated mill items. Some dedicated Chase collectors even have shower heads, faucet aerators, gutter pipe, and metal samples. Is anyone using Chase window screening?

Chase products are marked either on the item itself or on a screw or rivet. Because Chase sold screws, rivets, nails, etc. (all with their logo), not all items having these Chase-marked components were actually made at Chase. It should also be noted that during the 1930s, China produced good quality chromium copies; so when you're not absolutely positive an item is Chase, buy it because you like it, understanding that its authenticity may be in question. Remember that if a magnet sticks to it, it's not Chase. Brass and copper are not magnetic, and Chase did not use steel.

Prior to 1933 Chase made smoking accessories for the Park Sherman Co. Some are marked 'Park Sherman, Chicago, Illinois, Made of Chase Brass.' Others carry a Park Sherman logo. It is believed that the 'heraldic emblem' was also used during this period. Many items are identical or very similar to Chase-marked pieces. Produced in the 1950s, National Silver's 'Emerald Glo' wares look very similar to Chase pieces, but Chase did not make them. It is very possible that National purchased Chase tooling after the Chase Specialties line was discontinued.

Although Chase designer pieces and rarer items are still commanding good prices, the market has softened on the more common wares. This year's price guide will reflect this trend. The availabliity of Chase on the Internet has helped the collector, but has also contributed to the leveling off of values.

For further study we recommend *Chase Complete, Chase Catalogs 1934 & 1935, 1930s Lighting — Deco & Traditional by Chase,* and *The Chase Era, 1933 and 1942 Catalogs of the Chase Brass & Copper Co.*, all by Donald-Brian Johnson and Leslie Piña (Schiffer); *Art Deco Chrome, The Chase Era,* by Richard Kilbride; and *Art Deco Chrome* by James Linz (Schiffer). In the listings that follow, examples are polished unless noted satin. Our advisors for this category are Donna and John Thorpe; they are listed in the Directory under Wisconsin.

Key:
Ac — Ackerman
Ge — Gerth
HD — Helen Bishop Dennis
HL — Harry Layton
LG — Laurelle Guild
RK — Rockwell Kent
RW — Russel Wright
VN — designed by Von Nessen

Antelope Ash Receiver, frosted glass w/chrome trim, #881, 4½" . 115.00
Binnacle Light, wired, colored glass, #25002, from $40 to 50.00
Bomb Flashlight, polished nickel, A Mitchell, 3½" dia, $45 to...... 50.00
Bookends, spiral, blk/satin nickel finish, #17018 .... 250.00
Bookends, stylized soldier/brass ball, red jacket/blk helmet, 7¼".. 325.00
Brittany Bell, brass, #13002 .... 75.00
Bubble Cigarette Holder, open chrome ball/sq ft, #860, 2¼", $40 to.. 50.00
Bud Holder, 4-Tube; polished copper w/wht plastic collar, Ge, #11230.. 45.00
Butter dish, chrome w/wht, VN, #17067 .... 110.00
Candy jar, copper or satin copper w/brass knob, VN, #NS316, $150 to... 175.00
Cat Doorstop, Deco, tubular copper w/brass head, emb mk, 8½x4⅞" . 150.00
Circle Wall Bracket, brass, VN, #17033, 9" dia, from $450 to 500.00
Cocktail Canape Server, chrome, #28001..................................... 185.00
Colonel & Colonel's Lady Lamps, red/wht/blk figures, LG, 8¾", pr 300.00
Colonial Bookends, satin, blk nickel or copper, #11248, 5¼" 150.00
Compton Console Bowl, polished brass, HL, #15007.................. 125.00
Constellation Lamp, bronze helmet w/milk glass dome, VN, 8¾x7"..300.00
Coronet Coffee Set, pot+cr/sug+tray, #90121, from $600 to........ 650.00
Davy Jones Bookends, brass/walnut/Bakelite, wheel shape, #90142.50.00
Diplomat Tray, chrome/blk, VN, #17030, 10" dia........................ 240.00
Doric Cocktail Set, chrome, 12½" shaker +6 3" cups+tray 350.00

Drum Bank, #90156, 3½", from $80.00 to $90.00. (Photo courtesy Donna and John Thorpe)

Duplex Jelly Dish, chrome w/frosted glass, HL, #90062................. 25.00
Elephant Bookends, polished copper, #17043, VH, from $500 to. 550.00
Federal Plate, satin copper, #09007 .... 75.00
Festivity Tray, chrome, stepped hdls, #09018, 19½x12¼"............ 150.00
Fruit Basket, wireware, LG, #27028, 12½"................................... 300.00
Glow lamp, chrome w/blk, cone shade, #1001, 8" 100.00
Holiday Cocktail Set, chrome, shaker+4 cocktails+tray, #90064. 110.00
Ice Bowl, copper w/Bakelite hdls, RW, #28002, w/tongs.............. 135.00
Imperial Bowl, chrome w/brushed nickel base, #15003 .... 125.00
Lazy Boy Smoker's Stand, brass w/compo top, VN, 21½x11" 200.00
Nut Cracker Big 'n Small, copper or brass, HL, #90150, from $45 to .. 50.00
Planetarium Chandelier, 13" globe w/stars, M646, from $3,000 to. 3,500.00
Pretzelman Plate, copper, LG, #90038, from $95 to 110.00
Serving Fork & Spoon, chrome w/wht, HL, #90076, pr................ 45.00
Skyway Shakers, chrome/wht Bakelite, #17095, pr 35.00
Snack Server, 3 glass bowls w/chrome lids, in base, #90093, 14½". 75.00
Spheres Shakers, chrome, RW, #28004, pr..................................... 45.00
Squirrel Napkin Clip, copper w/wht, HL, #90107......................... 70.00
Stratosphere Smoking Stand, chrome, VN, 1937, #17076, from $350 to....400.00
Sugar Shaker, chrome, #90057 .... 50.00
Target Tray, chrome/wht, w/hdls, #09023, 12½" 300.00
Taurex Candlesticks, chrome or copper, VN, #24003, 7", pr, $125 to. 150.00
Tea Ball, chrome/wht, HL, #90118 .... 95.00
Triple Flower Stand, brass & copper, #11228, 14½x16" 175.00
Trophy Vase, chrome, #3005, 9"... 75.00
Two-In-Hand Tray, chrome/wht, VN, #17077 .... 100.00
Weather Vane, brass arrow, #90030, 12x12" 130.00
Wine cooler, chromium, child Bacchus in relief, R Kent, #27015, 9"... 600.00

Chelsea Dinnerware

Made from about 1830 to 1880 in the Staffordshire district of England, this white dinnerware is decorated with lustre embossings in the grape, thistle, sprig, or fruit and cornucopia patterns. The relief designs vary from lavender to blue, and the body of the ware may be porcelain, ironstone, or earthenware. Because it was not produced in Chelsea as the name would suggest, dealers often prefer to call it 'Grandmother's Ware.' For more information we recommend *Collector's Encyclopedia of English China* by Mary Frank Gaston, our advisor for this category. Mrs. Gaston is listed in the Directory under Texas.

Grape, bowl, 8" 35.00
Grape, cake plate, emb ribs, 10" dia, from $25 to 30.00
Grape, cake plate, w/copper lustre, sq, 10", from $25 to 30.00
Grape, coffeepot, stick hdl, 2-cup, 7" 75.00
Grape, creamer, 5½"... 55.00
Grape, cup & saucer, from $25 to.. 35.00
Grape, egg cup, 2¼", from $35 to 50.00
Grape, pitcher, milk; 40-oz 60.00
Grape, plate, 6", from $12 to 15.00
Grape, plate, 7" 18.00
Grape, plate, 8", from $22 to 25.00
Grape, plate, 9½" 22.50
Grape, teapot, octagonal, 8½", from $125 to 150.00
Grape, teapot, octagonal, 10" 165.00
Grape, teapot, 2-cup 75.00
Grape, waste bowl... 40.00
Sprig, cake plate, 9" 40.00
Sprig, cup & saucer... 40.00
Sprig, pitcher, milk 60.00
Sprig, plate, dinner 25.00
Sprig, plate, 7".. 18.00
Thistle, butter pat 15.00
Thistle, cake plate, 8¾", from $25 to 30.00
Thistle, cup & saucer, from $30 to 35.00
Thistle, plate, 6", from $6 to...8.00
Thistle, plate, 7".. 15.00
Thistle, sugar bowl, 8-sided, w/lid, 7½" 45.00

Chelsea Keramic Art Works

In 1866 fifth-generation Scottish potter Alexander Robertson started a pottery in Chelsea, Massachusetts, where his brother Hugh joined him the following year. Their father James left the firm he partnered to help his sons in 1872, teaching them techniques and pressing decorative tiles, an extreme rarity at that early date. Their early production consisted mainly of classical Grecian and Asian shapes in redware and stoneware, several imitating metal vessels. They then betrayed influences from Europe's most important potteries, such as Royal Doulton and Limoges, in underglaze and barbotine or Haviland painting. Hugh's visit to the Philadelphia Centennial Exposition introduced him to the elusive sang-de-boeuf or oxblood glaze featured on Ming porcelain, which he would strive to achieve for well over a decade at tremendous costs.

James passed away in 1880, and Alexander moved to California in 1884, leaving Hugh in charge of the pottery and his oxblood glaze experiments. The time and energy spent doing research were taken away from producing saleable artwares. Out of funds, Hugh closed the pottery in 1889.

Wealthy patrons supported the founding of a new company, the short-lived Chelsea Pottery U.S., where the emphasis became the production of Chinese-inspired crackleware, vases, and tableware underglaze-painted in blue with simplified or stylized designs. The commercially viable pottery found a new home in Dedham, Massachusetts, in 1896, whose name it adopted. Hugh died in 1908, and the production of crackleware continued until 1943.

The ware is usually stamped CKAW within a diamond or Chelsea Keramic Art Works/Robertson & Sons. Our advisors for this category are Suzanne Perrault and David Rago; they are listed in the Directory under New Jersey. See also Dedham Pottery.

Bottle, oxblood/slate gray, CKAW, 6½x4" 1,725.00
Ewer, cvd geometrics & scrolls, gr gloss, CKAW, ca 1885, 11¼".. 1,650.00
Lamp base, flowers emb on turq, cylindrical, 7", EX 150.00
Pilgrim flask, girl/geese, teal/gr, CKAW/Robertson-Sons, mfg flaws, 9"...1,800.00
Pitcher, appl vines, bl-gr on dk gr, CKAW, 1881, rpr, 10" 800.00
Plate, crackleware w/gr sponging to rim, experimental, CPUS, 3¾"... 450.00
Tile, emb floral, caramel w/gr tones, 1800s, 5¾" sq 1,430.00
Vase, Barbotine bird, wht on brn, pillow form, CKAW, 5¼x4¾".. 1,300.00
Vase, brn & oxblood lustre, 3¼x3¼" 850.00

Vase, burnished red clay with curled handles (one with firing split), $1,900.00. (Photo courtesy David Rago Auctions)

Vase, crab, bl on volcanic wht w/moss gr, experimental, 7½" 3,820.00
Vase, oxblood, bulbous w/long tapering neck, 7⅜" 2,940.00
Vase, oxblood lustre, 8¾x4" 7,200.00
Vase, oxblood w/red streaks/some crystalline, lt pitting, 8¾x4¼" .. 3,100.00
Vase, sailing ship, bl on wht crackle, CPUS/stamped rabbit, 6" .. 3,400.00

Cherokee Pottery

Made and sold in Oklahoma through tribal-owned facilities at an industrial development sponsored in part by the Bureau of Indian Affairs,

this pottery may be marked Cherokee in angular-style lettering or with the outline of an Indian head.

Bowl, cvd/scallop rim w/2 opposing Indian heads, 3 ft, EX color, 11" L....325.00
Bowl, snake effigy, 2 realistic snakes wrap sides, M Welch, 5¾" . 1,000.00
Pot, orange-blk, 3 V-shape devices cvd & punched to create dots, 5"... 100.00
Pot, orange-gray/sand-blk, cvd hdls, 3-legged, Maude Welch, 3¼" .450.00
Pot, pit-fire brns w/shell cvgs, Bigmeat, 3¼x3¼"............................. 80.00
Vase, punched geometric, pit-fired colors, Charlotte Bigmeat, 4¼".. 100.00

Chicago Crucible

For only a few years during the 1920s, the Chicago (Illinois) Crucible Company made a limited amount of decorative pottery in addition to their regular line of architectural wares. Examples are very scarce today; they carry a variety of marks, all with the company name and location. Our advisors for this category are Suzanne Perrault and David Rago; they are listed in the Directory under New Jerseey.

Vase, brn/gr mottle, cylinder neck over squat twisted body, 8x5". 510.00
Vase, floral stem, pk on dk gr matt, angle shoulder/narrowing body, 9" ..720.00
Vase, gr matt, long inverted trumpet neck, squat bowl body, 10½x7" . 780.00
Vase, gr matt w/emb grapevines, long neck w/scalloped rim, 10½x6". 1,080.00
Vase, gr mottled matt, cylinder neck over twisted lower body, 8".. 600.00
Vase, olive gr speckle, acorn body w/right-angle rim-to-width hdls, 7". 1,680.00

Children's Things

Nearly every item devised for adult furnishings has been reduced to child size — furniture, dishes, sporting goods, even some tools. All are very collectible. During the late seventeenth and early eighteenth centuries, miniature china dinnerware sets were made both in China and in England. They were not intended primarily as children's playthings, however, but instead were made to furnish miniature rooms and cabinets that provided a popular diversion for the adults of that period. By the nineteenth century, the emphasis had shifted, and most of the small-scaled dinnerware and tea sets were made for children's play.

Late in the nineteenth century and well into the twentieth, toy pressed glass dishes were made, many in the same patterns. Today these toy dishes often fetch prices in the same range or above those for the 'grown-ups'!

Children's books, especially those from the Victorian era, are charming collectibles. Colorful lithographic illustrations that once delighted little boys in long curls and tiny girls in long stockings and lots of ribbons and lace have lost none of their appeal. Some collectors limit themselves to a specific subject, while others may be far more interested in the illustrations. First editions are more valuable than later issues, and condition and rarity are very important factors to consider before making your purchase.

Our advisors for children's china and glassware are Margaret and Kenn Whitmyer; you will find their address in the Directory under Ohio. In the following listings, unless otherwise noted, our values are for examples in excellent condition. See also A B C Plates; Blue Willow; Clothing; Stickley; etc.

Key:
ds — doll size   hc — hardcover
dj — dust jacket   pic brds — pictorial boards

Books

Alice's Adventures in Wonderland, Lewis, Macrae Smith, 1931, hc . 30.00

America in Action...At Sea in Air, pop-up, Action Playbooks, 1942. 125.00
Aristocats, Tell-A-Tale Book, 1970...9.00
Bears' Vacation, Berenstain, Random Beginner Book, 1968, hc 15.00
Bedtime Book, M Watts, Winship illus, Western Publishing, 1963, hc, VG. 12.00
Blueberry Muffin, Thompson, Berry illus, Longmans Green & Co, 1951, hc .12.50
Bobbsey Twins: Merry Days..., LL Hope, Scott illus, Whitman, 1950, hc .6.00
Charlie Brown Christmas, Schulz, World Publishing, 1965 1st ed, VG . 10.00
Chuck Squirrel, Goldsmith Publishing, 1922, die-cut hc 30.00
Darling Fuzzy Wuzzy Kitten, Whitman, 1947, hc, VG 25.00
Donald Duck & His Cat Troubles, Disney, Whitman, 1948, hc, VG ..25.00
Farmer Al Falfa, Wonder Book #736, 1959, VG........................... 12.00
Father Tuck's ABC at the Zoo, Tuck & Sons Linen series, 1896.... 50.00
Gingerbread Man, Tell-A-Tale, 1953, VG 12.00
Hansel & Gretel, 7 pop-up pgs, Bancroft, 1961 .... 20.00
Here's to You Charlie Brown, C Schulz, 1970, hc, EX+ 8.00
Honey Bunch: Just a Little Girl, Thorndyke, Grosset Dunlap, 1923.. 12.50
If I Could Be, Whitman, 1953, soft cover 12.00
King's Stilts, Dr Seuse, Random House, 1939 1st ed, hc w/dj, NM ..75.00
Lassie & Blackberry Bog, Whitman, 1956, pic brds 25.00
Lazy Liza Lizard's Tricks, MC Rains, First Book Club Edition, 1953, dj ..165.00
Lillie's Bird Garden, no author credit, Leavit, NY, 1976, hc, G 27.50
Little Black Sambo, Whitman Tell-A-Tale, 1959, VG.................. 60.00
Little Elephant, JP Broderick, Rand McNally Jr Elf, 1959, hc........ 14.00
Littlest Christmas Tree, Wonder Book #525, 1954, VG 12.00
Lively Little Rabbit, Little Golden Book, 1950, VG 20.00
Mike Mulligan & ...Steam Shovel, Burton, Houghton Mifflin, 1939, hc.. 42.50
My Picture Story Book, Platt & Munk, 1941, hc........................... 40.00
Nancy's Mysterious Letter, Keene, Grosset & Dunlap, 1932, hc, VG..15.00
Noddy at the Seaside, E Blyton, Beek illus, 1953, hc w/dj............ 135.00
Open Up My Suitcase, Little Golden Book #207, A ed, 1954, VG ..18.00

The Outlaw of Torn, Edgar Rice Burroughs, Chicago: A.C. McClurg & Co, first editon, red cloth with gold stamping, pictorial dust jacket, NM, $3,000.00.

Pebbles Flintstone Runaway, Whitman Tell-A-Tale, 1964, NM.... 28.00
Peter Pan & Reddy Fox, Wonder Book #611, 1954, NM 25.00
Pooh Story Book, AA Milne, EH Shepard, EP Dutton, 1965, hc, VG+... 25.00
Pop-Up Minnie Mouse, 3 pop-ups, Blue Ribbon Books, 1933 ..... 175.00
Prayers for Little Children, MA Jones, Rand McNally, 1959, hc ... 22.50
Puppies, paintings by Diana Thorne, Saalfield #1072, 1935, VG... 28.00
Puppy Who Found a Boy, pic brds, Wonder Books, 1951, VG 10.00
Pussy Willow, Whitman Tell-A-Tale, 1948, hc, VG...................... 15.00
Rabbits Give a Party, Dermine, Wonder Books, 1974, hc, VG 25.00
Raggedy Ann Stories, Gruelle, MA Donohue, 1920, hc, VG 20.00
Scat Scat, SR Francis, Platt & Munk, 1940, hc 40.00
Sing Song of Sixpence, Clyne, pop-up, Mother Goose Playhouse series.. 25.00
Skippy & Others, M MacIntyre, MacMillan Co, 1944, hc, VG..... 25.00
Smokey Bear Saves Forest, Graham, Whitman Tell-A-Tale, 1971 ...8.00
Story of Dr Dolittle, Lofting, Tinkelman illus, NY, 1948, hc w/dj.. 28.00
Stuart Little, EB White, Williams illus, 1945, hc w/dj, VG 50.00
Things I Like, MW Brown, G Williams illus, Little Golden Book, VG ..5.00
Tim Tyler in Jungle, 3 pop-ups, L Young, King Features, 1933, VG 225.00

Tom Thumb, picture cover, Platt & Munk Made in USA, paper cover... 12.00
Your Friend the Policeman, Miss Frances, Ding Dong School, 1953, EX+ .8.00
3 Boy Scouts in Africa, Douglas & Oliver, Putnam Sons, 1928, hc, VG.. 40.00

China

Acorn, creamer, brn & wht, Cork Edge & Malkin, 2⅛" 22.50
Amherst Japan, saucer, England, mid-1800s, 4½" 15.00
Angel w/Shining Star, creamer, Germany, 3¾" 37.00
Archery, mug, lady shooting arrow, pk transfer, 2½" 120.00
Athens, tureen, bl & wht, Davenport, 1850s, 3½" 55.00
Banded Blue, canister, Germany, 2½" 30.00
Banded Blue, sugar bowl, w/lid, Germany, 4" 22.50
Barnyard Animals, sugar bowl, w/lid, Germany, 4" 22.50
Basket, creamer, flow bl, England 70.00
Basket, plate, Salem China, 6¼" 7.00
Blue Acorn, casserole, England, 5" 35.00
Blue Banded, creamer, Dimmock, 2¾" 25.00
Blue Banded, sugar bowl, w/lid, Dimmock, 3¾" 95.00
Blue Banded, teapot, Dimmock, 3¾" 90.00
Blue Banded Ironstone, bowl, 8-sided, England, 4" 25.00
Blue Banded Ironstone, server, mk Iron Stone, 2x3" 10.00
Blue Floral, washbowl & pitcher, England 225.00
Blue Marble, bowl, oval, England, 4½" 55.00
Blue Onion, egg whip, Germany, 4½" 180.00
Blue Onion, sugar bowl, w/lid, England 40.00
Blue Willow, bowl, England, 2" 42.50
Blue Willow, cake plate, Made in Japan, 5¼" 45.00
Blue Willow, casserole, oval, ribbed, England, 2" 50.00
Blue Willow, teapot, Made in Japan, 3¾" 75.00
Bluebird & Floral, dresser tray, hdls, England, 4¾" 45.00
Bridesmaid, mug, Germany, 2⅝" 120.00
Brundage Girls, creamer, Germany, 4" 32.00
Buster Brown, cup, Germany, 2½" 45.00
Butterfly, teapot, England, 4¼" 58.00
By the Mill, sugar bowl, brn & wht, w/lid, David Methvin & Sons..35.00
Calico, bowl, brn & wht, oval, England, 4" 35.00
Calico, tureen, brn on cream, 3¾".. 60.00
Catherine, mug, brn transfer, 2¾" 250.00
Chinaman (figural), creamer, Japan, 2¼" 42.00
Columbian Star, tea set, lt bl transfer, Ridgways, 11-pc, EX......1,200.00
Dimity, soup bowl, gr & ivory, England, 4¼" 12.00
Dr Franklin's Maxims, cup, bl transfer, unmk, 2¼x3" 480.00
Dr Franklin's Poor Richard, mug, blk transfer, 2¾".................... 100.00
Dutch Windmill, teacup & saucer, Germany, 2¼", 4⅝"................. 25.00
Fancy Loop, platter, cream & gr, England, 5" 26.00
Father Christmas & the Children, plate, Germany, 5" 25.00
Fishers, platter, dk gr & wht, CE&M, 3¾" 32.50
Flow Blue Dogwood, soup bowl, Minton, 4⅛" 48.00
Flowers That Never Fade, plate, children, blk transfer, 5", EX..... 180.00
Football, mug, blk transfer w/mc, 2½" 130.00
Forget-Me-Not, casserole, bl & wht, England, 4¾" 180.00
Forget-Me-Not, tureen, bl & wht, England, 3⅞" 125.00
Gaudy Floral, vegetable bowl, England, 4"............................... 55.00
Gaudy Ironstone, plate, England, 6"...................................... 55.00
Gaudy Ironstone, waste bowl, England, 2⅞" 120.00
Gold Floral, casserole, England, 5½" 55.00
Gold Floral, platter, bl band w/gold floral on wht, England, 5" 25.00
Greek Key, gravy boat, brn & wht, England, 4½" 32.00
Gumdrop Tree, cup & saucer, Southern Potteries, 2¼", 4½" 32.00
Holly, cup, Germany, 1900s... 25.00
Humphrey's Clock, soup bowl, bl & wht, Ridgways.................... 35.00
Humphrey's Clock, teapot, bl & wht, Ridgways, 4½" 85.00
Joseph, Mary & Donkey, creamer, Germany, 3" 42.50
Kite Fliers, gravy boat, bl & wht, England, 3½" 125.00

Lady Standing by Urn, teapot, purple & wht, England, 4½" 160.00
Lively Fern & Floral, soup bowl, gr & wht, 1850s, 4½" 25.00
Maiden-Hair-Fern, casserole, England, 5½" 35.00
Maiden-Hair-Fern, platter, Ridgways, late 1800s, 7¼" 25.00
Mary Had a Little Lamb, rolling pin, 9" 225.00
May, teapot, bulbous, bl & wht, England, 5" 75.00
Merry Christmas/Pink Lustre, sugar bowl, w/lid, Germany, 3⅝".... 40.00
Mickey Mouse, creamer, Made in Japan, 2" 27.00
Nursery Rhymes, cup & saucer, W&Co, 2", 5" 24.00
Orient, cup & saucer, bl & wht, England, 3" 28.00
Pagodas, plate, mc on wht (bl dominate), England, 4½" 13.00
Pastel Blue Majolica, compote, England, 3¼" 170.00
Pembroke, casserole, bl & wht, Bistro, England, 5¼" 55.00
Pink Lustre, pitcher & bowl, England, 3", 4½" 85.00
Pink Open Rose, plate, England, 4½" 7.00
Playful Cats, sugar bowl, w/lid, Germany, 2¾" 45.00
Playful Zoo Animals, creamer, Edwin M Knowles, 2¾" 15.00
Present for a Good Boy, mug, red transfer, lustre rim, Staffordshire.. 460.00
Prosper-Freedom, mug, brn transfer eagle & shield, 2½" 135.00
Punch & Judy, cup, bl & wht, England, 1⅞" 37.50
Rhodesia, casserole, floral w/gold, Ridgways, 1900s, 5½" 55.00
Rhodesia, tureen, floral w/gold, Ridgways, 1900s, 4¾" 65.00
Robinson Crusoe, plate, blk transfer/mc, 1920s, 6" 75.00
Roman Chariots, creamer, bl & wht, Cauldon, England, 2" 40.00
Scenes From England, plate, bl & wht, 3⅛" 45.00
Scenes From England, vegetable bowl, bl & wht, w/lid, England, 4" .135.00
Snow White, teapot, Disney, Made in Japan, ca 1937, 3¼" 70.00
Spirit of Children, platter, Jack & Jill, England, 5" 25.00
St Nicholas, teapot, Germany, 5½" 200.00
Standing Pony, saucer, gr lustre, Germany, 4¼" 6.00
Standing Pony, teapot, gr lustre, Germany, 6" 90.00
Stick Spatter, teapot, Staffordshire, 5" 80.00
Stick Spatter, waste bowl, Staffordshire, 2½" 80.00
Sunset, sugar bowl, w/lid, Made in Japan, 3⅛" 13.00
Tan Lustre & Wht, teapot, England, 5¼" 50.00
Teddy Bear, sugar bowl, w/lid, Germany, 4" 52.50
Twin Flower, bowl, flow bl, England, 4¾" 80.00
Twin Flower, plate, flow bl, England, 3¾" 25.00
Walley Ironstone, compote, England, 5¾" 400.00
Water Hen, waste bowl, bl & wht, England, 2½" 60.00

Furniture

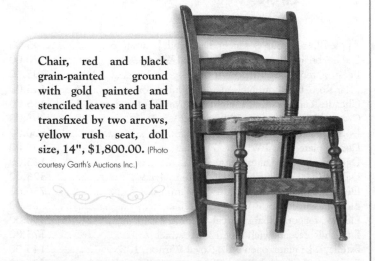

Chair, red and black grain-painted ground with gold painted and stenciled leaves and a ball transfixed by two arrows, yellow rush seat, doll size, 14", $1,800.00. (Photo courtesy Garth's Auctions Inc.)

Bed, mahog tall post w/canopy, acorn finials, 36x33x18½" 400.00
Bed, tramp art-type cvd headbrd w/3-color pnt, 1880s, Scandinavian, ds.. 60.00
Bed, 4-poster w/attached canopy, old red-brn stain, ds, 27x28x17" ..350.00

Blanket chest, cherry, 6-brd w/till, bracket base, rprs, 15x26x13" ...485.00
Blanket chest, curly maple/walnut, mellow rfn, rpl/rpr, 14x23x13" ..1,800.00
Blanket chest, pine, flowers on salmon pnt, European, ca 1893, 16x23"..285.00
Blanket chest, poplar w/old blk over red smoke decor, 14x22x10" ..525.00
Chair, bamboo Windsor w/thumb-bk posts, 4-spindle, grpt, 38" ..200.00
Chair, cut-out elephant figure ea side, rainbow on bk, 20th C, 22" 120.00
Chair, Egyptian Revival, animal figures/symbols, ebony/gilt, 1880s..2,200.00
Chair, horns form semicircle bk/arms/splayed legs, 20", +horn stool ...470.00
Chair, Windsor w/thumb-bk post, 4-spindle, bamboo trns, blk rpt, 28"..460.00
Chair, 5-spindle bk w/center medallion, grpt over gr, 30" 2,750.00
Chest, maple/pine w/old flame grpt, blk trn legs, 3-drw, 30x27x19"...3,585.00
Chest, poplar, 6-brd lift-off top, cut-out ends, MA, 1800s, 33" L.385.00
Cradle, bentwood top/24-spindle/scalloped rockers, wht rpt, 22x40x18".....515.00
Cradle, curly maple/walnut posts/shaped sides/scalloped rockers, 41" L..265.00
Cradle, hanging; mustard pnt/bl int/red knobs, NE, 1800s, 34" L ...500.00
Cradle, pine, hooded w/shaped footbrd & rockers, old red pnt, 10x17" .400.00
Cradle, pine, panel & post type w/hinged hood, 28x39x18", VG ...115.00
Cradle, swinging; 8 rtcl slats ea side w/circle cvgs, Vict, 38x41x19" ...180.00
Crib, curly maple w/trn spindles, acorn finials, rockers, 33x39x32"...350.00
Cupboard, pnt pine step-bk, raised panel doors above/below, 1850s, 16"...865.00
Cupboard, pnt pine step-bk, 2-drw, gr w/cream int, 1900s, 37x25x10"...315.00
Highchair, blk & red grpt w/yel striping, stencil on crest, PA, 34" .550.00
Highchair, ladderbk, blk pnt, 3-slat bk, cvd arms/trn supports, 1700s... 1,035.00
Highchair, mixed woods/curly maple legs, captain's style, rfn, 38" ..115.00
Highchair, Windsor rod-bk, maple, NE, 1810, rfn/rpr, 37" 500.00
Highchair, Windsor style, saddle seat, H stretcher, pnt, OH, 40". 350.00
Highchair on stand, elm Chpndl taste, rtcl splat, 1880s, 36x15"...1,500.00
Potty chair, red-pnt settee form, ME, early, 24" 175.00
Potty chair, shaped 1-brd sides w/cut-out handholds, bl pnt, 20" . 175.00
Rocker, serpentine crest, banister bk, spindle arms, rush seat, 25"...600.00
Rocker, Windsor w/old gr pnt, red arms, gold stencils, bamboo trn, 32"...750.00
Rocker, 2-slat bk, trn posts, woven seat, old gr pnt, ds, 14" 175.00
Sofa, classical mahog vnr w/uphl, NE, 1825, 17x32" 700.00

Glass

Acorn, butter dish, frosted, 4" 350.00
Acorn, spooner, 3⅛" 110.00
Acorn, sugar bowl, w/lid, 4¾" 200.00
Arched Panel, pitcher, cobalt, 3¾" 150.00
Austrian No 200, butter dish, chocolate 840.00
Austrian No 200, sugar bowl, w/lid, 3¾" 187.50
Baby Thumbprint, compote, w/lid, 4" 175.00
Banded Portland, pitcher, blush 56.00
Bead & Scroll, butter dish, amber, 4" 315.00
Bead & Scroll, spooner, cobalt, 2⅜" 155.00
Bead & Scroll, sugar bowl, w/lid, 4" 132.00
Beaded Swirl, spooner, amber, Westmoreland, 2¼" 150.00
Betty Jane, pie plate, McKee, #97, 4½" 12.00
Block, butter dish, bl 192.50
Braided Belt, butter dish, wht w/decor, 2¼" 315.00
Bucket (Wooden Pail), butter dish, 2¼" 280.00
Button Panel No 44, butter dish, w/gold trim, 4" 125.00
Buzz Saw No 2697, sugar bowl, w/lid, 2⅞" 34.00
Cherry Blossom, plate, pk, 5⅞" (+) 12.50
Cherry Blossom, sugar bowl, Delphite, 2⅝" (+) 50.00
Chicks & Pugs, mug, vaseline 75.00
Chimo, butter dish, 2⅜" (+) 130.00
Cloud Band, butter dish, 3¾" 125.00
Colonial Flute, punch cup, 1⅞" 14.00
Dewdrop, creamer, 2¾" 60.00
Diamond Ridge, butter dish 200.00
Doric & Pansy, creamer, pk, 2¾" 50.00
Doyle No 500, tray, bl, 6⅝" 80.00

Drum, mug, 2½" 40.00
Drum, spooner, 2⅝" 72.50
Dutch Boudoir, pitcher, milk glass, 2¼" 95.00
Fernland, butter dish, emerald gr, 2⅝" 54.00
Fernland, creamer, cobalt, 2⅜" 40.00
Fine Cut Star & Fan, butter dish, 2½" 36.50
Fine Cut Star & Fan, spooner, 2¼" 34.00
Galloway, tumbler, blush, US Glass, 2" 20.00
Grapevine w/Ovals, butter dish, 2½" 115.00
Hawaiian Lei, cake plate 52.50
Homespun, plate, 4½" 7.00
Homespun, teapot, pk, w/lid, Jeannette 125.00
Inverted Strawberry, master berry bowl, 1⅝" 65.00
Kidbake, casserole, wht opal, Fry, w/lid, #1938, 4½" 140.00
Kitten, banana dish, marigold 185.00
Kitten, cup, bl carnival, 2⅛" 200.00
Lamb, creamer, 2⅞" 85.00
Laurel, plate, French Ivory, 5⅞" 8.00
Laurel, sugar bowl, Scottie decal, 2⅜" 225.00
Lion, cup & saucer, crystal w/frosted head, Gillinder, 1¾", 3¼" 80.00
Mardi Gras, spooner 45.00
Moderntone, creamer, wht, 1¾" 17.50
Moderntone, teapot, maroon, w/lid, 3½" 100.00
Nearcut, pitcher, 3⅛" 32.50
Nursery Rhyme, berry set, 7-pc 227.00
Oval Star, berry set, 7-pc 100.00
Pattee Cross, pitcher, w/gold trim, 4½" 80.00
Pennsylvania, creamer, gr 110.00
Pert, spooner, 3" 130.00
Puritan, mug 16.00
Pyrexette, bread baker, 3x4¾" 24.00
Pyrexette, custard, 3½" 3.00
Rex (Fancy Cut), creamer, 2½" 28.50
Rex (Fancy Cut), pitcher, 3½" 62.50
Rooster, butter dish, 2¾" 200.00
Rose in Snow, mug, appl hdl 35.00
Sandwich Ivy, creamer, amethyst, 2⅜" 130.00
Sawtooth, creamer, 3½" 32.00
Sawtooth Band, sugar bowl, w/ruby stain, w/lid, 4⅛" 150.00
Sultan, creamer, chocolate, McKee, 2½" 320.00
Sunbeam (Twin Snowshoes), butter dish, 2" 147.50
Sunbeam (Twin Snowshoes), sugar bowl, w/lid, 3⅛" 122.50
Sunny Suzy, boxed set, 7-pc 150.00
Sunny Suzy, casserole, w/lid, 10-oz 12.00
Sweetheart, butter dish, 2" 22.00
Sweetheart, sugar bowl, w/lid, 3" 22.00
Tappan, sugar bowl, milk glass w/lid, 4" 30.00
Tulip & Honeycomb, sugar bowl, w/lid, Federal, 3¾" 35.00
Twist No 137, butter dish, frosted, 3⅝" 72.50
Wee Branches, cup & saucer, 1⅝", 3" 60.00
Whirligig No 15101, punch bowl, 4¾" 36.50
Wild Rose, candlestick, 4¼", ea 130.00
Wild Rose, punch bowl, milk glass 95.00
Wild Rose, sugar bowl, milk glass, 1¾" 60.00

Miscellaneous

Carriage, gr pnt w/red & yel decor, oak/iron, faux leather seat, 36" 500.00
Noah's ark, HP & stenciled wood, 7 wooden animals, mini, 2¾x7" 200.00
Noah's ark, pnt pine w/HP dove on roof, 28 cvd/HP animals, 23" L 1,200.00
Noah's ark, pnt pine w/2 figures+72 cvd animals, Germany, 1890s, 24" L 2,350.00
Noah's ark, 3-color pnt, Noah & 12 prs of animals, Germany, 20" l 525.00
Perambulator, wicker w/hide-covered horse, steel/rubber wheels, 55" L 2,585.00
Rocking horse, cvd/pnt wood, horsehair mane, leather tack, 53" L 750.00
Rocking horse, felt-covered w/hair, glass eyes/felt harness, 37" 1,380.00
Rocking horse, wood w/dapple pnt, red rockers, cloth saddle, 43" L 1,120.00
Sled, bentwood seat bk & runners, chamfered spindles, gr pnt, 32" 115.00
Sled, bl w/stenciled horse head, Paris Mfg, 27", G 290.00
Sled, pine brd w/red pnt & nautical scene, 22" L, VG 320.00

Chintz Dinnerware

'Chintz' is the generic name for English china with an allover floral transfer design. This eye-catching china is reminiscent of chintz dress fabric. It is colorful, bright, and cheery with its many floral designs and reminds one of an English garden in full bloom. It was produced in England during the first half of this century and stands out among other styles of china. Pattern names often found with the manufacturer's name on the bottom of pieces include Florence, Blue Chintz, English Roses, Delphinium, June Roses, Hazel, Eversham, Royalty, Sweet Pea, Summertime, and Welbeck, among others.

The older patterns tend to be composed of larger flowers, while the later, more popular lines can be quite intricate in design. And while the first collectors preferred the earthenware lines, many are now searching for the bone china dinnerware made by such firms as Shelley. You can concentrate on reassembling a favorite pattern, or you can mix two or more designs together for a charming, eclectic look. Another choice may be to limit your collection to teapots (the stacking ones are especially nice), breakfast sets, or cups and saucers.

Though the Chintz market remains very active, prices for some pieces have been significantly compromised due to their having been reproduced. For further information we recommend *Charlton Book of Chintz, I, II,* and *II,* by Susan Scott. Our advisor is Mary Jane Hastings; she is listed in the Directory under Illinois. See also Shelley.

Sunshine, basket, Royal Winton, 5", from $100.00 to $125.00. (Photo courtesy Carole Bess White and L.M. White)

Apple Blossom, cup & saucer, Diamond, James Kent 45.00
Bedale, breakfast-set toast rack, Royal Winton 70.00
Beeston, tennis set, Royal Winton, 2-pc 195.00
Briar Rose, trio, Lord Nelson, c/s+sq luncheon plate 145.00
Cheadle, cup & saucer, Caughley, Royal Winton, from $115 to 185.00
Cotswold, hot-water pot, Albans, 6x6½" 295.00
Dorset, breakfast set, Royal Winton 500.00
Dorset, plate, Royal Winton, 7" 50.00
DuBarry, pitcher, James Kent, 4½" 125.00
DuBarry, teapot, Diamond, James Kent, 4½x9½" 525.00
Eleanor, coffeepot, Albans, Royal Winton 750.00
Eleanor, saucer, Royal Winton 25.00
Eleanor, teapot, Albans, Royal Winton, 4-cup 350.00
English Rose, sandwich tray, 12x6" 175.00
Estelle, cake plate, open hdls, Royal Winton, 10⅛x9¾" 145.00
Evesham, cheese dish, Royal Winton, 6¼" L 495.00
Evesham, dish, open hdls, Royal Winton, 1¼x7x3¾" 275.00
Evesham, milk jug, globe shape, Royal Winton, rstr spout, 3¾" 295.00
Fireglow, breakfast set, Athena, rose-shaped shakers, Royal Winton 750.00

Fireglow, hot-water pot, Sexta, Royal Winton, lg....625.00
Floral Feast, nut dish, Wedgwood border, Royal Winton....45.00
Floral Feast, sugar bowl, w/hdls & lid, Royal Winton....75.00
Florita, bowl, fluted edge, James Kent, 5"....45.00
Florita, plate, Granville, James Kent, 9"....145.00
Florita, shell bowl, wavy edge, James Kent, 8⅜x6¾"....120.00
Hazel, bud vase, Clwyd shape, Royal Winton....195.00
Hazel, egg cup set, Seville, Royal Winton, 4 cups & tray....350.00
Hazel, nut scoop, Royal Winton, 5"....175.00
Hazel, plate, Royal Winton, 9"....65.00
Hazel, shell dish, Royal Winton, 5¼x4½"....75.00
Hazel, sugar bowl, Royal Winton....35.00
Heather, bud vase, Lord Nelson, 5"....95.00
Heather, platter, Lord Nelson, 12½x7½"....95.00
Heather, teapot, stacking; 3-pc, wrapped hdls, Lord Nelson....250.00
Julia, compote, Lily, Royal Winton....395.00
Julia, nut dish, cut-out hdl, Royal Winton....195.00
Julia, nut scoop, Royal Winton, rstr hdl, rare....195.00
Julia, plate, Ascot, Royal Winton, 6"....125.00
Julia, plate, Royal Winton, 7"....160.00
June Festival, creamer, red, Royal Winton....50.00
June Festival, cup, red, Royal Winton....20.00
Kew, cake plate, open hdls, Royal Winton....195.00
Kinver, bud vase, Royal Winton, 5¼"....115.00
Lilac Time, plate, Empire, 7"....65.00
Majestic, butter dish, rectangular, Royal Winton, stain....265.00
Majestic, cup & saucer, demitasse; can shape, Royal Winton....150.00
Majestic, nut dish, heart-shaped cut-out hdls, Royal Winton, 6⅝"....335.00
Majestic, plate, Athena, Royal Winton, 6"....125.00
Majestic, serving dish, Marina, 5-section, Royal Winton, 12x10¾"....295.00
Marguerite, cheese keeper, bl trim, Royal Winton, 7½x6¼"....250.00
Marguerite, jug, Globe, Royal Winton, 4½"....115.00
Marguerite, tray, Seville, bl trim, Royal Winton, 10x9¼"....145.00
Marina, cake plate, sq w/tab hdls, Lord Nelson, 10⅝x9⅛"....125.00
Marina, stacking teapot set, Lord Nelson....495.00
Marina, teapot, Lord Nelson, lg....395.00
Natwich, divided dish, Royal Winton, 9x6"....495.00
Old Cottage, breakfast set, Royal Winton....500.00
Old Cottage, cheese keeper, Rex, Royal Winton....250.00
Old Cottage, creamer & sugar bowl, Royal Winton, ind....55.00
Old Cottage, jug, Royal Winton, 4½"....215.00
Old Cottage, plate, Ascot, Royal Winton, 7¾"....55.00
Paisley, creamer & sugar bowl, James Kent....45.00
Pansy, cup & saucer, demitasse; Lord Nelson....45.00
Pansy, egg cup, Bucket, Crown Ducal....85.00
Pansy, plate, Art Deco, hdld, Crown Ducal, 8"....55.00
Pansy, tray, Lord Nelson, 8¼x5¼"....65.00
Pansy, trio, Lord Nelson....95.00
Peony, mayonnaise bowl & liner, Crown Ducal....135.00
Peony, plate, Crown Ducal, sq, 7"....85.00
Peony, teapot, Crown Ducal, 4-cup....435.00
Pink Chintz, plate, Crown Ducal, 9½"....250.00
Pink Chintz, relish tray, center hdl, 3-part, Crown Ducal....175.00
Primula, jug, Crown Ducal, 3¾"....95.00
Primula, oval dish, Crown Ducal, 9¾x8¾"....100.00
Rapture, sugar bowl, James Kent....45.00
Richmond, mint sauce w/undertray, Era, Royal Winton....260.00
Rosalynde, sugar bowl, James Kent....60.00
Rosalynde, toast rack, 4-slice, James Kent, rare....350.00
Rose Brocade, breakfast teapot, bl, Royal Winton....80.00
Rose DuBarry, creamer for stacking pot, Royal Winton....80.00
Rosetime, honeypot, w/lid & tray, Lord Nelson....175.00
Royalty, creamer & sugar bowl, Ascot, Royal Winton....275.00
Royalty, sugar bowl, Countess, Royal Winton, ind....35.00
Somerset, plate, Ascot, Royal Winton, sq, 6"....70.00
Somerset, plate, gold trim, Royal Winton, 8"....195.00
Spring, cake plate, Athena, Royal Winton....485.00
Spring Blossom, plate, bl trim, Crown Ducal, sq, 5¾"....125.00
Stratford, pepper shaker, Fife, Royal Winton, ea....55.00
Summertime, breadfast set, Countess, Royal Winton, NM....650.00
Summertime, jug, Dutch, Royal Winton, 3¾"....160.00
Summertime, nut dish, Royal Winton, ind....95.00
Summertime, tray, wrapped hdl, Royal Winton, 8x6"....495.00
Sunshine, bud vase, Royal Winton, 3¼"....10.00
Sunshine, compote, allover pattern, Lily, Royal Winton, 3x6"....175.00
Sunshine, cup, Countess, Royal Winton....45.00
Sunshine, plate, Athena, Royal Winton, 7"....85.00
Sweet Pea, bowl, rimmed soup; Royal Winton, 8"....85.00
Sweet Pea, candy dish, Royal Winton....150.00
Sweet Pea, compote, Royal Winton, 7x6½"....155.00
Sweet Pea, rimmed soup, Royal Winton, 8"....160.00
Sweet Pea, toast rack, 5-bar, Royal Winton....450.00
Triumph, plate, Athena, Royal Winton, 7"....120.00
Vera, creamer, Royal Winton....325.00
Victorian Rose, breakfast toast rack, Royal Winton....115.00
Victorian Rose, nut dish, Ascot, Royal Winton, ind....110.00
Victorian Rose, plate, Ascot, Royal Winton, 7"....85.00
Welbeck, cup & saucer, Royal Winton....175.00
Welbeck, plate, Royal Winton, 8¾"....190.00
White Crocus, teapot, Albans, Royal Winton, 2-cup....300.00

Chocolate Glass

Jacob Rosenthal developed chocolate glass, a rich shaded opaque brown sometimes referred to as caramel slag, in 1900 at the Indiana Tumbler and Goblet Company of Greentown, Indiana. Later, other companies produced similar ware. Only the latter is listed here. Our advisor for this category is Sandi Garrett; she are listed in the Directory under Indiana. See also Greentown.

Comb and brush tray, Venetian, McKee & Bros., 8x10", $425.00. (Photo courtesy Green Valley Auctions Inc.)

Bowl, Beaded Triangle, Royal, 4½"....350.00
Bowl, Geneva, McKee, oval, 10½"....275.00
Bowl, sauce; Water Lily & Cattails, Fenton, 4"....140.00
Bowl, Wild Rose w/Bowknot, McKee, 8½"....200.00
Box, jewel; Venetian, McKee....400.00
Box, powder; Orange Tree, Fenton, rnd....550.00
Butter dish, File, Royal....2,500.00
Butter dish, Fleur-de-Lis, Royal....750.00
Butter dish, Geneva, MeKee....500.00
Butter dish, Touching Squares, McKee....3,000.00
Butter dish, White Oak, McKee....6,000.00
Candleholder, griffin, ea....3,250.00
Carafe, Chrysanthemum Leaf....2,500.00

Celery holder, Chrysanthemum Leaf, 6" 900.00
Celery holder, Fleur-de-Lis, Royal, 5¾" 325.00
Celery tray, Jubilee, 10" 300.00
Compote, jelly; Geneva, McKee 125.00
Compote, jelly; Majestic, McKee 650.00
Compote, Melrose, Royal, 7¾" 225.00
Cracker jar, Chrysanthemum Leaf, w/lid 2,500.00
Creamer, Aldine, McKee 1,300.00
Creamer, Cattail & Water Lily, Fenton 475.00
Creamer, Rose Garland 1,350.00
Creamer, Wild Rose w/Scrolling, child sz, 2¾" 175.00
Cruet, Shield w/Daisy & Button, Royal 5,000.00
Dish, Honeycomb, rectangular, Royal, 6¾x4" 400.00
Flowerpot, Russell 1,000.00
Hatpin holder, Orange Tree, Fenton 700.00
Lamp, Cloverleaf 1,250.00
Mug, Swirl 600.00
Nappy, Navarre, w/hdl, McKee 300.00
Novelty, smoking set, McKee & Bros, 3-pc 1,100.00
Pitcher, File, Royal 2,000.00
Pitcher, Fleur-de-Lis, Royal 1,250.00
Pitcher, Rose Garland 3,000.00
Salt cellar, Honeycomb, Royal, master, 3½" 650.00
Shaker, Big Rib 500.00
Shaker, Geneva 375.00
Shaker, Wild Rose w/Bowknot, McKee 275.00
Spooner, Chrysanthemum Leaf 600.00
Spooner, Fleur-de-Lis, Royal 175.00
Spooner, Geneva, McKee 175.00
Sugar bowl, Water Lily & Cattails, w/lid, Fenton 600.00
Toothpick holder, Chrysanthemum Leaf 800.00
Toothpick holder, Kingfisher 1,000.00
Tray, Wild Rose w/Bowknot, McKee, 10½x8" 400.00
Tumbler, File, Royal Glass 600.00
Tumbler, Geneva, McKee, 3⅞" 110.00
Tumbler, Uneeda Milk Biscuit, Nat'l Biscuit Co, 5¾" 80.00
Vase, #400, Fenton, 6" 600.00
Vase, Water Lily & Cattails, Fenton, 6" 550.00

Christmas Collectibles

Christmas past… lovely mementos from long ago attest to the ostentatious Victorian celebrations of the season.

St. Nicholas, better known as Santa, has changed much since 300 A.D. when the good Bishop Nicholas showered needy children with gifts and kindnesses. During the early eighteenth century, Santa was portrayed as the kind gift-giver to well-behaved children and the stern switch-bearing disciplinarian to those who were bad. In 1822 Clement Clark Moore, a New York poet, wrote his famous *Night Before Christmas*, and the Santa he described was jolly and jovial — a lovable old elf who was stern with no one. Early Santas wore robes of yellow, brown, blue, green, red, white, or even purple. But Thomas Nast, who worked as an illustrator for *Harper's Weekly*, was the first to depict Santa in a red suit instead of the traditional robe and to locate him the entire year at the North Pole headquarters.

Today's collectors prize early Santa figures, especially those in robes of fur or mohair or those dressed in an unusual color. Some early examples of Christmas memorabilia are the pre-1870 ornaments from Dresden, Germany. These cardboard figures — angels, gondolas, umbrellas, dirigibles, and countless others — sparkled with gold and silver trim. Late in the 1870s, blown glass ornaments were imported from Germany. There were over 6,000 recorded designs, all painted inside with silvery colors. From 1890 through 1910, blown glass spheres were often decorated with beads, tassels, and tinsel rope.

Christmas lights, made by Sandwich and some of their contemporaries, were either pressed or mold-blown glass shaped into a form similar to a water tumbler. They were filled with water and then hung from the tree by a wire handle; oil floating on the surface of the water served as fuel for the lighted wick.

Kugels are glass ornaments that were made as early as 1820 and as late as 1890. Ball-shaped examples are more common than the fruit and vegetable forms and have been found in sizes ranging from 1" to 14" in diameter. They were made of thick glass with heavy brass caps, in cobalt, green, gold, silver, red, and occasionally in amethyst.

Although experiments involving the use of electric light bulbs for the Christmas tree occurred before 1900, it was 1903 before the first manufactured socket set was marketed. These were very expensive and often proved a safety hazard. In 1921 safety regulations were established, and products were guaranteed safety approved. The early bulbs were smaller replicas of Edison's household bulb. By 1910 G.E. bulbs were rounded with a pointed end, and until 1919 all bulbs were hand blown. The first figural bulbs were made around 1910 in Austria. Japan soon followed, but their product was never of the high quality of the Austrian wares. American manufacturers produced their first machine-made figurals after 1919. Today figural bulbs (especially character-related examples) are very popular collectibles. Bubble lights were popular from about 1945 to 1960 when miniature lights were introduced. These tiny lamps dampened the public's enthusiasm for the bubblers, and manufacturers stopped providing replacement bulbs.

Feather trees were made from 1850 to 1950. All are collectible. Watch for newly manufactured feather trees that have been reintroduced. For further information concerning Christmas collectibles, we recommend *Pictorial Guide to Christmas Ornaments and Collectibles* by George Johnson, available from Collector Books or your local bookstore.

Note: Values are given for bulbs that are in good paint, with no breaks or cracks, and in working order. When no condition is mentioned in the description, assume that values are for examples in EX/NM condition except paper items; those should be assumed NM/M.

Bulbs

Angel w/wings spread, wht plastic, Bradford, ca 1950, 5½", $8 to .. 10.00
Banana, clear glass, 2¾", from $20 to 30.00
Bear in red dress, celluloid, 3¾", from $70 to 80.00
Bozo the Clown, milk glass, Japan, ca 1950, 2½", from $30 to 35.00
Canary, milk glass, 4", from $15 to 20.00
Cat w/bow sitting, clear glass, Japan, 2¼", from $30 to 35.00
Dog, brn, Dresden, 1927, 3¾", from $90 to 100.00
Elephant w/trunk up, milk glass, 3", from $20 to 30.00
Flapper girl, milk glass, tall, Japan, ca 1950, from $55 to 65.00
Kewpie, milk glass, lg head, Japan, 2½", from $25 to 35.00
Lemon, clear glass, 1¾", from $10 to 12.00
Mother Goose rides goose, milk glass, Japan, 1950s, 3", from $50 to .. 65.00
Orange, Dresden, 3½", from $150 to 175.00
Owl-headed girl, frosted glass, 2½", from $75 to 90.00
Zeppelin, clear glass, American, 2¾", from $35 to 50.00

Candy Containers

Animal crackers box, print on cb, 3", from $15 to 25.00
Box, oval, Roman bust on lid, paper, 4½", from $150 to 175.00
Bucket w/Santa portrait, pk & silver, crepe paper, 4½", $40 to 50.00
Carrying case, emb paper w/metal key, 2", from $125 to 150.00
Cornucopia w/appl litho of sm girl in bl dress, 9¼", from $75 to .. 100.00
Mandolin, cb w/gold foil, ca 1925, 7½", from $80 to 110.00
Mantel clock, paper on cb, Russian, ca 1925, 2¾", from $60 to 75.00
Purse w/gold clover, wicker, Dresden, 1½", from $175 to 200.00
Roasted turkey, paper, 4½", from $50 to 75.00

Santa boots, pressed paper w/Venetian dew & Dresden trim, 1930-50, 6". 30.00
Sewing basket, wicker, 3½", from $200 to 225.00
St Nicholas' hat, cb covered w/fabric, 3¾", from $275 to 300.00
Watering can, printed paper on cb, 2½", from $200 to................. 225.00

Novelty Lighting

Bubble Lamps, USA Lite #107, ca 1950s, MIB, $150.00. (Photo courtesy Cindy Chipps and Greg Olson)

Bubble light, mini; Santa, 8-socket, ca 1955............................ 50.00
Bubble light, mini; Shooting Star, Good-Lite #820, 9-socket, ca 1948...375.00
Bubble light, Park Electric #607, 7-socket, 1950....................... 70.00
Candelabra, 3-socket, Good-Lite, ca 1948................................ 15.00
Candelabra, 5-socket, Raylite, #255, ca 1958............................ 50.00
Candelabra, 7-socket, Noma, #198, 1939................................. 95.00
Hurricane lamp, Thomas Co #707, ca 1960................................ 10.00
Lamp, motion; Merry Christmas, ca 1965, 11" 175.00
Lantern, Golden Christmas, Noma #940, 1958, 15"...................... 10.00
Music box, church window, Raylite #877MC, ca 1954, 11" 65.00
Music box, Santa on snowball, I'm Dreaming...Christmas, Rosbro, 6½"..150.00
Nativity scene, Glolite #315, ca 1949, 8"............................... 25.00
Santa behind fence, Harett-Gilmar, ca 1955, 7x7", from $45 to.... 55.00
Santa holding Merry Christmas sign, Royalite, 7½", from $45 to .. 55.00
Santa standing, General Products, ca 1950, 8¼", from $30 to........ 40.00
Socket set, Neon Flame, Thomas Co #F117, ca 1955.................... 35.00
Socket set, Pep-Mint-Stik, Leo Pollock #X3402, 7-socket, ca 1942...125.00
Socket set, Poinsettia, Noma #3165R, 20-socket, 1960................. 15.00
Star of Bethlehem, bulbs on tips of star, 4¼", from $8 to 10.00
Tree, metal, Cheer-O-Lite, Noma #615, 1936, 10"..................... 100.00
Tree, prewired, 17-socket, w/base, Noma #582, 1955, 30"........... 175.00
Tree, prewired, 2-socket, w/base, Glolite #112, ca 1949, 14"......... 20.00
Tree stand, CI, 8 mini sockets, USA, ca 1935, 13½" 95.00
Tree stand, plastic, Season's Greetings, Good-Lite, 1955, 13½" 40.00
Tree topper, angel, Royalite, 1940s-50s, 8½", MIB, from $20 to 25.00
Tree topper, Angel-Glo, Sunburst, 1950s, 9", from $15 to............. 20.00
Tree topper, Carillon Spire, Bradford, ca 1960, 13½", from $5 to 7.00
Tree topper, star, Glolite, 1940s-50s, 7½", MIB, from $15 to......... 20.00
Wall hanger, Christmas Bells, Glolite #103, 1955, 16"................. 30.00
Wall hanger, cross, wht, Noma #68, 1935, 10" 25.00
Wall hanger, Santa face, Noma, ca 1949, 15½", from $30 to 40.00
Wall hanger, snowman holding wreath, Royalite, ca 1955, 7½", $25 to. 35.00
Wall hanger, tree, Am, ca 1950, 14½", from $100 to................... 125.00
Wall hanger, 3 Wise Men, Vinylite, Raylite #377, ca 1954, 19"..... 30.00
Wreath, red cellophane, USA, ca 1945 .... 30.00
Wreath, Sno-Man, Noma #1103, 1956.................................... 50.00

Ornaments

Angel head in spun glass rosette, 4", from $20 to 30.00
Angel w/horn, wax w/pk satin dress, 6½", from $175 to.............. 200.00
Baby rattle, Merry Xmas, glass, 5", from $125 to...................... 150.00
Basket, glass w/metal cage, egg shape, hollow, 3½", from $150 to . 175.00
Basket, tin/lead, rectangular, w/lid, 4", from $80 to 100.00
Bear on swing, cotton, from $275 to 300.00

Bell, styrofoam w/red & gold beads, 3½", from $2 to 3.00
Bust of child, crepe-paper disks, 5", from $25 to 35.00
Butterfly, velour, German, 5", from $50 to 75.00
Chalet w/angel & deer, plastic, mk Western Germany, 2¼", from $5 to..6.00
Champagne bottle in pk bucket, floral decor, glass, Italian, 1950s, 4" ...150.00
Choir boy holding candle, pk plastic, Bradford, ca 1955-60, $20 to.... 25.00
Elf w/toy bear, plastic, 3¼", from $15 to................................. 20.00
Goldilocks head, glass, red ribbon in hair, 2½", from $100 to 125.00
Horse w/jockey, plastic, 3-D, Dresden, 3¼x3½", from $375 to 400.00
Jesus bust, glass, Germany, ca 1890, from $400 to...................... 450.00
Jesus bust on egg-shape bulb, glass, Germany, 3¼", from $225 to. 250.00
Lady w/baby, bl bodice & purple skirt, paper, Littaur & Boysen, 4¼"...75.00
Lincoln bust, glass, Radko, 1990s, 4¾", from $35 to 50.00
Mickey Mouse decal on silver ball, ca 1950s, from $15 to............. 20.00
Pear w/Mary & baby Jesus inside, wax, Germany, 2", from $150 to.. 175.00
Pears, spun cotton w/wire wrapping & fabric leaves, 2", from $20 to ...25.00
Santa holding tree, cotton batting w/wax face, 5", from $225 to . 250.00
Santa w/his sleigh & 2 reindeer, stamped brass, 3", from $25 to..... 30.00
Snow girl, cotton in glass ball, 3", from $10 to 15.00
Snowman, cotton, 5", from $60 to 80.00
Star, gold foil, ca 1950, from $3 to 5.00
Star w/paper Santa in middle, twisted wire & silver beads, 4", $35 to..45.00
Trolley, pressed cotton over cb, 14", from $175 to 200.00
Umbrella, closed, art glass, 4½", from $25 to 35.00
Wall clock, pk glass w/paper dial, Germany, 3¾", from $75 to 100.00

Miscellaneous

Bank, Santa at chimney, 7¾", from $200 to................................ 300.00
Calendar plate, 1909, Santa in dirigible, American China, 9½" .. 150.00
Chain, Inge-glas, man in crescent moon & star, from $75 to 100.00
Figurine, Santa drummer, celluloid face & hands, windup, 10½". 350.00
Flashlight, Santa face, Hong Kong, ca 1960 .... 20.00
Game, Rudolph the Red-Nosed Reindeer, Parker Brothers, 1948, $70 to....80.00
Jack-in-the-box, Santa Claus, Bradford, ca 1950, 3¾", from $35 to ..45.00
Kugel, berries, gold, 3¾", from $200 to 250.00
Kugel, orange, silver, 3½", from $350 to.................................. 400.00
Kugel, pine cone w/leaves, rare, 4¼", from $600 to 700.00
Lamp, kerosene; Santa, milk glass, 6" shade, 10", from $2,700 to... 3,000.00
Lantern, Santa, Hilco #222S, ca 1960 .... 25.00
Lapel pin, Rudolph, Hong Kong, ca 1960 .... 10.00
Light tester, Apco, Applied Products, ca 1930............................ 10.00
Lighting fuses, Noma, ca 1950...4.00
Nativity scene, chromolithograph paper, Made in Germany, ca 1900..150.00
Plaque, Santa & sleigh, CI, 14½", from $900 to 1,100.00
Santa holding candy cane, rubber, Hong Kong, ca 1965 .... 20.00
Snow, USA, pre-WWII, from $10 to 15.00
Stocking, net w/orig toys, ca 1939, 11", from $30 to 35.00
Tree, feather; paper-wrapped trunk, 25" 400.00
Tree topper, glass cone, 3 balls w/tinsel spray & wire wrap, 10-12" ...25.00

Chrysanthemum Sprig, Blue

This is the blue opaque version of Northwood's popular pattern, Chrysanthemum Sprig. It was made at the turn of the century and is today very rare, as its values indicate. Prices are influenced by the amount of gold remaining on the raised designs. Our advisors for this category are Betty and Clarence Maier; they're listed in the Directory under Pennsylvania. Unless noted otherwise, our values are for examples with excellent to near-mint gold.

Bowl, berry; ind, M gold, 2⅝x5x3¾", from $90 to 125.00
Bowl, master fruit; 8x5x10½" 450.00

Butter dish, from $900 to..1,200.00
Celery, from $275 to 375.00
Compote, jelly..45.00
Condiment tray, rare, VG gold, from $600 to 700.00
Creamer, from $300 to 375.00
Cruet, from $750 to 1,000.00

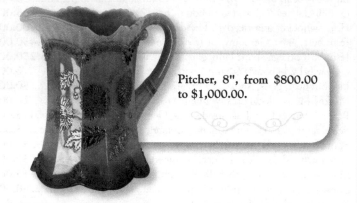

Pitcher, 8", from $800.00 to $1,000.00.

Shakers, pr from $350 to...400.00
Spooner, from $275 to 325.00
Sugar bowl, w/lid, 7", M gold, from $400 to...............475.00
Toothpick holder, 2¾", from $375 to 450.00
Tumbler, 3¾", from $90 to 125.00

Circus Collectibles

The 1890s — the golden age of the circus. Barnum and Bailey's parades transformed mundane city streets into an exotic never-never land inhabited by trumpeting elephants with jeweled gold headgear strutting by to the strains of the calliope that issued from a fine red- and gilt-painted wagon extravagantly decorated with carved wooden animals of every description. It was an exciting experience. Is it any wonder that collectors today treasure the mementos of that golden era? See also Posters.

Key:
BB — Barnum & Bailey   RB — Ringling Bros.

Banner, Side Show, Museum of Oddities...Curiosities, 1950s, 52x94", EX...525.00
Book, Route; Great Wallace Show, 1895, 134 pgs, 6¾x4½", VG+ ..340.00
Book, Route; Sells Bros, 1878, 16 pgs, 5½x3½", EX............60.00
Book, Route; Tom Mix Circus, 1937, 22 pgs, 10x7", EX 75.00
Booklet, ...History of Rosie's 5 Royal Midgets, 1926, 8 pgs, 9x6", EX...20.00
Cabinet card, female snake charmer, photo by Eisenmann, VG ..160.00
Check, RB & BB, to Ellis & Lowe Co, 5/48, 3½x8½", EX 125.00
Mug, lion on base, head tilts for lid, RB & BB on base, EX............10.00
Paperweight, RB & BB, Greatest Show on Earth, marble base, 1972, EX....45.00
Patch, RB Circus Museum, Sarasota FL, clown center, EX 8.00
Pennant, RB & BB, red on yel, w/clown, 1960s-70s, 9", EX.............6.00
Photo, Arturo Gaona Flying Trapeze Troupe, EX 30.00
Photo, Circus Clown Neil Kay, ca 1972, 10x8", EX 15.00
Photo, Dolly Jacobs (female lion tamer), 1937, 10x8", EX.............25.00
Photo, Great Levasseur, strong man, 1907, fr, 7x9" 85.00
Pin, RB & BB, Greatest Show on Earth, globe w/red border, 1" dia, EX ..13.00
Pitch card, Little Richard Miller, man w/no arms or legs w/guitar, EX...50.00
Postcard, RB & BB, elephant show, EX 10.00
Program, Al G Barnes Wild Animal Circus, 1936, 46 pgs, 11x8½", EX... 25.00
Program, Austen Bros Circus, 1979, EX..12.00
Program, Bertram Mills Circus, 1951-52, EX................................35.00
Program, Billy Smart's New World Circus, 24 pgs, 1955, 8¾x5", EX ... 15.00
Program, Blackpool Tower Circus, 1972, EX 30.00

Program, Cole Bros, 1942, 11x8½", EX..........................20.00
Program, King Bros Circus, 1953, EX.............................17.50
Program, Miller Bros & Arlington 101 Ranch Real West, 1915, EX ...90.00
Program, Nertram Mills Circus, man leading monkey band, 1953-54, EX...25.00
Program, Polak Bros Circus, bear on motorcycle, 1963-64, EX 10.00
Program, RB & BB, 1938, 11¼x8½", NM...........................50.00
Program, RB & BB, 1944, clown bowing to lady on horse, 11x8", EX...35.00
Program, RB & BB, 1949, 80 pgs, 11x8¼", VG+..................25.00
Stock certificate, RB & BB, 25 shares, 1970, 8x12", EX..........165.00
Tickets, RB & BB, 1946, set of 2, unused, EX.....................10.00
Tray, RB & BB, ticket design, glass, 1970s, 5¾x2½", EX 17.50
Wagon figure, cvd female above foliage, mc pnt, rprs, 19th C, 67", pr 3,225.00

Cleminson

A hobby turned to enterprise, Cleminson is one of several California potteries whose clever hand-decorated wares are attracting the attention of today's collectors. The Cleminsons started their business at their El Monte home in 1941 and were so successful that eventually they expanded to a modern plant that employed more than 150 workers. They produced not only dinnerware and kitchen items such as cookie jars, canisters, and accessories, but novelty wall vases, small trays, plaques, etc., as well. Though nearly always marked, Cleminson wares are easy to spot as you become familiar with their distinctive glaze colors. Their grayed-down blue and green, berry red, and dusty pink say 'Cleminson' as clearly as their trademark. Unable to compete with foreign imports, the pottery closed in 1963. For more information we recommend *Collector's Encyclopedia of California Pottery, Second Edition*, by Jack Chipman (Collector Books).

Bowl, Gram's on front, roses on brn wreath on lid, 2½" 30.00
Box, trinket; Miss in a Bathtub, 3½x5" 55.00
Clothes sprinkler bottle, Chinaman, 8½" 85.00
Cookie canister, Galagray 90.00
Cookie jar, Cookie Book, from $150 to...........................175.00
Cookie jar, Mother's Best..375.00
Cookie jar, Potbellied Stove, 9", from $140 to..................150.00
Creamer & sugar bowl, PA Dutch decor 18.00
Cup, child's; clown head, hat lid 80.00
Cup & saucer, My Old Man w/man sleeping, 5½", 8", from $15 to...20.00
Darning egg, lady w/Darn It on front, 5".........................50.00
Darning egg, winking sailor, 1 hand behind bk, 5" 100.00
Jar, vitamin; Daily Dose, w/lid, 5"..................................80.00
Pitcher, Distlefink, cylindrical, 5"..................................30.00
Pitcher, Distlefink, 9½" 45.00
Pitcher, watering can shape, wht w/bl & magenta floral decor, 5".. 35.00
Plaque, Family Tree, child & bunny at bottom, from $60 to 75.00
Plate, rooster crowing, yel decor rim, 9½"........................22.50
Razor blade bank, bell w/man shaving, 3½", from $30 to 40.00
Ring holder, wht & peach dog w/tail in air 30.00
Shakers, Cherry, 6", pr 40.00
Shakers, Distlefink, lg, pr 35.00
Shakers, Galagray rhumba couple, dk red trim, 6½", pr.............45.00
Spoon rest, Cherry 20.00
String holder, heart shape w/You'll Always Have a Pull w/Me.......45.00
Wall plaque, roses & butterflies, scalloped fluted border, 7" dia 40.00
Wall pocket, Antoine, chef's face, 7¼" 75.00

Clewell

Charles Walter Clewell was a metal worker who perfected the technique of plating an entire ceramic vessel with a thin layer of copper or bronze treated with an oxidizing agent to produce a natural deterioration of the surface. Through trial and error, he was able to control the degree of patina achieved. In the early stages, the metal darkened and if allowed to develop further formed a natural turquoise-blue or green corrosion. He worked alone in his small Akron, Ohio, studio from about 1906, buying undecorated pottery from several Ohio firms, among them Weller, Owens, and Cambridge. His work is usually marked. Clewell died in 1965, having never revealed his secret process to others.

Prices for Clewell have advanced rapidly during the past few years along with the Arts and Crafts market in general. Right now, good examples are bringing whatever the traffic will bear.

Lamp base, bronze brn w/gold undertones, emb floral, unmk, 14x5¼".. 400.00
Vase, brn to gr patina, trumpet neck, #290-215, 7¼" 535.00
Vase, copper w/strong gr at base, ovoid, #317, 7" 900.00
Vase, cvd tulips, shouldered bottle form, mk Owensart/Utopian, 8x5"... 600.00
Vase, deep gr verdigris, shouldered w/sm neck, #365-2-7, 6x4" 720.00
Vase, EX red & gr patina, classic form, mk 8-2-6, 15" 3,600.00
Vase, strong gr patina, bottle shape w/low width, #361, 10x4½", EX.. 1,080.00

Cliff, Clarice

Between 1928 and 1935 in Burslem, England, as the director and part owner of Wilkinson and Newport Pottery Companies, Clarice Cliff and her 'paintresses' created a body of hand-painted pottery whose influence is felt to the present time.

The name for the oevre was Bizarre Ware, and the predominant sensibility, style, and appearance was Deco. Almost all pieces are signed. There were over 160 patterns and more than 400 shapes, all of which are illustrated in *A Bizarre Affair — The Life and Work of Clarice Cliff*, published by Harry N. Abrams, Inc., written by Len Griffen and Susan and Louis Meisel.

Note: Non-hand-painted work (transfer printed) was produced after World War II and into the 1950s. Some of the most common names are 'Tonquin' and 'Charlotte.' These items, while attractive and enjoyable to own, have little value in the collector market.

Biscuit jar, Nuage, mc floral, 5¼" 400.00
Bowl, Latona (tree), ca 1930, 16⅜" 1,650.00
Charger, Killarney, geometrics, wide rim, 17¾" 1,115.00
Charger, Latona Tree, ribbed body, 18¼" 765.00
Flowerpot, geometric, mc on cream, Bizarre Ware, 7¾" 950.00
Ginger jar, mc geometric, rstr neck, 9½" 825.00
Jardiniere, water lily form, 1940s, 5x7" 165.00

Jug, Blue Chintz, 11½", $1,950.00. (Photo courtesy Skinner Inc. Auctioneers & Appraisers of Antiques & Fine Art)

Jug, Delecia Citrus, oranges & lemons, ribbed body, 12" 1,055.00
Jug, triangles & dmns, Athens shape, 6⅜" 585.00

Plate, Xanthic Harbor, 10" 650.00
Sandwich set, Fantasque floral, 11¾" 8-sided plate, +6 sm plates. 765.00
Sandwich set, Floreat, canted corners, 6 5⅝" plates+11¼" platter ..700.00
Shaker, Crocus, conical, 5¾", ea 700.00
Shaker, Nasturtium, conical, 5⅝" 700.00
Vase, Fantasque floral band on orange, flared rim, 7¾" 1,880.00
Vase, foliate design, #353, 7" 885.00
Vase, geometrics, mc on cream, ftd, #354, 6x5" 545.00
Vase, Inspiration, trees & bridge on teal, slim baluster, 8⅝" 750.00
Vase, Inspiration, trees & bridge on teal, swollen cylinder, 10".... 950.00
Vase, Inspirational Chrysanthemum, wide mouth & neck on cylinder, 8" ..950.00
Vase, Patina Country, mc on cream, ca 1930, 9¾" 1,300.00
Vase, Patina Tree, autumn tones, shaped rim, tapered cylinder, 6"... 585.00

Clifton

Clifton Art Pottery of Clifton, New Jersey, was organized ca 1903. Until 1911 when they turned to the production of wall and floor tile, they made artware of several varieties. The founders were Fred Tschirner and William A. Long. Long had developed the method for underglaze slip painting that had been used at the Lonhuda Pottery in Steubenville, Ohio, in the 1890s. Crystal Patina, the first artware made by the small company, utilized a fine white body and flowing, blended colors, the earliest a green crystalline. Indian Ware, copied from the pottery of the American Indians, was usually decorated in black geometric designs on red clay. (On the occasions when white was used in addition to the black, the ware was often not as well executed; so even though two-color decoration is very rare, it is normally not as desirable to the collector.) Robin's Egg Blue, pale blue on the white body, and Tirrube, a slip-decorated matt ware, were also produced.

Jardiniere, Indian Ware, abstract waves, blk/gray on red clay, 10". 600.00
Vase, Crystal Patina, dk celadon, bottle form, mfg flaw, 1906, 8". 660.00
Vase, Crystal Patina, gr, cylindrical neck, #115, 5¼" 400.00
Vase, Crystal Patina, tan, SP poppy o/l, bulbous base, #141, 1906, 7". 1,200.00
Vase, Crystal Patina, yel & gr drips on celadon, hdls, 5" 300.00
Vase, Indian Ware, blk & tan on red clay, #241, 1905-15, 10x13" ... 480.00
Vase, Indian Ware, blk on red clay, can neck, #218, 2¾" 215.00
Vase, Tirrube, floral, gray & wht on terra cotta, stick neck, 12" ... 850.00
Vase, Tirrube, heron & palm fronds, wht on terra cotta, #257, 12" ..1,550.00
Vase, Tirrube, rose w/gr foliage on terra cotta, #153, 7¾x5" 385.00

Clocks

In the early days of our country's history, clock makers were influenced by styles imported from Europe. They copied the European's cabinets and reconstructed their movements — needed materials were in short supply; modifications had to be made. Of necessity was born mainspring motive power and spring clocks. Wooden movements were made on a mass-production basis as early as 1808. Before the middle of the century, brass movements had been developed.

Today's collectors prefer clocks from the eighteenth and nineteenth centuries with pendulum-regulated movements. Bracket clocks made during this period utilized the shorter pendulum improvised in 1658 by Fromentiel, a prominent English clock maker. These smaller square-face clocks usually were made with a dome top fitted with a handle or a decorative finial. The case was usually walnut or ebony and was sometimes decorated with pierced brass mountings. Brackets were often mounted on the wall to accommodate the clock, hence the name. The banjo clock was patented in 1802 by Simon Willard. It derived its descriptive name from its banjo-like shape. A similar but more elaborate style was called the lyre clock.

The first electric novelty clocks were developed in the 1940s. Lux, who was the major producer, had been in business since 1912, making wind-up novelties during the '20s and '30s. Another company, Mastercrafter Novelty Clocks, first obtained a patent to produce these clocks in the late 1940s. Other manufacturers were Keebler, Westclox, and Columbia Time. The cases were made of china, Syroco, wood, and plastic; most were animated and some had pendulettes. Prices vary according to condition and rarity. Unless noted otherwise, values are given for eight-day time only clocks in excellent condition. Clocks that have been altered, damaged, or have had parts replaced are worth considerably less. Our advisor is Bruce A. Austin; he is listed in the Directory under New York.

Key:
br — brass	reg — regulator
dl — dial	rswd — rosewood
esc — escapement	T — time
mcr — mercury	S — strike
mvt — movement	wt — weight
pnd — pendulum	

Calendar Clocks

Ithaca #1 Reg, walnut 2-dl perpetual, rstr, 1880, 72" 24,000.00
Ithaca Hanging Office #4, rswd 30-day, 1 rstr dl, rfn, 1880, 28" .. 1,300.00
Ithaca No 0 Bank, oak, dbl dl, rstr base/top, 1880, 61" 4,600.00
Ithaca Parlor #3.5, blk dl, cut glass pnd, needs rstr, 1880, 19", G...1,650.00
LF & WW Carter, rswd rnd-drop Lewis, 1 rstr dl, pnd, 1865, 31" .1,500.00
New Haven Tampa, pressed oak, paper dl/sgn mvt, pnd missing, 1906, 38" .325.00
S Thomas Office #11, mahog 8-day, 1-wt, rpl top (G copy), 1892, 69" . 22,000.00
Waterbury #43, oak 8-day S perpetual, orig dls, rpl door, 1912, 28" .600.00
Welch, BB Lewis, dbl-dl perpetual, rswd vnr w/grpt, pnd, 56x24".4,150.00
Welch No 1 Drop Octagon, rswd 8-day TS, pnt dl, 1885, 25½", VG ...300.00
Welch Spring & Co Audran, walnut, dbl dl, 1880, 31", NM 4,500.00
Welch Spring & Co Audran Variant, walnut, dbl dl, old rfn, 1878, 28" ..3,000.00
Welch Spring & Co Gale Drop #2, 8-day S, moon phase dl, 1877, 30" .7,500.00
Welch Spring & Co Italian #3, rswd 8-day perpetual, 1872, 18¼" ...800.00

Novelty Clocks

Balloon, swinging arm, Fr Industrial series, 1890, 23" 29,600.00
Black boy w/banjo, bell alarm, Germany, ca 1890, 5½" dia 715.00
Boy w/wheel (clock in hub), bronze figural, Sterling Bronze Co, 1900s ...600.00
Candle Lighter, man strikes match/lights candle on hat, brass, 9½"...210.00
Cat w/rolling eyes, swinging tail, pressed wood, Lux, rpl/rprs, 8" . 145.00
Cowboy on bucking bronco, copper pnt on wht metal, Sessions, 14x11" . 135.00
Cowboy w/moving eyes, heavy plastic w/metal dial, Miken, Japan, 6"...145.00
Dog, CI figural, tail & tongue move, Austria, Meyers, 1880s, 6x7½" .. 2,200.00
Dog, wooden figural w/googly eyes, Germany, 1930s, 6x5½" 150.00
Dog & Doghouse, compo, Lux, 6", VG 160.00
Dog w/rotating eyes, cvd wood, Oswald Uhrenfabrik, 1930, 8".... 550.00
Elephant w/moving eyes, Miken logo at top, Japan, 5½x3" 125.00
Horses (4) w/covered wagon, driver's whip moves, w/lamp, Sessions.. 100.00
John Bull, moving eyes, pnt CI, Bradley & Hubbard, 15½" 1,100.00
Lighthouse automaton, Fr Industrial series, w/barometer, 1885, 17" .. 2,700.00
Log cabin, CI figural, 3 people & dog move, Meyers, 1870s, 7x7" .. 3,000.00
Man stands by bicycle w/clock in front wheel, brass, British, 1910s ...900.00
Man w/top hat, pressed wood, mc pnt, Lux, 6½x3¼"......................265.00
Middle-Eastern man kneeling, cvd wood, rolling eyes, Pat 1926, VG ..415.00
Monk, pressed wood, mc pnt, Lux, nonworking, VG 435.00
Monk rings bell atop clock, CI figural, Fr, ca 1900, 14x7½" 775.00
Monkey pushes cat (pnd) in swing hanging from tin bbl, Germany, 1890s...2,250.00
Old lady w/2 dogs in arms, 3rd barking at ft, Meyers, 1870, 10" .. 3,000.00
Skeleton acrobat, 8-day TS, New Haven, 1905, 19½" 3,500.00
Statue of Liberty, bronzed spelter, mystery swing, porc dl, 1905, 18"..3,200.00

Topsy, 30-hr winker, CI base, Bradley & Hubbard, 1860, rprs/rpt... 1,200.00
Waiter, pressed wood, mc pnt, Lux, 6¼x3⅜".................................375.00

Shelf Clocks

Ansonia Dorval, 8-day TS, 4-glass crystal reg, ca 1914, 8¾", VG . 145.00
Ansonia Duke, 8-day TS crystal reg, orig gilt, porc dl, 1904, 12". 725.00
Ansonia Floral, gilt-metal crystal reg, porc dl, 1914, 16½", EX+ ...2,500.00
Ansonia Hermes, bronze figural 8-day TS, porc dl, prof rstr, 1904, 12" ...500.00
Ansonia La Bretagne, porc, 8-day TS, porc dl, Royal Bonn, 1910, 15" ..775.00
Ansonia La Somme, porc w/HP floral on cream, 1910, scarce, 11" . 625.00

Ansonia La Vergne, Royal Bonn case, cleaned and polished, 11¾", $1,350.00. (Photo courtesy R. O. Schmitt Fine Arts)

Ansonia Marchionesse, 4-glass crystal reg w/open esc, 1914, 16"..1,000.00
Ansonia Osceola, gr porc, open esc, sm rpr, 1910s, 11½" 300.00
Ansonia Rosalind, 8-day TS, blk pnt on iron, paper dl, 1890, 12" ...275.00
Ansonia Roy, 8-day TS crystal reg, porc dl, pnd, 1914, 1½" 350.00
Ansonia Texas, walnut 8-day TS, rpl crest, clear tablet, 1880, 22"..125.00
Ansonia Viscount, 8-day TS crystal reg, gold pnt, porc dl, 1904, 15" ...425.00
Ansonia Winnipeg, porc 8-day TS w/gong, porc dl, cleaned, 12" ...250.00
Chelsea Mariner, ship's bell, br/bronze/mahog, 1970, 10".............550.00
D Pratt & Sons, mahog steeple, pnt wood dl, 1850, 24¾"............550.00
English Tambour, dk oak, gong strike, SP br dl, 1930s, 9" 50.00
Gilbert Amphion, walnut, etched mirror sides, gong, rfn, 1885, 25"..1,700.00
Gilbert Parisian, walnut case, paper dl, orig tablet, rfn, 1885, 24"...275.00
Ingraham, mosaic maple/walnut vnrs, TS, porc dl, rfn, 1885, 15"...650.00
Ingraham, walnut parlor, spirit level in base, rstr, 1890s, 24" 250.00
Ingraham Domino, blk enamel, TS, blk dl, rpl pnd, 1886, 16".....150.00
Ingraham Huron, rswd, TS, uncommon label, 1880, 16" 750.00
Ingraham Oriental, rswd, TS, paper dl, dk label, 1870, 17½" 900.00
Japy Freres, brass, TS, porc inserts in dl, 1890, 18½" 500.00
Jerome Dreadnaught, 30-hr T/alarm, rswd/mahog w/octagon top, 1880, 14"....125.00
Kienzle, 2-tune, 9-rod chime, pnd, appl shellac, 1950s, 9x31" 110.00
Kienzle Tambour, oak, TS, cathedral gong, rstr, 1920s, 8" 55.00
Kroeber Pompadour, enamel on iron (rpt), TS, rstr, 1900, 18"....200.00
Kroeber Topeka, walnut, TS, rpl hands, paper label, 1880, 24"....300.00
Kroeber Wabash, walnut, TS, etch tablet, pnd, rprs/rfn, 1875, 22" ..275.00
Marshall & Adams, mahog Emp, 2-wt, rpl dl, br mvt, 1845, 34" .. 625.00
New Haven San Pedro, oak Mission, gong, ca 1913, 19", G 175.00
Pons Emp style, cvd wht alabaster, cast pnd, sm losses, 1840, 23" .. 1,325.00
S Thomas, enameled, TS, emb/gilt dl, 1902, 10", VG....................50.00
S Thomas, mahog 30-hr TS, cvd eagle crest, half columns, 1835, 37"..475.00
S Thomas Atlas, walnut quarter-strike/3-train, 1885, 22½" 2,200.00
S Thomas Chicago, TS, ca 1885, 17", G..100.00
S Thomas Emp #23, TS crystal reg, porc dl, 1909, 11½" 300.00
S Thomas Gingerbread, walnut, TS, worn dl, ca 1890, 23"..........130.00
S Thomas Omaha, walnut 8-day TS, partial gallery, 1880, 19", VG..160.00
S Thomas Orchid #6, 5-day TS oval crystal reg, porc dl, 1909, 11" ...400.00
S Thomas Sons #8055, artist/flautist, spelter 8-day TS, 1870, 17", VG..225.00
S Thomas Tudor #3, rswd, TS/alarm, rstr/rpt, 1870s, 12" 180.00
Sessions, mahog tambour, TS, silvered dl, 1927, 10" 50.00
Smith & Goodrich, rswd steeple 30-hr fusee TS, Fenn Glass, 1847, 20"..4,600.00
Waltham, mahog w/lancet-arched silvered dl, rstr, 1920, 11" 80.00

Waterbury Beehive, mahog, TS alarm, rstr vnr, rprs, 1870s, 19", G..75.00
Waterbury Paris, walnut, TS, rfn, darkened dl, 1881, 24½"..........160.00
Welch, mahog steeple, 2 exceptional tablets, w/label, 1857, NM...1,350.00
Welch, walnut gingerbread, conquistadors on glass, pnd, rfn, 1885, 24"..230.00
Welch Cottage, rswd vnr w/pnt tablet (touched up), 30-hr, 1870s, 10"..55.00
Wm Johnson, mahog steeple, Boardman fusee TS, all orig, 1848, 20"....1,350.00

Tall Case Clocks

B Barlow, oak, sq br dl w/penny moon, pediment top, 1775, 84", VG..2,300.00
Balsattie Cupar, mahog Wm IV, steel face/quarter columns, 1820s, 80"...7,000.00
Benj Morris, PA, walnut w/string inlay, pnt moon dl, pnd, 90".7,475.00
CE Strieby, OH; cherry/poplar, bonnet top, br works, rprs, 102"..16,000.00
GW Russell, oak w/Asian decor, br dl, calendar mvt, 1890, 97"..3,000.00
Herschede #245, mahog quarter-chime, 3-wt, 1951, 86", M w/papers.1,600.00
Hoadley type, faux grpt mahog, ornate dl, tin can wts, 1825, 88"..2,100.00
I Brokaw, NJ; mahog w/3 br finials & inlay, late 18th C, 98"..10,000.00
J Fessler, Frederick Town; cherry/walnut, br works, pnd, 99"...12,000.00
J Walker, oak, br dl w/chereb spandrels, rolling moon, 1850, 86"..2,600.00
L Serberl, Wein; oak Alt Deutsch style, year-running br dl, 1890, 95". 6,500.00
Major T Chandler (att), NY, walnut/cherry w/cvd rosettes, HP face, 87". 4,000.00
R Winstanley, mahog 8-day bell S, sq pnt dl, cleaned, 1830, 86"...1,100.00
Read & Watson, OH; cherry w/cvd rosettes, 30-hr, pnd, rfn, 98".10,350.00
S Berry, London; Georgian chinoiserie, br face, 18th C, 84x17x9"..4,700.00
Sims, Georgian chinoiserie jappaning on faux tortoiseshell, 1750s, 82"..5,285.00
Waterbury Reg #69, mahog, Graham dead-beat esc, lyre pnd, 1905, 96"..7,600.00
WH Durfee #42 for Tiffany, quartersawn oak, 9-tube, 1895, 98"..22,500.00

Wall Clocks

Ansonia Capital, oak dbl-spring, lady's head finial, 1900, 55"...1,100.00
Ansonia Standard Reg, mahog, pnt dl, pnd, 1-wt, 1920, 37"....1,425.00
Becker Grand Sonnerie, walnut rod S w/emb br, 3-wt, 1890, 55"..1,900.00
Biedermeier Grand Sonnerie, 1-pc porc dl, 3-wt, old rfn, 1840, 46"..2,500.00
Chelsea, mahog banjo, tablet flakes, pnt dl, orig pnd/wt, 1913, 43"..1,350.00
E Howard #4 Banjo, grpt on cherry, rpl lower tablet, 1857, 32"...3,000.00
E Howard Reg #8, walnut figure-8, rfn/rstr, 1885, 44½"..............9,000.00
E Howard Reg #11, orig grpt, touchups to dl, 1871, 32", NM...9,000.00
E Howard Reg #41, walnut wt-driven, rfn otherwise orig, 1847, 48"..16,500.00
Fr Cartel, gilt bronze floral ormolu, prof cleaned, 1870, 23"......1,750.00
German cuckoo, 30-hr, bone hands, 3-wt, cvd quail, rprs, 1900, 24"..1,000.00
Gilbert Hampshire, spring-drive 8-day pnd banjo w/stencil, 1930, 22"..100.00
Gilbert Reg #21, cherry, 1-wt, front-hung pnd, rfn, 1880..........1,750.00
S Thomas Brookfield, mahog banjo, TS, silvered dl, 1859, 29"......70.00
S Thomas Drop Octagon, mahog, VG orig dl, ca 1885, 22".........225.00
S Thomas Queen Anne, oak, NP damascened pnd, rfn, 1902, 36"..900.00
S Thomas Reg #2, oak, sm flakes on dl, minor fading, 1900, 34"....1,500.00
S Thomas Reg #16, walnut 1-wt Railway, damascene bob, NP wt, 1890, 74"..15,000.00
S Thomas Reg #30, oak, minor rpt on dl, recabled mvt, 1905, 49"..3,500.00
Sessions #463-W, 110-volt banjo, eagle finial, 1950, 21"...............30.00
Sessions Halifax, mahog banjo, TS, pnt tablet, 1925, 27"..............75.00
Vienna Reg, oak gong S w/ornate cvgs, 2-wt, 1890, 55"............3,200.00
Waltham, mahog banjo, eagle finial, Mt Vernon tablet, 1-wt, 1925, 42".1,850.00
Waltham #1550, mahog mini banjo, tablet flakes, 1928, 21".......500.00
Waterbury Willard #3, gilt weight-driven banjo, rstr tablet, 1920, 42". 2,500.00

Cloisonne

Cloisonne is defined as 'enamel ware in which the surface decoration is formed by different colors of enamel separated by thin strips of metal. In the early original process, precious and semi-precious stones were crushed and their colors placed into the thin wire cells (cloisons) in selected artistic designs. Though a French word, cloisonne was first made in tenth century Egypt. To achieve the orginal result, many processes may be used. There are also several styles and variations of this art form. Standard cloisonne involves only one style, using opaque enamel within cloison borders. Besides metal, cloisonne is also worked into and on ceramics, glass, gold, porcelain, silver, and wood. Plique a jour is a style in which the transparent enamel is used between cloisons that are not anchored to a base material. In wireless cloisonne, the wires (cloisons) are pulled from the workmanship before the enamel is ever fired. Household items, decorative items, and ceremonial pieces made for royalty have been decorated with cloisonne. It has been made for both export and domestic use.

General cloisonne varies in workmanship as well as color, depending on the country of origin. In later years some cloisonne was made in molds, almost by assembly line. Examples of Chinese cloisonne made in the past 100 years or so seem to have brighter colors, as does the newer Taiwan cloisonne. In most of the Japanese ware, the maker actually studies his subject in nature before transfering his art into cloisonne form.

Cloisonne is a medium that demands careful attention to detail; please consult a professional for restoration. Our advisor for this category is Jeffery M. Person. Mr. Person has been a collector and dealer for 40 years. He is a speaker, writer, and appraiser on the subject of cloisonne. He is listed in the Directory under Florida.

Chinese

Basin, horses & waves, int w/foo dogs, Ming period, 18"...........7,650.00
Box, foo dogs & qilin circle rim, bat/peach reserve, 4½x9x8"......600.00
Figure, seated Quan Yin, bronze face/bib/hands/ft, 23".................820.00
Plate, foo dog surrounded w/5 red floral-design petals on turq, 12"...115.00
Teapot/wine server, foo lions on bl, rpl wire hdl, 1800s, 5½x7"....135.00
Vase, floral, mc on iron red, baluster, 1900-30, 9¼x4½"..............180.00
Vase, mc patterns, acorn form w/4 lg bronze buttresses, 1900, 14"..525.00
Vase, peonies, bl on geometric wht, tassel rim, stick neck, 15x7"....960.00

Japanese

Vase, slightly square, each side with birds or dragons, 18", EX, $4,100.00. (Photo courtesy James D. Julia Inc.)

Charger, flying crane on bl, 19th C, 14¼"....................................350.00
Vase, allover sm mc flowers w/gold on blk, bulbous, 15"...........1,600.00
Vase, birds & wisteria on dk bl, silver wire type, 1900s, 10", pr.1,295.00
Vase, birds on flowering tree, silver wire type, 1920s, 12½".......2,935.00
Vase, bl reserve w/lg bird & roses, bk: 2nd bird/floral reserve, 18"..4,000.00
Vase, finches & pk blossoms on gr, sm bruise, 12", pr...................500.00
Vase, flowering tree/bird/rooster/hen on blk, 7½", pr.................1,560.00
Vase, lg rooster, bk: hen, ovoid w/long neck, 6", pr....................3,000.00
Vase, orchid flowers on pale apricot, ca 1900, 9"........................585.00
Vase, pheasants/quail/sparrows/etc, gilt silver mts, 19th C, 9", pr..3,300.00
Vase, roosters/flowers/banana trees on yel, Meiji period, 27", pr..2,825.00

Clothing and Accessories

The field of collectable clothing is highly personalized and often confusing for the novice collector or nonspecialty dealer. Prices vary enormously from marketplace to marketplace. Four basic factors contribute to the valuation of clothing. They are:

1. Size. Larger sizes are more valuable as they can be worn or displayed on full-size mannequins. The rule of thumb here is 'The Bigger, The Better.' Adult clothes in tiny sizes are nearly impossible to sell and must be drastically discounted.

2. Condition. Even the smallest tear, rip, stain, or discoloration devalues a piece by as much as 75%.

3. Quality. High quality in construction, type of fabrics and trims, and design add greatly to the value of the piece. The more elaborate the piece, the higher the price.

4. Age. This is sometimes difficult to determine. Beware of reproductions and/or mismarked pieces. A good pictoral fashion reference book is recommended. A few clues to help in dating clothing are as follows:

If you see:	the date is:
machine stitching	after 1850
snaps	after 1912
zippers	after 1935
elastic	after 1915
boning or metal stays in bodice	before 1905
boning or metal stays, collar only	after 1904
tags on waistband	after 1870
tags on neckline	after 1905

For further information we recommend *Vintage Hats and Bonnets, 1770 – 1970*, by Susan Langley; *Ladies' Vintage Accessories* by LaRee Johnson Bruton; and *Antique & Vintage Clothing: A Guide to Dating and Valuation of Women's Clothing, 1850 – 1940*, by our advisor, Diane Snyder-Haug. (Ms. Snyder-Haug is listed in the Directory under Florida.) Vintage denim values are prices realized at Flying Deuce Auctions, who specialize not only in denims but Hawaiian shirts, souvenir jackets, and various other types of vintage clothing. They are listed in the Directory under Auction Houses. Our values are for items of ladies' clothing unless noted 'man's' or 'child's.' Assume them to be in excellent condition unless otherwise described.

Key:

cap/s — cap sleeves	ms — machine sewn
embr — embroidery	n/s — no sleeves
hs — hand sewn	plt — pleated
l/s — long sleeves	s/s — short sleeves

Cape, burgundy velvet with black beaded passementerie trimming, lined in black silk, Victorian, from $165.00 to $185.00.

All-in-one, wht linen & lace w/ribbon on yoke & armholes, 1910s ..165.00
Apron, wht dotted linen w/lace inserts & trim, ribbon ties, ca 1900....50.00
Bib, pk linen w/wht lace edge, embr flowers, ribbon tie, 1930s, 9x9" ...20.00
Bib, pk pastel linen w/much embr, 1930s, 8x11"............................. 20.00
Bloomers, wht cotton w/frills & pintucks, ca 1875, 33" L 45.00
Blouse, cream cotton w/lace yoke & l/s, boned collar, ca 1905 .... 150.00

Blouse, printed rayon, V neck, gathers at shoulders, s/s, 1940s 48.00
Blouse, wht linen w/embr/cutwork, high neck, l/s w/cuffs, ca 1905 .150.00
Blouse, wht nylon w/tucked rows, shawl collar, s/s w/cuffs, 1950s .. 38.00
Bodice, purple velveteen w/ivory lace, high collar, ¾-s, 1900s..... 125.00
Bonnet, child's, wht cotton w/10 ruched frills, bow on crown, 1905 .. 50.00
Bonnet, ivory linen w/wht scalloped lace, ca 1870, 18" around face .. 65.00
Boots, man's, brn leather high-top work type, brn laces, 1920s.... 100.00
Camisole, ivory lace w/pastel ribbons threaded through, 1930s 75.00
Camisole, wht batiste w/embr, silk straps, pk ribbons, ca 1906, 20" .. 75.00
Cape, red silk georgette, shoulder yoke, piped edge/fringe, 1920s....170.00
Cape, shoulder; Irish linen damask w/embr hairpins/brush/etc, 1920s ...60.00
Coat, blk cashmere, platter collar, open front, raglan ¾-s, 1950s . 115.00
Coat, dinner; blk faille, ¾-s w/cuffs, pockets, pk lining, 1950s 85.00
Coat, man's, brn suede w/notched lapels, much fringe, 1960s-70s...135.00
Dickey, ivory net w/embr, lace bands at neck/armholes, 1910s 55.00
Dress, baby's, wht silk organza, lace trim, s/s, w/slip, 1930s, 14" L. 85.00
Dress, bl brocade w/muslin underslip, fitted bodice/wide straps, 1950s.65.00
Dress, blk chiffon w/scooped neck, attached slip, ¾-s jacket, 1920s ...165.00
Dress, blk crepe w/V neck, dolman/s in gold bullion/blk brocade, 1930s..250.00
Dress, blk lace top w/elbow/s, full blk chiffon skirt, 1960s.............. 65.00
Dress, blk silk crepe, flat front, crochet lace, l/s, ca 1924.............. 125.00
Dress, blk silk crepe, rnd neck, pin tucks/ruching, l/s, fringe, 1920s . 245.00
Dress, blk silk crepe w/plunging neck, crossover top, no/s, 1920s... 75.00
Dress, brn serge wool w/ivory faille yoke, sm band collar, l/s, 1890s . 185.00
Dress, child's, wht cotton w/lace trim, l/s, box plts, 1900s, 24" L ... 95.00
Dress, cut velvet, l/s, draped bow at side of waist, ca 1930, 53" 165.00
Dress, floral silk, V neck, gathered shoulders, s/s, slim skirt, 1940s...85.00
Dress, girl's, cotton, Emp top w/ribbons/embr/lace, puff/s, 1900s.. 295.00
Dress, gold silk lace, yel slip, drop waist/tiered skirt, no/s, 1920s.. 265.00
Dress, gr irid taffeta, bustier bodice, attached crinoline, late 1940s .. 185.00
Dress, linen w/allover pin tucks, sweetheart neck, cap/s, 1950s 60.00
Dress, linen w/flower appliques/rhinestones, cummerbund, s/s, 1950s..85.00
Dress, navy crepe, sm collar/bead flowers/raglan batwing/s, 1930s . 95.00
Dress, pk bias cotton net, silk sash slides, tulle flounce, 1930s 185.00
Dress, pk chiffon w/silk slip, ruched bodice, plt skirt, 1950s, 54". 125.00
Dress, pk georgette, bertha collar, slip style w/flower bk, 1920s.... 225.00
Dress, pk rayon, scooped neck, V-neck bk, bias skirt, no/s, 1930s . 165.00
Dress, pk ribbed silk w/ribbons/beads/lace, ornate l/s, ca 1895 ..... 485.00
Dress, printed cotton, halter w/Peter Pan collar, full skirt, 1950s... 65.00
Dress, printed paper, wide neckline, no/s, 1960s.......................... 145.00
Dress, puckered rayon crepe, bias-cut bodice, l/s, bias skirt, 1930s ..245.00
Dress, purple silk, spaghetti straps, frill/bow on skirt, 1950s 155.00
Dress, purple velvet w/crewel embr, half/s, lace underskirt, ca 1912...375.00
Dress, silk brocade w/pin-tuck front/pigeon waist, puff/s/train, 1900s.. 495.00
Dress, silk chiffon w/lg fabric flower, l/s, dropped waist, 1920s 265.00
Dress, silk taffeta w/jet trim/blk ribbons, l/s, 1895 .... 575.00
Dress, striped batiste, scoop neck, s/s, gathered skirt, ca 1924........ 75.00
Dress, velvet, silk net s/s w/rhinestones, balloon skirt, 1930s 595.00
Dress, watered rayon taffeta w/V neck, dropped V waistline, 1920s...165.00
Dress, wedding; ivory satin/lace/gold embr silk netting, ca 1918.. 395.00
Dress, wht batiste w/lace/ribbon inserts, half/s, 1918, 40" 175.00
Dress, wht cotton w/lace inserts/pin tucks, elbow/s, ca 1905, 54".. 235.00
Dress, wht lawn w/lace inserts/pin tucks, l/s, tiny buttons, ca 1905 .. 325.00
Dress, wht net lace w/high neck, ¾-s, embr waistband, ca 1906... 245.00
Fur cape, brn mink w/mink tails along hemline, wide collar, 1940s ...595.00
Fur coat, sheared beaver, sm collar, l/s, silk lined, 1930s............... 225.00
Girdle, blk velvet, to be worn over bodice, laces up front, 1890s... 50.00
Gown, christening; wht cotton w/embr & frilled yoke, 1930s, 36" .. 125.00
Gown, christening; wht cotton w/embr yoke/lace, full skirt, 1860s, 41"... 185.00
Gown, christening; wht cotton w/embr/pin tucks/petticoat, 1860s, 38"...215.00
Halter top, cotton check, gathered center w/loop, 1940s 28.00
Halter top, textured cotton, waist sashes, ties at nape, 1950s......... 45.00
Hat, blk felt flat top w/narrow rise, button crown, yel net, 1940s... 65.00
Hat, blk straw ribbon toque w/allover fringe look, 1960s 17.00

Hat, gold & wht brocade turban, diagonal gathers, flat top, 1960s.... 18.00
Hat, ivory felt w/curved brim, wht plumes curve across front, 1940s.... 75.00
Jacket, blk net w/embr, pop-over point collar, peplum, pouf s/s, 1930s...65.00
Jacket, man's, red silk blend, shawl collar, 1 button, 1950s 165.00
Kimono, print on blk silk, red silk lining, 1930s, 43" 185.00
Lounger, bl patterned velvet, l/s, elastic waist, string belt, 1960s .. 58.00
Nightgown, peach silk w/hand-embr scalloped yoke, 1930s, 50"... 125.00
Nightgown, wht cotton w/lace & pin tucks, l/s w/cuffs, ca 1900, 48".. 125.00
Pajamas, man's, shantung silk, sm collar, l/s w/cuffs, 1930s............. 55.00
Pantaloons, wht cotton, split style w/embr/ribbons/drawstring, 1920s ...65.00
Pants, gray pinstripe wool, high waisted, flat front, cuffs, 1940s... 85.00
Petticoat, wht cotton & lace, 16" embr dbl frill, drawstring, 1900s.. 165.00
Petticoat, wht cotton w/lace frills/inserts, ca 1905, 39" front/45" bk ... 125.00
Shawl, blk silk w/blk embr roses, 1900s, 58x58"+9" fringe 175.00
Shawl, cream silk w/embr flowers/butterflies, 1920s, 48x48"+15" fringe .. 175.00
Shawl, purple silk w/lav & wht floral embr, 1920s, 52x52"+20" fringe ...350.00
Shirt, bl striped cotton, collar, pocket, l/s w/cuffs, 1950s 25.00
Shirt, boy's, cotton print, notched collar, button front, s/s, 1950s.. 45.00
Shirt, man's, cotton plaid, spread collar, button front, l/s, 1960s.... 35.00
Shirt, man's, cotton print, collar, pocket, l/s w/cuffs, 1970s............ 28.00
Shoes, alligator pumps, straps across vamp, 3" Cuban heels, 1940s...85.00
Shoes, baby's, wht leather, lace-up, Chubby, 1930s, 4", pr.............. 25.00
Shoes, blk twill pumps, rnd toe w/cutout, flat bow, 1930s 45.00
Shoes, brn leather oxfords w/faux alligator, 1½" chunk heels, 1930s.. 38.00
Shoes, navy leather platforms, open toes/sling bks, 3" sq heels, 1940s .85.00
Shoes, red leather pumps, peep toes/½" platform, 3¾" heels, 1950s .95.00
Shoes, silver lame sandals, cap toes, T-straps, 2½" Fr heels, 1930s . 95.00
Shoes, snakeskin sandals, open toes/ankle straps/3" heels, 1940s... 50.00
Shorts, ecru linen w/applique on pocket, mc buttons, 1940s.......... 35.00
Skirt, blk silk, 11" frill at botttom, 1890s, 42"......................... 120.00
Skirt, wht ribbed cotton, hook & eye closure, 1930s, 35" 95.00
Slip, gray silk w/net embr bodice & front, narrow straps, 1930s, 46".. 65.00
Socks, child's, red cotton w/wht embr, 1930s, pr from $10 to......... 15.00
Suit, man's, silk blend, 2-button front, notched lapels, 1980s 185.00
Suit, wool gabardine, notched collar, l/s w/cuffs, slim skirt, 1940s...145.00
Suit, wool gabardine, platter collar, princess w/sack bk, l/s, 1940s...160.00
Sweater, beige cashmere w/removable mink collar, l/s, lined, 1960s...150.00
Sweater, red faux mohair, boat neck, l/s, banded wrists, 1950s....... 55.00
Swimsuit, bl knit bikini, elastic runs through casing, 1960s 65.00
Swimsuit, cotton, sweetheart neck, narrow straps, bloomers, 1940s... 45.00
Swimsuit, printed cotton, gathered band at top, elastic straps, 1950s...65.00
Vest, man's, ivory brocade w/faint stripe, 2-pocket front, 1920s..... 65.00

Vintage Denim

Condition is very important in evaluating vintage denims. For this reason, in each of our descriptions, we will give a condition code just before the value. Be sure to access the condition of the garment you are dealing with objectively, then adjust our prices up or down as your assessment dictates. The term 'deadstock' refers to a top-grade item that has never been worn or washed and still has its original tags. 'Hedge' indicates the faded fold lines that develop on the front of denim jeans from sitting.

Bib overalls, Lee Jelt Denim House Tag, long L buttons, XL, deadstock .. 75.00
Jacket, JC Penney, 1-pocket, dk bl, sz 40, NM 70.00
Jacket, Lee 101J, indigo, minor wear, 1950s, EX........................... 120.00
Jacket, Levi 506E, 1-pocket, buckle-bk, red lines, sz 40, EX......... 860.00
Jacket, Levi 517XX 2nd edition, med bl, sz 42, EX+ 300.00
Jacket, workwear; Power House, dk bl, sz 40, NM 65.00
Jacket, Wrangle Blue Bell 1st model, 2-pocket, dk indigo, buckle bk, EX ..115.00
Jeans, Levi S-type E, super hege, 36x31", EX.................................. 40.00
Jeans, Levi 501, single-stitched, red lines, med color/hedge, rpr, sm, EX . 175.00
Jeans, Levi 501E, S-patch, very dk bl, 31x29", NM...................... 475.00

Jeans, Levi 501E, single-stitched, w/flashers, EX.......................... 525.00
Jeans, Levi 502E, single-stitched waistband, paper flashers, EX ... 400.00
Jeans, Levi 505, single-stitched, dk indigo, 40x32", NM 145.00
Jeans, Levi 516, flare legs, dk indigo, EX.................................... 185.00
Jeans, Levi 551 ZXX, G color/slight contrast, 38x34", EX............ 375.00
Jeans, Levi 646E, dk bl, 32x31", NM... 195.00
Shirt, Sears Roebuck, Western style, lg, EX.................................... 40.00
Shirt, Wrangler Blue Bell, wht denim Western style, 1960s, VG. 225.00
Tote bag, Levi E, 13x15", VG.. 20.00

Cluthra

The name cluthra is derived from the Scottish word 'clutha,' meaning cloudy. Glassware by this name was first produced by J. Couper and Sons, England. Frederick Carder developed cluthra while at the Steuben Glass Works, and similar types of glassware were also made by Durand and Kimball. It is found in both solid and shaded colors and is characterized by a spotty appearance resulting from small air pockets trapped between its two layers. See also specific manufacturers.

Bowl, wht w/pk int, no mk, 10".. 100.00
Plate, opal & amethyst mottle, att Kimball, 4¾" 250.00
Vase, brn, gr & yel, mk # K 1812-6, Kimball 6½" 350.00
Vase, gr mottle, bulbous w/flared rim, #1986-6K, Kimball, 6" 175.00

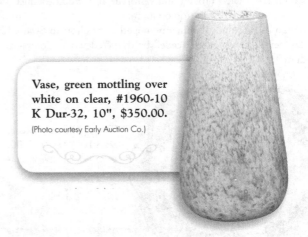

Vase, green mottling over white on clear, #1960-10 K Dur-32, 10", $350.00.
(Photo courtesy Early Auction Co.)

Vase, turq to gr decor on wht, crystal ft, shouldered, Kimball, 9". 300.00
Vase, wht, 2 horizontal ribs, Kimball, #20179 K Dee, 12x5" 150.00
Vase, yel & wht in clear, long neck, #1949, Kimball, 16"............. 350.00

Coalport

In 1745 in Caughley, England, Squire Brown began a modest business fashioning crude pots and jugs from clay mined in his own fields. Tom Turner, a young potter who had apprenticed his trade at Worcester, was hired in 1772 to plan and oversee the construction of a 'proper' factory. Three years later he bought the business, which he named Caughley Coalport Porcelain Manufactory. Though the dinnerware he produced was meant to be only everyday china, the hand-painted florals, birds, and landscapes used to decorate the ware were done in exquisite detail and in a wide range of colors. In 1780 Turner introduced the Willow pattern which he produced using a newly perfected method of transfer printing. (Wares from the period between 1775 and 1799 are termed 'Caughley' or 'Salopian.') John Rose purchased the Caughley factory from Thomas Turner in 1799, adding that holding to his own pottery which he had built two years before in Coalport. (It is from this point in the pottery's history that the wares are termed 'Coalport.') The porcelain produced there before 1814 was unmarked with very few exceptions. After 1820 some examples were marked with a '2' with an oversize top loop. The term 'Coalbrookdale' refers to a fine type of porcelain decorated in floral bas relief, similar to the work of Dresden.

After 1835 highly decorated ware with rich ground colors imitated the work of Sevres and Chelsea, even going so far as to copy their marks. From about 1895 until the 1920s, the mark in use was 'Coalport' over a crown with 'England A.D. 1750' indicating the date claimed as the founding, not the date of manufacture. From the 1920s until 1945, 'Made in England' over a crown and 'Coalport' below was used. Later the mark was 'Coalport' over a smaller crown with 'Made in England' in a curve below.

Each of the major English porcelain companies excelled in certain areas of manufacture. Coalport produced the finest 'jeweled' porcelain, made by picking up a heavy mixture of slip and color and dropping it onto the surface of the ware. These 'jewels' are perfectly spaced and are often graduated in size with the smaller 'jewels' at the neck or base of the vase. Some ware was decorated with very large 'jewels' resembling black opals or other polished stones. Such pieces are in demand by the advanced collector.

It is common to find considerable crazing in old Coalport, since the glaze was thinly applied to increase the brilliance of the colors. Many early vases had covers; look for a flat surface that would have supported a lid (just because it is gilded does not mean the vase never had one). Pieces whose lids are missing are worth about 40% less. Most lids had finials which have been broken and restored. You should deduct about 10% for a professional restoration on a finial.

In 1926 the Coalport Company moved to Shelton in Staffordshire and today belongs to a group headed by the Wedgwood Company. See also Indian Tree.

Tray, Ming Rose, 9¼x10", $135.00.
(Photo courtesy Cincinnati Art Galleries)

Bowl, Cairo, hdls, 9¾" 65.00
Bowl, rimmed soup; Ming Rose, 8" 75.00
Bowl, vegetable; Ming Rose, w/lid, 10¼" 295.00
Compote, flowers emb & HP, pierced lattice, ftd, 1814, rstr, 5x6" ...450.00
Creamer & sugar bowl, Blue Calico, ca 1881-90, 2¼", 1¾" 50.00
Cup & saucer, demitasse; Blue Calico, 2⅜x2", 4½" 50.00
Figurine, Clementine Debut in Paris, ltd ed, 8¼" 145.00
Figurine, Elizabeth Bennett, ltd ed, 8¾", from $225 to 250.00
Figurine, Emma Hamilton, ltd ed, 8½" 150.00
Figurine, Village School, 3x4¾x5¾" 110.00
Gravy boat, Ming Rose, 5x8½", +9¼" undertray 185.00
Pitcher, gold-lined leaves on wht, foliate ft & hdl, ca 1830, 10" ..975.00
Plate, bird in landscape, rich gilt & jewels, #202, 1881-1920, 8¾"..165.00
Plate, cake; floral sprays, pierced hdls, 1891-1920, 10¼x9½" 125.00
Plate, cake; Ming Rose, 11" 125.00
Plate, Hong Kong, #7708, ca 1800-30, 10½" 130.00
Plate, leaves/vines (underglaze bl), mc flowers/gilt vines, 1815, 9"..295.00
Plate, Winter Sheep, English Sunset, M Harnett, 9" 500.00
Platter, Ming Rose, 14" 125.00
Teapot, Athlone Blue, 9¼" 125.00

Teapot, florals, mc/gilt on cobalt, 1815, w/stand, 7" L 235.00
Teapot, flowers/fruited vines, pk on wht w/gold, ca 1825, 7" 400.00
Vase, appl/emb/HP flowers, ornate bl hdls w/gold, 1830s, 10x9" ...1,350.00
Vase, blk & wht rabbit on fan reserve on gold, #A3631, 1880s, 4¼"..600.00
Vase, floral band w/butterflies on cream, amphora form, 1895, 4½" .300.00

Coca-Cola

J.S. Pemberton, creator of Coca-Cola, originated his world-famous drink in 1886. From its inception the Coca-Cola Company began an incredible advertising campaign which has proven to be one of the most successful promotions in history. The quantity and diversity of advertising material put out by Coca-Cola in the last 100 years is literally mind-boggling. From the beginning, the company has projected an image of wholesomeness and Americana. Beautiful women in Victorian costumes, teenagers and schoolchildren, blue- and white-collar workers, the men and women of the Armed Forces, even Santa Claus have appeared in advertisements with a Coke in their hands. Some of the earliest collectibles include trays, syrup dispensers, gum jars, pocket mirrors, and calendars. Many of these items fetch prices in the thousands of dollars. Later examples include radios, signs, lighters, thermometers, playing cards, clocks, and toys — particularly toy trucks.

In 1970 the Coca-Cola Company initialed a multimillion-dollar 'image-refurbishing campaign' which introduced the new 'Dynamic Contour' logo, a twisting white ribbon under the Coca-Cola and Coke trademarks. The new logo often serves as a cut-off point to the purist collector. Newer and very ardent collectors, however, relish the myriad of items marketed since that date, as they often cannot afford the high prices that the vintage pieces command.

Beware of reproductions! The 1924, 1925, and 1935 calendars have been reproduced. They are identical in almost every way; only a professional can tell them apart. These are *very* deceiving! Watch for frauds: genuinely old celluloid items ranging from combs, mirrors, knives, and forks to doorknobs that have been recently etched with a new double-lined trademark. For more information we recommend *Petretti's Coca-Cola Collectibles Price Guide* and *B.J. Summers' Guide to Coca-Cola, B.J. Summers' Pocket Guide to Coca-Cola*, and *Collectible Soda Pop Memorabilia*, all by B.J. Summers.

Key:
cb — cardboard   sf — self-framed
CC — Coca-Cola   tm — trademark
dc — diecut

Reproductions and Fantasies

Still another area of concern deals with fantasy items. A fantasy item is a novelty made to appear authentic with inscriptions such as 'Tiffany Studios,' 'Trans Pan Expo,' 'World's Fair,' etc. In reality, these items never existed as originals. For instance, don't be fooled by a Coca-Cola cash register; no originals are known to exist! Large mirrors for bars are being reproduced and are often selling for $10.00 to $50.00.

Of the hundreds of reproductions (designated 'R' in the following examples) and fantasies (designated 'F') on the market today, these are the most deceiving.

Belt buckle, no originals thought to exist (F), up to 10.00
Bottle, dk amber, w/arrows, heavy, narrow spout (R)...................... 10.00
Bottle carrier, wood, yel w/red logo, holds 6 bottles (R)................ 10.00
Clock, Gilbert, regulator, battery-op, ¾-sz, NM+ (R) 175.00
Cooler, Glascock Jr, made by Coca-Cola USA (R) 250.00

Doorknob, glass etched w/tm (F)...3.00
Knife, bottle shape, 1970s, many variations (F), ea...........................5.00
Knife, fork or spoon w/celluloid hdl, newly etched tm (F)................5.00
Letter opener, stamped metal, Coca-Cola for 5¢ (F)........................3.00
Pocket watch, often old watch w/new face (R)............................ 10.00
Pocketknife, yel & red, 1933 World's Fair (F)...............................2.00
Sign, cb, lady w/fur, dtd 1911, 9x11" (F)....................................3.00
Soda fountain glass holder, word 'Drink' on orig (R)........................5.00
Thermometer, bottle form, DONASCO, 17" (R).........................10.00
Trade card, copy of 1905 'Bathtub' foldout, emb 1978 (R)..............15.00

The following items have been reproduced and are among the most deceptive of all:

Pocket mirrors from 1905, 1906, 1908, 1909, 1910, 1911, 1916, and 1920

Trays from 1899, 1910, 1913, 1914, 1917, 1920, 1923, 1925, 1926, 1934, and 1937

Tip trays from 1907, 1909, 1910, 1913, 1914, 1917, and 1920

Knives: many versions of the German brass model

Cartons: wood versions, yellow with logo

Calendars: 1924, 1925, and 1935

These fantasy items have been marketed:

Brass thermometer, bottle shape, Taiwan, 24"

Cast-iron toys (none ever made)

Cast-iron door pull, bottle shape, made to look old

Poster, Yes Girl (R)

Button sign, has 1 round hole while original has 4 slots, most have bottle logo, 12", 16", 20" (R)

Bullet trash receptacles (old cans with decals)

Paperweight, rectangular, with Pepsin Gum insert

1930 Bakelite radio, 24" tall, repro is lighter in weight than the original, of poor quality and cheaply made

1949 cooler radio (reproduced with tape deck)

Tin bottle sign, 40"

Fishtail die-cut tin sign, 20" long

Straw holders (no originals exist)

Coca-Cola bicycle with cooler, fantasy item: the piece has been totally made-up, no such original exists

1914 calendar top, reproduction, 11¼x23¾", printed on smooth-finish heavy ivory paper

Countless trays — most unauthorized (must read 'American Artworks; Coshocton, OH')

Centennial Items

The Coca-Cola Company celebrated its 100th birthday in 1986, and amidst all the fanfare came many new collectible items, all sporting the 100th-anniversary logo. These items are destined to become an important part of the total Coca-Cola collectible spectrum. The following pieces are among the most popular centennial items.

Bottle, gold-dipped, in velvet sleeve, 6½-oz................................. 75.00
Bottle, Hutchinson, amber, Root Co, ½-oz, 3 in case...................375.00
Bottle, International, set of 9 in plexiglas case 300.00
Bottle, leaded crystal, 100th logo, 6½-oz, MIB..........................150.00
Medallion, bronze, 3" dia, w/box...100.00
Pin set, wood fr, 101 pins..300.00
Scarf, silk, 30x30" 40.00
Thermometer, glass cover, 14" dia, M 35.00

Coca-Cola Originals

Bottle, Hutchinson, emb Birmingham Bottling Co, AL, 7", VG ..2,415.00
Bowl, Vernonware, Drink CC emb on gr ceramic, 1930s, 4x10", EX..230.00

Calendar, 1914, Betty, complete, 32x13", VG 920.00
Calendar, 1920, lady in yel dress w/golf course in distance, 32x12", G ...345.00
Carton insert, Take Home This Handy..., 1936, EX 175.00
Clock, Drink CC in Bottles, red/wht bull's-eye face, rnd, EX.......500.00
Clock, Drink CC in Bottles red dot on wht, wood fr, 1939, sq, 16", EX.425.00
Clock, Drink CC red fishtail, metal/glass, 1960s, 15x15", VG 150.00
Clock, Gilbert, oak w/paper dial, girl below, 1910, 37x19", VG..4,370.00
Clock, Ice Cold CC, octagonal, Silhouette Girl, 18", VG 1,600.00
Clock, light-up countertop, Serve Yourself, 1940s-50s, EX 750.00
Clock, regulator, oak, key-wound, 1980s, 23", M........................225.00
Coin purse, leather triangle shape w/Drink CC in gold, 1908, rare, EX .250.00
Cooler, Lunchbox, int tray, emb CC in Bottles, Progress, 9x14x18", VG.. 90.00
Cooler, picnic; metal, bottle-in-hand decal, 1940s-50s, 8x13x12", EX.450.00
Cooler, Westinghouse Jr, holds 51 bottles, 1935, 34x25".............800.00
Coupon, Hilda Clark, red/wht, 1901, 1½x3½", EX.....................475.00
Cuff links, bottle form, gold, mk 1/10, 10k, ¾", NM, pr 50.00
Decal, Drink CC Ice Cold, 1960, G...30.00
Dispenser, arched top, red, Drink CC on sides, 1930s, NM+ 1,500.00
Display, cb, Friends for Life, fishing boy, Rockwell, 1935, 36", VG ..2,500.00
Display, window; dc cb, girl drinks CC by cooler, 1939, 42x31", G.....570.00
Display, 3-D dc cb, button/soda jerk/patrons at counter, 1955, EX......500.00
Display bottle, clear glass, no cap, 1923, 20", M 225.00
Display rack, 6-Pack/25¢ red sign atop 3 wire tiers, 40s-50s, 47", EX ..225.00
Doll, Buddy Lee in uniform w/hat, compo, 1950s, EX+...............875.00
Door push, porc, Thanks Call Again for CC, yel/wht on red, 12", NM+..450.00
Door push, porc w/CC push plate, bright colors, 1940s-50s, 8x4" ...450.00
Drinking glass, flared, frosted 5¢ arrow logo, lg, G.......................475.00
Fan, Quality Carries On, bottle in hand, 1950, EX 65.00
Festoon, Autumn Girl, 5-pc, 1927, NM...................................3,500.00

Festoon, EX, $3,750.00. (Photo courtesy Morphy Auctions)

Festoon, Know Your State Tree, 3-pc, 1950s, EX (orig envelope) ...800.00
Festoon, Poppies, 5-pc, 1930s, unused, M (orig envelope) 1,100.00
Frisbee, plastic w/wave logo, 1960s, EX.....................................15.00
Game, Safety & Danger, 1938, complete, EX+............................100.00
Ice bucket, waxed cb, striped swag around top, EX+.....................50.00
Jug, clear glass w/diagonal paper label, 1910, 1-gal, EX 250.00
Lamp, Tiffany-style leaded glass, CC, chain hanger, 1920s, 16" dia, VG..4,800.00
Lampshade, ceiling; milk glass shaped globe w/red Drink CC, 18", EX...1,010.00
Lighter, bottle shape, 1950, M...30.00
Match holder, metal wall mt, wht w/red trim, CC Bottling Co, 1940s, G...400.00
Matchbook dispenser, metal tabletop, vertical, 1959, EX.............225.00
Menu, table; plastic holder w/paper insert for specials, 1950s, NM...50.00
Menu board, menu tabs either side of red button, 1950s, 14x60", NM...1,900.00
Menu board, metal, Silhouette Girl in lower corner, 1939, NM ..450.00
Menu board, tin sf chalkboard, Refresh Yourself, 1930s, VG 325.00
Note pad, leather cover, 1905, 4½x2¾", EX.................................225.00
Opener, steel, blk w/red, outing style, 1910s-20s, EX...................100.00
Pencil holder, ceramic 1896 dispenser form, 1960s, 7", EX 150.00
Playing cards, Drink CC, party scene, 1960, M 115.00
Playing cards, Welcome Friend!, 1958, MIB.................................175.00
Pocket mirror, girl w/bottle, 1916, oval, G....................................225.00

Pocket mirror, Wherever You Go You Will Find CC...Fountains 5¢, rnd, G..950.00
Postcard, CC girl, 1910, NM+.. 775.00
Postcard, Weldmech truck, 1930, EX.. 25.00
Pretzel bowl, aluminum w/3 cast CC bottle suports, 1930s, 4x9", VG.. 150.00
Service pin, 15 yrs, EX... 90.00
Sign, cb, Betty, 1914, 41x26", VG.. 650.00
Sign, cb, Bring Home the..., Santa at bench, 1956, 28x14", EX .. 225.00
Sign, cb, girl seated on diving board w/bottle, 1939, 29x60", EX. 750.00
Sign, cb, Have a Coke, bottle on iceberg, 1944, 20x36", NM...... 125.00
Sign, cb, Hospitality in Your..., lady serving tray, 1948, 20x36", G.. 250.00
Sign, cb, Play Refreshed/Have a Coke, girl/cooler, fr, 30x40", VG+ ..275.00
Sign, cb, Refreshed Through 70 Years, 2-sided, 1955, 28x56", EX ..300.00
Sign, cb, Things Go Better..., skaters, fr, 1960s, 24x40", EX 200.00
Sign, cb, We Sell CC Part of Every Day/Served../bottle, gold sf, 22" L...525.00
Sign, cb, Weissmuller & O'Sullivan, 1934, 29½x13½", EX+ 2,900.00
Sign, cb, Welcome Friend/graphics on 'oak,' beveled, 1957, 12x14", EX... 375.00
Sign, cb, Wherever You Go/bottle/travel/button, gold fr, 1950s, EX... 325.00
Sign, cb, Your Thirst Takes Wings, girl pilot, 1940s, 16x27", VG ...475.00
Sign, cb dc, lady w/6-pack, 60", EX 375.00
Sign, cb standup, military girl w/bottle, 1940s, 17", EX+ 600.00
Sign, cb standup, Santa, Greetings From CC, 1948, 14", NM+ ... 350.00
Sign, cb standup, Santa w/toy bag at ft, button logo, 1945, 13", EX...... 250.00
Sign, countertop; clock, Drink CC, Please Pay Cashier, 1950s, 20" L, G .. 460.00
Sign, crossing; porc 3-D policeman, Slow School Zone, 1950s, 63", VG.1,610.00
Sign, Edgebrite motion light-up, Pause, 1950s, 9x20", EX 850.00
Sign, fiberboard, Please Pay When Served, Kay Displays, 13" dia, VG...600.00
Sign, metal button, CC over bottle on red, 1950s, 48", EX........... 600.00
Sign, neon, CC Classic..., palm tree, 1980s, 28" dia, NM+ 1,500.00
Sign, neon, Coke w/Ice, 3-color, 1980s, EX 400.00
Sign, paper, Pause a Minute/Refresh..., girl/bottle, 1928, 20", EX..1,800.00
Sign, paper, Which?/CC or Goldelle Ginger Ale/lady, 1913, 24x18", EX+..11,000.00
Sign, paper (waxed), Go Refreshed, 3 military girls on gr, 20x57", EX....4,000.00
Sign, paper cutout, Home Refreshment/25¢ 6-pack, 1940s, 16x22", NM . 50.00
Sign, porc, Come In! Have a CC, yel & wht, 1940s, 54", NM..1,200.00
Sign, porc, Drink CC, Ingram-Richardson Co, 1915-20, 9x21", VG. 2,880.00
Sign, porc, Fountain Service, dc fr sign, 1930s, 14x27", VG+...1,000.00
Sign, porc, 2-sided dc, Fountain Service, 1933, 26x23", +scrolled arm...4,000.00
Sign, porc, 2-sided lollipop, Drink CC Refresh!, CI base, 65x30" dia......2,000.00
Sign, porc button, CC lettered over bottle, red, 24" dia, EX+...... 550.00
Sign, rvpt glass light-up on base, Brunoff, 1930s, 14x12", EX+.5,000.00
Sign, sidewalk; metal, fishtail/bottle, wht/gr stripes, 1960s, 33", EX...500.00
Sign, tin, ...Enjoy That Refreshing, fishtail/bottle, 53x18", VG+.. 300.00
Sign, tin, Cold Drinks, fishtail center, 1960s, 15x24", NM 300.00
Sign, tin, dc ribbon, Sign of Good Taste, 1957, 36", NM............. 275.00
Sign, tin, Drink CC above/below bottle, wht/red/gr, 1931, 14x6", EX+.625.00
Sign, tin, Drink CC/D&R, bottle at left, Dasco, 1920s, 11x35", VG..235.00
Sign, tin, Drink Delicious Refreshing/CC 5¢, Hilda Clark, rstr, 27" 60.95
Sign, tin, Drink..on red/bottle on wht, gr rim, 1934, 12x36", EX....235.00
Sign, tin, emb Christmas CC bottle to left, Robertson, 12x36", VG .. 200.00
Sign, tin, Ice Cold CC Sold Here/bottle, 1914, 20x28", EX...... 1,250.00
Sign, tin, red button/wht vertical, Serve...at Home/6-pack, 44x16", EX..875.00
Sign, tin, str-sided bottle emb, Shonk litho, 1914, 20x27", VG .. 1,920.00
Sign, tin bottle form, 1930s, 39", G+ 425.00
Sign, tin button, Drink CC/Sign of..., yel/wht letters, 1950s, 16", NM ..550.00
Sign, tin disk, Ice Cold CC Sold Here, red/gr rim, 1932, 20" dia, EX. 1,500.00
Sign, tin flange, Drink CC, bottle on yel dot, 1940s, 20x24", EX+ 550.00
Sign, tin flange, Grocery/fishtail logo/Refreshes You Best, 15x18", EX...300.00
Sign, tin triangle hanger w/filigree top, 2-sided, 1930s, 23", VG..700.00
Sign, trolley, cb, 4 seasons, 1923, 10x20", NM 4,000.00
Sign, trolley; cb, Drink CC/D&R, 2 girls/bottle, 1914, 11x21", EX ...3,000.00
Sign, wood, Refreshing/red dot, metal scrolled hanger, 8x24", EX ..165.00
Sign, wood, Silhouette Girl, metal hanger, 1940, G.................... 150.00
Sign, wood plaque/metal filigree top, 2 glasses, 1930s, 12x9", NM...675.00
Syrup bottle, Drink CC in wreath (frosted), metal cap, 1910, 13", EX.500.00

Syrup bottle, red on wht CC label, fancy pumpkin-shaped cap, 12", EX.775.00
Syrup jug, paper label w/Coke glass, 1950s, EX............................. 20.00
Thermometer, dc dbl-bottle gold version, 1942, 16", EX............. 525.00
Thermometer, dial, Drink CC in Bottles, red, 1950s, 12" dia, VG... 130.00

Thermometer, embossed tin with rolled edges, 1938, 16x7", NM, $300.00. (Photo courtesy Craig Stifter)

Thermometer, Masonite, Thirst Knows No Season, 1940s, 17", NM... 475.00
Thermometer, porc, Silhouette Girl, red & gr, 1939, 18", EX...... 625.00
Thermometer, tin, dbl bottles/wheat detail/Drink CC, 1940s, 16x7", EX. 375.00
Thermometer, tin bottle shape, 1950s, 17", EX 125.00
Thermometer, wood, Drink CC/D&R, 1905, 21", EX 500.00
Tip tray, 1903, VG 900.00
Tip tray, 1903, Victorian girl on purple ground, 4" dia, EX........1,440.00
Tip tray, 1906, girl drinks from glass, tin litho, 4½" 250.00
Tip tray, 1907, G+... 300.00
Tip tray, 1907, oval, 6", VG... 315.00
Tip tray, 1909, EX+.. 875.00
Tip tray, 1910, Hamilton King lady, oval, 6", VG........................ 345.00
Tip tray, 1910, NM+ 1,540.00
Tip tray, 1916, Elaine, VG+.. 115.00
Tip tray, 1916, EX+.. 275.00
Toy truck, Lincoln, metal, red pnt, 10 (of 12) cases, tarp, 15", EX . 1,050.00
Toy truck, Marx, metal, yel w/red, 6 plastic cases & dolly, 13", NMIB..900.00
Toy truck, Metalcraft, metal, red & yel, 10 glass bottles, 11", EX ... 1,250.00
Toy truck, Smith Miller, metal, 6 cases (24 bottles ea), 13", MIB .. 1,450.00
Wallet, leather, blk w/emb gold lettering, 1907, EX 100.00
Writing tablet, landmarks of the USA, 1960s, EX......................... 10.00

Trays

Values are given for trays in excellent plus condition (C8+). The 1934 Weismuller and O'Sullivan tray has been reproduced at least three times. To be original, it will have a black back and must say 'American Artworks, Coshocton, Ohio.' It was not reproduced by Coca-Cola in the 1950s.

All 10½x13½" original serving trays produced from 1910 to 1942 are marked with a date, Made in USA, and the American Artworks Inc., Coshocton Ohio. All original trays of this format (1910 – 1940) had REG TM in the tail of the C.

1897, Victorian Lady, 9¼" dia, VG..15,000.00
1901, Hilda Clark, 9¾", VG 4,000.00
1903, Hilda Clark, oval, 18½x15", EX 6,000.00
1905, Lillian Russell, glass or bottle, 10½x13¼", EX 3,500.00
1906, Juanita, glass or bottle, oval, 13¼x10½", EX..................2,200.00
1907, Relieves Fatigue, 10½x13¼", NM 4,000.00
1907, Relieves Fatigue, 13½x16½", EX 3,600.00
1908, Topless, Wherever Ginger Ale..., 12¼" dia, NM 9,500.00

1909, St Louis Fair, 10½x13¼", EX 1,800.00
1909, St Louis Fair, 13½x16½", NM.. 3,000.00
1910, Coca-Cola Girl, Hamilton King, 10½x13¼", EX+ 1,200.00
1914, Betty, oval, 12¼x15¼", EX+ 400.00
1914, Betty, 10½x13¼", EX+ 600.00
1916, Elaine, 8½x19", NM... 600.00
1920, Garden Girl, oval, 10½x13¼", EX+ 800.00
1921, Autumn Girl, oval, 10½x13¼", EX+ 800.00
1922, Summer Girl, 10½x13¼", NM... 1,100.00
1923, Flapper Girl, 10½x13¼", NM.. 500.00
1924, Smiling Girl, brn rim, 10½x13¼", NM................................ 650.00
1924, Smiling Girl, maroon rim, 10½x13¼", EX+..................... 1,050.00
1925, Party, 10½x13¼", NM... 650.00
1926, Golfers, 10½x13¼", EX+ 800.00
1927, Curbside Service, 10½x13¼", EX 850.00
1928, Bobbed Hair, 10½x13¼", NM... 750.00
1929, Girl in Swimsuit w/Glass, 10½x13¼", EX+......................... 550.00
1930, Swimmer, 10½x13¼", EX 425.00
1930, Telephone, 10½x13¼", NM... 650.00
1931, Boy w/Sandwich & Dog, 10½x13¼", NM.......................... 1,100.00
1932, Girl in Swimsuit on Beach, Hayden, 10½x13¼", EX+ 700.00
1933, Francis Dee, 10½x13¼", NM... 900.00
1934, Weismuller & O'Sullivan, 10½x13¼", NM 1,200.00
1935, Madge Evans, 10½x13¼", NM... 600.00
1936, Hostess, 10½x13¼", NM... 675.00
1937, Running Girl, 10½x13¼", NM... 425.00
1938, Girl in the Afternoon, 10½x13¼", NM 275.00
1939, Springboard Girl, 10½x13¼", NM....................................... 375.00

1940, Sailor Girl, 10½x13¼", NM, $450.00.

1941, Ice Skater, 10½x13¼", NM.. 450.00
1942, Roadster, 10½x13¼", NM+.. 500.00
1950s, Girl w/Wind in Hair, screen bkground, 10½x13¼", M...... 100.00
1950s, Girl w/Wind in Hair, solid bkground, 10½x13¼", NM 225.00
1955, Menu Girl, 10½x13¼", M.. 65.00
1957, Birdhouse, 10½x13¼", NM.. 125.00
1957, Rooster, 10½x13¼", NM.. 175.00
1957, Umbrella Girl, 10½x13¼", M... 375.00
1961, Pansy Garden, 10½x13¼", NM.. 30.00

Vendors

Though interest in Coca-Cola machines of the 1949 – 1959 era rose dramaticaally over the last decade, values currently seem to have leveled off. The major manufacturers of these curved-top, 5¢ and 10¢ machines were Vendo (V), Vendorlator (VMC), Cavalier (C or CS), and Jacobs. Prices are for machines in excellent or better condition, complete and working. A mint restored model will bring approximately double these values.

Cavalier, model #CS72, M rstr 3,200.00
Cavalier, model #C27, EX orig... 1,200.00
Cavalier, model #C51, EX orig... 1,100.00
Jacobs, model #26, EX 1,200.00
Vendo, model #23, EX orig... 900.00
Vendo, model #39, EX orig.. 1,100.00
Vendo, model #44, EX orig.. 3,250.00
Vendo, model #56, EX orig.. 1,400.00
Vendo, model #80, EX orig... 600.00
Vendo, model #81, EX orig.. 1,400.00
Vendorlator, model #27, EX orig 1,350.00
Vendorlator, model #27A, EX orig... 900.00
Vendorlator, model #33, EX orig 1,100.00
Vendorlator, model #44, EX orig 1,750.00
Vendorlator, model #72, EX orig 1,200.00

Coffee Grinders

These listings represent current values the collector will most likely encounter. Very rare examples have been eliminated, but we will continue to occasionally list mills that have set record prices in order to illustrate the effect condition has on pricing.

Please be aware that many coffee mill parts are being reproduced, and it is possible to restore mills to a very high degree of accuracy in relation to their original appearance. You can find accurate replacement wing nuts, labels, brass hoppers, decals, and iron or tin receiving cups. Note that there are several mills that show up on Internet auction sites on a fairly regular basis that are not old. These mills are either made from the old original molds with new names added, or molds have been made from an original mill and altered to include the new maker's name. One you may see will be labeled 'Ye Olde Coffee Mill'; another may be listed as 'Enterprise #2 with a removable, domed iron lid.' (To the knowlege of our advisor, no original Enterprise mill was ever made with such a lid.) Though neither of these mills is very old, they are worth collecting, as long as you know what it is you are buying. We are advised to beware of the possible reproduction of some of the glass receiving cups. Among them are the cup for the Kitchen Aid A-9 electric coffee mill originally produced in the 1930s. Due to an abundance of these cups without their mills, they seem highly suspect. Because some original cups sell from $125.00 to $500.00 each, unscrupulous sellers would certainly have a motive to market them as old instead of selling them as a replacement. As always, research is the key. We recommend joining online collector clubs, website chat rooms, and collector organizations to learn more. (See Association of Coffee Mill Enthusiasts listed under Clubs, Newsletters, and Catalogs in the Directory.) Our advisor for this category is Shane Branchcomb; he is listed in the Directory under Virginia.

Arcade #5, iron, wood bk brd, Pat June 94, EX 125.00
Arcade #777 IXL, ornate CI hopper, side crank, NM................... 425.00
Arcade Bell, ornate CI front, bell-shaped window, NM 800.00
Arcade Crystal #3, glass hopper, iron body, EX........................... 125.00
Arcade Crystal #3, w/orig mk glass cup, EX 250.00
Arcade Crystal #4, glass hopper, iron body, EX........................... 135.99
Arcade Crystal #9010, Art Deco, orig glass cup........................... 300.00
Arcade Favorite #7, iron, wall mt, on bk board, EX 95.00
Arcade Favorite #17, lg version of #7, EX.................................... 115.00
Arcade Imperial #999, box mill, orig label, NM 155.00
Arcade Jewel, rectangular glass hopper, tin lid, NM.................... 595.00
Arcade Our Baby, toy mill, paper label, NM................................ 135.00
Arcade Royal, CI, wall mt, iron receiving cup, EX....................... 115.00
Arcade Telephone, ornate CI face plate, NM............................... 650.00
Arcade X-Ray, CI grinder, wood box, glass front, EX 145.00
Belmont Hardware Lightning, tin canister, wall mt, EX............... 200.00
Bronson & Walton Ever-Ready No 2, w/cup, EX......................... 225.00

Bronson & Walton Silver Lake, glass, scarce, NM 800.00
Cavanaugh Bros, wood box, front fill, 1-lb, NM..........................300.00
Cavanaugh Bros, wood box, ornate CI legs, NM..........................700.00
Chatillon #11, same as Enterprise #1, side crank, EX 250.00
Coles No 00, CI, wall mt, w/cup, NM..350.00
Crescent #3, Rutland VT, CI, 2 wheels, EX..............................1,000.00
Crescent #4, Rutland VT, CI, nickel hopper, EX........................1,200.00
Crescent #7, iron hopper, 20" wheels, EX...............................1,300.00
Enterprise #0, CI, clamps to table, EX.......................................95.00
Enterprise #00, CI, w/CI cup, wall mt, NM...............................175.00
Enterprise #1, CI, counter, side crank, EX.................................175.00
Enterprise #2, CI, decals, 8¾" wheels, EX................................900.00
Enterprise #7, CI, counter, 17" wheels, EX.............................1,100.00
Enterprise #50, single wheel grist mill, NM...............................125.00
Enterprise #100, glass wall type w/mk cup, NM..........................225.00
Golden Rule, ornate CI front, wall mill by Arcade, NM..............425.00
Grand Union Tea Co (on flip-up lid), CI, Griswold, NM 750.00
Griswold, CI box, same as Grand Union Tea Co, NM 1,200.00
J Fisher, primitive PA box type, hand dvtls, EX.........................185.00
Landers, Frary & Clark #11, CI side crank, EX...........................175.00
Landers, Frary & Clark #20, CI, 8¾" wheels, EX........................975.00
Landers, Frary & Clark #24, orig mk hopper, NM 180.00
Logan & Strobridge #60 Acme, wall type, w/cup, NM.................250.00
Logan & Strobridge Franko American, wood box, EX.................115.00
Logan & Strobridge Queen, glass, wall mt, NM.........................625.00
National Specialty #0, CI w/CI lid, clamps to table, EX...............325.00
National Specialty #1, CI, rnd hopper, w/lid, EX........................325.00
National Specialty #1, CI, 8-sided hopper, w/lid, EX..................425.00
National Specialty #2, CI, 8¾" wheels, EX..............................1,200.00
National Specialty #7, CI, 16½" wheels, EX............................1,400.00
NCRA, rectangular, glass window, wall mt, 1915, EX 125.00
NCRA, rnd glass hopper, ca 1922, EX 115.00
Old 74, CI, parts mk 71, 72, 73, 74, ca 1840, NM.....................165.00
Parker #50 Eagle, side mill, brass label, EX.................................95.00
Parker #50 Farm, eagle emb in tin, EX.......................................85.00
Parker #200, CI, mk iron drw front, EX...................................1,100.00
Parker #260 Columbia, domed iron top, side crank, EX...............525.00
Parker #350, ornate CI, CI lid, on wood bk, NM 175.00
Parker #450, CI, side mt, orig rectangular cup............................275.00
Parker #555, wood, 1-lb box type, paper label, NM.....................155.00
Parker #1200, CI, orig pnt, 25½" wheels, EX...........................3,000.00

Russell & Erwin No. 90, iron, patented Sept. 28, 1875, and June 11, 1878, 5½", EX, $700.00; A. Kenrick & Sons, iron, English, ca. 1860, 6½", NM, $800.00; Landers, Frary & Clark, iron, ca. 1880, 4½", EX, $500.00. (Photo courtesy Shane Branchcomb)

Steinfeld, Simplex No 6, on wheels, nickel hopper, EX 1,000.00
Steinfeld, glass, wall type, mk lid & hopper, NM........................145.00

Sun #25 Success, rnd, wood box type, EX...................................275.00
Sun #94, stamped tin hopper, side mill, EX................................100.00
Sun #1080 1-lb Challenge, fast grinder, label, NM.......................145.00
Swift, Lane Bros #12, tin receiver, single 9" wheel, EX 550.00
Swift, Lane Bros #14, tin receiver, 15" wheels, EX 850.00
Waddel A-17, CI, sunflower design, wall mt, EX 300.00
Woodruff & Edwards Elgin National, 12" wheels, EX 850.00
Wrightsville Hardware, ca 1968, 6¾" wheels, NM......................250.00
Wrightsville Hardware Peerless #200, glass, EX...........................145.00
WWW Weaver, primitive PA box type, hand dvtls, EX..............250.00

Coin-Operated Machines

Coin-operated machines may be the fastest-growing area of collector interest in today's market. Many machines are bought, restored, and used for home entertainment. Older examples from the turn of the century and those with especially elaborate decoration and innovative features are most desirable.

The www.GameRoomAntiques.com website is an excellent source of information for those interested in coin-operated machines. Another source available is the Coin-Operated Collector's Association (www.coinopclub.org). See the Clubs, Newsletters, and Catalogs section of the Directory for publishing information. Jackie and Ken Durham are our advisors; they are listed in the Directory under the District of Columbia.

Arcade Machines

American Mutoscope/Biograph Clamshell Mutoscope #7598, CI, 33", +reel..8,000.00
Baby Jacks by Fields, pressed aluminum, EX 1,850.00
Baker 1¢ Kicker/Catcher, 1940s, EX 550.00
Benedict Happy Home, fortune teller, ca 1905, rstr, 66" 3,850.00
Booz-Barometer 5¢, comic front, 19x18", EX 300.00
Challenger, oak case, 36", EX..650.00
Columbia 3-Reel Bandit, 5¢, chrome/oak Deco case, no bk, 23" ..590.00
Egyptian Seeress 5¢, fortune teller, pnt plywood, 27", EX 700.00
Exhibit Supply Iron Claw Digger, Art Deco, VG 4,500.00
Frantz Kicker/Catcher, 1950s, EX...440.00
Hercules 1¢ Midget Baseball, oak w/CI front & marquee, EX...3,100.00
International Monkey Strength Tester, 92" 11,000.00
International Mutoscope, hand crank, metal trellis base, 53", +1 reel..1,850.00
King's 1¢ Horserace, countertop, 21", EX 2,300.00
Marvel Pop-Up Baseball, scoring skill, 1940s, EX.........................500.00
Mercury 5¢ Strength Tester, wood & cast aluminum, 17", VG....550.00
Panama Digger, cast-aluminum marquee, 65", EX.....................4,675.00
Peo Bat-a-Ball Baseball, 1930s, 16", VG 585.00
Pepsin Gum Fortune Teller, wooden, 22", G................................2,750.00
Radio Wave Shock Machine, 1940s, partial rstr.........................1,200.00
Slezek 1¢ Scale, 1920-30, 81", EX...1,875.00
Swami 1¢ Fortune Teller, w/napkin dispenser, no cards, 9x9", EX orig...300.00
Vending Machine Co Whiz Ball, 6 chutes/concentric rings, red case, 17"...415.00

Jukeboxes

The coin-operated phonograph of the early 1900s paved the way for the jukeboxes of the 1920s. Seeburg was first on the market with an automatic eight-tune phonograph. By the 1930s Wurlitzer was the top name in the industry with dealerships all over the country. As a result of the growing ranks of competitors, the '40s produced the most beautiful machines made. Wurlitzers from this era are probably the most popularly sought-after models on the market today. The model #1015 of 1946 is considered the all-time classic and even in unrestored condition often brings prices in excess of $6,500.00.

AMI A, mahog Art Deco case, 1946, G-............... 700.00
AMI C, mahog Art Deco case, 66", G 770.00
Seeburg DS-160, Art Deco style w/chrome trim, G..................... 800.00
Seeburg R, Art Deco, EX................................. 1,500.00
Seeburg SPS-2, Art Deco, G 500.00
Seeburg Symphonola, mahog case, rstr 1,450.00
Speaker, Wurlitzer, rare wall mount, 19½" dia, VG 1,045.00
Speaker, Wurlitzer #210, in mahog case, 17", EX 385.00
Speaker, Wurlitzer #3250, maple & mahog case, nickel grille, EX+ ...990.00
Speaker, Wurlitzer #4000 Star, 24" dia, VG......... 1,450.00
Speaker, Wurlitzer #4002, plastic & pnt steel, 24".......... 550.00
Speaker, Wurlitzer #4005, in mahog case, 16", VG 550.00
Speaker, Wurlitzer #4007, oval wall mt, 23x32", VG 3,850.00

Wurlitzer 'Victory,' 1942 – 1945, restored, $4,500.00.

(Photo courtesy Morphy Auctions)

Wurlitzer #700, 78 records, VG....................... 2,850.00
Wurlitzer #750, rstr 4,950.00
Wurlitzer #850, EX 14,300.00
Wurlitzer #850, Peacock, VG 18,000.00
Wurlitzer #1015, Bubbler, EX......................... 6,500.00
Wurlitzer P-12, 78 records, VG 465.00

Pinball Machines

Big Guns, Art Deco case, 52", VG 500.00
Criss Cross, floor model, G 330.00
Farfalla 25¢, floor model, colorful graphics, EX.... 300.00
Playball, floor model, wood case, VG................. 300.00
Star 35¢ Sit Down Pinball, wooden case, 29", VG 360.00
United 10¢ Empire Bowling, 97x34", VG............. 1,550.00
Williams Space Mission, floor model, early, G 175.00
World Series, wooden case, G 550.00

Slot Machines

Many people enjoy the fun of playing a slot machine in their home. Antique slots have become very collectible. The legality of owning a slot machine is different in each state. Also beware of reproduction or re-manufactured slot machines.

AC Novelty Multibell, wood & cast aluminum, NM 3,300.00
Buckley 5¢ Bonanza, oak & cast metal, non-prof rstr, VG 1,800.00
Buckley 25¢, oak & cast aluminum, working, VG.......... 1,800.00
Bull Durham 5¢, oak & cast aluminum, VG............ 2,000.00
Caille Midget Aristocrat Roulette, quartersawn oak case, EX.21,000.00
Caille Silver Cup, CI & NP, VG 17,500.00
Caille 5¢ Black Cat, upright, w/music, EX............ 33,000.00

Caille 5¢ 4-in-1, oak case w/NP, 19½", EX............ 3,850.00
Caille 25¢ Big Six, center pull, quartersawn oak case, 70", EX... 25,300.00
Jennings 1-¢ Chief Indian, Tic Tac Toe on marquee, 29x16x15", G..2,100.00
Jennings 10¢ Governor, oak & chrome, 27", EX....... 2,100.00
Mills Brownie, oak & CI, EX.......................... 8,250.00
Mills Dbl Dewey, 69", EX.............................. 12,000.00
Mills Golden Nugget Dbl Nickel, 1950s, EX.......... 2,250.00
Mills 1¢ Hightop, NM.................................. 2,750.00
Mills 5¢ Baseball, oak & NP, NM 8,800.00
Mills 5¢ Baseball, oak w/cast aluminum front, EX....... 7,150.00
Mills 5¢ Black Beauty, oak & cast aluminum, VG....... 1,100.00
Mills 5¢ Black Cherry, upright, oak & cast aluminum, EX........ 1,950.00
Mills 5¢ Blue Bell Hightop, VG........................ 2,050.00
Mills 5¢ Blue Black Cherry, rpt, VG 1,935.00
Mills 5¢ Bonus Hightop, oak & cast metal, EX 2,875.00
Mills 5¢ Bursting Cherry, EX.......................... 2,200.00
Mills 5¢ Castle Front, VG.............................. 2,200.00
Mills 5¢ Dutch Boy/Dutch Girl, oak & cast metal, NM........... 2,325.00
Mills 5¢ FOK, oak & cast aluminum, G............... 2,325.00
Mills 5¢ Golden Falls, oak & aluminum, 1946, 26", EX........... 2,300.00
Mills 5¢ Golden Falls, VG............................. 1,500.00
Mills 5¢ Hi-top, oak & cast aluminum, EX............ 1,500.00
Mills 5¢ Jewel Box, oak & cast aluminum, G......... 1,990.00
Mills 5¢ Operator Bell, quartersawn oak case w/aluminum face, VG... 2,050.00
Mills 5¢ Poinsettia, oak case w/aluminum face, 22", G 1,600.00
Mills 5¢ QT, wood & nickel, EX....................... 1,750.00
Mills 5¢ War Eagle, NM............................... 2,500.00
Mills 10¢ Blue Bell, wood & cast metal, G 2,100.00
Mills 10¢ Bursting Cherry, oak & cast aluminum, G.......... 2,200.00
Mills 10¢ Chrome Hightop, oak & nickel, EX 2,400.00
Mills 10¢ Hunting Scene Chief, EX.................... 2,500.00
Mills 10¢ Scarab, 7-slot, quartersawn oak & CI fr, 17"........... 55,000.00
Mills 15¢ Golden Nugget, oak & cast metal, EX 2,100.00
Mills 25¢ Black Cherry, VG 2,100.00
Mills 25¢ Castle Front, oak & aluminum, EX......... 2,500.00
Mills 25¢ Diamond Front, oak & cast metal, EX...... 2,400.00
Mills 25¢ Wild Deuce, oak & cast metal, rstr 1,875.00
Pace 10¢ All Star Comet, rstr, 1936................... 1,200.00
Pace 10¢ Comet 4-column, oak & NP, NM.............. 2,000.00
Watling 5¢ Cherry Front, NM.......................... 4,500.00
Watling 10¢ Treasury, wood & NP, VG 3,500.00
Watling 25¢ Baby Lincoln, oak case w/aluminum front, 3-reel, VG..1,325.00

Trade Stimulators

American Eagle 5¢, 3-reel, cast metal case, 10", EX 300.00
Baby Grand 5¢, cast aluminum & pnt steel, w/vendor, 10", EX .. 1,200.00
Banker 1¢, penny drop, EX............................. 3,200.00
Baseball Atlas Indicator, penny drop, mahog case, w/score card, EX... 990.00
Buckley Puritan Baby, 1932, 12", EX.................. 950.00
Deval Chicago, gumball vendor, 1933, 17", EX....... 1,100.00
Eclipse, pk case, cigar vendor, Pat 1894, 18½", EX 4,125.00
Field's Trip-l-Jax, oak w/aluminum facade, 18½", EX........ 825.00
Field's 1¢ 5 Jacks, penny drop, oak case, 19", EX 1,250.00
Groetchen Penny Smoke, 1937, 12", EX 700.00
Groetchen Zig Zag, 1936, 15", EX..................... 850.00
Mills Puritan Bell, rpl bk, 1926, 10", EX 600.00
Pace Cardinal, slot type, 1936, 12", EX............... 950.00
Pace Dandy Gum, 1930, 11", EX...................... 850.00
Pierce New Deal, 1934, 14", EX....................... 1,100.00
Rock-Ola 1¢ 4-Aces, gumball, VG..................... 2,750.00
Skilliard 5¢, cast metal & glass, 18½", VG 360.00
Wiz Ball, pnt steel & CI w/wooden base, marquee, 17", EX......... 600.00
3-Jack, mahog w/cast aluminum facade, 18", EX.............. 465.00

Vendors

Vending machines sold a product or a service. They were already in common usage by 1900 selling gum, cigars, matches, and a host of other commodities. Peanut and gumball machines are especially popular today. Older machines made of cast iron are especially desirable, while those with plastic globes have little collector value. When buying unrestored peanut machines, beware of salt damage.

Adam's Tuti-Fruiti Gum, quartersawn case, 32", EX 3,300.00
Am Vending Machine, aluminum/oak, stamps, patriotic theme, 22x10x9"..2,700.00
Baker Boy, gumball, Mannikin Vending Co, 16", EX 7,700.00
Blinkie Eye Wink & Smile 1¢, gumball, 17½", EX+...............31,000.00
Bluebird, gumball, NP & glass, 12", VG 465.00
Columbus M, cast metal & glass, rstr, 17" 185.00
Easy 5¢, gumball, CI base, marquee, EX.....................................2,100.00
Favorite 1¢ Horserace, oak case w/aluminum facade, 20", EX...2,850.00
Ford, gumball, CI, 11", VG... 85.00

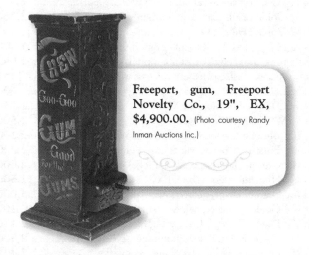

Freeport, gum, Freeport Novelty Co., 19", EX, $4,900.00. (Photo courtesy Randy Inman Auctions Inc.)

Freeport, Owl, CI w/wood base, 1910, 17", EX 4,950.00
Get-Em Hot 5¢, NP & glass, 21", VG... 165.00
Hamilton Mickey Mouse, gumball, porc & glass, 16", EX 2,100.00
Hance, gumball, countertop type w/CI base, 18", VG 2,500.00
Hershey's 5¢ (Candy Bars), metal, brn & wht, 18x9", NM 450.00
Hi-Low, gumball, CI base & lid, 17", EX 4,125.00
Honey Breath Balls, breath pellets, ca 1903, 8x12", EX 4,400.00
Jennings 1¢ Rockaway, gumball, 23", EX 2,400.00
JH Moore, gumball, quartersawn oak case, 24½", VG 4,125.00
Kenney & Sons Magic Clock Gum, 3 lever-op hands, chrome/pnt wood, 15"..500.00
Mansfield, gumball, etched glass w/CI base, repro marquee, 16"....1,500.00
Master, gumball, porc & cast aluminum, w/key, G.......................... 150.00
Northwestern, gumball, porc & glass, 15", VG 120.00
Pansy Gum & Fortune, tin & oak, G 7,700.00
Parker Pencils, CI & pnt steel, 9", EX.. 600.00
Price Collar Buttons, CI & glass, 11", EX 935.00
Pulver, clown, 21", VG+..1,450.00
Pulver, Cops & Robbers, red porc, VG 1,750.00
Pulver Kaola-Pepsin, gumball, CI & porc, EX 8,800.00
Ring Ding, gumball, tin & plastic, 12", G 100.00
Smiling Sam the Peanut Man, CI & aluminum, 13½", EX 4,400.00
Vendor-Bar Lil' Abner, pnt steel w/litho, 24", EX.....................1,045.00

Cole, A. R.

A second generation North Carolina potter, Arthur Ray Cole opened his own shop in 1926, operating under the name Rainbow Pot-
tery until 1941 when he adopted his own name for the title of his business. He remained active until he died in 1974. He was skilled in modeling the pottery and highly recognized for his fine glazes.

Bowl, brn gloss w/gr int, deeply scalloped, 2½x12", EX 35.00
Ewer, Rebecca, gr flambe, 20", EX..275.00
Ewer, Rebecca, wht w/mc line & drip decor, 19" 360.00
Jar, apothecary; royal bl, lg split hdls, 1930s, 9" 130.00
Jar, mottled wht/bl/yel/rose over teal, split 3-groove hdls, 10", EX ...175.00
Punch bowl, mirror blk, 13" dia, +12 tumblers, EX 90.00
Teapot, Halloween (orange w/blk highlighs), stamp mk, 4½x8", EX..215.00
Tumbler, turq matt, 4½".. 55.00
Vase, chrome red, prominent finger rings, rim-to-width hdls, 9".. 130.00
Vase, goggle-wheel decor, glossy/matt bl & brn, cylindrical, 11".... 60.00
Vase, lg 'eyes' in mc earth-tone glaze, mirror blk int/hdls, 19", pr...390.00
Vase, ochre/brn mottle, hdls extend above rim, attach at shoulder, 22" .420.00
Vase, organic gr matt, ovoid w/short flaring neck, shoulder hdls, 5"...150.00
Vase, rose, bulbous w/3 vertical rim-to-width hdls, Rainbow, 7x7½"..195.00

Compacts

The use of cosmetics before WWI was looked upon with disdain. After the war women became liberated, entered the work force, and started to use makeup. The compact, a portable container for cosmetics, became a necessity. The basic compact contains a mirror and a powder puff.

Vintage compacts were fashioned in a myriad of shapes, styles, materials, and motifs. They were made of precious metals, fabrics, plastics, and in almost any other conceivable medium. Commemorative, premium, patriotic, figural, Art Deco, plastic, and gadgetry compacts are just a few of the most sought-after types available today. Those that are combined with other accessories (music/compact, watch/compact, cane/compact) are also very much in demand. Vintage compacts are an especially desirable collectible since the workmanship, design, techniques, and materials used in their execution would be very expensive and virtually impossible to duplicate today.

Our advisor, Roselyn Gerson, has written six highly informative books: *Ladies' Compacts of the 19th and 20th Centuries*, *Vintage Vanity Bags and Purses*, *Vintage and Contemporary Purse Accessories*, *Vintage Ladies' Compacts*, *Vintage & Vogue Ladies' Compacts*, and *The Estee Lauder Solid Perfume Compact Collection*. She is listed in the Directory under New York. See Clubs, Newsletters, and Catalogs for information concerning the compact collectors' club and their periodical publication, *The Powder Puff*.

Arrowhead shape, wht metal, sunray/bl border, Woodworth, 3¼" ...90.00
Carryall, clutch, wht enamel w/blk polka dots, 4¼" 300.00
Clamshell, gold-tone w/bl stone thumb pc, Givenchy.................. 150.00
Cornucopia, gold-tone w/emb leaves, mirror/sifter/puff, 2x4½" ... 425.00
Envelope, gold-tone w/silver-tone flap & crest, mirror, Kreisler, 3"..90.00
Guitar shape, blk plastic strings, inner mirror, 5½x2" 225.00
Horseshoe, gold-tone w/blk enamel, mirror, Vanstyle, 2½x2⅜" 75.00
Necessaire, blk/ivorene Bakelite w/rhinestones, tassel, 4x1¾" dia...450.00
Octagon, bl enamel w/silver & bl pàte-de-verre center, Evans, 2¼"...100.00
Octagon, blk enamel w/wht Deco tulip on lid, Richard Hudnut, 2¼" ...90.00
Octagon, domed gr enamel case w/pk rose decor, Ripley & Gowen, 3⅛"..250.00
Octagon, gold-tone w/gr wreath on lid, dbl mirror, Djer-Kiss, 1⅞"....60.00
Oval, flattened, gold-tone, Deco lady's head on powder lid, Corday, 3".75.00
Owl shape, gold-tone w/faux emerald & dmn eyes, Italy, 2¾x2".. 400.00
Pendant, sterling w/blk onyx lid, silver cartouch, 3x1½" dia........ 300.00
Purse, brushed gold-tone w/mc stones in filigree plaque, w/chain, 2x3"..150.00
Rectangle, aqua enamel w/silver-tone gazelle, mirror, Evans, 3¼"...150.00
Rectangle, bl & wht enamel, monogram cartouch, Bourjois, 3", NMIB..125.00
Rectangle, cream enamel, gold on sides & crest on lid, Foster, 2½" ..75.00
Rectangle, Frigidaire crest on wht enamel, Elgin, ca 1938, 2¾" ... 150.00

Rectangle, glossy gold-tone w/logo on lid, 2 mirrors, Tre-Jur, 2", MIB .. 150.00
Rectangle, gold-tone on blk enamel, belt clip on bk, Rothley, 2⅛"....125.00
Rectangle, gold-tone w/bl enamel w/pk roses, Lampl, 3¼" 150.00
Rectangle, gold-tone w/blk enamel, mask in corner, Max Factor, 2¼"...70.00
Rectangle, gold-tone w/rhinestone pave bar opener, Bonita, 3½" .. 65.00
Rectangle, gold-tone w/silver-tone fr on lid, 2 mirrors, Lentheric, 3".. 100.00
Rectangle, gold-tone/gr enamel w/logo, Prince Matchabelli, 2¼", MIB... 100.00
Rectangle, padded wht leather lid w/gilt rococo decor, Marhill, 2¾" 45.00
Rectangle, red leather w/red & gr floral zigzag, Mondaine, 2¾" 75.00
Rectangle, wht metal w/blk champleve floral, unfr mirror, 2½" 75.00
Rectangle, wht metal w/emb oval flowerpot, 2 mirrors, Lachere, 2½". 100.00
Rectangle, wht metal w/2-tone gr enamel lid, chain strap, Evans, 3".. 250.00
Rnd, gold-tone, scalloped/domed case, fr mirror, Elgin American, 3" 90.00
Rnd, gold-tone/bl enamel w/roses & emb floral border, Evans, 2½".. 90.00
Rnd, gold-tone/champleve bl enamel/tulip motif, Richard Hudnut, 2⅝".. 75.00
Rnd, gr Lucite, lady on swing on marbleized irid lid, Fr, 2½"........ 200.00
Rnd, orange Bakelite, mirror, cord, 2 lipstick tubes, tassels, 2"..... 750.00
Rnd, wht metal, blk enamel lid w/silver moon & sun, Richard Hudnut, 2"..50.00
Rnd, wht metal, monogramed lid, emb hdl & sides, tassel, Elgin, 3⅛" . 100.00
Roulette wheel (spins) on brass lid, Majestic 150.00
Skyscraper, wht metal w/gr champleve skyscraper decor, Evans, 4½".. 250.00
Sq, Art Moderne mc lid, emb sides, pop-up fr mirror, rigid hdl, 3½" .. 250.00
Sq, bl leather on wht metal, Deco lady w/red & gilt accents, Vashe, 2" ... 100.00
Sq, bl silk-wrapped lid w/embr floral basket, Mondaine, 2½" 90.00
Sq, champleve gr enamel w/Art Moderne decor, mirror, Evans, 2½".. 150.00
Sq, gold-tone w/blk enamel, attached crest, hinged dbl mirrors, 2"... 55.00
Sq, gold-tone w/brushed hearts & enamel floral, Marathon, 1942, 2¾"... 80.00
Sq, gold-tone/gr enamel w/center snowflake & roses, La Mode, 2¼"... 90.00
Sq, pave case w/chrome int, fr mirror, Lampl, 3" 175.00
Sq, pk enamel w/bl florets & rhinestone corners on lid, Unique, 2½"...90.00
Sq, silver-tone, Nouveau relief, perfume combo, mirror, 2".......... 200.00
Sq, tan enamel w/brn strap accent, exterior push for lid release, 2"... 65.00
Sq, tortoise enamel lid on silver-tone, ultra thin, Bliss Bros, 2¾"... 75.00
Sq, wht metal w/brn enamel, emb bonsai lid, 2 mirrors, Vashe, 1½" .. 60.00
Sq, wht metal w/flower basket on lid, dbl mirrors, Langlois, 2" 65.00
Suitcase, ivory enamel w/gold-tone mts, travel decals, Cara Mia, 3"..175.00
Teardrop, gr enamel w/3-color lightning bolt, Elgin American, 3¼"....90.00
Vanity, book form, blk/red/Art Moderne eggshell enamel, Deere, 3", MIB... 200.00
Walnut, brass w/slate/mirror/compartments, loop for chain, 19th C... 225.00

Consolidated Lamp and Glass

The Consolidated Lamp and Glass Company of Coraopolis, Pennsylvania, was incorporated in 1894. For many years their primary business was the manufacture of lighting glass such as oil lamps and shades for both gas and electric lighting. The popular 'Cosmos' line of lamps and tableware was produced from 1894 to 1915. (See also Cosmos.) In 1926 Consolidated introduced their Martele line, a type of 'sculptured' ware closely resembling Lalique glassware of France. (Compare Consolidated's 'Lovebirds' vase with the Lalique 'Perruches' vase.) It is this line of vases, lamps, and tableware which is often mistaken for a very similar type of glassware produced by the Phoenix Glass Company, located nearby in Monaca, Pennsylvania. For example, the so-called Phoenix 'Grasshopper' vases are actually Consolidated's 'Katydid' vases.

Items in the Martele line were produced in blue, pink, green, crystal, white, or custard glass decorated with various fired-on color treatments or a satin finish. For the most part, their colors were distinctively different from those used by Phoenix. Although not foolproof, one of the ways of distinguishing Consolidated's wares from those of Phoenix is that most of the time Consolidated applied color to the raised portion of the design, leaving the background plain, while Phoenix usually applied color to the background, leaving the raised surfaces undecorated. This is particularly true of those pieces in white or custard glass.

In 1928 Consolidated introduced their Ruba Rombic line, which was their Art Deco or Art Moderne line of glassware. It was only produced from 1928 to 1932 and is quite scarce. Today it is highly sought after by both Consolidated and Art Deco collectors.

Consolidated closed its doors for good in 1964. Subsequently a few of the molds passed into the hands of other glass companies that later reproduced certain patterns; one such reissue is the 'Chickadee' vase, found in avocado green, satin-finish custard, or milk glass. For further information we recommend *Phoenix and Consolidated Art Glass, 1926 – 1980*, by Jack D. Wilson. Our advisor for this category is David Sherman; he is listed in the Directory under New York.

Ruba Rombic, vase, jade green, 9¼", $2,400.00.
(Photo courtesy David Rago Auctions)

Allover Ivy, pitcher, gr over wht casing 500.00
Bird of Paradise, candy box, purple wash, oval 325.00
Bird of Paradise, fan vase, yel wash, 10" 350.00
Bird of Paradise, vase, pk cased, 10" 400.00
Bird of Paradise, vase, sepia wash, fan form, 6" 135.00
Bittersweet, lamp, reverse ruby stain on crystal 100.00
Bittersweet, vase, bl/gr/orange on satin milk glass 120.00
Bittersweet, vase, gr cased 275.00
Bittersweet, vase, ruby stain on crystal 150.00
Blackberry, umbrella vase, amethyst wash 600.00
Blackberry, umbrella vase, gr cased 1,600.00
Catalonian, candlestick, rainbow: pk/bl/gr, ea 125.00
Catalonian, candlestick, yel, ea 45.00
Catalonian, plate, russet (rare color), 6" 100.00
Catalonian, vase, bl irid stretch, cased, fan shape, Regent line 225.00
Catalonian, vase, Nasturtium, russet (rare color) 325.00
Catalonian, vase, purple wash, pinched, 6" 145.00
Catalonian, whiskey jug, emerald gr 250.00
Chickadee, lamp, amber wash w/blk highlighting, 3-way lighting ..195.00
Chickadee, vase, purple cased 250.00
Chickadee, vase, sepia wash on crystal 150.00
Chrysanthemum, vase, bl on creamy milk glass, 12" 140.00
Chrysanthemum, vase, ruby-stain highlights in crystal, metal surmount.... 225.00
Chrysanthemum, vase, 3-color highlights on satin milk glass 175.00
Chrysanthemum, vase, 3-color on satin custard, 12" 175.00
Cockatoo, bowl, console; bl frosted crystal (rare color), 13" 395.00
Cockatoo, candlestick, purple wash, ea 275.00
Cockatoo, vase, straw opal, ormolu mts 450.00
Cockatoo, vase, yel cased 425.00
Con-Cora, cookie jar, violets on milk glass, 6½" 85.00
Dancing Girls, vase, bl highlights on satin milk glass, 12" 525.00
Dancing Girls, vase, glossy milk glass, no decor, 12" 250.00
Dancing Nymph, goblet, pk frosted 125.00
Dancing Nymph, platter, Rueben Blue, palace sz, 18" dia 2,500.00
Dancing Nymph, tumbler, ftd, gr frosted, 6½" 125.00
Dancing Nymph, vase, crystal, fan shape 125.00
Dancing Nymph, vase, opal on cream, w/label, 12" 300.00
Dogwood, lamp, 3-color on satin milk glass 125.00
Dogwood, vase, bl transparent over wht irid casing, Regent line . 650.00

Dogwood, vase, gold highlights on glossy milk glass, 11" 125.00
Dragon Fly, vase, gold on glossy custard, 7"........................... 175.00
Dragon Fly, vase, purple cased on straw opal, 7" 225.00
Dragon Fly, vase, reverse bl highlights on satin milk glass 165.00
Dragon Fly, vase, yel cased, 7" 195.00
Fish, tray, reverse ruby-stain highlights on crystal..................... 275.00
Fish, tray, yel wash 200.00
Five Fruits, goblet, yel wash 35.00
Five Fruits, pound box, reverse gold on milk glass 75.00
Five Fruits, tumbler, gr wash, ftd 30.00
Floral, vase, ruby stain on crystal..................................... 125.00
Floral, vase, 3-color on satin milk glass 125.00
Florentine, vase, gr, tumbler shape 75.00
Florentine, vase, gr, urn shape 250.00
Florentine, vase, gr, 7" 155.00
Foxglove, lamp, wht w/lav-bl flowers & gr leaves, orig mts, 10¼" . 125.00
Hummingbird, powder jar, amethyst, 3" dia............................. 225.00
Hummingbird & Orchids, candlestick, purple wash, ea 225.00
Iris, bowl, console; pk wash, 10¾" 165.00
Iris, jug, transparent gr over wht casing, ½-gal........................ 450.00
Jonquil, vase, red (rare color) 275.00
Katydid, vase, bl on satin milk glass, ovoid 165.00
Line 700, bowl, fruit; bl, 10" 175.00
Olive, vase, gold highlights on glossy milk glass 125.00
Pine Cone, vase, straw opal, 6½" 225.00
Pitcher, Guttate, pk cased w/camphor hdl, 9½" 250.00
Ruba Rombic, plate, service; Jungle Green, 10" 300.00
Ruba Rombic, toilet bottle, Smoky Topaz, 7¾" 1,200.00
Seagull, vase, gr cased, 11".. 650.00
Tropical Fish, vase, gr wash on crystal, 9" 300.00

Conta & Boehme

The Conta & Boehme company was in business for 117 years in the quaint town Poessneck, Germany (Thuringer district). Hand-painted dishes and pipe heads were their main products. However, in 1840, when the owner's two young sons took over the company, production changed drastically from dishes to porcelain items of almost every imaginable type.

For their logo, the brothers chose an arm holding a dagger inside a shield. This mark was either impressed or ink stamped onto the porcelain. Another mark they used is called the 'scissor brand' which looks just like it sounds, a pair of scissors in a blue or green ink stamp. Not all pieces were marked, many were simply given a model number or left completely unmarked.

England and the U.S. were the largest buyers, and as a result the porcelain ended up at fairs, gift shops, and department stores throughout both countries. Today their fairings are highly collectible. Fairings are small, brightly colored nineteenth-century hard-paste porcelain objects, largely figural groups and boxes. Most portray amusing if not risque scenes of courting couples, marital woes, and political satire complete with an appropriate caption on the base. For more information we recommend *Victorian Trinket Boxes* by Janice and Richard Vogel, and their latest book, *Conta & Boehme Porcelain*, published by the authors.

Conta & Boehme often produced their porcelain items in several different sizes (sometimes as many as nine). When ranges are used in our listings, it is to accomodate these different sizes (unless a specific size is given). Values are for items with no chips, cracks, or repairs. Our advisors for this category are Richard and Janice Vogel; they are listed in the Directory under South Carolina.

Fairings, Boxes

Dresser, boy & cat in seesaw, #3635 .... 200.00
Dresser, boy in bed putting on his trousers, #3576 .... 175.00

Dresser, boy on sled, #3614.. 300.00
Dresser, cats play on dresser top, #3564, from $175 to............... 225.00
Dresser, dog licking boy in face, #3569............................. 225.00
Dresser, girl & goose, #3621 .... 225.00
Dresser, girl w/kitten in bl chair, #5317, 6¾" 300.00
Dresser, man at desk, #2951 .... 250.00
Lg, boy & girl playing checkers, #3639 .... 550.00
Vintage, angel kneeling, #13 .... 125.00
Vintage, girl w/sheep, #255 .... 125.00
Vintage, Kiss Me Quick, bicyclists on lid, #2883 .... 225.00
3-spot, eagle w/American flag...................................... 300.00
3-spot, Sleeping Beauty, #273 .... 175.00
3-spot, Zouave soldiers (Crimean War)............................. 300.00

Fairings, Figurals

Fairings are small, brightly colored nineteenth-century hard-paste porcelain objects, largely figural groups and boxes. Most portray amusing if not risque scenes of courting couples, marital woes, and political satire complete with an appropriate caption on the base.

Animated Spirits, #3310, minimum value 500.00
Broken Hoop, #3343.. 275.00
Cancan, #3301 .... 400.00
Don't Awake the Baby, #3367 .... 400.00
Five O'Clock Tea, #3339 .... 112.00
God Save the Queen, #3307 .... 300.00
How Bridget Served the Tomatoes Undressed, #3362, minimum value .. 400.00
Looking Down Upon His Luck, #2863 .... 200.00
O'Do Leave Me a Drop, #3350..................................... 200.00
Out! By Jingo!, #3340, minimum value 500.00
Returning at One O'Clock in the Morning, #2857 .... 125.00
Sarah's Young Man, #2874... 125.00
Shamming Sick, #3358... 150.00
Tea Party, #3365.. 200.00
Walk In, man & lady at front door, from $900 to 1,000.00
Which Is Prettiest?, #3366... 175.00
Who Said Rats?, #3359... 150.00

Figurines

Birds (6 in series), Green Woodpecker, Pheasant, etc, ea from $50 to ... 80.00
Boy & girl, both w/parasols, #5316, 5¾", pr 125.00
Boy on bench, #470, 5¾", from $85 to 100.00
Courting couple, #1465, 7½", from $125 to 175.00
Elephant, #2376, 8½x11".. 1,500.00
Swinger, lady on swing, 8½", from $500 to 600.00
Toy, 3 Little Maids w/bonnet & muff on base, #5558, from $35 to ... 75.00

Nodders

Card Players, marked with Roman numeral II, 5¾", from $600.00 to $650.00. (Photo courtesy Janice and Richard Vogel/Hilma Irtz)

Candleholder, lady playing cards, head nods, unmk, 8", ea 175.00
Card Players (4), heads nod, #8587, from $500 to 600.00
Cat w/glass eye, unmk, 3½x6½" 500.00
Chess players (2), couple at table, heads nod, from $300 to 400.00
Colonial man standing beside birdcage, bird nods, #8630, from $450 to.... 500.00
Girl sitting in chair, head nods, #5317, from $250 to 300.00
Man & lady sit X-legged, head/tongue/hands nod, #5380, $750 to .. 950.00
Oriental couple, carrying bowl in ea arm, #7670, pr 450.00
Oriental couple, purple w/gold fans behind head, unmk, 6¼", pr.. 450.00

Piano Babies

Seated, butterfly on knee, #444, 5" 275.00
Seated, holding cup, #482, 7½" 350.00
Seated, holding fruit, #8266, from $175 to 275.00
Seated, holding sponge, #489, from $175 to 275.00
Seated, leaning on left hand, waving w/right, #487, from $400 to .. 500.00

Miscellaneous

Bank, man in robe seated in chair smoking pipe, slot in bk, unmk, 9".. 250.00
Basket w/realistic rose, #1276, 5¼", pr 75.00
Candleholder, girls dancing, w/hdl, #8311, ea 150.00
Candleholders, boy w/fiddle (girl holds dress out), #8306, pr 150.00
Candleholders, man (lady), #8330, pr from $175 to 225.00
Candleholders, owls, #670, pr from $175 to 225.00
Cigar holder, Enpassant, couple ready to kiss, #1693 .... 375.00
Cigar holder, frogs dueling, #3013, from $85 to 125.00
Cigar holder, red fox w/prey in mouth, #3025, 4" 125.00
Cigar holder, rooster beside basket & sm pail, #3063, from $125 to... 150.00
Compote, man (lady) w/sheep, pr, minimum value 500.00
Condiment set, dog w/basket on sides pulling cart, head nods 150.00
Condiment set, 3 pigs, unmk 150.00
Humidor, Asian lady's head w/bow, #6050, from $300 to 500.00
Humidor, dog's head, #2584, from $300 to 500.00
Humidor, owl, #6009, minimum value 1,000.00
Ink & penholder, vanity w/mirror, 2 covered wells, #3259, $100 to... 150.00
Inkwell, Erst Beten, lady urges child to pray, dog, from $600 to .. 1,000.00
Inkwell, mother holds baby while 2 children look on, unmk, 5".. 450.00
Lamp, oil; owl w/glass eyes, #5482, 6" 400.00
Matchbox, pitcher & washbowl on dresser, #476, 4½" 175.00
Matchbox, sailing vessel w/Bristol to London on side, #2133, 5½" .. 200.00
Matchstriker, boy (girl) w/hoop, #4192, ea from $150 to 200.00
Matchstriker, boy w/suitcase, #4204 .... 100.00
Matchstriker, lg frog on shell base, #1527, from $100 to 150.00
Menu holder, boy sits aside holding covered pot, shield mk, $150 to.. 200.00
Vase, boy (& girl) playing instruments, gr ink mk, 8½", pr 200.00
Wall pocket, angels holding cornucopia, shield mk, pr from $400 to.. 500.00

Cookbooks

Cookbooks from the nineteenth century, though often hard to find, are a delight to today's collectors both for their quaint formats and printing methods as well as for their outmoded, often humorous views on nutrition. Recipes required a 'pinch' of salt, butter 'the size of an egg' or a 'walnut,' or a 'handful' of flour. Collectors sometimes specialize in cookbooks issued as advertising premiums. Especially desirable are the figurals that were shaped like a jar, a slice of bread, or some other form relative to the product. Others with unique features such as illustrations by well-known artists or references to famous people or places are priced in accordance. Cookbooks written earlier than 1874 are the most valuable and when found command prices as high as $200.00; figurals usually sell in the $10.00 to $15.00 range.

Our listings are for examples in near-mint condition. As is true with all other books, if the original dust jacket is present and in nice condition, a cookbook's value goes up by at least $5.00. Right now, books on Italian cooking from before circa 1940 are in demand, and bread-baking is important this year. For further information we recommend *Collector's Guide to Cookbooks* by Frank Daniels. Our advisor for this category is Charlotte Safir; she is listed in the Directory under New York.

Key:
CB — Cookbook	prt — printing
dj — dust jacket	rb — ring binder
hb — hardbound	shb — spiral hardback
pb — paperback	spb — spiral paperback
pm — pamphlet	

Art of Cooking & Serving, Proctor & Gamble, hb, 1932, 252 pgs ... 15.00
Baking Made Easy, Margaret B Baker, Russell-Miller, pb, 1922, 55 pgs .. 15.00
Big Boy Barbecue Book, Tested Recipe Institute, spb, 1956, 62 pgs .. 5.00
Common Sense in the Kitchen, WA Henderson, Hurst & Co, hb, 1870.... 60.00
Dainty Desserts, Ida Bailey Allen, Buzza Co, pb, ca 1920, 57 pgs 100.00
Dessert Magic, General Foods, pb, 1944, 26 pgs 3.00
Everyday Foods, Houghton Mifflin, hb, 1944, 583 pgs 6.00
Fall & Winter Menus & Recipes for 2 or 4 or 6, pb, 1935, 31 pgs 6.00
Francatelli's Modern Cook, Charles Elme Francatelli, hb, 1876, 585 pgs .. 125.00
Gem Chopper CB, Sargent & Co, pb, 1902, 90 pgs 10.00
Helen Corbitt Cooks for Looks, Houghton Mifflin, hb w/dj, 1967 ... 8.00
I Hate To Cook Book, The; Peg Bracken, Crest Books, pb, 1965, 144 pgs .. 6.00
Idle Hour Cook Book, Chambers Gas Range Co, pb, 1927, 40 pgs ... 25.00
Jell-O Pudding Idea Book, General Foods, pb, 1968, 44 pgs 3.00

Jell-O, Desserts of the World, published by Genesee in 1909, 24 pages, $40.00. (Photo courtesy Frank Daniels)

Junior Jewish CB, Aunt Fanny, KTAV Publishing, hb, 1956, 64 pgs .. 15.00
Kitchen Fun, Louise Price Bell, Harter of Cleveland, hb, 1932, 28 pgs .. 60.00
Larkin Housewives' CB, Larkin Co, hb, 1923 .... 25.00
Liberace Cooks, Carol Truax, Doubleday, hb w/dj, 1970, 225 pgs .. 60.00
Mushroom Cookery, Rosetta Reitz, Gramercy, hb w/dj, 1945, 206 pgs .. 6.00
National Yeast Co, pb, 1885, 44 pgs 30.00
Old Favorite Honey Recipes, American Honey Institute, pb, 1945, 52 pgs.... 5.00
Our Home Cyclopedia, Frank S Burton, Mercantile, hb, 1889, 400 pgs.. 200.00
Pyrex Prize Recipes, Corning Glass Works, Greystone, hb, 1953, 128 pgs ... 20.00
Quantity Cookery, Lenore Richards & Nola Treat, hb, 1925, 200 pgs.. 8.00
Queen of Hearts CB, Peter Pauper Press, hb w/dj, 1955, 64 pgs........ 5.00
Rawleigh's 1916 Almanac, WT Rawleigh Co, pb, 98 pgs.............. 20.00
Thoughts for Buffets, Houghton Mifflin, hb, 1958, 425 pgs 6.00
Twentieth Century Home CB, Mrs Francis Carruthers, hb, 1906, 491 pages.. 40.00
Universal Simplifed Gas Cookery, Cribben & Sexton Co, pb, 1940, 53 pgs... 12.00
US Navy CB, Division of Naval Militia Affairs, pb, 1908, 62 pgs.... 20.00
Walt Disney's Mickey Mouse CB, Walt Disney Productions, hb, 1975 .. 15.00
Young Housekeeper's Friend, Mrs Mary Hooker Cornelius, hb, ca 1859 .200.00
Young Wife's Own CB, Mrs Jane Warren, Grand Union Tea Co, hb, 1890 ..40.00

Cookie Cutters

Early hand-fashioned cookie cutters command stiff prices at country auctions, and the ranks of interested collectors are growing steadily. Especially valuable are the figural cutters; and the more complicated the design, the higher the price. A follow-up of the carved wooden cookie boards, the first cutters were probably made by itinerant tinkers from leftover or recycled pieces of tin. Though most of the eighteenth-century examples are now in museums or collections, it is still possible to find some good cutters from the late 1800s when changes in the manufacture of tin resulted in a thinner, less expensive material. The width of the cutting strip is often a good indicator of age; the wider the strip, the older the cutter. While the very early cutters were 1" to 1½" deep, by the '20s and '30s, many were less than ½" deep. Crude, spotty soldering indicates an older cutter, while a thin line of solder usually tends to suggest a much later manufacture. The shape of the backplate is another clue. Later cutters will have oval, round, or rectangular backs, while on the earlier type the back was cut to follow the lines of the design. Cookie cutters usually vary from 2" to 4" in size, but gingerbread men were often made as tall as 12". Birds, fish, hearts, and tulips are common; simple versions can be purchased for as little as $12.00 to $15.00. The larger figurals, especially those with more imaginative details, often bring $75.00 and up. Advertising cutters and product premiums (usually plastic) are collectible as well, so are the aluminum cutters with painted wood handles. Hallmark makes cutters in plastic — many of them character related and often priced in the $15.00 to $35.00 range. The cookie cutters listed here are tin and handmade unless noted otherwise.

Cavalryman on horseback, tin, minor dents and rust, 10x9", $490.00. (Photo courtesy Garth's Auctions Inc.)

Acorn, flat bk, 4¾x4⅛"	120.00
Chimney sweep, flat bk, 8x6"	660.00
Eagle in profile w/wings raised, flat bk, 3⅞x4⅝"	120.00
Gingerbread man, flat bk w/appl hdl, 1870s-90s, 8x6¼"	95.00
Heart, flat bk, PA, ca 1870, 9"	175.00
Heart in hand, flat bk, 4½"	585.00
Horse running, flat bk w/appl hdl, 19th C, 5x8½"	100.00
Man in long coat & top hat, flat bk, 12½x5"	120.00
Man on horsebk, primitive style, flat bk, 8½"	660.00
Pig, flat bk, 3⅜x6⅛"	165.00
Rabbit seated, flat bk, 10½"	215.00
Rooster, fan tail, oversz comb, human ft, flat bk w/hole, 1820s, 3x4"	300.00
Rooster, flat bk, 6¼x6⅛"	120.00
Stag, flat bk, 6⅛x6½"	180.00

Cookie Jars

The appeal of the cookie jar is universal; folks of all ages, both male and female, love to collect 'em! The early '30s heavy stoneware jars of a rather nondescript nature quickly gave way to figurals of every type imaginable. Those from the mid to late '30s were often decorated over the glaze with 'cold paint,' but by the early '40s underglaze decorating resulted in cheerful, bright, permanent colors and cookie jars that still have a new look 50 years later.

Stimulated by the high prices commanded by desirable cookie jars, a broad spectrum of 'new' cookie jars are flooding the marketplace in three categories: 1) Manufactures have expanded their lines with exciting new designs specifically geared toward attracting the collector market. 2) Limited editions and artist-designed jars have proliferated. 3) Reproductions, signed and unsigned, have pervaded the market, creating uncertainty among new collectors and inexperienced dealers. One of the most troublesome reproductions is the Little Red Riding Hood jar marked McCoy. Several Brush jars are being reproduced, and because the old molds are being used, these are especially deceptive. In addition to these reproductions, we've also been alerted to watch for cookie jars marked Brush-McCoy made from molds that Brush never used. Remember that none of Brush's cookie jars were marked Brush-McCoy, so any bearing the compound name is fraudulent. For more information on cookie jars and reproductions, we recommend *The Ultimate Collector's Encyclopedia of Cookie Jars* by Fred and Joyce Roerig; they are listed in the Directory under South Carolina. Our advisors for this category are Fred and Joyce Roerig; they are listed in the Directory under South Carolina.

The examples listed below were made by companies other than those found elsewhere in this book; see also specific manufacturers.

Adam & Eve, FF Japan label, Fitz & Floyd, 1987	350.00
Baby Elephant, unmk, American Bisque, from $175 to	200.00
Baseball Boy, mk 875 USA on lid & base, California Originals, from $35	45.00
Basketball, For the Team, mk WH Hirsh MFG..., from $100 to	125.00
Beatrix Potter Rabbit, mk c Maddux of Calif, from $75 to	85.00
Beehive, mk WH Hirsh Mfg Made in USA, 10½", from $60 to	75.00
Bluebird Love Nest, Lefton #7525, 11", from $175 to	200.00
Bossie Cow, orange/yel floral, Lefton #6594, from $125 to	150.00
Buddha, mk USA DeForest of California #527, from $70 to	80.00
Buffalo Hunt, Omnibus Collections International, from $30 to	35.00
Camel, recumbent w/eyes closed, mk J 8 USA, Doranne of California	45.00
Castle, yel & pk, mk Cardinal USA #307, from $70 to	90.00
Cat w/Bell, yel w/wht spots, OCI Omnibus Korea label, from $25 to	35.00
Chipmunk, DeForest of California #514, from $45 to	50.00
Christmas Car, Fitz & Floyd, 8x15⅜x8½", from $300 to	325.00
Clown, mk 805 USA, American Bisque, from $250 to	275.00
Clown Head, Enesco Imports Japan E-5835, from $125 to	150.00
Coffee Grinder, mk 861 USA, California Originals, from $30 to	35.00
Coke Six-pack, mk Coca-Cola c 1996, Enesco, from $50 to	60.00
Cookie Crock, brn w/wht decor, mk Hull Ovenproof USA, from $20 to	25.00
Cookie Monster, mk c Muppets Inc 1970, from $35 to (+)	45.00
Cookie Safe, yel w/blk lid, mk Cardinal #309 USA, from $60 to	70.00
Cookie Thief, 1976 FF Stamp, Fitz & Floyd, from $50 to	60.00
Corvette, blk, ACC J9 c 1986 NAC USA, N Am Ceramics, $125 to	150.00
Country Sunflower Hampshire Hog, FF Taiwan label, Fitz & Floyd, $30 to	40.00
Cow w/Can of Milk, wht & pk, mk CJ-106, Doranne of California, $50 to	60.00
Cowboy Cats Miss Kitty, Omnibus Collections Int, from $35 to	45.00
Cuckoo Clock, brn, William H Hirsch Mfg, from $100 to	125.00
Davy Crockett, mk Sierra Vista of Calif..., rare	750.00
Deer, recumbent w/eyes closed, unmk, Doranne of California, $35 to	45.00
Dog, tongue out, mk 458, California Originals, from $30 to	35.00
Dragon, gr w/red eyes & tongue, Doranne of California, from $225 to	250.00
Duck w/Yarmulke, unmk, Doranne of California, from $50 to	60.00
Duckbilled Platypus, mk 790 USA, California Originals, from $100 to	125.00
Elf School House, red roof lid, unmk, from $40 to	50.00
Engine, DCJ32 c 1987 NAC USA, North Am Ceramics, from $45 to	50.00
Fat Lady, sitting, Made in Japan label, Fitz & Foyd, from $150 to	17,500.00
Fire Hydrant, red, mk CJ 50, Doranne of California, 1984, $50 to	60.00
Fire Truck, mk 841, California Originals, from $225 to	250.00
French Poodle, American Bisque, 1959, from $125 to	150.00

French Poodle, burgundy, mk USA, American Bisque, from $100 to .. 125.00
Frog w/Bow Tie, gr w/yel tie, mk 2645 USA, from $30 to 40.00
Garfield, standing, mk Garfield c 1982..., Enesco, from $100 to .. 125.00

Garfield on Stack of Cookies, Enesco, 1978, $200.00. (Photo courtesy Joyce and Fred Roerig)

Grandma, gold trim, unmk, American Bisque, from $175 to 225.00
Halloween Pumpkin, OCI Omnibus Taiwan label, 1989, from $20 to.. 25.00
Harvest Turkey, c OCI 1990 label, Omnibus Collections Int, from $30 to ..35.00
Hat Party Bear, FF Taiwan label, Fitz & Floyd, 1991, from $75 to . 85.00
Haunted House, F&F Taiwan label, Fitz & Floyd, from $100 to .. 125.00
Herman & Katnip, Harvey Famous Cartoons USA, Am Bisque, 1960...3,800.00
Humpty Dumpty, mk Clay Art Humpty Dumpty Series..., 1991, from $75 to . 85.00
Jocko the Monkey, yel hat, mk RRP Co Roseville O USA, from $325 to...375.00
Juggling Clown, red suit & hat, mk 876, California Originals, $45 to 55.00
Kittens & Yarn, American Bisque, lg, from $100 to 125.00
Le Chef Cuisine, Dept 56 label, from $100 to 125.00
Little Boy Blue, cold pnt, mk Hull Ware USA #968, 1940, 12½" .1,500.00
Little King, bib & crown, DeForest Of California, 1957 .... 800.00
Mickey Clock, Enesco WDE-219 label, from $525 to 575.00
Mickey Mouse Car, yel w/suitcase on top, mk c Walt Disney..., $400 to ..425.00
Midnight Snack, couple in night attire, Clay Art label, 1991, $40 to..50.00
Milk Wagon, mk USA 740, American Bisque, from $100 to....... 125.00
Mr & Mrs Pig, turnabout, unmk, APCO, from $175 to 200.00
Mrs Kringle, Christmas dress, Department 56 label, from $50 to... 60.00
Mushrooms on Stump, brn, mk 2956, California Originals, from $25 to. 30.00
Noah's Ark, mk 881 USA, California Originals, from $60 to 70.00
Nun, praying, mk DeForest of California, from $250 to 275.00
Owl, brn w/glasses, DeForest of California, from $30 to 35.00
Owl w/Guitar, mk Maurice c Calif USA 19c76 PG 62, from $100 to .. 125.00
Panda, c OCI label, Omnibus Collections, International, from $25 to..30.00
Pear, yel, mk 1971 Los Angelos Pottery #88, 11½", from $25 to.... 35.00
Pineapple, mk J 115, Doranne of California, from $25 to 35.00
Plaid Teddy, holiday decor, FF Korea label, Fitz & Floyd, 1991, $75 to... 100.00
Plaid Teddy, w/Christmas Tree, FF label, Fitz & Floyd, 1991, $60 to.. 70.00
Poodle, mk 19c60 DeForest of California USA, from $40 to 50.00
Professor Ludwig Von Drake, Walt Disney USA 1961, Am Bisque .1,200.00
Ragtime, man at piano, mk CA, Clay Art, 1995, from $40 to 50.00
Ricky Racoon, Cookie Bandit on yel shirt, Hallmark Cards, 1981, $75 to ..95.00
Road Hog, pig on red motorcycle, mk Clay Art..., 1995, from $45 to.. 55.00
Russian Santa, mk c OCI 1991, Omnibus Collections Internat'l, $30 to .. 35.00
School Bus, yel w/blk tires, mk Doranne California..., from $150 to..175.00
Sheriff Pig, gold trim, mk #363, Robinson-Ransbottom, from $175 to...200.00
Sherlock Hound, yel coat, c OCI label, Omnibus Collections Int, $35 to...45.00
Sitting Cat on Safe, brn, mk 2630, California Originals, from $30 to.. 35.00
Sitting Turtle, mk 2635 USA, California Originals, from $30 to... 35.00
Smiley Face, wht, wink/crooked smile, mk USA, Holiday Designs, $25 to.. 35.00
Snappy Gingerbread Boy, mk 6, DeForest of California, from $100 to... 125.00
Snow White, sitting w/bl bird & book, mk 866, Walt Disney USA... 2,000.00
Snowman, blk top hat, mk J 52 USA, Doranne of California, from $225 to..250.00

Southwest Santa, w/gifts, FF Japan label, Fritz & Floyd, 15", $175 to 200.00
Stagecoach, mk Sierra Vista Ceramics Pasadena Calif..., 1956, $150 to ..175.00
Strawberry, unmk, Doranne of California, from $25 to 35.00
Tat-L-Tale, bl polka-dot dress, Helen's Ware, from $700 to 750.00
Tuggle, brn boat, mk (DeForest of) California, from $100 to 125.00
Vegetable House, mk Dept 56 1990, from $50 to 60.00
Victorian Pig, couple, c OCI label, Omnibus, from $30 to............. 35.00
WC Fields, hat & cigar, mk CW (Cumberland Ware), scarce, from $775 to..850.00
Weather House, mk 19c60, DeForest of Calif USA, from $35 to... 45.00
Witch, bl dress & hat w/broom, unmk, Department 56 Inc, from $60 to...80.00
Yorkshire Terrier, bl bow, mk 937, California Originals, from $125 to .. 150.00
4x4 Pick-up, bl w/blk tires, mk Doranne, CA CJ 119..., from $225 to.. 250.00

Cooper, Susie

A twentieth-century ceramic designer whose works are now attracting the attention of collectors, Susie Cooper was first affiliated with the A.E. Gray Pottery in Henley, England, in 1922, where she designed in lustres and painted items with her own ideas as well. (Examples of Gray's lustreware is rare and costly.) By 1930 she and her brother-in-law, Jack Beeson, had established a family business. Her pottery soon became a success, and she was subsequently offered space at Crown Works, Burslem. In 1940 she received the honorary title of Royal Designer for Industry, the only such distinction ever awarded by the Royal Society of Arts solely for pottery design. Miss Cooper received the Order of the British Empire in the New Year's Honors List of 1979. She was the chief designer for the Wedgwood group from 1966 until she resigned in 1972. After 1980 she worked on a free-lance basis until her death in July 1995.

Key:
CW — Crown Works   HP — hand painted, painting
GP — Gray's Pottery   hs — hand signed

Bell, silver lustre floral, bone china, for Wedgwood, 4¼" 80.00
Bowl, animals incised under yel, 9½" 150.00
Bowl, cereal; Patricia Rose, rose on pk, CW, 6⅜", 4 for................. 35.00
Casserole, Hazelwood, autumn leaves & hazelnuts, w/lid, 9" dia ... 60.00
Casserole, Wedding Band, gray/rust on cream, w/lid, 5x9" 50.00
Coffee set, Dresden Spray, Rex shape, 7" pot+cr/sug+6 c/s......... 300.00
Coffee set, Moon & Mountains, pot+cr/sug+6 c/s, rare.............3,500.00
Coffee set, polka dots on dk red, pot+cr/sug+6 c/s...................... 250.00
Coffeepot, Wedding Ring, Kestrel shape, CW, 8" 95.00
Cup & saucer, coffee; Persian Bird, can form, ca 1929 .... 150.00
Cup & saucer, gr dots & lines on gray to wht, Deco, demitasse 25.00
Jug, abstracts on gr matt, 8½" 200.00
Jug, bird reserve w/silver o/l, bulbous, GP, 5½" 95.00
Jug, Gloria Lustre, HP foliage, GP, 4½" 145.00
Jug, Homestead, cottage scene on cream, 5½" 340.00
Jug, mc bands on wht, GP, 8½".. 40.00
Jug, Moons & Mountains, GP, 4¾" 400.00
Jug, rams leaping, lt gr, 8¼" 175.00
Marmalade jar, Dresden Spray, w/lid 25.00
Marmalade jar, Orchid, Kestral shape, 4" 110.00
Plaque, stylized feathers on dk burgundy, CW, 16" 350.00
Plate, Noah's Ark, animals, HP, rare, 7" 400.00
Plate, Nursery Ware, burro, yel & orange striped rim, 6½" 115.00
Platter, Hazelwood, autumn leaves & hazelnuts, 16" 125.00
Sandwich set, flowers & foxglove, red rim, GP, 1928, tray+6 sq plates ... 350.00
Tea set, Kestrel, floral sprays, 2 pots+cr/sug+plate+6 c/s+6 sm plates .. 1,500.00
Teapot, Deco flowers on wht to yel, CW, 5"................................ 165.00
Teapot, Wedding Ring, Kestrel shape, NM 50.00
Trio, Spiral Fern, 1930s, c/s+8¼" dessert plate............................ 55.00

Vase, bl-lined trumpet flowers & gr leaves on cream, 6½" 200.00
Vase, gr w/emb horizontal bands, #239, 10¼" 295.00
Vase, grooved teardrops in dbl band on cream, 1935, 8⅜" 275.00
Vase, squirrels in branches on yel ochre, ovoid, 11" 325.00

Coors

The firm that became known as Coors Porcelain Company in 1920 was founded in 1908 by John J. Herold, originally of the Roseville Pottery in Zanesville, Ohio. Though still in business today, they are best known for their artware vases and Rosebud dinnerware produced before 1939.

Coors vases produced before the late '30s were made in a matt finish; by the latter years of the decade, high-gloss glazes were also being used. Nearly 50 shapes were in production, and some of the more common forms were made in three sizes. Typical colors in matt are white, orange, blue, green, yellow, and tan. Yellow, blue, maroon, pink, and green are found in high gloss. All vases are marked with a triangular arrangement of the words 'Coors Colorado Pottery' enclosing the word 'Golden.' You may find vases (usually 6" to 6½") marked with the Colorado State Fair stamp and dated 1939. Please note: Prices for Coors, like many other collectibles, have taken a downward turn. Our prices here reflect those adjustments for today's current market.

Rosebud

Ashtray 185.00
Baker, lg 40.00
Bean pot, sm.. 65.00
Bowl, batter; lg.. 65.00
Bowl, cream soup; 4" 22.00
Bowl, mixing; hdls, 1½-pt 40.00
Bowl, mixing; 6-pt 50.00
Bowl, pudding; 2-pt 40.00
Bowl, pudding; 7-pt 75.00
Cake knife 85.00
Casserole, Dutch; 3¾-pt... 72.00
Casserole, French; 3¾-pt 45.00
Casserole, triple service; lg, 7-pt.. 55.00
Cup & saucer 50.00
Egg cup.. 55.00
Honey pot, no spoon.. 80.00
Loaf pan 40.00
Pitcher, w/lid, lg.. 150.00
Pitcher, water; w/stopper.. 120.00
Plate, 7¼" 8.00
Platter, 9¼".. 23.00
Saucer, 5½"... 5.00
Shakers, str sides, lg, pr 80.00
Sugar bowl, w/lid.. 40.00
Teapot, 2-cup, rare 150.00
Tumbler, ftd 125.00
Water server, cork stopper, 6-cup 120.00

Miscellaneous

Jardiniere, yel w/emb leaves, hdls, 4½x5½" 30.00
Vase, bl w/emb ribs, can neck, curved shoulder, 7" 40.00
Vase, Deco, sky bl w/wht int, integral hdls, 8x9" 75.00
Vase, tan w/aqua int, shouldered w/emb hdls, unmk, 6x5½" 45.00
Vase, turq w/wht int, shouldered, flared rim, mfg flaw, 12⅜" 60.00
Vase, wht w/gr int, emb ribs on bulbous body, can neck, 9" 42.50
Vase, yel w/slim trumpet neck, souvenir, 7⅞" 30.00

Copper

Handcrafted copper was made in America from early in the eighteenth century until about 1850, with the center of its production in Pennsylvania. Examples have been found signed by such notable coppersmiths as Kidd, Buchanan, Babb, Bently, and Harbeson. Of the many utilitarian items made, teakettles are the most desirable. Early examples from the eighteenth century were made with a dovetailed joint which was hammered and smoothed to a uniform thickness. Pots from the nineteenth century were seamed. Coffeepots were made in many shapes and sizes and along with mugs, kettles, warming pans, and measures are easiest to find. Stills ranging in sizes of up to 50-gallon are popular with collectors today. Mary Frank Gaston has compiled a lovely book, *Antique Brass and Copper,* with many full-color photos and current market values which we recommend for more information. Mrs. Gaston is listed in the Directory under Texas. See also Arts and Crafts, Roycroft, Stickley, and other specific categories.

Bucket, snake-form hdl, 9" dia.. 50.00
Candy pan, iron hdls, 14" dia 195.00
Coffeepot, Georgian, applewood hdl, 11", VG 345.00
Finial, ball form on stepped sq base, verdigris, 20½" 1,175.00
Fish poacher, emb rampant lion/fleur-de-lis, brass ears, 23" L....... 315.00
Funnel, 6x6" 35.00
Kettle, apple butter; dvtl, iron hdl, lg.. 100.00
Kettle, brass finial/swing hdl, sgn C Raborg, dvtl, dents, 6½"....1,495.00
Lavabo, Fr, ca 1830, lg, on pnt pine stand: 73x30x16" 2,000.00
Pail, jelly; tin lined, 11x12½" 325.00
Pitcher, water; emb geometrics, silver ice lip, Taxco, 7½x9" 750.00
Plaque, fisherman's profile in relief, 9½" dia in 12" sq copper fr ... 150.00
Pot, hand-hammered, tin lined, riveted hdls, Gallard Paris, 18x24" dia...500.00
Pot, heavy CI hdl, 4x8½" dia.. 125.00
Pot, 2 appl hdls, 10x21" dia 125.00

Steam washer, dated 1925, 19x17", NM, $175.00. (Photo courtesy Morphy Auctions)

Teakettle, dvtl, gooseneck spout, brass hdl on dome lid, 10¾" 490.00
Teakettle, dvtl, shaped & hinged hdl, sm dents, ca 1800, 8x13x9" ..225.00
Teakettle, dvtl, swivel hdl mk J Grimes Pittsburgh, rpr, 7" 400.00
Wash boiler, metal hdls w/wooden pulls, Behrens Mfg, w/lid, 12x13" ..165.00
Watering can, angular hdl, EX patina, 17x25" 75.00
Wine cooler, 4 paw ft, ca 1900, 12½x18" 250.00

Copper Lustre

Copper lustre is a term referring to a type of pottery made in Staffordshire after the turn of the nineteenth century. It is finished in a metallic rusty-brown glaze resembling true copper. Pitchers are found in abundance, ranging from simple styles with dull bands of color to those with fancy handles and bands of embossed, polychromed flowers. Bowls are common; goblets, mugs, teapots, and sugar bowls much less so. It's easy to find, but not in good condition. Pieces with hand-painted decoration and those with historical transfers are the most valuable.

Butter pat, cobalt & wht center scene, 4" 45.00
Creamer, bl band w/Gen Jackson Hero of New Orleans portraits, 5¾"...2,200.00
Cup & saucer, House, mini, 1¼" 25.00
Mug, bl band, 3" 100.00
Salt cellar, House band, pk int, ftd 85.00
Vase, shepherdess w/sheep (purple transfer), hdls, 7" 225.00

Coralene Glass

Coralene is a unique type of art glass easily recognized by the tiny grains of glass that form its decoration. Lacy allover patterns of seaweed, geometrics, and florals were used, as well as solid forms such as fish, plants, and single blossoms. (Seaweed is most commonly found and not as valuable as the other types of decoration.) It was made by several glasshouses both here and abroad. Values are based to a considerable extent on the amount of beading that remains. Our readers should know that recent coralene has raised bead decoration that is at least 10 millimeters thick.

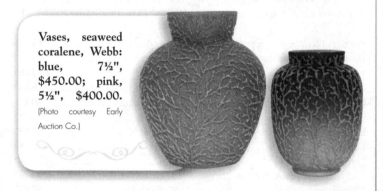

Vases, seaweed coralene, Webb: blue, 7½", $450.00; pink, 5½", $400.00. (Photo courtesy Early Auction Co.)

Bowl, peachblow w/yel seaweed, dk red int, everted cut rim, 7"... 400.00
Bowl, pk, Dmn Quilt w/gold fleur-de-lis, 4-lobe, 8" 450.00
Cup, pk shading to wht w/yel seaweed, frosted hdl, 3¾x3"........... 100.00
Rose bowl, yel-cased w/gold foliage, 3-ftd, 3⅝x5", NM 300.00
Vase, bicolor rainbow satin w/yel seaweed, smooth rim, 7½" 275.00
Vase, bl satin w/yel seaweed, pulled/ruffled rim, 8⅛" 150.00
Vase, lemon-cased w/wildflowers/butterfly, ruffled rim, 8¾".......... 325.00
Vase, reserve w/lady's portrait sgn T LeRoy, beading in scrolls, 20" ..1,840.00
Vase, rose Dmn Quilt w/yel wheat, slightly bulbous, 6½x5¼" 325.00
Vase, yel to wht w/yel seaweed, bulbous, flared neck, 7"............... 150.00

Cordey

The Cordey China Company was founded in 1942 in Trenton, New Jersey, by Boleslaw Cybis. The operation was small with less than a dozen workers. They produced figurines, vases, lamps, and similar wares, much of which was marketed through gift shops both nationwide and abroad. Though the earlier wares were made of plaster, Cybis soon developed his own formula for a porcelain composition which he called 'Papka.' Cordey figurines and busts were characterized by old-world charm, Rococo scrolls, delicate floral appliques, ruffles, and real lace which was dipped in liquefied clay to add dimension to the work.

Although on rare occasions some items were not numbered or signed, the 'basic' figure was cast both with numbers and the Cordey signature. The molded pieces were then individually decorated and each marked with its own impressed identification number as well as a mark to indicate the artist-decorator. Their numbering system began with 200

and in later years progressed into the 8000s. As can best be established, Cordey continued production until sometime in the mid-1950s. Boleslaw Cybis died in 1957, his wife in 1958.

Due to the increased availability of Cordey on the Internet over the last year, values of the more common pieces have fallen off. All items in our listings are considered to be in mint condition unless noted otherwise. Our advisor for this category is Sharon A. Payne; she is listed in the Directory under Washington.

#313, bust of lady, sgn MB Cybis 225.00
#914, clock, rococo scrolls & appl roses w/gold, Lanshire, 9½" 65.00
#1047, vase, rtcl top w/apple blossom band, 12", EX 75.00
#1949, bust of lady, drilled for lamp, 7" 60.00
#4027, lady w/parasol, 8" 80.00
#4049-P, lady, 10" 85.00
#4074, gentleman, lace shirt neck & cuffs, 13" 125.00
#4128, lady in lacy gown, curls, dbl bustle, 10½" 165.00
#5002, bust of lady in pk w/roses at base & in hair, 5¾" 45.00
#5009, bust of lady, bl Fedora-style hat, 6", from $45 to 40.00
#5011, bust of lady in wht w/lg collar, gold rose at base & hair, 6". 45.00
#5020, bust of man in pk w/lg wht curls, 2 roses at base, 6½" 60.00
#5025, bust of lady w/lace shawl, 6" 45.00
#5026, bust of madonna w/wht shawl, gold at base, 6" 45.00
#5034, Raleigh, bust of man, gr shirt, blk vest, 8½" 70.00
#5037, bust of lady (¾) in bl dress w/red roses in hair, 9½" 65.00
#5045, girl w/water jug, 10½" 65.00
#5047/#5048, man & lady, she w/grapes/jar, he w/flowers, 11", pr ...125.00
#5051, bust of lady in cream dress, bl ribbon at neck, bl hat w/roses .. 75.00
#5054, bust of lady (¾) in wht w/roses at base & in hair, 9" 75.00
#5059, bust of Victorian lady (¾), 9½".. 75.00
#5077, woman praying, 13" 90.00
#5084, Madame DuBarry in bl & pk, 11" 125.00
#5091, man holds coattail wide as if to bow, 10½"......................... 55.00
#5138, bust of lady w/bl bow on dress & bl Fedora hat, Papka curls, 6" .. 40.00
#7028, wall shelf, Art Nouveau nude w/cornucopia, 8x6½"........... 85.00
#9009, clock, appl roses, clockworks mk Lanshire, 13x11½".......... 65.00
Lamp, bluebird atop flowers & buds, floral-embr shade, ca 1940, 24" ..85.00
Lamps, ladies' high-button shoe, appl flowers, brass base, 30", pr. 125.00
Wall sconces (pr)+busts of lady & man, mid-1940s, 4 pcs 200.00

Corkscrews

The history of the corkscrew dates back to the mid-1600s, when winemakers concluded that the best-aged wine was that stored in smaller containers, either stoneware or glass. Since plugs left unsealed were often damaged by rodents, corks were cut off flush with the bottle top and sealed with wax or a metal cover. Removing the cork cleanly with none left to grasp became a problem. The task was found to be relatively simple using the worm on the end of a flintlock gun rod. So the corkscrew evolved. Endless patents have been issued for mechanized models. Handles range from carved wood, ivory, and bone to porcelain and repousse silver. Exotic materials such as agate, mother-of-pearl, and gold plate were also used on occasion. Celluloid lady's legs are popular.

For further information, we recommend *The Ultimate Corkscrew Book* and *Bull's Pocket Guide to Corkscrews* by Donald Bull, our advisor for this category. He is listed in the Directory under Virginia. In the following descriptions, values are for examples in excellent condition, unless noted otherwise.

Advertising, loop hdl w/emb Made for Franco's Wines..., from $60 to...80.00
Art, kissing birds pull, Just Anderson, Denmark, from $125 to.... 150.00
Art, man & satyr wrestling grapes pull, bronze, from $150 to 175.00
Barrel (closed), continually turning hdl, chrome, Italy, $30 to 40.00

Bow, folding, faceted, unmk, from $40 to 70.00
Bow, folding, w/cap-lifter frets, from $60 to 80.00
Bow, folding, w/corkscrew only, from $10 to 50.00
Can-opener combination, Re-Cap-O, Ransom Co, Detroit, from $10 to 15.00
Cellarman's, 2-finger simple oval hdl, Zeitz, from $50 to 60.00
Champagne knife combination w/folding screw & cleaning brush, $600 to...800.00
Clough's 1876 Pat, mk Williamson's on wire wrap, 3¾" hdl, $25 to... 35.00
Columbus, mk Industria Argentina Gaumen M Reg, from $75 to ..100.00
Cork lifter, single blade, mk Bte SGDG, from $400 to 500.00
Dbl-lever, A1, James Heeley & Sons, Birmingham...1888, from $125 to..175.00
Dbl-lever, clown figural, aluminum, Italy, 1950s-60s, from $150 to..200.00
Figural, Bar Bum, pnt aluminum or bronze, from $40 to 50.00
Figural, fish swallowing worm, cast metal, mk JB, from $50 to....... 60.00

Figural, lady's legs, metal and celluloid, German (Graff & Schmidt), 2¾", EX, $375.00.

(Photo courtesy Wm. Morford Auctions)

Figural, mouse (sm) w/corkscrew tail, Germany, from $100 to..... 125.00
Figural, red devil on triangular cap-lifter base, from $100 to........ 125.00
Figural, 2 horse heads of amber plastic as 2-finger pull, $90 to..... 100.00
Flynut, brass colored, hourglass bbl, Spain, from $50 to 60.00
Flynut, wooden embellishments riveted to hdl & flynut, from $100 to....125.00
Frame, George Willet's 1884, The Surprise, copper plated, from $75 to ..100.00
Frame, ornate casting, w/spring & wood hdl, from $200 to 300.00
Frame, ornate w/verdigris & gold-tone, rollover hdl, from $80 to ...100.00
Ivory hdl w/bulbous shank & gripper button, from $125 to.......... 250.00
Lazy tongs, Pullezi, Henry Armstrong's 1902 Pat, from $150 to ... 300.00
Lazy tongs, Zigzag, most common, many variations, from $30 to . 100.00
Murphy, acorn hdl w/fr mk R Murphy Boston, from $80 to 100.00
Needle, reciprocating pump action, Corkette, from $1 to.............. 10.00
Peg & worm, button, faceted or ball ends, ea from $75 to............ 200.00
Picnic, sheet metal swiveling cap lifter, English, in case, $25 to 30.00
Picnic, unmk brass hex head w/machined-in cap lifter, from $25 to 35.00
Pocket folder, over-the-top cap lifter, H Vaughan Pat 1924, $25 to ..50.00
Pocket folder, Tip Top, Williamson on Newark NJ, from $40 to.... 60.00
Prong puller, swivel cap lifter, For Crown Corks..., from $90 to ... 100.00
Rack & pinion, bbl-form w/Pat plate mk Dowler, from $800 to .. 1,400.00
Roundlet, machined & eng NP w/threaded case, from $150 to ... 250.00
Roundlet, mottled gr celluloid, from $100 to 125.00
Rundlet, gold w/worm shank, Germany/14k & initials, from $800 to.. 1,000.00
Single lever, Sperry, Pat 1878, from $2,500 to 3,500.00
Slide-out worm, German or Fr version of Jansen Pat, from $150 to...250.00
Spoon combination, SP, Pat Walker & Orr, 1932, from $100 to.. 125.00
Spring, Dunisch & Scholer's 1883 German Pat w/advertising, $100 to...150.00
T-hdl, bone, ivory, or brass, direct pull, mini, 1-2¾", $30 to......... 200.00
T-hdl, machined brass, mid-sz, from $60 to.................................... 70.00
T-hdl, metal, clawfoot hdl w/bulbed shank, from $100 to 125.00
T-hdl, metal, 2-finger grip, Jacques Perille, from $100 to.............. 150.00
Thomason, bbl eng w/Gothic windows, from $1,500 to 2,000.00
Traveling type, w/funnel, cap lifter & corkscrew, in case, $100 to...150.00
Tusk w/cvd long-beaked bird on branch, bell cap on shank, $450 to..600.00
Waiter's friend, cast mermaid figural, Davis Improved..., $1,000 to..1,200.00
Waiter's friend, w/bottle cap lifter, advertising, from $5 to............. 25.00
Whistle combination, metal roundlet, unscrews to open, from $300 to...350.00

Williamson's, Don't Swear, opener combination, Catalin sheath, $25 to.. 50.00
Wood T-hdl, direct pull w/brush & foil cutter, from $40 to.......... 275.00
2-finger pull, Commercial, from $30 to...................................... 80.00
3-finger pull (eyebrow) leather-wrapped hdl, from $75 to 100.00
4-finger pull, foil cutter/wire breaker at hdl, from $50 to................ 75.00
5-in-1 tool, Napier, lifter+corkscrew+funnel+measure+resealer, $50 to... 75.00

Cosmos

Cosmos, sometimes called Stemless Daisy, is a patterned glass tableware produced from 1894 through 1915 by Consolidated Lamp and Glass Company. Relief-molded flowers on a finely crosscut background were painted in soft colors of pink, blue, and yellow. Though nearly all were made of milk glass, a few items may be found in clear glass with the designs painted on. In addition to the tableware, lamps were also made.

All prices are for pieces in very good condition. Some roughness or 'fleabites' around the edges of most pieces (e.g. lamp globes, top of the covered butter dish) are acceptable, except for the tumblers where they severely reduce their value. Any cracks or significant chips reduce the values considerably. These are average 'selling' prices; some dealers may ask as much as 20% to 30% more but will often come down to close a sale. Our advisors for this category are Michael A. and Valarie Bozarth (info@ BeauxArtsUSA.com). They are listed in the Directory under New York.

Bottle, cologne; w/stopper, rare, 4¾" 275.00
Butter dish, underplate only 45.00
Butter dish, 5x8" 180.00
Condiment set, w/orig lids, rare.. 325.00
Creamer, 5" 90.00
Lamp, base only, 7" 105.00
Lamp, mini; base only, 3½"... 65.00
Lamp, mini; w/globe, 7½" 290.00
Lamp, w/globe, 16".. 425.00
Pickle castor, fr mk Toronto, rare 690.00
Pitcher, milk; 5" 250.00
Pitcher, water; 9"... 190.00
Shakers, w/orig lids, 2½", pr.. 130.00
Spooner, 4" 95.00
Sugar bowl, open.. 90.00
Sugar bowl, w/lid.. 165.00
Sugar shaker, rare.. 350.00
Syrup pitcher, rare, 6½" 325.00
Tumbler, 3¾"... 55.00
Water set, pitcher (9") w/six tumblers... 525.00

Cottageware

You'll find a varied assortment of novelty dinnerware items, all styled as cozy little English cottages or huts with cone-shaped roofs; some may have a waterwheel or a windmill. Marks will vary. English-made Price Brothers or Beswick pieces are valued in the same range as those marked Occupied Japan, while items marked simply Japan are considerably less pricey. All of the following examples are Price Brothers/Kensington unless noted otherwise.

Bank, dbl slot, 4½x3½x5" 80.00
Bell, minimum value.. 50.00
Biscuit jar, wicker hdl, Maruhon Ware, Occupied Japan, 6½"........ 80.00
Bowl, salad 50.00
Butter dish... 50.00
Butter dish, cottage int (fireplace), Japan, 6¾x5" 70.00
Butter dish, oval, Burlington Ware, 6" 60.00

Butter dish, rnd, Beswick, England, w/lid, 3½x6" 75.00
Butter pat, emb cottage, rectangular, Occupied Japan 20.00
Chocolate pot, from $85 to 110.00
Condiment set, mustard, 2½" s&p on 5" hdld leaf tray 75.00
Condiment set, mustard pot, s&p, tray, row arrangement, 6" 45.00
Condiment set, mustard pot, s&p, tray, row arrangement, 7¾" 45.00
Condiment set, 3-part cottage on shaped tray w/appl bush, 4½" 75.00
Cookie jar, pk/brn/gr, sq, Japan, 8½x5½" 60.00
Cookie jar, windmill, wicker hdl 145.00
Cookie jar/canister, cylindrical, 8½x5" 125.00
Cookie/biscuit jar, Occupied Japan 80.00
Covered dish, Occupied Japan, sm 35.00
Creamer, windmill, Occupied Japan, 2⅝" 25.00
Creamer & sugar bowl, 2½x4½" 40.00
Cup & saucer, chocolate; str-sided cup, 3½x2¾", 5½" 32.00
Cup & saucer, 2½", 4½" 35.00
Demitasse pot 90.00
Egg cup set, 4 on 6" sq tray 65.00

Gravy boat, rare, 7" long, $200.00.

Hot water pot, Westminster, England, 8½x4" 50.00
Marmalade 45.00
Marmalade & jelly, 2 conjoined houses 75.00
Mug, 3⅞" 40.00
Pin tray, 4", dia 20.00
Pitcher, emb cottage, lg flower on hdl 100.00
Pitcher, tankard; rnd, 7⅞" 80.00
Platter, oval, 11¾x7½" 60.00
Reamer, windmill, Japan 150.00
Sugar box, for cubes, 5¾" L 40.00
Tea set, Japan, child's, serves 4 .... 165.00
Teapot, Keele Street, w/creamer & sugar bowl 65.00
Teapot, Occupied Japan, 6½" 45.00
Teapot, Ye Olde Fireside, Occupied Japan, 9x5" 65.00
Teapot, 6¼" 45.00
Toast rack, 3-slot, 3½" 75.00
Toast rack, 4-slot, 5½" 85.00
Tumbler, Occupied Japan, 3½", set of 6 .... 65.00

Coverlets

The Jacquard attachment for hand looms represented a culmination of weaving developments made in France. Introduced to America by the early 1820s, it gave professional weavers the ability to easily create complex patterns with curved lines. Those who could afford the new loom adaptation could now use hole-punched pasteboard cards to weave floral patterns that before could only be achieved with intense labor on a draw-loom.

Before the Jacquard mechanism, most weavers made their coverlets in geometric patterns. Use of indigo-blue and brightly colored wools often livened the twills and overshot patterns available to the small-loom home weaver. Those who had larger multiple-harness looms could produce warm double-woven, twill-block, or summer-and-winter designs.

While the new floral and pictorial patterns' popularity had displaced the geometrics in urban areas, the mid-Atlantic, and the Midwest by the 1840s, even factory production of the Jacquard coverlets was disrupted by cotton and wool shortages during the Civil War. A revived production in the 1870s saw a style change to a center-medallion motif, but a new fad for white 'Marseilles' spreads soon halted sales of Jacquard-woven coverlets. Production of Jacquard carpets continued to the turn of the century.

Rural and frontier weavers continued to make geometric-design coverlets through the nineteenth century, and local craft revivals have continued the tradition through this century. All-cotton overshots were factory produced in Kentucky from the 1940s, and factories and professional weavers made cotton-and-wool overshots during the past decade. Many Jacquard-woven coverlets have dates and names of places and people (often the intended owner — not the weaver) woven into corners or borders.

Note: In the listings that follow, examples are blue and white and in excellent condition unless noted otherwise. When dates are given, they actually appear on the coverlet itself as part of the woven design.

Key: mdl — medallion

Jacquard

Biederwand, birds w/young, Christian & Heathen border, 1-pc, 86x82" ... 715.00
Biederwand, central mdl, red/bl/sage gr/natural, 1-pc, 90x83" 600.00
Biederwand, floral/star/birds, red/gr/bl/natural, 1-pc, 1950, 90x66" ... 635.00
Biederwand, Peace & Plenty, bl/natural, 1855, 90x72"+fringe 490.00
Biederwand, roses/grapevines, navy/teal/red/natural, sgn, 2-pc, 92x76" .. 550.00
Biederwand, stars/mdls, birds & tree border, Peace & Plenty, 2-pc, EX .. 490.00
Biederwand, stars/vines/flowers, red/2 bls/natural, 2-pc, 1849, 92x70" ... 500.00
Central mdl w/sm triangles, plume border, red/natural, 1-pc, 79x74" 300.00
Floral tile w/multiple borders, bl/red/gr/natural, 1-pc, 88x82"+fringe 260.00
Geometrics w/pine tree border, 2-pc, dbl weave, lt stains, 68x62" ... 100.00
Lily/acorn mdl, red/gr/navy/natural, 2-pc, summer/winter, 88x76" ... 925.00
Muir family symbol/thistles/bellflowers, 2-pc, dbl weave, 84x78" .. 200.00
Rose mdl, bird border, red/bl/natural, 2-pc, PA/1834, 85x62" 635.00
Rose mdls/grapevine borders, 4-color, 2-pc, sgn/1836, 76x92" 545.00
Roses/circles, 3 borders, red/gr/bl/natural, single weave, 90x82" .. 500.00
Silver dollar/eagles/stars, 2-pc, 73x84" 315.00
Star/fruit mdl, deer/state capitol borders, red/wht summer/winter, 90" ... 260.00
Stylized foliage, bl/red/olive wool, 1-pc, PA, 90x77"+fringe 500.00
Tulips/rosettes, floral borders, 2-pc, dbl weave, 1840, 90x75"+fringe .. 660.00

Overshot

Cloverleaves/checkerboards, red/gr/slate bl, 2-pc, PA, 64x68" 935.00
Geometric, navy/gold/natural, 2-pc, sm rstr, 92x90" 425.00
Geometric, red/blk, linen, 2-pc, 19th C, 83x72" 265.00
Geometric, rose/red/blk, linen, 3-part, NC, 19th C, 91x74" 275.00
Geometric, rust/navy/cream, 2-pc, 3 sides fringed, 1910s, 88x74" ... 470.00
Geometric floral, blk/cream, dtd 1840, 95x73" 450.00
Geometric w/border on 3 sides, bl/wht, 2-pc, 91x72" 480.00
Optical, dk bl/cream, wool & linen, 2-pc, NC, 95x74" 950.00
Optical, lt & dk bl, 2-pc, fringe on 3 sides, 96x70" 300.00
Optical, red/blk, 2-pc, minor wear, 88x76" 200.00

Cowan

Guy Cowan opened a small pottery near Cleveland, Ohio, in 1913, where he made tile and artware on a small scale from the natural red clay available there. He developed distinctive glazes — necessary, he felt, to cover the dark red body. After the war and a temporary halt in production, Cowan moved his pottery to Rocky River, where he made a commercial line of artware utilizing a highly fired white porcelain. Although he acquiesced to the necessity of mass production, every effort was made to ensure a product of highest quality. Fine artists, among them Waylande Gregory, Thelma Frazier, and Viktor Schreckengost, designed pieces which were often produced in limited editions, some of which sell today for prices in the thousands. Most of the ware was marked 'Cowan,' except for the 1930 mass-produced line called 'Lakeware.' Falling under the crunch of the Great Depression, the pottery closed in 1931.

The use of an asterisk (*) in the listing below indicates a nonfactory name that is being provided as a suggested name for the convenience of present-day collectors. One example is the glaze *Original Ivory, which is a high-gloss white that resembles undecorated porcelain. It was used on many of Cowan's lady 'flower figures' (Cowan's more graceful term for what some collectors call frogs). For more information, we recommend *Cowan Pottery and the Cleveland School,* by Mark Bassett and Victoria Naumann. Our prices are for marked examples in mint condition, unless noted otherwise.

Ashtray, Denset, Parchment, gr, W Gregory, #925, 5½" 55.00
Bookends, Boy & Girl, F Wilcox, *Orig Ivory, #519, 6½" 375.00
Bookends, kneeling camels, beige/brn crackle, A Blazys, 9x10" .. 3,900.00
Bookends, Sunbonnet Girl, gr crystalline, 7¼" 240.00
Bookends, toucan, blk/silver/bronze finish, Jacobson, 5¼" 2,800.00
Bookends, unicorn, mottled ochre & mahog gloss, 7¼", NM 400.00
Bowl, Columbine, #731, 5x16x11", from $75 to 125.00
Bowl, Logan, Dawn, RG Cowan, #537-A, 2½x7" 50.00
Bowl, Lohengrin, Azure, #B-11-B, 3¼x13¼x9½", from $55 to 75.00
Bowl, Nasturtium, #713-X, 4x13x9" 55.00
Bowl, Terpsichore, Hyacinth, W Gregory, #785-A, 9x12½x9" 90.00
Candelabrum figurine, Swirl Dancer, Special Ivory, #745, 9½" 650.00
Candlesticks, Apple Blossom Pink, #734, 4", pr 20.00
Candlesticks, Byzantine Angel, yel wash, #846, ca 1928, 9", pr... 220.00
Candlesticks, draped lady, Old Ivory, 1927, 12½", pr, NM 350.00
Candlesticks, low hdls, Larkspur, #528, 3½", pr 60.00
Candy box, R Josset, *Pippin Green, #X-14, 6¼" 250.00
Charger, leaping maids/foliage, leathery beige semi-matt, 13"... 1,140.00
Decanter, Arabian Night, #X-16, 10½", +4 matching cups 500.00
Figurine, Bird & Wave, Egyptian Blue, sm rstr, #749A, 12¼" 200.00
Figurine, dancer, Old Ivory, rstr, #792, 8" 300.00
Figurine, elephant w/tucked trunk on sq ft, orange matt, 4¾" 235.00
Figurine, flamingo, Oriental Red, W Gregory, #D-2-D, 11" 400.00
Figurine, Wildwood Stag, Caramel, W Gregory, #926, rstr, 13¼" .. 45.00

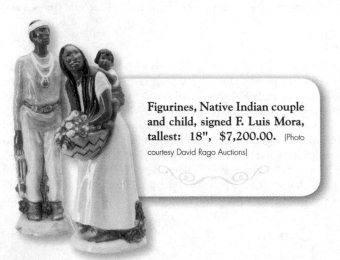

Figurines, Native Indian couple and child, signed F. Luis Mora, tallest: 18", $7,200.00. (Photo courtesy David Rago Auctions)

Flower frog, Art Deco nude w/draped scarf, wht, 7x5¼x4" 325.00
Flower frog, Awakening, Special Ivory, RG Cowan, #F-8, 9" 650.00
Flower frog, dancing nudes (2), *Orig Ivory, #685, 7½x6 14" 200.00
Flower frog, Mayflower Stag, Special Ivory, W Gregory, #905, 8¼"....500.00
Flower frog, Scarf Dancer, *Orig Ivory, RG Cowan, #686, 6" 200.00

Humidor, 6-sided w/goat finial, Oriental Red, E Eckhardt, 8" 300.00
Jar, strawberry; April Green, RG Cowan, #SJ-3, 12" 220.00
Lamp base, emb upright leaves, Antique Green, ftd, 11x7" 225.00
Lamp base, Oriental Red, W Atchley, #L-13, 10" 150.00
Plate, Thunderbird, Guave, A Blazys, #750, 15½", from $450 to. 600.00
Serving set, Colonial, Special Ivory, #X-24/#X-25/#X-33, cr/sug+tray ... 120.00
Vase, Copper, #544, 6" 120.00
Vase, dk bl drips on lt bl, flared rim, shouldered, 13¼" 450.00
Vase, floral (stylized), blk on yel to gr, bulbous, 9" 1,100.00
Vase, Sea Horse, Lapis, fan form, #715-B, 8", NM 120.00

Cracker Jack

Kids have been buying Cracker Jack since it was first introduced in the 1890s. By 1912 it was packaged with a free toy inside. Before the first kernel was crunched, eager fingers had retrieved the surprise from the depth of the box — actually no easy task, considering the care required to keep the contents so swiftly displaced from spilling over the side! Though a little older, perhaps, many of those same kids still are looking — just as eagerly — for the Cracker Jack prizes. Point of sale, company collectibles, and the prizes as well have over the years reflected America's changing culture. Grocer sales and incentives from around the turn of the century — paper dolls, postcards, and song books — were often marked Rueckheim Brothers (the inventors of Cracker Jack) or Reliable Confections. Over the years the company made some changes, leaving a trail of clues that often help collectors date their items. The company's name changed in 1922 from Rueckheim Brothers & Eckstein (who had been made a partner for inventing a method for keeping the caramelized kernels from sticking together) to The Cracker Jack Company. Their Brooklyn office was open from 1914 until it closed in 1923. The first time the Sailor Jack logo was used on their packaging was in 1919. The sailor image of a Rueckheim child (with red, white, and blue colors) was introduced by these German immigrants in an attempt to show support for the U.S.A. during the time of heightened patriotism after WW I. For packages and 'point of sale' dating, note that the word 'prize' was used from 1912 to 1925, 'novelty' from 1925 to 1932, and 'toy' from 1933 on.

The first loose-packed prizes were toys made of wood, clay, tin, metal, and lithographed paper (the reason some early prizes are stained). Plastic toys were introduced in 1946. Paper wrapped for safety purposes in 1948, subjects echo the 'hype' of the day — yo-yos, tops, whistles, and sports cards in the simple, peaceful days of our country, propaganda and war toys in the '40s, games in the '50s, and space toys in the '60s. Few of the estimated 15 billion prizes were marked. Advertising items from Angelus Marshmallow and Checkers Confections (cousins of the Cracker Jack family) are also collectible. When no condition is indicated, the items listed below are assumed to be in excellent to mint condition. 'CJ' indicates that the item is marked. Note: An often-asked question concerns the tin Toonerville Trolley called 'CJ.' No data has been found in the factory archives to authenticate this item; it is assumed that the 'CJ' merely refers to its small size. For further information see *Cracker Jack Toys, The Complete, Unofficial Guide for Collectors,* by Larry White. Our advisor for this category is Harriet Joyce; she is listed in the Directory under under Florida. Also look for *The Prize Insider* newsletter listed in the Directory under Clubs, Newsletters, and Catalogs.

Dealer Incentives and Premiums

Badge, pin-bk, celluloid, lady w/CJ label on bk, 1905, 1¼" 85.00
Blotter, CJ question mk box, yel, 7¾x3¾" 185.00
Book, pocket; riddle/sailor boy/dog on cover, RWB, CJ, 1919........ 14.00
Book, Uncle Sam Song Book, CJ, 1911, ea..................................... 18.00
Jigsaw puzzle, CJ or Checkers, 1 of 4, 7x10", in envelope.............. 35.00
Mirror, oval, Angelus (redhead or blond) on box 60.00

Pen, ink; w/nib, tin litho bbl, CJ 485.00
Puzzle, metal, CJ/Checkers, 1 of 15, 1934, in envelope, ea............. 12.00
Thimble, aluminum, CJ Co/Angelus, red pnt, rare, ea 120.00
Wings, Air Corps type, silver or blk, stud-bk, CJ, 1930s, 3", ea...... 35.00

Packaging

Box, popcorn; red scroll border, CJ 'Prize,' 1912-25, ea 300.00
Canister, tin, CJ Candy Corn Crisp, 10-oz.................................. 75.00
Canister, tin, CJ Coconut Corn Crisp, 10-oz................................ 65.00
CJ Commemorative canister, wht w/red scroll, 1980s 5.00

Prizes, Cast Metal

Badge, 6-point star, mc CJ Police, silver, 1931, 1¼" 55.00
Coins, Presidents, 31 series, CJ, mk cancelled on bk, 1933, ea 18.00
Pistol, soft lead, inked, CJ on bbl, early, rare, 2⅛" 180.00
Rocking horse, no rider, 3-D, inked, early, 1⅛"............................ 15.00
Spinner, early pkg in center, 'More You Eat...,' CJ, rare................ 295.00

Prizes, Paper

Book, Animals (or Birds) To Color, Makatoy, unmk, 1949, mini... 35.00
Book, Birds We Know, CJ, 1928, mini 90.00
Book, Twigg & Sprigg, CJ, 1930, mini 90.00
Disguise, glasses, hinged, w/eyeballs, unmk, 1933............................ 6.00
Fortune Teller, boy/dog on film in envelope, CJ, 1920s, 1¾x2½" ... 80.00
Hat, Me for CJ, early, ea 120.00
Magic game book, erasable slate, CJ, series of 13, 1946, ea 15.00
Movie, pull tab for 2nd picture, yel, early, 3", in envelope 125.00

Movie star cards, star's history on back, directions for child to write in the star's name on the front, very rare, 32 in the series, from $5.00 to $100.00 each. (Photo courtesy Harriet Joyce)

Sand toy pictures, pours for action, series of 14, 1967, ea 65.00
Transfer, iron-on, sport figure or patriotic, unmk, 1939, ea................ 6.00
Whistle, Blow for More, CJ/Angelus pkgs, 1928, '31 or '33, ea...... 45.00
Whistle, Razz Zooka, C Carey Cloud design, CJ, 1949.................... 25.00

Prizes, Plastic

Animals, standup, letter on bk, series of 26, Nosco, 1953, ea............ 2.00
Figure, circus; stands on base, 1 of 12, Nosco, 1951-54 .... 3.00
Palm puzzle, ball(s) roll into holes, dome or rnd, from 1966, ea........ 6.00
Palm puzzle, ball(s) roll into holes, sq, CJ, 1920s, ea 45.00
Ships in a bottle, 6 different, unmk, 1960, ea 4.00
Toys, take apart/assemble, variety, from 1962, unassembled, ea 8.00
WWII Cl Cloud punch-out war vehicles, CJ, series of 10, ea.......... 30.00

Prizes, Tin

Badge, boy & dog die-cut, complete w/bend-over tab, CJ 150.00

Bank, 3-D book form, red/gr/or blk, CJ Bank, early, 2" 120.00
Brooch or pin, various designs on card, CJ/logo, early, ea............. 125.00
Doll dishes, tin plated, CJ, 1931, 1¾", 1⅞", & 2⅛" dia, ea 35.00
Horse & wagon, litho die-cut, CJ & Angelus, 2⅛" 45.00
Horse & wagon, litho die-cut, gray/red mks, CJ, 1914-23, 3⅛" 350.00
Pocket watch, silver or gold, CJ as numerals, 1931, 1½" 30.00
Small box shape, electric stove litho, unmk, 1⅛" 80.00
Soldier, litho, die-cut standup, officer/private/etc, unmk, ea 17.00
Spinner, wood stick, Fortune Teller Game, red/wht/bl, CJ, 1½"..... 90.00
Spinner, wood stick, 2 Toppers, red/wht/bl, Angelus/Jack, 1½"...... 55.00
Tall box shape, Frozen Foods locker freezer, unmk, 1947, 1¾" 75.00
Tall box shape, grandfather clock, unmk, 1947, 1¾" 65.00
Train, engine & tender, litho, CJ Line/512 .... 95.00
Train, litho engine only, red, unmk, 1941 .... 10.00
Truck, litho, RWB, CJ/Angelus, 1931, ea................................... 45.00
Wagon shape: CJ Shows, yel circus wagon, series of 5, ea 175.00
Wheelbarrow, tin plated, bk leg in place, CJ, 1931, 2½" L 28.00

Miscellaneous

Ad, Saturday Evening Post, mc, CJ, 1919, 11x14" 18.00
Lunch box, tin emb, CJ, 1970s, 4x7x9"...................................... 30.00
Medal, CJ salesman award, brass, 1939, scarce............................. 125.00
Sign, bathing beauty, 5-color cb, CJ, early, 17x22" 600.00
Sign, Santa & prizes, mc cb, Angelus, early, lg 220.00
Sign, Santa & prizes, mc cb, CJ, early, lg 265.00

Crackle Glass

Though this type of glassware was introduced as early as the 1880s (by the New England Glass Co.), it was made primarily from 1930 until about 1980. It was produced by more than 500 companies here (by Benko, Rainbow, and Kanawah, among others) and abroad (by such companies as Moser), and its name is descriptive. The surface looks as though the glass has been heated then plunged into cold water, thus producing a network of tight cracks. It was made in a variety of colors; among the more expensive today are ruby red, amberina, cobalt, cranberry, and gray. For more information we recommend *Crackle Glass From Around the World* by Stan and Arlene Weitman, our advisors this category; they are listed in the Directory under New York. See also Moser.

Ashtray, dk bl, Viking, 1944-70, 7¼", from $35 to 45.00
Basket, bl w/crystal hdl, tall, Pilgrim, 1949-69, 5¼", from $75 to. 100.00
Bowl, cranberry w/floral decor, Moser, 1920s, 3¼", from $400 to. 425.00
Bowl, lt bl, scalloped rim, Blenko, 1960s, 2½", from $55 to 65.00
Candlesticks, bl, triple bulb cylinder, Rainbow, 1940s-60s, 6", pr....175.00
Candy dish, amberina, Kanawha, 1957-87, 3", from $55 to 65.00
Candy dish, topaz, crystal ribbed drop-over hdl, Hamon, 2¼x5½" ... 125.00
Creamer, bl, drop-over hdl, Rainbow, 1957-87, 3", from $40 to..... 50.00
Decanter, amber w/ship, uknown mfg, early 1900s, 8¼", from $350 to...450.00
Decanter, emerald gr, pinched, drop-over hdl, Biscoff, 1950s, 9¾"..150.00
Decanter, smoke gray, teardrop stopper, Pilgrim, 1950s, 11", $175 to.. 250.00
Hat, turquoise, Blenko, 1950s-60s, 3", from $50 to........................ 75.00
Ice bucket, crystal, wht metal hdl, unknown mfg, 5", from $100 to.125.00
Ladle, crystal w/amethyst hdl, Blenko, 1950s, 15" L, from $200 to .. 300.00
Perfume bottle, lt bl, flower stopper, unknown mfg, 4½", $75 to.. 100.00
Perfume bottle, rose crystal, w/rnd stopper, unknown mfg, 6¾" ... 125.00
Pitcher, amethyst, pulled-bk hdl, Hamon, 1940s-66, 5¼", from $70 to .. 80.00
Pitcher, bl, pulled-bk hdl, scalloped, Kanawha, 1957-87, 4", $45 to .. 55.00
Pitcher, mini; amberina, drop-over hdl, Pilgrim, 1949-69, 4", $50 to. 55.00
Pitcher, mini; mc, drop-over hdl, English, late 1800s, 4½", $150 to. 250.00
Pitcher, olive gr, pulled-bk hdl, ruffled rim, Blenko, 1960s, 8¼" .. 125.00

Pitcher, vaseline yel, pulled-bk hdl, waisted, Rainbow, 1940s-60s, 4" ..55.00
Rose bowl, topaz, deep folds at rim, Blenko, 1950s, 4½", $110 to....135.00
Tumbler, juice; gr, unknown mfg, 1920s, 4", from $30 to 50.00
Tumbler, ruby, pinched, Hamon, 1940s-70s, 6", from $85 to........ 100.00
Vase, cobalt satin, bulbous, unknown mfg, 6", from $110 to 120.00
Vase, crystal, block shape, Gillinder, 1930s-50s, 8", from $100 to ...150.00
Vase, crystal w/enameled mushrooms, England, 1900s, 6½", $250 to ...300.00

Vase, fish form, topaz, Hamon, 1940s – early 1970s, rare, from $125.00 to $150.00.

(Photo courtesy Stan and Arlene Weitman)

Vase, orange, ftd, scalloped rim, Blenko, 1940s-50s, 7", from $145 to...175.00
Vase, topaz w/underwater scene, 3-ftd, Moser, 1920s, 4", from $425 to.475.00

Cranberry Glass

Cranberry glass is named for its resemblance to the color of cranberry juice. It was made by many companies both here and abroad, becoming popular in America soon after the Civil War. It was made in free-blown ware as well as mold-blown. Today cranberry glass is being reproduced, and it is sometimes difficult to distinguish the old from the new. Ask a reputable dealer if you are unsure. For further information we recommend *American Art Glass* by John A. Shumann III, available from Collector Books or your local bookstore. See also Cruets; Salts; Sugar Shakers; Syrups.

Basket, Invt T'print, clear hdl, recent, 8x4¼" 85.00
Bowl, appl yel/clear decor, ftd, sq, 5" 175.00
Bowl, mc floral w/gold, clear scallops, brass ft, 5x6⅜" 195.00
Box, HP decor, hinged lid, ormolu base, 5" 150.00
Casket, jewelry; brass enclosure, 4x5½x3½" 200.00
Compote, mc floral w/gold berries, clear ped, 4x6⅛" 135.00
Creamer, ruffled rim, clear hdl, rigaree at neck, shell ft, 4¼" 145.00
Cruet, Baby T'print w/HP decor, clear hdl, cut clear stopper, 6½" ..225.00
Decanter, floral, ribbed, flared rim, hollow stopper, 9¼" 175.00
Decanter, wine; lt ribbing, clear ft/hdl/stopper, 12x3" 180.00
Epergne, single trumpet, crystal rigaree, 12" 230.00
Ewer, mc floral, clear hdl, 8½x4¼" 300.00
Pitcher, diagonal swirl, appl reed hdl, 8½" 115.00
Pitcher, ice bladder, 10x5" 210.00
Pitcher, Invt T'print, bulbous, clear hdl, 7x7", +4 3¾" tumblers.. 380.00
Pitcher, Invt T'print, bulbous, 8" 215.00
Pitcher, w/rainbow stripe of bl/yel, clear hdl, 9" 365.00
Plate, 8" 55.00
Smoke bell 120.00
Tumbler, bellflower eng, 1880s, 3¾" 125.00
Vase, ruffled rim, appl serpentine, 10½" 200.00
Vase, tulip form w/opal flutes, bronze base, 12x5" 450.00

Creamware

Creamware was a type of earthenware developed by Wedgwood in the 1760s and produced by many other Staffordshire potteries, including Leeds.

Since it could be potted cheaply and was light in weight, it became popular abroad as well as in England, due to the lower freight charges involved in its export. It was revived at Leeds in the late nineteenth century, and the type most often reproduced was heavily reticulated or molded in high relief. These later wares are easily distinguished from the originals since they are thicker and tend to craze heavily. See also Leeds; Wedgwood.

Bowl, rtcl basketweave sides, circular base, sm chips, 3¼x8½" 200.00
Charger, emb scalloped rim, ca 1800, 12" L 240.00
Charger, flowers in urn, mc w/bl feather scalloped rim, 19th C, 13"..1,025.00
Desk stand, cherub w/vase, horse & tree, 3 wells w/pots, 19th C, 12"...350.00
Inkwell, Black man's head w/wide open mouth, 1800s, 2½".........250.00
Jug, Bacchus & Ariadne emb scene, Copeland & Garrett, 1830s, 11"...395.00
Jug, Trellis Jug, emb oak leaves/branches, trunk hdl, Meigh, 8¼"....180.00
Teapot, house form w/goose neck, late 18th C, 5" 3,300.00
Tureen, emb/rtcl vines, brn HP/pine-cone finial, w/lid, 18th C, 18" ..325.00
Wall vase, putti emb on cornucopia form, stain/chip, 9½" 300.00
Waste bowl, cauliflower form, wht florets/lg leaves, 1770s, 5" dia..1,380.00

Crown Devon, Devon

Devon and Crown Devon were trade names of S. Fielding and Company, Ltd., an English firm founded after 1879. They produced majolica, earthenware mugs, vases, and kitchenware. In the 1930s they manufactured an exceptional line of Art Deco vases that have recently been much in demand.

Bowl, floral on red lustre, #2551, hairline, 8¾" 150.00
Bowl, galleon, mc w/gold on bl lustre, ped ft, 10¼" 80.00
Bowl, Oriental landscape & dragon on red w/gold, paper label, 9"... 200.00
Chamber pot, transfers w/gold on wht, 6x9½" 60.00
Cigar box, God Save the King, 1937 commemorative, musical, 8¼" L...600.00
Cigarette box, dog in doghouse, sm rstr, 8¾" 325.00
Entree dish, birds & foliage on Rouge Royale lustre, hexagonal 60.00
Figurine, Scottie dog, 10" 35.00
Flask, John Peel, hardwood stopper, fox hdl, musical, 9" 180.00
Ginger jar, chinoiserie scene on bl mottle w/gold, Fieldings, 6" ... 100.00
Ginger jar, peasants on brn w/gold, 9¼" 100.00
Jar, foliage on bl mottle w/gold, ftd baluster, 7½" 200.00
Jar, foliage/tree trunks on orange mottle w/gold, ovoid, 6½" 340.00
Jug, Auld Lang Syne, musical, 6".. 100.00
Jug, Captain Cook, kangaroo hdl, musical, ca 1930, 9", EX.......... 80.00
Jug, chinoiserie florals/branches on burgundy, 9" 110.00
Jug, Daisy Daisy, couple on bicycle, musical, 9" 250.00
Jug, exotic birds w/gold on red lustre, #5099, 8½" 240.00
Jug, floral on gray & blk panel on bright yel, ovoid, loop hdl, 6¼"....50.00
Jug, floral w/gold on Rouge Royale lustre, Fieldings, 5" 50.00
Jug, Sally portrait/street scene/song lyrics, musical, 8" 800.00
Jug, Widdicombe Fair, verse/related scenes, 7½" 140.00
Trinket dish, floral bands on gold, conical lid, ftd, 5½" 450.00
Vase, floral w/gr bands & gold, loop hdls, globular, 6½" 120.00
Vase, flowers & berries w/gold, blk int, hdls, sm ft, 6¼" 60.00
Vase, foliage/trees/buildings on gr fishscale w/gold, ovoid, 4¼" 900.00
Vase, galleon at sea on bl lustre w/gold, baluster, 9" 200.00
Vase, stylized foliage & butterflies on orange w/gold, Fieldings, 8" ..400.00
Vase, tropical fish on Rouge Royale lustre w/gold, 4-scallop, 10½"...325.00
Vases, Etna, roses baskets/swags, gold hdls, 10", pr 130.00
Washbowl & pitcher, medallions on cream, ca 1909, 15" dia, 13" ..375.00

Crown Ducal

The Crown Ducal mark was first used by the A.G. Richardson &

Co. pottery of Tunstall, England, in 1925. The items collectors are taking a particular interest in were decorated by Charlotte Rhead, a contemporary of Suzie Cooper and Clarice Cliff, and a member of the esteemed family of English pottery designers and artists. See also Chintz.

Biscuit barrel, Orange Tree, orig wicker hdl, 6x5½" 415.00
Bowl, Blue Bristol, oval, 10x7¼", pr... 225.00
Bowl, dragon w/brushed gold/mc abstracts, emb leaves ext, C Rhead, 10"...135.00
Bowl, Oriental Lanterns on blk, 1920s, 3½x9¾".......................... 140.00
Butter dish, Orange Tree, rectangular 130.00
Coffeepot, Britannia Rose 145.00
Coffeepot, Orange Tree, rare side hdl, 1930s, 6", NM 135.00
Jam pot, Orange Tree, w/lid & undertray 195.00
Jug, autumn foliage, C Rhead, #4921, 6½" 115.00
Jug, Firefly, orange/yel/gr, 8¼x4¼" 255.00
Lamp, boudoir; stylized flowers, C Rhead, #449?, ca 1935, 10".. 450.00
Mustard pot, Orange Tree.. 325.00
Plate, cake; Orange Tree.. 60.00
Reamer, Orange Tree, triangular, 2¼x5½"................................... 415.00
Shakers, Orange Tree, pr 225.00
Teapot, Britannia Rose, lg 185.00
Teapot, Orange Tree, 5" 135.00
Tureen, Orange Tree, scroll hdls, w/lid, 10" dia 250.00
Vase, Deco flowers, tube lined, C Rhead, 8½"............................. 175.00
Vase, jug form w/3 openings in side, Deco style, #4256/#206, 8½" ... 165.00
Vase, Manchu Dragon, C Rhead, 10¼".. 365.00
Vase, Oriental Lanterns on blk, 1924, 7" 100.00
Vase, Persian Rose, tube lined, C Rhead, #4318, ca 1936, 9"....... 325.00
Vase, Snowglaze, bl floral, C Rhead, 8½" 155.00

Crown Milano

Crown Milano was a line of decorated milk glass (or opal ware) introduced by the Mt. Washington Glass Co. of New Bedford, Massachussetts, in the early 1890s. It had previously been called Albertine Ware. Some pieces are marked with a 'CM,' and many had paper labels. This ware is usually highly decorated and will most likely have a significant amount of gold trim. The shiny pieces were recently discovered to have been called 'Colonial Ware'; these were usually marked with a laurel wreath and a crown. This ware was well received in its day, and outstanding pieces bring high prices on today's market. Our advisors for this category are Wilfred and Dolli Cohen; they are listed in the Directory under California.

Pitcher, Colonial, detailed depiction of a shore bird, heavy gold encrustation, 10", $4,500.00. (Photo courtesy Early Auction Co.)

Biscuit jar, Colonial, couple in period attire in gold reserve, 10"... 425.00
Biscuit jar, floral (pointillism), mc/gilt on cream to pk, SP mts, 8"... 575.00
Biscuit jar, floral/gold scroll medallions on emb opaque body, 7"... 400.00
Biscuit jar, gilt floral on yel to peach, ovoid, SP mts, 8" 460.00

Biscuit jar, mums, gold & earthtones on beige, lid mk MW, 10" .. 700.00
Biscuit jar, oak leaves/acorns, earth tones on pk to cream, SP lid, 8" .. 290.00
Biscuit jar, starfish/seaweed on hobnail sea gr, butterfly finial, 9"...1,100.00
Biscuit jar, thistles, pastel on cream, ovoid, simple metal mts, 8" .. 375.00
Biscuit jar, wild roses w/jewels on orange/yel mottle, SP mts, 8" W....635.00
Bride's bowl, pansies on gray/lav scrolling medallions, on stand, 12"...1,450.00
Creamer & sugar bowl, floral/gold scrolls, w/lid, 5"..................... 650.00
Creamer & sugar bowl, mc pansies on cream to yel, w/gold, 3¾" .. 250.00
Cup & saucer, Colonial, gold scroll medallions w/floral on opal, 5" W ..275.00
Ewer, gold branches/mauve & amber scrolls on opal, pk twist hdl, 14" ..850.00
Ewer, tapestry-like floral, red/gr on cream, brn hdl, shouldered, 12"...2,500.00
Jardiniere, fall leaves/berries, mc/gold on creamy opal, 8½" dia ... 400.00
Lamp, Colonial, mallards/gold leaves, ball shade, vasiform base, 36".. 4,500.00
Lamp, mums on 12" dome shade/font/cylinder std, ornate metal mts, 43" 10,000.00
Pitcher, gold mums on emb panels, bulbous w/cutaway rim, rope hdl, 9".1,200.00
Shaker, daisies on glossy bark texture, 2½", ea............................... 50.00
Shakers, daisies, squat/melon ribbed, 2½", pr............................. 100.00
Shakers, floral, ribbed ovoid w/4 sm ft, 2½", pr......................... 100.00
Syrup, chrysanthemums on wht, melon ribs, emb metal lid, 5½" .. 635.00
Tray, Colonial, pansies/gold on wht w/blk edge, 2 trn-up sides, 13"....750.00
Vase, Colonial, camel/Bedouins/distant pyramids, 3 neck hdls, 12x10"..4,500.00
Vase, Colonial, flowers/gilt on wht, squat, scroll hdls, w/lid, 9".... 865.00
Vase, Colonial, 4 mallards, gold reeds, scalloped/lobed, slim, 17" ... 3,450.00
Vase, daffodils on cream, cylindrical w/ring collar, 13" 550.00
Vase, floral bouquets/4 gold mythological medallions, wide/bulbous 7"...500.00
Vase, goldfish/seaweed on pastel ocean waves, rnd w/can neck, 11"...7,900.00
Vase, jack-in-pulpit; Colonial, floral, ftd, 12" 350.00
Vase, thistles/leaves/gilt on opal, wide dbl-bulb w/stick neck, 14" .. 1,700.00
Vase, 4 griffin medallions/vines, gold on opal, 4-sided w/hdls, 8x7"..1,400.00

Cruets

Cruets, containers made to hold oil or vinegar, are usually bulbous with tall, narrow throats, a handle, and a stopper. During the nineteenth century and for several years after, they were produced in abundance in virtually every type of glassware available. Those listed below are assumed to be with stopper and mint unless noted otherwise. See also specific manufacturers; Custard Glass; Opalescent Glass; other types of glass.

Alaska, bl or gr.. 265.00
Amberette, vaseline... 95.00
Amberina, Swirl, amber hdl/faceted stopper, bulbous, 6½" 330.00
Amberina w/bl overtones at rim, Coin Spot, bulbous body, 5½".. 345.00
Amethyst, Moorish design/gold panels, amber hdl/stopper, dimpled, 9"...1,035.00
Art, ruby stain.. 225.00
Bar & Diamond, ruby stain... 85.00
Beaded Comet Band 45.00
Beaded Shell, bl 75.00
Beaded Swirl, gr, US Glass, 7½" 110.00
Beaumont's Columbia, vaseline... 85.00
Beveled Diamond & Star, ruby stain... 125.00
Blooms & Blossoms (Mikado), vaseline....................................... 195.00
Bulging Loops, lemon yel cased, Consolidated 235.00
Buzz Saw, Cambridge 75.00
Cathedral, amethyst... 125.00
Citron, gold hummingbird, red/blk flowers, bl stopper/hdl, Harrach, 8".325.00
Columbian Coin (US Coin) 70.00
Cord Drapery, amber.. 275.00
Criss-Cross, cranberry opal, ca 1893-94 .... 1,375.00
Crystal Wedding, rare 145.00
Daisy & Button, amber, Hobbs... 125.00
Daisy & Fern, bl opal, 7½" 125.00
Dakota, ruby stain.. 325.00

Delaware, bl	225.00
Diamond Quilt, canary yel MOP, 6½"	300.00
Diamond Swag	65.00
Esther, ruby stain	275.00
Fancy Loop	60.00
Fern, cranberry opal, West Virginia Glass Co, ca 1894, 6½"	525.00
Fleur-de-Lis & Drape	60.00
Gonterman Swirl, amber	90.00
Heart w/Thumbprint	65.00
Hobnail, vaseline, Hobbs	85.00
Homestead (#63), Duncan	50.00
Intaglio, bl, Northwood	85.00
Inverted Feather	80.00
Inverted Thumbprint, cranberry, slim neck, ruffled, clear hdl/top	175.00
Locket on Chain, ruby stain	175.00
Marjorie (Sweetheart)	60.00
Millard, ruby stain	80.00
Peerless	65.00
Persian	50.00
Petticoat (Riverside), vaseline	95.00
Pineapple, New England Glass	195.00
Polka Dot, vaseline, Hobbs	85.00
Pressed Diamond, amber	55.00
Prince of Wales Plumes, ruby stain, Heisey, ca 1902, 6¾"	800.00
Priscilla, Fostoria	75.00
Queen, bl	90.00
Rising Sun	55.00
Romeo (Block & Fan)	60.00
Royal Crystal, ruby stain	110.00
Rubena Verde, Polka Dot, teepee form, Hobbs Brockunier, 7"	400.00
S-Repeat	70.00
Sawtooth	110.00
Semitar #2647, Cambridge	70.00
Shuttle	45.00
Snail	125.00
Startec	55.00
Sunk Honeycomb, ruby stain	85.00
Swag w/Brackets, sapphire bl, Jefferson Glass, ca 1903, 7"	135.00
Swirl, cased spatter w/MOP finish, ribbed spatter hdl, 8"	425.00
Tarentum's Virginia	60.00
Thousand Eye, vaseline	175.00
Tile (Optical Cube)	50.00
Truncated Cube, ruby stain	80.00
Vasa Murrhina, rose/yel spatter w/allover gold spangle, Hobbs, 7"	180.00
Victor	65.00
Winged Scroll, bl	85.00

Cup Plates, Glass

Before the middle 1850s, it was socially acceptable to pour hot tea into a deep saucer to cool. The tea was sipped from the saucer rather than the cup, which frequently was handleless and too hot to hold. The cup plate served as a coaster for the cup. It is generally agreed that the first examples of pressed glass cup plates were made about 1826 at the Boston and Sandwich Glass Co. in Sandwich, Cape Cod, Massachusetts. Other glassworks in three major areas (New England, Philadelphia, and the Midwest, especially Pittsburgh) quickly followed suit.

Antique glass cup plates range in size from 2⅝" up to 4¼" in diameter. The earliest plates had simple designs inspired by cut glass patterns, but by 1829 they had become more complex. The span from then until about 1845 is known as the 'Lacy Period,' when cup plate designs and pressing techniques were at their peak. To cover pressing imperfections, the backgrounds of the plates were often covered with fine stippling which endowed them with a glittering brilliance called 'laciness.' They were made in a multitude of designs — some purely decorative, others commemorative. Subjects include the American eagle, hearts, sunbursts, log cabins, ships, George Washington, the political candidates Clay and Harrison, plows, beehives, etc. Of all the patterns, the round George Washington plate is the rarest and most valuable — only four are known to exist today.

Authenticity is most important. Collectors must be aware that contemporary plates which have no antique counterparts and fakes modeled after antique patterns have had wide distribution. Condition is also important, though it is the exceptional plate that does not have some rim roughness. More important considerations are scarcity of design and color.

The book *American Glass* by George and Helen McKearin has a section on glass cup plates. The definitive book is *American Glass Cup Plates* by Ruth Webb Lee and James H. Rose. Numbers in the listings that follow refer to the latter. When attempting to evaluate a cup plate, remember that minor rim roughness is normal. See also Staffordshire; Pairpoint.

Note: Most of the values listed below are prices realized at auction. The more common varieties generally run between $35.00 to $75.00 in very good condition. Unless noted otherwise, our values are for examples in very good to excellent condition.

R-595, cabin, medium orange amber, perfect, 3¼", $450.00. (Photo courtesy Glass Works Auctions)

R-32, 16 even scallops, Sandwich, 3¼", NM	45.00
R-69, 16 even scallops, PA area, 3½"	45.00
R-80, mottled fiery opal w/bubbles, rope rim, 3¾"	250.00
R-89, deep fiery opal to lt opal rim, rope rim/top/bottom, 3¾"	65.00
R-90, opal to clear rim, rope rim, Sandwich, nicks, 3¾"	55.00
R-127-A, amethyst, 34 bull's-eye scallops, Midwestern, 3 9/16"	825.00
R-135-A, bl, 36 bull's-eye scallops, Midwestern, crack, 3⅜"	45.00
R-147-B, 16 scallops w/points between, Midwestern, flakes, 3"	55.00
R-163, lt gr, 34 scallops w/lines beneath, Midwestern, 3¼", NM	210.00
R-174, fiery opal opaque, 10 scallops, Sandwich, flake, 3⅝"	90.00
R-182, 40 bull's-eye scallops, Midwestern, bubble/flakes, 3¼"	75.00
R-183-B, 8-sided w/7 even scallops, Midwestern, 3½", EX	75.00
R-191-B, dk bl, 44 even scallops, Midwestern, roughness, 3"	330.00
R-212, 60 even scallops, Ft Pitt Glass Works, flakes, 3⅝"	120.00
R-216-C, lt opal, plain rim, Ft Pitt Glass Works, chips, 3⅝"	185.00
R-240-A, lt bl, 60 even scallops, Eastern, 3½", NM	1,325.00
R-243, opal, 19 lg scallops w/point between, Sandwich, 3½", NM	65.00
R-253, med bl-gr, 8 lg serrated scallops w/points between, 3 9/16", NM	90.00
R-262, dk cloudy bl, 66 even scallops, Sandwich, 3 5/16", EX	90.00
R-262, lt amethyst, 66 even scallops, Sandwich, 3 5/16", NM	190.00
R-269-D, 53 even stippled scallops, Sandwich, flake, 3 9/16"	45.00
R-277, dk peacock bl, 58 even scallops, Sandwich, 3⅜", EX	465.00
R-278, lav, 24 scallops w/points between, Eastern, chips, 2⅞"	120.00
R-284, 24 lg peacock eyes w/point between, flakes, 3¼"	65.00
R-296, lav tint, 53 even scallops, thick, Midwestern, chips, 3"	45.00
R-298, dk amethyst, plain rim, roughness, 3 15/16"	75.00
R-321-C, amethyst, 50 even scallops, Sandwich, chips, 3 1/16"	90.00
R-324, dk amethyst, 66 even scallops, Sandwich, flake, 3¼"	55.00
R-373, lt opal, 73 even scallops, Sandwich, flakes, 3⅜"	120.00
R-389, brilliant dk bl, plain rim, flakes, 3⅜"	120.00

R-440-B, opal, 24 lg scallops w/sm prs between, Sandwich, 3½", EX ... 90.00
R-465-H, dk amethyst, 59 even scallops, att NE, nicks, 3⁷⁄₁₆" 990.00
R-465-J, opal clambroth, 48 even scallops, att Sandwich, flake, 3½" ... 55.00
R-467-A, violet-bl, 48 even scallops, Sandwich, chips, 3⅝" 190.00
R-509, dk bl, 22 scallops w/point between, Sandwich, flakes, 3" .. 100.00
R-523-A, olive gr, 62 even scallops, Sandwich, 3", NM 145.00
R-561, 8-sided w/7 even scallops, rivet head in center, 3½", NM 935.00
R-565-B, peacock bl, 51 even scallops, Sandwich, flakes, 3⁹⁄₁₆" 100.00
R-591, 48 even scallops, Sandwich, chip/roughness, 3½" 135.00
R-615, 41 even scallops, chips, 3⁹⁄₁₆" 140.00
R-619-A, silver nitrate/amber stain, B Franklin, Sandwich, 3⁷⁄₁₆", NM...3,300.00
R-651-A, plain rim, Philadelphia area, flake, 3⁵⁄₁₆" 360.00
R-662, lt opal at shoulder, 79 even scallops, Sandwich, 3½", NM...145.00
R-667-F, clambroth tint w/smoke streak, 8-sided, very rare, 3½", NM .. 175.00
R-677-A, bl w/purple tones, 44 even scallops, Midwestern, 3³⁄₁₆", EX. 145.00
R-680, bright lilac, 44 even scallops, att Midwest, 3", NM 2,425.00
R-842, cameo sulfide Napoleon bust, 15 scallops, 3⅜", NM......... 230.00

Cups and Saucers

The earliest utensils for drinking were small porcelain and stoneware bowls imported from China by the East Indian Company in the early seventeenth century. European and English tea bowls and saucers, imitating Chinese and Japanese originals, were produced from the early eighteenth century and often decorated with Chinese-type motifs. By about 1810, handles were fitted to the bowl to form the now familiar teacup, and this form became almost universal. Coffee in England and on the Continent was often served in a can — a straight-sided cylinder with a handle. After 1820 the coffee can gave way to the more fanciful form of the coffee cup.

An infinite variety of cups and saucers are available for both the new and experienced collector, and they can be found in all price ranges. There is probably no better way to thoroughly know and understand the various ceramic manufacturers than to study cups and saucers. Our advisors for this category, Susan and Jim Harran, have written a series entitled *Collectible Cups and Saucers, Book I, II,* and *III*, published by Collector Books. Book III contains more than 800 full-color photos; it is divided into six collectible eras: cabinet cups, nineteenth and twentieth-century dinnerware, English tablewares, miniatures, Japanese tablewares, and art glass cups and saucers. The Harrans are listed in the Directory under New Jersey.

Breakfast, HP flowers w/gold trim on wht, Vienna Augarten, 1923-60s. 125.00
Breakfast, lady sitting transfer on yel, Rosenthal, 1901-33 .... 65.00
Chocolate, pk roses w/gold, scalloped base, Rosenthal, 1891-1907 ..70.00
Coffee, children transfer, loop hdl, Johann Haviland, 1938-present 50.00
Coffee, HP flowers & courting scene on cream & turq, Dresden, 1890......... 125.00
Coffee, HP flowers & gold scrolls, Empire-shaped cup, Limoges, 1900s . 115.00
Coffee, HP flowers on yel band, quatrefoil, Dresden, 1887-1914 .. 210.00
Coffee, lg yel roses on cobalt, angular hdl, Rosenthal, 1908-35 ..... 70.00
Coffee, lion transfer on wht, loop hdl, Germany, 1930-40s, from $25 to.. 35.00
Demi, cobalt w/gr clover & jewels, Lettin, 1900-30, from $40 to .. 55.00
Demi, gold Art Nouveau on cobalt fades to gr, RS Germany, 1904-20..90.00
Demi, gold flowers on gr, loop hdl, Royal Worcester, 1910, $55 to ..70.00
Demi, gold w/turq jewels, ftd, Dresden, 1900s, from $475 to........ 500.00
Demi, HP floral w/pearl jeweling, quatrefoil, Dresden, 1900-20... 165.00
Demi, lav w/gold, quatrefoil, ring hdl, Hutschenreuther, 1925-41 . 85.00
Demi, Wedgwood bl w/wht wreath & beads, Pompadour, Rosenthal, 1925-41. 45.00
Demi, wht w/silver o/l, angular hdl, Fraureuth, 1898-1935, $100 to ..125.00
Mini coffee, gold w/bl bird, can cup, ring hdl, Coalport, 1881-90...375.00
Mini tea, Autumn, Brambly Hedge series, Royal Doulton, 1990 ... 40.00
Mini tea, bl & wht landscape, fat loop hdl, Fenton, 1910, from $125 to.. 150.00
Mini tea, bl Jasperware, loop hdls, Wedgwood, 1980s, from $75 to.. 100.00
Mini tea, Christmas holly w/gold, pinched loop hdl, Blue Bird, 1960s ..65.00
Mini tea, gr flowers on wht w/gold trim, Gort, 1950s, from $90 to... 125.00
Mini tea, heavy gold flowers on wht, Limoges, 1896-1900, from $75 to .. 100.00
Mini tea, HP emb flowers, paneled cup, sq hdl, unmk, 1900, from $75 to ...100.00
Tea, Art Nouveau red peonies, pinched loop hdl, Limoges, 1891-96... 45.00
Tea, cream w/gold warrior on aqua border, R Wachter, 1930s 40.00
Tea, dk red w/gold, mc chintz int, Shelley, 1945-66, from $100 to... 125.00
Tea, gold Art Nouveau on wht, loop hdl, Hertel, 1969+, from $50 to...75.00
Tea, HP clovers, scalloped w/curled hdl, Herend, 1930s, from $60 to.. 75.00
Tea, HP courting scene medallion on cobalt & gold, Limoges, 1891-96.. 190.00
Tea, HP wht floral, 8-panel, angle hdl, Limoges, 1890s, from $40 to.. 50.00
Tea, red band w/floral, gold trim, Rosenthal, 1949-55, from $50 to .65.00
Tea, robins egg bl w/cartouches of roses, loop hdl, Furstenberg, 1950s ...45.00

Currier and Ives by Royal

During the 1950s dinnerware decorated with transfer-printed scenes taken from prints by Currier and Ives was manufactured by Royal China and distributed as premiums through A&P stores. Though it was also made in pink and green, blue is by far the easiest to find and the most popular collected. Pie plates have been found in black and brown, and other dinnerware items have been reported in black as well. Occasionally the blue line has been found decorated with a hand-painted pattern. Currier and Ives has long been a very popular collectible at malls and flea markets around the country. Included in our listings are pieces from Hostess sets by Royal which should be of great interest to collectors. The 11½" round platter with the 'Rocky Mountains' scene is very rare. This piece does not have tabs but is round like the 12" platter. An interesting note: There are six different (decal/shape) variations of the teapot. The glasses can be found in two different color types. There are also five or six different styles of covered casseroles. Our advisors for this category are Treva Jo and Jack Hamlin; they are listed in the Directory under Ohio.

Ashtray, 5½" 15.00
Bowl, cereal; 6¼" or 6⅝", ea 15.00
Bowl, cream soup; tab hdl, 7" 55.00
Bowl, dessert; 5½" 6.00
Bowl, soup; 8½" 10.00
Bowl, vegetable; deep, 10¼" 30.00
Bowl, vegetable; 9¼" 20.00
Butter dish, Fashionable (Summer) decal, ¼-lb 45.00
Butter dish, Road (Winter) decal, ¼-lb 35.00
Casserole, angle hdls, made in 4 different styles, w/lid 100.00
Casserole, tab hdls, knob turned 90 degrees, w/lid 200.00
Clock, 10" plate, bl #s, 2 decals, Charles Denning 300.00
Creamer, angle hdl 8.00
Creamer, rnd hdl, tall 75.00
Cup, angle hdl 4.00
Cup, rnd hdl, flared top 12.00
Gravy boat, tab hdls 65.00
Gravy boat, 2-spout 20.00
Gravy ladle, all wht, 2 styles 50.00
Lamp, candle; w/globe 375.00
Mug, coffee; lg 30.00
Mug, coffee; rnd hdl 50.00
Pie baker, 9 decals, 10" (depending on print) from $25 to 45.00
Plaque/spoon rest, wall hanging, very rare, 5x7" 250.00
Plate, bread & butter; 6½", from $3 to 5.00
Plate, calendar; 10" 20.00
Plate, chop; Getting Ice, 11¼" 35.00
Plate, chop; Rocky Mountains, no tab hdls, 11¼" 300.00
Plate, chop; 12¼" 30.00
Plate, dinner; 10" 5.00
Plate, luncheon; very rare, 9" 20.00

Plate, salad; rare, 7¼" 15.00
Plate, snack; w/cup well, very rare, 9" 175.00
Platter, oval, 13" 35.00
Platter, Rocky Mountains, tab hdls, 10½" dia 20.00
Platter, 13½" dia 150.00
Saucer, 6⅛" 2.00
Shakers, pr from $30 to 35.00
Sugar bowl, decal, angle hdls, w/lid 18.00
Sugar bowl, wht, no hdls, flared top, w/lid 65.00
Sugar bowl, wht, no hdls, str sides, w/lid 35.00
Teapot, 8 different styles & stamping, ea from $125 to 245.00
Tray, gravy boat; regular, 8" 20.00
Tray, gravy boat; wht tabs, 7" plate decal 100.00
Tumbler, iced tea; bl or wht, 12-oz, 5½" 15.00
Tumbler, juice; bl or wht, 5-oz, 3½" 15.00
Tumbler, old-fashioned; bl or wht, 7-oz, 3¼" 15.00
Tumbler, water; bl or wht, 8½-oz, 4¾" 15.00

Hostess Set Pieces

Bowl, candy; 7¾" 65.00
Bowl, dip; all wht, 4⅜" 65.00
Pie baker, 11" 60.00
Plate, cake; flat, 10" 35.00
Plate, cake; ftd, very rare, 10" 250.00
Plate, deviled egg; very rare, 10¾" 250.00
Plate, serving; 7¾" 20.00

Custard Glass

As early as the 1880s, custard glass was produced in England. Migrating glassmakers brought the formula for the creamy ivory ware to America. One of them was Harry Northwood, who in 1898 founded his company in Indiana, Pennsylvania, and introduced the glassware to the American market. Soon other companies were producing custard, among them Heisey, Tarentum, Fenton, and McKee. Not only dinnerware patterns but souvenir items were made. Today custard is the most expensive of the colored pressed glassware patterns. The formula for producing the luminous glass contains uranium salts which imparts the cream color to the batch and causes it to glow when it is examined under a black light. Our advisors for this category are Wilfred and Dolli Cohen; they are listed in the Directory under California.

Argonaut Shell, bowl, master berry; gold & decor, 10½" L 200.00
Argonaut Shell, butter dish, gold & decor 175.00
Argonaut Shell, compote, jelly; gold & decor, scarce 125.00

Argonaut Shell, gold and decor: Sugar bowl, 6½", $235.00; Creamer, 4½", $155.00.
(Photo courtesy John A. Shuman III)

Argonaut Shell, creamer, no gold 50.00
Argonaut Shell, pitcher, water; gold & decor 350.00
Argonaut Shell, spooner, gold & decor 75.00
Bead Swag, bowl, sauce; floral & gold 50.00

Bead Swag, goblet, floral & gold 65.00
Bead Swag, tray, pickle; floral & gold, rare 300.00
Bead Swag, wine, floral & gold 60.00
Beaded Circle, bowl, master berry; floral & gold 275.00
Beaded Circle, pitcher, water; floral & gold 450.00
Beaded Circle, spooner, floral & gold 125.00
Cane Insert, berry set, 7-pc 250.00
Cane Insert, table set, 4-pc 275.00
Cherry & Scales, butter dish, nutmeg stain 150.00
Cherry & Scales, creamer, nutmeg stain 95.00
Cherry & Scales, spooner, nutmeg stain, scarce 95.00
Cherry & Scales, tumbler, nutmeg stain, scarce 60.00
Chrysanthemum Sprig, bowl, master berry; gold & decor 250.00
Chrysanthemum Sprig, bowl, sauce; ftd, gold & decor 60.00
Chrysanthemum Sprig, butter dish, gold & decor 250.00
Chrysanthemum Sprig, compote, jelly; gold & decor 110.00
Chrysanthemum Sprig, creamer, gold & decor 75.00
Chrysanthemum Sprig, pitcher, water; gold & decor 375.00
Chrysanthemum Sprig, shakers, gold & decor, pr 250.00
Chrysanthemum Sprig, spooner, no gold 50.00
Chrysanthemum Sprig, toothpick holder, gold & decor 175.00
Chrysanthemum Sprig, toothpick holder, no decor 75.00
Chrysanthemum Sprig, tumbler, gold & decor 65.00
Dandelion, mug, nutmeg stain 175.00
Delaware, bowl, sauce; pk stain 65.00
Delaware, creamer, breakfast; pk stain 75.00
Delaware, tray, pin; gr stain 85.00
Diamond w/Peg, bowl, master berry; roses & gold 225.00
Diamond w/Peg, butter dish, roses & gold 175.00
Diamond w/Peg, creamer, ind; souvenir 50.00
Diamond w/Peg, mug, souvenir 50.00
Diamond w/Peg, napkin ring, roses & gold 75.00
Diamond w/Peg, pitcher, roses & gold, 5½" 175.00
Diamond w/Peg, toothpick holder, roses & gold 125.00
Diamond w/Peg, water set, souvenir, 7-pc 350.00
Diamond w/Peg, wine, souvenir 40.00
Everglades, butter dish, gold & decor 300.00
Everglades, cruet, EX gold & decor, rare 2,250.00
Everglades, spooner, gold & decor 160.00
Everglades, tumbler, gold & decor 100.00
Fan, bowl, master berry; good gold 295.00
Fan, butter dish, good gold 225.00
Fan, creamer, good gold 110.00
Fan, pitcher, water; good gold 300.00
Fan, spooner, good gold 100.00
Fan, sugar bowl, w/lid, good gold 125.00
Fan, water set, good gold, 7-pc 500.00
Fine Cut & Roses, rose bowl, fancy int, nutmeg stain 85.00
Fine Cut & Roses, rose bowl, plain int 69.00
Geneva, bowl, master berry; floral decor, ftd, oval, 9" L 110.00
Geneva, bowl, master berry; floral decor, rnd, 9" 130.00
Geneva, bowl, sauce; floral decor, rnd 50.00
Geneva, butter dish, no decor 145.00
Geneva, compote, jelly; floral decor 95.00
Geneva, cruet, floral decor 475.00
Geneva, pitcher, water; floral decor 275.00
Geneva, shakers, floral decor, pr 175.00
Geneva, sugar bowl, open, floral decor 85.00
Geneva, syrup, floral decor 500.00
Geneva, toothpick holder, floral w/M gold 175.00
Georgia Gem, bowl, master berry; good gold 135.00
Georgia Gem, bowl, master berry; gr opaque 115.00
Georgia Gem, celery vase, good gold 145.00
Georgia Gem, creamer, no gold 60.00

Georgia Gem, mug, good gold 45.00
Georgia Gem, shakers, good gold, pr 140.00
Grape (& Cable), bottle, scent; orig stopper, nutmeg stain 495.00
Grape (& Cable), bowl, banana; ftd, nutmeg stain 275.00
Grape (& Cable), bowl, sauce; nutmeg stain, ftd 50.00
Grape (& Cable), butter dish, nutmeg stain 250.00
Grape (& Cable), compote, jelly; open, nutmeg stain 125.00
Grape (& Cable), cracker jar, nutmeg stain 850.00
Grape (& Cable), humidor, bl stain, rare 950.00
Grape (& Cable), nappy, nutmeg stain, rare 60.00
Grape (& Cable), plate, nutmeg stain, 7" 50.00
Grape (& Cable), powder jar, nutmeg sain 350.00
Grape (& Cable), spooner, nutmeg stain 155.00
Grape (& Cable), tray, dresser; nutmeg stain, scarce, lg 375.00
Grape (& Cable), tumbler, nutmeg stain 75.00
Grape & Gothic Arches, bowl, master berry; pearl w/gold 200.00
Grape & Gothic Arches, butter dish, pearl w/gold 235.00
Grape & Gothic Arches, favor vase, nutmeg stain 80.00
Grape & Gothic Arches, goblet, pearl w/gold 75.00
Grape & Gothic Arches, pitcher, water; pearl w/gold 300.00
Grape & Gothic Arches, sugar bowl, w/lid, pearl w/gold 135.00
Grape & Gothic Arches, tumbler, pearl w/gold 65.00
Heart w/Thumbprint, creamer 90.00
Heart w/Thumbprint, lamp, good pnt, scarce, 8" 450.00
Honeycomb, wine 65.00
Horse Medallion, bowl, gr stain, 7" 85.00
Intaglio, bowl, sauce; gold & decor 50.00
Intaglio, compote, jelly; gold & decor 125.00
Intaglio, pitcher, water; gold & decor 225.00
Intaglio, shakers, gold & decor, pr 175.00
Intaglio, spooner, gold & decor 110.00
Intaglio, sugar bowl, w/lid, gold & decor 150.00
Intaglio, tumbler, gold & decor 65.00
Inverted Fan & Feather, bowl, master berry; gold & decor 275.00
Inverted Fan & Feather, bowl, sauce; gold & decor 75.00
Inverted Fan & Feather, butter dish, gold & decor 275.00
Inverted Fan & Feather, compote, jelly; gold & decor, rare 350.00
Inverted Fan & Feather, creamer, gold & decor 150.00
Inverted Fan & Feather, cruet, gold & decor, scarce, 6½" 1,100.00
Inverted Fan & Feather, pitcher, water; gold & decor 450.00
Inverted Fan & Feather, punch cup, gold & decor 250.00
Inverted Fan & Feather, spooner, gold & decor 150.00
Inverted Fan & Feather, sugar bowl, w/lid, gold & decor 225.00
Inverted Fan & Feather, tumbler, gold & decor 100.00
Jackson (Alaska Variant), bowl, master berry; good gold, ftd 150.00
Jackson (Alaska Variant), creamer, good gold 85.00
Jackson (Alaska Variant), pitcher, water; no decor 175.00
Jackson (Alaska Variant), tumbler, good gold 50.00
Louis XV, bowl, master berry; good gold 250.00
Louis XV, butter dish, good gold 175.00
Louis XV, cruet, gold decor, 6¾" 200.00
Louis XV, spooner, good gold 110.00
Louis XV, sugar bowl, w/lid, good gold 165.00
Maple Leaf, bowl, master berry; gold & decor, scarce 350.00
Maple Leaf, bowl, sauce; gold & decor, scarce 50.00
Maple Leaf, compote, jelly; gold & decor, rare 475.00
Maple Leaf, shakers, gold & decor, very rare, pr 1,500.00
Maple Leaf, sugar bowl, w/lid, gold & decor 250.00
Panelled Poppy, lamp shade, nutmeg stain, scarce 900.00
Peacock & Urn, bowl, ice cream; nutmeg stain, 10" 250.00
Punty Band, shakers, pr 125.00
Punty Band, tumbler, floral decor, souvenir 65.00
Ribbed Drape, bowl, sauce; roses & gold 45.00
Ribbed Drape, compote, jelly; roses & gold, rare 200.00

Ribbed Drape, creamer, roses & gold, scarce 180.00
Ribbed Drape, pitcher, water; roses & gold, rare 365.00
Ribbed Drape, shakers, roses & gold, rare, pr 400.00
Ribbed Drape, spooner, roses & gold 195.00
Ribbed Drape, tumbler, roses & gold 75.00
Ribbed Thumbprint, wine, floral decor 80.00
Ring Band, bowl, sauce; roses & gold 50.00
Ring Band, butter dish, roses & gold 225.00
Ring Band, compote, jelly; roses & gold, scarce 150.00
Ring Band, creamer, roses & gold 75.00
Ring Band, pitcher, roses & gold, 7½" 275.00
Ring Band, shakers, roses & gold, pr 155.00
Ring Band, spooner, roses & gold 75.00
Ring Band, table set, 4-pc 450.00
Ring Band, toothpick holder, roses & gold 155.00
Ring Band, tray, condiment; roses & gold 200.00
Singing Birds, mug, nutmeg stain 85.00
Tarentum's Victoria, butter dish, gold & decor, rare 350.00
Tarentum's Victoria, celery vase, gold & decor, rare 300.00
Tarentum's Victoria, creamer, gold & decor, scarce 135.00
Tarentum's Victoria, pitcher, water; gold & decor, rare 375.00
Tarentum's Victoria, spooner, gold & decor 135.00
Tarentum's Victoria, tumbler, gold & decor 75.00
Vermont, butter dish, bl decor 150.00
Vermont, vase, floral decor, jeweled 125.00
Wild Bouquet, bowl, sauce; gold & decor 60.00
Wild Bouquet, butter dish, gold & decor, rare, 11" L 250.00
Wild Bouquet, spooner, gold & decor 250.00
Wild Bouquet, tumbler, no decor 100.00
Winged Scroll, bowl, master berry; gold & decor, 11" L 175.00
Winged Scroll, butter dish, good gold 175.00
Winged Scroll, butter dish, no decor 125.00
Winged Scroll, cigarette jar, scarce 195.00
Winged Scroll, compote, ruffled, rare, 6¾x10¾" 495.00
Winged Scroll, hair receiver, good gold 135.00
Winged Scroll, shakers, bulbous, good gold, rare, pr 400.00
Winged Scroll, shakers, str sides, good gold, pr 250.00
Winged Scroll, sugar bowl, w/lid, good gold 175.00
Winged Scroll, tumbler, good gold 75.00

Cut Glass

The earliest documented evidence of commercial glass cutting in the United States was in 1810; the producers were Bakewell and Page of Pittsburgh. These first efforts resulted in simple patterns with only a moderate amount of cutting. By the middle of the century, glass cutters began experimenting with a thicker glass which enabled them to use deeper cuttings, though patterns remained much the same. This period is usually referred to as rich cut. Using three types of wheels — a flat edge, a mitered edge, and a convex edge — facets, miters, and depressions were combined to produce various designs. In the late 1870s, a curved miter was developed which greatly expanded design potential. Patterns became more elaborate, often covering the entire surface. The brilliant period of cut glass covered a span from about 1880 until 1915. Because of the pressure necessary to achieve the deeply cut patterns, only glass containing a high grade of metal could withstand the process. For this reason and the amount of handwork involved, cut glass has always been expensive. Bowls cut with pinwheels may be either foreign or of a newer vintage, beware! Identifiable patterns and signed pieces that are well cut and in excellent condition bring the higher prices on today's market. For more information, we recommend *Evers' Standard Cut Glass Value Guide* (Collector Books). See also Dorflinger; Hawkes; Libbey; Tuthill; Val St. Lambert; other specific manufacturers.

Basket, Eldorado, Pitkins & Brooks, std grade, 6", from $425 to..475.00
Basket, Sunbeam, Pitkins & Brooks, 7½", from $275 to..............325.00
Bell, Jewel, TB Clark & Co, sm, from $200 to..............250.00
Bonbon, Dorrance, TB Clark & Co, from $65 to..............80.00
Bonbon, Oriole, Pitkins & Brooks, std grade, 6", from $55 to........70.00
Bonbon/olive dish, Evelyn, JD Bergen, 6", from $70 to..............85.00
Bonbon/olive dish, Hawthorne, JD Bergen, 5x9", from $150 to...175.00
Bottle, cologne; Halle, Pitkins & Brooks, 6-oz, from $125 to.......150.00
Bottle, cologne; St Julien, Higgins & Seiter, 4-oz, from $50 to......60.00
Bowl, fruit or berry; Florida, Higgins & Seiter, 9¼x13½"............265.00
Bowl, Manhattan, TB Clark & Co, 7", from $75 to..............100.00
Bowl, salad; Venice, Pitkins & Brooks, 8", from $150 to............175.00
Bowl, Venus, TB Clark & Co, 10", from $300 to..............350.00
Butter tub & plate, Manhattan, TB Clark & Co, from $200 to...225.00
Butterette, Canton, Averbeck, 3½", from $25 to..............30.00
Candlestick, Victoria, JD Bergen, 10", ea from $175 to..............200.00
Carafe, Baltimore, JD Bergen, qt, from $200 to..............225.00
Carafe, Goldenrod, JD Bergen, qt, from $250 to..............300.00
Carafe, Trixy, Averbeck, qt, from $150 to..............175.00
Carafe, Webster, Higgins & Seiter, qt, from $125 to..............150.00
Carafe, Winola, TB Clark & Co, qt, from $100 to..............125.00
Celery dip, Pitkins & Brooks, 1½", from $10 to..............15.00
Celery tray, Aetna, Higgins & Seiter, 4½x12", from $75 to.........100.00
Celery tray, Diamond, Averbeck, 12", from $175 to..............200.00
Celery tray, Emerson, JD Bergen, 6x12", from $300 to..............350.00
Celery tray, Empress, Averbeck, 11¼", from $200 to..............225.00
Celery tray, TB Clark & Co, from $50 to..............75.00
Cheese dish, Manhattan, TB Clark & Co, from $250 to.............300.00
Comport, Crete, Pitkins & Brooks, 5", from $175 to..............200.00
Comport, Memphis, Pitkins & Brooks, 5", from $100 to.............125.00
Comport, Vienna, Averbeck, from $250 to..............300.00
Creamer, Glenwood, JD Bergen, from $50 to..............75.00
Creamer, Grace, JD Bergen, ½-pt, from $50 to..............60.00
Cruet, Garland, JD Bergen, ½-pt, from $175 to..............200.00
Cup, Kenwood, JD Bergen, from $35 to..............40.00
Cup, lemonade; w/hdl, TB Clark & Co, from $25 to..............30.00
Cup, Vienna, Averbeck, from $25 to..............30.00
Decanter, Ansonia, JD Bergen, 1-qt, from $250 to..............300.00
Decanter, Delmar, Pitkins & Brooks, from $125 to..............150.00
Decanter, Genoa, Averbeck, from $275 to..............325.00
Finger bowl, Belmont, Pitkins & Brooks, from $45 to..............50.00
Finger bowl, Georgia, Averbeck, from $35 to..............40.00
Goblet, Electric, JD Bergen, from $50 to..............55.00
Goblet, Radium, Averbeck, from $50 to..............60.00
Hair receiver, Hiawatha, Pitkins & Brooks, 5", from $125 to.......150.00
Horseradish jar, Imported, Pitkins & Brooks, from $25 to.............35.00
Ice cream tray, Oak Leaf, Pitkins & Brooks, 13", from $500 to....600.00
Ice tub, Amazon, JD Bergen, 4¾x7", from $250 to..............300.00
Ice tub, Webster, Higgins & Seiter, 4x4½", from $175 to..............200.00
Jug, Georgia, Averbeck, 3-pt, 9¾x7½", from $200 to..............250.00
Knife rest, Pitkins & Brooks, 5½", from $25 to..............30.00
Lamp, Chrysanthemum, Higgins & Seiter, 23", from $1,500 to.. 1,750.00
Lamp, electric; ARC, Pitkins & Brooks, 12½", from $500 to.......600.00
Nappy, Ambrose, JD Bergen, 7", from $150 to..............175.00
Nappy, Frisco, Averbeck, 6", from $75 to..............95.00
Nappy, Jewel, TB Clark & Co, 6", from $55 to..............70.00
Nappy, Mars, Pitkins & Brooks, 5", from $65 to..............75.00
Nappy, Monarch, Higgins & Seiter, 10", from $150 to..............175.00
Nut bowl, Sparkle, Pitkins & Brooks, std grade, 6", from $100 to...125.00
Oil bottle, Prism, JD Bergen, w/stopper, ½-pt, from $75 to..........100.00
Pickle dish, Marietta, Averbeck, 8", from $150 to..............175.00
Pin tray, Split & Hollow, JD Bergen, from $50 to..............75.00
Pitcher, Goldenrod, JD Bergen, 2-qt, from $350 to..............400.00
Plate, Boston, Averbeck, 7", from $70 to..............80.00
Plate, Lowell, Averbeck, 7", from $85 to..............95.00
Puff box, Aster, Pitkins & Brooks, std grade, 5", from $150 to.....175.00
Punch bowl, Marlow, JD Bergen, low ft, 12", from $900 to.......1,200.00
Punch bowl, Rajah, Pitkins & Brooks, ftd, 10", from $750 to......900.00

Punch bowl, unusual cuttings, 12x12", NM, $885.00. (Photo courtesy James D. Julia Inc.)

Salt dip, JD Bergen, rnd, 2", from $10 to..............12.00
Spooner, Napoleon, Higgins & Seiter, from $125 to..............150.00
Spooner, Prism, Averbeck, from $75 to..............95.00
Sugar bowl, Detroit, ftd, JD Bergen, from $75 to..............100.00
Sugar bowl, Emblem, JD Bergen, from $50 to..............60.00
Toothpick holder, Pitkins & Brooks, 2", from $25 to..............30.00
Tumbler, Goldenrod, JD Bergen, from $30 to..............35.00
Tumbler, Liberty, Averbeck, from $22 to..............25.00
Tumbler, Winola, TB Clark & Co, from $20 to..............22.00
Vase, Everett, Higgins & Seiter, 12", from $125 to..............150.00
Vase, Naples, Averbeck, 17", from $1,000 to..............1,200.00
Vase, Orient, TB Clark & Co, 9", from $175 to..............200.00
Vase, Trophy, JD Bergen, 6", from $30 to..............40.00
Whipped cream bowl, Irene, 3-hdl, JD Bergen, 6", from $100 to. 150.00
Whipped cream bowl, Liberty, Averbeck, 7x4½", from $125 to...150.00

Cut Overlay Glass

Glassware with one or more overlying colors through which a design has been cut is called 'Cut Overlay.' It was made both here and abroad. Watch for new imitations!

Bottle, scent; bl/wht/clear, punty & ovals, att Sandwich, 2⅛", NM...155.00
Bottle, scent; bl/wht/clear, waisted, SP cap, 3⅜"..............200.00
Bottle, scent; cobalt/clear, oval/groove cuttings, Sandwich, 9¾"...1,265.00
Bottle, scent; cobalt/clear, punty & loop, star-cut base, Sandwich, 6"...770.00
Bottle, scent; cobalt/wht/clear, loop/pyriform/punty cuttings, 6½"...400.00
Bottle, scent; purple/clear, dmns & grooves, silver cap, 3⅝", EX..165.00
Bottle, scent; spring gr/wht/clear w/gold trim, bulbous, 6¾".........115.00
Bottle, scent; wht/clear w/gold, Morrish windows, star-cut top, 8"...250.00
Bottle, scent; wht/gr opaque, scalloped panels w/gold, bbl form, 6"..115.00
Cigar holder, pk/wht, ovals/X-hatching, att Sandwich, 3⅛"..........90.00
Egg cup, cobalt/wht/clear, flute cuttings, att Sandwich, 2¾"..........80.00
Egg cup, rose/wht/clear, flute cuttings, att Sandwich, 2½"..............80.00
Stem, cobalt/wht/clear, ovals/punties/etc, att Sandwich, 5"..........50.00
Vase, hanging; powder bl/wht/clear, panel & punty cuttings, 6½x4"...500.00
Vase, wht to clear w/ovals & panels, HP floral/gilt, 16"..............600.00

Cut Velvet

Cut Velvet glassware was made during the late 1800s. It is characterized by the effect achieved through the execution of relief-molded patterns, often ribbing or diamond quilting, which allows its white inner casing to show through the outer layer.

Bottle, scent; Dmn Quilt, bl, ruffled rim, bulbous, 5¼"	600.00
Cup, Dmn Quilt, pk	130.00
Ewer, Dmn Quilt, pk, shouldered, 7½"	160.00
Finger bowl, Dmn Quilt, bl, 2½"	230.00
Lamp, Dmn Quilt, rose pk, opal glass ball shade, 17"	495.00
Pitcher, Dmn Quilt, deep sapphire bl, bl reeded hdl, 8¾x6"	400.00
Pitcher, Dmn Quilt, rose to wht, ewer form, 11"	425.00
Rose bowl, Dmn Quilt, pk, pinched rim, 3 clear frosted ft, 6¾"	550.00
Tumbler, Dmn Quilt, yel to wht, rose lining, scarce	130.00
Tumbler, Dmn Quilt, yel w/pk int, 4"	100.00
Vase, Dmn Quilt, dk to lt pk, ruffled 4-lobe top, Mt WA, 4¼x3"	225.00
Vase, Dmn Quilt, gr, stick neck, 6"	125.00
Vase, Dmn Quilt, lt gold, dbl-gourd w/curved neck, 13½"	650.00
Vase, Dmn Quilt, orange, ruffled/flared top, 9x6"	675.00
Vase, Dmn Quilt, robin-egg bl, stick neck, 7"	150.00
Vase, Dmn Quilt, royal bl, squat, 2" rim, 3"	200.00
Vase, Herringbone, ruffled/flared rim trn down on 2 sides, Mt WA, 8"	450.00
Vase, vertical ribs, pk & wht, 6"	180.00

Cybis

Boleslaw Cybis was a graduate of the Academy of Fine Arts in Warsaw, Poland, and was well recognized as a fine artist by the time he was commissioned by his government to paint murals in the Polish Pavilion's Hall of Honor at the 1939 World's Fair. Finding themselves stranded in America at the outbreak of WWII, the Cybises founded an artists' studio, first in Astoria, New York, and later in Trenton, New Jersey, where they made fine figurines and plaques with exacting artistry and craftsmanship entailing extensive handwork. The studio still operates today producing exquisite porcelains on a limited edition basis.

Apaloosa Colt, head erect, 1970s, 9¼"	325.00
Asian lady in ornate costume w/hands away, MB Cybis, 22"	225.00
Bear cub, 1985, 4½x6½"	50.00
Beaver Head (medicine man), wooden base, 11½", EX	450.00
Berengaria Consort to King Arthur, 15½"	600.00
Bicentennial Carousel Horse Ticonderoga, w/base, 13x12", EX	400.00
Boy w/sailor hat, blond hair & bl eyes, bust only, 10"	200.00
Brahma bull down on front legs, wht w/HP details, on base, 11½x14"	250.00
Carousel lion, ornate saddle, brass pole, on wooden base	325.00
Carousel Sugar Plum Pony, on base, 12¼"	750.00
Carousel tiger, 12x19½x3½"	575.00
Cinderella at ball, in finery, 8¼"	125.00
Cinderella seated (w/bare feet) holding broom, 7½"	100.00
Deermouse in clover, 1972, 3½"	125.00
Doves of Peace (2 wht doves), 11x11"	350.00
Elephant sitting, gray to wht, 5"	325.00
Eskimo boy's head, bust only, on wooden base, 10½"	100.00
Exodus Flight From Egypt, figure in long robe, 19"	200.00
First Flight, girl w/baby bird, wooden base, 1966, 4½"	50.00
Geisha, pk bsk, #13, 14"	275.00
George Washington, wht bsk bust, on wooden base, 12½"	250.00
Girl w/simple hat, ruffled bodice, holds flowers, ¾-figure, 10"	750.00
Great White Buffalo charging, grassy base, ltd ed, 13x17"	1,000.00
Horse head, ornate bridle & flowers, wht w/mc & gold, 12"	500.00
Horses, 2 prancing, ribbons in manes, 7½x12"	150.00
Indian hunter w/dead fawn, #53, on wooden base, 12¼"	300.00
Indian shaman on bearskin rug, #466, on wooden base, 12"	400.00
Indian youth, single feather in hair, bust only, 10"	75.00
Jester w/1 hand to hat, masked face, 16"	800.00

Kitten, curled up & asleep, 2¾x5¼", from $60 to	90.00
Lilies (2), wht w/gr foliage, #135, 16"	175.00
Madonna w/bl jay, 11½"	275.00
Moses the Lawgiver, 18¾", EX	375.00
Mother w/Child, lady w/golden crown holding baby, on base, 14"	850.00

Othello, #314, $1,000.00.

Pegasus Free Spirit, 1980	550.00
Pheasant, tail down, realistic, 15½x20"	400.00
Pollyanna, seated w/legs crossed, 7½", from $60 to	90.00
Priscilla, ltd ed, 14"	135.00
Queen Esther, 1974, 14"	100.00
Raccoon eating berries on limb, 7"	100.00
Sacajawea, Indian maiden w/baby, on wooden base, 12½", EX	500.00
Unicorn beside tree, #182, on base, 11¼x12"	150.00
Winged Fairy on Grasshopper, 5"	225.00

Czechoslovakian Collectibles

Czechoslovakia came into being as a country in 1918. Located in the heart of Europe, it was a land with the natural resources necessary to support a glass industry that dated back to the mid-fourteenth century. The glass that was produced there has captured the attention of today's collectors, and for good reason. There are beautiful vases — cased, ruffled, applied with rigaree or silver overlay — fine enough to rival those of the best glasshouses. Czechoslovakian art glass baskets are quite as attractive as Victorian America's, and the elegant cut glass perfumes made in colors as well as crystal are unrivaled. There are also pressed glass perfumes, molded in lovely Deco shapes, of various types of art glass. Some are overlaid with gold filigree set with 'jewels.' Jewelry, lamps, porcelains, and fine art pottery are also included in the field.

More than 70 marks have been recorded, including those in the mold, ink stamped, acid etched, or on a small metal nameplate. The newer marks are incised, stamped 'Royal Dux Made in Czechoslovakia' (see Royal Dux), or printed on a paper label which reads 'Bohemian Glass Made in Czechoslovakia.' (Communist controlled from 1948, Czechoslovakia once again was made a free country in December 1989. Today it no longer exists; after 1993 it was divided to form two countries, the Czech Republic and the Slovak Republic.) For a more thorough study of the subject, we recommend *Made in Czechoslovakia* and *Made in Czechoslovakia, Book 2*, by Ruth A. Forsythe. Other fine books are *Czechoslovakian Perfume Bottles and Boudoir Accessories* by Jacquelyne Y. Jones North, and *Czechoslovakian Pottery* by Bowers, Closser, and Ellis. In the listings that follow, when one dimension is given, it refers to height; decoration is enamel unless noted otherwise. See also Amphora; Erphila.

Baskets

Bl opaque w/crystal molded florals, blk hdl/rim, ca 1918-38, 7x6"	35.00

Mc spatter w/aventurine, crystal thorn hdl, 6x4¾" 85.00
Orange w/blk rim, blk hdl, ca 1920, 10x6½" 110.00
Red cased w/blk ruffle, crystal hdl, 7½" 48.00
Wht cased w/mc millefiori canes, ruffled rim, bl hdl, 9¾x4¾" 295.00

Cased Art Glass

Vase, autumn mottle w/yel int, handkerchief rim, 13x12" 40.00
Vase, orange cased in clear, slim w/flared ft, ruffled rim, 6¼" 35.00
Vase, orange w/blk swags, wht int, bulbous body, 10x7" 100.00
Vase, pk to wht, wide rolled rim, block-letter mk, 3x6" 80.00
Vase, threaded, purple on opal, purple int, 4x5" 260.00
Vase, wht cut to cobalt, HP floral, invt bell w/flared ft, 1950s, 9" .. 110.00
Vase, yel w/silver o/l baskets, cylindrical, 9¼x3" 35.00

Lamps

Boudoir, HP bridge & woods scene on bl frost, Ruckl, 12½" 185.00
Perfume, clear, cut decor, etched mk, 1930s, 5¼x3" 65.00
Shade, grapes/nuts/berries/etc, 3x6x6½", EX 150.00
Table, basket form, fruit/nuts in clear beaded metal fr, 9x7x5" 600.00
Table, basket form, mc flowers in clear beaded metal fr, 10" 540.00
Table, basket form, mc flowers/leaves in clear beaded metal fr, 12" .. 800.00
Table, basket form, mc fruit on clear beaded base, 12x8" 1,250.00
Table, Deco flowers HP on frost, conical shade, 1920s, 10½" 395.00

Mold-Blown and Pressed Bottles

Bl, faceted, jewels/metal front panel, faceted dauber, 4½" 780.00
Bl rayed/faceted butterfly-like body, jewels/metal mts, ornate dauber ... 1,200.00
Bl w/rayed lines, squat/ftd, dauber: nude w/rayed fan-like wing, 9" ... 2,040.00
Blk, squat, filigree metal+3 jade cabochons, clear dauber, Hoffman, 6" .. 1,920.00
Blk sq w/filigree metal & jade-set device at corner, Hoffman, 5" 2,400.00
Blk w/angle sides, pk enamel 'bib,' pointed/faceted pk dauber, 5" . 180.00
Blk w/etched Cupid in U-form panel, clear pointed dauber, 6" 270.00
Cl/frost fleur-de-lys-like form w/jewels & metal mts, 5½" 780.00
Clear 3-D maid ea side bell-form cavity w/HP porc medallion, 6" ... 1,080.00
Clear/frost sq body w/emb ½-figure nude, sq dauber, Ingrid, 8" 840.00
Clear/frosted, shaped sides w/emb flowes, butterfly dauber, 5" 180.00
Enameled glass elephant head form, w/atomizer, 4½" 720.00
Gr, 3 appl roses w/metal leaves, metal base band, faceted dauber, 5" ... 900.00
Ivory w/brn stain, textured/sq, w/lg flower basket dauber, Ingrid, 9" ... 1,440.00
Lapiz Blue, Iris pattern, gold neck, tiny dauber, 2½" 80.00
Malachite w/lg relief elephant, elephant dauber, Hoffman, 5" .. 2,400.00

Nude stopper showering flowers from a cornucopia embellished with Art Deco motifs, highlighted in black enamel, marked, 8¾", $1,200.00. (Photo courtesy Monsen & Baer)

Pk, jeweled blk metal ribbons, 4-sided, dauber w/head of man/lady, 5" ... 960.00
Pk sphere w/appl row of clear flowerheads, floral-spray dauber, 4" ... 480.00
Pk sq/dmn-cut skirt-shaped body w/lg flat pk bow dauber, 4½" 660.00
Pk/clear butterfly shape w/jewels & metal filigree, disk dauber, 3" ... 335.00
Pk/clear ribbed sq, sq (flat) dauber w/2 Classical maids, 5" 420.00
Purple frost, emb swirls/flowers, umbrella-shaped dauber, Ingrid, 7" ... 420.00
Vaseline, 4 canted sides, 2 filigree metal bands w/gr jewels, 5" .. 2,160.00
Yel, hand eng lady's head, 6-sided front/bk, w/atomizer, 5¾" 2,160.00

Opaque, Crystal, Colored Transparent Glass

Bottle, blk w/random red threading, matching stopper, 6x3¾" 195.00
Bowl, orange-red w/blk at flared rim, blk ball ft, 5¼x10¼" 160.00
Candy dish, mc mottle, amber ft, pointed finial, 1920s-30s, 8x5" ... 170.00
Cordial set, orange egg shape w/mc florals, holds 6 shots & decanter .. 50.00
Flower frog, owl figural, dk amber, 8 holes in base, 1940s, 4½" 20.00
Orange & red spatter w/red o/l, 3 emb ribs encircle body, 6x3¼" ... 60.00
Pk/gr/wht spatter, ruffled rim, 1950s, 5¼x4" 30.00
Vase, bud; orange w/dotted floral, blk trim, 1930s, 8¼" 80.00
Vase, cranberry w/controlled bubbles, flared rim w/blk, 1930s, 5" . 125.00
Vase, jack-in-pulpit; yel opaque w/blk trim at rim, 13½" 50.00
Vase, orange opaque w/mc mottle at ft, stepped shape, 6½x2¾" 52.50
Vase, orange w/mc spatter at bottom, ruffled rim, 6⅛" 35.00
Vase, peach trumpet form w/3 buttressed low hdls, 1930s, 7x3½" .. 95.00
Vase, red w/blk mottle, 3 emb ribs encircle body, 1930s, 6x3⅜" 40.00
Vase, red/gr/blk spider-web design, Kralik, 1920s, 7¾" 155.00
Vase, sky bl w/appl serpentine, blk trim at ruffled rim, 9¼" 100.00
Vase, yel opaque w/lady's silhouette in blk pnt, 1920s, 4½" 110.00
Vase, yel opaque w/3 blk buttressed ft, 1930s, 7⅜" 150.00

Pottery and Porcelain

Basket, appl rose to front, bird perched on rim, mc, 7x6½" 30.00
Basket, bl hdl & rim on yel, mc bird at side, wht int, 5x4", NM 30.00
Bottle, floral, mc on lt bl w/gold trim, sq, 1930s, 5x2½" 30.00
Bowl, Art Deco floral reserve on bl w/yel stripes, oval, 7¾" L 60.00
Bust, Deco lady's head, orange streaks in blond curls, 8¼x5½" 110.00
Casserole dish, floral swags, w/lid, Epiag, #9954, 3x10x9" 60.00
Creamer, cow seated, orange splotches on cream w/blk, 4¾" 25.00
Creamer & sugar bowl, bl-gray luster w/orange trim, w/lid 28.00
Creamer & sugar bowl, orange w/gr trim, vine hdl, 3¾" 25.00
Figure vase, bird on stump w/3 openings, mc, 5½" 30.00
Figure vase, bird on 2-sided holder, mc, 5½x3½" 20.00
Figure vase, parrot on limb w/2 openings, mc, 1940s, 5½" 50.00
Figurine, parrot on perch, bl/gr/yel/brns, #11702, 5½" 45.00
Flower frog, bird on stump, mc, red mk, 1948, 5" 60.00
Flower frog, woodpecker w/red crest, 6-hole base, #CO45, 6¼" ... 110.00
Pitcher, cow wearing orange jacket & gr pants, bell around neck, 4" .. 180.00
Pitcher, Deco floral on bl sponged w/blk trim, 4¾" 22.50
Pitcher, Deco geometrics, bl/orange/blk on wht, 4½" 18.00
Pitcher, floral, brn/orange/wht airbrushing, #3586, 9¾" 75.00
Pitcher, fruit emb, mc on bl, Bren mk, 7¼" 45.00
Pitcher, mc tulips on cream, bl trim, HP mk, 8½" 150.00
Pitcher, moose figural, brn tones, 5x5" 60.00
Pitcher, parrot figural, mc, 4½", NM 30.00
Pitcher, pelican figural, #5025, 6½" 78.00
Pitcher, red w/blk rim & hdl, trumpet neck, 7½" 36.00
Planter, floral reserve on lav w/vertical ribs, #7938, 4x7⅝x4" 20.00
Plaque, sailing ship, mc w/much detail, 13", NM 40.00
Spooner, orange/yel/gr/bl stripes on wht, 4 bl ft, 4½x4" 28.00
Vase, Deco floral on wht w/orange trim, fan form, #10852, 7¼x8¼" .. 32.00
Vase, Deco floral on red, cylindrical, Letovice #103K, 4½" 70.00
Vase, floral on cream, teardrop shape w/shell hdls, gold trim, 8" 25.00
Vase, roses w/gold on wht to rose-pk, ornate hdls, 8¾" 55.00
Wall pocket, bird on branch, 3 openings, mc, 5½x4½" 35.00
Wall pocket, bird on pine cones, airbrushed mc, 7½" 60.00
Wall pocket, bird perched on floral garland, #5946, 6x4¾" 110.00

D'Argental

D'Argental cameo glass was produced in France from the 1870s until about 1920 in the Art Nouveau style. Our advisor for this category is Don Williams; he is listed in the Directory under Missouri.

Vase, bleeding hearts on cobalt, bottle form, 5½" 500.00
Vase, floral, cranberry on terra cotta, wide teardrop form, 2½" 345.00
Vase, floral, red/red on sky bl, slim, 18" 1,095.00
Vase, floral cascade, crimson on citron, ovoid, 9¾", pr 3,450.00
Vase, foliage/pods, brn on camphor, ovoid, 12" 1,150.00
Vase, leaves/berries, russet over citron, 5" 745.00
Vase, lg trees/marsh beyond, brn/orange on lemon frost, base fp, 10".. 1,200.00
Vase, lily of the valley (padded), wht/gr on deep amber, 4¾" 1,840.00
Vase, orchids, amber/umber on lt yel, ovoid, 12" 1,450.00
Vase, palm trees/canoes/huts/mtns, brn on cream, 12" 2,070.00
Vase, trees/foggy scenic, plum/mauve/rose on wht, 12" 920.00
Vase, 2 oval panels w/lg fir trees, mtns in distance, ftd U-form, 12"..3,120.00

Daum Nancy

Daum was an important producer of French cameo glass, operating from the late 1800s until after the turn of the century. They used various techniques — acid cutting, wheel engraving, and handwork — to create beautiful scenic designs and nature subjects in the Art Nouveau manner. Virtually all examples are signed. Daum is still in production, producing many figural items. Our advisor for this category is Don Williams; he is listed in the Directory under Missouri.

Key: fp — fire polished

Cameo

Basket, rain/windblown trees, cut/pnt on frost to pk to gr, 7x6" ... 16,675.00
Basket, winter scene, cut/pnt on amber, amber hdl, 7" 15,000.00
Bottle, floral-cvd gr w/ribs, pnt floral, matching stopper, 6½" 1,325.00
Bottle, lily of the valley on amber, acid etched/gilded, ovoid, 7", NM .. 149.50
Bowl, exotic floral/foliage, dk gr on amethyst martele, 12 " L ... 6,325.00
Bowl, mushrooms, cut/pnt, red/brn on yel mottle, ft depicts grass, 4" . 2,875.00
Bowl vase, winter scene w/windmills, cut/pnt, oval, 4½x5¾" 5,465.00
Box, winter trees w/blkbirds on icy opal, 3x5½" dia 8,050.00
Creamer, winter trees/snow on mottled yel, 5½" L 2,588.00
Dish, oak leaves, orange on mottled ground w/3 appl bugs, sq, 5¾" .1,725.00
Lamp, fleet of sailboats on hat-form shade/vasiform base, 14".. 11,520.00
Lamp, rain/windblown trees on pointed dome shade/slim base, 14" .29,900.00
Lamp, trees, brn on orange, on hat-form shade & vasiform base, 17", NM .4,890.00
Lamp, trees/rain scene on hat-form shade & vasiform base, 13".. 35,650.00
Lamp, winter scene on amber onion shade & slim shouldered base, 28".10,350.00
Perfume lamp, flowers & appl dragonflies, gr/yel on bl to wine, 6" .. 16,100.00
Plaque, geese/tree, dk colors on sunset mottle, fr, 8½x12" 1,380.00
Salt cellar, winter scene w/blkbirds on frost, 1x2" L 2,300.00
Tumbler, Rat Who Withdrew From the World (Aesop), cut/pnt, 2" .. 635.00
Vase, autumn trees, red on yel mottle, red bun base, 16x5" 5,175.00
Vase, autumn trees on orange, sienna, ivory, 15x6" 3,960.00
Vase, berries/leaves, red/gr on amethyst/citron mottle, 22" 8,625.00
Vase, blown-out leaves & pods, purple on citron, 7x5" 5,400.00
Vase, crocus, red/wine on lav to gold martele, bulbous base, 12" ..16,675.00
Vase, Crow & Fox (Aesop), acid-etched enamel/gilt, bottle form, 8"... 3,220.00
Vase, Deco motif on orange w/blk speckles, 10x6" 1,610.00
Vase, floral, amethyst/wht on martele frost, fp, long bottle neck, 5"..5,750.00
Vase, floral, brn on frost to tangerine, pear shape, mfg flaw, 9"..1,290.00
Vase, floral, cut/pnt, orange on yel, ftd elongated trumpet form, 14"..3,450.00
Vase, floral, cut/pnt, pastels/gilt on frost, sphere w/long neck, 19"......4,715.00

Vase, floral, purple/gr on bl/purple/orange/cream mottle, ftd, 14" 3,910.00
Vase, floral (simple), lt purple on purple to clear to opal, 6x5" .1,065.00
Vase, floral (sm/simple), bl on cream to amethyst mottle, bulbous, 4" .. 1,995.00
Vase, floral stem, brn on orange mottled martele, ftd, 10" 2,760.00

Vase, floral stems, 10½",
$7,750.00. (Photo courtesy
Early Auction Co.)

Vase, fuchsia, cut/pnt on wht to dk bl, free-form rim, 6¾" 690.00
Vase, grapes, wine on yel/orange mottle, appl snails, cylindrical, 14"....21,850.00
Vase, mold-blown dense forest, dk colors on cranberry to pk frost, 12" ...5,465.00
Vase, pea pods/flowers, gr on bl w/clear stripes, 4-spout rim, 4x5" .. 1,150.00
Vase, rain/windblown tres, cut/pnt on frost/pk/gr, pillow form, 5x7" .10,350.00
Vase, rosehips/leaves, red/orange/gr on purple mottle, bun base, 20x6" 4,500.00
Vase, spring trees, pastels on pk mottle, above-rim hdls, slim, 14".. 7,475.00
Vase, trees (lacy/detailed), bl/purple on pastels, 12" 4,600.00
Vase, trees/lake, brn/gr on amber to frost, ftd/bulbous, 8x8" 2,300.00
Vase, trees/lake, dk gr on orange to citron, bulbous w/cup rim, 13" ..5,530.00
Vase, wild orchid/spider web/bee, cut/pnt on yel w/gilt, ftd cone, 6" ..8,625.00
Vase, windblown trees, brn on cream/butterscotch, classic form, 17".4,430.00
Vase, winter scene w/trees & snow, brn/wht on amber, 4-sided, 4¾"..2,500.00
Vase, winter trees/blkbirds, cut/pnt on icy opal, ftd, 10" 20,125.00
Vase, winter trees/snow at base on orange to yel mottle, slim, 20"... 11,500.00
Wall pocket, orchids/appl tendrils on gr to brn mottle, 5" 5,175.00

Miscellaneous

Bowl, orange/amethyst mottle, 4½" 290.00
Lamp, tall bullet-nose mauve/bl mottle shade w/bronze Brandt o/l, 18"...28,800.00
Plaque, La Danse, lady in flowing shawl, pate-sur-pate, 11" L 660.00
Tray, frog on gr/amethyst leaf, pate-sur-pate, 6" L 1,035.00
Vase, amber/gr/bl shaded w/gilt foil inclusions, ft V-shape, 13" .1,680.00
Vase, amethyst/bl/orange/wht mottle, amethyst int, slim w/bun ft, 17"...1,380.00
Vase, floral, violet enamel on pk to wht mottle, shouldered, 14"...2,875.00
Vase, gr mottle w/wht int, appl silver mica w/3-D scarab, cylinder, 5" ..900.00

De Vez

De Vez was a type of acid-cut French cameo glass produced by Cristallerie de Pantin in Paris around the turn of the century. Our advisor for this category is Don Williams; he is listed in the Directory under Missouri.

Cameo

Lamp, floral, brn on lt textured bl 11" dome shade/bulbous base, 14". 3,345.00
Vase, Alpine scene w/elk, pine-cone neck band, bl on yel, 11".1,560.00
Vase, cockatoo (bl/gr) on branch before forested swamp scene, 8" ... 1,500.00
Vase, floral vines, brn on gr-bl, stick neck, wide disk ft, 7½" 435.00

Vase, gondola/village, moonlit landscape, brn/red on lt yel, 10".. 1,560.00
Vase, landscape, cobalt on faded yel, 3½" 270.00
Vase, lg eagle/nest in tree, brn on pk frost, shouldered, 8" 840.00
Vase, mountain goat/fir trees, gr/bl/wht on shaded pk, slim form, 10". 1,560.00
Vase, Nouveau poppies, pk/gr on frost irid, flares to wide hip, 8" . 920.00
Vase, palm trees/mtns in bkground, bl/gr/yel on opal amber, 10" . 900.00
Vase, palm treess, bl on pk to yel, stick neck, 6" 375.00
Vase, pyramids/palm trees/boats, russet on camphor, slim form, 9½" ... 420.00
Vase, tree from top to bottom, fanned-out rim, slim, bl/gr, 11" 840.00
Vase, trees, village/mtns beyond, mauve/lt gr on lt yel to orange, 17" ... 1,920.00

De Vilbiss

Perfume bottles, atomizers, and dresser accessories marketed by the De Vilbiss Company are appreciated by collectors today for the various types of lovely glassware used in their manufacture as well as for their pleasing shapes. Various companies provided the glass, while De Vilbiss made only the metal tops. They marketed their merchandise not only here but in Paris, England, Canada, and Havana as well. Their marks were acid stamped, ink stamped, in gold script, molded in, or on paper labels. One is no more significant than another. Our advisor for this category is Randy Monsen; he is listed in the Directory under Virginia.

Key:
A — atomizer   B — bulb

Bottles

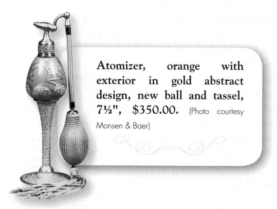

Atomizer, orange with exterior in gold abstract design, new ball and tassel, 7½", $350.00. (Photo courtesy Monsen & Baer)

Blk cylinder in gilt filigree metal stand w/sq base, gilt A, 3½" 425.00
Blk egg atop chromed metal cone-shaped base w/disk ft, 6" 325.00
Blk w/abstract gold, slim stem, disk ft, A w/rpl B, 7½" 185.00
Blk w/enamel & gilt floral, bell shape, A, in pyramid-shaped box, 4". 4,000.00
Clear w/bl int & gilt floral o/l, slim/disk ft, A, 7½" 950.00
Clear w/gilt pheasant, elongated, in gilt metal stand, A, 9" 650.00
Clear w/pk to bl int, jeweled filigree o/l, A, Imperial series, 8"..8,500.00
Coral & gold abstracts, gold stem/ft, A, orig B, 9⅜" 235.00
Deco mc leaves, slim gold stem & disk ft, A, orig B, 9½" 1,200.00
Frosted w/internal gr decor, disk ft, A w/rpl B, 6½" 110.00
Lt gr w/triangular windows & gold, disk ft, A w/rpl B & tassel, 8" ..115.00
Orange w/blk Deco enamel, long dauber, disk top, 4⅞"................ 195.00
Penguin, wht porc w/blk felt, sprayer is nose, Lenox, 4⅜" 265.00
Pk octagon w/gold lines, dauber disk top, 4½" 80.00
Pk w/gold bands, disk ft, A, w/rpl B, orig mk tag, 6½" 100.00
Red & gold enamel, slim w/blk acorn stopper, A, rpl B, 9½"........ 300.00

Miscellaneous

Ginger jar, amber w/gold pine needle design, w/A insert, 6⅜" 230.00
Tray, HP flowers & leaves on gold enamel, rectangular, 10½x7" .. 365.00

Decanters

Ceramic whiskey decanters were brought into prominence in 1955 by the James Beam Distilling Company. Few other companies besides Beam produced these decanters during the next 10 years or so; however, other companies did eventually follow suit. At its peak in 1975, at least 20 prominent companies and several on a lesser scale made these decanters. Beam stopped making decanters in mid-1992. Now only a couple of companies are still producing these collectibles.

Liquor dealers have told collectors for years that ceramic decanters are not as valuable, and in some cases worthless, if emptied or if the federal tax stamp has been broken. Nothing is further from the truth. Following are but a few of many reasons you should consider emptying ceramic decanters:

1) If the thin glaze on the inside ever cracks (and it does in a small percentage of decanters), the contents will push through to the outside. It is then referred to as a 'leaker' and worth a fraction of its original value.

2) A large number of decanters left full in one area of your house poses a fire hazard.

3) A burglar, after stealing jewelry and electronics, may make off with some of your decanters just to enjoy the contents. If they are empty, chances are they will not be bothered.

4) It is illegal in most states for collectors to sell a full decanter without a liquor license.

Unlike years ago, few collectors now collect all types of decanters. Most now specialize. For example, they may collect trains, cars, owls, Indians, clowns, or any number of different things that have been depicted on or as a decanter. They are finding exceptional quality available at reasonable prices, especially when compared with many other types of collectibles.

We have tried to list those brands that are the most popular with collectors. Likewise, individual decanters listed are the ones (or representative of the ones) most commonly found. The following listing is but a small fraction of the thousands of decanters that have been produced.

These decanters come from all over the world. While Jim Beam owned its own china factory in the U.S., some of the others have been imported from Mexico, Taiwan, Japan, and elsewhere. They vary in size from miniatures (approximately two-ounce) to gallons. Values range from a few dollars to more than $3,000.00 per decanter. Most collectors and dealers define a 'mint' decanter as one with no chips, no cracks, and label intact. A missing federal tax stamp or lack of contents have no bearing on value. All values are given for 'mint' decanters. A 'mini' behind a listing indicates a miniature. All others are fifth or 750 ml unless noted otherwise. Our advisor for this category is Roy Willis; he is listed in the Directory under Kentucky.

Aesthetic Specialties (ASI)

Cadillac, 1903, bl or wht 65.00
Chevrolet, 1914 .... 65.00
Golf, Bing Crosby 38th 50.00

Beam

Casino Series, Golden Gate, 1970 .... 18.00
Casino Series, Harold's Club Pinwheel 35.00
Casino Series, Reno Horseshoe Prima Donna or Cal Neva........... 10.00
Centennial Series, Alaska Purchase 9.00
Centennial Series, Key West 9.00
Centennial Series, Lombard 8.00
Centennial Series, Statue of Liberty, 1975.................................... 19.00
Executive Series, 1979 Mother of Pearl 16.00
Executive Series, 1981 Royal Filigree... 14.00

Executive Series, 1982 American Pitcher 18.00
Executive Series, 1983 Partridge Bell 35.00
Executive Series, 1984 Carolers Bell 25.00
Foreign Series, Australia, Galah Bird 24.00
Foreign Series, Australia, Kangaroo 18.00
Foreign Series, Fiji Islands 6.00
Organization Series, Ducks Unlimited, #6, 1980 .... 45.00
Organization Series, Ducks Unlimited, #7, 1981 .... 40.00
Organization Series, Ducks Unlimited, #9, 1983 .... 55.00
Organization Series, Ducks Unlimited, #10, 1984 .... 85.00
Organization Series, Elks, 1968 .... 5.00
Organization Series, Phi Sigma Kappa 25.00
Organization Series, Shriner Raja Temple 24.00
Organization Series, VFW 8.00
People Series, Cowboy 20.00
People Series, Emmett Kelly 35.00
People Series, George Washington 18.00
People Series, Martha Washington 12.00
State Series, Delaware 10.00
State Series, Kentucky, blk head stopper 25.00
State Series, Maine 9.00
State Series, Ohio 10.00
Wheels Series, Cable Car, 1968 .... 6.00
Wheels Series, Cable Car, 1983 .... 55.00
Wheels Series, Coal Tender for Grant 65.00
Wheels Series, Corvette, 1954, bl 125.00
Wheels Series, Corvette, 1955, copper 125.00
Wheels Series, Corvette, 1978, red, yel or wht 75.00
Wheels Series, Ford, 1913 Model T, blk or gr 48.00
Wheels Series, Ford, 1964 Mustang, blk 140.00
Wheels Series, Ford, 1964 Mustang, wht 75.00
Wheels Series, Golf Car 45.00
Wheels Series, Harold's Club Covered Wagon, 1974 ..... 35.00
Wheels Series, Mack Fire Engine 130.00
Wheels Series, Train, Caboose, gray 90.00
Wheels Series, Train, Caboose, red 75.00
Wheels Series, Train, Locomotive, Grant 75.00
Wheels Series, Train, Locomotive, JB Turner 125.00
Wheels Series, Train, Passenger Car 55.00
Wheels Series, Train, Wood Tender for General 150.00

Brooks

American Legion, Denver, 1971 .... 15.00
Amvets 10.00
Car, Auburn Boattail 30.00
Car, 1962 Corvette Mako Shark 32.00
Elk 24.00
Fire Engine 18.00
Indy Racer #21, 1970 .... 40.00
Keystone Kops 75.00
Man O' War 40.00
Phonograph 20.00
Pistol, Dueling 12.00
Setter With Bird, 1970 .... 17.00
Ticker Tape 10.00
Trail Bike 24.00
Train, Iron Horse 12.00
Vermont Skier 10.00
Whale, Killer 20.00

Dant, J.W.

American Legion 9.00

Field Birds, 8 diffrent, ea 10.00
Indy 500 .... 9.00
Owl, brn or red 15.00

Dickel, George

Golf Club 10.00
Powderhorn, amber, 1-qt 15.00
Powderhorn, dk, ⅘-qt 12.00

Famous Firsts

Coffee Mill 32.00
Roulette Wheel 32.00
Scale, Lombardy 30.00
Spirit of St Louis, midi 75.00
Spirit of St Louis, mini 50.00

Hoffman

Big Red Machine 50.00
Cats, 6 different, mini, ea 15.00
College Series, Helmet - Auburn 30.00
College Series, Helmet - Missouri 30.00
College Series, Mascot - Nevada Wolfpack 45.00
Mr Lucky Series, Blacksmith 38.00
Mr Lucky Series, Blacksmith, mini 15.00
Mr Lucky Series, Fireman, mini 25.00
Mr Lucky Series, Policeman 48.00
Mr Lucky Series, Policeman, mini 16.00
Race Car, AJ Foyt #2 .... 125.00
Wildlife Series, Doe & Fawn 45.00

Kontinental

Dentist 35.00
Dockworker 32.00
Innkeeper 28.00
Stephen Foster 28.00
Surveyor 35.00

Lionstone

Backpacker 30.00
Barber 42.00
Barber, mini 18.00
Camp Cook 25.00
Camp Follower 25.00
Canada Goose With Base 55.00
Chinese Laundryman 26
Clown, 6 different, ea 35.00
Country Doctor 24.00
Fisherman 38.00
Football Players 55.00
Johnny Lightning #1 .... 100.00
Johnny Lightning #2 .... 90.00
Meadowlark 24.00
Photographer 60.00
Photographer, mini 24.00
Rainmaker, mini 18.00
Riverboat Captain 25.00
Sheepherder 40.00
Telegrapher 25.00
Turbo Car, STP, red 55.00

McCormick

Abe Lincoln	35.00
Alexander Graham Bell	28.00
Elvis #1 White, plays Love Me Tender, mini	55.00
Elvis #3 Black, plays Can't Help Falling in Love	80.00
Elvis #3 Black, plays Can't Help Falling in Love, mini	48.00
Elvis Designer #1 Silver, plays Are You Lonesome Tonight?, mini	200.00
Elvis Designer #3 Gold Encore, plays It's Now or Never	300.00
Elvis Gold Tribute, plays My Way, mini	150.00
Elvis Teddy Bear, plays Let Me Be Your Teddy Bear	600.00
Hank Williams, Sr	125.00
Iwo Jima	150.00
Iwo Jima, mini	75.00

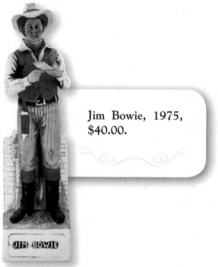

Jim Bowie, 1975, $40.00.

Jimmy Durante	70.00
King Arthur	48.00
Marilyn Monroe	550.00
Pony Express	50.00
Robert Peary	32.00
Shrine Dune Buggy	40.00
Telephone Operator	60.00

O.B.R.

Engine, General	18.00
Guitar, Music City	18.00
WC Fields Top Hat	60.00

Old Bardstown

Foster Brooks	28.00
Surface Miner	28.00
Tiger	30.00

Old Commonwealth

Coal Miner #1, w/shovel	90.00
Coal Miner #1, w/shovel, mini	27.00
Coal Miner #2, w/pick	40.00
Firefighter, Fallen Comrade	75.00
Firefighter, Fallen Comrade, mini	28.00
Firefighter, Modern Hero #1	70.00
Firefighter, Modern Hero #1, mini	25.00
Firefighter, Nozzleman #2	70.00

Old Fitzgerald

Irish, Blarney	12.00
Irish, Leprechaun, Plase God	28.00
Irish, Luck	26.00
Irish, Wish	22.00
Rip Van Winkle	28.00

Ski Country

Barrel Racer	95.00
Barrel Racer, mini	45.00
Birth of Freedom	125.00
Birth of Freedom, 1-gal	1,950.00
Bob Cratchit	60.00
Bob Cratchit, mini	35.00
Cardinals, Holiday	95.00
Ducks Unlimited, Pintail, 1978	120.00
Ducks Unlimited, Pintail, 1978, mini	38.00
Ducks Unlimited, Pintail, 1978, 1-gal	225.00
Ducks Unlimited, Widgeon, 1979	65.00
Ducks Unlimited, Widgeon, 1979, 1.75 liter	195.00
Eagle, Majestic	295.00
Eagle, Majestic, mini	140.00
Eagle, Majestic, 1-gal	1,800.00
Elk	225.00
Indian, Cigar Store	45.00
Indian, Cigar Store, mini	35.00
Indian, Northwest American, set of 6	260.00
Indian, Southwest Dancers, mini, set of 6	240.00
Jaguar	175.00
Jaguar, mini	50.00
Koala	50.00
Owl, Barred; wall plaque	150.00
Owl, Great Gray	90.00
Owl, Great Gray, mini	55.00
Pelican	65.00
Pelican, mini	35.00
Pheasant Standing, mini	65.00
Phoenix Bird	60.00
Ram, Big Horn; mini	40.00
Ruffed Grouse	70.00
Ruffed Grouse, mini	30.00
Skunk Family	65.00
Skunk Family, mini	35.00
Whitetail Deer	175.00
Wild Turkey	140.00

Wild Turkey

Series I, #1	195.00
Series I, #1, #2, #3, or #4, mini, ea	22.00
Series I, #2	135.00
Series I, #3 or #4, ea	60.00
Series I, #5, #6, #7, #8, mini, set of 4	160.00
Series I, #5, #6 or #7, ea	30.00
Series I, #8	45.00
Series II, Lore #1	25.00
Series II, Lore #2	35.00
Series II, Lore #3	45.00
Series II, Lore #4	55.00
Series III, #1, in flight	110.00
Series III, #1, in flight, mini	45.00
Series III, #2, Turkey & Bobcat	140.00

Series III, #2, Turkey & Bobcat, mini........................ 55.00
Series III, #3, Fighting Turkeys............................. 150.00
Series III, #3, Fighting Turkeys, mini 60.00
Series III, #4, Turkey & Eagle................................ 95.00
Series III, #4, Turkey & Eagle, mini 85.00
Series III, #5, Turkey & Raccoon 95.00
Series III, #5, Turkey & Raccoon, mini 45.00
Series III, #6, Turkey & Poults 95.00
Series III, #6, Turkey & Poults, mini 45.00
Series III, #7, Turkey & Red Fox 100.00
Series III, #7, Turkey & Red Fox, mini 60.00
Series III, #8, Turkey & Owl................................ 100.00
Series III, #8, Turkey & Owl, mini 60.00
Series III, #9, Turkey & Bear Cubs 100.00
Series III, #9, Turkey & Bear Cubs, mini 60.00
Series III, #10, Turkey & Coyote........................... 100.00
Series III, #10, Turkey & Coyote, mini 60.00
Series III, #11, Turkey & Falcon 100.00
Series III, #11, Turkey & Falcon, mini 60.00
Series III, #12, Turkey & Skunks 125.00
Series III, #12, Turkey & Skunks, mini 65.00

Decoys

American colonists learned the craft of decoy making from the Indians who used them to lure birds out of the sky as an important food source. Early models were carved from wood such as pine, cedar, balsa, etc., and a few were made of canvas or papier-mache. There are two basic types of decoys: water floaters and shorebirds (also called 'stick-ups'). Within each type are many different species, ducks being the most plentiful since they migrated along all four of America's great waterways. Market hunting became big business around 1880, resulting in large-scale commercial production of decoys which continued until about 1910 when such hunting was outlawed by the Migratory Bird Treaty.

Today decoys are one of the most collectible types of American folk art. The most valuable are those carved by such artists as Laing, Crowell, Ward, and Wheeler, to name only a few. Each area, such as Massachusetts, Connecticut, Maine, the Illinois River, and the Delaware River, produces decoys with distinctive regional characteristics. Examples of commercial decoys produced by well-known factories — among them Mason, Stevens, and Dodge — are also prized by collectors. Though mass-produced, these nevertheless required a certain amount of hand carving and decorating. Well carved examples, especially those of rare species, are appreciating rapidly, and those with original paint are more desirable. In the listings that follow, all decoys are solid-bodied unless noted hollow.

Key:

CG — Challenge Grade	OWP — original working paint
DDF — Dodge Decoy Factory	PDF — Peterson Decoy Factory
DG — Detroit Grade	PG — Premier Grade
MDF — Mason's Decoy Factory	SG — Standard Grade
OP — original paint	WDF — Wildfowler Decoy Factory
ORP — old repaint	WOP — worn original paint

Black duck, Charles Shang Wheeler, sleeping, never rigged, EX orig... 35,850.00
Black duck, J McLoughlin, glass eyes, Xd wings, wooden keel, EX OP...3,700.00
Black duck, PDF, rpt by MH Gould, trn head, glass eyes 125.00
Black duck, Sperry Decoy Co, glass eyes, EX OP, 1920s-30s 300.00
Black duck, WDF, Atlantic model, EX OP, ca 1950, sm dents 100.00
Black-Bellied Plover, Nantucket, hollow, split tail, tack eyes, VG ...3,750.00
Black-Bellied Plover, Phillip Fairbank Jr, split tail, antique EX OP .. 325.00
Black-Necked Stilt, Lloyd Johnson, glass eyes, EX OP/crazed/splits...4,175.00
Bluebell drake, Ward Bros, 1936 model w/trn head, OP, crack/dents .. 2,750.00

Bluebill drake, St Clair Flats, glass eyes, bottom brd, EX OP, shot ..700.00
Bluebill drake, Ward Bros, balsa w/trn cedar head, EX OP, 1948...2,100.00
Bluebill hen, MDF PG, WOP, lightly shot.................................2,300.00
Bluewing Teal pr, WDF, balsa body, EX OP, dents 550.00
Brant, Cobb Island VA, solid body, OWP w/varnish, slivers/checks ... 800.00
Brant, Paul Carter in Lincoln style, EX OP, brand.................. 175.00
Broadbill pr, MDF DG, glass eyes, EX OP, chips/crack 675.00
Bufflehead hen, James West, glass eyes, M OP........................ 600.00
Bufflehead hen, Ward Bros, cvd wings/fluted trn head, 1970, EX OP .. 3,050.00
Canada goose, AE Crowell, neck seam visible, EX OP, mini......2,000.00
Canada goose, Ward Bros, Bishop Head's Club style, 1930s, ORP...4,500.00
Canada goose, Ward Bros, 1936 model w/EX form, ORP, eye missing/shot..6,000.00
Canvasback drake, Lem & Steve Ward, ca 1936, worn OP w/some rpt ..4,250.00
Canvasback drake, MDF, ORP (some orig), checks/filler missing ...225.00
Canvasback drake, Ward Bros, 1948 model, balsa body, OP, dents/wear..3,150.00
Canvasback hen, PDF, WOP, 1890s, crack 250.00
Canvasback hen, Ward Bros, classic 1936 model w/trn head, rstr pnt 2,000.00
Eider drake, Nova Scotia, turtle-bk design, OP, crackling/checks ...125.00
Goldeneye drake, AE Crowell, trn head, cvd tail, glass eyes, EX OP.. 5,500.00
Goldeneye drake, Sam Collins, glass eyes, ORP, structurally sound ...150.00
Goldeneye hen, DDF, late 20th C, EX OP, chips/crack 1,000.00
Goldeneye hen, upstate New York area, head swivels, EX OWP, chip ...225.00
Goldeneye pr, AE Crowell, EX OP, fine patina, no brand or label, mini..3,950.00
Greenwing Teal drake, WDF, EX, OP, no brand 600.00
Gull, WDF, OP, Mt Pleasant stamp, NM 350.00
Hooded Merganser drake, AE Crowell, red breasted, early, EX OP..2,200.00
Hooded Merganser drake, Roe Terry, trn head, glass eyes, brand, M OP ... 150.00
Hudsonian Godwit, HN Gibbs, breeding plumage, intricate pnt. 550.00
Labrador duck, Long Island area, late 1800s, WOP, chips/shot 325.00
Mallard drake, Benjamin Schmidt, made in 2 pcs, EX OP, mini .. 400.00
Mallard drake, John McLoughlin, glass eyes, cvd Xd wing tops, M OP ..2,000.00
Mallard drake, MDF CG, OP w/shot/checks, rpr chip w/ORP..... 600.00
Mallard hen, MDF PG, early EX OP, prof rstr chips/shot 2,500.00
Merganser hen, Wquoit Decoy Co, tack eyes, narrow head, EX OP... 225.00
Pintail drake, Charles Perdew, glass eyes, OP w/added varnish, ca 1950...3,350.00
Pintail drake, in style of Ward Bros, solid body, 1930s style, OP.. 575.00
Pintail drake, WDF, balsa block, EX OWP, Chouteau brand, 1930s ..200.00
Red-Breasted Merganser, Ben Smith, natural wood, rpr/filler....... 950.00
Redhead drake, MDF PG, OP w/lt crazing, brand 800.00
Redhead drake, Ward Bros, balsa w/trn cedar head, OP, flakes/dents.. 2,200.00
Robin Snipe, MDF, nail bill, structurally M, prof rpt in orig style ...200.00
Scoter, DDF, EX OP, 1880s, missing filler...................................... 600.00
Shoveler drake, C Chauvin, raised wings, scratch pnt on head, EX OP... 75.00
White-Wing Scoter, Maine area, inlet head, EX OP, early 1900s, shot ..525.00
Widgeon drake, DDF, rare, 1890s, EX OP, missing filler 4,000.00
Widgeon pr, WDF, balsa, EX OP, rprs/touchups, unstamped, oversz...225.00
Wigeon hen, JJ West, glass eyes, detailed feather cvg, NM OP 360.00
Wood Duck drake, B Williams, preening, wings lifted, 1961, EX OP...425.00
Wood Duck drake, Ken Harris, glass eyes, EX OP, crack at neck .. 600.00
Yellowlegs, folding tin, EX OP, sm chips/rust 50.00

Dedham Pottery

Originally founded in Chelsea, Massachusetts, as the Chelsea Keramic Works, the name was changed to Dedham Pottery in 1895 after the firm relocated in Dedham, near Boston, Massachusetts. The ware utilized a gray stoneware body with a crackle glaze and simple cobalt border designs of flowers, birds, and animals. Decorations were brushed on by hand using an ancient Chinese method which suspended the cobalt within the overall glaze. There were 13 standard patterns, among them Magnolia, Iris, Butterfly, Duck, Polar Bear, and Rabbit, the latter of which was chosen to represent the company on their logo. On the very early pieces, the rabbits face left; decorators soon found the reverse position easier to paint, and the rabbits were turned to the right. (Earlier examples are worth from 10% to 20% more than identical pieces manufactured in later years.) In addition to the standard patterns, other designs were produced for special orders. These and artist-signed pieces are highly valued by collectors today.

Though their primary product was the blue-printed, crackle-glazed dinnerware, two types of artware were also produced: crackle glaze and flambe. Their notable volcanic ware was a type of the latter. The mark is incised and often accompanies the cipher of Hugh Robertson. The firm was operated by succeeding generations of the Robertson family until it closed in 1943. Our advisor for this category is Dale MacLean; he is listed in the Directory under Massachusetts. See also Chelsea Keramic Art Works.

Bowl, Butterfly, stamped/registered, 2x4½" 400.00
Bowl, Grape, stamped, 3½x7" 325.00
Bowl, Grape, stamped/registered, mfg flaw, 9" 325.00
Bowl, Rabbit, ftd, stamped, 2½x5½" 180.00
Bowl, Rabbit, stamped/registered, sq, 8½" 350.00
Bowl, Rabbit, stamped/registered, 3½x9" 425.00
Bowl, rice; Duck, stamped, 2x3½" 275.00
Bowl, soup; Rabbit (single ear), stamped/imp, 8½" 295.00
Chamberstick, Rabbit, stamped, 2½x7" 700.00
Charger, Rabbit (single ear), stamped/imp, 12" 600.00
Coffeepot, Rabbit, stamped, 5½x6½", NM 950.00
Compote, Rabbit, faint stain, stamped, 3½x5½" 275.00
Creamer, Horse Chestnut, stamped/registered, 3½x4½" 275.00
Creamer & sugar bowl, Rabbit, stamped/registered, 3½", 3" 425.00
Cup & saucer, bouillon; Elephant & Baby, stamped/registered, 2", 6" ..800.00
Cup & saucer, Rabbit, stamped, 2½" 225.00
Cup & saucer, Rabbit, stamped, 4x5", 6½" 275.00
Cup & saucer, Snowtree, 2¾x4½", 5½" 275.00
Dish, Rabbit, 5-sided, stamped/registered, 1½x7½" 450.00
Egg cup, Rabbit, chalice form, stamped, 2½x2" 375.00
Marmalade, Rabbit, flat lid w/knob finial, stamped, 4¾x4" 550.00
Medallion, Rabbit, slightly domed, sgn EM/2-36, 2" dia 325.00
Mug, Rabbit, stamped, flaw, 4½" 225.00
Nappy, Horse Chestnut, pre-1929 mk, sm stain, 6" 195.00
Nappy, Rabbit (pk & gr), stamped, 2x4" 195.00
Pitcher, Night & Morning, owl/rooster, stamped, 4¾" 450.00
Pitcher, Rabbit, cylindrical, stamped/registered, 4½x5" 550.00
Pitcher, Rabbit, looped hdl, bulbous, stamped, 6¾x7", NM 650.00
Pitcher, tankard; Rabbit, cylindrical, stamped/1931, 9x6" 750.00
Place-card holder, rabbit figural w/bl accents, stamped, 1½x2½" .. 500.00
Plate, Azalea, stamped/imp, 10" 300.00
Plate, Bird in Potted Orange Tree, stamped/imp, 8½" 400.00
Plate, Birds in Orange Tree, imp, 8½" 400.00
Plate, Butterfly, imp/registered, 6" 375.00
Plate, Clover, stamped, 10" 975.00
Plate, Crab, #2, stamped/imp, 8¾" 675.00
Plate, Crab, stamped, 6" 425.00
Plate, Crab w/Seaweed, stamped/imp, 6½" 425.00
Plate, Crab w/Seaweed (lg crab/heavy seaweed), stamped, 8½" ... 700.00
Plate, Dolphin, #2, stamped/imp, 8¾" 1,000.00
Plate, Double Turtle, stamped/imp, 6" 800.00
Plate, Duck, M Davenport, stamped/imp, 8½" 300.00
Plate, French Mushroom, Davenport, stamped/imp, 8½" 900.00
Plate, Goat & Putti, stamped/registered/imp rabbit, 9" 1,500.00
Plate, Grape, Davenport, stamped/imp, 9¾" 300.00
Plate, Grape, stamped, 8½" 250.00
Plate, Grape, stamped/1931/2 imp rabbits, 6" 175.00
Plate, Horse Chestnut, H Robertson, CPUS/stamped, 8½" 275.00
Plate, Iris, experimental pk, stamped/imp, 9¾" 275.00
Plate, Lily Pond, peppering, stamped, 10½" 250.00
Plate, Lobster, stamped/imp, 6½" 600.00

Plate, Lunar Moth, imp, 8½", NM 650.00
Plate, Magnolia, Davenport, stamped/imp, 9¾" 275.00
Plate, Magnolia, stamped, 10" 350.00
Plate, Mushroom, #2, lt pk overglaze, stamped/imp, 8½" 750.00
Plate, Mushroom, stamped/imp, 8½" 700.00
Plate, Pineapple, CPUS/imp, flake, 10" 800.00
Plate, Pineapple, Raised; #1, imp cloverleaf w/CPUS, 10" 950.00
Plate, Polar Bear, #1, Davenport, stamped/imp, 10" 950.00
Plate, Polar Bear, stamped, sm chips, 8½" 385.00
Plate, Pond Lily, stamped, 6" 175.00
Plate, Poppy, buds along border, stamped/imp, 6" 875.00
Plate, Poppy, stamped/imp, 8½" 700.00
Plate, Rabbit, CPUS, 10" 350.00
Plate, Rabbit, stamped, 8½" 225.00
Plate, Rabbit, stamped, 9¾" 300.00
Plate, Rabbit, w/Fairbanks House, stamped/registered, 1931, 9½" .. 1,765.00
Plate, River & Landscape, Hugh Robertson, lily border, stamped, 6" ... 1,500.00
Plate, Snow Tree, Davenport, stamped/imp, 6" 175.00
Plate, Snow Tree, stamped, 8½" 300.00
Plate, Snow Tree, stamped, 10" 350.00
Plate, Swan & Cattail, stamped/imp, 7½", NM 400.00
Plate, Tapestry Lion, #2, imp, 8½" 1,200.00
Plate, Turkey, stamped, edge chip, 8½" 265.00
Plate, Turkey, stamped, 9¾" 500.00
Plate, Turkey, stamped/registered, 8½" 475.00
Plate, Turtle, #2, stamped, chips to ft ring, 8½" 1,700.00
Plate, Upside Down Dolphin & Baby, CPUS, 10½" 700.00
Plate, Water Lily, stamped, 6" 175.00
Platter, Rabbit, stamped/2 imp rabbits, 12½" 875.00
Shakers, Rabbit, bulbous, stamped, 2⅝", pr. 400.00
Sugar bowl, Rabbit, Davenport, stamped/incised, 3½x4½" 325.00
Teapot, Rabbit, stamped, ca 1932, 4½" 900.00
Teapot, Rabbit, stamped, 6½" 975.00
Tray, celery; Rabbit, stamped/registered, 9¾" L 400.00
Tureen, Rabbit, 2 rabbit bands, ftd/hdld, rabbit finial, 8x8x11", EX ...2,185.00

Miscellaneous

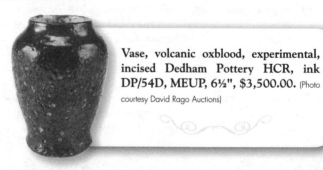

Vase, volcanic oxblood, experimental, incised Dedham Pottery HCR, ink DP/54D, MEUP, 6½", $3,500.00. (Photo courtesy David Rago Auctions)

Vase, brn flambe gloss, baluster, HCR/DP39F, 10x6" 1,450.00
Vase, bubbly oxblood over wht & bl crackle, WA, hairlines, 5½x4" ..2,400.00
Vase, gr & oxblood drip, can neck, H Robinson, 11" 5,500.00
Vase, gr matt w/orange-peel texture, HCR, 7½x4½" 2,400.00
Vase, mahog & oxblood flambe, HCR/DP24A, firing line, 8x6" ...2,750.00
Vase, textured/thick brn/gr, HCR/DP48C, 9x4½" 2,400.00
Vase, thick wht/beige drips on frothy gr, HCR/DP718, 8½x4½" ...2,875.00
Vase, volcanic chocolate/indigo/gr, bruise/chips, BW/DP32A, 7x4" ... 950.00
Vase, volcanic creamy buff, can neck, H Robinson, 10½x6" 1,200.00
Vase, volcanic mottled br/brn, HCR/DP10B, 8x6" 2,400.00

Degenhart

The Crystal Art Glass factory in Cambridge, Ohio, opened in 1947 under the private ownership of John and Elizabeth Degenhart. John had previously worked for the Cambridge Glass Company and was well known for his superior paperweights. After his death in 1964, Elizabeth took over management of the factory, hiring several workers from the defunct Cambridge Company, including Zack Boyd. Boyd was responsible for many unique colors, some of which were named for him. From 1964 to 1974, more than 27 different moulds were created, most of them resulting from Elizabeth Degenhart's work and creativity. Over 145 official colors were also developed. Elizabeth died in 1978, requesting that the 10 moulds she had built while operating the factory were to be turned over to the Degenhart Museum. The remaining moulds were to be held by the Island Mould and Machine Company, who (complying with her request) removed the familiar 'D in heart' trademark. The factory was eventually bought by Zack's son, Bernard Boyd. He also acquired the remaining Degenhart moulds, to which he added his own logo.

In general, slags and opaques should be valued 15% to 20% higher than crystals in color.

Bicentennial Bell, Charcoal	12.00
Bow Slipper, Amethyst	12.00
Chick Salt, Emerald Green, 2"	15.00
Daisy & Button Toothpick Holder, Cobalt Carnival	20.00
Forget-Me-Not Toothpick Holder, April Green	15.00
Forget-Me-Not Toothpick Holder, Ivory Slag (Dark)	25.00
Forget-Me-Not Toothpick Holder, Sparrow Slag	20.00
Forget-Me-Not Toothpick Holder, Vaseline	15.00
Gypsy Pot, Amberina (Dark)	20.00
Heart Toothpick Holder, Jade Green	25.00
Heart Toothpick Holder, Toffee Slag	25.00
Hen Covered Dish, Caramel Custard Slag, 3"	45.00
Hen Covered Dish, Emerald Green, 5"	30.00
Hen Covered Dish, Powder Blue Slag, 3"	45.00
Kat Slipper, Cobalt	15.00
Kat Slipper, Tomato	30.00
Lamb Covered Dish, Caramel Slag (Light), 5"	50.00
Lamb Covered Dish, Crown Tuscan	40.00
Lamb Covered Dish, Vaseline	30.00
Owl, Amberina (Dark)	45.00
Owl, Antique Blue	30.00
Owl, Caramel	60.00
Owl, Chad's Blue	40.00
Owl, Champagne	20.00
Owl, Concord Grape	35.00
Owl, Dark Amber Dichromatic	45.00
Owl, Ebony	50.00
Owl, Holly Green	25.00
Owl, Jade #1	55.00
Owl, Lavender Blue	35.00
Owl, Lemon Opal	30.00

Owl, Pink Lady	35.00
Pooch, Baby Pink Slag (Light)	25.00
Pooch, Bittersweet, 1976	35.00
Pooch, Buttercup Slag (Dark)	35.00
Pooch, Cobalt Carnival	35.00
Pooch, Crown Tuscan	15.00
Pooch, Daffodil Slag (dark)	60.00
Pooch, Dark Caramel Slag w/Green	30.00
Pooch, Dark Ivory Slag	40.00
Pooch, Light Powder Blue Slag	35.00
Pooch, Pink	15.00
Priscilla Doll, April Green	90.00
Priscilla Doll, Blue & White Slag	100.00
Priscilla Doll, Blue Lady	90.00
Priscilla Doll, Crown Tuscan	80.00
Priscilla Doll, Fawn	60.00
Priscilla Doll, Ivory	60.00
Priscilla Doll, Orchid	90.00
Priscilla Doll, Smoky Blue	60.00
Priscilla Doll, Vaseline	70.00
Robin Covered Dish, Bloody Mary, 5"	100.00
Robin Covered Dish, Fawn	40.00
Roller Skate, Sapphire Blue	20.00
Texas Boot Toothpick Holder, Amethyst	10.00
Texas Boot Toothpick Holder, Chocolate Slag, 1974	20.00
Turkey Covered Dish, Amberina, 1975, 5"	65.00
Turkey Covered Dish, Bittersweet, 5"	65.00
Turkey Covered Dish, Caramel Slag, 5"	75.00
Wildflower Candy Dish, Amber	16.00

Delatte

Delatte was a manufacturer of French cameo glass. Founded in 1921, their style reflected the influence of the Art Deco era with strong color contrasts and bold design. Our advisor for this category is Don Williams; he is listed in the Directory under Missouri.

Key: fp — fire polished

Cameo

Chandelier, grapevines, brn/orange, 18" bowl shade+3 pendant lilies	3,300.00
Vase, blackberries, polished reds on red to lemon & wht, bulbous, 6"	960.00
Vase, buckeye & foliage, brn on mottled pumpkin, 9½"	550.00
Vase, fruit on branches, bl on wht w/citron & burgundy mottle, 4"	515.00
Vase, lake scene, brn tones to frost, cylinder, metal base, 6"	600.00
Vase, orchids & leaves, purple/gr on pk, ovoid, 8x5"	2,150.00
Vase, thorny flowers, amethyst on citron, teardop, 7½"	550.00

Delft

Old Delftware, made as early as the sixteenth century, was originally a low-fired earthenware coated in a thin opaque tin glaze with painted-on blue or polychrome designs. It was not until the last half of the nineteenth century, however, that the ware became commonly referred to as Delft, acquiring the name from the Dutch village that had become the major center of its production. English, German, and French potters also produced Delft, though with noticeable differences both in shape and decorative theme.

In the early part of the eighteenth century, the German potter, Bottger, developed a formula for porcelain; in England, Wedgwood began producing creamware — both of which were much more durable. Unable to compete, one by one the Delft potteries failed. Soon only one remained.

Owl, Misty Blue, $35.00.

In 1876 De Porcelyne Fles reintroduced Delftware on a hard white body with blue and white decorative themes reflecting the Dutch countryside, windmills by the sea, and Dutch children. This manufacturer is the most well known of several operating today. Their products are now produced under the Royal Delft label.

For further information we recommend *Discovering Dutch Delftware, Modern Delft and Makkum Pottery,* by Stephen J. Van Hook (Glen Park Press, Alexandria, Virginia). Examples listed here are blue on white unless noted otherwise. See also specific manufacturers. Our advisor is Ralph Jaarsma; he is listed in the Directory under Iowa.

Bottle, England, florals on globular shape, slim neck, 18th C, 9" .. 1,175.00
Bottle, Liverpool, floral/foliage, mid-18th C, 9" 765.00
Bowl, England, Asian scenery, 18th C, 3⅞x11¾" 765.00
Bowl, England, floral spray/central band, 18th C, 4⅝" 1,100.00
Bowl, England, floral sprays/X-hatching/dots, 18th C, 6¾" 500.00
Bowl, England, flowers/insects/vines, ftd, 18th C, 10½", EX 885.00
Bowl, England, scrolled foliage/florals, 1740, 9" 585.00
Bowl, England, stylized flowers, lobed, mid-18th C, 2x8⅝", EX ... 475.00
Bowl, flower; English, attached pierced lid, vines/flowers, 1740, 9" .. 1,760.00
Char pot, England, fish on cylinder, 18th C, 8½", EX 2,700.00
Charger, England, Adam & Eve at tree, mc, ca 1700, 13½" 4,400.00
Charger, England, Chinaman/landscape, floral rim, mc, 1750s, 13½" ... 950.00
Charger, England, dragonfly medallions/flowers, 18th C, chips, 13" .. 1,650.00
Charger, England, floral sprays/borders, 18th C, 13" 1,100.00
Charger, England, flower garden/fence, 18th C, chip, 14" 950.00
Charger, Holland, flower garden, floral border, 18th C, 13½" ... 1,200.00
Charger, Holland, hunter & hounds, sm rpr, 18th C, 12" 1,175.00
Charger, Holland, Prince William, fruit/floral border, 18th C, 13½" .. 3,050.00
Plate, England, flower-filled urn, floral border, 18th C, 13", pr .. 2,350.00
Plate, England, pagodas & fisherman w/birds overhead, 12", NM. 750.00
Plate, Holland, peacock, early 18th C, 12⅜", EX 650.00
Teapot, England, flowers/birds panels, 18th C, 3¾" 4,400.00
Tobacco jar, Dutch, Rappe in cartouch, Indians w/pipes, mid-18th C, 8" 700.00
Tobacco jar, Holland, floral & scrolled foliage, oviform, B-P, 13" .. 765.00
Tobacco jar, Holland, sailor w/pipe/#7 cartouch, mid-18th C, 10" ... 2,350.00

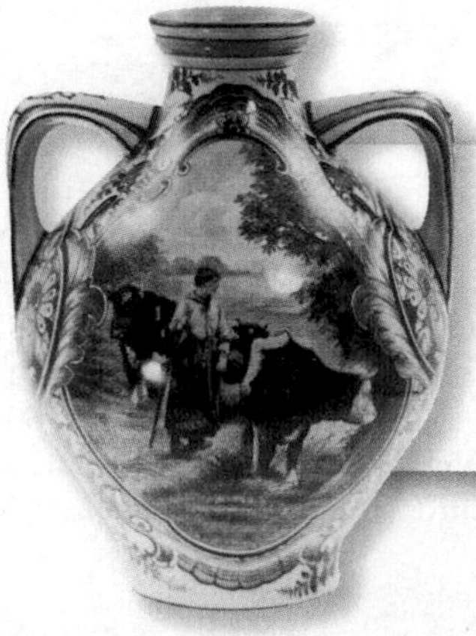

Vase, cattle reserve, back: floral, Dingendoy, pre-1891, 13", $595.00.

Vase, England, Chinese figures in landscape, 18th C, 10", EX .. 1,525.00
Wall pocket, England, cornucopia w/peonies, 18th C, chips, 7⅝" ... 700.00

Denver

The Denver China and Pottery Company began production in 1901 in Denver, Colorado. The founder, William A. Long, used materials native to Colorado to produce underglaze-decorated brownware as well as other artware lines. Several marks were used: an impressed 'Denver' (often with the Lonhuda Faience cipher inside a shield), an imprinted 'Denaura,' and an arrow mark.

Vase, nasturtiums emb on dk gr, squat top, 1903, 5½x6½" 2,400.00
Vase, poppies emb on gr matt, shouldered/waisted, Denura #169, 7" .. 2,280.00
Vase, speckled gray over gr, Denver, 1914, 6½" 240.00
Vase, swirls in brn/bl, swollen form, Denver, 6½" 425.00
Vase, underwater scene cvd on dk gr, squat, Denaura #171, 6x11", EX... 9,600.00
Vase, violets emb on robin's egg bl, Denaura, #184, 2½x5½", NM... 1,440.00

Denver White Pottery

In 1894 Frederick and Frank White settled in Denver, Colorado, and formed the F. J. White & Son Pottery Company. They located at 1434 Logan Street. After the death of Frederick in 1919, Frank moved the pottery to 1560 South Logan, where he remained until the company closed. He had a kiln set up at home and worked each day on the pottery, often selling his products in his front yard. On many occasions he was commissioned to produce specialty items for customers.

Each piece is hand thrown and many are dated. They are usually incised with the name Denver and the letter 'W' inside the capital 'D.' Many items are decorated with Colorado scenery. Though most pieces are matt glazed with a glossy interior, some later examples were completely glossy. The Whites would also add a small band to some of the ware, similar to what you see on Wedgwood pottery today. They created a line with swirled colors as well. On March 6, 1960, Frank White died at the age of 91.

Vase, med bl matt, simple ovoid form, 10½" 240.00
Vase, pine boughs, brn/gr/natural, Skiff, 5¾x4½" 675.00
Vase, pine tree, wht/cameo-style on bl-gray clay, firing line, 5½" .. 500.00
Vase, speckled gr, 3 sm angle hdls, 1914, 6½" 90.00

Depression Glass

Depression glass is defined by Gene and Cathy Florence, authors of several bestselling books on the subject, as 'the inexpensive glassware made primarily during the Depression era in the colors of amber, green, pink, blue, red, yellow, white, and crystal.' This glass was mass produced, sold through five-and-dime stores and mail-order catalogs, and given away as premiums with gas and food products.

The listings in this book are far from being complete. If you want a more thorough presentation of this fascinating glassware, we recommend *Collector's Encyclopedia of Depression Glass, Pocket Guide to Depression Glass, Elegant Glassware of the Depression Era, Glass Candlesticks of the Depression Era, Vol. 1* and *2,* and *Florences' Glassware Pattern Identification Guide, I – IV,* all by Gene and Cathy Florence, whose address is listed in the Directory under Kentucky. See also McKee; New Martinsville.

Adam, gr, bowl, oval, 10" 40.00
Adam, gr, vase, 7½" 125.00
Adam, pk, ashtray, 4½" 28.00
Adam, pk, shakers, 4", pr 90.00
Adam's Rib, irid, vase, 9¾" 150.00
Adam's Rib, non-irid, bowl, console; ped ft 55.00
Adam's Rib, non-irid, pitcher, lemonade; appl hdl 225.00
American Pioneer, gr, bowl, console; 10¾" 70.00
American Pioneer, gr, creamer, 3½" 22.00
American Pioneer, gr, saucer 5.00
American Pioneer, gr, tumbler, 8-oz, 4" 55.00
American Pioneer, pk, bowl, hdls, 5" 25.00
American Pioneer, pk, plate, 6" 12.50
American Pioneer, pk, tumbler, juice; 5-oz 40.00
American Pioneer, pk, whiskey, 2-oz, 2½" 50.00
American Sweetheart, Monax, creamer, ftd 15.00

American Sweetheart, Monax, plate, 15½" 250.00
American Sweetheart, Monax, sherbet, ftd, 4½" 19.00
American Sweetheart, pk, bowl, cream soup; 4½" 85.00
American Sweetheart, pk, pitcher, 80-oz 795.00
American Sweetheart, pk, tumbler, 10-oz, 4¾" 135.00
Aunt Polly, bl, bowl, berry; 4⅜" 14.00

Aunt Polly, blue: sugar bowl, $35.00; sugar bowl lid, $150.00. (Photo courtesy Gene and Cathy Florence)

Aunt Polly, bl, vase, ftd, 6½" 55.00
Aunt Polly, gr, bowl, pickle; oval, hdls, 7½" 10.00
Aunt Polly, gr, creamer 35.00
Aurora, cobalt, pk or gr, bowl, 4½" 62.00
Aurora, cobalt, pk or gr, creamer, 4½" 25.00
Aurora, cobalt, pk or gr, tumbler, 4¾" 26.00
Avocado, gr, bowl, salad; 7½" 72.00
Avocado, gr, sugar bowl, ftd 35.00
Avocado, pk, bowl, relish; ftd, 6" 30.00
Avocado, pk, plate, luncheon; 8½" 18.00
Beaded Block, gr, bowl, jelly; hdls, 4½" 20.00
Beaded Block, gr, pitcher, pt jug, 5½" 80.00
Beaded Block, opal, plate, sq, 7¾" 35.00
Beaded Block, opal, sugar bowl 50.00
Block Optic, gr, butter dish, 3x5" 50.00
Block Optic, gr, pitcher, 80-oz, 8" 105.00
Block Optic, gr, sherbet, 5 ½-oz, 3½" 6.00
Block Optic, gr, tumbler, 10-oz 20.00
Block Optic, pk, bowl, berry; 4½" 12.00
Block Optic, pk, ice bucket 80.00
Block Optic, pk, tumbler, 10-oz 18.00
Bowknot, gr, bowl, cereal; 5½" 38.00
Bowknot, gr, plate, salad; 7" 16.00
Cameo, gr, cookie jar, w/lid 60.00
Cameo, gr, decanter, w/stopper, 10" 215.00
Cameo, gr, platter, closed hdls, 12" 28.00
Cameo, gr, vase, 8" 65.00
Cameo, yel, bowl, vegetable; oval, 10" 30.00
Cameo, yel, cup 9.00
Cameo, yel, tumbler, 11-oz, 5" 110.00
Cherry Blossom, gr, sugar bowl 14.00
Cherry Blossom, gr or pk, mug, 7-oz 450.00
Cherry Blossom, gr or pk, plate, grill; 9" 30.00
Cherry Blossom, pk, bowl, hdls, 9" 50.00
Cherry Blossom, pk, plate, salad; 7" 24.00
Cherry Blossom, pk, sandwich tray, hdls, 10½" 30.00
Cherryberry, gr or pk, pickle dish 23.00
Cherryberry, gr or pk, pitcher, 7¾" 195.00
Cherryberry, gr or pk, sugar bowl, lg 25.00
Chinex Classic, decal decor, bowl, vegetable; 7" 40.00
Chinex Classic, ivory, plate, dinner; 9¾" 4.00
Circle, gr or pk, creamer 7.00
Circle, gr or pk, pitcher, 80-oz 40.00
Circle, gr or pk, sandwich tray, 10" 14.00

Cloverleaf, gr, bowl, 8" 125.00
Cloverleaf, gr, tumbler, ftd, 10-oz, 5¾" 30.00
Cloverleaf, yel, shakers, pr 130.00
Cloverleaf, yel or gr, plate, grill; 10½" 30.00
Colonial, gr, mug, 12-oz, 4½" 800.00
Colonial, gr, plate, sherbet; 6" 6.00
Colonial, gr, tumbler, lemonade; 15-oz 75.00
Colonial, pk, bowl, berry; 4½" 20.00
Colonial, pk, platter, oval, 12" 32.00
Colonial, pk, tumbler, juice; 5-oz, 3" 22.00
Colonial Block, gr or pk, butter dish 42.00
Colonial Block, gr or pk, tumbler, ftd, 5-oz 55.00
Columbia, crystal, bowl, cereal; 5" 17.00
Columbia, crystal, plate, chop; 11" 17.00
Columbia, pk, cup 25.00
Columbia, pk, saucer 10.00
Coronation, pk, bowl, berry; 4½" 65.00
Coronation, pk, pitcher, 68-oz, 7¾" 695.00
Coronation, red, cup 6.50
Coronation, red, nappy, hdls, 6½" 18.00
Cube, gr, shakers, pr 35.00
Cube, pk, bowl, deep, 4½" 9.00
Cube, pk, candy jar, w/lid, 6½" 30.00
Diamond Quilted, bl, cup 17.00
Diamond Quilted, bl, ice bucket 85.00
Diamond Quilted, bl, plate, sherbet; 6" 16.00
Diamond Quilted, gr, bowl, crimped edge, 7" 25.00
Diamond Quilted, gr, candleholders, pr 40.00
Diamond Quilted, gr, tumbler, ftd, 12-oz 20.00
Diamond Quilted, gr, tumbler, iced tea; 12-oz 9.00
Diana, amber, bowl, cream soup; 5½" 20.00
Diana, amber, platter, oval, 12" 15.00
Diana, pk, cup 18.00
Diana, pk, plate, bread & butter; 6" 4.00
Dogwood, gr, bowl, fruit; 10½" 295.00
Dogwood, gr, cake plate, heavy solid ft, 13" 145.00
Dogwood, pk, creamer, 3½" 20.00
Dogwood, pk, pitcher, decor, 80-oz, 8" 200.00
Dogwood, pk, plate, dinner; 9½" 28.00
Dogwood, pk, tumbler, decor, 5-oz, 3½" 195.00
Doric, gr, coaster, 3" 20.00
Doric, gr, tray, hdls, 10" 30.00
Doric, pk, bowl, hdls, 9" 30.00
Doric & Pansy, pk, bowl, hdls, 9" 25.00
Doric & Pansy, Ultramarine, plate, dinner; 9" 40.00
Doric & Pansy, Ultramarine, shakers, pr 350.00
Doric & Pansy, Ultramarine, tumbler, 9-oz, 4½" 90.00
English Hobnail, gr or pk, celery dish, 12" 35.00
English Hobnail, gr or pk, decanter, w/stopper, 20-oz .. 125.00
English Hobnail, gr or pk, egg cup 36.00
English Hobnail, gr or pk, pitcher, 38-oz 225.00
English Hobnail, gr or pk, tumbler, iced tea; 12-oz, 5" .. 32.00
Fancy Colonial, colors, bottle, water; no stopper 75.00
Fancy Colonial, colors, bowl, berry; hdls, 8" 65.00
Fancy Colonial, colors, butter dish 80.00
Fancy Colonial, colors, cake plate, 10½" 45.00
Fancy Colonial, colors, cocktail, shallow, 4½-oz 16.00
Fancy Colonial, colors, creamer, ftd 25.00
Fancy Colonial, colors, cup, punch; str edge 12.00
Fancy Colonial, colors, mayonnaise, w/liner, flat 50.00
Fancy Colonial, colors, oil bottle, w/stopper, 6¼-oz 65.00
Fancy Colonial, colors, pitcher, 3-pt 125.00
Fancy Colonial, colors, plate, salad; 7½" 20.00
Fancy Colonial, colors, shakers, pr 75.00

Fancy Colonial, colors, sherbet, low ft, 4½"	22.50
Fancy Colonial, colors, sugar bowl, w/lid, flat	30.00
Fancy Colonial, colors, tumbler, iced tea; 12-oz	20.00
Fancy Colonial, colors, tumbler, 4-oz	15.00
Fancy Colonial, colors, tumbler, 10-oz	18.00
Fancy Colonial, colors, vase, flared, low ft, 8"	65.00
Fancy Colonial, colors, vase, flat, bead base, ruffled rim, 12"	110.00
Fancy Colonial, colors, wine, deep, 2-oz	25.00
Fire-King Philbe, gr or pk, cookie jar, w/lid	950.00
Fire-King Philbe, gr or pk, plate, grill; 10½"	75.00
Fire-King Philbe, gr or pk, tumbler, water; 9-oz, 4"	105.00
Floral, gr, coaster, 3½"	11.00
Floral, gr, tumbler, lemonade; ftd, 9-oz, 5½"	60.00
Floral, pk, bowl, salad; 7½"	30.00
Floral, pk, sherbet	16.00
Floral & Diamond Band, gr, sugar bowl, sm	12.00
Floral & Diamond Band, pk, nappy, hdl, 5¾"	15.00
Florentine No 1, gr, ashtray, 5½"	22.00
Florentine No 1, gr, cup	8.00
Florentine No 1, yel, plate, grill; 10"	15.00
Florentine No 1, yel, tumbler, water; ftd, 10-oz, 4¾"	24.00
Florentine No 2, gr, bowl, cream soup; 4¾"	18.00
Florentine No 2, gr, compote, ruffled, 3½"	40.00
Florentine No 2, yel, butter dish	150.00
Florentine No 2, yel, plate, dinner; 10"	16.00
Florentine No 2, yel, tumbler, water; 9-oz, 4"	21.00
Flower Garden w/Butterflies, gr or pk, ashtray, w/matchbook holders	175.00
Flower Garden w/Butterflies, gr or pk, candleholders, 8", pr	135.00
Flower Garden w/Butterflies, gr or pk, cup	70.00
Flower Garden w/Butterflies, gr or pk, powder jar, flat	75.00
Flower Garden w/Butterflies, gr or pk, tray, oval, 5½x10"	60.00
Flute & Cane, crystal, bowl, pickle; oval, 6½"	16.00
Flute & Cane, crystal, celery, oval, 8½"	25.00
Flute & Cane, crystal, oil bottle, w/stopper, 6-oz	45.00
Flute & Cane, crystal, sugar bowl, w/lid	20.00
Fortune, pk, candy dish, w/lid, flat	30.00
Fortune, pk, plate, luncheon; 8"	30.00
Fortune, pk, tumbler, juice; 5-oz, 3½"	12.00
Fruits, gr, bowl, berry; 8"	95.00
Fruits, gr, pitcher, flat bottom, 7"	125.00
Fruits, pk, sherbet	12.00
Hex Optic, gr or pk, bowl, berry; lg, 7½"	15.00
Hex Optic, gr or pk, ice bucket, metal hdl	30.00
Hex Optic, gr or pk, shakers, pr	33.00
Hex Optic, gr or pk, whiskey, 1-oz, 2"	9.00
Holiday, pk, bowl, soup; 7¾"	55.00
Holiday, pk, pitcher, 52-oz, 6¾"	40.00
Holiday, pk, plate, dinner; 9"	18.00
Holiday, pk, sugar bowl	10.00
Holiday, pk, tumbler, ftd, 4"	40.00
Homespun, pk, bowl, closed hdls, 4½"	18.00
Homespun, pk, creamer, ftd	12.50
Homespun, pk, cup	13.00
Homespun, pk, tumbler, iced tea; 13-oz, 5½"	33.00
Homespun, pk, tumbler, 6-oz, 3⅞"	22.00
Indiana Custard, ivory, bowl, soup; flat, 7½"	28.00
Indiana Custard, ivory, sherbet	75.00
Iris, crystal, bowl, salad; 9½"	12.50
Iris, crystal, cup, demitasse	35.00
Iris, crystal, sandwich plate, 11¾"	35.00
Iris, crystal, tumbler, ftd, 6"	16.00
Iris, irid, bowl, sauce; 5"	25.00
Iris, irid, candleholders, pr	45.00
Iris, irid, plate, dinner; 9"	40.00

Iris, irid, wine, 4"	20.00
Jubilee, pk or gr, cheese & cracker set	175.00
Jubilee, pk or gr, sandwich tray, center hdl, 11"	130.00
Jubilee, pk or gr, vase, 12"	130.00
Jubilee, yel, bowl, fruit; hdls, 9"	125.00
Jubilee, yel, cake tray, hdls, 11"	35.00
Jubilee, yel, mayonnaise, w/plate & orig ladle	170.00
Laced Edge, bl or gr, bowl, 5"	30.00
Laced Edge, bl or gr, bowl, oval, 11"	136.00
Laced Edge, bl or gr, mayonnaise, 3-pc	135.00
Laced Edge, bl or gr, plate, bread & butter; 6½"	15.00
Laced Edge, bl or gr, sugar bowl	30.00
Laced Edge, bl or gr, tumbler, 9-oz	40.00
Lake Como, wht w/bl scenes, bowl, vegetable; 9¾"	40.00
Lake Como, wht w/bl scenes, platter, 11"	70.00
Laurel, ivory, candleholders, 4", pr	35.00
Laurel, ivory, champagne sherbet, 5"	30.00
Laurel, Jade, cup	15.00
Laurel, Jade, tumbler, flat, 9-oz, 4½"	75.00
Lincoln Inn, bl or red, bonbon, hdls, sq	15.00
Lincoln Inn, colors other than bl or red, finger bowl	12.50
Lorain, gr, bowl, salad; 7½"	60.00
Lorain, gr, creamer, ftd	16.00
Lorain, gr, plate, salad; 7¾"	14.00
Lorain, gr, relish, 4-part, 8"	25.00
Lorain, yel, bowl, berry; deep, 8"	175.00
Lorain, yel, cup	14.00
Lorain, yel, plate, dinner; 10½"	75.00
Lorain, yel, sugar bowl, ftd	65.00
Madrid, amber, bowl, vegetable; oval, 10"	18.00
Madrid, amber, cake plate, rnd, 11½"	20.00
Madrid, amber, pitcher, sq, 60-oz, 8"	60.00
Madrid, gr, bowl, soup; 7"	16.00
Madrid, gr, plate, relish; 10½"	16.00
Manhattan, crystal, ashtray, rnd, 4"	9.00
Manhattan, crystal, bowl, cereal; 5½"	110.00
Manhattan, crystal, compote, 5¾"	35.00
Manhattan, crystal, plate, dinner; 10½"	18.00
Manhattan, crystal, vase, 8"	25.00
Manhattan, pk, bowl, cereal; 5½"	225.00
Manhattan, pk, relish tray, 5-part, 14"	18.00
Mayfair Federal, amber, bowl, sauce; 5"	9.00
Mayfair Federal, amber, platter, oval, 12"	30.00
Mayfair Federal, gr, plate, dinner; 9½"	15.00
Mayfair Federal, gr, tumbler, 9-oz, 4½"	35.00
Mayfair/Open Rose, bl, pitcher, 37-oz, 6"	165.00
Mayfair/Open Rose, pk, bowl, cream soup; 5"	55.00
Mayfair/Open Rose, pk, celery, 10"	45.00
Mayfair/Open Rose, pk, plate, grill; 9½"	50.00
Mayfair/Open Rose, pk, relish, 4-part, 8⅜"	35.00
Mayfair/Open Rose, pk, tumbler, water; 9-oz, 4½"	35.00
Mayfair/Open Rose, pk, whiskey, 1½-oz, 2½"	130.00
Mayfair/Open Rose, pk or bl, sherbet, ftd, 4¾"	85.00
Miss America, crystal, butter dish	210.00
Miss America, crystal, comport, 5"	16.00
Miss America, pk, bowl, fruit; deep, str, 8¾"	90.00
Miss America, pk, relish, 4-part, 8¾"	25.00
Miss America, pk, sugar bowl	22.00
Moderntone, amethyst, cup	8.00
Moderntone, amethyst, sandwich plate, 10½"	35.00
Moderntone, amethyst, tumbler, 9-oz	25.00
Moderntone, cobalt, ashtray, w/match holder in center, 7¾"	150.00
Moderntone, cobalt, cheese dish, w/metal lid, 7"	350.00
Moderntone, cobalt, whiskey, 1½-oz	35.00

Mt Pleasant, amethyst, blk or cobalt, bonbon, rolled up hdls, 7" ... 23.00
Mt Pleasant, amethyst, blk or cobalt, bowl, scalloped, hdls, 8" 35.00
Mt Pleasant, amethyst, blk or cobalt, mayonnaise, 3-ftd, 5½" 25.00
Mt Pleasant, amethyst, blk or cobalt, plate, grill; 9" 20.00
New Century, gr, bowl, cream soup; 4¾" 22.00
New Century, gr, plate, breakfast; 7⅛" 13.00
New Century, gr, sugar bowl 12.00
New Century, gr, tumbler, 12-oz, 5½" 33.00
Newport, cobalt, bowl, cereal; 5½" 40.00
Newport, cobalt, sandwich plate, 11½" 40.00
No 610 Pyramid, gr, bowl, master berry; 8½" 60.00
No 610 Pyramid, gr, pitcher 265.00
No 610 Pyramid, pk, bowl, berry; 4¾" 25.00
No 610 Pyramid, pk, creamer 35.00
No 610 Pyramid, pk, sugar bowl 35.00
No 610 Pyramid, yel, ice tub 225.00
No 610 Pyramid, yel, tray, for creamer & sugar bowl 55.00
No 612 Horseshoe, gr, bowl, berry; 4½" 30.00
No 612 Horseshoe, gr, relish, ftd, 3-part 30.00
No 612 Horseshoe, yel, pitcher, 64-oz, 8½" 390.00
No 612 Horseshoe, yel, tumbler, ftd, 12-oz 185.00
No 616 Vernon, gr or yel, creamer, ftd 28.00
No 616 Vernon, gr or yel, cup 16.00
No 616 Vernon, gr or yel, plate, sandwich; 11" 25.00
No 616 Vernon, gr or yel, tumbler, ftd, 5" 35.00
No 618 Pineapple & Floral, amber, bowl, 4¾" 18.00
No 618 Pineapple & Floral, amber, plate, dinner; 9⅜" 13.00
No 618 Pineapple & Floral, crystal, cup 10.00
No 618 Pineapple & Floral, crystal, tumbler, 8-oz, 4½" 25.00
Normandie, amber, bowl, vegetable; oval, 10" 20.00
Normandie, amber, tumbler, iced tea; 12-oz, 5" 35.00
Normandie, amber, tumbler, juice; 5-oz, 4" 28.00
Normandie, pk, plate, salad; 7¾" 15.00
Old Cafe, pk, olive dish, oblong, 6" 10.00
Old Cafe, pk or red, cup 12.00
Old Cafe, red, tumbler, juice; 3" 22.00
Old Cafe, red, vase, 7½" 55.00
Old English, amber, gr or pk, compote, 3½x7" 25.00
Old English, amber, gr or pk, vase, fan shape, 7" 75.00
Oyster & Pearl, pk, sandwich plate, 13½" 20.00
Oyster & Pearl, red, bowl, rnd, 5½" 20.00
Parrot, amber, hot plate, 5" 995.00
Parrot, amber, saucer 18.00
Parrot, gr, bowl, soup; 7" 50.00
Parrot, gr, tumbler, 12-oz, 5½" 200.00
Patrician, amber, bowl, cream soup; 4¾" 14.00
Patrician, amber, cookie jar 80.00
Patrician, gr, shakers, pr 80.00
Patrick, pk, bowl, console; 11" 135.00
Patrick, pk, tray, hdls, 11" 65.00
Patrick, yel, candy dish, 3-ftd 225.00
Patrick, yel, mayonnaise, 3-pc 140.00
Pillar Optic, gr or pk, creamer, ftd 65.00
Pillar Optic, gr or pk, mug, 12-oz 35.00
Pillar Optic, gr or pk, pretzel jar, 130-oz 150.00
Pillar Optic, gr or pk, tumbler, whiskey; 1½-oz 14.00
Pillar Optic, Royal Ruby, plate, luncheon; 8" 30.00
Pillar Optic, Royal Ruby, sherbet, ftd 35.00
Pillar Optic, Royal Ruby, tumbler, ftd, 3-oz, 3½" 30.00
Pillar Optic, Royal Ruby, tumbler, ftd, 10-oz, 5½" 60.00
Primo, gr or yel, cake plate, 3-ftd, 10" 75.00
Primo, gr or yel, plate, dinner; 10" 30.00
Princess, gr, tumbler, iced tea; 13-oz, 5½" 50.00
Princess, gr or pk, platter, closed hdls, 12" 30.00

Princess, gr or pk, relish, plain, 7½" 200.00
Princess, pk, ashtray, 4½" 95.00
Queen Mary, pk, bowl, hdls, 5½" 20.00
Queen Mary, pk, compote, 5¾" 25.00
Raindrops, gr, sugar bowl, w/lid 40.00
Raindrops, gr, tumbler, 9½-oz, 4⅛" 9.00
Ribbon, blk, bowl, berry; 8" 40.00
Ribbon, blk, plate, luncheon; 8" 14.00
Ring, crystal, decanter, w/stopper 25.00
Ring, crystal, ice bucket 22.00
Ring, crystal & gr w/decor, shakers, 3", pr 55.00
Ring, crystal & gr w/decor, tumbler, cocktail; ftd, 3½" 12.00
Rock Crystal, crystal, bonbon, scalloped edge, 7½" 22.00
Rock Crystal, crystal, candy dish, rnd 75.00
Rock Crystal, crystal, parfait, low ft, 3½-oz 20.00
Rock Crystal, crystal, salt dip 60.00
Rock Crystal, crystal, sundae, low ftd, 6-oz 12.00
Rock Crystal, red, cake stand, ftd, 11x2¾" 125.00
Rock Crystal, red, cordial, 1-oz 45.00
Rock Crystal, red, finger bowl, plain edge, 5", w/7" plate 70.00
Rock Crystal, red, pitcher, w/lid, lg 895.00
Rock Crystal, red, plate, plain edge, 7" 25.00
Rock Crystal, red, tumbler, old-fashioned; 5-oz 60.00
Rose Cameo, gr, bowl, str sides, 6" 32.00
Rose Cameo, gr, plate, salad; 7" 15.00
Rosemary, amber, bowl, vegetable; oval, 10" 18.00
Rosemary, amber, plate, grill 10.00
Rosemary, gr, plate, dinner 15.00
Rosemary, gr, tumbler, 9-oz, 4½" 42.00
Roulette, gr, cup 6.00
Roulette, gr, plate, luncheon; 8½" 7.00
Roulette, gr, whiskey, 1½-oz, 2½" 16.00
Roulette, pk, tumbler, water; 9-oz, 4⅛" 30.00
Round Robin, gr, creamer, ftd 12.50
Round Robin, irid, sandwich plate, 12" 10.00
Royal Lace, bl, bowl, vegetable; oval, 11" 75.00
Royal Lace, bl, cookie jar 325.00
Royal Lace, bl, platter, oval, 13" 70.00
Royal Lace, pk, bowl, berry; 5" 40.00
Royal Lace, pk, candleholders, rolled edge, pr 160.00
Royal Ruby, red, pitcher, upright, 3-qt 42.00
Royal Ruby, red, punch bowl, w/stand 75.00
S Pattern, amber, pitcher, 80-oz 160.00
S Pattern, amber, tumbler, 12-oz, 5" 16.00
S Pattern, crystal, cake plate, heavy, 13" 50.00
S Pattern, crystal, saucer 2.00
Sandwich (Hocking), crystal, pitcher, ice lip, ½-gal 80.00
Sandwich (Hocking), crystal, plate, dinner; 9" 15.00
Sandwich (Hocking), gr, bowl, smooth or scalloped, 8" 110.00
Sandwich (Hocking), gr, pitcher, ice lip, ½-gal 495.00
Sandwich (Indiana), crystal, bowl, console; 11½" 20.00
Sandwich (Indiana), crystal, goblet, 9-oz 13.00
Sandwich (Indiana), pk, candlesticks, 3½", pr 45.00
Sharon, amber, shakers, pr 38.00
Sharon, pk, candy jar, w/lid 45.00
Sharon, pk, sugar bowl 14.00
Ships, bl & wht, ice bowl 40.00
Ships, bl & wht, tumbler, whiskey; 3½" 27.50
Sierra, gr, platter, oval, 11" 80.00
Sierra, gr, tray, serving; hdls 20.00
Sierra, pk, bowl, cereal; 5½" 17.00
Sierra, pk, pitcher, 32-oz, 6½" 140.00
Spiral, gr, bowl, mixing; 7" 15.00
Spiral, gr, pitcher, 58-oz, 7⅝" 40.00

Spiral, gr, tumbler, juice; 5-oz, 3"..4.50
Starlight, crystal, plate, dinner; 9".....................................8.00
Starlight, crystal, relish.. 15.00
Starlight, pk, bowl, cereal; 5½".. 14.00
Starlight, pk, bowl, closed hdls, 8½"................................ 20.00
Strawberry, gr or pk, olive dish, hdl, 5"........................... 20.00
Strawberry, gr or pk, plate, salad; 7½".............................. 18.00
Strawberry, gr or pk, tumbler, 9-oz, 3⅝"......................... 35.00
Sunburst, crystal, candleholders, dbl, pr.......................... 20.00
Sunburst, crystal, relish, 2-part...8.00
Sunburst, crystal, sandwich plate, 11¾"........................... 20.00
Sunburst, crystal, tray, oval, sm..9.00
Sunflower, gr, ashtray, center design only, 5".................. 12.00
Sunflower, gr, tumbler, ftd, 8-oz, 4¾"............................. 38.00
Sunflower, pk, plate, dinner; 9"....................................... 24.00
Swirl, pk, bowl, ftd, closed hdls, 10"............................... 35.00
Swirl, pk, coaster, 1x3½"... 15.00
Swirl, pk, plate, 7½".. 10.00
Swirl, pk, tumbler, 13-oz, 5⅛"... 60.00
Swirl, Ultramarine, bowl, console; ftd, 10½"................... 30.00
Swirl, Ultramarine, pitcher, ftd, 48-oz.........................2,000.00
Swirl, Ultramarine, shakers, pr... 48.00
Swirl, Ultramarine, vase, ftd, 8½"................................... 29.00
Tea Room, gr, bowl, banana split; ftd, 7½"..................... 165.00
Tea Room, gr, mustard, w/lid.. 310.00
Tea Room, gr, sundae, ruffled, ftd.................................. 135.00
Tea Room, gr, vase, 9½".. 130.00
Tea Room, pk, finger bowl.. 85.00
Tea Room, pk, parfait.. 115.00
Thistle, gr, cake plate, heavy, 13"................................... 235.00
Thistle, gr, saucer... 12.00
Thistle, pk, cup, thin... 28.00
Thistle, pk, plate, grill; 10½"... 30.00
Tulip, amethyst or bl, plate, 7½"..................................... 16.00
Tulip, crystal or gr, tumbler, juice.................................. 22.00
Twisted Optic, gr or pk, basket....................................... 60.00
Twisted Optic, gr or pk, pitcher, 64-oz........................... 45.00
Twisted Optic, gr or pk, server, sandwich; center hdl..... 22.00
Twisted Optic, gr or pk, tumbler, 12-oz, 5½"....................8.00
US Swirl, gr, butter dish... 100.00
US Swirl, gr, compote, 5½".. 35.00
US Swirl, pk or gr, creamer... 25.00
US Swirl, pk or gr, plate, salad; 7⅞".................................7.00
Victory, bl, bowl, flat edge, 12½".................................... 60.00
Victory, bl, platter, 12".. 75.00
Victory, pk, bowl, rolled edge, 11".................................. 25.00
Victory, pk, gravy boat, w/platter.................................... 200.00
Waterford, pk, bowl, berry; lg, 8½".................................. 28.00
Waterford, pk, plate, sandwich; 13¾"............................. 40.00
Windsor, pk, ashtray, 5¾".. 35.00
Windsor, pk, sherbet, ftd... 13.00

Derby

William Duesbury operated in Derby, England, from about 1755, purchasing a second establishment, The Chelsea Works, in 1769. During this period fine porcelains were produced which so impressed the King that in 1773 he issued the company the Crown Derby patent. In 1810, several years after Duesbury's death, the factory was bought by Robert Bloor. The quality of the ware suffered under the new management, and the main Derby pottery closed in 1848. Within a short time, the work was revived by a dedicated number of former employees who established their own works on King Street in Derby.

The earliest known Derby mark was the crown over a script 'D'; however this mark is rarely found today. Soon after 1782, that mark was augmented with a device of crossed batons and six dots, usually applied in underglaze blue. During the Bloor period, the crown was centered within a ring containing the words 'Bloor' above and 'Derby' below the crown, or with a red printed stamp — the crowned Gothic 'D.' The King Street plant produced figurines that may be distinguished from their earlier counterparts by the presence of an 'S' and 'H' on either side of the crown and crossed batons.

In 1876 a new pottery was constructed in Derby, and the owners revived the earlier company's former standard of excellence. The Queen bestowed the firm the title Royal Crown Derby in 1890; it still operates under that name today. See also Royal Crown Derby.

Figurine, man seated, doing tricks w/pug dog, mc/gilt, 1880, 5" .. 1,750.00
Hunt cup, head of fox, w/stand... 165.00
Mug, On the River Rhone, on cobalt w/gilt, 1850s, 4½".............. 325.00

Platter, ca 1830, 16" long, $600.00. (Photo courtesy David Rago Auctions)

Platter, crest/monogram, red/gilt vine decor, 1800s, 12¾" L......... 175.00
Urn, Moorish floral, cobalt on yel, baluster, late 19th C, 18"....... 950.00
Vase, gold floral on wht, long neck/ftd, rtcl shaped panel hdls, 10"..325.00

Desert Sands

As early as the 1850s, the Evans family living in the Ozark Mountains of Missouri produced domestic clay products. Their small pot shop was passed on from one generation to the next. In the 1920s it was moved to North Las Vegas, Nevada, where the name Desert Sands was adopted. Succeeding generations of the family continued to relocate, taking the business with them. From 1937 to 1962 it operated in Boulder City, Nevada; then it was moved to Barstow, California, where it remained until it closed in the late 1970s.

Desert Sands pottery is similar to Mission Ware by Niloak. Various mineral oxides were blended to mimic the naturally occurring sand formations of the American West. A high-gloss glaze was applied to add intensity to the colorful striations that characterize the ware. Not all examples are marked, making it sometimes difficult to attribute. Marked items carry an ink stamp with the Desert Sands designation. Paper labels were also used.

Bowl, sgn Evans, 2½x5½".. 20.00
Bowl, 2½x7½".. 30.00
Compote, ftd, sgn Evans, 7½x9¾", from $100 to......................... 125.00
Compote, ftd, unmk, 4¾x5⅝"... 35.00
Plate, 6½".. 25.00
Vase, ftd, flared rim, 6½"... 50.00

Documents

Although the word 'document' is defined in the general sense as 'anything printed or written, etc., relied upon to record or prove something...,' in the collectibles market, the term is more diversified with broadsides, billheads, checks, invoices, letters and letterheads, land grants, receipts, and waybills some of the most sought after. Some documents in demand are those related to a specific subject such as advertising, mining, railroads, military, politics, banking, slavery, nautical, or legal (deeds, mortgages, etc.). Other collectors look for examples representing a specific period of time such as colonial documents, Revolutionary or Civil War documents, early Western documents, or those from a specific region, state, or city.

Aside from supply and demand, there are five major factors which determine the collector-value of a document. These are:

1) Age — Documents from the eastern half of the country can be found that date back to the 1700s or earlier. Most documents sought by collectors usually date from 1700 to 1900. Those with twentieth-century dates are still abundant and not in demand unless of special significance or beauty.

2) Region of origin — Depending on age, documents from rural and less populated areas are harder to find than those from major cities and heavily populated states. The colonization of the West and Midwest did not begin until after 1850, so while an 1870s billhead from New York or Chicago is common, one from Albuquerque or Phoenix is not, since most of the Southwest was still unsettled.

3) Attractiveness — Some documents are plain and unadorned, but collectors prefer colorful, profusely illustrated pieces. Additional artwork and engravings add to the value.

4) Historical content — Unusual or interesting content, such as a letter written by a Civil War soldier giving an eyewitness account of the Battle of Gettysburg or a western territorial billhead listing numerous animal hides purchased from a trapper, will sell for more than one with mundane information.

5) Condition — Through neglect or environmental conditions, over many decades paper articles can become stained, torn, or deteriorated. Heavily damaged or stained documents are generally avoided altogether. Those with minor problems are more acceptable, although their value will decrease anywhere from 20% to 50%, depending upon the extent of damage. Avoid attempting to repair tears with tape — sell 'as is' so that the collector can take proper steps toward restoration.

Foreign documents are plentiful; and though some are very attractive, resale may be difficult. The listings that follow are generalized; prices are variable depending entirely upon the five points noted above. Values here are based upon examples with no major damage. Common grade documents without significant content are found in abundance and generally have little collector value. These usually date from the late 1800s to mid-1900s. It should be noted that the items listed below are examples of those that meet the criteria for having collector value. There is little demand for documents worth less than $5.00. For more information we recommend *Owning Western History* by Warren Anderson. Cheryl Anderson is our advisor; her address may be found in the Directory under Utah.

Key:
illus — illustrated   vgn — vignette
pp — pre-printed

Bank draft, Dakota Territory, maiden/building vgns on pk, 1883, 3x8" .. 15.00
Bank draft, IN, Brazil Bank bold title, 2 vgns, orange stamp, 1972 ... 14.00
Bank draft, NJ, Clinton Nat'l Bank, bold title, 2 vgns, ABNCo, 1888..14.00
Billhead, CO, coal delivery to mining camp, Black man/wagon vgn, 1912...12.50
Broadside, JW Fiske's Ornamental Iron Works, NY, late 1800s, 35x21"..1,880.00
Certificate, MO, boiler inspection Union Depot, pp, 1893, 8x9" 8.00
Certificate of Deposit, IN, 1st Nat'l Bank, ornate title/vgn, 1901 .....8.00
Certificate of Promotion, UT, bold/ornate title, 2 signatures, 1912... 14.00
Charges, Hays Co, TX, man stole pistol, 1907, 1-pg...................... 20.00
Check, City Nat'l Bank of Bridgeport CT, pp, issued, 1877, 3x7".....8.00
Check, MT Territory, 1st Nat'l Bank, miner vgn, orange tax stamp, 1880...14.00
Complaint, CA, gunman disturbs peace (varied charges), legal sz, 1909.. 10.00
Complaint, CA, man drunk/sleeping on sidewalks, legal sz, 1907.....9.00

Court order, MO, man confined to insane asylum, 1911, 2 legal-sz pgs .. 10.00
Indenture, Rigby Mining, AZ Territory, typed legal sz, 1912, 8-pg...16.00
Land grant, OH/1838, emb state seal/$1 stamp, 11x17" 60.00
Land grant, to TX militia man, sgn by Buchanan secretary, 1859, 16x10"...115.00
Letterhead, Co, US Senate, report, sgn Edward Wolcott, 1896 ..... 12.00
Letterhead, IL, Am Short-Horn Breeder's... re cows, purple, 1882, 1-pg.... 12.00
Letterhead, State Industrial Home for Girls, needs listed, 1895, 1-pg 8.00
Letterhead, WY lawyer, re court case, typed, 1896, 8x11"............. 18.00
Pay order, Columbia Mining, Indian maiden vgn, pp, 1859........... 30.00
Pay voucher, Goldfield Mowhawk Mining, lists payment, 1909, 3x7" ..8.00
Promissory note, NE, $165 at 10% interest, pp, 1881, 3x8" 10.00
Receipt, St John's Park, NY, NY Central & Hudson River, cargo, 1880 ...9.00
Receipt, St Louis MO, saddlery/harness, pp w/florals, 1895............ 12.50
Receipt, Tombstone, AZ Territory, Indian brave vgn, pp, 1905 ..... 20.00
Receipt, WA Land Co, along Puget Sound Electric Ry, town vgn, pp ...12.50
Survey, Harrisburg PA land track, 1829, 7x7½"+fr 265.00
Time check, Twin Buttes RR, AZ Territory, $1 day, pp, 1905 ....9.00

Dollhouses and Furnishings

Dollhouses were introduced commercially in this country late in the 1700s by Dutch craftsmen who settled in the east. By the mid-1800s, they had become meticulously detailed, divided into separate rooms, and lavishly furnished to reflect the opulence of the day. Originally intended for the amusement of adults of the household, by the late 1800s their status had changed to that of a child's toy. Though many early dollhouses were lovingly hand fashioned for a special little girl, those made commercially by such companies as Bliss and Schoenhut are highly valued.

Furniture and furnishings in the Biedermeier style featuring stenciled Victorian decorations often sell for several hundred dollars each. Other early pieces made of pewter, porcelain, or papier-mache are also quite valuable. Certainly less expensive but very collectible, nonetheless, is the quality, hallmarked plastic furniture produced during the '40s by Renwal and Acme, and the 1960s Petite Princess line produced by Ideal. For more information, see *Schroeder's Collectible Toys, Antique to Modern*. Our advisor for this category is Barbara Rosen; she is listed in the Directory under New Jersey. See also Miniatures.

Furniture

Acme/Thomas, rocker, yel w/gr or yel w/red, ea...................................4.00
Acme/Thomas, stroller, any color combo, ea 6.00
Allied/Pyro, corner cupboard; aqua 8.00
Allied/Pyro, hutch, aqua or red, ea...4.00
Allied/Pyro, nightstand, yel 4.00
Allied/Pyro, stove, wht, unmk 4.00
Best, cradle, bl..2.00
Casablanca, vanity w/mirror, brn..12.00
Fisher-Price, dresser w/mirror, wht 5.00
Fisher-Price, stove w/hood, yel 5.00
Ideal, chaise lounge, wht 18.00
Ideal, dishwasher, w/lettering 20.00
Ideal, highchair, collapsible, bl or pk, ea..25.00
Ideal, potty chair, pk, complete 15.00
Ideal Petite Princess, bed, #4416-4, bl, complete, w/orig box......... 30.00
Ideal Petite Princess, cabinet, Treasure Trove #4418-0....................10.00
Ideal Petite Princess, dressing table, #4417-2, bl, complete............20.00
Ideal Young Decorator, bathtub, corner; bl w/yel............................35.00
Ideal Young Decorator, chair, kitchen; wht......................................10.00
Ideal Young Decorator, playpen, pk...45.00
Jaydon, corner cupboard; red...5.00
Jaydon, nightstand, pk...4.00
Kage, refrigerator, wht w/blk & red trim 8.00

Lundby, fireplace, 3½x2¾" 15.00
Marx, hard plastic, patio barbecue, dk brn, ½" scale 8.00
Marx Little Hostess, coffee table, rnd, brn 8.00
Plasco, bed, yel spread & brn headboard 3.00
Plasco, buffet, any color 4.00
Plasco, toilet, turq w/wht 8.00
Reliable, chair, dining; rust 5.00
Reliable, highboy, rust 8.00
Renwal, baby bath, pk, duck decal 15.00
Renwal, blanket 5.00
Renwal, garbage can, yel w/red, decal 8.00
Renwal, hamper, ivory 2.00
Renwal, ironing board, bl 7.00
Renwal, kiddie car, bl w/red & yel 55.00
Renwal, kitchen clock, ivory 20.00
Renwal, radio, floor; brn 8.00
Sounds Like Home, shower curtain rod 2.00
Sounds Like Home, stove, electronic 12.00
Strombecker, bed, pk, 1940s, ¾" scale 8.00
Strombecker, floor lamp, unfinished, ¾" scale 10.00
Strombecker, sofa, gr flocked, 1940s, ¾" scale 18.00
Strombecker, television, paper screen, ivory, 1961, ¾" scale 20.00
Superior, dustpan, red, ¾" scale 8.00
Tomy-Smaller Homes, range top w/hood 18.00
Tomy-Smaller Homes, scale 15.00
Tomy-Smaller Homes, speakers 3.00
Tomy-Smaller Homes, throw rug 8.00
Tomy-Smaller Homes, vanity 15.00
Tootsietoy, club chair, bl 8.00
Tootsietoy, cupboard, non-opening doors, ivory 20.00
Tootsietoy, medicine cabinet, ivory 25.00
Tootsietoy, nightstand, bl 10.00
Tootsietoy, piano bench, yel w/tan seat 15.00
Tootsietoy, vanity, blk 18.00
Toysville (Renwal mold), hutch, tan 5.00

Houses

Bliss, 2-story, litho on wood w/glassine windows, 14½", G 550.00
Bliss, 2-story/2-room, litho on wood, rpt roof/rpl chimney, 24x18x11" ...1,450.00
Bliss, 2-story/2-room, Vict style, celluloid windows, 27x19", VG 725.00
German, kitchen only, tin w/oven/pump/accessories, 7" doll, 19" L. 300.00
Gottschalk, 2-story/2-room, bl roof, sm rprs/losses, 21x13x11" .2,750.00
Marx, 2-story/6-room, tin litho, 17x33x12"+58 pcs Marx furniture ...195.00
McLoughlin Bros, 2-story/2-room, cb w/litho on paper facade, VG ...240.00
Schoenhut, 3-story/6-room, wood & cb, gr roof, 21" 675.00
Unknown, 2-story/2 room, litho on wood, front porch, 13x9" 275.00
Vict, 2-story/4-room, pnt wood w/mica windows, 67x29x13" 430.00

Dolls

To learn to invest your money wisely as you enjoy the hobby of doll collecting, you must become aware of defects which may devaluate a doll. In bisque, watch for eye chips, hairline cracks and chips, or breaks on any part of the head. Composition should be clean, not crazed or cracked. Vinyl and plastic should be clean with no pen or crayon marks. Though a quality replacement wig is acceptable for bisque dolls, composition and hard plastics should have their original wigs in uncut condition. Original clothing is a must except in bisque dolls, since it is unusual to find one in its original costume.

It is important to remember that prices are based on condition and rarity. When no condition is noted, either in the line listing or the subcategory narrative, dolls are assumed to be in excellent condition.

In relation to bisque dolls, excellent means having no cracks, chips, or hairlines, being nicely dressed, shoed, wigged, and ready to to be placed into a collection. Some of our values are for dolls that are 'mint in box' or 'never removed from box.' As a general rule, a mint-in-the-box doll is worth twice as much (or there about) as one mint, no box. The same doll, played with and in only good condition, is worth half as much (or even less) than the mint-condition doll. Never-removed-from-box examples sell at a premium; allow an additional 10% to 20% over MIB prices for a doll in this pristine condition.

For a more thorough study of the subject, refer to *Collector's Guide to Dolls of the 1960s and 1970s* by Cindy Sabulis; *Collector's Encyclopedia of American Composition Dolls, 1900 – 1950, Vol. 1* and *2*, by Ursula R. Mertz; *Doll Values* by Linda Edward; *Encyclopedia of Bisque Nancy Ann Storybook Dolls, 1936 – 1947*, by Elaine M. Pardee and Jackie Robertson; *Horsman Dolls, The Vinyl Era*, by Don Jensen; and *The Complete Guide to Shirley Temple Dolls and Collectibles* by Tonya Bervaldi-Camaratta. Several other book are referenced throughout this category. All are published by Collector Books.

Key:
bjtd — ball-jointed	OC — original clothes
blb — bent limb body	o/m — open mouth
b/o — battery operated	p/e — pierced ears
c/m — closed mouth	pwt — paperweight
hh — human hair	RpC — replaced clothes
hp — hard plastic	ShHd — shouder head
jtd — jointed	ShPl — shoulder plate
MIG — Made In Germany	SkHd — socket head
NC — no clothes	str — straight
o/c/e — open closed eyes	trn — turned
o/c/m — open closed mouth	

American Character

For more information we recommend *American Character Dolls* by Judith Izen (Collector Books).

Sweet Sue Sophisticate, 19", MIB, $300.00. (Photo courtesy McMasters Harris Auction Company)

AC or Petite mk baby, compo & cloth, OC, 14", EX 185.00
AC or Petite mk baby, compo & cloth, OC, 18", EX 225.00
AC or Petite mk mama, compo & cloth, sleep eyes, hh wig, OC, 16, EX ...275.00
Annie Oakley, hp walker, OC w/embr skirt, 14", EX 400.00
Baby, hp & vinyl, bottle, 12", MIB 250.00
Bottletot, compo/cloth, p/e, o/m, OC, 1926, 13", EX 250.00
Bottletot, rubber drink/wet type w/bottle & diaper, 1936-38, 11", EX 75.00
Carol Ann Beery, compo Patsy type, o/c/e, c/m, OC, 1935, 19½", EX..785.00
Carol Ann Beery, compo Patsy type, o/e/c, c/m, OC, 1935, 13", EX..415.00

Cricket, vinyl, pre-teen w/bendable legs, 1964-66, OC, 9", EX ... 200.00
Eloise, cloth character, Christmas dress, 1950s, 15", EX.............. 360.00
Eloise, cloth character, orange yarn hair, OC, 1950s, 15", EX...... 260.00
Freckles, face changes, OC, 1966, 13", EX............ 40.00
Peggy, compo, scowling, p/e, pnt hair, OC, 1928, 13", EX............ 500.00
Sally, compo ShPl & cloth, S Temple look-alike, OC, 1934, 24", EX 375.00
Sally Joy, compo ShPl & cloth, o/c/e, curly wig, OC, 1934, 24", EX... 400.00
Sally Says, plastic & vinyl, talker, 1965, OC, 19", EX.................... 70.00
Sweet Sue, hp or hp & vinyl, 1953-61, OC, 15", EX.................... 225.00
Tiny Tears, all vinyl, 1963, MIB................................... 80.00
Tiny Tears, hp & vinyl, 1950-52, 8", MIB................................. 75.00
Toni, vinyl head, rooted hair, ca 1958, OC, 10½", EX 175.00
Toodles, vinyl, w/accessories & wardrobe, ca 1960, 11", MIB...... 285.00
Tressy, all vinyl, high heels, 1963-66, OC, 11", EX...................... 115.00
Whimsie, Trixie the Pixie, stuffed vinyl, pnt features, 1967, OC, EX ... 225.00

Annalee

Barbara Annalee Davis began making her dolls in the 1950s. What began as a hobby, very soon turned into a commercial venture. Her whimsical creations range from tiny angels atop powder puff clouds to funky giant frogs, some 42" in height. In between there are dolls for every occasion (with Christmas being her specialty), all characterized by their unique construction methods (felt over flexible wire framework) and wonderful facial expressions. Naturally, some of the older dolls are the most valuable (though more recent examples are desirable as well, depending on scarcity and demand), and condition, as usual, is very important. To date your doll, look at the tag. If made before 1986, that date is only the copyright date. (Dolls made after 1986 do carry the manufacturing date.) Dolls from the '50s have a long white red-embroidered tag with no date. From 1959 to 1964, that same tag had a date in the upper right-hand corner. From 1965 until 1970, it was folded in half and sewn into the seam. In 1970, a satiny white tag with a date preceded by a copyright symbol in the upper right-hand corner was used. In '75, the tag was a long white cotton strip with a copyright date. This tag was folded over in 1982, making it shorter. Our advisor for Annalee dolls is Jane Holt; she is listed in the Directory under New Hampshire. Values are for dolls in at least excellent condition.

1957, boy building boat, 10" 500.00
1963, monk, wht beard, blk hooded robe & skullcap, 10" 85.00
1970, monkey girl w/bow & muff, chartreuse, 10" 175.00
1971+, Santa & Mrs Claus, w/cape, 7", pr (made several yrs)........ 30.00
1972-85, teacher mouse (male or female), 7", ea 35.00
1975-76, colonial boy & girl mice, he w/flag/she knitting, 7", pr .. 125.00
1976, elephant, 18"... 250.00
1977, scarecrow, 10".. 60.00
1979, jogger mouse, 7" 25.00
1980, clown, 18".. 95.00
1980 only, disco mouse (boy or girl), 7" (made only 1 yr) 35.00
1981, monkey boy or girl on banana trapeze, 7", ea...................... 75.00
1981, wood-chopper mouse, ax in 1 hand, logs on shoulder, 7" 35.00
1984-86, Valentine bunny, 7".. 40.00
1985, ornament, Be Mine heart 5.00
1986, Logo Kid w/pin, 7" 100.00
1986, Valentine panda holding red heart, 10" (made only 2 yrs) ... 75.00
1987, duck in Santa hat, 5" 20.00
1989, kitten w/mittens, 10" 35.00
1990, elf, pk or yel, 22" 20.00
1991, cat, blk w/gr eyes, 12" (made only 1 yr)........................ 40.00
1991, spider, 12" (made only 1 yr)...................................... 45.00
1992, angel on cloud, 5" 20.00
1992, Back to School, Logo Kid w/pin, 7".............................. 45.00
1993, wizard mouse, 7"... 25.00
1994, Hershey kid, dressed in foil-like chocolate kiss, 7"............... 50.00

Armand Marseille

#231, Fany, RpC, ca 1912, 17", EX................................4,200.00
#256, bsk SkHd, o/m, glass eyes, wig, RpC, 12", EX 300.00
#310, Just Me, bsk SkHd, flirty eyes, wig, RpC, 1929, 9", EX....1,400.00
#341, My Dream Baby, bsk SkHd, cloth body, wig, RpC, 15", EX...475.00
#345, Kiddiejoy, bsk SkHd, glass eyes, cloth body, RpC, 1926, 16", EX..525.00
#351, My Dream Baby, bsk SkHd, cloth body, RpC, 12", EX 325.00
#360a, bsk SkHd, o/m, glass eyes, blb, wig, RpC, 24", EX 800.00
#370, Duchess, o/m, glass eyes, kid body, RpC, 12", EX 165.00
#370, Florodora, o/m, glass eyes, compo body, RpC, 13", EX 270.00
#370, Mabel, o/m, glass eyes, compo body, RpC, 27", EX............ 700.00
#370, My Playmate, o/m, glass eyes, kid body, RpC, 22", EX........ 700.00
#372, Kiddiejoy, ShHd, p/e, o/c/m, 2 teeth, kid body, RpC, 1925, 21"...1,025.00
#520, domed head, glass eyes, o/m, compo, RpC, ca 1910, 12", EX....775.00
#570, domed head, c/m, RpC, ca 1910, 12", EX 1,850.00
#1890, bsk Shd or SkHd, glass eyes, o/m/teeth, kid body, RpC, 12", EX ..150.00
#1894, bsk ShHd, glass eyes, compo body, o/m/teeth, RpC, 8", EX..325.99
#1899, bsk ShHd or SkHd, glass eyes, o/m/teeth, wig, RpC, 26", EX..450.00
Baby Gloria, solid dome, o/m, pnt hair, RpC, 15", EX................. 675.00
No mold #, child, bsk SkHd, o/m, glass eyes, jtd, wig, RpC, 17", EX... 400.00

Barbie Dolls and Related Dolls

Though the face has changed three times since 1959, Barbie is still as popular today as she was when she was first introduced. Named after the young daughter of the first owner of the Mattel Company, the original Barbie had a white iris but no eye color. These dolls are nearly impossible to find, but there is a myriad of her successors and related collectibles just waiting to be found.

For further information we recommend *Barbie, The First Thirty Years*, by Stefanie Deutsch; *Collector's Encyclopedia of Barbie Doll Exclusives, Barbie Doll Around the World*, and *Collector's Encyclopedia of Barbie Doll Collector's Editions*, all by J. Michael Augustyniak; *The Barbie Doll Years* by Patrick C. and Joyce L. Olds. *Barbie Fashion, Vol. I, II,* and *III*, by Sarah Sink Eames, give a complete history of the wardrobes of Barbie, her friends, and her family. *Schroeder's Toys, Antique to Modern*, is another good source for current market values. All these are published by Collector Books.

Barbie, American Girl, 1964, blond or brunette hair, NRFB, ea ...1,500.00
Barbie, Dorothy (Wizard of Oz), 1994, Hollywood Legends Series, NRFB...350.00
Barbie, Feelin' Groovy, 1987, NRFB.................................... 175.00
Barbie, Growin' Pretty Hair, 1971, NRFB.............................. 475.00
Barbie, Holiday, 1988, NRFB, minimum value..................... 500.00
Barbie, Knitting Pretty (pk), 1964, NRFB 1,265.00
Barbie, Nutcracker, 1992, Musical Ballet Series, NRFB 150.00
Barbie, Police Officer (wht or blk), 1993, Toys R Us, NRFB.......... 75.00
Barbie, Queen of Hearts, 1994, Bob Mackie, NRFB.................... 250.00
Barbie, Rockettes, 1993, FAO Schwarz, NRFB 120.00
Barbie, Serenade in Satin, 1997, Barbie Couture Collection, MIB....100.00
Barbie, Standard, 1967, any hair color, MIB, ea 475.00
Barbie, Theater Date, 1964, NRFB.................................... 660.00
Barbie, Winter Fantasy, 1990, FAO Schwarz, NRFB................. 200.00
Brad, Talking, 1970, NRFB.. 225.00
Casey, Twist 'n Turn, 1968, blond or brunette hair, NRFB.......... 300.00
Chris, 1967, any hair color, MIB 200.00
Christie, Fashion Photo, 1978, MIB.................................... 95.00
Christie, Twist 'n Turn, 1968, red hair, MIB 300.00
Francie, Twist 'n Turn, 1966, Black, 2nd issue, blk hair, MIB....1,500.00
Kelly, Yellowstone, 1974, brunette hair, NRFB..................... 575.00
Ken, Busy, 1972, NRFB 150.00
Ken, Crystal, 1984, NRFB 40.00
Ken, Live Action on Stage, 1971, NRFB................................ 150.00

Ken, Sport & Shave, 1980, MIB 40.00
Ken, Superstar, 1977, MIB.. 100.00
Midge, 30th Anniversary, 1992, porc, MIB, D2 .... 175.00
PJ, Live Action, 1971, orig outfit, M 150.00
PJ, Malibu (The Sun Set), 1971, blond hair, NRFP 100.00
Ricky, 1965, MIB 150.00
Skipper, Growing Up, 1976, MIB................................... 100.00
Skipper, Western, 1982, NRFB 40.00
Stacey, Talking, any hair color, MIB 400.00

Barbie Accessories and Gift Sets

Case, Barbie, Stacey, Francie & Skipper, pk hard plastic, rare, NM ... 100.00
Case, Barbie, vinyl w/Bubble-Cut head & Swirl Ponytail Barbie, VG ... 650.00
Case, Midge wearing Movie Date, bl vinyl, 1963, NM................. 125.00
Furniture, Barbie Dream Kitchen-Dinette, #4095, 1964, MIB..... 600.00
Furniture, Skipper & Scooter Double Bunk Beds & Ladder, MIB...100.00
Furniture, Susy Goose Mod-A-Go-Go Bedroom, 1966, NRFB.2,300.00
Gift Set, Ballerina Barbie on Tour, 1976, MIB........................... 175.00
Gift Set, Barbie Travel in Style, Sears Exclusive, 1968, MIB 1,500.00
Gift Set, Golden Groove Barbie, Sears Exclusive, 1969, NRFB.. 2,000.00
Gift Set, New 'n Groovy PJ Swingin' in Silver, MIB.................... 770.00
Gift Set, Tutti & Todd Sundae Treat, 1966, NRFB 500.00
House, Barbie Glamour Home, 1985, MIB 125.00
House, Jamie's Penthouse, Sears Exclusive, 1971, MIB 475.00
Outfit, Barbie, Barbie in Hawaii, #1605, 1964, NRFP............... 300.00
Outfit, Barbie, Beautiful Bride, #1698, 1967, NRFP 2,500.00
Outfit, Barbie, Cinderella, #872, 1964, NRFB 475.00
Outfit, Barbie, Dog 'n Duds, #1613, 1964, NRFP 350.00
Outfit, Barbie, Fraternity Dance, #1638, NRFP........................ 600.00
Outfit, Barbie, Friday Night Date, #979, 1960, NRFP 225.00
Outfit, Barbie, Gold 'n Glamour, #1647, NRFP 475.00
Outfit, Barbie, Groovin' Gauchos, #1057, 1971, NRFP 300.00
Outfit, Barbie, Masquerade, #944, 1963, NRFP 200.00
Outfit, Barbie, Midnight Blue, #1617, NRFP............................ 850.00
Outfit, Francie, Hip Knits, #1265, 1966, NRFP 225.00
Outfit, Holiday Dance, #1639, 1965, NRFP 625.00
Outfit, Ken, Army & Air Force, #797, 1963, NRFP 250.00
Room, Barbie's Full Country Kitchen, #7404, 1974, NRFB 100.00
Room, Full Firelight Living Room, 1974, MIB 100.00
Shop, Barbie & the Rockers Dance Cafe, 1987, MIB................... 50.00
Shop, Barbie Fashion Salon, Sears Exclusive, 1964, MIB............. 600.00
Shop, Barbie Unique Boutique, Sears Exclusive, 1971, MIB........ 185.00
Vehicle, Ken's Hot Rod, Sears Exclusive, 1964, red, MIB 900.00
Vehicle, Western Star Traveler Motorhome, 1982, MIB 50.00
Vehicle, 1957 Belair Chevy, 1989, 1st ed, aqua, MIB................. 150.00

Belton Type

Bru-type face, EX bsk, o/c/m, wig, RpC, 14", EX 2,400.00
Bru-type face, EX bsk, o/c/m or c/m, wig, RpC, 18", VG..........2,200.00
French-type face, bsk, o/c/m or c/m, wig, RpC, 9", EX 1,200.00
French-type face, bsk, o/c/m or c/m, wig, RpC, 12", EX 2,000.00
French-type face, bsk, o/c/m or c/m, wig, RpC, 24", EX 3,700.00
German-type face, bsk, o/c/m or c/m, wig, RpC, 18", EX 1,950.00
German-type face, bsk, o/c/m or c/m, wig, 9", VG 800.00
German-type face, bsk, o/c/m or c/m, wig, 12", VG...................900.00
German-type face, bsk, o/c/m or c/m, wig, 23", EX.................2,750.00
German-type face, bsk, o/c/m or c/m, wig, 25", VG.................2,250.00

Betsy McCall

The dolls listed are with complete, original outfits and have rooted hair unless noted otherwise.

Am Character, hp, sleep eyes, wig, Sunday Best OC, 8", EX........ 350.00
Am Character, vinyl, Patti Playpal-style body, 1959, OC, 36", EX .. 325.00
Am Character, vinyl, rooted hair, slim limbs, OC, 1959, 19-20", EX ...500.00
Horsman, vinyl & hp, sleep eyes, OC/accessories, 1974, 12½", EX...50.00
Horsman, vinyl/hp teen body, sleep eyes, c/m, OC, 1974, 29", EX...275.00
McCall Corp, vinyl, bl or brn sleep eyes, rooted hair, 1961, OC, 22" ...250.00
Rothchild, hp, sleep eyes, OC, 1986, 8", EX................................ 35.00
Uneeda, vinyl, rooted hair, brn or bl sleep eyes, OC, 1964, 11½" .. 95.00

Boudoir

Boudoir dolls, often called bed dolls, French dolls, or flapper dolls, were popular from the late teens through the 1940s. The era of the 1920s and 1930s was the golden age of boudoir dolls.

More common boudoir dolls are usually found with composition head, arms, and high-heeled feet. Clothes are nailed on (later ones have stapled-on clothes). Wigs are usually mohair, human hair, or silk floss. Smoking boudoir dolls were made in the late teens and early twenties. More expensive boudoir dolls were made in France, Italy, and Germany, as well as the U.S. Usually they are all cloth with elaborate sewn or pinned-on costumes and silk, felt, or velvet painted faces. Sizes of boudoir dolls vary, but most are around 30". These dolls were made to adorn a lady's boudoir or sit on a bed. They were not meant as children's playthings. Our advisor for this category is Bonnie Groves; she is listed in the Directory under Texas.

Anita, compo & cloth, pk floss hair, 1920s, EX 330.00
Anita, smoker, compo, 1925, all orig, 27", VG 385.00
Anita, trn head, all orig, 30", EX, minimum value 475.00
Anita smoker, compo, 1925, 25", VG, minimum value................ 375.00
Anita smoker, compo & cloth, all orig, 1920s, 30", G 135.00
Apache male, cloth, all orig, 26", VG, minimum value................ 300.00
Blossom, cloth, all orig, 1930s, 30", EX 400.00
Blossom, cloth, tagged, 30", G.. 115.00
Blossom, Pierrette, all orig, 1930s, 30", VG, minimum value....... 400.00
Bride, all orig, 1940s, 29", VG... 165.00
Bucilla kit for making boudoir doll costume, EX, minimum value ..200.00
Cloth, Gerling type, all orig, 1920s, 30", VG, minimum value 300.00
Cloth, long-faced egg head, RpC, 1920s, VG 200.00
Cloth, std quality, OC, 1920s, 16", EX, minimum value 265.00
Cloth, std quality, OC, 1920s, 32", EX, minimum value 325.00
Compo, OC, 1940, 28", EX, minimum value............................. 125.00
Compo, std quality, OC, 1930s, 28", EX, from $125 to 175.00
Compo & cloth, all orig, 1930s-40s, 25", NM 30.00
Cubeb smoker, compo, jtd, all orig, 1925, 25", EX, minimum value ..900.00
Etta, cloth, all orig, tagged, 1920s, NM................................... 900.00
Etta, cloth, all orig, 30", G, minimum value 350.00
French, cloth w/bsk arms & legs, all orig, 1920s, 27", VG........... 455.00
French, cloth w/bsk arms & legs, tagged, 18", VG, pr................. 395.00
French topsy-turvy, cloth w/bsk arms, 21", VG, minimum value .. 395.00
Gerbs, cloth, FR, all orig, 1920s, 25", EX, minimum value 375.00
Gerbs, cloth, FR, all orig, 1920s, 30", G, minimum value 300.00
Halloween, std quality, OC, 27", minimum value........................ 500.00
Lenci, Fadette, smoker, 25", VG, minimum value 3,000.00
Lenci, Pierrot, all orig, 26", VG..2,750.00
Lenci, salon lady, all orig, 25", EX, minimum value.................3,000.00
Lenci, Spanish, all orig, 1923, VG 2,025.00
Patriotic, standard quality, 1940s, 25", G, minimum value.......... 200.00
Ring lady, cloth w/floss hair, all orig, 1920s, 31", VG 300.00
Shoes, repro, 3" 22.50
Silk face, bsk arms & legs, Fr, 33", VG, from $300 to.................. 600.00
Smoker, cloth, OC, 1920s, 16", EX 300.00
Smoker, cloth, OC, 1920s, 25", EX 525.00

Sterling, all orig, 1930, 27", VG, minimum value........................ 200.00
Sterling, Halloween, all orig, 1930s, 28", G, minimum value....... 400.00
W-K-S, compo & cloth, all orig, 1930s, 25", G 50.00
W-K-S, compo head & hands, cloth body, nude, 1920s, G 40.00
W-K-S, Gypsy, all orig, 25", VG, minimum value 125.00
W-K-S, Remember Pearl Harbor, compo/cloth, all orig, 1940s, EX ...350.00

Bru

Bebe Automate (breather, talker), lever in torso, RpC, 19", VG ... 4,600.00
Bebe Marchant (walker), clockwork mechanism, RpC, 17", VG... 6,800.00
Bebe Teteur (nursing), o/m, key at bk of head, RpC, 20", VG... 12,000.00
Bru Jne, bsk swivel head, pwt eyes, o/c/m/teeth, RpC, 12", VG.... 10,000.00
Bru Jne, bsk swivel head, pwt eyes, o/c/m/teeth, RpC, 14", VG... 16,500.00
Bru Jne, bsk swivel head, pwt eyes, o/c/m/teeth, RpC, 17", EX..... 23,000.00
Bru Jne R, bsk swivel head, pwt eyes, c/m, hh wig, RpC, 21", EX.. 6,500.00
Bru Jne R, bsk swivel head, pwt eyes, o/m/teeth, RpC, 20", VG.. 2,250.00
Circle Dot Bebe, bsk swivel head, pwt eyes, o/c/m/teeth, RpC, 11", EX ..12,000.00
Circle Dot Bebe, bsk swivel head, pwt eyes, o/c/m/teeth, RpC, 26", VG.18,750.00
Fashion type, bsk swivel head, ShPl, spring in neck, RpC, 15", EX.3,300.00
Fashion type (smiler), swivel head, ShPl, spring in neck, RpC, 13", EX...3,000.00

Celebrity

For more information we recommend *Collector's Guide to Celebrity Dolls* by David Spurgeon.

Ashley & Mary Kate Olsen, Mattel, 1st ed, Dance & Horseback sets, MIB . 30.00
Boy George, LJN, 1984, rare, 11½", MIB...................................... 150.00
Brooke Shields, LJN, pk & gray casual outfit, 1982, 11½", MIB 55.00
Cher, Mego, pk evening gown, 1976, 12½", MIB 125.00
Cheryl Ladd, Mattel, 1978, 11½", MIB.. 85.00
Dick Clark, Juro, 1958, 26½", MIB 450.00
Dolly Parton, Goldberger, blk outfit w/silver boots, 1990s, 12", MIB... 75.00
Donny & Marie Osmond, Mattel, 1976, 12", MIB, ea.................... 85.00
Elizabeth Taylor, National Velvet, Madame Alexander, 1990, 12", MIB.100.00
Elvis Presley, Eugene, issued in 6 different outfits, 1984, 12", MIB.... 75.00
Farrah Fawcett-Majors, Mego, swimsuit, 1981, 12", MIB............... 50.00
Flip Wilson/Geraldine, Shindana, stuffed talker, 1970, 15", MIB .. 85.00
John Wayne, Great Legends, Effanbee, Guardian of the West, 1982, 18"....150.00
KISS, Mego, any from group, 1978, 12½", MIB, ea 350.00
Laurel & Hardy, Goldberger, denim overalls, 1986, 12", MIB, ea....... 55.00
Leann Rimes, Country Music Stars, Exclusive Premiere, 1998, MIB. 30.00
Lucille Ball, Effanbee, blk tails & top hat, 1985, 15", MIB 175.00
Lucille Ball, Hollywood Walk of Fame, CAL-HASCO INC, 1992, 20"...........350.00
Mae West, Great Legends, Effanbee, 1982, 18", MIB.................... 125.00
Marilyn Monroe, Tri-Star, pk gown & gloves, 1982, 16½", MIB.. 100.00
Marilyn Monroe, Tri-Star, 2nd issue, different face mold, 1982, MIB... 150.00
Muhammad Ali, Mego, 1976, 9", MOC 150.00
New Kids on the Block, Hasbro, In Concert, 5 different, 12", MIB.. 50.00
Prince William, Goldberg, christening gown, 1982, 18", MIB 150.00
Prince William, House of Nisbet, as baby, 1982, 18", MIB........... 200.00
Princess Diana, Danbury Mint, pk satin gown, 1988, 14", MIB ... 125.00
Princess Diana, Effanbee, Fan Club, wedding dress, 1982, 16½", MIB ...125.00
Princess Margaret, Dean's Rag Book Co, papier-mache over cloth, 1920s...350.00
Red Foxx, Shindana, stuffed talker, 1976, 16", MIB..................... 150.00
Rosie O'Donnell, Tyco, stuffed, w/outfit, 1997, 14", MIB.............. 40.00
Selena, Arm Enterprise, red jumpsuit, 1996, 11½", MIN 85.00
Sonny Bono, Mego, 1976, 12½", MIB.. 150.00
WC Fields, Knickerbocker, stuffed talker, 1972, 16", MIB 75.00

China

Child or boy, short blk or blond hairdo, exposed ears, RpC, 21", EX .. 2,650.00

Dolly Madison, 24", $725.00. (Photo courtesy McMaster Harris Auction Company)

French, pnt or glass eyes, cork pate, wig, kid body, RpC, 14", VG.. 2,350.00
Japanese, mk or unmk, blk or blond hair, RpC, 1910-20, 15", EX...190.00
Kling, mk w/bell & #, RpC, 13", VG 265.00
KPM, man or boy, glass eyes, RpC, 17", EX 2,650.00
KPM, ShPl, brn-haired man, RpC, 1869, 23", VG 7,000.00
Queen Victoria, young, RpC, 16", EX.....................................1,600.00
Swivel-neck, ShPl, flange type, 10", EX.................................2,100.00
1840 style, boy, smiling, side-parted brn hair, RpC, 21", VG 3,450.00
1840 style, Covered Wagon, center part w/sausage curls, RpC, 10", EX...275.00
1840 style, Covered Wagon, center part w/sausage curls, RpC, 25", EX...700.00
1850 style, Alice in Wonderland, snood/headband, RpC, 26", EX... 400.00
1850 style, bald head, hh or mohair wig, RpC, 12", VG.............. 475.00
1850 style, Greiner type, glass eyes, varied hairdos, RpC, 15", EX ..750.00
1850 style, Greiner type, glass eyes, varied hairdos, RpC, 21", EX.. 4,000.00
1850 style, Greiner type, pnt eyes, varied hairdos, RpC, 15"........ 750.00
1860 style, flat-top blk hair w/center part, side curls, RpC, 22", EX ...365.00
1860 style, flat-top blk hair w/center part, side curls, RpC, 7", EX ... 100.00
1860 style, highbrow w/curls, rnd face, RpC, 19", EX.................. 700.00
1860 style, Mary Todd Lincoln, blk hair, gold snood, RpC, 21", EX ..850.00
1860 style, w/grape cluster & leaves, RpC, 15", EX 1,325.00
1870 style, Adelina Patti, center part/ringlets, RpC, 25", EX....... 600.00
1870 style, bangs, as Highland Mary, blk hair, RpC, 19", EX 425.00
1870 style, Jenny Lind, blk hair in bun or coronet, RpC, 15", VG. 1,150.00
1870 style, ShHd, blk or blond hair, pk facial details, RpC, 18", EX..325.00
1880 style, Dolly Madison, blk hair ribbon, pnt eyes, RpC, 14", EX ..375.00
1880 style, molded curls allover, fat cheeks, RpC, 27", EX........... 675.00
1890 style, common low brow, printed body, RpC, 14", EX 155.00
1890 style, jeweled necklace, RpC, 20", EX............................... 325.00
1899-1933, Agness, Bertha, Daisy, etc, German mfg, RpC, 21", EX ..325.00

Cloth

A cloth doll in very good condition will display light wear and soiling, while one assessed as excellent will be clean and bright.

Alabama Indestructible, baby, pnt features, ca 1900-25, 22", VG .. 3,600.00
Alabama Indestructible, child, ca 1900-1925, 15", EX 1,800.00
Art Fabric Mills, Improved Life-Sz Doll, printed undies, 30", EX....400.00
Babyland Rag, Black, lithographed, 1893-1928, 24", EX.............. 800.00
Babyland Rag, Buster Brown, 1892-1928, 17", EX...................... 550.00
Babyland Rag, lithographed, 1893-1928, 14½", EX 335.00
Beecher, Black, 23", EX 5,600.00
Beecher, Missionary Ragbaby, 23", EX 5,000.00
Bing Art, cloth or felt, pnt hair, mk or unmk, 15", EX 650.00
Bing Art, cloth or felt, wig, 10", EX.. 350.00
Black, Mammy type, pnt or embr features, 1910-20s, 16", EX...... 285.00
Black, Mammy type, pnt or embr features, 1930s, 15", EX, minimum.. 165.00
Black, Topsy-Turvy, oil pnt, EX 650.00
Bruckner, printed, molded mask face, 1901-30+, 14", EX 325.00
Chad Valley, child, glass eyes, 1917-30+, 18", EX 775.00
Chad Valley, child, pnt eyes, 1917-30+, 18", EX 625.00

Chad Valley, Ghandi, 13", EX...675.00
Chad Valley, Princess Elizabeth, EX.................................1,700.00
Chad Valley, Story Book Doll, Red Riding Hood, 14", EX...........500.00
Chad Valley, train conductor, glass eyes, 18", EX......................1,000.00
Chase, baby, hospital type, RpC, 16", EX.............................575.00
Chase, child, molded bobbed hair, 16", EX.......................1,600.00
Columbian Doll, HP features, stitched fingers/toes, RpC, 15", VG..2,225.00
Columbian type, HP features, ca 1890+, 15", EX...............450.00
Deans Rag Book Co, child, litho face, 1905+, 9", EX.....................85.00
Deans Rag Book Co, child, mask face, 1905+, 12", EX................125.00
Deans Rag Book Co, Golliwog, 1905+, 13", EX...................250.00
Drayton, Dolly Dingle, printed features, 1923, RpC, 11".............385.00
Drayton, Peek-A-Boo, printed features, 1913-15, 15", EX..........275.00
Fangel, baby, flat printed face, 1920-30+, 17", EX.....................600.00
Gund, cloth mask face, pnt features, ca 1898, 19", EX................300.00
Krueger, child, oil-pnt mask face, yarn wig, 1917+, 20", EX.........240.00
Molly, child, mask face, 1929-30+, 17", EX............................150.00
Petzold, molded head, pnt features, wig, 1919-30+, 22", EX........775.00
Printed, Black child, ca 1876+, 16", EX.................................425.00
Printed, Santa/St Nicholas, cut/sewn printed cloth, ca 1876, 15", EX..325.00
Wellings, baby, molded face, oil-pnt details, 1926-30+, 22", EX..900.00

Effanbee

Bernard Fleischaker and Hugo Baum became business partners in 1910, and after two difficult years of finding toys to buy, they decided to manufacture dolls and toys of their own. The Effanbee trademark is a blending of their names, Eff for Fleischaker and bee for Baum. The company still exists today.

Ann Shirley, compo, OC, 1936-40, 27", EX..................................625.00
Baby Bud, compo, pnt features, o/c/m, RpC, 1918+, 6", EX.........195.00
Baby Dainty, compo/cloth, RpC, 1912+, 14", EX..........................245.00
Baby Grumpy, compo, pnt hair, pnt eyes, pouty, RpC, 1915+, 14½", EX..425.00
Barbara Lou, compo, o/m, separate fingers, OC, 1936-39+, 21", EX..900.00
Betty Bee, compo, sleep eyes, short tousel wig, OC, 1932, 22", EX....400.00
Brother or sister, compo/cloth, yarn hair, pnt eyes, OC, 1943, 6", EX...235.00
Bubbles, compo ShHd, o/c/m/teeth, heart necklace, RpC, 1924+, 16", VG...100.00
Champagne Lady, vinyl & hp, bl sleep eyes, rooted hair, OC, 21", EX.275.00
Grumpy Aunt Dinah, Black, cloth body, stocking legs, RpC, 14½", EX..425.00
Grumpykins, compo/cloth, RpC, 1927, 12", EX...........................300.00
Harmonica Joe, cloth body, rubber ball for air, RpC, 1923, 15", VG..85.00
Historical replica, compo, hh wig, OC, 1939+, 14", EX...............600.00
Honey Walker, hp walker, OC, 1952+, 19", EX.........................425.00
Johnny Tu-Face, compo w/face front & bk, RpC, 1912, 16", EX..325.00
Little Lady, compo, sleep eyes, wig, OC (formal), 1939+, 18", EX...325.00
MaMa, compo ShHd, pnt or sleep eyes, wig, OC, 1921+, 24", EX...400.00
Mary Jane, bsk head, sleep eyes, compo w/wooden limbs, RpC, 20"... 700.00
Patsy Ann, vinyl, sleep eyes, wht organdy dress, ltd ed, 1959, 15", EX..285.00
Patsy Babyette, compo, sleep eyes, OC, 1932, 9"..........................325.00
Patsy Joann, compo, OC, 1931, 16", EX.................................550.00
Patsy/Patricia, compo, pnt eyes, molded hair, OC, 1940, 15", EX...600.00
Polka Dottie, vinyl, molded pigtails on fabric body, OC, 1954, 21", EX..165.00
Suzanne, compo, sleep eyes, c/m, wig, OC, ca 1940, 14", EX.......325.00

Half-Dolls

Half dolls were never meant to be objects of play. Most were modeled after the likenesses of lovely ladies, though children and animals were represented as well. Most of the ladies were firmly sewn on to pincushion bases that were beautifully decorated and served as the skirts of their gowns. Other skirts were actually covers for items on milady's dressing table. Some were used as parasol or brush handles or as tops to candy containers or perfume bottles. Most popular from 1900 to about 1930, they will most often be found marked with the country of their origin,

usually Bavaria, Germany, France, and Japan. You may also find some fine quality pieces marked Goebel, Dressel and Kester, KPM, and Heubach.

Arms away, china or bsk, bald head w/wig, 4", VG.....................105.00
Arms away, holding item, 6", EX..275.00
Arms away, holding item, 6", VG..200.00
Arms away, mk by maker or mold #, 4", VG.............................150.00
Arms away, mk by maker or mold #, 8", EX............................400.00
Arms in, arms close to figure, bald head w/wig, 4", EX.................80.00
Arms in, decor bodice, necklace, etc, 3", EX...........................125.00
Arms in, hands attached, 3", EX..35.00
Arms in, mk by maker or mold #, 5", EX................................135.00
Arms in, papier-mache or compo, 4", EX.................................35.00
Jtd shoulders, china or bsk, molded hair, 7", EX.......................200.00
German mk, 4", EX..200.00
Japan mk, 6", EX...50.00
Man or child, 4", EX...120.00

Handwerck, Heinrich

#69, child, bsk SkHd, o/m, o/c/e or set eyes, wig, RpC, 15", EX...575.00
#69, child, bsk SkHd, o/m, o/c/e or set eyes, wig, RpC, 28", EX.....1,050.00
#78, bsk ShHd, o/m, kid body, wig, RpC, 14", EX......................235.00
#79, bsk ShHd, o/m, kid body, RpC, 14", EX............................235.00
#79, child, bsk ShHd, o/m, o/c/e or set eyes, wig, RpC, 40", EX.....3,400.00
#89, child, bsk ShHd, c/m, o/c/e or set eyes, wig, RpC, 18", 40", EX.....3,100.00
#89, child, bsk SkHd, o/m, p/c/e or set eyes, wig, RpC, 36", EX....2,000.00
#189, child, bsk SkHd, o/m, o/c/e, wig, RpC, 15", EX..................800.00
#199, child, bsk SkHd, o/m, o/c/e, wig, RpC, 15", EX.................625.00
No mold #, child, bsk SkHd, o/m, o/c/e or set eyes, RpC, 30", EX...1,100.00

Hertel, Schwab and Company

#127, character face, sleep eyes, o/m, RpC, 1915, 17", EX.........2,000.00
#130, baby, bsk head, o/m or o/c/m/teeth, sleep eyes, RpC, 9", EX...325.00
#134, character face, sleep eyes, c/m, RpC, 1915, rare, 15", VG. 15,000.00
#140, character, glass eyes, laughing o/c/m, RpC, ca 1912, 12", EX..3,400.00
#142, bsk head, o/m/teeth, sleep or pnt eyes, RpC, 22", EX.........900.00
#149, character, glass eyes, c/m, bjtd body, RpC, rare, 1912, 17", VG...9,500.00
#152, bsk head, molded hair, o/m, toddler body, RpC, 14", EX....600.00

Heubach, Ernst

#250, ShHd, o/m, kid body, RpC, 09", EX................................200.00
#250, ShHd, o/m, kid body, RpC, 32", EX................................900.00
#267, SkHd, glass eyes, o/m, 5-pc blb, wig, RpC, 11", EX.............250.00
#300, SkHd, glass eyes, o/m, 5-pc blb, RpC, 14", EX...................400.00
#320, SkHd, glass eyes, o/m, 5-pc blb, RpC, 14", EX...................400.00
#338, newborn, solid dome, glass eyes, c/m, cloth body, RpC, 12", EX.....425.00
#348, newborn, solid dome, glass eyes, c/m, cloth body, RpC, 15", EX.....700.00
#444, Black newborn, solid dome, glass eyes, cloth body, RpC, 12", EX....400.00
#1900, child, kid or cloth body, glass eyes, o/m, RpC, 26", EX.....650.00
#1900, pnt bsk, kid or cloth body, glass eyes, o/m, RpC, 12", EX.175.00

Heubach, Gebruder

#5689, character child, o/m, RpC, 14", EX...............................1,800.00
#5777, Dolly Dimple, o/m, RpC, 14", EX..................................2,300.00
#6688, character child, ShHd, solid dome, c/m, RpC, 10", EX....625.00
#6970, character child, glass eyes, c/m, RpC, 10", EX...............1,800.00
#7345, character child, pk-tinted c/m, sunburst, RpC, 17", VG..1,150.00
#7604, character child, o/c/m, intaglio eyes, RpC, 12", EX..........725.00
#7644, character child, pnt eyes, laughing o/c/m, RpC, 14", EX..865.00
#7911, character child, intaglio eyes, laughing o/c/m, RpC, 15", EX.1,200.00

#7972, character child, intaglio eyes, c/m, RpC, 20", EX 2,000.00
#8192, character child, sleep eyes, o/m, RpC, 13", EX 900.00
#8420, glass eyes, c/m, sq mk, RpC, 15", EX 2,800.00
#9055, character child, intaglio eyes, c/m, RpC, 11", EX 375.00
Heubach mk/no #, adult, o/m, glass eyes, RpC, 14", EX 4,500.00
Heubach mk/no #, o/c/m, dimples, RpC, 18", EX 4,450.00

Horsman

Angelove, plastic/vinyl, made for Hallmark, OC, 1974, 12" 25.00
Baby, compo, OC, 1930s-40s, 15" 125.00
Baby Butterfly (Oriental), compo head/hands, OC, ca 1913, 13" ...650.00
Betty Ann, vinyl head, hp body, OC, 1951, 16" 25.00
Betty Jane, all compo, OC, 25" 300.00
Bright Star, hp, OC, 1952+, 15" 450.00
Crawling Baby, vinyl, rooted hair, OC, 1967, 14" 25.00
Crissy, vinyl, brn hair that 'grows,' OC, 1969, 17½" 110.00
Dolly Rosebud (mama), compo head, dimples, o/c/e, OC, 1926-30, 18".175.00
Hansel & Gretel, vinyl & hp, rooted hair, c/m, OC, 1963, 15", pr ..200.00
Jackie, vinyl, rooted hair, c/m, OC, 1961, 25" 125.00
Jeanie Horsman, compo head/limbs, molded hair, o/c/e, OC, 1937, 14"..225.00
Naughty Sue, compo head, jtd, OC, 1937, 16" 400.00
Toni, hp, nylon wig, c/m, jtd, OC, 14" 450.00
Toni, hp, nylon wig, c/m, jtd, OC, 1949, 21" 700.00

Ideal

Two of Ideal's most collectible lines of dolls are Crissy and Toni. For more information, refer to *Collector's Guide to Ideal Dolls*, by Judith Izen (Collector Books).

April Shower, vinyl, battery-op actions, OC, 1969, 14", EX 28.00
Baby, compo, pnt or sleep eyes, wig, OC, 1913+, 16", minimum value.. 150.00
Baby Crissy, vinyl, auburn grow hair/2 pnt teeth, OC, 1973-76, 24", EX... 150.00
Baby Pebbles, vinyl w/soft body, OC, 1963-64, 16", MIB............. 265.00
Baby Snooks (Flexy), pnt hair, pnt eyes, o/c/m/teeth, 13½", EX ..325.00
Belly Button Baby, Black, vinyl head, pnt eyes, 1971, 9½", EX...... 45.00
Bonnie Play Pal, vinyl, bl sleep eyes, rooted hair, OC, 1959, 24", EX...275.00
Bonny Braids, vinyl/rubber, o/m/tooth, pnt hair, OC, 11½", EX ..125.00
Buster Brown, compo & cloth, tin eyes, OC, 1929, 16", EX 300.00
Child or toddler, compo, pnt or sleep eyes, wig, OC, 1915+, 18", EX. 200.00
Cinderella, compo, flirty eyes, o/m/teeth, hh wig, OC, 1938+, 16", EX.350.00
Crissy, vinyl, brn grow hair, swivel waist, OC, 1971, 17½", EX.... 110.00
Daddy's Girl, vinyl/plastic, swivel waist, bl sleep eyes, OC, 38", EX...1,200.00
Deanna Durbin, compo, brn sleep eyes, o/m/teeth, OC, 15", EX. 550.00
Dennis the Menace, printed cloth, OC, 1976, 7", EX 15.00
Flossie Flirt, compo/cloth, crier, tin flirty eyes, OC, 28" 400.00
Harmony, vinyl, battery-op, plays guitar, OC, 1972, 21", EX 200.00
Jiminy Cricket, compo/wood, OC & wooden umbrella, 1940, 8½" ...500.00
Judy Garland, compo teen, sleep eyes, o/m/teeth, long dress, 15", EX... 700.00
Kissy, vinyl, sleep eyes, rooted hair, OC, 1961-64, 22½", EX 155.00
Magic Skin baby, hp head/latex body/legs, sleep eyes, OC, 13-14", EX .50.00
Mama, compo, pnt or sleep eyes, crier, wig, 1921+, 24", minimum.. 350.00
Princess Beatrix, compo/cloth, flirty eyes, OC w/bonnet, 14", EX ..175.00
Saucy Walker, hp, flirty eyes/crier, o/c/m/teeth, OC, 1951-55, 16", EX ..225.00
Snow White, cloth w/mask face, hh wig, OC, 1938, 16", EX....... 550.00
Snow White, compo, flirty eyes, o/m/teeth, wig, OC, 1938+, 22", EX...650.00
Soozie Smiles, compo head w/2 faces, cloth body, orig romper, 15", EX...300.00
Tara, Black, vinyl, blk hair grows, sleep eyes, 1976, 15½", EX...... 390.00
Tickletoes, compo/rubber, squeaker, flirty eyes, o/m/teeth, 14", EX ..250.00

Jumeau

The Jumeau factory became the best known name for dolls during the 1880s and 1890s. Early dolls were works of art with closed mouths and paperweight eyes. When son Emile Jumeau took over, he patented sleep eyes with eyelids that drooped down over the eyes. This model also had flirty eyes that move from side to side and is extremely rare. Over 98% of Jumeau dolls have paperweight eyes. The less expensive German dolls were the downfall of the French doll manufacturers, and in 1899 the Jumeau company had to combine with several others in an effort to save the French doll industry from German competition.

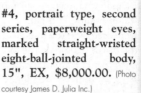

#4, portrait type, second series, paperweight eyes, marked straight-wristed eight-ball-jointed body, 15", EX, $8,000.00. (Photo courtesy James D. Julia Inc.)

Bebe, # over EJ, bsk SkHd, pwt/e, p/e, c/m, wig, RpC, 20", EX.....12,000.00
Bebe, Depoze E # J, bsk SkHd, pwt/e, p/e, c/m, wig, RpC, 23", EX. 6,625.00
Depose Jumeau & #, poured bsk head, pwt eyes, c/m, RpC, 23", EX..6,900.00
Fashion type, #d swivel head, c/m, pwt/e, p/e, kid body, RpC, 20", EX....4,600.00
Phonograph in torso, bsk head, o/m, RpC, rare, 24", VG........19,000.00
Portrait, almond eyes, wig, RpC, 13½" 12,500.00
Princess Elizabeth, bsk SkHd, c/m, flirty eyes, jtd, RpC, 18", EX...2,100.00
Tete Jumeau, bsk SkHd, glass eyes, c/m, wig, RpC, 32", EX 8,000.00
Tete Jumeau, child, bsk SkHd, glass eyes, c/m, wig, RpC, 32", EX....8,000.00
Tete Jumeau, poured bsk SkHd, glass eyes, c/m, RpC, 23", EX..5,000.00

Kammer and Reinhardt

#101, Peter or Marie, pnt eyes, c/m, jtd, RpC, ca 1909, 15", EX...3,200.00
#102, Elsa or Walter, pnt eyes, molded hair, c/m, RpC, rare, 14", VG..32,000.00
#109, Elise, pnt eyes, c/m, RpC, ca 1909, 14", EX 7,000.00
#114, Hans or Gretchen, pnt eyes, c/m, RpC, ca 1909, 18", EX.. 5,700.00
#115A, toddler, o/c/e, c/m, jtd compo, wig, RpC, 18", EX 5,500.00
#117, Mein Liebling, glass eyes, c/m, RpC, ca 1911, 15", EX....4,400.00
#123, Max, flirty o/c/e, laughing c/m, RpC, ca 1913, 16", VG ..1,450.00
#135, o/c/e, o/m, baby body, RpC, 13", EX................................... 850.00
#191, Dolly Face child, o/m, o/c/e, jtd, RpC, 30", EX................1,500.00
#192, child, c/m, o/c/e, jtd, RpC, 18", EX 2,800.00
#192, Dolly Face child, o/m, o/c/e, jtd, RpC, 18", EX................1,100.00
No mold # or K*R only, SkHd, glass eyes, c/m, flapper, RpC, 14", VG...2,400.00
No mold # or R*T only, SkHd, glass eyes, o/m, RpC, 19", EX 750.00

Kestner

Johannes D. Kestner made buttons at a lathe in a Waltershausen factory in the early 1800s. When this line of work failed, he used the same lathe to turn doll bodies. Thus the Kestner company began. It was one of the few German manufacturers to make the complete doll. By 1860, with the purchase of a porcelain factory, Kestner made doll heads of china and bisque as well as wax, worked-in-leather, celluloid, and cardboard. In

1895 the Kestner trademark of a crown with streamers was registered in the U.S. and a year later in Germany. Kestner felt the mark was appropriate since he referred to himself as the 'king of German dollmakers.'

#162, adult, bsk & compo, o/m, molded breasts, RpC, ca 1898, 18", EX..1,525.00
#208, character child, pnt eyes, RpC, 12", EX 3,300.00
#210, character baby, ShHd, o/c/e, o/c/m, RpC, ca 1912, 12", EX...700.00
#211, character baby, SkHd, glass eyes, o/m, bent legs, RpC, 8", EX..750.00
#237, Hilda, o/c/e, o/m, RpC, ca 1914, 13", EX 2,400.00
#243, Oriental baby, o/c/e, o/m, RpC, ca 1914, 13", EX 4,000.00
#263, character baby, SkHd, glass eyes, o/m, bent legs, RpC, 26", EX .. 1,650.00

Lenci

Characteristics of Lenci dolls include seamless, steam-molded felt heads, quality clothing, childishly plump bodies, and painted eyes that glance to the side. Fine mohair wigs were used, and the middle and fourth fingers were sewn together. Look for the factory stamp on the foot, though paper labels were also used. The Lenci factory continues today, producing dolls of the same high quality. Values are for dolls in excellent condition — no moth holes, very little fading. Dolls from the 1940s, 1950s, and beyond generally bring the lower prices; add for tags, boxes, and accessories. Mint dolls and rare examples bring higher prices. Dolls in only good condition are worth approximately 25% of one rated excellent.

Aviator, girl w/felt helmet, pre-1940, 18" 3,200.00
Baby, OC, pre-1940s, 22", EX 3,200.00
Bali dancer, OC, pre-1940, 15", EX 1,500.00
Child, hard face, less ornate OC, 1940s-50s, 15", EX 500.00
Child, softer face, ornate OC, 1920s-30s, 13", EX 1,750.00
Fadette, adult face, flapper body, OC, pre-1940s, 32", EX 2,600.00
Flirty glass eyes, OC, pre-1940, 15", EX 2,200.00
Mascotte, swing legs, OC, pre-1940, 8½", EX 325.00
Mendel, OC, pre-1940, 22", EX 3,700.00
Mini child, OC, pre-1940s, 9", EX 400.00
Modern, OC, ca 1979+, 13", EX 125.00
Modern, OC, ca 1979+, 26", EX 250.00
Pierrot, OC, pre-1940, 21", EX...2,000.00

Liddle Kiddles

From 1966 to 1971, Mattel produced Liddle Kiddle dolls ranging in size from ¾" to 4". They were all poseable and had rooted hair that could be restyled. There were various series of the dolls, among them Animiddles, Zoolery Jewelry Kiddles, Extraterrestrials, and Sweet Treats, as well as many accessories. Our advisor for this category is Paris Langford; she is listed in the Directory under Louisiana. Please send an SASE for information or contact Paris by e-mail: bbean415@aol.com.

Bunson Bernie, #3501, complete, 3", M 60.00
Florence Niddle, #3507, complete, 2¾", M 60.00
Freezy Sliddle, #3516, complete, 3½", M 60.00
Liddle Diddle, #3502, complete, 2¾", M 75.00
Liddle Kiddle Playhouses, complete, 1966-68, M, ea, minimum 50.00
Millie Middle, #3509, complete, 2¾", M 60.00
Rolly Twiddle, #3519, complete, 3½", M 200.00
Sizzly Friddle, #3513, complete, 3", M 65.00
Tea Party Kiddles, complete, 1970-71, 3½", M, ea 85.00
Telly Viddle, #3551, complete, 3½", M 100.00

Madame Alexander

Beatrice Alexander founded the Alexander Doll Company in 1923 by making an all-cloth, oil-painted face, Alice in Wonderland doll. With the help of her three sisters, the company prospered; and by the late 1950s there were over 600 employees making Madame Alexander dolls. The company still produces these lovely dolls today. For more information, refer to *Collector's Encyclopedia of Madame Alexander Dolls* and *Madame Alexander Collector's Doll Price Guide* by Linda Crowsey. Both are published by Collector Books. In the listings that follow, values represent dolls in mint condition.

Agatha, hp, red gown, Jacqueline, 1967, #2171, 21" 650.00
Alice in Wonderland, compo, Margaret or Wendy Ann, 1948-49, 21" ...950.00
Arlene Dahl, hp, Maggie, red wig, lav gown, 1950-51, 18" 7,000.00
Aunt Agatha, hp, checked taffeta gown, Wendy Ann, 1957, #434, 8" ..1,400.00
Ballerina, hp, Wendy Ann, 1953, #354, 8" 750.00
Belle Brummel, cloth, 1930s..800.00
Brenda Starr, hp, ballgown, 1964, 12" 450.00
Bridesmaid, hp, Wendy Ann, pk, bl or yel, 1953, 8" 900.00
Carmen, compo, Wendy Ann, extra makeup, 1939-42, 21" 1,400.00
Cinderella, hp, Classic Lissy, Literature series, 1966, 12" 950.00
Coco, plastic/vinyl, sheath-style ballgown, 1966, 21" 2,200.00
Edwardian, hp, Margaret, pk emb cotton, 1953, #2001A, 18" ..2,200.00
Estrella, hp, Maggie, lilac gown, 1953, 18"..............................1,200.00
Flower Girl, compo, Wendy Ann, 1956, #602, 8"........................950.00
Godey, compo, Wendy Ann, wht lace over pk satin, 1945-47, 21"..2,700.00
Goldilocks, hp, Maggie, 1951, 18"..1,200.00
Hulda, hp, Margaret, lamb's wool wig, 1949, 18" 1,900.00
Ice Skater, hp, Wendy Ann, 1955-56, #555, 8" 700.00
Jacqueline, hp/vinyl, street dress or suit w/hat, 1961-62, 21" 950.00
Juliet, compo, Wendy Ann, Portrait series, 1945-46, 21" 2,500.00
Klondike Kate, hp, Cissette, 1963, 10".....................................1,500.00
Lady in Red, Cissy, red taffeta, 1958, #2285, 20" 2,900.00
Lady Windermere, compo, extra makeup, Portrait series, 1945-46, 21"..2,500.00
Laughing Allegra, cloth, 1932 ....650.00
Little Minister, hp, Wendy Ann, 1957, #411, 8" 3,200.00
Little Victoria, Wendy Ann, 1953-54, #376, 7½-8" 1,200.00
Mambo, hp, Wendy Ann, 1955, #481, 8" 850.00
Melanie, hp, Wendy Ann, gr velvet, 1955-56, #633, 8" 1,300.00
Nana/Governess, hp, Wendy Ann, 1957, #433, 8" 2,000.00
Orphan Annie, plastic/vinyl, Mary Anne, 1965-66, #1480, 14" .. 300.00
Peggy Bride, hp, Margaret, lt blonde, 1950-51, 14-18", from $900 to... 1,400.00
Polly, plastic/vinyl, bridal gown, 1965, 17" 300.00
Queen, hp, Margaret, wht gown, cape w/fur trim, 1953, #2025, 18" ..1,800.00
Romeo, compo, Wendy Ann, 1949, 18"...................................1,300.00
Skater's Waltz, Cissy, 1955-56, 15-18" 650.00
Snow White, hp, Margaret, rare..1,200.00
Southern Belle or Girl, hp, Wendy Ann, striped gown, 1956, 8" ..1,100.00
Sweet Violet, hp, Cissy, 1951-54, 18".......................................875.00
Tiny Tim, cloth, early 1930s, 16"..700.00
Wendy Ann, compo, 1938-44, 17-21" 1,100.00
Zorina Ballerina, compo, Wendy Ann, extra makeup, 1937-38, 17".1,900.00

Mattel

For more information refer to *Talking Toys of the 20th Century* by Kathy and Don Lewis.

Baby Beans, vinyl head, bean-bag type, 1971-75, 12", M 70.00
Baby First Step, battery-op walker, rooted hair, OC, 18", M 150.00
Baby Love Light, battery-op, OC, 16", M 18.00
Baby Play-A-Lot, poseable, pull-string & switch, OC, 1972-73, 16", M...22.00
Baby Secret, vinyl face/hands, whispers 11 phrases, OC, 1966+, 18", M .75.00
Baby Tenderlove, realistic skin, wets, OC, 1970-73, 13", M 65.00
Baby Walk & See, OC, 18", M..18.00
Captain Kangaroo, talking, Sears only, OC, 1967, 19", M 50.00
Chatty Baby, viny, disc player, OC, 1962-64, 18", M 75.00
Cheerful Tearful, vinyl, blond hair, wets/cries, OC, 1966-67, 7", M...100.00

Drowsy, vinyl head, stuffed body, pull-string talker, OC, 15½", M ..**175.00**
Gramma, cloth, pnt face, says 10 phrases, Sears, OC, 1970-73, 11", M..**20.00**
Sunshine Family, Steve, vinyl, poseable, OC, 9", M.....................**40.00**
Talking Buffy, vinyl, holds 6" rag Mrs Beasley, OC, 10¾", M.......**350.00**
Tippee Toes, battery-op, rides accessory, OC, 1968-70, 17", M......**80.00**

Papier-Mache

Clown, pnt face, c/m, wig, cloth body, RpC, 8", EX **235.00**
French child in orig ethnic costume, 1920+, 9", EX.....................**125.00**
French type, ShHd, pnt blk hair, glass eyes, o/m/teeth, RpC, 13", EX..**1,000.00**
French type, ShHd, pnt blk hair, pnt eyes, o/m/teeth, RpC, 16", EX..**1,500.00**
German type, #1010, ShHd, pnt eyes, cloth body, RpC, 27", EX.**850.00**
German type, ShHd, glass eyes, molded hair, RpC, 12", EX.........**500.00**
Milliner's type, Apollo topknot, sm waist, kid body, RpC, 10", EX..**850.00**
Milliner's type, center part w/sausage curls, sm waist, RpC, 14", EX....**575.00**
Milliner's type, molded comb, side curls, sm waist, RpC, 16", EX..**3,300.00**
ShHd, molded/pnt hair, glass eyes, wood limbs, RpC, 1940-60s, 24", EX..**2,200.00**
ShHd, molded/pnt hair, pnt eyes, cloth torso, RpC, 1840-60s, 12", EX...**675.00**
ShHd, molded/pnt long curls, cloth/wood body, RpC, 1940-60s, 16", EX...**1,550.00**
ShHd w/mohair wig, glass eyes, EX quality, RpC, 1879-1900s, 18", EX...**700.00**
ShHd w/mohair wig, glass eyes, G quality, RpC, 1879-1900s, 10", EX.....**150.00**

Parian

Alice in Wonderland, molded headband or comb, RpC, 16", EX ...**625.00**
Dolly Madison, RpC, 22", EX...**1,600.00**
Lady, common hairdo, no decor, cloth body, RpC, 1850-90+, 10", EX ..**175.00**
Lady, common hairdo, no decor, cloth body, RpC, 1860-90+, 21", EX ..**425.00**
Lady, fancy hairdo, glass eyes, p/e, RpC, 1850-1900+, 20", EX .**2,700.00**
Lady, fancy hairdo, pnt eyes, p/e, RpC, 1850-1900+, 22", EX ...**1,700.00**
Man or boy, parted hair, pnt eyes, cloth body, RpC, 13", EX........**775.00**
Molded hat, blond or blk pnt hair, glass eyes, RpC, 14", EX **2,400.00**
Molded hat, blond or blk pnt hair, pnt eyes, RpC, 16", EX.......**2,300.00**

Schoenhut

Albert Schoenhut left Germany in 1866 to go to Pennsylvania to work as a repairman for toy pianos. He eventually applied his skills to wooden toys and later designed an all-wood doll which he patented on January 17, 1911. These uniquely jointed dolls were painted with enamels and came with a metal stand. Some of the later dolls had stuffed bodies, voice boxes, and hollow heads. Due to the changing economy and fierce competition, the company closed in the mid-1930s.

#101, girl, cvd hair (bob w/bow), rnd eyes/smile, RpC, 16", VG ...**2,200.00**
#104, girl, fine cvd hair w/braids, RpC, ca 1911-12, 16", EX.....**2,400.00**
#105, girl, short cvd hair bob, cvd ribbon, RpC, 1912-16, 21", EX...**2,100.00**
#107 or #107W (walker), toddler, RpC, 1913-26, 14", EX...........**750.00**
#109W (walker), toddler, o/c/e, RpC, 1921-23, 14", EX **800.00**
#110W, baby, bent limbs, o/c/e, o/m, RpC, 1921-23, 15", EX.......**625.00**
#200, boy, cvd hair, no iris outline, RpC, 1911-12, 16", EX **2,400.00**
#300, girl, long curly wig, dimple in chin, RpC, 16", EX...........**1,500.00**
#311, girl, heart-shaped face, bobbed wig, RpC, 1912-16, 14", EX...**825.00**
#402, boy, smiling, rnd eyes, RpC, 16", EX **1,500.00**
#407, wigged boy, face of #310 girl, RpC, 1912-16, 21", EX.........**825.00**
Circus clown, bsk head, RpC, 8", EX, from $150 to **300.00**
Girl, short cvd hair bob, no iris outline, RpC, 1912-23, 14", EX...**2,200.00**
Rolly-Dolly, from 9" to 12", EX, ea...**850.00**
Schnickel-Fritz, cvd hair, grinning o/c/m/teeth, lg ears, RpC, 15", EX..**3,000.00**

SFBJ

By 1895 Germany was producing dolls at much lower prices than the French dollmakers could, so to save the doll industry, several leading French manufacturers united to form one large company. Bru, Raberry and Delphieu, Pintel and Godshaux, Fleischman and Bodel, Jumeau, and many others united to form the company Society Francaise de Fabrication de Bebes et Jouets (SFBJ).

#060, Bluette, bsk SkHd, o/m/teeth, glass eyes, wig, RpC, 11⅜", EX ..**975.00**
#226, character, bsk SkHd, glass eyes, c/m, RpC, 20", EX.........**2,400.00**
#234, bsk SkHd, o/c/e, compo body, RpC, 18", EX.................**3,250.00**
#238, character, bsk SkHd, sm o/m, wig, RpC, 18", EX............**2,400.00**
#251, character, bsk SkHd, o/c/m/teeth/tongue, RpC, 15", EX .**1,500.00**
#301, bsk SkHd, o/m/teeth, glass eyes, wig, RpC, 24", EX.........**1,150.00**
Jumeau type, no mold #, o/m, RpC, 28", EX **2,700.00**

Shirley Temple

Prices are suggested for dolls that are in complete original outfits and made by the Ideal Toy Company unless noted otherwise.

Celluloid, 13", metal pate, o/c/e, dimples, tagged Dutch OC, 1937+, NM..**350.00**
Compo, 7½", molded brn curls, pnt eyes, o/c/m, Japan, OC, NM **300.00**
Compo, 11", o/c/e, o/m/teeth, mohair wig, tagged OC, 1934+, NM........**975.00**
Compo, 18", Baby Shirley, tagged OC, 1934+, NM **1,200.00**
Compo, 18", Hawaiian (Marama), blk yarn hair, OC (grass skirt), NM....**950.00**
Compo, 20", o/e/c, o/m/teeth, mohair wig, tagged OC, 1934+, NM..**1,100.00**
Vinyl, 12", o/c/e, o/c/m/teeth, rooted wig, tagged OC, 1957, NM...**350.00**
Vinyl, 15", o/c/e, rooted hair, jtd, Red Riding Hood outfit, 1961, EX..**250.00**
Vinyl, 17", Montgomery Wards reissue, MIB **225.00**

Simon and Halbig

Simon and Halbig was one of the finest German makers to operate during the 1870s into the 1930s. Due to the high quality of the makers, their dolls still command large prices today. During the 1890s a few Simon & Halbig heads were used by a French maker, but these are extremely rare and well marked S&H.

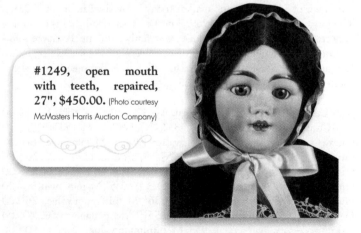

#1249, open mouth with teeth, repaired, 27", $450.00. (Photo courtesy McMasters Harris Auction Company)

#150, character face, intaglio eyes, c/m, RpC, ca 1912, 21", VG..... **15,500.00**
#151, pnt eyes, laughing c/m, RpC, ca 1912, 15", EX..............**15,000.00**
#530, ShHd child, RpC, ca 1910, 19", EX **685.00**
#719, child, o/c/e, c/m, p/e, compo/wood body, RpC, 18", EX..... **3,700.00**
#719, child, o/c/e, o/m, p/e, compo/wood jtd body, RpC, 18", EX **1,850.00**
#729, character laughing face, glass eyes, o/c/m, RpC, 16", EX......**2,550.00**
#749, SkHd, glass eyes, c/m, p/e, RpC, ca 1888, 21", EX...........**3,100.00**
#852, Oriental, swivel head, glass eyes, c/m, wig, RpC, 5½", EX **1,100.00**
#908, child, ShHd, o/m, RpC, 22", EX..................................**2,200.00**
#940, SkHd, glass eyes, o/m or c/m, kid body, RpC, 14", EX........**650.00**
#949, glass eyes, o/m, RpC, ca 1888, 31", EX............................**4,250.00**

#1009, o/c/e, o/m/teeth, p/e, kid body, wig, RpC, ca 1889, 19", EX.. 525.00
#1039, bsk SkHd, glass eyes, p/e, RpC, 17", EX 725.00
#1059, bsk SkHd, glass eyes, p/e, o/m, compo/wood body, RpC, 34", EX. 1,800.00
#1078, glass eyes, o/m, p/e, clockwork walker, RpC, 23", EX 2,900.00
#1079, Ondine, swimming doll, RpC, 16", VG 1,600.00
#1159, Gibson Girl, glass eyes, o/m, ca 1894, 20", EX............... 2,950.00
#1250, ShHd, glass eyes, o/m, kid body, RpC, 19", EX 800.00
#1294, character-face baby, glass eyes, o/m, RpC, 1910+, 16", EX .. 750.00
#1428, glass eyes, o/c/m, toddler, RpC, 16", EX 2,300.00
#1469, flapper adult, glass eyes, c/m, RpC, ca 1920, 15", EX..... 3,500.00
S&H w/no mold #, ShHd child, molded hair, RpC, 1870s, 19", EX.. 1,700.00

Steiner

Jules Nicholas Steiner established one of the earliest French manufacturing companies (making dishes and clocks) in 1855. He began with mechanical dolls with bisque heads and open mouths with two rows of bamboo teeth; his patents grew to include walking and talking dolls. In 1880 he registered a patent for a doll with sleep eyes. This doll could be put to sleep by turning a rod that operated a wire attached to its eyes.

Bebe, C series mks, bsk SkHd, pwt eyes, c/m, p/e, RpC, 34-38", EX. 13,000.00
Bebe, Series A, C, E, or G, bsk SkHd, pwt eyes, RpC, 14", EX. 6,000.00
Bebe le Parisien, SkHd w/cb pate, pwt eyes, wig, jtd, RpC, 10", EX. 3,600.00
Bebe w/figure mks, SkHd, glass eyes, c/m, p/e, wig, RpC, 13", EX .. 3,500.00
Bebe w/figure mks, SkHd, glass eyes, o/c/m, p/e, RpC, 27", EX. 4,500.00
Kicker, crying bebe, keywind, dome head, glass eyes, RpC, 18", VG. 1,650.00
Motchmann-type baby, dome head, glass eyes, c/m, wig, RpC, 14", EX... 4,800.00
Unmk Bebe, SkHd, pwt eyes, o/m/teeth, p/e, wig, RpC, 1870s, EX... 6,000.00

Vogue

This is the company that made the Ginny doll. Composition was used during most of the 1940s, but by 1948, hard plastic dolls were being produced. Dolls of the late 1950s often had vinyl heads and hard plastic bodies, but the preferred material throughout the decade of the '60s was vinyl. An original mint-condition composition Ginny would be worth a minimum of $450.00 on the market today (played-with, about $90.00). The last Ginny came out in 1969. Another Vogue doll that is becoming very collectible is Jill, whose values are steadily climbing. For more information, we recommend *Collector's Encyclopedia of Vogue Dolls* by Judith Izen and Carol Stover. Our advisor for Jill dolls is Bonnie Groves; she is listed in the Directory under Texas.

Baby Dear, vinyl & cloth, pnt eyes, squeaker, OC, 1960-64, 18", M... 225.00
Crib Crowd Baby, Sally, hp, pnt eyes, #832, OC, 1949, 8", M, $500 to.. 700.00
Ginny, Coronation Queen, hp, str-leg walker, 1954, 8", M, minimum... 800.00
Ginny, hp, bent-knee walker, OC, 1957-59, 8", from $175 to...... 200.00
Ginny, hp, str-leg walker, OC, 1954, 8", M.................................. 250.00
Ginny, Queen of Hearts, hp/strung, o/c/e, OC, 1950, 8", M, minimum. 500.00
Ginny, vinyl walker, bl o/c/e, OC, 1960, 36", M, minimum value... 250.00
Ginny, Wavette, hp/strung, o/c/e, #80, OC, 1951, 8", M, minimum value.. 400.00
Ginny accessory, gym set, ca 1955, M, minimum value................ 500.00
Ginny accessory, tablecloth, 1956-57, MIB 300.00
Ginny outfit, Sugar 'n Spice, #1352, 1960, MIB 75.00
Jan, vinyl, o/c/e, str legs, swivel waist, OC, 1959-60, 10½", M....... 75.00
Jill, #7403, MIB.. 200.00
Jill, All New; vinyl, rooted hair, high heels, OC, 1962, 10½", EX ... 76.00
Jill, Ginny, Jimmy, Jan booklet, 1958 .... 20.00
Jill, hp, nude, 10½", VG, minimum value....................................... 50.00
Jill, in basic leotard, VG 50.00
Jill, in red gown, scarce, EX 200.00
Jill, Sweetheart, vinyl, rooted hair, high heels, OC, 1963, M....... 175.00
Jill dress #3434, 1959, EX 75.00
Jill hat box, EX.. 20.00
Jill outfit #3236, 1959, EX 110.00
Jill shoes, EX 20.00
Jimmy, vinyl, jtd, pnt eyes, o/m, OC, 1958, 8", M 100.00
Li'l Lovable Imp, vinyl, o/c/e, str legs, OC, 1964-65, 11", M 65.00
Littlest Angel, vinyl & hp, bent-knee walker, OC, 1961-63, 10½", M.. 65.00
Patty, hp, o/c/e, mohair wig, OC, 1949-50, 14", M, from $250 to... 450.00
Toddles, Alpine Boy, compo, pnt eyes, OC, 1944-46, 8", M, $250 to... 300.00
Too Dear Brother, vinyl, o/c/e, c/m, OC, 1963-65, 23", M........... 350.00

Door Knockers

Door knockers, those charming precursors of the doorbell, come in an intriguing array of shapes and styles. The very rare ones come from England. Cast-iron examples made in this country were often produced in forms similar to the more familiar doorstop figures. Beware: Many of the brass door knockers being offered on Internet auctions are of recent vintage! Our values represent examples in excellent original condition with no damage, unless otherwise noted.

Birdhouse w/bird in oval, pnt CI, 3⅞x2⅞" 550.00
Bluebirds at birdhouse, pnt CI, Hubley, 3¾x1¾" 335.00
Boston terrier, brass, wreath w/Indian chief clapper, 3⅜" 85.00
Butterfly on oval, pnt CI, Pat...1926...Ill #70139, 3½", VG 500.00
Cardinal on branch, pnt CI, Hubley, 5x2⅞", NM........................ 400.00

Castle, cast iron, #630, 4", NM, $460.00. (Photo courtesy Morphy Auctions)

Cat scratching at door, pnt CI, rare, 3⅝x2⅝"............................ 1,450.00
Cherub w/roses & ribbon in oval, pnt CI, CJO (Judd) #622, 4½"... 500.00
Circus elephant, pnt CI, Albany Foundry, 6x5⅜"........................ 615.00
Cockatoo on branch in oval, pnt CI, Creations Co, 3¾x2½", NM.. 450.00
Cottage in trees w/road & porch, pnt CI, rare, 4x2½", minimum value. 800.00
Dove w/olive branch, pnt CI, detailed, rare, 4x3" 550.00
Eagle w/shield, pnt CI, CJO (Judd) #612, 4½x4½"...................... 850.00
Elephant holding log in trunk (knocker), CI, EX detail, 7⅜"....... 335.00
Flower basket, pnt CI, Hubley #13, 4x2⅞", NM........................... 175.00
Flowers in woven basket, pnt CI, floral clapper, 3⅞x2¾", VG 500.00
Girl in bonnet (facing left), pnt CI, CJO (Judd) #616, 4½x3"..... 450.00
Girl knocking, pnt CI, Hubley #143, 1921, NM.......................... 500.00
Girl knocking & holding Black doll, pnt CI, rare, 3¾x2¾"....... 1,000.00
Hound on trail, cold-pnt Viennese bronze, 1880s, 4x7", +wood plaque. 1,880.00
Medallion w/rose swag, pnt CI, Hubley #122, G 85.00
Morning glories in basket, pnt CI, CJO (Judd) #608, 3½x2¾", NM... 335.00
Pansies on branch, pnt CI, 5x3", VG 725.00
Parrot flying through ring, pnt CI, Hubley, 3¾x2⅞" 250.00
Parrot on branch, pnt CI, Hubley, 4⅝x2⅞", NM........................ 275.00
Parrot on ring, pnt CI, CJO (Judd), 3½x2¾", NM........................ 335.00
Pear & emb flowers, pnt CI, Hubley, 3½x3"................................. 445.00
Plum & emb flowers, pnt CI, Hubley, store label on bk, 3½x3" ... 255.00
Rooster (crowing) on branch, pnt CI, 4½x2⅞", NM...................... 395.00
Rooster on ring, pnt CI, CJO (Judd), 3½x2¾"............................ 280.00

Roses bouquet w/bow, pnt CI, 4½x2⅝" 450.00
Sarah W Symonds Cottage, pnt CI, Nichols House 1870... on base, 5½". 1,000.00
Snowy owl on branch, pnt CI, Hubley, 4¾x2⅞" 335.00
Woodpecker, pnt CI, Hubley #281, 3¾x2¾", MIB 300.00
Zinnia, pnt CI, LVL Pat Pend, 3⅝x2½", NM 395.00

Doorstops

Although introduced in England in the mid-1800s, cast-iron doorstops were not made to any great extent in this country until after the Civil War. Once called 'door porters,' their function was to keep doors open to provide better ventilation. They have been produced in many shapes and sizes, both dimensional and flat-backed. Doorstops retained their usefulness and appeal well into the 1930s. In some areas of the country, it it may be necessary to adjust prices down about 25%. Most of our listings describe examples in excellent original condition; all are made of cast iron. To evaluate a doorstop in only very good paint, deduct at least 35%. Values for examples in near-mint or better conditon sell at a premium, while prices for examples in poor to good paint drop dramatically.

Key:
B&H — Bradley & Hubbard
ff — full figured

Bathing Beauties, Deco style, Hubley #250, 10⅞x5½" 1,795.00
Cabin in Woods, National Foundry #78, 4⅝x10" 175.00
Chrysanthemum Flower Basket, Waverly Studio, 1926, 9x6¾" ... 335.00
Cocker Spaniel, Hubley, 6¾x11" 335.00
Colonial Lady, Pat Pend LVL, 10½x6⅛" 300.00
Colonial Man Holding Flowers, #821, 9x5¾" 450.00
Constitution Ship, #5 c 1926 by AM Greenblatt..., 8½x6½" 500.00
Cottage Well, C 1928 AA Richardson...#1, 5 18x8" 56.00
Daffodils & Mixed Flowers in Woven Basket, 11⅛x10¾" 850.00
Daisy Bowl, mc in wht bowl, Hubley #452, 7½x6", NM+ 225.00
Doberman Pinscher, Hubley, 7⅞x7⅝" 1,000.00
Doctor, souvenir of Hershey Motor Lodge, John Wright, 6⅜x3½" ... 450.00
Dwarf Gnome w/Lantern & Keys, ff, 10x5⅜" 350.00
Elephant, B&H #7799, 10½x11¾" 395.00
Flapper Girl, rare pk variation, Toledo Stove Co #8, 9⅜x4¾" ... 1,235.00
French Girl, Hubley #23, 9½x5½" 725.00
Fruit & Flowers, twisted hdl on basket, 13x7½" 175.00
German Shepherd Dog, wedge, Germany & P inside dbl triangle, 12½" .. 225.00
Girl Feeding Geese, rare, 9¾x11⅝" 2,250.00
Girl w/Bonnet, Waverly Studio, Pat Appld For..., 8x5½" 895.00
Gnome w/Barrel, pouring ale into his mug, ff, 14½x6½" 615.00

Golfer, CI, Hubley #238, 10", NM, $1,500.00. (Photo courtesy Morphy Auctions)

Harlow House, cottage w/oversz shingle roof, #1677, 5x5" 3,350.00
Highland Lighthouse, ff, Highland Light Cape Cod, 8x9⅜" 2,500.00
Horse w/Raised Nose, ff, 10x11" 675.00
House w/Woman, Eastern Specialty, 5¾x8½" 450.00
Indian Brave Bust, Carmen, rare, 5½x7½", VG 560.00
Jayhawk (KS University mascot), rare, 8⅜x6⅝" 675.00
Kitten on Pillow, National Foundry, 8x6" 60.00
Lady Holding Shawl, Albany Foundry, 11¾x6⅛" 500.00
Lighthouse w/Cottage, National Foundry, 6½x8" 560.00
Lilies of the Valley, w/lg bow, #189, 10½x7½" 335.00
Lincoln's Log Cabin, 4½x6½" 900.00
Marigolds, mc in bl & wht vase, Hubley #315, 7½x8" 335.00
Mary Quite Contrary, Littco, 12½x9½" 785.00
Mexican Guitar Player, #951, rare, 12" 3,075.00
Mill w/Bridge & Road, c 1926 Greenblatt...#3, 9¾x7½" 450.00
Mixed Flowers in French Woven Basket, pastels, Hubley #69, 10¾" .. 255.00
Mixed Flowers in Woven Basket, Hubley #8, 5⅝x4⅜" 150.00
Mixed Fruit in Basket, early casting, 7⅝x6", G 100.00
Modernistic Cat, Hubley, 9¾x5" 2,500.00
Monticello, Albany, 5½x8¾" 1,125.00
Old-Fashioned Lady, Hubley #296, 7¾x4" 175.00
Parlor Maid, Deco style, Hubley #268, 9½x3½" 2,800.00
Parrot on Stump, Blodgett Studio #1010, 12½x6½" 150.00
Poppies & Cornflowers, Hubley #265, 7½x6½" 399.99
Puppies in Barrel, c 1932 M Rosenstein..., Wilton, 7x7⅜" 1,795.00
Quail, Everett #4, mc pnt, 7½" 700.00
Rabbit in Top Hat & Tails, Nat'l Foundry #89, 10", VG 920.00
Sailor, bbl at ft, Littco, rare, 11½x5⅛" 4,480.00
Scottie Dog, ff, Hubley, 5x6½" 250.00
Siamese Cat, facing right, rare, 10½x6" 5,325.00
Silhouette Girl (Bridesmaid), Albany Foundry #5, 11½x10½" ... 7,850.00
Skunk, ff, tail over bk, 6⅜x8½" 895.00
Spanish Girl w/Fan, Waverly Studios Pat Appld..., 9½x5½" 500.00
Stagecoach, Creations Co, c 1930, 7⅜x8½" 250.00
Sulgrave Manor, c 1925 AM Greenblatt Studios, 8¾x10⅞" 1,795.00
Swallows, Hubley #480, 8½x7½" 950.00
Swan, dbl-sided, Spencer Guilford Conn, 7⅞x13½" 4,480.00
Swan, National Foundry, 5¾x4½" 725.00
Thoroughbred Horse, blk version, 7¾x10¾" 300.00
Two Kittens, Hubley #73, Grace Drayton, 7x5½" 500.00
Uncle Sam, red/wht/bl pnt, rare, 12⅛x5½" 12,325.00
Walking Duck w/Top Hat, dbl-sided, 7⅞x4½", VG 400.00
Wild Roses, Hubley #456, 7½x7⅜" 250.00
Windmill w/2 Cottages, c 1926 AM Greenblatt...#6, 11⅞x9", NM+ .. 1,900.00
Zinnias, urn-style vase, Hubley #267, 9¾x8½" 615.00

Dorchester Pottery

Taking its name from the town in Massachusetts where it was organized in 1895, the Dorchester Pottery Company made primarily utilitarian wares, though other types of items were made as well. By 1940 a line of decorative pottery was introduced, some of which was painted by hand with scrollwork or themes from nature. The buildings were destroyed by fire in the late 1970s, and the pottery was never rebuilt. In the listings that follow, the decorations described are all in cobalt unless otherwise noted. Our advisor for this category is Dale MacLean; he is listed in the Directory under Massachusetts.

Key:
CAH — Charles A. Hill (noted artist)
EHH — Ethel Hill Henderson
IM — in memory of

Basket, high-glaze wht, flared rim, paper label, 11¾x9½" 400.00
Bottle, scent; Tear Drop, CAH/Ricci, 5½x3¾" 325.00
Bottle, scent; Whale, scroll stopper, CAH, 5" 300.00
Bowl, Clematis, spongeware ext, sgn, stamped, 3⅛x8½" 400.00

Bowl, Eagle & Star, Nixon Inauguration commemorative, hdls, CAH..275.00
Bowl, Ship & Seascape, K Denisons, stamped, 2x5½" 175.00
Bowl, whale, CAH/N Ricci, 1⅛x3½" 125.00
Candy dish, Butterfly & Flower, sgn, stamped, 1½x6½" 275.00
Casserole, Colonial Lace (sgraffito), wht on med bl, CAH, 7½" dia ..275.00
Casserole, Half Scroll, CAH/N Ricci, stamped, 4¾x7½" 250.00
Charger, Ship, JM/N Ricci, stamped, 12½" 575.00
Coffee cup, Pine Cone 75.00
Coffee set, Blueberry, CAH, pot+mug+sugar bowl 400.00
Creamer & sugar bowl, Strawberry, Denisons/CAH, 3½", NM 250.00
Crock, Berry & Vine, unmk, 9¾x7", NM 250.00
Cup, Happy Day, clown's face, All Gone in bottom, mk, 2¾"...... 100.00
Foot warmer, Henderson; metal screw-type cap mk 1912, 11" 75.00
Jar, Whale, bulbous, C-hdl, 1950s, 5½" 175.00
Mug, Sacred Cod, CAH/EHH, 4½" 110.00
Pitcher, Pussy Willow, CAH/N Ricci, stamped, 5½x4½".............. 225.00
Pitcher, Whale, CAH/N Ricci, stamped, 5½x7" 250.00
Sugar bowl, Polka Dot, Robert Blake, 3½" 100.00
Sugar bowl, Pomegranate, blended bl, K Denisons, EX 125.00
Syrup pitcher, stripes/leaves/curvy lines, CAH/N Ricci, 4½" 160.00
Toby jug, Quaker Oats replica, early orig label, 8x7½" 350.00
Vase, Pine Cone, trumpet shape, CAH, 3½x3" 125.00

Dorflinger

C. Dorflinger was born in Alsace, France, and came to this country when he was 10 years old. When still very young, he obtained a job in a glass factory in New Jersey. As a young man, he started his own glassworks in Brooklyn, New York, opening new factories as profits permitted. During that time he made cut glass articles for many famous people including President and Mrs. Lincoln, for whom he produced a complete service of tableware with the United States Coat of Arms. In 1863 he sold the New York factories because of ill health and moved to his farm near White Mills, Pennsylvania. His health returned, and he started a plant near his home. It was there that he did much of his best work, making use of only the very finest materials. Christian died in 1915, and the plant was closed in 1921 by consent of the family. Dorflinger glass is rare and often hard to identify. Very few pieces were marked. Many only carried a small paper label which was quickly discarded; these are seldom found today. Identification is more accurately made through a study of the patterns, as colors may vary.

Hock goblet, gold decoration, cut stem, designed by Carl Prosch, original paper label, 7", $175.00. (Photo courtesy John A. Shuman III)

Bottle, scent; Marlboro, cut hobstar base, orig stopper 250.00
Bowl, Marlboro, 3½x9" 135.00
Candy jar, Kalana Poppy, w/lid, 7½x5½", EX 60.00
Carafe, Strawberry, Diamond & Fan, bulbous bottom, 8x5½" base dia ..135.00

Compote, Kalana Pansy, ruffled, teardrop stem, 5½x8" 870.50
Cruets, oil & vinegar; Hob Diamond, 7" 215.00
Decanter, Renaissance, pr 515.00
Pitcher, Hob Diamond, 9⅛" 465.00
Plate, oyster; Kalana Art #17, etched, 9", 8 for 275.00
Tumbler, gr cut to clear, 4" 300.00
Vase, gr cut to clear, trumpet form, 12" 475.00

Dragon Ware

Dragon Ware has always been fairly easy to find. Today, Internet auctions have made it even more so. It is still being produce and is often marketed in areas with a strong Asian influence and in souvenir shops in major cities around the United States and abroad.

As the name suggests, this china features a slip-painted dragon. Behind and around the moriage dragon (often done in a whitish color) are swirling clouds (rain), lines of color (water), fire, and in the dragon's clutch, a pearl — the dragon's most prized possession. (Although most dragon ware is ceramic, on rare occasion, you may find some beautiful examples of Dragon Ware executed in slip on glassware as well.) Gray (varying tones of gray and black) is the most common background color; however, it may also be done in shades of green, blue, orange, yellow, pink, white, pearl, and red. Sometimes the slip decoration will be applied in a flatter, slicker manner, rather than in the more traditional raised moriage style. On these pieces the dragon may be any color, and often the colors will be brighter and crisper. This style of painting is newer, seen on pieces from the 1940s and later.

Sometimes a three-dimensional dragon may act as the spout of a teapot or may seem to 'fly off' a vase; items with this type of modeling are a form of, but not actually considered, true Dragon Ware.

A lithophane is made by varying the density of the china in order to create an image when viewed with light behind it. They are often found in the bottom of coffee, demitasse, and sake cups and in this ware typically represet a geisha girl portrayed from the shoulders up. On rare occasions you may find nude ladies, usually only one, though groups of two and three may be found as well. Some cups have actual pictures in the bottom instead of lithophanes; these are newer.

Dragon Ware is divided into three categories. Nippon or Nippon quality pieces are the most desirable. The dragon and its background are typically done in vibrant, bold colors, and the slip work is well defined. Translucent jewels are often used for the dragon's eyes instead of the blue slip found on the more commonplace items. These pieces are usually executed in the gray tones; however, other colors have been used as well. Many pieces have a lustre interior. Nippon or Nippon-quality pieces with a recognizable Nippon mark command the highest prices.

Mid-century Dragon Ware was mass produced in the late 1930s, 1940s, and 1950s. Tea sets could be fond in the local drug store. These sets would serve up to six people and became popular in the days of bridge club and tea parties. Colors vary in this era of Dragon Ware, and interiors are sometimes painted in a goldish peach lustre. The slip work is not as detailed as it is on the earlier ware, and the onset of mass production techniques are evident. Many of these sets do not carry a mark, signature, or paper label, as they were brought to the states by servicemen who had been stationed in Japan. Other sets may have had only one or two marked pieces. Mid-century Dragon Ware falls in the mid-price range, although many of the pieces most popular with collectors were made during this era.

Turn-of-the-century pieces made from the 1970s up to the present time are obviously mass produced; the dragon often falls flat, without detail or personality. Background colors are no longer vibrant but lacklustre with a shiny appearance. Pastel pink, teal, orange, and green are commonly seen. These pieces are usually marked; however, some carried a paper label which may have been lost or removed. Dealers sometimes mistake unmarked pieces for the older ware and often sell them as such. Typically these pieces, if identified and priced correctly, would represent the lower end of the price spectrum.

These three styles are in addition to the typical gray pattern seen and positively recognized as Dragon Ware. Swirl: All the colors, including the background are actually slipped on, giving the effect of color having been 'drizzled' onto the surface. These pieces are usually made with white china, though on the occasion when the china body is more nearly a shade lighter than the drizzled paint, a 'squiggled' design is achieved. Cloud: These pieces have backgrounds that have been airbrushed on, achieving a flowing, soft, unified cloud effect. Solid: This type is first painted in a solid color before the dragon is applied. There may be slip painting (to represent the clouds, water, and fire) or airbrushing. Pearlized painting as well as lustre painting would fall under this category, as both techniques are, in effect, one overall color.

At the present time, the older pieces in colors other than gray are commanding the higher prices; so are the more unusual items. As always, condition is a major price-assessing issue, so be sure to check for damage before buying or selling. Overall, prices have softened over the past year, as is true with many collectibles. Our advisor for this category is Suzi Hibbard; she is listed in the Directory under California. In the following listings, all pieces listed are in the typical Dragon Ware style and from the Mid-century period unless noted otherwise.

Key:
HP — hand painted
lth — lithophane
MIJ — Made in Japan
MIOJ — Made in Occupied Japan
NQ — Nippon Quality
TD — traditional

Ashtray, blk, jewel eyes, HP Nippon, 3¾x5", from $125 to	200.00
Bell, pk, souvenir of Niagara Falls, 5¾x3", from $15 to	25.00
Console bowl, gray w/gold lustre, HP Japan, NQ, +2 sticks, $150 to	225.00
Cookie jar, blk swirl, glass eyes, Noritake, 8x5", from $350 to	500.00
Creamer & sugar bowl, orange & wht, 3½", from $25 to	40.00
Cup & saucer, coffee; bl TD, Dianan, no lth, from $25 to	45.00
Cup & saucer, coffee; blk cloud, HP Betsons, from $25 to	45.00
Cup & saucer, demitasse; bl swirl, MIJ, from $15 to	30.00
Cup & saucer, demitasse; dbl nude lth, TD, Niknoiko China, from $75 to	125.00
Cup & saucer, demitasse; google eyes, orange solid, from $25 to	45.00
Cup & saucer, demitasse; gr w/blk rim, HP, Shafford, from $30 to	45.00
Cup & saucer, demitasse; nude lth, gray TD, from $45 to	75.00
Cup & saucer, demitasse; orange cloud, MIOJ, from $20 to	40.00
Cup & saucer, gr solid, child sz, from $10 to	20.00
Dutch shoe, gray TD, from $15 to	30.00
Incense burner, gray TD, HP MIJ, 3½", from $15 to	25.00
Lamp, gray TD, jewel eyes, NQ, 7¾", from $150 to	225.00
Nappy, brn TD, HP MIJ, sq, 5½", from $20 to	40.00
Pitcher, yel cloud, MIJ, mini, 2⅞", from $15 to	25.00
Planter, orange solid, w/frog, MIJ, 5½", from $30 to	75.00
Plate, bl cloud, 7½", from $25 to	35.00
Saki cups, red cloud, whistling, set of 6, from $45 to	75.00
Saki set, bl cloud, geisha in plate center, Kutani, 8-pc, from $75 to	150.00
Saki set, bl cloud, whistling, kitten on decanter/plate, 8-pc, $125 to	175.00
Saki set, Orient China Japan, 7-pc, from $50 to	100.00
Saki set, wht solid, whistling, HP Japan, 5-pc, from $50 to	125.00
Shakers, bl cloud, unmk, pr from $10 to	30.00
Shakers, orange solid, pagoda style, Japan, 4", pr from $15 to	40.00
Snack set, brn cloud, gold dragon, RS MIJ, 2-pc, from $20 to	45.00
Table lighter, blk solid, from $50 to	100.00
Tea set, demitasse; gray TD, Nippon bl circle mk, NQ, 17-pc, $225 to	350.00
Tea set, demitasse; wht pearl, pearlized, Japan, newer, 17-pc, $50 to	100.00
Tea set, gray TD, MIOJ, 7½" pot+cr/sug+2 c/s, from $60 to	175.00
Tea set, gray TD w/gold, 7½", pot+cr/sug, from $45 to	70.00
Tea set, stacking, blk, MIJ, 5½x6½", from $30 to	50.00

Tea set, yel, child's, pot+c/s, 4-pc, from $45 to	65.00
Tea/coffee set, gr cloud, lth, dragon spout, 23-pc, $175 to	275.00
Teapot, gr cloud, 8x3", from $35 to	60.00
Teapot, gray, 6-sided, TT, 7½x4¾", from $45 to	60.00
Tidbit tray, gray TD, Nippon, 9x6½", from $100 to	225.00
Vase, aqua solid, Deco style, MIJ, 10½", from $100 to	175.00
Vase, bl cloud, wide mouth, 5", from $20 to	30.00
Vase, blk solid, MIJ, 6", from $25 to	50.00
Vase, gr swirl, unmk, 3¾", from $5 to	15.00
Vase, gray TD, glass eyes/ftd, HP Nippon w/wreath, NQ, 4⅜", $125 to	275.00
Vase, gray TD, jewel eyes, gr HP Nippon M in wreath, 10½", $400 to	550.00

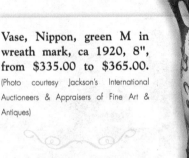

Vase, Nippon, green M in wreath mark, ca 1920, 8", from $335.00 to $365.00.
(Photo courtesy Jackson's International Auctioneers & Appraisers of Fine Art & Antiques)

Vase, orange SD, MIJ, 7½", from $30 to	75.00
Vase, orange SD, 4", from $20 to	50.00
Vase, orange/yel w/cloud, HP MIJ/MIOJ, 5", from $10 to	17.50
Vase, yel solid, MIJ, 5", from $7.50 to	20.00
Vase, yel swirl, MIJ, 5", from $15 to	50.00
Wall pocket, bl/orange lustre, Japan flower mk, 7", from $35 to	60.00
Wall pocket, orange solid, MIJ, 9", from $50 to	75.00
Watering can, gr solid, MIJ, 2½", from $7.50 to	15.00

Dresden

The city of Dresden was a leading cultural center in the seventeenth century and in the eighteenth century became known as the Florence on the Elbe because of its magnificent baroque architecture and its outstanding museums. Artists, poets, musicians, philosophers, and porcelain artists took up residence in Dresden. In the late nineteenth century, there was a considerable demand among the middle classes for porcelain. This demand was met by Dresden porcelain painters. Between 1855 and 1944, more than 200 painting studios existed in the city. The studios bought porcelain white ware from manufacturers such as Meissen and Rosenthal for decorating, marketing, and reselling throughout the world. The largest of these studios include Donath & Co., Franziska Hirsch, Richard Klemm, Ambrosius Lamm, Carl Thieme, and Helena Wolfsohn.

Most of the Dresden studios produced work in imitation of Meissen and Royal Vienna. Flower painting enhanced with burnished gold, courting couples, landscapes, and cherubs were used as decorative motifs. As with other hand-painted porcelains, value is dependent upon the quality of the decoration. Sometimes the artwork equaled or even surpassed that of the Meissen factory.

Some of the most loved and eagerly collected of all Dresden porcelains are the beautiful and graceful lace figures. Many of the figures found in the maketplace today were not made in Dresden but in other areas of Germany. For more information, we recommend *Dresden Porcelain Studios* by Jim and Susan Harran, our advisors for this category. They are listed in the Directory under New Jersey.

Basket, HP & appl flowers, rtcl rim, Thieme, 1901-60, 5" dia...... 175.00
Bowl, courting scenes/flower panels, rtcl rim, Klemm, 1888-1916, 9"... 175.00
Bowl, HP lovers in garden/garlands w/gold, Thieme, 1886-91, 9¾" L .. 250.00
Bowl, HP/appl flowers w/gold, rtcl rim, hdls, Thieme, 1901-14 ... 450.00
Bowl, serving; floral w/gold, irregular rim, Wolfsohn, 1886, 10x9" ... 225.00
Cake plate, HP flowers, emb basketweave rim, hdls, Thieme, 1950s, 11" . 150.00
Chocolate pot, HP florals/gold dots, branch hdl, F Hirsch, 1893-1930... 350.00
Coffee can & saucer, floral w/cobalt & gold, Wolfsohn, ca 1888 . 300.00
Coffee can & saucer, HP floral w/gold, swirled, Donath & Co, 1893-1916. 115.00
Compote, HP flowers & gold, rtcl rim/ft, Thieme, 1901-04, 3¾x8¾" . 400.00
Compote, HP/appl flowers/X-hatching, quartrefoil, Thieme, 1950s, 4x6" ... 100.00
Cup & saucer, coffee; HP cherubs, raised gold, Lamm, ca 1887 ... 650.00
Cup & saucer, demitasse; floral w/gold, Donath & Co, 1893-1916 .. 125.00

Figurine, plateau group, The Presentation, lace trim, $1,000.00. (Photo courtesy William J. Brinkley)

Figurine, Spanish lady, tiered lacy costume, appl flowers, ca 1900, 9" . 500.00
Figurines, monkey band, 1880s, from 4" to 6", 9 pcs...................... 825.00
Mint dish, alternating scenes/flowers on bl & wht, Klemm, 1898, 3" dia. 60.00
Napkin ring, flower garlands/gold trim, F Hirsch, 1893-1930......... 75.00
Plaque, Penitent Magdalene, T Lichtenberg, after Correggio, 7x4½" . 640.00
Plate, HP floral/gold rim, Tirschenreuth blank, F Hirsch, 1901-30, 6"... 60.00
Plate, lady's portrait & heavy gold paste, Schworz, 1908-14, 10½" ... 1,500.00
Plate, Lincoln portrait w/cobalt & gold, Hutchenreuther blank, 10½" ... 2,200.00
Plate, 10 HP figures around medallion on gold, Klemm, 1888-1916, 8"... 500.00
Platter, HP flowers/gold X-hatching, F Hirsch, 1901-14, 14¾x9¾" 356.00
Potpourri jar, courting scenes, rose finial, att Klemm, 1905-20s, 6" 350.00
Salt cellar, dbl pigs, floral w/gold, Wehsner, 1895-1918, 2¾" L ... 275.00
Shakers, flowers & gold, egg shape, Lamm, 1891-1914, pr 115.00
Soup tureen, floral w/gold rococo, Klemm, w/lid & 14" underplate . 1,500.00
Sugar bowl, flower garlands w/gold, hdls, w/lid, F Hirsch, 1901-30 .. 100.00
Teacup & saucer, figures in panels, bl & wht, Klemm, 1888-1916... 150.00
Teacup & saucer, flower band, pk ribs, gold trim, Lamm, 1887-91 .. 175.00
Teacup & saucer, star center w/flowers/cobalt/gold, Lamm, 1887-1914.. 275.00
Teacup & saucer, Watteau scenes/flowers, Hamann, 1891-92 ...... 150.00
Teapot, HP floral w/gold, globular, Donath & Co, 1893-1916, 6"... 300.00
Toast rack, HP flowers/X-hatching, 5 coils, F Hirsch, 1910-30 .... 275.00
Vase, courting scene medallion/gold fretwork, Klemm, 1888-1916, 9½" . 275.00
Vase, floral w/gold feathering, sm neck, Klemm, 1888-1916, 8" ... 200.00
Vase, HP scenes/flowers, emb leaves w/gold, rtcl, Thieme, 1901-60, 7".. 175.00

Dresser Accessories

Dresser sets, ring trees, figural or satin pincushions, manicure sets — all those lovely items that graced milady's dressing table — were at the same time decorative as well as functional. Today they appeal to collectors for many reasons. The Victorian era is well represented by repousse silver-backed mirrors and brushes and pincushions that were used to dis-play ornamental pins for the hair, hats, and scarves. The hair receiver — similar to a powder jar but with an opening in the lid — was used to hold long strands of hair retrieved from the comb or brush. These were wound around the finger and tucked in the opening to be used later for hair jewelry and pictures, many of which survive to the present day. (See Hair Weaving.) With the current interest in anything Art Deco, dresser sets from the 1930s and 1940s are especially collectible. These may be made of crystal, Bakelite, or silver, and the original boxes just as lavishly appointed as their contents. See also Celluloid.

Box, blk Bakelite lid on butterscotch Bakelite sides, blk ft, 4" dia... 325.00
Box, butterscotch Bakelite, ribbed sides, wood int, 1930s, 2x6x4" 325.00
Box, rouge; HP Nouveau floral on dk gr glass, hinged mts, 1½x2½" 100.00
Mirror & brush, SP, Nouveau maiden emerging from flower in relief 75.00
Set, butterscotch Bakelite w/HP flowers, 1940s+, hand mirror+long box.. 25.00
Set, cream Bakelite w/brn dots, 1930s-40s, mirror+3 brushes, MIB ... 165.00
Set, sterling, Art Nouveau style, 9 pc.. 300.00
Set, tan Bakelite w/brn Nouveau decor, mk DuPont, 7 pcs on tray.. 195.00

Dryden

World War II veteran, Jim Dryden founded Dryden Pottery in Ellsworth, Kansas, in 1946. Starting in a Quonset hut, Dryden created molded products which he sold at his father's hardware store in town. Using Kansas clay from the area and volcanic ash as a component, durable glossy glazes were created. Soon Dryden was selling pottery to Macy's of New York and the Fred Harvey Restaurants on the Santa Fe Railroad.

After 10 years, 600 stores stocked Dryden Pottery. However direct sales to the public from the pottery studio offered the most profit because of increasing competition from Japan and Europe. Using dental tools to make inscriptions, Dryden began to offer pottery with personalized messages and logos. This specialized work was appreciated by customers and is admired by collectors today.

In 1956 the interstate bypassed the pottery and Dryden decided to move to Hot Springs National Park to find a broader and larger tourist base. Again, local clays and quartz for the glazes were used. Later, in order to improve consistency, commercial clay (that fired bone white) and controlled glazes were used. Sometimes overlooked by collectors who favor the famous potteries of the past, Jim Dryden's son Kimbo, and grandsons Zach, Cheyenne, and Arrow, continue to develop new glazes and shapes in the studio in Hot Springs, Arkansas. Glazes comparable to those created by Fulper, Grueby, and Rookwood can be found on pottery for sale there. Dryden was the first to use two different glazes successfully at the same time.

In 2001 The Book Stops Here published the first catalog and history of Dryden pottery. The book shows the evolution of Dryden art pottery from molded ware to unique hand-thrown pieces; the studio illustrations show the durable and colorful glazes that make Dryden special. Visitors are always welcome at the Dryden Pottery, Hot Springs, Arkansas studio where they can watch pottery being made by the talented Dryden family.

Kansas pieces have a golden tan clay base and were made between 1946 and 1956. Arkansas pieces made after 1956 were made from bone white clay. Dryden pottery has a wide range of values. Many collectors are interested in the early pieces while a fast-growing number search for wheel-thrown and hand-decorated pieces made within the past 20 years. One-of-a-kind specialty pieces can exceed $500.00. Our advisor for this category is Ralph Winslow; he is listed in the Directory under Missouri.

Kansas Dryden (1946 – 1956)

Ashtray, souvenir, #17A 18.00
Bookends, horse, bl, 6½".. 125.00
Boot, souvenir, 4¾" 22.00

Bowl, console; yel, #44, 14"	22.00
Ewer, blk, #715, 11½"	35.00
Figurine, buffalo, souvenir, 1½"	175.00
Figurine, Girl Scout, GS on ped, lt gr, prof rpr, 7¾"	100.00
Figurine, panther, blk	98.00
Figurine, Scottie dog, 3¾"	40.00
Juice, set, gr, 7-pc	50.00
Leaf dish, Brookville Hotel, 5"	35.00
Pitcher, souvenir, #94, 6"	16.00
Planter, donkey, #2	27.00
Planter, elephant, Salina Kans, #313	56.00
Shakers, tall, 6¾", pr	25.00
Vase, gr ball form, #105, 4½x3½"	35.00
Vase, Madonna, #87, 4½"	45.00
Wall pocket, emb leaves, slate bl, #955, 5½x1½"	30.00
Wall pocket, ivy leaf, #956	25.00

Arkansas Dryden (1956 to Present)

Basket, metal holder, 5½"	16.00
Bowl, apple, 8½"	10.00
Crock, bean, drip glaze, w/lid, 5½"	17.50
Ewer/vase, brn abstracts on wht w/wht drips, long curved hdl, 11"	55.00
Figurine, lioness, 4½"	25.00
Leaf, bl, 9¾"	20.00
Mug, JK Dryden 82, 3¾"	22.00
Pitcher, wishbone hdl, 8"	18.00
Spoon rest, bird, drip glaze, 5" W	12.00
Teapot, JB Buck	25.00
Vase, drip glaze, 7¾"	28.00
Vase, fish, HP by Jim Dryden, mini	35.00
Vase, stippled, 5-necked, 5½"	35.00
Vase, TL, 5½"	16.00
Vase, vining decor on pk to gr top pk, wheel thrown, JK Dryden, 9"	40.00

Duncan and Miller

The firm that became known as the Duncan and Miller Glass Company in 1900 was organized in 1874 in Pittsburgh, Pennsylvania, a partnership between George Duncan, his sons Harry and James, and his son-in-law Augustus Heisey. John Ernest Miller was hired as their designer. He is credited with creating the most famous of all Duncan's glassware lines, Three Face. (See Pattern Glass.) The George Duncan and Sons Glass Company, as it was titled, was only one of 18 companies that merged in 1891 with U.S. Glass. Soon after the Pittsburgh factory burned in 1892, the association was dissolved, and Heisey left the firm to set up his own factory in Newark, Ohio. Duncan built his new plant in Washington, Pennsylvania, where he continued to make pressed glassware in such notable patterns as Bagware, Amberette, Duncan Flute, Button Arches, and Zippered Slash. The firm was eventually sold to U.S. Glass in Tiffin, Ohio, and unofficially closed in August 1955.

In addition to the early pressed dinnerware patterns, today's Duncan and Miller collectors enjoy searching for opalescent vases in many patterns and colors, frosted 'Satin Tone' glassware, acid-etched designs, and lovely stemware such as the Rock Crystal cuttings. Milk glass was made in limited quantity and is considered a good investment. Ruby glass, Ebony (a lovely opaque black glass popular during the '20s and '30s), and, of course, the glass animal and bird figurines are all highly valued examples of the art of Duncan and Miller.

Add approximately 40% to 50% to listed prices for opalescent items. Etchings, cuttings, and other decorations will increase values by about 50%. For further study we recommend *The Encyclopedia of Duncan Glass* by Gail Krause; she is listed in the Directory under Pennsylvania. Several Duncan and Miller lines are shown in *Elegant Glassware of the Depression Era* by Gene and Cathy Florence. Also refer to *Glass Animals* by Dick and Pat Spencer; they are listed under Illinois. Our advisor for this category is Roselle Shleifman; she is listed in the Directory under New York. See also Glass Animals and Figurines.

Canterbury, crystal, ashtray, 5"	12.00
Canterbury, crystal, basket, oval, hdl, 3½"	26.00
Canterbury, crystal, bowl, salad; 10x5"	30.00
Canterbury, crystal, candlestick, 6", ea	25.00
Canterbury, crystal, cigarette jar, w/lid, 4"	30.00
Canterbury, crystal, creamer, ind, 3-oz, 2¾"	9.00
Canterbury, crystal, decanter, w/stopper, 32-oz, 12"	80.00
Canterbury, crystal, marmalade, crimped, 4½x2¾"	20.00
Canterbury, crystal, oyster cocktail, 4½-oz, 4"	12.50

Canterbury, crystal, pitcher, 64-ounce, $250.00. (Photo courtesy Gene and Cathy Florence)

Canterbury, crystal, pitcher, martini; 32-oz, 9½"	80.00
Canterbury, crystal, plate, cake; hdl, 13½"	40.00
Canterbury, crystal, plate, 7½"	9.00
Canterbury, crystal, plate, 8½"	12.00
Canterbury, crystal, relish, rnd, 2-part, hdls, 6x2"	14.00
Canterbury, crystal, shakers, pr	22.50
Canterbury, crystal, tray, pickle & olive; 2-part, 9x4x1½"	17.50
Canterbury, crystal, tumbler, ice cream; #5115, ftd, 5-oz, 2½"	10.00
Canterbury, crystal, tumbler, iced tea; ftd, 13-oz, 6½"	20.00
Canterbury, crystal, tumbler, juice; ftd, 5-oz, 4½"	10.00
Canterbury, crystal, tumbler, water; #5115, ftd, 10-oz, 4½"	14.00
Canterbury, crystal, vase, cloverleaf, 3½"	15.00
Canterbury, crystal, vase, crimped, 5½"	20.00
Canterbury, crystal, vase, flared, 12"	80.00
Canterbury, crystal, vase, oval, 3½"	15.00
Canterbury, crystal, wine, #5115, 3½-oz, 6"	27.50
Caribbean, bl, bowl, salad; 9"	75.00
Caribbean, bl, cocktail shaker, 33-oz, 9"	300.00
Caribbean, bl, cordial, 1-oz, 3"	210.00
Caribbean, bl, ladle, punch	100.00
Caribbean, bl, plate, 14"	80.00
Caribbean, bl, sugar bowl	25.00
Caribbean, bl, vase, ruffled edge, ftd, 5¾"	55.00
Caribbean, crystal, champagne, ftd, ball stem, 6-oz, 4"	14.00
Caribbean, crystal, finger bowl, 4½"	16.00
Caribbean, crystal, pitcher, milk; 16-oz, 4¾"	95.00
Caribbean, crystal, plate, luncheon; 8½"	15.00
Caribbean, crystal, relish, rnd, 7-part, 12¾"	40.00
Caribbean, crystal, teacup	15.00
Caribbean, crystal, tray, rnd, 12¾"	25.00
Caribbean, crystal, vase, ruffled top, ftd, 9"	50.00
First Love, crystal, ashtray, #111, sq, 3½"	17.50
First Love, crystal, basket, #115, 9½x10x7½"	175.00
First Love, crystal, bowl, olive; #115, oval, 6x2½"	25.00
First Love, crystal, candy box, #106, 3-part, w/lid	90.00
First Love, crystal, cheese stand, #111, 3x5½"	25.00

First Love, crystal, claret, #5111½, 4½-oz, 6" 38.00
First Love, crystal, cocktail shaker, #5200, 16-oz 120.00
First Love, crystal, cruet, #25 .... 90.00
First Love, crystal, decanter, #5200, w/stopper, 32-oz 175.00
First Love, crystal, juice, #5111½, ftd, 5-oz, 5½" 18.00
First Love, crystal, mayonnaise, #115, 5½x2¾" 35.00
First Love, crystal, nappy, #111, hdl, 6x1¾" 22.00
First Love, crystal, pitcher, #5200 .... 175.00
First Love, crystal, plate, cake; #115, hdl, 13½" 50.00
First Love, crystal, plate, lemon; #111, hdl, 6" 14.00
First Love, crystal, plate, sandwich; #115, hdls, 11" 30.00
First Love, crystal, relish, #115, 10½x7" 37.50
First Love, crystal, rose bowl, #115, 3x5" 40.00
First Love, crystal, tray, celery; #91, 8¾" 30.00
First Love, crystal, tumbler, whiskey; #5200, 1½-oz, 2" 50.00
First Love, crystal, vase, #507, ftd, 12" 145.00
First Love, crystal, vase, bud; #506, 9" 80.00
Lily of the Valley, crystal, celery, 10½" 40.00
Lily of the Valley, crystal, cocktail 25.00
Lily of the Valley, crystal, mayonnaise 30.00
Lily of the Valley, crystal, mayonnaise liner 15.00
Lily of the Valley, crystal, tumbler, water; ftd 25.00
Lily of the Valley, crystal, wine 45.00
Nautical, bl, creamer 45.00
Nautical, bl, decanter 550.00
Nautical, bl, marmalade 75.00
Nautical, bl, plate, 8" 40.00
Nautical, bl, shakers, pr, w/tray 350.00
Nautical, bl, tumbler, bar; 2-oz 35.00
Nautical, bl, tumbler, orange juice; ftd 30.00
Nautical, crystal, ashtray, 3" 8.00
Nautical, crystal, candy jar, w/lid 295.00
Nautical, crystal, plate, cake; hdls, 6½" 12.00
Nautical, crystal, relish, 7-part, 12" 35.00
Nautical, crystal, tumbler, cocktail 12.00
Nautical, crystal, tumbler, whiskey & soda; 8-oz 12.00
Nautical, opal, candy jar, w/lid 695.00
Nautical, opal, decanter 695.00
Nautical, opal, ice bucket 300.00
Plaza, amber or crystal, bowl, vegetable; oval, 9" 28.00
Plaza, amber or crystal, candy dish, rnd, w/lid, 4½" 18.00
Plaza, amber or crystal, finger bowl, 4⅜" 6.00
Plaza, amber or crystal, parfait 12.00
Plaza, amber or crystal, plate, hdl, 10½" 18.00
Plaza, amber or crystal, shakers, pr 35.00
Plaza, amber or crystal, tumbler, tea; ftd 12.00
Plaza, amber or crystal, water 9.00
Plaza, gr or pk, bowl, cereal; 6½" 20.00
Plaza, gr or pk, bowl, console; flared, 14" 75.00
Plaza, gr or pk, cocktail 20.00
Plaza, gr or pk, cup 12.00
Plaza, gr or pk, pitcher, flat 100.00
Plaza, gr or pk, plate, luncheon; 8½" 15.00
Plaza, gr or pk, plate, salad; 7½" 12.00
Plaza, gr or pk, saucer champagne 17.50
Plaza, gr or pk, vase, 8" 65.00
Plaza, gr or pk, wine 22.00
Puritan, colors, bowl, console; rolled, 12" 55.00
Puritan, colors, bowl, 5" 12.50
Puritan, colors, creamer 17.50
Puritan, colors, cup 12.50
Puritan, colors, pitcher 135.00
Puritan, colors, plate, dinner; 10" 20.00
Puritan, colors, vase 65.00

Puritan, colors, water goblet 20.00
Sandwich, crystal, basket, w/loop hdl, 6½" 125.00
Sandwich, crystal, bonbon, heart shape, hdl, 5½" 15.00
Sandwich, crystal, bowl, console; oblong, 12" 40.00
Sandwich, crystal, bowl, fruit salad; 6" 12.00
Sandwich, crystal, bowl, grapefruit; w/rim liner, ftd, 5½" 15.00
Sandwich, crystal, cake stand, rolled edge, ftd, 11½" 75.00
Sandwich, crystal, candy box, flat, 5" 50.00
Sandwich, crystal, champagne, 5-oz, 5½" 15.00
Sandwich, crystal, cocktail, 3-oz, 4½" 10.00
Sandwich, crystal, compote, 2½" 12.00
Sandwich, crystal, creamer, ftd, 7-oz, 4" 10.00
Sandwich, crystal, plate, bread & butter; 6" 7.00
Sandwich, crystal, plate, cracker; w/ring, 13" 30.00
Sandwich, crystal, plate, dinner; 9½" 30.00
Sandwich, crystal, relish, oval, 2-part, 7" 22.00
Sandwich, crystal, relish, 3-part, 12" 45.00
Sandwich, crystal, sugar bowl, ftd, 9-oz, 3½" 9.00
Sandwich, crystal, tray, ice cream; rolled edge, 12" 55.00
Sandwich, crystal, tray, oval, 8" 18.00
Sandwich, crystal, tray, pickle; oval, 7" 15.00
Sandwich, crystal, vase, crimped, ftd, 5" 45.00
Sandwich, crystal, vase, ftd, 10" 80.00

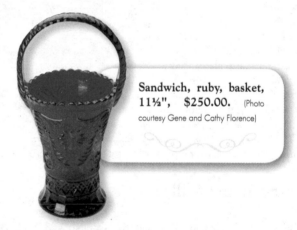

Sandwich, ruby, basket, 11½", $250.00. (Photo courtesy Gene and Cathy Florence)

Spiral Flutes, amber, gr or pk, bowl, bouillon; 3¾" 15.00
Spiral Flutes, amber, gr or pk, candleholder, 7½", ea 65.00
Spiral Flutes, amber, gr or pk, cigarette holder, 4" 35.00
Spiral Flutes, amber, gr or pk, creamer, oval 8.00
Spiral Flutes, amber, gr or pk, finger bowl, 4⅜" 7.00
Spiral Flutes, amber, gr or pk, parfait, 4½-oz, 5⅝" 16.00
Spiral Flutes, amber, gr or pk, pitcher, ½-gal 175.00
Spiral Flutes, amber, gr or pk, plate, dinner; 10⅜" 22.50
Spiral Flutes, amber, gr or pk, plate, luncheon; 8⅜" 4.00
Spiral Flutes, amber, gr or pk, platter, 13" 55.00
Spiral Flutes, amber, gr or pk, sherbet, tall; 6-oz, 4¾" 12.00
Spiral Flutes, amber, gr or pk, tumbler, flat, 8-oz, 4½" 25.00
Spiral Flutes, amber, gr or pk, tumbler, soda; flat, 7-oz, 4¾" ... 30.00
Spiral Flutes, amber, gr or pk, vase, 8½" 30.00
Tear Drop, crystal, ashtray, ind, 3" 7.00
Tear Drop, crystal, bonbon, 4 hdls, 6" 12.00
Tear Drop, crystal, bowl, gardenia; 13" 35.00
Tear Drop, crystal, bowl, salad; 9" 30.00
Tear Drop, crystal, butter dish, hdls, ¼-lb 28.00
Tear Drop, crystal, cake salver, ftd, 13" 55.00
Tear Drop, crystal, candy dish, heart shape, 7½" 22.50
Tear Drop, crystal, celery, 3-part, 12" 25.00
Tear Drop, crystal, claret, 4-oz, 5½" 20.00
Tear Drop, crystal, compote, ftd, 4¾" 12.00
Tear Drop, crystal, cordial, 1-oz, 4" 30.00

Tear Drop, crystal, creamer, 8-oz 8.00
Tear Drop, crystal, nut dish, 2-part, 6" 11.00
Tear Drop, crystal, pitcher, milk; 16-oz, 5" 50.00
Tear Drop, crystal, plate, canape; 6" 10.00
Tear Drop, crystal, plate, dinner; 10½" 35.00
Tear Drop, crystal, plate, torte; rolled edge, 14" 38.00
Tear Drop, crystal, shakers, 5", pr 25.00
Tear Drop, crystal, tumbler, iced tea; flat, 12-oz, 5½" .. 15.00
Tear Drop, crystal, tumbler, old-fashioned; flat, 7-oz, 3½" 12.00
Tear Drop, crystal, vase, fan shape, ftd, 9" 30.00
Terrace, amber or crystal, bowl, hdl, 9½x2½".......... 42.00
Terrace, amber or crystal, claret, #5111½, 4½-oz, 6" 45.00
Terrace, amber or crystal, cocktail, #5111½, 3½-oz, 4½" 22.50
Terrace, amber or crystal, pitcher 295.00
Terrace, amber or crystal, plate, sandwich; hdl, 11" 30.00
Terrace, amber or crystal, relish, 5-part, hdl, 12" 40.00
Terrace, amber or crystal, tumbler, water; 9-oz, 4" ... 17.50
Terrace, amber or crystal, vase, ftd, 10" 115.00
Terrace, cobalt or red, ashtray, sq, 3½" 25.00
Terrace, cobalt or red, bowl, trn-up edge, 4¾" 25.00
Terrace, cobalt or red, candy dish, hdl...................... 135.00
Terrace, cobalt or red, compote, w/lid, 8¾x5½" 425.00
Terrace, cobalt or red, plate, cracker; w/ring, hdl, 11" 100.00
Terrace, cobalt or red, relish, 5-part, w/lid, 12" 325.00
Terrace, cobalt or red, tumbler, shot; 2-oz 40.00

Durand

Durand art glass was made by the Vineland Flint Glass Works of Vineland, New Jersey. Victor Durand Jr. was the sole proprietor. Hand-blown art glass in the style of Tiffany and Quezal was produced from 1924 to 1931 through a division called the 'Fancy Shop.' Durand hired owner Martin Bach Jr. along with his team of artisans from the failed Quezal Art Glass and Decorating Co. in Brooklyn, New York, to run this division. Much Durand art glass went unsigned; when it was, it was generally signed Durand in silver script either within the polished pontil or across the top of a large letter V. The numbers that sometimes appear along with the signature indicate the shape and height of the object. Decorative names such as King Tut, Heart and Vine, Peacock Feather, and Egyptian Crackle became the company's trademarks. In 1926 Durand art glass was awarded a gold medal of honor at the Sesquicentennial International Exposition in Philadelphia; as a result, Durand took its place alongside Tiffany, Stueben, and Quezal as the epitome of American art glass. Our advisor for this category is Edward J. Meschi, author of *Durand — The Man and His Glass* (Antique Publications); he is listed in the Directory under New Jersey.

Bottle, scent; bl irid w/gold ft, allover gold threading, slim, 7½"....1,035.00
Candlestick, Coil, bl/gold on opal, baluster form, 10", ea..........1,035.00
Candy jar, Heart & Vine, gr on marigold, shouldered, dome lid, 9½"...3,450.00
Charger, Spanish Yellow w/gr lip wrap, optic ribs, 17½"...............230.00
Compote, feathers, opal on gr, ambergris ft w/knop stem, 5"........420.00
Finger bowl, ruby w/optic ribs, scalloped rim, +6" underplate......100.00
Ginger jar, feathers, marigold/gr on opal, 9"...........................7,000.00
Ginger jar, Heart & Vine, wht on bl irid, 9" 8,200.00
Lamps, King Tut, bl on marigold, bronze/glass base, 6".................350.00
Shade, bl/wht crackle on gold, 6½" 400.00
Shade, Lady Gay Rose, gold int, ribbed, 8x8½" 3,000.00
Torchiere, bl/wht crackle on gold, acanthus base w/baluster std, 16" ..700.00
Vase, bl irid, cylindrical flared rim & gold ft, #20120, 12"...........960.00
Vase, bl irid, ovoid beehive form, #1947, 13"..............................865.00
Vase, Coil, bl irid on dk bl, #1710, 8".....................................2,875.00
Vase, Coil, bl on gold, gold int, slim classic form, 10" 1,400.00

Vase, Coil, bl on marigold, 7"... 925.00
Vase, Coil, bl on opal, 10".. 1,375.00
Vase, Coil, gold on opal, wide shouldered form, 11"................1,325.00
Vase, Coil, gr on marigold, squat w/trumpet neck, #1990, 6"...1,095.00
Vase, Coil, opal on gold, gold int, slim classic form, 10" 1,150.00
Vase, crystal crackle alternating w/gr panels, shouldered, #1710, 7"...1,325.00
Vase, feathers, bl/wht on marigold w/allover threading, 6"........... 700.00
Vase, feathers, bl/wht on marigold w/allover threading, 10"...... 1,450.00
Vase, feathers, gr/wht on gr translucent w/cut flowers, shouldered, 9"...975.00
Vase, feathers, opal-tipped gold on Lady Gay Rose, shouldered, 11"..9,200.00
Vase, feathers, bl/wht on gold, 6" 1,100.00
Vase, floral & vine cuttings on ambergris w/bl bands, 10" 1,500.00
Vase, floral cuttings on ambergris irid, 6" 450.00
Vase, gold, beehive shape, 9"....................................... 750.00
Vase, gold, tapering ovoid w/flared rim, #20133, 12" 275.00
Vase, gold, wide pear form w/flaring rim, short ft, #1700, 8" 325.00
Vase, gold crackle, ovoid w/wide ribs & incurvate rim, #20122, 10"..2,300.00
Vase, gold w/random theading, bulbous, #2336, miniature........ 1,080.00
Vase, gold-orange irid, shouldered, #1721, 6½"............................ 345.00
Vase, Heart & Vine, gr on gold, gold int, classic form, 9"............. 920.00
Vase, Heart & Vine, wht on bright bl irid, shouldered, 11"....... 1,980.00
Vase, jack-in-pulpit; gold w/stretch border, #1984, 8½"............. 1,500.00
Vase, King Tut, gold on gr irid, flared pear form, short ft, #1700, 7" ...2,000.00
Vase, King Tut, opal on bl irid, corseted, #1717, 10", NM 975.00
Vase, King Tut, wht on dk bl, 6"....................................... 1,100.00
Vase, marigold irid w/bl hearts & vines, bulbous w/flared rim, 7" ..1,150.00
Vase, ruby to clear, ovals/t'print/X-hatching, trumpet neck, sgn, 17"..2,400.00

Vase, Moorish Crackle, green, #20121, 12", $4,800.00. (Photo courtesy Early Auction Co.)

Durant Kilns

The Durant Pottery Company operated in Bedford Village, New York, in the early 1900s. Its founder was Mrs. Clarence Rice; she was aided by L. Volkmar to whom she assigned the task of technical direction. (See also Volkmar.) The art and table wares they produced were simple in form and decoration. The creative aspects of the ware were carried on almost entirely by Volkmar himself, with only a minimal crew to help with production. After Mrs. Rice's death in 1919, the property was purchased by Volkmar, who chose to drop the Durant name by 1930. Prior to 1919 the ware was marked simply Durant and dated. After that time a stylized 'V' was added.

Bowl, band of modeled flowers, bl crackle w/oxblood int, 3x9", NM.. 450.00
Bowl, morning-glory shape, crackled Persian Blue, 1914, 3x5½" . 115.00
Bowl, volcanic Persian Blue w/finger ridges, wide/flared, '15, 15", EX... 600.00
Bowl on 3-dolphin ped, wht w/exposed red, 8x12½" 325.00

Candlestick, upright dolphin stem, wht crackle, 1916, 7½", EX, pr ...420.00
Plate, crackled gold lustre, mk D Volkmar '45, 10" 120.00
Stands/risers, sphinx facing outward ea end, gold cold pnt, 12" L, pr .. 335.00
Vase, curdled/volcanic wht on sheer amber, bulbous, 1923, 4x5½" 640.00
Vase, gray matt w/brn mottle, dk brn ft ring, 1936, 11", NM 660.00
Vase, volcanic wht curdling on sheer amber, bulbous, 1923, 4x6½" ...650.00

Easter

In the early 1900s to the 1930s, Germany made the first composition candy containers in the shapes of Easter rabbits, ducks, and chicks. A few were also made of molded cardboard. In the 1940s West Germany made candy containers out of molded cardboard. Many of these had spring necks to give a nodding effect. From the 1930s and into the 1950s, United States manufacturers made Easter candy containers out of egg-carton material (pulp) or pressed cardboard. Ducks and chicks are not as high in demand as rabbits. Rabbits with painted-on clothes or attached fabric clothes bring more than the plain brown or white rabbits. When no condition is mentioned in the description, assume that values reflect excellent to near mint condition for all but paper items; those assume to be in near mint to mint condition. Our advisor for this category is Jenny Tarrant; she is listed in the Directory under Missouri.

Note: In the candy container section, measurements given for the rabbit and cart or rabbit and wagon containers indicate the distance to the tip of the rabbits' ears.

Candy Containers

Advertising die-cut for Bunte Chocolates, cardboard, 21", $100.00 for the pair. (Photo courtesy Morphy Auctions)

German, begging rabbit, brn w/glass eyes, compo, 1900-30s, 5" 88.00
German, begging rabbit, brn w/glass eyes, compo, 1900-30s, 7" ...105.00
German, begging rabbit, brn w/glass eyes, compo, 1900-30s, 9" ...130.00
German, begging rabbit, mohair covered, compo, 1900-30s, 4" ...135.00
German, begging rabbit, mohair covered, compo, 1900-30s, 6" ...195.00
German, duck, yel w/glass eyes, compo, 1900-30s, 3" 75.00
German, duck, yel w/glass eyes, compo, 1900-30s, 5" 130.00
German, duck or chick, pnt-on clothes, compo, 1900-30s, 3-4" ..125.00
German, duck or chick, pnt-on clothes, compo, 1900-30s, 6" 185.00
German, duck or chick, pnt-on clothes, compo, 1900-30s, 7" 200.00
German, egg, molded cb, 1900-30, 3-7", from $65 to 45.00
German, egg, molded cb, 1900-30, 8" 65.00
German, egg, tin, 1900-10, EX, 2-3" 55.00
German, rabbit (dressed) in shoe, compo, 1900-30s, from $250 to .275.00
German, rabbit (dressed) on egg, compo, 1900-30s, from $250 to ..250.00
German, rabbit pulling fancy wood/moss wagon, brn compo, 1900-30s, 7" ..300.00
German, rabbit pulling wood cart, mohair covered, 1900-30s, 4" . 175.00
German, rabbit pulling wood cart, mohair covered, 1900-30s, 6" . 250.00
German, rabbit pulling wood wagon, brn compo, 1900-30s, 4" 150.00
German, rabbit pulling wood wagon, brn compo, 1900-30s, 6" 195.00

German, rabbit w/fabric clothes, compo, 1900-30s, 4" 250.00
German, rabbit w/fabric clothes, compo, 1900-30s, 6" 325.00
German, rabbit w/fabric clothes, compo, 1900-30s, 7", minimum value.. 350.00
German, rabbit w/glass beading, compo, 1900-30s, 6" 150.00
German, rabbit w/pnt-on clothes, compo, 1900-30s, 5" 200.00
German, rabbit w/pnt-on clothes, compo, 1900-30s, 7" 250.00
German, sitting rabbit, brn w/glass eyes, compo, 1900-30s, 6" ... 110.00
German, sitting rabbit, mohair covered, compo, 1900-30s, 4" 140.00
German, sitting rabbit, mohair covered, compo, 1900-30s, 5" 160.00
German, sitting rabbit, mohair covered, compo, 1900-30s, 6" 175.00
German, standing rabbit (Ma or Pa), pnt-on clothes, molded cb, 10½".250.00
German, walking rabbit, brn w/glass eyes, compo, 1900-30s, 6" ...110.00
German, walking rabbit, brn w/glass eyes, compo, 1900-30s, 8" ...150.00
German, walking rabbit, mohair covered, compo, 1900-30s, 4" ...150.00
German, walking rabbit, mohair covered, compo, 1900-30s, 6" ...225.00
German, walking rabbit, mohair covered, compo, 1900-30s, 7" ...245.00
US, begging rabbit, pulp, 1940-50, w/base 55.00
US, sitting rabbit, pulp, brn w/glass eyes, Burk Co, 1930 .... 85.00
US, sitting rabbit next to lg basket, pulp, 1930-50 .... 75.00
US, sitting rabbit w/basket on bk, pulp, 1940-50 .... 75.00
W German/US Zone, dressed duck or chick, cb, spring neck, 1940-50 .60.00
W German/US Zone, dressed rabbit, cb, spring neck, 1940-50 ...... 80.00
W German/US Zone, egg, molded cb, 1940-60, 3-8", from $25 to .. 40.00
W German/US Zone, plain rabbit, cb, spring neck, 1940-50 .... 60.00

Miscellaneous

Celluloid chick or duck, dressed, 3-5", M.. 45.00
Celluloid chick or duck, dressed, 6-8", M.. 75.00
Celluloid chicken pulling wagon w/rabbit, M............................... 125.00
Celluloid rabbit, dressed, 3-5", M.. 65.00
Celluloid rabbit, dressed, 6-8", M.. 75.00
Celluloid rabbit, plain, 3-5", M.. 20.00
Celluloid rabbit, plain, 6-7", M.. 30.00
Celluloid rabbit & chick in swan boat, M....................................... 150.00
Celluloid rabbit driving car, M.. 150.00
Celluloid rabbit pulling wagon, M.. 125.00
Celluloid rabbit pushing or pulling cart, lg, M.............................. 125.00
Celluloid rabbit pushing or pulling cart, sm, M 75.00
Celluloid windup toy, Japan or Occupied Japan, M...................... 150.00
Cotton batten rabbit w/paper ears, Japan, 1930-50, 2-5".............. 30.00
Cotton batten rabbit w/paper ears, Japan, 1930-50, 6" 45.00

Egg Cups

Egg cups, one of the fastest growing collectibles, have been traced back to the ruins of Pompeii. They have been made in almost every country and in almost every conceivable material (ceramics, glass, metal, papier-mache, plastic, wood, ivory, even rubber and straw). Popular categories include Art Deco, Black Memorabilia, Chintz, Personalities, Figurals, Golliwoggs, Railroadiana, Steamship, and Souvenir Ware.

Still being produced today, egg cups appeal to collectors on many levels. Prices range from the inexpensive to thousands of dollars. Those made prior to 1840 are scarce and sought after, as are the character/personality egg cups of the 1930s. For a more thorough study of egg cups we recommend *Egg Cups: An Illustrated History and Price Guide* (Antique Publications) by Brenda Blake, our advisor. You will find her address listed in the Directory under Maine.

Key:
bkt — bucket, a single cup   hoop — hoop, a single open
  without a foot   cup with waistline

dbl — 2-sided with small
    end for eating egg in shell,
    large end for mixing egg
    with toast and butter
fig — figural, an egg cup
    actually molded into the
    shape of an animal, bird,
    car, person, etc.

inst. dbl — large custard cup shape
    set — tray or cruet
    (stand, frame or basket)
    with two to eight cups
sgl — with a foot; goblet shaped

American

Dbl, Autumn Leaf, Autumn Leaf Collector's Club gift, 1997	68.00
Dbl, bl horizontal rings, Hankscraft	13.00
Dbl, bl tall ship, MA Hadley	25.00
Dbl, bride & groom, Cleminson, pr	60.00
Dbl, California Ivy, Metlox, ca 1965	32.00
Dbl, English Abbey, Taylor Smith & Taylor	35.00
Dbl, Jubilee, gr, Homer Laughlin, 1948	10.00
Dbl, Juvenile, chick, Roseville, ca 1917	270.00
Dbl, Juvenile, rabbit, Roseville, ca 1917	300.00
Dbl, Ming, Lenox	45.00
Dbl, Norma, Blue Ridge	35.00
Dbl, Robin Des Bois, Canonsburg Pottery Co - PV in circle	15.00
Sgl, turq, Lenox, ca 1911	55.00
Sgl, Valencia, Louise Bauer, Shawnee, 1937	25.00
Sgl, Vistosa, red, Taylor Smith & Taylor, ca 1940	45.00

Characters/Personalities

Dbl, Little Red Riding Hood, Columbia China	18.00
Fig, Dumbo pulling cart, Disney, ca 1950s	65.00
Fig, Fergie, Spitting Image, Luck & Flaw	58.00
Fig, Pink Panther sitting/holding cup, Royal Orleans, ca 1981	80.00
Fig, Pluto pulling cart, Disney, 1950s	65.00
Fig, Prince Andrew, Spitting Image, Luck & Flaw, ca 1986	70.00
Set, Muppets, Statler, Waldorf, Zoot & Sam, Sigma, ca 1981	175.00
Sgl, Anne of Green Gables, Crown Ashton, recent	12.00
Sgl, Garfield, Good Morning series	17.00
Sgl, Peter Rabbit, emb, gr jasper, Wedgwood	80.00
Sgl, Queen Elizabeth, 70th birthday, Coronet, 1996	15.00

English/Staffordshire

Bkt, Blue Aves, Royal Crown Derby	25.00
Bkt, Crocus, Clarice Cliff	75.00
Bkt, Golly at doorway pointing to display window, English, 1960s	40.00
Dbl, Cornish Kitchen Ware, bl stripes, TG Green, 1930s	36.00
Dbl, Dainty Blue, Shelley	95.00
Dbl, Rose Chintz, Johnson Bros	40.00
Set, flow bl, basket, 4 cups w/gold rim, Burleigh Ware, 1930s	135.00
Sgl, Abbey, flow bl, G Jones	100.00
Sgl, Amherst Japan, mc, Minton, ca 1830	185.00
Sgl, bl hens, Emma Bridgwater, current	15.00
Sgl, blk toast, printed: Egg Cup, Emma Bridgwater, current	15.00
Sgl, Blue Dawn, bl, Denby	17.00
Sgl, Cockatrice, pk, Minton	55.00
Sgl, dogs (3) playing musical instruments	55.00
Sgl, Gaudy Welsh, ca 1840	210.00
Sgl, gr transfer, panelled, Davenport, 19th C	72.00
Sgl, kingfisher, integral saucer, Longpark Torquay, 1920s	60.00
Sgl, Marguerite, chintz, Royal Winton	48.00
Sgl, mottoware, Longpark Torquay	35.00
Sgl, Victorian violets, Hammersley	15.00
Sgl, Vista, red, Mason's	25.00

Figurals

Baby chick, vintage,
$15.00.

Bluebird, Lefton	48.00
Butler holding cup on tray, Silver Crane Co, 1988	65.00
Car, gr convertible, Honiton	22.00
Car, pk & blk, mouse driver, St James	50.00
Cat, hdld, Portugal	15.00
Cat, salt attached to wht cup w/magnet, Rot Ceramic, Germany, 1980s	20.00
Chick in clown outfit, Foreign	50.00
Chick on seasaw, yel w/bl cup, molded window, Japan, ca 1930	20.00
Cowboy kewpie, blk hat & pants, red bandana	18.00
Donkey pulling cart, cobalt, Italy	20.00
Duck, bl, Fanny Farmer, 1930s	25.00
Face (male), Au Grand Dud Bethune, R Federic-Degeorges	38.00
Golly Sailor stands behind cup, Sailing Club, Silver Crane Co, 1987-94	40.00
Motorcycle, bl, Carter, Suffolk, England	17.00
Mr Shifter, PG Chimp, plastic, w/lid, ca 1958	25.00
Pirate, blk eye patch, 1980s	15.00
Quail, Goebel	40.00
Rabbit, repro Dedham, The Potting Shed, 1990	35.00
Rooster, brn drip glaze, Pfaltzgraff	32.00
Shoe, gr, Royal Art Pottery	15.00
Volkswagen, Devon Ceramics, ca 1959	22.00
Whistler bear, lustre, foreign, ca 1920s	125.00
Whistler duck, foreign, 1920s	110.00
2 big ft, blk & wht, Carlton, ca 1980	45.00

Glass

Dbl, amberina, mold blown, ca 1890	250.00
Dbl, Birch Leaf, bl, NF, ca 1878	70.00
Dbl, bl strings, Peloton	80.00
Dbl, Cape Cod, crystal, Imperial, ca 1932	32.00
Dbl, Chalaine Blue, McKee	25.00
Dbl, clambroth, ca 1970s	90.00
Dbl, English Hobnail, amber, Westmoreland, 1930s-40s	32.00
Dbl, Jade-ite gr	32.00
Dbl, Raindrop, amber	40.00
Dbl, Rock Crystal, ruby, McKee, 1920s	75.00
Fig, chicken, milk glass, John F Kemple	15.00
Fig, chicken, red & blk beak, Vallerysthal	30.00
Fig, duck, milk glass, Deco, Opalex, 1930s	14.00
Fig, swan, scalloped rim, Fenton	25.00
Set, covered hen w/6 chicken egg cups+master salt+tray, Vallerysthal	450.00
Sgl, amethyst, flared gallery rim, pressed, ca 1880	95.00
Sgl, cobalt, flared rim, blown, 1870s	100.00
Sgl, Colonial, #400, Heisey	38.00
Sgl, Cremax, bl to wht, ca 1940	6.00
Sgl, Kalonyal, Heisey, ca 1904	65.00
Sgl, leaf design, milk glass	7.00
Sgl, mercury glass w/gold-wash lining, ca 1910	75.00
Sgl, purple slag w/vertical ribs	70.00
Sgl, Rock Crystal, McKee	15.00

Metal

Hoop, graniteware, wht w/bl mottled Snow on the Mountain..... **160.00**
Hoop, graniteware, wht w/blk rim, 1930s........................ **75.00**
Set, christening, silver, +spoon+napkin ring, Birmingham, 1931, MIB .**145.00**
Set, christening, silver, +spoon+napkin ring, Mappin & Webb, 1993, MIB...**275.00**
Set, oak & SP, hdld cruet w/6 bkt egg cups **300.00**
Set, Sheffield SP, Georgian stand w/urn finial, 6 ftd cups, ca 1790 . **1,100.00**
Set, silver cruet w/4 cups in shape of riding boots, Victorian **1,750.00**
Set, SP, 2 cups, made in China, MIB.. **8.00**
Sgl, brass, cherub ped supports cup.. **35.00**
Sgl, copper, molded rim & base **9.00**
Sgl, silver, Bavarian style, 3 wooden ft, Mexican, Spratling, 1930s .. **150.00**
Sgl, silver, beaded rim, Birmingham, ca 1916 .... **55.00**
Sgl, silver, covered egg cutter, England, ca 1910 .... **225.00**
Sgl, silver w/2 emb egg spoons, Tiffany & Co **325.00**
Sgl, SP, w/integral saucer, France.. **20.00**
Sgl, wire, blk **12.00**
Sgl, wrought iron, ca 1850 .... **14.00**

Steamship/Cruise Ship

Bkt, Maid Line **20.00**
Bkt, Princess Cruise, floral, Dudson, 1999..**7.00**
Dbl, IOS line, bl flag & bands, Ridgways **80.00**
Dbl, Red Cross Line, bl flag, red bands.. **80.00**
Dbl, United Fruit, UFC logo **90.00**
Hoop, Coats & Clark, gr coat of arms, Dunn Bennet & Co........... **60.00**
Hoop, Cunard banner w/lion, bl transfer, ca 1910 .... **175.00**
Hoop, Hamburg-American Line (HAPAG) **40.00**
Hoop, Nordeutscher Lloyd Bremen, ca 1910 .... **250.00**
Hoop, Pacific Mail, maroon monogram **275.00**
Hoop, Queen Mary, Booths & Colcloughs.. **68.00**
Hoop, Union Castle Line, Edinburgh Castle, blk geometric rim, 1930s. **72.00**
Hoop, White Star Line, turq, Stoniers, early 1900s.................. **1,400.00**
Sgl, Cornuba, antique shape, Spode.. **175.00**
Sgl, HMS Aquitania, SP, pierced/scalloped rim, enameled crest.. **160.00**
Sgl, Swedish American Lines, bl flag... **28.00**

Elfinware

Made in Germany from about 1920 until the 1940s, these minia-ture vases, boxes, salt cellars, and miscellaneous novelty items are char-acterized by the tiny applied flowers that often cover their entire surface. Pieces with animals and birds are the most valuable, followed by the more interesting examples such as diminutive grand pianos and candleholders. Items covered in 'spinach' (applied green moss) can be valued at 75% to 100% higher than pieces that are not decorated in this manner. See also Salts, Open.

Slipper, any style shown, $45.00 each. (Photo courtesy Earlene Wheatley)

Basket, appl flowers & moss, dbl hdls that cross, 2¼x4" **50.00**
Basket, appl roses & leaves w/moss, 2x5" **55.00**
Box, dresser; appl flowers & moss, ca 1900, 1½x2½" **22.50**
Pitcher, appl flowers & moss, 2" **35.00**
Swan dish, appl overall flowers & moss, open bk, 2x2¼" **40.00**
Swan sleigh, appl flowers & moss, 2½x3½x2½" **45.00**
Teapot, appl flowers & moss, 2½" **50.00**
Vase, appl flowers & moss, angle hdl, 3" **50.00**
Vase, appl flowers & moss, loop hdls, 2".. **65.00**

Epergnes

Popular during the Victorian era, epergnes were fancy centerpieces often consisting of several tiers of vases (called lilies), candleholders, dishes, or a combination of components. They were made in all types of art glass, and some were set in ornate plated frames. Our advisor for this category is Barbara Aaronson; she is listed in the Directory under California.

Clear vase w/tall stem, scroll arms w/sm vases on ruffle bowl, 15x9" ..**235.00**
Cranberry lilies (3) attached to cranberry base, 20" **515.00**
Cut clear lily+2 bowls, bronze dore cherub std, ft w/3 lg beasts, 31".**3,055.00**
Gr vaseline opal, lg center vase & 2 hanging baskets, 23x19" dia. **550.00**
Millefiori fluted lilies (3), attached to matching 22" base, 24" **825.00**
Opal w/bl crests, 3 lilies w/clear rigaree+bowl, ruffled rims, 14" ... **520.00**
Silver, lily w/rtcl bowl supports 4 rtcl baskets, Scottish, 19"...... **1,440.00**
Turq opaline on ram's head holder on marble base, bronze mts, 6x4" .**475.00**

Erickson

Carl Erickson of Bremen, Ohio, produced hand-formed glassware from 1943 until 1960 in artistic shapes, no two of which were identical. One of the characteristics of his work was the air bubbles that were cap-tured within the glass. Both clear and colored glass was produced. Rather than to risk compromising his high standards by selling the factory, when Erickson retired, the plant was dismantled and sold.

Bowl, bl w/clear base w/controlled bubbles, att, 5½x8" **225.00**
Bowl, console; gr w/controlled bubbles, ftd, 1943-61.................... **350.00**
Bowl, nut; amethyst, 1943-61, 3½x3½"... **45.00**
Compote, smoke w/controlled-bubble clear triangular base, 5¼x6¼" ..**85.00**
Decanter, gr w/controlled bubbles, clear bubbled stopper, 15½"..... **70.00**
Pitcher, emerald gr w/clear bubbled paperweight base, 13", +stirrer...**125.00**
Pitcher, martini; gr to clear teapot shape, 5", +7" stirrer............... **100.00**
Top hat, amethyst, w/label, 4x6½" **150.00**
Vase, amber neck w/crystal controlled bubble base, 1943-61 .... **45.00**
Vase, bud; amber controlled bubble base, clear cylinder neck........ **35.00**
Vase, emerald gr w/clear bubbled paperweight base, 10⅛x6½" **115.00**
Vase, smoke, waisted, 7½x3⅛".. **30.00**

Erphila

The Erphila trademark was used by Ebeling and Ruess Co. of Phila-delphia between 1886 and the 1950s. The company imported quality porcelain and pottery from Germany, Czechoslovakia, Italy, and France. Pieces more readily found are from Germany and Czechoslovakia. A va-riety of items can be found and pieces such as figural teapots and larger figurines are moving up in value. There are a variety of marks, but all contain the name Erphila. One of the earlier marks is a green rectangle containing the name Erphila Germany. In general, Erphila pieces are scarce, not easily found.

Bust, Charles Dickens, 5x3½"...................... 40.00
Figurine, cherub holding goat by horns, gold mk, 5½"................... 45.00
Figurine, horse, wht gloss, head trn, Est 1886 mk, 4¼x3½"........... 85.00
Figurine, horses (2) prancing, Ebeling & Reuss, 9x9½x4"........... 160.00
Figurine, Russian wolfhound, blk/brn/wht, 4x5"................. 40.00
Figurine, Siamese cat, Ling on foil sticker, #9620, 11¼" L............ 75.00
Pitcher, terrier dog figural, blk/wht/pk, #6702B, 7¾", NM........... 55.00
Pitcher, toucan figural, blk/red/cream, Deco style, 9", NM........... 90.00
Teapot, cat figural, blk & wht w/pk bow, #6700B, 8"........... 135.00
Teapot, dachshund figural, brn tones, US Zone/#6703B, 8"........... 150.00
Teapot, elf figural, mc, pointed hat lid, foil label, 9¼x8½"........... 80.00
Teapot, pig figural, spotted, paper label, #AK722, 7½".................. 195.00
Vase, bird perched between lyre shape w/2 openings, 6⅞x6⅞"....... 60.00
Vase, Cubist decor, red/gr/wht, ftd, #3782, 8".................. 65.00

Eskimo Artifacts

While ivory carvings made from walrus tusks or whale teeth have been the most emphasized articles of Eskimo art, basketry and woodworking are other areas in which these Alaskan Indians excel. Their designs are effected through the application of simple yet dramatic lines and almost stark decorative devices. Though not pursued to the extent of American Indian art, the unique work of these northern tribes is beginning to attract the serious attention of today's collectors.

Basket, one-rod coiled, faded black and red chevron pattern, from Northern Athabascan and Eskimo sub-area, 4" loss of splint at rim, 8½", $550.00.
(Photo courtesy David Rago Auctions)

Awl/perforator, mineralized ivory chip, polished, 2¾"................... 12.00
Basket, seal gut design, w/lid, 1940s, 6x6"........................... 100.00
Basket, stylized snowflakes, w/lid, 1940s-50s, 6x5½"................... 200.00
Buttons, ivory, seal w/cvd circle designs on bk, 1890s, 1¼", 3 for. 175.00
Chopper, whalebone, polish on 1 face, 7¼"........................... 100.00
Cribbage board, ivory w/baleen & abalone inlay, ca 1910s-20s, 15" L.. 175.00
Cribbage board, ivory w/seal/geometric cvg, pegs/storage, 1920s, 11".. 200.00
Cvg, Eskimo hunter, ivory, Justin Tuilana, 1960s-70s, 3x2"........ 325.00
Cvg, hunter in kayak holding spear, Ellanna, 1940s, 1½x6"......... 325.00
Cvg, man holding seal, soapstone, 1960s, 9".......................... 130.00
Cvg, mask, ivory w/inlay baleen eyes, 1950s-60s, 2½x2x1".......... 150.00
Cvg, mythical being, ivory w/baleen eyes, 1930s, 4"................ 175.00
Cvg, mythical figure & seal head, ivory w/baleen inlay, 3"........... 170.00
Cvg, seal, ivory w/baleen eyes, 1940s, 1x5"........................ 150.00
Cvg, seal, pnt wood w/brass tack eyes, sgn Wankier, 1980s, 6x16x4".. 200.00
Cvg, seal w/baleen eyes atop human skull, ivory, 1940s, 4".......... 175.00
Cvg, seals (2), soapstone, 1960s, 6"................................ 130.00
Cvg, walrus, soapstone w/ivory tusks, 1950s, 4½x9"................. 250.00
Cvg, walrus mother w/calf on her bk, Koyuk, 1950s, 1¼x3½x2"... 250.00
Cvg, whale, ivory w/baleen eyes, G Slwook, 1960s-70s, 1½x5".... 150.00
Dance club, cvd wood w/dog-like head on end, 1900-20s, 20x4½".. 125.00
Drum, hide w/beaded design, hair trim, 1930s, 3x13", +beater.... 125.00
Gouge, ivory chip, mineralized & patinated, 2⅛".................. 15.00
Hairpin, ivory, decor at thick end, polished, 4⅜"................... 200.00
Halibut club, walnut tusk ivory, lg hole near end (wrist loop?), 22".. 500.00
Knife, mineralized bone, drilled hdl hold, prehistoric, 6⅝"......... 225.00

Mat, seal hide, complex design in center, 1920s, 29x31"............. 160.00
Net sinker, polished bone, 2⅞"................................... 50.00
Pendant, grizzly bear tooth, drilled, AK......................... 250.00
Tool, spatula shape, polished mammoth bone, 6½"................... 165.00

Eyewear

Collectors of Americana are beginning to appreciate the charm of antique optical items, and those involved in the related trade find them particularly fascinating. Anyone, however, can appreciate the evolution of technology apparent when viewing a collection of vintage eyewear, and at the same time admire the ingenuity involved in the design and construction of these glasses.

In the early 1900s the choice of an eyeglass frame was generally left to the optician, much as the choice of medication was left to the family doctor. By the 1930s, however, eyeglasses had emerged as fashion accessories. In 1939 Altina Sanders's 'Harlequin' frame (a forerunner of the 1950s 'Cat-Eyes'), won an American Design award. By the 1950s manufacturers were working overtime to enhance the allure of eyewear, hosting annual competitions for 'Miss Beauty in Glasses' and 'Miss Specs Appeal.'

Particularly sought after today are the flamboyant and colorful designs of the '50s and '60s. These include 'Cat-Eyes' with their distinctively upswept brow edges; 'highbrows,' often heavily jeweled or formed in the shape of butterfly or bird wings; and frames with decorative temples ranging from floral wreaths to musical notes. Many of today's collectors have such novel eyeglass frames fitted with their own prescription lenses for daily wear.

For further information on eyewear of this era, we recommend *Specs Appeal: Extravagant 1950s & 1960s Eyewear* (Schiffer) by Leslie Piña and Donald-Brian Johnson (our advisor for this category). Mr Johnson is listed in the Directory under Nebraska.

Key: Fr — France

Eyeglass stand, Lucite, bk-cvd red rose, from $15 to....................... 20.00
Eyeglasses, Batwing, gray, from $375 to.. 400.00
Eyeglasses, Bird Wing, nesting bird, from $600 to 650.00
Eyeglasses, blk/gold mesh, pearl/bl rhinestone brow clusters, $120 to. 140.00
Eyeglasses, Cat-Eye, blk w/silver aluminum inlay, Hudson, $175 to. 200.00
Eyeglasses, Cat-Eye, lt bl w/clear cutaways, rhinestone trim, $70 to... 80.00
Eyeglasses, Cat-Eye, pk & rhinestones, folding, from $100 to...... 120.00
Eyeglasses, child's, Graceline, pk w/gold strip laminate, from $30 to.. 40.00

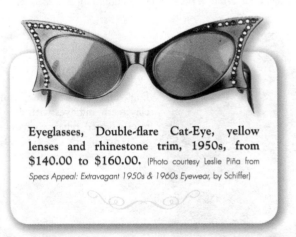

Eyeglasses, Double-flare Cat-Eye, yellow lenses and rhinestone trim, 1950s, from $140.00 to $160.00. (Photo courtesy Leslie Piña from *Specs Appeal: Extravagant 1950s & 1960s Eyewear*, by Schiffer)

Eyeglasses, Dbl-Pointed Cat-Eye, aurora rhinestones, Frame Fr, $200 to .225.00
Eyeglasses, Dior granny style/bl cloisonne rhinestones/pearls, $150 to..200.00
Eyeglasses, Dr Scholl's Health Glasses, from $25 to...................... 35.00
Eyeglasses, Earring Chains, yel or check fr, 1960s, from $120 to.. 160.00

Eyeglasses, elaborate highbrow fr, from $1,000 to 1,200.00
Eyeglasses, floral temple wreath trim, Tura, from $275 to 325.00
Eyeglasses, folding, bl & silver-gray, from $175 to 200.00
Eyeglasses, Granny style, faceted rosy pk lenses, 1960s, from $60 to .. 75.00
Eyeglasses, Headband style, butterscotch, from $250 to 275.00
Eyeglasses, Octette oversz 8-sided fr, Selecta, 1970s, from $50 to .. 60.00
Eyeglasses, Ram Horn highbrows, brn w/rhinestones, Qualite Fr, $550 to..600.00
Eyeglasses, silver-gray fr w/rhinestone swags, J Hasday, from $70 to..80.00
Eyeglasses, swan highbrows, wht pearlized, from $450 to 550.00
Eyeglasses, Triple-Flare Cat-Eye w/rhinestones, Fr, from $140 to. 160.00
Eyeglasses, Trucco Shallow Make Up Frames, demi-amber, Selecta, $50 to..60.00
Eyeglasses, Twist Cat-Eye fr in blk & clear, TWE, from $90 to 100.00
Eyeglasses, yel pearlized plastic, gold floral applique, Fr, $120 to.. 135.00
Lorgnette, Cat-Eye shape w/rhinestones, Hong Kong, 1950s, $70 to. 80.00
Lorgnette, gold-plated folding type, 1920, ca 1900, from $100 to . 110.00
Opera glasses, MOP & gold plate, lenses adjust, Lemaire, from $375 to. 395.00
Opera glasses, tortoiseshell, lenses adjust/hinged hdl, 1900s, $375 to.. 395.00
Sun glasses, bug-eye, Playboy Austria, from $80 to......................... 95.00
Sun glasses, folding, rhinestone decor, Japanese, from $130 to 150.00
Sun glasses, novelty, eyelash fringe trim, from $350 to................. 375.00
Sun glasses, Red Wings, Ray-Ban, from $60 to 70.00
Sun glasses, Schiaparelli design, yel-gold w/fruit clusters, $230 to...250.00
Sun glasses, Selecta 4000 White Pearl, from $55 to 65.00
Sun glasses, wraparounds, Polaroid, from $60 to............................ 70.00

Face Jugs

The most recognizable form of Southern folk pottery is the face jug. Rich alkaline glazes (lustrous greens and browns) are typical, and occasionally shards of glass are applied to the surface of the ware which during firing melts to produce opalescent 'glass runs' over the alkaline. In some locations clay deposits contain elements that result in areas of fluorescent blue or rutile; another variation is swirled or striped ware, reminiscent of eighteenth-century agateware from Staffordshire. Face vessels came in several forms as well. In America, from New England to the Carolinas, they were made as early as the 1840s. Collector demand for these unique one-of-a-kind jugs is at an all-time high and is still escalating. Choice examples made by Burlon B. Craig and Lanier Meaders range from $1,000.00 to over $5,000.00 on the secondary market. If you're interested in learning more about this type of folk pottery, contact the Southern Folk Pottery Collectors Society; their address is in the Directory under Clubs, Newsletters, and Catalogs. Our advisor for this category is Billy Ray Hussey; he is listed in the Directory under North Carolina.

Edgfield, South Carolina, white clay teeth and eyes with drawn pupils, glued repair to handle, ca. 1860s, 9", $24,700.00.
(Photo courtesy Garth's Auctions Inc.)

Brown, Charlie; crush glass glaze, cvd brows/lashes, china teeth, 15".130.00
Brown, Jerry; bl eyebrows/pupils/lashes/mustache, wht teeth, 1991, 12". 60.00

Craig, Burlon B; aqua over olive, cvd brows/pop eyes, smile/teeth, 20"...4,100.00
Craig, Burlon B; china teeth, Coke glass glaze, dripping 'beard,' 20"..1,900.00
Craig, Burlon B; wig stand, Egyptian Pharaoh, pointed head, 12".2,100.00
Ferguson, Bobby; dk gr, cvd eyebrows/lashes, china teeth, 3-hdl, 9". 375.00
Henson, Billy W; dbl monkey face, china teeth, 2-spout, EX mc, 13" ..350.00
Hewell, wht eye sockets/teeth, mustache, dk brn w/cobalt drips, 13".300.00
Hussey, Billy Ray; dbl face: Age/Youth, mc glaze/EX details, 10" .550.00
Hussey, Billy Ray; devil face, long tongue/china teeth, EX colors, 11"..800.00
Hussey, Billy Ray; pitcher, tall face, china teeth/EX mc, 20"........ 900.00
Lisk, Chas; dk olive, cvd waves/beard, china teeth, pop eyes, 19". 650.00
Lisk, Chas; swirlware, wht clay teeth/eyes w/bl pupils/unibrow, 10". 175.00
Meaders, AG; dk streaky olive, clay teeth, wht eyes w/blk pupils, 11"..375.00
Meaders, CJ II; devil, wht/bl eyes, sculpted chin/cheeks, 1988, 11" .275.00
Meaders, CJ II; olive, defined features/chin-cheek area, 1988, 10"..400.00
Meaders, Lanier; complete facial features front/bk, rock teeth, 10"..3,200.00
Meaders, Lanier; pleasant/well defined, wht/bl eyes, teeth, 1980s, 9".800.00
Miller, Eric; bull-headed, brn-blk Albany slip, 1980s, unsgn, 11".. 550.00

Fans

The Japanese are said to have invented the fan. From there it went to China, and Portuguese traders took the idea to Europe. Though usually considered milady's accessory, even the gentlemen in seventeenth-century England carried fans! More fashionable than practical, some were of feathers and lovely hand-painted silks with carved ivory or tortoise sticks. Some French fans had peepholes. There are mourning fans, calendar fans, and those with advertising. Fine antique fans (pre-1900) of ivory or mother-of-pearl are highly desirable. Those from before 1800 often sell for upwards of $1,000.00. Fans are being viewed as works of art, and some are actually signed by known artists.

Watercolored Indian court scene on ivory and silver, folding, 10½x20", $1,000.00. (Photo courtesy Neal Auction Company)

Celluloid brise, coral marbleized w/gilt, 1930s, 4½" 50.00
Feathers, maribou; on satin w/ivory sticks, Edwardian, 13" 95.00
Feathers, ostrich; aqua w/cvd ivory sticks & gold, 1900s, 11"......... 95.00
Feathers, ostrich; blk w/tortoise sticks, Vict, 9"............................ 115.00
Ivory, cvd w/figures in garden scenes, China, 19th C................. 1,000.00
Lace, HP cherubs scene, sgn A Cottinet, MOP ribs, 14x24"+fr.. 400.00
Litho, HP courtyard scene w/fountains/etc, eng MOP ribs, in 18x28" fr.. 300.00
MOP/lace, HP reserve w/3 figures, 1910, in gilt shadow-box fr, 13x22" ... 400.00
Paper, advertising, w/silver/red/blk florals, 1920s, 9½" 45.00
Paper, HP figures in brocade, gilt filigree/ivory sticks, 18th C, 11" . 1,000.00
Paper, HP figures on pnt bkground, ivory sticks, 19th C 525.00
Paper, HP figures/flowers, cut-out/pnt ivory sticks, China, 11x20". 2,700.00
Paper, HP Greek bldg/family in garden, ebony sticks/ormolu, 1810, 13"..650.00
Paper, HP Oriental figures, cvd/pierced ivory sticks, China, 19th C..825.00
Satin, cream w/HP bird/fruit, feather trim, ivory sticks, 1900s, 14"..125.00

Silk, ivory w/embr bird, pierced ivory sticks, 1900, 10" 200.00
Silk gauze, ivory w/embr flowers, ivory sticks, 1920s, 13" 150.00

Farm Collectibles

Country living in the nineteenth century entailed plowing, planting, and harvesting; gathering eggs and milking; making soap from lard rendered on butchering day; and numerous other tasks performed with primitive tools of which we in the twentieth century have had little first-hand knowledge. Our advisor for this category is Lar Hothem; his address is listed in the Directory under Ohio. Values listed below are for items in excellent original condition unless noted otherwise. See also Cast Iron; Lamps, Lanterns; Woodenware; Wrought Iron.

Pocket mirror, advertisement for Ohio brand farm machinery, celluloid, 1¾", EX, $650.00. (Photo courtesy Wm. Morford Auctions)

Book, Farm Machinery & Equipment, detailed illustrations, 1948, 520-pg . 40.00
Catalog, John Deere Plow Company, Catalog #1, 1912, 413 pgs . 535.00
Chain saw, 50V John Deere, 2-stroke, Kioritz Corp, 1960s, 16" bar .. 90.00
Chicken feeder, galvanized metal tray, Feed Purina..., 24" L 15.00
Chicken feeder, stoneware, James Mfg stencil, 2 interlocking pcs . 70.00
Chicken feeder/waterer, galvanized tin, 2-pc, 15x35" dia 15.00
Corn knife, 16" metal blade, 14" wooden hdl 12.00
Corn sheller, CI, bolts to solid surface, Black Hawk, ca 1903 .... 65.00
Corn sheller, CI, clamps down, wooden hdl, Black Beauty, Durbin .. 40.00
Corn sheller, CI, hand-held, mk Unique, 6x8½" across hdls 215.00
Corn sheller, gr pnt CI, mk John Deere, self standing, very heavy .. 120.00
Corn sheller, pnt CI, w/flywheel & manual hdl, self-standing, IHC mk. 75.00
Cow bell, wrought iron (smithy made), riveted, heavy clapper, 6" 15.00
Cream can, cast metal, locking lid, ca 1940s, 11¾x10¼" 60.00
Feed sack, roses in sqs, red/wht/lt bl, opened, 35x35" 32.50
Fence pliers, Cronk, long sq nose, cutters ea side of head 12.00
Fence stretcher, block & tackle type w/2 pulleys & 16' rope 17.50
Funnel, copper, ring for hanging, 16x11" 45.00
Funnel, galvanized metal, 18x11" 35.00
Hay saw, long blade, wooden hdl, 19th C, 36" 50.00
Hay trolley, CI, block rail type, bottom pulley, ca 1870s 50.00
Hay trolley, Louden Senior Fork Carrier w/bottom pulley, 18x15" ... 70.00
Horse collar, w/blk collar pad, adjusts from 25-28" 165.00
Implement seat, American Harrow Company, CI, 14x15⅝" 165.00
Implement seat, Furst & Bradley, CI, 18x15½" 70.00
Implement seat, Goulds, CI, blk & wht rpt, 14x17" 1,150.00
Implement seat, Grand Detour, CI 175.00
Jacket, Internat'l Harvester, red quilted w/lining, zipper, 1970s 25.00
Manual, Internat'l Harvester T-340 Tractor 80.00
Manual, John Deere JD 730 Tractor, 124-pg, 9½x6" 65.00
Manual, John Deere Model B, 1940s 65.00
Manual, Massey-Ferguson MF 85 Diesel Tractor 12.00
Manual, Operation Care & Repair of..., John Deere, 19th ed, 258-pg . 50.00
Milk can, cast metal, Solar on hdls, 40-qt, 24x13" 60.00
Milking stool, metal, 3-leg, 12x9¾" 45.00
Multi-tool, Never Stall Plier, w/wire cutters/wrench/screwdriver... 70.00

Oil bottle, Old Master, 1 Liquid Qt emb on clear glass, funnel top .. 35.00
Oiler, International Harvester, 3⅜" spout, 7⅛x3" dia 35.00
Pitch fork, 12-tine, wooden hdl & shaft (cvd from 1 pc) 65.00
Pith helmet, wht hard plastic w/Oliver decal on front, Hawley, 1950s . 115.00
Planter, potato; hand-held type, Acme, dtd Sept 11 1900, 33½" L .. 35.00
Plow, 1-bottom pull type, complete 100.00
Pulley, CI, 12x5x4¾", wheel dia: 3½" 40.00
Pump, hand; Baker...Evansville WI, 37" hdl 300.00
Pump, hand; FE Myers & Bro Co, lattice base, 40" hdl 485.00
Pump, hand; Red Jacket, Davenport IA, 53½" overall 200.00
Scale, Jacobs Detecto-Wate 20-Lb, rnd dial, hanging metal 16x13" tray . 55.00
Scythe, curved 58" wooden handle, 26" blade 70.00
Sheep shears, Sheer Steel WWC/W Wilkinson, 12" 15.00
Singletree, center hitch & clevis w/pin, 17" 22.50
Singletree, wooden w/center iron circle, hook ea end, 30" 45.00
Tire pump, John Deere #6886-C, fits power takeoff, ca 1950s 135.00
Tool box, CI, The Richardson Mfg Co Worcester MA, 4x11x5" . 150.00
Wagon, hay; Pekin, orig wooden 168x84" deck 675.00
Winnowing machine, pine w/mc pnt accents, CI crank, splits, 64" L. 260.00
Yoke, wooden, handmade, wooden loops remove, 46" L 95.00

Fenton

The Fenton Art Glass Company was founded in 1905 by brothers Frank L. and John W. Fenton. In the beginning they were strictly a decorating company, but when glassware blanks supplied by other manufacturers became difficult to obtain, the brothers started their own glass manufactory. This factory remains in operation today; it is located in Williamstown, West Virginia.

Early Fenton consisted of pattern glass, custard glass, and carnival glass. During the 1920s and 1930s, Fenton introduced several Depression-era glass patterns, including a popular line called Lincoln Inn, along with stretch glass and glassware in several popular opaque colors — Chinese Yellow, Mandarin Red, and Mongolian Green among them.

In 1939 Fenton introduced a line of Hobnail glassware after the surprising success of a Hobnail cologne bottle made for Wrisley Cologne. Since that time Hobnail has remained a staple in Fenton's glassware line. In addition to Hobnail, other lines such as Coin Spot, the crested lines, and Thumbprint have been mainstays of the company, as have their popular opalescent colors such as cranberry, blue, topaz, and plum. Their milk glass has been very successful as well. Glass baskets in these lines and colors are widely sought after by collectors and can be found in a variety of different sizes and shapes.

Today the company is being managed by third- and fourth-generation family members. Fenton glass continues to be sold in gift shops and retail stores. Additionally, exclusive pieces are offered on the television shopping network, QVC. Desirable items for collectors include limited edition pieces, hand-painted pieces, and family signature pieces. With the deaths of Bill Fenton (second generation) and Don Fenton (third generation) in 2003, family signature pieces are expected to become more desirable to collectors. Watch for special exclusive pieces to commemorate the company's 100th anniversary.

For further information we recommend *Fenton Art Glass, 1907 – 1939, Fenton Art Glass Patterns, 1939 – 1980, Fenton Art Glass Colors and Hand-decorated Patterns, 1959 – 1980,* and *Fenton Art Glass Hobnail Pattern* by Margaret and Kenn Whitmyer; *Fenton Glass, The Third Twenty-Five Years,* by William Heacock (with 1998 value guide); and *Fenton Glass: The 1980s Decade* by Robert E. Eaton, Jr. (1997 values). Additionally, two national collector clubs, the National Fenton Glass Society (NFGS) and the Fenton Art Glass Collectors of America (FAGCA) promote the study of Fenton art through their respective newsletters, *The Fenton Flyer* and *The Butterfly Net* (See Clubs, Newsletters, and Catalogs in the Directory). Our advisors for this category are Laurie and Richard

Karman; they are listed in the Directory under Illinois. See Also Carnival Glass; Custard Glass; Stretch Glass.

Apple Blossom, bonbon, #7428-AB, 1960-61, 8", from $40 to 50.00
Apple Blossom, cake plate, #7213-AB, 1960-61, from $180 to.... 200.00
Apple Crest, finger bowl, #202, 1941-43, from $25 to 30.00
Apple Crest, vase, dbl crimped, #192, 1942-43, 6", from $55 to 60.00
Aqua Crest, basket, #192, 1942-43, 7", from $95 to 125.00
Bell, Bride & Groom, wht satin, #9168-WS, 1977-79, from $20 to.25.00
Black Crest, plate, #7219-BC, 1970s, 6", from $14 to 16.00
Black Crest, vase, fan; #7356-BC, 1970s, 6¼", from $85 to.......... 100.00
Black Rose, candleholder, 2-pc, #7277-BR, 1954-55, ea from $95 to.120.00
Black Rose, vase, #7256-BR, 1953-55, 6", from $145 to............... 160.00
Block & Star, bonbon, milk glass, #5635-MI, 1955-59, from $10 to.. 12.00
Block & Star, tumbler, turq, #5647-TU, 1955-56, 12-oz, from $30 to .35.00
Block & Star, vase, milk glass, #5659-MI, 1955-56, 9", from $30 to .45.00
Blue Ridge, basket, #1921, ca 1939, 11", from $325 to 350.00
Blue Ridge, top hat, #1921, ca 1939, 10", from $200 to 225.00
Bubble Optic/Honeycomb, vase, Apple Green, #1350-AG, 1961-62, 5".. 50.00
Bubble Optic/Honeycomb, vase, coral, #1359-CL, 1961-62, 11½" . 200.00
Burmese, bowl, #7422-BR, 1970-72, 8", from $55 to 65.00
Burmese, pitcher, #7461-BR, 1970-72, from $40 to 45.00
Burred Hobnail, cup, child's, milk glass, 1950-52, from $35 to 45.00
Cactus, basket, milk glass, #3430-MI, 1959-60, 10", from $45 to.... 50.00
Cactus, cactus, milk glass, #3463-MI, 1959-61, from $30 to 32.00
Cactus, creamer & sugar bowl, milk glass, w/lid, 1959-61, from $38 to..47.00
Cactus, vase, topaz opal, ftd, #3460-TO, 1959-60, from $160 to . 180.00
Cased Lilac, vase, #7255-LC, 1955-56, 8½", from $75 to 85.00
Christmas plate, Mission of San Xavier Del Bac, wht satin, 1981.. 12.00
Christmas plate, Old Brick Church, bl satin, 1971, from $12 to 14.00
Coin Dot, basket, bl opal, #203, 1947-55, 7", from $85 to 95.00
Coin Dot, bl opal, tumbler, str sides, #1353, 1948-53, 9-oz, $35 to..40.00
Coin Dot, bowl, Fr opal, dbl crimped, #1523, 1947-49, 13", $85 to. 100.00
Coin Dot, candleholder, cranberry, #1524, 1947-54, ea from $125 to ..150.00
Coin Dot, chandelier, Fr opal, 6-light, from $500 to 600.00

Coin Dot, lamp, cranberry, with glass font, from $350.00 to $400.00. (Photo courtesy Margaret and Kenn Whitmyer)

Coin Dot, lamp, Honey Amber, #1406-HA, 1977-78, 20", from $150 to.175.00
Coin Dot, vase, cranberry, dbl crimped, #1934, 1947-50, 7", $115 to.135.00
Coin Dot, vase, honeysuckle, #1925, 1948-49, 6", from $110 to.. 125.00
Coin Dot, vase, topaz opal, #1442-TO, 1959-60, 10", from $210 to ..225.00
Crystal Crest, bonbon, dbl crimped, oval, #36, 1942, 4½" 30.00
Crystal Crest, compote, dbl crimped, ftd, flared, #206, 1942, 6" 40.00
Daisy & Button, basket, Colonial Amber, oval, #1939-CA, 1965-73..12.00
Daisy & Button, bell, custard, #1966-CU, 1972-80+, from $20 to...22.00

Daisy & Button, boot, bl satin, #1990-BA, 1973-77, from $20 to.. 22.00
Daisy & Button, bootee, bl pastel, #1994-BP, 1954-55, from $30 to .35.00
Daisy & Button, leaf ashtray, Colonial Blue, #1976-CB, 1968-70 . 14.00
Daisy & Button, vase, fan; gr pastel, ftd, #1959-GP, 1954-56, 9" ... 60.00
Diamond Lace, basket, Fr opal w/Aqua Crest, #1948, 1948-50, 12" ..375.00
Diamond Lace, compote, Fr opal w/Aqua Crest, ftd, #1948, 1949-50..85.00
Diamond Optic, barber bottle, #1771-RO, 1957-59, from $185 to.225.00
Diamond Optic, candy jar, Colonial Amber, #1780, 1962-65, from $25 to.35.00
Diamond Optic, creamer, ruby o/l, crystal hdl, #1924, 1942-46 ..... 38.00
Diamond Optic, jug, mulberry, #1353, 1927+, 70-oz, from $500 to . 550.00
Diamond Optic, tumbler, ruby o/l, #1353, 1942-49, 10-oz, from $25 to . 27.00
Diamond Optic, vase, Colonial Amber, threaded, 1977-78, 7", $26 to .28.00
Diamond Optic, vase, Colonial Blue, #1750, 1962-64, 10½" 50.00
Diamond Optic, vase, orange, #1751, 1963-65, 7", from $12 to..... 15.00
Dot Optic, vase, Fr opal, #186, 8", from $55 to............................. 65.00
Dot Optic, vase, Fr opal, crimped, #1354, 10", from $110 to 125.00
Emerald Crest, candleholder, #680, 1949-52, ea from $60 to......... 80.00
Emerald Crest, nut dish, ftd, #680, 1949-56, from $35 to............... 40.00
Fern, cruet, bl satin, #815, 1952-54, from $250 to....................... 300.00
Fern, vase, rose satin, #510, 1952-55, 8", from $100 to 125.00
Flame Crest, tidbit, 2-tier, #7294-FC, 1963, from $125 to 135.00
Gem, atomizer, Fr opal, from $25 to.. 35.00
Gem, atomizer, gr opal, from $35 to 45.00
Georgian, tumbler, gr, #6547-DG, 1953-45, 12-oz, from $7 to..........9.00
Gold Crest, jug, #982, 1943-44, 6", from $45 to 55.00
Gold Crest, vase, dbl crimped, regular, #196, 1943-44, 6", from $25 to.30.00
Goldenrod, vase, #7265-GD, 1956-57, 12", from $275 to 325.00
Grape, bell, bl opal, #9062-BO, 1980, from $35 to....................... 40.00
Grape, bell, topaz opal, #9062-TO, 1980, from $40 to 45.00
Hanging Heart, barber bottle, custard irid, #8960-CI, 1976, $175 to.200.00
Hanging Heart, cruet, turq irid, #8969-TH, 1976, from $175 to.. 195.00
Hanging Heart, pitcher, custard irid, #8964-CI, 1976, 70-oz, $280 to ..300.00
Hanging Heart, tumbler, turq irid, #8940-TH, 1976, 10-oz, from $55 to . 65.00
Historic America, finger bowl, Prairie Schooner, from $30 to........ 35.00
Historic America, goblet, Capitol in Washington, 6", from $45 to..55.00
Historic America, tumbler, Broadway NY, 5½", from $35 to........... 45.00
Hobnail, basket, bl opal, #389, 1941-44, 13½", from $350 to 450.00
Hobnail, basket, bl opal, #3834, 1940-55, 4½", from $40 to 50.00
Hobnail, basket, Wisteria opal, #3834, 1943-44, 4½", from $90 to .. 110.00
Hobnail, bell, milk glass, #3067, 1987-89, 6¾", from $30 to 40.00
Hobnail, bonbon, bl opal, 6-point star shape, #3921, 1953-55, 5" . 35.00
Hobnail, bowl, Fr opal, dbl crimped, #3927, 1940-56, 7", from $20 to ..25.00
Hobnail, bowl, topaz opal, dbl crimped, ftd, #3731, 1959-60, 10". 145.00
Hobnail, butter dish, Colonial Amber, #3977, 1959-60, ¼-lb, $25 to..35.00
Hobnail, candleholder, ruby, #3974, 1973-85, ea from $14 to........ 16.00
Hobnail, candy jar, turq, #3883, 1955-59, 5", from $50 to 60.00
Hobnail, compote, amber, ftd, #3920, 1959, 8", from $30 to 35.00
Hobnail, creamer & sugar bowl, milk glass, #3702, 1970-74, from $25 to . 30.00
Hobnail, epergne, Dusty Rose stretch, #3701, 1989, 4-pc, from $110 to..120.00
Hobnail, fan tray, bl opal, #389, 1941-51, 10½", from $30 to......... 35.00
Hobnail, honey jar, milk glass, #3886, 1953-60, 7¼", from $95 to ..120.00
Hobnail, jam set, bl opal, #3903, 1948-55, jar+lid+ladle+tray..... 120.00
Hobnail, jardiniere, gr, #3996, 1952-53, 6", from $30 to 25.00
Hobnail, pitcher, bl opal, ball jug, #3967, 1941-55, 80-oz, $225 to.275.00
Hobnail, puff box, bl opal, #3885, 1940-54, from $55 to............... 60.00
Hobnail, relish, divided, milk glass, #3740, 1959-60, 12", $225 to..250.00
Hobnail, relish, plum opal, heart shape w/ring hdl, #3733, 1984 . 165.00
Hobnail, sherbet, bl opal, sq, #3826, 1951-54, from $40 to............ 45.00
Hobnail, syrup pitcher, Wild Rose, #3762, 1961-63, 12-oz, from $40 to .. 50.00
Hobnail, water goblet, Fr opal, #3845, 1940-65, 8-oz, from $20 to ..25.00
Horizon, bowl, amber, #8126, 1959, 10½" w/walnut base, from $20 to..25.00
Horizon, candleholder, Jamestown Blue, w/insert, #8177, 1959, 8", ea..22.00
Horizon, vase, amber, #8157, 1959, 8½", from $20 to.................... 22.00
Ivory Crest, candlestick, cornucopia, #951, 1940-42, ea from $40 to. 45.00

Ivory Crest, vase, tulip; triangular, #1923, 1940-42, 7", from $32 to . **37.00**
Ivy, basket, #1924, 1949-52, 5", from $75 to **85.00**
Ivy, vase, #3003, 1950-51, 7", from $120 to **140.00**
Jacqueline, creamer & sugar bowl, Apple Green o/l, 1961-62, $45 to.. **55.00**
Jacqueline, pitcher, honey amber, #9166-HA, 1961-62, 48-oz, $50 to. **60.00**
Jacqueline, vase, bl opal, #9153-BN, 1960-61, 5", from $55 to **65.00**
Jacqueline, vase, tulip; pk opal, #9152-PN, 1960-61, 7", from $85 to . **100.00**
Lacy Edge, banana bowl, milk glass, #9024-MI, 1955-59, from $40 to. **50.00**
Lacy Edge, compote, bl pastel, #9028-BP, 1954-55, from $40 to **50.00**
Lacy Edge, lattice bowl, milk glass, #9031-MI, 1957-60, from $25 to .. **28.00**
Lacy Edge, plate, bl pastel, #360, 1954-55, 8", from $12 to **14.00**
Lacy Edge, plate, bl pastel, #9011-BP, 1954-55, 11", from $20 to... **25.00**
Lacy Edge, plate, rose pastel, #360, 1954-55, 8", from $12 to......... **14.00**
Lacy Edge, plate, rose pastel, #9011-RP, 1954-55, 11", from $20 to . **25.00**
Lacy Edge, shell, turq, #9030-TU, 1955-56, from $12 to................ **15.00**
Lacy Edge/Scroll & Eye, compote, gr pastel, 1955-56, from $35 to... **45.00**
Lamb's Tongue, candy jar, bl pastel, #4381-BP, 1954-55, from $90 to . **110.00**
Lamb's Tongue, creamer & sugar bowl, gr pastel, #4301, 1954-55 . **65.00**
Lamb's Tongue, shakers, rose pastel, #4306-RP, 1954-55, pr from $50 to . **75.00**
Lily of the Valley, basket, Cameo opal, #8437, 1979-80+, from $40 to.. **50.00**
Lily of the Valley, bud vase, Cameo opal, #8458-CO, 1979-80+, $18 to.. **25.00**
Love Bird, vase, custard satin, #8258-CU, 1974-65, from $30 to... **35.00**
Mandarin, vase, blk, #8251-BK, 1968-70, from $110 to.............. **135.00**
Mandarin, vase, orange satin, #8251-OE, 1968, from $120 to **140.00**
Modern Swirl, ashtray, gr, #9175-GN, 1960-63, 5", from $8 to...... **10.00**
New World, bowl, salad; Dusk, #7323-KV, 1953, 12", from $140 to.. **180.00**
New World, wine bottle, Dusk, #7367, 1953, from $175 to **225.00**

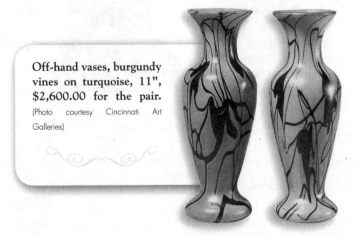

Off-hand vases, burgundy vines on turquoise, 11", $2,600.00 for the pair. (Photo courtesy Cincinnati Art Galleries)

Patriot Red, bell, Patriot's, #8467-PR, 1975-76, from $30 to **35.00**
Patriot Red, stein, Bicentennial, #8446-PR, 1975-76, from $27 to.. **32.00**
Peach Crest, basket, #192, 1942-49, 10½", from $160 to **185.00**
Peach Crest, bowl, 8-point, #1522, 1940-41, 10", from $75 to....... **85.00**
Peach Crest, creamer, #1924, 1943-48, from $42 to **50.00**
Peach Crest, vase, #7459-PC, 1959-62, 9", from $75 to **85.00**
Peach Crest, vase, triangular, #711, 1949-50, 5½", from $35 to **40.00**
Persian Medallion, chalice, custard satin, 1972-74, from $25 to.... **30.00**
Persian Medallion, compote, 1972-80+, from $18 to **22.00**
Plated Amberina, basket, #1637-PA, 1962-64, 7", from $120 to.. **140.00**
Plated Amberina, vase, #1650-PA, 1962-64, 10½", from $150 to . **170.00**
Polka Dot, basket, cranberry, #2237-CR, 1956, 7", from $200 to. **225.00**
Polka Dot, butter/cheese dish, cranberry, #2277-CR, 1955-56, $400 to. **500.00**
Polka Dot, creamer, ruby o/l, #2461-RO, 1956-59, from $25 to..... **35.00**
Polka Dot, shakers, cranberry, #2206-CR, 1955-56, pr from $140 to. **160.00**
Polka Dot, sugar shaker, ruby o/l, #2493-RO, 1956-57, from $100 to . **125.00**
Polka Dot, vase, cranberry, #2259-CR, 1955-56, 8½", from $300 to .. **325.00**
Polka Dot, vase, Jamestown Blue, pinched, #2452-JT, 1959-59, 8".. **75.00**
Polka Dot, vase, ruby o/l, #2453-RO, 1959-60, 10", from $140 to .. **160.00**
Poppy, student lamp, milk glass, #9100-MI, 1975-77, 19", from $230 to.. **250.00**

Poppy, vase, rose satin, #9154-RS, 1974-78, 7", from $40 to......... **50.00**
Priscilla, bowl, bl, cupped, 1950+, 9", from $32 to **37.00**
Priscilla, sugar bowl, crystal, 1950+, from $8 to............................ **10.00**
Priscilla, tumbler, gr, ftd, 1950+, 12-oz, from $30 to..................... **35.00**
Rib Optic, creamer & sugar bowl, cranberry, #1604-CR, 1953-55 .. **225.00**
Rib Optic, cruet, bl satin, #815, 1952-55, from $200 to **250.00**
Rib Optic, cruet, lime opal, #1669-LO, 1953-54, from $200 to ... **230.00**
Rib Optic, ivy ball & base, gr opal, #1622-GO, 1950s, from $100 to.. **150.00**
Rib Optic, shakers, cranberry, #1605-CR, 1953-59, pr from $110 to . **140.00**
Rib Optic, vase, rose satin, #0510, 1952-54, 8", from $90 to........ **110.00**
Rib Optic, vase, rose satin, #1925, 1952-55, 6", from $90 to........ **110.00**
Rib Optic, wine, lime opal, #1647-LO, 1953-54, from $140 to.... **160.00**
Ring Optic, bottle, Stiegel Blue opal, hdld, ca 1939, 6", from $60 to. **75.00**
Ring Optic, candlestick, Fr opal, #1523, ca 1939, ea from $35 to.. **50.00**
Ring Optic, vase, cranberry, #510, ca 1939, 8", from $100 to....... **125.00**
Rose, ashtray, Colonial Amber, #9271-CA, 1966-70, from $4 to...... **5.00**
Rose, ball lamp, Wild Rose o/l, #9207-WR, 1967-69, 22", from $190 to. **210.00**
Rose, basket, Colonial Blue, #9235-CB, 1967-70, 9", from $45 to. **50.00**
Rose, candleholder, Colonial Green, #9270-CG, 1967-69, ea from $5 to. **8.00**
Rose, candy box, Colonial Pink, oval, #9282-CP, 1965-67, $25 to.. **30.00**
Rose, compote, lime sherbet, #9222-LS, 1974-77, from $20 to...... **22.00**
Rose, goblet, milk glass, #9246-MI, 1967-69, 9-oz, from $8 to....... **10.00**
Rose, lamp, milk glass, #9204-MI, 1967-69, 24", from $120 to.... **150.00**
Rose, vase, handkerchief; Colonial Amber, #9254-CA, 1968-70, $10 to.. **12.00**
Rose Crest, bowl, dessert; deep, #680, 1946-48, from $22 to.......... **25.00**
Rose Crest, plate, #680, 12", from $65 to....................................... **75.00**
Silver Crest, ashtray, #7377-SC, 1960-65, from $35 to **45.00**
Silver Crest, bottle, cologne; squat, #192, 1943-49, from $55 to ... **60.00**
Silver Crest, candleholder, squat, #192, 1943-49, ea from $25 to .. **28.00**
Silver Crest, finger bowl, #202, 1943-48, from $16 to **18.00**
Silver Crest, tidbit, 3-tier, 1956-60, from $65 to............................ **75.00**
Silver Crest, vase, #7262, 1956-67, 12", from $100 to **145.00**
Silver Crest, vase, dbl crimped, #711, 1949-72, 6", from $28 to..... **30.00**
Silver Crest/Apple Blossom, bowl, #6423-AB, 1969-71, 9½", $55 to .. **65.00**
Silver Crest/Spanish Lace, basket, #3537-SC, 1968-80, 10", $125 to . **150.00**
Silver Crest/Violets in Snow, basket, #7436-DV, 1968-80+, sm, $65 to . **85.00**
Silver Crest/Violets in Snow, swan, #5161-DV, 1978-80+, from $40 to . **42.00**
Snowcrest, bowl, amber, #1522, 1951-52, 11", from $60 to........... **70.00**
Snowcrest, hurricane lamp, ruby, #3198-RS, 1951-54, from $150 to . **185.00**
Snowcrest, vase, bl, #1925, 1950-51, 5", from $40 to **50.00**
Snowcrest, vase, dk gr, #3005, 1950-53, 7½", from $80 to.............. **85.00**
Spiral Optic, barber bottle, topaz opal, 1939, from $350 to.......... **375.00**
Spiral Optic, basket, cranberry, #1923, 1938+, 6", from $125 to.. **140.00**
Spiral Optic, pitcher, Cameo opal, #3164-CO, 1979-80, 44-oz...... **85.00**

Spiral Optic, pitcher, wisteria opal, #1353, from $700.00 to $800.00. (Photo courtesy Margaret and Kenn Whitmyer)

Spiral Optic, top hat, gr opal, #1924, 1939, 4", from $45 to........... **55.00**
Spiral Optic, top hat, Stiegel Blue, #1924, 1939, 4", from $45 to .. **55.00**
Spiral Optic, vase, #3264-CR, 1956-60, 11½", from $185 to **220.00**
Spiral Optic, vase, bl opal, #3157-BO, 1979-80, 6½", from 20 to .. **30.00**

Spiral Optic, vase, cornucopia; Fr opal, #1523, 1939, from $75 to . 95.00
Spiral Optic, vase, cranberry, crimped, triangular, #187, 1938+, 7"..115.00
Swirl, ashtray, Colonial Amber, #7075-CA, 1977-78, 5½", from $8 to..10.00
Swirl, bowl, bl pastel, #7021-BP, 1954-55, 11", from $55 to...........65.00
Swirl, candleholder, gr pastel, #6073-GP, 1954-56, ea from $40 to...50.00
Swirl, creamer & sugar bowl, milk glass, #7006-MI, 1954-55.........35.00
Swirl, shakers, bl pastel, #7001-RP, 1954-55, pr from $35 to..........40.00
Swirl, vanity set, rose pastel, #7005-RP, 1954-55, 3-pc, from $85 to ... 105.00
Swirl, vase, turq, #7056-TU, 1955-58, 6", from $25 to..................30.00
Swirled Feather, bottle, cologne; bl satin, 1953-55, from $200 to . 250.00
Swirled Feather, candy jar, cranberry satin, 1953-54, from $500 to.600.00
Swirled Feather, fairy lamp, Fr satin, 1953-55, from $175 to........200.00
Swirled Feather, puff box, gr satin, 1953-55, from $185 to...........225.00
Teardrop, bowl, milk glass, #6929-MI, 1957-59, 9", from $20 to.... 25.00
Teardrop, condiment set, Goldenrod, #6909-GD, 1957+, from $200 to......225.00
Teardrop, shakers, milk glass, #6906-MI, 1955-67, pr from $18 to. 20.00
Teardrop, shakers, turq, #6906-TU, 1955-57, pr from $35 to.........40.00
Threaded Diamond Optic, vase, Springtime Green, 1977-78, 7", $27 to.. 32.00
Thumbprint, ashtray, Colonial Amber, #4469-CA, 1957-70, 6½" 8.00
Thumbprint, bud vase, Colonial Green, tall, #4453-CG, 1963-75 ..10.00
Thumbprint, cake plate, Colonial Blue, ftd, #4421-CB, 1964-67 .. 40.00
Thumbprint, candy box, Colonial Amber, oval, #4486-CA, 1963-69...15.00
Thumbprint, cocktail goblet, Colonial Pink, 1962-65, from $12 to.14.00
Thumbprint, relish, Colonial Green, divided, 1966-689, 8½"........ 10.00
Thumbprint, tumbler, Colonial Amber, #442-CA, 1962-70, 12-oz .12.00
Valencia, basket, Colonial Amber, #8338-CA, 1970-73, 8", from $20 to..25.00
Valencia, cigarette lighter, Colonial Blue, #8399-CB, 1969-72 ..... 25.00
Valencia, sherbet, Colonial Green, #8343-CB, 1970-72, from $6 to .8.00
Valencia, tumbler, iced tea; crystal, #8349-CY, 1970-72, from $4 to .5.00
Valencia, vase, swung; Colonial Amber, #8352-CA, 1969-73, lg, $22 to.25.00
Vasa Murrhina, basket, bl mist, #6437-BM, 1964-65, 11", from $110 to .130.00
Vasa Murrhina, creamer, rose mist, #6464-RM, 1964-66, from $40 to.45.00
Vasa Murrhina, vase, Autumn Orange, #6458-AO, 1965-68, 11", $75 to. 85.00
Vasa Murrhina, vase, bl mist, #6459-BM, 1964-65, 14", from $110 to .145.00
Vasa Murrhina, vase, gr aventurine w/bl, #6459-GB, 1964-67, 14".135.00
Violets in Snow/Spanish lace, basket, 1974-80+, 8½", from $125 to .140.00
Waffle, basket, milk glass, #6137-MI, 1960-61, from $40 to........... 45.00
Waffle, candy box, gr opal, #6180-GO, 1960-61, from $75 to........ 85.00
Waffle, vase, bl opal, #6152-BO, 1960-61, 4", from $35 to............. 45.00
Water Lily, basket, bl satin, #8434-BA, 1977-80+, 7", from $45 to..55.00
Water Lily, bowl, crystal velvet, crimped, ftd, 1978-80, from $27 to.30.00
Water Lily, bud vase, bl satin, #8456-BA, 1978-80+, from $25 to . 27.00
Water Lily, bud vase, lav satin, #8456-LN, 1978-79, from $30 to .. 40.00
Water Lily, pitcher, bl satin, #8464-BA, 1976-80, 36-oz, from $40 to..45.00
Wave Crest, candy box, coral, #6080-CL, 1960s, from $95 to 115.00
Wave Crest, candy box, milk glass, #60800-MI, 1956-60, from $40 to..45.00
Wheat Sheaf, vase, bl opaque o/l, #5858-OB, 1962-63, 8", from $50 to. 60.00
Wide Rib Optic, bowl, Fr opal, crimped, #1522, ca 1939, 10", $35 to .45.00
Wild Rose w/Bowknot, pitcher, milk glass, #2865-MI, 1961, 32-oz .50.00
Wild Rose w/Bowknot, vase, Apple Green, #2855, 1961, 5", from $35 to...45.00

Fiesta

Fiesta is a line of dinnerware that was originally produced by the Homer Laughlin China Company of Newell, West Virginia, from 1936 until 1973. It was made in 11 different solid colors with over 50 pieces in the assortment. The pattern was developed by Frederick Rhead, an English Stoke-on-Trent potter who was an important contributor to the art-pottery movement in this country during the early part of the century. The design was carried out through the use of a simple band-of-rings device near the rim. Fiesta Red, a strong red-orange glaze color, was made with depleted uranium oxide. It was more expensive to produce than the other colors and sold at higher prices. During the '50s the color

assortment was gray, rose, chartreuse, and dark green. These colors are relatively harder to find and along with medium green (new in 1959) command the highest prices.

Fiesta Kitchen Kraft was introduced in 1939; it consisted of 17 pieces of kitchenware such as pie plates, refrigerator sets, mixing bowls, and covered jars in four popular Fiesta colors. As a final attempt to adapt production to modern-day techniques and methods, Fiesta was restyled in 1969. Of the original colors, only Fiesta Red remained. This line, called Fiesta Ironstone, was discontinued in 1973.

Two types of marks were used: an ink stamp on machine-jiggered pieces and an indented mark molded into the hollow ware pieces.

In 1986 HLC reintroduced a line of Fiesta dinnerware in five colors: black, white, pink, apricot, and cobalt (darker and denser than the original shade). Since then yellow, turquoise, seafoam green, 'country' blue, lilac, persimmon, sapphire blue, chartreuse, gray, juniper, cinnabar, plum, sunflower yellow, shamrock, tangerine, scarlet, peacock, heather, and the newest color, evergreen, have been added. For more information we recommend *Collector's Encyclopedia of Fiesta, Tenth Edition,* by Sharon and Bob Huxford, and *Post 86 Fiesta* by Richard Racheter, both by Collector Books.

Note: More than ever before, condition is a major price-assessing factor. Unless an item is free from signs of wear, smoothly glazed, and has no distracting manufacturing flaws, it will not bring 'book' price.

Dinnerware

Candleholders, tripod; cobalt, from $550.00 to $700.00 for the pair.

Ashtray, '50s colors, from $55 to 75.00
Ashtray, red, cobalt or ivory, from $45 to....................................... 60.00
Ashtray, yel, lt gr or turq, from $35 to.. 50.00
Bowl, covered onion soup; cobalt or ivory, from $600 to..............675.00
Bowl, covered onion soup; red, from $625 to................................. 700.00
Bowl, covered onion soup; turq, minimum value......................8,000.00
Bowl, covered onion soup; yel or lt gr, from $525 to.....................625.00
Bowl, cream soup; '50s colors, from $60 to..................................... 75.00
Bowl, cream soup; med gr, minimum value..................................4,000.00
Bowl, cream soup; red, cobalt or ivory, from $45 to........................ 60.00
Bowl, cream soup; yel, lt gr or turq, from $30 to.............................. 45.00
Bowl, dessert; 6", '50s colors, from $35 to 45.00
Bowl, dessert; 6", med gr, from $650 to 700.00
Bowl, dessert; 6", red, cobalt or ivory, from $40 to........................ 50.00
Bowl, dessert; 6", yel, lt gr or turq, from $30 to.............................. 45.00
Bowl, fruit; 4¾", '50s colors, from $30 to 35.00
Bowl, fruit; 4¾", med gr, minimum value.....................................550.00
Bowl, fruit; 4¾", red, cobalt or ivory, from $25 to........................ 30.00
Bowl, fruit; 4¾", yel, lt gr or turq, from $20 to.............................. 25.00
Bowl, fruit; 5½", '50s colors, from $35 to 40.00
Bowl, fruit; 5½", med gr, from $65 to 70.00
Bowl, fruit; 5½", red, cobalt or ivory, from $25 to.......................... 30.00
Bowl, fruit; 5½", yel, lt gr or turq, from $20 to.............................. 25.00

Bowl, fruit; 11¾", red, cobalt, ivory or turq, from $250 to............300.00
Bowl, fruit; 11¾", yel or lt gr, from $225 to................................275.00
Bowl, ftd salad; red, cobalt, ivory or turq, from $350 to.............475.00
Bowl, ftd salad; yel or lt gr, from $275 to..................................375.00
Bowl, ind salad; 7½", med gr, from $100 to................................120.00
Bowl, ind salad; 7½", red, turq or yel, from $80 to....................100.00
Bowl, nappy; 8½", '50s colors, from $50 to.................................60.00
Bowl, nappy; 8½", med gr...150.00
Bowl, nappy; 8½", red, cobalt, ivory or turq, from $45 to...............50.00
Bowl, nappy; 8½", yel or lt gr, from $30 to...................................35.00
Bowl, nappy; 9½", red, cobalt, ivory or turq, from $60 to...............70.00
Bowl, nappy; 9½", yel or lt gr, from $55 to...................................60.00
Bowl, Tom & Jerry; ivory w/gold letters, from $250 to.................260.00
Bowl, unlisted salad; red, cobalt, or ivory, minimum value........2,000.00
Bowl, unlisted salad; yel, from $80 to..100.00
Candleholders, bulb; red, cobalt, ivory or turq, pr from $120 to ..130.00
Candleholders, bulb; yel or lt gr, pr from $80 to.........................110.00
Candleholders, tripod; red, ivory or turq, pr from $550 to............700.00
Candleholders, tripod; yel or lt gr, pr from $450 to.....................600.00
Carafe, red, cobalt, ivory or turq, from $275 to..........................300.00
Carafe, yel or lt gr, from $250 to...285.00
Casserole, French; standard colors other than yel....no established value
Casserole, French; yel, from $250 to..300.00
Casserole, w/lid, '50s colors, from $250 to.................................275.00
Casserole, w/lid, med gr, minimum value...............................1,000.00
Casserole, w/lid, red, cobalt or ivory, from $180 to....................200.00
Casserole, w/lid, yel, lt gr or turq, from $150 to........................175.00
Coffeepot, demi; red, cobalt, ivory or turq, from $500 to.............600.00
Coffeepot, demi; yel or lt gr, from $350 to.................................400.00
Coffeepot, regular, '50s colors, from $300 to.............................350.00
Coffeepot, regular, red, cobalt or ivory, from $230 to..................265.00
Coffeepot, regular, yel, lt gr or turq, from $180 to......................220.00
Compote, sweets; red, cobalt, ivory or turq, from $125 to............135.00
Compote, sweets; yel or lt gr, from $95 to..................................110.00
Compote, 12", red, cobalt, ivory or turq, from $180 to................220.00
Compote, 12", yel or lt gr, from $160 to....................................175.00
Creamer, ind; red, minimum value..325.00
Creamer, ind; yel, from $60 to...80.00
Creamer, regular, '50s colors, from $25 to....................................30.00
Creamer, regular, med gr, from $90 to..120.00
Creamer, regular, red, cobalt or ivory, from $25 to........................30.00
Creamer, regular, yel, lt gr or turq, from $20 to............................25.00
Creamer, stick hdld, red, cobalt, ivory or turq, from $55 to...........65.00
Creamer, stick hdld, yel or turq, from $45 to................................60.00
Cup, demitasse; '50s colors, from $325 to...................................400.00
Cup, demitasse; red, cobalt or ivory, from $80 to........................100.00
Cup, demitasse; yel, lt gr or turq, from $70 to...............................80.00
Egg cup, '50s colors, from $140 to..160.00
Egg cup, red, cobalt, or ivory, from $60 to....................................70.00
Egg cup, yel, lt gr or turq, from $55 to..65.00
Lid, for mixing bowl #1-#3, any color, from $600 to....................750.00
Lid, for mixing bowl #4, any color, minimum value.................1,000.00
Marmalade, red, cobalt, ivory or turq, from $365 to....................400.00
Marmalade, yel or lt gr, from $350 to...375.00
Mixing bowl, #1, red, cobalt, ivory or turq, from $275 to............300.00
Mixing bowl, #1, yel or lt gr, from $220 to.................................250.00
Mixing bowl, #2, red, cobalt, ivory or turq, from $125 to............150.00
Mixing bowl, #2, yel or lt gr, from $100 to.................................125.00
Mixing bowl, #3, red, cobalt, ivory or turq, from $125 to............150.00
Mixing bowl, #3, yel or lt gr, from $110 to.................................140.00
Mixing bowl, #4, red, cobalt, ivory or turq, from $150 to............185.00
Mixing bowl, #4, yel or lt gr, from $110 to.................................145.00
Mixing bowl, #5, red, cobalt, ivory or turq, from $190 to............235.00
Mixing bowl, #5, yel or lt gr, from $175 to.................................200.00

Mixing bowl, #6, red, cobalt, ivory or turq, from $260 to............300.00
Mixing bowl, #6, yel or lt gr, from $230 to.................................265.00
Mixing bowl, #7, red, cobalt, ivory or turq, from $400 to............500.00
Mixing bowl, #7, yel or lt gr, from $325 to.................................450.00
Mug, Tom & Jerry; '50s colors, from $80 to..................................90.00
Mug, Tom & Jerry; ivory w/gold letters, from $55 to......................65.00
Mug, Tom & Jerry; red, cobalt or ivory, from $70 to.......................80.00
Mug, Tom & Jerry; yel, lt gr or turq, from $50 to..........................60.00
Mustard, red, cobalt, ivory or turq, from $250 to........................300.00
Mustard, yel or lt gr, from $240 to...275.00
Pitcher, disk juice; gray, minimum value...............................2,000.00
Pitcher, disk juice; Harlequin Yellow, from $65 to.........................75.00

Pitcher, disk juice; red, from $450.00 to $550.00.

Pitcher, disk juice; yel, from $45 to...50.00
Pitcher, disk water; '50s colors, from $200 to.............................275.00
Pitcher, disk water; med gr, minimum value............................1,500.00
Pitcher, disk water; red, cobalt or ivory, from $150 to.................175.00
Pitcher, disk water; yel, lt gr or turq, from $100 to.....................125.00
Pitcher, ice; red, cobalt, ivory or turq, from $130 to...................145.00
Pitcher, ice; yel or lt gr, from $100 to.......................................125.00
Pitcher, jug, 2-pt; '50s colors, from $120 to...............................140.00
Pitcher, jug, 2-pt; red, cobalt or ivory, from $95 to.....................105.00
Pitcher, jug, 2-pt; yel, lt gr or turq, from $70 to...........................80.00
Plate, cake; red, cobalt, ivory or turq...................................1,200.00
Plate, cake; yel or lt gr..1,000.00
Plate, calendar; 1954 or 1955, 10", from $45 to............................55.00
Plate, calendar; 1955, 9", from $45 to..55.00
Plate, chop; 13", '50s colors, from $90 to....................................95.00
Plate, chop; 13", med gr..500.00
Plate, chop; 13", red, cobalt or ivory, from $45 to........................55.00
Plate, chop; 13", yel, lt gr or turq, from $40 to............................50.00
Plate, chop; 15", '50s colors, from $135 to................................150.00
Plate, chop; 15", red, cobalt or ivory, from $90 to......................100.00
Plate, chop; 15", yel, lt gr or turq, from $70 to............................80.00
Plate, compartment; 10½", '50s colors, from $60 to......................70.00
Plate, compartment; 10½", red, cobalt or ivory, from $40 to.........45.00
Plate, compartment; 10½", yel, lt gr or turq, from $35 to.............40.00
Plate, compartment; 12", red, cobalt or ivory, from $55 to...........60.00
Plate, compartment; 12", yel or lt gr, from $40 to........................50.00
Plate, deep; '50s colors, from $50 to..55.00
Plate, deep; med gr, from $130 to..145.00
Plate, deep; red, cobalt or ivory, from $50 to................................60.00
Plate, deep; yel, lt gr or turq, from $35 to....................................40.00
Plate, 6", '50s colors, from $7 to...10.00
Plate, 6", med gr, from $30 to...45.00
Plate, 6", red, cobalt or ivory, from $5 to......................................7.00
Plate, 6", yel, lt gr or turq, from $4 to..6.00
Plate, 7", '50s colors, from $10 to...12.00
Plate, 7", med gr, from $30 to...45.00
Plate, 7", red, cobalt or ivory, from $8 to....................................10.00
Plate, 7", yel, lt gr or turq, from $7 to..9.00

Plate, 9", '50s colors, from $20 to 25.00
Plate, 9", med gr, from $60 to 75.00
Plate, 9", red, cobalt or ivory, from $15 to.......................... 20.00
Plate, 9", yel, lt gr or turq, from $10 to 15.00
Plate, 10", '50s colors, from $45 to 50.00
Plate, 10", med gr, minimum value.................................... 125.00
Plate, 10", red, cobalt or ivory, from $35 to........................ 40.00
Plate, 10", yel, lt gr or turq, from $30 to............................ 40.00
Platter, '50s colors, from $50 to 60.00
Platter, med gr, from $175 to 225.00
Platter, red, cobalt or ivory, from $50 to.............................. 55.00
Platter, yel, lt gr or turq, from $40 to................................... 45.00
Relish tray, gold decor, complete, from $220 to 250.00
Relish tray base, red, cobalt, ivory or turq, from $90 to 100.00
Relish tray base, yel or lt gr, from $80 to.......................... 100.00
Relish tray center insert, red, cobalt, ivory or turq, from $50 to..... 70.00
Relish tray center insert, yel or lt gr, from $50 to................. 60.00
Relish tray side insert, red, cobalt, ivory or turq, from $50 to........ 60.00
Relish tray side insert, yel or lt gr, from $45 to................... 55.00
Sauceboat, '50s colors, from $60 to 75.00
Sauceboat, med gr, from $200 to 225.00
Sauceboat, red, cobalt or ivory, from $60 to......................... 70.00
Sauceboat, yel, lt gr or turq, from $40 to.............................. 45.00
Saucer, demitasse; '50s colors, from $70 to 100.00
Saucer, demitasse; red, cobalt or ivory, from $15 to 20.00
Saucer, demitasse; yel, lt gr or turq, from $15 to 20.00
Saucer, regular, '50s colors, from $3 to 5.00
Saucer, regular, med gr, from $10 to 15.00
Saucer, regular, orig colors, from $2 to 3.00
Shakers, '50s colors, pr from $50 to 60.00
Shakers, med gr, pr from $175 to 225.00
Shakers, red, cobalt or ivory, pr, from $25 to 30.00
Shakers, yel, lt gr or turq, pr from $22 to 25.00
Sugar bowl, ind; turq, from $400 to.................................... 500.00
Sugar bowl, ind; yel, from $125 to...................................... 175.00
Sugar bowl, w/lid, '50s colors, from $70 to 80.00
Sugar bowl, w/lid, med gr, from $225 to............................. 250.00
Sugar bowl, w/lid, red, cobalt or ivory, from $60 to 70.00
Sugar bowl, w/lid, yel, lt gr or turq, from $50 to................... 60.00
Syrup, red, cobalt, ivory or turq, from $400 to 425.00
Syrup, yel or lt gr, from $375 to... 400.00
Teacup, '50s colors, from $35 to 40.00
Teacup, med gr, from $60 to 75.00
Teacup, red, cobalt or ivory, from $25 to.............................. 40.00
Teacup, yel, lt gr or turq, from $15 to 20.00
Teapot, lg; red, cobalt, ivory or turq, from $300 to 350.00
Teapot, lg; yel or lt gr, from $250 to 300.00
Teapot, med; '50s colors, from $250 to............................... 300.00
Teapot, med; med gr, minimum value 1,500.00
Teapot, med; red, cobalt or ivory, from $200 to 250.00
Teapot, med; yel, lt gr or turq, from $150 to 200.00
Tray, figure-8; cobalt, from $90 to...................................... 100.00
Tray, figure-8; turq, from $350 to...................................... 400.00
Tray, figure-8; yel, from $500 to.. 600.00
Tray, utility; red, cobalt, ivory or turq, from $45 to.................. 50.00
Tray, utility; yel or lt gr, from $40 to................................... 45.00
Tumbler, juice; chartreuse, or dk gr, minimum value 750.00
Tumbler, juice; red, cobalt or ivory, from $45 to 50.00
Tumbler, juice; rose, from $55 to 60.00
Tumbler, juice; yel, lt gr or turq, from $40 to 45.00
Tumbler, water; red, cobalt, ivory or turq, from $80 to 90.00
Tumbler, water; yel or lt gr, from $70 to............................... 80.00
Vase, bud; red, cobalt, ivory or turq, from $100 to...................... 125.00
Vase, bud; yel or lt gr, from $75 to.....................................115.00

Vase, 8", red, cobalt, ivory or turq, from $650 to 800.00
Vase, 8", yel or lt gr, from $600 to 700.00
Vase, 10", red, cobalt, ivory or turq, from $800 to 1,100.00
Vase, 10", yel or lt gr, from $800 to 1,000.00
Vase, 12", red, cobalt, ivory or turq, from $1,400 to 1,900.00
Vase, 12", yel or lt gr, from $1,100 to 1,500.00

Kitchen Kraft

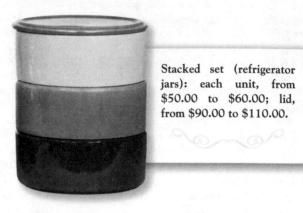

Stacked set (refrigerator jars): each unit, from $50.00 to $60.00; lid, from $90.00 to $110.00.

Bowl, mixing; 6".. 60.00
Bowl, mixing; 8".. 80.00
Bowl, mixing; 10"... 110.00
Cake plate 35.00
Cake server, from $150 to 175.00
Casserole, ind; from $150 to 160.00
Casserole, 7½"... 75.00
Casserole, 8½"... 85.00
Covered jar, lg, from $350 to 375.00
Covered jar, med, from $275 to 300.00
Covered jar, sm, from $300 to 325.00
Covered jug, lg, from $275 to 300.00
Covered jug, sm, from $300 to 320.00
Fork, from $150 to 160.00
Metal frame for platter.. 15.00
Pie plate, spruce gr 150.00
Pie plate, 9".. 40.00
Pie plate, 10".. 40.00
Platter, from $60 to 75.00
Platter, spruce gr.. 150.00
Shakers, pr from $120 to 150.00
Spoon, from $150 to 200.00
Spoon, ivory, 12", from $400 to.. 500.00
Stacking refrigerator lid, ivory, from $200 to 225.00
Stacking refrigerator unit, ivory, from $200 to.................... 210.00

Fifties Modern

Postwar furniture design is marked by organic shapes and lighter woods and forms. New materials from war research such as molded plywood and fiberglass were used extensively. For the first time, design was extended to the masses, and the baby-boomer generation grew up surrounded by modern shape and color, the perfect expression of postwar optimism. The top designers in America worked for Herman Miller and Knoll Furniture Company. These include Charles and Ray Eames, George Nelson, and Eero Saarinen.

Unless noted otherwise, values are given for furnishings in excellent condition; glassware and ceramic items are assumed to be in mint condition. This information was provided to us by Richard Wright. See also Italian Glass.

Key:

alum — aluminum	plwd — plywood
cntl — cantilevered	rswd — rosewood
fbrg — fiberglass	ss — stainless steel
lcq — lacquered	uphl — upholstered
lm — laminated	vnr — neneer

Chest, gentleman's; George Nakashima/Widdicomb, burl veneer panels, branded, 56" tall, $5,700.00. (Photo courtesy David Rago Auctions)

Chair, van der Rohe/Knoll, BRNO, brn leather, 32", 4 for........1,880.00
Chair, van der Rohe/Knoll, BRNO, ss tube fr/leather uphl, 31", 9 for..2,115.00
Chair, van der Rohe/Thonet, chromed ss tubes, MR533, canvas seat/bk..550.00
Chair, Wegner style/Denmark, oak w/curved crest rail/3-dowel bk, 8 for.3,360.00
Chair, Wegner/Denmark, Wishbone, ebonized fr w/rush seat, 28", pr...600.00
Chair, West/Lee, Egg, molded fbrg shell, reuphl, 50x40" 840.00
Chest, Dunbar, mahog, 6-drw w/fitted top drw, 33x42", pr........3,290.00
Chest, Nelson/Miller, blk pnt, 3-drw, bentwood legs, 35x34" ...1,295.00

Clock, George Nelson/Howard Miller, #2203, 15"diameter, $3,500.00.
(Photo courtesy David Rago Auctions)

Clock, table; Miller, sq red Bakelite, brass base w/ball ft, 6x5".....300.00
Coat rack, Glaxo, anodized alum over 15" dia iron base, 68".......420.00
Compote, E Sottass Jr/Bitossi, ceramic, Hollywood series, blk/wht, 7"..660.00
Console, Italian, wht lcq over wood, 3 drw, curved legs, rfn, 72" L ..1,020.00
Desk, Alvar Aalto, molded birch plwd, composite top, 45" L ...1,880.00
Desk, Dunbar, door on left, 3 drws on right, woven privacy panel, 72"..700.00
Desk, Nelson/Miller, Action Office, alum fr, lm top, 3-drw, 50" W..1,020.00
Desk, Quistgaard/Dansk, teak, hinged gallery folds down, 4 drws, 64" L.1,440.00
Desk, Wormley/Drexel, elm, leather top w/2 sliding compartments, 56"..480.00
Dresser, Baughmann/Coggin, blk lcq, 2 banks of 3 drw, brass trim, 64" ..285.00
Globe, Wormley/Dunbar, walnut fr/tripod base, ss supports, 33x22"..2,880.00
Ice bucket, Jacobsen/Stelton, Cylinda, ss cylinder w/hdls, 4x9"... 180.00
Jewelry cabinet, McCobb, bleached mahog, 2 sm over 1 long drw, 8x20".360.00
Jewelry chest, Nelson/Miller, walnut, 2 rows of 3 drw, alum ped, 30" W.4,900.00
Knife sharpener, Nelson/Carvel Hall, blk plastic, made by Briddell. 120.00
Lamp, Dunbar, 4-sided base w/24 1¼" Tiffany tiles, 14x5" sq, EX.15,525.00
Lamp, floor; Hans-Agne Jakobsson, louvered alum cylinder shade, 36".780.00
Lamp, floor; Rispal/France, cord laced through walnut J-form, 2 shades.2,000.00
Lamp, Gambone, geometrics, bl/blk on ivory, 3 pinched sides, 21"..1,560.00
Lamp, Nouguchi style, cylinder shade, conforming chrome/cork base, 58".360.00
Lamp, Ponti (att), leather-wrap brass std w/tripod base, 24", +shade..900.00
Light, ceiling; tube-like hub radiating 6 1-socket spheres, 21" dia...120.00
Magazine stand, Dunbar, walnut, 4-shelf, 24x16x28" 3,525.00
Mirror, molded plastic w/marble finish, 4 rows of bars/Vs, 55x38"...265.00
Nightstand, Nelson/Miller, walnut w/blk legs, door over drw, 25x18" ..500.00
Ottoman, tubular chromed fr w/blk leather uphl, rstr, 14x24x19"...235.00
Plaque, Pidena/Mexico, bl composite w/inset steel & bronze, 32x12" ..660.00
Rocker, Eames/Miller, gray fbrg, wirework base w/wood rockers, 27", VG.1,115.00
Rug, Fields/USA, wool, pk/turq/wine areas/blk lines on gray, 102x96".840.00
Rug, Panton/Mirax, 3 mc sqs on cream, 101x71", VG 1,800.00
Rug, Unica Vaev, Geometri I, 89x89"...2,250.00
Sculpture, Chihuly, gr/bl w/red rim, folded base+w/?-form 2nd pc, 13"W .6,600.00
Sculpture, Messerschmidt, Pipeline #8, clear acrylic tubes, 50".....145.00
Sculpture vase, Pomodoro/Alessi, chromed orb w/cutout, red int, 7".1,200.00
Serving cart, Wegner/Tuck, teak w/11" drop sides, shelf, 29" W ..180.00
Sideboard, Knoll/Knoll, walnut w/4 wht doors, shelves/drws w/in, 75"...2,760.00
Sideboard, Nakashima, walnut, 2 sliding doors, oak int, 32x60x20".12,925.00
Sideboard, Wormley/Dunbar, lt mahog, 2 doors+2 banks of 4 drws over 1..3,600.00
Sideboard, Wormley/Dunbar, 3 drws over 3 sliding burlap doors, 82". 2,820.00
Sofa, H Probber, armless, 1 tufted seat cushion+9 in bk, 11" 1,175.00
Sofa, Hvidt/Molgaard-Nielsen, leather uphl, marble table surface, 112" ..1,680.00
Sofa, Thayer Doggin, walnut fr w/6 legs, 3 uphl bk cushions+seat, 101"..235.00

Armchair, J Risom, walnut w/blk leather webbed seat, 32", pr..1,000.00
Barstool, Buck/OD Mobler A-S, teak w/rswd ftrest, low vinyl bk/seat..720.00
Bedroom set, Drexel, elm w/ebonized wood legs, 3-pc.................660.00
Bench, Badsen & Larsen, teak fr w/reuphl leather seat & bkrest, rfn.1,140.00
Bench, McGuire/San Francisco, rawhide straps on wood fr, 45" L, pr..420.00
Bench, Nelson/Miller, Platform, birch slat top w/open sq blk legs, 72".660.00
Bench, Nelson/Miller, Platform, ebonized slat top/open sq legs, 68" L..540.00
Bench, Wormley/Dunbar, solid sap walnut top, 4 bentwood legs 78" L..1,080.00
Bowl, Prestini, trn mahog, flared str sides, 4x7½" 2,160.00
Cabinet, Knoll/Knoll, walnut w/2 sliding grasscloth doors, rfn, 72" L.1,560.00
Cabinet, Nakashima, walnut free-form 72" L top/sliding doors over drws.1,920.00
Cabinet, Nelson/Miller, Basic, walnut, 2-door (& 1 3-drw), 24x34", pr.600.00
Cabinet, Nelson/Miller, Basic, walnut 5-drw w/ebonized legs, 40x40". 1,020.00
Cabinet, Nelson/Miller, Steelframe, glass over wht lm top & 2 yel drws..960.00
Cabinet, Nelson/Miller, Thin Edge, rswd w/alum legs, doors/drws, 56" L.6,000.00
Cabinet, Nelson/Miller, Thin Edge, rswd 4-drw w/alum legs, 30x34". 3,000.00
Cabinet, Nelson/Miller, Thin-Edge, rswd w/2 doors, alum pulls, 34".2,100.00
Cabinet, Risom/Risom, walnut, 2 doors ea side 2 drws+drop-down, 60"..660.00
Cabinet, Wormley/Dunbar, mahog w/4 burl doors, open shelves, 84x66". 8,400.00
Chair, B Mathsson/K Mathsson, Eva, bentwood w/woven 1-pc seat/bk, 44"..900.00
Chair, Breuer/Thonet, B-11, chromed ss & blk pnt, canvas seat/bk, 35"..1,645.00
Chair, Cherner/Plycraft, wide bentwood arms/padded triangular bk, 31"..650.00
Chair, dining; Nakashima/Knoll, birch, C-bk over 8 dowels, 5 for. 1,680.00
Chair, dining; Robsjohn Gibbings/Widdicomb, maple, 2 arm+4 sides. 1,800.00
Chair, dining; Wormley/Dunbar, mahog w/caned bk, uphl seat, 4 for. 265.00
Chair, Eames/Miller, DKR, wire 1-pc seat/bl, blk Eiffel-Tower base . 300.00
Chair, Eames/Miller, DKW, wireware w/dowel legs, bikini pads, 33"..350.00
Chair, Jacobsen/Hansen, Oxford #3291, alum swivel base, 51".1,410.00
Chair, Jacobsen/Hansen, Series 7, orange lcq, chrome legs, 8 for. 940.00
Chair, lounge; +ottoman, Eames/Miller, #607/671, rswd plwd/leather. 2,640.00
Chair, lounge; Dux #72, continuous bk rail over 7 slats, 22x30x30" ..200.00
Chair, lounge; Wormley/Dunbar, sandalwood, bentwood sides, 31", pr..7,640.00
Chair, lounge; Wormley/Dunbar, uphl mahog, armless, 32" 1,000.00
Chair, Nakashima, C-curve rail, 3 pr spindles, grass seat, 6 for..10,575.00
Chair, Nakashima, Conoid, hickory/walnut, curved crest over 8 spindles.8,800.00
Chair, Nelson/Miller, coconut, pnt ss/chrome legs, 32x41".......3,055.00
Chair, side; Frankel, curved chair rail over wide slat, uphl seat, 29".300.00
Chair, side; Peter Hvidt (att), teak fr w/rush seat & bk, 32", pr ...300.00
Chair, side; Rohde/Miller, birch legs w/uphl seat & bk, 33x25", 4 for. 450.00
Chair, van der Rohe/Knoll, Barcelona, Xd flat metal bar base, 29", pr. 3,820.00

Stool, Barcelona, tufted vinyl on chrome legs w/X-stretcher, 15x18" sq. 375.00
Table, Bellman/Knoll, Popsicle, 24" dia birch plwd top/3 blk legs fold .. 900.00
Table, coffee; Baughman/Coggin, olive burl vnr, apron/legs 1 pc, 48" . 500.00
Table, coffee; Frankl/Johnson, 48x24" cork top, 2 canted 3-panel legs . 1,320.00
Table, coffee; mahog/ebonized hardwood, 3-part top, block base, 56" L. 470.00
Table, coffee; Nakashima, walnut, 40" dia on Xd base, butterfly joints. 8,800.00
Table, coffee; Noguchi, IN-50, birch w/2 connected J-shapes, glass top . 4,800.00
Table, coffee; Noguchi style, 2 birch J-shape supports, glass top, 65" . 450.00
Table, coffee; Rison/Rison Design, walnut w/cutout over magazine rack . 840.00
Table, coffee; Saarien/Knoll, 36" dia walnut top/wht enamel ped base . 780.00
Table, coffee; Wormley/Dunbar, top w/6 Tiffany tiles, 77" L, VG.. 13,225.00
Table, coffee; Wormley/Dunbar, walnut, 5-brd top, loop legs, 84". 1,645.00
Table, coffee/magazine; Brown-Saltman, walnut w/blk/wht lm hinged top. 1,140.00
Table, dining; H Probber, oval rswd top over ebony base, +2 leaves .. 1,000.00
Table, dining; Jalk/Jeppesen, teak w/contrast trim, 5th leg drops down .. 1,140.00
Table, dining; Nakashima, 4 butterflies join exposed free edge, 36" L. 31,725.00
Table, dining; Nelson/Miller, ebonized birch w/2 deep drop leaves, rfn .. 450.00
Table, dining; Nogucki/Knoll, 48" dia birch plwd top/CI & wire base .. 840.00
Table, dining; Rhode/Miller, 72x40" walnut checkerbrd vnr top/blk base. 1,020.00
Table, dining; Robsjohn Gibbings/Widdicomb, 72x40" mahog top/2 Xd legs .. 1,800.00
Table, end; Wormley/Dunbar, mahog/satinwood/glass wedge shapes, pr .. 1,880.00
Table, end; Wormley/Dunbar, top inset w/2 Tiffany tiles, 23x25x21", VG .. 7,475.00
Table, game; Rhode/Miller, Palado, inlaid checkerbrd, 32x32" 900.00
Table, Intrex, Monoform, rnd blk marble top, composite base, 22x22" .. 120.00
Table, occasional; Frankl/Johnson, 18x30" cork top, mahog fr w/shelf . 720.00
Table, occasional; Rhode/Troy Sunshade, 2 step-bk blk lcq tiers/ss fr .. 660.00
Table, occasional; Saarinen, 22" dia wht marble top/wht metal ped, 21" . 265.00
Table, occasional; Wormley/Dunbar, dk mahog fr w/27" dia rswd top .. 1,680.00
Table, occasional; Wormley/Dunbar, limed mahog, Asian legs, 15x15" . 335.00
Table, occasional; Wormley/Dunbar, walnut on mahog fr, shelf, 28x19" . 240.00
Table, side; Nakashima, shaped walnut 3-sided top, dowel legs, 17" .. 3,400.00
Table, side; Wormley/Dunbar, 22" dia stone top/mahog 3-ftd ped, pr . 3,290.00
Table, sq glass 26" top, continuous alum frwork:vertical sides/C ends . 700.00
Table, Wegner/Tuck, teak 40x24" top, Xd legs ea end, brass stretcher .. 960.00
Table, Weinberg, wrought-wirework horse w/glass insert 2,160.00
Table/desk, walnut vnr 59x30" top over 2 open sq-shape legs, G ... 60.00

Tray, Russel Wright, Oceana, 18" long, $850.00. (Photo courtesy David Rago Auctions)

Tray table, Nelson/Miller, molded ash plwd 15" sq, chromed ss base, pr . 1,800.00
Vanity, McCobb/Calvin, Conoisseur, mahog, lift top w/mirror, 28x44" . 58.50
Vase, Conover, Bacel, cvd designs/lines, gray on wine, 14x14" . 3,000.00
Vase, Osolnik, cedar, squat orb w/very sm neck, 3" 390.00
Wall panel, Panton, red plastic, 4 w/1 lg bubble+2 w/4 smaller, set . 600.00
Wall sculpture, brass rods w/cast metal & enamel geometrics, 17x36" .. 440.00
Wall sculpture, handwrought nails radiate around central hub, 37" dia . 150.00

Finch, Kay

Kay Finch and her husband, Braden, operated a small pottery in

Corona Del Mar, California, from 1939 to 1963. The company remained small, employing from 20 to 60 local residents who Kay trained in all but the most requiring tasks, which she herself performed. The company produced animal and bird figurines, most notably dogs, Kay's favorites. Figures of 'Godey' type couples were also made, as were tableware (consisting of breakfast sets) and other artware. Most pieces were marked, but ink stamps often came off during cleaning.

After Kay's husband, Braden, died in 1962, she closed the business. Some of her molds were sold to Freeman-McFarlin of El Monte, California, who soon contracted with Kay for new designs. Though the realism that is so evident in her original works is still strikingly apparent in these later pieces, none of the vibrant pastels or signature curliques are there. Kay Finch died on June 21, 1993.

For further information we recommend *Kay Finch Ceramics, Her Enchanted World* (Schiffer), written by our advisors for this category, Mike Nickel and Cynthia Horvath; they are listed in the Directory under Michigan.

Note: Original model numbers are included in the following descriptions — three-digit numbers indicate pre-1946 models. After 1946 they were assigned four-digit numbers, the first two digits representing the year of initial production. Unless otherwise described, our prices are for figurines decorated in multiple colors, not solid glazes.

Ashtray, Bloodhound (head), #4773, 6½x6½" 65.00
Ashtray, Swan, #4958, 4½" 25.00
Bank, Lion, #5921, 8" 300.00
Brooch, Afghan (head), 2x3" 175.00
Candlesticks, turkey figures, #5794, 3¾", pr 150.00
Covered dish, Swan, #4957, 6" 75.00
Cup, Kitten Face, Toby, 3" 75.00
Cup, Missouri Mule, natural colors, 4¼" 95.00
Egg box, 9x8" 125.00
Figurine, Angel sitting, #4802, 4½" 125.00
Figurine, Bull, #621, 6½" 175.00
Figurine, Chanticleer, rooster, #129, 11" 250.00
Figurine, Cubby & Tubby, playful bears, #3837/#4848, 4¼", pr 225.00
Figurine, Dachshund pup, #5320, 8" 450.00
Figurine, Dickey Bird, Mr & Mrs, #4905a/#4905b, ea 90.00
Figurine, Dog Show Maltese, #5833, 2½" 500.00
Figurine, Donkey standing, Florentine White, #839, 9½" 100.00
Figurine, Godey Man & Lady, #122, 9½", pr.................................... 75.00
Figurine, Guppy, fish, #173, 2½" 75.00
Figurine, Hannibal, angry cat, #180, 10½" 450.00
Figurine, Madonna kneeling, #4900, 6" 75.00
Figurine, Mehitable, playful cat, #181, 8½" 225.00
Figurine, Mermaid, #161, 6½" 175.00
Figurine, Mumbo, sitting elephant, #4840, 4½" 90.00
Figurine, Pajama Girl, #5002, 5½" 225.00
Figurine, Peep & Jeep, ducks, #178a/#178b, pr.............................. 60.00

Figurine, Pekingese, #154, 14" long, $275.00.

Figurine, Pheasant, pk lustre w/gold, #5020, rare, 18" L, pr.......... 600.00
Figurine, Polly Penguin, #467, 4¾" 90.00
Figurine, Sassy, pig looking up, #166, 3¾x4" 50.00
Figurine, Scandi Boy & Girl, #126/#127, 5¼", pr 60.00
Figurine, Tootsie, #189, 3¾" 30.00
Figurine, Yorky Pup, #170 or #171 .... 400.00
Figurine, 3 Wise Men, mottled tan, #5590/#5591/#5592, 10", set of 3 . 150.00
Plaque, Starfish, #5790, 9" 100.00
Plate, Santa face, 6½" 50.00

Salt and pepper shakers, Pup and Puss, 6", $250.00 each. (Photo courtesy Jack Chipman)

Shakers, stallion heads, 5", pr 75.00
String holder, dog w/bow over left ear, wall mt, 4½x4" 300.00
Toby mug, Santa, w/hat lid, 5½" 100.00
Tureen, Turkey, platinum/gray, #5361, 9", w/ladle 200.00
Vase, South Sea Girl, #4912, 8¼" 100.00
Wall pocket, Santa, #5373, 9½" 225.00

Findlay Onyx and Floradine

Findlay, Ohio, was the location of the Dalzell, Gilmore, and Leighton Glass Company, one of at least 16 companies that flourished there between 1886 and 1901. Their most famous ware, Onyx, is very rare. It was produced for only a short time beginning in 1889 due to the heavy losses incurred in the manufacturing process.

Onyx is layered glass, usually found in creamy white with a dainty floral pattern accented with metallic lustre that has been trapped between the two layers. Other colors found on rare occasions include a light amber (with either no lustre or with gilt flowers), light amethyst (or lavender), and rose. Although old tradepaper articles indicate the company originally intended to produce the line in three distinct colors, long-time Onyx collectors report that aside from the white, production was very limited. Other colors of Onyx are very rare, and the few examples that are found tend to support the theory that production of colored Onyx ware remained for the most part in the experimental stage. Even three-layered items have been found (they are extremely rare) decorated with three-color flowers. As a rule of thumb, using white Onyx prices as a basis for evaluation, expect to pay five to ten times more for colored examples.

Floradine is a separate line that was made with the Onyx molds. A single-layer rose satin glassware with white opal flowers, it is usually valued at twice the price of colored Onyx.

Chipping around the rims is very common, and price is determined to a great extent by condition. Unless noted otherwise, our prices are for examples in near-mint condition.

Floradine

Bowl, fluted, squat bulbous base, 4" 750.00
Bowl, low, 5¾"... 1,000.00
Celery vase, fluted cylinder neck, bulbous body, 6½"............. 1,000.00

Creamer, bulbous, 4⅝" 900.00
Mustard pot 1,250.00
Spooner, 4¾" 900.00
Sugar bowl, bulbous, w/lid, 5½" 1,100.00
Sugar shaker 1,500.00

Onyx

Bowl, wht w/raspberry decor, fluted top, 2½x4½" 2,000.00
Bowl, wht w/silver decor, 2¾x8", from $400 to 500.00
Butter dish, wht w/silver decor, 3x6" 1,250.00
Celery vase, wht w/silver decor, 6¾" 485.00

Covered dish, 5½" diameter, $1,000.00.

Creamer, wht w/silver decor, 4½", from $435 to 485.00
Mustard, wht w/raspberry decor, hinged metal lid, 3¼" 2,900.00
Mustard, wht w/silver decor, 3½" 600.00
Pitcher, apricot w/orange decor, 4½" 4,200.00
Pitcher, water; wht w/silver decor, 8" 1,300.00
Shaker, wht w/silver decor, Pat 2/23/1889, 2⅝" 800.00
Spooner, raisin w/wht decor, 4" 2,250.00
Spooner, wht w/orange decor, 4" 1,500.00
Spooner, wht w/silver decor, 4", from $450 to 500.00
Sugar bowl, wht w/silver decor, w/lid, 5½" 650.00
Sugar shaker, wht w/silver decor, brass mts, 5½" 335.00
Sugar shaker, wht w/silver decor, sterling cap, 6¼", from $600 to . 700.00
Syrup, gr (unusual color) w/silver decor................................3,000.00
Syrup, wht w/silver decor, 7¾", from $850 to...................... 950.00
Toothpick holder, wht w/silver decor, rare 1,300.00
Tumbler, wht w/apricot decor, lt line unseen from w/in, bbl 2,300.00
Tumbler, wht w/silver decor, bbl shape, 3½" 250.00
Tumbler, wht w/silver decor, thin str sides (rare), 3¾"...............1,250.00
Vase, wht w/silver decor, 9", VG 800.00

Firefighting Collectibles

Firefighting collectibles have always been a good investment in terms of value appreciation. Many times the market will be temporarily affected by wild price swings caused by the 'supply and demand principle' as related to a small group of aggressive collectors. These collectors will occasionally pay well over market value for a particular item they need or want. Once their desires are satisfied, prices seem to return to their normal range. It has been noticed that during these periods of high prices, many items enter the marketplace that otherwise would remain in collections. This may (it has in the past) cause a price depression (due again to the 'supply and demand principle' of market behavior).

The recent phenomena of Internet buying and selling of firefighting collectibles and antiques has caused wild swings in prices for some fire collectibles. The cause of this is the ability to reach into vast international markets. It appears that this has resulted in a significant escalation in prices paid for select items. The bottom-line items still languish price wise but at least continue to change hands. This marketplace continues to be active, and many outstanding items have appeared recently in the fire antiques and collectibles field. But when all is said and done, the careful purchase of quality, well-documented firefighting items will continue to be an enjoyable hobby and an excellent investment opportunity.

The earliest American fire marks date back to 1752 when 'The Philadelphia Contributionship for the Insurance of Houses From Loss By Fire' (the official name of this company, who is still in business) used a plaque to identify property they insured. Early fire marks were made of cast iron, sheet brass, lead, copper, tin, and zinc. The insignia of the insurance company appeared on each mark, and they would normally reward the volunteer fire department who managed to be the first on the scene to battle the fire. First used in Great Britain about 1780, English examples were more elaborate than U.S. marks, and usually were made of lead. Most copper and brass fire marks are of European origin. By the latter half of the nineteenth century, they became nearly obsolete, though some companies continued to issue them for advertising purposes. Many of these old fire marks are being reproduced today in cast iron and aluminum.

Fire grenades preceded the pressurized metal fire extinguishers used today. They were filled with a mixture of chemicals and water and made of glass thin enough to shatter easily when thrown into the flames. Many varieties of colors and shapes were used. Not all grenades contain salt-brine solution, some, such as the Red Comet, contain carbon tetrachloride, a powerful solvent that is also a health hazard and an environmental threat. (It attacks the ozone layer.) It is best to leave any contents inside the glass balls. The source of grenade prices are mainly auction results; current retail values will fluctuate.

Today there is a large, active group of collectors for fire department antiques (items over 100 years old) and an even larger group seeking related collectibles (those less than 100 years old). Our advisors for this category (except grenades) are H. Thomas and Patricia Laun; they are listed in the Directory under New York. They will be glad to return your phone call as soon as possible. Our fire grenades advisor is Willy Young; he is listed in the Directory under Nevada. In the following listings, values are for items in at least excellent to near-mint condition unless otherwise noted.

Alarm box, Gamewell (NY), CI, #52, w/mechanism/plaque, 17" ...235.00
Alarm box, Gamewell #51, Pat Jan 1 1924 .... 185.00

Alarm box, Gamewell, 1930s, restored, 16", $275.00. (Photo courtesy Morphy Auctions)

Alarm box, Garl Electric Co, orig weight/mechanism/code wheel, 1900s. 350.00
Axe, Plum #6, 35" w/12" head 45.00
Axe, Viking style, early, VG 275.00
Badge, Allentown Fire Department-14-172, steel shield, 2⅛" 60.00
Badge, Brockton Fire Dept #563, silver, mk Sterling 65.00
Badge, Lowell FD, silver w/high eagle helmet/trumpets/etc 65.00

Badge, Philadelphia Centennial Expo, silver-tone, 1876, 2x2½" ... 80.00
Badge, presentation, EX Chief...NY, 10k gold, dbl-sided, 1947.... 100.00
Badge, Whitman FD H&L 1 Foreman, eng 40.00
Badge, 2nd Deputy...Chief, Hartford CT, eagle atop, 10k gold..... 285.00
Bed key 150.00
Bell, apparatus; brass, w/bracket & finial, 10" 500.00
Bell, jumper; solid brass, 7" dia 235.00
Bell, muffin; brass, trn wood w/whalebone separator, 3½" 300.00
Bell, NP, w/clapper, on wrought-iron bracket, 11" 295.00
Belt, parade; leather w/UNION cutouts, red & wht, VG 80.00
Book, American La France Operator's Manual, 1920s 150.00
Boots, American La France, red logo on blk rubber, pull hoops ... 135.00
Bracket, Dietz King lantern, nickel & brass 185.00
Bracket, Dietz Queen lantern (or similar), EX 125.00
Bucket, pnt leather, Balden Fire Club 1822, w/rings, 13" 1,725.00
Bucket, pnt leather, blk w/gold letters: C Goodall No 1, rpr, VG... 425.00
Bucket, pnt leather, First Church...1821 on gr, 12½", VG 575.00
Bucket, pnt leather, No 1/Federal FS/1789/name, missing hdl, 12"..3,750.00
Bucket, pnt leather, No 2 SA Ward 1827 on blk, w/hdl, 10½"... 1,450.00
Bucket, pnt leather gr w/blk RRB lettering, 12x8", VG 435.00
Buckeye Roto Ray, complete & working 950.00
Clip, London Assurance, NY branch, early 35.00
Drawing, chemical horse-drawn wagon, pen & ink, dtd 1935, 10x20" ..150.00
Extinguisher, American La France, apparatus, polished brass, 2½-gal...475.00
Extinguisher, American La France, dry powder, sm 12.00
Extinguisher, Anthes, CCL4, w/bracket 10.00
Extinguisher, brass/copper, child's apparatus type 475.00
Extinguisher, Elkhart emb label, copper & brass, 2½-gal 100.00
Extinguisher, Interstate Dry Powder, chimney type 30.00
Extinguisher, Kontrol, brass, by Stemple 105.00
Extinguisher, Presto, in bucket 25.00
Extinguisher, Presto, polished brass 20.00
Extinguisher, Pyrene, CCL4, pump type 15.00
Extinguisher, Rough Rider, American La France, apparatus type.. 235.00
Extinguisher, Seaco, Seagrave, chrome-plated, apparatus type..... 400.00
Extinguisher, Shur Spray, ceiling mt, empty, 1-gal 40.00
Extinguisher, various manufacturers, copper & brass, 2½", VG 35.00
Extinguisher, Waterloo, Chemical Dry Powder, Reed & Campbell, 20-oz...75.00
Fire alarm key, w/chain & shaped brass fob eng Boston..., 5" 1,060.00

Fire mark, Baltimore Equitable Society, old gold and black paint, dated 1776, ca. 1837, restored corner, 9¾x10½", $875.00.

(Photo courtesy Garth's Auctions Inc.)

Fire mark, FA, CI w/old rpt, oval w/emb hydrant & hose, 1800s, 12"...300.00
Fire mark, FA, CI w/orig patina, oval w/emb hydrant & hose, 1800s, 12" ...600.00
Fire mark, FI Co, CI w/emb fire pump, 1800s, 15" dia 325.00
Fire mark, Fr-style horn/envelope/crown, S Bourlean, CI, 20" dia ...90.00
Fire mark, Globe, CI, globe emb over Globe, rnd, 7½x7¼" 600.00
Fire mark, horseshoe w/eagle atop & eye/chain/clasped hands w/in, CI...100.00
Fire trumpet, SP w/eng floral/hose nozzle/etc/presentation, 20" ... 900.00
Gong, combination indicator; Gamewell, 3-digit display/rvpt panel, 39"..5,290.00
Gong, Edwards Transformer Bell, 2-coil, rpt, 8" dia, 15" 55.00
Gong, Gamewell, 8" brass ball, wooden 21" case 2,200.00

Gong, Gamewell house type, brass, Pat 1866, 10" dia w/5x10" bracket..115.00
Gong, Gamewell Moses Crane style w/brass plaque, 10" brass bell, 24"..2,700.00
Gong, turtle; Louis Bills, brass, CI base, 6" 85.00
Grenade, Carbona, amber glass, 8-sided, w/paper label 65.00
Grenade, Combination Ladder Co, acid, bottle type........................5.00
Grenade, Harden, aqua-gr, quilted, pt..165.00
Grenade, Harden's Star, cobalt, qt...500.00
Grenade, Harden's Star, 3 in wire frs, museum quality repro, 3-qt...115.00
Grenade, Harden's Star (orig), lt bl glass 110.00
Grenade, Harkness, Indigo Blue..550.00

Grenade, Hayward Hand Grenade Fire Extinguisher – New York, medium grass green, original embossed neck foil, 6", $1,000.00.
(Photo courtesy Glass-Works Auctions)

Grenade, Hawyard's Diamond, cobalt (lt), pt 650.00
Grenade, Hayward's, aqua, pleated, ⅔-qt 250.00
Grenade, Hayward's Pleated, clear, 1-pt.......................................250.00
Grenade, Hayward's Pleated, plum amethyst, 1-pt.......................750.00
Grenade, Hayward's...1871, med golden yel amber, 3 on base, 6½"..325.00
Grenade, HSN, dk amber 450.00
Grenade, Letson & Honegger's, aqua 2,500.00
Grenade, PSN, dk amber 750.00
Grenade, Red Comet Safety, hanger type w/metal cover...............35.00
Grenade, Shur Stop, Automatic Fireman on the Wall, glass..........60.00
Helmet, aluminum, high eagle, leather frontispc............................275.00
Helmet, aluminum, low front, metal frontispc: Lieut WFD, w/liner ..125.00
Helmet, brass w/brass front: fire ball/castle, VG...........................125.00
Helmet, leather, high eagle, aluminum frontispc: #1, Cairns, w/liner ...450.00
Helmet, leather, high eagle, frontispc: Chief, sm rpr 450.00
Helmet, leather, high eagle, Phoenix Hose 5 HFD........................825.00
Helmet, leather, red high eagle/pnt shield Hose Co 4 HFD 235.00
Helmet, leather (blk), 6" front/neck strap/stitched/pnt shield, Cairns..180.00
Helmet, leather (wht), 6" front, pnt/transfer shield Chief BFD, Cairns..210.00
Helmet, leather (wht), 8-comb, Chief of Dept, Boston FD finial, Cairns..800.00
Helmet, salesman's sample, red frontispc, Cairns, mini 250.00
Horn, brass, 7" dia bell & silk cord, 15".......................................415.00
Ladder, American La France, wooden, folding attic type 235.00
Lantern, Dewey Mill, blk pnt 75.00
Lantern, Dietz Fire King, loop hdl, missing slide-off cage, 15" 75.00
Lantern, Dietz Fire King, red pnt, tin w/copper tank, 14", G 140.00
Lantern, Dietz King, nickel & brass 220.00
Lantern, Dietz Mill, orig red pnt 65.00
Lantern, Dietz Mill, removable shield..145.00
Lantern, Dietz Queen, brass...950.00
Lantern, Eclipse, complete w/manufacturer's bracket 1,250.00
Lantern, Grether, Dayton OH, electric, hand type.......................145.00
Lantern, steam gauge, brass (like Queen) 935.00
Lantern, wrist; fixed globe etched Volunteer 2, burner, brass cage....1,060.00
Lantern, wrist; SP, eng RAPFD on globe, 13", VG......................650.00
Lithograph, firefighters/steamer/water tower, Buchanan & Lyall, 18x23"..385.00
Nozzle, brass, AJ Morse Boston, lg shutoff hdls, 21½", pr............175.00
Nozzle, brass, shutoff valve mk C Callahan's...1885, 5½" 35.00
Nozzle, brass & copper, flow control by AJ Morse Boston MA, 1917...110.00

Nozzle, brass & copper, play pipe, Boston Coupling Co, VG 70.00
Nozzle, brass w/bl wrap, American La France, 1⅛" str bore tip, 30" ...120.00
Nozzle, combination; Rockwood, aluminum, 1½" 35.00
Nozzle, fog; brass, shutoff, Akron, 9½" 35.00
Nozzle, fog; Elkhart, 1½"...15.00
Nozzle, hand tub; leather-covered pipe, 42"..................................650.00
Nozzle, leather-wrap hdls, Callahan tip, E-45, 1920s, pr 470.00
Nozzle, NP brass, 36½" 200.00
Nozzle holder, metal, lg..65.00
Photo, firefighters in uniform, w/roof-hooks, ladders, etc, 11x17", fr...210.00
Photo, steam fire engine, Boston FD, 7½x9½"+mat 150.00
Play pipe, brass, mk Metacomet Mill, 1880s, 41½" 185.00
Play pipe, Larking, w/leather hdls..145.00
Play pipe, Seagrave, w/leather hdls, 2½" 400.00
Play pipe, steamer; NP brass, 43", pr 385.00
Play pipe, Underwriters, brass w/cord wrapping............................55.00
Print, albumen; Ruins of Great Fire...Boston, JP Soule, 12x39"+fr ..470.00
Register, Gamewell, brass, #1174, ½", batwing winding key, 1902, 9"...180.00
Sector box, Gamewell #4, w/mechanism, CI case w/slant fist motif, 14"...235.00
Siren, Sterling Siren Fire Alarm Co #12, 6-volt, 1920s-30s 55.00
Spanner wrench, 6-function, 4 house fittings/1 hex in center, P1699..60.00
Trumpet, emb florals/high-eagle helmet/etc, 19th C, 18" 1,050.00
Trumpet, eng/etched SP w/repousse Derby-style bell/lion's heads, 25" 1,880.00
Wrench, brass, 7-function, 12¾x3¼" 98.00

Fireglow

Fireglow is a type of art glass that first appears to be an opaque cafe au lait, but glows with rich red 'fire' when held to a strong source of light.

Bottle, atomizer; floral panels, 6" 75.00
Compote, bird/flowers, gold/beaded shaped scalloped rim, 8" 120.00
Lamp base, bird/flowers, slim baluster form, 26"...........................135.00
Pitcher, flowers, wht/brn/bl, melon ribbed, 8" 125.00
Pitcher, morning-glory vine/butterfly, angle hdl, 7" 80.00
Vase, autumn flowers/leaves, earth tones, trumpet top w/bun ft, 18"..310.00
Vase, bird/flowering leafy branch, brn/wht enamel, stick neck, 11"..110.00

Vase, brown and white floral decor, Sandwich, 9", $165.00. (Photo courtesy John A. Shumann III)

Vase, butterfly/flowers, ruffled, stepped rings at shoulder, ftd, 10" .. 90.00
Vase, courting pr reserve on long can neck, stepped bulb body, 12"..85.00
Vase, flowers in bl/yel, elongated body on bun ft, 12", pr 125.00
Vase, flowers on spherical body & cylinder neck, 14", pr 180.00

Fireplace Implements

In the colonial days of our country, fireplaces provided heat in the winter and were used year round to cook food in the kitchen. The implements that were a necessary part of these functions were varied and have become treasured collectibles, many put to new use in modern homes as decorative accessories. Gypsy pots may hold magazines; copper and brass kettles, newly polished and gleaming, contain dried flowers or green plants. Firebacks, highly ornamental iron panels that once reflected heat and protected masonry walls, are now sometimes used as wall decorations. By Victorian times the cook stove had replaced the kitchen fireplace, and many of these early utensils were already obsolete; but as a source of heat and comfort, the fireplace continued to be used for several more decades. See also Wrought Iron.

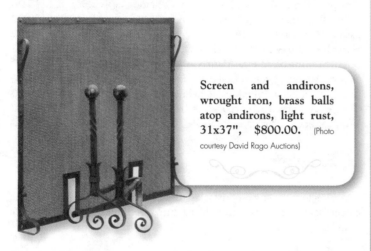

Screen and andirons, wrought iron, brass balls atop andirons, light rust, 31x37", $800.00. (Photo courtesy David Rago Auctions)

Andirons, brass, columnar w/orb finial, 1820s, 15" 500.00
Andirons, brass, faceted top/pierced brass ft, 24" 345.00
Andirons, brass, steeple/ball top/arched spur legs, Boston, 1800s, 18". 265.00
Andirons, brass Baroque style, lobed stem/scroll legs, 1800s, 30" ..2,000.00
Andirons, brass Fed w/dbl-lemon top, 21", VG 375.00
Andirons, CI Gothic-Revival, spire/pinnacle/scroll legs, 16x8" ... 650.00
Andirons, gilt bronze/CI, rtcl urn w/foliate finial, 1900s, 25".... 1,880.00
Fender, brass fr w/scrolled ends, wire work, 6½x41" 315.00
Fender, brass fr w/3 finials, wire work, 1800s, 16x35x14" 765.00
Fender, brass fr w/4 ball finials, 3 ball ft, wire work, 16x32x11" ... 150.00
Fender, brass Louis XVI style, 4 urns/swags, central gallery, 41" L. 500.00
Fender, brass screen w/jewel inlays, acorn finials to railing, 11x40"..1,200.00
Fender, brass w/cast wolf heads, scrolled foliage, 7x60x14" 375.00
Fender, brass w/pierced foliage, stylized paw ft, 8x41".................. 120.00
Fender, brass/iron, molded ribs, ribbed ft, 1800s, 8x45x13" 295.00
Fender, serpentine iron base w/wire body, 3 brass finials, 15x47x14"..800.00
Fire bk, CI, central motif: maid w/hand mirror, foliate surrounds, 32".. 460.00
Mantel, Cerrara marble, bust-cvd keystone/rope twists/etc, 53x23x14"..5,875.00
Screen, mahog Emp w/ormolu mts, inset w/needlepoint, 1800s, 47x29" . 1,880.00
Tongs, brass w/serpents' heads & designs, 6¼x2½x¾"..................... 60.00

Fischer

Ignaz and Emil Fisher were art pottery designers and producers from Hungary. Ignaz Fisher founded a workshop in Budapest, Hungary, in 1866. He had previously worked for M.F. Fisher, owner of the famous Herend factory, also in Hungary. His first products included domestic items that utilized a cream-colored clay; styles were copied from the Herend factory. His ware is recognized by the pale yellow, soft-lead glaze, usually decorated with painted ethnic Hungarian designs.

Emil Fischer took the business over from his father around 1890. The workshop was closed in 1908 and reopened for only a short time. Production from this period was influenced by the high-style designs of the Zsolnay factory in Pecs, Hungary. Unable to compete, they turned to the manufacture of building materials. Marks (incised and painted): Fisher J. Budapest; initials: F.E. under a crown.

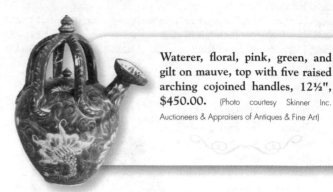

Waterer, floral, pink, green, and gilt on mauve, top with five raised arching cojoined handles, 12½", $450.00. (Photo courtesy Skinner Inc. Auctioneers & Appraisers of Antiques & Fine Art)

Bowl, heavy rtcl, pastels w/bl scrolling devices, #1478, 3x19"...... 450.00
Bowl, scrolling rim w/animal at side, satyr w/dolphins as ft, 20" .. 500.00
Bowl vase, 2 girls/butterflies (3X) on yel, 3 long hdls, rtcl, 6x8" 95.00
Ewer, rtc florals & guilloche, baluster, serpentine spout, 1900s, 20". 650.00
Ewer, rtcl body w/shaped floral reserves, 3-D dragon hdl, rstr, 18". 450.00
Lamp base, cranes/fans reserves on blk w/leafage, gilt mts, 18" 385.00

Fisher, Harrison

Harrison Fisher (1875 – 1934), noted illustrator and creator of the Fisher Girl, was the son of landscape artist, Hugh Antoine Fisher. His career began in his teens in San Francisco where he did artwork for the Hearst papers. Later in New York his drawings of beautiful American women attracted much attention and graced the covers of the most popular magazines of the day such as *Puck, Ladies' Home Journal, Saturday Evening Post,* and *Cosmopolitan.* He also illustrated novels, and his art books are treasured. His drawings appeared on thousands of postcards and posters. His creation of the Fisher Girl and his panel of six scenes of the *Greatest Moments in a Woman's Life* made him the most sought-after and well-paid illustrator of his day.

Book, American Girl, Scribner's Sons, 1909, tall folio (17½"), EX.360.00
Book, Hearts & Masks by MacGrath, Fisher illustrations, 1905, EX.25.00
Book, The Harrison Fisher Book, full-pg drawings, Scribner, NY, '07, G. 85.00
Candy tin, Dancing Girl, ca 1920-30, Tindeco, 10" dia 60.00
Magazine, Ladies' Home Journal, print: A Girl's Number, 1908, EX..130.00
Magazine cover, Cosmopolitan, ca 1920, in fr, pr 60.00
Pencil drawing, woman in big hat w/terrier, '11, 10x10", in pk oval mt..720.00
Postcard, And Yet Her Eyes Can Look Wise, unlisted publisher, NM .. 120.00
Postcard, Good Little Indian (girl), Russian publisher 180.00
Postcard, The Rose, Russian publisher, NM.................................. 240.00
Postcard grouping, Greatest Moments in a Girl's Life, 8x24" fr.... 110.00
Poster, I Summon You to Comradeship, WWI, 10x30", EX 310.00
Print, bookplate; Am Indians, 8x10", in new fr, pr 65.00
Print, bookplate; lot of 4, 8x11½" 35.00
Print, bookplate; lot of 4, 11x14" 110.00
Print, Honeymoon, c Scribner's, 16x12", orig gold pinstripe mat & fr..110.00
Print, lady w/devil, in gold fr 65.00
Print, officer & seated lady, 15½x21½".. 240.00
Print, Proposal, c Scribner's, 16x12", orig gold pinstripe mat & fr...110.00
Print, You Will Marry...Man, sight: 20x16"+mat, glass & fr 120.00
Watercolor, Portrait of a Lady & Her Suitor, sgn/1909, 24x19". 10,800.00
Watercolor & gouache on sketching brd, Dutch Girl, 1909, 14x11" .3,000.00

Fishing Collectibles

Collecting old fishing tackle is becoming more popular every year. Though at first most interest was geared toward old lures and some reels, rods, advertising, and miscellaneous items are quickly gaining ground. Values are given for examples in excellent or better condition and should be used only as a guide. For more information we recommend *Fishing Lure Collectibles: An Encyclopedia of the Early Years, 1840 to 1940*, by Dudley Murphy and Rick Edmisten; *Fishing Lure Collectibles: An Encyclopedia of the Modern Era, 1940 to Present*, by Dudley Murphy and Deanie Murphy; *Captain John's Fishing Tackle Price Guide* by John A. Kolbeck; *Modern Fishing Lure Collectibles, Vol. 1 – 5*, and *Field Guide to Fishing Lures*, by Russell Lewis; *Spring-Loaded Fish Hooks, Traps & Lures* by William Blauser and Timothy Mierzwa; *The Pflueger Heritage* by Wayne Ruby; and *The Fred Arbogast® Story* by Scott Heston. These books are all published by Collector Books. Our advisor for this category is Dave Hoover; he is listed in the Directory under Indiana.

Advertising die-cut for Pflueger Fishing Tackle, Frank Ross art, Enterprise Mfg. Akron, Ohio, 16", NM, $1,350.00. (Photo courtesy Morphy Auctions)

Creel, split willow, single ribs, leather 167.50
Decoy, cvd/pnt wood fish, wooden dorsal fin/2 tin side fins, 12" .. 175.00
Decoy, cvd/pnt wood fish w/cvd gills, tin fins, tack eyes, 12 .... 250.00
Fly Casting Line, Gladding's Saline, early celluloid pack, 4x4", NM+ .. 100.00
Lure, Big Bud #9410, Budweiser can, 1970s, 2¾", from $15 to 20.00
Lure, Cobra #9930, 2 trebles, 1964, 3¾", from $8 to 12.00
Lure, Creek Chub, Castrola #3100, 3 trebles, 1927-41, 3⅝", $85 to .. 100.00
Lure, Creek Chub, Cheekie C-100, 1975-78, 1⅞", from $25 to 40.00
Lure, Creek Chub, Close Pin #5000, 2 trebles, 1936-46, 3½", $400 to. 600.00
Lure, Creek Chub, Flip Flap #4400, 1934-41, 3¼", from $50 to 60.00
Lure, Creek Chub, Plunking Dinger #6200, 1939-53, 4", from $65 to. 75.00
Lure, Creek Chub, Salt Spin Darter #7700, 1955-59, 5¾", $125 to . 150.00
Lure, Creek Chub, Spinning Deepster #9600, 2 trebles, 1953-55, 2⅛" ... 55.00
Lure, Creek Chub, Surf Darter #7600, 2 trebles, 1955-59, 7", $125 to.. 150.00
Lure, Creek Chub, Tarpon Pikie #4000, 2 single hooks, 1933-61 . 275.00
Lure, Creek Chub, Tiny Tim #6400, diving lip, 1941-54, 1¾", $40 to. 50.00
Lure, Creek Chub, Wiggler #100, 2 trebles, 1906-1964, 3½", $50 to ... 60.00
Lure, Dying Quiver #9200, 2 trebles, 1958, 3¾", from $8 to 12.00
Lure, Flaptail Jr #7110, 1 treble, glass eyes, 1937, 3", from $40 to.. 50.00
Lure, Hair Mouse, deerskin & hair, 1938, 2½", from $175 to 225.00
Lure, Heddon, Ace #190, cast brass, 1927-40, 1¾", from $10 to 15.00
Lure, Heddon, Basser #8500, pnt eye, 1922-50, 4", from $35 to 45.00
Lure, Heddon, Commando #2020, spinning tail, 1968, 4¼", from $10 to.. 15.00
Lure, Heddon, Crackleback #8050, gr w/yel crackle, 1970s, 3", $20 to. 25.00
Lure, Heddon, Dowagiac Minnow #150, 5 trebles, 2 spinners, 3⅝" ... 125.00
Lure, Heddon, Drop Zara, dressed drop hook, 1980s, 4¼", from $10 to. 15.00
Lure, Heddon, Early Japanese Color Zara Spooks, 1978, 4¼", $50 to .. 75.00
Lure, Heddon, Experimental Musky Mouse, 2 trebles, '83, 3½", $125 . 175.00
Lure, Heddon, Giant Laptail #7050, 2 trebles, 1937, 6¾", $40 to.. 50.00
Lure, Heddon, Giant Vamp #7550, 3 trebles, 1939, 5⅝", from $40 to. 50.00
Lure, Heddon, Hedd Plug, yel w/blk stripes, 1980s, 4½", from $30 to.. 40.00

Lure, Heddon, King Zig-Wag #8350, jtd body, 1940, 5", from $30 to .. 40.00
Lure, Heddon, Laguna Runt L-10, 2 trebles, 1939, 2⅝", from $40 to... 50.00
Lure, Heddon, Meadow Mouse Spook #9800, 1956, 2⅞", from $10 to.. 15.00
Lure, Heddon, Punkinseed #740, 2 trebles, 1940, 2½", from $70 to.. 80.00
Lure, Heddon, Tiger #1020, 2 trebles, 1960s, 3¼", from $20 to 25.00
Lure, Heddon, Wounded Spook #9140, propellers, 1970s, 3¼", $10 to. 15.00
Lure, Hi-Jacker #9355, 2 trebles, 1980s, 2¾", from $10 to 15.00
Lure, Paw Paw, Aristocrat Shiner #8500, propellers, 1942, 4", $20 to.. 25.00
Lure, Paw Paw, Bass Caster, 2 trebles, 1940, 2¾", from $70 to 80.00
Lure, Paw Paw, Mouse, olive gr, treble, 1935, 2½", from $100 to . 150.00
Lure, Paw Paw, Old Wounded Minnow #2500, propeller, 1940s, 3½" . 25.00
Lure, Paw Paw, Slim Jim Senior, 2 propellers, 3 trebles, 1963, 3¾" .. 15.00
Lure, Paw Paw, Spoon Belly Wobbler, 3 trebles, 1940, 5⅜", $230 to.. 260.00
Lure, Paw Paw, Weedless Wow #75, frog w/rubber legs, 1960, 1¾" . 50.00
Lure, Pflueger, #3195, red striped bk, EX 490.00
Lure, Pflueger, Ballerina Minnow #5400, 1952, 4¼", from $25 to .. 30.00
Lure, Pflueger, Gay Blade, gr & yel, 1 dbl & 1 treble, 1967, 2¾" 5.00
Lure, Pflueger, Tantrum Minnow #8400, 3 trebles, 1952, 4", from $25 to.. 30.00
Lure, Pflueger, The Jerk, bl & yel, 1965, 3⅜", from $10 to 15.00
Lure, Salmon River-Runt #8850, scoop lip, glass eyes, 1939, 5", $80 to .100.00
Lure, Shakespeare, Baby Popper, 2 trebles, 1940, 2⅛", from $35 to .45.00
Lure, Shakespeare, Slim Jim #6552, 2 propellers, 1937, 4¼", $25 to. 35.00
Reel, bait casting; Diawa TDE1Hi, EX.. 80.00
Reel, Julios Vom Hofe, Pat Jan 14, 1902, 4½", VG...................... 100.00
Reel, Plate Wind, brass, 6½x3¼", VG.. 110.00
Reel, spinning; Fin Nor #3, blk die-cast w/gold spool, VG........... 121.00
Reel, trout; Hardy Perfect, gray enamel w/wht agate line, 3⅝", VG. 165.00
Rod, fly; Greenheart, 3-pc w/2 tips, w/reel/line/leader/fly, 9', NM. 150.00
Rod, fly; split bamboo, 3-pc w/2 tips & Chubb tip tube, ca 1930, 9'. 125.00
Rod, fly; Winchester #6086, 9', VG 250.00
Rod, Viscount Gray Perfection, 2-pc w/1 tip, 11½', NM w/bag.... 125.00
Trap, wood slats & woven strings, 6-sided, 1940s, 3x5x5" 38.00

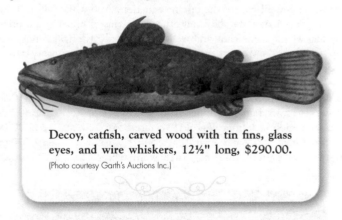

Decoy, catfish, carved wood with tin fins, glass eyes, and wire whiskers, 12½" long, $290.00.
(Photo courtesy Garth's Auctions Inc.)

Flags

Over the past few years the popularity of vintage flags has grown dramatically, and prices have risen greatly as a result. The pending restoration of the Fort McHenry Flag (The Star Spangled Banner) has also created greater public interest in flag collecting.

The brevity and imprecise language of the first Flag Act of 1777 allowed great artistic license for America's early flag makers. This resulted in a rich variety of imaginative star formations which coexisted with more conventional row patterns. In 1912 inviolate design standards were established for the new 48-star flag, but the banners of our earlier history continue to survive:

The 'Great Star' pattern — configured from the combined stars of the union, appeared in various star denominations for about 50 years, then gradually disappeared in the post-Civil War years.

The utilitarian 'scatter' pattern — created through the random placement of stars, is traceable to the formative years of our nation and remained a design influence through most of the nineteenth century.

The 'wreath' pattern — first appearing in the form of simple single-wreath formations, eventually evolved into the elegant double- and triple-wreath medallion patterns of the Centennial period.

Acquisition of specific star denominations is also a primary consideration in the collecting process. Pre-Civil War flags of 33 stars or less are very scarce and are typically treated as 'blue chip' items. Civil War-era flags of 34 and 35 stars also stand among the most sought-after denominations. Market demand for 36-, 37-, and 38-star flags is strong but less broad-based, while interest in the unofficial 39-, 40-, 41-, and 42-star examples is largely confined to flag aficionados. The very rare 43 remains in a class by itself and is guaranteed to attract the attention of the serious collector.

Row-patterned flags of 44, 45, and 46 stars still turn up with some frequency and serve as a source of more modestly priced vintage flags. Ordinary 48-star flags flood the flea markets and are priced accordingly, while the short-lived 49 is regarded as a legitimate collectible. Thirteen-star flags, produced over a period of more than 200 years, surface in many forms and must be assessed on a case-by-case basis.

Many flag buffs favor sizes that are manageable for wall display, while others are attracted to the more monumental proportions. Allowances are typically made for the normal wear and tear — it goes with the territory. But severe fabric deterioration and other forms of excessive physical damage are legitimate points of negotiation.

The dollar value of a flag is by no means based upon age alone. The wide price swings in the listing below have been influenced by a variety of determining factors related to age, scarcity, and aesthetic merit. In fact, almost any special feature that stands out as unusual or distinctive is a potential asset. Imprinted flags and inscribed flags; eight-point stars, gold stars, and added stars; extra stripes, missing stripes, tricolor stripes, and war stripes are all part of the pricing equation. And while political and military flags may rank above all others in terms of prestige and price, any flag with a significant and well-documented historical connection has 'star' potential (pardon the pun). Our advisor for this category is Ryan Cooper; he is listed in the Directory under Massachusetts.

13 stars, hand/machine sewn, Centennial.................................... 850.00
13 stars, str rows, hand/machine sewn, Civil War era, 40x50" .. 1,800.00
15 stars, Union Jack from War of 1812, rare, 35x62"...............23,000.00
16 stars, Great Star, hand sewn, 1850s, 54x78"..........................9,500.00
20 stars, oval pattern, ship's flag, 1818, worn, 64x128".............. 6,500.00

25 stars, oval pattern w/central star, ship's flag, 96x200" 6,700.00
26 stars, Great Star, embr on sewn silk, 30x43" 8,500.00
29 stars, entirely hand sewn, poor condition, 43x68" 4,500.00
31 stars, Great Star, hand-sewn silk, 168" 4,000.00
31 stars, Scatter Star pattern, hand sewn, 45x68"......................4,480.00
33 stars, Great Star, hand-sewn muslin, 60x96"..........................5,000.00
33 stars, in rows, printed bunting, 28x44", G- 1,200.00
34 stars, Great Star, printed cotton, 25x39"...............................3,500.00
34 stars, random pattern, hand sewn, 66x140"...........................1,600.00
35 stars, dbl-wreath pattern, printed, sized muslin, 19x28" 1,500.00
35 stars, row pattern, hand/machine sewn, 96x180"..................1,500.00
36 stars, inscr parade flag, muslin print, 6x9" 350.00
37 stars, medallion pattern, printed/sewn muslin, 48x87" 550.00
37 stars, printed silk, 32x40"..300.00
37 stars, row pattern, stitched bunting, 30x48"............................600.00
38 stars, printed silk w/ribbon ties, 30x47"..................................350.00
38 stars, row pattern, hand/machine-stitched bunting, 71x116".. 450.00
38 stars, unique wreath pattern, sewn, 89x134"........................1,200.00
38 stars, 1776-1876 pattern, printed linen, 27½x46"..................1,800.00
39 stars, row pattern, all machine-stitched bunting, 40x84" 450.00
39 stars (6-5 pattern), printed gauze bunting, 19x34"...................200.00
40 stars, row pattern, hand-sewn bunting, lg, 98x204"................270.00
40 stars, row pattern, printed/sewn British import, 55x106".........250.00
42 stars, sewn cotton, from Ft Hamilton NY, 120x177" 275.00
43 stars, machine-sewn bunting, extremely rare, 29x70"...........1,500.00
44 stars, triple-wreath pattern, printed cotton, 23x26"..................350.00
45 stars, machine-sewn cotton bunting, 80x108"............................55.00
45 stars, row pattern variant, printed muslin, 9x13".......................25.00
46 stars, printed silk, GAR Post in gold, 32x45"............................350.00
48 stars, all crocheted, dtd 1941, 20x38"..85.00
48 stars, printed cotton w/GAR surprint, 11x16" 40.00
48 stars, USN Union Jack, machine-sewn wool, 23x33"..................35.00
48 stars in gold, sewn WWII casket flag, 58x118"...........................95.00
49 stars, 3 uncut flags, printed cotton sheet, 37x36".......................25.00
50 stars, hand-knitted coverlet w/fringe, 30x51" 30.00

Florence Ceramics

Figurines marked 'Florence Ceramics' were produced in the '40s and '50s in Pasadena, California. The quality of the ware and the attention given to detail has prompted a growing interest among today's collectors. The names of these lovely ladies, gents, and figural groups are nearly always incised into their bases. The company name is ink stamped. Examples are evaluated by size, rarity, and intricacy of design. For more information we recommend *Collector's Encyclopedia of California Pottery, Second Edition*, by Jack Chipman; *The Florence Collectibles* by Doug Foland; and *The Complete Book of Florence Ceramics: A Labor of Love* by Sue and Jerry Kline and Margaret Wehrspaun. Our advisor for this category is Jerry Kline; he is listed in the Directory under Tennessee.

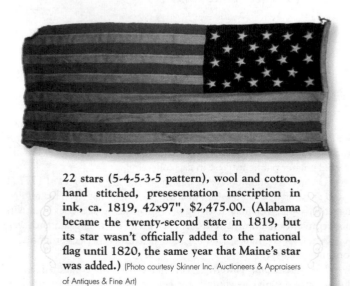

22 stars (5-4-5-3-5 pattern), wool and cotton, hand stitched, presesentation inscription in ink, ca. 1819, 42x97", $2,475.00. (Alabama became the twenty-second state in 1819, but its star wasn't officially added to the national flag until 1820, the same year that Maine's star was added.) (Photo courtesy Skinner Inc. Auctioneers & Appraisers of Antiques & Fine Art)

Vivian, 10", from $350.00 to $400.00.
(Photo courtesy Doug Foland)

Adeline, fancy, 8¼", from $250 to...300.00
Amelia, 8¼", from $200 to..225.00
Anita, brocade, rare, 15", from $3,000 to..............................3,500.00
Ann, pk & wht w/gold trim, 6", from $40 to..............................50.00
Ava, flower holder, 10½", from $200 to......................................225.00
Baby, flower holder, 10½", from $275 to....................................325.00
Beth, 7½", from $125 to...150.00
Bride, rare, 8¾", from $1,800 to..2,000.00
Butch, 5½", from $175 to..200.00
Carmen, rare, 12½", from $,2750 to..3,000.00
Caroline, brocade, rare, 15", from $3,000 to...........................3,500.00
Charles, 8¾", from $225 to..275.00
Cindy, 8", from $425 to..475.00
Claudia, 8¼", from $225 to..275.00
Colleen, hands out, 8", from $275 to...300.00
Darleen, 8¼", from $825 to..900.00
Deborah, rare, 9¼", from $675 to..750.00
Delia, yel, hand showing, 7¼", from $325 to..............................375.00
Don, prom boy, 9½", from $275 to...300.00
Edward, 7", from $300 to..350.00
Emily, flower holder, 8", from $40 to..50.00
Eve, 8½", from $375 to...425.00
Fair Lady, rare, 11½", from $3,250 to......................................3,500.00
Gary, 8½", from $125 to..140.00
Grace, bl, plain, 10", from $175 to...200.00
Halloween Child, 4", from $600 to...700.00
Jennifer, 7¾", from $450 to...500.00
Jim, child, 6¼", from $125 to..150.00
John Alden, 9¼", from $200 to..250.00
Joy, child, 6", from $125 to...150.00
Joyce, 9", from $500 to...600.00
Kathy, wht dress w/pk & bl flowers, flower holder, 7", from $60 to...70.00
Kiu, 11"..250.00
Leading Man, 10½", from $400 to..475.00
Lillian, 7¼", from $125 to...140.00

Lillian Russell, hands out, lace on top of dress, applied flowers along bottom of dress, fine details, 13¼", from $2,000.00 to $2,500.00. (Photo courtesy Doug Foland)

Louise, 7½", from $125 to..140.00
Madonna, 10½", from $350 to..375.00
Margo, rare, 8½", from $650 to..700.00
Mary, seated, 7½", from $500 to..575.00
Masquerade, rare, 8¼", from $800 to...900.00
Master David, rare, 8", from $500 to..550.00
Nita, 8", from $500 to..550.00
Oriental couple, in aqua & wht, 7¾", pr from $125 to.................140.00
Pamela, 7¼", from $350 to...400.00
Pinkie, 12", from $300 to..350.00
Rebecca, aqua dress w/violet trim, 7", from $200 to....................250.00
Sherri, 8½", from $450 to...500.00
Summer, 6¼", from $400 to..450.00

Suzanne, wht dress w/gold trim, matching hat, 9¼", from $550 to..600.00
Vase, wht on pk, scrolling neck band, acanthus band below, 4", $40 to..50.00
Violet, wall pocket, w/gold, 7", from $125 to...............................140.00
Winkin & Blynkin, fancy, 5½", pr, from $400 to..........................450.00
Yvonne, plain, 8¾", from $425 to...500.00

Florentine Cameo

Although the appearance may look much like English cameo, the decoration on this type of glass is not wheel cut or acid etched. Instead a type of heavy paste — usually a frosty white — is applied to the surface to create a look very similar to true cameo. It was produced in France as well as England; it is sometimes marked 'Florentine.'

Vase, flowers and butterflies on Prussian Blue, 9", from $300.00 to $375.00. (Photo courtesy Cincinnati Art Galleries)

Vase, apple blossoms, wht on cranberry, 10", pr...........................250.00
Vase, classical maiden, wht on topaz to peach satin, sq, 11", NM.180.00
Vase, Roman chariot/driver, winged creature, wht on cobalt, ftd, 11".265.00

Flow Blue

Flow Blue ware was produced by many Staffordshire potters; among the most familiar were Meigh, Podmore and Walker, Samuel Alcock, Ridgways, John Wedge Wood (who often signed his work Wedgewood), and Davenport. It was popular from about 1825 through 1860 and again from 1880 until the turn of the century. The name describes the blurred or flowing effect of the cobalt decoration, achieved through the introduction of a chemical vapor into the kiln. The body of the ware is ironstone, and Oriental motifs were favored. Later issues were on a lighter body and often decorated with gilt. For further information we recommend *Gaston's Flow Blue China, the Comprehensive Guide*, by Mary Frank Gaston (Collector Books); she is listed in the Directory under Texas.

Abbey, chocolate pot, Geo Jones, 10"...235.00
Acorn, soup plate, Furnivals Ltd, 10"...60.00
Addison, toureen, w/lid, Rigby & Stevenson, 1910s, 7½x12"......495.00
Agra, bone dish, F Winkle & Co, 3½x6"..75.00
Alaska, creamer, Grindley, 5¼"..150.00
Albert, plate, Dudson Wilcox & Till Ltd, 7"....................................40.00
Albion, soup plate, W&E Corn, 10"...65.00
Aldine, tureen, ftd, w/lid, Grindley, 8x12".....................................375.00
Alma, plate, Wm Alsager Adderley & Co, ca 1900, 9"...............125.00
Amoy, berry bowl, Davenport, 5½"...80.00
Amoy, creamer, Davenport, 6"..300.00
Amoy, pitcher, att Adams, 7"...80.00
Amoy, plate, Davenport, 9¼"..150.00
Amoy, teapot, Davenport, 9½"...1,200.00
Anemone, platter, 23x17"...895.00

Anemone, sauce bowl, ped ft, hdls, Lockhart & Arthur.............. 500.00
Argyle, tray, 6-sided, Ford & Sons, 6¼x9" 225.00
Arundal, salad bowl, Doulton, silver trim 275.00
Ashburton, demitasse cup, ped base, WH Grindley 70.00
Aster, vegetable bowl, Upper Hanley Pottery, 10" 160.00
Astoria, plate, Johnson Bros, 10¼" 90.00
Aurora, vegetable bowl, ftd, w/lid, Morley & Co, 7½x11¼"......... 500.00
Ayr, platter, W&E Corn, 10¼x7½" 235.00
Baltic, plate, Grindley, 10" 90.00
Bay, bowl, Ford & Sons.. 70.00
Beatrice, gravy boat, gold trim, John Maddock; 9" L 100.00
Beauty Roses, plate, Grindley, 9"... 65.00
Bejapore, platter, Geo Phillips, 18x14" 1,200.00
Bejapore, tureen, Geo Phillips, 15x12" 1,400.00
Bentick, platter, Ridgways, 17x14"... 1,000.00
Bentick, tureen, polychromed, w/lid, Cauldon 800.00
Blue Rose, tray, oval, Grindley, 10" 200.00
Bolingbroke, plate, gold trim, Ridgways, 10" 80.00
Bombay, demitasse cup, Furnival.. 70.00
Botanical, toothbrush holder, w/lid, Minton................................. 450.00
Bouquet, cuspidor, Furnivals, 2½x8" 1,000.00
Bouquet, plate, Alcock, 9".. 90.00
Burmese, serving dish, gold trim, Rathbone, 13½x9" 500.00
Buttercup, toothbrush holder, Doulton, 6"................................... 275.00
California, cup, ftd, att Podmore, Walker & Son, 3" 120.00
California, plate, Podmore, Walker & Co, 10" 140.00
Campion, chamber pot, w/lid 450.00
Campion, mustache cup, Grindley, 3½".. 200.00
Campion, waste jar, Grindley 600.00
Canton, demitasse cup, Maddock, 2½" 110.00
Carlton, teapot, John & Geo Alcock, 8½"..................................... 800.00
Cashmere, cup & saucer, Ridgways & Morley, 2¼", 5¾" 140.00
Cashmere, plate, Morley, 9"... 200.00
Cashmere, plate, paneled rim, Morley, 10⅜"................................ 225.00
Cashmere, plate, scalloped, Morley, 10½"................................... 300.00
Cecil, plate, Till & Sons, 9½".. 90.00
Celeste, platter, Alcock, 10x7"... 350.00
Celestial, pitcher, Ridgways, ca 1841, 7" 800.00
Celtic, plate, Grindley, 9" 90.00
Chen-Si, plate, 12-sided, JM Meir, 6⅝" 75.00
Chen-Si, vegetable bowl, att Meir, 8½x6⅛".................................. 250.00
Cherubs, plate, polychromed center, English, 9" 75.00
Chinese, pitcher, Dimmock, 9" 550.00
Chinese Gem, plate, ET Troutbeck, 1844-46, 9½" 75.00
Chinoiserie, bowl, ftd, Ashworth, ca 1870, 13x9" 225.00
Chiswick, plate, scalloped rim, Ridgways, 10" 85.00
Chiswick, vegetable bowl, gold trim, w/lid, Ridgways, 8½" 225.00
Chusan, punch bowl, unmk, 7x12" 1,800.00
Chusan, sugar bowl, w/lid, Clementson, 8" 800.00
Cimerian, soup plate, Maddock, 11" 160.00
Circassia, bowl, ped base, w/lid, Alcock, 8x15" 600.00
Claremont, plate, gold trim, Johnson Bros, 10" 85.00
Claremont, waste bowl, Johnson Bros, 3" 120.00
Clarence, soup bowl, Grindley, 7½" 70.00
Clarendon, platter, plain wht center, Henry Alcock, 18x13½" 450.00
Clayton, soup bowl, plain wht rim & center, Johnson Bros, 7½" ... 60.00
Clematis, vase, ped ft, high hdls, 8"... 450.00
Cleopatra, cake stand, wide ped ft, att E Walley, 2⅝x11¾" 1,000.00
Clifton, pitcher, Grindley, 8½" 450.00
Coburg, cup plate, John Edwards, 4½" 140.00
Coburg, ladle for tureen, gold trim, Barker & Kent, 7"................ 140.00
Coburg, plate, John Edwards, 8" 130.00
Coburg, platter, scalloped edge, gold trim, B&K, 13x10½" 325.00
Coburg, soup tureen, gold trim, 4¾x7½" 275.00
Coburg, underplate for tureen, gold trim, 6x8½" 175.00
Colonial, platter, Meakin, 17½x14" 300.00
Conway, plate, New Wharf Pottery, 9".. 95.00
Coral, soup plate, Johnson Bros, 9" 70.00
Corey Hill, pitcher, polychromed, gold trim, unmk, 11" 375.00
Countryside, teapot, gold trim, HJ Wood...................................... 500.00
Crescent, gravy boat & underplate, Grindley, 4x9" 17,500.00
Crescent, soup plate, gold trim, Grindley.. 85.00
Crescent, tureen, gold trim, w/lid, Grindley, 7x14" 600.00
Crescent, vegetable bowl, gold trim, Grindley, 8x10".................. 175.00
Crumlin, platter, Myott & Son, 12x9" 195.00
Crumlin, soup plate, Myott, Son & Co, 9" 85.00
Dahlia, cup & saucer, w/copper lustre, 2⅞", 5¾" 75.00
Dahlia, platter, canted corners, EC (Challinor), 8¼x10¾" 325.00
Dahlia, sugar bowl, ped ft, hdls, w/lid, att Challinor, 7½" 550.00
Daisy, butter pat, Burgess & Leigh.. 30.00
Delmar, plate, Grindley, 9¾" 100.00
Delph, cup, ped ft, 3" 120.00
Devon, platter, Meakin, 14x10" 275.00
Devon Floral & Swags, platter, Meakin, ca 1895, 17½x13" 295.00
Doreen, soap dish, w/lid, Grindley 300.00
Doreen, washbowl & pitcher set, hexagonal, Grindley 1,600.00
Douglas, vegetable bowl, w/lid, Ford & Sons, 8x11".................... 350.00
Dresden, platter, Johnson Bros, 6x12"... 200.00
Duchess, washbowl, Wood & Son, 17¼"....................................... 750.00
Eagle, platter, canted corners, Podmore Walker & Co, 10½x13½" .450.00
Eileen, soup plate, Grindley, 10" 80.00
Elsie, creamer, New Warf Pottery 95.00
Fallow Deer, serving dish, sq w/curved corners, w/lid, Wedgwood...375.00
Ferrara, pitcher, Wedgwood, 6" 325.00
Ferrara, tea bowl, Wedgwood, 3" 165.00
Fisherman, pitcher, att Podmore Walker, 5½".............................. 250.00
Flanders, creamer, ca 1900, 3¼" 160.00
Flanders, platter, Grimwades, ca 1890, 15½x12" 225.00
Floral, vegetable bowl, oblong, w/lid, T Hughes & Son 300.00
Floral & Scroll, waste bowl, ftd, Germany mk, 3¼x6⅛"................. 75.00
Fulton, plate, Johnson Bros, 10" 90.00
Garland, chamber pot, Adams & Co, 5¼x9"................................. 400.00
Genevese, plate, Johnson Bros, 9¼" 150.00
Geranium, plate, Podmore, Walker & Co, 9½" 140.00
Gironde, berry bowl, Grindley, 12½".. 395.00
Gladiolus, pitcher, cylindrical, Doulton, 9".................................... 700.00
Hague, serving tray, tab hdls, Wedgwood, 8x17½"....................... 500.00
Harvard, plate, Alfred Meakin, 10" 90.00
Hizen, plate, GL Ashworth, 10½" 100.00
Hong Kong, waste bowl, Meigh.. 450.00
Indian, cup plate, Pratt, 4⅛" 70.00
Indian, pitcher, 11", EX 350.00
Indian (deer), plate, ca 1880, 10" 95.00
Indian Jar, platter, Furnival, 13½x10½".. 200.00

Irene, plate, gold trim, Wedgwood & Co., 10", $65.00.

Iris, cheese dish, w/lid, Doulton, 9½x9" 600.00
Iris, soup bowl, Staffordshire, 8" 78.00
Ivy, pitcher, gold trim, unmk, 8" 500.00
Japan, teapot, ped ft, T Fell 900.00
LaBelle, bowl, oval, Wheeling Pottery, 3¼x11¼x9¼" 300.00
Lakewood, tureen, w/lid & ladle, Wood 750.00
Manilla, teapot, Podmore Walker, 9½x9" 900.00

Nankin, teapot, un-marked, attributed to Cauldon, from $800.00 to $1,000.00. (Photo courtesy Mary Frank Gaston)

Non Pareil, platter, Burgess & Leigh, 17¾" L 600.00
Normandy, cup & saucer, Johnson Bros 120.00
Onion, plate, Allertons, 8" 85.00
Oregon, vegetable bowl, sq, w/lid, Mayer, 8½x11", EX 575.00
Orleans, platter, unmk, 16x14" 500.00
Peach, platter, Johnson Bros, 17x14" 400.00
Persian, plate, Johnson Bros, 10" 90.00
Peruvian, plate, John Wedge Wood, 10½" 175.00
Richmond, berry dish, Johnson Bros, 5½" 25.00
Richmond, platter, Ford & Sons, ca 1900, 12x9" 250.00
Rock, plate, Challinor, 8½" 110.00
Rose, jardiniere, Myott Son & Co, 7x10" 650.00
Roseville, biscuit jar, John Maddock, 8" 280.00
Scinde, coffeepot, 8-sided, scroll hdl, Alcock, EX 1,000.00
Scinde, plate, Alcock, 10¼" 150.00
Scinde, soup bowl, Alcock, 9½" 125.00
Seville, platter, Wood & Son, 12½x9" 400.00
Shanghae, relish, 1-hdl, Furnival 250.00
Swallow, plate, gold rim, Grove & Stark, 10" 85.00
Temple, washbowl, Podmore Walker, 5x14¾" 400.00
Thistle, bowl vase, gold trim/sponging 275.00
Togo, plate, Winkle & Co, 9" 140.00
Tonquin, bone dish, Alcock, 6" 85.00
Touraine, pitcher, milk; sm 450.00
Trent, plate, New Wharf Pottery, 10" 80.00
Turkey, plate, Cauldon, 10" 150.00
Tyne, saucer, Bridgwood & Son, 5½" ....: 25.00
Venice, plate, Upper Hanley Pottery, 10" 80.00
Vernon, platter, Ridgways, 12½x9½" 375.00
Vintage, jug, relief molded, ca 1840, 7" 295.00
Wagon Wheel, creamer, w/copper lustre, unmk, 3¼x4¼" 125.00
Wagon Wheel, mug, 3" 125.00
Waverly, gravy boat, Grindley, 7" 135.00
Willow, washbowl & pitcher, Doulton, set 2,000.00
Yeddo, soup bowl, Arthur J Wilkinson, 7½" 95.00
York, plate, Couldon England, 9" 75.00

Flue Covers

When spring housecleaning started and the heating stove was taken down for the warm weather season, the unsightly hole where the stovepipe joined the chimney was hidden with an attractive flue cover. They were made with a colorful litho print behind glass with a chain for hanging. In a 1929 catalog, they were advertised at 16¢ each or six for 80¢. Although scarce today, some scenes were actually reverse painted on the glass itself. The most popular motifs were florals, children, animals, and lovely ladies. Occasionally flue covers were made in sets of three — one served a functional purpose, while the others were added to provide a more attractive wall arrangement. They range in size from 7" to 14", but 9" is the average.

Baby Lambs, 7½", from $85.00 to $95.00. (Photo courtesy Jim Meckley II)

Boy (sm) stands w/finger in his mouth, red hat, w/chain, 9½" 135.00
Boys (2) w/dachshund dogs, 1920s, 6¼" 35.00
Children (2 girls & 1 boy) playing among flowers, Germany, 9½" . 95.00
Collie dog portrait, facing left, w/chain, Germany, 9½" 160.00
Courting couple in landscape, 9½" 95.00
Girl in floral hat & coat, much finery, blond curls, 8" 125.00
Girl in gr hat, curly brn hair, holds flowers, 7½" 185.00
Girl in red w/dk hair holds cat, dog beside, Germany, 9⅝" 195.00
Girl w/puppies & dog, Germany, 9⅝" 225.00
Girl w/red flowers in dk hair, red dress, Germany, 7½" 125.00
Girls (1 in pk, 2nd in red) dancing, orig chain, 9½" 165.00
Lady in oversz hat, flowers on hat & at bosom, Germany, 9½" 75.00
Lady in purple gazes at 3 cherub/children (1 w/wings), 9½" 85.00
Lady sitting on wall by flower garden, advertising, 7x5" 60.00
Lady w/dk hair, scarf loosely draped around her, 14¼" 185.00
Naval officer & lady w/ship scene beyond, w/chain, 7⅞" 100.00
Renoir-like cherub in thoughtful pose, 7" 100.00
Roses, cream to pk, crimped fr, metal chain, 7¼x8½" 135.00
Winter scene w/farmhouse, figure in snow, Germany, 6½x9" 95.00

Folk Art

That the creative energies of the mind ever spark innovations in functional utilitarian channels as well as toward playful frivolity is well documented in the study of American folk art. While the average early settler rarely had free time to pursue art for its own sake, his creativity exemplified itself in fashioning useful objects carved or otherwise ornamented beyond the scope of pure practicality. After the advent of the Industrial Revolution, the pace of everyday living became more leisurely, and country folk found they had extra time. Not accustomed to sitting idle, many turned to carving, painting, or weaving. Whirligigs, imaginative toys for the children, and whimsies of all types resulted. Though often rather crude, this type of early art represents a segment of our heritage and as such has become valued by collectors.

Values given for drawings, paintings, and theorems are 'in frame' unless noted otherwise. See also Baskets; Decoys; Frakturs; Samplers; Trade Signs; Weather Vanes; Wood Carvings.

Articulated dancers, 2 men on wide springboard, wood w/mc pnt, 16x16" ... 600.00
Biplane model, wood/tin/found parts, worn pnt, 20x25"+metal stand ... 285.00

Calligraphic drawing, eagle and rattlesnake, pennants stream from eagle's mouth lettered: Three things bear mighty sway with man, the sword, the scepter, and the pen; 20x26", in modern frame, $1,265.00. (Photo courtesy James D. Julia)

Diorama, farmhouse & winter trees, horse-drawn carriage, 12x22x22"..350.00
Diorama, log cabin scene w/outhouse/split log fence/trees, 20x27"..175.00
Diorama, 4 figures tipping outhouse, cvd wood w/mc pnt, 16x26"..400.00
Footstool, uphl carpet top, deer-horn ft, 1900s, 13" H..................125.00
House, wood w/mc pnt, pierced porch rails, rooms inside, 21x20x18".2,400.00
Lawn ornament, collie seated, mc pnt, 2-sided, 1930s-40s, 21"......85.00
Oil on board, irises & leaves on gray, detailed, 20x14"+1" fr.........95.00
Paper cutout, hearts/flowers/birds/unicorn, late, well done, 14x19"+fr..315.00
Stone cvg, half-fig, pnt, 1800s, minor chps, 6" dia....................1,645.00
Theorem on board, flower basket on creamy wht, alligatored 19x24" fr.400.00
Theorem on cloth, floral arrangement watercolor, good fr, 8x11".135.00
Theorem on paper, basket of fruit/flowers, 1800s, 10x14", VG.....350.00
Theorem on paper, fruit & butterfly watercolor, 17x13"+old fr....435.00
Theorem on paper, fruit spilling from basket on table, NY, 23x27"+fr.3,100.00
Theorem on velvet, bowl of fruit, stenciled, EX color, gilt fr, 16x19"..550.00
Theorem on velvet, fruit nested in vines, mc on tan, freehand, 12x14".460.00
Watercolor on paper, lady in parlor w/dog at ft, naive style, 13x11"...1,265.00
Watercolor on paper, lady in wht bonnet/blk dress, reeded 5x4" fr..700.00
Watercolor on paper, man in frock coat, naive style, 10x8¼"+gilt fr..1,000.00
Watercolor on velvet, lady w/book & canary, castle beyond, 12x16"+fr.3,450.00
Whirligig, duck, cvd pnt pine/cut-out sheet-iron wings, 1900, 26x37".650.00
Whirligig, gardener hoeing, nearby shrubs, cvd/pnt wood, 21x19"..585.00
Whirligig, man & lady w/rolling pin, tin/wood, worn pnt, 38"+base..375.00
Whirligig, man milking cow, pnt wood, late, 14x16", EX..............75.00
Whirligig, man plays fiddle/sits on bbl, wood, mc pnt, 1940s, 17x36".265.00
Whirligig, man swinging ax while 2nd uses bucksaw, wood w/mc pnt, 23".110.00
Whirligig, policeman in uniform, wood, red/wht/bl revolving arms, 24".800.00
Whirligig, soldier w/rotating paddle arms, cvd/pnt pine, 1890s, 33".30,550.00

Fostoria

The Fostoria Glass Company was built in 1887 at Fostoria, Ohio, but by 1891 it had moved to Moundsville, West Virginia. During the next two decades, they produced many lines of pressed patterned tableware and lamps. Their most famous pattern, American, was introduced in 1915 and was produced continuously until 1986 in well over 200 different pieces. From 1920 to 1925, top artists designed tablewares in colored glass — canary (vaseline), amber, blue, orchid, green, and ebony — in pressed patterns as well as etched designs. By the late '30s, Fostoria was recognized as the largest producer of handmade glassware in the world. The company ceased operations in Moundsville in 1986.

Many items from both the American and Coin Glass lines have been reproduced by Lancaster Colony. In some cases the new glass is superior in quality to the old. Since the 1950s, Indiana Glass has produced a pattern called 'Whitehall' that looks very much like Fostoria's American, though with slight variations. Because Indiana's is not handmade glass, the lines of the 'cube' pattern and the edges of the items are sharp and untapered in comparison to the fire-polished originals. Three-footed pieces lack the 'toe' and instead have a peg-like foot, and the rays on the bottoms of the American examples are narrower than on the Whitehall counterparts. The Home Interiors Company offers several pieces of American look-alikes which were not even produced in the United States. Be sure of your dealer and study the books suggested below to become more familiar with the original line.

Coin Glass reproductions flood the market. Among items you may encounter are an 8" round bowl, 9" oval bowl, 8¼" wedding bowl, 4½" candlesticks, urn with lid, 6¼" candy jar with lid, footed comport, sugar and creamer; there could possibly be others. Colors in production are crystal, green, blue, and red. The red color is very good, but the blue is not the original color, nor is the emerald green. Buyer beware! For further information see *Elegant Glassware of the Depression Era* by Gene and Cathy Florence, and *The Fostoria Value Guide*, by Milbra Long and Emily Seate. See also Glass Animals and Figurines.

Alexis, crystal, butter dish 75.00
Alexis, crystal, creme de menthe, 2½-oz 15.00
Alexis, crystal, finger bowl, flat edge 15.00
Alexis, crystal, horseradish jar, w/spoon.......................... 60.00
Alexis, crystal, nappy, 4½" 12.50
Alexis, crystal, nut bowl 15.00
Alexis, crystal, pitcher, ice; 64-oz 85.00
Alexis, crystal, pitcher, 32-oz 75.00
Alexis, crystal, spooner 30.00
Alexis, crystal, toothpick holder 30.00
Alexis, crystal, tray, pickle 22.50
Alexis, crystal, tumbler, water 15.00
Alexis, crystal, tumbler, whiskey 15.00
Alexis, crystal, vase, ftd, 9" 65.00
Alexis, crystal, water bottle 85.00
American, crystal, ashtray, oval, 3⅞" 9.00
American, crystal, ashtray, sq, 2⅞" 7.50
American, crystal, bell..495.00
American, crystal, bottle, cologne; w/stopper, 6-oz, 5¾" 72.50
American, crystal, bowl, sq, hdl, 4½" 11.00

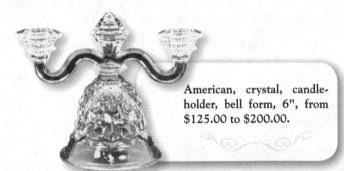

American, crystal, candleholder, bell form, 6", from $125.00 to $200.00.

American, crystal, creamer, 9½-oz.................................... 12.50
American, crystal, cup, flat...7.50
American, crystal, hat, 3" 27.50
American, crystal, ice bucket, w/tongs.............................. 60.00
American, crystal, marmalade, w/lid & chrome spoon 50.00
American, crystal, picture frame 15.00
American, crystal, pitcher, flat, 1-qt................................. 30.00
American, crystal, plate, salad; 7" 10.00
American, crystal, plate, sandwich; sm center, 9" 14.00
American, crystal, plate, torte; 18" 135.00
American, crystal, platter, oval, 12" 55.00
American, crystal, spooner, 3¾" 35.00
American, crystal, sugar shaker 65.00

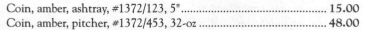

American, crystal, toothpick holder................................ 20.00
American, crystal, tray, rectangular, 5x2½"................... 80.00
American, crystal, tray, rnd, 12"................................... 150.00
American, crystal, tumbler, juice; #2056, ftd, 5-oz, 4¾" 12.00
American, crystal, tumbler, tea; #2056½, str sides, 12-oz, 5" 18.00
American, crystal, urn, sq, ped ft, 6".......................... 30.00
American, crystal, vase, bud; flared, 6"....................... 18.00
American, crystal, vase, flared, 10"............................. 90.00
Baroque, bl, ashtray... 22.00
Baroque, bl, bowl, fruit; 5"... 38.00
Baroque, bl, compote, 6½"... 55.00
Baroque, bl, plate, 8½"... 22.50
Baroque, bl, rose bowl, 3¾"...................................... 110.00
Baroque, bl, tray, oval, 12½"..................................... 85.00
Baroque, crystal, bowl, salad; 10½"............................ 35.00
Baroque, crystal, bowl, vegetable; oval, 9½"................ 40.00
Baroque, crystal, ice bucket....................................... 60.00
Baroque, crystal, platter, oval, 12".............................. 40.00
Baroque, crystal, tumbler, cocktail; ftd, 3½-oz, 3"........ 12.00
Baroque, crystal, vase, 7".. 60.00
Baroque, yel, bowl, 3 ftd, 7"...................................... 25.00
Baroque, yel, candlestick, 4", ea................................. 35.00
Baroque, yel, creamer, ftd, 3¾"................................. 20.00
Baroque, yel, pitcher, 6½".. 450.00
Baroque, yel, saucer..6.00
Baroque, yel, tidbit, 3-toe, flat.................................. 30.00
Brocade, Grape, bl, candy box, #2331, 3-part............. 185.00
Brocade, Grape, bl, compote, #2327, twist stem, 7"..... 75.00
Brocade, Grape, gr, compote, #2362, stack disk stem, ftd, 11" 100.00
Brocade, Grape, gr, sugar pail, #2378.......................... 40.00
Brocade, Oakleaf, crystal, bowl, #2375, hdls, 10"........ 80.00
Brocade, Oakleaf, crystal, mayonnaise, #2315 .... 55.00
Brocade, Oakleaf, crystal, vase, #4105, scalloped rim, 6"........ 65.00
Brocade, Oakleaf, crystal, whipped cream pail, #2378.......... 90.00
Brocade, Oakleaf, ebony, bowl, #2395, scroll hdl, 10" 145.00
Brocade, Oakleaf, ebony, vase, #4103, bulbous, 3" or 4".......... 75.00
Brocade, Oakleaf, gr or rose, bowl, centerpc; #2375½, oval 135.00
Brocade, Oakleaf, gr or rose, ice bucket, #2378 .... 145.00
Brocade, Oakleaf, gr or rose, plate, #2283, 7".............. 25.00
Brocade, Oakleaf, gr or rose, urn, #2413, w/lid 200.00
Brocade, Oakwood, orchid or azure, bowl, centerpc; #2375, 11".. 195.00
Brocade, Oakwood, orchid or azure, cocktail, #877, 3½-oz 65.00
Brocade, Oakwood, orchid or azure, mayonnaise, #2315 .... 35.00
Brocade, Oakwood, orchid or azure, tumbler, #877, ftd, 9-oz 85.00
Brocade, Palm Leaf, rose or gr, candlestick, #2375, 3", ea 75.00
Brocade, Palm Leaf, rose or gr, plate, #2419, sq, 8"...... 35.00
Brocade, Palm Leaf, rose or gr, tray, #2342, octagonal, center hdl. 140.00
Brocade, Paradise, gr or orchid, tumbler, tea; #877, ftd, 12-oz........ 65.00
Brocade, Paradise, gr or orchid, vase, #4100, 8"........... 95.00
Brocade, Paradise, gr or orchid, vase, #4103, optic, 5" or 6"........... 75.00

Coin, amber, ashtray, #1372/123, 5"........................... 15.00
Coin, amber, pitcher, #1372/453, 32-oz....................... 48.00

Coin, blue, ashtray, #1372/124, 10", $50.00. (Photo courtesy Gene and Cathy Florence)

Coin, bl, creamer, #1372/680 .... 16.00
Coin, bl, cruet, #1372/531, 7-oz................................ 165.00
Coin, crystal, shakers, #1372/652, 3¼", pr 25.00
Coin, crystal, tumbler, juice; #1372/81, 9-oz................ 22.00
Coin, gr, candleholders, #1372/316, 4½", pr 50.00
Coin, ruby, bowl, #1372/179, 8"................................ 45.00
Coin, ruby, candleholders, #1372/326, 8", pr 100.00
Colony, crystal, ashtray, sq, 3½"................................ 16.00
Colony, crystal, bowl, cream soup; 5"......................... 55.00
Colony, crystal, candlestick, 7", ea............................. 37.50
Colony, crystal, ice bucket.. 90.00
Colony, crystal, pitcher, milk; 16-oz........................... 58.00
Colony, crystal, plate, dinner; 9"............................... 25.00
Colony, crystal, sugar bowl, 3½".................................9.00
Colony, crystal, vase, bud; flared, 6".......................... 15.00
Fairfax #2375, amber, ashtray, 2½"...............................6.00
Fairfax #2375, amber, bottle, salad dressing 75.00
Fairfax #2375, amber, celery, 11½".............................. 15.00
Fairfax #2375, amber, ice bucket................................ 50.00
Fairfax #2375, amber, shakers, ftd, pr 30.00
Fairfax #2375, gr or topaz, bowl, cereal; 6"................. 15.00
Fairfax #2375, gr or topaz, butter dish 100.00
Fairfax #2375, gr or topaz, claret, 4-oz, 6"................. 33.00
Fairfax #2375, gr or topaz, vase, 8"........................... 60.00
Fairfax #2375, rose, bl or orchid, baker, oval, 9".......... 45.00
Fairfax #2375, rose, bl or orchid, creamer, tea.............. 25.00
Fairfax #2375, rose, bl or orchid, plate, salad; 7½"....... 10.00
Fairfax #2375, rose, bl or orchid, relish, 11½".............. 22.00
Fairfax #2375, rose, bl or orchid, tumbler, ftd, 9-oz, 5¼" 22.00
Fuchsia, crystal, bonbon, #2470................................. 33.00
Fuchsia, crystal, bowl, #2470, 12".............................. 90.00
Fuchsia, crystal, candlestick, #2470, 5½", ea................ 55.00
Fuchsia, crystal, cordial, #6004, ¾-oz......................... 65.00
Fuchsia, crystal, oyster cocktail, #6004, 4½-oz............. 14.00
Fuchsia, crystal, parfait, #6004, 6"............................. 30.00
Fuchsia, crystal, plate, luncheon; #2440, 8"................. 20.00
Fuchsia, crystal, sugar bowl, #2440, ftd 20.00
Fuchsia, crystal, sweetmeat, #2470............................. 30.00
Fuchsia, crystal, tumbler, #6004, ftd, 9-oz.................. 16.00
Fuchsia, Wisteria, compote, #2470, tall, 6".................. 125.00
Fuchsia, Wisteria, tumbler, #7004, ftd, 12-opz.............. 65.00
Fuchsia, Wisteria, wine, #6004, 2½-oz......................... 50.00
Glacier, crystal, ice bucket.. 65.00
Glacier, crystal, tray, sq, 10"..................................... 55.00
Hermitage, amber, gr or topaz, bowl, cereal; #2449½, 6" 10.00
Hermitage, amber, gr or topaz, compote, #2449, 6" 17.50
Hermitage, amber, gr or topaz, plate, sandwich; #2449, 12" 12.50
Hermitage, amber, gr or topaz, vase, ftd, 6"................. 30.00
Hermitage, azure, bowl, soup; #2449½, 7"................... 22.00
Hermitage, azure, decanter, #2449, w/stopper, 28-oz 165.00
Hermitage, azure, ice tub, #2449, 6".......................... 60.00

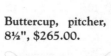

Buttercup, pitcher, 8½", $265.00.

Hermitage, crystal, cup, #2449, ftd....6.00
Hermitage, crystal, finger bowl, #2449½, 4½"....4.00
Hermitage, crystal, mug, #2449, ftd, 9-oz....15.00
Hermitage, wisteria, bowl, #2449, ftd, 10"....100.00
Hermitage, wisteria, shakers, #2449, 3⅜", pr....90.00
Hermitage, wisteria, tumbler, cocktail; #2449, ftd, 4-oz, 3"....18.00
June, crystal, bowl, bouillon; #2375, ftd....18.00
June, crystal, compote, #2400, 5"....30.00
June, crystal, decanter....425.00
June, rose or bl, ashtray....55.00
June, rose or bl, cup, demitasse....100.00
June, rose or bl, plate, canape....55.00
June, topaz, platter, 15"....125.00
June, topaz, tray, center hdl, 11"....40.00
June, topaz, whipped cream pail....160.00
Kashmir, bl, bowl, fruit; 5"....25.00
Kashmir, bl, cup, #2350½....20.00

Kashmir, blue, sandwich server, $40.00. (Photo courtesy Gene and Cathy Florence)

Kashmir, bl, vase, 8"....185.00
Kashmir, yel or gr, bowl, soup; 7"....26.00
Kashmir, yel or gr, pitcher, ftd....335.00
Kashmir, yel or gr, plate, salad; 8"....8.00
Lafayette, burgundy, relish, 3-part, 7½"....45.00
Lafayette, burgundy, tray, oval, hdls, 8½"....45.00
Lafayette, crystal or amber, bowl, cream soup....22.50
Lafayette, Empire Green, mayonnaise, 2-part, 6½"....55.00
Lafayette, Empire Green, tray, lemon; hdls, 5"....33.00
Lafayette, Regal Blue, bonbon, hdls, 5"....35.00
Lafayette, Regal Blue, plate, torte; 13"....115.00
Lafayette, rose, gr or topaz, creamer, ftd, 4½"....22.00
Lafayette, rose, gr or topaz, sugar bowl, ftd, 3⅝"....22.00
Lafayette, wisteria, bowl, cereal; 6"....45.00
Narcissus, crystal, bowl, floral; #1519, ftd, 11"....50.00
Narcissus, crystal, claret, #3408, 4½-oz....32.00
Narcissus, crystal, plate, #1519, 7"....12.00
Narcissus, crystal, vase, #1519, rnd, ftd, 7"....85.00
Navarre, crystal, bonbon, #2496, ftd, 7⅜"....26.00
Navarre, crystal, bowl, #2496, ftd, hdl, 5"....20.00
Navarre, crystal, compote, #2496, 4¾"....37.50
Navarre, crystal, cordial, #6016, 1-oz, 3⅞"....50.00
Navarre, crystal, cup, #2440....20.00
Navarre, crystal, ice bucket, #2496, 4⅜"....110.00
Navarre, crystal, plate, cake; #2440, oval, 10½"....60.00
Navarre, crystal, plate, luncheon; #2440, 8½"....18.00
Navarre, crystal, shakers, #2375, ftd, 3½", pr....110.00
Navarre, crystal, tumbler, #6106, 10-oz, 5⅜"....23.00
Navarre, crystal, tumbler, juice; #6106, ftd, 5-oz, 4⅝"....22.00
Navarre, crystal, vase, #2470, ftd, 10"....185.00
Navarre, crystal, vase, #4128, 5"....135.00
New Garland, amber or topaz, bonbon, hdls....15.00
New Garland, amber or topaz, bowl, fruit; 5"....10.00
New Garland, amber or topaz, celery, 11"....22.00
New Garland, amber or topaz, goblet, #6002....22.00
New Garland, amber or topaz, pitcher, ftd....225.00
New Garland, amber or topaz, tumbler, #6002, ftd, 13-oz....15.00
New Garland, rose, cup, demitasse; #2419....22.00
New Garland, rose, finger bowl, #4121....15.00
New Garland, rose, oyster cocktail, #6002....20.00
New Garland, rose, platter, 15"....80.00
New Garland, rose, vase, 8"....95.00
Pioneer, azure or orchid, ashtray, lg, deep....20.00
Pioneer, azure or orchid, compote, 8"....40.00
Pioneer, bl, bowl, salad; 10"....40.00
Pioneer, bl, plate, 9"....20.00
Pioneer, bl, sugar bowl, flat....15.00
Pioneer, crystal, amber or gr, bowl, cereal; 6"....12.00
Pioneer, crystal, amber or gr, creamer, flat....9.00
Pioneer, crystal, amber or gr, platter, 12"....25.00
Pioneer, crystal, amber or gr, sugar bowl, #2350½, ftd....9.00
Pioneer, ebony, ashtray, 3¾"....15.00
Pioneer, ebony, cup, #2350½, ftd....12.50
Pioneer, ebony, plate, salad; 7"....9.00
Pioneer, ebony, saucer....4.00
Pioneer, rose or topaz, creamer, #2350½, ftd....12.00
Pioneer, rose or topaz, egg cup....25.00
Pioneer, rose or topaz, relish, rnd, 3-part....15.00
Priscilla, amber or gr, plate, 8"....8.00
Priscilla, amber or gr, tumbler, ftd....12.00
Priscilla, bl, ashtray, sq, 3"....12.50
Priscilla, bl, creamer....15.00
Rogene, crystal, cocktail, #5082, 3-oz....16.00
Rogene, crystal, jug, #318, 7"....150.00
Rogene, crystal, plate, 5"....6.00
Rogene, crystal, vase, rolled edge, 8½"....100.00

Romance, bowl, #2594, 13½", $55.00.

Royal, amber or gr, bowl, almond; #4095....30.00
Royal, amber or gr, bowl, fruit; #2350, 5½"....15.00
Royal, amber or gr, butter dish, #2350....295.00
Royal, amber or gr, creamer, flat....18.00
Royal, amber or gr, egg cup, #2350....28.00
Royal, amber or gr, nappy, #2350, 8"....30.00
Royal, amber or gr, parfait, #869, 5½-oz....30.00
Royal, amber or gr, pitcher, #1236....350.00
Royal, amber or gr, pitcher, #5000, 48-oz....295.00
Royal, amber or gr, plate, dinner; #2350, 10½"....28.00
Royal, amber or gr, plate, luncheon; #2350, 8½"....8.00
Royal, amber or gr, shakers, #5100, pr....65.00
Royal, amber or gr, tumbler, #5000, ftd, 2½-oz....30.00
Royal, amber or gr, vase, #2292, flared....110.00
Seville, amber, bowl, #2315, low ft, 7"....18.00
Seville, amber, egg cup, #2350....25.00
Seville, amber, pickle, #2350, 8"....13.50
Seville, amber, plate, chop; #2350, 13¾"....30.00

Seville, amber, shakers, #5100, pr.................................. 50.00
Seville, gr, bowl, vegetable; #2350 .... 27.50
Seville, gr, oyster cocktail, #870 .... 15.00
Seville, gr, pitcher, #5084, ftd.................................. 295.00
Seville, gr, sugar bowl, #2350½, ftd 13.50
Seville, gr, vase, #2292, 8" 95.00
Sun Ray, crystal, bowl, flared, 9½" 30.00
Sun Ray, crystal, decanter, w/stopper, 18-oz 70.00
Sun Ray, crystal, plate, sandwich; 12" 32.00
Sun Ray, crystal, salt dip 12.50
Sun Ray, crystal, tray, sq, 10" 40.00
Sun Ray, crystal, vase, 7" 50.00
Trojan, rose, celery, #2375, 11½" 48.00
Trojan, topaz, creamer, tea; #2375½ 50.00

Trojan, topaz, ice bucket, #2374, $90.00. (Photo courtesy Gene and Cathy Florence)

Trojan, topaz, vase, #4105, 8" 195.00
Versailles, bl, cup, demitasse; #2375 .... 75.00
Versailles, bl, plate, canape; #2375, 6" 30.00
Versailles, bl, whipped cream pail, #2378.................. 250.00
Versailles, gr, ashtray, #2350 .... 25.00
Versailles, gr, bowl, #2394, ftd, 12" 80.00
Versailles, gr, compote, #5098, 3" 35.00
Versailles, pk or yel, bowl, bouillon; #2375, ftd............ 25.00
Versailles, pk or yel, sugar bowl, #2375½, ftd 20.00
Versailles, pk or yel, vase, #2417, 8" 235.00
Woodland, crystal, bottle, salad dressing; #2083, w/stopper 85.00
Woodland, crystal, decanter, #300, 32-oz.................... 75.00
Woodland, crystal, finger bowl, #766, 4½" 12.00
Woodland, crystal, plate, sherbet; #840, 5" 5.00
Woodland, crystal, tumbler, tea; #889, 14-oz, 5½" 14.00
Woodland, crystal, water, 9-oz.................................... 15.00

Fostoria Glass Specialty Company

The Fostoria Glass Specialty Company was founded in Fostoria, Ohio, in 1899. In 1910 they were purchased by General Electric. The new owners had an interest in developing a high-quality lustre-type art glass able to compete with the very successful glassware produced by Tiffany. They hired Walter Hicks, who had previously worked for Tiffany, to help develop the line they called Iris. Their efforts were extremely successful. The art glass they developed was cased and iridescent, very similar to Steuben's Aurene. Colors included green, tan, white, blue, yellow, and rose. It was made in several patterns, including Heart and Leaf, Leaf and Tendrils, Heart and Spider Webbing, and Lustred Dot. Although the main thrust of their production was lamp shades, vases and bowls were made as well. Iris was made for only four years, since gold was required in its production and manufacturing costs were very high. It was marked with only a paper label, without which identification is sometimes difficult. Look for a pronounced, well-finished pontil that shows the glass layers represented. Most items show a layer of white which Fostoria called Calcite, as did Steuben. Very little has been written on the history of this company, but for more information refer to *The Col-*

lector's Encyclopedia of Art Glass by John Shuman III (Collector Books) and *Fostoria Ohio Glass, Vol. II,* by Melvin L. Murray (self published).

Our advisor for this category is Frank W. Ford; he is listed in the Directory under Massachusetts.

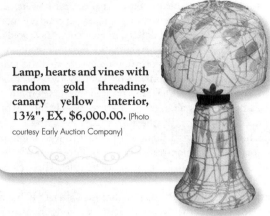

Lamp, hearts and vines with random gold threading, canary yellow interior, 13½", EX, $6,000.00. (Photo courtesy Early Auction Company)

Frackelton, Susan

Born in Milwaukee, Wisconsin, in 1848, Susan worked at her her family's pottery import business where as a young adult she began experimenting with china painting, potting, and glazing, and gradually became well known for her efforts in creating a unique type of art pottery, most of which was salt-glazed stoneware with underglaze blue designs taken from nature. More often than not, these pieces combined dimensional applications in combination with the hand painting. Some of her pieces were painted on the inside as well. She was awarded a gold medal at the 1893 Columbian Exposition for her stoneware creations and was greatly admired by her contemporaries.

Though salt-glazed stoneware had for many decades been a mainstay of Wisconsin pottery production, Susan was recognized as the first to apply these principals to the manufacture of art pottery.

In addition to her artistic accomplishments, Susan also developed a gas-fired kiln specifically for use in the home.

She retired and moved to Chicago in 1904, where she died in 1932.

Key: stw — stoneware

Bowl, salt-glazed stoneware, clusters of applied blue grapes and vines, interior painted: Love Is the Sweet Wine of Life, MNCWL 1902, signed, 6½x14", $18,000.00. (Photo courtesy David Rago Auctions)

Bowl, stw w/appl indigo poppies/HP butterfly, 2¼x4¾", EX 1,800.00
Jar, stw w/appl indigo wreath on cvd floral, SF/1898, w/lid, 5x5", EX . 7,800.00
Punch bowl, stw w/lg clusters of appl bl grapes, motto, '02, 14" 18,000.00
Vase, stw w/appl roses over indigo leaf band, 3½x6", EX 4,500.00
Vase, stw w/cvd/appl roses & stems, indigo on cream, 6x4½" .. 25,000.00
Vase, stw w/HP indigo roses/stylized crosses, #108, 3¾", EX 2,520.00
Vase, stw w/salt glaze, indigo oak leaves, 8x4 " 10,800.00

Frakturs

Fraktur is a German style of black letter text type. To collectors the fraktur is a type of hand-lettered document used by the people of German descent who settled in the areas of Pennsylvania, New Jersey, Maryland, Virginia, North and South Carolina, Ohio, Kentucky, and Ontario. These documents recorded births and baptisms and were used as bookplates and as certificates of honor. They were elaborately decorated with colorful folk-art borders of hearts, birds, angels, and flowers. Examples by recognized artists and those with an unusual decorative motif bring prices well into the thousands of dollars; in fact, some have sold at major auction houses well in excess of $100,000.00. Frakturs made in the late 1700s after the invention of the printing press provided the writer with a prepared text that he needed only to fill in at his own discretion. The next step in the evolution of machine-printed frakturs combined woodblock-printed decorations along with the text which the 'artist' sometimes enhanced with color. By the mid-1800s, even the coloring was done by machine. The vorschrift was a handwritten example prepared by a fraktur teacher to demonstrate his skill in lettering and decorating. These are often considered to be the finest of frakturs. Those dated before 1820 are most valuable.

The practice of fraktur art began to diminish after 1830 but hung on even to the early years of the twentieth century among the Pennsylvania Germans ingrained with such customs. Our advisor for this category is Frederick S. Weiser; he is listed in the Directory under Pennsylvania. (Mr. Weiser has provided our text, but being unable to physically examine the frakturs listed below cannot vouch for their authenticity, age, or condition. When requesting information, please include a self-addressed stamped evelope.) These prices were realized at various reputable auction galleries in the East and Midwest and should be regarded as minimum values. Buyers should be aware that there are many fakes on the market, a real problem for beginning collectors. Know your dealer. Unless otherwise noted, values are for examples in excellent condition. Note: Be careful not to confuse frakturs with prints, calligraphy, English-language marriage certificates, Lord's Prayers, etc.

Key:
lp — laid paper   wc — watercolored
pr — printed   wp — wove paper
p/i — pen and ink

Birth Records

Watercolor on laid paper in yellow, red, and green ink: records the birth of a daughter in 1801, Northampton Co., Pennsylvania, good color, 13x16", in frame with old red and black paint, $3,565.00. (Photo courtesy Garth's Auctions Inc.)

P/i/lp, arches/vines/flowers/parrots/whirlwind, NY, 1821, 15x18"+fr... 2,350.00
P/i/wc, lg/sm hearts, birds/tulips, Berks Co PA, 1807, 13x16", G . 445.00
P/i/wc, 2 hearts/12 stippled lambs by fence/tulips, 1834, 13x16", EX .1,060.00
P/i/wc/lp, angels/hearts, PA, 1812, in 15x18" grpt fr.................... 700.00
P/i/wc/lp, birds/flowers/text, PA, 10x9⅜"+grpt fr 1,265.00
P/i/wc/lp, heart/tulips, att Brechall, 1793, 14x17" 865.00
P/i/wc/lp, hearts/flowers/German text, PA, 1850s, 12x17"+folky fr ..2,185.00
P/i/wc/lp, ladies under arch w/urns, att H Young, PA/1850, 16x14"+fr. 6,000.00
P/i/wc/lp, pin-prick roosters/flowers, att J Rhule, 1826, 10x9"...... 460.00
P/i/wc/lp, ships/buildings/eagle/banners, sm rstr, 16x13"+fr........2,415.00
P/i/wc/lp, tulips/flowers/dmns/German text, 12x17"+grpt fr......1,600.00

Miscellaneous

Bookplate, p/i/wc, roses/carnation/text, 1834, 8½x6½"+fr 115.00
Bookplate, p/i/wc/lp, German text/florals/stripes, 7¼x6¼"+fr 115.00
Bookplate, p/i/wc/lp, sgn/1817, 4¾x5" curly maple fr 430.00
P/i/wc, birds/flowers, 10", 10x9½" rpt grpt fr 1,265.00
P/mc ink, Christmas Present for...Parents, sgn/1831, 17x15" 575.00
Vorschrift, p/i/wc/lp, panels w/verse, symbols/tree, sgn/1820, 8x12" .2,300.00

Frames

Styles in picture frames have changed with the fashion of the day, but those that especially interest today's collectors are the deep shadow boxes made of fine woods such as walnut or cherry, those with Art Nouveau influence, and the oak frames decorated with molded gesso and gilt from the Victorian era. The last few years have seen the middle- to late-Victorian molded composition-on-wood frames finally being recognized as individual works of art. While once regulated to to the trash heap, they are now being rescued and appreciated.

As is true in general in the antiques and collectibles fields, the influence of online trading is greatly affecting prices. Many items once considered difficult to locate are now readily available on the Internet; as a result, values have declined. Our advisor for this category is Michael Hinton; he is listed in the Directory under Pennsylvania.

Note: Unless another date is given, frames described in the following listings are from the nineteenth century.

Alligator hide covered, easel bk, 6⅜x5¾x1¼" 465.00
Beadwork birds & flowers, scalloped top, easel bk, 7½", EX 175.00
Brass, oval, convex glass, 14x20".. 70.00
Brushed aluminum, beveled glass, 14x12½" 65.00
Cast brass, Cupid design, 20x12"... 250.00

Cast iron, double, white and pastel paint, Judd Co. #9120, $225.00. (Photo courtesy Morphy Auctions)

CI, eagle at top/flag/anchor/etc, mc pnt, Judd #9447, WWI era, 13x9"..150.00

CI, emb floral w/rtcl, mc pnt, Judd #8003, 6x4¼" 150.00
Gesso w/corn cob & scrolled leaf design, 6" W, 37x47" 600.00
Gesso w/flower sprays, sgn Samuel Little, 6" W, 30x36" 300.00
Gesso w/leaves & flowers, red velvet liner, 7" W, 23x31" 300.00
Gilt bronze, Louis XVI style, floral crest/geometric borders, 15x11".1,500.00
Giltwood, Italian rococo, projecting rtcl foliage/shell, 15x9" 300.00
Giltwood, ornate corners w/floral/shell, Pat 1870, 40x35" 1,410.00
Tabernacle style, gilt crown & capitals, bl frieze columns, 22x17" ..330.00
Walnut crisscross, cvd leaves at corners, Vict, 22x28" 175.00
Walnut/burl/gilt Renaissance, stepped/reeded outer fr, 70x56" 850.00

Frances Ware

Frances Ware, produced in the 1880s by Hobbs, Brockunier and Company of Wheeling, West Virginia, is a term refering to the decoration or finish used in the production of some of their glassware lines. Hobnail (Dewdrop) is the most commonly found of these lines, though Swirl and on occasion Quartered Block with Stars were also finished with the frosted surface and amber-stained band that defines the Frances Ware indication. Though collectors in general tend to regard examples in crystal with simply an amber-stained band as Frances Ware, according to *Hobbs, Brockunier & Co. Glass* by Nelia and Tom Bredehoft, this is incorrect. The company called this finish 'decorated #7.' To evaluate examples in crystal with amber stain, deduct 10% from the values given below, which are for the frosted finish.

Hobnail, bowl, ftd, berry pontil, 6x10" 150.00
Hobnail, bowl, nappy, sq, 4½" 25.00
Hobnail, bowl, no flange, sq, 9" 85.00
Hobnail, bowl, oblong, 8" 75.00
Hobnail, bowl, shell ft, 8" ....:........... 250.00
Hobnail, bowl, sq, 7½" 70.00
Hobnail, bowl, sq, 8" 75.00
Hobnail, bowl, 2½x5½" 30.00
Hobnail, bowl, 7½", from $65 to 75.00
Hobnail, bowl, 8" dia 75.00
Hobnail, bowl, 10" 90.00
Hobnail, butter dish, from $80 to 120.00
Hobnail, celery vase 125.00
Hobnail, chandelier, amber font, brass fr, 14" dia 950.00
Hobnail, creamer, from $40 to 60.00
Hobnail, cruet, from $425 to 500.00
Hobnail, finger bowl, 4", from $25 to 35.00
Hobnail, molasses can 375.00
Hobnail, pickle jar 175.00
Hobnail, pitcher, milk 160.00

Hobnail, pitcher, water; square top, 8½", $195.00. (Photo courtesy John A. Shuman III)

Hobnail, sauce dish, sq, 4" 28.00
Hobnail, shakers, very rare, pr 300.00

Hobnail, sugar bowl, w/lid, from $65 to 80.00
Hobnail, syrup, pewter lid.. 375.00
Hobnail, toothpick holder/toy tumbler 60.00
Hobnail, tray, cloverleaf, 12", from $90 to 125.00
Hobnail, tumbler, water.. 45.00
Hobnail, vase, ruffled top... 165.00
Quartered Block w/Stars, bowl, oval, 10" 65.00
Quartered Block w/Stars, butter dish.. 95.00
Quartered Block w/Stars, goblet.. 140.00
Quartered Block w/Stars, sugar bowl, w/lid................................. 75.00
Swirl, bowl, 4" 25.00
Swirl, bowl, 8" 90.00
Swirl, butter dish... 95.00
Swirl, celery, ind.. 35.00
Swirl, cruet, from $250 to 295.00
Swirl, mustard jar, from $90 to 125.00
Swirl, pitcher, water... 225.00
Swirl, plate, 6".. 30.00
Swirl, shakers, pr 165.00
Swirl, sugar bowl, w/lid.. 80.00
Swirl, sugar shaker, orig lid 195.00
Swirl, syrup, Pat dtd 295.00
Swirl, toothpick holder.. 160.00
Swirl, tumbler 45.00

Franciscan

Franciscan is a trade name used by Gladding McBean and Co., founded in northern California in 1875. In 1923 they purchased the Tropico plant in Glendale where they produced sewer pipe, gardenware, and tile. By 1934 the first of their dinnerware lines, El Patio, was produced. It was a plain design made in bright, attractive colors. El Patio Nouveau followed in 1935, glazed in two colors — one tone on the inside, a contrasting hue on the outside. Coronado, a favorite of today's collectors, was introduced in 1936. It was styled with a wide, swirled border and was made in pastels, both satin and glossy. Before 1940, 15 patterns had been produced. The first hand-decorated lines were introduced in 1937, the ever-popular Apple pattern in 1940, Desert Rose in 1941, and Ivy in 1948. Many other hand-decorated and decaled patterns were produced there from 1934 to 1984.

Dinnerware marks before 1940 include 'GMcB' in an oval, 'F' within a square, or 'Franciscan' with 'Pottery' underneath (which was later changed to 'Ware'). A circular arrangement of 'Franciscan' with 'Made in California USA' in the center was used from 1940 until 1949. At least 40 marks were used before 1975; several more were introduced after that. At one time, paper labels were used.

The company merged with Lock Joint Pipe Company in 1963, becoming part of the Interpace Corporation. In July of 1979 Franciscan was purchased by Wedgwood Limited of England, and the Glendale plant closed in October 1984.

Note: Due to limited space, we have used a pricing formula, meant to be only a general guide, not a mechanical ratio on each piece. Rarity varies with pattern, and not all pieces occur in all patterns. Our advisor for this category is Shirley Moore; she is listed in the Directory under Oklahoma. See also Gladding McBean.

Coronado, 1936 – 1956

Both satin (matt) and glossy colors were made including turquoise, coral, celadon, light yellow, ivory, and gray (in satin); and turquoise, coral, apple green, light yellow, white, maroon, and redwood in glossy glazes. High-end values are for maroon, yellow, redwood, and gray. Add 10 – 15% for gloss.

Bowl, casserole; w/lid, from $45 to 90.00
Bowl, cereal; from $10 to 15.00
Bowl, cream soup; w/underplate, from $25 to 40.00
Bowl, fruit; from $6 to 12.00
Bowl, nut cup; from $8 to 12.00
Bowl, onion soup; w/lid, from $25 to 40.00
Bowl, rim soup; from $14 to 25.00
Bowl, salad; lg, from $20 to 35.00
Bowl, serving; oval, 10½", from $20 to 33.00
Bowl, serving; 7½" dia, from $12 to 18.00
Bowl, serving; 8½" dia, from $10 to 17.00
Bowl, sherbet/egg cup; from $10 to 15.00
Butter dish, from $25 to... 35.00
Cigarette box, w/lid, from $40 to 75.00
Creamer, from $8 to 12.00
Cup & saucer, demitasse; from $20 to 32.00
Cup & saucer, jumbo 32.00
Demitasse pot, from $100 to.. 150.00

Fast-stand gravy boat, from $25.00 to $35.00.

Jam jar, w/lid, from $45 to 60.00
Pitcher, 1½-qt, from $25 to 45.00
Plate, chop; 12½" dia, from $18 to 32.00
Plate, chop; 14" dia, from $20 to 30.00
Plate, crescent hostess; w/cup well, no established value
Plate, crescent salad; lg, no established value
Plate, ind crescent salad; from $22 to........................... 32.00
Plate, 6½", from $5 to 8.00
Plate, 7½", from $7 to 10.00
Plate, 8½", from $8 to 11.00
Plate, 9½", from $10 to 15.00
Plate, 10½", from $12 to 18.00
Platter, oval, 10", from $12 to 20.00
Platter, oval, 13", from $24 to 36.00
Platter, oval, 15½", from $25 to 45.00
Relish dish, oval, from $12 to 25.00
Shakers, pr from $15 to 30.00
Sugar bowl, w/lid, from $10 to 20.00
Teacup & saucer, from $8 to 12.00
Teapot, from $75 to... 95.00
Tumbler, water; no established value
Vase, 5¼" 65.00
Vase, 6¾", no established value
Vase, 8½", no established value
Vase, 9½", no established value

Desert Rose

Ashtray, ind.. 15.00
Ashtray, oval 95.00
Ashtray, sq... 150.00
Bell, Danbury Mint 95.00
Bell, dinner 95.00

Bowl, bouillon; w/lid, from $195 to............................ 295.00
Bowl, cereal; 6" 15.00
Bowl, divided vegetable 45.00
Bowl, fruit 10.00
Bowl, mixing; lg 175.00
Bowl, mixing; med 165.00
Bowl, mixing; sm 155.00
Bowl, porringer 175.00
Bowl, rimmed soup 25.00
Bowl, salad; 10" 95.00
Bowl, soup; ftd 25.00
Bowl, vegetable; 8" 32.00
Bowl, vegetable; 9" 40.00
Box, cigarette 95.00
Box, egg 145.00
Box, heart shape 145.00
Box, rnd. 165.00
Butter dish 45.00
Candleholders, pr... 95.00
Candy dish, oval, from $150 to 225.00
Casserole, 1½-qt 75.00
Casserole, 2½-qt, minimum value 295.00
Coffeepot 125.00
Coffeepot, ind, from $300 to 395.00
Compote, lg... 75.00
Compote, low 125.00
Cookie jar 295.00
Creamer, ind 40.00
Creamer, regular 20.00
Cup & saucer, demitasse 35.00
Cup & saucer, jumbo 30.00
Cup & saucer, tall 35.00
Cup & saucer, tea 10.00
Egg cup 35.00
Ginger jar 225.00
Goblet, ftd.. 225.00
Gravy boat 38.00
Hurricane lamp, from $250 to 325.00
Jam jar 125.00

Long 'n narrow, 15½x7¾", $495.00.

Microwave dish, oblong, 1½-qt 195.00
Microwave dish, sq, 1-qt 150.00
Microwave dish, sq, 8" 95.00
Mug, bbl, 12-oz 45.00
Mug, cocoa; 10-oz 95.00
Mug, 7-oz.. 35.00
Napkin ring... 50.00
Piggy bank, from $195 to 295.00

Pitcher, milk	65.00
Pitcher, syrup	75.00
Pitcher, water; 2½-qt	125.00
Plate, chop; 12"	50.00
Plate, chop; 14"	95.00
Plate, coupe dessert	65.00
Plate, coupe party	125.00
Plate, coupe steak	145.00
Plate, divided; child's, from $125 to	195.00
Plate, grill, from $75 to	95.00
Plate, side salad	35.00
Plate, TV; from $95 to	125.00
Plate, 6½"	7.00
Plate, 8½"	12.00
Plate, 9½"	20.00
Plate, 10½"	18.00
Platter, turkey; 19"	295.00
Platter, 12¾"	35.00
Platter, 14"	45.00
Relish, 3-section	65.00
Relish/pickle dish, oval, 10"	28.00
Shaker & pepper mill, pr, from $195 to	295.00
Shakers, rose bud, pr	22.50
Shakers, tall, pr, from $75 to	95.00
Sherbet	20.00
Soup ladle	75.00
Sugar bowl, open, ind	45.00
Sugar bowl, regular	25.00
Tea canister	295.00
Teapot	125.00
Thimble	75.00
Tidbit tray, 2-tier	95.00
Tile, in fr	50.00
Tile, sq	50.00
Toast cover	195.00
Trivet, rnd, from $150 to	195.00
Tumbler, juice; 6-oz	45.00
Tumbler, 10-oz	30.00
Tureen, soup; flat bottom	595.00
Tureen, soup; ftd, either style	695.00
Vase, bud	95.00

For other hand-painted patterns, we recommend the following general guide for comparable pieces (based on current values):

Daisy	-20%
October	-20%
Cafe Royal	Same as Desert Rose
Forget-Me-Not	Same as Desert Rose
Meadow Rose	Same as Desert Rose
Strawberry Fair	Same as Desert Rose
Strawberry Time	Same as Desert Rose
Fresh Fruit	Same as Desert Rose
Bountiful	Same as Desert Rose
Desert Rose	Base Line Values
Apple	+10%
Ivy	+10%
Poppy	+50%
Original (small) Fruit	+50%
Wild Flower	200% or more!

There is not an active market in Bouquet, Rosette, or Twilight Rose, as these are scarce, having been produced only a short time. Our estimate would place Bouquet and Rosette in the October range (-20%) and Twilight Rose in the Ivy range (+20%).

There are several Apple items that are so scarce they command higher prices than fit the formula. The Apple ginger jar is valued at $600.00+, the 4" jug at $195.00+, and any covered box in Apple is at least 50% more than Desert Rose.

Apple Pieces Not Available in Desert Rose

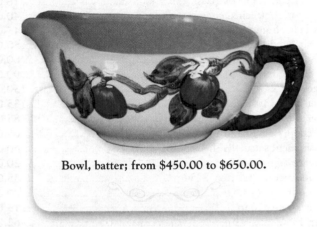

Bowl, batter; from $450.00 to $650.00.

Bowl, str sides, lg	55.00
Bowl, str sides, med	45.00
Casserole, stick hdl & lid, ind	65.00
Coaster, from $25 to	35.00
Jam jar, redesigned	425.00
Shaker & pepper mill, wooden top, pr from $295 to	395.00
½-apple baker, from $150 to	195.00

El Patio, 1934 – 1954

This line includes a few pieces not offered in Coronado, and the colors differ; but per piece, these two patterns are valued about the same.

Franciscan Fine China

The main line of fine china was called Masterpiece. There were at least four marks used during its production from 1941 to 1977. Almost every piece is clearly marked. This china is true porcelain, the body having been fired at a very high temperature. Many years of research and experimentation went into this china before it was marketed. Production was temporarily suspended during the war years. More than 170 patterns and many varying shapes were produced. All are valued about the same with the exception of the Renaissance group, which is 25% higher.

Bowl, vegetable; serving, oval	50.00
Cup	20.00
Plate, bread & butter	18.00
Plate, dinner	30.00
Plate, salad	25.00
Saucer	12.00

Starburst

Ashtray, ind	20.00
Ashtray, oval, lg, from $50 to	75.00
Bowl, divided, 8", from $25 to	35.00
Bowl, fruit; ind, 5"	15.00
Bowl, oval, 8"	35.00
Bowl, salad; ind, from $20 to	25.00
Bowl, soup/cereal; from $15 to	25.00
Bowl, vegetable; 8½"	45.00
Butter dish, from $50 to	65.00

Candlesticks, pr from $175 to	200.00
Canister/jar, w/lid, from $150 to	225.00
Casserole, 8½", from $100 to	120.00
Coffeepot, from $175 to	225.00
Creamer, from $22 to	25.00
Cruet, vinegar or oil; ea from $80 to	110.00
Cup & saucer, from $15 to	18.00
Gravy boat, w/attached undertray, from $35 to	40.00
Gravy ladle, from $35 to	45.00
Jam dish, w/hdl 1 side, 8", from $40 to	50.00
Mug, sm	60.00
Mug, tall, 5", from $80 to	90.00
Pepper mill	150.00
Pitcher, water; 10"	135.00
Pitcher, 7½", from $70 to	85.00
Plate, chop; from $55 to	65.00
Plate, crescent salad; 9½" L, from $50 to	60.00
Plate, dinner; from $15 to	20.00
Plate, luncheon; 9½", from $25 to	35.00
Plate, 6", from $7 to	9.00
Plate, 8", from $10 to	15.00
Platter, 13"	62.00
Platter, 15"	65.00

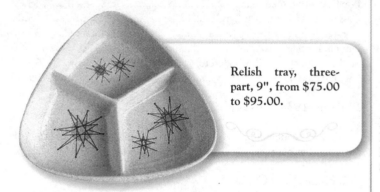

Relish tray, three-part, 9", from $75.00 to $95.00.

Shakers, bullet shape, sm, 2½", pr, from $25 to	35.00
Shakers, bullet shape, 3½", pr from $50 to	65.00
Snack/TV tray w/cup rest, 12½", from $80 to	110.00
Sugar bowl, from $30 to	35.00
Teapot, 5½x8½", from $175 to	225.00
Tumbler, 6-oz, from $40 to	50.00

Frankart

During the 1920s Frankart, Inc., of New York City, produced a line of accessories that included figural nude lamps, bookends, ashtrays, etc. These white metal composition items were offered in several finishes including verde green, jap black, and gunmetal gray. The company also produced a line of caricatured animals, but the stylized nude figurals have proven to be the most collectible today. With few exceptions, all pieces were marked 'Frankart, Inc.' with a patent number or 'pat. appl. for.' All pieces listed are in very good original condition unless otherwise indicated. Our advisor for this category is Walter Glenn; he is listed in the Directory under Georgia.

Aquarium, nudes (3), kneel/encircle 10" fishbowl, 10½"	1,750.00
Ashtray, bk-to-bk nudes hold rack of 4 rnd trays, 8"	600.00
Ashtray, nude grows from leaves to hold tray above, 25"	1,650.00
Ashtray, nude seated w/matchbox holder, 5½"	675.00
Ashtray, nude stands/leans against circle, tray at ft, 7"	500.00
Bookends, horse (stylized) prancing, 7"	350.00

Bookends, lady w/fan support books, 10"	300.00
Bookends, Modernistic female head, 6"	475.00
Bookends, nude kneeling, bk supports books, 6"	525.00
Candy dish, majorette, 1 knee supports dish, 10"	975.00
Cigarette box, nudes bk-to-bk hold 4" rectangular glass box, 9"	1,250.00
Clock, nudes (2) kneel & hold 10" dia glass clock, 12½"	4,500.00
Lamp, nude as butterfly w/frosted glass wings, 10¼"	2,850.00
Lamp, nude dancer silhouettes against rectangular glass panel, 11"	1,275.00
Lamp, nude holds rod above, glass panel hangs by rings, 13"	1,750.00
Lamp, nude kneels before 4" bubble ball, 8"	1,200.00
Lamp, nude stands atop frosted glass panel, light below, 10"	1,050.00

Lamp, two nudes hold tiered shade aloft, 20", $2,350.00.
(Photo courtesy Fontaine's Auction Gallery)

Lamp, nudes (2) stand, face ea other through glass rods, 12"	1,750.00
Lamp, nudes (4) stand & surround sq glass cylinder, 13"	2,250.00
Mirror, nude stands & holds 6" gold-bk mirror, 15"	1,250.00
Smoke stand, nude stands atop arch, mtd to sq base, 22"	1,150.00

Frankoma

John Frank opened a studio pottery in Norman, Oklahoma, in 1933, creating bowls, vases, etc., which bore the ink-stamped marks 'Frank Pottery' or 'Frank Potteries.' At this time, only a few hundred pieces were produced. Within a year, Mr. Frank had incorporated. Though not everything was marked, he continued to use these marks for two years. Items thus marked are not easy to find and command high prices. In 1935 the pot and leopard mark was introduced.

The Frank family moved to Sapulpa, Oklahoma, in 1938. In November of that year, a fire destroyed everything. The pot and leopard mark was never re-created, and today collectors avidly search for items with this mark. The rarest of all Frankoma marks is 'First Kiln a Sapulpa 6-7-38' which was applied to only about 100 pieces fired on that date.

Grace Lee Frank worked beside her husband, creating many limited edition Madonna plates, Christmas cards, advertising items, birds, etc. She died in 1996.

Clay is important in determining when a piece was made. Ada clay, used through 1954, is a creamy beige color. In 1955 they changed over to a red brick shale from Sapulpa. Today most clay has a pinkish-red cast, though the pinkish cast is sometimes so muted that a novice might mistake it for Ada clay.

Rutile glazes were created early in the pottery's history; these give the ware a two-tone color treatment. However the US government closed the rutile mines in 1970 and Frank found it necessary to buy this material from Australia. The newer rutile produced different results, especially noticeable with their Woodland Moss glaze.

Upon John Frank's death in 1973, their daughter Joniece became president. Though the pottery burned again in 1983, the building was quickly rebuilt. Due to so many setbacks, however, the company found it necessary to file chapter 11 in order to remain in control and stay in business.

Mr. Richard Bernstein purchased Frankoma in 1991. Sometime in 2001, Mr. Bernstein began to put the word out that Frankoma Pottery Company was for sale. It did not sell and because of declining sales, he closed the doors on December 23, 2004. The company sold July 1, 2005, to another pottery company owned by Det and Crystal Merryman of Las Vegas, Nevada. They took possession the next day and began bringing life back into the Frankoma Pottery once more. Today they are producing pottery from the Frankoma molds as well as their own pottery molds, which goes by the name of 'Merrymac Collection,' a collection of whimsical dogs.

Frank purchased Synar Ceramics of Muskogee, Oklahoma, in 1958; in late '59, the name was changed to Gracetone Pottery in honor of Grace Lee Frank. Until supplies were exhausted, they continued to produce Synar's white clay line in glazes such as Alligator, Woodpine, White Satin, Ebony, Wintergreen, and a black and white straw combination. At the Frankoma pottery, an 'F' was added to the stock number on items made at both locations. New glazes were Aqua, Pink Champagne, Cinnamon Toast, and black, known as Gunmetal. Gracetone was sold in 1962 to Mr. Taylor, who had been a long-time family friend and manager of the pottery. Taylor continued operations until 1967. The only dinnerware pattern produced there was Orbit, which today is hard to find. Other Gracetone pieces are becoming scarce as well. If you'd like to learn more, we recommend *Frankoma and Other Oklahoma Potteries* by Phyllis Boone (Bess), our advisor; you will find her address in the Directory under Oklahoma.

Cookie jar, swan lid, Prairie Green, silver overlay rim, 10", from $900.00 to $1,000.00.
(Photo courtesy Phyllis Boone [Bess])

Ashtray, Oklahoma shape, Prairie Green, ASA '66 OSU Stilwater, 5½" .. 12.00
Ashtray, 4-leaf clover, Brown Satin, #223 .... 20.00
Baker, Lazybones, Autumn Yellow, w/candle-warmer base, 3-qt 60.00
Baker, Westwind, Brown Satin, w/lid, #6VS, 5½x9¼ 50.00
Bean pot, Lazy Bones, Desert Gold, Sapulpa clay, 2-qt, 6½" 50.00
Bowl, lug soup; Lazy Bones, Desert Gold, 5x6½" 10.00
Bowl, soup; Woodland Moss, hdl, #45C, 2½x4⅞" 10.00
Candleholder, Brown Satin, flower form, 5" L 15.00
Candleholder, triple, blk, #306, 3½x8⅛", ea 20.00
Candlesticks, Autumn Yellow, #305, 5¼x4¼x2¼", pr 40.00
Carafe, Desert Gold, Sapulpa clay, 8" 40.00
Casserole, Lazy Bones, hdls, w/lid, #4V, 7x9¾" L 50.00
Christmas card, 1944, from $500 to 600.00
Christmas card, 1947-48, from $95 to 115.00
Christmas card, 1949, from $85 to 95.00

Christmas card, 1950-51, from $125 to 150.00
Christmas card, 1952, Donna Frank, from $150 to 200.00
Christmas card, 1952, from $125 to 140.00
Christmas card, 1953, from $90 to 110.00
Christmas card, 1954 .... 110.00
Christmas card, 1957 .... 70.00
Christmas card, 1958-60 .... 65.00
Christmas card, 1969-71 .... 40.00
Christmas card, 1972 .... 35.00
Christmas card, 1973-75 .... 30.00
Christmas card, 1976-82 .... 25.00
Creamer, Wagon Wheel, Desert Sand, Ada clay, 2⅜" 12.50
Creamer, Wagon Wheel, Sorghum Brown, SD souvenir 15.00
Cup, Mayan Aztec, Desert Gold, Ada clay, sm 20.00
Cup & saucer, demitasse; Plainsman, Brown Satin, Ada clay 20.00
Dealer sign, Frankoma Pottery, Terra Rose, 1955-57 .... 55.00
Egg plate, Prairie Green, #819 .... 75.00
Gravy boat, Westwind, Desert Gold, Sapulpa clay, side hdl 35.00
Jar, honey; Mayan Aztec, Prairie Green, #7JH, 35th Anniversary, 9"..25.00
Jug, Canteen, Desert Gold, w/stopper, Ada clay 115.00
Leaf dish, Leaf Green, 1⅝x9¼x4¾" 15.00
Leaf dish, Prairie Green, 3-compartment, 1965-91, 12x6½" 38.00
Mug, Donkey, Chocolate Brown, 1979 .... 30.00
Mug, Donkey, Desert Gold, 1979 .... 15.00
Mug, Donkey, Kerry Edwards, red, 2005 .... 35.00
Mug, Donkey, yel, 1975 .... 30.00
Mug, Elephant, Nat'l Republican Women's Club, 1968, 5-oz 60.00
Mug, Elephant, Prairie Green, 1972 .... 30.00
Mug, Plainsman, Woodland Moss, #5C 15.00
Mug, Wagon Wheel, Prairie Green, Sapulpa clay, #94C, 5-oz 15.00
Pitcher, eagle emb, White Sand, #555, 2½x2¾" 48.00
Pitcher, honey; Prairie Green, #8, 1950s, 6¾" 17.50
Planter, Flame Red, ped ft, 6" 40.00
Planter, mallard duck w/open bk, Brown Satin, Sapulpa clay......... 55.00
Plate, Christmas, Laid in a Manger, White Sand, 1969 .... 20.00
Plate, Easter, He Is Not Here..., Oral Roberts Assn, White Sand, 1972 . 15.00
Plate, Plainsman, Woodland Moss, Sapulpa clay, 6" 8.00
Plate, Teenager of Bible, David the Musician, Desert Gold, 1974, 7" .. 20.00
Plate, Wagon Wheel, Prairie Green, Sapulpa clay, #94FL, 10" 10.00
Plate, Wagon Wheel, Prairie Green, Sapulpa clay, #94G, 7" 7.00
Platter, Plainsman, Brown Satin, Sapulpa clay, 1948, 9¾x6" 15.00

Sculpture, Deer group, Prairie Green, designed by Joseph Taylor, 8", $5,000.00. (Photo courtesy Phyllis Boone [Bess])

Sculpture, Fan Dancer, Rubbed Bisque, pk clay 60.00
Sculpture, Greyhound, Prairie Green, #827, 15" L 360.00
Sculpture, Indian Maiden, Prairie Green, #123 .... 65.00
Sculpture, Nude #3, Prairie Green, Sapulpa clay, #GS53/105, 11½"..195.00
Sculpture, Trojan Horse, Desert Gold, Ada clay, #162, mini.......... 60.00
Sculptures, Farmer Boy & Girl, mc HP, Ada clay, 7", 5¾", pr 315.00
Swan dish, Desert Gold, closed tail, #228, 5½x8" 32.00
Teapot, Wagon Wheel, Prairie Green, 2-cup 50.00

Teapot, Westwind, Desert Gold, Sapulpa clay, #6T, 6¼" 25.00
Toby jug, Uncle Sam, Flame Red, 1976 .... 40.00
Toby mug, Cowboy, White Sand, 1977 .... 25.00
Trivet, American's Stars & Stripes, red, 1976 Bicentennial 20.00
Trivet, Historic Route 66 New Mexico, Terra Cotta, 6" 22.00
Tumbler, Plainsman, Prairie Green, 12-oz 15.00
Vase, Brown Satin, Sapulpa clay, octagonal, #38, 1967, 6" 20.00
Vase, Cactus, Prairie Green, #4, 7" 45.00
Vase, collector; V-1, from $125 to 150.00
Vase, collector; V-2, 1970, 12", from $80 to 90.00
Vase, collector; V-3, 1971 .... 85.00
Vase, collector; V-4, 1972 .... 85.00
Vase, collector; V-5, 1973, 13" 85.00
Vase, collector; V-6, from $80 to 90.00
Vase, collector; V-7, 13" 80.00
Vase, collector; V-8, w/stopper, 13" 75.00
Vase, collector; V-9, w/stopper, 13" 65.00
Vase, collector; V-10 & V-11, ea from $40 to 50.00
Vase, collector; V-12, 13" 65.00
Vase, collector; V-13 .... 65.00
Vase, collector; V-14, from $75 to 80.00
Vase, cornucopia; Prairie Green, Sapulpa clay, #57, 1962-91 .... 45.00
Vase, Jade, emb rings, puma mk, 1936-38, 4¼" 275.00
Wall mask, Tragedy, Prairie Green, 9" 70.00
Wall pocket, cowboy boot, Winter White, 6⅝" 50.00

Fraternal

Fraternal memorabilia is a vast and varied field. Emblems representing the various organizations have been used to decorate cups, shaving mugs, plates, and glassware. Medals, swords, documents, and other ceremonial paraphernalia from the 1800s and early 1900s are especially prized. Our advisor for Odd Fellows is Greg Spiess; he is listed in the Directory under Illinois. Information on Masonic and Shrine memorabilia has been provided by David Smies, who is listed under Kansas. Assistance concerning Elks collectibles was provided by David Wendel; he is listed in the Directory under Missouri.

Eagles

Match safe, eagle w/wings spread, silver-tone metal, 2¾x1½" 35.00
Ring, 10k yel gold, eagle, FOE in blk enamel on sides 215.00
Watch fob, cvd pearlescent eagle w/gold-tone chain 30.00

Elks

Whiskey nip, china, elk's tooth with brown wash, embossed with name of bar, its address, and beer advertisement, ca. 1890 – 1910, from $125.00 to $175.00.

Doorknob, brass, Roman numeral clock at 11th hour emb, EX 60.00
Lapel pin, 10k yel gold, elk emb, Schickerling Pat, ½x⅝" 22.50
Medal, Delegate emb on pin, Washington...1908 on bl ribbon, 4"...20.00

Postcard, Icebergs? Yes Bring Me a Few, Atlantic City, comic, 1907.15.00
Tankard, HP elk & symbols on wht ironstone, slim, 11½" 75.00
Watch fob, 14k yel gold w/bl & wht enameling, 1⅝" 60.00

Masons

Buckle, 10-12k rolled gold, emb symbols, ca 1860, 2⅜x2" 50.00
Hat, beaver skin, blk & wht feathers, Superior Uniform..., 1930s.. 50.00

Plaque, relief carved with polychrome paint, $1,980.00 for a pair (only one shown). (Photo courtesy Aston Macek Auctions)

Pocket watch, triangular 14k gold case w/eng symbols, Hiram, 15-jewel..1,800.00
Ring, 10k wht gold w/gold symbols in red stone 50.00
Ring, 14k yel gold, 32nd Degree, red stone 150.00
Sword, Battle of Crusades eng on scabbard, Henderson Ames Co ..125.00
Sword, pictorial etched blade, ivory grip, 1900s, 35" 100.00
Watch fob, dbl-headed eagle, 14k yel gold, 1½" 125.00
Watch fob, 14k gold mesh band & emblem locket w/.40ct Euro dmn, enamel .865.00

Odd Fellows

Arc of Covenant, wooden box w/carrying rods, pnt symbols, 9x36x12"..750.00
Box, walnut w/symbolic inlay, burl molding, late 19th C, 10x21x12". 350.00
Cornucopia, cvd/pnt wood, mts to wall, OH, 19th C, 20" 2,235.00
Cvg, Indian head, varnished wood, hollowed int, ca 1900, 12"........195.00
Fob, Maltese cross, gold filled w/enamel, ca 1900, 1⅝x1" 90.00
Hourglass, pnt wood, represents flight of time, OH, 19th C, 10". 1,050.00
Podium, walnut/pine, orig pnt w/heart/hand/star/etc, 38x34x16", pr.635.00
Pole, ceremonial; cvd serpent, blk/gold pnt, OH, 19th C, 65¼" ..880.00
Ring, yel & wht gold FLT & 3 rings w/red/wht/bl enameling....... 215.00
Robe, red velvet w/much gold cording, snap front, 1900s, EX 70.00
Scepter, cvd/pnt wood, gilt finial & rings, OH, 19th C, 36"......1,000.00
Staff, cvd/pnt heart & hand, gold trim, OH, 19th C, 74"........12,925.00

Shrine

Lapel pin, silver w/sword/other symbols, faux dmns........................ 15.00
Postcard, Phila United...Hospital, real photo, 1940s-50s, unused 6.00
Shield, crescent/star/scimitar, mc pnt on wood, 24x20½" 300.00

Miscellaneous

Eastern Star, ring, 14k wht gold filigree, ¾x⅝" top 275.00
Knights of Columbus, sword, Linch & Kelly, w/sash & cloth case ..125.00
Order of Red Men, badge, bronze/celluloid, w/ribbon, PA, 1880s, EX .95.00

Fraunfelter

Charles Fraunfelter organized his company in Zanesville, Ohio, in

1915. It was known as the Ohio Pottery Company until 1923. During this period their main product was a line of utilitarian articles for chemical laboratories made of hard-paste porcelain. In 1918 they used the same body to produce a brown and white line called 'Petruscan.' By 1920 a line of hotel ware was added. The company reorganized in 1923 and became known and Fraunfelter China Company; but after the death of Fraunfelter in 1925, the business fell into hard times and eventually closed altogether in 1939.

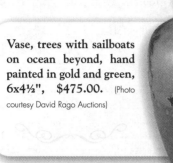

Vase, trees with sailboats on ocean beyond, hand painted in gold and green, 6x4½", $475.00. (Photo courtesy David Rago Auctions)

Coffee set, Deco floral, electric pot+cr/sug w/lid+2 cups w/metal frs..800.00
Coffeepot, Deco-style, gr & wht w/platinum trim 65.00
Syrup, Modernistic, Royal Rochester, 5½" 615.00
Syrup, red poppies w/gr stripe on ivory, Royal Rochester, 5¼" 225.00
Teapot, Art Deco, gr & wht w/platinum trim, Manning-Bowman, 11" L . 50.00
Teapot, cobalt w/thick gold trim, 7½x10" 35.00
Teapot, red poppies w/gr stripe on ivory, Royal Rochester, 6¾x9". 225.00
Vase, brn/orange mottle, wide shoulders, 4" 40.00
Vase, gray MOP w/gold inlay at top, #98, ca 1927, 6½"................. 60.00
Vase, landscape, lustered gray glazes, Lessell, 4½x5" 840.00
Vase, royal bl, baluster, partial label, 4½x3" 40.00

Fruit Jars

As early as 1829, canning jars were being manufactured for use in the home preservation of foodstuffs. For the past 25 years, they have been sought as popular collectibles. At the last estimate, over 4,000 fruit jars and variations were known to exist. Some are very rare, perhaps one-of-a-kind examples known to have survived to the present day. Among the most valuable are the black glass jars, the amber Van Vliet, and the cobalt Millville. These often bring prices in excess of $20,000.00 when they can be found. Aside from condition, values are based on age, rarity, color, and special features. Unless noted otherwise, values are given for clear glass jars. Our advisor for this category is John Hathaway; he is listed in the Directory under Maine.

Acme (on shield w/stars & stripes), pt 2.00
Atlas E-Z Seal, amber, qt 65.00
Atlas E-Z Seal, aqua, qt 1.50
Atlas E-Z Seal, aqua, ½-pt 15.00
Atlas E-Z Seal, ½-gal 3.00
Atlas Mason Patent, qt...3.00
Atlas Whole Fruit, qt...2.00
Ball Eclipse, base Pat 7-14-08, qt...4.00
Ball Eclipse Wide Mouth, pt...1.00
Ball Ideal, rnd, ½-gal...3.00
Ball Ideal, sq, pt 3.00
Ball Ideal Pat'd July 14 1908, bl, qt..2.00

Ball Improved, aqua, ½-gal 15.00
Ball Mason, bl, pt..2.00
Ball Perfect Mason, bl, 40-oz 25.00
Ball Sanitary Sure Seal, bl, qt..5.00
Ball Special, bl, qt.. 10.00
Ball Sure Seal, bl, pt..3.00
Canadian Jewel, Made in Canada, qt...4.00
Clark's Peerless, aqua, qt... 10.00
Clark's Peerless, aqua, ½-gal 25.00
Cleveland Fruit Juices, Cleveland Ohio, ½-gal................................4.00
Corona Jar, Made in Canada, pt..3.00
Crown (crown), aqua, ½-gal...7.00
Crown Crown (ring crown), aqua, qt... 17.00
Crown Mason, pt..2.00
Daisy FE Ward & Co (in circle), aqua, qt 15.00
Double Safety, qt..1.00
Double Safety (Script), ½-pt... 12.00
Double Seal, pt.. 28.00
Drey Improved Ever Seal, pt...2.00
Drey Square Mason (in carpenter's sq), ½-gal............................... 20.00
Economy, base: Portland Ore..., qt 4.00
Empire (in stippled cross), pt...5.00
Eureka (script), base: Eureka Jar Co..., lt gr, qt 25.00
Franklin Dexter Fruit Jar, aqua, whittled, qt 70.00
Gem (CFJ Co), aqua, ½-gal... 30.00

Gilberds Improved (star) Jar, aqua, smooth base, ground lip, original glass lid embossed Gilberds Improved Jar Cap, Jamestown, N.Y., Pat. July 31, 83, Oct. 13, 1885, reproduction wire closure, pint, $700.00. (Photo courtesy Glass-Works Auctions)

Gilberds (star) Jar, aqua, qt.. 350.00
Globe, aqua, pt.. 60.00
Green Mountain (in fr), qt... 12.00
Hazel Preserve Jar, ½-pt.. 35.00
Home-pack, qt..2.00
Ivanhoe (base), pt..4.00
Jewel Jar, Made in Canada, pt 10.00
Kerr Self Sealing Mason, amber, qt 40.00
King (on banner below crown), qt... 10.00
Knox (K in keystone) Mason, regular zinc lid, qt 2.00
Leotric (in circle), aqua, pt...5.00
Lockport Mason AQ Co, qt... 15.00
Magic TM Mason Jar, qt...1.00
Mason Arched Ball, bl, qt... 50.00
Mason's Cross Improved, aqua, midget... 50.00
Mason's Cross Patent Nov 30th 1858, aqua, ½-gal 15.00
Mason's H Patent Nov 30th 1858, aqua, qt 50.00
Mason's Patent, aqua, ½-gal... 10.00
Mason's Patent Nov 30th 1858, aqua, qt..4.00
Mason's 5 Patent Nov 30th 1858, base: WFM, aqua, ½-gal........... 50.00
Mason's 6 Patent Nov 30th 1858, aqua, qt 20.00
Mason's 11 Patent Nov 30th 1858, aqua, qt 50.00
Mason's 14 Patent Nov 30th 1858, aqua, qt 40.00
Mason's 20 (underlined) Patent Nov 30th 1858, aqua, qt............... 25.00
Mason Star Jar, qt..1.00

Masons CFJ Patent Nov 30th 1858, lt gr 50.00
Mid West Canadian Made, qt 14.00
Mountain Mason, qt 30.00
Ohio (sm HI) Quality Mason, ½-gal 25.00
Old North Bridge, Williamsburg Capitol, Valley Forge, qt 3.00
Pacific Mason, base: PC in broken rectangle, qt 40.00
Presto, ½-pt 35.00
Presto Supreme Mason, pt 1.00
Presto Supreme Mason, ½-gal 5.00
Princess (in shield, in fr), pt 50.00
Putnam (on base), amber, qt 65.00
Root (looped Os), aqua, qt 10.00
Sealfast, base: Foster, ½-pt 15.00
Security Seal FG Co (in triangles), qt 8.00
Sure Seal (in fancy script in circle), bl, pt 3.00
TF (mono base), ½-gal 2.00
Tight Seal Rev: Pat'd July 14 1908, bl, pt 4.00
Trademark Banner Registered (in banner), pt 10.00
Trademark Keystone Registered, qt 6.00
Trademark Lightning, base: Putnam, aqua, 24-oz 65.00
Trues Imperial Brand, Portland ME, pt 9.00
Victory (in shield) on lid, qt...4.00
Widemouth Telephone Jar, aqua, pt 10.00

Fry

Henry Fry established his glassworks in 1901 in Rochester, Pennsylvania. There, until 1933 when it was sold to the Libbey Company, he produced glassware of the finest quality. In the early years they produced beautiful cut glass; and when it began to wane in popularity, Fry turned to the manufacture of occasional pieces and oven glassware. He is perhaps most famous for the opalescent pearl art glass called 'Foval.' It was sometimes made with Delft Blue or Jade Green trim in combination. Because it was in production for only a short time in 1926 and 1927, it is hard to find. See also Kitchen Collectibles, Glassware.

Bowl, console; Green Jade with silver overlay, 4½x9½", $575.00; Candlesticks, 10", $800.00 for the pair. (Photo courtesy Early Auction Co.)

Baker, pearl ovenware, 9" sq 30.00
Bell, amber, needle etched, 7½" 45.00
Bottle, scent; Foval, elongated, Delft Blue ft, rnd dauber, 8" 460.00
Bottle, scent; Foval, eng floral, Delft Blue top w/intaglio, 3½" 690.00
Bottle, scent; Foval, eng floral, Jade stopper w/intaglio, 3½" 400.00
Bottle, scent; Foval, rnd w/short neck, Jade Green stopper, 4" 200.00
Bowl, cut, Lyton, sawtooth rim, 4x8" 80.00
Bowl, Foval, gr festooning, Jade Green ft, 8" 975.00
Bowl, Foval, onion form w/2 sqd Jade Green ft, #823, 4" 400.00
Bowl, fruit; cut, Orient, ftd, 9".. 175.00

Brown Betty, pearl ovenware, 9", from $55 to.............................. 65.00
Candleholder, blk, wide flat ft, 3", ea 18.00
Casserole, blk w/silver resist, w/lid, pre-1933, 1½-qt in NP fr 215.00
Casserole, pearl ovenware, w/lid, 7" sq, in metal holder, from $85 to ...95.00
Chicken roaster, pearl ovenware, #1946, 14" 60.00
Compote, Foval, corset shape, Delft Blue ft/lip wrap, #353, 10" ..460.00
Compote, Foval, Jade Green ft, emb silver band at rim, 8" W 575.00
Compote, Foval, Jade Green stem, silver o/l scrolls at rim, 7" 345.00
Compote, Foval, silver o/l scrolls at wide flaring rim, 5" 460.00
Cordial, bl w/clear stem, 4½" 55.00
Creamer & sugar bowl, Foval, festooning, Delft Blue hdls, 3½" ... 400.00
Cup, coffee; pearl ovenware.. 27.05
Cup & saucer, Foval, Jade Green hdl, 4 for.................................. 325.00
Goblet, Diamond Optic, azure, 7" 35.00
Mug, lemonade; Foval, Jade Green hdl 75.00
Pie plate, pearl ovenware, #1916, 9" 30.00
Pitcher, Celeste Blue, bubbles/rim threading, bl hdl, 9", +underplate. 150.00
Platter, fish; eng, 11", from $60 to 65.00
Relish, cut, Asteroid, oblong, 13" 150.00
Sherbet, Foval, Delft Blue stem & ft 120.00
Teapot, Foval, Jade Green finial/hdl/spout, 6", +4 c/s+cr/sug 575.00
Teapot, Foval, silver o/l paneled Dutch scene, Delft Blue hdls, +9 pcs. 1,285.00
Tumbler, iced tea; Japanese Maid etch, cherry blossom hdl, ftd, 5" .115.00
Vase, Foval, Delft Blue ft/lip wrap, U-form w/wide flared lip, 6" ..425.00
Vase, Foval, enameled rim, tapering w/Delft Blue raised disk ft, 8" .575.00
Vase, Foval, Jade Green connector, ftd, #830, 8" 285.00
Vase, jack-in-pulpit; Foval, Jade Green lip wrap, #821, slim, 10". 520.00

Fulper

Throughout the nineteenth century the Fulper Pottery in Flemington, New Jersey, produced utilitarian and commercial wares. But it was during the span from 1902 to 1935, the Arts and Crafts period in particular, that the company became prominent producers of beautifully glazed art pottery. Although most pieces were cast rather than hand decorated, the graceful and classical shapes used together with wonderful experimental glaze combinations made each piece a true work of art.

The company also made dolls' heads, Kewpies, figural perfume lamps, and powder boxes. Their lamps with the colored glass inserts are extremely rare and avidly sought by collectors. Examples prized most highly by collectors today are those produced before the devastating fire in 1929 and subsequent takeover by Martin Stangl (see Stangl Pottery).

Several marks were used: a vertical in-line 'Fulper' being the most common in ink or incised, an impressed block horizontal mark, Flemington, Rafco, Prang, and paper labels. Unmarked examples often surface and can be identified by shape and glaze characteristics. Values are determined by size, desirability of glaze, and rarity of form. Our advisor for this category is Douglass White; he is listed in the Directory under Florida.

Pilgrim flask, banded glazes of green over Mirror Black over frothy Butterscotch Flambe, 10", NM, $1,200.00. (Photo courtesy Cincinnati Art Galleries)

Bookends, books, 1 open/1 lying flat, gr/tan, 5" 375.00
Bowl, gr crystalline w/concentric rings, ink stamp, 3½x9½" 400.00
Candle shield, purple mottled matt, 7½" 175.00
Candlesticks, ivory melds into brn, bl at trumpet ft, 10", pr 300.00
Flower holder, frothy gr w/bl & rose, mushroom style, 8¼x5½" ... 175.00
Jar, Mirror Black, shouldered, w/lid, 14x9", EX 1,440.00
Lamp base, bl flambe crystalline, 3-hdl, bulbous, 8x8", 18" overall .. 250.00
Lantern, w/rivets & straps as if copper, glass panels, 13x11", EX ... 5,400.00
Vase, bl flambe crystalline, classic form, imp mk, 16½" 3,000.00
Vase, bl/brn flambe, right-angle hdls, rnd body flaring at base, 7x9" ... 420.00
Vase, bl/mauve streaky gloss/matt, trumpet form, 5¾" 120.00
Vase, brn matt, angle hdls, ink stamp, 4½" 380.00
Vase, brn/tan flambe, long flared top/squat bottom, 10½x6¼" 480.00
Vase, Cat's Eye flambe, 16x5" 4,800.00
Vase, Cat's-Eye flambe, 7-sided, kiln pull, 9¾x5½" 650.00
Vase, Cucumber Crystalline, burst bubbles, 9¼" 385.00
Vase, gr crystalline, bulbous base, rim-to-hip hdls, 6x6" 250.00

Vase, Green Flambe over blue gloss over blue matt, 10", $1,000.00. (Photo courtesy Cincinnati Art Galleries)

Vase, gr gloss/matt drip, bulbous w/hdls, 4⅜" 235.00
Vase, gr/turq crystalline, 7¾", EX 210.00
Vase, indigo/cobalt/brn/tan flambe, waisted, 7½x4½" 325.00
Vase, ivory flowing to mirror blk flambe w/cobalt, 3½x3" 225.00
Vase, ivory to brn & mirror blk flambe, ovoid, 6x3½" 125.00
Vase, ivory to mauve frothy flambe, bullet shape, grinding chip, 13x8" .. 3,360.00
Vase, khaki gr & cobalt flambe, flared rim, waisted, 7¼x5" 250.00
Vase, pk, flared sides, ring hdls, 13" 700.00
Vase, purple/bl mottled matt, right-angle rim hdls, shouldered, 8x5" . 300.00

Furniture

Aside from its obvious utility, furniture has always been a symbol indicating wealth, taste, and social position. Each period of time has wrought distinct changes in style, choice of wood, and techniques — all clues that the expert can use to determine just when an item was made. Regional differences as well as secondary wood choice give us clues as to country and locale of origin.

The end of the Civil War brought with it the Industrial Revolution and the capability of producing man-made furniture. With this came the Victorian period and the many revival styles.

Important to the collector (and dealer) is the ability to recognize furniture on a 'good, better, best' approach. Age alone does not equal value. During a recessionary market the 'best' of forms always seem to do well. The 'better' or middle market will show a drop in value, and the 'good' or lower end of the marketplace will suffer the most. Many of this year's values emphasize what has been going on in the marketplace. Pre-auction estimates appear to be closer to actual selling prices as there is less speculation. Uncertainty has leveled out among collectors

and dealers, and they are paying more attention to the details of quality items and current fashion. The classics are still in vogue, with a strong showing in the metropolitan markets. Good collectible reproductions of the twentieth century are still gaining in popularity in the common and median marketplaces. Country pieces (or 'high country') items are gaining ground and value in rural areas across the country. English and continental furniture, currently more affordable, are strong choices for younger collectors. Prices for 'floor ready' upholstered items continue to rise.

Items that have sold at auction for at least 25% lower than their normal market values will be designated with (*). Items listed in the lines that are designated with (**) are pieces in the best of form and of museum quality.

Please note: If a piece actually dates to the period of time during which its style originated, we will use the name of the style only. For example: 'Hepplewhite' will indicate an American piece from roughly the late 1700s to 1815. The term 'style' will describe a piece that is far removed from the original time frame. 'Hepplewhite style' refers to examples from the turn of the century. When the term 'repro' is used it will mean that the item in question is less than 30 years old and is being sold on a secondary market. When only one dimension is given, for blanket chests, dry sinks, settees, sideboards, sofas, and tables, it is length, unless otherwise noted.

Condition is the most important factor to consider in determining value. It is also important to remember that *where* a piece sells has a definite bearing on the price it will realize, due simply to regional preference. To learn more about furniture, we recommend *Heywood-Wakefield Modern Furniture* by Steve and Roger Rouland; *The Marketplace Guide to Oak Furniture* by Peter S. Blundell; and *Early American Furniture* by John Obbard. In the listings that follow, items are in good condition unless noted otherwise. See also Art Deco, Art Nouveau; Arts and Crafts; Fifties Modern; Limbert; Nutting, Wallace; Shaker; Stickley; Wright.

Our advisor for this category is Suzy McLennan Anderson, CAPP of Bachelorhill Antiques and Appraisals of Walterboro, South Carolina. Her mailing address is listed in the Directory under South Carolina. Requests that do not include a SASE regretfully can no longer be answered.

Key:	
* — auction price but 25% under the norm	Geo — Georgian
	grpt — grainpainted
** — museum quality	hdbd — headboard
: — over (example, 1 do:2 drw)	hdw — hardware
bj — bootjack	Hplwht — Hepplewhite
brd — board	mar — marriage
Co — country	mahog — mahogany
cvd, cvg — carved, carving	NE — New England
c&b — claw and ball	QA — Queen Anne
do — door	R/R — Renaissance Revival
drw — drawer	rswd — rosewood
Emp — Empire	trn — turning, turned
Fed — Federal	uphl — upholstered/upholstery
Fr — French	vnr — veneer
ftbd — footboard	Vict — Victorian
G — good	W/M — William and Mary

Armoires, See Also Wardrobes

Cherry LA, later cornice:2 panel do, 3-drw int, 1790s, 79x49x22" .. 8,225.00
Mahog Emp style w/brass inlay, dbl mirrored do, 70x54x20" 1,650.00
N European pnt w/mc foliage on bl-gr, 2-do, dtd 1812, 71x56" .. 2,115.00
Walnut Co Fr, arched crown:2 arched do:3 drw:apron, 83x51x19" .. 1,265.00

Beds

Campaign, pnt iron Directoire-style, scrolled hd/ftbd, 40x80x55" ... 1,400.00

Canopy, cherry Sheraton style, Wheeler repro, 70" posts............. 925.00
Canopy, old red pnt on tall post w/notched hdbd, 60x64x48" 650.00
CI w/cast floral/shell ornaments, gold pnt details, 51x70x55" 700.00
Half tester, cvd walnut Am, serpentine tester/arched hdbd, 110x86x67".4,500.00
Half tester, walnut Vict rococo, arched hdbd, ornate, 110x73x61"..7,300.00
Poster, mahog Fed w/scrolled-ear hdbd, foliate cvgs, 88x74x55" . 2,000.00
Rope, mixed woods, trn posts w/acorn finials, ball ft, 53x72x55".660.00
Rope, scrolled hdbd, cannonball finials, orig red pnt, 60x70x53"....700.00

Tall post, bird's-eye maple with applied walnut rose, 73" headboard, $4,325.00. (Photo courtesy Neal Auction Co. Auctioneers & Appraisers of Fine Art)

Tall post, mahog Am Fed, hdbd: scrolled acanthus, 94x56x82" .8,500.00
Tall post, mahog Centennial, broken arch hdbd:trn spindles, 84x74x57". 1,000.00
Tester, curly/str-grain maple Sheraton, scalloped hdbd, 58x42" . 1,700.00
Tester, mahog Am rococo, arched hdbd w/ornate cvg, 110x72x60" .5,000.00
Tester, scrolled/paneled hdbd, grpt w/alligatoring, 78x71x52" 400.00
Trundle, cherry/poplar, cannonball posts, scalloped hdbd, 18x65x46"..375.00
Walnut/burl Am Eastlake, scalloped crest, low ftbd, 89x65" 600.00

Benches

Bucket, red/brn pnt, 3-tier w/half-canted top section, 35x37" ..2,015.00
Fire-bk, pine Co, tongue & grooved, shaped sides, rfn, 69x72" 465.00
Fireside, stripped pine, shaped ends & arms, rpl hinges, 50x55" .. 325.00
Garden, bronze, bk/seat as planks w/branch-like scroll arms/legs, 63". 3,000.00
Mahog late Fed, horsehair damask padded seat, scroll legs, 13x50x20"...1,200.00
Railway, red-pnt Windsor style, spindle bk, metal arms, rpt, 96" . 275.00
Settle, mixed wood Co, arrow-bk spindles, grpt w/stencil, 33x82" . 1,500.00
Settle, oak European, 4-arch panel bk:roped seat:trn legs, 69" 835.00
Settle, pine Co, boldly shaped crest, gr pnt w/mc stencil, 36x82" . 770.00
Wagon, 2-seat (rpl) ladderbk, 2 horizontal slat bks, trn posts, 31x37". 445.00
Water, old red pnt, angled sides, cutouts form ft, 2-shelf, 46x41x14" .1,150.00
Window, fruitwood Louis XV-style, scrolled arms:serpentine seat, 33" . 425.00
Windsor, yel pnt/decor, bamboo-trn spindle bk/stretchers, NE, 82" L ** .5,000.00

Blanket Chests, Coffers, Trunks, and Mule Chests

Camphorwood w/rows of brass tacks, Chinese Export, 1800s, hdls, 40" L.765.00
Dome top, pine w/yel/blk smoke-pnt decor, gr traces, cracks, 10x28x14"..515.00
Dower, pnt Scandinavian w/rosemaling on bl-gray pnt, 1789, 34x52x27" ..1,080.00

Grpt faux mahog w/mustard-lined panels, 6-brd, 8 drws w/in, 22x42x21"..1,150.00
Grpt simulated bird's-eye maple, lift top, scalloped molding, 42" L.800.00
Leather over camphorwood, Chinese Export, brass studs/mts, 36" L... 355.00
Mule, bl/dk bl pnt, 6-brd, thumb-molded top/end battens, 45".3,680.00
Mule, pine w/bl-gr:red, 6-brd, 1-drw, bold molding, 41x38x18" .2,530.00
Pine, 6-brd:long drw, worn pnt, scalloped sides, 33x45x18"...3,675.00
Pine NY, dvtl & molded, mc floral on red pnt, rprs, 19x43x18".3,000.00
Pine w/ea side & lid deeply cvd, 6-brd, bracket base, 37" L, VG.. 600.00
Pine w/lt bl pnt, 6-brd, lift top, bracket base, NE, 1780s, 42" L ... 885.00
Pnt, potted flowering vine on red, sgn JP, NY, rpr/rpl, 43".........3,100.00

Red-painted pine, six-board, ring-turned legs, ca. 1830, Ohio or Kentucky, 49" long, $3,760.00. (Photo courtesy Skinner Inc. Auctioneers & Appraisers of Antiques & Fine Art)

Red-pnt 6-brd w/molded edge, dvtl, strap hinges, 1800, 48" 575.00
Steamer trunk, Louis Vuitton, leather w/wood straps, 1920s, 31" L .3,170.00
Walnut, dvtl case w/sq-cut nails, rpl hinges/ft, w/till, 13x25x11". 575.00
Walnut Sheraton Co w/inlay, wrought-iron hinges, 21x32x16" . 2,900.00
Walnut/poplar Chpndl, dvtl case/drws, strap hinges/till, 38x50x23"..1,350.00
Yel pine, paneled case:2 dvtl drws:bracket ft, w/till, 26x48x18" ... 550.00

Bookcases

Mahog, cvd baluster end posts on claw ft, 1910, 58x77x20" 1,200.00
Mahog, Paine Co, 2 sliding glass do, fluted columns w/trn ft, 55x36" . 635.00
Mahog Hplwht-style, 2 glazed do, simple styling, Fr bracket ft, 87x50"..3,000.00
Mahog step-bk, 3-part, 2 glazed do:2 do, removable crown, 92x46", VG .. 1,150.00
Mahog Wm IV breakfront, 4 Gothic-arch do:4 panel do, 1830s, 98x97x23".8,900.00
Oak, 3-section stacking w/drw base, 1920x, lt water damage, 47x25". 885.00
Oak, 4-stack w/desk unit, 3 glass do sections, 62x34x16" 475.00
Walnut, heavy lion paw ft/rope-cvd borders w/3-D nudes, 70x52". 2,000.00

Bureaus, See Also Chests

Mahog, bombe front:4 grad drw:bracket ft, rfn, 35x38x22".......4,115.00
Mahog Fed w/inlay, bowfront, 4 grad cockbeaded drw, Fr ft, rfn, 38x40"..2,350.00
Mahog Louis XVI style w/cvg & leather top, center drw+2 side, 64".. 1,900.00
Mahog/rswd/flame birch vnr Fed bowfront w/inlay, 4-drw, NH, 37x42" **..14,000.00
Maple/bird's-eye maple/mahog Fed, elliptical front, 4-drw, rfn, 43x42"...6,400.00

Cabinets

China, oak, dbl front doors, side lites angled, pressed frieze, 64x42".1,035.00
China, oak w/EX cvg, lg 3-D lady ea side, fish/shells, etc, 71x49".. 11,500.00
Corner, cherry w/bl-pnt int, 12-pane do:2 panel do, bracket ft, 82x40" ..3,400.00
Corner, mahog Geo III, glazed do w/criss-X mullions:panel do, 85x40"..3,100.00
Curio, Fr style, arched top, gilt w/HP courting scene, 71x34" 690.00

Curio, Fr style, mahog serpentine do w/ormolu, HP figure panel, 60x27"..800.00
Curio, Vernis Martin, ormolu glass fr, rose borders, 3-shelf, 56".1,300.00
Mahog Regency style, shelves/mirror bk:3 drw+4 do w/grill, 67x48"..880.00
Marquetry w/extensive inlay, bombe w/step-bk top, 4-shelf int, 78x47".2,400.00
Music, serpentine, 1 drw:lg do w/faux 2-drw bottom, burl vnr, 51x26".635.00
On stand, W/M, scenic marquetry, 5-drw unit ea side do, twist trn, 54".1,325.00
Spice, oak Georgian, X-banded do over pigeonholes/sm drw, 29x25".825.00
Spice, tabletop, 10-drw, 5 rows of 2, ea w/porc knob, 1850s, 15x15x7"..745.00
Vitrine, Fr style, bowfront w/do, 2 curved side windows, HP, 55x27".460.00
Vitrine, walnut Austrian Biedermeier, oval-panel dbl do, 78x48".2,850.00

Candlestands

Cherry Co, trn ped:tripod base:snake ft, rfn, rprs, 27x16x15" 260.00
Cherry Fed, cloverleaf 22x17" tilt top, trn post, arch legs, 28" 575.00
Cherry Fed w/dished top:drw:vase:support:tripod, old rfn, CT, 27x17"..4,115.00
Cherry QA, 'whirling tray' top:trn std:3 snake ft, rfn, 25x16x16" .1,325.00
Curly maple/cherry Fed w/chip cvg, oval top:tripod base, NE, 26x22x18"...775.00
Hickory/mixed woods Windsor, dish top, platform base:3 ft, 36x16".3,000.00
Mahog Fed, top w/reeded edge:trn shaft:3 arched legs, 19x24x16".1,295.00
Mahog QA, 13" 8-sided top:trn shaft:3 snake legs w/pad ft, rstr, 25".375.00
Mahog tilt-top, 1-brd 8-sided top:trn post:tripod base, rfn, 29".... 350.00
Mahog/cherry Fed w/inlay, sq top:vase:trn support:tripod, 36x17" .1,765.00
Maple tilt-top, brn & yel grpt w/scrubbed top, mid-19th C, 28x23" dia.1,785.00
Pine/birch Co, 8-sided top:X-ftd base, pnt on ring trns, rprs, 23" ..1,035.00

Chairs

Windsor, low back, crest rail screwed to two-piece arm rail, older apple green paint with trace of darker green underneath, 28", $3,450.00. (Photo courtesy Garth's Auctions Inc.)

Arm, ivory pnt Louis XVI style w/loose cushion, 19th C, rstr, 37", pr .. 1,650.00
Arm, Jacobean w/trn stretcher base, scrolled arms, reuphl, 47".2,750.00
Arm, maple/ash NH banister-bk w/fishtail crest, rush seat, 42"....975.00
Arm, rswd Am rococo, Rosalie w/Grapes pattern by Belter, 1850s .4,400.00
Arm, Windsor, knuckle arm, by DT Smith/11-99, blk pnt, 45" ...375.00
Club, Chesterfield, scrolled arms, tufted leather, 29", pr............2,500.00
Corner, elm Irish Georgian, tall headrest, Marlborough legs, 40x21" . 1,500.00
Corner, walnut Italian R/R, cvd lion masks/foliage 415.00
Gentleman's, walnut Vict, open arms, tufted bk, finger cvg, 40x24" ..375.00
Side, blk pnt ladder-bk, 3-slat bk, trn arms/stretcher, 1700s, 45" ..2,415.00
Side, mahog English Chpndl, pierced splat, reuphl/rfn, 36" 230.00
Side, mahog English QA, reuphl balloon seat, rfn/rprs, 40" 925.00
Side, mahog Geo III, scroll crest/openwork splat, c&b ft, 1775 .1,115.00
Side, QA Co, yoked crest:solid splat:rush seat:trn legs, 40", pr 700.00
Side, rswd Am rococo, Stanton Hall, JW Meeks, 1860, pr........5,200.00

Side, rswd w/fruit & floral crests, C-scroll stiles, att Belter, pr...2,350.00
Side, Walnut Co QA, crest:vase splat:rush seat:Spanish ft, 41", pr ..1,600.00
Side, walnut W/M, heavily trn legs/stretchers, uphl bk/seat, 40", pr ..1,700.00
Side, walnut/mahog Chpndl, curved crest:pierced splat:slip seat, 36". 145.00
Walnut Black Forest, goats inlay/cvd lion's heads to arms, 42" .1,600.00
Windsor arm, D-shaped comb w/9 spindles, 1830s, 38" 980.00
Windsor arm, Prince of Wales Plume splat w/heart cutout, 39" .3,450.00
Windsor bow-bk arm, 7-spindle, pine seat, old gr pnt, 37" 1,750.00
Windsor comb-bk arm, 7-spindle, cvd/shaped arms, blk pnt, 38" ... 2,415.00
Windsor comb-bk arm, 8-spindle, curved/shaped crest, trn, 43".. 1,725.00
Windsor fan-bk side, 7-spindle, arched crest w/uptrn ears, rfn, 39" ..1,200.00
Windsor fan-bk side, 9-spindle, dk gr over lt gr rpt, EX trn, 37".2,875.00
Windsor knuckle-arm style, 7-spindle, chip-cvd ears, blk pnt, 45"..375.00
Windsor sack-bk arm, trn/splay legs, well cvd, old pnt, 38"........3,625.00
Windsor-style continuous arm, brace-bk w/comb, crackled pnt, 44"..575.00
Windsor-style fan-bk side w/bold trns, saddle seat, yel/red pnt..... 360.00
Windsor-style sack-bk arm, 7-spindle, boldly trn, rfn, 37" 460.00
Wing, Chpndl style, cabriole legs w/c&b ft, silk reuphl/rfn, 44" ... 350.00
Wing, Chpndl style, flame-stitch style uphl, 20th C, 47" 400.00
Wing, mahog Chpndl, naive form, wht uphl w/brass tacks, 47" .1,895.00
Wing, mahog Chpndl style, str legs, old bl uphl, 43" 345.00
Wing, mahog QA style, quilted floral reuphl, pad ft, 46" 635.00
Wing, mahog/oak w/scalloped bk/scrolled arms/str front, reuphl, 48" . 1,600.00
Wing-bk Am Fed, trn mahog legs w/brass cuffs, 1820s, 36x22".2,100.00

Chair Sets

Dining, Louis XVI-style w/cream pnt, caned seat, 8 side+2 arm.. 3,000.00
Dining, mahog Chpndl style, pierced splat, reuphl/rprs, 6 side+2 arm.. 1,380.00
Side, Co QA style, yoke crest, red w/gr splint seat, OH, 40", 4 for..575.00
Side, decorated (extensive) York Co PA, mc tulips etc, lyre bk, 6 for.3,410.00
Side, decorated PA, flowers on brn, keyhole splats, 1830s, 6 for.. 1,400.00
Side, Fr Provincial, scroll & floral crest/rtcl splat/rush seat,12 for.. 1,765.00
Side, Hitchcock pillow-bk w/gold stencil on blk ground, 34", 8 for..1,125.00
Side, mahog Emp, vase bk w/cvd leaf crests, serpentine rail, 5 for...400.00
Side, mahog Emp-style w/ormolu mts, needlepoint seat, 35", 8 for ..6,000.00
Side, mahog Geo III, tall bk, bl leather uphl, 4 for 3,250.00
Side, mahog Geo III style, rtcl ladder-bk:uphl seat, 38", 12 for .8,225.00
Side, mahog Regency, paneled crest:rtcl splat, trn legs, 8 for 4,700.00
Side, QA w/extensive floral & bird inlay, serpentine seats, 4 for. 1,150.00
Side, rswd Am rococo, Rosalie w/Grapes pattern by Belter, 4 for.....5,300.00
Side, walnut Chpndl, yoke crest:vase splat:slip seat, 39", 4 for..8,000.00
Side, walnut Geo III style, serpentine crest:pierced splat, 39", 4 for...500.00
Windsor birdcage side, 7-spindle, bamboo trn, 36", 4 for 925.00

Chests (Antique), See Also Dressers

Birch Sheraton, 4 grad drw:high trn ft, att NE, 40x39x20" 460.00
Campaign, camphor wood w/flush brass mts, 2-part, 1850s, 44x42x20" ..1,150.00
Cherry Chpndl, 4 grad drw w/beaded edges, rfn/rpl, PA, 33x38x22" .7,750.00
Cherry Sheraton bowfront, 4 grad drw, reeded corners, rfn, 43x42x23" ..1,725.00
Cherry w/3-panel figured birch drw faces (4), ¾-reed columns, 38x40" ..7,475.00
Cherry/birch Chpndl, 4 overlapping beaded-edge drw, rfn/rpl, 32x34x18" ..1,600.00
Cherry/birch/pine NH, cornice:6 dvtl grad drws, old red pnt, 61x39x20" .4,300.00
Cherry/curly maple Fed, cornice:3 drw:5 grad dvtl drw:Fr ft, 66x44" .4,300.00
Cherry/poplar/chestnut Chpndl, 4 dvtl drw, rpl brasses, 36x40x23".4,875.00
Curly maple Fed bowfront, 4 dvtl drw:shaped apron, rfn/rprs, 37x41x21" .3,450.00
Curly maple/cherry Co, 4-drw, paneled sides, trn columns, 44x43x20"..800.00
Figured walnut Biedermeier, wide banding, 4-drw, scalloped ft, 40x52"..2,200.00
Grpt pine, 6-brd, burnt umber/ochre w/yel striping, 1820s, 18x39x18" ..1,060.00
High, cherry Chpndl, 6 grad dvtl drw, att N Lombard, 53x37x41" ** .17,250.00
Mahog Sheraton bowfront, reeded ¾-columns/dbl-scroll bksplash, 46"..1,000.00
Mahog/chestnut Hplwht, 2-brd top w/string inlay, 4 dvtl drw, 39x39x21"...3,795.00
Mahog/figured vnr bowfront w/4 dvtl drw, appl bead, rpr ft, 41x45x22".1,100.00

Maple Sheraton bowfront, crest w/brass rosettes:4 drw, rfn, 45x44x22"* .525.00
Maple/pine NE, overhang top:4 grad drws:bracket base, rpr, 35x41x20"..4,600.00
On chest, cherry/maple/poplar Chpndl, cornice:5 drw:3 in base, 75x40".. 6,900.00
On chest, cherry/pine Chpndl, bonnet top:3 short:4 grad drw:4, 84x38".. 12,650.00
On chest, walnut Geo, molded cornice:3 short+3 L drws:3 drws, 73x40" .3,800.00
On frame, mahog Irish Geo III w/broken arched pediment, 6-drw, 71x30"..8,000.00
On stand, oak W/M w/all drw fronts cvd w/floral scrolls, 56x38" ..2,100.00
Pine Co, 1-brd top:5 grad drw w/thumb molding, rpl brasses, 44x38x20"..435.00
Walnut Co Fr, serpentine front w/3 cvd drw, rprs, 36x49x20"..2,500.00
Walnut/oak/pine English Chpndl, 1-brd:4 grad drws:bracket ft, 32x32" .3,000.00
Walnut/oak/pine English Chpndl, 4-drw, bracket ft w/scallops, 32x32"..2,990.00

Cupboards, See Also Pie Safes

Cherry Chpndl, 12-pane do:2 drw:panel do, att G Woltz, 2-pc, 92x47"..10,000.00
Cherry Emp, 4 do:3 drw:4 panel do, scrolled front, 101x85x24" ...5,750.00
Cherry/pine/poplar Co, cornice:2 6-pane do, pnt int, 2-pc, 83x55x19"..1,950.00
Cherry/poplar, bold cornice:2 6-pane do & 3-pane panel, 2-pc, 83x63"..7,200.00
Chimney, yel pine Co w/old red wash, 2 panel do, sq nails, 80x36x20"..2,300.00
Chimney corner, pine/Co, 1-pc repro w/sq nails/alligatored pnt, 70x25"...800.00
Corner, cherry Co, cornice:9-pane do:2 panel do, sq nails, 78x36x23"..2,300.00
Corner, cherry/pine, flat panel do (2:2), scalloped apron, 86x42" .1,400.00
Corner, cherry/pine, 2-pc, 4 panel do (2:2), rfn/rprs, 86x42x18" .1,450.00
Corner, grpt pine/poplar PA, 9-pane do:step-out:drw:2-panel do, 78x36" .4,300.00
Corner, mahog Geo III, cornice:dbl do:plinth base w/2 do, 90x48" .4,400.00
Corner, pine Co, raised panel do:raised panel do, rfn, KY, 90x36"* .1,100.00
Corner, pine Co, 2-pc, 4 arched panel do, rfn, 81x37x19" 1,850.00
Corner, walnut Chpndl Co, cornice:4 panel do:apron, old rfn, 76x36" ..3,750.00
Grpt, do w/6 flame-decor simulated panels, cut-out base, 1800s, 84x48" .1,140.00

Hoosier cabinet, oak with enameled top, foldout flour bin, early twentieth century, 70x40", $500.00. (Photo courtesy Jackson's International Auctioneers & Appraisers of Fine Art & Antiques)

Hutch, pine, top w/stepped shelves & wainscot bk:2 drw+2 do, 87x63"..520.00
Jelly, grpt PA or OH, do w/4 inset panels, 3-shelf, cornice, 62x40" 3,740.00
Linen, cherry Fed, 2 panel do:4 drw:bracket ft..........................3,350.00
Linen, mahog English Wm IV, 2 panel do:4 drw:trn ft, 82x48" .3,400.00
Linen, mahog Geo III, tablet-form banded panels:3 drw, 82x51" .4,200.00
Linen, pine, 2-panel do:3 drw:bracket ft, 68x43" 1,550.00
Linen, pine Co, 2 panel do:3 grad drw, red pnt traces, 1-pc, 68x44"..1,550.00
Oak/walnut Welsh, cornice:3 shelves:base w/5 drw, sm rprs, 86x90x19"..5,000.00
Pine Co, cornice:panel do:3 dvtl drw:shaped ft, H hinges, 72x39x20"..925.00
Pine Co, 1-pc 1-panel do:3 dvtl drw, molded cornice, rpl/rfn, 72x39"..920.00
Pine Co, 2 raised panel do:2, worn orig pnt, sm rprs, 84x54" 635.00
Pine Co step-bk, open top:panel do, pegs/sq nails, old pnt, 75x38"..1,150.00
Pine NE, open scalloped-edge 4-shelf top:2 drw, scalloped base, 75x46"..920.00
Poplar/pine/walnut Co w/red pnt, 2 6-pane do:base w/2 do+2 drw, 84x52"..2,500.00

Poplar/walnut, 2-pc, cornice:2 6-pane do:2 drw:2 do, red stain, 84x52"..2,500.00
Walnut Co step-bk, cornice:2 6-pane do:2 drw:2 panel do, 80x54x21"..2,000.00

Desks

Birch/pine Chpndl, slat lid:4 drw:ogee bracket ft, 42x42", G.......865.00
Birch/pine Fed oxbow, slant lid:4 grad drw, rfn, 46x41x22".......2,250.00
Blk lacquer & gilt Chinese Export Regency style, 1820, 53x24" ...3,675.00
Bureau-plat, much ormolu/marquetry, cabriole legs/paw ft, 48"..2,465.00
Butler's, mahog Sheraton, drws:pullout top:3 grad drws, 57x46x23"..2,100.00

Cherry Chippendale slant-lid desk, Connecticut, ca 1790, 44x40", $3,175.00. (Photo courtesy Skinner Inc. Auctioneers & Appraisers of Antiques & Fine Art)

Chpndl, slant lid, step-down int w/many drws & fan, serpentine, 44x42"...16,000.00
Clerk's, mahog Am Fed, base w/drw, ring-trn reeded legs, 64x35".3,800.00
Lap, campaign, mahog w/brass straps/shield/inlay, 6¾x10x21", G 460.00
Mahog cylinder kneehole, 2 banks of 3 drw, 1850s, 42x53" 1,295.00
Mahog Geo III slant front, 4-do, bracket ft, 1790, 42x43" 1,880.00
Mahog Regency style, oval reeded top w/leather, kneehole, 71" ...4,400.00
Mahog/bird's-eye maple Hplwht tambour, folding writing top, 42x40x19"....2,185.00
Maple w/VG figure Co Chpndl, drop front/fitted int/bracket ft, 42x36"..3,450.00
Maple/pine Co Chpndl, dvtl case:slant lid:6 dvtl drw, 42x36x18" .3,450.00
Partner's, walnut w/cvd openwork scrolled ends, 3-drw, pullouts, 55"*...700.00
Roll-top, walnut Vict w/burl, S-roll, 5 dvtl drw/1 do, 56x52x25"..3,100.00
Walnut, 3-D Hercules supports, front panel:cvd chariot scene, 67" W ..2,300.00
Walnut Chpndl, slant lid:4 grad drw, rpl brasses, 44x39" 1,325.00

Dressers (Machine Age), See Also Chests

Deco, pnt mahog, mirror, chrome, D Deskey, 72x42x19" 960.00
Deco, waterfall vnr w/losses, rnd mirror, 73" 275.00
Maple/bird's-eye maple faux bamboo Am Esthetic, RJ Horner Co, 75x48"..4,400.00
Oak Art Nouveau, swing mirror, 2-do base 300.00

Dry Sinks

Gr-rpt open int, open top:drw:do, wood latch/knob, 30x28x17"..520.00
Pnt (gray) pine NE, 1 panel do, built w/no bk, 27x29x17"........1,785.00
Poplar Co w/red wash, bksplash:shelf:drw:2 do, sq nails/PA, 36x45x17"* .925.00
Poplar w/red wash, shaped bksplash:recessed top & shelf, drws, 34x64" .1,400.00
Poplar/pine Co w/red wash, 2-pc step-bk, 2 do:3 drw:sink:2 do, 89x61" .5,500.00
Walnut/poplar Co w/old layered pnt, gallery:shelf:2 sm drw:2 do, 43"..1,750.00

Hall Pieces

Chair, oak Elizabethan, arched bk w/rtcl splat, spiral legs, 49x22" ..415.00
Chair, Oak Regency, paneled bk, pnt lion & arm crests 200.00
Chair, walnut Fr Gothic cvd/rtcl bk/stretchers, 1850s, 48", pr ..4,450.00
Console table, giltwood Geo III, serpentine marble:skirt, 35x59" . 21,150.00
Console table, mahog Am rococo, marble:cvd floral cartouch/legs, 50" .1,000.00
Console table, oak Vict, cvd details, heavy scroll supports, bun ft.. 1,000.00
Console table, walnut Vict, 3-drw cvd legs, bell pulls, 34x43x17" ..425.00
Corner console table, rswd Am rococo, marble:much cvg, 36x27x25", pr .1,650.00
Hall tree, oak, cvd crest:mirror:chair w/cvd bk splat below, 80x22x15"..260.00

Hall tree, walnut with marble top, arched crest, and carved back panel, 87x47x13", from $1,800.00 to $2,200.00. (Photo courtesy Fontaine's Auction Gallery)

Stand, Black Forest, cvd bear & cub, 81" 7,000.00
Stand, iron, Vict tree form w/candle sockets, 82" 3,500.00
Tree, oak, half mirror, openwork, ca 1920, 80" 300.00
Tree, Oak Vict, cvd shell crest, lift seat, 82" 760.00

Highboys

Cherry QA, cornice w/secret compartment:2 drw:3:base w/1 drw:3, 72x40" ..4,000.00
Cherry QA, swan-neck crest w/3 flame finials, acorn drops, rfn, 82" ..12,340.00
Cherry QA style w/fan cvgs, 5 grad drws:long drw:3 short drws, repro . 3,225.00
Cherry/pine QA, cvd fans in top & base drws, rfn/rstr, 66x39" .2,300.00
Cherry/poplar QA, 10 overlapping drw (2 concave), rstr/old rfn, 73x38". 14,950.00
Curly maple QA, 5 drw:1 long:3 short drw:cabriole legs, 39x42x22" **..31,625.00
Maple QA, cove moldings:concealed frieze drw, scalloped skirt, 64x36"..7,250.00
Maple/pine QA, 4 grad drw:2:cabriole legs, rpl batwing brasses, 73x39" .7,000.00
Walnut X-banded Geo tallboy, flat top:3 short+3 L drws, 66x40" .4,110.00

Lowboys

Curly maple QA style, early 20th-C repro, 31x34x20".............. 2,500.00
Mahog Chpndl, cvd shell, c&b ft, PA, 29x31x21" ** 98,000.00
Oak English Chpndl, 1-brd:3 dvtl dr:apron, rprs, 28x32x20" 550.00
Walnut English QA, 2-brd top:3 dvtl drw:cabriole legs, rfn, 28x35x20".1,950.00
Walnut Geo, molded top:cockbeaded drws:cabriole legs w/pad ft, 30" W . 3,200.00
Walnut QA, scalloped skirt, trifid ft, 28x21x21" 28,000.00

Pie Safes

Hanging, pine Co, punched tin do, old bl pnt:bl-gray, rprs, 23x26x26"....2,500.00
Heart pine, tin panels w/Masonic symbols, red pnt traces, 40x45" 940.00
Poplar Co, 12 punched star tins, drw, sq nails, old red pnt, 48x39" ..1,850.00

Poplar Co w/orig bl pnt, dbl do w/tin tulip-punched inserts, 50x39x18".... 4,600.00
Walnut/poplar Co, 8 punched tin panels, dvtl drw, rfn, 50x42" . 1,600.00

Secretaries

Cherry Co Chpndl, 2 raised panel do w/fitted int:slant lid:4-drw, 73" . 4,300.00
Cherry/pine Co Chpndl, 2-pc, bookcase top, later stain, 74x36x19" .4,350.00
Cherry/poplar Co Hplwht, dbl do:slant lid:4 grad drw, 88x40x21"...2,100.00
Curly maple Chpndl style, fan cvgs, fine 20th-C repro, 79x37x22" .2,875.00
Mahog Chpndl, split ped, panel do:4 drw:bracket ft, 95" 8,150.00
Mahog Chpndl style, 2 1-pane do:slant lid:serpentine base w/4 drw, 90" .6,325.00
Mahog Fed, inlaid do:4 drw:Fr ft, 2-part, 34x34x20" 1,850.00
Mahog Geo III, bookcase top w/dbl do:hinged drop front:2 do, 93x50x24"..8,500.00
Mahog Late Fed w/bookcase top:foldout top:drws:dbl do:paw ft.. 6,000.00

Settees

Beechwood Louis XV style, cvd extended crest rail/leg, 1800s, 81"....3,000.00
Mahog Emp style, rolled-bk str crest w/bronze ormolu mts, 64" . 3,200.00
Mahog Geo II style, cvd cabriole legs w/c&b ft, 1800s, 53" L ...3,500.00
Mahog Geo style, dbl scroll bk, cvd apron, c&b ft, leather uphl, 55".. 2,200.00
Mahog Sheraton style, dbl-shield bk, silk reuphl, ca 1900, 37" .1,035.00
Mahog w/tufted bk uphl, cabriole legs, brass castors, 32x57x30".. 315.00
Walnut, bk: 2 open oval medallions w/cvd beading, uphl seat, 39x39"...6,635.00
Walnut Vict w/finger cvg, medallion bk, 36x56" 300.00
Wingbk, stretcher base, dk bl uphl, 20th C, 48x54x27" 400.00

Settles, See Benches

Shelves

Corner, maple w/red wash, 3-tier, bowfront, 3-tier, 40x11" 285.00
Crock, pine, 3-tier semicircular shelves, tan pnt, 39x47x20", VG ..300.00
Etagere, mahog Fed, sq form w/3 shelves:drw, brass mts, 53x21" ...1,645.00
Etegere, walnut Vict, crest:mirror amid shelves:2 shelves, 79x46"....1,475.00
Mahog Geo III w/inlay, 3 bowfront tiers/3 sm drw, 30x19x8".......880.00
Maple, 3-tier w/scroll ends, 1800s, 28x23x8" 765.00
Pine w/3 plate shelves, molded lip/rails, scalloped ends, 6x48x37"...500.00

Sideboards

Oak Victorian with curved glass and applied carvings, original finish, 51x59", $950.00. (Photo courtesy Jackson's International Auctioneers & Appraisers of Fine Art & Antiques)

Cherry Fed style w/tiger-maple inlay, handmade repro, 39x44x22"..1,840.00
Cherry/figured mahog Fed, 1-brd top:3 drw:4 arched panel do, 45x73"..1,495.00
Mahog English bowfront, 1-brd top:5 drw:8 tapered legs, 33x65x33". 1,200.00
Mahog Fed/Sheraton, bowed center, flame vnr, lion-mask hdw, 76"..6,000.00
Mahog Geo III bowfront, frieze drw:arch amid 2 drws, 32x40x22" .2,500.00
Mahog Geo IV, bksplash:shelf:drw& 2 do:trn legs, 48x72x26"..4,000.00
Mahog Hplwht w/inlay, serpentine front, 3 drw:4 do:fine legs, 72" **.23,000.00
Mahog Regency, step-down top centers 2 1-do cabinets w/cvgs, 109" L.4,100.00
Mahog vnr Vict, 5 flame-grain drws w/string inlay:4 do, 48x85x25"..1,150.00
Mahog w/inlay Geo III, serpentine top/case, 2 banks of 2 do, 36x48x25"..6,465.00
Oak, EX cvd w/lion's faces, mirror, sides w/slanted do+2:2 drw, 80x72"..1,150.00

Sofas

Chpndl Centennial camelbk w/mahog base, 1st half 20th C, 79" .1,265.00
Curly maple Co, serpentine bk, scrolled arms, reuphl, OH, 88" L. 550.00
Mahog Am classical w/cvd Grecian elements, att Quervelle, 71" . 5,300.00
Mahog Chpndl reproduction by Kittinger, 78" L......................2,185.00
Mahog Chpndl style, camelbk:scrolled arms:c&b ft, reuphl, 38x66"..550.00
Mahog Duncan Phyfe, serpentine crest w/fan, rswd panels to arms, 79".1,175.00
Mahog Emp, rnded crest w/cvd rosettes, cvd ft, rprs, 33x100x22" .1,380.00
Mahog Fed, canted crest rail w/cvg, scroll arms, red reuphl, 35x75"..7,950.00
Mahog Regency w/brass inlay, lyre-shape front trim, scroll ft, 76" .3,000.00
Mahog Sheraton, reed top rail:reuphl:trn legs, 33x74" 1,000.00
Mahog Vict, eagle centers foliate crest/phoenix heads on arms, 65" .1,200.00
Mahog/bird's-eye vnr w/inlay Co, lg scroll ft, att Thos Day, 93", G..690.00
Parcel-gilt Italian neoclassical, 3-pc bk w/alternate openwork, 108"..4,700.00
Recamier, mahog Wm IV w/foliate cvg, scrolled arm, silk uphl, 36x78".2,950.00

Stands

Cherry/curly maple, 2 dvtl drw, rpr, 28x18x21" 375.00
Cherry/curly maple Co, 2 dvtl drw, sm rpr, G color, 28x21x18"...375.00
Cherry/poplar Sheraton, dvtl drw:trn legs, soft rfn, 29x21x19"....300.00
Fern, pine w/mc pnt, relief-cvd petal designs, wire nails, 32x10x10"..650.00
Flame birch Hplwht, 1 drw, sq tapered legs, 20x18x17" 380.00
Grpt (mustard/brn) Sheraton, 1-drw, trn splay legs, 28x22x22" .1,555.00
Grpt Hplwht, splay legs, ME, 27x16x16", VG 345.00
Marquetry Louis XV/XVI style w/marble top, serpentine, ormolu mts, pr.440.00
Music, elm Geo III, tilt top:tripod:slipper ft, rpr/rfn, 30x20x15"..635.00
Red-pnt Fed, 1-drw, sq/tapering legs, NE, 1820s, 28x19x18" 300.00
Sewing, mahog Dutch w/inlay, 8-sided lift top, fitted int, 30x23x20" .765.00
Sewing, mahog/pine Sheraton w/inlay, dvtl drw, rpl bag, rfn, 39x19x14".4,150.00
Sewing, pine, 2-brd top:drw:pullout bag:trn legs, rprs, 30x20x19"...375.00
Walnut Hplwht, 2-brd top:drw:tapered legs w/inlay, att PA, 28x18x18"..1,500.00

Stools

Footstool, old red-brn pnt, scrolled aprons, cut-out ft, 7x15x7" ...285.00
Footstool, pine w/blk grpt on red w/wht stripes, att ME, 6x16x6" .460.00

Footstool, walnut with molded apron and legs, late nineteenth century, 14x22", **, $275.00.

(Photo courtesy Robert W. and Harriet Swedburg)

Gout, mahog Regency w/uphl adjustable ftrest, 16½x20x13".......415.00
Gout, pnt/gilt, scroll-shaped top w/oval scenic vignette, 1850s ..2,500.00
Joint, oak w/stretcher base, cvd edge & apron, pegged, 23x19x12"..285.00
Mahog/walnut Geo, shaped apron, sq legs, tufted modern uphl, 19x20x16"..2,015.00
Piano, mahog Regency w/needlepoint uphl, early 19th C, 21x15x15"..1,500.00
Red pnt, 1 drw w/'wing' ea side, 13x18x8" 115.00
Red/brn pnt, scroll-cut aprons w/cut-out ft on sides, 7x7x15"......285.00
Tall, pine w/dk stain, dished seat:splayed trn legs, 29" 230.00
Walnut W/M, twist/trn & blk legs, needlepoint uphl, 21x18x16", pr ..3,000.00

Tables

Tea, mahogany Chippendale, tilt top, carved knees, claw and ball feet, 30" diameter, $15,275.00.

(Photo courtesy Skinner Inc. Auctioneers & Appraisers of Antiques & Fine Art)

Adirondack, 25" dia top w/pinwheel design, branch supports, 29"......650.00
Baker's, pnt scrub top w/2 breadbrd slides:2 lg utensil drws, 45"..175.00
Banquet, cherry, D-top/rectangle leaves, trn legs, rfn/rpr, pr: 82".985.00
Card, mahog Fed fold-over Duncan Phyfe style, 4 cvd scroll legs, 36"..800.00
Card, mahog w/inlay Hplwht style, Kaplan Co, 36" 400.00
Center, CI Italian w/marble top, acanthus-molded support, 29x42" dia....475.00
Center, mahog w/38" marble top (rstr), triangle column w/cvd swans .2,645.00
Chair/table, red-stained birch, 48" dia tilt top, NE, 1780s 4,995.00
Chair/table, scrubbed w/red pnt traces, 47" dia top, 27" 1,265.00
Cricket, pine Co, rnd top:apron:triangular shelf:3 legs, rfn, 29x30" ...575.00
Dining, mahog Duncan Phyfe style w/inlay, 2-pc, rfn, 29x75x47"+leaf..575.00
Display, mahog w/line & shell inlay, glass do, 42x14", VG...........345.00
Dressing, cherry w/mahog drw fronts NE Sheraton, 2 drw:1, 35x31x18"..550.00
Dressing, mc stencil on mustard, wood knobs, bk splat, ME, 32x32x15" .1,050.00
Dressing, rswd Louis Philippe, inset mirror, drw, 1830s, 32x39x21" .7,885.00
Drop-leaf, cherry QA, rnd 1-brd top/leaves, pad ft, open: 42x41"..3,700.00
Drop-leaf, cherry QA, 1-brd top:str apron, att MA, 27x42x13"+leaves..3,750.00
Drop-leaf, mahog Duncan Phyfe style, 1 drw, reeded edge, open: 56"...800.00
Drop-leaf, mahog QA, swing-leg, pad ft, rfn top, 28x42+15" leaves ..1,600.00
Drop-leaf, mahog Wm IV, drw, spiral legs w/brass ft, 1800s, open: 69"..800.00
Drop-leaf, mahog/oak English QA, 1-brd top:swing legs, rfn, 29x57x48"..700.00
Drop-leaf, mahog/oak QA, 2 swing legs, 28x41"+2-brd leaves.....700.00
Drop-leaf, maple Co QA, 1-brd:swing legs, rosehead nails, 27x42x42"..6,900.00
Drop-leaf/gate-leg, mahog English QA style, trn legs, 20th C, 40x18" .575.00
Drum, mahog Regency, rnd top:4 frieze drw:trn std:4 legs, 30x48"..4,115.00
Dumbwaiter, mahog Geo III, 3 grad drop-leaf tops, 3-leg, 49x22"....1,400.00
Farm, pine Co w/oak base, tapered legs, rprs, 39x84x39" 500.00
Farm, red pnt, 2-brd top w/2 rnded drop leaves, simple trn, 72", VG..800.00
Game, curly maple/maple/pine, 1-brd top:drw, swing-leg support, NE .3,450.00
Game, inlaid w/checkerbrd, Biedermeier, 30" dia top...................940.00
Game, mahog Fed w/acanthus cvg, appl plaque on apron, rfn, 29x36x18" .8,900.00
Hutch, pine Co, scrubbed 2-brd top, red pnt w/gr traces, 30x60x44"..2,400.00
Library, oak Vict Baroque, bold cvgs/huge scroll-cvd ft, 54"......5,875.00
Library, trestle type w/extensively cvd apron & legs, 1900, 72"..1,380.00

Nesting, oak English, cvd panels on aprons, mortise & peg, set of 3 ... 750.00
Pembroke, cherry Fed, arched X-stretcher, 2-brd, 28x37x42" ...3,165.00
Pembroke, cvd mahog Regency, fitted end drw, trn legs, 1810, open: 39" . 3,290.00
Pembroke, mahog Geo III, rectangle leaves, drw, sq legs, 1700s, 20" .650.00
Pembroke, mahog Geo III, 1 drw+1 faux drw, D-leaves, open: 38" ..1,610.00
Pembroke, mahog Sheraton, scalloped leaves, att Allison NY, 34"....5,200.00
Pietra dura/giltwood Italian, inset w/doves etc, 29x29" 2,000.00
Sawbuck, pine, scrubbed top/bl-pnt base, NE, 1800s, 47" L 440.00
Sawbuck, pine w/gray & wht pnt traces, 2-brd top, sq nails, 68" ..515.00
Tavern, cherry/pine QA Co, 1-brd top:dvtl drw, putty rstr, 27x41x27"..1,150.00
Tavern, curly maple/chestnut, 2-brd top:dvtl drw w/lock:apron, 39" L...2,300.00
Tavern, maple/pine NE, 1-brd scrubbed top:blocked legs, rpr, 27x31x22". 1,800.00
Tavern, pine, 1-drw, overhang top:trn legs, rpr/wear, 34x22" 920.00
Tavern, pine Co, 1-brd top:apron:trn maple legs w/blk rpt, 25x30x20" ..1,850.00
Tavern, pine NE, 2-brd scrubbed top/breadbrd ends, red pnt, drw, 44". 3,000.00
Tavern, pine/maple Co, 1-brd top w/molding, drw, rprs, 27x34x22" ... 925.00
Tea, maple QA, 2-brd top:scalloped aprons:shaped ft, rfn, 25x29x22" . 8,915.00
Tea, oak Geo III tilt-top, 3-brd top:cabriole legs:snake ft, 29x27x29" . 450.00
Tilt top, mahog Geo, top:trn stem:tripod base w/pad ft, 13" dia. 1,175.00
Tilt top, mahog Geo III, birdcage:spiral twist:3 cabriole legs, 35" .. 2,940.00
Tilt top, mahog Regency, trn ped:sabre legs, 28x40x28" 950.00
Trestle, pine Co, 2-brd top:reeded details:shoe ft, 20th C, 54" 465.00
Work, cherry Sheraton, 2-brd top:drw:trn legs, red stain, 30x30x29" . 400.00
Work, curly maple Co, 2-brd top:2 drws, string inlay, rprs, 38x50x30" . 3,750.00
Work, walnut/poplar, 3-brd top:middle drw:trn legs/ball ft, 29x77x35"...1,150.00
Work, walnut/poplar QA, lift top:3 drw:apron:trn legs, rprs, 80"...5,000.00

Wardrobes

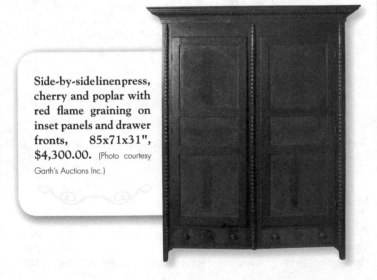

Side-by-side linen press, cherry and poplar with red flame graining on inset panels and drawer fronts, 85x71x31", $4,300.00. (Photo courtesy Garth's Auctions Inc.)

Curly maple/figured cherry Co, cornice:2 panel do, rfn/rpl, 80x70" ...925.00
Mahog Edwardian w/inlay, 2 mirror do, 3-section, 83x79x28" ..1,300.00
Mahog Geo III, dbl do:5 grad drw:Fr bracket ft, fitted int, 88x48x23" . 5,250.00
Mahog Geo III style, dbl do:2 short drw+3 L drw, 80x49" 4,900.00
Mahog/rswd w/much inlay, lg reserves w/putti, knock-down, 75x95" ... 1,840.00
Pine Co, dbl do w/inset panels, pegged/sq nails, worn red pnt, 84x50" ... 345.00

Washstands

Basswood Sheraton Co, yel pnt w/HP foliage, cut-out top:drw, 37x17" sq... 1,000.00
Cherry Co, dvtl scalloped gallery, trn legs, rfn, 37x28x19"........... 375.00
Corner, Am Fed, scalloped bksplash:open top:apron & shelf, 39x29x22"....265.00
Corner, cherry/pine Co, hinged drw swings out, cutout on top, rfn/rprs.175.00
Curly maple Sheraton, dvtl drw w/rnded front:shelf, rfn, 36x25x18".. 1,100.00
Inlaid kingwood Louis XVI style, serpentine marble top/ormolu, 36" W .1,645.00
Mahog Am Fed w/Ionic columns, frieze drw, 37x30x20" 1,000.00

Mahog burl vnr/pine Sheraton, cutout & 2 drw, shelf, rfn, 39x20x18"*....230.00
Mahog corner English, bowfront:dvtl drw:2 false fronts:shelf, 36x22" ..200.00
Mahog Fed, marble top/reeded gallery/stiles/trn legs/ball ft, 33x27"**..5,285.00
Mahog late Fed, shaped gallery/cut-out top, incurvate stretcher, 20" W..1,175.00
Mahog late Georgian, divided hinged top:shelf for bowl:drw:2 do ...1,100.00
Mahog w/inlay Italian neoclassic, do flanked by 2 drw ea side, 35x34" ..2,200.00
Poplar/butternut Co, smoke decor ivory pnt w/stripes, drw, 35x20x16" .4,375.00
Walnut Vict marble-top, 1 drw w/fruit-cvd pull:do, 30x20x17" .1,150.00
Yel-pnt/decor, scroll bkbrd/cut-out shelf, drw below, trn legs, 20" W .. 470.00

Miscellaneous

Bed steps, mahog w/string inlay Regency, lift top, drw/do, 27x20" ...2,000.00
Bed steps, mahog w/trn ft, molded pilasters, hinged lid, 19x18x17", VG...300.00
Bin, pine Co, mortised/pinned, pegged battens, rfn/rprs, 35x35x16" ..175.00
Butler's tray on stand, mahog, trn legs/stretchers, 31x29x19"........635.00
Canterbury, burl mahog/rswd Regency style, rtcl gallery/panels, 36x22"...1,000.00
Canterbury, mahog Boston classical, lyre front/bk:drw:4ft, 22x17x17". 4,800.00

Canterbury, mahogany George III-style Regency, 24x18x14", $2,950.00.
(Photo courtesy Skinner Inc. Auctioneers & Appraisers of Antiques & Fine Art)

Canterbury, mahog Geo III, 4 divisions & trough in top, drw, 18x22"....1,035.00
Canterbury, rswd Wm IV, scroll-rtcl gallery/sides/basket, 41x24" ... 1,880.00
Canterbury, walnut Vict, barley-twist supports, trn legs, 19x25x16" ..765.00
Cellarette, brass-banded Regency, hexagon top, zinc lined, 24x19x16"..2,350.00
Cellarette, burl vnr w/brass/rswd/MOP inlay, hinged lid, 11x13x10" .650.00
Cellarette, mahog Regency w/brass mts, lion mask/ring hdls, 23x26x16".. 1,880.00
Cellarette on stand, mahog Regency, 8-sided, gilt-bronze mts ..3,235.00
Fireplace screen, mahog w/15" oval embr insert, tripod base, 52" . 175.00
Folio stand, mahog Wm IV, drop-down sides, leaf-cvd trestle base, 50" ..2,235.00
Globe, Cary's New Celestial, 9", on 3-ftd walnut stand, 24", VG..1,725.00
Ladder, library; dk oak, fits to slide on track, ca 1900, 71x20" 150.00
Lectern, rswd Regency, gilt eagle support:fluted std, base w/3 paw ft... 7,345.00
Parlor suite, giltwood Louis XVI style, silk uphl, sofa & 2 chairs ...2,350.00
Parlor suite, Louis XVI-style settee+2 side/2 armchairs, EX uphl . 575.00
Parlor suite, rswd Am rococo, sofa+4 side/2 armchairs, mid-19th C ..3,800.00
Peat bucket on stand, mahog Geo III style, slatted supports, 18x14" ..265.00
Podium, slant lid w/herringbone design, 3-shelf, shoe ft, 20th C, 39" ..70.00
Screen, cvd wooden fr, 3-part ea w/glass:uphl inset, 58x54".........575.00
Screen, giltwood Louis XV style, 5-panel, 1880s, 56x17" 175.00
Tea cart, mahog Geo style, glass top/drop leaf/shelf/trn legs, 27" L... 240.00
Tea trolley, brass w/2 ebonized oak trays, rtcl galleries, 1900, 28" L..700.00

Galena

Potteries located in the Galena, Illinois, area were generally plain utility wares with lead glaze and often found in a pumpkin color with some slip decoration or splashes of other colors. These potteries thrived from the early 1830s until sometime around 1860. In the listings that follow, all items are made of red clay unless noted otherwise.

Bowl, mixing; redware, 9¾" 200.00
Crock, redware, mottled gr/orange, ovoid w/raised rim, 9x9¾", NM .. 360.00
Figurine, King Charles spaniel, redware w/brn & yel slip, 9⅛" ..1,850.00
Jar, redware, mottled gr/amber/orange, no lid, 8", NM 450.00
Jug, redware, lt salmon & lt yel glaze, appl strap hdl, 7½", EX 210.00
Jug, redware w/orange spots on burnt orange, att, 9" 175.00
Pot, redware, mottled gr/orange, ovoid w/raised rim, 7½", EX...... 360.00

Galle

Emile Galle was one of the most important producers of cameo glass in France. His firm, founded in Nancy in 1874, produced beautiful cameo in the Art Nouveau style during the 1890s, using a variety of techniques. He also produced glassware with enameled decoration, as well as some fine pottery — animal figurines, table services, vases, and other objets d'art. In the mid-1880s he became interested in the various colors and textures of natural woods and as a result began to create furniture which he used as yet another medium for expression of his artistic talent. Marquetry was the primary method Galle used in decorating his furniture, preferring landscapes, Nouveau floral and fruit arrangements, butterflies, squirrels, and other forms from nature. It is for his cameo glass that he is best known today. All Galle is signed. Our advisor for this category is Don Williams; he is listed in the Directory under Missouri.

Key: fp — fire polished

Cameo

Vase, mold-blown plums in natural colors on citron to green, 16", $10,000.00. (Photo courtesy James D. Julia Inc.)

Bowl, leaves/berries, amethyst on gr, 4".. 865.00
Hall light, hydrangeas, tangerine on yel/cream frost, acorn shape, 12" 4,315.00
Letter seal, leaves, red on red mottle & clambroth, beetle on top, 4".... 660.00
Vase, berries/leaves, brn/gr on salmon to frost, ground rim, 18"... 2,530.00
Vase, clematis vines, purple on yel to wht, bulbous, sm neck & ft, 17"....2,640.00
Vase, falling leaves, red on red & clear, 7" 4,390.00
Vase, floral, gray-gr/lav on peach to frost to salmon, ground top, 19" .. 2,990.00

Vase, floral, purple/bl on camphor, banjo shape, 7" 1,200.00
Vase, floral/leaves, cranberry on citron, spherical, 12x10".........6,120.00
Vase, floral/leaves, cut/pnt on transparent brn, cylinder, 14".....2,645.00
Vase, floral/leaves, muted gold on frost to gold, chalice form, 10" .. 5,175.00
Vase, floral/leaves, orange on yel to frost, teardrop shape, 5½".....5,750.00
Vase, fuchsia stalk, dk amber on soft yel to frost, slim, 20".......4,315.00
Vase, fuchsia/foliage, pastels on lt gr, slim ovoid w/bulb top, 9" .. 3,600.00
Vase, irises, lav on amber to frost, 8" 2,185.00
Vase, irises, lt gr/lav/wht on frost/orange, incurvate cylinder, 22".3,965.00
Vase, leaves/buds, soft gr to frost, cylindrical w/bun base, 23" 2,020.00
Vase, leaves/seed pods, gr/chartreuse on salmon to frost, 15x4" .. 2,185.00
Vase, mold-blown hyacinths, bl/purple on frost to bl, 12x5" 8,625.00
Vase, mold-blown leaves/sea pods, purple on yel, ovoid on ring ft, 7"... 1,150.00
Vase, mold-blown plums, dk colors on citron, shouldered, 15½"...5,175.00
Vase, scenic (EX detail), brn on amber to turq mottle, fp, bulbous, 8" .. 12,650.00
Vase, trees, brn on amber to frost to peach, ovoid w/long neck, 13"...2,990.00
Vase, trees, brn/gr on frost, bulbous, 5¾".................................1,840.00
Vase, trees, brn/gr on salmon to frost, bulbous w/cup rim, 13" ..3,900.00
Vase, trees, mtns/lake beyond, dk bl on yel to frost to bl, 17x9" ...10,925.00
Vase, trees/peacock on fence, mtns/lake, wine on bl to citron, 14x10" ..24,150.00
Vase, trees/shrubs, brn/gr on salmon to frost, folded rim, 7x6" ..2,990.00
Vase, trumpet vines, dk red/cinnamon on bright yel, 14x9" 6,325.00

Enameled Glass

Vase, mums, yellow and green on amber with ribbing, 5¼", $1,100.00. (Photo courtesy Early Auction Co.)

Bottle, scent; amber w/Queen Anne's Lace, rnd w/short neck, 4" .. 1,680.00
Bowl, tulips, wine/rose/gr on gr frost w/gilt, 3-lobe rim, 6¾" 2,760.00
Vase, tiny flowers/ladybugs, mc on pale lilac, 3¾"........................ 205.00

Marqueterie-Sur-Verre

Pitcher, magnolias on martele clear to wht, pk hdl, 9¾" 8,400.00
Vase, floral, ovoid w/cvd leaves, resting on leafy bronze ft, 7" ...6,240.00
Vase, leaves/flowers, gray/orange on yel-amber, ruffled lip/ft, 11"... 60,375.00

Marquetry, Wood

Etagere, 2 sq shelves w/leaves fruitwood inlay, buttresses, 44x20x19" ... 4,800.00
Table, daffodils on top & bottom tier, sgn in marquetry, 27x22x13" ... 1,500.00
Table, side; foliage inlay on oak, shelf, 29x22¼x15" 3,000.00
Tables, nesting; nature studies, set of 4, lg: 30x23" 6,900.00
Tea table, tulips/floral/parquetry, folding, 29x27x20"................3,600.00

Pottery

Card tray, 'card'/floral center on bl mottle, 2 rolled-in sides, 12" ...1,840.00
Inkwell, free-form w/HP nautical scene: rowboat/6 men/ship beyond, 12"..1,435.00
Pitcher, lg dragonfly on crackled/gold-leaf embedded ground, 7", EX... 2,700.00
Pitcher, peasant smoking pipe, 12x7".. 865.00
Vase, farmyard/chickens, 4-ftd pillow form, sgn EG/#244/ 12" L, NM 2,000.00
Vase, sunflower form w/thistles & X of Lorraine in bl on wht, 6½" ...985.00

Gambling Memorabilia

Gambling memorabilia from the infamous casinos of the West and items that were once used on the 'Floating Palace' riverboats are especially sought after by today's collectors.

Box, gaming; mahog w/inlay, hinged lid, holds 2 chip racks+3 decks.. 225.00
Counter, cvd ivory w/floral medallion, etch 0-9, 2¼" dia 150.00
Crap table, tabletop type from 1890s saloon, 8¼x73x45" 125.00
Dice, orange mottled Bakelite, 2x2", pr 40.00
Dice, wood w/gr & wht pnt, 3x3", pr 60.00
Dice bowl, famille verte dragons on cream, China, 18th C, 8½"... 650.00
Dice game, Winkle, wooden countertop type w/flip paddle, Pat 93, 5" H....300.00
Poker chip, horse head eng on ivory, red border, late 1800s 45.00
Poker chip, Pequop Hotel Wells Nevada $1, gold letters on red clay... 90.00
Poker chip caddy, gr & yel swirled Catalin, blk hdl, 10-compartment.........125.00
Poker chip carousel, brn Catalin, Drueke Co...MI #509, 15" dia........ 70.00
Poker chips, Royal Flush, 1870s, 180 mc chips in wooden box w/inlay....650.00
Poker chips, Spirit of St Louis, set of 198 (red/wht/bl) in holder .. 100.00
Poker chips, 200 Bakelite (red/butterscotch/gr) in Bakelite caddy ... 175.00
Punch board, Big Top Tommy, 16" 50.00

Roulette wheel, Ten for One, gilt and painted cards and racehorses, ca 1890, 24x24", $2,250.00. (Photo courtesy Skinner Inc. Auctioneers & Appraisers of Fine Art)

Wheel, bright mc pnt on wood, 1950s, 30", EX............................. 250.00
Wheel, horserace theme, pnt wood, 24" dia, 32" 375.00
Wheel, wood on iron base, orig pnt, Dailey Mfg, ca 1910, 60" dia, 86"...1,250.00

Gameboards

Gameboards, the handmade ones from the eighteenth and nineteenth centuries, are collected more for their folk art quality than their relation to games. Excellent examples of these handcrafted 'playthings' sell well into the thousands of dollars; even the simple designs are often expensive. If you are interested in this field, you must study it carefully. The market is always full of 'new' examples. Well-established dealers are often your best sources; they are essential if you do not have the expertise to judge the age of the boards yourself. Our advisor for this category is Louis Picek; he is listed in the Directory under Iowa.

Checkers, blk & red pnt on hand-planed pine, gallery edge, 29x19" .350.00
Checkers, blk/bl pnt on wood, reverse: fantasy figure, 19th, 18x18" ..4,400.00
Checkers, brn/cream pnt wood, appl molding, 1800s, 18x31"...... 585.00
Checkers, red/blk/yel pnt pine brd, pnt wear, 18x18" 750.00
Checkers, red/yel sqs placed together w/in frwork under glass, 19" sq ... 400.00
Checkers/parcheesi, mc pnt on pine, alligatored, 21x22" 925.00
Checkers/parcheesi, old mc pnt on pine, 27x19", EX 575.00
Checkers/unknown, mc pnt on wood, appl molding, ca 1900, 10x20"...2,450.00
Cribbage brd, walnut w/inlaid 5-point stars & eagles, 14x3" 325.00
Goose, spiral field w/63 spaces, mc pnt on wood, early 19th C, 25x26" ...16,450.00

Games

Collectors of antique games are finding it more difficult to find their treasures at shows and flea markets. Most of the action these days seems to be through specialty dealers and auctions. The appreciation of the art on the boards and boxes continues to grow. You see many of the early games proudly displayed as art, and they should be. The period from the 1850s to 1910 continues to draw the most interest. Many of the games of that period were executed by well-known artists and illustrators. The quality of their lithography cannot be matched today. The historical value of games made before 1850 has caused interest in this period to increase. While they may not have the graphic quality of the later period, their insights into the social and moral character of the early nineteenth century are interesting.

Twentieth-century games invoke a nostalgic feeling among collectors who recall looking forward to a game under the Christmas tree each year. They search for examples that bring back those Christmas-morning memories. While the quality of their lithography is certainly less than the early games, the introduction of personalities from the comic strips, radio, and later TV created new interest. Every child wanted a game that featured their favorite character. Monopoly, probably the most famous game ever produced, was introduced during the Great Depression. For further information, we recommend *Schroeder's Collectible Toys, Antique to Modern*, available from Collector Books.

Advance to Boardwalk, Parker Bros, 1985, NMIB 15.00
Air Defense Target Game, Wolverine, tin, 18" L, VG................. 275.00
American Boys, McLoughlin Bros, Boy Scouts, 1913, VGIB....... 290.00
Aquanauts, Transogram, 1961, NMIB....................................... 75.00
Auto Racing Game, Milton Bradley, 1962, VGIB....................... 125.00

Bagatelle, McLoughlin Bros., 1890s, VG+, $400.00. (Photo courtesy Paul Fink)

Bamboozle, Milton Bradley, 1962, NMIB 30.00
Base Ball, Pan Am Toy Co, 1920s, NMIB.................................. 400.00
Baseball Challenge, Tri-Valley Games, 1980, NMIB..................... 30.00
Baseball Game, Hustler, tin & wood, spring-activated roller, 14x9", VG..110.00
Bash!, Milton Bradley, 1965, NMIB... 20.00
Battle of Manila, board game, Parker Bros, incomplete, VGIB.... 565.00
Blow Your Cool, Whitman, 1969, NMIB.................................... 15.00
Boots & Saddles, Chad Valley, 1960, EXIB 40.00
Bop the Beetle, Ideal, 1963, EXIB... 40.00
Bowling Game, Singer, early, VGIB...1,035.00
Broadcast Football, J Pressman & Co, 1934, incomplete in G- box..30.00
Candyland, Milton Bradley, 1955, NMIB.................................... 20.00
Clue, Parker Bros, 1972, NMIB.. 10.00
Commercial Traveler, McLoughlin Bros, EXIB............................ 330.00
Dash for the North Pole, McLoughlin Bros, 1897, EXIB..........2,760.00
Deputy (The), Milton Bradley, Bell, 1960, NMIB.......................... 50.00

Diner's Club Credit Card Game, Ideal, 1961, MNIB.................... 40.00
Dogfight, Milton Bradley, 1962, EXIB................................. 85.00
Don't Spill the Beans, 1967, EXIB 25.00
Dream House, Milton Bradley, 1968, EXIB............................. 40.00
Election, Singer, early political concerns, rare, EXIB 3,450.00
Electric Sports Car Race, Tudor, 1959, NMIB 75.00
Electric Target Game, Marx, 1950s, unused, EXIB 300.00
Escort Game of Guys & Gals, Parker Bros, 1955, unused, MIB...... 30.00
Farmer Jones Pigs, McLoughlin Bros, VGIB 130.00
Game of Famous Men, Parker Bros, VGIB............................. 50.00
Game of Flags, McLoughlin Bros, VGIB.............................. 75.00
Game of Golf, JH Singer, VGIB..................................... 550.00
Game of Innocence, Parker Bros, 1888, GIB 100.00
Game of Nosey, McLoughlin, VGIB 175.00
Game of Steeple Gase, Milton Bradley, 1917, VGIB.................. 110.00
Gee-Wiz Horse Race, Wolverine, EX 100.00
Going to the Klondike, Game of; McLoughlin Bros, 1890s, EXIB.....4,600.00
Hoopla, Ideal, 1966, NMIB.. 60.00
Hot Wheels Wipe Out Race Game, Mattel, 1968, NMIB............. 50.00
Identipops, Playvalue, 1969, VGIB 200.00
Magnetic Fish Pond, McLoughlin Bros, 1890s, VGIB................ 400.00
Merry Go Round, Parker Bros, EXIB................................ 400.00
Monopoly, Chas B Darrow, Parker Bros, wht box lid, 1933, VGIB ...85.00
Monopoly, Parker Bros, 1964, lg maroon box 65.00
Motor Carriage, board game, Parker Bros, 1899, incomplete, EXIB...665.00
Mystery Date, Milton Bradley, 1965, NMIB 175.00
New Game of Hunting, 4 metal game pcs/15 animals/spinner, VGIB..850.00
Playing Department Store, Milton Bradley, VGIB 400.00
Pop the Chutes Target Game, NN Hill, NMIB....................... 225.00
Pop Yer Top! Game of Suspense, Milton Bradley, 1968, EXIB....... 40.00

Rival Policeman, McLoughlin Bros., 1896, EX, $4,500.00. (Photo courtesy Paul Fink)

Roulette Wheel, Marx, NMIB....................................... 50.00
Spot Shot Marble Game, Wolverine, 1930s, NM...................... 50.00
Stanley Africa Game, Bliss, EXIB 7,475.00
Steeple Chasing, McLoughlin Bros, incomplete, VGIB.............. 200.00
Stop Thief, Parker Bros, 1979, NMIB............................. 50.00
Tiny Time Game of Beautiful Things, Parker Bros, 1970, MIB...... 50.00
Touchdown Football, Wilder, GIB 75.00
Town & Country Traffic, Ranger Steel, 1940s, EXIB............... 50.00
Train for Boston, Parker Bros, 1900, EXIB...................... 865.00
Turn Over, Milton Bradley, EXIB................................. 65.00
Voodoo Doll Game, Schaper, 1967, EXIB........................... 30.00
Which Witch?, Milton Bradley, 1970, NMIB....................... 130.00
Young America Target, Parker Bros, VGIB........................ 275.00

Personalities, Movies, and TV Shows

Amazing Spider-Man, Milton Bradley, 1966, EXIB.................. 50.00
Angela Cartwright Buttons & Bows, Transogram, EXIB............. 75.00
Babe Ruth's Baseball Game, Milton Bradley, EXIB............... 500.00
Barbie Queen of the Prom, Mattel, 1960, NMIB.................. 55.00
Barney Google & Spark Plug Game, Milton Bradley, 1923, EXIB..100.00
Bat Masterson, Lowell, 1958, NMIB............................. 65.00
Beatles Flip Your Wig Game, Milton Bradley, 1964, NMIB........ 125.00
Brady Bunch, Whitman, 1973, MIB.............................. 100.00

Buck Rogers, three boards, no game pieces, EX, $460.00. (Photo courtesy Morphy Auctions)

Captain & the Kids, Milton Bradley, 1947, NMIB...................... 85.00
Creature From the Black Lagoon, Hasbro, 1963, EXIB 350.00
Dangerous World of James Bond 007, Milton Bradley, 1965, NMIB ...60.00
Dick Tracy Card Game, Whitman, 1934, EXIB........................ 75.00
Disneyland Game, Transogram, 1954, EXIB 65.00
Emergency, Milton Bradley, 1973, NMIB 40.00
Flipper Flips, Mattel, 1965, NMIB 70.00
Fugitive, Ideal, 1964, NMIB...................................... 75.00
Game of Red Riding Hood, Parker Bros, 1895, VGIB................. 150.00
Gene Autry Bandit Trail Game, Kenton, EXIB....................... 200.00
Hawaiian Eye, Lowell, 1960, VGIB................................. 130.00
Hopalong Cassidy Game, Marx, 1950s, EXIB......................... 115.00
Jack & Jill, Milton Bradley, 1966, VGIB.......................... 100.00
Lone Ranger Silver Bullets, Whiting, 1956, MIB................... 150.00
Lost in Space, Milton Bradley, 1965, NMIB........................ 75.00
Mission Impossible, Ideal, 1967, EXIB............................ 120.00
Monster Old Maid, cards, Milton Bradley, 1964, EXIB.............. 65.00
Nancy Drew Mystery Game, Parker Bros, 1957, NMIB................. 160.00
Outer Limits, Milton Bradley, 1964, EXIB......................... 240.00
Peter Potamus Game, Ideal 1964, NMIB............................. 70.00
Popeye Carnival (3 Games in 1), Toymaster, NMIB 200.00
Prisoner of Zelda, Parker Bros, 1896, EXIB....................... 125.00
Red Ryder Target Game, Daisy, VGIB 75.00
Rin-Tin-Tin (Adventures of), Transogram, 1955, EXIB.............. 50.00
Robin Hood (Adventures of), Betty-B, 1956, EXIB 65.00
Rocky & His Friends, Milton Bradley, 1960, EXIB.................. 75.00
Rudolph the Red-Nosed Reindeer, Parker Bros, 1948, EXIB........ 200.00
Scarlett O'Hara - One of Her Problems, Marietta Games/MGM, 1939, EXIB..75.00
Sea Hunt, Lowell, 1961, EXIB..................................... 75.00
Smokey Bear Forest Prevention Bear, Ideal, 1961, NMIB............ 95.00
Snoopy & the Red Baron, Milton Bradley, 1970, MIB................ 55.00
Stagecoach West Adventure Game, Transogram, 1961, NMIB 90.00
Star Trek, Milton Bradley, 1979, EXIB............................ 45.00
Superman (Adventures of), Milton Bradley, 1942, EXIB............ 225.00
Superman Game, Hasbro, 1965, EXIB................................ 90.00
Tim Holt Rodeo Dart Games, American Toys, unused, NMIB 100.00

Tom & Jerry Adventure in Blunderland, Transogram, 1965, EXIB...55.00
Tom Sawyer & Huck Finn (Adventures of), Stoll & Edwards, VGIB..125.00
Top Cat, Cadaco-Ellis, 1961, NMIB 70.00
Twiggy, Milton Bradley, 1967, EXIB...65.00
Uncle Remus Shooting Gallery, American B&B Novelties, 1917, VGIB..690.00
Uncle Sam's Mail, Milton Bradley, GIB...................................90.00
Untouchables, Marx, 1950s, NMIB 220.00
Untouchables Target Game, Marx, 1950s, NM 350.00
Voyage to the Bottom of the Sea Card Game, Milton Bradley, 1964, NMIB...50.00
Wagon Train, Milton Bradley, 1960, EXIB 50.00
Walt Disney's Fantasyland, Parker Bros, 1950, MIB 50.00
Walter Johnson Baseball Game, VGIB 200.00
Wanted Dead or Alive, Lowell, 1959, EXIB 110.00
Who Framed Rodger Rabbit?, Milton Bradley, 1987, NMIB.......130.00
Wild Bill Hickok's Calvary & Indians Game, Built Rite, 1955, NMIB..40.00
Wilder's Football Game, GIB 125.00
Wonder Woman, Hasbro, 1967, NMIB....................................60.00
Woody Woodpecker Game, Milton Bradley, 1959, MIB...............50.00
Wyatt Earp, Transogram, 1958, EXIB.....................................70.00
Yogi Bear Score-A-Matic Ball Toss, Transogram, EXIB..............65.00
Zamboola, Norstar, VGIB..275.00
Zorro, Parker Bros/Walt Disney, 1966, EXIB............................55.00

Garden City Pottery

Founded in 1902 in San Jose, California, by the end of the 1920s this pottery had grown to become the largest in Northern California. During that period production focused on stoneware, sewer pipe, and red clay flowerpots. In the late '30s and '40s, the company produced dinnerware in bright solid colors of yellow, green, blue, orange, cobalt, turquoise, white, and black. Royal Arden Hickman, who would later gain fame for the innovative artware he modeled for the Haeger company, designed not only dinnerware but a line of Art Deco vases and bowls as well. The company endured hard times by adapting to the changing needs of the market and during the '50s concentrated on production of garden products. Foreign imports, however, proved to be too competitive, and the company's pottery production ceased in 1979.

Because none of the colored-glazed products were ever marked, to learn to identify the products of this company, you'll need to refer to *Sanford's Guide to Garden City Pottery* by Jim Pasquali. Values apply to items in all colors (except black) and all patterns, unless noted otherwise. Due to relative rarity, 20% should be added for any item found in black.

Vase, 4½x10", $70.00; candleholders, $35.00 for the pair. (Photo courtesy Jim Pasquali)

Bean pot, Deco, w/lid, lg..85.00
Bean pot, plain, 1-qt 25.00

Bowl, Bulb, 10" 45.00
Bowl, mixing; Wide-Ring, solid color, #3 (mid sz)........................30.00
Bowl, nappy, #4...25.00
Bowl, soup; plain, solid color 35.00
Bowl, Succulent, 11"..60.00
Casserole, narrow or wide rings, solid color, 7", ea.......................35.00
Cookie jar, Deco style, solid color, 7½".......................................75.00
Crock, 2-gal..45.00
Cup, punch 15.00
Frog, sm 15.00
Jardiniere, ribbed solid color, 10"...45.00
Mug, chowder; solid color, w/lid...45.00
Oil jar, hand thrown, mini..150.00
Pitcher, 2-qt 55.00
Plate, artichoke; solid color 40.00
Plate, dinner; solid color, 9" 20.00
Ramekin, solid color, 3" 20.00
Teapot, Deco style, solid color, 4-cup...75.00
Vase, Deco, 4½x10" 65.00
Vase, Ribbed Cylinder, 8" 35.00
Water cooler, crockery..75.00

Gardner Porcelain

Models of wonderfully complicated and detailed subjects illustrating people of many nations absorbed in day-to-day activities were made by this company from the turn of the nineteenth century until well past the 1850s. The factory was founded in 1765 near Moscow, Russia, by an Englishman by the name of Francis Gardner. They are still in business today.

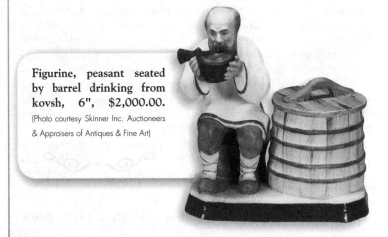

Figurine, peasant seated by barrel drinking from kovsh, 6", $2,000.00. (Photo courtesy Skinner Inc. Auctioneers & Appraisers of Antiques & Fine Art)

Figurine, blind beggar, can in right hand, hat in left, 1870, 5¾".. 2,000.00
Figurine, boxer, fighting pose, boxing gloves/typical garb, 1840, 8"..5,875.00
Figurine, boys (2) cracking colored eggs, basket at ft, 6" 880.00
Figurine, cat reclining, looking upwards, right paw raised, 1860, 4" L..1,000.00
Figurine, coachman, hands to hips, long bl coat, 1845, 7⅜"......4,700.00
Figurine, dog by tree trunk (pen holder), rococo base, 1820s, 2½"...1,290.00
Figurine, drunken man being aided by wife, child at side, 7".....3,300.00
Figurine, girl carries lg flower basket in both hands, 1820, 5"....3,800.00
Figurine, girl leans over pail of mushrooms, 1800s, 4½" 4,100.00
Figurine, hound seated on rectangular base, 1850s, att, 3x6" 940.00
Figurine, lad stands/holds tree branch, 1850s, 4" 2,820.00
Figurine, lady, fashionably dressed, from a set of 6, 1820, 8" 5,550.00
Figurine, lady on sofa pulls up hose, boy kneels at side, 1940, 2"..5,580.00
Figurine, man standing, bsk, 1850s, 3¼" 1,645.00
Figurine, man w/bow & arrow, game in left hand, 1840, 6½"...3,800.00

Figurine, mother & child (seated), she w/cloth, child w/smoother, 4" ..765.00
Figurine, nude in draped peignoir adjusts stockings, 1850s, 7½" ...11,750.00
Figurine, old man stands, hands in pockets, 1850s, 9" 3,290.00
Figurine, peasant girl in regional dress shields eyes from sun, 9".. 1,175.00
Figurine, peasant lady breast-feeding baby, 8", EX 300.00
Figurine, peasant lady dancing, floral apron, 8" 1,175.00
Figurine, peasant lady on bench feeds baby, child beside, 5½" ..1,250.00
Figurine, peasant man, seated/eating, 1860, 4¾" 1,880.00
Figurine, peasant man & lady in local costumes, 1850s, 5½", pr.. 3,150.00
Figurine, peasant woman seated on bench, jar/pot w/lids at ft, bsk, 6" 2,115.00
Figurine, Spaniard standing/wearing short coat over shoulders, 7¾"..8,225.00

Gas Globes and Panels

Gas globes and panels, once a common sight, have vanished from the countryside but are being sought by collectors as a unique form of advertising memorabilia. Early globes from the 1920s (some date back to as early as 1912), now referred to as 'one-piece' (Type 4) globes, were made of molded milk glass and were globular in shape. The gas company name was etched or painted on the glass. Few of these were ever produced, and this type is valued very highly by collectors today.

A new type of pump was introduced in the early 1930s; the old 'visible' pumps were replaced by 'electric' models. Globes were changing at the same time. By the mid-teens a three-piece (Type 3) globe consisting of a pair of inserts and a metal body was being produced in both 15" and 16½" sizes. Collectors prefer to call globes that are not one-piece or metal frame 'three-piece glass' (Type 2). Though metal-framed globes with glass inserts (Type 3) were most popular in the 1920s and 1930s, some were actually made as early as 1914. Though rare in numbers, their use spans many years. In the 1930s Type 2 globes became the the replacements of the one-piece globe and Type 3 globes. The most recently manufactured gas globes are made with a plastic body that contains two 13½" glass lenses. These were common in the 1950s but were actually used as early as 1932. This style is referred to as Type 1 in our listings. Values here are for examples with both sides in excellent condition: no chips, wear, or other damage. Our advisor for this category is Scott Benjamin; he is listed in the Directory under Ohio. For more information we recommend *Value Guide to Gas Station Memorabilia* by B.J. Summers and Wayne Priddy.

Note: Standard Crowns with raised letters are one-piece globes that were made in the 1920s; those made in the 1950s (no raised letters), though one-piece, are not regarded as such by today's collectors.

Type 1, Plastic Body, Glass Inserts (Inserts 13½") — 1931 – 1950s

Aro Flight, dk bl/wht/orange-red...1,250.00
Dino Supreme, sm dinosaur, red/wht/gr, EX................................250.00
Dixie, plastic band, EX 250.00
Fleet-Wing, EX 400.00
Kendal Deluxe, Capco body w/red pnt, 13½", EX 350.00
Malco, orig bl-gr Capco fr, EX 2,000.00
New State 88, EX...1,000.00
Phillips 66 Flite-Fuel, EX 450.00
Pure, blk on milk glass, orig Capco fr, 1960s, EX 375.00
Road King, knight on horse, red on wht, Capco fr, 1950s, EX ..1,350.00
Sinclair H-C Gasoline, red & gr on wht, EX 250.00
Skelly Keotane, EX..250.00
Spur, oval body, EX...350.00
Sunray Ethyl Corp, EX..1,600.00
Texaco Diesel Chief, Capco body, 13½", EX................................1,350.00
Viking, pictures Viking ship, EX...2,800.00

Type 2, Glass Frame, Glass Inserts (Inserts 13½") — 1926 – 1940s

Aerio, w/airplane 12,000.00
Amoco, Gill body, 13½", EX 500.00
Atlantic, red/wht/bl, ca 1966, EX 500.00
Atlantic Hi-Arc, red/wht/bl, Gill fr, ca 1936.................................650.00
Barnsdall Be Square Gasoline, 2 lenses in wide body, EX.............600.00
Bay Ethyl, Gill glass, EX 750.00
Capitol Gasoline Ethyl Corp, EX 500.00

Clark, EX, $350.00.
(Photo courtesy Collector's Auction Service)

Col-Tex Service Gasoline, 5-color, EX+ 1,250.00
Derby's Flexgas Ethyl, threaded base, Gill fr, 1940s, EX 850.00
Esso, EX 325.00
Frontier Gas, Double Refined, EX 400.00
Globe Gasoline, metal base ring, EX...2,000.00
Hustol, yel & blk on milk glass, wide fr, EX 450.00
Lion, Knix Knox, metal base, EX 3,000.00
Marine Gasoline, sea horse, red/turq/wht, 1940s, NM.................3,000.00
Never Nox Ethyl, EX..650.00
Pitman Streamlined, Gill body, 13½", EX...................................12,000.00
Pure, EX 500.00
Sinclair Dino, ray glass fr or 3-pc glass 300.00
Sinclair H-C Gasoline, red/wht/gr, EX...600.00
Sky Chief, Gill body, 13½", EX 650.00
Sohio Diesel Supreme, orig wide fr, EX 500.00
Standard Crown, gr crown, tractor fuel, rare, EX..........................1,500.00
Standard Crown, wht, red or gold, EX, ea....................................450.00
Texaco Ethyl, EX 2,000.00
Tydol A Ethyl, red/blk on milk glass, Gill fr, ca 1946, EX 1,450.00
United Hi-Test Gasoline, red/wht/bl, EX......................................450.00
WNAX, w/radio station pictured, EX 5,000.00

Type 3, Metal Frame, Glass Inserts (Inserts 15" or 16½") — 1915 – 1930s

Aero Mobilgas, new metal body, rare, 15", EX...........................2,800.00
Atlantic Ethyl, 16½", EX...950.00
Blue Anti-Knock Gasoline, Interstate Oil Gas, EX...................1,200.00
Bluebird Anti-Knock Gasoline, bl on milk glass, 1930s, 15", EX ..3,500.00
Conoco Gasoline, silhouette figure on yel, 1913-29 ....6,000.00
Farmer's Union High Octane, red/wht/bl, high profile metal body, 15"..1,000.00
Humble Oils, red/bl/wht, orig red fr, NM....................................2,500.00
Mobilgas, red Pegasus, blk letters, 16½", EX 850.00
Mohawk Gasoline, Indian's portrait, red version, 1930s, EX...12,000.00
Phillips Benzo, low-profile metal body, 15", EX 4,500.00
Purol the Pure Oil, bl & wht, 15", EX+ 800.00
Red Star Gasoline, blk w/red star on wht, new fr, 1920s, 15", EX... 1,400.00
Rocor Gasoline, eagle, blk & yel on milk glass, ca 1939, EX.....1,800.00
Signal, old stoplight, 15", EX...8,000.00
Texaco Leaded, glass globe, EX...5,000.00

Type 4, One-Piece Glass Globes, No Inserts, Co. Name Etched, Raised or Enameled — 1912 – 1931

Imperial Premier Gasoline, red & yel on milk glass, rpt 1,500.00
Newport Gasoline Oils, orange & gr on milk glass, VG 2,850.00
Pierce Pennant, etched, EX 3,500.00
Sinclair Gasoline, etched, orig pnt, 1920s, VG+ 1,850.00
Sinclair Gasoline baked on milk glass, ca 1926-29, EX 1,750.00
Sinclair HC Gasoline, red/wht/blk on milk glass, 1927-29, EX..2,000.00
Super Shell, clam shape, EX 1,800.00
Texaco Ethyl, EX 2,500.00
That Good Gulf..., emb, orange & blk letters, EX 1,500.00
White Eagle, detailed eagle, 20¾", EX 2,500.00

Gaudy Dutch

Inspired by Oriental Imari wares, Gaudy Dutch was made in England from 1800 to 1820. It was hand decorated on a soft-paste body with rich underglaze blues accented in orange, red, pink, green, and yellow. It differs from Gaudy Welsh in that there is no lustre (except on Water Lily). There are 17 patterns, some of which are War Bonnet, Grape, Dahlia, Oyster, Urn, Butterfly, Carnation, Single Rose, Double Rose, and Water Lily.

Values hinge on condition, strength of color, detail, and variations to standard designs. Our values are based on near-mint to mint condition items, with only minimal wear or scratches. Even a piece rated excellent may bring from 60% to 75% less than these prices. We have used the term 'chain' to refer to a border device less detailed than one with distinguishable hearts or leaves, as the latter will bring higher prices. When ranges are used, the higher side will represent an item with better than average color and execution.

Butterfly, plate, bl band w/wavy line+inner leaf border, 8" 2,200.00
Butterfly, plate, yel ovals in bl band+inner leaf border, 8", $2,200 to .3,100.00
Butterfly, tea bowl & saucer, yel chain in bl band, from $1,500 to..2,000.00
Butterfly, waste bowl, yel chain in bl band border, 3½x6⅜", VG 1,400.00
Carnation, plate, yel chain in bl band+inner leaf border, 9½" ..1,650.00
Carnation, plate, yel chain in bl band+waves border, 6¾" 960.00
Carnation, soup bowl, yel ovals in bl band+inner leaf border, 10" ...1,080.00
Carnation, sugar bowl, yel chain in bl band border, w/lid, 5x6", VG ..780.00
Carnation, waste bowl, yel chain in bl band border, 3x6½", VG... 480.00
Dahlia, tea bowl & saucer, bl band, red hearts border, sm flakes to ft .. 4,500.00
Double Rose, creamer, helmet shape, shaped hdl, 5" 1,375.00
Double Rose, plate, 10"..1,560.00
Double Rose, platter, 10" L 7,200.00
Double Rose, soup plate, 9" 540.00
Double Rose, teapot, rectangular, 6¼", from $2,400 to..............3,200.00
Dove, plate, bl band w/wavy lines+inner leaf border, 9¾" 880.00
Dove, plate, yel chain on bl band+waves border, 8⅜" 525.00
Dove, tea bowl & saucer, narrow bl rim band 540.00
Grape, bowl, yel chain on bl band border, shallow, 9¾" 840.00
Grape, cup plate, yel chain on bl band, 3½" 990.00
Grape, pitcher, yel chain on bl band border, 4¾" 2,000.00
Grape, plate, yel chain on bl band border, 7", from $440 to.........510.00
Grape, soup plate, yel chain on bl band border, sm mfg flaw, 7"...495.00
Grape, tea bowl & saucer, flared sides, yel chain on bl band border ...780.00
Grape, teapot, 7"; creamer, 4½"; sugar bowl, w/lid, 5½", all EX..2,400.00
Grape, toddy plate, yel heart chain on bl band border, 4½" 1,500.00
Grape, waste bowl, yel chain on bl band border, VG....................400.00
Leaf, tea bowl & saucer, yel heart chain on bl band border, VG .4,200.00
Oyster, creamer, 4¼", EX, from $1,100 to 1,550.00
Oyster, plate, 8¼", from $500 to..600.00
Oyster, tea bowl & saucer, w/King's Rose, pk band w/hearts & swags, EX....400.00

Oyster, teapot, w/King's Rose+bright yel flower, EX, 5x9½"......2,700.00
Oyster, waste bowl, 6¼" 1,200.00
Primrose, toddy plate, yel hearts on bl band+wavy border, 4⅝", EX..4,550.00
Single Rose, coffeepot, acanthus leaf spout/hdl, rpr, 11", $2,800 to..3,000.00
Single Rose, creamer, yel chain on bl band border, EX, 4¼" 720.00
Single Rose, plate, exceptional detail, pale pk flowers, 8⅜" 1,800.00
Single Rose, plate, yel chain on lt bl band border, 8⅛" 535.00
Single Rose, soup bowl, yel ovals on bl band border, 9⅞"............840.00
Single Rose, tea bowl & saucer, yel heart chain on bl band border, EX..475.00
Single Rose, teapot, 6¾" 3,850.00
Single Rose, waste bowl, yel heart/bl band border inside rim, 3x6".. 700.00
Sunflower, plate, bl band w/waves+inner leaf border, 9¾".........1,000.00
Sunflower, plate, 2 wavy lines+bl band border, from $350 to 350.00

Sunflower, sugar bowl with lid, 5½", $1,600.00; Oyster, teapot, paneled borders, 6", $2,530.00. (Photo courtesy Garth's Auctions Inc.)

Sunflower, tea bowl & saucer, bl band w/waves, from $500 to 660.00
Sunflower, teapot, bl/dk brn band w/waves border, prof rstr, 10" ..5,700.00
Urn, plate, yel chain on bl band+waves border, 7½" 1,020.00
Urn, waste bowl, paneled floral border inside, 3½x6½" 2,150.00
War Bonnet, bowl, shallow, 8⅛"..960.00
War Bonnet, cup plate, 3¼"..1,400.00
War Bonnet, pitcher, 5¾" 3,000.00
War Bonnet, soup plate, 7"..500.00
War Bonnet, sugar bowl, w/lid, prof rstr, 5x5"..............................575.00
War Bonnet, toddy plate, #d/red artist mk, 4⅝"............................725.00
Zinnia, plate, dk brn-lined bl band w/leaf chain, Riley, 8¼"......3,000.00

Gaudy Welsh

Gaudy Welsh was an inexpensive hand-decorated ware made in both England and Wales from 1820 until 1860. It is characterized by its colors — principally blue, orange-rust, and copper lustre — and by its uninhibited patterns. Accent colors may be yellow and green. (Pink lustre may be present, since lustre applied to the white areas appears pink. A copper tone develops from painting lustre onto the dark colors.) The body of the ware may be heavy ironstone (also called Gaudy Ironstone), creamware, earthenware, or porcelain; even style and shapes vary considerably. Patterns, while usually floral, are also sometimes geometric and may have trees and birds. Beware! The Wagon Wheel pattern has been reproduced. Our advisor for this category is Cheryl Nelson; she is listed in the Directory under Texas.

Note: Prices are rising. Each day more collectors enter the field. For the first time British auction houses are picturing and promoting Gaudy Welsh. Demand for Columbine, Grape, Tulip, Oyster, and Wagon Wheel is slow. We should also mention that the Bethedsa pattern is very similar to a Davenport jug pattern. No porcelain Gaudy Welsh was made in Wales.

Anglesey, jug, 7"..575.00
Betws-y-Coed, jug, 7"..695.00
Billingsley Rose, cake plate, 9½".........................250.00
Blinking Eye, waste bowl, 6"................................275.00
Buckle Cockle, plate, 4"...75.00
Capel Curig, jug, 7½"..550.00
Castle, cup & saucer...245.00
Celyn, teapot, 8½"..800.00
Chinoiserie, tyg, 5½"...600.00
Corbaea, jug, 7"..650.00
Corn Laws, bowl, ftd, dtd 1846, 10½"..............1,700.00
Dimity, cup & saucer..130.00
Ducks, jug, 5½"...750.00
Fern, cup & saucer..150.00
Fruit, cup & saucer..275.00
Grape, sucrier, 7"...130.00
Harmony, jug, 6"..500.00
Herald, jug, 7½"..825.00
Kyoto, cake plate, 9½"..265.00
Lotus, sucrier, 5¼"..275.00
New Quay, plate, 6½"...295.00
Oyster, cup & saucer...45.00
Oyster, teapot, 8½"...235.00
Poinsettia, cup & saucer.......................................300.00
Prestatyn, jug, 8¼"...600.00
Repousse Name, mug, rare, 3½"........................1,100.00
Schrimp, sucrier, 5"..300.00
Strawflower, jug, 6"...500.00
Teahouse, jug, 5"..400.00
Vine, plate, 7½"...295.00
War Bonnet, cup & saucer....................................275.00

Geisha Girl

Geisha Girl porcelain was one of several key Japanese china production efforts aimed at the booming export markets of the U.S., Canada, England, and other parts of Europe. The wares feature colorful, kimono-clad Japanese ladies in scenes of everyday Japanese life surrounded by exquisite flora, fauna, and mountain ranges. Nonetheless, the forms in which the wares were produced reflected the late nineteenth- and early twentieth-century Western dining and decorating preferences: tea and coffee services, vases, dresser sets, children's items, planters, etc.

Over 100 manufacturers were involved in Geisha Girl production. This accounts for the several hundred different patterns, well over a dozen border colors and styles, and several methods of design execution. Geisha Girl Porcelain was produced in wholly hand-painted versions, but most were hand painted over stencilled outlines. Be wary of Geisha ware executed with decals. Very few decaled examples came out of Japan. Rather, most were Czechoslovakian attempts to home in on the market. Czech pieces have stamped marks in broad, pseudo-Oriental characters. Items with portraits of Oriental ladies in the bottom of tea or sake cups are *not* Geisha Girl Porcelain, unless the outside surface of the wares are decorated as described above. These lovely faces, formed by varying the thickness of the porcelain body, are called lithophanes and are collectible in their own right.

The height of Geisha Girl production was between 1910 and the mid-1930s. Some post-World War II production has been found marked Occupied Japan. The ware continued in minimal production during the 1960s, but the point of origin of the later pieces was not only Japan but Hong Kong as well. These productions are discerned by the pure whiteness of the porcelain; even, unemotional borders; lack of background washes and gold enameling; and overall sparseness of detail. A new wave of Nippon-marked reproduction Geisha emerged in 1996. If the

Geisha Girl productions of the 1960s – 1980s were overly plain, the mid-1990s repros are overly ornate. Original Geisha Girl porcelain was enhanced by brush strokes of color over a stenciled design; it was never the 'color perfectly within the lines' type of decoration found on current reproductions. Original Geisha Girl porcelain was decorated with color washes; the reproductions are in heavy enamels. The backdrop decoration of the current reproductions feature solid, thick colors, and the patterns feature too much color; period Geisha ware had a high ratio of white space to color. The new pieces also have bright shiny gold in proportions greater than most period Geisha ware. The Nippon marks on the reproductions are wrong. Some of the Geisha ware created during the Nippon era bore the small precise decaled green M-in-Wreath mark, a Noritake registered trademark. The reproduced items feature an irregular facsimile of this mark. Stamped onto the reproductions is an unrealistically large M-in-Wreath mark in shades of green ranging from an almost neon to pine green with a wreath that looks like it has seen better days, as it does not have the perfect roundness of the original mark. Other marks have also been reproduced. Reproductions of mid-sized trays, chunky hatpin holders, an ornate vase, a covered bottle, and a powder jar are among the current reproductions popping up at flea and antique markets.

Our advisor for this category is Elyce Litts; she is listed in the Directory under New Jersey.

Berry set, Dragonboat, cobalt border w/gold, master+6 ind bowls.. 85.00
Berry set, Garden Bench, red/pine gr border w/gold, 10"+4 5½" bowls..34.00

Biscuit jar, Basket of Mums, $65.00. (Photo courtesy Elyce Litts)

Bonbon/mint dish, Temple B, red border w/int gold lacing, 2⅜x5¼" ...17.50
Bowl, berry; Pointing F, red maple leaves/gold border, Kutani, 10" ..50.00
Bowl, Footbridge B, red border w/gold buds, 9½"............................34.00
Bowl, Parasol C, red border w/gold buds, rtcl rim, MIJ, 7½"...........16.00
Bowl, Pointing Q, red butterfly border, foliate/rtcl rim, 7½"...........18.00
Bowl, salad; Garden Bench A, red border, 9-lobed, 7¼"................25.00
Bowl, Samurai Dance, red border w/gold, 10".................................38.00
Bread dish, Bamboo Trellis, red border w/gold lacing, 3x9¾".........32.00
Cocoa set, Temple B, red/orange border w/gold, pot+6 c/s...........150.00
Cracker jar, Spider Puppet, cobalt w/gold border, ftd & lobed.......65.00
Cup & saucer, Mother & Son A, diapered border, child sz.............12.00
Jar, sachet; Fan C, red border w/gold, hdls, ftd, 6½".......................75.00
Lemonade set, Bellflower, brn border w/trim, pitcher+5 mugs.....135.00
Plate, Gardening, Fort Deerborn Brand advertising, scalloped, 4¾"..14.00
Platter, Ikebana Party, red & gold border, 9½", NM 38.00
Platter, Temple Vase, bl w/gold border, red int border, flaw, 11x10"..35.00
Powder jar, Court Lady, cobalt border w/gold, unmk, 2½x4½" dia ...35.00
Relish, Chrysanthemum Garden, red border/gold, hdls, Kutani, 4½x7"...16.00
Relish, scenic/ladies reserves, red border w/gold lacing, hdls, 9¼x5".. 24.00
Tea set, River's Edge, mc 3-banded border w/gold, pot+cr/sug+6 c/s ...125.00

Tea set, River's Edge, pine gr border, MIJ, teapot+cr/sug 55.00
Tea set, Torii, geometric yel/gr border w/gold, HP MIJ, 8"pot+cr/sug...45.00
Teacup & saucer, River's Edge, mc border, MIJ 12.00
Teapot, Bamboo Trellis, lightly lobed, red border, Japan, 4½x7¾" ...25.00
Vase, Parasol, red border & ft rim, 3¾" 12.00

Georgia Art Pottery

In Cartersville, Georgia, in August 1935, W.J. Gordy first fired pottery turned from regional clays. By 1936 he was marking his wares 'Georgia Pottery' (GP) or 'Georgia Art Pottery' (GAP) and continued to do so until 1950 when he used a 'Hand Made by WJ Gordy' stamp (HM). There are different configurations of the GAP mark, one being a three-line arrangement, another that is circular and thought to be the earlier of the two. After 1970 his pottery was signed. Known throughout the world for his fine glazes, he won the Georgia Governor's Award in 1983. Examples of his wares are on display in the Smithsonian. His father W. T. B. and brother D. X. are also well-known potters.

Pitcher, mottled green and gold glaze, 4½", $125.00.

Bowl, brn w/gr mottled int, 1½x6" 75.00
Candleholder, Mountain Gold, ring hdl, WJ Gordy, 1987, ea........ 85.00
Dipper, Albany slip, GAP mk, 3¼x9" 250.00
Urn, brn matt, appl hdls, ftd, WJ Gordy, 6¾x7½" 150.00

German Porcelain

Unless otherwise noted, the porcelain listed in this section is marked simply 'Germany.' Products of other German manufactures are listed in specific categories. See also Bisque; Pink Paw Bears; Pink Pigs; Elfinware.

Plaque, nude sits among rocks, Berlin, 4x5½", in brass frame (not shown), $1,000.00.

(Photo courtesy Early Auction Co.)

Bottle, lad w/ruffled collar, bl smock, yel trousers, w/instrument, 8" ...135.00
Cup & saucer, chocolate; titled street scene on lav, paw ft, 5¾" ..325.00
Figurine, dogs (3) in various poses on grassy base, 1800s, 5⅜"...3,290.00
Figurine, pug, seated, brn/blk, 1880s, 9", facing pr.....................3,000.00
Figurine, pug on tasseled pillow, brn/gr/gilt, 1880s, 8½" 555.00
Figurine, pugs (3) at play, bell-adorned bl ribbon collar, 1900, 3"..2,560.00
Jardiniere, sm lion masks/foliage cartouches on bl w/gilt, waisted, 7".. 800.00
Plaque, Penitent Magdalene, after Batoni, ca 1857, 6"+fruitwood fr ..500.00
Plaque, Reflection (bust of young lady), Wagner, 4x2½"+gilt fr...200.00
Plaque, Vestalin, seated, holding oil lamp, 1890s, 8x6"+giltwood fr ..940.00
Plate, animals after fables, med bl/gilt rim, 1880s, 10", 7 for 880.00
Vase, dense foliate rondels on cobalt w/gilt 1880s, 10", pr 585.00
Vase, rococo style w/appl birds/insects/pine branches, 19th C, 5" ...200.00

Gladding McBean and Company

This company was established in 1875 in Lincoln, California. They first produced only clay drainage pipes, but in 1883 architectural terra cotta was introduced, which has been used extensively in the United States as well as abroad. Sometime later a line of garden pottery was added. They soon became the leading producers of tile in the country. In 1923 they purchased the Tropico Pottery in Glendale, California, where in addition to tile they also produced huge garden vases. Their line was expanded in 1934 to included artware and dinnerware.

At least 15 lines of art pottery were developed between 1934 and 1942. For a short time they stamped their wares with the Tropico Pottery mark; but the majority was signed 'GMcB' in an oval. Later the mark was changed to 'Franciscan' with several variations. After 1937 'Catalina Pottery' was used on some lines. (All items marked 'Catalina Pottery' were made in Glendale.) For further information we recommend *Collector's Encyclopedia of California Pottery, Second Edition*, by Jack Chipman (Collector Books). See also Franciscan Ware.

Bowl, batter; Cocinero, gr, 5x9" 35.00
Bowl, mixing; Cocinero, yel, #24, 1930s, 3½x7", from $25 to........ 32.00
Bowl, Redwood, stick hdl w/finger ridges, GMB, 5" 12.00
Bowl, Sandalwood, pk blush w/wht int, platinum trim, 11" 65.00
Bowl, sunbonnet form, pk, Catalina Pottery, 4½x10x8½" 32.00
Bowl, Sunkist, gr, scalloped/ribbed, 3½x10"................................... 60.00
Carafe, orange w/wooden hdl, GMcB stamp, 1934-38, 9" 75.00
Carafe, yel, wood hdl attaches at neck, Catalina Rancho, 9".......110.00
Charger, tangerine, GMcB in oval, 12"... 30.00
Cup & saucer, Sandalwood, pk blush w/creamy wht, platinum trim .. 15.00
Mug, assorted colors, in metal fr w/hdl, GMcB, 3¾", set of 6......... 85.00
Pitcher, clear over wht clay, w/lid, 5½x5" 115.00
Pitcher, pineapple shape, coral, 7¼"... 145.00
Plate, rolled edge, solid color, Catalina Pottery, 10" 15.00
Platter, Montecito, coral, 16x12" 38.00
Pot, serving; bl w/wht int, 2 bowls inside, w/lid, oval mk, 5½x9" ..240.00
Tray, tan w/bl int, scalloped/lobed rectangle, Catalina Pottery, 10" L ...400.00
Umbrella stand, emb leaf panels on wht, 4 buttresses at rim, 19x11"..275.00
Vase, Cielito, ruby w/wht int, GMcB #114, 8¾"...........................200.00
Vase, Cielito, wht w/Glacier Blue int, 4x2¼" 30.00
Vase, Cielito, wht w/turq gloss int, trumpet form, 4¾x4¾" 40.00
Vase, shell form, wht w/pk int, 5½x9" 65.00
Vase, wht, emb branches, Catalina Pottery #C636, 7¼x8"............. 45.00
Vase, yel w/oxblood int, lobed gourd form, Catalina Pottery #C-252, 6"..60.00

Glass Animals and Figurines

These beautiful glass sculptures have been produced by many major companies in America — in fact, some are still being made today. Heisey,

Fostoria, Duncan and Miller, Imperial, Paden City, Tiffin, and Cambridge made the vast majority, but there were many other companies involved on a lesser scale. Very few marked their animals.

As many of the glass companies went out of business, their molds were bought by companies still active, who have used them to produce their own line of animals. While some are easy to recognize, others can be very confusing. For example, Summit Art Glass now owns Cambridge's 6½", 8½", and 10" swan molds. We recommend *Glass Animals, Second Edition*, by Dick and Pat Spencer, if you are thinking of starting a collection or wanting to identify and evaluate the glass animals and figural-related items that you already have. The authors are our advisors for this category and are listed in the Directory under Illinois.

Cambridge

Bashful Charlotte, flower frog, crystal, 11½" 125.00
Bashful Charlotte, flower frog, Dianthus, 6½" 225.00
Bashful Charlotte, flower frog, Moonlight Blue, 11½", minimum value .. 950.00
Bird, crystal satin, 2¾" L 20.00
Bird on stump, flower frog, gr, 5¼", minimum value 400.00
Bridge hound, ebony, 1¼" 40.00
Buddha, amber, 5½" 350.00
Draped Lady, flower frog, crystal frost, 13¼" 150.00
Draped Lady, flower frog, Dianthus, 13¼" 225.00
Draped Lady, flower frog, gr frost, 8½" 125.00
Draped Lady, flower frog, ivory, oval base, 8½", minimum value ... 1,000.00
Draped Lady, flower frog, Moonlight Blue, 13¼", minimum value ... 1,000.00
Eagle, bookend, crystal, 5½x4x4", ea 80.00
Heron, crystal, lg, 12" 150.00
Mandolin Lady, flower frog, crystal 200.00
Mandolin Lady, flower frog, lt emerald 350.00
Melon Boy, flower frog, Dianthus, minimum value 850.00
Rose Lady, flower frog, amber, 8½" 200.00
Rose Lady, flower frog, dk amber, tall base, 9¾" 250.00
Rose Lady, flower frog, gr, 8½" 200.00
Seagull, flower block, crystal 50.00
Swan, Carmen, #3 style, 8½" 350.00
Swan, Crown Tuscan, 8½" 145.00
Swan, ebony, 3" 85.00
Swan, ebony, 8½" 275.00
Swan, ebony, 10½" 325.00
Swan, emerald, 3" 55.00
Swan, milk glass, #3 style, 8½" 175.00
Swan, milk glass, 6½" 125.00
Swan, punch bowl (15") & base, crystal, +12 cups 3,000.00
Swan, yel, 8½" 250.00
Turkey, gr, w/lid 550.00
Turtle, flower holder, ebony 200.00
Two Kids, flower frog, amber satin, 9¼" 350.00
Two Kids, flower frog, crystal, 9¼" 200.00

Duncan and Miller

Sailfish, crystal, Line #30/Pall Mall, 5½", from $175.00 to $200.00. (Photo courtesy Lee Garmon and Dick Spencer)

Donkey, cart & peon, crystal, 3-pc set 650.00
Dove, crystal, head down, w/o base, 11½" L 125.00
Duck, ashtray, red, 7" 375.00
Goose, crystal, fat, 6x6" 225.00
Swan, candleholder, red, 7", ea 85.00
Swordfish, bl opal, rare 500.00
Tropical fish, ashtray, pk opal, 3½" 60.00

Fenton

Airedale, Rosalene, 1992 issue for Heisey 65.00
Alley cat, Teal Marigold, 11" 115.00
Butterfly on stand, Lime Sherbet, 1989 souvenir, 7½" 30.00
Butterfly on stand, ruby carnival, 1989 souvenir, 7½" 35.00
Filly, Rosalene, head front, 1992 issue for Heisey 65.00
Fish, red w/amberina tail & fins, 2½" 60.00
Peacock, bookends, crystal satin, 5¾", pr 350.00
Turtle, flower block, amethyst, 4" L 75.00

Fostoria

Bird, candleholder, crystal, 1½", ea 15.00
Cardinal head, Silver Mist, 6½" 200.00
Deer, bl, sitting or standing, ea 30.00
Deer, milk glass, sitting or standing, ea 30.00

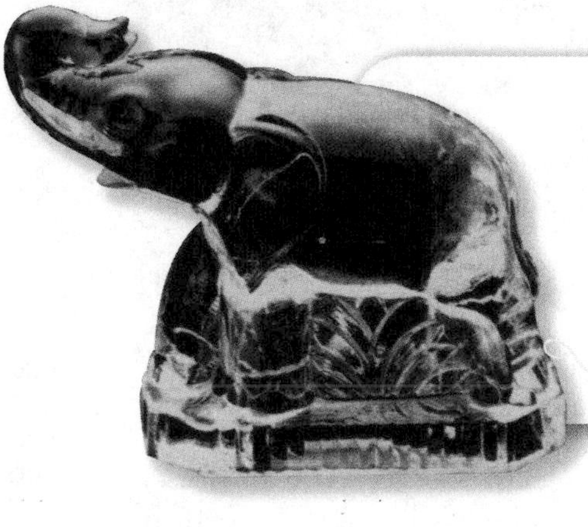

Elephant bookend, crystal, 6½", each from $65.00 to $75.00. (Photo courtesy Lee Garmon and Dick Spencer)

Lady bug, bl, lemon or olive gr, 1¼", ea 25.00
Pelican, amber, 1987 commemorative 55.00
Seal, topaz, 3⅞" 65.00

Heisey

Airedale, crystal 1,400.00
Bull, crystal, mk, 4x7½" 2,200.00
Colt, crystal, rearing 225.00
Duck, ashtray, Moongleam 250.00
Elephant, amber, lg or med, ea 2,400.00
Fish, bowl, crystal, 9½" 450.00
Giraffe, crystal, head bk 200.00
Irish setter, ashtray, crystal 25.00
Mallard, crystal, wings down 275.00
Mallard, crystal, wings up 175.00
Rabbit, paperweight, crystal, 2¾x3¾" 140.00
Rooster, amber, 5⅝" 2,500.00
Rooster, crystal, 5½x5" 450.00
Rooster head, cocktail, crystal 45.00
Rooster head, cocktail shaker, 1-qt 85.00
Show horse, crystal 1,250.00
Sparrow, crystal 90.00

Swan, pitcher, crystal 650.00
Tropical fish, crystal, 12" 2,000.00
Wood duck, crystal, standing 225.00

Imperial

Airedale, caramel slag 90.00
Bulldog-type pup, milk glass, 3½" 65.00

Candle Servant, Cathay line, frosted crystal, signed Virginia B. Evans, from $200.00 to $250.00 each.

Chick, milk glass, head down 15.00
Colt, amber, balking 100.00
Donkey, caramel slag 40.00
Donkey, Ultra Blue 45.00
Elephant, caramel slag, sm 60.00
Fish, candlestick, Sunshine Yellow, 5", ea 25.00
Flying mare, amber, NI mk, extremely rare 1,250.00
Mallard, caramel slag, wings down 150.00
Mallard, lt bl satin, wings down 25.00
Owl, milk glass 55.00
Piglet, ruby, standing 20.00
Rabbit, paperweight, Horizon Blue, 2¾" 90.00
Scolding bird, Cathay Crystal 175.00
Terrier, Parlour Pup, amethyst carnival, 3½" 45.00
Tiger, paperweight, Jade Green, 8" L 80.00
Wood duckling, Sunshine Yellow satin, floating 20.00

L.E. Smith

Elephant, crystal, 1¾" 6.00
Horse, bookend, amber, rearing, ea 38.00
King Fish, aquarium, gr, 7¼x4x15" 450.00
Rooster, butterscotch slag, ltd ed, #208 .... 90.00
Swan, milk glass w/decor, 8½" 35.00

New Martinsville

Chick, frosted, 1" 25.00
Gazelle, crystal w/frosted base, leaping, 8¼" 45.00
Piglet, crystal, standing 150.00
Porpoise on wave, orig 350.00
Rooster w/crooked tail, crystal, 7½" 50.00
Seal, candleholders, crystal, lg, pr 120.00
Swan, sweetheart candy dish, red, 5" 30.00
Wolfhound, crystal, 7" 70.00
Woodsman, crystal, sq base, 7⅜" 80.00

Paden City

Bunny, cotton-ball dispenser, crystal frost, ears bk 225.00
Bunny, cotton-ball dispenser, pk frost, ears up 350.00
Eagle, bookends, crystal, pr 500.00
Horse, crystal, rearing 275.00
Pheasant, Chinese; bl 175.00
Pheasant, Chinese; crystal, 13¾" 90.00
Pheasant, lt bl, head bk, 12" 200.00
Polar bear on ice, crystal, 4½" 50.00
Pony, crystal, 12" 110.00
Pouter pigeon, bookend, crystal, 6¼", ea 100.00
Rooster, Barnyard; crystal, 8¾" 110.00
Rooster, Chanticleer, crystal, 9½" 100.00
Squirrel on curved log, crystal, 5½" 40.00

Tiffin

Cat, Sassy Suzie, blk satin w/pnt decor, #9448, 11" 175.00
Cat, Sassy Suzie, milk glass, minimum value 450.00
Fawn, flower floater, Copen Blue 300.00

Fish, crystal, 9½x10", from $300.00 to $385.00.

Fish, crystal, solid, 8¾x9" 325.00
Pheasants, Copen Blue, paperweight bases, male & female pr 500.00

Viking

Angelfish, amber, 7x7" 90.00
Angelfish, milk glass, pr 475.00
Bird, moss gr, tail up, 12" 45.00
Bird, Orchid, 9½" 100.00
Cat, gr, sitting, 8" 45.00
Dog, orange 45.00
Duck, crystal, fighting, head up or down, Viking's Epic Line, ea 40.00
Duck, crystal, standing, Viking's Epic Line, 9" 55.00
Duck, orange, rnd, ftd, 5" 30.00
Duck, ruby, rnd, ftd, 5" 35.00
Egret, amber, #1315, 12" 40.00
Egret, orange, 12" 50.00
Jesus, crystal w/Crystal Mist, flat bk, 6x5" 50.00
Owl, amber, Viking's Epic Line 20.00
Rabbit, amber, 6½" 35.00
Rabbit (Thumper), crystal, 6½" 25.00

Rooster, avocado, Viking's Epic Line..45.00
Swan, bowl, amber, 6"..20.00
Swan, Yellow Mist, paper label, 6" 20.00

Westmoreland

Wren on Perch, Light Blue Mist on milk glass base, $45.00. (Photo courtesy Lee Garmon and Dick Spencer)

Bird in flight, Amber Marigold, wings out, 5" W 45.00
Butterfly, crystal, 4½"...30.00
Butterfly, pk, 2½"...25.00
Owl, dk bl, shiny eyes, 5½"..40.00
Pouter pigeon, any color, 2½", ea..20.00
Robin, crystal, 5⅛"..15.00
Robin, pk, 5⅛"..22.00
Robin, red, 5⅛"...26.00
Turtle, ashtray, crystal...8.00
Turtle, flower block, gr, 7 holes, 4" L.......................................50.00
Turtle, paperweight, Green Mist, no holes, 4" L 20.00
Wren, Pink Mist, 2½"..25.00
Wren, smoke, 3½"..25.00

Miscellaneous

Blenko, owl, paperweight, amber 30.00
Co-Operative Flint, elephant, pk, 4½x7"...................................275.00
Haley, Lady Godiva, bookend, crystal, 1940s, ea 40.00
Indiana, horse head, bookends, milk glass, 6", pr.......................60.00
Indiana, pouter pigeon, bookend, crystal frost, ea......................35.00
LG Wright, trout, crystal..150.00
LG Wright, turtle, amber..80.00
Pilgrim, whale, crystal, #924, w/labels, in 1964 World's Fair box ...35.00
Viking for Mirror Images, baby seal, ruby...................................65.00
Viking for Mirror Images, police dog, ruby................................100.00

Glidden

Genius designer Glidden Parker established Glidden Pottery in 1940 in Alfred, New York, having been schooled at the unrivaled New York State College of Ceramics at Alfred University. Glidden pottery is characterized by a fine stoneware body, innovative forms, outstanding hand-milled glazes, and hand decoration which make the pieces individual works of art. Production consisted of casual dinnerware, artware, and accessories that were distributed internationally.

In 1949 Glidden Pottery became the second ceramic plant in the country to utilize the revolutionary Ram pressing machine. This allowed for increased production and for the most part eliminated the previously used slip-casting method. However, Glidden stoneware continued to reflect the same superb quality of craftsmanship until the factory closed in 1957. Although the majority of form and decorative patterns were

Mr. Parker's personal designs, Fong Chow and Sergio Dello Strologo also designed award-winning lines.

Glidden will be found marked on the unglazed underside with a signature that is hand incised, mold impressed, or ink stamped. Interest in this unique stoneware is growing as collectors discover that it embodies the very finest of Mid-Century High Style. Our advisor is David Pierce; he is listed in the Directory under Ohio.

Ashtray, Gulfstream Blue, #4006..22.00
Bowl, cobalt, #15...15.00
Bowl, cobalt, #26...34.00
Bowl, Green Mesa, #4013...96.00
Bowl, Gulfstream Blue, #4012..195.00
Bowl, Turquoise Matrix, #22..10.00
Butter pat, #19..19.00
Casserole, Alfred Stoneware, Saffron, #806...............................31.00
Casserole, Fish, Charcoal & Rice, #412...................................110.00
Casserole, Fish, Viridian, #412...120.00
Creamer, Sandstone, #453..15.00
Creamer & sugar bowl, High Tide, #1430/#1440, w/lid................90.00
Cup & saucer, Turquoise Matrix, #141/#142...............................14.00
Planter, cobalt, #128..18.00
Plate, cake; Gulfstream Blue, ped ft, #4763...............................69.00
Plate, Chi-Chi Poodle, #65...17.00
Plate, Circus, lion tamer, #35..16.00
Plate, High Tide, #435..18.00
Plate, Lamb, #35...19.00
Plate, Marine Fantasia, #31...26.00
Plate, Menagerie, tiger, #35..7.00
Plate, Mexican Cock, #35..8.00
Plate, Turquoise Matrix, #31..20.00
Plate, Turquoise Matrix, #31B..26.00
Saucer, Turquoise Matrix, #142..11.00

Server, Laizy Daizy, $65.00. (Photo courtesy David Pierce)

Tray, divided relish; Turquoise Matrix, #280..............................31.00
Tumbler, Chi-Chi Poodle, #1127...6.00
Tumbler, cobalt, #1127...12.00
Tumbler, Will-o-The-Wisp, #1127...19.00
Vase, cobalt #2..38.00
Vase, Turquoise Matrix, #2..28.00

Goebel

F.W. Goebel founded the F&W Goebel Company in 1871, located in Rodental, West Germany. They manufactured thousands of different decorative and useful items over the years, the most famous of which are the Hummel figurines first produced in 1935 based on the artwork of a Franciscan nun, Sister Maria Innocentia Hummel.

The Goebel trademarks have long been a source of confusion because all Goebel products, including Hummels, of any particular time period bear the same trademark, thus leading many to believe all Goebels are Hummels. Always look for the Hummel signature on actual Hummel figurines (these are listed in a separate section).

There are many other series — some of which are based on artwork of particular artists such as Disney, Charlot Byj, Janet Robson, Harry Holt, Norman Rockwell, M. Spotl, Lore, Huldah, and Schaubach. Miscellaneous useful items include ashtrays, bookends, salt and pepper shakers, banks, pitchers, inkwells, perfume bottles, etc. Figurines include birds, animals, Art Deco pieces, etc. The Friar Tuck monks and the Co-Boy elves are especially popular.

The date of manufacture is determined by the trademark. The incised date found underneath the base on many items is the mold copyright date. Actual date of manufacture may vary as much as 20 years or more from the copyright date. Our advisors for this category are Gale and Wayne Bailey; they are listed in the Directory under Georgia.

Most Common Goebel Trademarks and Approximate Dates Used

1.) Crown mark (may be incised or stamped, or both): 1923 – 1950

2.) Full bee (complete bumble bee inside the letter 'V'): 1950 – 1957

3.) Stylized bee (dot with wings inside the letter 'V'): 1957 – 1964

4.) Three-Line (stylized bee with three lines of copyright info to the right of the trademark): 1964 – 1972

5.) Goebel bee (word Goebel with stylized bee mark over the last letter 'e'): 1972 – 1979

6.) Goebel (word Goebel only): 1979 – present

Our advisors for this category are Gale and Wayne Bailey; they are listed in the Directory under Georgia.

Cardinal Tuck (Red Monk)

Tray, TMK-4, small, $100.00.

Bank, #SD29, TMK-3	80.00
Creamer, #S141 2/0, TMK-3, 2½"	40.00
Creamer, #S141/0, TMK-3, 4"	65.00
Decanter, TMK-5, 10"	240.00
Mug, TMK-2, 5¼", NM	75.00
Pourer	230.00
Spoon holder, #RF142, TMK-2, 3x3¾"	125.00

Charlot BYJ Redheads and Blonds

At Work, BYJ-74, TMK-5, 4¾"	160.00
Baby Sitter, BYJ-66, TMK-6	85.00
Bachelor Degree Boy, BYJ-50, TMK-5	45.00
Bird Watcher, BYJ-84, TMK-5, 5½"	145.00
Bongo Beat, BYJ-65, TMK-4, 4¼"	85.00
Boy w/duck, BYJ-10, TMK-6	125.00
Damper on the Camper, BYJ-72, TMK-6, 3¾"	135.00
Dating & Skating, BYJ-52, TMK-3, 4½"	85.00
Forbidden Fruit, BYJ-20, TMK-4, flaw, from $70 to	80.00
Gangway, BYJ-28, TMK-4, 4½"	60.00
Guess Who, BYJ-40, 4¾"	115.00
Lazy Day, BYJ-78, TMK-5, 4¼x5¼"	90.00
Let It Rain, BYJ-51, TMK-4	180.00
Mother & Child, BYJ-37, TMK-3, 6¼"	90.00
Off Key, BYJ-22, TMK-5	85.00
Prayer Girl, BYJ-17, TMK-4, 5¼"	45.00
Putting On the Dog, BYJ-25, TMK-4	115.00
Roving Eye, boy & dog, BYJ-2, TMK-3	60.00
Say Aaah, BYJ-58, TMK-4, 5½"	72.00
Sleepy Head, BYJ-11, TMK-4	50.00
Stolen Kiss, BYJ-18, TMK-4	60.00
Super Service, BYJ-39, TMK-5	85.00
Swinger, BYJ-62, TMK-4, 5¼"	85.00
Trim Lass, BYJ-49, TMK-4, 4½"	85.00
Trouble Shooter, BYJ-67, TMK-4	98.00

Co-Boy Figurines

Al the Trumpet Player, TMK-6	50.00
Ben the Blacksmith, 1980, 8"	85.00

Bob the Bookworm, Well #510, 1970, from $60.00 to $75.00.

Brum the Lawyer, 1970	60.00
Chuck riding pig, 1986	195.00
Dealer plaque, Well #516, 8x6"	75.00
Doc, gnome, TMK-6	75.00
Flips the Fisherman, Well #508, TMK-5, 7½x5½"	60.00
Gerd the Driver, 1979	60.00
Greg the Gourmet, TMK-6	60.00
Greta the Happy Housewife, TMK-6	45.00
Hermann the Butcher, TMK-6, 7½"	95.00
Jack the Pharmacist, Well #517, TMK-6	75.00
Mike the Jam Maker, Well #502, TMK-4	75.00
Nick the Nightclub Singer, TMK-6	70.00
Porz the Mushroom Muncher, Well #511, 1970	58.00
Sam the Gourmet, TMK-4	90.00
Ted the Tennis Player, TMK-6, 7¼"	58.00
Toni the Skier, Well #522, TMK-6	50.00
Wine Steward - Taster, Wells #521, TMK-4	52.00

Cookie Jars

Cat, TMK-5, from $100 to 125.00
Dog, TMK-5, from $100 to 125.00
Friar Tuck, K-29, TMK-5 .... 250.00
Owl, #607/36, 15" 125.00
Panda Bear, TMK-5, from $70 to 125.00
Pig, TMK-5, from $100 to 125.00

Friar Tuck (Brown Monk)

Ashtray, #ZF43/0, TMK-3, 2¾x3" 110.00
Bank, 3 monks surround bbl, mk West Germany, 1957, 2¾" 350.00
Clock, 125th Anniversary, 1996, 6½x8" 335.00
Condiment set, TMK-5, 4¾" jar w/2⅜" shakers on 5½x4¾" tray ... 52.50
Creamer & sugar bowl, #S141/0 & #Z37, TMK-3 .... 45.00
Egg timer, #E104, TMK-3, 3" 80.00
Jar, #Z37, TMK-3, 4½" 42.50
Mug, TMK-2, 4½" 40.00
Oil bottle, O on collar, #M80C, TMK-4, 5" 75.00
Pitcher, #S141/111, 8¼" 150.00
Razor blade bank, toes showing, #X103, TMK-3, 4½" 125.00
Shakers, #P153, TMK-3, 2", pr 60.00
Shakers, 2¾", 2½", pr in wicker bsket 50.00
Stein, w/lid, #T74/3, 1957, 7" 215.00
Vinegar bottle, Fussen on collar, #M80, TMK-4, 5¼" 75.00

Shakers

Bears, 3", pr 25.00
Clowns, 2¾", pr 25.00
Ducks, 1½", pr 20.00

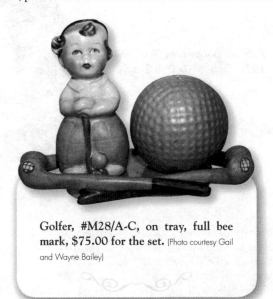

Golfer, #M28/A-C, on tray, full bee mark, $75.00 for the set. (Photo courtesy Gail and Wayne Bailey)

Onion & radish tops, TMK-3, 3", pr 35.00
Peppers, 1 gr & 1 red, pr 32.00
Rabbits, bright mc details, W Goebel, W Germany, 4", pr 55.00
Squirrel & pine cone, on leaf-shaped tray, #M36/A, B & C 65.00
Turkeys, #P-98, pr 42.50

Miscellaneous

Figurine, Baltimore Oriole, #6852807, TMK-6, 3x2¼" 30.00
Figurine, bird w/crest, #3893825, 1984, 10½", NM 85.00
Figurine, boxer pup, silver label/bl stamp, 3x4" 32.00

Figurine, Chardonnere bird, #CV33, TMK-3, 3x4" 33.00
Figurine, flapper-style lady, Fashion on Parade series, 1986, 8", MIB.. 90.00
Figurine, girl & lt bl kitten, #608, TMK-2, 2x2" 18.00
Figurine, koala bear climbing up tree trunk, #36518-08, 3⅜" 28.00
Figurine, lamb, creamy wht w/pk & brn details, #32048, TMK-6, 2½"..26.00
Figurine, Marie Antoinette, TMK-6, 9" 75.00
Figurine, Ol' Swimming Hole, #11608-14, TMK-4, 5½" 45.00
Figurine, owl, #38316-08, TMK-5, 3½" 24.00
Figurine, poodle, blk, #KT161, TMK-5, 3" 20.00
Figurine, red bird w/brn wings & tail, #38504, TMK-5, 3x4½" 39.00
Figurine, robin fledgling, #38011, TMK-6, 2x2¾" 28.00
Figurine, Waxwing, #CV80, TMK-5, 6¾" 50.00
Figurine, Whoosit in blk hat, #11711, TMK-6, 4" 22.00
Figurine, zebra, Serengetti Collection, 1980s, 4½x7½" 85.00
Mug, clown figural, #7431514, TMK-6, 5½" 29.00
Plate, bl titmouse, Wildlife Series #2, 1974, 7½" 15.00

Goldscheider

The Goldscheider family operated a pottery in Vienna for many generations before seeking refuge in the United States following Hitler's invasion of their country. They settled in Trenton, New Jersey, in the early 1940s where they established a new corporation and began producing objects of art and tableware items. (No mention was made of the company in the Trenton City Directory after 1950, and it is assumed that by this time the influx of foreign imports had taken its toll.) In 1946 Marcel Goldscheider established a pottery in Staffordshire where he manufactured bone china figures, earthenware, etc., marked with a stamp of his signature. Larger artist-signed examples are the most valuable with the Austrian pieces bringing the higher prices. Also buyers should know that the 1920s era terra cotta items, masks, busts, and figures are really costly now, while religious items have fallen in value.

A wide variety of marks has been found: 1.) Goldscheider USA Fine China; 2.) Original Goldscheider Fine China; 3.) Goldscheider USA; 4.) Goldscheider-Everlast Corp.; 5.) Goldscheider Everlast Corp. in circle; 6.) Goldscheider Inc. in circle; 7.) Goldcrest Ceramics Corp. in circle; 8.) Goldcrest Fine China; 9.) Goldcrest Fine China USA; 10.) A Goldcrest Creation; and 11.) Created by Goldscheider USA. Our co-advisors are Randy and Debbie Coe (listed in the Directory under Oregon) and Darrell Thomas (listed under Wisconsin).

Key:
D — Dakon   WW — Weiner Werkstatte
L — Lorenzl

American

Lady in long dress, marked Created by Goldscheider USA Everlast, 15½", $150.00. (Photo courtesy David Rago Auctions)

Ann Boleyn, gr & maroon outfit, #1199, mk 7, 10¾" 195.00
Bust, lg pk hibiscus in bl/gr hair, EX Deco detail, Baldwin, mk 5, 12". 350.00
Bust, Madonna, gray w/maroon, #664, mk 9, 6¾x4½" 65.00
Cat, Persian type, EX detail, orange/wht fur, 1950s, 4" L 45.00
Dog, Great Dane, blk/wht, EX lifelike qualities, 9½" 75.00
Lady, hand on head, other holding dress, #257, mk 3, 6¼" 75.00
Mandarin Dancers, she dancing, (he w/drums), Urbach, 1950s, 14", pr ..185.00
Oriental man w/lute, gray, #822, USA, mk 5, 10½" 125.00
Southern Belle, floral dress, holds hat, #500, mk 5, 10" 150.00
Wedding Bells, girl in wht dress, 7" 48.00

Austrian

Boy w/bouquet of flowers, Wein, 5⅝" 300.00
Bust, lady w/red wavy hair, flower in hand, Wein, sm rstr, 9x6" ... 550.00
Bust of maiden, terra cotta, Cherc, early 20th C, 18" 7,000.00
Butterfly girl, flower-filled urn on blk base, Lorenzl, rstr, 16" 2,710.00
Clock, nude maiden figure, cutouts of planets/stars, Wein, 37" .. 4,300.00
Girl w/butterfly-wing skirt, bass drum at ft, #5282, Wein, 12x9x5" .. 725.00
Lady dancer w/skirt wide, alabaster, Lorenzl, 1930s, 16" 2,000.00
Lady in long floral dress holds parasol, Lorenzl, #7642, Wein, 13" ..800.00
Lady's head, forest gr accents, #0177, ca 1925, 12½" 1,000.00
Lady's head, wht face, brn curls w/gilt, Wein, 12x7" 850.00
Lady stands on 1 leg, arms out/skirt wide, Lorenzl, Wein, 15", NM..1,000.00
Lady w/lg hat, skirts raised, oval base, #6511, 15⅜" 1,800.00

Mid-eastern dancer, signed Laurenthal, #5281/518/12__, Goldscheider Wein Made in Austria, piece missing from headband, 17", $900.00. (Photo courtesy Bertoia Auctions)

Peasant lady dancing, full sleeves, short skirt, Wein, rpr, 16x17" .. 450.00
Wall mask, woman w/hands to cheek, pastels, Wein, 12¾x8¼" ... 100.00

Gonder

Lawton Gonder grew up with clay in his hands and fire in his eyes. Gonder's interest in ceramics was greatly influenced by his parents who worked for Weller and a close family friend and noted ceramic authority, John Herold. In his early teens Gonder launched his ceramic career at the Ohio Pottery Company while working for Herold. He later gained valuable experience at American Encaustic Tile Company, Cherry Art Tile, and the Florence Pottery. Gonder was plant manager at the Florence Pottery until fire destroyed the facility in late 1941.

After years of solid production and management experience, Lawton Gonder established the Gonder Ceramic Art Company, formerly the Peters and Reed plant, in South Zanesville, Ohio. Gonder Ceramic Arts produced quality art pottery with beautiful contemporary designs which included human and animal figures and a complete line of Oriental pottery. Accentuating the beautiful shapes were unique and innovative glazes developed by Gonder such as flambe (flame red with streaks of yellow), 24k gold crackle, antique gold, and Chinese crackle. (These glazes bring premium prices.)

All Gonder is marked with the company name and mold number. They include 'Gonder U.S.A' in block letters, 'Gonder' in script, 'Gonder Original' in script, and 'Gonder Ceramic Art' in block letters. Paper labels were also used. Some of the early Gonder molds closely resemble RumRill designs that had been manufactured at the Florence Pottery; and because some RumRill pieces are found with similar (if not identical) shapes, matching mold numbers, and Gonder glazes, it is speculated that some RumRill was produced at the Gonder plant. In 1946 Gonder started another company which he named Elgee (chosen for his initials LG) where he manufactured lamp bases until a fire in 1954 resulted in his shifting lamp production to the main plant. Operations ceased in 1957.

Ashtray, dk red-maroon w/wht foam at edge, #219, 10" L 60.00
Ashtray, Trojan horse head at side, Sea Swirl, #548, 6⅞" L........... 27.50
Bank, sheriff figural, gr, 9x7", NM 65.00
Console set, shell vase, mc drip, #521, +pr #521C candleholders.. 40.00
Cookie jar, brn drips on cream, #P-24... 35.00

Ewer, light aqua-tan, 11", $60.00.

Figurine, panther, tan mottle, #210, 19", NM.................................. 80.00
Figurines, Bali man (& woman) water carrier, tropical gr, 13", pr.. 55.00
Figurines, Oriental man (& lady), w/yoke, yel, 14x10¾", pr 70.00
Ginger jar, emb dragons on Chinese Turq crackle, #533, w/lid, 9¼" .. 70.00
Lamps, storks (2), lt lilac & brn, #562, 16½" 135.00
Pitcher, bl & wht vertical & pk horizontal stripes, 8"..................... 75.00
Pitcher, burgundy w/combed effect, swirling integral hdl, 8½"....... 75.00
Teapot, yel crackle w/drips, #P-31, 6½x10½" 40.00
Vase, brn runs on yel, twist hdls, #H-5, 9x5¾"............................... 42.00
Vase, cornucopia, bl-gray w/pk mottle undertones, #H-14, 9½"..... 32.00
Vase, gold & bl crackle, bulb base w/scalloped rim, #E-49, 6½" 30.00
Vase, leaves emb on mc mottle on turq, #E-66, 6¼" 35.00
Vase, peachy-pk w/bl-gr mottle, emb ribs, hdls, #H-33, 12" 32.00
Vase, peacock feathers, pk w/gr flecks, #K-15, 12" 55.00
Vase, red flambe, bottle form, 9"... 85.00
Vase, scalloped shell, bl mottle w/pk int, #J-60, 8x11½" 32.00
Vase, shell ewer form, mustard yel, #508, 13⅜"............................. 28.00
Vase, starfish, pistachio & pk, #H-79, 8x6".................................... 32.00
Vase, Sunshine Yellow over pk, twist hdls, #H-5, 9x6".................... 35.00
Vase, Trojan horse head, MOP, 10¼x7¾".. 50.00
Vase, 2 leaves form body, pk & gray mottled, 11" 25.00
Vase, 3 leaves form body, purple-brn, #504, 11¼x9"....................... 40.00

Goofus Glass

Goofus glass is American-made pressed glass with designs that are either embossed (blown out) or intaglio (cut in). The decorated colors were aerographed or hand applied and not fired on the pieces. The various patterns exemplify the artistry of the turn-of-the-century glass crafters. The primary production dates were ca 1908 to 1918. Goofus was produced by many well-known manufacturers such as Northwood, Indiana, and Dugan.

When no condition is given, our values are for examples in mint original paint. Our advisor for this category is Steven Gillespie of the *Goofus Glass Gazette;* he is listed in the Directory under Missouri. See also Clubs, Newsletters, and Catalogs.

Basket, Diamond & Daisy, 6½", EX.. 55.00
Bowl, Butterfly, red & gold, ruffled, 2½x10½", EX+...................... 65.00
Bowl, Carnation, La Belle & Roses in Snow, sq, 5½" 12.00
Bowl, Cherry, red & gold, Dugan, 2¼x10⅛" 65.00
Bowl, Cherry, ruffled rim, 3¼x10", NM.................................. 75.00
Bowl, Hearts, 7" 45.00
Bowl, Jeweled Heart, 2x9", NM 45.00
Bowl, Poppy, red & gold, ftd, 4x9", EX 60.00
Bowl, Poppy, Two Fruits & Olympic Torch, pattern decor, rare, 9".. 130.00
Bowl, Rose, 5-sided (hard to find) 110.00
Bread tray, The Last Supper.. 35.00
Cake plate, Acorn & Leaf, 12".. 30.00
Cake plate, Wild Flower, crackle glass border, 12"................... 25.00
Compote, Butterfly, 6⅞x10¼", EX...................................... 70.00
Dish, Hearts, rolled rim, 10" 50.00
Lamp, Cabbage Rose, matching chimney, 12" 150.00
Lamp, oil; Grape & Leaves, minor flaking, 13¼" 275.00
Lamp, oil; Nosegay, #2, EX orig pnt 250.00
Lamp, oil; Wild Rose, Riverside, finger loop, 15" overall 250.00
Plate, Butterfly, Dugan, rare, 11" 125.00
Plate, Chrysanthemum, frosted ground, 6¼", EX....................... 45.00
Plate, Hearts, 10" 45.00
Plate, Little Bo Peep, minor gold flaking, 6½" 80.00
Plate, rose in base amid 8 long-stemmed roses, red/gold, 10¾", EX... 55.00
Plate, Temple of Music, Pan Am Expo Buffalo NY, 7¼", EX.......... 60.00
Relish plate, Rose, glass hdls, 7".................................. 50.00
Shakers, Vintage, dk gr & gold on milk glass, G orig lids, 3¾", pr....55.00
Tray, Fruit, sq, 8½" 50.00

Tray, The Lord's Supper, 7x11", $65.00.

Vase, Cabbage Rose, 15" 95.00
Vase, Magnolia Blossoms, filigree top & bottom, 9½" 75.00

Vase, Peacock, red & gold, 15¼" 100.00
Vase, Poppy, red flower w/gold leaves, 10".......................... 15.00
Vase, Poppy, 5" 15.00
Vase, Tree Flowers (uncommon), 14½" 95.00
Vase, Victorian Vase & Rose Buds, 14½" 85.00

Goss and Crested China

William Henry Goss received his early education at the Government School of Design at Somerset House, London, and as a result of his merit was introduced to Alderman William Copeland, who owned the Copeland Spode Pottery. Under the influence of Copeland from 1852 to 1858, Goss quickly learned the trade and soon became their chief designer. Little is known about this brief association, and in 1858 Goss left to begin his own business. After a short-lived partnership with a Mr. Peake, Goss opened a pottery on John Street, Stoke-on-Trent, but by 1870 he had moved his business to a location near London Road. This pottery became the famous Falcon Works. Their mark was a spread-wing falcon (goss-hawk) centering a narrow, horizontal bar with 'W.H. Goss' printed below.

Many of the early pieces made by Goss were left unmarked and are difficult to discern from products made by the Copeland factory, but after he had been in business for about 15 years, all of his wares were marked. Today, unmarked items do not command the prices of the later marked wares.

Adolphus William Henry Goss (Goss's eldest son) joined his father's firm in the 1880s. He introduced cheaper lines, though the more expensive lines continued in production. Shortly after his father's death in 1906, Adolphus retired and left the business to his two younger brothers. The business suffered from problems created by a war economy, and in 1936 Goss assets were held by Cauldon Potteries Ltd. These were eventually taken over by the Coalport Group, who retained the right to use the Goss trademark. Messrs. Ridgeway Potteries bought all the assets in 1954 as well as the right to use the Goss trademark and name. In 1964 the group was known as Allied English Potteries Ltd. (A.E.P.), and in 1971 A.E.P. merged with the Doulton Group.

Sir F. A. Gore Ouseley Jug, goshawk mark, 2", $110.00. (Photo courtesy quarryman.2)

Ancient Saxon Font in Avebury Church Near Calne Wilts, 1880s...485.00
Ancient Warwick Font at Troy House Monmouth Rich, heraldic shields...265.00
Army Water Bottle Used at...Waterloo, 14th Battalion County of London ...255.00
British Tank, Dartmouth in Devon 80.00
Cherbourg Milk Can, Leicester Regiment, w/lid 195.00
Hindhead Sailor's Stone, full inscription, ca 1930................. 175.00
Jug, Allied Flags: England, France, Belgium, Russia, 4¾" 155.00
Ludlow Sack Bottle, Crystal Palace bl transfer 200.00
Maltese Urn, Royal Berkshire Regiment.............................. 175.00
Painswick Pot, St John Ambulance Brigade & St John Ambulance Assoc....395.00
Queen Victoria's Shoe, Plymouth.................................... 75.00
Robert Burns Cottage, nightlight, 3⅛x5⅞" at base.................. 90.00

Roman Urn, Worcestershire Regiment 135.00
Shakespeare's House, nightlight 110.00
Silchester Urn, Coldstream Guards 135.00
Welsh Antiquities, bowl, 3¾" 85.00
William Shakespeare Bust, ca 1910 .... 135.00
Winchester Bushel, 1½x3" dia 245.00

Other Crested China

Sutherland, Dainty Ware cup, WWI Flags of Principal Allies, 2¾", $95.00.
(Photo courtesy quarryman.2)

Alexandra, Zeppelin, Plymouth crest, 2x5" 55.00
Arcadia, match holder & striker, Bexhill on Sea, 2½x3" 50.00
Arcadia, Super Zeppelin, Arms of Whitney, 2x5" 130.00
Arcadia, Zeppelin Airship, Hastings, 5¼" 20.00
Carlton, Field Gun, City of York 65.00
Carlton, Lucky White Heather (swan), Edinburgh, 3¼" 55.00
Carlton, Lusitania Ship, Blackpool 125.00
Carlton, Monitor Warship, Kidderminster (Worcestershire), 5½" L..115.00
Carlton, Oast House, Hastings 45.00
Carlton, Open Car, Hampton Wick Middlesex, 4½" L 60.00
Carlton, Stephenson's Rocket, Darlington 115.00
Carlton, Tommy in Trench Hut, Shrapnel Villa, Haddington 125.00
Shelley, creamer & sugar bowl, Dumfries, 2¼", 1¾" 70.00
Shelley, Silver Rose Bowl, Arms of Cardinal Wolsey, 2" 20.00

Gouda

Gouda is an old Dutch market town in the province of South Holland, famous for producing Gouda cheese. Gouda's ceramics industry had its beginnings in the early sixteenth century and was fueled by the growth in the popularity of smoking tobacco. Initially learning their craft from immigrant potters from England who had settled in the area, the clay pipe makers of Gouda were soon regarded as the best. While some authorities give 1898 (the date the Zuid-Holland factory began operations) as the initial date for the manufacturing of decorative pottery in Gouda, C.W. Moody, author of *Gouda Ceramics* (out of print), indicates the date was ca 1885. Gouda was not the only town in the Netherlands making pottery; Arnhem, Schoonhoven, and Amsterdam also had earthenware factories, but technically the term 'Gouda pottery' refers only to pieces made within the town of Gouda. Today, no Gouda-style factories are active within the city's limits, but in the first quarter of the twentieth century there were several firms producing decorative pottery there — the best known being Zuid, Regina, Zenith, Ivora, and Goedewaagen. At present Royal Goedewaagen is making three patterns of limited editions. They are well marked as such.

This information was provided to us by Adela Meadows; she is listed in the Directory under California. For further information we recommend *The World of Gouda Pottery* by Phyllis T. Ritvo (Front & Center Press, Weston, Massachussets).

Bottles, liqueur; Holland, Dutch man & lady, Bols, 10", pr 200.00
Candlestick, Holland, Damascus III, Raap, 4 hdls, PZH, 8¼", ea. 200.00

Candlestick, Holland, Plate, sgn ADW, 4 hdls, PZH, 8¼", ea...... 175.00
Candlesticks, dots & triangles, Arnhem, #342, 9x4½", pr........... 260.00
Candlesticks, Holland, Blanca, rtcl top, PZH, 15¼", pr 400.00
Clock, Holland, thistles/foliage, Bordewijk, PZH, #103, 13x5".. 2,900.00
Decanter, Holland, floral panels/crown top, sgn P, PZH, #3031, 11¾".. 125.00
Figurine, Holland, stork, mc sponging, PZH, 12¼x5" 700.00
Jug, flowers & pea-pod leaves, PZH, #1201, 1918, 10½x4½" 435.00
Jug, Holland, Damascus pattern, abstracts, #1-19-0, 7x4½" 250.00
Lamp base, Holland, Ivory Mat 20, floral, prof rpr, Ivory #181, 14x7" .. 200.00
Plaque, gazelle & shrubbery, PZH, #1950-11E, 1¾x9" dia............ 285.00
Plaque, Holland, Attractive HP... & flowers, A Smit, 4¾x7¼" 150.00
Plaque, Holland, exotic bird on branch, G Veerman, #1165, 1922, 12"..2,100.00
Plaque, Holland, Nouveau floral, sgn JR, PZH, 16" dia 950.00
Plaque, Holland, trumpet flowers, sgn J, PZH, 1928, 15", NM 150.00
Plaque, Sourac, stylized fruit & abstracts, PZH, 1929, 12½" 350.00
Tazza, Regina, Pochara pattern, floral, 1922, 5¾x10½" 400.00
Tray, Beek, abstracts, PZH, #646, X, 1925, 12" 200.00
Vase, bud; Holland, Appel pattern, fruit, 1922, 8½" 100.00
Vase, Holland, Abuca, globular, PZH, #4442, 7½x8" 275.00
Vase, Holland, Archipel, abstracts, #1/860, 11¾x5" 225.00
Vase, Holland, bird on branch, W van Maaren, PZH, 1919, 8x4½" ..275.00
Vase, Holland, butterflies, D van der Bree, PZH, 1920s, 12½x5¼".....375.00
Vase, Holland, Dec Breetvelt, sunflower, 1926, 7½x4" 350.00
Vase, Holland, floral, J Kalmeijer, #39/103, 17½x7" 325.00
Vase, Holland, Hurh, abstracts, 1930, 11¼x6"........................... 460.00
Vase, Holland, iris on gloss, J Kalmeijer, hdls, PZH, 10¼x6"........ 500.00
Vase, Holland, Mabapan, abstracts, trophy shape w/hdls, PZH, 9x5"... 80.00
Vase, Holland, Mero, abstracts, #1052, 1926, 10½x7¼" 200.00
Vase, Holland, orchids & abstracts, stick neck, Ivory, #183, 6¼" .. 175.00
Vase, Holland, pansies/abstracts, slim neck, PZH, #619/2, 11½"..250.00
Vase, Holland, Polo, sgn HS, trumpet neck, Arhem, 13x4¾" 150.00
Vase, Holland, tulips, sgn W, pinched long neck, PZH, 1910s, 11½".. 400.00
Vase, Holland, tulips, stick neck, low hdls, PZH, #320/278, 13x6" 275.00
Vase, Nouveau design w/yel flowers, integral hdls, PZH, 1901, 20"..4,450.00
Vase, Rozenburg-style floral, pastels on ivory, basket shape, 14" .. 2,400.00

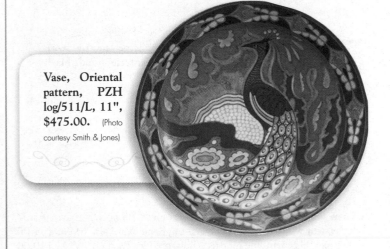

Vase, Oriental pattern, PZH log/511/L, 11", $475.00. (Photo courtesy Smith & Jones)

Grand Feu

The Grand Feu Art Pottery existed from 1912 until about 1918 in Los Angeles, California. It was owned and operated by Cornelius Brauckman, who developed a method of producing remarkably artistic glaze effects achieved through extremely high temperatures during the firing process. The body of the ware, as a result of the intense heat (2,500 degrees), was vitrified as the glaze matured. Brauckman signed his ware either with his name or 'Grand Feu Pottery, L.A. California.' His work is regarded today as being among the finest art pottery ever produced in the United States. Examples are rare and command high prices on today's market.

Bowl vase, yel-speckled indigo/dk brn on red clay, 4½x7½" 5,400.00
Vase, brn 3-color flambe, shouldered, BR #1730, 7½x5" 9,000.00
Vase, celadon mottle on red clay, long rstr hairline, 8¾x4½" 1,320.00
Vase, purple/gr semi-matt crystalline, squat w/long neck, 7", NM... 15,500.00
Vase, tan/brn mottled crystalline, shouldered, 7x3½" 7,200.00

Graniteware

Graniteware, made of a variety of metals with enamel coatings, derives its name from its appearance. The speckled, swirled, or mottled effect of the vari-colored enamels may look like granite — but there the resemblance stops. It wasn't especially durable! Expect at least minor chipping if you plan to collect.

Graniteware was featured in 1876 at Philly Expo. It was mass produced in quantity, and enough of it has survived to make at least the common items easily affordable. Condition, color, shape, and size are important considerations in evaluating an item; cobalt blue and white, green and white, brown and white, and old red and white swirled items are unusual, thus more expensive. Pieces of heavier weight, seam constructed, riveted, and those with wooden handles and tin or matching graniteware lids are usually older. Pieces with matching granite lids demand higher prices than ones with tin lids.

For further study we recommend *The Collector's Encyclopedia of Graniteware, Book 2,* by our advisor, Helen Greguire. It is available from the author and Collector Books. For information on how to order, see her listing in the Directory under South Carolina. For the address of the National Graniteware Society, see the section on Clubs, Newsletters, and Catalogs.

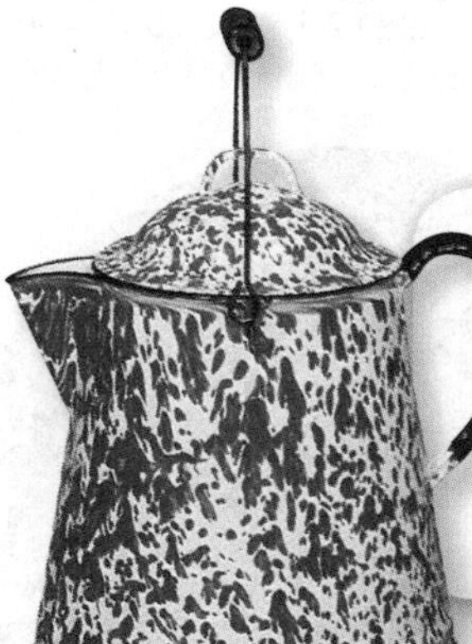

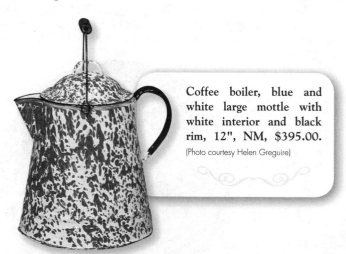

Coffee boiler, blue and white large mottle with white interior and black rim, 12", NM, $395.00.
(Photo courtesy Helen Greguire)

Ashtray, wht, red & cream w/bl emb advertising, Whirlpool, 8", NM.. 155.00
Ashtray, wht w/blk trim, emb advertising Polar Ware, 4⅝", M 155.00
Baking pan, bl & wht fine mottle, 2 hdls, oblong, 2¼x12¾", VG ... 120.00
Baking pan, red & wht swirl, bl trim, molded hdls, old, 2x10x15", VG..3,650.00
Bean pot, bl & wht lg swirl, blk trim & hdls, w/lid, 5½x6¼", M .. 265.00
Bed pan, bl & wht lg mottle inside & out, oblong, 2⅛x10¾", VG... 115.00
Bed pan, gray lg mottle, w/lid, Nesco Royal label, 13½x19½", M.... 115.00
Bowl, mixing; lav bl & wht lg mottle, blk trim, 4x9¾", VG.......... 65.00
Bowl, mixing; yel & wht lg swirl, blk trim, 6x12¼", NM 60.00
Bread pan, lav cobalt bl & wht lg swirl, bl trim, 8½" L, VG......... 295.00
Bread pan, lt bl & wht med mottle, wht int, seamed ends, 3x6", VG... 165.00
Bucket, bl & wht lg swirl, wht int, blk trim & lid, wire hdl, 6x6", NM .. 295.00
Bucket, water; bl & wht lg swirl, wht int, blk trim, 8⅜x10", M ... 340.00
Candlestick, cobalt bl & wht lg swirl, finger ring, 2¼x5", VG 995.00
Candlestick, Save All; gray med mottle, center prongs, 2x6⅜", VG... 425.00
Canister, tea; gray med mottle, seamless, w/tin lid, 6x4¾", NM... 650.00
Coaster, olive gr/wht mottle, advertising, Enterprise Enamel, 4", NM.. 255.00
Coffee biggin, gray lg mottle, wooden hdl, seamed, 9¾", NM...... 325.00
Coffee biggin, gray sm mottle, NP, 5-pc, 14¼", M 795.00
Coffee boiler, bl & wht lg swirl, blk trim, seamed, 10½x9", NM.. 395.00
Coffeepot, apple gr, dk gr trim, emb, Vollrath label, 7½x4⅝"....... 225.00
Coffeepot, bl & wht wavy mottle, bl trim & hdl, 9¼x5¾", NM... 450.00
Coffeepot, cobalt bl & wht lg swirl, wht int, blk trim, 10x6¾", M ... 425.00
Coffeepot, lt brn & wht med relish, bl trim, 5½x3½", VG 245.00
Colander, bl & wht mottle, blk trim & hdls, ftd, 3½x9½", VG.... 260.00
Cream can, bl & wht lg swirl, bl trim, Blue Diamond Ware, 8x4", NM... 975.00
Cream can, gray lg mottle, tin lid, seamed, Savory Inc, 7x4¼", M ... 245.00
Cream can, gray med mottle, w/lock lid, wire bail, 5¾x3¼", NM ...310.00
Creamer, gr & wht relish, bl trim, riveted hdl, 4½x3¾", VG 195.00
Creamer, red & wht lg mottle, blk trim, squatty, 1960s, 3¼x4", M ... 65.00
Cup, dk bl & wht med mottle relish, bl trim, hdl, 2⅜x4", VG....... 55.00
Cup, spit; gray med mottle, riveted hdl & thumb lift, 3x4", VG.. 295.00
Custard cup, wht, blk trim, Vollrath label, 2x3½", M 30.00
Dessert plate, bl & wht lg mottle inside & out, blk trim, 7", VG... 70.00
Dipper, bl & wht lg swirl, wht int, blk trim, cup shape, 2⅜x4", NM ... 275.00
Dishpan, bl & wht lg mottle, wht int, bl hdl & trim, rnd, 5x18", VG .. 175.00
Double boiler, bl & wht lg swirl, blk trim, seamed, 7x6⅝", NM... 325.00
Double boiler, gray med mottle, L&G Mfg Co, 11¾", VG 115.00
Dough bowl, bl & wht mottle, Geuder Paeschke & Frey, 5½x14", M .. 185.00
Egg plate, bl & wht lg mottle, wht int, blk hdls, 1x6¼", VG........ 245.00
Flask, coffee; gray lg mottle, Nesco... label, 6¼x2x4⅜", NM 475.00
Fruit press, gray & wht lg mottle, emb Presse Fruits A5, 9x5x10", NM.... 295.00
Fry pan, lav bl & wht lg swirl, blk trim & hdl, 2x10", VG 350.00
Fry pan, lt bl & wht lg swirl, CI base, 2¼x11½", NM 420.00
Fudge pan, yel & wht lg swirl, blk trim, 1x6x8¼", VG 95.00
Funnel, bl & wht lg swirl, blk trim & hdl, 4½x3¼", NM............. 410.00
Funnel, gray med mottle, Central Stamping Co, 4x3¾", M 75.00
Gravy boat, bl & wht fine mottle, bl trim & hdl, ftd, 4½x5⅝", NM ..425.00
Kettle, Berlin-style, lt gray med mottle, bl trim & hdls, w/lid, 9x11" .. 125.00
Kettle, gray lg mottle, seamless, w/lid, 6½x9", VG 110.00
Kettle, milk; wht w/blk trim, hdl, US Stamping Co, 9½x6¼", VG .. 130.00
Kettle, perserving; bl & wht lg swirl, Azure Enamelware, 5x11", M...325.00
Ladle, sauce; wht w/blk trim & hdl, 9x2½" dia, M......................... 35.00
Ladle, side snipe; solid wht, riveted hdl, 14½x4½" dia, NM......... 140.00
Ladle, soup; bl & wht med swirl, wht int/blk hdl, 13⅜x3⅝" dia, M.... 110.00
Measure, aqua gr & wht swirl, bl trim, strap hdl, seamed, 5x3⅝", NM ... 450.00
Measuring cup, bl & wht med mottle, hdl, ¼-C grad measure, VG ... 165.00
Milk can, wht w/gr trim & hdl, Savory label, 6¼x5", NM 110.00
Milk pan, bl & wht med mottle, side pouring lip, 3¼x9", VG 155.00
Muffin pan, bl & wht lg swirl, wht int, blk trim, 11⅜x14½", VG... 1,550.00

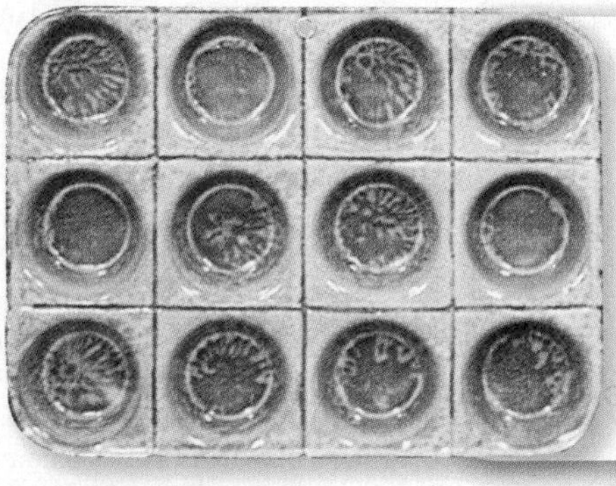

Muffin pan, gray large mottle, underside has straps that hold the cups in place, 12½x9", G+, $265.00. (Photo courtesy Helen Greguire)

Mug, cobalt bl & wht lg swirl, wht int, blk trim, 3x4", NM 95.00
Mug, farmer's; bl & wht lg swirl, wht int, blk trim, 4½x4¼", VG.. 240.00
Mug, lt gray & wht lg marble, wht int, 4⅛x4", VG 75.00
Mug, red & wht lg swirl, wht int, blk trim & hdl, ca 1960, 3x3½", M ...45.00

Paperweight, man figural, lt gray, emb advertising, 3½x2⅝", VG .. 225.00
Pie plate, blk w/wht flecks, eagle, General Housewares Co, 10", M .. 55.00
Pie plate, red & wht swirl, wht int, bl trim, old, ⅞x9¾", NM 625.00
Pie plate, solid red, shallow, 1x8", VG 40.00
Pitcher, gr lg mottle, Double Coated Puritain label, 6½", M 425.00
Pitcher, milk; gray lg mottle, weld hdl, squatty, 7x4½", NM 295.00
Pitcher, water; red & wht swirl, wht int, dk bl trim, old, 9x6", NM ... 5,775.00
Pitcher & bowl, bl & wht lg mottle, blk trim, 2-pc, 11¼x6¼", NM...... 865.00
Plate, red & wht swirl inside & out, blk trim, 1960s, 10¼", NM.... 45.00
Platter, bl & wht lg swirl, Blue Diamond Ware, 11x14", NM....... 365.00
Potato kettle, lt bl & wht mottle, str style, w/lid, 6¾x8⅜", VG ... 295.00
Preserving kettle, bl & wht mottle, gray int, blk trim, 8x17¼", VG... 165.00
Pudding pan, blk & wht lg swirl, blk trim, 3⅛x 9¾", M 295.00
Pudding pan, deep red & wht lg swirl, 2x6½x8½", NM........ 170.00
Pudding pan, dk gr & wht lg mottle, wht int, dk bl trim, 2x8½", VG... 165.00
Refrigerator dish, solid red, blk trim, w/red lid, 3¼x8x5", NM....... 35.00
Roaster, lt bl & wht swirl, blk hdl, rnd, w/lid, 5¾x11¾", M 250.00
Saucepan, bl & wht mottle, Paragon Lion Brand, 3⅜x6⅜", VG 95.00
Saucepan, red & wht lg swirl, blk trim & hdl, 1940, 2⅜x5⅜", M... 95.00
Saucepan, wht w/cobalt trim & hdl, Tru-Blu label, 2½x6⅜", M..... 40.00
Saucer, bl & wht mottle/bl trim, Geuder Paeschke & Frey label, 6", M . 170.00
Scoop, solid wht, seamless, 2¾x2⅜x9¼", VG 110.00
Skimmer, solid red, blk hdl, Made in Poland label, 14½" L, VG.... 45.00
Slop bucket, bl & wht med mottle, wht int, w/lid, 9½x10¼" NM... 250.00
Spoon, bl & wht lg mottle, blk hdl, 13" L, VG........ 110.00
Stew pan, bl & wht med swirl, blk riveted hdl, 3⅛x10⅛", NM.... 185.00
Stew pan, bl & wht mottle, wht int, blk trim, deep, 2x9", NM.... 185.00
Strainer, wht w/bl trim, kettle hdl, fancy perforation, 5½" dia, VG... 65.00

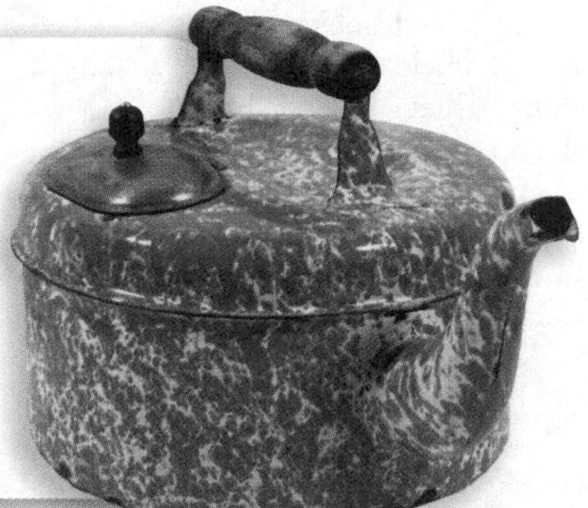

Teakettle, blue and white large mottle, embossed 'Savory' on top, hinged copper cover embossed 'Pat'd 1903,' G+, $495.00. (Photo courtesy Helen Greguire)

Teakettle, bl & wht lg swirl, wht int, blk trim, 8x7¼", VG 295.00
Teakettle, bl & wht med swirl, blk hdl & trim, seamed, 7x9½", VG... 310.00
Teakettle, red & wht swirl, wht int, wooden bail, old, 7x9¼", NM.. 1,350.00
Teakettle, solid red, bl int, blk trim, 7¼x9¼", M 240.00
Teapot, bl & wht lg mottle, wht int, seamed, 11¾x7⅛", VG 165.00
Teapot, deep red & wht lg swirl, wht int, blk trim, 7¾x4¾", NM ... 195.00
Teapot, gray lg mottle, Geuder Paeschke & Frey Co, 8x5¼", M .. 215.00
Teapot, gray med mottle, squatty, seamless, 4¼x3⅜", VG 395.00
Teapot, red & wht lg mottle, wht int, red trim, old, 8¾x5¼", NM... 750.00
Tray, gray lg mottle, oblong, L&G Mfg Co, 9½x13⅝", NM......... 175.00
Tube cake mold, lt bl & wht swirl, blk trim, 8-sided, 3½x8", VG.... 180.00
Washbowl, bl & wht lg swirl, bl trim, Blue Diamond Ware, 3x12", NM... 250.00
Washbowl, bl & wht lg swirl, wht int, blk trim, 3⅝x13¾", NM... 225.00
Washbowl, solid wht, eyelet for hanging, 2¾x10½", M 45.00

Green Opaque

Introduced in 1887 by the New England Glass Works, this ware is very scarce due to the fact that it was produced for less than one year. It is characterized by its soft green color and a wavy band of gold reserving a mottled blue metallic stain. It is usually found in satin; examples with a shiny finish are extremely rare. Values depend to a large extent on the amount of the gold and stain remaining.

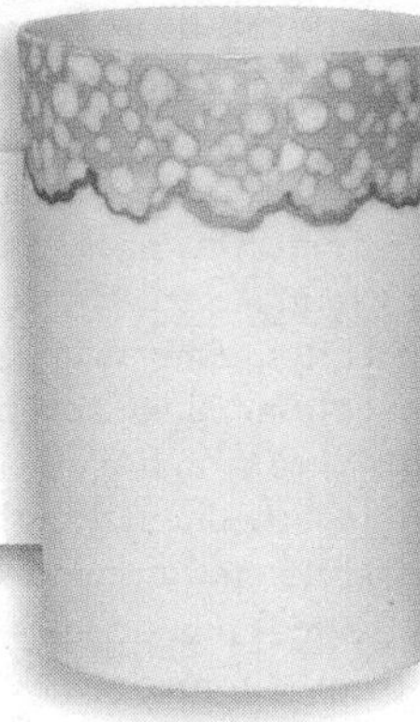

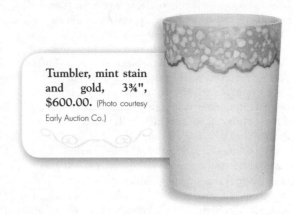

Tumbler, mint stain and gold, 3¾", $600.00. (Photo courtesy Early Auction Co.)

Bowl, w/lid, EX stain, 6" dia, from $900 to 1,000.00
Bowl, w/lid, M stain & gold, appl finial, 6" dia 3,500.00
Celery vase, blk mottling, VG gold, 6¼"........ 750.00
Creamer, EX stain & gold........ 950.00
Cruet, M stain & gold, orig stopper........ 1,950.00
Mug, M stain & gold, 2½" 700.00
Punch cup, worn stain & gold, 2½"........ 225.00
Shaker, M stain & gold, 2½"........ 400.00
Spooner, EX stain & gold, 4" 925.00
Sugar bowl, EX stain & gold, 5½" W 920.00
Toothpick holder, EX stain, 2⅜", from $325 to........ 375.00
Toothpick holder, M stain & gold........ 1,150.00
Tumbler, EX gold & stain, 3¾" 400.00
Tumbler, lemonade; w/hdl, M stain & gold, 5" 950.00

Greenaway, Kate

Kate Greenaway was an English artist who lived from 1846 to 1901. She gained worldwide fame as an illustrator of children's books, drawing children clothed in the styles worn by proper English and American boys and girls of the very early 1800s. Her book, *Under the Willow Tree*, published in 1878, was the first of many. Her sketches appeared in leading magazines, and her greeting cards were in great demand. Manufacturers of china, pottery, and metal products copied her characters to decorate children's dishes, tiles, and salt and pepper shakers as well as many other items.

What some collectors/dealers call Kate Greenaway items are not actual Kate Greenaway designs but merely look-alikes. Genuine Kate Greenaway items (metal, paper, cloth, etc.) must bear close resemblance to her drawings in books, magazines, and special collections. Our advisor for this category is James Lewis Lowe; he is listed in the Directory under Pennsylvania. See also Napkin Rings.

Biscuit jar, ceramic, boy w/tinted features, w/lid........ 165.00
Book, A Apple Pie, Warne, 1940, w/dust jacket, VG........ 30.00
Book, Almanack for 1884, printed by Edmund Evans, EX 135.00
Book, Good-Night Stories for Little Folks, NY & London, no date, EX+.... 65.00
Book, Kate Greenaway Pictures, London, Warne, 1st ed, 1921, VG .. 300.00
Book, Kate Greenaway's Book of Games, Routledge, 1st ed, 1889, NM.. 475.00
Book, Marigold Garden, London, 1888, VG........ 60.00
Book, Pictures & Rhymes for Children..., paperbk, McLoughlin, ca 1900... 65.00
Book, Ring-Round-a-Rosy, red cover, cloth, Saalfield, 1907, EX+ .. 100.00
Book, Sunshine for Little Children, 1884, EX 80.00
Book, Under the Window, Routledge, 1st ed, orig cloth 165.00
Butter pat, children playing transfer, pre-1910 .... 40.00

Button, Autumn from Almanack, metal silhouette, ½".................. 40.00
Button, Johnny at Fence Post, metal, ¾" 30.00
Button, Little Bo Peep, flat or cupped metal, ⅝-¾", from $20 to.... 25.00
Button, Miss Pelicoes, metal silhouette, rear or front view, 1¼"..... 40.00
Button, Pretty Patty Sitting on Fence, cupped metal silhouette, ¾"... 20.00
Button, Pretty Patty Sitting on Fence, metal, ¾"........................... 20.00
Button, Ring the Bells Ring, 4 girls in queue, gold on glass, ⅝" 30.00
Button, Ring the Bells Ring, 4 girls in queue, silver on glass, ⅞" ... 40.00
Button, Spring from Almanack, glass, 1" 40.00
Button, Spring from Almanack, wht metal on brass, ¾" 40.00
Button, Summer from Almanack, glass, ¾"................................... 20.00
Button, Summer from Almanack, metal silhouette, 1"................... 25.00
Button, 2 Girls Sitting on Rail, metal, ¾" 50.00
Calendar, chromolithograph, Routledge, 1884, 7⅜x9½", EX 60.00
Cup & saucer, children transfer, pk lustre trim, pre-1910............. 125.00
Figurine, girl (seated) tugs on lg hat, bsk, pre-1910, sm.................. 75.00
Inkwell, boy & girl, bronze 215.00
Paperweight, CI, Victorian girl in lg bonnet, pre-1910, 3x2¾" 110.00
Pickle castor, bl; SP fr w/2 girls, blown-out florals....................... 455.00
Scarf, children on silk, early, EX.. 65.00
Toothpick holder, SP, girl holds amberina cup, ornate base, 5" 785.00
Wall pocket, ceramic, 6 girls on open-book form, 6x9x3" 137.00

Greentown Glass

Greentown glass is a term referring to the product of the Indiana Tumbler and Goblet Company of Greentown, Indiana, ca 1894 to 1903. Their earlier pressed glass patterns were #75 (originally known as #11), a pseudo-cut glass design; #137, Pleat Band; and #200, Austrian. Another line, Dewey, was designed in 1898. Many lovely colors were produced in addition to crystal. Jacob Rosenthal, who was later affiliated with Fenton, developed his famous chocolate glass in 1900. The rich, shaded opaque brown glass was an overnight success. Two new patterns, Leaf Bracket and Cactus, were designed to display the glass to its best advantage, but previously existing molds were also used. In only three years Rosenthal developed yet another important color formula, Golden Agate. The Holly pattern was designed especially for its production. The dolphin covered dish with a fish finial is perhaps the most common and easily recognized piece ever produced. Other animal dishes were also made; all are highly collectible. There have been many repros — not all are marked! The symbol (+) at the end of some of the following lines was used to indicate items that have been reproduced. Our advisor for this category is Sandi Garrett; she is listed in the Directory under Indiana. See the Pattern Glass section for clear pressed glass; only colored items are listed here.

Animal dish, bird w/berry, chocolate (+) 1,000.00
Animal dish, bird w/berry, Golden Agate 2,000.00
Animal dish, cat on hamper, amber, tall 350.00

Animal dish, cat on hamper, teal blue, $450.00.

Animal dish, cat on hamper, wht opaque, tall 550.00
Animal dish, dolphin, beaded, cobalt 1,500.00
Animal dish, dolphin, chocolate, smooth rim 350.00
Animal dish, dolphin, emerald gr, beaded rim 850.00

Animal dish, dolphin, golden Agate, beaded edge, $300.00. (Photo courtesy Early Auction Co.)

Animal dish, dolphin, teal bl, sawtooth rim (+) 925.00
Animal dish, fighting cocks, Nile Green............................3,000.00
Animal dish, hen, cobalt 500.00
Animal dish, hen, wht opaque 225.00
Animal dish, rabbit, wht opaque (+)... 225.00
Animal pitcher, heron, chocolate 650.00
Animal pitcher, squirrel, chocolate 550.00
Austrian, butter dish, canary 500.00
Austrian, creamer, chocolate, 4¼"... 135.00
Austrian, pitcher, water; canary 525.00
Austrian, plate, canary, sq.. 250.00
Austrian, rose bowl, canary, lg 325.00
Brazen Shield, cake stand, bl, 9⅜" 250.00
Brazen Shield, goblet, bl.. 250.00
Brazen Shield, relish tray, bl 125.00
Brazen Shield, spooner, bl.. 130.00
Brazen Shield, tumbler, bl... 75.00
Cactus, bowl, chocolate, 5¼".. 80.00
Cactus, butter dish, chocolate 150.00
Cactus, butter/cheese dish, chocolate, ped ft 800.00
Cactus, celery vase, chocolate, 7½", NM 500.00

Cactus, compote, chocolate, 9¼", $285.00.

Cactus, cruet, chocolate, w/stopper.. 135.00
Cactus, sauce dish, chocolate, flat 125.00
Cactus, syrup, chocolate, metal thumb-lift lid, 6"........................ 200.00
Cactus, tumbler, bl-wht opal rim.. 700.00
Cactus, vase, chocolate, 6" 550.00
Cord Drapery, bowl, amber, hand fluted, ftd, 8¼" 225.00
Cord Drapery, bowl, amber, w/fluted top, 8" 200.00
Cord Drapery, bowl, cobalt, ftd, 8¼" 350.00
Cord Drapery, butter dish, cobalt, 4¾" 450.00
Cord Drapery, compote, cobalt, w/lid, 8½" 375.00
Cord Drapery, creamer, emerald gr, 4¼" 175.00
Cord Drapery, mug, emerald gr, ftd.. 225.00
Cord Drapery, sauce bowl, amber, ftd, 3⅞" 95.00

Cord Drapery, tray, water; emerald gr 325.00
Cupid, butter dish, chocolate 700.00
Cupid, creamer, chocolate 375.00
Cupid, spooner, Nile Green 425.00
Cupid, sugar bowl, chocolate, w/lid 550.00
Cupid, sugar bowl, wht opaque, w/lid 150.00
Dewey, creamer, Nile Green, 5" 375.00
Dewey, parfait, chocolate, no lid 225.00
Dewey, pitcher, canary 175.00
Dewey, plate, emerald gr 60.00
Dewey, sugar bowl, emerald gr, w/lid, 4" 125.00
Dewey, tumbler, amber 40.00
Early Diamond, dish, amber, rectangular, 8x5" 225.00
Early Diamond, dish, cobalt, rectangular, 8x5" 275.00
Early Diamond, pitcher, amber 350.00
Early Diamond, tumbler, chocolate 225.00
Greentown Daisy, creamer, chocolate, w/lid 175.00
Greentown Daisy, sugar bowl, emerald gr frost 115.00
Greentown Daisy, sugar bowl, wht opaque, w/lid 80.00
Herringbone Buttress, bowl, amber, 5¼" 350.00
Herringbone Buttress, cordial, emerald gr, 3¾" 325.00
Herringbone Buttress, cracker jar, emerald gr 425.00
Herringbone Buttress, nappy, emerald gr 225.00
Herringbone Buttress, plate, emerald gr, 7¼ 350.00
Herringbone Buttress, vase, emerald gr, 6" 225.00
Herringbone Buttress, wine, olive gr, 4" 225.00
Holly, toothpick holder, Rose Agate 4,500.00
Holly Amber, bowl, rnd, 7½" 550.00
Holly Amber, butter dish, ped ft 3,000.00
Holly Amber, cake stand 3,000.00
Holly Amber, compote, low ped base, 4½x4", EX 1,350.00

Holly Amber, creamer, $850.00.

Holly Amber, cruet, w/stopper 2,250.00
Holly Amber, mug, 4" (+) 650.00
Holly Amber, mustard pot, open, 3¼" 1,000.00
Holly Amber, pickle dish, oval w/tab hdls, 8¾" 400.00
Holly Amber, sauce dish, 4½" 225.00
Holly Amber, toothpick holder, 2½" 325.00
Holly Amber, tray, rnd, 9¼" 1,500.00
Holly Amber, tumbler, 4" 450.00
Mug, deer & oak tree, chocolate 1,750.00
Novelty, cuff set, chocolate 2,250.00
Novelty, trunk, chocolate 1,800.00
Pattern #75, tumbler, iced tea; chocolate 450.00
Teardrop & Tassel, pitcher, amber 325.00
Toothpick holder, witch head, chocolate (+) 1,500.00

Grueby

William Henry Grueby joined the firm of the Low Art Tile Works at the age of 15 and in 1894, after several years of experience in the pro-

duction of architectural tiles, founded his own plant, the Grueby Faience Company, in Boston, Massachusetts. Grueby began experimenting with the idea of producing art pottery and had soon perfected a fine glaze (soft and without gloss) in shades of blue, gray, yellow, brown, and his most successful, cucumber green. In 1900 his exhibit at the Paris Exposition Universelle won three gold medals.

Grueby pottery was hand thrown and hand decorated in the Arts and Crafts style. Vertically thrust tooled and applied leaves and flower buds were the most common decorative devices. Tiles continued to be an important product, unique (due to the matt glaze decoration) as well as durable. Grueby tiles were often a full inch thick. Many of them were decorated in cuenca, others were impressed and filled with glaze, and some were embossed. Later, when purchased by Pardee, they were decorated in cuerda seca.

Incompatible with the Art Nouveau style, the artware production ceased in 1907, but tile production continued for another decade. The ware is marked in one of several ways: 'Grueby Pottery, Boston, USA'; 'Grueby, Boston, Mass.'; or 'Grueby Faience.' The artware is often artist signed. Our advisors for this category are Suzanne Perrault and David Rago; they are is listed in the Directory under New Jersey.

Bowl, gr, alligatored effect, leaf logo, 1¾x4½" 700.00
Bowl, gr, horizontal panels, int swirl, 2¾x8" 450.00
Bowl vase, bl-gr, leaves (delicate/rnded), R Erickson, 2¼x5" 2,040.00
Bowl vase, gr, wide leaves, sgn, sm rpr, 5" 1,440.00
Bowl vase, indigo, faint band of rings under rim, 3x5" 1,140.00
Jardiniere, gr, leaves, R Erickson, #8/4, 6x11", NM 3,900.00
Jardiniere, gr, leaves, stress cracks/nicks, 12x19" 15,275.00
Paperweight, scarab, deep azure bl, 2½" 500.00
Tile, cellist at work, bl & caramel on red clay, 6" 480.00
Tile, horses frieze, ivory on bl, gr below, A LeBoutillier, KC, 6", EX ... 2,640.00
Tile, lion & trees, 4-color, 4" 1,000.00
Tile, mermaid grooming her hair, brn on yel, #65, 6" 775.00
Tile, ship, ivory/brn on dk gr, in hammered copper mt, 6" 1,200.00
Tile, St Geo & dragon, bl/gr/ochre/cream, 9" 7,650.00
Tile, The Pines, pines/mtn range, shades of gr/brn, sgn RD, 6" .. 3,480.00
Tile, unicorn, blk on gr, sm nick, unmk, 6" 1,800.00
Tile frieze, water lilies, ivory/yel/lt gr on dk gr, set of 6, ea 6" 4,500.00
Vase, azure bl w/gray flecks, bulbous, 4x3½" 600.00
Vase, gr, emb panels, #06, 5x7" 1,100.00
Vase, gr, flared rim, 5½x2¾" 550.00

Vase, green, leaves and amber buds, signed Ruth Erickson, 6½ x 7¼", $20,000.00.
(Photo courtesy David Rago Auctions)

Vase, gr, leaves, squat, sm rpr, 5" 1,200.00
Vase, gr, leaves (2 rows), pumpkin shape, rstr, 4½x5½" 1,920.00
Vase, gr, leaves (3) w/yel buds, M Seaman, 8½x4½" 2,280.00
Vase, gr, leaves w/yel buds, R Erickson, 11½x5½" 10,500.00
Vase, gr, long oval panels between inverted leaves w/long stems, 8x5" ... 1,920.00

Vase, gr, narcissus (brn/cream), bulbous, W Post, 10"..............16,450.00
Vase, gr, quatrefoils/leaves, W Post, squat pear form, 5x5½", NM ..3,900.00
Vase, gr, short leaves at wide base, stems/buds on long neck, 7" ..1,800.00
Vase, gr, 5-panel, cylinder neck, 7x4¼".....................................2,300.00
Vase, gr (curdled), leaves, short & tall alternate, sgn, 11½" 7,200.00
Vase, gr (feathered), leaves, gourd shape, ER, 8x7", NM...........7,800.00
Vase, gr (feathered), long stems/leaves, bulbous base, 7x4½" ...2,400.00
Vase, gr (feathered), wide leaves, R Erickson, 3¼x4¾"..............1,080.00
Vase, gr (leathery), 2nd row of leaves cup rim, label, 13x8½" .12,000.00
Vase, gr (suspended), leaves/buds, sgn RE, 11¼".......................4,800.00
Vase, gr-bl (curdled), 6¾" 750.00
Vase, lt bl, leaves, sm rim rstr, 7¾x4"......................................3,600.00
Vase, purple-brn, leaves, 2 sm rpr chips, 11½x5½"....................2,520.00

Gustavsberg

Gustavsberg Pottery, founded near Stockholm, Sweden, in the late 1700s, manufactured faience, creamware, and porcelain in the English taste until the end of the nineteenth century. During the twentieth century, the factory has produced some inventive modernistic designs, often signed by their artists. Wilhelm Kage (1889 – 1960) is best remembered for Argenta, a stoneware body decorated in silver overlay, introduced in the 1930s. Usually a mottled turquoise, Argenta can also be found in cobalt blue and white. Other lines included Cintra (an exceptionally translucent porcelain), Farsta (copper-glazed ware), and Farstarust (iron oxide geometric overlay). Designer Stig Lindberg's work, which dates from the 1940s through the early 1970s, includes slab-built figures and a full range of tableware. Some pieces of Gustavsberg are dated. Our advisors for this category are Suzanne Perrault and Dave Rago; they are listed in the Directory under New Jersey.

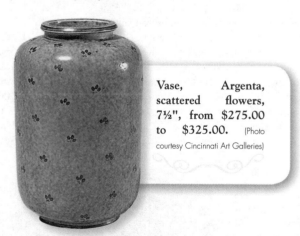

Vase, Argenta, scattered flowers, 7½", from $275.00 to $325.00. (Photo courtesy Cincinnati Art Galleries)

Bowl, appl flowers & leaves, wht, Kage, 1930, X, 3½x7½", EX 70.00
Bowl, Argenta, concentric rings on turq, Kage, #1055, 3⅜" H....... 85.00
Bowl, Argenta, fish on turq, #1094, 1⅝x4⅞" 125.00
Bowl, Argenta, floral int on turq, conical, sm ft, 3½" 110.00
Bowl, Argenta, mermaid medallion on turq, shaped rim w/2 bands, 11" ... 180.00
Bowl, bl & yel irid w/geometric designs, crazing, 5x10"................ 500.00
Bowl, center; bl w/pk int, pnt swirls, gold hdls, Ekberg, 5x9" 200.00
Candlesticks, bl irid w/gold trim, tulip sockets, Ekberg, 3½", pr.. 130.00
Charger, Argenta, mermaid on turq, sm chip, 2¾x18" 1,000.00
Figurine, horse, 'fat' body w/brn spots, Lindberg, 5½x6"............. 375.00
Figurine, nude woman on ped, parian, Hasselberg, #19B, 19", NM ...750.00
Plaque, fish in multiple directions, red/ivory/charcoal, bl trim, 11" .. 300.00
Plaque, stylized horse w/tooled details, brn/bl/bl-gr, label, 13x19"...300.00
Plate, Argenta, floral on turq, 6½".. 70.00
Vase, Argenta, figure w/bow on turq, Kage, #1207, ca 1925, 10¾"...1,500.00
Vase, Argenta, fish on turq, flared cylinder, 6" 195.00

Vase, Argenta, flowers on turq, cylindrical, #1029H, 6" 125.00
Vase, Argenta, foliage on grid on turq, rectangular w/hdls, 6"...... 265.00
Vase, Argenta, tulips on blk gloss, slim, 7"................................. 100.00
Vase, sgraffito floral, bl on bl-wht, Ekberg, 1911, 12¾"............1,400.00

Vase, squeeze-bag florals, artist signed, 1910, 6¾", from $700.00 to $800.00.
(Photo courtesy David Rago Auctions)

Hadley, M. A.

Founded by artist-turned-potter Mary Alice Hadley, this Louisville, Kentucky, company has been producing handmade dinnerware and decorative items since 1940. Their work is painted freehand in a folksy style with barnyard animals, whales, sailing ships, and several other patterns. The palette is predominately blue and green. Each piece is signed with Hadley's first two initials and her last name, and her artwork continues to be the inspiration for modern designs. Among collectors, horses and other farm animals are popular subject matter. Older pieces are generally heavier and, along with the more unusual items, command the higher prices. Our advisor for this category is Lisa Sanders; she is listed in the Directory under Indiana.

Bean pot, Bouquet, 7" 30.00
Bean pot, cow & pig, pitcher form w/spout, w/lid, 7" 50.00
Bowl, mixing; rooster, 4x8½"... 40.00

Bowl, salad; farmer and his wife, 11", from $35.00 to $45.00. (Photo courtesy Michael Sessman)

Butter dish, cow, rectangular, 2x7½" 30.00
Candleholder, angel w/harp & shamrock, 2" halo for candle, 10", ea ..25.00
Casserole, Bouquet, w/hdls, 5x12"... 40.00
Casserole, pig & cow, The End inside, w/lid, 5½x5¾" 40.00
Cookie jar, Goodies & flower, 6x5" dia 40.00
Creamer & sugar bowl, frog, w/lid, 2½".................................... 30.00
Cup & saucer, jumbo; Dad, The End inside cup 25.00
Flower arranger, horse head, 9".. 90.00
Mug, cat, flared, lg.. 20.00
Pie plate, sailboat 35.00
Pie plate, Way to a Man's Heart 35.00
Pitcher, ship & whale, 28-oz, 5¼x5".. 27.50

Plate, barn, tall ship, or any animal, 11", ea................................... 25.00
Platter, farmer & wife, 13".. 35.00
Platter, rabbit, 13¾x9"... 35.00
Wall pocket, flowers, conical, 8x7½x3½"................................ 40.00
Water cooler, horse, brass spout, w/lid, 12".................................. 150.00

Hagen-Renaker

Hagen-Renaker Potteries was founded in a garage in Culver City, California, in 1945. By 1946 they had moved to a Quonset hut in Monrovia, California, where they produced hand-painted dishes decorated with fruits and vegetables or animal designs. These dishes were usually signed 'HR Calif' in paint on the back. In 1948 the company began producing miniature animal figurines, which quickly became their bestselling line. Remarkably, this is still true, and some of the old miniatures from the '50s are still being produced today.

In 1952 Hagen-Renaker introduced a new larger line of animal figurines called Designer's Workshop. These pieces were designed by many remarkable artists. Their design, mold detail, and painting were amazing. They made hundreds of different Designer's Workshop pieces — birds, cats, dogs, farm animals, horses, insects, and wildlife — that actually looked more like real animals than pottery renditions. Their horses are particularly prized by collectors.

When Disneyland opened in 1955, Hagen-Renaker made many Disney pieces and continued producing them until 1960. Walt Disney was particularly impressed, saying that Hagen-Renaker made the finest three-dimensional figurines he had ever seen. Hagen-Renaker made these groups of figurines: Alice in Wonderland, Bambi, Cinderella, Dumbo, Fantasia, Mickey Mouse & Friends, Peter Pan, Sleeping Beauty, a few miscellaneous pieces, and two sizes of Snow White and the Seven Dwarfs. Most of the Disney pieces were minis, but they also produced larger items, including banks and cookie jars. A chamber pot was also produced that Walt Disney gave to employees with new babies, pink for girls and blue for boys. A second larger set of Fantasia pieces was made in 1982.

The late 1950s and early 1960s was a very difficult time for all American potteries. Most were forced to close due to cheap Japanese imports. Many of these imports were unauthorized copies of American-made pieces. The company initiated new products and cost-cutting measures, trying to compete with these imports. They introduced many new lines including Little Horribles, Rock Wall plaques and trays (glazed with brightly colored primitive animals similar to cave drawings), Zany Zoo pieces, and Black Bisque animals. They also tried Aurasperse, a cold paint that didn't have to be fired in a kiln, thus saving time and money. The problem with this paint was that it washed off very easily. Because these pieces weren't long in production, they are treasured today due to their scarcity. Even with these new lines, paints, and many other cost-saving efforts, Hagen-Renaker was still forced to shut down; however, the shutdown lasted only a few months. Shortly after reopening, the company moved to San Dimas, California, where they still operate today.

In 1908 Hagen-Renaker bought the Freeman-McFarlin factory in San Marcos, California, and operated that factory for six years. They specialized in making large Designer's Workshop pieces. Some were new designs while others were Freeman-McFarlin's, but the majority were re-issued Designer's Workshop pieces. Most of these old molds had to be reworked, so many of the pieces from the San Marcos era vary slightly from the earlier products. Hagen-Renaker continued to produce Freeman-McFarlin pieces using the glazes and colors that company originally favored, usually white or gold leaf. They also made some items in new colors. In many cases, it is impossible to make a distinction between products of the two companies.

In the late '80s, Hagen-Renaker started Stoneware and Specialty lines which are larger than the minis and smaller than the Designer's Workshop pieces. The Stoneware line was short lived, but they still make the Specialty pieces. Recently, Hagen Renaker issued a line of dogs called the Pedigree line, which are actually redesigns of Designer's Workshop. The current Hagen-Renaker line consists of 45 Specialty pieces, 13 Pedigree dogs, and 206 miniatures. The company has recently issued limited editions of larger horses as well. Some are new designs while others are re-issues of the old Designer's Workshop horses. Currently, 14 of these larger horses are available in various colors with more to come. Our advisors for this category are Ed and Sheri Alcorn; they are listed in the Directory under Florida. Feel free to visit their Hagen-Renaker Online Museum where you will find over 2,500 Hagen-Renaker items pictured.

Black Bisque, pigeon, blk & wht, #15, 1959, 3"............................. 50.00
Black Bisque, rooster, bl-gr enamel on blk, #21, 1959, 3¾".......... 200.00
Butter pat, Rooster design, #610, 1946-49, 3½" dia....................... 45.00
Designer's Workshop, Banty hen, #747, rare, 1962-67, 4¼"......... 235.00
Designer's Workshop, Banty rooster, wht, rare, #766, 1962-67, 5½" ..250.00
Designer's Workshop, Beep, duckling, #573, 1954-56, 2"............... 25.00
Designer's Workshop, Bernie, fireside dachshund, #1545, 1957-68, 14x7" ..250.00
Designer's Workshop, cat reclining, blk & wht, #121, 1985-86, 7x12"...300.00
Designer's Workshop, chick seated, #747, 1980s, 1⅝".................... 25.00
Designer's Workshop, Comet, greyhound, gray, #1003, 1954-55, 3¼" ...65.00
Designer's Workshop, Diana, Doberman sitting, #1539, 1957-67, 5¾" ..200.00
Designer's Workshop, Edna, chick w/head up, #618, 1967, 1½"... 145.00
Designer's Workshop, Fez, rearing stallion, wht, #612, 1955-57, 8½".. 900.00
Designer's Workshop, Fez, rearing stallion reissue, blk, #612, current ... 260.00
Designer's Workshop, Kelso, famous racehorse, #772, 1965-74, 6½"... 400.00
Designer's Workshop, Lipizzaner horse rearing, wht/#653, '57-84, 6½" ..300.00

Designer's Workshop, Love Appaloosa, 1964 – 1968, 4¾", $400.00.
(Photo courtesy Ed and Sheri Alcorn)

Designer's Workshop, Nubian goat kid walking, #78, 1984-86, 3" ...60.00
Designer's Workshop, pheasant standing/long legs, #691, 1962+, 5½" ...200.00
Designer's Workshop, pig mama, recumbent, #55, 1984-86, 3x8".. 50.00
Designer's Workshop, Scamper, Morgan foal, brn, #562, 1954-58, 5"... 125.00
Designer's Workshop, Sespe Violette, Belgian, chestnut, #567, '54+, 5" ..1,200.00
Designer's Workshop, Siamese cat climbing, #525, 1952-78, 6½".. 35.00
Designer's Workshop, Siamese cat watching tail, #526, 1952-54, 3".. 30.00
Disney miniature, Bacchus from Fantasia, 1957, 1¾"................... 225.00
Disney miniature, Bluebird from Sleeping Beauty, 1959-60,½"...... 85.00
Disney miniature, Jaq, mouse from Cinderella, 1956-57, 1¾"...... 200.00
Disney miniature, Peter Pan, 1957-60, 1¾"............................... 125.00
Disney miniature, Ruffles, cocker pup from Lady & Tramp, 1955-59, ⅝".. 40.00
Disney miniature, Tinkerbell, shelf sitter, 1957-60, 1½"............... 400.00
Geranium Leaf, tray, #302, 1946-49, 5"................................. 75.00
Little Horribles, Guitar Player, #436, 1959, 1½".......................... 150.00
Little Horribles, Helping Hand, #396, 1959, 1"........................... 60.00
Little Horribles, Little Blue Man, #390, 1958-59, 1¼"................. 50.00
Little Horribles, Patient, couch shape, #395, 1959, 1⅜".............. 225.00
Miniature, Abyssinian cat, A-2044, 1989-90, 1½"........................ 35.00
Miniature, Arabian foal, #3348, 2001-02, 2¾".............................. 30.00
Miniature, Arabian horse prancing, wht, A-297, 1956-73, 3¼"..... 75.00
Miniature, badger baby, A-851, 1984-86,½"................................. 30.00
Miniature, bloodhound sniffing, A-2062, 1989-92, 1⅜"................ 20.00

Miniature, Blue-footed Booby, #2019, 2½" 85.00
Miniature, border collie, A-3208, 1996-98, 1⅜" 10.00
Miniature, budgie in hoop, A-2030, 1988-91, 2½" 25.00
Miniature, cardinal on branch, #2054, 1989, 2¼" 35.00
Miniature, cat lying w/ball, A-2047, 1989, 2½" 35.00
Miniature, cat papa, fluffy, gray (rare color), A-353, 1968-69, 1¾" .. 150.00
Miniature, chickadee mama, gray bsk, A-288, 1950s, 1¼" 20.00
Miniature, circus seal baby w/ball, blk, A-259, 1955-56, 1" 30.00
Miniature, cocker spaniel carrying newspaper, A-255, 1956-57, 1¾" ... 20.00
Miniature, coyote, A-3016, 1991-2002, 2½" 12.00
Miniature, donkey baby w/ears out, A-304, 1956 only, 1" 50.00
Miniature, fox mama, #3321, 2000-06, 4" 40.00
Miniature, frog playing banjo, #3180, current, 2¾" 17.00
Miniature, goat papa, gray (rare color), A-237, 1969 only, 2½" ... 125.00
Miniature, great white shark, A-3145, 1994-99, 1¼x4" 15.00
Miniature, Guernsey bull, A-3200, 1996-97, 1¾" 10.00
Miniature, hackney, A-2085, 1990-93, 2¾" 40.00
Miniature, hawk on branch, brn, A-3060, 1992-94, 2¼" 25.00
Miniature, hummingbird, #3128, 1993-96, 2" 45.00
Miniature, Indian pony, pinto, A-3110, 1993-current, 2" 8.00
Miniature, meerkat, A-3278, 1998-current, 1⅝" 6.00
Miniature, Morgan foal scampering, palomino, A-391, 1959-67, 2" ... 130.00
Miniature, mustang turning, buckskin, A-360, 1958-59, 2¾" 150.00
Miniature, o'possum baby, A-838, 1983-84, ⅜" 25.00
Miniature, Scottish Fold tom cat, gray, A-2041, 1989-90, 1¼" 20.00
Miniature, Shar Pei w/balloon, A-2022, 1988-2001, 1½" 10.00
Miniature, wart hog, A-3167, 1995-96, 1¼" 15.00
Miniature, worm in apple, #3105, 1993-94, 2" 30.00
Plaque, Corbina, 1959-60, 20x8½" 150.00
Plaque, fawn, 1959, 10½x5½" 200.00
Plaque, rooster mosaic, 1959, 12x18" 200.00
Plaque, Victorian lady, oval, sgn HR Calif, #560, 1946-49, 5" 50.00
Zany Zoo, Yak, Aurasperse finish, purple, 1960 only, 1⅞" 250.00

Hagenauer

Carl Hagenauer founded his metal workshops in Vienna in 1898. He was joined by his son Karl in 1919. They produced a wide range of stylized sculptural designs in both metal and wood.

Candelabra, bronze, bird and grapevine motif, marked WHW, 13½x10", $9,200.00. (Photo courtesy David Rago Auctions)

Candelabra, brass, 4-branch, rnd base, WHW mk, 11¾x12¾", pr ..900.00
Candlestick, 3 bent NP tubes form U-shape & support 2 holders, 5", ea... 1,500.00
Coffee/tea service, chrome & nickel w/ebonized wood hdls, 4-pc .. 3,000.00
Figurine, dachshund seated w/tail up, ebonized wood, NP base, 11" ..7,650.00
Figurine, female dancer, teak/brass, ca 1930, sm rstr, 23½"........9,000.00

Figurine, head of lady wearing scarf, blk patina on bronze, 9½"... 1,200.00
Figurine, horse head, olive wood, cvd features, brass base, 13x14x4" .. 1,700.00
Figurine, horse rearing, wood w/brass tail & base, WHW mk, 11x10x3" .. 2,000.00
Figurine, man dancing (simplistic), bronze w/dk patina, 2" 180.00
Figurine, soccer player, brass, WHW mk, 3¼x2¼"..................... 275.00
Figurines, wooden w/legs stretched out, SP ft, 4⅞x5½", pr........1,385.00
Lamp, figural bronze stem on dome base, w/ribbed linen shade, 22x10"...6,500.00
Lamps, wood/brass base, grass shade, 8½x6", pr 1,800.00
Locomotive engine, brass, WHW mk, 1930s, 9⅜x9⅝"..............3,600.00
Mask, stylized lady's face, bronze, WHW mk, 10".....................2,300.00
Mirror, stylized nude female kneels & holds rnd mirror, chrome, 12x7"...1,000.00

Hair Weaving

A rather unusual craft became popular during the mid-1800s. Human hair was used to make jewelry (rings, bracelets, lockets, etc.) by braiding and interlacing fine strands into hollow forms with pearls and beads added for effect. Wreaths were also made, often using hair from deceased family members as well as the living. They were displayed in deep satin-lined frames along with mementoes of the weaver or her departed kin. The fad was abandoned before the turn of the century. The values suggested below are for mint condition examples. Any fraying of the hair greatly lowers value.

See also Mourning Collectibles.

Key: p-w — palette work   t-w — table work

Stickpin, table-worked hair in lyre motif set in gold mounting, 1850 – 1880s, 1x⅞", $235.00. (Photo courtesy C. Jeanenne Bell, G.G.)

Bracelet, coiling snake w/gold head & tail w/garnet eyes, 1840-80 ..775.00
Bracelet, t-w braided rows (3), gold locket clasp, 1850-70 .... 525.00
Bracelet, t-w hair w/elastic weave, gold bbl clasp, 1850-80s, 3¾x7" ...425.00
Brooch, gold w/braided hair under crystal fr by pearls 185.00
Brooch, p-w braid under beveled glass, enameled jet fr, 1850s, 1⅜" ...295.00
Brooch, p-w flowers on milk glass ground in gold oval, 1850s, 2"....325.00
Brooch, p-w willow scene in oval gold mt, 1840-60s, 1⅞x1½".....425.00
Brooch, t-w tubes form bow in gold-filled mt, 1850-80s, 2¾" L...300.00
Earrings, t-w elongated drops w/gold mts, 1840-70s, 2⅝" 425.00
Earrings, t-w 2 openweave bells w/gutta percha details, 1850s-70s....475.00
Necklace, t-w balls w/2 wrapped wood balls, gold mts, 1840-60s .. 900.00
Necklace, t-w choker, gold snake head & tail clasp, 1840-60 ...... 550.00
Pendant, gold cross w/compartment for braided hair, 1850-80s, 2½" ..650.00
Pendant/locket, ornate gold-filled mt, hair swirl under glass, 2¾" 395.00
Ring, t-w braid w/hollow gold mt w/shield, 1840-80, ⅝" W 275.00
Stickpin, gold & enamel w/center compartment, 1840-80s, from $150 to ..200.00
Watch chain, t-w twisted tubes (2), gold-filled mts, 1830-50, 9" .. 150.00

Hall

The Hall China Company of East Liverpool, Ohio, was established in 1903. Their earliest products were whiteware toilet seats, mugs, jugs, etc. By 1920 their restaurant-type dinnerware and cooking-ware had become so successful that Hall was assured of a solid future. They continue today to be one of the country's largest manufacturers of this type of product.

Hall introduced the first of their famous teapots in 1920; new shapes and colors were added each year until about 1948, making them the largest teapot manufacturer in the world. These and the dinnerware lines of the '30s through the '50s have become popular collectibles. For more thorough study of the subject, we recommend *Collector's Encyclopedia of Hall China, Third Edition,* by Margaret and Kenn Whitmyer; their address may be found in the Directory under Ohio.

Blue Blossom, ball jug, #4, from $145.00 to $185.00. (Photo courtesy Margaret and Kenn Whitmyer)

Blue Bouquet, bowl, fruit; D-style, 5½"	11.00
Blue Bouquet, cake plate	52.00
Blue Bouquet, gravy boat, D-style	65.00
Blue Bouquet, platter, oval, 13¼"	50.00
Blue Bouquet, pretzel jar	285.00
Blue Bouquet, tray, metal, rectangular	60.00
Cameo Rose, bowl, cream soup; E-style, 5¼"	85.00
Cameo Rose, creamer, E-style	11.00
Cameo Rose, plate, E-style, 10"	25.00
Cameo Rose, sugar bowl, E-style, w/lid	20.00
Century Fern, casserole	65.00
Century Fern, gravy boat	32.00
Century Fern, relish, 4-part	42.00
Century Fern, sugar bowl, w/lid	22.00
Century Garden of Eden, ladle	22.00
Century Garden of Eden, teapot, 6-cup	170.00
Century Sunglow, bowl, vegetable; divided	45.00
Century Sunglow, cup	7.50
Century Sunglow, relish, 4-part	42.00
Christmas Tree & Holly, bowl, plum pudding; 4½"	30.00
Christmas Tree & Holly, cup	22.00
Christmas Tree & Holly, saucer	4.00
Christmas Tree & Holly, tidbit, 2-tier	125.00
Crocus, bowl, salad; 9"	22.00
Crocus, bowl, vegetable; rnd, D-style, 9¼"	45.00
Crocus, creamer, Art Deco	35.00
Crocus, cup, D-style	15.00
Crocus, mug, flagon style	90.00
Crocus, plate, D-style, 10"	110.00
Crocus, teapot, Medallion	110.00

Fantasy, baker, from $150.00 to $190.00.
(Photo courtesy Margaret and Kenn Whitmyer)

Gaillardia, casserole, Radiance	37.00
Gaillardia, coffeepot, Terrace	55.00
Gaillardia, plate, D-style, 7¼"	10.00
Gaillardia, saucer, D-style	2.00
Gaillardia, shaker, hdld, ea	25.00
Game Bird, bowl, fruit; 5½"	14.00
Game Bird, plate, 6½"	11.00
Game Bird, plate, 9¼"	45.00
Game Bird, platter, oval, 13¼"	80.00
Golden Oak, bowl, cereal; 6"	8.00
Golden Oak, bowl, soup; flat, 8½"	10.00
Golden Oak, custard, str-sided	8.00
Golden Oak, teapot, E-style	125.00
Heather Rose, bowl, vegetable; w/lid	45.00
Heather Rose, cake plate	20.00
Heather Rose, cookie jar, Flare-Shape	85.00
Heather Rose, jug, Rayed	25.00
Heather Rose, mug, Irish coffee	20.00
Heather Rose, pie baker	27.00
Heather Rose, platter, oval, 15½"	30.00
Homewood, bowl, fruit; D-style, 5½"	6.00
Homewood, plate, D-style, 9"	12.00
Homewood, shaker, hdld, ea	22.00
Homewood, sugar bowl, Art Deco	30.00
Mums, baker, Fr	40.00
Mums, bowl, oval, D-style, 10¼"	45.00
Mums, jug, Simplicity	220.00
Mums, pie baker	55.00
Mums, platter, oval, D-style, 13¼"	45.00
Mums, stack set, Radiance	150.00
No 488, bowl, salad; 9"	40.00
No 488, butter dish, Zephyr, 1-lb	650.00
No 488, cocotte, hdld	55.00
No 488, coffeepot, drip; #691	500.00
No 488, condiment jar, Radiance	500.00
No 488, mug, Tom & Jerry	30.00
No 488, soup tureen	350.00
No 488, sugar bowl, Modern, w/lid	50.00
Orange Poppy, bean pot, New England, #4	145.00
Orange Poppy, bowl, soup; flat, C-style, 8½"	35.00
Orange Poppy, casserole, #101, oval, 9½"	75.00
Orange Poppy, cup, C-style	30.00
Orange Poppy, drip jar, Radiance, w/lid	37.00
Orange Poppy, jug, #5, Radiance	45.00
Orange Poppy, plate, C-style, 6"	8.00
Orange Poppy, saucer, C-style	5.00
Orange Poppy, spoon	120.00
Orange Poppy, teapot, Donut	450.00
Pastel Morning Glory, cake plate	55.00
Pastel Morning Glory, creamer, New York	27.00
Pastel Morning Glory, cup, St Denis	40.00
Pastel Morning Glory, petite marmite	70.00
Pastel Morning Glory, shaker, Teardrop, ea	22.00
Pastel Morning Glory, teapot, Medallion	225.00
Prairie Grass, bowl, cereal; 6¼"	10.00
Prairie Grass, cup	8.00
Prairie Grass, plate, 8"	10.00
Prairie Grass, saucer	2.00
Prairie Grass, sugar bowl, w/lid	22.00
Primrose, cake plate	20.00
Primrose, creamer	9.00
Primrose, cup	7.00
Primrose, pie baker	25.00
Primrose, saucer	1.50

Red Poppy, bowl, oval, D-style, 10¼" 55.00
Red Poppy, bowl, Radiance, 6" 20.00
Red Poppy, leftover, sq 250.00
Red Poppy, pie baker 65.00
Red Poppy, plate, D-style, 7¼" 9.50

Red Poppy, sugar bowl with lid, from $22.00 to $25.00; creamer, from $18.00 to $22.00.

(Photo courtesy Margaret and Kenn Whitmyer)

Sears' Arlington, creamer 9.00
Sears' Arlington, plate, 10" 8.00
Sears' Arlington, saucer 1.50
Sears' Brown-Eyed Susan, jug, Rayed 19.00
Sears' Brown-Eyed Susan, saucer 1.50
Sears' Brown-Eyed Susan, teapot, Aladdin 250.00
Sears' Fairfax, bowl, fruit; 5¼" 4.50
Sears' Fairfax, cup 5.00
Sears' Fairfax, platter, oval, 15½" 30.00
Sears' Monticello, bowl, cream soup; 5" 90.00
Sears' Monticello, gravy boat, w/underplate 30.00
Sears' Monticello, plate, 6½" 4.00
Sears' Mount Vernon, bowl, cereal; 6¼" 10.00
Sears' Mount Vernon, cup 7.00
Sears' Mount Vernon, sugar bowl, w/lid 22.00
Serenade, baker, Fr; fluted 20.00
Serenade, bowl, fruit; D-style, 5½" 5.50
Serenade, coffeepot, Terrace 75.00
Serenade, cup, D-style 9.00
Serenade, custard, Radiance 20.00
Serenade, plate, D-style, 6" 4.00
Serenade, sugar bowl, Art Deco, w/lid 35.00
Serenade, teapot, Aladdin 300.00

Shaggy Tulip, bean pot, New England #3, from $185.00 to $220.00. (Photo courtesy Margaret and Kenn Whitmyer)

Silhouette, ball jug, #3 .... 135.00
Silhouette, bowl, Medallion, 6" 14.00
Silhouette, bread box 85.00
Silhouette, jug, Simplicity 160.00
Silhouette, pretzel jar 150.00

Silhouette, shaker, Five Band, ea 20.00
Silhouette, sifter 60.00
Silhouette, teapot, Streamline 285.00
Silhouette, wastebasket 75.00
Springtime, bowl, rnd, D-style, 9¼" 28.00
Springtime, coffeepot, Washington 40.00
Springtime, creamer, E-style 27.00
Springtime, gravy boat, D-style 27.00
Springtime, jug, #6, Radiance 25.00
Tulip, bowl, salad; 9" 20.00
Tulip, custard, Thick Rim 20.00
Tulip, drip jar, Thick Rim, w/lid 35.00
Tulip, waffle iron 125.00
Wildfire, bean pot, tab-hdld 450.00
Wildfire, bowl, oval, D-style 30.00
Wildfire, casserole, tab-hdld 40.00
Wildfire, custard, str sides 25.00
Wildfire, jug, #5, Radiance 60.00
Wildfire, plate, D-style, 7" 450.00
Wildfire, teapot, Aladdin 140.00
Yellow Rose, baker, Fr; fluted 27.00
Yellow Rose, casserole, Radiance 45.00
Yellow Rose, creamer, Norse 25.00
Yellow Rose, stack set, Radiance 110.00

Zeisel Designs, Hallcraft

Tomorrow's Classic Arizona, casserole, 1¼-qt 37.00
Tomorrow's Classic Arizona, egg cup 50.00
Tomorrow's Classic Arizona, shaker, ea 16.00
Tomorrow's Classic Bouquet, bowl, fruit; 5¾" 7.00
Tomorrow's Classic Bouquet, bowl, salad; lg, 14½" 45.00
Tomorrow's Classic Bouquet, coffeepot, 6-cup 120.00
Tomorrow's Classic Bouquet, jug, 3-qt 45.00
Tomorrow's Classic Bouquet, plate, 6" 5.00
Tomorrow's Classic Bouquet, saucer 2.50
Tomorrow's Classic Bouquet, sugar bowl, w/lid 25.00
Tomorrow's Classic Bouquet, teapot, 6-cup 215.00
Tomorrow's Classic Buckingham, bowl, cereal; 6" 9.00
Tomorrow's Classic Buckingham, ladle 25.00
Tomorrow's Classic Buckingham, vase 95.00
Tomorrow's Classic Caprice, ashtray 9.00
Tomorrow's Classic Caprice, creamer 14.00
Tomorrow's Classic Caprice, ladle 22.00
Tomorrow's Classic Caprice, marmite, w/lid 35.00
Tomorrow's Classic Caprice, platter, 17" 38.00
Tomorrow's Classic Caprice, vase 80.00
Tomorrow's Classic Dawn, bowl, celery; oval 24.00
Tomorrow's Classic Dawn, casserole, 2-qt 65.00
Tomorrow's Classic Dawn, cup, AD 27.50
Tomorrow's Classic Dawn, jug, 1¼-qt 37.00
Tomorrow's Classic Dawn, plate, 8" 9.50
Tomorrow's Classic Dawn, saucer 2.50
Tomorrow's Classic Fantasy, creamer 15.00
Tomorrow's Classic Fantasy, onion soup, w/lid 42.00
Tomorrow's Classic Fantasy, teapot, 6-cup 195.00
Tomorrow's Classic Fantasy, vinegar bottle 75.00
Tomorrow's Classic Flair, bowl, cereal; 6" 10.00
Tomorrow's Classic Flair, cup, AD 27.50
Tomorrow's Classic Flair, egg cup 55.00
Tomorrow's Classic Flair, saucer 2.50
Tomorrow's Classic Flair, vase 95.00
Tomorrow's Classic Frost Flowers, coffeepot, 6-cup ... 110.00
Tomorrow's Classic Frost Flowers, plate, 11" 13.00

Tomorrow's Classic Frost Flowers, shaker, ea.................................. 16.00
Tomorrow's Classic Frost Flowers, vase 90.00
Tomorrow's Classic Harlequin, ashtray.. 10.00
Tomorrow's Classic Harlequin, gravy boat 45.00
Tomorrow's Classic Harlequin, ladle 25.00
Tomorrow's Classic Lyric, ashtray 10.00
Tomorrow's Classic Lyric, bowl, cereal; 6" 10.00
Tomorrow's Classic Lyric, butter dish 170.00
Tomorrow's Classic Lyric, plate, 6" 5.50
Tomorrow's Classic Mulberry, bowl, salad; lg, 14½" 45.00
Tomorrow's Classic Mulberry, creamer 16.00
Tomorrow's Classic Mulberry, jug, 3-qt 42.00
Tomorrow's Classic Mulberry, platter, 17" 40.00
Tomorrow's Classic Peach Blossom, ashtray 9.00
Tomorrow's Classic Peach Blossom, bowl, celery; oval 24.00
Tomorrow's Classic Peach Blossom, candlestick, 8", ea 45.00
Tomorrow's Classic Peach Blossom, ladle....................................... 22.00
Tomorrow's Classic Peach Blossom, shaker, ea................................ 19.00
Tomorrow's Classic Pine Cone, bowl, fruit; 5¾" 6.50
Tomorrow's Classic Pine Cone, bowl, salad; lg, 14½" 35.00
Tomorrow's Classic Pine Cone, creamer 15.00
Tomorrow's Classic Pine Cone, egg cup 45.00
Tomorrow's Classic Pine Cone, marmite, w/lid................................ 37.00
Tomorrow's Classic Pine Cone, plate, 11" 13.00
Tomorrow's Classic Pine Cone, platter, 15" 32.00
Tomorrow's Classic Pine Cone, sugar bowl, AD; open 15.00
Tomorrow's Classic Pine Cone, vinegar bottle................................ 80.00
Tomorrow's Classic Spring/Studio 10, ashtray................................... 9.00
Tomorrow's Classic Spring/Studio 10, bowl, coupe soup; 9" 13.00
Tomorrow's Classic Spring/Studio 10, butter dish.......................... 180.00
Tomorrow's Classic Spring/Studio 10, candlestick, 4½", ea 30.00
Tomorrow's Classic Spring/Studio 10, casserole, 2-qt 50.00
Tomorrow's Classic Spring/Studio 10, cup 7.00
Tomorrow's Classic Spring/Studio 10, jug, 1¼-qt............................ 28.00
Tomorrow's Classic Spring/Studio 10, plate, 6"............................... 5.50
Tomorrow's Classic Spring/Studio 10, platter, 12¼" 28.00
Tomorrow's Classic Spring/Studio 10, saucer 2.00
Tomorrow's Classic Spring/Studio 10, teapot, 6-cup.................... 190.00
Tomorrow's Classic Spring/Studio 10, vase 80.00

Teapots

Airflow, Dresden, solid color, from $65 to.................................... 75.00
Airflow, ivory, gold special, from $110 to.................................... 130.00
Airflow, Orchid, from $250 to 300.00
Aladdin, blk, gold label, from $225 to... 250.00
Aladdin, Chinese Red, solid color, from $165 to.......................... 180.00

Aladdin, Marine, standard gold, from $75.00 to $90.00.
(Photo courtesy Margaret and Kenn Whitmyer)

Aladdin, pk, standard gold, from $80 to... 90.00
Albany, Blue Turquoise, gold label, from $150 to 175.00
Albany, Emerald, gold special, from $100 to................................. 125.00
Albany, ivory, standard gold, from $45 to 55.00
Art Deco, bl, Danielle, from $200 to.. 210.00
Art Deco, gr, Adele, from $175 to.. 200.00

Art Deco, maroon, Damascus, from $225 to 250.00
Baltimore, Chinese Red, solid color, from $300 to 350.00
Baltimore, ivory, gold label, from $100 to 125.00
Bellevue, red, 2- to 4-cup, from $35 to.. 45.00
Boston, blk, old gold design, 4- to 8-cup, from $35 to................... 45.00
Boston, Canary, solid color, 1- to 3-cup, from $25 to.................... 30.00
Boston, cobalt, gold label, 4- to 8-cup, from $85 to...................... 95.00
Boston, Marine, standard gold, 1- to 3-cup, from $50 to 60.00
Cleveland, Cadet, solid color 50.00
Cleveland, Orchid, standard gold, from $800 to.......................... 1,000.00
French, Blue Turquoise, standard gold, 10- to 12-cup, from $65 to ... 70.00
French, Chartreuse, solid color, 1- to 3-cup, from $32 to 37.00
French, Dresden, gold label, 4- to 8-cup, from $55 to.................... 65.00
Globe, cobalt, solid color, from $200 to 250.00
Hollywood, blk, solid color, from $35 to 40.00
Hollywood, Orchid, standard gold, from $100 to.......................... 125.00
Hook Cover, Cadet, gold label, from $50 to 60.00
Hook Cover, Chinese Red, solid color, from $200 to 225.00
Illinois, Canary, standard gold, from $175 to 200.00
Illinois, pk, solid color, from $155 to 175.00
Indiana, maroon, solid color, from $300 to 350.00
Indiana, Warm Yellow, standard gold, from $350 to 450.00
Kansas, Emerald, solid color, from $400 to.................................. 500.00
Los Angeles, Marine, solid color, from $55 to 65.00
Los Angeles, Monterey, gold label, from $85 to 95.00
Melody, Chinese Red, solid color, from $250 to 275.00
Melody, Warm Yellow, standard gold, from $190 to...................... 220.00
Moderne, Delphinium standard gold, from $60 to........................ 70.00
Moderne, Dresden, solid color, from $45 to 55.00
Musical, Orchid, from $500 to 550.00
Nautilus, Canary, gold special, from $260 to................................ 300.00
Nautilus, cobalt, standard gold, from $340 to 365.00
New York, Camellia, solid color, 1- to 4-cup, from $30 to............. 35.00
Newport, ivory, solid color, from $30 to 35.00
Ohio, blk, standard gold, from $200 to 225.00
Ohio, Stock Green, solid color, from $120 to 140.00
Philadelphia, Old Rose, solid color, from $35 to........................... 40.00
Sundial, Citrus, solid color, from $250 to.................................... 290.00
Sundial, Dresden, standard gold, from $85 to 95.00

Hallmark

Hallmark introduced a line of artplas (molded plastic) ornaments in 1973 which quickly became popular with collectors. The Hallmark Keepsake Ornament Collectors Club was organized in 1987 and offered exclusive limited edition ornaments to club members only. Hallmark has produced miniature ornaments since 1988 and added a line of Easter (now known as Spring) ornaments beginning in 1991. All these ornaments are very collectibles.

Betsy Clark, 1st in series, 1973, MIB, from $100 to...................... 120.00
Betsy Clark, 2nd in series, 1974, MIB, from $80 to 100.00
Betsy Clark, 3rd in series, 1975, MIB, from $65 to 85.00
Betsy Clark, 4th in series, 1976, MIB, from $65 to 85.00
Carousel, 1st in series, Toys, 1978, MIB, from $325 to 365.00
Carousel, 2nd in series, Angels, 1979, MIB, from $125 to............. 150.00
Carousel, 3rd in series, Sleigh, 1980, MIB, from $125 to.............. 150.00
Carousel, 4th in series, Skaters, 1981, MIB, from $100 to............. 125.00
Frosty Friends, 1st in series, Cool Yule, 1980, MIB, from $400 to ... 450.00
Frosty Friends, 2nd in series, Husky Igloo, 1981, MIB, from $300 to.. 350.00
Frosty Friends, 3rd in series, Icicle, 1982, MIB, from $165 to....... 195.00
Heavenly Angel, 1st in series, 1991, MIB, from $10 to.................. 15.00
Heavenly Angel, 2nd in series, 1992, MIB, from $10 to................. 15.00
Heavenly Angel, 3rd in series, 1993, MIB, from $8 to 12.00

Lionel Train, 1st in series, 700 Hudson, 1996, MIB, from $40 to... 50.00
Lionel Train, 2nd in series, Santa Fe, 1997, MIB, from $20 to....... 25.00
Lionel Train, 3rd in series, Pennsylvania, 1998, MIB, from $20 to...25.00

Puppy Love, first in series, 1991, from $40.00 to $50.00.

Rocking Horse, 1st in series, Dappled, 1981, MIB, from $400 to . 450.00
Rocking Horse, 2nd in series, Black, MIB, from $225 to 275.00
Rocking Horse, 3rd in series, Russet, 1983, MIB, from $215 to ... 245.00
Rocking Horse, 4th in series, Appaloosa, MIB, from $50 to........... 75.00
Star Trek, 1st in series, Starship Enterprise, 1991, MIB, from $285 to .. 315.00
Star Trek, 2nd in series, Shuttlecraft Galileo, 1992, MIB, from $20 to... 30.00
Star Trek, 3rd in series, Enterprise Next Generation, 1993, MIB... 35.00
Thimble, 1st in series, Mouse, 1978, MIB, from $100 to 125.00
Thimble, 2nd in series, Soldier, 1979, MIB, from $90 to.............. 115.00
Thimble, 3rd in series, Elf, 1980, MIB, from $90 to...................... 115.00
12 Days of Christmas, 1st in series, Partridge, 1984, MIB, $200 to...235.00
12 Days of Christmas, 2nd in series, Doves, 1985, MIB, from $60 to... 70.00
12 Days of Christmas, 3rd in series, Hens, 1986, MIB, from $30 to...40.00

Halloween

Though the origin of Halloween is steeped in pagan rites and superstitions, today Halloween is strictly a fun time, and Halloween items are fun to collect. Pumpkin-head candy containers of papier-mache or pressed cardboard, noisemakers, postcards with black cats and witches, costumes, and decorations are only a sampling of the variety available.

Here's how you can determine the origin of your jack-o'-lantern:

American 1940 – 1950s	German 1900 – 1930s
items are larger	items are generally small
made of egg-carton material	made of cardboard or composition
bottom and body are one piece	always has a cut-out triangular nose; simple, crisscross lines in mouth; blue rings in eyes
	have attached cardboard bottoms

For further information we recommend *More Halloween Collectibles* and *Anthropomorphic Vegetables and Fruits of Halloween* by Pamela E. Apkarian-Russell (Schiffer). Other good reference books are *Halloween in America* by Stuart Schneider and *Halloween Collectables* by Dan and Pauline Campanelli.

Our advisor for this category is Jenny Tarrant; she is listed in the Directory under Missouri. See Clubs, Newsletters, and Catalogs for information concerning the *Trick or Treat Trader*, a quarterly newsletter. Unless noted otherwise, values are for examples in excellent to near mint condition except for paper items, in which case assume the condition to be near mint to mint.

American

Most American items were made during the 1940s and 1950s, though a few date from the 1930s as well. Lanterns are constructed either of flat cardboard or the pressed cardboard pulp used to make the jack-o'-lantern shown on the left.

Jack-o'-lantern, pressed cb pulp w/orig face, 4-4½", from $95 to.. 110.00
Jack-o'-lantern, pressed cb pulp w/orig face, 5-5½", from $115 to ...125.00
Jack-o'-lantern, pressed cb pulp w/orig face, 6-6½", from $130 to ...135.00
Jack-o'-lantern, pressed cb pulp w/orig face, 7" 150.00
Jack-o'-lantern, pressed cb pulp w/orig face, 8", minimum value.. 175.00
Lantern, cat, pressed cb pulp w/orig face................................. 175.00
Lantern, cat (full body), pressed cb pulp, 7x6½".......................... 350.00
Lantern, cb w/tab sides, any.. 75.00

Lantern, pumpkin man, pressed cardboard pulp with original face, 8", NM+, $350.00. (Photo courtesy Morphy Auctions)

Plastic Halloween car 250.00
Plastic pumpkin stagecoach, witch & cat.................................... 450.00
Plastic witch holding blk cat w/wobbling head, 7" 275.00
Plastic witch on rocket, horizontal, 7" 300.00
Plastic witch on rocket, vertical, 7".. 300.00
Plastic witch on rocket, 4" 95.00
Tin noisemaker, bell style 35.00
Tin noisemaker, can shaker 35.00
Tin noisemaker, clicker.. 35.00
Tin noisemaker, frying-pan style.. 35.00
Tin noisemaker, horn 35.00
Tin noisemaker, sq spinner 35.00
Tin noisemaker, tambourine, Chein.. 75.00
Tin noisemaker, tambourine, Kirkoff... 95.00
Tin noisemaker, tambourine, Ohio Art, 1930s, 6" dia 75.00

Celluloid (German, Japanese, or American)

Blk cat, plain, M 150.00
Egg-shape house, M 400.00

Long-leg veggie rattle, M 300.00
Owl, plain, M 85.00
Owl on pumpkin, M 125.00
Owl on tree, M 200.00
Pumpkin-face man, M 350.00
Pumpkin-face pirate, M 400.00
Scarecrow, M 200.00
Witch, plain, M 200.00
Witch in auto, M 450.00
Witch in corncob car, M 450.00

Witch on motorcycle, $325.00. (Photo courtesy Morphy Auctions)

Witch pulling cart w/ghost, M 400.00
Witch pulling pumpkin cart w/cat, M 400.00
Witch sitting on pumpkin, M 350.00

German

As a general rule, German Halloween collectibles date from 1900 through the early 1930s. They were made either of composition or molded cardboard, and their values are higher than American-made items. In the listings that follow, all candy containers are made of composition unless noted otherwise.

Candy container, blk cat walking, glass eyes, head removes, 3-4" ...225.00
Candy container, blk cat walking, glass eyes, head removes, 5-6" ...250.00
Candy container, cat, 3-5" 175.00
Candy container, cat sitting, glass eyes, 4-6" 200.00
Candy container, cat walking, w/mohair, 5" 350.00
Candy container, lemon-head man, pnt compo, 7" 575.00
Candy container, pumpkin-head man (or any vegetable), on box, 3" ..175.00
Candy container, pumpkin-head man (or any vegetable), on box, 4" ..185.00
Candy container, pumpkin-head man (or any vegetable), on box, 5" ..225.00
Candy container, pumpkin-head man (or any vegetable), on box, 6" ..275.00
Candy container, witch, pumpkin people, devil, etc, solid figure, 4" 150.00
Candy container, witch, pumpkin people, devil, etc, solid figure, 5" 175.00
Candy container, witch, pumpkin people, devil, etc, solid figure, 6" ..200.00
Candy container, witch, pumpkin people, devil, ghost, etc, 3" 225.00
Candy container, witch or pumpkin man, head removes, 4" 225.00
Candy container, witch or pumpkin man, head removes, 5" 350.00
Candy container, witch or pumpkin man, head removes, 6" 400.00
Candy container, witch or pumpkin man, head removes, 7" 450.00
Die-cut, bat, emb cb, M, from $95 to 125.00
Die-cut, cat, emb cb, from $55 to 95.00
Die-cut, cat (dressed), emb cb 150.00
Die-cut, devil, emb cb, from $95 to 150.00
Die-cut, jack-o'-lantern, emb cb 65.00

Die-cut, pumpkin head (Mickey Mouse style) playing saxophone, 27", EX, $200.00. (Photo courtesy Morphy Auctions)

Die-cut, pumpkin man or lady, emb cb, 7½" 125.00
Jack-o'-lantern, compo w/orig insert, 3" 225.00
Jack-o'-lantern, compo w/orig insert, 4" 250.00
Jack-o'-lantern, compo w/orig insert, 5" 350.00
Jack-o'-lantern, molded cb w/orig insert, 3" 95.00
Jack-o'-lantern, molded cb w/orig insert, 4" 125.00
Jack-o'-lantern, molded cb w/orig insert, 5" 155.00
Jack-o'-lantern, molded cb w/orig insert, 6" 185.00
Lantern, cat, cb, molded nose, bow under chin, 3" 250.00
Lantern, cat, cb, molded nose, bow under chin, 4" 300.00
Lantern, cat, cb, molded nose, bow under chin, 5" 450.00
Lantern, cat, cb, simple rnd style 225.00

Lantern, face of white cat, composition with original papers, very rare, 5", EX, $500.00. (Photo courtesy Morphy Auctions)

Lantern (ghost, skull, devil, witch, etc), molded cb, 3-4", minimum .. 300.00
Lantern (ghost, skull, devil, witch, etc), molded cb, 5"+, minimum ... 350.00
Lantern (skull, devil, witch, etc), compo, 3", minimum value 300.00
Lantern (skull, devil, witch, etc), compo, 4", minimum value 400.00
Lantern (skull, devil, witch, etc), compo, 5", minimum value 450.00
Noisemaker, cat (3-D) on wood rachet 95.00
Noisemaker, cb figure (flat) on rachet 95.00
Noisemaker, cb paddle w/die-cut face 95.00
Noisemaker, devil (3-D) on wood rachet 95.00
Noisemaker, pumpkin head (rnd, 3-D) on wood rachet 95.00
Noisemaker, tin frying-pan paddle, Germany, no rust or dents, 5" L 75.00
Noisemaker, tin horn, Germany, 3" 75.00
Noisemaker, veggie (3-D) horn (w/pnt face) 125.00
Noisemaker, veggie or fruit (3-D) horn (no face), ea 55.00
Noisemaker, witch (3-D) on wood rachet 115.00
Noisemaker, wood & paper tambourine w/pumpkin face 150.00

Hampshire

The Hampshire Pottery Company was established in 1871 in Keene, New Hampshire, by James Scollay Taft. Their earliest products were redware and stoneware utility items such as jugs, churns, crocks, and flowerpots. In 1878 they produced majolica ware which met with such success that they began to experiment with the idea of manufacturing art pottery. By 1883 they had developed a Royal Worcester type of finish which they applied to vases, tea sets, powder boxes, and cookie jars. It was also utilized for souvenir items that were decorated with transfer designs prepared from photographic plates.

Cadmon Robertson, brother-in-law of Taft, joined the company in 1904 and was responsible for developing their famous matt glazes. Colors included shades of green, brown, red, and blue. Early examples were of earthenware, but eventually the body was changed to semiporcelain. Some of his designs were marked with an M in a circle as a tribute to his wife, Emoretta. Robertson died in 1914, leaving a void impossible to fill. Taft sold the business in 1916 to George Morton, who continued to use the matt glazes that Robertson had developed. After a temporary halt in production during WWI, Morton returned to Keene and re-equipped the factory with the machinery needed to manufacture hotel china and floor tile. Because of the expense involved in transporting coal to fire the kilns, Morton found he could not compete with potteries of Ohio and New Jersey who were able to utilize locally available natural gas. He was forced to close the plant in 1923.

Interest is highest in examples with the curdled, two-tone matt glazes, and it is the glaze, not the size or form, that dictates value. The souvenir pieces are not of particularly high quality and tend to be passed over by today's collectors. Our advisors for this category are Suzanne Perrault and David Rago; they are listed in the Directory under New Jersey.

Bowl, gr, artichoke form, E Robertson, #24, 3x4¾" 380.00
Bowl, gr, emb water lily leaves & buds, #57, 3¼x10" 450.00
Bowl, gr/yel, water lily buds, incurvate rim, #57, 3x10" 850.00
Lamp, gr, emb feathers, long plain neck, simple ldgl shade, 18" .. 3,050.00
Lamp, gr, emb water lily, orig burner, pierced metal shade, 16x13" .. 1,000.00
Lamp base, gr, emb tulips, 11x5¾" 1,300.00
Lamp base, gr, Greek key pattern, 10x9½" 840.00

Lamp base (factory), green with swirl pattern, impressed mark, 10x9½", $840.00. (Photo courtesy David Rago Auctions)

Pitcher, gr, organic form w/leafy top, unmk, 8x7" 300.00
Vase, bl, cvd vertical leaves, bulbous, 8" 960.00
Vase, bl & blk crackle w/graphite touches, #95, 7⅛" 550.00

Vase, bl & wht mottle, emb floral w/oblong leaves, #33, 6¾x4"... 550.00
Vase, bl & wht mottle, globular, #54/1, 4¼x4½" 300.00
Vase, bl mottle, trumpet neck, #124/M, 9¼x6½" 850.00
Vase, bl w/wht drips, emb cattails, #112, 4¼x6" 650.00
Vase, brn, emb wide vertical mottled leaves, 7" 840.00
Vase, brn & gr mottle (rare), emb floral w/oblong leaves, #33, 7x4" ... 425.00
Vase, brn mottle, pinched neck, incised panels/swirls, #105/M, 7¾"... 325.00
Vase, butterscotch mottle, emb floral, #130/M, 7½x6" 950.00
Vase, caramel streaks on gr, #18/1, 4⅞" 265.00
Vase, curdled gr over rose, squiggled pattern, #52, 6⅝" 300.00
Vase, frothy bl matt, 12x5" 900.00
Vase, gr, #2-H, 14¾" 1,020.00
Vase, gr, emb corn & husk, #15, 6x5½" 550.00
Vase, gr, emb feathers, rtcl rim, #140/M, 3¾x4" 375.00
Vase, gr, emb lg petal-like panels on sides, squat, 6½" 775.00
Vase, gr, emb panels, #129/M, 6x7" 425.00
Vase, gr, emb panels on melon form, #96/M, 3x4¾" 375.00
Vase, gr, ruffled rim, #125, 3¾x3½" 275.00
Vase, gr (flowing), cylinder, incurvate rim, #38, 7½" 325.00
Vase, gr & frothy wht, emb water lilies, imp/M, 7¼x5" 550.00
Vase, gray & blk mottle on bl bl, cylinder neck, #10, 11½"......... 550.00
Vase, hunter gr to cucumber gr, gourd shape, 3¾x3½" 450.00
Vase, natural bsk, emb intertwining lily vines, flaw, 8¼x5½" 200.00
Vase, ochre matt, gourd shape, incised mk/M, 3¾x3½" 550.00
Vase, plum to gray, emb water lily buds & leaves, #42/M, 7x4½" .. 1,400.00
Vase, purple/blk/gray mottle, #106, 7½x4" 850.00
Vase, sea green & bl mottle, emb floral, #33, 6¾x4" 600.00
Vase, tan & mocha matt swirl, cylindrical, #105/M, 7½x3¾"....... 300.00
Vase, yel w/cvd broad leaves, shouldered, 8½x6", NM 450.00

Handel

Philip Handel was best known for the art glass lamps he produced at the turn of the century. His work is similar to the Tiffany lamps of the same era. Handel made gas and electric lamps with both leaded glass and reverse-painted shades. Chipped ice shades with a texture similar to overshot glass were also produced. Shades signed by artists such as Bailey, Palme, and Parlow are highly valued.

Teroma lamp shades were created from clear blown glass blanks that were painted on the interior (reverse painted), while Teroma art glass (the decorative vases, humidors, etc. in the Handel Ware line) is painted on the exterior. This type of glassware has a 'chipped ice' effect achieved by sand blasting and coating the surface with fish glue. The piece is kiln fired at 800 degrees F. The contraction of the glue during the cooling process gives the glass a frosted, textured effect. Some shades are sand finished, adding texture and depth. Both the glassware and chinaware decorated by Handel are rare and command high prices on today's market. Many of Handel's chinaware blanks were supplied by Limoges.

Key: chp — chipped/lightly sanded

Handel Ware

Unless noted china, all items in the following listing are glass.

Jar, Teroma, birds flying in bamboo thicket on dk gr, unmk, 8", VG... 2,000.00
Jar, Teroma, sub-tropical scene on chipped sand, #4202, 9x6" ..3,600.00
Vase, floral stalk, red/gr on ivory w/emb fleur-de-lis, metal rim, 12" ...575.00
Vase, Teroma, autumn trees on textured frost, #4211, 6" 840.00
Vase, Teroma, birds/lg trees, Bragg, #4217, 12x5" 2,100.00
Vase, Teroma, mtns/trees & lake, vivid colors, ftd, #4218, 10"... 1,900.00
Vase, Teroma, trees/distant mtns, incurvate cylinder, 8" 1,150.00
Vase, Teroma, trees/lake, wide shouldered cylinder, 8", from $1,600 to..1,800.00

Vase, Teroma, birch trees in woodland scene, signed Broggi, 9½", $1,400.00. (Photo courtesy Fontaine's Auction Gallery)

Lamps

Base only, textured bronze on ft molded as Chinese stand, 25" 585.00
Base only, tree trunk w/roots on rnd ft, 3-arm spider, 11" 646.00
Boudoir, lava-decor 10" shade/rnd base, aqua w/quartz coloration, 14" ..1,035.00
Desk, cylindrical 11" shade pnt w/cornucopia band; arm on base adjusts... 1,300.00
Desk, Mosserine 7" shade w/Arts & Crafts floral border; harp std, 19" 1,725.00
Desk, o/l 12" cylinder shade w/pine needles; adjustable arm pivots .. 1,765.00
Floor, gold 7" shade w/blown-out floral border; std adjusts, 56" . 1,320.00
Floor, o/l 25" 8-panel shade w/loop border; std w/4 lg ball ft, 65" ..6,325.00
Hanging, HP parrots, indigo/gr/orange on gold, 10" ball shape, w/mts. 3,600.00
Table, HP 18" parrots/butterflies/stenciled leaves shade; mc std (VG).. 10,638.00
Table, ldgl 20" geometric 4-panel shade w/tree o/l, std w/2 uprights.... 15,600.00
Table, ldgl 22" cattail shade; mk leaf-emb vasiform std, 28" 51,000.00
Table, ldgl 26" Gothic-arch panel 26" shade (EX); mk std, 31" ... 3,600.00
Table, o/l 16" shade, trees in apron; ribbed/fluted std................ 3,525.00
Table, o/l 18" shade w/grapevine border; unmk tree-trunk std, 25" ..3,525.00
Table, o/l 18" 6-panel shade w/dandelions; bronze-metal std w/tag, 23" ..5,100.00
Table, o/l 20" Hawaiian tropics shade; 4-ftd emb trumpet base, 24" . 5,750.00
Table, o/l 22" 6-panel shade w/cattail border; mk std w/sq ft, 28" 5,100.00
Table, rvpt chp 16" hydrangea shade; bronzed pear-shape base, 22" 14,950.00
Table, rvpt chp 18" Dutch scene #7067 shade; simple mk std, 23" .. 3,360.00
Table, rvpt chp 24" dusky scenic #6625 18" shade; std w/tag, 24" 7,800.00
Table, rvpt 12" mushroom-cap shade w/floral; std w/cleaned patina, 18" . 1,800.00

Table lamp, reverse-painted 18" exotic bird #7036 shade with chipped ice exterior signed RC; Chinese base, 24", $14,375.00. (Photo courtesy James D. Julia Inc.)

Table, rvpt 18" jungle bird #6674 shade; std w/rtcl Chinese ft, 23" ...17,825.00
Table, rvpt 18" jungle bird shade; floral-pnt vasiform base, 23", EX ..13,225.00

Table, rvpt 18" scenic shade #5889/JB; 4-ftd bronze rattan-emb std..10,800.00
Table, rvpt 18" scenic w/floral border shade (EX); sgn vasiform std, 27"..4,885.00
Table, rvpt 18" shade #6529 w/Japanese scene; ribbed/flaring std ..6,465.00

Harker

The Harker Pottery was established in East Liverpool, Ohio, in 1840. Their earliest products were yellow ware and Rockingham produced from local clay. After 1900 whiteware was made from imported materials. The plant eventually grew to be a large manufacturer of dinnerware and kitchenware, employing as many as 300 people. It closed in 1972 after it was purchased by the Jeannette Glass Company. Perhaps their best-known lines were their Cameo wares, decorated with white silhouettes in a cameo effect on contrasting solid colors. Floral silhouettes are standard, but other designs were also used. Blue and pink are the most often found background hues; a few pieces are found in yellow. For further information we recommend *The Best of Collectible Dinnerware* by Jo Cunningham (Schiffer). Our advisor for this category is Ted Haun; he is listed in the Directory under Indiana.

Amy, bowl, cereal; 6" 8.00
Amy, creamer, 6-oz.. 20.00
Amy, cup & saucer, ftd... 15.00
Amy, plate, luncheon; 9" 10.00
Bouquet, bowl, rimmed soup; 8½" 8.00
Bouquet, cup & saucer... 15.00
Bouquet, plate, dinner; 10" 15.00
Bouquet, plate, luncheon; 9" 9.00
Bouquet, plate, sq, 8½" 7.00
Bouquet, platter, 14" L 30.00
Cameo, cup, bl swirl shape, 2½" 12.00
Cameo, plate, bl swirl shape, 9½" 18.00
Cameo, plate, bread & butter; bl swirl shape, 6" 3.00
Cameo, platter, bl swirl shape, 13½" L 30.00

Deco Dahlia, platter, 9½", $16.00.

Garden Trail, bowl, dessert/fruit; 5½" 7.00
Garden Trail, coaster, 4¾" 3.00
Garden Trail, creamer.. 17.50
Garden Trail, plate, bread & butter; 6" 4.00
Garden Trail, sugar bowl, w/lid.. 20.00
Ivy Wreath, bowl, coupe soup; 7½" 8.00
Ivy Wreath, bowl, divided vegetable; 10½" 40.00
Ivy Wreath, cup & saucer 10.00
Ivy Wreath, sugar bowl, w/lid 15.00
Magnolia, bowl, rimmed fruit; 5½" 7.00
Magnolia, bowl, vegetable; 8½" 30.00
Magnolia, plate, dinner; 10" 12.00
Magnolia, platter, 13" L 50.00
Petit Point, bowl, lugged cereal; 6⅞".....................................7.50

Petit Point, creamer, 8-oz 18.00
Petit Point, plate, bread & butter; 6" 4.00
Petit Point, plate, dinner; 10" 15.00
Petit Point, platter, 12" L 38.00
Snowleaf, cup & saucer 10.00
Snowleaf, plate, salad; 7¼" 6.00
Snowleaf, platter, 11½" L 12.00
White Rose, bowl, rimmed soup; bl, 7¾" 14.00
White Rose, cup & saucer, bl, 2⅜" 32.00
White Rose, plate, luncheon; 9" 14.00
White Rose, platter, bl, 14" L 50.00
Woodsong, creamer 22.00
Woodsong, cup & saucer 20.00
Woodsong, plate, dinner; 10" 15.00
Woodsong, plate, salad; 7¼" 7.00
Woodsong, sugar bowl, w/lid 30.00

Harlequin

Harlequin dinnerware, produced by the Homer Laughlin China Company of Newell, West Virginia, was introduced in 1938. It was a lightweight ware made in maroon, mauve blue, and spruce green, as well as all the Fiesta colors except ivory (see Fiesta). It was marketed exclusively by the Woolworth stores, who considered it to be their all-time bestseller. For this reason they contracted with Homer Laughlin to reissue Harlequin to commemorate their 100th anniversary in 1979. Although three of the original glazes were used in the reissue, the few serving pieces that were made were restyled, and collectors found the new line to be no threat to their investments. In fact, it is becoming collectible on its own.

The Harlequin animals, including a fish, lamb, cat, penguin, duck, and donkey, were made during the early 1940s, also for the dime-store trade. Today these are very desirable to collectors of Homer Laughlin china.

Pricing is very color driven. Our values are for the more desirable colors: maroon, dark green, gray, spruce, and chartreuse. For blue, rose, red, and light green, values are approximately 70% to 80% of those listed; yellow and turquoise, about 50% to 60%. Some pieces of light green are very hard to find, such as the regular ashtray, the individual creamer, the egg cup, and the candleholders. Medium green is prized in Harlequin just as it is in the Fiesta line. For the light green items listed above or for pricing on medium green, refer to *Collector's Encyclopedia of Fiesta, Tenth Edition*, by Sharon and Bob Huxford (Collector Books).

Animals, any, from $125 to 225.00
Animals, maverick, w/ or w/out gold trim, from $40 to 60.00
Animals, non-standard color, minimum 500.00
Animals, standard color, donkey or cat, from $195 to 225.00
Ashtray, basketweave or regular, from $45 to 50.00
Ashtray/saucer, from $100 to 125.00
Bowl, '36s, from $35 to 45.00
Bowl, '36s oatmeal, from $15 to 20.00
Bowl, cream soup; from $35 to 40.00
Bowl, cream soup; med gr, minimum value 1,100.00
Bowl, fruit; 5½", from $9 to 11.00
Bowl, ind salad; from $25 to 30.00
Bowl, mixing; Kitchen Kraft, lt gr, 6", from $60 to 80.00
Bowl, mixing; Kitchen Kraft, mauve bl, 8", from $75 to ... 100.00
Bowl, mixing; Kitchen Kraft, red, 6", from $125 to 150.00
Bowl, mixing; Kitchen Kraft, yel, 10", from $110 to 125.00
Bowl, nappy, 9", from $35 to 45.00
Bowl, oval baker, from $30 to 35.00
Butter dish, cobalt, ½-lb, from $135 to 150.00

Butter dish, ½-lb, from $95 to 125.00
Candleholders, spruce, maroon, mauve blue, red, pr 250.00
Casserole, w/lid, from $150 to 175.00
Creamer, high lip, any color, ea from $125 to 165.00
Creamer, ind; from $35 to 40.00
Creamer, novelty; from $25 to 35.00
Creamer, regular; from $15 to 20.00
Cup, demitasse; gray, chartreuse, or dk gr, from $100 to ... 120.00
Cup, demitasse; maroon or spruce, from $75 to 95.00
Cup, lg, any color but med gr, ea from $175 to 225.00
Egg cup, dbl; from $25 to 35.00
Egg cup, single; from $25 to 35.00
Marmalade, from $275 to 300.00
Marmalade, lt gr, minimum value 450.00
Marmalade, rose, minimum value 350.00
Nut dish, basketweave, from $45 to 55.00
Nut dish, basketweave, lt gr, from $65 to 75.00
Nut dish, basketweave, rose, from $55 to 65.00
Perfume bottle, either color, either sz, ea, minimum value ... 975.00
Pitcher, service water; from $75 to 90.00
Pitcher, 22-oz jug; from $50 to 65.00
Plate, deep; from $15 to 20.00
Plate, deep; med gr, minimum value 95.00
Plate, 6", from $7 to 9.00
Plate, 7", from $9 to 11.00
Plate, 9", from $12 to 15.00
Plate, 10", from $25 to 30.00
Platter, med gr, 11", minimum value 300.00
Platter, med gr, 13", minimum value 375.00
Platter, 11", from $20 to 25.00
Platter, 13", from $25 to 35.00

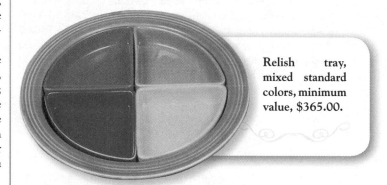

Relish tray, mixed standard colors, minimum value, $365.00.

Sauceboat, from $25 to 30.00
Saucer, demitasse; from $20 to 25.00
Saucer, demitasse; med gr, minimum value 175.00
Saucer, from $4 to 5.00
Shakers, pr from $50 to 70.00
Sugar bowl, w/lid, from $30 to 40.00
Sugar bowl, w/lid, med gr, minimum value 135.00
Syrup, spruce, mauve bl, or red, from $300 to 375.00
Syrup, yel, from $225 to 275.00
Teacup, from $8 to 12.00
Teapot, from $75 to 125.00
Tumbler, from $35 to 50.00

Hatpin Holders

Most hatpin holders were made from 1860 to 1920 to coincide with the period during which hatpins were popularly in vogue. The taller types were required to house the long hatpins necessary to secure the large hats that were in style from 1890 to 1914. They were usually porcelain, either decorated by hand or by transfer with florals or scenics, although some were clever figurals. Glass examples are rare, and those of slag or carnival glass are especially valuable.

For information concerning the American Hatpin Society, see the Clubs, Newsletters, and Catalogs section of the Directory. Our advisor for this category is Virginia Woodbury; she is listed in the Directory under California (SASE required).

Austria, flowers & buds, pastels w/gr & gold borders, attached tray....150.00
Austria, swan scene on aqua w/gold, bell shape, 1890s, 5½" 150.00
Bavaria, acorns & leaves on branch, hdls, scalloped top, 4¾" 95.00
Bavaria, pk roses on wht to pk, gold twining hdl, rnd top/sq base, 5".. 120.00
Benedict Karnak, brass, emb Egyptian decor, 6-hole top, 4½"........ 82.50

Limoges, floral with gold trim, Lozeyras, Rosenfield and Lehman mark #3, 1920s, $115.00. (Photo courtesy Virginia Woodbury)

McKee (unmk), clear glass, 6-sided, 6" 95.00
Nippon, geishas in garden, Mt Fuji beyond, 5x3" :.......................... 30.00
Nippon, roses reserves (2 sides), gold dots, 4-sided, 4¾"................. 60.00
Noritake, man on camel/palms/desert, HP mk, 4½" 200.00
Northwood, Grape & Cable, amethyst, 6½" 300.00
Northwood, Grape & Cable Banded, gr carnival, 6½" 225.00
Northwood, Orange Tree, amethyst carnival, 6½"....................... 180.00
Royal Bayreuth, cavaliers drinking, attached tray, 4¼"................. 425.00
Royal Bayreuth, pk poppy figural w/gold, 4⅜x3⅛"....................... 160.00

Hatpins

A hatpin was used to securely fasten a hat to the hair and head of the wearer. Hatpins, measuring from 7" to 12" in length, were worn from approximately 1850 to 1920. During the Art Deco period, hatpins became ornaments rather than the decorative functional jewels that they had been. The hatpin period reached its zenith in 1913 just prior to World War I, which brought about a radical change in women's head-dress and fashion. About that time, women began to scorn the bonnet and adopt 'the hat' as a symbol of their equality. The hatpin was made of every natural and manufactured element in a myriad of designs that challenge the imagination. They were contrived to serve every fashion need and complement the milliner's art. Collectors often concentrate on a specific type: hand-painted porcelains, sterling silver, commemoratives, sporting activities, carnival glass, Art Nouveau and/or Art Deco designs, Victorian gothics with mounted stones, exquisite rhinestones, engraved and brass-mounted escutcheon heads, gold and gems, or simply primitive types made in the Victorian parlor. Some collectors prefer the long pin-shanks while others select only those on tremblants or nodder-type pin-shanks.

If you are interested in collecting or dealing in hatpins, for information concerning a national collectors' club see Clubs, Newsletters, and Catalogs. Our advisor for this category is Virginia Woodbury; she is listed in the Directory under California. (SASE required.)

Sterling elephant figural (1x1"), on 8¼" steel pin, from $350.00 to $450.00.
(Photo courtesy Virginia Woodbury)

Amethyst faceted stone amid wht & lav rhinestones, 1890s, 1½"...125.00
Amethyst faceted stones w/foil bks in silver-tone dome fr, 1½"....250.00
Brass flower form w/hinged top (compact), 1½x1⅝" on 8" pin.....685.00
Brass w/HP dog's head under glass dome, 1890s, 1¼" 195.00
Carnival glass, Dragonflies Variant, gold pnt on blk, 1½"............110.00
Celluloid, cvd red 5-petal flower rests on gold-tone fr 45.00
Cobalt glass ball w/floral silver o/l, ca 1900, ¾" 115.00
Porc, lily-of-valley enamel bands on ornate 10k gold fr, 1¼"..........70.00
Porc disk w/lady transfer, HP details, 1½" in 6-prong fr, 1890s.....300.00
Satsuma, butterflies & gold dots, ¾" dia, 6" steel pin...................120.00
Satsuma, floral & crane w/gold, brass mts, ca 1900, 1½" oval.......430.00
Sterling lion's head w/2 ruby eyes, EX patina...............................95.00

Haviland

The Haviland China Company was organized in 1840 by David Haviland, a New York china importer. His search for a pure white, non-porous porcelain led him to Limoges, France, where natural deposits of suitable clay had already attracted numerous china manufacturers. The fine china he produced there was translucent and meticulously decorated, with each piece fired in an individual sagger.

It has been estimated that as many as 60,000 chinaware patterns were designed, each piece marked with one of several company back-stamps. 'H. & Co.' was used until 1890 when a law was enacted making it necessary to include the country of origin. Various marks have been used since that time including 'Haviland, France'; 'Haviland & Co. Limoges'; and 'Decorated by Haviland & Co.' Various associations with family members over the years have resulted in changes in management as well as company name. In 1892 Theodore Haviland left the firm to start his own business. Some of his ware was marked 'Mont Mery.' Later logos included a horseshoe, a shield, and various uses of his initials and name. In 1941 this branch moved to the United States. Wares produced here are marked 'Theodore Haviland, N.Y.' or 'Made In America.'

Though it is their dinnerware lines for which they are most famous, during the 1880s and 1890s they also made exquisite art pottery using a technique of underglaze slip decoration called Barbotine, which had been invented by Ernest Chaplet. In 1885 Haviland bought the formula and hired Chaplet to oversee its production. The technique involved mixing heavy white clay slip with pigments to produce a compound of the same consistency as oil paints. The finished product actually resembled oil paintings of the period, the texture achieved through the application of the heavy medium to the clay body in much the same manner as an artist would apply paint to his canvas. Primarily the body used with this method was a low-fired faience, though they also produced stoneware. For further information we recommend Mary

Frank Gaston's *Collector's Encyclopedia of Limoges Porcelain, Third Edition* (the first two editions are out of print), which shows examples and marks of the Haviland Company. Mrs. Gaston is listed in the Directory under Texas.

Bowl, autumn-like floral w/gold, rectangular, H&Co, 1890s, 9x7½"... 175.00
Bowl, brn flowers w/yel trim, scalloped rim, H&Co, 12x8" 95.00
Bowl, floral w/gold, rectangular, w/lid & hdls, H&Co, 10" 225.00
Cake plate, Dubarry (Dresden-like floral), hdls, Theodore, 10¾"...175.00
Chamberstick, Moss Rose, ring hdl, bl trim, H&Co 225.00
Chocolate pot, floral on wht to brn, gold hdl, H&Co, 12" 250.00
Coffeepot, anchor design, braided hdl, H&Co, 9½" 375.00
Coffeepot, rose sprays w/gold, H&Co, 9¾" 350.00
Compote, pk bands on wht, ftd, Fabrique Par..., 1840s, 4½x9" 700.00
Cup & saucer, bl floral w/mc accents on Vermicelle blank, H&Co...65.00
Cup & saucer, Papillon (butterfly), HP holly & berries, H&Co .. 100.00
Leaf bowl, garden theme w/fruit/beetle/rabbit, Theodore, 12" ..7,000.00

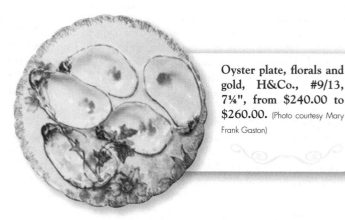

Oyster plate, florals and gold, H&Co., #9/13, 7¼", from $240.00 to $260.00. (Photo courtesy Mary Frank Gaston)

Pitcher, penguin figural, Deco style, Sandoz, 7" 600.00
Plate, floral bouquets, brushed gold at rim, Theodore, 10" 75.00
Plate, floral center w/pk border, H&Co, 9½" 100.00
Plate, game birds in brush, H&Co, 9½" 120.00
Plate, peacocks on flowering limbs w/gold, H&Co, 1887, 8" 125.00
Plate, pk roses scattered, gold scalloped trim, H&Co, 10" 50.00
Plate, roses w/wht & gold accents, Naudin, H&Co, 9½" 350.00
Plate, shellfish; pk rose garlands & brushed gold, Theodore, 8¼"....240.00
Plate, Silver Anniversary on Ranson blank, H&Co, 10" 55.00
Platter, drippings well, gold trim at rim, Theodore, 14½x12"....... 350.00
Platter, floral bouquets, brushed gold at rim, Theodore, 12x7"..... 175.00

Ramekin, Drop Rose, 3¼" diameter, on 5¼" underplate, $150.00; Sherbet, $130.00.

Sugar bowl, Moss Rose, emb rope decor, bl trim, w/lid, H&Co, 7½" .. 185.00
Teapot, birds & leaf on basket weave, H&Co, 6" 275.00

Tureen, sauce/gravy; floral w/gold, w/lid, attached tray, H&Co..... 165.00
Tureen, soup; bl floral sprays w/gold, w/lid & hdls, Theodore....... 500.00
Tureen, vegetable; Old Blackberry, w/lid, hdls, H&Co...Wis 375.00
Vase, morning glories, dbl style w/center hdl, H&Co, 1850s, 6" ...1,400.00
Vase, roses/peonies on gr, moon flask form, late 19th C, 11" 585.00

Hawkes

Thomas Hawkes established his factory in Corning, New York, in 1880. He developed many beautiful patterns of cut glass, two of which were awarded the Grand Prize at the Paris Exposition in 1889. By the end of the century, his company was renowned for the finest in cut glass production. The company logo was a trefoil form enclosing a hawk in each of the two bottom lobes with a fleur-de-lis in the center. With the exception of some of the very early designs, all Hawkes was signed. (Our values are for signed pieces.)

Bowl, hobstar & spoked button cuttings, 11"................................ 550.00
Candlesticks, intaglio flowers on clear, bl cups & ft, 1920s, 9", pr...300.00
Candy dish, floral intaglio w/lattice, sterling finial, 5¼x9" dia 150.00
Carafe, water; strawberries/fans/star cuttings, notched neck, 7" ... 200.00
Cocktail shaker, intaglio pheasant & fruited vines, silver mts, 12"... 150.00
Jar, grapevine cuttings on bright bl, ftd, silver repousse lid, 4¾" .. 200.00

Pitcher, China Aster, 8x16", $2,000.00.

Pitcher, poinsettias, cuttings & notches, tall hdl, 11".................. 210.00
Vase, dmn cuttings, flared sides, silver ft, 1950s, 15", pr 850.00
Vase, fans & trellis cuttings, trumpet shape w/silver stem/ft, 10"... 200.00
Vase, gr satin w/wht enameled branch, gold rim, 1920s, 13" 275.00
Vase, intaglio fruit, silver ft, 9¾x4½"................................... 325.00

Head Vases

Vases modeled as heads of lovely ladies, delightful children, clowns, famous people — even some animals — were once popular as flower containers. Most of them were imported from Japan, although some American potteries produced a few as well. For more information, we recommend *Head Vases* by Kathleen Cole; *Collecting Head Vases* by David Barron; and *The World of Head Vase Planters* by Mike Posgay and Ian Warner. Our advisor for this category is Larry G. Pogue (L&J Antiques and Collectibles); he is listed in the Directory under Texas.

Baby girl w/kitten, bow in hair, Enesco, 5½" 65.00
Child w/pk bow in blond hair, lg bow at neckline, eyes open, 6½"....98.00
Geisha girl, open fan to chin, gold eyelashes, unmk, 4¾".............. 55.00
Girl, blond in wht head scarf, thick lashes, Velco #6686, 5½" 195.00
Girl child holding gift, hat w/daisies, gold trim, Japan, 5½" 65.00
Girl holding doll, blond w/pk bow, USA #810, 6½" 55.00

Girl with green leaf on head, scalloped bodice, Velco #6690, 5", $195.00.
(Photo courtesy Larry Pogue)

Girl w/umbrella, blond in aqua plaid, 3½"+umbrella 250.00
Girl w/umbrella, blond in gr striped outfit, #52/271, 5" (8" overall)...215.00
Girl w/umbrella, brunette in gr outfit w/pk & blk hat, Japan, 5½" ..215.00
Girl w/umbrella, brunette w/purple bows in hair, 5" (8" overall).....215.00
Girl w/umbrella in pk & wht plaid outfit, pk ribbon bonnet, 5"... 160.00
Jackie Kennedy, Inarco #E-1852...1964, 6" 995.00
Lady, blond, bl bodice, pearls, hand to throat, Enesco, 8" 380.00
Lady, blond, daisies at neck/pearl earrings/gloved hand, #C6428, 6"... 215.00
Lady, blond, daisy at neck, pearl earrings, bl gloved hand, Enesco, 6"... 230.00
Lady, blond, gloved hand, pearl bracelet, Napco #C2589B, 5½".. 245.00
Lady, blond, gr bodice, pearls, hand up, red polish, Ardco, 7½".. 325.00
Lady, blond, ruffled neckline, pearls, thick lashes, Japan #C5939, 6" .. 215.00
Lady, blond curls, hand to face, thick lashes, Ardco, 6" 215.00
Lady, blond flip, gloved hand to chin, picture hat, Lefton #2251, 6"... 195.00
Lady, blond frosted hair, gr bodice/leaf pin/pearls, Napco #C7472, 6" ...200.00
Lady, blond frosted hair/hand to face, Relpo #K1402, 7", +orig flowers..445.00
Lady, blond in flat-brim hat, blk bodice, pearls, #5047, 7" 305.00
Lady, blond in flat-brim hat, hands to face & chest, #2703, 6½"..275.00
Lady, blond in flat-brim hat, hands Xd at chin, pearls, #434, 4½"...195.00
Lady, blond in flat-brim hat, hands Xd at chin, Ruben #494, 4½"...195.00
Lady, blond in flat-brim hat w/red feather, Lefton #2359, 7½" 325.00
Lady, blond in gr, pearls, gloved hand to face, Relpo ##K1633, 7¼"...320.00
Lady, blond in gr flat-brim hat & bodice, dangle earrings, Japan, 7" ...295.00
Lady, blond in red flat-brim hat & jacket, Relpo #K1009B, 5½"..225.00
Lady, blond updo, pearls, wht bodice, #3855, 4½" 170.00
Lady, blond w/pk rose in hair, pearls, hand to face, Inarco #E-779, 6"... 245.00
Lady, brn flip, gr bodice w/wht & gold flower, Napco ##C6987, 10½"...930.00
Lady, colonial, wht curls w/gold, eyes open, Relpo #K1335, 8" 380.00
Lady, frosted blond, gr hat & bodice, pearls, Napco #C7498, 10½"....865.00
Teen girl, blond, wht & blk bodice w/butterfly, Napco #CE6060, 3½"...149.00
Teen girl, blond curls atop head, dangle pearl earrings, #3855, 4½"...175.00
Teen girl, blond dk bl bodice, bl eyes, pearls, Ardco, 6" 185.00
Teen girl, blond in gr hat w/wht bow, thick lashes, Lefton #3515, 8"..315.00
Teen girl, blond in ponytail, blk top hat, pearls, 6", +orig flowers ...210.00
Teen girl, blond w/brn bow, lace collar, bl eyes, Japan #T1576, 6"..245.00
Teen girl, blond w/long hair, scalloped bodice, pearls, Enesco, 6" ...215.00
Teen girl, frosted blond, blk bodice, pearls, Napco #C747, 8" 395.00
Teen girl, frosted blond, dangle earrings, Napco #C7293, 5¾"..... 195.00
Teen girl, frosted blond, gr bodice, pearls, Inarco #E-1062, 6½"... 260.00
Teen girl, frosted blond in bl bodice, pearls, unmk, 6", +orig flowers... 230.00
Teen girl, frosted blond w/gr bow & bodice, Napco #C8497, 7" .. 270.00
Teen girl, glasses on top of head, 2 ponytails, unmk, 7½" 375.00
Uncle Sam, allover gr, unmk, 6½" 45.00

Heino, Otto and Vivika

Born in East Hampton, Connecticut, in 1915, Heino served in the Air Force during WWII. He had always been interested in various crafts, and through the Air Force, he was able to take classes in England, where he learned the basics of silversmithing, painting, and ceramics. He had

the oportunity to visit Bernard Leach's studio, where he was fascinated to see the inert clay come to life under the absolute and total control of the potter. Returning to America he met Vivika, the woman who was to become his wife. She was already well advanced in the trade, and Otto became her student. They eventually moved to California and until her passing in 1995 worked together to become a team well known for producing large bowls, vases, bottles, and jars glazed in fantastic textures and rich colors, often decorated with organic forms or calligraphic images.

Otto is still working at his studio in Ojai, California.

In the listings that follow, all pieces are signed by both Otto and Vivika unless otherwise noted.

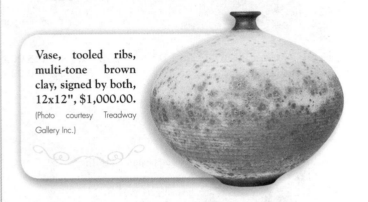

Vase, tooled ribs, multi-tone brown clay, signed by both, 12x12", $1,000.00.
(Photo courtesy Treadway Gallery Inc.)

Bowl, stylized fish, cvd/emb, brn/wht speckled stoneware, 6x17" ..1,440.00
Charger, Oriental-style mums pnt in indigo on wht stoneware, 23"...660.00
Jar, ribbed, horizontal wht line on mahog matt, rstr lid, 18x13".. 1,200.00
Jardiniere, wht reserves w/blk devices on brn, stoneware, 9x12" ...1,560.00
Plate, mc splotches pnt at rim on wht stoneware, sgn only Otto, 12"... 180.00
Platter, leafy branches, cvd/pnt, wht on brn/indigo matt, sq, 17x18".. 1,920.00
Vase, ridged, ivory/yel/brn volcanic speckle, 7x9" 960.00

Heintz Art Metal Shop

Founded by Otto L. Heintz in Buffalo, New York, ca 1909, the Heintz Art Metal Shop (HAMS) succeeded the Art Crafts Shop (begun in 1903) and featured a new aesthetic. Whereas the Art Craft Shop offered products of hammered copper with applied color enamel and with an altogether somewhat cruder or more primitive and medieval-looking appearance, HAMS presented a refined appearance of applied sterling silver on bronze. Most pieces are stamped with the manufacturer's mark — the letters HAMS conjoined within a diamond, often accompanied by an Aug. 27, 1912, patent date — although paper labels were pasted on the bottom of lamp bases. Original patinas for Heintz pieces include a mottled brown or green (the two most desirable), as well as silver and gold (less desirable). Desk sets and smoking accessories are common; lamps appear less frequently. The firm, like many others, closed in 1930, a victim of the Depression. Silvercrest, also located in Buffalo, produced products similar though not nearly as valuable as Heintz. Please note: Cleaning or scrubbing original patinas will diminish value. Our advisor for this and related Arts & Crafts subjects is Bruce A. Austin; he is listed in the Directory under New York.

Bowl, center; rose branch, hdls, 5½x11x9" 325.00
Box, leaves & berries, 3½" L 400.00
Candlesticks, Greek key bands, HAMS 12", pr 600.00
Frame, leaves & berries, #1055, 5x6" 350.00
Inkwell, lid w/water lily, lily-pad ftd base, 5" W.......................... 425.00
Inkwell & blotter corners, leaves & berries................................... 400.00
Lamp, floral, silk-lined 9" cone shade, 9½" 700.00

Lamp, poppies, sterling on bronze, large paper label, 9x10", $1,600.00. (Photo courtesy David Rago Auctions)

Vase, cattails, cylindrical, #3608A, ca 1915, 10" 125.00
Vase, floral, flared ft, 9¼" 300.00

Vase, poppies, sterling on bronze with verdigris patina, 11", NM, $700.00. (Photo courtesy David Rago Auctions)

Heisey

A. H. Heisey began his long career at the King Glass Company of Pittsburgh. He later joined the Ripley Glass Company which soon became Geo. Duncan and Sons. After Duncan's death Heisey became half-owner in partnership with his brother-in-law, James Duncan. In 1895 he built his own factory in Newark, Ohio, initiating production in 1896 and continuing until Christmas of 1957. At that time Imperial Glass Corporation bought some of the molds. After 1968 they removed the old 'Diamond H' from any they put into use. In 1985 HCA purchased all of Imperial's Heisey molds with the exception of the Old Williamsburg line.

During their highly successful period of production, Heisey made fine handcrafted tableware with simple, yet graceful designs. Early pieces were not marked. After November 1901 the glassware was marked either with the 'Diamond H' or a paper label. Blown ware is often marked on the stem, never on the bowl or foot. For more information we recommend *Heisey Glass, 1896 – 1957*, by Neila and Tom Bredehoft. For information concerning Heisey Collectors of America, see the Clubs, Newsletters, and Catalogs section of the Directory. See also Glass Animals and Figurines.

Charter Oak, crystal, sherbet, #3362, low ft, 6-oz 10.00
Charter Oak, crystal, tumbler, #3362, flat, 10-oz 10.00
Charter Oak, Flamingo, bowl, flower; #116 Oak Leaf, 11" 50.00
Charter Oak, Flamingo, plate, luncheon; #1246 Acorn & Leaves, 8" .. 15.00
Charter Oak, Hawthorne, plate, dinner; #1246 Acorn & Leaves, 10½" .. 70.00
Charter Oak, Hawthorne, plate, salad; #1246 Acorn & Leaves, 6" ... 20.00
Charter Oak, Marigold, cocktail, #3362, 3-oz 40.00
Charter Oak, Marigold, luncheon goblet, #3362, low ft, 8-oz 60.00
Charter Oak, Moongleam, coaster, #10 Oak Leaf 25.00

Charter Oak, Moongleam, parfait, #3362, 4½-oz 35.00
Chintz, crystal, bowl, mint; ftd, 6" 20.00
Chintz, crystal, bowl, vegetable; oval, 10" 20.00
Chintz, crystal, cup 15.00
Chintz, crystal, mayonnaise, dolphin ft, 5½" 35.00
Chintz, crystal, tumbler, water; #3389, 9-oz 17.50
Chintz, crystal, vase, dolphin ft, 9" 95.00
Chintz, Sahara, bowl, jelly; ftd, hdls, 6" 35.00
Chintz, Sahara, cocktail, #3389, 3-oz 35.00
Chintz, Sahara, compote, oval, 7" 85.00
Chintz, Sahara, ice bucket, ftd 155.00
Chintz, Sahara, plate, dinner; sq or rnd, 10½", ea 85.00
Chintz, Sahara, sugar bowl, ind 30.00
Chintz, Sahara, tumbler, soda; #3389, 8-oz 24.00
Crystolite, crystal, ashtray, oblong, 4x6" 85.00
Crystolite, crystal, bonbon, hdls, 7½" 15.00
Crystolite, crystal, bottle, cologne; w/#108 stopper, 4-oz 75.00
Crystolite, crystal, bowl, dessert; 5½" 14.00
Crystolite, crystal, bowl, nut; ind, hdl, 3" 20.00
Crystolite, crystal, candy box, 7" 60.00
Crystolite, crystal, cigarette box, 4½" 40.00
Crystolite, crystal, cigarette lighter 30.00
Crystolite, crystal, mayonnaise, oval, hdl, 6" 40.00
Crystolite, crystal, plate, salad; 7" 15.00
Crystolite, crystal, plate, sandwich; 12" 45.00
Crystolite, crystal, plate, torte; 14" 50.00
Crystolite, crystal, punch ladle, glass 35.00
Crystolite, crystal, sugar bowl, rnd 40.00
Crystolite, crystal, tumbler, juice; blown, 5-oz 30.00
Crystolite, crystal, vase, ftd, 6" 40.00
Empress, Alexandrite, bowl, mint; dolphin ft, 6" 325.00
Empress, Alexandrite, creamer, ind 210.00
Empress, Alexandrite, tray, celery; 10" 150.00
Empress, cobalt, bowl, floral, dolphin ft, 11" 400.00
Empress, cobalt, grapefruit, w/sq liner 35.00
Empress, cobalt, plate, sq, 8" 80.00
Empress, Flamingo, ashtray 175.00
Empress, Flamingo, nappy, 8" 35.00
Empress, Flamingo, shakers, pr 100.00
Empress, Moongleam, bowl, cream soup 50.00
Empress, Moongleam, oyster cocktail, 2½-oz 30.00
Empress, Moongleam, plate, 8" 24.00
Empress, Sahara, cup 30.00
Empress, Sahara, oil bottle, 4-oz 125.00
Empress, Sahara, vase, flared, 8" 150.00
Greek Key, crystal, bowl, almond; ftd, 5" 40.00
Greek Key, crystal, bowl, punch; ftd, 15" 400.00
Greek Key, crystal, burgundy, 3½-oz 125.00
Greek Key, crystal, candy dish, 1-lb 170.00
Greek Key, crystal, claret, 4½-oz 170.00
Greek Key, crystal, cordial, ¾-oz 225.00
Greek Key, crystal, creamer 50.00
Greek Key, crystal, cup, punch; 4½-oz 20.00
Greek Key, crystal, egg cup, 5-oz 80.00
Greek Key, crystal, jar, horseradish; w/lid, sm 130.00
Greek Key, crystal, nappy, 6½" 35.00
Greek Key, crystal, oil bottle, w/#6 stopper, 6-oz 80.00
Greek Key, crystal, pitcher, 1-qt 210.00
Greek Key, crystal, plate, 4½" 20.00
Greek Key, crystal, plate, 10" 110.00
Greek Key, crystal, straw jar, w/lid 425.00
Greek Key, crystal, tray, oblong, 15" 300.00
Greek Key, crystal, tumbler, flared rim, 13-oz 100.00
Greek Key, crystal, tumbler, flared rim, 5-oz 50.00

Greek Key, crystal, tumbler, str sides, 12-oz	100.00
Ipswich, cobalt, bowl, flower; ftd, 11"	450.00
Ipswich, cobalt, candlestick, 1-light, 6", ea	400.00
Ipswich, crystal, creamer	35.00
Ipswich, crystal, oil bottle, w/#86 stopper, ftd, 2-oz	125.00
Ipswich, crystal, plate, sq, 7"	30.00
Ipswich, Flamingo, candy jar, w/lid, ½-lb	325.00
Ipswich, Flamingo, finger bowl, w/underplate	90.00
Ipswich, Flamingo, tumbler, soda; ftd, 12-oz	80.00

Ipswich, Moongleam, candlestick, footed, with vase and prisms, rare, $450.00. (Photo courtesy Gene and Cathy Florence)

Ipswich, Moongleam, cocktail shaker, w/#86 stopper & strainer, 1-qt	800.00
Ipswich, Moongleam, plate, sq, 8"	75.00
Ipswich, Moongleam, saucer champagne, knob stem, 5-oz	70.00
Ipswich, Moongleam, tumbler, soda; ftd, 8-oz	90.00
Ipswich, Sahara, oyster cocktail, ftd, 4-oz	50.00
Ipswich, Sahara, pitcher, ½-gal	550.00
Ipswich, Sahara, sugar bowl	90.00
Kalonyal, crystal, bottle, molasses; hdl, 13-oz	185.00
Kalonyal, crystal, bowl, flared, 8"	65.00
Kalonyal, crystal, bowl, shallow, 6"	35.00
Kalonyal, crystal, cake plate, ftd, 9"	275.00
Kalonyal, crystal, champagne, 6½-oz	65.00
Kalonyal, crystal, cordial, 1¼-oz	300.00
Kalonyal, crystal, creamer, hotel	70.00
Kalonyal, crystal, cup, punch; 3½-oz	26.00
Kalonyal, crystal, egg cup, 9½-oz	75.00
Kalonyal, crystal, pickle jar, w/lid	195.00
Kalonyal, crystal, pitcher, ½-gal	350.00
Kalonyal, crystal, plate, 5½"	30.00
Kalonyal, crystal, sherbet, scalloped, 3½-oz	40.00
Kalonyal, crystal, spooner, tall	65.00
Kalonyal, crystal, sugar shaker	145.00
Lariat, crystal, basket, ftd, 8½"	165.00
Lariat, crystal, bowl, flower; oval, 13"	35.00
Lariat, crystal, bowl, nut; ind, 4"	32.00
Lariat, crystal, bowl, punch; 7-qt	130.00
Lariat, crystal, candy dish, w/lid, 7"	90.00
Lariat, crystal, cheese dish, w/lid, 8"	60.00
Lariat, crystal, coaster, 4"	10.00
Lariat, crystal, cocktail, pressed, 3½-oz	18.00
Lariat, crystal, cordial, dbl loop, 1-oz	195.00
Lariat, crystal, cup, punch	8.00
Lariat, crystal, oil bottle, w/#133 stopper, hdl, 4-oz	180.00
Lariat, crystal, oyster cocktail, blown, 4½-oz	15.00
Lariat, crystal, plate, deviled egg; rnd, 13"	290.00
Lariat, crystal, plate, dinner; 10½"	125.00
Lariat, crystal, plate, salad; 8"	22.00
Lariat, crystal, plate, sandwich; hdls, 14"	50.00

Lariat, crystal, saucer	5.00
Lariat, crystal, shakers, pr	200.00
Lariat, crystal, tray, rnd, center hdl w/ball finial	165.00
Lariat, crystal, tumbler, juice; ftd, 5-oz	22.00
Lariat, crystal, wine, pressed, 3½-oz	22.00
Minuet, crystal, bowl, #1514, oval, 12"	65.00
Minuet, crystal, bowl, jelly; ftd, hdls, 6"	30.00
Minuet, crystal, bowl, pickle & olive; 13"	45.00
Minuet, crystal, candelabra, w/prisms, 1-light, pr	110.00
Minuet, crystal, cocktail, #5010, 3½-oz	35.00
Minuet, crystal, creamer, dolphin ft	42.50
Minuet, crystal, finger bowl, #3309	50.00
Minuet, crystal, ice bucket, dolphin ft	175.00
Minuet, crystal, plate, luncheon; 8"	30.00
Minuet, crystal, plate, sandwich; rnd, hdls, 12"	150.00
Minuet, crystal, plate, torte; #1511 Toujours, 14"	60.00
Minuet, crystal, tumbler, water; #5010, low ft, 9-oz	35.00
Minuet, crystal, vase, #5013, 5"	50.00
Minuet, crystal, wine, #5010, 2½-oz	50.00
New Era, crystal, bottle, rye; w/stopper	140.00
New Era, crystal, champagne, 6-oz	15.00
New Era, crystal, cordial, 1-oz	40.00
New Era, crystal, cup	15.00
New Era, crystal, pilsner, 12-oz	45.00
New Era, crystal, plate, bread & butter; 5½x4½"	20.00
New Era, crystal, plate, 10x8"	75.00
New Era, crystal, relish, 3-part, 13"	35.00
New Era, crystal, saucer, AD	12.50
New Era, crystal, tumbler, soda; ftd, 5-oz	10.00
New Era, crystal, tumbler, soda; low ft, 10-oz	14.00
Octagon, crystal, basket, #500, 5"	500.00
Octagon, crystal, bowl, mint; #1229, 6"	10.00
Octagon, crystal, cup, #1231	5.00
Octagon, crystal, platter, 12¾" L	20.00
Octagon, crystal, tray, celery; 12"	10.00
Octagon, Flamingo, bonbon, #1229, sides up, 6"	40.00
Octagon, Flamingo, creamer, #500	30.00
Octagon, Flamingo, plate, 6"	8.00
Octagon, Flamingo, saucer, #1231	8.00
Octagon, Flamingo, tray, #500, 6" L	15.00
Octagon, Hawthorne, bowl, cream soup; hdls	40.00
Octagon, Hawthorne, bowl, grapefruit; 6½"	35.00
Octagon, Hawthorne, plate, luncheon; 8"	25.00
Octagon, Hawthorne, sugar bowl, #500	50.00
Octagon, Marigol, ice tub, #500	150.00
Octagon, Marigold, bowl, nut; ind, hdls	65.00
Octagon, Marigold, plate, muffin; #1229, sides up, 12"	45.00
Octagon, Moongleam, bowl, vegetable; 9"	30.00
Octagon, Moongleam, mayonnaise, #1229, ftd, 5½"	35.00

Octagon, Moongleam, muffin plate, #1229, from $32.00 to $38.00. (Photo courtesy Neila and Tom Bredehoft)

Octagon, Moongleam, plate, hors d'oeuvres; #1229, 13" 45.00
Octagon, Moongleam, saucer, AD 10.00
Octagon, Moongleam, tray, celery; 9" 25.00
Octagon, Sahara, candlestick, 1-light, 3", ea 30.00
Octagon, Sahara, plate, bread; 7" 10.00
Octagon, Sahara, plate, 10½" 30.00
Octagon, Sahara, tray, celery; 9" 20.00
Old Sandwich, cobalt, beer mug, 18-oz 380.00
Old Sandwich, cobalt, claret, 4-oz 150.00
Old Sandwich, cobalt, creamer, 12-oz 575.00
Old Sandwich, cobalt, tumbler, bar; ground bottom, 1½-oz 100.00
Old Sandwich, crystal, ashtray, ind 9.00
Old Sandwich, crystal, comport, 6" 60.00
Old Sandwich, crystal, finger bowl 12.00
Old Sandwich, crystal, tumbler, toddy; 6½-oz 20.00
Old Sandwich, Flamingo, beer mug, 12-oz 300.00
Old Sandwich, Flamingo, decanter, w/#98 stopper, 1-pt 185.00
Old Sandwich, Flamingo, shakers, pr 65.00
Old Sandwich, Flamingo, tumbler, iced tea; ftd, 12-oz 45.00
Old Sandwich, Moongleam, bowl, popcorn; cupped, ftd 135.00
Old Sandwich, Moongleam, oil bottle, w/#85 stopper, 2½-oz 180.00
Old Sandwich, Moongleam, pitcher, reg, ½-gal 185.00
Old Sandwich, Moongleam, tumbler, 10-oz 45.00
Old Sandwich, Sahara, candlestick, 6", ea 110.00
Old Sandwich, Sahara, cocktail, 3-oz 32.00
Old Sandwich, Sahara, creamer, 18-oz 190.00
Old Sandwich, Sahara, tumbler, juice; 5-oz 15.00

Plantation, crystal, candle-block, #1567, 3", $110.00.
(Photo courtesy Gene and Cathy Florence)

Pleat & Panel, crystal, nappy, 4½" 6.00
Pleat & Panel, crystal, pitcher, 3-pt 45.00
Pleat & Panel, crystal, plate, 6" 4.00
Pleat & Panel, crystal, platter, oval, 12" 15.00
Pleat & Panel, crystal, vase, 8" 30.00
Pleat & Panel, Flamingo, bowl, chow chow; 4" 11.00

Pleat and Panel, Flamingo, compotier, from $125.00 to $135.00. (Photo courtesy Neila and Tom Bredehoft)

Pleat & Panel, Flamingo, cup 15.00
Pleat & Panel, Flamingo, plate, bread; 7" 8.00
Pleat & Panel, Flamingo, sugar bowl, hotel; w/lid 30.00
Pleat & Panel, Flamingo, tray, spice; compartments, 10" 25.00
Pleat & Panel, Moongleam, bowl, jelly; hdls, 5" 17.50
Pleat & Panel, Moongleam, marmalade, 4¾" 35.00
Pleat & Panel, Moongleam, plate, dinner; 10¾" 52.00
Pleat & Panel, Moongleam, saucer champagne, 5-oz 18.00
Pleat & Panel, Moongleam, tumbler, tea; ground bottom, 12-oz ... 30.00
Provincial/Whirlpool, crystal, bonbon, hdls, upturned sides, 7" 12.00
Provincial/Whirlpool, crystal, marmalade 45.00
Provincial/Whirlpool, crystal, oil bottle, w/#1 stopper, 4-oz 45.00
Provincial/Whirlpool, crystal, plate, bread; 7" 10.00
Provincial/Whirlpool, crystal, tumbler, juice; ftd, 5-oz 14.00
Provincial/Whirlpool, Limelight Green, bowl, nut/jelly; ind 40.00
Provincial/Whirlpool, Limelight Green, nappy, 5½" 40.00
Provincial/Whirlpool, Limelight Green, plate, luncheon; 8" 50.00
Provincial/Whirlpool, Limelight Green, relish, 4-part, 10" 150.00
Provincial/Whirlpool, Limelight Green, sugar bowl, ftd 95.00
Queen Ann, crystal, bowl, cream soup 18.00
Queen Ann, crystal, bowl, pickle/olive; 2-part, 13" 20.00
Queen Ann, crystal, bowl, preserve; hdls, 5" 15.00
Queen Ann, crystal, bowl, vegetable; oval, 10" 30.00
Queen Ann, crystal, cup, bouillon; hdls 20.00
Queen Ann, crystal, jug, ftd, 3-pt 100.00
Queen Ann, crystal, mayonnaise, w/ladle, ftd, 5½" 30.00
Queen Ann, crystal, oil bottle, 4-oz 40.00
Queen Ann, crystal, oyster cocktail, 2½-oz 15.00
Queen Ann, crystal, plate, hors d'oeuvres; hdls, 13" 60.00
Queen Ann, crystal, plate, muffin; upturned sides, 12" 35.00
Queen Ann, crystal, plate, sq, 6" 5.00
Queen Ann, crystal, plate, 4½" 5.00
Queen Ann, crystal, plate, 7" 8.00
Queen Ann, crystal, plate, 9" 12.00
Queen Ann, crystal, platter, 14" 30.00
Queen Ann, crystal, saucer, sq 5.00
Queen Ann, crystal, sherbet 15.00
Queen Ann, crystal, sugar bowl, dolphin ft, 3 hdls 30.00
Queen Ann, crystal, tray, celery; 13" 20.00
Queen Ann, crystal, tray, hors d'oeuvres; 7-part, 10" 60.00
Queen Ann, crystal, tray, pickle & olive 15.00
Queen Ann, crystal, tumbler, ground bottom, 8-oz 20.00
Queen Ann, crystal, tumbler, tea; ground bottom, 12-oz 20.00
Queen Ann, crystal, vase, flared, 8" 55.00
Ridgeleigh, crystal, ashtray, rnd 14.00
Ridgeleigh, crystal, bottle, cologne; 4-oz 130.00
Ridgeleigh, crystal, bowl, lemon; w/lid, 5" 65.00
Ridgeleigh, crystal, cocktail shaker, w/#86 stopper, #1 strainer, 1-qt .. 300.00
Ridgeleigh, crystal, compote, flared, low ft, 6" 25.00
Ridgeleigh, crystal, cup, punch 12.00
Ridgeleigh, crystal, decanter, w/#95 stopper, 1-pt 210.00
Ridgeleigh, crystal, ice tub, hdls 100.00
Ridgeleigh, crystal, mustard, w/lid 80.00
Ridgeleigh, crystal, oil bottle, w/#103 stopper, 3-oz 50.00
Ridgeleigh, crystal, pitcher, ball shape, ½-gal 380.00
Ridgeleigh, crystal, plate, sq, 7" 28.00
Ridgeleigh, crystal, plate, torte; ftd, 13½" 45.00
Ridgeleigh, crystal, puff box, w/lid, 5" 90.00
Ridgeleigh, crystal, salt cellar, ind 13.00
Ridgeleigh, crystal, shakers, pr 45.00
Ridgeleigh, crystal, sherry, blown, 2-oz 90.00
Ridgeleigh, crystal, tray, celery & olive; divided, 12" 50.00
Ridgeleigh, crystal, wine, pressed 40.00
Saturn, crystal, ashtray 10.00

Saturn, crystal, creamer 25.00
Saturn, crystal, plate, torte; 15" 30.00
Saturn, crystal, rose bowl, lg 40.00
Saturn, crystal, shakers, pr 45.00
Saturn, Zircon Limelight, parfait, 5-oz 110.00
Saturn, Zircon Limelight, sugar bowl 180.00
Saturn, Zircon Limelight, tumbler, soda; 12-oz 85.00
Saturn, Zircon Limelight, tumbler, 10-oz 80.00
Saturn, Zircon Limelight, vase, flared, 8½" 225.00

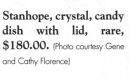

Stanhope, crystal, candy dish with lid, rare, $180.00. (Photo courtesy Gene and Cathy Florence)

Stanhope, crystal, mayonnaise, hdls........................... 35.00
Stanhope, crystal, saucer... 10.00
Stanhope, crystal, shakers, #60 top, pr...................... 125.00
Stanhope, crystal, tumbler, soda; #4083, 12-oz 25.00
Sunburst, crystal, bottle, molasses; 13-oz................. 175.00
Sunburst, crystal, cake plate, ftd, 9" 165.00
Sunburst, crystal, egg cup, ftd 65.00
Sunburst, crystal, oil bottle, 6-oz 85.00
Sunburst, crystal, pickle jar, w/stopper 145.00
Sunburst, crystal, pitcher, str sides, ½-gal 175.00
Sunburst, crystal, plate, torte; 13" 35.00
Sunburst, crystal, spooner 90.00
Sunburst, crystal, toothpick holder 135.00
Sunburst, crystal, tray, pickle; 6" 35.00
Twist, Alexandrite, bowl, nasturtium; rnd, 8" 450.00
Twist, Alexandrite, ice bucket, w/metal hdl.............. 300.00
Twist, Alexandrite, saucer 140.00
Twist, crystal, baker, oval, 9" 25.00
Twist, crystal, pitcher, 3-pt..................................... 95.00
Twist, crystal, plate, sandwich; hdls, 12" 30.00
Twist, Flamingo, nappy, 4" 30.00
Twist, Flamingo, sugar bowl, ftd 30.00
Twist, Flamingo, tray, celery; 13".............................. 50.00
Twist, Marigold, bonbon, ind.................................... 40.00
Twist, Marigold, oyster cocktail, ftd, 3-oz 50.00
Twist, Marigold, tumbler, soda; ftd, 9-oz................... 60.00
Twist, Moongleam, bottle, French dressing 110.00
Twist, Moongleam, comport, tall, 7" 120.00
Twist, Moongleam, plate, dinner; 10½".................... 100.00
Twist, Sahara, oil bottle, w/#78 stopper, 4-oz 90.00
Twist, Sahara, plate, ground bottom, 8" 20.00
Twist, Sahara, shakers, ftd, pr 140.00
Victorian, crystal, bottle, rye; 27-oz....................... 160.00
Victorian, crystal, jug, 54-oz.................................. 400.00
Victorian, crystal, plate, cracker; 12"....................... 75.00
Victorian, crystal, tumbler, old-fashioned; 8-oz......... 35.00
Victorian, crystal, vase, 5½"..................................... 60.00
Victorian, crystal, wine, 2½-oz................................. 30.00
Waverly, crystal, bowl, salad; 7".............................. 20.00
Waverly, crystal, butter dish, sq, 6".......................... 65.00

Waverly, crystal, plate, luncheon; 8" 10.00
Waverly, crystal, tumbler, juice; #5019, blown, ftd, 5-oz......20.00
Waverly, crystal, vase, fan shape, ftd, 7" 45.00
Yeoman, crystal, bowl, banana split; ftd 7.00
Yeoman, crystal, pitcher, qt 70.00
Yeoman, Flamingo, bowl, lemon; rnd, w/lid, 5" 20.00
Yeoman, Hawthorne, bowl, berry; hdls, 8½" 35.00
Yeoman, Hawthorne, saucer 10.00
Yeoman, Marigold, bottle, cologne; w/stopper 180.00
Yeoman, Marigold, plate, cheese; hdls........................ 25.00
Yeoman, Moongleam, champagne, 6-oz 22.00
Yeoman, Moongleam, vase, #516-2, 6" 60.00
Yeoman, Sahara, platter, oval, 12"............................. 19.00
Yeoman, Sahara, tumbler, 8-oz 20.00

Herend

Herend, Hungary, was the center of a thriving pottery industry as early as the mid-1800s. Decorative items as well as tablewares were made in keeping with the styles of the times. One of the factories located in this area was founded by Moritz Fisher, who often marked his wares with a cojoined MF. Items described in the following listings may be marked simply Herend, indicating the city, or with a manufacturer's backstamp.

Rothschild Bird, serving dish, $200.00. (Photo courtesy Garth's Auctions Inc.)

Chanticleer, bowl, rimmed soup; 8" 75.00
Chanticleer, candleholder, ea 55.00
Chanticleer, cup & saucer, ftd 75.00
Chanticleer, teapot, 4-cup 200.00
Chinese Bouquet, cache pot, 6x7¾" 100.00
Chinese Bouquet, coffeepot, cr/sug w/lid, oval 16" tray.......270.00
Chinese Bouquet, cup & saucer, demitasse 30.00
Chinese Bouquet, dish, sq, pierced rim, 1½x7x7" 40.00
Chinese Bouquet, plate, 9" 48.00
Chinois, cache pot, 8"... 400.00
Fortuna, fish platter, 19½"...................................... 175.00
Fortuna, salt cellar, dbl.. 200.00
Fortuna, tureen, w/lid 750.00
Peach Tree, covered dish, 4½" 55.00
Queen Victoria, box, yel rose finial, 3⅛" dia 100.00
Queen Victoria, candelabra, 3-light, 8⅞", pr 500.00
Queen Victoria, dessert stand, 2-tier, rtcl rims, 14¾".......600.00
Queen Victoria, pendant, 2" dia............................... 30.00
Queen Victoria, teapot, 6½" 275.00
Queen Victoria, tureen, w/bird finial, 12¾", +15" platter.......600.00
Queen Victoria, urn, ovoid, scrolled hdls, domed lid, ped ft, 20" ..900.00
Queen Victoria, washbowl & pitcher, 14¼", 15" 1,000.00
Rothschild Bird, bowl, w/lid, 4x3½"......................... 100.00
Rothschild Bird, cake plate, hdls, 11"...................... 250.00

Rothschild Bird, candy bowl, 3x4½" dia 70.00
Rothschild Bird, candy dish, 1 hdl, 1915-30, 2½x8x7" 75.00
Rothschild Bird, chocolate pot, 6" 200.00
Rothschild Bird, dresser box, 3x4" dia 80.00
Rothschild Bird, jardiniere, #6300/35, 16x16" 425.00
Rothschild Bird, marmalade, w/lid & underplate, 5" 100.00
Rothschild Bird, platter, 16" L, from $275 to 325.00
Rothschild Bird, salt cellar, dbl; shaped center hdl, 6" L 80.00
Rothschild Bird, vase, baluster, 5" 100.00
Rothschild Bird, vase, 7¾x4" 150.00

Miscellaneous

Figurine, boy riding swan, #5415, 3" 100.00
Figurine, elephant w/trunk up, gr fishnet on wht, #52141/#2540, 3½" ... 170.00
Figurine, man seated on Tokaj bbl & lifting glass, 7⅛x5x4" 150.00
Figurine, nude woman kneeling w/snake, rpr, #5722/s, 9¾" 225.00
Figurine, peasant lady w/fish in apron, yel bonnet, 10¼" 175.00
Figurine, tiger growling, natural coloring, 5¾x18" 700.00
Vase, plums on branch, hdls w/gold, w/lid, 10½x6½" 125.00

Heubach

Gebruder Heubach is a German company that has been in operation since the 1800s, producing quality bisque figurines and novelty items. They are perhaps most famous for their doll heads and piano babies, most of which are marked with the circular rising sun device containing an 'H' superimposed over a 'C.' Items with arms and hands positioned away from the body are more valuable, and color of hair and intaglio eyes affect price as well. Our advisor for this category is Grace Ochsner; she is listed in the Directory under Illinois. See also Dolls, Heubach.

Babies (2) in wht sit on grassy base, 4½x5", from $800 to 975.00
Baby girl (nude) on knees, blond hair, 6½" 575.00
Baby playing w/toes, mk, 9" L 725.00
Baby sitting, detailed dress, intaglio eyes, 2 teeth, 8½", NM 725.00

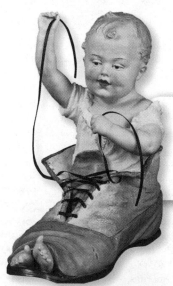

Baby sitting in shoe, replaced shoelace, 12", $875.00. (Photo courtesy McMasters Harris Auction Company)

Baby standing nude in father's brn shoes, #84, 8" 700.00
Baby w/molded hair, intaglio eyes, seated in wht gown, 11" 500.00
Bather in gr china tub, ft to mouth, 4½x5½" 900.00
Boy & girl fishing, wooden poles, 8½", pr 475.00
Boy & girl in beaded costumes, intaglio eyes, on base, rprs, 14" .. 1,000.00
Boy in nightshirt w/pug dog, 7", from $1,500 to 1,700.00

Child in Easter bunny outfit by egg, 6x3¼" 625.00
Child praying w/cross on chain around neck, blond, 11" 395.00
Dog, gray & wht short-haired terrier down on front paws, 9" L ... 250.00
Dog at side of pin tray, 3" H 45.00
Dog on haunches, wht w/tan collar, 9x3⅝" 375.00
Dutch boy holding cap to head, 6", from $300 to 400.00
Girl dancing & swinging skirt, tambourine at ft, 11" 500.00
Girl curtsying on base, 12x6½" 400.00
Girl in nightgown curtsying, roses at ft, 11" 475.00
Girl seated on wicker stool holds dress wide, intaglio eyes, 12" 400.00
Girl w/upturned bonnet, frilly dress, seated w/legs out, 5¾" 175.00
Lady w/flowing dress, bl scarf, blond hair, #9031, 8", pr 500.00
Man & lady, fine pk attire w/gold trim, #62/#00, 14", pr 850.00
Santa on stump, crepe-paper clothes, seated on cb candy container, 9" ... 850.00
Vase, Nouveau lady w/flowing veils on lav, ca 1884, 7" 495.00

Higgins

Acclaimed contemporary glass artists Frances and Michael Higgins founded their Chicago-area studio in 1948. They are credited with rediscovering and refining the ancient craft of glass fusing, resulting in 'modern miracles with everyday glass.'

Essentially, fusing can be described as the creation of a 'glass sandwich.' On one piece of enamel-coated glass, a design is either drawn with colored enamels or pieced with glass segments. Over this, another piece of enameled glass is laid. Placed on a mold, the object is then heated. Under heat the glass 'slumps' into the shape of the mold. The design is fused between the outer glass pieces with additional layers often adding to the texture and color complexity.

The Higginses applied their fusing technique to everything from tableware such as bowls, plates, and candleholders, to ashtrays, jewelry, vases, mobiles, sculptures, lamps, clocks, and even 'rondelay' room dividers. Higgins buyers in the 1950s were immediately attracted to the novelty of fused glass, the colorful 'modern' designs, and the variety of items available. Today collectors can also appreciate the artistry and skill involved in the creation of Higgins glass and the imaginative genius of its makers.

In 1957, Michael and Frances Higgins became associated with Dearborn Glass Company of Chicago. Dearborn marketed Higgins designs to a mass audience, greatly increasing the couple's 'brand-name' recognition. Following a brief association in 1965 with Haeger Potteries, the Higginses opened their own studio in Riverside, Illinois. Michael Higgins died in 1999, Frances Higgins in 2004. The studio continues today under the direction of their longtime associates and designated successors, Louise and Jonathan Wimmer, still creating glass objects in the distinctive Higgins style.

Higgins's pieces are readily identifiable by an almost-always-present lower-case signature. From 1948 until 1957, pieces were engraved on the reverse with the name 'higgins,' or the complete artist name. In 1951, a raised 'dancing man' logo was also added. Dearborn and Haeger pieces (1957 – 1965) are denoted either by a gold 'higgins' signature on the surface, or by a signature in the colorway. Since 1966 the marking has been an engraved 'higgins' on the reverse, sometimes accompanied by the artist's name. Following the death of Frances Higgins, pieces have been signed 'higgins studio.'

The Higgins Glass Studio is located at 33 East Quincy Street, Riverside, IL 60546 (708-447-2787, www.higginsglass.com). For more information we recommend *Higgins: Adventures in Glass,* and *Higgins: Poetry in Glass* (Schiffer), both by our advisor, Donald-Brian Johnson, and Leslie Piña. Mr. Johnson is listed in the Directory under Nebraska.

Ashtray, Balloons, rogue (free-form), longest side: 9", from $175 to .. 200.00
Ashtray, Barbaric Jewels, circular, 8½" dia, from $100 to 150.00

Ashtray, Country Garden (floral), rectangular, 5x7", from $75 to...100.00
Ashtray, Forget-Me-Not, rectangular, 7x10", from $125 to 150.00
Ashtray, Mandarin, rectangular, 10x14", from $150 to................ 175.00
Ashtray, Rose, 7x10", from $150 to.. 175.00
Bonbon, Arabesque Apple, scalloped, metal base, 7¼" dia, $250 to ..275.00
Bowl, Blueray, gold decor at scalloped rim, 7¼", from $125 to..... 175.00
Bowl, common circular shape, production pc, 12¼", from $225 to ..350.00
Bowl, common squarish shape, production pc, 7", from $125 to 225.00
Bowl, Daisy, 8¼", from $175 to.. 200.00
Bowl, One Man Band (Jonathan Wimmer), 24", from $3,250 to..3,500.00
Bowl, Pointille, bl/gold, 17", from $650 to.............................. 700.00
Bowl, Stardust, yels & grs, crimped rim, 11½", from $150 to 200.00
Bowl, Wide Stripe, chartreuse & wht w/gold sea urchins, 17", $600 to..650.00
Candleholders, Delphinium Blue, 2½", pr from $100 to.............. 150.00
Candleholders, dinner; 8½", pr from $350 to.............................. 400.00
Cigarette box, Keys, glass base, 7x4", from $200 to 225.00
Clock, Rhapsody (Roman Stripe pattern), 16¼" L, from $500 to ...550.00
Jewelry, coral nugget necklace w/brass spirals, +earrings, $900 to... 1,000.00
Jewelry, ivory pendant w/embedded jewels/central coral design, $200 to... 250.00
Jewelry, Shards pendant & earrings, from $450 to 500.00
Mobile, Dingle-Dangle box mobile, 16½x12½", from $900 to ..1,000.00
Mobile, Jumping Jane & Johnny people-mobiles, 23" L, pr from $850 to .900.00
Mobile, 23x36" L, from $1,500 to 1,750.00
Plaque, October Tree (Louise Wimmer), 9", from $125 to 150.00
Plate, Arabesque, bl, 12¼", from $225 to.................................... 250.00
Plate, Buttercup, golden yel & orange, 13¼", from $225 to 250.00
Plate, Chance Encounter (Jonathan Wimmer), 17", from $1,000 to.. 1,250.00
Plate, Fruit, sq, 14", from $200 to... 225.00

Pi Plate, Michael Higgins, 15", from $2,750.00 to $3,000.00. (Photo courtesy Leslie Piña from Higgins: Poetry in Glass, Schiffer)

Plate, Sunrise to Sunset (Jonathan Wimmer), 11", from $900 to........ 1,000.00
Platter, abstract butterflies, 20", from $1,350 to.......................... 1,500.00
Rondelay circles, daisy & winegold, 9" dia, ea from $150 to 200.00
Sculpture, Flower, bl w/glass leaves, wire stem, 27" L, from $400 to...450.00
Sculpture, Sparkler, bl & gold panel, brass stand, 9x5", $1,000 to.. 1,100.00
Sculpture, Walkpast Eye (Michael Higgins), 10x11", from $2,500 to ..2,750.00
Server, relish; Classic Line, 15" dia, from $350 to......................... 375.00
Trifle dish, studio coral pattern, 10x16", from $450 to................. 500.00
Vase, Classic Line dropout, bl, heavy, gold at base, 7½x7", $600 to ...650.00
Vase, Small Chips (Frances Higgins), 6", from $1,000 to 1,100.00
Vase, wht daisy border dropout, 5½" dia, from $200 to................. 250.00

Hilton Pottery

The Hilton family was involved in pottery making in the Catawaba Valley of North Carolina as early as the end of the Civil War. The branch responsible for items marked 'Hilton' was established in 1935 by Ernest Hilton in Marion. The wares they produced were of the typical 'Jugtown' variety, high glazed and hand thrown. Ernest died in 1948, and the pottery closed in 1953.

Bottle, lg cobalt splotches on gray, crazing, att, 9½" 480.00
Creamer, daisies, wht/gr heavy slip, 4½", EX............................... 420.00
Figurine, African American man, wht hair, Bible in left hand, rpr, 7".. 1,800.00
Figurine, lady, long bl dress/yel hat, bag in right arm, rpr, 8" 1,320.00
Figurine, opera singer, blk dress w/lg bl flower, hands clasped, 6"...1,080.00
Pitcher, cabins/trees/river/mtns beyond, 9½", EX 1,320.00
Pitcher, cobalt top over dk gray, ovoid w/waisted neck, unmk, 6½" ...240.00
Salt cellar, clear glaze w/cobalt areas, att, 1¾x2¼".......................... 95.00
Vase, barn/fence/house, brn/wht on tan, cylindrical w/step-bk neck, 5" .510.00
Vase, farmhouse, fence & barn, mtns beyond, bl/cream, 5x6½", NM.....450.00
Vase, oak limb w/2 acorns, brn tones on cream, Mrs FW Hilton, 3¾"....600.00
Vase, red pnt w/fruit decal, 16x12x9" 135.00
Vase, rural landscape w/cabin, bridge, sgn Clara, rpr, 10" 480.00
Vase, salt-glazed cobalt w/orange peel texture by CB Maston, 6x7"...275.00

Historical Glass

Glassware commemorating particularly significant historical events became popular in the late 1800s. Bread trays were the most common form, but plates, mugs, pitchers, and other items were also pressed in clear as well as colored glass. It was sold in vast amounts at the 1876 Philadelphia Centennial Exposition by various manufacturers who exhibited their wares on the grounds. It remained popular well into the twentieth century.

In the listings that follow, L numbers refer to a book by Lindsey, a standard guide used by many collectors. Our advisor for this category is Darlene Yohe; she is listed in the Directory under Arkansas. See also Bread Plates; Pattern Glass.

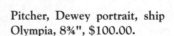

Pitcher, Dewey portrait, ship Olympia, 8¾", $100.00.

Ale glass, Centennial.. 60.00
Bottle, Century of Progress 1833-1933, skyscraper/cabin, 6x6"...... 38.00
Bust, Dewey, Manila 1898, 5"... 145.00
Bust, MJ Owens, frosted, 4¾" 138.00
Butter dish, Lincoln Drape 145.00
Butter dish, US Grant, Patriot & Soldier.................................... 60.00
Celery, HMS Pinafore, Actress.. 170.00
Celery, Independence Hall 65.00
Compote, Actress, Jenny Lind... 85.00
Creamer, Peace & Plenty, milk glass, pontil scar, 4⅝" 500.00
Creamer or spooner, Washington Centennial............................... 70.00
Flask, McKinley & Hobart, Distilled Protection, 7" 475.00
Goblet, Emblem Centenial, L-61 .... 45.00
Goblet, Liberty Bell, Gillinder, 1876, 6⅛x3½ 48.00

Goblet, Philadelphia Centennial, 6¼x3" 65.00
Hat, 1908 Presidential Campaign, milk glass w/red pnt 125.00
Lamp, Goddess of Liberty, 1887 Centennial 125.00
Mug, Assassination 60.00
Mug, Centennial, waisted 90.00
Mug, Columbus/Washington, L-2 .... 175.00
Mug, Our Country's Martyrs, Lincoln & Garfield, 2⅝x2¼" 110.00
Mug, Protection & Prosperity, Maj Wm McKinley, 3¼" 75.00
Mug, Tennessee, L-102 .... 55.00
Mustard dish, Dewey bust, Xd flags on lid, milk glass, 4¼" 55.00
Paperweight, Shakespeare, frosted, Gillinder 150.00
Pitcher, Liberty Bell, John Hancock, milk glass 595.00
Pitcher, Lincoln Drape 400.00
Plate, Admiral Dewey, 7" 95.00
Plate, flag w/eagles & fleur-de-lis border, milk glass, 7¼", NM 30.00
Plate, Last Supper 55.00
Plate, Old State House, L-32 .... 50.00
Plate, Pope Leo, milk glass, L-240 .... 40.00
Plate, Present From the Isle of Man, 10" 60.00
Plate, Union, 6½" 60.00
Spooner, Liberty Bell 50.00
Sugar bowl, US Grant, Patriot & Soldier 25.00
Tumbler, Lincoln Drape 60.00
Tumbler, McKinley, L-337 .... 50.00

Hobbs, Brockunier, and Company

Hobbs and Brockunier's South Wheeling Glass Works was in operation during the last quarter of the nineteenth century. They are most famous for their peachblow, amberina, Daisy and Button, and Hobnail pattern glass. The mainstay of the operation, however, was druggist items and plain glassware — bowls, mugs, and simple footed pitchers with shell handles. See also Frances Ware.

Vase, Hobnail, ruby over frost, 9½", $95.00. (Photo courtesy Cincinnati Art Galleries)

Bar bottle, Polka Dot, ruby 225.00
Bowl, Daisy & Button, Old Gold, sq, 6½" 40.00
Bowl, Dew Drop, sapphire, shell ft, 8" 250.00
Bowl, Maltese & Ribbon, Old Gold, sq, 7" 45.00
Butter dish, Daisy & Button, crystal w/amber stain, sm 125.00
Celery dish, Polka Dot, ruby amber 140.00
Creamer, Polka Dot, sapphire, cylindrical neck & top 95.00
Cruet, Polka Dot, rubena verte, teepee form, 7" 285.00
Cruet, Vasa Murrhina, rose/yel spatter w/gold spangle, bulbous, 7" .. 175.00
Finger bowl, Daisy & Button, crystal w/amber stain 45.00
Finger bowl, Dew Drop, canary 25.00
Finger bowl, Maltese & Ribbon, crystal 30.00
Jug, Dew Drop, Marine Green, #3 .... 160.00
Match safe, Daisy & Button, crystal (no stain) 85.00
Molasses can, Dew Drop, Old Gold 300.00

Molasses can, Polka Dot, Old Gold, 12-oz 135.00
Nappy, Maltese & Ribbon, canary, 4½" 20.00
Pitcher, Hobnail, amberina, rnd w/sq mouth, 8" 400.00
Pitcher, Hobnail, ruby opal, clear reed hdl, 8" 325.00
Pitcher, Maltese & Ribbon, sapphire, ½-gal 135.00
Plate, Daisy & Button, canary, 7" 25.00
Sugar bowl, Dew Drop, canary, w/lid 65.00
Sugar bowl, Polka Dot, Marine Green, w/lid 140.00
Tankard, Daisy & Button, crystal w/amber stain, 2-qt 175.00
Toothpick holder, Daisy & Button, amberina, 3 ft, 3" 145.00
Tumbler, Dew Drop, sapphire 45.00
Whiskey, Daisy & Button, Old Gold 30.00

Holt Howard

Novelty ceramics marked Holt Howard were produced in Japan from the 1950s into the 1970s, and these have become quite collectible. They're not only marked, but most are dated as well. There are several lines to reassemble — the rooster, the white cat, figural banks, Christmas angels, and Santas, to name only a few — but the one that most Holt Howard collectors seem to gravitate toward is the pixie line. For more information see *Garage Sale and Flea Market Annual* (Collector Books).

Key: KK — Kozy Kitten

Ashtray, KK, gr & wht pillow w/brass match holder, 1958 .... 85.00
Ashtray, Starry-eyed Santa 35.00
Bank, Coin Kitty Bobbing Head, 5½", from $175 to 200.00
Bell, winking Santa, 1958, 4", from $12 to 15.00

Bottle, French Dressing; winking chef, $175.00. (Photo courtesy Pat and Ann Duncan)

Butter dish, KK, 2 kittens peek from under lid, 7", from $90 to ... 110.00
Butter dish, Rooster, emb rooster, ¼-lb, from $35 to 45.00
Candleholder, Ponytail Princess, fan before face, 1959, 4", $50 to ... 60.00
Candleholder, Santa in antique car w/stoplight candle ring, 1959, pr ... 65.00
Candleholder, Santa in converible, 1959, 3½", ea 25.00
Candleholders, holly w/leaves, set of 4, MIB 25.00
Candleholders, horse w/red hearts & flowers, 1964, 4¼", pr 50.00
Candleholders, Santa w/gift bag, candles go in bags, 3½", pr 30.00
Candleholders/bell, 3 Wise Men, 3½", set from $65 to 85.00
Candy dish, Santa head, beard forms dish, 1959, 7x4" 35.00
Cheese crock, KK, Stinky Cheese on side, 2 kissing cats on lid, 1958 ... 60.00
Cheese crock, wht w/holly decor, Mr & Mrs Santa on lid, 4½" 40.00
Christmas ornaments, Santa holding 4 different things, set of 8, MIB ... 55.00
Cocktail onions jar, Pixie Ware, gr head finial, 1958 .... 150.00
Coffee jar, Pixie Ware, Instant Coffee, yel head finial w/spoon, 1960 ... 250.00
Coffeepot, Rooster, wht w/rooster decor, electric, 1960, from $45 to ... 55.00
Creamer & sugar bowl, KK, head sugar/body creamer, $125 to 150.00

Cups, tomato w/leaf-shaped hdl, 6 for............................ 24.00
Egg cup, Rooster, dbl, from $9 to................................. 12.00
Figurine, girl holding Christmas tree in left hand, 5½"......... 30.00
Figurines, pheasants, wings spread, 1958, 3: 10x8", 7x5½", 5½x4"...80.00
Groceries clip, face in front, H Japan H sticker, 2½x2¼"........ 80.00
Head vase, Christmas decor, 1959, 4"............................ 60.00
Jam 'n Jelly jar, Pixie Ware, yel head finial, w/spoon, from $75 to....85.00

Jar, Instant Coffee; Pixie, from $245.00 to $285.00. (Photo courtesy Pat and Ann Duncan)

Lamp, oil; Holly Girl, unused wick, 7"......................... 60.00
Letter holder, KK, wire spring on bk, 1958, 7", from $40 to..... 50.00
Lunch set, gr lettuce leaf plate w/red tomato cup, 1962, set of 4.... 50.00
Marmalade jar, Pixie Ware, yel head finial, 5½", minimum value ...800.00
Martini shaker, butler (Jeeves), 9", from $175 to.............. 200.00
Mayonnaise jar, Pixie Ware, orange head finial w/spoon, 1959, $200 to..235.00
Memo minder, KK, full-bodied cat, legs cradle note pad, 7", $60 to... 75.00
Mug, KK, cat on side, w/squeaker, 8-oz, from $35 to.............. 45.00
Mustard jar, Pixie Ware, scowling yel head spoon finial, from $85 to.. 110.00
Napkin holder, Rooster, from $20 to............................. 30.00
Napkin rings, wht mice on holly leaves, ⅞", set of 4............ 35.00
Pitcher, juice; orange (fruit) wht, slim, 1962, 7⅞"............ 60.00
Pitcher, KK, wht w/kitten, 1960, 7½", from $100 to............. 120.00

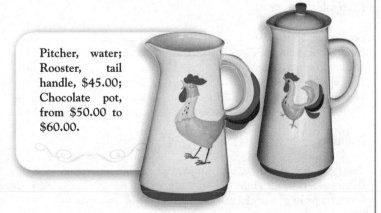

Pitcher, water; Rooster, tail handle, $45.00; Chocolate pot, from $50.00 to $60.00.

Planter, doe & fawn, wht w/gold trim, 1960, 7¼x5".............. 35.00
Planter, Santa Express, Santa riding train, 6x7½"............. 45.00
Punch set, Santa, 6x7¾" bowl, 8 mugs & ladle................. 235.00
Recipe box, kitchen items & food w/rooster pop-up inside, 3½x5¼" ... 60.00
Relish jar, Pixie Ware, crabby gr head spoon finial, 1959, $200 to ..250.00
Sewing box, KK, kitten on pillow, tape measure tongue, 1958....... 50.00
Shakers, angel girls, 1 w/bells, other w/hands in muff, 1959, pr 40.00
Shakers, chick on egg cup, 1959, 3¾", 4-pc..................... 42.00
Shakers, Pixie Ware, Salty & Peppy, wooden side hdls, pr from $125 to.. 150.00
Shakers, Ponytail Princess, 3½-4", pr from $35 to............. 45.00

Shakers, Santa winking, w/label, pr........................... 30.00
Snack set, lettuce leaf plate & tomato cup, 8-pc, serves 4............. 35.00
Spoon rest, Rooster, 1961, 4x3½".............................. 15.00
Spoons, Pixie Ware, set of 4................................. 700.00
Tea bag holders, teapot shape, set of 4 in metal rack 35.00
Tray, Santa face, starry eyed, 1959, 1x6" dia 45.00
Twine holder, rooster head on burlap sack, 8x10", MIP............ 85.00
Vase, KK, full-bodied cat, male or female, 6½", ea $65 to 80.00
Vase, Rooster, figural, 6¼", from $25 to....................... 35.00
Vase, speckled gr, lg split-lip rim, 1958, 8".................... 75.00
Wall pocket, anthropomorphic sunflower, lg...................... 35.00
Wall pocket, KK, full-bodied cat w/hook tail, 7x3", $45 to............ 60.00

Homer Laughlin

The Homer Laughlin China Company of Newell, West Virginia, was founded in 1871. The superior dinnerware they displayed at the Centennial Exposition in Philadelphia in 1876 won the highest award of excellence. From that time to the present, they have continued to produce quality dinnerware and kitchenware, many lines of which are very popular collectibles. Most of the dinnerware is marked with the name of the pattern and occasionally with the shape name as well. The 'HLC' trademark is usually followed by a number series, the first two digits of which indicate the year of its manufacture. For further information we recommend *Collector's Encyclopedia of Fiesta, 10th Edition*, by Sharon and Bob Huxford; and *The Collector's Encyclopedia of Homer Laughlin China* by Joanne Jasper (both available from Collector Books). Another fine source of information is *Homer Laughlin, A Giant Among Dishes*, by Jo Cunningham (Schiffer). Our advisors for Virginia Rose are Jack and Treva Hamlin; they are listed in the Directory under Ohio.

Our values are base prices, and apply to decaled lines only — not solid-color dinnerware. Very desirable patterns on the shapes named in our listings may increase values by as much as 75%. See also Blue Willow; Fiesta; Harlequin; Riviera.

Century

For English Garden, Sun Porch, and Mexicana lines, double the values listed below. Some items from these lines are rare (for instance, the teapot in Sun Porch) and no market value has been established for them.

Plate, English Garden (rare pattern), 7", $26.00.

Baker, 9", from $14 to....................................... 20.00
Bowl, deep, 1-pt, from $23 to................................ 32.00
Bowl, nappy, 8", from $22 to................................. 26.00
Bowl, oval, 8", from $20 to.................................. 25.00
Butter dish, from $125 to................................... 150.00

Coffeecup, demitasse; from $28 to............................ 38.00
Cup, coffee; from $10 to................................... 15.00
Jug, w/lid, 2½-pt, from $85 to.......................... 100.00
Jug, ⅝-pt, from $55 to.................................... 65.00
Muffin cover, rare, from $65 to........................... 75.00
Platter, 10", from $22 to.................................. 26.00
Platter, 15", from $32 to.................................. 42.00

Debutante

For Suntone, add 20%; add 25% for Karol China gold-decorated items.

Platter, Dogwood, 13", from $16.00 to $20.00.

Bowl, coupe soup; from $6 to.............................. 8.00
Bowl, fruit 5.00
Casserole, w/lid, from $30 to............................. 35.00
Chop plate, 15", from $16 to.............................. 20.00
Creamer, from $9 to....................................... 12.00
Dish (platter), 11", from $12 to.......................... 14.00
Pie server, from $20 to................................... 30.00
Teapot, from $40 to....................................... 50.00

Eggshell Georgian

Teapot, Rambler Rose, $95.00.

Bowl, fruit; 5", from $4 to................................ 8.00
Bowl, oatmeal; 6", from $10 to............................ 15.00
Casserole, w/lid, from $60 to............................. 85.00
Pickle dish, from $6 to................................... 8.00
Plate, rim soup; deep; from $15 to........................ 18.00
Plate, 10", from $15 to................................... 18.00
Shakers, pr from $35 to................................... 60.00

Eggshell Nautilus

Bowl, 9", from $14 to..................................... 16.00

Bowl, cream soup; from $10 to............................. 15.00
Bowl, rim soup; deep, from $12 to......................... 18.00
Bowl, 15", from $16 to.................................... 26.00
Creamer, from $15 to...................................... 25.00
Cup & saucer, AD; from $13 to............................. 20.00
Egg cup, dbl (Swing)...................................... 16.00

Gravy boat and undertray, Aristocrat, from $30.00 to $35.00.

Plate, 8", from $9 to..................................... 12.00
Sugar bowl, w/lid, from $20 to............................ 30.00

Empress

Add 25% for solid colors. See also Bluebird China.

Baker, 8", from $10 to.................................... 12.00
Bone dish, from $6 to..................................... 8.00
Bowl, cream soup; from $12 to............................. 16.00
Bowl, 10", from $12 to.................................... 16.00
Celery tray, 11", from $20 to............................. 25.00
Creamer, 5-oz, from $12 to................................ 16.00
Jug, 24s, 27-oz, from $26 to.............................. 28.00
Ladle, rare, from $18 to.................................. 22.00
Oyster tureen, 8", from $45 to............................ 50.00
Plate, 10", from $9 to.................................... 12.00
Platter, 8", from $12 to.................................. 16.00
Platter, 17", from $30 to................................. 35.00
Teacup, from $6 to.. 8.00

Marigold

Bowl, deep, 5", from $10 to............................... 12.00
Bowl, flat soup; from $12 to.............................. 18.00
Creamer, from $18 to...................................... 23.00
Egg cup, dbl; from $14 to................................. 16.00
Plate, sq, 8", from $14 to................................ 19.00
Plate, 10", from $10 to................................... 12.00

Nautilus

Baker, 10", from $22 to................................... 28.00
Baker (oval bowl), 9", from $12 to........................ 16.00
Bowl, coupe soup; from $6 to.............................. 8.00
Bowl, fruit; from $5 to................................... 8.00
Bowl, 15½", from $16 to................................... 24.00
Plate, 9", from $8 to..................................... 12.00
Sugar bowl, w/lid, from $20 to............................ 28.00

Rhythm

Add 25% for American Provincial.

Bowl, coupe soup; from $8 to.............................. 10.00
Bowl, 13½", from $14 to................................... 18.00

Creamer, from $14 to.. 20.00
Plate, 10", from $9 to.. 12.00

Platter, American Provincial, 12", from $20.00 to $22.00.

Spoon rest, from $100 to... 125.00
Sugar bowl, w/lid, from $20 to... 25.00

Swing

Add 30% for Oriental patterns and Mexicali.

Baker, from $25 to... 32.00
Bowl, nappy, rnd, from $25 to 35.00
Bowl, oatmeal; from $6 to... 10.00
Butter dish (Jade), from $40 to... 50.00
Casserole, w/lid, from $35 to.. 45.00
Cup, demitasse; from $10 to.. 18.00
Egg cup, dbl, from $12 to... 18.00
Plate, rimmed soup; deep, from $15 to 18.00
Sugar bowl, w/lid, from $14 to.. 18.00
Teapot, from $85 to... 125.00
Tray, utility; from $14 to.. 18.00

Virginia Rose

Use the high end of the price range to evaluate popular patterns such as JJ59, VR128, Spring Wreath, and Wild Rose.

Baker, 9", from $18 to... 26.00
Bread plate, rare, from $20 to 25.00
Cup & saucer, from $12 to... 15.00
Jug, 5", from $65 to 80.00

Milk pitcher, Bouquet, 5½", $90.00 to $100.00.

Mixing bowls, set of 3, from $115 to 145.00
Mug, coffee; from $50 to.. 100.00

Plate, 8", rare, from $15 to... 18.00
Platter, 11½", from $18 to... 26.00
Sauceboat, from $23 to... 30.00
Shakers, Kitchen Kraft, scarce, pr from $160 to........................ 185.00

Wells

Add 25% for solid colors Sienna Brown, French Rose, or Leaf Green.

Bowl, bouillon; from $10 to... 12.00
Bowl, oatmeal; from $14 to... 18.00
Cake plate, from $18 to... 24.00
Casserole, from $35 to 45.00
Cup, demitasse; from $22 to.. 30.00
Egg cup, dbl; from $18 to... 22.00
Jug, 24s, w/lid, from $60 to... 70.00
Muffin cover, from $55 to.. 75.00
Platter, 15", from $18 to.. 22.00
Teacup & saucer, from $9 to.. 14.00
Teapot, from $50 to.. 60.00

Hoya Crystal Inc.

Hoya Cristal Inc. originated in 1946 in the town of Hoya, Japan. They were manufacturers of fine crystal. Upon learning that General McArthur partook of a glass or two of scotch every evening, Hoya designed a double old-fashioned glass especially for him and presented it to him for his enjoyment during the evening cocktail hour. Today, Hoya Crystal is one of the world's largest and most respected crystal companies. Our advisor for this category is William L. Geary; he is listed in the Directory under Sweden.

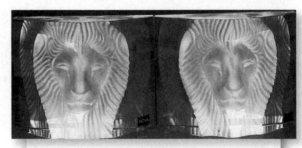

Bookends, lion head motif, 4x5x3", $210.00. (Photo courtesy Du Mouchelles)

Book, crystal, presented in open format, 3".................................. 195.00
Clock, gold colored, cased in clear rectangle, 6¾" 375.00
Frame, octagonal, lg, pr... 215.00
Sculpture, eagle, crystal, on rectangular base, 7¼"...................... 500.00
Vase, Aster, crystal w/vertical cuts, detailed X-cuts at top, 16¾" ...7,900.00
Vase, Imperial, crystal w/bl at base, 6-sided, 9" 665.00

Hull

The A. E. Hull Pottery was formed in 1905 in Zanesville, Ohio, and in the early years produced stoneware specialities. They expanded in 1907, adding a second plant and employing over 200 workers. By 1920 they were manufacturing a full line of stoneware, art pottery with both airbrushed and blended glazes, florist pots, and gardenware. They also produced toilet ware and kitchen items with a white semiporcelain body. Although these continued to be staple products, after the stock market crash of 1929, emphasis was shifted to tile production. By the mid-'30s interest in art pottery production was growing, and over the next 15 years, several lines of matt pastel floral-decorated patterns were designed, consisting of vases, planters, baskets, ewers, and bowls in various sizes.

The Red Riding Hood cookie jar, patented in 1943, proved so successful that a whole line of figural kitchenware and novelty items was added. They continued to be produced well into the '50s. (See also Little Red Riding Hood.) Through the '40s their floral artware lines flooded the market, due to the restriction of foreign imports. Although best known for their pastel matt-glazed ware, some of the lines were high gloss. Rosella, glossy coral on a pink clay body, was produced for a short time only; and Magnolia, although offered in a matt glaze, was produced in gloss as well.

The plant was destroyed in 1950 by a flood which resulted in a devastating fire when the floodwater caused the kilns to explode. The company rebuilt and equipped their new factory with the most modern machinery. It was soon apparent that the matt glaze could not be duplicated through the more modern equipment. The new plant concentrated on high-gloss artware lines such as Parchment and Pine and Ebb Tide. Figural planters and novelties, piggy banks, and dinnerware were produced in abundance in the late '50s and '60s. By the mid-'70s dinnerware and florist ware were the mainstay of their business. The firm discontinued operations in 1985.

Our advisor, Brenda Roberts, has compiled two lovely books, *The Collector's Encyclopedia of Hull Pottery* and *The Collector's Ultimate Encyclopedia of Hull Pottery,* both with full-color photos and current values, available from Collector Books.

Special note to Hull collectors: Reproductions are on the market in all categories of Hull pottery — matt florals, Red Riding Hood, and later lines including House 'n Garden dinnerware.

Blossom Flite, candleholder, #T-11, 3", ea from $45 to 65.00
Blossom Flite, ewer, #T-13, 13½", from $165 to 210.00
Blossom Flite, honey pot, #T-1, 6", from $65 to 105.00
Blossom Flite, teapot, #T-14, 8", from $140 to 195.00
Blossom Flite, vase, basket, #T-4, 8½", from $170 to 210.00
Bow-Knot, candleholder, #B-17, 4", ea from $140 to 175.00

Capri, basket, #F-38, 1961, 6½", from $40 to.............................. 60.00
Capri, basket, leaf, 12¼", from $50 to 75.00
Capri, candy dish, w/lid, unmk, 8½", from $50 to 75.00
Capri, ewer, #87, 12", from $135 to.. 185.00
Capri, swan, #23, 8½", from $50 to 75.00
Capri, vase, #58, 13¾", from $55 to 75.00
Cinderella Kitchenware (Blossom), bowl, mixing; #20, 5½", $25 to.. 35.00
Cinderella Kitchenware (Blossom), teapot, #26, 42-oz, from $140 to... 180.00
Cinderella Kitchenware (Bouquet), cookie jar, unmk, 10½", $140 to .. 180.00
Cinderella Kitchenware (Bouquet), pitcher, #29, 32-oz, from $25 to 35.00
Continental, ashtray, #A-3, 12", from $40 to 60.00
Continental, flower bowl, #69, 9¼", from $40 to.......................... 60.00
Continental, flower dish, #51, 15½", from $25 to 40.00
Continental, vase, #64, 10", from $50 to 80.00
Dogwood, candleholder, #512, 3¾", ea from $135 to.................... 155.00
Dogwood, console bowl, #511, 11½", from $285 to 395.00
Dogwood, teapot, #507, 6½", from $300 to................................. 400.00
Dogwood, vase, #516, 4¾", from $75 to 95.00
Ebb Tide, basket, #E-11, 16½", from $210 to 265.00
Ebb Tide, console bowl, #E-12, 15¾", from $215 to 260.00
Ebb Tide, teapot, #E-14, 6½", from $235 to 265.00
Floral, bowl, cereal; #50, 6", from $14 to 18.00
Floral, bowl, mixing; #40, 9", from $45 to..................................... 65.00
Floral, casserole, ind; #47, open, 5", from $15 to 20.00
Floral, cookie jar, #48, 8¾", from $110 to 160.00
Heritageware, cookie jar, #A-18, 9½", from $100 to..................... 125.00
Heritageware, cruet, oil or vinegar; 6¼", ea from $25 to 35.00
Heritageware, grease jar, #A-3, 5¾", from $30 to.......................... 45.00
Heritageware, mug, 3¼", from $8 to 10.00
Heritageware, pitcher, #A-7, 4½", from $18 to 25.00
Heritageware, shaker, 3½", ea from $15 to 18.00
Imperial, duck planter, wht matt, #F-69, 1985, 10", from $25 to ... 35.00
Imperial, ewer, #F-480, 1965, 10½", from $45 to 75.00
Imperial, jardiniere, spiral, unmk, 1960, 10x12", from $155 to 210.00
Imperial, Victorian vase, #B-37, 1974, 9", from $10 to.................. 16.00
Iris, candleholder, #411, 5", ea from $125 to................................ 155.00
Iris, console bowl, #409, 12", from $280 to 340.00

Bow-Knot, ewer, #B-15, 13½", from $950.00 to $1,250.00. (Photo courtesy Brenda Roberts)

Iris, ewer, #401, 13½", from $500.00 to $625.00. (Photo courtesy Brenda Roberts)

Bow-Knot, teapot, #B-20, 6", from $450 to.................................. 650.00
Camellia, console bowl, #116, 12", from $300 to.......................... 375.00
Camellia, creamer, #111, 5", from $125 to................................... 150.00
Camellia, ewer, #128, 4¾", from $130 to 165.00
Camellia, jardiniere, #114, 8¼", from $325 to.............................. 395.00
Camellia, wall pocket, #125, 8½", from $400 to 525.00

Iris, jardiniere, #413, 5½", from $175 to... 205.00
Iris, vase, #404, 8½", from $210 to 250.00
Iris, vase, bud; #410, 7½", from $165 to 210.00
Lusterware, bulb bowl, unmk, 7½", from $60 to............................. 75.00
Lusterware, candleholder, unmk, 9", ea from $60 to...................... 95.00
Lusterware, flower frog, unmk, 4½", from $20 to 30.00
Lusterware, pitcher, unmk, 5¾", from $65 to................................. 85.00
Lusterware, vase, unmk, 12", from $80 to 120.00

Magnolia, gloss; console bowl, #H-23, 13", from $125 to 165.00
Magnolia, gloss; creamer, #H-21, 3¾", from $50 to 70.00
Magnolia, gloss; ewer, #H-3, 5½", from $60 to 85.00
Magnolia, matt; basket, #10, 10½", from $375 to 425.00
Magnolia, matt; sugar bowl, open, #25, 3¾", from $55 to 80.00

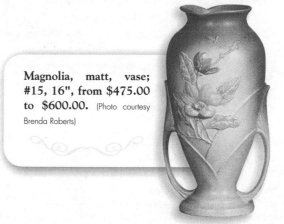

Magnolia, matt, vase; #15, 16", from $475.00 to $600.00. (Photo courtesy Brenda Roberts)

Magnolia, matt; vase, #17, 12¼", from $300 to 385.00
Mardi Gras/Granada, basket, #65, 8", from $100 to 145.00
Mardi Gras/Granada, teapot, #33, 5½", from $235 to 310.00
Mardi Gras/Granada, vase, #207, 7½", from $50 to 80.00
Novelty, dachshund figural, 1952, 14", from $175 to 225.00
Novelty, dancing girl, #955, 1938, 7", from $50 to 75.00
Novelty, giraffe planter, #115, 8", from $50 to 75.00
Novelty, jubilee ashtray, #407, 1957, 11½", from $30 to 45.00
Novelty, kitten planter, #61, 7½", from $40 to 55.00
Novelty, kitten w/spool planter, #89, 1951, 6", from $25 to 35.00
Novelty, lovebirds planter, #93, 1953, 6", from $40 to 60.00
Novelty, parrot w/cart planter, #60, 6", from $45 to 65.00
Novelty, peacock vase, #73, 1951, 10½", from $35 to 50.00
Novelty, pigeon planter, #91, 1955, 6", from $30 to 50.00
Novelty, poodle planter, #114, 8", from $50 to 75.00
Novelty, rooster planter, #53, 1953, 5¾", from $100 to 135.00
Novelty, scroll basket, #56, 6", from $50 to 80.00
Novelty, swan ashtray, #70, 1951, 4", from $14 to 20.00
Novelty, twin geese planter, #95, 1951, 6½", from $50 to 80.00
Novelty, unicorn vase, #99, 1952, 11½", from $95 to 110.00
Novelty, wishing well planter, #101, 1951, 7¾", from $40 to 60.00
Orchid, basket, #305, 7", from $600 to 800.00
Orchid, console bowl, #314, 13", from $340 to 440.00
Orchid, ewer, #311, 13", from $625 to 725.00
Orchid, vase, bud; #306, 6¾", from $175 to 225.00
Parchment & Pine, creamer, #S-12, 3¾", from $20 to 35.00
Parchment & Pine, sugar bowl, #S-13, 3¾", from $20 to 35.00
Parchment & Pine, vase, #S-4, 10", from $75 to 100.00
Poppy, basket, #601, 9", from $600 to 700.00
Poppy, jardiniere, #608, 4¾", from $165 to 200.00
Poppy, vase, #607, 10½", from $400 to 500.00
Poppy, wall pocket, #609, 9", from $310 to 410.00
Rosella, basket, #R-12, 7", from $260 to 310.00
Rosella, ewer, #R-7, 9½", from $1,200 to 1,500.00
Rosella, sugar bowl, #R-4, w/lid, 5½", from $150 to 170.00
Rosella, wall pocket, #R-10, 6½", from $150 to 175.00
Serenade, bowl, fruit; #S-15, 7", from $140 to 180.00
Serenade, casserole, #S-20, w/lid, 9", from $120 to 165.00
Serenade, vase, bud; #S-1, 6½", from $50 to 70.00
Stoneware, batter bowl, #25-3, 9", from $95 to 135.00
Stoneware, cookie jar, #300-20, 11", from $90 to 125.00
Sunglow, basket, #84, 6¼", from $95 to 145.00

Sunglow, bowl, mixing; #50, 5½", from $16 to............................... 25.00
Sunglow, casserole, #51, w/lid, 7½", from $60 to 80.00
Sunglow, shaker, #54, 2¾", ea from $15 to 20.00
Water Lily, basket, #L-14, 10½", from $400 to 510.00
Water Lily, candleholder, #L-22, 4½", ea from $85 to 125.00
Water Lily, creamer, #L-19, 5", from $80 to 110.00
Water Lily, sugar bowl, #L-20, w/lid, 5", from $80 to 110.00
Water Lily, teapot, #L-18, 6", from $245 to 300.00
Water Lily, vase, #L-15, 12½", from $475 to 600.00
Wildflower, basket, #W-16, laced hdl, 10½", from $375 to........... 425.00
Wildflower, console bowl, #W-21, 12", from $225 to................... 265.00
Wildflower, vase, #W-5, 6½", from $95 to 135.00
Wildflower (# series), bonbon, hdl, #65, 7", from $375 to........... 475.00
Wildflower (# series), sugar bowl, #74, 4¾", from $240 to........... 275.00
Wildflower (# series), teapot, #72, 8", from $850 to 1,150.00
Woodland, gloss; ewer, #W-3, 5½", from $80 to.......................... 120.00
Woodland, gloss; jardiniere, #W-7, 5½", from $135 to 210.00
Woodland, gloss; vase, #W-1, 5½", from $75 to 100.00
Woodland, matt; basket, #W-9, 8¾", from $250 to 300.00
Woodland, matt; ewer, #W-6, 6½", from $180 to......................... 240.00
Woodland, matt; teapot, #W-26, 6½", from $450 to 550.00
Woodland, matt; vase, #W-18, 10½", from $260 to 350.00

Dinnerware

Avocado, creamer, 4½", from $15 to 22.00
Avocado, mug, 3½", from $5 to.. 7.00
Avocado, plate, dinner; 10¼", from $8 to 10.00
Avocado, platter, oval, 11", from $20 to 25.00
Avocado, stein, 6", from $6 to 10.00
Country Belle, canister, 6¼", from $25 to 35.00
Country Belle, mug, clear glaze, no stamp, 5", from $4 to 6.00
Country Belle, pitcher, 3½", from $25 to 35.00
Country Belle, teapot/coffee server, 9", from $65 to 95.00
Crestone, coffee server, 11", from $75 to................................... 125.00
Crestone, pitcher, 38-oz, from $25 to 35.00
Crestone, plate, luncheon; 9⅜", from $6 to 8.00
Crestone, sugar bowl, w/lid, 4¼", from $20 to 25.00
Gingerbread Man, cookie jar, Flint, 9", from $135 to 210.00
Gingerbread Man, server, 10", from $60 to 80.00
Heartland, bowl, mixing; 8", from $25 to..................................... 30.00
Heartland, bowl, soup/salad; 8", from $15 to 20.00
Heartland, pie plate, 11", from $35 to 45.00
Heartland, plate, dinner; 10¼", from $15 to 22.00
Heartland, platter, oval, from $20 to 30.00
Mirror Almond, bowl, vegetable; 11" L, from $20 to..................... 30.00
Mirror Almond, casserole, ind; Fr hdl, 5½", from $10 to 15.00
Mirror Almond, mug, 3¼", from $3 to 4.00
Mirror Almond, ramekin, from $20 to 25.00
Mirror Brown, bowl, 6½", from $4 to 6.00
Mirror Brown, canister, Coffee, 7", from $100 to......................... 125.00

Mirror Brown, casserole, chicken, 8", from $85.00 to $125.00.

Mirror Brown, casserole, chicken, 9", from $135 to...................... 170.00
Mirror Brown, cheese shaker, 6½", from $30 to 40.00
Mirror Brown, egg plate, 9¼", from $75 to................................ 100.00
Mirror Brown, jug/creamer, 4¼", from $15 to............................ 22.00
Mirror Brown, planter, duck, #F69, 10", from $30 to.................... 40.00
Mirror Brown, shakers, 3¾", pr from $16 to.............................. 24.00
Mirror Brown, teapot, 6", from $25 to...................................... 35.00
Mirror Brown, vase, cylindrical, 6", from $25 to......................... 35.00
Mirror Brown Ringed Ware, ashtray, #18, 7", from $20 to 30.00
Mirror Brown Ringed Ware, bowl, batter; 10½", from $35 to 45.00
Mirror Brown Ringed Ware, canister, 6", from $100 to 135.00
Rainbow, plate, dinner; 10½", from $8 to.................................. 10.00
Rainbow, plate, luncheon; 8½", from $6 to................................. 8.00
Rainbow, tray, soup & sandwich; 9¾", w/5" mug, from $20 to 25.00
Tangerine, coffee mug, experimental, 3½", from $20 to 30.00
Tangerine, gravy boat/syrup, 6", from $45 to............................... 65.00
Tangerine, leaf dish, 12", from $45 to....................................... 65.00
Tangerine, shakers, 4", pr from $16 to...................................... 24.00
Tangerine, tray, toast 'n cereal; 9¾", w/6½" bowl, from $20 to....... 25.00

Hummel

Hummel figurines were created through the artistry of Berta Hummel, a Franciscan nun called Sister M. Innocentia. The first figures were made about 1935 by Franz Goebel of Goebel Art Inc., Rodental, West Germany. Plates, plaques, and candy dishes are also produced, and the older, discontinued editions are highly sought collectibles. Generally speaking, an issue can be dated by the trademark. The first Hummels, from 1935 to 1949, were either incised or stamped with the 'Crown WG' mark. The 'Full Bee in V' mark was employed with minor variations until 1959. At that time the bee was stylized and represented by a solid disk with angled symetrical wings completely contained within the confines of the 'V.' The Three-Line mark, 1964 – 1972, utilized the stylized bee and included a three-line arrangement, 'c by W. Goebel, W. Germany.' Another change in 1972 saw the 'Stylized Bee in V' suspended between the vertical bars of the 'b' and 'l' of a printed 'Goebel, West Germany.' Collectors refer to this mark as the 'Last Bee' or 'Goebel Bee.' The mark in use from 1979 to 1990 omits the 'Bee in V.' The New Crown mark, in use from 1991 to 1999 is a small crown with 'WG' initials, a large 'Goebel,' and a small 'Germany,' signifying a united Germany. The current Millennium Mark came into use in the year 2000 and features a large bee. For further study we recommend *Hummel, An Illustrated Handbook and Price Guide*, by Ken Armke; *Hummel Figurines and Plates, A Collector's Identification and Value Guide*, by Carl Luckey; *The No. 1 Price Guide to M.I. Hummel* by Robert L. Miller; and *The Fascinating World of M.I. Hummel* by Goebel. These books are available through your local book dealer. See also Limited Edition Plates.

Key:
CM — Crown Mark   NC — New Crown Mark
cn — closed number   oe — open edition
FB — Full Bee   SB — Stylized Bee
LB — Last Bee   tw — temporarily withdrawn
MB — Missing Bee   3L — Three-Line Mark

#II/111, Wayside Harmony, table lamp, FB, 7½" 315.00
#II/112, Just Resting, table lamp, CM, 7½"................................ 420.00
#III/058, Playmates, box, CM, 6¾" 525.00
#III/063, Singing Lessons, box, CM, 5¾" 525.00
#III/069, Happy Pastime, box, CM, 6½" 525.00
#III/110, Let's Sing, box, MB, 5¼" 140.00
#2, Little Fiddler, CM, 6"... 490.00
#3, Book Worm, FM, 5½".. 420.00

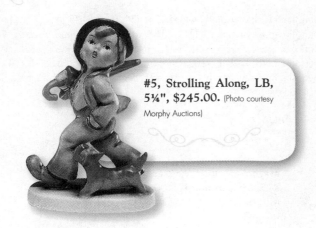

#5, Strolling Along, LB, 5¼", $245.00. (Photo courtesy Morphy Auctions)

#5, Strolling Along, FM, 5" 350.00
#6/II, Sensitive Hunter, FB, 7" 665.00
#7/III, Merry Wanderer, CM, 11"..2,310.00
#8, Book Worm, CM, 4" 490.00
#9, Begging His Share, SB, 5½" 245.00
#11 2/0, Merry Wanderer, 3L, 4½" 140.00
#12/I, Chimney Sweep, CM, 6"... 490.00

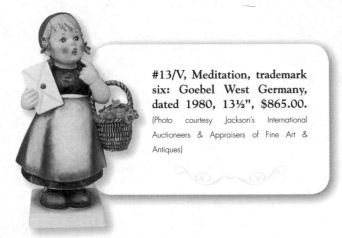

#13/V, Meditation, trademark six: Goebel West Germany, dated 1980, 13½", $865.00.
(Photo courtesy Jackson's International Auctioneers & Appraisers of Fine Art & Antiques)

#13 2/0, Meditation, SB, 4¼" 155.00
#14, Book Worm, bookends, boy & girl, CM, 5½" 420.00
#15/I, Hear Ye, Hear Ye, CM, 6¼"... 490.00
#16, Little Hiker, CM, 5½".. 455.00
#17/2, Congratulations, FM, 8" 3,850.00
#19, Prayer Before Battle, ashtray, CM, 5½".............................3,500.00
#20, Prayer Before Battle, FB, 4¼" 245.00
#21/I, Heavenly Angel, FB, 7".. 315.00
#22/I, Angel w/Bird (Angel Sitting), font, CM, 4¼"..................... 350.00
#23/I, Adoration, 3L, 6½"... 315.00
#24/I, Lullaby, candleholder, FB, 3½x5"................................... 245.00
#25, Angelic Sleep, candleholder, CM, 3½x5" 385.00
#26/I, Child Jesus, font, CM, 3¼x6"... 210.00
#27/3, Joyous News, FB, 4¾x4¼".. 700.00
#28, Wayside Devotion, CM, 8¾"...1,190.00
#29, Guardian Angel, font, CM, 2½x5¾" 910.00
#32/0, Little Gabriel, CM, 5" 315.00
#33, Joyful, ashtray, FB, 3¾x6" 210.00
#34, Singing Lesson, ashtray, CM, 3½x6¼" 315.00
#35, Good Shepherd, font, CM, 2¾x5¾".................................... 280.00
#36/I, Child w/flowers, font, CM, 3½x4½"................................. 280.00
#37, Herald Angels, candleholder, FB, 2¾x4", ea......................... 280.00
#42/0, Good Shepherd, CM, 6".. 525.00
#43, March Winds, SB, 5".. 185.00
#44A, Culprits, table lamp, CM, 9".. 350.00

#48/II, Madonna, plaque, CM, 4¾x5¾" 385.00
#49 3/0, To Market, CM, 4" 350.00
#50/0, Volunteers, FB, 5¾" 350.00
#52/0, Going to Grandma's, CM, 4¾" 525.00
#53, Joyful, LB, 3½" 105.00
#55, Saint George, CM, 6¾" 700.00
#56A, Culprits, CM, 6½" 595.00
#57/I, Chick Girl, FB, 4¼" 315.00
#58/0, Playmates, CM, 4" 350.00
#60 A&B, Farm Boy & Goose Girl, bookends, CM, 4¾" 665.00
#62, Happy Pastime, ashtray, CM, 3½x6¼" 315.00
#65/0, Farewell, FB, 4" 4,200.00
#67, Doll Mother, FB, 4½" 280.00
#68/0, Lost Sheep, SB, 5½" 210.00
#70, Holy Child, FB, 7" 265.00
#71, Stormy Weather, FB, 6½" 560.00
#72, Spring Cheer, CM, 5¼" 350.00
#74, Little Gardener, 3L, 4" 350.00
#75, White Angel, font, CM, 4" 160.00
#80, Little Scholar, 3L, 5½" 190.00
#81/0, School Girl, SB, 5" 210.00
#82/0, School Boy, CM, 5½" 420.00
#83, Angel Serenade (w/Lamb), FB, 5½" 350.00
#84/V, Worship, FB, 12¾" 1,050.00
#85, Serenade, CM, 7¼" 875.00
#86, Happiness, CM, 4¾" 280.00
#89/II, Little Cellist, FB, 7½" 560.00
#90B, Adoration (w/out shrine), bookend, 4" 3,500.00
#92, Merry Wanderer, plaque, SB, 4½x5" 160.00
#94 3/0, Suprise, CM, 4" 315.00
#95, Brother, CM, 5½" 420.00
#96, Little Shopper, SB, 4¾" 145.00
#97, Trumpet Boy, CM, 4½" 280.00
#98, Sister, FB, 5¾" 245.00
#99, Eventide, FB, 4¼x5" 420.00
#100, Shrine, lamp, CM, 7½" 5,600.00
#101, To Market, table lamp, SB, 7½" 350.00
#109, Happy Traveler, FB, 7½" 560.00
#110, Let's Sing, FB, 4" 230.00
#111/I, Wayside Harmony, SB, 5¼" 280.00
#112, Just Resting, CM, 5½" 490.00
#113, Heavenly Song, candleholder, CM, 3½x4¾", ea 4,200.00
#115, Girl w/Nosegay, advent candlestick, CM, 3½" 140.00
#118, Little Thrifty, bank, FB, 5¼" 280.00
#119, Postman, CM, 5¼" 420.00
#123, Max & Moritz, 3L, 5¼" 200.00
#124/I Hello, CM, 7" 560.00
#125, Vacation Time, plaque, CM, 4⅜x5¼" 420.00
#127, Doctor, CM, 5" 315.00
#128, Baker, CM, 5" 420.00
#129, Band Leader, FB, 5½" 245.00
#132, Star Gazer, CM, 4¾" 420.00
#133, Mother's Helper, SB, 5" 210.00
#134, Quartet, plaque, CM, 5½x6¼" 560.00
#135, Soloist, FB, 4¾" 210.00
#136/V, Friends, SB, 11" 1,120.00
#137A, Child in Bed (looking left), plaque, CM, 3x3" 3,500.00
#138, Tiny Baby in Crib, plaque, CM, 2¼x3" 2,800.00
#139, Fitting Butterfly, plaque, FB, 2½x2½" 140.00
#142, Apple Tree Boy, CM, 6½" 560.00
#142/X, Apple Tree Boy, 3L, 30" 11,200.00
#143, Boots, CM, 6¾" 630.00
#145, Little Guardian, CM, 4" 280.00
#146, Angel Duet, font, FB, 3½x4¾" 85.00
#150, Happy Days, FB, 6¼" 630.00
#151, Madonna Holding Child, bl, CM, 12½" 1,400.00
#152, Umbrella Boy, FB, 8" 1,680.00
#152B, Umbrella Girl, CM, 8" 2,800.00
#153, Auf Wiedersehen, CM, 7" 630.00
#154, Waiter, FB, 6½" 385.00
#166, Boy w/Bird, ashtray, CM, 3¼x6" 315.00
#167, Angel w/Bird, font, CM, 3¼x4⅛" 175.00
#169, Bird Duet, CM, 4" 290.00
#172/0, Festival Harmony (Flute), 3L, 8" 280.00
#172/0, Festival Harmony (Mandolin), 3L, 8" 280.00
#174, She Loves Me, She Loves Me Not, SB, 4¼" 205.00
#176, Happy Birthday, CM, 5½" 595.00
#177, School Girls, FB, 9½" 2,100.00
#178, The Photographer, CM, 5" 525.00
#179, Coquettes, FB, 5" 350.00
#184, Latest News, FB, 5" 385.00
#186, Sweet Music, SB, 5" 210.00
#192, Candlelight, candleholder, FB, 7", ea 560.00
#193, Angel Duet, CM, 5" 945.00

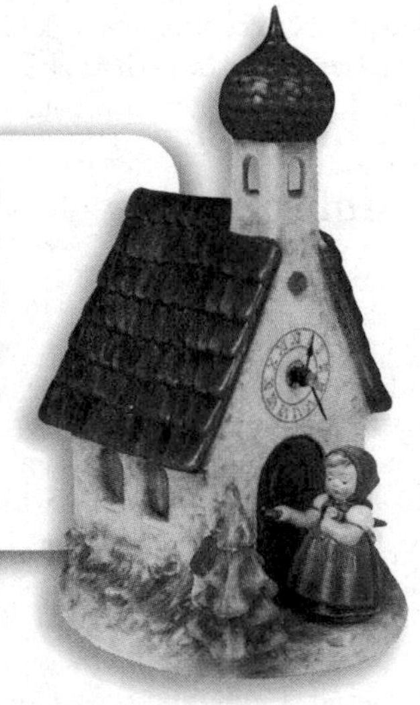

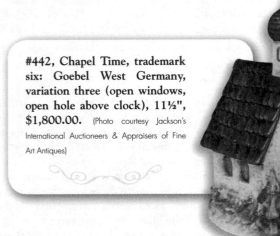

#442, Chapel Time, trademark six: Goebel West Germany, variation three (open windows, open hole above clock), 11½", $1,800.00. (Photo courtesy Jackson's International Auctioneers & Appraisers of Fine Art Antiques)

Hutschenreuther

The Porcelain Factory C.M. Hutschenreuther operated in Bavaria from 1814 to 1969. After the death of the elder Hutschenreuther in 1845, his son Lorenz took over operations, continuing there until 1857 when he left to establish his own company in the nearby city of Selb. The original manufactory became a joint stock company in 1904, absorbing several other potteries. In 1969 both Hutschenreuther firms merged, and that company still operates in Selb. They have distributing centers in both France and the United States.

Figurine, Baron Munchausen flying on gold fire ball, 5x4½" 400.00
Figurine, bison, F Diller, ca 1970, 12½x17" 500.00
Figurine, boxer dog in show stance, 9¾x11" 350.00
Figurine, children (3) dancing in circle, ivory w/gold, Tutter, 8½" .. 180.00
Figurine, doe & fawn, Achtziger, 10x8" 475.00
Figurine, fox hunter on jumping horse, Granget, 1950s-60s, 9x10" 385.00
Figurine, fox terrier up on bk legs, Tutter, 7¼x3¼x2½" 325.00
Figurine, jockey on racing horse, Granget, 1950s-60s, 7½x10" 385.00
Figurine, man in red tights, short cape, spike helmet, Tutter, 9" .. 300.00
Figurine, nude lady down on knee, graceful arms up, Werajea, 11" .. 350.00
Figurine, nude lady standing w/1 leg on gold ball, arms extended, 10" .. 150.00
Figurine, nude maiden sits & holds flowers, fawn beside, 9" 100.00

Figurine, putto balancing ball on ft, wht porc, 6" 70.00
Figurine, 2 ladies dancing on gold ball, arms joined/outstretched, 9" .. 200.00
Plaque, brunette lady w/low-cut pk bodice, E Volk, 5¾x4"+fr... 1,275.00

Plaque, monk in wine cellar, 6x4", $660.00. (Photo courtesy Leslie Hindman Auctioneers)

Plaque, Ruth Harvesting Grain, after Landell, 9x6"+gilt openwork fr.. 1,750.00
Plate, fruits in center, simple gold rim, 10⅝" 25.00
Plate, lady w/brn flowing hair, pk low-cut bodice, ca 1870-90, 10x8" ... 585.00
Vase, floral reserve on gr w/gold, 4-scallop rim, slim, 12½" 75.00

Imari

Imari is a generic term which covers a broad family of wares. It was made in more than a dozen Japanese villages, but the name is that of the port from whence it was shipped to Europe. There are several types of Imari. The most common features a design with panels of birds, florals, or people surrounding a central basket of flowers. The colors used in this type are underglaze blue with overglaze red, gold, and green enamels. The Chinese also made Imari wares which differ from the Japanese type in several ways — the absence of spur marks, a thinner-type body, and a more consistent control of the blue. Imari-type wares were copied on the Continent by Meissen and by English potters, among them Worcester, Derby, and Bow. Unless noted otherwise, our values are for Japanese ware.

Temple jar, relief dragons, brocade patterns, 1800s, 19", $600.00. (Photo courtesy Skinner Auctions)

Bowl, emblems surround central dragon, gilt scrolls, 19th C, 14" 565.00
Charger, Chinese women/children, 19th C, 22" 500.00
Charger, flower basket center, sq w/scalloped rim, 19th C, 17¼" ... 1,765.00
Charger, geishas in gardens, radiating panels, 1870s, 15½" 800.00
Charger, geometric borders, 19th C, 18½" 880.00

Charger, mtns w/huts reserves & medallions, 19th C, 19" 200.00
Charger, radiating panels w/florals/scrolls/etc, 13⅜" 175.00
Ink stand, fan shaped, 2 fixed wells, sm rstr, ca 1880, 3x9x7" 500.00
Jar, cobalt & iron red decor, cvd wooden base, w/lid, 15½", pr... 600.00
Teapot, house & water reserves, China, ca 1740, 5x7¼" 600.00
Vase, 2 panels w/bird & flowers, 4-sided, 1850s, 12", NM 500.00

Imperial Glass

The Imperial Glass Company was organized in 1901 in Bellaire, Ohio, and started manufacturing glassware in 1904. Their early products were jelly glasses, hotel tumblers, etc., but by 1910 they were making a name for themselves by pressing quantities of carnival glass, the iridescent glassware that was popular during that time. In 1914 NuCut was introduced to imitate cut glass. The line was so popular that it was made in crystal and colors and was reintroduced as Collector's Crystal in the 1950s. From 1916 to 1924, they used the lustre process to make a line called Art Glass, which today some collectors call Imperial Jewels. Free-Hand ware, art glass made entirely by hand using no molds, was made from 1923 to 1924. From 1925 to 1926, they made a less expensive line of art glass called Lead Lustre. These pieces were mold blown and have similar colors and decorations to Free-Hand ware.

The company entered bankruptcy in 1931 but was able to continue operations and reorganize as the Imperial Glass Corporation. In 1936 Imperial introduced the Candlewick line, for which it is best known. In the late 1930s the Vintage Grape Milk Glass line was added, and in 1951 a major ad campaign was launched, making Imperial one of the leading milk glass manufacturers.

In 1940 Imperial bought the molds and assets of the Central Glass Works of Wheeling, West Virginia; in 1958 they acquired the molds of the Heisey Company and in 1960 the molds of the Cambridge Glass Company of Cambridge, Ohio. Imperial used these molds, and after 1951 they marked their glassware with an 'I' superimposed over the 'G' trademark. The company was bought by Lenox in 1973; subsequently an 'L' was added to the 'IG' mark. In 1981 Lenox sold Imperial to Arthur Lorch, a private investor (who modified the L by adding a line at the top angled to the left, giving rise to the 'ALIG' mark). He in turn sold the company to Robert F. Stahl, Jr., in 1982. Mr. Stahl filed for Chapter 11 to reorganize, but in mid-1984 liquidation was ordered, and all assets were sold. A few items that had been made in '84 were marked with an 'N' superimposed over the 'I' for 'New Imperial.' For more information we recommend *Imperial Glass Encyclopedia, Vol I, II,* and *III*, edited by James Measell. See also Candlewick; Carnival Glass; Glass Animals and Figurines; Slag Glass; Stretch Glass.

Amelia/Line 671, clambroth, bowl, nappy, 6" 20.00
Amelia/Line 671, clambroth, celery vase, ftd 80.00
Amelia/Line 671, clambroth, tumbler, lemonade; flared rim, 4½" . 30.00
Amelia/Line 671, rubigold, compote, crimped rim 35.00
Amelia/Line 671, rubigold, goblet, wine 50.00
Amelia/Line 671, smoke, pitcher, milk or hotel 80.00
Amelia/Line 671, smoke, plate, luncheon; 9½" 70.00
Amelia/Line 671, smoke, tumbler, 4" 40.00
Beaded Block, See Depression Glass
Cape Cod, crystal, basket, crimped, hdl, #160/221/0, 9" 235.00
Cape Cod, crystal, bottle, cordial; #160/256, 18-oz 125.00
Cape Cod, crystal, bowl, console; #160/75L, 13" 42.50
Cape Cod, crystal, bowl, dessert; tab hdl, #160/197, 4½" 24.00
Cape Cod, crystal, bowl, ftd, #160/137B, 10" 75.00
Cape Cod, crystal, bowl, jelly; #160/33, 3" 12.00
Cape Cod, crystal, bowl, oval, #160/221, 10" 80.00
Cape Cod, crystal, bowl, salad; #1608D, 11" 60.00
Cape Cod, crystal, butter dish, #160/161, ¼-lb 45.00

Cape Cod, crystal, butter dish, hdl, #160/144, 5" 30.00
Cape Cod, crystal, cake stand, ftd, #160/67D, 10½" 50.00
Cape Cod, crystal, candleholder, single, #160/170, 3", ea 17.50
Cape Cod, crystal, candleholder, twin, #160/100, ea 95.00
Cape Cod, crystal, carafe, wine; #160/185, 26-oz 225.00
Cape Cod, crystal, compote, #160/48B, 7" 37.50
Cape Cod, crystal, compote, ftd, w/lid, #160/140, 6" 85.00
Cape Cod, crystal, cookie jar, wicker hdl, #160/195, 5" 150.00
Cape Cod, crystal, cordial, #1602, 1½-oz 6.00
Cape Cod, crystal, cruet, w/stopper, #160/119, 4-oz 25.00
Cape Cod, crystal, decanter, bourbon; #160/260 .... 100.00
Cape Cod, crystal, decanter, w/stopper, #160/163, 30-oz 65.00
Cape Cod, crystal, epergne, plain center, 2-pc, #160/196.......... 265.00
Cape Cod, crystal, ice bucket, #160/63, 6½" 195.00
Cape Cod, crystal, jar, peanut; hdl, w/lid, #160/210, 12-oz.......... 75.00
Cape Cod, crystal, jar, pokal; #160/133, 10" 85.00
Cape Cod, crystal, ladle, marmalade; #160/130 .... 10.00
Cape Cod, crystal, marmalade, 3-pc, #160/89/3 .... 32.50
Cape Cod, crystal, pepper mill, #160/236 .... 30.00
Cape Cod, crystal, pitcher, milk; #160/240, 1-pt 55.00
Cape Cod, crystal, plate, hdls, #160/145D, 11½" 40.00
Cape Cod, crystal, platter, #160/124D, 13½" L 80.00
Cape Cod, crystal, puff box, #1601 .... 60.00
Cape Cod, crystal, relish, oval, 3-part, #160/55, 9½" 25.00
Cape Cod, crystal, salt cellar, #160/61 .... 20.00
Cape Cod, crystal, shakers, ftd, #160/117, pr 20.00
Cape Cod, crystal, sugar bowl, ftd, #160/31 .... 15.00
Cape Cod, crystal, tray, creamer/sugar; sq, w/lid, #160/25/26 .... 160.00
Cape Cod, crystal, tray, pastry; center hdl, #160/68D, 11" 70.00
Cape Cod, crystal, tumbler, tea; ftd, #160, 12-oz 12.00

Cape Cod, crystal, tumbler, 14-ounce, $32.00.

Cape Cod, crystal, vase, fan shape, #160/87F, 8" 235.00
Cape Cod, crystal, vase, ftd, #160/110B, 6½" 70.00
Crocheted Crystal, crystal, basket, 12" 75.00
Crocheted Crystal, crystal, bowl, salad; 10½" 30.00
Crocheted Crystal, crystal, cake stand, ftd, 12" 40.00

Crocheted Crystal, crystal, candleholder, 2x6", each $20.00.
(Photo courtesy Gene and Cathy Florence)

Crocheted Crystal, crystal, creamer, flat 30.00
Crocheted Crystal, crystal, epergne, ftd bowl, center vase, 11" 130.00
Crocheted Crystal, crystal, plate, 9½" 12.50
Crocheted Crystal, crystal, plate, 17" 40.00
Crocheted Crystal, crystal, punch bowl, 14" 65.00
Crocheted Crystal, crystal, relish, 3-part, 11½" 25.00
Crocheted Crystal, crystal, sugar bowl, flat 30.00
Crocheted Crystal, crystal, tumbler, iced tea; ftd, 12-oz, 7⅛" 25.00
Crocheted Crystal, crystal, tumbler, juice; ftd, 6-oz, 6" 20.00
Crocheted Crystal, crystal, vase, 4-ftd, 5" 35.00
Crocheted Crystal, crystal, vase, 8" 35.00
Crocheted Crystal, crystal, water goblet, 9-oz, 7⅛" 25.00
Diamond Quilted, See Depression Glass
Fancy Colonial, any color, bottle, water; no stopper.......... 75.00
Fancy Colonial, any color, butter dish.......... 80.00
Fancy Colonial, any color, champagne, deep, 6-oz 21.00
Fancy Colonial, any color, cocktail, shallow, 3-oz.......... 20.00
Fancy Colonial, any color, custard cup, flared edge 17.50
Fancy Colonial, any color, pitcher, 3-pt 150.00
Fancy Colonial, any color, sugar bowl, w/lid 35.00
Fancy Colonial, any color, tumbler, 10-oz 18.00
Free-Hand, vase, drag loops, gr on gold-fleck citron, shouldered, 6"...350.00
Free-Hand, vase, hearts/vines, bl/orange irid, 3 pulled rim hdls, 7" 135.00
Free-Hand, vase, hearts/vines, wht on gr irid, orange int 10" 1,165.00

Free-Hand, Vase, marbleized swirl, 10", $400.00. (Photo courtesy Early Auction Co.)

Free-Hand, vase, vines, dk irid purples, 4 extended-rim hdls, 11" ...660.00
Monticello, crystal, bonbon, hdl, 5½" 12.00
Monticello, crystal, bowl, lily; 5" 20.00
Monticello, crystal, bowl, vegetable; 8" 25.00
Monticello, crystal, butter tub, 5½" 35.00
Monticello, crystal, compote, 5¼" 12.50
Monticello, crystal, mayonnaise set, 3-pc 35.00
Monticello, crystal, plate, 12" 35.00
Monticello, crystal, punch bowl, belled rim 65.00
Monticello, crystal, sherbet 10.00
Monticello, crystal, vase, flat, 10½" 40.00
Mt Vernon, crystal, bowl, lily; 8" 20.00
Mt Vernon, crystal, butter dish.......... 30.00
Mt Vernon, crystal, plate, 8".......... 10.00
Mt Vernon, crystal, shakers, pr 22.00
Mt Vernon, crystal, sugar bowl, w/lid, ind 16.00
Mt Vernon, crystal, tidbit, 2-tier 30.00
Mt Vernon, crystal, tumbler, iced tea; 12-oz 12.50
Olive, bl or red, bowl, fruit; ped ft, 9".......... 35.00
Olive, bl or red, bowl, shallow; 9" 35.00
Olive, bl or red, compote, 6" 20.00
Olive, bl or red, sugar bowl.......... 16.00

Olive, emerald or pk, bowl, flared, ftd, 6½"	16.00
Olive, emerald or pk, bowl, fruit tray, 9"	20.00
Olive, emerald or pk, bowl, shallow, 7"	15.00
Olive, emerald or pk, compote, 6½"	12.50
Square, crystal, pk or gr, bowl, soup/salad; 7"	20.00
Square, crystal, pk or gr, cup	20.00
Square, crystal, pk or gr, plate, salad; 8"	15.00
Square, crystal, pk or gr, server, center hdl, 10½"	40.00
Square, ruby, bowl, nappy, 4½"	20.00
Square, ruby, creamer, ftd	35.00
Square, ruby, plate, dessert; 6"	10.00
Square, ruby, shakers, sq, ftd, pr	75.00
Square, ruby, sugar bowl, ftd	35.00

Imperial Porcelain

The Blue Ridge Mountain Boys were created by cartoonist Paul Webb and translated into three-dimension by the Imperial Porcelain Corporation of Zanesville, Ohio, in 1947. These figurines decorated ashtrays, vases, mugs, bowls, pitchers, planters, and other items. The Mountain Boys series were numbered 92 through 108, each with a different and amusing portrayal of mountain life. Imperial also produced American Folklore miniatures, 23 tiny animals one inch or less in size, and the Al Capp Dogpatch series. Because of financial difficulties, the company closed in 1960.

American Folklore Miniatures

Cat, 1½", from $50 to	65.00
Cow, 1¾", from $60 to	75.00
Hound dogs, from $60 to	75.00
Plaque, store ad, Am Folklore Porcelain Miniatures, 4½"	250.00
Sow, from $60 to	75.00

Blue Ridge Mountain Boys by Paul Webb

Planter, #110, hillbilly sits by tree stump with jug and snake, from $40.00 to $60.00.

Ashtray, #92, 2 men by tree stump, for pipes, from $50 to	75.00
Ashtray, #101, man w/jug & snake, from $50 to	70.00
Ashtray, #103, hillbilly & skunk, from $55 to	80.00
Ashtray, #105, baby, hound dog & frog, from $50 to	75.00
Ashtray, #106, Barrel of Wishes, w/hound, from $45 to	65.00
Box, cigarette; #98, dog atop, baby at door, sq, from $80 to	100.00
Dealer's sign, Handcrafted Paul Webb Mtn Boys, rare, 9", from $200 to	250.00
Decanter, #100, outhouse, man & bird, from $50 to	75.00
Decanter, #104, Ma leaning over stump, w/baby & skunk, from $75 to	100.00
Decanter, man, jug, snake, & tree stump, Hispch Inc, 1946, from $50 to	75.00
Figurine, #101, man leans against tree trunk, 5", from $50 to	75.00
Figurine, man on hands & knees, 3", from $50 to	75.00
Figurine, man sitting, 3½", from $50 to	80.00
Figurine, man sitting w/chicken on knee, 3", from $50 to	75.00
Jug, #101, Willie & snake, from $40 to	60.00

Mug, #94, Bearing Down, 6", from $40 to	60.00
Mug, #94, dbl baby hdl, 4¼", from $40 to	60.00
Mug, #94, ma hdl, 4¼", from $40 to	60.00
Mug, #94, man w/bl pants hdl, 4¼", from $40 to	60.00
Mug, #94, man w/yel beard & red pants hdl, 4¼", from $40 to	60.00
Mug, #99, Target Practice, boy on goat, farmer, 5¾", from $40 to	60.00
Pitcher, lemonade; from $80 to	110.00
Planter, #81, man drinking from jug, sitting by washtub, from $40 to	60.00
Planter, #100, outhouse, man & bird, from $60 to	80.00
Planter, #105, man w/chicken on knee, washtub, from $60 to	80.00
Shakers, Ma & Old Doc, pr from $40 to	65.00

Indian Tree

Indian Tree is a popular dinnerware pattern produced by various potteries from the early 1800s to recent times. Although backgrounds and borders vary, the Oriental theme is carried out with the gnarled, brown branch of a pink-blossomed tree. Among the manufacturers' marks, you may find represented such notable firms as Coalport, S. Hancock and Sons, Soho Pottery, and John Maddock and Sons. See also Johnson Brothers.

Platter, Pullman logo, Buffalo China, 11" long, from $65.00 to $95.00.

Basket, #581/4, HJ Woods, 8x4x6"	60.00
Bonbon, fluted, Coalport, 6¼"	35.00
Bowl, Aynsley, 2¾x8¾"	60.00
Bowl, cereal/coupe; scalloped rim, Coalport, 1⅝x6"	30.00
Bowl, cream soup; scalloped, Spode	45.00
Bowl, fruit; 8-sided, Coalport, 5"	15.00
Bowl, serving; Copeland Spode, 10" L	45.00
Bowl, vegetable; Coalport, w/hdls & dome lid, 7x12"	185.00
Bowl, vegetable; John Maddock & Sons, ca 1935, w/lid, 8" dia	55.00
Butter pat, scalloped, #2/916, 4¼"	25.00
Cake plate, sq w/hdls, Spode, 9¼x10¾"	95.00
Cake stand, Coalport, 3½x8"	110.00
Candy dish, scalloped edge, gr mk, 5¼" L	20.00
Cheese dish, scalloped, ftd, dome lid, Coalport	85.00
Coffeepot, paneled sides, bud finial, Livesley Powell & Co, EX	330.00
Compote, ribbed, Copeland, 5½x11"	250.00
Cup & saucer, gold trim, Coalport, mini, 1", 2¼" dia	180.00
Dinner service, Coalport, serves 10+8 serving pcs, 144-pc	750.00
Gravy boat, Copeland Spode, 8" L, +underplate	75.00
Jar, Sadler, fancy shape, w/lid, 4½"	55.00
Mug, smooth rim, Coalport, 3¾"	35.00
Mustard pot, w/lid, Spode, 2¾"	80.00
Pitcher, Coalport, 4¾"	65.00
Pitcher, smooth rim, Coalport, 12-oz, 5½"	80.00

Plate, cookie; Coalport, 10½"...................................... 55.00
Plate, luncheon; Minton, #5185, 9¼", set of 8............................. 100.00
Plate, sq, Coalport, 7½".. 25.00
Platter, Ashworth, 14½"... 90.00
Platter, Handcock & Sons, 17"..................................... 75.00
Platter, Spode, 15"... 80.00
Shakers, egg shape, Spode, 3", pr................................. 85.00
Teapot, Coalport, 7"... 150.00
Teapot, hexagonal body, Sadler, 6x9¾"............................ 90.00
Teapot, spode, 7x11".. 175.00
Tray, mc w/gold accents, Coalport, 10¾x8½"....................... 85.00
Trivet, sq, Coalport, 6".. 75.00

Inkwells and Inkstands

Receptacles for various writing fluids have been used since ancient times. Through the years they have been made from countless materials — glass, metal, porcelain, pottery, wood, and even papier-mache. During the eighteenth century, gold or silver inkstands were presented to royalty; the well-known silver inkstand by Philip Syng, Jr., was used for the signing of the Declaration of Independence, and proud possessions of men of letters. When literacy vastly increased in the nineteenth century, the dip pen replaced the quill pen, and inkwells and inkstands were widely used and produced in a broad range of sizes in functional and decorative forms from ornate Victorian to flowing Art Nouveau and stylized Art Deco designs. However, the acceptance of the ballpoint pen literally put inkstands and inkwells 'out of business.' But their historical significance and intriguing diversity of form and styling fascinate today's collectors. It should be noted here that many cast white-metal inkwells have lost much of their value. Collectors and antique dealers are leaning toward more valuable materials such as brilliant cut glass, silver, and copper. See also Bottles, Ink.

Glass, German helmet, deep puce with gold detail, marked G.E.S. Etzligh Geschutzt with eagle on base, 3½", $150.00. (Photo courtesy American Bottle Auctions)

Brass, chestnut leaf & nut w/ladybug, hinged lid, glass insert, 1900s... 250.00
Brass, classic column, early 1900s, 3½" W 70.00
Brass, classical contour type, swivel lid, distressed, 19th C, 2½" 60.00
Brass, teapot form w/appl brass flowers/etc, brass insert, 1890s, 2"...125.00
Bronze, 3-D couple, he w/scythe, she w/jug, sgn Curomko, dore, 12" L..500.00
Bronzed metal, lady's head in center of shamrock, unmk 65.00
Bronzed wht metal, bison center, 2 wells, ca 1900, 7" L 225.00
Bronzed wht metal, 2 owls on branch, Meriden SP Co, 7½" L, VG...350.00
Cast iron, god's head, glass eyes, ca 1900, 4½" 125.00
Cast iron, stag's head, orig pnt, brass patinated lid, 5½" 175.00
Chrome base w/blk pnt, blk Bakelite pen holder/lid, Deco style, 1920s...185.00
CI w/blk finish, rococo style, pressed glass well, ca 1900, 5¼" W .. 140.00
Compo base (blk), chrome well w/glass insert, Deco style, 3⅜x5" ...80.00
Copper, chased floral, pierced, Nouveau style, 1900-15, 5¼" L..... 140.00
Faience, mc coat of arms on heart form, 3 quill holes, Fr, 1900s, 3" ...180.00
Gilt bronze, Cupid holds bird, hinged lid, glass liner, Paris, 4x6x5"....250.00
Glass, bl, hand-blown, cut facets/brass mts, late 1800s, Am, 3x2⁹⁄₁₆"..500.00
Glass, blk amethyst, hand-blown, cut facets, brass mts, sq, 2¾" ... 400.00

Glass, brilliant bl, hinged brass mts, 8-sided, Am, 1900-10, 2¾".. 450.00
Glass, Cane cuttings, brass mts, sq, Am?, 1890-1900, 2" 145.00
Glass, clear w/appl gr threads, blown, brass mts, European, 4" dia...190.00
Glass, Daisy & Button, lt gr cube, Am, 1890-1900, 2¼" 75.00
Glass, Dmn pattern, olive-amber, blown 3-mold, att Keene, 2x2¾"..415.00
Glass, gr hand-blown funnel type, ped ft, Simons...1845, 3¾" dia...800.00
Glass, guilloche pattern, brass flame finial, sq, Fr, 1880s, 3" 95.00
Glass, swirls/zippers, sterling ball lid/ft ring w/repousse floral, 5".. 400.00
Glass, Thousand Eye, vaseline, brass/enamel lid, sq, 1890s, 2⅛x2".. 140.00
Glass, vaseline, hand blown, cut 3-tier body, brass mts, 19th C, 2¾".. 600.00
Glass, wheat cuttings, SP top w/emb florals, sq sides, ca 1900...... 185.00
Porc, Arabic man seated & holding pipe, opens at waist, Germany, 4" .. 80.00
Porc, bellhop picking up package, Deco, Fish/Fulper, 1920s, 4¾"....400.00
Porc, bird beside nest w/snake stealing eggs, Staffordshire, 2¾" ... 150.00
Porc, dish w/attached well, HP floral, dome lid, Fr, 1890s, 3¼x6"...175.00
Porc, rtcl hexagon, floral transfer, porc insert, Japan, 1900s, 2¾".. 160.00
Porc, sq rococo style w/HP floral/gold, sq, Germany, 1890s, 3½"..200.00

Pot metal, Black man's head, 4½", $920.00. (Photo courtesy Morphy Auctions)

Pottery, 3-lion ped on triangular ft, mc majolica, Italy, 1878, 3".. 350.00
Soapstone, hand-cvd, sq, Am, early 20th C, 2½" 35.00
SP, rectangular on bun ft, hinged dome lid w/beaded borders, 4x6x2" ...65.00
Sterling, hammered w/repousse floral, monogram, sq, mk Bond, 2x2½"..230.00

Insulators

The telegraph was invented in 1844. The devices developed to hold the electrical transmission wires to the poles were called insulators. The telephone, invented in 1876, intensified their usefulness; and by the turn of the century, thousands of varieties were being produced in pottery, wood, and glass of various colors. Even though it has been rumored that red glass insulators exist, none have ever been authenticated. There are amber-colored insulators that appear to have a red tint to the amber, and those are called red-amber. Many insulators are embossed with patent dates. Of the more than 3,000 types known to exist, today's collectors evaluate their worth by age, rarity, color and, of course, condition. Aqua and green are the most common colors in glass, dark brown the most common in porcelain. Threadless insulators (for example, CD #701.1), made between 1850 and 1865, bring prices well into the hundreds, sometimes even the thousands, if in mint condition.

In the listings that follow, the CD numbers are from an identification system developed in the late 1960s by N.R. Woodward. Those seeking additional information about insulators are encouraged to contact Line Jewels NIA #1380 (whose address may be found in the Directory under Clubs, Newsletters, and Catalogs) or attend a club-endorsed show. (For information see Directory under Florida for Jacqueline Linscott Barnes.) In the listings that follow those stating 'no name' have no company identification, but do have embossed numbers, dots, etc. Those stating 'no embossing' are without raised letters, dots, or any other markings. Please note: Our values are for insulators in mint condition.

Key:
* (asterisk) — Canadian   RB — rough base
BE — base embossed   RDP — round drip points
CB — corrugated base   SB — smooth base
CD — Consolidated Design   SDP — sharp drip points
FDP — flat drip points

CD 24, (crown emb), The United States Light & Heating Company, aqua.... 75.00
CD 100, Surge, RDP, clear..4.00
CD 102, NEGMCo, SB, yel-gr... 200.00
CD 106, Ericksson, RDP, yel-olive gr... 550.00
CD 112, Lynchburg No 31, RDP, aqua..5.00
CD 121, Maydwell-16W, SDP, straw.. 50.00
CD 122.4, Hemingray-E2, SB, lemon.. 100.00
CD 125, W.U./5, SB, bl... 50.00
CD 127.4, (no emb), SB, dk aqua 350.00
CD 130.1, Cal Elec Works/Patent, SB, lt cobalt...........................5,000.00
CD 131.4, LGT & Co, SB, aqua 125.00
CD 133, City Fire Alarm, SB, lt aqua 125.00
CD 134, BGMCo, SB, lt purple 150.00
CD 136.5, Boston Bottle Works - Pat Oct 15 72, SB, aqua.......3,000.00
CD 136.5, Boston Bottle Works - Pat Oct 16 72, SB, lime gr ...5,500.00
CD 139.9, McLaughlin, SB, aqua.. 700.00
CD 140, Jumbo, SB, aqua.. 250.00
CD 140, Jumbo, SB, dk aqua.. 400.00
CD 141.7, WR Twiggs, SB, clear..20,000.00
CD 141.8, JF Buzby/Pat'd May 6/1890, SB, aqua 20,000.00
CD 141.9, Emminger's, BE, lt aqua 20,000.00
CD 143.5, T-HE Co, SB, aqua 125.00
CD 145, BGMCo, SB, lemon.. 400.00
CD 145, BGMCo, SB, lt purple 250.00
CD 145, HGCo/Petticoat, SB, aqua..2.00
CD 150, Barclay, SDP, aqua..7,500.00
CD 154, Hemingray-42, RDP, ice gr 100.00
CD 154, Hemingray-42, SB, Hemingray Blue 30.00
CD 154, Maydwell-42/USA, RDP, straw 2.00
CD 155, Kerr DP 1, SB, clear 2.00
CD 158, Boston Bottle Works/Patent Applied For, SB, aqua........ 700.00
CD 160, (star), SB, lt yel olive gr 75.00
CD 160, Brookfield/New York, SB, gr..5.00
CD 160.6, Am Tel & Tel Co, SB, aqua.. 300.00
CD 160.6, Am Tel & Tel Co, SB, lt aqua 300.00
CD 161, California, SB, purple 30.00
CD 162, BGMCo, SB, purple... 300.00
CD 162, California, SB, sage gr 5.00
CD 162, Hamilton Glass Co, RB, lt aqua 30.00
CD 162, Westinghouse, SB, lt gr 600.00
CD 162, WFGCo, SB, lt purple 40.00
CD 190 & CD 191, Hemingray-50, SB, aqua 40.00
CD 190 & CD 191, Two Piece/Transposition, SB, milky aqua, pr...400.00
CD 194 & CD 195, Hemingray-54-A & Hemingray-54-B, purple .. 150.00
CD 196, HCGo, SDP, purple...2,500.00
CD 196, HGCo, SDP, ice bl 75.00
CD 196, HGCo, SDP, lt aqua 50.00
CD 196, HGCo, SDP, lt purple 5,000.00
CD 196, HGCo, SDP, milky aqua 1,000.00
CD 197, Hemingray-53, CB, clear 2.00
CD 208, California, SB, lt purple 125.00
CD 217, Armstrong's 51 C3, SB, root beer amber 10.00
CD 231, Hemingray-820, CB, clear 25.00
CD 250, NEGMCo, RB.. 30.00
CD 250, NEGMCo, SB, aqua..15,000.00
CD 251, NEGMCo, RB, aqua.. 30.00
CD 254, No 3 Cable, RB, aqua 40.00

CD 262, No 2 Columbia, SB, lt bl aqua....................................... 175.00
CD 267.5, NEGMCo, SB, emerald gr 200.00
CD 269, Jumbo, SB, aqua.. 500.00
CD 292.5, Boston/'Knowles 6,' SB, aqua..................................... 300.00

CD 302, Hemingray, round drip points, aqua, $75.00.

CD 317, Chambers/Pat Aug 14 1877, SB, lt aqua 500.00
CD 701.1, (no emb), SB, citrine 3,000.00
CD 724, Chester, NY, BE, cobalt 5,000.00
CD 729.4, Mulford & Biddle/83 John St NY, SB, aqua............. 1,250.00
CD 735, Chester/NY, SB, aqua 600.00
CD 736, NY & ERR, SB, lt gr aqua..3,500.00
CD 742.3, MTCo, BE, lt teal bl 1,500.00

Irons

History, geography, art, and cultural diversity are all represented in the collecting of antique pressing irons. The progress of fashion and invention can be traced through the evolution of the pressing iron. Over 700 years ago, implements constructed of stone, bone, wood, glass, and wrought iron were used for pressing fabrics. Early ironing devices were quite primitive in form, and heating techniques included inserting a hot metal slug into a cavity of the iron, adding hot burning coals into a chamber or pan, and placing the iron directly on hot coals or a hot surface.

To the pleasure of today's collectors, some of these early irons, mainly from the period of 1700 to 1850, were decorated by artisans who carved and painted them with regional motifs typical of their natural surroundings and spiritual cultures. Beginning in the mid-1800s, new cultural demands for fancy wearing apparel initiated a revolution in technology for types of irons and methods to heat them. Typical of this period is the fluter which was essential for producing the ruffles demanded by the nineteenth-century ladies. Hat irons, polishers, and numerous unusual iron forms were also used during this time, and provided a means to produce crimps, curves, curls, and special fabric textures. Irons from this era are characterized by their unique shapes, odd handles, latches, decorations, and even revolving mechanisms.

Also during this time, irons began to be heated by burning liquid and gaseous fuels. Gradually the new technology of the electrically heated iron replaced all other heating methods, except in the more rural areas and undeveloped countries. Even today the Amish communities utilize gasoline fuel irons.

In the listings that follow, prices are given for examples in best possible as-found condition. Damage, repairs, plating, excessive wear, rust, and missing parts can dramatically reduce value. For further information we recommend *Irons by Irons*, *More Irons by Irons*, and *Even More Irons by Irons* by our advisor Dave Irons; his address and information for ordering these books are given in the Directory under Pennsylvania.

Alcohol, Geo L Marion...NY, ca 1897, w/trivet, 6", from $150 to ..200.00
Box, pieced construction, hinged gate, Fr, 1700s, 6½", $200 to ... 300.00
Box, str sides, hinged gate, English, 1850s, 5½", from $150 to 200.00

Clamp-on fluter, Companion, blk pnt, ca 1875, 5" roll, from $200 to .. 300.00
Combination, charcoal, Pat'd Aug 23, 1904 Pat Pend, fluter rocker hdl.. 200.00
Combination, fluter clamps on sadiron, Pat July...'74, 8½", $300 to ... 500.00

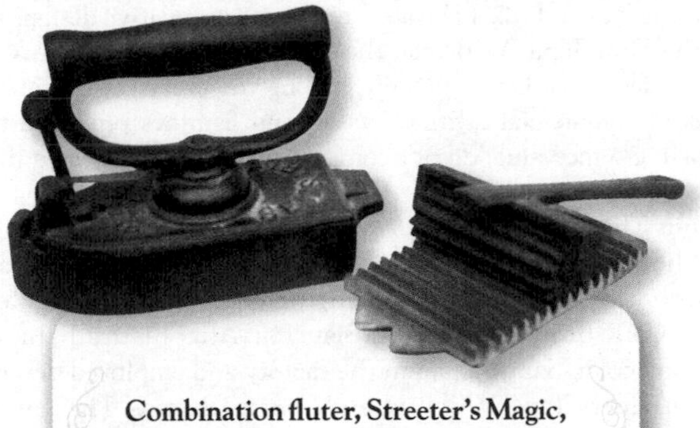

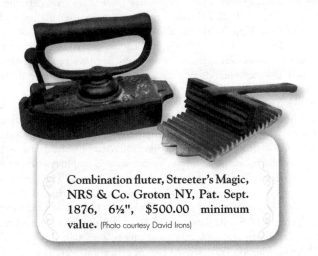

Combination fluter, Streeter's Magic, NRS & Co. Groton NY, Pat. Sept. 1876, 6½", $500.00 minimum value. (Photo courtesy David Irons)

Dragon-head trn chimney, Pomeroy Peckover...Sept 7, 1854, 11", minimum.. 500.00
Flatiron, CI, Ober #6, Pat Mar 19 '12, 6", from $50 to 70.00
Flatiron, CI w/floral top, ca 1900, 7", from $75 to 100.00
Flatiron, cold hdl slips into iron base, late 1800s, 6", $150 to 200.00
Flatiron, wrought iron, made from 1 pc, mid-1800s, 5", $75 to 100.00
Gas jet, WF Shaw's Pat Sept 1 1857, 6¼", from $150 to 200.00
Goffer, triple; trn std/supports, bbl plugs, 1850s, 14", minimum .. 1,000.00
Goffering, single, iron bbl & std, CI base, European, 1890s, 8¼" .. 200.00
Goffering, triple; w/candleholder, brass std, 1850s, 9", minimum ... 1,000.00
Kerosene, Tilley Model DN, Made in UK, blk Bakelite, 1950s, 7½" ... 150.00
Natural gas, Clark's Fairy...#374..., bl enamel/plastic hdl, 6½" 150.00
Ox tongue, slug or gas jet, lift-up gate, Aver Wein, 1900s, 8" 150.00
Polisher, Enterprise Mfg Co of PA, Pat Oct 1 67, Jan 16 77, 5½" ... 70.00
Polisher, rnd bottom, Carron 2, late 1800s, 4⅝", from $75 to 100.00
Slug, brass w/dolphin posts, openwork lyre, Europe, 1800s, 7", minimum.... 750.00
Slug, CI swan, Pat Apd For, David Barns NY Dec 11, 1877, 7", minimum... 1,000.00
Slug, iron w/ornate brass cut-work top, hinged gate, 1880s, 7⅝" .. 750.00
Sm, charcoal, tall chimney, European, late 1800s, 3½", $200 to .. 300.00
Sm, CI swan, Ray M Harpel, Sinking...PA, ca 1900, 3⅛", $300 to .. 500.00
Sm, goffer, brass bbl, English, ca 1900, 3⅜", from $150 to 200.00
Sm, hollow grip, Russian, late 1800s, 3¼", from $100 to 150.00
Sm, wrought, late 1800s, 4", from $70 to 100.00
Sm, wrought, 1820 (rare date), 3¼", from $150 to 200.00
Smoothing board, common wooden type w/trn hdl, late 1800s, 24" ... 100.00
Tall chimney, vulcan face damper, E Bless R Drake Pat'd 1852, 6¾" .. 150.00

Ironstone

During the last quarter of the eighteenth century, English potters began experimenting with a new type of body that contained calcinated flint and a higher china clay content, intent on producing a fine durable whiteware — heavy, yet with a texture that would resemble porcelain. To remove the last trace of yellow, a minute amount of cobalt was added, often resulting in a bluish-white tone. Wm and John Turner of Caughley and Josiah Spode II were the first to manufacture the ware successfully. Others, such as Davenport, Hicks and Meigh, and Ralph and Josiah Wedgwood, followed with their own versions. The latter coined the name 'Pearl' to refer to his product and incorporated the term into his trademark. In 1813 a 14-year patent was issued to Charles James Mason, who called his ware Patented Ironstone. Francis Morley, G.L. Asworth, T.J. Mayer, and other Staffordshire potters continued to produce ironstone until the end of the century. While some of these patterns are simple to the extreme, many are decorated with in-mold designs of fruit, grain, and foliage on ribbed or scalloped shapes. In the 1830s transfer-printed designs in blue, mulberry, pink, green, black, and some two-tone became popular; and polychrome versions of Oriental wares were manufactured to compete with the Chinese trade. See also Mason's Ironstone. Our advise for this category comes from Anne Miller, her address is listed in the Directory under Illinois.

Bone dish, Crescent, Wilkinson, 3x6¼", EX 55.00
Bowl, Crescent Pottery, 3¼x9⅞" 85.00
Bowl, punch; Ceres, Elsmore & Forster, 6½x11" at hdls 335.00
Bowl, ribbed, J&G Meakin, 1890s, 3¼x 8¼", NM 75.00
Bowl, sauce; w/lid, Red Cliff..., ca 1960, 6½x4¾" 130.00
Bowl, soup; Full Ribbed, Pankhurst, 8¾" 32.00

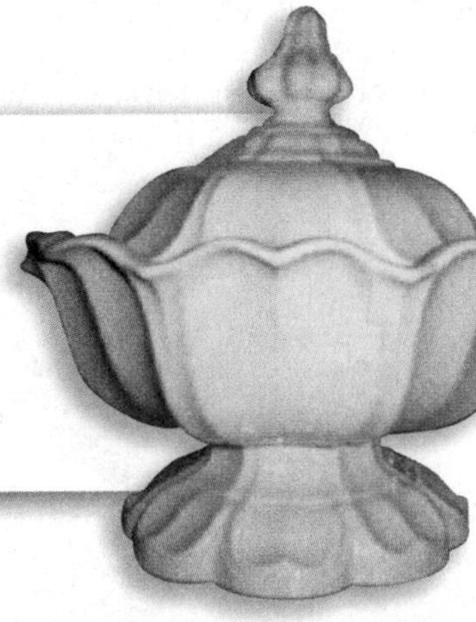

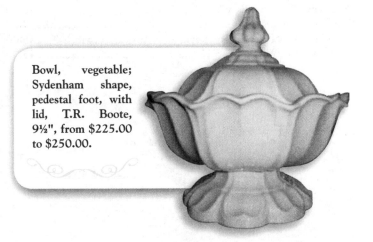

Bowl, vegetable; Sydenham shape, pedestal foot, with lid, T.R. Boote, 9½", from $225.00 to $250.00.

Bowl, waste; J&G Meakin, 3½x5¾" 28.00
Bowl, Wheat & Daisy, Bishop & Stonier, 1890s, 9" 45.00
Butter dish, Fig, Davenport, ca 1853, 5½x6½", NM 295.00
Cake stand, scalloped apron, fluted column, Shaw, 7x13" 300.00
Chamber pot, wicker basket design/acanthus leaves, Meakin 155.00
Coffeepot, Laurel Wreath, Elsmore & Forster, 12" 250.00
Coffeepot, Lily, Burgess 275.00
Compote, fluted, Burgess, heavy crazing, 11x6½" 200.00
Creamer, octagonal w/paneled sides, Meigh & Son, 5⅛" 85.00
Gravy boat, Fig, J Wedgwood, ca 1856 .... 110.00
Gravy boat, floral design at thumb rest, Pankhurst, ca 1870, 9" L ... 110.00
Invalid feeder, WT&C Germany, 7¼" L 35.00
Jelly/pudding mold, Grimwades, ca 1900, 4¾x6⅞" 75.00
Jug, Cable & Ring, ca 1875-90, 6¼" 85.00
Ladle, sauce; flower on hdl, paneled bowl, unmk 65.00
Mold, tiger lilies, late 1800s, 2½x7x5½" 295.00
Mustard cup, w/lid, Knowles Taylor & Knowles, ca 1920, 3½" 75.00
Pitcher, Acanthus Leaf, Warranted mk, 10" 145.00
Pitcher, Baltic, ped ft, GF Bowers, ca 1855, 11¼" 285.00
Pitcher, bulbous w/emb decor at hdl & spout, J Wedgwood, 8½" .. 200.00
Pitcher, Cable & Ring, Anthony Shaw & Son, 12½x7¾" 175.00
Pitcher, Fuchsia, Geo Jones, ca 1850, 19" 315.00
Pitcher, Gothic, 8-panel, Davenport, #38, 9½" 185.00
Pitcher, Hawthorn's Fern, Wood & Hawthorn, ca 1891, 12¼x8" ... 185.00
Pitcher, Laurel Wreath, Elsmore & Forster, sm rpr, 8" 165.00
Pitcher, President, J Edwards, 8⅝" 155.00
Pitcher, Ribbon, Edwin Knowles, 1923, 8¼" 115.00
Pitcher, Tracery, Johnson Bros, 11½" 170.00
Pitcher, Union, TR Boote, 7" 185.00
Pitcher, Wheat & Clover, Turner & Tomkinson, ca 1860-72, 12" .. 200.00
Plate, Bellflower, Edwards, 9¾" 55.00
Plate, Sydenham, T&R Boote, 10½" 40.00

Platter, Chas Meakin Warranted, oval, 13½x9½" 65.00
Platter, Crown Potteries, 14x10½" 36.00
Platter, De Soto, Thos Hughes, 11⅝x9" 65.00
Platter, Framed Leaf, Pankhurst, ca 1850, 17", NM 95.00
Platter, LS&S, ca 1870-80, 18x13", NM 65.00
Platter, Maddock, 16x11" 60.00
Platter, Wheat, Jacob Furnival, ca 1860, 17¾x12½" 165.00
Relish, Ceres, w/rope hdls, Elsmore & Forster 78.00
Shaving mug, Berlin Swirl 165.00
Soap dish, Cable & Ring, w/insert, Meakin, 1890s, 6½", EX 145.00
Soup plate, Budded Vine, Meakin, ca 1869, 10¼" 75.00
Soup plate, plain, rnd, Wilkinson, 10" 40.00
Sugar bowl, Iona, w/lid, Powell & Bishop, 1886, 7½" 90.00
Sugar bowl, President, w/lid, John Edwards, ca 1856, 7" 195.00
Sugar bowl, Sydenham, w/lid, T&R Boote, ca 1854, 8x6", NM 75.00
Sugar bowl, Wheat, hdls, w/lid, 8" 340.00
Teapot, Corn & Oats 275.00
Teapot, Full Panel Gothic, octagonal, John Alcock, ca 1848, 8¼" 245.00
Teapot, Wheat, Wilkinson, 8½" 245.00

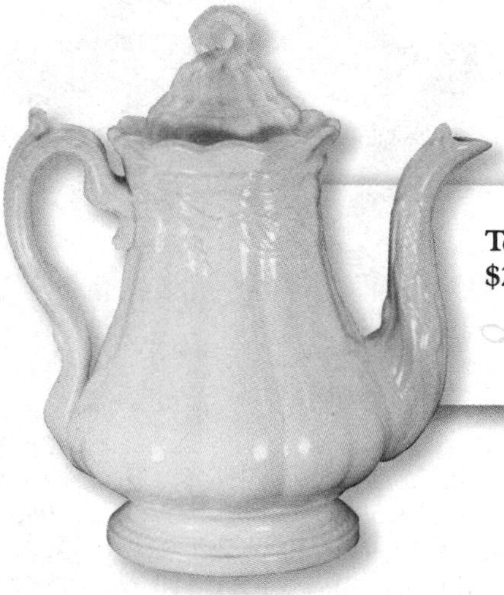

Teapot, Wheat, 11", $245.00.

Tureen, Gothic, 10-sided, w/lid, Joseph Heath, 7½x9¾x8¼", NM 275.00
Tureen, Maddock & Gater, w/lid & ladle, 6x8" 225.00
Tureen, Octagonal, w/acorn finial, ladle, 13½" H 150.00
Tureen, sauce; Baltic, J Meir & Son, ca 1855, w/lid & ladle 215.00
Tureen, sauce; President, John Edwards, 1855, w/lid & ladle 295.00
Tureen, soup; Sydenham, w/lid, T&R Boote, sm rpr, 13" 100.00
Tureen, vegetable; President, w/lid, J Edwards, 9x10" 235.00
Wash pitcher, Corn & Oats 175.00
Washbowl, Hyacinth, unmk, 13" 120.00
Washbowl, Jacob Furnival, 6½x15¾" 85.00
Washbowl, New York, Clementson, 13½" 165.00
Washbowl & pitcher, Sydenham, T&R Boote, 12¼", 4¾x13⅜" 495.00
Washbowl & pitcher, Wheat 375.00
Waste bowl, Tuscan, unmk, 3⅛x5¼" 80.00

Italian Glass

Throughout the twentieth century, one of the major glassmaking centers of the world was the island of Murano. From the Stile Liberte work of Artisi Barovier (1890 – 1920s) to the early work of Ettore Sottsass in the 1970s, they excelled in creativity and craftsmanship. The 1920s to 1940s featured the work of glass designers like Ercole Barovier for Barovier and Toso and Vittorio Zecchin, Napoleone Martinuzzi, and Carlo Scarpa for Venini. Many of these pieces are highly prized by collectors.

The 1950s saw a revival of Italy as a world-reknown design center for all of the arts. Glass led the charge with the brightly colored work of Fulvio Bianconi for Venini, Dino Martens for Aureliano Toso, and Ercole Barovier for Barovier and Toso. The best of these pieces are extremely desirable. The '60s and '70s have also seen many innovative designs with work by the Finn Tapio Wirkkala, the American Thomas Stearns, and many other designers. Unfortunately, among the great glass, there was a plethora of commercial ashtrays, vases, and figurines produced that, though having some value, do not compare in quality and design to the great glass of Murano.

Venini: The Venini company was founded in 1921 by Paolo Venini, and he led the company until his death in 1959. Major Italian designers worked for the firm, including Vittorio Zecchin, Napoleone Martinuzzi, Carlo Scarpa, and Fulvio Bianconi. After his death, his son-in-law, Ludovico de Santillana, ran the factory and employed designers like Toni Zucchieri, Tapio Wirkkala, and Thomas Stearns. The company is known for creative designs and techniques including Inciso (finely etched lines), Battuto (carved facets), Sommerso (controlled bubbles), Pezzato (patches of fused glass), and Fascie (horizontal colored lines in clear glass). Until the mid-'60s, most pieces were signed with acid-etched 'Venini Murano ITALIA.' In the '60s they started engraving the signatures. The factory still exists.

Barovier: In the late 1920s, Ercole Barovier took over the Artisti Barovier and started designing many different vases. In the 1930s he merged with Ferro Toso and became Barovier and Toso. He designed many different series of glass including the Barbarico (rough, acid-treated brown or deep blue glass), Eugenio (free-blown vases), Efeso, Rotallato, Dorico, Egeo (vases incorporating murrine designs), and Primavera (white etched glass with black bands). He designed until 1974. The company is still in existence. Most pieces were unsigned.

Aureliano Toso: The great glass designer Dino Martens was involved with the company from about 1938 to 1965. It was his work that produced the very desirable Oriente vases. This technique consisted of free-formed patches of green, yellow, blue, purple, black, and white stars and pieces of zanfirico canes fused into brilliantly colored vases and bowls. His El Dorado series was based on the same technique but was not opaque. He also designed pieces with alternating groups of black and white filigrana lines. Pieces are unsigned.

Seguso: Flavio Poli became the artistic director of Seguso in the late 1930s and remained until 1963. He is known for his Corroso (acid-etched glass) and his Valve series (elegant forms of two to three layers of colored glass with a clear glass casing).

Archimede Seguso: In 1946 Archimede Seguso left the Seguso Vetri D'Arte to open a new company and designed many innovative pieces. His Merlatto (thin white filigrana suspended three dimensionally) series is his most famous. The epitome of his work is where a colored glass (yellow or purple) is windowed in the merlotti. His Macchia Ambra Verde is yellow and spots on a gold base encased in clear glass. The A Piume series contained feathers and leaves suspended in glass. Pieces are unsigned.

Alfredo Barbini: Barbini was a designer known for his sculptures of sea subjects and his amorphic-shaped vases with an inner core of red or blue glass with a heavy layer of finely incised outer glass. He worked in the 1950s to the 1960s, and some pieces are signed.

Vistosi: Although this glassworks was started in the 1940s, fame came in the 1960s and 1970s with the birds designed by Allesandro Pianon and the early work of the Memphis school designer, Ettore Sottsass. Pieces may be signed.

AVEM: This company is known for its work in the 1950s and 1960s. The designer, Ansolo Fuga, did work using a solid white glass with inclusions of multicolored murrines.

Cenedese: This is a postwar company led by Gino Cenedese with Alfredo Barbini as designer. When Barbini left, Cenedese took over the design work and also used the free-lanced designs of Fulvio Bianconi. They are known for their figurines and vases with suspended murrines.

Cappellin: Venini's original partner (1921 – 1925), Giacomo Cappellin, opened a short-lived company (1925 – 1932) that was to become extremely important. His chief designer was the young Carlo Scarpa who was to create many masterpieces in glass both for Cappellin and then Venini.

Ettore Sottsass: Sottass founded the Memphis School of Design in the 1970s. He is an extremely famous modern designer who designed several series of glass for the Vistosi Glass Company. The pieces were created in limited editions, signed and numbered, and each piece was given a name.

Basket, bl & wht latticinio ribbons in clear, clear hdl, Venini, 8" ...215.00
Bottle, clear w/red serpentine & stopper, Moretti, 9½" 425.00
Bowl, clamshell w/raised ridges, Grosse Costolature, Barovier, 8x10" ... 5,200.00
Bowl, dk purple swirls in clear, red scalloped rim, unmk, 6x13" dia.. 150.00
Bowl, gr Bullicante, flattened ovoid, Toso, 3½x8" 60.00
Bowl, merlatto/incalmo, gr/wht/clear, Seguso, 2½x4¾" 385.00
Bowl, twisted amethyst base on clear, Venini Italia Laura, 16½".. 900.00
Candleholder, clear flower w/metallic gold foil, Seguso, 5" dia, ea ..145.00
Candlesticks, bl opal w/appl bl wafers & spiral threading, 10½", pr ...125.00

Chandelier, flower clusters on metal frame, Murano, 26", $4,250.00.

(Photo courtesy David Rago Auctions)

Chandelier, 12 cups, portrait medallions, smoky quartz, Venetian, 42"...3,525.00
Chandelier, 4-tier, clear/smoky accents, pendants, Venini, 38"..2,350.00
Compote, gold mica on clear swirl, appl roses/gr stem, Barovier, 8x11"..360.00
Cruet, mc millefiori, frosted reeded hdl, Fratelli Toso, 6½" 325.00
Ewer, gr dolphin w/gold mica, appl clear details/hdls, Salviati, 9"..125.00
Frame, clear spiral w/gr trim, brass trim, Venini Murano, 14x12"....825.00
Goblet, twisted amethyst & wht ribbons, clear ft w/gold flecks, 5½".. 50.00
Mirror, rope-twist glass-rod borders/appl flowers, mica, 27x24"....585.00
Sculpture, bird, 3 grs in clear, high tail, Murano, 1950s, 18½" 100.00
Sculpture, duck, blk/gold/silver shards cased in clear, Artas, 11" L..460.00
Sculpture, fish on ped, mc stripes, gold fins, Murano, 1950s, 10¾"....60.00
Sculpture, gr cased w/controlled bubbles on body, 15½"................. 75.00
Sculpture, owl, red & blk cased in clear, V Nason, 4⅞x2½"........... 35.00
Sculpture, pelican, crystal w/amber lines in open wings, Zanetti, 14" ...245.00
Sculpture, red/gr/clear/gold flecks/appl threads, Barovier Seguso, 11" ... 175.00

Sculpture, rooster in lattimo glass with applied details, marked Venini/Murano/Italia, 8x9", $2,700.00.

(Photo courtesy David Rago Auctions)

Vase, amethyst spirals on cerulean bl, sheared angle top, Seguso, 10" ... 250.00

Vase, Athena Catterdrale, lozenge-shaped tesserae, no mark, 11x7", $8,500.00.

(Photo courtesy David Rago Auctions)

Vase, bl Dmn Quilt w/wht int, ruffled trumpet neck, Murano, 14x7½".. 40.00
Vase, Corroso, bl w/mica/controlled bubbles, Barovier Seguso, 10".......225.00
Vase, face, bl to wht cased w/appl mc features, 1970s, 12¾"...2,000.00
Vase, lt gr w/appl tendrils, rnd ft, 8" dia top, Venini, 12", pr........ 400.00
Vase, mc broken stripes on cased wht, Murano, 9" 135.00
Vase, mc millefiori, flared rim, 8x5½" 375.00
Vase, Pezzato, purple/amber/gray, sgn Italy/Murano, 10x7" 4,485.00
Vase, Pezzato mc patchwork, manner of Bianconi, 11⅜"...........3,800.00
Vase, pk/gr latticinio ribbons w/gold speckles, clear hdls & ft, 9" 200.00
Vase, red & gr striped ribbons, flared cylinder, Venini Murano, 11"...525.00
Vase, red mottled ball form w/gold flecks/splashes, 1950s, 6x5" ... 250.00
Vase, ruby/gr/clear stripes, conical, Venini, dtd '82, 8½" 500.00
Vase, sections of fine lines: pk, blk or aqua, Lino Tagliapietra, 23" ...4,025.00
Vase, yel triangular form w/ribbed swirls, unmk, 9½"................... 125.00
Vases, pk mottle w/gold flecks, clear dolphin hdls, AVEM, 9½", pr.. 385.00

Ivory

Ivory has been used and appreciated since Neolithic times. It has been a product of every culture and continent. It is the second most valuable organic material after pearls. Ivory is defined as the dentine portion of mammalian teeth. Commercially the most important ivory comes from elephant and mammoth tusks, walrus tusks, hippo teeth, and sperm whale teeth. The smaller tusks of boar and warthog are often used whole.

Ivory has been used for artistic purposes as a palette for oil paints, as inlay on furniture, and especially as a medium for sculptures. Some are in the round, others in the form of plaques. Ivory also has numerous utilitarian uses such as cups and tankards; combs; handles for knives and medical tools; salt and pepper shakers; chess, domino, and checker pieces; billiard balls; jewelry; shoehorns; snuff boxes; brush pots; and fans.

There are a number of laws domestically and internationally to protect endangered animals including the elephant, walrus, and whale. However ivory taken and used before the various enactment dates is legal within the country in which it is located, and can be shipped internationally with a permit. Ivory from mammoths, hippopotamus, wart hogs, and boar is excepted from all bans. Prices have risen slightly over the previous several years for the majority of ivory items with the exception of jewelry, which has fallen in price, and better European and Japanese ivory carvings which have increased substantially over the last 18 months. Prices are lowest for African and Indian ivories. As with all collectibles, the very best pieces will appreciate most in the years to come. Small, poorly carved pieces will not appreciate to any extent. Our advisor for this category is Robert Weisblut; he is listed in the Directory under Florida.

Bicycle, spokes, hand brakes, headlight, etc, China, 1990s, 4x6½" .. 750.00
Bust of Voltaire on marble plinth, France, 19th C, 10" 9,500.00
Candle screen, angels, irregular floral rim, European/19th C, 20x6" .. 8,500.00
Chalice, ivory & silver, high relief stags, European/19th C, 10½x2" .. 1,500.00
Children, cvg, Communist Chinese era, 9½" 1,250.00
Clock, 5 musical nymphs, Dieppe, Fr, late 19th C, 8½x6" 8,000.00
Lantern, Chinese, late 19th C, 28" 7,500.00
Narwhal tusk shakers, scrimshawed, 2½", pr 350.00
Plate, sectioned floral rim/goddess center, Japanese, early 20th C, 8" .. 2,200.00
Snuff bottle, deep relief, China, 19th C, 5" 1,250.00

Study of a rose branch, Japan, early twentieth century, 13" long, $1,750.00.
(Photo courtesy Robert Weisblut)

Triptych, Marie Antoinette, scenes w/in skirt, Fr, late 19th C, 9x5" .. 2,500.00
Village scene, Japanese, ca 1900, 5½" 2,000.00
Walrus sailing vessel w/full sails, Eskimo, 1950s, 10" 1,850.00
Woman w/parasol, European, Late 19th C, 7x3" 1,400.00
Woman w/weaving implements, Chinese, early 20th C, 9" 675.00

Jack-in-the-Pulpit Vases

Popular novelties at the turn of the century, jack-in-the-pulpit vases were made in every type of art glass produced. Some were simple, others elaborately appliqued and enameled. They were shaped to resemble the lily for which they were named.

Yellow with pink interior, English, 12¾", $150.00. (Photo courtesy Early Auction Co.)

Bl opal w/lt gr petals & stem, ca 1870-80, 8" 180.00
Cranberry opal to clear ruffle w/HP floral, Moser, 16", pr 865.00
Cranberry w/encrusted gold motif, gold-trimmed clear disk ft, 13" .. 60.00
Gold irid w/threaded design, 8" 325.00
Gr-gold irid flower, swirled/pulled stem, stepped bulb, Radke, 14" .. 300.00
Mc vertical latticinio & ribbon canes, Italy, 7" 250.00

Opaline to cranberry to mahog at crimped rim, Sandwich, 1870s-80s, 9" 275.00
Pastel gr satin w/vertical ribs, 5½" 125.00
Pk to wht w/appl ft, ruffled top, Italy, 12" 110.00
Rainbow pinwheel on face, camphor leaf-form ped, 6¼" 675.00
Red-crested milk glass, fluted edge, Boston & Sandwich, 5" 65.00
Robin's egg bl to pearl gray, bulbous body, 6" 185.00
Vaseline opal w/ribbing; SP ftd base w/'S' hdls, 8", pr.............. 225.00
Wht opal w/bl stripe at crimped edge, 4½" 100.00
Wht w/yel-to-rose quilted int, HP base/int w/daisies, ruffled, 9" .. 550.00

Jervis

W. P. Jervis began his career as a potter in 1898. By 1908 he had his own pottery in Oyster Bay, New York. His shapes were graceful; often he decorated his wares with sgraffito designs over which he applied a matt glaze. Many piece were incised 'Jervis' in a vertical arrangement. The pottery closed around 1912.

Goblet, mistletoe, gr & wht on teal bl, minute flecks, 4x3" 2,650.00
Pitcher, cats/cattails, bl/yel/gr on dk ground, hairline, 5x7" 1,560.00
Pitcher, irises in panels, textured olive gr, 5⅛" 1,560.00
Pitcher, stylized trees, matt ochre & gray, obscured mk, 4½x5" .. 1,450.00
Planter, gr matt, hdls, #197, 7¾x11½" 960.00

Vase, Queen Anne's lace, white on indigo, blue, incised Jervis, 6x6", NM, $1,885.00. (Photo courtesy David Rago Auctions)

Vase, goose in flight, wht on indigo, 4x4" 1,560.00
Vase, leaves (Grueby style), mint gr matt, 7x3½" 2,760.00

Jewelry

Jewelry as objects of adornment has always been regarded with special affection. Today prices for gems and gemstones crafted into antique and collectible jewelry are based on artistic merit, personal appeal, pure sentimentality, and intrinsic value. Note: In general, diamond prices vary greatly depending on cut, color, clarity, etc., and to assess the value of any diamond of more than a carat in weight, you will need to have information about all of these factors. Values given here are for diamond jewelry with a standard commercial grade of diamonds that are most likely to be encountered.

Our advisor for fine jewelry is Rebecca Dodds-Metts; her address may be found in the Directory under Florida. Marcia 'Sparkles' Brown is our advisor for costume jewelry and the author of *Unsigned Beauties of Costume Jewelry*; *Signed Beauties of Costume Jewelry, Book 1* and *2*; *Coro Jewelry, and Rhinestone Jewelry* (Collector Books); she is also the host of the videos *Hidden Treasures*. Mrs. Brown is listed in the Directory under Oregon. Other good references are *Collect-*

ing *Costume Jewelry 101* and *Collecting Costume Jewelry 202* by Julia C. Carroll; *Inside the Jewelry Box: A Collector's Guide to Costume Jewelry, Vol. 1* and *2*, by Ann Mitchell Pitman; *Brillant Rhinestones* and *20th Century Costume Jewelry* by Ronna Lee Aikens; *Collectible Costume Jewelry* by Cherri Simonds; *Costume Jewelry*, and *Collectible Silver Jewelry* by Fred Rezazadeh; and *100 Years of Collectible Jewelry* and *Fifty Years of Collectible Fashion Jewelry* by Lillian Baker (all available from Collector Books). See also American Painted Porcelain; Hair Weaving.

Key:

B — Bakelite	gt — goldtone
C — Catalin	k — karat
ca — cellulose acetate	L — Lucite
cab — cabochon	lm — laminate
clu — celluloid	pl — plastic
ct — carat	plat — platinum
dmn — diamond	r — resin
dwt — penny weight	r'stn — rhinestone
Euro — European cut	stn — stone
fct — faceted	t — thermoset
fl — filigree	tw — total weight
gf — gold filled	wg — whie gold
gp — gold plated	yg — yellow gold
grad — graduated	ygf — yellow gold filled
gw — gold washed	

Bracelet, amethyst beads, rnd & cvd as flowers, 3-strand, 7" 60.00
Bracelet, bangle; gr/brn jade w/cvd lizards................................. 60.00
Bracelet, bangle; 14k yg w/appl wire decor & 7 6x8mm opals, 17dwt... 400.00
Bracelet, bangle; 14k yg w/3 rubies & 2 dmns, ea 3½mm dia 330.00
Bracelet, Kalo, sterling w/line & circle design, pr...................... 1,120.00
Bracelet, lg nephrite beads w/clusters of rose quartz beads, 8" 175.00
Bracelet, plat w/5 lg aquamarines tw 40ct & O-links w/dmns tw 2.5ct.. 4,320.00
Bracelet, plat w/52 Euro dmns tw 5.0cts & 5.0ct tw sapphires .. 5,750.00
Bracelet, Tiffany & Co, 18k yg links w/16 5½mm lapis beads ... 1,725.00
Bracelet, watch slide; 13 sqs w/various untested stones & seed pearls ... 375.00
Bracelet, wg w/135 dmns, 7ct tw, +14 marquis & 4 pear-cut sapphires ... 2,300.00
Bracelet, 9k mesh 'belt' w/ball trim, 'buckle' closure, Victorian, 7" .. 230.00
Bracelet, 10k wg, 17 sq-cut rubies tw 6.65, dmn spacers tw 1ct, in row.. 2,585.00
Bracelet, 14k wg, sq links & flowers all set w/dmns tw 3.50ct ... 1,725.00
Bracelet, 14k wg, 2 'fingers' 1 side/3 on other, hinged, tw 2.51ct dmn.. 1,265.00
Bracelet, 14k yg, 2-row: interlocking figure-8 links & leaves, 17dwt..... 145.00
Bracelet, 14k yg, 2-strand, dmn-set buckle & belt-tip, 20 dmn tw .50ct... 1,035.00
Bracelet, 14k yg belt w/appl horseshoe/buckle/ball & chain, tiny split . 230.00
Bracelet, 14k yg w/5 14k gold charms, some w/mc stones, 54.5dwt... 1,035.00
Bracelet, 14k yg/wg encrusted w/tw .84ct dmns+sapphires tw 1ct, Deco.. 1,440.00
Bracelet, 18k wg, dmn marquis flowers alternate w/rnd dmns tw 3ct .2,415.00
Bracelet, 18k wg, sq links w/sq pk sapphires tw 3ct+275 dmns tw 2ct .. 2,585.00
Bracelet, 18k wg, V-links set w/186 dmns (SI2-I1/G-I) tw 2.50ct .. 1,150.00
Bracelet, 18k wg, 14 sq links+rnd clasp, 6.33 tw sapphires+2.47 dmns..... 4,600.00
Bracelet, 18k wg, 9 bl sapphires tw 4ct+53 dmn tw 4ct, row arrangement ..3,165.00
Brooch, Kalo, sterling, floral pin #79, 2", +domed beaded earrings .. 235.00
Brooch, Tiffany, 18k yg walking lion w/emerald eyes, 16dwt, 2" L .. 1,265.00
Brooch, yg bee w/3 sapphires+2 sm rubies+8 dmns+3 seed pearls, 1½".. 520.00
Brooch, 14k w/micro-mosaic dam w/trees in onyx oval, 1½" L 230.00
Brooch, 14k w/yg branch w/2 bees, 1.30ct tw dmn+.15ct yel dmn+2 pearls.. 1,035.00
Brooch, 14k wg circle w/14 dmn tw 2.75ct, 1" dia....................... 3,565.00
Brooch, 14k wg Deco-style oval w/tw .44ct dmns & 3 rubies tw .90, 2" L... 575.00
Brooch, 14k wg dmns: 2.07+1.22+1.60ct+76 sm dmns w/tw 2cts.. 8,850.00
Brooch, 14k wg dragonfly w/pave single-cut dmns, 1⅛x1½"........... 865.00
Brooch, 14k wg dragonfly w/shaded bl sapphires tw 1.31ct, 1½" .. 745.00
Brooch, 14k wg fl dmn shape w/55ct bl topaz & 100 wht dmns tw 1ct .. 865.00
Brooch, 14k wg oval w/bow to side, 41 dmn tw 1.33cts, 1½" L 690.00

Brooch, 14k y/wg bow set w/.50ct yel marquis dmn+19 dmns tw 1.0, 2" L..1,440.00
Brooch, 14k yg, micro-mosaic Roman ruins scene in onyx & yg rope fr..865.00
Brooch, 14k yg, 15mm garnet+36 rose-cut dmns, symetrical surround, 2"..345.00
Brooch, 14k yg dbl oval w/bow at side set w/5.5mm rnd amethyst, 1½"..200.00
Brooch, 14k yg enamel dragonfly w/.18ct tw dmns, 1½x⅝" 435.00
Brooch, 14k yg spray w/wg swirl center set w/30 dmn tw .50, 1½" L..520.00
Brooch, 14k yg stork paved w/.59cts dmns+1.25cts sapphires, 1¾"....865.00
Brooch, 18k bumblebee w/17 dmn tw .66ct & 5 rubies .85ct tw, 1⅛"..240.00
Brooch, 18k wg dragonfly, dmn body tw .15ct, wings: amethysts tw .98ct ...1,265.00
Brooch, 18k yg, 4 crystal cabs w/imp & rvpt cockfights linked together.460.00
Brooch, 18k yg dmn-set fr .30ct tw around cvd/pierced gr jade, 1½"..520.00
Brooch, 18k yg koala w/.50ct tw dmn accents, ruby 1.5mm eyes, 13.6dwt..1,300.00
Brooch, 18k yg peacock w/pave dmns/bl sapphires/emeralds, 3½"...920.00
Brooch, 18k yg rampant lion w/5 .15ct dmns, 2 1.2mm rubies, 6.7dwt ..550.00

Brooch/pendant, 18k gold with a 1½x1¼" nephrite jade cabochon, 48 pearls and four single-cut diamonds, nineteenth century, 4" long, from $700.00 to $1.000.00.

Cross, 14k rose gold w/132 rnd & princess dmns tw 3.30ct, 2"..1,600.00
Cross, 18k wg, stylized/cut-out, allover tsavorite garnets & dmns, 2" .700.00
Cuff links, Tiffany, 14k, ea sq w/4 sapphires & 4 textured sqs, ¾"....375.00
Earrings, wg w/cartouch-form drops, 2ct tw dmns, 1¼" 1,140.00
Earrings, 14k wg, ea w/bl sapphire tw 4.30ct in ring of tw .90ct dmns... 600.00
Earrings, 14k wg, ea w/oval ruby tw 1.54ct+.14ct dmns in 3-band mt ..400.00
Earrings, 14k wg, ea w/12mm Tahitian gray pearl, brn/wht dmn enhancer.1,095.00
Earrings, 14k wg, oval/baguette rubies tw 3.39cts/dmn surround tw .20 ...480.00
Earrings, 14k wg dangles, ea w/pear emerald tw .58ct+96 dmns tw .96ct... 900.00
Earrings, 14k wg w/6x8mm bl sapphire w/in 2 rows sm dmns tw .61ct ...800.00
Earrings, 18k yg floral mt w/2.50ct tw dmns/2 sm sapphires/6 emeralds ..3,680.00
Earrings, 18k yg w/garnet & opal, oval, Fr hooks, Vict, ⅞"........... 500.00
Necklace, G Jensen, silver bellflower drop over MOP cab+3 gr stn cabs... 8,900.00
Necklace, Kalo, silver, 13 links in cherry & leaf design, 15" 1,000.00
Necklace, pearls, blk 10mm cultured, 14kt wg/yg clasp w/tiny dmns, 14".. 2,950.00
Necklace, pearls, pk 11mm cultured, w/14k yg clasp, 14" 1,200.00
Necklace, pearls, pk 7-7½mm cultured, 2 rows sterling clasp, 17"...285.00
Necklace, pearls, 10-10½mm blk, 14k yg clasp, 24"...................... 400.00
Necklace, pearls, 7-7½mm, 2-strand, 14k yg clasp w/dmn & sapphire..635.00
Necklace, pearls, 7-7½mm, 3-strand, 14k wg clasp w/rubies & dmns.. 920.00
Necklace, pearls, 9½-10mm cultured/freshwater, 14k yg clasp, 36" 115.00
Necklace, rutile quartz beads w/tiny gold spacers, 18k yg clasp, 18" 115.00
Necklace, wg chandelier pendant w/7 baguette dmns+12 .5ct tw, 14"....1,200.00
Necklace, 102 plat sq links ea w/dmn, tw 4.5cts, tw: 39.93 grams, 15"...5,405.00
Necklace, 14k gold bar chain, ea bar w/swirl drop w/dmn in 4-6mm range...1,150.00
Necklace, 14k wg, 2-row dmn 'bib' of 19 vertical bars, 386: tw 27ct...10,925.00
Necklace, 14k wg links w/9 blk-silver Tahitian pearls, 9mm-11.5mm, 17"..635.00
Necklace, 14k yg dmn-cut rope w/solid center w/.32ct tw dmns, Italy..290.00
Necklace, 14k yg ovals/stars alternate, tw 10.60ct dmns+10.26 emeralds..6,900.00
Necklace, 14k yg w/boar tusk mtd in gold at tip & bk, sq snake chain ..40.00
Necklace, 18k wg, dmn links form V, w/23 dmn drops, tw 3cts, 17" ..1,495.00
Necklace, 18k yg curbed link chain w/tw .55ct dmn-fr octagon pendant.. 575.00
Necklace, 18k yg link chain w/dmn & oval dangles ea w/sm dmn tw 3.5ct ..1,380.00

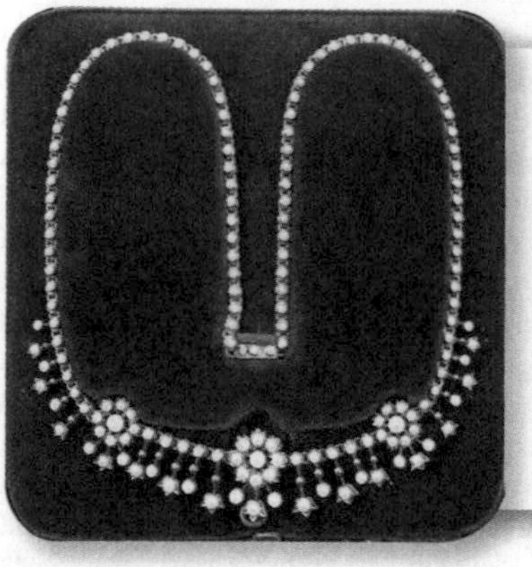

Necklace, 160 pearls ranging from 2mm to 3.7mm set in metal base, English, in original D. J. Welby London box, $1,200.00. (Photo courtesy Jackson's International Auctioneers & Appraisers of Fine Art & Antiques)

Pendant, 14k yg w/pear-cut 12.5ct aquamarine+2 rows sm dms tw 2.25ct..920.00
Pendant, 18k yg crown form w/garnet/pearls, 1", on 18" yg box chain..400.00
Pendant, 1899 $20 gold Liberty head coin w/14k rope border, 1½" dia..635.00
Pendant, 1927 Liberty coin in plat fr w/33 2.7mm dmns tw 2.33ct..980.00
Pin, plat open dmn shape w/flower w/67 dmns tw 1.5ct & 28 rubies tw .8..2,070.00
Ring, man's, 10k wg w/32 pave-set single-cut dmns, top: ⅝x⅞" ... 290.00
Ring, man's, 14k yg, 3 dmns in row on top: 5.5mm, 4.1mm ea side, ⅝"..865.00
Ring, man's, 14k yg w/1.2ct mine-cut dmn 1,400.00
Ring, man's, 18k wg, mine-cut sq 1ct dmn & 2 4.5mm synthetic sapphires..865.00
Ring, plat, openwork rectangle mt w/3 dmns (3mm to 4mm)+25 single-cuts..920.00
Ring, plat, row of 3 dmn tw 1.40ct (SI1/H) 2,300.00
Ring, plat, w/brilliant-cut dmn & 4 sm dmns, .3ct tw 500.00
Ring, plat, .50ct yel/brn dmn circled w/36 Euro dmn tw 1.25ct.....2,590.00
Ring, plat w/13ct sq emerald & 40 2ct tw dmns 5,700.00
Ring, plat w/3.99 dmn (VS2/K), pear dmn ea side tw .60cts...16,390.00
Ring, plat w/4.4ct dmn solitaire (VS1/J-K) flanked by .08ct baguettes . 13,225.00
Ring, plat/rose gold, 13 grad dmns in dbl fan form, 2.25ct tw ...1,500.00
Ring, wg w/.57ct mine-cut (GH/I1) dmn, Deco-style fl mt 600.00
Ring, wg w/2.5ct star sapphire & sm dmns, Deco style.............1,585.00
Ring, 9k yg, ⅝x½" crystal cab w/rvpt dog face, Vict........................ 70.00
Ring, 14k wg, .92ct oval tanzanite, 3 sm dmns above/below+14 baguettes...575.00
Ring, 14k wg, cushion amethyst+2 half-moon citrines, tw stns: 10.79ct..345.00
Ring, 14k wg, 1.54ct bl sapphire w/in 2 rows dmn tw .31ct, crown: ¾" ..400.00
Ring, 14k wg fl, center cross w/bl sapphires tw .26ct+tw .23ct dmns..400.00
Ring, 14k wg w/12x15mm colorless sapphire 175.00
Ring, 14k wg w/2.85ct dmn solitaire (VS2/L-M)....................5,635.00
Ring, 14k wg w/3 .25ct dmns in diagonal+bar on ea side w/tiny dmn .. 550.00
Ring, 14k wg ¾" floral cluster mt w/7 dmns tw 3.18ct (SI1-I1/I-J) . 1,150.00
Ring, 14k yg, amethyst, 22x15mm, +4 sm dmn tw .12ct............. 385.00
Ring, 14k yg, wide textured band, 'buckle' set w/18 single-cut dmns .. 260.00
Ring, 14k yg w/cushion-cut purple amethyst in dmn surround tw .35ct...575.00
Ring, 14k yg w/2.66ct dmn (VS1/L-M)+.10ct dmn ea side.......5,750.00
Ring, 14k yg w/5.7ct oval brilliant emerald & 2 brilliant dmns.. 3,300.00
Ring, 14k yg w/6.5x16.8mm apple gr jadeite saddle.................. 400.00
Ring, 18k wg, .65ct rnd cut dmn amid 6 .77ct tw dmns, w/.9ct dmn band..2,000.00
Ring, 18k wg, onyx upright bar ea side panel w/6 sm dmns, crown: ⅞" ..345.00
Ring, 18k wg, 1.1ct marquis bl sapphire w/2 sm baguette dmns ea side ..345.00
Ring, 18k wg fl w/.50ct Euro dmn ea side .50ct ruby..................... 980.00
Ring, 18k wg fl w/5.4mm rnd dmn+triangle bl sapphires on 4 sides...550.00
Ring, 18k wg w/1.85ct emerald cab, wide pave crown w/100 dmn tw 1ct. 300.00
Ring, 18k yg, .5ct emerald-cut emerald, 14 rnd/8 baguette dmns ..4,465.00
Ring, 18k yg, 14mmx8mm oval garnet w/surround of 12 sm garnets, ¾" ... 75.00
Ring, 18k yg flower mt w/dmn cluster center, enameled petals w/sm dmns...920.00
Ring, 18k yg granulated dome w/1.15ct center dmn+6 dmn tw .60, 7.3dwt ...2,185.00
Ring, 18k yg w/.76ct dmn (I1/G-H), bypass mt w/17 baguettes tw .66ct ...920.00
Ring, 18k yg w/1.20ct marquis dmn (SI1/J-K)+.60cts baguettes.....1,870.00
Ring, 18k yg w/12.4ct oval emerald & 2 rnd brilliant dmns......4,400.00
Ring, 18k yg w/3.5ct oval sapphire+14 baguettes+10 rnd dmns.. 2,300.00
Ring, 18k yg/wg, 3.05ct Euro dmn (Fancy Yellow) & 36 sm .70ct tw dms.. 19,000.00
Ring, 18k yg/wg w/.5ct brilliant cut dmn+2 sm heart-shaped sapphires..1,000.00
Slide chain, 14k yg dbl link chain, cameo/seed pearl-set slide, .30dwt....690.00
Tie tack, 14k wg, Oriental letter set w/19 single-cut dmns, ⅞x⅞" ...290.00
Watch chain, 10k yg, graduated links, fob w/faceted topaz, 14" ... 190.00
Watch chain, 10k yg, heavy long oval links, amethyst in 1x½" fob..... 340.00

Costume Jewelry

Rhinestone jewelry has become a very popular collectible. Rhinestones are foil-backed, leaded crystal, faceted stones with a sparkle outshining diamonds. Copyrighting jewelry came into effect in 1955. Pieces bearing a copyright mark (post-1955) are considered 'collectibles,' while pieces (with no copyright) made before then are regarded as 'antiques.' Fur clips are two-pronged, used to anchor fur stoles. Dress clips have a spring clasp and are used at the dress neckline. Look for signed and well-made, unmarked pieces for your collections and preserve this American art form. Our advisor for costume jewelry is Marcia Brown (see introductory paragraphs for information on her books and videos).

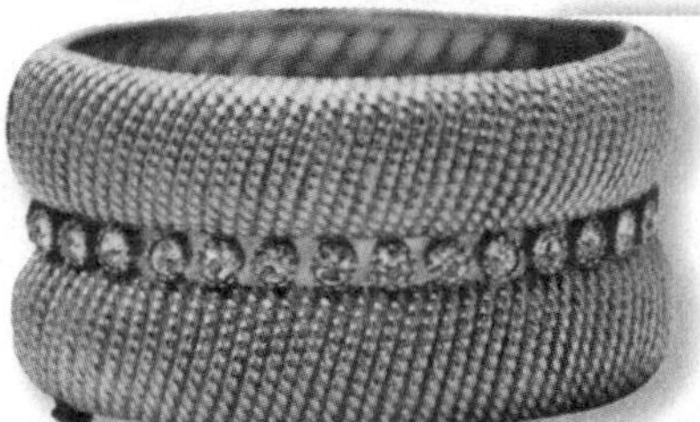

Bracelet, cuff; Castlecliff, gold-tone with diamante rhinestones, 1½", from $125.00 to $145.00. (Photo courtesy Marcia Brown)

Bracelet, cuff; KJ Lane, g-t w/eng dmns, from $100 to................. 135.00
Bracelet, cuff; unsgn, silver-tone twisted rope design, heavy, $50 to... 70.00
Bracelet, Eisenberg, clear chaton r'stns in 2 szs/3 rows, dbl clasp... 165.00
Bracelet, Harwood, g-t expansion w/bl r'stns, from $55 to 75.00
Bracelet, Monet, tailored g-t links.. 45.00
Bracelet, Renoir, copper loops form links...................................... 48.00
Bracelet, S Coventry, 8 ocean-theme charms on gold-tone chain....48.00
Bracelet, unsgn, chaton-cut r'stns in 2 rows, rhodium plated, $115 to.. 135.00
Bracelet, Vendome, faux pearls, 6-strand, r'stn clasp, from $50 to....70.00
Bracelet & earrings, Eisenberg, clear r'stns, 7½x¾", 1¼" 300.00
Brooch, Boucher, bird on branch, bl enamel/r'stns, 3¾", $500 to. 750.00
Brooch, Boucher, r'stns in rhodium-plated bow, 1950, 2½", $70 to.. 100.00
Brooch, Boucher, Skye terrier, g-t w/enamel details, 1½" 60.00
Brooch, BSK, fish, yel & gr enamel, 1955-60s, 2", from $45 to...... 55.00
Brooch, Cadoro, g-t birds form Christmas tree 255.00
Brooch, Capri, mc r'stns on cap, gr enameling................................ 48.00
Brooch, Castlecliff, crown, sterling w/3 pearls/red & clear r'stns.. 225.00
Brooch, Doddz, golden cameo on faux hematite oval w/in r'stn fr ...30.00
Brooch, Eisenberg, clear crystals/bl r'stns on gp body 135.00
Brooch, Florenza, starfish, lav & purple r'stns 85.00
Brooch, H Carnegie, flower, mc enamel w/detailed stamen, 1¾" ... 95.00
Brooch, H Carnegie, wreath, gp w/gr & red cabs.......................... 85.00
Brooch, Hobe, bow, sterling w/lav crystal in flower center........... 425.00
Brooch, Hobe, flower w/gr prong-set aurora borealis r'stns, 3¾"..... 90.00
Brooch, Hollycraft, butterfly, mc enamel, 1960s, 2¼", from $35 to..45.00
Brooch, JJ, cat, gp w/articulated tail 20.00
Brooch, JJ, dolphin & clamshell, pewter finish w/bl enamel 40.00
Brooch, Kandall & Marcus, r'stn waterfall, 1940s, 5¼", $45 to 60.00
Brooch, Kramer, horse, gp w/diamante r'stn trim, chain tassel tail. 90.00
Brooch, Lisner, butterfly, g-t w/r'stns, 1950s, 2¼", $70 to 100.00
Brooch, Monet, bee, silver-tone w/wire (harp-like) wings............. 55.00
Brooch, Monet, sunburst, g-t w/fringe, 1960s, 2¾" 10.00
Brooch, Sandor, daisy, mc enameling w/pnt butterfly 42.00
Brooch, Star Novelty, branch, SP w/diamante r'stns 190.00

Brooch, Staret, Burma red chatons topped by red and crystal pave ribbons, **$180.00.** (Photo courtesy Marcia Brown)

Brooch, Trifari, bird, g-t w/baguette r'stns, 3x2", $65 to 90.00
Brooch, Trifari, crescent w/golden r'stns, 2x1¾", from $60 to 80.00
Brooch, Trifari, goose, g-t w/diamante r'stns 145.00
Brooch, Trifari, key, silver w/r'stns, 1947, 2½", from $95 to.......... 135.00
Brooch, Trifari, leaves, g-t w/glued-in pearls, 2¼", $60 to 80.00
Brooch, Trifari, Plume, faux pearls on gold feather, 2", from $15 to..20.00
Brooch, Trifari, pod, g-t w/faux pearls 180.00
Brooch, Trifari, rose, g-t w/10 sm r'stns, 1960s, 2½", $70 to 100.00
Brooch, Trifari, 4 amber r'stn flowers beside gold swirl, 2½" 60.00
Brooch, Trifari Pat Pend, poodle, faceted r'stn belly, mini, $65 to....100.00
Brooch, unsgn, flower, blk/wht enamel, 1960s, 1x3½", from $25 to....45.00
Brooch, Vendome, flower, bl enamel w/gr leaves, 1960s, 3½", $35 to ..55.00
Brooch, Weiss, butterfly, enameled.. 58.00
Brooch, Weiss, frog, pk enamel w/gr spots..................................... 80.00
Brooch, Weiss, rose, pk enamel fr w/pk r'stns................................. 80.00
Brooch & earrings, Barclay, bl r'stns in silver-tone rectangle fr....... 55.00
Brooch & earrings, Emmons, Deco gp triangle w/bl r'stn, Deco style...75.00
Brooch & earrings, Florenza, amber r'stn amid sm aurora borealis stns ...100.00
Brooch & earrings, Judy Lee, faux bl moonstone clusters............... 68.00
Brooch & earrings, KJ Lane, crown, gp w/diamante r'stns............... 70.00
Brooch & earrings, orange & gold beaded snowflake....................... 80.00
Brooch & earrings, Schreiner, cut citrine stones/olive gr crystals.. 300.00
Brooch & earrings, Trifari, leaf, pave diamante rstns..................... 135.00
Choker, Laquepaque FCS Plata 925 Mexico, dbl chain w/silver half-orbs...345.00
Clip, Eisenberg, r'stns in varied shapes on wht metal, 1930s, 2¾" ...250.00
Cuff links, Swank, purple cab in g-t fr, matching tie bar, MIB 100.00
Earrings, Boucher, diamante r'stns w/faux pearl center................. 100.00
Earrings, Coro, lg red r'stn amid sm pk stns, 1948-55, 1", from $8 to....12.00
Earrings, Hollycraft, star, bl r'stns on SP 6-point fr....................... 60.00
Earrings, Kramer, diamante r'stns in tic-tac-toe pattern 68.00
Earrings, Ledo, flower, gr r'stns, 1" clips, from $20 to..................... 30.00
Earrings, TARA, 3 faux pearls/3 aurora borealis r'stns, 1" clips 65.00
Necklace, Boucher, g-t collar w/mc jewels, 15", from $100 to...... 200.00
Necklace, Boucher, gr pearl & clear beads, 5-strand........................ 55.00
Necklace, Coro, bl glass ribbed stns w/bl r'stns, 1950s, $65 to....... 75.00
Necklace, Hobe, bl & clear beads, 4-strand 85.00
Necklace, Joseff of Hollywood, SP chain w/3 owls' heads 295.00
Necklace, Karmer, g-p w/diamante r'stns & pave work.................. 110.00
Necklace, KJ Lane, pearls, 3-strand, mk clasp................................ 110.00
Necklace, M Haskell, pk glass beads, 3-strand choker, 16", $150 to...250.00
Necklace, M Haskell, wht chalk beads, 3 long strands 125.00
Necklace, Pomeroy's, red seed beads, 30-strand, 15", from $120 to..190.00
Necklace, R De Mario, faux pearls, 3-strand w/pearl/r'stn center, 12" ... 175.00
Necklace, Robert Originals, lav/purple/pk beads, 5-strand, lg clasp....325.00
Necklace, Trifari, 2 sunflowers w/r'stn centers on snake chain 65.00
Necklace, unsgn, aurora borealis crystals, 1-strand choker, $65 to. 85.00
Necklace, unsgn, blk jet glass beads, hand strung/knotted, 22" 175.00
Necklace, unsgn, herringbone chain w/gr cabochon drop, from $60 to..120.00
Necklace, Weiss, diamante r'stn bib 275.00
Necklace, Whiting & Davis, gold mesh fabric bib style 110.00

Necklace & bracelet, Hollycraft, bl r'stns & seed pearls 165.00
Necklace & bracelet, Lisner, SP floral design w/pk r'stns............... 65.00
Necklace & earrings, mc diamante r'stn locket on dbl g-t chain..325.00
Necklace & earrings, Napier, diamante r'stns leaves, 3½" earrings....235.00
Necklace & earrings, Park Lane, opaline oval in r'stn fr on chain.48.00
Necklace & earrings, Schiaparelli, bl crackled cabs/aurora borealis...280.00
Necklace & earrings, Trifari, faux pearls, 3-strand........................ 140.00
Parure, Hobe, wht beads/diamante rondels, springe wire bracelet...250.00

Parure, Miriam Haskell, five-color beadwork, $4,950.00. (Photo courtesy Marcia Brown)

Ring, E Taylor/Avon, amethyst teardrop r'stn/turq seed pearls 60.00
Ring, S Coventry, amethyst-color stone & sm faux pearls.............. 32.00
Stick pin, M Haskell, flower, antique gold w/sm r'stns.................. 135.00

Plastic Jewelry

Barrette, A Bonaz, Galalith w/gold-leaf trim, 1920, from $125 to...150.00
Bracelet, B, blk w/cvd flowers & plain brass sqs, linked bk, 1935..185.00
Bracelet, B, mc segments, elastic stretch, 1935, from $150 to....... 250.00
Bracelet, B, red & chrome-plated links on metal chain, 1930, $250 to..295.00
Bracelet, bangle; B, apricot w/cvg, 1" W, from $55 to.................... 75.00
Bracelet, bangle; B, maroon w/chrome band, 1935, from $55 to.... 85.00
Bracelet, bangle; clu, scalloped w/HP roses, 1920, from $45 to...... 55.00
Bracelet, bangle; L, pearlized wht saucer shape, from $35 to.......... 45.00
Bracelet, bangle; Lea Stein, ca lm, 1960-80, from $200 to........... 250.00
Bracelet, bangle; Lea Stein, ca snake, 1960-80, from $85 to 125.00
Bracelet, cuff; ca, nautical buckle design, wide, 1930, from $200 to...300.00
Bracelet, cuff; t pl, blk, simple, 1935, from $35 to 50.00
Bracelet, cuff; t pl, blk hinged style w/lg r'stns, 1945-50, $110 to.. 125.00
Bracelet, L, red sq links, 1950s, from $45 to................................ 55.00
Bracelet, L & pearlized wht pl & rhodium, 1965, from $25 to....... 35.00
Brooch, Art, pl, cattails, gr w/golden leaves, 3x2", +clip earrings .. 35.00

Brooch, Bakelite, Black figure, jointed, 4¼", $635.00. (Photo courtesy Skinner Inc. Auctioneers & Appraisers of Antiques & Fine Art)

Brooch, B, horse head, butterscotch w/metal studs, glass eye, chain...350.00
Brooch, B, leaves, cvd w/HP accents, 1930s, from $55 to 75.00

Brooch, B, Maltese cross, dk amber, 1935, lg, from $45 to 65.00
Brooch, B, red & blk w/much cvg, 1925, from $125 to 150.00
Brooch, B, sword, blk w/chrome, from $75 to 100.00
Brooch, Coro, pl, flowers, wht on gp w/r'stn centers, 2½", $30 to .. 40.00
Brooch, H Carnegie, B, rooster, mc w/metal accents, from $300 to . 350.00
Brooch, Lea Stein, lm ca, pearlized blk rectangle, 1960-80, $75 to .. 100.00
Brooch, pl, bird, scratch-cvd w/r'stn eye, 1935, from $55 to 65.00
Brooch, S Coventry, t pl, turq w/glass stns, 1960, from $55 to 65.00
Brooch, Trifari, L, Jelly Belly frog, sterling w/gold wash, 2¾" 700.00
Brooch, W Germany, L/pl/glass, bead cluster, 1960-70, from $65 to .. 75.00
Buckle, B & metal, 2-pc, 1935, from $95 to 125.00
Buckle, clu, HP fruit on bl, 1920, from $125 to 135.00
Buckle, pl, blk 2-pc daisy pattern, 1930, from $35 to 40.00
Clip, C, brn & gr bar w/metal triangle set w/r'stns, 1936-40, $50 to .. 80.00
Clip, C, ivory & gr zigzag Deco design on triangle, 1936-41, $75 to .. 100.00
Comb, clu, amber w/pave set r'stns, 1925, very lg, from $135 to .. 150.00
Earrings, B, orange triangular drop, heavy, 1935, from $55 to 75.00
Earrings, B, pnt transparent pendant balls, 1950, from $55 to 75.00
Earrings, L, cvd & pnt w/r'stns, clip-style button, 1935, from $55 to .. 65.00
Earrings, Missoni, r, gr w/chrome disk center, 1980, from $100 to ... 150.00
Earrings, molded + pl, clip type, 1950, from $25 to 50.00
Earrings, pl, button type, red w/r'stns, 1935, from $45 to 55.00
Earrings, pl, flower w/r'stn center, screw-bk button, 1960, $10 to .. 20.00
Earrings, t pl set in rhodium, 1950, from $10 to 15.00
Necklace, B, mc beads, 2-strand, 1930s, from $300 to 350.00
Necklace, Belgium, B, carnelian w/mesh chrome, 1930, from $300 to ... 350.00
Necklace, Galalith & metal w/cvd beads, Egyptian revival pendant .. 150.00
Necklace, H Carnegie, B & chrome, sardine in a can pendant, $195 to .. 250.00
Necklace, KJ Lane, t pl, faux jade/coral/jet/pearls, 6-strand, $225 to .. 275.00
Necklace, pl lm w/pulverized gemstones/cvd cinnabar, 1970, $275 to .. 300.00
Necklace, t pl, faux jade/onyx stns, channel-set r'stns, 20", up to ... 400.00
Necklace, t pl, turq w/wood & pnt cork, 1950, from $35 to 45.00

Parure, Coro, L, confetti rectangles, 16" choker+1" clip earrings... 48.00

Johnson Brothers

A Staffordshire-based company operating since well before the turn of the century, Johnson Brothers has produced many familiar lines of dinnerware, several of which are becoming very collectible. Some of their patterns were made in both blue and pink transfer as well as in polychrome, and many of their older patterns are still being produced. Among them are Old Britain Castles, Friendly Village, His Majesty, and Rose Chintz. However, the lines are less extensive than they once were.

Values range from a low base price for patterns that are still in production or less collectible to a high that would apply to very desirable patterns such as Tally Ho, English Chippendale, Wild Turkeys, Strawberry Fair, Historic America, and Harvest Fruit. Mid-range lines include Coaching Scenes, Millsteam, Old English Countryside, Rose

Bouquet (and there are others). These prices apply only to pieces made before 1990. Lines currently in production are being sold in many retail and outlet stores today at prices that are quite different from the ones we suggest. While a complete place setting of Old Britain Castles is normally about $50.00, in some outlets you can purchase it for as little as half price. For more information on marks, patterns, and pricing, we recommend *Johnson Brothers Dinnerware Pattern Directory and Price Guide* by Mary J. Finegan, who is listed in the Directory under North Carolina.

Bowl, cereal/soup; rnd, sq or lug, ea from $10 to 20.00
Bowl, soup; rnd or sq, 7", from $12 to 25.00
Bowl, vegetable; oval, from $30 to 50.00
Butter dish, from $50 to 80.00
Chop/cake plate, from $50 to 80.00
Coffee mug, from $20 to 25.00

Coffeepot, Friendly Village, $90.00.

Demitasse set, 2-pc, from $20 to 30.00
Egg cup, from $15 to 30.00
Pitcher/jug, from $45 to 55.00
Plate, dinner; from $14 to 30.00
Plate, salad; sq or rnd, from $10 to 18.00
Platter, med, 12-14", ea from $45 to 55.00

Platter, Wild Turkey, 20", minimum value, $300.00.

Sauceboat/gravy, from $40 to 48.00
Shakers, pr, from $40 to 48.00
Sugar bowl, open, from $30 to 40.00
Teacup & saucer, from $15 to 30.00
Teapot, from $90 to 100.00
Turkey platter, 20½", from $200 to 300.00

Josef Originals

Figurines of lovely ladies, charming girls, and whimsical animals marked Josef Originals were designed by Muriel Joseph George of Arcadia, California, from 1945 to 1985. Until 1960 they were produced in California, but costs were high and copies of her work were being made in Japan. To remain competitive, she and her partner, George Good, found a company in Japan to build a factory and produce her designs to her specifications. Muriel retired in 1982; however, Mr. Good continued production of her work and made some design changes on some figurines. The company was sold in late 1985; the name is currently owned by Dakin/Applause, and a limited amount of figurines with the Josef Originals name are being made. Those made during the ownership of Muriel are the most collectible. They can be recognized by these characteristics: The girls have a high-gloss finish, black eyes, and most are signed on the bottom. As of the late 1970s, bisque finish was making its way into the lineup, and by 1980 glossy girls were fairly scarce in the product line. Brown-eyed figurines date from 1982 through 1985. Applause uses a red-brown eye, although they are starting to release 'copies' of early pieces that are signed Josef Originals by Applause or by Dakin. The animals were nearly always done in a matt finish and bore paper labels only. In the mid-1970s they introduced a line of fuzzy flocked-coat animals with glass eyes. Our advisors, Jim and Kaye Whitaker (see the Directory under Washington, no appraisal requests please) have written three books: *Josef Originals, Charming Figurines, Revised Edition*; *Josef Originals, A Second Look*; and *Josef Originals, Figurines of Muriel Joseph George*. These are all currently available, and each has no repeats of items shown in the other books. Please note: All figurines listed here have black eyes unless specified otherwise. As with many collectibles, values have been negatively impacted to a measurable extent since the advent of the Internet.

Basket Pet, 6 in series, bsk finish, Japan, 3½", ea 15.00
Birthday Girls, 1-16, Japan, 7", ea 25.00
Careers, 6 in series, Japan, 7", ea 75.00
Christmas Choir Boys, 2 different sets of 3, Japan, 5½", ea set 60.00
Christmas Music Box Angel, Japan, 7" 35.00
Colonial Days, 6 in series, Japan, 9½", ea.. 115.00
Doll of the Month (tilt head), California, 3¼", ea............................. 35.00
Ecology Girls, 6 in series, Japan, 4¼", ea... 40.00
Elephant, sitting, Japan, 3¾", from $25 to 30.00
Favorite Music Box, 6 in series, Japan, 6½", ea 85.00
First Date, young lady in gr gown holding fan, Japan, 9" 95.00
Fuzzy Animals, various species & poses, ea from $5 to 10.00
Hunter, beautiful standing horse, Japan, 6"..................................... 25.00
Kennel Club, 6 in series, Japan, 4", ea.. 15.00

Lara's Theme, music box, 6", $70.00. (Photo courtesy Jim and Kaye Whitaker)

Love Makes the World Go Round, 6 in series, Japan, 9", ea 95.00

Love Theme Music Box, 6 in series, couple on base, 6¼", ea 75.00
Mary Ann & Mama, California, 4", 7", pr 135.00
Mermaid, lipstick holder, wht w/beige trim, Japan, 6½" 85.00
Mice, Christmas, Japan, 2¾", ea... 9.00
Monkey Family, various poses, Japan, 3", ea 12.00
Mother's World, 6 in series, doing chores, Japan, 7½", ea.............. 95.00
Nursery Rhyme, 6 in series, Japan, 4", ea 45.00
Ostrich Mama, Japan, 5"... 30.00
Persian Cat, sitting, Japan, 4½" 15.00
Persian Cat Family, set of 4, Japan, mini, 1½-2", complete set 20.00
Persian Mama Cat w/Kitten, Japan, 8" 35.00

Pixies, various poses, $25.00 each.
(Photo courtesy Jim and Kaye Whitaker)

Romance Music Box, 6 in series, brn eyes, Japan, 6½", ea.............. 75.00
Rose Garden, 6 in series, brn eyes, Japan, 5¼", ea 65.00
Santa Music Box, several styles, Japan, 7", ea 65.00
Siamese Cat Family, 4-pc mini set by Josef, Japan, 1-2", complete set....20.00
Smail Family, set of 4, mini, Japan, ¾-1½", complete set............... 20.00
Small World, 6 in series, brn eyes, Japan, 4½", ea........................... 25.00
Story Angel, 6 in series, Japan, 5½", ea.. 40.00
Sweet Sixteen, 6 in series, Japan, 7", ea 95.00
Taffy, made in various colors, California, 4½", ea 45.00
Three Kings, Japan, 8½-11", set of 3 .... 70.00
Wee Ching & Wee Ling, boy w/dog, girl w/cat, often copied, California .. 45.00
White Colonial Days, 6 in series, Japan, 9", ea................................ 75.00
World Greatest, 6 in series, Japan, 4½", ea....................................... 15.00
Zodiac Series, various colors, California, 3½" 25.00

Judaica

The items listed below are representative of objects used in both the secular and religious life of the Jewish people. They are evident of a culture where silversmiths, painters, engravers, writers, and metal workers were highly gifted and skilled in their art. Most of the treasures shown in recently displayed exhibits of Judaica were confiscated by the Germans during the late 1930s up to 1945; by then eight Jewish synagogues and 50 warehouses had been filled with Hitler's plunder. Judaica is currently available through dealers, from private collections, and the annual auction held in Israel, New York City, and Boston.

Our advisor for this category is Arthur M. Feldman, executive director of the Sherwin Miller Museum of Jewish Art (Tulsa); he is listed in the Directory under Oklahoma.

Box, charity; brass building form w/2 slots, 2 doors on body, 6½" ..1,650.00
Box, charity; silver well form w/dome lid, eng text, Russia, 1895, 6"..2,950.00
Box, etrog, silver w/emb foliage/scrolls, Germany, 5¾"................. 800.00
Box, etrog, silver w/emb fruit/text, German style, 20th C, 4½"....585.00
Box, marriage; eng marriage scene on pewter, Mazel Tov, 19th C, 4¼"..235.00

Box, spice; silver, fruit finial, 3-part int, Germany, ca 1900, 2½" ...1,175.00
Broadside, Warning to Inhabitants of Jerusalem, 3 languages, 1938...200.00
Candelabra, brass, 7-light, w/bobeches, cast supports, 18", pr 200.00
Cup, Kiddush, plain silver, flared rim, Dutch, ca 1927, 3½" 765.00
Cup, Kiddush, silver & parcel gilt scrollwork, Europe, 1890s, 2¾"..585.00
Cup, Kiddush; silver, Remember the Sabbath..., ftd, Germany, 1900s, 5"..1,500.00
Hanukah lamp, brass, openwork bkplate w/lions/crown/etc, Poland, 10"..585.00
Matzoh bag, embr silk, lion/crown/foliage, Europe, 1900s, 15" dia..175.00
Megillah, brass case w/serpentine thumb-pc, Persia, 1900s, 14" .2,700.00
Megillah, silver repousse case w/flattened onion top, Balkan, 10"..2,700.00

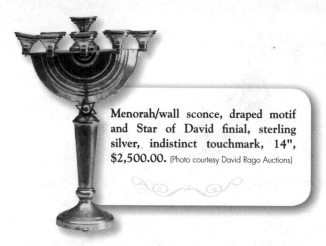

Menorah/wall sconce, draped motif and Star of David finial, sterling silver, indistinct touchmark, 14", $2,500.00. (Photo courtesy David Rago Auctions)

Mezuzah, silver w/cvd ivory front, scrolled bkplate, Poland, 6½" .. 325.00
Mezuzah, silver-gilt & HP foliage, wood bk, Russian type, 6⅜"....325.00
Palm branch holder, enameled brass, Near Eastern, 19th C, 28"..1,525.00
Plate, Havdalah, HP porc w/gold, Germany, ca 1900, 9½" 300.00
Plate, Seder order & w/floral sprays on porc, Germany, 1900s, 10"..585.00
Poster, United Jewish Appeal, Their Fight Is Our Fight..., 22x14"...765.00
Spice container, silver articulated fish form, red eyes, 10" L.........585.00
Spice tower, silver & silver filigree, Berlin, late 19th C, 12", VG..550.00
Torah binders, HP linen, Alsace-Lorraine, late 19th C, pr...........470.00
Torah pointer, bone, trn shaft, spice compartment, 1900s, 12" 700.00
Torah pointer, silver, flattened knop, Poland, 1800s, 9"+loop & chain ..825.00
Torah shield, silver, cartouch w/crown/ark/etc, Am, 1936, 13" 700.00
Torah shield, silver/silver gilt, tablet/bells, Germany/1900, 12"... 2,450.00

Jugtown

The Jugtown Pottery was started about 1920 by Juliana and Jacques Busbee, in Moore County, North Carolina. Ben Owen, a young descendant of a Staffordshire potter, was hired in 1923. He was the master potter, while the Busbees experimented with perfecting glazes and supervising design and modeling. Preferred shapes were those reminiscent of traditional country wares and classic Oriental forms. Glazes were various: natural-clay oranges, buffs, Tobacco-spit Brown, Mirror Black, white, Frog Skin Green, a lovely turquoise called Chinese Blue, and the traditional cobalt-decorated salt glaze. The pottery gained national recognition, and as a result of their success, several other local potteries were established. The pottery closed for a time in the late 1950s due to the ill health of Mrs. Busbee (who had directed the business after her husband died in 1947) but reopened in 1960. Jugtown is still in operation; however, they no longer use their original glaze colors which are now so collectible and the circular mark is slightly smaller than the original.

Bean pot, orange, cord-style shoulder hdls, w/lid, Owen, 1930s, 6½".110.00
Bean pot, Tobacco Spit Brown, flared rim, appl strap hdls, 1940s, 6"..85.00
Bowl, center; orange, tapered form, 4¼x11⅞"..............................300.00
Bowl, Chinese Blue, hemispherical, 4½x8"..................................900.00

Bowl, Chinese Blue, Oriental translation, EX glaze, 1930s, 5x7"..950.00
Bowl, Chinese Blue, oxblood at rim & along long glaze 'waves,' 8x15"..2,500.00
Bowl, Oriental White, waves/mottling, angular sides, Ben Owen, 4x11"..110.00
Inkwell, Chinese Blue w/frog-skin int, 1930s, 3x3½" 180.00
Jug, glossy frog-skin Albany slip, groove-top rnd hdl, 1930s, 5" ...100.00
Pie pan, orange w/gr spotting, ruffled rim, 2¼x9½"......................120.00
Pitcher, chicken figural, salt glazed, 1992, 8¼" 180.00
Pitcher, orange, wide hdl w/finger-groove top, smoothed ends, 1925, 9"..110.00
Platter, orange, concentric rings, Ben Owen, late 1920s, 15" L, EX ...130.00
Teapot, orange, domed lid, att Ben Owen, 1930s, 7¼x10" 450.00
Tray, orange, shaped sides form hdls, Ben Owen, 11x13" 200.00
Vase, Chinese Blue w/oxblood, unglazed lower area, frog-skin int, 4x5"..850.00
Vase, Chinese White, flared rim, bulbous body, 9½".....................270.00
Vase, Chinese White on upper half, flat shoulder, 3½" 215.00
Vase, Sung, Oriental translation, butter/orange, Owen, hdls, 6" ...1,050.00

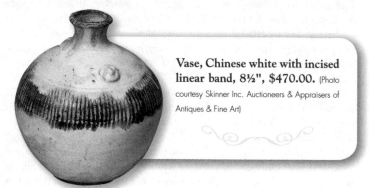

Vase, Chinese white with incised linear band, 8½", $470.00. (Photo courtesy Skinner Inc. Auctioneers & Appraisers of Antiques & Fine Art)

Kayserzinn Pewter

J. P. Kayser Sohn produced pewter decorated with relief-molded Art Nouveau motifs in Germany during the late 1800s and into the twentieth century. Examples are marked with 'Kayserzinn' and the mold number within an elongated oval reserve. Items with three-dimensional animals, insects, birds, etc., are valued much higher than bowls, plates, and trays with simple embossed florals, which are usually priced at $100.00 to about $200.00, depending on size. Copper items are rarely found, but one is listed below. Assume that all other items are made of pewter.

Claret jug, five cups and tray (14½"), $1,150.00.
(Photo courtesy Treadway Gallery Inc.)

Candelabrum, 3-light, bat w/wings wide tops std, #4506, 12" ...1,950.00
Figurine, working man w/lg basket, #d, 9½" 215.00
Match holder/ashtray, Nouveau floral, #4385, 2¾x5x4½" 70.00
Pitcher, devil's face flanked by irises, #4061P, ca 1900, 12½x9" ...180.00
Stein, copper w/dog's head medallion, #27/4400/P, w/lid, 12½", VG ..$180.00
Tankard, Imperial eagle emb, head spout, #4015, 13½x7", EX.....365.00
Tray, boar in center, rim w/pea pods & pine cones, 20" L.............250.00
Tray, emb Nouveau decor, low w/basket-like hdl, #44?0, 6¾x12½x9"..75.00
Tray, 2 shell-like lobes w/Nouveau floral, 2-part, side hdl, 11x8" ..150.00

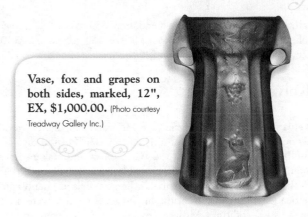

Vase, fox and grapes on both sides, marked, 12", EX, $1,000.00. (Photo courtesy Treadway Gallery Inc.)

Vase, Nouveau flowers & leaves, #23/4092P, hdls, 10x7½" 115.00
Vase, 3 mask/acorn hdls, animals around body, #4318, 9½" 1,150.00

Keeler, Brad

Keeler studied art for a time in the 1930s; later he became a modeler for a Los Angeles firm. By 1939 he was working in his own studio where he created naturalistic studies of birds and animals which were marketed through giftware stores. They were decorated by means of an airbrush and enhanced with hand-painted details. His flamingo figures were particularly popular. In the mid-'40s, he developed a successful line of Chinese Modern housewares glazed in Ming Dragon Blood, a red color he personally developed. Keeler died of a heart attack in 1952, and the pottery closed soon thereafter. For more information, we recommend *The Collector's Encyclopedia of California Pottery, Second Edition,* by Jack Chipman (Collector Books).

Bowl, Lobster Ware, leafy form w/lobster on lid, 6x8¾x6½" 60.00
Bowl, Lobster Ware (no lobster), gr leaves, #858, 4½x12" 20.00
Bowl, wht w/strawberries on lid, 6" dia 35.00
Box, Dragon Blood, man at cart etched on lid, 4x5½" 65.00
Cookie jar, fish figural, turq w/wht belly, #130, 7x13½" 165.00
Creamer & sugar bowl, fish figural, w/lid, #147/#148.................... 150.00
Dish, fish figural, #10, 6½x5½" 45.00

Divided dish, Lobster Ware, red lobster handle, 11½", $60.00. (Photo courtesy Jack Chipman)

Figurine, bird, rose colored, #18, 8¼" 50.00
Figurine, cat in basket, 3¾" 50.00
Figurine, cat playing on bk, blk, #779, 3½x7", from $45 to 55.00
Figurine, cockatoo on perch, 8½x3" 75.00
Figurine, cocker spaniel puppy seated w/front legs up, #748, 4½" .. 50.00
Figurine, flamingo, wings spread & raised, #47, 10½", from $140 to ...160.00
Figurine, flamingo standing on grassy base w/head up, 9¾", $75 to .. 90.00
Figurine, hen pheasant, #21, 6½" 45.00
Figurine, peahen, mc pastels, head up, #717, 10½" 200.00
Figurine, rabbit, wht w/pk accents, #608, 5" 80.00
Figurine, Siamese cat seated w/tail curled, #969, 12", from $65 to. 85.00
Figurine, tabby cat, #923, 8", from $45 to 55.00

Pitcher, fish figural, mouth spout, tail hdl, #147, 5" 70.00
Pitcher, fish figural, mouth spout, tail hdl, 8", from $100 to 125.00
Plate, rooster figural, mc, #233, 6½x7" 40.00
Platter, fish figural, #138, 18½" L.. 150.00
Platter, Lobster Ware, lobster on gr leaves, #867, 12x10" 45.00
Platter, rooster w/plumed tail figural, #231, mk BBK, 11¼"............ 60.00
Shakers, crabs, ruby red, pr 125.00
Shakers, Lobster Ware, figural, red, 3½", pr 50.00
Vase, bud; Oriental man & woman, #610/#611, 4½", 3¾", pr...... 110.00
Vase, 2 budgies on cornucopia-like form, yel to wht, #854, 5x7" ... 45.00

Figurine, duck, 7x7", $25.00.

Keen Kutter

Keen Kutter was the brand name chosen in 1870 by the Simmons Firm for a line of high-grade tools and cutlery. The trademark was first applied to high-grade axes. A corporation was formed in 1874 called Simmons Hardware Company. In 1922 Winchester merged with Simmons and continued to carry a full line of hardware plus the Winchester brand. The merger terminated in March of 1929 and converted back to the original status of Simmons Hardware Co. It wasn't until July 1, 1940, that Simmons Hardware Co. was purchased by Shapleigh Hardware Company. All Simmons Hardware Co. trademark lines were continued, and the business operated successfully until its closing in 1962. Today the Keen Kutter logo is owned by the Val-Test Company of Chicago, Illinois. For further study we recommend *Collector's Guide to E. C. Simmons Keen Kutter Cutlery Tools,* an illustrated price guide by our advisors for this category, Jerry and Elaine Heuring, available at your favorite bookstore or public library. The Heurings are listed in the Directory under Missouri. See also Knives. Unless otherwise noted, values are for examples in at least excellent condition.

Apple parer, CI, Pat May 24 1898, from $75 to 95.00
Axe, broad; Bob Taylor Canada pattern, EC Simmons, 12" cutting edge....200.00
Axe box, for 4½-lb hollow bevel axe head, sliding top, 2x9½x6"... 75.00
Book, How To Read a Keen Kutter Square, from $50 to 75.00
Calendar, tin, pad type w/store name & location, from $75 to..... 125.00
Case, salesman's sample; 15x14x8½" 125.00
Chopper, butcher's; from $30 to 35.00
Clock, plastic, Shapleigh's, 10" dia.. 275.00
Corkscrew, 3 styles, ea.. 20.00
Dental snips, K11D, 7½", from $15 to.. 20.00
Drill, electric; KK200, ¼" 30.00
File, bastard; sq or rnd, 14", ea from $5 to......................................8.00
Fork, barn/ensilage; 8-tine, wooden hdl, from $40 to 45.00
Hammer, bill-poster's; K55 .... 50.00
Hammer, blacksmith's/riveter's; str-pein, from $100 to................ 125.00
Hatchet, claw; w/label, M... 275.00
Hatchet, poll claw; plain 35.00
Hoe, weeding; K3C4½ from $25 to 30.00
Knife, lunch slicer, K33, 8" blade, from $15 to 20.00

Knife, roast beef slicer, 12", from $15 to.......................... 20.00
Lawn mower, push type w/wooden hdl, from $30 to........................ 40.00
Level, mason's; KK25, adjustable, brass button w/logo, from $65 to... 95.00
Marking gauge, wooden, K25 .... 40.00
Milter box, complete w/saw, from $275 to 350.00
Plane, K31, wooden bottom, 24", from $35 to.......................... 45.00
Plane, scrub; K240, from $150 to 200.00
Pliers, combination; K51, center cutters, 10", 8" or 6", ea, $25 to.. 35.00
Pliers, KK7, pistol grip, mk Pat Applied For Shapleigh..., $125 to ..175.00
Pliers, rnd nose, 5¼", from $30 to.. 40.00
Plumb bob, hexagonal, 6-oz or 7-oz, ea 65.00
Pocketknife, #882, Barlow pattern, blk bone hdl, from $25 to....... 50.00
Pot fork, K8101, cocobola hdl, from $30 to 40.00

Puzzle, cardboard, MIB, $1,000.00.

Rake, garden; 12 teeth, from $15 to 20.00
Rasp, wood; half-round, various szs, ea from $7 to 12.00
Razor, str; metal hdl w/KK written on bk, lady on front, Germany .. 250.00
Rule, zigzag; K603, 36" 6-fold, yel enamel, from $175 to.............. 250.00
Saw, hack; K188A, adjustable 8-12", from $35 to...................... 45.00
Saw, 1-man crosscut; #309, emblem on blade, from $150 to 200.00
Saw clamp, folding pattern, 3x12", from $100 to..................... 150.00
Scissors, 7", from $4 to...8.00
Screwdriver, mk Special, 4", from $40 to 50.00
Screwdriver, wood hdl w/brass ferrule, 2½x9", ea from $30 to........ 40.00
Shears, barber's; 7" 10.00
Shears, mule; 10½", from $20 to....................................... 30.00
Shipping tape, roll, mk Keen Kutter, from $75 to...................... 80.00

Sign, cardboard, 13x10", $40.00. (Photo courtesy B. J. Summers)

Slaw cutter 45.00
Square, K10, long tongue, 8", from $35 to 45.00
Square, KF100, EC Simmons, from $25 to................................ 35.00
Thermometer, yel border, Shapleigh, rnd, from -30 to 120 degrees 300.00
Vise, KC/412, combination pipe swivel base, from $225 to.......... 275.00
Wrench, alligator; K40, combination bolt wrench, from $20 to 40.00

Wrench, automobile; K96, w/pry on end, from $55 to 65.00
Wrench, crescent; Shapleigh, 4", from $300 to 350.00
Wrench, pipe; wooden hdl, 8", from $20 to 25.00

Kelva

Kelva was a trademark of the C. F. Monroe Company of Meriden, Connecticut; it was produced for only a few years after the turn of the century. It is distinguished from the Wave Crest and Nakara lines by its unique Batik-like background, probably achieved through the use of a cloth or sponge to apply the color. Large florals are hand painted on the opaque milk glass; and ormolu and brass mounts were used for the boxes, vases, and trays. Most pieces are signed. Our advisors for this category are Dolli and Wilfred Cohen; they are listed in the Directory under California.

Whiskbroom holder, floral on blue, ornate ormolu backplate, $750.00. (Photo courtesy Dolli and Wilfred Cohen)

Biscuit jar, daisies on peach, SP lid/hdl, rare 750.00
Box, Bishop's Hat, wild roses on gr, w/grayed border, 3x4" 500.00
Box, floral, pk on wht, scalloped edge, 3½x8" 300.00
Box, floral on bl w/beading, 3½x8" 495.00
Box, lilies, wht on pk, sq, 5¾" 635.00
Box, roses, pk on gr, fuchsia trim, wht dots, mk, 3½x6" 700.00
Box, roses on bl & cream w/gold, sq, 8" 1,150.00
Box, wild roses, pk on gr, hinged lid, sq, 2¾x4" 425.00
Napkin ring, floral on waisted hexagon form, rare 450.00
Shakers, floral on gr, gr enamel top, 3", pr.............................. 900.00
Tray, Crown mold, floral on moss gr, 6" dia 350.00
Vase, floral, pk w/gold scrolls on bl mottle, 8" 700.00
Vase, floral on gr, SP ormolu ft, 14" 1,500.00
Vase, floral on rose, trumpet form w/4 ormolu ft, 6x2" 450.00
Vase, lg floral bouquet on gr/pk (shiny), 8x3" 950.00
Vase, roses w/wht dots on marbled bl, hexagonal, 13" 1,250.00

Kenton Hills

Kenton Hills Porcelain was established in 1940 in Erlanger, Kentucky, by Harold Bopp, former Rookwood superintendent, and David Seyler, noted artist and sculptor. Native clay was used; glazes were very similar to Rookwood's of the same period. The work was of high quality, but because of the restrictions imposed on needed material due to the onset of the war, the operation failed in 1942. Much of the ware is artist signed and marked with the Kenton Hills name or cipher and shape number.

Ashtray, fish form, gr majolica, 8¾".. 240.00
Ashtray, horse head figural, ivory matt, #182, 5½", pr 175.00

Bookends, turtle form, purple gloss, J Bechtold, #118, ca 1940, 6" ... 600.00
Box, gr w/emb geometrics on lid, label, D Seyler, #159, 3½x6" 275.00
Candlestick, rooster figural, turq gloss, sgn, #1990, 9½", EX 250.00
Figurine, Evening Star, female seated, wht, #156, rare, 9⅛" 700.00
Figurine, Madonna holding Child, wht gloss, D Seyler, 13¾" 390.00
Lamp base, Art Deco foliage & geometrics, flared rim, Hentschel, #90 .. 1,020.00
Lamp base, horses, brn on cream, orig fittings, 10" 700.00
Lamp base, stylized floral on bl, A Stratton, 9¾" 190.00

Lamp base/vase, lotus blossom, signed AS (Alza Stratton), #90, 12½", $800.00. (Photo courtesy Cincinnati Art Galleries)

Paperweight, Suzanne, head of sleeping lady, goldstone, D Seyler, #157 .. 360.00
Sculpture, female face, pk matt, D Seyler, #152, 6½" 360.00
Sculpture, female face, 3-color, D Seyler, #152, 6½" 400.00
Vase, brn drip on yel, D Seyler, #103, 6" 500.00
Vase, designs emb on gr, #111, 5¼" 400.00
Vase, dots & lines emb on pk matt, Wm Hentschel, #127, 6½" ... 275.00
Vase, draped nudes, brn on cream, D Seyler, drilled, 10" 240.00
Vase, floral, mc on gourd form, C Haupt, #87, 6¼" 700.00
Vase, leaves, brn on yel, experimental, Wm Hentschel, 9" 360.00
Vase, leaves emb on bl, Wm Hentschel, #136, 6¼" 160.00
Vase, magnolias, pk on frothy caramel, sgn KH, #88, 9¼x5½" 550.00
Vase, Spanish Red w/goldstone accents, #108, 8x4" 325.00
Vase, stylized flowers & seed pods, D Seyler, 12½" 660.00
Vase, yel matt, incurvate rim, H Bopp, ca 1940, 4¼" 120.00

Kentucky Derby Glasses

Kentucky Derby glasses are the official souvenir glasses sold at Churchill Downs filled with mint juleps on Derby Day. Many folks from all over the country who attend the Derby take home the souvenir glass, and thus the collecting begins. The first glass (1938) is said to have either been given away as a souvenir or used for drinks among the elite at the Downs. This one, the 1939 glass, two glasses from 1940, the 1940 – 1941 aluminum tumbler, the 'Beetleware' tumblers from 1941 to 1944, and the 1945 short, tall, and jigger glasses are the rarest, most sought-after glasses, and they command the highest prices. Some 1974 glasses incorrectly listed the 1971 winner Canonero II as just Canonero; as a result, it became the 'mistake' glass for that year. Also, glasses made by the Federal Glass Company (whose logo, found on the bottom of the glass, is a small shield containing an F) were used for extra glasses for the 100th running in 1974. There is also a 'mistake' and a correct Federal glass, making four to collect for that year. Two glasses were produced in 1986 as the mistake glass has an incorrect 1985 copyright printed on it. Another mistake glass was produced in 2003 as some were made with the 1932 winner Burgoo King listed incorrectly as a Triple Crown winner instead of the 1937 winner of the Triple Crown, War Admiral.

The 1956 glass has four variations. On some 1956 glasses the star which was meant to separate the words 'Kentucky Derby' is missing making only one star instead of two stars. Also, all three horses on the glass were meant to have tails, but on some of the glasses only two have tails making two tails instead of three. To identify which 1956 glass you have, just count the number of stars and tails.

In order to identify the year of a pre-1969 glass, since it did not appear on the front of the glass prior to then, simply add one year to the last date listed on the back of the glass. This may seem to be a confusing practice, but the current year's glass is produced long before the Derby winner is determined.

The prices on older glasses remain high. These are in high demand, and collectors are finding them extremely hard to locate. Values listed here are for absolutely perfect glasses with bright colors, all printing and gold complete, no flaws of any kind, chipping or any other damage. Any problem reduces the price by at least one-half. Our advisor for this category is Betty Hornback; she is listed in the Directory under Kentucky.

1938 .... 4,000.00
1939 .... 6,500.00
1940, aluminum 1,000.00
1940, French Lick, aluminum 1,000.00
1940, glass tumbler, 2 styles, ea, minimum value 10,000.00
1941-44, plastic, Beetleware, ea from $2,500 to 4,000.00
1945, jigger, gr horse head, I Have Seen Them All 1,000.00
1945, regular, gr horse head facing right, horseshoe 1,600.00
1945, tall, gr horse head facing right, horseshoe 450.00
1946-47, clear frosted w/frosted bottom, L in circle, ea 100.00
1948, clear bottom, gr horsehead in horseshoe & horse on reverse .. 225.00
1948, frosted bottom, gr horse head in horseshoe & horse on reverse ... 250.00
1949, He Has Seen Them All, Matt Winn, gr on frosted 225.00
1950, gr horses running on track, Churchill Downs behind 450.00
1951, gr winner's circle, Where Turf Champions Are Crowned ... 650.00
1952, Gold Derby Trophy, Kentucky Derby Gold Cup 225.00
1953, blk horse facing left, rose garland 200.00
1954, gr twin spires 225.00
1955, gr & yel horses, The Fastest Runners, scarce 200.00
1956, 1 star, 2 tails, brn horses, twin spires 275.00
1956, 1 star, 3 tails, brn horses, twin spires 400.00
1956, 2 stars, 2 tails, brn horses twin spires 200.00
1956, 2 stars, 3 tails, brn horses, twin spires 250.00
1957, gold & blk on frosted, horse & jockey facing right 125.00
1958, Gold Bar, solid gold insignia w/horse, jockey & 1 spire 175.00
1958, Iron Leige, same as 1957 w/'Iron Leige' added 225.00

1959, gold and black on frosted glass, $100.00. (Photo courtesy Betty Hornback/ Photographer Dean Langdon)

1961, blk horses on track, jockey in red, gold winners 110.00
1962, Churchill Downs, red, gold & blk on clear 70.00
1963, brn horse, jockey #7, gold lettering 70.00
1964, brn horse head, gold lettering 25.00

1965, brn twin spires & horses, red lettering 85.00
1966-68, blk, blk & bl respectively, ea 65.00
1969, gr jockey in horseshoe, red lettering 65.00
1970, gr shield, gold lettering 70.00
1971, gr twin spires, horses at bottom, red lettering 55.00
1972, 2 blk horses, orange & gr print 55.00
1973, wht, blk twin spires, red & gr lettering 60.00
1974, Federal, regular or mistake, brn & gold, ea 200.00
1974, Libbey, mistake, Canonero in 1971 listing on bk 18.00
1974, regular, Canonero II in 1971 listing on bk 16.00

1975, $16.00.

1976, plastic tumbler or regular glass, ea 16.00
1977 .... 14.00
1978-79, ea 16.00
1980 .... 22.00
1981-82, ea 15.00
1983-85, ea 12.00
1986 .... 14.00
1986 (1985 copy) 20.00
1987-89, ea 12.00
1990-92, ea 10.00
1993-95, ea 9.00
1996-98 ....8.00
1999-2000, ea 6.00
2001-03, ea 5.00
2003, mistake, 1932 incorrectly listed as Derby Triple Crown Winner .. 6.00
2004-2007, ea 4.00

Keramos

Keramos (Austria) produced a line of decorative items including vases, bowls, masks, and figurines that were imported primarily by the Ebeling & Ruess Co. of Philadelphia from the late 1920s to the 1950s. The figurines they manufactured were of high quality and very detailed, similar to those made by other Austrian firms. Their glazes were very smooth, though today some crazing is present on older pieces. Most items were marked and numbered, and some bear the name or initials of the artist who designed them. In addition to Ebeling & Ruess (whose trademark includes a crown), other importers' stamps and labels may be found as well. Knight Ceramics employed a shield mark, and many of the vases produced through the 1940s are marked with a swastika; these pieces are turning up with increasing frequency at shops as well as Internet auction sites. Although the workmanship they exhibit is somewhat inferior, the glazes used during this period are excellent and are now attracting much attention among collectors. Masks from the 1930s are bringing high prices as well. Beware of reproduction masks online.

Detail is a very important worth-assessing factor. The more detailed the art figures are, the more valuable. Artist-signed pieces are quite

scarce. Many artists were employed by both Keramos and Goldscheider. The molds of these two companies are sometimes very similar as well, and unmarked items are often difficult to identify with certainty. Items listed below are considered to be in excellent, undamaged condition unless otherwise stated. Our advisor for this category is Darrell Thomas; he is listed in the Directory under Wisconsin.

Bookends, mc geometrics on cube form, W/KK/Keramos, 3½x4x4" ..780.00
Bowl, center; 3 penguin supports, w/flower frog, WK mk, #d, 10x11"...660.00
Figurine, beagle w/head & tail up, Vienna mk, 8x9½" 45.00
Figurine, boy plays violin, bird perched on shoulder, Wein, 8¾"..175.00
Figurine, boy walking w/ice skates on arm, Wein, 8½" 115.00
Figurine, dancer w/swirled skirt, Dakon, Knight Ceramics, #2119, 8" ..600.00
Figurine, elephant, cherry red crackle, Austria, 5x5½" 630.00
Figurine, flamingos (2) on grassy base, Wein, ca 1950s, 12x9" 65.00
Figurine, girl w/flower basket in hand, flower in other, Dakon, 7¾" ...155.00
Figurine, lady in gr & wht w/sm brn handbag, Wein, 8¼" 75.00
Figurine, Madonna & Child, F Barwig, Austria, #442-A, 9½" 240.00

Figurine, nude on pier, #46, 8¾", EX, $250.00.
(Photo courtesy Cincinnati Art Galleries)

Figurine, tiger cubs (2) playing, Wein, 5x9" 60.00
Vase, mermaid on 5 open branches, clam base, Weiner Kunst, 10"....540.00

Kew Blas

The Union Glass Company was founded in 1854, in Somerville, Massachusetts, an offshoot of the New England Glass Co. in East Cambridge. They made only flint glass — tablewares, lamps, globes, and shades. Kew Blas was a trade name they used for their iridescent, lustered art glass produced there from 1893 until about 1920. The glass was made in imitation of Tiffany and achieved notable success. Some items were decorated with pulled leaf and feather designs, while others had a monochrome lustre surface. The mark was an engraved 'Kew Blas' in an arching arrangement.

Candlesticks, gold, optic ribs, wide base, 8", pr 485.00
Vase, bud; drag loops, gold on ivory, wide trumpet base, 6" 540.00
Vase, feathers, gold on ivory, gold int, appl lip, 9" 720.00
Vase, feathers, gold w/gr tips on gold, cylindrical, 8x4" 720.00
Vase, feathers, gold/gr on alabaster, ovoid, Wm Blake, 4¼" 460.00
Vase, feathers, gold/gr on opal, shouldered, 8¾" 1,200.00
Vase, feathers, gr/gold on opal, ca 1920, slim form, 8" 575.00
Vase, gold, poppy bud form, 10¼".. 180.00
Vase, gold, shouldered cylinder w/flaring scalloped rim, 5"........... 345.00
Vase, gold pulled diagonals on opal, conical w/flared rim, 4" 275.00
Vase, hooked gold free-forms on swirled/marbled gr/ivory/gold, 10x5"....1,320.00
Vase, opal w/gr & amber-gold lustre bands, cylinder, 4-lobe rim, 10" .. 300.00

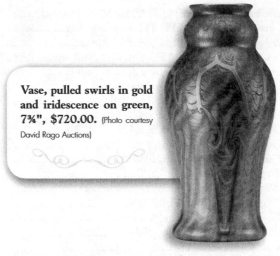

Vase, pulled swirls in gold and iridescence on green, 7¾", $720.00. (Photo courtesy David Rago Auctions)

Vase, undulating bands, gr/gold on opal, cylinder w/3-lobe rim, 11" ... 575.00
Vase, zippers, gr/gold on creamy yel, sm rim, shouldered, 6"......1,150.00

Kindell, Dorothy

Yet another California artist that worked during the prolific years of the 1940s and 1950s, Dorothy Kindell produced a variety of household items and giftware, but today she is best known for her nudes. One of her most popular lines consisted of mugs, a pitcher, salt and pepper shakers, wall pockets, bowls, a creamer and sugar set, and champagne glasses, featuring a lady in various stages of undress, modeled as handles or stems (on the champagnes). In the set of six mugs, she progresses from wearing her glamorous strapless evening gown to ultimately climbing nude, head-first into the last mug. These are relatively common but always marketable. Except for these and the salt and pepper shakers, the other items from the nude line are scarce and rather pricey. Collectors also vie for her island girls, generally semi-nude and very sensuous.

Ashtray, Beachcombers, 4 legs under lg sombrero, 6", from $60 to ... 70.00
Ashtray, Hawaiian hula girl in 7" dia blk tray, 4½" 530.00
Ashtray, nude lady w/hair over eyes & legs apart, on sq tray 160.00
Box, Hawaiian girl finial, 5x4x6½", from $400 to 500.00
Champagne glass, nude stem, made in series, ea from $135 to 150.00
Creamer & sugar bowl, nude hdls, 3½x3", from $250 to 300.00
Figurine, collie dog w/head turned, 6x7" 35.00
Figurine, nude seated w/red scarf on arm & head, 1½x4½", $250 to ..300.00
Figurine, nude w/flowers in hair, lying on bk, 9x9¼" 175.00

Figurine, Polynesian dancer, 13½", $265.00.

Figurine, Scottish terrier, 5x4¼", NM 35.00

Head vase, Polynesian lady w/long neck, in gr & gold, 1950s, 7".. 115.00
Ice bucket, nude hdl ea side, 11x4½" 150.00
Lamp base, Polynesian man on knees, gr headpc, 13½x9¼" 275.00
Mug, bearded man, bl cap, smiling face, 4" 90.00
Mug, nude w/red ballerina shoes as hdl 175.00
Mugs, nude figural hdl, series of 6, ea from $30 to 38.00
Pitcher, nude lady hdl, 9x5½" 275.00
Shakers, drum shape w/nude lady hdl, 3", pr.................................. 50.00

Wall pocket, lady removing her gown by cup, rare, from $200.00.

King's Rose

King's Rose was made in Staffordshire, England, from about 1820 to 1830. It is closely related to Gaudy Dutch in body type as well as the colors used in its decoration. The pattern consists of a full-blown, orange-red rose with green, pink, and yellow leaves and accents. When the rose is in pink, the ware is often referred to as Queen's Rose.

Bowl, int w/wide pk band, deep, 5½" 500.00
Cake plate, Queen's Rose, floral rim band, rose in center, 10" 200.00
Coffeepot, dome lid, minor wear, 11¾" 700.00
Pitcher, milk; pearlware, 5⅜" 300.00
Plate, orange stripes on rim, 8¼" 250.00
Plate, Queen's, 4-color, vine border, scalloped, 8" 180.00

Plate, soft paste with pink lustre 'lacing' and green teardrop designs encircling border, 5¼", $125.00. (Photo courtesy A&B Auctions)

Plate, toddy, 4¾" 275.00
Plate, 7½" 150.00
Tea bowl & saucer, Queen's, ca 1815 .... 120.00
Tea bowl & saucer, red rose, vine border...................................... 245.00
Tea bowl & saucer, wide pk band, 3¾", 6⅜" 250.00
Teapot, Queen's, 6" 400.00

Kitchen Collectibles

During the last half of the 1850s, mass-produced kitchen gadgets were patented at an astonishing rate. Most were ingeniously efficient.

Apple peelers, egg beaters, cherry pitters, food choppers, and such were only the most common of hundreds of kitchen tools well designed to perform only specific tasks. Today all are very collectible.

For further information we recommend *Kitchen Glassware of the Depression Years* and *Anchor Hocking's Fire-King & More, Second Edition*, both by Gene and Cathy Florence; *Kitchen Antiques, 1790 – 1940*, by Kathryn McNerney; and *Hot Kitchen & Home Collectibles of the 30s, 40s, and 50s* by C. Dianne Zweig. See also Appliances; Butter Molds and Stamps; Cast Iron; Cookbooks; Copper; Glass Knives; Molds; Pie Birds; Primitives; Reamers; String Holders; Tinware; Trivets; Wooden Ware; Wrought Iron.

Cast-Iron Bakers and Kettles

Be aware that cast-iron counterfeit production is on the increase. Items with phony production numbers, finishes, etc., are being made at this time. Many of these new pieces are the popular miniature cornstick pans. To command the values given below, examples must be free from damage of any kind or excessive wear. Waffle irons must be complete with all three pieces and the handle. The term 'EPU' in the description lines refers to the Erie PA, USA mark. The term 'Block TM' refers to the lettering in the large logo that was used ca 1920 until 1940; 'Slant TM' refers to the lettering in the large logo ca 1900 to 1920. 'PIN' indicates 'Product Identification Numbers,' and 'FW' refers to 'fuel writing.' Victor was Griswold's first low-budget line (ca 1875). Skillets #5 and #6 are uncommon, while #7, #8, and #9 are easy to find. See also Keen Kutter; Clubs, Newsletters, and Catalogs.

Aebleskiver pan, unmk, makes 7, 2x9"+hdl 75.00
Biscuit pan, Barstow Stove Co, makes 12 dmn shapes, 1x11½x7½" ... 85.00
Bread pan, Wagner, hdls, 13½x4⅜" 145.00
Broiler, dbl; Griswold #875/#876, top: 9¼", base: 16¾x12¼" 225.00
Cake mold, Santa, Griswold, #897 & #898 on hdls, 12" 300.00
Cake pan, Wagner #1508, rectangular, 13¾x10"+hdls 375.00
Cake pan, Wagner #1510, 2½x17x11¾" 225.00
Chicken fryer, Wagner, sq, w/lid, 3x10x10"+hdl 155.00
Dutch oven, Griswold #6 Tite Top, Slant TM, smooth lid, w/trivet 285.00
Dutch oven, Griswold 10 Tite Top, PIN 2553A, w/trivet 235.00
Dutch oven, Griswold #310 Tite-Top, flanged lid, ftd, 1920 .... 350.00
Gem pan, GF Filley #8, makes 11 rectangles, 1¼x13x6" 255.00
Griddle, Wagner #1126, wire bail, 16" dia 65.00
Griddle, Wagner #1168, 21½x9¼" 90.00
Grill, Griswold #18, 'cookie sheet' pattern #1108, 16¾x10" 225.00
Grill/griddle, Griswold Gas Vapor, PIN 774, 12" dia 200.00
Hot plate, Griswold #33, 3-burner, w/gas valves, 4-leg 215.00
Kettle, #7, w/bail, 7¾x9¼" 145.00
Kettle, #20, 13x20½" 225.00
Muffin pan, Piqua Ware, 9-cup, ca 1925, 2⅝x10½x10½" 135.00
Muffin pan, WC Davis & Co Cin'ti, makes 10 6-sided muffins 320.00
Roaster, Oval; Griswold #7, FW lid, w/trivet 600.00
Roaster, Oval; Wagner #3 Drip Drop Baster, heat rings, w/lid, 1922 ... 100.00
Roaster, Oval; Wagner #5 Drip Drop, PIN 265, FW lid 100.00
Roaster, Rnd; Wagner #6, smooth top lid, bail hdl 110.00
Saucepan, Griswold #737, 2-spout, PIN 737, 2-qt 200.00
Skillet, egg; Griswold #129, sq w/hdl in corner, enamel int, 1950s ... 315.00
Skillet, Erie #6, Erie TM, w/heat ring 180.00
Skillet, Griswold #0, Block TM, Erie PA/562, ca 1950 .... 315.00
Skillet, Griswold #1, Erie #411 Toy, ca 1900, rare, 4⅜" dia 5,875.00
Skillet, Griswold #2, Block TM, no heat ring, from $400 to 500.00
Skillet, Griswold #2, Slant TM, w/heat ring 365.00
Skillet, Griswold #4, Block TM/Erie #702A, 1920s 375.00
Skillet, Griswold #5, Erie #348, NPCI, w/heat ring 300.00
Skillet, Griswold #6A, Erie TM 255.00
Skillet, Griswold #7, Victor/EPU TM, PIN 21B 35.00
Skillet, Griswold #8, Block/EPU TM, PIN 1008, 1932-40 .... 400.00
Skillet, Griswold #8, Victor/EPU TM, ca 1920-35 .... 50.00
Skillet, Griswold #9, Victor/EPU TM, PIN 723 .... 45.00
Skillet, Griswold #10, lg Block/EPU TM, PIN 716B, w/heat ring ... 180.00
Skillet, Griswold #12, Erie #719, low dome lid w/FW 200.00
Skillet, Griswold #14, slant TM, w/heat ring 200.00
Skillet, Griswold #15, oval, Block TM, w/lid 915.00
Skillet, Griswold #15, oval, Slant/EPU TM 450.00
Skillet, Griswold #20, Block TM, Erie USA 728, 2-hdl 675.00
Skillet, Griswold #719, Slant TM, 13" 650.00
Skillet, Piqua Ware #14, 2-spout, 14¾" dia 250.00
Skillet, Wagner #2A, 6" dia 60.00
Skillet, Wagner #9, PIN 1059 .... 80.00
Skillet, Wagner #14, PIN 1064, 15" dia 225.00
Skillet, Wagner #1365, mini, 1x4¾" dia+hdl 85.00
Skillet, Wapak #3, Indian TM, ca 1903-26 .... 85.00
Skillet, Wapak #7, Indian TM 200.00
Skillet, Wapak #8, Indian TM 70.00
Skillet lid, Wagner #10 Drip Drop, FW 65.00

Stick pan, Wagner 'A - Stick Pan,' 13" long, from $50.00 to $65.00.

Teakettle, AT Nye & Son #7, Marietta O 1867, 6½x9½" 85.00
Teakettle, Griswold, Erie Spider & Web TM on sliding lid, #8 on spout ... 325.00
Vienna roll pan, Griswold #6, raised letters, makes 6 .... 175.00
Wall clock, frying pan w/windup works, Griswold/Erie Up to..., 14½" 4,400.00
Wheat/cornstick pan, Griswold #27, PIN 638, 11x6" 235.00

Egg Beaters

Egg beaters are unbeatable. Ranging from hand-helds, rotary-crank, and squeeze power to Archimedes up-and-down models, egg beaters are America's favorite kitchen gadget. A mainstay of any kitchenware collection, over the recent years egg beaters have come into their own — nutmeg graters, spatulas, and can openers will have to scramble to catch up! At the turn of the century, everyone in America owned an egg beater. Every household did its own mixing and baking — there were no preprocessed foods. and every inventor thought he/she could make a better beater. Thus American ingenuity produced more than 1,000 egg beater patents, dating back to 1856, with several hundred different models being manufactured dating back to the nineteenth century. As true examples of Americana, egg beaters enjoyed a steady increase in value for quite sometime, though they have leveled off and even decreased in the past few years, due to a proliferation of Internet sales. Some very rare beaters will bring more than $1,000.00, including the cast-iron, rotary crank 'Dodge Race Course egg beater.' But the vast majority stay under $50.00. Just when you think you've seen them all, new ones always turn up, usually at flea markets or garage sales. For further information, we recommend our advisor (author of the definitive book on egg beaters) Don Thornton, who is listed in the Directory under California (SASE required).

A&J, metal beater w/wooden hdl fits on 4-cup gr glass measure, 1923 ..82.50
A&J Ecko #7216...USA, crank type fits on clear 5½" dia pitcher .. 40.00
Borden, metal push-pull top on clear glass jar dtd 1915 .... 35.00
Brevetto #1920, aluminum, push-pull type, 13¼" 50.00
Holt's Patented, wire crank, fluted beaters, 8½" 95.00
Keystone, push-pull type fits on clear glass Westmoreland base, 11" .. 52.50
Lyon, dbl blades, crank type, Pat Sept 7, 1897 .... 80.00

Master Pat. Aug. 24, '09, 10½", $500.00. (Photo courtesy Diane Thornton ©1994)

Maynard, crank stype w/pk hdls, 1950s 35.00
Monroe Bros...Mass, CI, table mt, Pat April 19 1859 & Oct 16 1860 .. 400.00
New Keystone, fits on sq glass jar, crank hdl, 11" 95.00
PD&Co, crank hdl, 3¾" dia wire end, Pat Dec 1 85, 10" 350.00

Glass

Batter jug, gr, Jenkins, from $225 to 250.00
Batter jug, pk, New Martinsville, from $125 to 135.00
Bowl, mixing; amethyst, Hazel-Atlas, 9⅝", from $45 to 50.00
Bowl, mixing; Chalaine Blue, 9", from $125 to 135.00
Bowl, mixing; fired-on color, McKee, 6", from $22 to 28.00
Bowl, mixing; iridized, Federal, 9½", from $35 to 38.00
Butter dish, amber, Federal, 1-lb, from $35 to 40.00
Canister, crystal, emb Tea, from $55 to 65.00
Canister, Jade-ite, 10-oz, from $50 to 55.00
Creamer, Colonial Block, from $200 to 225.00
Cruet, gr, Hazel-Atlas, from $45 to 50.00
Cruet, oil/vinegar; amber, Fostoria, ea from $55 to 65.00
Funnel, Radnt, from $45 to 50.00
Gravy boat, bl, Imperial, from $75 to 85.00
Ice bucket, gr, McKee, from $40 to 45.00
Ice bucket, pk elephant, from $45 to 55.00
Knife, Aer-Flo, gr, 7½" 70.00
Knife, Block, crystal, 8¼" 22.00

Knife, Block, green, from $45.00 to $50.00. (Photo courtesy Gene and Cathy Florence)

Knife, Dur-X, 3-leaf, gr, 9¼" 40.00
Knife, Dur-X, 5-leaf, bl, 9¼" 45.00
Knife, plain hdl, pk, 9¼" 70.00
Knife, Star, pk, 9¼" 20.00
Knife, Stonex, gr, 8½" 80.00
Knife, Westmoreland, crystal, pnt hdl, thumb guard, 9¼" 45.00
Knife, 3-Star, crystal, 9¼" 15.00
Ladle, crystal, Fostoria, from $18 to 20.00
Measuring cup, amber, Tufglas, from $300 to 325.00
Measuring cup, cobalt, Hazel-Atlas, 3-spout, from $300 to 350.00
Measuring cup, crystal, Hazel-Atlas, 4-cup, from $28 to 30.00
Measuring cup, gr, Federal, solid hdl, from $40 to 45.00
Measuring cup, red flashed, Glasbake, from $55 to 65.00
Mug, red, from $35 to 40.00
Napkin holder, gr, Paden City, from $150 to 160.00
Pitcher, crystal, Fry, from $250 to 275.00
Reamer, elephant-decorated base, Fenton, from $110 to 125.00
Refrigerator dish, bl & wht, Pyrex, 4¼x6¾", from $20 to 25.00
Rolling pin, amethyst, from $120 to 135.00
Rolling pin, Chalaine Blue, from $500 to 600.00

Rolling pin, cobalt, blown, from $180.00 to $200.00. (Photo courtesy Gene and Cathy Florence)

Rolling pin, pk, screw-on wooden hdls, from $450 to 500.00
Salt box, crystal, emb Salt, Flintext, from $125 to 135.00
Shakers, Modern Tulips, Hocking, ea, from $24 to 26.00
Spoon holder, mk Clamborne, from $45 to 55.00
Straw holder, cobalt, from $200 to 225.00
Sugar shaker, cobalt, Paden City, from $900 to 950.00
Sugar shaker, opaque yel, Hocking, from $40 to 45.00
Syrup jug, amber, Cambridge, from $55 to 60.00
Tea kettle, white, Glasbake, from $40 to 45.00
Water bottle, Royal Ruby, Hocking, from $225 to 250.00

Miscellaneous

Apple peeler, Domestic Landers Frary & Clark...1873, clamps to table ..260.00
Apple peeler, Goodell Bonanza, orig gr pnt on CI, clamps to table 275.00
Apple peeler, Reading, CI, crank hdl, clamps to table, Pat 1867 .. 125.00
Apple peeler, Reading Hardware Works, CI, clamps to table 225.00
Apple peeler, Union Pat Pending, clamps to table, ca 1895, 9x8" ..265.00
Bowl, mixing; mc plastic (confetti), Texasware, #118, 4½x10" 78.00
Bread box, wht porc w/red Bakelite hdl, vented bk, 6x18x9" 75.00
Cake cutter/server, yel Bakelite hdl, 3¾" tines, 11" 7.50
Can opener, CI bull's head type, tail folds under body, 1890s, 6" ... 22.00
Can opener, Daisy Universal, CI w/wooden hdl, wall mt 25.00
Can opener, Joy Kan Kutter, scissors type, 1926 .... 40.00
Can opener, metal, mts to wall & swivels, Made in St Louis USA ..22.00
Carrier, cake; tin litho, red roses, plain red lid, wht inner lid 45.00
Carrier, pie/cake; tin litho, red apples on wht, bail hdl 38.00
Chopper, single crescent-shaped blade, 2 wooden hdls, 9x12½" 90.00
Chopper, single curved blade, extended wooden hdl, 6x7½" 60.00
Chopper, single oblong blade, wood hdl, 6x8" 45.00
Churn, Blanchard No 3, pine w/yel pnt/stencil, side crank, 32x18x14" ...180.00
Churn, Dazey #10, beveled edge, 1-qt, EX, from $550 to 700.00

Churn, Dazey #20, EX, from $100 to 150.00
Churn, Dazey #30, Pat 1922, EX, from $150 to 175.00
Churn, Dazey #30, Pat 1922, M 250.00
Churn, Dazey #40, EX, from $100 to 125.00
Churn, Dazey #60, EX, from $120 to 150.00
Churn, Dazey #80, EX, from $150 to 175.00
Clock/wall pocket, red/wht, Telechron #2H33, 1950s, 5¾x8¾" 35.00
Colander, aluminum w/pierced star pattern, 3-ftd, hdls 27.50
Colander, gr enamelware w/dk gr trim, 4¾x9⅞"+hdls 30.00
Colander, wht enameling w/red trim & hdls, ftd 50.00
Crimper, aluminum, spoon-like shape, unmk, 5" 40.00
Cutter, cheese; wht enamel, Corcoran Tru Cut, 1928, 5x12x8" 45.00
Cutter, cheese; wire held in fr, Bakelite hdl, Clem-Brand, 8x3" 25.00
Cutter, vegetable; scalloped tin blade, wooden hdl, 1930s, 6" 7.50
Dough scraper, forged iron, made in 1 pc w/solid hdl, 3½" 40.00
Dough scraper, forged iron w/wooden hdl, early 1900s, 2x5½" 30.00
Food mill, Foley #101, metal w/red wood hdl, 7¼" dia, EX, +booklet 17.50
French fry cutter, Ekco, wire grid, lever type, 1950s, MIB, $25 to .. 45.00
French fry cutter, Heuck, wires in metal fr, 3x5" 12.00
Grater, nutmeg; tin, w/sliding lid for storage, 1¼x6½x2½" 15.00
Grater, punched tin, half rnd, 6x3¾" 25.00
Grater, wires cross in metal fr, Made in USA, 9x5½"+4" hdl 20.00
Jar lifter, curved wire w/thumb push, single wood hdl, 1900s 12.50
Juicer/extractor, Hamilton Beach #32, lever action, gr porc base ... 70.00
Juicer/press, Wear-Ever, aluminum, squeeze type 50.00
Knife sharpener, stainless steel disks w/wooden hdl, Made in USA .. 20.00
Knife sharpener, steel w/hardwood hdl, Forschner, 12" 26.00
Measuring cups, Foley, stainless steel saucepan shape, set of 4" 28.00
Meat tenderizer, CI, 1¾" sq grid w/hdl, 7" L 36.00
Meat tenderizer, wooden mallet type w/gr pnt wood hdl, 1930s 15.00
Meat tenderizer, 2 iron heads w/red pnt wood hdl, 9" 10.00
Meat tenderizer/maul, wooden mallet type w/red hdl, mk Munising, NM ... 48.00
Noodle cutter, Acme Mincer, rotary blades, wooden hdl, 1930s, 8", MIB 15.00
Noodle cutter, metal rotary type w/red wooden hdl 25.00
Pastry blender, Androck, arched wires held by wooden hdl 12.00
Potato masher, wire ware w/red wooden hdl, 9½x4" 15.00
Ricer/press, metal cone shape on stand w/wooden pestle, NM 40.00

Roaster, Guardian Ware, glass lid, 12" long, from $65.00 to $75.00.

Scoop, Androck, metal w/red Bakelite hdl, 1950s, ¼-cup 38.00
Scoop, coffee; aluminum, Wagner, 1-tablespoon, 3⅝" L 28.00
Scoop, turq hard plastic, Made in USA, ca 1950s, 1-cup 5.00
Sifter, Androck Handi-Sift, lady w/pie, red hdl, 1950s, EX 45.00
Sifter, Hunter's Sifters/FJ Meyers Mfg Co, tin, 6" 30.00
Sifter, Victor, red angled stripes, red & wht stars, 6½" 25.00
Spatula, Androck, flexible metal w/red Bakelite hdl, 10⅛" 18.00
Spoon, slotted; Androck, metal w/red Bakelite hdl, 1940s, 12" 15.00
Teakettle, shiny aluminum dome shape w/red bird whistle cap 70.00

Knife Rests

Recording the history of knife rests has to begin in Europe. There is a tin-glazed earthenware knife rest at the Henry Francis Dupont Winterthur Museum, It's dated 1720 – 1760 and is possibly Dutch. Many types have been made in Europe — porcelain, Delft, majolica, and pottery. European companies made knife rests to match their dinnerware patterns, a practice not pursued by American manufacturers. Research has found only one company, Mackenzie-Childs of New York, who made a pottery knife rest.

Several scholars feel that porcelain knife rests originated in Germany and France; from there, their usage spread to England. Though there were glasshouses in Europe making pressed and cut glass, often blanks were purchased from American companies, cut by European craftsmen, and shipped back to the States. American consumers regarded the European cut glass as superior. When economic woes forced the Europeans to come to the U.S., many brought their motifs and patterns with them. American manufacturers patented many of the designs for their exclusive use, but in some cases as the cutters moved from one company to another, they took their patterns with them.

Knife rests of pressed glass, cut crystal, porcelain, sterling silver, plated silver, wood, ivory, and bone have been collected for many years. Signed knife rests are especially desirable. It was not until the Centennial Exhibition in Philadelphia in 1876 that the brilliant new cut glass rests, deeply faceted and shining like diamonds, appeared in shops by the hundreds. There were sets of twelve, eight, or six that came in presentation boxes. Sizes vary from 1¼" to 3¼" for individual knives and from 5" to 6" for carving knives. Glass knife rests were made in many colors such as purple, blue, green, vaseline, pink, and cranberry. These colors have been made in Europe.

There are many items of glass and pottery that resemble knife rests but are actually muddlers, toothpick holders (sanitary types that allow you to pick the toothpicks up by the centers), and paperweights. Collectors should be familiar with these and able to recognize them for what they are. It is important to note that prices may vary from one area of the country to another and from dealer to dealer. For further information we recommend our advisor, Beverly Schell Ales; she is listed in the Directory under California.

Ceramic, bl floral transfer on wht, unmk England, ca 1840s, 1¼x4" .. 70.00
Ceramic, Blue Onion, att Meissen, 2⅞" 110.00
Glass, cut; bl, rest bar between 2 oval open salts, 4 sm ft, 4⅜" 125.00
Glass, cut; Chardon, etched leaves, Lalique #13628, 4¾" 75.00
Glass, cut; dmns cut on dumbell shape, 6-sided bar, Hawkes, 3" .. 100.00
Glass, cut; radial circles, Waterford, 2½x3¼" 45.00
Glass, cut; Russian pattern, 1⅝x6" 510.00
Glass, cut; starbursts on spool shape, Waterford, 2x2⅜" 35.00
Glass, cut; 4-sided bar w/dmn-cut ends, 4" 85.00

Glass, pressed; amber, ca. 1963, Val St. Lambert Belquique, $100.00. (Photo courtesy Beverly Schell Ales)

Glass, pressed; frosted lion head ea end 70.00
Glass, pressed; gold irid twisted rope w/sq ends, Quezal, 3⅞" 540.00
Glass, pressed; wht opal w/bee on end, Sabino 45.00
Majolica, branch w/fungi, EX color & detail, 3¼" 275.00
Porc, fox figural, wht w/HP details, Germany, 1920s, 5¼" 45.00
Silver, cherub faces away ea end of bar, Meriden, 3⅜" 30.00
Sterling silver, geometric eng & monogram, Lung, 1½x3¼" 40.00

Knives

Knife collecting as a hobby began in earnest during the 1960s when government regulations required for the first time that knife companies mark their products with the country of origin. The few collectors and dealers aware of this change at once began stockpiling the older knives made before this law was enacted. Another impetus to the growing interest in this area came with the Gun Control Act of 1968, which severely restricted gun trading. Frustrated gun dealers transferred their attention to knives. Today there are collectors' clubs in many of the states.

The most sought-after pocketknives are those made before WWII. However, as time goes on knives no older than 20 years are collectible if in mint condition. Most collectors prefer knives in 'as found' condition. Do *not* attempt to clean, sharpen, or in any way 'improve' on an old knife.

Please note: Length is measured with blades *closed*. Our values are for knives in used/excellent condition (unless specified 'mint'). Most old knives are usually not encountered in mint condition. Therefore to give a mint price could mislead the novice collector. If a knife has been used, sharpened, or blemished in any way, its value decreases. It is common to find knives made in the 1960s and later in mint condition. Knives made in the 1970s and 1980s may be collectible in mint condition, but not in used condition. Therefore a used knife 30 years old may be be worth no more than a knife for use. For further information refer to *The Standard Knife Collectors Guide*, *Big Book of Pocket Knives*, and *Remington Knives* by Ron Stewart and Roy Ritchie; and *The Case Cutlery Dynasty: Tested XX* by Brad Lockwood (all are published by Collector Books). *Sargent's American Premium Guide to Knives and Razors, Identification and Values, 6th Edition*, by Jim Sargent is another good reference. Our advisor for this category is Bill Wright, author of *Theatre-Made Military Knives of World War II* (Schiffer). Mr. Wright is listed in the Directory under Indiana.

Key:

alum — aluminum	jack — jackknife
bd — blade	lb — lockback
gen — genuine	pat — pattern
imi — imitation	wb — winterbottom

A Davy & Sons (Sheffield England), 2-bd, Liberty & Union bolster ... 700.00
Aerial Cutlery Co, 2-bd jack, bone hdl, 3⅜" 60.00
Anheuser-Busch, red & gold emb hdl, w/peephole & picture 375.00
Barnett Tool Co, bone hdl, bd+punch+pliers 175.00
Boker, Henrich (German), 1-bd, bone hdl, 4½" 65.00
Boker (German), 4-bd congress, bone hdl, 4" 125.00
Boker (USA), 3-bd stockman, imi pearl hdl, 4" 40.00
Boker (USA), 4-bd congress, bone hdl, 3¾" 65.00
Bulldog Brand (Germany), 3-bd whittler, gen abalone hdl, 5⅛", M ... 150.00
Case, Tested XX, 5202½, 2-bd, gen stag hdl, 3⅜" 100.00
Case, Tested XX, 6220, 2-bd, rough blk hdl, peanut pat, 2⅜" 100.00
Case, Tested XX, 6392, 3-bd, gr bone hdl, stockman pat, 4" 175.00
Case, Tested XX, 8383, 2-bd, gen pearl hdl, whittler pat, 3½" 500.00
Case, Tested XX, 61093, 1-bd, gr bone hdl, toothpick pat, 5" 200.00
Case, Tested XX, 62031½, 2-bd, gr bone hdl, 3¾" 150.00
Case, Tested XX, 62100, 2-bd, gr bone hdl, saddlehorn pat, 4⅜" .. 500.00
Case, XX, 2-bd, bone hdl, muskrat pat, 3⅜" 150.00
Case, XX, 3347hp, 3-bd, yel compo hdl, stockman pat, 3⅜" 85.00
Case, XX, 5254, 2-bd, gen stag hdl, trapper pat, 4⅛" 300.00
Case, XX, 5375, 3-bd, gen red stag hdl, long pull, stockman, 4¼" ... 600.00
Case, XX, 6185, 1-bd, bone hdl, doctor's pat, 3¾" 125.00
Case, XX, 62009, 1-bd, bone hdl, barlow pat, 3⅜" 40.00
Case, XX, 6231½, 2-bd, bone hdl, 3¾" 75.00
Case, XX, 6250, 2-bd, bone hdl, sunfish pat, 4½" 200.00

Case, XX, 6265 Sab, folding hunter knife, $100.00; Russell Granddaddy, Barlow, $200.00; Remington, R1123, Bullet, $750.00. (Photo courtesy Bill Wright)

Case, XX, 6294, 2-bd, bone hdl, cigar pat, 4¼" 250.00
Case, XX, 6308, 3-bd, bone hdl, whittler pat, 3¼" 100.00
Case, XX, 6488, 4-bd, bone hdl, congress pat, 4⅛" 500.00
Case, XX, 6565sab, 2-bd, bone hdl, folding hunter pat, 5¼" 125.00
Case, XX USA, 10 dots, 6111½, 1-bd, bone hdl, lb, 4⅜", M 325.00
Case, XX USA, 52131, 2-bd, gen stag hdl, canoe pat, 3⅝", M 350.00
Case, XX USA, 5354, 2-bd, gen stag hdl, trapper pat, 4⅛", M 375.00
Case Bros, Little Valley NY, 2-bd, wood hdl, 3¼" 125.00
Case Bros, Springville NY, 8250, 2-bd, pearl hdl, sunfish pat 3,000.00
Cattaraugus, D2589, 4-bd, bone hdl, Official Scout emblem, 3½" ... 200.00
Cattaraugus, 3-bd+nail file, gen pearl hdl, lobster gun stock, 3" 150.00
Cattaraugus, 12839, 1-bd, bone hdl, King of the Woods, 5⅜" 500.00
Cattaraugus, 22346, 2-bd, wood hdl, jack pat, 3⅜" 85.00
Cattaraugus, 22919, 2-bd, bone hdl, cigar pat, 4¼" 300.00
Cattaraugus, 32145, 3-bd, bone hdl, stockman pat, 3⅜" 200.00
Challenge Cutlery, 1-bd, bone hdl, lb pat, 4¾" 200.00
Challenge Cutlery, 3-bd, bone hdl, cattle pat, 3⅜" 125.00
Diamond Edge, 2-bd, bone hdl, jack, 3⅜" 75.00
Diamond Edge, 2-bd, pearl celluloid hdl, gun stock, 3" 100.00
Frost Cutlery Co (Japan), 3-bd, bone hdl, lb whittler pat, 4" 15.00
H&B Mfg Co, 3-bd, buffalo horn hdl, whittler pat, 3⅜" 150.00
Hammer Brand, NY Knife Co, 2-bd, bone hdl, 3⅜" 85.00
Hammer Brand, 1-bd, bone hdl, NYK on bolster, lb, 5¼" 375.00
Hammer Brand, 1-bd, tin shell hdl, powder-horn pat, 4¾" 25.00
Hammer Brand, 2-bd, bone hdl, dog-leg pat, 3¾" 225.00
Hammer Brand, 2-bd, wood hdl, jack, 3¾" 85.00
Henckels, JA; 3-bd, bone hdl, whittler pat, 3¼" 65.00
Henckels, JA; 4-bd, bone hdl, congress pat, 4" 150.00
Hibbard, Spencer, Bartlett & Co, 2-bd, bone hdl, barlow, 3⅜" 85.00
Hibbard, Spencer, Bartlett & Co, 2-bd, bone hdl, dog-leg pat, 3⅜" ... 110.00
Holley Mfg Co, 1-bd, wood hdl, 5" 140.00
Holley Mfg Co, 3-bd, pearl hdl, whittler pat, 3¼" 225.00
Holley Mfg Co, 4-bd, bone hdl, congress pat, 3½" 375.00
Honk Falls Knife Co, 1-bd, bone hdl, 3" 125.00
I*XL (Sheffield England), 4-bd, gen stag hdl, congress, 4" 350.00
I*XL (Sheffield), 2-bd, wood hdl, heavy jack, 4" 125.00
Imperial Knife Co, 2-bd, bone hdl, dog-leg pat, 3⅜" 50.00
Imperial Knife Co, 2-bd, mc hdl, 3¼" 35.00
John Primble, Belknap Hdw Co, 3-bd, bone hdl, 4" 75.00
John Primble, Belknap Hdw Co, 4-bd, bone hdl, 3¾" 85.00

John Primble, India Steel Works, 2-bd, gen stag hdl, 4¼" 500.00
John Primble, India Steel Works on bolster, celluloid hdl, 3" 125.00
Ka-Bar, Union Cutlery, knife & fork, bone hdl, 5¼" 350.00
Ka-Bar, Union Cutlery, 2-bd, gen stag hdl, dog head, 5¼" 300.00
Ka-Bar, Union Cutlery, 3-bd, bone hdl, whittler pat, 3¾" 150.00
Ka-Bar, 2-bd, gen stag hdl, Old Time Trapper, 4⅛" 85.00
Ka-Bar, 3-bd, bone hdl, cattle pat, 3⅜" 100.00
Keen Kutter, EC Simmons, 1-bd, bone hdl, lb, 4¼" 200.00
Keen Kutter, EC Simmons, 1-bd, bone hdl, 3¼" 50.00
Keen Kutter, EC Simmons, 2-bd, bone hdl, trapper, 3⅞" 250.00
Keen Kutter, EC Simmons, 2-bd, colorful celluloid hdl, 3⅜" 70.00
Keen Kutter, EC Simmons, 2-bd, pearl hdl, doctor pat, 3⅜" 250.00
Keen Kutter, EC Simmons, 2-bd, wood hdl, jack, 3¼" 75.00
Keen Kutter, EC Simmons, 3-bd, bone hdl, whittler pat, 3⅜" 75.00
Keen Kutter, 1-bd, bone hdl, TX toothpick, 5" 125.00
Keen Kutter, 2-bd, bone hdl, barlow, 3⅜" 75.00
Keen Kutter, 2-bd, bone hdl, folding hunter, 5¼" 125.00
LF&C, 2-bd, jigged hard rubber hdl, jack, 3⅜" 75.00
LF&C, 3-bd, gen pearl hdl, whittler pat, 3½" 125.00
Maher & Grosh, 2-bd, bone hdl, jack, 3⅜" 150.00
Marbles, 1-bd, gen stag hdl, Safety Folding Hunter, lg 700.00
Marbles, 1-bd, gen stag hdl, Safety Folding Hunter, sm 500.00
Miller Bros, 2-bd, bone hdl, jack, 3½" 100.00
Miller Bros, 2-bd, screws in bone hdl, 4¼" 500.00
Miller Bros, 3-bd, gen stag hdl, stockman, 4" 350.00
Miller Bros, 3-bd, screws in gen pearl hdl, 3⅜" 250.00
Morley, WH & Sons; 3-bd, bone hdl, whittler pat, 3¼" 65.00
MSA Co, Marbles, 2-bd, pearl hdl, sunfish pat, rare, 4" 3,500.00
Napanoch Knife Co, X100X, 1-bd, bone hdl, very rare, 5⅜" 2,500.00
Napanoch Knife Co, 2 lg bds, bone hdl, 3⅜" 250.00
Napanoch Knife Co, 4-bd, bone hdl, 3¼" 150.00
Northfield Knife Co, 2-bd, bone hdl, dog-leg pat, 3¾" 500.00
Northfield Knife Co, 2-bd, bone hdl, jack, 3⅜" 165.00
Pal, 2-bd, bone hdl, easy-open, 3¾" 85.00
Pal, 3-bd, bone hdl, jack, 3⅜" 60.00
Parker, Eagle (Japan), 1-bd, bone hdl, lb, 4½", M 25.00
Parker, Eagle (Japan), 4-bd, gen abalone hdl, congress, 3⅜", M ... 100.00
Queen, #18, 2-bd, wb bone hdl, jack, 3¹¹⁄₁₆" 50.00
Queen, #19, 2-bd, wb bone hdl, trapper, 4⅛" 150.00
Remington, R173, 2-bd, bone hdl, teardrop jack, 3¾" 150.00
Remington, R555, 2-bd, candy stripe celluloid hdl, 3¼" 125.00
Remington, R775, 2-bd, red/wht/bl hdl, 3½" 185.00
Remington, R1153, 2-bd, bone hdl, jack, 4½" 250.00
Remington, R1225, 2-bd, wht compo hdl, 4¼" 125.00
Remington, R1306, (old) gen stag hdl, lb, silver bullet, 4⅝" 600.00
Remington, R3054, 3-bd, gen pearl hdl, stockman, 4" 300.00
Remington, RB43, 2-bd, bone hdl, barlow, 3⅜" 75.00
Remington, RS3333, 4-bd, bone hdl, scout shield, 3¾" 125.00
Robeson, Shuredge, 2-bd, gen pearl hdl, jack, 3½" 150.00
Robeson, Shuredge, 2-bd, strawberry bone hdl, jack, 3¾" 100.00
Robeson, Shuredge, 3-bd, bone hdl, stockman, 3⅜" 125.00
Rodgers, Jos & Sons, multi-bd, stag hdl, sportsman's 350.00
Rodgers, Jos & Sons, 2-bd, gen stag hdl, jack, 3⅜" 125.00
Rodgers, Jos & Sons, 3-bd, bone hdl, stockman, 4" 150.00
Russell, 2-bd, bone hdl, barlow, 3⅜" 175.00
Russell, 2-bd, bone hdl, barlow, 5" 250.00
Schatt & Morgan (current), 1-bd, w/bone hdl, lb, 5¼", M 100.00
Schatt & Morgan (old), 2-bd, bone hdl, jack, 3⅜" 150.00
Schrade Walden, 2-bd, peach seed bone hdl, 4¼" 250.00
Schrade Walden, 3-bd, peach seed bone hdl, 3⅜" 75.00
Ulster Knife Co, 1-bd, bone hdl, barlow, 5", M 200.00
Ulster Knife Co, 4-bd, imi bone hdl, scout/campers 30.00
Wade & Butcher (Germany), 3-bd, gen stag hdl, whittler pat 125.00
Wade & Butcher (Sheffield England), 4-bd, gen stag hdl, 4" 500.00

Walden Knife Co, 1-bd, bone hdl, toothpick pat, 5" 150.00
Wards, 4-bd, bone hdl, cattle pat, 3⅜" 85.00
Winchester, 1920, (old) 1-bd, bone hdl, 5¼" 650.00
Winchester, 2046, (old) 2-bd, celluloid hdl, jack, 3¾" 85.00
Winchester, 2904, (old) 2-bd, bone hdl, trapper, 3⅞" 350.00
Winchester, 2974, (old) 2-bd, bone hdl, dog-leg jack, 3½" 125.00
Winchester, 3350, (old) 3-bd, gen pearl hdl, whittler pat, 3¼" 125.00
Winchester, 3960, (old) 3-bd, bone hdl, stockman, 4" 275.00
Winchester, 3971, dtd 89 (1989), 3-bd, bone hdl, whittler pat, M.... 75.00

Sheath Knives

Over the past several years knife collectors have noticed that the availability of quality old pocketknives has steadily decreased. Many collectors have now started looking for sheath knives as an addition to their hobby. In many cases, makers of pocketknives also made quality hunting and sheath knives. Listed below is a small sampling of collectible sheath knives available. Length is given for overall knife measurement; price includes original sheath and reflects the value of knives in excellent used condition.

Case, (XX) 515-5, stacked leather hdl, 9" 35.00
Case, (XX) 523-5, gen stag hdl, 9¼" 85.00
Case (Bradford PA), bk of tang: Case's Tested XX, 8¼" 150.00
Case (WR & Sons), bone hdl, Bowie knife, 11" 400.00
Case (XX USA), gen stag hdl, Kodiak hunter, 10¾" 125.00
Case (XX), V-44, blk Bakelite hdl, WWII, 14½" 350.00
Cattaraugus, gen stag hdl, alum pommel, 10¼" 85.00
Cattaraugus, 225Q, stacked leather hdl, WWII, 10⅜" 45.00
I*XL (Sheffield), Bowie knife, ca 1845, 14" 2,000.00
I*XL (Sheffield), leather hdl w/stag, ca 1935, 10" 100.00
Ka-Bar, Union Cutlery Co, jigged bone hdl, 9¾" 150.00
Ka-Bar, Union Cutlery Co, leather hdl w/stag, 8½" 125.00
Ka-Bar, USMC, stacked leather hdl, WWII, 12¼" 100.00
Keen Kutter, EC Simmons, K1050-6, Bowie knife, 10" 500.00
Marbles, Ideal, all gen stag hdl, 10" 275.00
Marbles, Ideal, stacked leather hdl w/alum, 9" 100.00
Marbles, Ideal, stacked leather hdl w/stag, 11⅜" 500.00
Marbles, Woodcraft, stacked leather hdl w/alum, 8¼" 125.00
Randall, Springfield MA, leather hdl, WWII, 13" 1,750.00
Randall, stacked leather hdl w/alum, 10¼" 300.00
Remington, RH36, stacked leather hdl w/alum, 10½" 150.00
Remington, RH40, stacked leather hdl w/alum, rare, 14½" 1,500.00
Remington, RH73, gen stag hdl, 8" 75.00
Ruana, alum w/elk horn hdl, skinner, current, 7½" 100.00
Ruana, RH; alum w/elk horn hdl, ca 1980, 6½" 200.00
Ruana, RH; M stamp, alum w/elk horn hdl, skinner, 9¼" 275.00
Winchester, W1050, jigged bone hdl, Bowie knife, 10" 750.00
Wragg, SC (Sheffield); stag hdl, Bowie knife, 13½" 1,500.00

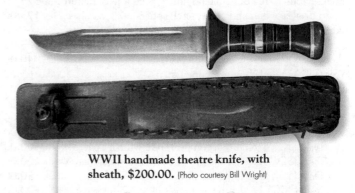

WWII handmade theatre knife, with sheath, $200.00. (Photo courtesy Bill Wright)

WWII, theater knife, mc Bakelite hdl, 12" 200.00
WWII, theater knife, mc hdl, Bowie knife, 12¾" 125.00
WWII, theater knife, mc hdl, dagger, 11" 100.00
WWII, theater knife, Plexiglass hdl w/picture, 12" 175.00

Kosta

Kosta glassware has been made in Sweden since 1742. Today they are one of that country's leading producers of quality art glass. Two of their most important designers were Elis Bergh (1929 – 1950) and Vicke Lindstrand, artistic director from 1950 to 1973. Lindstrand brought to the company knowledge of important techniques such as Graal, fine figural engraving, Ariel, etc. He influenced new artists to experiment with these techniques and inspired them to create new and innovative designs. In 1976 the company merged with two neighboring glasshouses, and the name was changed to Kosta Boda. Today's collectors are most interested in pieces made during the 1950s and 1960s.

Bottle, purple w/bl & gr spatters, rnd w/1 flat side, #47267, 7¼" .. 500.00
Bottle, scent; clear oval w/rnd cuts, amber int, Boda, #95120, 3⅛" . 115.00
Bottle, scent; rnd cuts on side, int amber oval, Monalos, #95120, 3" .. 115.00
Bowl, boat shape, med bl opaque cased in clear, LS618/90, 6½" 55.00
Paperweight, bl swirls in clear w/bubbles, Bergh #90962, 2¾" dia ... 125.00
Tumbler, equestrian & floral etching, stemmed, 6¼" 150.00
Vase, amber cased w/clear, appl ft, LH1711, 5½" 155.00

Vase, Autumn, Vicke Lindstrand, 6½", $2,350.00. (Photo courtesy Skinner Inc. Auctioneers & Appraisers of Antiques & Fine Art)

Vase, blk w/wht lines, LH1116/HD234, 4¾" 290.00
Vase, clear w/blk ribbon, LH1241, 5x4¼" 100.00
Vase, encased coiled snake below bubble at rim, Unik 1280, 6¼" ... 425.00
Vase, encased gr seaweed w/bubbles, teardrop shape, L111803, 7¾" .. 110.00
Vase, gr opaque w/brn ribs, gr ft, V Lindstrand, #146, 2⅞x5⅜" 585.00
Vase, gr w/2 etched figures/geometrics, Unik B.197B Vallien, 5¾" ... 950.00
Vase, pnt face, swollen form w/hair at rim, UH Vallien, #48746, 10" ... 600.00
Vase, sea gr w/bl spirals cased in heavy crystal, V Lindstrand, 8" . 470.00

KPM Porcelain

The original KPM wares were produced from 1823 until 1847 by the Konigliche Porzellan Manfaktur, located in Berlin, Germany. Meissen used the same letters on some of their porcelains, as did several others in the area. The mark contains the initials KPM. Watch for items currently being imported from China; they are marked KPM with the eagle but the scepter is not present. Our advisor for this category is Don Williams; he is listed in the Directory under Missouri.

Bowl, fruit/floral spray, rocaille rim, boat shape, 1880s, 15" L 265.00
Figurine, Athena, on later claw-ftd porc base, 15¾", EX 400.00
Figurine, English setter, recumbent, #9805, ca 1914-17, 3½x9" ... 400.00
Figurine, Hercules, mc on later claw-ft porc base, 15" 825.00
Figurine, reclining nude on mossy bank, oval base, 20th C, 16" L.... 1,295.00
Jar, Chinese couples/flowers w/gold, ftd egg shape, 1890s, 6½", pr... 525.00
Jug, castle ruins by river, ovoid w/narrow neck, 1890s, 12¼" 365.00
Plaque, angels (nude/seminude), 6½x8½"+ornate fr: 14x16" 4,657.00
Plaque, Angels Kiss, 2 figures in clouds, ca 1900, 5½x7½" 3,600.00
Plaque, boy eating bread at knee of lady stroking his hair, 15x13" . 3,825.00
Plaque, Chicken Sellers, outdoor scene, 19th C, 11x7"+fr........ 1,900.00
Plaque, Christopher Columbus in chains, oval, 9x7"+fr: 13x15"... 2,250.00
Plaque, Eros/Psyche embrace by pond's edge, 6x9"+fr: 11x14" .. 6,000.00
Plaque, FX Tallmaier of Munich, after Denner, 7x10"+ornate fr: 15x17" .. 2,000.00
Plaque, gypsy maiden w/tambourine in red velvet, #330/200, 18x11" .. 4,500.00
Plaque, Jesus healing lady among attendants, Wirkner, 16x12"+fr.. 11,750.00
Plaque, lady (brunette) w/wine goblet, 7x5" 2,600.00
Plaque, lady stands w/bottle, sgn, 19th C, 12x6" 3,000.00
Plaque, lady w/long brn hair, sgn Wagner, oval, 9x7"+ornate fr .. 8,635.00
Plaque, lady w/red drape, profile bust, Una Gitana, 4x5"+new fr .. 1,490.00
Plaque, lady w/serving tray, long wht apron, ca 1870, 9½x6⅜" ... 4,500.00

Plaque, Madonna Addoloato, after Carl Dolei, 1890, 12x10½", $4,000.00. (Photo courtesy Jackson's International Auctioneers & Appraisers of Fine Art & Antiques)

Plaque, Madonna & Child, after Raphael, 22x18"+architectural fr.. 13,000.00
Plaque, maid in prayer before Gothic bldgs, sgn Koch, 17x12"+fr.. 7,475.00
Plaque, maid stands by fence in moonlight, after Bodnhausen, 9x6"+fr... 4,995.00
Plaque, maid stands by harp, tambourine in hand, Wagner, 6x9"+mat/fr.... 3,738.00
Plaque, maid w/long curly hair gazing upward, oval, 11x8"+blk fr.. 2,245.00
Plaque, maids stand w/jug, cherub on wall behind, 7x10"+fr: 16x19"... 2,250.00
Plaque, nude lying by waterside/monk looking upward, 7x10"+wood fr .. 5,175.00
Plaque, Outdoor Hike, 19th C, 7x9½" 4,000.00
Plaque, Pearl Fisherman's Dream, late 19th C, 6x8⅞" 5,000.00
Plaque, Princess Lamballe (bust), 7x5"+ornate gilt scrollwork fr... 1,750.00
Plaque, Princess Louise, sgn Echkardt, 12¾x7½"+scrolled gilt fr... 5,000.00
Plaque, Psyche in the Moonlight, Wallther, 6x9"+fr: 15x18" ... 5,500.00
Plaque, Self Portrait, after Vigee le Brun, 1880s, 5½x5½"+fr 470.00
Plaque, seminude, cattails/pond, 6½x10"+mat & gilt fr: 13x15" ... 4,600.00
Plaque, Sistine Madonna, after Raphael, 8x10"+ornate fr: 15x18" .. 4,500.00
Plaque, St Jerome kneeling at altar w/book, 11x9"+fr: 17x15" .. 4,000.00
Plaque, young woman in hat & scarf (bust), oval, 7x5"+gilt fr... 1,750.00
Plate, Das Beandenburger Thor, acanthus scrolls, late 19th C, 9¾" ... 355.00
Tureen, soup; appl flowerheads/gilt, twig hdls/rim, 1880s, 16" L .. 235.00
Urns, campagna; courting scenes/courtiers/flowers, 20th C, 17", pr ... 1,175.00

Kutani

Kutani, named for the Japanese village where it originated, was first produced in the seventeenth century. The early ware, Ko Kutani, was made for only about 30 years. Several types were produced before 1800, but these are rarely encountered. In the nineteenth century, kilns located in several different villages began to copy the old Kutani wares. This later, more familiar type has large areas of red with gold designs on a white ground decorated with warriors, birds, and flowers in controlled colors of red, gold, and black.

Beaker, landscape w/brocade/fans, Kabaruagi-sei, 3½" 250.00
Bottle, sake; figures in landscapes/brocade w/gold & red, 8" 225.00

Bowl, fruit and animal motifs, 1700s, 7", $1,200.00. (Photo courtesy Du Mouchelles)

Charger, figures & landscapes w/gold & iron red, 14¾" 200.00
Charger, heron on floral branch, Meiji, ca 1830, 15¼" 485.00
Charger, landscape scenic, bl/yel/brn/gr, ca 1830, 15" 455.00
Figurine, lady in kimono holds child w/fan, Meiji, 14", EX 500.00
Figurine, tiger w/smiling face, 19th C, 7" 450.00
Plate, bamboo shoots amid folded screens/falling flowers, Edo, 8" . 1,000.00
Vase, figures in garden, geometrics/roundels, early 1900s, 15" 225.00
Vase, florals, gold on red, baluster, 20th C, 11½" 80.00
Vase, shishi lion panels/phoenix birds, stick neck, 1830s, 16" 450.00
Wine pot, One Hundred Poets, late 19th C, 9" 300.00

Labels

Before the advent of the cardboard box, wooden crates were used for transporting products. Paper labels were attached to the crates to identify the contents and the packer. These labels often had colorful lithographed illustrations covering a broad range of subjects. Eventually the cardboard box replaced the crate, and the artwork was imprinted directly onto the carton. Today these paper labels are becoming collectible — not only for the art, but also for their advertising appeal. Our advisor for this category is Cerebro; their address is listed in the Directory under Pennsylvania.

Can, Advona Red Kidney Beans, McCord Bracy Co, bowl of beans, EX.. 12.00
Can, Apollo, peaches in reserve, goddess playing lyre, gold emb, EX... 15.00
Can, Broadway Tomatoes, NY street scene, M 9.00
Can, Crystal Baking Powder, angel in apron w/cat, grapes, EX 8.00
Can, Dixie Maid Syrup, girl eating waffles, pouring syrup, M 12.00
Can, Easter Sliced Peaches, bowl of peaches, white lilies, 1935, EX .. 25.00
Can, Horseshoe Pure Ground Black Pepper, sm yel horseshoe, M 5.00
Can, Ibex Bartlett Pears, ibex on mountain, M 40.00
Can, Ko-We-Ba Shrimp, yel butterfly in reserve, shrimp on lettuce, EX.. 25.00
Can, Luzianne Tea, woman holding cup of tea, London Bridge behind, G.. 6.00
Can, Mephisto, devil holding can, bowl of peas, M 8.00
Can, OK Brand Tomatoes, buck near stream, lg tomato, EX 15.00
Can, Queen of the Meadow Sugar Corn, maiden carrying pail, M ...7.00
Can, Robin Hood Hawaiian Pineapples, Robin Hood w/bow, pineapple, EX.. 40.00
Cigar box, inner; Al-U-Pa, Alaskan map, Croger, 1909, EX 50.00
Cigar box, inner; Bantam, Worth Fighting For, 2 fighting cocks, VG.. 85.00
Cigar box, inner; Colonial Orator, Patric Henry portrait, 1900, M... 12.00
Cigar box, inner; Don Pablo, portrait reserve, Klingenber, G 500.00
Cigar box, inner; Fernand, blind WWI soldier, M 45.00

Cigar box, inner; Hedad, star of David, EX.............................. 20.00
Cigar box, inner; Imperiales, king's portrait, Harris Litho, M......... 15.00
Cigar box, inner; Marguerite, lady by red curtain, Since 1887..., EX.. 45.00
Cigar box, inner; Primeros, elephant's head, cigar in trunk, EX..... 15.00
Cigar box, inner; Royal Brand, well dressed Black man w/cigar, M... 12.00
Cigar box, inner; Surveyer, man w/horse & tools, EX 45.00
Cigar box, outer; Buffalo, cowboy on wht horse, Belgium, M 20.00
Cigar box, outer; Curly Boy, blond boy w/bl bow at neck, Harris, EX.. 15.00
Cigar box, outer; Empire, classical lady on couch, VG 25.00
Cigar box, outer; Flor De Sevilla, Spanish drinking scene, M........ 15.00
Cigar box, outer; General Terry, Civil War officer, 1895, M.......... 175.00
Cigar box, outer; Lady Dainty, lady holding fan, Harris, VG 30.00
Cigar box, outer; Lord Wolseley, military portrait, VG 35.00
Cigar box, outer; Natcheza, Indian chief's portrait, M 30.00
Cigar box, outer; 2 nude figures & coat of arms, G 30.00

Crate, apple; Best Strike Apples, Pajaro Valley, 9x11", $35.00. (Photo courtesy Cerebro)

Crate, apple; Del Rio, Spanish couple among letters of name, 1932, EX ... 45.00
Crate, cranberry; Mayflower Brand, sailing ship reserve, NJ, M 10.00
Crate, fruit; Blue Boy Concord Grapes, boy & grapes, EX 5.00
Crate, grapes; Parra Superior, wht & yel chicks carrying grapes, M... 12.00
Crate, onions; Barraca Brand, farmhouse, lg onion, VG 15.00
Crate, orange; Amor, woman leaning over crate, EX 35.00
Crate, orange; Gilda, stunning woman in wht dress, M.................. 20.00
Crate, orange; Gold Coast, orange as setting sun, CA, 1930, M 20.00
Crate, orange; Josefa Gil, 2 Victorian girls playing w/ball, VG 50.00
Crate, orange; Marquita, Senorita w/orange in hand, CA, M 50.00
Crate, orange; Mireille, smiling girl w/braids, Spain, M 30.00
Crate, orange; Navajo, Indian brave's portrait, Schmidt, CA, 1930, M.. 45.00
Crate, orange; OranG Outang, ape w/oranges, Spain, EX 35.00
Crate, pear; Eskimo brand, man in furs & carrying snowshoes, VG .. 35.00
Crate, peas; King Tut Farms, King Tut in reserve, peas on vines, VG 45.00

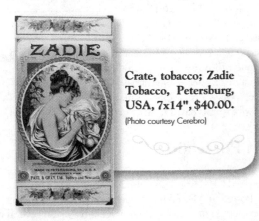

Crate, tobacco; Zadie Tobacco, Petersburg, USA, 7x14", $40.00. (Photo courtesy Cerebro)

Labino

Dominick Labino was a glassblower who until mid-1985 worked in his studio in Ohio, blowing and sculpting various items which he signed and dated. A ceramic engineer by trade, he was instrumental in developing the heat-resistant tiles used in space flights. His glassmaking shows his versatility in the art. While some of his designs are free-form and futuristic, others are reminiscent of the products of older glasshouses. Because of problems with his health, Mr. Labino became unable to blow glass himself; he died January 10, 1987. Work coming from his studio since mid-1985 has been signed 'Labino Studios, Baker,' indicating ware made by his protegee, E. Baker O'Brien. In addition to her own compositions, she continues to use many of the colors developed by Labino.

Vase, ruby, free-form, 1973, 7", $550.00. (Photo courtesy Early Auction Co.)

Bowl, clear to gr marbleized opaque, bun base, 1978, 2x4⅝" 360.00
Mortar & pestle, cinnamon-orange, 1979, 3x5" 390.00
Sculpture, arrow head shape, gr, 1972, 9¾" 880.00
Sculpture, dolphin, clear bl, 1979 .... 240.00
Vase, amethyst-bl, bulbous, 1976, 13" 115.00
Vase, Ariel, angelfish & dolphins in lt aqua, 3-1971, 5½" 450.00
Vase, Ariel, gr w/sculptured air traps, onion form, 1978, 3¼" 285.00
Vase, Ariel, smoky amber w/crimson clouds, 1968, 13⅝" 420.00
Vase, clear cased w/gray/yel/wht swirls at base, sq, 1976, 5½" 440.00
Vase, cobalt w/lg cornered medallions at shoulder, 1967, 5" 285.00
Vase, crimson/bl alternating stripes, elongated teardrop, 1981, 13".. 460.00
Vase, dk brn & olive gr teardrop, 1965, 5x5" 175.00
Vase, emerald & wht abstracts cased in clear, Baker 11-1985, 4½" .. 325.00
Vase, gr irid w/appl patterns at shoulder, 3-1970, 5⅞" 600.00
Vase, purple/gr w/lg int bubbles, teardrop, 1976, 5½" 365.00
Vase, robin's egg bl, raised ribbing, elongated pear, 1971, 9" 350.00
Vase, wht/cobalt/yel pulled chevron-like design, 1982, 5½" 475.00

Lace, Linens, and Needlework

Two distinct audiences vie for old lace and linens. Collectors seek out exceptional stitchery like philatelists and numismatists seek stamps or coins — simply to marvel at its beauty, rarity, and ties to history. Collectors judge lace and linens like figure skaters and gymnasts are judged: artist impression is half the score, technical merit the other. How complex and difficult are the stitches and how well are they done? The 'users' see lace and linens as recyclables. They seek pretty wearables or decorative materials. They want fashionable things in mint condition, and have little or no interest in technique. Both groups influence price.

Undiscovered and underpriced are the eighteenth-century masterpieces of lace and needle art in techniques which will never be duplicated. Their beauty is subtle. Amazing stitches often are invisible without magnification. To get the best value in any lace, linen, or textile item, learn to look closely at individual stitches, and study the design and technique. The finest pieces are wonderfully constructed. The stitches are beautiful to look at, and they do a good job of holding the item together. Unless noted otherwise, values are for examples in at least excellent condition.

Key: embr — embroidered

Bedcover, wht linen w/hand embr, scalloped edge, 1900s, 92x78" ..355.00
Blanket, homespun/hand loomed, brn/wht rows, Acadian, 1800s, 80x66" .3,000.00

Centerpiece, drawnwork linen, 24x24", $35.00. (Photo courtesy www.dewittco.com — vintage textiles & ephemera)

Coasters, wht organdy w/embr florals, 1930s, 3½", 9 for 65.00
Collar, Irish crochet lace, ca 1900, 15" inside neck, 5" W 85.00
Collar, wht Irish crochet w/raised lace flowers, 1930s, 18x3" 45.00

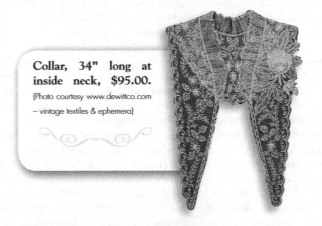

Collar, 34" long at inside neck, $95.00. (Photo courtesy www.dewittco.com – vintage textiles & ephemera)

Curtain, ivory net lace w/Battenburg lace trim, 1930s, 108x50" .. 195.00
Curtains, wht cotton Broderie Anglaise w/ruffled bottom, 85x50", pr .. 250.00
Doily, ivory Madeira lace, 1930s, 5x11" 25.00
Doily, linen center w/5" handmade lace edge, ca 1900, 17" 45.00
Doily, wht crochet w/heavy beading, 1930s, 4½" 50.00
Doily, wht linen damask w/3½" lace edge, 1890s, 10x12½" 50.00
Doily, wht voile w/embr flowers, scalloped edge, 1930s, 5½", pr 45.00
Duvet cover, wht linen w/pk & wht embr, 1930s, 50x67" 60.00
Handkerchief, hand-embr monogram, 1" crocheted edge, 11x11" ...25.00
Handkerchief, wht linen w/embr & lace trim, 11x11" 30.00
Handkerchief, wht linen w/lace inserts, crocheted edge, 12x12" ... 30.00
Handkerchief, wht linen w/2" Bedforshire bobbin-lace edge, 11x11" 65.00
Mantilla, blk lace bows & garlands edge ea side, ca 1900, 68x17" ...145.00
Modest front, wht Irish crochet lace, 2" ruff, 15" V front, ca 1900....75.00
Napkins, cream linen w/Alencon lace in 1 corner, 1930s, 17", 12 for...175.00
Napkins, ivory Madeira linen w/floral-embr corner, 1930s, 19", 12 for. 165.00
Napkins, wht linen damask w/embr wreath & leaves, 1920s, 23x23", 8 for...80.00
Napkins, wht linen w/drawn-work, 1920s, 17"+2" fringe, 12 for.. 125.00
Napkins, wht linen w/embr flowers & scallops, 1930s, 17x17", 6 for . 50.00
Napkins, wht silk damask, wht-on-wht stripe, ca 1930s, 30x20", 6 for ... 50.00
Needlework, silk embr lady at Shakespeare's tomb, oval, 1900s, 15"+fr...880.00
Needlework, silk embr of lady gathering flowers, HP details, 12x11"+fr ..635.00
Nightdress case, wht linen w/embr & lace, ribbon bows, 1900s, 14x19" 70.00
Pillowcases, wht cotton w/cutwork & lt bl embr, 1930s, 30x21", pr... 60.00
Pillowcases, wht linen w/scallops, cutwork/embr, 1920s, 34x19", pr .. 70.00
Place mats, wht linen/organdy, oval, 1920s, 19" L, +8 napkins, 8 for.. 165.00

Runner, ivory Fr Alencon lace, ca 1920, 24x14½" 80.00
Runner, wht Battenburg lace, ca 1900-10, 72x17" 120.00
Runner, wht embr & cutwork Madeira w/scalloped edge, 1930s, 54x15" . 60.00
Runner, wht linen & lace w/embr flower garlands, ca 1930, 44x12" .. 80.00
Runner, wht linen w/Battenburg edge all around, ca 1930, 104x14".. 95.00
Runner, wht linen w/chemical lace & embr baskets, lace trim, 48x18".. 50.00
Runner, wht linen w/drawn work, 1930s, 44x11" 45.00
Runner, wht linen w/embr baskets, ca 1900, 52x17" 70.00
Runner, wht linen w/embr baskets, narrow lace trim, 1930s, 16x10".. 40.00
Runner, wht linen w/fancy openwork along edge, 1930s, 42x17" 65.00
Runner, wht linen w/floral punch work, scalloped edge, 1920s, 56x22".. 65.00
Runner, wht linen w/hand embr, 3" tassel ea corner, 1930s, 50x16".. 65.00
Runner, wht linen w/lace inserts & 2" lace border, 1920s, 42x16" . 60.00
Runner, wht Madeira linen w/ivory cutwork & embr, 1930s, 31x15" ..50.00
Runner, wht pina cloth w/bl lattice design/embr inserts, 1930s, 46x15"... 55.00
Shawl, metallic & net lace, blk & gold, 1930s, 22x50" 175.00
Table topper, wht linen w/embr cameos/etc, lace insets, 1930s, 27" dia..165.00
Table topper, wht linen w/lace inserts & border, 1930s, 35" dia..... 65.00
Tablecloth, bl linen w/wht applique flowers, 1930s, 42x42", +6 napkins..110.00
Tablecloth, embr baskets/cutwork, scalloped, 1900s, 50" dia........ 175.00
Tablecloth, ivory heavy Quaker lace, ca 1920, 94x70" 125.00
Tablecloth, lt gray linen w/applique floral, 1930s, 76x65", +8 napkins...135.00
Tablecloth, pk linen w/floral-embr organdy surround, 1930s, 32x32" ..70.00
Tablecloth, wht Fr Alencon lace (fine pattern), 1930s, 108x72" . 345.00
Tablecloth, wht hand-embr linen w/cutwork, 8" lace edge, 1910s, 96x76"..325.00
Tablecloth, wht linen w/bl embr & openwork, scalloped, 1900s, 68" dia ..185.00
Tablecloth, wht linen w/cutwork & embr, Masonic symbols, 1930s, 37x37"..125.00
Tablecloth, wht linen w/cutwork baskets/embr flowers, 1900s, 44" dia...165.00
Tablecloth, wht linen w/drawn thread work, 1900s, 32x32"........... 70.00
Tablecloth, wht linen w/embr baskets, scalloped, 1900s, 88x68" .. 250.00
Tablecloth, wht linen w/embr figures, 1930s, 43x43"...................... 65.00
Tablecloth, wht linen w/lace inserts, 4" lace edge, 1900s, 44x44"...125.00
Tablecloth, wht linen w/needle-lace inserts/cutwork/embr, 1900, 46x46"...145.00
Tablecloth, yel linen w/6" Fr Alencon ivory lace, 45" sq, +6 napkins...325.00
Tapestry, Orientals at various pursuits, Flemish, 1700s, 70x59"...4,100.00
Tea cosy, wht lace w/peach silk ribbon insert & lace, 1900, 10x15"..50.00
Towel, lt bl linen w/embr floral tree & flowers, 1930s, 19½x13½"....30.00
Towel, lt yel organdy & linen w/embr inserts, 1930s, 17x11", pr ... 50.00
Towel, wht linen w/embr angel playing violin, 1930s, 21x14", pr.. 55.00
Towel, wht linen w/embr bird & strawberries, 1920s, 22½x15"...... 45.00
Towel, wht linen w/pastel embr flowers, scalloped edge, 1920s, 28x20" ... 40.00
Towel, wht linen w/woven challice & bird border, 1910s, 23x16" ...47.50
Towel, wht linen w/woven duck band, ca 1920, 22x14" 35.00
Towel, wht linen w/5" scalloped lace border, ca 1900, 24x15" 48.00

Lachenal, Edmond

Lachenal was born in France in 1855. From the age of 15, he was tutored in the trade by such icons as Theodore Deck and later collaborated with that era's major artisans including Rodan, Emile Decouer, Dejean, and others.

He established a studio at Malakoff, Paris, in 1880, relocating seven years later in Chatillon-sous-Bagneux. He produced sculptural pieces as well as vessles decorated with naturalistic themes and is especially noted for his glazes and stonewares. He is recognized today as an important ceramic artist of the Art Deco period.

His son Raoul succeeded him in 1904, and though his methods included a more mechanized approach, he nevertheless became well known for his stoneware which he decorated with geometric and Far Eastern designs.

Bud vase, emb stylized leaves, bright bl vellum, sgn, 6" 720.00
Charger, stylized rabbits/central lion, cvd/pnt in turq slip, 11", NM...600.00

Figurine, young woman, seated, pastels, sgn, minor rstr, 9" 180.00
Vase, burgundy/lt bl flambe, shaped rnd body w/stick neck, 7"........ 95.00
Vase, icy mc glazes, gr crystalline w/in, swirl body/vine hdls, 5"... 360.00

Vase, white band with ram's head handles on turquoise background with pate-sur-pate florals, 11", $900.00. (Photo courtesy Jackson's International Auctioneers & Appraisers of Fine Art & Antiques)

Lacy Glass

Lacy glass became popular in the late 1820s after the development of the pressing machine. It was decorated with allover patterns — hearts, lyres, sheaves of wheat, etc. — and backgrounds were completely stippled. The designs were intricate and delicate, hence the term 'lacy.' Although Sandwich produced this type of glassware in abundance, it was also made by other eastern glassworks as well as in the Midwest. By 1840, its popularity on the wane and a depressed economy forcing manufacturers to seek less expensive modes of production, lacy glass began to be phased out in favor of pressed pattern glass. For more information refer to *Sandwich Glass* by Ruth Webb Lee. When no condition is indicated, the items listed below are assumed to be without obvious damage; minor roughness is normal. See also Salts, Open; Sandwich.

Cup & saucer, stippled w/dbl arch border, dmn-point base, saucer: 7" .. 110.00
Dish, Nectarine & Star, 8-sided, 6" L, EX............................... 135.00
Inkstand, faceted dmns, 3 cups for wells, 5x8", EX 110.00
Plate, anthemion border, roses/foliage center, 8-sided, 7" 390.00
Plate, central star w/in dbl dmn bands w/in floral/scroll border, 7" ... 100.00
Sugar bowl, cobalt, stippled w/shells & scrolls, Fr, w/lid, 5", EX... 240.00
Tazza, Daisy, heavy glass, 3½" H 420.00
Tray, 8 arches/flowers/fleur-de-lis to shoulder+18 bull's eyes, 6" L....240.00

Lalique

Having recognized her son's talent at an early age, Rene Lalique's mother apprenticed him at the age of 21 to a famous Paris jeweler. In 1885 he opened his own workshop, and his unique style earned him great notoriety because of his use of natural elements in his designs — horn, ivory, semiprecious stone, pearls, coral, enamel, even plastic or glass.

In 1900 at the Paris Universal Exposition at the age of 40, he achieved the pinnacle of success in the jewelry field. Already having experimented with glass, he decided to focus his artistic talent on that medium. In 1907 after completing seven years of laborious work, Lalique became a master glassmaker and designer of perfume bottles for Francois Coty, a chemist and perfumer, who was also his neighbor in the Place Vendome area in Paris. All in all he created over 250 perfume bottles for Roger et Gallet, Coty, Worth, Forvil, Guerlain, D'Orsay, Molinard, and many others. In the commercial perfume bottle collecting field, Rene Lalique's are those most desired. Some of his one-of-a-kind experimental models have gone for over $100,000.00 at auction in the last few years. At the height of production his factories employed over 600 workers.

Seeking to bring art into every day life, he designed clocks, tableware, stemware, chandeliers, inkwells, bowls, statues, dressing table items, and, of course, vases. Lalique's unique creativity is evident in his designs through his polishing, frosting, and glazing techniques. He became famous for his use of colored glass in shades of blue, red, black, gray, yellow, green, and opalescence. His glass, so popular in the 1920s and 1930s, is still coveted today.

Lalique's son Marc assumed leadership of the company in 1948, after his father's death. His designs are made from full lead crystal, not the demi-crystal Rene worked with. Designs from 1948 on were signed only Lalique, France. The company was later taken over by Marc's daughter, Marie-Claude, and her designs were modern, clear crystal accented with color motifs. The Lalique company was sold in 1995, and Marie-Claude Lalique retired shortly thereafter.

Condition is of extreme importance to a collector. Grinding, polished out chips, and missing perfume bottle stoppers can reduce the value significantly, sometimes by as much as 80%.

Czechoslovakian glassware bearing fradulent Lalique signatures is appearing on all levels of the market. Study and become familiar with the various Lalique designs before paying a high price for a fraudulent piece. Over the past five years Lalique-designed glass has been showing up in a deep purple-gray color. These are clear glass items that have been 'irradiated' to change their appearance. Buyer beware. Our advisor for this category is John Danis; he is listed in the Directory under Illinois.

Key:
cl/fr — clear and frosted   RL — signed R. Lalique
L — signed Lalique   RLF — signed R. Lalique, France
LF — signed Lalique France

Ashtray, Canard, upright duck, jade gr opal, RL, 2¾" H 900.00
Ashtray, Grenade, wheel cut, dk amber, RLF, 5½" dia 1,050.00

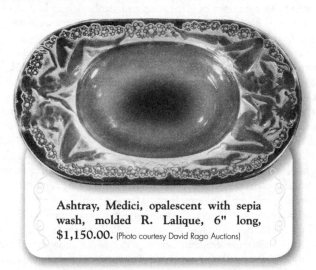

Ashtray, Medici, opalescent with sepia wash, molded R. Lalique, 6" long, $1,150.00. (Photo courtesy David Rago Auctions)

Ashtray w/Statuette De la Fontaine, topaz, RL/288, 4½" 1,600.00
Bottle, Ambre D'Orsay, women in long gowns ea corner, blk, L, 5"...1,495.00
Bottle, Ameile, bulbous w/rows of overlapping feathers, RLF/520, 3"...800.00
Bottle, Arys, feathers, pillow form, bl wash, RL, 4¾", NM............. 80.00
Bottle, Arys, vertical rows of flowers, fr, cylindrical, 7", EX....... 1,035.00
Bottle, Arys, 8 panels, ea separated w/beaded line, slender, L, 5" .. 690.00
Bottle, Camelia, D'Orsay, cl w/bl flower, RL, 4" 1,600.00
Bottle, Corail Rouge/Forvile, cl/fr w/coral pnt, RLF, 4", M in G box .. 3,400.00
Bottle, Dans la Nuit, rnd w/allover stars, bl, moon stopper, 3"..... 345.00
Bottle, Helen, fr w/4 brn-wash sq relief panels w/ladies, RLF, 9"....2,800.00
Bottle, Imprudence, horizontal rings, RL, 3".................................. 360.00
Bottle, La Violette, sheaf of violets, cl/fr w/violet pnt, RL, 3¼"... 4,400.00
Bottle, Le Lys, cl w/sepia-washed allover flowers, disk form, RL, 4"..720.00
Bottle, Lentilles, wavy vines, cl/fr w/gray wash, RL, 3" dia........1,410.00
Bottle, Olives, cl w/sepia wash on vertical ribs/bosses, RL, 4" ..10,200.00

Bottle, Serpent, cl w/fr serpent-head stopper, RL, 3¼" 2,100.00
Bottle, sq flat-sided body, butterfly stopper, L, 3¼" 800.00
Bottle, Unjourviendra, stars/circles border stopper, oval, RL, 8"..800.00
Bowl, Dauphins, fish in swirling waves, opal, RLF, 12" 1,200.00
Bowl, fish against strong waves, RLF, 9¾"................................ 950.00
Bowl, Merienthal, swirling berries, opal, RL, 7"........................... 360.00
Bowl, Nonnettes, 3 prs of birds, opal, RLF, 8½" 1,050.00

Bowl, Ondines Ouvertes, opalescent, molded R. Lalique and wheel-cut France, 8", $1,900.00. (Photo courtesy David Rago Auctions)

Bowl, Rosace, radiating petals, bl, RLF, 12" 2,400.00
Bowl, Volubulis, morning glories, opal, RLF, 1921, 8½" 585.00
Box, Cheveux de Venus, leaves/roots, gray wash, L, 1910, 2¾" dia..1,650.00
Box, cigar; Sultane, cl/fr w/sepia wash, nude sits atop lid, RLF, 6" H...18,360.00
Box, Coquilles, radiating fan panels, opal w/gray wash, RLF, 3" dia..... 780.00
Box, Dahlia, flower-head lid, lt gr wash, RLF, 5" dia 690.00
Box, Dux Figurines, 2 nudes/flowers, gray wash, RL, 2¾" 1,750.00
Box, Hirondelles, many birds on lid, dmns on sides, gray wash, RLF, 4"...1,100.00
Box, Pommier du Japon, Arys, floral branches, blk w/gray, RL, 3" dia..1,400.00
Box, Rambouillet, exotic birds on lid, cl/fr w/gray wash, RL, 3" dia...720.00
Box, Tokio, exotic flower-head lid, yel amber, L, 6⅝" dia..........1,440.00
Box, Trois Figurines, 3 nudes, cl/fr w/sepia wash, RLF, 3¾" dia 650.00
Box, Trois Figurines, 3 nudes, leafy bands on body, RLF, 3¾" dia.250.00
Bracelet, Cerisier, 14 elasticized links, blk w/wht patina, RLF, 1928...3,800.00
Brooch, Figurine Se Balancant, nude on vine, cl/fr, RL, 2¼" L.2,100.00
Brooch, Trois Soleils, 3 flower heads, bl foil/gilt metal bk, L, 2"...585.00
Candlesticks, St Gall, 2 wide grad tiers, RL, 1934, 5½" dia, pr 350.00
Chandelier, Passiflore, spherical w/6 5-sided panels, amber, 18", VG...69,150.00
Clock, Moineaux, birds, cl/fr/sepia wash, rpl face/movement, 8½" L..1,440.00
Clock, Six Hirondelles Perchees, cl/fr, windup, RL, 5½"...........3,000.00
Frame, Quatre Perruches, facing parakeet prs, cl/fr, RL, 4x4"....1,320.00
Jar, Epines, intertwining vines on cl w/bl wash, RL, w/lid, 4".......550.00
Lamp, grad rows of relief floral stems, gr ball form, metal mt, RL, pr..2,250.00
Letter seal, Canard, duck, cl/fr w/sepia wash, RL, 2½"..............1,100.00
Letter seal, Dindon, turkey, deep topaz, RLF, 2⅛".........................960.00
Letter seal, Renard, fox, topaz, RL, 1¾" 650.00
Letter seal, Statuette Drapee, draped nude, opal, RL, 2½" 2,640.00

Letter seal, Tete D'Aigle, eagle's head, blk w/wht wash, RL, 3⅛" ..1,400.00
Liqueur glass, Pouilly, cl/fr w/bl wash, RL, 2¾" 120.00
Mascot, Archer, cl/fr on chrome collar & later stand, RL, 4¾" ..2,400.00

Mascot, Epson, chrome collar and marble socle, molded R. Lalique France, 7" long, $21,000.00.

(Photo courtesy David Rago Auctions)

Mascot, Faucon, RL, 6" 2,640.00
Mascot, Hirondelle, bird, cl/fr w/amethyst tint, RL, 6" 2,680.00
Mascot, Saint Christophe, cl/fr w/sepia wash, RLF, 4½" 1,440.00
Mascot, Sanglier, wild pig, topaz, RL, 3½" L 1,500.00
Mascot, Tete de Coq, head of rooster, cl/fr w/blk glass base, LF, 8" ...1,560.00
Mirror, hand; Narcisse Couche, cl/fr w/gray wash, RLF, 11½" L ..3,600.00
Pendant, Sorbier, triangular w/cherries, electric bl, L, 2" L 600.00
Perfume burner, Sirenes, nudes/sea fauna, bl wash, L, 1920, 6¾"...5,100.00
Statuette, Cygnes, swans, 1 w/head up/1 feeding, cl/fr, LF, 14" L, pr...3,600.00
Statuette, Figurine Avec Guirlande de Fruits, cl/fr/sepia, RL, 8" ...9,000.00
Statuette, Floreal, kneeling nude w/flowers, cl/fr w/blk glass ft, 4"...180.00
Statuette, Floreal, kneeling nude w/flowers, LF, 1970s, 3" 235.00
Statuette, Hirondelles, pr birds, cl/fr w/bronze stand, RL, 14"...8,400.00
Statuette, Voilee Mains Jointes, standing maid, opal, RL, 11" ..1,150.00
Tray, Epines, swirling branches, cl/fr, RL, 1920, 12" dia 600.00
Vase, Ajaccio, sleeping impalas/stars, bl wash, cylindrical, RLF, 8"...2,300.00
Vase, Archers, males w/bows, gray wash, bulbous, RLF, 10½"....8,050.00
Vase, Avallon, birds/cherries, deep bl wash, cylindrical, RLF, 5½"....2,000.00
Vase, Bachantes, dancing nudes, amber wash, U-form, RLF, 9½"... 8,400.00
Vase, Boulouris, band of birds, cl/fr, flared sides, LF, 5" 540.00
Vase, Ceylan, parakeet prs, opal, cylindrical, RL, 9½" 9,200.00
Vase, Dahlias, cl/fr, bulbous, RL, 1923, 5" 4,700.00

Vase, Danaides, clear with blue wash, raised block letters: R. Lalique, 7", $4,140.00.

(Photo courtesy James D. Julia Inc.)

Vase, deer standing against dense foliage, amethyst, LF, 7x5" 400.00
Vase, Dentelle, hobnail ribs, cl/fr, bottle shape, RL, 7½" 780.00
Vase, Domremy, emb flower heads, bl patina, bulbous, RLF, 8½" ..1,725.00

Vase, Domremy, thistles relief, cased opal, shoudered, RLF, 8"..1,800.00
Vase, Domremy, thistles relief, deep amber, shouldered, RLF, 8" ...3,600.00
Vase, Domremy, thistles relief, gr w/wht wash, shouldered, RLF, 8"..4,500.00
Vase, Espalion, ferns, electric bl, bulbous, RLF, 7" 3,360.00
Vase, fleurets all over, opal, U-shape, RL, 7x7"........................3,105.00
Vase, Formose, school of fish, aqua patina, spherical, RL, 6½" ..4,025.00
Vase, Gui, berries branches, opal w/pea gr wash, spherical, RLF, 7"..2,000.00
Vase, Honfleur, cl U-form w/leaf-rtcl brn-wash buttress hdls, RLF, 6"... 1,600.00
Vase, Ibis, panels w/wheat, lt bl wash, RLF, flaring sides, 6½"....... 120.00
Vase, Monnaie du Pape, rnd leaves/stems, med bl wash, RLF, 9x7"..2,585.00
Vase, Perles, rows of draped pearls, opal, ovoid, RLF, 5" 1,645.00
Vase, Perruches, pr of parakeets, red, bulbous, RLF, 10" 25,875.00
Vase, Plumes, feathers, cl/fr/bl wash, bulbous, RLF, 8" 1,320.00
Vase, Plumes, ostrich plumes, red-brn wash, bulbous, RL, 8" 2,160.00
Vase, Poissons, lg fish, opal w/sepia wash, spherical, RLF, 9" 4,500.00
Vase, roses/thorns, cl/fr, tumbler form, LF, 9½" 585.00
Vase, Saint-Mark, zippers/concave panels, bl wash, V-shape, RLF, 7"... 3,220.00
Vase, Tournai, oval panels w/leaves, ovoid, teal gr, RL, 5" 1,880.00
Wine goblet, Rapace, bird stem, cl/violet, RLF, 4⅝" 1,320.00

Lamps

The earliest lamps were simple dish containers with a wick that hung over the edge or was supported by a channel or tube. Grease and oil from animal or vegetable sources were the first fuels used. Ancient pottery lamps, crusie, and Betty lamps are examples of these early types. In 1784 Swiss inventor Ami Argand introduced the first major improvement in lamps. His lamp featured a tubular wick and a glass chimney. During the first half of the nineteenth century, whale oil, burning fluid (a highly explosive mixture of turpentine and alcohol), and lard were the most common fuels used in North America. Many lamps were patented for specific use with these fuels.

Kerosene was the first major breakthrough in lighting fuels. It was demonstrated by Canadian geologist Dr. Abraham Gesner in 1846. The discovery and drilling of petroleum in the late 1850s provided an abundant and inexpensive supply of kerosene. It became the main source of light for homes during the balance of the nineteenth century and for remote locations until the 1950s.

Although Thomas A. Edison invented the electric lamp in 1879, it was not until two or three decades later that electric lamps replaced kerosene household lamps. Millions of kerosene lamps were made for every purpose and pocketbook. They ranged in size from tiny night or miniature lamps to tall stand or piano lamps. Hanging varieties for homes commonly had one or two fonts (oil containers), but chandeliers for churches and public buildings often had six or more. Wall or bracket lamps usually had silvered reflectors. Student lamps, parlor lamps (now called Gone-With-the-Wind lamps) and patterned glass lamps were designed to complement the popular furnishing trends of the day. Gaslight, introduced in the early nineteenth century, was used mainly in homes of the wealthy and public places until the early twentieth century. Most fixtures were wall or ceiling mounted, although some table models were also used.

Few of the ordinary early electric lamps have survived. Many lamp manufacturers made the same or similar styles for either kerosene or electricity, sometimes for gas. Top-of-the-line lamps were made by Pairpoint, Tiffany, Bradley and Hubbard, and Handel. See also these specific sections.

When buying lamps that have been converted to electricity, inspect them very carefully for any damage that may have resulted from the alterations; such damage is very common, and when it does occur, the lamp's value may be lessened by as much as 50%. Lamps seem to bring much higher prices in some areas than others, especially the larger cities. Conversely, in rural areas they may bring only half as much as our listed values. One of our advisors for lamps is Carl Heck; he is listed in the

Directory under Colorado. Jeff Bradfield (in Virginia) is our advisor for pattern glass lamps. See also Stained Glass.

Note: When only one color is given in a two-layer cut overlay lamp description, the second layer is generally clear; in three-layer examples, the second will ususally be white, the third clear. Exceptions will be noted.

Key: col — cut overlay

Aladdin Lamps

From 1908 Aladdin lamps with a mantle became the mainstay of rural America, providing light that compared favorably with the electric light bulb. They were produced by the Mantle Lamp Company of America in over 18 models and more than 100 styles. During the 1930s to the 1950s, this company was the leading manufacturer of electric lamps as well. Still in operation today, the company is now known as Aladdin Mantle Lamp Co., located in Clarksville, Tennessee. For those seeking additional information on Aladdin Lamps, we recommend *Aladdin — The Magic Name in Lamps, Aladdin Electric Lamps Collector's Manual & Price Guide #5,* and *Aladdin Collector's Manual and Price Guide #22,* all written by our advisor for Aladdins, J. W. Courter; he is listed in the Directory under Kentucky. Mr. Courter has also published a book called *Angle Lamps, Collector's Manual and Price Guide.* Kerosene lamp values are for lamps with correct burners.

Bed, B-45, Whip-o-Lite shade, EX, from $75 to 100.00
Bedroom, P-58, ceramic, from $30 to 40.00
Boudoir, G-42, Allegro, Alacite, from $40 to 50.00
Bridge, #7092, swing-arm, reflector, from $125 to 150.00
Floor, #3451, Type B, from $150 to 200.00
Floor, #3625, reflector, candle arms, from $175 to 250.00
Floor, #4898C, Circline, fluorescent, trigger ring, from $200 to... 250.00
Glass Urn, G-379, Alacite, tall ribbed urn w/top, from $250 to... 300.00

Hopalong Cassidy, with original tags, NMIB, $1,100.00. (Photo courtesy Morphy Auctions)

Pinup, G-354, Alacite, from $125 to 150.00
Table, G-178, Opalique, from $150 to 200.00
Table, M-475, ceramic w/blk iron base, from $30 to 40.00
Table, P-408, planter, from $40 to 50.00
Table, W-503, wood & ceramic, from $40 to 60.00

Aladdin Lamps, Kerosene

Aladdinette candle lamp, glass chimney (2 shapes), ea from $200 to... 250.00
Caboose, Model B, B-400, brass font, from $175 to 250.00

Floor, Model B, bronze, #1258, 1934-35, from $150 to 225.00
Foreign Table Model 12, London, nickel, from $50 to 75.00
Shade, Aladdinite Parchment, vase/floor, EX, 20-20½" dia, $350 to..450.00
Table, Model #10, nickel, correct flame spreader #10, from $300 to ..400.00
Table, Model #12, str side, bronze or nickel, M, from $75 to........ 100.00
Table, Model A, Venetian, peach, EX, from $100 to 150.00
Table, Model B, Victoria, ceramic, w/oil fill, B-25, EX, from $550 to.. 650.00
Table, Model B, Washington Drape, P353P, pk-tint crystal, from $150 to...200.00
Table, Model B, wht Moonstone, B-85, 1937, from $300 to 375.00
Table, Model B-61, Short Lincoln Drape, amber crystal, EX, $3,000 to...3,500.00

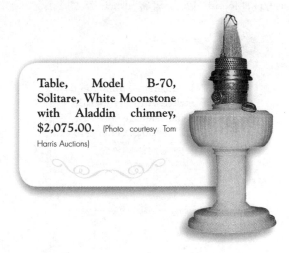

Table, Model B-70, Solitare, White Moonstone with Aladdin chimney, $2,075.00. (Photo courtesy Tom Harris Auctions)

Angle Lamps

The Angle Lamp Company of New York City developed a unique type of kerosene lamp that was a vast improvement over those already on the market; they were sold from about 1896 until 1929 and were expensive for their time. Nearly all Angle lamps are hanging lamps and wall lamps. Table models are uncommon. Our Angle lamp advisor is J. W. Courter; he is listed in the Directory under Kentucky. See the narrative for Aladdin Lamps for information concerning popular books Mr. Courter has authored. Old glass pieces for Angle lamps are scarce to rare; unless noted otherwise, the lamp values that follow are for examples with no glass.

Gas adaptor, polished brass, no glass, EX...................................... 850.00
Glass, chimney top, wht, petal-top, EX.. 85.00
Glass, chimney top, wht, ribbed, EX 75.00
Glass, elbow globe, clear w/floral bouquet band, EX..................... 250.00
Hanging, #254, rose floral, 2-burner, polished brass, lamp only, EX.. 1,000.00
Hanging, #263, polished brass, old glass, EX 475.00

Hanging, #352, Fleur-de-Lis, polished brass, with three milk glass chimneys, $850.00 (value minus glass chimneys: $550.00). (Photo courtesy Tom Harris Auctions)

Hanging, Classic, antique gold, cast tank, 2-burner, NM 2,250.00
Hanging, Leaf & Vine, 2-burner, nickel, EX................................. 400.00
Wall, #103, plain can, nickel, EX.. 200.00

Wall, #185, pinwheel, antique brass, EX 400.00
Wall, Classic #3, antique gold, cast tank, no glass, EX 1,200.00
Wall, MW 966-NF, Leaf & Vine, nickel, 2-burner, EX 350.00
Wall cone, #101, tin, blk pnt, no glass, EX 200.00

Banquet Lamps

Col (2-layer), bl, Moorish Windows/Quatrefoil & Punty, Sandwich, 15" . 3,300.00
Col (2 layer), bl, Moorish Windows/Quatrefoil & Punty, Sandwich, 20" .. 7,975.00
Col (2-layer), gr, cut/frosted 5" shade, #2 Jones burner, 30¾" .11,000.00
Col (3-layer), pk, Moorish Windows, Sandwich, 28½" 9,000.00

Cranberry font and etched cranberry shade, some damage to base, 32", $400.00. (Photo courtesy Jackson's International Auctioneers & Appraisers of Fine Art & Antiques)

Gilt brass & glass, T'print font w/dbl burner, etch star globe, 35" ...415.00
Gilt metal std, HP globe w/gold griffins, 19th C, 32" 425.00
Putti bronzed std w/HP floral globe, electrified, ca 1900, 25" 240.00
Red cased w/HP gold wreaths, electrified, 36" 900.00

Chandeliers

Brass, 12-arm, cranberry cut-to-clear vase and bowl, ram's head masks, 45x30", $7,100.00. (Photo courtesy Neal Auction Co. Auctioneers & Appraisers of Fine Art)

Brass, 6-arm, trn std/leafy scroll arms, crest w/eagles/urns, 29x29" 470.00
Brass, 12-light, trefoil hanging ring w/drop, 18th C, 34x23" 600.00
Brass, 2 tiers w/12 arms & candle sockets, post w/globe, 26x28" ..450.00
Bronze, Am rococo, 3-arm, etched orb shades, 43" 5,875.00
Bronze, Baroque-style, 2-tier, ea w/9 arms, cartouch drops, 20th C 2,999.99
Bronze 'basket of roses' w/5 frosted glass rose-shape shades, 27x12" ...250.00
Bronze, Regency style, 8-arm, very ornate, foliate scrolls, 43x46" ..3,200.00
Crystal, Baccarat style, 6-light basket form w/pendants, 46x36" ...1,525.00
Gilt bronze, Louis XV style, 11 lights/3 tiers of leafy arms, 31x29" ...2,000.00
Gilt bronze/blk tole pnt, Emp style 6-light, pendant chains, 33x25" ... 600.00

Gilt bronze/crystal, Louis XVI style, 16-light, pendants, 34x28" 2,825.00
Gilt/patinated bronze, Bell Epoque, 4-light, acanthus mts, 55x21" ..1,295.00
Gilt/patinated metal, Directoire style, 5-light, 20th C, 18x14" 525.00
Glass, 8 electric socket, scrolls/chains/pendants/prisms, 27x30" ... 800.00
Pnt wrought iron w/scrolls/leaves, 23-light, bud sockets, 60x42" .. 525.00
Porc, Dresden style, 4-arm, putti/maids as std, encrusted florals, 20" 200.00
Tole/gilt bronze, Emp style w/6 swan arms, bellflower finial, 11x20" 525.00
Wrought iron, Renaissance Revival, 13-light/scrolled cage, 47x42" .3,800.00
Wrought iron, rococo style, 6-arm, scrolled cage w/leaves, 33x23" 125.00
Wrought iron, 8-arm, twist supports/floral cups, acanthus, 59x59" 940.00
Wrought iron w/gr patina, scrolling arms/leaves/floral cups, 40x32" 350.00

Decorated Kerosene Lamps

Bl & wht latticinio threads on clear w/blk glass base, Lutz, 9¾" .. 1,760.00
Col (2-layer), bl to wht, Moorish Windows, 2-step marble base, 15" 770.00

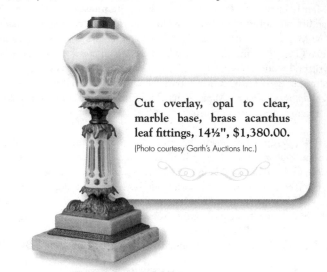

Cut overlay, opal to clear, marble base, brass acanthus leaf fittings, 14½", $1,380.00. (Photo courtesy Garth's Auctions Inc.)

Col (2-layer), ruby, floral, 2-step marble base, Sandwich, 11" 600.00
Col (2-layer), ruby, floral band, gr/wht col stem, NE Glass, 10" .. 3,100.00
Col (2-layer), ruby, geometrics, bl alabaster base w/gold, 14" 9,900.00
Col (2-layer), wht to bl alabaster, Quatrefoil, clambroth font, 12" ...770.00
Col (2-layer), wht to emerald, 2-step marble base, 12½" 715.00
Col (2-layer), wht to ruby, floral/acorns/berries, marble base, 12" ...550.00
Col (2-layer), wht to ruby, Moorish Windows, gilt Baroque base, 14" ..500.00
Col (2-layer), wht to ruby, Star & Quatrefoil, wht opal base, 14" ...660.00
Col (3-layer), gr, opaque wht glass base, Sandwich, 1860s, 12" 770.00
Col (3-layer), red, Star & Quatrefoil, marble base, 13" 715.00
Nailsea, wht loops on clear, 1-step marble base, Lutz, 8¾" 935.00

Fairy Lamps

Burmese, red berries on green stems, clear insert marked Clarke Cricklite, base marked Thomas Webb & Son, 7", $1,950.00. (Photo courtesy Early Auction Co.)

Bl & wht verre moire, 3-lobe ruffled bowl, 1880s, 8" dia 510.00
Bl satin Dmn Quilt, Clarke cup, pyramid sz 210.00

Burmese, down-trn crimped base, Webb, 6¼" 600.00
Burmese, floral, crimped base, Webb, 6" 1,100.00
Burmese, floral (complex), Webb, Clarke cup, 7" 1,800.00
Burmese, oak leaves on shade, down-trn crimped base, Webb, 7" .. 2,450.00
Cranberry overshot, swirled shade/ruffled base, clear cup, 6" 400.00
Millefiori, swirled mc canes, Venetian, 4¾" 285.00
Nailsea, bl/wht, in Clarke cup, 4¼x4" 265.00
Nailsea, citron/wht, ruffled base, Clarke Cricklite cup, 6¼" 500.00
Queen Victoria Dmn Jubilee, cobalt, emb portrait 4 sides 325.00
Red Nailsea, ruffled base, Clarke cup, 7" 750.00
Wht opal Dmn Quilt, Clarke Cricklite cup, 4½" 200.00

Gone-With-the-Wind Lamps

Arabic camel rider and palm trees on shade and base with blown-out lion's heads, 22", $795.00. (Photo courtesy Fontaine's Auction Gallery)

Amberina Hobnail shade, oil burner, 7x7", complete w/chain pulley ... 600.00
Cranberry Coin Dot, orig brass mts & chains, 13½x8" 400.00
Cranberry Hobnail shade w/prisms, Dmn Quilt lower globe, 34x14".. 600.00
Floral on beige ball shade & base, all orig, 23x11" 115.00
Gilt chinoiserie on beige ball shade & base, 24½" to chimney top ... 275.00
Opaque wht shade w/floral transfer, Bradley & Hubbard font, 36x13½".. 300.00
Pk Bristol shade & font, gold-tone emb heart fr, 39x13½" 425.00
Pk opaque HP floral ball shade, wht-metal cherub figural base 550.00
Roses on shaded gr, 10" shade w/gr bead fringe, brass mts, 24" 180.00

Hanging Lamps

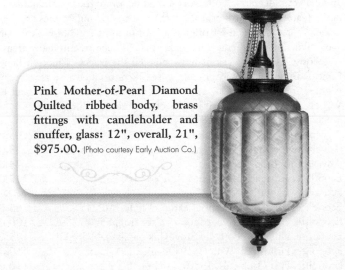

Pink Mother-of-Pearl Diamond Quilted ribbed body, brass fittings with candleholder and snuffer, glass: 12", overall, 21", $975.00. (Photo courtesy Early Auction Co.)

Blown, bulbous w/flared rim, cut/eng florals, brass mts, 18x12" .. 2,760.00

Opal w/Delft Dutch windmills/ships, brass chains, S-scroll straps, 9".. 800.00
Pk opal swirl ruffled 9" shade; etched red-brass fr w/scrolled straps... 350.00

Lanterns

Bronze neoclassic style w/acanthus & scrolls, curved glass panels, 36".. 1,100.00
Carriage, brass w/glazed sides, dome cap w/ball finial, 24x12x15" ...150.00
Giltwood Italian, hexagonal w/scrollwork, 41x23", pr 6,170.00
Glass tumbler w/tin candle socket in tin fr, sm smoke bell, 11".... 315.00
Patinated bronze w/glass panes, central shaft/pendant, 36x14x14", pr... 600.00
Pillar-mold globe w/punched tin top, oil burner, Pittsburgh, 13" 1,600.00
Tin top/base w/star piercings, 8-sided cylindrical globe, 13", VG. 175.00

Lard Oil/Grease Lamps

Betty, dbl; iron, 2 shallow pans on hook w/swivel ring, 1750s, 6" 150.00
Betty, iron, ornate hanger, scalloped finial, 12¾x7" 315.00
Betty, iron, shallow pan, ornate acorn-shaped top, 1780s, 9½" 175.00
Iron, basket-shaped holder on 8" harpoon-like hook, 1770s 250.00
Iron, pear-shaped pan mtd on 11" spike, EX patina, ca 1770 .... 180.00
Iron, 4-spout, 1750s, 5½x3½x3½", w/8" hanger 175.00
Pewter, unmk saucer base, dents/scratches, 10½x6½" dia 70.00

Miniature Lamps

Miniature oil lamps were originally called 'night lamps' by their manufacturers. Early examples were very utilitarian in design — some holding only enough oil to burn through the night. When kerosene replaced whale oil in the second half of the nineteenth century, 'mini' lamps became more decorative and started serving other purposes. While mini lamps continue to be produced today, collectors place special value on the lamps of the kerosene era, roughly 1855 to 1910. Four reference books are especially valuable to collectors as they try to identify and value their collections: *Miniature Lamps* by Frank and Ruth Smith, Schiffer Publishing, 1968 (referred to as SI); *Miniature Lamps II* by Ruth Smith, Schiffer Publishing 1982 (SII); *Miniature Victorian Lamps* by Marjorie Hulsebus (source of the H numbers below), Schiffer Publishing, 1996; and *Price Guide for Miniature Lamps* by Marjorie Hulsebus, Schiffer Publishing, 1998 (contains 1998 values for all the above books). References in the following listings correlate with each lamp's plate number in these books.

Cranberry swirl with white casing, knob marked P&A Mfg. Co. Victor, 8½", $1,500.00. (Photo courtesy Morphy Auctions)

Amber, ribbed swirl/cut stars, Foreign burner, Stevens & Wms, SI-553 ...5,175.00
Amethyst w/wht floral & gold, Hornet burner, SI-262 variant, 8¾" ..350.00
Bl cased w/mc floral, Nutmeg burner, SI-386, 8" 975.00
Bl o/l, berries & leaves, clear glass hdl, SII-413, 9¼", VG 230.00

Bl opaque w/fired-on leaves/coralene fruit, Foreign burner, SI-358, VG ..515.00
Bl satin MOP, Raindrop, Acorn burner, SI-601, 8" 750.00
Bl satin MOP, ribbed swirl w/crystal ft, Foreign burner, SI-595, 9" ...1,265.00
Cat, wht porc w/red ball, mc base, SI-496, 6½" 575.00
Columbus, milk glass shade & base, Nutmeg burner, SI-491, VG/EX.. 8,625.00
Cranberry Nailsea, wafer ft, Foreign burner, unlisted, 7" 3,450.00
Cranberry w/amber raspberry prunts, Foreign burner, SI-figure XI, 9"...925.00
Cranberry w/optic rib panels, Nutmeg burner, SI-440, 9" 295.00
Frosted ribbed swirl w/mc floral, silver base, Foreign burner, SI-556...925.00
Gr cased, Florette, Nutmeg burner, SI-388, 7", VG 460.00
Honey amber/wht spatter w/wide swirl ribs, Nutmeg burner, SI-294, 6" ..465.00
Log, bl opaline, Hornet burner, Atterbury, SI-50, 3½"+chimney ..1,380.00
Mc spatter, beaded & ribbed, Hornet burner, SI-367, 9" 350.00
Milk glass, panels w/mc flowers & gold, Nutmeg burner, SII-267, 8¾"...300.00
Milk glass w/fired-on satin pnt/mc floral, Hornet burner, SI-218, VG ..300.00
Milk glass w/mc floral, Foreign burner, SI-355, 9½" 400.00
Milk glass w/N & S Am maps, Pan Am Expo 1901, SI-309, 8½"... 1,600.00
Owl, milk glass, mc details, Acorn burner, SI-497, 8" 750.00
Pig w/corn in mouth, brn pottery, SI-500, rare, 3⅜" 14,950.00
Pk opaline font & shade, gr ped ft, Foreign burner, SI-562, 12½"..1,725.00
Pk opaline shade & base, 5 crystal ft, Nutmeg burner, SI-536, 8½"..1,150.00
Pk Satin MOP, Dmn Quilt, crystal ft, Foreign burner, SI-594/595, 9" ..2,245.00
Red irid w/emb decor, Nutmeg burner, SI-423, 9¼" 575.00
Red satin w/emb decor, Nutmeg burner, SI-399, 7¾", VG 200.00
Rubena w/emb ivy & swirl, Nutmeg burner, SI-431, 6" 425.00
Santa, milk glass w/HP decor, Acorn burner, 9¼".....................5,500.00
Shoe, emb Pat date on sole, Hornet burner, SI-51, 3" to collar.... 575.00
Wht Nailsea w/bl top, Foreign burner, Kempton, 3-pc, unlisted, 9".4,600.00
Yel, reverse swirl, candy ribbon skirt, Foreign burner, 7" 1,725.00
Yel cased ribbed swirl w/emb medallions, Acorn burner, SI-547, 8½" ..1,900.00
Yel cased w/gold floral, Nutmeg burner, SI-391, 8½" 460.00
Yel satin MOP, Dmn Quilt, frosted ft, Foreign burner, SI-594, 9½"..1,035.00

Moss Lamps

Moss lamps, a unique blend of Plexiglas and whimsical design, enjoyed their heyday during the 1940s and 1950s. Created by Moss Mfg. Co. of San Francisco, the lamps were the brainchild of company co-owner Thelma Moss and principal designers Duke Smith and John Disney. Plexiglas was initially used to offset World War II metal rationing, but its adaptability and translucence made it an ideal material for the imaginative and angular Moss designs. Adding to the novelty of Moss lamps were oversize 'spun glass' shades and revolving platforms which held figurines by many top ceramic firms of the day, including Hedi Schoop, Ceramic Arts Studio, Lefton, and Dorothy Kindell. Later additions to the Moss lamp line incorporated everything from clocks and music boxes to waterwheels and operating fountains. The 'Moss Fish Tank Bar' even combined the functions of lamp, aquarium, and bar, all in one unit!

Moss ceased production in 1968, but the company's lamps remain in great demand today, as eye-catching accent pieces for retro decorating schemes. Moss lamps are also cross-collectibles, for those interested in figural ceramics. For further information we recommend *Moss Lamps: Lighting the '50s* (Schiffer) by Donald-Brian Johnson and Leslie Piña. Mr Johnson is our advisor for this category; he is listed in the Directory under Nebraska. See also Clubs, Newsletters, and Catalogs.

#T 434, Harlequinade Boy & Girl (Lefton) music box lamp, 29", $275 to..300.00
#T 476, Siamese Dancer (deLee) on base, 30", from $200 to....... 225.00
#T 569, Birdcage-style hanging lantern, 28", from $225 to 250.00
#T 688, Leaf lamp, late 1940s, 27", from $75 to 100.00
#T 689, Marilyn table lamp w/dbl rotating shades, from $375 to .. 400.00
#X 2404, Cocktail Girl floor lamp, pk Plexiglas, 61", from $525 to....550.00
#XT 802, Ballet Man (Decoramic) table lamp, 40", from $175 to ..200.00
#XT 805, Asian Dancer (Lefton) table lamp, 29", from $175 to..200.00

#XT 807, Phantasy Lady (Hedi Schoop), 29½", from $250 to 275.00
#XT 807, Poodle Girl (H Schoop), revolving platform, 31½", $275 to..300.00
#XT 811, Girl w/Basket (Yona) table lamp, 24", from $200 to 225.00
#XT 826, Turbaned Man w/Scimitar table lamp, 31", from $125 to ..150.00
#XT 827, Marilyn figure on base, starry Plexiglas, 32", from $375 to ..400.00
#XT 853, Bali Dancer (Yona) fountain lamp, 52", from $1,200 to...1,300.00
#XT 856, Adonis & Aphrodite (Ceramic Arts Studio), 31", from $950 to ..1,000.00
#XT 858, Aquarium lamp, 27", from $400 to 500.00
#77A, Tami lamp, ceramic base, 2-tone bl drip, 1960s, 51", from $50 to ... 75.00
#2249, floor lamp w/wood base, 63½", from $375 to.................... 400.00
#2293, Leaning Lena floor lamp, fluorescent stem, 55", from $275 to...300.00
#2310, Mr Mambo (Decoramic) floor lamp, 28" sq fringed shade, $600 to...625.00
#2314, floor lamp w/glitter panel, starburst bulbs, 60", from $325 to..350.00
#2326, Leaf floor-to-ceiling, birdcage lanterns, up to 108", $225 to ...250.00
#3006, Triangular Clock lamp w/side planters, from $175 to 200.00
#5002, Dancer (H Schoop) wall plaque lamp w/planters, 35" W, $350 to..400.00
#5007, Native Man (Consolidated) wall plaque, from $300 to 350.00
#6001, Fish Tank Bar, from $2,400 to 2,500.00

Mr. Mambo floor lamp, 28" square red-fringed shade, Decoramic Kilns figurine (5"), from $600.00 to $625.00. (Photo by Leslie Piña from *Moss Lamps: Lighting the '50s*, Schiffer)

Motion Lamps

Animated motion lamps were made as early as 1920 and as late as 1980s. They reached their peak during the 1950s when plastic became widely used. They are characterized by action created by the heat of a light bulb which causes the cylinder to revolve and create the illusion of an animated scene. Some of the better-known manufacturers were Econolite Corp., Scene in Action Corp., and LA Goodman Mfg. Co. As with many collectible items, prices are guided by condition, availability, and collector demand. Collectors should be aware that reproductions of lamps featuring cars, trains, sailing ships, fish, and mill scenes are being made. Values are given for original lamps in mint condition. Any damage or flaws seriously reduce the price. As has been true in many areas of collecting, Internet auctions have affected the prices of motion lamps. Erratic ups and downs in prices realized have resulted in a market that is often unpredictible. Our advisors for motion lamps are Kaye and Jim Whitaker; they are listed in the Directory under Washington.

Advertising, Coor's Beer, wall mt, ca 1960s, 15"............................ 55.00
Advertising, Hamm's Beer, wall mt, coastal area scene, 1963 .... 45.00
Advertising, 7-Up, 13"... 75.00
Econolite, Antique Car, #768, 11", from $100 to 135.00
Econolite, Butterfly, #753, 11"... 150.00
Econolite, child's lamp, various carousel styles, 10", ea 85.00
Econolite, Christmas Tree, paper, 2 szs, ea from $50 to 100.00
Econolite, Fireplace, Potbelly Stove, blk or silver, 1958, 11" 145.00
Econolite, Fish (Fresh Water), 1950s, 11".................................... 110.00
Econolite, Fish (Tropical), 1950s, 11" (+).................................... 110.00
Econolite, Fountain of Youth, #861, 11"....................................... 95.00

Econolite, Hawaiian Scene, #701, 11" 175.00
Econolite, Mill Stream, 1956, 11" (+) 110.00
Econolite, Miss Liberty, #769, 11" 225.00
Econolite, Old Mill, #765, 11" 125.00
Econolite, Sailboats, Mayflower, etc, 1954, 14" (+) 120.00
Econolite, Seattle World's Fair, 1962, 11" 170.00
Econolite, Snow Scene, #766 or #767, 11", ea 115.00
Econolite, Truck & Bus, 1962, 11" 150.00
Elvgrin Pin-up Girls 375.00
Gritt, Indian Maiden or Chief, ea 150.00
Gritt, Village Blacksmith 125.00
LA Goodman, Davy Crockett 150.00
LA Goodman, Firefighters, 11" 150.00
LA Goodman, Ocean Creatures by Sunken Ship, 14" 125.00
LA Goodman, Oriental Fantasy, 11" 100.00
LA Goodman, Trains, 1950s, 11" 95.00
LA Goodman, Waterfall - Campfire, 11" 75.00
National Co, Forest Fire, 10" 125.00
National Co, Off Tardmouth, 13" 175.00
Roto-Vue Jr, Econolite, Forest Fire, #FF, 10" 75.00
Roto-Vue Jr, Econolite, Fountain of Youth, 10" 95.00
Roto-Vue Jr, Econolite, Niagara Falls, #NF, 10" 55.00

Roto-Vue Jr., Forest Fire, 1949, 10", $75.00. (Photo courtesy Jim and Kaye Whitaker)

Roto-Vue Jr, Merry Go Round, red, yel or bl, 1949, 10" 90.00
Scene in Action, Colonial Fountain, 13" 135.00
Scene in Action, Flames, 10" 135.00
Scene in Action, Japanese Twilight, 13" 150.00
Scene in Action, Marine Scene, 10" 150.00
Scene in Action, Serenader, 13" 150.00
Scene in Action, Ship/Lighthouse, 1931, 10" 135.00
Visual Effects Co, Bar Is Open, 1970, 15" 25.00
Visual Effects Co, Budweiser, 1970, 15" 45.00
Visual Effects Co, Op Art Lamp, 1970s, 13" (+) 50.00

Pattern Glass Lamps

The letter/number codes in the following descriptions refer to *Oil Lamps, Book I, II,* and *III,* by Catherine Thuro (book, page, item number or letter). Our advisor for this section is Jeff Bradfield who is listed in the Directory under Virginia.

Acorn, fine-rib bkground, 1860s, T2-67g, 9" 300.00
Aries, ornate hdl, hand lamp, TI-199h, 5¾", from $75 to 85.00
Basketweave w/Medallions, ftd hand lamp, T2-109g 325.00
Bigler, sapphire bl, sq base, stand lamp, NE Glass, 10¼" 2,300.00
Blackberry, bl alabaster/clambroth, wht 1-step glass ft, 8" 660.00

Blocked Fern, wht opaque base, TI-103e, 8¾", from $110 to 130.00
Chadwick, pressed, wht opaque pressed base, T2-79i, from $225 to ... 275.00
Chieftain, figural stem, Atterbury, TI-123a, 10⅝" 200.00
Clarissa, 3-pc straw-holder style, P&A Victor burner, TI-pg 285, 17" ... 360.00

Coolidge Drape, clear, TII-125H, 18", $50.00. (Photo courtesy Morphy Auctions)

Dexter, opaque base, TI-168f, 9⅜", from $150 to 175.00
Ellipse, semi-opaque fiery opal, fiery opal hex base, stand lamp, 6" ... 2,400.00
Essex, broad rib front, leaded glass base, TI-90c, 6¼" 75.00
Heart-Top Panel, transfer/pnt stem on wht opaque base, T2-32a 400.00
Hobbs Fruit Medallion, all glass, T3-117f, minimum value 150.00
Lowell Loop, hand lamp, TI-273j, 6¼" 140.00
Melon, leaded glass, stand lamp, 1860s, TI-88c, from $80 to 100.00
Pineapple & Fan, P&A Victor burner, TII-123L, 17", VG 500.00
Plume, hand lamp, T2-99x 125.00
Princess Feather, cobalt bl, TI-279i, 9½" (watch for repros) 475.00
Ring & Oval, violet-bl, hex base, stand lamp, Sandwich, 8¼" .. 3,950.00
Ring Punty, leaded glass base, TI-85e, 8⅝", from $140 to 180.00
Star & Punty, alabaster/clambroth, hex base, stand lamp, Sandwich, 10" 2,200.00
Star Brooch, sq pressed base, T2-75h, 8", from $200 to 300.00
Star Oval Panel, stand lamp, TI-99h, 8½", from $70 to 100.00
Triple Flute & Bar, etched/frosted 4" Oregon shade, marble base, 11" .. 440.00
Triple Flute & Bar, fiery opal font, bl alabaster/clambroth base, 13" ... 1,045.00
Tulip, alabaster/clambroth font, bl alabaster/clambroth base, 12⅜" 825.00
Waffle & Thumbprint, wide flat base, T2-62a, 10⅛", from $175 to 275.00
Waisted Loop, dk amethyst, 1-pc w/hex base, stand lamp, NE Glass, 9" .. 2,300.00
Wave, amber Beaded Bar base, Atterbury, TI-140e, 9¼", from $95 to .. 110.00
3-Printie, sapphire bl, sq base, stand lamp, 7⅝" 2,950.00
3-Printie, wht opaq, fiery opal hex base, stand lamp, 7⅜" 3,000.00

Perfume Lamps

One catalog from the 1950s states that a perfume lamp 'precipitates and absorbs unpleasant tobacco smoke in closed rooms; freshens air in rooms, and is decorative in every home — can be used as a night lamp or television lamp.' An earlier advertisement reads 'an electric lamp that breathes delightful, delicate fragrance as it burns.' Perfume-burner lamps can be traced back to the earliest times of man. There has always been a desire to change, sweeten, or freshen air. Through the centuries the evolution of the perfume-burner lamp has had many changes in outer form, but very little change in function. Many designs of incense burners were used not only for the reasons mentioned here, but also in various ceremonies — as they still are to this day. Later, very fine perfume burners were designed and produced by the best glasshouses in Europe. Other media such as porcelain and metal also were used. It was not until the early part of the twentieth century that electric perfume lamps came into existence. Many lamps made by both American and European firms during the '20s and '30s are eagerly sought by collectors.

From the mid-1930s to the 1970s, there seems to have been an explosion in both the number of designs and manufacturers. This is especially true in Europe. Nearly every conceivable figure has been seen as a perfume lamp. Animals, buildings, fish, houses, jars, Oriental themes, people, and statuary are just a few examples. American import firms have purchased many different designs from Japan. These lamps range from replicas of earlier European pieces to original works. Except for an occasional article or section in reference books, very little has been written on this subject. The information contained in each of these articles generally covers only a specific designer, manufacturer, or country. To date, no formal group or association exists for this area of collecting.

Fulper, ballerina in pk tutu seated on pk base, 1920s, 6", $200 to....250.00
Germany, porc, lizard, mc on wht base, glass eyes, Deco style, 7"....425.00
Germany, terrier sitting & begging, brn airbrushing, 7" 155.00
Goebel, lady dressed as butterfly, ca 1923-49, 12" 1,150.00
Goebel W Germany, Chinese lantern, mc w/gold dragon top, 7½"..175.00
Irice, lady w/fan, appl flowers on skirt, 6¾" 55.00
Limoges, lady sits on steps w/flower basket, 5½" 275.00
Noritake, lady seated by flower basket, mc, ca 1925, 5¾" 125.00
Rosenthal, puppy standing in grass, Deco style, 6x5" 625.00

Two fish, 6½", $100.00. (Photo courtesy Monsen & Baer)

Reverse-Painted Lamps

Jefferson, 18" shade w/trees/road/house sgn/#1897; gr glass base, 22" .. 2,040.00
Jefferson, 18" woodland scene w/bl sky #2680 shade; vasiform base, 24"..1,725.00
Moe Bridges, 15" nasturtium sgn shade (EX); sgn bronze std, 21" 1,985.00
Moe Bridges, 15" trees/lake shade; blk-patina std w/linear decor, 20" ... 1,645.00
Moe Bridges, 18" birds of paradise shade; ftd bottle std w/2 supports..5,175.00
Moe Bridges, 18" trees shade w/distant mtns; tapering bronze std, 22"....3,165.00

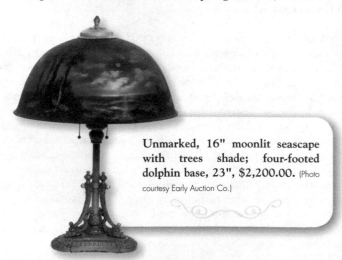

Unmarked, 16" moonlit seascape with trees shade; four-footed dolphin base, 23", $2,200.00. (Photo courtesy Early Auction Co.)

Unmk, 17" galleons dome shade (EX); simple std w/sqd stem & ft, 21"...800.00
Unmk, 20" scenic shade/base, ea w/6 gilt metal-fr panels, 24" ..2,700.00

Student Lamps, Kerosene

Am Student Lamp on font insert, milk glass shade, 22¼" 460.00
Brass, dbl, cased gr shades, electrified, 28x22"..............................300.00
Brass, dbl, cased pk shades, electrified, 1870s, 22x26" 1,700.00

Brass, double, Harvard base, cased ruby shades, 23", $1,950.00. (Photo description James D. Julia Inc.)

Brass, dbl, wht umbrella shades, Cosmos Brenner tank, 17".........375.00
Brass, Imperial German...Pat 1884, orange shade 300.00
Cast metal floral base, gr pulled-feather 9" shade, 21" 475.00

TV Lamps

When TV viewing became a popular pastime during the 1940s, TV lamps were developed to provide just the right amount of light — not bright enough to compromise the sharpness of the picture, but just enough to prevent the eyestrain it was feared might result from watching TV in a darkened room. Most were made of ceramic, and many were figurals such as cats, owls, ducks, and the like, or made in the shape of Conestoga wagons, sailing ships, seashells, etc. Some had shades and others were made as planters. Few were marked well enough to identify the maker without some study. *TV Lamps to Light the World* by John A. Shuman III (Collector Books) provides many photos and suggested value ranges for those who want more information. All lamps listed below are ceramic unless otherwise described. See also Maddux; Morton Pottery; Rosemeade; other specific manufacturers.

Exotic bird, gold spray trim, #L-701, 13x12", from $75.00 to $85.00. (Photo courtesy Peggy and John Scott)

Banana leaves, mc pastels, Lane, 1958, 14½x11"..........................225.00
Bluebirds (2) before fiberglass panel, Lane, 1959, 10½".................. 90.00
Cat (Deco style) stands before planter, Miramar of CA, 1955, 12" ..135.00
Cocker spaniel & pup w/glass eyes, Made in CA, 11x12x5½"........ 75.00
Dachshund on wooden base before 2 paper screens, 10¼x10¼"...125.00
Deer (2) on planter base, Lane, 1959, 13x14x8".......................... 70.00

Fawn on planter base, Lane, 1959, 12½x14x8" 70.00
Flamingos (2) on planter base, Lane, 14x15½x5½" 250.00
Horse jumping on grassy base, yel-gr & deep gr, unmk, 9½x13x6¼" .. 55.00
Horse on rocky planter base, Lane, #P80, 1959, 13½" 85.00
Marlin jumping, mc pastels, on planter base, Lane 215.00
Mermaid among flowers & foliage, wht w/gold, unmk, 11½x9" ... 100.00
Mermaid seated by fish, gr w/wht foam, shaded bulb beside, 7x10x4"....65.00
Monkeys (2), wht w/glass eyes, Van Res Ceramics, 11x6" 110.00
Nude Deco-style lady (brass) stands before glass in fr, 9¼x5¼" 135.00
Palm tree (cvd koa wood) before parchment shade, 10x6½" 80.00
Panther (blk) on rocky planter base, Lane, 1959, 10½x14x8" 70.00
Panther stalking, creamy wht, 4¼x21½" 70.00
Rooster stands w/head turned, colorful tail, Lane, 15x11½" 135.00
Roses, mc pastels, Lane, 1960, 9½x11½x10", NM 85.00
Siamese cats (2), realistic w/glass eyes, Claes...1954, 12x10" 110.00
Siamese cats (3) w/marble eyes, Made in CA USA, 11" 125.00

Whale Oil/Burning Fluid Lamps

Bl, rnd/squat w/appl loop hdl, tooled brass collar, 6x3" 90.00
Clear blown ball font, 2-tube burner, peg lamp, NE Glass, 4½" ... 440.00
Clear blown ball font w/dbl-knop stem, saucer base, 7½" 1,400.00
Clear invt pear font on cylinder w/ovals & swags, 12x5" 1,410.00
Clear invt pear font on lacy sq ped ft, 7x2½" 470.00
Col (2-layer), pk, finely cut, 2-tube burner, peg lamp, 5" 1,200.00
Col (2-layer), powder bl, 2-tube burner, Sandwich, peg lamp, 5" ... 1,045.00
Col (2-layer), ruby, pear-shaped font, 2-tube burner, peg lamp, 5½" ..660.00
Fiery opal mold-blown paneled font, hex base, stand lamp, 7½" . 2,650.00
Heliotrope onion form, ribbed font/base, Sandwich, 13½"........3,200.00
Teal gr blown font, clear waterfall base, tin burner, Sandwich, 7¼" ...6,000.00

Miscellaneous

Metal overlay 18" shade; similar base, 25", $1,150.00.

(Photo courtesy Early Auction Co.)

Argand, ewer-on-lily font on stone base, frosted/cut shade, 23", pr ..1,440.00
Astral, brass fluted shaft/stepped marble base, prisms, cut shade, 30" .. 2,000.00
Gilt brass, acanthus stds, urn-shaped fonts, cut/etched shades, 21" ..1,800.00
O/l 14" shade w/Aladdin lamp silhouette in 4 panels, riveted base, 23"..2,585.00
Partner's desk, brass, sq base/tapered post, rectangle shades, 15x15"...260.00
Slag glass 13" bent panel shade; figural lady std, 21"...................... 520.00

Lang, Anton

Anton Lang (1875 – 1938) was a German studio potter and an actor in the Oberammergau Passion Plays early in the twentieth century. Because he played the role of Christ three times, tourists brought his pottery back to the U.S. in suitcases, which accounts for the prevalence of smaller examples today. As the only son in the family, he took up his father's and grandfather's trade. Following the successful completion of an apprenticeship in his father's workshop in 1891, Lang worked for master potters in Wolfratshausen, Munich, and Stuttgart to better learn his craft. Returning to Oberammergau in 1898, Lang resumed working with his father. The next year the village elders surprised everyone by selecting Lang to play the role of Christ in the 1900 Passion Play. He proved to be a popular choice with the audience and became an international celebrity.

In 1902 Lang married Mathilde Rutz. In that same year, with the help of an assistant and an apprentice, he built his own workshop and a kiln. In the early days Mathilde helped in the pottery as a decorator until Lang could afford to employ girls from the local art school.

During 1923 – 1924 Anton Lang and the other 'Passion Players' toured the U.S. selling their crafts. Lang would occasionally throw pottery when the cast passed through a pottery center such as Cincinnati, where Rookwood was located. The pots thrown at Rookwood are easy to identify as Lang hand signed the side of each piece and they have a 1924 Rookwood mark on the bottom. Lang visited the U.S. only once, and contrary to popular belief, he was never employed by Rookwood. His pottery, marked with his name in script, is fairly scarce and highly valued for its artistic quality.

His son Karl (1903 – 1990) was also a gifted potter. Karl apprenticed with his father and then completed his training at the national ceramic school in Landshut. He took over the day-to-day operations of the pottery while his father was touring America. Over time Karl became the chief designer and was responsible for creating most of the modern pieces and inventing many new glazes. Only pieces bearing a hand-written signature (not a facsimile) are certain to be Anton Lang originals instead of the work of Karl or the Langs's assistants. Anton and Karl also made pieces together; Karl might design a piece and Anton decorate it. In 1925 Karl went to Dresden to study with sculptor Arthur Lange. Under the influence of the famous artist Ernst Barlach, Karl designed his greatest work, the 'Wanderer in the Storm.' This large figure depicts a man dressed in a long coat and hat resisting a violent wind. Between 1925 and 1930, four or five examples of the 'Wanderer' were made in the Lang workshop in Oberammergau. One of the three known examples has only a 'KL' (Karl Lang) mark. The other two are unmarked or the mark is obscured by the glaze. At least two additional 'Wanderers' were produced at a later date, probably after WWII. They are marked with the 'Anton Lang' shop mark, a facsimile of Anton's signature, and are much cruder in appearance than the originals. Underneath they have two horizontal supports carrying the weight of the figure; the originals have only one horizontal support. The later versions appear to have been made from a mold taken from one of the originals.

In 1936 Karl Lang was put in charge of the complete operation of the pottery and enlarged and modernized the enterprise. He continued to operate the workshop as the Anton Lang pottery after his father's death in 1938. The pottery is now owned and operated by Karl's daughter, Barbara Lampe, who took over for her father in 1975. The facsimile 'Anton Lang' signature was used until 1995 when the name was changed to Barbara Lampe Pottery. Her mark is an interlocked 'BL' in a circle. Pieces with a facsimile signature and an interlocked 'UL' in a circle were made by Lampe's former husband, Uli Lampe, and date from 1975 to 1982. The 'Anton Lang' mark is not sharp on pieces made in 1975 and later. The brick red clay used in their manufacture can be seen on the bottoms as well as three lighter circular tripod marks. The later pieces are considerably heavier than the earlier work. Our advisor for this category is Clark Miller; he is listed in the Directory under Minnesota.

Bowl, aqua, 3-hdl, 2x8"... 50.00
Bowl, floral, red & bl on gr, real signature, 2x4⅛" 65.00

Candleholder, turq, 6¼x5" 30.00
Cup, girl carrying basket & flowers, mc, 3" 45.00
Egg cup, floral (simple), mc on bl, 2⅝" 45.00
Figurine, cat w/ball on base, tan/orange/gr/brn streaks, 8½x8" 120.00
Holy water font, lamb w/flag & cross, gr, 7½" 100.00
Medallion, ivory style, autographed/dtd 1925 on bk, 2x1½" 90.00
Pitcher, fuzzy horizontal stripes, cream/bl/brn/yel, 4¼x3" 50.00
Pitcher, ocher & yel w/gr & terra cotta, 4" 50.00
Pitcher, red flambe, slightly bulbous, 7" 48.00
Plaque, Jesus w/cross in relief, mc, 5" dia. 32.50
Time magazine, Anton Lang on cover, Dec 17, 1923 .... 20.00
Vase, floral, brn/yel/red, late mk (ca 1975-95), 6¾x3" 16.00
Vase, Nubian Black, signature at shoulder, Rookwood mk, 1924, 3⅝" ...660.00

Vase, pendant floral, hand thrown, signed, 16", $1,250.00.
(Photo courtesy Clark Miller)

Vase, stylized design in bl & aqua, flared form, 7" 250.00
Vase, turq, 3 rim-to-hip hdls, 9½" 240.00
Wall pocket, girl in pinafore & winged cherub, mc, 6¼x3½" 90.00

Le Verre Francais

Le Verre Francais was produced during the 1920s by Schneider at Epinay-sur-Seine in France. It was a commercial art glass in the cameo style composed of layered glass with the designs engraved by acid. Favored motifs were stylized leaves and flowers or geometric patterns. It was marked with the name in script or with an inlaid filigrane. Our advisor for this category is Don Williams; he is listed in the Directory under Missouri.

Cameo

Bowl, Deco motif, orange/red/gr on wht mottle, ped ft, Charder, 10x12" .. 4,600.00
Compote, mushrooms, red/brn on yel mottle, ped ft, 8x12" 2,300.00
Jardiniere, stemed curlicues, orange/gr on wht mottle, U-form, 11x12"..5,462.00
Vase, bellflowers (lg spire), red/mauve on mottle, bun ft, 15" ...2,520.00
Vase, dahlia, lav to purple on pk/mauve, shouldered w/ogee sides, 24". 4,600.00
Vase, fence-like design on bell-form body w/cone neck, bl, 4" .. 1,680.00
Vase, floral/trailing stems, orange on orange to gr, ftd, 10" 1,645.00
Vase, freesia, orange/bright bl on frost to lt bl, coupe shape, 15" ...3,335.00
Vase, fruit, orange on yel, shouldered, bun base, 12" 1,440.00
Vase, fuchsia, rust/dk bl w/red neck band on frost/bl mottle, ftd, 12" . 3,335.00
Vase, grapes, orange/gr on yel mottle, long neck, 13" 1,440.00
Vase, horseshoe crab, rose/gr on orange, 8" 530.00
Vase, leafy stems, brn/wht/orange on fiery orange, elongated/ftd, 21" ... 4,025.00
Vase, leaves/fruit, brn on orange mottle, slim/shouldered/ftd, 18" .. 2,300.00
Vase, leaves/stylized flowers, orange/gr on bright bl, 11" 2,020.00
Vase, money plant, gr/orange/brn on peach, ovoid, 15" 2,760.00

Vase, nightshade, tortoiseshell mottle on orange/yel, faceted/ftd, 15" ... 2,520.00
Vase, pansies/long stems, flaring funnel form w/bun ft, 15" 3,240.00
Vase, snails/branches, brn to orange on mottled yel, pear form, 15" ..4,500.00

Vase, stylized grapes, Charder, 15", $3,450.00.

Vase, swan pr, purple on yel/orange mottle, lav hdls/ftd, Charder, 8" .. 9,485.00
Vase, swan pr ea side, amethyst on ivory, knob over bun base, 10" 2,375.00

Leach, Bernard

An English artist, Bernard Leach studied traditional pottery in China and Japan from 1909 until 1920. He returned home a superior potter, one who would revolutionize the craft through his technique and materials. His ceramics are marked with a 'BL' seal and a 'S' seal for St. Ives, where his pottery was located in England. Our advisors for this category are Suzanne Perrault and David Rago; they are listed in the Directory under New Jersey.

Bowl, snail on branch HP on beige, sm rstr, BL, St Ives, 5x12" ... 2,650.00
Bowl, terra cotta w/dk glazed int, domed lid w/loop hdl, St Ives, 10" .. 150.00
Pilgrim flask, dk tenmoku w/khaki, ftd flattened form, 1960s, 14".. 4,000.00
Pitcher, running gr ash w/vertical cuttings, strap hdl, 1966, 13"....8,150.00
Vase, brn gloss drips over unglazed base, BL, St Ives, 4½x3½" ..2,850.00
Vase, brn/blk mottle w/incised kangi script, St Ives, 4¾x4¼"....4,000.00
Vase, fish, brn on gray bottle form, 15x5½" 9,600.00

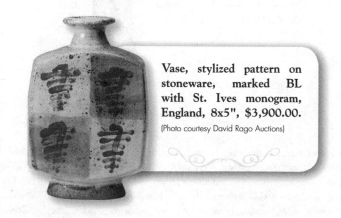

Vase, stylized pattern on stoneware, marked BL with St. Ives monogram, England, 8x5", $3,900.00.
(Photo courtesy David Rago Auctions)

Leeds, Leeds Type

The Leeds Pottery was established in 1758 in Yorkshire and under varied management produced fine creamware, often highly reticulated and transfer printed, shiny black-glazed Jackfield wares, polychromed pearlware, and figurines similar to those made in the Staffordshire area. Little of the early ware was marked; after 1775 the impressed 'Leeds Pottery' mark was used. From 1781 to 1820, the name 'Hartley Greens & Co.' was added. The pottery closed in 1898. Today the term 'Leeds' has become generic and is used to encompass all polychromed pearlware and creamware, wherever its origin. Thus similar wares of other potters (Wood for instance) is often incorrectly called 'Leeds.' Unless a piece is marked or can be definitely attributed to Leeds by confirming the pattern to be authentic, 'Leeds-type' would be a more accurate nomenclature.

Bank, cottage flanked by 2 figures, mc, 19th C, rstr, 5" 540.00
Bowl, eagle transfer (burgundy), bl feather edge, ca 1810, 8" 1,325.00
Bowl, peafowl, 5-color w/spatter trees, flakes/hairline, 3½x7¼" ... 1,200.00
Bowl, Push...Bowl Round Boys, floral, 4-color, 1800s, 3¾x9½" ... 1,000.00
Can, floral band, 4-color, simple C-scroll hdl, ca 1840, 4¾", VG+... 125.00

Charger, four-color peacock, scalloped feather edge, 13", $1,800.00. (Photo courtesy Garth's Auctions Inc.)

Pepper pot, bl feather edge at shoulder, bl star on top, 19th C, 4"...240.00
Plaque, Cleopatra portrait, cream on gr, late 19th C, 14⅜" 645.00
Plate, dahlia & acorns, 4-color, gr feather edge, 7¾", NM 585.00
Shell dish, bl feather edge, emb lady's head in bowl, 4½x4¼" 390.00
Teapot, floral, 3-color on wht, ovoid, dome lid, 4", EX 450.00
Vase, quintal; floral, bl on wht, 5-spout w/feather edge, 19th C, 8".. 500.00

Lefton

The Lefton China Company was the creation of Mr. George Zoltan Lefton who migrated to the United States from Hungary in 1939. In 1941 he embarked on a new career and began shaping a business that sprang from his passion for collecting fine china and porcelains. Though his funds were very limited, his vision was to develop a source from which to obtain fine porcelains by reviving the postwar Japanese ceramic industry, which dated back to antiquity. As a trailblazer, George Zoltan Lefton soon earned the reputation as 'The China King.'

Counted among the most desirable and sought-after collectibles of today, Lefton items such as Bluebirds, Miss Priss, Angels, all types of dinnerware and tea-related items are eagerly acquired by collectors. As is true with any antique or collectible, prices may vary, dependent on location, condition, and availability. For additional information on the history of Lefton China, its factories, marks, products, and values, readers should consult the *Collector's Encyclopedia of Lefton China, Books I, II, and III*, and *Lefton Price Guide* by Loretta DeLozier.

Ashtray, Miss Priss, #1524, 6" 60.00
Ashtray, White Holly, leaf shape, #6056, 7" 20.00
Baby set, Bluebirds, bowl & mug, #435/284, set 125.00
Bank, Green Holly, bell shape, #158 .... 35.00
Bookends, ducks, #2229 .... 95.00
Bookends, tigers, #6663 .... 40.00

Bowl, Lily of the Valley w/sponge gold, ftd, #284 .... 350.00
Box, egg shape, pk w/flowers, #4741, 3¼" 18.00
Candy box, Green Holly, #159, 6" 30.00
Coffeepot, Yuletide Holly, #7802 .... 135.00
Comport, Rose Chintz, #650 .... 55.00
Cookie jar, Dainty Miss, #040 .... 250.00
Cookie jar, Miss Priss, #1502 .... 185.00
Cookie jar, Pennsylvania Dutch, #3702 .... 200.00
Creamer & sugar bowl, Bluebirds, #290 .... 95.00
Creamer & sugar bowl, Brown Heritage Fruit, #20592 .... 75.00
Cup & saucer, demitasse; English Holly, #7951 .... 20.00
Cup & saucer, demitasse; Rose Heirloom, #1378 .... 35.00

Cup and saucer, roses and gold, #975, from $30.00 to $40.00. (Photo courtesy Loretta DeLozier)

Cup & saucer, tea; Blue Paisley, #2339 .... 22.00
Cup & saucer, tea; White Holly, #6067 .... 25.00
Egg cup, Miss Priss, #1510 .... 65.00
Figurine, American Children, girl w/book, #1110, 5½" 40.00
Figurine, bride & groom in boat, wht w/pk roses, #990, 6¼" 200.00
Figurine, Chinese lady, #10600, 8" 150.00
Figurine, clown w/monkey & organ grinder, #7111, 8" 90.00
Figurine, George Washington, #1108, 8" 95.00
Figurine, Kewpie sitting on leaf, #2992, 3½" 32.00
Figurine, Louise, #5743, 7½" 150.00
Figurine, Marguerite & Edward, #345, 8", pr 200.00
Figurine, old man & woman w/golf clubs, #302, 8", pr 85.00

Hanging lantern, Green Holly, 9x4½", $50.00. (Photo courtesy Doug Dezso)

Jam jar, Bluebirds, #436 .... 95.00
Jam jar, Bossie the Cow, #6509 .... 30.00
Jam jar, Brown Heritage Floral, w/tray, #2761 .... 85.00
Lamp, electric; Floral Bisque Bouquet, #5055, 11" 95.00
Mug, Miss Priss, #1503, 4" 75.00
Mug, White Holly, #6066 .... 12.00
Music box, angel w/Christmas tree, O' Holy Night, #04573, 7½".. 55.00
Nappy, Floral Chintz, #8041 .... 18.00
Nappy, floral design, #486, 6¾" 30.00
Nappy, Poinsettia, #4394 .... 20.00
Nappy, violets w/gold, #2334 .... 35.00

Pitcher, Bluebirds, #287, 4½" 95.00
Pitcher, Poinsettia, #4389, 6¼" 150.00
Planter, egg w/sm yel chick, #7880, 4½" 15.00
Planter, Santa on reindeer, #1496, 6" 30.00
Plate, Brown Heritage Fruit, #2222, 9" 40.00
Plate, Floral Chintz, #8036, 7" 15.00
Plate, Green Holly, #161, 6" 16.00
Plate, Rose Chintz, #658, 7" 28.00

Platter, Bluebird, #50/155, 9" long, $75.00.

Platter, Green Holly, #2369, 18" 95.00
Relish, White Holly, #6057 .... 30.00
Shakers, Bluebirds, #282, pr 50.00
Shakers, Brown Heritage Fruit, #2760 .... 30.00
Shakers, Christmas candles, #1556, 4" 22.00
Shakers, Green Holly, #1353, pr 22.00
Shakers, Rose Chintz, #665 .... 28.00
Tea bag holder, Rose Chintz, #1793 .... 35.00

Teapot, Dainty Miss, #321, from $100.00 to $125.00. (Photo courtesy Loretta DeLozier)

Teapot, Green Holly, #1357 .... 15.00
Teapot, mini; Brown Heritage Floral, #476 .... 60.00
Teapot, Miss Priss, #1516 .... 165.00
Teapot, Rose Chintz, #3185 .... 60.00
Teapot, White Christmas, #603 .... 80.00
Tidbit, Rose Chintz, #649 .... 85.00
Tidbit, White Holly, #6065 .... 60.00
Tray, Green Holly, #1348 .... 40.00
Tray, White Christmas, tree shape, #1368, 11" 40.00
Vase, Brown Heritage Floral, #2763, 5½" 22.00
Vase, Christy, #438, 6¼" 18.00
Wall plaque, Christy, #448, 7½" 20.00
Wall pocket, Miss Priss, #1509 .... 150.00
Wall pocket, Mr & Mrs Bluebirds, #283, pr 350.00

Legras

Legras and Cie was founded in St. Denis, France, in 1864. Production continued until the 1930s. In addition to their enameled wares, they made cameo art glass decorated with outdoor scenes and florals executed by acid cuttings through two to six layers of glass. Their work is signed 'Legras' in relief and in enamel. Our advisor for this category is Don Williams; he is listed in the Directory under Missouri.

Cameo

Bowl, dogwood, cut/pnt on spring gr w/gold rim decor, 10" 2,300.00
Bowl, winter scene w/trees & snow on orange/gr, att, 7½" 650.00
Vase, autumn leaves, purple on shaded orange, cylindrical, 12" .. 1,200.00
Vase, autumn trees/lake, charcoal on pale amber to yel, slim, 22" ... 920.00
Vase, branches, amethyst on pk texture, ovoid w/flared rim, 7" ... 400.00
Vase, country bridge in summer on pk/gr opal, pillow form, 4" 850.00
Vase, Deco geometrics, cobalt to frost, 8¾" 395.00
Vase, floral, brn/purple on wht/bl/purple, 3-sided pear form, 8" ... 360.00

Vase, forest scene, 24", $2,200.00. (Photo courtesy Cincinnati Art Galleries)

Vase, lake scene in summer, pk to amethyst, flat sided/corseted, 5" .. 800.00
Vase, lg tree/sailboats beyond, gr/wht on lemon-orange, 7½" 1,560.00
Vase, trees/sailboats, cut/pnt on amber enamel over clear, slim, 16" ... 515.00
Vase, trees/shrubs, gr over wht & rust, 9x4" 575.00
Vase, 3 lg Deco fountains, amethyst on pk mottle, elongated pear, 15" .. 425.00

Lenox

Walter Scott Lenox, former art director at Ott and Brewer, and Jonathan Coxon founded The Ceramic Art Company of Trenton, New Jersey, in 1889. By 1906 Cox had left the company, and to reflect the change in ownership, the name was changed to Lenox Inc. Until 1930 when the production of American-made Belleek came to an end, they continued to produce the same type of high-quality ornamental wares that Lenox and Coxon had learned to master while in the employ of Ott and Brewer. Their superior dinnerware made the company famous, and since 1917 Lenox has been chosen the official White House China. The dinnerware they produced is listed here; see Ceramic Art Company for examples of their belleek.

Dinnerware

Angelina, bowl, cream soup; w/plate 60.00
Angelina, plate, dinner; 10" 45.00
Angelina, plate, salad; 8½" 30.00
Apple Blossom, bowl, cream soup; w/plate 60.00
Apple Blossom, cup & saucer, demitasse 30.00
Apple Blossom, cup & saucer, 2¼" 30.00
Apple Blossom, plate, luncheon; 9" 25.00

Arcadia, bowl, rimmed soup 30.00
Arcadia, cup & saucer, ftd 35.00
Arcadia, plate, dinner; 10½" 25.00
Arcadia, plate, salad; 8" 18.00
Bancroft, cup & saucer, ftd 32.00
Bancroft, plate, bread & butter; 6" 12.00
Bancroft, plate, salad; 8" 25.00
Celeste, creamer, 3½" 45.00
Celeste, cup & saucer, flat 18.00
Celeste, plate, dinner; 10½" 27.50
Celeste, plate, salad; 8" 20.00
Countess, coffeepot, 4-cup 200.00
Countess, creamer 75.00
Countess, cup & saucer, demitasse; ftd 35.00
Countess, plate, luncheon; 9" 30.00
Countess, sugar bowl, w/lid 85.00
Empress, bowl, vegetable; oval, 9½" 75.00
Empress, cup & saucer, ftd 35.00
Empress, plate, dinner; 10½" 30.00
Empress, platter, oval, 16" 185.00
Fountain, bowl, vegetable; oval, w/lid 200.00
Fountain, cup, bouillon; ftd, 5½" 28.00
Fountain, cup & saucer, demitasse 32.00
Fountain, cup & saucer, flat 40.00
Fountain, plate, dinner; 10½" 90.00
Golden Wreath, bowl, vegetable; oval, 9½" 70.00
Golden Wreath, cup & saucer, ftd 22.00
Golden Wreath, plate, luncheon; 9" 25.00
Golden Wreath, sugar bowl, w/lid 70.00
Joan, bowl, rimmed soup 45.00
Joan, plate, bread & butter; 6" 15.00
Joan, plate, dinner; 10½" 60.00
Lenox Rose, bowl, rimmed soup 42.00
Lenox Rose, cup & saucer, ftd 25.00
Lenox Rose, plate, dessert; 7" 18.00
Lenox Rose, plate, dinner; 10½" 27.50
Moonlight, bowl, coupe cereal; 5¼" 20.00
Moonlight, creamer 32.00
Moonlight, plate, luncheon; 9" 17.50
Moonlight, platter, oval, 17" 130.00
Peachtree, bowl, vegetable; oval, 9½" 80.00
Peachtree, creamer 70.00
Peachtree, cup & saucer 20.00
Peachtree, plate, 8" 18.00
Pembrook, candleholder, ea 25.00
Pembrook, cup & saucer, cream soup 110.00

Pembrook, plate, dinner; 10" 45.00
Roselyn, bowl, vegetable; 8" 165.00
Roselyn, creamer, 8-oz 50.00
Roselyn, cup & saucer 20.00
Roselyn, plate, 8" 20.00
Roselyn, platter, oval, 16" 135.00
Springfield, bowl, vegetable; 9½" 125.00
Springfield, plate, dinner; 10½" 32.00
Springfield, platter, oval, 14" 200.00
Springfield, sugar bowl, w/lid 100.00
Victoria, bowl, fruit; 6½" 18.00
Victoria, bowl, vegetable; oval, 9¾" 115.00
Victoria, cup & saucer, ftd 30.00
Victoria, plate, dinner; 10½" 30.00
Wheat, bowl, coupe cereal; 5¼" 30.00
Wheat, cup & saucer, 2", 3⅞" 22.50
Wheat, gravy boat, attached underplate 90.00
Wheat, platter, 17½" L 135.00

Wheat, teapot, from $90.00 to $125.00. (Photo courtesy Tom Harris Auctions)

Miscellaneous

Basket vase, wht w/2 openings, gold trim, #81/R86, 5x6½" 55.00
Candleholders, Charleston, 2¾x4¾", pr. 35.00
Candleholders, wht w/22k gold trim, scroll designs, 1950s, 8", pr. .. 50.00
Christmas tree votive holder (for 5), ivory w/jewels & gold, 12", MIB .. 65.00
Figurine, Carousel Tiger King, 5¾x8½" 150.00
Figurine, First Waltz, lady w/fan, 8", from $50 to 75.00
Figurine, Lions Africa, dtd 1988, 6x8½" 100.00
Loving cup, oxblood w/3 hdls, sterling collar, Bigelow & Kennard, 6" .. 180.00
Pitcher, 2 cranes/flowers, mc/gold on ivory, gold hdl, CAC, 10" ... 2,760.00
Swan, Lenox Rose on side, ca 1930-52, 4" L 65.00
Toby jug, Theodore Roosevelt as African explorer, 1908, 7⅝" ... 1,650.00
Vase, flowers/ferns, Wm Morley, CAC/Tiffany Co, 15x7" 3,480.00
Vase, irises, Wm Morley, gold scroll hdls, CAC, 13x8", NM 4,500.00

Pembrook, cup and saucer, demitasse; ca. 1930s, from $60.00 to $70.00. (Photo courtesy Jim and Susan Harran)

Vase, ivory with embossed scrolling leaves, 11", from $35.00 to $40.00.

Libbey

The New England Glass Company was established in 1818 in Boston, Massachusetts. In 1892 it became known as the Libbey Glass Company. At Chicago's Columbian Expo in 1893, Libbey set up a 10-pot furnace and made glass souvenirs. The display brought them worldwide fame. Between 1878 and 1918, Libbey made exquisite cut and faceted glass, considered today to be the best from the brilliant period. The company is credited for several innovations — the Owens bottle machine that made mass production possible and the Westlake machine which turned out both electric light bulbs and tumblers automatically. They developed a machine to polish the rims of their tumblers in such a way that chipping was unlikely to occur. Their glassware carried the patented Safedge guarantee. Libbey also made glassware in numerous colors, among them cobalt, ruby, pink, green, and amber. Our advisors for this category are Don and Anne Kier; they are listed in the Directory under Ohio. See also Amberina.

Candleholder, opalescent camel stem, 5", $165.00. (Photo courtesy Gene and Cathy Florence)

Bottle, scent; cobalt cut to clear w/peacock on branch, ftd, 8"..... 515.00
Compote, amethyst flower-form bowl, clear ft & stem, 7x7"..... 1,200.00
Compote, cut, hobstars w/cane, notched teardrop stem, cut ft, 9¾x6" ... 150.00
Compote, wht w/gr pulled petals, clear ft, Nash, 4⅜x11¾" 425.00

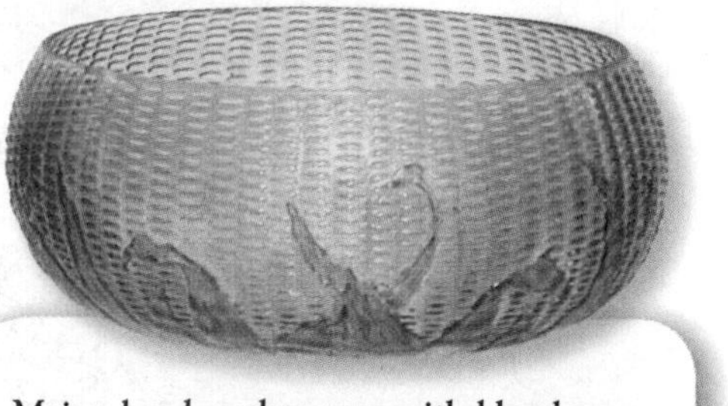

Maize, bowl, amber corn with blue leaves, 9", $285.00. (Photo courtesy Early Auction Co.)

Maize, bowl, gr husks on oyster wht, 4x8¾" 235.00
Maize, butter dish, bl husks on irid 650.00
Maize, butter dish, bl husks w/gold outlines, 6½x7" 850.00
Maize, butter dish, gr husks on custard 225.00
Maize, celery vase, bl leaves on amber, 5½" 175.00
Maize, celery vase, gold-tipped gr husks on oyster wht, 6½" 225.00
Maize, celery vase, gr husks on custard 140.00
Maize, celery vase, gr on wht, 6¾" 200.00
Maize, celery vase, lt gold irid on clear, 6⅝" 150.00
Maize, condiment set, gr husks on custard, 3-pc+tray, metal lids .. 395.00
Maize, condiment set, shakers+mustard jar+tray, gr on wht, metal lids .. 695.00
Maize, pickle castor, amber stain, SP fr 595.00
Maize, pickle castor, gr husks on custard, SP fr 495.00
Maize, shakers, bl husks w/gold edge on custard, pr 185.00
Maize, sugar shaker, bl husks w/gold edge on custard, 5½" 325.00
Maize, sugar shaker, gold husks on oyster wht, 5½" 325.00
Maize, syrup, bl husks, gold irid cob, pewter lid, 6" 550.00
Maize, syrup, gr husks on custard, pewter lid, 7½" 300.00
Maize, toothpick holder, gr husks w/gold edge on custard 500.00
Maize, tumbler, bl husks on irid 110.00
Maize, tumbler, gr husks on irid 110.00
Maize, vase, yel/gold husks on custard, 6½" 210.00
Pitcher, cut, hobstars/canes/prisms/etc, stepped neck, 8⅝" 750.00
Punch bowl, brilliant cuttings, scalloped rim, 12½" 400.00
Stem, champagne flute, bear, wht opal, 5½" 210.00
Stem, claret, bear, blk, 5½" 235.00
Stem, claret, bear, wht opal, 5½" 250.00
Stem, cocktail, kangaroo, wht opal, 6", set of 4 .... 735.00
Stem, cordial, monkey, wht opal, 5" 145.00
Stem, cordial, whippet/greyhound, wht opal, 5" 175.00
Stem, goblet, cat, frosted, 7" 225.00
Stem, goblet, cat, wht opal, 7" 200.00
Stem, goblet, monkey, wht opal 170.00
Stem, sherbet, squirrel, wht opal, 4" 135.00
Stem, wine, giraffe, wht opal, 6" 175.00
Stem, wine, kangaroo, moonstone, 6" 195.00
Stem, wine, kangaroo, wht opal 230.00
Stem, wine, monkey, frosted, 5" 150.00
Stem, wine, squirrel, wht opal, 4" 95.00
Toothpick holder, floral on opal to bl, lobed w/can neck, beaded rim ... 165.00
Toothpick holder, peachblow, hat form w/ribbed body, 2" 375.00
Vase, amberina, optic ribs, ovoid w/rim-to-shoulder hdls, 9" 635.00
Vase, amethyst cut to clear w/intaglio flowers, crystal ft, 14" 1,380.00

Vase, intaglio flowers, marked, 14", $1,380.00. (Photo courtesy James D. Julia Inc.)

Vase, optic t'prints/leaves, clear w/flowing lilac threads, Nash, 9" ... 475.00
Wines, crystal w/Prussian Blue festoons at rim, 4¾", pr 225.00

Lightning Rod Balls

Used as ornaments on lightning rods, the vast majority of these balls were made of glass, but ceramic examples can be found as well. Their average diameter is 4½", but it can vary from 3½" up to 5½". Only a few of the 400 pattern-and-color combinations are listed here. The most common are round and found in sun-colored amethyst or milk glass. Lightning rod balls are considered mint if they have no cracks or holes and if any collar damage can be covered with a standard cap. Some patterns are being reproduced without being marked as such, and new patterns are being made as well. Collectors are cautioned to look for signs of age (stains) and learn more before investing in a 'rare' lightning rod ball. Our advisor is Rod Krupka, author of a book (out of print) on this subject. He is listed in the Directory under Michigan.

Amber, Electra Round, 5x4½", $100.00. (Photo courtesy Rod Krupka)

Amber, Dodd & Struthers, faint stain, 5¾x5¾"	60.00
Amber, Raised Quilt, 5½x5"	145.00
Amber, WC Shinn Mfg Co, aluminum caps, 5¼x4½"	120.00
Bl opaque, National, belted, aluminum caps, 5¼x4½"	120.00
Bl opaque, plain rnd, 4½"	35.00
Bl opaque, rnd w/vertical ribs, pr	60.00
Bl opaque, Shinn-System, aluminum caps, 5¼x4½"	40.00
Blk amethyst, plain rnd, 4½"	375.00
Cobalt, acorn pennant, w/orig cap, 5⅜"	675.00
Cobalt, D&S, 5¼x4"	215.00
Cobalt, Flat Quilt, chips to 1 collar	215.00
Cobalt, plain rnd, 4½"	95.00
Gr opaque, plain rnd, 5¼x5"	95.00
Gr transparent, plain, rnd, 4½"	175.00
Milk glass, Electra Cone, bold emb, 5x4½"	40.00
Milk glass, Hawkeye, 5x4⅜"	65.00
Milk glass, Maher, heavy, aluminum caps, 5¾x5"	250.00
Milk glass, Moon & Star	45.00
Milk glass, plain rnd, 4½", from $25 to	40.00
Ruby, Ribbed Grape, aluminum caps, 5x4⅜"	425.00
Ruby, rnd, 5x4½"	100.00
Silver mercury, National Round, correct tube, brass caps, 5x4½"	400.00
Sun-colored amethyst, Moon & Star, 5x4½"	95.00
Sun-colored amethyst, National Belted, 5¼x4½"	200.00
Sun-colored amethyst, plain rnd, 5x4½"	25.00

Limbert

Charles P. Limbert formed his firm in 1894 in America's furniture capital, Grand Rapids, Michigan, and from 1902 until 1918, produced a line of Arts & Crafts furniture. While his wide-ranging line of furniture is not as uniformly successful as Gustav Stickley, the Limbert pieces that do exhibit design excellence stand among the best of American Arts & Crafts examples. Pieces featuring cutouts, exposed construction elements (e.g., key and tenon), metal and ebonized wood inlays, and asymmetric forms are among the most desirable. Less desirable are the firm's Outdoor Designs that show exposed metal screws and straight grain, as opposed to quartersawn oak boards. His most aesthetically successful forms mimic those of Charles Rennie Mackintosh (Scotland) and, to a lesser extent, Jo-

seph Hoffmann (Austria). Usually signed with a rectangular mark (a paper label, branded in the wood, or a metal tag) showing a man planing wood, and with the words Limbert's Arts Craft Furniture Made in Grand Rapids and Holland. The firm continued to produce furniture until 1944. Currently, only his Arts & Crafts-style furniture holds any interest among collectors.

Please note: Furniture that has been cleaned or refinished is worth less than if its original finish has been retained. Our values are for pieces in excellent original condition unless noted otherwise. Our advisor for this and related Arts & Crafts categories is Bruce A. Austin; he is listed in the Directory under New York.

Key: b — brand

Armchair, 5-slat bk, open arms, plank seat, b, rfn, 39x27x20"	325.00
Bed, #51170, horizontal rail over 5 vertical slats, 47x43" W	475.00
Bed, str rail over 11 slats of 3 alternating widths, b, wear, single	500.00
Bookcase, #340, 2 doors, ea w/vertical mullion, rpr/rfn, 46x32", VG	1,200.00
Bookcase, 1 door, corbels under shaped top, rfn, 58x30x14"	4,500.00
Chair, side; #1921, 2-slat rail over 3-slat bk, 38", 6 for	1,800.00
Chair, side; oak w/shaped crest rail, triangular bk, 39½"	560.00
Chair, side; 3-slat bk, arched bk rail, leather seat, b, 36", 4 for	1,440.00
Chest of drawers, #476, 2 sm over 2 long drw, mirror pivots, 66x35"	2,800.00
China cabinet, #448, 2 doors, ea w/vertical mullion, rfn, 61x46"	2,400.00
China cabinet, 1 door, 3 sm panes over lg 1, side shelves, 57x44x16"	6,000.00
China cabinet, 1 door w/3 sm mullions, arched plate rail, 62x34", VG	2,400.00
China cabinet, 2 doors, ea w/vertical mullion, unmk, rpl/rfn, 61x40"	1,200.00
China cabinet, 2 doors ea w/2 sm mullions, plate rail, 62x46"	2,600.00
Daybed, spade cutouts to plank sides, spring cushions, 23x75x26"	2,600.00
Desk, #139, bookshelf under top ea side/central drw, 42" L	1,400.00
Hall tree, #230, revolving top w/copper hooks, 4-leg base, 68"	800.00
Magazine stand, #304, 2-slat sides, 4 shelves, invt V toebrd, 43x16"	1,500.00
Magazine stand, 5-shelf, 2 sq cutouts ea side, trapezoidal, 40x24", VG	2,400.00
Plant stand, Ebon-Oak, apron panels w/caning, corbels under 14" top	1,800.00
Porch swing, 7-slat bk, 1-slat sides, shaped crest rail, gr stain, b	2,600.00
Rocker, curved crest rail/2 slats, flat arms, spring seat, b, 32", VG	375.00
Rocker, Ebon-Oak, geometric inlay, 3 bk slats, 1-slat sides, 34"	2,400.00
Server, #0402, mirror bk, 2 short drw over lg 1, unmk/#d, 49x54"	1,500.00
Server, #1404 1/2, plate rail, 2 drws, 2-shelf, b, 44x40x18"	1,300.00
Settle, drop arm, 5-slat sides, wide plank apron, rfn, 76"	6,600.00
Settle, even-arm, 8-slat bk/3 ea side, pyramid posts, reuphl, 60" L	1,800.00
Stand, #240, arched aprons, sq shelf, 30x20x20"	2,800.00
Table, #100, 23" octagon top, wide legs w/spade cutouts, rfn, 29" H	600.00
Table, #146, oval 45" top, slab sides, ea w/2 cutouts, rfn	2,700.00
Table, #251, 17" cut-corner top, flared plank base w/cutouts, rfn, 17"	1,800.00
Table, console; cut-away front corners, 2-drw, shaped skirt, b, 66" L	8,500.00
Table, Ebon-Oak, 45" dia top, X-stretchers, VG, +2 9" leaves	2,600.00
Table, game; #118, 36" sq top/splay legs w/X-stretchers, rfn	1,300.00
Table, lamp; #148, 30" dia top, cutouts to wide lower stretcher, rfn	2,100.00

Table, lamp; canted cut-out sides, lower shelf, refinished, minor stains, 45x30x30", $3,240.00. (Photo courtesy David Rago Auctions)

Table, library; #164, overhang top, 2-drw, corbels, b, wear, 48".... 950.00
Table, library; Ebon-Oak, geometric inlay, sq copper knobs, 42" L, VG..2,600.00
Table, library; like #1141, 1 drw, arched supports, rfn, 42" L..... 1,200.00
Table, 22" dia top, 4 tapering legs w/X-stretcher, rfn, 6"........... 1,500.00

Limited Edition Plates

Current values of some limited edition plates remained steady, while many others have fallen. Prices charged by plate dealers in the secondary market vary greatly; we have tried to suggest an average. Since Goebel Hummel plates have been discontinued, values have started to decline. While those who are trying to complete the series continue to buy them, few seem interested in starting a collection. As for the Danish plates, Royal Copenhagen and Bing and Grondahl, more purchases are for plates that commemorate the birth year of a child or a wedding anniversary than to add to a collection.

Bing and Grondahl

1895, Behind the Frozen Window, from $5,500 to 6,000.00
1896, New Moon, from $2,000 to 2,200.00
1897, Christmas Meal of Sparrows, from $1,250 to 1,400.00
1898, Roses & Star, from $750 to 800.00
1899, Crows Enjoying Christmas, from $1,200 to.................... 1,500.00
1900, Church Bells Chiming, from $800 to 900.00
1901, 3 Wise Men, from $300 to 350.00
1902, Gothic Church Interior, from $300 to 325.00
1903, Expectant Children, from $250 to..................................... 300.00
1904, View of Copenhagen From Fredericksberg Hill, from $100 to .. 125.00
1905, Anxiety of the Coming Christmas Night, from $100 to..... 135.00
1906, Sleighing to Church, from $80 to.. 90.00
1907, Little Match Girl, from $90 to 110.00
1908, St Petri Church, from $85 to 90.00
1909, Yule Tree, from $85 to 90.00
1910, Old Organist, from $75 to 85.00
1911, Angels & Shepherds, from $75 to 85.00
1912, Going to Church, from $75 to 85.00
1913, Bringing Home the Tree, from $75 to 85.00
1914, Amalienborg Castle, from $70 to 80.00
1915, Dog on Chain Outside Window, from $95 to 100.00
1916, Prayer of the Sparrows, from $70 to 80.00
1917, Christmas Boat, from $70 to... 80.00
1918, Fishing Boat, from $70 to 80.00
1919, Outside the Lighted Window, from $65 to.......................... 75.00
1920, Hare in the Snow, from $65 to 75.00
1921, Pigeons, from $65 to 75.00
1922, Star of Bethlehem, from $65 to 75.00
1923, Hermitage, from $65 to... 75.00
1924, Lighthouse, from $60 to.. 70.00
1925, Child's Christmas, from $60 to 70.00
1926, Churchgoers, from $60 to.. 70.00
1927, Skating Couple, from $60 to 70.00
1928, Eskimos, from $60 to... 65.00
1929, Fox Outside Farm, from $70 to 90.00
1930, Tree in Town Hall Square, from $80 to 90.00
1931, Christmas Train, from $80 to 90.00
1932, Lifeboat at Work, from $75 to 85.00
1933, Korsor-Nyborg Ferry, from $60 to..................................... 70.00
1934, Church Bell in Tower, from $60 to...................................... 70.00
1935, Lillebelt Bridge, from $60 to 70.00
1936, Royal Guard, from $75 to 85.00
1937, Arrival of Christmas Guests, from $80 to 90.00
1938, Lighting the Candles, from $110 to 125.00

1939, Old Lock-Eye, The Sandman, from $150.00 to $160.00.

1940, Delivering Christmas Letters, from $180 to 185.00
1941, Horses Enjoying Meal, from $175 to 195.00
1942, Danish Farm on Christmas Night, from $165 to................. 175.00
1943, Ribe Cathedral, from $165 to.. 180.00
1944, Sorgenfri Castle, from $100 to.. 110.00
1945, Old Water Mill, from $110 to 115.00
1946, Commemoration Cross, from $85 to 95.00
1947, Dybbol Mill, from $90 to 100.00
1948, Watchman, from $80 to 90.00
1949, Landsoldaten, from $85 to 95.00
1950, Kronborg Castle at Elsinore... 125.00
1951, Jens Bang, from $80 to 90.00
1952, Old Copenhagen Canals & Thorsvaldsen Museum, from $85 to... 95.00
1953, Royal Boat.. 100.00
1954, Snowman, from $90 to 95.00
1955, Kaulundborg Church, from $90 to 95.00
1956, Christmas in Copenhagen 135.00
1957, Christmas Candles, from $110 to 125.00
1958, Santa Claus, from $90 to 100.00
1959, Christmas Eve, from $85 to 95.00
1960, Village Church, from $125 to.. 140.00
1961, Winter Harmony, from $85 to 95.00
1962, Winter Night, from $75 to 85.00
1963, Christmas Elf, from $75 to 85.00
1964, Fir Tree & Hare, from $40 to 50.00
1965, Bringing Home the Tree, from $35 to 45.00
1966, Home for Christmas, from $35 to 40.00
1967, Sharing the Joy, from $30 to 40.00
1968, Christmas in Church, from $30 to 40.00
1969, Arrival of Guests, from $25 to 30.00
1970, Pheasants in Snow, from $20 to.. 25.00
1971, Christmas at Home, from $20 to 25.00
1972, Christmas in Greenland, from $20 to................................... 25.00
1973, Country Christmas, from $15 to... 20.00
1974, Christmas in the Village, from $15 to 20.00
1975, The Old Water Mill, from $15 to.. 20.00
1976, Christmas Welcome, from $15 to 20.00
1977, Copenhagen Christmas, from $15 to.................................... 20.00
1978, A Christmas Tale, from $15 to 20.00
1979, White Christmas, from $20 to.. 25.00
1980, Christmas in the Woods, from $20 to 25.00
1981, Christmas Peace, from $20 to... 25.00
1982, The Christmas Tree, from $20 to 25.00
1983, Christmas in Old Town, from $20 to.................................... 25.00
1984, Christmas Letter, from $20 to.. 25.00
1985, Christmas Eve, Farm, from $20 to 25.00
1986, Silent Night, from $25 to 35.00
1987, Snowman's Christmas, from $25 to 35.00
1988, In King's Garden, from $30 to 40.00

1989, Christmas Anchorage, from $35 to 45.00
1990, Changing Guards, from $30 to 40.00
1991, Copenhagen Stock Exchange, from $50 to 60.00
1992, Pastor's Christmas, from $50 to 60.00
1993, Father Christmas in Copenhagen, from $55 to 65.00
1994, Day in Deer Park, from $60 to 65.00
1995, Towers of Copenhagen, from $60 to 65.00
1996, Winter at the Old Mill, from $60 to 65.00
1997, Country Christmas, from $60 to 65.00
1998, Santa the Storyteller, from $60 to 65.00
1999, Dancing on Christmas Eve, from $60 to 65.00
2000, Chirstmas at Bell Tower, from $60 to 65.00

M. I. Hummel

1971, Heavenly Angel, from $275.00 to $300.00.

1972, Hear Ye, Hear Ye, from $45 to 55.00
1973, Glober Trotter, from $80 to 100.00
1974, Goose Girl, from $45 to 55.00
1975, Ride Into Christmas, from $45 to 55.00
1976, Apple Tree Girl, from $45 to 55.00
1977, Apple Tree Boy, from $40 to 50.00
1978, Happy Pastime, from $40 to 50.00
1979, Singing Lesson, from $35 to 45.00
1980, School Girl, from $35 to 45.00
1981, Umbrella Boy, from $35 to 45.00
1982, Umbrella Girl, from $50 to 60.00
1983, The Postman, from $100 to 125.00
1984, Little Helper, from $45 to 55.00
1985, Chick Girl, from $45 to 55.00
1986, Playmates, from $75 to 85.00
1987, Feeding Time, from $135 to 150.00
1988, Little Goat Herder, from $70 to 80.00
1989, Farm Boy, from $70 to 80.00
1990, Shepherd's Boy, from $70 to 80.00
1991, Just Resting, from $75 to 95.00
1992, Meditation, from $80 to 100.00
1993, Doll Bath, from $80 to 100.00
1994, Doctor, from $80 to 100.00
1995, Come Back Soon, from $65 to 75.00

Royal Copenhagen

1908, Madonna & Child, from $3,750 to 4,000.00
1909, Danish Landscape, from $225 to 250.00
1910, Magi, from $175 to 195.00
1911, Danish Landscape, from $175 to 195.00
1912, Christmas Tree, from $175 to 195.00
1913, Frederik Church Spire, from $150 to 175.00
1914, Holy Spirit Church, from $150 to 175.00

1915, Danish Landscape, from $150 to 175.00
1916, Shepherd at Christmas, from $125 to................... 150.00
1917, Our Savior Church, from $115 to 135.00
1918, Sheep & Shepherds, from $100 to 125.00
1919, In the Park, from $100 to 125.00
1920, Mary & Child Jesus, from $95 to 110.00
1921, Aabenraa Marketplace, from $80 to 100.00
1922, 3 Singing Angels, from $80 to 100.00
1923, Danish Landscape, from $80 to 100.00
1924, Sailing Ship, from $115 to 135.00
1925, Christianshavn Street Scene, from $80 to 100.00
1926, Christianshavn Canal, from $80 to 100.00
1927, Ship's Boy at Tiller, from $100 to 135.00
1928, Vicar's Family, from $90 to 110.00
1929, Grundtvig Church, from $80 to 100.00
1930, Fishing Boats, from $100 to 120.00
1931, Mother & Child, from $100 to 125.00
1932, Frederiksberg Gardens, from $80 to 100.00
1933, Ferry & Great Belt, from $125 to 165.00
1934, Hermitage Castle, from $175 to 200.00
1935, Kronborg Castle, from $200 to 250.00
1936, Roskilde Cathedral, from $200 to 250.00
1937, Main Street of Copenhagen, from $275 to 300.00
1938, Round Church of Osterlars, from $300 to 375.00
1939, Greenland Pack Ice, from $500 to 550.00
1940, Good Shepherd 550.00
1941, Danish Village Church, from $425 to 475.00
1942, Bell Tower, from $475 to 500.00
1943, Flight Into Egypt, from $550 to 600.00
1944, Danish Village Scene, from $300 to 350.00
1945, Peaceful Scene, from $500 to 550.00
1946, Zealand Village Church, from $250 to 250.00

1947, Good Shepherd, from $275.00 to $300.00.

1948, Nodebo Church, from $175 to 195.00
1949, Our Lady's Cathedral, from $175 to 195.00
1950, Boeslunde Church, from $225 to......................... 250.00
1951, Christmas Angel, from $350 to 375.00
1952, Christmas in Forest, from $60 to 75.00
1953, Frederiksberg Castle, from $100 to 125.00
1954, Amalienborg Palace, from $100 to 125.00
1955, Fano Girl, from $145 to 165.00
1956, Rosenborg Castle, from $120 to 135.00
1957, Good Shepherd, from $90 to 110.00
1958, Sunshine Over Greenland, from $100 to 115.00
1959, Christmas Night, from $125 to 145.00
1960, Stag, from $80 to.. 100.00
1961, Training Ship, from $80 to 100.00
1962, Little Mermaid, from $150 to 175.00
1963, Hojsager Mill, from $50 to.................................. 65.00

1964, Fetching the Tree, from $45 to	55.00
1965, Little Skaters, from $45 to	50.00
1966, Blackbird, from $45 to	50.00
1967, Royal Oak, from $35 to	40.00
1968, Last Umiak, from $35 to	40.00
1969, Old Farmyard, from $35 to	40.00
1970, Christmas Rose & Cat, from $20 to	30.00
1971, Hare in Winter, from $20 to	25.00
1972, In the Desert, from $20 to	25.00
1973, Train Home Bound, from $20 to	25.00
1974, Winter Twilight, from $20 to	25.00
1975, Queen's Palace, from $20 to	25.00
1976, Danish Watermill, from $20 to	25.00
1977, Immervad Bridge, from $20 to	25.00
1978, Greenland Scenery, from $20 to	25.00
1979, Choosing Tree, from $30 to	40.00
1980, Bringing Home Tree, from $30 to	35.00
1981, Admiring Tree, from $30 to	35.00
1982, Waiting for Christmas, from $40 to	50.00
1983, Merry Christmas, from $40 to	50.00
1984, Jingle Bells, from $40 to	50.00
1985, Snowman, from $40 to	50.00
1986, Wait for Me, from $40 to	50.00
1987, Winter Birds, from $40 to	50.00
1988, Christmas Eve Copenhagen, from $50 to	65.00
1989, Old Skating Pond, from $50 to	70.00
1990, Christmas in Tivoli, from $70 to	80.00
1991, St Lucia Basilica, from $70 to	80.00
1992, Royal Coach, from $50 to	60.00
1993, Arrival Guests by Train, from $200 to	225.00
1994, Christmas Shopping, from $50 to	60.00
1995, Christmas at Manorhouse, from $300 to	325.00
1996, Lighting Street Lamps, from $50 to	75.00
1997, Roskilde Cathedral, from $50 to	75.00
1998, Welcome Home, from $135 to	150.00
1999, Sleigh Ride, from $50 to	75.00
2000, Trimming the Tree, from $50 to	75.00

Limoges

From the mid-eighteenth century, Limoges was the center of the porcelain industry of France, where at one time more than 40 companies utilized the local kaolin to make a superior quality china, much of which was exported to the United States. Various marks were used; some included the name of the American export company (rather than the manufacturer) and 'Limoges.' After 1891 'France' was added. Pieces signed by factory artists are more valuable than those decorated outside the factory by amateurs. The listings below are hand-painted pieces unless noted otherwise.

For a more thorough study of the subject, we recommend you refer to *Collector's Encyclopedia of Limoges Porcelain, Third Edition* (with beautiful illustrations and current market values), by our advisor, Mary Frank Gaston; she is listed in the Directory under Texas. Limoges porcelain is totally French in origin, but one American china manufacturer, The Limoges China Company, marked its earthenware 'Limoges' to reflect its name. For information concerning this American earthenware, we recommend *American Limoges* by Raymonde Limoges. Both this book and Mrs. Gaston's are available from Collector Books.

Biscuit jar, courting scene reserve, ornate gold, Laviolette/LS&S, 8"	450.00
Bowl, blkberries w/gold, 3-ftd, Klingenberg & Dwenger, 7¾"	375.00
Bowl, vegetable; floral transfer w/gold, w/lid, Lanternier, 12x8"	200.00

Box, Cupid in pate-sur-pate reserve on lid, 6" long, $300.00. (Photo courtesy Leslie Hindman Auctioneers)

Cake plate, floral transfer w/gold, pierced hdls, Bawo & Dotter, 11"	165.00
Cake plate, roses on yel, gold trim, hdls, T&V, 10½", from $120 to	145.00
Celery tray, blkberries/flowers, Goodrich, Coiffe, 15½"	325.00
Chamberstick, daisies on turq, T&V, from $225 to	275.00
Chocolate pot, fruit on gr, gold hdl, Blakeman & Henderson, 8"	600.00
Chocolate pot, gold/gr floral on wht, T&V, 10", from $550 to	650.00
Cup & saucer, bouillon; holly & berries, T&V, from $150 to	175.00
Cup & saucer, floral on wht, Pouyat, Pat Dec 1892, from $60 to	75.00
Ewer, orchids, pk on cream, much appl gold scrolling/ft, ribbed, 16"	800.00
Ferner, gr leaves on wht w/gold sponging, 4-ftd, D&Co, 5x8½"	500.00
Fish set, fish/crustaceans, Martin, 24" platter+10 9" plates	800.00
Jardiniere, roses on gr, Mel, B&Co, 9x11", from $500 to	600.00
Jardiniere, roses w/gold, elephant-head hdls, Pouyat, 9x12", $2,000 to	2,200.00
Leaf dish, floral on lt gr w/gold, gold hdl, D&Co, 6½x7", $120 to	140.00
Oyster plate, floral reserves, shell forms, gilt borders, 8", 8 for	700.00
Pitcher, cider; berries & leaves, artist sgn, Lanternier, 9"	375.00
Pitcher, cider; raspberries on pastel, squat, Guerin, 6¾", $400 to	450.00
Pitcher, floral on cream, bamboo hdl, D&Co, 8", from $300 to	325.00
Plaque, cavalier smoking, Coudert, gold rim, Borgfeldt, 10½"	450.00
Plaque, dog's portrait, Coudert, Borgfeldt, 10", from $275 to	300.00
Plaque, Indian portrait, Luc, Borgfeldt, 10", from $550 to	650.00
Plaque, lady & cherub on pier, T&V, 8x6", from $2,000 to	2,400.00

Plaque, naval battle, T&V, 13" diameter, in gilt frame, $700.00. (Photo courtesy Early Auction Co.)

Plaque, pears (1 hole/2nd split), scalloped rim, Coiffe, 10", $200 to	225.00
Plaque, red & pk roses w/gold, gold scalloped rim, Flambeau, 8½"	165.00
Plaque, Soul's Awakening, after J Sant, 7x9", in fr: 14x11"	700.00
Plate, cherub w/flower, gold border, D&Co, 9", from $200 to	225.00
Plate, cherubs in clouds, gold scrolls, Ahrenfeldt, 9½", $375 to	475.00
Plate, cherubs in lt pk on wht w/gold border, Redon, 9", from $200 to	250.00
Plate, courtship scene w/roses, Pouyat, Pat Dec 6 1898, 9", $175 to	225.00
Plate, dinner; birds of paradise/floral branches, Bawo & Dotter	65.00
Plate, fish on gr, Duca, Flambeau, 9½", from $200 to	225.00
Plate, game bird, Rene, Flambeau, 9½", from $175 to	200.00
Plate, game bird & daisies, Luc, Blakeman & Henderson, 8½"	225.00
Plate, grape clusters w/gold, Blakeman & Henderson, 8½", $150 to	175.00
Plate, pk roses w/gold scrolls, Borgfeldt, 9½", from $150 to	175.00
Plate, windmill & river scene, E Vidal, Bawo & Dotter, 9", $350 to	400.00

Platter, fish scenic, gold beaded rim, L Straus & Sons, 19".........1,100.00
Tankard, grapes, mc on lav, slim, Pouyat, 12", from $500 to 600.00
Tankard, roses on dk gr, ornate gold hdl, T&V, 15", from $1,400 to ..1,600.00
Toast tray, gold leaves on wht, Klingenberg & Dwenger, 7½" L..... 85.00
Tray, swan & lily pad scenic, Guerin, 16½x12", from $175 to...... 200.00
Vase, floral, lav/gr w/gold lines, gold hdls, Gibus & Redon, 6" 400.00
Vase, floral, Moorish style w/gold hdls, Bawo & Dotter, 7", $650 to...750.00
Vase, floral w/gold, ftd letter-holder style, Bawo & Dotter, 6" 365.00
Vase, irises on gr w/gold, slim, sm gold hdls, Guerin, 15", $1,200 to...1,400.00
Vase, lady's portrait reserve on gr, Pouyat, ETS 1888, 13", $1,400 to .1,600.00
Vase, poppies, orange on peach to gr, M Muller, WG&Co, cylinder, 11"..170.00

Lithophanes

Lithophanes are porcelain panels with relief designs of varying degrees of thickness and density. Transmitted light brings out the pattern in graduated shading, lighter where the porcelain is thin and darker in the heavy areas. They were cast from wax models prepared by artists and depict views of life from the 1800s, religious themes, or scenes of historical significance. First made in Berlin about 1803, they were used as lamp shade panels, window plaques, and candle shields. Later steins, mugs, and cups were made with lithophanes in their bases. Japanese wares were sometimes made with dragons or geisha lithophanes. See also Dragon Ware; Steins.

Candleholder, shepherd, metal columnar stem/scroll base, German, 8x6" ..450.00
Candleholder, woods/castle, CI figural stem (boy w/flowers), KPM, 8" .. 750.00
Lamp, 6x9½" shade w/5 mc panels; gilt metal base w/2 urns, 16" ... 1,035.00
Panel, 2 ladies w/bird, arched top, Belleek, 19th C, 6" 600.00
Panel (5") of child reading, in ormolu fr on ornate ped............. 1,000.00

Screen, child reading (5"), ormolu pedestal frame, $1,200.00. (Photo courtesy Noel Barrett Antiques & Auctions)

Little Red Riding Hood

Though usually thought of as a product of the Hull Pottery Company, research has shown that a major part of this line was actually made by Regal China. The idea for this popular line of novelties and kitchenware items was developed and patented by Hull, but records show that to a large extent Hull sent their whiteware to Regal to be decorated. Little Red Riding Hood was produced from 1943 until 1957. Buyers need to be aware that reproduction Little Red Riding Hood has flooded the markets. Reproductions are distinguished by inferior detail and decoration. Many reproduction molds carry the original patent number. For further information we recommend *The Collector's Ultimate Encyclopedia of Hull*

Pottery by our advisor Brenda Roberts, and *The Ultimate Collector's Encyclopedia of Cookie Jars* by Joyce and Fred Roerig. Both are published by Collector Books.

Bank, wall hanging, $1,200.00. (Photo courtesy Pat and Ann Duncan)

Bank, standing, 7", from $900 to 1,350.00
Butter dish, from $350 to.. 400.00
Canister, cereal 1,375.00
Canister, coffee, sugar or flour; ea from $600 to 700.00
Canister, salt 1,100.00
Canister, tea 700.00
Casserole, red w/emb wolf, RRH, Grandma & axe man, 11¾", $1,800 to ..2,500.00
Cookie jar, closed basket, from $450 to 650.00
Cookie jar, full skirt, from $750 to 850.00
Cookie jar, open basket, from $400 to............................. 500.00
Cracker jar, unmk, from $600 to 750.00
Creamer, side pour, from $150 to................................. 225.00
Creamer, top pour, no tab hdl, from $400 to...................... 425.00
Creamer, top pour, tab hdl, from $350 to......................... 375.00
Dresser jar, 8¾", from $450 to................................... 575.00
Lamp, from $2,000 to...2,650.00
Match holder, wall hanging, from $400 to 650.00
Mustard jar, w/orig spoon, from $375 to.......................... 460.00
Pitcher, 7", from $450 to.. 675.00
Pitcher, 8", from $550 to.. 850.00
Planter, wall hanging, from $400 to 500.00
Shakers, Pat design 135889, med sz, pr (+) from $800 to............. 900.00
Shakers, 3¼", pr from $95 to 140.00
Shakers, 5½", pr from $180 to 235.00
Spice jar, sq base, ea from $650 to 750.00
String holder, from $1,800 to 2,500.00
Sugar bowl, crawling, no lid, from $300 to........................ 450.00
Sugar bowl, standing, no lid, from $175 to........................ 225.00
Sugar bowl, w/lid, from $350 to.................................. 425.00
Sugar bowl lid, minimum value 175.00
Teapot, from $400 to.. 450.00
Wolf jar, red base, from $925 to 1,000.00
Wolf jar, yel base, from $750 to 850.00

Liverpool

In the late 1700s Liverpool potters produced a creamy ivory ware, sometimes called Queen's Ware, which they decorated by means of the newly perfected transfer print. Made specifically for the American market, patriotic inscriptions, political portraits, or other American themes were applied in black with colors sometimes added by hand. (Obviously their loyalty to the crown did not inhibit the progress of business!)

Before it lost favor in about 1825, other English potters made a similar product. Today Liverpool is a generic term used to refer to all ware of this type.

Coffee can, quail (3) among plants & rocks, reeded hdl, bl transfer...240.00
Jug, allegorical: planning city of Washington, blk transfer, 10"..3,300.00
Jug, Apotheosis/Lady Liberty/eagle/ship, blk transfer, 1800.......2,100.00
Jug, Behold Our Support, blk transfer, 1800s, 7"..........................660.00
Jug, Emblem of America, Native Americans, blk transfer, 8"....2,400.00
Jug, Farmers in Arms/Weavers Arms, 1796, blk transfer, 8¼"..1,325.00
Jug, Geo Washington w/globe & flag, Sam'l Kelton, blk transfer, 10"..2,100.00
Jug, Masonic emblems (2), blk transfer, 1780s, 6½"......................435.00

Jug, Washington, LaFayette, and the Republican emblem, 5", VG, $750.00. (Photo courtesy Neal Auction Co. Auctioneers & Appraisers of Fine Art)

Jug, 3-masted Am ship, Farmer's Arms, blk w/mc, rpr, 19th C, 9"..2,150.00
Plate, Washington His Country's Father, blk transfer, 1800s, 6x5½"...210.00

Lladro

Lladro porcelains are currently being produced in Labernes Blanques, Spain. Their retired and limited edition figurines are popular collectibles on the secondary market.

August Moon, Oriental lady serving tea, #5122, retired, 9½" 180.00
Ballerina, seated, #4559, retired, 13¾"..240.00
Blowing Boy, boy stands w/cheeks puffed out, #4869, retired, 7¾"...60.00
Celestial Journey, winged horse pulls coach, #1848, retired 1,550.00
Chrysanthemum, geisha w/fan, #4990, retired, 11½"...................275.00
Dog & Cat, girl holds cat, dog on hip, #5032, retired...................300.00
Dog in basket, #1128, retired in 1971, 7½".................................360.00

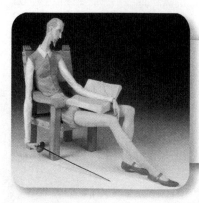

Don Quixote, issued in 1969, 14½", from $750.00 to $800.00. (Photo courtesy Jackson's International Auctioneers & Appraisers of Fine Art & Antiques)

English Lady, lady w/parasol, #5324, ca 1985, 10½"....................180.00
Exquisite Scene, girl smelling flower, #1313, retired, 11", MIB....390.00
Feeding My Rabbit, girl w/rabbit at ft, retired in 1993, 9"............120.00
For You, boy gives flower to lady, #5453, retired..........................330.00
Girl Kissing, #4873, retired, 7¾", MIB...150.00
Gossips, 2 women on sidewalk whispering, #4984, retired 1978..480.00

The Grandfather, retired 1979, 12", $325.00. (Photo courtesy Jackson's International Auctioneers & Appraisers of Fine Art & Antiques)

Gypsy Woman, stands beside brn bear, #4919, retired, 15", MIB..600.00
Kiyoko, Oriental lady kneeling w/flowers, #1450, retired.............330.00
Lady Empire, lady leaning on chair, #4719, retired, 18", MIB......600.00
Lady of the East (bust), #1488, retired in 1993, 9¾"....................390.00
Lady w/Bread Basket, puppy at her ft, #1034, 11½" 150.00
Lady w/Shawl, holds umbrella/walks dog, #4914, retired, 17", MIB...300.00
Lovers in the Park, couple on bench, #1274, retired, 11½", MIB..570.00
Medic, man in hospital attire, #6282, retired, 14", MIB...............150.00
Milanese Lady, lady w/umbrella, #5323, ca 1985, retired, MIB....150.00
Mother w/Pups, poodle w/puppies, #1257, retired, 6"...................375.00
Naughty Dog, pup pulling girl's skirt, #4982, retired, 7¾", MIB..240.00
Nude Torso, wht matt, J Huerta, #4512, ca 1969, retired, 12"......390.00
Nuns (2) stand side by side, #2075, retired, 13½"........................285.00
One Two Three, boy & girl look at shoe, #5426, retired, 10½", MIB..150.00
Parisian Lady, lady w/parasol, #5321, ca 1985, retired, 10", MIB...130.00
Poetry, seated beauty, Tonjos, retired, 16¼", MIB........................425.00
Puppy Love, boy & girl, #1127, retired, 10"................................150.00
See Saw, children on teeter-totter, #4867, retired........................180.00
Serenity, couple w/sheep, #4903, retired 1979, 14½"...................480.00
Shepherdess Sleeping, girl holding lamb, retired in 1981.............660.00
Spring Flirtation, lady w/flowers, retired, 11"..............................270.00
Two Elephants, lg & sm, #1151, retired, 12x10½"........................360.00
Wild Goose Chase, girl reaching out to goose, #5553, retired, 6x7½"...120.00

Lobmeyer

J. and L. Lobmeyer, contemporaries of Moser, worked in Vienna, Austria, during the last quarter of the 1800s. Most of the work attributed to them is decorated with distinctive enameling; favored motifs are people in eighteenth-century garb. Our advisor for this category is Don Williams; he is listed in the Directory under Missouri.

Goblets, four-lobed, intaglio scrolls, gilt and hand-painted pictorial medallions, 6", $300.00 for the pair. (Photo courtesy Early Auction Co.)

Bowl, cranberry to clear w/Nouveau floral, 1910s, 3¾" H 515.00
Candy dish, amber cut to clear, florals/geometrics, w/lid, 10" 120.00
Cordial, pk band, gilt rim on quatrefoil bowl, leaf decor stem, 4⅜"..200.00
Decanter, romantic scene/crest, faceted neck w/jewels, w/stopper, 10"....1,680.00
Goblet, floral/peacock eyes on cranberry bowl/disk ft, clear stem, 6" ..500.00
Vase, mc floral w/gold swans & rim, cut panels, att, 6" 90.00
Wine, Colonial man/florals/gilt, sgn, 5⅜".. 675.00

Locke Art

By the time he came to America, Joseph Locke had already proven himself many times over as a master glassmaker, having worked in leading English glasshouses for more than 17 years. Here he joined the New England Glass Company where he invented processes for the manufacture of several types of art glass — amberina, peachblow, pomona, and agata among them. In 1898 he established the Locke Art Glassware Co. in Mt. Oliver, a borough of Pittsburgh, Pennsylvania. Locke Art Glass was produced using an acid-etching process by which the most delicate designs were executed on crystal blanks. All examples are signed simply 'Locke Art,' often placed unobtrusively near a leaf or a stem. Some pieces are signed 'Jo Locke' and some are dated. Most of the work was done by hand. The business continued into the 1920s. For further study we recommend *Locke Art Glass, Guide for Collectors*, by Joseph and Janet Locke, available at your local bookstore.

Our advisor for this category is Richard Haigh; he is listed in the Directory under Virginia.

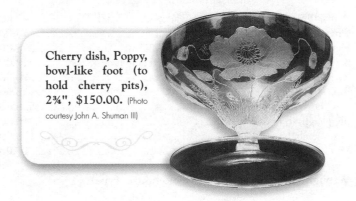

Cherry dish, Poppy, bowl-like foot (to hold cherry pits), 2¾", $150.00. (Photo courtesy John A. Shuman III)

Champagne, Poppy, 6" 95.00
Cup, ice cream; Kalana Poppy, ftd.. 95.00
Goblet, Ivy 95.00
Oyster cocktail, seaweed/coral/3 oysters, fire-polished rim, 3⅝" ... 195.00
Salt cellar, Vintage, ped ft, 2¼x1¼" 100.00
Sherbet, Daisy, on optic ribbed blank, 3¼" 85.00
Sherbet, Vintage, saucer base 85.00
Tankard, poppies/fern fronds/grasses, waisted, 8" 650.00
Tumbler, brandy; flowers & leaves, rare, 3¼" 195.00
Vase, long-stemmed roses, scalloped/ruffled rim, faint ribs, 7" 650.00
Vase, Rose, flared rim, 6¼".. 290.00
Wine, floral, dbl-knob stem, rnd ft, 5¾"................................ 125.00

Locks

The earliest type of lock in recorded history was the wooden cross bar used by ancient Egyptians and their contemporaries. The early Romans are credited with making the first key-operated mechanical lock. The ward lock was invented during the Middle Ages by the Etruscans of Northern Italy; the lever tumbler and combination locks followed at various stages of history with varying degrees of effectiveness. In the eighteenth century the first precision lock was constructed. It was a device that utilized a lever-tumbler mechanism. Two of the best-known of the early nineteenth-century American lock manufacturers are Yale and Sargent, and today's collectors value Winchester and Keen Kutter locks very highly. Factors to consider are rarity, condition, and construction. Brass and bronze locks are generally priced higher than those of steel or iron. Our advisor for this section is Joe Tanner; he is listed in the Directory under California. See also Railroadiana.

Key: bbl — barrel   st — stamped

Brass Lever Tumbler

Automatic, emb, flat key, 2⅛" 30.00
Blue Grass w/bell emb on front, 3⅛" 300.00
Chubbs, Patent London, st, 6⅛" 350.00
Cleveland, emb on front, 4-way, 2¼" 70.00
Cleveland, emb on front, 4-way, 3⅛" 55.00
Cotterill, st High Security key, 5⅛x3⅛" 500.00
Eagle Lock Co, word Eagle emb on front, scrolled, 3" 50.00
Fagoma, Fagoma emb in shield on front, 3" 125.00
GW Nock, fancy etch, st, 2⅞" 400.00
Mercury, Mercury emb on body, 2¾" 75.00
Our Very Best, DVB emb on body, 2⅞" 300.00
Roeyonoc, Roeyonoc st on body, 3¼" 60.00
Siberian, Siberian emb on shackle, 2½" 120.00
Spade, emb on front, mk Pat 25 1896, 2½" 60.00
Tower & Lyon NY, st, 3" 25.00
W Bohannan & Co, SW emb in scroll on front, 2⅜" 40.00
1898, emb, 2¾" 40.00

Combinations

Canton, Canton OH emb on face, 3⅜".....................................1,600.00
Corbin Sesamee 4-Dial Brass Lock, St Sesamee, 2¾" 15.00
Iowa Lock & Mfg emb on lock, 3½".. 100.00
Number or letter disk, st, 3-disk, brass, 2½" 150.00
Number or letter disk, st, 4-disk, iron, 4½" 325.00
Rochester Safety Lock emb on bottom, 1½x2" 145.00
Sorel Limited Canada, st, brass, 3¼" 450.00
Turman's Keyless, st, brass, 2¼" 160.00

Eight-Lever Type

Blue Chief, st, steel, 4½" 40.00
Excelsior, st, steel, 4¾" 30.00
Mastadon, st, brass, 4½" 30.00
Reese, st, steel, 4¾" 15.00

Iron Lever Tumbler

Airplane, st, 2¾" 60.00
Bull, word Bull emb on front, 2⅝" 30.00
Dragon, word Dragon & dragon emb on front, 2⅞"................... 25.00
HC Jones (trick lock), st, 4¼" 900.00
King Korn, words King Korn emb on body, 2 7/8" 70.00
Nineteen O Three, 1903 emb on front, 3⅞"...............................350.00
Rugby, football emb on body, 3" 20.00
Unique, word Unique emb on front, 3¼"................................... 150.00
Woodland, emb, 2⅜" 30.00

Lever Push Key

Aztec, emb 6-Lever, 2⅛".. 600.00
Celtic Cross, emb cross on face, brass, 2¼" 700.00

Columbia, emb Columbia 6-Lever, brass push-key type, 2¼" 35.00
Duke, emb 6-Lever, 2⅛" 65.00
Empire, emb, 6-Lever, brass, 2½" 20.00
HS&Co, 6-Lever, emb, brass, 2¼" 150.00
McIntosh, emb, 6-Lever, iron, 2½" 425.00
Nugget, 4-Lever, emb, brass, 2" 75.00
Vulcan, emb, iron, 2¾" 20.00

Logo — Special Made

Anaconda, st, brass, 2⅞" 60.00
City of Boston Dept of Schools, st, brass, 2⅞" 110.00
Conoco, st, brass, 2⅝" 25.00
Delco Products, st, brass 20.00
Hawaiian Elec, st brass, 3" 40.00
Heart-shape brass lever type st Board Education, bbl key, 3½" 65.00
Lilly, st, brass, 2½" 65.00
Ordinance Dept, st, brass, 2⅞" 75.00
Public Service Co, st, brass, 2⅞" 20.00
Sq Yale-type brass pin tumbler, st Shell Oil Co on body, 3⅛" 25.00
Standard Oil Co, st, brass, 2⅝" 25.00
Texaco, emb, brass, 2¾" 150.00
University of Okla, st, brass, 2⅞" 200.00
USBIR, st, brass, 3¾" 80.00
USMC, st, brass, 2½" 150.00
Zoo, st, iron, 2½" 25.00

Pin-Tumbler Type

Corbin, emb, iron, 2¾" 20.00
Corbin, st, brass, 2½" 50.00
Hope, emb Hope on body, brass, 2½" 20.00
Nrarvck (Russian), st, iron, 4" 400.00
Sargent, emb, iron, 2¾" 15.00
Segal, emb Segal on shackle, iron, 3¾" 30.00
Yale, emb Yale on body, Made in England on shackle, brass, 3" 30.00
99 Miller, emb 99, brass, 1¾" 80.00

Scandinavian (Jail House) Type

Backalaphknck (Russian), st, iron, 5" 600.00
R&E Co, emb, iron, 3¼" 40.00

Scandinavian Star, 3¾", $200.00. (Photo courtesy Joseph and Pamela Tanner)

Six-Lever Type

Eagle, Eagle Six-Lever st on body, brass 18.00
Miller, Six-Lever, st, brass, 3⅞" 20.00
Olympiad Six-Lever, st, iron, 3¾" 25.00
SHCo Simmons Six-Lever, emb, iron, 3⅝" 200.00

Story and Commemorative

Canteen, US emb on lock, lock: canteen shape, 2" 900.00

Dan Patch, iron, 1⅞" 250.00
National Hardware Co (NHCo), emb, iron, 2½" 325.00
North Pole, brass, 2⅞" 250.00
NY to Paris Lindbergh's Flight, brass, warded, 2⅝" 600.00
Russell & Erwin (R&E), emb Aztec figure, iron, 2¼" 650.00
Russell & Erwin (R&E), emb Diana, iron, 2⅞" 1,500.00
Russell & Erwin (R&E), emb mailbox, iron, 3⅛" 850.00
Russell & Erwin (R&E), emb Masonic symbols, iron, 3⅛" 1,500.00
Russell & Erwin (R&E), emb vase, iron, 3¼" 1,700.00
1901 Pan Am Expo, brass, emb w/buffalo, 2⅝" 650.00

1904 St. Louis World's Fair, embossed medallion, iron and brass, $600.00. (Photo courtesy Joseph and Pamela Tanner)

Warded Type

Army, iron pancake ward key, emb letters, 2½" 40.00
Cruso Chicken, emb, brass, 2¾" 35.00
Hex, iron, sq lock case, emb US on bk, 2⅛" 95.00
Navy, iron pancake ward key, bk: scrolled emb letters, 2½" 40.00
Red Cross, brass sq case, emb letters, 2" 10.00
Rex, steel case, emb letters, 2⅝" 18.00
Safe, brass sq case, emb letters, 1⅞" 8.00
Shapleigh, st, brass, 2" 18.00
Texas, emb, brass, 2½" 175.00
Van Guard, emb, iron, 2⅞" 18.00

Wrought Iron Lever Type (Smokehouse Type)

DM&Co, bbl key, 4¼" 20.00
MW&Co, bbl key, 2⅝" 10.00
R&E, 4½" 40.00
VR, 3½" 30.00
WT Patent, 3¼" 20.00

Loetz

The Loetz Glassworks was established in Klostermule, Austria, in 1840. After Loetz's death the firm was purchased by his grandson, Johann Loetz Witwe. Until WWII the operation continued to produce fine artware, some of which made in the early 1900s bears a striking resemblance to Tiffany's. In addition to the iridescent Tiffany-style glass, he also produced threaded glass and some cameo. The majority of Loetz pieces will have a polished pontil. Our advisor for this category is Don Williams; he is listed in the Directory under Missouri.

Basket, silver o/l floral & web on gr w/red fanned-out rim, 20" .. 8,625.00
Compote, bl/wht striated w/appl irid snake wrapping stem & bowl, 9" .. 115.00
Lamp, bl irid 12" globe shade w/gr int; metal base as 2 fruiting trees ... 7,475.00
Lamp, red feathers on bl oil-spot 7"dome shade; metal base w/gargoyles ..2,645.00

Lamp, sm bell shade w/zippers, yel/orange; twisted harp std, 17" ...3,335.00
Vase, amber w/gold irid, ruffled trumpet top, bun base, 12" 270.00
Vase, amber w/gold irid & appl chain-like loops, 9½" 660.00
Vase, amethyst w/bl irid oil spots, ruffled top, 10" 720.00
Vase, bold mc irid swirl lily in gilt metal holder w/3-D child, 15"..1,725.00
Vase, bronze w/oil spots, purple/gr irid, bulbous, 6" 400.00
Vase, cobalt w/oil spots, appl trailing prunts & ft, bulbous, 5" ..2,000.00
Vase, fish head, rim is mouth, random purple threads on gold, 5½"..1,095.00
Vase, gold w/gold butterflies w/wings of red & bl jewels, 8" 690.00
Vase, gold w/platinum oil spots, irregular rim, tree trunk shape, 5x7" ... 700.00
Vase, gr irid shading to flared bl ft, cylinder w/fan rim, 24" 200.00
Vase, gr w/irid bl oil spots, bun base, trumpet top, 8½" 430.00
Vase, gr-gold irid w/tight wavy lines in rust/cream, ftd cylinder, 10" ...1,495.00
Vase, jack-in-pulpit; gr w/bl Rusticana motif, elephant ear face, 16" .. 2,300.00
Vase, jack-in-pulpit; vaseline w/gold int, appl leaf above ft, 14", EX ... 575.00
Vase, Papillion w/platinum ribbons, base w/silver o/l band, 8x5"......2,500.00
Vase, Phänomen Cytisus, oil spots/waves/swirls of gr on yel, 4½" 1,725.00

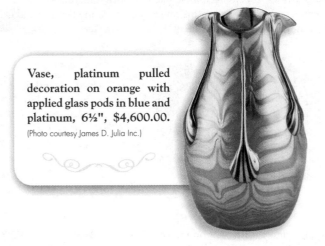

Vase, platinum pulled decoration on orange with applied glass pods in blue and platinum, 6½", $4,600.00.
(Photo courtesy James D. Julia Inc.)

Vase, purple/silver oil spots, 6 pulled hdls, silver rim, 5x8" 2,500.00
Vase, red w/oil spots & gold waves, cylinder w/shaped rim & ft, 6".. 400.00
Vase, silver o/l, silver gr to burgundy Titania, slim, 8¾" 2,250.00
Vase, silver o/l floral, amber oil spots w/purple/bl/gr swirls, 6"....2,650.00
Vase, silver o/l floral on rust to yel w/irid silver webbing, 8½" ...4,140.00
Vase, silver o/l orchids & straps on feathered/oil-spotted ground, 5"..3,450.00
Vase, silver o/l vines on gold ovoid w/pinched sides, ruffled rim, 5" ...635.00
Vase, silver o/l vining floral, rich bl irid on bl, 6½" 1,375.00
Vase, swirled/lined waves on deep bl/purple irid, bulbous 6½" 690.00
Vase, Titania, orange w/variegated gr irid to gray, clear cased, 8"...1,095.00

Lomonosov Porcelain

Founded in Leningrad in 1744, the Lomonosov porcelain factory produced exquisite porcelain miniatures for the Czar and other Russian nobility. One of the first factories of its kind, Lomonosov produced mainly vases and delicate sculptures. In the 1800s Lomonosov became closely involved with the Russian Academy of Fine Arts, a connection which has continued to this day as the company continues to supply the world with these fine artistic treasures. In 1992 the backstamp was changed to read 'Made in Russia,' instead of 'Made in USSR.'

Afghan hound, 6¼x7¼" 100.00
Badger, 4½" L 35.00
Bulldog, seated, 1950-60, 8⅜" 250.00
Carrying Watermelons, peasant w/melons, 1937, 5½" 1,600.00
Collie, seated, Made in USSR, 7" 35.00

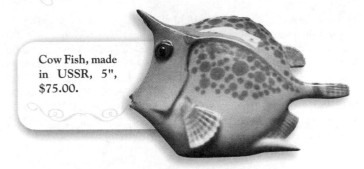

Cow Fish, made in USSR, 5", $75.00.

Giraffe baby seated, 5x6" 45.00
Girl seated before lg open book, holds doll, 1950s, 2½" 50.00
Great Dane, recumbent, brn tones, 5x9½"..................................... 50.00
Hippopotamus, 2¾x9" 35.00
Lenin bust, wht, 7"...45.00
Leopard grooming itself, 1950-60, 8¼" L 120.00
Shaliapin, male figure in robe, ca 1940, 11½" 4,800.00
Tabby kitten, gray stripes, 5½" 30.00
Zebra baby, recumbent, 3x3" 45.00

Longwy

The Longwy workshops were founded in 1798 and continue today to produce pottery in the north of France near the Luxembourg-Belgian border under the name 'Societe des Faienceries de Longwy et Senelle.' The ware for which they are best known was produced during the Art Deco period, decorated in bold colors and designs. Earlier wares made during the first quarter of the nineteenth century reflected the popularity of Oriental art, cloisonne enamels in particular. Examples are marked 'Longwy,' either impressed or painted under glaze. Our advisors for this category are Suzanne Perrault and David Rago; they are listed in the Directory under New Jersey.

Bowl, Chinese Art Deco floral, footed, #1252/223, 3x10½", $1,325.00. (Photo courtesy David Rago Auctions)

Bowl, crown/sailing ship/trefoils/branches/banner, #F3038, 5" 200.00
Box, Deco florals on turq, bow-tie shape, #1504, 2x5x4¾"........... 240.00
Box, floral, stylized/mc on wht crackle, 3¾" dia 125.00
Cake plate, Ceylon, stylized birds/gr clouds, 13", +server............. 850.00
Charger, nature scene w/birds & vines, D206, 14"........................ 660.00
Charger, Primavera, fruit still life on wht crackle, Levy, 3x15".... 1,325.00
Charger, Primavera, goddess & fish, Levy, 15" 2,760.00
Figurine, elephant standing, off-wht w/brn crazing, 7¼x9" 550.00
Figurine, Ketupa Zeylonensis, fish owl, gr/purple lustre, 13x7", NM ..2,160.00
Lamp, kerosene; Persian, brass cap/ft, electrified, 11" 995.00
Pin dish, flowers/leaves on bronze faux bamboo fr, 3½x5½" 55.00
Planter, floral, brass base w/elephant ft, metal insert, 8¾x11" ...2,150.00
Stamp holder/inkwells (2), bird & flowers on turq, w/3 lids 775.00
Trivet, bird w/in floral border on bl, 8-sided, 10" 395.00

Trivet, Primavera, Deco flowers, 1930-40s, 8".............................185.00
Trivet, Primavera, Deco lady in landscape, mc, 1920s, 8⅛" sq.....450.00
Vase, Art Deco flowers/geometrics, ftd invt cone, ca 1920s, 14⅝"..2,500.00
Vase, floral on bl, slim neck w/bl & yel ring, #1443, 9x4"...........215.00
Vase, modeled as 3 owls, purple lustre, #5286, 12x7", NM........5,400.00
Vase, parrot/exotic landscape, HP on lustre, #5919/1/36/48, 19x7", EX..9,600.00
Vase, Primavera, blk raised decor on bright bl, bottle form, 11¾"...775.00
Vase, Primavera, fruit/geometrics on ivory crackle, pillow form, 12"...2,040.00
Vase, sunflowers HP in landscape, mc lustre, #7879/36/18, 17x8", EX....8,400.00

Lonhuda

William Long was a druggist by trade who combined his knowledge of chemistry with his artistic ability in an attempt to produce a type of brown-glazed slip-decorated artware similar to that made by the Rookwood Pottery. He achieved his goal in 1889 after years of long and dedicated study. Three years later he founded his firm, the Lonhuda Pottery Company. The name was coined from the first few letters of the last name of each of his partners, W. H. Hunter and Alfred Day. Laura Fry, formerly of the Rookwood company, joined the firm in 1892, bringing with her a license for Long to use her patented airbrush-blending process. Other artists of note, Sarah McLaughlin, Helen Harper, and Jessie Spaulding, joined the firm and decorated the ware with nature studies, animals, and portraits, often signing their work with their initials. Three types of marks were used on the Steubenville Lonhuda ware. The first was a linear composite of the letters 'LPCO' with the name 'Lonhuda' impressed above it. The second, adopted in 1893, was a die-stamp representing the solid profile of an Indian, used on ware patterned after pottery made by the American Indians. This mark was later replaced with an impressed outline of the Indian head with 'Lonhuda' arching above it. Although the ware was successful, the business floundered due to poor management. In 1895 Long became a partner of Sam Weller and moved to Zanesville where the manufacture of the Lonhuda line continued. Less than a year later, Long left the Weller company. He was associated with J. B. Owens until 1899, at which time he moved to Denver, Colorado, where he established the Denver China and Pottery Company in 1901. His efforts to produce Lonhuda utilizing local clay were highly successful. Examples of Denver Lonhuda are sometimes marked with the LF (Lonhuda Faience) cipher contained within a canted diamond form.

Pitcher, 5-petal flowers at waisted neck, Spaulding, rpr, 6"...........240.00
Vase, Aburamu & Iskan (Biblical couple), sgn ADF, bulbous, 11"...1,680.00
Vase, band of hooked fish at shoulder, tiny rim/wide shoulder, 8"...600.00
Vase, blackberries on brn, Mary Taylor, #341, 8½", NM...............480.00
Vase, daisies on celadon & orange, sgn TS, integral hdls, 3¼x5½"..210.00
Vase, floral, J Spaulding, long slim neck, #206, 7⅜".....................200.00
Vase, floral on low shoulder, Steel, slim trumpet neck, #265, 11"....240.00
Vase, lg 5-part leaves, shield mk, 8"...360.00

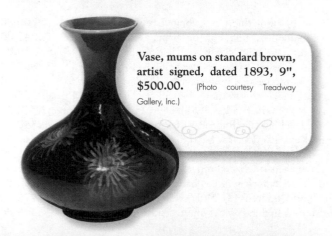

Vase, mums on standard brown, artist signed, dated 1893, 9", $500.00. (Photo courtesy Treadway Gallery, Inc.)

Vase, spider mum, J Spaulding, loop hdls, #174, 1893, 4½x6"......500.00
Vase, upright leaves/tulips emb on matt gr, 8½x5", EX.............1,560.00

Losanti

Mary Louise McLaughlin, who had previously experimented in trying to reproduce Haviland faience in the 1870s and 'American faience' (a method of inlaying color by painting the inside of the mold before the vessel was cast) in the mid-1890s, developed a type of hard-paste porcelain in which the glaze and the body fused together in a single firing. Her efforts met with success in 1900, and she immediately concentrated on glazing and decorating techniques. The ware she perfected was called Losanti (after the early name for Cincinnati), most of which was decorated with Nouveau florals, either carved or modeled. Examples are marked with several ciphers, one resembling a butterfly, another with the letters MCL superimposed each upon the other, and L. McL in a linear arrangement. Other items were marked Losanti, sometimes in the Oriental manner. Our advisors for this category are Suzanne Perrault and David Rago; they are listed in the Directory under New Jersey.

Vase, carved acanthus leaves on sheer celadon, signed Lonsanti, 4", $4,800.00. (Photo courtesy David Rago Auctions)

Bowl, sgraffito wreath, wht on indigo, MCL #65, 2½x4½", EX....900.00
Vase, oak leaves (inlaid/appl), cream/gr on bl/wht patches, 7"..10,500.00
Vase, robin's egg bl mottle, sgn MCL #18, rstr, 7x4¾"..................510.00

Lotton

Charles Lotton is a contemporary glass artist who began blowing glass full time in January 1973. He developed his own glass formulas and original designs, becoming famous for his Multi-flora design and his unique lamps. He has work on display in many major museums and collections, among them the Smithsonian, the Art Institute of Chicago, the Museum of Glass at Corning, and the Chrysler Museum. Every piece is made freehand, decorated with hot glass, and has a polished pontil. Charles' three sons, David, Daniel, and John each learned the art from their father and established their own studios. John stopped blowing glass in 2002, and his work is becoming scarce. David's sons, Jeremiah and Joshua are now beginning their careers in glass. Daniel's 16-year-old son, Tim, is also venturing into his initial designs. Scott Bayless, not a relative, and Charles's nephew, Jerry Heer, each produce unique designs signed with their names, the year, and Lotton Studios. All of the artists produce distinctive work. They sell their work at craft shows and at their showrooms in Crete, Illinois, as well as their gallery on Michigan Avenue in Chicago, and in art galleries across the US. For further information read *Lotton Art Glass* by Charles Lotton and Tom O'Conner. Our advisors are Gerald and Sharon Peterson; they are listed in the Directory under Washington.

Key:
CL — Charles Lotton   JL — John Lotton
DL — David Lotton   JoL — Joshua Lotton
DnL — Daniel Lotton   SB — Scott Bayless

JH — Jerry Heer   TL — Tim Lotton
JhL — Jeremiah Lotton

Bottle, Wisteria, blk/Gold Ruby, Oriental, CL, '05, 9¾x7¼" 2,200.00
Bowl, asters, pk/crystal w/Verre-de-Soie int, globular, DnL, '04, 8x8" . 1,100.00
Bowl, Cynthia flowers, lav/Neodymium crystal, DnL, '06, 8¾x10½".. 4,200.00
Bowl, Drop Leaf, gold/cobalt irid, trn collar, CL, '04, 5¼x6½"..1,600.00
Bowl, flower branches, pk/crystal, globular, JL, '02, 7½x8¾" 3,200.00
Bowl, King Tut, cobalt irid, JH, '03, 2½x3¼" 250.00
Bowl, leaves, pk/Selenium Red irid, collar, JH, '04, 3¾x5½"........ 350.00
Bowl, leaves/vine, pk/gold/irid cobalt, JL, '94, 4½x6" 400.00
Bowl, leaves/vine, pk/gold/opal w/cobalt int, collar, JH/'04, 3¼x5"...350.00
Bowl, leaves/vines, 3-color/crystal w/pk crush, free-form, JL, 8x17" ...2,250.00
Bowl, magnum; Egyptian symbols, blk/Verre de Soie, JL, '01, 7½x9".3,200.00
Bowl, magnum; long-stem flowers, pk/bl/opal w/bl int, JL, '00, 9x12" .. 4,600.00
Bowl, Multi-flora, lav/opal/mc crush, collared bowl, CL, '06, 7¼x9" 3,800.00
Bowl, Multi-flora, pk/cobalt w/aventurine int, trn collar, CL, '99, 8".... 3,000.00
Bowl, Multi-flora, pk/opal Cypriot/mc crush/orange int, CL, '00, 8".... 4,400.00
Bowl, Multi-flora, pk/yel/blk, collared bowl, CL, '06, 8x10½"...5,000.00
Bowl, pulled leaves, gr/Sunset, DL, '05, 3¾x6⅜" 350.00
Bowl, Tulipticus, lav/crystal, Sunset int, DnL, '05, 5x8"............1,100.00
Candlestick, morning glories, purple/Sunset, JhL, '02, 3¾x2¼" ... 150.00
Lamp, Antheriums, pk/opal w/red int, DnL, '98, 27x14½"........4,500.00
Lamp, Fern, pk/Selenium Red, ruffled, DnL, '92, 19½x12⅜".....3,000.00
Lamp, floral, pk/opal w/gr int, DnL, '89, mini, 11½x7".............1,400.00
Lamp, floral, pk/Selenium Red, mushroom, DnL, '02, 12½x7½".. 1,600.00
Lamp, floral/feathers, pk/cobalt/fuchsia, mushroom, DnL, '00, 16x8"... 1,800.00
Ornament, Zipper, gr/irid pk, DnL, '99, 3¼" dia 145.00
Paperweight, calla lilies, blk/wht/crystal, SB, '04, 2¾x3"........... 175.00
Paperweight, calla lilies, pk/Verre de Soie, fet, SB, '05, 4¼"......... 300.00
Paperweight, calla lilies (6), mc/crystal, '04, 4x4".................... 350.00
Paperweight, eggshell design, crystal/opal, SB, '04, 4¼x2".......... 200.00
Paperweight, Erlacher eng, irid gold to cobalt, DL, '93, 2¼x2½"... 600.00
Paperweight, flowers, pk/purple/crystal/ruby crush, DL, '01, 5⅜x6".. 900.00
Paperweight, flowers, pk/wht/crystal w/irid veil, JL, 2000, 8½" .5,400.00
Paperweight, Multi-flora, crystal/3 pk irid veils, CL, '03, 7x6¾"....3,200.00
Paperweight, orchids, purple/yel/crystal, DL, '98, 3¼x3¾" 200.00
Paperweight, orchids (3), mc/crystal, SB, mk prototype, '02, 3x3¼" ... 350.00
Paperweight, orchids (3), wht/lav/crystal, 3-lobe, SB, '03, 2½x3" ...175.00
Paperweight vase, hollyhocks/flower, purple/gr/clear/yel veil, DL, 8" ..650.00
Paperweight vase, orchids, purple/fuchsia/crystal, DL, '97, 6x3½"...450.00
Pendant, flower, lav/Verre de Soie, DL, '98, 1½x1⅛".................... 125.00
Pendant, scarab form, irid w/blk border, DL, '02, 2½x2" 125.00
Perfume, Antheriums, pk/Verre de Soie, DnL, '94, 7½x5" 600.00
Perfume, leaves, pk/Verre de Soie, teardrop stopper, JH, '05, 5½" . 275.00
Perfume, leaves/vine, pk/gold/opal w/gold ruby crush, JH, '00, 4½"....325.00
Sculpture, Bridal Veil, crystal w/3 irid veils, DL, '98, 11¼x7" 850.00
Sculpture, Cypriot w/silver lava draping, TL, '06, 6½x5¼" 250.00
Sculpture, free-form basket, int gr leaves/crimson spray, DL/'93, 13" .. 400.00
Sculpture, purple core/gr leaf & vine/crystal w/Sunset irid, DL, 11x7"....800.00
Sculpture, reeds/orchids, yel/gr/purple/crystal, DL, '05, 10½x7" .. 2,200.00
Sculpture, threading, Copper Blue/crystal, TL, '05, 6½x11½"...... 250.00
Sculpture, threading, pk/gr/crystal, TL, '06, 8¼x20"..................... 350.00
Vase, bl-blk branches in Mandarin Red, CL, 1973, 7½" 600.00
Vase, Blue Wisteria w/gold swirling feathers, bulbous, CL, 1987, 7"...700.00
Vase, Clematis, purple/crystal, DL, '03, 7¼x4¼" 500.00
Vase, Cynthia flowers, pk/wht/apple gr crystal, collar, DnL, '06, 13"..4,200.00
Vase, Cypriot, hearts & vines, bl irid on opal w/gold, CL, 1981, 9x6" ..850.00
Vase, Cypriot, moonscape, wht on bl, irid lava flow rim, CL, 1977, 7"...400.00
Vase, Cypriot, pitted bl irid w/flowing gold lava, CL, 1977, 6x5" .. 600.00
Vase, Fern, pk & bl irid, DnL, 1997, 7¼x7½" 1,200.00
Vase, irid leaves/vines on antique ivory, CL, 1973, 10¼" 1,100.00
Vase, jack-in-pulpit; no decor, yel, DL, '02, 9¼x2⅞" 275.00
Vase, jack-in-pulpit; Verre de Soie Cypriot, DL, '02, 10¼x3½"....350.00

Vase, jack-in-the-pulpit, Wisteria, opal with selenium interior, vividly stretched collar, Charles, 2001, 14x11", $2,200.00. (Photo courtesy Gerald and Sharon Peterson)

Vase, Lava, raspberry, cocoon form, CL, 1988, 6¾" 1,150.00
Vase, Lava Drape, gr/Cobalt Cypriot irid, CL, '01, 5¼x4" 600.00
Vase, leaf & vine, blk w/gr crush, JhL/JoL, '06, 3¼x3¾"............. 225.00
Vase, long-stem flowers, pk/crystal, free-form, JL, '01, 18x16"...2,700.00
Vase, magnum; long-stem flowers, crystal, JL, 2000, 16¾x5½"..2,600.00
Vase, Mandarin Red w/bl irid King Tut pattern, bulbous, CL, 1976, 7" ..1,000.00
Vase, Mandarin Yellow w/irid bl swags, bulbous, sgn Lotton, 1974, 10"...550.00
Vase, Multi-flora, orange/dk gr on deep translucent gr, CL, 1977, 9" .. 1,200.00
Vase, Multi-flora, pk/bl on amber irid, elongated pear, CL, 1977, 10"...800.00
Vase, Multi-flora, pk/tan on ruby translucent, slim, DL, 1993, 11"...550.00
Vase, Multi-flora, rose/gr on pk, cylindrical, CL, 1980, 8" 800.00
Vase, Multi-flora, sapphire bl, CL, 1987, 6" 485.00
Vase, Multi-flora on lilac, CL, 1987, 7½" 1,100.00
Vase, paperweight; calla lilies, wht/crystal, SB, '06, 9¼x6"........1,200.00

Vase, peacock feathers on bing cherry with aventurine interior, Charles, 2001, 10½x8", $2,800.00. (Photo courtesy Gerald and Sharon Peterson)

Vase, Primo Web, Blue Aurene at rim & base, DL, 1988, 7⅜" 485.00
Vase, pulled feathers, bl on wht, CL, 1974, 6" 515.00
Vase, pulled feathers/loops, cobalt/opal w/cobalt int, JhL, '02, 8x3" ...325.00
Vase, reverse pull, yel/purple on opal, JhL, '02, 6⅜x2¾".............. 275.00
Vase, silvery bl & cobalt loops on amethyst, stick neck, 1974, 11"...500.00
Vase, swirled feathers, gr/bl on cranberry, bottle form, CL, 1987, 10" ...700.00
Vase, threading, blk/yel/opal w/lt gr int, DL, 2000, 4¼x5½" 250.00
Vase, threading, dk gr w/lt gr wide collar, DL, '05, 3¼x4" 275.00
Vase, twisted reverse pull, blk/silver/red irid, DnL, '02, 5x4".....1,200.00
Vase, vine/leaves, gr/silver/coral irid, DnL, '03, 9¼x7½" 1,600.00
Vase, watermelon striped, emerald gr, SB, '05, 6¾x3½"................ 325.00

Lotus Ware

    Isaac Knowles and Issac Harvey operated a pottery in East Liverpool, Ohio, in 1853 where they produced both yellow ware and Rockingham.

In 1870 Knowles brought Harvey's interests and took as partners John Taylor and Homer Knowles. Their principal product was ironstone china, but Knowles was confident that American potters could produce as fine a ware as the Europeans. To prove his point, he hired Joshua Poole, an artist from the Belleek Works in Ireland. Poole quickly perfected a Belleek-type china, but fire destroyed this portion of the company. Before it could function again, their hotel china business had grown to the point that it required their full attention in order to meet market demands. By 1891 they were able to try again. They developed a bone china, as fine and thin as before, which they called Lotus. Henry Schmidt from the Meissen factory in Germany decorated the ware, often with lacy filigree applications or hand-formed leaves and flowers to which he added further decoration with liquid slip applied by means of a squeeze bag. Due to high production costs resulting from so much of the fragile ware being damaged in firing and because of changes in tastes and styles of decoration, the Lotus Ware line was dropped in 1896. Some of the early ware was marked 'KT&K China'; later marks have a star and a crescent with 'Lotus Ware' added. Non-factory decorated pieces are usually lower in value. Our advisor for this category is Mary Frank Gaston; she is listed in the Directory under Texas.

Bowl, appl cherry blossoms & leaves, ruffled/beaded rim, 4¼x5½" ... 650.00
Bowl, appl floral branches, netting, 3¾x4¾" 175.00
Bowl, Columbia, mc roses sgn Milford, filigree disks on sides, 4½" ... 400.00
Chocolate jug, emb florals, no enameling or gold, 9" 550.00
Creamer, floral, mc w/gold fishnet & hdl, 3¼x4½" 350.00
Creamer & sugar bowl, Valenciennes, gold fishnet on wht to pk, w/lid.. 600.00
Ewer, Etruscan, floral, pk/yel/gr on gr-gray mottle, 10" 600.00
Ewer, rtcl, melon ribs, beaded slim neck, 10" 1,850.00
Jar, flower form w/swirled petals, scalloped rim, 5¼x5¼" 450.00
Jar, Luxor, rtcl raised medallions/tassels & cords, 4-ftd, 7", EX..... 800.00
Jug, Valenciennes, gold fishnet, floral inside spout, squat, 3¾" 400.00
Pin tray, draped nude w/lg fan behind, HP finish, 6" L, from $1,200 to...1,500.00

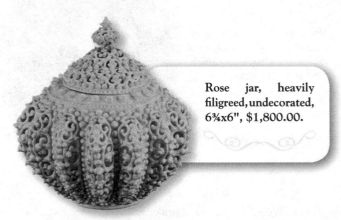

Rose jar, heavily filigreed, undecorated, 6¾x6", $1,800.00.

Shell tray, HP berries & leaves sgn WW, 8¾x8½" 500.00
Shell tray, Victorian lady transfer, gold trim, 7½x8¾", $500 to 600.00
Vase, Cremonian, wht w/appl flowers on celadon body, 6¼" 1,200.00
Vase, Egyptian, Victorian ladies' portrait w/gold, 15" 3,500.00
Vase, lily form w/pk & wht petals at base, Nouveau style, 8¾" 1,200.00
Vase, Old Man of Mtn, Venetian, purple violets, gold, w/hdls, 8"...800.00
Vase, Tuscan, HP flowers & leaves w/filigree, non-factory, 8½".. 2,000.00
Vase, Tuscan, wht ware, ornate filigree designs/appl flowers, 8½" ... 1,800.00
Vase, wild roses on wht, ornate gold hdls, stick neck, 9¾" 600.00

Lu Ray Pastels

Lu Ray Pastels dinnerware was introduced in the early 1940s by Taylor, Smith, and Taylor of East Liverpool, Ohio. It was offered in assorted colors of Persian Cream, Sharon Pink, Surf Green, Windsor Blue, and Chatham Gray in complete place settings as well as many service pieces. It was a successful line in its day and is once again finding favor with collectors of American dinnerware. For further information we recommend *Collector's Guide to Lu Ray Pastels* by Bill and Kathy Meehan. Our advisor for this category is Shirley Moore; she is listed in the Directory under Oklahoma.

Bowl, coupe soup; flat 18.00
Bowl, cream soup 70.00
Bowl, fruit; Chatham Gray, 5" 16.00
Bowl, fruit; 5" 6.00
Bowl, lug soup; tab hdls 24.00
Bowl, mixing; 5½" 125.00
Bowl, mixing; 7" 125.00
Bowl, mixing; 8¾" 125.00
Bowl, mixing; 10¼" 150.00
Bowl, salad; any color other than yel 65.00
Bowl, salad; yel... 55.00
Bowl, vegetable; oval, 9½" 25.00
Bowl, 36s oatmeal 60.00
Bud vase 400.00
Butter dish, any color other than Chatham Gray, w/lid 60.00
Butter dish, Chatham Gray, rare color, w/lid 90.00
Calendar plates, 8", 9" & 10", ea 40.00
Casserole 140.00
Chocolate cup, AD; str sides 80.00
Chocolate pot, AD; str sides 400.00
Coaster/nut dish 65.00
Coffee cup, AD 22.50
Coffeepot, AD 200.00
Creamer 10.00
Creamer, AD, ind 40.00
Creamer, AD, str sides, ind, from chocolate set 92.00
Egg cup, dbl.. 30.00

Epergne, $125.00.
(Photo courtesy Joyce Stewart)

Jug, water; ftd 150.00
Muffin cover.. 140.00
Muffin cover, w/8" underplate 165.00
Nappy, vegetable; rnd, 8½" 25.00
Pickle tray 28.00
Pitcher, bulbous w/flat bottom, any color other than yel 125.00
Pitcher, bulbous w/flat bottom, yel 95.00
Pitcher, juice 200.00
Plate, cake 70.00
Plate, Chatham Gray, rare color, 7".. 16.00
Plate, chop; 15" 38.00
Plate, grill; 3-compartment.. 35.00
Plate, 6" 3.00

Plate, 7".. 12.00
Plate, 8".. 25.00
Plate, 9".. 10.00
Plate, 10".. 25.00
Platter, oval, 11½".. 20.00
Platter, oval, 13".. 24.00
Relish dish, 4-part.. 125.00
Sauceboat... 28.00
Sauceboat, fixed stand, any color other than yel.... 35.00
Sauceboat, fixed stand, yel................................. 27.50
Saucer, coffee; AD 12.50
Saucer, coffee/chocolate 30.00
Saucer, cream soup 28.00
Saucer, tea.. 2.00
Shakers, pr.. 18.00
Sugar bowl, AD; str sides, w/lid, from chocolate set 92.00
Sugar bowl, AD; w/lid, ind 40.00
Sugar bowl, w/lid.. 15.00
Teacup.. 8.00
Teapot, curved spout, w/lid............................... 125.00
Teapot, flat spout, w/lid..................................... 160.00
Tumbler, juice 50.00
Tumbler, water 80.00

Lunch Boxes

Early twentieth-century tobacco companies such as Union Leader, Tiger, and Dixie sold their products in square, steel containers with flat, metal carrying handles. These were specifically engineered to be used as lunch boxes when they became empty. (See Advertising, specific companies.) By 1930 oval lunch pails with colorful lithographed decorations on tin were being manufactured to appeal directly to children. These were made by Ohio Art, Decoware, and a few other companies. In 1950 Aladdin Industries produced the first 'real' character lunch box — a Hopalong Cassidy decal-decorated steel container now considered the beginning of the kids' lunch box industry. The other big lunch box manufacturer, American Thermos (later King Seely Thermos Company) brought out its 'blockbuster' Roy Rogers box in 1953, the first fully lithographed steel lunch box and matching bottle. Other companies (ADCO Liberty; Landers, Frary & Clark; Ardee Industries; Okay Industries; Universal; Tindco; Cheinco) also produced character pails. Today's collectors often tend to specialize in those boxes dealing with a particular subject. Western, space, TV series, Disney movies, and cartoon characters are the most popular. There are well over 500 different lunch boxes available to the astute collector. For further information we recommend *The Illustrated Encyclopedia of Metal Lunch Boxes* by Allen Woodall and Sean Brickell. In the following listings, unless specific information to the contrary is included in the description, assume the lunch boxes to be made of metal and values to reflect the worth of boxes that are complete with their original vacuum bottles. The low side of our range represents examples in excellent condition; the high side represents mint.

A-Team, plastic, 1980s, from $15 to...................... 20.00
Adams Family, 1970s, from $25 to 40.00
Annie Oakley & Tag, 1950s, from $225 to 325.00
Barbie Lunch Kit, vinyl, 1960s, from $300 to 400.00
Battle of the Planets, 1970s, from $50 to 75.00
Beatles, 1960s, from $450 to.................................. 600.00
Benji, plastic, 1970s, from $20 to 30.00
Campbell Kids, 1970s, from $125 to 175.00
Casper the Friendly Ghost, vinyl, 1960s, from $400 to 500.00
Chuck Conners, 1960s, Cowboy in Africa, from $150 to..... 200.00
Chuck E Cheese, plastic, 1990s, from $25 to 35.00
Daniel Boone, Aladdin, 1950s, from $300 to................. 350.00

Davy Crockett, green rim: Lunch box, from $150.00 to $200.00; Metal Thermos bottle, from $55.00 to $100.00. (Photo courtesy Carole Bess White and L. M. White)

Deputy Dawg, vinyl, 1960s, from $325 to 375.00
Disneyland, 1950-60s, from $150 to 200.00
Donny & Marie, vinyl, 1970s, from $80 to 120.00
Dr Seuss, plastic, 1990s, from $20 to 25.00
Evel Knievel, 1970s, from $50 to 100.00
Fat Albert, plastic, 1970s, from $20 to 30.00
Flintstones, 1960s, from $125 to............................. 175.00
Flying Nun, 1960s, from $100 to.............................. 150.00
Garfield, plastic, 1980s, from $15 to 20.00
GI Joe, 1960s, from $80 to...................................... 130.00
Hogan's Heroes, dome top, 1960s, from $200 to........... 300.00
Holly Hobbie, plastic, 1989, from $20 to 25.00
Holly Hobbie, vinyl, 1970s, from $50 to 75.00
Huckleberry Hound & Friends, 1960s, from $100 to.......... 175.00

The Incredible Hulk, 1978: Lunch box only, from $30.00 to $60.00; Plastic Thermos bottle, from $5.00 to $15.00. (Photo courtesy Carole Bess White and L. M. White)

James Bond 007, 1960s, from $150 to 225.00
Jetson's, dome top, 1960s, from $900 to 1,400.00
Jr Deb, vinyl, 1960s, from $100 to............................. 150.00
Jurassic Park, w/recalled thermos, plastic, 1990s, from $25 to 30.00
Keebler Cookies, plastic, 1980s, from $30 to 50.00
Kermit the Frog, dome top, 1980s, from $30 to 40.00
Knight Rider, 1980s, from $20 to 40.00
Krofft Supershow, 1970s, from $50 to 100.00
Laugh-In, 1971, from $75 to................................... 150.00
Little Orphan Annie, dome top, 1970s, from $35 to 45.00
Lost in Space, dome top, 1960s, from $350 to 450.00
Mardi Gras, vinyl, 1970s, from $50 to 110.00

Mary Poppins, 1960s, from $50 to.............................100.00
Mickey Mouse & Donald Duck, 1950s, from $75 to..............150.00
Muppet Babies, plastic, 1980s, from $15 to...................25.00
Nancy Drew Mysteries, 1970s, from $30 to.....................60.00
Nestle Quik, plastic, 1980s, from $25 to.....................30.00
Osmonds, 1970s, from $15 to..................................25.00
Our Friends, 1980s, from $200 to............................400.00
Pathfinder, 1959, from $300 to..............................400.00
Pepsi, plastic, 1980s, from $30 to...........................40.00
Pink Panther, vinyl, 1980s, from $75 to.....................100.00
Pony Express, 1950s, from $225 to...........................275.00
Return of the Jedi, 1980s, from $30 to.......................60.00
Robin Hood, 1950s, from $125 to.............................200.00
Rocky & Bullwinkle, plastic, 1990s, from $75 to.............125.00

Secret Wars, 1980s: Lunch box, from $50.00 to $75.00; Plastic Thermos bottle, from $18.00 to $28.00. (Photo courtesy Carole Bess White and L. M. White)

Sesame Street, 1970s, from $25 to............................50.00
Smokey Bear, 1970s, from $225 to............................300.00
Smurfs, dome top, plastic, 1980s, from $20 to................30.00
Snoopy, brunch bag, vinyl, 1970s, from $75 to...............125.00
Snoopy & Woodstock, dome top, plastic, 1970s, from $20 to....30.00
Soupy Sales, vinyl, 1960s, from $300 to.....................375.00
Strawberry Shortcake, vinyl, 1980, from $75 to..............135.00
Three Little Pigs, 1980s, from $40 to........................80.00
Thundercats, 1980s, from $25 to..............................50.00
Tick, The; plastic, 1990s, from $25 to.......................50.00
Tic-Tac-Toe, vinyl, 1970s, from $50 to.......................75.00
Tom & Jerry, plastic, 1990s, from $10 to.....................20.00
Underdog, 1970s, from $350 to...............................750.00
US Mail/Zippy, dome top, 1969, from $35 to...................65.00
Voyage to the Bottom of the Sea, 1960s, from $175 to........250.00
Wagon Train, 1960s, from $100 to............................200.00
Winnie the Pooh, 1970s, from $150 to........................200.00
Wonder Woman, vinyl, 1970s, from $100 to....................150.00
Yellow Submarine, 1968, from $250 to........................500.00
Yogi Bear & Friends, 1960s, from $85 to.....................135.00
Young Astronauts, plastic, 1980s, from $20 to................30.00
Ziggy, vinyl, 1979, from $50 to..............................75.00

Lundberg Studios

This small studio has operated in Davenport, California, since 1970, when founder James Lundberg (now deceased) began making quality handcrafted glassware using a variety of techniques — some reminiscent of Tiffany. Their production includes vases, lamps, paperweights, perfume bottles, and marbles. Each piece they make is signed with the studio's name, the artist's name, a registration number, and the date.

Lamp, 3-lily, feathered shades; gr/gold on opal, Buffalo base, 12".375.00
Vase, angelfish/plants, mc in clear, Steven, #072402, 1986, 5¾"..660.00
Vase, bl irid, bulbous w/stick neck, 12".....................200.00

Vase, Evening Star Magnum Heart, gold interior, 2000, #061327, 13", $865.00. (Photo courtesy Early Auction Co.)

Vase, feathers, brn w/bl on gold, 1978 #LS101276, 10".........540.00
Vase, feathers, gr on gold, gr-trimmed rim, #062707, 11"......380.00
Vase, gold irid, flared rim, 2002, 8"........................185.00
Vase, paperweight; fuchsia blossoms in clear, #011423, 1988, 6"...660.00
Vase, pulled feathers, gr on gold irid, flared rim, #LS050734, '81, 5"..125.00

Maddux of California

One of the California-made ceramics now so popular with collectors, Maddux was founded in the late 1930s and during the years that followed produced novelty items, TV lamps, figurines, planters, and tableware accessories.

Ashtray, gr oval w/3 rests, #7180, 1½x10½x4½".................15.00
Ashtray, hippopotamus w/wide mouth open, #1152?, 4x4".........25.00
Ashtray, red w/blk speckles, swirled free-form, #701.........10.00
Ashtray, spear-like shape, gr/brn/red, #756, 11½"............17.50

Cookie jar, Squirrel Hiker, from $175.00 to $200.00. (Photo courtesy Ermagene Westfall)

Figurine, cockatoo w/wings out on flower base, 11¼x10½", $65 to..75.00
Figurine, cockatoos (2)on branch, lt yel & gr, 10½x10", from $50 to..65.00
Figurine, flamingo, #445, 6x6¼"..............................40.00
Figurine, flamingo, standing, beak touching S-curve neck, #309, 9½"...70.00
Figurine, flamingo, wings spread, #723, 7"...................50.00
Figurine, road runner, red to orange, tail up, 16⅜x7x3½".....35.00
Nightlight, chihuahua figural, #E-21855-M, 8x5½"............. 90.00
Planter, birds (2) before open stump, #528...................35.00
Planter, flamingo, #504, 10½x6x5½"...........................50.00
Planter, flamingo w/wings wide, #515, 10¾x7"................165.00

Planter, swan, pk to wht, #510, 11x7½" 15.00
Plaque, Aquarius emb on yel, 1967, 3⅜" 25.00
Plaque, exotic lady's face, gold pnt, #616, 8½" 125.00
Snack server, gr w/emb ribs, 2-compartment, #3151, 1½x11x6¼"....15.00
TV lamp, basset hound, #2990A, from $75 to 90.00
TV lamp, horse & colt, wht glossy, 11x12" 50.00
TV lamp, mallard duck, #893, 7½", from $50 to 65.00
TV lamp, pheasant, gray/yel/pk/gr/wht/blk, 11x11", NM 45.00
TV lamp, swan, shiny wht, 12x9x5¾", from $35 to 45.00
Vase, swan figural, wht glossy, wings form body of vase, 12¼x4¼" ...30.00

Magazines

Magazines are collected for their cover prints and for the information pertaining to defunct companies and their products that can be gleaned from the old advertisements. Other things factor in as well. Some of these factors are mentioned in our description lines. For further information we recommend *Old Magazines* by Richard E. Clear. See also Movie Memorabilia; Parrish, Maxfield.

Key:
M — in original wrapper
NM — spine intact, edges of pages clean and straight
EX/VG — average as-found condition

Life, 1968, April 12, Martin Luther King cover and article on his death, EX, $35.00.

After Dark, 1977, February, Arnold Schwarzenegger cover, EX 55.00
American Home, 1962, Summer, A-frame house on cover, EX 10.00
American Woman, 1918, March, fashionable lady on cover, EX... 12.50
Bazaar, 1966, July, fashion cover, EX 35.00
Black Hood Detective, 1941, September, Black Hood art cover, VG... 155.00
Circus, 1969, June, Frank Zappa cover, Morrison interview, EX .. 180.00
Collier's National Weekly, 1905, January, Parrish cover, VG 80.00
Double Detective, 1939, October, EX 80.00
Esquire, 1945, September, Tunnel of Love cover, EX 45.00
Gala, 1950, May-June, Marilyn Monroe cover, Vol 1, #1, VG 65.00
Good Housekeeping, 1932, March, Jessie Willcox Smith art cover, EX... 45.00
Grecian Guild Pictorial, 1958, June, male models, blk & wht, EX.... 75.00
Heavy Metal, 1977, April, robot cover, NM/M 50.00
High Heel, 1937, May, lady walking dog in wind on cover, EX...... 37.50
High Times, 1980, June, Mick Jagger cover, EX.......................... 50.00
Hit!, 1949, September, Marilyn Monroe cover, NM 300.00
Hit!, 1949, September, Marilyn Monroe cover, VG 65.00
Household, 1928, Charlotte Becker cover, EX............................. 20.00
Jayne Mansfield for President, 1964, Jayne on cover, EX................ 40.00
Life, 1922, April 27, Music Hath Charms by Kilvert cover, EX 75.00
Life, 1922, April 6, Morning cover by Parrish, cover only, NM 75.00
Life, 1922, February 2, Lyendecker butterfly lady cover, EX 375.00
Life, 1936, December 7, ski scene cover, Hitler bio, EX 65.00
Life, 1936, December 14, Archbishop of Canterbury cover, NM... 65.00

Life, 1936, December 21, Lord Beaverbrooks' grandaughter cover, NM .. 65.00
Life, 1936, November 30, West Point cadet cover, VG................ 50.00
Life, 1938, July 11, Shirley Temple Goes East cover, NM 35.00
Life, 1941, December 22, American flag cover, WWII coverage, VG ...80.00
LIfe, 1942, March 30, Shirley Temple Grows Up, NM................... 25.00
Life, 1952, April 7, Marilyn Monroe cover, EX 175.00
Life, 1953, May 25, Marilyn Monroe & Jane Russell cover, EX 60.00
Life, 1957, Ernie Kovacs cover, Churchill article, VG................ 50.00
Life, 1959, April 20, Marilyn Monroe cover, EX 75.00
Life, 1961, August 18, Mantle & Maris on cover, EX 35.00
Life, 1962, April 13, Taylor/Burton cover, Mantle/Maris cards, EX...70.00
Life, 1965, February 5, Winston Churchill's funeral cover, NM..... 28.00
Look, 1960, May 10, Princess Margaret cover, EX 20.00
Maxim, 1977, girl in Indian's shirt on cover, EX+ 65.00
McCall's, 1910, Queen of Fashion cover art, EX 20.00
Movie Stars Parade, 1946, June, Lana Turner cover, EX 75.00
Movie Stars Parade, 1948, July, Esther Williams, cover, NM 25.00

Movie World, 1956, June, Marilyn Monroe cover, Jane Russell article, NM, $90.00.

New Yorker, 1930, August 9, archery artwork cover, EX 155.00
New Yorker, 1937, October 9, circus cover, EX 50.00
Photoplay, 1945, August, Diana Lynn cover, EX 27.50
Photoplay, 1948, September, Alan Ladd cover, EX......................... 35.00
Playboy, 1953, December, Marilyn Monroe cover, NM, from $800 to....1,000.00
Playboy, 1954, April, blond centerfold, EX................................. 200.00
Playboy, 1954, April, Fahrenheit 451 (Bradbury) feature, NM 275.00
Playboy, 1954, February, sweetheart of month/centerfold, EX...... 300.00
Playboy, 1954, March, brunette centerfold, VG 300.00
Playboy, 1954, March, Joanna Arnold cover, EX 300.00
Playboy, 1954, May, w/centerfold, NM 200.00
Playboy, 1954, September, jazz band art cover, L Armstrong article, EX ..200.00
Popular Science, 1959, November, car cover, EX 10.00
Private Peeks, 1957, Betty Page cover, Vol 2, EX 160.00
Private Peeks, 1978, Betty Page cover, some color photos, Vol 1, EX ...215.00
Radio & Television Mirror, 1940, August, Barbara Stanwyck cover, EX.. 15.00
Ring, 1937, September, Schmeling & Joe Louis cover, VG............ 80.00

Rolling Stone, 1969, May 3, Issue #32, EX, $25.00. (Photo courtesy www.gasolinealleyantiques.com)

Rolling Stone, 1981, October 1, Yoko Ono cover, VG.................. 20.00
Saturday Evening Post, 1927, February 19, Rockwell cover, EX ..200.00
Saturday Evening Post, 1933, December 16, Rockwell cover, EX ...165.00
Saturday Evening Post, 1935, May, lady's portrait, NM.................. 30.00
Saturday Evening Post, 1936, October 24, Rockwell cover, EX ... 140.00
Saturday Evening Post, 1951, April 7, Harley-Davidson cover, EX...70.00
Saturday Evening Post, 1962, October 6, Pope John XXIII on cover, EX.. 25.00
Screen Album, 1946, August/September, Cornel Wilde cover, NM.. 30.00
Screenland, 1934, October, Shirley Temple cover, VG.................. 50.00
Screenland, 1965, January, Elvis art cover, NM.................... 40.00
Silver Screen, 1944, February, Merle Oberon cover, EX................ 30.00
Suspense, 1959, September, horror cover, #4, EX........................ 200.00
Teen Set, 1966, November, John Lennon & others on cover, EX.. 55.00
Thriller, 1962, February, Wild 1st issue, Vol 1, EX........................ 60.00
Time, 1930, Sept 22, Robert Jones Jr (golfer) cover, EX............. 185.00
Time, 1947, November 22, Jackie Robinson cover, EX 55.00
Time, 1969, August 1, Ted Kennedy cover/article, EX 25.00
Time, 1975, October 27, Bruce Springsteen cover, EX................. 175.00
True, 1952, December, racing cover, EX 7.50

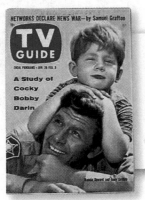

TV Guide, 1961, January 28, Andy Griffith and Ron Howard, EX, $25.00.
(Photo courtesy www.gasolinealleyantiques.com)

Vanity Fair, 1935, February, Japan's rising sun cover, Dali art, EX.. 55.00
Vogue, 1914, March, fashion lady & exotic bird cover, EX 80.00
Vogue, 1915, August 4, Steinmetz cover of 2 fashionable ladies, EX....65.00
Vogue, 1916, September, Dryden fashion lady cover, EX 80.00
Vogue, 1919, December, Plank art cover, EX................................ 100.00
Vogue, 1934, April, lady w/umbrella on cover, VG 45.00
Vogue, 1960, November 1, lady in gr cover by Irving Penn, NM... 65.00
Woman's Day, 1949, November, baby cover, NM.......................... 30.00
Woman's Day, 1950, June, mother tossing baby in air on cover, NM... 30.00
Woman's Day, 1950, March, baby on cover, NM.......................... 30.00
Young Physique, 1959, August, male models, EX 60.00
Young Physique, 1962, October, male models, EX......................... 70.00

Majolica

Majolica is a type of heavy earthenware, design-molded and decorated in vivid colors with either a lead or tin type of glaze. It reached its height of popularity in the Victorian era; examples from this period are found in only the lead glazes. Nearly every potter of note, both here and abroad, produced large majolica jardinieres, umbrella stands, pitchers with animal themes, leaf shapes, vegetable forms, and nearly any other design from nature that came to mind. Not all, however, marked their ware. Among those who sometimes did were Minton, Wedgwood, Holdcroft, and George Jones in England; Griffin, Smith and Hill (Etruscan) in Phoenixville, Pennsylvania; and Chesapeake Pottery (Avalon and Clifton) in Baltimore.

Color and condition are both very important worth-assessing factors. Pieces with cobalt, lavender, and turquoise glazes command the highest prices. For further information we recommend *The Collector's Encyclo-pedia of Majolica* by Mariann Katz-Marks (see Directory, Pennsylvania). Unless another condition is given, the values that follow are for pieces in mint condition. Our advisor for this category is Hardy Hudson; he is listed in the Directory under Florida.

Basket, Blackberry & Basketweave, vine hdl 350.00
Bowl, shell/coral/seaweed, oval, ftd, Wardle, 10" 450.00
Bowl, waste; Wild Rose & Rope, 5½".. 200.00
Bread tray, Wheat, cobalt center, 13".. 500.00
Butter dish, Shell & Seaweed, w/insert, Etruscan......................... 800.00
Butter dish, Water Lily, Samuel Lear.. 375.00
Butter pat, floral, Wedgwood.. 200.00
Butter pat, Geranium, gr.. 115.00
Butter pat, Honeycomb & Fern, Holdcroft................................... 325.00
Butter pat, Maple Leaf on Plate, pk... 150.00
Butter pat, Pansy, mc, Etruscan... 175.00
Butter pat, Pansy & Leaf, att Holdcroft 250.00
Butter pat, pk fan shape, Eureka.. 150.00
Butter pat, Pond Lily, mottled 125.00
Butter pat, Shell & Seaweed, Etruscan... 250.00
Cache pot, Bamboo w/Ribbon & Bow, w/stand, Minton, #4880, 8"..1,200.00
Cake plate, Napkin, Etruscan, cobalt accent, 12½" 475.00
Cake stand, Pear & Apple, 4½x9".. 400.00
Cake stand, Shell & Seaweed, Etruscan, 5x9¼" 850.00
Candleholder, lady frog figural, Continental, 8", ea..................... 315.00
Candleholder, Seaweed & Shell, Palissy style, Portugal, 6½", ea . 100.00
Candlestick, putto & cattail figural, Wedgwood, 10", ea.............. 550.00
Celery vase, lily form, Etruscan, scarce, 8½" 1,900.00
Centerpc, putto atop shell, EX color, Minton, #1539, 18" 2,500.00
Cheese keeper, Basketweave & Floral, Victoria Pottery Co, 8½" .. 700.00
Cheese keeper, lily/daisy/wheat/fern, Etruscan, scarce, 11" dia..1,600.00

Cheese keeper, picket fence, George Jones, $2,200.00.
(Photo courtesy Majolica Auctions, Strawser Auction Group)

Cheese keeper, Primrose, Wedgwood, 10"...................................1,000.00
Cheese keeper, Water Lily, Cattail & Dragonfly, Geo Jones, 11"...9,000.00
Comport, Overlapping Begonia Leaf, pk trim, 6x10¼" 350.00
Comport, Tobacco Leaf & Rosette, low, Holdcroft, 8½" 350.00
Creamer, Bamboo & Fern, Wardle, 4¾"....................................... 160.00
Creamer, Corn, pewter lid, Etruscan, 5" 375.00
Creamer, Ribbon & Bow, Fielding.. 250.00
Creamer, Sunflower, pk, Etruscan, 4"... 400.00
Creamer, Wild Rose, butterfly spout, Etruscan, 4½" 140.00
Cup & saucer, Bird & Fan, Fielding.. 350.00
Cup & saucer, Shell & Seaweed, Etruscan.................................... 300.00
Cup & saucer, Wild Rose & Rope.. 150.00
Dessert dish, owl on fan shape w/cobalt trim, 7½" 175.00
Figurine, boy w/shell, Continental, 8"... 200.00
Figurine, fox & rabbit, George Jones, 4½" 1,200.00
Figurine, frog singing, Jerome Massier, 4¾"................................ 500.00
Finger bowl, Water Lily, Etruscan, shape #M1 .... 275.00
Flower holder, putti (2) at sides of tub, Holdcroft, 10" 1,200.00

Garden seat, twig form ft, George Jones, 18" 6,500.00
Humidor, frog w/pipe figural, red smoking jacket, Continental, 8"..700.00
Humidor, frog w/red smoking jacket, 6¼" 500.00
Humidor, monkey's head figural, Mafra, 6" 250.00
Humidor, Shell & Seaweed, Etruscan 1,800.00
Jardiniere, cattail, cobalt mottle, Minton, 10x10" 1,200.00

Jardiniere, Magnolia & Bee, bamboo ft, cobalt, George Jones, 12" ..3,000.00
Jardiniere, Stork & Cattail, cobalt, ftd, Holdcroft, 13"..............1,800.00
Marmalade, Apple Blossom & Napkin, Albino, George Jones 200.00
Match striker, kangaroo figural, 5" 200.00
Match striker, pig figural, Continental, 6"................................... 450.00
Mug, rabbit w/rabbit hdl, Fr, 3½" 325.00
Mug, Water Lily, cobalt rim, Etruscan 275.00
Pitcher, bear w/drum figural, Holdcroft 900.00
Pitcher, Calla Lily, cobalt, 10" 650.00
Pitcher, Fan & Scroll, Fielding, 6½" 375.00
Pitcher, Fern, Etruscan, 8" 700.00
Pitcher, floral & wheat on turq, 6-sided, att Holdcroft, 9½"......... 450.00
Pitcher, goat on yel ground, 8" 300.00
Pitcher, heron & fish figural, Minton, #1241, 21".....................6,600.00
Pitcher, Hummingbird & Basketweave, Fielding, 8½"................. 400.00
Pitcher, Pine Cone, Wedgwood, 9½" 350.00
Pitcher, rat w/umbrella, Fr, 7¾" 1,250.00
Pitcher, robin on leafy branch, cobalt, George Jones, 6¼" 2,200.00
Pitcher, Shell & Seaweed, Etruscan, 5" 400.00
Pitcher, Shell & Seaweed, Etruscan, 6" 500.00
Pitcher, shell form, Fielding, 8½" 650.00
Pitcher, shell/coral/seaweed/waves, Wardle, 8" 1,100.00
Plaque, snake w/frog, lizards/shells/ferns, Palissy, 12½" 900.00
Plate, Boy on Bicycle, Fr, 7½"... 150.00
Plate, Cauliflower, Etruscan, 9" 350.00
Plate, Cauliflower, Wedgwood, 8¼" 250.00
Plate, Flying Fish & Cattail, 8½" 300.00
Plate, Maple Leaf & Basket, pk rim, Etruscan, 9" 300.00
Plate, Napkin on Basket, Morley & Co, 8¾" 200.00
Plate, oyster; 6 fish heads surround center well, Wedgwood, 7¼" ..1,000.00
Plate, oyster; 9-well, pk & turq alternate, 9" 400.00
Plate, Pear & Apple, 8¼" 250.00
Plate, Shell & Seaweed, Etruscan, 9¼" 350.00
Plate, Strawberry & Apple, Etruscan, 9" 275.00
Platter, Banana Leaf on Basket, 13½" 350.00
Platter, Begonia Leaf on cobalt, 11¾" 350.00
Platter, Corn, 13"... 450.00
Platter, Eat Thy Bread w/Thankfulness, Begonia Leaf, 12½"........ 350.00
Platter, fish atop vegetation, Wedgwood, Argenta, 25¼" 1,500.00
Platter, Leaf & Fern, 12".. 350.00

Platter, Pear & Apple, 13" 425.00
Platter, shell/coral/seaweed/waves, oval, Wardle, 13" 450.00
Platter, Sunflower & Classical Urn, Samuel Lear, 14½" 375.00
Platter, Wild Rose & Rope, turq w/cobalt center, 15" 425.00
Salt cellar, Lily, Etruscan... 275.00
Salt cellar, Pond Lilly, Holdcroft 250.00
Sugar bowl, Shell & Fishnet, coral hdls, Fielding 700.00
Sugar bowl, Strawberry, pk, twig ft, Minton, 2½" 2,200.00
Syrup, Bamboo, pewter lid, Etruscan, 8" 600.00
Syrup, Bamboo & Blackberry, pewter lid, 6" 350.00
Syrup, coral, pewter lid, Etruscan, 6½" 450.00
Syrup, Sunflower, cobalt, pewter lid, Etruscan, 8" 650.00
Tea set, Shell & Seaweed, Wardle, teapot+cr/sug 1,250.00
Teapot, Bird & Fan, Fielding, 8" 350.00
Teapot, Blackberry & Bark, Holdcroft, 4½" 550.00
Teapot, monkey & coconut figural, Minton, #1844.....................4,500.00
Teapot, Shell & Seaweed, Etruscan, crooked spout 750.00
Tile, fruit & flowers, Minton #1125, 8" 500.00
Tray, Dragonfly, fan shape, cobalt, 10"....................................... 350.00
Tray, rabbit on cabbage leaf figural, Minton, 10" 2,100.00
Vase, boy climbing tree figural, Holdcroft, 7".............................. 550.00
Vase, cat w/basket figural, 5".. 400.00
Vase, frog on lily pad figural, 5¾" 175.00
Vase, laurel swags, supported by 2 putti, cobalt, Wedgwood, 11"...1,200.00
Waste bowl, Honeycomb, turq, Holdcroft, 5" 250.00

Malachite Glass

Malachite is a type of art glass that exhibits strata-like layerings in shades of green, similar to the mineral in its natural form. Some examples have an acid-etched mark of Moser/Carlsbad, usually on the base. However, it should be noted that in the past 30 years there have been reproductions from Czechoslovakia with a paper label. These are most often encountered.

Ashtray, panthers relief, 2½x7½".. 150.00
Ashtray, 3 figural horses support bowl, 3x5"................................ 85.00
Basket, allegorical scenes in relief, integral hdl, 5½" 65.00
Bottle, scent; lg finial: nude/leaves, sq body w/leaves, Czech, 4½"...180.00
Bottle, scent; 3-lobe floral finial, body molded as a zinna, 5¾"..... 300.00
Box, lg Buddha on lid, blk-pnt compo base, 9x6x4" 80.00
Box, lg horse on lid, 7".. 165.00
Box, nude holding hourglass emb on lid, Zodiac symbols, 2¼x5x4"...180.00
Box, nudes intwined in vines on lid & base, 4" dia...................... 100.00
Figurine, stylized lady, long skirt blowing in wind, 9" 60.00
Obelisks, gilt metal mts w/classical masks, Continental, 28", pr.. 2,600.00

Tray, reclining nude molded on edge of pool, 8" L 120.00
Vase, nudes & foliage in high relief, flared rim, ftd, Moser, 8", pr 625.00
Vase, nudes & foliage in high relief, shouldered, Czech, 5", pr 240.00
Vase, seminude in 4 panels, plain & ribbed sqs, Ingrid, 9x7", EX .. 360.00

Mantel Lustres

Mantel lustres are decorative vases or candleholders made from all types of glass, often highly decorated and usually hung with one or more rows of prisms. In the listings that follow, values are given for a pair, unless otherwise noted.

White cut to cranberry with gilt and enameled flowers, jeweled drops with prism terminals, Bohemian, 13½", $1,900.00. (Photo courtesy Neal Auction Co. Auctioneers & Appraisers of Fine Art)

Bl Bristol ruffled squat body on slim trumpet std, 2-pc cut prisms, 9" .. 360.00
Brass figural lady on marble base, 3-light, long tiered prisms, 18" .. 195.00
Clear star-cut glass slim std w/long 2-pc prisms, 11", 4 for 390.00
Cobalt cut to clear w/optic windows, incurvate rim, 4-pc prisms, 9" ... 575.00
Cranberry, tulip form w/floral medallions & gilt, 10 prisms, 12" .. 1,750.00
Cranberry w/floral & gilt, 2 rows bk-cut Albert prisms, knop std, 14" ... 500.00
Gilt brass w/warrior figures, 3-light, marble base, 17x6x4" 475.00
Gilt bronze Regency w/cast dolphins, prisms, marble base, 15x7" .. 2,350.00
Gr opalene w/gold & pk medallions, 8 long prisms, scalloped top, 7" .. 145.00
Gr w/wht cut/pnt o/l, scalloped top/slim std, 2-pc cut prisms, 14" .. 1,020.00
Pk cased w/gold, ruffled, wide body on lobed std, 2-pc prisms, 11" ..225.00
Pk o/l w/gilt floral & butterflies, crenelated top, 2 rows prisms, 14" 900.00
Red Bohemian glass, grapes & leaves, long glass prisms, 13" 600.00
Red o/l, eng ovals, long prisms, Bohemian, 10¾" 200.00
Red o/l, foliage/deer eng, flared top, 2-pc prisms, Bohemian, 12x7" 900.00
Ruby w/gilt foliage, vasiform, long 2-pc prisms, 11" 600.00
Wht cut to clear ovals & Xs, mc/gold florals, prisms, Bohemian, 13" .. 350.00
Wht w/ruby-flashed cut/pnt o/l, long 2-pc prisms, Bohemian, 12" ..660.00

Maps and Atlases

Maps are highly collectible, not only for historical value but also for their sometimes elaborate artwork, legendary information, or data that since they were printed has been proven erroneous. There are many types of maps including geographical, military, celestial, road, and railroad. Nineteenth-century maps, particularly of U.S. areas, are increasing in popularity and price. Rarity, area depicted (i.e. Texas is more sought after than North Dakota), and condition are major price factors. World globes as a form of round maps are increasingly sought after, especially lighted and black ocean globes. Any tape other than archival tape hurts the value of maps — better still torn than badly mended. Our advisor for this category is Murray Hudson; he is listed in the Directory under Tennessee. Unless otherwise noted, our values are for maps in excellent condition.

Key: hc — hand colored

Atlases

Bradford Comprehensive..., Boston, 1st TX map, 1836, VG.....5,000.00
Colton's...of the World, NY, Vol II, 63 map sheets (non-US), 1856..1,750.00
Cram's Unrivaled...of the World, Chicago, 1897, 486-pg............. 325.00
Johnson's New Illustrated..., NY, 1864, 123-pg.........................2,250.00

Louisiana history, published by Jean Mariette, Paris, 1728, full calf with raised bands and gilt letters, 30 maps, charts, and plates, 10x7¾", $5,580.00. (Photo courtesy Early Auction Co.)

Peoria Star's Handy...World, Peoria IL, 1911, 86 maps, 106-pg...... 85.00
Rand McNally & Co's New Census...World, Chicago/NY, 1911, 177-pg, VG ...125.00
Rand McNally & Co...Unrivaled...World, Chicago/NY, 1910, 357-pg..175.00
Tunison's Peerless Universal..., Jacksonville, IL, 1886, 208-pg..... 800.00
Wm Higgins, Orr & Smith, London, 51 maps, 1836, 12x10½"....300.00

Maps

Amerique Meridionale, R de Vaugondy, Paris, hc, 1750, 5¾x6", G ..90.00
Amerique Meridionale (S Am), Vaugondy, hc details, 1700s, 22x30"..300.00
Asie, R de Vaugondy, Paris, 1750, shows Wall of China, 5¾x6⅛", G ...150.00
CO, from Rand-McNally Atlas, mc w/mining camps/etc, 1915, 14x11" ...25.00
Dbl hemisphere, R de Vaugondy, outline color, 2-pg, 1786, 29x39"......750.00
Deux Continents, Buffer, Paris, ca 1760, 9¼x11¾", G 125.00
Johnson's S Am, AJ Johnson, Johnson & Browning, NY, 1862, 24x17", VG..90.00
KY, Carey's Am Edition...1795, hc details, 9½x20", EX 475.00
L'Amerique 1762, NA w/mc highlights, cartouch w/palm tree, 12x18"+fr..230.00
Mitchell's Map of OH, red leather cover w/gilt, 1833, 15¼x13" .. 300.00
Mitchell's Map of VA, book form, 1842, loose from cover, 13x16" .. 500.00
N Am, T Jefferys, Ballard, London, 1758, modern color, 7¼x9", G 200.00
NB, from Rand-McNally atlas, ethnic communities, 1915, 14x11" ...17.50
NC & SC, HS Tanner, Philadelphia, 1928, 23x31"+bird's-eye maple fr..1,950.00
New Engelland (sic)/NY/NJ/Pensilvania (sic), hc, 1740s, 8x12" .. 650.00
Noua Terrae-Mariae Tabula, Ogilby, London, 17th C, 16x17", EX..3,000.00
Oceania (Australia, South Seas, etc), hand drawn, sgn/1863, 11x14"..345.00
Orbis Veteribus Notus, D'Anville, hc highlights, 1756, 22½x32" ...750.00
S Am, AH Jaillot, political divisions at end of 17th C, 23x35" ... 800.00
S Am, Ettling, Weekly Dispatch Atlas, London map, 1861, 24x17", G ..175.00

Sicily, by Nicolaum Visscher, published in Amsterdam, hand colored, ca. 1680, G, 20x22", in reverse-painted frame (G), $325.00. (Photo courtesy James D. Julia Inc.)

Solis Circa Orbem Terrarum Spiralis Revoltio, A Cellarius/1708, 18x21"...1,235.00
Strait of Magellan, Henrick Hondius, ships/whales/etc, 1635, 17x21"..530.00
United States, JH Young, SA Mitchell, 1837, darkened, 9x15", VG..525.00
UT, from Rand-McNally Atlas, mining camps/ghost towns, 1895, 14x11"...40.00
Voightland (Germany), J Blaeu, Amsterdam, hc, 20x15½", VG..400.00
World, T Bowen, London, copper eng, mc, 1779, 11x18¼"+fr, VG ..900.00

Marblehead

What began as therapy for patients in a sanitarium in Marblehead, Massachusetts, has become recognized as an important part of the Arts and Crafts movement in America. Results of the early experiments under the guidance of Arthur E. Baggs in 1904 met with such success that by 1908 the pottery had been converted to a solely commercial venture. Simple vase shapes were sometimes incised with stylized animal and floral motifs or sailing ships. Some were decorated in low relief; many were plain. Matt glazes in soft yellow, gray, wisteria, rose, tobacco brown, and their most popular, Marblehead blue, were used alone or in combination. They also produced fine tiles decorated with ships, stylized floral or tree motifs, and landscapes. Early examples were lightly incised and matt-painted (these are the most valuable) on 1" thick bodies. Others, 4" square and thinner, were matt-painted with landscapes in indigoes, in the style of Arthur Wesley Dow.

The Marblehead logo is distinctive — a ship with full sail and the letters 'M' and 'P.' The pottery closed in 1936. Our advisors for this category are Suzanne Perrault and David Rago; they are listed in the Directory under New Jersey. Unless noted otherwise, all items listed below are marked and in the matt glaze.

Bowl, bl, flared rim, mk, sm flaw, 3¼x8¼" 180.00
Bowl, lotus w/raised leaves, bl, flared rim, 8½" 235.00
Bowl vase, yel, flared cylinder, 3½x5½" 720.00
Chamberstick, gr, 3 loop hdls, label, 5" 265.00
Jar, dk gr speckled, stilt pulls to lid, 6x4"..................................1,680.00
Plaque, evergreens, ochre/gr/turq/indigo, 10x6"+Arts & Crafts fr ... 66,000.00
Teapot, geometric band, blk on dk gr, AEB/HT, low tab hdl, 6x6".....9,000.00

Teapot, geometrics, black on dark green, ship stamp and AEB/HT, 6x6", $9,000.00. (Photo courtesy David Rago Auctions)

Tile, sailboat in calm water, 3 tones of bl-gray, 6¼" 4,200.00
Tile, squirrel w/acorn, brn/gr on mustard, 6" 4,500.00
Vase, amber mottle, spherical, invt rim, A Baggs, 3½x2¼" 600.00
Vase, bl w/purple highlights, swollen cylinder, 5¼" 420.00
Vase, bl-gray, swollen cylinder, 5".. 340.00
Vase, butterflies/flowers, mc on mustard, bbl shape, 4½x4", NM ...5,100.00
Vase, carnations (long stems), blk on dk gr, H Tutt, 4½x3½"....3,900.00
Vase, cats stalking, lt bl on dk bl, invt rim, ca 1907, 7½x10"..10,500.00
Vase, dk bl, squat, 2½x5" 300.00
Vase, floral, bl & brn on gr, H Tutt, rstr chps, 5¼x6½" 3,900.00

Vase, floral, bl on gray speckled, H Tutt, 8¾x4" 2,000.00
Vase, floral, indigo on gray, cylindrical, experimental, 2" 1,650.00
Vase, floral band on gr, wide mouth, H Tutt/A Baggs, 4⅜" 2,500.00
Vase, foliage, dk brn on gr, 5¼x3½", NM 1,560.00
Vase, foliage (at neck) on gr, 4x4¼" 2,640.00

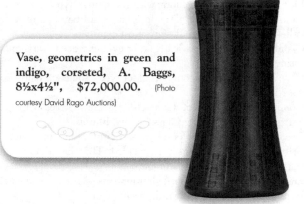

Vase, geometrics in green and indigo, corseted, A. Baggs, 8½x4½", $72,000.00. (Photo courtesy David Rago Auctions)

Vase, gr, cylindrical, 3½x2¼" 325.00
Vase, gr textured, flaring at rim, 7½" 420.00
Vase, gr w/textured finish, swollen cylinder, paper label, 6⅞"....1,500.00
Vase, grapevine band, gr/brn on mustard, 5x3¼" 1,800.00

Vase, grapevines carved in purple and green, yellow ground, 5", $2,530.00. (Photo courtesy David Rago Auctions)

Vase, grapevines, long parallel stems, 5-color, cylindrical, HT, 5"...5,875.00
Vase, gray w/bl int, ovoid, 9x5", NM.. 325.00
Vase, indigo speckled, baluster form, 9x5" 840.00
Vase, lav-gray, ovoid w/sm flared rim, nick, 6x5¼" 390.00
Vase, leaves, brn on speckled burnt sienna, 6½" 7,200.00
Vase, leaves on gr, ship mk/MT, 3¾x4¼" 2,760.00
Vase, oatmeal w/striations, swollen cylinder, flaw, 3¼" 250.00
Vase, ochre, curdled/speckled squat/integral hdls, 2½" 540.00
Vase, salmon pk, swollen cylinder, 7" 360.00
Vase, trees on dk bl, H Tutt, tall cylinder, 9¼x5".......................9,000.00
Vase, wisteria branches, brn on lt brn, H Tutt, 7x5" 2,400.00
Wall pocket, lovebirds on branch, speckled gr/red on indigo, 5x7" ..2,250.00

Marbles

Marbles have been popular with children since the mid-1800s. They've been made in many types from a variety of materials. Among some of the first glass items to be produced, the earliest marbles were made from a solid glass rod broken into sections of the proper length which were placed in a tray of sand and charcoal and returned to the fire. As they were reheated, the trays were constantly agitated until the marbles were completely round. Other marbles were made of china, pottery, steel, and natural stones. Below is a listing of the various types, along with a brief description of each.

Agates: stone marbles of many different colors — bands of color alternating with white usually encircle the marble; most are translucent.

Ballot Box: handmade (with pontils), opaque white or black, used in lodge elections.

Bloodstone: green chalcedony with red spots, a type of quartz.

China: with or without glaze, in a variety of hand-painted designs — parallel bands or bull's-eye designs most common.

Clambroth: opaque glass with outer evenly spaced swirls of one or alternating colors.

Clay: one of the most common older types; some are painted while others are not.

Comic Strip: a series of 12 machine-made marbles with faces of comic strip characters, Peltier Glass Factory, Illinois.

Crockery: sometimes referred to as Benningtons; most are either blue or brown, although some are speckled. The clay is shaped into a sphere, then coated with glaze and fired.

End of the Day: single-pontil glass marbles — the colored part often appears as a multicolored blob or mushroom cloud.

Goldstone: clear glass completely filled with copper flakes that have turned gold-colored from the heat of the manufacturing process.

Indian Swirls: usually black glass with a colored swirl appearing on the outside next to the surface, often irregular.

Latticinio Core Swirls: double-pontil marble with an inner area with net-like effects of swirls coming up around the center.

Lutz Type: glass with colored or clear bands alternating with bands which contain copper flecks.

Micas: clear or colored glass with mica flecks which reflect as silver dots when marble is turned. Red is rare.

Onionskin: spiral type which are solidly colored instead of having individual ribbons or threads, multicolored.

Peppermint Swirls: made of white opaque glass with alternating blue and red outer swirls.

Ribbon Core Swirls: double-pontil marble — center shaped like a ribbon with swirls that come up around the middle.

Rose Quartz: stone marble, usually pink in color, often with fractures inside and on outer surface.

Solid Core Swirls: double-pontil marble — middle is solid with swirls coming up around the core.

Steelies: hollow steel spheres marked with a cross where the steel was bent together to form the ball.

Sulfides: generally made of clear glass with figures inside. Rarer types have colored figures or colored glass.

Tiger Eye: stone marble of golden quartz with inclusions of asbestos, dark brown with gold highlights.

Vaseline: machine-made of yellowish-green glass with small bubbles.

Prices listed below are for marbles in near-mint condition unless noted otherwise. Polished marbles have greatly reduced values. For a more thorough study of the subject, we recommend *Antique and Collectible Marbles, 3rd Edition*, and *Big Book of Marbles, Third Edition*, both by Everett Grist (published by Collector Books); you will find his address in the Directory under Tennessee.

Akro Agate, bl slag, ½-1" 1.00
Akro Agate, Carnelian oxblood, ½-1" 175.00
Akro Agate, corkscrew, ½-1" 2.00
Akro Agate, limeade corkscrew, ½-1" 30.00
Akro Agate, Royal (patched opaque on colored base), ⅝-1", from $2 to 10.00
Akro Agate, translucent oxblood swirl, ⅝-¾", from $75 to 250.00
Akro Agate, wht opaque w/transparent colored corkscrew 20.00
Akro Agate, 3-colored corkscrew, from $10 to 35.00
Banded Opaque, gr w/red bands, wht & bl streaks, 1¾", EX 160.00
Banded Swirl, wht opaque w/red & bl swirls, 1¾" 2,200.00
Blk opaque w/4 bright bl bands, end-of-day clambroth, ⅝" 360.00
China, decorated, HP over glaze for 2nd firing, ⅝" 100.00
China, decorated, unglazed, geometrics & flowers, ¾" 125.00
Christensen Agate, blk opaque base w/orange & yel triangular patch 250.00
Christensen Agate, clear Cobra, ⅝", NM+ 145.00
Christianson Agate, yel/gr/grn swirl w/single seam, 11/16" 240.00
Clay, common, ⅝" .... .50
Clay, common, 1¾" 5.00
Clear w/goldstone flakes, wht & yel spiral bands, ⅝" 60.00
Clear w/red & gr core, wht & gold flake outer bands, ⅝" 180.00
Comic, Andy Gump, 11/16", M 85.00
Comic, Betty Boop, 11/16", M 275.00
Comic, Herbie, 11/16", M 100.00
Comic, Little Orphan Annie, 11/16", M 100.00

Comic, Moon Mullins, 11/16", NM, $325.00.
(Photo courtesy Morphy Auctions)

Comic, Sandy, 11/16", M 90.00
Comic, Smitty, 11/16", M 275.00
Indian Swirl, bl/yel/red, sm air blow-out, 13/16" 275.00
Indian Swirl, blk w/earth-toned swirls, ⅝" 150.00
Jackson, 2-color swirl 2.00
Jackson, 3-color swirl, from $2 to 25.00
Joseph Swirl, bright bl w/red strands, ⅝" 300.00
Lutz, blk opaque w/yel bands, ⅞" 480.00
Lutz, butterscotch w/lt bl bands, ¾" 360.00
Lutz type, bl opaque w/gold swirl & wht borders, ⅝" 350.00
Lutz type, clear w/gold swirls, bl & wht borders, ⅝" 125.00
Lutz type, coreless w/lt gr bands, ⅞" 210.00
Lutz type, orange banded, ⅞" 265.00
Lutz type, red ribbon core, single gold swirl w/wht border, ⅝" 300.00
Lutz type, yel bands, 1⅛" 420.00
Marble King, gr & wht cat eye 10.00
Marble King, mc rainbow 4.00
Marble King, watermelon 400.00
Millefiori flowers, tight pattern, pontil mk, 1½", EX 575.00
Onion Swirl, bl/wht/orange panels, 2 5/16" 330.00
Onionskin, clear/yel/red/wht/gr alternating core, 1⅝" 295.00
Onionskin, pk w/silver mica, bl & yel spots, 1¾", EX 360.00
Onionskin, red/pk/bl/wht/yel/blk swirled flecks, 1¾" 750.00
Onionskin, yel & red w/mica, 2 7/16", +Lucky Boy bag 660.00
Onionskin, 2 wht panels w/bl streaks & 2 yel w/red streaks, 2¼" 1,125.00
Opaque Swirl, horizontal dbl pk lines, 2¼" 420.00
Opaque Swirl Lutz-type, bl/yel/gr, ¾" 325.00
Peltier Glass, NLR Revel, much aventurine, 11/16", M 200.00
Peppermint Swirl, much mica, ¾" 540.00
Sulfide, baby in basket (Moses in Bulrushes?), 1¾" 800.00
Sulfide, bear, standing, 1 5/16", VG 145.00
Sulfide, bird (baby eagle?) w/stumpy tail, 1¾" 350.00
Sulfide, bird (prairie chicken?), 1¾" 300.00
Sulfide, boy in top hat & dress clothes, gr glass, 1¾" 4,000.00
Sulfide, buffalo, little detail, 1¾" 300.00
Sulfide, crucifix, well centered, 2 3/16" 330.00
Sulfide, dog (Nipper), 1¾", EX 350.00
Sulfide, doves (facing pr), EX details, gr glass, 1¾" 5,000.00
Sulfide, eagle flying, 1 13/16" 265.00

Sulfide, elephant, head erect, 'bang' tail, 1¾" 300.00
Sulfide, elephant standing, sea gr glass, 1¾" 400.00
Sulfide, elephant w/long trunk, 1¼" 140.00
Sulfide, girl sitting in chair, bubble around figure, 1⁹⁄₁₆", VG........ 260.00
Sulfide, gnome, 1½", EX 615.00
Sulfide, Indian head, rare, 1⅛" ....: 240.00
Sulfide, man (politician) standing on stump, 1¼", VG................. 450.00
Sulfide, number 1, fine delineation, 1¾" 400.00
Sulfide, owl w/wings spread, details to feathers, 1¾" 350.00
Sulfide, parrot, 1⅝" 330.00
Sulfide, peacock, tricolor in clear glass, 1¾" 8,000.00
Sulfide, Santa Claus in short coat, 1¾" 1,300.00
Sulfide, sheep, recumbent, 2", EX 88.00
Sulfide, squirrel standing, 1¾", EX 170.00
Swirl, bl/pk/gr w/wht solid core, yel outer bands, 2¹³⁄₁₆" 360.00
Swirl, dbl ribbon red/yel/lt & dk bl/wht/pk core, ⅝" 100.00
Swirl, gr transparent core w/red & wht swirls & yel threads, ⅝" 75.00
Swirl, gr/bl/wht/yel strands, solid core, wht/yel bands, 1⅜" 180.00
Swirl, orange solid core, red & wht outer swirls, ¹³⁄₁₆" 120.00
Swirl, red solid core w/4-color swirls, 2⅝" 910.00
Swirl, transparent swirl ribbon core w/lg core, 1⁹⁄₁₆" 2,500.00

Swirl, tri-color, 2¼",
NM, $635.00. (Photo
courtesy Morphy Auctions)

Swirl, yel/gr/bl/pk, solid wht core, wht outer bands, 1½" 180.00
Swirl/Dbl-Ribbon, pk/bl/wht & pk/yel/gr, yel & wht outer bands, 1¾" ..210.00
Vitro Agate, 3-color helmet type, ea from $3 to 6.00
Wht clambroth w/gr/pk/bl swirls, ⅞" 275.00

Marine Collectibles

Vintage tools used on sea-going vessels, lanterns, clocks, and memorabilia of all types are sought out by those who are interested in preserving the romantic genre that revolves around the life of the sea captains, their boats, and their crews; ports of call; and the lure of far-away islands. See also Steamship Collectibles; Telescopes; Scrimshaw; Tools.

Awl, bone w/fish hdl, circular pewter inlays, 5" 285.00
Binnacle, J Hand, brass, compass by Ritchie, dome top, 1940s, 39x10"..1,500.00
Binnacle, K White, Boston, brass & wood, free standing, 52x34" 1,440.00
Binnacle, Ludolph, teakwood & brass, electric compass light, 61x32" ...840.00
Chest, old gr pnt w/stars, dvtl w/fitted int, becket hdls, 16x37x17"..1,295.00
Chest, orig gr pnt on wood, rope beckets, 19th C, 17x32x17" 425.00
Chest, star/pinwheel inlay, 6-brd, dvtl, till, 16x30x15" 865.00
Chest, teakwood w/ebony/ivory/boxwood star & string inlay, 31"...765.00
Chest, tropical woods w/brass mts/hdls, 3 trays, 19th C, 21x39x21" ..660.00
Chronometer, Hamilton #2E12684, 2-day, 3-part mahog/brass case, 8x8"..1,175.00
Chronometer, McLachland London #326, 2-day, 4" Roman dial, EX..1,650.00
Chronometer, Morris Tobias #809, in 7¼" mahog case w/brass mts ...2,400.00
Chronometer, Richard Hornby & Son #1341, 2-day, 4" dial, 7" ..2,100.00
Chronometer, Ulysse Nardin #4347, 2-day, mahog/brass case, 1947, 7x7"..2,950.00
Chronometer, Ulysse Nardin #5673, in 7½" mahog case w/brass mts ..2,550.00
Chronometer, Whyte Thompson & Co #5330, 2-day, 4" dial, 7", EX..1,800.00
Compass, FW Lincoln Jr, 5½" dia floating card, pnt, in 10" red case..... 1,000.00

Compass, Gyro-Compass Repeater, Sperry Gyroscope...NY #7382, EX ..235.00
Compass, Ritchie #12393, 4" dia liquid card, Pat 1870, mahog case, 7"...150.00
Compass, S Thaxter, floating 6" card w/Am flag, in pine case, 10".....295.00
Harpoon, Arctic-style w/dbl flue, 27½", VG 360.00
Harpoon, toggle; smithy made, orig red pnt traces, 31½" 900.00
Helmet, deep sea diving; AJ Morse #512, 4-light w/tinned surface ..3,000.00

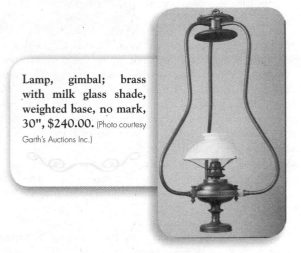

Lamp, gimbal; brass
with milk glass shade,
weighted base, no mark,
30", $240.00. (Photo courtesy
Garth's Auctions Inc.)

Lantern, concave metal fr w/blk pnt, electrified, 1900, 12x12", pr... 150.00
Lantern, Daniel Mahoney & Sons, brass/ribbed glass/red glass int, 26" 330.00
Lantern, signal; brass, unmk, sm dents, 14" 180.00
Lithograph, 2-masted ship in Boston Harbor, dtd 1867, 17x21", +fr..175.00
Log, Aikokuseiki High Speed, 3" enamel dial scaled to 100 miles ..480.00
Marking gauge, cvd whalebone, sailor made, 19th C, 8" 2,450.00
Model, Charles Morgan whaling ship, 29", w/info on orig ship.... 300.00
Model, 3-masted clipper under full sail, in 16x36x25" case.......... 850.00
Octant, Middleton & Griby-Hull, brass w/ivory scales, EX in case .600.00
Octant, Sargent, ebony T-frame, 2-hole peepsite, 1820s, EX in case..800.00

Octant, Spencer, Browning
& Co., London, wood, ivory,
and brass, 1850, in 13x14"
case, $585.00. (Photo courtesy
Skinner Inc. Auctioneers & Appraisers of
Antiques & Fine Art)

Oil on canvas, Am Screw Steamer, A Jacobsen 1889, 23x35"+gesso fr..1,650.00
Oil on canvas, Schooner Edward H Cole, SFM Badger, ca 1900, 18x32"+fr....11,165.00
Porthole, brass w/hinged glass door, ca 1920, 24x27", VG 600.00
Porthole, brass w/hinged glass door, 1940s, 21" dia, VG............... 360.00
Quadrant, FB Roberts, ivory inlays, ca 1800, 12", EX in case....... 720.00
Sextant, box; Stanley, brass, military mks, 1917, screw lid 75.00
Sextant, box; Troughton & Simms, brass, 3", in case 265.00
Sextant, box; W&W Jones, brass, magnifier/mirror/shades, 3", in case ..700.00
Sextant, H Hughes & Son, London, lattice fr on tripod, 19x11", in case..1,950.00
Sextant, McMillan & Talbot, brass, w/mirror/lenses, 9½", in case ..350.00
Sextant, Spencer/Browning, brass, shades & 3 telescopes, 8", in case...765.00
Sextant, Thos Evans Esq London, brass, complete, 10", in case...400.00
Sextant, Troughton & Simms Ltd #7315, bronzed finish, 2½", in case...300.00
Sextant, vernier; Thos Jones, ebony/bone, 10", in mahog case 825.00
Trunk, seaman's; Chinese export, leather covered w/brass tacks, 31", G ..375.00

Wheel, ship's; walnut w/8 spokes & hdls, worn varnish, 44" 315.00
Wheel, ship's; wood w/brass hub & bands, 24" dia 450.00

Martin Bros.

The Martin Bros. were studio potters who worked from 1873 until 1914, first at Fulham and later at London and Southall. There were four brothers, each of whom excelled in their particular area. Robert, known as Wallace, was an experienced stonecarver. He modeled a series of grotesque bird and animal figural caricatures. Walter was the potter, responsible for throwing the larger vases on the wheel, firing the kiln, and mixing the clay. Edwin, an artist of stature, preferred more naturalistic forms of decoration. His work was often incised or had relief designs of seaweed, florals, fish, and birds. The fourth brother, Charles, was their business manager. Their work was incised with their names, place of production, and letters and numbers indicating month and year.

Though figural jars continue to command the higher prices, decorated vases and bowls have increased a great deal in value. Our advisors for this category are Suzanne Perrault and David Rago; they are listed in the Directory under New Jersey.

Bird jar, droopy beak, sleepy eyes, ebony wood base, 1888, 10¼" .. 11,165.00
Bird jar, lg beak, ruffled look to brow, mc w/bl, ca 1900, 10" 7,050.00
Face jug, 2-faced, earth tones, ca 1898, 8" 10,575.00
Jar, grotesque, w/lid, head rstr, 1888, 8x5" 15,600.00
Jardiniere, grotesque storks among plants, ca 1892, 9½" 5,585.00
Jug, fish & vegetation, globular, 1886, 8¼" 5,585.00
Jug, fish & vegetation, Welcome My Friends... at spout, 1887, 15¼".. 12,925.00
Pencil holder, Scotsman, 3½x3" 900.00
Pitcher, Bellarmine figural, brn, 14¼x6¼" 5,100.00
Pitcher, grotesque sea creatures, 1895, rstr glaze flakes, 7x6" 3,480.00
Pitcher, Renaissance glyphs, cobalt & wht, 7x6½" 1,450.00

Spoon warmer, grotesque, cobalt and teal, 8¾x9", $6,600.00. (Photo courtesy David Rago Auctions)

Vase, birds & foliage, brn & bl on tan, #44.4.S2RW, 9¾" 1,550.00
Vase, crabs cvd on amber, disk shape w/integral hdls, 1903, 8x5", EX... 800.00
Vase, dragons on dk brn, 1901, 11½x3¾" 3,600.00
Vase, grotesque sea creatues, gray, amber & bl, 7¼x6" 3,120.00
Vase, orchids/hummingbirds/dragonflies, #10-1898, 9½" 4,200.00
Vase, Renaissance floral, 1999, rstr rim/shoulder, 7¾x3" 1,140.00
Vase, sea creatures in habitat, brn on cream, #7-1907, mini, 2¾"..1,300.00
Vase, thistles on amber, 1905, 10¼x5" 2,880.00

Mary Gregory

Mary Gregory glass, for reasons that remain obscure, is the namesake of a Boston and Sandwich Glass Company employee who worked for the company for only two years in the mid-1800s. Although no evidence actually exists to indicate that glass of this type was even produced there, the fine colored or crystal ware decorated with figures of children in white enamel is commonly referred to as Mary Gregory. The glass, in fact, originated in Europe and was imported into this country where it was copied by several eastern glasshouses. It was popular from the mid-1800s until the turn of the century. It is generally accepted that examples with all-white figures were made in the U.S.A., while gold-trimmed items and those with children having tinted faces or a small amount of color on their clothing are European. Though amethyst is rare, examples in cranberry command the higher prices. Blue ranks next; and green, amber, and clear items are worth the least. Watch for new glass decorated with screen-printed children and a minimum of hand painting. The screen effect is easily detected with a magnifying glass.

Box, sapphire bl, young lady on lid, in rope-twist/4-ftd fr w/hdls, 7" ..230.00
Decanter, amber w/bl hdl & stopper, mc scrolls, sq, 9", +6 cordials..975.00
Humidor, cranberry, colonial man, emb lid mk Darby Silver, 7"..225.00
Jar, cranberry, child on lid, floral on cylinder body, 2¼" H 145.00
Jar, dresser; bl opaque, girl w/flower, brass mts, 1½x2¼" dia.......... 150.00
Pitcher, gr, optic ribs, boy w/anchor, late 19th C, 6"..................... 90.00
Stein, amber, w/child, optic ribbed, pewter/glass flip lid, 4"........... 75.00
Tumbler, bl, boy (girl), amber ft, ca 1880, 6¼", pr 180.00
Vase, amethyst, girl w/butterfly net, ftd, 19th C, 10½" 150.00
Vase, cranberry, girl at water trough, gilt traces, baluster, 8", pr ... 540.00
Vase, cranberry opal, sprite dancing/butterfly, 4 clear ft, 9½" 1,020.00
Vase, gr, boy w/flower, slim, 9½x2¾" 90.00
Vase, gray, girl holding fishing line, gold rim & ft, 13", NM......... 390.00

Mason's Ironstone

In 1813 Charles J. Mason was granted a patent for a process said to 'improve the quality of English porcelain.' The new type of ware was in fact ironstone which Mason decorated with colorful florals and scenics, some of which reflected the Oriental taste. Although his business failed for a short time in the late 1840s, Mason re-established himself and continued to produce dinnerware, tea services, and ornamental pieces until about 1852, at which time the pottery was sold to Francis Morley. Ten years later, Geo. L. and Taylor Ashworth became owners. Both Morley and the Ashworths not only used Mason's molds and patterns but often his mark as well. Because the quality and the workmanship of the later wares do not compare with Mason's earlier product, collectors should take care to distinguish one from the other. Consult a good book on marks to be sure. The Wedgwood Company now owns the rights to the Mason patterns.

American Marine, tureen, brn, slotted lid, hdls, early mk, 5x12".. 595.00
Bamboo, jug, mc, octagonal, ca 1818, child sz, 2¾", NM 125.00
Bandana, mug, mc, ca 1840, 4¾x3½", NM 250.00
Black Chinese, cup & saucer, 2¼", 5¼".................................... 38.00
Black Chinese, washbowl & pitcher, 1850s, 15¾", 12½" 235.00
Colored Pagoda, chamber pot, mc, ca 1830, 10½" 200.00
Colored Pheasants, jug, mc, cobalt/gold serpent hdl, 1840s, 4½" .. 275.00
Colored Pheasants, vase, mc, sq w/bulbous midsection, 1840s, 7x3⅛"..175.00
Double Landscape, compote, mc, ca 1862, 5¾x10½x4" 325.00
Floral Basket & Butterfly, dish, mc, ca 1862, 10⅛x9⅛", EX 125.00
Fruit Basket, toast rack, mc, pre-1923 mk 55.00
Japan, dish, mc, scalloped, emb leaf hdls, ca 1818, 9½" L............. 300.00
Japan, jug, mc, octagonal, branch hdl, ca 1818, 5¼x5" 375.00
Japan, mug, mc, ca 1818, 4⅛x5½", NM 275.00
Mandalay, plate, mc, ca 1813-25, 8½".. 30.00
Orange Leaf, dish, mc w/emb swags & gold o/l, 1913-25, 11⅛" L ...325.00
Orange Leaf, plate, mc w/gold o/l, paneled border, 1813-25, 8½"....150.00
Pagoda, chamber pot, mc, serpent hdl, ca 1840, 5¾x10¼"........... 225.00
Strathmore, bowl, mc, Pat mk, 2½x9½" 110.00

Strathmore, cake plate, mc, sq, 1938 mk, 9¼" 75.00
Vase Japanned, plate, mc, scalloped, ca 1840, 8¼", 4 for 175.00
Vista, bowl, brn, oval, ca 1920, 8½x6½" 50.00
Vista, bowl, nesting; red, octagonal, 1925-30 mk, 3¼x6½" 125.00
Vista, bowl, red, Pat mk, 10" 100.00
Vista, butter dish, red, rectangular, crown mk, 7⅛" 165.00
Vista, coffeepot, red, Pat mk, 9x8" 65.00
Vista, dish, brn, sq, Pat mk, 1¼x4¼" 25.00
Vista, egg cup, dbl; red, 1890-1900 .... 38.00
Vista, jug, hydra; brn, ca 1890s mk, 4½" 50.00
Vista, jug, hydra; red, 1900-20s, 6" 95.00
Vista, mayonnaise, red, early mk, w/liner 125.00
Vista, pitcher, bl, 1925-30 mk, 7" 75.00
Vista, plate, brn, 1890-1900 mk, 7¾" 25.00
Vista, platter, brn, crown mk, 15½x12½" 100.00
Vista, platter, red, hdls, Pat mk, 11x9¼" 60.00
Vista, platter, red, late 1900s, rpr, 15x12¼" 175.00
Vista, tureen, red, Pat mk, 10½x14", +lid & ladle 450.00
Watteau, jug, milk; brn, ca 1900-20, 3½" 60.00
Willow, jug, Pat mk, 6½" 125.00

Massier, Clement

The Massier family's work in ceramics goes back in France to the middle eighteenth century. Clement, his brother Delphin, and their cousin Jerome, brought about a renaissance of the ceramics industry in Vallauris, in the south of France. Clement apprenticed and worked under his father until his father's death, after which he set up his own pottery in nearby Golfe-Juan. Artistic director Lucien Levey-Dhurmer introduced Massier to Spanish iridescent glazes in 1887; and through the use of bronze, brass, and gold salts, Massier developed his own. He won the pottery an award at the Paris Exposition Universelle in 1889.

Jacques Sicard, one of his artists, took the glaze formula with him to the Weller Pottery in Zanesville, Ohio, closely replicating the overall floral patterns he had learned in France. This particular type of glaze proved difficult to fire on both continents, seldom yielding the perfectly crisp decoration and smooth lustre desired. Perfectly fired pieces sell quickly and for a premium.

Bowl, cornflowers on pale yel, 5-hdld, CM, 3½x5⅛" 300.00
Bowl, volcano scene, purple/yel/brn/gr lustre, CM, 1900, 13" ... 2,400.00
Vase, Afghan, mc lustre, CM, ca 1890, 20" 3,600.00
Vase, appl silver leafy vines mts on lustre, 5⅛" 2,400.00
Vase, butterflies, gold on brn, CM, ca 1900, 9¾" 800.00
Vase, chestnuts/leaves/branches on lustre, shouldered, CM, 12" ... 5,500.00

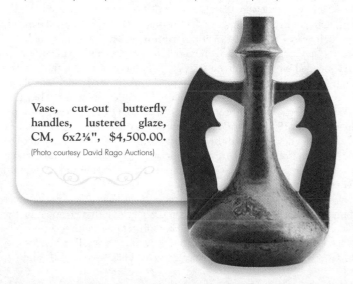

Vase, cut-out butterfly handles, lustered glaze, CM, 6x2¼", $4,500.00. (Photo courtesy David Rago Auctions)

Vase, floral, gold/purple/gr lustre, stick neck, sm rstr, CM, 12" 550.00
Vase, floral, 4-color w/lustre, conical, rpr, CM, 6⅜" 400.00
Vase, lake scene, earthy tones, bulbous, CM, 8¼x8½" 3,600.00
Vase, organic form w/emb nude, mc irid, CM, 8x12" 4,200.00

Match Holders

John Walker, an English chemist, invented the match more than 100 years ago, quite by accident. Walker was working with a mixture of potash and antimony, hoping to make a combustible that could be used to fire guns. The mixture adhered to the end of the wooden stick he had used for stirring. As he tried to remove it by scraping the stick on the stone floor, it burst into flames. The invention of the match was only a step away! From that time to the present, match holders have been made in amusing figural forms as well as simple utilitarian styles and in a wide range of materials. Both table-top and wall-hanging models were made — all designed to keep matches conveniently at hand. The prices in this category are very volatile due to increased interest in this field and the fact that so many can be classified as a cross or dual collectible. Caution: As prices for originals continue to climb, so do the number of reproductions. Know your dealer. See also Advertising.

Advertising, American Steel Farm Fences, litho tin, 5x3½", VG .. 95.00
Advertising, JH Leshler Tailors, CI turtle, 1½x5½x3" 140.00
Advertising, Lyell...Fertilizers, CI bag form on ashtray base, 6x6" .. 40.00

Advertising, Vulcan Plow Co., Hagerstown Maryland, 8", EX, $750.00. (Photo courtesy Morphy Auctions)

Brass, Apollo-like image in relief, w/striker, 5x4x2" 40.00
Bronze, man seated on rim of staved bbl, on sq base, 6½" 90.00
CI, alligator w/hinged compartment on bk, 8½" L 90.00
CI, log cabin form, 2½x4" 135.00
CI, Pilgrim's face, emb wheat shocks at sides, wall mt, 6x4½x2" 40.00
CI, Pioneers, man w/gun stands on 8-sided tray, leans on cup, 5" .. 80.00
CI, Victorian styling w/lift top, Parker Pat design, 1870s, 6x4" 200.00
Majolica, tan w/emb Nouveau masks/scrolls, w/8" candleholder on tray .. 50.00
NP CI, lady's boot, striker at front of base, 5½x4½x3", EX 50.00
Porc, devil's head figural, red, Germany, 2" 120.00
Pot metal, Gordon bust figural, striker on bk, early 1900s, 5", EX ... 130.00
Pottery, pig at dressing table w/mirror, wht/gold, Staffordshire, 5" 45.00

Match Safes

Before the invention of the safety match in 1855, matches were carried in small pocket-sized containers because they ignited so easily. Aptly called match safes, these containers were used extensively until about 1920, when cigarette lighters became widely available. Some incorporated added features (hidden compartments, cigar cutters, etc.), some were figural, and others were used by retail companies as advertising giveaways. They were made from every type of material, but silver-plated styles abound. Both the advertising and common silver-plated cases generally fall in the $50.00 to $100.00 price range.

Beware of reproductions and fakes; there are many currently on the market. Know your dealer. See also Advertising.

Advertising, figural pnt/CI fly, Use Insectolene..., 4½", EX 210.00
Advertising, Vulcanite Portland Cement Co, celluloid trim, sales chart..450.00
Brass, coiled snake w/glass eyes, 1¾" 720.00
Brass, emb Nouveau floral, 2⅞x½" 60.00
Brass, man riding horse in relief, ca 1890-1910, 3x1½" 75.00
Brass, owl form w/bl eyes, 2½" 120.00
Celluloid, domino form, blk/wht 180.00
Enamel, dog's portrait on silver, match-striker base, 2¼x1¾" 425.00
EPNS, enameled English crest... 85.00
German silver, Nouveau motif w/emb & scalloped radiating devices ..50.00
German silver, sq w/emb diagonals under rococo scroll device 65.00
Gold (14k), simple vining floral, oval monogram reserve............. 660.00
Metal/wood, pistol form w/cigar cutter, ca 1890, 4¾" L................ 450.00
Nickel on brass, book form w/Isle of Man symbol, coin holder 60.00

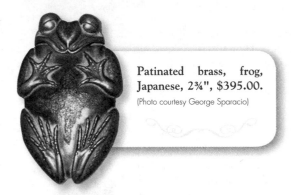

Patinated brass, frog, Japanese, 2¾", $395.00.

(Photo courtesy George Sparacio)

Silver, Nouveau cherubs in relief, Sterling, 2⅝x1⅝".................... 300.00
Silver, Nouveau lady's head (repousse), Sterling, 2⅝x1¾" 500.00
Silver, rococo border, beaded oval center, Sterling, #260, VG 160.00
Souvenir, Reading PA: tower on Mt Penn, bk: pagoda, metal w/photo..270.00
SP, advertising, emb hunting scene, ca 1910, 2¾x1½".................... 35.00
Stering, 4 cherubs pulling wishbone, 5th on hinged lid, monogram ..360.00
Sterling, cherub resting on garden bench, scrollwork border, monogram ..660.00
Sterling, floral in high relief.. 180.00
Sterling, leafage emb, 'chain' device at sides of kidney shape, Gorham...1,320.00
Sterling, Nouveau maid's head, entwining vines/florals, 2⅝" 600.00
Sterling, nude boy w/pipe, rococo scrolls/floral, monogram.......... 450.00
Sterling, nude maid, repousse scene, rococo shield form, monogram ..385.00
Sterling, quail eng on oval, monogram 180.00
Sterling, rococo border, monogram in lg shaped reserve, dtd 1917...165.00
Sterling, rococo scrolls, fan devices, R&R 85.00
Sterling, 2 cherubs/rococo scrolls, Unger Bros #2563 .... 300.00

Mauchline Ware

Mauchline ware is the generic name for small, well-made, and useful wooden souvenirs and giftware from Mauchline, Scotland, and nearby locations. It was made from the early ninteenth century into the 1930s. Snuff boxes were among the earliest items, and tea caddies soon followed. From the 1830s on, needlework, stationery, domestic and cosmetic items were made by the thousands. Today, needlework items are the most plentiful and range from boxes of all sizes made to hold supplies to tiny bodkins and buttons. Napkin rings, egg cups, vases, and bowls are just a few of the domestic items available.

The wood most commonly used in the production of Mauchline ware was sycamore. Finishes vary. Early items were hand decorated with colored paints or pen and ink. By the 1850s, perhaps even earlier, transferware was produced, decorated with views associated with the place of purchase. These souvenir items were avidly bought by travelers for themselves as well as for gifts. Major exhibitions and royal occasions were also represented on transferware. An alternative decorating process was initiated during the mid-1860s whereby actual photos replaced the transfers. Because they were finished with multiple layers of varnish, many examples found today are still in excellent condition.

Tartan ware's distinctive decoration was originally hand painted directly on the wood with inks, but in the 1840s machine-made paper in authentic Tartan designs became available. Except for the smallest items, each piece was stamped with the Tartan name. The Tartan decoration was applied to virtually the entire range of Mauchline ware, and because it was favored by Queen Victoria, it became widely popular. Collectors still value Tartan ware above other types of decoration, with transferware being their second choice. Other types of Mauchline decorations include Fern ware and Black Lacquer with floral or transfer decorations.

When cleaning any Mauchline item, extreme care should be used to avoid damaging the finish. Mauchline ware has been reproduced for at least 25 years, especially some of the more popular pieces and finishes. Collectors should study the older items for comparison and to learn about the decorating and manufacturing processes.

Bottle, Robert Burns portrait, trn w/cork top & screw lid 160.00
Bowl, Ripley's Point, Cloverdale-on-the-Lake George, 1½x3" 30.00
Box, Burns Monument, book form, for playing cards...................... 85.00
Box, Fern Ware, ca 1875, 1⅝x4⅜x3½".. 160.00
Box, Mountain House, Catskills Mtn, NY, 1894, ¾x1⅞" dia 145.00
Box, Tartan ware, McIntosh plaid, 3 cards on lid, 2-compartment.....165.00
Clock bank, Burns Cottage/poem, 4½x3x2½"................................ 125.00
Egg cup, Tartan ware, Stuart, blk ft, w/orig bone spoon............... 310.00
Pincushion, Betsi River, Frankfort MI, sliding top, 2x3½x2½"....... 40.00
Pincushion, Tartan ware, ca 1875, 1⅝" dia 85.00
Saucepan, Burns Monument, w/lid, 1¾x4" 110.00
Stamp box, Plymouth Rock, hinged lid, 1¼x2¾x1¾"..................... 30.00
Stamp box, Tartan ware, Stuart, 2¼x1¼" 315.00
Tray, State Dept Building, Washington,½x3¼"................................ 25.00
Tumbler, Mountain Home, Catskill Mtn NY, 2¼x2"..................... 115.00

McCoy

The third generation McCoy potter in the Roseville, Ohio, area was Nelson, who with the aid of his father, J. W., established the Nelson McCoy Sanitary Stoneware Company in 1910. They manufactured churns, jars, jugs, poultry fountains, and foot warmers. By 1925 they had expanded their wares to include majolica jardinieres and pedestals, umbrella stands, and cuspidors, and an embossed line of vases and small jardinieres in a blended brown and green matt glaze. From the late '20s through the mid-'40s, a utilitarian stoneware was produced, some of which was glazed in the soft blue and white so popular with collectors today. They also used a dark brown mahogany color and a medium to dark green, both in a high gloss. In 1933 the firm became known as the Nelson McCoy Pottery Company. They expanded their facilities in 1940 and began to make the novelty artware, cookie jars, and dinnerware that today are synonymous with 'McCoy.' More than 200 cookie jars of every theme and description were produced.

More than a dozen different marks have been used by the company; nearly all incorporate the name 'McCoy,' although some of the older items were marked 'NM USA.' For further information consult *The Collector's Encyclopedia of McCoy Pottery* by Sharon and Bob Huxford; or *McCoy Pottery Collector's Reference & Value Guide, Vols. I, II, and III,* by Margaret Hanson, Craig Nissen, and Bob Hanson (all published by Collector Books). Also available is *Sanfords Guide to McCoy Pottery* by Martha and Steve Sanford. (Mr. Sanford is listed in the Directory under California.)

Alert! Stimulated by the high prices commanded by desirable cookie jars, a broad spectrum of 'new' cookie jars have flooded the marketplace in three categories: 1) Manufacturers have expanded their lines with exciting new designs to attract the collector market. 2) Limited editions and artist-designed jars have proliferated. 3) Reproductions, signed and unsigned, have pervaded the market, creating uncertainty among new collectors and inexperienced dealers. After McCoy closed its doors in the late 1980s, an entrepreneur in Tennessee tried (and succeeded for nearly a decade) to adopt the McCoy Pottery name and mark. This company reproduced old McCoy designs as well as some classic designs of other defunct American potteries, signing their wares 'McCoy' with a mark which very closely approximated the old McCoy mark. Legal action finally put a stop to this practice, though since then they have used other fraudulent marks as well: Brush-McCoy (the compound name was never used on Brush cookie jars) and B.J. Hull.

Still under pressure from Internet exposure and the effects of a slow economy, the cookie jar market remains soft. High-end cookie jars are often slow to sell. Our advisor for McCoy cookie jars is Judy Posner; she is listed in the Directory under Florida.

Cookie Jars

Animal Crackers	100.00
Apollo Age	500.00
Apple, 1950-64	50.00
Apples on Basketweave	70.00
Asparagus	50.00
Astronauts	500.00
Bananas	95.00

Barnum's Animals, $150.00.

Barrel, Cookies sign on lid	75.00
Baseball Boy	95.00
Basket of Eggs	40.00
Basket of Potatoes	40.00
Bear, cookie in vest, no 'Cookies'	85.00
Betsy Baker (+)	95.00
Black Kettle, w/immovable bail, HP flowers	40.00
Black Lantern	65.00
Blue Willow Pitcher	55.00
Bobby Baker	65.00
Bugs Bunny	125.00
Burlap Bag, red bird on lid	50.00
Caboose	95.00
Cat on Coal Scuttle	125.00
Chairman of the Board (+)	550.00

Chef Head	125.00
Chilly Willy	65.00
Chipmunk	125.00
Christmas Tree	350.00
Churn, 2 bands	35.00
Circus Horse, blk	150.00
Clown Bust (+)	75.00
Clown in Barrel, yel, bl or gr	85.00
Clyde Dog	95.00
Coalby Cat	195.00
Coca-Cola Can	75.00
Coca-Cola Jug	55.00
Coffee Grinder	45.00
Coffee Mug	45.00
Colonial Fireplace	85.00
Cookie Bank, 1961	125.00
Cookie Barrel, from $35 to	45.00
Cookie Boy	225.00
Cookie Cabin	80.00
Cookie Jug, dbl loop	35.00
Cookie Jug, single loop, 2-tone gr rope	35.00
Cookie Jug, w/cork stopper, brn & wht	40.00
Cookie Log, squirrel finial	45.00
Cookie Mug	45.00
Cookie Pot, 1964	40.00
Cookie Safe	45.00
Cookstove, blk or wht	35.00
Corn, row of standing ears, yel or wht, 1977	85.00
Corn, single ear	150.00
Covered Wagon	95.00
Cylinder, w/red flowers	45.00
Dalmatians in Rocking Chair (+)	150.00
Davy Crockett (+)	300.00
Dog in Doghouse	150.00
Dog on Basketweave	75.00
Drum, red	90.00
Duck on Basketweave	75.00
Dutch Boy	65.00
Dutch Girl, boy on reverse, rare	250.00
Dutch Treat Barn	50.00
Eagle on Basket, from $35 to	50.00
Early American Chest (Chiffoniere)	65.00
Elephant	150.00
Elephant w/Split Trunk, rare, minimum value	200.00
Engine, blk	125.00
Flowerpot, plastic flower on top	350.00
Football Boy (+)	125.00
Forbidden Fruit	90.00
Fortune Cookies	50.00
Freddy Gleep (+), minimum value	350.00
Friendship 7	125.00
Frog on Stump	75.00
Frontier Family	55.00
Fruit in Bushel Basket	65.00
Gingerbread Boy	75.00
Globe	195.00
Grandfather Clock	75.00
Granny	95.00
Hamm's Bear (+)	175.00
Happy Face	80.00
Hen on Nest	95.00
Hillbilly Bear, rare, minimum value (+)	900.00
Hobby Horse, brn underglaze (+)	150.00
Hocus Rabbit	45.00

Honey Bear, rustic glaze	80.00
Hot Air Balloon	40.00
Ice Cream Cone	45.00
Indian, brn (+)	250.00
Indian, majolica	350.00
Jack-O'-Lantern	400.00
Kangaroo, bl	250.00
Keebler Tree House	70.00
Kettle, bronze, 1961	40.00
Kissing Penguins	75.00
Kitten on Basketweave	90.00
Kittens (2) on Low Basket	600.00
Kittens on Ball of Yarn	85.00
Koala Bear	85.00
Kookie Kettle, blk	35.00
Lamb on Basketweave	90.00
Lemon	75.00
Leprechaun, minimum value (+)	1,800.00
Liberty Bell	75.00
Little Clown	75.00
Lollipops	80.00
Mac Dog	95.00
Mammy, Cookies on base, wht w/cold pnt (+)	150.00
Mammy w/Cauliflower, G pnt, minimum value (+)	1,100.00
Milk Can, Spirit of '76	45.00
Modern	65.00
Monk	50.00
Mother Goose	95.00
Mouse on Clock	40.00
Mr & Mrs Owl	90.00
Mushroom on Stump	55.00
Nursery, decal of Humpty Dumpty, from $70 to	80.00
Oaken Bucket, from $25 to	45.00
Orange	55.00
Owl, brn	70.00
Pear, 1952	85.00
Pears on Basketweave	70.00
Penguin, yel or aqua	95.00
Pepper, yel	40.00
Picnic Basket	75.00
Pig, winking	250.00
Pine Cones on Basketweave	70.00
Pineapple	80.00
Pineapple, Modern	90.00
Pirate's Chest	95.00
Popeye, cylinder	150.00
Potbelly Stove, blk	30.00
Puppy, w/sign	85.00
Quaker Oats, rare, minimum value	500.00
Raggedy Ann	110.00
Red Barn, cow in door, rare, minimum value	150.00
Rooster, wht, 1970-1974	60.00
Rooster, 1955-57	95.00
Round w/HP Leaves	40.00
Sad Clown	85.00
Snoopy on Doghouse (+), mk United Features Syndicate	125.00
Snow Bear	75.00
Spaniel in Doghouse, bird finial	175.00
Stagecoach, minimum value	650.00
Strawberry, 1955-57	65.00
Strawberry, 1971-75	45.00
Teapot, 1972	60.00
Tepee, slant top	250.00
Tepee, str top (+)	200.00

Thinking Puppy, #0272	40.00
Tilt Pitcher, blk w/roses	50.00
Timmy Tortoise	45.00
Tomato	60.00
Touring Car	75.00
Traffic Light	50.00
Tudor Cookie House	95.00
Tulip on Flowerpot	100.00
Turkey, gr, rare color	200.00
Turkey, natural colors	200.00
Upside Down Bear, panda	50.00
WC Fields	125.00
Wedding Jar	90.00
Windmill	100.00
Wishing Well	40.00
Woodsy Owl	150.00
Wren House, side lid	125.00
Yellow Mouse (head)	45.00
Yosemite Sam, cylinder	125.00

Miscellaneous

Beverage server, Brocade, 1956, on stand, from $60 to	80.00
Bookends, Bird, pastel bl, 1940s, 6", from $175 to	250.00
Candy boat, Gondola, Sunburst Gold, 3½x11½", from $40 to	50.00
Dripolator coffee maker, 3-pc, 1943, 7", from $50 to	60.00
Ferner, Butterfly, pastel, braided rim, 3½x9", from $250 to	300.00
Ferner, Hobnail, pastel matt, 1940s, 5½", from $25 to	35.00
Flower holder, Pigeon, yel or rose, 4x3½", from $100 to	125.00
Flowerpot, Hobnail, pastel matt, 1940s, 5", from $40 to	50.00
Jardiniere, Basketweave, chartreuse or yel, 1950s, 6", from $40 to	50.00
Jardiniere, Basketweave, gr or wht, 7½", from $60 to	75.00
Jardiniere, Butterfly, coral, 3½", from $50 to	60.00
Jardiniere, Fish, brn spray, 1958, 7½", from $300 to	400.00
Jardiniere & ped, Berries & Leaves, Onyx, brn, 7", 6½", $250 to	275.00
Lamp, Model-A pick-up truck, Sunburst Gold, 1956, from $85 to	100.00
Paperweight, Football, gold trim, 1940s, scarce, from $100 to	150.00
Pitcher, ball jug, yel or wht, 1940s, 7", from $35 to	50.00
Planter, Basket, ivory & gr, 1957, 5¼x9", from $40 to	50.00
Planter, Bird of Paradise, pk w/gold trim, 1946, 4½x12½", $65 to	80.00
Planter, Clown & Pig, wht w/mc details, 1951, 8½", from $80 to	100.00
Planter, Football, antiqued finish, 1957, 4½x7", from $75 to	100.00

Planter, Frog With Umbrella, ca 1954, 6½x7½", from $125.00 to $175.00.

(Photo courtesy Bill and Betty Newbound)

Planter, Kitten, yarn ball & basket beside, pastel, 6", from $50 to	60.00
Planter, Lamb, alphabet block at ft, cold-pnt details, 1954, 4½x5"	75.00
Planter, Mary Ann Shoe, pastel, 1940s, 5" L, from $25 to	40.00
Planter, Panther, blk, gr or yel, 1950, 5½x16", from $40 to	50.00
Planter, Poodle, pk or lime gr, 1956, 7½x7½", from $60 to	75.00
Planter, Rabbit & Stump, yel & purple, from $100 to	150.00
Planter, Shell, spiky, pastel matt, 1940s, 7½x5½", from $50 to	60.00
Planter, Stork, baby in bag, gr, NM mk, 1940s, rare, 7", minimum	1,500.00

Planter, Swan, Sunburst gold w/pk int, 4½x6", from $65 to 80.00
Planter, Wild Rose, lav, yel, bl or pk, 1952, 3½x8", from $40 to 50.00
Planter, Zebra, blk & wht, 1956, 6½x8½", from $650 to 800.00
Planting vase, Shell, wht matt, 1941, 6", from $25 to 35.00
Strawberry jar, maroon, brn or gr, w/3 chains, 1953, 6x7", $40 to.. 45.00
Sugar bowl, Grecian Line, w/lid, 1956, 4½", from $35 to 45.00
Teapot, Daisy, shaded brn/gr/wht, 1940s, from $40 to 50.00
Vase, Chrysanthemum, pk or yel, 1950, 8", from $110 to............. 140.00
Vase, Contrasting Leaf, chartreuse, 1955, 9", from $175 to......... 225.00
Vase, Double Tulip, wht w/pk decor, 1948, 8", from $75 to.......... 100.00
Vase, Grape, bl & yel (rare), 1951, 9", from $200 to 300.00
Vase, Heart, variety of colors, 1940s, 6", from $60 to 75.00
Vase, Magnolia, pk tint w/gr leaves, 1953, 8¼", from $160 to...... 190.00
Vase, Parrot, brn tones, 1940s, 7½", from $50 to 80.00
Vase, Rustic, emb grapes, bl, turq or yel, 8", from $25 to............... 40.00
Vase, Sunflower, yel, gr or chartreuse, 1954, 9", from $40 to.......... 60.00
Wall pocket, Lady w/Bonnet, EX/NM cold pnt, from $50 to 60.00
Wall pocket, Leaves & Berries, cobalt (scarce color), from $250 to...300.00
Wall pocket, Lily Bud, aqua pastel, from $225 to 275.00
Wall pocket, Square Flower, coral, from $35 to 45.00

McCoy, J. W.

The J. W. McCoy Pottery Company was incorporated in 1899. It operated under that name in Roseville, Ohio, until 1911 when McCoy entered into a partnership with George Brush, forming the Brush-McCoy Company. During the early years, McCoy produced kitchenware, majolica jardinieres and pedestals, umbrella stands, and cuspidors. By 1903 they had begun to experiment in the field of art pottery and, though never involved to the extent of some of their contemporaries, nevertheless produced several art lines of merit.

The company rebuilt in 1904 after being destroyed by fire, and other artware was designed. Loy-Nel Art and Renaissance were standard brown lines, hand decorated under the glaze with colored slip. Shapes and artwork were usually simple but effective. Olympia and Rosewood were relief-molded brown-glaze lines decorated in natural colors with wreaths of leaves and berries or simple floral sprays. Although much of this ware was not marked, you will find examples with the die-stamped 'Loy-Nel-Art, McCoy,' or an incised line identification.

Corn Line, jug, ca 1915, 9x4½", NM 150.00
Corn Line, salt pot, #56, 6½x5½", NM 165.00
Loy-Nel-Art, cuspidor, pansies, chips, 6¾x8" 160.00
Loy-Nel-Art, jardiniere, daffodils, 4-ftd, 8½x11" 265.00
Loy-Nel-Art, jardiniere, floral, 4-ftd, 7¾x13" 200.00
Loy-Nel-Art, pillow vase, floral, unmk, flake, 5x5½" 75.00
Loy-Nel-Art, pitcher, open roses, sm rstr, 8¼" 95.00

Loy-Nel-Art, vase, floral, 11", $225.00.

Loy-Nel-Art, vase, floral, shoulder-to-hip hdls, 10½" 210.00
Loy-Nel-Art, vase, floral, sm loop hdls, #02, 12¼", NM.............. 190.00
Olympia, jardiniere, #70, 7½"... 120.00
Olympia, vase, invt cone w/3" W base, 9"................................. 140.00
Sylvan (Avenue of Trees), jardiniere, gr, #233, 5½x6½".............. 175.00

McKee

McKee Glass was founded in 1853 in Pittsburgh, Pennsylvania. Among their early products were tableware of both the flint and non-flint varieties. In 1888 the company relocated to avail themselves to a source of natural gas, thereby founding the town of Jeannette, Pennsylvania. One of their most famous colored dinnerware lines, Rock Crystal, was manufactured in the 1920s. Production during the '30s and '40s included colored opaque dinnerware, Sunkist reamers, and 'bottoms up' cocktail tumblers as well as a line of black glass vases, bowls, and novelty items. All are popular items with today's collectors, but watch for reproductions. The mark of an authentic 'bottoms up' tumbler is the patent number 77725 embossed beneath the feet. The company was purchased in 1916 by Jeannette Glass, under which name it continues to operate. See also Animal Dishes with Covers; Carnival Glass; Depression Glass; Kitchen Collectibles; Reamers.

Bottoms Up, tumbler, frosted, 3¾", from $80 to 100.00
Bottoms Up, tumbler, Jade-ite, 3¾"+4" Jade-ite coaster, $125 to.. 135.00
Bottoms Up, tumbler, lt caramel, 3¾"+4" lt caramel coaster........ 110.00

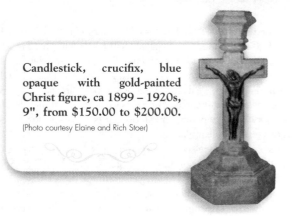

Candlestick, crucifix, blue opaque with gold-painted Christ figure, ca 1899 – 1920s, 9", from $150.00 to $200.00.

(Photo courtesy Elaine and Rich Stoer)

Candlesticks, Loop, ca 1870-91, 9½x4¾", NM, pr...................... 75.00
Card receiver, Fancy Arch, rolled on 2 sides, 6½" L 50.00
Compote, Sunburst (Aztec Sunburst), ca 1910, 7½x6¼" 30.00
Covered dish, Baby Moses, milk glass, reed base, 3x4" 120.00
Lamp, Danse de Lumiere, nude, gr satin, 11¼x4¾" 780.00
Orange bowl, Innovation Line #412, milk glass, ca 1918, 14½"..... 80.00
Pitcher, Pressed Leaf, oak leaves around lower half, 9½" 75.00
Pitcher, Sunburst, ca 1910, 4⅛"... 35.00
Vase, Champion, ca 1894, 10"... 30.00

Medical Collectibles

The field of medical-related items encompasses a wide area from the primitive bleeding bowl to the X-ray machines of the early 1900s. Other closely related collectibles include apothecary and dental items. Many tools that were originally intended for the pharmacist found their way to the doctor's office, and dentists often used surgical tools when no suitable dental instrument was available. A trend in the late 1800s toward self-medication brought a whole new wave of home-care manuals and 'patent' medical machines for home use. Commonly referred to as 'quack' medical gimmicks, these machines were usually ineffective and occasionally dangerous. Our advisor for this category is Jim Calison; he is listed in the Directory under New York.

Book, Confederate Military Surgery, Aryes & Wade, 1863, marbleized bk....**2,185.00**
Cabinet, apothecary; walnut/oak, 32 dvtl drws w/rvpt labels, 76x35x12"..**1,035.00**
Cabinet, dental; walnut/maple w/22 sm & 5 lg drws, 2 doors, 59x45x18".....**975.00**
Cabinet, Harvard Dental Co, oak, 6 drop & roll-front compartments, 61"..**3,175.00**
Case, optometrist's; lenses & frs in fitted case w/tray, 4x22".........**235.00**
Case, slide display; mahog w/glass paneled door, brass hdl, 12x10"..**375.00**
Case, slide; mahog w/2 drw & 12 trays w/bone knobs/175 slides, 9x8x8"..**515.00**

Chest, apothecary, mahogany with 16 similar glass bottles, 10x6x8½", $575.00. (Photo courtesy Garth's Auctions Inc.)

Chest, apothecary; pine w/8 sm drw, shaped bksplash, +11 jars, 23x22"....**865.00**
Dental drill, CI floor model w/flywheel & ft pedal, blk pnt, 57" ..**150.00**
Dr's lady, reclining Oriental figure, cvd ivory, 6¼"+wooden stand......**485.00**
Dr's lady, reclining Oriental figure, cvd ivory, 12⅛"+wooden stand ...**1,100.00**
Etui, fish-skin covered, w/silver rule/scoop/scalpel+others, 3¾" L ...**890.00**
Etui, lancet; silver-mtd shagreen, 4 lancets w/tortoiseshell mts, 3"...**650.00**
Jar, apothecary; Et de Saponai, blk/gilt on wht porc, 1850s, 11x5"...**350.00**
Jar, Leeches emb on clear glass, sm blister, 10½x8"......................**115.00**
Jar, Leeches on banner label, cobalt on pottery, Royal Doulton, 9½"..**8,625.00**
Jar, Leeches/crown/banner on moss gr, porc, dome lid, 9½" **5,975.00**
Kit, bloodletting; varied tools in mahog case w/fitted int, 4x10x6"..**1,200.00**
Kit, enema; Weiss...62, dbl-action pump, ebony hdl, +accessories+case ..**400.00**
Kit, mortician's; 16+ instruments, many mk Savigny, +10x5" case ..**575.00**
Kit, surgeon's; fitted mahog case w/28 early instruments, 16"....**1,850.00**
Kit, surgeon's; 27 ivory-hdld instruments & saw/etc, +mahog 16" case....**10,350.00**
Kit, surgeon's; 30+ Civil War era tools w/ebonized hdls, +mahog case...**3,735.00**
Kit, surgeon's; 40+ instruments, many mk Tiemann, +fitted walnut case..**6,900.00**
Kit, surgeon's; 8 instruments & glass vial, various makers, +8" case ...**230.00**
Kit, vampire killing; Prof Blomberg's New..., ca 1900, complete in box .**5,465.00**
Lamp, microscope; Bockett...London, oil burner, 9¾", +wood case ...**575.00**
Lamp, microscope; brass V-shaped post, glass font, oil burner, 15" **150.00**
Lamp, microscope; Collins London, brass w/glass font, oil burner, 17" ...**400.00**
Machine, electro-therapeutic; GA Supplee, coil/rosewood-hdl terminal..**120.00**
Medicine chest, traveling; leather, 6 bottles, dtd 5/1/99, 10" L **180.00**
Microtome, brass & steel, for slicing specimens, 4½" **550.00**
Otoscope, Am Optical Co, EX in 10" case......................................**75.00**
Phrenology head, porc, LN Fowler, 11½", +Fowler's instruction book....**575.00**
Quack device, Midland Electricity Is Life, shocker, oak case, NM ...**8,250.00**
Quack device, Mills Shocker, CI & oak case, 23", VG............**15,400.00**
Smith's New Outline Map of Human System, American Manikin No 2, 44"**350.00**
Sphygmograph, Millikin & Downe #1412, NP clockwork mechanism, 3" ..**180.00**
Table, examination; walnut, 2-drw/1-door base, WD Allison...Ind, rfn..**465.00**
Test set for urinary analysis, Whitall Tatum, w/contents, +11" case.**235.00**
Tooth key, dbl claw, steel shaft, trn ebony hdl, 6" **235.00**
Tooth key, single claw, locking-pin & trn wood hdl, 6".................**210.00**

Meissen

The Royal Saxon Porcelain Works was established in 1710 in Meissen, Saxony. Under the direction of Johann Frederick Bottger, who in 1708 had developed the formula for the first true porcelain body, fine ceramic figurines with exquisite detail and tableware of the highest quality were produced. Although every effort was made to insure the secrecy of Bottger's discovery, others soon began to copy his ware; and in 1731 Meissen adopted the famous crossed swords trademark to identify their own work. The term 'Dresden ware' is often used to refer to Meissen porcelain, since Bottger's discovery and first potting efforts were in nearby Dresden. See also Onion Pattern.

Basket, fruit; floral sprays w/gold, rtcl, 19th C, 12¾" **355.00**
Bowl, floral w/gilded & molded rim w/shell cartouch, 1880s, 11", pr..**235.00**
Bowl serving; blanc-de-chine w/appl foliage, w/lid 13", +tray......**500.00**
Candlesticks, vestal masks, courting scenes, 20th C, 8⅞", pr ...**1,880.00**
Cup & saucer, Dresden city scene/Bastey mtn scene w/cobalt, 2⅝" ...**1,645.00**

Ewer, ocean scene, putto handle surmount, Neptune seated on a shell near mermaid, dolphins at base, 1870, losses and restorations, 26", $6,300.00. (Photo courtesy Neal Auction Co. Auctioneers & Appraisers of Fine Art)

Figurine, Aphrodite on knoll w/urn, 2 cherubs beside, 20th C, 5x6".**1,645.00**
Figurine, blk fox slinking across ovoid naturalistic base, 7"........**1,175.00**
Figurine, cherubs (4) grouped around fire, early 20th C, 6⅝"...**1,525.00**
Figurine, cherubs (4) w/floral wreaths & garlands, ca 1900, 6¾" ...**1,645.00**
Figurine, dog w/shaggy hair, seated/looking right, ca 1900, 8"...**1,880.00**
Figurine, girl, nude/crouching w/unstrung bow, 1910, 5½"...........**940.00**
Figurine, girl w/fruit bowl, 18th-C garb, early 20th C, 5" **235.00**
Figurine, lady/cherub/2 ladies-in waiting/children, 1900s, 12"..**6,450.00**
Figurine, parrot, gr/bl/purple on wht base, 1920s, 5¾"..................**325.00**
Figurine, pug, wht w/blk face/tips, collar w/bells, she w/pup: 9", pr...**6,450.00**
Figurine, pug seated, brn/blk enamel, 1880s, 5"..........................**1,175.00**
Figurine, pugs (2) in grass, brn/gr, w/bl ribbons & bells, 2½", pr..**1,000.00**
Figurine, seated lady having her hand kissed by Blackamoor, 11" .**3,525.00**
Figurine, Spring allegorical, 1880s, 8", EX **600.00**
Platter, fish; sm floral sprays/gilt quatrefoils/burgundy rim, 22".....**120.00**
Potpourri, heavily encrusted w/flowers, putto finial, hdls/ftd, 21" ..**3,000.00**
Vase, cobalt/gilt, looped dbl snake hdls, fluted ft, 1880s, 16" **380.00**

Mercury Glass

Silvered glass, commonly called mercury glass, was a major scientific achievement of the nineteenth century. It was developed by the glass industry, who was searching for an inexpensive substitute for silver. Though very fragile, it was lightweight and would not tarnish. Mercury glass was made with two thin layers, either blown with a double wall or joined in sections, with the space between the walls of the vessel filled with a silvering compound, the perfecting of which involved much experimentation. Colored glass was also silvered. Green, blue, and amber were favored. Occasionally, colors were achieved using clear glass by adding certain chemicals to the compound. Besides hollow ware items, flat surfaces were silvered as well, through a process whereby small facets were cut on the underneath side, then treated with the silvering compound. Sometimes mercury glass was decorated by engraving; it was also hand painted. Besides decorative items such as vases and candlesticks, for instance, utilitarian items — doorknobs, curtain tiebacks, and reflectors for lamps — were also popular. Silvered Christmas ornaments were produced in large quantities.

Condition is an issue, though opinions are divided. While some prefer their acquisitions to be in mint condition, others accept items with flaked silvering. Watch for reproductions marked Made in China. In the listings that follow, all examples are silver unless noted another color. For more information we recommend *Pictorial Guide to Silvered Mercury Glass* by Diane Lytwyn (Collector Books).

Bird, wire clip at ft, 4½x1", 4 for	45.00
Bottle, fluted body, rectangular base, 1850s, 14"	765.00
Bottle, liquor; crest on front, 57 on bottom, cork stopper, 11x3"	18.00
Bottle, scent; spherical, w/dauber, 2½x2" dia	30.00
Bowl, 3 clear appl ft, 4¾x9½"	125.00
Candlestick, baluster, ca 1860-75, 9", pr	200.00
Deer, hand blown, 4x3x1½"	95.00
Gazing ball, Dithridge, ca 1867-75, 7" dia, +matching stand	800.00
Lamp, table; urn form, 1950s era, 22x8"	235.00
Mug, clear appl hdl, 3"	40.00
Ornament, bird, 5x8½"	25.00
Ornament, bird w/wire clip, 4½x1", 4 for	45.00
Salt cellar, HP floral on ftd egg form, 1850s, 3⅛x2"	100.00
Toothpick holder	50.00
Vase, HP bird, 7½"	70.00
Vase, HP orange bird w/yel wings, flowers, 9½"	90.00
Witch ball, w/stand, scarce, 18"	240.00

Merrimac

Founded in 1897 in Newburyport, Massachusetts, the Merrimac Pottery Company primarily produced gardenware. In 1901 they introduced a line of artware, covered mostly in semi-matt green glaze, somewhat in the style of Grueby's, but glossier and with the appearance of a second tier below the top, feathered one. Marked examples carry an impressed die-stamp or a paper label, each with the firm name and the outline of a sturgeon, the meaning of the Native American word, Merrimac. Our advisors for this category are Suzanne Perrault and David Rago; they are listed in the Directory under New Jersey.

Vase, green matt, tooled and applied underwater plants, unmarked, signed E. B., 8x4¾", NM, $3,750.00. (Photo courtesy David Rago Auctions)

Pitcher, gr, snake hdls, unmk, 8¼x4½"	840.00
Vase, gr (feathered), paper label, 4x5"	2,160.00

Vase, gr/brn mottle, paper label, 10x4½"	2,280.00
Vase, gr/gunmetal (feathered), wide cylinder, 6x4¾", NM	2,040.00
Vase, gr/gunmetal mottle, 3 sm rim hdls, 15x6"	18,000.00
Vase, gr, w/hdls, illegible mk, 4x4½"	840.00
Vase, gr (feathered), paper label, 4x5"	2160.00
Vase, leaves, gr, bulbous, fish mk, 4½x6"	1,680.00
Vase, mustard, fish mk, 9½x4¾"	3,480.00

Metlox

Metlox Potteries was founded in 1927 in Manhattan Beach, California. Before 1934 when they began producing the ceramic housewares for which they have become famous, they made ceramic and neon outdoor advertising signs. The company went out of business in 1989. Well-known sculptor Carl Romanelli designed artware in the late 1930s and early 1940s (and again briefly in the 1950s). His work is especially sought after today.

Some Provincial dinnerware lines can be confusing. There are two 'rooster' lines, Red Rooster (red, orange, and brown) and California Provincial (dark green and burgundy), and there are three 'homestead' lines, Colonial Heritage (red, orange, and brown like the Red Rooster pieces), Homestead Provincial (dark green and burgundy like California Provincial), and Provincial Blue (blue and white). For further information we recommend *Collector's Encyclopedia of Metlox Potteries, Second Edition,* by our advisor Carl Gibbs, Jr.; he is listed in the Directory under Texas.

Cookie Jars

Ballerina Bear, yel & wht, from $75 to	85.00
Bear, Uncle Sam, minimum value	850.00
Beaver, unmk, from $150 to	175.00
Black Santa, from $575 to	625.00
Brownie Scout, blond hair, hat is lid, rare, minimum value	750.00

Calf Head, says 'Moo,' no mark, from $225.00 to $275.00. (Photo courtesy Ermagene Westfall)

Calico Cat, yel w/pk bow, from $90 to	110.00
Circus Bear, from $175 to	225.00
Clown, wht, 3-qt, from $150 to	175.00
Cookie Girl, unmk, from $50 to	60.00
Cub Scout, unmk, rare, minimum value	750.00
Downy Woodpecker, sits atop lg acorn, from $160 to	180.00
Ferdinand Calf, brn tones, from $500 to	550.00
Katy Cat, wht w/bl eyes, pk nose, from $85 to	95.00
Little Piggy, floral decor on wht, yel hdl on lid, from $60 to	75.00
Little Red Riding Hood, Poppytrail Calif, rare, minimum value	1,250.00
Lucy Goose, from $35 to	45.00
Mammy Scrub Woman, unmk, minimum value	1,500.00
Mrs Rabbit, from $100 to	125.00
Noah's Ark, from $45 to	65.00
Nun, wht w/bl trim, holds cookies, from $100 to	125.00

Nut & Chipmunk Barrel, unmk, from $40 to 50.00
Owl, unmk, from $40 to 45.00
Panda Bear, blk & wht, unmk, from $75 to 85.00
Polka Dot Topsy, from $550 to 575.00
Rabbit on Cabbage, unmk, from $75 to 80.00
Rex, pk dinosaur, c '87, from $100 to 150.00
Salty Pelican, US Diving Team, bl hat & neckerchief, from $150 to.. 175.00
Scottie Dog, blk, from $100 to 125.00
Squirrel on Pinecone, Made in USA, from $65 to 75.00
Teddy Bear, bl sweater, holding cookie, unmk, from $40 to 45.00
Uncle Sam Bear, minimum value 850.00
Walrus, bl cap & neckerchief, from $70 to 80.00
Watermelon, from $250 to 300.00

Dinnerware

California Apple, creamer, 6-oz, $23 to 25.00
California Apple, cup, 6-oz, from $10 to 11.00
California Apple, plate, bread & butter; 6½", from $8 to 9.00
California Apple, saucer, 6", from $3 to 4.00
California Confetti, gravy boat, from $40 to 45.00
California Confetti, pitcher, milk; from $75 to 85.00
California Confetti, plate, salad; from $12 to 14.00
California Confetti, sugar bowl, w/lid, from $32 to 35.00
California Confetti, tumbler, from $38 to 40.00
California Ivy, bowl, cereal; 6¾", from $18 to 20.00
California Ivy, mug, 7-oz, from $28 to 30.00
California Ivy, pitcher, lg, 2½-qt, from $70 to 75.00
California Ivy, tumbler, 13-oz, from $35 to 38.00

California Mobile, Freeform shape: Plate, dinner; from $32.00 to 35.00.

California Provincial, casserole, w/chicken lid, 1-qt, 10-oz, $185 to ..200.00
California Provincial, cruet, oil or vinegar; w/lid, 7-oz, from $42 to.....45.00
California Provincial, egg cup, from $40 to 45.00
California Provincial, mug, lg, w/lid, 1-pt, from $65 to 70.00
California Provincial, plate, dinner; 10", from $18 to 20.00
California Provincial, platter, oval, med, 11", from $45 to 50.00
Camellia, bowl, fruit; 6⅛", from $12 to 15.00
Camellia, creamer, from $22 to 25.00
Camellia, plate, bread & butter; 6½", from $7 to 8.00
Camellia, plate, luncheon; 9", from $10 to 12.00
Camellia, sugar bowl, w/lid, from $25 to 30.00
Colonial Heritage, bowl, cereal; from $14 to 16.00
Colonial Heritage, coffee carafe, w/lid, from $120 to 130.00
Colonial Heritage, egg cup, from $25 to 28.00
Colonial Heritage, pepper mill, from $40 to 45.00
Colonial Heritage, pitcher, sm, from $40 to 45.00
Colonial Heritage, plate, dinner; from $13 to 14.00
Colonial Heritage, platter, oval, extra lg, from $75 to 80.00
Colonial Heritage, saucer, from $3 to 4.00
Delphinium, bowl, rim soup; from $18 to 20.00

Delphinium, creamer, from $22 to 25.00
Delphinium, cup, from $9 to 10.00
Delphinium, plate, chop; 13", from $35 to 40.00
Delphinium, plate, dinner; 10", from $12 to 15.00
Delphinium, saucer, from $3 to 4.00
Delphinium, vegetable dish, 10", from $35 to 40.00
Homestead Provincial, ashtray, 10", from $35 to 40.00
Homestead Provincial, bowl, salad; 11⅛", from $100 to 110.00
Homestead Provincial, cup, 6-oz, from $13 to 14.00
Homestead Provincial, plate, luncheon; 9", from $28 to 30.00
Homestead Provincial, platter, turkey; 22½", from $300 to 325.00
Homestead Provincial, salt box, from $110 to 120.00
Homestead Provincial, sugar bowl, w/lid, 8-oz, from $35 to 38.00
Jamestown, bread server, from $50 to 55.00
Jamestown, butter dish, from $45 to 50.00
Jamestown, creamer, from $28 to 30.00
Jamestown, pitcher, sm, from $32 to 35.00
Jamestown, plate, dinner; from $11 to 12.00
Jamestown, plate, luncheon; from $12 to 14.00
Jamestown, teapot, w/lid, from $100 to 110.00
Navajo, baker, oval, from $40 to 45.00
Navajo, mug, cocoa; 8-oz, from $20 to 22.00
Navajo, pepper mill, from $35 to 40.00
Navajo, plate, salad; from $3 to 4.00
Navajo, shakers, pr from $16 to 18.00
Navajo, tumbler, 10-oz, from $35 to 38.00
Provincial Blue, bread server, 9½", from $75 to 80.00
Provincial Blue, candleholder, ea from $55 to 60.00
Provincial Blue, coffeepot, w/lid, 7-cup, 42-oz, from $125 to 135.00
Provincial Blue, gravy boat, 1-pt, from $45 to 50.00
Provincial Blue, pitcher, sm, 1½-pt, from $65 to 70.00
Provincial Blue, soup tureen, w/lid, from $475 to 500.00
Provincial Rose, cup, from $8 to 9.00
Provincial Rose, plate, bread & butter; from $6 to 7.00
Provincial Whitestone, gravy boat, 1-pt, from $30 to 32.00
Provincial Whitestone, plate, salad; 7½", from $8 to 9.00
Provincial Whitestone, platter, oval, med, 11", from $30 to 35.00
Provincial Whitestone, sugar bowl, w/lid, 8-oz, from $20 to 22.00
Red Rooster, ashtray, lg, 8¼", from $25 to 28.00
Red Rooster, bowl, fruit; 6", from $12 to 14.00
Red Rooster, butter dish, from $60 to 65.00
Red Rooster, coffee carafe, w/lid, 6-cup, 44-oz, from $42 to 45.00
Red Rooster, pitcher, lg, 2¼-qt, from $75 to 85.00
Red Rooster, plate, salad; 7½", from $10 to 12.00
Rooster Bleu, coffeepot, w/lid, 6-cup, 42-oz, from $90 to 100.00
Rooster Bleu, creamer, 6-oz, from $20 to 22.00
Rooster Bleu, platter, oval, lg, 13½", from $40 to 45.00
Rooster Bleu, shakers, ea from $11 to 12.00
Sculptured Daisy, plate, dinner; 10½", from $12 to 13.00
Sculptured Daisy, sugar bowl, w/lid, 8-oz, from $28 to 30.00
Sculptured Daisy, teapot, w/lid, 7-cup, from $90 to 100.00
Sculptured Daisy, vegetable dish, divided, 10", from $35 to 40.00
Sculptured Grape, bowl, cereal; 7⅜", from $16 to 18.00
Sculptured Grape, pitcher, lg, 2¼-qt, from $75 to 80.00
Sculptured Grape, tumbler, 12-oz, from $35 to 38.00
Sculptured Zinnia, cup, 7-oz, from $11 to 12.00
Sculptured Zinnia, platter, oval, med, 12½", from $40 to 45.00
Sculptured Zinnia, shakers, pr from $12 to 13.00
Shoreline, pitcher, from $65 to 70.00
Shoreline, saucer, from $3 to 4.00
Tickled Pink, mug, 12-oz, from $20 to 22.00
Tickled Pink, plate, dinner; 10", from $12 to 13.00
Woodland Gold, butter dish, oval, from $50 to 55.00
Woodland Gold, cup, 7-oz, from $9 to 10.00

Woodland Gold, pitcher, sm, 1½-pt, from $40 to 45.00
Woodland Gold, sauceboat, 1¼-pt, from $35 to 40.00

Disney

Alice in Wonderland, #292, from $350 to 400.00
Bambi, #202, from $140 to 165.00
Bruno (Cinderella), sitting, #288, from $175 to 200.00
Cinderella, peasant, from $450 to 500.00
Dumbo standing, from $200 to 225.00
Figaro sitting, from $175 to 225.00
Flower (Bambi), med, #258, from $75 to 100.00
Huey w/bat, from $250 to 275.00
Mickey Mouse, #212, from $350 to 400.00
Minnie Mouse, #213, from $275 to 300.00
Nana (Peter Pan), from $225 to 250.00
Prince Charming, from $350 to 400.00
Thumper, sm, #262, from $100 to 125.00
Unicorn (VK Fantasia), from $250 to 325.00
Wendy (Peter Pan), #247, from $350 to 400.00

Miniatures

Canary, 4", from $60 to.. 100.00
Dinosaur, 4½", from $350 to 450.00
Dove, 6¼", from $40 to 60.00
Fawn, 5½", from $50 to 80.00
Fish, 5½", from $125 to 175.00
Hippopotamus, from $125 to 175.00
Horse, 4½", from $125 to 175.00
Pig, 3½", from $75 to 125.00
Squirrel, 2", from $75 to 125.00

Nostalgia Line

Reminiscent of the late nineteenth and early twentieth centuries, the Nostalgia line contained models of locomotives, gramophones, early autos, stage coaches, and baby carriages. There were also wagons and carts pulled by horses or donkeys, sometimes with separate drivers and passengers. The line was produced from the late 1940s through the 1960s.

Cadillac, Antique Automobiles, from $75 to................................ 85.00
Locomotive, from $60 to 65.00
Old Mill Ensemble, 2-pc, from $200 to 225.00
Trolley Car, from $85 to... 95.00
Victrola, from $60 to.. 65.00

Poppets

From the mid-'60s through the mid-'70s, Metlox produced a line of 'Poppets,' 88 in all, representing characters ranging from royalty and professionals to a Salvation Army group. They came with a name tag; some had paper labels, others backstamps.

Angelina, angel, 7⅝", from $55 to.. 65.00
Conchita, Mexican girl, 8¾", from $60 to 70.00
Doc, 7", from $40 to.. 50.00
Effie, cymbal lady, 7¾", from $75 to 85.00
Florence, nurse, 8", from $45 to 55.00
Grace, princess, from $45 to 55.00
Huck, fishing boy, 6½", from $45 to 55.00
Joy, bell ringer, 6½", from $40 to 50.00
Melinda, girl tennis player, 6¼", from $45 to 55.00
Nellie, girl w/bird, 8⅝", from $55 to.. 65.00

Penelope, nursemaid, 7¾", from $40 to...................................... 50.00
Ralph, bather man, 11¾", from $45 to 55.00
Suzie, girl w/purse, 7", from $45 to 55.00
Zelda, choral lady No 1, 7¾", from $75 to 85.00

Romanelli Artware

Figurine, cowboy, 10¾", minimum value...................................... 500.00
Figurine, cowgirl, 9½", from $300 to 375.00
Figurine, rooster, 8¼", from $100 to 125.00
Flower holder, dancing girl, 10", from $250 to 275.00
Mug, High Life, from $100 to... 125.00

Vase, Sagittarius, 7½", from $175.00 to $200.00. (Photo courtesy Carl Gibbs, Jr.)

Vase, sailfish, 9", from $140 to.. 160.00
Vase, sea horse, 9¼", from $175 to 200.00
Wall plaque, prancing horse, 15", from $325 to............................ 375.00

Mettlach

In 1836 Nicholas Villeroy and Eugene Francis Boch, both of whom were already involved in the potting industry, formed a partnership and established a stoneware factory in an old restored abbey in Mettlach, Germany. Decorative stoneware with in-mold relief was their specialty, steins in particular. Through constant experimentation, they developed innovative methods of decoration. One process, called chromolith, involved inlaying colorful mosaic designs into the body of the ware. Later underglaze printing from copper plates was used. Their stoneware was of high quality, and their steins won many medals at the St. Louis Expo and early world's fairs. Most examples are marked with an incised castle and the name 'Mettlach.' The numbering system indicates size, date, stock number, and decorator. Production was halted by a fire in 1921; the factory was not rebuilt.

Key:
L — liter   PUG — print under glaze
POG — print over glaze   tl — thumb lift

#101, stein, relief: choir, ornate pewter lid, 1L, NM 200.00
#171, stein, etched: people around body, inlaid lid, .25L............. 120.00
#485, stein, relief: musicians, inlaid lid, .5L 200.00
#1036, stein, threading/glazed: repeating design, inlaid lid, l3L ... 300.00
#1044, plaque, PUG: Hamburg, Deichthorfleeth, 12" 365.00
#1044, plaque, PUG: Hamburg, Jungfernstieg, 12" 275.00
#1044-094, plaque, PUG: Altes Stadthor Cochem, 12" 200.00
#1044-512, plaque, PUG: Bratwurst Glocklein Nurnberg, 12" 360.00
#1044-9027, plaque, PUG: fox, worn gold, 14" 665.00
#1164, stein, etched: drinking scene, Warth, pewter lid, .5L 240.00
#1317, stein, etched: crest w/lion, inlaid lid, .5L 345.00
#1370, stein, relief: verse, old rpl pewter lid, .5L 70.00
#1403, stein, etched; bowling, inlaid lid, .5L, NM....................... 185.00

#1410, plaque, etched and glazed, EX, $8,200.00. (Photo courtesy Andre Ammelounx)

#1436, vase, etched/glazed: repeating pattern, 4½" 240.00
#1467, stein, relief: 4 scenes w/people, inlaid lid, .5L 130.00
#1526, stein, relief: Yale University, pewter lid, .5L 185.00
#1526-1502, stein, PUG: soldiers, inlaid lid, .5L, NM 225.00
#1527, stein, etched: cavaliers drinking, pewter lid, horn tl, 1L ... 375.00
#1655, stein, etched; dancing scene, inlaid lid, .5L 575.00
#1662, stein, etched: workman drinking, pewter lid, 1889, .5L 240.00
#1695, stein, etched: hunters, inlaid lid, .5L 675.00
#1786, stein, etched: St Florian extinguishing fire, dragon hdl, .5L ...725.00
#1796, stein, etched: drunken cavalier, Warth, inlaid lid, .5L 365.00
#1803, stein, etched/glazed: repeating design, inlaid lid, .25L 265.00
#1888, punch bowl, relief: Prussian eagle, inlaid lid, 6L 865.00
#1909, stein, transfer/HP: 4F, pewter lid, .4L 120.00
#1909-0727, stein, PUG: dwarfs bowling, Schlitt, pewter lid, .3L ...300.00
#1909-1008, stein, PUG: man w/harp, Schlitt, pewter lid, rpr, .5L ..275.00
#1909-1179, stein, PUG: Gesang, pewter lid, .5L 465.00
#1909-1180, stein, PUG: Tanz, pewter lid, .5L 385.00
#1909-1288, stein, PUG: fox drinking beer, pewter lid, .5L 475.00
#1940, stein, etched: brewmeister, Warth, inlaid lid, 3L 1,150.00
#2002, stein, etched: Munchen, Munic child pewter lid, .5L 365.00
#2003, stein, etched: 3 cavalier scenes, inlaid lid, .5L 500.00
#2089, stein, etched: man w/winged barmaid, Schlitt, inlaid lid, .5L.. 775.00
#2092, stein, etched: dwarf adjusting clock, inlaid lid, .5L 1,000.00
#2094, stein, etched: scene w/musicians, inlaid lid, .5L 415.00
#2097, stein, etched: musical design, inlaid lid w/hairline, .5L 215.00
#2140, stein, transfer/HP: 4F Turner, relief pewter lid, .5L 365.00
#2171, pokal, etched: musical design, Etruscan style, w/lid, 7¾".. 425.00
#2172, vase, etched: 3 ladies, Etruscan, 8" 345.00
#2177-960, stein, PUG: jester, Schlitt, pewter lid, .25L 225.00
#2184-966, stein, PUG: dwarfs, inlaid lid, .3L 250.00
#2192, stein, etched: Etruscan, inlaid lid, Schlitt, .5L 725.00
#2205, stein, etched, Diana & hunters, inlaid squirrel lid, .5L..1,800.00
#2230, stein, etched: man drinking w/barmaid, Schlitt, inlaid lid, .5L..575.00
#2286, stein, etched: Gasthaus lid (inlaid), rpr base chip, 3L 815.00
#2327, beaker, transfer/HP: Student Society, .25L 195.00
#2327-0426, beaker, PUG: Hamburg Jungfernstieg, .25L 100.00
#2327-1200, beaker, PUG: Indiana, .25L 100.00
#2327-1200, beaker, PUG: Munchen, .25L 105.00
#2327-1273, beaker, PUG: drunken man, .25L 200.00
#2327-1287, beaker, PUG: donkey barmaid feeds fox gentleman, .25L..215.00
#2368-1095, beaker, PUG: man smoking, flaw, .25L 80.00
#2373, stein, etched: St Augustine FL, alligator hdl, inlaid lid, .5L....725.00
#2382, stein, etched; Thirsty Rider, Schlitt, inlaid lid, .5L 535.00
#2414, clock, etched: Art Nouveau, brass floral metal work, 23" ..2,415.00
#2440, stein, Capodimonte style, old rpl pewter lid, .5L 175.00
#2441, stein, etched: man playing dice, inlaid lid, .5L 485.00
#2442, plaque, cameo: Roman warriors at sea, Stahl, 19" dia 690.00
#2443, plaque, cameo: ladies, Stahl, flaw, 18" 400.00
#2531, stein, etched: men in house, Quidenus, inlaid lid, .5L 575.00
#2568, vase, cvd/pnt: birds in landscape, Chevrolon, 14" 840.00
#2581, stein, etched: choir, Quidenus, inlaid lid, .5L, NM 215.00

#2583, stein, etched: Blk Whale of Ascolon, Quidenus, rpr lid, 1L....315.00
#2690, stein, etched: drinking scene, Quidenus, inlaid lid, 1.4L ...1,450.00
#2715, stein, cameo/etched: 3 couples, inlaid lid, .5L 725.00
#2716, stein, etched: Gasthaus scene, Quidenus, inlaid lid, .5L... 500.00
#2719, stein, etched/glazed: baker occupation, inlaid lid, .5L ...1,950.00
#2720, stein, etched/glazed: cabinetmaker occupation, inlaid lid, .5L ..1,500.00
#2721, stein, etched/glazed: carpenter occupation, inlaid lid, .5L...2,300.00
#2727, stein, etched/glazed: printer occupation, inlaid lid, .5L .2,650.00
#2729, stein, etched/glazed: blacksmith occupation, inlaid, lid, .5L...4,600.00
#2730, stein, etched/glazed: butcher occupation, inlaid lid, .5L .. 4,600.00
#2767, stein, etched: Munich child, Schlitt, pewter strap rpr, .5L...500.00
#2780, stein, etched: cavalier & lady, inlaid lid, tl rpr, .5L 230.00
#2805, plaque, etched: deer, Art Nouveau, H Gradl, 15" 1,200.00
#2833E, stein, etched: soldiers in forest, inlaid lid, .5L 515.00
#2863, cruet, glazed relief, 5½" 125.00
#2905, vase, etched: Art Nouveau, rim rpr, 9½" 260.00
#2917, stein, etched/relief: Munchen, rpl figural lid, 1L 925.00
#3024, stein, relief: cavalier, inlaid lid, 1.8L 400.00
#3084, stein, etched: postman drinking, pewter lid, 3.1L 1,100.00
#3104, butter dish, etched: Art Nouveau, 3¼x5", NM 230.00
#3322IV, creamer, etched: Art Nouveau, 4¼" 275.00
#3340, bowl, etched: floral, 6½x6" 345.00
#5241, plaque, etched: Delft, 15¼" 240.00
#7025, plaque, phanolith: Lohengrin, Stahl, 15¼x12" 1,400.00
#7042, plaque, phanolith: people at table, Stahl, rpr, 15½x12" ..1,850.00
No #, decanter, PUG: leaf design, w/stopper, 8½" 120.00
No #, figure, nude boy removing thorn from ft, parian, 6¾" 625.00

Microscopes

The microscope has taken on many forms during its 250-year evolutionary period. The current collectors' market primarily includes examples from England, surplus items from institutions, and continental beginner and intermediate forms which sold through Sears Roebuck & Company and other retailers of technical instruments. Earlier examples have brass main tubes which are unpainted. Later, more common examples are all black with brass or silver knobs and horseshoe-shaped bases. Early and more complex forms are the most valuable; these always had hardwood cases to house the delicate instruments and their accessories. Instruments were never polished during use, and those that have been polished to use as decorator pieces are of little interest to most avid collectors. Unless otherwise described, all examples in the following listing are in excellent condition and retain their original cases.

A Pritchard...London, brass, tripod base, w/accessories 1,850.00
Bate, brass solar, rack-&-pinion focus projection lens, 15½" 3,820.00
Beck Star, compound, brass tube, rack-&-pinion focus, 10½" 500.00
Busch, brass compound, rack-&-pinion focus on tube, CI U-ft, 11" ..150.00
Chas Baker, brass student, coarse focus+fine adjustment on nosepc, 15" ...590.00
Culpeper type, brass tube, circular ft, rack-work focus, 10" 1,525.00
Culpeper type, vertical rack-&-pinion focus, circular stage, 11" ..825.00
Davis, brass compound, tube unscrews for storage, 16", +accessories ..825.00
Duboscq, projecting, brass horizontal tube, CI tripod base, 18"...2,115.00
Ellis-pattern, brass, rack-work adjustment w/forceps, 4¼" W 700.00
Ernst Leitz, petrographic, rack-&-pinion focus, brass tube 415.00
French, student's compound, brass, rack-work, swivel magnifier, 9½"...165.00
Gould type, brass, tapered tube/substage mirror, 7", +mahog case ...470.00
Griffith Club, Bausch & Lomb, brass, rack-&-pinion focus, rnd ft, 11"..3,000.00
J Swift, brass compound, ½", 1" & 2" objectives in canisters, 14" . 235.00
Kezor & Bendon, brass compound, 1 eyepc+¼" & 1" objectives, 17"...500.00
Leitz, compound, lacquered brass tube & pillar, U-ft, 10" 300.00
Martin-pattern drum, brass, rack-work focus/sprung stage/live box, 10"..470.00
Moritz Pillischer #470, brass, rack-work+fine screw adjustments, 16"...885.00

Newton, brass compound, nosepc adjusts w/screw, 4-stop aperture, 14" ...**885.00**
Newton, brass compound, tube unscrews, nosepc fine focusing, 14" **470.00**
Nuremberg Culpeper type, paper-covered tube+2 draw tubes, 1800s, 13" ...**1,410.00**
R&J Beck, binocular body tube, eng tripod ft, 15" **650.00**
R&J Beck #15909, brass, Wenham-pattern tube/1 eyecpc+2 objectives,12" ..**500.00**
R&J Beck Economic #9821, eyepc/objective, 11" (closed) **355.00**
R&J Beck London, brass, w/accessories, +mahog 20x12x9" case ..**4,715.00**
Reichert Heimdal, folding field, blk enamel tube, brass eyepc, 7½" ..**180.00**
TH McCallister, brass, fusee chain focus, U-ft, 11" **235.00**
W&S Jones, brass solar, 2½" condensing lens+projection lens, 12" ...**1,880.00**

Militaria

Because of the wide and varied scope of items available to collectors of militaria, most tend to concentrate mainly on the area or areas that interest them most or that they can afford to buy. Some items represent a major investment and because of their value have been reproduced. Extreme caution should be used when purchasing Nazi items. Every badge, medal, cap, uniform, dagger, and sword that Nazi Germany issued is being reproduced today. Some repros are crude and easily identified as fakes, while others are very well done and difficult to recognize as reproductions. Purchases from WWII veterans are usually your safest buys. Reputable dealers or collectors will normally offer a money-back guarantee on Nazi items purchased from them. There are a number of excellent Third Reich reference books available in bookstores at very reasonable prices. Study them to avoid losing a much larger sum spent on a reproduction. Our advisor for this category is Ron L. Willis; he is listed in the Directory under Washington.

Key: insg — insignia

Imperial German

Cap, visor, officer, lt bl-gray w/yel felt band, 2 insg.......................**250.00**
Helmet, spike; Fusilier battalion officer, silver death head **2,750.00**
Helmet, spike; leather w/brass mts, chin strap, G **525.00**

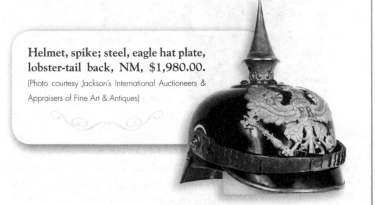

Helmet, spike; steel, eagle hat plate, lobster-tail back, NM, $1,980.00.
(Photo courtesy Jackson's International Auctioneers & Appraisers of Fine Art & Antiques)

Inkwell, officer's spike helmet shape, blown blk glass w/gold, 3½" ...**160.00**
Medal, Johannitter Order, gold-tone metal cross w/enamel **325.00**
Medal, Order of Griffen, red enamel inlay, breast cross................**750.00**
Medal, Order of St Michael, enamel on silver, w/ribbon, EX **275.00**
Medal, Service Cross 1st Class, brass-tone metal, 1914................**150.00**
Medal, 25 Yr commemorative of defeat of France, SP, 2½"+ribbon ..**50.00**
Pipe, porc bowl, spike helmet lid, Wilhelm I & II, decals, 33" L..**300.00**

Third Reich

Badge, Tank Battle, eagle/swastika/tank, zinc, late issue................**75.00**

Binoculars, Kriegsmarine, blk body, Dientsglas 10x50, +case.......**750.00**
Breeches, olive gr, tropics type **125.00**
Dagger, Alles fur Deutschland/#ZM M7-68 etched on blade, 1941, 8½"...**475.00**
Dagger, Luftwaffe officer, 2nd pattern, Holler, 10" +scabbard **425.00**
Drum, side; wht metal w/mc pnt, Sonor, dtd 1935, VG...............**250.00**
Flag, blk swastika & wht disk on red cloth, 40x60" **165.00**
Helmet, M35, SS rune decal, pnt steel, w/leather liner, chin strap...**1,200.00**
Helmet, M35, steel body w/broken brn/blk camo, w/liner/strap...**350.00**
Helmet, M40, SS dbl decal, leather liner & chin strap, EX.......**1,200.00**
Helmet, 1935 pattern, pnt skull w/dbl DRK decals, w/liner, EX...**350.00**
Helmet, 1943 pattern, gr pnt shell, excavated relic......................**250.00**
Knife, Blut & Ehre etched on blade, plated hilt, inlaid grips, 5½"...**275.00**
Sidecap, Africa Korps, tan w/cloth eagle/swastika, pk piping.......**300.00**

Japanese

Badge, Order of Rising Sun, 4th Class, silver-gilt/enamel **325.00**
Belt, Army officer, leather w/brass buckle & keepers, G...............**140.00**
Cap, visor; Army type 45, olive gr w/red band, yel star, WWII era...**100.00**
Cap, visor; olive gr wool w/yel star, WWII era, NM.....................**165.00**
Dog tag, Imperial Army officer, name & rank, 1¾x1¼"..................**50.00**
Flag, red sun & rays on wht silk, gold & wht fringe, WWII era, 38x44" ..**250.00**
Flag, red sun on wht, WWII era, 42x49", EX..............................**120.00**
Flag, signal; Navy, yel & red triangles, WWII era, 64½x52" **75.00**
Flight suit, Navy, fur lined, internal belt, WWII era.....................**300.00**
Hat, visor; Navy submarine officer, bullion badge, WWII era, VG ..**125.00**
Helmet, Army aviator, leather, missing fleece liner, WWII era, VG ...**300.00**
Helmet, sun; Imperial Army, canvas over cb, yel star, WWII era..**215.00**
Poster, Sino-Japanese War, naval scene, 1930s, 54x78"................**650.00**
Tunic, Army Model 1938, summer service, dtd 1941, G **100.00**
Tunic, Army private, olive wool, orig buttons/patches, WWII era, VG...**175.00**

Russia/Soviet

Cap, visor; Navy, blk wool w/wht piping, red star device, WWII.. **100.00**
Cap, visor; Navy, wht cotton crown, blk band w/anchor/star, WWII **40.00**
Hat, Army, olive gr wool w/fleece lining, red star, WWII era.......**150.00**
Hat, Army field, dk olive gr wool, pointed crown, WWII era, VG ..**110.00**
Hat, Army officer, brn sable fur w/satin line, red star, 1970s **50.00**
Medallion, silver, commemorative, Defeat of Napoleon in 1812 ... **60.00**
Statue, Stalin leading workers in revolt, bronze, dtd 1941, 15"....**250.00**

United States

Boots, Infantry, brn leather, 2-buckle, orig laces, WWII, pr.........**125.00**
Canteen, tinned iron, pewter spout, Civil War relic, G **90.00**
Canteen, wooden cask w/stepped spout, Revolutionary War era, 12x7"..**200.00**
Cap, forage; dk bl wool, blk leather visor, ca 1858.......................**950.00**
Cap, Navy enlisted, bl wool, oilcloth sweatband, 1920s.................**25.00**
Collar disk, enlisted, bronze, nat'l shield/spoked gear, WWI..........**20.00**
Collar disk, enlisted, silver winged shield on brass field, WWII, EXIB...**20.00**
Drum, bentwood w/brass tacks/red-pnt rim, Meacham & Co, 1880s, 17" dia...**560.00**
Flight suit, Navy, camo lightweight nylon, WWII era....................**60.00**
Goggles, flight; Air Force M1944 pattern, blk rubber fr, WWII era ..**75.00**
Hat, visor; Navy officer, dk bl wool/mohair band, embr insg, WWI...**150.00**
Helmet, fighter pilot, leather, WWII era......................................**150.00**
Helmet, Navy pilot, brn leather, WWII-Korea type **75.00**
Insignia, Infantry enlisted, brass, horn form, Civil War era...........**30.00**
Jacket, Union Artillery, dk bl wool w/red trim, Civil War **900.00**
Kepi, Militia officer, bl wool, brass buttons, Indian Wars **400.00**
Overcoat, Army officer, brn wool, short style, WWII....................**50.00**
Photo, Gen Patton, blk & wht, WWII era, 9x7"...........................**45.00**
Shako, leather w/orange/lt bl pom-pom, Civil War era, lacks frontplate..**400.00**
Shoes, Army, brn leather ankle boots w/brass grommets, WWI era, NM..**125.00**

Telephone; field; Army, blk Bakelite receiver, side crank, WWII .. 50.00
Trousers, Army, olive drab wool, side pockets, compo buttons, WWII era...25.00
Trousers, Infantry, dk bl wool, japanned buttons, Span-Am War 125.00
Uniform, Army enlisted, khaki cotton shirt & trousers, WWII 50.00
Vest, Air Force Type A-9, pile lined, WWII era 70.00

Milk Glass

Milk glass is today's name for milk-white opaque glass. The early glassmaker's term was Opal Ware. Originally attempted in England in the eighteenth century with the intention of imitating china, milk glass was not commercially successful until the mid-1800s. Pieces produced in the U.S.A., England, and France during the 1870 – 1900 period are highly prized for their intricate detail and fiery, opalescent edges. For further information we recommend *Collector's Encyclopedia of Milk Glass* by Betty and Bill Newbound. (CE numbers in our listings refer to this publication.) Another highly recommended book is *The Milk Glass Book* by Frank Chiarenza and James Slater. The newest reference, published in 2001, is *Milk Glass Imperial Glass Corporation* by Myrna and Bob Garrison. Our advisor for this category is Rod Dockery; he is listed in the Directory under Texas. See also Animal Dishes with Covers; Bread Plates; Historical Glass; Westmoreland.

Key:
B — Belknap   G — Garrison
CE — Newbound   MGB — Milk Glass Book

Basket, Lace Edge, Imperial, G-190-1723, 7¾", from $35 to 40.00
Bottle, barber; mk Witch Hazel, CE-2, 7", from $70 to 90.00
Bottle, dresser; draped scroll w/gold, rose-shaped finial, CE-14, 10" ... 45.00
Bowl, candy; English Hobnail, ftd, Westmoreland, CE-96a, 5½x6" ..35.00
Bowl, shell-shaped, lacy edge, Fenton, CE-23, 5⅜", from $18 to .. 20.00
Box, cuff; Three Kittens, Westmoreland, CE-39b, 5½x4½", $75 to ..85.00
Box, powder; emb floral, Fostoria, CE-41a, 4¾x4", from $40 to..... 45.00
Box, salt; w/wood lid, CE-59b, 6¼" dia, from $100 to 125.00
Butter dish, Wild Rose, CE-82, from $70 to 75.00
Cake stand, sq, Indiana, CE-108, 6¾x10⅜", from $15 to 18.00
Candlestick, Dolphin, Westmoreland, CE-65b, 9¼", ea from $35 to...40.00
Candlestick, emb tassels on sides, rope hdl, CE-64, ea from $30 to......35.00

Candy dish, pocket watch, Imperial, ca. 1958 – 1960, 5¾" diameter, from $40.00 to $50.00. (Photo courtesy Bill and Betty Newbound)

Compote, Atlas, Atterbury, lacy edge, B-104, 8¼", from $100 to....125.00
Covered dish, Battleship Maine, HP, MGB-178, 8" L, from $150 to .. 175.00
Covered dish, picnic basket, Westmoreland, CE-167, 5", from $50 to...60.00
Decanter, wine; Grape, Imperial, G-1950-163/PG-93, 11½".......... 50.00
Jar, cracker; Cherry Thumbprint, Westmoreland, CE-183, 7¾" ... 120.00
Jar, mustard; Tyrolean Bears, Westmoreland, CE-190, 4⅛", $125 to ..130.00
Ladle, curved hdl & ice lip, CE-223, 14" L, from $50 to 60.00

Lamp, Acanthus, emb decor, CE-225, 8¼", from $245 to 250.00
Lamp, Mission Octagon, US Glass, CE-244a, 6½", from $100 to....125.00
Pitcher, Water Lily, Fenton, CE-319, 7", from $70 to.................... 75.00
Plate, bread; Diamond Grille, Atterbury, CE-338, 12", from $55 to... 60.00
Plate, Cardinal, beaded edge, Westmoreland, CE-246d, 7½" dia ... 25.00
Plate, Tree Kittens, Westmoreland, B-106, 7", from $35 to........... 40.00
Shakers, Grape Cluster, 3", CE-284, pr+5½x2⅜" tray, from $28 to...35.00
Sugar bowl, Cow & Wheat, CE-295a, 3⅛x4⅞", from $80 to 90.00
Tray, pin; Rose Garden, CE-344d, 6¾x9⅝", from $12 to 15.00
Vase, Bird, Consolidated, CE-388, 15½", from $130 to 145.00
Vase, Mephistopheles, Vallerysthal, CE-368, 9½", from $60 to...... 80.00
Wall plaque, Eagle & Shield, MarCor, CE-251, 15" dia, from $45 to ..50.00

Millefiori

Millefiori was a type of art glass first produced during the 1800s. Literally the term means 'thousand flowers,' an accurate description of its appearance. Canes, fused bundles of multicolored glass threads such as are often used in paperweights were cut into small cross sections, arranged in the desired pattern, refired, and shaped into articles such as cruets, lamps, and novelty items. It is still being produced, and many examples found on the market today are fairly recent in manufacture. See also Paperweights.

Compote, satin finish, frosted ft, 6½" dia 120.00
Cup & saucer, red/wht/yel/blk, pk trim, 20th C............................. 75.00
Frame, artist's palette shape w/ornate mc border, ca 19th C, 7x6⅝"...210.00
Lamp, bronze dancer stands beside mc 4½" ball shade, 8½" 660.00
Lamp, red flowers on bl & wht, matching shade & shaft, 17" 240.00
Toothpick holder, ruffled rim, 2¾"... 95.00
Tray, concentric rows of canes in clear, star-cut center, 11" dia ..3,500.00
Vase, bulbous body, twisted neck, ruffled/scalloped rim, 2½x2¼"... 90.00
Vase, cylindrical w/5 faint folds, Venetian, 2½"............................. 60.00

Vase, Fratelli Toso, 3x2", $225.00. (Photo courtesy fastgril)

Vase, gourd shape w/ornate appl hdls, 2½x2"................................. 60.00
Vase, lg mc canes w/lava design, Italy, 8" 95.00

Miniature Paintings

Miniature works of art vary considerably in value depending on many criteria: as with any art form, those that are signed by or can be attributed to a well-known artist may command prices well into the thousands of dollars. Collectors find paintings of identifiable subjects especially interesting, as are those with props, such as a child with a vintage toy or a teddy bear or a soldier in uniform with his weapon at his side. Even if none of these factors come to bear, an example exhibiting fine details and skillful workmanship may bring an exceptional price. Of course, condition is important, and ornate or unusual frames also add value. When no medium is described, assume the work to be watercolor on ivory; if no signature is mentioned, assume them to be unsigned.

Bearded man, blk/wht on copper, sgn AG, 1900, oval, 4¾x3½" .. **175.00**
Blond lady w/bl eyes, identified, ca 1830, 4⅛x3¾"+fr................... **300.00**
Cavalier (2nd: woman w/ruff), style of A Van Dyck, 3x2½", pr ... **235.00**
Elizabethan man, on copper, 5x3"+Fr-style brass fr w/crest, 7x6" .. **460.00**
Girl, blk dress/wht collar, sgn AM/1828, on porc, 3x2½"+burl fr... **750.00**
Girl, EX details, Fr enamel sgn Mulis, 6x6"+2-door leather case... **200.00**
Girl, identified, pnt by ED Spritts(?), oval, 2x2½" **210.00**
Girl, pk dress on gr chair, on paper, JS Ellsworth/1854, 4x4"+fr.. **1,150.00**
Girl w/short hair, pendant, BZ Richter 1915 label, porc, 3x2"+fr...**380.00**
Gleaners, enamel on copper, 6x7"+ornate brass fr w/decorative crest... **375.00**
Lady, eyes closed/yel halo, sgn FP, 1½x1"+fold-out leather case..... **95.00**
Lady in chair, lace/jewelry, on paper, sgn/'52, oval, 4x3"+fr **260.00**
Lady w/leg-o'-motton sleeved dress, watercolor/ink on paper, 5x4"+fr.. **490.00**
Lady w/upswept hair, oil on tinned sheet iron, 5" dia+metal fr **650.00**
Man, powdered hair, high-collared coat, 3"+gilt fr **700.00**
Man in blk coat & ascot, ruby ring, 1875, 4¾x3¾" **120.00**
Man in blk hood/robe, on porc, 3x2½"+cvd walnut fr w/oval window... **130.00**
Mary Queen of Scots, ul Gifend (sic), 1880s, 3" L+gilt metal fr .. **530.00**
Noblewoman, high-neck gown, wc on paper, 2¾"+gold-filled fr w/MOP...**175.00**
Noblewoman, powdered wig, sash/jewls, sgn Rosmanol, 4x3" **450.00**
Noblewoman, rose in hair done in ringlets, wht lacy dress, 5½" fr....... **230.00**
Noblewoman, veil & pearls, sgn Girard, 6"+ivory & tortoise-shell fr . **300.00**
Noblewoman (identified) w/lace collar, pearls & medal, 5"+brass fr... **300.00**
Noblewoman in period dress, identified, sgn A Roi, 4x3" **285.00**

Miniatures

There is some confusion as to what should be included in a listing of miniature collectibles. Some feel the only true miniature is the salesman's sample; other collectors consider certain small-scale children's toys to be appropriately referred to as miniatures, while yet others believe a miniature to be any small-scale item that gives evidence to the craftsmanship of its creator. For salesman's samples, see specific category; other types are listed below. See also Dollhouses and Furnishings; Children's Things.

Andirons, brass Fed form w/trn fronts & iron dogs, 9x7", pr **1,095.00**
Armoire, mahog, 2 doors/ball ft, segmented panel sides, 22x13x7".. **1,060.00**
Blanket chest, curly maple/poplar, cut-out bracket ft, inlay, 11½" **2,875.00**

Blanket chest, four-color decor on original brown, chip-carved moldings, interior with open till, 15" wide, $12,650.00.
(Photo courtesy Garth's Auctions Inc.)

Blanket chest, pine w/gr pnt, blk & wht trim, tin/wire hinges, 7x15"... **865.00**
Blanket chest, red-glk grpt on front panel, sq nails, dvtl, 8x12x7"....**1,375.00**
Bucket, staved, brass bands, mustard pnt, wire bail, 3¾" **750.00**
Bucket, staved, brass bands, wire bail, E Murdock...Mass, 3¾".....**800.00**
Chamber pot, yellowware, unmk, ca 1880, 1¾"............................ **175.00**
Chest, cherry/poplar, 3-drw, paneled sides, dry red stain, 12x12x8" ...**400.00**
Chest, curly maple/cherry, half-trn pilasters, dvtl drws, 23x20x13"..**3,350.00**

Chest, mahog Hplwht w/pinstriping, serpentine front, Fr ft, 16x17" **2,030.00**
Chest, mahog/mahog flame vnr w/2 dvtl drws, rprs/rpl, 8⅜x9¾x5".. **800.00**
Chest, mahog/oak/pine Hplwht w/red stain, 3 dvtl drw, rprs, 12x13x6"...**600.00**
Chest, mahog/poplar w/serpentine front, 4 grad drw, trn ft, 13x11x7".. **1,150.00**
Chest, pine w/orig red grpt case, 3 mustard grpt drws, 1850s, 13x15x8"..**2,500.00**
Cupboard, jelly; 2 drw over 2 do, pine w/gray pnt over red, 17x13x8"....**490.00**
Cupboard, pine step-bk w/EX patina, 3-shelf/1-do, sq nails, 17x8x6" . **1,150.00**
Dry sink, drainboard over drw/2 doors/metal pulls/orig pnt, 19x25x13"..**1,095.00**
Gazebo, gray pnt w/red trim, octagonal, 1800s, 13x12", +2 benches .. **1,400.00**
Mule chest, walnut/poplar, 2-drw/bracket ft, wire nails, rfn, 12x13x7"... **490.00**
Settee, Windsor, cvd/pnt wood, swollen spindles, plank seat, 8x12x5".**235.00**
Trammel, wrought-iron w/scrolled details, 8¾-12" **700.00**

Minton

Thomas Minton established his firm in 1793 at Stoke on Trent and within a few years began producing earthenware with blue-printed patterns similar to the ware he had learned to decorate while employed by the Caughley Porcelain Factory. The Willow pattern was one of his most popular. Neither this nor the porcelain made from 1798 to 1805 was marked (except for an occasional number series), making identification often impossible.

After 1805 until about 1816, fine tea services, beehive-shaped honey pots, trays, etc., were hand decorated with florals, landscapes, Imari-type designs, and neoclassic devices. These were often marked with crossed 'Ls.' It was Minton that invented the acid gold process of decorating (1863), which is now used by a number of different companies. From 1816 until 1823, no porcelain was made. Through the 1920s and 1930s, the ornamental wares with colorful decoration of applied fruits and florals and figurines in both bisque and enamel were usually left unmarked. As a result, they have been erroneously attributed to other potters. Some of the ware that was marked bears a deliberate imitation of Meissen's crossed swords. From the late '20s through the '40s, Minton made a molded stoneware line (mugs, jugs, teapots, etc.) with florals or figures in high relief. These were marked with an embossed scroll with an 'M' in the bottom curve. Fine parian ware was made in the late 1840s, and in the 1850s Minton experimented with and perfected a line of quality majolica which they produced from 1860 until it was discontinued in 1908. Their slogan was 'Majolica for the Millions,' and for it they gained widespread recognition. Leadership of the firm was assumed by Minton's son Herbert sometime around the middle of the nineteenth century. Working hand in hand with Leon Arnoux, who was both a chemist and an artist, he managed to secure the company's financial future through constant, successful experimentation with both materials and decorating methods. During the Victorian era, M. L. Solon decorated pieces in the pate-sur-pate style, often signing his work; these examples are considered to be the finest of their type. After 1862 all wares were marked 'Minton' or 'Mintons,' with an impressed year cipher.

Many collectors today reassemble the lovely dinnerware patterns that have been made by Minton. Perhaps one of their most popular lines was Minton Rose, introduced in 1854. The company itself once counted 47 versions of this pattern being made by other potteries around the world. In addition to less expensive copies, elaborate hand-enameled pieces were also made by Aynsley, Crown Staffordshire, and Paragon China. Solando Ware (1937) and Byzantine Range (1938) were designed by John Wadsworth. Minton ceased all earthenware production in 1939.

See also Majolica; Parian.

Dinnerware

April, bowl, rimmed soup; 7⅞" **40.00**
April, cup & saucer, ftd... **20.00**
April, plate, dinner; 10¾" **30.00**

April, platter, 14⅞" L 120.00
Avondale, cup & saucer, ftd 35.00
Avondale, plate, salad; 7⅝" 27.50
Avondale, sugar bowl 45.00
Chatham, cream soup, ftd, w/saucer 50.00
Chatham, cup & saucer, ftd 35.00
Chatham, plate, salad; 7¾" 27.00
Clivedon, bowl, rice, 4" 10.00
Clivedon, bowl, rimmed soup; 8" 28.00
Clivedon, bowl, vegetable; oval, w/lid 185.00
Clivedon, plate, dinner; 10⅝" 22.00
Diana, bowl, cream soup; ftd, w/saucer 50.00
Diana, cup & saucer 35.00
Diana, plate, dinner; 10¾" 30.00
Diana, plate, salad; 7¾" 22.00
Emperor's Garden, bowl, fruit/dessert 20.00
Emperor's Garden, bowl, rimmed soup; 8" 48.00
Emperor's Garden, plate, salad; 8" 35.00
Grosvenor, bowl, vegetable; oval, /wlid 300.00
Grosvenor, coffeepot, 5-cup 225.00
Grosvenor, creamer, 10-oz 55.00
Grosvenor, cup & saucer, ftd 30.00
Lady Hamilton, bowl, coupe cereal 30.00
Lady Hamilton, bowl, cream soup; ftd, w/saucer 40.00
Lady Hamilton, plate, dinner; 10½" 30.00
Lady Hamilton, plate, luncheon; 9" 32.00
Marlborough, bowl, rimmed soup; lg 70.00
Marlborough, cup & saucer, ftd 25.00
Marlborough, plate, dinner; 11" 40.00
Marlborough, platter, 16" L 220.00
Marlborough, teapot 175.00
Portland Rose, creamer 115.00
Portland Rose, cup & saucer, ftd 100.00
Portland Rose, plate, dinner 95.00
Portland Rose, sugar bowl, w/lid 200.00
Seaforth, bowl, coupe cereal; lg 40.00
Seaforth, cookie plate, 9½" 35.00
Seaforth, cup & saucer, flat, 2¼" 35.00
Seaforth, cup & saucer, oversz 40.00
Seaforth, sugar bowl 75.00
Versailles, coffeepot, 5-cup 230.00
Versailles, creamer 35.00
Versailles, cup & saucer, ftd 25.00
Versailles, plate, dessert 25.00
Versailles, plate, dinner 65.00

Miscellaneous

Charger, parakeets on red ground with flowers, ca. 1877, 14", $1,095.00.
(Photo courtesy Skinner Inc. Auctioneers & Appraisers of Antiques & Fine Art)

Charger, birds on floral branches on yel, 1872, 13½" 825.00
Jardinieres, floral/foliage, enamel/slip, Secessionist, 1900s, 11", pr.... 1,300.00
Plaque, Jasper, Endymion on Rock Latmos, solid lt bl, 1919, 13x10" .. 1,295.00
Plate, garland rim w/pk & gr floral swags, gilt inner rim, 9", 9 for ... 530.00
Plate, portrait of a youth, earthenware, Ellen Welby, 1877, 10" ... 700.00
Tile/plaque, cavalier in relief, yel, late 19th C, 12" L 325.00
Vase, birds/flowering branches, wht on med bl, shouldered, 1875, 7" .. 700.00
Vase, mother & child/nymph, snake hdls, pearlware, 1870s, 15" ... 1,295.00

Mirrors

The first mirrors were made in England in the thirteenth century of very thin glass backed with lead. Reverse-painted glass mirrors were made in this country as early as the late 1700s and remained popular throughout the next century. The simple hand-painted panel was separated from the mirrored section by a narrow slat, and the frame was either the dark-finished Federal style or the more elegant, often-gilded Sheraton.

Mirrors changed with the style of other furnishings; but whatever type you purchase, as long as the glass sections remain solid, even broken or flaking mirrors are more valued than replaced glass. Careful resilvering is acceptable if excessive deterioration has taken place. In the listings that follow, items are from the nineteenth century unless noted otherwise. The term 'style' (example: Federal style) is used to indicate a mirror reminiscent of, but made well after, the period indicated. Obviously these retro styles will be valued much lower than their original counterparts. As with most other items in antiques and collectibles, the influence of online trading is greatly affecting prices. Many items once considered difficult to locate are now readily available online. Our advisor for this category is Michael Hinton; he is listed in the Directory under Pennsylvania.

Key:
Chpndl — Chippendale
Emp — Empire
Fed — Federal
QA — Queen Anne
vnr — veneer

Burl walnut QA, scroll/rtcl crest w/gilt shell, foliate sides, 45x24" 2,100.00
Cheval, mahog Am Late Fed in Gothic style, 1830s, 70x37x22" .. 5,200.00
Cheval, mahog classical, blocked/cvd supports, scroll ft, 63x24" ... 825.00
Dressing, polished steel, rtcl w/floral, scroll ft, Pat 1890, 18x16" ... 300.00
Fed w/rvpt panel: church/home/man on sailboat, 3-reed columns, 43x21" .. 450.00
Giltwood, eagle crest/pendant husk, wheat as candle arms, rnd, 44" .. 6,500.00
Giltwood, ornate cornice/stepped molded frieze, florals, 76x61" ... 3,985.00
Giltwood, shell/scroll-cvd rtcl crest, 8-sided, 8-panel border, 47x33" .. 2,800.00
Giltwood Italian rococo, rtcl scrolls/leaves/shells, 74x50" 7,000.00
Giltwood Louis XVI-style sunburst, cloud & cherub masks, 19th C, 23" .. 1,400.00
Giltwood Regency bull's-eye, ebonzied rabbet, 19th C, 23 " dia .. 2,000.00
Mahog & figured vnr Chpndl, scalloped crest, sm rprs, 42" 500.00
Mahog Chpndl, scrollwork all around, gilt eagle atop, 36x18" 350.00
Mahog Chpndl style w/scrolled crests & bottom, rpt gold liner, 33x17" .. 250.00
Mahog English Chpndl, Prince of Wales crest, rprs, 32" 250.00
Mahog Fed w/flame grpt, molded crest, rfn/rpl, 44⅝x21" 600.00
Mahog flame-gr vnr Chpndl style, 20th C, 40" 250.00
Mahog ogee w/gilt outer fr & liner, 1920s, Buckley & Co, 49x24" .. 2,350.00
Mahog QA style w/eagle crest, gilt gesso liner, ca 1900, 47x21" .. 500.00
Mahog vnr QA w/gilt & molded liner, 38½x16¼" 600.00
Mahog/giltwood Chpndl, scalloped/rtcl w/phoenix bird, 1780s, 30x14" .. 880.00
Mahog/pine Chpndl, alligatored finish, sm rpr, att NY, 26x14" ... 400.00
Maple/curly maple, broken arch crest w/cvd eagle finial, rpr, 51" 250.00
Overmantel, gilt/ebonized, ring-trn half columns, rosettes, 20x42" .. 2,000.00
Overmantel, giltwood, candle shelf/2 columns ea side, ornate, 54x60" 1,355.00
Part-ebonized fruitwood Biedermeier, arched crest/fan inlay, 48x22" 1,880.00
Pier, giltwood, lg pediment cornice w/acorns/swags/etc, 56x33" .. 5,100.00
Pier, giltwood, plain fr, Hudson & Smith, 1820s, 84x36" 7,050.00
Pier, giltwood, rectangular w/spiral moldings, mercury glass, 54x35" .. 400.00
Pier, giltwood Am classical, corners w/shells/scrolls, 1820, 62x30" ... 4,100.00

Pier, giltwood Fed, beveled molded fr, early 19th C, 65x42" 2,350.00
Pier, maple w/split columns/acanthus capitals, rvpt above, 50x28" ..1,600.00
Walnut/parcel gilt, scroll pediment w/lg cvd plume, Italian, 60x52" ..7,500.00

Mocha

Mochaware is utilitarian pottery made principally in England (and to a lesser extent in France) between 1780 and 1840 on the then prevalent creamware and pearlware bodies. Initially, only those pieces decorated in the seaweed pattern were called 'Mocha,' while geometrically decorated pieces were referred to as 'Banded Creamware.' Other types of decorations were called 'Dipped Ware.' During the last 40 to 50 years the term 'Mocha' has been applied to the entire realm of 'Industrialized Slipware' — pottery decorated by the turner on his lathe using coggle wheels and slip cups. It was made in numerous patterns — Tree, Seaweed or Dandelion, Rope (also called Earthworm or Loop), Cat's-eye, Tobacco Leaf, Lollypop or Balloon, Marbled, Marbled and Combed, Twig, Geometric or Checkered, Banded, and slip decorations of rings, dots, flags, tulips, wavy lines, etc. It came into its own as a collectible in the latter half of the 1940s and has become increasingly popular as more and more people are exposed to the rich colorings and artistic appeal of its varied forms of abstract decoration. (Please note: Values hinge to a great extent on vivid coloration, intricacy of patterns and unusual features.)

The collector should take care not to confuse the early pearlware and creamware Mocha with the later kitchen yellow ware, graniteware, and ironstone sporting Mocha-type decoration that was produced in America by such potters as J. Vodrey, George S. Harker, Edwin Bennett, and John Bell. This type was also produced in Scotland and Wales and was marketed well into the twentieth century.

Our values are prices realized at auction, where nearly every example was in exceptional condition. Unless a repair, damage, or another rating is included in the description, assume the item to be in NM condition.

Bowl, waste; earthworm, 3-color on orange, dk brn bands 300.00
Creamer, brn/wht marbleized, gr band at rim, wht ft, 19th C, EX ..2,600.00
Creamer, seaweed, blk on lt gray, tooled gr band, 4½" 1,000.00
Goblet, tobacco leaves, brn & wht on chocolate, banded ft, 4" ..6,000.00
Jug, brn/bl/tan/wht marbleized, bl band, chips, 8"......................2,600.00
Jug, earthworm, brn & wht on lt bl, med bl/brn bands, stain, 4" ...1,500.00
Jug, earthworm, brn on tan, bl/brn/gr bands, 7", EX 500.00
Jug, earthworm (allover), brn/wht on rust, gr/brn bands, rpr, 7½" ..1,100.00
Jug, geometrics, brn on tan, gr/orange stripes, crack, 9½"..........4,100.00
Jug, polka dots, 3-color on tan, 3-color bands, rpr, 7⅜" 1,080.00
Jug, seaweed, brn on lt orange, dk brn & gr bands, leaf hdl, 7"...1,140.00
Muffineer, earthworm, brn & wht on bl w/brn bands, EX 2,700.00
Mug, brn broken bands & thin blk bands, 3", EX........................ 575.00
Mug, checkerboard band, bl & wht, brn splotches inside, 4¾" 600.00
Mug, earthworm, bl/mc on brn, bl/brn bands, cylindrical..........3,600.00
Mug, earthworm, brn/wht on dk brn (2 bands), brn bands, EX.2,400.00
Mug, earthworm, gray/brn/wht on orange, gr/brn bands, flakes, 4¾"..2,200.00
Mug, seaweed, brn on bl, gr/brn bands, 5⅞" 1,080.00
Mug, seaweed, brn on tan, bl & brn bands, 6" 300.00
Mug, tobacco leaf, brn/wht on caramel, brn band, cylindrical, 6"..........6,240.00
Pepper pot, earthworm, slate bl w/burnt orange bands, 4¼" 3,000.00
Pepper pot, seaweed, dk brn on orange, gr/brn bands, 4" 1,025.00

Molds

Food molds have become popular as collectibles — not only for their value as antiques, but because they also revive childhood memories of elaborate ice cream Santas with candy trim or barley-sugar figurals adorning a Christmas tree. Ice cream molds were made of pewter and came in a variety of shapes and styles with most of the detail on the inside of the mold. Chocolate molds were made in a wider variety of shapes, showing more detail on the outside of the mold, making it more decorative to look at. They were usually made of tin or copper, then nickel-plated to keep them from tarnishing or rusting as well as for sanitary reasons. (Many chocolate molds have been recently reproduced. These include Christmas trees and Santa Claus figures as well as some forms of rabbits. They are imported from Europe and may affect the market.) Hard candy molds were usually metal, although primitive maple sugar molds (usually simple hearts, rabbits, and other animals) were carved from wood. Cake molds were made of cast iron or cast aluminum and were most common in the shape of a lamb, a rabbit, or Santa Claus. Our advisors for this category are Dale and Jean Van Kuren; they are listed in the Directory under New York.

Chocolate Molds

Babies (standing in 2 rows of 9 ea), 6¼x8¾" overall..................... 145.00
Baby carriage, Holland, 3".. 60.00
Chick emerging from egg, 2-pc, w/clips, 4" 60.00
Chick pulling bunny in egg wagon, 2-pc, Germany, #3055, 5¼x6¼"...65.00
Chicken, hinged 2-pc, #290 .... 70.00
Chicken on nest, France, #1305, 2-sided w/removable base, 8x8", VG.......120.00
Cigar, rolled tobacco look, 2-pc, w/clips, 2½x10" 42.00
Donkey standing w/head trn to 1 side, 2-pc, 4½x6¼" 85.00
Easter rabbits (5) in row, 12" L... 70.00
Heart shape w/Merry Christmas emb in center, 8x7" 45.00
Indian chief, sgn W Jeacock, Coyote 95.00
Lovebirds facing ea other on base, #40, 1920s, 2¾" 95.00
Mandolin, detailed, H Walie Berlin, 2-pc w/clips, 1¾x8½x4"...... 125.00
Parrot on perch, CC Marque de Fabrique, 3-pc, 10¾x4½" 360.00
Porcupine, EX details, 2-pc, 10½" L...480.00
Rabbit, 2-pc, 5" 35.00
Rabbit (4) in fr, NY, 9x7" overall 145.00
Rabbit seated, hinged, 9" 60.00
Rabbit w/basket, 2-pc, Alton R_ #6231, 7x8¼" 60.00
Rifle, 2-pc, w/wire hanging clip, 12x3".. 120.00

Santa, 8½", G, $120.00.
(Photo courtesy Morphy Auctions)

Sedan, 4-pc w/clips, 7¼", VG 120.00
St Nicholas, detailed, 2-pc, #2041, 4½" 55.00
Turkey w/tail spread, 2-pc, old clips, Made in USA, 4x3½" 90.00

Ice Cream Molds

Asparagus bunch tied w/string, CC 823 France, 3½x3" 65.00
Bell w/cherub, hinged, 3½" dia.. 100.00
Bowl, dessert; 3-pc, E&Co, 5x12x8¼".. 140.00

Castle on hillside, 2-pc, 11"... 280.00
Chick emerging from egg, hinged, 3" 120.00
Crown & peak pattern, copper/tin, Birmingham #578, 3½x4½".. 120.00
Elephant, hinged, 3" 70.00
Geo Washington profile, hinged, 3½x3x1½" 100.00
Heart, 2-pc, S&Co, 8" 300.00
Hen sitting, 2-pc, Germany, 10" 140.00
Oyster plate, 2-pc, Pat Appl For, 9" dia............................ 450.00
Pear, hinged, E&C #249, 4" 30.00
Rabbit running, 2-pc, 3" 70.00
Rabbit seated, 2-pc, 12" 500.00
Ring, copper/tin, 3-tiered, 5x10" 100.00
Rose, hinged, 2-pc, 9½", VG 170.00
Santa Claus, hinged, E&Co, 11" 420.00
Star w/10 stars (waving), hinged, E&Co #1075, 2½x3½x1⅜" 90.00
Stork w/baby, hinged, #1151, 5" 85.00
Tin, fish in arched shape, 2½x20x3½" 30.00
Tin, lamb & cross, geometric sides, 19th C, 5x11" dia 360.00
Watermelon w/slice removed, S&Co, 4-pc, 9½" W..................... 420.00

Miscellaneous

Copper, roses and leaves, 6" diameter, $250.00. (Photo courtesy Mary Frank Gaston)

Copper, flower form, 1800s, 7½", EX 60.00
Copper/tin, emb fruit, Kreamer, 7" 30.00
Copper/tin, lg thistle, hanging tab, rectangular, 6" L.................. 110.00
Tin, grape cluster, rectangular, 2-pc, England, 4½x6x4" 35.00

Monart

Scottish glassmaker, John Moncrief was fascinated by the technique of suspending colored enamels within the molten glass during the glass-making process. Recognizing the potential of the process (which he had observed while in France), he began his own business in Perth, Scotland, in 1924. The glassware he created was called Monart. Several commercial lines were along the fine artware pieces designed with scrolls or feathers suspended within the glass. Nearly all examples are unmarked, most having originally carried a paper label.

Bowl, bl mottle w/swirling amethyst rim, 9" 550.00
Bowl, lt gr w/aventurine, emb ribs, flared rim, 13" 250.00
Vase, bl/citron/heather/teal mottle, bulbous, 8½" 725.00
Vase, burnt orange mottle w/gr splashes, 9" 900.00
Vase, peach & purple mottle w/3 whorls, gold flecks, 7¼"............ 425.00
Vase, red mottle w/aventurine, amethyst rim, cylinder neck, 13¾"..2,000.00
Vase, red mottle w/bubbles, yel mottle rim, ovoid, 13½" 1,200.00

Monmouth

The Monmouth Pottery Company was established in 1892 in Mon-
mouth, Illinois. It was touted as the largest pottery in the world. Their primary products were utilitarian: stoneware crocks, churns, jugs, water coolers, etc. — in salt glaze, Bristol, spongeware, and Albany brown. In 1906 they were absorbed by a conglomerate called the Western Stoneware Company. Monmouth Pottery Co. became their #1 plant and until 1930 continued to produce stoneware marked with the Western Stoneware Company's maple leaf logo. Items marked 'Monmouth Pottery Co.' were made before 1906. Western Stoneware Co. introduced a line of artware in 1926. The name chosen for the artware was Monmouth Pottery. Some stamps and paper labels add ILL to the name. All the ware in this category was produced from 1892 through 1906 when the Monmouth Pottery Co. became part of the Western Stoneware Company and ceased to exist as the original entity.

Bowl, salt glazed, brn int, mk, 2-gal.. 200.00
Churn, #3, cobalt on salt glaze, 3-gal, 13" 250.00
Churn, #4, cobalt on salt glaze, 16½" 250.00
Churn, #5, cobalt on salt glaze, 5-gal 325.00
Churn, Bristol, Maple Leaf mk, 2-gal 250.00
Churn, cobalt on salt glaze, 6-gal 400.00
Churn, salt glaze, mini, 4"... 1,200.00
Churn, 2 Men in a Crock stencil, 5-gal.................................... 1,000.00
Cooler, ice water; bl & wht spongeware, mini 1,500.00
Cooler, ice water; bl & wht spongeware, w/lid & spigot, 8-gal..1,500.00
Cow & calf, brn, Monmouth Pottery Co, mk 5,000.00
Crock, Bristol, mini, 2½" 600.00
Crock, Bristol, 10-gal... 100.00
Crock, Bristol, 20-gal... 200.00
Crock, Bristol, 60-gal...2,000.00
Crock, Bristol Monmouth Pottery Co, bl stencil, 1-qt 250.00
Crock, Bristol w/Albany slip int, 4-gal....................................... 85.00
Crock, Bristol w/Maple Leaf mk, 2½x3¼" 40.00
Crock, Bristol w/Maple Leaf mk, 2-gal...................................... 75.00
Crock, early dull Bristol w/cobalt stencil 300.00
Crock, salt glaze, Albany slip int, 3-gal 95.00
Crock, salt glaze, hand decor, mk, 2-gal 250.00
Crock, salt glaze, unmk, 2-gal 60.00
Crock, stencil, bl on dk brn Albany slip, 3-gal........................ 400.00
Crock, stencil, bl on dk brn Albany slip, 6-gal........................ 600.00
Crock, 2 Men in a Crock stencil, 10-gal................................... 700.00
Dog, Monmouth Pottery Co, mk, Albany slip 8,000.00
Hen on nest, bl & wht spongeware 1,200.00
Jug, Bristol, bl stencil (early rectangle), 5-gal 250.00
Jug, Bristol, Maple Leaf mk, 5-gal.. 200.00
Jug, Bristol w/Albany slip top, mini, 2½" 500.00
Letterhead, 1898 letter 45.00
Pig, Bristol, Monmouth Pottery Co, mk................................. 1,500.00
Pig, brn, mk Monmouth Pottery Co, mk................................. 1,000.00
Snuff or preserve jar, wax seal.. 350.00
Tobacco jar, monk, brn Albany slip.......................................3,000.00

Mont Joye

Mont Joye was a type of acid-cut French cameo glass produced by Cristallerie de Pantin in Paris around the turn of the century. It is accented by enamels. Our advisor for this category is Don Williams; he is listed in the Directory under Missouri.

Rose bowl, cyclamen on textured frost, gilt 6-scallop rim, 4" 575.00
Vase, floral, gold on textured ruby, gilt rim, 4-sided, 6½", pr 460.00
Vase, heavily enameled flowers on amethyst w/optic ribs, ruffled, 4".....345.00
Vase, horse chestnuts, brn/silver/gilt on mauve frost, long neck, 27"..4,200.00
Vase, irises, purple/wht/mauve w/yel stamens, gilt trim, cylinder, 12" ...750.00
Vase, irises, 1 on ea of 4 sides, purple on textured crystal, 12"......690.00

Vase, pansies, enameled, applied bumblebee (later addition), 14", $1,095.00. (Photo courtesy James D. Julia Inc.)

Vase, sunflowers, silver/gold on textured clear, trumpet form, 10" ...350.00
Vase, violets & gold leaves, stalactite gilt rim, stick neck, 14" 600.00

Moorcroft

William Moorcroft began to work for MacIntyre Potteries in 1897. At first he was the chief designer but very soon took over their newly created art pottery department. His first important design was the Aurelian Ware, part transfer and part hand painted. Very shortly thereafter, around the turn of the century, he developed his famous Florian Ware, with heavy slip, done in mostly blue and white. Since the early 1900s there has been a succession of designs, most of them very characteristic of the company. Moorcroft left MacIntyre in 1913 and went out on his own. He had already well established his name, having won prizes and gold medals at the St. Louis World's Fair as well as in Paris. In 1929 Queen Mary, who had been collecting his pottery, made him 'Potter to the Queen,' and the pottery was so stamped up until 1949. William Moorcroft died in 1945, and his son Walter ran the company until recent years. The factory is still in existence. They now produce different designs but continue to use the characteristic slipwork. Moorcroft pottery was sold abroad in Canada, the United States, Australia, and Europe as well as in specialty areas such as the island of Bermuda.

Moorcroft went through a 'Japanese' stage in the early teens with his lovely lustre glazes, Oriental shapes and decorations. During the mid-teens he began to produce his most popular Pomegranate Ware and Wisteria (often called 'Fruit'). Around that time he also designed the popular Pansy line as well as Leaves and Grapes. Soon he introduced a beautiful landscape series called variously Hazeldine, Moonlit Blue, Eventide, and Dawn. These wonderful designs along with Claremont (Mushrooms) seem to be the most sought after by collectors today. It would be possible to add many other designs to this list. During the 1920s and 1930s, Moorcroft became very interested in highly fired Flambe (red) glazes. These could only be achieved through a very difficult procedure which he himself perfected in secret. He later passed the knowledge on to his son.

Dating of this pottery is done by knowledge of the designs, shapes, signatures, and marks on the bottom of each piece; an experienced person can usually narrow it down to a short time frame. Prices escalated for this 'rediscovered' pottery in the late 1980s but has now leveled off. This is true mainly of the pre-1935 designs of William Moorcroft, as it is items from that era that attract the most collector interest. Prices in the listings below are for pieces in mint condition unless noted otherwise; no reproductions are listed here. Advisors for this category are Wilfred and Dolli Cohen; they are listed in the Directory under California.

Biscuit jar, Eventide, SP lid/hdl, MIE, 6½x5½", NM 2,500.00
Biscuit jar, rose garlands on wht, SP rim/hdl/lid, Macintyre, 1910s..750.00

Bowl, Freesia on washed bl, ca 1935, 12" 765.00
Bowl, mixed flowers, loop hdls, ftd, Macintyre, ca 1907, 5⅛" ...1,400.00
Bowl, Moonlit Blue Landscape, SP rim, ca 1925, 8⅜" 1,500.00
Bowl, Pansy, purple/cream, 8"...1,000.00
Bowl, Pomegranate on dk bl, w/hdls, MIE, 11" W 400.00
Box, Clematis, Royal Warrant label, 1¾x4¾"...............................145.00
Box, Clematis, Royal Warrant label, 9¼" dia................................360.00
Candlesticks, Poppy on cobalt, ca 1925, 7⅞", pr 1,175.00
Case, Orchid on cobalt, mid-20th C, 8¼"....................................700.00
Compote, Hibiscus, coral on brn, 3⅝" H 90.00
Ginger jar, Hibiscus, rose on gr, label, 8½".................................300.00
Lamp, berries & leaves on flambe, ca 1945-49, 11"+mts 600.00
Lamp, dragon, purple/red on ivory, base: 10".............................210.00
Pitcher, Florian, Anemone on wht, Macintyre, #447667/M2645, 5"..565.00
Pitcher, flowers & ribbons on cream, 1912, 5½" 235.00
Plate, Moonlit Blue Landscape, ca 1925, 7¼"...........................1,175.00
Trade sign, rectangular shallow tray, blk letters on cream, 8" L....350.00
Vase, Anemone, mc on cobalt, ca 1950s, 8⅛"..............................475.00
Vase, Anemone, red/bl/wht on wht to bl, bulbous, 6" 465.00
Vase, brick red w/foliate roundels on shouldered cylinder, Liberty, 8" ...250.00
Vase, Claremont, toadstools on washed bl, ca 1915, 7¼" 3,000.00
Vase, Eventide, rust/orange trees, 6"..1,920.00

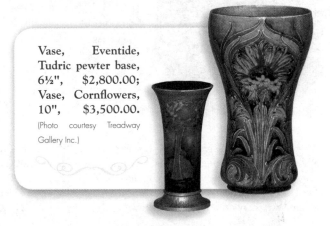

Vase, Eventide, Tudric pewter base, 6½", $2,800.00; Vase, Cornflowers, 10", $3,500.00. (Photo courtesy Treadway Gallery Inc.)

Vase, Florian, lg peacock feathers, bl on wht, 6" 1,200.00
Vase, Florian, lilac on wht, Macintyre, early 20th C, 8¾" 1,060.00
Vase, Florian, shades of bl on wht, lg bl hdls, 12" 1,440.00
Vase, Freesia, red/gr on red, orb shape, late, 5" 350.00
Vase, grapes & leaves on washed bl, ca 1930, 8¼" 600.00
Vase, Hibiscus, pk/bl on brn, #10/111.80, 12½"...........................300.00
Vase, Hibiscus, washed bl, mid-20th C, 10" 650.00
Vase, Hibiscus on gr, 10"..150.00
Vase, landscape, bl/wht, cylinder w/pewter base, MIE #281, 11x5"..3,240.00
Vase, Orchid, flambe, flared rim, Royal Warrant label, 9¼" 775.00
Vase, Orchid on cobalt, ca 1925, 9⅞" 650.00
Vase, Pansy on cobalt, ca 1925, 7¾"...500.00
Vase, Pomegranate, bottle shape, ca 1930, 6" 600.00
Vase, Pomegranate, classic shape, 6¼" 565.00
Vase, Pomegranate, mc on cobalt, bottle shape, ca 1925, 12" 765.00
Vase, Pomegranate on dk bl, w/hdls, Burslem England #5, 8½x7½"...1,200.00
Vase, Wisteria, banded decor w/cobalt bands, ca 1930, 6¼" 1,000.00
Vase, Wisteria & Fruit, mc on cobalt, ca 1930, 10" 650.00

Moravian Pottery and Tile Works

The Moravian Pottery and Tile Works, Doylestown, Pennsylvania, was founded by Dr. Henry Chapman Mercer in 1898. He discovered the art and science of tile making on his own, without training from the existing American or European tile industry. This, along with his diverse talents as an author, anthropologist, historian, and artist, led Dr. Mercer to create something very unique. He approached tile design with an historic point of view, and he created totally new production methods that ultimately became widely accepted by manufacturers of handcrafted tile. The subject matter for the designs he preferred included nature and the arts, colonial tools and artifacts, storytelling, and medieval themes. Both of these 'new' approaches to design and production allowed Dr. Mercer to become extremely influential in the development of pottery and tile in the Arts & Crafts Movement in America.

After Mercer's death in 1930, the Tile Works was managed by Frank Swain until 1954. In 1967 it was purchased by the Bucks County Dept. of Parks & Recreation. Tiles are being produced there today in the handmade tradition of Mercer; they are marked with a conjoined MOR and dated. Collectors look for the early tiles (mostly pre-1940), the preponderance of which bear no backstamps. These tiles were made using both red and white clays and are also referred to as 'Mercer' tiles. Our advisor for this category is Suzanne Perrault; she is listed in the Directory under New Jersey.

Medallion, Autumn, MR, 16¾", from $3,000.00 to $4,000.00. (Photo courtesy David Rago Auctions)

Box, Vicca of Stowe, bl & ivory w/red showing, no lid, 3¾", EX... 840.00
Medallion, bird on floral branch, 5-color, rstr, 17½" dia 6,000.00
Tile, Birds of Tintern Abbey, ivory on bl, diagonal, 5½" 300.00
Tile, Persian Antelope, ivory & bl w/red clay showing, nicks, 5¾" .. 575.00
Tile, steamboat, ivory on gr w/red clay showing, chips to fr, 6¼"... 275.00

Morgan, Matt

From 1883 to 1885, the Matt Morgan Art Pottery of Cincinnati, Ohio, produced fine artware, some of which resembled the pottery of the Moors with intense colors and gold accents. Some of the later wares were very similar to those of Rookwood, due to the fact that several Rookwood artists were also associated with the Morgan pottery. Some examples were marked with a paper label, others were either a two- or three-line impression: 'Matt Morgan Art Pottery Co.,' with 'Cin. O.' sometimes added.

Bowl, sparrows/bamboo, brn on tan gloss, spherical w/3 ball ft, 5½" ..360.00
Bowl vase, marsh birds/cvd beetle on mottled gr, scroll hdls, 10x13".. 1,200.00
Charger, pr lg wht cranes on brn/rust, att, 17" 3,000.00
Vase, bamboo shoots/sparrows on lt to dk gr w/gilt rim, bulbous, 8"...360.00
Vase, floral/butterfly, pk/gr on yel w/gilt, shoulder hdls, 5", NM... 300.00
Vase, lg swallows/bamboo on dk gr to pumpkin w/gilt trim, bulbous, 8" .480.00
Vase, relief Moresque panels, brn over terra cotta, pear form, 17"...420.00

Morgantown Glass

Incorporated in 1899, the Morgantown Glass Works experienced many name changes over the years. Today 'Morgantown Glass' is a generic term used to identify all glass produced there. Purchased by Fostoria in 1965, the factory was permanently closed in 1971.

Golf Ball is the most recognized design with crosshatched bumps equally distributed along the stem (very similar to Cambridge #1066, identified with alternating lines of dimples between rows of crosshatching). For further information we also recommend *Elegant Glassware of the Depression Era* by Gene and Cathy Florence (Mr. and Mrs. Florence's books are published by Collector Books).

American Beauty, crystal, champagne, 6-oz 20.00
American Beauty, crystal, compote, 5x8" 37.50
American Beauty, crystal, finger bowl, #2927, 4⅜" 45.00
American Beauty, crystal, pitcher, 48-oz, 8" 195.00
American Beauty, crystal, plate, #1511, 7½" 12.50
American Beauty, crystal, tumbler, water; 9-oz, 7" 32.50
Golf Ball, colors other than Steigel Green or Spanish Red, bell.... 60.00
Golf Ball, colors other than Steigel Green or Spanish Red, compote, 6"... 300.00
Golf Ball, colors other than Steigel Green or Spanish Red, urn, 6½" ..65.00
Golf Ball, Steigel Green or Spanish Red, cafe parfait, 4-oz, 6½" .. 100.00
Golf Ball, Steigel Green or Spanish Red, champagne, 5" 32.00
Golf Ball, Steigel Green or Spanish Red, claret, 4½-oz, 5¼" 38.00
Golf Ball, Steigel Green or Spanish Red, creamer 175.00
Golf Ball, Steigel Green or Spanish Red, pilsner, 11-oz, 9⅛" 165.00
Golf Ball, Steigel Green or Spanish Red, tumbler, juice; ftd, 5-oz, 5"...30.00
Golf Ball, Steigel Green or Spanish Red, tumbler, wine; ftd, 4⅜".. 35.00
Queen Louise, crystal w/Anna Rose, cocktail, 3-oz 400.00
Queen Louise, crystal w/Anna Rose, finger bowl, ftd.................. 250.00
Queen Louise, crystal w/Anna Rose, plate, salad........................ 150.00
Queen Louise, crystal w/Anna Rose, saucer champagne, 5½-oz ... 395.00
Queen Louise, crystal w/Anna Rose, tumbler, ftd, 9-oz 395.00
Queen Louise, crystal w/Anna Rose, wine, 2½-oz....................... 400.00
Sunrise Medallion, bl, creamer.. 325.00
Sunrise Medallion, bl, finger bowl, ftd 85.00
Sunrise Medallion, bl, plate, 8⅜" 25.00
Sunrise Medallion, crystal, cup.. 40.00
Sunrise Medallion, crystal, plate, salad; 7½" 15.00
Sunrise Medallion, crystal, tumbler, ftd, 4-oz, 2½"..................... 25.00
Sunrise Medallion, gr or pk, cordial, 1½-oz.............................. 225.00
Sunrise Medallion, gr or pk, saucer 17.50
Sunrise Medallion, gr or pk, water, 9-oz, 7¾" 55.00
Tinkerbell, Azure or gr, cocktail, 3½-oz................................... 125.00
Tinkerbell, Azure or gr, finger bowl, ftd................................... 100.00
Tinkerbell, Azure or gr, plate, finger bowl liner.......................... 30.00
Tinkerbell, Azure or gr, saucer champagne, 5½-oz 125.00
Tinkerbell, Azure or gr, sherbet, 5½-oz................................... 100.00
Tinkerbell, Azure or gr, vase, ruffled top, ftd, #36 Uranus, 10" 350.00
Tinkerbell, Azure or gr, wine, 2½-oz....................................... 175.00

Mortens Studios

Oscar Mortens was already established as a fine sculptural artist when he left his native Sweden to take up residency in Arizona. During the 1940s he developed a line of detailed animal figures which were distributed through the Mortens Studios, a firm he co-founded with Gunnar Thelin. Thelin hired and trained artists to produce Mortens's line, which he called Royal Designs. More than 200 dogs were modeled and over 100 horses. Cats and wild animals such as elephants, panthers, deer, and elk were made, but on a much smaller scale. Bookends with sculptured dog heads were shown in their catalogs, and collectors report finding wall plaques on rare occasions. The material they used was a plaster-type composition with wires embedded to support the weight. Examples were marked 'Copyright by the Mortens Studio,' either in ink or decal. Watch for flaking, cracks, and separations. Crazing seems to be present in some degree in many examples. When no condition is indicated, the items listed below are assumed to be in near-mint condition, allowing for minor crazing.

Beagle sitting, brn/wht/blk, 3¼" 65.00
Boxer male standing, brn w/blk muzzle, 6½x6", from $60 to 75.00
Boxer pup, head down on front legs, tail up, 2½x4" 55.00
Boxer pup, recumbent, 6" 60.00
Boxer pup seated & looking up, 3x4", from $45 to 55.00
Bulldog puppy seated, brn & wht, 3" 65.00
Chihuhua standing, brn, 3¾x4½", from $65 to 75.00
Cocker spaniel puppy sitting, red-brn, 3" 40.00
Collie standing, 8" L, from $60 to 75.00
Dachshund head, wall plaques, facing pr, from $200 to 250.00
Elephant w/trunk down, 2¼x4", from $150 to 175.00
German shepherd pup seated w/head up, brn tones, 3½x2¼" 50.00
Hereford bull, 4x7¼" 45.00
Horse, blk w/wht glaze & socks, 7¼", from $70 to 85.00
Pointer dog in hunting stance, red-brn, 3¾x6½", from $50 to 60.00
Spaniel puppy seated, blk & wht, 3" 65.00

Morton Pottery

Six potteries operated in Morton, Illinois, at various times from 1877 to 1976. Each traced its origin to six brothers who immigrated to America to avoid military service in Germany. The Rapp brothers established their first pottery near clay deposits on the south side of town where they made field tile and bricks. Within a few years, they branched out to include utility wares such as jugs, bowls, jars, pitchers, etc. During the 90 years of pottery operations in Morton, the original factory was expanded by some of the sons and nephews of the Rapps. Other family members started their own potteries where artware, gift-store items, and special-order goods were produced. The Cliftwood Art Pottery and the Morton Pottery Company had showrooms in Chicago and New York City during the 1930s. All of Morton's potteries were relatively short-lived operations with the Morton Pottery Company being the last to shut down on September 8, 1976. For a more thorough study of the subject, we recommend *Morton's Potteries: 99 Years* and *Morton Potteries: 99 Years, Vol. II,* by Doris and Burdell Hall; their address can be found in the Directory under Illinois.

Morton Pottery Works — Morton Earthenware Co. (1877 – 1917)

Baker, deep yel ware, 8" dia 50.00
Bowl, rice nappy, brn Rockingham, fluted, 10" 65.00
Bowl, rice nappy, yel ware, fluted, 8" 80.00
Coffeepot, dripolator, brn Rockingham, sm infuser, 10-cup 90.00
Jardiniere, brn, Rockingham, 7" 40.00
Marble, gr, 3" 25.00
Milk jug, cobalt, fancy appl hdl, #36s, 1-pt 50.00
Miniature, milk jug, cobalt, 4¼" 60.00
Pie baker, yel ware, 7" 75.00
Stein, emb German decor, brn spray, 8½" false bottom w/bell clapper .60.00
Teapot, Rebecca in shield, brn Rockingham, bulbous, 2½-pt 50.00

Cliftwood Art Potteries, Inc. (1920 – 1940)

Bean pot, Old Rose, ind 15.00
Beer set, chocolate drip, bbl-shape pitcher+6 mugs 225.00
Bookends, elephant, bl/mulberry, 3¼", pr 125.00
Bowl, bulb; bl/gray, deep, 6" 24.00
Candlesticks, blk semi-lustre, 7", pr 50.00
Creamer, cow figural, tail hdl/mouth spout, chocolate drip, 3¾x6" ..85.00
Figurine, American eagle, natural-colors spray glaze, 8½" 150.00
Flower bowl insert, water lily pad #2, med bl, 2x6" 24.00
Jar, Pretzels emb on brn drip, bbl shape, w/lid 65.00
Lamp, bulb w/emb lovebirds, jade gr, w/harp, 20" 60.00

Planter, police dog, open bk, wht matt, 5" 30.00
Shakers, stove top, yel/gr drip over wht, 5", pr 30.00
Vase, wht matt/old rose spray, dolphin base, 9" 75.00

Midwest Potteries, Inc. (1940 – 1944)

Candleholder, lime gr, Jack-be-nimble type, hdl, 7" 24.00
Figurine, Afghan hound, wht w/gold decor, 7" 45.00
Figurine, cockatoo, yel w/gr drip, on ped, 6" 24.00
Figurine, gull in flight, wht w/gold, 12" 35.00
Figurine, pony, yel w/gold decor, 3½" 24.00

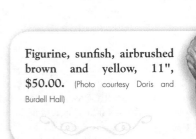

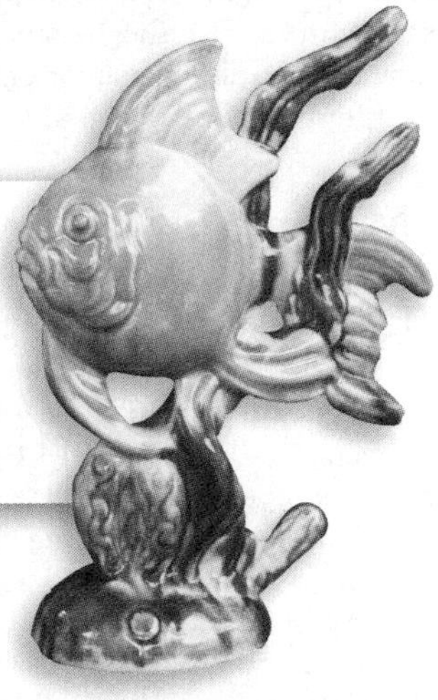

Figurine, sunfish, airbrushed brown and yellow, 11", $50.00. (Photo courtesy Doris and Burdell Hall)

Pitcher, cow, tail hdl, wht w/gold, 4½" 25.00
Pitcher, duck figural w/cattail hdl, brn/gray spray, 10" 40.00
Planter, elephant, bl/yel drip, 4" 12.00
Planter, elephant, bl/yel drip, 5½x6¾" 20.00

Morton Pottery Company (1922 – 1976)

Ashtray, hexagon, bl, Dirksen, 3¾" 30.00
Bank, acorn, brn 40.00
Bank, log cabin school, brn 35.00
Bank, Scottie dog, blk, 7" 22.00
Cookie jar, Clown, straw hat lid 75.00
Creamer/sugar bowl, hen & rooster, wht w/brushed blk, red cold pnt ..45.00
Figurine, donkey, political; gray, mk Kennedy, 2¼x2¼" 80.00
Figurine, hound dog, wht/brn/blk, #583, 3¼x4½" 15.00
Figurine, Scottish terrier, wht/brn spray, 7½x7" 15.00
Grass grower, sailor 30.00
Stein, brn Rockingham, cylindrical, emb advertising 28.00

American Art Potteries (1947 – 1963)

Bottle, crown shape, yel/gray spray, 6" 24.00
Figurine, Afghan hounds, bl, 15", pr 55.00
Figurine, rooster, gray/blk spray, #305, 8" 24.00
Honey jug, 14k gold, #50G, 5½" 25.00
Planter, baby buggy, wht, decor, 5½x7" 20.00
Tray, butterfly shape, pk w/mauve spray, #135G, 1x7x6¼" 25.00
Vase, cowboy boot, gray/pk, #312, 5½" 20.00
Vase, pitcher, wht w/rust speckling, 14" 24.00

Mosaic Tile

The Mosaic Tile Company was organized in 1894 in Zanesville, Ohio, by Herman Mueller and Karl Langenbeck, both of whom had years of previous experience in the industry. They developed a faster, less-costly method of potting decorative tile, utilizing paper patterns rather than copper molds. By 1901 the company had grown and expanded with offices in many major cities. Faience tile was introduced in 1918, greatly increasing their volume of sales. They also made novelty ashtrays, figural boxes, bookends, etc., though not to any large extent. Until they closed during the 1960s, Mosaic used various marks that included the company name or their initials — 'MT' superimposed over 'Co.' in a circle.

Box, recumbent dog on lid, bl gloss, 3⅞x8⅜" 190.00
Figurine, bear on base, dk gr-bl, MTC logo, 6x9½" 150.00
Figurine, buffalo, wht, unmk, flake, 8¼x13x4⅞" 180.00
Paperweight, German shepherd on base, taupe, prof rstr, 6x10"... 120.00
Pin tray, hunting dog on point, dk gr & gunmetal gray gloss, 5x8"... 180.00
Pin tray, turtle figural, lt bl, 4½" L 30.00

Moser

Ludwig Moser began his career as a struggling glass artist, catering to the rich who visited the famous Austrian health spas. His talent and popularity grew and in 1857 the first of his three studios opened in Karlsbad, Czechoslovakia. The styles developed there were entirely his own; no copies of other artists have ever been found. Some of his original designs include grapes with trailing vines, acorns and oak leaves, and richly enameled, deeply cut or carved floral pieces. Sometimes jewels were applied to the glass as well. Moser's animal scenes reflect his careful attention to detail. Famed for his birds in flight, he also designed stalking tigers and large, detailed elephants, all created in fine enameling.

Moser died in 1916, but the business was continued by his two sons who had been personally and carefully trained by their father. The Moser company bought the Meyr's Neffe Glassworks in 1922 and continued to produce quality glassware.

When identifying Moser, look for great clarity in the glass; deeply carved, continuous engravings; perfect coloration; finely applied enameling (often covered with thin gold leaf); and well-polished pontils. Our advisor for this category is Don Williams; he is listed in the Directory under Missouri. Items described below are enameled unless noted otherwise. If no color is mentioned in the line, the glass is clear.

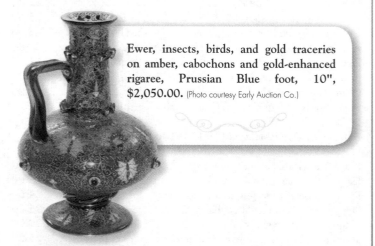

Ewer, insects, birds, and gold traceries on amber, cabochons and gold-enhanced rigaree, Prussian Blue foot, 10", $2,050.00. (Photo courtesy Early Auction Co.)

Basket, cranberry w/allover leaves/insects, lg appl amber leaves, 12" .. 1,950.00
Bottle, scent; cranberry w/gold medallions & mc scrolls, 4½" 575.00
Bottle, scent; gr w/allover gold scrolls, bulbous, faceted stopper, 7".. 115.00
Bowl, cameo Deco floral on dk amber sgn HH; silver rim, boat form, 11". 800.00
Bowl, marquetry, clear w/gr intaglio floral, gold-trimmed gr rim, 6" ...735.00
Box, emerald gr, wht-dotted shields between 4 floral reserves, 6" W..150.00
Box, gr w/gilt panels & mc decor, dome flip lid, 5½" dia 200.00

Candlesticks, amber w/gold Grecian warriors frieze, columnar, 7", pr ... 250.00
Chalice, gr w/much gold, window panels w/mc floral, gilt metal ft, 12"..690.00
Cheese dish, gr w/gold & mc flowers, gold peacock-eye band, 7x9"...635.00
Compote, cranberry cut to clear w/3 deer, w/label, 7x9" 520.00
Creamer, cranberry, bl/red jewels on gold panels, amber hdl, 3" .. 325.00
Cup & saucer, lime gr w/allover gold scrolls, 2½" 70.00
Decanter, bl-lav etched w/stag, paneled/flaring, w/stopper, 18"....500.00
Decanter, cranberry w/floral, gilt bands/scrolls, 8", +4 tumblers...780.00
Dish, cranberry w/mc acanthus scrolls & peacock eyes, 3 ft, 3" W..115.00
Ewer, med bl w/allover floral, appl bird/acorns, ftd, 18", EX......5,500.00
Ewer, med bl w/mc floral, clear scroll ft/hdl, cornucopia body, 11" ...575.00
Finger bowl, clear to cranberry w/allover gold scrolls, ribbed, +plate .. 200.00
Finger bowl, gr w/overall gold scrolls, melon ribs, +6" underplate......325.00
Goblet, gold w/Moorish medallions w/wht scrolls, floral, 4½" 285.00
Goblet, ruby w/overall gold leaves, 5½" 345.00
Jewel casket, amethyst cased w/gold beads/swags, ca 1895, 2x8x3" .. 700.00
Letter holder, clear, sides cut to follow intaglio flowers, 8x9" L.. 650.00
Mug, clear w/portrait of Queen Louise in gold scroll fr, 5" 115.00
Pitcher, cranberry, gold coralene leaves/wht branches, 9", +4 tumblers..900.00
Pitcher, gr w/mc floral+overall amethyst scrolls, ftd, R Briggs, 9" 840.00
Pitcher, tankard; cranberry, wht floral/gold coralene, clear hdl, 11" ...375.00
Pitcher, tankard; gr, gold/mc scrolls, rows of peacock eyes, ftd, 12"...1,250.00
Plate, clear w/rtcl crenelated border, etched castle scene, 12"...... 140.00
Powder horn, amethyst w/bl & yel ferns, metal mts/chain, 8½" L. 520.00
Tumbler, cranberry w/mc flowers/gold scrolls, ped ft, 5½", pr 285.00
Vase, amber craquelle w/2 gr fish/crimson seaweed, ovoid, 6" 400.00
Vase, amber w/all-over gilt/mc scrolls, bl hdl/ft, rigaree/jewels, 10" ..2,050.00
Vase, amethyst, gold warrior frieze, ribbed, 9x4" 360.00
Vase, bl, stacked 4-lobed faceted form, cylindrical, 9½" 330.00
Vase, bud; intaglio stemmed tulip, optic ribs, cylindrical, 12" 115.00
Vase, clear to amethyst w/sculptured eagle/gold reeds, optic rib, 14"..3,500.00
Vase, clear w/floral-eng ruby-flash medallions & gold, 5x5" 420.00
Vase, cranberry w/panels of dmn cuts/florals/gold scrolls, ftd, 11"....450.00
Vase, gold scrolls w/allover birds/floral, hdls/prunts, ftd, 11" 1,600.00
Vase, gold/silver encrusted bands/mc leaves, 3 scrolling ft, 4" 230.00
Vase, lily; gr w/gilt panels of scrolling flowers, 4¾" 160.00
Vase, lt gr w/2 lg raised mc fish/seaweed, shouldered, 9" 920.00
Vase, multi-faceted cylinder w/waisted gilt/jewel band, red ft, 11" ... 150.00
Vase, Royo Art, bl w/mc fighting horsemen/foliage, ftd, 14" 285.00
Vase, rubena w/pk & yel mums/gold tracery, optic ribs, 9½", pr ... 600.00
Wine, Diplomat pattern, Alexandrite-type, 5", set of 10........... 1,035.00
Wine, gr bowl w/mc leaves & jewels, baluster stem w/prunts, 8" . 365.00
Wine, gr w/gilt, mc scrolling leaves, faceted under cup, 8" 285.00

Moss Rose

Moss Rose was a favorite dinnerware pattern of many Staffordshire and American potters of the mid-1800s. In America the Wheeling Pottery of West Virginia produced the ware in large quantities, and it became one of their bestsellers, remaining popular well into the '90s. The pattern was colored by hand; this type is designated 'old' in our listings to distinguish it from the more modern Moss Rose design of the twentieth century, which we've also included. It's not hard to distinguish between the two. The later ware you'll recognize immediately, since the pattern is applied by decalcomania on stark white backgrounds. It has been made in Japan to a large extent, but companies in Bavaria and other regions of Germany have produced it as well. Today, there is more interest in the twentieth century items than in the older ware. In the listings that follow, when no manufacturer is given, assume that item to have been made in twentieth-century Japan.

Ashtray, sm..6.00
Bowl, salad; fluted edge, Royal Albert, 9½"................................. 85.00
Bowl, scalloped hdls & ft, oval, Rosenthal, 4x9¼x13⅝"............... 145.00

Bowl, soup; scalloped rim, 7½" 10.00
Bowl, vegetable; oval, Rosenthal Pompadour, 2½x11¼x10¼" 65.00
Bud vase, 3½" 15.00
Chocolate pot 23.00
Coffeepot, Pompadour, Rosenthal, 11" 150.00
Creamer & sugar bowl, gold trim, w/lid, 1940s, pr 35.00
Cup & saucer, Rosenthal, 2¾", 5½" 70.00
Lamp/nightlight, Aladdin style, Wales/Made in Japan, 1950s, 7½" ... 25.00
Mustard jar, ovoid, w/lid & orig spoon 15.00
Pin dish, gold trim, 6¼" 24.00
Plate, dinner; pearlized, gold trim, Japan label, 1960, 10½" 12.50
Plate, luncheon; scalloped rim, 9" 8.00
Platter, oblong, Rosenthal, 6¾x14¼" 50.00
Platter, Ucagco, rare, 12", from $65 to 85.00
Shakers, bublous bottom w/slim neck, sterling tops, Rosenthal, 5", pr ... 85.00
Shakers, ftd, Royal Rose Japan, 4", pr 40.00
Smoke set, flat tray w/4 ashtrays & lighter 40.00
Sugar bowl, cup shape w/lg hdls, dome lid, 4¾" 15.00
Sugar shaker, 6x3" 45.00
Tea set, stacking; creamer & sugar bowl set atop teapot 30.00
Teapot, Rosenthal, 7½" 70.00
Tidbit, 3-tiered, Johann Haviland 50.00
Tray, emb design, open hdls, Rosenthal, 12¼" 65.00
Tray, Pompadour, Rosenthal, 13x10" 65.00
Tray, sandwich; tab hdld, sq, 6¾x11½" 45.00
Tray, tab hdls, scalloped sides, Rosenthal, 8½x13¼" 40.00
Tray, tea; rtcl segments along rim, pierced hdls, Rosenthal, 11" ... 35.00
Vase, conical w/flared rim, Rosenthal, Sheffield Silver base, 8½" ... 145.00

Mother-of-Pearl Glass

Mother-of-Pearl glass was a type of mold-blown satin art glass popular during the last half of the nineteenth century. A patent for its manufacture was issued in 1886 to Frederick S. Shirley, and one of the companies who produced it was the Mt. Washington Glass Company of New Bedford, Massachusetts. Another was the English firm of Stevens and Williams. Its delicate patterns were developed by blowing the gather into a mold with inside projections that left an intaglio design on the surface of the glass, then sealing the first layer with a second, trapping air in the recesses. Most common are the Diamond Quilted, Raindrop, and Herringbone patterns. It was made in several soft colors, the most rare and valuable is rainbow — a blend of rose, light blue, yellow, and white. Occasionally it may be decorated with coralene, enameling, or gilt. Watch for twentieth-century reproductions, especially in the Diamond Quilted pattern. See also Coralene; Stevens and Williams.

Basket, Dmn Quilt, rainbow, ruffled rim, vaseline hdl, mk Pat, 9" .. 1,300.00
Basket, Herringbone, rose pk/gr int, frosted tepee hdl, Mt WA, 9x11" ... 570.00
Biscuit jar, Herringbone, pk w/gold ferns, ovoid, SP mts, 7½" 920.00
Bottle, scent; Dmn Quilt, butterscotch w/daisies, faceted stopper, 6" .. 450.00

Bowl, Diamond Quilt, rainbow, clear rigaree collar and thorn handles, stylized feet, 9½x10", NM, $7,750.00. (Photo courtesy Early Auction Co.)

Bowl, Dmn Quilt, tan w/bl int, crimped 4-lobe rim, emb lobes, 12" L .. 700.00
Creamer & sugar bowl, Coinspot, peach to caramel w/camphor hdls, 5" .. 700.00
Epergne, Dmn Quilt, rainbow, bowl on baluster std above 3 rose bowls ... 11,400.00
Ewer, Dmn Quilt, pk, melon ribbed, camphor hdl, Stevens & Wms, 12" . 825.00
Ewer, Dmn Quilt, rainbow, 3-lobe rim, thorny camphor hdl, ftd, 6½" .. 1,095.00
Ewer, Herringbone, rainbow, ruffled rim, 9" 950.00
Ewer, Herringbone, rainbow, 3-lobe rim, frosted hdl, 6", pr 690.00
Hall chandelier, Dmn Quilt, pk shaded, cylinder w/lg ribs, 12", +mts ... 975.00
Marmalade, Peacock Eye, pk, floral, 6" 290.00
Pitcher, Dmn Quilt, apricot, frosted hdl, bulbous, 9" 225.00
Pitcher, Dmn Quilt, rainbow, long neck w/tri-fold rim, camphor hdl, 7" . 650.00
Rose bowl, Dmn Quilt, rainbow, clear vertical ribs, mk Pat, 3½" .. 1,380.00
Rose bowl, Dmn Quilt, rainbow, trefoil body, rigaree rim/3-ft, Pat, 4" .. 1,550.00
Sugar shaker, Dmn Quilt, butterscotch, rtcl metal dome lid, 6x5" .. 260.00
Sweetmeat, Flower & Acorn, wht w/floral & gold, 5½" 350.00
Underplate, Dmn Quilt, red, pie-crust rim, Stevens & Wms, 4½" .. 200.00
Vase, Bridal Ribbon, wht w/4-fold rim, intaglio/gilt decor, 8" 520.00
Vase, Dmn Quilt, butterscotch, clear rigaree scalloped rim, 4" ... 140.00
Vase, Dmn Quilt, pk, stick neck, 7½" 165.00
Vase, Dmn Quilt, red w/yel dmns, squat w/long ruffled fan neck, 6" .. 290.00
Vase, Federzeichnung, brn w/gold flecks, ovoid 7" 1,400.00
Vase, Moire, pk w/gold floral, shouldered, deeply ruffled rim, 9½" ... 435.00
Vase, Zipper, yel, bulbous w/can neck, att S&W, 8" 145.00

Movie Memorabilia

Movie memorabilia covers a broad range of collectibles, from books and magazines dealing with the industry in general to the various promotional materials which were distributed to arouse interest in a particular film. Many collectors specialize in a specific area — posters, pressbooks, stills, lobby cards, or souvenir programs (also referred to as premiere booklets). In the listings below, a one-sheet poster measures approximately 27" x 41", three-sheet: 41" x 81", and six-sheet: 81" x 81". Window cards measure 14" x 22". Lobby and title cards measure 11" x 14", while an insert poster is 36" x 14". Our advisor for this category is Robert Doyle; he is listed in the Directory under New York. See also Autographs; Cartoon Art; Magazines; Paper Dolls; Personalities; Rock 'n Roll Memorabilia; Sheet Music.

Insert card, Animal Farm, G Orwell, 1955, NM+ 100.00
Insert card, Born Yesterday, J Holliday/W Holden/B Crawford, VG+ .. 75.00
Insert card, Desert Fury, B Lancaster w/others, 1947, VG+ 100.00
Insert card, Happy Go Lucky, D Powell/B Hutton/others, 1943, EX+ .. 65.00
Insert card, Ring of Fire, M Spillane, 1954, EX 50.00
Insert poster, Abbott & Costello Meet the Mummy, 1955, EX 500.00
Insert poster, Arsenic & Old Lace, C Grant, 1944, EX 415.00
Insert poster, Sleeping Beauty, Disney, 1959, EX 125.00
Lobby card, College Holiday, M Raye, VG+ 75.00
Lobby card, Dial M for Murder, 1954, EX 85.00
Lobby card, Don't Bother To Knock, #7, M Monroe, 1952, EX ... 75.00
Lobby card, Forbidden Planet, #4, 1956, EX 525.00
Lobby card, Key Largo, #4, H Bogart/L Bacall, 1947, VG+ 350.00
Lobby card, King Kong vs Godzilla, #8, 1963, EX 225.00
Lobby card, Mummy's Tomb, #2, 1944, EX 85.00
Lobby card, Nothing But Trouble, #3, Laurel & Hardy, 1945, EX .. 90.00
Lobby card, Rancho Notorious, M Dietrich, 1952, VG+ 20.00
Lobby card, Rear Window, J Stewart, 1954, EX 175.00
Lobby card, Singin' in the Rain, #5, G Kelly, 1952, EX 65.00
Lobby card, Sunset Boulevard, Wm Holden, 1950, EX 165.00
Lobby card, Voice in the Night, T McCoy, 1934, EX 50.00
Lobby card, War of Worlds, #3, G Barry, 1953, EX 100.00
Lobby card set, Prisoner of War, R Reagan, 1954, VG/EX 100.00
Lobby card set, Rocky, #1-8, S Stallone, 1977, M 90.00

Lobby card set, The Spy Who Loved Me, Bob Peak artwork, 1977, NM .. 50.00
Lobby card set, Young Man w/a Horn, #1-8, K Douglas, 1950, EX ... 280.00
Poster, Ace of Cactus Range, Art Mix, 1924, 41x27", VG 350.00
Poster, Anatomy of Murder, J Stewart/L Remick, 1959, 3-sheet, VG+ .. 950.00
Poster, Aristocats, Disney, 1971, 1-sheet, EX 125.00
Poster, Batman, A West, 1966, British quad, 30x40", EX 300.00
Poster, Beast w/a Million Eyes, 1955, 1-sheet, EX 450.00
Poster, Blaze Away, Big Boy G Williams, 1922, 41x27", VG 440.00
Poster, Blue Hawaii, E Presley, 1961, 1-sheet, EX 500.00
Poster, Broken Arrow, J Stewart, 1950, 1-sheet, EX 500.00
Poster, Citizen Kane, O Wells, blk/wht/red, 1930s, 24x18", EX ... 735.00
Poster, Dead Reckoning, H Bogart/L Scott, 1955 reissue, ½-sheet, EX ... 125.00
Poster, Dive Bomber, E Flynn/F MacMurray, 1941, rstr 450.00
Poster, Flash Gordon Conquers the Universe, 1940, 1-sheet, EX .. 4,700.00
Poster, Flying Tigers, J Wayne, 1942, ½-sheet, EX 220.00
Poster, Foxy Brown, P Grier, 1974, 1-sheet, EX 220.00
Poster, Godzilla King of the Monsters, R Burr, 1956, 1-sheet, EX .. 1,800.00
Poster, Going My Way, Bing Crosby, 1944, VG 150.00
Poster, Harvey, James Stewart, 1950, 1-sheet, EX 1,000.00
Poster, Headless Horseman, W Rogers, 1922, 41x27", VG 2,150.00
Poster, High Society, B Crosby, 1956, 3-sheet, EX 295.00
Poster, Hold That Lion, 3 Stooges, 1947, 1-sheet, EX 1,850.00
Poster, Hondo, J Wayne, 1953, ½-sheet, G+ 350.00
Poster, I Was a Teenage Frankenstein, 1957, 1-sheet, VG+ 275.00
Poster, If You Knew Susie, E Cantor/J Davis, 1947, 3-sheet, VG+ .. 100.00
Poster, Judgement at Nuremberg, profiles of cast, 1961, 40x30", EX .. 100.00
Poster, Lady Sings the Blues, D Ross, 1972, 1-sheet, EX 40.00
Poster, Lost in Alaska, Abbott & Costello, 1952, 1-sheet, EX 215.00
Poster, Love Me Tender, Elvis playing guitar, 1956, 1-sheet, EX .. 500.00
Poster, Mad Max, M Gibson, 1980, 1-sheet, NM 175.00
Poster, Madam, S Loren, 1962, 1-sheet, EX+ 50.00
Poster, Magic Town, J Stewart/J Wymen, 1947, 3-sheet, VG+ 100.00
Poster, Malcom X, documentary, 1972, 1-sheet, NM 100.00
Poster, Man Who Fell to Earth, D Bowie, 1976, British quad, 30x40", M ... 215.00
Poster, Mars Attacks the World, 1938, 1-sheet, EX 820.00
Poster, Mexican Hayride, Abbott & Costello, 1948, 36x14", EX. 110.00
Poster, Munsters Go Home, Munster cast, 1966, 2-sheet, VG+ ... 150.00

Poster, Mysterious Lady, Greta Garbo and Conrad Nagel, professional restoration, 41x27", $4,500.00.

Poster, No Time for Love, C Cobert/F McMurry, 1943, 1-sheet, VG ... 76.00
Poster, North by Northwest, Cary Grant, 1959, 1-sheet, EX 450.00
Poster, Ocean's 11, D Martin, 1960, 1-sheet, EX 515.00
Poster, Outwitted, Texas Gunman, Reelcraft Pictures, 1917, 41x27", G .. 825.00
Poster, Painted Hills, Lassie, 1-sheet, 1951, VG+ 125.00
Poster, Pale Face, B Hope, 1948, 1-sheet, EX 610.00
Poster, Pillow Talk, R Hudson/D Day, 1959, 1-sheet, EX 360.00
Poster, Remember Pearl Harbor, D Barry, 1943, 1-sheet, rare, VG+ .. 150.00
Poster, Reservoir Dogs, 1992, 1-sheet, EX 275.00
Poster, Rings on Her Fingers, G Tierney/H Fonda, 1942, 1-sheet, EX .. 250.00
Poster, Rock Around the Clock, B Haley/others, 1956, ½-sheet, G+ ... 150.00

Poster, Rumba, C Lombard/G Raft, 1935, ½-sheet, G+ 650.00
Poster, Second Fiddle, G Hunter/M Astor, 1923, 41x27", EX ... 1,450.00
Poster, Sherlock Holmes in Washington, B Rathbone, 1942, 1-sheet, EX ..850.00
Poster, Showdown, Wm Boyd as Hopalong Cassidy, 1940, 1-sheet, EX.650.00
Poster, Slattery's Hurricane, V Lake/R Windmark, 1949, ½-sheet, VG 65.00
Poster, Summer Storm, L Darnell/G Sanders, 1944, 1-sheet, EX .. 250.00
Poster, Tangled Trails, N Hart, 41x27", G 495.00
Poster, The Birds, R Taylor, 1963, 1-sheet, EX 300.00
Poster, The Mummy's Curse, 1944, L Chaney, 1-sheet, EX 710.00
Poster, The Sisters, B Davis/E Flynn, 1938, 1-sheet, rare, EX 400.00
Poster, The Wild Bunch, Wm Holden, 1969, 1-sheet, EX 175.00
Poster, Untamed, P Morison/R Milland/A Tamiroff, 1940, 1-sheet, VG+ ..200.00
Poster, Watch the Rhine, B Davis/P Lucas, 1943, 1-sheet, EX 450.00
Poster, Winter Meeting, B Davis, 1948, 3-sheet, EX 190.00
Poster, Yellow Rolls Royce, I Bergman/R Harrison, 1965, 1-sheet, EX ..75.00
Poster, You Only Live Twice, S Connery, 1967, 6-sheet, EX 375.00
Poster, You're My Everything, D Dailey/A Baxter, 1949, 1-sheet, EX ..50.00
Poster, Zulu, M Cane, 1963, rare, 40x30", EX 250.00
Poster, 40 Horse Hawkins, H Gibson, Universal, 1924, 41x27", VG .. 465.00
Press photo, An Affair To Remember, D Kerr/C Grane, 1957, 8x10", EX..150.00
Press photo, Streetcar Named Desire, Brando/Leigh, 1951, 7¼x9½", EX. 300.00
Pressbook, Black Raven, G Zucco, 1943, EX 45.00
Souvenir book, On a Clear Day, B Streisand, EX 25.00
Title card, Black Widow, G Rogers/G Tierney/G Raft, 1954, EX ... 25.00
Title card, Eyes of Texas, R Rogers, 1948, VG+ 80.00
Title card, Fort Apache, J Wayne, 1948, VG+ 200.00
Title card, Sands of Iwo Jima, J Wayne, 1950, VG+ 200.00
Window card, Carousel, S Jones/G MacRae, 1956, VG+ 50.00
Window card, China, A Ladd/L Young, 1943, VG 75.00
Window card, Daddy Long Legs, F Astaire/L Caron, 1955, VG+ .. 50.00
Window card, Desiree, M Brando/J Simmons/M Overon, 1954, VG+ ..100.00
Window card, Dragnet, J Webb, 1954, VG+ 100.00
Window card, Giant, E Taylor/J Dean/R Hudson, 1956, rare, VG+...175.00
Window card, I'm No Angel, M West/C Grant, 1933, rare, EX... 750.00
Window card, I Married a Witch, V Lake, 1942, EX 475.00
Window card, Little Colonel, S Temple/L Barrymore, 1935, G ... 300.00
Window card, Psycho, A Perkins/J Leigh, 1960, G+ 150.00
Window card, Ten Commandments, artwork of Moses w/tablet, 1923, rstr .650.00
Window card, The Great Escape, S McQueen, 1963, EX 195.00
Window card, The Searchers, J Wayne, 1956, EX 245.00
Window card, The World Changes, P Muni, 1933, VG 250.00

Mt. Washington

The Mt. Washington Glass Works was founded in 1837 in South Boston, Massachusetts, but moved to New Bedford in 1869 after purchasing the facilities of the New Bedford Glass Company. Frederick S. Shirley became associated with the firm in 1874. Two years later the company reorganized and became known as the Mt. Washington Glass Company. In 1894 it merged with the Pairpoint Manufacturing Company, a small Brittania works nearby, but continued to conduct business under its own title until after the turn of the century. The combined plants were equipped with the most modern and varied machinery available and boasted a work force with experience and expertise rival to none in the art of blowing and cutting glass. In addition to their fine cut glass, they are recognized as the first American company to make cameo glass, an effect they achieved through acid-cutting methods. In 1885 Shirley was issued a patent to make Burmese, pale yellow glassware tinged with a delicate pink blush. Another patent issued in 1886 allowed them the rights to produce Rose Amber, or amberina, a transparent ware shading from ruby to amber. Pearl Satin Ware and Peachblow, so named for its resemblance to a rosy peach skin, were patented the same year. One of their most famous lines, Crown Milano, was introduced in 1893. It was an opal glass either free blown or pattern molded, tinted a delicate color and decorated with enameling and gilt. Royal Flemish was patented in 1894 and is considered the rarest of the Mt. Washington art glass lines. It was decorated with raised, gold-enameled lines dividing the surface of the ware in much the same way as lead lines divide a stained glass window. The sections were filled in with one or several transparent colors and further decorated in gold enamel with florals, foliage, beading, and medallions. For more information, see *Mt. Washington Art Glass* by Betty B. Sisk (Collector Books). See also Amberina; Cranberry; Salt Shakers; Burmese; Crown Milano; Mother-of-Pearl; Royal Flemish; etc.

Biscuit jar, blown-out mums ea corner, yel on brn, lid mk MW, 10" ..625.00
Biscuit jar, floral on cream to opal, melon ribbed, metal mts, 6" W.. 175.00
Biscuit jar, floral on pnt Burmese, Albertine label, 10" w/hdl....... 835.00
Box, floral on pk to gr w/gold, blown-out mold, metal hdw, 6x7½"..1,150.00
Bride's basket, cameo flower baskets/etc, pk/opal, Pairpoint fr, 11"...975.00
Condiment set, Ribbed Pillar floral shakers+mustard, Rogers Bros caddy....210.00
Cruet, floral on cream/bl, squat/ribbed, long neck, ribbed stopper, 7" ... 1,035.00
Lamp base, cameo griffins/fountains, yel on opal, Bradley-Hubbard mt..550.00
Pitcher, Verona, violet cluster, mc w/gilt, optic ribs, 8½" 360.00
Shade, torchiere; Napoli, floral/scrolls, mc/gold, flared cylinder, 11"..385.00
Shaker, Cockle Shell, clear w/purple flowers & gr leaves, 3" 565.00
Shaker, Palmer Cox Brownie, 2⅝" 330.00
Shakers, Tomato, floral, 2", pr 150.00
Sugar shaker, Egg, cut w/dmn & fan, 4¼" 475.00
Sugar shaker, Egg, floral sprays, 4½" 230.00
Sugar shaker, Fig, pk floral/gr leaves on yel 'bark,' 4" 240.00

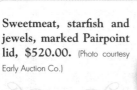

Sweetmeat, starfish and jewels, marked Pairpoint lid, $520.00. (Photo courtesy Early Auction Co.)

Toothpick holder, allover floral on opal satin, onion form, 2¼"...375.00
Toothpick holder, floral on cream to pk, ovoid w/short collar, 2¾" ..265.00
Toothpick holder, floral on gr opal Swirl, random folds to cut rim, 2" ..2,750.00
Tumbler, Lava, mc shards in blk, rare form, 3½" 4,830.00
Vase, Lava, mc shards in blk, curled hdls, 9" 3,450.00
Vase, Verona, lg dragon/floral, cylinder w/pointed scallops, #910, 10"..2,430.00
Vase, wht/yel mums, cylinder w/7 crenelated scallops, flared base, 12" ...345.00

Mulberry China

Mulberry china was made by many of the Staffordshire area potters from about 1830 until the 1850s. It is a transfer-printed earthenware or ironstone named for the color of its decorations, a purplish-brown resembling the juice of the mulberry. Some pieces may have faded out over the years and today look almost gray with only a hint of purple. (Transfer printing was done in many colors; technically only those in the mauve tones are 'mulberry'; color variations have little effect on value.) Some of the patterns (Corean, Jeddo, Pelew, and Formosa, for instance) were also produced in Flow Blue ware. Others seem to have been used exclusively with the mulberry color. Our advisor for this category is Mary Frank Gaston; she is listed in the Directory under Texas.

Alpine Amusements, platter, Davenport, 14½" 675.00
Asia, plate, Heath, 9" 200.00
Athens, plate, Adams, 10¼" 100.00
Avon, pitcher, 11" 65.00
Beauties of China, undertray, Mellor Venables, 10x7¼"..............150.00
Bochara, plate, 12-sided, Edwards, 9" 95.00
Bochara, sauce tureen, Edwards, w/lid & ladle............................650.00
Brunswick Star, plate, 7½" 125.00
Bryonia, cup & saucer...35.00
Canova, sauce tureen, w/lid, +8x6¼" undertray, Mayer..............600.00
Castle Garden, plate, medallion/floral border, 7⅞" 85.00
Castle Scenery, plate, Furnival, 7½" 65.00
Castle Scenery, sugar bowl, w/lid, Furnival 275.00
Corea, tea bowl & saucer...120.00
Corean, bowl, soup; Podmore Walker, 9¾" 125.00
Corean, compote, 9x11" 325.00
Corean, cup & saucer 75.00
Corean, plate, 8" 80.00
Corean, platter, Podmore Walker, 16x12¼", NM 325.00
Corean, posset cup, Podmore Walker, 3" 125.00
Corean, sauce tureen, ftd, Podmore Walker, 7½x7", +8½" tray....450.00
Corean, teapot 600.00
Cyprus, plate, Davenport, 9¼" 95.00
Cyprus, teapot, 10" 350.00
Excelsior, plate, Wooliscroft, 8½" 65.00
Flora, tea bowl & saucer..110.00
Foliage, gravy boat 140.00
Foliage, plate, 12-sided, 10¼" 80.00
Foliage, platter, A Walley, 15¼" 300.00
Fruit Basket, plate, 10½" 90.00
Gondola, plate, Davenport, 7¼" 70.00
Hollins College, plate, Wedgwood, 10⅜" 70.00
Hong, pitcher, 2-qt 500.00
Hong, plate, 12-sided, T Walker, 9" 125.00
Japonica, creamer, 5¼x6½" 175.00
Jeddo, bowl, sauce 45.00
Jeddo, cup & saucer, Adams 140.00
Jeddo, plate, Adams, 7½" 75.00
Jeddo, plate, Adams, 9¼" 120.00
Jeddo, teapot, Adams 475.00
Lucerne, plate, JW Pankhurst, 9½" 80.00
Marble, pitcher, 8" 325.00
Marble, plate, 9½" 40.00
Neva, cup, no hdl, Challinor 50.00
Ning-Po, plate, Hall, 9½" 110.00
Ning-Po, platter, Hall, 10¾x8" 175.00
Nonpareil, pitcher, Mayer, 7½" 595.00
Panama, platter, Challinor, 13½x10½"......................................250.00
Park Scenery, plate, Wallace, 9¼" 110.00
Pelew, mitten relish, Challinor...125.00
Peruvian, platter, Wedgwood, 18x14⅛" 400.00
Peruvian, sauce tureen & underplate, Wedgwood, 7½x7¼", 8½" ..400.00
Pomerania, plate, Ridgway, 10" 165.00
Rhone Scenery, plate, Mayer, 9¼" 95.00
Rose, pitcher, Walker, 2-qt 375.00
Rose, plate, Challinor, 10"...75.00
Rose, platter, TF&Co, 11x8½" 125.00
Royal Festoon, tea bowl & saucer, 2⅜x3½", 5½" 125.00
Sardinia, platter, Hall, 15¼x12¼" 375.00
Singan, creamer, 8-panel, 5¾" 250.00
Singan, plate, 10-sided, T Goodfellow, 10" 125.00
Tillenburg, teapot, prof rstr, 1840s, EX......................................295.00
Vincennes, plate, Alcock, 9½" 90.00
Washington Vase, teapot, 8-sided, Podmore Walker, 9½x8½" 425.00

Muller Freres

Henri Muller established a factory in 1900 at Croismare, France. He produced fine cameo art glass decorated with florals, birds, and insects in the Art Nouveau style. The work was accomplished by acid engraving and hand finishing. Usual marks were 'Muller,' 'Muller Croismare,' or 'Croismare, Nancy.' In 1910 Henri and his brother Deseri formed a glassworks at Luneville. The cameo art glass made there was nearly all produced by acid cuttings of up to four layers with motifs similar to those favored at Croismare. A good range of colors was used, and some later pieces were gold flecked. Handles and decorative devices were sometimes applied by hand. In addition to the cameo glass, they also produced an acid-finished glass of bold mottled colors in the Deco style. Examples were signed 'Muller Freres' or 'Luneville.' Our advisor for this category is Don Williams; he is listed in the Directory under Missouri.

Cameo

Chandelier, roses, red on yel to frost, chains w/emb hangers, 15", VG 3,500.00
Lamp, boudoir; cap shade & flared base w/dk mottle band on yel, 12"....1,500.00
Lamp, desert oasis on bullet-shaped shade; slim base, brn on rust, 26" 5,400.00
Vase, birch trees/mtns, Fluogravure, flat-sided bottle form w/hdls, 9" 6,750.00
Vase, butterflies/leaves, cut/pnt on yel-orange to purple w/foil, 6" ..2,400.00
Vase, butterflies/leaves on yel to purple w/int decor, 15x4" 2,070.00
Vase, Deco fish, red on frost w/silver & gold mica, 6x4½" 230.00
Vase, floral, burgundy on camphor, tubular w/flaring ft, 17" 1,065.00
Vase, floral, dk gr on wht, thick neck, bun base, 13½"...............1,610.00

**Vase, floral, 14",
$4,485.00.** (Photo courtesy
Early Auction Co.)

Vase, lg leaves, brn on tan/frost/amber, Fluogravure, spherical, 2"...290.00
Vase, lg peonies & buds, red on yel mottle, tapered sides, bun ft, 15".. 5,290.00
Vase, lg roses, red/brn on yel mottle, 16x4"................................2,990.00
Vase, mums, brn on amber mottle, bulbous, 12" 2,530.00
Vase, poppies/leaves, red/wine on citron to bl mottle, ovoid, 14" ... 4,250.00
Vase, ships in harbor/trees, brn/amber on shaded bl, bulbous, 13" ..2,590.00
Vase, Tibetan man/falling snow, cut/pnt on gr to brn, 10".........5,175.00
Vase, trees, brn/umber on orange, ftd urn form, 6" 690.00
Vase, trees, brn/yel against orange sky, Fluogravure, ftd, 9" 3,605.00
Vase, trees, multiple layers: purple & teal on peach, bulbous, 2".. 780.00
Vase, trees/distant lake, brn on lt gr, slim 10" 1,275.00
Vase, windmill/cabins/lg trees, brn on yel to butterscotch, ftd, 15" ..960.00

Miscellaneous

Lamp, sm cone wht/pk mottle shade hangs from ftd hoop w/spirals, 11" ...285.00
Shade, maize to orange & bl mottle, gilded leaf/fruit hdw, 16" dia ... 750.00

Vase, chevrons/dmns, yel/orange on clear w/mica, cylindrical, 12" .. 960.00
Vase, paperweight style: sunset hues w/gold flecks, shouldered, 12".. 1,020.00

Muncie

The Muncie Pottery was established in Muncie, Indiana, by Charles O. Grafton; it operated there from 1922 until about 1935. The pottery they produced is made of a heavier clay than most of its contemporaries; the styles are sturdy and simple. Early glazes were bright and colorful. In fact, Muncie was advertised as the 'rainbow pottery.' Later most of the ware was finished in a matt glaze. The more collectible examples are those modeled after Consolidated Glass vases — sculptured with lovebirds, grasshoppers, and goldfish. Their line of Art Deco-style vases bear a remarkable resemblance to the Consolidated Glass Company's Ruba Rombic line. Vases, candlesticks, bookends, ashtrays, bowls, lamp bases, and luncheon sets were made. A line of garden pottery was manufactured for a short time. Items were frequently impressed with MUNCIE in block letters. Letters such as A, K, E, or D and the numbers 1, 2, 3, 4, or 5 often found scratched into the base are finishers' marks. In our listings the first number in the description is the shape number, taken from old company catalogs or found on examples of the company's pottery. (These numbers are preceded by a number sign.)

Bookends, owl, bl on rose, #256, 5"................................375.00
Bottle, gr on lilac, #411, 5½"..125.00
Bowl, bl on rose, #169, 7½"..150.00
Bowl, console; Spanish line, gr on lilac, #276, 11", +2 #277 sticks... 200.00
Candlesticks, gr on rose, #149, unmk, 6", pr 100.00
Canoe w/flower frog, gr matt on rose, #253, unmk, 11½" 100.00
Ewer, blk gloss, #136, mk Muncie-1, 12"..........................125.00
Lamp, Dancing Nudes, gr matt, #U33, 28½" overall 500.00
Lamp base, lovebirds on yel gloss, 8"..............................325.00
Lamp base, lt gr on gr, att, 10" 150.00
Pitcher, gr drip, #466, 5½"...200.00
Pitcher, juice; bittersweet, #494, 6½"..............................150.00
Vase, bl drip on peach-skin gloss, hdls, #427, mk A, 7"...............200.00
Vase, bl on gr, #445, 7"..150.00
Vase, blk gloss, #445, 7¼", EX.......................................50.00
Vase, gr, #102, unmk, 8" 225.00
Vase, gr gloss on yel, #112, 8"....................................100.00
Vase, gr on lilac, #181, 7½"...200.00
Vase, gr on lilac, #490, 5"...50.00
Vase, gr on pumpkin, hand thrown, #410, unmk, flakes, 6"..........275.00
Vase, gr on rose, #423, unmk, 9" 275.00
Vase, gr on wht, #134, unmk, 7" 50.00
Vase, lt bl on wht, #119, unmk, 9" 175.00
Vase, matt gr over rose, waisted, #215, E-4, 12" 275.00
Vase, Rombic, bl on gr, #309, 7"....................................600.00
Vase, Rombic, bl on gr, #312, 5"....................................275.00
Vase, Rombic, gr on pumpkin, #301, 6" 550.00
Vase, Rombic, gr on rose, #312, unmk, 5"...........................275.00
Vase, Rombic, ming gr/lav, 4x5"......................................495.00
Vase, sea green gloss, #102 impressed bkwards, unmk, 8½" 50.00
Vase, wht on bl, #U5, 6"..100.00
Wall pocket, gr airbrushed over rose, shape #266, mk 3E, 9" 300.00

Musical Instruments

The field of automatic musical instruments covers many different categories ranging from watches and tiny seals concealing fine early musical movements to huge organs and orchestrions which weigh many hundreds of pounds and are equivalent to small orchestras. Music boxes, first made in the early nineteenth century by Swiss watchmakers, were produced in both disc and cylinder models. The latter type employs a cylinder with tiny pins that lift the teeth in the comb of the music box (producing a sound much like many individual tuning forks), and music results. The value of a cylinder music box depends on the length and diameter of the cylinder, the date of its manufacture, the number of tunes it plays (four or six is usually better than 10 or 12), whether it has multiple cylinders, if it has extra instruments (like bells, an organ, or drum), and its manufacturer. Nicole Freres, Henri Capt, LeCoultre, and Bremond are among the the most highly regarded, and the larger boxes made by Mermod Freres are also popular. Examples with multiple cylinders, extra instruments (such as bells or an organ section), and those in particularly ornate cabinets or with matching tables bring significantly higher prices. Early cylinder boxes were wound with a separate key which was inserted on the left side of the case. These early examples are known as 'keywind' boxes and bring a premium. While smaller cylinder boxes are still being made, the larger ones (over 10" cylinders) typically date from before 1900. Disc music boxes were introduced about 1890 but were replaced by the phonograph only 25 years later. However, during that time hundreds of thousands were made. Their great advantage was in playing inexpensive interchangeable discs, a factor that remains an attraction for today's collector as well. Among the most popular disc boxes are those made by Regina (USA), Polyphon, Mira, Stella, and Symphonion. Relative values are determined by the size of the discs they play, whether they have single or double combs, if they are upright or table models, and how ornate their cases are. Especially valuable are those that play multiple discs at the same time or are incorporated into tall case clocks.

Player pianos were made in a wide variety of styles. Early varieties consisted of a mechanism which pushed up to a piano and played on the keyboard by means of felt-tipped fingers. These use 65-note rolls. Later models have the playing mechanism built in, and most use 88-note rolls. Upright pump player pianos have little value in unrestored condition because the cost of restoration is so high. 'Reproducing' pianos, especially the 'grand' format, can be quite valuable, depending on the make, the size, the condition, and the ornateness of the case; however the market for 'reproducing' grand pianos has been very weak in recent years. 'Reproducing' grand pianos have very sophisticated mechanisms and are much more realistic in the reproduction of piano music. They were made in relatively limited quantities. Better manufacturers include Steinway and Mason & Hamlin. Popular roll mechanism makers include AMPICO, Duo-Art, and Welte.

Coin-operated pianos (Orchestrions) were used commercially and typically incorporate extra instruments in addition to the piano action. These can be very large and complex, incorporating drums, cymbals, xylophones, bells, and dozens of pipes. Both American and European coin pianos are very popular, especially the larger and more complex models made by Wurlitzer, Seeburg, Cremona, Weber, Welte, Hupfeld, and many others. These companies also made automatically playing violins (Mills Violin Virtuoso, Hupfeld), banjos (Encore), and harps (Whitlock); these are quite valuable.

Collecting player organettes is a fun endeavor. Roller organs, organettes, player organs, grind organs, hand organs — whatever the name — are a fascinating group of music makers. Some used wooden barrels or cobs to operate the valves, or metal and cardboard discs or paper strips, paper rolls, metal donuts, or metal strips. They usually played from 14 to 20 keys or notes. Some were pressure operated or vacuum type. Their heyday lasted from the 1870s to the turn of the century. Most were reed organs, but a few had pipes. Many were made in either America or Germany. They lost favor with the advent of the phonograph, as did the music box. Some music boxes were built with little player organs in them. Any player organette in good working condition with rolls will be worth from $200.00 to $600.00, depending on the model. Generally the more keying it has and the larger and fancier the case, the more desirable it is. Rarity plays a part too. There are a handfull of individuals who make new music

rolls for these player organs. Some machines are very rare, and music for them is nearly impossible to find. For further information on player organs we recommend *Encyclopedia of Automatic Musical Instruments* by Bowers.

Unless noted, prices given are for instruments in fine condition, playing properly, with cabinets or cases in well-preserved or refinished condition. In all instances, unrestored instruments sell for much less, as do those with broken or missing parts, damaged cases, and the like. On the other hand, particularly superb examples in especially ornate case designs and those that have been particularly well kept will often command more. Our advisor for mechanical instruments is Martin Roenigk; he is listed in the Directory under Arkansas.

Key: c — cylinder   d — disc

Mechanical

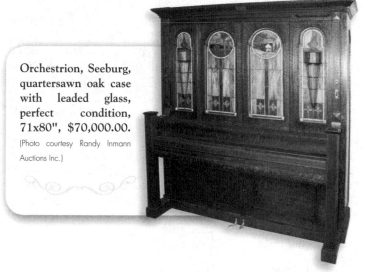

Orchestrion, Seeburg, quartersawn oak case with leaded glass, perfect condition, 71x80", $70,000.00. (Photo courtesy Randy Inmann Auctions Inc.)

Accordion, Tanzbaer 16-note, inlaid walnut, 11", +6 rolls	950.00
Box, BA Bremond, 16" c, 4 mandolin airs, rosewood w/inlay	4,850.00
Box, Bermond Forte Piano #11717, 6 airs, boxwood w/red int, 13" c	2,350.00
Box, Bremond Mandoline #1496118, rosewood vnr w/inlay, 13" c, 20" L	2,585.00
Box, Bremond Organocleide #15416, 6 airs, walnut vnr/inlay, 17" c	12,925.00
Box, Capital Model C, 7" tapering cuffs, Pat 1889, oak case, 27½" W	5,500.00
Box, console; Stella, 17" d, mahog w/appl cvg, dbl combs, 29x36x22"	6,000.00
Box, Cuendet #7803, coin-op, 8 patriotic airs, 6½" c, 17" L	885.00
Box, Ducommun Girod Bells-In-Sight #7679, rosewood w/inlay, 13" c	2,115.00
Box, Empress, dbl comb, 12" d, mahog 4-ftd case, 11x21x18", EX	2,100.00
Box, F Nicole, 8" c, 6 airs, fruitwood case, 15" W	1,500.00
Box, Heller Mandoline, 15" c, 16 airs, zither attachment, 28½", EX	1,800.00
Box, L'Epee Harmoniphone, 11" c, 17-key, rosewood case w/inlay, EX	1,800.00
Box, Mermod Freres Ideal Guitar, 4 11" c, 6 airs, golden oak, 28"	2,585.00
Box, Mermod Freres Sublime Harmony Piccolo, 16"c/3 combs/8 airs, rprs	2,200.00
Box, Mira, 18½" d, dbl combs, cvd console, rstr	10,500.00
Box, Nicole, 12" c, key-wind, 6 airs, EX	1,600.00
Box, Nicole Freres #26639, key-wind, walnut w/ebony stringing, 6" c	1,765.00
Box, Nicole Freres, 11" c, key-wind, 6 airs, grpt case, 18" W	1,500.00
Box, Nicole Freres, 12" c, lever-wind, 6 airs, rosewood case, 1873, EX	1,800.00
Box, Paillard Orchestral #4821, 12 airs, inlaid burr walnut, 17" c	4,000.00
Box, Pillard #79989, 12 airs, rswd w/inlay & ormolu, 17" c	1,530.00
Box, Polyphon, 24" d, burled walnut, coin-op, 79x33", EX	15,500.00
Box, Polyphon Emerald, 22¼"d/2-comb/16 bells, top folds, 28½" W	22,500.00
Box, Regina, 15½" d, dbl combs, automatic changer, EX	21,000.00
Box, Regina, 20¾" d, flat front, automatic changer	18,500.00
Box, Reginaphone, 20¾" d, NP horn, matching base	9,500.00
Box, S Troll Fils Changeable Orchestral #3607, 4 6 airs, 16" c, walnut	15,500.00

Box, snuff; #284, La Traviata Polka+2nd, blk compo, engine trn, 3¾" ... 400.00
Box, snuff; Nicole, God Save the Queen, tortoiseshell/rvpt case, 3" L .. 350.00
Box, snuff; 1 air, brass repousse case w/swags, emb/pnt lid, 3¼" L .. 210.00
Box, Stella, 25¾" d, dbl combs, walnut case, ca 1900, 77" 18,000.00
Kalliope, horserace panorama, 20" d, coin-op, walnut case, 94", NM .. 17,600.00
Nickelodeon, Chicago Electric A Roll, EX 1,500.00
Nickelodeon, Peerless #44, rfn oak case, M rstr, +20 rolls 8,000.00
Nickelodeon, Western Electric, 2-tier mahog case, 64x44x22" .. 5,875.00
Orchestrelle, Aeolian Y, mahog, 58-note, M rstr, +12 rolls 5,000.00
Orchestrion, Seeburg G, quartersawn oak/ldgl, 71x80", working, EX. 65,000.00
Organ, band; N Tonawanda Military, 18 brass trumpets, VG .. 19,000.00
Organ, band; Wurlitzer #125 Military, 40-note/35-pipe, 74x41x30"+rolls .. 16,450.00
Organ, band; Wurlitzer #153, rstr 38,000.00
Organ, bbl; Astor (att), 21-key, 3-bbl, 30 airs, mahog case, 57" .. 1,400.00
Organ, Grand Roller, 15" roller cob, 32-note 3,700.00
Organ, monkey; Molinari, 20-key, EX 4,000.00
Organ, paper roll; Improved Celestina, EX stencils, EX, +1 roll .. 700.00
Organette, Gem roller organ, 6 wooden rollers 500.00
Organette, Horton's Autophone, 22-note, Pats 1877 & 78, 9¾" W . 400.00
Piano, Cremona A, 25¢ play, takes O rolls (10 airs), ca 1920 ... 2,400.00
Piano, grand; Chickering Ampico, 1916, rfn, 68", EX 3,500.00
Piano, grand; Knabe Ampico, 64", M 2,500.00
Piano, grand; Mason & Hamlin B Ampico, rstr, 84" 8,000.00
Piano, grand; Steinway Duo-Art XR, rstr 4,500.00
Piano, grand; Steinway Louis XV Duo-Art, ca 1924, M rstr 13,000.00
Piano, grand; Welte-Mignon, Louis XV style, 1919, 72", M rstr . 7,500.00
Piano, Seeburg L #53638, coin-op, mahog w/gilt putto capitals, 53" .. 3,200.00
Piano orchestrion, Lion-Healy, w/pipes, EX 7,500.00
Piano orchestrion, Webner Unika 88-note, cvd oak/mirror doors, 75x68" . 24,000.00
Piano orchestrion, Welte Briscovia A #5160, oak w/inlay, 96x66" ... 70,500.00
Violin, Mills Dbl Virtuoso, M 55,000.00

Non-Mechanical

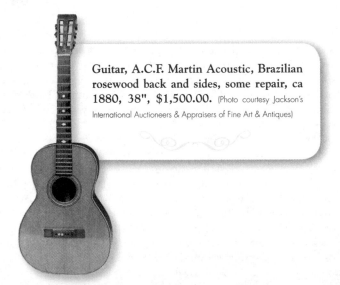

Guitar, A.C.F. Martin Acoustic, Brazilian rosewood back and sides, some repair, ca 1880, 38", $1,500.00. (Photo courtesy Jackson's International Auctioneers & Appraisers of Fine Art & Antiques)

Accordion, Capri, Sonola Musette, 41 treble keys/120 brass buttons, EX . 275.00
Accordion, Titano Tube Chamber Organette, MOP keyboard, EX, +case ... 400.00
Accordion, Virtuoso, ivory keys, 120 buttons, Pat 1931, EX, +case ... 335.00
Banjo, B&D Tenor, maple neck, EX, +hard-shell case 550.00
Banjo, Bacon & Day Senorita, 5-string, rpl bridge, EX, +case 565.00
Banjo, Gibson Mandolin, hinged trap door, ca 1925, EX, +case ... 900.00
Banjo, Gretsch Broadkaster, 4-string, ca 1927, EX, +case 700.00
Banjo, Ome Vintage Series Juniper, 5-string, inlay neck, EX 1,650.00
Banjo, WA Coles Eclipse, open bk/pearlized forms, 1890s, EX, +case .. 1,465.00
Clarinet, H Bettoney E-flat, SP metal, EX, + hard case 475.00
Clarinet, Selmer Paris, metal 2-pc body w/separate bell, NM, +case .. 1,100.00

Cornet, Boston 3-flat Leader Pattern, rotary valve, 1870+, VG .. 2,000.00
Cornet, FE Olds & Son, brass w/SP trim, 16½", EX, +hard case 325.99
Cornet, Frank Holton, SP, w/Blessing 7c mouthpc, Pat Oct 17 11, EX .. 300.00
Cornet, Reynolds Emperor, lg bore, brass w/nickel silver trim, 1969, M. 425.00
Drum, bentwood hoops & rope tension, blk pnt, 19th C, 14" dia, VG .. 115.00
Drum set, Gretsch Maple Shell, bass+tom+2 floor toms, ca 1983, EX 1,750.00
Drum set, Gretsch Round Badge, bass+tom+floor tom+snare, 1960s, EX .. 2,250.00
Drum set, Ludwig champagne sparkle, bass+3 toms+snare, 1966, EX 1,500.00
Drum set, Rogers gr sparkle, 22" kick+tom+floor tom+snare, 1980s, EX .. 2,100.00
Drum set, Slingerland Agate Bl, bass+2 toms+floor tom+snare, '70s, EX+ ... 850.00
Flute, GL Penzell NY, Grenadilla, German silver, prof rstr 775.00
Flute, Rudall Carte & Co, wood w/silver keys, open G, ca 1900, +case .. 1,575.00
Guitar, Fender Jaguar, F tuners, 1977, +case 3,550.00
Guitar, Fender Stratocaster, Olympic White, 1975, +case 3,950.00
Guitar, Fender Telecaster Deluxe, prototype, 1972, NM 12,500.00
Guitar, Gibson Dove, pearl inlay, ivory pegs, 1960s, +case 7,850.00
Guitar, Gibson Les Paul SG body style, ebony block tailpc, 1962, +case .. 9,750.00
Guitar, Gibson Les Paul Standard Sunburst, 1974, +case 1,775.00
Guitar, Gibson Moderne, gold hardware, 1983, rare, NM 4,400.00
Guitar, Gibson Sunburst J-45 flat top, 1951, EX, +case 2,400.00
Guitar, Gretch #6131 Jet Firebird, Filtertron pickups, 1964, +case 2,900.00
Guitar, Martin D-18 Acoustic, rpl bridge pins, 1954, EX+ 4,900.00
Guitar, Martin 000-28 Ltd Ed Golden Era, 6-string, 1996, +case .. 2,600.00
Guitar, Sunburst Stratocaster, pre-CBS L series, rosewood, 1985, NM .. 16,750.00
Harmonica, Hohner Chromonica DeLuxe, 6½", +red & gold case .. 115.00
Harmonica, Hohner Preciosa, dbl sided, 1930s, 6", +Deco case ... 115.00
Harp, J Erat, London; mahog & burl vnr, ca 1805-07, 66", +case .. 5,175.00
Harp, T Dodd & Son, gilt Vict decor/animal paw ft/winged women, 67x32" .. 3,680.00
Keyboard, Fender Rhodes Mark 1, 73-key, 1975, +worn case ... 1,050.00
Keyboard, Roland XP-80 Synth Workstation, 64 voices, 1996, +case .. 900.00
Keyboard, Wurlitzer #200A, chrome legs, pedal assembly, 1960s-70s ... 600.00
Mandolin, Gibson Flatiron 1SB, sunburst finish, 1970s-80s, +case .. 525.00
Mandolin, Lyon & Healy Style C, maple bk & sides, 1920s, rpr, EX . 865.00
Organ, Farfisa mini compact, 16-8-4 tone, Fender Bassman Amp, 1960s 800.00
Organ, Hammond B3 w/JR20 Tone cabinet & bench, 1950s, EX+ ... 3,000.00
Piano, baby grand; Steinway & Sons, ebonized, ca 1900, rfn, 72x57" .. 14,000.00
Piano, grand; Baldwin SF, Renner hammers, unused, 1988, 84" ... 17,000.00
Piano, grand; Steinway, flame mahog, Model O, 1906, 70" W .. 8,225.00
Piano, grand; Steinway, mahog, 1901, 1980s rstr, 93x64" 65,000.00
Piano, grand; Steinway & Sons Model B Semi Concert, 1923, 82" .. 18,000.00
Piano, grand; Steinway & Sons Model M, mahog w/gold, 1985, 67" ... 16,000.00
Saxophone, Conn Silver 10M Naked Lady, 1936, +hard case .. 2,750.00
Saxophone, Selmer Mark VI Alto, 1964, +soft case 4,100.00
Saxophone, Selmer Mark VI Tenor w/high F-sharp key, +hard case .. 4,000.00
Trombone, CG Conn Model 42H, 8" eng bell, 1929, +case 1,100.00
Trombone, FE Olds Super, brass, #3 mouthpc, 1940s, +case 275.00
Trumpet, Bach Stradivarius Model 37, SP, 19", +hard case 650.00
Trumpet, Conn Connstellation B, NP, 1956, +bag 565.00
Trumpet, Conn Director, tri-color, E-Z Tone mouthpc, VG+ 235.00
Trumpet, Conn Pan-American, brass, 1947, +case 225.99
Trumpet, King Liberty #567, silver 600.00
Trumpet, Martin Committee Model, gold-tone, 2 mutes, VG+case .. 1,400.00
Violin, N Lupot Cremona, curly maple/spruce, 2-pc bk, 1857, 14"+bow .. 2,115.00

Mustache Cups

Mustache cups were popular items during the late Victorian period, designed specifically for the man with the mustache! They were made in silver plate as well as china and ironstone. Decorations ranged from simple transfers to elaborately applied and gilded florals. To properly position the 'mustache bar,' special cups were designed for the 'lefties.' These are the rare ones! Our advisor for this category is Robert Doyle; he is listed in the Directory under New York.

Bamboo & Fern, gr & yel majolica, Wardle, +saucer 180.00
Bl rose panels w/gold on wht, Wileman, Shelley, 1896, +6⅛" saucer .. 850.00
Floral & Basket, aqua & brn, majolica, Wedgwood, +saucer........ 225.00
Floral emb on pk to wht, beveled mirror on front, unmk, 3" 30.00
Floral HP on wht swirled cylinder, unmk, ca 1880, 3¼" 65.00
Floral reserves on aqua to wht w/gold, CT Austria, +saucer........... 25.00
Flowers & swags w/gold on wht, Nippon mk, 2½x3½" 50.00
Indian chief decal on wht porc, gold trim, unmk, 3½" 90.00
Nouveau floral on aqua & wht, swirled body, ornate gold hdl, unmk...35.00
Oriental floral in gold, ornate hdl, unmk England, 1880s, +saucer .. 150.00
Roses, mc on lt bl china, Brandenburg mk, 3½" 28.00

Nailsea

Nailsea is a term referring to clear or colored glass decorated in contrasting spatters, swirls, or loops. These are usually white but may also be pink, red, or blue. It was first produced in Nailsea, England, during the late 1700s but was made in other parts of Britain and Scotland as well. During the mid-1800s a similar type of glass was produced in this country. Originally used for decorative novelties only, by that time tumblers and other practical items were being made from Nailsea-type glass. See also Lamps, Fairy.

Bottle, gemel; clear w/wht loopings, flattened ovoid, 8¼x3" 110.00
Bottle, gemel; gray w/wht loopings, elongated ovoid, 19th C, 9¼"... 175.00
Flask, milk glass w/red & bl loopings, plump ovoid form, 6½"...... 600.00
Gazing ball, clear w/wht loopings, on baluster stand, 14", pr.....2,750.00
Jug, aquamarine w/wht loopings, bulbous, pulled spout, 1850s, 6½" ..4,175.00
Jug, clear w/bl loopings, crude hdl, disk ft, late 19th C, 7½", EX... 165.00
Powder horn, clear w/wht loopings & bl-gr stripes, ring neck, 12"... 175.00
Sweetmeat, cranberry w/wht loopings, SP mts, 5" W 300.00
Sweetmeat, lime/wht swirl on melon ribbing, SP mts, 5¾" 150.00
Vase, amethyst w/wht loopings, ftd valuster, late 18th C, 8x4½"...1,750.00

Nakara

Nakara was a line of decorated opaque milk glass produced by the C. F. Monroe Company of Meriden, Connecticut, for a few years after the turn of the century. It differs from their Wave Crest line in several ways. The shapes were simpler; pastel colors were deeper and covered more of the surface; more beading was present; flowers were larger; and large transfer prints of figures, Victorian ladies, cherubs, etc., were used as well. Ormolu and brass collars and mounts complemented these opulent pieces. Most items were signed; however, this is not important since the ware was never reproduced. Our advisors for this category are Dolli and Wilfred R. Cohen; their address is listed in the Directory under California.

Ashtray, floral on gr, 3 gilt metal rests, 6" dia................................ 195.00
Bonbon tray, Dmn Swirl, geometric scrolling/beadwork on bl 450.00
Box, Bishops's Hat (scarce), floral on pk/yel, wht beadwork, 7" dia....795.00
Box, blown-out stemmed rose on flip lid, pk hexagonal body, 3" H ...850.00
Box, Collars & Cuffs, Gibson girl transfer 2,950.00
Box, courting couple reserve on peach, 6" dia 1,150.00
Box, floral (stylized) lid w/beadwork, hexagon, unmk, 4" dia....... 230.00
Box, floral on bl, ca 1890, 8" dia... 900.00
Box, floral/wht beadwork rim on shaded bl, no emb, 8" dia.......... 800.00
Box, Kate Greenway figures on lid, pk shades w/wht beadwork, 4" W.. 500.00
Box, ladies in Greco-Roman garden transfer, 8" dia 2,500.00
Box, lady's portrait in reverse on bl w/wht enamel, 5" dia 900.00
Box, lady's portrait on pk, emb rococo scrolls, 5½x8¼" dia 2,750.00
Box, mums, pk/wht on shades of bl, beadwork accents, 3¼" W....350.00
Box, robin's egg, bl w/tan accents & wht beadwork, hexagon, 4"....515.00
Box, roses, red/wht, on pk to gr w/wht beadwork, 6" dia 700.00

Box, roses on pale bl, metal base 3x3¾" dia.................................. 750.00
Box, violets on yel, 3¾" dia 350.00
Box, X in wht beadwork/bl floral on pk to yel, mirror, 5" dia 575.00
Box, 2 ladies in meadow in wht-dotted reserve on pk w/floral, 8" W .. 975.00
Cigar holder, floral on gr/wht, ormolu hdld rim/base w/4 ft, rare..630.00
Cracker jar, floral on rose w/gold, gold metal hdl & lid 895.00
Humidor, floral, pk/wht on dk bl, Tobacco at lower front............ 775.00
Humidor, frog reading paper on bl, Tobacco, metal lid, 6¾" 1,950.00
Humidor, owl/tree transfer on shades of brn, Cigars on lid, rare, 6"....1,500.00

Humidor, reserve with transfer of lady, 7¾", $1,000.00. (Photo courtesy Dolli and Wilfred R. Cohen)

Jardiniere, pk floral on gr, gold trim.. 625.00
Mustard pot, bl w/wht-outlined cream half-circles, SP lid/spoon, 3"... 350.00
Smoke set, floral on gr, cigar holder+2 ash bowls+match holder on ft..800.00
Sweatmeat, fall leaves on bl, shaped body, metal lid/hdl, 5½" W .. 325.00
Tray, floral, pk/wht on pk to gr, ormolu rim w/pointed hdls, 6" L .. 150.00
Tray, wht beadwork/floral on pk to yel, mirror in ormolu frwork.. 750.00
Vase/ornament, floral reserve on pk, ormolu rim/collar/hdls/ft, sm... 425.00

Napkin Rings

Napkin rings became popular during the late 1800s. They were made from various materials. Among the most popular and collectible today are the large group of varied silver-plated figurals made by American manufacturers. Recently the larger figurals in excellent condition have appreciated considerably. Only those with a blackened finish, corrosion, or broken and/or missing parts have maintained their earlier price levels. When no condition is indicated, the items listed below are assumed to be all original and in very good to excellent condition. Check very carefully for missing parts, solder repairs, marriages, and reproductions.

A timely warning: Inexperienced buyers should be aware of excellent reproductions on the market, especially the wheeled pieces and cherubs. However, these do not have the fine detail and patina of the originals and tend to have a more consistent, soft pewter-like finish. There may also be pitting on the surface. These are appearing at the large, quality shows at top prices, being shown along with authentic antique merchandise. Beware! Our advisor for this category is Barbara Aaronson; she is listed in the Directory under California.

Key:
gw — gold washed   SH&M — Simpson, Hall, &
R&B — Reed & Barton   Miller

Baseball player, ball in right hand, sq base, Pairpoint #83 ....1,500.00
Bear holding rifle, oval base w/woodland decor, #200..........................750.00
Bird on horseshoe base, emb triangular holder, Pairpoint #70, $200 to ..350.00
Boy lying bk barefoot holds ring, oval shield base, Wilcox #01549 ..500.00
Bull by hexagon holder, Knickerbocker #1248, from $200 to 350.00
Bulldog w/collar by doghouse holder, Simpson...#207, 4 ftd, $350 to..500.00
Cat on sq pillow-shaped base, Meriden Silver Plate...#293 .... 750.00

Cat sitting beside holder on oval ftd base, Meriden...#232, $350 to...500.00
Cherub, lg (4⅛"), sitting w/bk to ring, 4 ball ft, Pairpoint #7.......750.00
Cherub w/legs crossed sits on 2-ftd base, w/glass vase, Pairpoint #10...750.00
Chick on coop holder, 4 ball ft, Tufts #1633, from $200 to..........350.00
Cockatoo on sunflower stem, book-shaped ring, Derby #370, $200 to...350.00

Cow on floral-embossed mound stands by bucket, $500.00. (Photo courtesy Morphy Auctions)

Crane, lg, standing on 1 ft, rnd woodland base, Meriden #163, $350 to..500.00
Deer, ruffled-edge ring, sq fringed rug base, Toronto #1205................650.00
Dog barks at bird atop holder, Homan Silver...#131, from $200 to ..350.00
Dog w/wishbone in mouth, fancy cast base, Derby #303, from $200 to....350.00
Fox under holder, grapes over head, Meriden Britannia #331 .... 1,200.00
Frog wearing boots, ring w/fluted & beaded edge, Pelton #110................650.00
Girl riding chariot by ring, rubena glass s&p, Wm Rogers #231.. 1,500.00
Girl w/flowers by holder w/cinched-in center, Derby #319 ....550.00
Girls carries basket by ring, low base, R&B #1492......................... 750.00
Gnomes w/beards carry barrel ring on poles, SH&M #016........................1,500.00
Goat pulls holder mtd on wheels, Meriden Britannia Co #212..................650.00
Grapes topped w/leaf on side of wine barrel, Standard... #733, $350 to..550.00
Greenway boy by rustic fence, 4-ball ftd base, Tufts #1598, $500.00 to...700.00
Greenway girl in front of ornate holder, Rockford #120, from $350 to...500.00
Greenway girl pets goat on rope by holder, oval base, Meriden #0236. 1,200.00
Greenway girl pushes boy on sled, sq holder, SH&M #037 ....1,500.00
Horse, lg & saddled, w/front hoofs on holder, ball ft.........................650.00
Horseshoe, lg, emb Bonheur on front, Tufts #1540, from $200 to ...250.00
Jester w/left arm out leans on ring, long oval base, Meriden #0258..900.00
Leaf w/scallop edge & stem hdl, 3-flower decor, Toronto #1145, $200 to..350.00
Lion holds open ornate ring w/medallion on top, unmk.................550.00
Mouse w/long tail by ring, plain rnd ftd base, #01501, from $200 to..350.00
Oriental fans on ring sides, mtd on sq block, oval base, Meriden #485...250.00
Owl, great horned; lg, by holder on plain base, Meriden #156..... 500.00
Parakeet on hdl w/scrolled ft, ring mtd on 2 wheels, unmk.................750.00
Peacock w/trn head on clip, mk Happy New Year...1935, R&B, $200 to..350.00
Rabbit by log holder, woodland decor, SH&M #210...........................600.00
Rifles crossed to support emb holder, Meriden #335, from $200 to 350.00
Rooster, lg & standing on shovel hdl, Meriden #181 (+)........................550.00
Saddlebags+2 swords form base, holder w/bulbous center, #291.................450.00
Sailor holding rope to anchor, w/pitcher bud vase, R&B #1357 .. 700.00
Sheep, scroll-edge base, holder w/decor band, Meriden #0279..................550.00
Sparrow, emb floral holder, emb base border, unmk, from $200 to ..350.00
Squirrel, ring on 2 balls, emb base, Knickerbocker #7, from $200 to..350.00
Squirrels, pr w/nuts holding ring w/tails, Bridgeport #211, $200 to 350.00
Stool supporting woodland-decor ring, R&B #1585, from $200 to 350.00
Swan pulling ring on 2 wheels, fine details, Meriden #334 .... 1,200.00

Nash

A. Douglas Nash founded the Corona Art Glass Company in Long Island, New York. He produced tableware, vases, flasks, etc. using delicate artistic shapes and forms. After 1933 he worked for the Libbey Glass Company.

Bowl, Chintz, red w/turq stripes, 7½x10" 780.00
Bowl, gold irid, wide flat rim, ribbed, #515, 1⅛x4" 265.00
Compote, amber irid w/bl overtones, att, 4x5¼" 230.00
Compote, Chintz, radiating bands of ruby on lt gr, 8" dia 390.00
Plate, Chintz, orange & clear radiating design, unmk, 6½" 115.00
Vase, bl irid, lt ribbing, elongated pear form, #526, 5½" 480.00
Vase, Chintz, brn/gr bands, wide clear ft, bulbous, unmk, 7½" 860.00
Vase, Chintz, red w/turq stripes, bulbous, 8" 960.00
Vase, Chintz, vertical rows of loopings, gold w/bl-gray, #57, 12" ...4,200.00
Vase, gold w/molded 'veins,' slim form, #532, 12" 360.00

Natzler, Gertrude and Otto

The Natzlers came to the United States from Vienna in the late 1930s. They settled in Los Angeles where they continued their work in ceramics, for which they were already internationally recognized. Gertrude created the forms; Otto formulated a variety of interesting glazes, among them volcanic, crystalline, and lustre. Our advisors for this category are Suzanne Perrault and David Rago; they are listed in the directory under New Jersey.

Bowl, beige semimatt, folded rim, sm nick, 2½x8"........................ 550.00
Bowl, chartreuse, folded sides, rstr chip, 3¾x8¼".........................3,000.00
Bowl, chartruse & brn volcanic, rstr line, 3x9½" 2,600.00
Bowl, gray & amber microcrystalline, hemispherical, 3½x6" 1,000.00
Bowl, ivory/brn volcanic, rstr line, 3x9½" 500.00
Bowl, lt yel & umber hare's fur matt, hemispherical, rstr chip, 7"..1,400.00
Bowl, multi-tone gray reduction glaze w/fissures, low, wide, 11" .. 4,000.00
Bowl, pumpkin flambe, vertical streaks, nick, 1¾x6½"................. 200.00
Bowl, raspberry copper-reduction w/melt figures, chip, 5x6¼" ..3,500.00
Bowl, sang reduction glaze w/slight irid, 3¼" 1,500.00
Bowl, teal & oxblood gloss w/melt fissures, 3¾x5½" 3,250.00
Dish, frothy uranium red, 1x5" 1,300.00
Vase, thick textured red clay body, lt gr int, 2½" 2,000.00

Vase, blue-green striated volcanic glaze, label: K874, 18", $54,000.00. (Photo courtesy David Rago Auctions)

Naughties and Bathing Beauties

These daring all-bisque figurines were made in various poses, usually in one piece, in German and American factories during the 1920s. Admired for their fine details, these figures were often nude but were also made with molded-on clothing or dressed in bathing costumes. Items below are all in excellent undamaged condition. Our advisors for this category are Don and Anne Kier; they are listed in the Directory under Ohio.

Action figure, Germany, 5" 450.00
Action figure, Germany, 7½" 700.00
Action figure, w/wig, Germany, 7" 650.00
Elderly woman in suit w/legs crossed, rare, 5¼" 1,400.00

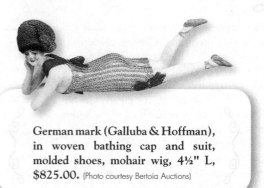

German mark (Galluba & Hoffman), in woven bathing cap and suit, molded shoes, mohair wig, 4½" L, $825.00. (Photo courtesy Bertoia Auctions)

Glass eyes, 5" 400.00
Glass eyes, 6" 650.00
Japan mk, 3" 40.00
Japan mk, 5-6", ea 65.00
Japan mk, 9" 95.00
Painted eyes, 3" 165.00
Painted eyes, 6" 325.00
Swivel neck, 5" 700.00
Swivel neck, 6" 750.00
With animal, 5½" 1,200.00
2 molded together, 4½-5½", ea 1,600.00

New Geneva

In the early years of the nineteenth century, several potteries flourished in the Greensboro, Pennsylvania, area. They produced utilitarian stoneware items as well as tile and novelties for many decades. All failed well before the turn of the twentieth century.

Figurine, Egyptian hawk, brn glazed wings & crest, 5¼" 925.00
Flowerpot, tulips & foliage, attached saucer, ring hdls, 8¾" 495.00
Mug, allover Albany glaze, tooled rim, att, 6⅜" 150.00
Pitcher, floral, umber slip on redware, flakes, 7" 700.00

New Martinsville

The New Martinsville Glass Company took its name from the town in West Virginia where it began operations in 1901. In the beginning years pressed tablewares were made in crystal as well as colored and opalescent glass. Considered an innovator, the company was known for their imaginative applications of the medium in creating lamps made entirely of glass, vanity sets, figural decanters, and models of animals and birds. In 1944 the company was purchased by Viking Glass, who continued to use many of the old molds, the animals molds included. They marked their wares 'Viking' or 'Rainbow Art.' Viking ceased operations and was purchased by Kenneth Dalzell, who continued making birds and animals. These pieces were at first unmarked, but later productions used an acid stamp. Production has again ceased, leaving the Dalzell/Viking animals to fall in the $50.00 to $60.00 range. Values for cobalt and red items are two to three times higher than for the same item in clear. See also Depression Glass; Glass Animals and Figurines.

Addie, blk, cobalt, jade or red, bowl, vegetable; flared rim, lg 35.00
Addie, blk, cobalt, jade or red, plate, luncheon 12.50
Addie, blk, cobalt, jade or red, saucer 5.00
Addie, blk, cobalt, jade or red, tumbler, water; ftd, 9-oz 22.50
Addie, crystal or pk, creamer, ftd 12.00
Addie, crystal or pk, sugar bowl, open, ftd 10.00

Janice, bl or red, basket, #4552, 11" 225.00
Janice, bl or red, bowl, oval, 11" 95.00
Janice, bl or red, bowl, salad; scalloped top, 12" 85.00
Janice, bl or red, oil bottle, w/stopper, #4583, 5-oz 100.00
Janice, bl or red, plate, 13" 60.00
Janice, bl or red, relish, 2-part, hdls, 6" 37.50
Janice, bl or red, sugar bowl, 6-oz 20.00
Janice, bl or red, vase, ftd, 7" 75.00
Janice, crystal, bonbon, hdls, 6x4" 20.00
Janice, crystal, bowl, fruit; ruffled top, 12" 50.00
Janice, crystal, cup, #4580 .... 8.00
Janice, crystal, mayonnaise, hdls, 6" 18.00
Janice, crystal, plate, cheese; swan hdl, #4528-25J, 11" 22.50
Janice, crystal, shakers, pr 40.00
Janice, crystal, vase, ball, 9" 55.00
Lions, amber or crystal, bowl, cream soup; ftd, hdls, #34 .... 20.00
Lions, amber or crystal, candleholder, #37, ea 25.00
Lions, amber or crystal, creamer, #37 .... 15.00
Lions, amber or crystal, sugar bowl, #37 .... 15.00
Lions, blk, compote, cheese 35.00
Lions, blk, creamer, #34 .... 35.00
Lions, blk, plate, 8" 30.00
Lions, blk, saucer, #34 .... 10.00
Lions, gr or pk, candlestick, #34, ea 35.00
Lions, gr or pk, candy dish, w/lid 75.00
Lions, gr or pk, plate, cracker; 12" 30.00
Lions, gr or pk, sugar bowl, #34 .... 25.00
Meadow Wreath, crystal, bonbon, hdls, 7" 18.00
Meadow Wreath, crystal, candlestick, 2-light, rnd ft, ea 42.50
Meadow Wreath, crystal, cheese & cracker, #42/26, 11" 50.00
Meadow Wreath, crystal, ladle, punch; #4226 .... 55.00
Meadow Wreath, crystal, plate, 11" 35.00
Meadow Wreath, crystal, sugar bowl, ftd, tab hdls, #42/26 .... 15.00
Meadow Wreath, crystal, tray, creamer & sugar; oval, #42/26 .... 15.00
Meadow Wreath, crystal, vase, crimped, #4232/26 .... 60.00
Moondrops, bl or red, ashtray 30.00
Moondrops, bl or red, bowl, soup; 6¾" 90.00
Moondrops, bl or red, butter dish 475.00
Moondrops, bl or red, cup 15.00
Moondrops, bl or red, decanter, 11¼" 110.00
Moondrops, bl or red, sugar bowl, 2¾" 15.00
Moondrops, colors other than bl or red, bowl, berry; 5¼" 12.00
Moondrops, colors other than bl or red, bowl, vegetable; oval, 9¾" .. 45.00
Moondrops, colors other than bl or red, creamer, mini; 2¾" 11.00
Moondrops, colors other than bl or red, mug, 12-oz, 5⅛" 27.50
Moondrops, colors other than bl or red, plate, salad; 7⅛" 10.00
Moondrops, colors other than bl or red, tumbler, 9-oz, 4⅞" 15.00
Radiance, amber, bonbon, 6" 15.00
Radiance, amber, plate, luncheon; 8" 10.00
Radiance, amber, tray, oval 25.00
Radiance, bl or red, bowl, celery; 10" 45.00
Radiance, bl or red, compote, 5" 32.00
Radiance, bl or red, shakers, pr 95.00

Radiance, crystal, mayonnaise, three-piece, from $35.00 to $45.00.

Newcomb

The Newcomb College of New Orleans, Louisiana, established a pottery in 1895 to provide the students with first-hand experience in the fields of art and ceramics. Using locally dug clays — red and buff in the early years, white-burning by the turn of the century — potters were employed to throw the ware which the ladies of the college decorated. From 1897 until about 1910, the ware they produced was finished in a high glaze and was usually surface painted. After 1905 some carving was done as well. The letter 'Q' that is sometimes found in the mark indicates a pre-1906 production (high glaze). After 1912 a matt glaze was favored; these pieces are always carved. Soft blues and greens were used almost exclusively, and decorative themes were chosen to reflect the beauty of the South. The year 1930 marked the end of the matt-glaze period and the art-pottery era.

Various marks used by the pottery include an 'N' within a 'C,' sometimes with 'HB' added to indicate a 'hand-built' piece. The potter often incised his initials into the ware, and the artists were encouraged to sign their work. Among the most well-known artists were Sadie Irvine, Henrietta Bailey, and Fannie Simpson.

Newcomb pottery is evaluated to a large extent by era (early, transitional, or matt), decoration, size, and condition. In the following descriptions, unless noted otherwise, all decoration is carved and painted on matt glaze. The term 'transitional' defines a period of a few years, between 1910 and 1916, when matt glazes were introduced as waxy, with green finishes. One can tell a 'transitional' piece by the use of ink marks with matt glazes. Our advisors for this category are Suzanne Perrault and David Rago; they are listed in the Directory under New Jersey.

Key: hg — high glaze

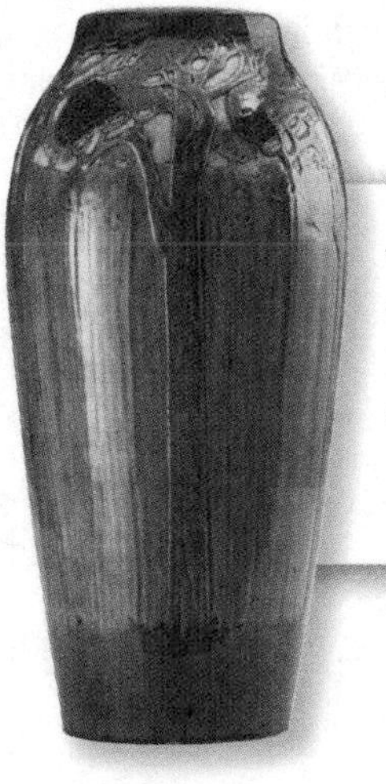

Vase, high glaze, carved, pine trees, Sadie Irvine, 1909, 15x7½", $96,000.00. (Photo courtesy David Rago Auctions)

Bowl, floral band on bl, AF Simpson, #90, 1918, 3" 1,300.00
Bowl, floral stalks/leaves, H Bailey, narrow flat ft, 6", NM 750.00
Bowl, trumpet flowers, AF Simpson, #268/IA67, flake, 9".........1,765.00
Bowl vase, iris band on bl to pk, AF Simpson, 1917, 4½x8" 2,760.00
Bowl vase, moon/moss/oaks, S Irvine, bulbous, 4½x6½" 3,100.00
Bowl vase, roses at shoulder, AF Simpson, very bulbous, 4x5" ..1,800.00
Charger, Newcomb Chapel/oak-leaf border, Delft style, SE Bres, #97, 9" ..5,400.00
Pitcher, crocus at rim, M LeBlanc, flaring sides, 7½" 1,320.00
Pitcher, daffodils, rose pk/bl, S Irvine, 1919, 6" 1,175.00
Pitcher, floral at top, wht/gr on bl, AF Simpson, cylindrical, 5x4" ..720.00
Pitcher, sailboats on Lake Pontchartrain, S Irvine, 1918, 4x5" ..3,480.00
Planter, tree scenic, MW Summey, transitional, 1910, 4x11" ...3,360.00
Teapot, jasmine bands, wht on bl, AF Simpson, 5x9", +4 c/s+cr/sug, EX....12,000.00
Trivet, floral, pk/bl, S Irvine, #R195, 4½" dia 480.00
Trivet, jasmine band around rim, AF Simpson, label, 6" dia 1,920.00
Vase, bayou scene against pk sky, S Irvine, 1919, 3½x4" 2,880.00
Vase, cornflowers on dk bl, M Morel, 1910, sm rstr, 10½x5" 2,880.00
Vase, crocuses in yel, M LeBlanc, 3-hdl, 8½x9½" 21,600.00
Vase, daffodils in bl, Ada Lonnegan, 1903, 5x8½" 1,800.00
Vase, daisies & tendrils, AF Simpson, #KX98/25Y, 4½x7¼" 1,700.00
Vase, floral, AF Simpson/J Meyer, flared cylinder, 1912, 6⅝" 1,325.00
Vase, floral, wht/yel/lt gr on dk/lt bl, C Littlejohn, 5½".............1,200.00
Vase, floral (heart-shaped) on bl matt, sgn A, X12, 3x4" 1,200.00
Vase, floral (long-stem), wht on bl tones, corseted, 1919, 8x3½" ..2,040.00
Vase, floral (long-stem), C Payne, slim, 1908, hairline, 6⅜" 2,650.00
Vase, floral clusters on leafy stems, wht/bl/gr, H Joor, 14", NM... 36,000.00
Vase, floral panels, G Blethen, #18OV90, 5x5½" 3,000.00
Vase, floral stalks/tall leaves alternate, H Bailey, 5½", NM........1,440.00
Vase, foliage (stylized) at bulbous base, MO Delavigne, 1902, 6x4"...3,120.00
Vase, freesia at top, AF Simpson, bulbous, 1919, label, 4x5".....2,160.00
Vase, fruit trees, M Ross, collar neck, chip/line rstr, 5x6"..........4,200.00
Vase, geometrics (repeating), cobalt on lt bl, bulbous, Q, 4⅝" 2,150.00
Vase, gulf-stream glaze, baluster, 1940-47, 5¾" 475.00
Vase, gunmetal, vertical ridges/dimples, JM stamp, 5¾x5½" 1,200.00
Vase, hg, split pods, M & E LeBlanc, 1901, 3¾x5¼" 16,800.00
Vase, jonquils, pk/gr/bl, AF Simpson, shouldered, 6".................1,800.00
Vase, jonquils (full-length), AF Simpson, long body/squat base, 9" .3,600.00
Vase, leaves (tall/Xd at rim), lt gr semi-matt, NC/HJ/A/G9/TP80, 10x6"....2,760.00
Vase, moon/moss/cyprus trees, AF Simpson, 6½".......................4,100.00
Vase, moon/moss/oak trees, AF Simpson, 1925, 6x3½" 3,900.00
Vase, moon/moss/trees, S Irvine, 7½x6½" 6,000.00
Vase, moon/moss/trees, S Irvine & S Henderson, #49/TB78, 6½x8" .. 5,000.00
Vase, moon/palm trees, AF Simpson, 6½x5"..............................8,400.00
Vase, morning glories, pk/gr, S Irvine/J Meyer, 1924, 10¾" 3,235.00
Vase, morning glories in lg panels, cylindrical, 1928, 8" 2,880.00
Vase, moss/oak trees, AF Simpson, 8" 4,200.00
Vase, moss/oak trees against vermillion sky, NC/4/RA72, 5x3"... 3,900.00
Vase, moss/oak trees in sunlit landscape, S Irvine, 1913, 8x11".. 11,400.00
Vase, moss/trees, AF Simpson, #115, 1921, 12½" 15,000.00
Vase, pine cones half way down, H Bailey, shouldered, 13".....12,000.00
Vase, poinsettia in bl, M LeBlanc, 1904, 6x8............................11,400.00
Vase, poppy pods in bl, L Nicholson, 1905, 10½x5"..................13,200.00

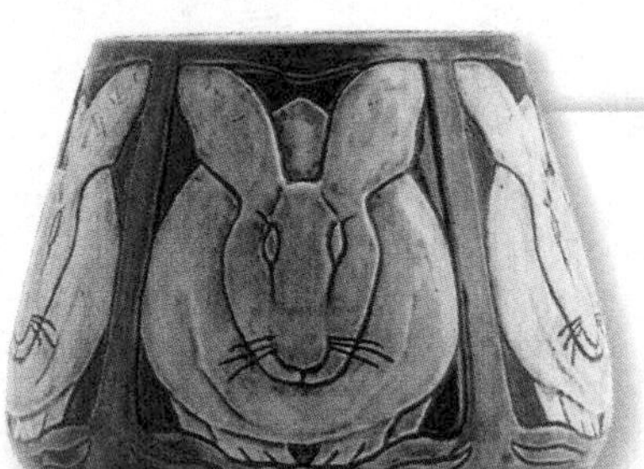

Vase, rabbits, incised and glossy, M. LeBlanc, 1902, 7½x9½", $84,000.00. (Photo courtesy David Rago Auctions)

Vase, trees (stylized), dk on lt bl, NC/N41/JM/U, 1902, 8x5¾" .. 7,800.00
Vase, trees (windswept/bending) w/ivory sky, NC/JM/Ke32/237, 6x3" ..3,120.00
Vase, trumpet flower at waisted neck, AF Simpson, neck hdls, 5x4" .. 1,560.00

Newspapers

People do not collect newspapers simply because they are old. Age has absolutely nothing to do with value — it does not hold true that the older the newspaper, the higher the value. Instead, most of the value is determined by the historic event content. In most cases, the more important to American history the event is, the higher the value. In over 200 years of American history, perhaps as many as 98% of all newspapers ever published do not contain news of a significant historic event. Newspapers not having news of major events in history are called 'atmosphere.' Atmosphere papers have little collector value. (See price guide below.) To learn more about the hobby of collecting old and historic newspapers, visit this Internet website: www.historybuff.com/. The e-mail address for the NCSA is help@historybuff.com/. See Newspaper Collector's Society of America in Clubs, Newsletters, and Catalogs for more information.

1836, Texas declares independence, from $60 to 85.00
1845, Annexation of Texas, from $35 to... 45.00
1846, Start of Mexican War, from $25 to 35.00
1846-1847, Major battles of Mexican War, from $25 to.................. 30.00
1850, Death of Zachary Taylor, from $45 to 65.00
1859, John Brown executed, from $40 to 85.00
1860, Lincoln elected 1st term, from $115 to 225.00
1861, Lincoln's inaugural address, from $140 to 275.00
1861-1865, Atmosphere editions: Confederate titles, from $110 to...165.00
1861-1865, Atmosphere editions: Union titles, from $7 to............ 12.00
1861-1865, Civil War major battle, Confederate report, $225 to.. 390.00
1861-1865, Civil War major battle, Union 1st report, $60 to...... 120.00
1862, Emancipation Proclamation, from $85 to 225.00
1863, Gettysburg Address, from $165 to....................................... 380.00
1865, April 29 edition of Frank Leslie's, from $225 to.................. 325.00
1865, April 29 edition of Harper's Weekly, from $200 to 300.00
1865, Capture & Death of J Wilkes Booth, from $85 to............... 165.00
1865, Fall of Richmond, from $85 to 275.00
1865, NY Herald, April 15 (Beware: reprints abound), from $700 to... 1,200.00
1865, Titles other than NY Herald, Apr 15, from $300 to 500.00
1866-1900, Atmosphere editions, from $3 to 5.00
1876, Custer's Last Stand, later reports, from $30 to 80.00
1876, Custer's Last Stand, 1st reports, from $100 to 250.00
1880, Garfield elected, from $30 to... 40.00
1881, Gunfight at OK Corral, from $175 to.................................. 400.00
1882, Jesse James killed, later report, from $60 to....................... 120.00
1882, Jesse James killed, 1st report, from $165 to 385.00
1889, Johnstown flood, from $25 to 40.00
1892, Lizzie Borden crime & trial, from $40 to 85.00
1900, James Jeffries defeats Jack Corbett, from $20 to.................. 35.00
1900-1936, Atmosphere editions, from $2 to 3.00
1901, McKinley assassinated, from $45 to..................................... 100.00
1903, Wright Brother's flight, from $200 to 500.00
1904, Teddy Roosevelt elected, from $25 to 35.00
1906, San Francisco earthquake, other titles, from $25 to 50.00
1906, San Francisco earthquake, San Francisco title, from $300 to ...500.00
1912, Sinking of Titanic, later reports, from $45 to..................... 115.00
1912, Sinking of Titanic, 1st reports, from $150 to 350.00
1918, Armistice, from $25 to... 85.00
1924, Coolidge elected, from $20 to 30.00
1927, Babe Ruth hits 60th home run, from $50 to 125.00
1927, Lindbergh arrives in Paris, 1st reports, from $65 to 125.00
1929, St Valentine's Day Massacre, from $100 to 225.00
1929, Stock market crash, from $75 to.. 180.00
1931, Al Capone found guilty, from $40 to 80.00
1931, Jack 'Legs' Diamond killed, from $30 to 45.00
1932, FDR elected 1st term, from $20 to 30.00
1933, Hitler becomes Chancellor, from $20 to 55.00
1934, Dillinger killed, from $100 to 250.00
1937, Amelia Earhart vanishes, from $30 to................................... 85.00
1937, Hindenburg explodes, from $75 to 150.00
1939-45, WWII major battles, from $20 to..................................... 50.00
1940, FDR elected 3rd term, from $20 to....................................... 30.00
1941, December 8 editions w/1st reports, from $30 to.................... 50.00
1941, Honolulu Star-Bulletin, December 7, 1st extra (+), from $300 to..600.00
1944, D Day, from $25 to... 60.00
1945, FDR dies, from $20 to.. 55.00

1948, Chicago Daily Tribune, Nov 3, Dewey Defeats Truman, from $500 to...800.00
1952, Eisenhower elected 1st term, from $20 to 25.00
1957, Soviets launch Sputnik, from $5 to....................................... 15.00
1958, Alaska joins union, from $15 to 25.00
1960, JFK elected, from $30 to 45.00
1963, JFK assassination, Nov 22, Dallas title, from $45 to 65.00
1963, JFK assassination, Nov 22, titles other than Dallas, from $3 to ...7.00
1967, Super Bowl I, from $15 to.. 30.00
1968, Assassination of Martin Luther King, from $20 to............... 35.00
1968, Assassination of Robert Kennedy, from $3 to 5.00
1969, Moon landing, from $5 to... 12.00
1974, Nixon resigns, from $15 to 20.00

Nicodemus

Chester R. Nicodemus was born near Barberton, Ohio, August, 17, 1901. He started Pennsylvania State University in 1920, where he studied engineering. Chester got a share of a large paper route, a job that enabled him to attend Cleveland Art School where he studied under Herman Matzen, sculptor, and Frank Wilcox, anatomy illustrator. He graduated in 1925. That fall Chester was hired to begin a sculpture department at the Dayton Art Institute.

Nicodemus moved from Dayton to Columbus, Ohio, in 1930 and started teaching at the Columbus Art School. During this time he made vases and commissioned sculptures, water fountains, and limestone and wood carvings. In 1941 Chester left the field of teaching to pursue pottery making full time, using local red clay containing a large amount of iron. Known for its durability, he called the ware Ferro-Stone. He made teapots and other utility wares, but these goods lost favor, so he started producing animal and bird sculptures, nativity sets, and Christmas ornaments, some bearing Chester's and his wife Florine's names as personalized cards for his customers and friends. His glaze colors were turquoise or aqua, ivory, green mottle, pink pussy willow, and golden yellow. The glaze was applied so that the color of the warm red clay would show through, adding an extra dimension to each piece. His name is usually incised in the clay in an arch, but paper labels were also used. Chester Nicodemus died in 1990. For more information we recommend *Sanfords Guide to Nicodemus, His Pottery and His Art*, by James Riebel.

Ashtray, fraternity lettering in brn on bl, #275, 4½" dia............... 110.00
Bowl, Clintonville Woman's Club Inc w/3-leaf clover, yel, 1x3¾"....60.00
Dish, Buckeye, egg shaped, 7x5½"... 115.00
Figurine, bear seated, brn, Ellen Jennings, mini,¾" 660.00
Figurine, boy w/frog held up in right hand, ivory, 1932, 19"......3,575.00
Figurine, bunny w/ears folded bk, pnt eyes, 4" 62.50
Figurine, goldfinch, yel w/blk features, 2¾"................................... 50.00
Figurine, koala bear, terra cotta, on mottled brn post, 2½"........... 210.00

Figurine, owl, 5", from $85.00 to $95.00.

Figurine, raccoon, brn w/pnt face, tail & ft, sgn Chester, 7½"...... 145.00
Jar, golden yel, knobbed lid, 4⅜" 80.00

Jug, brn mottle, 3" dia..70.00
Jug, Great Smoky Mountains in brn on yel, bulbous, #60, 4½" dia ...55.00
Paperweight, World Neighbors in relief on brn, 3½" dia.............100.00
Pitcher, golden yel, 4½"...100.00
Planter, elephant figural, yel, 4½" L...............................75.00
Teapot, gr mottle w/brn rim, w/lid, 6-cup, 6½"......................145.00

Niloak

During the latter part of the 1800s, there were many small utilitarian potteries in Benton, Arkansas. By 1900 only the Hyten Brothers Pottery remained. Charles Hyten, a second generation potter, took control of the family business around 1902. Shortly thereafter he renamed it the Eagle Pottery Company. In 1909 Hyten and former Rookwood potter Arthur Dovey began experimentation on a new swirl pottery. Dovey had previously worked for the Ouachita Pottery Company of Hot Springs and produced a swirl pottery there as early as 1906. In March 1910, the Eagle Pottery Company introduced Niloak — kaolin spelled backwards.

In 1911 Benton businessmen formed the Niloak Pottery corporation. Niloak, connected to the Arts and Crafts Movement and known as 'mission' ware, had a national representative in New York by 1913. Niloak's production centered on art pottery characterized by accidental, swirling patterns of natural and artificially colored clays. Many companies through the years have produced swirl pottery, yet none achieved the technical and aesthetic qualities of Niloak. Hyten received a patent in 1928 for the swirl technique. Although most examples have an interior glaze, some early Mission Ware pieces have an exterior glaze as well; these are extremely rare.

In 1934 Hyten's company found itself facing bankruptcy. Hardy L. Winburn, Jr., along with other Little Rock businessmen, raised the necessary capital and were able to provide the kind of leadership needed to make the business profitable once again. Both lines (Eagle and Hywood) were renamed 'Niloak' in 1937 to capitalize on this well-known name. The pottery continued in production until 1947 when it was converted to the Winburn Tile Company.

Of late, poor copies of Niloak Missionware swirl and Hywood pieces have been seen at flea markets and on the Internet. These pieces even bear a Niloak mark, but this is a 'fantasy' mark. To the experienced eye, the pieces are blatantly bogus. Buyer beware!

Virtually all of Niloak Missonware/swirl pottery is marked with die stamps. The exceptions are generally vases, wall pockets, lamp bases, and whiskey jugs. The terms 'first' and 'second art marks' used in the listings refer to specific die-stamped trademarks. The earlier mark was used from 1910 to 1925, followed by the second, very similar mark used from then until the end of Mission Ware production. Letters with curving raised outlines were characteristic of both; the most obvious difference between the two was that on the first, the final upright line of the 'N' was thin with a solid club-like terminal.

Be careful not to confuse the swirl production of the Evans Pottery of Missouri with Niloak. The significant difference is the dark brown matt interior glaze of Evans pottery. For further information we recommend *Collector's Encyclopedia of Niloak Pottery* by David Edwin Gifford (Collector Books). Our advisor for this category is Lila Shrader; she is listed in the Directory under California.

Key:
FHN — 1st Hywood mark NB — Niloak (block letters)
 (black circular stamp) NI — Niloak (impressed)
IH — incised Hywood   NL — Niloak (in low relief)

Mission Ware

Ashtray, sides slope outwards, 3 rests, 2nd art mk, 1¾x4¾"..........148.00
Ashtray, top hat form, 3 rests, 2nd art mk, 1½x5" dia.................295.00

Ashtray/match holder, for loose matches, unmk, 1½x4"..............125.00
Bowl, attached center flower frog, 2nd art mk, 1¾x8".................220.00
Bowl, console; cream/tan/rust, 2nd art mk, 3x10"......................525.00
Bowl, flower; flat, str sides, 2nd art mk, 2½x6½".....................110.00
Bowl, fruit; 2nd art mk, 2½x9½".......................................470.00
Bowl, incurvate rim, 1st art mk, 2¼x8"................................118.00
Candleholder w/finger ring, 2nd art mk, 4½x5¼".......................265.00
Candlestick, grooved top, flared base, 1st art mk, 7¼", ea...........300.00
Compote, flared ped ft, w/lid, unmk, 6"..............................725.00
Cup, punch; 1st art mk, 2½"...100.00
Flower frog, unmk, 3" dia...62.00
Humidor, str sides, pierced lid w/ball-like knob, 2nd art mk, 7"...680.00
Jardiniere, rolled/tailored collar, 2nd art mk, 13x14"..............1,990.00
Jug, str sides, narrowing neck w/rolled collar, 2nd art mk, 6½".....770.00
Jug, whiskey; Pensacola/Golden Corn, mini, 3¼"......................100.00
Lamp, complete w/hardware, wiring, early 1930s shade, 22"...........300.00
Lamp base, rolled collar, closed on top, drilled, 2nd art mk, 14½"...650.00
Pitcher, delicate appl hdl, Patent Pend'g, 8".......................1,240.00
Plate, collection; unmk, 1¾x9¼".......................................200.00
Powder jar, knobbed lid, 2nd art mk & Niloak sticker, 4½" dia ...285.00
Stein/mug, bbl shape, 1st art mk, 4½"................................465.00
Tankard, graceful appl hdl, flared base, 1st art mk, 13".............2,000.00
Tumbler/shot glass, 2nd art mk, 2¼"..................................188.00
Vase, brn/bl/tan/cram, gourd shape, 1st art mk, 9"...................590.00
Vase, bud; stick neck, flared base, 2nd art mk, 7"...................190.00
Vase, classic shape w/rolled collar, 1st art mk, 9½".................335.00
Vase, conical w/flared ft, 1st art mk, 9½"...........................455.00
Vase, conical w/flared ft, 2nd art mk, 9½"...........................350.00
Vase, cream/tan/lt brn, gourd shape, 1st art mk, 8"..................325.00
Vase, cylindrical, 2nd art mk, 6½x3".................................145.00
Vase, cylindrical, 2nd art mk, 9½x3½"................................295.00
Vase, fan shape w/flared base, 2nd art mk, 6¾".......................255.00
Vase, gr w/rust, bulbous w/rolled collar, 2nd art mk, 6".............295.00
Vase, high shoulder, rolled-in collar, 2nd art mk, 9½"...............250.00
Vase, high shoulder, rolled-in collar, 2nd art mk, 10¼"..............375.00
Vase, orange-rust w/cream, classic shape, 1st art mk, 8".............375.00
Vase, rolled-in collar, 2nd art mk, mini, 3¼"........................100.00
Vase, rose bowl shape, 1st art mk, 5x7"..............................140.00
Vase, rose bowl shape w/perforations at top, 2nd art mk, 4½"......275.00

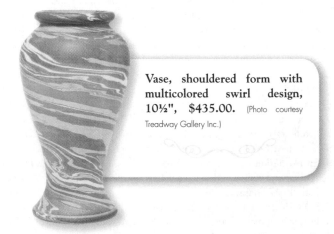

Vase, shouldered form with multicolored swirl design, 10½", $435.00. (Photo courtesy Treadway Gallery Inc.)

Vase, squat w/narrow rolled neck, 2nd art mk, 3¼x6½"................425.00
Vase, std shape w/lip flaring to 6½", 2nd art mk, 12½"...............665.00
Vase, teardop w/narrow 2" neck opening, 1st art mk, 10½".........475.00

Miscellaneous

Bean pot, deep-seated lid w/knob, hdls, blk stamp, 7¼"..............880.00
Bowl, console; fluted, sm scroll hdls, matt, NI, 3x14"...............155.00

Bowl, Peter Pan seated on edge, glossy, NL, 7½" 75.00
Cookie jar, deep seated lid, sm tab hdls, Ozark Blue, unmk, 9½" .. 185.00
Cow creamer, Bouquet dinnerware, matt, NI 28.00
Cow creamer, glossy, sticker, 4x6" 145.00
Cup & saucer, Bouquet dinnerware, matt, NI 28.00
Ewer, stylized daffodil, Ozark Dawn, sticker only, 10½" 60.00
Figure, pooch seated w/ears extended, brn matt, NI, 2", from $70 to ... 95.00
Figurine, razorback hog, Arkansas, maroon matt, NB, 5¼" 245.00
Figurine, retriever seated, Ozark Blue, NI, 4½" 80.00
Figurine, rooster standing, red-brn gloss, NB, 6" 50.00
Figurine, Southern Belle standing, lt gr matt (unusual), 7½" 90.00
Flower frog, turtle w/pierced shell, glossy, NB, 4¾" L 110.00
Jug, Fox Red, rolled-in collar, 2nd art mk, 8" 110.00
Jug, slight spout, NI, mini, 3¾" 85.00
Mug, Bouquet dinnerware, matt, NI, 3½", from $8 to 18.00
Mug, Souvenir of..., glossy, sticker, 3½x4", from $8 to 18.00
Novelty, army tank, open turret, matt, WWII era, NB, 2¼x4" 38.00
Pitcher, bull's-eye style, sm ped ft, bl matt, FHN, 10" 60.00
Planter, clown w/donkey, from Alley's Stars of the Big Top, 6¼" ... 40.00
Planter, deer (free-standing), matt, NL, 10" 155.00
Planter, deer (stylized) in grass, matt, 8x9" 30.00
Planter, deer in grass, matt, NL, 8" 50.00
Planter, elephant (stylized) w/trunk up, matt, 4¼" 34.00
Planter, fox seated w/plumed tail over bk, bl matt, NB, 5x6½" 50.00
Planter, rabbit, long-eared, 6½x4" 55.00
Planter, satyr w/flute staring into ribbed bowl, glossy, NB, 7½" 50.00
Planter, Siberian polar bear, wht gloss, NL, 3½" 60.00
Platter, Bouquet dinnerware, unmk, 13x10" 38.00
Shakers, bullet shape, Niloak foil label, 3¼" 72.00
Shakers, chicks, ducks, geese, penguins, etc, glossy, pr from $8 to .. 25.00
Shakers, ducks, geese, penguins, etc, matt, pr from $10 to 40.00
Strawberry jar, matt, NL, 6½" 28.00
Tea set, glossy, Niloak stickers, 4-cup pot+cr/sug w/lid 165.00
Toothpick holder, airplane shape, wht matt, 2x5" wingspan 90.00
Vase, Art Deco, pleated diagonal design w/sq ft, Peacock Blue, IH, 8" .. 200.00
Vase, Art Deco vertical/horizontal lines at collar & base, NB, 10" ... 195.00
Vase, Grecian urn-like w/graceful hdls, flared base, matt, NI, 7" 48.00
Vase, minimal vertical decor, high shoulder, hdls, Ozark Blue, NI, 12" ..370.00
Vase, minimal vertical decor, sm ft, Ozark Blue, NI, 7" 70.00

Vase, Ozark Dawn II, 7½", from $30.00 to $40.00. (Photo courtesy David Edwin Gifford)

Vase, Stoin glaze, elongated hdls, FHN, 8½" 225.00
Vase, Winged Victory, glossy, WWII Niloak Victory mk, 7" 25.00
Wall pocket, last entry was 228.00
Wall pocket, rolled rim, somewhat rnd, drilled, 2nd art mk, 6½" .. 228.00
Wall pocket, Starved Rock Hotel etched, drilled, unmk, 7¼" 260.00
Wishing well, open design, matt, NL, 8½" 110.00

Nippon

Nippon generally refers to Japanese wares made during the period from 1891 to 1921, although the Nippon mark was also used to a limited extent on later wares (accompanied by 'Japan'). Nippon, meaning Japan, identified the country of origin to comply with American importation restrictions. After 1921 'Japan' was the acceptable alternative. The term does not imply a specific type of product and may be found on items other than porcelains. For further information we recommend *Van Patten's ABC's of Collecting Nippon* by our advisor Joan Van Patten; you will find her address in the Directory under New York. In the following listings, items are assumed hand painted unless noted otherwise. Numbers included in the descriptions refer to these specific marks:

Key:
#1 — Patent   #5 — Rising Sun
#2 — M in Wreath   #6 — Royal Kinran
#3 — Cherry Blossom   #7 — Maple Leaf
#4 — Double T Diamond in   #8 — Royal Nippon, Nishiki
   Circle   #9 — Royal Moriye Nippon

Ashtray, horses heads (2) in relief, 4 rests, gr #2, 5½" 650.00
Basket, flowers, gr & gold borders, ring hdl, #7, 6" L, from $225 to .. 275.00
Basket vase, roses reserve on gr w/gold o/l, #7, 8½", from $800 to ... 900.00
Bowl, Indian in canoe scene, triangular, gr #2, 7½", from $250 to .. 300.00
Celery dish, mums reserves on cobalt w/much gold, #7, 13¼" L . 900.00
Child's trio, children dancing, c/s+sm plate, #5, from $85 to 110.00
Condensed milk container, roses w/gold, w/saucer, #2, 5", $250 to .. 300.00
Creamer & sugar bowl, floral w/gold/bl eagle border, w/lid, #2 ..... 180.00
Ewer, coralene irises/leaves, beaded hdl, #1, 10½", from $1,000 to .. 1,300.00
Ewer, lady's portrait w/gold & pk ivy o/l, unmk, 9", from $1,500 to..2,000.00
Ferner, lion's portraits, brn tones, 3 buttresses, #2, 5¾" 675.00
Humidor, bulldog in relief on keg form, gr #2, 7", from $1,200 to .. 1,500.00
Humidor, bulldog portraits, 4-ftd, gr #2, 5½", from $1,000 to ... 1,300.00
Humidor, Egyptian figures in relief, brns, gr #2, 6¼", $3,500 to .. 4,000.00
Humidor, Indian chief in relief, mc, #2, 7", from $4,000 to....... 5,000.00
Humidor, old fisherman w/sm boat & basket, gr #2, 7¼", $8,000 to .. 10,000.00
Humidor, owl in flight before bl sky, #2, 3¾", from $400 to 475.00
Humidor, playing cards on brn, sq, #2, 5½", from $750 to........... 875.00
Humidor, waves crashing on island shore, #2, 7", from $850 to ... 900.00
Lamp, wisteria on wht w/cobalt & gold, Nippon mk, 13½", $2,000 to ...2,500.00
Letter holder, open flowers on cream to rust, #3, 4½x7¼" 350.00
Matchbox holder, man on camel in desert scene, #2, 3¼", $250 to.. 300.00
Matchbox holder, owl on branch, rust borders, #2, 3½", $350 to .. 400.00
Mug, horse & 2 dogs (Captive Horse), gr #2, 5½", from $350 to .. 400.00
Mug, stag in forest, brn tones, gr #2, 5½", from $300 to 400.00

Nightlight, two-part rabbit on stump, inset glass ruby eyes, green M in wreath mark, 6¾", $3,290.00. (Photo courtesy Jackson's International Auctioneers & Appraisers of Fine Art & Antiques)

Pitcher, roses, mc on yel w/much gold, illegible mk, 8½", $575 to ..700.00
Plaque, child's face in relief, bl #5, 6", from $75 to 100.00
Plaque, Dutchman w/dog in sq reserve on brn, gr #2, 10" dia, $400 to ... 500.00
Plaque, fox hunt scene, gr #2, 8¾", from $325 to......................... 400.00
Plaque, Indian chief on running horse in relief, gr #2, 10½" 950.00
Plaque, lion & lioness (Raiders) in relief, gr #2, 10½", $600 to.... 800.00
Plaque, man in cart, gr #2, 11", from $700 to.............................. 800.00

Plaque, man w/horse & plow, gr #2, 10¼", from $500 to 600.00
Plaque, Newfoundland dog, brn tones, gr #2, 10¼" W, from $2,400 to..2,800.00
Plaque, owl in woods scene, gr #2, 8¾" dia, from $350 to 400.00
Plaque, Sitting Bull portrait, ornate borders, #2, 10½", $2,400 to.. 2,800.00
Plaque, storks (3) among rushes, brn tones, gr #2, 8½", $200 to .. 300.00
Plaque, Sunbonnet Babies, moriage grain, #7, 10", from $500 to....600.00
Plaque, swan swimming on moonlit pond, #2, 10", from $400 to....475.00
Plaque, windmill scene, brn tones, #2, 9", from $150 to............... 200.00
Plaque, 2 men by wall in desert scene, #2, 10¼", from $400 to 475.00
Plate, cobalt w/gold lacy scrolls, #2, 8½", from $225 to 275.00
Plate, cobalt w/heavy gold, unmk, 7½", from $150 to................... 200.00
Stein, Dutch people walking dog, #2, 7", from $700 to 800.00
Toothbrush holder, desert scene, hangs, #2, 4⅛", from $350 to.... 425.00
Trivet, Dutch girl w/umbrella, bl & wht, gr #2, 5¾", from $200 to... 250.00
Urn, coralene floral on bl, gold hdls & ft, w/lid, #1, 15", $3,600 to ..4,000.00
Vase, autumn scene w/stream, gold hdls, #2, 15", from $2,000 to...2,500.00
Vase, cherry trees gold band on cobalt, hdls, #7, 7½", $1,000 to ...1,200.00
Vase, coach scene, hdls, gr #2, 7½", from $700 to......................... 800.00
Vase, coralene lilies w/cobalt & gold, hdls, #1, 10¾", $1,300 to .. 1,600.00
Vase, coralene pastel poppies w/gold, ftd, #1, 8¼", from $1,200 to...1,400.00
Vase, Egyptian lady's portrait reserve, flared rim, #2, 8", $400 to... 550.00
Vase, fighting frogs, integral moriage hdls, ftd, unmk, 6", $3,000 to .3,500.00
Vase, gold mums o/l on cobalt, gold hdls, slim, #7, 12¼", $1,400 to.1,700.00

Vase, lady's portrait framed by moriage flowers, Art Nouveau styling, blue mark, 10½", from $4,500.00 to $5,200.00. (Photo courtesy Joan Van Patten)

Vase, Madame Lebrun portrait w/gold o/l, #7, 7¼", from $1,200 to..1,400.00
Vase, moriage cockatoo in pines, ornate hdls, #7, 9¾", $1,200 to.....1,500.00
Vase, moriage dragon on brn, #2, 5", from $250 to 300.00
Vase, moriage flying swans, brn tones, hdls, #7, 14", from $1,700 to..2,000.00
Vase, moriage long-stem flowers, hdls, #7, 9", from $600 to 800.00
Vase, moriage swans in sunset, shouldered, #7, 8", from $1,150 to . 1,350.00
Vase, moriage winter cottage in relief, gr #2, 9½", from $1,900 to...2,200.00
Vase, mountainside brambles, bulbous, #2, 6¾", from $1,050 to 1,200.00
Vase, mtn scene w/cobalt & gold trim, hdls, slim, #7, 10", $1,500 to.. 2,000.00
Vase, mums on gold w/beading, uptrn hdls, bl #7, 11¼", $2,000 to....2,500.00
Vase, New England winter scene, gold hdls, #2, 7", from $600 to ...700.00
Vase, pastoral scene w/gold & jeweling, hdls, #2, 15½", $1,800 to ...2,000.00
Vase, Queen Louise portrait on aqua w/jewels/gold, #7, 12", $4,000 to...4,600.00
Vase, roses & gold beading, slim, hdls, bl #7, 12", $1,000 to .. 1,200.00
Vase, swans in flight, encrusted gold, slim, #7, 7¾", $800 to 950.00
Vase, tapestry hunt scene, hdls, #7, 7½", $1,600 to 1,900.00
Vase, water lilies band on cobalt w/gold, #7, 8¾", from $450 to... 550.00
Vase, windmill/bldg on wht, red-beaded gold bands top/bottom, hdls, 6"..115.00
Vase, wisteria on sponge tapestry, gilt hdls/neck collar, 7"............ 405.00
Whiskey jug, sailboat scenic, gr hdl, #2, 6", from $850 to 1,000.00
Wine jug, Galle-style scenic, bl #7, 11", from $2,000 to............2,500.00

Nodders

So called because of the nodding action of their heads and hands,

nodders originated in China where they were used in temple rituals to represent deity. At first they were made of brass and were actually a type of bell; when these bells were rung, the heads of the figures would nod. In the eighteenth century, the idea was adopted by Meissen and by French manufacturers who produced not only china nodders but bisque as well. Most nodders are individual; couples are unusual. The idea remained popular until the end of the nineteenth century and was used during the Victorian era by toy manufacturers. See also Conta and Boehme.

Betty Boop, pnt celluloid, tin base, Fleisher Studios, Japan, NMIB....950.00
Black boy w/chalkboard, pnt bsk, rpr, 5", VG 75.00
Black child on potty, pnt bsk, unmk, 4" 210.00
Blackamoor lady seated w/fan in hand, pnt bsk, pre-Nippon, 4" .. 250.00
Cow, pnt bsk, metal collar, att Germany 60.00
Donald Duck, pnt celluloid, band driven, 6", EX........................... 425.00
Foxy Grandpa in horse-drawn wagon, pnt CI, Kenton, 6¼" L, VG ...450.00
Geisha in kimono seated, Banko Ware, 4x3½" 135.00
Happy Hooligan, pnt wood, mk DRGM (Germany), ca 1915, 9", EX...300.00
Happy Hooligan in cart pulled by horse, rpt CI, 6", VG 180.00
Lady in Persian dress w/orange & blk enamel, Germany, 1920s, 7½".. 500.00
Mickey Mouse, pnt celluloid, Borgfeldt, 7", EX 575.00
Mule, pnt CI, head nods, rust, 10½x11½x3" 90.00
Oriental man seated, laughing, head/hands nod, Meissen, 19th C, 14"...10,000.00
Oriental man sits w/robe apart, mc porc, head/hands nod, 5½" ... 725.00
Pluto, celluloid, tan w/blk & red details, orig tag, 8" L 450.00

Reindeer, clockwork, Germany, 12x14", $4,250.00. (Photo courtesy Morphy Auctions)

Nordic Art Glass

Finnish and Swedish glass has recently started to develop a following, probably stemming from the revitalization of interest in forms from the 1950s. (The name Nordic is used here because of the inclusion of Finnish glass — the term Scandinavian does not refer to this country.) Included here are Flygsfors, Hadeland, Holmegaard, Iittala, Maleras, Motzfeldt, Nuutajarvi, Pukeberg, Reijmyre, and Strombergshyttan. Our suggested prices are fair market values, developed after researching the Nordic secondary markets, the current retail prices on items still being produced, and American auction houses and antique stores. Our advisor for this category is William L. Geary; he is listed in the Directory under Sweden.

Flygsfors Glass Works, Sweden

Flygsfors Glass Works was established in 1888 and continued in production until 1979 when the Orrefors Glass Group, which had acquired this entity, ceased operations. The company is well known for art glass designed by Paul Kedelv, who joined the firm in 1949 with a contract to design light fittings, a specialty of the company. Their 'Coquille' series, which utilizes a unique overlay technique combining opaque, bright colors, and 'Flamingo' have become very desirable on today's secondary market. Other internationally known artists/designers include Prince Sigvard Bernadotte and the Finnish designer Helene Tynell.

Bowl, bl & wht, sculptural w/trn ends, Coquille, 11½"................. 195.00
Bowl, blk & wht sting-ray design, unmk, 8".................................. 150.00
Dish, gr & wht free-form w/wht stripe around, #69 Coquille, 4½"..95.00
Lamp, gr, tall hollow form, 4-sided base, unmk, 21" 135.00
Vase, raspberry & wht w/pulled ends, #57 Coquille, 6x9⅜" 175.00
Vase, Scorpio (Zodiac), smoked gray, Berndt...#61, 8" 145.00

Hadeland Glassverk, Norway

Glass has been produced at this glassworks since 1765. From the beginning, their main product was bottles. Since the 1850s they have made small items — drinking glasses, vases, bowls, jugs, etc. — and for the last 40 years, figurines, souvenirs, and objects of art. Important designers include Willy Johansson, Arne John Jutrem, Inger Magnus, Severin Brorby, and Gro Sommerfelt.

Bowl, olive gr w/prunts at rim, ped ft, #393 SP, 10¾" 325.00
Pitcher, crystal w/horizontal lines, rnd, S Petterson, 1932............. 75.00
Sculpture, crystal w/eng faun/hearts, A Faun's..., WS/GS/AV, 7½" ..465.00

Vase, #2129, WJ (Willy Johansson), $520.00. (Photo courtesy Cincinnati Art Galleries)

Vase, bl-gray, rnd w/air bubbles throughout, Johansson, #58, 5" 95.00
Vase, orange w/gr/yel/raspberry dots, stemmed/ftd, Gro, 7¼" 105.00

Holmegaard Glassvaerk, Denmark

This company was founded in 1825. Because of a shortage of wood in Denmark, it became necessary for them to use peat, the only material available for fuel. Their first full-time designers were hired after 1923. Orla Juul Nielson was the first. He was followed in 1925 by Jacob Band, an architect. Per Lukin became the chief designer in 1941. His production and art glass incorporates a simple yet complex series of designs. They continue to be popular among collectors of Scandinavian glass. During 1965 the company merged with Kastrup and became Kastrup Holmegaard AS; a merger with Royal Copenhagen followed in 1975.

Vase, clear w/eng deer, Michael Bang design, 8⅜" 175.00
Vase, crystal cylinder w/flared rim, Per Luken logo, 1960, 11½"... 125.00
Vase, dk gr teardrop encased in clear, Per Luken logo, 1958, 6½" ...155.00
Vase, gr w/wht int, flared from base to top 145.00
Vase, lt gray, Per Luken logo, #14405, 7½"................................... 125.00

Iittala Glass Works, Finland

This glassworks was founded in 1881; it was originally staffed by Swedish workers who produced glassware of very high quality. In 1917 Ahiststrom OY bought and merged Iittala with Karhula Glass Works. After 1945 Karhula's production was limited to container glass. In 1946 Tapio Wirkkala, the internationally known artist/designer, became Iitta-

la's chief designer. Timo Sarpeneva joined him in 1950. Jointly they successfully spearheaded the promotion of Finnish glass in the international markets, winning many international awards for their designs. Today, Oiva Toikka leads the design team.

Bowl, Aalto, clear bowl/plate in clear glass, Alvar Aalto, 2x15"..335.00
Carafe, flared top w/vertical cuts w/2 indents, Tapio Wirkkala..., 6" ..175.00
Sculpture, willow grouse, mc, Oiva Toikka, mk, 4¼x6"................ 120.00
Set, clear flower form consisting of 2 plates+2 bowls, Alvar Aalto...1,130.00
Vase, Claritas, clear w/6 lg bubbles towards base, T Sarpeneva, 7½" ... 675.00

Vase, TW (Tapio Wirkkala), 10½", $1,840.00. (Photo courtesy David Rago Auctions)

Maleras Glass Works, Sweden

The first glassworks at Maleras was founded in 1890. The city of Maleras was an important railway junction in Smaland, the Kingdom of Crystal, where articles from many of the glasshouses were shipped to the Swedish cities of Stockholm, Goteborg, and Malmo. During the 1940s the company built a reputation throughout Sweden as one of the leading manufacturers of lead crystal. In 1975 the company joined the Royal Krona Group. Six years later, under the leadership of Mats Jonasson, the glassblowers and members of the community bought the factory from the existing management. During the last 20 years, the company has produced first-class crystal sculptures of wildlife, which are sold around the world. Mats Jonasson is the master designer, and his wildlife images and engraving techniques are superb. Two other designers, artists Erika Hoglund and Lars Goran Tinback, are also important elements in this company's success.

Necklace, pendant w/image of lady, mc, blk chain 125.00
Sculpture, Arome, crystal, Erika Hoglund.................................... 150.00
Sculpture, Fighting Roosters, cast & colored, ltd ed of 99.........3,000.00
Sculpture, guitar, red w/gold string, cased in clear, 6¼" 95.00
Sculpture, Lg Celia, cast & colored form w/floral motif............... 120.00

Benny Motzfeldt, Norwegian Glass Artist

Benny Motzfeldt, a graduate of the Arts and Crafts School of Oslo, Norway, started her career in glass in 1954 by responding to an ad for a designer of engraving and decoration at Christiania Glassmagasin and Hadeland Glassverk. After several years at Hadeland, she joined the Plus organization and managed their glass studio in Frederikstad. She is acknowledged as one of the leading exponents of Norwegian art glass and is recognized internationally. She challenged the rather sober Norwegian glass designs with a strong desire to try new ways, using vigorous forms and opaque colors embedded with silver nitrate patterns.

Bowl, clar w/lt bl-gr towards top, BM #70.................................... 135.00
Cordial, crystal, long stem w/X-cuttings at base of ea stem, 4 for... 80.00

Vase, clear w/colored granules, tall neck, flared rim, Plus Norway...115.00
Vase, gr base w/bl towards top, short neck 95.00
Vases, metallic charcoal, rnd w/short neck, Randafjord Glasverk, pr .. 110.00

Nuutajarvi Glass Works, Finland

Bottle, dk gr w/prunts at base, long neck, company label 65.00
Bowl, sparkling gr, dbl-walled, O Toikka.. 120.00
Bowl, thick walls, encased free-form bubbles, 1½x2" 75.00
Sculpture, ibis, red, O Toikka 2005, 7x10"................................... 400.00
Vase, dk gray cased in clear, sgn, 8" 105.00
Vase, oxblood cased in clear, ftd, K Franck, 6½" 195.00

Pukeberg Glass Works

This glassworks was founded in 1871 by a master glassblower, C. W. Nystrom, formerly a master glassblower at Kosta Glass Works. In 1894 a Stockholm lamp company purchased the company and retained ownership until 1968 when it went into bankruptcy. This company (AB Arvid Bohlmarks Lampfabrik) manufactured shades and globes. Many talented people were involved with the company. In 1935 Uno Westerberg, a famous architect, designed domestic and ornamental wares. Goran Warff joined the company in 1957 and stayed until 1964, when he left with his wife Ann to go to the Kosta Glass Works. The famous artist Eva Englund started her glass career in 1964. She experimented with the material and created new and unique sculptures in glass, Edward Hald lured her to Orrefors 1973. Another icon of Swedish glass, Erick Hoglund, joined the company in 1978 and stayed until 1981. Various other artists have free-lanced with the company over the years and made important contributions to Swedish glass design.

The company has experienced many economic difficulties with changing ownership, but it has always been focused on encouraging new talented artists to experiment with design. Andris Nolendorf and his partners purchased the company and have brought innovative concepts to this glassworks. The Design School of Kalmar University now has space at the glassworks, and a museum is being set up to house the largest collection of design material in Sweden. Along with these changes, Micke Johansson, a young, talented artist and master glassblower, joined the firm in 2004. A master at 23, Micke brings with him his special knowledge of glass as well as his artistic talents which he uses in designing and making art and decorative glass.

Candlestick, clear, rnd, holds 3 sm candles, Uno Westerberg 35.00
Candlestick, rnd cast form w/grape cluster in center, 10½" 28.00
Plate, rondel form, red & wht ovals, blk rim, R Sinnemark, 12" .. 110.00
Sculptures, fish, cast, 4", pr 65.00
Vase, bl w/3-tiered ft, 5¾" 55.00

Reijmyre Glass Works

The Reijmyre Glass Works was founded in 1810. During the early days the company produced window glass, domestic glassware, pharmaceutical and technical vessels. It became the leading producer of cut and engraved glass. Pressed glass became a mainstay of the company and lasted 100 years until the 1930s. The company management encouraged innovation: in 1872 a gas-fired furnace was installed, a cracking-off machine in 1877, and the first etching machine in Sweden in the 1880s. In the 1890s, the company management recognized the need to bring artists into the glasshouse. The company hired many Swedish artists including A. E. Boman, Alf Wallander, Edvin Ollers, Monica Bratt, and Paul Kedelv. As a result they became one of the leading glasshouses in Sweden at the turn of the twentieth century. The company continues today producing domestic and art glass, utilizing some of the leading glass designers in Sweden.

Carafe, clear w/waves design (matching stopper), Berit Johannson .. 70.00
Snap glasses, red w/rnd cup & stem w/ft, Monica Bratt, 4", set of 4 .. 55.00
Tumblers, ea a different clear color, company label, set of 6 .... 65.00
Vase, gr, body formed by 2 lg spheres, 7" 140.00

Strombergshyttan, Sweden

The original factory, Lindefors, was founded in 1876. Although the factory was modernized in the 1920s, it closed in 1931. In 1933 Edvard Stromberg bought the factory; Gerda Stromberg designed for the company until 1942. In 1945 the factory was purchased by Stromberg's son Eric and his wife Asta. She designed for them until 1976. Edvard worked with Eric, who was a chemist, and together they developed a new color of glass with a distinctive bluish-silver hue which became the factory's speciality. Gunnar Nylund, famous for his copper wheel-engraved forms, was at the glassworks from 1952 until 1975. After a renovation in 1962, the factory suffered a serious fire and due to economic conditions was sold to Orrefors Glass Works; it operated under that title until it closed in 1979.

Bowl, clear, cut/eng corners, #398/C798....Strand, AS, 5½x7¼".. 210.00
Ice bucket, brn cased in clear, silver hdl, 5" 105.00
Vase, blown, symmetrical, clear cased, pointed rim, B8515.......... 180.00
Vase, clear w/many facets, B 940, 6"... 365.00
Vase, clear w/many stone-wheel cuts, B1172, 6"........................... 395.00

Noritake

The Noritake Company was first registered in 1904 as Nippon Gomei Kaisha. In 1917 the name became Nippon Toki Kabushiki Toki. The 'M in wreath' mark is that of the Morimura Brothers, distributors with offices in New York. It was used until 1941. The 'tree crest' mark is the crest of the Morimura family. The company has produced fine porcelain dinnerware sets and occasional pieces decorated in the delicate manner for which the Japanese are noted. (Two dinnerware patterns are featured below, and a general range is suggested for others.)

In the following listings, examples are hand painted unless noted otherwise. Numbers refer to these specific marks:

Key: #1 — Komaru   #2 — M in Wreath

Azalea

The Azalea pattern was produced exclusively for the Larkin Company, who gave the lovely ware away as premiums to club members and their home agents. From 1916 through the 1930s, Larkin distributed fine china which was decorated in pink azaleas on white with gold tracing along edges and handles. Early in the '30s, six pieces of crystal hand painted with the same design were offered: candleholders, a compote, a tray with handles, a scalloped fruit bowl, a cheese and cracker set, and a cake plate. All in all, 70 different pieces of Azalea were produced. Some, such as the 15-piece child's set, bulbous vase, china ashtray, and the pancake jug, are quite rare. One of the earliest marks was the Noritake 'M in wreath' with variations. Later the ware was marked 'Noritake, Azalea, Hand Painted, Japan.' Our advisor for Azalea is Linda Williams; she is listed in the Directory under Massachusetts.

Basket, mint; Dolly Varden, #193... 185.00
Bonbon, #184, 6¼" 60.00
Bowl, #12, 10" 38.00
Bowl, candy/grapefruit; #185 .... 340.00
Bowl, cream soup; #363 .... 135.00

Bowl, deep, #310.. 60.00
Bowl, fruit; #9, 5¼" 8.00
Bowl, fruit; scalloped, glass 95.00
Bowl, fruit; shell form, #188, 7¾" 325.00
Bowl, oatmeal; #55, 5½" 25.00
Bowl, soup; #19, 7⅛"... 28.00
Bowl, vegetable; divided, #439, 9½" 280.00
Bowl, vegetable; oval, #101, 10½" 55.00
Bowl, vegetable; oval, #172, 9¼" 42.00
Butter chip, #312, 3¼" 80.00
Butter tub, w/insert, #54 .... 30.00
Cake plate, #10, 9¾" 35.00
Candleholders, glass, 3½", pr 100.00
Candy jar, w/lid, #313 .... 625.00
Casserole, gold finial, w/lid, #372 .... 325.00
Casserole, w/lid, #16 .... 70.00
Celery tray, #444, closed hdls, 10" 275.00
Celery/roll tray, #99, 12" 35.00
Cheese/butter dish, #314 .... 125.00
Cheese/cracker, glass 75.00
Child's set, #253, 15-pc... 2,500.00
Coffeepot, demitasse; #182 .... 600.00
Compote, #170 .... 110.00
Compote, glass 80.00
Condiment set, #14, 5-pc 52.00
Creamer & sugar bowl, #7 .... 38.00
Creamer & sugar bowl, demitasse; open, #123............ 110.00
Creamer & sugar bowl, gold finial, #401 .... 155.00

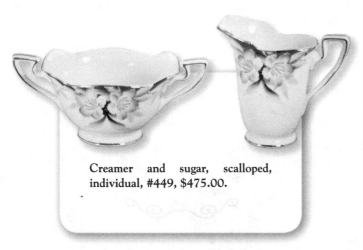

Creamer and sugar, scalloped, individual, #449, $475.00.

Creamer & sugar shaker, berry; #122..................... 150.00
Cruet, #190 .... 180.00
Cup & saucer, #2.. 15.00
Cup & saucer, bouillon; #124, 3½"........................... 25.00
Cup & saucer, demitasse; #183 .... 150.00
Egg cup, #120... 35.00
Gravy boat, #40 .... 40.00
Jam jar set, #125, 4-pc.. 155.00
Mayonnaise set, scalloped, #453, 3-pc................... 500.00
Mustard jar, #191, 3-pc 60.00
Olive dish, #194.. 25.00
Pickle/lemon set, #121 .... 24.50
Pitcher, milk jug; #100, 1-qt 180.00
Plate, #4, 7½"... 10.00
Plate, bread & butter; #8, 6½" 8.00
Plate, breakfast/luncheon; #98 .... 18.00
Plate, dinner; #13, 9¾" 18.00
Plate, grill; 3-compartment, #38, 10¼" 210.00
Plate, salad; 7⅝" sq... 65.00

Plate, scalloped sq, salesman's sample.................... 950.00
Plate, tea; #4, 7½"... 10.00
Platter, #17, 14" 60.00
Platter, #56, 12" 50.00
Platter, cold meat/bacon; #311, 10¼" 185.00
Platter, turkey; #186, 16" 450.00
Refreshment set, #39, 2-pc 38.00
Relish, #194, 7⅛" 52.00
Relish, oval, #18, 8½" 20.00
Relish, 2-part, #171 .... 45.00
Relish, 2-part, loop hdl, #450 .... 280.00
Relish, 4-section, #119, rare, 10" 160.00
Saucer, fruit; #9, 5¼" 10.00
Shakers, bell form, #11, pr 40.00
Shakers, bulbous, #89 .... 40.00
Shakers, ind, #126, pr 28.00
Spoon holder, #189, 8" 110.00
Syrup, #97, w/underplate & lid................................. 98.00
Tea tile 65.00
Teapot, #15 .... 150.00
Teapot, gold finial, #400 .... 380.00
Toothpick holder, #192... 80.00
Vase, bulbous, #452.. 1,200.00
Vase, fan form, ftd, #187 .... 225.00
Whipped cream/mayonnaise set, #3, 3-pc 35.00

Tree in the Meadow

Another of their dinnerware lines has become a favorite of many collectors. Tree in the Meadow is a scenic hand-painted pattern which features a thatched cottage in a meadow with a lake in the foreground. The version accepted by most collectors will have a tree behind the cottage and will not have a swan or a bridge. The colors resemble a golden sunset on a fall day with shades of orange, gold, and rust. This line was made during the 1920s and 1930s and seems today to be in good supply. A fairly large dinnerware set with several unusual serving pieces can be readily assembled. Our advisor for Tree in the Meadow is Linda Williams; she is listed in the Directory under Massachusetts.

Basket, Dolly Varden 95.00
Bowl, cream soup; 2-hdl.. 75.00
Bowl, fruit; shell form, #210 .... 285.00
Bowl, oatmeal 25.00
Bowl, oval, 9½" 48.00
Bowl, oval, 10½" 45.00
Bowl, soup 38.00
Bowl, vegetable; 9".. 35.00
Butter pat 25.00
Butter tub, open, w/drainer 35.00
Cake plate, open hdl.. 35.00

Candy jar, hexagonal, with lid, $395.00. (Photo courtesy Linda Van Patten)

Candy dish, octagonal, w/lid, 5½" 395.00
Celery dish 35.00
Cheese dish 95.00
Coffeepot, demitasse 250.00
Compote 95.00
Condiment set, 5-pc 45.00
Creamer & sugar bowl, berry 110.00
Creamer & sugar bowl, demitasse 125.00
Cruets, vinegar & oil; cojoined, #319 .... 275.00
Cup & saucer, breakfast 18.00
Cup & saucer, demitasse 60.00
Egg cup 30.00
Gravy boat 40.00
Jam jar/dish, cherries on lid, 4-pc 110.00
Lemon dish 15.00
Mayonnaise set, 3-pc 48.00
Plate, dessert; 6½" 8.00
Plate, dinner; 9¾" 75.00
Plate, rare, 7⅝" sq 95.00
Plate, salad; 8" 12.00
Platter, 10" 125.00
Platter, 11¾x9" 58.00
Platter, 13¾x10¼" 65.00
Relish, divided 30.00
Snack set (cup & tray), 2-pc 60.00
Tea tile 75.00
Teapot 95.00
Vase, fan form 95.00

Various Dinnerware Patterns, ca. 1933 to Present

So many lines of dinnerware have been produced by the Noritake company that to list them all would require a volume in itself. And while many patterns had specific names, others did not, and it is virtually impossible to identify them all. Outlined below is a general guide for the more common pieces and patterns. The high side of the range will represent lines from about 1933 until the mid-1960s (including those marked 'Occupied Japan'), while the lower side should be used to evaluate lines made after that period.

Bowl, berry; ind, from $8 to 12.00
Bowl, soup; 7½", from $12 to 16.00
Bowl, vegetable; rnd or oval, ca 1945 to present, from $28 to 38.00
Butter dish, 3-pc, ca 1933-64, from $40 to 50.00
Creamer, from $18 to 28.00
Cup & saucer, demitasse; from $12 to 17.50
Gravy boat, from $35 to 60.00
Pickle or relish dish, from $18 to 28.00
Plate, bread & butter; from $8 to 12.00
Plate, dinner; from $15 to 30.00
Plate, luncheon; from $14 .... 18.00

Plate, salad; Madera #5106 MM-38, ca. 1933 – 1940, $15.00. (Photo courtesy Aimee Neff Alden)

Platter, 12", from $25 to 40.00
Shakers, pr, from $15 to 25.00
Sugar bowl, w/lid, from $18 to 30.00
Tea & toast set (sm cup & tray), from $18 to 28.00
Teapot, demitasse pot, chocolate pot, or coffeepot, ea from $45 to ... 85.00

Miscellaneous

Ashtray, Deco-style lady smoking, #2, 1¾" 200.00
Ashtray, Indian chief portrait, geometric rim, 6-sided, #2, 6½" 250.00
Basket vase, red w/floral int, gold hdl, #2, 5½" 140.00
Bowl, river scenic on yel, gold hdls, #2, 7" 60.00
Cake plate, exotic birds, pk border w/gold, #2, 8¼" 70.00
Candy jar, river reserve & band on gold lustre, #2, 6½" 225.00
Chocolate pot, gold o/l on wht, #2, 9" 200.00
Chocolate set, exotic bird w/gold, #2, 8¾", pot+6 c/s 350.00
Compote, floral on cream w/gold hdls, ftd, #2, 9¾" 80.00
Condensed milk container, Deco floral w/gold, #2, 5¼", +tray 160.00
Egg cup, windmill & river scenic, earth tones, #2, 3½" 40.00
Game set, deer in forest, geometric border, #2, 16" platter+8 plates... 2,200.00
Humidor, horse w/in horseshoe in relief, brn tones, #2, 7" 700.00
Humidor, lion killing python in relief on red, #2, 6¾" 850.00
Humidor, owl on branch w/acorns in relief, 6¾" 635.00
Mustard set, roses, pk & yel on wht, #2, 3", 4-pc 35.00
Nightlight, lady praying figural, lustre dress, #2, 9¾" 2,700.00
Plaque, elk in relief, brn tones, #2, 10½" 600.00
Plaque, river scenic w/swans, earth tones, #2, 6½" 115.00
Punch set, peacock reserve w/gold on pk, #2, 9x16" bowl+8 cups.. 1,200.00
Shaving mug, river scenic, earth tones w/gold, #2, 3¾" 120.00
Spooner, river scenic w/red-roofed cottage, #2, 8" L 70.00
Tea set, floral on blk w/gold, #2, 6" pot+cr/sug 165.00
Toast rack, bl lustre w/bird finial, #2, 5½" L 125.00

Tray, lady clown with balloon, green mark, 10½" long, from $250.00 to $300.00. (Photo courtesy Joan Van Patten)

Vase, bird by tree trunk, mc lustres, #2, 5⅛" 375.00
Vase, peacock feathers on tan, ruffled rim, slim, #1, 8", pr 180.00
Vase, Wedgwood type, wht flowers on bl, hdls, #1, 9½" 475.00
Wall pocket, musician w/wide ruffled collar on lustre, #2, 6" 300.00

Norse

The Norse Pottery was established in 1903 in Edgerton, Wisconsin, by Thorwald Sampson and Louis Ipson. A year later it was purchased by A. W. Wheelock and moved to Rockford, Illinois. The ware they produced was inspired by ancient bronze vessels of the Norsemen. Designs were often incised into the red clay body. Dragon handles and feet were favored decorative devices, and they achieved a semblance of patina through the application of metallic glazes. The ware was marked with model numbers and a stylized 'N' containing a vertical arrangement of the remaining letters of the name. Production ceased after 1913. Our advisor for this category is John Danis; he is listed in the Directory under Illinois.

Bowl, band of owls, #30, X, 3¾" 395.00
Bowl, incised decor, appl ornament along shoulder, 3-ftd, 4x8" ... 300.00

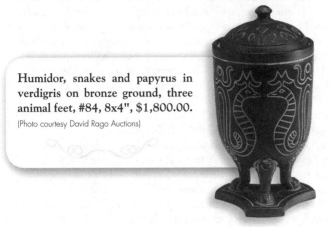

Humidor, snakes and papyrus in verdigris on bronze ground, three animal feet, #84, 8x4", $1,800.00.

(Photo courtesy David Rago Auctions)

Pedestal, hammered/tooled designs of women, #98, 19x12", EX ...1,440.00
Vase, appl salamander #25, 11½x7" 1,500.00
Vase, geometrics, verdigris on blk, dragon hdls/ft, 14" W 1,050.00
Vase, geometrics/waves/invt Vs in shoulder band, 9½x9" 575.00
Vase, shouldered, 2 dragon hdls & 3 dragon-head ft, #70, 4x7½" 600.00
Vase, tepees/water, baluster, nicks, 9½x8" 800.00

North Dakota School of Mines

The School of Mines of the University of North Dakota was established in 1890, but due to a lack of funding it was not until 1898 that Earle J. Babcock was appointed as director, and efforts were made to produce ware from the native clay he had discovered several years earlier. The first pieces were made by firms in the east from the clay Babcock sent them. Some of the ware was decorated by the manufacturer; some was shipped back to North Dakota to be decorated by native artists. By 1909 students at the University of North Dakota were producing utilitarian items such as tile, brick, shingles, etc. in conjunction with a ceramic course offered through the chemistry department. By 1910 a ceramic department had been established, supervised by Margaret Kelly Cable. Under her leadership, fine artware was produced. Native flowers, grains, buffalo, cowboys, and other subjects indigenous to the state were incorporated into the decorations. Some pieces have an Art Nouveau – Art Deco style easily attributed to her association with Frederick H. Rhead, with whom she studied in 1911. During the '20s the pottery was marketed on a limited scale through gift and jewelry stores in the state. From 1927 until 1949 when Miss Cable announced her retirement, a more widespread distribution was maintained with sales branching out into other states. The ware was marked in cobalt with the official seal — 'Made at School of Mines, N.D. Clay, University of North Dakota, Grand Forks, N.D.' in a circle. Very early ware was sometimes marked 'U.N.D.' in cobalt by hand. Our advisor for this category is William M. Bilsland III; he is listed in the Directory under Iowa.

Ashtray, Old Faithful, geyser image on ¼-circle base, Sather #13 .... 280.00
Bowl, caramel at rim to chicory bl, Erickson, 3½x4¾" 100.00
Bowl, fruit band, McCosh, flared, 1949, 1½x9¼" 175.00

Bowl, geometrics on bl, #252, 3x7" 520.00
Bowl, Prairie Rose on pk, M Cable, #152, 2⅝x5½" 450.00
Bowl, Russian Olive pattern, Clark, bl-gray/ivory, low, 1942, 7½" ..375.00
Bowl, tulips, bl on ivory, 5½" 850.00
Carafe, turq, Sioux calendar motif, Mattson 199, 7½" 675.00
Coaster, coyote cvd on gr matt, ink stamp, 3½" 275.00
Humidor, waves of gr drip on tan, HB, UND mk, 5¾" 400.00
Lamp base, birds on branches, mc on shaded bl, JSG/MMc/25, 17" ...300.00
Vase, bl shading to gr to yel, incurvate rim, 3½" 480.00
Vase, cowboy & bronco, tan mottle, J Mattson, 7¼" 2,275.00

Vase, cowboys and lassos against a mountainous background, excised by Julia Mattson, 4x3½", $4,200.00.

(Photo courtesy David Rago Auctions)

Vase, cowboys on horses relief on brn, JM210, J Mattson, 8x5" .. 3,120.00
Vase, cowboys/horses/lassos cvg, ivory/bl-gray, JM, 4¼x3½" 4,200.00
Vase, Indian Travois (cvd depiction in band), Cable/Huckfield, 7x6" ..5,700.00
Vase, pine trees, multi-tone gr matt, Huck, 9¼" 6,000.00
Vase, sheaves of wheat cvd on bl-gray, ELH-750 S Sorlie, 9x6" .. 6,600.00
Vase, tulips, lt & dk brn, shouldered cylinder, #45, 2/47, 8" 2,000.00

North State

In 1924 the North State Pottery of Sanford, North Carolina, began small-scale production, the result of the extreme fondness Mrs. Rebecca Copper had for potting. With the help of her husband Henry and the abundance of suitable local clay, the pottery flourished and became well known for lovely shapes and beautiful glazes. They shared the knowledge they gained from their glaze experiments with the ceramic engineering department of North Carolina University, and during summer vacation they often employed some of the university students. Salt-glazed stoneware was produced in the early years but was quickly abandoned in favor of Henry's vibrant glazes. Colors of copper red, Chinese Red, moss green, and turquoise blue were used alone and combination, producing bands of blending colors. Some swirl ware was made as well. The pottery was in business for 35 years; most of its ware was sold in gift and craft shops throughout North Carolina. Items in the following descriptions are earthenware unless noted stoneware within the line.

Pitcher, runny red on gr/yel mottle, blistered, 8½" 540.00
Refrigerator pitcher, Chinese blue upper half, high arched hdl, 8½" ..360.00
Teapot, yel, 6¾x7½x5", EX 300.00
Vase, bright bl over gold-yel to warm butter/orange, hdls, Owens, 10" ...375.00
Vase, cobalt w/dripping, salt-glazed stoneware, filled crack, 8x6" .. 390.00
Vase, cobalt/jade/burgundy mingled over pumpkin, crimp rim, 4½" ..140.00
Vase, lt & dk bl over dk red over tan, 8½" 360.00
Vase, lt purple/wht w/some runs, bulbous, mfg flaws, 6x6" 270.00
Vase, runny bl w/wht & brn highlights, blistered/volcanic, hdls, 9x10" ...480.00
Vase, salt glaze & cobalt, flared/ftd U-shape, 5", NM 150.00
Vase, swirled brn & tan, glaze to int only, 7x5½" 360.00
Vase, turq drippings over foamy bl w/some red clay showing, 6x6x5" ...420.00
Vase, warm orange modified red lead glaze, O hdls, 3 stilt mks, 6" ...70.00
Vase, yel crackle, ovoid w/widely spaced rings, long hdls, 10½" ... 300.00

Northwood

The Northwood Company was founded in 1896 in Indiana, Pennsylvania, by Harry Northwood, whose father, John, was the art director for Stevens and Williams, an English glassworks. Northwood joined the National Glass Company in 1899 but in 1901 again became an independent contractor and formed the Harry Northwood Glass Company of Wheeling, West Virginia. He marketed his first carnival glass in 1908, and it became his most popular product. His company was also famous for its custard, goofus, and pressed glass. Northwood died in 1923, and the company closed. See also Carnival, Custard, Goofus, Opalescent, Pattern Glass.

Bowl, berry; Intaglio, bl or gr, lg 65.00
Bowl, berry; Leaf Mould, vaseline, lg.. 325.00
Bowl, berry; Leaf Mould, vaseline, sm.. 90.00
Bowl, berry; Ribbon Star & Bows, amethyst, sm........................ 40.00

Bowl, Cosmos, green with gold trim, $60.00. (Photo courtesy Bill Edwards and Mike Carwile)

Bowl, sauce; Posies & Pods, emerald gr w/gold 25.00
Butter dish, Regent/Leaf Medallion, gr w/gold, from $345 to....... 395.00
Butter dish, Teardrop Flower, gr w/gold.................................... 185.00
Celery vase, Leaf Mould, ruby, 7¾" 675.00
Celery vase, Leaf Mould, vaseline, 7¾" 225.00
Compote, Cosmos, amethyst 110.00
Compote, jelly; Intaglio, bl or gr 50.00
Compote, Ribbon Star & Bows, bl or gr 75.00
Compote, sweets; Ribbons & Overlapping Squares, gr w/gold 150.00
Compote, Wildflower, gr.. 40.00
Creamer, Royal Oak, crystal & frosted... 60.00
Creamer & sugar bowl, Mikado, frosted w/mc floral, from $145 to .. 165.00
Cruet, Royal Ivy, rubena, 6½", from $400 to............................... 450.00
Pickle castor, opal-cased red spatter w/mica, Leaf Mold; Empire SP, fr.. 600.00
Pitcher, Dandelion, bl w/gold, tall, slender, water sz, from $350 to... 400.00
Pitcher, Leaf Mould, vaseline 900.00
Pitcher, Oriental Poppy, gr w/gold, tankard form, from $300 to... 350.00
Pitcher, Posies & Pods, clear w/ruby stain & gold, 8", from $125 to...150.00
Pitcher, Regent/Leaf Medallion, gr w/gold, water sz, from $400... 450.00
Pitcher, Royal Ivy, rubena, ribbed, frost hdl, 8"............................ 350.00
Plate, Cosmos, gr or bl w/gold 68.00
Plate, Ribbon Star & Bows, bl or gr, sm 40.00
Sugar bowl, Intaglio, bl or gr 60.00
Sugar shaker, Royal Ivy, frosted rainbow craquelle, from $500 to....600.00
Sugar shaker, Royal Ivy, frosted w/amber stain, NM................. 1,200.00
Sweetmeat, draped swags, swirled rose/gr/bl, SP mts, 6½" 475.00
Toothpick holder, Leaf Mould, vaseline...................................... 350.00
Toothpick holder, Leaf Umbrella, bl 240.00
Tumbler, Panelled Holly, gr w/gold, 4¼", from $65 to 75.00
Tumbler, Regent/Leaf Medallion, cobalt w/gold, 4", from $55 to... 85.00
Vase, pull-up, opal-cased red/yel/bl, urn w/ruffled rim, hdls, 11" .. 690.00
Vase, red/multi pulled diagonal swirls on opal, camphor hdls, 8¾"....850.0

Norweta

Norweta pottery was produced by the Northwestern Terra Cotta Company of Chicago, Illinois. Both matt and crystalline glazes were em-ployed, and terra cotta vases were also produced. It was made for approximately 10 years, beginning sometime before 1907. Not all was marked.

Lamp base, modeled as a tulip w/4 buttress leaves, bl/gr/yel, 12x8" ..2,040.00
Vase, gray-purple crystalline mottle, baluster, #106, 12x5½".....1,950.00
Vase, lt bl crystalline on tan, shouldered, 8⅜" 1,200.00

Nutcrackers

The nutcracker, though a strictly functional tool, is a good example of one to which man has applied ingenuity, imagination, and engineering skills. Though all were designed to accomplish the same end, hundreds of types exist in almost every material sturdy enough to withstand sufficient pressure to crack the nut. Figurals are popular collectibles, as are those with unusual design and construction. Patented examples are also desirable. For more information, we recommend *Nutcrackers* by Robert Mills.

Dachshund, CI, 5x9" on 8x2½" wood base, EX 15.00
Dog, tail hdl, CI, Made in England, 9½" 35.00
Dog standing, brn-pnt CI, on wood base mk 1918 Undsderfer, 5½x11"... 35.00
Eagle head, pnt CI, lever operates lower jaw, 7x7½x3", EX........... 25.00
Elephant, CI, 2-part, orig red pnt w/mc details, twine tail, 5x9½" ...50.00
Elf, ornate cvd wood, Black Forest, 8⅛" 120.00
Fish, tall fin on bk (hdl), metal w/spring in jaw, EX 110.00
Forest Ranger, wooden, att Anri, 1950s, 9½" 125.00
Monkeys w/coconuts, tails wrapped around hdl, SP, 5¾"............... 55.00
Owl on branch, screw type, metal, 6", EX..................................... 20.00

Parrot, realistic original paint on cast iron, 10" long, $50.00. (Photo courtesy Morphy Auctions)

Squirrel, CI, tail operates front legs, 10x9" 190.00
Squirrel, tail hdl, CI, 4¾" 100.00
Squirrels facing ea other hdls, CI, 6⅛", EX 40.00
St Bernard, Old Dog Tray on base, metal, 6x12½", EX................. 25.00
Swiss (Black Forest), bear, full figure w/glass eyes, EX 435.00
Wolf head, NP CI, lever operates lower jaw, Pat 1880, 5x9½" 50.00

Nutting, Wallace

Wallace Nutting (1861 – 1941) was America's most famous photographer of the early twentieth century. A retired minister, Nutting took more than 50,000 pictures, keeping 10,000 of his best and destroying the rest. His popular and bestselling scenes included exterior scenes (apple blossoms, country lanes, orchards, calm streams, and rural American countrysides), interior scenes (usually featuring a colonial woman working near a hearth), and foreign scenes (typically thatch-roofed cottages). His poorest selling pictures, which have become today's rarest and most highly collectible, are classified as miscellaneous unusual scenes and include categories not mentioned above: animals, architecturals, children, florals, men, seascapes, and snow scenes. Process prints are 1930s machine-produced reprints of 12 of Nutting's most popular pictures. These have minimal value and can be detected by using a magnifying glass.

Nutting sold literally millions of his hand-colored platinotype pictures between 1900 and his death in 1941. He started in Southbury, Connecticut, and later moved his business to Framingham, Massachusetts. The peak of Wallace Nutting picture production was 1915 – 1925. During this period Nutting employed nearly 200 people, including colorists, darkroom staff, salesmen, and assorted office personnel. Wallace Nutting pictures proved to be a huge commercial success and scarcely an American household was without one by 1925.

While attempting to seek out the finest and best early American furniture as props for his colonial interior scenes, Nutting became an expert in early American antiques. He published nearly 20 books in his lifetime, including his 10-volume *State Beautiful* series and various other books on furniture, photography, clocks, stools, chairs, settles, settees, tables, stands, desks, mirrors, beds, chests of drawers, cabinet pieces, and treenware. He made furniture as well, which he clearly marked with a distinctive paper label that was glued directly onto the piece, or a block or script signature brand which was literally branded into the furniture.

The overall synergy of the Wallace Nutting name — on pictures, books, and furniture — has made anything 'Wallace Nutting' quite collectible. Our advisor for this category is Michael Ivankovich, author of many books on Nutting: *The Collector's Guide to Wallace Nutting Pictures* and corresponding price guide, *The Alphabetical and Numerical Index to Wallace Nutting Pictures*, *Collector's Guide to Wallace Nutting Furniture*, *The Guide to Wallace Nutting Furniture*, *Collector's Value Guide to Early 20th Century Prints*, *The Guide to Wallace Nutting-Like Photographers of the Early 20th Century*, and *The Hand-Painted Pictures of Charles Henry Sawyer*. Mr. Ivankovich is also expert in Bessie Pease Gutmann, Maxfield Parrish, and R. Atkinson Fox and has written *Guide to Popular Early 20th Century Prints*, containing a wealth of information on their work. Mr. Ivankovich is listed in the Directory under Pennsylvania. Prices below are for pictures in good to excellent condition. Mat stains or blemishes, poor picture color or frame damage can decrease value significantly.

Wallace Nutting Books

Clock Book	75.00
Connecticut Beautiful	35.00
Furniture of the Pilgrim Century	100.00
Ireland Beautiful	50.00
Maine Beautiful, 1st ed	45.00
New York Beautiful, 2nd ed	45.00
Photographic Art Secrets	200.00
Virginia Beautiful	50.00
Wallace Nutting Biography	100.00

Wallace Nutting Pictures

Among October Birches, 16x20"	295.00
Birch Grove, 9x11"	165.00
Bit of Sewing, 11x14"	325.00
Cup of Cheers, 11x14"	295.00
Dream & Reality, 12x20"	195.00
Eames House	1,250.00
Fruit Luncheon, 11x14"	275.00
Guardian Mother	2,800.00
Hawthornside, 13x16"	475.00
Heart of Maine, 16x20"	375.00
Honeymoon Stroll, 10x12"	175.00
Justifiable Vanity	150.00
Little River, 13x22"	250.00
Maple Sugar Cupboard, 12x16"	325.00
Memory of Childhood	160.00
Neighborhood News, 11x14"	325.00
Nuttinghame Nook	210.00

The Old Stage Road, $285.00.
(Photo courtesy Michael Ivankovich)

Orchard Heights, 11x14"	315.00
Priscilla's Cottage, 17x14"	375.00
River's Song, 11x14"	185.00
Story of Chivalry, 10x12"	295.00
Untitled, swirling seas, 7x9"	185.00
White & Gold, 13x16"	195.00

Wallace Nutting Furniture

Armchair, child's, #211	2,700.00
Brewster armchair, script band, #411	1,000.00
Butterfly table, #625	2,200.00
Candlestand, 3-leg, #17	1,125.00

Chair, Windsor, writing arm, New England turnings, #451, $1,760.00.
(Photo courtesy Michael Ivankovich)

Chaise lounge, adjustable bk, 43x75x23"	965.00
Comb-bk armchair, #415	1,500.00
Curly maple candlestick (single), imp brand, #31, ea	175.00
Game table w/rotating top	850.00
Maple crane bracket table, script brand, #619	685.00
Maple drop-leaf chair, #603	950.00
New England ladder-bk armchair, #492	770.00
Pennsylvania Windsor comb-bk armchair, block brand, #412	1,400.00
Pilgrim armchair, #493	1,050.00
Rushed maple stool, block brand, #168, 22"	425.00
Stand, 4-leg, #653	500.00
Wild Rose side chair, #365	440.00
Windsor rocking chair, #477	700.00
Windsor side chair, fan-bk, old finish, brand/label, 44"	1,100.00
Windsor side chari, fan-bk, script brand/paper label, #326	550.00
Windsor tenon arm chair, #422	1,500.00
Windsor writing armchair, #4451	2,750.00
Windsor writing chair, #451	1,600.00
Windsor 4-leg stool, #145	150.00

Occupied Japan

Items marked 'Occupied Japan' were produced during the period from the end of World War II until April 18, 1952, when the occupation ended. By no means was all of the ware exported during that time marked 'Occupied Japan'; some was marked 'Japan' or 'Made In Japan.' It is thought that because of the natural resentment felt by the Japanese toward the occupation, only a fraction of these wares carried the 'Occupied' mark. Even though you may find identical 'Japan'-marked items, because of its limited use, only those with the 'Occupied Japan' mark are being collected to any great extent. Values vary considerably, based on the quality of workmanship. Generally, bisque figures command much higher prices than porcelain, since on the whole they are of a finer quality.

Our advisor for this category is Florence Archambault; she is listed in the Directory under Rhode Island. She represents the Occupied Japan Club, whose mailing address may be found in the Directory under Clubs, Newsletters, and Catalogs. All items described in the following listings are common ceramic pieces unless noted otherwise.

Ashtray, Georgia, shape of state, from $12.50 to 15.00
Ashtray, Wedgwood type, bl & wht, 2⅝" 10.00
Basket, pk w/angel on hdl, red mk, 5", from $55 to 60.00
Bell, Dutch girl figure in orange lustre skirt, sm 20.00
Book, Japan Tourist Bureau, hardcover, various subjects, from $35 to.. 50.00
Bookends, penguins, 4" 25.00
Bowl, oval w/open latticework, floral center, gold trim 15.00
Box, cigarette; emb roses on lid, red mk, from $15 to 20.00
Box, cigarette; wht w/bl floral decor, Rossetti, Chicago 20.00
Candy dish, metal, 3-part, center hdl, from $15 to 20.00
Child's tea set, 4 place settings, 13 pcs 65.00
Child's tea set, 6 place settings, 26 pcs 125.00
Cigarette lighter, metal knight figural, from $10 to 25.00
Coasters, papier-mache, set of 8 in rnd box 35.00
Crumb pan, metal, emb NY scene, from $10 to 15.00
Cup & saucer, bird & floral on blk, Lenwile China, Adarlt 6194 .. 25.00
Cup & saucer, cottage scene, lustre 20.00
Cup & saucer, lg pk roses, high gold hdl, scalloped rims, $12.50 to... 25.00
Cup & saucer, wht w/chintz-like floral decor, Merit 20.00

Cups and saucers: Floral, Trimont China, from $15.00 to $18.00; Tower and arched wall, Maruta, from $20.00 to $22.00. (Photo courtesy Gene and Cathy Florence)

Dinnerware, complete set for 12 w/all major serving pcs 500.00
Dinnerware, complete set for 8+cr/sug+gravy+2 lg/1 sm platter .. 350.00
Dinnerware, 3 szs of plates, service for 4 w/berries+soups+cr/sug..... 150.00
Doll, celluloid, Betty Boop type, under 8" 50.00
Egg timer, Dutch girl stands beside sand timer, complete, 3½" 30.00
Figurine, Black band member, 2¾" 20.00
Figurine, Black shoeshine boy, 5½", from $50 to 55.00
Figurine, boy & girl on fence, cat at ft, 4", pr 35.00
Figurine, boy in short pants w/suitcase, Maruyama, 5" 20.00
Figurine, boy playing mandolin, 5" 15.00
Figurine, boy w/parrot, red mk, 5" 15.00
Figurine, children under umbrella, Hummel type, 6" 75.00
Figurine, coach (yel) led by 2 wht horses, 3" 10.00
Figurine, colonial couple at piano, 4" 22.50
Figurine, colonial lady w/dog & gun, 6" 35.00
Figurine, colonial man, bsk, pastels, 15½", from $150 to 175.00
Figurine, dog beside lamp, 2" 8.00
Figurine, dog pushing 2 puppies in basket-like buggy, 3" 12.50
Figurine, dog sitting upright w/pipe & hat, 3½" 10.00
Figurine, East Indian man & lady in wht, red mk, 6⅛", pr 35.00
Figurine, East Indian man winding turban, 6" 20.00

Figurine, equestrian, 10½", from $175.00 to $200.00. (Photo courtesy Gene and Cathy Florence)

Figurine, fisher boy w/basket & pole, Ucagco, 7" 40.00
Figurine, gardening boy & girl on base, Hummel type, Paulux, 5½" .. 60.00
Figurine, girl w/doll, blond standing, 4¼", from $12.50 to 15.00
Figurine, horse w/rider, bsk, mk Andrea HP, 10¼" 250.00
Figurine, lady holding skirt wide to curtsy, 4¼" 15.00
Figurine, man beside lady playing cello, Maruyama, 3½" 25.00
Figurine, man in turban, 6" 20.00
Figurine, man playing mandolin for lady on base, 4¾" 20.00
Figurine, Oriental boy & girl kissing, lying on tummies, pr 40.00
Fishbowl decoration, cat poised to hang from rim of bowl, from $20 to ... 25.00
Ice bucket, lacquerware, 7⅝", from $50 to 60.00
Incense burner, Oriental figure, 4¼" 20.00
Jewelry box, silver-tone metal, emb scrolls, ftd, 3½x4½" 20.00
Lamp, bulbous bottle form w/hdls, wht w/appl roses, gold decor, 8½" .. 40.00
Lamp, Oriental boy seated on books reading, detailed pnt glaze 40.00
Music box, geisha dancer, 4-drw, 12x5" 175.00
Pie bird, Mammy, high gloss, from $125 to 150.00
Pitcher, chicken form, wht w/red, blk & brn accents 25.00
Planter, lady stands beside lg open flower, bsk, Paulex, 6" 75.00
Plate, roses, mc on shaded ground, 7", from $25 to 35.00
Salt box, wooden lid, Ucagco, 5x5" 50.00
Vase, angel boy supports flower-form vase, pastels, 7½", $55 to...... 60.00

Ohr, George

Finding his vocation late in life, George Ohr set off in a two-year learning journey around 1880, visiting as many potteries as he could find in the 16 states he traveled through, including the Kirkpatrick brothers' Anna Pottery and Susan Frackelton's studio. Upon his return George built his Pot-Ohr-y, took a wife, made babies — some flesh, some clay. After a devestating fire destroyed a large section of the town in 1893, George rebuilt his homestead and studio and seemed to gain inspiration from new surroundings. His 'Mud Babies' became paper-thin, full of movement, wild ear-shaped handles, impish snakes, suggestive shapes, and inventive glazes. Ohr threw out the rules of folk pottery's sponge-glazing, covering only a section of a vessel with a particular color or pattern, mixing dead-matt greens or purples with bright yellow flambes, and topping it all in brown gunmetal drips. This was accomplished among the derisive smiles and lack of understanding he encountered from a society accustomed to the propriety of neo-Japanese wares such as Rookwood and Trenton Belleek or the plainness of salt-glazed stoneware.

About the time he decided to move away from branding his pots with one version or another of 'GEORGE E OHR, Biloxi, Miss.' and start signing them 'as if it were a check,' Ohr also came to the realization that he did not care to glaze them anymore. He appreciated the qualities of unadorned fired clays and enjoyed mixing different types, which he often dug from neighboring Tchoutacabouffa river. His shapes became increasingly more abstract and modern, probably ostracizing him even more from a potential clientel, to whom he would relent to sell only his entire output of thousands of pieces at once.

Today George Ohr's legacy shines as the unequaled, unrivaled product of the preeminent art potter — iconaclast, inventive, multi-faceted, the first American abstract artist. Our advisors for this category are Suzanne Perrault and David Rago; they are listed in the Directory under New Jersey.

Vase, red and green mottle, ribbon handles, 8½", $84,000.00. (Photo courtesy David Rago Auctions)

Ashtray/match holder, gunmetal/gr on yel, floriform, 1¾x4¾x4"	1,920.00
Bank, blk-gr to cobalt at base, slot along dome, 2½x3"	700.00
Bowl, amber, lobed/pointed & pinched rim, 1¼x3"	1,800.00
Bowl, bl/gr/pk sponged, scalloped trn-down rim, 2¼x4", NM	5,100.00
Bowl, blk & pumpkin speckled, spherical, 2¼x4½"	1,100.00
Bowl, bsk, deep in-body twist, Mud from...N.0.St 1905, 3x4"	4,200.00
Bowl, bsk, flat shoulder, dimpled lower body, 3x6", NM	1,560.00
Bowl, bsk red clay, dimpled w/prunts, 1 dk area, 1906, 3x5½", NM	1,560.00
Bowl, caramel/gr/oatmeal, swirled, 2x3½"	1,400.00
Bowl, dk gr, squat w/'bow tie' pinched dimple front/bk, 2¼x4"	2,280.00
Hat, gr-speckled gloss, wide torn/floppy/folded brim, 2½x6"	2,520.00
Hat, gunmetal brn, folded rim w/1" glaze chip, 3x5½"	840.00
Mug, gunmetal gray, bulbous upper body, pinched below, 5x4¾"	1,100.00
Mug, pk/bl-gr/gr bands, lg C hdl 1 side, ring hdl opposite, 4x5½"	10,200.00
Mug, puzzle; amber gloss, rabbit hdl, 3¼x4¼"	1,680.00
Mug, tan/gunmetal/gr sponge on raspberry & gray, hdls differ, rstr, 4"	5,700.00
Pitcher, bl gloss on thin red clay, sm rstr, 3"	1,800.00
Pitcher, marbleized bsk, pinched section is spout, angle hdl, 4x4"	4,500.00
Strawberry planter, gunmetal, rtcl w/circles & triangles, 11x8"	2,160.00
Vase, bottle gr/raspberry mottle, crimped/folded rim, ftd, 5x5"	11,400.00
Vase, brn bsk, bulbous w/dimpled front, folded can top, 5x6"	4,200.00
Vase, bsk, folded rim, bulbous bottom, 1906, Red GSTRR Pier Clay, 3"	1,560.00
Vase, bsk, folded/crimped rim, protruding band around waist, 4½"	1,140.00
Vase, buff bsk, bulbous w/deep twist below cylinder top, ftd, 6x5"	2,520.00
Vase, Burnt Baby, deep red remnants, 3 stacked lobes, hairlines, 3"	960.00
Vase, Burnt Baby, olive gr remnants, pinched rim/dimpled body, 3¼"	1,200.00
Vase, gr speckled, spherical, 2¼x3¾"	1,680.00
Vase, gunmetal brn, crimped/folded rim, appl notched band, rstr, 4x3"	2,040.00
Vase, indigo/amber sponged bands on amber, 1-pinch front/bk, 6x4½"	7,200.00
Vase, raspberry/gr matt over bl/gr semimatt, twist in neck, 7x4"	16,800.00
Vase, red scroddled bsk, irregular form, pinched rim, 1906, 2x3"	2,280.00
Vase, scroddled bsk, bowl shape w/pinched side-section hdl, 3x6", EX	2,160.00
Vase, thin gr, crumpled/folded top, dimpled body, 3½x4	9,600.00
Water jug, wht bsk, ring hdl top center, nipple on ea shoulder, 6x5"	1,920.00

Old Ivory

Old Ivory dinnerware was produced from 1882 to 1920 by Herman Ohme, of Lower Salzbrunn in Silesia. The patterns are referred to by the numbers stamped on the bottom of most pieces. There are some early patterns with no number, but these seem to be stamped with a blank name. The factory mark most often seen is a small fleur-de-lis sometimes having either Silesia, Germany, or Prussia under it. The handwritten numbers are artist identification or manufacturing numbers, not the pattern number. Patterns #16 and #84, being the easiest to find, have seen a decline in value with the popularity of Internet sales. The patterns with flowers in pink, lavender, yellow, and some pieces with fruit decor bring higher prices at this time. These are still on the soft ivory background, Worn gold and any damage will certainly reduce the value of any item unless it is extremely rare. Holly patterns remain very desirable and command 70% to 200% more than the more common patterns. Beware of copy-cat pieces produced by other manufacturers. They are not included in this listing. Also note that portrait vases have retained their high prices, even with the finding of more and different shapes.

The clear glazed hotel ware by Ohme is steadily climbing in popularity and price. We have included some pieces in this finish for comparison. There are many more shapes and patterns of the clear glaze than the Old Ivory. Even a few experimental pieces have shown up. One such piece is a tapestry (similar to Royal Bayreuth tapestry) pickle dish.

For more information, we recommend *Collector's Encyclopedia of Old Ivory China, The Mystery Explored,* by Alma Hillman (our advisor), David Goldschmitt, and Adam Szynkiewicz. Ms. Hillman is listed in the Directory under Maine.

Basket, #134, oblong, 8", from $300 to	425.00
Biscuit/cracker jar, #16, 8", from $400 to	500.00
Bowl, porringer; #39, 6¼", from $400 to	600.00
Bowl, vegetable; #75, w/lid, 10½" dia, from $1,000 to	1,500.00
Cake plate, #34, open hdls, 10" or 11", ea from $175 to	275.00
Charger, #82, Empire, 13", from $500 to	800.00
Chocolate pot, #12, 9½", from $700 to	800.00
Coffeepot, #84, Deco variant, from $1,200 to	1,500.00
Compote, #84, 9", from $700 to	1,200.00
Creamer, #16 or #84, 3½", from $40 to	50.00

Cup and saucer, bouillon; with lid, #118, rare, from $300.00 to $400.00. (Photo courtesy Alma Hillman)

Cup & saucer, cider; #16, 3", from $300 to	500.00
Cup & saucer, mustache; #53, 3½", from $900 to	1,200.00
Cup & saucer, tea; #7, 3¼", from $65 to	85.00

Cup & saucer, tea; #63, Clarion, from $185 to 300.00
Gravy boat, #16, 8½", from $600 to 800.00
Plate, coupe; #75, 6¼", from $50 to 75.00
Plate, dessert; #113, 7½", from $95 to 150.00
Plate, luncheon; #10, 8½", from $95 to 115.00
Platter, #16, 21", from $500 to 600.00
Platter, #34, 28", from $1,500 to 2,000.00
Powder jar, #16 or #84, w/lid, from $400 to 600.00
Shakers, #22, 2¾", pr from $400 to 600.00
Spittoon, #429, from $1,200 to 1,500.00
Spooner, #11, 4", from $250 to 400.00
Teapot, #200, 8½", from $400 .... 600.00
Trinket box, portrait, 3", from $500 to 1,000.00
Vase, many szs, from $400 to 1,800.00

Clear-Glazed Hotelware by Hermann Ohme

Because of climbing values for Old Ivory, interest is growing for the clear-glazed pieces by Ohme, which are still reasonable, though escalating in price. It was produced between 1882 and 1928 in Niedersalzbrunn, Selesia, Germany (now Western Poland). The body of the ware was white, and many of the Old Ivory patterns and shapes were utilized. It is often marked with the blue fleur-de-lis stamp. In comparison, while an Old Ivory open-handled cake plate might sell for $125.00 to $145.00, a comparable clear-glazed example might go for $45.00 to $55.00 with the same mark.

Child's dishes, teapot+plate+creamer+c/s, from $150 to 250.00
Chocolate pot, Worcester blank, from $65 to 150.00
Creamer, Dresden decor, from $60 to 70.00
Creamer & sugar bowl, Eglantine blank, from $35 to 75.00
Cup & saucer, Clairon blank, from $10 to 35.00
Cup & saucer, mustache; Eglantine blank, from $100 to 250.00

Demitasse pot, creamer, and sugar bowl, Elysee blanks, from $175.00 to 250.00.

(Photo courtesy Alma Hillman)

Egg cup, Eglantine blank, from $30 to 40.00
Gravy boat, Deco blank, from $35 to 50.00
Plate, Beaded blank, fruit decor, 7½", from $45 to 75.00
Plate, dinner; Alice blank, 9¾", from $25 to 45.00
Plate, Dresden decor, 8", from $40 to 50.00
Ramekin set, Quadrille blank, from $45 to 65.00
Shakers, Louis XVI blank, pr from $20 to 40.00
Spittoon, from $150 to 300.00
Teapot, Clairon blank, from $150 to 350.00
Teapot, Dresden decor, sm, from $250 to 350.00
Teapot, Dresden Swirl, from $350 to 450.00
Vase, Elysee blank, 14", from $200 to 300.00

Old Paris

Old Paris porcelains were made from the mid-eighteenth century until about 1900. Seldom marked, the term refers to the area of manufacture rather than a specific company. In general, the ware was of high quality, characterized by classic shapes, colorful decoration, and gold application.

Apothecary jar, blk-lettered/mc decor labels, w/lids, 10", 5 for... 1,470.00
Candlestick, lady praying, foliate std, pnt bsk, 9", ea.................... 125.00
Clock, mantel; lady in repose, scrolled body/legs, 1850s, 13¼x7x3"...300.00
Clock, mantel; man & lady stand ea side of dial, gilt/florals, 17x11"..490.00
Clock, mantel; ornate scrolls/2 seated figures on base, 1850s, 13x7x3"...300.00
Clock, mantel; shells & scrolls, 2 youths sit astride front, 20x14" .. 1,175.00
Coffee set, peach/wht/gold dmn band, 1820s, serves 6, 16 pcs ..1,295.00
Corbeille, rtcl, oval w/gilt banding, 1840s, 9¼x10½x14" 200.00
Cup & saucer, baskets of roses/gilt arabesques, For My Dear..., 4x6"..120.00
Cup & saucer, cafe-au-lait; floral on bl w/gold, rstr saucer, 1830s..150.00
Figurine, American Indian warrior (& maiden), att J Petit, 17"/16", pr .525.00

Garniture vases, in the manner of Jacob Petit, figural reserves, applied flowerheads, rare violet ground with gilt, now lamps, ca. 1850 – 1860, 14", $4,000.00 for the pair.

(Photo courtesy Neal Auction Co. Auctioneers & Appraisers of Fine Art)

Jardiniere, romantic reserve on bl w/floral, hdls, 1850s, 5¾x12" .. 160.00
Teapot, cherubs/roses on magenta w/gilt, bird-head spout, 9x11", EX...295.00
Teapot, gilt bellflower border, 8½", +cr/sug 325.00
Teapot, 2 men smoking/drinking on puce brick-like ground, 8"...295.00
Tureen, gilt/red bands, fruit finial, scroll hdls, 1800, +14" tray..... 470.00
Urn, figure scenes HP on gilt, low uptrn hdls/sq base, 1850s, 8", pr..1,530.00
Vase, appl maidens/putti/etc, pnt florals/diapering, rprs, 16x10", pr ...480.00
Vase, appl/molded birds/fuchsias on dk bl, florals/gilts, 17x10", pr ..650.00
Vase, floral reserve w/gold, floral hdls/acanthus leaf rim, 14x10x7" ..1,400.00
Vase, lady in floral bower reserve, mc w/gold, #CF354, 1860s, 14x9".. 200.00
Vase, Persian couple/scenic reserve on bl, florals/gilt, 16" 350.00
Vase, rtcl tulip over 3 lily forms, gilt/appl floral, J Petit, 17", pr... 1,410.00
Vase, spill; scenic reserve on gr, J Petit, ca 1835-50, 3x3x2¾"...... 415.00

Old Sleepy Eye

Old Sleepy Eye was a Sioux Indian chief who was born in Minnesota in 1780. His name was used for the name of a town as well as a flour mill. In 1903 the Sleepy Eye Milling Company of Sleepy Eye, Minnesota, contracted the Weir Pottery Company of Monmouth, Illinois, to make steins, vases, salt crocks, and butter tubs which the company gave away to their customers. A bust profile of the old Indian and his name decorated each piece of the blue and gray stoneware. In addition to these four items, the Minnesota Stoneware Company of Red Wing made a mug with a verse which is very scarce today.

In 1906 Weir Pottery merged with six others to form the Western Stoneware Company in Monmouth. They produced a line of blue and white ware using a lighter body, but these pieces were never given as flour premiums. This line consisted of pitchers (five sizes), steins, mugs, sugar bowls, vases, trivets, and mustache cups. These pieces turn up only rarely in other colors and are highly prized by advanced collectors. Advertising items such as trade cards, pillow tops, thermometers, paperweights, letter openers, postcards, cookbooks, and thimbles are considered very valuable. The original ware was made sporadically until 1937. Brown steins and mugs were produced in 1952. Our advisor for this category is Jim Martin; he is listed in the Directory under Illinois.

Barrel, flour; orig paper label, 1920s 1,000.00
Barrel, grapevine-effect banding 2,500.00
Barrel, oak w/brass bands 3,000.00
Barrel label, mk Chief/Strong Bakers, image in center, 16", NM .. 175.00
Barrel label, mk Cream, red circle, many repros 170.00
Blanket, horse; w/logo, EX 1,000.00
Butter crock, Flemish bl & gray 600.00
Cabinet, bread display; Old Sleepy Eye etched in glass 950.00
Calendar, 1904, NM 375.00
Cookbook, Indian on cover, Sleepy Eye Milling Co, 4¾x4" 200.00
Cookbook, loaf-of-bread shape, NM 120.00
Coupon, for ordering cookbook 200.00
Dough scraper, tin/wood, To Be Sure, EX 300.00
Fan, die-cut image of Old Sleepy Eye, EX+ 200.00
Flour sack, cloth, mc Indian, red letters 345.00
Flour sack, paper, Indian in blk, blk lettering, NM 125.00
Hot plate/trivet, bl & wht 2,000.00
Ink blotter 125.00
Letter opener, bronze 500.00
Match holder, pnt 800.00
Match holder, wht 850.00
Mug, bl & gray, 4¼" 300.00
Mug, bl & wht, 4¼" 150.00
Mug, verse, Red Wing, EX 1,200.00
Mustache cup, bl & wht, very rare 3,000.00
Paperweight, bronzed company trademk 300.00
Pillow cover, Sleepy Eye & tribe meet President Monroe 350.00
Pillow cover, trademk center w/various scenes, 22", NM 800.00
Pin-bk button, Indian, rnd face 250.00
Pitcher, bl & gray, 5" 300.00
Pitcher, bl & wht, #1, ½-pt 150.00
Pitcher, bl & wht, #2, 1-pt 200.00
Pitcher, bl & wht, #3, w/bl rim, 1-qt 800.00
Pitcher, bl & wht, #3, 1-qt 275.00
Pitcher, bl & wht, #4, ½-gal 300.00
Pitcher, bl & wht, #5, 1-gal 350.00
Pitcher, bl on cream, 8", M 220.00
Pitcher, brn on yel, Sesquicentennial, 1981, from $100 to 125.00
Pitcher, standing Indian, good color 1,000.00
Postcard, colorful trademk, 1904 Expo Winner 185.00

Postcard, Indian Artist, one of nine in series, EX, $100.00.

Ruler, wooden, 15" 700.00
Salt crock, Flemish bl & gray, 4x6½" 500.00

Sheet music, in fr 200.00
Sign, cb easel-back, portrait, prof rstr, 12x7¼", EX+ 1,050.00
Sign, emb tin litho, ...Flour & Cereal Products, profile, rstr, 28x19" .. 760.00
Sign, self-fr tin, Old Sleepy Eye Flour, 20x24" 3,000.00
Sign, self-fr tin, portrait w/multiple scenes on border, 24x20", G ... 2,300.00
Sign, tin litho die-cut Indian, ...Flour & Cereals, 13½" 1,650.00
Spoon, demitasse; emb roses in bowl, Unity SP 60.00
Spoon, Indian-head hdl 70.00
Stein, bl & wht, 7¾" 500.00
Stein, Board of Directors, all yrs, 40-oz 265.00
Stein, Board of Directors, 1969, 22-oz 350.00
Stein, brn, 1952, 22-oz 150.00
Stein, brn & wht 1,000.00
Stein, brn & yel, Western Stoneware mk 1,000.00
Stein, chestnut, 40-oz, 1952 .... 200.00
Stein, cobalt 800.00
Stein, Flemish bl on gray 500.00
Stein, ltd edition, 1979-84, ea 125.00
Sugar bowl, bl & wht, 3" 600.00
Vase, cattails, all cobalt 700.00
Vase, cattails, bl & wht, good color, 9" 500.00
Vase, cattails, brn on yel, rare color 1,000.00
Vase, cattails, gr & wht, rare 1,500.00
Vase, Indian & cattails, Flemish bl & gray, 8½" 250.00

O'Neill, Rose

Rose O'Neill's Kewpies were introduced in 1909 when they were used to conclude a story in the December issue of *Ladies' Home Journal*. They were an immediate success, and soon Kewpie dolls were being produced worldwide. German manufacturers were among the earliest and also used the Kewpie motif to decorate chinaware as well as other items. The Kewpie is still popular today and can be found on products ranging from Christmas cards and cake ornaments to fabrics, wallpaper, and metal items. In the following listings, 'sgn' indicates that the item is signed Rose O'Neill. Values are for examples in excellent condition with no chips. The copyright symbol, ©, is also a good mark. Unsigned items can be of interest to collectors; many are authentic and collectible, some are too small to sign. Our advisors for this category are Don and Anne Kier; they are listed in the Directory under Ohio.

Handkerchief, Kewpie Hankies, MIB, from $30.00 to $40.00. (Photo courtesy Barbara Guggenheim and Helene Guarnaccia)

Book, Jell-O Girl, Rose O'Neill, 1916, EX 40.00
Book, Loves of Edwy, leather cover, 432 pgs, 1904, VG 850.00
Boutonniere, bsk Kewpie, lapel stud on bk, 2" 65.00
Bowl, Kewpies playing, Germany, Royal Rudolstadt, 1⅝x6" 100.00
Box, pin; bsk, Kewpies playing, Germany, 4¼" 245.00
Box, trinket; jasperware w/3 Kewpies on ea side, 4 on lid, 3¼" 130.00

Candy container, blk Kewpie finial, jtd arms, Germany, 1930s, 5¼"..400.00
Candy container, bsk, Kewpie, 4"..500.00
Dish, 2 Kewpies inside w/Baby on border, Czechoslovakia, 5½" ..155.00
Figurine, Black Ho-Ho (buddha-like) seated in robe, 1940, 5½"...100.00
Inkwell, bsk, w/writer Kewpie, 4½"..500.00
Kewpie, bsk, action figure, Aviator, 8½"...................................850.00
Kewpie, bsk, action figure, Cowboy, #7863 on ft, 1960s, 6x4"......215.00
Kewpie, bsk, action figure, Cowboy, Germany, 10".....................800.00
Kewpie, bsk, action figure, Farmer, Germany, 6½"....................900.00
Kewpie, bsk, action figure, Fireman, #7863 on ft, 1960s, 6x4" 185.00
Kewpie, bsk, action figure, Governor seated in chair....................325.00
Kewpie, bsk, action figure, Minister, 5"...................................250.00
Kewpie, bsk, action figure, reading book, 3¾"............................440.00
Kewpie, bsk, action figure, Sailor, USN on hat, 4½"...................300.00
Kewpie, bsk, action figure, seated, holds roses, Germany, 2¾x1¼" ...320.00
Kewpie, bsk, action figure, seated w/blk cat in lap, 3¼"................600.00
Kewpie, bsk, immobile, bl wings, pnt hair, Germany, 2½"............135.00
Kewpie, compo, jtd shoulders, Jesco, 1966, 24", EXIB.................295.00
Kewpie, compo, Scootles, orig romper/shoes, Cameo Dolls Co, 1925, 15"..400.00
Kewpie, Doodle Dog, bsk, blk & wht w/bl wings, 6"..................1,530.00
Kewpie, hard plastic, ca 1950, 8½", MIB....................................385.00
Kewpie, nude holding drawstring bag, #4882, 4½" 1,195.00
Kewpie, soap figure w/cotton batting, RO Wilson 1917, 4", NM ..110.00
Paper dolls, Ragsy & Ritzy, ca 1912, 12" dolls, VG.......................75.00
Perfume bottle, seated Kewpie, #31 Germany, 2¼".....................180.00
Pitcher, cream; 2 Kewpies playing horsey, Royal Rudolstadt, 3½" ..185.00
Pitcher, jasperware, Kewpies playing, Germany, 4¼"...................245.00
Plate, Kewpies on bl & gr, Royal Rudolstadt, 7"...........................95.00
Plate, 2 Kewpies w/holly, 2 sm tab hdls, 5"................................170.00
Plate, 3 Kewpies in center w/3 on border, Bavarian, 5⅛" 125.00
Soap figure, Kewpie, RO Wilson, 1917, 4"..................................110.00
Talcum container, Kewpie, celluloid, jtd shoulders, c O'Neill, Japan..285.00
Tea set, Kewpies, Rose O'Neill Kewpie Germany, 6" pot+cr/sug...575.00
Vase, Kewpie sits in gr wicker chair w/hole in bk, 3¼" 490.00
Vase, Kewpie soldier stands at base of tree, 6½"..........................335.00

Onion Pattern

The familiar pattern known to collectors as Onion acquired its name through a case of mistaken identity. Designed in the early 1700s by Johann Haroldt of the Meissen factory in Germany, the pattern was a mixture of earlier Oriental designs. One of its components was a stylized peach, which was mistaken for an onion; as a result, the pattern became known by that name. Usually found in blue, an occasional piece may also be found in pink and red. The pattern is commonly associated with Meissen, but it has been reproduced by many others including Villeroy and Boch, Hutchenreuther, and Royal Copenhagen (whose pattern is a variation of the standard design).

Many marks have been used, some of them fraudulent Meissen marks. Study a marks book to become more familiar with them. In our listings, 'Xd swords' indicates first-quality old Meissen ware. Meissen in an oval over a star was a mark of C. Teichert Stove and Porcelain Factory of Meissen; it was used from 1882 until about 1930. Items marked simply Meissen were produced by the State's Porcelain Manufactory VEB after 1972. The crossed swords indication was sometimes added. Today's market abounds with quality reproductions.

Blue Danube is a modern line of Onion-patterned dinnerware produced in Japan and distributed by Lipper International of Wallingford, Connecticut. At least 100 items are available in porcelain; it is sold in most large stores with china departments.

Bowl, flowered stem hdl, gold trim, Xd swords, w/lid, 4¼x4½".......60.00
Bowl, fruit; Blue Danube, 5½", from $10 to...................................14.00

Bowl, hdld, w/lid, Xd swords, 5¾x6"..155.00
Bowl, muffin; 5-sided, rtcl rim, Blue Danube, 7½"........................45.00
Bowl, rimmed soup; mk Meissen w/star, 9", set of 4....................115.00
Bowl, rimmed soup; Xd swords, 1⅞x9"...50.00
Bowl, rtcl, Xd swords, sq, 1¾x9½"..100.00
Bowl, serving; Blue Danube, 10" L...50.00
Bowl, soup; Blue Danube, 1½x7½", set of 5...................................85.00
Bowl, spaghetti; Blue Danube, 12", from $50 to.............................60.00
Bowl, triangular, #27, Xd swords, 1¾x11"......................................90.00
Bowl, Xd swords, sq, 1¼x8¼"...140.00
Box, scalloped edge, Xd swords, 2½x4¾".......................................60.00
Canister, Instant Tea, w/sm hdl, Xd swords, 7½"............................70.00
Casserole, oval, Blue Danube, w/lid, 9½"..60.00
Casserole, w/lid, Blue Danube, 1½-qt, 7¼" dia...............................55.00

Compote, lattice rim with five floral reserves, blue under-glaze crossed swords mark, #87/90a, $300.00. (Photo courtesy DuMouchelles)

Compote, ped ft, rtcl rim, Xd swords, 5¼x9½"...............................55.00
Creamer, Blue Danube, 2¾"...18.00
Dish, vegetable; divided, Blue Danube, 3x8x11", from $35 to.........45.00
Gravy boat, attached underplate (6x10"), Xd swords, 4¼x8⅜".......70.00
Gravy boat, w/lid & attached underplate, Made in Germany......160.00
Gravy separator, Xd swords, 8"...50.00
Inkwell, w/lid, Meissen w/star, 3x3⅞", +1x7¼" saucer..................65.00
Kitchen utensil, 5-point porc star on wooden hdl, 12"...................50.00
Measuring cups, ¼, ⅓, ½ & 1-cup, Xd swords, set of 4...................50.00
Meat tenderizer, 3¼x3¼", 13½" L hdl...90.00
Pastry wheel, wooden hdl, ca 1900, 7"...60.00
Pitcher, T-87, Xd swords, 5¾"...95.00
Pitcher, Xd swords, 4½"..50.00
Plate, bread & butter; Meissen w/star, 6" dia, set of 4...................80.00
Plate, dinner; Blue Danube, 10⅜"..20.00
Plate, dinner; Hutschenreuther, 1½x10"...45.00
Plate, rtcl rim, gold trim, Xd swords, 2x11"...................................75.00
Plate, rtcl rim, Xd sword, 6"..50.00
Plate, rtcl rim, Xd swords, 8"...65.00
Platter, cheese; hole for hanging, Xd swords, 10¼", from $45 to....55.00
Platter, fish; oval, Xd swords, 21" L...370.00
Platter, Meissen w/star, 12" L..65.00
Platter, orange accents, Meissen w/star, 15x10"............................85.00
Platter, scalloped edge, gold trim, Xd swords, #163/4, 14x10"......140.00
Salt cellar, lady sits on base/holds bowl, Xd swords, #2872, 8" L..375.00
Salt cellar, wooden lid, Villery & Boch, 1890s, 8¾".....................210.00
Strainer, wooden hdl, Xd swords, 9⅛x2⅝" dia bowl.......................70.00
Tablecloth, Blue Danube, cloth, 124x104"......................................65.00
Teapot, Blue Danube, 4¾"...55.00
Teapot, Blue Danube, 6½x9½"..65.00
Tidbit, 3-tiered, Blue Danube, 6½", 8½" & 10", from $65 to..........75.00
Tray, sandwich; rtcl hdls, Blue Danube, #135, 14½x7⅛"...............90.00
Tureen, soup; w/lid, Blue Danube banner mk, 6¾x10¾".............140.00
Wine taster, stick hdl, mk RA, Xd swords, 3¾" dia (+hdl)...........145.00

Opalescent Glass

First made in England in 1870, opalescent glass became popular in America around the turn of the century. Its name comes from the milky-white opalescent trim that defines the lines of the pattern. It was produced in table sets, novelties, toothpick holders, vases, and lamps. Note that American-made sugar bowls have lids; sugar bowls of British origin are considered to be complete without lids. For further information we recommend *Standard Encyclopedia of Opalescent Glass* by Bill Edwards and Mike Carwile (Collector Books). See also Sugar Shakers; Syrup Pitchers; etc.

Buttons and Braids, tumbler, blue, $80.00.
(Photo courtesy Tom Harris Auctions)

Abalone, bowl, gr	35.00
Acorn Burrs (& Bark), bowl, sauce; wht	30.00
Ala-Bock, candy dish, vaseline or canary	100.00
Alaska, bowl, master; bl	145.00
Alaska, bowl, master; wht	75.00
Albany Reverse Swirl, water bottle, wht	115.00

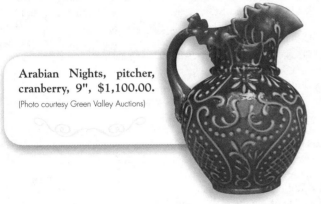

Arabian Nights, pitcher, cranberry, 9", $1,100.00.
(Photo courtesy Green Valley Auctions)

Arabian Nights, pitcher, wht	285.00
Argonaut Shell (Nautilus), bowl, sauce; bl	45.00
Argonaut Shell (Nautilus), compote, jelly; vaseline or canary, mk	125.00
Ascot, biscuit jar, bl	175.00
Ascot, biscuit jar, vaseline or canary	160.00
Band & Rib (Threaded Optic), rose bowl, wht	30.00
Barbells, bowl, gr	40.00
Barbells, vase, gr	50.00
Basketweave (Open Edge), nappy, bl	35.00
Beaded Block, celery vase, gr	75.00
Beaded Cable, rose bowl, gr, ftd	60.00
Beaded Fleur-de-Lis, compote, wht	45.00
Beaded Stars & Swag, plate, advertising; bl	450.00
Beatty Honeycomb, creamer, wht	50.00
Beatty Honeycomb, tumbler, bl	50.00
Beatty Rib, bowl, master; bl	55.00
Beatty Rib, tumbler, wht	30.00
Beatty Swirl, bowl, sauce; wht	20.00
Beatty Swirl, celery vase, bl	75.00
Beatty Swirl, spooner, wht	45.00
Beaumont Stripe, pitcher, vaseline or canary	350.00
Blown Drapery, vase, gr	85.00
Blown Twist, pitcher, cranberry	900.00
Blown Twist, tumbler, cranberry	125.00
Brideshead, butter dish, bl	100.00
Brideshead, tray, oval, bl	125.00
Bubble Lattice, toothpick holder, wht	150.00
Bulbous Base Coinspot, syrup, wht	110.00
Bull's Eye, bowl, bl	50.00
Buttons & Braids, bowl, cranberry	110.00

Cane & Diamond Swirl, tray, vaseline or canary, stemmed	70.00
Cane Rings, bowl, bl, 8½"	75.00
Casbah, compote, wht	45.00
Chippendale, basket, vaseline or canary	80.00
Chippendale, plate, vaseline or canary, 6¼"	95.00
Chrysanthemum Base Swirl, cruet, wht	200.00
Chrysanthemum Swirl, bl, bl hdl, faceted crystal stopper, 6¾"	150.00
Circled Scroll, butter dish, bl	475.00
Circled Scroll, creamer, gr	95.00
Circled Scroll, sugar bowl, gr	150.00
Colonial Stairsteps, creamer, bl	100.00
Compass, rose bowl, wht	90.00
Conch & Twig, wall pocket, bl, vaseline or canary	110.00
Consolidated Criss-Cross, shakers, gr or cranberry, ea	135.00
Contessa, basket, bl	60.00
Coral Reef, bottle, bitters; bl	200.00
Coral Reef, bottle, bitters; wht	125.00
Coronation, pitcher, bl, vaseline or canary	200.00
Crown Jewels, pitcher, bl	250.00
Crown Jewels, platter, bl	110.00
Daffodils, hand lamp, gr	300.00
Daisy & Fern, butter dish, cranberry	300.00
Daisy & Fern, cruet, bl, faceted stopper, 7½"	250.00
Daisy & Fern, vase, wht	100.00
Daisy & Fern, wht, bulbous w/clear hdl & faceted stopper, 7"	100.00
Daisy & Plume, basket, wht, rare	85.00
Daisy & Plume, rose bowl, bl, ftd	60.00
Daisy in Criss-Cross, pitcher, bl	450.00
Daisy May (Leaf Rays), nappy/bonbon, gr	45.00
Diamond & Daisy (Caroline), basket, bl	100.00
Diamond Maple Leaf, bowl, gr, hdls	70.00
Diamond Optic, compote, bl	50.00
Diamond Spearhead, butter dish, gr	275.00
Diamond Spearhead, butter dish, wht	175.00
Diamond Spearhead, carafe, water; vaseline or canary	350.00
Diamond Wave, pitcher, cranberry, w/lid	175.00
Diamond Wave, vase, cranberry, 5"	85.00
Diamonds, tumbler, cranberry	70.00
Dolly Madison, creamer, bl	90.00
Dolphin & Herons, tray, novelty; wht, ftd	100.00
Double Greek Key, tray, pickle; bl	200.00
Dragon Lady (Dugan's Diamond Compass), rose bowl, wht	90.00
Drapery, Northwood's, spooner, wht	55.00
Drapery, Northwood's, vase, bl	140.00
Duchess, butter dish, vaseline or canary	175.00
Dugan Peach Intaglio, compote, wht	100.00
Dugan's Honeycomb, bowl, bl, various shapes, rare, ea	85.00
Dugan Strawberry Intaglio, bowl, fruit; wht, stemmed	85.00
Elipse & Diamond, tumbler, cranberry	115.00
Elson Dewdrop #2, bowl, sauce; wht	15.00
Elson Dewdrop #2, cruet, wht	90.00

English Drape, vase, bl... 65.00
English Ripple, tumbler, bl, vaseline or canary 80.00
Everglades, creamer, wht 45.00
Everglades, shakers, bl, pr 220.00
Fan, creamer, gr 60.00
Fan, tumbler, gr 75.00
Feathers, vase, bl 35.00
Fenton #220 (Stripe), tumbler, gr, w/hdl 35.00
Fenton #370, nappy, amber 55.00
Fern, cruet, bl 225.00
Fern, cruet, wht 150.00
Fern, toothpick holder, cranberry, rare 475.00
Field Flowers, compote, vaseline or canary, 2 szs 250.00
Fish-in-the-Sea, vase, wht, scarce 150.00
Flora, bowl, master; wht 80.00
Flora, butter dish, bl 425.00
Fluted Scrolls (Klondyke), epergne, bl, sm 125.00
Fluted Scrolls (Klondyke), spooner, bl 55.00
Four Pillars, vase, gr 70.00
Frosted Leaf & Basketweave, creamer, vaseline or canary 135.00
Gonterman (Adonis) Hob, cruet, amber 425.00
Gonterman (Adonis) Swirl, pitcher, bl 110.00
Gonterman (Adonis) Swirl, spooner, amber 125.00
Grape & Cable w/Thumbprints, bowl, gr 175.00
Greely (Hobbs), finger bowl, bl 225.00
Harrow, cordial, bl, vaseline or canary, stemmed 35.00
Harrow, creamer, vaseline or canary 70.00
Hearts & Flowers, compote, wht 85.00
Herringbone, tumbler, cranberry 150.00
Herringbone, tumbler, wht 65.00
Hobnail (Hobbs), bottle, bitters; bl 150.00
Hobnail 4-Footed, spooner, cobalt 60.00
Hobnail-in-Square (Vesta), butter dish, wht 200.00
Honeycomb (Blown), bowl, bl 75.00
Honeycomb (Blown), cracker jar, wht 250.00
Honeycomb & Clover, bowl, master; gr, Fenton 60.00
Idyll, sugar bowl, gr, scarce 250.00
Inside Ribbing, celery vase, vaseline or cranberry 60.00
Intaglio, compote, jelly; bl 50.00
Intaglio, shakers, wht, pr 90.00
Intaglio (Dugan), nappy, wht, 6-9" 45.00
Interior Swirl, rose bowl, bl 100.00
Inverted Fan & Feather, bowl, master; bl 300.00
Inverted Fan & Feather, spooner, wht 150.00
Inverted Fan & Feather, sugar bowl, wht 225.00
Jackson, pitcher, bl 300.00
Jackson, powder jar, gr 80.00
Jewel & Fan, bowl, banana; bl 125.00
Jewel & Fan, bowl, gr 55.00
Jewel & Flower, creamer, vaseline or canary 95.00
Jewel & Flower, pitcher, wht 250.00
Jewelled Heart, bowl, sauce; bl 45.00
Jewelled Heart, compote, bl or gr 150.00
Jewelled Heart, toothpick holder, wht 300.00
Jewels & Drapery, vase, aqua 75.00
Keyhole, rose bowl, bl or gr 175.00
Lady Chippendale, compote, cobalt, tall 100.00
Late Coinspot, pitcher, gr 150.00
Lattice Medallions, rose bowl, wht 50.00
Leaf & Beads, bowl, bl, ftd or dome 60.00
Leaf Mold, bowl, master; cranberry 140.00
Leaf Mold, sugar bowl, cranberry 300.00
Leaf Mold, tumbler, cranberry 100.00
Lords & Ladies, butter dish, bl 100.00

Lords & Ladies, celery boat (in wire basket), bl 200.00
Lords & Ladies, plate, vaseline or canary, 7½" 125.00
Lustre Flute, butter dish, wht 200.00
Maple Leaf, compote, jelly; bl 75.00
Maple Leaf, compote, jelly; gr 65.00
Mavis Swirl, bottle, bitters; bl 100.00
Mavis Swirl, bottle, bitters; wht 85.00
Melon Swirl, pitcher, bl 375.00
National Swirl, pitcher, bl or gr 275.00
Old Man Winter, basket, bl, lg ftd 150.00
Opal Loops, flask, wht 195.00
Opal Loops, glass pipe, wht 180.00
Opal Loops, vase, wht 110.00
Over-All Hobnail, bowl, sauce; bl 40.00
Over-All Hobnail, spooner, bl 100.00
Over-All Hobnail, tumbler, wht 25.00
Overlapping Leaves (Leaf Tiers), plate, wht, ftd 195.00
Palm Beach, creamer, vaseline or canary 140.00
Panelled Flowers, nut cup, bl, ftd 60.00
Panelled Holly, bowl, wht 135.00
Panelled Holly, butter dish, wht 250.00
Panelled Holly, creamer, bl 125.00
Pearl Flowers, rose bowl, gr, ftd 60.00
Piasa Bird, bowl, wht 45.00
Piasa Bird, plate, wht, ftd 60.00
Picket, planter, bl 75.00
Pine Cone, plate, wht 75.00
Poinsettia, bowl, fruit; gr, 2 szs, ea 110.00
Polka Dot, syrup, cranberry 725.00
Polka Dot, tumbler, bl 70.00
Popsicle Sticks, shade, wht 35.00
Prince William, creamer, bl 100.00
Princess Diana, compote, bl, metal base 150.00
Pussy Willow, vase, vaseline or canary, 4½" 60.00
Queen's Spill, vase, spill; bl, 4" 90.00
Quilted Wide Stripe, finger bowl, cranberry 70.00
Ray, vase, bl 55.00
Regal, Northwood's, butter dish, gr 175.00

Regal, Northwood's, butter dish, white, $100.00. (Photo courtesy Tom Harris Auctions)

Regal, Northwood's, pitcher, wht 150.00
Reverse Swirl, bottle, water; wht 100.00
Reverse Swirl, custard cup, cranberry 150.00
Ribbed (Opal) Lattice, bowl, master; bl 70.00
Ribbed (Opal) Lattice, tumbler, cranberry 150.00
Ribbed Pillar, bowl, berry; cranberry, lg 95.00
Ribbed Pillar, shakers, cranberry, pr 135.00
Ribbed Spiral, vase, vaseline or canary, squat, 4-7" 75.00
Ribbon Swirl, spitton, gr 175.00
Richelieu, compote, jelly; bl 75.00
Richelieu, tray, bl 50.00
Ring Handle, ring tray, gr 150.00
Ring Handle, shakers, bl, pr 100.00

Roulette, bowl, novelty; bl 50.00
Roulette, bowl, novelty; wht 30.00
Roulette, plate, bl or gr 60.00
Ruffles & Rings, nut bowl, gr 40.00
Ruffles & Rings w/Daisy Band, bowl, wht, ftd 60.00
S-Repeat, tumbler, bl 65.00
Scottish Moor, celery vase, bl 65.00
Scroll w/Acanthus, cruet, vaseline or canary 350.00
Seaweed, bowl, master; wht 40.00
Seaweed, creamer, cranberry 225.00
Shell (Beaded Shell), bowl, sauce; gr 65.00
Shell & Dots, nut bowl, bl... 45.00
Shell & Dots, rose bowl, wht 35.00
Smooth Rib, bowl, wht, on metal stand................................100.00
Snowflake, oil lamp, bl..325.00
Somerset, dish, bl, oval, 9"... 40.00
Somerset, pitcher, juice; vaseline or canary, 5½" 90.00
Spanish Lace, butter dish, bl...425.00
Spanish Lace, water bottle, vaseline or canary......................325.00
Spatter, vase, bl, 9"... 95.00
Speckled Stripe, shakers, wht, pr..100.00
Spool, compote, bl or gr.. 50.00
Stars & Stripes, bottle, bitters; cranberry 350.00
Stars & Stripes, bottle, bitters; wht 100.00
Stippled Scroll & Prism, goblet, gr, 5" 30.00
Stripe, bowl, wht... 60.00
Stripe (Wide), cruet, wht 175.00
Sunburst-on-Shield (Diadem), creamer, bl 100.00
Swag w/Brackets, bowl, master; bl... 85.00
Swag w/Brackets, spooner, gr.. 80.00
Swirl, cruet, red, tri-fold rim, camphor hdl, clear stopper, Hobbs, 7"..225.00
Swirl, custard cup, cranberry 75.00
Swirl, finger lamp, wht..350.00
Swirling Maze, bowl, salad; gr... 90.00
Target Swirl, tumbler, cranberry 95.00
Thousand Eye, celery vase, wht...100.00
Thousand Eye, sugar bowl, wht 100.00
Three Fruits & Meander, bowl, wht, ftd................................ 65.00
Tokyo, compote, jelly; wht 30.00
Tokyo, creamer, gr... 65.00
Tokyo, vase, bl... 55.00
Tree of Love, plate, wht, 2 szs, rare, ea 135.00
Twigs, vase, bl, sm, 5½" 65.00
Twigs, vase, vaseline or cranberry, panelled, 7"..................... 85.00
Twist (Miniatures), sugar bowl, vaseline or canary 150.00
Twister, bowl, bl.. 50.00
Twister, plate, bl..100.00
Victoria & Albert, butter dish, wht..110.00
War of Roses, compote, bl, w/metal stand.............................150.00

Water Lily & Cattails, relish, gr, hdls...................................... 60.00
Waves, plate, novelty; gr..100.00
Wild Bouquet, spooner, gr 150.00
Wild Grapes, bowl, wht 40.00
Wild Rose, bowl, banana; amethyst 80.00
William & Mary, cake plate, bl, stemmed 150.00
Windows (Plain), bottle, bitters; cranberry 325.00
Windows (Swirled), cruet, cranberry, clear hdl/faceted stopper, 7" ..325.00
Windows (Swirled), mustard jar, wht 55.00
Windows (Swirled), tumbler, bl 85.00
Wishbone & Drapery, plate, gr 60.00
Wreath & Shell, celery vase, bl..225.00
Wreath & Shell, spooner, bl...130.00
Zipper & Loops, vase, bl, ftd.. 65.00

Opaline

A type of semiopaque opal glass, opaline was made in white as well as pastel shades and is often enameled. It is similar in appearance to English Bristol glass, though its enamel or gilt decorative devices tend to exhibit a French influence.

Bottle, dresser; appl cameo portrait w/gold, ca 1880, 8" 100.00
Bottle, scent; HP scene on turq, gilt-brass mts & fr 295.00
Box, medallion w/peasants on pk, egg form, brass mts, PMB, 4" ..300.00

Dresser box, Russian peasants in carriage, ormolu feet, $350.00.
(Photo courtesy Early Auction Co.)

Jewel casket, HP floral/jewels on wht, hinged lid, 3½x4½x3½"....695.00
Pitcher, HP floral, cobalt hdl, ca 1900, 8½", +3 matching cups ...525.00
Vase, HP floral on wht, gourd form, 12"..195.00

Orient & Flume

A Victorian home built in the late 1890s between Orient and Flume streets in Chico, California, was purchased by Douglas Boyd in 1972 and converted into a glass studio. Due to his on-going success in producing fine, contemporary art glass reminiscent of masters such as Tiffany, Loetz, and Steuben, the business flourished and about a year later had become so successful that larger quarters were required nearby. Today, examples of their workmanship are found in museums and galleries all over the world.

Bottle, scent; pk orchid cased in crystal, G Held, 7", +box 260.00
Figurine, bear, bl irid, GGT3, w/label, 3"......................................200.00
Vase, Acorn, gr oak leaves on gold, gr int, dk irid ft, 10", +box ...635.00
Vase, bamboo stems/butterflies, paperweight, Sillars/Beyers, 11", +box..725.00
Vase, Black-eyed Susan cased in crystal, 6", +box 400.00
Vase, calla lily bouquet in crystal, paperweight type, Beyers, 7", +box..365.00
Vase, echinacea blossoms in crystal, B Sillars, 6", +orig box 345.00
Vase, fish/seagrass cased in crystal, S Beyers, 7", +box 345.00

Water Lily, bonbon dish, blue, rare shape, $36.00. (Photo courtesy Bill Edwards and Mike Carwile)

Water Lily & Cattails, bonbon, amethyst 45.00
Water Lily & Cattails, bonbon, bl... 45.00

Vase, gold, shouldered bowl form w/incurvate rim, 2¼" H, +box... 65.00
Vase, Hawthorne, millefiori style on bl, shouldered, 10", +box.... 750.00
Vase, Hawthorne on crystal, paperweight type, 6¾", +box........... 250.00
Vase, irises on crystal, ftd, E Alexander, 10", +box 285.00
Vase, orchids, bl/wine in crystal, paperweight type, G Held, 6", +box..230.00
Vase, pk dogwood on crystal, G Held, sgn/#d, 5½", +box............. 635.00
Vase, pk orchids on crystal, paperweight type, G Held, 6", +box .. 150.00
Vase, red dogwood on heavy crystal, paperweight type, G Held, 6", +box...265.00
Vase, red fuchsias/gr stems in clear, paperweight type, 7", +box... 285.00
Vase, red irises on cobalt cased, bulbous, E Alexander, 7½", +box.635.00
Vase, strawberries in cased crystal, spherical, E Alexander, 5", +box..145.00
Vase, strawberries on cobalt, paperweight type, E Alexander, 5", +box..325.00

Orientalia

The art of the Orient is an area of collecting currently enjoying strong collector interest, not only in those examples that are truly 'antique' but in the twentieth-century items as well. Because of the many aspects involved in a study of Orientalia, we can only try through brief comments to acquaint the reader with some of the more readily available examples. We suggest you refer to specialized reference sources for more detailed information. See also specific categories.

Key:
Ch — Chinese   hdwd — hardwood
cvg — carving   Jp — Japan
drw — drawer   Ko — Korean
Dy — Dynasty   lcq — lacquer
E — export   mdl — medallion
FR — Famille Rose   rswd — rosewood
FV — Famille Verte   tkwd — teakwood
gb — guard border

Blanc de Chine

Bowl, flowering prunus branch, thick stem & ft, 18th C, 12½".. 1,350.00
Cup, rhino horn shape w/relief pine/prunus/dragon/etc, 18th C, 5"...500.00
Figurine, Guandi Kangxi, snake & tortoise in front of him, 7⅞"...3,200.00
Figurine, Madonna & Child on cloud base, Kangxi, 15"...........4,000.00

Blue and White Porcelain

Bowl, floral, ftd, Aria Ware, Jp, 19th C, 6x8¾"............................. 800.00
Bowl, horse & waves mdl, floral reserves, Ch, Ming Dy, 5½" 355.00
Bowl, South Sea Island scene, geometric border, 1910, 6½" H 400.00
Bowl, stylized floral scrolls, Ch, 1821-51, sm rpr, 6"................... 525.00
Brush pot, figures in landscape, cylindrical, 18th C, 7¼x8".......2,350.00
Garden seat, dragons/flowers, pierced coins, Ch, 19th C, 19", pr..2,235.00
Jar, Hundred Antiques, cracked ice ground, 1662-1722, 9½" 1,000.00
Plate, floral, Hundred Antiques, Ch, 18th C, 9", pr 595.00
Tureen, floral motifs/borders, peach finial, 1770, 13" L.............. 1,175.00
Vase, cobalt flowers, elephant mask hdls, Ch'ien Lung era, 10½".. 12,925.00
Vase, Ku form w/Hua decor at mouth & ft, Immortals, 17th C, 14"..3,800.00
Vase, 8 Precious Emblems/lotus, mask hdls, Ch, ca 1800, 19" ... 1,295.00

Bronze

Buddha, X-legged figure w/brass finish, 8½" 900.00
Drums, ritual; archaic form, 18x22" 4,100.00
Figure, Quan Yin, elaborate bird headdress, holding lotus, ftd, 42"...8,225.00
Figure, seated Buddha, gr/brn patina, 21x12"............................. 900.00
Figure, seated Quan Yin, cloisonne robe, 22½" 825.00
Figure, warrior standing w/hands clasped, gilt/red pnt, 1700s, 15"...500.00

Jardiniere, encircled with a dragon, Meiji Period, 37" diameter, $3,000.00. (Photo courtesy Neal Auction Co. Auctioneers & Appraisers of Fine Art & Antiques)

Mirror, landscape/cranes/turtles, straw-wrap hdl, mk, 1800s, 7" dia....275.00
Temple bell, mythological figure hdl, allover relief, Meiji Dy, 18"...850.00
Urn, dragonfly/botanical relief, Meiji Dy, 9", EX 900.00

Celadon

Censer, dk gray-gr, tripod ft, pierced brass lid, Jp, 19th C, 5x4" ... 325.00
Plate, foliate edge, exposed brick red, brn ft, ca 1735-96, 9½" ..3,000.00
Vase, eng lotus flowers/clouds, Maebyong, Ko, 12th C, rpr, 14".. 16,450.00
Vase, pear shape w/animal mask rings, Lung Chuan, Ming Dy, 9¾"...700.00
Vase, pear shape w/flared rim, emb/eng decor, Ch, 6¼" 175.00

Furniture

Armchair, teakwood, carved bats on knees, dragon arms and back (ivory signature panel below), 45", $575.00. (Photo courtesy Garth's Auctions Inc.)

Armchair, rswd, bk splat cvd w/peaches, Ch, late 19th C 200.00
Cabinet, altar; Huang Hua Li w/rtcl panels, 2-door, 18th C, 34x36" .. 2,235.00
Cabinet, cvd/lcq 2-door type w/simple cvgs, Ch, late 1800s, 54x39x18" ... 450.00
Cabinet, K'ang; Huang Hua Li, 5-drw, dbl doors, 17th C, 18x56x15"..825.00
Cabinet, K'ang; Hung Mu w/butterfly brasses, Ch, 18th C, 7x56x5".. 700.00
Cabinet, russet lcq, iron mts, Jp, ca 1900, 35x41x15"................... 475.00
Cabinet, single case type w/iron mts, Jp, late 19th C, 40x45x16" ...300.00
Chair, side; Huang Hua Li w/cane seats, Ch, 18th C, pr 18,800.00
Chairs, official's hat; cane seats, much cvg, Ch, 17th C, 47", pr ..99,500.00
Coffee table, tkwd, floral aprons, soapstone inserts, Ch, 20x36x23"...300.00
Desk, rswd, pedestal type w/3 sections, Ch, 19th C, 34x54x23"... 880.00
Screen, 4-panel (ea 38x19"), cvd wood w/ivory/MOP/horn/lcq scenes, Jp..2,950.00
Screen, 4-panel: bl w/mc flowers & birds, brass-capped ft, 72" 460.00
Screen, 6-panel, w/cvd figures HP on blk lcq, 20th C, 72x102" 515.00
Screen, 8-panel: cvd/mc battle scenes, bk: court scene, 70x126"...7,000.00
Stool, rswd, horse-hoof ft, Ch, 19th C 235.00
Table, game; teakwood/faux bamboo, 1910, 32x38x38" 2,000.00
Table, Huang Hua Li, molded tray top/folding base w/scrolls, 28x29x18"....2,350.00
Table, painting; Huang Hua Li Hunah bk braces, Ch, 17th C, 34x70x33"..44,650.00
Table, russet lcq, scroll legs, brass mts, Jp, 18th C, 24x32x12" 385.00
Tables, gilt & red lcq, early 20th C, tallest: 28", nesting set of 4..550.00

Hardstones

Amethyst, cvg, peaches & children, Ch, 19th C, 6" 765.00
Jade, censer, celadon, pierced top w/cvd flowers, mask rings, Ch, 6x8"..5,580.00
Jade, cup stand, gray w/straitions, archaic dragons, Ch, Ming Dy, 7"..2,250.00
Jade, cvg, celadon, dragon, Ch, Ming Dy, 4" 825.00
Jade, cvg, celadon w/brn, caparisoned horse, Ch, 19th C, 4" ...3,525.00
Jade, cvg, celadon w/brn, kylin w/bow in mouth & cub beside, Ch, 5"...5,285.00
Jade, cvg, wht w/russet mks, conjoined cups w/mask hdls, Ch, 3" .. 1,295.00
Jade, cvg, yel-gr, pr of rams, 5½" 700.00

Jade, group of three gods, polished, with wood base, 21", $465.00. (Photo courtesy Jackson's International Auctioneers & Appraisers of Fine Art & Antiques)

Jade, jar, med gray, cranes/rams, w/lid, Ch, ca 1800, 3¾"...........7,650.00
Jade, jardiniere, gr, stylized cloud/scrolls, Asia, 8x12", pr 800.00
Jade, nephrite; cvg, figure on rock/monkey/tiger, gray mottle, 2⅜".. 750.00
Jade, panel, translucent wht, 3 Buddhist symbols, 19th C, 4¾x3¼"...825.00
Jade, paperweight, celadon, mtn w/pines, Ch, 19th C, 4" 150.00
Jade, vase, gray-wht, sq w/Kylin hdl, Ch, 18th C, 6½" 3,815.00
Jade, vase, lt gr, lotus flowers/Buddha's-hand citrons, Ch, 19th C, 6".. 2,585.00
Jade, water coupe, gray, bamboo/pine/prunus friezes, Ch, 19th C, 8" .. 585.00
Marble, fragment, Buddhist divinity in relief, Ch, ca 618-920, 7"...400.00
Rose quartz, cvg, Hsi Wang Mu w/peach branch & peacock, 1900s, 12"..325.00

Netsukes

A netsuke is a miniature Japanese carving made with two holes called the Himitoshi, either channeled or within the carved design. As kimonos (the outer garment of the time) had no pockets, the Japanese man hung his pipe, tobacco pouch, or other daily necessities from his waist sash. The most highly valued accessory was a nest of little drawers called an Inro, in which they carried snuff or sometimes opium. The netsuke was the toggle that secured them. Although most are of ivory, others were made of bone, wood, metal, porcelain, or semiprecious stones. Some were inlaid or lacquered. They are found in many forms — figurals the most common, mythological beasts the most desirable. They range in size from 1" up to 3", which was the maximum size allowed by law. Many netsukes represented the owner's profession, religion, or hobbies. Scenes from the daily life of Japan at that time were often depicted in the tiny carvings. The more detailed the carving, the greater the value.

Careful study is required to recognize the quality of the netsuke. Many have been made in Hong Kong in recent years; and even though some are very well carved, these are considered copies and avoided by the serious collector. There are many books that will help you learn to recognize quality netsukes, and most reputable dealers are glad to assist you. Use your magnifying glass to check for repairs. In the listings that follow, netsukes are ivory unless noted otherwise; 'stain' indicates a color wash.

Demon snatching fan from Okame's hand, 19th C, 2¼" 475.00
Dutchman holding rooster, red stain, ca 1800, 4" 1,295.00
Kinko sennin on carp, sgn Seiichi, red stain, 19th C, 2" 880.00
Kinko sennin on carp, staghorn, 19th C, 2½" 175.00

Manju type w/pierced gourds, 19th C, 2" 125.00
Mask, artist sgn, 19th C, 1½"... 175.00
Miller w/2 children, late 19th C, 1¾" 585.00
Mouse nibbling on candle, 19th C,½" 560.00
Okame drinking in her bath, 19th C, 1" 385.00
Shoki smoking pipe w/demon, Hakumei, 19th C, 1½" 265.00

Porcelain

Chinese export ware was designed to appeal to Western tastes and was often made to order. During the eighteenth century, vast amounts were shipped to Europe and on westward. Much of this fine porcelain consisted of dinnerware lines that were given specific pattern names. Rose Mandarin, Fitzhugh, Armorial, Rose Medallion, and Canton are but a few of the more familiar.

Basket, scenic w/nobles, gilt bands, rtcl sides, 1795, +11" rtcl stand...7,050.00
Candlestick, E, FR, widely spaced florals & insects, 1760s, 11", ea.....1,175.00
Charger, E, FR, flower vase/reserves/chrysanthemums, 1850s, 13½"..1,100.00
Cup, E, flower tree w/orange border, strap hdl, dome lid, 1800s, 7 for...980.00
Figurine, immortal, E, FR, yel robe, w/peach spray, on base, 1880, 9"...240.00
Figurine, Kylin w/child (& 1 w/ft on ball) on ped, turq, 1890, 12", pr..530.00
Jug, cider; armorial/floral sprigs, bl/mc on wht, twist hdl, 8x7"..1,880.00
Pitcher, E, FR, outdoor genre scene w/gilt, ftd, 1760, 9".............. 415.00
Plate, E, armorial, floral center, sprigs on flat rim, 1770s, 9"......... 650.00
Plate, E, armorial (att Blunt), floral border, 8-sided, 7½".............. 650.00
Plate, E, FR, court scene reserve, floral border, 19th C, 11" 615.00
Platter, E, FR, floral sprays/gilt borders 1700s, 13x10" 825.00
Punch bowl, E, Cabbage, Ch, late 19th C, 6½x16" 1,880.00
Punch bowl, E, crests/florals w/gold, Ch, 18th C, 6x14"...........2,000.00
Punch bowl, floral mdls, banded rim, bl on wht, 1800s, 14", VG. 885.00
Shakers, butterflies on wht, fluted bell form, 1900, 3", pr 300.00
Teapot, butterfly frieze, gilt, squat oval form, 1900, 5x6".............. 370.00
Teapot, E, continuous genre scene, lobed baluster, 1730, 5x3".....415.00

Temple jars, flowering tree and peacocks by waterfall, block chop mark, 19", EX, $3,450.00 for the pair. (Photo courtesy Jackson's International Auctioneers & Appraisers of Fine Art & Antiques)

Vase, continuous dragon/floral decor on turq, 1890, 10x7" 645.00
Vase, E, panels of Immortals on turq, rtcl, 1850s, 9x5"................ 550.00
Vase, FR, floral/gilt on sq body w/can neck, ormolu ft, 14", pr .. 1,750.00
Vase, scenic w/nobles/bldgs, sm floral reserves, w/lid, 1775, 23x10"..3,400.00
Vase, 3 rows of elaborately robed figures, mc on wht, hdls, 1800s, 17"..850.00

Rugs

The 'Oriental' or Eastern rug market has enjoyed a renewal of interest as collectors have become aware of the fact that some of the semi-antique rugs (those 60 to one 100 years old) may be had at a price within the range of the average buyer. Unless noted otherwise, values are for rugs in excellent or better condition.

Bidjar, 6-sided mdl on red w/allover mc pattern, late 20th C, 100x80" .. 575.00
Bokara, repeated central motif, bl on red, 116x62" 470.00
Caucasian Soumak, repeating dmns, bl/pk on rose, 1910, 80x62" .. 1,560.00

Cloud Band Karabaugh, ivory border and blue medallions on salmon, 56x73", $3,680.00. (Photo courtesy Garth's Auctions Inc.)

Dagestan, people/roosters/horses on red, mc borders, 63x51" 7,200.00
Heriz, dk bl border, ivory spandrels on red, 208x116" 2,875.00
Heriz, lg mdl in rose on red w/ivory corners, 144x108" 865.00
Heriz, 3 mdls on red, Herati border, semi-antique, 60x72" 1,765.00
Kashan, lt plum w/dk bl borders, lt wear, 215x109" 3,450.00
Kashan, red w/lg mdl, 7 gb, late 20th C, 156x112" 750.00
Kazak, geometric borders w/bl mdl on red, lt wear, 56x44" 1,495.00
Kermin, lg red mdl, outer portion w/allover pattern, 150x110", VG .. 635.00
Mashad, floral mdl on dk bl w/floral spray, 3 gb, 1960s, 156x112" ... 750.00
Melez, red primary & multiple borders, red ground, rprs, 67x44" .. 2,415.00
NW Persia, gr spandrels on rust w/ivory border, 129x44" 700.00
Persian Qashqai, serrated/floral mdls on red/bl, 98x60" 1,000.00
Persian Serapi, lg mdl w/geometrics, red/ivory/bl, antique, 190x108" . 22,325.00
Persian Serapi, serrated/floral mdls, red/bl/ivory/blk, 250x190" .. 1,527.00
Sarouk, burgundy ground w/wide midnight bl borders, 77x48" .. 1,550.00
Sarouk, red w/flower design, wide blk border, 1960s, 94x30", EX .. 345.00
Sarouk, wine w/allover floral & 2 lg mdls, 196 knots per inch, 78x50" ... 800.00
Sarouk type, bl w/allover floral, 3 gb, 144 knots per inch, 60x37", G .. 800.00
Sarouk type, bl w/floral groups, floral gb, 144 knots per inch, 79x51" ... 3,565.00
Sarouk type, sq w/lg floral mdl, 144 knots per inch, 45x45", VG 1,150.00
Serapi, Abrash red border, salmon spandrels on ivory gb, 166x120" ... 24,150.00
Shiraz, geometric mdl on red, late 20th C, 113x80" 1,100.00
Shirvan, wide bl primary border, ivory ground, 70x43" 1,500.00
Tabriz, ivory w/trees & flowers, lg mdl, 1950s, 152x115", VG 230.00
Tabriz, red w/allover flowers, mutiple gb, 120x98" 635.00

Snuff Bottles

The Chinese were introduced to snuff in the seventeenth century, and their carved and painted snuff bottles typify their exquisite taste and workmanship. These small bottles, seldom measuring over 2½", were made of amber, jade, ivory, and cinnabar; tiny spoons were often attached to their stoppers. By the eighteenth century, some were being made of porcelain, others were of glass with delicate interior designs tediously reverse painted with minuscule brushes sometimes containing a single hair. Copper and brass were used but to no great extent.

Agate, rnd form, carnelian & silver stopper, Ch, 19th C, 2¼" 175.00
Amber w/dk swirls, well hollowed, Ch, 19th C, 2¼" 250.00
Amethyst, relief phoenixes & flowers, Ch, early 1900s, 2¾" 355.00
Cloisonne, dragons & flowers on turq, Ch'ien Lung mk, 2¼" 500.00
Cloisonne, dragons on red, cylindrical, Ch, 19th C, 2¾" 825.00
Cloisonne, Hundred Antiques, flattened rectangle, 2¼" 1,175.00
Cloisonne, phoenixes/foo dogs/garnet/seed pearl, flattened form .. 325.00
Jade, gr w/scholars & mystical pavilion, Ch, ca 1800, 2½" 995.00
Jade, lt celadon color w/coral glass stopper, 19th C, 2½" 4,995.00
Jade w/pebble-skin area & cvd Immortal, coral lid, Ch, 19th C, 2" ... 880.00
Milk glass w/HP birds/flowers, Ku Yuch Hsuan type, 19th C, 2" 1,525.00
MOP, cvd boatman/farmer scenes, Ch, ca 1900, 2¼" 585.00
Peking glass, yel w/eng poems & gold inlay, 2" 1,050.00
Pk over butterscotch glass, kylin design, Ch, ca 1900, 2" 355.00
Porc, pebble shape w/HP butterflies, coral stopper, Ch, 19th C, 2¼" .. 585.00
Rock crystal, eng orchids & lotus, well hollowed, Ch, 19th C, 2¼" ... 125.00
Rock crystal, lion mask hdls, finely hollowed, Ch, 19th C, 2" 525.00
Silver, Ju-i shape w/inlaid gold wire characters, 19th C, 2½" 500.00
Silver w/enamel decor, 2-compartment, hinged, Ch, 19th C, 1½" ... 565.00
Smoky quartz, finely hollowed, tourmaline stopper, 19th C, 2¼" .. 175.00

Textiles

Coat & trousers, orange silk w/embr, Ch, 19th C 100.00
Panel, castle scene w/boats/water wheel, Jp, 19th C, 33x27" 4,400.00
Panel, gold embr on blk, Mihrab, India, 19th C, 84x41" 125.00
Panel, mc flowers w/metal threads & lacework, Turkey, 19th C, 70x15" ... 1,100.00
Robe, bl silk w/embr gold dragons, Ch, 19th C 4,400.00
Robe, gold brocade silk w/bl figures, Jp, 19th C, VG 355.00
Robe, orange silk w/floral embr, Ch, early 20th C 450.00

Woodblock Prints

Framed prints are of less value than those not framed, since it is impossible to inspect their condition or determined whether or not they have borders or have been trimmed.

Asakusa Kinryusan Temple, Hiroshige, ca 1856, 21x17" 115.00
Bamboo Wood, Yoshida Hiroshi, ca 1939, 16¼x11" 800.00
Chrysanthemum, Ohno Bakufu, 20th C, 15⅛x10¼" 300.00
Fish (5), S Watanabe, 1961 ltd ed, 18x21½" 480.00
Ichicawa Sadaniji as K Narukami, Natori Shunsen, 1926, 16x11" ... 725.00
In a Temple Yard, Yoshida, 1935, 16x10⅝" 540.00
Maruyama Park in Kyoto, Yoshida Hiroshi, 10⅝x16" 425.00
Moonlight by River Tama, Hiroshige, ca 1838, 17⅜x21⅜" 350.00
Pomegranite & Parrot, Ohara Koson, 1920s, 10⅜x7⅜" 450.00
Ryogoka in E Capital, A Hiroshige, ca 1858, 14x9" 385.00

Samurai with Geisha, Tutgawa Toyokuni (1769 – 1825), with seal, 13x9½", $235.00. (Photo courtesy Leslie Hindman)

Stage Town Nagakubo, Hiroshige, 19th C, 7x11"+18x24" fr 150.00
Sumo Wrestlers, Utagawa Kunisada/Toyokuni III, 1850, 8x16" ... 400.00
Yotsuya, evening landscape, Tschucya Koitsu, 1935, 15⅝x10½" .. 480.00

Orrefors

Orrefors Glassworks was founded in 1898 in the Swedish province of Smaaland. Utilizing the expertise of designers such as Simon Gate, Edward Hald, Vicke Lindstrand, and Edwin Ohrstrom, it produced art glass of the highest quality. Various techniques were used in achieving the decoration. Some were wheel engraved; others were blown through a unique process that formed controlled bubbles or air pockets resulting in unusual patterns and shapes. (Remember: When no color is noted, the glass is crystal.)

Bottle, scent; melon form, elongated stopper, 8½" 145.00
Bowl, nude/flora, E Hald, rectangular, 8" 175.00
Bowl, Ravenna, trapped rectangles/1 in bl surround, Palmqvist, '53, 7" ... 765.00
Vase, Ariel, girl & dove, bl in clear w/amber, Ohrstrom, #292-E3, 7" ... 2,115.00
Vase, Ariel, int bl bubbles, rows of various szs, Lundin, #4361, 6x4" 1,725.00
Vase, bl netting in clear, Palmqvist, Kraka #526, 8¾" 500.00
Vase, clear w/bl int decor & bubbles, S Palmqvist, #322, 11⅞" 940.00
Vase, dk gray cased, ovoid w/long neck, #3538/173, 11½" 300.00
Vase, Graal, bl int decor, I Lundin, D275-67, 6" 1,525.00

Vase, Kraka, clear with blue interior decoration, controlled bubbles, Sven Palmqvist, #322, 12", $1,140.00. (Photo courtesy Skinner Inc. Auctioneers & Appraisers of Antiques & Fine Art)

Vase, ovoid w/long neck, smoke in clear, #3538/173, 11½" 225.00
Vase, seminude dancer w/veiled skirt etched, sgn/#256B4D, 14" .. 890.00
Vase, Thunderstorm, cobalt, detailed scene, E Hald, #1914-44, 4⅝" .. 1,525.00

Ott and Brewer

The partnership of Ott and Brewer began in 1865 in Trenton, New Jersey. By 1876 they were making decorated graniteware, parian, and 'ivory porcelain' — similar to Irish Belleek though not as fine and of different composition. In 1883, however, experiments toward that end had reached a successful conclusion, and a true Belleek body was introduced. It came to be regarded as the finest china ever produced by an American firm. The ware was decorated by various means such as hand painting, transfer printing, gilding, and lustre glazing. The company closed in 1893, one of many that failed during that depression. In the listings below, the ware is Belleek unless noted otherwise. Our advisor for this category is Mary Frank Gaston; she is listed in the Directory under Texas.

Bust of Jesus, parian, Isaac Broome, 1876, 16x9" 3,600.00
Ewer, orchid, bl on wht w/gold, rtcl hdl/base/neck ring, 17x8" ... 2,280.00
Pitcher, floral w/gold, water lily hdl, gourd shape, 9¼x7½" 1,000.00
Vase, bird on branch (detailed), pastels/gold on gr matt, 10x6" .. 7,200.00
Vase, floral/gilt, ovoid w/rtcl basket hdl, 4 ft, lid gone/rstr, 14x8" 840.00
Vase, nasturtiums on cobalt, gilt filigree hdls, 10x7½" 6,250.00
Vase, tea roses, mc w/gold on wht, gold dolphin-head hdls, rstr, 18" ... 900.00

Overbeck

Four genteel ladies set up the Overbeck pottery around 1911 in the unlikely area of Cambridge City, Indiana. Margaret, Hannah, Elizabeth, and Mary would produce high-quality hand-thrown vases featuring vertical panels excised with floral, landscape, or figural decoration, at first with an Arts & Crafts stylization, then moving on to a more modern, Art Deco geometry. Mary, holding up the fort starting in 1937, increasingly turned to the production of hand-sized figurines in period dress, which she would often give to children visiting the pottery. The operation closed in 1955. Most vases and figurines are stamped OBK, sometimes with the addition of a first-name initial. In the last couple of years, some convincing copies have been appearing on the market. Collectors should buy with a guarantee of authenticity or otherwise take their chances. Our advisors for this category are Suzanne Perrault and David Rago; they are listed in the Directory under New Jersey.

Bowl, stylized floral cvg, caramel matt, Mary Frances, 2x6" 2,400.00
Drawing, pen/ink, Calendar 1903: Salvia, mat/fr, Hannah, 8x5" ..2,280.00
Drawing, pen/ink, frog fruit plant, Hannah, mat/fr, 11x3½" 4,200.00
Figurine, dog panting, wht w/blk & brn spots, 3" 480.00
Figurine, farmer's wife w/apples in basket, goggle eyes, 4¼" 535.00
Figurine, farmer w/watermelon, brn floppy hat, 5⅛" 700.00
Figurine, lady in pk w/umbrella, 4¼" 240.00
Figurine, man in frock coat w/top hat, OBK, 4" 250.00
Figurine, Southern belle, bl w/red, OBK, 3⅜" 265.00
Figurine, Southern belle w/goggle eyes, OBK, 4⅛" 315.00
Figurines, Geo & Martha Washington, OBK, 3⅞", 3⅜", pr........2,280.00
Pitcher, stylized floral, bl-gray on lt brn matt, OBK/F, 4¾x9½" ..3,600.00
Vase, birds/floral, rose cut bk to ivory, E/MF, 5x3½" 6,000.00
Vase, floral, cvd/pnt, mauve/gr on tan, 2½x2¾" 6,000.00
Vase, floral, pastel on tan, E/H bruise/line, 11⅞" 13,800.00
Vase, floral panels, gr on taupe, OBK/E, 4½x3¼" 2,850.00
Vase, pine cones, Mustard & gr, Elizabeth & Hannah, E/H, 8¾x4¾"............$16,800.00

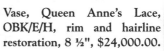

Vase, Queen Anne's Lace, OBK/E/H, rim and hairline restoration, 8 ½", $24,000.00. (Photo courtesy David Rago Auctions)

Overshot

Overshot glass originated in sixteenth century Venice, and the ability to make this ware eventually spread to Bohemia, Spain, and elsewhere in Europe. Sometime prior to 1800, the production of this glass seems to have stopped. The Englishman Apsley Pellatt, owner of the Falcon Glass Works, is credited with reviving this decorative technique around 1845 – 1850. He acknowledged the origin of this technique by calling his product 'Venetian Frosted Glass' or 'Anglo-Venetian Glass.' Later it would be called by other names, such as Frosted Glassware, Ice Glass, or Craquelle Glass.

It is important to understand the difference between crackle glass and overshot glass. All crackle is not overshot, and all overshot is not crackle. However, most overshot is also crackle glass. Two different processes or steps were involved in making this glassware.

Crackle glass was produced by dipping a partially blown gob of hot glass in cold water. The sudden temperature change caused fissures or cracks in the glass surface. The gob was then lightly reheated and blown into its full shape. The blowing process enlarged the spaces between fissures to create a labyrinth of channels in varying widths. When cooled in the annealing lehr, the surface of the finished object had a crackled or cracked-ice effect.

Overshot glass was made by rolling a partially inflated gob of hot glass on finely ground shards of glass that had been placed on a steel plate called a marver. The gob was then lightly reheated to remove the sharp edges of the ground glass and blown to its final shape. Most overshot pieces were immersed in cold water before application of the ground glass, and such glassware can be considered both crackle and overshot. Sometimes an object was blown to full size before being rolled over the glass shards. As Barlow and Kaiser explained in *The Glass Industry in Sandwich, Vol. 4*, 'The ground particles adhered uniformly over the entire surface of the piece, showing no roadways, because the glass was not stretched after the particles had been applied. Overshot glass produced by this second method is much sharper to the touch' (page 104). Overshot glass produced by the first method — with the 'roadways' — has been mistaken for the Tree of Life Pattern. However, this pattern is pressed glass, whereas overshot is either free-blown or mold-blown. Overshot pieces could be further embellished, requiring a third decorative technique at the furnace, such as the application of vaseline glass designs or fine threads of glass that were picked up and fused to the object. The latter decorative style, called Peloton, was patented in 1880 by Wilhelm Kralik in Bohemia.

Boston & Sandwich, Reading Artistic Glass Works, and Hobbs Brockunier were among the companies that manufactured overshot in the United States. Such products were quite utilitarian — vases, decanters, cruets, bowls, water pitchers with ice bladders, lights, lamps, and other shapes. Colored overshot was produced at Sandwich, but research has shown that the applied ground glass was always crystal. Czechoslovakia is known to have made overshot with colored ground glass. Many such pieces are acid stamped 'Czechoslovakia.' Undamaged, mint-condition overshot is extremely hard to find and expensive. Our advisors for this category are Stan and Arlene Weitman; they are listed in the Directory under New York.

Atomizer, melon ribbed swags/HP flowers w/gold, cranberry flashed, 5"... 60.00
Basket, appl rope hdls, 6½x10½" L 425.00
Basket, cranberry to clear, thorn hdl, rectangular, 10x7½" 750.00

Bowl, crystal with red snake on lid, with underplate, ca. 1880s, 5½" tall, from $850.00 to $1,000.00. (Photo courtesy Stan and Arlene Weitman)

Bowl, rubena, on wht metal ped ft, 6½x8½" 180.00
Compote, tall ft, 7¼x6¾" 475.00
Goblet, blown, gold rim, 6" 20.00
Pitcher, bl, bulbous body, bl hdl, 7¼" 525.00
Pitcher, champagne; cranberry, clear hdl & rigaree, ice bladder, 12"... 500.00

Pitcher, cranberry to clear, bulbous body, clear hdl, 5¼" 525.00
Pitcher, cranberry to clear, cylindrical, low hdl, 7" 750.00
Pitcher, lemonade; emb swirl, twist hdl, 9", +6 tumblers.............. 650.00
Pitcher, Sandwich, 4½"... 350.00
Pitcher, tankard; bright bl, amber rigaree rim/reed hdl, Sandwich, 10"...285.00
Pitcher, tankard; cranberry, clear reeded hdl, 9⅜x4½"................. 995.00
Pitcher, tankard; cylindrical, appl rigaree at opening, 10¼" 950.00
Pitcher, wine; wht, slim elegant form w/clear ft, 11½"................... 875.00
Rose bowl, amethyst, clear thorn legs, 5x4½" 425.00
Rose bowl, rubena, 6x5" 275.00
Tumbler, gr to clear, 3¾x2¾" 100.00
Tumbler, rubena 145.00
Vase, clear w/appl vaseline flower, sq sides, vaseline ft, 12" 1,200.00
Vase, metallic gold, indented sides, slight twist to 6" neck, 10" 60.00

Owen, Ben; Master Potter

Ben Owen worked at the Jugtown Pottery of North Carolina from 1923 until it temporarily closed in 1959. He continued in the business in his own Plank Road Pottery, stamping his ware 'Ben Owen, Master Potter,' with many forms made by Lester Fanell Craven in the late 1960s. His pottery closed in 1972. He died in 1983 at the age of 81. The pottery was re-opened in 1981 under the supervision of Benjamin Wade Owen II. One of the principal potters was David Garner who worked there until about 1985. This pottery is still in operation today with Ben II as the main potter.

Bowl, centerpc; salt glaze w/cobalt int, Ben Owen III, 1993, 5x9½" .. 60.00
Bowl, Frogskin Green w/t'prints, circular stamp, 4x7¾" 180.00
Bowl, salt glaze w/dogwood decor, ftd, 2¾x8¾", NM.................... 360.00
Candlesticks, Frogskin Green, Ben Owen Master Potter, 11¾", pr ..450.00
Dish, orange, Ben Owen Master Potter, crazing/chip, 2½x12¼" 70.00
Jar, burnt orange, 4 open hdls, Ben Owen Master Potter, 12x8" ..510.00
Tureen, Tobacco Spit, domed lid w/acorn finial, strap hdls, chip, 12" ...275.00
Vase, foamy bl w/red highlights, egg shape, 6x4¾" 660.00
Vase, Frogskin Green, high shoulders, Ben Owen Master Potter, 8½" ..360.00
Vase, Hang Dynasty style, Chinese Blue w/strong red, hdls, 10½"..5,100.00
Vase, mottled foamy wht, egg shape, Ben Owen Master Potter, 4½"..325.00
Vase, runny bl w/scattered red, high shoulders, ...Master Potter, 8"..1,550.00

Owens Pottery

J. B. Owens founded his company in Zanesville, Ohio, in 1891, and until 1907, when the company decided to exert most of its energies in the area of tile production, made several quality lines of art pottery. His first line, Utopian, was a standard brown ware with underglaze slip decoration of nature studies, animals, and portraits. A similar line, Lotus, utilized lighter background colors. Henri Deux, introduced in 1900, featured incised Art Nouveau forms inlaid with color. In time, the Brush McCoy Pottery acquired many of Owens's molds and reproduced a line similar to Henri Deux, which they called Navarre. (Owens pieces were usually marked Henri Deux and have a heavier body and coarser feel to the glaze than similar McCoy pieces.) Other important lines were Opalesce, Rustic, Feroza, Cyrano, and Mission, examples of which are rare today. The factory burned in 1928, and the company closed shortly thereafter. Values vary according to the quality of the artwork and subject matter. Examples signed by the artist bring higher prices than those that are not signed. For further information we recommend *Owens Pottery Unearthed* by Kristy and Rick McKibben and Jeanette and Marvin Stofft. Mrs. Stofft is listed in the Directory under Indiana.

Aborigine, vase, abstracts, brn tones, JBO, #27, 5½" 135.00
Coralene Opalesce, pitcher, autumn leaves on gr w/gold beads, 12x6"...600.00

Coralene Opalesce, vase, bronzed flower on gr ground, Lessell, 6x4" .. 600.00
Feroza, vase, red lustre, hdls at shoulder, unmk, 7x7" 300.00
Henri Deux, vase, Nouveau maid, wide bottom flanked by 2 lg hdls, 12" 540.00
Lotus, vase, carnations, wht on shaded ground, F Ferrell, 13x3¾"...840.00
Lotus, vase, floral, purple & gr on wht, #220, X, 8⅝" 300.00
Matt Green, vase, emb swirls in panels, sq, unmk, 5¾x4" 250.00
Matt Green, vase, geometric band near rim, #218, 6½x5" 570.00
Matt Utopian, vase, autumn leaves on dk brn, C Excel, 14½x4½" ..450.00
Mission, vase, dk gr w/cold-pnt dk brn matt drips, oak stand, 12x5"..1,680.00
Soudaneze, vase, poppy, wht on blk, CL, #220, 8¾x5" 900.00
Tile, leaping stag/moon/pine trees, 4-color, 12x18", NM..........3,120.00
Tile, sailboat/waves, 6-color cuenca, 11½x18", EX 2,520.00

Tile, swans on water lily pond, 12x18", $5,100.00. (Photo courtesy David Rago Auctions)

Utopian, vase, carnations, rim rpr, 12x4¼" 180.00
Utopian, vase, horse's head, bottle shape, 8½x5", EX 1,080.00
Utopian, vase, pansies, cylindrical, #219, 8⅛" 95.00
Utopian, vase, roses, yel & orange on brn, #1069, 8", NM 120.00
Venetian, vase, emb sylized Nouveau floral, gold, hdls, 10x10".... 480.00

Paden City Glass

Paden City Glass Mfg. Co. was founded in 1916 in Paden City, West Virginia. It made both mold-blown and pressed wares and is most remembered today for its handmade lines in bright colors with fanciful etchings. A great deal of Paden City's business was in supplying decorating companies and fitters with glass; therefore, Paden City never identified their glass with a trademark of any kind, and the company's advertisements were limited to trade publications, rather than retail. In 1948 the management of the company opened a second plant to make utilitarian, machine-made wares such as tumblers and ashtrays, but the move was ill-advised due to a glut of similar merchandise already on the market. The company remained in operation until 1951 when it permanently closed the doors of both factories as a result of the losses incurred by Plant No. 2. (To clear up an often-repeated misunderstanding, dealers and collectors alike should keep in mind that The Paden City Glass Mfg Co. had absolutely no connection with the Paden City Pottery Company, other than their identical locale.)

Today Paden City is best known for its numerous acid-etched wares that featured birds, but many other ornate etchings were produced. Fortunately several new books on the subject have been published, which have provided names for and increased awareness of previously undocumented etchings. Currently, collectors especially seek out examples of Paden City's most detailed etching, Orchid, and its most appealing etching, Cupid. Pieces in the company's plainer pressed dinnerware lines, however, have remained affordable, even though some patterns are quite scarce. After several years of rising prices, Internet auction sites have increased the supply of pieces with more commonly found etchings such as Peacock & Rose, causing a dip in prices. However, pieces bearing documented etchings on shapes and/or colors not previously seen combined continue to fetch high prices from advanced collectors.

Below is a list of Paden City's colors. Names in capital letters indicate original factory color names where known, followed by a description of the color.

Amber — several shades
Blue — early 1920s color, medium shade, not cobalt
Cheriglo — pink
Copen, Neptune, Ceylon — various shades of light blue
Crystal — clear
Ebony — black
Emeraldglo — thinner dark green, not as deep as Forest Green
Forest Green — dark green
Green — various shades, from yellowish to electric green
Mulberry — amethyst
Opal — white (milk glass)
Primrose — amber with reddish tint (rare)
Rose — dark pink (rare)
Royal or Ritz Blue — cobalt
Ruby — red
Topaz — yellow

Collectors seeking more information on Paden City would do well to consult the following: *Paden City, The Color Company*, by Jerry Barnett (out of print, privately published, 1979); *Colored Glassware of the Depression Era 2* by Hazel Marie Weatherman (Glassbooks, 1974); *Price Trends to Colored Glassware of the Depression Era 2* by Hazel Marie Weatherman (Glassbooks, Editions in 1977, 1979, and 1981). Also available are: *Paden City Company Catalog Reprints from the 1920s* (Antique Publications, 2000); *Paden City Glassware* by Paul and Debora Torsiello and Tom and Arlene Stillman (Schiffer, 2002); *Paden City Glass Company* by Walker, Bratkovich & Walker (Antique Publications, 2003); and *Encyclopedia of Paden City Glass* by Carrie and Gerald Domitz (Collector Books, 2004). There is also a quarterly newsletter currently being published by the Paden City Glass Collectors Guild; this group is listed the Directory under Clubs, Newsletters, and Catalogs. Our advisor for this category is Michael Krumme; he is listed in the Directory under California. If no color is listed, assume the item item to be crystal.

Ardith, amber, ice bucket, from $100 to 125.00
Ardith, blk, ivy ball, from $95 to.. 120.00
Ardith, blk, vase, 10", from $175 to 200.00
Ardith, Cheriglo or gr, creamer, from $50 to 65.00
Ardith, Cheriglo or gr, pitcher, 10", from $300 to 375.00
Ardith, Cheriglo or gr, tray, center hdl, 10¼", from $75 to 100.00
Ardith, cobalt or ruby, cup, from $85 to....................................... 100.00
Ardith, cobalt or ruby, plate, luncheon; 8½", from $75 to............. 85.00

Ardith, yellow, cup and saucer, from $85.00 to $95.00. (Photo courtesy Carrie and Jerry Domitz)

Black Forest (etched), amber, bowl, console; 11" 95.00
Black Forest (etched), amber, whipped cream pail 95.00
Black Forest (etched), blk, bowl, fruit; 11" 150.00
Black Forest (etched), blk, vase, 6½" 195.00
Black Forest (etched), crystal, batter jug.................................... 250.00
Black Forest (etched), gr, compote, low ft, 4" 75.00

Black Forest (etched), gr, plate, luncheon; 8" 40.00
Black Forest (etched), pk, champagne, 6-oz, 4¾" 30.00
Black Forest (etched), pk, pitcher, 80-oz, 9" 500.00
Black Forest (etched), pk, plate, hdls, 11" 65.00
Black Forest (etched), red, cup & saucer 175.00
Black Forest (etched), red, decanter, bulbous, stopper, 28-oz, 8½" ..395.00
Crow's Foot, amber, bowl, sq, 11" 30.00
Crow's Foot, amethyst, plate, rnd, 8" 4.50
Crow's Foot, blk, creamer, flat 6.50
Crow's Foot, crystal, bowl, sq, rolled edge, 11" 32.50
Crow's Foot, crystal, sugar bowl, flat 5.50
Crow's Foot, pk, cup, ftd 6.00
Crow's Foot, Ritz Blue, bowl, ftd, 10" 32.50
Crow's Foot, Ritz Blue, cup, flat 6.00
Crow's Foot, Ritz Blue, platter, 12" 15.00
Crow's Foot, Ritz Blue, vase, flared, 11¾" 70.00
Crow's Foot, Ruby Red, bowl, cream soup; ftd, flat 25.00
Crow's Foot, Ruby Red, creamer, ftd 12.50
Crow's Foot, Ruby Red, gravy boat, ped ft 140.00
Crow's Foot, Ruby Red, plate, dinner; 10½" 80.00
Crow's Foot, Ruby Red, saucer, rnd, 6" 3.50
Crow's Foot, Ruby Red, tumbler, 4¼" 75.00
Crow's Foot, yel, plate, 5¾" 2.00
Crow's Foot, yel, server, sandwich; rnd, center hdl 32.50
Crow's Foot, yel, vase, cupped, 10¼" 45.00
Cupid (etched), gr or pk, bowl, console; 11" 200.00
Cupid (etched), gr or pk, bowl, fruit; 10¼" 235.00
Cupid (etched), gr or pk, bowl, oval, ftd, 8½" 275.00
Cupid (etched), gr or pk, cake plate, 11¾" 215.00
Cupid (etched), gr or pk, compote, 6¼" 225.00
Cupid (etched), gr or pk, creamer, ftd, 5" 150.00
Cupid (etched), gr or pk, cup 225.00
Cupid (etched), gr or pk, ice bucket, 6" 325.00
Cupid (etched), gr or pk, plate, 10½" 150.00
Cupid (etched), gr or pk, saucer 50.00
Cupid (etched), gr or pk, sugar bowl, ftd, 5" 150.00
Cupid (etched), gr or pk, tray, oval, ftd, 10⅞" 250.00
Cupid (etched), gr or pk, vase, 10" 335.00
Delilah Bird, amber, yel or Primrose, bowl, ftd, 4½x11", $300 to. 400.00
Delilah Bird, amber, yel or Primrose, plate, hdls, 10", from $150 to ... 175.00
Delilah Bird, bl or ruby, bowl, berry; 4½", from $75 to 85.00
Delilah Bird, bl or ruby, cheese & cracker set, 10" plate, $250 to.... 300.00
Delilah Bird, bl or ruby, sugar bowl, 2¾", from $50 to 70.00
Delilah Bird, crystal, bowl, console; 12", from $125 to 150.00
Delilah Bird, crystal, candlestick, keyhole, 5", ea from $100 to ... 125.00
Delilah Bird, ebony, vase, 6", from $225 to 275.00
Delilah Bird, gr or pk, bowl, sq, w/hdls, 12", from $250 to 300.00
Delilah Bird, gr or pk, cup, from $65 to.................................... 85.00
Emerald Glo, Emerald Green, bowl, salad; w/metal base, fork & spoon ... 55.00
Emerald Glo, Emerald Green, bowl, salad; 10" 30.00
Emerald Glo, Emerald Green, casserole, w/metal lid 45.00
Emerald Glo, Emerald Green, cheese dish, w/metal lip & top 65.00
Emerald Glo, Emerald Green, ice bucket, w/metal holder & tongs... 70.00
Emerald Glo, Emerald Green, marmalade, w/metal lid & spoon.... 25.00
Emerald Glo, Emerald Green, server, w/metal-covered center, 5-part.. 65.00
Emerald Glo, Emerald Green, sugar bowl, w/metal lid & liner 25.00
Emerald Glo, Emerald Green, syrup, w/metal lid & liner 45.00
Gazebo (etched), bl, bowl, bead hdls, 9" 75.00
Gazebo (etched), bl, candleholders, dbl, #444, pr.......................... 50.00
Gazebo (etched), bl, candy dish, heart shape, w/lid..................... 250.00
Gazebo (etched), bl, cheese dish, w/lid, #555 .... 265.00
Gazebo (etched), bl, plate, bead hdls, 12½" 85.00
Gazebo (etched), bl, relish, 3-part, #555, 9¾" 65.00
Gazebo (etched), bl, server, center hdl, #555, 11" 85.00

Gazebo (etched), bl, vase, 12" 450.00
Gazebo (etched), crystal, bowl, fan hdls, 9" 42.00
Gazebo (etched), crystal, cake stand 55.00
Gazebo (etched), crystal, candy dish, clover shape, flat................ 85.00
Gazebo (etched), crystal, cocktail shaker, w/glass stopper 135.00
Gazebo (etched), crystal, creamer 20.00
Gazebo (etched), crystal, plate, 10¾" 40.00
Gazebo (etched), crystal, sugar bowl 20.00
Gazebo (etched), crystal, vase, 10¼" 95.00
Gothic Garden (etched), colors, bowl, ftd, 10" 90.00
Gothic Garden (etched), colors, bowl, oval, hdl, 10½" 110.00
Gothic Garden (etched), colors, bowl, tab hdl, 9" 75.00
Gothic Garden (etched), colors, cake plate, ftd, 10½" 85.00
Gothic Garden (etched), colors, candy dish, flat..................... 135.00
Gothic Garden (etched), colors, compote, deep top, tall 70.00
Gothic Garden (etched), colors, creamer 45.00
Gothic Garden (etched), colors, plate, tab hdl, 11" 65.00
Gothic Garden (etched), colors, sugar bowl 45.00
Largo, amber or crystal, ashtray, rectangular, 3" 16.00
Largo, amber or crystal, bowl, crimped, 7½" 22.50
Largo, amber or crystal, bowl, 7½" 20.00
Largo, amber or crystal, cake plate, ped ft 35.00
Largo, amber or crystal, cup 15.00
Largo, amber or crystal, sugar bowl, ftd 22.00
Largo, amber or crystal, tray, serving; 3-ftd, 10¾" 25.00
Largo, bl or red, bowl, tab hdls, 9" 75.00
Largo, bl or red, bowl, 5" 25.00
Largo, bl or red, candy dish, flat, 3-part, w/lid 95.00
Largo, bl or red, compote, cracker 25.00
Largo, bl or red, plate, 6⅝" 15.00
Largo, bl or red, saucer 10.00
Largo, bl or red, tray, relish; 5-part, 14" 100.00
Maya, crystal, bowl, non-flared, 9½" 30.00
Maya, crystal, cake plate, ped ft.. 35.00
Maya, crystal, cheese dish, w/lid 75.00
Maya, crystal, compote, plain rim, 6½x10" 32.50
Maya, crystal, plate, mayonnaise; 7" 10.00
Maya, crystal, plate, 6⅝" 8.00
Maya, crystal, sugar bowl, flat 20.00
Maya, crystal, tray, serving; 3-ftd, 13¾" 25.00
Maya, lt bl or red, bowl, flared rim, 7" 35.00
Maya, lt bl or red, bowl, 4¾x12¾" 80.00
Maya, lt bl or red, candleholder, ea 55.00
Maya, lt bl or red, compote, fluted rim 75.00
Maya, lt bl or red, creamer, flat 50.00
Maya, lt bl or red, mayonnaise, 3-ftd 40.00
Maya, lt bl or red, tray, tab hdl 60.00
Nerva, crystal, bowl, cereal; 6½", from $18 to 22.00
Nerva, crystal, cake plate, 12", from $75 to 100.00
Nerva, crystal, cup, from $20 to 25.00
Nerva, crystal, sugar bowl, 3⅝", from $20 to 25.00
Nerva, ruby, bowl, fruit; hdls, 10", from $75 to 95.00

Nerva, ruby, candlestick, double, from $50.00 to $65.00 each. (Photo courtesy Carrie and Jerry Domitz)

Nerva, ruby, candy dish, w/lid, 6⅞", from $100 to 125.00
Nerva, ruby, relish, 3-part, 6½x11", from $65 to........................... 85.00
Orchid (etched), bl or red, bowl, hdls, 8½"................................... 135.00
Orchid (etched), bl or red, bowl, sq, 4⅞" 55.00
Orchid (etched), bl or red, candleholders, 5¾", pr 195.00
Orchid (etched), bl or red, compote, 6⅝x7" 135.00
Orchid (etched), bl or red, creamer... 100.00
Orchid (etched), bl or red, ice bucket, 6" 195.00
Orchid (etched), bl or red, plate, sq, 8½"..................................... 125.00
Orchid (etched), bl or red, sugar bowl 100.00
Orchid (etched), bl or red, vase, 8".. 275.00
Party Line, bl, candleholders, 4¼x3¾", pr...................................... 35.00
Party Line, Cheri Glo, compote, ftd, 3x9" 15.00
Party Line, gr, sherbet, low ft, 4½-oz, 3¼" 20.00
Party Line, gr, vase, fan 50.00
Party Line, pk, creamer 25.00
Party Line, pk, sugar bowl 25.00
Party Line, pk, vase, fan, 7" 53.00
Peacock & Rose/Nora Bird, amber, bowl, console; 12", from $100 to... 150.00
Peacock & Rose/Nora Bird, amber, candlestick, mushroom, ea from $65 to.85.00
Peacock & Rose/Nora Bird, amber, ice bucket, 6¼", from $125 to.....150.00
Peacock & Rose/Nora Bird, amber, tray, center hdl, 12½" L, $75 to ..100.00
Peacock & Rose/Nora Bird, bl, candy dish, flat, 6½", from $450 to....550.00
Peacock & Rose/Nora Bird, bl, compote, ftd, 10", from $600 to.. 650.00

Peacock and Rose/ Nora Bird, green, candy dish, 7", from $165.00 to $200.00. (Photo courtesy Carrie and Jerry Domitz)

Peacock & Rose/Nora Bird, lt bl, sugar bowl, from $125 to 150.00
Peacock & Rose/Nora Bird, pk or gr, cake plate, from $200 to 225.00
Peacock & Rose/Nora Bird, pk or gr, ice bucket, 4", from $100 to ..125.00
Peacock & Rose/Nora Bird, pk or gr, pitcher, 8½", from $1,000 to... 1,500.00
Peacock & Rose/Nora Bird, pk or gr, tumbler, 4", from $150 to... 200.00
Peacock & Rose/Nora Bird, pk or gr, vase, 10", from $100 to 150.00
Peacock Reverse (etched), colors, creamer, flat, 2¾" 100.00
Peacock Reverse (etched), colors, plate, luncheon; 8½" 60.00
Peacock Reverse (etched), colors, plate, sherbet; 5¾" 25.00
Peacock Reverse (etched), colors, sherbet, 4⅝x3⅜" 65.00
Peacock Reverse (etched), colors, tumbler, flat, 10-oz, 4" 95.00
Peacock Reverse (etched), colors, vase, 10".................................. 250.00
Penny Line, Ritz Blue, wine, 3-oz.. 23.00
Penny Line, ruby, goblet, 5".. 13.00

Pairpoint

The Pairpoint Manufacturing Company was built in 1880 in New Bedford, Massachusetts. It was primarily a metalworks whose chief product was coffin fittings. Next door, the Mt. Washington Glassworks made quality glasswares of many varieties. (See Mt. Washington for more information concerning their artware lines.) By 1894 it became apparent to both companies that a merger would be to their best interest.

From the late 1890s until the 1930s, lamps and lamp accessories were an important part of Pairpoint's production. There were three main types of shades, all of which were blown: puffy — blown-out reverse-painted shades (usually floral designs); ribbed — also reverse painted; and scenic — reverse painted with scenes of land or seascapes (usually executed on smooth surfaces, although ribbed scenics may be found occasionally). Cut glass lamps and those with metal overlay panels were also made. Scenic shades were sometimes artist signed. Every shade was stamped on the lower inside or outside edge with 1) The Pairpoint Corp., 2) Patent Pending, 3) Patented July 9, 1907, or 4) Patent Applied For. Bases were made of bronze, copper, brass, silver, or wood and are always signed. (In our listings all information before the semicolon pertains specifically to the shade.)

Because they produced only fancy, handmade artware, the company's sales lagged seriously during the Depression, and as time and tastes changed, their style of product was less in demand. As a result, they never fully recovered; consequently part of the buildings and equipment was sold in 1938. The company reorganized in 1939 under the direction of Robert Gundersen and again specialized in quality hand-blown glassware. Isaac Babbit regained possession of the silver departments, and together they established Gundersen Glassworks, Inc. After WWII, because of a sharp decline in sales, it again became necessary to reorganize. The Gundersen-Pairpoint Glassworks was formed, and the old line of cut, engraved artware was reintroduced. The company moved to East Wareham, Massachusetts, in 1957. But business continued to suffer, and the firm closed only one year later. In 1970, however, new facilities were constructed in Sagamore under the direction of Robert Bryden, sales manager for the company since the 1950s. In 1974 the company began to produce lead glass cup plates which were made on commission as fund-raisers for various churches and organizations. These are signed with a 'P' in diamond and are becoming quite collectible. See also Burmese; Napkin Rings.

Glass

Biscuit jar, blueberries/flowers on mauve, melon ribs, mk lid, 9½"...550.00
Biscuit jar, floral, pk on gr-pnt opal, lion cartouch hdls, 8" W 300.00
Biscuit jar, gold flowers on gr, wide melon ribs, SP mk mts, 7" W . 550.00
Biscuit jar, shaped wht reserves w/lilacs on gr, ornate metal mts, 8" ...395.00
Biscuit jar, ships/distant shoreline, faceted sides, mk lid, 9" 450.00
Candlesticks, amethyst cut w/grapevines, baluster form, 11", pr .. 395.00
Cocktail mixer, eng roster/2 garlands, silver rim, 7" 230.00
Compote, gr w/clear bubble-ball stem on raised gr ft, 7x11" 80.00
Compote, peaches, HP/rvpt; floral-emb Nouveau SP stand, 11", VG ..520.00
Compote, Rosaria, Dmn Quilt, clear stem, 4¾x9½" 200.00
Compote, vaseline, tall stem, rnd ft, 7x8" 115.00

Dresser box, opal glass with hand-painted flowers, metal mounts marked Pairpoint, $525.00. (Photo courtesy Jackson's International Auctioneers & Appraisers of Fine Art & Antiques)

Ice bucket, 3-masted boat eng on clear, SP rim & hdl, 6" 115.00
Vase, cut crystal, bubble-ball connector, ftd trumpet form, 13x7" ...230.00

Lamps

Boudoir, rvpt 7" 4-sided Vassar shade w/floral; 3-D cherub std, 14"..575.00
Chandelier, pk 14" sgn bowl w/heavy lace-like enamel w/cherubs, +mts.3,165.00
Puffy 6½" rose bonnet shade; tree-trunk std, 11", EX 2,875.00
Puffy 9" Papillon shade w/butterflies & roses; simple Pairpoint std.....1,000.00
Puffy 9" shade w/4 shaped floral sides; #3086 4-sided std w/flared ft ...2,900.00
Puffy 10" red rose bouquet shade (NM); std #3088: 4 ogee sides w/vines.5,750.00
Puffy 10" Torino shade rvpt w/peonies; 4-sided ornately emb #B2053 std.5,175.00
Puffy 12" apple tree/bees/butterfly sgn shade; sgn tree base, 26"....28,750.00
Puffy 12" rose bouquet shade; SP std #3040 w/floral base, worn, 20"..5,175.00
Puffy 14" butterflies/roses shade; 3-D flower above base of std, 20". 4,800.00
Puffy 14" orange tree/butterfly sgn shade; sgn tree-trunk std, 24" .46,000.00
Puffy 15" 3-color poppy shade; triangular base w/appl poppies, 22".20,700.00
Puffy 16" begonia shade; organic std #32082 w/brass finish, 23" ...51,750.00

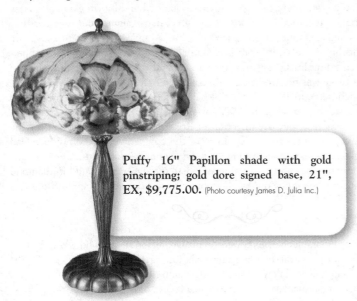

Puffy 16" Papillon shade with gold pinstriping; gold dore signed base, 21", EX, $9,775.00. (Photo courtesy James D. Julia Inc.)

Puffy 21" butterfly/dogwood Stratford shade; Pairpoint #D3084 std, EX..4,000.00
Radio, flat panel shade w/Deco floral sits in brass-plated fr, 11"... 1,600.00
Radio, 8-sided panel: butterflies/tulips; Pairpoint std #E3036, 14" ..575.00
Rvpt 8" rose shade HP outside w/blk lines around florals; #B3023 std.....1,265.00
Rvpt 12" palm shade w/sunset, HP obverse w/trees/bldg; palm-tree std ..6,600.00
Rvpt 14" Venetian Harbor Chesterfield shade; Pairpoint tree-trunk std ..4,000.00
Rvpt 15" Garden of Allah 4-scene sgn shade; simple sgn/#d std, 23".. 5,465.00
Rvpt 16" nautical Venetian panel Lansdowne shade; copper std...1,725.00
Rvpt 17" birds/flowers shade w/wide shoulder & deep border; #3070 std.4,115.00

Paper Dolls

No one knows quite how or when paper dolls originated. One belief is that they began in Europe as 'pantins' (jumping jacks). During the nineteenth century, most paper dolls portrayed famous dancers and opera stars such as Fanny Elssler and Jenny Lind. In the late 1800s, the Raphael Tuck Publishers of England produced many series of beautiful paper dolls. Retail companies used paper dolls as advertisements to further the sale of their products. Around the turn of the century, many popular women's magazines began featuring a page of paper dolls.

Most familiar to today's collectors are the books with dolls on cardboard covers and clothes on the inside pages. These made their appearance in the late 1920s and early 1930s. The most collectible (and the most valuable) are those representing celebrities, movie stars, and comic-

strip characters of the '30s and '40s. When no condition is indicated, the dolls listed below are assumed to be in mint, uncut, original condition. Cut sets will be worth about half price if all dolls and outfits are included and pieces are in very good condition. If dolls were produced in die-cut form, these prices reflect such a set in mint condition with all costumes and accessories. For further information we recommend *20th Century Paper Dolls Identification and Values* (Collector Books), *Tomart's Price Guide to Lowe and Whitman Paper Dolls*, and *Tomart's Price Guide to Saalfield and Merrill Paper Dolls*, all by Mary Young, our advisor for this category; she is listed in the Directory under Ohio. We also recommend *Schroeder's Collectible Toys, Antique to Modern*; and *Paper Dolls of the 1960s, 1970s, and 1980s* by Carol Nichols (both from Collector Books).

Angel Face, Gabriel #293, 1950s.. 20.00
At Home Abroad Dolls, Platt & Munk Co #240, 1937.............. 100.00
Baby Brother & Sister, Whitman #1956, 1961 .... 50.00
Baby Kim, Whitman #1969, 1960-62.................................... 25.00
Beth Ann, Whitman/Western #1955, 1970 .... 45.00
Betsy McCall, Avalon/Standard Toykraft #85, 1960 .... 35.00
Betty & Barbara, Milton Bradley #4382, 1934........................ 50.00
Bewitched, Magic Wand #114, 1965.................................... 65.00
Bobby & Betty, Burton #550, 1934 .... 75.00
Bradley's Jointed Doll w/Embossed Dresses, Milton Bradley #4279, 1910s..80.00
Caroline, Jaymar #971, 1950s-early 1960s 35.00
Century Dolls, Platt & Munk Co #243, 1960 .... 65.00
Chatty Cathy, Whitman/Mattel #1961, 1963 .... 55.00
Cindy & Mindy, Whitman #1974, 1960 .... 35.00
Cleopatra, Blaise #1000, ca 1963 .... 25.00
Country Weekend w/Kathy & Jill, Reuben H Lilja #913, ca 1950...20.00
Cutie Paper Dolls, Milton Bradley #4053, 1940s.................... 40.00
Darling Dot, Gabriel #12, ca 1911 .... 100.00
Dolls From Fairyland, Nourse Co, 1921 .... 85.00
Dolly & Her Dresses, McLoughlin #0540, ca 1914................... 100.00
Dolly Darling, EP Dutton #2739, early 1900s 100.00
Dolly Dingle's Travels, John H Eggers series 2, 1921 .... 75.00
Dozen Cousins, Whitman #2090, 1960................................. 50.00
Earnest & Justin Tubb, Jenson, 1946................................... 60.00
Fairy Tale & Flower Paper-Dolls, MA Donohue #675, ca 1913 ... 100.00
I'm Debra Dee the Bride, Lisbeth Whiting #189, 1963 .... 25.00
Ideal Doll Book, McLoughlin Bros #235 Y2, 1907 .... 100.00
Jackie & Caroline, Magic Wand #107, early 1960s 50.00
Johnny Jones, Goldsmith #2005, 1930.................................. 30.00
Junior, Fish-Lyman #4, 1920.. 75.00
Little Ballerina, Whitman #1963, 1961 .... 25.00
Little Colonel Doll Book, LC Page & Co, 1910 .... 200.00

Little Dick and His New Outfit (small 7" doll), J. W. Spear & Sons (distributed by Selchow & Righter), 1920s, $80.00. (Photo courtesy Mary Young)

Little Folks Crepe Paper Doll Outfit, American Toy Works #902, 1930s .. 50.00
Little Folks Doll's Set, Milton Bradley #4727, 1910s...................... 75.00
Little Red School House Kindergarten, McLoughlin #549, 1940 ...100.00
Miss America, Reuben H Lilja #900, 1941 .... 75.00

Modern Dolls a Plenty, Gabriel #895, ca 1933 .... 90.00
Modern Girls Sewing Set, American Toy Works #400, 1930s........ 35.00
My Fair Lady, Avalon/Standard Toykraft #401, 1960s.................... 50.00
Nursery Favorite, MA Donohue #672, 1913............................. 75.00
Patsy, Childrens Press #3002, 1946 .... 30.00
Peg, Nan, Kay & Sue, Whitman/Western #1995, 1966.................. 40.00
Round About Dolls on Parade, McLoughlin #2992, 1941............. 80.00
Santa's Workshop, Whitman #1989, 1960.............................. 75.00
Sapphire, Queen of Night Clubs, Reuben H Lilja #907, 1940s....100.00
Shirley Temple, Gabriel #303, ca 1961 .... 60.00
Sister Helen, Kaufmann & Strauss #12, 1915........................... 75.00
Tina & Trudy, Whitman #1952, 1967...................................... 40.00
Toni, Merry Mfg Co #6501, 1960s... 30.00
Town & Country, Gabriel #894, 1930s 90.00

Paperweights

Glass paperweight collecting has grown in intensity over the past 25 years. Perhaps it is because there are many glass artists who today are creating beautiful examples that generally sell for less than $100.00. Hundreds of glass artisans and factories in the United States, China, Mexico, Italy, and Scotland produce these 'gift range' paperweights. Collectors have the option of choosing strictly from that price range, or they can choose to buy more costly pieces that sometimes range into the thousands of dollars. Additionally, astute collectors are beginning to piece together collections of old Chinese paperweights first imported into this country during the 1930s — unrefined imitations of the lovely French weights of the mid-1800s. When viewed more than 70 years later, their beauty and craftsmanship is very evident. Of particular note are the weights containing an opaque white glass disk hand painted with charming and sometimes quite intricate designs. Other weights gaining in popularity (and still relatively inexpensive) are motto weights (No Place Like Home, Remember Me, Happy Birthday, etc.) and those made of English bottle glass — especially examples with sulfide inclusions. Plaque weights, such as those created by Degenhart, and Liverpool-process weights made by Mosser are disappearing from the marketplace into the hands of collectors. With the demise of Perthshire Paperweights (Scotland), collectors are seeking out high-end, very limited edition 'Collection' and Christmas paperweights. There is strong interest in advertising paperweights because they are abundant and relatively inexpensive. Collectors who have a larger budget for these exquisite 'glass balls' may choose to purchase only antique French paperweights from the classic period (1845 – 1860), the wonderful English or American weights from the 1840s, or examples of the high quality contemporary workmanship of today's master glass artists.

Baccarat, St. Louis, Clichy, Pantin, and St. Mande (names synonymous with classic French paperweights) as well as some American factories discontinued production between the 1880s and 1910 when paperweights fell out of favor. In the 1950s Baccarat and St. Louis revived paperweight production, creating very high quality, limited-production weights. St. Louis discontinued paperweights several years ago. In the 1960s many American glass studios began to spring up due to the development of smaller glass furnaces that allowed the individual glassmaker more freedom in design and fabrication from the fire to the annealing kiln. Such success stories are evident in the creative glass produced by Lundberg Studios, Orient & Flume, and Lotton Studios, to name only a few.

Many factors determine value, particularly of antique weights, and auction-realized prices of contemporary weights usually differ from issue price. Be cautious when comparing weights that may seem very similar in appearance; their values may vary considerably. Size, faceting, fancy cuts on the base, the inclusion of a seemingly innocuous piece of frit, or a tear in a lampworked leaf are some conditions that can affect cost. Of course, competition among new collectors has greatly influenced prices, as have Internet auction sales. Some paperweights heretofore purported to be 'rare' now appear with some frequency on Internet auctions, driving down their prices. However, as the number of collectors multiply, the supply of antique weights decrease, forcing prices upwards. Fine antique paperweights have steadily increased in value as has the work of many now-deceased contemporary pioneer glass artists (i.e., Paul Ysart, Joe St. Clair, Charles Kazian, Del Tarsitano, and Ray Banford).

The dimension given at the end of the description is diameter. Prices are for weights in perfect or near-perfect condition unless otherwise noted. Our advisors for this category are Betty and Larry Schwab, The Paperweight Shoppe; they are listed in the Directory under Illinois. See Clubs, Newsletters, and Catalogs in the Directory for the Paperweight Collector's Associations, Inc., with chapters in many states. They offer assistance to collectors at all levels. The values for cast-iron weights are prices realized at auction.

Key:
con — concentric	jsp — jasper
(d) — deceased	latt — latticinio
fct — facets, faceted	mill — millefiori
gar — garland	o/l — overlay
grd — ground	sil — silhouette

Ayotte, Rick

Bird on branch on clear bl grd, 1983, 3", from $350 to................. 450.00
Blueberry Morning, blueberries & flowers, 1990, 4⅞", $1,400 to...1,600.00
Chickadees (2) on holly w/berries, snow grd, 1990, 3½", $350 to ...450.00
Morning glories & blueberries, 1990, 4⅞", from $1,400 to........1,600.00
Salamander on woodland grd, 1989, 3¼", from $800 to............1,000.00
Seagulls, 1 on branch/2 in flight, ca 1980, 3", from $400 to.........500.00

Baccarat, Antique

Con mil complex canes w/several arrowhead canes, 2¼", EX, $500 to.600.00
Dbl Clematis w/bud on muslin, con ring of canes, repolished, 3⅛" ..2,000.00
Dog rose, pk/wht w/11 leaves, star-cut base, 1850s, 2⅝", $2,000 to ..3,000.00
Pansy, purple/yel w/gr leaves, 1850s, 2½", from $400 to 500.00
Primrose, bl & wht w/several leaves, star-cut base, 2⅜", $1,600 to ...2,100.00

Primrose with center of white stardust canes around red bull's-eye, from $1,200.00 to $1,800.00. (Photo courtesy Garth's Auctions Inc.)

Sand, rock weight, tan/brn/gr on clear base, 2", from $100 to...... 150.00
Scattered mill canes on muslin, 11 figural/animal canes, B1847, 3" ..2,550.00
Scattered mill on muslin grd, 10 figural/animal canes, B1848, 3¼" 2,650.00

Baccarat, Modern

Con mill canes in 8 mc rings, 20th C, 3", from $400 to 475.00
DuPont dbl trefoil mill on clear grd, early 20th C, 3", from $200 to ..250.00
Floral mill rings in pk/bl/gr, 200th Anniv pc, bruise, 2½", $100 to...150.00
JF Kennedy sulfide, dbl o/l, bl/wht, 3", from $100 to 175.00
Scrambled wht filigree canes w/mc swirls, 20th C, 3", from $300 to ..500.00
Sulfide, Harry S Truman, 1973, 1⅝", from $50 to.........................100.00

Banford, Bob and Ray (deceased)

Bee & flower on bl grd, 2½", from $400 to **475.00**
Flower, wht & gold on mosaic grd w/snake, Bob...'72, 1½", $300 to ..**400.00**
Mixed flowers, mc w/gr leaves on clear, upright/fct, 3¾", $600 to ...**800.00**
Rose w/cobalt & aventurine grd, 1½", from $250 to **400.00**
Roses, 2 pk w/sm bud among leaves, sgn B, 1½x2", from $250 to.. **400.00**

Caithness

Bl & wht gar, A Scott, 1987, 2¼", from $100 to **150.00**
Butterfly, purple/pk on dk bl, Manson, 1998 ltd ed, 3", from $200 to.. **350.00**
Mayfly & 2 pk flowers, Manson, 3", MIB, from $200 to **250.00**
Night Vision, M Thomson, 1993, 3", from $100 to **150.00**
Night Vision, spherical, M Thomson, 1993 ltd ed, 3", from $100 to..**150.00**

Clichy, Antique

Barber pole chequer B, rose to side, ca 1848, 2⅝", from $2,500 to....**3,200.00**
Chequer w/turq/pk/wht rose canes w/latt, repolished, 2⅝", $900 to.**1,300.00**
Close-pack mill basket w/2 mc roses/yel rose cane, 2⅛", $4,500 to..**5,500.00**
Patterned mill trefoil gar on dk pk, repolished, 3¼", from $900 to..**1,300.00**
Queen Victoria sulfide w/in 3-row con mill circles, 3", from $1,800 to. **2,200.00**
Swirl, bl & wht w/central cane lustre, 3", from $2,800 to...........**3,200.00**
Swirl, pk/wht w/central bl cane, 3", from $1,500 to...................**2,200.00**

Lundberg Studios

Amethyst flower blossom w/4 gr leaves on wht, 1983, 2¾", $400 to ..**500.00**
Apple blossoms on cobalt grd, D Salazar, 1989, 2½", from $275 to..**375.00**
Beta Fish, D Salazar, 1989, 2½", from $400 to **500.00**
Button mushrooms (3)/grasses/sandy grd, Steven/1989, 2½", $800 to.. **1,000.00**
Dragonfly/floral branch in clear, D Salazar, 1989, 2¾", $700 to.... **800.00**
Lady slipper orchid w/gr leaves on wht opal, 1984, 2¾", $300 to . **400.00**
Pk dahlia w/4 tiers of petals & 6 gr leaves, 1983, 2¾", $450 to **600.00**
Yel daffodils (2) w/gr leaves on blk, 1984, 2¾", from $450 to....... **600.00**

New England Glass, Antique

Clematis w/5 gr leaves, dbl swirl wht latt, 1860s, 2⅝", $1,200 to...**1,500.00**
Con mill canes on latt/running hare canes, repolished, 2¾", $300 to ...**500.00**
Con mill pk & rose canes on wht latt grd, 2¾", from $500 to **800.00**
Fruit on wht latt grd, some polishing, 3", from $200 to **350.00**
Pears (5) & leaves/4 sm veggies on latt grd, 2¼", from $400 to....**600.00**

Orient & Flume

Octopus on coral encrusted with sea forms, Dave Smallhouse, signed and numbered, in original box, 3½", from $400.00 to $600.00. (Photo courtesy Early Auction Co.)

Floral, irid on navy bl, 1979, 3¾", from $200 to **350.00**
Flower/vines in clear, swirled bl cushion, 1978, 2¾", from $250 to .. **350.00**
Herons w/fledglings on bl grd, 1983, 3⅛", from $300 to **400.00**
Threaded/pulled geometrics, mc irid, #847N, 1975, 3", MIB, $200 to....**300.00**

Perthshire

Bouquet, mc on blk & cobalt spiral bed, 1988, 3", MIB, from $400 to ...**600.00**
Bouquet in floral pentagon/purple cushion, fcts, 1972, 2¾", $400 to .. **600.00**
Dahlia, pk/4-tiered, fct, sq, 1972, 2x2⅛", MIB, from $400 to....... **600.00**
Forget-me-nots/leaves on wht optic twist grd, '76, 3", MIB, $400 to..**600.00**
Orchids (3)/yel bow/dragonfly, 1/5 fct, P cane, 3⅛", from $400 to ..**600.00**

Sandwich Glass

Flower (10-petal) w/3 leaves on latt grd, 2", from $450 to **650.00**
Poinsettia, 10-petal w/3 gr leaves on swirled latt, 3", NM, $500 to .. **800.00**

Poinsettia on latticinio, ground pontil, antique, 3", EX, from $400.00 to $500.00. (Photo courtesy James D. Julia Inc.)

Poinsettia w/gr leaves on bl jsp w/Lutz rose cane, 2½", $500 to.... **800.00**
Weedflower, petals, gold-stone center cane, 2¾", from $1,000 to... **1,300.00**

Stankard, Paul

Blueberries/moth/blossoms, 3 word canes, PS '95, 3", from $3,200 to... **4,000.00**
Blueberries/pk & yel flowers/root/4 word canes, PS '96, 3", $3,500 to .. **4,500.00**
Flowers & buds on desert grd, 3", from $1,000 to **1,400.00**
St Anthony's Fire, mixed bouquet, ca 1970, 3", from $900 to... **1,200.00**
Wildflowers/berries/bumblebees, PS '95, 3", from $1,500 to...... **2,000.00**

Tarsitano, Delmo

Lizard & 3 flowers on pebbled grd, 3¾", from $1,500 to **1,800.00**
Peaches (2) on branch w/leaves, 7 fcts, 2½", from $1,500 to..... **1,800.00**
Snake curled around flower on pebbled grd, 3½", from $1,500 to... **2,000.00**
Strawberries (2) & blossoms w/leaves, 3", from $1,000 to **1,400.00**

Trabucco, Victor

Mixed floral bouquet, magnum, 5", from $1,200 to **1,800.00**
Pk flowers (2) & 3 buds w/gr leaves, 1988, 2½", from $300 to...... **400.00**
Violets w/bright gr stems & leaves, 1984, 3", from $250 to **350.00**

Cast Iron

Bunny, realistic pnt, 3x2½", NM **300.00**
Elephant trumpeting on base, mc pnt, 2-pc casting, 5x4" **70.00**
Fido, blk/wht/red pnt, Hubley #126, 1½", NM **140.00**
Fox, realistic pnt, Hubley, rare, 2⅛x1⅜", NM **1,140.00**
Kitty w/bow, wht w/pk, Hubley #195, NM.................................. **265.00**
Lady skier, mc pnt, Hubley, 3x3¼", EX **395.00**
Peter Rabbit, in pk overalls, Hubley, 3x1¼", VG........................ **600.00**
Pheasant, realistic pnt, Hubley, 2¾x3½", NM **300.00**
Quail (2), realistic pnt, Hubley, 2¾x2⅞", NM............................ **400.00**
Skater, girl w/arm raised, mc pnt, Hubley, 3x1½" **275.00**

Miscellaneous

Chinese, bl clematis w/bud/gr foliage on latt, 2½", from $150 to.....**200.00**

Mosser, Currier & Ives print, Liverpool-transfer process, $100 to ...200.00
Rosenfeld, K; floral bouquet on purple grd, 2000, 3¼", $350 to .. 650.00
Smith, Hugh; cattails on gr/wht textured grd, mini, 2", from $175 to...250.00

Papier-Mache

The art of papier-mache was mainly European. It originated in Paris around the middle of the eighteenth century and became popular in America during Victorian times. Small items such as boxes, trays, inkwells, frames, etc., as well as extensive ceiling moldings and larger articles of furniture were made. The process involved building layer upon layer of paper soaked in glue, then coaxed into shape over a wood or wire form. When dry it was painted or decorated with gilt or inlays. Inexpensive twentieth-century 'notions' were machine processed and mold pressed. See also Christmas; Candy Containers.

Box, letter; rose & gold rocaille on ochre, Jennens & Bettridge, 8" .885.00
Box, MOP floral inlay, gold leaf, pnt, 1850, 2½x9x7" 200.00
Box, writing; MOP inlay house/church, gilt, slant lid, 1850, 16" L .. 1,175.00
Figurine, polar bear, wht w/red & blk, Ol' King Cole, 20¼" 500.00
Sewing stand, MOP inly, on vasiform ped/scroll ft, 1850s, 29x15x11" ...400.00
Tables, nesting; blk w/mc MOP castles, Jennens & Bettridge, 3 for.... 4,995.00
Tea table, tilt top w/bird & dog reserve w/in floral border, 28x27x23" 850.00
Tray, bl flowers/gilt vines/gr leaves, late 19th C, 24¼" 1,000.00
Tray, blk w/MOP floral/gilt scrolls, att Jennens & Bettridge, 31" L.. 1,175.00
Tray, floral bouquet (lg/lush) w/abalone inlay, gilt, 1890s, 30" L.. 2,000.00
Tray, floral bouquet on blk w/gold swags, abalone chips, 31" 1,175.00
Tray, hoho birds/flowering trees/scrolls on dk red, 1890s, 31" dia .. 1,880.00
Tray, peacock/fountain/hoho bird, Jennens & Bettridge, 32" 2,235.00
Tray, scene titled: Milk Maid, B Walton & Co, lacquered, 26x20" .. 2,100.00
Tray, Tudor int w/man & dog by fireplace, 1880s, 29x23" 1,800.00
Trays, sponged blk lacquer, gilt decor, set of 3: 32", 25", 18" 235.00

Parian Ware

Parian is hard-paste unglazed porcelain made to resemble marble. First made in the mid-1800s by Staffordshire potters, it was soon after produced in the United States by the U.S. Pottery at Bennington, Vermont. Busts and statuary were favored, but plaques, vases, mugs, and pitchers were also made.

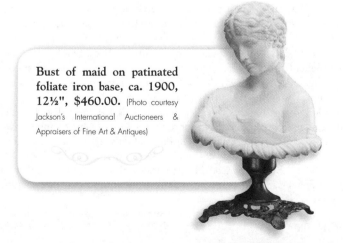

Bust of maid on patinated foliate iron base, ca. 1900, 12½", $460.00. (Photo courtesy Jackson's International Auctioneers & Appraisers of Fine Art & Antiques)

Bust, Benjamin Franklin, Isaac Broome, Ott & Brewer, 9x6", EX.. 2,500.00
Bust, Charles Sumner on rnd waisted socle, J McD&S, Equality..., 12"..585.00
Bust, Daphne on waisted socle, M Wood, Copeland, 1865, 14½" ...700.00
Bust, Disraeli on rnd socle, EW Wyon Sculpt, Robinson&Leadbeater, 15"..525.00

Bust, Duke of Wellington, S Keys & Mountford, ca 1870, 11"..... 115.00
Bust, Jenny Lind on waisted rnd socle, J Durham SC, Copeland, 8"..235.00
Bust, John Andrew, att Robinson & Leadbeater, J McD&S Boston, 12"..645.00
Bust, John Milton on waisted socle, Copeland, 14" 350.00
Bust, Juno on rnd waisted socle, Copeland, 1896, 24" 4,995.00
Bust, Prince Albert on waisted rnd socle, JS Westmacott, Copeland, 11"....440.00
Bust, Queen Victoria, Robinson & Leadbeater, 1887, 20½"...... 2,115.00
Bust, Virgin Mary, Isaac Broome, Ott & Brewer, 1876, 16x9".... 3,600.00
Bust, Wendell Phillips, M Milmore, att Robinson & Leadbeater, 10" .. 525.00
Bust of a child, Isaac Broome, Ott & Brewer, 7x5" 1,560.00
Busts, Awake (& Asleep) on sq base, J Westmacott, Copeland, 9", pr.. 940.00
Busts, Miranda (& Ophelia), Copeland, Crystal Palace Art Union, 12", pr.415.00
Ewer, Triton seated at shoulder w/monster's horns, Mayer, 1850s, 14"..825.00
Figure, Comus on rocky base w/goblet in hand, Copeland, 1860s, 13" .885.00
Figure, Diana seated/holding dead bird, hound at ft, Minton, 1863, 14" ..1,300.00
Figure, draped nude seated on rocky base clasping knee, 1870s, 16" ..415.00
Figure, girl reading, P MacDowell, Copeland, 1869, 13¼" 500.00
Figure, Hermione, w/gold & enamel, WC Marshall, ca 1860, 16" ..440.00
Figure, Highland Mary, seated, Art Union of Great Britain, 14".....235.00
Figure, Jason seated w/walking stick & satchel, Minton, 1860, 16"....700.00
Figure, Lady Godiva, R Monti, Copeland, 1876, 21"................. 1,175.00
Figure, Penelophan, Beggar Maid, W Brodie RSA, Copeland, 27"..940.00
Figure, Peter Paul Rubens wearing cap, on plinth, 1880s, 16"...... 350.00
Figure, Robert Bruce, W Beattie, England, ca 1875, 19¾" 525.00
Figure, water nymph seated on rock, Copeland, 18"..................... 765.00
Group, Amphitrite (sea goddess) w/Cupid blowing conch shell, 22".. 300.00
Group, Aphrodite & Edos, she kneeling/embracing him, 23x12" .. 1,500.00
Group, Finding of Moses, Wm Beattie, Wedgwood, 19x16x9", EX 175.00
Group, Issac & Rebekah, Wm Beattie, Wedgwood, 20x14".........700.00
Group, Night: draped figure/sleeping baby, R Monti, Copeland, 21".. 7,600.00

Parrish, Maxfield

Maxfield Parrish (1870 – 1966), with his unique abilities in architecture, illustrations, and landscapes, was the most prolific artist during 'the golden years of illustrators.' He produced art for more than 100 magazines, painted girls on rocks for the Edison-Mazda division of General Electric, and landscapes for Brown & Bigelow. His most recognized work was 'Daybreak' that was published in 1923 by House of Art and sold nearly 2,000,000 prints. Parrish began early training with his father who was a recognized artist, studied architecture at Dartmouth, and became an active participant in the Cornish artist colony in New Hampshire where he resided. Due to his increasing popularity, reproductions are now being marketed. In our listings, values for prints apply to those that are in their original frames (or very nice and appropriate replacement frames) unless noted otherwise. Bobby Babcock, our advisor for this category, is listed in the Directory under Colorado

Ad, Saturday Evening Post, Edison-Mazda Lamps, full sheet, 1924 .. 85.00
Ad poster, Ferry Seeds, Jack & the Beanstalk, 1923, cropped, 19" ...2,500.00
Book, Knave of Heart, spiral-bound, 1925, EX 1,000.00
Book, Mother Goose on Prose, by L Frank Baum, 1st ed, 1897, EX...1,400.00
Book, Sapphire Story Book, Penrhyn W Coussens, hardbk w/jacket, 1917..210.00
Book, Tanglewood Tales, 1st Edition, 1910, EX............................ 225.00
Calendar, Contentment, 1928, Edison-Mazda, w/pad, 38½x18½", EX..1,500.00
Calendar, Golden Hour, 1929, Edison-Mazda, partial pad, 21⅜x9⅜" ...210.00
Calendar, Golden Hour, 1929, w/pad, 37½x18", EX................. 2,000.00
Calendar, Lampseller of Bagdad, 1923, full pad, 37½x18", EX ..2,900.00
Calendar, Moonlight, 1934, Edison-Mazda, full pad, 19⅛x8½", EX...925.00
Calendar, Old Glen Mill, 1954, 21½x16½", EX........................... 200.00
Calendar, Prince Agib, Dodge Pub, 1925, 8x6" 150.00
Calendar, Reveries, 1928, Edison-Mazda, no pad, 38½x18½", EX...750.00
Calendar, Solitude, 1932, Edison-Mazda, full pad, 19⅛x18½" 650.00

Calendar, Spirit of the Night, 1919, Edison-Mazda, full pad, 19x9½"... 4,500.00
Calendar, Spirit of Transportation, 1928, 10x5⅜", EX 400.00
Calendar, Sunrise, 1933, full pad, 19x8½", EX.......................... 400.00
Calendar, Venetian Lamplighter, 1924, full pad, 19x8½", EX .. 1,350.00
Calendar, Vicobello, 1934, full pad, rare, 7x4⅞"........................... 550.00
Calendar top, Egypt, 1922, Edison-Mazda, 20⅝x16¾" 875.00
Calendar top, Enchantment, Edison-Mazda, 14⅞x12" 350.00
Calendar top, Golden Hours, 1929, 19x14¼" (w/fr), NM 500.00
Calendar top, Prometheus, 1920, 23¾x14⅜", EX 2,000.00
Calendar top, Venetian Lamplighter, 1924, 23⅝x14⅛", EX 1,500.00
Chocolate box, Crane, textured cb w/Rubaiyat image insert, 11x7x1", EX ..950.00
Display, Get Together, GE light bulbs, 1920s, 26½x16x3" 2,600.00
Display, house & car, GE light bulbs, cb foldout, 1930s, 26½x16x3" .. 2,600.00
Greeting card, winter landscape, Brown & Bigelow 75.00
Magazine, Circus Bedquilt, Ladies' Home Journal, 1905, 16x11¼", NM... 60.00
Magazine cover, A Man of Letters, Life, Jan 5, 1922 .... 150.00
Magazine cover, Balloon Man, Collier's, Dec 12-26, 1908 .... 125.00
Magazine cover, Boar's Head, Collier's, Dec 16, 1905.................. 125.00
Magazine cover, Milking Time, Collier's, May 19, 1906, EX 75.00
Magazine insert, Pandora's Box, 1908, 9x11" 85.00
Menu, Broadmoor Hotel, 1920s, 11x15"...................................... 200.00
Playing cards, Dawn, Edison-Mazda, MIB.................................... 300.00
Playing cards, Ecstasy, Edison-Mazda, 1930, M in wrapper........... 275.00
Playing cards, Waterfall, 1931, EXIB... 175.00
Postcard, Pied Piper, 7x7" foldout, 1915 .... 175.00
Postcard, The Billboard/A Bolt on Nature..., 3½x5⅝" 150.00
Poster, Century Magazine, 1902, 14x20"...................................1,900.00
Poster, New Hampshire, Winter, 1939, 24x29"............................ 850.00
Print, Atlas, 1908, 11½x9½".. 325.00
Print, Autumn, 1905, 10x12" 250.00
Print, Cleopatra, 1917, 24½x28" 2,300.00
Print, Daybreak, Brett Litho Co, gilt fr w/dbl mat, 18x30".......... 575.00
Print, Evening Shadows, Brown & Bigelow, 1940, 13x17½" 400.00

Print, Lute Players, 1926, 16x13", $325.00. (Photo courtesy Wm. Morford Auctions)

Print, Pied Piper, 6¾x21"...1,200.00
Print, Prince, 1928, 10x12" 185.00
Print, Romance, 1925, 18x27", EX...1,500.00
Triptych, Daybreak flanked by Stars & Hilltop, 12x32", EX 1,500.00

Pate-De-Verre

Simply translated, pate-de-verre means paste of glass. In the manufacturing process, lead glass is first ground, then mixed with sodium silicate solution to form a paste which can be molded and refired. Some of the most prominent artisans to use this procedure were Almaric Walter, Daum, Argy-Rouseau, and Decorchemont. See also specific manufacturers.

Bowl, 2 demonic masks ea side/laurel leaves, gr, Decorchemont, 2x3"....1,325.00

Figurine, bust of lady w/scarf over hair, Despret, 3¼"..................... 485.00
Paperweight, frog on lily pad, gr/bl, Decorchemont, 5½" L 1,725.00
Paperweight, gr rodent w/lg bl eyes on pk disk, 4" dia 2,590.00
Paperweight, mouse atop rock, Decorchemont, 2¼" L 1,435.00
Plaque, Ave Maria, profile, orange/gr mottle, JD, 4½" dia 645.00

Pate-Sur-Pate

Pate-sur-pate, literally paste-on paste, is a technique whereby relief decorations are built up on a ceramic body by layering several applications of slip, one on the other, until the desired result is achieved. Usually only two colors are used, and the value of a piece is greatly enhanced as more color is added.

Plaque, couple by Cupid in cradle, Louis Solon, 6½x7", $7,600.00. (Photo courtesy Skinner Inc. Auctioneers & Appraisers of Antiques & Fine Art)

Plaque, Aurora, bl/wht, WA Bougeureau, ca 1890, 6½x3½"+fr.. 3,400.00
Vase, cherubs reserve w/gold, baluster, 1890-1910, 8⅝".............7,200.00
Vase, draped figure among branches, flared cylinder, 16¾"........1,650.00
Vase, maid/garden, wht/gr w/gilt rim/ft, flat sides, G Jones, 9", pr... 1,645.00

Pattern Glass

Pattern glass was the first mass-produced fancy tableware in America and was much prized by our ancestors. From the 1840s to the Civil War, it contained a high lead content and is known as 'Flint Glass.' It is exceptionally clear and resonant. Later glass was made with soda lime and is known as non-flint. By the 1890s pattern glass was produced in great volume in thousands of patterns, and colored glass came into vogue. Today the highest prices are often paid for these later patterns flashed with rose, amber, canary, and vaseline; stained ruby; or made in colors of cobalt, green, yellow, amethyst, etc. Demand for pattern glass declined by 1915, and glass fanciers were collecting it by 1930. No other field of antiques offers more diversity in patterns, prices, or pieces than this unique and historical glass that represents the Victorian era in America.

Our advisor for this category is Darlene Yohe; she is listed in the Directory under Arkansas. For a more thorough study on the subject, we recommend *Standard Encyclopedia of Pressed Glass, 1860 – 1930, Identification & Values*, by Bill Edwards and Mike Carwile, available from Collector Books. See also Bread Plates; Cruets; Historical Glass; Salt and Pepper Shakers; Salts, Open; Sugar Shakers; Syrups; specific manufacturers such as Northwood.

Note: Values are given for open sugar bowls and compotes unless noted 'w/lid.'

Acorn, butter dish.. 90.00
Acorn, egg cup 25.00
Acorn, sugar bowl 35.00
Acorn Band, pitcher... 85.00

Acorn Band, sugar bowl...30.00
Actress, bowl, 6-9½"..90.00
Actress, cake stand, 9-10"...150.00
Actress, celery vase...145.00
Actress, cheese dish..275.00
Ada, butter dish...75.00
Ada, cruet...45.00
Ada, pitcher...95.00
Ada, tumbler...25.00
Adam's Apollo, lamp..75.00
Adam's Apollo, lamp, amber......................................110.00
Adam's Plume, bowl, ftd, bl or gr.................................50.00
Adam's Plume, sauce bowl...10.00
Adonis, cake plate, vaseline...60.00
Adonis, compote, w/lid, bl or gr...................................45.00
Adonis, relish tray..10.00
Alabama, honey dish, w/lid, rare..................................75.00
Alabama, toothpick holder, bl or gr............................150.00
Alaska, cruet...185.00
Alaska, rose bowl...45.00
Alaska, tray, jewel; bl or gr..50.00
Almond, decanter, wine...65.00
Almond, tray, wine...30.00
Almond Thumbprint, cordial..20.00
Almond Thumbprint, decanter.....................................45.00
Amaryllis, bowl, 8"...45.00
Amazon, claret...25.00
Amazon, egg cup..20.00
Amberette, cake stand, gr or bl..................................145.00
Amberette, cake stand, vaseline.................................165.00
Amberette, pickle dish, bl or gr....................................40.00
Amberette, pickle dish, vaseline...................................45.00
Amberette, See Also Klondike
Amboy, butter dish...65.00
Amboy, spoon dish...15.00
American Beauty, berry bowl, lg...................................35.00
American Beauty, jelly compote....................................30.00
Arcadia Lace, candy dish, w/lid....................................35.00
Arcadia Lace, plate, 11"...30.00
Arched Fluer-De-Lis, plate, sq, ruby stain....................50.00
Arched Fluer-De-Lis, vase, bl or gr...............................75.00
Arched Forget-Me-Not Bands, jam jar..........................30.00
Arched Forget-Me-Not Bands, spooner.........................25.00
Arched Ovals, mug, ruby stain......................................35.00
Arched Ovals, toothpick holder, bl or gr.......................35.00
Arrowhead, butter dish, vaseline................................110.00
Arrowhead, pickle dish...20.00
Art, fruit basket, 10"..65.00
Art, milk pitcher, bl or gr..165.00
Art, plate, 7"..20.00
Ashburton, bowl, amethyst...55.00
Ashburton, champagne, amber......................................25.00
Ashburton, compote...30.00
Ashburton, pitcher, bl or gr..115.00
Ashman, bread tray...30.00
Ashman, tumbler...20.00
Atlanta, shaker, ea..20.00
Atlanta, toothpick holder..30.00
Atlanta, wine..25.00
Baby Face, creamer...110.00
Baby Face, salt dip...60.00
Balder, See Pennsylvania
Ball & Swirl, pitcher, wht opaque...............................100.00
Ball & Swirl, plate, 6"..25.00

Baltimore Pear, bowl, w/lid, 5-9"..................................60.00
Baltimore Pear, cake plate..30.00
Band & Diamond Swirl, vase, 6"...................................65.00
Banded Fleur-De-Lis, milk pitcher................................60.00
Banded Raindrops, goblet, amber.................................80.00
Banded Raindrops, plate, 7½-9"....................................30.00
Bar & Diamond, celery vase..20.00
Bar & Diamond, decanter, ruby stain............................65.00
Bar & Diamond, shakers, ea..25.00
Bar & Diamond, wine, ruby stain..................................25.00
Barberry, cordial..35.00
Barley, platter, oval, scarce...70.00
Barred Forget-Me-Not, creamer....................................25.00
Barred Forget-Me-Not, plate, hdls, amber.....................30.00
Bead Column, berry bowl, sm.......................................10.00
Bead Swag, cup, vaseline..40.00
Bead Swag, saucer, bl or gr..20.00
Bead Swag, toothpick holder, ruby stain.......................40.00
Bead Swag, tumbler, milk glass.....................................40.00
Beaded Arch Panels, mug...30.00
Beaded Arch Panels, sugar bowl...................................35.00
Beaded Band, syrup..50.00
Beaded Tulip, jam jar...40.00
Beaded Tulip, water tray...25.00
Bearded Head, See Viking
Beaumont's Columbia, celery vase, ruby stain..............30.00
Beaumont's Columbia, salt dip.....................................20.00
Bellflower, champagne..90.00
Bellflower, whiskey tumbler..135.00
Bird & Harp, mug, purple slag......................................80.00
Bird & Strawberry, plate, chop....................................150.00
Birds at Fountain, compote, w/lid................................135.00
Birds at Fountain, mug, mini..65.00
Bleeding Heart, cake stand, 9-11".................................45.00
Bleeding Heart, pickle tray...25.00
Blockade, finger bowl...20.00
Blockade, nappy, 4½-6"...30.00
Box Pleat, tumbler...10.00
Brazilian, carafe...40.00
Brazilian, cracker jar, 7-9"..40.00
Brittanic, banana stand, ruby stain.............................110.00
Brittanic, custard cup...10.00
Broken Arches, punch bowl, vaseline..........................400.00
Broken Arches, punch cup, vaseline..............................30.00
Bryce Hobnail, mug..35.00
Bryce Hobnail, pickle dish..25.00
Buckingham, basket..45.00
Buckingham, pitcher...85.00
Buckingham, tumbler..20.00
Bull's-Eye & Daisy, creamer..25.00
Bull's-Eye & Daisy, shakers, ea.....................................30.00

Bull's Eye & Fan, creamer, #15090, clear with gold, $30.00. (Photo courtesy Gene and Cathy Florence)

Bull's-Eye Band, See Reverse Torpedo
Butterfly & Thistle, bowl, scarce, 9"... 50.00
Buttressed Loop, bowl, w/lid 50.00
Buttressed Loop, compote... 30.00
Cabbage Rose, basket, hdl 75.00
Cabbage Rose, wine 25.00
Cambridge #2351, jug, squat 55.00
Cambridge #2467, punch bowl, w/base 145.00
Cane, berry bowl, amber, lg 30.00
Cane, finger bowl, vaseline 30.00
Cane, honey dish, bl or gr 25.00
Caprice, cigarette box 45.00
Caprice, goblet 30.00
Carnation, pickle dish 15.00
Chain, cordial 15.00
Chain, pitcher 65.00
Chandelier, finger bowl 35.00
Chandelier, sugar shaker 130.00
Checkerboard, cake plate, ruby stain 45.00
Checkerboard, spooner 25.00
Church Windows, celery vase 25.00
Church Windows, jelly compote, w/lid 45.00
Circular Saw, butter dish 55.00
Classic, bowl, w/lid, 7" 150.00
Classic, marmalade jar, w/lid 375.00
Clover, pitcher 65.00
Clover, shakers, ea 20.00
Colorado, bowl, bl or gr, lg 45.00
Comet, butter dish 55.00
Comet, mug 25.00
Compact, See Snail
Connecticut, plate 20.00
Coral Gables, cruet 55.00

Cord Drapery, cup, from $18.00 to $22.00. (Photo courtesy Gene and Cathy Florence)

Cottage, banana stand 35.00
Cottage, relish tray... 15.00
Cradled Prisms, sugar bowl 30.00
Crow's Foot, See Yale
Crystal Rock, tumbler... 10.00
Crystal Wedding, claret 25.00
Crystal Wedding, syrup, ruby stain 90.00
Currier & Ives, lamp, 9½" 100.00
Curved Star, cake stand 35.00
Cut Block, celery vase, ruby stain... 40.00
Cut Log, mustard jar 30.00
Dahlia & Fan, plate, 11" 35.00
Daisy & Bluebell, spooner 40.00
Daisy & Bluebell, wine 25.00
Daisy & Button (Hobbs), egg cup, amber 25.00
Daisy & Button Basket, bride's basket, vaseline......................... 115.00
Daisy & Button w/Thumbprint, bowl, bl or gr, 6"...................... 25.00
Dart, sugar bowl 30.00
Deer Alert, pitcher... 375.00
Delaware, pin tray, ruby stain 80.00

Delaware, pomade box, bl or gr 250.00
Diamond Lattice, plate 25.00

Diamond Point Loop, plate, square, green, $35.00. (Photo courtesy Bill Edwards and Mike Carwile)

Diamond Swag, spoon tray 25.00
Diamond Swirl, shakers, ea... 20.00
Doric, See Feather
Double Beetle Band, celery vase 20.00
Double Pinwheel, berry bowl, sm 15.00
Double Pinwheel, compote, w/lid 95.00
Double Pinwheel, tumbler 20.00
Double Ribbon, bread plate 20.00
Double Ribbon, pickle dish 25.00
Drapery, egg cup 30.00
Drapery, sugar bowl 35.00
Duncan #13, mug 40.00
Duncan's Late Block, bowl, sq 40.00
Duncan's Late Block, rose bowl 45.00
Early Excelsior, ale glass... 55.00
Early Excelsior, spillholder 80.00
Edgewood, butter dish.. 50.00
Edgewood, carafe 65.00
Egyptian, plate, pyramids.. 125.00
Elephant, See Jumbo
Emerald Green Herringbone, See Florida
Esther, caster set, ruby stain 165.00
Etta, nappy 20.00
Evangeline, pitcher 70.00
Eyewinker, vegetable bowl.. 35.00
Falling Leaves, dish, oval 15.00
Fan Band, wine 20.00
Fandango, cookie jar, tall.. 50.00
Fandango, custard cup 10.00
Fashion, orange bowl, w/base... 45.00
Fashion, salver, 8-12" 50.00
Feather, milk pitcher, bl or gr 175.00
Feather, toothpick holder, ruby stain 60.00
Federal #1910, berry bowl, sm 15.00
Federal #1910, mayonnaise set 45.00
Finecut & Block, finger bowl, amber.. 60.00
Finecut & Block, perfume bottle, bl or gr 100.00
Finecut & Panel, bread tray.. 30.00
Finecut Hearts, bowl, rare, 8-9".. 425.00
Fishscale, condiment tray 35.00
Fishscale, relish 20.00
Flamingo, butter dish.. 125.00
Flora, compote, bl or gr 45.00
Florida, pickle dish... 20.00
Florida, wine, gr or bl 75.00
Flower Medallion, sugar bowl... 30.00
Flute & Cane, champagne 15.00
Flute & Cane, vase 25.00

Framed Jewel, goblet, ruby stain 50.00
Framed Jewel, toothpick holder 40.00
Frosted Lion, cheese dish, w/lid, rare 400.00
Frosted Stork, bowl, 9" 60.00
Frosted Stork, water tray, 11-15½" 110.00
Fuchsia, mug 35.00
Garden of Eden, cake stand 45.00
Garden of Eden, platter, Our Daily Bread 85.00
Garfield Drape, compote 45.00
Garfield Drape, relish 25.00
Gem, See Nailhead
Globe & Star, celery vase 20.00
Globe & Star, sugar bowl 45.00
Gonderman Swirl, creamer, amber 35.00
Good Luck, See Horseshoe
Gooseberry, mug, milk glass 45.00
Gooseberry, syrup 65.00
Grand, cordial 15.00
Grand, waste bowl 20.00
Grape & Festoon, bowl 35.00
Grape Bunch, egg cup 25.00
Grapevine Basket, basket, metal hdl, bl or gr 80.00
Grasshopper, butter dish, amber 100.00
Grasshopper (deduct 50% if no insect present)
Greentown Squirrel, pitcher, rare 265.00
Grogan, butter dish 50.00
Grogan, spooner 20.00
Hairpin, compote 40.00
Hand, mug 55.00
Hand, wine 20.00
Hanover, cheese dish, w/lid 85.00
Hartley, bread plate 30.00
Heart & Sand, pitcher 90.00
Heart & Sand, tumbler 20.00
Heart Plume, pickle dish 20.00
Heavy Diamond, bowl, lg 30.00
Heavy Diamond, molasses can, vaseline 65.00
Heisey's #1250, cracker jar 50.00
Heisey's #1250, spoon tray 35.00
Hickman, bonbon, sq 20.00
Hickman, custard cup 15.00
Hobnail w/Fan, dish, oblong, amber 25.00
Hobnail w/Fan, tray, bl or gr 35.00
Hobstar, cookie jar, w/lid 40.00
Hobstar, plate, 10½" 25.00
Hops & Barley, See Wheat & Barley
Horseshoe, platter 35.00
Huber, bitters bottle 75.00
Hummingbird, cheese plate 35.00
Hummingbird, goblet, vaseline 65.00
Hummingbird, pitcher, amber 135.00
Illinois, ice cream bowl 25.00
Illinois, puff box 40.00
Illinois, straw holder 50.00
Indiana, bowl, oval, 7-9" 30.00
Indiana, ice tub 45.00
Indiana, pitcher 85.00
Intaglio Butterflies, compote, 7½" 55.00
Ivanhoe, cake salver 45.00
Ivanhoe, nappy 20.00
Jabot, creamer 20.00
Jacob's Ladder, cologne bottle 110.00
Jacob's Ladder, cruet 95.00
Jersey Swirl, bowl, vaseline 45.00

Jeweled Butterflies, milk pitcher, scarce 125.00
Job's Tears, See Art
Jubilee, butter dish 65.00
Jumbo, pitcher 700.00
Jumbo, sugar bowl, Barnum Head 475.00
King's Crown, claret, ruby stain 45.00
King's Crown, honey dish, sq 85.00
Klondike, pitcher 375.00
Knotted Beads, vase, red 125.00
Kokomo, decanter, ruby stain 100.00
Kokomo, wine 15.00
Lacy Daisy, puff box 35.00
Lacy Daisy, rose bowl 25.00
Laverne, berry bowl, lg 45.00
Laverne, pitcher 60.00
Leaf, See Maple Leaf
Leaf & Rib, celery vase, amber 30.00
Leaf & Rib, pitcher, bl or gr 100.00

Leaf and Star/#711, goblet, New Martinsville Glass Co., 1916, $30.00. (Photo courtesy Gene and Cathy Florence)

Leafy Scroll, spooner 25.00
Liberty, cordial 20.00
Loop, bitters bottle 80.00
Loop, egg cup 25.00
Lorne, butter dish, vaseline 145.00
Louisa, bowl, ftd 40.00
Lustre Rose, fernery 35.00
Magna, pickle tray 15.00
Magna, pitcher 85.00
Maltese, basket, 5" 55.00
Manhattan, plate, 5" 20.00
Manhattan, straw holder 60.00
Maple Leaf, dish, sq, 10" 30.00
Maple Leaf, tray, oblong, vaseline 80.00
Maple Leaf, tumbler, amber 40.00
Mardi Gras, bonbon, ruby stain 165.00
Mardi Gras, pomade jar 40.00
Melrose, milk pitcher 55.00
Melton, butter dish 55.00
Memphis, decanter, w/stopper 175.00
Memphis, punch bowl, w/base, regular 375.00
Millard, cup, ruby stain 25.00
Millard, plate 20.00
Minerva, bread plate 35.00
Minerva, platter, oval 50.00
Mitted Hand, bowl, 6" 75.00
Monkey, creamer 85.00
Monkey, pitcher, opal 1,000.00
Moon & Star, oil lamp 165.00

Mulberry, tray, rare, 8x13¼" 350.00
Nailhead, cake stand 35.00
Nailhead, cordial 15.00
Nailhead, dinner plate 25.00
New Hampshire, biscuit jar, ruby stain 150.00
New Hampshire, olive dish 15.00
Niagara, cracker jar 30.00
Niagara, syrup 55.00
Notched Panel, bowl, sq 20.00
Notched Panel, relish 15.00
Notched Panel, toothpick holder 20.00
Oaken Bucket, See Wooden Pail
Octagon, tumbler 20.00
Octagon, vase, ped ft 30.00
Old Colony, butter dish 45.00
Old Colony, celery vase 20.00
Old Colony, plate 15.00
Oregon, carafe 45.00
Oregon, cruet 60.00
Oregon, syrup 55.00
Paddle Wheel, jelly compote 25.00
Paddle Wheel, shakers, ea 20.00
Palm Beach, creamer 25.00
Palm Beach, pitcher 125.00
Palmette, cake stand 140.00
Palmette, salt dip, master 25.00

Panelled Cane, spooner, clear with gold, $20.00. (Photo courtesy Gene and Cathy Florence)

Panelled Dewdrop, pickle jar 20.00
Panelled Dewdrop, relish 15.00
Panelled Heather, salad bowl, ftd 30.00
Pavonia, compote, w/lid, 5-10" 70.00
Pavonia, mug, ruby stain 60.00
Pennsylvania, biscuit jar 75.00
Pennsylvania, pitcher, bl or gr 250.00
Persian, celery dish 15.00
Persian, cup 10.00
Pert, goblet, amber 40.00
Pert, water tray, vaseline 95.00
Pheasant, butter dish 245.00
Pheasant, creamer 80.00
Pigs in Corn, goblet, rare 500.00
Plume, cake stand 65.00
Plume, lamp 95.00
Polar Bear, pickle dish 95.00
Polar Bear, tray 200.00
Portland, basket, hdl 50.00
Portland, cruet 65.00
Prayer Rug, See Horseshoe
Pressed Diamond, berry bowl, sm 10.00
Pressed Diamond, custard cup, amber 15.00

Primrose, cake stand, vaseline 60.00
Primrose, cordial, bl or gr 35.00
Primrose, egg cup, milk glass 30.00
Priscilla, biscuit jar 45.00
Prism, compote 25.00
Prism, tumbler 10.00
Queen, claret, amber 40.00
Queen Anne, casserole, 7-8" 45.00
Queen Anne, shakers, ea 15.00
Rainbow, carafe 60.00
Rainbow, cigar jar 40.00
Rainbow, salt dip 30.00
Rainbow, wine tray 35.00
Raindrop, cake plate, amber 50.00
Raindrop, egg cup, vaseline 50.00
Red Block, bowl, ruby stain 75.00
Red Block, spooner, ruby stain 70.00
Reverse Torpedo, banana dish 35.00
Reverse Torpedo, plate 25.00
Rexford, cake stand 45.00
Ribbon, champagne 80.00
Ribbon, waste bowl 50.00
Rising Sun, bonbon, ftd 15.00
Rising Sun, vase 20.00
Robin Hood, milk pitcher, bl or gr 20.00
Robin Hood, pickle dish 15.00
Roman Key, egg cup 20.00
Roman Key, wine 15.00
Rose Point Band, bowl, ftd 25.00
Rose Point Band, creamer 20.00
Rose Sprig, dish, oblong 20.00
Rose Sprig, plate, vaseline, 6-10" 50.00
Roseland, pitcher 45.00
Roses in Snow, plate, 11" 45.00
Royal Crystal, cologne, ruby stain 85.00
Royal Crystal, cracker jar 65.00
Royal Ivy, See Northwood
Royal Oak, See Northwood
Ruby Thumbprint, See King's Crown
S-Repeat, pitcher, chocolate 900.00
S-Repeat, tray 50.00
Sandwich Star, cordial, vaseline 375.00
Sandwich Star, decanter, amethyst 550.00
Sawtooth, pomade jar 55.00
Sawtooth, wine 35.00
Sawtooth Band, See Amazon
Scalloped Skirt, berry bowl, bl or gr, sm 20.00
Scalloped Skirt, toothpick holder, amethyst 65.00
Scroll w/Flowers, pitcher 70.00
Sedan, mug 40.00
Sedan, relish tray 20.00
Sequoia, finger bowl 20.00
Sequoia, pickle jar 35.00
Sheaf & Block, shakers, ea 25.00
Shell & Jewel, cake stand 50.00
Sheraton, butter dish, amber 65.00
Sheraton, platter, oblong, 8 panels, bl or gr 45.00
Singing Birds, celery vase 20.00
Slick Willie, vase 25.00
Snail, cake basket, 10" 100.00
Snail, rose bowl, 3-7" 50.00
Snail, vase, ruby stain 100.00
Spirea, sugar shaker, bl or gr 70.00
Spirea Band, compote, amber, w/lid 45.00

Spirea Band, goblet, vaseline.. 50.00
Star & Crescent, pickle dish.. 15.00
Star & File, custard cup 15.00
Star Medallion, claret 15.00
Sterling, comport 35.00
Sterling, punch bowl.. 150.00
Strawberry & Cable, sweetmeat, w/lid 95.00
Strawberry & Cable, tumbler 20.00
Sunbeam, sauce 15.00
Sunflower, butter dish 55.00
Sunken Teardrop, pitcher 95.00
Sunken Teardrop, shakers, ea 20.00
Swan w/Tree, goblet... 90.00
Swan w/Tree, pitcher 235.00
Sydney, celery vase.. 35.00
Tacoma, banana dish, ruby stain.. 80.00
Tape Measure, sugar bowl 30.00
Teardrop, candlesticks, ea.. 25.00
Teardrop, pitcher... 65.00
Teasel, cracker jar... 40.00
Teasel, honey jar, w/lid.. 55.00
Texas, plate, ruby stain... 150.00
Texas, water bottle 125.00
Theatrical, See Actress
Thousand Eye, cologne, amber 40.00
Thousand Eye, inkwell, amber 70.00
Thousand Eye, jelly glass, vaseline 45.00
Three Face, biscuit jar... 350.00
Three Face, pitcher.. 400.00
Three Face, salt dip, ind 45.00
Three Panel, bowl, 8½-10" 30.00
Three Panel, cruet, amber 225.00
Three Panel, sugar bowl, bl or gr 65.00
Thunderbird, See Hummingbird
Tile, bread tray 30.00
Tile, olive dish.. 15.00
Tile, pitcher.. 75.00
Tiptoe, pickle dish... 15.00
Togo, berry bowl, ruby stain, lg 45.00
Tree of Life, honey plate 25.00
Tree of Life, See Portland
Tree of Love, bowl... 25.00
Tree of Love, plate, ruffled 30.00
Truncated Cube, decanter 70.00
Tulip, jug, qt 50.00
US Coin, ale glass, amber 50.00
US Coin, pitcher, frosted coins, 9½" 1,200.00
US Comet, celery vase, vaseline 50.00
US Sheraton, pin tray 20.00
Venetian, vase, 9" 95.00
Viking, egg cup... 35.00
Volunteer, plate, rare 450.00
Waffle & Star Band, butter dish 50.00
Waffle & Star Band, toothpick holder 40.00
Washington Centennial, bowl, 7-9" 35.00
Washington Centennial, milk pitcher 125.00
Weston, cake stand 35.00
Weston, sugar bowl 25.00
Wheat & Barley, mug, amber 35.00
Wheat & Barley, shakers, vaseline, ea.................................. 45.00
Willow Oak, creamer... 30.00
Willow Oak, plate, bl or gr 60.00
Wooden Pail, pitcher, amber 125.00
Wooden Pail, sugar pail, open, vaseline 50.00

Wyoming, compote, w/lid... 50.00
Wyoming, wine 40.00
X-Logs, bowl, oval... 25.00
X-Ray, cruet 65.00
X-Ray, syrup, bl or gr.. 250.00
Yale, celery vase 20.00
Yale, relish, oval 15.00
York, banana bowl... 35.00
Zenith, shakers, ea.. 20.00
Zipper Slash, pitcher... 85.00
Zippered Heart, bowl, berry; sm... 10.00
Zippered Heart, sherbet 15.00
Zippered Windows, wine 20.00

Paul Revere Pottery

The Saturday Evening Girls was a group of young immigrant girls headed by philanthropist Mrs. James Storrow who started meeting with them in the Boston library in 1899 for lectures, music, and dancing. Mrs. Storrow provided them with a kiln in 1906. Finding the facilities too small, they soon relocated near the Old North Church and chose the name Paul Revere Pottery. Under the supervision of Ms. Edith Brown, the girls produced simple ware. Until 1915 the pottery operated at a deficit, then a new building with four kilns was constructed on Nottingham Road. Vases, miniature jugs, children's tea sets, tiles, dinnerware, and lamps were produced, usually in soft matt glazes often decorated with wax-resist (cuerda seca) or a black-outlined stylized pattern of flowers, landscapes, or animals. Examples in black high gloss may also be found on occasion. Several marks were used: 'P.R.P.'; 'S.E.G.'; or the circular device, 'Boston, Paul Revere Pottery,' with the horse and rider. The pottery continued to operate; and even though it sold well, the high production costs of the handmade ware caused the pottery to fail in 1946. Our advisors for this category are Suzanne Perrault and David Rago; they are listed in the Directory under New Jersey.

Bowl, daffodils, mc on gr grass & bl, SEG/4-19/SG, 8½"...........3,000.00
Bowl, daffodils on yel, SEG/FI/6-14, 2½x8½" 1,920.00
Bowl, geese, wht/brn on yel, SEG/217, 4¼x10½", EX 5,100.00
Bowl, geese & trees band, 5-color, flared, stamp/label, 5x11½"... 15,500.00
Bowl, lotus blossoms, mc on yel, low, EM/6/1, 8½".....................400.00

Bowl, Midnight Ride of Paul Revere, interior band reads: A Voice in the Darkness, A Knock at the Door, and A Word That Shall Echo Forever More, PRP/6-41/LS, 3x7", $8,820.00. (Photo courtesy David Rago Auctions)

Bowl, pine trees landscape band on bl, circular stamp, 2¾x6¼" .. 1,650.00
Bowl, sailboats, wht/brn on bl, SEG/IG/157.7.11, 4x10½", EX .. 5,400.00
Bowl, trees band, tan on yel, sgn by SEG news editors, 2½x7", EX ..1,080.00

Bowl, trees band, tan/gr/bl/brn, SEG/11-16, 2½x8½" 2,800.00
Creamer, ducks on bl band, SEG/2-2-15, bruise, 3¼x3½" 725.00
Cup, trees band, bl/gr on wht, SEG/JG, 4½" dia..........................540.00
Mug, trees landscape/verse, sgn/SG/1912, 4" 3,750.00
Plate, chicks (3), Janice Her Plate, 4-color, PRP/5-4-40, 7½" 395.00
Plate, landscape medallion on bl-gray, FG/circular stamp, 12"..1,080.00
Plate, lotus blossoms on wht & bl, SEG/4-14/RM, 7½" 475.00
Plate, wht border w/blk ring & bl center, SEG/3-21/EG, 6⅜" 200.00
Saucer, water lilies band on ivory, mk, 6"..................................145.00
Tile, fox & grapes, mustard on gr, SEG/FR338.5'10/label, sq, 5¼"....2,880.00
Tile, tulip, gr/bl/wht/ocher, EM/6-25, 4½" dia...........................420.00
Vase, bl matt, cylindrical, PRP/9-23/FL, 6½" 175.00
Vase, bl mottle w/gr drips, incurvate rim, PRP/?-26, 7x5½".........660.00
Vase, daffodils band, yel/bl/gr on gr, shouldered, stamped mk, 13" ..10,000.00
Vase, repeated landscape on bl, 4-sided, SEG/JMD/AP/12-20, 4x2½"....1,440.00
Vase, trees band, dk gr & brn w/bl & wht sky, EM/6-26, 4¼x4" .. 2,650.00
Vase, trees band on purple-gray, SEG/LS2-17, 5¾x4½" 1,560.00
Vasw, trees band on yel, SEG/514, 8x3" 3,120.00
Vase, trees on yel, SEG/4-19, 7¾x3½".......................................3,900.00
Vase, yel matt, ovoid, incurvate rim, 1924, 8½".........................1,050.00

Pauline Pottery

Pauline Pottery was made form 1883 to 1888 in Chicago, Illinois, from clay imported from the Ohio area. The company's founder was Mrs. Pauline Jacobus, who had learned the trade at the Rookwood Pottery. Mrs. Jacobus moved to Edgerton, Wisconsin, to be near a source of suitable clay, thus eliminating shipping expenses. Until 1905 she produced high-quality wares, able to imitate with ease designs and styles of such masters as Wedgwood and Meissen. Her products were sold through leading department stores, and the names of some of these firms may appear on the ware. Not all are marked; unless signed by a noted local artist, positive identification is often impossible. Marked examples carry a variety of stamps and signatures: 'Trade Mark' with a crown, 'Pauline Pottery,' and 'Edgerton Art Pottery' are but a few.

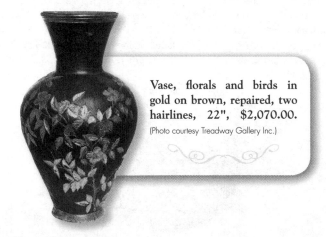

Vase, florals and birds in gold on brown, repaired, two hairlines, 22", $2,070.00.

(Photo courtesy Treadway Gallery Inc.)

Jardiniere, bl ribbons/HP flower garlands on ivory, #90, 4¼x5½" .. 420.00
Jug, monk HP in Barbotine on cream gloss, crown mk, 8x5" 780.00
Lamp base, wild roses, pk on brn, factory hole, metal base, 13", NM..450.00
Pitcher, reserve: bearded man w/cup & pipe, leaves surround, 10x8" .. 2,880.00
Vase, ivory w/gilt floral, pk/gold bands, 3-lobe stick neck, att, 12".......275.00

Peachblow

Peachblow, made to imitate the colors of the Chinese Peachbloom porcelain, was made by several glasshouses in the late 1800s. Among them were New England Glass, Mt. Washington, Webb, and Hobbs, Brockunier and Company (Wheeling). Its pink shading was achieved through action of the heat on the gold content of the glass. While New England's peachblow shades from deep crimson to white, Mt. Washington's tends to shade from pink to blue-gray. Many pieces were enameled and gilded. While by far the majority of the pieces made by New England had a satin (acid) finish, they made shiny peachblow as well. Wheeling glass, on the other hand, is rarely found in satin. In the 1950s Gundersen-Pairpoint Glassworks initiated the reproduction of Mt. Washington peachblow, using an exact duplication of the original formula. Though of recent manufacture, this glass is very collectible.

Claret jug, Wheeling, rigaree colar, amber reed hdl, #322, 9½"... 4,600.00
Creamer, Drape, sqd rim, crystal reeded hdl, 4½" 345.00
Creamer & sugar bowl, NE Glass, optic ribs, loop hdls, 5", 3½"...690.00
Creamer & sugar bowl, Wheeling, SP lid & Manhattan leaf-emb caddy, 10"..2,760.00
Cruet, Wheeling, amber faceted stopper, reed hdl, bulbous, 7" ..1,200.00
Decanter, Wheeling, pilgrim flask form, amber rope-twist hdl, 10"....1,500.00
Finger bowl, NE Glass, ruffled rim, 5" 345.00
Finger bowl, simple coupe form, 4", set of 6..................................285.00
Perfume, Mt WA, ribbed pillar form w/bl faceted stopper, floral, 5" ...1,400.00
Pitcher, tankard; Wheeling, amber hdl, sm closed surface bubble, 10"....4,800.00
Pitcher, Wheeling, sq mouth, dk amber hdl, 8" 1,350.00
Punch cup, Mt WA, flattened Hobnail, 2¾" 460.00
Shaker, NE Glass, pillar form, 4" 345.00
Sugar bowl, Mt WA, ftd ovoid, 3" W 1,025.00
Sugar bowl, raspberry to wht, ribbed, lg wht hdls, 4½" W 120.00
Tazza, Gundersen, EX color, petal rim, swirled ball below bowl, 7x7"...288.00
Toothpick holder, Libbey, hat form w/ribbed body, 2" 375.00
Tumbler, lemonade; Mt WA, Dmn Quilt, shiny, 4¾" 285.00
Tumbler, NE Glass, shiny, 3¾"...185.00
Vase, Bohemian, Morrish mc/gold motif, shouldered bottle form, 11", pr .800.00
Vase, jack-in-pulpit; Mt WA, 12"..1,725.00
Vase, lily; Gundersen, EX color, 9"...175.00
Vase, lily; NE Glass, shiny, tri-fold, 6½" 240.00
Vase, lily; NE Glass, 3-fold rim, 9" 600.00
Vase, lily; NE Glass, 3-fold rim, 18" 1,095.00
Vase, Morgan; Wheeling, glass griffin holder, 10"......................2,500.00
Vase, Mt WA, classic shape w/hdls, ftd, 6½" 520.00
Vase, Mt WA, daisies, gourd shape, 9" 4,600.00
Vase, Mt WA, Desert Series, lg bl elephant/natives, shoulder hdls, 13"....20,700.00
Vase, Mt WA, lt bl to pk, yel floral, dbl-gourd bottle form, 8"...2,100.00
Vase, Mt WA, orchids, gold rim, gourd shape, 8"......................1,095.00
Vase, Mt WA, Queen's pattern, rnd w/stick neck, 5¾x3"..........9,775.00
Vase, Webb, gold ginkgo/butterflies, shouldered, 11"....................460.00
Vase, Webb, gold prunus, dbl gourd, 7" 600.00
Vase, Wheeling, bulbous w/stick neck, #13 in catalog, 11" 800.00
Vase, Wheeling, elongated teardrop w/stick neck, 9" 520.00
Vase, Wheeling, rigaree ring at base of stick neck, 8"................1,150.00
Vase, Wheeling, satin, bulbous w/stick neck, 10" 1,000.00
Vase, Wheeling, shouldered, #6 in catalog, 8¼" 1,150.00

Peking Cameo Glass

The first glasshouse was established in Peking in 1680. It produced glassware made in imitation of porcelain, a more desirable medium to the Chinese. By 1725 multilayered carving that resulted in a cameo effect lead to the manufacture of a wider range of shapes and colors. The factory was closed from 1736 to 1795, but glass made in Po-shan and shipped to Peking for finishing continued to be called Peking glass. Similar glassware was made through the first half of the twentieth century. Our advisor for this category is Jeff Person; he is listed in the Directory under Florida.

Bowl, ducks & lotus plants, gr to wht, early 20th C, 8¼" 150.00
Jar, floral, rose-red on wht, 20th C, w/lid, 3x2" 60.00
Vase, butterflies, red on wht, classic shape, 20th C, 12x5", pr...... 145.00
Vase, butterflies & pond lilies, turq on wht, 20th C, 13x5½", pr.... 80.00
Vase, floral, cobalt on wht, baluster, late 1800s, 9½" 285.00
Vase, flowering trees/bird, emerald gr on wht, 20th C, 6", pr 145.00
Vase, horses prancing, cobalt on wht, ovoid, ca 1900, 8" 150.00
Vase, kingfishers/lotus, blk to wht, late 19th C, 8½", pr 575.00

Peloton

Peloton glass was first made by Wilhelm Kralik in Bohemia in 1880. This unusual art glass was produced by rolling colored threads onto the transparent or opaque glass gather as it was removed from the furnace. Usually more than one color of threading was used, and some items were further decorated with enameling. It was made with both shiny and acid finishes.

Vase, blue with pastel strings, 8", $300.00. (Photo courtesy Cincinnati Art Galleries)

Butter dish, clear w/mc strings, 6½x9" 500.00
Pitcher, amber w/red/bl/yel/wht strings, amber reed hdl, 7½" 250.00
Pitcher, clear w/mc strings, clear hdl, 4½" 185.00
Pitcher, clear w/mc strings, 5½" 200.00
Tumbler, clear w/gr strings, 3¼x2⅝" 175.00
Vase, clear w/cranberry strings, ftd, 7¾" 385.00

Pennsbury

Established in the 1950s in Morrisville, Pennsylvania, by Henry Below, the Pennsbury Pottery produced dinnerware and novelty items, much of which was sold in gift shops along the Pennsylvania Turnpike. Henry and his wife, Lee, worked for years at the Stangl Pottery before striking out on their own. Lee and her daughter were the artists responsible for many of the early pieces, the bird figures among them. Pennsbury pottery was hand painted, some in blue on white, some in multicolor on caramel. Pennsylvania Dutch motifs, Amish couples, and barbershop singers were among their most popular decorative themes. Sgraffito (hand incising), was used extensively. The company marked their wares 'Pennsbury Pottery' or 'Pennsbury Pottery, Morrisville, PA.'

In October of 1969 the company closed. Contents of the pottery were sold in December of the following year, and in April of 1971, the buildings burned to the ground. Items marked Pennsbury Glenview or Stumar Pottery (or these marks in combination) were made by Glenview after 1969. Pieces manufactured after 1976 were made by the Pennington Pottery. Several of the old molds still exist, and the original Pennsbury Caramel process is still being used on novelty items, some of which are produced by Lewis Brothers, New Jersey. Production of Pennsbury dinnerware was not resumed after the closing. Our advisor for this category is Shirley Graff; she is listed in the Directory under Ohio. Note: Prices may be higher in some areas of the country — particularly on the East Coast, the southern states, and Texas. Values for examples in the Rooster patterns apply to both black and red variations.

Ashtray, Pennsbury Inn, 8" 45.00
Ashtray, Solebury National Bank, 5" 30.00
Ashtray, Sommerset, 1804-1954, 5" dia 30.00
Bank, Hershey Kiss, brn, 4" 20.00
Bank, jug, pig decor, cork top, 7" 55.00
Bookends, eagle, 8" 185.00
Bowl, Dutch Talk, 9" 85.00
Bowl, pretzel; Eagle, 12x8" 85.00
Bowl, pretzel; Red Barn, 12x8" 150.00
Butter dish, Folk Art, 5x4" 35.00
Candleholders, Rooster, saucer type, pr 60.00
Candy dish, Hex, heart shaped, 6x6" 35.00
Casserole, Rooster, w/lid, 10¼x8¼" 100.00
Chip & dip, Rooster, 11" 85.00
Coaster, Doylestown Trust Co, 1896-1958, 5" dia 25.00
Coaster, Gay Ninety, 5" dia 35.00
Coaster, Quartet, face of Olson, 5" dia 30.00
Coffeepot, Hex, 6-cup, hearts in design, 8½" 40.00
Coffeepot, Rooster, 2-cup, 6" 55.00
Compote, Rooster, ftd, 5" 40.00
Cookie jar, Red Barn.. 225.00
Cruets, oil & vinegar; Rooster, pr 150.00
Desk basket, Lafayette, train decor, 4" 60.00
Desk basket, Two Women Under Tree, 5" 50.00
Display sign, bird atop, 4½x5" 175.00
Dresser tray, tulips w/pastel shades, sgn ET (Ester Titus), 7¼x4".... 35.00
Figurine, Bluebird, #103, 4" 150.00
Figurine, Cardinal, #120, 6½" 175.00
Figurine, Chickadee, #111, 3½" 120.00
Mug, coffee; Eagle, 3¼" 20.00
Mug, coffee; Rooster 25.00
Mug, Irish coffee; horse decor w/gold trim 40.00
Pie plate, Rooster, 9" 40.00
Pitcher, Blue Dowry, 5" 55.00
Pitcher, Folk Art (later called Brown Dowry), 5" 50.00
Plaque, Baltimore & Ohio RR Veterans, Phili 1955, 7½x5½"........ 50.00
Plaque, General, train decor, 11x8".. 55.00
Plaque, Greater Lower Bucks County Week June 7-13, 1953, 8" dia...45.00
Plaque, It's Making Down, 4" 25.00
Plaque, Mother Serving Pie, 6" dia.. 35.00
Plaque, Stourbridge Lion, 1829, 11x8".. 55.00
Plaque, The Bark, Charles W Morgan ship, 11x8" 110.00
Plaque, The Flying Cloud, dtd 1851, 9½x7" 110.00
Plate, Amish, 9" 40.00
Plate, Boy & Girl, w/primary colors, 11" 95.00
Plate, Eagle, 8" 50.00
Plate, Harvest, 8" 40.00
Plate, Peahen Over Heart, 11" 85.00
Plate, Two Birds Over Heart, 11" 85.00
Shakers, pitcher shape, Amish couple, pr from $30 to 45.00
Snack set, Rooster, tray & cup, from $20 to.................................... 25.00
Sugar bowl, Rooster, w/lid 30.00
Tray, Church of the Redeemer, Longport NJ, 1908-1958, 8" dia.... 50.00
Tray, Fidelity Mutual Life, 75th Anniversary, plum colored, 7x6".. 40.00
Wall pocket, floral in heart shape w/bl border, 6½" 50.00

Pens and Pencils

The first metallic writing pen was patented in 1809, and soon machine-produced pens with steel nibs gradually began replacing the quill. The first fountain pen was invented in 1830, but due to the fact that the ink flow was not consistent (though leakage was), they were not manufactured commercially until the 1880s. The first successful commercial producers were Waterman in 1884 and Parker with the Lucky Curve in 1888. The self-filling pen of the early 1900s featured the soft, interior sack which filled with ink as the metal bar on the outside of the pen was raised and lowered. Variations of the filling mechanisms were tried until 1932 when Parker introduced the Vacumatic, a sackless pen with an internal pump. Unless noted otherwise, prices below are for pens in near mint or better condition which have been professionally restored to full operating capacity. For unrestored as-found pens, approximagely one third should be deducted from the values below. For more information we recommend *Fountain Pens, Past & Present,* by Paul Erano (Collector Books). Our advisor for this category is Gary Lehrer; he is listed in the Directory under Connecticut. For those interested in purchasing pens through catalogs, our advisor, Mr. Lehrer publishes extensive catalogs.

Key:

AF — aeromatic filler	HR — hard rubber
BF — button filler	LF — lever filler
CF — capillary filler	NP — nickel plated
CPT — chrome-plated trim	NPT — nickel-plated trim
ED — eyedropper filler	PF — plunger filler
GF — gold-filled	PIF — piston filler
GFT — gold-filled trim	

Fountain Pens

Aiken Lambert, 1900, #2, ED, GF Gopheresque (rare), med, NM ..600.00
C Stewart, 1938, #15, LF, gr pearl, NPT, NM 75.00
C Stewart, 1950, #74, twist filler, red herringbone, fretwork band, NM...200.00
C Stewart, 1951, #27, LF, silver candy-strip, GFT, NM 175.00
C Stewart, 1951, #55, LF, gr marble, GFT, NM 150.00
C Stewart, 1952, #27, LF, Tiger's Eye, GFT, NM 250.00
C Stewart, 1955, #55, LF, bl marble, GFT, NM 200.00
C Stewart, 1955, #58, LF, gr pearl web, GFT, NM 185.00
C Stewart, 1956, #76, gr herringbone, GFT, NM 200.00
C Stewart, 1956, #85, LF, bl pearl w/gold veins, GFT, NM 150.00
Carters, 1928, #6 sz INX, LF, coral, GFT, NM 825.00
Carters, 1928, #6 sz INX, LF, Ivory Pearltex, GFT, NM 500.00
Carters, 1928, #7 sz INX, bl pearl, GFT, NM 600.00
Chilton, 1924, #6 sleeve filler, blk, GFT, NM 300.00
Conklin, 1918, #20, CF, blk chased HR, GFT, NM 175.00
Conklin, 1918, #40, crescent filler, blk chased HR, GFT, NM ..25,000.00
Conklin, 1927, #2, LF, wht w/blk veins (rare), GFT, NM 300.00
Conklin, 1927, Endura Lg, LF, blk, GFT, NM.............................. 450.00
Conklin, 1927, Endura Lg, LF, sapphire bl, GFT, NM 650.00
Conklin, 1927, Endura Oversz, blk, HR, long cap/section, GFT, NM.. 1,200.00
Conklin, 1927, Endura Standard, LF, Cardinal, GFT, NM 225.00
Conklin, 1930, Endura Symetric Oversz, LF, blk/bronze, GFT, NM...350.00
Conklin, 1932, Nozac, PF, gr pearl w/blk stripe, GFT, NM 300.00
Crocker, 1910, #2, blow filler, blk chased HR, NM 200.00
Crocker, 1932, #2, hatchet filler, blk chased HR, GFT, NM 175.00
Dann, 1921, #2, pump fill, blk HR, GFT, NM 200.00
Eclipse, 1931, #2, LF, Mandarin Yellow w/jade ends, GFT, NM ... 100.00
Esterbrook, 1949, LJ Pen, LF, red, NM 35.00
Esterbrook, 1949, SJ Pen, LF, red, NM 30.00
Esterbrook, 1950, Pastel Pen, LF, wht, NM.................................. 75.00
Esterbrook, 1950, Relief #12, Tiger's Eye web, GFT, NM 275.00
Leboeuf, 1928, #4, sleeve fill, Green Pearltex, GFT, NM 450.00
Leboeuf, 1932, #8, sleeve fill, Green Pearltex, GFT, NM 1,500.00
Mabie Todd, 1925, #44 Eternal, LF, blk, NM 150.00
Mabie Todd, 1925, #44 Eternal, LF, jade, NM 225.00
Mabie Todd, 1938, Blackbird, bulb filler, gr & gold spiral, GFT, NM .175.00
Mabie Todd, 1939, #4, LF, silver pearl snakeskin, NM 275.00
Mabie Todd, 1947, Swan #3240, LF, dk gr, GFT, NM................. 125.00
Montblanc, 1927, #1266, PIF, chrome plate flute, NM................ 200.00

Montblanc, 1935, #20, blk, GFT, NM 600.00
Montblanc, 1935, #20, Coral Red, GFT, NM 750.00
Montblanc, 1935, #25, blk, GFT, NM 750.00
Montblanc, 1935, #25, Coral Red, GFT, NM 900.00
Montblanc, 1935, #30, blk, GFT, NM 850.00
Montblanc, 1935, #30, Coral Red, GFT, NM 1,100.00
Montblanc, 1937, #134, blk w/long window, NM 650.00
Montblanc, 1937, #333½, PIF, blk, GFT, NM............................. 450.00
Montblanc, 1939, #139, PIF, blk, GFT & silver trim, NM 3,000.00
Montblanc, 1941, #25 Masterpiece, PIF, 12-sided marble, GFT, NM .. 1,500.00
Montblanc, 1947, #136, PIF, blk, GFT, NM 1,000.00
Montblanc, 1950, #146, PIF, gr stripe, GFT, NM...................... 1,250.00
Montblanc, 1950, #246, PIF, blk, GFT, short window, NM 450.00
Montblanc, 1950, #642N, silver striped, brushed chrome cap w/GFT, NM .800.00
Montblanc, 1952, #142, PIF, blk GFT, NM 350.00
Montblanc, 1955, #124, PF, GF, fluted, M 2.50
Montblanc, 1955, #82, PIF, GF pinstripe 275.00
Moore, 1925, L-96, dk bl, GFT, NM 400.00
Moore, 1925, L-96, LF, maroon/burgundy, GFT, NM 500.00
Moore, 1946, #2, LF, gr pearl web, GFT, NM 125.00
Parker, 1918, Black Giant, ED, blk HR, NP clip, NM 1,500.00
Parker, 1921, Duofold Jr, BF, red HR, bandless cap, NM 300.00
Parker, 1921, Duofold Sr, BF, red HR, bandless cap, MIB..........1,500.00
Parker, 1928, Duofold Sr, BF, Mandarin Yellow, GFT, NM 1,750.00
Parker, 1930, Duofold Special, BF, red, GFT, EX 250.00
Parker, 1932, BF, blk, bandless, NM 75.00
Parker, 1932, Thrift Time, BF, gray marble, GFT, NM 200.00
Parker, 1935, Victory, BF, bl marble, GFT, NM 300.00
Parker, 1937, Vacumatic Oversz, blk, GFT, NM 350.00
Parker, 1937, Vacumatic Oversz, brn banded, GFT, NM 450.00
Parker, 1937, Vacumatic Oversz, gr banded, GFT, NM 500.00
Parker, 1937, Vacumatic Oversz, gr banded, NPT, NM 400.00
Parker, 1937, Vacumatic Oversz, red banded, GFT, NM 650.00
Parker, 1939, Duofold Jr, BF, silver geometric, NPT, NM 125.00
Parker, 1939, Vacumatic Slender, red laminated, GFT, NM......... 125.00
Parker, 1945, Vacumatic Major, silver laminated, NPT, dbl jeweled, EX...175.00
Parker, 1946, #51, AF, forest gr, brushed lustraloy cap, M 125.00
Parker, 1946, NS (New Style) Duofold, gray, NPT, NM 300.00
Parker, 1948, #51, AF, Buckskin, GF cap w/pinstripe & plain panels, NM..200.00
Parker, 1948, #51, AF, plum, GF cap, NM 175.00
Parker, 1950, #51, Mark II, AF, rare later version, NM 150.00
Parker, 1951, #51, plum, brushed lustraloy cap, NM 175.00
Parker, 1957, #61, wick fill, blk, 2-tone lustraloy cap, NM.......... 100.00
Parker, 1960, #45, cartridge/converter, bronzed/anodized, M 100.00
Parker, 1965, #75, sterling silver crosshatch (flat ends), NM 175.00
Parker, 1965, #75 Spanish Treasure LE, sterling silver crosshatch, MIB..1,600.00
Parker, 1970, #T-1 (Titanium), M 750.00
Parker, 1970, #T-1 Titanium Ball (ballpoint) Pen, M 300.00
Parker, 1970, #75 Titanium, M 800.00
Parker, 1975, #75, sterling silver crosshatch (dimpled ends), NM....150.00
Parker (Valentine), 1935, #32, BF, burgundy pearl web, GFT, rare, NM .150.00
Pelikan, 1937, #100N, gr pearl, GFT, NM 300.00
Pelikan, 1937, #100N, tortoise w/matching cap/derby, NM 1,100.00
Pelikan, 1938, #100N, gr pearl, chased GF band/clip, NM 325.00
Pelikan, 1938, #100N, tortoise w/red cap, NM 1,100.00
Pelikan, 1938, IBIS, PIF, blk, GFT, NM 175.00
Pelikan, 1950, #400, PIF, brn stripe, GFT, NM 185.00
Pelikan, 1950, #400, PIF, gr stripe, GFT, NM 175.00
Pelikan, 1950, #400, PIF gr V stripe, gr cap/tuning knob/section, NM...450.00
Salz, 1920, Peter Pan, LF, dk red w/blk veins, GFT, NM 75.00
Salz, 1925, Peter Pan, LF, blk, HR, GFT, rare longer length, NM ..60.00
Salz, 1925, Peter Pan, LF, tan/brn Bakelite, GFT, NM 60.00
Sheaffer, 1930, Lifetime Balance Lg, LF, brn stripe, GFT, NM..... 325.00
Sheaffer, 1930, Lifetime Balance Lg, LF, Carmine Red stripe, GFT, NM ..600.00

Sheaffer, 1930, Lifetime Balance Lg, LF, ebonized pearl, GFT, NM ...500.00
Sheaffer, 1930, Lifetime Balance Lg, LF, gr stripe, GFT, NM 350.00
Sheaffer, 1930, Lifetime Balance Lg, LF, Roseglow stripe, GFT, NM .1,200.00
Sheaffer, 1936, Feather Touch #8 Lg Balance, gray marble, NM.. 750.00
Sheaffer, 1937, Standard Sz Lifetime Balance, LF, blk, GFT, NM.. 75.00
Sheaffer, 1942, Lifetime Triumph, PF, silver laminated, NPT, EX.. 75.00
Sheaffer, 1950, Triumph Snorkle, GF, NM 100.00
Sheaffer, 1952, Clipper Snorkle, sage gr, chrome cap w/GFT, MIB.. 150.00
Sheaffer, 1954, Valiant Snorkle, burgundy, NM 50.00
Sheaffer, 1954, Valiant Snorkle, pk, NM 100.00
Sheaffer, 1958, Lady Skripsert, gold-plated, jeweled ring, EX 35.00
Sheaffer, 1959, PFM I, blk, blk cap, CPT, NM............................. 175.00
Sheaffer, 1959, PFM II, blk, stainless steel cap, NM 200.00
Sheaffer, 1959, PFM II, burgundy, stainless steel cap, GFT, NM.. 200.00
Sheaffer, 1959, PFM III, blk, blk cap, GFT, NM......................... 200.00
Sheaffer, 1959, PFM III, gray (rare), GFT, NM............................ 375.00
Sheaffer, 1959, PFM III Demonstrator, transparent, GFT, blk shell, NM.. 1,000.00
Sheaffer, 1959, PFM IV, blk, GF cap, GFT, NM 400.00
Sheaffer, 1959, PFM V, blk polished chrome cap, GFT, NM........ 350.00
Soennecken, 1952, 111 Extra, PIF, gr herringbone, NM 900.00
Soennecken, 1952, 111 Superior, PIF, golden weave, NM 600.00
Soennecken, 1952, 222 Extra, PIF, blk....................................... 450.00
Soennecken, 1952, 222 Superior, PIF, silver lizard, NM 375.00
Wahl Eversharp, 1920, #0, LF, GF pinstripe, NM....................... 55.00
Wahl Eversharp, 1927, Gold Seal, LF, rosewood, NM 200.00
Wahl Eversharp, 1929, #2, LF, rosewood, GFT, NM................... 175.00
Wahl Eversharp, 1929, Equipoised, LF, blk & pearl, GFT, NM.... 350.00
Wahl Eversharp, 1929, Oversz Deco Band, LF, blk, GFT, NM 450.00
Wahl Eversharp, 1929, Oversz Deco Band, LF, Lapis, GFT, NM.. 900.00
Wahl Eversharp, 1929, Oversz Deco Band, woodgrain, GFT, NM..650.00
Wahl Eversharp, 1934, #2 Doric, LF, blk & pearl, NPT, NM 300.00
Wahl Eversharp, 1942, Skyline Jr, LF, bl Moderne stripe, GFT, NM..125.00
Wahl Eversharp, 1951, Symphony, LF, blk, GFT, M w/orig label . 100.00
Waterman, 1910, #18S Safety ED, blk, HR, rare, M 2,600.00
Waterman, 1915, #52, LF, blk chased HR, NPT, NM................... 150.00
Waterman, 1920, #52½ V, LF, Cardinal HR, GFT, NM............... 200.00
Waterman, 1920, #554½ LEC, LF, GF Gothic eng, NM 375.00
Waterman, 1924, #452, LF, sterling Gothic, NM........................ 350.00
Waterman, 1924, #54, LF, blk HR, GFT, NM 175.00
Waterman, 1925, #058, blk HR, GFT, NM................................. 900.00
Waterman, 1925, #552½, ED, Secretary in GF filigree, NM 400.00
Waterman, 1926, #7, LF, red ripple w/red band, GFT, NM+ 400.00
Waterman, 1927, #7, LF, red ripple, pk band, 1st yr model, NM.. 500.00
Waterman, 1929, Patrician, LF, moss agate..............................1,250.00
Waterman, 1929, Patrician, LF, Nacre (blk & pearl), GFT, M color .. 2,250.00
Waterman, 1929, Patrician, LF, Onyx (red cream), GFT, M color. 2,500.00
Waterman, 1930, #94, LF, bl & cream, NPT, NM 225.00
Waterman, 1930, #94, LF, brn & cream (mahog), GFT, NM 250.00
Waterman, 1930, #94, LF, red ripple HR, GFT, NM 400.00
Waterman, 1940, #2 Model 513, LF (England), GFT, NM 125.00
Waterman, 1940, 100 yr, blk, smooth cap/bbl, GFT, NM............. 400.00

Mechanical Pencils

Anonymous, rifle shape, cocking mechanism, eng Rin Tin Tin, NM ..75.00
Autopoint, 1945, 2-color (blk & bl), w/clip, M............................. 15.00
Conklin, 1929, Symetric, gr marble, GFT, EX 50.00
Cross/Tiffany 1990, sterling silver pinstripe, clip: Tiffany, MIB.... 100.00
Eversharp, 1940, blk snakeskin-pattern leather cover, GFT, NM.. 100.00
Montblanc, 1924, #6, octagonal, blk HR, rare, lg, NM 1,350.00
Montblanc, 1930, #92 Repeater, blk HR, NPT, NM 125.00
Montblanc, 1939, #392 Repeater, blk HR, NM............................ 80.00
Parker, 1929, Duofold Jr, jade, GFT, NM 50.00
Parker, 1929, Duofold Jr, Mandarin Yellow, GFT, NM 250.00

Parker, 1930, Duofold Vest Pocket, burgundy, GFT, w/opener taper, NM ...250.00
Parker, 1948, Duofold Repeater, gray, GFT, NM.......................... 150.00
Sheaffer, 1925, Balance, deep jade, GFT, NM+ 50.00
Sheaffer, 1925, Balance, gr marble, GFT, NM+ 40.00
Sheaffer, 1959, PRM III, blk, GFT, M w/orig decal...................... 175.00
Wahl Eversharp, 1929, Oversz Deco Band, blk & pearl, GFT, NM.. 175.00
Wahl Eversharp, 1939, Coronet, blk w/smooth GF cap, NM....... 100.00
Waterman, 1925, blk HR, GFT, M... 100.00
Waterman, 1928, #52½ V, olive ripple, GFT, NM 85.00

Sets

Parker, 1940, Vacuum Jr, gr/bronze/blk stripes, GFT, NM 175.00
Parker, 1957, GF, alternating pinstripes & panels, M 200.00
Sheaffer, 1925, #3-25 Tall, blk plastic, GFT, NM 100.00

Sheaffer, ca. 1932, Lifetime Balance pen and pencil set in pearl and black plastic, lever filler, split cap bands; Set: $350.00; Pen only, $250.00. (Photo courtesy Paul Erano)

Sheaffer, 1936, Junior, LF, gray marble, NPT, NM 100.00
Sheaffer, 1952, Clipper Triumph Snorkle, bright red, chrome caps, MIB.. 200.00
Sheaffer, 1958, Lady Skripsert, GF filigree & bl, MIB 45.00
Sheaffer, 1959, PFM III, blk, GFT, MIB...................................... 325.00
Wahl Eversharp, #4, GF w/chased wave pattern, NM 175.00
Waterman, 1925, #52, LF, red ripple, GFT, NM 250.00

Personalities, Fact and Fiction

One of the largest and most popular areas of collecting today is character-related memorabilia. Everyone has favorites, whether they be comic-strip personalities or true-life heroes. The earliest comic strip dealt with the adventures of the Yellow Kid, the smiling, bald-headed Oriental boy always in a nightshirt. He was introduced in 1895, a product of the imagination of Richard Fenton Outcault. Today, though very hard to come by, items relating to the Yellow Kid bring premium prices.

Though her 1923 introduction was unobtrusively made through only one newspaper, New York's *Daily News*, Little Orphan Annie, the vacant-eyed redhead in the inevitable red dress, was quickly adopted by hordes of readers nationwide, and before the demise of her creator, Harold Gray, in 1968, she had starred in her own radio show. She made two feature films, and in 1977 'Annie' was launched on Broadway.

Other early comic figures were Moon Mullins, created in 1923 by Frank Willard; Buck Rogers by Philip Nowlan in 1928; and Betty Boop, the round-faced, innocent-eyed, chubby-cheeked Boop-Boop-a-Doop girl of the early 1930s. Bimbo was her dog and KoKo her clown friend.

Popeye made his debut in 1929 as the spinach-eating sailor with the spindly-limbed girlfriend, Olive Oyl, in the comic strip *Thimble Theatre*, created by Elzie Segar. He became a film star in 1933 and had his own radio show that during 1936 played three times a week on CBS. He obligingly modeled for scores of toys, dolls, and figurines, and especially those from the '30s are very collectible.

Tarzan, created around 1930 by Edgar Rice Burroughs, and Captain Midnight, by Robert Burtt and Willfred G. Moore, are popular heroes with today's collectors. During the days of radio, Sky King of the Flying Crown

Ranch (also created by Burtt and Moore) thrilled boys and girls of the mid-1940s. Hopalong Cassidy, Red Rider, Tom Mix, and the Lone Ranger were only a few of the other 'good guys' always on the side of law and order.

But of all the fictional heroes and comic characters collected today, probably the best loved and most well known is Mickey Mouse. Created in the late 1920s by Walt Disney, Micky (as his name was first spelled) became an instant success with his film debut, Steamboat Willie. His popularity was parlayed through windup toys, watches, figurines, cookie jars, puppets, clothing, and numerous other products. Items from the 1930s are usually copyrighted 'Walt Disney Enterprises'; thereafter, 'Walt Disney Productions' was used.

For more information we recommend *Schroeder's Collectible Toys, Antique to Modern,* available from Collector Books. See also Autographs; Banks; Big Little Books; Children's Books; Comic Books; Cookie Jars; Dolls; Games; Lunch Boxes; Movie Memorabilia; Paper Dolls; Pin-Back Buttons; Posters; Puzzles; Rock 'n Roll Memorabilia; Toys. When no condition is noted in the description, assume the value is for examples in excellent to near-mint condition.

A-Team, Blowgun Gliders, Arco, 1983, MOC 45.00
Addams Family, Lurch figure, plastic, Remco, 1960s, 5", MIB 275.00
Addams Family, Morticia hand puppet, vinyl head, cloth body ... 225.00
Alvin & Chipmunks, Simon, cloth, musical, Knickerbocker, 1963, 13".. 75.00
Amos & Andy, figure set, wood, pnt names on front, 6" 350.00
Animal Crackers, Grandpa Turtle bank, ceramic, 5" 55.00
Aristocats, Colorforms, 1960s, MIB 50.00
Atom Ant, punch-out playset, Whitman, unused, EXIB................. 75.00
Atom Ant, push-button puppet, Kohner, 1960s 125.00
Augie Doggie, figure, jtd rubber, lt bl collar, Bucky, 1970s, 8" 75.00
Baba Looey, doll, plush/vinyl, w/orange sombrero, Knickerbocker, 1959... 50.00
Baby Huey, hand puppet, cloth w/vinyl head, Gund, 1950s........... 75.00
Bambi, figure, celluloid, w/metal stand, WD, 1940s, 4" 75.00
Bambi, push-button puppet, Kohner, 1960s..................................... 25.00
Barney Google, hand puppet, cloth w/vinyl head & cigar, Gund, 1950s... 100.00
Barney Google & Spark Plug, bank, pnt CI w/emb name on side, 7½" .. 85.00
Barney Google & Spark Plug, figure, wood, Schoenhut, 10½" 250.00
Bat Masterson, figure, Gene Barry labels, Kaynee, MIB 160.00
Batman, bank, ceramic, wht base w/red name, Lego, 1966, 7" 65.00
Batman, Bat Grenade, shaped like bat, National Periodicals, 1966, MOC... 140.00
Batman, costume, Ben Cooper, 1969, NMIB.................................. 60.00
Batman, hand puppet, plastic body w/molded head, Ideal, 1966.......... 50.00
Batman, Joker bank, plastic, bust figure w/emb name, Mego, 1974, 8" ... 60.00
Batman, Oil Painting by Numbers, NPP, 1965, NMIB................. 140.00
Batman, Utility Belt, complete w/accessories, Remco, MIB.......... 950.00
Batman & Robin, scissors, Chemtoy, 1973, MOC........................ 25.00
Battlestar Galactica, Atomic Yo-Yo, plastic, Larami, 1978............. 35.00
Battlestar Galactica, Colorforms Adventure Set #2359, 1978, MIB .. 75.00
Beany & Cecil, Beany hand puppet, cloth body w/vinyl head, ca 1950... 75.00
Beetle Bailey, Miss Buxley figure, cloth, Sugar Loaf, 1990s, 15"..... 20.00
Beetle Baily, doll, printed cloth w/name, vinyl head, Gund, 1960 ..150.00
Ben Casey, Paint-by-Number Water Color, Transogram #1825, 1962, MIB...175.00
Bert, bank, vinyl, NY Vinyl, 1971, 13".. 25.00
Bert, rag doll, #2601, Knickerbocker, 1975, 10", MIB 35.00
Bert & Ernie, lamp, w/instruments, graphical shade, 1970s, 16" 35.00
Betty Boop, figure, celluloid, jtd, pk heart dress, Japan, prewar, 8" ..390.00
Betty Boop, nodder figure, celluloid w/rnd tin base, Japan, prewar, 7" ..950.00
Beverly Hillbillies, car, plastic, Ideal, NMIB.............................. 880.00
Beverly Hillbillies, Ellie May doll, Unique Art, 1964, 12", MIB..200.00
Beverly Hillbillies, Jane Hathaway doll, Japan, 1960s, 11½", MIB...400.00
Big Bird, jack-in-the-box, Big Bird pops up w/guitar, Playskool, 10"... 25.00
Big Bird, lamp, figure in nest reading, wood base, 20" 40.00
Big Bird, Make Your Own Marionette, Friends Industries, 1977, MIB...40.00
Bo-Peep, doll, jtd, mohair wig, w/hat & lamb, Vogue, 8" 550.00
Bob Hope, hand puppet, cloth w/vinyl head, Zany, 1940s............ 125.00

Bob McNutt, doll, oilcloth w/printed features, Averill, 1920s, 34".......... 100.00
Bonzo, figure, stuffed velvet, jtd, Chad Valley, 1920s, 22" 1,000.00
Boo Boo, doll, cloth w/felt hair & tie, Knickerbocker, 1973, 7", NRFB.. 50.00
Bozo the Clown, figure, cloth w/soft vinyl head, 1972, 12" 25.00
Brady Bunch, Fishing Puzzle & Game, Larami, 1973, MOC.......... 45.00
Brady Bunch, gum cards, complete set of 88, rare, 1969................ 600.00
Buck Rogers, map of the solar system, 1933, 18x25", VG 200.00
Buck Rogers, Twiki Robot Signal Flasher, b/o figure, 9½", MIB ... 125.00
Bugs Bunny, bookends, figure w/cart, pk base, Holiday Fair, 1970, 7" ...50.00
Bugs Bunny, figure, cloth, Uncle Sam attire, Dakin, 1976, 11" 25.00
Bugs Bunny, figure, plush & vinyl, toothy grin, Mattel, 1960s, 15" 25.00
Bugs Bunny, figure, vinyl, Dakin Goofy Gram, 1971, 12" 38.00
Bugs Bunny, flashlight, plastic figure, 1940s, 5"............................ 25.00
Bugs Bunny, gumball machine, plastic head w/gray ears, Tarrson, 10" ...25.00
Bugs Bunny, hand puppet, cloth w/vinyl head, Zany, 1950s 65.00
Bugs Bunny, push-button puppet, Kohner, 1960s 30.00
Bullwinkle, bank, brn vinyl, by tree trunk, 11½" 100.00
Buttercup & Spare Ribs, doll set, cloth, 1920s, 18" & 12" 900.00
Captain America, hand puppet, vinyl, Imperial, 1978, MIP 55.00
Captain Kangaroo, doll, Mattel, 1960s, MIB 150.00
Captain Kangaroo, squeeze toy, pnt vinyl, 1950s, 8", MIB 65.00
Carrot Top, hand puppet, cloth w/vinyl head, Zany, 1940s 125.00
Casper, pull-toy, w/xylophone on 4-wheel base, 1950-60s, 10x9"......... 275.00
Casper, squeeze toy figure, Sutton, 1972, 7" 28.00
Cat in the Hat, bookends, emb red plastic figure, 14" 28.00
Cat in the Hat, figure, plush, Eden, 1979, 24" 45.00
Charlie Brown, figural brush & comb, Avon, 1971, NMIB 25.00
Charlie Brown, figure, cloth, Rag Doll, Ideal, 1960-70s, MIP 35.00
Charlie Brown, figure, plastic, jtd, 1960s, 7" 35.00
Charlie Brown, figure, vinyl, Hungerford, 1950s, 9" 75.00
Charlie Brown, gyroscope, figure atop globe, Aviva, 1970s, 8½", MIB...40.00
Charlie Brown, marionette, vinyl, jtd, Pelham, 1980s, 8", MIB... 100.00
Charlie Chaplin, pitcher, porc figural face, spout at hat, 9", VG+ ...60.00

Charlie McCarthy, alarm clock, Gilbert, VG, $800.00. (Photo courtesy Morphy Auctions)

Chilly Willy, vinyl bank, figure on skis, Royalty Ind, 1970s, 8½" ... 35.00
Cindy Bear, doll, plush w/vinyl face, Knickerbocker, 16" 250.00
Clarabell, bank, flocked plastic figure, Straco, 1970s, 9"................ 35.00
Clarabell, hand puppet, cloth w/vinyl head & googly eyes.............. 75.00
Clarabell, push-button puppet, Kohner #188, VG........................ 150.00
Davy Crockett, Dart Gun Target, Knickerbocker, MIB.................. 80.00
Davy Crockett, doll, plastic, w/rifle, Fortune Toy/WDP, '50s, 7", EXIB..100.00
Davy Crockett, lamp, chalkware figural base, w/scenic shade, 18", VG..100.00
Dennis the Menace, figure, cloth/vinyl, Mighty Star, 13", MIB..... 38.00
Dennis the Menace, figure, vinyl, walking pose, Hall Syndicate, 8"..40.00
Dennis the Menace, hand puppet, cloth w/vinyl head, 1959 .... 60.00
Deputy Dawg, figure, cloth w/vinyl head, Ideal/Terrytoons, 1960s, 14" .. 75.00
Dick Tracy, hand puppet, cloth w/vinyl head, Ideal, 1961.............. 85.00
Dick Tracy, Handcuffs for Junior, 1940s, NMOC 85.00
Dick Tracy, Sparkle Paints, Kenner, 1963, MIB............................ 75.00
Dick Tracy, Talking Phone, Marx, 1967, NMIB 92.00
Dick Tracy, Wrist Radio, leather band, Da-Myco, 1940s, EXIB ... 300.00

Donald Duck, doll, cloth w/name on chest, vinyl head, Gund, 1960s ...35.00
Donald Duck, figure, compo, movable head, Knickerbocker, 1930s, 5½"..400.00
Donald Duck, hand puppet, bl & wht cloth w/vinyl head, Gund, 1950s... 45.00
Donald Duck, tape measure, figural, celluloid, 2½"........................ 925.00
Donald Duck, watering can, litho tin, Ohio Art, 1930s, 6"............. 50.00

Donald Duck, wristwatch, WS Time, NMIB, $975.00. (Photo courtesy Morphy Auctions)

Donny Osmond, nodder, paper-mache, w/microphone 150.00
Dopey, hand puppet, cloth w/vinyl head, Gund, 1950s 65.00
Droop-A-Long Coyote, hand puppet, cloth w/vinyl head, Ideal, 1960s... 100.00
Droopy Dog, hand puppet, cloth w/vinyl head, Zany, 1950s 85.00
Dudley Do Right, figure, bendable vinyl, Wham-O, 1972............. 20.00
Dumbo, figure, squeeze rubber, Dell, 1950s, 5" 25.00
Dumbo, hand puppet, cloth w/name on chest, vinyl head, Gund, 1960s .. 55.00
Elmer Fudd, figure, jtd vinyl, blk coat/red shoes & hat, Dakin, 8"....25.00
Elmer Fudd, figure, vinyl, hunting attire & gun, Dakin, 1968, 7".. 100.00
Emmett Kelly Jr, ventriloquist doll, Horsman, 1978, MIB............. 50.00
Fat Albert, hand puppet, vinyl w/molded head, Ideal, 1973, NM+.. 150.00
Felix the Cat, figure, cloth, cowboy attire, Gund, 1930s, 24".......... 1,232.00
Felix the Cat, figure, plush, jtd, Steiff, ca 1927, 9½".................5,600.00
Felix the Cat, figure, wood, name on chest, Schoenhut, 8".......... 560.00
Felix the Cat, hand puppet, plush body & head w/felt ears 600.00
Felix the Cat, magic slate, red, Lowe #3068, 1950s 50.00
Felix the Cat, push toy, blk & wht pnt wood, jtd arms & legs, VG..250.00
Ferdinand the Bull, hand puppet, cloth w/compo head, 1938...... 200.00
Flash Gordon, Strat-O-Wagon, wooden wheels & hdl, Wyandotte, 1940s, 6"..95.00
Flintstones, Bamm-Bamm figure, cloth, Knickerbocker, 1970s, 8", MIB..45.00
Flintstones, Bamm-Bamm push-button puppet, Kohner, 1960s 75.00
Flintstones, Barney bank, figure on rock base, vinyl, 1994, 6"........ 12.00
Flintstones, Barney figure, cloth & vinyl, Knickerbocker, 16½" 100.00
Flintstones, Barney hand puppet, cloth w/vinyl head, Knickerbocker ...75.00
Flintstones, Barney marionette, furry outfit, Knickerbocker, 12" ... 35.00
Flintstones, Barney nightlight, plastic figural, Levito, 1975, 4"...... 15.00
Flintstones, Betty figure, plastic, gr dress, Imperial, 1976, 3".......... 10.00
Flintstones, Dino figure, plush w/vinyl head, Gund, 1960s, 10"..........75.00
Flintstones, Dino push-button puppet, Kohner, 1960s 50.00
Flintstones, Fred bank, w/golf club, vinyl, 7¾" 85.00
Flintstones, Fred figure, cloth w/vinyl head, Knickerbocker, 11"..125.00
Flintstones, Fred push-button puppet, flexing muscles, Kohner 65.00
Flintstones, Pebbles figure, squeeze vinyl, Sanitoy, 1979, 6"........... 25.00
Flintstones, Pebbles hand puppet, cloth w/vinyl head, Ideal, 1966 ...75.00
Flintstones, pencil topper, any character, mk Hong Kong, 1970s, 1½"..12.00
Flintstones, Wilma bank, holding Pebbles, 1970s, 11" 40.00
Flintstones, Wilma figure, squeeze vinyl, w/2-wheel cart, 1960s, 9"..60.00
Flipper, figure, plush, gray & wht w/sailor attire, Knickerbocker, 17"...35.00
Flub-A-Dub, push-button puppet, Kohner, 1950s, NMIB 175.00
Flying Nun, doll, Hasbro, 1967, rare, 4½", MIB............................. 175.00
Foghorn Leghorn, Looney Tunes, jtd vinyl figure, Dakin, 1970............55.00
Gabby Hayes, cannon ring 250.00
Gabby Hayes, Champion Shooting Target, Hacker/Ind, 1950s, NMIB...225.00
Garfield, bank, basketball player figure, Enesco, 1980s, 5½"........... 35.00
Garfield, comb & brush set, orange plastic figural w/blk trim, Avon.. 12.00

Garfield, gumball machine, But It Will Cost..., Superior Toy, 1970-80s... 35.00
Garfield, ornament, ceramic, wearing Santa hat, Enesco, 1980s, 3"... 18.00
Garfield, snow dome, Happy Holidays on base, Enesco, 4½", MIB ...25.00
Gene Autry, doll, comp/cloth outfit/felt hat, Terry Lee, 16"......... 500.00
Gene Autry, flashlight, Cowboy Lariat, EXIB.............................. 100.00
Gene Autry, record player, plastic, Flying A decal, Columbia, 13", VG...250.00
Gene Autry, toy guitar, plastic, Emenee, 32", NMIB.................... 225.00
Gene Autry, wristwatch, Wilane, 1948, NMIB.............................. 400.00
Geppetto, wood fiber figure, sitting on box, Multiproducts, 1940s, 5"..55.00
Gomer Pyle, gum cards, set of 66 blk & wht images, 1960s........... 80.00
Goofy, figure, plush w/orange shirt & pk vest, Mattel, 17" 100.00
Goofy, hand puppet, cloth, bow on neck, vinyl head w/hat, Gund, 1950s...75.00
Green Hornet, Colorforms Cartoon Kit, Greenway Productions, 1966... 55.00
Green Hornet, playing cards, 52 cards w/40 action photos, 1966, NMIB.. 100.00
Grizzly Adams, figure, Mattel, 9½", MIB....................................... 85.00
Groucho Marx, hand puppet, cloth w/vinyl head, detective outfit, VG... 85.00
Gumby, Astronaut Adventure Costume, plastic playset, Lakeside, 1965 . 22.00
Gumby, figure, w/up, vinyl, Lakeside, 1966, 4" 45.00
Gumby, Pokey figure, bendable rubber, red w/blk, Jesco, 9½"......... 12.00
Hansel & Gretel, witch marionette, yel hair, Pelham #5048, NMIB.. 100.00
Happy Hooligan, doll, wood w/cloth outfit, Schoenhut, 8½", EXIB..2,500.00
Happy Hooligan, marionette, wood w/cloth outfit, Schoenhut, 1920s, 10"..450.00
Heckle & Jeckle, bank, pnt wood figure, Famous Terry Toon, 8", VG+.150.00
Herietta Hippo, doll, New Zoo Revue, cloth w/vinyl head, 1970s..100.00
Honey West, doll, Gilbert, 1965, rare, 11½", MIB........................ 400.00
Hopalong Cassidy, bank, plastic bust, Savings Club Ohio S&L, 4"...50.00
Hopalong Cassidy, doll, rubber head, w/gun & holsters, 1950s, 21" .300.00
Hopalong Cassidy, motion lamp, plastic, Econolite, 10" 500.00
Howdy Doody, doll, stuffed body, compo head & hands, clothed, 19", G .250.00
Howdy Doody, figure, compo w/pnt hair, Effanbee, 1950s, 23", EXIB...345.00
Howdy Doody, figure, pnt wood, name decal on chest 225.00
Howdy Doody, marionette, Peter Puppet Plaything, EXIB............ 200.00
Howdy Doody, Mr Bluster marionette, wood & compo, Peter Puppet...200.00
Howdy Doody, push-button puppet, Kohner, 1950s, EXIB........... 175.00
Howdy Doody, ring, flasher, 1950... 50.00
HR Pufnstuf, hand puppet, cloth w/vinyl head, Remco, 1970...... 150.00
Huckleberry Hound, figure, squeeze vinyl, policeman attire, Dell, 10" ..55.00
Huckleberry Hound, push-button puppet, Kohner, 1960s.............. 55.00
Hulk Hogan, vinyl doll, cloth outfit, 1980s, 18", MIB.................. 100.00
Ignatz, figure, beaded wood w/bendable arms & legs, 1920s, 6½"............250.00
Incredible Hulk, bank, vinyl, breaking through wall, Renzi, 1977, 10"..... 25.00
Incredible Hulk, hand puppet, vinyl w/molded head, Imperial, 1978 ....35.00
Jerry Mahoney, hand puppet, vinyl w/molded head...................... 125.00
Jerry Mahoney, ventriliquist doll, Juro Novelty, 1950s, 25"........... 150.00
Jetson, George figure, cloth w/vinyl head, Knickerbocker, 1963.......... 125.00
Jetsons, Judy figure, cloth w/vinyl head, Knickerbocker, 1963 ....150.00
Jetsons, Orbity, Elroy & Astro nightlight, bsk, Giftique, 1980s, 6" ...35.00
Jiminy Cricket, figure, beaded wood, Ideal, 1940, 9" 410.00
Jiminy Cricket, hand puppet, cloth w/vinyl head, Gund, 1960s 75.00
Joe Palooka, bop bag, vinyl w/boxer image, Ideal, 1952, 44"......... 68.00
Katnip, hand puppet, cloth w/vinyl head, Gund, 1950s 75.00
King Kong, bank, vinyl, figure walking on building, Relic Art Ltd .. 150.00
King Kong, costume, Ben Cooper, 1976, MIB 95.00
King Kong, pennant, felt, Kong on World Trade Center, 1970s, 25" L...75.00
Kojak, doll, Excel Toy Corp, 1976, 8", MOC................................. 150.00
Koko the Klown, figure, cloth w/vinyl head, Gund, 1962, scarce. 200.00
Krazy Kat, doll, purple & wht cloth, yel ribbon, Averill, 1930s, 18"...950.00
Krazy Kat, figure, wood bead type, w/yel toothy grin, Chein, 7½"...785.00
Krazy Kat, toy tea set, litho tin, 16-pc, Chein.............................. 125.00
Laurel & Hardy, figure, vinyl w/cloth shirt, Dakin, 1970s, 8", MIP, ea...50.00
Laurel & Hardy, hand puppet, cloth & vinyl, Knickerbocker, 1965, ea.65.00
Laurel & Hardy, vinyl doll, 1950s, 13", VG, ea 70.00
Lil' Abner, bank, Can O' Coins, 1953, 5" 125.00
Lil' Abner, Daisy Mae bank, compo, on Dogpatch base, 1975, 8".. 55.00

Lil' Abner, Mammy Yokum figure, vinyl, Baby Barry Toy, 1950s, 14"..........100.00
Linus, bendable vinyl figure, 1960s, 5½" 25.00
Linus, doll, cloth, Ideal, 1960s, 8", MIP.. 40.00
Linus, squeeze toy, vinyl, Hungerford, 1950s, 9" 65.00
Little Audrey, doll, compo, felt hat/shoes/socks, 1950s, 14" 275.00
Little Audrey, doll, vinyl w/cloth dress & bow, Juro Novelty, 12½"....175.00
Little Audrey, hand puppet, cloth w/vinyl head, Gund, 1950s....... 75.00
Little Lulu, doll, cloth, Western attire w/wht holster, 16" 275.00
Little Lulu, doll, cloth w/red dress, Gund, 1972, 6½", MIB........... 75.00
Little Orphan Annie, Jack Set, Arcade, 1935, NRFP.................. 175.00
Little Red Riding Hood, Grandma hand puppet, MPI Toys, 1960 ...85.00
Little Red Riding Hood, hand puppet, cloth & vinyl, MPI Toys, 1960.. 85.00
Little Red Riding Hood, marionette, red & wht clothes, Hazelle, 15".. 100.00
Little Red Riding Hood, Wolf marionette, Hazelle, 15" 150.00
Little Red Riding Hood, Wolf puppet, cloth, vinyl head, MIP Toys, 1960 ..125.00
Lone Ranger, doll, compo head & hands, Dollcraft Novelty Co, 15".....600.00
Lone Ranger, horseshoe set, rubber, Gardner, NMIB..................... 85.00
Lone Ranger, toy binoculars, plastic, Harrison, EXIB.................. 135.00
Lucy, figure, cloth w/printed features & hair, Ideal, 7½", NRFP..... 40.00
Lucy, figure, vinyl, Hungerford, 1950s, 9" 75.00
Maggie & Jiggs, dolls, wood w/cloth outfits, Schoenhut, 7", 9", NRFB...2,750.00
Magilla Gorilla, figure, felt w/vinyl head, Ideal, 1960s, 7½" 55.00
Magilla Gorilla, hand puppet, cloth w/name, vinyl head, Ideal, 1960s... 100.00
Magilla Gorilla, push-button puppet, Kohner, 1960s..................... 75.00
Mary Poppins, doll, cloth, w/umbrella, name on apron, Gund, 1960s .. 125.00
Mickey Mouse, Cut-Out Scissors, WDE, 1930s, NMOC 250.00
Mickey Mouse, figure, wood, jtd bead body, pie eyes, 1930s, 7" 550.00
Mickey Mouse, push-button puppet, Kohner, 1960s..................... 45.00
Mickey Mouse, stuffed figure, felt hands/shoes, Dean's/England, 8" 375.00
Mickey Mouse, stuffed figure, felt hands/shoes, Dean's/England, 12" .. 1,050.00
Mickey Mouse, toy flute, litho tin, SFC/Italy, 1930s, 10", VG 115.00
Minnie Mouse, figure, ceramic, pk/wht skirt/turq shoes, 1960s, 6" 40.00
Minnie Mouse, marionette, wood & compo, Peter Puppet..., 1950s, 12" .. 75.00
Miss Kitty, costume, Halco, EXIB.. 125.00
Miss Piggy, hand puppet, Fisher-Price, 1978, MIB........................ 35.00
Mister Magoo, doll, cloth w/vinyl head & hat, Ideal, 1960s, 16" .. 100.00
Mr Ed, doll, cloth w/vinyl head, Knickerbocker, 1962 .... 100.00
Munsters, Herman doll, cloth w/vinyl head & hands, Mattel, 1964, 12"... 50.00
Munsters, Herman doll, cloth w/vinyl head/etc, Presents, 13" 35.00
Munsters, Lily hand puppet, cloth w/vinyl head, Ideal, 1964....... 150.00
Mushmouse, figure, felt w/vinyl head, red vest, Ideal, 1960s, 9" 75.00
Mutt & Jeff, drum, litho tin, Converse, 13" dia 300.00
Nancy, doll, cloth, Knickerbocker, 1973, 6½", MIB 40.00
Olive Oyl, doll, plush w/vinyl head, Gundikins, 1950s, 9" 50.00
Olive Oyl, doll, vinyl, swivel joints, Multiple Toys, 1960s, 9"........ 55.00
Olive Oyl, hand puppet, cloth w/vinyl head, Gund, 1950s 50.00
Olive Oyl, push-button puppet, plastic, Kohner, 1960s.................. 75.00
Oswald the Rabbit, doll, plush, name on chest, Irwin, 1930s, 17"...........450.00
Paddington Bear, cloth figure, Edin Toys, 1970s, 13" 20.00
Pepe Le Pew, figure, vinyl, You're a...Stinker, Goofy Gram, 1971, 9" ... 75.00
Peppermint Patty, bank, leaning on baseball bat, Determined, 1972, 7" .. 65.00
Peppermint Patty, doll, cloth, 7", MIP 40.00
Peter Pan, push-button puppet, Kohner, 1960s............................. 25.00
Phantom of the Opera, nodder, gr face, Universal....................... 200.00
Pink Panther, bank, plastic, golfer figure emb on yel bank, 9x4x2½".....50.00
Pink Panther, doll, plush, blk satin jacket, Might Star, 1987, 16".. 25.00
Pink Panther, figure, vinyl, jtd arms, Dakin, 1971, 8".................... 28.00
Pink Panther, gumball machine, plastic, Tarrson, 1970s, 8" 30.00
Pink Panther, marionette, compo w/clothes, JJK Assoc, 1960-70s, 12" .. 75.00
Pink Panther, mug, ceramic head, Royal Orleans, 1980s, 4½" 50.00
Pinocchio, figure, wood & compo, pnt bead body, Ideal, 8", VG+.. 100.00
Pinocchio, hand puppet, Knickerbocker, 1962 .... 50.00
Pixie, doll, jtd vinyl, Hanna-Barbera, Knixies/Knickerbocker, 1962, 6"... 40.00
Pixie & Dixie, squeeze toy, rubber, on cheese wedge, Dell, 1960s, 6"... 40.00

Pluto, figure, plush w/posable ears & tail, Gund, 1940-50s, 9x13"...150.00
Popeye, bath toy, vinyl figure in boat, Stahlwood, 1950s, 5¼x6¼"....40.00
Popeye, Christmas Tree set, 8-pc, ea w/Mazda lamp, Reliance, 1930s...175.00
Popeye, doll, felt w/cloth outfit/wooden pipe, can under arm, 11", VG....150.00
Popeye, figure, pnt wood, w/pipe, completely rstr, 13".................440.00
Popeye, figure, vinyl, jtd, Cameo, 1950s, 13½" 125.00
Popeye, figure, wood w/compo head, Ideal, 15", VG 450.00
Popeye, game, Popeye the Juggler, tin w/glass top, Bar-Zim Toys, 1929 .. 95.00
Popeye, lamp, die-cast metal boat w/figure in smokestack, 7", G .. 230.00
Popeye, marionette, cloth w/vinyl head/plastic hands, Gund, 1950s, 12".. 75.00
Popeye, music box, litho tin, Mattel, 11"................................... 825.00
Popeye, Thimble Theatre Mystery Playhouse, Harding, 1959, EXIB.. 990.00
Porky Pig, bank, bsk figure w/arms behind bk, 1940s, 5", G+ 75.00
Porky Pig, bank, ceramic, mk That's All Folks!, Good Co, 1989, 8".. 50.00
Porky Pig, figure, plush, Gund, 1950, 14"................................... 75.00
Porky Pig, squeeze toy, rubber, Sun Rubber, 1940s, 7" 50.00
Porky Pig & Petunia, pull toy, paper litho on wood, Brice Novelty #920 .. 110.00
Princess Summerfall Winterspring, push-button puppet, Kohner, 1949...275.00
Punch & Judy, hand puppet set, pnt wood w/clothes, Punch, 18" 3,300.00
Quick Draw McGraw, Modelcast 'n Color set, Standard Toycraft, 1960, VG.. 50.00

Raggedy Ann and Andy, bookends, painted cast iron, 6", $7,590.00.
(Photo courtesy Morphy Auctions)

Raggedy Ann & Andy, Andy toothbrush, b/o, Janex, 1973, MIB.. 45.00
Raggedy Ann & Andy, bank, vinyl w/red yarn hair, Royalty, 1974, 9"..35.00
Raggedy Ann & Andy, hand puppet, yarn hair, Knickerbocker, 1960s .50.00
Raggedy Ann & Andy, rag doll, Knickerbocker, 1970s, 6½" ea, MIP..35.00
Raggedy Ann & Andy, rag doll, Knickerbocker, 1979, 12", NMIB...75.00
Ricochet Rabbit, hand puppet, cloth w/vinyl head, Ideal, 1960s 100.00
Road Runner, figure, compo, grassy base, Holiday Fair, 1970s, 8" .. 50.00
Road Runner, figure standing w/legs together, Dakin, 1968 .... 25.00
Rocky & Friends, bank, ceramic, Rocky/Bullwinkle/Mr Peabody, 5x7", M..175.00
Rocky Squirrel, doll, plush w/vinyl head, 1966, rare, 9½", VG 150.00
Rocky the Squirrel, figure, vinyl, jtd, Dakin, 1970s, 6½", MIB....... 75.00
Roy Rogers, bank, metal boot form, Almar Metal Arts Co, 1950s, 5½"... 75.00
Roy Rogers, flashlight, tin, Signal Siren, Usalite, 7", MIB 150.00
Roy Rogers, telescope, plastic, H George, 9", MIB 200.00
Roy Rogers, Woodburning Set, Burn-Rite, complete, EXIB......... 175.00
Santa Claus, push-button puppet, Kohner, 1960s 75.00
Schroeder, doll, vinyl, Beethoven sweater, Pocket Dolls, 1970s, 7½"...35.00
Schroeder, squeeze toy, vinyl, Hungerford, 1950s, 8"................... 125.00
Scooby Doo, figure, plush, seated, Sutton, 1970, 8" 28.00
Skippy, figure, pnt bsk, stands on rnd base, Crosby, 1930s, 5½"...... 50.00
Sleeping Beauty, squeeze toy, w/rabbit, Dell, 1959, 5" 40.00
Sleeping Beauty, tea set, plastic, Worchester Toy Co, 1959, EXIB..250.00
Sluggo, doll, cloth, Knickerbocker, 1970s, 6½", MIB 40.00
Sluggo, squeeze toy, w/boxing gloves, Dreamland, 1955, 10" 75.00
Smurfs, push-button puppet, standing on sq base, TM, 1970s........ 40.00
Smurfs, toy telephone, w/rotary dial, HG Toys, 1980s, 10", VG+.. 28.00
Snagglepuss, figure, pk vinyl, Dakin, 1971, 7½", MIP................... 68.00
Snoopy, bank, pnt compo, fireman's attire, 6" 50.00
Snoopy, bank, pnt compo, Racer, 1970s, 4x5" 50.00
Snoopy, bank, pnt compo, The Express Truck, 1970s, 4" 55.00

Snoopy, doll, cloth, w/jeans & name on red shirt, Ideal, 8", MIP .. 38.00
Snoopy, doll, vinyl, jtd, astronaut, Determined, 1969, 9", G.......... 50.00
Snoopy, doll, vinyl, jtd, Determined, 9" 25.00
Snoopy, Pound-a-Ball, Child Guidance, 1978, 17x13", EXIB........ 50.00
Snoopy, Soaper, plastic, Kenner, 1975, MIB 45.00
Snoopy as Joe Cool, push-button puppet, Ideal, 1970 .... 75.00
Snow White, figure, compo, Knickerbocker, 1940, 12", VG+ 75.00
Snuffy Smith, doll, cloth w/vinyl head, Gund, 1950s................... 100.00
Soupy Sales, hand puppet, yel cloth w/vinyl head, Gund, 1965... 225.00
Sparkle Plenty (Dick Tracy), doll, compo w/yel yarn hair, Ideal, 13" .. 350.00
Speedy Gonzalez, bank, vinyl, standing on cheese, Dakin, 9½" 75.00
Spider-Man, costume, Ben Cooper, 1972, NMIB 35.00
Spider-Man, kazoo, plastic head shape, Straco, MOC................... 50.00
Superman, costume, Ben Cooper, complete w/comic book, EXIB...225.00
Superman, flicker rings, plastic w/various scenes, 1966, ea.......... 150.00
Superman, hand puppet, cloth w/vinyl head, Ideal, 1960s 100.00
Superman, Oil Painting by Numbers, Hasbro, 1965, NMIP......... 225.00
Superman, record player, suitcase style, 1978, 12x9½" 160.00
Superman, string puppet, cloth w/vinyl head, Madison, 1978, MIB ..125.00
Superman, wallet, brn w/emb mc image, Croydon, 1950s 75.00
Superman, wallet, yel vinyl, snap closure, Mattel, 1966................. 88.00
Superman, water pistol, plastic, Multiple Toys, 1960s, MIP 175.00
Tasmanian Devil, bank, vinyl figure standing, 1970s, 6" 50.00
Tasmanian Devil, bank, vinyl figure w/closed mouth, Dakin, 5", NM+... 150.00
Three Stooges, hand puppet, any character, molded heads, 1950s, ea .. 150.00
Tom & Jerry, bank, ceramic, Tom holds sleeping Jerry, Gorham, 6"..45.00
Tom & Jerry, figure set, plastic, Marx, 1973, 9" & 6", MIB............. 65.00
Tom & Jerry, Jerry figure, plastic, showing muscles, Marx, 1973 ....28.00
Tom & Jerry, Jerry hand puppet, cloth w/vinyl head, Zany, 1950s, VG .85.00
Tom & Jerry, kaleidoscope, litho metal, Green Monk, 1970s......... 28.00
Tom & Jerry, pull toy, plastic, figures on mc platform, Combex, 7"..50.00
Tom & Jerry, Tom doll, cloth, 2 mice in creel, Italian, 1960s, 18" 725.00
Tom & Jerry, Tom figure, plastic, hands on hips, Marx, 1973, 6" 28.00
Tom & Jerry, water gun, vinyl figure, Marx, 1970s, 6", NMIB, ea .. 50.00
Tonto, soap figure, Kerk Guild, 1939, 4", EXIB............................. 50.00
Top Cat, Kite Fun Book, PG&E premium, 16 pgs 35.00
Tweety Bird, figure, cloth, seated, Mighty Star, 1971, 18" 12.00
Tweety Bird, figure, vinyl, swivel head & ft, Dakin, 1969, 6" 25.00
Tweety Bird, mug, ceramic head, Applause, 1989, w/tag................ 12.00
Tweety Bird, pull toy, figure atop wagon, Broce, 1950s, 9½" 125.00
Tweety Bird, squeeze toy, vinyl, in diaper, Oak Rubber, 1940s, 6"..25.00
Underdog, costume, Collegeville, 1974, MIB 40.00
Underdoy, bank, vinyl, standing w/hands on hips, Play Pals, 1973, 11".. 75.00
Universal Monsters, Mummy figure, vinyl, jtd, Imperial, 7½" 22.00
Wile E Coyote, figure, vinyl, Dakin Goofy Gram, 1971, 11".......... 45.00
Wile E Coyote, figure, vinyl, jtd, Dakin, 1960s, 9½", MIP 45.00
Winnie the Pooh, Magic Slate, Western Publishing, 1965............. 50.00
Witch (of Hansel & Gretel), marionette, jtd mouth, Pelham, 14", NMIB... 135.00
Wizard of Oz, figure, vinyl, 50th Anniversary ed, Multi Toys, MIB, ea... 25.00
Wizard of Oz, Scarecrow hand puppet, vinyl molded head, 1960s 20.00
Wonder Woman, Flashmite, Jane X, 1976, MOC 75.00
Woody Woodpecker, figure, plastic, standing, Imco, 1977, 10" 45.00
Woody Woodpecker, hand puppet, cloth w/vinyl head, 1950s.......... 75.00
Yogi Bear, bank, pnt compo, seated w/harmonica, 5½".................. 75.00
Yogi Bear, camera, blk plastic, image on side, Hong Kong, 3½", NMIB.. 35.00
Yogi Bear, doll, plush w/vinyl face, Knickerbocker, 1959, 18½" 50.00
Yogi Bear, hand puppet, brn cloth w/vinyl head, bl hat.................. 65.00
Yogi Bear, iron-on transfer, Yogi on bl circle, Holoubek, 1976, 8x6".. 18.00
Yogi Bear, push-button puppet, Kohner, 1960s 65.00
Ziggy, figure, cloth, writing on shirt, Knickerbocker, 1978, 8"........ 12.00
Zorro, bowl & plate, Sun-Valley Melmac, 1950-60s, 5" & 6" dia, set .. 40.00
Zorro, costume, Ben Cooper #233/WDP, deluxe ed, 1950s, scarce, EXIB . 100.00
Zorro, Target Shoot, Lido/WDP, MIB 225.00
Zorro, tote bag, red vinyl 275.00

Peters and Reed

John Peters and Adam Reed founded their pottery in Zanesville, Ohio, just before the turn of the century, using the local red clay to produce a variety of wares. Moss Aztec, introduced about 1912, has an unglazed exterior with designs molded in high relief and the recesses highlighted with a green wash. Only the interior is glazed to hold water. Pereco (named for Peters, Reed and Company) is glazed in semi-matt blue, maroon, cream, and other colors. Orange was also used very early, but such examples are rare. Shapes are simple with in-mold decoration sometimes borrowed from the Moss Aztec line. Wilse Blue is a line of high-gloss medium blue with dark specks on simple shapes. Landsun, characterized by its soft matt multicolor or blue and gray combinations, is decorated either by dripping or by hand brushing in an effect sometimes called Flame or Herringbone. Chromal, in much the same colors as Landsun, may be decorated with a realistic scenic, or the swirling application of colors may merely suggest one. Vivid, realistic Chromal scenics command much higher prices than weak, poorly drawn examples. (Brush-McCoy made a very similar line called Chromart. Neither will be marked; and due to the lack of documented background material available, it may be impossible make a positive identification. Collectors nearly always attribute this type of decoration to Peters and Reed.) Shadow Ware is usually a glossy, multicolor drip over a harmonious base color but occasionally seen in overall matt glaze. When the base is black, the effect is often iridescent.

Several other lines were produced, including Mirror Black, Persian, Egyptian, Florentine, Marbleized, etc., and an unidentified line which collectors call Mottled-Marbleized Colors. In this high-gloss line, the red clay body often shows through the splashed-on multicolors. At one time, the brown high-glaze artware line with 'sprigged' decoration was attributed to Peters and Reed. However, this line has recently been re-attributed to Weller pottery by the Sanfords in their latest book on Peters and Reed pottery. This conclusion was drawn due to the overwhelming number of shapes proven to be Weller molds. Since the decoration was cut out and applied, however, it is possible that Peters and Reed or yet another Zanesville company simply contracted for the Weller greenware and added their own decoration and finishes. In 1922 the company became known as the Zane Pottery. Peters and Reed retired, and Harry McClelland became president. Charles Chilcote designed new lines, and production of many of the old lines continued. The body of the ware after 1922 was light in color. Marks include the impressed logo or ink stamp 'Zaneware' in a rectangle.

Vase, Moss Aztec, 12x5½", $500.00. (Photo courtesy Smith & Jones Inc.)

Bowl, Landsun, bl & wht, low, 2½x8" 90.00
Bowl, Wilse Blue, emb dragonfly, 2x5⅛" 55.00

Doorstop, cat, Mirror Black w/gr eyes, Zaneware, chips, 11¼" 240.00
Figure, frog, gr matt, open mouth, unmk, 2¾x3¾" 100.00
Figurine, dog, ivory, unmk, 13⅝" 540.00
Floor vase, Shadow Ware, spattered blk/yel on orange, 24", NM .. 420.00
Jardiniere, Landsun, swirled bl, #12-6, nicks/bruise, 4¾" 190.00
Jardiniere & ped, Moss Aztec, bands of poppies, 29", EX 480.00
Planter, Moss Aztec, Greek figures, sgn Ferrell, nicks, 5¼x12½" .. 300.00
Umbrella stand, Moss Aztec, Springtime, #520, 21⅝" 600.00
Vase, camouflage pattern, earth tones, flared rim, unmk Zaneware, 12" . 140.00
Vase, camouflage pattern w/marbleized gr tones, unmk Zaneware, 9" . 110.00
Vase, Chromal, mtn/lake scene (realistic), unmk, 9½x4½", NM . 330.00
Vase, Marbleized, blk/gr/ivory/russet, corseted, 8x5½" 60.00
Vase, Marbleized, brn/bl/yel/blk, shouldered, unmk, 8" 120.00
Vase, Marbleized, swirled brn/gr/yel/orange, unmk, flakes, 12¼" 90.00
Vase, Shadow Ware, bl & gr drips on brn, unmk, 6¾", NM 160.00
Vase, Shadow Ware, bl/blk/yel drips on caramel, shouldered, 7½" .. 190.00
Vase, Shadow Ware, bls/brns on lt brn, cylindrical, 8⅞" 275.00
Vase, Shadow Ware, mc drips on tan, shouldered, #3, Zaneware, 8½" .. 550.00
Wall pocket, Moss Aztec, floral, sgn Ferrell, 9½x6¼" 200.00

Pewabic

The Pewabic Pottery was formally established in Detroit, Michigan, in 1907 by Mary Chase Perry Stratton and Horace James Caulkins. The two had worked together following Ms. Perry's china painting efforts, firing wares in a small kiln Caulkins had designed especially for use by the dental trade. Always a small operation which relied upon basic equipment and the skill of the workers, they took pride in being commissioned for several important architectural tile installations. Some of the early artware was glazed a simple matt green; occasionally other colors were added, sometimes in combination, one over the other in a drip effect. Later Stratton developed a lustrous crystalline glaze. (Today's values are determined to a great extent by the artistic merit of the glaze.) The body of the ware was highly fired and extremely hard. Shapes were basic, and decorative modeling, if used at all, was in low relief. Mary Stratton kept the pottery open until her death in 1961. In 1968 it was purchased and reopened by Michigan State University; it is still producing today. Several marks were used over the years: a triangle with 'Revelation Pottery' (for a short time only); 'Pewabic' with five maple leaves; and the impressed circle mark. Our advisors for this category are Suzanne Perrault and David Rago; they are listed in the Directory under New Jersey.

Vase, green and indigo curdled lustre, two paper labels, stamped, two drill holes, 12½", $1,725.00. (Photo courtesy David Rago Auctions)

Candleholder, bl crystalline, ruffled saucer base, 4¼" 300.00
Pitcher, gr crystalline, cylindrical, 3x4" 310.00
Plate, rooks, gold/blk lustre, 10" 4,800.00
Tile paperweight, fish, brn on gr w/red showing through, sq, 2¾" .. 60.00
Vase, bl irid w/faint ribs, burst glaze bubbles, 6" 720.00
Vase, bl matt w/silver irid patches, bulbous, 7⅛" 725.00
Vase, bl w/lustre drips, Detroit, 11½x11" 2,400.00
Vase, bl w/tan splashes, paper label, ca 1910, 5½" 950.00
Vase, bl-gr matt, Pewabic w/maple leaves, 7x4¾" 1,200.00
Vase, bright bl lustre, bulbous, 8x6½" 960.00
Vase, cobalt top over gold lustre, baluster, 4x3" 660.00
Vase, copper red over mauve, slightly bulbous, faint line, 10⅝" .. 3,300.00
Vase, fire orange, faint horizontal rings, bulbous, 8x7" 1,440.00
Vase, gr & purple lustre, shouldered, 9¼x8½" 1,300.00
Vase, gr matt/beige, geometric, Pewabic w/maple leaves, 14½x11" .. 4,500.00
Vase, gr-brn metallic drip over yel, bulbous/ftd, label, 5½" 1,080.00
Vase, lav metallic lustre, bulbous, 4" 550.00
Vase, mustard matt w/brn drip, Detroit, 10½x6¾" 1,920.00
Vase, Persian Blue mottle, shouldered, low ft, 11x8" 1,080.00
Vase, purple/bl/gr lustre, rim rstr, 9½x6" 360.00
Vase, streaky metallic, orb w/short collar rim, label, 3½" 660.00
Vase, volcanic blk/bl/purple, bulbous body, chip, 15½" 4,800.00
Vase, volcanic cobalt/bl-gray/purple lustre, bulbous, 9¼x5¾" ... 1,800.00
Vase, volcanic orange, bulbous, 3x3" 180.00
Vase, wht over indigo (experimental), 2¾" 660.00

Pewter

Pewter is a metal alloy of tin, copper, very small parts of bismuth and/or antimony, and sometimes lead. Very little American pewter contained lead, however, because much of the ware was designed to be used as tableware, and makers were aware that the use of lead could result in poisoning. (Pieces that do contain lead are usually darker in color and heavier than those that have no lead.) Most of the fine examples of American pewter date from 1700 to the 1840s. Many pieces were melted down and recast into bullets during the American Revolution in 1775; this accounts to some extent why examples from this period are quite difficult to find. The pieces that did survive may include buttons, buckles, and writing equipment as well as the tableware we generally think of. After the Revolution makers began using antimony as the major alloy with the tin in an effort to regain the popularity of pewter, which glassware and china was beginning to replace in the home. The resulting product, known as britannia, had a lustrous silver-like appearance and was far more durable. While closely related, britannia is a collectible in its own right and should not be confused with pewter.

Key: tm — touch mark

Basin, Parks Boyd tm, 9" 300.00
Charger, Thomas D Boardman partial tm, sm ding, 13⅛" 375.00
Coffeepot, A Griswold eagle tm, wooden wafer finial, rpr, 10¼" .. 150.00
Coffeepot, A Griswold tm, blk rpt on hdl, 11¼" 400.00
Coffeepot, F Porter tm, bulbous w/domed lid, worn blk on hdl, 11⅜" ... 200.00
Coffeepot, Josiah Danforth partial tm, minor dent, 11" 395.00
Flagon, unmk Am, scrolled hdl, 3-wafer spire finial, 12" 460.00
Flagon, unmk Continental, stamped cartouch, 19th C, 8" 120.00
Lamp, R Gleason tm, 5¾"+whale-oil burner 235.00
Mug, JW tm, horizontal ribs, hollow hdl 80.00
Pitcher, Rufus Dunham tm, lt pitting/dents/sm rpr, 6½" 230.00
Platter, warming; Made in London tm, divided well, hdls, 21x15½" .. 175.00
Porringer, att Richard Lee, shield hdl, well-done patch, 5" 180.00
Porringer, Roswell tm on hdl, pitting, 3¼" 90.00
Tall pot, HB Ward & Co tm, banded body, paneled spout, 11½" .. 175.00
Tall pot, Lyman tm, sm dents/rpr, ca 1844-52, 11¼" 230.00
Tall pot, unmk Am, scrolled hdl, wafer finial, 11½" 350.00
Tankard, Bailey & Brainard tm, tooled hdl w/lady's head, 1840s, 15" ... 200.00
Teapot, Boardman lion tm, soldered rpr on ft, 8½" 200.00
Teapot, Curtiss tm, ftd pear shape, rpr, 8" 175.00
Teapot, McQuilkin partial tm, sm dents, worn blk on hdl, 8⅝" ... 175.00

Pfaltzgraff

Pfaltzgraff has operated in Pennsylvania since the early 1800s making redware at first, then stoneware crocks and jugs, yellow ware and spongeware in the '20s, artware and kitchenware in the '30s, and stoneware kitchen items through the '40s. To collectors, they're best known for their Gourmet Royal (circa 1950s), a high-gloss dinnerware line of solid brown with frothy white drip glaze around the rims, and their giftware line called Muggsy, comic-character mugs, ashtrays, bottle stoppers, children's dishes, pretzel jars, cookie jars, etc. It was designed in the late 1940s and continued in production until 1960. The older versions have protruding features, while the features of later examples were simply painted on.

Their popular Village line, an almond-glazed pattern with a brown-stenciled folk-art tulip design, was basically discontinued several years ago, and is today very collectible. Until the company closed in spring of 2007, Yorktown and Folk art were still being manufactured on a very limited basis; both of these lines are now attracting much interest as well. (In general, use Village prices to help you evaluate those two lines.) For more information on their dinnerware, we recommend *Flea Market Trader* and *Garage Sale and Flea Market Annual*, both by Collector Books. Keep in mind that our values are for mint examples. Crazing and/or scratches affect values drastically. Our advisor for the Muggsy line is Judy Posner; she is listed in the Directory under Florida.

Planter, elephant form, brown drip, hard to find, from $90.00 to $110.00.

Christmas Heritage, bowl, soup/cereal; #009, 5½", from $4 to 7.00
Christmas Heritage, butter tub 65.00
Christmas Heritage, casserole, w/lid, 2-qt, from $50 to 65.00
Christmas Heritage, mug, ped ft 20.00
Christmas Heritage, pie plate, 9" 35.00
Christmas Heritage, pitcher, paneled, str sides, 32-oz, 7½" 65.00
Christmas Heritage, plate, dinner; #004, 10" 25.00
Christmas Heritage, platter, 16" 50.00
Christmas Heritage, punch bowl, paneled, 10" 85.00
Christmas Heritage, teapot, lighthouse shape, 8½" 65.00
Christmas Heritage, tray, Christmas tree shape, 10½" 75.00
Gourmet Royale, bean pot, #11-3, 3-qt................................. 25.00
Gourmet Royale, bowl, mixing; 10", from $20 to 25.00
Gourmet Royale, bowl, spaghetti; shallow, #219, 14", from $15 to ... 20.00
Gourmet Royale, bowl, vegetable; 8⅛" 12.50
Gourmet Royale, casserole, hen on nest, 2-qt, from $50 to........... 60.00
Gourmet Royale, casserole, stick hdl, 2-qt, from $12 to 15.00
Gourmet Royale, chip 'n dip, #306, 2-pc set, w/stand, from $22 to... 25.00
Gourmet Royale, creamer, #382 ....4.00
Gourmet Royale, cup & saucer..5.00
Gourmet Royale, jug, #384, 32-oz, from $18 to 25.00
Gourmet Royale, plate, Give Us This Day..., 10" 45.00
Gourmet Royale, plate, salad; 6¾" 2.00
Gourmet Royale, platter, #17, 16".................................... 35.00
Gourmet Royale, shakers, #317/#318, 4½", pr 7.00

Gourmet Royale, souffle dish, #393, 5-qt, +underplate, from $50 to.. 60.00
Gourmet Royale, teapot, #701, 6x10" 25.00
Gourmet Royale, tray, 3-part, 15½" L................................. 20.00
Gourmet Royale, trivet, rnd w/tab hdls, ornate design 10.00
Heritage, casserole, str sides, glass lid, 3-qt, 9¾" 28.00
Heritage, fondue pot w/hdl, #522H, +warmer stand, 7x11½" 32.00
Heritage, lazy Susan, 4-pc, wooden base, from $55 to 75.00
Heritage, mug, ftd 7.00
Heritage, plate, dinner; 10¼" 5.00
Heritage, punch bowl, 6 cups & ladle 75.00
Heritage, soup tureen, #002-160, 3½-qt, +ladle & underplate, $45 to 60.00
Heritage, teapot, lighthouse shape, 8", from $50 to 65.00
Heritage, vase, bud; 6½" 18.00
Village, beverage server, #490, from $18 to................................. 22.00
Village, bowl, fruit; #008, 5" 3.00
Village, bowl, mixing; enamelware, set of 4, w/lids 50.00
Village, bowl, pasta; 12" 50.00
Village, cookie jar, glass w/ceramic lid, 10½" 45.00
Village, garlic keeper, 5x4½" 30.00
Village, ice bucket, metal liner 55.00
Village, picture frame, 3½x5" 38.00
Village, shakers, pr from $10 to 15.00
Village, soap dispenser, 6" 28.00
Village, table light, clear glass shimney on candleholder base, #620 .. 13.00
Village, vase, cylindrical, 7½" 45.00

Phoenix Bird

Blue and white Phoenix Bird china has been produced by various Japanese potteries from the early 1900s. With slight variations the design features the Japanese bird of paradise and scroll-like vines of Kara-Kusa, or Chinese grass. Although some of their earlier ware is unmarked, the majority is marked in some fashion. More than 125 different stamps have been reported, with 'Made in Japan' the one most often found. Coming in second is Morimura's wreath and/or crossed stems (both having the letter 'M' within). The cloverleaf with 'Japan' below very often indicates an item having a high-quality transfer-printed design. Among the many categories in the Phoenix Bird pattern are several shapes; therefore (for identification purposes), each has been given a number, i.e. #1, #2, etc. Post-1970 items, if marked at all, carry a paper label. Compared to the older ware, the coloring of the 1970s items is whiter and the blue more harsh; the design is sparse with more ground area showing. Although collectors buy later pieces, the older is, of course, more highly prized and valued.

The Flying Turkey is a pattern very similar to Phoenix Bird. Though there are several differences, the phoenix bird's head is facing back or to the right, while the turkey faces forward and has a heart-like border design. Values are given for this line as well.

Because of the current over-supply of Phoenix Bird's 'everyday' pieces on eBay in the last year or two, versus today's 'demand' for the latter, most collectors' 'wants' are not as great as they used to be, and the market shows it. As in the past it's the very 'hard-to-find' shapes that still bring the higher prices today. However, for the new collector, today's 'over-supply' is a great opportunity to build an inexpensive, useable collection. Therefore, the advanced collector must persevere, keeping tuned-in to various Internet sites for unique shapes and/or titles that sellers use to find rare shapes to add to their collection. For further information we recommend *Phoenix Bird Chinaware, Books I – V*, written and privately published by our advisor, Joan Oates; her address is in the Directory under Michigan. Join Phoenix Bird Collectors of America (PBCA) and receive the *Phoenix Bird Discoveries* newsletter, an informative publication that will further your appreciation of this chinaware. See Clubs, Newsletters, and Catalogs for ordering information.

Bisquit jar, Flying Turkey, scalloped, HP, 4¾x8¼" 200.00
Bowl, berry; 16 scallops, 1⅝x4¾" 33.00
Bowl, cereal; Myott & Son, 6½" 12.00
Bowl, fruit; 5 scallops, 2¼x9¼" 52.00
Bowl, sauce; w/heart border (HoWo), 3¼x5¾" 45.00
Chamberstick #1, scalloped hdl, 2x5" 85.00
Chocolate pot #1, 8¾" 200.00
Coffeepot #1, 6½x6¼" 60.00
Creamer #18 .... 12.00
Pitcher, buttermilk; 6⅜x6⅝" at spout 65.00
Plate #11, wicker encased, 6", 5½" to top of hdl, 7" dia overall.... 100.00
Reamer pitcher B, w/unmatched reamer top (all wht) 45.00
Ring box A, 1½x2⅝" 25.00
Tea strainer #3, 2-pc 35.00
Teapot #19, Myott & Son 275.00
Tumbler, lemonade/water; flared top, 3¾x3⅜" 20.00
Tureen, Rice A 130.00
Tureen #1, oval, on sm oval platter, child sz, 7¾x5¼" 65.00

Phoenix Glass

Founded in 1880 in Monaca, Pennsylvania, the Phoenix Glass Company became one of the country's foremost manufacturers of lighting glass by the early 1900s. They also produced a wide variety of utilitarian and decorative glassware, including art glass by Joseph Webb, colored cut glass, Gone-With-the-Wind style oil lamps, hotel and barware, and pharmaceutical glassware. Today, however, collectors are primarily interested in the 'Sculptured Artware' produced in the 1930s and 1940s. These beautiful pressed and mold-blown pieces are most often found in white milk glass or crystal with various color treatments or a satin finish. Phoenix did not mark their 'Sculptured Artware' line on the glass; instead, a silver and black (earliest) or gold and black (later) foil label in the shape of the mythical phoenix bird was used.

Quite often glassware made by the Consolidated Lamp and Glass Company of nearby Coraopolis, Pennsylvania, is mistaken for Phoenix's 'Sculptured Artware.' Though the style of the glass is very similar, one distinguishing characteristic is that perhaps 80% of the time Phoenix applied color to the background leaving the raised design plain in contrast, while Consolidated generally applied color to the raised design and left the background plain. Also, for the most part, the patterns and colors used by Phoenix were distinctively different from those used by Consolidated. In 1970 Phoenix Glass became a division of Anchor Hocking which in turn was acquired by the Newell Group in 1987. Phoenix has the distinction of being one of the oldest continuously operating glass factories in the United States. For more information refer to *Phoenix and Consolidated Art Glass, 1926 – 1980*, written by our advisor, David Sherman, who is listed in the Directory under New York. See also Consolidated Glass.

Dancing Girl, vase, light blue on satin milk glass, reverse decorated, partial label, rare, 11½", $750.00.
(Photo courtesy David Sherman)

Bluebell, vase, brn shadow, 7" 125.00
Bluebell, vase, peach & gr (reverse decor) on milk glass, 7" 150.00
Cosmos, vase, gr on milk glass, 7½" 145.00
Cosmos, vase, lav pearlized, 7½" 185.00
Cosmos, vase, wht on brn (brn shadow), 7½" 100.00
Dancing Girl, vase, red pearlized, 12" 625.00
Dancing Girl, vase, tan shadow on wht satin, 12" 250.00
Diving Girl, banana boat, orange w/frosted design 425.00
Fern, vase, brn on milk glass, 7" 135.00
Fern, vase, burgundy on wht satin, 7" 110.00
Fern, vase, Reuben Blue on milk glass, 7" 195.00
Fern, vase, wht frost, 7" 75.00
Fern, vase, yel & gr (reverse decor) on milk glass, 7" 115.00
Freesia, vase, tan w/frosted design, fan shape, 8" 175.00
Lace Dew Drop, tumbler, pk on milk glass, 6" 35.00
Lacy Dewdrop, candy dish, bl on wht, w/lid, 6" dia 95.00
Lacy Dewdrop, pitcher, gray highlights on milk glass 175.00
Lily, vase, yel wash, 3-crimp, 9" 325.00
Madonna, vase, lt bl on milk glass, 10" 165.00
Madonna, vase, tan shadow, 10" 195.00
Philodendron, vase, gray w/frosted design, 11½" 175.00
Philodendron, vase, wht on sky bl, 11½" 165.00
Phlox, candy dish, bl frosted 200.00
Primrose, vase, crystal w/wht wash, 8¾" 595.00
Screech Owls/Reuben Line, vase, bl, orig label 300.00
Thistle, vase, gr frosted, 18" 525.00
Thistle, vase, gr shadow, paper label, 18" 600.00
Tiger Lily, bowl, pk frosted, 11½" 350.00
Zodiac, vase, slate bl over milk glass 950.00

Phonographs

The phonograph, invented by Thomas Edison in 1877, was the first practical instrument for recording and reproducing sound. Sound wave vibrations were recorded on a tinfoil-covered cylinder and played back with a needle that ran along the grooves made from the recording, thus reproducing the sound. Very little changed to this art of record making until 1885, when the first replayable and removable wax cylinders were developed by the American Graphophone Company. These records were made from 1885 until 1894 and are rare today. Edison began to offer musically recorded wax cylinders in 1889. They continued to be made until 1902. Today they are known as brown wax records. Black wax cylinders were offered in 1902, and the earlier brown wax cylinders were discontinued. These wax two-minute records were sold until 1912. From then until 1929, only four-minute celluloid blue amberol record cylinders were made. The first disc records and disc machines were offered by the inventor Berliner in 1894. They were sold in America until 1900, when the Victor company took over. In the 1890s all machines played 7" diameter disc records; the 10" size was developed in 1901. By the early 1900s there existed many disc and cylinder phonograph companies, all offering their improvements. Among them were Berliner, Columbia, Zonophone, United States Phono, Wizard, Vitaphone, Amet, and others.

All Victor I's through VI's originally came with a choice of either brass bell, morning-glory, or wooden horns. Wood horns are the most valuable, adding $1,000.00 (or more) to the machine. Spring models were produced until 1929 (and even later). After 1929 most were electric (though some electric-motor models were produced as early as 1910). Unless another condition is noted, prices are for complete, original phonographs in at least fine to excellent condition. Note: Edison coin-operated cylinder players start at $7,000.00 and may go up to $20,000.00 each. All outside-horn Victor phonographs are worth at least $1,000.00 or more, if in excellent original condition. Machines that are complete, still retaining all their original parts, and with the original finish still in good condition are the most sought after, but those that have been carefully restored with their original finishes, decals, etc., are bringing high prices as well.

Key:
cyl — cylinder   NP — nickel plated
mg — morning glory   rpd — reproducer

Aeolian Vocalion, disc, upright oak case, 42x20¾x18¼" 275.00
Boston Talking Machine Little Wonder, mica soundbox, pnt metal, 11"..825.00
Bremon, interchangeable cyl, mahog w/walnut inlay case, 40"+49" base..5,225.00
Brooks #901, disc, floor model, cvd mahog case, 46" 300.00
Cameraphone, 78 rpm disc, orig rpd, tortoiseshell resonator, oak ... 360.00
Columbia Disc, sq base, crank hdl, metal mg horn, Pat May 4, 1886 ... 1,900.00
Columbia Graphophona A, cyl, rpl brass horn, oak case.......... 4,800.00
Columbia Graphophone AA, orig horn & rpd, oak case, 1901..2,000.00
Columbia Graphophone AQ, floating mica rpd, blk tin horn, VG..325.00
Columbia Graphophone B, cyl, w/horn, oak case, 1897 .... 525.00
Columbia Graphophone BF, 6" cyl, rpl horn, oak case w/transfers, 1906... 1,300.00
Columbia Graphophone BV Royal, cyl, aluminum horn, oak, ca 1908.1,050.00
Columbia Graphophone Q, cyl, blk tin horn, oak case w/stencil. 425.00
Columbia Graphophone QA, NP open works, NP horn, Pat 1897, 10"...645.00
Edison Amberola VIII, cyl, oak table-top, +9 rolls 480.00
Edison Amberola XXX, cyl, stained oak case w/speaker grill........ 540.00
Edison Chippendale Diamond, disc, mahog case, 50" 360.00
Edison Fireside A, cyl, C rpd, 2-4 min, brass cygnet horn, orig decals...660.00
Edison Fireside A, cyl, 20" red horn, oak case.......................... 420.00
Edison Gem A, cyl, B rpd, 2-min, no horn, oak case 840.00
Edison Gem B, cyl, B rpd, 2-4 min, blk cygnet horn, rfn oak 850.00
Edison Gem B, cyl, C rpd, 2-min, rpl horn, oak case, 1905 .... 1,300.00
Edison Gem C, C rpd, blk case w/gold, blk horn, ca 1905 .... 500.00
Edison Home, cyl, brass mg horn, oak case w/decals, +65 cyls 900.00
Edison Home A, B rpd, oak w/gilt mg floral-pnt horn, transfer, 19" dia..885.00
Edison Home A, C rpd, gr oak base w/banner, red mg horn 585.00
Edison Home A, cyl, 2-min, automatic rpd, oak case, conical brass horn.. 1,550.00
Edison Home A, H rpd, 4-min, papier-mache Phono Mega horn, 23", +cyl..470.00
Edison Home D, H rpd, brass horn, oak case, ca 1908.................. 950.00

Edison Home, morning glory horn, $885.00. (Photo courtesy Morphy Auctions)

Edison N American M, cyl, automatic rpd, mahog case, Pat 1888..21,000.00
Edison Standard A, C rpd, gr oak case, brass horn, +40 cyl, VG... 445.00
Edison Standard A, cyl, C rpd, 2-min, aluminum horn, 1901 ...1,050.00
Edison Standard B, H rpd, 4-min, oak w/transfer, dome lid/horn. 355.00
Edison Standard C, C rpd/combo gears, red-lacquer mg horn, +2nd horn ..425.00
Edison Standard Flat Top, C rpd, 2-min, brass horn, oak case...... 950.00
Edison Standard Rnd Top, cyl, oak case, pnt/gilt mg horn, ca 1903 ...800.00
Edison Triumph, C rpd, 4-min, decagon horn.............................. 995.00
Edison Triumph A, cyl, C rpd, 2-min, crane, brass horn, oak case....2,650.00
Edison Triumph B, cyl, mg horn, oak case 1,050.00
MacDonald AB, cyl (2" & 5"), Eagle rpd, aluminum horn, orig decals...1,650.00
Modernola, disc, fringed ostrich-feather shade, walnut case, 47x22" .6,600.00

Peter Pan, 78 rpm disc, mica rpd, box camera style, ca 1920........ 240.00
Rosenfeld, quartersawn oak, coin-op, 72" 18,750.00
Talk-a-Phone, disc, cvd oak case, 10" turntable, 30" brass bell horn ..2,150.00
Victor E, Exhibition rpd, 7" turntable, oak traveling arm, blk horn .995.00
Victor Gramophone VV-IV, hornless, Exhibition soundbox, oak 2-door ..85.00
Victor I, disc, mg horn, quartersawn oak case 880.00
Victor II, disc, blk & brass horn, oak case 825.00
Victor III, disk, quartersawn oak horn & case............................2,550.00
Victor III, external 30" brass bell horn, oak case, 14x18x14", VG.. 1,380.00
Victor IV, disc, tiger oak case, pnt mg horn, all orig 2,000.00
Victor Orthophonic VV-47, disc, orig rpd, upright mahog case, 38"..300.00
Victor V, disc, oak case, blk mg horn, all orig 1,440.00
Victor V, disc, quartersawn oak horn & base, 31", VG 2,650.00
Victor V, Exhibition rpd, bl/gold transfer, oak case & horn.......3,000.00
Victor VI, disc, mahog horn & stand, 66", NM 7,750.00
Zonophone, cyl, oak table model w/24" outside brass horn 3,240.00
Zonophone, disc, beaded mahog case, 24" wood horn, Pat 1908, VG.. 2,400.00

Photographica

Photographic collectibles include not only the cameras and equipment used to 'freeze' special moments in time but also the photographic images produced by a great variety of processes that have evolved since the daguerrean era of the mid-1800s. For the most part, good quality images have either maintained or increased in value. Poor quality examples (regardless of rarity) are not selling well. Interest in cameras and stereo equipment is down, and dealers report that average-priced items that were moving well are often completely overlooked. Though rare items always have a market, collectors seem to be buying only if they are bargain priced. Our advisor for this category is John Hess; he is listed in the Directory under Massachusetts. Unless noted otherwise, values are for examples in at least near-mint condition.

Albumens

These prints were very common during the nineteenth century. The term comes from the emulsion of silver salts and albumen that was used to coat the paper they were printed on.

Battleship Maine as it lays in bottom of Havana harbor, Hoy, 10x7"...35.00
Chinese junk & sm boats in Shanghai harbor, 8x10½" 235.00
Columbo (Ceylon) river scene, 1890s, 7½x10" 90.00
Martinique Black man w/dead snake on stick, 5½x4½" 70.00
Nude woman stands beside rocks, Marconi, 1870s, 10x7½" 175.00
Ox cart going through village in Argentina, Rimathe, 6x8" 90.00
Scene of explosion, mining disaster, Silver Valley ID, 1899, 7x9"....65.00
Sudanese lady w/breast exposed, pierced nose, 1880, 5½x4""......... 45.00

Ambrotypes

An ambrotype is a type of photograph produced by an early wet-plate process whereby a faint negative image on glass is seen as positive when held against a dark background.

Half plate, boy in Civil War uniform w/weapon, hand colored, +case....1,000.00
Half plate, man seated w/musical instrument, pk cheeks, in fr.....265.00
Whole plate, 2 sisters, 1 stands on chair/2nd sits on table, Brady.. 975.00
4th plate, man in Western garb w/long rifle, +Union case 375.00
4th plate, sisters in fine winter attire, dtd 1858, +case................. 185.00
4th plate, 2 hunters w/shotguns, tinted cheeks, arched mat, +case ..235.00
4th plate, 2 instrument makers at work, gilt mat, +leather fr....... 500.00
6th plate, boy w/gold watch chain & jewelry holds a dag of himself, VG..115.00
6th plate, military cadet sits w/sword in hand, shako at side, +case.. 350.00

6th plate, NH volunteer, ruby, IN Teague/NH, gilt mat, +case 175.00
9th plate, Confederate soldier w/beard, gold foil mat, +case 215.00
9th plate, Union militia sergeant, ruby tinted, brass mat, +case .. 265.00

Cabinet Photos

When the popularity of Carte De Visites began to wane in the 1880s, a new fascination developed for the cabinet card, a larger version measuring about 4½x6½". These photos were produced by a variety of methods. They remained popular until the turn of the century.

Baseball team w/umpires & managers, 1890s, 9x11" 300.00
Black lady in Victorian finery, fine jewelry & hat, 6x4¼", VG 115.00
Black man w/eyeglasses in graduation cap, Boston, 6½x4¼" 95.00
Gen Adlai Stevenson formal portrait, NY photographer, 6½x4¼" ...80.00
Gen Lew Wallace in close-up portrait, 6½x4¼" 195.00
Girl w/long curls posed w/pug dog in studio setting 100.00
Honus Wagner in auto driver's seat w/other figures, ca 1910, 5x7"... 465.00
Hump (Indian chief) & 2 wives, MT Territory, Huffman, 1870s . 650.00
Keystone cop, Philadelpha PA, 1880, 6x4" 140.00
Lady Randolph Churchill close-up portrait, Mendelsohn, 1880s . 125.00
Last photo of Gen Grant 4 Days Before Death, Gilman, 1885 ..... 220.00
Stanley (explorer) in high boots, map on lap, Gurney, NY, 1880s ..235.00

U.S. Grant, framed by a 15x13" woodcut template of his initials, from $500.00 to $700.00. (Photo courtesy Early American History Auctions)

Cameras

Collectible high-quality cameras are not easy to find. Most of the pre-1900 examples will be found in the large format view cameras or studio camera types. There are quite a few of these that can be found in well-worn condition, but there is a large difference in value between an average-wear item and an excellent or mint-condition camera. It is rare indeed to find one of these early cameras in mint condition.

The types of cameras are generally classified as follows: large format, medium format, early folding and box types, 35 mm single-lens-reflex (SLR), 35mm rangefinders, twin-lens reflex (TLR), miniature or subminiature, novelty, and even a few others. Collectors may specialize in a type, a style, a time period, or even in high-quality examples of the same camera.

In the 1900 to 1940 period, large quantities of various makes of box cameras and folding bellows type cameras were produced by many manufacturers, and the popular 35mm camera was introduced in the 1930s. Most have low values because they were made in vast numbers, but mint-condition cameras are prized by collectors. In the 1930 to 1955 period, the 35mm rangefinders and the SLR's and TLR's became the cameras of choice. The most prized of these are the early German or Japanese rangefinders such as the Leica, Canon, or Nikon. Earlier, German optics were favored, but after WWII, Japanese cameras and optics rivaled and/or even exceeded the quality of many German optics.

Now there are thousands of different cameras to choose from, and collectors have many options when selecting categories. Quality is the

major factor; values vary widely between an average-wear working camera and one in mint condition, or one still in the original box and unused. This brief list suggests average prices for good working cameras with average wear. The same camera in mint condition will be valued much higher, while one with excessive wear (scratches, dents, corrosion, poor optics, nonworking meters or rangefinders) may have little value.

Buying, selling, and trading of old and late vintage cameras on the Internet, both in direct transactions and via e-mail auctions, have tremendously affected the number of cameras that are available to collectors today. As a result, values have fluctuated as well. Large numbers of old, mass-produced box cameras and folding cameras have been offered; many are in poor condition and have been put up for sale by persons who know nothing about quality. So in general, prices have dropped, and it is an excellent buyer's market at the present, except for the mint quality offerings. Many common models in poor to average condition can be bought for $1.00 to $10.00. The collector is advised to purchase only quality cameras that will enhance his collection. To date, no appreciable collector's market has developed for most old movie cameras or projectors. The Polaroid type of camera has little value, although a few models are gaining in popularity among collectors, and values are expected to increase. Today's new camera market is dominated by digital cameras. The initial effect on yesterday's film cameras has been dramatic, reducing both demand and prices of regular and film-type cameras. There is no immediate collector's market for digital cameras. Many fakes and copies have been made of several of the classic cameras such as the German Leica, and caution is advised in purchasing one of these cameras at a price too good to be true. Consult a specialist on high-priced classics if good reference material is not available. Our advisor for this category is Gene Cataldo; he is listed in the Directory under Alabama (e-mail: genecams@ aol.com). SASE required for information by mail.

Agfa, box type, 1930-50, from $5 to 20.00
Agfa, Karat-35, 1940 .... 35.00
Aires, 35III, 1958, from $15 to 35.00
Ansco, Cadet 5.00
Ansco, Memar, 1954-58 .... 20.00
Ansco, Super Speedex, 3.5 lens, 1953-58, from $100 to 150.00
Argus A, early model, 35mm Bakelite, 1936-41, from $20 to 30.00
Argus A2F, 1940, from $10 to 20.00
Argus C4, 2.8 lens w/flash 30.00
Asahiflex 1, 1st Japanese SLR 500.00
Bell & Howell Dial 35, from $25 to 40.00
Bolsey B2 .... 20.00
Burke & James, Cub, 1914 .... 20.00
Canon AE-1, from $50 to 100.00
Canon F-1, from $125 to 200.00
Canon III, 1952, from $150 to 250.00
Canon L-1, 1956-57 .... 400.00
Canon Rangefinder IIF, ca 1954, from $200 to 300.00
Canon S-II, 1947-49, from $200 to 350.00
Canon TL, from $30 to 50.00
Canon VT, 1956-57, from $200 to 300.00
Canon 7, 1961-64, from $200 to 400.00
Canon 7s Rangefinder, w/F1.2 lens, 1964-67, from $350 to 500.00
Canonet QL1, from $25 to 40.00
Compass Camera, 1938, from $1,000 to 1,300.00
Conley 5x7", folding plate, 1908-17, from $150 to 250.00
Contessa 35, 1950-55, from $100 to 150.00
Detrola Model D, Detroit Corp, 1938-40 .... 20.00
Eastman Baby Brownie Special, 1939-54, from $1 to 10.00
Eastman Kodak Baby Brownie, Bakelite, from $5 to 10.00
Eastman Kodak Medalist, 1941-48, from $100 to 175.00
Eastman Kodak No 2C Brownie Box, 1917-34, from $7 to 15.00
Eastman Kodak Retina IIa, from $55 to 75.00

Eastman Kodak Retina IIIC, from $225 to.......................325.00
Eastman Kodak Signet 35...35.00
Eastman Kodak 35, 1940-51, from $20 to........................35.00
Eastman View Camera, early 1900s, from $100 to.............200.00
Edinex, by Wirgen, Germany, 1930s-50s...........................30.00
Exakta VX, 1951, from $75 to..85.00
FED 1, USSR, postwar, from $30 to.................................50.00
Fuijca AX-3, from $50 to..75.00
Fujica ST-701..60.00
Graflex Speed Graphic, various szs, ea from $60 to...........200.00
Herbert-George, Donald Duck, 1946................................25.00

Hit, subminiature novelty from Japan, many variations and names, from $15.00 to $30.00. (Photo courtesy C.E. Cataldo)

Kine Exakta 1, Ihagee, Dresden, 35mm Rangefinder, from $175 to ...250.00
Kodak, vest pocket folding automatic, 1912-14, from $30 to 50.00
Kodak Brownie Target Six-20, 1952, from $1 to 10.00
Kodak Medalist 1, 1941-48, from $100 to 150.00
Kodak No 2 Folding Pocket Brownie, 1904-07 ....25.00
Kodak Retina 1a, Type (o15), 1952, from $50 to.................75.00
Kodak Tourist II, 1951-58, from $12 to.............................15.00
Konica Autoreflex TC, various models, ea from $40 to.........70.00
Konica III Rangefinder, 1956-59, from $90 to....................110.00
Leica IID, 1932-38, from $200 to....................................400.00
Leica IIIa, 1935-50, from $200 to...................................350.00
Leica IIIc, gray (ball-bearing model), 1942, from $2,500 to......4,500.00
Leica IIIF, 1950-56, from $200 to...................................400.00
Linex Stereo, by Lionel, 1954, from $80 to........................120.00
Mamiya-Sekor 500TL, 1966...20.00
Mercury Model II CX, 1945, from $25 to 35.00
Minolta HiMatic Series, various models, ea from $10 to.......25.00
Minolta SRT-202, from $50 to 90.00
Minolta XD-11, 1977, from $90 to...................................130.00
Minolta 35, early Rangefinder models, 1947-50, ea from $250 to ...400.00
Minox B, chrome, 1958-71, from $80 to...........................125.00
Minox II, made in Wetzlar, Germany, from $200 to 300.00
Nikkormat (Nikon), various models, ea from $60 to.............150.00
Nikon F, SLR, w/finder & lens, 1960s, from $125 to............350.00
Nikon FM...135.00
Nikon S Rangefinder, 1951-54, from $450 to.....................800.00
Nikon SP Rangefinder, 1958-60, from $1,500 to.............2,000.00
Nr3A Folding Pocket Kodak, ModB-4, red bellows, 1903-15, from $40 to...60.00
Olympus OM-1, from $50 to 80.00
Olympus OM-10, from $40 to 60.00
Olympus Pen EED, 33mm half-fr, 1967-72, from $50 to 80.00
Olympus Pen F, compact half-fr SLR, from $100 to.....................200.00
Olympus-35, many models, from $30 to............................80.00
Orion Works 6x9 Plate, 1921-28, from $60 to.....................100.00
Pentax ME, from $50 to...75.00
Pentax Spotmatic, many models, ea from $40 to.................100.00
Petri-7, 1961 ....20.00
Plaubel-Makina II, 1933-39...200.00
Polaroid 110, 110A, 110B, ea from $20 to 40.00
Praktica FX, 1952-57..30.00

Praktica Super TL..40.00
Realist Stereo, 3.5 lens..80.00
Regula, King, interchangable lens, various models, ea from $40 to...60.00
Ricoh Singlex, 1965, from $50 to....................................70.00
Rollei 35, mini, Singapore, from $80 to.............................150.00
Rolleicord II, 1936-50, from $70 to..................................90.00
Rolleiflex SL35M, 1978, from $75 to................................100.00
Samoca 35, 1950s..25.00
Spartus Press Flash, 1939-50...10.00
Tessina, mini, from $300 to 500.00
Tower 50, Sears, w/Cassar lens 20.00
Univex-A, Univ Camera Co, 1933.....................................25.00
Voigtlander Bessa, w/Rangefinder, 1936............................140.00
Voigtlander Prominent 1, 35mm Rangefinder, 1952-58, from $150 to...200.00
Voigtlander Vitessa T, 1957, from $110 to..........................175.00
Yashica A, TLR..35.00
Yashica FX-70...60.00
Yashicaflex TLR, Yashikor 80mm lens, from $175 to.............250.00
Zeiss Baldur Box Tengor, Frontar lens, 1935, from $35 to 125.00
Zeiss Contax III, 1936-42, from $175 to 350.00
Zeiss Ikon Juwell, 1927-39..500.00
Zenit A, USSR, from $20 to...35.00
Zorki-4, USSR, Rangefinder, 1956-73, from $35 to...............50.00

Cartes De Visites

Among the many types of images collectible today are carte de visites, known as CDVs, which are 2¼" x 4" portraits printed on paper and produced in quantity. The CDV fad of the 1800s enticed the famous and the unknown alike to pose for these cards, which were circulated among the public to the extent that they became known as 'publics.' Note: A common portrait CDV is worth only about 50¢ unless it carries a revenue stamp on the back; those that do are valued at about $2.00 each.

Black Teeth's Daughter, Sioux girl/finery, NB/1880, 4x2½", $200 to... 300.00
Chinaman in silk jacket, Western hat, studio pose, IL, 1890s........ 95.00
Dog seated on ornate ped in studio, ca 1879, 4x2⅜" 45.00
George Peabody Philanthropist, seated in studio, 4x2¾" 20.00
Indian man w/cartridge belt across chest, 1860s, 4x2⅜" 225.00
John Jennings Modern Sampson, man lifts 2 other men, 4x2½", $45 to.. 75.00
John Keats, Fred Bruckmann London, VG+................................. 150.00
Lincoln seated in chair facing left, arm on table........................ 200.00
Postmortem of lovely young woman, English, ca 1880, EX 45.00
Shaker lady w/wht bonnet, simple shawl, Kimball, NH, 4x2⅜" ... 160.00
Ulysses S Grant as Lieutenant General, 1865, 4½x2½", EX......... 100.00
Union soldiers at cards/drinking before adobe building, guns aside.. 750.00
USD Grant in uniform as Lieutenant General seated in chair, NY... 30.00
Ute Chief Curecanti & 2 Indian women, Chamberlin, ca 1865, 4x2½" ... 360.00
Yellow Man, Native American in studio, 1900s, 5x4", EX........... 350.00

Daguerreotypes

Among the many processes used to produce photographic images are the daguerreotypes (made on a plate of chemically treated silver-plated copper) — the most-valued examples being the 'whole' plate which measures 6½" x 8½". Other sizes include the 'half' plate, measuring 4½" x 5½", the 'quarter' plate at 3¼" x 4¼", the 'sixth' plate at 2¾" x 3¼", the 'ninth' at 2" x 2½", and the 'sixteenth' at 1⅜" x 1⅝". (Sizes may vary slightly, and some may have been altered by the photographer.)

Half plate, couple in wedding portrait, ca 1850, +case, from $325 to.. 450.00
Half plate, husband & wife seated together, paper mt, +early case... 400.00
Half plate, lady in finery w/lace cuffs & collar, hand to face, +case.. 400.00
Half plate, Washington Irving portrait of Whitehurst painting, +case... 565.00

Whole plate, gentleman in top hat, scratches, 8½x6½", $1,500.00. (Photo courtesy Garth's Auctions Inc.)

Whole plate, multi-portrait, 5 rows of 6 males, +leather case ... 2,940.00
4th plate, sm brother & sister seated side by side, tinted, +case ... 300.00
4th plate, US Naval officer stands in full uniform by column, +case..550.00
6th plate, beautiful young mother & baby, Southworth & Hawes, +case.. 1,000.00
6th plate, curly-haired dog in chair, ca 1860, GA, +leather case... 1,100.00
6th plate, lady w/tinted cheeks & pendant, +leather case............ 150.00
6th plate, man in casket w/man at ea side, +leather case 1,200.00
6th plate, mother & baby in tinted pk, Gurney, NY, ca 1850, +case... 665.00
6th plate, well-dressed young mulatto man, JP Ball, +case.......... 500.00

Photos

Photogravure, Cheyenne Warriors, Curtis, 1905, 12x16", +mat & fr ... 600.00
Photogravure, John Ruskin portrait, Hollyer/Collis, 1890s, 5x4"... 35.00
Photogravure, Picking Blueberries - Cree, full bookplate, Curtis, 1926.. 155.00
Photogravure, Selawik girl in fur coat, full bookplate, Curtis, 1928 ... 195.00
Sepia tone, Cliff Dwellers, in landscape, Curtis copy, ca 1925, 9x7" ... 100.00
Sepia tone, lady seated by table & curtain, PA, 1860s, 7⅜x5⅜"..... 20.00
Sepia tone, lady stands beside car, ca 1942, 2½x4½" 10.00
Sepia tone, Plains Indian warrior/wife, 1910s, in Victorian fr, 10x8" ... 125.00
Sepia tone, Pueblo Indian in traditional dress, R Price, 1920s, 13x9" ... 120.00
Silver gelatin print, Face in Shadows, SM Wright, 1940s, 6¾x4¾" .. 18.00
Silver gelatin print, Goats on Michigan Beach, E Steichen, 7x9".. 2,000.00
Silver gelatin print, Jim Thorpe in NY Giants uniform, 1913, 5x4" ..585.00
Silver gelatin print, Little Girl w/Dog, E Steichen, 4½x3½" 840.00

Stereoscopic Views

Stereo cards are photos made to be viewed through a device called a stereoscope. The glass stereo plates of the mid-1800s and photo prints produced in the darkroom are among the most valuable. In evaluating stereo views, the subject, date, and condition are all-important. Some views were printed over a 30- to 40-year period; 'first generation' prices are far higher than later copies, made on cheap card stock with reprints or lithographs, rather than actual original photographs. It is relatively easy to date an American stereo view by the color of the mount that was used, the style of the corners, etc. From about 1854 until the early 1860s, cards were either white, cream-colored, or glossy gray; shades of yellow and a dull gray followed. While the dull gray was used for a very short time, the yellow tones continued in use until the late 1860s. Red, green, violet, or blue cards are from the period between 1865 until about 1870. Until the late 1870s, corners were square; after that they were rounded off to prevent damage. Right now, quality stereo views are at a premium.

Baptist University, Florence AL, RM Williams 80.00
Calculating Machine at US Centennial Expo 1876 .... 80.00
Central Pacific RR bridge, NV, F Durgan, 1870............................ 215.00
Chief Geronimo w/bow & arrows, Universal View Co, 1904....... 310.00
Confederate artillery pc in firing position, horse beyond, $130 to ... 200.00

Crippled Locomotive in Richmond, wreckage, #6258................... 75.00
First World War set, Keystone View Co, approximately 300, 3 volumes ... 445.00
Flood Aftermath, Brattleboro VT, yel mt, 1869............................ 80.00
Fort Denham panoramic view, 1870s 35.00
Gen Stonewall Jackson portrait, Taylor & Huntington................ 255.00
Indian Encampment Grand Island (Lake Superior), yel mt 100.00
Looking Across Trukee Meadows Toward Sierra..., train, #288, ca 1870... 250.00
Private Box at Ford's Theatre...Lincoln..., Anthony, #3403, $225 to .. 300.00
River trestle bridge, Florence AL, Williams................................ 80.00
Roosevelt planting tree, Ft Worth TX, 1905 .... 80.00
Samuel FB Morse portrait, J Gurney & Son, 1871....................... 135.00
Sherman's Army...Washington DC, orange mt, Brady, #3398, 1865..335.00
Union Officer's House, Charleston SC, Anthony, #3101, 1860s.. 150.00

Tintypes

Tintypes, contemporaries of ambrotypes, were produced on japanned iron and were not as easily damaged.

Full plate, Civil War soldier in infantry overcoat, HP 260.00
Full plate, group of 3 children, full-length 95.00
Full plate, lady in hoop skirt stands by chair, HP, 1860s, +fr 100.00
Full plate, postmortem of baby in long gown on ornate pillow..... 230.00
Full plate, soldier seated before 32-star flag, oval card mt............ 500.00
4th plate, Civil War officer seated, +thermplastic case................ 245.00
6th plate, baseball players (2) w/striped socks, 1 holds bat, NY ... 300.00
6th plate, boy seated w/dog, +broken case 150.00
6th plate, lady in finery seated w/dog at side, gold-tone mat 150.00
6th plate, 3 men w/shotguns, hatchets & knives in studio pose ... 385.00
9th plate, Am Indian chief (unknown) seated w/weapons, ca 1880...180.00
9th plate, Black girl (about 2 yrs old) in finery seated, +G- case 215.00
9th plate, Black lady holding dead child, tinted cheeks 195.00
9th plate, Union soldier seated before US flag, MA volunteer, +fr .. 300.00
9th plate, 3 ladies (sisters?) peeling potatoes/cooking, seated....... 210.00

Union Cases

From the mid-1850s until about 1880, cases designed to house these early images were produced from a material known as thermoplastic, a man-made material with an appearance much like gutta percha. Its innovator was Samuel Peck, who used shellac and wood fibers to create a composition he called Union. Peck was part owner of the Scoville Company, makers of both papier-mache and molded leather cases, and he used the company's existing dies to create his new line. Other companies (among them A.P. Critchlow & Company; Littlefield, Parsons & Company; and Holmes, Booth, & Hayden) soon duplicated his material and produced their own designs. Today's collectors may refer to cases made of this material as 'thermoplastic,' 'composition,' or 'hard cases,' but the term most often used is 'Union.' It is incorrect to refer to them as gutta percha cases.

Sizes may vary somewhat, but generally a 'whole' plate case measures 7" x 9⅛" to the outside edges, a 'half' plate 4⅞" x 6", a 'quarter' plate 3¾" x 4¾", a 'sixth' 3⅛" x 3⅝", a 'ninth' 2⅜" x 2⅞", and a 'sixteenth' 1¾" x 2". Clifford and Michele Krainik and Carl Walvoord have written a book, *Union Cases*, which we recommend for further study. Another source of information is *Nineteenth Century Photographic Cases and Wall Frames* by Paul Berg. Values are for examples in excellent condition unless noted otherwise.

Half plate, American Country Life, VG 310.00
Half plate, Wedding Procession, +ambrotype of couple 495.00
4th plate, Angel w/Stag, VG 175.00
4th plate, Chasse Au Faucon, +tintype of boy by corner chair 125.00
4th plate, Music Lessons, +tintype of young man w/tinted cheeks... 135.00
4th plate, Washington Monument, w/G- ambrotype.................... 350.00
6th plate, Belt Buckle & Chain, Littlefield Parsons, K-161............ 85.00

6th plate, Civil War soldier, mk Union Now & Forever, K-370... 200.00
6th plate, Eagle at Bay, +tintype of seated lady 175.00
6th plate, Faithful Hound, +2 daguerrotypes 225.00
6th plate, Farmer's Dream, +ambrotype of seated man 125.00
6th plate, Geometric, w/glass window, K-355 .... 110.00
6th plate, Magnified Circle, R-233, +daguerrotype 30.00
6th plate, Mixed Flower Bouquet, +daguerrotype of bearded man ...85.00
6th plate, Rebecca at the Well, +ambrotype bust of man 125.00
6th plate, Scroll/Geometric, +ambrotype of bride 80.00
6th plate, Ten Dollar Piece w/floral border, +ambrotype of lady .. 225.00
6th plate, The Hunter, Littlefield Parsons, +ambrotype of seated lady.. 175.00
6th plate, Union & Constitution, K-373 .... 125.00
9th plate, Chess Players, R-41 variant... 100.00
9th plate, Geometrics/Scrolls, Littlefield Parsons, K-478 .... 75.00
9th plate, Twice Armed, Civil War infantryman w/Warner pistol ..400.00
9th plate (dbl), Family Party, K-560.. 165.00

Miscellaneous

Photo album, celluloid, gilt-tipped pages, gilt hardware, containing 16 cabinet card photos, $225.00. (Photo courtesy Jackson's International Auctioneers & Appraisers of Fine Art & Antiques)

Magic lantern, child's; Jean Schoenner, rnd brass lamp house, 12" .. 120.00
Stanhope viewer, monocular form, ivory 50.00
Stereoscope, A Becker's Pat Apr 7 1857, walnut, on ped, 15", $400 to.. 700.00
Stereoscope, Brewster pattern, mahog w/bone fittings, 6" 440.00
Stereoscope, Gaumont, wooden table type, rack & pinion movement, 1920 ..765.00
Stereoscope, Holmes pattern Perfecscope, HC White, 22 cards, +case.. 195.00
Stereoscope, Monarch Keystone, wooden hand-held type, 1900s.. 65.00
Stereoscope, Schneck pattern, reversible, NP, velvet covered, 13", VG... 295.00
Stereoscope, walnut w/ground-glass scene, fretwork, 16" 295.00

Piano Babies

A familiar sight in Victorian parlors, piano babies languished atop shawl-covered pianos in a variety of poses: crawling, sitting, on their tummies, or on their backs playing with their toes. Some babies were nude, and some wore gowns. Sizes ranged from about 3" up to 12". The most famous manufacturer of these bisque darlings was the Heubach Brothers of Germany, who nearly always marked their product; see Heubach for listings. Watch for reproductions. These guidelines are excerpted from one of a series of informative doll books by Patsy Moyer, published by Collector Books. Values are for examples in near-mint condition. See also Conta and Boehm.

Blk, bsk, 4", EX quality 600.00
Blk, bsk, 4", med quality, unmk 500.00
Blk, bsk, 5", EX quality 600.00
Blk, bsk, 8", EX quality 600.00
Blk, bsk, 8", med quality 550.00
Blk, bsk, 9", EX quality 675.00
Blk, bsk, 12", EX quality 675.00
Blk, bsk, 12", med quality 600.00
Blk, bsk, 14", EX quality 900.00
Blk, bsk, 16", EX quality 1,000.00
Blk, bsk, 16", med quality 900.00
Bsk, may not have pnt finish on bk, unmk, 4", med quality 410.00
Bsk, may not have pnt finish on bk, unmk, 8", med quality 375.00
Bsk, may not have pnt finish on bk, unmk, 12", med quality 500.00
Bsk, molded hair, unjtd, molded-on clothes, 4", EX quality 500.00
Bsk, molded hair, unjtd, molded-on clothes, 4", med quality 425.00
Bsk, molded hair, unjtd, molded-on clothes, 6", EX quality 675.00

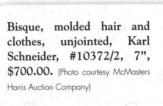

Bisque, molded hair and clothes, unjointed, Karl Schneider, #10372/2, 7", $700.00. (Photo courtesy McMasters Harris Auction Company)

Bsk, molded hair, unjtd, molded-on clothes, 8", EX quality 825.00
Bsk, molded hair, unjtd, molded-on clothes, 8", med quality 500.00
Bsk, molded hair, unjtd, molded-on clothes, 9", EX quality 800.00
Bsk, molded hair, unjtd, molded-on clothes, 12", EX quality 900.00
Bsk, molded hair, unjtd, molded-on clothes, 16", EX quality 1,095.00
Bsk, w/animal/pot/flowers/etc, 4", EX quality 500.00
Bsk, w/animal/pot/flowers/etc, 5", EX quality 500.00
Bsk, w/animal/pot/flowers/etc, 8", EX quality 600.00
Bsk, w/animal/pot/flowers/etc, 10", EX quality 700.00
Bsk, w/animal/pot/flowers/etc, 12", EX quality 800.00
Bsk, w/animal/pot/flowers/etc, 16", EX quality, minimum value... 950.00

Picasso Art Pottery

Pablo Picasso created some distinctive pottery during the 1940s, marking the ware with his signature.

Bowl, bird, brn on wht, Edition Picasso mk, 6" 900.00
Pitcher, face, blk/brn/bl on cream, Madoura, 5" 1,800.00
Pitcher, wide mc brush strokes form eyes at spout, 'hands' below, 5" ..1,765.00
Plate, face, gr/bl/blk on wht, Madoura, 10", NM 2,050.00
Platter, cvd facial features highlighted in dk bl on yel, 12x15"..6,325.00
Platter, lady's face, blk & wht, Madoura, 15⅜" L 3,900.00
Platter, man's face, blk/yel/gr/pk/bl/cream, Madoura, 1948, 15⅜" L..3,250.00
Vase, face on tripod, blk/bl/gr/gray/wht, Madoura, 1951, 29½" ... 32,375.00
Vase, red/blk/wht abstract, hdls, Madoura, 22½" 14,400.00

Pickard

Founded in 1895 in Chicago, Illinois, the Pickard China Company was originally a decorating studio, importing china blanks from European manufacturers. Some of these early pieces bear the name of those companies as well as Pickard's. Trained artists decorated the wares with hand-painted studies of fruit, florals, birds, and scenics and often signed their work. In 1915 Pickard introduced a line of 24k gold over a dainty floral-etched ground design. In the 1930s they began to experiment with the idea of making their own ware and by 1938 had succeeded in developing a formula for fine translucent china. Since 1976 they have issued an annual limited edition Christmas plate. They are now located in Antioch, Illinois.

The company has used various marks. The earliest (1893 – 1894) was a double-circle mark, 'Edgerton Hand Painted' with 'Pickard' in the center. Variations of the double-circle mark (with 'Hand Painted China' replacing the Edgerton designation) were employed until 1915, each differing enough that collectors can usually pinpoint the date of manufacture within five years. Later marks included the crown mark, 'Pickard' on a gold maple leaf, and the current mark, the lion and shield. Work signed by Challinor, Marker, and Yeschek is especially valued by today's collectors.

Bonbon boat, Honeysuckle Design, Passoni, Bavaria blank, 1905-10, 7" .. 225.00
Bowl, carnation/raised gold, sgn Fischer, Limoges blank, 1905-10, 9" ... 425.00
Bowl, floral, sgn A Roy, scalloped/hdls, T&V blank, 1903-05, 9½" ...225.00
Bowl, seashells w/spider web, sgn Kriesche, 1905-10, 9" 250.00
Bowl, Thistles in Paste, Fischer, J&C blank, 1905-10, 10½" 365.00
Bowl, Tulip Conventional, sgn PG, JPL France blank, 1903-05, 9" ...350.00
Cake plate, Trumpet Fowers & Trellis, D&Co blank, 1905-10, 10½". 150.00

Chalice, Plain Hopps and Matte Green pattern, signed Hessler, ca. 1905 – 1910, 11¼", $1,300.00. (Photo courtesy Joy Luke Fine Arts Brokers & Auctioneers)

Coffee set, Cornflower Conventional, Rosenthal blank, pot+4 c/s+tray..1,200.00
Coffeepot, Etched Gold Peacock on Blue, unsgn, 1919-22, +cr/sug w/lid....475.00
Coffeepot, Oleta, floral border, Germany blank, 1918-19, +cr/sug..475.00
Compote, Rose & Daisy, much gold, 2-pc, 1925-30, 6" dia 145.00
Jug, lemonade; peaches on gr, sgn S Heap, CAC blank, 1903-05, 8"..500.00
Mug, Falstaff, gold trim, sgn Gasper, 1905-10, 7".......................650.00
Mug, monk w/tankard & candle, Aldrich, Limoges blank, 1898-1903, 6" ..700.00
Mustard boat, White Poppy & Daisy, Gasper, w/lid, 1912-18 ...... 275.00
Nut dish, Rose & Daisy, gold, 3-compartment, center hdl, 1930-38, 6" ... 45.00
Plate, cherry spray, rococo gold, sgn MP, CA France blank, 1903-05, 8"..200.00
Plate, chrysanthemums, sgn Brun, Limoges blank, 1905-10, 8¾".. 100.00
Plate, dessert; floral spray/lav border, sgn Mark, 1912-18, 8" 100.00
Plate, Rean Carnations & Gold, Rean, Haviland blank, 1905-10, 8½"...250.00
Plate, Triple Tulip, sgn Yeschek, Bavaria blank, 1912-18, 8½" 275.00
Plate, Twin Lilies, sgn Walter, hdls, Bavaria blank, 1910-12, 11" 275.00
Plate, vellum scenic w/gr & gold border, sgn Marker, 1925-30, 11"....350.00
Sugar/cracker jar, amaryllis w/etched gold, Beutlich, w/lid, 1905-10..495.00
Vase, bud; cow scenic, Aldrich, ca 1903-05, 6".........................1,000.00
Vase, Calla Lilly, sgn Marker, shouldered, slim, 1905-10, 11" ... 575.00
Vase, Flora Geometrica, sgn Kriesche, slim, 1905-10, 12" 700.00
Vase, Japanese lady w/comb, unsgn, Willets blank, 1903-05, 12" ... 2,100.00
Vase, Praying Mohammedan, Farrington, RC Bavaria blank, 1903-04, 14"..3,000.00
Vase, seagull on bl, Motzfeldt, Aladdin's lamp form, 1903-05, 7½" ..500.00
Vase, St Denis; tulips w/gold, Lemke, 1903-05, 8" 300.00
Vase, tulips, orange on maroon, Challinor, 1938-present, 6¾"..... 450.00
Vase, twin poppies on gold border, Gasper, shouldered, 1905-10, 7¼"..425.00

Pickle Castors

Affluent Victorian homes seemed to have something for every purpose, and a pickle castor was not only an item of beauty but of practicality. American Victorian pickle castors can be found in old catalogs dating from the 1860s through the early 1900s. (Those featured in catalogs after 1900 were made by silver manufacturers that were not part of the International Silver Company which was formed in 1898 — for instance, Reed and Barton, Tufts, Pairpoint, and Benedict.) Catalogs featured large selections to choose from, ranging from simple to ornate. Inserts could be clear or colored, pattern glass or art glass, molded or blown. Many of these molds and design were made by more than one company as they merged or as personnel took their designs with them from employer to employer. It is common to see the same insert in a variety of different frames and with different lids as viewed in these old catalogs.

Pickle castors are being reproduced today. Frames are being imported from Taiwan. New enameling is being applied to old jars; and new or old tumblers, vases, or spooners are sometimes used as jars in old original frames. Beware of new mother-of-pearl jars. The biggest giveaway in this latter scenario is that old glass is not perfect glass. In the listings below, the description prior to the semicolon refers to the jar (insert), and the remainder of the line describes the frame. Unless noted 'rstr' (restored), the silver plate is assumed to be in very good original condition. When tongs are present, they will be will be indicated. Glass jars are assumed to be in near-mint condition. Our advisor for this category is Barbara Aaronson; she is listed in the Directory under California.

Key: R&B — Reed and Barton

Amberina, ribbed Coinspot; Meriden 4-ftd leaf-emb fr, 9", +tongs..1,000.00
Clear Illinois, sq; Toronto emb fr, 9", +fork 150.00
Clear ribbed tree bark w/pk floral, Mt WA; Toronto rtcl fr, 12" ...850.00
Clear w/emb birds; R&B floral-emb fr w/half-heart hdls, +tongs... 400.00
Cobalt Invt T'print w/wht daisies; emb metal fr, 10", +tongs.......690.00
Cranberry opal, Honeycomb, cylinder; J Morch 4-ftd rtcl fr, 12", +fork ...460.00
Cranberry w/bl floral; Pairpoint leaf/fruit-emb ft, 10", +tongs 450.00
Cranberry w/floral, Mt WA; James Tuft fr w/griffins/roses, 13", +tongs 950.00
Cranberry w/optic ribbing & floral; Knickerbocker #179, +tongs ...425.00
Frosted pumpkin form w/SP cucumber lid; Wilcox leaf-emb fr, 10", +fork ..450.00
Lt bl Dmn Quilt MOP; Wm Rogers floral-emb/rtcl ftd fr, 11", +tongs. 1,200.00
Pomona, bl cornflowers/amber leaves; Meriden rtcl fr w/cherub, +tongs... 1,350.00
Vaseline Daisy & Button, cylinder; Pairpoint mts, 10", +fork 450.00

Royal Flemish, Mt. Washington, molded blown with enameled mums; reticulated Pairpoint frame, 10", with tongs, $2,500.00. (Photo courtesy Early Auction Co.)

Pie Birds

A pie bird or pie funnel (pie vent) is generally made of pottery, glazed inside and out. Most are 3" to 5" in height with arches at the base to allow steam to enter. The steam is then released through a single exit hole at the top. The English pie funnel was as tall as the special baking dish was deep and held the crust even with the dish's rim, thereby lifting the crust above the filling so it would stay crisp and firm. These dishes came in several different sizes, which accounts for the variances in the heights of the pie birds.

The first deviations from the basic funnels were produced in the mid-1930s to late 1940s: the Clarice Cliff (signed Midwinter or Newport) pie bird (reg. no. on white base) and the signed Nutbrown elephant. Shortly thereafter (1940s – 1960s), figures of bakers and colorful birds were created for additional visual baking fun. From the 1980s to present, many novelty pie vents have been added to the market for the enjoyment of both the baker and collector. These have been made by commercial (including Far East importers) and local enterprises in Canada, England, and the United States. A new category for the 1990s includes an array of holiday-related pie vents. Basic tip: Older pie vents were air brushed, not hand painted.

Incense burners (i.e., elephants and Oriental people), one-hole pepper shakers, dated brass toy bird whistles, egg timers (missing glass timer), and ring holders (i.e., elephant with clover on his tummy) should not be mistaken for pie vents. Our advisor for this category is Linda Fields; she is listed in the Directory under Tennessee.

Bear in gr jacket, w/hat & shoes, England, 4½" 55.00
Benny the Baker, w/pie crimper & cake tester, Cardinal, from $125 to.. 135.00
Bird, mc, Morton Pottery.. 20.00
Bird, mouth open, arched base, brn, English, 4½" 88.00
Bird, thin neck, Scotland, 1972, 4¼", from $75 to 90.00
Bird w/gold beak, floral transfers on wht body, 4½", from $175 to...200.00
Black boy kneeling in prayer, blk pants, England, 4" 55.00
Black clown, plain bl top & hat, stands on drum, Made in England, 5". 45.00
Black lady w/polka-dot muff, England, 3¾" 45.00
Blackbird, wht head, teardrop eyes, Australia, from $40 to 60.00
Bugs Bunny, California, 4"... 27.00
Bumble Bee, mc, California, 5" 35.00
Cutie Pie, Josef (or Lorrie Design), hen in bonnet, from $125 to.. 150.00
Dragon, gr, England, 4¼" 75.00
Duck, long neck, yel, unmk, 5".. 75.00
Dutch girl, multipurpose kitchen tool, from $150 to 195.00
Eagle, mk Sunglow, golden color, from $75 to 85.00
Elephant, trunk up, sitting on blk stand, England, 4" 65.00
Fox in jacket, cap & tie, mc, emb England, 4" 45.00
Fred the Flour Grater, (orig has) dots for eyes, from $65 to 75.00
Funnel, terra cotta, mk Wales.. 35.00
Gobbler's Mountain, Arkansas, solid colors, few made, 1994-95, $50 to.. 75.00
Golliwog, striped pants, mc, England, 4¾".................................... 55.00
Meadowlark, ltd ed, Sandhurst...Minnesota, 4¾", MIB.................. 50.00
Patches, rose/yel/turq on wing, Morton, common, 5", from $25 to ...30.00
Pie Boy, gr sombreros on outfit, from $350 to 400.00

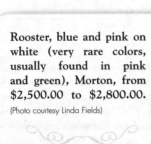

Rooster, blue and pink on white (very rare colors, usually found in pink and green), Morton, from $2,500.00 to $2,800.00.

(Photo courtesy Linda Fields)

Rooster, wht w/brn/bl/lav, Cleminson, 4½" 55.00
Rooster on stump, wht, Made in England, 4¾" 45.00
Servex Chef, Australia, 1938, from $150 to.................................. 165.00
Songbird, Chick Pottery (Le Pere), cream & blk w/gold, from $125 to..150.00
Toucan, mc, England, 5¾" 45.00
Woodpecker on stump, mc, California, 6¾" 36.00
3-fruits series, peach, apples & cherries, Japan, 2½", ea, $350 to.. 400.00

Pierce, Howard

William Manker, a well-known ceramist, hired Howard Pierce to work for him in 1938. After three years, Pierce opened a small studio of his own in LaVerne, California. Not wanting to compete with Manker, Pierce began designing miniature animal figures, some of which he made into jewelry. Today, his pewter brooches, depending on the type of animal portrayed, sell for as much as $275.00. Howard married, and he and his wife Ellen (Van Voorhis) opened a small studio in Claremont, California. In the early years, he used polyurethane to create animal figures — mostly roadrunners on bases, either standing or running; or birds on small, flat bases. Pierce quickly discovered that he was allergic to the material, so a very limited number of polyurethane pieces were ever produced; today these are highly collectible.

The materials used by Pierce during his long career were varied, probably to satisfy his curiosity and showcase his many talents. He experimented with a Jasperware-type body, bronze, concrete, gold leaf, porcelain, Mt. St. Helens ash, and others. By November 1992, Pierce's health had continued to worsen, and he and Ellen destroyed all the molds they had created over the years. After that they produced smaller versions of earlier porcelain wares, and they developed a few new items as well. Pierce died on February 28, 1994. Much of his work quickly appreciated in value, and items not seen before began to appear on the market.

Bowl, blk w/bl drip, mk Pierce 1991, 4x6¼" 125.00
Creamer & sugar bowl, maroon w/wht drip, mk #1XS, open, 2".. 100.00

Dish, sea green mottle with brown exterior, dated 1981, 12", minimum value, $150.00. (Photo courtesy Darlene Hurst Dommel)

Figurine, bison, gray w/dk mane & head, unmk, 9" 175.00
Figurine, coyotes (2) howling, 7x4" & smaller, pr.......................... 88.00
Figurine, dinosaur, off-wht, dtd 1991, 5½x4½" 100.00
Figurine, hippo, gr speckled, 10½" L 250.00
Figurine, horse, brn w/tan flying mane, blk ink stamp, 8½x7½" ... 150.00
Figurine, horse standing, wht frothy drip over red, 8½x10½" 435.00
Figurine, Madonna & Child, creamy wht & earth tones, 7¾" 70.00
Figurine, owls, gr/blk/wht/tan tones, 5¼", 3", pr 55.00
Figurine, owls (2) on dead limb, brn/gray speckled, sgn/'85, 10¾x5"... 100.00
Figurine, parakeets (3) on brn agate, 3½x6½" 85.00
Figurine, quail, brn tones, 6x5½"... 35.00
Figurine, rabbit crouching, brn speckled, 5½" 90.00
Figurine, rattlesnake, W shape, brn, 3x6" 100.00
Figurine, road runner, speckled brn/gr/wht, 4¾x12¼x3" 55.00
Figurine, sparrows, 4", pr.. 48.00

Figurine, St Francis w/birds, soft gray & blk, 12" 60.00
Figurine, Stellar's Jay, bl/wht/blk/gray, 6½" 65.00
Figurine, tiger stalking, blk ink stamp, rare, 2x12", minimum value ... 300.00
Figurine, unicorn, spotty brn w/dk brn highlights, 5½x5¼" 150.00
Flower frog, hummingbird, bl 125.00
Magnet, quail, brn, 4x2" 75.00
Planter, bl w/pale bl border & 4 wht deer, 2½x9¾" 125.00
Planter, turtle, sqs w/in sqs around rim, gray/brn, 3¾x6x4" 60.00
Vase, coral in rnd cutout, dk gr/wht/gray, cornucopia shape, 8x7" ... 135.00
Vase, gr w/wht fish insert, cornucopia shape 8x7" 125.00

Pierrefonds

Pierrefonds is a small village in France, best known today as the place to see a castle once owned and inhabited by Napoleon III. Pottery collectors, however, know it better as the location of The Societe Faienciere Heraldique de Pierrefonds studio, which became famous for stoneware art pottery often finished in flambe or crystalline glazes. The pottery was founded in 1903 by Comte Hallez d'Arros, who was also an innovative contributor to the advancement of photography. The ware they produced was marked with a helmet between the letters P (for Pierrefonds) and H (for Hallez).

Bowl, gr/brn crystalline, low w/sharp shoulder, 2½x13" 420.00
Dish, bl mottle, w/gilt metal 3-D bird, rim & leaf, 4" 120.00
Lamp, yel/bl crystalline, lt ribbing, sm appl device ea side, 31x6" ... 540.00

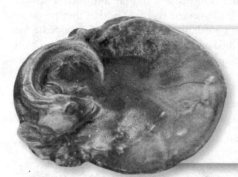

Pen tray, green, blue, and black crystalline, fish in relief at side, #578, 7¾" long, $1,080.00. (Photo courtesy Cincinnati Art Galleries)

Pitcher, bl/ochre crystals on bl, tan & mauve, 7" 140.00
Vase, bl crystalline, ovoid, 5¾x4½" 275.00
Vase, bl w/strong crystalline effect, 6-panel, widens at base, 10", NM ... 160.00
Vase, bl/brn crystalline drips on buff clay, stick neck, 9", pr 325.00
Vase, bl/gr drip, 15½x3½" 325.00
Vase, bl/tan crystalline, pear form w/sm shoulder hdls, 3" 65.00
Vase, brn/bl crystalline, bulbous, 9x7", NM 240.00
Vase, frothy bl crystalline, sqd neck-to-width hdls, 7½" 265.00

Pietra-Dura

From the Italian Renaissance period, Pietra-Dura is a type of mosaic work used for plaques, tabletops, frames, etc., that includes pieces of gemstones, mother-of-pearl, and the like.

Box, bird on flowering branch, Romanelli label, 6x4x2½", EX 500.00
Box, floral inlay panels, gilt-metal fr, scroll ft, 4½x9x6½" 1,700.00
Picture, lizard/scenic, trompe l'oeil, 20th C, 7x6"+modern ft 880.00
Plaque, architectural street, R Casini, blk slate surround, 11x9"+fr .. 2,900.00
Plaque, mixed flowers in vase, sgn Tirenze, ca 1885, 20x15" ... 16,800.00
Sugar shaker, paneled sides, threaded top, 6x4" 450.00
Table, mc birds top, ornate cvg, 3-leg, 1850s, 31x20½" 4,700.00

Pigeon Blood

Pigeon blood glass, produced in the late 1800s, may be distinguished from other dark red glass by its distinctive orange tint.

Ewer, ornate gold floral, bird & butterfly, att Webb, 8" 200.00
Vase, blown gourd shape w/narrow ruffled top, 7" 75.00
Vases, HP floral, cylindrical, 1880s, 10½", pr 275.00
Water set, Bulging Loops, 9" pitcher w/clear hdl+6 tumblers 550.00

Pigeon Forge

Douglas J. Ferguson and Ernest Wilson started their small pottery in Pigeon Forge, Tennessee, in 1946. Using red-brown and gray locally dug clay and glazes which they themselves formulate, bowls, vases, and sculptures are produced there. Their primary target was the tourist trade. Since Ferguson's death in 2000, the pottery is no longer in operation. Note: 'PFP' in the listings indicates a 'Pigeon Forge Pottery' mark.

Bowl, gray & wht crackle glaze, w/lid, Ferguson, 3½x5" 85.00
Bust, eagle, speckled brn & blk on cream, D Ferguson, 1987, 4¾" ... 90.00
Candlestick, gr matt, PFP St John, 5⅛", ea 30.00
Creamer & sugar bowl, wht w/brn drip, w/sugar lid, 2½", 3" 30.00
Figurine, bear seated, blk matt, D Ferguson, 4" 30.00
Figurine, bird, gray w/brn beak, PFP, 3¼", from $25 to 40.00
Figurine, chipmunk, speckled brn, dk brn eyes, PFP, 5½" L 25.00
Figurine, frog on base, brn & wht, mk, 2¼x3½" 45.00
Figurine, mother bear on bk w/cub on her belly, brn, PFP, 4¼" 80.00
Figurines, owls (2), brn & wht, 4½", 2½", pr 35.00
Figurines, raccoon family (3-pc set), brn tones, 6½", 6", 3½" 150.00
Jug, speckled brn on redware, ovoid, mk, 5" 40.00
Mug, gray w/gr pine tree, PFP 35.00
Tile, owl center, D Ferguson, 5½x5½" 65.00
Vase, brn, slightly folded/shaped rim, 3½x3¼" 27.50
Vase, wedding; dbl neck w/1 hdl above, blk w/wht specks, PFP, 8" ... 45.00

Vases, 4" and 4½", from $35.00 to $45.00 each. (Photo courtesy DuMouchelles)

Pilkington

Founded in 1892 in Manchester, England, the Pilkington pottery experimented in wonderful lustre glazes that were so successful that when they were displayed at exhibition in 1904, they were met with critical acclaim. They soon attracted some of the best ceramic technicians and designers of the day who decorated the lustre ground with flowers, animals, and trees; some pieces were more elaborate with scenes of sailing ships and knights on horseback. Each artist signed his work with his personal monogram. Most pieces were dated and carried the company mark as well. After 1913 the company became known as Royal Lancastrian. Their Lapis Ware line was introduced in the late 1920s, featuring intermingling tones of color under a matt glaze. Some pieces were very simply decorated while others were painted with designs of stylized leafage, scrolls, swirls, and stripes. The line continued into the '30s. Other pieces of this period were molded and carved with animals, leaves, etc., some of which were reminiscent of their earlier wares. The company closed in 1938 but reopened in 1948. During this period their mark was a simple P within the outline of a petaled flower shape.

Bowl, swirled royal bl, 1914, firing flaw, 8⅝" 100.00
Charger, Lancastrian Lustre, galleon, WS Mycock, ca 1900, 15⅝"..3,815.00
Floral, lav on red, R Joyce, bulbous body, 5⅞" 400.00
Vase, animals & flowers, mc lustre on yel, bulbous, 5½" 480.00
Vase, dragon, gold on amber to red, flecks, P/208/5/England, 10½"..2,250.00
Vase, floral, gold lustre w/dk red flowers on cream ground, 4½" ... 940.00
Vase, floral, red on cream w/linear designs, stick neck, 1915, 4½"...800.00
Vase, gr-amber matt, bulbous, P mk, 12x7" 385.00
Vase, ivy vine, cobalt on ultramarine, melon ribs, #3063, 8½".....650.00
Vase, oxblood, bulbous body, #2495, 1910, glaze flaw, 4¼" 100.00
Vase, Pro Patria, knight/shield/foliage on bl, Mycock, 1923, 7¾"..1,900.00
Vase, raspberry pk, slim ovoid w/short neck, 1909, 7¾" 280.00

Vase, red with blue drip, marked, 11", $920.00. (Photo courtesy Treadway Gallery Inc.)

Vase, Sea Maiden on red lustre, R Joyce/W Crane, #2472, rpr, 10¼" ... 2,400.00
Vase, Secessionist, arabesques/etc, gr/orange/yel, Mycott, #2089, 13"... 1,000.00

Pillin

Polia Pillin was born in Poland in 1909. She came to the U.S. as a teenager and showed an interest and talent for art, which she studied in Chicago. She married William Pillin, who was a poet and potter. They ultimately combined their talents and produced her very distinctive pottery from the 1950s to the mid-1980s. She died in 1993. Polia Pillin won many prizes for her work, which is always signed Pillin with the loop of the 'P' over the full name. Some undecorated pieces are signed W&P, to indicate her husband's collaboration. Her work is prized for its art, not for the shape of her pots, which for the most part are simple vases, dishes, bowls, and boxes. Wall plaques are rare. She pictured women with hair reminiscent of halos, girls, an occasional boy, horses, birds, and fish. After viewing a few of her pieces, her style is unmistakable. Some of her early work is very much like that of Picasso. Her pieces are somwhat difficult to find, as all the work was done without outside help, and therefore limited in quantity. In the last few years, more and more people have become interested in her work, resulting in escalating prices. Our advisors for this category are Dolli and Wilfred Cohen; they are listed in the Directory under California.

Bowl, lady w/2 cats on wht, irregular shape, 2¾x8" 1,500.00
Bowl, 2 ladies on brn, 6½x7½" 1,100.00
Box, lady w/lute on yel, 3x4¾x6½" 600.00

Charger, two women, one with lute, second with bird, 11" square, $2,200.00. (Photo courtesy David Rago Auctions)

Cordial pitcher, birds on antique wht, slim, rstr, 13", +2 cups...... 840.00
Dish, 2 dancing harlequins on brn, 6" dia 350.00
Jug, blistered yel/brn gloss, 7¾x5½" 275.00
Plaque, 2 ladies by tree w/bird, rectangular, 11" L..................... 2,000.00
Plate, lady w/chicken & birds, mc on bl, 8½" 1,650.00
Tray, lady's portrait (lg/detailed), sm nick, 8¼x6" 1,325.00
Vase, abstract figure on all 4 sides, 11½x3¾"............................. 975.00
Vase, birds on horizontal striations, earth tones, cylinder, 7" 495.00
Vase, br w/yel goldstone effect, bulbous, 8", NM 800.00
Vase, cat/rooster, trees/female dancers on marigold, 4½x3¾" 1,000.00
Vase, complex geometrics, mc w/blk, bulbous, 6½x6" 600.00
Vase, fish (3), spherical, closed mouth, 2¾x3½" 550.00
Vase, gr crystalline w/brn mottle drip, 5¾x3½" 340.00
Vase, horse & 2 ladies, wht on peacock & rust, 9x7"..................... 850.00
Vase, horses (4) prancing on gr to pk, spherical, 4¾" 585.00
Vase, ladies, 1 w/birds, 2nd w/horse, bottle shape, 6½x2½" 650.00
Vase, ladies (2) & lg deer on brn, sm rstr, 5x4¼" 500.00
Vase, ladies (4), 4-sided, 10¼" 1,950.00
Vase, lady, chicken & deer, cylindrical, 4½" 450.00
Vase, lady (full-length), cylindrical, 14¾x3", NM 1,895.00
Vase, lady & horse, 6" 625.00
Vase, lady holding bird, 2nd bird beside; bk: lady, 6¾" 650.00
Vase, lt to dk brn crystalline, bulbous w/can neck, 8½" 270.00
Vase, rooster on bl, cylindrical, 7" 495.00
Vase, scarlet flambe gloss, spherical w/short neck, 9½x7" 425.00

Pin-Back Buttons

Buttons produced up to the early 1920s were made of a celluloid covering held in place by a ring (or collet) to the back of which a pin was secured. Manufacturers used these 'cellos' to advertise their products. Many were of exceptional quality in both color and design. Many buttons were produced in sets featuring a variety of subjects. These were given away by tobacco, chewing gum, and candy manufacturers, who often packed them with their product as premiums. Usually the name of the button maker or the product manufacturer was printed on a paper placed in the back of the button. Often these 'back papers' are still in place today. Much of the time the button maker's name was printed on the button's perimeter, and sometimes the copyright was added. Beginning in the 1920s, a large number of buttons were lithographed on tin; these are referred to as tin 'lithos.' Nearly all pin-back buttons are collected today for their advertising appeal or graphic design. There are countless categories to base a collection on.

The following listing contains non-political buttons representative of the many varieties you may find. Values are for pin-backs in near-mint condition, unless noted otherwise. Our advisor for this category is Michael J. McQuillen; he is listed in the Directory under Indiana.

Boston Red Sox, Ted Williams portrait, mc on yel, 1⅛"............... 60.00
Buster Keaton, bust die-cut, enamel on metal, EX......................... 17.50
Clutch Cargo, blk/wht/red, 1950s, 1⅛", M on card 45.00
Field & Stream Honor Badge, turkey in center, emb metal.......... 135.00
Hopalong Cassidy, Mary Jane Bread, portrait on red, EX 40.00
James McAleer, Mgr St Louis Browns (1902-07), blk & wht, ⅞", EX .. 190.00
King & Smead's Shirts & Overalls, boy w/wagon, 1897, 1¾", EX.. 70.00
Lone Ranger & horse on TV shape, blk & wht, ⅞x1", EX............ 12.50
Lone Ranger on rearing horse, red letters on wht, 1930s, 1¼", EX...70.00
Michigan State..., Rose Bowl, Jan...1966, red/wht/gr, 3⅜" 15.00
Patty (Peanuts Character), blk on creamy wht, late 1950s, 1" 10.00
Pride of USA, Lindbergh portrait, blk & wht, EX 42.50
Red Comb Poultry Feed, rooster in center, red/wht/bl, 1¼", VG ... 12.50
Red Indian Cut Plug, package on wht cello, clip attachment, 1¾", EX..110.00
Riddler (Batman's enemy), portait on red, 1966, EX 12.50
Stargell Stars Shine, Sportsalute..., portrait on yel, 1980, 3¾" 20.00
The American, touring car on gr cello, 1¾", EX.......................... 325.00
The Bus Driver Jackie Gleason, portrait on yel, 1955, EX.............. 27.50

The Flash, Fastest Man Alive, reader survey award, 1942, $635.00. (Photo courtesy Morphy Auctions)

The Golden Rule & Santa portrait, mc on wht, Orange Mfg Corp...NJ, EX..75.00
Twin City Tractors Built in 4 Szs, red tractor, ca 1910s, 1½", VG ...120.00
USS Maine, blk & wht ship, Whitehead & Hoag, 1896, 1¼", EX....35.00
Violet (Peanuts character), blk on yel-cream, ca late 1950s, 1" 10.00
Welcome Home Lindy, portrait, ⅞", +red/wht/bl ribbon, EX 25.00
Yellow Kid #25, High Admiral Cigarettes, 1896, EX...................... 55.00

Pine Ridge

In the mid-1930s, the Bureau of Indian Affairs and the Work Progress Administration offered the Native Americans living on the Pine Ridge Indian Reservation in South Dakota a class in pottery making. Originally, Margaret Cable (director of the University of North Dakota ceramics department) was the instructor and Bruce Doyle was director. By the early 1950s, pottery production at the school was abandoned. In 1955 the equipment was purchased by Ella Irving, a student who had been highly involved with the class since the late 1930s. From then until it closed in the 1980s, Ella virtually ran the pot shop by herself. The clay used in Pine Ridge pottery was red and the decoration reminiscent of early Native American pottery and beadwork designs. A variety of marks and labels were used.

Bowl, avocado gr gloss, Reed, 2¼x7", from $40 to 50.00
Bowl, brn gloss, bulbous, O Cottier, X mk, 3¼x6½" 110.00
Bowl, dk bl gloss, Ella Irving, 4½x6¾"... 100.00
Bowl, dk bl gloss, Ramona W Knee, 2¾x4" 75.00
Bowl, incised geometrics, milky transparent on tan, Cottier, 3x6"..350.00
Cup & saucer, bl-gr, Ella Cox, 2", 5½", from $50 to 75.00
Jardiniere, brn w/gray-bl flow, O Cottier, mk Sioux Indian, 5x9".. 400.00
Mug, gr, B Talbot, 3½", from $30 to 50.00
Plate, incised geometric star, cream on red-brn, Irving, 7" 250.00
Vase, incised geometrics, cream & red-brn, 7¼x5½", from $450 to.. 500.00

Pink Lustre Ware

Pink lustre was produced by nearly every potter in the Staffordshire district in the late eighteenth and first half of the nineteenth centuries. The application of gold lustre on white or light-colored backgrounds produced pinks, while the same over dark colors developed copper. The wares ranged from hand-painted plaques to transfer-printed dinnerware.

Teapot, Staffordshire, ca. 1920, 6x10", $265.00. (Photo courtesy DuMouchelles)

Bowl, Ship Caroline (transfer), Adams, 4¾x10"........................... 165.00
Creamer, lg red rose/gr leaves/lav sprigs on wht, lustre rim, 4", NM... 45.00
Creamer, wide mc floral band to body, wide lustre neck band, 4¼" ...40.00
Mug, child's; cows/bldg transfer, inscribed name & Burn 1824/poem, 5"... 720.00
Mug, landscape in pk on ivory, lustre bands, porc, 5" 90.00
Pitcher, hunters/dogs, mc/emb, soft paste, 6¾" 210.00
Plate, Gen Jackson, Hero of New Orleans transfer, 3 lustre rings, 9"..1,200.00
Pot, Fulton Steamboat, Success to the Coal Trade/poem, can form, 6"...1,020.00
Teabowl & saucer, pk sprig in gr-lined wht reserve, 2½", 5" 45.00
Teabowl & saucer, strawberries, pk lustre highlights, #449............. 85.00
Waste bowl, pk/bl erratic lines on wht, lustre trim, 3¼x6" 35.00

Pink-Paw Bears

These charming figural pieces are very similar to the Pink Pigs described in the following category. They were made in Germany during the same time frame. The cabbage green is identical; the bears themselves are whitish-gray with pink foot pads. You'll find some that are unmarked while others are marked 'Germany' or 'Made in Germany.' In theory, the unmarked bears are the oldest, made prior to 1890 when the McKinley Tariff Act required imports to be marked with the country of origin. Those marked 'Made In' were probably produced after the revision of the Act in 1914. Our advisor for this category is Mary 'Tootsie' Hamburg; she is listed in the Directory under Illinois.

1 by bean pot.. 135.00
1 by graphophone 150.00
1 by honey pot.. 145.00
1 by top hat.. 125.00
1 in front of basket... 135.00
1 in roadster (car identical to pk pig car) 225.00
1 on binoculars... 175.00
1 peaking out of basket 135.00
1 sitting in wicker chair 150.00
2 in hot air balloon 175.00
2 in purse.. 165.00
2 in roadster 225.00
2 on pin dish 175.00
2 on pin dish w/bag of coins.. 160.00
2 peering in floor mirror.. 150.00
2 sitting by mushroom 160.00
2 standing in washtub 150.00
3 in roadster 250.00
3 on pin dish 160.00

Pink Pigs

Pink Pigs on cabbage green were made in Germany around the turn of the century. They were sold as souvenirs in train depots, amusement parks, and gift shops. 'Action pigs' (those involved in some amusing activity) are the most valuable, and prices increase with the number of pigs. Though a similar type of figurine was made in white bisque, most serious collectors prefer only the pink ones. They are marked in two ways: 'Germany' in incised letters, and a black ink stamp 'Made in Germany' in a circle. The unmarked pigs are the oldest, made prior to 1890 when the McKinley Tariff Act required imports to be marked with the country of origin. Those marked 'Made In' were probably produced after the revision of the Act in 1914. Pink Pigs may be in the form of a match holder, salt cellar, a vase, a stickpin holder, and (the hardest to find) a bank.

At this time three reproduction pieces have been found: a pig by an outhouse, one playing the piano, and one poking out of a large purse. These not difficult to spot because they are found in a rough, poor quality porcelain in a darker green. Our advisor for this category is Mary 'Tootsie' Hamburg; she is listed in the Directory under Illinois.

1 at telephone, 1 inside, 4½" 175.00
1 at trough, gold trim, 4½" 95.00
1 beside lg pot emb Boston Baked Beans, match holder, 4" W 135.00
1 beside shoe 115.00
1 beside stump, camera around neck, toothpick holder 185.00
1 beside wastebasket 110.00
1 coming through gr fence, post at sides, open for flowers 125.00
1 driving touring car 210.00
1 holding cup by fence 140.00
1 in Japanese submarine, Japan imp on both sides 175.00
1 on cushion chair w/fringe, 3" 195.00
1 on key playing piano 225.00

One riding train, $235.00. (Photo courtesy Tom Harris Auctions)

1 sitting on log, mk Germany 175.00
1 standing in front of cracked open egg 135.00
1 standing in oversz opera-house box, gold trim, 3½" 250.00
1 talking on old-fashioned telephone, gold trim, 3½" 250.00
1 w/basketweave cradle, gold trim, 3½" W 140.00
1 w/binoculars, brn/gr coat & hat, lg money bag, 5" 160.00
1 w/devil pulling on hose 225.00
1 w/flag, 2 Black children in skiff, match holder w/striker 500.00
1 w/front ft in 3-part dish containing 3 dice, 1 ft on dice 175.00
1 w/grandfather clock, 7" 250.00
1 w/lg umbrella, picnic basket & water bucket, 5¼" 150.00
1 w/red lobster pulling leg 185.00
1 w/tennis racket stands beside vase, Lawn Tennis, 3¾" 180.00
1 w/typewriter, Gentlemen 165.00
1 wearing chef's costume, holds frypan, w/basket 275.00
2, fat couple sitting, A Fine Looking Couple 200.00
2, mother & baby in bl blanket in tub, rabbit on board atop 175.00
2, mother & baby in cradle, Hush a Bye..., gold trim, 3¼x3¼" 225.00
2, mother in tub gives baby a bottle, lamb looks on, 4x3½" 175.00

2, mother looks at baby in cradle, Hush-a-Bye-Baby..., old MIG mk .. 185.00
2, 1 cutting hair of 2nd, A Little Bit Off the Top, 3x3½" 250.00
2, 1 lg (Scratch My Back) & 1 sm (Me Too), match holder, 5" ... 155.00
2 at confession, 4½" 145.00
2 at pump, bank, Good Old Annual, 3¾" 170.00
2 at pump & trough, 3¼" W 170.00
2 at wishing well 165.00
2 by eggshell 95.00
2 by washtub, toothpick holder, souvenir of White City, 3¾" W .. 135.00
2 coming out of woven basket, 3" W 115.00
2 courting in touring car, trinket holder, 4½" W 225.00
2 dancing, in top hat, tux & cane 175.00
2 in bed, Good Night on footboard, 4x3x2½" 165.00
2 in carriage 175.00
2 in front of oval washtub w/hdls, 3" W 135.00
2 in open trunk, 3¾" 125.00
2 in purse 115.00
2 looking in phonograph horn, tray, 4½" W 200.00
2 on cotton bale, 1 peers from hole, 1 over top 175.00
2 on seesaw on top of pouch bank 175.00
2 on tray hugging, 3x4½" 125.00
2 singing, receptacle behind, gold trim, 4½" 365.00
2 sitting at table playing card game 'Hearts' 225.00
2 sitting by heart-shaped opening, trinket holder, 4" W 110.00
2 teeter-tottering over log bank, 3½" L 125.00
2 under toadstool 125.00
2 w/accordion camera, tray, 4½" W 150.00
3, mother w/2 babies, The Dinner Bell, planter, 3¾" W 145.00
3, 1 on lg slipper playing banjo, 2 dancing on side 195.00
3, 2 sit in front of coal bucket, 3rd inside 175.00
3 (center pig w/accordion) on tray, gold trim, 6½" L 530.00
3 dressed up on edge of dish 150.00
3 in horseless carriage, 4½" W 150.00
3 in trolley car, conductor at front, 4¼x3¼" 175.00
3 piglets behind oval trough, mk, 2¾x2½x1¾" 135.00
3 piglets in egg-shaped basin, Triplets of Fancy, mk Germany 110.00
3 sitting at trough, 4½" 100.00
3 w/baby carriage, father & 2 babies, Wheeling His Own 225.00
3 w/carriage, mother & 2 babies, mk Germany 195.00
4, mother pushing cart w/3 babies, clovers on wheels, vase, 3½" ... 195.00
4, 3 piglets in cart, 1 wheeling, More the Merrier 110.00

Pisgah Forest

The Pisgah Forest Pottery was established in 1920 near Mount Pisgah in Arden, North Carolina, by Walter B. Stephen, who had worked in previous years at other locations in the state — Nonconnah and Skyland (the latter from 1913 until 1916). Stephen, who was born in the mountain region near Asheville, was known for his work in the Southern tradition. He produced skillfully executed wares exhibiting an amazing variety of techniques. He operated his business with only two helpers. Recognized today as his most outstanding accomplishment, his Cameo line was decorated by hand in the pate-sur-pate style (similar to Wedgwood Jasper) in such designs as Fiddler and Dog, Spinning Wheel, Covered Wagon, Buffalo Hunt, Mountain Cabin, Square Dancers, Indian Campfire, and Plowman. Stephen is known for other types of wares as well. His crystalline glaze is highly regarded by today's collectors.

At least nine different stamps mark his wares, several of which contain the outline of the potter at the wheel and 'Pisgah Forest.' Cameo is sometimes marked with a circle containing the line name and 'Long Pine, Arden, NC.' Two other marks may be more difficult to recognize: 1) a circle containing the outline of a pine tree, 'N.C.' to the left of the trunk and 'Pine Tree' on the other side; and 2) the letter 'P' with short uprights in the middle of the top and lower curves. Stephen died in 1961, but the work was continued by his associates. Our advisor for this category is R.J. Sayers; he is listed in the Directory under North Carolina.

Bowl vase, turq crackle, wht int w/red reduction border, 5x7" 95.00
Bowl vase, turq crackle over wine, rose int, 4x5" 80.00
Candlestick, aqua, rose int, 1950s, 2¾", ea 45.00
Creamer & sugar bowl, rose w/in & w/out, ca 1920s, w/lid, 2" 85.00
Jug, aubergine feldspathic, rnd hdl w/sq end, 6" 50.00
Jug, lt turq w/dense crackle, 1940, 5½" 50.00
Jug, turq over wine, incised shoulder lines, 1941, 5" 50.00
Teapot, turq crackle, ovoid w/str spout, 1943, hairlines, 7" L 100.00
Vase, Cameo, celadon crystalline, sowers/reapers on gr band, 17", EX 2,160.00
Vase, Cameo, wagon scenes/Indians/tepees on dk bl, aqua below, 8", pr ..2,040.00
Vase, crystalline, aqua/gold on gold over mint w/gold flecks, 6" ... 275.00
Vase, crystalline, wht/brn/bl/ochre flambe, mk Long Pine, 1955, 18x9"...2,520.00
Vase, crystalline (full blown), tan on creamy gr, gray int, 4x5" 300.00

Vase, three-handled, dated 1930, small firing line, 17", $1,200.00; Vase, Cameo-style people around Christmas tree, signed Stephen, dated, 8", $1,300.00.

(Photo courtesy Treadway Gallery Inc.)

Vase, turq crackle, rose int, bulbous w/tab hdls, 1932, 7" 350.00
Vase, turq crackle, wht int, Asheville mispelled on mk, 1935, 3½"...80.00
Vase, turq over wine, rose int, shouldered, 1938, 9½"................... 250.00

Playing Cards

Playing cards can be an enjoyable way to trace the course of history. Knowledge of the art, literature, and politics of an era can be gleaned from a study of its playing cards. When royalty lost favor with the people, kings and queens were replaced by common people. During the periods of war, generals, officers, and soldiers were favored. In the United States, early examples had portraits of Washington and Adams as opposed to kings, Indian chiefs instead of jacks, and goddesses for queens. Tarot cards were used in Europe during the 1300s as a game of chance, but in the eighteenth century they were used to predict the future and were regarded with great reverence.

The backs of cards were of no particular consequence until the 1890s. The marble design used by the French during the late 1800s and the colored wood-cut patterns of the Italians in the nineteenth century are among the first attempts at decoration. Later the English used cards printed with portraits of royalty. Eventually cards were decorated with a broad range of subjects from reproductions of fine art to advertising.

Although playing cards are now popular collectibles, prices are still relatively low. Complete decks of cards printed earlier than the first postage stamp can still be purchased for less than $100.00. In the listings that follow, decks are without boxes unless the box is specifically mentioned. For more information we recommend *Collecting Playing Cards* by Mark Pickvet (Collector Books). Information concerning the American An-

tique Deck Collectors Club, 52 Plus Joker, may be found in the Directory under Clubs, Newsletters, and Catalogs.

Key: J — joker   XC — extra card

Advertising

Bacardi Rum, MIB 10.00
BF Goodrich, industrial products, MIB...................................4.00
Biba Fashion House, fashion ladies on bks, 1960s, 52+2 J, MIB 80.00
Brand name, 75 years or older, MIB.......................................8.00
Bristol Cigarettes, MIB 6.00
Busch Beer, MIB..8.00
Buster Brown, w/his dog Tige, cartoon on face, ca 1906, 52+J, EX ...60.00
Cracker Barrel Restaurant, MIB...8.00
Firestone, The People Tire People, MIB 10.00
Franklin Cigars, Ben Franklin, gold edges, 1900, 52+J, G 100.00
International Harvester, dbl deck, 1 red, 1 blk, w/logos, EXIB....... 35.00
Johnson Outboard Motors, 1951, MIB..................................... 50.00
Massey Harris, man & dog by tractor, 52+J, EXIB...................... 40.00
Old Master Coffee, lady on tobbogan, mid-1920s, EXIB............... 40.00
Packard, 2 decks, score pad & pencil in leather case, C, EX 90.00
Pepsi-Cola Bottling Co, red rose & bud, 52+J, NMIB.................. 210.00
Primo Hawaiian Beer, MIB.. 10.00
Pure Oil, dbl deck, truck/office, ca 1945, M (NM box) 50.00
Reddy Kilowatt, face on power plug, USPC, MIB 40.00

Rubberset Shaving Brush, 1920s, $35.00. (Photo courtesy Mark Pickvet)

Snap-On Tools, MIB..8.00
Soft drink, modern, 1970s+, MIB...6.00
Standard Oil Co, 1932, MIB 50.00
Studebaker, 100 Years, 1852-1952, dbl deck, EXIB...................... 45.00

Pinups

Al Moore, Esquire, dbl deck, M (sealed)................................... 125.00
Elvgren, lady w/puppies, Berman Sales Co, Brown & Bigelow, VG ..25.00
Elvgren, nude w/towel, 1940s-50s, MIB (sealed) 40.00
Elvgren, service station adv, Brown & Bigelow, EX...................... 95.00
Elvgren Cuties, Seasons Greetings, dbl deck, EX........................ 110.00
Esquire, girl in jungle-print bikini, 1948, dbl deck, 52+J+poem, EXIB..50.00
Esquire, nude redhead seated in flowers, dbl deck, 1943, MIB 85.00
Girl in scanty outfit, Hires Rootbeer, 1950s, EXIB 12.00
Girl on couch, Auburn Esso Service, 1960, EXIB......................... 30.00
Marilyn Monroe, Golden Dream pose, 1950s, MIB...................... 80.00
Marilyn Monroe, New Wrinkle, 1950s, MIB 80.00
Nude model, modern, 1970s+, MIB...5.00
Nude model, 1940s & earlier, MIB... 20.00
Nude model, 1950s-60s, MIB 12.00
Playboy, Playmates, 1968, MIB (cb sleeve)................................ 50.00
Tennis girl, Admiral Cigarettes #999, 52+J, EXIB........................ 80.00
53 Vargas Girls, 52+2J, 1950s, NMIB 60.00

Souvenir

Atlanta Olympics, 1966, M in vinyl case... 15.00
Boblo Island, amusement park, NMIB...3.00
Buffalo Bills, MIB..6.00
California, poppy flower bks, Reider, 1944, G............................... 75.00
Chicago Bears, MIB...6.00
Duke Blue Devils, University, MIB...5.00
Grand Teton Nat'l Park, WY, G.. 75.00
Harold's Club, Reno NV, Harold's Club or Bust w/wagon bks, M .. 15.00
Historical Facts About TX, mid-1960s, M (sealed) 24.00
Homes of Longfellow & Emerson, dbl deck, ea: 52+2J, EX............ 25.00
Kennedy Space Center, MIB..4.00
Maine lighthouses, MIB...4.00
NY State, scenic bks, Brown & Bigelow, 1950s, dbl deck, M (sealed) ...45.00
Paris, city scenes in fr, M in plastic case.. 20.00
Republican Nat'l Convention 2000, dbl deck, MIP 12.50
Ringling Bros Barnum & Bailey Circus World, scenic bks, EX 12.50
Souvenir of Las Vegas...Fremont Street at Night, M (sealed).......... 22.00
St Regis, geisha bks, plastic coated, dbl deck, MIB....................... 16.00
Tourist, modern, MIB 4.00
Tourist trade, 75 yrs or older, G 50.00
USPC Congress #602, Spanish lady in oval, Madrid, 1906, 52, EXIB..235.00
Yellowstone Nat'l Park, photo faces, 1920s, 52+J+XC, EXIB 45.00

Transportation

Am Airlines DH-4, single-wing plane, 1972, MIB 10.00
Boston & Maine RR, MIB...8.00
Braniff International, wht lettering, MIB..4.00
British United Airways, bl & gold bk w/logo, EXIB 55.00
C&O for Progress, MIB 6.00
Caribbean Cruise Lines, flag, MIB..6.00
Delta Air Lines, Washington, Jefferson Memorial, MIB................. 10.00
Frisco RR, Pigs Are Beautiful, 52+2J, ca 1980, NMIB................... 65.00
Georgia Railroad, Old Reliable 1834, MIB.......................................6.00
Grand Trunk Railway, Victorian lady, travel views, 52+J, EX (VG box) ... 85.00
Hiawatha Trains, 50th Year, 1935-85, M (sealed)........................... 40.00
Missouri Pacific Lines, 2 engines, 52+J, EXIB............................... 40.00
Norfolk & Western Railway, train, MIB (sealed) 60.00
Northern Pacific RR, Yellowstone Park Line, C, VGIB 100.00
NY/New Haven/Hartford RR, train station, 52+J, EXIB................ 80.00
Ozark Flies Your Way, NY, Statue of Liberty, MIB.........................8.00
P&O Branch Service Steamers, steamer Barrabool (1922-36), Goodal, EXIB ..50.00
Pan Am, jet in sky, dbl deck, 1957, 52+2J ea, EX........................... 50.00

Pan American World Airways, $6.00. (Photo courtesy Mark Pickvet)

Santa Fe, 2 trains, desert, bridge, several styles, MIB, ea 30.00
TWA, Lockheed 749 jet bks, USPC, 1970, MIB........................... 10.00

Miscellaneous

Alf Cooke's Universal, fairy silhouette/full moon bks, 1925, NMIB .. 45.00

Aquarius the Water Bearer, zodiac sign, 1960s, MIB 10.00
Bicycle, rider bks, Russell & Morgan, 1890, G 475.00
Bicycle #808, USPC, 1890s-early 1900s, G 85.00
Bicycle #808, USPC, 1910s-30s, G 75.00
Bicycle #808, USPC, 1940s-50s, G 75.00
Clinton/Gore, 54 caricatures, Politicards, 2000, M (sealed) 8.50
Combat vehicle identification, 1985, MIB..................................... 10.00
Congress, poodle on bl, Cell-U-Tone, M 25.00
Donkey Kong Jr, Ralson cereal premium, MIB...............................8.00
Duratone, fighting cocks, dbl deck, 52+2J ea, VG....................... 110.00
Hundred dollar bill design, US, Ben Franklin, MIB 4.00
Kem, Guiding Star (astrology signs), c 1947, MIP (sealed).......... 145.00
Kem, Seville, geometric blocks, ca 1947, MIB w/KEM booklet 50.00
NASCAR, Dale Earnhardt commemorative, dbl deck, M in tin case .25.00
Norman Rockwell paintings, winter, dbl deck, MIB...................... 12.00
Piatnik of Austria, bird bks, gold edged, 1950s, dbl deck, mini, MIB ...40.00
Poodle w/bl bow on bks, Western Publishing, M (sealed) 15.00
Port Scenes by Lionel Barrymore, Brown & Bigelow, 1960s, dbl deck, M .45.00
Russell Blue Ribbon #929, Oreole on Ace of Spades, bl tax stamp, EXIB .60.00
Seabees Can Do/Phoebee The Female Seabee, dbl deck, NM in G box.. 55.00
Smiley Face, lg yel face, MIB..5.00
Streamline Pinochle, US Government issue, linen finish, 1940s, MIB .6.00
Thomas Kincade, dbl deck, M in cb art box 12.00
Trip or Trap, drug info, WR Spence MD, Spenco, 1960s, 52+2J, MIB..40.00
Virgo, symbol on bl, 52+J+1 Virgo XC, EXIB.............................. 15.00
Waddingtons, classical lady & dragon bks, 1930s, 52+J, EXIB........ 35.00
Waldorf Playing Cards, Victorian lady photo bks, 52+J, EXIB....... 80.00
Washington/Lincoln portrait bks by Eisenhower, 1960s, dbl deck, EXIB... 60.00
WW Russell, Russell's Regents, Georgian, ca 1906, 52+J, EXIB..125.00

Political

Many of the most valuable political items are those from any period which relate to a political figure whose term was especially significant or marked by an important event or one whose personality was particularly colorful. Posters, ribbons, badges, photographs, and pin-back buttons are but a few examples of the items popular with collectors of political memorabilia. Political campaign pin-back buttons were first mass produced and widely distributed in 1896 for the president-to-be William McKinley and for the first of three unsuccessful attempts by William Jennings Bryan. Pin-back buttons have been used during each presidential campaign ever since and are collected by many people. Some of the scarcest are those used in the presidential campaigns of John W. Davis in 1924 and James Cox in 1920.

Contributions to this category were made by Michael J. McQuillen, monthly columnist of *Political Parade*, which appears in *AntiqueWeek* newspapers; he is listed in the Directory under Indiana. Our advisor for this category is Paul J. Longo; he is listed under Massachusetts. See also Autographs; Broadsides; Historical Glass; Watch Fobs.

Badge, Bryan 1908 Kern on horseshoe shape.................................. 50.00
Badge, Harrison/Morton jugate, mechanical gilt eagle, ca 1888 ..725.00
Ballot, lists Zachary Taylor/Millard Fillmore/etc, VA, 1848, 6⅜x4" ...200.00
Bandana/handkerchief, Cleveland/Thurman, cotton, 1888, 24x22"..110.00
Blow-up doll, Ronald Reagan, rubber head, plastic torso, 1987, 30" 40.00
Book, Cartoons Tell the Story, Landon/Knox, 1936, 16-pg, VG.... 30.00
Broadside, anti-Martin Van Buren Views, 1840s, 2-pg, 42x32" overall...1,450.00
Brooch, Andrew Jackson, missing bk clasp, ca 1832, 1x⅞".......2,000.00
Car plaque, Hoover for President, portrait, mc, rust/pnt loss, 4" dia... 75.00
Cigarette case, GOP/elephant/1948, gold enamel on metal........... 45.00
Cuff link, Benjamin Harrison portrait, cello, ca 1888, ⅝", 1 only .. 50.00
Drum, Grover Cleveland our Next.../portrait on side, 37", VG... 5,175.00
Lantern, Jackson Forever, pierced tin, dome top, ca 1824, 18", EX..4,995.00
Lapel pin, I'm a Yellow Dog Democrat, dog's portrait...................... 28.00

License plate, Landon, Barrows, White, 1936, 6x9" 65.00
Medallion, McKinley/Bryan, Sound Money/Free Silver, mechanical, 1½" ..50.00
Novelty, pottery log cabin, Harrison campaign, brn pnt, ca 1840, 5x6" ..1,150.00
Paper dolls, First Family, Reagan family, 1981, uncut, lt wear 30.00
Pendant, Henry Clay, portrait emb on metal 155.00
Pennant, WH Taft Inauguration, eagle/portrait/etc on bl 100.00
Photo, Wm McKinley parade w/lg banner, men on horsebk, etc, 6x7" ..65.00
Plate, B Disreali portrait, ceramic, Wallis Cimson & Co, 9½" 45.00
Plate, Rosalyn Carter portrait, mc on wht porc, 8¼" 15.00
Postcard, Our 25 Presidents, emb portraits, ca 1907, VG 35.00
Postcard, Socialism banner & soccer scene, May Day 1904, VG .. 75.00
Poster, Gov Reagan a Proven Winner, red/wht/blk, 1968, 28x22" ...90.00
Poster, JF Kennedy portrait, blk/red/wht/bl vinyl, 24x18" 45.00
Poster, Kennedy/Johnson, portraits, red/wht/bl, 1960, 11x16" 145.00
Poster, LBJ for the USA, blk/wht, 1964, 20½x13" 45.00
Poster, Reagan Country, portrait in cowboy hat, mc, 1980 .... 45.00
Poster, Roosevelt/Truman jugate, Allied Printing Co, 1944, 15x11", G... 95.00
Poster, Wm Jennings Bryan portrait among flags, paper litho, 30x20" ..1,500.00
Radio, Jimmy Carter in peanut, plastic, 7½" 75.00
Ribbon, parade marshal, Wm Jennings Bryan button in center, 9½" L..80.00
Scarf, B Harrison for President on flag, red/wht/bl silk, 1888, 18x19" ..125.00
Stickpin, bear figural (T Roosevelt) 30.00
Tie clasp, Gene McCaffry, mc enameling on metal, 1974 .... 5.00
Token, Geo B McClellan for President, emb portrait on brass 130.00
Token, Henry Clay, bust w/in wreath emb on dk metal 55.00
Token, MA for Justice, Freedom of Speech..., wht metal 45.00
Token, Republican Candidate 1860 Abraham Lincoln, brass, drilled hole ..70.00
Tray, Pres Wm McKinley portrait, oval, tin litho, ca 1896-1900, VG... 150.00

Tray, William McKinley, tin, 17x12", VG, $80.00.

Tumbler, Eventually Why Not?, elephant/mule on keg, glass, '32, 3½" ..150.00
Watch fob, Charles Evans Hughes emb on metal, 1908, 1½" 375.00
Wristwatch, G Wallace caricature on face, 1⅜" dia 85.00

Pin-back Buttons

Ax form, promoting prohibition, 1¾" 55.00
Bryan/Cowherd jugate, blk & wht portraits, 1895, ⅞" 245.00
Churchill/FD Roosevelt portraits, Victory..., red/wht/blk, 1940s.... 85.00
Clinton/Gore Inauguration Day, mc, 1993, 3⅜" 10.00
Coxsure, cream letters on gray, ⅝" 70.00
Dewey for Students, red/wht/bl, cello, 1¼" 55.00
FD Roosevelt/Boston Mayor JM Curley portraits, red/wht/bl, 2¼" ... 300.00
Gimme Jimmy, wht on gr, 1½" 6.00
Go Go Goldwater in '64, blk & yel, 1964, 3½" 14.00
I Like Ike, state of FL, red/wht/bl, ¾" 45.00
McKinley/Roosevelt, 4 Years More of Full Dinner Pail, cello, ⅞" 215.00
McKinley/Roosevelt portrait reserves, eagle/flag, cello, ⅞" 70.00

McKinley/Roosevelt portraits on red/wht/bl, cello, 1¼" 80.00
Mondale, wht lettering on bl, 1¼" 5.00
Nixon/Agnew portraits, blk/red/wht/bl, 1968, 1⅛" 10.00
Nixon/Agnew portraits, mc flasher, 1968, 2½" 12.50
RF Kennedy/Wm Fulbright jugate, blk on yel, cello, 1968, 6" 250.00
Roosevelt (Teddy) & portrait, Progressive Candidate 395.00
Taft portrait, cello, oval, 1¼" 80.00
Texas for Bush (Geo Sr), portrait on state, mc, 2½" 40.00
Theodore Roosevelt, Welcome & color portrait, w/red/wht/bl ribbons..165.00

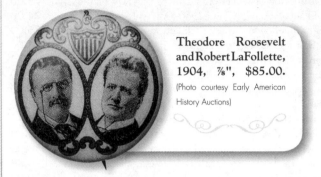

Theodore Roosevelt and Robert LaFollette, 1904, ⅞", $85.00.
(Photo courtesy Early American History Auctions)

Theodore Roosevelt portrait, blk & wht, 1¼", VG...................... 80.00
Theodore Roosevelt portrait in dmn, sepia-tone/red/wht/bl, 1¼" .. 75.00
WH Taft portrait w/in wreath, mc, 1¼" 100.00
When the Swallows Homeward..., prohibition cause, cello, 1904, 1"...115.00
Who Hoover, bl & wht litho, ¾", VG.. 40.00
Wings for Willkie America, plain, red/wht/bl 20.00

Pomona

Pomona glass was patented in 1885 by the New England Glass Works. Its characteristics are an etched background of crystal lead glass often decorated with simple designs painted with metallic stains of amber or blue. The etching was first achieved by hand cutting through an acid resist. This method, called first ground, resulted in an uneven feather-like frost effect. Later, to cut production costs, the hand-cut process was discontinued in favor of an acid bath which effected an even frosting. This method is called second ground.

Card holder, 1st ground, bl cornflowers, ruffled, scalloped ft, 6" L...425.00
Celery vase, 1st ground, bl cornflowers, ruffled amber rim/ft, 5"... 500.00
Creamer & sugar bowl, 1st ground, amber ruffled rims/hdls, 6", 5"... 375.00
Cruet, 1st ground, amber lip/scalloped ft, spherical w/long neck, 8"...400.00
Finger bowl, 2nd ground, etched berries, amber rim, 5" 90.00
Pitcher, 1st ground, bl cornflowers, amber branch ft, ovoid, 8" ..4,300.00
Pitcher, 1st ground, Invt T'print, 4-spout, amber rim/hdl, 4½" 240.00
Tumbler, lemonade; 2nd ground, bl cornflower band, 6" 275.00
Vase, 1st ground, bl cornflowers, scalloped ft/ruffled rim, 5".........300.00

Poole Pottery

Recognizing the area's potential for pottery making — readily available clay and accessible transportation in and out of the town — Jesse Carter purchased an old pottery in Poole, Dorset, England, in 1873. The pottery he opened still exists there today. Primarily they made tile; but through various changes in management and the evolution that followed, by the 1920s they were also producing art ware, stoneware, and dinnerware, through a subsidary called Carter Stabler and Adams. Items from the 1920s and 1930s are highly collectible today. In 1964 Carter Stable and Adams became part of the Pilkington group, changing its name to Poole Pottery Limited.

Bowl, allover bluebirds/flowers, Hilda Hampton, #965, ca 1940, 9½"... 120.00
Bowl, stylized floral cluster HP on wht, T Carter, 1920s, 4x10" 45.00
Candleholders, floral sprig on ivory, 6-sided, CSA #931, 2½", pr... 65.00
Charger, antelope, trees behind, Deco, R Sommerfelt, 16" 600.00
Charger, Delphis, abstracts, vivid orange/yel/dk brn, #54, 16" 295.00
Charger, layered branching free-forms, orange/blk/bl/turq, 15" 300.00
Charger, radiating lines, brn tones, G Sydenham, 13¾" 210.00
Figurine, bird on apple, brn tones, BLA, 4¼" 65.00
Figurine, bird on tree stump, brn tones, BL Adams, 6½" 225.00
Figurine, group of 3 monkeys, brn mottle, Deco styling, rstr 360.00
Tray, pulled feathers in tan/brn/bl/ivory, 12" L............................. 120.00
Vase, allover flowers/birds, mc on wht, artist sgn, 13½" 720.00
Vase, Atlantis, flat wide rim, emb leafy bands, G Sydenham, 6¾" ..410.00
Vase, brilliant yel/orange/red flambe-type glaze, ovoid, 9¾" 120.00
Vase, Deco florals on lt pk, ovoid, sgn, 7½" 325.00
Vase, Deco florals on wht, mc banded neck, 1920s, 10½"............. 720.00
Vase, Delphis, abstracts, mc on fiery orange, UW, 15½" 225.00
Vase, geometrics/flowers, brn tones on buff, CSA, 13½" 1,440.00
Vase, mc enameled sponging, flared cylinder, ca 1970, 9½".......... 100.00
Vase, Native American style, terra cotta on buff, CSP, 4" 120.00

Postcards

Postcards are often very difficult to evaluate, since so many factors must be considered — for instance the subject matter or the field of interest they represent. For example: a 1905 postcard of the White House in Washington D.C. may seem like a desirable card, but thousands were produced and sold to tourists who visited there, thus the market is saturated with this card, and there are few collectors to buy it. Value: less than $1.00. However, a particular view of small town of which only 500 were printed could sell for far more, provided you find someone interested in the subject matter pictured on that card. Take as an example a view of the courthouse in Hillsville, Virginia. This card would appeal to those focusing on that locality or county as well as courthouse collectors. Value: $5.00.

The ability of the subject to withstand time is also a key factor when evaluating postcards. Again using the courthouse as an example, one built in 1900 and still standing in the 1950s has been photographed for 50 years, from possibly 100 different angles. Compare that with one built in 1900 and replaced in 1908 due to a fire, and you can see how much more desirable a view of the latter would be. But only a specialist would be aware of the differences between these two examples.

Postcard dealers can very easily build up stocks numbering in the hundred thousands. Greeting and holiday cards are common and represent another area of collecting that appeals to an entirely different following than the view card. These types of cards range from heavily embossed designs to floral greetings and, of course, include the ever popular Santa Claus card. These were very popular from about 1900 until the 1920s, when postcard communication was the equivalent of today's quick phone call or e-mail. Because of the vast number of them printed, many have little if any value to a collector. For instance, a 1909 Easter card with tiny images or a common floral card of the same vintage, though almost 100 years old, are virtually worthless. It's the cards with appeal and zest that command the higher prices. One with a beautiful Victorian woman in period clothing, her image filling up the entire card, could easily be worth $3.00 and up. Holiday cards designed for Easter, Valentines Day, Thanksgiving, and Christmas are much more common than those for New Year's, St. Patrick's Day, the 4th of July, and Halloween. Generally, then, they can be worth much less; but depending on the artist, graphics, desirability, and eye appeal, this may not always be true. The signature of a famous artist will add significant value — conversely, an unknown artist's signature adds none.

In summary, the best way to evaluate your cards is to have a knowledgeable dealer look at them. For a list of dealers, send a SASE to the

International Federation of Postcard Dealers, c/o Juanita Clemens, 462 Freeman Rd., Greensburg, PA 15601. Do not expect a dealer to price cards from a list or written description as this is not possible. For individual questions or evaluation by photocopy (front and back), you may contact our advisor, Jeff Bradfield, 90 Main St., Dayton, VA 22821. You **must** include a SASE for a reply. For more information we recommend *The Collector's Guide to Postcards* by Jane Wood and *Vintage Postcards for the Holidays* by Robert and Claudette Reed (Collector Books).

Halloween, child with birds and bats over cauldron, $40.00.

Posters

Advertising posters by such French artists as Cheret and Toulouse-Lautrec were used as early as the mid-1800s. Color lithography spurred their popularity. Circus posters by the Strobridge Lithograph Co. are considered to be the finest in their field, though Gibson and Co. Litho, Erie Litho, and Enquirer Job Printing Co. printed fine examples as well. Posters by noted artists such as Mucha, Parrish, and Hohlwein bring high prices. Other considerations are good color, interesting subject matter and, of course, condition. The WWII posters listed below are among the more expensive examples; 70% of those on the market bring less than $65.00. Values are for examples in excellent condition to near mint unless noted otherwise. See also Movie Memorabilia; Rock 'n Roll.

Advertising

Cat's Paw, Foster Rubber Co., 42x30", $1,095.00. (Photo courtesy Wm. Morford Auctions)

Century Cocoanut, lady w/banner, Mayer & Ottman, 1880s, 26x15"..450.00
Infallible Smokeless...Powder, man shooting, 1914, 30x20"......... 600.00
Louisville Slugger Bats, Ty Cobb images, blk/wht, 17¾x13¼"........ 70.00
Mandeville & King Superior Flower Seeds, lady w/flowers, 27x17" ...300.00
Marlin Firearms, man on horse, 1960s repro, easel-bk, 30x20" 275.00
McClellan's Diptheria Remedy, It Never Fails, baby, 21x14" 40.00
Mobil Oil, race cars in montage on wht, Pegasus logo, 1980s, 20x28"..250.00
No-Nox Gas Wakes Up Slow Starters, man & alarm clock, 40x27"..135.00
Pabst Brewing Co, factory scene, 13 Am flags, 1890s, 33x45"+fr, VG+..1,350.00
Peace & Goodwill Plug Smoking, dog & cat, linen, 23x14" 130.00

Peters Big Game Ammunition, caribou scene, Goodwin, 30x20".. 2,700.00
Red Man First in America, Indians & trader, 20x13", VG 100.00
Remington UMC, Bear Doing Camp, RC Edwards, Am Litho, 1919, 24x15"... 675.00
Star Soap, Liberty Rose, red roses, Heinmuller, 1901, 23x15" 60.00

Circus

Key: B&B — Barnum & Bailey

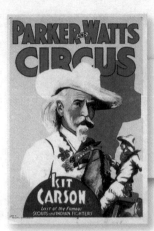

Parker & Watts Circus, Kit Carson, 1930s, 41x27", VG, $245.00. (Photo courtesy James D. Julia Inc.)

B&B, Big Free Street Parade, 24½x16¾" 300.00
B&B, Greatest Show on Earth, 2 portraits, 25x17", VG 245.00
B&B, wide-angle circus view, Strohberg, 1894, 28x75"............. 3,250.00
Buffalo Bill's Wild West, Sells Floto Circus, horseman, 40x25"... 4,000.00
Christy Bros Wild Animal Show, crowd & wagons w/animals, 30x44".. 975.00
Cole Bros, Ken Maynard, shown w/horse, 53x18" 1,500.00
Laugh w/Dolly, mc on canvas, Schulman, 48x58" 400.00
Parkway Shows, clown/rides/game, 41x27" 1,200.00

Magic

Chang & Fak-Hong's United Magicians Presents the Bhuda (sic), 25x17"... 165.00
George the Supreme Master Triumphant Am Tour, 27x20" 600.00
Man before Oriental figure, question mks at sides, 35x38" 170.00
T Nelson Downs King of Koins, ca 1900, 21x14", G 185.00
Thurston the Great..., Do Spirits Come Back?, Otis, 40x26" 2,050.00

Theatrical

Al G Field Minstrels, man in blackface, Otis, 40x25½", VG 765.00
Hilsen's Minstrels, comic characters, ca 1890, 40x27", G 725.00
Hoyt's Midnight Bell, children throw snowballs at trustee, 43x29".. 350.00
Jesse James, people in int cabin scene, Donaldson, 28x41" 1,500.00
Nomadie, Polar Bear Hunt in Arctic, Hiner, 1900s, 40x26" 275.00
On the Mississippi, dock scene, Hayworth, 1894, 27½x38" 650.00
Supremes at Lincoln Center Philharmonic Hall, 1965, 38x25" ... 900.00

Travel

Fly TWA San Francisco, Golden Gate Bridge, 1950s, 40x25" 425.00
Gibralter, Algier, Palma, palm scenic, ca 1920, sm rstr, 38x25" ... 300.00
Greece, Roman statue & Constellation airplane, TWA, 1950s, 1-sheet... 225.00
London, Transworld Airlines, queen's guard, newer plane, 40x25".. 450.00
New York Fly TWA, mc color blocks form cityscape, Klein, 40x25".. 445.00
Vence (Venice) Cite Des Arts..., lovers, Chagal, 1954, 28x20" ... 950.00

War

Save for Security, Buy Defense...red/wht/bl, 1941, 28x22", VG........... 145.00

WWI, Buy Liberty Bonds, Lincoln profile, 30x20", VG+.............. 50.00
WWI, Come On!, doughboy w/gun, Whitehead, 30x20"............. 100.00

WWI, I Want You for the U.S. Army, James Montgomery Flagg illustration, Leslie-Judge Co., New York, 40x30", $3,300.00. (Photo courtesy James D. Julia Inc.)

WWI, Invest in...Victory Liberty Loan, naval scene, Shafer, 28x39", VG...350.00
WWI, Joan of Arc Saved France, H Coffin, 1918, 30x20", G 165.00
WWI, Joan of Arc Saved France, lady w/sword, US Litho, 30x20", VG ... 90.00
WWI, Join Now, Red Cross nurse, Anderson, 28¼x22¼" 100.00
WWI, Look After My Folks, Navy scene, Brangwyn, 1917, 41½x28", VG..275.00
WWI, Remember the Bond, war scene, Powers Litho, 25x19" 90.00
WWI, USA Bonds Weapons for Liberty, Leyendecker, 1917, 30x20".. 425.00
WWI, Victory Liberty Loan, For Home &..., soldier/family, 30x20" .. 90.00
WWI, Victory Liberty Loan, They Thought We Couldn't Fight, 30x20" ...100.00
WWI, Victory Loan Flyers, biplanes, Sackett & Wilhelm, 30x20" ..100.00
WWI, WMCA His Home Over There, Herter, 41x28" 60.00
WWII, Americans! Share the Meat, blk/wht/red, 1942, 25x20", VG..135.00
WWII, Four Freedoms, N Rockwell, 1943, 40x30", EX+, set of 4..1,100.00
WWII, I'll Carry Mine Too!, lady w/bags, Valentino, 28x22" 100.00
WWII, I Want You...US Army/Enlist Now, Uncle Sam, 1940, 38x25" ..900.00

Pot Lids

Pot lids were pottery covers for containers that were used for hair dressing, potted meats, etc. The most common were decorated with colorful transfer prints under the glaze in a variety of themes, animal and scenic. The first and probably the largest company to manufacture these lids was F. & R. Pratt of Fenton, Staffordshire, established in the early 1800s. The name or initials of Jesse Austin, their designer, may sometimes be found on exceptional designs. Although few pot lids were made after the 1880s, the firm continued into the twentieth century. American pot lids are very rare. Most have been dug up by collectors searching through sites of early gold rush mining towns in California. In the following listings, all lids are transfer printed. Minor rim chips are expected and normally do not detract from listed values. When no condition is given, assume that the value is based on an example in such condition.

Barker's Eye Salve Cures in 48 Hours, blk transfer, 1⅞" 365.00
Bears at School, mc, Pratt, 3", VG 115.00
Burgess Genuine Anchovy Paste, blk transfer, 1890s, 3⅜", +base.. 80.00
Courting couple in garden, mc, 4¼", +wooden fr 65.00
Creme de Savon Dulcifie...Paris, blk transfer 125.00
Embarking for the East, Crimea War Series, mc, Pratt, M............ 165.00
First Appeal, romantic couple, mc, Pratt, 4" 165.00
Fishbarrow, figures in street scene, lace border, Pratt, 4¼".......... 100.00
Good Dog, dog retriving from water, mc, chips, 5" 100.00
HO Mitchell Otto of Rose Cold Cream, gr transfer, 2¾", +base.. 115.00
Holborn Viaduct, figures/houses/buildings, mc, Pratt, 4" 150.00
James Areca Nut Tooth Paste, Jameson & Curtis, blk transfer, 3", VG..125.00

Mending the Nets Pegwell Bay Kent, Pratt, pre-1862, +base, VG. 75.00
Oriental Tooth Paste, Jewsbury & Brown Chemists, blk transfer, 3"..140.00
Osbourne House, Isle of Wright, paddle steamer scene, mc, Pratt, 5"...200.00
Otto of Rose Cold Cream, Baildon & Son..., blk transfer, 2⅜".... 115.00
Pegwell Bay Near Ramsgate, mc scene, Pratt............................ 225.00
Return From Stag Hunting, hunt scene, mc, Pratt, 5" 185.00
Rivals, 2 men, lady & dog, mc, 1870s, +6¼" mahog fr 240.00
Snap Dragon, figures around table, chip, 3", +base..................... 135.00
Trysting Place, couple, mc, Pratt, 3⅛"...................................... 130.00
Wood's Areca Nut Tooth Paste, blk transfer, 3", +base 125.00
Youth & Age, mc figures, Mayer, ca 1850-60, 4" 215.00

Powder Horns and Flasks

Though powder horns had already been in use for hundreds of years, collectors usually focus on those made after the expansion of the United States westward in the very early 1800s. While some are basic and very simple, others were scrimshawed and highly polished. Especially nice carvings can quickly escalate the value of a horn that has survived intact to as high as $1,000.00 or more. Those with detailed maps, historical scenes, etc., bring even higher prices. Metal flasks were introduced in the 1830s; by the middle of the century they were produced in quantity and at prices low enough that they became a viable alternative to the powder horn. Today's collector regards the smaller flasks as the more desirable and valuable, and those made for specific companies bring premium prices.

Flask, brass, cannon & flags, 8½" 275.00
Flask, brass, deer & leaves, 9" 225.00
Flask, brass, Eagle, Ames, 9" 400.00
Flask, brass, Eagle & US banner, sgn Batty, dtd 1847, 9"............. 300.00
Flask, brass, emb hunter under tree, 9½" 100.00
Flask, brass, emb hunting scene w/man, horse & dogs, 8½".......... 175.00
Flask, brass, horns (musical) along base, 10" 400.00
Flask, brass, horses, spring broken, 8½" 150.00

Flask, embossed stag, fox, and oak leaves, possibly German, 8¼", $65.00. (Photo courtesy Jackson's International Auctioneers & Appraisers of Fine Art & Antiques)

Horn, concentric rings, iron/brass loops, brass mts, 1870s, 8" 70.00
Horn, copper & brass, emb anthemia, spring-loaded, 1845, 8" 310.00
Horn, cvd spout flange, flat wood base, short plug, 1880s, 5¾" 35.00
Horn, eagle (metal) appl to polished horn, 21" 150.00
Horn, eagle/E Pluribus Unum/man w/Mason's compass, 1854, w/plug, 13"...3,150.00
Horn, eagle/shield/dogs/man w/pipe, OH, 1856, w/plug, 8".........975.00
Horn, horn & tin, Indian hunting scene w/deer, 12" 50.00
Horn, maps/Masonic symbols/name/1763, brass plug, 10¾" 2,235.00
Horn, semi-flat body, cvd spout, cvd dmns, missing plug, 1870s, 9" ..25.00
Horn, wood base w/brass stud, missing plug, 1890s, 6" 30.00

Horn, 1843 Blackhawk w/Am Indian & dogs hunting deer, wooden plug, 12"..3,750.00
Horn, 1849 w/Am eagle/banner/hunter & dogs w/deer, w/plug, 12"..3,000.00
Horn, 3-masted British ships/serpents/etc, 1762, w/plug, 12"....5,875.00
Horn, 4 men/house/eagle/shield/stars, GW Mann 1847, w/plug, 9"...2,000.00

Pratt

Prattware has become a generic reference for a type of relief-molded earthenware with polychrome decoration. Scenic motifs with figures were popular; sometimes captions were added. Jugs are most common, but teapots, tableware, even figurines were made. The term 'Pratt' refers to Wm. Pratt of Lane Delph, who is credited with making the first examples of this type, though similar wares were made later by other Staffordshire potters. Pot lids and other transferwares marked Pratt were made in Fenton, Staffordshire, by F. & R. Pratt & Co. (See Pot Lids.)

Plate, scene with waterfall and ruins, 8", from $125.00 to $150.00. (Photo courtesy Mary Frank Gaston)

Cup, caudal; sailing ships transfer, hdls, ca 1860, 4⅛x4" 135.00
Figurine, man in spotted coat & striped hat, 1790-1810, 3½"......235.00
Flask, Great Exhibition of 1851 Hyde Park London, mc transfer, rpr.. 650.00
Plaque, lady & Cupid by table w/ewer emb, mc on wht oval, ca 1800, 8".525.00
Plaque, Toby Philpot amid taverners emb, mc on wht, 1800s, 9¾"....1,525.00
Plate, Lend a Bite, 2 men eating, watched by man w/monkey & dog, 7"... 30.00
Plate, 4 boys w/birds in nest, blk transfer, mc rim, 1830s, 7½" 150.00

Primitives

Like the mouse that ate the grindstone, so has collectible interest in primitives increased, a little bit at a time, until demand is taking bites instead of nibbles into their availability. Although the term 'primitives' once referred to those survival essentials contrived by our American settlers, it has recently been expanded to include objects needed or desired by succeeding generations — items representing the cabin-'n-corn-patch existence as well as examples of life on larger farms and in towns. Through popular usage, it also respectfully covers what are actually 'country collectibles.' From the 1600s into the latter 1800s, factories employed carvers, blacksmiths, and other artisans whose handwork contributed to turning out quality items. When buying, 'touchmarks,' a company's name and/or location and maker's or owner's initials, are exciting discoveries.

Primitives are uniquely individual. Following identical forms, results more often than not show typically personal ideas. Using this as a guide (combined with circumstances of age, condition, desire to own, etc.) should lead to a reasonably accurate evaluation. For items not listed, consult comparable examples. Authority Kathryn McNerney has compiled two lovely books on primitives and related topics: *Primitives, Our American Heritage*, and *Antique Tools, Our American Heritage*. See also Butter Molds and Stamps; Boxes; Copper; Farm Collectibles; Fireplace

Implements; Kitchen Collectibles; Molds; Tinware; Weaving; Woodenware; and Wrought Iron.

Barrel, staved w/old red pnt & laced vines, ME stencil, 22x16" ... 400.00
Bedwarmer, brass pan, wrought-iron hdl & ring, rprs, 44" L 350.00
Bedwarmer, brass w/flower-eng dome lid, hook hdl, 41x12" dia ... 375.00
Bedwarmer, brass w/punched rosettes & circles, trn grpt hdl, 42" L ...165.00
Bedwarmer, punched pewter, pierced lid, trn wood hdl, 26¼" L .. 560.00
Bellows, cvd oak w/coat of arms, brass nozzle, rpl leather, 45" 200.00
Bucket, staved, iron bands & Y-shape straps, red pnt, 12x13", VG .. 345.00
Bucket, staved w/metal bands, trn lid, bail hdl, salmon pnt, 11x14" ..315.00
Bucket, staved w/2 metal bands, wire hdl, bl pnt, 6¾" 375.00
Candle mold, pewter/cherry wood, 24-tube, J Calverly..., 18x21x7" ..1,950.00
Candle mold, tin, 24-tube, dbl strap hdls, 11" 165.00
Candle mold, tin, 33-tube (unusual), strap hdls, dents, 10x13x5" ...500.00
Candle mold, tin, 36-tube, gray pnt, 11x8" 175.00
Candle mold, tin, 48-tube, strap hdls, 11x10", VG 660.00
Churn, Windsor style, gr pnt, w/rockers, boat-shaped compartment, 36" .. 145.00
Dough box, yel-pnt pine, canted, 4 splay legs, 1800s, NE, 20x20x16" ..300.00
Firkin, staved, copper/iron tacks, pegged hdl, dk red pnt, 10x10" ...515.00
Firkin, staved, swing hdl, worn salmon pnt, 7½x8¾" 800.00
Firkin, staved, 3 fingered bands, gr pnt, swing wood hdl, 12x11", G ..230.00
Firkin, staved oak, 3 flat iron bands, hdls, 25½", VG 200.00
Firkin, staved pine w/3 wooden bands, fitted lid, yel pnt, 12½" ... 460.00
Firkin, staved w/lapped hoops, cvd swing hdl, bl pnt, 1800s, 15" .. 700.00
Firkin, staved w/wire staples, yel & red-brn pnt, 14" 115.00
Flax break, hickory & oak, mortised, age splits, 34x58x30" 115.00
Footwarmer, mortised/pegged wooden fr w/punched tin, 6x9x8" .. 175.00
Hourglass, cvd wood w/blown glass, gr pnt, 19th C, 6½" 2,450.00
Keg, staved bbl-form, iron bands, early 19th C, 6½" 120.00
Mortar, ash burl, age splits, 5¾x6", +curly maple pestle 175.00
Mortar, birch w/red traces, ovoid top, split, 8", +pestle 230.00
Mortar, CI, slightly tapered, 1700s, 5", +10" CI pestle 120.00
Mortar, trn lignum vitae, 6⅛x54½", +pestle 150.00
Niddy-noddy, chip-cvd central shaft, 19x11" 115.00
Niddy-noddy, shaft cvd w/Oriental writing etc, 20x12" 345.00
Rack, drying; pine w/old red stain, 3-bar, mortised ft, 37x34" 145.00
Rack, herb-drying; 4 slats, side posts ending in shaped dbl ft, 41x33" ...145.00
Spoon mold, bronze, 2-part, EX verdigris patina, 9" 300.00
Tinderbox, tin, finger loop/candle socket on lid, no striker, 4" dia ..145.00

Washboard, cast iron, with heart cutout, Pennsylvania, 1800s, 22½x12½", $2,600.00. (Photo courtesy Skinner Inc. Auctioneers & Appraisers of Antiques & Fine Art)

Yarn winder, bl-pnt X-form swivels on 8-side shaft, 4-ftd base, 46x27". 295.00
Yarn winder, 4-arm, blk pnt, exposed click counter, 39" 150.00

Prints

The term 'print' may be defined today as almost any image printed on paper by any available method. Examples of collectible old 'prints' are Norman Rockwell magazine covers and Maxfield Parrish posters and calendars. 'Original print' refers to one achieved through the efforts of the artist or under his direct supervision. A 'reproduction' is a print produced by an accomplished print maker who reproduces another artist's print or original work. Thorough study is required on the part of the collector to recognize and appreciate the many variable factors to be considered in evaluating a print. Prices vary from one area of the country to another and are dependent upon new findings regarding the scarcity or abundance of prints as such information may arise. Although each collector of old prints may have their own varying criteria by which to judge condition, for those who deal only rarely in this area or newer collectors, a few guidelines may prove helpful. Staining, though unquestionably detrimental, is nearly always present in some degree and should be weighed against the rarity of the print. Professional cleaning should improve its appearance and at the same time help preserve it. Avoid tears that affect the image; minor margin tears are another matter, especially if the print is a rare one. Moderate 'foxing' (brown spots caused by mold or the fermentation of the rag content of old paper) and light stains from the old frames are not serious unless present in excess. Margin trimming was a common practice; but look for at least ½" to 1½" margins, depending on print size. When no condition is indicated, the items listed below are assumed to be in very good to excellent condition. See also Nutting, Wallace; Parrish, Maxfield. For more information we recommend *Beaux Arts Pocket Guide to American Art Prints* by Michael Bozarth.

Audubon, John J.

Audubon is the best known of American and European wildlife artists. His first series of prints, 'Birds of America,' was produced by Robert Havell of London. They were printed on Whitman watermarked paper bearing dates of 1826 to 1838. The Octavo Edition of the same series was printed in seven editions, the first by J.T. Bowen under Audubon's direction. There were seven volumes of text and prints, each 10" x 7", the first five bearing the J.J. Audubon and J.B. Chevalier mark, the last two, J.J. Audubon. They were produced from 1840 through 1844. The second and other editions were printed up to 1871. The Bien Edition prints were full size, made under the direction of Audubon's sons in the late 1850s. Due to the onset of the Civil War, only 105 plates were finished. These are considered to be the most valuable of the reprints of the 'Birds of America Series.' In 1971 the complete set was reprinted by Johnson Reprint Corp. of New York and Theaturm Orbis Terrarum of Amsterdam. Examples of the latter bear the watermark G. Schut and Zonen. In 1985 a second reprint was done by Abbeville Press for the National Audubon Society. Although Audubon is best known for his portrayal of birds, one of his less-familiar series, 'Vivaparous Quadrupeds of North America,' portrayed various species of animals. Assembled in corroboration with John Bachman from 1839 until 1851, these prints are 28" x 22" in size. Several Octavo Editions were published in the 1850s. Our advisor for this category is Michael Bozarth; he is listed in the Directory under New York.

Pied Oyster Catcher, Havell/45, 1834, sheet: 12½x19½", $3,000.00. (Photo courtesy Neal Auction Co. Auctioneers & Appraisers of Fine Art)

American Coot, Havell/419, 1830, sight: 16x25" 7,200.00
Black-Billed Cuckoo, Havell/32, 1828, sight: 18¾x26½" 2,950.00
Black-Footed Ferret, Bowen, Royal Octavo/93, 6x10"+mat & 15x18" fr 775.00
Black-Throated Diver, Amsterdam/346 & 70, 1971, sheet: 27x40" ...675.00
Black-Winged Hawk, Bien/16, 36x26" unmtd 365.00
Dusky Duck, Royal Octago/386, 6½x10¾" unmtd 270.00
Fish Crow, Havell, #CXLVI, 1927-38, 38x25⅝"+mat & fr 1,500.00
Green Heron, Amsterdam/333 & #67, 1971, sheet: 26x40" 560.00
Hooded Merganser Male & Female, Havell, 1830, 22x28" 8,900.00
Lewis Marmot, Bowen Imperial/107, 21⅝x27⅜" unmtd 230.00
Portfolio facsimile: Birds of Am, Abbeville, NY, 1985, 435 plates ...23,500.00
Purple Gullinule, Adult Male in Spring Plumage, Havell, 1830, 16x24" .. 4,300.00
Red-Bellied Squirrel, Bowen/38, 26¾x21"+fr 600.00
Spotted Grouse, Amsterdam/176 & 67, offset color, 1971, sheet: 26x40" . 560.00
Swift Fox, Havell/11, JT Bowen, 1844, 24¾x21"+mat & fr 750.00
Tell-Tale Godwit or Snipe (Male & Female), Havell, 1830, 24x18" .3,750.00
Tropic Bird, Havel, 1835, prof cleaned/rstr, lg folio+fr 4,950.00
Trumpeter Swan, Amsterdam/376 & 76, 1971, sheet: 27x40" 765.00
Velvet Duck, Havell, London, 1835, sight: 21x30½" 1,900.00

Currier and Ives

Nathaniel Currier was in business by himself until the late 1850s when he formed a partnership with James Merrit Ives. Currier is given credit for being the first to use the medium to portray newsworthy subjects, and the Currier and Ives views of nineteenth-century American culture are familiar to us all. In the following listings, 'C' numbers correspond with a standard reference book by Conningham. Values are given for prints in very good condition; all are colored unless indicated black and white. Unless noted 'NC' (Nathaniel Currier), all prints are published by Currier and Ives. Our advisor for this category is Michael Bozarth; he is listed in the Directory under New York.

Am Co Life, Summers Evening, NC, C-124, lg folio 4,400.00
Am Country Life - October Afternoon, NC, C-122, lg folio 2,070.00
Am Country Life - Pleasures of Winter, NC, C-123, lg folio 3,225.00
Am Country Life - Summers Evening, C-122, lg folio 2,250.00
Am Farm Scenes - Autumn, 1853, C-133, NC, lg folio 3,400.00

American Field Sports: Retrieving, 1857, large folio, $2,350.00. (Photo courtesy Garth's Auctions Inc.)

Am Forest Game, 1866, C-156, lg folio 1,000.00
Am River Scenery - View on Androscoggin ME, C-190, lg folio .. 500.00
Arkansas Traveler, 1870, C-270, sm folio 275.00
Beauties of Billiards, lg folio 1,600.00
Bombardment & Capture of Fort Henry, TN; C-590, sm folio 300.00
Burning of Chicago, 1871, C-738, sm folio 600.00
Cares of a Family, C-815, sm folio 800.00
Coming in 'On His Ear,' 1875, C-1221, sm folio 250.00
Cooling Stream, C-1246, med folio 450.00
Cutter Genesta RYS, C-1338, lg folio 1,100.00
Darktown Fire Brigade - To the Rescue, sm folio 400.00
Declaration Committee, 1876, C-1530, sm folio 300.00
Easter Flowers, 1869, C-1655, sm folio 50.00
Feeding the Swans, C-1939, sm folio 275.00
First Trot of the Season, 1870, C-1998, sm folio 2,000.00
Gen Z Taylor Rough & Ready, NC, 1846, C-2330, sm folio 125.00
Grand National Whig Banner, NC, 1844, C-2511, sm folio 400.00
Great St Louis Bridge Across Mississippi..., undtd, C-2648, sm folio .. 825.00
Hero & Flora Temple, NC, 1856, C-2800, lg folio 2,000.00
Home in the Wilderness, C-2861, sm folio 635.00
Home on the Mississippi, 1876, C-2876, sm folio 500.00
Hooked, 1874, C-2928, sm folio 1,800.00
James K Polk Eleventh President of US, NC, sm folio 225.00
John Brown the Martyr, 1870, C-3254, 16¼x13½"+fr 1,265.00
Lake in the Woods, C-3409, sm folio 200.00
Leaders, 1888, C-3471, lg folio 1,000.00
Life in the Country - Morning, C-3508, lg folio 700.00
Life of a Fireman - Jump Her Boys..., 1954, C-3519, lg folio 600.00
Life of a Fireman - Metropolitan System, 1866, C-3516, lg folio ...1,000.00
Life of a Fireman - New Era..., 1861, C-3517, lg folio 700.00
Life of a Sportsman - Camping in the Woods, 1872, C-3523, sm folio .400.00
Little Snowbird, undtd, C-3719, sm folio 250.00
Magic Lake, C-3870, med folio 150.00
Mating in the Woods, 1871, C-4079, sm folio 525.00
Mountain Stream, C-4246, med folio 550.00
Niagara Falls, C-4456, NC, lg folio 725.00
Old Ford Bridge, C-4559, sm folio 200.00
Old Mill in Summer, C-4571, sm folio 300.00
Old Oaken Bucket, 1872, C-4577, sm folio 200.00
Partridge Shooting, C-4714, lg folio 4,485.00
Partridge Shooting, C-4717 (similar), lg folio, +cvd fr 3,000.00
President Lincoln at Home, 1865, 14x11" 325.00
Quail Shooting, NC, 1852, C-4989, lg folio 4,485.00
Race on the Mississippi, 1870, C-05042, sm folio 550.00
Road Side Mill, 1870, C-5175, sm folio 325.00
Snipe Shooting, NC, C-5577, lg folio 3,600.00
Starting Out on His Mettle, 1878, C-5711, sm folio 300.00
Summer in the Country, C-5861, sm folio 200.00
Sunny Side on the Hudson, C-5893, sm folio 175.00
Sylvan Lake, C-5939, sm folio 200.00
Tacony & Mac, NC, 1853, C-5943, lg folio 2,800.00
Valley Valls, Virginia; C-6355, sm folio 225.00
Western River Scenery, 1866, C-6620, med folio 1,250.00
Wild Duck Shooting, NC, C-6669, lg folio 3,900.00
Windsor Castle & Park, C-6720, med folio 200.00
Winter Evening, NC, 1854, C-6734, lg folio 8,150.00
Woodcock Shooting, NC, C-6774, lg folio 4,000.00

Erte (Romain de Tirtoff)

Aladdin & His Bride, signed in pencil, 25½x32" 450.00
Bride, portrait of lady in ornate headdress, 18x13½" 475.00
Enchanted Melody, 1985, 37x26" 1,400.00
Giuletta, ca 1983, 21⅞x17½" 1,050.00
Liberty at Night w/Fireworks, NY skyline, ltd ed of 300, 31x23" .. 800.00
Paresseuse, ca 1980, 25⅜x18" 750.00
Reflections, lady smoking, ca 1976, 20x15" 480.00
Show Girl in Elaborate Costume, silkscreen, 29¼x21" 1,450.00

Fox, R. Atkinson

A Canadian who worked as an artist in the 1880s, R. Atkinson Fox moved to New York about 10 years later, where his original oils were widely sold at auction and through exhibitions. Today he is best known, however, for his prints, published by as many as 20 print makers. More than 30 examples of his work appeared on Brown and Bigelow calendars, and it was used in many other forms of advertising as well. Though he was an accomplished artist able to interpret any subject well, he is today best known for his landscapes. Fox died in 1935. Our advisor for Fox prints is Pat Gibson whose address is listed in the Directory under California.

Canadian Landscape, #140, 1930s, 14x20"+orig bl & gold fr 175.00
Dawn, #1, 18x30"+orig ornate gold fr 275.00
Dreamland, #41, 1920-30s, 12x8"+orig ornate fr 60.00
Garden of Romance, #40, 13½x21½"+orig simple fr 160.00
Glorious Vista, #6, 18x30"+orig simple fr 175.00

**Oriental Dreams, #575, 10x13",
$175.00.** (Photo courtesy Pickering's Prints in Studio City; Joanne Pickering)

Promenade, #10, 8x12"+Deco fr 75.00
Shower of Daisies, #77, 10x24"+orig simple fr 120.00
Spirit of Youth, #4, 1926, 9x15"+orig simple fr 100.00

Gutmann, Bessie Pease

Delicately tinted prints of appealing children sometimes accompanied by their pets, sometimes asleep, often captured at some childhood activity are typical of the work of this artist; she painted lovely ladies as well and was a successful illustrator of children's books. Her career spanned the five decades of the 1900s, and she recorded over 800 published artworks. Our advisor for this cagegory is Dr. Victor J.W. Christie; he is listed in the Directory under Pennsylvania.

The Bedtime Story, #712, 14x21", $750.00. (Photo courtesy Dr. J. W. Christie)

Aeroplane, The; #266/#695, 14x21" 900.00
Always, #744, 14x21" 2,600.00
American Girl, The; #220, 13x18" 500.00

An Anxious Moment, #714, 14x21" 650.00
Annunciation, #705, 14x21" 1,200.00
Awakening, #664, 14x21" 125.00
Baby's First Birthday, #618, 14x21" 750.00
Baby's First Christmas, #158 .... 500.00
Betty, #787, 14x21" 250.00
Billy, 3790, 14x21" 270.00
Blossom Time, #654, 14x21" 800.00
Blue Bird, The; #265/#666, 14x21" 650.00
Bobby, #789, 14x21" 225.00
Brown Study, A; #611, 14x20" 1,500.00
Bubbles, #779, 14x21" 350.00
Butterfly, The; #632, 14x18" 210.00
Call to Arms, A; #806, 14x21" 850.00
Caught Napping, #153, 9x12" 2,000.00
Chip of the Old Block, #728, 14x21" 600.00
Chuckles, #799, 11x14" 150.00
Chums, #665, 14x21" 350.00
Contentment, #781 .... 90.00
CQD, #149, 9x12" 450.00
Cupid, After All My Trouble; #608, 16x20" 800.00
Cupid's Reflection, #602, 14x21" 800.00
Daddy's Coming, #644, 14x21" 495.00
Divine Fire, #722, 14x21" 700.00
Double Blessing, A; #643, 14x21" 500.00
Fairest of the Flowers, The; #659, 14x21" 700.00
Feeling, #19, 6x9" 250.00
First Dancing Lesson, The; #713, 14x21" 825.00
Friendly Enemies, #215, 11x14" 155.00
Going to Town, #797, 14x21" 650.00
Goldilocks, #771, 14x21" 1,100.00
Good Morning, #801, 14x21" 250.00
Guest's Candle, The; #651, 14x21" 500.00
Hearing, #22, 6x9" 250.00
His Majesty, #793, 14x21" 320.00
His Queen, #212, 14x20" 700.00
Home Builders, #233/#655, 14x21" 235.00
How Miss Tabitha Taught School, Dodge Publishing Co, 11x16" .. 900.00
In Arcady, #701, 14x21" 700.00
In Disgrace, #792, 14x21" 200.00
In Slumberland, #786, 14x21" 120.00
Kitty's Breakfast, #805, 14x21" 350.00
Knit Two - Purl Two, #657, 14x21" 850.00
Little Bit of Heaven, A; #650, 14x21" 125.00
Little Bo Peep, #200, 11x14" 150.00
Little Mother, #803, 14x21" 450.00
Lorelei, #645, 14x21" 1,700.00
Love's Blossom, #223, 11x14" 100.00
Love's Harmony, #791, 14x21" 400.00
Lullaby, The; #819, 14x21" 2,100.00
Madonna, The; #674, 14x21" 2,100.00
May We Come In, #808, 14x21" 385.00
Merely a Man, #218, 13x18" 800.00
Message of the Roses, The; #641, 14x21" 400.00
Mighty Like a Rose, #642, 14x21" 200.00
Mine, #798, 14x21" 225.00
Mischief Brewing, #152, 9x12" 2,000.00
Mothering Heart, The; #351, 14x21" 700.00
My Honey, #765, 14x21" 1,200.00
New Pet, The; #709, 14x21" 950.00
Nitey Nite, #826, 14x21" 175.00
Now I Lay Me, #620, 14x21" 1,800.00
Off to School, #631, 14x21" 1,200.00
On Dreamland's Border, #692, 14x21" 155.00

On the Up & Up, #796, 14x21"............................295.00
Our Alarm Clock, #150, 9x12" 250.00
Perfect Peace, #809, 14x21" 500.00
Popularity (Has Its Disadvantages), #825, 14x21" 150.00
Poverty & Riches, #640, 14x21" 700.00
Priceless Necklace, A; #744, 14x21"................1,600.00
Rosebud, A; #780, 14x21" 320.00
Seeing, #122, 11x14" 250.00
Smile Worth While, A; #180, 9x12" 800.00
Snowbird, #777, 14x21" 650.00
Springtime, #775, 14x21" 750.00
Star From the Sky, A; #817, 14x21" 175.00
Sunbeam in a Dark Corner, A; #638, 14x21" 2,200.00
Sunkissed, #818, 14x21" 125.00
Sweet Innocence, #806, 11x14" 150.00
Symphony, #702, 14x21" 650.00
Tabby, #172, 9x12" 600.00
Taps, #815, 14x21" 550.00
Television, #821, 14x21" 110.00
Thank You, God, #822, 14x21" 175.00
To Have & To Hold, #625, 14x21" 800.00
To Love & To Cherish, #615, 14x21" 265.00
Tom, Tom the Piper's Son, #219, 11x14" 175.00
Tommy, #788, 14x21" 175.00
Touching, #210, 11x14" 150.00
Vanquished, The; #119, 9x12" 750.00
Verdict: Love for Life, The; #113, 9x12"..............550.00
When Daddy Comes Marching Home, #668, 14x21"......3,800.00
Who's Sleepy, #816, 14x21" 260.00
Winged Aureole, The; #700, 14x21".....................500.00
Wood Magic, #703, 14x21" 750.00

Icart, Lewis

Louis Icart (1888 – 1950) was a Parisian artist best known for his boudoir etchings in the '20s and '30s. In the '80s prices soared, primarily due to Japanese buying. The market began to readjust in 1990, and most etchings now sell at retail between $1,400.00 and $2,500.00. Value is determined by popularity and condition, more than by rarity. Original frames and matting are not important, as most collectors want the etchings restored to their original condition and protected with acid-free mats.

Beware of the following repro and knock-off items: 1. Pseudo engravings on white plastic with the Icart 'signature.' 2. Any bronzes with the Icart signature. 3. Most watercolors, especially if they look similar in subject matter to a popular etching. 4. Lithographs where the dot-matrix printing is visible under magnification. Some even have phony embossed seals or rubber stamp markings. Items listed below are in excellent condition unless noted otherwise. Our advisor is William Holland, author of *Louis Icart: The Complete Etchings* and *The Collectible Maxfield Parrish*; he is listed in the Directory under Pennsylvania.

Before Christmas, 1922, sheet: 24x19", $7,000.00.
(Photo courtesy Butterfield and Butterfield)

Apache Dancer, 1929, sight: 20x13¼" 1,600.00
Conchita, 1929, 20½x13¼" 1,050.00
Des Grieux, 21x14"...1,650.00
Fair Model, 1940s, 18¾x11" 2,400.00
Faust, 21x14"..1,000.00
Flower Seller, 22x27"...1,250.00
Il Pleut Berge, 21x14"...1,800.00
Joy of Life, 1929, 23x15"...................................3,850.00
Lady w/whippet at window, 12x16" oval 1,200.00
Laziness, 1925, 15x19" 1,200.00
Leda & Swan, lacquered w/EX color, 19¾x30½" 650.00
Lis, 29x20"..2,400.00
Louise, 1926, 20x13⅛"......................................1,900.00
Orange Seller, 1929, 19x14¼" 1,000.00
Orchides, 29x20"..3,800.00
Poem, 1928, 18x21¾"...1,950.00
Vitesse, 1933, 16x26"...3,250.00
Winged Victory, ltd ed, 30½x23".......................3,150.00
Winter, 10x6"..1,600.00

Kurz and Allison

Louis Kurz founded the Chicago Lithograph Company in 1833. Among his most notable works were a series of 36 Civil War scenes and 100 illustrations of Chicago architecture. His company was destroyed in the Great Fire of 1871, and in 1880 Kurz formed a partnership with Alexander Allison, an engraver. Until both retired in 1903, they produced hundreds of lithographs in color as well as black and white. Unless noted otherwise, values are for prints in excellent condition.

Battle of Atlanta, 1882, 22x28⅜"......................425.00
Battle of Chattanooga, 1888, lg folio 385.00
Battle of Gettysburg, 1884, 21½x27½"...............900.00
Battle of Kenesaw Mountain, 1891, 17¼x25¾" 240.00
Battle of New Orleans, Chicago, 1890, 22¼x28⅜".........385.00
Battle of New Orleans, Jan 8, 1815, sight: 19½x26" 720.00

Battle of Princeton (George Washington leading the charge), matted and framed, 27x34", $300.00.
(Photo courtesy Garth's Auctions Inc.)

Battle of Williamsburg, 12893, 17¼x25¼" 240.00
Chicago in Early Days, 1893, 22x28⅛", VG 575.00
Col Theodore Roosevelt USV, Chicago, 1898, 23½x18" 600.00
Declaration of Independence, Chicago, 1890, 22¼x28⅜".........180.00
General TJ Jackson, Chicago, 27½x21½" 540.00

Max, Peter

Born in Germany in 1937, Peter Max came to the United States in 1953 where he later studied art in New York City. His work is colorful and his genre psychedelic. He is a prolific artist, best known for his designs from the '60s and '70s that typified the 'hippie' movement.

Brown Lady, lithograph, 1990, 36x27", +fr 3,250.00
Flag w/Heart II, lithograph, 2003, 24x28"...............................1,750.00
Mexico, serigraph, 1970 ltd edition, 30x22", +fr 3,250.00
Mickey Mouse Suite, serigraph, Disney, 1995 ltd ed, 16x14" 3,750.00
Red Flowers, lithograph, 1999, 28x21".....................................1,650.00
Sailing New Worlds, lithograph, 1976 ltd ed, 13x11½", +fr.......4,000.00
Seated Lady, serigraph, 1979 ltd ed, 20x23", +fr 1,650.00
Space Rainbow, serigraph, 1978 ltd ed, 22x30", +fr..................1,575.00
Zero Amarillo, serigraph, 1984 ltd ed, 26x20", +mat & metal fr ...2,750.00

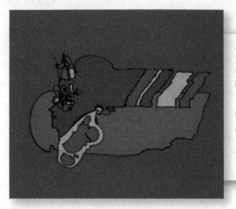

Witnessing From Above, print, signed and numbered, 15x17", $185.00. (Photo courtesy Leslie Hindman Auctioneers)

McKenney and Hall

John Ridge a Cherokee, Greenough, 1838, sight: 16x12" 480.00
Kee-She-Waa Indian Chief, 1837-44, 20x14"................................ 600.00
Keokuk, Chief of Sacs & Foxes, hand colored, Greenough, 20x14" ..1,530.00
Ki-On-Twog-Ky, Bowen, EC Biddle, 1837, 20¼x14⅝" 850.00
Mon-Ka-Ush-Ka, Bowen, EC Biddle, 18⅞x13½" 700.00
Po-Ca-Hon-Tas, Rice & Clark, 1842-44, 15½x11¼".................... 325.00
Red Jacket, 19th C, 30x13½" 950.00
Wa-Na-Ta, JT Bowen, Greenough, 1838, 20¼x14⅝" 1,100.00
Winnebago Hoowanneka, Rice & Clark, 1837-44, full sheet 450.00

Yard-Longs

Values for yard-long prints are given for examples in near mint condition, full length, nicely framed, and with the original glass. To learn more about this popular area of collector interest, we recommend *Those Wonderful Yard-Long Prints and More*, *More Wonderful Yard-Long Prints, Book 2*, and *Yard-Long Prints, Book 3*, by our advisors Bill Keagy, and Charles and Joan Rhoden. They are listed in the Directory under Indiana and Illinois respectively. A word of caution: Watch for reproductions; know your dealer.

American Beauty Roses, Newton A Wells, c 1894 .... 325.00
American Beauty Roses, Paul DeLongpre, c 1896 .... 350.00
American Farming magazine, lady in yel/parasol, EH Lister, c 1918 ..400.00
American Girl, Pabst, c 1914 .... 550.00
Bridal Favors, Mary E Hart 300.00
Butterick pattern lady, ad for Butterick Transfers, etc, c 1930 ...... 600.00
Clay, Robinson & Co's Flower Girl Souvenir, calendar on front, c 1911... 500.00
Ducklings, ducks around pool of water, WM Carey 400.00
Hope, Union Pacific Tea Co, c 1898.. 500.00
In Grandmother's Garden, Charles C Curran, c 1909 .... 500.00
Jack Roses & Lilacs, Paul DeLongpre, c 1897 .... 325.00
Kittens (4) climbing tree, Helena Maguire 400.00
Metropolitan Life Insurance Co, 4 stages of life, c 1907 .... 475.00
Pabst Extract, different nationality baby for ea month, c 1904 .... 450.00
Pompeian Beauty art panel, ad & calendar on bk, c 1913 .... 550.00
Schlitz Malt Extract, titled Priscilla, calendar on front, c 1910.... 600.00

Selz Good Shoes, copyright Selz, Schwab & Co., calendar and advertising for Hugh's Clothing Company (Dependable Clothes Merchants) of Sabetha, Kansas (this was 'made to order' and may be found with various business advertisements), $500.00. (Photo courtesy Bill Keagy and Charles and Joan Rhoden)

Selz Good Shoes, lady in red shawl, Earl Chambers, c 1929......... 650.00
Stockman Bride for Nat'l Stockman & Farmer Magazine, c 1911...500.00
Sunbonnet Babies or PA NY Short Line, c 1882, minimum value... 500.00
Unknown, lady in pk hat/calendar at bottom, Knowles Hare Jr, 1917.. 500.00
White Roses, Paul DeLongpre... 350.00
Yard of Cherries, Guy Bedford, c 1906 .... 300.00
Yard of Pansies, Grace Barton Allen 275.00
Yard of Puppies, Guy Bedford, mostly blk & wht, 9 puppies........ 350.00
Yard of Youth, 8 children, Youth's Companion, FL Martini 350.00

Purinton

With its bold colors and unusual shapes, Purinton Pottery is much admired by today's dinnerware collectors. In 1939 Bernard Purinton purchased the East Liverpool Pottery in Wellsville, Ohio, and re-named it the Purinton Pottery Company. One of its earliest lines was Peasant Ware, featuring simple shapes and bold, colorful patterns. It was designed by William H. Blair, who also designed what have become the company's most recognized lines, Apple and Intaglio. The company was extremely successful, and by 1941 it became necessary to build a new plant, which they located in Shippenville, Pennsylvania. Blair left Purinton to open his own pottery (Blair Ceramics), leaving his sister Dorothy Purinton (Bernard's wife) to assume the role of designer. Though never a paid employee, Dorothy painted many one-of-a-kind special-occasion items that are highly sought after by today's collectors who are willing to pay premium prices to get them. These usually carry Dorothy's signature.

Apple was Purinton's signature pattern; it was produced throughout the entire life of the pottery. Another top-selling pattern designed by Dorothy Purinton was Pennsylvania Dutch, featuring hearts and tulips. Other long-term patterns include the Plaids and the Intaglios. While several other patterns were developed, they were short-lived. One of the most elusive patterns, Palm Tree, was sold only through a souvenir store in Florida owned by one of the Purinton's sons. In addition to dinnerware, Purinton also produced a line of floral ware, including planters for NAPCO. They did contract work for Esmond Industries and RUBEL, who were both distributors in New York. They made the Howdy Doody cookie jar and bank for Taylor, Smith & Taylor; both items are highly collectible.

The pottery was sold to Taylor, Smith & Taylor in 1958 and closed in 1959 due to heavy competition from foreign imports. Most items are not marked, but collectors find their unusual shapes easy to identify. A small number of items were ink stamped 'Purinton Slip-ware.' Some of the early Wellsville pieces were hand signed 'Purinton Pottery,' and several have emerged carrying the signature 'Wm. H. Blair' or simply 'Blair.' Blair's pieces command a premium price. See Clubs, Newsletters, and Catalogs in the Directory for information concerning *Purinton News and Views*.

Apple, bottles, Oil & Vinegar; 1-pt, 9½", pr 95.00
Apple, bowl, fruit; scalloped border, 12" 45.00
Apple, bowl, vegetable; 8½" 30.00
Apple, canister, tall, oval, 9", ea from $50 to 60.00
Apple, creamer & sugar bowl, open, mini 30.00
Apple, Dutch jug, 2-pt, 5¾" 35.00
Apple, marmalade 40.00
Apple, planter, rum jug shape, 6½" 55.00
Apple, relish, 3 rnd sections 25.00
Apple, shakers, stacking, 2¼", pr 95.00
Blue Pansy, basket planter, 6¼" 65.00
Brown Intaglio, creamer & sugar bowl, w/lid 20.00
Brown Intaglio, platter, 12" 20.00
Cactus, shakers, rnd, 2¾", pr 200.00
Cactus, teapot, 4-cup, rare 235.00
Fruit, shakers, range style, red trim, 4", pr 30.00
Heather Plaid, chop plate, 12" 35.00
Howdy Doody cookie jar 350.00
Intaglio, gravy pitcher, TS&T mold, 3¾" 45.00
Intaglio, mug, beer; 16-oz, 4¾" 18.00

Intaglio, tidbit tray, 10" diameter, $50.00. (Photo courtesy Susan Morris-Snyder)

Ivy - Red, coffeepot, 8-cup 25.00
Ivy - Red Blossom, pitcher, 2-pt, 6¼" 25.00
Ivy - Yellow Blossom, cornucopia vase, 6" 25.00
Maywood, cup & saucer, 2½" & 5½" 15.00
Maywood, shakers, mini jug, pr 35.00
Ming Tree, cup & saucer 30.00
Ming Tree, sprinkler can, 7" 50.00
Mountain Rose, plate, dinner; 9½" 40.00
Normandy Plaid, canister, apartment sz, 5½" 45.00
Normandy Plaid, Dutch jug, 5-pt 45.00
Palm Tree, honey jug, 6¼" 75.00
Peasant Garden, chop plate, 12" 150.00
Pennsylvania Dutch, honey jug, 6¼" 75.00
Pennsylvania Dutch, shakers, mini jug, pr 60.00
Petals, bowl, fruit; 12" 85.00
Petals, jug, 5-pt, 8" 85.00
Provincial Fruit, bowl, fruit; 12" 95.00
Saraband, bowl, range; w/lid, 5½" 20.00
Saraband, plate, dinner; 9¾" 10.00
Saraband, teapot, 6-cup, 6½" 25.00
Seafoam, shakers, 3", pr 55.00
Tea Rose, platter, meat; 12" 50.00
Tionesta Park, shakers, range style, souvenir, 4", pr 175.00
Turquoise Intaglio, plate, dinner; 9½" 20.00
Windflower, jardiniere, 5" 30.00

Purses

Purses from the early 1800s are often decorated with small, brightly colored glass beads. Cut steel beads were popular in the 1840s and remained stylish until about 1930. Purses made of woven mesh date back to the 1820s. Chain-link mesh came into usage in the 1890s, followed by the enamel mesh bags carried by the flappers in the 1920s. Purses are divided into several categories by (a) construction techniques — whether beaded, embroidered, or a type of needlework; (b) material — fabric or metal; and (c) design and style. Condition is very important. Watch for dry, brittle leather or fragile material. For those interested in learning more, we recommend *More Beautiful Purses* and *Combs and Purses* by Evelyn Haertigi of Carmel, California; and *100 Years of Purses, 1880s to 1980*, by Ronna Lee Aikins. Unless otherwise noted, our values are for examples in 'like-new' condition, showing very little if any wear.

Key: W&D — Whiting & Davis

Beaded, blk, Bags by Jose..., 1930-40s, 6x11½", from $40 to 90.00
Beaded, blk, floral needlework, beaded hdl, 7x10", from $250 to .. 350.00
Beaded, blk, Made in Japan by Bonni Int'l, 1930-40s, 6x8", $25 to .. 55.00
Beaded, blk, red & wht floral, string closure, 1940s, 12x14", $35 to.... 75.00
Beaded, blk & silver, drawstring closure, fringe, 1900s, 7x9", $205 to. 275.00
Beaded, blk dbl bead loops, chain dbl loop hdl, 1900s, 6x8", $205 to... 275.00
Beaded, blk satin w/beaded diamond pattern, Kane - M-M, 1950s ... 65.00
Beaded, cream w/floral accent, Corde-Bead in gold, 1950s, $80 to .. 120.00
Beaded, gold palm tree design, Newey Pat 201430-22, 1950-60s, 5x8" .. 115.00
Beaded, mc floral, w/silver-tone ornate fr, 1890s, 6x9", from $935 to.. 1,335.00
Beaded, silver & wht, silver chain & fr, 1950s, 4½x7¼", $75 to .. 115.00
Beaded, sm blk & silver check pattern, silver-tone fr, fringe, 1900s ... 240.00
Beaded, wht, hdl, mk Corde-Bead by Lumured, 1950s, 7x9", $65 to.. 95.00
Beaded, wht & crystal, clutch, Lumured, 1940s, from $40 to 80.00
Beaded, wht & lime, chain drawstring, fringe, 1950s, 10x9", $45 to.. 90.00
Crocheted, gr, silver-tone fr & chain, 1930-40s, 10x7", from $50 to.. 90.00
Crocheted, pk, cream plastic fr, 3" chain, 1930s, 8x9", from $45 to.. 75.00
Enid Collins, Flower Basket V, jeweled flowers on blk, M w/tag .. 950.00
Enid Collins, It Grows on Trees, jeweled tree/birds/coins, NM 365.00
Enid Collins, Summertime, jeweled bugs/flowers, dtd 1966, MIP 515.00
Enid Collins, Tropical Treat, jeweled tropic scene, 2-hdl, 13x11x4" .. 425.00
Fabric, mc floral, celluloid elephant on snap, Made in Japan, 1960s .. 105.00
Fabric, wht w/mc floral, Margaret Smith Gardiner..., 13x10", $60 to. 100.00
Leather, alligator, tri-fold, gold-tone twist-clasp, from $200 to 300.00
Leather, alligator, whipstitch border, gold-tone base & clasp; 7x8" .. 125.00
Leather, alligator, wht stitching, 1940s, 9½x10", $175 to 205.00
Leather, envelope style, whipstitch border, 1910, 5x8", from $120 to.. 160.00
Leather, gold-tone clasp & fr, Mecker Joplin, 1945, 6x11" 195.00
Leather, snakeskin, blk & brn, 4 sm ft, gold-tone clasp, 1950s, 7x10" 75.00

Leather, tooled, open pockets outside, zipper, ca. 1950s, 11" wide, from $160.00 to $240.00.

(Photo courtesy Ronna Lee Aikins)

Lucite, butterscotch & clear w/cvd flower on lid, 2-hdl, 5x7x4" .. 275.00
Lucite, gold & silver-tone woven metal, tortoiseshell top, clear hdl ..145.00
Lucite, gold confetti in clear, Gilli Orig NY, 1950s, 7¾" L........... 360.00
Lucite, lemon pearlized w/aurora borealis stones, 4½x9x4"+hdl .. 315.00
Lucite, wht seed beads, needlework rose, Midas of Miami, 1950s, 4x8"..175.00
Mesh, Alumesh eggshell, celluloid fr & hdl, 1930s, 9½x10", $65 to ..115.00
Mesh, eggshell, leather border & hdls, 1950s, 9x19", from $65 to...105.00
Mesh, floral, clasp w/bl glass tips, Germany, 1900-1915, 5x4½" ... 160.00
Mesh, gold-tone, Whiting & Davis..., 4" chain, 1940s, 7x5", $90 to .130.00
Mesh, loop design, ball drops, German Silver, 1900-1910, 4½x6"...175.00
Mesh, silver-tone, Whiting & Davis, 5" chain, 5½x5", from $75 to...115.00
Satin, gold w/mc rhinestones, clutch, Exclusively for LA Regale. 115.00
Satin, gr, crystal on gold-tone leaf clasp, After Five R, 1950s 85.00
Sequined, silver clutch, Made in Czechoslovakia, late 1930s, 4x8" ..50.00
Straw, Bahama Blue floral decor, rnd, dbl braided straw hdls, 1945...65.00
Straw, brn leather straps & snap, mk Mantessa handmade..., 1955, 8x11"...75.00
Straw, fan shape, 2 embr flowers, hdls, 1955, 10¾" H.................. 90.00
Straw, seashells in plastic on side, Atlas Hollywood Florida, 1950s..125.00
Straw, sq w/gr & cream tapestry on sides, 5¼" gold hdls, 1945....... 70.00
Straw, wht, bamboo hdl, mk Made in Japan, 1955, 5½x12½" 45.00
Straw, wht Lucite front, top & hdl, Stylecraft Miami, 1945, 9x10"...100.00
Suede, dk bl, 4½" hdl, Blenendavis, 1940s, 7x9½"....................... 100.00
Tapestry, floral, emb metal fr w/jewels, 1900s, 6x6" 165.00
Tapestry, floral, tortoiseshell Bakelite fr & chain hdl, 1940s, 9x14" ..75.00
Tapestry, floral, vinyl hdl, gold-tone fr, 1950s, 8x13", from $35 to 75.00
Vinyl, bone, gold rope trim, gold-tone fr & snap, 1950s, 8½x10½"...60.00
Vinyl, brn, gold-tone fr & snap, dbl hdls, 1950s, 7x10½" 55.00

Puzzles

'Jigsaw' puzzles have been around almost as long as games. The first examples were handcrafted from wood, and they are extremely difficult to find. Most of the early examples featured moral subjects just as the board games did. By the 1890s jigsaw puzzles had become a major form of home entertainment. During the Depression years jigsaw puzzles were set up on card tables in almost every home. The early wood examples are the most valuable. Cube puzzles, or blocks, were often made by the same companies as the board games. Again, early examples display the finest quality lithography. While all subjects are collectible, some (such as Santa blocks) often command prices higher than games from the same period. In the miscellaneous subcategory below, all listing are for jigsaw puzzles (that are complete) unless noted otherwise.

Personalities, Movies, and TV Shows

Aquaman, jigsaw, w/Mera, Whitman, 1968, 100 pcs, EXIB 30.00
Flip the Frog, jigsaw, Saalfield, 1932, set of 4, EXIB 75.00

Flintstones, Whitman, 1964, VG-, from $60.00 to $70.00.

(Photo courtesy Morphy Auctions)

Gulliver's Travels, jigsaw, Saalfield, 1930s, set of 3, EXIB............. 125.00
Lady & the Tramp, fr-tray, Whitman, 1954, EX+ 25.00
Marvel Superheroes, jigsaw, Milton Bradley, 1967, 100 pcs, EXIB...50.00
Monkees Greatest Hits, jigsaw, Suns Out Inc, 19x19", MIB 15.00
Pink Panther, jigsaw, Whitman, 100 pcs, EXIB 25.00
Superman, fr-tray, various scenes, Whitman, 1966, EX+, ea 30.00
Thunderball/J Bond 007, jigsaw, M Bradley, 1965, over 600 pcs, NMIB.. 50.00
Wizard of Oz, jigsaw, Departure From Oz, Jaymar, 1970s, 19x19", EXIB .. 55.00
Zorro, fr-tray, beside tree, Whitman, 1957, 15x11½", NM 40.00

Miscellaneous

Afternoon Tea, Parker Bros, plywood, 1930s, 516 pcs, 16x19", rpl box..220.00
Automobile Scroll Puzzle, McLoughlin Bros NY, 1903, 18½x25", EXIB ..300.00
Bamboo Walk (Asian farm scene), Parker Bros, 1930s, 7x10", EXIB...40.00
Cattle in Pasture, Dupre, plywood, 1930s, 188 pcs, 10x14", rpl box.....45.00
Colonial Picture (WA & colonists), wood, 1910-20, 380 pcs, rpl box..120.00
High Society (stylized carriage), plywood, Par Co, 1950s, 17x25", +box...1,200.00
Indian Paradise, cb, RA Fox, 1930s, 250 pcs, 10x13½", EXIB........ 15.00
Lagoon at Night (Venice), Saybold, 1930s, 500 pcs, EXIB........... 110.00
Little Convalescent, Parker Bros, 1931, 385 pcs, EX in G box 225.00
Moses in Bulrushes, plywood, Parker Bros, 1930s, 12x16½", EXIB 150.00
My Garden Is a Glory, plywood, Strauss, 15½" dia, EXIB.............. 50.00
Out for a Sail, plywood, Parker Bros, 1932, 7x10", EXIB 50.00
Pride of the Litter, plywood, Strauss, 1930s, EXIB........................ 60.00

Santa, three puzzles included, Milton-Bradley, 19x13", NMIB, $3,165.00. (Photo courtesy Morphy Auctions)

St Nicholas, Santa & reindeer, McLoughlin Bros, NY, 1890, EXIB...650.00
Trouble on the Trail, cb, Tuco/Deluxe, 1940s, 15x19½", EXIB 16.00
Twilight Express, cb litho, Milton Bradley, EX in 18x13" litho box ...225.00
Union Forever, litho wood, HM Zeller, 1967, in slide-lid box 375.00
Washington at Valley Forge, plywood, Strauss, 1930s, 9x12", EXIB .. 25.00
White Squadron, McLoughlin Bros, 1892, 9½x9½", NMIB......... 375.00

Pyrography

Pyrography, also known as wood burning, Flemish art, or poker work, is the art of burning designs into wood or leather and has been practiced over the centuries in many countries.

In the late 1800s pyrography became the hot new hobby for thousands of Americans who burned designs inspired by the popular artists of the day including Mucha, Gibson, Fisher, and Corbett. Thousands of wooden boxes, wall plaques, novelties, and pieces of furniture that they purchased from local general stores or from mail-order catalogs were burned and painted. These pieces were manufactured by companies such as The Flemish Art Company of New York and Thayer & Chandler of

Chicago, who printed the designs on wood for the pyrographers to burn. This Victorian fad developed into a new form of artistic expression as the individually burned and painted pieces reflected the personality of the pyrographers. The more adventurous started to burn between the lines and developed a style of 'allover burning' that today is known as pyromania. Others not only created their own designs but even made the pieces to be decorated. Both these developments are particularly valued today as true examples of American folk art. By the 1930s its popularity had declined. Like Mission furniture, it was neglected by generations of collectors and dealers. The recent appreciation of Victoriana, the Arts and Crafts Movement, the American West, and the popularity of turn-of-the-century graphic art has rekindled interest in pyrography which embraces all these styles.

Key: hb — hand burned

Bedroom set, hb/pnt, Wm Rogers/Forusville PA, 1904-07, 3-pc ...4,000.00
Box, flatware; factory burned/pnt poinsettias, Rogers, 9x11x5".... 195.00
Box, hb/pnt lady petting horse amid flowers, 1920s, 1⅛x13x4½"... 70.00
Box, lady w/flowing hair, Flemish Art Co, 1909, 11¼x4¼" 120.00
Box, Miller Bros Steel Pens, 1900, stamped to look hb, 7" L, +contents.. 45.00
Catalog, Thayer-Chandler, Chicago, 1904, 92 pgs, 12 in full color...27.00
Checker/backgammon brd, red & gr decor/glass bead insets, 30x15" . 1,550.00

Checker board, 'America's Champion, C.F. Barker,' dated 1905, hinged, 15x15", $475.00. (Photo courtesy Garth's Auctions Inc.)

Chest, blanket; hb/pnt swans/lady's head/flower/etc, ca 1890....... 850.00
Cue holder, hb pool-hall scene, folk art, unique 650.00
Etching set, Snow White, Disney/Marks, 1938, electric pen, complete ... 175.00
Frame, hb/pnt cherries, standing type, 7½x6", EX 85.00
Frame, owls in tree, 2 Is Company, 2 oval cutouts 145.00
Humidor, trees & landscape on lid, gold & bl pnt on pine, 3x9x6".. 295.00
Knife rack, hb Lizzie Borden w/axe, 5 hooks below, rare............... 550.00
Mirror, hand; grapes, 1920s, 8½x4½" 65.00
Mirror, hand; hb/pnt lady's head w/flowing hair, 13¼x6¾"........... 180.00
Panel, basswood, burned/pnt orange, Thayer-Chandler, 16x30"..465.00
Pedestal, hb/pnt Nouveau flowers & vines, 45" 400.00
Ping-Pong paddle, Gibson girl, ca 1905, 11¼x5½" 160.00
Plaque, cvd/burned/pnt strawberry basket, 3-ply, 12" dia............... 70.00
Plaque, girl bathing puppies, #854, 14½" 125.00
Plaque, Nouveau lady w/cherries, 19½"..................................... 150.00
Plaque, Oddfellows, hb IOOF in center, early 1900s, 16x10"........ 87.00
Ribbon holder, hb/pnt Sunbonnet babies (3), 5x12".................... 160.00
Screen, birds & foliage, mc pnt, 3-part, 63x73" 400.00
Table, hb/pnt daisies & scrolls, lower shelf, 16½x11x11" 315.00
Tie rack, factory stamp, HP soldier/nurse/sailor, WWI motto 125.00

Quezal

The Quezal Art Glass and Decorating Company of Brooklyn, New York, was founded in 1901 by Martin Bach. A former Tiffany employee, Bach's glass closely resembled that of his former employer. Most pieces were signed 'Quezal,' a name taken from a Central American bird. After Bach's death in 1920, his son-in-law, Conrad Vohlsing, continued to produce a Quezal-type glass in Elmhurst, New York, which he marked 'Lustre Art Glass.' Examples listed here are signed unless noted otherwise.

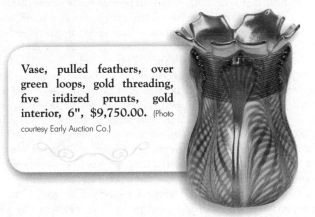

Vase, pulled feathers, over green loops, gold threading, five iridized prunts, gold interior, 6", $9,750.00. (Photo courtesy Early Auction Co.)

Compote, floriform; feathers, gr w/gold on opal, stretched rim, 5".. 1,800.00
Cup & saucer, gold, loop hdl w/curlicue at base, 4", +saucer........ 365.00
Finger bowl, gold, optic ribs, scalloped rim, +6" underplate......... 300.00
Finger bowl, gold, optic ribs, shouldered/tapered w/everted rim, 4".. 230.00
Shade, feathers, dk on lt gr w/allover platinum zipper decor, 8" .. 2,700.00
Shade, feathers, gr on gold, gold int, flared tulip shape, 5" 270.00
Shade, feathers, gr w/gold tips on opal, optic ribs, lily form, 9" 635.00
Shade, feathers, gr/gold on opal, ruffled, 4¾" 335.00
Shade, feathers, gr/gold on wht, gold int, ovoid w/flared rim, 6".. 300.00
Shade, gold, bowl form w/ruffled rim, 5" dia 240.00
Shade, hall; feathers, gr/gold on wht, scalloped, 12x4".............. 1,955.00
Sherbet, Coil, bl on gold, 3¼x3¾" 345.00
Vase, Agate, red-amethyst shoulders & bottom, chartreuse center, 7".. 3,200.00
Vase, bl irid, bulbous w/flaring flat rim, 6" 520.00
Vase, bl irid, elongated w/disk ft, 7" 480.00
Vase, bud; gold cylinder in metal holder w/3-leaf support & ft, 8" ..285.00
Vase, bud; gold w/amethyst highlights, scalloped/flared top, 6".... 515.00
Vase, Coil, bl on opal, gold int, cylinder w/incurvate rim, 6¾".... 1,035.00
Vase, feathers, gold on opal, gr/gold feathers on doughnut rim, 4"..1,440.00
Vase, feathers, gold/gr on opal, dripped gold extends to waist, 6" .. 2,300.00
Vase, feathers, gr/gold on opal, appl gold seashell drippings, 5½" ..6,300.00
Vase, feathers, gr/tan/gold on opal, ruffled w/doughnut ft, 5" .. 2,500.00
Vase, feathers/coils, gr/gold on opal, long gold neck w/feathers, 7"...6,600.00
Vase, feathers/hooks, gold/gr on ivory gold int, squat w/long neck, 9" .. 1,800.00
Vase, floriform; feathers, gr on cream, zipper ft, gold int, 7" 3,165.00
Vase, gold, slim trumpet form in bronze ft emb w/entwined snakes, 19"..3,165.00
Vase, gold w/bl highlights, appl silver floral trim, D1198, 9" 800.00
Vase, gr w/bl irid, shouldered, 7" 690.00
Vase, hooked swirls, bl/yel on opal, gold int, shouldered/bulbous, 6"..1,650.00
Vase, jack-in-pulpit; feathers, bl on gold, optic ribs, 8" 1,500.00
Vase, lily; gold, 3-fold rim, ftd, #981, 4" 400.00

Quilts

Quilts, though a very practical product, nevertheless represent an art form which expresses the character and the personality of the designer. During the seventeenth and eighteenth centuries, quilts were considered a necessary part of a bride's hope chest; the traditional number required to be properly endowed for marriage was a 'baker's dozen'! American colonial quilts reflect the English and French taste of our ancestors. They would include the classifications known as Lindsey-Woolsey and the central medallion applique quilts fashioned from imported copper-plate printed fabrics.

By 1829 spare time was slightly more available, so women gathered in quilting bees. This not only was a way of sharing the work but also gave them the opportunity to show off their best handiwork. The hand-dyed and pieced quilts emerged, and they are now known as sampler, album, and friendship quilts. By 1845 American printed fabric was available.

In 1793 Eli Whitney developed the cotton gin; as a result, textile production in America became industrialized. Soon inexpensive fabrics were readily available, and ladies were able to choose from colorful prints and solids to add contrast to their work. Both pieced and appliqued work became popular. Pieced quilts were considered utilitarian, while appliqued quilts were shown with pride of accomplishment at the fair or used when itinerant preachers traveled through and stayed for a visit. Today many collectors prize pieced quilts and their intricate geometric patterns above all other types. Many of these designs were given names: Daisy and Oak Leaf, Grandmother's Flower Garden, Log Cabin, and Ocean Wave are only a few. Appliqued quilts involved stitching one piece — carefully cut into a specific form such as a leaf, a flower, or a stylized device — onto either a large one-piece ground fabric or an individual block. Often the background fabric was quilted in a decorative pattern such as a wreath or medallions. Amish women scorned printed calicos as 'worldly' and instead used colorful blocks set with black fabrics to produce a stunning pieced effect. To show their reverence for God, the Amish would often include a 'superstition' block which represented the 'imperfection' of Man!

One of the most valuable quilts in existence is the Baltimore album quilt. Made between 1840 and 1860 only 300 or so still exist today. They have been known to fetch over $100,000.00 at prominent auction houses in New York City. Usually each block features elaborate applique work such as a basket of flowers, patriotic flags and eagles, the Oddfellow's heart in hand, etc. The border can be sawtooth, meandering, or swags and tassels.

During the Victorian, period the crazy quilt emerged. This style became the most popular quilt ever in terms of sheer numbers produced. The crazy quilt was formed by random pieces put together following no organized lines and was usually embellished by elaborate embroidery stitches. Fabrics of choice were brocades, silks, and velvets.

Another type of quilting, highly prized and rare today, is trapunto. These quilts were made by first stitching the outline of the design onto a solid sheet of fabric which was backed with a second having a much looser weave. White was often favored, but color was sometimes used for accent. The design (grapes, flowers, leaves, etc.) was padded through openings made by separating the loose weave of the underneath fabric; a backing was added and the three layers quilted as one.

Besides condition, value is judged on intricacy of pattern, color effect, and craftsmanship. Examine the stitching. Quality quilts have from 10 to 12 stitches to the inch. A stitch is defined as any time a needle pierces through the fabric. So you may see five threads but 10 (stitches) have been used. In the listings that follow, examples rated excellent have minor defects, otherwise assume them to be free of any damage, soil, or wear. Also assume that all the stitching is hand done; any machine work will be noted. Values given here are auction results; retail may be somewhat higher. For more information we recommend *Vintage Quilts, Identifying, Collecting, Dating, Preserving, and Valuing*, by Bobbie Aug, Sharon Newman, and Gerald Roy.

Key: ms — machine sewn   qlt — quilted, quilting

Amish

Basket, cotton sateen, blk qlt, OH, 1923, lt stains, 90x65" 575.00
Hole in the Barn Door, rows of dmns, bl/purple/blk, MO, 1940, 58x84" . 175.00
Irish Triple Chain, bl/purple, 2 borders, ms but hand qlt, 52x40".. 575.00
OH Star w/Pinwheel center, mc mixed fabrics, early 20th C, 82x72"... 750.00
Scraps patchwork pattern, bl/gray/lav/purple, grid qlt, 90x78" 360.00
Sm Dmns, brn/bl/gr/blk, cotton/wool, MO, 1950s, 80x60" 520.00
Sunshine & Shadow, mc cottons, blk plumes/dmns qlt, 78x78" .. 375.00
Triangular patchwork w/pinwheel flowers on blk, bl borders, 35x35" ... 360.00

Appliqued

Acorn & Leaf, gr & brn on wht cotton, OH/1844, 96x93" 2,750.00
Basket, mc w/bl Star calico border, bl Star bk, stain, 1880s, 34x27" ... 360.00
Brick Walk Path, mc cottons, machine binding, striped bk, 1890s, lg .. 780.00
Cherry trees & yel birds, embr details, patterned qlt, 92x80" 695.00
Cockscombs & Urns, floral wreaths/vine borders, hearts/rosettes qlt, EX . 800.00

Double Six-Point Star and Floral, chintz and calico prints, designs stuffed and appliqued to white cotton ground, ca. 1842, 135x125", $18,800.00.
(Photo courtesy Skinner Inc. Auctioneers & Appraisers of Antiques & Fine Art)

Flowers, 7 staggered rows, red/br on wht, vine border, 1850s 575.00
Hawaiian Pineapple, cream w/gr central medallion, ca 1900, 93x94"... 600.00
Irish Chain, mc on red w/dbl border, brn calico bk, 1880s, full sz.... 780.00
NC Lily, mc on 34 wht blocks set on diagonal, floral border, 86x86" .. 925.00
Pomegranates among gr foliage, red/yel/wht, patterned qlt, 80x76" ... 550.00
President's Wreath, mc on wht pieced sqs, vine border, 86x86" . 2,750.00
Stars (12), mc on bl ground, dbl border, PA, 1900s, 82x82" 660.00
Sunflowers, mc on wht, fine qlt, pencil mks, 90x72" 540.00
Tulips in urns/vines, EX qlt, red border (some period rprs), 83x70".. 960.00
Wreath (16), swag border, mc cotton solids, ca 1900, 85x84" ... 1,750.00

Mennonite

Bricks, bk: Bars, cotton, PA, 190, 79x79", VG 445.00
Evening Stars, red & gold on dk gr, calico bk, 1880s, 85x85", VG.. 540.00
Penny, 4½" mc circles, wool & cotton, feather qlt, 1880s, 77x68" ... 1,550.00
Star Medallion, red & yel, initials, PA, 1880s, full sz, VG........... 480.00
Trip Around the World, mc cottons, gr bking, PA, 88x75" 540.00
Variable Stars, mc w/red/gr border, chambray/calico bk, 1890s, 75x72" ... 600.00

Pieced

Album, 25 signature sqs w/red border, 1870s, 84x83" 1,800.00
Album Cross, red on wht, dmns/hex motif qlt, unwashed, 91x76"..360.00
Alternating sqs w/star centers, mc prints/red/yel, plaid bk, 75x70"... 330.00
Basket, mc w/red ground, chintz border, PA, 1900s, full sz 1,080.00
Baskets, red & yel, signature, ca 1900, 86x85", EX...................... 480.00
Baskets (tiny), mc scraps, gr bk, ca 1880s, 91x90", VG 850.00
Broken Dishes, mc silks w/zigzag border, 70x72", VG................... 420.00
Broken Star w/Zigzag Border, red & tan on wht, bl binding, 81x79"... 795.00
Carpenter's Star, red/yel/gr, ca 1880, unused, 97x94" 2,000.00
Court House Steps Log Cabin Variation, mc wools, 1870s, full sz...600.00
Dbl 6-Point Star w/floral applique, cotton/calicos, 1840s, 134x125" ..21,000.00
Dmn patchwork w/maroon floral bk, PA, 1890s, full sz 360.00
Drunkard's Path, red & wht, 2 borders, red binding, 1891, 82x80" 550.00
Eagle/shield/stars, red/wht/bl w/applique, pattern qlt, 1940s, 74x66" . 670.00
Irish Chain, cotton prints, gr border/yel binding, circle qlt, 81x82"...360.00
Joseph's Coat of Many Colors, red/bls/grs/yels, PA, 1880s, 82x81" ... 2,700.00
Log Cabin, mc w/yel border, ca 1890s, full sz 330.00
Log Cabin Courthouse Steps, red/lilac w/brn border, machine qlt, 1900.460.00

Log Cabin Variation, brn & wht w/brn bk, PA, 1890s, 92x91" 960.00
Lone Star, mc calicos, printed foliage border, 84x84", EX 300.00
Lone Star, mc cotton solids, printed bk, EX qlt, ca 1894, 80x82"....420.00
Mariner's Compass, mc, appliqued to yel bkground, 1890s, 73x72" ...540.00
Mariner's Compass, mc, overall fading/deterioration, 1840s, 100x99", G..720.00
Mc cotton prints in sqs alternate w/red print strips, ms, 90x82"... 310.00
Robbing Peter To Pay Paul, bl & wht glazed cotton, 86x80" 670.00
Rolling Stone, mc w/bl/red/gr calico borders, ca 1900, 99x98" 540.00
Rolling Stone, red & yel calicos/mc, sgn/1852, sm stain, VG ...1,020.00
Sawtooth, red & wht, vine w/feather qlt, 82x82" 625.00
Star of Bethlehem, mc cotton prints, brn border, patterned qlt, 92x91"...600.00
Star of Bethlehem, mc cotton sateen on gr, feather qlt, 20th C, 72x74" ..1,050.00
Stars, mc on pk w/gr sashing, ms, 84x70", NM 550.00
Stars Upon Stars, mc cotton prints, feathered wreath qlt, 1893, 90x88"..720.00
Stars/triangles, navy/wht, triple border, qlt plumes, 81x76" 550.00
Streak of Lightning, paisley bk, wool/cotton, PA, 1900, 73x81" ..400.00
Touching Stars, mc calicos, late 19th C, 91x89" 1,450.00
Triangles w/Zigzag border, PA, crib sz, 38x38" 840.00
Trip Around the World, mc cottons, 1890s, 83x82", EX 1,140.00
Triple Irish Chain, bl/red/gr, mc qlt, 1880s, unused, 84x83" 720.00
Variable Star/Flying Geese, bl/wht, qlt dmns/floral, stain/rpr, 74x68" ... 360.00
Wild Goose Chase, dbl sawtooth border, NY State, 1880s, 104x102", G.. 320.00
Zigzags, mc & red prints, dbl pk border, slight fading, 84x83"...... 375.00
4-Patch in 10-Patch, red & bl X pattern, PA, NM 840.00
4-Patch in 9-Patch, scrap style, PA, ca 1890, 79x79", VG 420.00
9-Patch, mc prints, brn print border/bk, clamshell qlt, stain, 84x76" .. 360.00

Quimper

Quimper pottery bears the name of the Breton town in northwestern France where it has been made for over 300 years. Production began in 1690 when Jean-Baptiste Bousquet settled into a small workshop in the suburbs of Quimper, at Locmaria. There he began to make the hand-painted, tin enamel-glazed earthenware which we know today as faience. By the last quarter of the nineteenth century, there were three factories working concurrently: Porquier, de la Hubaudiere (the Grand Maison), and Henriot. All three houses produced similar wares which were decorated with scenes from the everyday life of the peasant folk of the region. Their respective marks are an AP or a P with an intersecting B (similar to a clover), an HB, and an HR (which became HenRiot after litigation in 1922). The most desirable pieces were produced during the last quarter of the nineteenth century through the first quarter of the twentieth century. These are considered to be artistically superior to the examples made after World War I and II with the exception of the Odetta line, which is now experiencing a renaissance among collectors here and abroad.

Most of what was made was faience, but there was also a history of utilitarian gres ware (stoneware) having been produced there. In 1922 the Grande Maison HB revitalized this ware and introduced the line called Odetta, examples of which seemed to embody the bold spirit of the Art Deco style. The companion faience pieces of this period and genre are classified as Modern Movement examples and frequently bear the name of the artist who designed the mold. These artist-signed examples are dramatically increasing in value.

Currently there are two factories still producing Quimper pottery. La Societe Nouvelle des Faienceries de Quimper is owned by Sarah and Paul Jenessens along with a group of American investors. Their mark is a stamped HB-Henriot logo. The other, La Faiencerie d'art Breton, is operated by the direct descendents of the de la Hubaudiere and Henriot families. Their pieces are marked with an interlocked F and A conjoined with an inverted B. Other marks include HQF which is the Henriot Quimper France mark and HBQ, the HB Quimper mark. If you care to learn more about Quimper, we recommend *Quimper Pottery: A French Folk Art Faience* by Sandra V. Bondhus, our advisor for this category, whose address can be found in the Directory under Connecticut.

Benitier, Vierge et l'Enfant, Porquier, 8" 300.00
Bottle, snuff; man w/pipe/floral sprays, book shape, HB, 2¾x3" ... 250.00
Bowl, red petals/bl dots in garland, geometric center, HBQ, 1½x4" ..20.00
Box, lady w/basket, flow bl acanthus border, shield shape, HBQ, 4½" ..200.00
Cache pot, Breton couple/flower garlands, HenRiot 76, 5x8", EX ..230.00
Candy box, peasant man w/pipe/forest/Crest of Britany, HR 10, 3½x5" ..250.00
Chamberstick, Breton w/flower branch, att AP, sq, 5", NM 160.00
Charger, geometric snowflakes, bl tones, HQ 90, 11¼" 80.00
Coffeepot, Breton man w/pipe/Crest of Brittany/ermine tails, HB, 9" ..225.00
Compote, Mistletoe (hdls), couple in meadow, HRQ, 11½x7" 400.00
Creamer, peasant lady/floral sprays, HR 8, 3½", NM 50.00
Figurine, Breton man w/bagpipes, HBQ, flake, 3¼" 125.00
Figurine, man w/bottle assisted by wife, A Galland, pk clay, 3¼" .. 250.00

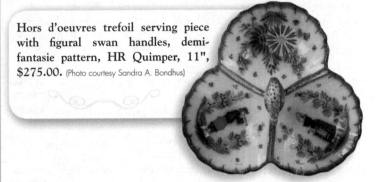

Hors d'oeuvres trefoil serving piece with figural swan handles, demi-fantasie pattern, HR Quimper, 11", $275.00. (Photo courtesy Sandra A. Bondhus)

Inkwell, dbl; grandmother w/pipe, bagpipe form, decor riche, HR, 7x7"..500.00
Inkwell, dbl; man w/cup, demi-fantasie, HQF 95, 3½x6¾" 250.00
Jardiniere, girl seated w/flowers, loop hdls, ftd, HB, 5x9" L 300.00
Jardiniere, lady/musician, demi-fantasie, swan figural, HQF 95, 4" .. 150.00
Jardiniere, pique fleurs chest w/false drws, HRQ, sm rpr.............1,350.00
Match holder, Breton musician, envelope shape, unmk, 4½x2¼"...155.00
Menu card holder, Breton crest/ermine tails, scalloped 175.00
Pipe rack, bagpipe form w/4 openings, Crest of Brittany, HQF 75, 10"...350.00
Pitcher, sponged fir tree/bl dots & sponging, HBQ, doll sz, 2½"..... 50.00
Plate, bl croisille lattice/stars/mc bands, HBQ, ca 1900, 9⅛" 125.00
Plate, Breton man (lady), 12-pointed rim, HenRiot, 8½", pr 450.00
Plate, butterfly, a la touche bands, HBQ, 7" 175.00
Plate, crab among branches, cobalt border, HRQ, 8¾" 850.00
Plate, delphiniums/roses/bird, linear border, HB (early), 8" 350.00
Plate, lady w/grasses ea side/floral sprays, HQ 123, 8½" 80.00
Plate, luncheon; naive man w/glass, HB, 19th C, 7¾" 100.00
Plate, piper between flower branches, curled rim, HR, 8x6"......... 300.00
Plate, Sevellec Breton Life, peasants & church, HQ 133, 9½" 200.00
Platter, facing peasant couple, decor riche, HQ, 17¾x13", NM ... 300.00
Platter, peasant couple & fir tree, HBQ, 11x8" 200.00
Tray, couple w/basket & pipe, decor riche, hdls, HB, 11", NM 160.00
Tray, man w/flute, demi-fantasie, hdls, HQF 96, 8½" 75.00
Trivet, Breton musicians, decor riche, HRQ, sq, 9¾" 225.00
Trivet, peasant man, florals w/bluets, gr sponging, HQF 122, EX .. 100.00
Vase, Breton w/walking stick/crest, fleur-de-lis shape, HR, 10x6", EX .325.00
Vase, peasant lady/Crest of Brittany/fleur-de-lis, HR, 8x7"........... 475.00
Vase, tulipiere; lady w/chevrette, ermine tails, 3-tube, HB, 7x7"... 145.00
Wall pocket, demi-fantasie lady, bagpipe form, HRQ, 10½"......... 200.00
Wall pocket, man w/horn & flower, conical, 19th C, 10½" 180.00
Wall pocket, peasant couple/a la touche border, dbl cone, unmk, 11x7"..400.00

Radford, Alfred

Pottery associated with Albert Radford (1882 – 1904) can be categorized by three periods of production. Pottery produced in Tiffin, Ohio,

(1896 – 1899) consists of bone china (no marked examples known) and high-quality jasperware with applied Wedgwood-like cameos. Tiffin jasperware is often impressed 'Radford Jasper' in small block letters. At Zanesville, Ohio, Radford jasperware was marked only with an incised, two-digit shape number, and the cameos were not applied but rather formed within the mold and filled with a white slip. Zanesville Radford ware was produced for only a few months before the Radford pottery was acquired by the Arc-en-Ciel company in 1903. Production in Zanesville was handled by Radford's father, Edward (1840 – 1910), who remained in Zanesville after Albert moved to Clarksburg, West Virginia, where the Radford Pottery Co. was completed shortly before Albert's death in 1904. Jasperware was not produced in Clarksburg, and the molds appear to have been left in Zanesville, where some were subsequently used by the Arc-en-Ciel pottery. The Clarksburg, West Virginia, pottery produced a standard glaze, slip-decorated ware, Ruko; Thera and Velvety, matt glazed ware often signed by Albert Haubrich, Alice Bloomer, and other artists; and Radura, a semimatt green glaze developed by Albert Radford's son, Edward. The Clarksburg plant closed in 1912.

Jardiniere, Ruko, poppies, hdls, #207-12, 16" W 285.00
Jardiniere & pedestal, Ruko, poppies, rpr, 30" 735.00
Lamp base, Jasper, cherubs w/instruments, #14, 6¾" 135.00
Vase, floor; simple floral, bl/rose on olive, minor rim flakes, 22" .. 635.00
Vase, Jasper, A Lincoln medallion, bk: eagle, #12, 7" 350.00
Vase, Jasper, cherubs/eagles, wht on lt olive, #23, 9½", NM......... 230.00
Vase, Jasper, 2 cherubs w/lion, lt gr w/dk brn lava top/base, #15, 7" ...165.00
Vase, lg mums, wht/lt bl on soft olive gr, sgn A Haubrich, 13x7".. 920.00
Vase, Thera, gooseberries/leaves, pk/bl on gr matt, TC/#1455, 11x4"...535.00
Vase, Thera, lg standing egret, wht on mint gr, A Haubrich, #1452, 14"... 1,200.00
Vase, Velvety, berries/leaves on dk gr, A Haubrich, bottle form, 11x4" ..575.00
Vase, Velvety, blackberries/leaves on dk gr, A Haubrich, 11x4"... 540.00
Vase, Velvety, heron in stream, wht on dk bl, A Haubrich, 20" .. 3,850.00

Vase, Velvety, white mums on bright matt blue with gold highlights in background, signed Albert Haubrich, 14", $2,675.00.
(Photo courtesy Cincinnati Art Galleries)

Radios

Vintage radios are very collectible. There were thousands of styles and types produced, the most popular of which today are the breadboard and the cathedral. Consoles are usually considered less marketable, since their size makes them hard to display and store. For those wishing to learn more about the subject, we recommend *Collector's Guide to Antique Radios* by John Slusser and the staff of Radio Daze, available through Collector Books.

Unless otherwise noted in the descriptions, values are given for working radios in near mint to mint condition. Our advisor for this category is Dr. E. E. Taylor; he is listed in the Directory under Indiana. See also Plastics.

Key:
BC — broadcast　　　　　　　　R/P — radio-phonograph
b/o — battery-operated　　　　　s/r — slide rule
LW — long wave　　　　　　　　SW — short wave
pb — push button　　　　　　　tbl/m — table model
phono — phonograph

Acratone, 1938, cathedral, wood, BC, from $300 to 350.00
Addison, A2A, tbl/m, plastic Deco style, BC, 1940, from $300 to.. 350.00
Adler, 325, console, wood, BC, 1930, from $150 to 180.00
Admiral, AZ593, console, wood, BC, 1936, from $75 to 85.00
Admiral, 218, portable, leatherette, BC, 1958, from $35 to.......... 45.00
Aetna, 500, tombstone, wood, BC, SW, 1935, from $90 to......... 110.00
Airline, 14BR-514B, tbl/m, pnt plastic, Deco, BC, 1941, from $85 to.. 105.00
Airline, 84KR-2510A, end table, wood, BC, 1948, from $85 to.... 95.00
American Bosch, 46, Little Six tbl/m, walnut, BC, from $150 to.... 160.00
Arvin, 40, Mighty Mite tbl/m, metal, BC, 1938, from $85 to 95.00
Arvin, 952P1, portable, plastic, BC, 1956, from $30 to................. 35.00
Atwater Kent, 60, console, wood, BC, 1929, from $200 to 230.00

Atwater Kent, #82 cathedral, wood with Gothic cutouts, twisted columns, broadcast, 1922, from $440.00 to $500.00. (Photo courtesy John Slusser and the staff of Radio Daze)

Atwater Kent, 206, cathedral, wood, BC, SW, 1934, from $380 to.. 430.00
Belmont, 6D111, tbl/m, streamline, plastic, BC, 1946, from $150 to.. 180.00
Bendix, 55L3U, tbl/m, plastic, BC, from $45 to 55.00
Bulova, 100, tbl/m, clock-radio, plastic, BC, 1957, from $40 to..... 50.00
Coronado, 1070A, tbl/m, wood, BC, SW, 1940, from $65 to......... 75.00
Crosley, 7H2, tombstone, wood, BC, SW, 1934, from $150 to..... 180.00
Crosley, 25AY, console, walnut, BC, SW, 1940, from $130 to 160.00
Crosley, 167, cathedral, wood, BC, SW, 1936, from $180 to........ 200.00
Delco, R-1228, tbl/m, plastic, BC, 1947, from $55 to.................... 65.00
Detrola, 4D, cathedral, wood, BC, 1934, from $200 to 230.00
Dewald, 615, tbl/m, wood, BC, SW, 1935, from $75 to................. 85.00
Emerson, F-133, tbl/m, 2-tone wood, BC, SW, 1936, from $95 to ..115.00
Emerson, 45, tombstone, walnut, BC, SW, 1934, from $120 to...... 150.00
Emerson, 54, tbl/m, plastic Deco style, BC, 1940, from $85 to 105.00
Emerson, 263W, tbl/m, plastic, BC, 1936, from $85 to................. 115.00
Emerson, 358, tbl/m, wood, BC, SW, 1937, from $75 to 95.00
Emerson, 511, Moderne tbl/m, plastic, BC, 1946, from $55 to....... 65.00
Eveready, 1, tbl/m, gumwood w/maple finish, BC, 1927, from $120 to... 150.00
Farnsworth, GT-050, tbl/m, plastic Deco style, BC, 1948, from $120 to.. 150.00
General Electric, J-72, cathedral, wood, BC, 1932, from $200 to....230.00
General Electric, K-105, console, wood, BC, SW, 1933, from $150 to... 180.00
General Electric, 636, portable, plastic, BC, b/o, 1955, from $35 to .. 40.00
Kadette, S947, Kadette Jr tbl/m, plastic, BC, 1933, from $320 to ...350.00
Knight, 68B-151K, tbl/m, wood, BC, b/o, from $50 to 65.00
Lafayette, M31-71, cathedral, wood, BC, 1935, from $140 to...... 160.00
Majestic, 31, cathedral, walnut, BC, 1931, from $240 to 270.00
Majestic, 463, Century Six tbl/m, walnut, BC, 1933, from $200 to ...230.00
Majestic, 886, Park Avenue console, BC, SW, 1933, from $800 to.. 900.00
Motorola, 48L11Q, portable, plastic, BC, 1949, from $35 to 45.00
Motorola, 57R4, tbl/m, pk plastic, BC, 1957, from $75 to 85.00

Philco, 17B, cathedral, wood, BC, SW, 1933, from $240 to 300.00
Philco, 38-4XX, console, wood, BC, SW, 1938, from $120 to 150.00
Philco, 39-71T, portable, cloth-covered, BC, b/o, 1939, from $30 to 35.00
Philco, 41-290X, console, wood, BC, SW, 1941, from $120 to 140.00
Philco, 71B, cathedral, wood, BC, 1932, from $240 to 300.00
Philco, 655B, tombstone, wood, BC, SW, 1936, from $130 to 150.00
RCA, 9K1, console, wood, BC, SW, 1936, from $120 to 150.00
RCA, 15X, tbl/m, mahog plastic, BC, 1940, from $40 to 50.00
RCA, 103, tombstone, wood, BC, SW, 1934, from $85 to 95.00
Silvertone, 1403, cathedral, wood, BC, 1931, from $270 to 300.00
Silvertone, 2005, tbl/m, red plastic, BC, 1953, from $20 to 25.00
Silvertone, 7050, console, wood, BC, SW, 1941, from $120 to.... 140.00
Westinghouse, H-138, console-R/P, wood, BC, SW, 1946, from $75 to... 85.00
Westinghouse, H-474T5, portable, plastic, BC, b/o, 1955, from $35 to ... 40.00
Westinghouse, WR-6, console, wood, BC, 1930, from $120 to.... 150.00
Zenith, G-516W, tbl/m, plastic, BC, 1950, from $45 to 50.00
Zenith, K-731, tbl/m, wood, BC, FM, 1963, from $40 to............... 50.00
Zenith, 5-R-216, tbl/m, wood, BC, 1937, from $120 to............... 140.00
Zenith, 6-D-612 W, tbl/m, wht plastic, BC, 1942, from $50 to 65.00
Zenith, 6-S-152, console, wood, BC, SW, 1936, from $240 to 270.00

Catalin/Bakelite Radios

Addison, A2A, tbl/m, BC, 1940, from $300 to............................. 350.00
Addison, B-2E, tbl/m, mahog & ivory, 10½", EX.......................... 500.00
Addison, R5-A1, tbl/m, burgundy & butterscotch, 10", VG........ 360.00
Admiral, 4L28, tbl/m, BC, 1958, from $20 to.............................. 50.00
Air Castle, 106B, tbl/m, streamline, BC, 1947, from $120 to....... 150.00
Air King, 66, tombstone, BC, 1935, minimum value 3,000.00
Airline, 14BR-514B, tbl/m, pnt, BC, 1941, from $85 to 105.00
Bendix, 526C, tbl/m, Catalin, gr/blk, BC, 1946, minimum value ...650.00
Crosley, V, tbl/m, wood/Bakelite, BC, 1922, from $240 to 300.00
DeWald, A-501, tbl/m, butterscotch, 10", VG+ 300.00
Emerson, AU-190, tombstone, Catalin, BC, SW, 1938, minimum value ... 1,200.00
Fada, L-56, tbl/m, gr & butterscotch, 9", EX................................ 1,200.00
Fada, 53, tbl/m, Catalin, BC, 1938, minimum value 900.00
Fada, 115, tbl/m, butterscotch & red, bullet form, 10½", EX..... 1,200.00
Fada, 652, tbl/m, butterscotch w/ivory knobs, 11", EX 385.00
Fada, 1000, tbl/m, butterscotch on butterscotch case, bullet form, EX....1,200.00
Fada, 1000, tbl/m, maroon & butterscotch, bullet form, 10½", EX... 1,100.00

Fada Model 1000, maroon with butterscotch trim, 10½" wide, VG, $920.00. (Photo courtesy Tom Harris Auctions)

Garod, 6AU1, tbl/m, red w/butterscotch grille & knobs, 11½", EX 800.00
Stewart Warner, 62T-36, marbleized & butterscotch, 13", EX 525.00

Novelty Radios

Archie, jukebox shape, Vanity Fair, 1977, 6", M 50.00
Bullwinkle, 1969, 12", NM.. 150.00

Casper the Friendly Ghost, Harvey Cartoons/Sutton, 1972 .... 50.00
Charlie McCarthy, brn Bakelite w/Charlie on front, Majestic, 1930s, EX...500.00
Dick Tracy, Creative Creations, wristband type, 1970s, AM, EX 225.00
Hopalong Cassidy, red, electric, Arvin, 1950s, model #441T, EX...350.00
Incredible Hulk, Marvel Comics, 1978, 7"....................................... 75.00
King Kong, Amico, 1986, 13", M... 35.00
Masters of the Universe, mouth moves w/music, 5½", EX+ 50.00
R2-D2 Robot, Kenner, figural, AM, MIB...................................... 150.00
Snoopy Doghouse, Determined, 1970s, 6x4", NMIB..................... 55.00
Snow White & the Seven Dwarfs, Emerson, 1938, 8x8", VG...... 500.00
Superman Exiting Phone Booth, Vanity Fair, 1970s, b/o, AM, EX+.... 50.00

Transistor Radios

Post-World War II baby boomers, now in their fifties, are rediscovering prized possessions of youth, their pocket radios. The transistor wonders, born with rock 'n roll, were at the vanguard of miniaturization and futuristic design in the decade which followed their introduction to Christmas shoppers in 1954. The tiny receiving sets launched the growth of Texas Instruments and shortly to follow abroad, Sony and other Japanese giants.

The most desirable sets include the 1954 four-transistor Regency TR-1 and colorful early Sony and Toshiba models. Certain pre-1960 models by Hoffman and Admiral represented the earliest practical use of solar technology and are also highly valued. To avoid high tariffs, scores of two-transistor sets, boys' radios, were imported from Japan with names like Pet and Charmy. Many early inexpensive transistor sets could be heard only with an earphone. The smallest sets are known as shirt-pocket models while those slightly larger are called coat-pockets. Early collectible transistor radios all have civil defense triangle markings at 640 and 1240 on the frequency dial and nine or fewer transistors. Very few desirable sets were made after 1963. Model numbers are most commonly found inside.

Admiral, 4P21, horizontal, 4 transistors, AM, 1957, from $50 to.....60.00
Admiral, 7M12, horizontal, 7 transistors, AM, 1958, from $50 to ...60.00
Airline, GEN-1207A, horizontal, 8 transistors, AM, 1961, from $20 to.... 30.00
Bendix, 420, Navigator, horizontal, 9 transistors, AM 80.00
Cameo, 7866, horizontal, 7 transistors, AM, 1962 .... 40.00
Columbia, 400G, vertical, 4 transistors, AM, 1960 .... 55.00
Crosley, TR-333, vertical, 3 transistors, AM, 1959...................... 150.00
Delmonico, TR-7C, horizontal, w/watch, 7 transistors, AM, 1963 ..65.00
Emerson, 844, horizontal, leather, 6 transistors, AM, 1956............ 45.00
Emerson, 888, Titan, vertical, 8 transistors, AM, 1963 .... 80.00
General Electric, P831A, vertical, 6 transistors, AM, 1960 .... 30.00
Grundig, Transworld Ambassador, horizontal, AM 35.00
Harpers, 2TP-110, vertical, AM... 85.00
Hitachi, WH-822MB, horizontal, 8 transistors, AM, 1960 .... 35.00
ITT, 1011, horizontal, 10 transistors, AM, 1963............................ 25.00
Juliette, LR-57, lamp/radio, 7 transistors, AM, 1968 .... 35.00
Lafayette, FS-223, horizontal, 7 transistors, AM, 1962 .... 40.00
Maco, AB-175M, horizontal, 7 transistors, AM, 1962 .... 30.00
Mitsubishi, 6X-720, vertical, AM.. 55.00
Motorola, 6X28B, horizontal, 6 transistors, AM, 1959.................. 95.00

Motorola, 6X31C, AM, metal and plastic, 4x6½x2", $50.00. (Photo courtesy Sue and Marty Bunis)

Olympic, 771, horizontal, 6 transistors, AM, 1959 .... 75.00
RCA, 1-BT-32, Transicharg Deluxe, horizontal, 7 transistors, 1958...100.00
Realistic, 90L613, vertical, 9 transistors, AM 150.00
Realtone, TR-2021, horizontal, 10 transistors, AM, 1963 .... 30.00
Seminole, 1001, horizontal, 10 transistors, AM, 1963 .... 45.00
Sony, TFM-151, vertical, 15 transistors, AM/FM, 1959 .... 110.00
Sony, TR-624, horizontal, 6 transistors, AM, 1962 .... 50.00
Toshiba, 5TR-221, vertical, AM 275.00
United Royal, PTR-81B, vertical, 8 transistors, AM, 1962 .... 40.00
Westinghouse, H-588P7, horizontal, 7 transistors, AM, 1957........ 85.00
Zenith, Royal 500N, horizontal, AM, 1965 .... 45.00
Zenith, Royal 555, Sun Charger, horizontal, AM, 1966 .... 225.00

Railroadiana

Collecting railroad-related memorabilia has become one of America's most popular hobbies. The range of collectible items available is almost endless; not surprising, considering the fact that more than 185 different railroad lines are represented. Some collectors prefer to specialize in only one railroad, while others attempt to collect at least one item from every railway line known to have existed. For the advanced collector, there is the challenge of locating rarities from short-lived railroads; for the novice, there are abundant keys, buttons, and passes. Among the most popular specializations are dining-car collectibles — flatware, glassware, dinnerware, etc., in a wide variety of patterns and styles. Railroad blankets are also collectible. Most common are Pullman blankets. The early ones had a cross-stitch pattern; these were followed by one in a solid cinnamon color; both are marked clearly with the Pullman name. In the 1920s, Pullman put out a blue blanket marked Pullman, specifically for the use of Black porters. There is one in the Sacramento railroad museum. Other railroads had their own 'marked' blankets that are even more desirable, such as the Soo line, the Chessie, and one marked Pheasant (which was a private car on the Milwaukee Line that was reserved to carry special parties for hunting trips).

Another name among railroad dining collectors is Fred Harvey. (See information about a new book on this subject.) From 1893 until after WWII, Fred Harvey masterminded all the dining halls and dining cars on the Santa Fe Railroad System from Chicago to the west coast. (A little known fact, he also had dining facilities on the Frisco railroad.) He had his famous Harvey girls, as portrayed by Judy Garland, and a lot of personal dining china, silver, and linens marked with his 'FH.' Fred Harvey's operations, not heretofore known, extended well beyond WWII and into the 1960s, having dining facilities in California, Death Valley, and the east.

Berth keys have become scarce and expensive as more and more collectors purchase private rail cars. This is also true of 'window lifters,' specially designed pry bars made of wood used to ram the windows open in the old wood coaches. Most recently Otto Mears (of Silverton Colorado railroad fame) 1893 silver filigree railroad passes have surfaced. They are very scarce; made to the individual with possibly only 100 issued. These are appraised at $12,000.00 and have recently sold for near $11,000.00.

As is true in most collecting fields, scarcity and condition determine value. There is more interest in some railway lines than in others; generally speaking, it is greater in the region serviced by the particular railroad. American collectors prefer American-made products and items with ties to American railroads. For example, English switch lanterns, though of superior quality, usually sell at lower prices, as does memorabilia from Canadian railways such as Canadian Pacific or Canadian National.

Reproductions abound in railroadiana collectibles — from dinnerware and glassware to lanterns, keys, badges, belt buckles, timetables, and much more. Railroad police badges replicas have glutted the market. They are professionally made and only the expert is able to differentiate the replica from the original. Beware of 'fantasy' shot glasses. Repro hand-executed, reverse-painted glass signs have been abundant throughout

the country, most of them read 'Santa Fe,' but some say 'Whites Only.' Lately, markets in the east have been inundated with Baltimore & Ohio reproductions: menus, glass water carafes, demitasse sets in the George Washington theme, and more. Watch for a Union Pacific brass spittoon, tall, somewhat weighted, and with a Union Pacific medallion on the front. The Union Pacific never had one like this. Railroad drumheads are coming out of collections. A drumhead is a large (approximately 24" diameter) glass sign in a metal case. They were used on the back end of all railroad observation cars to advertise a special train or a presidential foray, etc. They're now beginning to surface, and a good one like the Flying Crow from the Kansas City Southern Railroad will go for $2,500.00, as will many others. When items of this value come out, the counterfeiters are right there. It is important to 'Know Thy Dealer.' For a more thorough study, we recommend *Fred Harvey: Behind the Scenes at Newton, Florence and Hutchinson* by our co-advisor, John 'Grandpa' White (see the Directory for ordering information.) The values noted for most of our dinnerware, glassware, linen, silverplate, and timetables are actual selling prices. However, because prices are so volatile, the best pricing sources are often monthly or quarterly 'For Sale' lists. Two you may find helpful may be ordered from Golden Spike, P.O. Box 422, Williamsville, NY 14221, and Grandpa's Depot, 6720 E. Mississippi Ave., Unit B, Denver, CO 80224. Our co-advisors for this category are Lila Shrader (See Directory, California) and Grandpa's Depot (see Colorado). See also Badges.

Key:
BL — bottom logo	PTA — patent applied for
BS — bottom stamped	ScL — Scammell's Lamberton
FBS — full back stamp	SL — side logo
FPC — Fraunfelter China	TL — top logo
NBS — no back stamp	TM — top mark

Dinnerware

Many railroads designed their own china for use in their dining cars or company-owned hotels or stations. Some railroads chose to use stock patterns to which they added their name or logo; others used the same stock patterns without the added identification. A momentary warning: The railroad dinnerware market has fallen considerably, only the rare and scarce items are saleable; otherwise don't speculate in dining china. For more information, we recommend *Restaurant China*, Vols. 1 and 2, by Barbara J. Conroy (Collector Books).

Ashtray/matchbox holder, MKT, Blue Bonnet, Buffalo, BS, 5½" .. 465.00
Bouillon cup, CMStP&P, Peacock, NBS, 3¾", +5¼" underplate .. 300.00
Bouillon cup, GN, Mtns & Flowers, NBS, 4½" dia....................... 100.00
Bouillon cup, NP, Yellowstone SL, hdls 460.00
Bouillon cup, NYC&StL, Nickel Plate Road, Bellevue, SL, 3¾" 80.00
Bowl, sauce; MKT, Blue Bonnet, Buffalo BS, 5" 165.00
Bowl, sauce; UP, Winged Streamliner, TL, NBS, Sterling, 4½" 16.00
Butter pat, ACL, Palmetto, TM & BS, Buffalo, 3¼" 195.00
Butter pat, ATSF, Bleeding Blue, TL, Albert Pick, 3½".............. 535.00
Butter pat, ATSF, California Poppy, Bauscher, FBS, 1922, 3½".... 100.00
Butter pat, B&O, Centenary, BS, Shenango, from $10 to.............. 30.00
Butter pat, Boston & Albany, Berkshire, TL, 3½" 190.00
Butter pat, Boston & Albany, Pittsfield, TL, 3⅜" 450.00
Butter pat, CB&Q, Violets & Daisies, NBS, 3½", from $10 to 32.00
Butter pat, CMStP&P, Peacock, NBS, 3" 60.00
Butter pat, GRGW, Blue Adam, NBS, 3" 40.00
Butter pat, Louisville & Nashville, Regent, NBM, 3⅝"............... 280.00
Butter pat, Newfoundland Government Ry, Newfoundland, 3¼" ...215.00
Butter pat, NYNH&H, Shoreline, TL, Greenwood China, 3½".. 565.00
Butter pat, UP, Historical, TL, NBS, 3⅜" 315.00
Butter pat, UP, Portland Rose, NBS, 3½".................................... 375.00
Chocolate pot, ATSF, Mimbreno, FBS, 6" 195.00

Coffeepot, Chicago, Rock Island, and Pacific, La Salle pattern, Rock Island stamp, from $375.00 to $450.00.

(Photo courtesy Barbara J. Conroy)

Compote, ATSF Santa Fe, Mimbreno, ped ft, NBS, 3x7" 1,200.00
Compote, C&A, Lincoln, ped ft, triangular TL, 3x6" 1,745.00
Creamer, ATSF, California Poppy, BM, ind, 3¼" 230.00
Creamer, Fred Harvey, Webster, no hdl, NBS, 2" 20.00
Creamer, MKT, Katy Ornaments w/hdl, NBS, 3¼" 45.00
Creamer, Pittsburgh & Lake Erie, Youngstown, SL, NBS, 2¾" 485.00
Creamer, UP, Harriman Blue, Overland shield BM, 2" 185.00
Cup, demitasse; Canadian Pacific, Blue Maple Leaf, SL, NBS, 2¼" ... 130.00
Cup, demitasse; CRI&P, El Reno, SL, NBM, 2¼" 275.00
Cup, demitasse; GN, Glory of West (w/o Rocky), 2¼", from $480 to... 585.00
Cup & saucer, D&RGW, Main Line, SL & TL, Lamberton-Sterling... 130.00
Cup & saucer, demitasse; UP, Desert Flower, both BS 90.00
Cup & saucer, UP, Portland Rose, NBS 685.00
Egg cup, Boston & Albany/NY Central, Berkshire, SL, 2⅜" 465.00
Egg cup, GN, Glory of West (w/o Rocky), NBS, 2⅜" 465.00
Egg cup, GN, Oriental, BM, 2⅜" 595.00
Egg cup, SP, PMFWF, BM, Made Expressly for..., 2⅜" 470.00
Horseradish, ATSF, Mimbreno, w/lid, BS, 2¼" 398.00
Hot food cover, WP, Feather River Route, SL, 6⅛" 145.00
Plate, Alaska RR, Mt McKinley, TL, 7½" 500.00
Plate, ATSF Santa Fe, Turquoise Room, BM, 10¼" 1,225.00
Plate, C&NW, Flambeau 'The 400,' TM, Shenango, 10½" 1,275.00
Plate, C&O, Greenbriar, gr band w/gold trim, BS, 10¼" 110.00
Plate, CMStP&P, Traveler, NBS, 9½" 75.00
Plate, CRI&P, LaSalle, TL & BS, Buffalo, 9" 95.00
Plate, D&RGW, Main Line, TL, NBS, Lamberton-Sterling, 9¾".. 85.00
Plate, GN, Glory of the West (w/Rocky), FBM, 9½" 315.00
Plate, grill; B&O, Centenary, Thomas Viaduct, Lamberton, 10¾"... 695.00
Plate, grill; MOPAC, St Albans, divided, NBS, 9⅞" 32.00
Plate, Maine Central, Bangor, TL, 5½" 385.00
Plate, N&W, Cavalier, TL, 8¼" 425.00
Plate, NYC, Mercury, TL, BS, 9½", from $55 to 80.00
Plate, rimmed soup; Lehigh Valley, Asa Packer, BM, 8½" 535.00
Plate, rimmed soup; SL&SF, Denmark, NBS, Syracuse, 9" 20.00
Plate, service; C&NW, Flambeau 'The 400,' TM & BS, 10½" 600.00
Plate, service; C&O, George Washington, BS, Buffalo, 10½" 185.00
Plate, service; C&O, Nature Study Poppies, NBS, 10½" 375.00
Plate, service; FH, Fred Harvey Service, blk & gold, TL, 10½" 265.00
Plate, service; MP, State Capitols/Diesel, FBM, 10½", from $150 to... 210.00
Plate, soup; Alaska RR, McKinley, no rim, TL, 7¼" 390.00
Plate, SP, Prairie Mountain Wildflowers, FBS, 5½", from $40 to.... 60.00
Plate, UP, Desert Flower, BM, MM-2 (1958), 6½" 25.00
Plate, Virginian Ry, Virginian, TL, 9" 3,300.00
Platter, ATSF, Bleeding Blue, rectangular, tab hdls, TL, 10¾x6½"... 520.00
Platter, CNRy Hotels, Quetico, TL, 11x8½" 32.00
Platter, GN, Mountains & Flowers, BS, 9x7" 80.00
Platter, ME Central, Kennebec, TL, NBS, 8¼x5¾" 185.00
Platter, MKT, Bluebonnet, BM, Buffalo, 11x8" 225.00
Platter, NP, Yellowstone, TL, Shenango, 7x5½" 175.00
Platter, SP, Imperial, TL & BS, 9½x6½" 235.00
Platter, UP, BS: Columbine State Flower of CO, 8x5½" 315.00
Relish dish, CMStP&P, Traveler, NBS, 10x4¾", from $65 to 115.00

Relish dish, Grand Rapids & IN, Fishing Line, TL, 4¼x5" 1,400.00
Sauceboat, ATSF, Griffon, hdl, BM: Made Expressly for..., 3¾" ... 790.00
Sauceboat, SP, Prairie Mountain Wildflowers, w/hdl, BS, 6" 100.00
Sherbet, ATSF Santa Fe, California Poppy, ped ft, NBS, 3½" 70.00
Teacup & saucer, NP, Garnet, BS 900.00
Teapot, GM&O, Rose, SL, 5¼" 500.00
Teapot, IL Central, Louisiane, SL, 4¾" 945.00

Glass

Ashtray, CMStP&P, Hiawatha silk screen, Art Deco style, 3½x2½" .. 100.00
Bottle, seltzer; Fred Harvey El Tovar in bl enamel SL, 11" 180.00
Bottle, whiskey; New Haven (bottled for), Jack Daniels, 1/10th pt ...230.00
Carafe, C&O, w/tl & BM hinged lid, holder & hdl, Internat'l, 6¾" ..300.00
Cordial, CN, stemmed, acic-etched SL, 3½" 45.00
Cruet, GN, acid-etched Rocky logo, orig stopper, 5½" 800.00
Goblet, water; GN interlocking, wht enamel, ftd, 5¼" 42.50
Pitcher, NP, YPL SL, Internat'l silver fr, hinged lid/base SL, 10" ...2,000.00
Roly-poly, IC enamel dmn SL & diesel enamel SL, 2¾x2¾" 18.00
Salt cellar, CO & Southern, etched logo, heavy cut glass, 1½x2¼" ...255.00
Shakers, SP, cylindrical w/SP flat screw tops, SL, 3¼", pr 190.00
Shot glass, B&O, acid-etch Capitol Dome w/bellflower wreath SL, 2⅛" .. 115.00
Shot glass, PRR emb in bottom, dbl sz, 3" 120.00
Swizzle stick, ATSF Santa Fe, Turquoise Room SL, bl, 4¾" 65.00
Swizzle stick, UP in wht enamel speed writing on cobalt, 4¾" 50.00
Swizzle stick/stirrer, CMStP&P, Hiawatha/Nothing Faster on Rails, 5".. 38.00
Tumbler, ATSF, etched SL Santa Fe w/in banner w/tassels, 3⅝" .. 335.00
Tumbler, IC dmn enamel SL, 5½" 125.00
Tumbler, juice; WP, wht enamel SL, 3½" 45.00
Wine stem, ATSF, etched SL Santa Fe w/in banner w/tassels, 4" .. 285.00
Wine stem, B&O, acid-etched SL Linking 13 Great States..., 5½" ...55.00

Keys

B&M, Slaymaker, brass, hollow bbl 30.00
Berth, 2-color brass, T-shape unmk, 3x4" 40.00
Caboose, unmk, Adlake, solid long bbl, 3¾" 8.00
CRR, brass 22.50
Shanty, GNRR, hollow bbl, 1¾" 15.00
SOO Line, Adlake, brass, hollow bbl 30.00

Lamps

Switch: Handland, single blue lens, marked UPRR, 13", $100.00; Adlake, two light blue and two dark blue lenses, marked PRR, 14", $175.00.

(Photo courtesy Jackson's International Auctioneers & Appraisers of Fine Art & Antiques)

Inspector's, Dietz Acme, unmk globe, complete 90.00
Inspector's, NYC, Acme, clear etched globe, 19x9" 95.00
Signal, Adlake, 2 red/2 gr Kopp lenses, complete, 16¼" 265.00

Signal, SP, Adlake, 2 red/2 bl lenses, 13½x11" 300.00
Station, Dietz Pioneer post type, clear globe, 25x13" 600.00
Switch, PRR, Handlan, 2 bl/2 amber lenses, complete, 18x12" ... 245.00

Lanterns

Before 1920 kerosene brakemen's lanterns were made with tall globes, usually 5⅜" high. These are most desirable to collectors and are usually found at the top of the price scale. Short globes from 1921 through 1940 normally measure 3½" in height, except for those manufactured by Dietz, which are 4" tall. (Soon thereafter, battery brakemen's lanterns came into widespread usage; these are not highly regarded by collectors and are generally not railroad marked.) All lanterns should be marked with the name or initials of the railroad — look on the top, the top apron, or the bell base (if it has one). Globes may be found in these colors (listed in order of popularity): clear, red, amber, aqua, cobalt, and two-color. Any lantern's value is enhanced if it has a colored globe.

Key: A&W — Adams and Westlake

B&M, Armspear, clear emb 5⅜" globe, orig pot/burner, Pat 1890s... 255.00
B&O, Keystone, Safety First/LOCO clear 5½" globe, complete... 285.00

Cast iron and porcelain with an all-glass globe, minor paint loss, 17", $250.00. (Photo courtesy Randy Inman Auctions Inc.)

CMStP&P, A&W, mk collar & red globe, insert pot, bb, 9½"+hdl.. 155.00
D&H, Dressel, mk chimney, red emb 5⅜" globe, complete 255.00
E&J Detroit MI, oil burner, 2 rnd/2 sq jeweled lights, Pat 1908, pr .. 200.00
Erie, CT Ham, emb clear globe, blk pnt on brass, Pat Dec 26 93 .. 825.00
GTR, A&W Adlake Reliable, emb cobalt 5¼" globe w/hairline .. 450.00
LA&SL, Adlake Reliable, wire ring base, clear 5⅜" globe, Pat 1909 .. 735.00
NYC, Dietz #6, red CNX emb globe, orig burner, bb, 10"+hdl 265.00
P&LE RR, NYC Lines globe, insert burner, bb, 9¾"+hdl............. 110.00
Pullman, A&W conductor's, worn NP brass fr, oil burner, bb...... 350.00
Santa Fe, A&W NY & Chicago, emb clear globe, bb, 1912, NM... 185.00

Linens and Uniforms

Over the years the many railroad companies took great pride in their dining car table presentation. In the very early years of railroad dining car service, the linens used at the tables were of the finest quality white damask. Most railroads would add their company's logo, name, initials, or even a spectacular scene that would be woven into the cloth (white on white). These patterns were not evident unless the fabric was held at a particular angle to the light. The dining car staff's attire generally consisted of heavily starched blinding white jackets with shiny buttons.

In later years, post-World War II, color began to be used for table linens. Florida railroads created some delightfully colorful items for the table as well as for headrest. The passenger train crew, the conductor, and the brakemen, were generally attired in black suits, white shirts, and black ties. Their head gear generally bore a badge denoting their position.

These items have all become quite collectible. Sadly, however, replicas of badges and pins have been produced as well as 'fantasy' items (items that do not replicate an older item but are meant to mislead or deceive).

Key:
RBH — reinforced button holes   w/w — white on white damask

Bath mat, GN in red script on heavy wht toweling, 21x33"........... 36.00
Blanket, CP w/beaver center logo, 100% wool, wht w/brn, 74x54" ...155.00
Cap, operator's, Pacific Electric mc logo on silver-tone badge...... 350.00
Hat, chef's, FH, Harvey in bl stripe, cotton mushroom type, 10"... 72.00
Hat, conductor's, ATSF, blk wool w/bl/wht enamel & brass badge... 180.00
Hat, conductor's, GN, wool, GN Rocky pin (enamel on brass) ... 380.00
Jacket, cook's, CI&L, Monon embr script on pocket, wht cotton.. 40.00
Napkin, Santa Fe center script logo w/oak leaves, w/w, 23x23" 64.00
Napkin, SP, Daylight, coastal scenes, mc, 19x19" 26.00
Tablecloth, ATSF, Santa Fe script logo w/oak leaves, w/w, 46x46"..110.00
Tablecloth, C&S, elaborate center belt logo, w/w, 54x54" 75.00
Tablecloth, CP, elaborate center CP Dining Cars logo, w/w, 63x52"..115.00
Tablecloth, SOO, elaborate center logo, Irish linen, 36x36", M w/tags.. 75.00
Tablecloth, SOO, elaborate center logo, w/w, Simtex, 54x64"....... 70.00
Towel, hand; B&M RR, 8-28 woven on red center stripe, wht huck, 19x22" .. 15.00
Towel, hand; NP, mc Monad logo on wht huck, 13x17" 13.00
Towel, hand; PRR woven in script on red vertical center stripe 17.00

Locks

Brass switch locks (pre-1920) were made in two styles: heart-shaped and Keen Kutter style. Values for the heart-shaped locks are determined to a great extent by the railroad they represent and just how its name appears on the lock. Most in demand are locks with large embossed letters; if the letters are small and incised, demand for that lock is minimal. For instance, one from the Union Pacific line (even with heavily embossed letters) may go for only $45.00, while the same from the D&RG railroad could go easily sell for $250.00. Old Keen Kutter styles (brass with a 'pointy' base) from Colorado & Southern and Denver & Rio Grande could range from $600.00 to $1,200.00. Steel switch locks (circa 1920 on) with the initials of the railroad incised in small letters — for example BN, L&H, and PRR — are usually valued at $20.00 to $28.00.

General use, B&ORR, Corbin, brass, w/key & chain 72.50
Mail car, GNRy US Mail Car, sm brass heart shape 75.00
Signal, ATSF on bottom edge, Eagle Lock Co...USA on shackle .. 35.00
Signal, GNRy on front, RACO on side, w/hex wrench-like key.... 30.00
Switch, B&MRR on shackle bk, Wilson Bohannon on shackle front...85.00
Switch, BN Inc, Adlake... 10.00

Switch, C&NW, Adlake, $16.00.

Switch, D&SF, Eagle Lock Co...USA, brass heart shape................ 85.00
Switch, DTRR, Adlake... 22.00
Switch, MOPAC, Adlake, w/chain & brass key 55.00
Switch, MW&Co, brass heart shape, w/key................................. 60.00
Switch, N&WRy, Slaymaker, lg S on top of hasp, EX 75.00

Switch, NP, tapered bbl 50.00
Switch, PCRR, Adlake, unused...................................... 15.00
Switch, UP, Switch CSI, Adlake, brass heart shape...................... 215.00
Telegraph Dept, NYNH&H, Yale, Tel'g Dept emb on body, brass ...20.00
Water service, D&RG, F-S Hdw Co, w/key................................ 150.00

Silver-plated Flatware

Key: R&B — Reed & Barton

Corn holders, GN, BM, pr... 290.00
Fork, dinner; Canadian Government Ry, Waverly, TM, Rogers, 6¾" ..37.00
Fork, seafood; Southern Ry, DeSota, TM, Internat'l, 5¾" 27.00
Ice tongs, ATSF, Albany, SL Santa Fe in script, 7½" 188.00
Knife, dinner; GN SL, Zephyr, Internat'l, 9" 20.00
Knife, dinner; SOO, Empire, TL, Gorham, 9¾" 55.00
Ladle, Pullman, Roosevelt, BM, curved hdl, Gorham, 7½" 65.00
Spoon, cream soup; CB&Q, Belmont, BR TM monogram, R&B, 5½" . 28.00
Spoon, grapefruit; CA Zephyr, Century, BM, Internat'l, 6"............ 42.00
Spoon, mustard; NYC, Century, BM, Internat'l, 3⅝" 50.00
Spoon, soup; Pullman, Roosevelt, BM, 5¾" 30.00
Sugar tongs, GN, Cromwell, SL, Internat'l, 4½" 188.00
Sugar tongs, NYP&NRR, Westfield, SL, Internat'l, 4½" 100.00
Teaspoon, SP Del Monte Hotel, Art Nouveau decor, TM, Gorham, 6" ..22.00

Silver-plated Hollow Ware

The value of silver plate, hollow ware, or flatware, is influenced by the location of the logo or railroad name and, of course, by condition. A side- or top-marked piece is preferable to one with a bottom mark. Examine a prospective purchase carefully. Some unmarked flatware has been 'enhanced' with a rather crude stamping of the railroad's name. Authentic railway markings were done at the time of manufacture and were generally executed in a flawless manner.

Bowl, New Haven, Art Deco rtcl decor, BM, Internat'l, 5"............ 38.00
Bread tray, UP The Overland Route TL, Internat'l, 11½"............ 160.00
Butter pat, CRI&P, BM, Wallace, 3½"...................................... 42.50
Candleholder, PRR, TL & BM, Internat'l, 1½x3¾", ea................ 135.00

Coffeepot, CB&Q RR, individual, 5", $85.00.

Coffeepot, CN, wooden hdl, SL, Rogers, 5¾" 200.00
Coffeepot, SP, hinged lid w/ball & wing logo+SL, Internat'l, 10" ...550.00
Creamer, PRR, graceful spout & hdl, Keystone SL, R&B, 2¾" 185.00
Crumber, Pullman, BM, Gorham, 5¾x9"................................... 80.00
Gravy, Lehigh Valley, hammered finish, SL, 2½"......................... 315.00
Hot food cover, GN, fancy knob, oval, BM, 5x7"......................... 65.00
Ice bucket, NYC, Internat'l, BS, 5½x9½" (hdl-to-hdl) 215.00
Ice cream, C&A, ped ft, ornate SL, R&B, 4½".......................... 700.00

Menu holder, Monon, Deco, w/pencil holders, SL/BM/Internat'l, 4½x6" ...995.00
Napkin holder, Erie, rtcl, ftd, SL, R&B, 5x5½" 425.00
Relish dish, SP, fr w/ball & wing SL, w/lid, R&B........................ 300.00
Sauceboat, SAL, SM & BM, Internat'l, 7½"............................... 115.00
Seafood server, SAL, bowl, ring, holder & glass insert, TM & BM ..210.00
Soup tureen, ATSF, w/lid & spoon, all pcs TM, Gorham & Internat'l...360.00
Sugar bowl, UP Overland SL, lid w/knob, tab hdls, Internat'l, 3½" ...190.00
Syrup, UP, hinged lid & attached drip tray, BM, Internat'l, 5"....... 62.00
Teapot, ACL, hinged lid, SL & BM, Internat'l, 4½" 340.00
Teapot, PRR, appl Keystone SL, hinged lid, R&B, 5" 235.00
Teapot, Seaboard eng SL, hinged lid w/sculptured knob, Internat'l, 5"...280.00
Vase, bud; CPR, elaborate SL, 6-sided, weighted, Elkington, 7¼"...300.00
Wine bucket, CN System SL, Rogers, 11½" to top of swivel hdl ... 40.00

Switch Keys

Switch keys are brass with hollow barrels and round heads with holes for attaching to a key ring. They were used to unlock the padlocks on track-side switches when the course of the tracks had to be changed. (Switches were padlocked to prevent them from being thrown by accident or vandals, a situation that could result in a train wreck.) A car key used to open padlocks on freight cars and the like is very similar to the switch key, except the bit is straighter instead of being specifically curved for a particular railroad and its accompanying switch locks. A second type of 'car' key was used for door locks on passenger cars, Pullmans, etc.; this type was usually of brass, but instead of having a hollow barrel, they were shaped like an old-fashioned hotel door key. In order for a key to be collectible, the head must be marked with a name, initials, or a railroad identification, with 'switch' generally designated by 'S' and 'car' by 'C' markings. Railroad, patina 'not polished,' and the presence of a manufacturer's mark other than Adlake all have a positive effect on pricing and collectibility.

B&M RR, brass, #2939, 2".. 25.00
D&RGW, Adlake, steel.. 25.00
DL&W RR, Fraim #9615, brass... 30.00
Indiana Harbor Belt, brass 50.00
KCFS&M RR, brass.. 145.00
M&NW RR, steel.. 365.00
OSL, A&P Co Chicago, #1762S... 37.50

PCRR, $20.00.

Santa Fe Route, #6136S, brass.. 60.00
SC&NW, brass, 2" 30.00
SP Lines CS-25.. 40.00
UPRR Bohannan, brass, 2⅛" 155.00

Miscellaneous

Timetables and railroad travel brochures continue to gain in popularity and offer the collector vast information about the glory days of railroading. Annual passes continue to be favored over trip and one-time passes. Their value is contingent upon the specific railroad, its length of run, and the appearance of the pass itself. Many were tiny works of art enhanced with fancy calligraphy and decorated with unique vignettes. Pocket calendars are popular as well as railroad playing cards. Pins, badges, and uniform buttons bearing the name or logo of a railroad are also sought after. The novice needs to be cautious about signs (metal as well as cardboard) and belt buckles. Reproductions flourish in these areas.

Key:
dd — double deck   hb — hardback
sd — single deck

Accident report #3991 by ICC re ATSF, Lomas IL, 1963, 9-pg, 8½x11".. 230.00
Ashtray, ATSF, Deco chrome/blk Bakelite, floor-standing/weighted..325.00
Ashtray, Monon TM, alligator's open mouth receives ashes, detailed, 9" .. 58.00
Ashtray/match holder, C&O, Washington silhouette, Buffalo, 4½x7" ..100.00

Badge, Berkshire Street Railway, $65.00.

Badge, breast; SP, Police/AZ, 6-point star, sterling, Irvine/Jachiens..4,495.00
Badge, breast; UP Waiter Instructor, blk Bakelite, 2⅛" dia 125.00
Badge, hat; D&RG Conductor, brass, 4⅛x1⅛" 360.00
Blotter, desk; ATSF, Chico holding Santa Fe logo, unused, 16x20" ..38.00
Blotter, ink; CRI&P, IA NB Ltd to Chicago, unused, 3½x8" 30.00
Book, A History of TX RRs, sgn CG Reed, 2nd ed hardbk, 1946, 800-pg..130.00
Book, Poor's Manual of Railroads...US, hardbk, 1882, 1,150-pg .. 155.00
Book, UP System Official Ry Guide, hardbk, 1922, 1,500-pg, 7½x11" .. 155.00
Booklet, ATSF, All Private...Streamliner, graphics, 1930s, 9-pg, 5x7" .. 70.00
Booklet, PRR, Division of Maps, Office Chief Engineer, 1964, 14 maps.. 55.00
Box, fare; LA Transit Ry, Johnson Fare Box Co, 24x8x8" 300.00
Builder's plate, Baldwin Locomotive Works, Phila, CI, 1942, 9¼" dia ..1,580.00
Bulletin board, MKT, dtd 190_, for chalk notations, 36x25" 1,950.00
Button, Grand Trunk RR, GTR/Canada, Chanteloup, Montreal, brass, ⅝"..6.00
Calendar, ATSF, celluloid, 1938, pocket sz 200.00
Calendar, B&O, Mt Vernon pictured, much info, 1930, 28x22"..200.00
Calendar, GN, Winold Reiss Evening Star Woman, 13 sheets, 1954, 33x16"....58.00
Calendar, NPYPL logo, card stock, 1949, pocket sz 98.00
Calendar, PRR, Grif Teller mining scene, complete, 1940, 28½" sq...170.00
Calendar postcard, GN, Sept 1914, oversz 9x12" folds to 9x6" 385.00
Catalog, Baldwin Steam Locomotive parts, hardbk, 1924, 9½x11"..698.00
Cigarette lighter, NYC&StL, Nickel Plate Road, Zippo-like 23.00
Drink markers, SP, colored plastic, fits on glass edge, TL, 6 for 17.00
Globe, C&NW RR emb SL, gr glass, extended, 5⅜".................2,100.00
Handkerchief, NYC, style of red bandana w/NYC logos, 22x22" ... 25.00
Jack, Duff Barrett RR jack used by gandy dancers, 22" 60.00
Jug, GN, Property of..., stoneware, 1-gal, 13"................................ 200.00
Luggage token, MStP&SSMRy, brass, 1½" dia 36.00
Magazine, employee; L&N RR, March, 1942 .... 12.00
Magazine, employee; MOPAC Lines, February, 1953 .... 75.00
Magazine, employee; SP, obit for LD Hoisington, January, 1959.... 55.00
Manual, GN Dining Car Operations, 1967, 100+ pgs in 3-ring binder..500.00
Manual, MP, diesel freight locomotive, fold-out diagrams, 1944.. 500.00
Manual, Union Switch & Signal Co, hardbk, 1937 .... 180.00

Matchbook, Central of GA, Serving the Southeast, 1950s, unused.. 13.00
Matchbox, ATSF logo, Turquoise Room, no matches, 1x2¼" 22.00
Medal, B&O, 1827-1927, bronze, Medallic Art Co, 2¾" 200.00
Menu, New Haven, Yankee Clipepr, card stock, 1930, 9½x5¾" folded ...180.00
Menu, PRR, Train to 1931 World Series, photo cover, PRR/TAT, 9x6" .. 90.00
Menu, UP, child's, die-cut squirrel, mc.. 30.00
Napkin, C&O, Chessie logo in corner, mc on wht paper, unused, $4 to.....8.00
Pamphlet, MP Iron Mtn Rte Sunshine Special, pictures, 1920, 15-pg ...150.00
Pamphlet, Shooting & Fishing...Bangor & Aroostook Ry, 1895, 37-pg.270.00
Pamphlet, Souvenir...Salt Lake Rte, die-cut orange, 1912, 40-pg .. 30.00
Paperweight, Bangor & Aroostook, train wheel shape, TM, 3½" dia.. 260.00
Paperweight, PRR, die-cut CI PRR Keystone logo on weighted ped, 3½"..155.00
Pass, annual; DT&FW RR, 1889, 2¾x3½" 550.00
Pass, annual; Gila Valley Globe & NRy, 1905, 2¼x3½" 200.00
Pass, annual; Quebeck & Lake St John Ry, graphics/map, cardstock, 1903...575.00
Pass, lifetime; IC, 40 Years of Service, 1959, w/case 24.00
Pass, trip; C&O, paper, issued 8/1/38, expired 10/30/38, 3x6"........ 10.00
Photo, D&RGW, Rocky Mtn Scenery, hand-tinted, plaque on oak fr, 29x24"..300.00
Pin, lapel; Wabash, Follow the Flag Banner logo, red/bl enamel,⅞"... 10.00
Pin-bk button, GN, ND Development Tour, space for name, 1890s, 4" ..145.00
Pin-bk button, PRR Keystone w/photo ID, 1938, 1¾" 50.00
Playing cards, BR/Nat'l Park Line, dbl deck, orig case.................. 275.00
Playing cards, N&W, Powhatan Arrow+Pocahontas, dbl deck, +slipcase....148.00
Postcard, Artillery loaded on Mexican military train, real photo, 1913..150.00
Postcard, Key Route Inn, Oakland CA, chrome, unused 6.00
Postcard, Milwaukee Depot, Louistown MT, real photo, horses/early auto ..85.00
Postcard, real photo of train wreck, Muskegon MI, 1900s, unused...35.00
Poster, SP, Carlsbad Caverns Nat'l Park, 1930s, 16x23", VG 155.00
Print, annual; Alaska RR, Denali Park Station, 1988, 21x23" 30.00
Shaving kit, UP shield TL, dbl-edge razor, blades in faux leather case...55.00
Shaving mug, RR engineer's, HP mc scene of train crossing bridge/name ... 1,300.00

Sign, Bamberger Railroad, Utah, yellow, black, and red porcelain, 15" diameter, $635.00.
(Photo courtesy Morphy Auctions)

Sign, WP, Feather River logo, porc on metal, 8 grommets, 24x24" ..415.00
Souvenir dish, Yakima WA RR depot, Wheelock China, 5½x4½" ...85.00
Spittoon, SAL, CI w/wht porc collar, emb SL, 8" dia................... 155.00
Stepstool, BR SM, gridded top, stainless steel, 17x20" 735.00
Stereoview, CP, 155-View...Forks...American River, 3¼x6¾" 185.00
Stereoview, Pike's Peak view, train, 1900s.................................... 15.00
Swizzle stick, Chicago Milwaukee Electroliner, plastic, 5⅜" 10.00
Telegraph key & sounder, T&P BM, Bunnell, brass on wood base, 100 ohms ...155.00
Ticket puncher, PRR, SM, spring action, 5¼" L 160.00
Timetable, public; CRI&P, 1/1906, 36-pg, 1-pg maps, folds to 9x4"... 90.00
Timetable, public; SP, 14 panels, map, 1890 .... 200.00
Timetable, public; UP The Overland.../Exposition 1898 in Omaha, 42-pg..128.00
Track chart, SP, SF to LA coast route, 1980, 49-pg, 8½x11" 200.00
Watch fob, Brotherhood...Trainmen, enamel/brass bezel/strap, 1911...68.00
Water can, KCS SM, galvanized, spigot, strap hdl/bale hdl, 18½" ...45.00
Wax sealer, D&H, Whitehall NY, wood hdl, brass seal 270.00
Whistle, PRR, 3-chime, brass, side-mt, 21x6", 32" overall........2,655.00

Razors

As straight razors gain in popularity, prices of those razors also increase. This carries with it a lure of investment possibilities which can encourage the novice or speculator to make purchases that may later prove to be unwise. We recommend that before investing serious money in razors, you become familiar with the elements which make a razor valuable. As with other collectibles, there are specific traits which are desirable and which have a major impact on price.

The following information is based on the second edition of *The Standard Guide to Razors* by Roy Ritchie and Ron Stewart (available from R&C Books, Box 2421, Hazard KY 41702, $12.95 +$2.50 S&H). It describes the elements most likely to influence a razor's collector value and their system of calculating that value. (Their book is a valuable reference guide to both the casual and serious collector of razors.)

There are four major factors which determine a razor's collector value. These are the brand and country of origin, the handle material, the art work found on the handles or blades, and the condition of the razor. Ritchie and Stewart freely admit that there are other factors that may come into play with some collectors, but these are the major components in determining value. They have devised a system of evaluation which is based on these four factors.

The most important factor is the value placed on the brand and country of origin. This is the price of a common razor made by (or for) a particular company. It has plain handles, probably made of plastic, no art work, and is in collectible condition. It is the beginning value. Hundreds of these values are provided in the 'Listings of Companies and Base Values' chapter in the book.

The second category is that of handle material. This covers a wide range of materials, from fiber on the low end to ivory on the high end. The collector needs to be able to identify the different handle materials when he sees them. This often takes some practice, since there are some very good plastics that can mimic ivory quite successfully. Also, the difference between genuine celluloid and plastic can become significant when determining value. A detailed chart of these values is supplied in the book. The listing below can be used as a general guide.

The third category is the most subjective. Nevertheless, it is an extremely important factor in determining value. This category is artwork, which can include everything from logo art to carving and sculpture. It may range from highly ornate to tastefully correct. Blade etching as well as handle artistry are to be considered. Perhaps what some call the 'gotta have it' or the 'neatness' factors properly fall into this category. You must accurately determine the artistic merits of your razor when you evaluate it relative to this factor. Again, the book we referenced earlier provides a more complete listing of considerations than is used here.

Finally, the condition is factored in. The book's scales run from 'parts' (10% +/-) to 'Good' (150% +/-). Average (100% +/-) is classified as 'Collectible.' See chart D for details concerning condition guidelines for evaluation.

Samplings from charts:

Chart A: Companies and Base Values:

Abercrombie & Finch, NY	14.00
Aerial, USA	25.00
Boker, Henri & Co, Germany	14.00
Brick, F; England	12.00
Case Mfg Co, Spring Valley NY	50.00
Chores, James; England	13.00
Dahlqres, CW; Sweden	14.00
Diane, Japan	10.00
Electric Co, NY	15.00
Faultless, Germany	100.00
Fox Cutlery, Germany	11.00
Fredericks (Celebrated Cutlery), England	13.00
Gilbert Bros, England	12.00
Griffon XX, Germany	11.00
Henckels, Germany	15.00
Holly Mfg Co, CT	30.00
International Cutlery Co NY/Germany	11.00
IXL, England	15.00
Jay, John; NY	12.00
KaBar, Union Cut Co, USA	30.00
Kanner, J; Germany	11.00
Kern, R&W; Canada/England	12.00
LeCocltre, Jacque; Switzerland	12.00
Levering Razor Co, NY/Germany	18.00
McIntosh & Heather, OH	12.00
Merit Import Co, Germany	11.00
Monthoote, England	12.00
National Cut Co, OH	15.00
Oxford Razor Co, Germany	10.00
Palmer Brothers, Savannah, GA	25.00
Primble, John; Indian Steel Works, Louisville KY	25.00
Queen City NY	30.00
Querelle, A; Paris France	12.00
Quigley, Germany	12.00
Radford, Joseph & Sons; England	12.00
Rattler Razor Co, Germany	10.00
Robeson Cut Co, USA	30.00
Salamander Works, Germany	11.00
Soderein, Ekilstuna Sweden	12.00
Taylor, LM; Cincinnati OH	15.00
Tower Brand, Germany	16.00
Ulmer, Germany	12.00
US Barber Supply, TX	12.00
Vinnegut Hdw Co, IN	11.00
Vogel, Ed; PA	10.00
Wade & Butcher, England	20.00
Weis, JH; Supply House, Louisville KY	17.00
Yankee Cutlery Co, Germany	12.00
Yazbek, Lahod; OH	11.00
Zacour Bros, Germany	11.00
Zepp, Germany	12.00

Chart B, as described below, is an abbreviated version of the handle materials list in *The Standard Guide to Razors*. It is an essential category in the use of the appraisal system developed by the authors.

Genuine Ivory	600%
Tortoise Shell	500%
Pearl	400%
Stag	400%
Jigged Bone	350%
Smooth Bone	300%
Celluloid	250%
Composition	150%
Plastic	100%

Chart C deals with the artistic value of the razor. As pointed out earlier, this is a very subjective area. It takes study to determine what is good and what is not. Taste can also play a significant role in determining the value placed on the artistic merit of a razor. The range is from exceptional to nonexistent. Categories generally are divided as follows:

Exceptional	650%
Superior	550%
Good	400%
Average	300%

Minimal	200%
Plain	100%
Nonexistant	0%

Chart D is also very subjective. It determines the condition of the razor. You must judge accurately if the appraisal system is to work for you.

Good	150%

Does not have to be factory mint to fall within this category. However, there can be no visible flaws if it is to be calculated at 150%.

Collectible	100%

May have some flaws that do not greatly detract from the artwork or finish.

Parts	10%

Unrepairable, valuable as salvageable parts.

Razors may fall between any of these categories, ie. collectible to 112%.

Now to determine the value of your razor, multiply A times B, then multiply A times C. Add your two answers and multiply this sum times D. The answer you get is your collector value. See the example below.

(A) Brand & Origin Base Value	(B) Handle Material % Value	(C) Artwork % Value	(D) Condition % Value	(E) Collector Value
Wade & Butcher England $20.00	Iridescent Pearl Handles 20 x 400%= $80.00	Carved Handles 20 x 350%= $70.00	Cracked handle at pin Collectible 80%	$80+$70= $150 $150 x 80%= $120.00

Reamers

The largest producer of glass reamers was McKee, who pressed their products from many types of glass — custard; Delphite and Chalaine Blue; opaque white; Skokie Green; black; caramel and white opalescent; Seville Yellow; and transparent pink, green, and clear. Among these, the black and the caramel opalescents are the most valuable. Prices vary greatly according to color and rarity. The same reamer in crystal may be worth three times as much in a more desirable color.

Among the most valuable ceramic reamers are those made by American potteries, for example the Spongeband reamer by Red Wing, Coorsite reamers, and figural reamers. China one- and two-piece reamers are also very desirable and command very respectable prices.

A word about reproductions: A series of limited edition reamers is being made by Edna Barnes of Uniontown, Ohio. These are all marked with a 'B' in a circle. Other reproductions have been made from old molds. The most important of these are Anchor Hocking two-piece two-cup measure and top, Gillespie one-cup measure with reamer top, Westmoreland with flattened handle, Westmoreland four-cup measure embossed with orange and lemons, Duboe (hand-held darning egg), and Easley's Diamonds one-piece.

For more information concerning reamers and reproductions, contact or the National Reamer Collectors Association (see Clubs, Newsletters, and Catalogs). Be sure to include an SASE when requesting information.

Ceramic

Anthropomorphic, peach w/smiling face, #1K3358, 1950s, 4¾".... 35.00
Cat face, pk/bl/blk, yel hat forms reamer, side hdl, 5¾", NM 50.00

Clown face, Made in Japan, ca. 1940s, 4½", $245.00. (Photo courtesy Larry Pogue)

Clown sitting cross-legged, gr w/wht ruffled coat & hat, Germany, 5".. 300.00
Cup, 2-pc, yel & wht spatter design, Stangl, 6¼" 75.00
House w/thatched roof, reamer lid, HP, Japan, 5⅛x4½" dia 45.00
Lemon & leaf decor, gr trim & hdl, Made in Germany #2887, 3".. 55.00
Majolica grapevines/fence on ivory, sq pitcher w/reamer top, Japan ... 225.00
Mexican taking siesta, 2-pc, mc, Japan, 4¾" 200.00
Orange for Baby, 2-pc, bl flowers, Goebel, 3½" 135.00
Teapot, 2-pc, yel, tan & wht, England/Shelly, 3½" 125.00

Glass

Cambridge, cobalt bl, sm, ftd, from $1,000 to 1,200.00
Cambridge, cobalt bl, sm tab hdl, from $375 to 395.00
Cambridge, gr, sm, ftd, from $550 to 600.00
Federal, amber, ribbed, loop hdl, from $25 to 30.00
Federal, pk, tab hdl, seed dam, from $125 to............................... 135.00
Federal, yel-amber, tab hdl, from $300 to 325.00
Fenton, blk, 2-cup pitcher & reamer set, from $1,000 to 1,200.00
Fenton, China White, from $700 to 800.00
Fenton, Pearl opal wht, from $40 to 45.00
Foreign (emb), gr or pk, 2-pc, from $135 to................................ 145.00
Fry, Amber, from $375 to 395.00
Fry, Azure Blue, str sides, from $1,800 to 2,000.00
Fry, Canary Yellow, fluted, loop hdl, from $350 to 375.00
Fry, Emerald Green, fluted, from $500 to 550.00
Hazel-Atlas, cobalt, 2-cup pitcher & reamer set (+), from $325 to.. 350.00
Hazel-Atlas, gr, tab hdl, from $28 to 30.00
Hazel-Atlas, gr, 4-cup pitcher, ftd, 2-pc, from $45 to.................... 70.00
Hazel-Atlas, pk, lg tab hdl, from $45 to 48.00
Hocking, flashed blk, ribbed, loop hdl, from $35 to....................... 38.00
Hocking, gr, 2-cup pitcher w/reamer top, from $65 to................... 70.00
Hocking, Indiana Amber, from $325 to 350.00

Hocking, Mayfair Blue, two-cup measuring cup with reamer top, from $1,600.00 to $1,800.00. (Photo courtesy Gene Florence)

Hocking, pk, 2-cup pitcher, ribbed, from $65 to 70.00
Indiana Glass, amber, hdl w/spout opposite, from $275 to 300.00
Indiana Glass, pk, 6-sided cone, vertical hdl, from $175 to.......... 195.00
Sunkist, bl turq, from $395 to.. 450.00
Sunkist, blk, from $600 to 650.00
Sunkist, Delphite, emb McK, 6", from $750 to............................ 800.00
Sunkist, Mustard, from $500 to 550.00

Sunkist, wht, emb McK, from $25 to 30.00
US Glass, bl, 2-cup pitcher & reamer set, from $750 to 800.00
US Glass, crystal, vertical ribs, slick hdl, from $35 to 40.00
US Glass, pk, pitcher w/reamer top, from $275 to 295.00
Valencia, pk, emb LINDSEY, from $450 to 500.00
Valencia, red-orange slag, emb Fleur-de-Lis, from $375 to 400.00
Westmoreland, frosted crystal, 2-pc, from $75 to 95.00
Westmoreland, pk, 2-pc, from $225 to 245.00
Westmoreland, pk w/decor, 2-pc, from $225 to 245.00
Westmoreland, sun-colored amethyst, 2-pc, from $75 to 95.00

Records

Records of interest to collectors are often not the million-selling hits by 'superstars.' Very few records by Bing Crosby, for example, are of any more than nominal value, and those that are valuable usually don't even have his name on the label! Collectors today are most interested in records that were made in limited quantities, early works of a performer who later became famous, and those issued in special series or aimed at a limited market. Vintage records are judged desirable by their recorded content as well; those that lack the quality of music that makes a record collectible will always be 'junk' records in spite of their age, scarcity, or the obsolescence of their technology.

Records are usually graded visually rather than aurally, since it is seldom if ever possible to first play the records you buy at shows, by mail, at flea markets, etc. Condition is one of the most important determinants of value. For example, a nearly mint-condition Elvis Presley 45 of 'Milk Cow Blues' (Sun 215) has a potential value of over $1,500.00. A small sticker on the label could cut its value in half; noticeable wear could reduce its value by 80%. A mint record must show no evidence of use (record jackets, in the case of EPs and LPs, must be equally choice). Excellent condition denotes a record showing only slight signs of use with no audible defects. A very good record has noticeable wear but still plays well. Records of lesser grades may be unsaleable, unless very scarce and/or highly sought-after.

While the value of most 78s does not depend upon their being in appropriate sleeves (although a sleeveless existence certainly contributes to damage and deterioration!), this is not the case with most EPs (extended play 45s) and LPs (long-playing 33⅓ rpm 'albums'), which must have their jackets (cardboard sleeves), in nice condition, free of disfiguring damage, such as writing, stickers, or tape. Often, common and minimally valued 45s might be collectible if they are in appropriate 'picture sleeves' (special sleeves that depict the artist/group or other fanciful or symbolic graphic and identify the song titles, record label, and number), e.g. many common records by Elvis Presley, The Beatles, and The Beach Boys.

Promotional copies (DJ copies) supplied to radio stations often have labels different in designs and/or colors from their commercially issued counterparts. Labels usually bear a designation 'Not for Sale,' 'Audition Copy,' 'Sample Copy,' or the like. Records may be pressed of translucent vinyl; while most promos are not particularly collectible, those by certain 'hot' artists, such as Elvis Presley, The Beach Boys, and The Beatles are usually premium disks.

Many of the most desirable and valuable 45s have been 'bootlegged' (counterfeited). For example, there are probably more fake Elvis Presley *Sun* records in circulation than authentic copies — certainly in higher grades! Collectors should be alert for these often deceptive counterfeits.

Our advisor for this category is L. R. Docks, author of *American Premium Record Guide,* which lists 60,000 records by over 7,000 artists in its sixth edition. He is listed in the Directory under Texas. In the listings that follow, prices are suggested for records that are in excellent condition; worn or abused records may be worth only a small fraction of the values quoted and may not be saleable at all.

Blues, Rhythm and Blues, Rock 'n Roll, Rockabilly

Ace, Sonny; If My Teardrops Could Talk, TNT 153, 45 rpm 15.00
Admirals, Close Your Eyes, King 4782, 45 rpm 30.00
Alexander, Texas; Sittin' on a Log, Okeh 8624, 78 rpm 50.00
Alexander Brothers, St Louis Blues, Champion 16499, 78 rpm ... 100.00

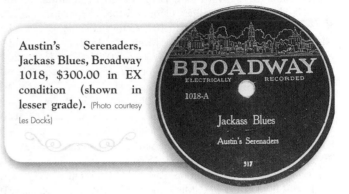

Austin's Serenaders, Jackass Blues, Broadway 1018, $300.00 in EX condition (shown in lesser grade). (Photo courtesy Les Docks)

Banjo Joe, Jonestown Blues, Paramount 12588, 78 rpm 200.00
Barefoot Bill, One More Time, Columbia 14561-D, 78 rpm 175.00
Barrix, Billy; Cool Off Baby, Chess 1662, 45 rpm 300.00
Bowshier, Little Donnie; Rock & Roll Joys, Dess 7002, 45 rpm 90.00
Burston, Clara; Pay With Money, Gennett 7319, rpm 70 .... 300.00
Cadillacs, Gloria, Josie 765, 45 rpm 75.00
Cannon & Woods, Fourth & Beale, Brunswick 7138, 78 rpm 150.00
Cardinals, Shouldn't I Know, Atlantic 938, 45 rpm 100.00
Charles, Ray; I'm Movin On, Atlantic 2043, 45 rpm 30.00
Coleman, Jaybird; Mill Log Blues, Gennett 6226, 78 rpm 400.00
Conway, Ben; Sing Song Blues, Herwin 93014, 78 rpm 250.00
Daly, Terry; You Don't Bug Me, Mark 122, 45 rpm 20.00
Dash, Frankie; Rock Rhythm Roll, Cool 106, 45 rpm 60.00
Davis, Walter; Santa Claus, Bluebird 6125, 78 rpm 45.00
Dickson, Pere; Red Hot Papa, Victor 23335, 78 rpm 200.00
Earls, Whoever You Are, Rome 115, 45 rpm 10.00
Eddie & Oscar, Flying Crow Blues, Victor 23324, 78 rpm 400.00
Edwards, Tenderfoot; Seven Sister Blues, Paramount 12873, 78 rpm ... 300.00
Encores, When I Look at You, Checker 760, 45 rpm 100.00
Falcons, I Miss You Darling, Cash 1002, 45 rpm 60.00
Fiestas, Good News, #1074, 45 rpm 10.00
Foster, Jim; It Won't Be Long, Champion 15453, 78 rpm 300.00
Foster, Rudy; Corn Trimmer Blues, Paramount 12981, 78 rpm 300.00
Gems, You're Tired of Love, Drexel 904, 45 rpm 200.00
Georgia Bill, Stomp Down Rider, Okeh 8936, 78 rpm 300.00
Gowdy, Ruby; Florida Flood Blues, Gennett 6708, 78 rpm 500.00
Guitar Slim, Things That I Used To Do, Specialty 2120, LP, 45 rpm .. 80.00
Hall, Larry; Sandy, Strand 1005, LP, 45 rpm 40.00
Heartbreakers, Heartbreaker, RCA Victor 4327, 45 rpm 100.00
Hound Head Henry, My Silver Dollar Mama, Vocalion 1288, 78 rpm .. 150.00
Inspirators, If Loving You Is Wrong, Treat 502, 45 rpm 75.00
Irby, Jerry; Clickety Clack, Daffan 108, 45 rpm 20.00
Jackson, Sadie; Original Black Bottom Dance, Columbia 14181-D, 78 rpm... 80.00
James, Skip; Blues, Paramount 13066 22-20, 78 rpm 300.00
Jan & Dean, Jan & Dean, Dore 101, LP, 45 rpm 100.00
Jenkins, Bo Bo; Democrat Blues, Chess 1565, 45 rpm 60.00
Kelly, Jimmy; Little Chickie, Cobra 5028, 45 rpm 20.00
Kelly, Willie; Kelly's Special, Victor 23259, 78 rpm 200.00
King, Eddie; Shakin' Inside, JOB 1122, 45 rpm 50.00
Kyle, Charlie; Walking Blues, Victor 38625, 78 rpm 200.00
Lamplighters, Part of Me, Federal 12149, 45 rpm 50.00
Lee, Jerry; Smiling Blues, Herwin 93014, 78 rpm 250.00
Lewis, Bobby; Mumbles Blues, Mercury 71245, 45 rpm 8.00

Lewis, Furry; Creeper's Blues, Vocalion 1547, 78 rpm 300.00

Louis, Joe Hill; Dorothy May, Checker 763, 45 rpm..................... 150.00

Maiden, Sidney; Honey Bee Blues, Imperial 5189, 45 rpm 40.00

Martin, Sara; Kitchen Man Blues, QRS 7043, 78 rpm 300.00

Marvellos, Calypso Mama, Theron 117, 45 rpm.......................... 125.00

Mayes, Ethel; Goin' Down to the Levee, Harmograph 842, 78 rpm ..150.00

McTell, Kate; Drive Away Blues, Victor V38580, 78 rpm 300.00

Moss, Teddy; Rocky Luck Blues, Gennett 7158, 78 rpm 300.00

Nelson, Willie; Night Life, Bellair 107, 45 rpm 20.00

Neville, Aaron; Show Me the Way, Minit 618, 45 rpm 10.00

Noble, George; Oh My Death Bed, Vocalion 02954, 78 rpm 200.00

Ogletree, Louis; Tell It Like It Is, Parrot 822, 45 rpm 40.00

Old Man Oden, Silk Worm Blues, Decca 7412, 78 rpm 40.00

One Arm Slim, Howling Man Blues, Bluebird 7806, 78 rpm 40.00

Orchids, Oh Why, King 4661, 45 rpm 100.00

Parakeets, Teenage Rose, Atlas 1071, 45 rpm 40.00

Paul, Ruby; Red Letter Blues, Paramount 12592, 78 rpm 100.00

Platters, Only You, Mercury 70633, 45 rpm 10.00

Quintones, More Than a Notion, Park 57-112, 45 rpm 40.00

Railroad Bill, M & O Blues, Melotone 12373, 78 rpm 80.00

Ravens, White Christmas, Mercury 70505, 45 rpm 25.00

Regals, Run Pretty Baby, Aladdin 3266, 45 rpm 35.00

Reynolds, Blind Willie; Third Street Woman Blues, Victor 23258, $2,000.00.

(Photo courtesy Les Docks)

Rogers, Mae; My Time Blues, Champion 16530, 78 rpm 250.00

Scarlets, Kiss Me, Red Robin 138, 45 rpm 100.00

Self, Ronnie; Big Fool, Columbia 40875, 45 rpm 20.00

Sloppy Henry, Canned Heat Blues, Okeh 8630, 78 rpm 100.00

Sluefoot Joe, Rocky Road Moan, QRS 7091, 78 rpm 200.00

Smith, Bessie; After You've Gone, Columbia 14197-D, 78 rpm..... 50.00

Taylor, Edna; Good Man Blues, Paramount 12057, 78 rpm 200.00

Temptations, Standing Alone, King 5118, 45 rpm 50.00

Terry, Larry; Hep Cat, Testa 0006, 45 rpm 80.00

Thomas, Sippie; I'm a Mighty Tight Woman, Victor V-38502, 78 rpm...250.00

Tune Blenders, Oh Yes I Know, Federal 12201, 45 rpm 30.00

Uncle Skipper, Look What Shape I'm In, Decca 7455, 78 rpm 30.00

Vaughn, Bobby; Good Good Lovin', Whiz 503, 45 rpm 12.00

Videls, Be My Girl, Rhody 2000, 45 rpm 20.00

Vincent, Walter; Overtime Blues, Brunswick 7141, 78 rpm 150.00

Virgial, Otto; Bad Notion Blues, Bluebird 6213, 78 rpm 25.00

Walker, Jackie; Peggy Sue, Imperial 5473, 45 rpm 15.00

Wallace, Sippie; Mail Train Blues, Okeh 8345, 78 rpm 200.00

Washington, Lizzie; East Coast Blues, Champion 15303, 78 rpm....150.00

Watkins, Bill; I Got Troubles, Tip-Toe 14321, 45 rpm 30.00

Williams, Hank; I Saw the Light, MGM 3331, LP, 45 rpm 70.00

Williamson, Sonny Boy; Drink On Little Girl, Bluebird 8992, 78 rpm .. 10.00

Yas Yas Girl, Love Shows Weakness, Vocalion 04094, 78 rpm 12.00

York, Rusty; Shake 'Em Up Baby, King 5103, 45 rpm 15.00

Young, Billie; You Done Played Out Blues, Victor 23339, 78 rpm ..350.00

Young, Faron; My Sweet Garden of Prayer, Capitol 1185, LP, 45 rpm ...20.00

Zircons, Return My Love, Winston 1022, 45 rpm 20.00

Country and Western

Allen Brothers, Pile Drivin' Papa, Victor 23578, 78 rpm 50.00

Arkansas Charlie, Old Zip Coon, Vocalion 5384, 78 rpm 15.00

Arthur & Rexroat, White Rose, Vocalion 5335, 78 rpm 30.00

Augusta Trio, Down Yonder, Champion 15729, 78 rpm 20.00

Bang Boys, When Lulu's Gone, Vocalion 03372, 78 rpm 40.00

Banjo Joe, Engineer Joe, Columbia 15238-D, 78 rpm 30.00

Barlow, Jerry; Just Thinkin of You, Lyric 703, 78 rpm 6.00

Bird, Connie; Little Mamie, Gennett 6929, 78 rpm 50.00

Blalock & Yates, Pride of the Ball, Columbia 15576-D, 78 rpm..... 40.00

Blue Boys, Memphis Stomp, Okeh 45314, 78 rpm 100.00

Bowman Sisters, Old Lonesome Blues, Columbia 15621-D, 78 rpm.. 20.00

Brown, Jimmy; Keep a Light in Your Window..., Champion 16812, 78 rpm...50.00

Buckeye Boys, Duck Foot Sue, Champion 16168, 78 rpm 10.00

Buddy Baker, Box Car Blues, Victor 21549, 78 rpm 15.00

Burnette & Miller, Twenty-One Years, Superior 2764, 78 rpm 20.00

Cain, Albert; Runnin' Wild, Okeh 45567, 78 rpm 40.00

Carter Brothers & Son, Saddle Up the Grey, Okeh 45202, 78 rpm ..25.00

Carver Boys, Simpson County, Paramount 3233, 78 rpm 100.00

Crazy Hill Billies Band, Going Down the Road..., Okeh 45579, 78 rpm.. 40.00

Dalhart, Vernon; Jesse James, Herwin 75507, 78 rpm 50.00

Davis, Eva; Wild Bill Jones, Columbia 129, 78 rpm 10.00

Deckers, That Little Boy of Mine, Paramount 3323, 78 rpm.......... 20.00

Elkins' Stringed Steppers, Speed, Okeh 45079, 78 rpm 75.00

Elm City Quartet, Tree Song, Champion 16827, 78 rpm 10.00

Farley, JD; Bill Was a Texas Lad, Victor V40269, 78 rpm 35.00

Ferguson, John; Railroad Daddy, Challenge 159, 78 rpm 15.00

Fletcher & Foster, Travelin' North, Champion 16121, 78 rpm 50.00

Gaydon, Whit; Tennessee Coon Hunt, Victor V40315, 78 rpm 25.00

Georgia Wildcats, She's Waiting for Me, Victor 23640, 78 rpm 50.00

Harper & Hall, Life's Railway to Heaven, Superior 2799, 78 rpm....20.00

Hart Brothers, Miner's Prayer, Paramount 3162, 78 rpm 15.00

Hawkins', Ted & Mountaineers; Roamin Jack, Columbia 15752-D, 78 rpm..75.00

Irwin, Harvey; Sunny Tennessee, Okeh 45052, 78 rpm................. 15.00

Jarvis & Justice, Muskrat Rag, Brunswick 358, 78 rpm 15.00

Johnson, James; Papa Please Buy Me an Airship, Columia 15453-D, 78 rpm .. 15.00

Johnson Brothers, Sweet Nellie Brown, Victor 20662, 78 rpm 16.00

Knowles, Bert; Blue Undertaker's Blues No 2, Okeh 45427, 78 rpm.. 30.00

Kutter, Don; Two Little Orphans, Challenge 326, 78 rpm 10.00

Lake, Slim; Peach Picking Time in Georgia, Superior 2819, 78 rpm.... 100.00

Lancaster, GE; Tennessee Yodel, Superior 2538, 78 rpm 40.00

Mack, Bill; Big Bad Daddy, Imperial 8151, 78 rpm 10.00

Martin, John; Gobos Pal, Superior 2658, 78 rpm 30.00

Martin Melody Boys, Donald Rag, Columbia 15413-D, 78 rpm..... 40.00

Narmour & Smith, Limber Neck Blues, Okeh 45548, 78 rpm 100.00

Nichols Brothers, She's Killing Me, Victor 23582, 78 rpm 100.00

Norris, Land; Getting Into Trouble, Okeh 45058, 78 rpm 25.00

Oaks, Charlie; Poor Little Joe, Vocalion 5072, 78 rpm...................8.00

Owens Brothers, Harvest Field, Victor V40309, 78 rpm 20.00

Ozark Rambler, Wreck of the 1262, Paramount 3322, 78 rpm 20.00

Pickard, Obed; Kitty Wells, Columbia 15141-D, 78 rpm 12.00

Pierce, Webb; In the Jailhouse, Pacemaker 1015, 78 rpm 15.00

Puckett, Holland; Drunken Hiccoughs, Gennett 6189, 78 rpm 15.00

Quadrillers, Cumberland Blues, Paramount 3009, 78 rpm 20.00

Rector Trio, Skyland Rag, Columbia 15658-D, 78 rpm 50.00

Ritter, Tex; Oregon Trail, Champion 45154, 78 rpm 12.00

Roark, Shortbuckle & Family; Rye Straw, Gennett 7221, 78 rpm....30.00

Rodgers, Jessie; Give Your Love, Bluebird 6196, 78 rpm 10.00

Shore's Southern Trio, Goin' Crazy, Gennett 6927, 78 rpm 40.00

Steve's Hot Shots, Sour Apple Cider, Victor 23699, 78 rpm.......... 50.00

Tommie & Willie, By My Side, Champion 16240, 78 rpm 15.00

Turner, Lemuel; Jake Bottle Blues, Victor V40052, 78 rpm 30.00

Wallace, Jerry; Hand Me Down My Walking Cane, Superior 2677, 78 rpm...20.00

Watts & Wilson, Chain Gang Special, Paramount 3019, 78 rpm...100.00
White, Reuben; Old Sefus Brown, Challenge 336, 78 rpm 10.00
Wooten, Kyle; Choking Blues, Okeh 45526, 78 rpm................. 50.00
Yates, Ira & Eugene; Sarah Jane, Columbia 15581-D, 78 rpm........ 50.00
Zack & Glenn, Love's Old Sweet Song, Okeh 45240, 78 rpm 8.00

Jazz, Dance Bands, Personalities

Alabama Harmony Boys, Sweet Patootie, Silvertone 5139, 78 rpm ..200.00
Alabama Washboard Stompers, I Need Lovin', Vocalion 1635, 78 rpm.... 30.00
Andrews Sisters, Just a Simple Melody, Decca 1496, 78 rpm 12.00
Arcadian Serenaders, Yes Sir Boss, Okeh 40562, 78 rpm 60.00
Bailey's Lucky Seven, Flag That Train, Gennett 5710, 78 rpm 15.00
Baker, Belle; Cheer Up, Bruswick 4843, 78 rpm 8.00
Baltimore Bellhops, Hot & Anxious, Columbia 2449-D, 78 rpm .. 20.00
Barbecue Joe & His Hotdogs, Shake That Thing, Champion 16192, 78 rpm...250.00
Beasley, Irene; Baby's Back Today, Victor V40092, 78 rpm 10.00
Bell, Anna; Kitchen Woman Blues, QRS 7008, 78 rpm................. 150.00
Bernard, Mike; That Peculiar Rag, Columbia A1313, 78 rpm 20.00
California Poppies, What a Wonderful Time, Sunset 506/507, 78 rpm...500.00
Calloway, Cab & His Orchestra; Little Town Gal, Victor 24494, 78 rpm....12.00
Campus Boys, She My Girlfriend?, Banner 6124, 78 rpm...................8.00
Checker Box Boys, Am I Blue?, Broadway 1287, 78 rpm 8.00
Clifford's Louisville Jug Band, Get It Fixed Blues, Okeh 8269, 78 rpm... 100.00
Cotton Pickers, Hot Heels, Cameo 9207, 78 rpm 15.00
Dixieland Jug Blowers, Florida Blues, Victor 20403, 78 rpm 50.00
Dodds & Parham, Oh Daddy, Paramount 12471, 78 rpm 150.00
Duerson, Herve; Easy Drag, Gennett 7191, 78 rpm 200.00
Eddie's Hot Shots, That's a Serious Thing, Victor V-38046, 78 rpm .. 50.00
English, Peggy; Sweet Man, Vocalion 15132, 78 rpm 15.00
Etting, Ruth; It's Been So Long, Brunswick 7646, 78 rpm.............. 12.00
Five Rhythm Kings, Minnie the Moocher, Victor 23269, 78 rpm .. 60.00
Fuller, Bob; Growin' Old Blues, Ajax 17117, 78 rpm 40.00
Garland, Judy; You Can't Have Everything, Decca 1463, 78 rpm .. 10.00
Gold, Lou & His Orchestra; Everything Is Hotsy..., Banner 1544, 78 rpm...15.00
Handy, Katherine; Loveless Love, Paramount 12011, 78 rpm........ 60.00
Henderson, Edmonia; Dead Man Blues, Vocalion 1043, 78 rpm.. 250.00
Ink Spots, Swing Gate Swing, Victor 24876, 78 rpm 50.00
Jelly Whippers, SOB Blues, Herwin 92018, 78 rpm...................... 200.00
Jimmie's Joys, No No Nora, Golden 1858, 78 rpm 300.00
King David's Jug Band, Rising Sun Blues, Okeh 8913, 78 rpm..... 150.00
Kopp, Howard; Calico Rag, Columbia A2241, 78 rpm.................. 20.00
Lee, Julia; He's Tall & Dark & Handsome, Brunswick 4761, 78 rpm...100.00
Lee's Black Diamonds, Piggly Wiggly Blues, Broadway 1294, 78 rpm . 300.00
Levee Serenaders, Midnight Mama, Vocalion 1154, 78 rpm........ 200.00
Mapp, Eddie; Riding the Blues, QRS 7078, 78 rpm...................... 200.00
Memphis Bell-Hops, Animal Crackers, Challenge 135, 78 rpm 70.00
Memphis Melody Players, A Blues Serenade, Challenge 234, 78 rpm...70.00

Nowlin, Sam; So What, Champion 16828, 78 rpm..................... 150.00
Original Atlanta Footwarmers, Hot Licks, Bell 585, 78 rpm.......... 50.00
Oscar's Chicago Swingers, Try Some of That, Decca 7201, 78 rpm ..15.00
Perkins, Alberta; Levee Man, Ajax 17125, 78 rpm....................... 30.00
Powell's Jazz Monarchs, Laughing Blues, Okeh 8333, 78 rpm 200.00
Queen City Blowers, Stomp Off Let's Go, Champion 15030, 78 rpm ...75.00
Rainey, Ma & Her Georgia Band, Dream Blues, Paramount 12238, 78 rpm.....75.00
Rainey, Ma & Her Georgia Band, Misery Blues, Paramount 12508, 78 rpm..200.00
Rhythm Wreckers, September in the Rain, Vocalion 3608, 78 rpm ..8.00
Seminole Syncopators, Blue Grass Blues, Okeh 40228, 78 rpm ... 120.00
Six Black Diamonds, Dixie Flyer Sam, Banner 1428, 78 rpm 15.00
State Street Swingers, Swing Cat Swing, Vocalion 03364, 78 rpm ...25.00
Thomas' Devils, Boot It Boy, Brunswick 7064, 78 rpm................ 150.00
Troy Harmonists, Great Scott, Perfect 108, 78 rpm...................... 75.00
University Sextette, What a Man!, Lincoln 2517, 78 rpm.............. 10.00
Varsity Eight, Charleston Cabin, Cameo 577, 78 rpm.....................8.00
Washboard Serenaders, Kazoo Moan, Victor V38127, 78 rpm..... 150.00
Washingtonians, Rainy Nights, Puritan 11437, 78 rpm 100.00
Young's Creole Jazz Band, Tin Roof Blues, Paramount 20272, 78 rpm..150.00
Zutty & His Band, Royal Garden Blues, Decca 465, 78 rpm.......... 10.00

Red Wing

The Red Wing Stoneware Company, founded in 1878, took its name from its location in Red Wing, Minnesota. In 1906 the name was changed to the Red Wing Union Stoneware Company after a merger with several of the other local potteries. For the most part they produced utilitarian wares such as flowerpots, crocks, and jugs. Their early 1930s catalogs offered a line of art pottery vases in colored glazes, some of which featured handles modeled after swan's necks, snakes, or female nudes. Other examples were quite simple, often with classic styling. After the addition of their dinnerware lines in 1935, 'Stoneware' was dropped from the name, and the company became known as Red Wing Potteries, Inc. They closed in 1967. For more information we recommend *Red Wing Collectibles* and *Red Wing Stoneware* by Dan DePasquale, Gail Peck, and Larry Peterson (Collector Books).

Cookie Jars

Be aware that there is a very good reproduction of the King of Tarts. Except for the fact that the new jars are slightly smaller, they are sometime difficult to distinguish from the old.

Pierre (chef), blue, brown, green, or pink, unmarked, $150.00. (Photo courtesy Ermagene Westfall)

Napoleon, Phil and His Orchestra, Five Pennies Fox Trot, Edison 52147, EX+, from $100.00 to $150.00. (Photo courtesy Les Docks)

New Orleans Pepsters, The Rackett, Van Dyke 81843, 78 rpm 30.00
Noble, Ray & His Orchestra; Down by the River, Victor 24879, 78 rpm.. 15.00

Dutch Girl (Katrina), yel w/brn trim, from $125 to...................... 150.00
Friar Tuck, cream w/brn, mk, from $175 to................................. 200.00
Friar Tuck, gr, mk, from $250 to 300.00
Friar Tuck, yel, unmk, from $90 to 110.00

Grapes, gr, from $150 to 175.00
Jack Frost, short, unmk, from $550 to 600.00
King of Tarts, mc, mk (+), from $850 to 950.00
King of Tarts, pk w/bl & blk trim, mk, from $750 to 850.00
King of Tarts, wht, unmk, minimum value 500.00
Peasant design, emb/pnt figures on aqua, short, from $75 to 90.00
Peasant design, emb/pnt figures on brn, tall, from $90 to 125.00
Pineapple, yel 100.00

Dinnerware

Dinnerware lines were added in 1935, and today collectors scramble to rebuild extensive table services. Although interest is obvious, right now the market is so volatile, it is often difficult to establish a price scale with any degree of accuracy. Asking prices may vary from $50.00 to $200.00 on some items, which indicates instability and a collector market trying to find its way. Sellers seem to be unfamiliar with pattern names and proper identification of the various pieces that each line consists of. There were many hand-decorated lines; among the most popular are Bob White, Tropicana, and Round-up. But there are other patterns that are just as attractive and deserving of attention. Ray Reiss has published a book called *Red Wing Dinnerware, Price and Identification Guide,* which shows nearly 100 patterns on its back cover alone.

Town and Country, designed by Eva Zeisel, was made for only one year in the late 1940s. Today many collectors regard Zeisel as one of the most gifted designers of that era and actively seek examples of her work. Town and Country was a versatile line, adaptable to both informal and semiformal use. It is characterized by irregular, often eccentric shapes, and handles of pitchers and serving pieces are usually extensions of the rim. Bowls and platters are free-form comma shapes or appear tilted, with one side slightly higher than the other. Although the ware is unmarked, it is recognizable by its distinctive shapes and glazes. White (often used to complement interiors of bowls and cups), though an original color, is actually more rare than Bronze (metallic brown, also called gunmetal), which enjoys favored status; Gray is unusual. Other colors include Rust, Dusk Blue, Sand, Chartreuse, Peach, and Forest Green. Pieces have also shown up in Mulberry and Ming Green and are considered quite rare. (These are Red Wing Quartette colors!)

Eva Zeisel gave permission to reissue a few select pieces of Town and Country; these were made by World of Ceramics. In 1996 salt and pepper shakers were reproduced in new colors not resembling Red Wing colors. In 1997 the mixing bowl and syrup were reissued. All new pieces are stamped EZ96 or EZ97 and are visibly different from the old, as far as glaze, pottery base, and weight. Charles Alexander (who is listed in the Directory under Indiana) advises us on the Town and Country market.

Key:
c/s — cobalt on stoneware   RW — Red Wing
MN — Minnesota   RWUS — Red Wing Union
NS — North Star   Stoneware

Bob White, bowl, vegetable; 9⅜" 28.00
Bob White, casserole, metal lid, 1-qt 50.00
Bob White, cruet, cork stopper, 10" 85.00
Bob White, cup & saucer 10.00
Bob White, pitcher, slim, 4" 80.00
Bob White, plate, salad; 8" 18.00
Bob White, platter, oval, 13½" 26.00
Bob White, relish tray, 4 rim sections, 1 in center, 12" dia 125.00
Bob White, tumbler, 5x3" 75.00
Brittany, plate, dinner; 10" 30.00
Brittany, shakers, pr 28.00
Brittany, teapot, 4-cup 75.00
Capistrano, bowl, coupe soup; 8¼" 16.00

Capistrano, gravy boat 34.00
Capistrano, plate, dinner; 11" 15.00
Capistrano, sugar bowl, w/lid 30.00
Country Garden, bowl, vegetable; 9¼" 30.00
Country Garden, creamer 18.00
Country Garden, cup & saucer 12.00
Country Garden, platter, oval, 15" 50.00
Granada, butter dish, ¼-lb 28.00
Granada, coffeepot 42.50
Granada, plate, dinner; 10½" 12.00
Granada, sugar bowl, w/lid 18.00
Lexington, bowl, cream soup 15.00
Lexington, cup & saucer 9.00
Lexington, sugar bowl, w/lid 22.50
Lute Song, gravy boat, stick hdl, w/lid 40.00
Lute Song, plate, dinner; 10⅜" 15.00
Lute Song, platter, oval, 12¾" 30.00
Lute Song, teapot, 4-cup 150.00

Magnolia, bowl, nappy, from $12.00 to $15.00.

Normandy, casserole, 1-qt 80.00
Normandy, cup & saucer 15.00
Normandy, plate, salad; 7" 7.50
Normandy, shakers, pr 22.00
Round-Up, cup & saucer 35.00
Round-Up, platter, oval, 13⅝" 125.00
Round-Up, shakers, pr 75.00
Smart Set, bowl, lug soup; 8¼" 26.00
Smart Set, plate, dinner; 11" 50.00
Smart Set, platter, oval, 19⅞" 120.00
Smart Set, relish, 3-part 60.00
Town & Country, baker, Peach, oval, 10⅞" 60.00
Town & Country, bowl, serving; Bronze, 9" 80.00
Town & Country, pitcher, 2-pt 165.00
Town & Country, plate, dinner; Sand, 10⅝" 18.00
Town & Country, shaker, Schmoo shape, ea 60.00
Town & Country, sugar bowl, Dusk Blue 30.00
Two Step, bowl, vegetable; 9" 30.00
Two Step, plate, bread & butter; 6¼" 5.00
Two Step, plate, dinner; 10¼" 14.00
Two Step, sugar bowl, w/lid 26.00

Stoneware

Batter jar, Albany slip, high, MN, 1-gal 100.00
Bean pot, bailed; Albany slip & wht, RW, ½-gal, from $75 to 95.00
Bowl, beater; Albany slip, RW, from $50 to 60.00
Bowl, mc spatter, Albany slip, RW, 1-qt, from $50 to 75.00
Churn, #6/bird, c/s, unmk, 6-gal 1,500.00
Churn, #6/butterfly, c/s, RW, 6-gal 1,750.00
Churn, molded seam; #3/leaf, MN, 3-gal, from $1,600 to 1,900.00
Cooler, #5/flower/Ice Water, c/s, RW, 6-gal 9,000.00

Crock, #2/dbl P, c/s, MN, 2-gal..................................200.00
Crock, #5/2 elephant-ear leaves, c/s, unmk, 5-gal.....................1,400.00
Crock, #10/birch leaves (dbl set), c/s, RW oval, 10-gal, $1,300 to....1,600.00
Crock, butter, salt glaze, RW, 10-lb, from $60 to.........80.00
Cuspidor, molded seam, Albany slip, unmk 125.00
Jar, preserve/snuff; Albany slip, MN, ½-gal 60.00
Jug, beehive; #4/red wing, c/s, RWUS, 4-gal 700.00
Jug, common, Albany slip, molded bottom seam, NS, 1-gal, from $175 to...200.00
Jug, common, salt glaze, MN, 1-gal 325.00
Jug, fancy, wht w/brn ball top, RW, ½-pt 175.00
Jug, molded seam; Albany slip, stylized bird in RW mk, 2-gal, $150 to...175.00
Jug, shoulder; brn & salt glaze, dome top, MN, 1-gal.....................200.00
Jug, shoulder; brn & salt glaze, funnel top, MN, 2-gal, $125 to....150.00
Jug, shoulder; wht, funnel top, MN, 2-gal 75.00
Jug, shouldered syrup; wht, MN, ½-gal, from $55 to.....................75.00
Pitcher, dk gr w/emb rim, MN, sm, from $400 to.....................450.00

Salt and pepper shakers, Sponge Band, 4½", $700.00 for the pair. (Photo courtesy Buffalo Bay Auction Co.)

Spittoon, wht w/bl sponging, waisted, unmk 650.00
Washbowl & pitcher, lt bl on wht, emb lily decor, RW 875.00

Redware

The term redware refers to a type of simple earthenware produced by the Colonists as early as the 1600s. The red clay used in its production was abundant throughout the country, and during the eighteenth and nineteenth centuries redware was made in great quantities. Intended for utilitarian purposes such as everyday tableware or use in the dairy, redware was simple in design and decoration. Glazes of various colors were used, and a liquid clay referred to as 'slip' was sometimes applied in patterns such as zigzag lines, daisies, or stars. Plates often have a 'coggled' edge, similar to the way a pie is crimped or jagged, which is done with a special tool. In the following listings, EX (excellent condition) indicates only minor damage. Our advisor for this category is Barbara Rosen; she is listed in the Directory under New Jersey.

Bank, hen on nest, wht & dk brn vertical squiggles, 3¼" 235.00
Bowl, brn daubs, incised line, coggled rim, 3⅛x7" 400.00
Bowl, brn sponging, coggled band, flakes, 5½x13" 345.00
Bowl, lt orange w/dk brn dashes, shallow, sloping sides, crackled, 8"..60.00
Bowl, orange w/blk speckles, PA type, 1¾x6" 100.00
Bowl, scallops & flower in yel slip, PA, wear/damage, 3½x10½" ..230.00
Charger, yel slip wavy lines w/gr speckles, coggled rim, 11½".......865.00
Charger, 5 sets of wavy yel slip lines/gr speckles, wear, 12"...........865.00
Figurine, cat seated on block, gray/gr glaze, rprs, att OH, 10" 800.00
Figurine, dog seated, cast, mottled blk w/brn-gold & red pnt, 6¾" ...115.00
Food mold, jumping fish, brn daubs, chips, 10"...........................175.00
Jar, apple butter; dk brn runs, slightly ovoid, flakes, 5¾" 260.00
Jar, brn splotches, incised lines, cylindrical, 1830-60, 11" 350.00
Jar, canning; brn splotches on neck/shoulder, chips, 8¾x5¾".......200.00
Jar, canning; mottled w/orange & gr tints, tin lid, chip, 5⅝"........230.00
Jar, daubs of manganese, ribbed basket hdl, no lid, PA, 7½", EX ...2,530.00
Jar, dk brn-red w/some mottling, cvd shoulder lines, ovoid, 11x9"...345.00
Jar, gr w/orange lines that resemble cracks, ear hdls, 7x6" 175.00

Jar, lt gr, ovoid, not fitted for cover, 9x7" 1,495.00
Jar, manganese flecks, pinched hdls, ovoid, flakes, 8x7" 315.00
Jar, olive gr w/manganese streaks/orange halos, chip, 9½".........1,998.00
Jar, orange/rust w/3 incised shoulder lines, cylindrical, 12" 290.00
Jug, gr splotches, ovoid w/incised lines at shoulders, chips, 11"....880.00
Jug, gr w/orange highlights, ovoid w/rim-to-width hdl, 6".........1,265.00
Jug, incised eagle/shield/banner, coggled neck band, strap hdl, 7" ..2,350.00
Jug, puzzle; cut-out heart/trefoils/1753, ca 1753, rpr, 5⅜"..........2,465.00

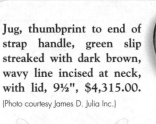

Jug, thumbprint to end of strap handle, green slip streaked with dark brown, wavy line incised at neck, with lid, 9½", $4,315.00.

(Photo courtesy James D. Julia Inc.)

Loaf pan, crisscross yel slip, coggled rim, flakes, 13x10½".............150.00
Loaf pan, foliate yel slip, coggled rim, 3x16x12"........................1,100.00
Loaf pan, 4 yel wavy lines & sm leaves, coggled rim, sm rpr, 2x16x11" ..980.00
Loaf pan, 5 sets of wavy yel slip lines/coggled, sm chips/wear, 10x15"...1,265.00
Lofa pan, S-curve yel slip decor, coggled rim, chips, 2x13x9" 360.00
Milk pan, orange w/brn streaks, sloping sides/rolled rim, 4x14" ...345.00
Milk pan, wavy yel slip designs, flakes, 12¾"............................375.00
Pie plate, combed yel slip lines, coggled rim, 8"........................350.00
Pie plate, crisscross yel slip wavy lines, coggled rim, flakes, 8"......490.00
Pie plate, flags & wavy lines in yel slip, coggled rim, flakes, 8"......600.00
Pie plate, yel slip lines, coggled rim, roughness, 9¾"....................300.00
Pitcher, brn mottled, coggled rim & neck band, strap hdl, 7⅜" ...500.00
Pitcher, daubed manganese vertical stripes, gallery rim, strap hdl, 7"..230.00
Pitcher, dk brn daubs, incised ring, ribbed hdl, 6", EX..................800.00
Pitcher, gr/brn streaks, cvd wavy line at neck, w/lid, 9", VG.....4,315.00
Pitcher, incised bird on potted plant, coggled neck, att Medinger, 7" ...880.00
Pitcher, manganese & gr brush decor, strap hdl, hairline, 8⅝" ..3,300.00
Pitcher, peppery brn, att New England, 1850s, 4½".....................175.00
Plate, wavy yel slip lines on dk red, coggled rim, flakes, 9½" 325.00
Pot, orange w/sm red dots w/in & w/out, rim unglazed, 5x5½".....175.00

Regal China

Located in Antioch, Illinois, the Regal China Company openned for business in 1938. Products of interest to collectors are James Beam decanters, cookie jars, salt and pepper shakers, and similar novelty items. The company closed its doors sometime in 1993. The Old MacDonald Farm series listed below is especially collectible, so are the salt and pepper shakers.

Note: Where applicable, prices are based on excellent gold trim. (Gold trim must be 90% intact or deductions should be made for wear.) Our advisor for this category is Judy Posner; she is listed in the Directory under Florida. See also Decanters.

Cookie Jars

Alice in Wonderland, Walt Disney, minimum value.................2,500.00
Cat, from $425 to...475.00
Churn Boy...175.00
Clown, gr collar 450.00

Davy Crockett 400.00
Diaper Pin Pig 350.00
Dutch Girl 600.00
Dutch Girl, peach trim 720.00
FiFi Poodle, minimum value 500.00
Fisherman, from $650 to 720.00
French Chef, from $475 to 525.00
Goldilocks (+), from $200 to 300.00
Harpo Marx 1,080.00
Hubert Lion, minimum value 1,000.00
Humpty Dumpty, red 175.00
Little Miss Muffet, from $200 to 275.00
Majorette 350.00
Oriental Lady w/Baskets, from $725 to 775.00

Peek-a-Boo, from $925.00 to $975.00. (Photo courtesy Joyce and Fred Roerig)

Quaker Oats 95.00
Rocking Horse, from $275 to 325.00
Three Bears 175.00
Toby Cookies, unmk, from $675 to 725.00
Tulip, from $200 to 225.00
Uncle Mistletoe 765.00

Old McDonald's Farm

Butter dish, cow's head 135.00
Canister, flour, cereal, coffee; med, ea, from $225 to 245.00
Canister, pretzels, peanuts, popcorn, chips, tidbits; lg, ea, $270 to .. 315.00
Canister, salt, sugar, tea; med, ea from $110 to 135.00
Canister, soap, cookies; lg, ea from $315 to 375.00
Cookie barn 175.00
Creamer, rooster, from $65 to 75.00
Grease jar, pig, from $110 to 135.00
Pitcher, milk; from $180 to 200.00
Shakers, boy & girl, pr 75.00
Shakers, churn, gold trim, pr 100.00
Shakers, feed sacks w/sheep, pr from $80 to ... 110.00
Spice jar, assorted lids, sm, ea from $110 to 135.00
Sugar bowl, hen 85.00
Teapot, duck's head 200.00

Shakers

A Nod to Abe, 3-pc nodder, from $200 to ... 250.00
Bendel, bears, wht w/pk & brn trim, pr 75.00
Bendel, bunnies, wht w/blk & pk trim, pr 75.00
Bendel, kissing pigs, gray w/pk trim, lg, pr from $250 to ... 275.00
Bendel, love bugs, burgundy, lg, pr 125.00
Bendel, love bugs, gr, sm, pr 65.00

Cat, sitting w/eyes closed, wht w/hat & gold bow, pr 225.00
Clown, pr 250.00
Dutch Girl, pr from $200 to 225.00
FiFi, pr 250.00
Fish, mk C Miller, 1-pc 55.00
French Chef, wht w/gold trim, pr 250.00
Humpty Dumpty, pr 75.00
Peek-a-boo, red dots, lg, pr (+) from $350 to ... 400.00
Peek-a-boo, red dots, sm, pr from $125 to 150.00
Peek-a-boo, wht solid, sm, pr 175.00
Pig, pk, mk C Miller, 1-pc 75.00
Tulip, pr 35.00
Van Tellingen, bears, brn, pr from $25 to 28.00
Van Tellingen, boy & dog, Black, pr 75.00
Van Tellingen, boy & dog, wht, pr 65.00
Van Tellingen, bunnies, solid colors, pr from $28 ... 32.00
Van Tellingen, ducks, pr 25.00
Van Tellingen, Dutch boy & girl, from $45 to 50.00
Van Tellingen, Mary & lamb, pr from $40 to 50.00
Van Tellingen, sailor & mermaid, from $100 to ... 125.00

Relief-Molded Jugs

Early relief-molded pitchers (ca 1830s – 1840s) were made in two-piece molds into which sheets of clay were pressed. The relief decoration was deep and well defined, usually of animal or human subjects. Most of these pitchers were designed with a flaring lip and substantial footing. Gradually styles changed, and by the 1860s the rim had become flatter and the foot less pronounced. The relief decoration was not as deep, and foliage became a common design. By the turn of the century, many other types of pitchers had been introduced, and the market for these early styles began to wane.

Watch for recent reproductions; these have been made by the slip-casting method. Unlike relief-molded ware which is relatively smooth inside, slip-cast pitchers will have interior indentations that follow the irregularities of the relief decoration. Values below are for pieces in excellent condition. Our advisor for this category is Tim Sublette; he is listed in the Directory under Ohio. Tim wishes to extend his appreciation to Kathy Hughes, who has devoted so much of herself to this section of the book and is now enjoying her retirement.

Key: Reg — Registered

Amphitrite, bl & wht, Charles Meigh, ca 1857, 10¾" 695.00
Babes in the Woods, polychrome, ca 1855, 8½" 250.00
Battle of Acre, lav & wht, Alcock, ca 1845, 5" 295.00
Blue Tulip, stippled w/silver lustre, Dudson, ca 1860, 6¾" 195.00
Dancing Amorini, bl & wht, Minton, Reg Mar 20, 1845, 8" 495.00
Deer scene, wht, ca 1840, 8¾" 125.00
Floral, bl on wht parian, unmk, ca 1865, 6¾" 70.00
Hunt scene, Georgian brn & wht, ca 1820, 7½" 795.00
Lady on horseback, wht, limb hdl, ca 1840, 6" 395.00
Leaves, maroon & gr on wht parian, Staffordshire, ca 1860, 5" ... 125.00
Medici, gold trim, hexagonal, Ridgway #274, ca 1840, 7¼" 395.00
Oriental, mothers & children, bl & wht, 8-sided, ca 1810, 3¾" ... 250.00
Pan pattern, figural hdl, creamy wht, Ridgway, ca 1830 .... 395.00
Pilgrimage to Canterbury, wht, ca 1845, 7½" 295.00
Prunus, polychrome on wht, cane hdl, Britannia lid, Brownhills, 7½" .. 250.00
Queen Victoria Golden Jubilee, Dudson, 1897, 8½", NM 300.00
Ranger in outdoor scene, wht, Jones & Walley, ca 1840, 9" 395.00
Shakerspeare's Bust, lt bl w/brn speckling, ca 1870, 4" 195.00
Sylvan, vines on wht, Ridgway & Abington, Reg Feb 10, 1849, 8" ... 295.00
Tam-O-Shanter, creamy wht, Ridgway, ca 1835, 5½" 195.00

Tulip, Dudson, ca. 1860, 8", $250.00. (Photo courtesy Kathy Hughes)

Turq/& wht stripes above red base, Livesley, Powell & Co, 1865, 8½" ... 195.00
Two Dancers, polychrome, Reg April 21, 1842, 8" 250.00
Vintage, wht, J&MP Bell, ca 1855, 7¼" 350.00
Willie, lt tan, Ridgway, ca 1851, 6½" 225.00

Restraints

Since the beginning of time, many things from animals to treasures have been held in bondage by hemp, bamboo, chests, chains, shackles, and other constructed devices. Many of these devices were used to hold captives who awaited further torture, as if the restraint wasn't torturous enough. The study and collecting of restraints enables one to learn much about the advancement of civilization in the country or region from which they originated. Such devices at various times in history were made of very heavy metals — so heavy that the wearer could scarcely move about. It has only been in the last 60 years that vast improvements have been made in design and construction that afford the captive some degree of comfort. Our advisor for this category is Joseph Tanner; he is listed in the Directory under California.

Key:
bbl — barrel   lc — lock case
d-lb — double lock button   NST — non-swing through
K — key   ST — swing through
Kd — keyed   stp — stamped

Foreign Handcuffs

Deutshce Polizei, ST, middle hinge, folds, takes bbl-bit K.............. 80.00
East German, heavy steel, NP single lg hinge, NST, bbl K........... 120.00
English, Chubb Arrest, steel, ST, multi-bit solid K...................... 275.00
English, Chubb Escort, steel multi-bit lever................................ 300.00
Flash Action Manacle, like Bean Giant w/ST, K-way center 500.00
Flexibles, steel segmented bows, NST Darby type, screw K.......... 300.00
French Revolved, oval, ST, takes 2 Ks: bbl & pin tumbler........... 190.00
German, 3-lb steel set, 2⅝" thick, center chain, bbl K 175.00
German Clejuso, sq lc, adjusts/NST, d-lb on side, bbl K............. 100.00
German Darby, adjusts, well finished, NST, sm.......................... 120.00
Hiatt English, figure-8 (w/chain), steel, screw K...................... 85.00
Hiatt English, solid-state figure 8, screw K 95.00
Hiatt English Darby, like US CW Darby, stp Hiatt & #d 75.00
Hiatt English Model 2000/2010/2015, modern st/chain between,ea........ 125.00
Hiatt English non-adjust screw K Darby style, uses screw K 120.00
Italian, stp New Police, modern Peerless type, ST, sm bbl K.......... 35.00
Russian modern ST, blued bbl K, unmk, crude 100.00
Spanish, stp Alcyon/Star, modern Peerless type, ST, sm bbl K....... 40.00

Foreign Leg Shackles

East German, aluminum, lg hinge, cable amid 4 cuffs, bbl key..... 150.00
Hiatt English combo manacles, handcuff/leg irons w/chain 325.00
Hiatt Plug leg irons, same K-ing as Plug-8 cuffs, w/chain 600.00

U.S. Handcuffs

Adams, teardrop lc, bbl Kd, NST, usually not stp 350.00
American Munitions, modern/rnd, sm bbl Kd, ST bow, stp 45.00
Bean Cobb, mk Pat 1899, 1 link between cuffs............................ 180.00
Bean Giant, sideways figure-8, solid center lc, dbl-bit K............. 800.00
Cavenay, looks like Marlin Daley but w/screw K, NST 300.00
Civil War padlocking type, various designs w/loop for lock 225.00
Elias Rickert (ER), screw K, 1878 .... 900.00
H&R Bean, mk H&R Arms Co, steel, 2 lg links between, sm flattish K... 250.00
H&R Super, ST, shaft-hinge connector takes hollow titted K 150.00
Judd, NST, used rnd/internally triangular K, stp Mattatuck 250.00
Kimbel, screw K at top side, 1964..3,000.00
Marlin Daley, NST, bottle-neck form, neck stp, dbl-titted K 400.00
Mattatuck, mk Mfg by...Mfg Co Waterbury CT, stork, propeller type K .. 150.00
Palmer, 2" steel bands, 2 K-ways (top & center), NST stp 650.00
Peerless, ST, takes sm bbl K, stp Mfg'ered by S&W Co 75.00
Phelps, NST, twist chain between cuffs, Tower look-alike 800.00
Providence Tool Co, stp, NST, Darby screw K style 350.00
Romer, NST, takes flat K, resembles padlock, stp Romer Co........ 600.00
Strauss, ST, takes lg solid bitted K, stp Strauss Eng Co................. 120.00
Tower bar cuffs, cuffs separate by 10-12" steel bar...................... 300.00
Tower Detective Pinkerton, NST, sq lc, bbl-bitted K, no stp 300.00
Tower-Bean, NST, sm rnd lc, takes tiny bbl-bitted K, stp............. 175.00
Walden 'Lady Cuff,' NST, takes sm bbl K, lightweight, stp 800.00

U.S. Leg Shackles

Bean Cobb, mk Patented 1899, steel.. 375.00
Civil War or prison ball & chain, padlocking or rivet type 700.00
FR, screw K 950.00
H&R Bean, mk H&R Hdw Co, steel, takes sm flattish K............. 400.00
H&R Supers, as handcuffs.. 700.00

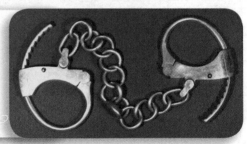

Judd, 1904, takes hollow key that has triangular shape inside, $375.00. (Photo courtesy Joseph and Pamela Tanner)

Mattatuck, mk Mfg by Mattatuck...Waterbury CT, steel, takes flat K...800.00
Oregon boot, break-apart shackle on above-ankle support........3,000.00
Peerless Big Guy, modern ST, bbl K 60.00
Strauss, as handcuffs... 200.00
Tower ball & chain, leg iron w/chain & 6-lb to 50-lb ball 700.00
Tower Detective, as handcuffs (imitation)................................. 250.00

Various Other Restraining Devices

African slave Darby-style cuffs, heavy iron/chain, handmade 200.00
African slave Darby-style leg shackles, heavy/hand forged........... 220.00
African slave padlocking or riveted forged iron shackles.............. 170.00
Darby neck collar, rnd steel loop opens w/screw K 500.00
English figure-8 nipper, claws open by lifting top lock tab........... 120.00

Gale finger cuff, knuckle duster, non-K, mk GFC..........................300.00
German nipper, twist hdl opens/closes cuff, stp Germany/etc 75.00
Hiatt High Security, hinged bbl K & pin-tumbler K (2 Ks) 150.00
Jay Pee, thumb cuffs, mk solid body, bbl K.....................................20.00
Korean, hand chain model, blk, bbl K...60.00
Korean, hand hinged model, blk, bbl K...70.00
Mighty-Mite, thumb cuffs, solid body, ST, mk, bbl K 225.00
New Model Russian, chain bbl K, blued 125.00
New Model Russian, hinged, bbl key, blued......................................140.00
Phillips Nipper, claw, flip lever on top to open 140.00
Thomas Nipper, claw, push button on top to open.........................150.00
Tower Lyon, thumb cuffs, solid body, NST, dbl-bit center K 400.00

Reverse Painting on Glass

Verre eglomise is the technique of painting on the underside of glass. Dating back to the early 1700s, this art became popular in the nineteenth century when German immigrants chose historical figures and beautiful women as subjects for their reverse glass paintings. Advertising mirrors of this type came into vogue at the turn of the century. Our values are for examples in at least excellent condition.

Albert von England, military uniform w/medal & epaulettes, 12x9", VG...335.00
Capitol Bldg, WA DC, pedestrians/cars, oval, several dk spots, 19x13"..195.00
Frigate, 18th-C ship at sea, gold-leaf fr, 10½x12½".........................485.00

George Washington, attributed to W. M. Prior, 25x20" (not including gilt frame), paint chipping, some restoration, $690.00. (Photo courtesy Early American History Auctions)

Geo WA, formal portrait, att Wm Matthew Prior, 24x20", +Martha, pr.1,000.00
Geo WA, 4" waist-up profile silhouette, cherubs above, oval, 12x10"..2,875.00
Jack Randall (boxer) w/record of wins, 1820, 20x15"+fr..............175.00
Lady (¾-view) in wht gown w/bl shawl holding bouquet, 16x12"......950.00
Lady combing hair at vanity table, EX detail/sm flakes, 12x10" fr...485.00
Lady in exotic costume, much jewelry, sgn MR, 13x11"...............100.00
Lady w/gold jewelry, wht dress w/leg-o'-mutton sleeves, 15x12" fr..300.00
Mirror, oval w/ornate rvpt fr w/cupids, openwork pediment, 39x25", VG...700.00
Oriental beauty in woodland setting, Chinese Export, 1800s, 31x20"..400.00
Oriental gent & child, ornate red/mc robes, simple fr, 20x14" 920.00
Shipwreck at shore in storm, men dragging salvage, 6x8"+giltwood fr...230.00
Titanic sinks in night scene w/iceberg & lifeboats, flakes, 17x30"+fr...85.00
Trees by stream, house in bkground, simple dk fr, 19x23"...............85.00

Rhead

Frederick Hurten Rhead was born in 1880 in Hanely, Staffordshire, England into a family of prominent ceramists. He went on to became one of the most productive artisans in the history of the industry. His career began in England at the Wardel Pottery. At only 19 years of age, he was named art director there. He left England in 1902 at the age of 22, and came to America.

He was associated with many companies during his career in America — Weller, Vance/Avon Faience, Arequipa, A.E. Tile, and lastly Homer Laughlin China. He organized his own pottery in Santa Barbara, California, ca 1913. Admittedly more of a designer than a potter, Rhead hired help to turn the pieces on the wheel but did most of the decorating himself. The process he favored most involved sgraffito designs inlaid with enameling. Egyptian and Art Nouveau influences were evidenced in much of his work. The ware he produced in California was often marked with a logo incorporating the potter at the wheel and 'Santa Barbara.' Our advisors for this category are Suzanne Perrault and David Rago; they are listed in the Directory under New Jersey. See also Roseville; Weller; Vance/Avon Faience.

Bowl, carp (wax resist/mc) on wide blk flange, bl int, ftd, 3½x10"..15,600.00
Bowl, wht pods on matt bl-gray, squeeze-bag, Santa Barbara, 8"...3,500.00
Charger, Elizabethan lady, sgn, Pinder Bourne & Co mk, 1875, 16"..1,300.00
Pepsi-Cola dispenser, squeeze-bag trees/rabbits, rare, 16", NM..7,500.00
Umbrella stand, emb trees w/squirrels fr panel w/birds, 22", EX.5,400.00
Vase, cvd trees, gr matt, University City, UC 1911 5045, 9x5"..5,100.00
Vase, gr semi-matt brn mottle over brn clay, Santa Barbara, 7x4", EX....2,475.00
Vase, spades (squeeze-bag), yel on gr, Arequipa, 8x4" 9,000.00

Vase, trees carving, multicolor on blue, marked Rhead, Santa Barbara, potter at the kiln mark, 11x6", $516,000.00. (Photo courtesy David Rago Auctions)

Vase, waves (squeeze-bag), sheer gr, Santa Barbara, 4", NM 3,240.00
Vase, 3 witches dancing, dk scene w/sky bl top, Wardle, #2122, 12", VG....475.00

Richard

Richard, who at one time worked for Galle, made cameo art glass in France during the 1920s. His work was often multilayered and acid cut with florals and scenics in lovely colors. The ware was marked with his name in relief. Our advisor for this category is Don Williams; he is listed in the Directory under Missouri.

Cameo

Bottle, scent; floral/stems, charcoal on med bl, new atomizer, 6" ..475.00
Bowl, continuous scene of house/trees/ships on river, 3x12" 475.00
Covered dish, holly, dk bl on orange, 3 scroll ft, 5x6", EX 650.00
Vase, flamingos in lily pond, pendant foliage, brn on ivory, 6" 900.00
Vase, floral/leaves, royal bl on orange, 3 bl hdls, 4x3½"................365.00
Vase, flowers/insects, brn tones on orange, slim/ftd, 10¼" 700.00
Vase, foliage, gr on yel, cylindrical w/doughnut bottom, 3¼".......200.00
Vase, lake/mtns/trees, slim w/wide mushroom-cap top, 8½".........590.00
Vase, orchids/foliage, dk/lt raspberry on cream, slim, 11½" 800.00
Vase, tree, village/river beyond, brn on lt orange, shouldered, 8".800.00
Vase, tree w/boats & mtns on red, slanted pinched rim, 6x3½" ...600.00

Vase, tree w/mtns/ships/bldgs beyond, 3 detailed cvgs, bulbous, 15"..**2,000.00**
Vase, trees/coastal bldgs, brn on orange, slim w/bun ft, 12" **590.00**
Vase, wisteria, cobalt on orange, slim/elongated, 15" **520.00**

Riviera

Riviera was a line of dinnerware introduced by the Homer Laughlin China Company in 1938. It was sold exclusively by the Murphy Company through their nationwide chain of dime stores. Riviera was unmarked, lightweight, and inexpensive. It was discontinued sometime prior to 1950. Colors are mauve blue, red, yellow, light green, and ivory. On rare occasions, dark blue pieces are found, but this was not a standard color. For further information we recommend *Collector's Encyclopedia of Fiesta* by Sharon and Bob Huxford, available from Collector Books.

Batter set, standard colors other than red, complete, from $175 to ..**225.00**
Bowl, baker; 9", from $15 to **20.00**
Bowl, fruit; 5½", from $6 to **10.00**
Bowl, nappy; 7¼", from $20 to **25.00**
Bowl, oatmeal; 6", from $25 to **32.00**
Butter dish, cobalt, ½-lb, from $125 to.. **150.00**
Butter dish, cobalt, ¼-lb, from $200 to.. **250.00**
Butter dish, colors other than cobalt, ½-lb, from $100 to............. **125.00**
Butter dish, ivory, ¼-lb, from $120 to.. **150.00**
Butter dish, turq, ¼-lb, from $225 to... **250.00**
Casserole, from $85 to **100.00**
Creamer, from $11 to **13.00**
Jug, w/lid, from $90 to **110.00**
Pitcher, juice; mauve bl, from $100 to.. **130.00**
Pitcher, juice; red, from $120 to **145.00**
Pitcher, juice; yel, from $75 to **90.00**
Plate, deep, from $15 to **20.00**
Plate, 6", from $3 to **5.00**
Plate, 7", cobalt, from $20 to **25.00**
Plate, 7", from $4 to **8.00**
Plate, 9", from $15 to **18.00**
Plate, 10", from $50 to **60.00**
Platter, closed hdls, 11¼", from $20 to **25.00**
Platter, oval well, 11½", from $15 to **22.00**
Platter, oval well, 15", from $40 to **50.00**
Sauceboat, from $18 to **20.00**
Saucer, from $2 to **4.00**
Shakers, pr from $15 to **20.00**
Sugar bowl, w/lid, from $18 to **20.00**
Syrup, w/lid, from $100 to **150.00**
Teacup, from $6 to **9.00**
Teapot, from $125 to **150.00**
Tumbler, hdl, from $35 to **50.00**
Tumbler, juice; from $25 to.. **35.00**

Robineau

After short-term training in ceramics in 1903, Adelaide Robineau (with the help of her husband Samuel) built a small pottery studio at her home in Syracuse, New York. She was adept in mixing the clay and throwing the ware, which she often decorated by incising designs into the unfired clay. Samuel developed many of the glazes and took charge of the firing process. In 1910 she joined the staff of the American Women's League Pottery at St. Louis, where she designed the famous Scarab Vase. After this pottery failed, she served on the faculty of Syracuse University. In the 1920s she worked under the name of Threshold Pottery. She was also the founder and publisher of *Keramic Studio* magazine. Her work was

and is today highly acclaimed for the standards of excellence to which she aspried. Our advisors for the category are Suzanne Perrault and David Rago; they are listed in the Directory under New Jersey.

Bowl, gr flambe w/gold crystalline int, 1921, 1x4" **2,160.00**
Bowl vase, cafe-au-lait & verdigris crystalline, AB/184/5, 3x4", NM.. **3,000.00**
Candlestick, flowing brn/orange matt, sq rtcl at flared base, 6x3½"..**1,440.00**
Tile, rooster w/lg fan tail, mc cuenca w/some crystalline, 6½" ...**6,600.00**
Vase, purple/celadon cyrstalline flambe, 1919, AR/1919, 5x3¼", ...**5,290.00**
Vase, brn crystalline, AR/rnd stamp, sm chip, 7x2"................. **10,800.00**
Vase, cabinet; bl crystalline, ink mk, 2¼x2"................................ **1,200.00**
Vase, cabinet; bl/ivory crystalline, Y/AR, 2¾x2¼".................... **2,400.00**
Vase, cabinet; ivory crystalline, 2¼x2"..................................... **1,200.00**
Vase, celadon crystalline, bottle shape, 1919, AR, 4½x3½" **5,800.00**
Vase, cobalt crystalline, squat, RP'5/481, 4¼x6"...................... **2,580.00**

Vase, fine purple and celadon crystalline flambe, signed AR and dated 1919, 5x3¼", $5,290.00. (Photo courtesy David Rago Auctions)

Vase, indigo/oxblood crackle, shouldered, 3½" **2,760.00**
Vase, lg bl crystals on celadon, cvd AR medallion on front, 5x2½" ..**13,200.00**
Vase, pk/ivory crystals, AR in circle/27 1912, 4½x1¾" **7,800.00**
Vase, turq crystalline, medallion w/956 05, paper label, 2¾".....**7,800.00**

Robj

Robj was the name of a retail store that operated in Paris for only a few years, from about 1925 to 1931. Robj solicited designs from the best French artisans of the period to produce decorative objects for the home. These were executed mostly in porcelain but there were glass and earthenware pieces as well. The most well known are the figural bottles which were particularly popular in the United States. However, Robj also promoted tea sets, perfume lamps, chess sets, ashtrays, bookends, humidors, powder jars, cigarette boxes, figurines, lamps, and milk pitchers. Robj objects tend to be whimsical, and all embody the Art Deco style. Items listed below are ceramic unless noted otherwise. Our advisors for this category are Randall Monsen and Rod Baer; their address is listed in the Directory under Virginia.

Bottle, Cointreau, clown in wht w/red details, 10½" **2,200.00**
Bottle, Curacao, bl jacket, wht bottom w/thin bl stripes, 10".......**550.00**
Bottle, Curacao, red jacket, red-striped wht bottom, 10" **650.00**
Bottle, General De Brigade, 10" **1,410.00**
Bottle, Kummel Cursky De Cointreau, bl coat w/wht fur trim, 10½" ... **2,300.00**
Bottle, L'Ecuyere, gr military-style jacket, wht bottom, w/purse, 12"..**3,720.00**
Bottle, La Cantinere, 12½"... **2,585.00**
Bottle, lady in apron over gr dress, 10½" **1,975.00**
Bottle, Les Trois Matelots, 3 back-to-back sailors in bl, 11" **4,200.00**
Bottle, man in top hat, red jacket, w/riding crop, 12½".............**2,000.00**
Bottle, MP, Military Police, in khaki attire, 10½".....................**1,500.00**

Bottle, Paysanne Revolutionnaire, 10½".....................................2,800.00
Bottle, Vieux Marc de Champane, in red-trimmed blk robe/hat, 10" ...765.00
Bottle, Vodka, Red Russian, 10½" 995.00
Jar, pointed hat as lid, bottom w/facial features, gold crackle, 9"..250.00
Lamp, perfume; mottled glass shade, wrought-iron tower base, 9"...475.00

Roblin

The intimate and short-lived Roblin pottery was founded at the turn of the last century in San Francisco by descendants of the Robertson family, Scottish ceramicists for generations, and California potter Linna Irelan. Its name came from the contraction of Robertson and Linna, and its product from their joined experience and tastes. The two shared a fondness for local clays, which Alexander Robertson threw along classical shapes. Mrs. Irelan embellished them with painted and applied decoration, often minimal beading, sometimes with applied lizards or mushrooms. Most were stamped Roblin along with a bear drawing. The company was forced to close after the great earthquake of 1906. Our advisors for this category are Suzanne Perrault and David Rago; they are listed in the Directory under New Jersey.

Vase, brn drips on celadon flambe, trumpet top, low angle width, 2x3"..1,920.00
Vase, bsk w/lt spatter of brn, lt tooling at neck, 2x2"....................420.00
Vase, bsk w/multi-tone tan & brn finish, 2" 540.00

Vase, cloverleaves, white on brown, glaze bubbles, signed Linna Irelan, 5x4", $3,600.00. (Photo courtesy David Rago Auctions)

Vase, gunmetal, cylindrical w/random prunt, AWR/BMN/L Irelan, 4" ..780.00
Vase, tan/brn mottled bsk, rope band at shoulder, ovoid/ftd, 2" ...540.00

Rock 'n Roll Memorabilia

Memorabilia from the early days of rock 'n roll recalls an era that many of us experienced firsthand; these listings are offered to demonstrate the many and various aspects of this area of collecting. Beware of reproductions! Many are so well done even a knowledgeable collector will sometimes be fooled. Unless otherwise noted, our values are for examples in near-mint to mint condition. Our advisor for this category is Bob Gottuso, author of Beatles, KISS and Monkees sections in *Garage Sale Gold II* by Tomart. He is listed in the Directory under Pennsylvania. See also Decanters.

Aerosmith, blanket, Get Your Wings tour, 50x71", EX 200.00
Aerosmith, guitar pick, pearlescent, Nine Lives tour, EX...............35.00
Aerosmith, jersey, red/blk/wht, Nine Lives tour, 1997....................75.00
Alice Cooper, doll skewered on tip of sword, ca 1973, 41x5".......480.00
Alice Cooper, poster, Alice at Aladdin, blk/wht/red, 1977, 1-sheet+fr...240.00
Alice Cooper, program, Mad House tour, 1978, EX........................35.00
Beatles, animation cel, group in band uniforms beneath rainbow, 9x10"...1,700.00

Beatles, concert ticket, Suffolk Downs Racetrack, MA, 1966........75.00
Beatles, game, Flip Your Wig, Milton Bradley, 1964, complete, EX+..175.00
Beatles, lunch box, tin litho, w/glass thermos, 1966-67, EX.........800.00
Beatles, lunch box, Yellow Submarine, King Features, 1968, VG ...250.00
Beatles, Lux soap, 3 bars, 1967, unopened, MIB..........................450.00
Beatles, model kit, Geo Harrison unassembled figure, Revell, MIB....450.00
Beatles, notebook, group in doorway of bl brick building, 10½x8"...75.00
Beatles, paperback book, All About the Beatles, 1964, 96-pg, EX...10.00
Beatles, pennant, We Luv You, red on wht felt, ca 1964, 29", EX. 120.00
Beatles, picture sleeve, Can't Buy Me Love/You Can't Do That, 1964, VG .250.00
Beatles, picture sleeve, I'll Cry Instead, 45 rpm, EX 75.00
Beatles, poster, movie, Help!, 1965, 1-sheet, 27x41".....................600.00
Beatles, puzzle, Beatles in Pepperland, Jaymar, 650 pcs, 1968, EXIB..125.00
Beatles, record carrier, red vinyl w/mc group photo, blk hdls, UK...250.00
Beatles, wig, Lowell Toy Mfg, M in EX pkg..................................100.00
Bee Gees, Andy Gibbs doll, Disco Dancin', 1979, 8", M in VG box ...45.00
Bee Gees, poster, Barry Gibbs in blk, 1979, 34x22"........................40.00
Bee Gees, program, many photos, Atlantic Records, 1976, EX......35.00
Bee Gees, tour book, color photos, 1976, EX..................................40.00
Bill Haley, sheet music, Rock-A-Beatin' Boogie, photo cover, 1954, EX...20.00
Black Sabbath, T-shirt, Heaven & Hell Tour 80...........................100.00
Bobby Darin, sheet music, Dream Lover, EX 20.00
Bruce Springsteen, backstage pass, Solo Acoustic tour, EX 30.00
Creedence Clearwater Revival, tour book, hardcover, 1969, EX ...85.00
Dave Clark 5, button, Fan-Fair '67, red & wht, 1967, 1¾", VG.....20.00
Dave Clark 5, concert program, 1970s, EX 20.00
Dave Clark 5, promo photo, blk & wht, 1960s, 8x10", EX................8.00
David Bowie, postcard, RCA Fan Club membership, 1970s 35.00
David Bowie, poster book, Labyrinth, 1980s, holds 8 17x11" posters...30.00
David Bowie, tour book, Diamond Dogs, 1974, 20-pg, 9x12", EX..65.00
David Cassidy, 3-ring binder, Westab, 1972, from $40 to 50.00
Def Leppard, book, Animal Instinct, 1987, 1st ed, EX 40.00
Def Leppard, jacket, blk leather, Rock of Ages design, Wilson 160.00
Def Leppard, T-shirt, 4 members (after Clark's death) shown, 1992, EX..20.00
Dino, Desi & Billy, fan card, 1960s, 5x7"..30.00
Donny & Marie, Magic Slate, 1977, EX 25.00
Donny & Marie, promo photo, mc, as teenagers, 8x10".................15.00
Donny & Marie, record case, portrait, mc on yel vinyl, 1977 ....20.00
Doors, poster, Pay Attention, Rick Griffin, 1967.........................135.00
Doors, tour program, 1968-69, 24-pg, EX+ 315.00
Doors/Grateful Dead, poster, Fillmore, W Wilson, 1967, 1st printing ..400.00

Eagles, belt buckle, 1977, 3½", $65.00. (Photo courtesy www.gasolinealleyantiques.com)

Elton John, belt buckle, in style of Peter Max, 2¼x3¼", EX 40.00
Elton John, rubber stamp, Blues Moves, 2¼x4" 40.00
Elton John, T-shirt, Don't Shoot Me, I'm Only the Piano Player, EX..40.00
Elton John, T-shirt, portrait on blk, 1970s 15.00
Elvis, All Elvis, unofficial biography, Daily Mirror, 1962...............18.00
Elvis, bust, wht porc, EP 1935-77, Goebel, from $50 to 60.00
Elvis, doll, Burning Love, wht jumpsuit, World Doll, 1984, 21", MIB...70.00
Elvis, earrings, Loving You..., gold-fr portrait, pierced bks, MIP (+)...225.00
Elvis, handkerchief, My Best/song titles/portrait, EPE, 1956, NM ..150.00
Elvis, magazine, Elvis Monthly 1962 Special, photo cover, 60+pgs, EX... 12.00
Elvis, menu, Las Vegas Hilton Hotel, w/rainbow on blk, 1976, NM...225.00

Elvis, pin-bk, portrait/guitar flasher, blk/wht, 1956, 2½", EX.......... 30.00
Elvis, scrapbook, EP Solid Gold Memories, Ballentine, 1977, 218-pg....55.00
Elvis, table lamp, bust w/wht costume/turq scarf, ceramic, 1970s.. 110.00
Elvis, thimble, EP's Graceland, heart cap, pewter, 1"...................... 50.00
Elvis, tour book, in wht jumpsuit on cover, 1976, EX.................... 30.00
Elvis, wallet, red vinyl, EPE, dtd 1956, EX................................. 300.00
Jackson 5, tour/program book, 1972, 22-pg, 10x13", EX................ 55.00
Jimi Hendrix, tour book, Electric Church, 1969, 24-pg, 12x12", EX .. 225.00
KISS, belt buckle, prism logo, Pacifica Mfg, 1978....................... 75.00
KISS, book, The Real Story, oversz, 1979, EX 40.00
KISS, Colorforms, complete w/instruction sheet, EXIB 90.00
KISS, model kit, KISS Custom Chevy Van, AMT, 1977, MIB (sealed)..170.00
KISS, pencils, 1978, set of 4, MIP 65.00
KISS, poster, group on Harleys, logo upper left, 1979, 21x30" 35.00
KISS, poster, portraits on pk, blk light, MH Stein, 1976, 28x20", VG ..65.00
KISS, poster, 1977 KISS Alive II tour, 58x42", M (sealed).......... 300.00
KISS, stuffed toy, Peter Criss, Dynasty Collection 18", MIB........ 100.00
KISS, T-shirt, Gene Simmons on blk, wht ¾-sleeves, 1980s, EX 35.00
KISS, T-shirt, portraits on bl, 1983-84 tour 45.00
Led Zeppelin, jacket, studded blk leather, Wilson 90.00
Led Zeppelin, poster, Bonzo Dog Band/R Kirk, 2nd printing, 22x14"... 165.00
Pearl Jam, floor mat, stick figure/'ten' on blk rubber, promo item.. 110.00
Pink Floyd, concert program, The Wall, 1980 Am tour, EX........... 45.00

Pink Floyd, patch, 2x5", unused, $15.00. (Photo courtesy www.gasolinealley.com)

Ricky Nelson, postcard, fan club photo, 1960s 35.00
Rolling Stones, book, Rolling Stones, R Palmer, Doubleday, 1983 ...20.00
Rolling Stones, program, Jagger w/arms raised, 1972 tour, EX........ 35.00
Rolling Stones, tour book, girl pointing on cover, 1978, EX 25.00
Rolling Stones, tour/program book, photo cover, 1965, 16-pg, EX....65.00

Rockingham

In the early part of the nineteenth century, American potters began to prefer brown- and buff-burning clays over red because of their durability. The glaze favored by many was Rockingham, which varied from a dark brown mottle to a sponged effect sometimes called tortoiseshell. It consisted in part of manganese and various metallic salts and was used by many potters until well into the twentieth century. Over the past two years, demand and prices have risen sharply, especially in the east. See also Bennington.

Bean pot, dk tortoiseshell, flat lid w/mushroom finial, 5" 95.00
Bed pan, oval w/spout 1 end, 15" L 125.00
Biscuit jar, acanthus leaf arched panels, mask hdls, dome lid, 9".. 425.00
Biscuit jar, vining blackberries around body & on lid, 7¾x5½"....650.00
Bowl, octagonal, ca 1850s, 9x7x2", EX 85.00
Bowl, rope band over arched panels, deep w/str flared sides, 12".. 125.00
Bowl, str flared sides, 1800s, 3x11" 100.00
Bowls, nesting; 4" to 9½", set of 6... 450.00
Coffeepot, dk brn, curvilinear design, acorn finial, 10" 675.00

Cooler, brn w/gr streaks, att Woodward & Vodrey, 1848-79 .... 800.00
Creamer, cow standing on oval base, tail curled over bk, 6¾"...... 475.00

Cuspidor, paneled mold, 7x13½", $175.00. (Photo courtesy Garth's Auctions Inc.)

Custard, att J Patterson & Sons (OH), 6-oz, from $18 to.............. 22.00
Figurine, dog seated, free-standing front legs, curly coat, 11x11" .. 895.00
Figurine, spaniel seated on base, free-standing front legs, OH, 11"...895.00
Figurine, spaniel seated on raised base, lt brn, 1850, 10" 795.00
Flask, boot form, laced up 1 side, removable spout, rpr, 7x7" 400.00
Flask, fish form, EX details, stands vertically, rprs, 9".................. 475.00
Hatpin holder, figural lady wearing hat, long cloak, 5½", NM 120.00
Inkwell, young girl sleeping, hat beside, 4¾" L 125.00
Mold, fluted pinwheel, 9" 80.00
Mug, 3-D frog w/in, cylindrical w/C hdl, att E Liverpool, 4"........ 495.00
Pitcher, eagle, spread wings, arrows in talons in front panel, 9" ... 700.00
Pitcher, floral, 4½" 50.00
Pitcher, hounds/stag, lg full-figure hound as hdl, Harker Taylor, 11" ... 850.00
Pitcher, hunting scene in relief, 8½" 1,150.00
Pitcher, Miss Liberty in US flag holding pike, star/ribbon banner, 8".. 700.00
Pitcher, neck band w/emb design, 7½" 60.00
Pitcher, Pillar & Scroll, 7" 150.00
Pitcher, sm cow/foliage on lower body, incurvate neck, 8" 80.00
Pitcher, 2 horsemen/3 hounds/stag/appl name, gr frog w/in, Perth, 10"...1,750.00
Plate, berries & leaves, Hautin & Boulanger, 1800s, 8", from $35 to...65.00
Pot, melon ribs, dome lid, curved stem-like hdl, 7½" 590.00
Shaving/barber's dish, incised name/1850 on bk, 6¼" L............... 800.00
Teapot, Rebecca at the Well, ca 1850, sm.................................... 90.00
Washboard, yel/brn, overall wear, E Liverpool OH origin, 22x12"...600.00

Rockwell, Norman

Norman Rockwell began his career in 1911 at the age of 17 doing illustrations for a children's book entitled *Tell Me Why Stories*. Within a few years he had produced the *Saturday Evening Post* cover that made him one of America's most beloved artists. Though not well accepted by the professional critics of his day who did not consider his work to be art but 'merely' commercial illustration, Rockwell's popularity grew to the extent that today there is an overwhelming abundance of examples of his work or those related to the theme of one of his illustrations.

The figurines described below were issued by Gorham. For Rockwell listings by Rockwell Museum and Museum Collections Inc. (formerly Rockwell Museum), see last year's edition of *Schroeder's Antiques Price Guide*. Our advisor for this category is Barb Putratz; she is listed in the Directory under Minnesota.

A Tough One, 1983 .... 95.00
Adventures Between Adventures, 1972....................................300.00
Antique Dealer, 1983.. 195.00
At the Vets, Gorham Miniature, 1981 .... 55.00
At the Vets, 1974.. 110.00
Baby Sitter, Gorham Miniature, 1987....................................... 90.00
Batter Up, Gorham Miniature, 1984... 76.00

Beguiling Buttercup, 1977 .... 115.00
Best Friends, Gorham Miniature, 1986 .... 45.00
Blasting Out, 1983 .... 95.00
Boy & His Dog, 4 Seasons set, complete 1,200.00
Boy Meets His Dog, Gorham Miniature, 1981................... 110.00
Canine Solo, 1982 .... 100.00
Captain, 1974 .... 115.00
Careful Aim, Gorham Miniature, 1984 .... 80.00
Careful Aim, 1981 .... 25.00
Checking Good Deeds, 1982, 3½" 25.00
Choosing Up, 1978 .... 175.00
Christmas Goose, ltd ed of 7,500 .... 150.00
Closed for Business, 1980 .... 240.00
Coal-Seasons Coming, 1980 .... 240.00
Confrontation, Gorham Miniature, 1988 .... 90.00
Cool Aid, 1979 .... 260.00
Country Pedlar, 1985 .... 100.00
Dad's Boy, 4 Seasons set, complete 1,050.00
Day Dreamers, 1975.. 175.00
Day in the Life of a Boy, 1980 .... 115.00
Day in the Life of a Boy III, 1982 .... 120.00
Day in the Life of a Girl II, 1981 .... 115.00
Diary, Gorham Miniature, 1988 .... 95.00
Disastrous Daring, 1976 .... 275.00
Downhill Daring, Gorham Miniature, 1981 .... 80.00
Downhill Daring, 1973 .... 250.00
Drum for Tommy, ltd ed of 7,500, 1986............................ 100.00
Expert Salesman, ltd ed of 1,500, 1983 .... 225.00
Final Speech, 1984... 100.00
First Annual Visit, 1980 .... 185.00
Fishing, Gorham Miniature, 1984 .... 80.00
Flying High, 1973 .... 250.00
Football Season, Gorham Miniature, 1986 .... 70.00
Four Ages of Love, 4 Seasons set, complete 900.00
Gaily Sharing Vintage Times, 1977 .... 130.00
Gay Blades, Gorham Miniature, 1981................................. 75.00
Ghostly Gourds, 1977... 300.00
God Rest Ye Merry Gentlemen, 1976 ....1,400.00
Goin' Fishing, Gorham Miniature, 1984............................. 70.00
Going On Sixteen, 4 Seasons set, complete....................... 750.00
Grand Pals, 4 Seasons set, complete...............................1,050.00
Grandpa & Me, 4 Seasons set, complete........................... 700.00
Helping Hand, 4 Seasons set, complete 950.00
Home for the Holidays, 1988.. 140.00
Horse Trader, 1985... 100.00
In His Spirit, Gorham Miniature, 1984............................... 70.00
In His Spirit, 1981 .... 250.00
Jolly Coachman, Gorham Miniature, 1984......................... 45.00
Lazy Days, 1982 .... 100.00
Life w/Father, 4 Seasons set, complete 70.00
Little Angel, Gorham Miniature, 1986............................... 70.00
Marriage License, Gorham Miniature 85.00
Marriage License, 1976, 6¼".. 310.00
Me & My Pal, 4 Seasons set, complete 1,100.00
Missed, 1978 .... 245.00
Morning Walk, Gorham Miniature, 1986 .... 75.00
New Arrival, Gorham Miniature, 1985 .... 50.00
New Year Look, 1979... 260.00
No Swimming, 1974 .... 160.00
Oh Yeah, 1978 .... 245.00
Old Sign Painter, Gorham Miniature, 1986........................ 90.00
Old Sign Painter, ltd ed of 7,500, 1984 .... 120.00
Pensive Pals, 1975.. 175.00
Pilgrimage, 1978 .... 190.00

Pride of Parenthood, 1972 .... 300.00
Prom Dress, Gorham Miniature, 1987 .... 90.00
Puppet Maker, 1985 .... 195.00
Runaway, 1978 .... 105.00
Santa's Friend, ltd ed of 7,500, 1985 .... 150.00
Santa's Friend, 1983, 3½" 25.00
Season's Greetings, Gorham Miniature, 1986..................... 65.00
Serenade, 1983 .... 170.00
Shared Sucess, 1984 .... 100.00
Shoulder Ride, Gorham Miniature, 1986............................ 65.00
Snow Sculpture, Gorham Miniature, 1981 .... 80.00
Soaring Spirits, 1977... 250.00
Springtime, Gorham Miniature, 1987 .... 250.00
Summer Vacation, pewter, 1980.. 105.00
Sweet Serenade, Gorham Miniature, 1981 .... 60.00
Sweet Serenade, 1978 .... 190.00
Sweet Song So Young, 1974 .... 225.00
Tackled, 1976 .... 110.00
To Love & To Cherish, Gorham Miniature, 1985 .... 50.00
Traveling Salesman, ltd ed of 1,500, issued at $175, 1981 ... 210.00
Triple Self Portrait, 1980, 10½" 500.00
Trout Dinner, Gorham Miniature, 1983............................. 80.00
Weighing In, 1974 .... 150.00
Welcome Mat, Gorham Miniature, 1986 .... 90.00
Winter, Bringing Home the Tree, pewter, 1980 .... 105.00
Young Man's Fancy, Gorham Miniature, 1981 .... 75.00
Young Man's Fancy, 1976.. 275.00
Yuletide Reckoning, ltd ed of 7500, 1984 .... 100.00
Yuletide Reckoning, 1981, 3½" 25.00

Rogers, John

John Rogers (1829 – 1904) was a machinist from Manchester, New Hampshire, who turned his hobby of sculpting into a financially successful venture. From the originals he meticulously fashioned of red clay, he had bronze master molds made from which plaster copies were cast. He specialized in five different categories: theatrical, Shakespeare, Civil War, everyday life, and horses. His large detailed groupings portrayed the life and times of the period between 1859 and 1892. In the following listings, examples are assumed to be in very good to excellent condition unless otherwise noted. Many examples will be in poor condition, be sure to adjust prices accordingly.

Bubbles..2,000.00
Charity Patient 650.00
Coming to the Parson... 660.00

The Council of War, Patented March 31, 1868, 24", NM, $2,645.00. (Photo courtesy James D. Julia Inc.)

Courtship in Sleepy Hollow, Pat date 550.00
Elder's Daughter 475.00
Favored Scholar 780.00
Fighting Bob, 1889 .... 1,100.00
Frolic at the Old Homestead, 1887 .... 900.00
It Is So Nominated in the Bond 1,500.00
Matter of Opinion 600.00
Parting Promise, 22x10x9" 635.00
Photographer, 1878 .... 4,000.00
Rip Van Winkle on the Mountain 575.00
School Days, 22x12x8" 800.00
Speak for Yourself John 500.00
Tap on the Window 525.00
Uncle Ned's School, wht pnt, 20x15x9" 1,035.00
Watch on the Santa Maria 1,000.00
Wounded Scout, 23x11x9", from $700 to 1,000.00

Rookwood

The Rookwood Pottery Company was established in 1879 in Cincinnati, Ohio, by Maria Longworth Nichols. From a wealthy family, Ms. Nichols was provided with sufficient financial backing to make such an enterprise possible. She hired competent ceramic artisans and artists of note, who through constant experimentation developed many lines of superior art pottery. While in her employ, Laura Fry invented the airbrush-blending process for which she was issued a patent in 1884. From this, several lines were designed that utilized blended backgrounds. One of their earlier lines, Standard, was a brown ware decorated with underglaze slip-painted nature studies, animals, portraits, etc. Iris and Sea Green were introduced in 1894 and Vellum, a transparent mat-glaze line, in 1904. Other lines followed: Ombroso in 1910 and Soft Porcelain in 1915. Many of the early artware lines were signed by the artist. Soon after the turn of the twentieth century, Rookwood manufactured 'production' pieces that relied mainly on molded designs and forms rather than freehand decoration for their aesthetic appeal. The Depression brought on financial difficulties from which the pottery never recovered. Though it continued to operate, the quality of the ware deteriorated, and the pottery was forced to close in 1967.

Unmarked Rookwood is only rarely encountered. Many marks may be found, but the most familiar is the reverse 'RP' monogram. First used in 1886, a flame point was added above it for each succeeding year until 1900. After that a Roman numeral added below indicated the year of manufacture. Impressed letters that related to the type of clay utilized for the body were also used — G for ginger, O for olive, R for red, S for sage green, W for white, and Y for yellow. Artware must be judged on an individual basis. Quality of the artwork is a prime factor to consider. Portraits, animals, and birds are worth more than florals; and pieces signed by a particularly renowned artist are highly prized.

Our advisors for this category are Suzanne Perrault and David Rago; they are listed in the Directory under New Jersey.

Black Opal

Vase, holly leaves & berries on blk, S Sax, #900D, 1906, 6¼" ..7,200.00
Vase, Moorish decor, L Epply, #1920, 1922, 9½" 4,000.00
Vase, stylized floral, L Epply, #324, 1925, 17", NM 4,700.00

Cameo

Bowl, floral branch, E Abel, #549, Wy, W, 1890, 1½x6½" 300.00
Coffeepot, daffodil, AM Valentien, #843/W, 1891, 9" 800.00
Cup & saucer, floral on red, #460P, 1889, 2¼" 300.00
Pitcher, wild roses, AM Valentien, #522/W, 1890, 7" 600.00
Plate, Endymion, EP Chanch, 1890, 7½", VG 110.00

Vase, wisteria branch in white pate-sur-pate on matt indigo, A. R. Valentien, 1893, 14½", $13,200.00.
(Photo courtesy David Rago Auctions)

French Red

Vase, floral, S Sax, #942E, P, X, 1917, 4⅝" 1,075.00
Vase, floral (EX art), S Sax, #703, 1922, X, 5¾x7¼" 8,000.00
Vase, stylized flowers, S Sax, #356F, 1922, 5½" 9,900.00
Vase, stylized flowers, S Sax, #977, 1923, 10⅝" 21,000.00

Glaze Effect

Bowl, bl/gr/brn, #6313, 1932, 2¾x8¼" 120.00
Vase, bl & dk pk over striated brn, #6315, 1932, 6¼" 480.00
Vase, bl crystalline drips on dk gray, #3617-C, 1932, 6¾" 500.00
Vase, bl/brn/yel, #6307, 1932, 3" 425.00
Vase, gr/brn/bl, E Menzel, S, 1953, 7" 425.00

High Glaze

Planter, floral, E Barrett, #6292C, 1945, 7⅝" 425.00
Vase, abstract irises, L Epply, #6043, X, 1930, 7" 975.00
Vase, floral branches on ivory, L Epply, #5316, 1932, 4x4¼" 475.00
Vase, geometrics on cream, J Harris, #1780, X, 1930, 6½" 850.00
Vase, jellyfish, J Wareham, 1952, 12" 1,200.00
Vase, scenic, M McDonald, #2544, 1942, 8" 3,000.00
Vase, stars & lightning bolts, M McDonald, #6194D, 1931, 6⅛" ..4,150.00

Iris

Vase, clover blossoms, F Rothenbusch, #926, W, 1903, 8⅜" 1,800.00
Vase, clover blossoms, S Sax, #30E, W, 1906, 8x3¼" 2,000.00
Vase, crocuses, C Lindemann, #30F, W, 1906, 6¼" 1,200.00
Vase, crocuses, L Asbury, #917C, W, X, 1908, 7⅜" 1,325.00
Vase, cvd tulips, wht/buff on olive & dk bl, JD Wareham, drilled, 12" ..19,200.00
Vase, fish (3 lg), J Wareham, drilled, #907C, 1901, 13⅞" 1,100.00
Vase, floral, C Baker, #914, 1900, 5" 1,200.00
Vase, floral, C Schmidt, #924, W, 1901, tight line, 5⅝" 565.00
Vase, floral, M Nourse, #932CC, W, X, 1904, 9¾" 1,450.00
Vase, floral, S Sax, #935D, W, 1902, 7¼" 3,150.00
Vase, hawthorn blossoms, unknown artist, #920, X, 1903, 6⅛" 360.00
Vase, honeybees & clover, C Schmidt, 1902, 6½" 4,400.00
Vase, hydrangeas, S Coyne, #604D, W, 1908, 7" 4,500.00
Vase, irises, C Schmidt, drilled, 1906, 13½" 5,275.00
Vase, lotus blossom & bud on stems, S Sax, #829a, W, X, 1902, 9⅛" ..4,250.00
Vase, milkweed pods on charcoal to wht, F Rothenbusch, 1903, 9x6" ..3,600.00
Vase, morning glories, E Lincoln, #900C, W, 1904, 7⅝" 4,200.00
Vase, mushrooms, C Schmidt, #917B, 1907, 9⅝" 46,800.00
Vase, Nouveau poppies, silver bl on wht to dk bl, L Asbury, 1908, 9x4" ..1,560.00
Vase, orchids, A Valentien, drilled, #932B, 1902, 14¾" 15,500.00
Vase, orchids, C Schmidt, #1358C, W, 1908, 10⅝", NM 9,800.00

Vase, parrot tulips, L Asbury, #1357B, W, 1908, 13" 1,450.00
Vase, red hot pokers on blk, S Sax, drilled/seconded, 1905, 12" .. 3,480.00
Vase, roses, F Rothenbusch, #604D, W, 1904, 7" 950.00
Vase, roses (2 lg), S Sax, #937CC, W, 1907, 9½" 3,000.00
Vase, tulips, S Sax, #941C, 1906, 9½" 4,800.00
Vase, wild roses, C Lindemann, #604E, W, 1906, 5⅞" 2,450.00

Limoges

Bowl, porridge; bats/grasses/clouds, H Horton, #87R, 1883, 6¼" .. 385.00
Charger, butterfly/tree in night scene, M Daly, #205, W, 1885, 8¾" .. 1,325.00
Ewer, swallows in flight, pastels, M Daly, 1886, 12x6" 900.00
Perfume jug, autumn landscape, A Valentien, #61G, 1882, 4½" ... 650.00
Perfume jug, birds on pk, M Rettig, #60, 1883, 4¾" 180.00
Pitcher, insects/foliage, gilt accents, A Valentien, ftd orb, 9" 1,880.00
Pitcher, reeds & bats on tan, N Hirshfield, bulbous, 1882, 8x7" .. 900.00

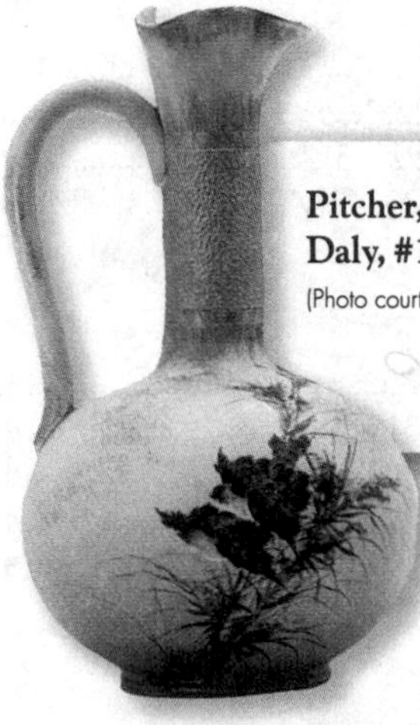

Pitcher, swallows in flight, Matt Daly, #101A, 1886, 12", $900.00. (Photo courtesy David Rago Auctions)

Plate, birds & bamboo w/gold, N Hirschfeld, #140, 1883, 6½" 265.00
Ramekin, bird & grasses w/cobalt, M Daly, G, 1883, 1⅝x4½" 550.00
Vase, field daisies, A Valentien, hdls, 1882, 10¼" 950.00
Vase, Oriental grasses w/gold, M Rettig, R, 1883, rstr rim, 7¾" 500.00

Matt

Note: Both incised mat and painted mat are listed here. Incised mat descriptions are indicated by the term 'cvd' within the line; all others are hand-painted matt ware.

Bowl, cvd/pnt floral, E Lincoln, #2106C, 1920, 2½x10" 575.00
Candleholders, floral, H Moos, #2666, 1924, 7½", pr 600.00
Charger, poppy & gr leaves, J Wareham, #577BZ, 1902, 12¼" .. 3,250.00
Mug, cvd floral on bl, R Fechheimer, #1071, V, 1905, 5⅝" 1,650.00
Vase, abstract floral, K Jones, #2724, 1928, 6" 385.00
Vase, buttercups & geometrics, W Rehm, #6110, 1929, 8½" 780.00
Vase, cvd bellflower band on brn, C Todd, 1915, 7x4" 1,440.00
Vase, cvd dragonflies, S Coyne, #911E, 1904, 4¼" 1,450.00
Vase, cvd floral, E Lincoln, #112, 1918, 6½" 850.00
Vase, cvd floral accents, combed areas below, W Hentschel, 1913, 11x5" ... 2,280.00
Vase, cvd grapes & vines, purple/gr on royal bl, C Todd, 1920, 13x8" .. 2,760.00
Vase, cvd lotus, wht on gr, R Fechheimer, 1906, 6½x5" 1,560.00
Vase, cvd nasturtiums, R Fechheimer, #905F, 1906, 5⅜x3" 625.00
Vase, cvd oak leaves/acorn neck band, red/gr, R Fechheimer, 1906, 6x5" .. 1,200.00
Vase, cvd peacocks, bl/brn, C Todd, #808, 1912, 21¾" 6,750.00
Vase, cvd pine-cone neck band on brn/red, R Fechheimer, 1906, 6x5" .. 1,800.00
Vase, cvd stylized vertical vines on gr, #56Z, 1903, 6" 650.00
Vase, cvd stylized windmills, frothy gr, Wm McDonald, 1901, 8x6" .. 1,080.00
Vase, cvd/pnt seaweed/fish, W Hentschel, #438, 1911, 5¾x9" .. 3,150.00
Vase, dogwood blossoms, E Lincoln, #905F, X, 1926, 6" 850.00
Vase, exotic blooms, M McDonald, S, 1935, 6¾" 1,100.00
Vase, field clovers, B Cranch, #725, W, 5⅛" 385.00
Vase, floral, M McDonald, textured wht, S, 1939, 7x4½" 650.00
Vase, floral, red/yel on brn, S Toohey, 1901, seconded glaze flaw, 6" .. 1,440.00
Vase, floral on bl, C Crabtree, #1356E, 1923, 7⅛" 100.00
Vase, floral shoulder, V Tischler, #270, 1924, 11⅞", NM 2,500.00
Vase, fuchsias, C Todd, #2033D, 1919, 10" 1,800.00
Vase, irises, A Valentien, #194BZ, 1901, 11½" 12,750.00
Vase, irises, J Jensen, #614C, 1929, 12⅝" 2,650.00
Vase, Japanese Iris, H Wilcox, #578CZ, 1903, 10¼" 20,500.00
Vase, lg mums, amber on indigo mottle, H Wilcox, 1901, 8½x4", NM .. 5,100.00
Vase, lotus blossoms, bl on brn, W Hentschell, #6240C, 1930, 13¼" ... 7,800.00
Vase, maple leaves/pods, maroon/red on blk, O Reed, #952C, 1905, 10" .. 9,800.00
Vase, oak leaves & acorns, E Lincoln, #1369B, 1928, 15" 3,850.00
Vase, roses, E Lincoln, #2032C, 1931, 11⅝" 3,000.00
Vase, stylized thistles on cerulean bl, L Abel, #913C, 1921, 9½" ... 1,100.00
Vase, tulips & foliage, E Barrett, #2724, 1943, 5⅝" 700.00
Vase, wisteria (EX art), E Lincoln, #950D, 1923, 9½" 2,400.00

Porcelain

Bowl vase, Jewel, lg birds/blooming branches, ET Hurley, 1929, 5x6" .. 1,440.00
Lamp base, landscape, M McDonald, #14B, 1937, 17½x7" 2,700.00
Vase, birds & foliage, ET Hurley, #2301B, 1927, 13⅝" 1,800.00
Vase, cherry blossom branch on wht, L Epply, 1919, #2191, 5x4" .. 1,080.00
Vase, chevrons, mc, L Holtkamp, #922D, 1951, 7⅜" 900.00
Vase, floral, L Holtkamp, #2984A, 1953, 15½" 850.00
Vase, floral branch, W Hentschel, #2194, P, 1905, 8⅝" 600.00
Vase, Jewel, birds/branches on emerald gr, A Conant, 1920, 9½x4" .. 2,280.00
Vase, Jewel, birds/flowering branch on raspberry, ET Hurley, 1925, 10" .. 1,680.00
Vase, Jewel, lg indistinct floral on bl, J Jensen, 1934, 6½x4" 1,080.00

Vase, Jewel, Oriental landscape with sailboats and prunus tree on three panels, Arthur Conant, #2103, 1919, 5¼", $5,000.00. (Photo courtesy David Rago Auctions)

Vase, leaves & berries, L Epply, #2466, 1920, 8" 9,600.00
Vase, lilies, K Shirayamadani, #890C/#6032, 1945, 5⅝" 1,675.00
Vase, magnolia, wht on indigo, J Jensen, 1944, 9x5" 1,920.00
Vase, mergansers/lagoon/mountains, A Conant, #807, 1920, 13¼" .. 12,000.00
Vase, Nativity scene, J Jensen, #6604D, 1944, 7½" 7,500.00
Vase, pk w/abstract int, ET Hurley, flared rim, #2260E, 1929, 4⅛" ... 850.00
Vase, 2 cranes/flowering tree/mountains, S Sax, #2372, 1920, 16⅝" ... 21,000.00

Sea Green

Vase, catfish & ripples, ET Hurley, #907D, 1903, 10¼" 10,000.00
Vase, crocuses & leaves, S Sax, partial #, G, 1900, 6⅝" 3,150.00
Vase, cvd pond lilies, MA Daly, #836, G, X, 1898, 11" 6,500.00
Vase, floral, M Daly, #750C, X, 1897, 5¼" 360.00

Standard

Ewer, floral, A Sprague, #433, W, L, 1891, 7" 600.00
Ewer, floral, C Steinle, #738C, 1899, 7⅞" 550.00
Ewer, floral on shaded pk, L Asbury, silver hdl, #566D, 1895, 6¾" ... 785.00
Ewer, silver o/l poppies mk Gorham, poppies by M Nourse, 1892, 11"....3,000.00
Humidor, American Indian's portrait, G Young, #812, 1898, 4¾".. 1,925.00
Humidor, Antonio Jose Governor of Nambe, S Markland, #801, 1898, 5"..600.00
Mug, American Indian, F Sturgis Laurence, #65-6, 1898, 5x5".. 1,700.00
Mug, Black man & son, H Wilcox, #323, W, ly (lt yel), 1890, 5⅞" ...385.00
Pitcher, irises, C Schmidt, #456, 1900, 4¼" 850.00
Tankard, floral, R Fechheimer, #564D, 1898, 8⅞", NM................ 600.00
Vase, autumn leaves, S Toohey, #664D, 1899, 9⅛" 600.00
Vase, blooming branch, AR Valentien, 1886, 16x6" 900.00
Vase, dogwood blossoms, K Shirayamadani, #459, A, W, L, 1890, 11½"... 3,150.00
Vase, dogwood branches, H Altman, #30, 1903, 6¼x3" 300.00
Vase, floral, A Valentien, #806B, 1898, 10¾" 1,000.00
Vase, floral, M Mitchell, bulbous upper body, #909C, 1903, 9x4¾" ...500.00
Vase, floral, M Nourse, #906B, 1901, 6⅞", NM 950.00
Vase, floral spray, K Hickman, #387B, 1897, 6½" 360.00
Vase, hawthorne branches/flowers, A Valentien, #S888, 1890, 18"...3,225.00
Vase, hickory nuts, K Shiraymadani, #488F, W, L, 1890, 10⅝"... 2,600.00
Vase, jonquils, E Lincoln, #935C, 1903, 9" 2,275.00
Vase, nasturtiums, AM Valentien, bottle neck, #611, 1898, 10x7" ..600.00
Vase, nasturtiums, M Mitchell, #909C, 1903, 9", NM................ 550.00
Vase, pansies, C Steinle, #950F, 1906, 5¾x2¾" 475.00
Vase, poppies, A Sprague, #732B, 1900, 10⅜", NM 950.00
Vase, portrait of Sarah Siddons, G Young, 1903, 9x4"..............3,120.00
Vase, Sculptor (portrait), G Young, #892B, 1902, 10¼x5" 1,900.00
Vase, tulips, S Toohey, #556C/ST, 1900, 11x5" 750.00
Vase, wild rose, I Bishop, #745E, 1900, 8x4" 325.00
Whiskey jug, hops, E Lincoln, #512B, 1901, 6" 575.00

Tiger Eye

Vase, exotic bird, W McDonald, #S1353, 1898, 8¼" 2,400.00
Vase, frog, AR Valentien, #806D, 1898, 6¼" 600.00
Vase, holly leaves/florals, P Conant, #551, 1916, 7", NM.......... 1,300.00
Vase, iris buds, H Wilcox, #589E, 1894, 8¼x3¼" 2,000.00
Vase, swan, W McDonald, #562, R, 1892, 9½", NM 500.00

Vellum

Jar, apple blossoms, ETH, #1321E, 1919, 3⅞" 235.00
Lamp base, stylized decor on cylinder, 1919V, 18½" 525.00
Plaque, Gathering Clouds, E Diers, 6x8"+orig gilt fr 7,800.00
Plaque, misty lanscape, F Rothenbush, 1914, 9x15"+VG orig fr ...8,400.00
Plaque, pines & stream, L Asbury, 1929, 11¼x6¾"....................8,400.00

Plaque, snowy forest, ET Hurley, 1920, 7¾x9¾" 7,800.00
Plaque, stream & trees, F Rothenbusch, 1922, 10x12" 9,600.00
Plaque, trees & stream, L Asbury, 1926, 9¼x14½"+fr.............17,000.00
Plaque, Western mtn snow scene, muted wht/bl/gr, E Diers, 7x9"+fr... 11,000.00
Plaque, winter scene, MG Denzier, 1915, 5¼x8¼" 450.00
Plaque, winter scene at dusk, F Rothenbusch, 1912, 6x8"+orig fr .. 5,700.00
Plaque, woodland w/lake & mtns, CJ McLaughlin, 1915, 4x6"+fr...3,650.00
Vase, abstract floral on yel matt, E Lincoln, #1120, V, 1919, 5" ... 600.00
Vase, bluebells, M McDonald, #7873, 1923, 5½x3½" 750.00
Vase, Canadian geese fly above indigo body, L Asbury, 1916, 8x4½".. 1,920.00
Vase, cherry blossoms, K Jones, #356F, 1926, 5½x3" 550.00
Vase, clematis, H Wilcox, #1369E, X, 1918, 7½" 550.00
Vase, clematis, M McDonald, #6194D, 1939, 6⅛" 1,000.00
Vase, daisies, bl-gray on ivory, F Rothenbusch, 1907 9x3¾"......1,140.00
Vase, floral, S Sax, #950E, V, 1907, 6".....................................1,150.00
Vase, floral band, E Diers, #999D, V, 1907, 9⅛" 1,675.00
Vase, forget-me-nots, M McDonald, 1937, #6644E, 6¼x2¾" 650.00
Vase, geese, moon & trees, S Coyne, #1356E, V/G, 1911, 7¼".3,000.00
Vase, grape clusters, S Coyne, #614D, 1915, 11x5½" 1,400.00
Vase, hilly landscape, F Rothenbusch, #2032D, V, 1920, 9¾" ...2,650.00
Vase, lily of the valley, C Schmidt, #907E, 1912, 7¾x3" 700.00
Vase, mums/etc, pastels on shaded bl, L Asbury, #614, 1928, 13x6"...5,100.00
Vase, phlox, Lenore Asbury, #2523, V, 17¾" 18,500.00
Vase, phlox (repeating), S Sax, #904CC, 1908, 10" 4,200.00
Vase, pk roses, F Rothenbusch, 1912, 7x4" 840.00
Vase, poppies, red/bl, S Sax, #932D, 1917, 9".........................7,200.00
Vase, scenic (rather dk), E McDermott, 1916, 8x3½".................1,200.00
Vase, scenic (sm scale), S Coyne, 1914, 6½x3½" 1,320.00
Vase, scenic band, S Sax, #1356D, GV, V, 1911, 8⅞ 2,400.00
Vase, shoreline, F Rothenbusch, #1658E, V, 1919, 8".................1,200.00
Vase, stylized floral, S Sax, #952E, 1911, 7¾" 1,925.00
Vase, stylized floral, W Hentchel, 1916, 6¼x3½"........................ 500.00
Vase, stylized poppies inside & out, H Wilcox, #1369E, 1925, 6"....780.00
Vase, swan scenic, C Schmidt, #531D, V, 1915, 10"...............23,400.00
Vase, trees, F Rothenbusch, #944A, V, 1920, 17¾" 13,000.00
Vase, trees, F Rothenbusch, 1913, 9½x5".................................2,280.00
Vase, trees, L Epply, #1660B, GV, 1911, chip, 13" 6,000.00
Vase, wisteria, E Diers, #892C, V, 1919, 9" 4,250.00
Vase, wisteria, ET Hurley, #907F, 1941, 7¾" 3,275.00
Vase, wolf/moon/trees, S Coyne, #1661, V/G, 1909, 8⅜"..........6,500.00

Wax Mat

Jardiniere, pine cones inside, E Lincoln, sqd funnel form, 1926, 4x6"...600.00
Vase, exotic flowers, E Lincoln, #833, 1923, 10x4½" 1,500.00
Vase, fan-shaped flower band, red/yel on raspberry, E Lincoln, 6x3" ..840.00
Vase, floral, J Jensen, #256E, 1943, 6⅝", NM................................ 600.00

Plaque, pines over a valley, Lorinda Epply, 1916, original frame, 9x7", $9,000.00. (Photo courtesy David Rago Auctions)

Vase, hollyhocks, Kataro Shirayamadani, 1939, 10", $4,300.00. (Photo courtesy David Rago Auctions)

Vase, man on antelope/bird/vegetation, W Hentschel, #6080, 1929, 13"....8,600.00
Vase, tall leaves, amber/red/bl-gr, E Barrett, 1924, 9x5" 1,140.00
Vase, water lilies, pastels on lav, S Coyne, #2969, 8x6" 1,200.00

Miscellaneous

Bookend, #2502, 1921, 2 boys reading book, tan matt, X, ea.......360.00
Bookends, #2444D, 1927, elephant, ivory matt, 4¾".................360.00
Bookends, #2446, 1921, girl on bench, pk w/gr tinge, 5⅜"...........325.00
Bookends, #6014, 1927, horse head, bronze finish, McDonald, 6" ..300.00
Bowl, #2151, 1915, gr-brn, incurvate rim, 3½x9½" 85.00
Bowl, #2713-E, 1924, tan w/pk int, 4⅞x10" 120.00
Bust, #2026, 1922, lady, ivory matt, 7½" 1,000.00
Figurine, #6900, 1959, Madonna w/halo, ivory, 12" 240.00
Flower frog, #2338, 1927, ivory matt, mild peppering, 6⅛" 350.00
Inkwell, #2034, 1919, oak leaves emb on pk/gr matt, 3¼" sq 300.00
Inkwell, #998, 1917, rook at side, dk bl, rpr insert, 7¼" 725.00
Paperweight, #1623, 1922, rook, tan matt 300.00
Paperweight, #1623, 1925, rook, bl & tan matt, 3x4" 725.00
Paperweight, #1855, 1912, 2 geese, brn matt, 4".................515.00
Paperweight, #2628, 1922, elephant w/clowns at head, NM........600.00
Paperweight, #2677, 1929, monkey, gray-gr matt, 3½" 400.00
Paperweight, #2792, 1930, clipper ship, bl matt crystalline, 3¾" ..360.00
Paperweight, #2810, 1930, rook near acorn, bl matt, 4"...........1,100.00
Paperweight, #6160, 1931, rabbit, gr matt 450.00
Paperweight, #6490, 1934, elephant, bl matt, X, 4"...............325.00
Paperweight, no #, 1935, book, Commercial Clubs of..., ¾x3½"..360.00
Pencil holder, #1795, 1923, rook, blk over bl matt, 4⅝".........480.00
Planter, #2842, 1927, turq, 5⅝"................................135.00
Plaque, 1903, Four-Master Bound In, S Laurence, glossy, fr, 10x14"...36,000.00
Potpourri jar, #2506, 1922, med bl w/clay showing through, 2½"....180.00

Tile, medallion with scrub oak tree, marked Rookwood Faience, minor chip, 8", $2,400.00. (Photo courtesy David Rago Auctions)

Tile panel, 45 comprise landscape, +14 molding tiles+1 row borders, EX....22,800.00
Trivet, #1683, 1920, grapes, mc, chips, 5⅝x5⅝" 265.00
Trivet, #2043, 1925, parrot, mc, 5½" 400.00
Trivet, #2350, 1916, sea gulls, bl matt, 1916..................425.00
Urn, #5635, 1937, cherub in chariot, ivory matt, 6½" 140.00
Vase, #1660C, 19??, hand-modeling, oatmeal matt, 11"...........1,450.00
Vase, #1711, 1917, tulips, 10" 550.00
Vase, #1746, 1910, bl & gr drips on gr matt, 5¾"................725.00
Vase, #1747, 1910, yel-tan, 6" 300.00
Vase, #1815, 1922, rooks in band, gr to pk, 6⅝" 450.00
Vase, #2095, 1919, gr over bl matt, 6-lobed, 4¾" 240.00
Vase, #2097, 1921, swans, bl, 3½" 250.00
Vase, #2122, 1924, tan & bl crystalline, 4½" 240.00
Vase, #2136, 1921, feathers, rose w/mint gr mottle, 6⅛", NM......150.00
Vase, #2283, 1921, brn matt, 5⅜"...............................130.00
Vase, #2320, 1921, stylized flowers, gr, 7½" 335.00
Vase, #2375, 1921, peacock feathers, bl, 9"....................450.00
Vase, #2522, 1922, nudes, gray-gr, 4⅞"........................480.00

Vase, #2557, 1921, gr to pk, hdls, 5" 150.00
Vase, #256F, 1920, purple gloss, 5½"............................435.00
Vase, #2814, 1924, yel matt, 6⅛"...............................240.00
Vase, #2985, 1927, leaves, bl matt, 3½" 200.00
Vase, #581E, 1910, yel, 10¼"...................................395.00
Vase, #604D, 1914, tulips alternate w/leaves on lined panels, 7"...1,680.00
Vase, #6053, 1933, bl, glaze miss, 7½" 125.00
Vase, #6254, 1932, gr, angle hdls, 4⅝" 170.00
Vase, #6545, 1935, lilies on tan, 3½" 130.00
Vase, #6610, 1937, pk, rim-to-hip hdls, 9¾" 180.00
Vase, #6833, 1954, lotus blossoms, 6¼" 95.00
Vase, #750C, 1907, yel matt, bottle neck, 6" 360.00
Vase, #952D, 1906, geometric tulips on red/bl matt, cylinder, 9" ..1,680.00

Rorstrand

The Rorstrand Pottery was established in Sweden in 1726 and is today Sweden's oldest existing pottery. The earliest ware, now mostly displayed in Swedish museums, was much like old Delft. Later types were hard-paste porcelains that were enameled and decorated in a peasant style. Contemporary pieces are often described as Swedish Modern. Rorstrand is also famous for their Christmas plates.

Bowl, brn/blk mottle on porc, Gunnar Nyland, swooping rim, 6x11" ..175.00
Dish, 3 stylized blk/wht birds on shaded aqua, Bengtson, 1960s, 9"..125.00
Ewer, majolica w/bird/floral/cupids, metal neck/hdl/ft, 22", pr 590.00
Figurine, cat, seated/stylized, lt brn, B Vallien, 5" 90.00
Figurine, dolphin, tail curved high, brn haresfur, Gunnar Nylund, 9"...185.00
Figurine, hippopotamus, brn/gunmetal mottle, Gunnar Nylund, 7" L..265.00
Figurine, penguin, wht mottle, Gunnar Nylund, 6" 80.00
Pitcher, milk; Mon Amie, rows of 4-petal bl flowers on wht, 3½"..110.00
Plaque, lg 4-lobe leaf design, dk gr/red on bl matt, Kavalkad, 12x12"..200.00
Plate, Christmas, Bringing Home the Tree, 1968, MIB..............325.00
Plate, dinner; Mon Amie, 4-petal dk bl floral rim band on wht.....90.00
Teapot, majolica, gr fluting above wht band w/florals, +cr/sug.....250.00
Tray, Picknick, mc fish/vegetables/herbs on wht, #33, 17" L........225.00
Vase, allover X-d hobnails on dk bl, cylindrical w/sm rim, Nylund, 12"...260.00
Vase, beige mottle, oval w/flat flared rim, Gunnar Nylund, 8" 135.00

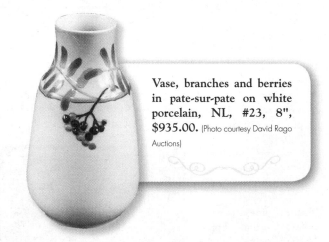

Vase, branches and berries in pate-sur-pate on white porcelain, NL, #23, 8", $935.00. (Photo courtesy David Rago Auctions)

Vase, brn matt to dk orange, spherical, Gunner Nyland, 2¾" 80.00
Vase, cvd lilies, purple/wht on lt gray, KL/15893/EG, 8x3" 750.00
Vase, cvd lines, brn mottle, angled shoulder/body, Stalhane, 1958, 14"..225.00
Vase, cvd/raised leather-like motif on porc, Vallien, 9x7" 175.00
Vase, Diatreta, o/l twigs & leaves, 2 frogs at rim, dk bl/brn, 6¾"....1,125.00
Vase, floral, pate-sur-pate, pastels, w/simple silver o/l, 8"............535.00
Vase, floral, sculpted/appl, Nouveau style, pastels, Lundstrom, 7" ...325.00
Vase, grapes/vines underglaze on off-wht, 1920s, now lamp, 12"..245.00

Vase, long-stemmed leaves, lav/gr on creamy wht, C/M monogram, 3½"....750.00
Vase, ochre/apricot/gunmetal microcrystalline, Stalhane, 12x3" .475.00
Vase, pansies w/raised petals form rtcl neck on ivory, RR/NL, 10" ...2,100.00
Vase, poppies, cvd/relief, pastels on ivory, porc, Ewerlos, 4" 365.00
Vase, porc w/layers of rose/lt ochre mottle, Stalhane, 20", EX ..1,175.00
Vase, roses (3 long-stem), appl petals, pastels, KI, 10" 1,400.00
Vase, simple pastel floral on blk, porc, RE, 4" 350.00
Vase, snowy twilight tree scene, glossy, NL, rpr drill hole, 18" ..5,000.00

Rose Mandarin

Similar in design to Rose Medallion, this Chinese Export porcelain features the pattern of a robed mandarin, often separated by florals, ladies, genre scenes, or butterflies in polychrome enamels. It is sometimes trimmed in gold. Elaborate in decoration, this pattern was popular from the late 1700s until the early 1840s.

Bottle, genre scenes in oval panels, bulbous w/long neck, 14" 825.00
Bowl, central scene, scalloped foliate edge, gilt trim, 20" 950.00
Bowl, ormolu rim w/angle hdls, trumpet stem, sq base, 1880s, 10" H.. 1,400.00
Bowl, oval w/skirted base, 10½" L, EX, on cvd wooden base........265.00
Charger, central genre scene, gilt, 14"..800.00
Cup & saucer, spur hdl, 6¼" saucer 280.00
Dish, genre scene, shaped rim on sq form, 9x9" 725.00
Garden seat, hexagonal, curved panels, extensive decor, gilt, 19", pr.. 7,500.00
Garden seat, hexagonal, 4 scenes/pierced medallions, 19" H 700.00
Mantel garniture, 2 vases & 3 urns w/foo dog finials, 1770, 10"....10,415.00
Picher, cider; continuous scene, twisted twig hdl, no lid, 8", EX.. 595.00
Pitcher, paneled genre scenes, roses on rim int, gilt, 7½" 725.00
Plate, dignitaries/pagoda, gilt, butterfly/peony band, 9¾", 8 for... 4,000.00
Plate, genre scene in center, ca 1830, 6", 4 for..............................300.00

Platter, fish; ca. 1800s, 24" long, $2,500.00. (Photo courtesy Skinner Inc. Auctioneers & Appraisers of Antiques & Fine Art)

Platter, genre center, wide butterfly/floral border, 12"..................650.00
Punch bowl, ca 1850, 5½x13", on rosewood stand, 4½" 1,385.00
Punch bowl, continuous genre scene, gilt/red rim int, 5x12" 2,150.00
Punch bowl, continuous genre scene, 16", on cvd rosewood stand ..3,200.00
Punch bowl, paneled genre scenes, gilt, 6x14"...........................1,400.00
Tray, several figures in center (1 w/gilt robe), gilt/rose rim, 11" L....245.00
Tureen, continuous genre scene, gilt, w/lid, 15" L, +undertray 650.00
Vase, continuous courtyard scenes, ring/foo lion mask hdls, 13", pr..3,800.00
Vase, paneled genre scenes, shaped reserves, gilt, w/lid, 10", pr... 1,175.00

Rose Medallion

Rose Medallion is one of the patterns of Chinese export porcelain produced from before 1850 until the second decade of the twentieth century. It is decorated in rose colors with panels of florals, birds, and but-

terflies that form reserves containing Chinese figures. Pre-1850 ware is unmarked and is characterized by quality workmanship and gold trim. From about 1850 until circa 1860, the kilns in Canton did not operate, and no Rose Medallion was made. Post-1860 examples (still unmarked) can often be recognized by the poor quality of the gold trim or its absence. In the 1890s the ware was often marked 'China'; 'Made in China' was used from 1910 through the 1930s.

Bough pot, tapered 4-sided body/conforming ft, gilt hdls, 1860, 8", EX..530.00
Bowl, figures in reserves, late 19th C, 4x10½" 450.00
Bowl, flower/figure reserves, scalloped, hdls, late 19th C, 1⅜x10". 325.00
Bowl, mandarin scenes, rtcl sides, 4x10¼x9½" 500.00
Bowl, rtcl bamboo sides, 3½x10x9", +17x13" underplate.............800.00
Bowl, smooth rim, late 19th C, 4x9¾" 350.00
Bowl, vegetable; ftd, 19th C, 2⅞x14" L..440.00
Bowl, vegetable; w/lid, 19th C, 3½x10¼" 400.00
Box, birds & mandarin scene, gold trim on orange peel, 3x8x4"..235.00
Box, brush; rectangular, compartmented, 19th C, 2½x7½x4", pr.. 700.00
Coffeepot, dome lid, wide cylindrical body, 1850, 8x7"...............425.00
Dish, butterfly form, scalloped edges, 4x10x12" 525.00
Pitcher, mtn village scene reserves, molded leaf on hdl, 6¾" 300.00
Plate, chop; early to mid-19th C, 13⅜" 585.00
Plate, hot water; 19th C, 2½x11½" 200.00
Plates, w/gilt, 1870, 8", set of 6...430.00
Platter, landscape scenes w/boats/mtn, 14½x11½", EX................260.00
Platter, lobed trefoil, late 19th C, 13¾" dia....................................425.00
Platter, 18¼" L 880.00
Platter, 19th C, 16¼" L 500.00
Punch bowl, late 19th C, 5¼x13⅛"...700.00
Punch bowl, late 19th C, 6⅝x16"..1,295.00
Tureen, vegetable; rectangular w/shaped corners, gilt, 1870, 11" L ..470.00
Urn, baluster form, foo dog finial, rosewood base, 18", pr...........1,400.00
Vase, baluster form, foo dog head-&-ring hdls, 19th C, 14¾", pr ..1,525.00
Vase, gilt foo dog hdls, scalloped baluster, 14", pr.....................1,400.00
Vase, gilt salamander hdls/foo dogs on shoulder, 18" 885.00
Vase, Ku-form, China late 19th C, 15⅜"...650.00

Vases, domestic scenes, manuscript scrolls, etc., ca. 1800s, 23", $4,600.00 for the pair. (Photo courtesy Neal Auction Co. Auctioneers & Appraisers of Fine Art)

Rosemeade

Rosemeade was the name chosen by Wahpeton Pottery Company of Wahpeton, North Dakota, to represent their product. The founders of the company were Laura A. Taylor and R. J. Hughes, who organized the firm in 1940. It is most noted for small bird and animal figurals, either in high gloss or a Van Briggle-like matt glaze. The ware was marked 'Rosemeade' with an ink stamp or carried a 'Prairie Rose' sticker. The pottery closed in 1961. Our advisor for this category is Bryce L. Farnsworth; he is listed in the Directory under North Dakota.

Ashtray, cocker spaniel head on bk of 7" blk oval, minimum value ... 1,000.00
Ashtray, miniature fighting cock on Minnesota tray, 5" L, from $300 to ... 350.00
Ashtray, 2-tiered platform w/cock pheasant, 6½" L, from $300 to ... 350.00
Bank, Maltese Cross Ranch cabin, 2x3½", from $350 to ... 400.00
Covered dish, mallard duck form, 4½x6½", from $300 to ... 350.00
Creamer & sugar bowl, hen & drake mallards, from $125 to ... 200.00
Figurine, bison, recumbent, 2x3¾", minimum value ... 500.00
Figurine, cowboy boot, brn, 2x1¾", from $50 to ... 75.00
Figurine, dove, closed bk, 4½x6¼", from $250 to ... 300.00
Figurine, jackrabbit, solid, matt rose, 3¼x1¾", from $250 to ... 300.00
Figurine, mallard drake, seated, 6¼x6", from $250 to ... 300.00
Figurines, cocks fighting, red w/dk feathers, 4¾x6", 5x6½", pr ... 200.00
Figurines, raccoon, 1x2½", 1¼x1½", pr from $250 to ... 300.00
Flower frog, sea horse, bl matt, 10¼x3¾", from $200 to ... 250.00
Hors d'oeuvres, cock strutting, 3¾x2¾", from $100 to ... 125.00
Jam jar, bbl form w/apple finial, 5", from $125 to ... 150.00
Paperweight, teddy bear seated, 3½", from 300 to ... 350.00
Pitcher, bulbous, wine gloss, 2⅝", from $35 to ... 50.00
Planter, bird on wood log, matt pastels, 3x6" L, from $45 to ... 65.00
Planter, dove w/1 outstretched wing, wht, 4½x6¼", from $125 to .. 150.00

Planter, horse figural, bronze, 7" long, $125.00. (Photo courtesy Steve Shonek)

Plaque, pheasant hen: 4¾x7", cock: 6x7½", pr, minimum value .. 1,000.00
Shakers, brook trout, 1¾x5", pr from $200 to ... 225.00
Shakers, chow chow head, russet, pr from $50 to ... 65.00
Shakers, dalmatian heads, 3", pr from $100 to ... 125.00
Shakers, eagle, matt pastel gr & yel, 2¾", pr from $350 to ... 400.00
Shakers, mallard ducks, 1x1¾", pr from $150 to ... 175.00
Shakers, palomino horse head, 1½", pr from $50 to ... 75.00
Shakers, pheasants, hen: 1⅛x2½", cock: 2¼x2½", pr ... 275.00
Shakers, puppy begging, solid bl, 3", pr from $75 to ... 85.00
Shakers, sailboat, 3½x3¾", pr minimum value ... 400.00
Shakers, Trojan seed corn, ear figural, 4½", pr from $450 to ... 600.00
Spoon rest, Fort Lincoln State Park, 8¾", from $100 to ... 125.00
Spoon rest, prairie rose, 4¼", from $75 to ... 100.00
Spoon rest, turkey gobbler, rare, 5½", minimum value ... 500.00
Tea bell, elephant seated, trunk curled over head, 4", from $150 to ... 200.00
Tray, outline of state of Indiana, 5¼", from $100 to ... 125.00
Vase, fluted 6-section wide pillow form, gr, rose or ivory, 4½x7" ... 80.00
Wall pocket, leaf-on-leaf mold, pastel matt, 4½", from $50 to ... 75.00

Rosenthal

In 1879 Phillip Rosenthal established the Rosenthal Porcelain Factory in Selb, Bavaria. Its earliest products were figurines and fine tablewares. The company has continued to operate to the present decade, manufacturing limited edition plates.

Biscuit jar, houses & trees, bl & wht Delft style, 6½" ... 180.00
Charger, fantasy Oriental on horsebk, mc/dk bl, Bjorn Winblad, 13", pr ... 250.00
Charger, rooster/poppies, earth tones, sgn/#1293, 1900, 18" ... 6,465.00
Coffeepot, Pompadour, rococo style w/sm moss roses, 11", +cr/sug .. 225.00
Cup & saucer, bird, mc on wht, #288, 1911, NM ... 650.00
Cup & saucer, courting scenes/floral panels HP on yel, w/lid, cup: 4" ... 100.00
Figurine, Black servant in turban & wht suit carrys fruit, Meisel, 7" .. 195.00
Figurine, child carrying lamb, MH Fritz #473, 6" ... 150.00
Figurine, child pulls towel away from sm dog, MH Fritz #496, 6" .. 125.00
Figurine, dancer, open bolero exposes breasts, blk tights, 10" ... 565.00
Figurine, dapple gray stallion/naturalistic base, 20th C, Karner, 7" .. 120.00
Figurine, German shepherd seated, F Diller, brn tones, 8" ... 125.00
Figurine, girl seated/reading to animals, she in bl/wht, 4" ... 190.00
Figurine, mallard duck pr, W Zugel, 6½x8½" ... 125.00
Figurine, nude child stands before seal pup, MM Fritz, 5¾" ... 115.00
Figurine, nude satyr carrying gilt bowl of grapes, A Coosmann, 15" ... 1,850.00
Figurine, nude sipping water in cupped hands, Wenck, 7¼" ... 535.00
Figurine, nude w/upswept hair, LFG, 20th C, 8½" ... 250.00
Figurine, puppy seated, brn (HP), 6x7x5" ... 110.00
Figurine, St Bernard, F Diller, #K262, tan/wht, printed mk, 16" L ... 585.00
Figurine, St Bernard sleeping, F Diller, #K262, 20th C, 12" L ... 350.00
Figurines, fan-tailed doves, wht gloss w/yel ft on base, 7", 6", pr .. 265.00
Miniature tea set, Maria, wht porc w/imp floral, pot: 5½", 10-pc .. 125.00
Vase, cobalt, bulbous w/long neck & flared rim, 1914, 8" ... 180.00
Vase, Indian sitting on river bank (HP), Cannon, tumbler form, 4" .. 225.00
Vase, pheasant, brn/gold/blk, NK/54, bulbous/ftd, 1896, 13" ... 1,880.00
Vase, tulip reserves, lt/dk bl, ftd orb w/bottle-form neck, 1896, 16" .. 825.00

Roseville

The Roseville Pottery Company was established in 1892 by George F. Young in Roseville, Ohio. Finding their facilities inadequate, the company moved to Zanesville in 1898, erected a new building, and installed the most modern equipment available. By 1900 Young felt ready to enter into the stiffly competitive art pottery market. Roseville's first art line was called Rozane. Similar to Rookwood's Standard, Rozane featured dark blended backgrounds with slip-painted underglaze artwork of nature studies, portraits, birds, and animals. Azurean, developed in 1902, was a blue and white underglaze art line on a blue blended background. Egypto (1904) featured a matt glaze in a soft shade of old green and was modeled in low relief after examples of ancient Egyptian pottery. Mongol (1904) was a high-gloss oxblood red line after the fashion of the Chinese Sang de Boeuf. Mara (1904), an iridescent lustre line of magenta and rose with intricate patterns developed on the surface or in low relief, successfully duplicated Sicardo's work. These early lines were followed by many others of highest quality: Fudjiyama and Woodland (1905 – 1906) reflected an Oriental theme; Crystalis (1906) was covered with beautiful frost-like crystals. Della Robbia, their most famous line (introduced in 1905), was decorated with carved designs ranging from florals, animals, and birds to scenes of Viking warriors and Roman gladiators. These designs were worked in sgraffito with slip-painted details. Very limited but of great importance to collectors today, Rozane Olympic (1905) was decorated with scenes of Greek mythology on a red ground. Pauleo (1914) was the last of the artware lines. It was varied — over 200 glazes were recorded — and some pieces were decorated by hand, usually with florals.

During the second decade of the century until the plant closed 40 years later, new lines were continually added. Some of the more popular of the middle-period lines were Donatello, 1918; Futura, 1928; Blackberry, 1933; and Pine Cone, 1936. The floral lines of the later years have become highly collectible. Pottery from every era of Roseville production — even its utility ware — attest to an unwavering dedication to quality and artistic merit.

Examples of the fine art pottery lines present the greatest challenge to evaluate. Scarcity is a prime consideration. The quality of artwork varied from one artist to another. Some pieces show fine detail and good color, and naturally this influences their values. Studies of animals and portraits bring higher prices than the floral designs. An artist's signature often increases the value of any item, especially if the artist is one who is well recognized.

The market is literally flooded with imposter Roseville that is coming into the country from China. An experienced eye can easily detect these fakes, but to a novice collector, they may pass for old Roseville. Study the marks. If the 'USA' is missing or appears only faintly, the piece is most definitely a reproduction. Also watch for lines with a mark that is not correct for its time frame; for example, Luffa with the script mark, and Woodland with the round Rozane stamp from the 1917 line.

For further information consult *Collector's Encyclopedia of Roseville Pottery, Vol 1 and 2,* by Sharon and Bob Huxford and Mike Nickel (Collector Books). Other books on the subject include *Collector's Compendium of Roseville Pottery, Volume I, II,* and *III,* by R. B. Monsen (see Directory, Virginia); and *Roseville in All Its Splendor With Price Guide* by Jack and Nancy Bomm (self-published). Our advisor for this category is Mike Nickel; he is listed in the Directory under Michigan.

Apple Blossom, vase, #388-10, bl, 10", from $300 to 350.00
Apple Blossom, vase, #392-15, gr or pk, 15½", from $550 to 650.00
Apple Blossom, window box, #368-8, 2½x10½", from $200 to 225.00
Artcraft, jardiniere, tan, 4", from $200 to 250.00
Artwood, planter, #1054, 8½", from $85 to 95.00
Artwood, vase, #1057-8, 8", from $85 to 95.00
Azurean, mug, #4, from $350 to 400.00

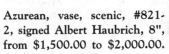
Azurean, vase, scenic, #821-2, signed Albert Haubrich, 8", from $1,500.00 to $2,000.00.
(Photo courtesy Cincinnati Art Galleries)

Baneda, candleholders, #1087, pk, 5½", pr from $500 to 550.00
Baneda, center bowl, #234, pk, 3x11", from $475 to 550.00
Baneda, vase, #235, gr, 5", from $750 to 825.00
Baneda, vase, #610, gr, 7", from $725 to 800.00
Baneda, wall pocket, pk, 8", from $3,000 to 3,500.00
Bittersweet, candlesticks, #851-3, 3", pr from $150 to 175.00
Bittersweet, planter, #828-10, 10½", from $150 to 175.00
Bittersweet, vase, #874-7, 7", from $125 to 150.00
Bittersweet, wall pocket, #866-7, 7½", from $225 to 275.00
Blackberry, hanging basket, 4½x6½", from $600 to 700.00
Blackberry, vase, 6", from $400 to 450.00
Blackberry, wall pocket, 8½", from $1,500 to 1,700.00
Bleeding Heart, basket, #360-10, bl, 9½", from $350 to 400.00
Bleeding Heart, plate, #381-10, gr or pk, from $150 to 175.00
Bleeding Heart, vase, #964-6, gr or pk, 6½", from $125 to 150.00
Bushberry, bowl vase, #411-6, bl, 6", from $300 to 350.00
Bushberry, candleholders, #1447-2CS, orange, 2", pr from $125 to ... 150.00
Bushberry, dbl cornucopia, #155-8, bl, from $200 to 225.00
Bushberry, mug, #1-3½, bl, 3½", from $200 to 225.00
Bushberry, vase, #157-8, bl, 8", from $250 to 275.00
Bushberry, vase, bud; #152-7, orange, 7½", from $125 to 150.00
Cameo II, flowerpot, 5½", from $200 to 250.00
Cameo II, jardiniere, 8", from $375 to 450.00
Cameo II, wall pocket, 9½", from $250 to 300.00

Capri, ashtray, #598-9, 9", from $40 to 50.00
Capri, bowl, #529-9, 9", from $20 to 30.00
Capri, planter, #582-9, 9", from $50 to 60.00
Carnelian I, wall pocket, 9½", from $200 to 250.00
Carnelian II, ewer, 12½", from $800 to 900.00
Carnelian II, planter, 3x8", from $125 to 150.00
Carnelian II, vase, 8", from $225 to 275.00
Clemana, bowl, #281, bl, 4½x6½", from $250 to 275.00
Clemana, flower frog, #23, tan, 4", from $150 to 175.00
Clemana, vase, #280, gr, 6½", from $350 to 400.00
Clemana, vase, #750, bl, 6½", from $250 to 275.00
Clematis, center bowl, #458-10, brn or gr, 14", from $175 to 200.00
Clematis, flower frog, #50, bl, 4½", from $95 to 110.00
Columbine, candleholders, #1146-4½, bl or tan, 5", pr from $175 to 200.00
Columbine, hanging basket, pk, 8½", from $375 to 425.00
Columbine, vase, #151-8, pk, from $275 to 325.00
Corinthian, bowl, #121, 5", from $60 to 75.00
Corinthian, bowl, ftd, #256, 4½", from $100 to 125.00
Corinthian, hanging basket, #336, 8", from $200 to 250.00
Corinthian, jardiniere, #601, 7", from $125 to 150.00
Cosmos, center bowl, #374-14, bl, 15½", from $275 to 325.00
Cosmos, center bowl, #374-14, gr, 15½", from $250 to 300.00
Cosmos, hanging basket, #361, gr, 7", from $300 to 350.00
Cosmos, vase, #950-8, tan, 8", from $250 to 300.00
Creamware, pitcher, floral decal, 8", from $250 to 275.00
Cremona, vase, #356, 8", from $200 to 250.00
Dahlrose, candlesticks, #1069, 3½", pr from $175 to 225.00
Dahlrose, hanging basket, #343, 7½", from $250 to 300.00
Dahlrose, vase, bud; #78, from $175 to 225.00
Dahlrose, window box, #377, 6x12½", from $450 to 500.00
Dawn, bowl, #318-14, gr, 16", from $200 to 225.00
Dawn, ewer, #834-16, pk or yel, 16", from $600 to 700.00
Dawn, vase, #833-12, gr, 12", from $350 to 400.00
Dogwood I, vase, #140, 14½", from $700 to 750.00
Dogwood I, vase, dbl bud; 8", from $175 to 200.00
Dogwood II, bowl, #151, 4", from $125 to 150.00
Dogwood II, jardiniere, #608, 6", from $150 to 175.00
Donatello, basket, 7½", from $300 to 350.00
Donatello, bowl, 8x3", from $100 to 125.00
Donatello, compote, 9½", from $150 to 175.00
Donatello, cuspidor, 5½", from $250 to 300.00
Dutch, mug, shaving; 4", from $125 to 150.00
Dutch, pitcher, 7½", from $225 to 275.00
Dutch, plate, 11", from $100 to 125.00
Dutch, teapot, 6½", from $400 to 450.00
Earlam, candlesticks, #1080, 4", pr from $500 to 600.00
Earlam, planter, #89, 5½x10½", from $400 to 450.00
Earlam, vase, #515, 4", from $325 to 350.00
Egypto, creamer, 3½", from $350 to 400.00
Egypto, vase, bud; 5½", from $400 to 450.00
Falline, candleholders, #1092, bl, 4", pr from $800 to 900.00
Falline, center bowl, #244, bl, 11", from $450 to 500.00
Falline, center bowl, #244, tan, 11", from $300 to 350.00
Ferella, vase, #505, red, 6", from $800 to 900.00
Ferella, vase, #505, tan, 6", from $600 to 700.00
Florane, basket, 8½", from $200 to 250.00
Florane, bowl, 5", from $100 to 125.00
Florane, bowl, 10", from $30 to 35.00
Florane, planter, 6", from $25 to 30.00
Florane, pot, 5", from $25 to 30.00
Florane, vase, 14", from $90 to 115.00
Florentine, ashtray, #17-3, 5", from $125 to 150.00
Florentine, bowl, #257-8, 9", from $85 to 100.00
Florentine, vase, dbl bud; #41-6, 4½", from $100 to 125.00

Foxglove, flower frog, #46, bl, 4", from $125 to 150.00
Foxglove, tray, #419, gr or pk, 8½", from $200 to 225.00
Foxglove, vase, #47-8, pk, 8½", from $225 to 275.00
Fuchsia, candlesticks, #1132, brn/tan, 2", pr from $125 to 150.00
Fuchsia, center bowl, #351-10, bl, 3½x12½", from $375 to 425.00
Fuchsia, vase, #891-6, gr, 6", from $200 to 225.00
Fuchsia, vase, #898-8, gr, 8", from $375 to 425.00
Futura, fan vase, #82, 6", from $450 to 500.00
Futura, window box, #376, 5x15½", from $1,750 to 2,000.00
Gardenia, basket, #610-12, 12", from $300 to 350.00
Gardenia, tray, #631-14, 15", from $200 to 250.00
Gardenia, vase, #638-8, 8", from $150 to 175.00
Holland, mug, 4", from $60 to 75.00
Holland, pitcher, 12", from $400 to 500.00
Imperial I, basket, #7, 9", from $200 to 250.00
Imperial I, planter, 14x16", from $300 to 350.00

Imperial I, umbrella stand, 20", from $750.00 to $800.00. (Photo courtesy Treadway Gallery Inc.)

Imperial II, bowl, #198, 4½", from $350 to 400.00
Imperial II, vase, #466, 4", from $550 to 650.00
Iris, center bowl, #362-10, bl, 3½x12½", from $225 to 250.00
Iris, center bowl, #362-10, pk or tan, 3½x12½", from $200 to 225.00
Iris, pillow vase, bl, #922-8, 8½", from $325 to 375.00
Iris, vase, #924-9, pk or tan, from $350 to 400.00
Ivory II, candlesticks, #1122-5, 5½", pr from $75 to 95.00
Ivory II, hanging basket, 7", from $75 to 100.00
Ivory II, vase, #274-6, 6½", from $75 to 95.00
Ixia, center bowl, #330-7, 3½x10½", from $125 to 150.00
Ixia, hanging basket, 7", from $200 to 250.00
Jonquil, candlesticks, #1082, 4", pr from $400 to 450.00
Jonquil, vase, #531, 12", from $900 to 1,000.00
Jonquil, vase, #541, 7", from $350 to 400.00
Juvenile, bowl, bear, 6", from $700 to 750.00
Juvenile, creamer, duck w/boots, high gloss, 3", from $250 to 300.00
Juvenile, custard, rabbit, 2½", from $250 to 300.00
Juvenile, egg cup, chicks, 3½", from $200 to 250.00
Juvenile, mug, fat puppy, 3½", from $500 to 600.00
Juvenile, plate, skinny puppy, 8", from $125 to 150.00
Juvenile, plate, sunbonnet girl, rolled edge, 8", from $150 to 175.00
Juvenile, pudding dish, rabbit, 1½x3½", from $250 to 275.00
Juvenile, sugar bowl, goose, 3", from $600 to 700.00
La Rose, jardiniere, #604, 6½", from $150 to 175.00
La Rose, vase, #236, 4", from $125 to 150.00
Laurel, vase, #676, gold, 10", from $400 to 450.00
Laurel, vase, #676, gr, 10", from $650 to 700.00
Laurel, vase, #676, russet, 10", from $500 to 550.00
Luffa, candlesticks, #1097, 5", pr from $500 to 600.00
Luffa, jardiniere, #631, 7", from $350 to 400.00

Luffa, vase, #689, 8", from $650 to 750.00
Lustre, basket, 6", from $200 to 250.00
Lustre, bowl, 5", from $95 to 125.00
Lustre, candlestick, 10", ea from $100 to 125.00
Magnolia, ashtray, #28, bl, 7", from $150 to 175.00
Magnolia, flower frog, #182-5, brn or gr, 5½", from $95 to 110.00
Magnolia, planter, #388-6, bl, 8½", from $85 to 95.00
Ming Tree, ashtray, #599, 6", from $75 to 85.00
Ming Tree, basket, #509-12, 13", from $275 to 300.00
Ming Tree, vase, #583-10, 10½", from $175 to 200.00
Ming Tree, window box, #569-10, 4x11", from $125 to 150.00
Mock Orange, planter, #932, 4x10½", from $125 to 150.00
Mock Orange, window box, #956-8, 8½x4½", from $100 to 125.00
Moderne, compote, #397-6, 6", from $225 to 250.00
Moderne, vase, #787, 6½", from $150 to 175.00
Mongol, mug, 3-hdl, over-fired, 6", from $600 to 700.00
Mongol, vase, 5", from $450 to 500.00
Montacello, basket, #332, tan, 6", from $600 to 700.00
Montacello, vase, #557, turq, 5", from $350 to 400.00
Morning Glory, candlesticks, #1102, gr, 5", pr from $650 to 750.00
Morning Glory, center bowl, #270, ivory, 4½x11½", from $350 to... 375.00
Morning Glory, vase, #723, ivory, 5", from $275 to 325.00

Morning Glory, vase, 9½", from $1,200.00 to $1,300.00. (Photo courtesy Smith & Jones Inc.)

Moss, bowl vase, #290, gr/pk or gr/orange, 6", from $350 to 400.00
Moss, candlesticks, #1109, bl, 2", pr from $150 to 175.00
Mostique, compote, 7", from $300 to 350.00
Mostique, vase, 6", from $150 to 200.00
Mostique, wall pocket, 10½", from $250 to 300.00
Olympic, pitcher, Pandora Brought to Earth, 7", from $4,000 to... 5,000.00
Orian, center bowl, #275, red, 5x12", from $375 to 400.00
Orian, vase, #733, yel, 6", from $250 to 275.00
Orian, vase, #737, turq, 7½", from $475 to 500.00
Pauleo, vase, #340, 19", from $1,500 to 2,000.00
Pauleo, vase, 20½", from $2,000 to 2,500.00
Peony, basket, #379-12, 11", from $250 to 275.00
Peony, bookends, #11, 5½", from $200 to 250.00
Peony, bowl, #430-10, 11", from $100 to 125.00
Peony, flower frog, #47, 4", from $85 to 95.00
Peony, mug, #2-3½, 3½", from $100 to 125.00
Peony, pitcher, #1326-7½, 7½", from $275 to 325.00
Peony, tray, 8", from $75 to 100.00
Peony, vase, #68-14, 14", from $300 to 350.00
Persian, hanging basket, 9", from $500 to 600.00
Persian, wall pocket, 11", from $500 to 600.00
Pine Cone, ashtray, #499, brn, 4½", from $175 to 200.00
Pine Cone, basket, #353-11, bl, 11", from $950 to 1,100.00
Pine Cone, bowl, bl, #320-5, 4½", from $250 to 300.00
Pine Cone, pitcher, #485-10, gr, 10½", from $350 to 400.00
Pine Cone, tumbler, #414, bl, 5", from $375 to 425.00

**Pine Cone vase, #907, 7",
from $300.00 to $350.00.**

(Photo courtesy Cincinnati Art Galleries)

**Wisteria, vase, 8", from
$900.00 to $1,000.00.**

(Photo courtesy Smith & Jones Inc.)

Pine Cone, window box, #431-15, gr, 3½x15½", from $175 to 200.00
Poppy, basket, #348-12, pk, 12½", from $500 to 550.00
Poppy, bowl, #336-10, pk, 12", from $225 to 275.00
Poppy, ewer, #880-18, gray/gr, 18½", from $550 to 650.00
Primrose, vase, #760-6, bl or pk, from $150 to 175.00
Raymor, butter dish, #181, 7½", from $75 to 100.00
Raymor, gravy boat, #190, 9½", from $30 to 35.00
Raymor, pitcher, water; #189, 10", from $100 to 150.00
Rosecraft Blended, vase, bud; #36-6, from $90 to 110.00
Rosecraft Blended, vase, 12½", from $150 to 175.00
Rosecraft Hexagon, candlestick, bl, 8", ea from $575 to 625.00
Rosecraft Hexagon, vase, dbl bud; gr, 5", from $475 to 525.00
Rosecraft Panel, jar, brn, w/lid, 10", from $550 to 600.00
Rosecraft Panel, window box, gr, 6x12", from $550 to 600.00
Rosecraft Vintage, bowl, 3", from $100 to................................... 125.00
Rosecraft Vintage, vase, 12", from $500 to................................... 550.00
Rozane, ewer, floral, #870-4, 11" 500.00
Rozane, mug, floral, H Rhead, 4½" 200.00
Rozane, vase, berries, Mitchel, 14" 500.00
Rozane Light, vase, floral, M Timberlake, 8" 550.00
Rozane Light, vase, roses, H Pillsbury, bulbous, 9" 1,500.00
Russco, vase, #108, heavy crystals, 7", from $200 to 225.00
Russco, vase, #109, 8½", from $120 to 150.00
Russco, vase, dbl bud; #101, 8½", from $100 to 125.00
Silhouette, dbl planter, #757-9, 5½", from $125 to...................... 150.00
Silhouette, vase, #781-6, 6", from $90 to 110.00
Snowberry, basket, #1BK-12, bl or pk, 12½", from $350 to 375.00
Snowberry, flowerpot, #1PS-5, bl or pk, 5½", from $225 to 250.00
Sunflower, center bowl, 3x12½", from $800 to 900.00
Sunflower, jardiniere, #619, 6", from $900 to........................... 1,000.00
Teasel, vase, #881-6, dk bl or rust, 6", from $150 to................... 175.00
Thorn Apple, hanging basket, 7", from $300 to 350.00
Thorn Apple, vase, triple bud; #1120, 6", from $200 to 250.00
Topeo, center bowl, bl, 3x11½", from $200 to 250.00
Topeo, vase, red, 15", from $1,500 to.. 2,000.00
Tourmaline, bowl, #A-152, 8", from $75 to 100.00
Tourmaline, candlesticks, #1089, 5", pr from $175 to.................. 200.00
Tuscany, wall pocket, 7", from $275 to.. 325.00
Velmoss, #718, bl, 8", from $300 to.. 350.00
Velmoss, bowl, #266, gr, 3x11", from $175 to 225.00
Velmoss Scroll, bowl, #C7, 3", from $100 to................................ 125.00
Velmoss Scroll, vase, 5", from $125 to 150.00
Water Lily, flower frog, #48, bl, 4½", from $110 to 130.00
Water Lily, vase, #78-9, rose w/gr, from $250 to 300.00
White Rose, basket, #362-8, 7½", from $200 to............................ 250.00
White Rose, vase, #987-9, 9", from $150 to 200.00
Wincraft, center bowl, #227-10, 4x13½", from $125 to............... 150.00
Wincraft, dealer sign, 4½x8", from $4,000 to............................ 4,500.00
Wincraft, mug, 4½", from $75 to 100.00
Wisteria, vase, #680, tan, 8½", from $550 to.............................. 600.00
Wisteria, vase, #682, bl, 10", from $1,500 to............................ 1,750.00

Woodland, vase, 6", from $450 to 500.00
Woodland, vase, 10", from $850 to 900.00
Zephyr Lily, center bowl, #479-14, brn, 16½", from $225 to 250.00
Zephyr Lily, pillow vase, #206-7, gr, 7", from $175 to.................. 200.00

Rowland and Marsellus

Though the impressive backstamp seems to suggest otherwise, Rowland and Marsellus were not Staffordshire potters but American importers who commissioned various English companies to supply them with the transfer-printed crockery and historical ware that had been a popular import commodity since the early 1800s. Plates (both flat and with a rolled edge), cups and saucers, pitchers, and platters were sold as souvenirs from 1890 through the 1930s. Though other importers — Bawo & Dotter and A. C. Bosselman & Co., both of New York City — commissioned the manufacture of similar souvenir items, by far the largest volume carries the R. & M. mark, and Rowland and Marsellus has become a generic term that covers all twentieth-century souvenir china of this type. Their mark may be in full or 'R. & M.' in a diamond. Though primarily made with blue transfers on white, other colors may occasionally be found as well. Our advisors for this category are Angi and David Ringering; they are listed in the Directory under Oregon.

Key:
r/e — rolled edge   v/o — view of
s/o — souvenir of

Bowl, English castle, floral border, 8½" 25.00
Creamer, Plymouth, mk as Burbank.. 45.00
Cup & saucer, Alaska-Yukon-Pacific Expo, 1909 .... 120.00
Pitcher, American Independence 1776, 6½"................................. 250.00
Pitcher, American Pilgrims, #527014, 6¼" 250.00
Plate, American Authors, 9½" 65.00
Plate, Battle of Lake Erie, fruit & flower border................................ 50.00
Plate, Bethlehem PA, Moravian College, v/o, 9"............................. 35.00
Plate, Bridgeport CT, r/e, 6-scene border, 10" 55.00
Plate, Chicago, Marshall Field & Co, coupe, v/o, 6" 45.00
Plate, Cincinnati OH, v/o, 9".. 45.00
Plate, Countess Grosvenor & Sir Thomas Laurence, 10¼" 150.00
Plate, Denver, coupe, v/o, 10" 60.00
Plate, Early Mission CA, coupe, s/o, Parmelee/Horham, 6" 40.00
Plate, Hermitage, fruit & flower border, 9¾"................................... 50.00
Plate, Jackson MS, New Capitol Building, r/e, s/o, 10" 75.00
Plate, Longfellow's Early Home, r/e, 10".. 60.00
Plate, Lookout Mountain TN, s/o, r/e, 10"...................................... 70.00
Plate, Los Angeles CA, r/e, 10¼" 75.00

Plate, New Bedford MA, r/e, s/o, 10" 70.00
Plate, Niagara Falls, r/e, 10" 50.00
Plate, Plymouth MA, 4 versions made, coupe, 10" 50.00
Plate, Portland OR, s/o, coupe, 10" 60.00
Plate, Richfield Springs NY, r/e, 10" 60.00
Plate, Ride of Paul Revere, fruit & flower border, r/o, 9¾" 50.00
Plate, Seattle WA, r/e, s/o, 10" 85.00
Plate, Syracuse NY, Indian, r/e, s/o, 10¼" 140.00
Plate, Thomas Jefferson, St Louis World's Fair, r/e, 10" 150.00
Plate, Topeka KS, capital w/6-scene border, s/o, r/e, 10" 75.00
Plate, Tucson AZ, 5 scenes, coupe, v/o, 6" 40.00
Plate, Waterbury CT, r/e, s/o, 10" 75.00
Sugar bowl, Plymouth American Pilgrims 65.00
Tumbler, Ashville, s/o 95.00
Tumbler, Plymouth, 1906, v/o 65.00
Tumbler, Thousand Islands, v/o 85.00

Royal Bayreuth

Founded in 1794 in Tettau, Bavaria, the Royal Bayreuth firm originally manufactured fine dinnerware of superior quality. Their figural items, produced from before the turn of the century until the onset of WWI, are highly sought after by today's collectors. Perhaps the most abundantly produced and easily recognized of these are the tomato and lobster pieces. Fruits, flowers, people, animals, birds, and vegetables shapes were also made. Aside from figural items, pitchers, toothpick holders, cups and saucers, humidors, and the like were decorated in florals and scenic motifs. Some, such as the very popular Rose Tapestry line, utilized a cloth-like tapestry background. Transfer prints were used as well. Two of the most popular are Sunbonnet Babies and Nursery Rhymes (in particular, those decorated with the complete verse).

Caution: Many pieces were not marked; some were marked 'Deponiert' or 'Registered' only. While marked pieces are the most valued, unmarked items are still very worthwhile. Our advisor for this category is Harold Brandenburg; he is listed in the Directory under Kansas.

Figurals

Pitcher, apple, blue mark, water size, 6", $285.00. (Photo courtesy Jackson's International Auctioneers & Appraisers of Fine Art & Antiques)

Ashtray, clown, gr, bl mk, 4¾" 385.00
Ashtray, robin, bl mk, 6" 475.00
Bowl, grapes, wht lustre, bl mk, 9" L 150.00
Box, tomato, #8913, unmk, 3" dia 50.00
Candlestick, nautilus shell, bl mk, 2¾x6", ea 250.00
Candy dish, grape, wht bl mk 65.00
Card box, Queen of Hearts & Devil, bl mk, 2¼x3¾x1¾" 700.00
Cracker jar, grapes, wht MOP, from $350 .... 225.00
Cup & saucer, demitasse; devil, red, bl mk 3,000.00
Cup & saucer, demitasse; Devil & Dice, bl mk 200.00
Cup & saucer, demitasse; tulip 535.00
Cup & saucer, demitasse; violet 455.00
Dish, lobster, w/lid, bl mk, 4¾x5x4" 200.00

Humidor, eagle, blk mk, 5" 600.00
Humidor, elk's head, bl mk, 6x7¾" 750.00
Inkwell, elk, w/lid, gr mk 550.00
Match holder, clown, wall mt, blk mk, 5¼" 375.00
Match holder, Devil & Cards, bl mk, wall mt, from $500 to 575.00
Mug, Devil & Cards, bl mk, 4¾" 300.00
Mustard pot, tomato, w/ladle & underplate 115.00
Pitcher, alligator, albino, unmk, cream sz 325.00
Pitcher, alligator, bl mk, milk sz 450.00
Pitcher, Art Nouveau, yel, bl mk, water sz, 6" 1,500.00
Pitcher, bull, blk w/red horns, bl mk, cream sz 150.00
Pitcher, butterfly, open wings, bl mk, cream sz, 3¾" ... 295.00
Pitcher, cat, blk, bl mk, cream sz, 4¾" 150.00
Pitcher, chrysanthemum, bl mk, cream sz, 3¾" 300.00
Pitcher, clown, red, bl mk, cream sz, 3¾" 215.00
Pitcher, coachman, bl mk, cream sz 150.00
Pitcher, cow, bl mk, cream sz, 3¾" 225.00
Pitcher, crow, blk, bl mk, cream sz 185.00
Pitcher, dachshund, bl, bl mk, cream sz, 3½" 600.00
Pitcher, devil, blk, bl mk, water sz, 6½" 1,200.00
Pitcher, devil, red, bl mk, water sz, 6½" 3,500.00

Pitcher, Devil and Cards, blue mark, milk size, $325.00. (Photo courtesy Jackson's International Auctioneers & Appraisers of Fine Art & Antiques)

Pitcher, Devil & Cards, bl mk, water sz, 7" 450.00
Pitcher, duck, bl mk, water sz, 6¾" 600.00
Pitcher, eagle, bl mk, cream sz 150.00
Pitcher, elk, bl mk, cream sz 125.00
Pitcher, elk, bl mk, water sz 400.00
Pitcher, frog, unmk, ca 1920, cream sz, 4" 125.00
Pitcher, geranium, pearlized, Deponiert, water sz, 6¼" 1,400.00
Pitcher, grapes, lav MOP, bl mk, cream sz 100.00
Pitcher, kangaroo, brn, bl mk, cream sz 5,000.00
Pitcher, lady bug, bl mk, water sz, 6½" 3,100.00
Pitcher, lamplighter, gr, bl mk, milk sz, 5½" 275.00
Pitcher, lettuce & lobster, bl mk, cream sz, 4" 100.00
Pitcher, lobster, bl mk, 4" 100.00
Pitcher, milkmaid, red, bl mk, cream sz, 4" 300.00
Pitcher, oak leaf, bl mk, cream sz 150.00
Pitcher, Old Man of the Mountain, gr mk, cream sz, 3¾" 75.00
Pitcher, orange, bl mk, milk sz, 4½" 225.00
Pitcher, owl, bl mk, cream sz, 3¾" 265.00
Pitcher, parakeet, red, unmk, cream sz 265.00
Pitcher, parrot/parakeet, mc, unmk, water sz, 6½" 750.00
Pitcher, poodle, bl, bl mk, cream sz, 3½" 500.00
Pitcher, poppy, wht MOP, bl mk, cream sz 200.00
Pitcher, rabbit, bl mk, cream sz, 4½" 2,450.00
Pitcher, rooster, blk w/red comb, unmk, 7" 1,175.00
Pitcher, rooster, wht w/red, bl mk, cream sz 300.00
Pitcher, rosebud, bl mk, cream sz, 4" 200.00
Pitcher, Santa, Deponiert, no hdl, milk sz, 5¼" 2,150.00
Pitcher, shell w/coral hdl, unmk, cream sz 125.00
Pitcher, spiky shell, pearl lustre, bl mk, cream sz, 4½" 95.00

Pitcher, sunflower, Deponiert, cream sz, 4½"...................................450.00
Pitcher, turtle, bl mk, milk sz, 2½"..450.00
Pitcher, water buffalo, gray, cream sz..155.00
Plate, lobster, unmk, 7½"...70.00
Plate, lobsters (3) on leaves, bl mk, 5½"..25.00
Powder jar, spiky shell, gr mk, 3½x4¼" L..95.00
Shaker, cherry, red, bl mk, ea...330.00
Shakers, chile pepper, long, unmk, pr...250.00
Shakers, lemon, unmk, pr...600.00

Shoe, fabric laces, 2x6" long, EX, $110.00.

Sugar bowl, grapes, purple, w/lid, bl mk 100.00
Sugar bowl, poppy, orchid, bl mk, w/lid, lg.....................................235.00
Sugar bowl, tomato, bl mk, w/lid, 3⅞"..75.00
Tea strainer, pansy, bl mk, 5¾"...550.00
Teapot, maple leaves, Depose, 5x6½"..800.00
Teapot, poppy, red, bl mk..295.00
Tray, dresser; clown, yel, bl mk...1,000.00
Wall pocket, grapes, various colors, gr, bl mk, 9x5½"....................175.00
Wall pocket, tomato, wall mt, bl mk, 9½"...845.00

Nursery Rhymes

Note: Items with printed verses bring premium prices.

Bell, Jack & Beanstalk, w/rhyme, bl mk...350.00
Bowl, Jack & Jill, bl mk, 5¾"...140.00
Box, Jack & Jill, bl mk...250.00
Candlestick, Jack & Jill, ring hdl, bl mk..225.00
Coffeepot, Jack & Jill, bl mk..450.00
Dutch shoe, Little Bo Peep, bl mk...450.00
Hatpin holder, Miss Muffet, unmk...900.00
Leaf dish, Little Jack Horner, bl mk..75.00
Pitcher, Jack & the Beanstalk, no verse, bl mk, cream sz, 3½"......125.00
Pitcher, Jack & the Beanstalk, w/verse, bl mk, water sz, 6"...........600.00
Pitcher, Little Miss Muffet, w/verse, bl mk, milk sz, 4¾"...............235.00
Plate, Little Bo Peep, bl mk, 6¼"...125.00
Sugar bowl, Little Boy Blue, w/verse, bl mk....................................275.00
Vase, Babes in the Woods (boy), bl mk, 4".......................................250.00

Scenics and Action Portraits

Bowl, 2 musicians, 3-ftd, gold trim, bl mk, 2x5".............................65.00
Box, peacock scene, bl mk...160.00
Candleholder, lady & chickens, bl mk, 4½", ea................................90.00
Candlestick, frog & bee, frog on bk, hdl, bl mk, 7".........................450.00
Charger, goose girl, bl mk, 13"...150.00
Creamer & sugar bowl, girl in lg hat & fur muff, gold trim, bl mk...225.00
Cup & saucer, demitasse; boys & turkeys, unmk............................110.00
Dish, boy w/donkey, clover shape, bl mk, 4½".................................125.00
Hair receiver, storks (4) on yel, bl mk, 2¾"....................................350.00
Hatpin holder, Brittany girl, unmk, 4½"..1,000.00
Humidor, jester, Welcome Is the Best Cheer, ladies', bl mk, 5".. 1,000.00
Loving cup, cattle in landscape, 3 gold hlds, bl mk, 3¾"................145.00
Mug, cavalier, 3-hdl, bl mk...85.00

Pin tray, polar bears, w/molded cork, bl mk, 4¾x3½"...............3,000.00
Pitcher, castle scene w/roses, bl mk, cream sz.................................95.00
Pitcher, cattle in pastoral scene, milk sz, 4¼".................................95.00
Pitcher, Corinthian, blk, bl mk, milk sz, 5".....................................95.00
Pitcher, fisherman, bl mk, milk sz..95.00
Pitcher, hunter w/dog in landscape w/flying birds, bl mk, water sz, 6"...295.00
Pitcher, man & turkeys, w/gold, cylindrical w/vertical-pinch spout, 6". 325.00
Pitcher, sailing scene, gray & wht tones, bl mk, cream sz.............125.00
Pitcher, Sand Babies, bl mk, cream sz, 4¼"....................................150.00
Pitcher, The Hunt, boat shape, bl mk, cream sz................................90.00
Pitcher, youth herding turkeys, bl mk, 4¾".....................................125.00
Plaque, men in boat fishing, gold border, bl mk, 9½"....................165.00

Plate, Arab on horse, green mark, 9", $60.00. (Photo courtesy Jackson's International Auctioneers & Appraisers of Fine Art & Antiques)

Plate, girl walking her dog, bl mk, 7½"..95.00
Plate, musicians, bl mk, 7½"..75.00
Toothpick holder, goose girl, 3-hdl, bl mk......................................215.00
Toothpick holder, penguin on yel, tricorner, bl mk, 2¾".................325.00
Toothpick holder, woman w/horse, unmk.......................................175.00
Toothpick holdler/vase, birds, silver-gilt rim, 3-hdl, bl mk, 3¼"...170.00
Vase, cows & trees, bl mk, 6"..145.00
Vase, highland sheep, hdls, bl mk, 4"...95.00
Vase, hunting scene, low hdls, bl mk, 3"..150.00
Vase, lady w/candle on brn, bl mk, 8"...150.00
Vase, sailboats, flower borders, bl mk, 8¾"....................................125.00
Vase, swan, hdls, bl mk, 4½"...150.00

Sunbonnet Babies

Bells, various activities, ltd ed, 3½", ea..50.00
Bowl, cereal; sweeping, bl mk, 5¼"...195.00
Bowl, washing, bl mk, 9"...200.00
Cake plate, washing, bl mk, 10¼"..225.00
Cheese dish, w/lid, mini, 1½x3½x2¼"..650.00
Coffeepot, ironing, bl mk, 6¼"...450.00
Hair receiver, washing, 4-leg, bl mk..395.00
Pitcher, cleaning, bl mk, cream sz, 3¼"...200.00
Pitcher, scrubbing floor, bl mk, cream sz..200.00
Pitcher, sweeping, bl mk, cream sz..200.00
Plates, various activities, ltd ed, 1974, ea..50.00
Sugar bowl, fishing, w/lid, bl mk...325.00
Sugar bowl, washing, w/lid, bl mk...250.00
Vase, fishing, low gold hdls, bl mk, 2¾x3½"...................................350.00
Vase, ironing, ruffled top, bl mk, 3⅝"..175.00

Tapestries

Basket, floral, silver tapestry, bl mk, 5x5 2¼"............................1,000.00
Box, dresser; colonial scene, bl mk, 2¼x3¼"..................................200.00
Box, pin; courting scene, bl mk, 2½x4½" L.....................................175.00
Box, Rose Tapestry, wht, bl mk, 3"..225.00

Creamer, Rose Tapestry, 3¼" 125.00
Hatpin holder, Rose Tapestry, ftd, bl mk, 4⅜" 200.00
Hatpin holder, Rose Tapestry, 3-color, bl mk, 4½" 275.00
Hatpin holder, violets, bl mk 375.00
Nappy, sheep scenic, cloverleaf w/hdl, bl mk 125.00
Pincushion, Rose Tapestry, slipper form, gr mk, 2½x5" 345.00
Pitcher, goats in meadow, bl mk, milk sz, 4" 225.00
Pitcher, Rose Tapestry, corseted, bl mk, cream sz, 3⅝" 200.00
Pitcher, 2 polar bears in Arctic waters, bl mk, 7" 1,900.00
Shoe, Rose Tapestry, pk, bl mk, 4½" L 275.00
Shoe, violets, low style, orig laces, gr mk 600.00
Vase, castle scene, bottle neck, bl mk, 3½" 200.00
Vase, Rose Tapestry, bl mk, 5¼x3¼" 175.00
Vase, silver rose top on tapestry, bl mk, 9" 1,200.00
Vase, The Bathers, bl mk, 8¼" 450.00

Royal Bonn

Royal Bonn is a fine-paste porcelain, ornately decorated with scenes, portraits, or florals. The factory was established in the mid-1800s in Bonn, Germany; however, most pieces found today are from the latter part of the century.

Clock, floral case, Ansonia open escapement movement, 12", $1,960.00. (Photo courtesy Fontaine's Auction Gallery)

Charger, sailboat, intricate border, bl/wht Delft style, 14" 85.00
Clock, La Don, mill scene, Ansonia works, 12x9x4½" 500.00
Clock, La Roca, florals, Ansonia works, 11½x14x5", EX 850.00
Clock, La Tour, floral on wht, Ansonia works, 11x9" 400.00
Jar, tapestry texture w/castle & floral, cylinder, SP dome lid, 8½" ...195.00
Vase, bust portrait: nude in gauzy drape on shaded brn, sgn Duren, 8".. 485.00
Vase, floral on wht, ornate gold hdls, w/lid, 14" 190.00
Vase, lady's portrait in gold reserve on wht, gold trim, Duren, 9". 160.00
Vase, lg pond lilies on bkground shading to bl at top & bottom, 9x9".. 725.00
Vase, maid in classic attire on brn, gilt rim/hdls/neck band, 7" 420.00
Vase, peony HP on emb waisted Nouveau form w/hdls, pastels, 14".. 250.00
Vase, young lady standing, mc on gr, elongated teardrop, 12" 145.00
Vase, 2 floral ovals on red w/much gold, cylinder w/sm neck, 8".. 325.00

Royal Copenhagen

The Royal Copenhagen Manufactory was established in Denmark in about 1775 by Frantz Henrich Muller. When bankruptcy threatened in 1779, the Crown took charge. The fine dinnerware and objects of art produced after that time carry the familiar logo, the crown over three wavy lines. For further information we recommend *Royal Copenhagen Porcelain, Animals and Figurines* by Robert J. Heritage (Schiffer). See also Limited Edition Plates.

Bonbon, arched lizard on lid, #320/23, squat/rnd, 1910, 4" 1,645.00
Bonbon, monkey crouching on lid, #11, 1920m 5" 1,300.00

Bonbon, pigeon on lid, A Petersen, #368, 1910, 10½" 880.00
Bonbon, rabbit on lid, JF, #1694/1437, 1925, 7" 440.00
Box, lid modeled as a bird half w/in a wicker basket, #302, 4½" L...235.00

Creamer and sugar bowl with lid, Flora Danica, 2¾", $1,825.00. (Photo courtesy Bonhams & Butterfield)

Dish, Flora Danica, twig hdl on dome lid, oval, modern, 6" L...1,175.00
Figurine, basset puppy, P Herold, 1920s, 6¾" 175.00
Figurine, bird dog standing, brn/wht, J Grunt, #4852, 1930, 10".. 175.00
Figurine, cherub drinking, A Malinowski, #2195, 20th C, 3" 120.00
Figurine, cockerel, C Thomsen, #1126, 1925, 4" 145.00
Figurine, collie lying down, head erect, P Herold, #1701, 1970, 11" L....265.00
Figurine, cow grooming calf, recumbent, H Lykke, #800, 11" 385.00
Figurine, dachshund, K Moller, #1238/1450, 1913, 7¾" L 350.00
Figurine, dog chewing bone, C Thomsen, #704, 1910, 9" L......... 325.00
Figurine, elephant pr, K Kyln, #802, 1910, 11" L 645.00
Figurine, elk, recumbent, K Kyhn/GG, #2813, 1970, 9" L 235.00
Figurine, farmer between 2 horses, A Lochner, #2119, 1936, 9½"...585.00
Figurine, female lion lies w/front paws out, head up, #804-50, 12" L... 345.00
Figurine, fox howling, E Nielsen, #946, 1910, 10½" 300.00
Figurine, fox standing on hollow base, E Nielsen, #546, 1920s, 6"... 765.00
Figurine, foxes (vixen & 2 pups), P Herold, #1788, 1925, 4" 385.00
Figurine, geese pr, P Herold, #2068, 1970, 8¾" 470.00
Figurine, goat & kid, C Thomsen, early 20th C, 7" L 470.00
Figurine, Great Dane, P Herold, #1679, 1975, 8¾" L 400.00
Figurine, guillemot, natural colors, early 20th C, 11" 350.00
Figurine, guinea pig, JA Heuch, #503, 1910, 3" 470.00
Figurine, hippopotamus stands/mouth open, M Prinsesse, #309, 1930, 14"...2,000.00
Figurine, horse, windswept, L Jensen, #1362, dtd 1912, 12" L...... 530.00
Figurine, jaguar cub crouching, J Grut, #4659, 1980, 8" L........... 350.00
Figurine, ladies (2) gossip, 1 w/basket, D Thomsen, #1319, 1960, 12"..300.00
Figurine, lamb seated, K Kyhn, #2720, 1925, 3" 265.00
Figurine, leopard crouching/snarling, J Jensen, #1343, 1910, 9½" L...880.00
Figurine, lioness, lying/looking ahead, L Jensen, #804, 1949, 12" L ...235.00
Figurine, lioness grooming, natural colors, #2051, 1950s, 9" 295.00
Figurine, long-eared owl, P Herold, #1331, 1911, 14" 555.00
Figurine, lynx crouching, P Herold, #1329, 1940, 6" L................ 500.00
Figurine, marmot, upright, natural colors, sgn G, #1096, 7¾" 800.00
Figurine, monkey pr, 1 comforting other, C Thomsen, #415, 1920s, 5"..200.00
Figurine, monkey seated, A Pederson, #1454/431, 1930, 5" 265.00
Figurine, monkeys (3) sit/embrace, K Kyhn, #940, 1910, 6" 325.00
Figurine, musk ox, recumbent, A Nielsen, #1442, 1910, 8" L...1,350.00
Figurine, Pan kneeling w/frog on knee, C Thomsen, #1713, 1925, 4½"...300.00
Figurine, Pan riding turtle, C Thomsen, #585, 20th C, 3¾"......2,352.00
Figurine, Pan w/goat, C Thomsen, #1012/498, 1935, 5".............. 200.00
Figurine, Pan w/rabbit, C Thomsen, #439, 1961, 5" 175.00
Figurine, Pan w/rabbit sits on pedestal, C Thomsen, #456, 1963, 8"... 200.00
Figurine, Pan w/snake, C Thomsen, #1712, 1940, 4¼"................ 200.00
Figurine, Pan wrestling bear cub, C Thomsen, #648, 1965, 6" 300.00
Figurine, Pan wrestling lg rabbit, K Kyhn, #1036, 1910, 5".......1,115.00
Figurine, parrot on tall plinth w/garland, bl/wht, C Thomsen, 12" ..2,115.00

Figurine, pheasant cock & hen, A Nielson, #862, 1970, 5¾".......200.00
Figurine, raccoon, head trn right, W Timyn, #5401, 1981, 4".......300.00
Figurine, serval (spotted African cat), seated, H Liisberg, 1923, 9"..940.00
Figurine, tiger mother/2 playful cubs, J Grut, #4687, 1980, 10" L...1,765.00
Figurine, wht mink crouching, #4654, 1980, 7" L.........................175.00
Figurine, woman puts potatoes in basket, C Thomsen, #1549, 1975, 11"..300.00
Figurine, woman w/hoe, C Thomsen, #1528, 1950, 10½".............175.00
Inkwell, frog wrapped w/snake, Nielsen, Michaelsen silver mts, 11"..2,350.00
Jar, Flora Danica, twig hdls, orb shape w/flat lid, modern, 4½"......555.00
Plate, Flora Danica, floral specimen, modern, 5⅝", 10 for.........2,585.00
Plate, Flora Danica, floral specimen, modern, 7½", 10 for.........3,170.00
Plate, Flora Danica, floral specimen, modern, 10", 10 for..........4,995.00
Sauceboat, Flora Danica, ovoid w/attached underplate, twig hdl, 9" L...2,350.00
Tazza, Flora Danica, triangular w/rnd corners, trumpet base, 5"...940.00
Tray, dragonfly appl to side, spider/web in bowl, #9/15, 6½" L......400.00
Tray, moth on side, 1890s, 5"...350.00
Tray, 3-D lizard on side of rim, Pedersen, #552/287, 5" L.............700.00
Tureen, Flora Danica, twig hdls/finial, +underplate, 11" H.......4,995.00
Vase, appl butterfly wings above rim, #646/328, 1920s, 4"...........875.00
Vase, bats at shoulder, blk on purple to lt gray, J Meyer, #10732, 21"..5,875.00
Vase, bats/pine branch, #1406/45A, globular, 1925, 4"...............295.00
Vase, bleeding hearts, sq bottle shape, #457/135, 1920, 6"..........235.00
Vase, butterfly wings, #646/328, 1920s, 4".....................................875.00
Vase, daffodils, wht on dk gr, #496240, 4-panel ovoid, 1920s, 6½"...175.00
Vase, magnolias on pk, U-form, ftd/flared rim, 1935, #8626/411, 11"...150.00
Vase, moths, cobbled ground, rtcl rim/scalloped shoulder, #346/218,10"...885.00
Vase, narcissus on dk gr, Michaelsen silver o/l on neck, #496/61, 9"...470.00
Vase, orchid stem on wht, #214/245, rim-to-shoulder hdls, 13"...470.00
Vase, orchid stem/leaves, #2640/137, 1956, 12".........................235.00
Vase, poppies/dragonfly, gray tones, #2652/2308, bulbous, 1930, 11"..175.00
Vase, sheep/landscape, G Rode, #131B, 1933, 22½".................1,645.00
Vase, turkey ea side, M Host, sqd/ftd pillow form, #8786, 20th C, 8"..470.00
Vase, waterscape w/distant farmhouse, K Sorensen, 1926, 23".....700.00

Royal Copley

Royal Copley is a decorative type of pottery made by the Spaulding China Company in Sebring, Ohio, from 1942 to 1957. They also produced two other major lines — Royal Windsor and Spaulding. Royal Copley was primarily marketed through five-and-ten cent stores; Royal Windsor and Spaulding were sold through department stores, gift shops, and jobbers. Items trimmed in gold are worth 25% to 50% more than the same item with no gold trim. For more information we recommend *Collecting Royal Copley Plus Royal Windsor & Spaulding* by our advisor for this category, Joe Devine; he is listed in the Directory under Iowa.

Figurines, drake, 8½", and mallard hen, 6¼", first pair in Game Birds of North America series, from $150.00 to $175.00 pair. (Photo courtesy Glenn Hovinga)

Ashtray, leaping deer, pk, mk USA, from $35 to 40.00
Ashtray, rooster emb, Spaulding, mk AD Priolo USA, from $55 to...65.00

Bank, farmer pig, eyes closed, paper label, 5½", from $90 to........100.00
Bank, teddy bear, blk & wht, pk sucker & bow, paper label, 8", $175 to..195.00
Coaster, Dutch couple in garden, metal rim, unmk, from $35 to...40.00
Coaster, hunting dog, chrome rim, unmk, from $35 to..................40.00
Coaster, hunting dog, unmk, from $35 to 40.00
Creamer, duck, paper label, Spaulding, 4½", from $30 to..............35.00
Creamer, leaves form body, gr stamp on base, 3"...........................30.00
Figurine, banty rooster, paper label, 6½", from $60 to 75.00
Figurine, dove, various colors, paper label, 5", from $12 to 15.00
Figurine, hen, ft not showing, paper label, 7", from $50 to............60.00
Figurine, lady dancing, yel dress, scarce, 8", from $125 to 150.00
Figurine, mallard baby, paper label, 5½", from $18 to....................20.00
Figurine, parrot, yel, paper label only, 8", from $50 to...................60.00
Figurines, cat, blk w/red bow, paper label, 8", from $85 to.............95.00
Lamp, child praying, paper label, 7¾", from $75 to 85.00
Lamp, Oriental girl, red dress, holding bl basket, 7½", $75 to..........80.00
Lamp, rooster, paper label, Spaulding, 9½", from $125 to 150.00
Pitcher, Floral Beauty, red on bl, gr stamp or emb mk, 8", $75 to...80.00
Plant holder, metal, leaf design, paper label, from $20 to 25.00
Planter, angel, red, paper label, 8", from $40 to 45.00
Planter, bl hummingbird on red flower, paper label, 5¼", $70 to....75.00
Planter, blossom, yel on gr, gr stamp, from $10 to.........................12.00
Planter, cat w/yel cello, paper label, 7½", from $125 to 150.00
Planter, coach, paper label, 3¼x6", from $20 to............................30.00
Planter, elf w/lg stump, red hat w/dk gr clothes, paper label, $40 to..45.00
Planter, floral arrangement, ftd, gr stamp, 3½x7", from $10 to.......12.00
Planter, girl w/wide brim hat, hand by cheek, emb mk, 7½", $40 to...45.00
Planter, Joyce decal, ftd, hdls, gold stamp, from $12 to 15.00
Planter, nuthatch on stump, paper label, 5½", from $30 to.............35.00
Planter, Oriental boy w/lg basket on bk, paper label, 8", $45 to.....50.00
Planter, Plain Jane, emb mk, 3¼", from $10 to 12.00
Planter, poodle w/bow posing, paper label, 5¼", from $55 to 65.00
Planter, ribbed, emb mk on bottom, 3½", from $8 to.....................10.00
Vase, Carol's Corsage, lt gr w/yel floral, gr stamp, 7", from $18 to..20.00
Vase, cornucopia decal, gold trim, mk emb Royal Copley, from $25 to..30.00
Vase, fish, gray w/red top & bl stripe, paper label, 6", $100 to...........1.25
Vase, Marjorie decal, ftd, hdls, Spaulding, gold stamp, 10", $90 to...100.00
Vase, Virginia, gold-trimmed hdls, 7", from $12 to.........................15.00
Wall pocket, Blackmoor prince, wht & yel, emb mk, 8", from $40 to...45.00
Wall pocket, decal on plaque shape, paper label, 8 ", from $65 to....75.00
Wall pocket, Turner Crossing the...Amsterdam Holland, 8", $60 to..70.00

Royal Crown Derby

The Royal Crown Derby company can trace its origin back to 1848. It first operated under the name of Locker & Co. but by 1859 had became Stevenson, Sharp & Co. Several changes in ownership occurred until 1866 when it became known as the Sampson Hancock Co. The Derby Crown Porcelain Co. Ltd. was formed in 1876, and these companies soon merged. In 1890 they were appointed as a manufacturer for the Queen and began using the name Royal Crown Derby.

In the early years, considerable 'Japan ware' decorated in Imari style, using red, blue, and gold in Oriental patterns was popular. The company excelled in their ability to use gold in the decoration, and some of the best flower painters of all time were employed. Nice vases or plaques signed by any of these artists will bring thousands of dollars: Gregory, Mosley, Rouse, Gresley, and D'esire Leroy. We have observed porcelain plaques decorated with flowers signed by Gregory selling at auction for as much as $12,000.00. If you find a signed piece and are not sure of its value, if at all possible, it would be best to have it appraised by someone very knowledgeable regarding current market values.

As is usual among most other English factories, nearly all of the vases produced by Royal Crown came with covers. If they are missing, deduct

40% to 45%. There are several well illustrated books available from antique booksellers to help you learn to identify this ware. The back stamps used after 1891 will date every piece except dinnerware. The company is still in business, producing outstanding dinnerware and Imari-decorated figures and serving pieces. They also produce custom (one only) sets of table service for the wealthy of the world.

Bowl, center; pheasant & floral on wht, gold rim, A 73 XXXIII .. 340.00
Bowl, cream soup; Imari, #2451, w/hdls, +underplate, set of 8..... 650.00
Bowl, Olde Avesbury, octagonal, 4x10" 210.00
Candlesticks, Old Imari, #1128, 10", NM, pr.............................. 925.00
Candlesticks, Olde Avesbury, Asian pheasants/gilt, sq base, 11", pr...425.00
Creamer & sugar bowl, Old Imari, #1128 XLIII, w/lid, 3¾", 6" W ... 165.00

Cup and saucer, Imari pattern with gilt, ca. 1929, from $75.00 to $90.00. (Photo courtesy Jim and Susan Harran)

Figurines, she w/lamb, he w/dog, bocage behind, scroll base, 7", pr.. 550.00
Plate, cake; Old Imari, #1128 XL, 10" 135.00
Plate, Imari, #2451, ca 1898, 9" 175.00
Platter, Old Imari, #1128 XLIII, 16" 265.00
Tray, Old Imari, #1128 MMV, oval, w/hdls, 15½" L 550.00
Tray, pin; Old Imari, #1128, 3x3¾x1" 60.00
Urn, lt/pk areas w/gilt & swags, gold hdls, dome lid, 1895, 7", pr 550.00
Vase, floral, bronzed/silver/gilt on yel, w/lid, ca 1894, 14½" 2,115.00
Vase, floral in ornate gold reserve on dk bl, gold hdls/ft, Leroy, 8" .. 6,350.00
Vase, fruit & foliage, mc w/gold, w/hdls & lid, ca 1891, 6½" 650.00
Vase, Old Imari, #1128, much gilt, lg gold hdls, 9" 635.00

Royal Doulton

The range of wares produced by the Doulton Company since its inception in 1815 has been vast and varied. The earliest wares produced in the tiny pottery in Lambeth, England, were salt-glazed pitchers, plain and fancy figural bottles, etc. — all utility-type stoneware geared to the practical needs of everyday living. The original partners, John Doulton and John Watts, saw the potential for success in the manufacture of drain and sewage pipes and during the 1840s concentrated on these highly lucrative types of commercial wares. Watts retired from the company in 1854, and Doulton began experimenting with a more decorative product line. As time went by, many glazes and decorative effects were developed, among them Faience, Impasto, Silicon, Carrara, Marqueterie, Chine, and Rouge Flambé. Tiles and architectural terra cotta were an important part of their manufacture. Late in the nineteenth century at the original Lambeth location, fine artware was decorated by such notable artists as Hannah and Arthur Barlow, George Tinworth, and J. H. McLennan. Stoneware vases with incised animal drawings, gracefully shaped urns with painted scenes, and cleverly modeled figurines rivaled the best of any competitor.

In 1882 a second factory was built in Burslem which continues even yet to produce the famous figurines, character jugs, series ware, and table services so popular with collectors today. Their Kingsware line, made from 1899 to 1946, featured flasks and flagons with drinking scenes, usually on a brown-glazed ground. Some were limited editions, while others were com-

memorative and advertising items. The Gibson Girl series, 24 plates in all, was introduced in 1901. It was drawn by Charles Dana Gibson and is recognized by its blue and white borders and central illustrations, each scene depicting a humorous or poignant episode in the life of 'The Widow and Her Friends.' Dickensware, produced from 1911 through the early 1940s, featured illustrations by Charles Dickens, with many of his famous characters. The Robin Hood series was introduced in 1914; the Shakespeare series #1, portraying scenes from the Bard's plays, was made from 1914 until World War II. The Shakespeare series #2 ran from 1906 until 1974 and was decorated with featured characters. Nursery Rhymes was a series that was first produced in earthenware in 1930 and later in bone china. In 1933 a line of decorated children's ware, the Bunnykin series, was introduced; it continues to be made to the present day. About 150 'bunny' scenes have been devised, the earliest and most desirable being those signed by the artist Barbara Vernon. Most pieces range in value from $60.00 to $120.00.

Factors contributing to the value of a figurine are age, demand, color, and detail. Those with a limited production run and those signed by the artist or marked 'Potted' (indicating a pre-1939 origin) are also more valuable. After 1920 wares were marked with a lion — with or without a crown — over a circular 'Royal Doulton.'

Animals and Birds

Airedale, Ch'Cotsford Topsail, HN1023 .... 250.00
Alsatian, AK13 .... 115.00
Birds, 2 cockatoos, wht, perched on bl to brn rock base, early, 8" . 400.00
Boxer, Warlord of Mazelaine, AHN2643, med 125.00
Brittany Spaniel, HN1002, 9x6" 275.00
Bull Terrier, HN1100 .... 385.00
Bulldog, HN1043, standing 485.00
Cairn Terrier, AK11, sitting 95.00
Cairn Terrier, HN1034 .... 435.00
Cat, HN2539 .... 95.00
Cat, Lucky, K12 .... 69.00
Cat, sleeping, HN2581 .... 115.00
Cat, striped, HN2584 .... 95.00
Chestnut Mare & Foal, HN2533.. 800.00
Cocker Spaniel, HN1036, med 129.00
Dachshund, Shrewd Saint, AK8, med.. 125.00
English Setter, HN1051... 325.00
English Setter, pheasant in mouth, HN2529, 8½x11x4½" 500.00
Gordon Setter, HN1081 .... 795.00
Horse, brn w/wht nose/left sock, right leg raised, 9" L 110.00
Horse, wht, running, DA245 Milton Limited Edition.................. 245.00
Palomino, right leg lifted, wht sock on left front ft, 6¾" L 50.00
Pekingese, HN1012 JC 90.00
Persian cat, HN2539, sitting 135.00

Scottish Terrier, HN1016, 5" long, $125.00 to $140.00. (Photo courtesy Candace Sten Davis and Patricia J. Baugh)

Sealyham, AK4... 245.00
Sealyham, K3, begging... 120.00
St Bernard, AK19 .... 90.00
Terrier With Bone, HN1159 .... 100.00

Bunnykins

Aussie Surfer, DB133	175.00
Basketball Player, DB262	150.00
Boy Skater, DB152, from $40 to	65.00
Captain Cook, DB251	225.00

Chimney Sweep, DB6, 1972, 4", from $65.00 to $75.00; As Queen of the May, DB83, from $75.00 to $90.00.

Christmas Surprise, DB146	45.00
Deep Sea Diver, DB273	95.00
Detective, DB193	150.00
Fireman, DB75	50.00
Firemen, DB187	120.00
Flemenco Dancer, DB256	35.00
Friar Tuck, DB246	35.00
Gardener, DB156	40.00
Gladiator, DB326	42.00
Groom, DB102, from $70 to	90.00
Harry, DB73	90.00
Ice Hockey, DB282	199.00
Judy, DB235	160.00
Juliet, DB283	35.00
King Arthur, DB304	45.00
Little Bo Peep, DB220	235.00
Maid Marian, DB245	29.00
Mandarin, DB252	175.00
Matador, DB218	165.00
Mrs Bunnykins at Easter Parade, DB19	65.00
Out for a Duck, DB160	275.00
Partners in Collecting, DB151	125.00
Punch, DB234	150.00
Randolf the Ringmaster, DB330	45.00
Rugby Player, DB318	200.00
Santa, DB17	60.00
Schoolmaster, DB60	75.00
Sightseer, DB215	95.00
Sister Mary Barbara, DB334	42.00
Storytime, DB9	70.00
Tino the Trixstar, DB330	45.00
Town Crier, DB259	175.00
Uncle Sam, DB50	75.00
Uncle Sam, DB175	200.00
Wee Willie Winkie, DB270	100.00

Character Jugs

Arriet, D6208 lg	149.00
Arriet, D6236, sm	95.00
Angler, D6866, sm	100.00
Anne Boleyn, D6651, mini	98.00
Athos, D6439, lg	149.00
Auld Mac, D5932, lg	80.00

Bacchus, D6499, lg	129.00
Blacksmith, D5671, lg	95.00

Busker, D6775, 1987, large, $150.00.

Buzfuz, D5838, med	195.00
Cardinal, D6129, mini	45.00
Catherine of Aragon, D6643, lg	125.00
Cavalier, D6114, lg	149.00
Choir Singer, DB223	69.00
Collector, D6796, lg	235.00
Confucius, D7003, lg	595.00
D'Artagnan, D6691, lg	135.00
Dick Turpin, D5485, lg	145.00
Dick Turpin, D6528, horse hdl, lg	245.00
Elf, D6942, mini	95.00
Falstaff, D6519, mini	45.00
Fat Boy, D6142, tiny	79.00
Fortune Teller, D6874, lg	295.00
Gardener, D6867, lg	185.00
Gardener, D6967	179.00
Gondolier, D6595, mini	295.00
Gone Away, D6538, sm	65.00
Granny, D5521, lg	85.00
Gulliver, D6566, mini	295.00
Guy Fawkes, D6861, lg	145.00
Jester, D5556, sm	145.00
John Doulton, D6656, 2 o'clock, sm	55.00
John Peel, D6130, mini	50.00
John Shorter, D6880, sm	195.00
Long John Silver, D6335, lg	139.00
Lord Nelson, D6336, lg	395.00
Merlin, D6529, lg	100.00
Merlin, D6536, sm	80.00
Mine Host, D6470, mini	40.00
Mr Pickwick, D5839, med	200.00
Night Watchman, D6576, sm	145.00
Old Charley, D5420, lg	85.00
Old King Cole, D6036, lg	295.00
Old King Cole, D6037, sm	100.00
Othello, D6673, lg	189.00
Paddy, D5753, lg	139.00
Paddy, D5768, sm	45.00
Pharoah, D7028, lg	695.00
Pied Piper, D6403, lg	95.00
Poacher, D6429, lg	85.00
Punch & Judy, D6946, lg	385.00
Rip Van Winkle, D6438, lg	100.00
Rip Van Winkle, D6517, mini, from $50 to	70.00
Robin Hood, D6252, mini	60.00
Romeo, D6670, lg	95.00
Sailor, D6875, sm	95.00
Sairey Gamp, D5528, sm	45.00

Sam Weller, D5821, sm 95.00
Sam Weller, D6064, lg.................................... 100.00
Santa Claus, D6704, lg 145.00
Santa Claus, D6705, sm 80.00
Simon the Cellarer, D5504, lg.......................... 145.00
Sir Henry Doulton, D7054, lg 295.00
Sleuth, D6631, lg 80.00
Tam O'Shanter, D6640, mini 88.00
Tony Weller, D6044, mini 45.00
Town Crier, D6537, sm, from $80 to 100.00

Veteran Motorist, D6633, Doulton & Co., Limited, 1972, 7½", from $100.00 to $135.00.

Vicar of Bray, D5615, lg................................. 200.00
Walrus & Carpenter, D6600, lg......................... 200.00
WC Fields, D6674, lg...................................... 180.00

Figurines

A' Courting, HN 2004 .... 935.00
Abigail, HN4044 .... 395.00
Adrienne, HN2152... 175.00
Afternoon Tea, HN1747 .... 495.00
Alfred the Great, HN3821 .... 395.00
Ankhesenamun, HN4190.................................... 795.00
Ann, HN2739... 145.00
Anna of the Five Towns, HN3865 .... 295.00
Anthea, HN1669..1,895.00
Antoinette, HN2426... 189.00
Ariel, HN3831... 395.00
Artful Dodger, M55 .... 69.00
At Ease, HN2473.. 325.00
Automne, HN3068..1,150.00
Autumn Breezes, HN1934................................. 395.00
Autumn Breezes, HN3736................................. 290.00
Autumntime, HN3621 .... 495.00
Baby's First Christmas, HN4427......................... 110.00
Balloon Girl, HN2818....................................... 395.00
Barbara, HN1432...1,800.00
Beachcomber, HN2487...................................... 195.00
Bedtime Story, HN2059 .... 365.00
Bess, HN2002 .... 295.00
Betsy, HN2111... 475.00
Blacksmith of Williamsburg, HN2240 .... 250.00
Blithe Morning, HN2021, from $235 to 285.00
Blithe Morning, HN2065................................... 265.00
Bon Voyage, HN3866.. 195.00
Bormoir, HN2918... 395.00
Bride, HN2166... 195.00
Buttercup, HN2309 .... 195.00
Buttercup, HN3268 .... 145.00
Camelia, HN2222... 295.00
Captain Cuttle, M77 .... 75.00

Captain Hook, HN3639..................................... 250.00
Carpenter, The; HN2678 .... 425.00
Carpet Seller, HN1464, hand closed.................... 295.00
Celeste, HN2237.. 195.00
Charlie Chaplin, HN2771................................... 465.00
Charmaine, HN1568......................................1,800.00
Chloe, HN1470.. 875.00
Christine, HN1840..1,200.00
Christine, HN2792.. 195.00
Christmas Morn, HN1992.................................. 195.00
Clarinda, HN2724.. 200.00
Cleopatra, HN2868......................................2,000.00
Coachman, HN2282.. 545.00
Country Love, HN2418...................................... 265.00
Cradle Song, HN2246 .... 395.00
Cup of Tea, The; HN2322 .... 270.00
Cymbals, HN2699 .... 695.00
Daffy Down Dilly, HN1713 ....1,495.00
Daisy, HN1961... 695.00
Darling, HN4140 .... 150.00
Daydreams, HN1731... 245.00
Debutante, HN2210.. 300.00
December, HN3329 .... 39.00
Delight, HN 1772 .... 325.00
Dinky Doo, HN2120.. 80.00
Drummer Boy, HN2679...................................... 495.00
Elaine, HN2791... 215.00
Elaine, HN3214... 120.00
Elegance, HN2264..1,820.00
Eliza, HN3179... 26.50
Elizabeth Bennett, HN3845 .... 500.00
Enchantment, HN2178...................................... 195.00
Ermine Coat, HN1981....................................... 395.00
Fair Lady, HN2835, coral dress.......................... 135.00
Fair Lady, HN3336... 235.00
Farewell to Daddy, HN4363 .... 295.00
Father Christmas, HN3399 .... 375.00
Favourite, The; HN2249 .... 250.00
Flower of Love, HN2460.................................... 185.00
Flower of Love, HN3970.................................... 210.00

Fortune Teller, HN2159, 6½", $500.00.

Fragrance, HN3250... 235.00
Gay Morning, HN2135....................................... 345.00
Giselle, HN2139.. 375.00
Gollywog, HN2040.. 465.00
Grandma, HN2052.. 465.00
Gwynneth, HN1980... 345.00

Gypsy Dance, HN2230	325.00
Hannah, HN3369	175.00
Helen, HN3601	215.00
Helen of Troy, HN4497	350.00
Hello Daddy, HN3651	95.00
Her Ladyship, HN1977	450.00
Homecoming, HN3285	595.00
Hostess of Williamsburg, HN2209	255.00
In the Stocks, HN2163	895.00
Jacqueline, HN2333	235.00
Jane, HN2806	275.00
Janette, HN3415	345.00
Jemma, HN3168	235.00
Jessica, HN3850	275.00
Jester, HN2016	295.00
Judge, HN2433	165.00
Julia, HN2705	235.00
Julia, HN4124	235.00
Juliet, HN3453	585.00
Kelly, HN3305	175.00
Kirsty, HN2381	100.00
Kirsty, HN3213	135.00
Lady Charmian, HN1949, from $235 to	265.00
Lady From Williamsburg, HN2228	190.00
Laird, The; HN2361	215.00
Land of Nod, HN4174	165.00
Laura, HN4665	200.00
Lise, HN3474	595.00
Little Miss Muffet, HN2727	135.00
Lobster Man, HN2317	195.00
Lorraine, HN3118	195.00
Love Letter, The; HN2149	395.00
Loyal Friend, HN3358	365.00
Lunchtime, HN2485	295.00
Make Believe, HN2224	135.00
Marguerite, HN1928	685.00
Marie, HN1370, 2nd version	89.00
Marie Sisley, HN3475	595.00
Masquarade, HN2251	350.00
Master, HN2325	189.00
Master Sweep, HN2205	695.00
Mayor, HN2280	345.00
Miranda, HN3037	250.00
Miss Demure, HN1402	295.00
Mr Micawber, M42	79.00
My Best Friend, HN3011	235.00
My Love, HN2339	195.00
My Pet, HN2238	195.00
Newsboy, HN2244	495.00
Nicole, HN4527	250.00
Ninette, HN2379	195.00
Noelle, HN2179	350.00
Officer of the Line HN2733	395.00
Old Balloon Seller, HN2129	295.00
Old Country Roses, HN3692	400.00
Old Meg, HN2494	235.00
Oliver Twist, M89	80.00
Paisley Shawl, HN1392	495.00
Pantalette, HN1362	695.00
Partners, HN3991	265.00
Pauline, HN3643	195.00
Penelope, HN1901	495.00
Pied Piper, HN2102	295.00
Polly Peachum, HN550	595.00

Primrose, HN3710	250.00
Prince of Wales, HN2884	500.00
Prue, HN1996	465.00
Queen Anne, HN3141	395.00
Queen Victoria, HN4475	385.00
Rachel, HN2936	225.00
Railway Sleeper, HN4118	295.00
Roseanna, HN1926	495.00
Rosie, HN4094	175.00
Sailor's Holiday, HN2442	365.00
Sairey Gamp, M46	100.00
Sally, HN2265	250.00
Sally, HN2741	195.00
Sara, HN3249	195.00
Seafarer, HN2455	295.00
Silversmith of Williamsburg, HN2208	180.00
Slapdash, HN2277	295.00
Sleeping Beauty, HN3079	295.00
Southern Belle, HN2229	140.00
Southern Belle, HN3244	245.00
Spring Morning, HN1923	798.00
Stephanie, HN3759	200.00
Suitor, The; HN2132	450.00
Summertime, HN3478	295.00
Sunday Best, HN2698	125.00
Sunday Best, HN3128	145.00
Susan, HN3871	235.00
Suzette, HN1487	595.00
Taking Things Easy, HN2680	295.00
Tall Story, HN2248	439.00
Thanks Doc, HN2731	295.00
Tina, HN3494	275.00
Tony Weller, M47	95.00
Top O' the Hill, HN1849	250.00

Town Crier, HN2119, 8½", from $250.00 to $285.00.

Tupence a Bag, HN2390	300.00
Twilight, HN2256	180.00
Uriah Heep, HN2101	495.00
Vanessa, HN1836	2,000.00
Veneta, HN2722	195.00
Victoria, HN3416	375.00
Viking, HN2375	235.00
Vivienne, HN2073	325.00
Wigmaker of Williamsburg, The; HN2239	195.00
Will He, Won't He, HN3275	300.00
Winter's Walk, HN4690	385.00
Young Melody, HN3654	100.00

Flambe

Unless another color is noted, all flambe in the listing that follows is red.

Bowl, Sung Ware, pheasant on orange flambe, Noke, 1900s, 11"... **3,815.00**
Compote, Sung, much bl, Noke/Moore, w/lid (no finial), 2¾" H.... **725.00**
Figurine, rabbit, 1 ear up, 2¾" **100.00**
Figurine, upright trout, 12½" **650.00**
Jar, red/yel/blk, slightly globular, H Nixon, ca 1932, 7¾" **380.00**
Vase, camels & palm trees, woodcut, bulbous, 5½" **325.00**
Vase, church/trees/fence, woodcut, Noke, 8x4" **465.00**
Vase, cottage in wooded lot, woodcut, stick neck, 15½" **545.00**

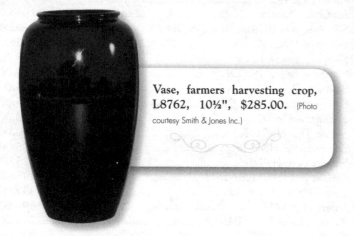

Vase, farmers harvesting crop, L8762, 10½", $285.00. (Photo courtesy Smith & Jones Inc.)

Vase, forest scene w/deer, woodcut, #1619, 11" **240.00**
Vase, shepherd/flock, woodcut, bulbous shoulder, 5½" **300.00**
Vase, silver o/l floral, 9¾" **345.00**
Vase, veined, bl highlights, bulbous pear form w/shaped rim, 4" .. **140.00**
Vase, veined, bottle form w/V-notched rim, 8" **265.00**
Vase, 2 cows in river/field of daisies, woodcut, 5x3¼" **300.00**

Lambeth

Bowl, grapes & fruit clusters, HP, ped ft, 1890, 6½x9" **600.00**
Flask, toby; moon shape, flat sides w/toby relief, 1890s, 7¾" **415.00**
Flowerpots, scalloped rims, floret bands, late 19th C, 7¾", pr **300.00**
Pitcher, Columbus portrait medallion (appl), 2-tone brn, 6½", NM .. **60.00**
Pitcher, Greek coins relief encircled by sayings, #573, 6" **125.00**
Pitcher, Natural Foliage, ovoid, #5188, 9" **325.00**
Sauceboat, marqueterie w/cherub ea ind, gold trim, 9" L **2,475.00**
Vase, geometric floral on bl, #573, 1883, 12⅝" **1,080.00**
Vase, shaped ovals w/bird against bl/gr mottle, HEH/1884, 11x7" .. **975.00**
Vase, symetrical/opposing scrolls & stylized flowers, stick neck, 7x5".. **235.00**

Series Ware

Bowl, Coaching Days, D2416, 3¾x8" **185.00**
Bowl, Dickensware, Artful Dodger, D5175, 10" **200.00**
Charger, Tony Weller, Dickensware, 13" **135.00**
Cup & saucer, Coaching Days, 4½" **45.00**
Dish, vegetable; Coaching Days, D2716, w/lid, 12½" L **300.00**
Jar, Jackdaw of Rhiems, 2 monks above rockwork band, w/lid, 5½" .. **185.00**
Mug, As the Wind Blows, So Set Your Sail, D3597, 5½" **80.00**
Pitcher, Coaching Days, 3½x5¾" **80.00**
Pitcher, Fat Boy, Dickensware, 6½" **235.00**
Pitcher, Fox Hunting, cylindrical w/elongated hdl, D5104, 5½" .. **165.00**
Pitcher, monks at table, 4-sided, D2561, Noke, inside crazing, 6½" .. **145.00**
Pitcher, Oliver Twist, sq cottage w/2 figures, 6" **135.00**

Pitcher, tankard; Blue Children, lady playing guitar, 13" **1,000.00**
Pitcher, tankard; Coaching Days, D2716, 12x7" **365.00**
Plate, Canterbury Pilgrims, 10½" **45.00**
Plate, Coaching Days, Man Opening Gate for Coach, 7" **70.00**
Plate, Coaching Days, 10", EX, set of 12 .... **450.00**
Plate, Dickensware, Poor Jo, D3516, 10" **100.00**
Plate, Dr Johnson at Cheshire Cheese, D6377, 13½" **55.00**
Plate, Gibson Girl, She Contemplates the Cloister, 10½" **85.00**
Plate, Gibson Girl, She Goes to the Dress Ball..., 10½" **95.00**
Plate, Gnomes, group under roots of lg tree, 1927, 9½" **300.00**
Plate, Queen Elizabeth at Old Moreton 1589, 10½" **38.00**
Plate, Shakespearean Characters in Setting, Juliet, 10½" **100.00**
Plate, The Hunting Man, TC #1049, 10½" **50.00**
Plate, Widow & Her Friends, She Becomes a Trained Nurse, 10½" ... **110.00**
Rose bowl, Coaching Days, brass wireware insert, 4½x5½" **120.00**
Syrup pitcher, Sam Weller, Dickensware, w/metal lid, 4½" **265.00**
Vase, Dickensware, Barnaby Rudge, 4¾" **210.00**
Vase, Dickensware, Night Watchman, 4¼" **185.00**

Stoneware

Bowl, chicken form, detailed feather pnt, MV Marshall, #896, 12" L .. **5,500.00**
Figurine, Steeplechase, frogs on mice, mc, ca 1885, 6" L........... **7,650.00**
Figurine, Trumpet Blowers, sm & lg mouse play horn, 1885, 3¼" .. **1,525.00**
Jug, cat reserves/florals/foliage, Barlow, late 1800s, 7⅜" **4,400.00**
Jug, horses band, earth tones, H Barlow, ca 1890, 12" **1,055.00**
Menu holder, Potters, mice at clay/at wheel, 1885, 4", VG **2,825.00**
Sauceboat, boar figural, tail hdl, MV Marshall, ca 1885, 7¼"....**5,285.00**
Vase, bands of sm wht flowers separated by purple foliage, Pope, 13" .. **745.00**
Vase, dog reserves & birds, brn tones, H Barlow, 1880s, 11½", pr..... **3,815.00**
Vase, flowers in V-shape wht reserves, pk tones, MV Marshall, 15x5"....**1,875.00**
Vase, flowers on trellises on ovoid body, trumpet neck, Simmance, 26"..**2,850.00**
Vase, flowers/foliage, rose/gr on wht, MV Marshall, #557, 15x3½" **800.00**
Vase, flowers/foliage, wht tube lining, FA Butler/Huskinson, #208, 15"..**1,465.00**
Vase, foliage (stylized/upright), tube lined, FA Butler, #583, 15x7"..**3,650.00**
Vase, foliage/fleur-de-lis, MV Marshall, bulbous, 1907, 13".......**1,600.00**
Vase, folige/scroll reserves, purple/brn, MV Marshall, #108, 16" ...**1,950.00**
Vase, mountain goats in field, H Barlow, 15½x7" **3,000.00**
Vase, rabbits & tall trees frieze, MV Marshall, 1903, 16x4" **1,100.00**
Vase, swirling Nouveau foliage, gr/wht, MV Marshall, 1905, 24"..**7,300.00**
Vase, 3-D gr dragon at neck, flambe-type glaze, MV Marshall, 9", NM..**2,100.00**
Watch stand, 3 shells surround bird, mc, 1890s, 5½" **2,350.00**

Miscellaneous

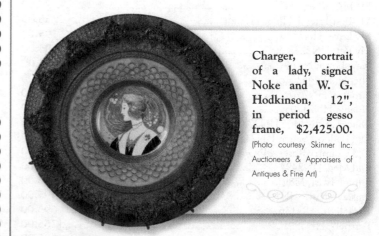

Charger, portrait of a lady, signed Noke and W. G. Hodkinson, 12", in period gesso frame, $2,425.00. (Photo courtesy Skinner Inc. Auctioneers & Appraisers of Antiques & Fine Art)

Bowl, soup; Sherborne, #D5915, set of 12................................. **150.00**
Humidor, water lilies, wht tube-lined on dk bl w/brn linear bands, 6" .. **165.00**
Jug, Kingsware, full-length man in kilt & full regalia, sm spout, 9" .. **350.00**

Match holder, Good Luck, swastikas/horseshoes/mums, #7138, 3¾" .. 165.00
Pitcher, Chine, floral, bl/gilt wht/brn, dk brn neck, lid, Slater, 7" ... 110.00
Pitcher, Kingsware, man holding stein, 4¾" 175.00
Pitcher, sailboats, dk brn/amber on bottle-gr mottle, 10x10", NM ... 325.00
Plate, dinner; E9433, 10½", set of 12 .... 150.00
Plate, Much Ado About Nothing, bl transfer, 10½" 100.00
Punch bowl, grapevines at rim, ftd, ca 1900, 7¾x4½" 435.00
Tankard, Kingsware, man w/tankard, sgn Noke, silver rim, 4" 250.00
Toby, Kingsware, Charles Noke design, 7" 400.00
Vase, cafe-au-lait crystalline gloss, gourd shape, 6¾x6" 98.00
Vase, Chine, dk bl w/central band: yel/wht gr flowers on brn, 7" .. 110.00
Vase, Church & Trees, underglaze, A Eaton, factory hole, 18x7" 935.00
Vase, floral cluster, tube-lined/3-color on plain beige ground, MB, 6". 195.00
Vase, spade leaves/upright flowers, highly stylized, bl tones, 6x5" . 485.00
Vase, Titanian, Kingfisher, bird on bamboo on lt bl, H Allen, 10x3" .. 700.00
Vase, Titanian, sm bl crystals on darker bl ground, #4-18, 6" 250.00

Royal Dux

The Duxer Porzellan Manufactur was established by E. Eichler in 1860. Located in what is now Duchcov, Czechoslovakia, the area was known as Dux, Bohemia, until WWI. The war brought about changes in both the style of the ware as well as the mark. Prewar pieces were modeled in the Art Nouveau or Greek Classical manner and marked with 'Bohemia' and a pink triangle containing the letter 'E.' They were usually matt glazed in green, brown, and gold. Better pieces were made of porcelain, while the larger items were of pottery. After the war the ware was marked with the small pink triangle but without the Bohemia designation; 'Made in Czechoslovakia' was added. The style became Art Deco, with cobalt blue a dominant color.

Bowl, 2 draped nudes form hdl, pastel w/gold, 12x14¼" L, NM ... 750.00
Bowl, 3 ladies dance about stem, emb lilacs/gilt, 19½" 420.00
Bust, Art Deco girl in stylish hat, sgn E Strobach, Bohemia, 7x3" .. 210.00
Bust, lady w/ruffled/pleated bonnet & collar, appl flower, 20", NM.. 720.00
Card tray, figural maid holds lg shallow bowl, wht, 6¾" 210.00

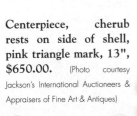

Centerpiece, cherub rests on side of shell, pink triangle mark, 13", $650.00. (Photo courtesy Jackson's International Auctioneers & Appraisers of Fine Art & Antiques)

Compote, maid stands on base picking fruit from 'tree' bowl, 26", VG 500.00
Compote, seashell supported by tree, ocean wave base, gold trim, 15" 700.00
Figurine, Art Deco nude, long dk bl/gold drape around hips, #3040, 10". 390.00
Figurine, Bedouin basket-bearer, gr robe, 1910, 14", NM, pr........ 765.00
Figurine, boy w/2 geese/basket (girl w/basket/2 pails), 12"/13", pr ... 175.00
Figurine, elaborate French attire, he w/violin, #298/298, 19", pr..... 420.00
Figurine, elephant trumpeting, long tusks, 8" 180.00
Figurine, female on horsebk, very stylized, wht porc, 14x11" 150.00

Figurine, girl holds cape wide, arms/midriff/legs exposed, pk mk, 15".. 720.00
Figurine, he w/goat (she w/lamb), now lamps, 26", pr 720.00
Figurine, hunter on horse, horn in left hand, 3 dogs below, pk mk, 17"..720.00
Figurine, hunting dog w/bird in mouth, 14" L............................... 65.00
Figurine, maid on horse, very stylized, wht porc, pk triangle, 14x12" .. 120.00
Figurine, man in stylish attire & flowers (she w/fan), 25", pr 1,920.00
Figurine, Rebecca at the Well, reaching for jug w/left hand, 18", NM.. 165.00
Figurine, seminude in bl skirt strides w/bowl in left arm, #3342, 11"..... 420.00
Figurine, shepherd blowing horn, animal-skin wrap, sheep below, 15". 275.00
Figurine, squirrel (upright) on base, brn tones, 10"......................... 50.00
Figurine, water bearers, classical gowns, she: #671, 24", pr, EX 500.00
Figurine, young man w/lute, long shirt/knee pants, pastels, 13" ... 275.00
Group, Arab on camel/2nd on base w/bags, dk bl/gilt on wht, 24" ... 420.00
Group, Art Deco dancers in dk bl w/gold gaze at ea other, 12½"... 330.00
Group, couple in colonial attire chat at tea table, 13x15", EX..... 265.00
Group, Harlequin w/lute kisses hand of lady in hoop skirt, pk mk, 12"...420.00
Group, masquerade ball harlequin dancers (pr), 20"................. 1,080.00
Group, Pax et Labor, mother kneels, lifts child to man in apron, 27" ...840.00
Group, 2 ladies, 1 sits/1 stand by bench, #1874, Bohemia, 13x10".. 690.00
Vase, muse w/harp appl to shoulder/cherub below, #2294, 18", EX. 840.00
Vase, organic form w/appl fruit, leaves extend from rim, 18" 210.00

Royal Flemish

Royal Flemish was introduced in the late 1880s and was patented in 1894 by the Mt. Washington Glass Company. Transparent glass was enameled with one or several colors and the surface divided by a network of raised lines suggesting leaded glasswork. Some pieces were further decorated with enameled florals, birds, or Roman coins.

Biscuit jar, lg Roman coins, SP lid, ovoid, 6½" 1,700.00
Biscuit jar, mums/earthtone panels, sq, SP lid mk MW, 10" overall ... 2,000.00
Ewer, armorial shields on shoulder, scrolls/lines, rope hdl, 9x7" .. 2,700.00
Jar, 5 Roman coins/gold sections, gold-scrolled red lid w/crown, 10" .. 6,350.00

Jug, rampant lion medallions, reverse with cross, ornate gilt-decorated neck band, with lid, 14", $6,000.00. (Photo courtesy Early Auction Co.)

Lamp base, lg gold griffin w/shield, mc sections, ornate brass ft, 23"...1,035.00
Pickle castor, wht/yel mums on frost; Pairpoint fr w/rtcl floral+tongs.. 3,150.00
Pitcher, fish/sea life, pk-scrolled top, gold sections/rope hdl, 9" .. 14,950.00
Pitcher, lions in shield below gold crown, floral scrolls at neck, 12"...5,650.00
Toothpick holder, mums, wht/yel on amber, paneled/beaded rim, 1½"...865.00
Vase, dragon centers dividing line, bk: dragon's head, 8x7" 2,280.00
Vase, floral roundels/scrolls, cup-like crown top, neck hdls, 9½" ...5,520.00
Vase, griffin, gold on gold-lined sections in red tones, ovoid, 5½"...920.00

Vase, lg scrolling/rtcl hdls & rim, florals on wht below, #6992, 13" .. **1,600.00**
Vase, peacock, gold w/jewels, thin neck: wine w/gold scrolls, 13".....**5,465.00**
Vase, Roman coins, onion form w/cupped 3-lobed rim w/red floral, 8"..**2,750.00**
Vase, 5 Roman gold coins, panels, 4-sided w/rim-to-shoulder hdls, 9x8"..**3,680.00**

Royal Haeger, Haeger

In 1871 David Henry Haeger, a young son of German immigrants, purchased a brick factory at Dundee, Illinois. David's bricks rebuilt Chicago after their great fire in 1871. Many generations of the Haeger family have been associated with the ceramic industry, that his descendants have pursued to the present time. Haeger progressed to include artware in their production as early as 1914. That was only the beginning. In the '30s they began to make a line of commercial dinnerware that was marketed through Marshall Fields. Not long after, Haeger's artware was successful enough that a second plant in Macomb, Illinois, was built.

Royal Haeger was their premium line beginning in 1938 and continued in to modern-day production. The chief designer in the '40s was Royal Arden Hickman, a talented artist and sculptor who also worked in mediums other than pottery. For Haeger he designed a line of wonderfully stylized animals, birds, high-style vases, and human figures, all with extremely fine details. His designs are highly regarded by collectors today.

Paper labels have been used throughout Haeger's production. Some items from the teens, twenties and thirties will be found with 'Haeger' in a diamond shape in-mold script mark. Items with 'RG' (Royal Garden) are part of their Flower-Ware line (also called Regular Haeger or Genuine Haeger). Haeger has produced a premium line (Royal Haeger) as well as a regular line for many years, it just has changed names over the years.

Collectors need to be aware that a certain glaze can bring two to three times more than others. Items that have Royal Hickman in the mold mark or on the label are usually higher valued than without his mark. The current collector trend has leaned more towards the mid-century modern styled pieces of artware. The most desired items are ones done by glaze designers Helmut Bruchman and Alrun Osterberg Guest (presently employed by Haeger). These items are from the late '60s into the very early '80s. For those wanting to learn more about this pottery, we recommend *Haeger Potteries Through the Years* by our advisor for this category, David Dilley (L-W Books); he is listed in the Directory under Indiana.

#47, Bowl, Chartreuse, 2½x13¼" 15.00
#57, Swan flower frog, gr/wht/beige, unmk, 1918, 4x3x3¼" 40.00
#257, Vase w/relief design, Briar Agate, 9¼" 15.00
#329-H, Lily bowl, yel-orange w/dk tips, 16¼" L 30.00
#336, Candleholders, Blue Crackle, 3¾", pr 20.00
#613, Hen, 10½", from $15 to 20.00
#2069, Ashtray, White Earth Graphic Wrap, 1970s, 8¼" 10.00
#3003, Compote, Cotton White & Turquoise, 12" L 15.00
#3212, Double cornucopia, sq base, 16" L, from $6 to 8.00
#3622, Bookends, Chartreuse, 7x4¾x5" 35.00
#4165, Vase, Peasant Orange w/blk int, 11⅜x4⅝" 20.00
#5015-H, Owl hanging basket, Bennington Brown Foam, 8½x7".. 60.00
#6140, Sailfish TV lamp, Silver Spray, unmk, 9x9¼x3¾" 50.00
#8183-X, Pitcher vase, orange/yel w/dk spots, 12¼" 15.00
#8300, Toe Tapper, brn textured, 8", from $35 to 50.00
R-36, Swan vase, neck up, cutouts around base, 16"....................... 35.00
R-103, Horse, Green Briar, 8¼x5⅛x3¾" 60.00
R-110, Elephant planter, 11½", minimum value........................... 150.00
R-160, Inebriated Duck, upright, 10" L, from $18 to...................... 20.00
R-166, Greyhound, head down, Gunmetal, 1940s, 9" 150.00
R-220, Dbl birds candleholders, Cloudy Blue, unmk, 5¼", pr 50.00
R-222, Round Spiral vase w/seated frog, 12", from $18 to............. 22.00
R-284, Trout vase, Mauve Agate, 7x9" L 60.00

R-287, Wren house, w/birds, Mauve Agate, 9¼x7¼x4¼".............. 75.00
R-313, Tiger, Amber, 12¾" L.. 75.00
R-352, Bowl, ftd rectangle, Black Mistique, 14½" L 60.00
R-358, Bowl, ftd, Mallow & Ebony, 3½x17½x8" 40.00
R-379, Bull, Mallow, ca 1941, 6½x12x3½" 500.00
R-435, Rooster Pheasant, Mauve Agate, 12x13" 50.00
R-451, Mare & Foal, Amber, 13" L, minimum value.................. 225.00
R-457, Triple leaf dish w/bird finial, Mauve Agate, 8½" 50.00
R-481, Seashell on ftd vase, Silver Spray & Chartreuse................ 75.00
R-492, Modernistic horse head vase, 15½", from $25 to 30.00
R-555, Pei Tung vase, 13", minimum value 300.00
R-579, Block candleholder (dbl tier), Green Briar, 2x2", ea 20.00
R-579, Dbl-Tier Block candleholder, Green Briar, unmk, 2¼", ea.....20.00
R-616, Tulip vase, 8", from $8 to... 10.00
R-657, Gondolier planter, Green Agate, 19" L.............................. 75.00

R-721, Indian on horse before cactus, Desert Red, $200.00.
(Photo courtesy David Dilley/Snyder's Antiques)

R-733, Panther, 13" L, from $12 to 15.00
R-819, Acanthus Leaf bowl, 14" L, from $8 to............................... 10.00
R-873, Free-form ashtray, Green Agate... 15.00
R-988, Basket bowl, 15" L, from $12 to... 15.00
R-1364, Rococo bookends, 6", pr from $18 to 20.00
R-1405, Mare figurine, 7½", from $15 to... 18.00
R-1446, Basket planter, Turquoise Blue, 9x6½" dia 15.00
R-1499, Ruffled Top vase, 7½", from $7 to..9.00
R-1718, Boomerang ashtray, orange, 1¾x13½x8"........................ 15.00
R-1752-W, Eccentric vase, Cotton White & Turquoise, 16¾"....... 40.00
R-1915, 1-Stem vase, Mandarin Orange, foil label, 15¼x3⅛"........ 30.00

Royal Rudolstadt

The hard-paste porcelain that has come to be known as Royal Rudolstadt was produced in Thuringia, Germany, in the early eighteenth century. Various names and marks have been associated with this pottery. One of the earliest was a hay-fork symbol associated with Johann Frederick von Schwarzburg-Rudolstadt, one of the first founders. Variations, some that included an 'R,' were also used. In 1854 Earnst Bohne produced wares that were marked with an anchor and the letters 'EB.' Examples commonly found today were made during the late nineteenth and early twentieth centuries. These are usually marked with an 'RW' within a shield under a crown and the words 'Crown Rudolstadt.' Items marked 'Germany' were made after 1890.

Boat, winged eagle at helm, scrollwork base, ca 1867-1918, 13" L 180.00
Bust, elegant lady w/pearls, beaded gown, scrolled base, 11½" 155.00
Bust, young blonde lady draped in bl scarf, floral corset, #4204, 13"...165.00
Candlesticks, Venus on elaborate ftd std, Cupid on 2nd, rpr, 12", pr..240.00

Centerpc, cornucopia w/lg 3-D spreadwing bird atop, ornate ft, 15" L..330.00
Charger, scenic w/terraces & house, 13" 50.00
Ewer, birds/foliage/gilt on wht, scrolled rim/ft, gold scroll hdl, 14"..180.00
Ewer, ferns, red/gr on peach to ivory w/gold, stick nek, 13"............ 75.00
Ewer, sm HP floral on wht w/gold trim, angled fluted rim, 10½".... 85.00
Ewer, violets/gilt on wht, ornate rtcl hdl & neck band, 14" 210.00
Figurine, parrot, bright bl/pk, on wht spool-like base, ENS, 15", pr....570.00
Figurine, wolfman playing piano supported by lg monkey, #V20407, 4"..120.00
Figurine, 2 cherubs frolick w/in basket of flowers, ornate ped ft, 6" .. 300.00
Jar, floral/peacock panels w/gilt scrollwork, lion finial, 11", EX.... 300.00
Jar, potpourri; lid & body w/rtcl scrolls, pastels w/gilt, 10" 150.00
Lamp, banquet; disk thrower w/horse, frosted ball shade, 22" 360.00
Oyster plate, 6 pk wells on turq ground, ivory center cup, majolica ..100.00
Plate, roses, lt pk on wht w/gold, gold hdls, 10" 35.00
Tray, roses/gold vines, canted corners, scalloped rim, 8" 115.00
Vase, flock of sheep, openwork long feather-like hdls, 16" 110.00
Vase, floral, pastel on wht w/gold, gold dragon hdls, slim neck, 12" ..90.00
Vase, floral sprays, scroll hdls, early 1900s, 18⅝"............................ 175.00
Vase, florals all around body, fluting above/below, gold hdls/rim, 8" ...120.00
Vase, upright cornucopia w/3-D bird on rim, seated boy below, 9" ... 150.00

Royal Vienna

In 1719 Claude Innocentius de Paquier established a hard-paste porcelain factory in Vienna where he made highly ornamental wares similar to the type produced at Meissen. Early wares were usually unmarked; but after 1744, when the factory was purchased by the Empress, the Austrian shield (often called 'beehive') was stamped on under the glaze. In the following listings, values are for hand-painted items unless noted otherwise. Decal-decorated items would be considerably lower.

Note: There is a new resurgence of interest in this fine porcelain, but an influx of Japanese reproductions on the market has affected values on genuine old Royal Vienna. Buyer beware! On new items the beehive mark is over the glaze, the weight of the porcelain is heavier, and the decoration is obviously decaled. Our advisor for this category is Madeleine France; she is listed in the Directory under Florida.

Box, 2 ladies in sq gold reserve, gold on red ground, 5¾" dia 780.00
Charger, Wotan & Brunhilda, she kneeling, red rim w/gold & jewels, 15"..1,440.00
Cup, portrait of maid in gold reserve on dk bl, gold hdl 360.00
Cup & saucer, lady & child reserve, harps in gilt border, 1820 .... 400.00
Cup & saucer, Phaedra & Hippolyte/maroon panels, gilt hdl/rim ...235.00
Ewer, centaurs/maids/cherubs on bl, red lip/shoulder, sq base, 15"...840.00

Ewer, lady and cherub, blue beehive mark, 5", $450.00.

(Photo courtesy Early Auction Co.)

Ewer, mythological scene in gold reserve on cobalt ea side, 23" .. 2,250.00
Ewer, neoclassic continuous scene on gold band, much gilt on dk bl, 8"..390.00
Figurine, French military officer, formal attire, 11", pr.................. 900.00
Plaque, Cupid & Cephisa, burgundy/gilt bkground, rtcl gilt fr, 9x7"..1,800.00
Plate, classical figures, gr rim w/gold-trimmed wht stations, 9" 75.00
Plate, classical figures, red/gilt rim, F Ahn, 9".............................. 110.00
Plate, Hector Departing for Battle, Balgne, much gold, 9⅝" 550.00
Plate, Marie Antoinette, Wagner, gilt/flowers on lt gr rim, 10".... 980.00
Plate, Schafende Genius, 2 red/2 wht gold-trimmed sections in rim, 12"..160.00
Platter, battle scene, dk bl w/gilt shaped border, 14" L 540.00
Snuff box, courting couple on lid, gilt metal int, oval, 3½" L....... 330.00
Stein, monk holding bbl, Grutzner, beehive mk, .5L, NM 2,200.00
Stein, monk holding bbl, Grutzner, cobalt w/gold, .3L, NM 1,815.00
Tea caddy, soldier/lady dance, P Heel, floral/gilt on dk bl, sq, 6"..630.00
Tete-a-tete, gold mums on wht on royal bl, sugar w/animal ft, 6-pc.1,560.00
Tray, Hector Taking Leave..., after Restout, LL, rtcl rim, 12" L..1,950.00
Urn, continuous figural panel on gr, Ahne, simple hdls/ft, 21"...1,500.00
Urn, garden scene band on red w/gilt, lg gold hdls, lid, 10", pr .1,020.00
Vase, Anemone (portrait), much gold on copper ground, hdls, 11"..3,200.00
Vase, Comtesse Du Barry in gold reserve on red, ovoid, 4¾"........ 570.00
Vase, Daphne in gold reserve on bl, gold floral hdls, stick neck, 12"..1,900.00
Vase, portrait of a lady, Wagner, maroon w/much gilt, 3½" 630.00
Vase, portrait of lady in lg cocked hat on wine w/much gold, hdls, 6"..480.00
Vase, portrait of lady on lt bl w/in elaborated gold reserve, 5"...... 450.00

Roycroft

Near the turn of the twentieth century, Elbert Hubbard established the Roycroft Printing Shop in East Aurora, New York. Named in honor of two seventeenth-century printer-bookbinders, the print shop was just the beginning of a community called Roycroft, which came to be known worldwide. Hubbard became a popular personality of the early 1900s, known for his talents in a variety of areas from writing and lecturing to manufacturing. The Roycroft community became a meeting place for people of various capabilities and included shops for the production of furniture, copper, leather items, and a multitude of other wares which were marked with the Roycroft symbol, an 'R' within a circle below a double-barred cross. Hubbard lost his life on the *Lusitania* in 1915; production at the community continued until the Depression.

Interest is strong in the field of Arts and Crafts in general and in Roycroft items in particular. Copper items are evaluated to a large extent by the condition and type of the original patina. The most desirable patina is either the dark or medium brown; brass-wash, gunmetal, and silver-wash patinas follow in desirability. The acid-etched patina and the smooth (unhammered) surfaced Roycroft pieces are later (after 1925) developments and tend not to be attractive to collectors. Furniture was manufactured in oak, mahogany, bird's-eye maple, and occasionally walnut or ash; collectors prefer oak. Books with Levant binding, tooled leather covers, Japan vellum, or hand illumining are especially collectible; suede cover and parchment paper books are of less interest to collectors as they are fairly common. In the listings that follow, values reflect the worth of items in excellent to near-mint original condition unless noted to the contrary. Our advisor for this category is Bruce Austin; he is listed in the Directory under New York.

Key: h/cp — hammered copper

Ashtray, oak w/h/cp details, tapering post/rnd ft, 2-tier, 32", VG.. 700.00
Bed, head/ftbrds w/vertical slats, Mackmurdo ft, 49x55x80" 6,000.00
Book, Book of Job, full Levant, incised/gilded, w/sleeve, 8x6", M . 4,200.00
Bookcase, 16-pane door, shaped side posts, cvd mk, 57x40".......9,000.00
Bookends, brass, wide band w/scroll base on sq platform, 5x4" 210.00
Bookends, h/cp, raised stylized floral, arched top, 5x3¾"............. 480.00

Bookends, h/cp, trillium pattern on verdigris medallions, 5x3¾" .. 325.00
Bookrack, Little Journeys, cut-out half-rnd ends, +14 books, VG ... 275.00
Bowl, copper w/brass lacquered 'rays,' 4¾x12" 240.00
Bowl, h/cp, rolled incurvate rim, 3 ft, new patina, 4x10" 1,250.00
Box, h/cp w/silver sqs, suede liner, D Hunter, lock/key, 2x6½x3", M .. 9,500.00
Bracelet, cuff; hammered sterling w/quatrefoil in woodgrain pattern .. 300.00
Candelabrum, h/cp, 3-arm w/scroll ft, 1906, 14¾" 5,000.00
Candelabrum, h/cp, 6 bobeches on horizontal bar, twisted stem, 14" ... 1,200.00
Candlesticks, brass-washed h/cp, Princess w/pyramid base, 7", pr... 750.00
Candlesticks, h/cp, pencil std, floriform base, unmk, 8", pr 690.00
Candlesticks, h/cp, riveted curled hdls/trumpet base, 2½x3¾", pr... 510.00
Candlesticks, h/cp, 3 curved strap legs, dome base, 9", pr.......... 7,200.00
Chair, side; mahog w/waisted bk splat, new leather/tacks, X mk, 44x17"... 1,200.00
Chair, side; tacked-on leather bks/seats, rfn/rpl leather, 41", pr ... 1,200.00

Chair, straddle seat, orb and cross mark, 35x24x22", $1,700.00. (Photo courtesy David Rago Auctions)

Chair, 4 vertical bk slats, Mackmurdo ft, new seats, 38x18x17", 4 for .. 2,000.00
Dresser, 4-drw w/integrated mirror, Mackmurdo ft, 62x44x26" .. 10,800.00
Dressing table, 1-drw, integrated mirror, Mackmurdo ft, 56x39x18"...7,800.00
Footstool, mahog w/orb, 4-leg, drop-in embr seat, rfn, 14x17" L, VG... 850.00
Footstool, oak, tapered legs, tacked-on new leather, cvd orb, 10x15" L... 750.00
Frame, h/cp, ea corner emb w/quatrefoils, 5¾x8" 840.00
Lamp, h/cp 7" dome shade (sm dent), bell-shape harp, slim std, 16"...2,200.00
Lamp, h/cp 8" helmet shade w/mica windows; sq woodgrain base, 14"...3,000.00
Lamp, hp/c 10" shade, leaf extends from center to past mica apron, 14"...4,500.00
Magazine stand, 3-shelf, canted sides, arched top, 38x18x16"...3,000.00
Mat, leather w/emb stylized flowers & leaves, 10", VG 1,560.00
Plate, geometric rim, red/blk on wht, Dard Hunter/1926, Buffalo, 10"... 120.00
Plate, vegetable; designed by D Hunter, Buffalo, 6¾x8", 5 for 780.00
Sconces, h/cp, oval w/candle shield at top, cup at base, 8½", pr... 780.00
Sideboard, short ldgl doors over mirror bk, base:2 doors/4 drw, 76x66".. 42,000.00
Stand, Little Journeys; 2-shelf, shoe-ft base, tag, 26x26x14" 700.00
Table, lamp; 30" dia top, Mackmurdo ft, X-stretcher, rfn 3,900.00
Table, library; dbl-arrow stretcher under overhang top, 42", VG...2,400.00
Telephone, h/cp & Bakelite, Property of American Bell..., 12".. 5,500.00
Tray, h/cp, emb stylized floral, w/hdls, rpr/wear, 9½x23" 390.00
Tray, h/cp, riveted hdls, new patina, mk, 16" 400.00
Vanity, bird's eye maple, mirror pivots, drw, 58x39", +chair (reuphl) ... 14,400.00
Vase, h/cp, Ali Baba bottle form, gr patina, 15x8", VG............. 2,000.00
Vase, h/cp, Am Beauty, Grove Park Inn, 22x8" 5,100.00
Vase, h/cp, Am Beauty, riveted base, cylinder neck, new patina, 19".. 2,700.00
Vase, h/cp, angled shoulder, sm shallow dent, mk, 5x5" 720.00
Vase, h/cp, rtcl top, 4-sided/tapering, lt cleaning, 7x2½"........... 6,000.00
Vase, h/cp w/appl silver sqs, cylinder w/4 full-length buttresses, 9"... 3,700.00
Vase, h/cp w/rtcl top, appl silver panel w/R, D Hunter, 7x2½".. 9,600.00
Waiter's stand, folding, w/chain link, from Roycroft Inn, brn pnt, 30"... 1,020.00

Rozenburg

Some of the most innovative and original Art Nouveau ceramics were created by the Rozenburg factory at the Hague in The Netherlands between 1883 and 1914, when production was ceased. (Several of their better painters continued to work in Gouda, which accounts for some pieces being similar to Gouda.) Rozenburg also made highly prized eggshell ware, so called because of its very thin walls; this is eagerly sought after by collectors. T.A.C. Colenbrander was their artistic leader, with Samuel Schellink and J. Kok designing many of the eggshell pieces. The company liquidated in 1917. Most pieces carry a date code. Our advisor for this category is Ralph Jaarsma; he is listed in the Directory under Iowa.

Bowl, bl & brn clovers repeat on ivory-gray, JW Rossom, rstr ft, 4x7" .. 200.00
Candleholder, naturalistic morning glories, bl on brn, stork mk, 6" ... 145.00
Jar, exotic florals, strong mc, stork mk, w/cone-shape lid, 6" 780.00
Plaque, trees/thatched-roof cottage, after van Borselan, 11x16".. 1,800.00
Plaque (20 6¼" tiles), old-world street scene w/people, after Mauve... 3,300.00
Plate, Queen holding orb of earth & palm frond, Dutch Royal House, 11"...1,200.00
Tile, fisherman in barge by windmill, subtle mc, #358/VB, in fr, 3x6". 480.00
Tile, shepherd/flock by barn in winter, after VerMeulen, #594, 6x6" .720.00
Vase, birds/pansies, strong mc, Jugendstil, #649, rstr, 13" 1,200.00
Vase, exotic floral, slim neck, #454, ca 1899, chip rpr, 15½x6½". 1,000.00
Vase, exotic floral/foliage, bl/gr/brn/wht, stork mk, 3¾x5" 195.00
Vase, floral, mc on dk bl, wide baluster form, 19" 2,280.00
Vase, frogs & lily pads on wht, sm lip chip, early 20th C, 7" 2,500.00
Vase, irises, rust/yel on wht eggshell, long-neck pear shape, 6" .3,000.00
Vase, long-stemmed irises/daisies on wht eggshell, #558, 9x3½" . 6,900.00
Vase, Nouveau floral, strong mc, thick integral hdls, 11" 5,500.00
Vase, pansies/butterflies, yel/purple on teal/olive, stick neck, 11".. 510.00
Vase, stylized irises, strong mc, ovoid w/waisted stepped-in neck, 4" ..240.00
Vase, tulips on mc ground, integral rim-to-shoulder hdls, #1082, 8x7" ... 720.00

Rubena

Rubena glass was made by several firms in the late 1800s. It is a blown art glass that shades from clear to red. See also Art Glass Baskets; Cruets; Sugar Shakers; Salts; specific manufacturers.

Bowl, lt vertical ribs, 9", in metal fr w/scrolls & leaves................. 125.00
Celery vase, bird & flowers, SP holder, 8" 750.00
Cheese dish, Invt T'print lid w/daisies & faceted knob, 9" dia..... 460.00
Ice bucket, enameled decor, silver bail hdl................................. 130.00
Pitcher, floral, 3-fold rim, clear reed hdl, 8¾" 230.00
Pitcher, Invt T'print, 4-sided rim, water sz................................ 200.00
Pitcher, Lincoln Drape, crystal cased, reeded hdl, 5½" 75.00
Rose bowl, 4"... 250.00
Tumbler, Invt T'print.. 30.00
Tumbler, Invt T'print, floral enamel.. 100.00
Vase, gold spider mums, cylindrical, 9¾"...................................... 145.00
Vase, Invt T'print w/HP flowers/birds, Aurora SP fr, 8", NM 335.00

Rubena Verde

Rubena Verde glass was introduced in the late 1800s by Hobbs, Brockunier, and Company of Wheeling, West Virginia. Its transparent colors shade from red to green. See also Art Glass Baskets; Cruets; Sugar Shakers; Salts.

Bowl, allover floral enameling, appl rigaree, 11½" L..................... 265.00
Butter dish, Invt T'print dome on vaseline Daisy & Button tray, 7⅝" ..335.00
Creamer, appl vaseline leaves, vaseline hdl & ft, 4¾x3" 135.00

Cruet, Inverted Thumbprint, 7", $450.00. (Photo courtesy Early Auction Co.)

Decanter, optic ribs on spherical body, gr knop & stopper, 14" 135.00
Pitcher, Coin Spot, ovoid w/sq rim, vaseline hdl, Hobbs Brockunier, 8" .. 200.00
Pitcher, Invt T'print, reeded hdl, sq rim, 7¾" 250.00
Pitcher, optic panels, flared top, ovoid body, att Hobbs, 6¾" 275.00
Pitcher, optic ribs, ovoid w/sq cased rim, vaseline hdl, 9" 230.00
Pitcher, vaseline hobs/hdl, Hobbs Brockunier, 8" 400.00
Rose bowl, florals & gold scrolls, 8-crimp, 4x4¼" 235.00
Vase, Drape, gr ruffled rim, 11" 435.00
Vase, floral spray, hexagonal cranberry top, bulbous bottom, 4½" ... 165.00

Ruby Glass

Produced for over 100 years by every glasshouse of note in this country, ruby glass has been used to create decorative items such as one might find in gift shops, utilitarian bottles and kitchenware, figurines, and dinnerware lines such as were popular in the Depression era. For further information and study, we recommend *Ruby Glass of the Twentieth Century* by our advisor, Naomi Over; she is listed in the Directory under Colorado.

Basket, Hobnail pattern, Fenton, #3837, 1985-86, 7" 33.00
Basket, metal hdl & decor, Westmoreland, 5" 22.00
Bonbon, swan w/crystal neck, New Martinsville, 8½" 27.50
Bookend, pillow design, Blenko, 1982, 5½", ea 16.50
Bowl, Barred Oval pattern, Fenton, 1984-86, 8½" 33.00
Bowl, Holly & Berry, Fostoria, 1980s, 13" 49.50
Bowl, punch; apple shape w/gr stem, dk ruby, Heisey, 1984, 9" 88.00
Cake plate, Tally Ho, Cambridge, 1930-34, 14½" 100.00
Candleholder, Heirloom, Cambridge, 1930-34, 10", ea 88.00
Candy dish, Everglade, Cambridge, 1930s, 3" 16.50
Creamer, Argus, Fostoria, 1967, 6-oz 33.00
Creamer, Popeye & Olive pattern, Paden City, #994, 1932, 3" 22.00
Decanter, Mt Vernon, w/stopper, Cambridge, 1930-34, 40-oz 93.50
Decanter, pinched, w/stopper, Blenko, 1930-53, 9" 27.50
Dish, chicken form, w/lid, Degenhart Crystal, 1970s, 2½" 12.00
Figurine, butterfly, Westmoreland, 1987-88, 2¼" 12.00
Figurine, potbellied stove, Mosser, 1982, 2½" 16.50
Goblet, Georgian, Fenton, 8-oz 44.00
Goblet, Penny Line, Paden City, #991, 1932, 8-oz 22.00
Lamp, oil; Moon & Star, LG Wright, 1970s, 12" 65.00
Mug, Fenton, 8-oz 27.50
Nut dish, Scroll & Eye, ruby carnival, Fenton, 1980, 5" 49.50
Oil cruet, English Hobnail, w/stopper, Westmoreland, 1980, 6½" 66.00
Pitcher, Northwood's Beaded Shell, ruby carnival, Mosser, 1997 .. 165.00
Plate, American, Fostoria, 1980, 14" 82.50
Plate, Christmas; Holly & Berry, Fostoria, 1980, 12½" 66.00

Plate, Doric, lace edge, Westmoreland, 1981, 12½" 181.50
Reamer, ruby carnival, Fenton, 6" 49.50
Sherbet, Argus, Fostoria, 1967, 8-oz 27.50
Sherbet, Mt Vernon, Cambridge, 1930-34, 6½-oz 24.50
Sugar bowl, English Hobnail, Westmoreland, 1980, 2⅛" 44.00
Toothpick holder, Beaded Oval, Degenhart Crystal, 1970s, 2½" 38.50
Toothpick holder, Rose, Blenko, 1980s, 2" 16.50
Tray, Regina, Paden City, #210, 1936, 10½x4¼" 27.50
Vase, bud; Barred Oval, Fenton, #8351, 1984-86, 8½" 20.00
Water, Rosette base, Blenko, 1930-53, 4-oz 9.50
Wine, Argus, Fostoria, 1967, 4-oz 27.50

Rugs

Hooked rugs are treasured today for their folk-art appeal. Rug making was a craft that was introduced to this country in about 1830 and flourished its best in the New England states. The prime consideration when evaluating one of these rugs is not age but artistic appeal. Scenes with animals, buildings, and people; patriotic designs; or whimsical themes are preferred. Those with finely conceived designs, great imagination, interesting color use, etc., demand higher prices. Condition is, of course, also a factor. Our values reflect the worth of hooked rugs in at least excellent condition, unless otherwise noted. Other types of rugs may be listed as well. This information will be given within the lines. Marked examples bearing the stamps of 'Frost and Co.,' 'Abenakee,' 'C.R.,' and 'Ouia' are highly prized. See also Orientalia, Rugs.

Bird/leaves/flowers, mc wool on burlap, on 19x18" stretcher 260.00
Canada geese (3), trees beneath, Grenfell, 27x40" 4,560.00
Cardinal on branch w/leaves, mc border, 1930s, 16x18" 85.00
Collie dog in landscape, crocheted edges, 20th C, 26x43" 475.00
Dog lying before flowers/trees, bright mc, Frost design, 56x30", VG .. 1,150.00
Floral sprays inside grid pattern, 1900s, 180x98" 530.00
Floral/geometric blocks alternate, wool, 1950s, rpr/losses, 108x70" 415.00
Folky cat w/lg smile on tan, geometric border, mc, 27x35" 1,725.00
Geometric/8-point star/plants, 1920s, edge losses, 40x25" 400.00
Holstein cow on bl w/brn trees, mc borders, 25x45" 1,850.00
House w/trees, floral border, wool, demilune, pre-1950, 34x20" ... 120.00
House/sky/duck/sunrise, mc wool on burlap, sm stain, 17x24"+fr .. 150.00
Houses/landscape, mc w/brn & blk border, 21x37" 115.00
Lion pr/foliate ground, bright colors, cotton/wool, 1880s, 62x32" .. 4,400.00
Native Americans/tepees/etc, mc dyed jersey, 1950s, 70x17" 765.00
Oak leaves over 16 striped sqs, geometric border, 107x32" 230.00
Penny, brn & orange geometrics on bl w/pk embr, thread loss, 40x26" .. 175.00
Penny, brn/navy/gr felt circles sewn to plaid wool ground, 31x36" 315.00
Pinwheel, mc on tan w/variegated field, minor edge loss, 26x25"+fr.. 550.00
Random stripes, mc, shaggy wool on burlap, 22x38", VG 150.00
Random stripes, mc cotton & wool rags, 3 joined panels, 105x120" .. 150.00
Spaniel, wool/cotton/jersey strips on burlap, 1900s, 21x35+fr 235.00
Tree of Life, tree & flowers, wool on burlap, rpr/rebound, 59x34" ... 150.00
United States, ea w/mc picture, sgn E Pailes MA, 44x69" 1,095.00

RumRill

George Rumrill designed and marketed his pottery designs from 1933 until his death in 1942. During this period of time, four different companies produced his works. Today the most popular designs are those made by the Red Wing Stoneware Company from 1933 until 1936 and Red Wing Potteries from 1936 until early 1938. Some of these lines include Trumpet Flower, Classic, Manhattan, and Athena, the Nudes.

For a period of months in 1938, Shawnee took over the production of RumRill pottery. This relationship ended abruptly, and the Florence

Pottery took over and produced his wares until the plant burned down. The final producer was Gonder. Pieces from each individual pottery are easily recognized by their designs, glazes, and/or signatures. It is interesting to note that the same designs were produced by all three companies. They may be marked RumRill or with the name of the specific company that made them. Our advisors for this category are Leo and Wendy Frese; they are listed in the Directory under Texas.

Bookends, polar bear, wht, #396, 7x3x4", NM.............................. 300.00
Bowl, peach, squat/wide ribs, #E12, +pr candleholders, 4¾" 30.00
Floor vase, celadon, 24" 120.00

Head of a woman, Art Deco styling, #1001, 11", $350.00.

(Photo courtesy Treadway Gallery Inc.)

Jardiniere, cream to brn, scroll hdls, spiral fluted rim, #274, 4½" ... 20.00
Jardiniere, wht semigloss, emb shoulder band, sqd hdls, #589, 5½x5" ..35.00
Party server, gr/brn matt, 3 graduated tiers, largest: 10" dia 50.00
Pitcher, Nakomis glaze, ball type w/bar hdl, w/stopper, #50, 7x8½"....235.00
Planter, bright pk w/emb dmns/ribs, wide fan top, #H360, 5½x10"...22.00
Planter, log form, brn/gr bsk finish.. 18.00
Planter, pk w/peach int, oak leaves relief under waisted top, 8" dia... 26.00
Planter, wht semigloss, lg arch hdl over 2-lobe leafy base, #H39.... 26.00
Vase, bl, 3-tier flower form, bulbous top, ftd, 13x7" 62.00
Vase, gr mottle, elongated cone form, fluted at bottom & disk ft, 8".. 32.00
Vase, gr mottle, spherical w/flared rim & elephant hdls, #215, 6x7" .. 80.00
Vase, ivory to gr, ribbed sphere w/sqd rim hdls widens at base, #299 .. 45.00
Vase, peach, V shape (Victory), 8¾x8" 30.00
Vase, Scarlet/Bay, spherical w/rim-to-width hdls, #320, 5½".......... 60.00
Vase, Seadrift Blue, Neo-Classic, graduated balls as hdls, #564, 9"....90.00
Vase, tan w/gr int, spherical w/3 openings, Deco style, #601, 8" 85.00
Vase, turq, duck-bill throat, 2 upright scroll hdls, #H21, 8¾" 24.00
Vase, wht w/gr int, wide flat rim over urn form w/lg hdls, 5½" 60.00

Ruskin

This English pottery operated near Birmingham from 1889 until 1935. Its founder was W. Howson Taylor, and it was named in honor of the renowned author and critic, John Ruskin. The earliest marks were 'Taylor' in block letters and the initials 'WHT,' the smaller W and H superimposed over the larger T. Later marks included the Ruskin name.

Ginger jar, yel pearl lustre w/pk highlights, 1923, w/lid, 5½" 300.00
Vase, abstract florals/gr vines, pastels on yel, dtd 1914, 13".......... 900.00
Vase, bl/gr flambe, long trumpet neck over squat body, 5½" 510.00
Vase, bl/violet crystalline (intense colors), bulbous w/can neck, 9"..1,100.00
Vase, indigo flambe crystalline w/celadon & amber neck, 1931, 4½"..385.00
Vase, lav lustre, shouldered/cylindrical, can neck, 7½" 360.00
Vase, maroon/bl flambe mottle on gray, lobed trumpet form, rpr, 6½" ..480.00

Vase, ochre crystalline, 9x4¼" 490.00
Vase, orange lustre, 1925, minor wear/scratch, 10x4" 540.00
Vase, pk/purple lustre flambe, ovoid, 5¾" 420.00
Vase, purple/gr/red crystalline (EX colors), cylindrical, 1910, 10" .. 2,250.00
Vase, silver o/l poppies on red & purple mottle, 9¼x3¾" 2,600.00
Vase, wht/bl/rose mottle w/gunmetal & gr speckles, cylindrical, 6x4" .. 2,600.00
Vase, yel lustre w/wht areas, bulbous w/long neck, 1915, 9½" 180.00

Russel Wright Dinnerware

Russel Wright, one of America's foremost industrial designers, also designed several lines of ceramic dinnerware, glassware, and aluminum ware that are now highly sought-after collectibles. His most popular dinnerware then and with today's collectors, American Modern, was manufactured by the Steubenville Pottery Company from 1939 until 1959. It was produced in a variety of solid colors in assortments chosen to stay attune with the times. Casual (his first line sturdy enough to be guaranteed against breakage for 10 years from date of purchase) is relatively easy to find today — simply because it has held up so well. During the years of its production, the Casual line was constantly being restyled, some items as many as five times. Early examples were heavily mottled, while later pieces were smoothly glazed and sometimes patterned. The ware was marked with Wright's signature and 'China by Iroquois.' It was marketed in fine department stores throughout the country. After 1950 the line was marked 'Iroquois China by Russel Wright.'

American Modern

To calculate values for American Modern, at the least, double the low values listed for these colors: Canteloupe, Glacier Blue, Bean Brown, and White. Chartreuse is represented by the low end of our range; Cedar, Black Chutney, and Seafoam by the high end; and Coral and Gray near the middle.

Bowl, lug fruit; from $15 to.. 20.00
Carafe, from $225 to 250.00
Coffee cup cover, minimum value.. 200.00
Ice box jar, from $250 to 275.00
Pitcher, water; tall, from $135 to 150.00
Saucer, demitasse; from $25 to 30.00
Sugar bowl, stacking, from $15 to 18.00
Teapot, restyled, from $175 to 200.00

Glass

Morgantown Modern is most popular in Seafoam, Coral, and Chartreuse. In the Flair line, colors other than crystal and pink are rare and expensive. Seafoam is hard to find in Pinch; Canteloupe is scarce so double the prices for that color, and Ruby Flair is very rare.

Bartlett-Collins Eclipse, dbl old-fashioned, from $22 to................. 35.00
Bartlett-Collins Eclipse, tumbler, cocktail; 3", from $15 to............ 20.00
Imperial Flare, tumbler, juice; 6-oz, from $45 to 50.00
Imperial Flare, tumbler, water; 11-oz, from $50 to 65.00
Imperial Pinch, tumbler, iced tea; 14-oz, from $30 to.................... 35.00
Imperial Twist, tumbler, water; from $35 to 50.00
Old Morgantown/Modern, dessert dish, 2x4", from $35 to 45.00
Old Morgantown/Modern, pilsner, 7", from $140 to 160.00
Snow Glass, bowl, sherbet/fruit; from $55 to 750.00
Snow Glass, tumbler, any sz (5-oz, 12-oz or 14-oz), ea from $200 to 225.00

Highlight

Bowl, divided vegetable; minimum value....................................... 200.00

Bowl, soup/cereal; 2 szs, ea from $30 to 35.00
Dish, salad or vegetable; rnd, ea from $100 to 150.00
Plate, dinner; from $35 to 40.00
Platter, oval, sm, from $50 to 75.00
Shakers, either sz, pr from $100 to 150.00

Iroquois Casual

To price Sugar White, Charcoal, and Oyster, use the high end of the pricing range. Canteloupe commands premium prices, and even more valuable are Brick Red and Aqua.

Bowl, fruit; 9 ½-oz, 5½", from $12 to 14.00
Bowl, soup; 11½-oz, from $20 to 25.00

Butter dish, restyled, rare color, from $225.00 to $275.00.

Coffeepot, demitasse; w/lid, from $100 to 125.00
Cover for soup/cereal, from $30 to 35.00
Gravy stand, from $15 to 20.00
Plate, dinner; 10", from $12 to 15.00
Teapot, restyled, from $200 to 225.00

Spun Aluminum

Russel Wright's aluminum ware may not have been especially well accepted in its day — it tended to damage easily and seems to have had only limited market appeal — but today's collectors feel quite differently about it, as is apparent in the suggested values noted in the following listings.

Beverage set, pitcher+6 tumblers+tray, from $450 to 550.00
Bowl, from $75 to 95.00
Coffee set, percolator+cr/sug, wooden finials, 9", 3¾", 3" 1,300.00
Gravy boat, from $150 to 200.00
Peanut scoop, from $75 to 100.00
Pitcher, w/rnd hdl, from $175 to 225.00
Tea set, from $500 to 700.00
Wastebasket, from $125 to 150.00

Sterling

Ashtray, from $75 to 100.00
Bowl, bouillon; 7-oz, from $18 to 20.00
Pitcher, water; 2-qt, from $125 to 150.00
Platter, oval, 13⅝", from $30 to 32.00
Relish, divided, 16½", from $65 to 70.00
Teapot, 10-oz, from $125 to 150.00

Miscellaneous

Bauer, vase, apricot mottle w/blk int, teardrop opening, bulbous, 9" ..800.00
Chase, pitcher, beer; Devonshire, #90025, from $225 to 250.00
Chrome, smoking stand, from $500 to 700.00
Country Garden, ladle, from $125 to 175.00

Everlast Gold Aluminite, creamer, from $50 to 60.00
Everlast Gold Aluminite, sugar bowl, from $65 to 75.00
Fabric, napkin 15.00
Flair, bowl, fruit 18.00
Flair, tumbler 18.00
Home Decorator, tumbler, from $15 to 18.00
Ideal Adult Kitchenware, jug, water; lg, from $50 to 75.00
Knowles Esquire, bowl, soup/cereal; 6¼", from $16 to 18.00
Knowles Esquire, plate, dinner; 10¾", from $15 to 18.00
Meladur, plate, dinner; 9", from $10 to 12.00
Oceana, bowl, salad; flat shell, from $500 to 600.00
Pinch cutlery, butter spreader, from $100 to 110.00
Pinch cutlery, iced tea spoon, from $100 to 125.00
Residential, cup & saucer, from $9 to 13.00
Theme Formal, coffeepot, from $600 to 650.00
White Clover, bowl, vegetable; w/lid, 8¾", from $75 to 100.00
White Clover, plate, chop; Clover decor, 11", from $40 to 50.00
Wood accessory, relish, 2-compartment, from $300 to 400.00

Russian Art

Before the Revolution in 1917, many jewelers and craftsmen created exquisite marvels of their arts, distinctive in the extravagant detail of their enamel work, jeweled inlays, and use of precious metals. These treasures aptly symbolized the glitter and the romance of the glorious days under the reign of the Tsars of Imperial Russia. The most famous of these master jewelers was Carl Faberge (1852 – 1920), goldsmith to the Romanovs. Following the tradition of his father, he took over the Faberge workshop in 1870. Eventually Faberge employed more than 500 assistants and set up workshops in Moscow, Kiev, and London as well as in St. Petersburg. His specialties were enamel work, clockwork automated figures, carved animal and human figures of precious or semiprecious stones, cigarette cases, small boxes, scent flasks, and his best-known creations, the Imperial Easter eggs — each of an entirely different design. By the turn of the century, his influence had spread to other countries, and his work was revered by royalty and the very wealthy. The onset of the war marked the end of the era. Very little of his work remains on the market, and items that are available are very expensive. But several of his contemporaries were goldsmiths whose work can be equally enchanting. Among them are Klingert, Ovchinnikov, Smirnov, Ruckert, Loriye, Cheryatov, Kuzmichev, Nevalainen, Adler, Sbitnev, Third Artel, Wakewa, Holmstrom, Britzin, Wigstrom, Orlov, Nichols, and Plincke. Most of them produced excellent pieces similar to those made by Faberge between 1880 and 1910.

Perhaps the most important bronze Russian artist was Eugenie Alexandrovich Lanceray (1847 – 1887). From 1875 until 1887, he modeled many equestrian groups of falconers and soldiers ranging in height from about 20" to 30". Some of them bear the Chopin foundry mark; they are presently worth from $4,000.00 up. Other excellent artists were Schmidt Felling (nineteenth century), who specialized in mounted figures of cossacks wearing military uniforms, and Nicholas Leiberich (late nineteenth century), who also specialized in equestrian groups. Most of the pieces made by the above artists were signed and had the foundry mark (Chopin, Woerfell, etc.).

Russian porcelain is another field where Imperial connections have undoubtedly added to the interest of collectors and museums worldwide. The most important factories were Imperial Russian Porcelain, St. Petersburg (or Petrograd or Leningrad, 1744 – 1917); Gardner, Moscow (1765 – 1872); Kuznetsoff, St. Petersburg and Moscow (1800 – 1900); Korniloff, St. Petersburg (1800 – 1900); and Babunin, St. Petersburg (1800 – 1900).

Key: lcq — lacquer   t-oz — troy ounce

Badge, cross, gold/enamel, crest, bk: #22 & 1789, 1¾" 5,000.00
Beaker, copper enamel, Nicholas II coronation commemorative, 1896, 4" .500.00
Bowl, silver w/gold wash, eng crest, St Petersburg, 1785, 7", 14-t-oz ... 880.00

Bowl, silver-gilt and enamel, Fyodor Ruckert, $9,500.00. (Photo courtesy Jackson's International Auctioneers & Appraisers of Fine Art & Antiques)

Box, cigarette; silver niello, Kremlin view, Moscow, 1856, 5⅜" ... 650.00
Box, cigarette; silver w/mc scroll, hardstone latch, 1908-17, 4" L ... 825.00
Box, silver w/mc enameling, Ovchinnikov, dtd 187?, 1¼x3" ... 1,850.00
Box, tobacco; silver w/eng Turkish scene, St Petersburg, 1881, 3x6x4" ... 4,700.00
Bronze, figure of boy reclining on stomach w/horn & crop, 1880s, 7" L ... 2,468.00
Buckle, lav enamel bordered w/rose-cut dmns & seed pearls, Faberge, 3" .. 8,050.00
Case, cigarette; silver w/bl stone/sm dmn melee/sapphires, 20th C, 4" ... 3,000.00
Chalice, parcel gilt silver w/porc saints plaques, Moscow, 1768, 13" .. 16,450.00
Crucifix, silver over wood, chased/emb scenes, 1854, 13¾" 2,235.00
Cup & saucer, silver gilt/enamel mums, brn/wht on blk, 1890, 2¾", 5" 265.00
Dish, gold-washed silver/clear glass, navette form, hdls, 1900s, 14" L ... 3,000.00
Egg, porc, after the Imperial, roses/vines, Alexandra monogram, 3½" .. 4,400.00
Figurine, shepherd boy w/dog, HP porc, Kornilov, 9¾" 2,950.00
Icon, bearded saint w/book receiving word of God, 20th C, 10x8" .. 500.00
Icon, male saint in red robe, emb gilt-metal riza, 18th C, 10x8" 1,175.00
Icon, St Nicholas Miracle Worker, gilt metal riza, 19th C, 11x9" ... 350.00
Kovsh, silver w/mc floral, rope-twist rims, 1808-17, 6" L, 5-oz .. 2,465.00
Lamp, hanging; Ecclesiastic, silver/mc enamel, 1900s, 8" L, 42-oz ... 8,800.00
Salt cellar, enameled silver, 3 ball ft, Orest Kurlikov, 1" 200.00
Salt cellar, silver, as a bread roll on napkin, 1890s, 6½" L 1,525.00
Spoons, demitasse; enameled bowls/hdls, JE/84 silver, 4", set of 12 .. 690.00
Tankard, silver w/emb cherubs, domed lid, St Petersburg, 1790s, 8" .. 21,150.00
Tea set, silver, 2 pots+cr/sug w/lid+waste bowl, Petrograd, NM... 3,000.00

Sabino

Sabino art glass was produced by Marius-Ernest Sabino in France during the 1920s and 1930s. It was made in opalescent, frosted, and colored glass and was designed to reflect the Art Deco style of that era. In 1960, using molds he modeled by hand, Sabino once again began to produce art glass using a special formula he himself developed that was characterized by a golden opalescence. Although the family continued to produce glassware for export after his death in 1971, they were never able to duplicate Sabino's formula.

Bonbon dish, 3 nude mermaids on interior of lid, clear, 6½" dia, EX .. 240.00
Bottle, scent; swirled ribs/dmns, opal, spherical body, #62-H, 6", pr... 85.00
Bowl, Les Poissons, in-mold koi/bubbles, opal/clear, 15" 1,320.00
Bowl, 3 ballerinas superimposed over lg flowers, opal, 14" 780.00
Box, 3 nudes on lid, opal/clear, 1⅞x9", NM 360.00
Bust, Praying Madonna, opal, 4" 60.00
Figurine, Branch of Birds, 5 sparrows, opal, 7x6" 660.00
Figurine, dragonfly, opal, 6x5¼" 195.00
Figurine, Feeding Sparrow, opal, 3½x5" 60.00
Figurine, nude holding sheer cape wide, head trn left, opal, 9½" .. 390.00
Figurine, Ondine, fish, opal, 4" L.. 65.00
Figurine, owl on stump, opal, 4½" 170.00
Figurines, chicks, opal, lg: 3", pr 92.00

Plate, 1819 Grand Prix de Gravure en Medailles, opal, ltd ed, 8½" .. 80.00
Vase, Carangues, rows of upright fish in relief, opal, sq ft, 5" 150.00
Vase, Deco panels of interlocking Vs, bl, octagon top, 12½" 1,080.00
Vase, floral spray in low relief on clear cylinder, 4½x3¾" 120.00
Vase, honeybees/honeycomb on geometrics, opal, spherical, 7" ... 345.00
Vase, rows of lappets, ea w/3-line petals, sepia wash, bulbous, 6" 395.00
Vase, stacked V panels on ftd rnd body, frosted, octagon rim, 9" 270.00

Salesman's Samples and Patent Models

Salesman's samples and patent models are often mistaken for toys or homemade folk art pieces. They are instead actual working models made by very skilled craftsmen who worked as model-makers. Patent models were made until the early 1900s. After that, the patent office no longer required a model to grant a patent. The name of the inventor or the model-maker and the date it was built is sometimes noted on the patent model. Salesman's samples were occasionally made by model-makers, but often they were assembled by an employee of the company. These usually carried advertising messages to boost the sale of the product. Though they are still in use today, the most desirable examples date from the 1800s to about 1945. Many small stoves are incorrectly termed a 'salesman's sample'; remember that no matter how detailed one may be, it must be considered a toy unless accompanied by a carrying case, the indisputable mark of a salesman's sample.

Animal trap, JH Morris, sprung brass jaws, mahog case, 1880, 8"..2,115.00
Barbecue grill, metal, w/grate & cover, working, 14", EX 300.00
Beer cooler, A Hammer, mahog w/tin trough, Sept 1852, 9½" L... 325.00
Bootjack, Wm W Cansley, hinged at center, fancy CI fr, 1895, 11" L .. 530.00
Bow saw, cvd Gothic leaf motifs ea end, trn stiles, 9½" blade ... 1,530.00
Brick maker, tin w/3 (orig had 4) wheels & roller, 20" L 150.00
Carburator, ST McDougall, gilt-metal valves, Jan 3, 1865, 9x10"..420.00
Compass plane, punchwork designs, cvd date 1834, wedge mk Charff, 6"...120.00
Cradle, self-rocking, open spring motor, crank w/seesaw action, 13" L... 150.00
Furnace, The Holland, metal, 9½" 120.00
Furnace, WH Churchman, pnt metal doors/flues/jets, wood casing, 10x6"... 235.00
Lawn chair/chaise lounge, vinyl cushions, 1950s, 9x22", NM........ 30.00
Oil-dispensing machine, nickel over brass, working, ca 1901, 8", EX... 1,000.00
Piano, G Bothurr, dbl-hinged top, 19 wht+13 blk keys, fancy, 23" W.. 3,680.00
Plow, 1-bottom, wood & iron, 11", on wooden stand.................. 280.00
Pool table, felt top, w/balls, no stick, 28x17" 55.00
Printing press, E Braidwood, mahog fr w/pulley drive, 1868, 10" .. 325.00
Queen Washing Machine, wood/metal 3-legged bucket w/top crank, 10", NM...4,200.00
Safe, The Opener Safe Co, pressed tin/CI/NP, blk/gold pnt, 19", EX.. 220.00
Sanitary closet, Rex, quartersawn oak, serpentine front, lift lid, 8"... 2,300.00
Sombrero, woven fibers w/fancy work on brim, 1930s, 3x8"........... 80.00
Spittoon, Beco Ware, wht porc, 2x3½" dia, EX 400.00
Stone dressing machine, N Jenkins, Mar 1, 1888, 4¼" dia 210.00
Sunbeam Stove No 1044C, cast metal, in orig box, 14x11x12", EX..500.00
Swimming pool, detailed above-ground type, in 28x24" case.... 1,080.00
Ventilator, H Doerge, NP flue/rotating fan, 1895, 8" 325.00
Watchmaker's lathe, mahog w/hand-cranked shaft, 13" L............ 385.00
Windmill, Challenge, brass w/wood base, working, salesroom sample, 39"..6,785.00

Salt Shakers

John Mason invented the screw-top salt shaker in 1858. Today's Victorian salt shaker collectors have a wide range of interests, and their collections usually reflect their preference. There are many possible variables on which to base a collection. You may prefer shakers made of clear pattern glass, art glass, specific types of glass (custard, ruby stain, Burmese, opaque, chocolate), or glass of a particular color (cranberry, green, blue, or amber, for instance). Some collectors search for examples made by only one maker (in particular Mt. Washington, Dithridge, Northwood, Hobbs Brockunier, and C. F. Monroe). Others may stick to decorated shakers, undecorated examples, or any combination thereof that captures their fancy. If you would like to learn more about Victorian glass salt shakers, we recommend *Early American Pattern Glass* by Reilly and Jenks. Unless noted otherwise, values are for examples in at least near-mint condition with near-mint decorations (when applicable). Unless 'pr' is specified, the value is for a single shaker. See also specific companies.

Victorian Glass

Alaska, cobalt, Northwood, ca 1897, 2⅜" 250.00
Artichoke, Fostoria's (AKA Valencia); clear/frosted, Fostoria, 2⅝" .. 80.00
Atterbury Twin, wht opal, 2-pc mold, ca 1877-82, 5" 105.00
Bale, bl w/HP flowers, Pairpoint, 1894-1900, 2⅜" 200.00
Barrel, Arabesque; opaque w/ornate HP geometrics, Moser, 3⅛" .. 540.00
Beaded Embroidery, wht opal w/gr & yel ovals, 1898-1906, 3½" .. 175.00
Beaded Panel, Concave; wht opal w/HP roses, 1900-06 .... 30.00
Bulb, Ringed Base; cranberry w/HP floral, att Europe, 1888-91, 3" .. 125.00
Champion (aka Fan w/Cross Bars), clear w/ruby stain, McKee, 2⅞" .. 85.00
Chick on Pedestal, yel opaque to lt gr on milk glass, CF Monroe 600.00
Christmas Barrel, purple, pewter top sgn Alden, Boston, Pat.., 2½" ... 120.00
Chrysanthemum Base Variant, cranberry opal, Buckeye, 1888-91, 3⅛" .. 195.00
Coin Dot, Phoenix; clear apricot opal, ca 1885-87, 2¾" 2,580.00
Corn, pk opaque triple cased, Dithridge, 1894-1901, 3⅛" 150.00
Cotton Bale, butterscotch variegated, Consolidated, 1894-95, 2½" ... 180.00
Creased Side Panel, rubena satin w/HP floral, 1883-95, 2¾" 160.00
Cylinder, Optic Honeycomb; bluina, 1886-95, 2¾" 160.00
Delaware (4-petal flower), rose flashed w/gold, US Glass, 1899, 2⅝" .. 200.00
Diamond Mosaic, bl opaque, emb RD 307899 on base, 1895-1908, 4⅝" .. 32.00
Elongated Bulb Variant, wht opal w/floral transfer, CF Monroe, 3⅛" ... 70.00
Elvira's Butterfly Variant, rubena stain w/HP decor, 1886-91, 2½" ... 225.00
Famous, clear, Co-op, 1899, pr 60.00
Flower Blooming, opal, Eagle Glass Co 55.00
Flower Tracery, red & gilt goofus on opal, Eagle, 1899-1905, 2½" .. 30.00
Hobb's Block, frosted amber stained, Hobbs Brockunier, ca 1890, 3" ... 80.00
Honeycomb, Intaglio Pillar; bl w/HP berries, Mt WA/Pairpoint, 3⅝" .. 190.00

Intaglio, green with hand-applied gold, 3", $70.00 each.
(Photo courtesy Mildred and Ralph Lechner)

Ivy Scroll, Jefferson; bl w/gold leaves, 30-rib, 1900-05, 2¾" 130.00
Leaf Umbrella, med bl, Northwood, 3" 185.00
Lobed Heart, cranberry w/HP floral, Mt WA/Pairpoint, 1894, 2¼" .. 200.00
Paneled Holly, wht opal w/HP gold, Northwood, 1907-08, 3" 190.00
Pleat Band (aka Panel, Ten), chocolate, Indiana, ca 1898, 3⅛" ... 900.00
Pseudo Pomona, clear frost w/3 fish, ca 1889-91, 2⅝" 150.00
Star of Bethlehem (Nearcut Star), ruby stain, Cambridge, 1909, 2⅞" ... 72.00
Strawberry Delight, bl opaque, Dithridge & Co, ca 1890s 150.00
Swag w/Brackets Variant, gr opal, Jefferson, ca 1904, 3" 125.00
Tulip Spray, wht opaque w/emb decor, 1899-1910, 3⅛" 21.00
Westmoreland #1775, columnar, Pat May 24 1910, 3" 18.00
Zippered Block, clear w/ruby stain, Geo Duncan, ca 1887, 2⅞" 85.00
Zippered Borders, ruby-stained thin glass, 1898-1903, 3½" 80.00

Novelty Advertising

Those interested in novelty shakers will enjoy *Florences' Big Book of Salt and Pepper Shakers* by Gene and Cathy Florence. It's available at your local library or from Collector Books. Note: 'Mini' shakers are no taller than 2". Instead of having a cork, the user was directed to 'use tape to cover hole.' Our advisor for novelty salt shakers is Judy Posner; she is listed in the Directory under Florida. See also Regal; Rosemeade; Occupied Japan; Shawnee; other specific manufacturers.

Anthracite Bit Co, rotary bit, rotating, plastic, 1959, 3", pr 125.00
Big Boy, ceramic w/pnt details, Japan, crazed, 4¾", pr 60.00
Budweiser Beer, Bud Man, ceramic, Ceramarte, 3½", pr 45.00
Camel Cigarettes, Max & Ray (camels), hard plastic, 1993, 4¼", pr ... 50.00
Chicken of the Sea, fish, 1 aqua/1 yel, pottery, 2x2¾", pr 19.00
Colonel Sanders KFC, bust of colonel, plastic, 1972, 3¾", ea 35.00
Dairy Queen, girl, pottery, Dairy Queen on flat bk, Japan, 4", pr .. 150.00
Evinrude, boat motor, bl plastic w/decal & clear stand, 3¾", pr ... 225.00
Fingerhut, truck, 1¾x3¾", 2-pc 30.00
Golden Guernsey Dairy, milk bottle, glass/metal lid, 1930s, 3⅜", pr .. 65.00
Greyhound, bus, pottery, Japan, 1960s, 1½x3¼", pr 45.00
Gunther Beer, bottle, foil label on brn glass, Baltimore, 4", pr 22.00
Hersey Kiss, candy, pottery, blk w/silver S or P, Japan, 2⅝", pr 15.00
Homepride Flour, Flour Fred spiller, hard plastic, Airfix, 2⅛", pr ... 45.00
John Deere, combination shaker (salt 1 side/pepper other), plastic, 4" .. 45.00
Kellogg's, Snap & Pop, porc, blk Japan mk, 2½", NM, pr 45.00
Koppitz Beer, bottle, decal on amber glass, Muth, Buffalo, 3¼", pr .. 25.00
Lennie Lennox (Lenox Furnaces), pottery w/decals, 5", EX, pr 85.00
M&M, candy men, 1 yel/1 red, plastic, 1991, 3¾", pr 28.00
Millie & Willie, Kool cigarettes, plastic, Mold & Die Works, 3½", pr . 20.00
Old Strasburg RR, conductor & engineer, pottery, Japan, 4¼", pr . 65.00
Pillsbury Dough Boy & Poppie, ceramic, 1988, 4", pr 28.00
Possum Hollow Whiskey, bottle, glass w/metal lid, 3¾", pr 18.00
Quaker Oats, building, pottery, Japan, 3⅛", pr 35.00
RCA, 1 is Nipper, 2nd is gramophone, plastic, 2-pc 15.00
Rice a Roni, cable car, pottery, ca 1970s, 2-pc 24.00
Schmidt's Beer, can, cardboard 6-pack, 1½", in orig case 20.00
Tappan, chef, pottery, Japan, 4⅛", pr 18.00
Vess Soda, bottle, decals on glass, 1 clear/1 gr, plastic tops, pr 25.00

Novelty Animals, Fish, and Birds

Bear, 1 in Navy hat, 1 w/life preserver, CA pottery, 4", pr 45.00
Black cat, crouching, pottery, wood stopper, no mk, 2x2", pr 25.00
Bluebird, bone china, Lego, 2½x2½", pr 28.00
Burrow, bucket (shaker) on ea side, ceramic, bl/wht, Japan, 5", 3-pc ... 18.00
Cat ice skater, ceramic, unmk, 4½", pr 10.00
Dachshund, begging/sitting, brn pottery, Marston, 5", 4", pr 38.00
Dog, tall/slim w/long ears, brn spots, pottery, 6½", pr 15.00
Dog playing Ping-Pong, ceramic, 1950s, Japan, 2¾", pr 19.00
Dog w/nodding head, pottery, vintage Japan, 3½", ea 60.00
Dolphin, pottery, souvenir, EW Japan, 5¼" L, pr 28.00
Fish, pr on tray, pottery, Shorter & Son England, 1950s, 3x4", 3-pc .. 36.00
Flamingos, 1 preening/1 feeding, ceramic, Japan paper label, 4", pr .. 15.00
Goose & the Golden Egg, plastic goose contains 2 egg shakers, 3½" ... 18.00
Iguanodon dinosaurs, necks entwined, pottery, Japan, 4½", pr 55.00
Koala bear, bone china, no mk (Japan), 1970s, 2", pr 19.00
Pekingese, ceramic, Goebel W Germany, P209, 1968, 3", pr 28.00
Puppy dog, seated, bow tie, gr vest, yel pants, pottery, Japan, 5", pr .. 24.00
Rabbit mom & baby, pottery, she w/umbrella, Japan, 4", pr 22.00
Scottie dog, seated, Deco style, aluminum, tail screws off, 2¾", pr ... 28.00

Novelty Character and Disney

Aladdin & lamp, pottery, he: 4¼" w/jewels, Japan, 1960s, 2-pc 29.00
Barbar elephant & girlfriend, ceramic, vintage, 3½", pr 55.00
Betsy Ross & Paul Revere, pottery, 1960s, Japan label, 4½", pr...... 30.00
Betty Boop (carhop on skates) & Bimbo (in car), ceramic, Vandor, pr .. 30.00
Betty Boop & Bimbo in (wood) boat, ceramic, Vandor, 1981, 5" L, 3-pc.. 65.00
Bonzo (dog), pottery, wht w/much gold, 1930s, 3", pr 30.00
Buddha, full figure, gold glaze, Japan, 3¾", pr 22.00
Charlie McCarthy bust, pottery, Japan, lt pnt wear, 3", pr 80.00
Cinderella's slipper on pillow, pottery, Applause, 2¾x3" L, 2-pc.... 30.00
Crows Preacher & Dandy (Disney), pottery, Japan, 3¾", pr 75.00
Donald Duck, pottery, Dan Brechner, 1961, WD-32/WDP/Japan, 5", pr.. 95.00
Donald Duck, 1 w/pipe, 1 w/flowers, pottery, 1950s, Japan, 2¾", pr .. 28.00
Dopey (Snow White's dwarf), pottery, gr Japan mk, 4", pr 55.00
Ginghman Dog & Cat, pottery, 1950s, 4½", pr.............................. 29.00
Jack & Jill, pottery, Kreiss, 1957, Japan label, 4", pr 39.00
Jimmy Carter peanut, smiling, w/shoes, Japan label/#H693, 3½", pr.. 25.00
John Alden & Priscilla, pottery, 1950s, gr Japan mk, 4¾", pr......... 25.00
Leo & Gino Garabaldi busts (wrestler team), pottery, 1950s, 3¼", pr.. 39.00
Mammy & Pappy Yokum, pottery, Japan label/#2611, glued rpr, 4", pr .. 95.00
Mickey & Minnie Mouse, chef hats, ceramic, Hoan/WDC/Taiwan, 4¼", pr..30.00
Mona Lisa in photo fr, ceramic, Vandor, 1992, 4x3½x3", 2-pc, w/box...32.00
Mother Goose, pottery, Josef labels, 3½", pr................................. 39.00
Pinocchio & girlfriend, porc, 1940s, Japan, he: 4¾", pr.................. 75.00
Pluto, seated, pottery, wht w/blk & red cold-pnt, '40s, 3¼", pr 30.00
Pooh & Rabbit, pottery, Enesco, 1960s, 3½", 4", pr....................... 65.00
Popeye & Olive Oyl, pottery, HP, 1960s-70s, unmk, 6¼", pr........... 95.00
Queen of Hearts & Jester, pottery, Japan #6440, 4¼", pr............... 45.00
Raggedy Ann & Andy, pottery, vintage import, 4", pr 40.00
Robin Hood sitting atop rock (shaker), pottery, Japan, 4½", 2-pc.. 28.00
Rudolph head, pottery, #4370, vintage, 3", pr............................... 28.00
Santa & Mrs Claus sit on wood bench, pottery, Japan label, 4½", pr ...25.00
Santa & reindeer, stylized, pottery, National Ceramics label, pr 18.00
Santa face, ceramic, wht w/worn cold pnt, TX-#1231, 3", pr......... 18.00
Yosemite Sam, pottery, Warner Bros, 1960, Lego label, 4", pr........ 75.00

Novelty People

Amish lady w/pie, he w/slice, pottery, Japan label/H763, 4¾", pr .. 24.00
Army & Navy servicemen, pottery, 1940-50s, 2¾", pr 28.00
Black boy riding hippo, pottery, ca 1940s-50s, Japan, 2-pc........... 145.00
Black child on cabbage, pottery, Japan, 1950s, 2½x3", 2-pc 55.00
Black lady (bust), bowl on head/bone in hair, pottery, Japan, 4", pr... 45.00
Boy & girl, Hummel-like, ceramic, Occupied Japan, 4½", pr 25.00
Boys in space suits, arms raised, pack on bk, pottery, Japan, 4", pr ...40.00
Chef bust (winking), pottery, Japan label, 3¼", pr.......................... 20.00
Children, red hats, bl & yel attire, ceramic, Goebel/Germany, 3", pr...35.00
Choir boy w/songbook, pottery, 1950s, 4¾", pr.............................. 22.00
Clown acrobat supports the 2nd in handstand, pottery, Japan, 6", pr...40.00
Colonial boy w/Bill of Rights, Betsy Ross w/flag, ceramic, 4½", pr. 15.00
Cowboy & girl, he in chaps holds gun & bottle, ceramic, 4¼", pr . 15.00
Dear God kids, ceramic, Enesco, w/hang tag & label, 1982, 4", pr. 45.00
Dutch girl & windmill, (from a series), pottery, Japan, 4¼", 2-pc .. 34.00
Eskimo & igloo, pottery, 1950s, Japan, he: 4½", 2-pc 24.00
Fireman, #1 w/dog, #2 w/ax, pottery w/some cold pnt, Japan, 4", pr... 15.00
Golliwog driving car, pottery, Made in England, car: 4½" L, 2-pc ...110.00
Graduates, thick eyeglasses, diploma under arm, pottery, Japan, 3", pr ... 15.00
Indian boy & girl, pottery, 1960s, Japan label, 4¼", pr 22.00
Lion tamer sits & talks w/lion (2nd shaker), pottery, Japan, 3", pr....25.00
Maid & Chef (Salt w/spoon, Pep w/knife), pottery, Japan, 1950s, 3", pr...150.00
Mammy & Chef waving, pottery, HP, Japan, 1950s, 2½", pr 30.00
Man & lady, he (huge nose) & she (lg bosom) interlock, pottery, 5", pr.. 45.00
Man pulling fruit cart (w/'fruit' shakers), pottery, 1950s, 4x5", 3-pc... 23.00

Mexican couple, from $18.00 to $20.00; Cactus, from $15.00 to $18.00. (Photo courtesy Helene Guarnaccia)

Mexicans, he w/guitar, she w/fan, chartreuse, pottery, c UC, 4", pr...20.00
Moon man & rocket ship, ceramic, Enesco, 1950s, ship: 4¼", 2-pc .60.00
Pirate & treasure chest, pottery, solid colors, 1950s, 3½", 2-pc 22.00
Policeman w/club, rnd face, wht w/pnt details, pottery, Japan, 4", pr...25.00
Scottish children, pottery, Josef/Scotland labels, 4¼", pr............... 38.00
Zodiac girl (from a series), pottery, Japan, 4½", pr 35.00

Miscellaneous Novelties

Accordion, ceramic, Arcadia, ea 22.00
Anthropomorphic foot, pottery, 1950s, Japan label, 3½", pr 16.00
Basket of clothes & iron, OH turnpike souvenir, ceramic, Japan, 2-pc..18.00
Bible, ceramic, Arcadia, ea 14.00
Christmas candle w/holly & bow, ceramic, Lefton #1556, 4¼", pr...18.00
Flowerpot w/2 roses (shakers), plastic, 1950s, USA, 8", 3-pc 15.00
Flying saucer, pottery, 1950s, Coventry, 1¼x2½x3", pr.................. 24.00
Golf bag & ball, ceramic, Japan label/H-#151, bag: 3¼", 2-pc 16.00
Guitar (1-pc salt & pepper) on stand, plastic, Pat Pend, 5¼", 2-pc...17.00
Hay Wagon, pottery, Arcadia, 1¼", ea 22.00
Ice cream cones (2 shakers on stand), plastic, 1950s, 4¼", 3-pc..... 16.00
Jack in the box, pottery, 1950s, 4", pr.. 28.00
Skull nodders on base w/HP Niagara Falls, lusterware, Pat TT, 3-pc.. 45.00
Spouting Geyser Saratoga Springs NY scene, ceramic, Royal Winton, pr....20.00
Victrola crank phonograph, ceramic, Napco, 1950s, 3¼", pr 20.00
Wanted poster on cactus, pottery, 1950s, 3¼", pr 18.00
Washington monument, metal, 2¾" pr on tray w/emb DC scene, Japan...20.00

Salts, Open

Before salt became refined, processed, and free-flowing as we know
it today, it was necessary to serve it in a salt cellar. An innovation of the
early 1800s, the master salt was placed by the host and passed from person
to person. Smaller individual salts were a part of each place setting. A
small silver spoon was used to sprinkle it onto the food.

If you would like to learn more about the subject of salts, we recommend *The Open Salt Compendium* by Sandra Jzyk and Nina Robertson
and *5,000 Open Salts*, written by William Heacock and Patricia Johnson,
with many full-color illustrations and current values. In the listings below, the numbers refer to the Heacock and Johnson book and *The Glass
Industry in Sandwich* by Raymond Barlow and Joan Kaiser. See also Blown
Glass; Blown Three-Mold Glass.

Key: EPNS — electroplated nickel silver   HM — hallmarked

Animals, Figurals, and Novelties

Bird & egg, pressed glass, mold mks 22.00
Chair, Russian silver-gilt/cloisonne, Vasilly Agafonov, 1900, 2½"..2,040.00

Daisy blossom, James W Tufts SP, 1¼" dia, pr 65.00
Elephant, Russian silver, ivory tusks/ruby eyes, faux Faberge mk, 4-oz .. 510.00
Frogs, sterling w/glass eyes, Cartier, +4 matching frog pepper shakers ... 4,550.00
Ivory, wide band w/open-cvd natives, lg head finial, Angolan, 16" .. 450.00
Ladies stand back-to-back, common lower body ea w/cup, Quimper, 8", NM .. 180.00
Lady in gown w/lg collar stands on base w/cup, gilt trim, KPM 75.00
Lady lifts cellar in ea hand, mc on French faience, Quimper style, 7" .. 120.00
Lady seated w/basket, Wedgwood majolica, 7" 600.00
Oriental man kneels on 1 knee, holds shaped cellar, Herend, 3" 95.00
Putto holding shell while riding dolphin, majolica, Geo Jones, 7" . 1,150.00
Putto on arched base w/2 cups & scroll ft, KPM, 1800s, 4¾x5" ... 350.00
Viking ship, sea creature's head ea end, sterling w/cobalt liner, 3" L ... 135.00

Art Glass

Cranberry w/clear pinwheel, vaseline rigaree to rim/waist, SP ftd fr ... 145.00
Daum Nancy, cameo vines & berries, gilt accents, 1¼x2" 780.00
Daum Nancy, enameled windmill/sailboats on opal mottle, 7¾" dia ... 630.00
Gr opal, ribbed w/tooled rigaree, in 3-ftd silver fr mk JD & S EPNS ... 140.00
Quezal, gold w/magenta highlights, bl-gr highlights to int, 2½" dia ... 315.00
Steuben, clear, ped ft, 2x2¾" 120.00
Steuben, gold w/reddish int, mk Aurene #3067/label, +Gorham spoon .. 315.00
Steuben verre de soie, fleur-de-lis mk, 1⅝", +Gorham spoon 120.00
Tiffany, bl pastel cased w/irid opal, lt ribs/scallops, 3", +mk spoon .. 1,150.00
Tiffany, deep bl irid, finger-crimped rim, 2½" dia 330.00
Tiffany, gold w/much irid, deeply tooled w/spirals & ridges, #6417 .. 315.00

China and Porcelain

Doulton Lambeth stoneware, raised/incised floriate design, sq base, 4" .. 230.00
Dutch Delft, mc scrolls/foliage, octagonal top & base, sgn, 2½" .. 1,840.00
Dutch Delft, typical bl/wht, octagonal rim/ft, de Berg, 1¾", EX ... 960.00

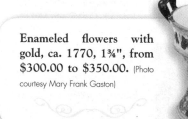

Enameled flowers with gold, ca. 1770, 1¾", from $300.00 to $350.00. (Photo courtesy Mary Frank Gaston)

Flower form, porc, pk w/gilt int, 2" dia, 12 for 60.00
Geo Jones majolica, sm pk floral stems on lt bl, pk int, EX 520.00
Herend, dbl cups w/central ring hdl, bl bands/gilt sprigs, 4" L 55.00
Herend, dbl w/center loop hdl, HP birds/flowers, 5½" L, pr 135.00
Mason's ironstone, bl transfer Canton scenes, lion's paw ft, 6x6" ... 95.00
Meissen Blue Onion, 2 joined cups, center hdl 50.00
Redware w/manganese splotches, 2x3½" dia 330.00
Royal Copenhagen Flora Danica, oval, set of 6 .... 1,000.00

China, Pottery, and Porcelain

Belleek, HP, ruffled top, rnd, mk, HJ-1310, ind 35.00
Delft, seated lion holds dbl cups, mc, 1800s, 3x4" L, EX 430.00
Elfinware, heavy decor, sgn Germany, HJ-1270, ind 30.00
Elfinware, swan, Germany, ornate, HJ-1039 .... 35.00
Haviland, pattern decor, HJ-1400, ind 30.00
Nippon, celery salt, HJ-1714, ind 12.00
Pickard, sq, HJ-1569, ind 45.00
Royal Bayreuth, claw figural, HJ-1667, ind 85.00

Royal Bayreuth, poppy figural, HJ-1790 .... 95.00
Royal Doulton, pottery w/gold swirls, bl int 75.00

Lacy Glass

When no condition is indicated, the items below are assumed to be without obvious damage; minor roughness is normal.

BF-1B, Basket of Flowers, clambroth, Sandwich, 1830-40, 2⅛" ... 200.00
BF-1D, Basket of Flowers, fiery opal violet-bl, ftd, Sandwich, 2⅛" ... 4,400.00
BT-4B, Lafayet (sic) Steamboat, Sandwich, 1830-45, 1½x3⅝", EX ... 165.00
BT-8, Lafayet (sic) Steamboat, wht opaque opal, Sandwich, 1⅝", EX .. 230.00
CN-1A, Crown, dk cobalt, 4 scroll ft, Sandwich, 1830-45, 2⅛" .. 1,595.00
DD-1, Dmn, scalloped rim, att Pittsburgh, 1835-60, 1¾", EX 440.00
EE-3B, Eagle & Shield, 4-ftd, Sandwich, 1830-45, 2⅛", NM 100.00
EE-8, Eagle & Ship, chain rim, Sandwich, 1830-45, chip, 1⅞" 300.00
GA-2, Gothic Arch, violet-bl w/some opal, Sandwich, 1835-45, 1¾", G .. 440.00
GA-3, Gothic Arch, scalloped rim, 4-ftd, Pittsburgh, 1835-45, 1¾" .. 255.00
GA-4A, Gothic Arch & Heart, Sandwich, 1835-45, 1¾", EX 75.00
JY-1A, lt gr, scalloped, star base, Jersey, 1835-50, 1¾", EX 200.00
LE-2, Lyre, lav-bl opaque w/lt mottle, Sandwich, 1835-45, 1⅞", NM .. 7,700.00
MV-1, aquamarine, scallop & point rim, att Mt Vernon, 1¾", NM .. 90.00
MV-1B, cobalt, scallop & point rim, Sandwich or Mt Vernon, 1¾", EX .. 155.00
NE-3, scallop & point rim, NE Glass, 1835-50, 2", NM 145.00
NE-6, lt gr, star under base, scallop & point rim, 1835-50, 2", NM .. 125.00
OG-19, oblong, 4 paw ft, att Fr, 1835-50, 2", G- 45.00
OL-10 variant, serrated scalloped rim, 1835-50, 1¼", NM 600.00
OL-14, Star in Dmn, med amethyst, Sandwich, 1830-50, 1¾", G- .. 200.00
OL-16, Dmn Rosette & Swag, bright red amber, Sandwich, 1½", NM .. 1,325.00
OL-27, Strawberry Dmn w/Corner Ovals, att NE Glass, 1½", NM .. 175.00
OL-35, Gothic Arch & Magnet Oval, 1835-50, 1½", G 90.00
OO-10, Octagon, dk cobalt, att NE Glass, 1835-50, 1½", NM 825.00
OP-2B, Strawberry Dmn, opal, paw ft, Sandwich, 2", NM 385.00
OP-12, clambroth w/bl-gr tint, oval ped, Sandwich, 1¾", NM 150.00
OR-8, octagon, att Sandwich, 1¾", NM 110.00
PO-5, Peacock Eye, bright sapphire bl, Sandwich, 1830-45, 1½", NM .. 4,295.00
PP-1, Peacock Eye, ped ft, Pittsburgh area, 2¾", NM 300.00
PP-2, Peacock Eye, violet-bl, Sandwich, 1830-45, 2", EX 360.00
RP-7, deep scallops, Sandwich, 1835-50, 2¼", NM 100.00
RP-18, plain rim, 16 rays in base, att Sandwich, 1940-60, 1¾" 100.00
SC-5, cobalt, scrolled ft, att Sandwich, 1835-50, 1¾", NM 660.00
SD-2, Strawberry Dmn & Fan, 4 hairy paw ft, att Sandwich, 2" 90.00
SD-4D, Waves & Strawberry Dmn, scalloped, Sandwich, 1828-40, 2", NM .. 55.00
SN-1C, Stag's Horn, gray-bl, 20 rays under base, 1835-50, 1¾", NM ... 155.00

Pressed Pattern Glass, Clear

Atlanta (Lion), master 55.00
Daisy & Button, LG Wright, HJ-875 to HJ-876, repro, ind, ea 8.00
Engish Hobnail, HJ-2680, ind 10.00
Euchre, HJ-3018 to HJ-3021, ind, ea 12.00
Heisey, Fandango, HJ-2673, ind 30.00
Horseshoe, HJ-3741, ind 30.00
King's Crown, plain, HJ-2776 .... 25.00
Panelled Grape Band, HJ-3516, master 35.00
Sawtooth Circle, HJ-3540, master 30.00
Scalloped/panelled cups in cherub silver o/l holders, pr 125.00
Snail, HJ-2656, ind 22.00
Washington's Centennial, HJ-2518, ind 20.00

Pressed Pattern Glass, Colored

Amber, triangular, HJ-524 .... 15.00
Degenhart, bl, mk, HJ-931 .... 45.00

French, cobalt, HJ-2086, dbl 65.00
Intaglio, polo players, gr, HJ-224 .... 18.00

Silver Plate

Lattice holder, cobalt liner, HJ-653, ind, VG.................................. 20.00
Oval, cranberry liner, ftd lattice holder, HJ-317, VG 65.00
Oval w/bl glass liner, 4 paw ft, +pepper shaker & spoon, Barker Ellis ..30.00
Overshot cranberry liner, sq fr, HJ-4215 to HJ-4217, ea.............. 150.00
Sheffield, chased florals, curved ft, set of 4 w/spoons 345.00
Sheffield, oval w/rtcl band top & base, monogrammed, shell ft, 1⅞" .. 185.00

Sterling and Continental Silver

Austria-Hungary, ca 1840, 3x4¼", $225.00. (Photo courtesy Patricia Johnson)

Austrian, dbl w/trumpet bud vase, figural dragon ea side, etched, 7" ... 200.00
Birmingham (English), oval w/rtcl band, cobalt liner, +spoon, 4 for... 210.00
Boat w/cherub on 1 end, ornately chased, scroll ft, Continental, 3" H...250.00
Bowl w/dbl-star cut-out sides, ruby-flashed liner, +spoon, 4 for.... 180.00
Bread roll w/hinged top on folded napkin, Russian, .875, 6½" L ...1,495.00
Chased florals at rim, ftd, +4" pepper caster, Kirk & Sons, 5-oz ... 250.00
Danish, bl guilloche enamel int, matching mushroom-form pepper, boxed..270.00
English, mug shape w/slot in lid for spoon, no liner, 1898, 1½x2".. 65.00
English, simple design, ftd, +pepper shaker, mustard, 2 spoons, boxed ... 180.00
Frank M Whiting Co, Georgian Shell w/cobalt liner & spoon, +pepper... 95.00
French, dbl, loop-hdl connector chased as tied branches, 4x5½" .. 105.00
French, Martial Fray, Napoleon III 1st std .950, 2 glass cups on stand ..510.00
Geo Jensen, bowl w/simple hdl, ball ft, #110, +spoon, 3 for......... 450.00
Geo Jensen, openwork acorn hdls, mk Dessin/JR, cobalt liner, 6 for... 840.00
George III by James & Elizabeth Bland, ovoid on oval ft, +spoon, pr. 335.00
Gorham cup form, rtcl floral sides, lid w/slot for spoon, cobalt liner.... 240.00
London, rectangular w/gadrooned rim, ftd, 3½" L 145.00
Rococo stand w/fleur-de-lys between 2 cobalt glass cups, Florentine..175.00
Rope twist at rim, lion head/paw ft, w/hdl & lid, Meka Denmark.. 75.00
Russian, boat w/lion & ring hdls, ftd, gilt int, Yashiov, 3¾" L 290.00
Russian, cloisonne exterior: arches/flowers, rope rim, mk 84, 2" dia...330.00
Russian, troika emb on cup w/sq raised base, 84 silver, 1908-07, 2-oz ...460.00
Russian enamel kovish, w/spoon, sgn MC, 84 silver, 1908, 2½" L...720.00
S Kirk & Son, fruit-repousse dish w/3 ball ft, 2½", +repousse spoon .. 65.00
Scalloped, porc disk w/flowers in base, Continental, 1700s, 4" dia....60.00
Tiffany, wht cloisonne flowers w/red centers, ftd, BC 1887, 2½" dia....240.00
Tiffany & Co, Windham pattern, gilt int, #17668A/#164, monogram..65.00
Victorian, rococo scrolls/cartouches, ornate hdls, cut glass liner.... 85.00
Watrous, ftd heart shape w/emb rim, +spoon................................. 120.00
Wm Spratling, bowl on rnd ft, 1940-44, 1x1½", +mk spoon, pr ..270.00

Samplers

American samplers were made as early as the colonial days; even earlier examples from seventeenth-century England still exist today. Changes in style and design are evident down through the years. Verses

were not added until the late seventeenth century. By the eighteenth century, samplers were used not only for sewing experience but also as an educational tool. Young ladies, who often signed and dated their work, embroidered numbers and letters of the alphabet and practiced fancy stitches as well. Fruits and flowers were added for borders; birds, animals, and Adam and Eve became popular subjects. Later houses and other buildings were included. By the nineteenth century, the American Eagle and the little red schoolhouse had made their appearances. Many factors bear on value: design and workmanship, strength of color, the presence of a signature and/or a date (both being preferred over only one or the other, and earlier is better), and, of course, condition.

ABCs, faded mc on linen, sgn/1799, sewn to brd, 12x8" 260.00
ABCs/#s/divided rows, silk on linen, sgn/1812, 15x8"+modern fr...350.00
ABCs/#s/peacock/parrot/dogs/stag/flowers, wool on linen, 19x17", VG...400.00
ABCs/berry vines/zigzags/drawnwork, silk on linen, 1802, 18x20"+fr...435.00
ABCs/birds/potted flowers, dbl-sided, sgn, 11x8"+burl vnr fr.......635.00
ABCs/buildings/willows, silk on linen, sgn/1816, 19x19"+fr........700.00
ABCs/dogs/pines/strawberries, silk on linen, PA/1815, 15x11"+fr ...2,500.00
ABCs/fancy stitches in lines, silk on linen, sgn/1735, 9x9"+fr.....925.00
ABCs/flowers/plant/lions, mc silk on linen, sgn/1811, 20x21"+fr...4,875.00
ABCs/house/vines/flowers, silk on linen, sgn/1818, ribbon edge, 22x22" ..575.00
ABCs/initials/house/berries, wool on linen, sgn/1834, 19x18"+fr ...700.00
ABCs/numbers/birds/flowers, wool on linen, sgn/1843, 15x12"+fr...400.00
ABCs/numbers/heart/initials, silk on cotton, sgn/1803, 18x9"+fr...435.00
ABCs/verse, silk pastels on linen, sgn/1799, 11x15", VG.............550.00
ABCs/verse/vines/flowers/etc, silk on linen, sgn/1827, PA, 18x15"+fr...1,850.00
ABCs/verse/vining border, silk on linen, minor losses, 9½x11"+fr.....500.00
ABCs/verses/crowns/hearts/etc, silk on linen, 1768, stain, 20x15"+fr...975.00
ABCs/vines/house/fence/etc, silk on linen, sgn/1816, 10x13"+fr ... 1,200.00
Adam & Eve/trees/hunter/dog/stag, silk on linen, sgn/1824, 15x15"+fr...1,600.00
Alphabet, verse, butterflies/crowns, vine border, sgn/1827, 17x15"..1,800.00
Alphabets/potted plant/lion, silk on linen, sgn/1828, 21x20", EX.. 4,880.00
Couple/crowns/stars/etc, silk on linen, PA German, 17x14"+fr .. 1,035.00
Family record/hearts/baskets/etc, silk on wool, 1850, 17x15"+fr, VG.. 635.00

Family register, silk thread on linen, signed and dated 1828, modern frame, with provenance, 24x22", $3,100.00. (Photo courtesy Garth's auctions Inc.)

Flowers/birds/stars/etc, wool on canvas, sgn/1844, 12x11"+grpt fr ..600.00
House/mother & child (2X)/pot w/flowers, EX color, sgn/ca 1815, 21x18"...6,000.00
Star amid flowers/2 deer/etc, wool on linen, 1837, 21x21"+vnr fr...925.00
Verse/animals/trees/flowers, silk on wool, sgn/1815, 15x14"+fr ... 1,785.00
Verse/birds/dogs/flowers/crown, silk on linen, 1818, 17x14".........515.00

Sandwich Glass

The Boston and Sandwich Glass Company was founded in 1825 by Deming Jarves in Sandwich, Massachusetts. Their first products were blown and molded, but eventually they perfected a method for pressing glass that led to the manufacture of the 'lacy' glass which they made until about 1840. Up until the closing of the factory in 1888, they made a wide variety of not only flint pattern glass, but also beautiful fancy glass such as cut, overlay, overshot, opalescent, and etched. Today colored Sandwich commands the highest prices, but it all is becoming increasingly rare and expensive. Invaluable reference books are George and Helen McKearin's *American Glass* and Ruth Webb Lee's publications. The best book for identifying Sandwich candlesticks and their later wares is *The Glass Industry in Sandwich* by Raymond Barlow and Joan Kaiser. Our advisor for this category is Elizabeth Simpson; she is listed in the Directory under Maine. See also Cup Plates; Salts, Open; other specific types of glass.

Candlestick, apple gr dolphin w/hex base, 1855-70, 6¾x4⅛", ea . **715.00**
Candlestick, emerald gr, hexagonal, 1840-1860, att, 7½x3⅜", ea.. **1,750.00**
Candlestick, socket on hex base, 1835-60, 9x3⅞", NM, ea **90.00**
Candlesticks, bl & clambroth, hexagonal socket, ca 1845, 8⅜", pr.. **600.00**
Candlesticks, canary yel, columnar shaft, stepped base, 9⅜", pr... **900.00**
Candlesticks, knop center, stepped sq base, 10", pr, EX............... **525.00**
Candlesticks, Petal & Loop, canary, 1840-60, 7x4¼", pr............. **250.00**
Candlesticks, starch bl on dolphin clambroth base, 10x3½", pr .. **1,000.00**
Candlesticks, vaseline, dolphin std, stepped base, 1847-70, 10", pr.. **1,175.00**
Creamer, GI-30, cobalt, tooled rim/appl hdl w/EX curl, 1825-40, 4⅜"....**6,325.00**
Creamer, GV-3, ribbed hollow hdl, rayed base, pontil, 1825-35, 4¾"... **1,875.00**
Creamer, Heart & Scale, electric bl, 1835-50, 4½"...................**2,200.00**
Cruet, dk cobalt, slim neck w/ring, cobalt stopper, 1825-35, 7¼"....**330.00**
Cup, amethyst, Dmn Scroll & Lily, 1835-50, child's, 1x1⅛", NM.. **1,045.00**
Curtain pins, Rosette, fiery opal, orig shanks, 5", pr **120.00**
Decanter, sapphire bl, 8-flute, bar lip, 1840-60, chip, 10¾".......... **600.00**
Ewer & basin, fiery opal, thorn hdl, 1840-55, child's, 2¾", 3⅛" ... **2,750.00**
Flat iron, bubbly sapphire bl, 1850-70, child's, ⅞x1⅜", EX........ **1,375.00**
Hat, GIII-13, cobalt, folded rim, rayed base, ca 1825-35, 2¼"...... **415.00**
Jar, pomade; bear figural, wht opaque, 1850-87, 3¾", NM............ **80.00**
Jar, pomade; cavalier figural, starch bl, ETS & Co NY, w/lid, 3¾" ..**825.00**
Jar, pomade; clambroth, unpatterned base, w/lid, 2⅝" **65.00**
Jug, fiery opal purple-bl, dmn scroll w/lilies, child's, 1⅝", EX **4,180.00**
Jug, opal, Dmn Scroll w/Lily, scalloped ft, 1835-50, child's, 1⅝".. **300.00**
Nappy, 11-concave dot base, folded rim, 1820-40, 1⅜x5¾" **65.00**
Plate, teal w/many bubbles, stars & scrolls, child's, 2½" **75.00**
Platter, canary, 20-panel, 1835-50, flakes, child's, 2⅝x1⅞"............ **65.00**
Salt cellar, cobalt, flared rim, 1825-35, 1½x2⅜", EX.................... **200.00**
Sugar bowl, Gothic Arch, bl opaque, 8-sided, w/lid, 5x3" **850.00**
Sugar bowl, Gothic Arch, deep electric bl, w/lid, 1840-50, 5¼x5"...**2,100.00**
Tumbler, rayed/ring base, cylindrical, 1825-35, 2¾x2¼".............. **185.00**
Vase, tulip; dk peacock gr, scalloped, 8-sided ft, 1845-65, 9¾" .. **3,750.00**
Wine, GII-19, conical w/button stem, 1820-40, 4x2".................. **255.00**

Santa Barbara Ceramic Design

Established in 1976 by current director Raymond Markow (after three years of refining his decorative process), Santa Barbara Ceramic Design arose less auspiciously than the 'Ohio' potteries — no financial backing and no machinery beyond that available to ancient potters: wheel, kiln, brushes, and paint. The company produced intricate, colorful, hand-painted flora and fauna designs on traditional pottery forms, primarily vases and table lamps. Although artistically aligned with turn-of-the-century art potteries, the techniques used were unique and developed within the studio. Vibrant glaze stains with wax emulsion were applied by brush over a graduated multicolor background, then enanced by elaborate sgraffito detailing on petals and leaves. In the early 1980s, a white stoneware body was incorporated to further brighten the color palette, and during the last few years sgraffito was replaced by detailing with a fine brush.

Early pieces were thrown. Mid-1980 saw a transition to casting, except for experimental or custom pieces. Artists were encouraged to be creative and often given individual gallery exhibitions. Custom orders were welcomed, and experimentation occurred regularly; the resulting pieces are the most rare and seldom appear today. Limited production lines evolved, including the Collector Series that featured an elaborate ornamental border designed to enhance the primary design. The Artist's Collection was a numbered series of pieces by senior artists, usually combining flora and fauna.

The company's approach to bold colors and surface decoration influenced many contemporary potters and inspired imitation in both pottery and glass during the craft renaissance of the 1970s and 1980s. Several artists successfully made use of the studio's designs and techniques after leaving. Authentic pieces bear the artist's initials, date, and 'SBCD' marked in black stain and, if thrown, the potter's inscription.

Markow employed as many as three potters and 12 decorators at a given time. The ware was marketed through craft festivals and wholesale distribution to art and craft galleries nationwide. An estimated 100,000 art pottery pieces were made before a transition in the late 1980s to silk-screened household and garden items, which remain in production today.

Though less than 30 years old, Santa Barbara Ceramic Design's secondary market has seen upwards of 1,000 pieces change hands; these are often viewed as bargains compared to their Rookwood and Weller Hudson counterparts. For artist/potter marks visit johnguthrie.com. Our advisor is John Guthrie; he is listed in the Directory under South Carolina.

Bowl, #5107, birds, Alvaro Suman, 1978, 10" **133.00**
Bud vase, eucalyptus, Gary Ba-Han, 1983, 6" **104.00**
Candlestick, #5116, bearded iris, Margie Gilson, 1982, 7", ea **75.00**
Lamp, #5117, hibiscus, Allison Atwill, 1983, 10½"....................... **63.00**
Lamp, #5117, poppy, Shannon Sargent, 1980, 10½" **203.00**
Lamp, #5118, iris, unsgn, ca 1984, 11".. **195.00**
Lamp, #5119, morning glory, Laurie Linn-Ball, 1986, 15½"......... **295.00**
Lamp, #5119, nasturtium, Margie Gilson, 1982, 15½" **37.00**
Lamp, #5119lg, bouquet, Laurie Linn, 1982, 17"......................... **495.00**
Lamp, #7125, iris, Gary Ba-Han, 1984, 18" **375.00**
Lamp, apple blossom, Gary Ba-Han, 1984, 13", pr **650.00**
Lamp, apple blossom, Michelle Foster, ca 1983, 7"....................... **165.00**
Mug, #5121, orchid, Barbara Rose, ca 1978, 5"............................. **44.00**
Mug, #5121, tiger lily, William Pacini, 1984, 5" **63.00**
Oil lamp, #1102, bird, Nancy Looker, 1979, 6½"............................ **255.00**
Pitcher, #5106, hibiscus, Christine Adcock, 1980, 8½"................ **158.00**
Pitcher, #5106, poppy, Dorie Knight, 1979, 9".............................. **265.00**
Plate, #5114, orchid, Zetta, 1981, 7".. **110.00**
Plate, #5114, tulip, Eleyna Dhyansky, 1980, 7".............................. **147.00**
Platter, #4118cs, apple blossom, Shannon Sargent, 1982, 15" **275.00**
Vase, #4113, columbine, Laurie Cosca 1981, 10" **275.00**
Vase, #5101, duck, Anne Collinson, 1979, 6-7" **363.00**
Vase, #5101, japanese iris, Laurie Cosca, 1979, 6-7"..................... **125.00**
Vase, #5101, morning glory, Laurie Linn-Ball, 1986, 6" **215.00**
Vase, #5101, pansy, Laurie Cosca, 1979, 3½".................................. **99.00**
Vase, #5101, penguin, Alvaro Suman, 1979, 6-7" **200.00**
Vase, #5101, tiger lily, Allison Atwill, 1982, 7" **100.00**
Vase, #5101, tiger lily, Gary Ba-Han, 1983, 6½"........................... **175.00**
Vase, #5101, tulip, Michelle Foster, 1981, 6-7"............................ **180.00**
Vase, #5101, water lily, Kat Corcoran, 1980, 5¾".......................... **82.00**
Vase, #5101cs, morning glory, Laurie Linn, 1981, 6"..................... **175.00**
Vase, #5102, bearded iris, Dorie Knight-Hutchinson, 1981, 9".... **412.00**
Vase, #5102, bearded iris, Itoko Takeuchi, 1983, 9" **310.00**
Vase, #5102, Japanese iris, Dorie Knight-Hutchinson, 1982, 9"... **357.00**
Vase, #5102, poppy, Laurie Linn-Ball, 1985, 9" **240.00**
Vase, #5102, trumpet lily, Laurie Cosca, 1980, 9"......................... **125.00**
Vase, #5102, wisteria, Dorie Knight, ca 1978, 9" **129.00**
Vase, #5102, wisteria, Shannon Sargent, 1985, 9"......................... **125.00**
Vase, #5103, experimental, Laurie Linn-Ball, 1985, 8" **104.00**
Vase, #5103, orchid, Allison Atwill, 1981, 8½"............................. **281.00**

Vase, #5103, orchid, Mary Favero, 1981, 8" 251.00
Vase, #5103cs, poppy, Laurie Cosca, 1982, 9" 250.00
Vase, #5104cs, poppy, Shannon Sargent, 1983, 14" 1,425.00
Vase, #5133, iris, Shannon Sargent, 1984, 20" 1,500.00
Vase, #6112, fuchsia/bird, Dorie Knight-Hutchinson, 1984, 10" .. 425.00
Vase, #6114a, pansy, Dorie Knight-Hutchinson, 1984, 8" 275.00
Vase, #7111, bouquet, Nancy Looker, 1979, 11" 51.00
Vase, #7116, columbine, Suzanne Tormey, 1980, 14" 381.00
Vase, #7116, iris, Dorie Knight, 1981, 12" 280.00

Vase, #7116cs, Bearded Iris, by Shannon Sargent, 1982, vase by Bob Osif, 11x9", $1,200.00. (Photo courtesy John Guthrie)

Vase, #7116cs, bouquet, Itoko Takeuchi, 1986, 12" 325.00
Vase, #7116cs, morning glory, Mary Favero, 1982, 12" 298.00

Sarreguemines

Sarreguemines, France, is the location of Utzschneider and Company, founded about 1800, producers of majolica, transfer-printed dinnerware, figurines, and novelties which are usually marked 'Sarreguemines.' In 1836, under the management of Alexandre de Geiger, son-in-law of Utzschneider, the company became affiliated with Villeroy and Boch. During the 1850s and 1860s, two new facilities with modern steam-fired machinery were erected. Alexandre's son Paul was the next to guide the company, and under his leadership two more factories were built — one at Digoin and the other at Vitry le Francois. After his death in 1931, the company split but was consolidated again after the war under the name of Sarreguemines-Digoin-Vitry le Francois. Items marked 'St. Clement' were made during the period from 1979 to 1982, indicating the group who owned the company for that span of time. Today the company is known as Sarreguemines-Batiment.

Bowl, unglazed pierced faience, floral relief, #151/eagle, 19" L..... 660.00
Character jug, Black man's face, red bow tie, #H-7, #3884 .... 1,080.00
Character jug, Colonial man, curls over ears, #4502, 6½" 210.00
Character jug, dbl face (2nd inverted at base), #2313, hdl rpr, 8¾" ... 100.00
Character jug, Eyes Ouvertes, man w/goatee, #3612, 8" 300.00
Character jug, jester, 2-tone gr hat, bl int, #658, 7" 120.00
Character jug, man w/receding hairline, #3320, 7", EX 180.00
Character jug, Paul Kruger, man w/wht beard, G3185, 7", VG 95.00
Character jug, Puck, wine/burgundy turban, bl int, 7", NM 95.00
Character jug, smiling man's face, bl cap band, #3181, 8" 180.00
Character jug, 2-faced (2nd inverted below 1st), turq, 8½" 115.00
Compote, bird & floral transfer on ironstone, 7x11" 165.00
Figurine, penguin, wht w/blk head, orange ft, on gr base, 10", EX... 510.00
Humidor, man w/rosy nose & cheeks, blk top hat, #3388, 7", EX ... 180.00
Pitcher, cat sitting, mouth is spout, wht w/blk nose, 8", EX 300.00
Pitcher, dog sitting w/mouth open, blk/wht, majolica, #3677, rpr, 9".. 275.00
Pitcher, elephant sitting, gray, #4470, 10" 900.00
Pitcher, gorilla head as top portion, #3322, 9" 150.00

Pitcher, lg owl on branch, pk/blk ground, stamped Bussard, 9" 125.00
Pitcher, monkey sitting, joined hands form spout, #3676, 8", NM ... 325.00
Pitcher, parrot sitting, pk/wht w/brn details, #3566, 7½" 360.00
Pitcher, pelican, mouth open wide, yel/wht/blk, 8", NM 660.00
Pitcher, pig sitting, wht w/pk ears/nose, #G3318, 9½" 410.00
Pitcher, ram's head as body, brn/wht w/bl int, 9x9½" 685.00
Planter, majolica, oak leaves & acorns, rectangular, 10", NM 420.00
Plaque, Printemps (Spring), 6 birds in border, mk/#d, 15", NM ... 350.00
Plate, majolica, asparagus emb on gr, w/side section, 9½" 75.00
Platter, majolica, 3 high-relief birds on dk bl/brn/gr, #571, 24" L .. 2,400.00
Platter, street scene w/2 groups of men, sgn H Loux, 15" L 120.00
Stein, fish/sausages/radish by verse, cat hdl, #2668, 1L 1,325.00
Stein, man feeds baby at table, pewter lid, rpr strap, .5L 600.00
Stein, relief: drunken man w/monkey & cat, porc lid w/deer, #2888, 1L.. 1,000.00
Stein, relief: man w/beer at table, couple on pewter lid, 1L 300.00
Tray, girl figural w/umbrella & basket, #4089, 8" L 95.00
Vase, Art Deco waves/disected circles, blk/red/wht/bl on lt gray, 5x5".. 510.00
Vase, dbl bud; circular body disjoined at top, vines/beading/gilt, 6" ... 325.00
Vase, gr crystalline, mtd in classical ormolu, 11½x5" 210.00
Vase, intricate floral in panels, dk bl/wht/gilt, ovoid, 17x10" 450.00
Vase, Japanesque birds/floral, 4-sided/shouldered w/hdls, 12", pr... 325.00
Vase, Japanesque floral vines on ivory, intricate neck band, 24", VG ... 480.00
Vase, majolica, modeled as a shell, crab ea side, rim rpr, 9" 240.00
Vase, stylized floral, ornate neck band, yel/bl on brn, 12", pr 480.00
Washbowl & pitcher, lt enamel, much gilt on cobalt, turq int, 17", 13" .. 575.00

Satsuma

Satsuma is a type of fine cream crackle-glaze pottery or earthenware made in Japan as early as the seventeenth century. The earliest wares, made at the original kiln in the Satsuma province, were enameled with only simple florals By the late eighteenth century, a floral brocade (or nishikide design) was favored, and similar wares were being made at other kilns under the direction of the Lord of Satsuma. In the early part of the nineteenth century, a diaper pattern was added to the florals. Gold and silver enamels were used for accents by the latter years of the century. During the 1850s, as the quality of goods made for export to the Western world increased and the style of decoration began to evolve toward becoming more appealing to the Westerners, human forms such as Arhats, Kannon, geisha girls, and samurai warriors were added. Today the most valuable pieces are those marked 'Kinkozan,' 'Shuzan,' 'Ryuzan,' and 'Kozan.' The genuine Satsuma 'mon' or mark is a cross within a circle — usually in gold on the body or lid, or in red on the base of the ware. Character marks may be included.

Caution: Much of what is termed 'Satsuma' comes from the Showa Period (1926 to the present); it is not true Satsuma but a simulated type, a cheaper pottery with heavy enamel. Collectors need to be aware that much of the 'Satsuma' today is really Satsuma style and should not carry the values of true Satsuma. Our advisor for this category is Clarence Bodine; he is listed in the Directory under Pennsylvania.

Bowl, courtiers, cobalt borders, Japan, early 20th C, 5½" 265.00
Bowl, figures before Mt Fuji, 19th C, 10" 475.00
Bowl, samurai w/gold, foliate edge, Japan, ca 1900, 6" 325.00
Cup, sake; ancient Egyptian boat, early 20th C, 5½" 120.00
Figure, Kannon seated on rock throne holding lotus, rprs, 19th C, 12"..765.00
Moon flask, 7 Gods of Luck & Hundred Poets, Japan, late 1800s, 9½"..525.00
Plate, Hundred Rakans, foliate form, Japan, 19th C, 9½" 300.00
Plate, One Hundred Birds, early 20th C, 9¼" 645.00
Tureen, parrots & chrysanthemums, urn form w/dome lid, 19th C, 12x13" .700.00
Vase, birds/flowers/butterflies in panels, sq, Meiji period, 12" 650.00
Vase, dragons & brocade, sgn Senzan, integral hdls, 7x6" 1,400.00
Vase, emb/pnt peonies, Makuzu Kozan, Meiji period, 8½" 3,250.00

Vase, figures in fan-shaped reserves, Japan, early 20th C, 5".........150.00
Vase, floral, trumpet mouth, dragon hdls, Meiji period, 25".........450.00
Vase, flowering branch, oviform, Japan, 19th C, 13"...................700.00
Vase, men's faces/geishas w/dragon, elephant-head hdls, 9½", pr ..525.00
Vase, moriage butterflies & flowers, Japan, late 19th C, 14".........385.00
Vase, tied money bag/chrysanthemums, Meiji period, 5¾"...........175.00
Vase, women & brocade, trumpet mouth/shishi hdls, Japan, ca 1900, 29" ..400.00
Vase, 6 Orientals, mc w/extensive gold, bk: 3 warriors, 24x12"....510.00
Wine pot, women in garden scenes, early 20th C, 4¾"................265.00

Scales

In today's world of pre-measured and pre-packaged goods, it is difficult to imagine the days when such products as sugar, flour, soap, and candy first had to be weighed by the grocer. The variety of scales used at the turn of the century was highly diverse; at the Philadelphia Exposition in 1876, one company alone displayed over 300 different weighing devices. Among those found today, brass, cast-iron, and plastic models are the most common. Fancy postal scales in decorative wood, silver, marble, bronze, and mosaic are also to be found.

A word of caution on the values listed: These values range from a low for those items in fair to good condition to the upper values for items in excellent condition. Naturally, items in mint condition could command even higher prices, and they often do. Also, these are retail prices that suggest what a collector will pay for the object. When you sell to a dealer, expect to get much less. The values noted are averages taken from various auction and other catalogs in the possession of the society members. Among these, but not limited to, are the following: Malter & Co., Inc., Encino, CA; Auktion Alt Technic, Auction Team, Koln, Germany.

For those seeking additional information concerning antique scales we recommend *Scales, A Collector's Guide*, by Bill and Jan Berning (Schiffer). You are also encouraged to contact the International Society of Antique Scale Collectors, whose address can be found in the Directory under Clubs, Newsletters, and Catalogs. Visit the society website at www.isasc.org. Our advisor for this category is Jerome R. Katz; he is listed in the Directory under Pennsylvania.

Key:
ap — arrow pointer	h — hanging
bal — balance	hcp — hanging counterpoise
bm — base metal	hh — hand held
br — brass	l+ — label with foreign coin values
Brit — British	lb w/i — labeled box with instructions
Can — Canadian	lph — letter plate or holder
Col — Colonial	pend — pendulum
CW — Civil War	PP — Patent Pending
cwt — counterweight	st — sterling
Engl — English	tt — torsion type
eq — equal arm	ua — unequal arm
Euro — European	wt — weight
FIS — Fairbanks Infallible Scale Co.	

Analytical (Scientific)

Am, eq, mahog w/br & ivory, late 1800s, 14x16x8", $200 to 400.000

Assay

Am, eq, mahog box w/br & ivory, plaque/drw, 1890s, $400 to ..1,000.00

Coin: Equal Arm Balance, American

Blk japanned metal, eagle on lid, late 19th C, $300 to.................400.00
Col, oak 6-part box, Col moneys, Boston, 1720-75, $800 to.....1,800.00
Post Col to CW, oak 6-part box, l+, 1843, $400 to.................1,000.000

Coin: Equal Arm Balance, English

Charles I, wooden box w/11 Brit wts, 1640s, $900 to................1,500.00
1-pc wood box, rnd wts, label, Freeman, 1760s, $250 to 450.00
6-pc oak box, coin wts label, Thos Harrison, 1750s, $200 to 450.000

Coin: Equal Arm Balance, French

Solid wood box, 12 sq wts, J Reyne, Bourdeau, 1694, $400 to...1,000.00
Solid wood box w/recesses, 5 sq wts, A Gardes, 1800s, $250 to ...800.00
1-pc oval box, nested/fractional wts, label, 18th C, $250 to.........400.00
1-pc oval box, no wts, label of Fr/Euro coins, 18th C, $150 to 250.00
1-pc walnut box, nested wts, Charpentier label, 1810, $275 to.....675.00

Coin: Equal Arm Balance, Miscellaneous

Amsterdam, 1-pc box, 32 sq wts, label, late 1600s, $850 to 2,500.00
Cologne, full set of wts & full label, late 1600s, $1,200 to 2,800.00
German, wood box, 13+ wts beneath main wts, label, 1795, $650 to...900.00

Counterfeit Coin Detectors, American

Allender Pat, lb w/i, cwt, Nov 22, 1855, 8½", $350 to 650.00
Allender PP, rocker, labeled box, cwt, 1850s, 8½", $450 to..........750.00
Allender PP, rocker, no box or cwt, 1850s, 8½", $250 to..............375.00
Allender PP, space for $3 gold pc, lb w/i, cwt, 1855, $350 to 750.00
Allender Warranted, rocker, no box or cwt, 1850s, 8½", $350 to..475.00
FIS, steelyard, combination detector & postal scale, from $900 to...1,200.00
McNally-Harrison Pat 1882, rocker, cwt, JT McNally, $275 to ...500.00
McNally-Harrison Pat 1882, rocker, cwt & box, FIS, $400 to 750.00
McNally-Harrison...1882, rocker, CI base, no cwt/box, $250 to ..400.00
Thompson, Z-formed rocker, Berrian Mfg, 1877 Pat, $175 to......350.00
Troemner, rocker, for 25¢ & 50¢ silver coins, from $300 to 500.00

Counterfeit Coin Detectors, Dutch

Rocker, Ellinckhuysen, brass, +copy of 1829 Patent, $700 to ...1,000.00

Counterfeit Coin Detectors, English

Folding, Guinea, self-rising, labeled box, 1850s, $175 to.............225.00
Folding, Guinea, self-rising, wood box/label, ca 1890s, $125 to...175.00
Rocker, simple, no maker's name or cb, end-cap box, $85 to 125.00
Rocker, w/maker's name & cb, end-cap box, $120 to 150.00

Egg Scales/Graders, 1930s – 1940s

Acme Egg Grade, Specialty Mfg St Paul MN, aluminum, from $30 to..50.00
Brower Mfg Save All, sheet steel (cheaply made), Steelyard bal, $50 to..75.00
Jiffy Way, Minneapolis MN, steel w/mc bands, pend bal, common, $30 to..50.00
Reliable, rocker bal, all brass, wooden base, 2½x13¾", $75 to 100.00
Unique..., Specialty Mfg, sheet steel/aluminum, pend bal, $30 to....50.00
Zenith, CI, aluminum, brass pointer, pend bal, from $50 to...........75.00

Postal

In the listings below an asterisk (*) was used to indicate that any one of several manufacturers' or brand names might be found on that particular set of scales. Some of the American-made pieces could be marked Pelouze, Lorraine, Hanson, Kingsbury, Fairbanks, Troemner, IDL, Newman, Accurate, Ideal, B-T, Marvel, Reliance, Howe, Landers-Frary-Clark, Chatillon, Triner, American Bank Service, or Weiss. European/U.S.-made scales marked with an asterisk (*) could be marked Salter, Peerless, Pelouze, Sturgis, L.F.&C., Alderman, G. Little, or S&D. English-made scales with the asterisk (*) could be marked Josh. & Edmd. Ratcliff, R.W. Winfield, S. Mordan, STS (Samuel Turner, Sr.), W.&T. Avery, Parnall & Sons, S&P, or H.B. Wright. There may be other manufacturers as well.

Brit/Can Bal, eq, br or CI on base, *, 4-15", $100 to	750.00
Engl Bal, eq/Roberval, gilt or st, on stand, *, 3-8", $500 to	2,500.00
Engl Bal, eq/Roberval, plain to ornate, *, 3-8", $100 to	2,500.00
Engl Spring, candlestick, br or st, *, 3½-15", $100 to	500.00
Engl Spring, CI, br or NP fr, Salter, ozs/lbs, 7-10", $25 to	200.00
Engl Steelyard, ua, 1- or 2-beam, h lph, *, 4-15", $100 to	1,500.00
Euro pend, gravity, br, CI or NP fr on base, oz/grams, $75 to	350.00
Euro pend, gravity, 2-arm, bm, br or NP, *, 6-9", $50 to	300.00
Euro/US Spring, br or NP, pence/etc, h or hh, *, 4-17", $10 to	100.00
US pend, gravity, metal, pnt face, ap, hcp, sm, $20 to	100.00
US Spring, pnt base metal, *, 2½-8", $10 to	80.00
US Spring, pnt bm, *, mtd on inkstand, 2½-8", $200 to	400.00
US Spring, pnt bm, rnd glass-covered face, *, 8-10", $25 to	100.00
US Spring, SP, oblong base, *, 2½-8", $100 to	200.00
US Spring, st, oblong base, *, 2½-8", $200 to	500.00
US Steelyard, ua, CI, *, 5"-13" beam, 4½-12" base, $25 to	100.00

Schafer and Vater

Established in 1890 by Gustav Schafer and Gunther Vater in the Thuringia region of southwest Germany, by 1913 this firm employed over 200 workers. The original factory burned in 1918 but was restarted and production continued until WWII. In 1972 the East German government took possession of the building and destroyed all of the molds and the records that were left.

You will find pieces with the impressed mark of a nine-point star with a script 'R' inside the star. On rare occasions you will find this mark in blue ink under glaze. The items are sometimes marked with a four-digit design number and a two-digit artist mark. In addition or instead, pieces may have 'Made in Germany' or in the case of the Kewpies, 'Rose O'Neill copyright.' The company also manufactured items for sale under store names, and those would not have the impressed mark.

Schafer and Vater used various types of clays. Items made of hard-paste porcelain, soft-paste porcelain, Jasper, bisque, and majolica can be found. The glazed bisque pieces may be multicolored or have an applied colored slip wash that highlights the intricate details of the modeling. Gold accents were used as well as spots of high-gloss color called jewels. Metallic glazes are coveted. You can find the Jasper in green, blue, pink, lavender, and white. New collectors gravitate toward the pink and lavender shades.

Since Schafer and Vater made such a multitude of items, collectors have to compete with many cross-over collections. These include shaving mugs, hatpin holders, match holders, figurines, figural pitchers, Kewpies, tea sets, bottles, naughties, etc.

Reproduction alert: In addition to the crudely made Japanese copies, some English firms are beginning to make figural reproductions. These seem to be well marked and easy to spot. Our advisor for this category is Joanne M. Koehn; she is listed in the Directory under Texas.

Bottle, concave front w/lady on seal, 4½x3¾"	415.00
Bottle, Never Drink Water, naughty boy/frogs, 5¼"	95.00
Creamer, bear in wht coat & muff, 5"	225.00
Creamer, Black boy w/wide eyes, frowning, 1930s, 3½", NM	180.00

Creamer, Dutch lady kneeling & screaming, mouth is spout, mc, 3¼x2"	90.00
Creamer, girl w/basket on bk carries pitcher, mc, 3½"	145.00
Creamer, Oriental lady kneels, mouth is spout, bl wash, 4¼"	175.00
Decanter, bearded man sits on bbl & smokes pipe, bl wash, 6½"	325.00
Decanter, clown w/drunken lady in arms, legs stopper, bl wash, rpr	120.00
Decanter, woman praying, basket in arms & cross around neck, 9½"	650.00
Figurine, Black lady holding sign: We Want the Vote, 7½"	850.00
Figurine, Black man singing w/lg open mouth & holding music, 4"	100.00
Figurine, Black man w/bug on nose, 4¼"	360.00
Figurine, Golfer, man in early golfing costume, 7½"	385.00
Figurine, Hitchy Koo, Black man's face, top hat, comic, 4"	275.00
Figurine, native boy on seated elephant, mc, 3", VG	130.00
Figurine, Snookums, baby w/wht w/bl trim, 3"	250.00
Figurine, You Made Me Love You, smiling Black couple, 3½x3½"	275.00
Figurines, Mr Adam & Mrs Eve (Black), 7½", pr	1,000.00
Flask, A Wee Scotch, Scottish girl w/bagpipes on bottle, 4¼"	90.00
Flask, clown holding lady, crown mk w/R, 5"	320.00
Flask, Fire Water, fireman w/hose at side of lg bottle, 4⅝"	285.00
Flask, lady seated on keg w/stein in hand, 5¼x3"	680.00
Flask, lady standing on turtle, 5½x3½"	410.00
Flask, One of the Boys, drunken man sits in champagne glass, 5½"	180.00
Flask, Sir John Flastaff, w/stein & sword, 9"	370.00
Flask, Stop the Vote, policeman w/long arm, cork hand, 7¼"	750.00

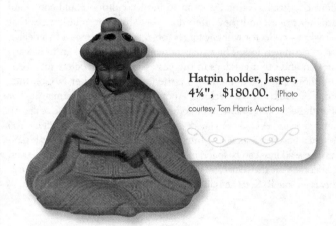

Hatpin holder, Jasper, 4¼", $180.00. (Photo courtesy Tom Harris Auctions)

Match holder, boy's face & 2 smiling feet, 3¼x4"	65.00
Match holder, Your Good Old Pal, man's face & hands, 3¼"	150.00
Match holder/ashtray, Very Fine View, ladies' (2) showing legs, 1920s	155.00
Vase, bud; Under the Mistletoe, smiling Black lady under greenery, 5"	275.00

Scheier

The Scheiers began their ceramics careers in the late 1930s and soon thereafter began to teach their craft at the University of New Hampshire. After WWII they cooperated with the Puerto Rican government in establishing a native ceramic industry, an involvement which would continue to influence their designs.

Artwork, mixed media/tinted wax, lg face/figure in brain area, 18x20"	1,175.00
Artwork, mixed media/tinted wax, 3 abstract figures, 12x18"	1,050.00
Bowl, aqua w/mahog rim, glossy, 2x4"	250.00
Bowl, figure w/man & woman's heads, caramel & bl, 5x8"	1,800.00
Bowl, frothy wht & mahog, flambe int, 3¾x5½"	475.00
Bowl, gunmetal blk w/drips, gray int, 2¼x4½"	300.00
Bowl, ivory w/yel streaks, emb ribs, #14, 3¾x5"	375.00
Bowl, mahog & pumpkin w/cobalt, sm ft, 3½x6¾"	600.00
Bowl, man & snake, burgundy/frothy wht/mocha, 1x6¾"	225.00
Bowl, Raku fired, 5x7"	350.00
Bowl, sgraffito stylized figures, brn, 6x7½"	1,880.00

Bowl, sgraffito stylized motif on maroon-brn, 3½x7" 2,115.00
Bowl, squiggled lines & animals, bl on red clay, 6⅛x11⅞" 3,200.00
Bowl, woman, child, fish & serpent, cobalt/lav/wht, 4x8" 1,500.00
Bowl, woman, serpent & child, cobalt/gr/brn, 1½x7½" 350.00
Totem pole, 2-pc: sm figure above lg figure holding child, 10", EX...530.00
Tray, sgraffito stylized mother & child, bl, 10" dia 880.00
Tureen, wht accents on tan, hdls, w/lid, 9x14" 200.00
Vase, aqua, cobalt on flared lip, sm ft, 6¾x3½", EX 150.00

> **Vase, primitive females, bronzed gunmetal, #91, ca. 1991, 12½", $4,600.00.**
>
> (Photo courtesy David Rago Auctions)

Vase, woman, child & fish, teal gr/chartreuse/mint gr, ftd, 12x5¾" ..1,600.00
Vase, woman & fish, caramel & cobalt, ovoid, 5x4" 750.00

Schlegelmilch Porcelain

For information about Schlegelmilch Porcelain, see Mary Frank Gaston's book, *R. S. Prussia Popular Lines*, which addresses R. S. Prussia molds and decorations and contains full-color illustrations and current values. Mold numbers appearing in some of the listings refer to this book. Assume that all items described below are marked unless noted otherwise. Our advisor for this category is Mary Frank Gaston; she is listed in the Directory under Texas.

Key:
BM — blue mark   SM — steeple mark
GM — green mark   RM — red mark

E.S. Germany

Fine chinaware marked 'E.S. Germany' or 'E.S. Prov. Saxe' was produced by the E.S. Schlegelmilch factory in Suhl in the Thuringia region of Prussia from sometime after 1861 until about 1925.

Bowl, bird on limb, Prov Saxe, GM, sq, 6" 60.00
Bowl, pansies & flowers, steeple mold #3, circle mk 125.00
Butter pat, ladies & child, rtcl gold rim, 3¼" 125.00
Chocolate pot, Napoleon portrait 375.00
Cup & saucer, demitasse; woman & roses, MOP lustre, ornate....175.00
Lobster dish, tail forms hdl, florals/gilt, BM, 10" 85.00
Vase, lady w/doves, much gold/turq beads, Tiffany finish, hdls, 6½" ..425.00
Vase, lady w/swallows, ornate gold hdls & trim, 13½", from $800 to ..1,000.00
Vase, maidens (4), cobalt & gold trim, 13½", minimum value..3,500.00

R.S. Germany

In 1869 Reinhold Schlegelmilch began to manufacture porcelain in Suhl in the German province of Thuringia. In 1894 he established another factory in Tillowitz in upper Silesia. Both areas were rich in resources necessary for the production of hard-paste porcelain. Wares marked with the name 'Tillowitz' and the accompanying 'R.S. Germany' phrase are

attributed to Reinhold. The most common mark is a wreath and star in a solid color under the glaze. Items marked 'R.S. Germany' are usually more simply decorated than R.S. Prussia. Some reflect the Art Deco trend of the 1920s. Certain hand-painted floral decorations and themes such as 'Sheepherder,' 'Man With Horses,' and 'Cottage' are especially valued by collectors — those with a high-gloss finish or on Art Deco shapes in particular. Not all hand-painted items were painted at the factory. Those with an artist's signature but no 'Hand Painted' mark indicate that the blank was decorated outside the factory.

Basket, pheasants on yel, Deco mold, GM, 5" 250.00
Bowl, Cottage II scene on brn tones, 10½" 300.00
Bowl, roses, hdls, BM, sq, 8½" 55.00
Cake plate, flower clusters & roses on gr, RSP mold #205............200.00
Celery tray, yel-to-wht roses, 14x6½" 55.00
Coffeepot, roses, gold trim, BM, 8½" 95.00
Cup, floral on pearlized ground, emb swirls, BM, 3½"....................40.00
Fernery, floral, ftd, SM, 3½x6½" dia 180.00
Hair receiver, wht floral, pierced hdls, 2½" 75.00
Nightlight, owl, brn/yel, BM, 5½" 900.00
Pitcher, milk; roses, GM, 5½" 140.00
Plate, peonies, wht on shaded gr, 8⅜" 50.00
Sugar bowl, Chinese pheasants, w/lid, 4" 350.00
Toothpick holder, lilies, RM, 2¼"...75.00
Tray, bun; woman w/oxen at country house, purple/pk/yel, 13" ...300.00
Vase, Nightwatch by Rembrandt, gold hdls/trim, ftd, 8¾" 900.00
Vase, peonies & snowballs, RS Suhl mold #3, 8¼" 300.00

R.S. Poland

'R.S. Poland' is a mark attributed to Reinhold Schlegelmilch's factory in Tillowitz, Silesia. It was in use for a few years after 1945.

Bowl, crowned cranes, 5¾" 465.00
Bowl, lav & wht flowers, Tiffany trim, scalloped, 11", from $400 to...600.00
Cup & saucer, dainty flowers on wht, gold rim, from $150 to 200.00
Cup & saucer, flowers, dainty/pk on wht to gr, 2½" H 60.00
Ewer, windmill scene, ornate hdl, RS Germany mold, 5½" 500.00
Vase, blk swans, bulbous, RM, 6" 1,000.00
Vase, clematis on brn to cream, gold hdls, 10", from $300 to.......400.00
Vase, lg pale rose on shaded cream to brn, baluster, 7⅜" 350.00
Vase, lg peach roses on shaded brn, Nouveau hdls, mold #956, 12" ...550.00
Vase, long-stemmed roses, gold hdls, cobalt at base, 9¾"..............800.00
Vase, peasant ladies in landscape, cylinder w/bottle neck, 4" 275.00
Vase, pk roses, gold band, shouldered, mk, 6½", from $300 to......400.00
Vase, roses & garlands, gold trim, 6½", from $300 to....................400.00
Vase, roses on wht to gr, ornate gold hdls/ft/rim, 9" 550.00
Vase, Sheepherder scene, gold hdls, 6"..500.00

R.S. Prussia

Art porcelain bearing the mark 'R.S. Prussia' was manufactured by Reinhold Schlegelmilch in the early 1900s in a Germanic area known until the end of WWI as Prussia. The vast array of mold shapes in combination with a wide variety of decorations is the basis for R.S. Prussia's appeal. Themes can be categorized as figural (usually based on a famous artist's work), birds, florals, portraits, scenics, and animals.

Bowl, barnyard scene w/cobalt & gold, RM, 10".........................3,000.00
Bowl, floral w/wht shadow flowers/opal jewels/gold, mold #82, 11"..325.00
Bowl, Madame Lebrun I, much gold, 10 petal ft, mold #29, 10½"..2,400.00
Bowl, Madame Recamier, Tiffany finish, mold #339, 11" 1,800.00
Bowl, Old Man in the Mountain, oval, mold #14, 13x8½" 1,100.00
Bowl, roses on cream to bl w/gold/jewels, mold #85, 10"..............350.00

Bowl, three swans, bluebirds, green wreath mark, 11", $350.00.

(Photo courtesy Early Auction Co.)

Bowl, Winter, emb floral on lt lav, mold #25, 10" 2,200.00
Cake plate, ducks w/peacock, shadow trees w/gold, mold #304, 9½" .. 900.00
Cake plate, portrait medallions at rim, floral center, mold D14, 11" ..1,200.00
Celery tray, roses, pk on watered silk w/gr touches, mold #13, 12x6" .. 275.00
Celery tray, Sheepherder I scene/Swallows, mold #304, 12x6" 700.00
Chocolate pot, wht floral/gr leaves on cobalt, ornate gold hdl, 12" ..2,250.00
Cracker jar, Cottage scene, Point & Clover mold, 7¼" 650.00
Cracker jar, swans & pines on pearl lustre, mold #633, 5½" 650.00
Creamer & sugar bowl, Castle scene/Mill scene, mold #644, w/lid ..650.00
Creamer & sugar bowl, swan on satin, shadow flowers, mold #452, w/lid....400.00
Leaf dish, poppies on irid & satin, Leaf mold variation 10B, 9" ... 325.00
Pitcher, cider; magnolias on dk rose, wht hdl w/gold, mold #537, 6"..425.00
Plate, Madame Lebrun (bl ribbon), cobalt w/gold trim, RM, 8½" .. 3,200.00
Plate, Mill scene on turq, gold at rim, mold #90, 8½" 500.00
Plate, roses, mc on wht w/gold, Acorn mold, 10¼" 375.00
Plate, Roses & Snowballs w/cobalt & gold, Point & Clover mold, 6½"...375.00
Plate, Spring, red & bold rim, mold #343, 9" 2,200.00
Plate, turkey w/pines, gold trim, Popcorn mold #92, 8" 550.00
Tankard, Autumn, mold #526, ornate hdl, 13½" 3,600.00
Tankard, pheasant w/pines, gold trim, mold #569, 12¼" 1,000.00
Tankard, poppies w/rust-brn at top, mold #583, 11" 775.00
Tankard, roses, mc w/deep rose-pk at base, Ball Foot mold, 14½" ...950.00
Toothpick holder, Roses & Snowballs, hdls, Icicle mold, 2½" 250.00
Tray, bun; daffodils on cobalt w/gold, scalloped, open hdls, 12½" L....450.00
Vase, Spring on pearl lustre, ornate gold hdls, mold #924, 10¼" ...1,000.00

R.S. Suhl

Porcelains marked with this designation are attributed to Reinhold Schlegelmilch's Suhl factory.

Dish, lav & wht flowers, gold trim, w/hdls, 8⅛" 160.00
Sugar bowl, open flowers on shaded gr, gold trim, Friedrich II, w/lid... 150.00
Vase, Crowned Cranes, mold #2, 10½" 2,000.00
Vase, maidens (4), gold uptrn hdls, 14½" 2,600.00
Vase, maidens reserve, floral tapestry, gold hdls & trim, 7".......... 600.00
Vase, ostriches, hdls, mk, 8¾" 1,600.00
Vase, parrots, crown crane on bk, ring hdls, 14" 5,000.00
Vase, parrots & ostriches, cobalt, o/l gold enamel, mold #14, 8½"..4,000.00
Vase, poppies, gold hdls & trim, Friedrich II, GM, 8", from $600 to ..800.00
Vase, women w/sheep, gold hdls, 11" 1,400.00

R.S. Tillowitz

R.S. Tillowitz-marked porcelains are attributed to Reinhold Schlegelmilch's factory in Tillowitz, Silesia.

Butter dish, China Blau, 3¾x6⅝" 600.00
Chocolate pot, daisies on wht, script mk, 8½", from $350 to 400.00
Coffeepot, yel & wht striped, ribbed, 8½" 250.00
Cup & saucer, daisies on wht, script mk, 3", 4", from $50 to........ 100.00
Plate, mc floral bouquets, 1931, 7⅝" 20.00

Relish tray, Bird of Paradise, gold trim, GM, 9¼", from $250 to .. 300.00
Vase, floral, gold angle hdls, 14" 1,400.00

Schneider

The Schneider Glass Company was founded in 1914 at Epinay-sur-Seine, France. They made many types of art glass, some of which sandwiched designs between layers. Other decorative devices were applique and carved work. These were marked 'Charder' or 'Schneider.' During the '20s commercial artware was produced with Deco motifs cut by acid through two or three layers and signed 'LeVerre Francais' in script or with a section of inlaid filigrane. Our advisor for this category is Don Williams; he is listed in the Directory under Missouri. See also Le Verre Francais.

Bowl, cranberry to cream mottle, 4½" 145.00
Bowl, rust/bl mottle w/yel mottled int, 12" 500.00
Charger, orange rim w/brn & gr swirl center, 16", NM................. 235.00
Compote, red to orange to wine center, clear to wine stem, red ft, 7"... 2,115.00
Ewer, raspberry mottle on orange, purple hdl, rnd w/waisted neck, 7" .. 1,250.00
Pitcher, red w/bl mottling at base, yel spout int, blk hdl, 12" 2,000.00
Vase, dk brn mottle over orange w/yel highlights, brn ft, slim, 18"..2,000.00
Vase, heavily mottled orange/red/yel w/wht accents, shouldered, 12"... 1,600.00
Vase, orange/yel/brn mottle funnel form on purple stem/ft, 12" .. 1,600.00
Vase, pk/bl/purple mottle, baluster w/bun ft, 14" 1,560.00
Vase, pk/red/purple mottle on purple ped ft, 7¾" 480.00
Vase, wht frosted bowl w/bl ribs, appl amber connector/bl ft, 10x10" ... 2,300.00

Cameo

Vase, abstract floral, dk bl on orange frost, inlaid cane, 13x10" ... 1,550.00
Vase, fruiting branches, cinnabar on amber frost, slim w/bun ft, 16"..2,520.00
Vase, leaves, wine w/yel highlights on frost, slim wine ft, 5½" ..2,645.00
Vase, pr swans, purple on orange/yel mottle, bun ft, Charder, 10"..3,480.00
Vase, sunflowers, lt gr/wht on frost & clear, elongated w/disk ft, 14"..2,760.00

Schoolhouse Collectibles

Schoolhouse collectibles bring to mind memories of a bygone era when the teacher rang her bell to call the youngsters to class in a one-room schoolhouse where often both the 'hickory stick' and an apple occupied a prominent position on her desk. Our advisor for this category is Kenn Norris; he is listed in the Directory under Texas.

Book, Elson Basic Readers (1st appearance of Dick & Jane), 1930, EX .200.00
Book, Fun w/Dick & Jane, hardcover, scarce lg type edition, 1946, EX ...200.00
Book, Fun w/Dick & Jane, hardcover primer, ca 1946-47, EX+ ... 115.00
Book, New Fun w/Dick & Jane, hardcover, 1951, M.................... 135.00
Book, Viens Voir (Fr version of Dick & Jane), red wrappers, 1940, EX..250.00
Desk, child's; pnt poplar/pine, lift top, sm gallery, 30x20x19" ...1,000.00
Desk, master's; cherry/pine Hplwht, dvtl drw, rfn, VA, 37x33x27" .. 515.00
Desk, master's; poplar w/dry red stain, slant lid, sq nails, 40x32x19" ..800.00
Desk, master's; walnut & poplar w/red grpt, slant lid, drw, 42x30x22" ..865.00
Globe, celestial; Rand McNally, papier mache, edited by Dr Lee, 16" .. 120.00
Globe, GW Bacon, 12 colored gores, 1912 & 1926 expeditions, 14x8".325.00
Globe, Rand McNally, gores on plaster sphere, mahog stand, 35x12" ..200.00
Globe/starfinder, Rand McNally, 1930, cast brass base w/claw ft, 16" ...590.00
Pencil sharpener, Bakelite, Dumbo decal on cream, rectangular, 1¼"..40.00
Pencil sharpener, Bakelite, elephant figural, 1940s, 1¼x1½" 60.00
Pencil sharpener, Bakelite, Snow White decal, WD Ent, ca 1937 .... 75.00
Pencil sharpener, celluloid, wht w/orange beak, Made in Japan... 145.00
Pencil sharpener, lead, Santa figural, Made in England, 1⅞x⅞" 85.00
Pencil sharpener, metal, vending cart, crank hdl 60.00

Pencil Boxes

Among the most common of school-related collectibles are the many classes of pencil boxes. Generally from the period of the 1870s to the 1940s, these boxes were made in hundreds of different styles. Materials included tin, wood (thin frame and solid hardwood), and leather; fabric and plastics were later used. Most pencil boxes were in a basic, rectangular configuration, though rare examples were made to resemble other objects such as rolling pins, ball bats, nightsticks, etc. They may still be found at reasonable prices, even though collectors have recently taken a keen interest in them. All boxes listed below are in very-good to near-mint condition. For further information we recommend *School Collectibles of the Past* by Lar and Sue Hothem.

Wood frame, Jack and Jill on lid, 7¾" long, $40.00. (Photo courtesy the Sue Hothem collection)

Cb litho, Mickey Mouse & Donald Duck, Dixon #2917, 1930s......... 35.00
Pnt wood, dk gr w/mustard panels, sliding lid, 8" L 550.00
Tin, advertising giveway, Security Shoes, sliding lid, 8" 38.00
Tin, Scholar's Companion, Pat 1874, 7¼" 85.00
Tin litho, Boy Scouts at camp scene, cb liner, ¾x7¾x3½"............. 55.00
Wood litho, Mother Goose, 1930s, 1⅜x7⅞x2⅜" 60.00
Wooden, simple slide w/ruler built into top, 1900s, 1x9¾x2½"...... 20.00
Wooden, 2-tier, 4 pencil slots/3 compartments, HP lid, 1900s, 9" L .. 65.00
Wooden, 4-level, 1 compartment ea, floral decor, 9¼" 70.00

Schoop, Hedi

In the 1940s and 1950s one of the most talented artists working in California was Hedi Schoop. Her business ended in 1958 when a fire destroyed her operation. It was at that time that she decided to do freelance work for other companies such as Cleminson Clay. Schoop was probably the most imitated artist of the time and she answered some of those imitators by successfully suing them. Some imitators were Kim Ward, Ynez, and Yona. Schoop was diversified in her creations, making items such as shapely women, bulky-looking women and children with fat arms and legs, TV lamps, and animals as well as planters and bowls. Schoop used many different marks including the stamped or incised Schoop signature and also a hard-to-find sticker. 'Hollywood, Cal.' or 'California' were occasionally used in conjunction with the Hedi Schoop name. For further information we recommend *Collector's Encyclopedia of California Pottery, Second Edition*, by Jack Chipman; he is listed in the Directory under California.

Bell, lady calling w/hands to face, 4½" 85.00
Bookends, girl holding purse reviews image in mirror behind her, 8".. 235.00
Box, brn rectangle, 1⅝x6¾x4", w/2¼" pk & wht poodle on lid.... 295.00
Box, brn triangle, 1½x8x8", w/2¼" pk & wht poodle on lid......... 235.00
Candleholder, dancing girl kneels, holds lotus flower (cup), 10", ea .. 90.00
Candleholder/bowl, duck figural, raspberry w/gold accents 65.00
Console bowl, 2 ducks bk-to-bk, candleholder heads, wht w/gold, 13" L.. 135.00

Dish, lady w/skirt forming bowl, holds lg rose in hands, 7x11½".... 95.00
Figurine, Chinese Musician, Young China Line, 11", from $70 to...90.00
Figurine, cowboy dancing w/coy lady in ruffled skirt, 10½" 135.00
Figurine, geisha dancer w/umbrella, gold trim, #228, 11½" 125.00
Figurine, lady in gray dress/scarf, opening at right hand, 12¾"..... 125.00
Figurine, lady kneeling, opening in apron, 8½" 65.00
Figurine, lady w/basket on head, opening in skirt on right, 12½"... 75.00
Figurine, little girl w/jump rope, platinum trim, 8¾x6" 120.00
Figurine, madonna kneels/cradles nude baby, #43, 7x5" 150.00
Figurine, Oriental lady w/arm on tearful boy, 2 open baskets, 9".... 85.00
Figurine, Oriental man (lady), ea w/bucket, 12½", pr from $125 to ...150.00
Tray, blk cat peeks out from behind tree, #18, sq, NM 100.00
Tray, face of wht cat w/amber eyes, sq, 7½x7½" 90.00
Tray, pk & wht poodle pnt on glossy blk triangle, 7" 125.00

Scouting Collectibles

Boy Scouts

Scouting was founded in England in 1907 by a retired Major General, Lord Robert Baden-Powell. Its purpose is the same today as it was then — to help develop physically strong, mentally alert boys and to teach them basic fundamentals of survival and leadership. The movement soon spread to the United States, and in 1910 a Chicago publisher, William Boyce, set out to establish scouting in America. The first World Scout Jamboree was held in 1920 in England. Baden-Powell was honored as the Chief Scout of the World. In 1926 he was awarded the Silver Buffalo Award in the United States. He was knighted in 1929 for distinguished military service and for his scouting efforts. Baden-Powell died in 1941. For more information you may contact our advisor, R. J. Sayers, author of *Guide to Scouting Collectibles*, whose address (and ordering information regarding his book) may be found in the Directory under North Carolina. (Correspondence other than book orders requires SASE please.)

Axe/hatchet, Official Voyageur, eng BSA emblem, 9" hdl, EX in sheath.. 135.00
Book, Ben - Hur, BSA emblem on hardcover, 1913, 560 pgs, VG ...60.00
Book, Wisdom of the Woods, D Beard, Woodcraft Series, 1926, EX ...60.00
Bugle, brass, Rexcraft, 1930-40, 17", VG 70.00
Camera, Agfa Ansco Memo Camera, gr, 1927, G........................ 215.00
Camera, Eastman Kodak, folds out, 1920s, NM in case............... 175.00

Game, Boy Scout's Progress, Parker Brothers, 1924, $200.00. (Photo courtesy Don and R.C. Raycraft)

Handbook, Boy Scout Official, red cover, 498 pgs, 1916, VG 250.00
Handbook, Boy Scouts of Am, Seton, Doubleday, Page & Co, 1910, VG..775.00
Handbook, BSA Handbook for Boys, red softcover, 1911, VG 215.00
Knife, Case Tested XX, etched BSA, 4-blade, compo hdl, 1920-40, NM .250.00
Knife, Western, leathered hdl, 4½" blade, 8⅝", M in scabbard..... 175.00
Lapel pin, Press Club, bl enamel w/gold 1st Class emblem & quill, mini... 550.00
Medal, Silver Beaver Award, silver figural, 1950s, 1½x1x1", +ribbon. 175.00
Neckerchief, emblem in 2 corners, red & wht, Nat'l Jamboree, 1937, EX ...95.00
Neckerchief, Yahnundasis 465 Area II, 1981, M 75.00
Patch, Buffalo, felt, rectangular, 1926-28, 1½x1⅜" 100.00
Patch, Camp Bird (tepee) 1944, red felt arrowhead shape 150.00
Patch, Camp Shawondosse, emb leather, 1935, 3", EX.................. 40.00
Patch, Honor Camper Nicholet Area Council, 1944, EX 50.00

Patch, Senior Patrol Leader Honors, 2 bl chevrons on wht, 1930s...110.00
Pin, Assistant Scoutmaster, Be Prepared, gold-tone/gr enamel, 1" ..130.00
Pocketknife, Scout Is Clean, 1-blade, Franklin Mint, 7½", M in bag...75.00
Puzzle, wooden litho camp scene of scout signaling, 1930s, 154-pc, EX .115.00
Watch fob, emb Scout w/Am flag, red/wht/bl enamel on brass 80.00
Woodcarving set, 5 varied chisels, Cattaragus, M in wood box w/emblem ..95.00

Girl Scouts

Collecting Girl Scout memorabilia is a hobby that is growing nation-wide. When Sir Baden-Powell founded the Boy Scout movement in England, it proved to be too attractive and too well adapted to youth to limit its great opportunities to boys alone. The sister organization, known in England as the Girl Guides, quickly followed and was equally successful. Mrs. Juliette Low, an American visitor to England and a personal friend of the father of scouting, realized the tremendous future of the movement for her own country, and with the active and friendly cooperation of the Baden-Powells, she founded the Girl Guides in America, enrolling the first patrols in Savannah, Georgia, in March 1912. In 1915 national headquarters were established in Washington, D.C., and the name was changed to Girl Scouts. The first national convention was held in 1914. Each succeeding year has shown growth and increased enthusiasm in this steadily growing army of girls and young women who are learning in the happiest ways to combine patriotism, outdoor activities of every kind, skill in every branch of domestic science, and high standards of community service. Today there are over 400,000 Girl Scouts and more than 22,000 leaders. Mr. Sayers is also our Girl Scout advisor.

Badge, For Merit, emb bronze, ca 1920-25, 1" dia, +3" ribbon 325.00
Belt, gold-tone chain links w/4 gold-tone charms, 1972-73, 40", EX ...65.00
Beret, gr cloth w/metal emblem on front, 1950s, EX 22.50
Book, Brave Girls, HC Philmus, hardbk, 1947, VG 40.00
Book, Girls Scouts of Eagles Wing, Vandercook, 1921, EX 28.00
Bookends, eagle & 7 stars on shield, compo, Permo #061, 1952, MIB...70.00
Bracelet, gold-plated brass w/emb symbol, cuff style, ca 1930s-40s, EX..75.00
Bracelet, 12k gold-filled w/6 various charms, 1960s, EX 45.00
Camera, Instant Load 900W, gr, Eastman Kodak Patents..., 5" L .100.00
Camera, Official GS, Herbert George Co #620, 3x3½x3¼", EX 40.00
Card, membership; pre-printed both sides, 1919, 4⅛x3¼", EX 10.00
Catalog, Girl Scout Equipment, 1957, EX 30.00
Doll, cloth, yarn hair, orig uniform, Georgene, 1940s, 14", M 400.00
Doll, hard plastic, pnt eyes, wig, orig uniform, Terri Lee, 16", M .450.00
Doll, Jr Girl Scout, vinyl, jumper/etc, Effanbee, 1970s, 11", MIB ..75.00
Flashlight, Nat'l Equipment Service, 1950s, MIB 30.00
Hat, gr cloth w/blk GS, gr ribbon w/bow, w/tags, MIB 60.00
Medal, Girl Scouts War Service, emb metal, 1918, 1¼" 525.00
Necklace, gold-plated locket w/emb eagle & 7 stars, 1950s, MIB ..65.00
Pin-bk, 10k yel gold, emb GS & eagle, ⅞x⅞" 50.00
Pin-bk, Golden Eaglet (3 variations), 10K-B mk on bk, ½x½" 500.00
Pocketknife, symbol on gr hdl, blade & 3 tools, 3⅜", NM 30.00
Ring, silver w/emb emblem on top, Sterling, EX 85.00
Ring, 10k yel & rose gold, emb symbol, NM.................................40.00
Sheet music, Girl Scouts Are We, J Rivenburg, 1941, EX..............15.00
Stamp set, Girl Power, 8-pc, retired, MIB.....................................50.00
Statue, copper-bronze Scout figural, M Dauigerfield, 1960s, 8x4" ..30.00
Uniform, tan, top, skirt & bloomers (3-pc), ca 1920, VG 250.00
Wristwatch, silver-tone case, windup, Timex, leather band, EX 25.00

Scrimshaw

The most desirable examples of the art of scrimshaw can be traced back to the first half of the nineteenth century to the heyday of the whaling industry. Some voyages lasted for several years, and conditions on board were often dismal. Sailors filled the long hours by using the tools of their trade to engrave whale teeth and make boxes, pie crimpers (jagging wheels), etc., from the bone and teeth of captured whales. Eskimos also made scrimshaw, sometimes borrowing designs from the sailors who traded with them.

Beware of fraudulent pieces; fakery is prevalent in this field. Many carved teeth are of recent synthetic manufacture (examples engraved with information such as ship's or captain's names, dates, places, etc., should be treated with extreme caution) and have no antique or collectible value. A listing of most of these plastic items has been published by the Kendall Institute at the New Bedford Whaling Museum in New Bedford, Massachusetts. If you're in doubt or a novice collector, it's best to deal with reputable people who guarantee the items they sell. Our advisor for this category is John Rinaldi; he is listed in the Directory under Maine. See also Powder Horns.

Busk, bone w/flowers/stars/hearts, splits, 14" 800.00
Busk, bone w/inked pinwheels/stars/flowers, 11¼" 575.00
Busk, whalebone, church/tower/flags, 19th C, 14¼" 880.00
Cane, eagle cvd whale-ivory 3½" hdl, ebony shaft/ivory tip, 1840s+ .. 1,675.00
Jagging wheel, whale ivory, serpent-form hdl, leaf-form fork, 5¼" .. 1,295.00
Rolling pin, teak w/whale ivory 4¼" hdls, ca 1830-40, 20" 1,875.00

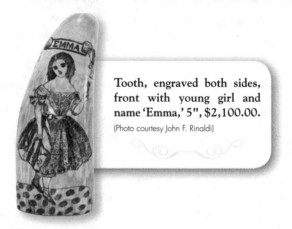

Tooth, engraved both sides, front with young girl and name 'Emma,' 5", $2,100.00.

(Photo courtesy John F. Rinaldi)

Tooth, lady w/plumed hat, Liberty w/Am flag, cracks, 19th C, 5" .. 1,765.00
Tooth, mother w/daughter (hair in ringlets), age split, 6⅝".......4,250.00
Tooth, panel: man presents lady a miniature portrait by window, 6", VG 985.00
Tooth, queen in royal robes, man in frock coat, pinprick art, 6".. 1,150.00
Tooth, soldiers (2/19th C), 2 eagles/landscape, 19th C, 6"........2,235.00
Tooth, warship firing, warship hiding behind rocks, whalers, 6¾" ..9,775.00
Tooth, whaleship/boats, monument/eagle, red wax, E Burdett, 5¾" ...55,000.00
Tooth, 2-masted ship/2 sm 2-masted ships/eagle/Am flag, 1880s, 7"...11,165.00
Yardstick, flowers/leaves/vines/tree/etc, 1830-40, rpr, 21¼x¾" 875.00

Sebastians

Prescott W. Baston first produced Sebastian Miniatures in 1938 in his home in Arlington, Massachusetts. In 1946 Baston bought a small shoe factory in Marblehead, Massachusetts, and produced his figurines there for the next 30 years. Over the years Baston sculpted and produced more than 750 different pieces, many of which have been sold nationwide through gift shops. Baston and The Lance Corporation of Hudson, Massachusetts, consolidated the line in 1976 and actively promoted Sebastians nationally. Many of Baston's commercial designs, private commissions, and even some open line pieces have become very collectible. Aftermarket price is determined by three factors: 1) current or out of production status, 2) labels, and 3) condition. Copyright dates are of no particular significance with regard to value.

Mr. Baston died in 1984, and his son Prescott 'Woody' Baston, Jr. continued the tradition by taking over the designing. To date Woody has sculpted over 250 pieces of his own. After numerous changes in the company that held manufacturing and distribution rights for Sebastions, Woody and his wife Margery are now sculpting and painting the Sebastian Miniatures out of their home in Massachusetts. By personally producing the pieces, Sebastions are the only collectible line that is produced from design to finished product by the artist. Sebastian Miniatures have come full cycle. Our advisor for this category is Jim Waite; he is listed in the Directory under Illinois.

Alexander Hamilton, MIB	25.00
Captain John Smith, 1940s	32.00
Charles Dickens, standing behind table w/open book	32.00
Colonial Watchman, Marblehead label	55.00
Coronaro & Senora, 1960, 3¼"	35.00
George Washington, Marblehead era, 4"	95.00
James Madison, MIB	38.00
Jell-O Cow Pitcher, 6 orig fruit flavors on wht, 1956	55.00
Jell-O! A Fine Treat for All!, Santa scene	175.00
Old South Union Church Weymouth MA, 1989	25.00
Our Lady of Good Voyage, 1952, 4¼", NM	55.00
Parade Rest, 1953, 4¼"	25.00
Pocahontas, 1940s	25.00
Sampling the Stew, gr label, 2½"	15.00
Shepherds, 1954 Nativity pc	35.00
Spirit of 76	25.00
Thomas A 'Stonewall' Jackson, standing in gray uniform	32.00
Uncle Sam in Orbit, Marblehead era, 1960	285.00
William Shakespeare, Sebastian Collectors Society, 1988	25.00

Sevres

Fine-quality porcelains have been made in Sevres, France, since the early 1700s. Rich ground colors were often hand painted with portraits, scenics, and florals. Some pieces were decorated with transfer prints and decalcomania; many were embellished with heavy gold. These wares are the most respected of all French porcelains. Their style and designs have been widely copied, and some of the items listed below are Sevres-type wares.

Bucket, ice cream; floral, feather-edge lid, w/insert, ca 1782, 7"	1,400.00
Bust, Henry IV, after Bachelier, draped armor, ca 1870, 14x9x5½"	1,775.00
Coffee set, Napoleonic scenes/landscapes, pot+cr/sug+12 c/s+6 plates	12,925.00
Cup & saucer, Chateau de Chantilly w/cobalt/gold, 1850s, 3", 5½"	825.00
Figurine, Forging of Arrows, Cupid & cherub, wht porc, ca 1860, 13"	960.00
Figurine, La Rosee, nude seated on rocky base, wht bsk, 30"	1,880.00
Figurine, 3 cherub accountants w/scroll & 2 w/ledger, ca 1900, 9"	2,000.00
Figurine, 3 cherubs in scientific activities, ca 1900, 8"	2,450.00
Figurine, 3 cherubs representing agriculture, ca 1900, 8¾"	2,475.00
Garniture, scenic reserves/ormolu mts, Japy Freres clock, 20", +2 urns	5,875.00
Lamp base, huntsman/lady, jewels/scrolls, bronze ft, 19th C, 18", pr	2,000.00
Platter, exotic birds on pk w/gold, ca 1774, 12⅝"	1,880.00
Tureen, floral reserves on bl w/gold, w/lid & tray, 16x24x15"	1,880.00
Urn, couple/cherubs, Quentin, brass mts, w/lid, 20th C, 31"	2,650.00
Urn, figure scene reserve on dk bl w/much gold, gold hdls, 18", pr, EX	1,150.00
Urn, huntsman/shepherdess w/gold, 19th C, 37"+ornate stand, 57"	11,165.00
Urn, ormolu swan-head hdl/floral swags, gilt bronze base/lid, 18", pr	3,885.00
Urn, 2 maids/Cupid at well, pastels on wht, sgn Fuchs, bronze mts, 48"	17,250.00
Vase, couple reserve, wht on bl w/ornate gilt hdls, ftd, 1850s, 12", V	300.00
Vase, hunting scene reserves, cobalt w/gold, bronze mts, 32x17"	6,500.00

Sewer Tile

Whimsies, advertising novelties, and other ornamental items were sometimes made in potteries where the primary product was simply tile.

Desk set, lion w/tree trunks, Romig Clay Products, 1928, 5x9x6"	1,495.00
Eagle, hand molded w/incised feathers, sgn, dtd 1925, 8⅛", VG	285.00
Frog, hand tooled, smiling face, att OH, 9"	550.00
Lion, hand tooled w/full mane/smiling face, 7x10⅛", EX	285.00
Lion reclining on rectangular base, 7x9"	315.00
Lion reclining on scalloped base, dk brn pnt, att OH, 6x10", VG	200.00
Lion reclining on scalloped base, tooled features, 1929, 5½x9"	400.00
Owl, molded, on rnd base, pumpkin orange, seam separations, 10½"	175.00
Rabbit, bank, 6¼x10½"	115.00
Spaniel seated w/paw raised, brn lustre, OH, 19th C, 8⅞"	1,175.00
Stump w/lion family, hollow, handmade w/gr glaze, 8", EX	230.00
Tree trunk planter, simulated bark & 3 branches, 37x15" dia	550.00
Tree trunk planter, Uhrichsville Fire Clay Co, 38x14"	460.00

Sewing Items

Sewing collectibles continue to intrigue collectors, and fine nineteenth-century and earlier pieces are commanding higher prices due to increased demand and scarcity. Complete needlework boxes and chatelaines in original condition are rare, but even incomplete examples can be considered prime additions to any collection, as long as they meet certain criteria: boxes should contain fittings of the period; the chains of the chatelaine should be intact and contemporary with the style; and the individual holders should be original and match the brooch. As nineteenth-century items become harder to find, new trends in collecting develop. Needle books, many of which were decorated with horses, children, beautiful ladies, etc., have become very popular. Some were giveaways printed with advertisements of products and businesses. Even early pins are collectible; the first ones were made in two parts with the round head attached separately. Pin disks, pin cubes, and other pin holders also make interesting additions to a sewing collection.

Tape measures are very popular — especially Victorian figurals. These command premium prices. Early wooden examples of transferware and Tunbridge ware have gained in popularity, as have figurals of vegetable ivory, celluloid, and other early plastics. From the twentieth century, tatting shuttles made of plastics, bone, brass, sterling, and wood decorated with Art Nouveau, Art Deco, and more modern designs are in demand — so are darning eggs, stilettos, and thimbles. Because of the decline in the popularity of needlework after the 1920s (due to increased production of machine-made items), novelty items were made in an attempt to regain consumer interest, and many collectors today also find these appealing.

Watch for reproductions. Sterling thimbles are being made in Holland and the U.S. and are available in many Victorian-era designs. But the originals are usually plainly marked, either in the inside apex or outside on the band. Avoid testing gold and silver thimbles for content; this often destroys the inside marks. Instead, research the manufacturer's mark; this will often denote the material as well. Even though the reproductions are well finished, they do not have manufacturers' marks. Many thimbles are being made specifically for the collectible market; reproductions of porcelain thimbles are also found. Prices should reflect the age and availability of these thimbles. Our advisor for this category is Kathy Goldsworthy; she is listed in the Directory under Washington. For more information we recommend *Sewing Tools & Trinkets* by Helen Lester Thompson and *Antique & Collectible Buttons, Volumes I* and *II*, by Debra Wisniewski.

Awl, steel & bone, 4¼"	22.50
Bodkin, cvd ivory w/inset 'jewels,' 3½"	225.00
Bodkins, cvd bone, 3¼", 3", pr	35.00
Box, burl walnut w/MOP inlay, ca 1860s, 5x9¾x6¾", EX	595.00
Box, olive wood, hinged lid w/center hdl, 1900s, 3x7x4"	100.00
Box, roses decal on wood, J&P Coats ad in lid, 2¼x3¾" dia	85.00
Box, spool; lady's portrait on wood, Brook's label, 2¼x4¼"	88.00
Button, Bakelite Scottie dog, lg, from $18 to	25.00

Button, glass vest type w/rosette shank, from $5 to 8.00
Button, japanned brass w/eng, from $4 to 6.00
Button, reverse-cvd/pnt Lucite flower, lg 25.00
Button, silvered brass, dog portrait, TW&W Paris, med 12.00
Caddy, Peaseware, 2-pc step-bk, pincushion top, metal posts, 6x4"....215.00
Caddy, walnut w/trn details, spire finial, varnish, 9x8½" 265.00
Caddy, wood, sq w/appl ft, dvtl drw, pincushion top, 9x7x7" 485.00
Clamp, gilt brass, pincushion top, sm mirror on side, 6" 395.00
Darner, ebonized wooden egg shape w/ornate silver hdl, 1890s.... 100.00
Darner, milk glass w/dk maroon splotches cased in clear, 6" 175.00
Darner, wood, mushroom shape w/metal ring to hold sock 25.00
Dress form, adjustable, w/iron claw-ft base, 60" 75.00
Gauge, sewing/knitting; Singer, older type, 6" 8.00
Kit, celluloid bodkin/SP scissors/knife/2 sm tools, 1900s, EX in case....65.00
Measure, celluloid, bear walking, 1930-50, Japan 175.00
Measure, celluloid, bird w/2 chicks, mc on wht, Japan, 1930s+, 2¼" .. 160.00
Measure, celluloid, clown's head, sm blk hat is pull, Germany 325.00
Measure, celluloid, country cottage, 1920, 2x1¼" 195.00
Measure, celluloid, elephant w/basket on bk, Germany, 1¼x1⅝".. 265.00
Measure, celluloid, flamingo, pk, w/tape in base, 2⅝"...................... 75.00
Measure, celluloid, fruit basket, cloth tape, unmk Japan 125.00
Measure, celluloid, Indian boy in headdress, red pants 135.00
Measure, celluloid, kangaroo w/joey, pk, 2¾x2⅜" 80.00
Measure, celluloid, parrot's head, mc on wht, Germany, 1⅜" 315.00
Measure, celluloid, parrot's head, mc on wht, unmk 265.00
Measure, celluloid, pig, pk w/red hat, Japan, 1¼x2½" 55.00
Measure, celluloid, purse w/jeweled clasp, Japan, 1½x1½" 225.00
Measure, celluloid, sailboat, mc on wht, Japan, 2x2" 235.00
Measure, celluloid, spaniel dog, wht/blk/red, 1930s-50s, Japan 225.00
Measure, ceramic, lion, velvet crown cushion, tape at bk, 1950s... 15.00
Measure, metal, egg form, yel pnt, fly at top is pull, 1¾x2½" 85.00

Measure, metal fish with spring mechanism, from $150.00 to $175.00. (Photo courtesy Morphy Auctions)

Measure, metal, table lamp, gr shade w/fringe, brn base, 1930s, 2¼"..155.00
Measure, pierced bone w/ivory spindle, silk tape, 1850-90, 1" dia.. 70.00
Measure, plated copper, shoe, 3 Feet in 1 Shoe emb on side, 2¼" L...225.00
Measure, porc, child w/flowers, tape in base, Germany.................. 185.00
Measure, porc, fisherman, mc, pull at bk, Germany...................... 245.00
Measure, tin plate, early car, rubber tires, 1900s, 2½" L................ 385.00
Needle case, cvd oak, opens from center, late 1800s, 4x½" dia 45.00
Needle case, Mauchline Tartan Ware, Prince Charlie, 1880s, 2" .. 165.00
Needle holder, trn wood, sponge pnt, ftd, ball finial, 4½x1½" 400.00
Pincushion, gold-plated, shoe, WA DC souvenir, early 1900s........ 95.00
Pincushion, lustreware, pelican figural, mc, Japan, 2½x3¼" 40.00
Pincushion, porc, poodle, head & tail nodder, cushion bk, Florenza.. 65.00
Pincushion, wool, circus seal w/ball on nose, straw filled, 5" L....... 50.00
Scissors, embr; silver, Nouveau decor hdls/body, F&B Sterling, 4" ...110.00
Scissors, embr; silver, wild roses emb, 4" 60.00
Scissors, embr; sterling stork figural, ca 1900, 3¾" 40.00
Sewing bird, brass, ornate clamp, EX rstr, 5" 150.00
Sewing bird, brass, 2 red pincushions, w/clamp, 1850s, 5¼" 175.00
Sewing bird, steel, orig blk pnt, figural worm clamp, 4"................ 295.00
Tatting shuttle, cvd bone, 1900s, 3" 25.00
Thimble, German .800 silver, amethyst glass top, fancy border ... 110.00
Thimble, German .925 silver, red stone cap, ribbed w/ribbon-like band.. 60.00
Thimble, glass, cranberry stain, bird cuttings, West Germany, 1¼"...20.00

Thimble, gold-filled, Flower & Leaf Band, Stern & Co.................. 50.00
Thimble, porc, HP robin/flowers/gilt, Worcester, unmk, pre-1900..225.00
Thimble, porc, Jasperware, bl w/wht unicorn, Wedgwood............ 125.00
Thimble, porc, Jasperware, Kings & Queens of England, Wedgwood, ea.50.00
Thimble, silver w/all-over HP flowers on turq, JS&S Birmingham, 1978.. 70.00
Thimble, sterling w/emb gold animals, unmk 325.00
Thimble, 10k gold, fancy emb band centers 2 plain bands............. 60.00
Thimble, 14k gold, apex w/sm shield, bands: 1 plain/1 fancy/1 faceted ..220.00
Thimble, 14k gold, mk T&CO (Tiffany), monogram..................... 165.00
Thimble, 14k rose gold w/eng name, dtd Dec 25, 1900 .... 95.00
Thimble case, vegetable ivory, acorn form, 2x1" 65.00
Tracing wheel, Bakelite, Dritz 12.50

Sewing Machines

The fact that Thomas Saint, an English cabinetmaker, invented the first sewing machine in 1790 was unknown until 1874 when Newton Wilson, an English sewing machine manufacturer and patentee, chanced upon the drawings included in a patent specification describing methods of making boots and shoes. By the middle of the nineteenth century, several patents were granted to American inventors, among them Isaac M. Singer, whose machine used a treadle. These machines were ruggedly built, usually of cast iron. By the 1860s and 1870s, the sewing machine had become a popular commodity, and the ironwork became more detailed and ornate. Though rare machines are costly, many of the old oak treadle machines (especially these brands: Davis, Home, Household, National, New Home, Singer, Weed, Wheeler & Wilson, and Willcox & Gibbs) have only nominal value. Machines manufactured after 1875 are generally very common, as most were mass produced. Values for these later sewing machines range from $50.00 to $100.00. For more information see *The Encyclopedia of Early American Sewing Machines* by Carter Bays. Our advisor for this category is Peter Frei; he is listed in the Directory under Massachusetts. In the listings that follow, unless noted otherwise, values are suggested for machines in excellent working order.

Bel Air, ft-operated, 1930s, EX in solid wood cabinet 60.00
Child's, Baby Brother, gray-gr metallic, Japan, 1960s, from $75 to... 100.00
Child's, Casige, Deco decor, cam drive, MIG - British Zone, $75 to ... 100.00
Child's, Cornet, heavy metal, wht rabbit in circle, 9"................... 170.00
Child's, Faultless, iron/steel, floral decor, early 1900s, 8x9"..........255.00
Child's, Gateway Rotar Model N-8, orig red, lt rust 75.00
Child's, Genero, Gurlee Stitch Mistress, manual, 1940s-50s, 7" .. 125.00
Child's, KAYanEE Sew Master, hand-operated, wood base............. 50.00

Child's, Lindstrom, early, VG, $230.00. (Photo courtesy Morphy Auctions)

Child's, Little Comfort Improved, Smith & Egge, 1897.............. 175.00
Child's, Marx Sew Big, die-cast metal w/plastic table, 1960s 75.00
Child's, Olympia, manual or battery-operated, Japan 35.00
Child's, plastic, crystal/pk/wht, battery-operated, 7½x120x4"........ 45.00
Child's, Singer, Sewhandy Model 50D, electric, 1960s, +box 75.00

Child's, Stitchwell, CI/steel/wood, hand crank, 6x9x4", EX, +crate ..350.00
Florence, CI, belt-driven, Pat Nov 12, 1850, plain stand 160.00
Frisby, hand-crank, England, ca 1850s, 9x18", +case 195.00
Goodrich, treadle, quartersawn oak cabinet................................ 200.00
Grover & Baker #10574, flywheel-operated, +13" rosewood case . 880.00
Jones Electric Serial #2640, +case 450.00
Precision Built De Luxe, EX enamel & gold, +bl case 160.00
Singer, blk japanning w/gold decals, 1940s, +case 125.00
Singer, leather sewing, floor model, heavy 300.00
Singer, Pat 1846, MOP inlay in head, walnut fold-out case 800.00
Singer 221 Featherweight, gold graphics, NM 375.00
Wheeler & Wilson, 625 Broadway, EX 200.00
Wilcox & Gibbs, CI 13" bedplate, Pat dates to 1871, EX............. 300.00
Wilcox & Gibbs Automatic Noiseless, vintage decor, EX in mahog case . 300.00

Shaker Items

The Shaker community was founded in America in 1776 at Niskeyuna, New York, by a small group of English 'Shaking Quakers.' The name referred to a group dance which was part of their religious rites. Their leader was Mother Ann Lee. By 1815 their membership had grown to more than 1,000 in 18 communities as far west as Indiana and Kentucky. But in less than a decade, their numbers began to decline until today only a handful remain. Their furniture is prized for its originality, simplicity, workmanship, and practicality. Few pieces were signed. Some were carefully finished to enhance the natural wood; a few were painted. Other methods were used earlier, but most Shaker boxes were of oval construction with overlapping 'fingers' at the seams to prevent buckling as the wood aged. Boxes with original paint fetch triple the price of an unpainted box; number of fingers and overall size should also be considered.

Although the Shakers were responsible for weaving a great number of baskets, their methods are not easily distinguished from those of their outside neighbors, and it is nearly impossible without first-hand knowledge to positively attribute a specific example to their manufacture. They were involved in various commercial efforts other than woodworking — among them sheep and dairy farming, sawmilling, and pipe and brick making. They were the first to raise crops specifically for seed and to market their product commercially. They perfected a method to recycle paper and were able to produce wrinkle-free fabrics. Our advisor for this category is Nancy Winston; she is listed in the Directory under New Hampshire. Standard two-letter state abbreviations have been used throughout the following listings. Painted pieces are in original paint unless noted repainted.

Key:
bj — bootjack   ML — Mt. Lebanon
CB — Canterbury   SDL — Sabbathday Lake
EF — Enfield   WV — Watervliet
NL — New Lebanon

Basket, blk ash, dbl-wrapped rim, invt bottom, 1850s, 13½x13½" ..450.00
Basket, sewing; 4-finger, copper tacks, torn lining, SDL, 3x9x6" 345.00
Basket, splint, rnd rim/sq base, upright hdl, NY, 19th C, 13x9½"....550.00

Basket, woven splint with leather lining, New Hampshire or Maine, #20 in ink, nineteenth century, 22" long, $400.00. (Photo courtesy Skinner Inc. Auctioneers & Appraisers of Antiques & Fine Art)

Bench, milk; pnt pine, splayed legs w/V cutouts, CB, 19th C, 13x37x12"...825.00
Blanket chest, pine, 2 lidded tills, hinged top, red pnt, NY, 52".. 1,400.00
Box, seed; red pnt on pine, hinged lid, wire hdl, dvtl, bl label 900.00
Box, wood; chrome yel pnt on pine/maple, dvtl, SDL, 1840s, 33x27x18"...32,500.00
Box, 2-finger, gr-pnt maple (lt wear), copper tacks, Harvard MA, 5" L ..825.00
Box, 2-finger, mellow natural, copper tacks, 3¼" 635.00
Box, 3-finger, golden brn, copper tacks, sm loss, 11".................... 700.00
Box, 3-finger, gr pnt, copper tacks, 8x11"................................. 1,035.00
Box, 3-finger, red grpt, copper tacks, 2⅝x5" L 500.00
Box, 4-finger, natural finish, copper tacks, 13½" 1,100.00
Box, 4-finger, olive gray pnt over stain, copper tacks, 4¼x11" 575.00
Box, 4-finger, red-brn stain on maple/pine, copper tacks, 1890s, 3x7" .. 700.00
Bracket, lamp; pine, mortise & tenon, early brn, 19th C, 12x15x12" ... 300.00
Bucket, sap; yel pnt on staved pine w/2 iron hoops, yel int, EF, 9x12" .. 445.00
Bucket, sponging on yel, pine staves, 2 iron hoops, wire hdl, EF, 10" .. 725.00
Bucket, wooden staves w/2 bl metal hoops, mini, 3½x4½" 1,000.00
Candlestand, birch, trn shaft, snake legs, pnt traces, EF, 24x14" dia..3,000.00
Carrier, cutlery; oak, pierced hdl, wire-hinged lid, 19th C, 7x12x8"..475.00
Chair, arm; yel/red traces on maple, 2-slat, tilters, NL, 26", 3 for ..3,500.00
Chair, side; birch/cherry, 3-slat, cane seat, old red, EF, 1830s, 41" .. 2,000.00
Chair, side; maple, 3 arched slats, 2-color tape seat, WV, 39" 350.00
Chest, cherry drw fronts (4) on poplar, bracket base, OH, 46x39x19"....2,000.00
Chest, pine, 4 short over 3 long drws, orig stain, WV, 1840s 5,000.00
Cupboard, pine, rpt yel, 2 2-brd doors, rpl knobs, 76x31x18" 900.00
Cupboard, poplar stepbk, 2-door w/2-drw/2 door base, rpt, OH, 90x46"..2,000.00
Desk, poplar/pine, hinged lid, 4 grad drws, rfn, ML, 51x23x16" .. 1,875.00
Footstool, trn legs/stretchers, dk varnish, rprs, ML, 6x11⅜x12".. 400.00
Grinder, herb; CI boat shape & wheel, trn maple hdls, 1820-40s, 7x15".450.00
Ladder, fruit picking; canted sides w/15 rungs, bl pnt, NY, 1840s, 20' ...500.00
Measure, ash/pine w/iron rim, lug hdls, SDL, 19th C, 7⅝x14½" .. 200.00
Rocker, #0, recent webbed tape bk & seat, pnt traces, NL, 23".. 315.00
Rocker, #1, dk walnut, tape bk & seat, NY decal, child's, 29½"... 1,800.00
Rocker, #4, 3-slat bk w/acorn pommels, rpl rush seat, 1880s, 35½" .. 350.00
Rocker, #5, 4-slat, acorn finials, shaped arms, tape seat, 38½"...... 465.00
Rocker, #7, 4-slat ladder-bk w/acorn finials, shaped arms, 42½"... 600.00
Rocker, arm; #0, old dk stain, ML, late 19th C.......................... 1,650.00
Rocker, arm; #5, 3-slat bk, arms w/mushroom caps, rpl tape seat, ML... 435.00
Rocker, arm; #7, 4-slat bk, shawl bar, ML, 41"............................. 975.00
Rocker, arm; birch, 3-slat bk, splint seat, orig red-brn, ME, 41" .. 3,500.00
Rocker, arm; maple/hickory/oak, 4-slat, rush seat, OH, 44" 700.00
Rocker, maple, 3-slat bk, splint seat, att F Wells, WV, 36"........2,825.00
Shelves, corner, tiered, wood, EF, 30x20x9⅛".............................4,750.00
Slate chalkboard, mortise & tenon wood fr, 19th C, 8½x6½" 60.00
Stand, pine/birch, 16" sq top, sq legs, red stain, 1830s, 26" 2,115.00
Stool, revolving; maple, Windsor style, old rfn, 1860s, 30x17" dia.. 550.00
Stove, CI, rnded sides, front hinged door, tapered legs, 20x34x12".. 600.00
Swift, maple w/yel traces, trn cup on top, 19th C, 25-30" 395.00
Table, drop-leaf; figured cherry, old varnish, OH, 1840s, 29x39x44"..1,100.00
Table, tailor's; 1-brd pine top/cherry legs/hickory supports, EF, 36" .. 435.00
Table, work; pine, 1-drw, tapered legs, orig red, MA, 1830s, 26x17" sq..1,400.00
Table, work; 3-brd top, 3 dvtl drws, orig red on base, att ML, 62x31".. 4,000.00
Tray, cherry, appl molding, ML, 1830-50, 16x22" 700.00
Washstand, poplar, dvtl shelf, 2 towel pegs, old rpt, NY, 26x29x14"..500.00
Yarn winder, cherry w/iron spokes, adjustable arm, 21x15x6" dia....700.00

Shaving Mugs

Between 1865 and 1920, owning a personalized shaving mug was the order of the day, and the 'occupationals' were the most prestigious. The majority of men having occupational mugs would often frequent the barber shop several times a week, where their mugs were clearly visible for all to see in the barber's rack. As a matter of fact, this display was in many ways the index of the individual town or neighborhood.

During the first 20 years, blank mugs were almost entirely imported from France, Germany, and Austria and were hand painted in this country. Later on, some china was produced by local companies. It is noteworthy that American vitreous china is inferior to the imported Limoges and is subject to extreme crazing. Artists employed by the American barber supply companies were for the most part extremely talented and capable of executing any design the owner required, depicting his occupation, fraternal affiliation, or preferred sport. When the mug was completed, the name and the gold trim were always added in varying degrees, depending on the price paid by the customer. This price was determined by the barber who added his markup to that of the barber-supply company. As mentioned above, the popularity of the occupational shaving mug diminished with the advent of World War I and the introduction by Gillette of the safety razor. Later followed the blue laws forcing barber shops to close on Sundays, thereby eliminating the political and social discussions for which they were so well noted.

Occupational shaving mugs are the most sought after of the group which would also include those with sport affiliations. Fraternal mugs, although desirable, do not command the same price as the occupationals. Occasionally, you will find the owner's occupation together with his fraternal affiliation. This combination could add anywhere between 25% to 50% to the price, which is dependent on the execution of the painting, rarity of the subject and detail. Some subjects can be done very simply; others can be done in extreme detail, commanding substantially higher prices. It is fair to say, however, that the rarity of the occupation will dictate the price. Mugs with heavily worn gold lose between 20% and 30% of their value immediately. This would not apply to the gold trim around the rim, but to the loss of the name itself. Our advisor for this category is Burton Handelsman; he is listed in the Directory under New York.

Decorative, frog smoking pipe & holding fishing pole, gold trim ..1,200.00
Decorative, frogs on high-wheel bicycles (comic), 3⅝" 1,500.00
Decorative, ornate drapery/flowers/name w/gold, unmk, 3⅝" 85.00
Decorative, 3 Oriental beauties, name in gold, 3⅞", EX 420.00
Occupational, baker standing at lg ovens, sm chip, 3¾".............. 300.00
Occupational, bakers (2) in wht reserve, name/gold scrolls on pk, 4" ... 790.00
Occupational, bar scene w/5 figures, detailed/much gold, 3½" 600.00
Occupational, barber shaving man, detailed scene, EX gold, 3⅝" .. 1,200.00
Occupational, bartender & 2 customers in bar scene, unmk, 3¾" ...360.00
Occupational, baseball scene, 3¾" 1,650.00
Occupational, blacksmith shoeing horse, gold trim, 3⅝".............. 950.00
Occupational, butcher w/tools & runaway steer, gold trim, 3⅝" .. 650.00
Occupational, early open touring car, 3½" 715.00
Occupational, fire department hose reel, 3¾" 990.00
Occupational, flagman waving flag at train, KPM 950.00
Occupational, horsedrawn coal cart & driver, Leonard Vienna, 4".. 145.00
Occupational, hunting scene, T&V Limoges, 3½" 215.00
Occupational, man driving sm horsedrawn delivery cart, EX color, 4" ...415.00
Occupational, man in buggy driving 2 horses, 3⅝" 780.00
Occupational, man in early open car, rpr to base rim, 3½" 480.00
Occupational, man sitting at roll-top desk, 5" 415.00
Occupational, man standing by bull, 3¼" 500.00
Occupational, mason laying brick wall of house, worn gold, 3¾".. 265.00
Occupational, mortar & pestle, gold trim, 3⅝", EX 120.00
Occupational, painting tools, gold trim, 3½" 360.00
Occupational, printing press, much gold at rim, 3½".................... 660.00
Occupational, railroad car, gold trim, 3½" 330.00
Occupational, railroad tracks, name in gold, 3½" 500.00
Occupational, saloon scene, EX color & detail, 3½" 600.00
Occupational, shining light bulb, 3½"... 600.00
Occupational, skull & crossbones, 3½" 110.00
Occupational, telegraph operator, floral trim, 3½", EX................ 170.00
Occupational, trolley car, brn & blk w/name in gold, 4" 220.00
Occupational, trolley car w/2 men in bl uniforms, name in gold, 3⅝" .. 1,020.00
Occupational, 2 men singing, 3¼".. 150.00

Shawnee

The Shawnee Pottery Company operated in Zanesville, Ohio, from 1937 to 1961. They produced inexpensive novelty ware (vases, flowerpots, and figurines) as well as a very successful line of figural cookie jars, creamers, and salt and pepper shakers. They also produced three dinnerware lines, the first of which, Valencia, was designed by Louise Bauer in 1937 for Sears & Roebuck. A starter set was given away with the purchase of one of their refrigerators. Second and most popular was the Corn line. The original design was called White Corn. In 1946 the line was expanded and the color changed to a more natural yellow hue. It was marketed under the name Corn King, and it was produced from 1946 to 1954. Then the colors were changed again. Kernels became a lighter yellow and shucks a darker green. This variation was called Corn Queen. Their third dinnerware line, produced after 1954, was called Lobsterware. It was made in either black, brown, or gray; lobsters were usually applied to serving pieces and accessory items.

For further study we recommend these books: *The Collector's Guide to Shawnee Pottery* by Janice and Duane Vanderbilt, who are listed in the Directory under Indiana; and *Shawnee Pottery* by our advisors for this category, Jim and Bev Mangus; they are listed in Ohio.

Cookie Jars

Cottage, mk USA 6, 6¾", minimum value 1,500.00
Dutch Boy (Jack), gold & decals, mk USA, from $450 to........... 475.00
Dutch Girl (Jill), bl skirt, gold & decals, mk USA, from $375 to...400.00
Dutch Style, gr, mk USA, 8¼", from $145 to 165.00
Great Northern Girl, wht, mk Great Northern USA 1026, from $400 to....475.00
Jack, striped pants, gold & decals, mk USA, from $400 to........... 450.00
Jack, striped pants, mk USA from $190 to................................. 200.00
Jo Jo the Clown, mk Shawnee 12, 9½", from $475 to.................. 500.00
Little Chef, mc, mk USA, 8½", from $150 to ....:175.00

Muggsy, gold and decals, marked USA or Pat Muggsy USA, minimum value, $800.00. (Photo courtesy Ermagene Westfall)

Owl, mk USA, 11½", from $150 to.. 175.00
Smiley the Pig, bl neckerchief, mk USA, from $150 to............... 175.00
Smiley the Pig, roses, gold & decals, mk USA, from $650 to....... 700.00
Smiley the Pig, w/fly, gold & decals, mk USA, from $800 to 1,000.00
Winnie the Pig, gr, mk Shawnee USA 61, minimum value 1,200.00
Winnie the Pig, w/apples, from $525 to 550.00

Corn Line

Bowl, mixing; King, mk Shawnee 5, 5", from $22 to 25.00
Bowl, vegetable; King or Queen, mk Shawnee 95, 9", from $50 to ...55.00
Casserole, King, lg, mk, Shawnee 74, from $50 to.......................... 60.00
Creamer, Queen, mk Shawnee 70, from $24 to 26.00
Plate, King or Queen, mk Shawnee 68, 10", from $35 to 40.00
Popcorn set, Queen, mk Shawnee 68, 10", from $35 to.................. 40.00

Relish tray, Queen, mk Shawnee 79, from $25 to 30.00
Snack set, Queen, from $350 to 365.00
Sugar shaker, King, mk USA, from $55 to................................. 60.00
Teapot, King or Queen, mk Shawnee 75, 30-oz, from $75 to 85.00

Kitchenware

Canister, HP allover gold, 2-qt, mk USA, from $75 to................. 100.00
Casserole, fruit; mk Shawnee USA 83, from $45 to 50.00
Creamer & sugar bowl, Snowflake, 7-oz, set from $25 to............... 35.00
Grease jar, Fern, w/lid, from $55 to 60.00
Grease jar, Snowflake, w/lid, 3½-oz, from $40 to 45.00
Ice server, Pink Elephant, w/blk or wht collar, ea from $200 to ... 250.00
Matchbox holder, Fern, from $110 to 120.00
Pitcher, Flower & Fern, 4-cup, from $22 to 24.00
Pitcher, Tulip, ball shape, mk USA, 48-oz, from $100 to 150.00
Shakers, Boy Blue & Bo Peep, gold trim, sm, pr from $50 to 55.00
Shakers, Chanticleer, lg, pr from $45 to................................... 50.00
Shakers, cottage, sm, pr from $350 to 375.00
Shakers, Farmer Pigs, gold, sm, pr from $100 to....................... 110.00
Shakers, flower cluster, gold, sm, pr from $55 to 60.00
Shakers, flowerpot, all-gold center, sm, pr from $55 to.................. 60.00
Shakers, Jack & Jill, gold & decals, lg, pr from $200 to................ 225.00
Shakers, Laurel Wreath, lg, pr from $25 to 30.00
Shakers, Muggsy, lg, pr minimum value 175.00
Shakers, Muggsy, sm, pr from $55 to 60.00
Shakers, owl, gr eyes, unmk, sm, pr from $20 to 25.00
Shakers, Smiley, gr neckerchief, lg, pr from $125 to.................... 135.00
Shakers, Smiley & Winnie, clover bud, lg, pr from $200 to 235.00
Shakers, watering cans, sm, pr 26.00
Teapot, elephant, mk USA, 5-cup, from $125 to......................... 135.00
Teapot, Fern, 2-cup, from $75 to 85.00
Teapot, horsehoe design, mk USA, 8-cup, from $40 to.................. 45.00
Teapot, Snowflake, 8-cup, from $60 to 65.00
Utility jar, bucket, w/lid, rnd, mk USA, from $80 to..................... 85.00

Lobsterware

Bowl, baker; open, mk 917, 7", from $35 to............................... 40.00
Bowl, salad; mk 922, from $30 to 35.00
Casserole, Fr; mk 900, 10-oz 20.00
Creamer jug, mk 921, from $45 to.. 50.00
Shakers, claw, mk USA, pr from $35 to 40.00
Shakers, full body, mk USA, pr from $200 to 225.00
Spoon holder, dbl, mk USA 935, 8½", from $225 to..................... 250.00

Valencia

Ashtray... 18.00
Bowl, fruit; w/hdls, 5".. 22.00
Candleholder, bulb style, ea.. 22.00
Coffeepot, regular, no lid, from $35 to 40.00
Creamer, mk Valencia... 20.00
Fork, from $40 to 45.00
Pitcher, ice; mk USA, from $35 to.. 40.00
Plate, chop; 13", from $20 to.. 25.00
Punch bowl, 12", from $45 to.. 50.00
Relish tray, from $130 to... 135.00
Teacup & saucer.. 22.00
Vase, bud.. 20.00

Miscellaneous

Bank, Howdy Doody, mk Bob Smith USA, 6½", from $500 to.... 550.00

Figurine, deer, head up, unmk 100.00
Figurine, donkey, unmk, 6½".. 12.00
Flowerpot w/saucer, flared petals, mk Shawnee USA 466, 5"......... 18.00
Planter, baby skunk, mk Shawnee 512 .... 35.00
Planter, birds on driftwood, mk Shawnee 502, from $45 to............ 50.00
Planter, chick & egg, mk Shawnee USA 730, from $35 to 40.00
Planter, dog & jug, mk USA 610 .... 12.00
Planter, dove & planting dish, w/gold, mk Shawnee 2025 .... 45.00
Planter, hound dog, mk USA 12.00
Planter, rabbit w/turnip, mk USA 703 .... 35.00
Vase, butterfly, mk USA 680, 6"... 16.00
Vase, leaf, w/gold, mk USA 822, 6½"....................................... 40.00
Wall pocket, Scottie dog's head, unmk, from $65 to..................... 75.00
Wall pocket, star shape, mk USA 35.00

Shearwater

Since 1928 generations of the Peter, Walter, and James McConnell Anderson families have been producing figurines and artwares in their studio at Ocean Springs, Mississippi. Their work is difficult to date. Figures from the '20s and '30s won critical acclaim and have continued to be made to the present time. Early marks include a die-stamped 'Shearwater' in a dime-sized circle, a similar ink stamp, and a half-circle mark. Any older item may still be ordered in the same glazes as it was originally produced, so many pieces on the market today may be relatively new. However, the older marks are not currently in use. Currently produced Blacks and pirates figurines are marked with a hand-incised 'Shearwater' and/or a cipher formed with an 'S' whose bottom curve doubles as the top loop of a 'P' formed by the addition of an upright placed below and to the left of the S. Many are dated, '93, for example. These figures are generally valued at $35.00 to $50.00 and are available at the pottery or by mail order. New decorated and carved pieces are very expensive, starting at $400.00 to $500.00 for a six inch pot.

Bookends, pelican, Shoal Blue, after W Anderson design, 9¾" ... 720.00
Bowl, bronze, flared sides, thrown by P Anderson, ca 1930s, 4x9" ..540.00
Bowl, outline of a bird/waves, 4-color on wht, att W Anderson, 8" ...3,600.00
Bowl, waves, blk/cobalt/wht/brn, att W Anderson, 2x6"...........3,820.00
Bowl, 3 tiers of scrolls, blk on wht, salmon int, M Anderson, 4x9" 3,600.00
Bowl vase, Earth/Sea/Sky, emb on turq, W Anderson design, 6x7" .6,000.00
Bust, Mayan boy, beige/celadon mottle, 7" 415.00
Figurine, Black couple dancing, 5¾" 60.00
Figurine, Black lady dancing, 5" 42.00
Figurine, Head Down Goose, Old Field Series, gr/bl, 5x9" 840.00
Figurine, owl, mottled gr/bl running glaze, crescent mk, 7x5".....275.00
Figurine, seagull, incised SP-9Z, 5x9"..................................... 180.00
Figurine, stout woman w/basket on head, turq/bl/yel, 6" 210.00
Figurine, woman cradling infant, cobalt/rutile runny glazes, 7".... 510.00

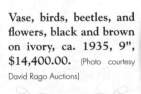

Vase, birds, beetles, and flowers, black and brown on ivory, ca. 1935, 9", $14,400.00. (Photo courtesy David Rago Auctions)

Vase, cvd faces/figures, P Findeisen, 8x2½" 480.00
Vase, Earth/Sea/Sky, emb on gr/tan, W Anderson design, 12x7" .. 10,800.00
Vase, gr/brn matt, hand-thrown, ftd, 6½" 240.00
Vase, lt purple, elongated w/melon ribs, 6¼" 360.00
Vase, lt turq, ovoid w/flared rim, 7¾" 530.00
Vase, prominent finger rings on upper half, wht, P Anderson, 6x3½"... 420.00
Vase, sea gr mottle, ovoid, 8" 415.00

Sheet Music

Sheet music is often collected more for its colorful lithographed covers, rather than for the music itself. Transportation songs (which have pictures or illustrations of trains, ships, and planes), ragtime and blues, comic characters (especially Disney), sports, political, and expositions are eagerly sought after. Much of the sheet music on the market today is valued at under $5.00; some of the better examples are listed here. For more information refer to *The Sheet Music Reference and Price Guide, Second Edition*, by Anna Marie Guiheen and Marie-Reine A. Pafik. Values are given for examples in at least near-mint condition.

At the Five & Ten Cent Store, Marvin Lee & Jean Walz, 1915 .... 15.00
Ballad of John & Yoko, John Lennon & Paul McCartney, 1969.... 25.00
Boy Scouts' Dream, V Paul Jones, 1915 .... 25.00
Carnival King, Ralph K Elicker & ET Paull, 1911 .... 35.00
Coal Smoke, Clarence H St Johns, 1904 .... 15.00
Cuban Independence, CD Henninger, 1898.............................. 15.00
Daddy Wants Someone Too, Rowe, 1909 .... 15.00
Dashing Cavaliers, ET Paull, 1938....................................... 35.00
Dixie Daisy, Halsey K Mohr, 1911....................................... 10.00
Drink Up, Boys; Arthur West, 1890....................................... 15.00
Elite Syncopations, Scott Joplin, 1902 .... 50.00
Every Little Dog Must Have His Day, Chauncey Olcott, 1902 ...... 10.00
Excelsior Rag, Joseph F Lamb, 1909..................................... 15.00
Fallen by the Wayside, Charles K Harris, 1892......................... 15.00
First Heart Throbs, Rich Eilenberg, 1902 .... 15.00
Flirting in the Twilight, Kemble & Braham, 1870..................... 15.00
For Your Country & My Country, Irving Berlin, 1917 .... 15.00
Gay Chauffeur, Valentine, transportation theme, 1907................. 20.00
Girl Who Is Loved by All, Tony Stanford, 1897.......................... 15.00

Golden Girl of My Dreams, Geo Spink, cover artist: Barbelle, 1927, $10.00.
(Photo courtesy Anna Marie Guiheen and Marie-Reine A. Pafik)

Goodnight Moonlight, Ed Rose & Frank Magine, 1929................. 15.00
Heaven's Artillery, Harry J Lincoln & J Dittmar, 1914................. 30.00
Hello Baby, Edward Harrigan & David Braham, 1884.................. 15.00
Hobomoko, Ernest Reeves, Indian, 1907 .... 25.00
I Dreamt My Daddy Came Home, Joe Darcey & Lew Porter, 1919 .. 15.00
I Saw Mommy Kissing Santa Claus, Tommie Connor, 1952 .... 10.00
Jockey Hat & Feather, Julia Brodwig, 1860............................. 50.00
Judy, Hoagy Carmichael & Sammy Lerner, 1934....................... 10.00
Keep On Walking, Irving Berlin, 1913 .... 15.00
Kentucky Babe, RH Buck & Geibel, 1897................................ 15.00

Lady Bird, Cha, Cha, Cha, Norman Rockwell cover, 1968............ 25.00
Lazy Luke, George L Philpot, 1905 .... 15.00
Love Among the Roses, Delahanty & Coffin, 1869 .... 15.00
Oh! That Cello, Charlie Chaplin, 1916 .... 15.00
Put My Little Shoes Away, Mitchell & Pratt, 1873 .... 15.00
Sleepy Song, Carrie Jacobs Bond, 1912.................................. 15.00
Sweet Meats, Percy Wenrich, 1907 .... 25.00
Sweet Suzanne, Jos Geo Gilbert, 1928.....................................5.00
Sweetheart's a Pretty Name When It Is Y-O-U, Leslie & Piantadosi, 1909... 15.00
Swipsey Cake Walk, Arthur Marshal & Scott Joplin, 1900 .... 50.00
Take a Little Tip From Father, Irving Berlin & Ted Snyder, 1912.. 15.00
Take Me Around Again, Ed Rose & Kerry Mills, 1907 .... 10.00
Tess of the Storm Country, Patrick/Allan, Pickford photo, 1915 ... 16.00
Thanks for the Lobster, Clarence Jones, 1914 .... 10.00
That Old Irish Mother of Mine, Jerome/Von Tilzer/Mack, 1920.......6.00
They've Won Every Nation's Battles But Their Own, Shields & Ball, 1910...15.00
Underneath the Cotton Moon, Sam Lewis & George Meyer, 1913.. 15.00
Up Dar in de Sky, Davis, Black Face, 1892 .... 25.00
Victory, TA Wilson Bard & MK Jerome, WWI, 1918 .... 10.00
Voice of the Violet, C Olcott, musical: Old Limrick Town, 1902 .. 15.00
We'll Do Our Share, Brown/Harriman/Egan, WWI, cover artist: Walton....10.00
We're All Going Calling on the Kaiser, Caddigan & Brennen, 1918..25.00
What's the Use of Going Home?, Clarke/McCarthy/Monaco, artist: Symbol.. 10.00
When I Get Back Again to Bonnie Scotland, Harry Lauder, 1908 ... 10.00
Where the Blue of the Night Meets Gold of the Day, Turk/Crosby/Ahlert... 15.00
Yacht Club, Barker, 1895, transportation theme............................ 10.00
Yesterday, Chas Harrison & Monte Wilhite, 1926 ....7.00
You'll Have To Get Off & Walk, Dave Reed, 1907, transportation theme..20.00
You're a Grand Old Flag, Geo Cohan, movie: Yankee Doodle Dandy, cast.12.00
Your Kiss, Auld & Cates, movie: To Catch a Thief, photo: Kelly/Grant....3.00
Zip-A-Dee-Doo-Dah, Wrubel & Gilbert, movie: Song of the South (Disney).. 15.00
Ziz-March, Feltman & ET Paull, 1907, artists: Paull & March 5.00

Shelley

In 1872 Joseph Shelley became partners with James Wileman, owner of Foley China Works, thus creating Wileman & Co. in Stoke-on-Trent. Twelve years later James Wileman withdrew from the company, though the firm continued to use his name until 1925 when it became known as Shelley Potteries, Ltd. Like many successful nineteenth-century English potteries, this firm continued to produce useful household wares as well as dinnerware of considerable note. In 1896 the beautiful Dainty White shape was introduced, and it is regarded by many as synonymous with the name Shelley. In addition to the original Dainty (six-flute) design, other lovely shapes were produced: Ludlow (14-flute), Oleander (petal shape), Stratford (12-flute), Queen Anne (with eight angular panels), Ripon (with its distinctive pedestal), and the 1930s shapes of Vogue, Eve, and Regent. Though often overlooked, striking earthenware was produced under the direction of Frederick Rhead and later Walter Slater and his son Eric. Many notable artists contributed their talents in designing unusual, attractive wares: Rowland Morris, Mabel Lucie Attwell, and Hilda Cowham, to name but a few.

In 1966 Allied English Potteries acquired control of the Shelley Company, and by 1967 the last of the exquisite Shelley China had been produced to honor remaining overseas orders. In 1971 Allied English Potteries merged with the Doulton group.

It had to happen: Shelley forgeries! Chris Davenport, author of *Shelley Pottery, The Later Years*, reports seeing Mocha-shape cups and saucers with the Shelley mark. However, on close examination it is evident that the mark has been applied to previously unmarked wares too poorly done to have ever left the Shelley Pottery. This Shelley mark can actually be 'felt,' as the refiring is not done at the correct temperature to allow it to be fully incorporated into the glaze. (Beware! These items are often seen on Internet auction sites.)

Some Shelley patterns (Dainty Blue, Bridal Rose, Blue Rock) have been seen on Royal Albert and Queensware pieces. These companies are part of the Royal Doulton Group.

Note: Measurements for objects with lids are measured to the top of the finial unless stated otherwise. Be aware that Rose Spray and Bridal Rose are the same pattern. Our advisor for this category is Lila Shrader; she is listed in the Directory under California.

Key:
MLA — Mabel Lucie Attwell RPFMN — Rose, Pansy, Forget-Me-Not
QA — Queen Anne shape   W — Wileman, pre-1910

Ashtray, Lily of the Valley, 3 rests, #13822, 5½" dia 23.00
Bell, Dainty Blue, wht hdl w/bl decor, 5½" 265.00
Biscuit barrel, Oriental decor, w/lid, Late Foley, 5½" 95.00
Bowl, cereal; Dainty Yellow, #052/Y, 6¼" 55.00
Bowl, rimmed soup; Primrose Chintz, Oleander shape, 7½" 100.00
Bowl, slop; Fern print, Lily shape, #5900, W, 3½x6" 92.00
Butter dish, Rosebud, Dainty shape, ¼-lb 225.00
Butter dish, RPFMN, Dainty shape, rnd w/dome lid 135.00
Butter pat, Campanula, Dainty shape, #13886, 3¾" 110.00
Butter pat, Dainty Mauve, not Dainty shape, #051/M, 3¼" 100.00
Butter pat, Heather, 3¼" 36.00
Butter pat, Rose Trellis, pk trim, 3¼" 30.00
Butter pat, Wild Anemone, Dainty shape, 3¼" 138.00
Cake plate, Rosebud, Dainty shape, ped ft, #13426, 3¼x9" 160.00
Cake stand, Blue Iris, QA, enameled bl iris+fruit, #11561, 8½" ... 550.00
Cake stand, Dainty Blue, 4⅞x8⅞" 265.00
Candy/sweet dish, Blue Iris, Dainty shape w/tab hdls, #11561, 5x4" .. 185.00
Candy/sweet dish, Paisley, Dainty shape w/tab hdls, 5x4" 188.00
Candy/sweet dish, Pansy Chintz, Dainty shape, 4¾" dia 36.00
Chamber pot, Butterfly decor, w/hdl, #8265, Late Foley, 11½" dia ... 88.00
Cheese dome & base, Blue Rock, Dainty shape, #13591, 4¾x8¼" ... 635.00
Child's feeding dish, Pussy Cat, Where Have You Been..., MLA, 8½" .. 162.00
Children's ware, creamer, Little Boy Blue, W, 4" 55.00
Children's ware, teapot, duck w/bl jacket, striped scarf, MLA, 7¼" 400.00
Cigarette holder, Lilac Time, Dainty shape, #14293, 2" 44.00
Coffeepot, Archway of Flowers, cobalt, #11627, 7¼" 825.00
Coffeepot, Rock Garden, long slim hdl, minimal graceful spout, 7½" ... 250.00
Coffeepot, Rosebud, Dainty shape, #13426, 7" 200.00
Cream soup, Bridal Rose, Oleander shape, hdls, w/liner 20.00
Creamer, Wild Flower, Regent shape, #13668, 3½" 60.00
Creamer & sugar bowl, Dainty Blue, #051/28, from $78 to 110.00
Creamer & sugar bowl, pk floral transfer, Alexandra shape, w/lid, W ... 160.00
Creamer & sugar bowl, Primrose Chintz, Cambridge shape 55.00
Creamer & sugar bowl, Trees & Sunset, QA, #11828 .... 58.00
Crested ware, airplane/biplane, City of London, 5¾" L 180.00
Crested ware, fishing creel, Hythe, A Good Catch, 3¾" L 12.00
Crested ware, Kathleen Mavourneen figurine, Maidenhead, 4¼" ... 265.00
Crested ware, Patrol Boat Hastings, skipper at wheel, 4½" L 55.00
Crested ware, Richmond Surrey, dog in kennel, 3" 24.00
Cup & saucer, Baker Chocolate, lady w/gold, Mocha shape, Late Foley .. 27.00
Cup & saucer, bl baskets of flowers w/garlands/gold trim, Ludlow shape .. 72.50
Cup & saucer, blk chintz w/rich gold, Ripon shape, #14156 ..... 1,115.00
Cup & saucer, Blue Daisy Chintz, Henley shape, #13204 .... 58.00
Cup & saucer, Blue Rock, Canterbury shape, #13591, 1¾" 115.00
Cup & saucer, Dainty Mauve, #051/M 125.00
Cup & saucer, Dainty Pink, #051/P 100.00
Cup & saucer, Dainty Pink, Dainty shape, #14075/P, mini 1,075.00
Cup & saucer, Dainty Yellow, #051/Y 345.00
Cup & saucer, demitasse; 'letter j' decor/mc flowers, Mode shape .. 112.00
Cup & saucer, Heavenly Blue, Ripon shape, #14165 .... 175.00
Cup & saucer, HP Oriental flowers on blk matt w/gold, Ripon shape .. 82.00
Cup & saucer, lav w/Hulmes Lowestoft chintz in cup, Oleander, #14033 .. 150.00

Cup & saucer, Lilac Time, Dainty shape, #14293 .... 110.00
Cup & saucer, Primrose, Westminster shape, #13430, mini 295.00
Cup & saucer, Serenity, Westminster shape, #13908, mini 200.00
Cup & saucer, Summer Glory, lav w/#13418 in cup, ftd Oleander shape .. 110.00
Cup & saucer, Violets, Dainty shape, #1381, mini, 1⅜" 800.00
Cup & saucer, Wine Grape, Westminster shape, #13907, mini ... 345.00
Cup & saucer, Yutoi, Canterbury shape, #13868, mini, 1⅝" 110.00
Egg cup, Wildflowers, Dainty shape, no ped, #13668, 1¾" 22.50
Egg cup set, Lilac Time, Dainty shape, #14293, 4 sm 1¾" cups+stand .. 425.00
Figurine, Boo-Boo (elf-like) w/watering can, MLA, 3¾" 645.00
Figurine, Toucan perched on rock, blk/gr/bl, 8" 515.00
Ginger jar, Harmony, cream/tan/brn/gray, w/lid, 8½" 30.00
Gravy/sauceboat, Rambler Rose, Dainty shape, #13900, 6¾" 82.00
Gravy/sauceboat, Sheraton, #13291, w/liner (2 pcs) 65.00
Horseradish pot, Dainty White, slotted, 2½", +spoon & underplate .. 65.00
Hot water pot, Blossom, Dainty shape, w/lid, #13429, 5½" 60.00
Jug, Fern print, Lily shape, #5900, W, 4½" 100.00
Jug, storks on tangerine, Art Deco, #8589, 4½" 30.00
Loving cup, Edward VIII, hdls, 1937, 4½" 50.00
Mold, food/jelly; graceful flowing form, utilitarian ware, 5¾" 25.00
Mold, food/jelly; spirals, 5x7", from $20 to 35.00
Mug, coronation; George VI & princesses, 1927, 3", MIB 12.50
Mustache cup & saucer, cartouch scenes of seasons, Wileman, pre-1892 .. 74.00
Mustard pot, Shamrocks, plain shape, w/slotted lid, 4", +underplate ... 58.00
Napkin rings, Bridal Rose, Rosebud, Primrose, Violets, set of 4 ... 200.00
Plate, bread & butter; Blue Iris, QA, #11561, 6¼" 20.00
Plate, bread & butter; Georgian, #13289, 6" 25.00
Plate, bread & butter; Primrose Chintz, 6" 24.00
Plate, chop; American Brookline, Dainty shape, 13½" 210.00
Plate, dinner; Daffodil Time, butter yel border, 10¾" 30.00
Plate, dinner; Dainty Mauve, #051/M, 10¾", from $125 to 185.00
Plate, salad/dessert; Dainty Green, 8¼", from $110 to 240.00
Plate, salad/dessert; Maytime Chintz, 8" 70.00
Plate, salad/dessert; Wind Flower, Dainty shape, #14032, 8¼" 32.50
Platter, Begonia, Dainty shape, #13427, 12x9" 90.00
Platter, Georgian, rich gold trim, #13289, 12x9" 65.00
Powder dish, emb high-gloss fruit on lid, matt body, #8615, 5" 160.00
Ring holder, blk cloisonne, #8320, 3¼" dia 135.00
Rose bowl, Kingfisher, mc birds on blk matt, #8656, 6½" 85.00
Sign, display; Shelley in block letters, porc, Deco era, 1¼x3⅛" ... 290.00
Tea & toast set, Regency, Dainty shape, cup+8" rnd tray 45.00
Tea & toast set, Rosebud, Dainty shape, #13426, cup+5x8" oval tray .. 65.00
Tea & toast set, Shamrocks, Dainty shape, #14114, cup+8" dia tray .. 75.00
Teapot, blk cloisonne, QA, #2087, 5½" 240.00
Teapot, children peek from under big top, Helen Cowhan 425.00
Teapot, Cloisello w/gold trim, recessed lid, #6332, Late Foley, 4½" ... 70.00
Teapot, Dainty Blue, #051/28, 6½" 425.00
Teapot, Dainty White, 6½", from $100 to 145.00
Teapot, Drifting Leaves w/platinum trim, 6¼" 130.00
Teapot, Primrose Chintz, Henley shape, #13586, 6½" 185.00
Teapot, Shamrock, Dainty shape, graceful spout, #14114, 5¼" 250.00
Teapot, Stocks, #13428, 6" 185.00
Teapot, Wild Flowers, Dainty shape, #13668, 6½" 355.00
Teapot stand, Dainty White, oval, 6½" 75.00

Teapot with underplate, Bands and Lines, Regent shape, $250.00. (Photo courtesy Skinner Inc. Auctioneers & Appraisers of Antiques & Fine Art)

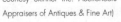

Toast rack, Stocks, Oleander shape, 3 bars, #13428, 4¼x6" 118.00
Tray, sandwich; Harebell, Oleander shape, tab hdls, 11½x4½"....... 75.00
Trio, Block pattern, Vogue shape, #11785, c/s+6½" plate.............. 420.00
Trio, bright HP flowers, Mode, butterfly hdl, #11757, c/s+6½" plate..395.00
Trio, Cameo Print, Snowdrop shape, #9334, W, c/s+7¼" plate 110.00
Trio, Dainty Brown, #051/48, c/s+8" plate 190.00
Trio, Garland of Flowers on pk, QA, #11312, c/s+5½" sq plate..... 175.00
Trio, Georgian w/gr border/gold, Richmond shape, #13360, c/s+8" plate .. 50.00
Trio, Harebell, Oleander shape, #13590, c/s+7" plate.................... 35.00
Trio, Indian Peony, Gainsborough, enamel decor, #13216, c/s+8" plate 60.00
Trio, Marguerite w/rich gold, Ripon shape, #13455, c/s+8" plate.............. 130.00
Trio, Paradise, Daisy shape, W, #6237, c/s+7" plate 85.00
Trio, Summer Glory Chintz on ivory, Henley shape, #13455, c/s+7" plate..115.00
Tureen & stand, Sunrise & Tall Trees, QA, hdls, w/lid, #11678.... 185.00
Vase, HP mc roses band on blk matt, #8103, 13" 90.00
Vase, Intarsio, tall slim neck, ball-shape base, #3006, W, 7¾" 400.00
Vase, Jazz Circles, mc on blk matt, Art Deco, 5¾" 60.00
Vase, Moonlight, slim, 5x2¾" (neck opening)............................. 150.00
Wall pocket, Harmony Drip, yel & orange shades, #8742, 7" 92.00

Silhouettes

Silhouette portraits were made by positioning the subject between a bright light and a sheet of white drawing paper. The resulting shadow was then traced and cut out, the paper mounted over a contrasting color and framed. The hollow-cut process was simplified by an invention called the Physiognotrace, a device that allowed tracing and cutting to be done in one operation. Experienced silhouette artists could do full-length figures, scenics, ships, or trains freehand. Some of the most famous of these artists were Charles Peale Polk, Charles Wilson Peale, William Bache, Doyle, Edouart, Chamberlain, Brown, and William King. Though not often seen, some silhouettes were completely painted or executed in wax. Examples listed here are hollow-cut unless another type is described and assumed to be in excellent condition unless noted otherwise.

Key:
c/p — cut and pasted   l — laid paper
fl — full length   p — profile
hc — hand colored   wc — water color

Boy, ink p, gold inked hair, identified, 1818, 6¼x5½"+fr.............. 200.00
Elderly lady knitting at table, ink & gouache, fl, foxing, 12x10".. 800.00
Facing couple: man w/open book, lady w/fan, paper on silk, 9x13".. 470.00
Girl wearing bonnet holds bird, fl, c/p, hc, J Gapp, 1835, 11x9"+fr....435.00
Lady in bonnet w/lacy accents, p, 7½x5½"+fr............................... 325.00
Lady in dress & pantaloons, fl, eglomise mat & fr, 5" 435.00
Lady sitting, fl, c/p, ink-wash bkground, faint stain, 14x9⅜" 250.00
Lady w/fancy bonnet, p, foxing/stains, 6x4" gilt fr 115.00
Lady w/hair comb on wood-block print body, fl, c/p, 6x5" fr 460.00
Lady w/red flower, p to waist, c/p, wc details, 5x5" brass fr 300.00
Man, bust-length p, c/p, wc/graphite details, early 1800s, 3x2"+fr ..765.00
Man, paper on silk, Peale's Museum, +gilt Carvers & Gilders fr: 8x10"..940.00
Man, wc/ink p on l, bl wc coat, identified/1824, 6x5" fr 230.00
Man holding top hat, fl, c/p, ink details, Hubbard/1862, 16x12"... 800.00
Man standing, fl, c/p, blk/gold ink details, Herve, 14x11" fr......... 800.00

Silver

Coin Silver

During colonial times in America, the average household could not afford items made of silver, but those fortunate enough to have accumula-

tions of silver coins (900 parts silver/100 parts alloy) took them to the local silversmith who melted them down and made the desired household article as requested. These pieces bore the owner's monogram and often the maker's mark, but the words 'Coin Silver' did not come into use until 1830. By 1860 the standard was raised to 925 parts silver/75 parts alloy and the word 'Sterling' was added. Coin silver came to an end about 1900.

Key: t-oz — troy ounce

Albert Coles, NY; ladle, eng/chased scrolls/flowers, wood hdl, 17"...2,585.00
Am, teapot, plain oval w/reeded borders, str spout, eng crest, 11-t-oz...250.00
Am, teaspoons, fiddle hdl, rnd shoulders, oval bowl, 5½", 3 for ... 120.00
Baldwin Gardiner, NY; beaker, beaded bands/acanthus at lip, 3½"... 700.00
Ball Black & Co, sugar bowl, repousse acorns/oak leaves, 6x6"..1,120.00
Caldwell & Co, Phila; sugar bowl, pear form w/scroll hdls, lid, 10x9"...590.00
David Kinsey, OH; teaspoons, uptrn hourglass hdl, shouldered, 10 for...150.00
E&D Kinsey, OH; soup spoon, uptrn wavy fiddle-type hdl, set of 6....235.00
Eoff & Shephard, NY City; teapot, lobed pear w/repousse floral, 9"...800.00
Gorham, beaker, shield w/name, engine-trn decor, 1860, 3¾x3" .650.00
Gorham, tazza, Renaissance Revival, 3 creatures as legs, 32-t-oz...2,350.00

Hyde & Goodrich, New Orleans; water pitcher, repousse panels, presentation, hollow-cast scroll handle, 11", 27 troy ounce, $4,600.00. (Photo courtesy Neal Auction Co. Auctioneers & Appraisers of Fine Art)

Jesse Churchill, Boston; beaker, reeded band at base, mongram, 3" ...1,120.00
John McMullin, Phila; cream pot, beaded rim/eng bands, 5½" 825.00
Jones Ball & Poor, Boston; tea caddy, repousse cartouch, 1840s, 6" ...700.00
Obadiah Rich, Boston; repousse floral/scrolls, leaf-cap spout, 7x11"..1,295.00
Paul Revere, tablespoon, eng w/initials, 8¾", EX...................... 8,625.00
Samuel Wilmot, SC; pitcher, repousse/chased floral, scroll hdl, 12"...1,645.00
Wm Forbes, salver, laurel band, 4 scroll ft, 1855, 15x11", 26-t-oz... 1,650.00

Flatware

Silver flatware is being collected today either to replace missing pieces of heirloom sets or in lieu of buying new patterns, by those who admire and appreciate the style and quality of the older ware. Prices vary from dealer to dealer; some pieces are harder to find and are therefore more expensive. Items such as olive spoons, cream ladles, lemon forks, etc., once thought a necessary part of a silver service, may today be slow to sell; as a result, dealers may price them low and make up the difference on items that sell more readily. Many factors enter into evaluation. Popular patterns may be high due to demand though easily found, while scarce patterns may be passed over by collectors who find them difficult to reassemble. If pieces are monogrammed, deduct 20% (for rare, ornate patterns) to 30% (for common, plain pieces). Place settings generally come in three sizes: dinner, place, and luncheon, with the dinner size generally more expensive. In general, dinner knives are 9½" long, place knives, 9" to 9⅛", and luncheon knives, 8¾" to 8⅞". Dinner forks measure 7⅜" to 7½", place forks, 7¼" to 7⅜", and luncheon forks, 6⅞" to 7⅛". Our advisor for this category is Rick Spencer; he is listed in the Directory under Utah.

Acorn, Geo Jensen, pickle fork, 2-tine, 6"	114.00
Adolphus, Mt Vernon, chip beef fork, gold wash	64.00
Adolphus, Mt Vernon, dessert/pickle fork	32.00
Afterglow, Oneida, salad fork	18.00
Afterglow, Oneida, teaspoon	14.00
Alexandra, D&H, iced tea spoon	28.00
Barocco, Wallace, butter knife, flat hdl	32.00
Barocco, Wallace, place spoon, 6⅞"	37.00
Bead, Whiting, fish serving knife, 10½"	140.00
Belle Rose, Oneida, cream ladle	16.00
Belle Rose, Oneida, place spoon	35.00
Blossomtime, Int'l, cheese serving knife	20.00
Blossomtime, Int'l, salad fork	21.00
Burgundy, Reed & Barton, butter knife, hollow hdl	24.00
Burgundy, Reed & Barton, cocktail fork	21.00
Candlelight, Towle, butter knife, hollow hdl	20.00
Candlelight, Towle, cocktail fork	15.00
Celeste, Gorham, pastry knife, hollow hdl	29.00
Celeste, Gorham, sauce ladle	20.00
Chateau Rose, Alvin, sugar spoon	14.00
Chateau Rose, Alvin, 4-pc dinner place setting, modern blade	83.00
Chippendale, Towle, dessert spoon, 6¾"	30.00
Danish Baroque, Towle, cold meat fork, 9¼"	59.00
Danish Baroque, Towle, tablespoon	60.00
Dawn Star, Wallace, place fork, 7¼"	22.00
Dawn Star, Wallace, place spoon, 7¼"	23.00
Fontana, Towle, iced tea spoon	19.00
Fontana, Towle, place fork	24.00
Forget Me Not, Stieff, cream soup spoon, 6½"	40.00
Forget Me Not, Stieff, vegetable serving spoon, 8½"	112.00
Georgian, Towle, beef serving fork, 6½"	225.00
Georgian, Towle, youth fork	75.00
Gossamer, Gorham, cocktail fork	29.00
Gossamer, Gorham, sugar spoon	22.00
Grand Baroque, Wallace, service for 10+11 servers, in chest	1,700.00
Homewood, Stieff, place spoon, 6⅝"	32.00
Imperial Queen, Whiting, berry fork, 2-tine	52.00
Imperial Queen, Whiting, soup/oyster ladle, 10½"	400.00
Impero, Wallace Italian, dinner knife, modern blade, 9½"	24.00
Irene, International, pierced olive spoon, 8"	80.00
John Alden, Watson, teaspoon	12.00
King Edward, Gorham, flat hdl butter spreader	170.00
King Edward, Gorham, steak knife	30.00
Kingsley, Kirk, 4-pc place setting	75.00
Leonore, Manchester, luncheon fork, 7"	21.00
Melrose, Gorham, cold meat fork	22.00
Melrose, Gorham, luncheon fork, 7⅛"	21.00
Melrose, Gorham, tablespoon	56.00
Mythologique, Gorham, ladle, gilt bowl, Gorham, 1899, 12½"	700.00
Mythologique, Gorham, service for 12, Gorham, 50 pcs	3,235.00
Old English, Towle, parfait/sherbet spoon, 6⅜"	33.00
Peachtree Manor, Towle, place fork, 7¼"	22.00
Peachtree Manor, Towle, tablespoon	48.00
Rosecrest, Alvin, cream soup	15.00
Rosecrest, Alvin, tablespoon	29.00
Royal Rose, International, pie server, hollow hdl	40.00
Stieff Rose, Steiff, lettuce fork	75.00
Stieff Rose, Steiff, butter spreader, flat hdl	16.50
Stieff Rose, Steiff, salad fork	25.00
Washington, Wallace, mayonnaise ladle	35.00
Washington, Wallace, pickle fork, 7½"	25.00
William & Mary, Lunt, cold meat fork	35.00
William & Mary, Lunt, grapefruit spoon	19.00
William & Mary, Lunt, teaspoon, 6"	14.00

Hollow Ware

Until the middle of the nineteenth century, the silverware produced in America was custom made on order of the buyer directly from the silversmith. With the rise of industrialization, factories sprung up that manufactured silverware for retailers who often added their trademark to the ware. Silver ore was mined in abundance, and demand spurred production. Changes in style occurred at the whim of fashion. Repousse decoration (relief work) became popular about 1885, reflecting the ostentatious preference of the Victorian era. Later in the century, Greek, Etruscan, and several classic styles found favor. Today the Art Deco styles of this century are very popular with collectors.

In the listings that follow, manufacturer's name or trademark is noted first; in lieu of that information, listings are by country or item. See also Tiffany, Silver.

A Rasch, Philadelphia; pitcher, eng/emb floral, ftd baluster, 13"	9,400.00
AT, London; creamer, helmet shape, sq base, eng shield, 1796, 3-t-oz	200.00
B&M, service plate, eng Greek key banded wide rims, 12", set of 12	2,235.00
Bigelow Kennard & Co, pitcher, chased/emb foliage, 1900s, 8", 32-t-oz	1,765.00
Black Starr Frost, crumber, monogram/foliage scrolls/shells, +tray	500.00
Cartier, bowl, oval, short openwork ft w/'lazy S' design, 5x12"	1,410.00
CE Adler, goblet, bell form on trumpet base, 20th C, 7", 8 for	400.00
Chatterley, Birmingham; punch bowl, repousse floral, ca 1791, 7x11"	925.00
China, man stands on sm cart w/pole balancing basket & castor, 3"	440.00
CK 925, center bowl, ribbed body/ft, flower-topped hdls, 34" L, 164-t-oz	2,300.00
Dominick & Haff, sugar shaker, rococo repousse, dome lid, 6½", pr	1,500.00
Elkington & Co, claret jug, ewer form, Minerva mask, 1875, 31-t-oz	2,235.00
Elkington & Co, tea tray, oval w/shaped & scalloped rim, hdls, 31"	3,000.00
Emes/Barnard, London; teapot, Geo III, mushroom finial, 1811, 12-t-oz	385.00
FD, mug, repousse, gold-wash int, 4¼"	375.00
French, chocolate pot, rooster form, fruit/etc emb, 1780s, 9x9"	4,890.00
Georg Jensen, bowl, flared rim, ftd, #17B/Nissen, 5⅛", 9-t-oz	1,000.00
GMCo, Birmingham; kettle on stand, invt pear shape, swing hdl, 15"	8,800.00
Goodnow & Jenks, Colonial Revival, fluted/slender forms, 6-pc	3,200.00
Gorham, tea service, orb w/molded spreading ft, 20th C, 5-pc	1,000.00
Gorham, tea/coffee, eng flowers, 2 pots/bowl+cr/sug, +29" SP tray	1,150.00
Grogan, center bowl, down-trn rim w/leaves, rnd ftd base, 15" dia	800.00
Hester Bateman, pepper pot, baluster w/acorn finial, bead trim, 5¾"	750.00
J Sanders, London; salver, Geo II, shell rim, 1743, 13-t-oz	585.00
JC Ltd, coffee service, rococo repousse lower portion, 1954, 7-pc	2,350.00
Joseph Angell, teapot, Geo III, leaves relief to body/ft, crest, 6x10"	1,000.00
Joseph Clare, London; caudle cup, Geo I, cherub mask, 1718, 4⅜"	3,000.00
Kirk & Son, EX repousse, 3 pots/warmer/waste bowl+cr/sug+tray,281-t-oz	16,000.00
Kirk & Son, hot water pot, repousse, tall goat-head hdls, 13x11", EX	4,000.00
Lion w/N, box, repousse putto musician on lid, chased body, 2½", pr	345.00

London, cake basket, bright cut, George III, 1781, 11x14", $2,875.00. (Photo courtesy Neal Auction Company Auctioneers & Appraisers of Fine Art)

London WBJ (Messrs Barnard), punch bowl, repousse, ftd, 10x17"	6,720.00
MF Hirsch, coffee/tea service, Blossom design, 7-pc, 203-t-oz	3,985.00
MH&Co, tureen, chased w/ram's head ea side, +underplate & lid, 42-t-oz	1,495.00

N (Fr), bowl, repousse musicians, int: flowers, hdls, 13" L 690.00
Oriental, pitcher w/lid, appl dragon/shield, 12", +12 cups, 87-t-oz...1,200.00
R Sibley, London; kettle on stand, serpentine spout, 1820s, 57-t-oz...995.00
RB (R Bigge?), London; tankard, Georgian, ear hdl, 1724, 26-t-oz...2,465.00
RB (Robert Breading), serving dish, gadrooned w/leaf hdls, w/lid, 14". 1,320.00
RD, DH (Robert & David Hennell), bowl, scroll band, monogram, 4x7" ..840.00
Reed & Barton, center bowl, Salem, lobed rim, 1941, 4x12", 32-t-oz.. 300.00
Reed & Barton, coffee/tea set, dmn pattern, 2 pots+cr/sug 1,645.00
Robert Hennell, cake basket, Geo III, rtcl ft/oval rim, crest, 15" L..3,800.00
S Kirk & Son, bowl, repousse foliage, stem/ft, 1880-90, 10", 26-t-oz. 1,115.00
S Kirk & Son, serving dish, dolphin hdls, w/lid, 1880-90, 15½" L..5,000.00
S&J Crespell, London; shafing dish, Geo III, w/lid, 1768, 56-t-oz..2,115.00
SH (English), coffeepot, paneled pear form w/eng crest/elks, 1802, 12"..1,320.00
Shreve & Co, San Francisco; bowl, emb iris, lobed rim, 20th C, 13".. 415.00
T Whipplham, mug, baluster w/eng crest, 1750-51, 3¾" 585.00
Tane, Mexico City; coffee/tea set, chased balusters, 5-pc, 118-t-oz..3,250.00
Tenney, basket, repousse hdl: boy climbs beanstalk, ftd, 6x7" 485.00
TP in crown w/in oval, tray, Chpndl, 3 animal hoof ft, 6" dia....... 520.00
V in shield w/crown, pounce pot, egg shaped/rtcl, 8-side base, 6" ...180.00
W Fountain, London; saucepan, Geo III, tapered cylinder, 1802, 4" dia. 350.00
Whiting, pitcher, hammered finish, high loop hdl, 1918, 9", 21-t-oz. 585.00
WL, London; oval w/ribbed sides, 1726 mk, 9" L 5,635.00
Wm Chawner, London; ladle, soup/punch; Geo IV, 1826, 13", 6-t-oz..575.00
Wm Hunter, London; pitcher, Geo II, pear shape, 1749, 32-t-oz ..9,985.00
Wm Spratling, coffeepot, stepped dome lid, wooden hdl, 7", +cr/sug... 2,935.00
Wm Spratling, pot, long spout, wooden side hdl, 6¾", +cr/sug .. 1,880.00
WP (English), bowl, crest/lions eng, oval w/hinged hdls, 11" L, EX, pr ..4,320.00

Silver Overlay

The silver overlay glass made since the 1880s was decorated with a cut-out pattern of sterling silver applied to the surface of the ware.

Bottle, scent; gr w/floral o/l, worn silver lid stuck in place, 2½" 90.00
Decanter, cranberry, heavy o/l of grapes & leaves dtd 1877, 14", EX..2,415.00
Decanter, crystal, floral vines/cartouch o/l, ball body/finial, 6x5".. 550.00
Decanter, crystal, grapes/leaves o/l on body & stopper, flared, 9"...1,610.00
Decanter, crystal, scroll/initaled reserve o/l, Gorham, flat sides, 9". 1,300.00
Decanter, gr, floral o/l at neck, wide gr-cut-to-clear base, 10"....3,220.00
Decanter, gr, pineapples/leaves o/l, simple silver stopper, 11"....2,300.00
Decanter, perfume; crystal w/heavy scroll & floral o/l, #1346, 6x6"..720.00
Jar, blk w/o/l Deco bird & floral, ftd, w/lid, att Cambridge, 10".... 185.00
Pitcher, cranberry, heavy trellis/vine o/l, eagle mk, 10", +wine stem..900.00
Vase, bl w/floral o/l, 4-lobe rim, long neck w/low width, 8".......... 750.00
Vase, bud; cranberry w/floral & bow o/l, bulbous top, Alvin, 8"...950.00
Vase, crystal frost w/floral o/l, #52/99 Sterling, 7¾" 300.00
Vase, gr w/Nouveau iris o/l, chased/eng, int diaper pattern, 12" .. 1,650.00
Wine, ruby w/grapes o/l & shield-like logo, Pat PO32, 4¾" 425.00

Silverplate

Silverplated flatware is becoming the focus of attention for many of today's collectors. Demand is strong for early, ornate patterns, and prices have continued to rise steadily over the past five years. Our values are based on pieces in excellent or restored/resilvered condition. Serving pieces are priced to reflect the values of examples in complete original condition, with knives retaining their original blades. If pieces are monogrammed, deduct from 20% (for rare, ornate patterns) to 30% (for common, plain pieces). Our advisor for this category is Rick Spencer; he is listed in the Directory under Utah. For more information we recommend *Silverplated Flatware, Revised Fourth Edition*, by Tere Hagan. See also Railroadiana; Silverplate.

Flatware

Adam, Community, fruit knife 9.00
Adam, Community, luncheon fork, 7" 6.00
Ancestrial - 1847, Rogers, butter spreader, flat hdl 8.00
Ancestrial - 1847, Rogers, 3-pc roast carving set 100.00
Avon-1847, Rogers, beef serving fork................................ 16.00
Baroque, Godinger, pierced tablespoon...............................6.00
Berkshire - 1847, Rogers, berry spoon 29.00
Berkshire - 1847, Rogers, jelly trowel 46.00
Berwick, Rogers, dinner fork, 7¼" 10.00
Berwick, Rogers, salad serving fork.................................... 46.00
Caprice, Nobility, sugar spoon 4.00
Classic Plume, Towle, flat pie server................................. 14.00
Classic Plume, Towle, tablespoon..9.00
Columbia - 1847, International, cake lifter w/gold-wash tines....... 52.00
Coronation, Community, cream soup spoon, 6⅞" 7.00
Daybreak, Rogers, cereal spoon 6.00
Daybreak, Rogers, fork, 7⅛"..7.00
Dresden Rose, Reed & Barton, dinner fork, 7½"................6.00
First Love - 1847, Rogers, chip beef fork 11.00
First Love - 1847, teaspoon...4.00
Floral, Wallace, bouillon soup spoon, 4⅝" 16.00
Georgian, Community, cream soup spoon, 7" 9.00
Georgian, Community, sauce ladle...................................... 12.00
Grenoble/Gloria, Rogers, curved baby spoon...................... 26.00
Grenoble/Gloria, Rogers, pastry fork................................. 38.00
Heraldic - 1847, Rogers, meat serving fork 14.00
Invitation, Gorham, salad fork 11.00
Invitation, Gorham, sugar spoon...5.00
Lady Empire, Nobility, gravy ladle..................................... 14.00
Londontown, Oneida, tablespoon.. 11.00
Londontown, Oneida, 4-pc grill set.................................... 16.00
Marquise - 1847, Rogers, butter spreader, flat hdl................8.00
Marquise - 1847, Rogers, teaspoon 4.00
May Queen, Holmes & Edwards, pierced tablespoon...................... 15.00
May Queen, Holmes & Edwards, salad fork........................6.00
Milady, Community, cream soup spoon, 6⅞" 6.00
Milady, Community, grill fork 5.00
Modern Art, Reed & Barton, sugar tongs 40.00
Nenuphar, American, beef serving fork 32.00
Nenuphar, American, lunch fork, 7" 10.00
Old Colony - 1847, Rogers, dinner fork, 7½".....................6.00
Old Colony - 1847, Rogers, jelly server............................. 14.00
Old Colony - 1847, Rogers, salad fork............................... 12.00
Orange Blossom, Rogers, flat pie/cake server...................... 46.00
Patrician, Community, jelly serving spoon.......................... 12.00
Patrician, Community, lg berry serving spoon..................... 36.00
Paul Revere, Community, bouillon soup spoon 7.00
Queen Bess - 1946, Oneida, gravy ladle 15.00
Regal, Dirilyte, cold meat fork.. 14.00
Regal, Dirilyte, teaspoon..4.00
Remembrance - 1847, Rogers, rnd soup spoon, 7"................9.00
Reverie, Nobility, tomato server... 13.00
Rex, Reed & Barton, sugar tongs.. 18.00
Sharon - 1847, Rogers, sauce ladle 13.00
Silver Artistry, Community, pierced tablespoon 12.00
South Seas, Community, pastry server 16.00
South Seas, Community, pierced nut spoon.........................8.00
Torun, Dansk, cake knife... 17.00
Torun, Dansk, casserole serving spoon, 11"........................ 25.00
Tudor - 1904, International, pickle fork, long hdl 17.00
Vintage - 1847, Isco, cheese scoop 170.00
Vintage - 1847, Isco, olive spoon, 8¼"............................. 44.00

Violet, SG Rogers, cake server, hollow hdl 30.00
Violet, SG Rogers, teaspoon.. 6.00
White Orchid, Community, dinner fork 10.00
White Orchid, Community, oval soup spoon......................... 7.00
Wildwood, Oneida, ladle, 11".. 63.00
Windsong, Nobility, butter spreader, flat hdl 7.00
Windsong, Nobility, pickle fork.. 8.00
Windsong, Nobility, seafood fork 7.00
Winsome - 1959, Community, meat fork 16.00
Winsome - 1959, Community, pierced tablespoon 15.00
Youth, Holmes & Edwards, grill knife, modern blade............. 4.00
Youth, Holmes & Edwards, master butter knife 3.00

Hollow Ware

B&R Brower & Rusher, NY; warming dish, w/hdls & lid, 8x15x10"..650.00
Elkington & Co, soup tureen, plain oval form, ftd/hdls, 1885, 11x10". 1,000.00
English, bowl, lobed body, ringed hdls, ftd, 9½x13½x15" 850.00
English, centerpc, navette form w/rtcl sides, lion-face hdls, 4x16x8" .. 250.00
English, gravy pitcher, domed lid, fruitwood hdl, 19th C, 6⅜" 585.00
English, wine coaster, floral/leaf borders, crested, 5x9", pr.......... 1,250.00
English, wine coaster, shell & scroll rim, hardwood base, 2x7", pr ..295.00
HB, ewer, emb Bacchic band, mask spout, domed lid, 1873, 8¾".. 295.00
Munday John St Oxford St, kettle w/stand, allover eng foliage, 15", VG..320.00

Plateado, Emilia Castillo, Mexico, water pitcher, monkey with hardstone cabochon eyes as handle, 10½", $2,500.00. (Photo courtesy David Rago Auctions)

Reed & Barton, compote, birdcage support, swing hdl w/fox head, 8½"..150.00
Reed & Barton, flower basket, fluted/rtcl sides, #5548, 1920, 19" ...440.00
Reed & Barton, flower basket, rtcl ft/sides, #6650, 1920, 21".......300.00
Reed & Barton, tea service, medallion w/lady's head & Greek key, 7-pc.460.00
Silver City, candlesticks, shaped ovals w/floral vines, 1900, 10", pr..... 175.00
Unmk, cake basket, lobed bowl w/grapes/flower panels, swing hdl, 8x11"..300.00
Unmk, egg server, sq tray w/central hdl, 6 leaf-like cups, 1900, 8x8" .. 200.00
Unmk, entree, gadroon/shell borders, inset shield, w/lid, 7x12x10", pr....300.00
Unmk, fish platter, Geo III, oval w/gadrooned edge, eng crown/CP, 34"..290.00
Unmk, hot water urn, Adam style, 24x12" 880.00
Unmk, hot water urn, Georgian, lion mask hdls, 1810s, 17"........ 885.00
Unmk, kettle on stand, Victorian, rtcl/eng, shell ft, heater, 15"...235.00
Unmk, supper server, 2 entrees w/lids, castor, 2 sauce bowls, 10x24".550.00
Unmk, tray, eng florals, rtcl gallery, 4 bun ft, hdls, 20" 90.00
Unmk, tray, rtcl rim, cast grapevines, eng flat surface, 28x18" 300.00
Unmk, venison platter/warming dish, rococo repousse, dome lid/ftd, 26".2,350.00
Unmk, well & tree platter w/shells/leaves, dome lid, reservoir, 20x15" ..750.00
Unmk, wine coaster, shell/scroll borders, wood base, 2¼" dia, pr .. 490.00
Unmk, wine cooler, bbl form, lion masks/drop ring hdls, 8x10", pr..2,465.00

Sheffield

Candelabra, Edwardian, 5-light/4 scrolling arms, sq base, 20", pr ..5,500.00
Candelabra, Geo III, 3-light, late 18th C, 17", pr....................... 2,885.00

Candleabrum, Corinthian column w/4 arms, flame finials, 26", ea... 400.00
Candlesticks, columnar stem/Corinthian capital/eng motto, 13", pr..825.00
Candlesticks, Corinthian capital nozzles, bobeches, 1760s, 14", 4 for. 2,115.00
Coffee/tea set, Georgian style, 2 pots+cr/sug, 1892-93, 52-t-oz.... 650.00
Coffeepot, dome lid, shaped/cvd wood hdl, TB&S, 7" 175.00
Cruet set, rococo floral sprays ea side, mask ft, James Dixon, 11x8" ...415.00
Entree dish & warmer, cast floral bands, ornate hdls, 14" L, pr ..2,100.00
Hot water urn, Georgian, orig burner, ivory hdl, 1810s, 22"......... 950.00
Hot water urn, Regency, classical borders, scroll hdls, 15x18" 850.00
Kettle on stand, Geo style, partly lobed sq form, Atkin Bros, 14" ...110.00
Punch bowl, scrolls/floral swags, early 20th C, 6x9" 435.00
Salver, Greek key borders, inset shield, rtcl rim, J Dixon & Sons, 12"....500.00
Server, heated tray w/tureen+3 bowls w/lids+mustard+3 s/p+3 open salts...1,600.00
Tea caddy, Adam style, urn finial/4 bun ft, hinged lid, 5x5x3" 200.00
Tray, eng castle, rtcl gallery, hdls/6 sm ft, KH&Co, 32" L............. 750.00
Tray, Regency w/gadroon border, shell/scroll hdls, crest, 3x27x17" ..200.00
Tureen, game; stag finial, tiered lid, paw ft, 1890s, 9½" 350.00
Tureen, revolving; ram's heads/swags/etc, Martin, Ebenezar Hall, 16" L..1,200.00
Vase, wirework w/ruby glass inserts, cast floral swags, 19", pr 1,110.00
Venison dome, H Wilkinson, Greek key border, beaded hdl/rim, 12x20"...300.00
Warming stand, crested rnd plate on hot water base, drop ring hdls, 9" ..175.00
Wine coaster, crested buttons/acanthus borders, wood bottom, 2x6", pr..2,500.00
Wine cooler, shell/acanthus rim, low uptrn hdls, fluted/ftd, 10x10" ...1,235.00

Sinclaire

In 1904 H. P. Sinclaire and Company was founded in Corning, New York. For the first 16 years of production, Sinclaire used blanks from other glassworks for his cut and engraved designs. In 1920 he established his own glassblowing factory in Bath, New York. His most popular designs utilize fruits, flowers, and other forms of nature. Most of Sinclaire's glass is unmarked; items that are carry his logo: an 'S' within a wreath with two shields.

Bowl, cut, 13 hobstars (various szs) in vessica panels, 4x8", NM . 120.00
Bowl, fruit; cut starbursts, eng floral rim band, ftd, 7x13x9"......3,100.00
Candlesticks, amber, slim/twisted std, wide bobeche, 10", pr 300.00
Candlesticks, gr, slim std, 16", pr.. 575.00
Compote, amber, flared rim, ring around std, ca 1918, 4½x12½" . 180.00
Compote, etched flowers/scallops/dots, shallow, wreath mk, 7x7". 130.00
Decanter, wheat cutting on clear, open doughnut shape, 10½".... 175.00
Plate, electric bl w/eng rim band, 8½".. 35.00
Teapot, cut starbursts/eng flowers, ca 1917, 4½x9x6" 5,300.00
Vase, electric bl, optic ribs, ftd, mk S, ca 1920, 6x7¾" 300.00
Vase, electric bl w/etched floral band at fan top, ftd, 13½x11".....210.00
Vase, etched verticals/2 reserves w/flower baskets, waisted, 9", EX... 120.00

Sitzendorf

The Sitzendorf factory began operations in Germany in the mid-1800s, adopting the name of the city as the name of their company. They produced fine porcelain groups, figurines, etc., in much the same style and quality as Meissen and the Dresden factories. Much of their ware was marked with a crown over the letter 'S' and a horizontal line with two slash marks.

Bowl, florals/gilt on wht, 2 leafy sections w/center hdl, 14" L 120.00
Candelabra, lady (& man) as std, 5-light top pc lifts off, 16", pr..780.00
Candelabrum, base w/2 children playing in tree, 3-light, 10", ea . 100.00
Comport base, 3-D man/lady flank floral-encrusted std, gilt, 14" .275.00
Figurine, boy w/ice skates in knee britches, long jacket, hat, 6"..... 65.00
Figurine, dandy in fine uniform on goat, ea wearing glasses, 7" L. 195.00
Figurine, Godey's Fashion for May 1863, 6¾", EX 65.00

Figurine maid with lamb, blue crown S mark, twentieth century, small repair, 19", $440.00. (Photo courtesy Jackson's International Auctioneers & Appraisers of Fine Art & Antiques)

Figurine, Napoleon on rearing horse crossing Alps, 16" 840.00
Figurines, boy (& girl), vase on opposing shoulders, bl tones, 10", pr.190.00
Figurines, extremely ornate attire, much appl lace etc, 18", pr..... 215.00
Group, couple dancing, she w/fan, he w/hat at side, appl lace, 9", EX... 180.00
Group, courting pr, appl flowers to lady's uplifted skirt, 7" 135.00
Group, lady w/her maid primping before mirrored table, att, 15".. 540.00
Group, 3 maids in wheeled chariot pulled by pr winged dogs, 17" L .515.00
Group, 3 musicians, dancing pr & 4 watchers on platform, 9x14x21".. 660.00
Group, 3 seminude children, center 1 on goat, 1 w/instrument, 8½".. 575.00
Inkstand, 2 cherubs sit between wells, ftd scrolled base, 10" L 180.00
Lamp base, courting reserve/appl florals, 3-D maids as hdls, rtl base...720.00

Skookum Dolls

Representing real Indians of various tribes, stern-faced Skookum dolls were designed by Mary McAboy of Missoula, Montana, in the early 1900s. The earliest of McAboy's creations were made with air-dried apple faces that bore a resemblance to the neighboring Chinook Indian tribe. The name Skookum is derived from the Chinook/Siwash term for large or excellent (aka Bully Good) and appears as part of the oval paper labels often attached to the feet of the dolls. In 1913 McAboy applied for a patent that described her dolls in three styles: a female doll, a female doll with a baby, and a male doll. In 1916 George Borgman and Co. partnered with McAboy, registered the Skookum trademark, and manufactured these dolls which were distributed by the Arrow Novelty Co. of New York and the HH Tammen Co. of Denver. The Skookum (Apple) Packers Association of Washington state produced similar 'friendly faced' dolls as did Louis Ambery for the National Fruit exchange. The dried apple faces of the first dolls were replaced by those made of a composition material. Plastic faces were introduced in the 1940s, and these continued to be used until production ended in 1959. Skookum dolls were produced in a variety of styles, with the most collectible having stern, lined faces with small painted eyes glancing to the right, colorful Indian blankets pulled tightly across the straw- or paper-filled body to form hidden arms, felt pants or skirts over wooden legs, and wooden feet covered with decorated felt suede or masking tape. Skookums were produced in sizes ranging from a 2" souvenir mailer with a cardboard address tag to 36" novelty and advertising dolls. Collectors highly prize 21" to 26" dolls as well as dolls that glance to their left. Felt or suede feet predate the less desirable brown plastic feet of the late 1940s and 1950s. Unless noted otherwise, our values are for skookums in excellent condition. Our advisor for this category is Glen Rairigh; he is listed in the Directory under Michigan.

Baby, looks left, cradle brd, beaded body/head covering, 10½"..1,100.00
Baby, mc blanket, leather headband w/pnt decor, 4" 30.00

Baby mailer, 1½¢ postcard attached, feather/ribbon binding, 4" ... 100.00
Baby/child in loop basket, blanket wrap, necklace, 14" 200.00
Boy, brn ft w/pnt decor, Bully Good label, 6½" 100.00
Boy, brn suede ft w/decor, headband, 10" 150.00
Boy, mc blanket, felt pants, leather shoes, 6½", VG 50.00
Chief w/headdress, paper tape shoes w/decor, 12½" 250.00
Family, chief & female w/baby, clothes match, 15", 14" 600.00
Female, w/baby, w/blanket, worn paper tape ft, 12½", VG 150.00
Female w/baby, w/blanket, purple felt ft/skirt, necklace, 11½" 200.00
Girl, cotton-wrapped legs, beaded ft decor, headband, 9½" 150.00
Girl, cotton-wrapped legs, pnt suede ft covers, Bully Good, 6½"... 100.00
Girl, w/blanket/skirt, leather shoes, label, 6½" 125.00
Mailer, baby in bl & yel cotton, Grand Canyon, 10-1-52 .... 25.00
Mailer, baby in patterned cotton on yel cb 25.00
Mailer, baby in red bandana on yel cb.. 55.00

Slag Glass

Slag glass is a marbleized opaque glassware made by several companies from about 1870 until the turn of the century. It is usually found in purple or caramel (see Chocolate Glass), though other colors were also made. Pink is rare and very expensive. It was revived by several American glassmakers, L.E. Smith, Westmoreland, and Imperial among them. The listings below reflect values for items with excellent color.

Blue, Marquis & Marchioness of Lorne, butter dish, Henry Greener.. 685.00
Caramel, bookends, Scottie dog, Imperial, 6½x5" 300.00
Caramel, bowl, ftd, Imperial, 4½x8½" 45.00
Caramel, Pansy, nappy w/hdl, Imperial, 5" 35.00
Green, bell, Imperial, 5¾" 65.00
Green, Paneled Grape, #1881, canister, ftd, w/lid, Westmoreland 10".. 175.00
Green, shade, 6 panels in metal fr w/crown, 7¾x13½" 115.00
Jade Green, Rose, candleholders, Imperial #160, 3½", pr 55.00
Orange, bowl, flared rim, 3¼x9½" 45.00
Pink, Invt Fan & Feather, bowl, fruit; 5x9", from $750 to......... 1,000.00
Pink, Invt Fan & Feather, butter dish, 6" dia 1,500.00
Pink, Invt Fan & Feather, pitcher, 8" 2,500.00
Pink, Invt Fan & Feather, punch cup, from $285 to..................... 315.00
Pink, Invt Fan & Feather, spooner 475.00
Pink, Invt Fan & Feather, sugar bowl, w/lid............................ 1,000.00
Purple, bell, Imperial, #720, ca 1850, 6" 55.00
Purple, box, duck (#823) or dog (#822), Imperial, ea.................. 185.00
Purple, butterfly, Westmoreland, lg 50.00
Purple, cardinal, solid, Westmoreland.. 35.00
Purple, Cherry, goblet, LG Wright, 6½" 45.00
Purple, Colonial ashtray, Westmoreland 30.00
Purple, creamer & sugar bowl, rose in flowerpot emb, Imperial, 3" ...85.00
Purple, Hobnail, bell, Fenton #2667, 5½" 50.00
Purple, jar, peacock head emb, Sowerby's Ellison Glass Works, 2½" ..90.00
Purple, Pansy #757, basket, split hdl, Westmoreland..................... 35.00
Purple, pitcher, windmill/cottage/fisherman, Imperial #340, 6½"... 50.00
Purple, toothpick holder, Sowerby, 1880s 125.00
Purple, vase, fish form, Heppel & Co, 1882, 5" 235.00
Ruby, basket, Imperial, #300, ca 1969-74, 9½" 55.00
Ruby, cat on rib base, Westmoreland, 5½" 145.00
Ruby, Open Rose, bowl, Imperial, 3¼x9" 45.00
Ruby, vase, nudes emb on urn form, Imperial #132, 8½x3¾" 115.00

Smith Bros.

Alfred and Harry Smith founded their glassmaking firm in New Bedford, Massachusetts. They had been formerly associated with the Mt.

Washington Glass Works, working there from 1871 to 1875 to aid in establishing a decorating department. Smith glass is valued for its excellent enameled decoration on satin or opalescent glass. Pieces were often marked with a lion in a red shield.

Biscuit jar, flowers w/7 gr jewels & gold on melon ribs, SP lid, 7"....600.00
Biscuit jar, pk floral/gr leaves on cream w/undulating bl lines, 8" W ..385.00
Biscuit jar, pk roses/gr leaves on cream, melon ribs, SP mts, 8" W ..430.00
Bottle, scent; floral on melon ribs, lion-mk metal lid, ovoid, 5"... 225.00
Bowl, daisies on biscuit ground, rampant lion mk, 3½" H 300.00
Jar, gold-lined floral on melon ribs, red mk, 5¼" dia 350.00
Sweetmeat, water lily on melon ribs, floral-rtcl mk metal lid, 6" dia ..235.00
Vase, pansies in lav/pk/bl on opal w/gold scrollwork, 8½" 425.00
Vase, rose branch/butterflies/bee, cream to wht, w/label, 10x6½" ... 2,000.00
Vase, wisteria on opal w/gold, melon ribs, bulb w/doughnut top, 9" ...460.00

Snow Babies

During the last quarter of the nineteenth century, snow babies — little figures in pebbly white snowsuits — originated in Germany. They were originally made of sugar candy and were often used as decorations for Christmas cakes. Later on they were made of marzipan, a confection of crushed almonds, sugar, and egg whites. Eventually porcelain manufacturers began making them in bisque. They were popular until WWII. These tiny bisque figures range in size from 1" up to 7" tall. Quality German pieces bring very respectable prices on the market today. Beware of reproductions. Our advisor for this category is Linda Vines; she is listed in the Directory under California.

Babies (2) on snowball plant Am flag at apex, open bk, Germany, 3¼"... 360.00
Baby feeding seal w/baby bottle, Germany, 2" 250.00
Baby in sled pulled by huskies, Germany, 2" 275.00
Baby inside igloo, Santa on top, Germany, 2" 225.00
Baby on red & silver airplane, Germany, 2" 175.00
Baby playing musical instrument, Germany, 2" 150.00
Baby w/drum & cymbal, mk German US Zone, 2" 90.00
Baby w/seal & red ball, Germany, 2" 225.00
Boy & girl on yel toboggan, Germany, 2" 150.00
Boy & girl sliding down the snow on brick wall, Germany, 2½" .. 250.00
Carollers, 3 w/snow hats & lantern on snow base, Germany, 2" .. 210.00
Penguins (3) walking down brick wall, Germany, 2½" 175.00
Santa atop gray elephant, Germany, 2½" 275.00
Santa driving yel car, toys in bk, Germany, 2" 210.00
Santa nodder, Germany, 3"... 110.00
Santa riding on snow bear, Germany, 2½" 225.00
Santa riding yel train, pixie in bk, Germany, 3"........................... 200.00
Snow bear sitting or walking, Germany, 2½" 110.00
Snow man sitting, blk top hat, Germany, 2" 80.00
Snow man sitting, red hat w/pompom, Germany, 1½"..................... 75.00
Snow mother pushing twins in red carriage-sled, Germany, 2½".. 375.00

Snuff Boxes

As early as the seventeenth century, the Chinese began using snuff. By the early nineteenth century, the practice had spread to Europe and America. It was used by both the gentlemen and the ladies alike, and expensive snuff boxes and bottles were the earmark of the genteel. Some were of silver or gold set with precious stones or pearls, while others contained music boxes. See also Orientalia, Snuff Bottles.

Birchbark w/stained decor, wood base, top removes, oval, 3" L...... 60.00
Blk compo case/engine-trn base & lid: Paris, #284, musical, 3¾" L.. 700.00

Blk-banded agate, oval, metal mts, late 19th C, ¾x2x1½" 125.00
Burlwood w/gilt soldier medallion on lid, shell lined, 3½" dia...... 210.00
Gilt on silver w/allover eng, rectangular, 2⅜" L........................... 450.00
Papier mache, metal oval on apex of hinged lid, oval, 18th C, 2x3" ..210.00
Pewter w/brass insert of colonial man, att Germany, 3x1½" 240.00
Silver, pressed sailing ship/sailor/lighthouse, Pat Parker 1860, 3" L... 70.00
Tortoiseshell, Geo Washington portrait on lid, 2¾" dia 2,500.00
Tortoiseshell, rvpt lid: equestrian, 1-air, F Nicole, 2½" cylinder .. 4,700.00
Tortoiseshell w/painting on ivory of lady w/teacup on lid, 1780s .. 660.00
Wood, Le General Lafayette & portrait on lid, worn, ca 1824 ..2,650.00

Soap Hollow Furniture

In the Mennonite community of Soap Hollow, Pennsylvania, the women made and sold soap; the men made handcrafted furniture. Rare today, this furniture was stenciled, grain painted, and beautifully decorated with inlaid escutcheons. These pieces are becoming very sought after. When well kept, they are very distinctive and beautiful. The items described in these listings are in excellent condition unless otherwise described. Assume that all painted decoration is original to the piece unless 'rpt' (repainted) is noted. Our advisor for this category is Anita Levi; she is listed in the Directory under Pennsylvania.

Blanket chest, grpt w/blk lid, fruit/florals w/gold, 1882.............. 2,900.00
Blanket chest, grpt w/silver/gilt stencil, poplar, ET/1859, 23x44x19" .. 7,185.00
Blanket chest, red & blk, gold stencil, CW/1874, 25x45x18" ...6,700.00
Blanket chest, red & blk, gold stencil, decals, JC/1874, 10x17x9" ...5,060.00
Blanket chest, red & blk, gold stencil, MH/1871, 25x15x10", VG ..7,500.00
Blanket chest, red/gr pnt w/yel stripes/stencil, SH, 1868, 24x49".. 19,250.00
Chest, 6-drw, brn w/mustard & decals, blk top & sides, Sala 2,300.00
Chest, 6-drw, cherry w/red stain/ebonized trim, 45x37" 2,750.00
Chest, 6-drw, cherry/poplar w/blk & red pnt, stencil, 1861, 55x39x21"..7,475.00
Chest, 6-drw, dk red w/silver stencil, 56x42x21" 9,500.00
Chest, 6-drw, mc pnt/stencil, dtd 1859, 47x37x20" 14,000.00
Chest, 6-drw, no pnt or decor, EX wood, G 650.00
Chest, 7-drw, foliate stencil, 1851, 55x41"..............................1,350.00
Chest, 7-drw, grpt w/blk, gold stencil, MH/1887, 47½x39½" ..18,000.00
Chest, 7-drw, red & gr pnt w/gold stencil, SM 1867, 54x41" 8,000.00
Cradle, maroon grpt, gilt stencil, mustard trim..........................1,100.00
Cupboard, corner; maroon w/blk, stencil, 1856 ....15,500.00
Cupboard, Dutch; 4 doors/2 drws, stencil/old rpt, 1875, 84x65".. 8,000.00
Cupboard, red & gr pnt/striping/stencil, poplar, 2-pc, 87x64"..35,200.00
Desk, 5-drw base, red/yel/blk, pine/poplar, 1870, 33x21x15"...33,350.00
Dresser, Emp style, columns on 3 drws, HF/1874......................2,200.00
Frame, cross pcs, gr/yel striping, 15½x19¾" 1,000.00
Rope bed, red & brn finish on cherry, rare 2,300.00
Sewing chest, 1-drw, red pnt w/floral, 1875, rare, 12x8", EX...10,300.00
Sewing stand, pnt poplar, dvtl drw/porc knob, 876/LAY, 15x9x7"..4,600.00

Soapstone

Soapstone is a soft talc in rock form with a smooth, greasy feel from whence comes its name. (It is also called Soo Chow Jade.) It is composed basically of talc, chlorite, and magnetite. In colonial times it was extracted from out-croppings in large sections with hand saws, carted by oxen to mills, and fashioned into useful domestic articles such as footwarmers, cooking utensils, inkwells, etc. During the early 1800s, it was used to make heating stoves and kitchen sinks. Most familiar today are the carved vases, bookends, and boxes made in China during the Victorian era. Our advisor for this category is Clarence Bodine; he is listed in the Directory under Pennsylvania.

Bookends, bird of paradise pecking on flowers on base, 5½" 125.00
Censer, foo dog on lid, animal-head hdls, spherical, on flat stand, 8".. 120.00
Figurine, bamboo & flowering tree, 3-color, 13x9" 300.00
Figurine, bird in rtcl flower garden, integral ftd ornate base, 14".. 125.00
Figurine, Buddha on throne, early 20th C, 8x6"+wood stand 150.00
Figurine, hillside temple, red/blk streaks, ca 1900, 6¼x9¾" 100.00
Figurine, ptarmigan bird, 3x1¼" 50.00
Figurine, Quan Yin, rockwork platform, 1880s, now 14" lamp..... 300.00
Lamp base, Lohan stands on beach, branch in hand, metal base, 10"...250.00
Pagoda, 7-tier w/bird finial, attached cvd bells, 23"+28" wooden case..375.00
Screen, table; flowers & birds on oval, cvd stand, 10¼x7" 50.00
Seals, foo dog atop, sgn, 18th C, 7½", EX, pr 240.00
Vase, dbl; centered by phoenix bird/foliage, 8x8x3", G 90.00

Soda Fountain Collectibles

Dispenser, Clayton's Grape Smack, 15½", $14,300.00.

(Photo courtesy Randy Inman Auctions Inc.)

The first soda water sales in the United States occurred in the very late 1790s in New York and New Haven, Connecticut. By the 1830s soda water was being sold in drug stores as a medicinal item, especially the effervescent mineral waters from various springs around the country. By this time the first flavored soda water appeared at an apothecary shop in Philadelphia.

The 1830s also saw the first manufacturer (John Matthews) of devices to make soda water. The first marble soda fountain made its appearance in 1857 as a combination ice shaver and flavor-dispensing apparatus. By the 1870s the soda fountain was an established feature of the neighborhood drug store. The fountains of this period were large, elaborate marble devices with druggists competing with each other for business by having fountains decorated with choice marbles, statues, mirrors, water fountains, and gas lamps.

In 1903 the fountain completed its last major evolution with the introduction of the 'front' counter service we know today. (The soda clerk faced the customer when drawing soda.) By this time ice cream was a standard feature being served as sundaes, ice cream sodas, and milk shakes. Syrup dispensers were just being introduced as 'point-of-sale' devices to sell various flavorings from many different companies. Straws were commonplace, especially those made from paper. Fancy and unusual ice cream dippers were in daily use, and they continued to evolve, reaching their pinnacle with the introduction of the heart-shaped dipper in 1927.

This American business has provided collectors today with an almost endless supply of interesting and different articles of commerce. One can collect dippers, syrup dispensers, glassware, straw dispensers, milk shakers, advertising, and trade catalogs. Assume that our prices are for examples with the corrrect pump, unless otherwise noted. (Note: The presence of a 'correct' pump enhances the value of a syrup dispenser by 25%.) When no condition is given, values are for items in excellent condition.

Collectors need to be made aware of decorating pieces that are actually fantasy items: copper ice cream cones, a large copper ice cream dipper, and a copper ice cream soda glass. These items have no resale value. Our advisors for this category are Joyce and Harold Screen; they are listed in the Directory under Maryland. See also Advertising; Coca-Cola.

Bottle, syrup; Lime Juice & Cola label, glass w/metal cap, 10½" 80.00
Cone rack, glass & brass, 14½" 360.00
Container, Carnation Malted Milk, gr letters on milk glass, 6", VG ..100.00
Dipper, Bohlig Mfg, aluminum & wht metal, squeeze hdl, 1908, 10" L..1,140.00
Dipper, Dan Dee sandwich maker, NP brass, plunger style, Pat 1920... 2,500.00
Dipper, Fletcher #28, polished NP & brass w/wood hdl, EX+ 250.00
Dipper, Jewel sandwich maker, wht metal, wood hdl, last Pat 5-4-26.. 2,000.00
Dipper, sandwich; NP brass, 6-sided, angle hdl, unmk, 8" 900.00
Dipper, Schupfer & Eaton, NP brass w/wooden hdl, Pat 1930, 9½".. 3,000.00
Dispenser, Birchola, ceramic, ball shape, 14", NM 3,300.00
Dispenser, Birchola, porc keg form, 16"..................................... 2,550.00
Dispenser, Buckeye Root Beer, ceramic.................................... 1,900.00

Dispenser, Dixie-Dew, glass top w/worn decal, 16" 165.00
Dispenser, Emerald Isle, gr glass shamrock top/wht milk glass base, NM..775.00
Dispenser, Fowler's Cherry Smash, wht ceramic, 15", EX................. 2,800.00
Dispenser, Fowler's Cherry Smash 5¢, ceramic ball, orig pump, 16", NM..5,500.00
Dispenser, Grape-Crush, purple glass keg w/top pump, 14" 1,150.00
Dispenser, Green Muscadine porc bbl form, 15" 750.00
Dispenser, Hires, porc w/metal top, ca 1920, 15x7" dia 400.00
Dispenser, Iced Nestea, ribbed glass bbl w/orig lid & spigot, 14x9" ...75.00
Dispenser, Jersey Creme, porc, 12" 3,800.00
Dispenser, Johnston's Cold Fudge, crockery w/galvanized tin lid, 10" ... 145.00
Dispenser, Kirsch's, holds cones in clear glass, clear lid, 8x12" dia ..400.00
Dispenser, Magnus Root Beer, milk glass keg w/blk lid & label, 15"...325.00
Dispenser, Mission Real Fruit, glass/nickel fountain-glass shape, 13" .. 155.00
Dispenser, Moxie, clear & milk glass w/orig spigot, 1917, 8x10", NM ..200.00
Dispenser, Ward's Lemon-Crush, stoneware lemon, 14"............. 2,000.00
Display, die-cut cb, boy/girl at counter, 16x16", EX+ 575.00
Flavor board, Abbotts DeLuxe Ice Cream, 1950s, 19½x8½" 30.00
Fountain glass, Moxie, red ad on clear glass, flared rim, 4" 35.00
Frostie Root Beer, tin sign, Drink..., Frostie figure, 12x23".......... 160.00
Jar, Borden's Malted Milk, glass w/metal lid, bl on wht label, 9".. 600.00
Jar, Carnation Malted Milk, red/wht porc w/metal lid, 9", EX+.. 475.00
Jar, Crispo Ice Cream Cones, clear glass, 11x9" dia 125.00
Jar, Thompson's Malted Milk, gray enameled porc, 10", EX+ 675.00
Juicer, Sunkist, aluminum & porc, electric 200.00
Mug, Buckeye Root Beer, ceramic, yel w/blk lettering, 6½" 40.00
Mug, Dr Swett's Original Root Beer, portrait, ceramic, 6"............ 130.00
Mug, Drink Hires Root Beer, boy pointing, porc, Mettlach, 4".... 240.00
Mug, Lash's Root Beer, ceramic, bl & wht stripes/blk letters, 6½" . 50.00
Mug, Murry Co Soda Water Flavor, figures emb, ceramic, 6" 120.00
Mug, Root Beer/3 men drinking, bl on cream, ceramic, 4"........... 100.00
Pitcher, Bardwell's Root Beer, cobalt on stoneware, pewter lid, 14" .1,100.00
Popcicle maker, metal compartments, makes 24, hdls, 17" L, VG....60.00
Pump, Nehi, chrome, 19" 250.00
Sign, Allen's Red Tame Cherry, 2-sided die-cut cb hanger, 6x6".....375.00
Straw dispenser, clear ribbed glass, brass lid & insert, 11½" 70.00
Straw holder, clear glass, emb V panels, scalloped top, 7¾" 50.00
Straw holder, cut, clear, glass lid, 13" 550.00
Straw holder, Grape Smash, purple pyro on clear glass, 11½" ... 1,325.00
Syrup bottle, Ho-Vie 5¢ label, metal cap, 12½"............................ 300.00
Syrup bottle, Ward's Orange-Crush label, metal cap, 12"............. 650.00
Table, oak top w/CI base, ca 1900, 28x41" dia............................ 1,500.00
Table, oak w/CI base, old pnt, ca 1900, 29½x36", VG 700.00
Trade sign, Safe-T Cup, paper compo ice cream in cone, 20th C, 21"..150.00
Tray, Always Eat Quality Ice Cream, boy/girl, 13" dia 200.00
Tray, Fearson's Ice Cream, girl in red tam w/ice cream, 15x10".... 225.00
Tray, Noaker Ice Cream Co, boy/girl eating ice cream, 13" dia, EX+.. 700.00

Tray, Zipp's Cherri-O Soda, tin litho, bird/glass, 12" 660.00
Warmer, Bowey's Hot Fudge, metal, 7", VG 100.00

Spangle Glass

Spangle glass, also known as Vasa Murrhina, is cased art glass characterized by the metallic flakes embedded in its top layer. It was made both abroad and in the United States during the latter years of the nineteenth century, and it was reproduced in the 1960s by the Fenton Art Glass Company. Vasa Murrhina was a New England distributor who sold glassware of this type manufactured by a Dr. Flower of Sandwich, Massachusetts. Flower had purchased the defunct Cape Cod Glassworks in 1885 and used the facilities to operate his own company. Since none of the ware was marked, it is very difficult to attribute specific examples to his manufacture. See also Art Glass Baskets; Fenton.

Basket, bl w/mica crimped-edge body w/clear twist hdl, 5½x7½" .. 375.00
Bride's bowl, yel/wht swirl w/overall silver mica & bl daisies, 11" ... 125.00
Ewer, pk w/overall clear casing, wht liner, ornate clear hdl, 9½" 225.00
Rose bowl, rose/maroon/gilt, crimped rim, 3¼x4" 175.00
Sweetmeat, cranberry w/yel spatter & gold aventurine, SP emb lid, 6".. 275.00
Tumble-up, pk to wht w/mica flecks, carafe & tumbler, 7" 195.00
Vase, pk w/flecked gold dmn pattern, fine horizontal ribs, 5x5" ... 400.00
Vase, pk/bl sections alternate, spiral crystal rigaree at neck, 9" 135.00
Vase, yel on wht w/silver flecks, wht int, 8½" 165.00
Vase, yel w/brn streaks & gold mica, dbl gourd, ruffled fan rim, 11" ... 100.00

Spatter Glass

Spatter glass, characterized by its multicolor 'spatters,' has been made from the late nineteenth century to the present by American glass houses as well as those abroad. Although it was once thought to have been made entirely by workers at the 'end of the day' from bits and pieces of leftover scrap, it is now known that it was a standard line of production. See also Art Glass Baskets.

Candlesticks, dk mc, baluster w/diagonal ribs, raised ft, 9", pr 100.00
Pitcher, gold-tan/amber, amber hdl, spherical w/ruffled lip, 9" 120.00
Pitcher, gr/wht w/clear reed hdl, Phoenix, 8½" 125.00
Pitcher, pastel colors, swirl mold, clear hdl, ball shape, 7¾" 130.00
Pitcher, pk/yel, wht int, swirled mold, 4-corner lip, 7½" 90.00
Pitcher, wht/pk, bulbous w/crimped rim, 9", +8 tumblers............. 460.00
Vase, cranberry/wht, Ribbed Pillar, 6x5" 80.00

Spatterware

Spatterware is a general term referring to a type of decoration used by English potters as early as the late 1700s. Using a brush or a stick, brightly colored paint was dabbed onto the soft-paste earthenware items, achieving a spattered effect which was often used as a border. Because much of this type of ware was made for export to the United States, some of the subjects in the central design — the schoolhouse and the eagle patterns, for instance — reflect American tastes. Yellow, green, and black spatterware is scarce and highly valued by collectors. In the descriptions that follow, the color listed after the item indicates the color of the spatter. The central design is identified next, and the color description that follows that refers to the design. When no condition code is present, assume that the item is undamaged and has only very light wear.

Biscuit jar, rainbow w/HP floral, SP lid & bail, 7½x5" 635.00

Pitcher, bl, Adams Rose, red, stain/flakes, 8" 460.00
Plate, bl, Peafowl, bl/gr/red, 9⅜", EX 300.00
Plate, bl, Peafowl, red/gr, 10-panel, 8⅛" 350.00
Plate, bl, Peafowl, red/gr/yel, 7½" 175.00
Plate, bl (band), Peafowl, red/yel/gr on bl center, 9¾" 360.00
Plate, cobalt, Peafowl, gr/yel/red, 14-sided, 7½" 275.00
Plate, rainbow, bl/gr, 8¼" 800.00
Plate, rainbow, bull's-eye, purple/blk, 9½" 1,500.00
Plate, rainbow, bull's-eye, red/gr, flake, 9⅝" 750.00
Plate, rainbow, red/bl, 8¼" 550.00
Plate, red, Primrose, purple/gr w/yel center, lt stain, 8" 150.00
Plate, red (allover), Peafowl, bl/gr/red, Adams, 8½" 400.00
Platter, brn/purple, bull's eye, brn/purple, 13½x10¼" 3,700.00
Saucer, gr, boat, red/blk/gr, 6" 850.00
Saucer, red, deer, brn-blk, 6" 175.00
Saucer, red, Peafowl, red/yel/bl/gr, 6" 175.00
Saucer, red, Schoolhouse, red/brn/gr 575.00
Sugar bowl, bl, Peafowl, bl/gr/red, octagonal, w/lid, 7½", EX 480.00
Sugar bowl, rainbow, red/gr, paneled, mismatched lid, stain, 7¼"... 575.00
Tea bowl & saucer, bl, Peafowl, gr/red/yel, EX 100.00
Tea bowl & saucer, rainbow, red/bl 650.00
Tea bowl & saucer, rainbow, tulip, yel/purple, hairlines............. 2,500.00
Tea bowl & saucer, red, Holly Berry, gr/red, EX 150.00
Tea bowl & saucer, red, Peafowl, bl/gr/red 300.00
Tea bowl & saucer, red, Peafowl, bl/yel/gr, EX 240.00
Tea bowl & saucer, red, Primrose, purple/yel/gr 775.00
Tea bowl & saucer, wht, Tic Tac Toe, gr/red 550.00
Tea bowl & saucer, yel, Cockscomb, red/gr, stains/flakes 1,600.00
Tea bowl & saucer, yel, Tulip, red/bl/gr 1,035.00
Teapot, brn, Peafowl, bl/yel/red, hairline/chip/stains................... 200.00
Teapot, rainbow, purple/bl/brn, w/Adams Rose, stained spout, 6" ... 390.00
Teapot, red, Peafowl, bl/yel/gr, bulbous/shouldered, low dome lid, 7".. 900.00
Teapot, red, Thistle, bl/gr in wht reserve, bulbous, low dome lid, 7" ..2,650.00
Teapot, red (allover), Peafowl, bl/red/long gr tail, on gr grass, 7"...2,400.00

Spelter

Spelter items are cast from commercial zinc and coated with a metallic patina. The result is a product very similar to bronze in appearance, yet much less expensive.

Bookends, Diana w/dog & bow on base, Fugere, 1920s 1,800.00
Candle arbor, knight stands & holds staff w/4 candle arms, 1880s, 34" ..750.00
Candleholder, nude figural, Nouveau style, Hur Yon 1921, 12", ea.. 135.00
Clock, lady holding tambourine on base w/clock, 1880s, 35x18x7"...450.00
Figurine, allegorical maiden leans on anchor, after Moreau, 1900s, 25"...235.00
Figurine, classical maiden, multi-patinated, late 19th C, 21"....... 700.00
Figurine, Don Juan in full costume w/sword, bronze patina, 21" .. 115.00
Figurine, lady banjo player, bronze patina/resin face & hands, 8¼".. 250.00
Figurine, man, well dressed & w/sword, bronze patina, 1920s, 20"..300.00
Figurine, sailor standing on sailboat, 2 Paris mks, 22½x11" 125.00
Figurine, Spirit of Am Dough Boy, WWI soldier w/grenade, rpr, 11½" ..100.00
Figurine, 2 children on stump w/turtle head protruding from water, 17"..200.00
Inkwell, fisherman's head, cap lifts to reveal well, wooden base, 6".. 150.00
Lamp, bird figural, w/grapes (gr glass shade) in beak, 18¼" 325.00
Lamp, gent in Elizabethan attire holds torch aloft, pnt, 45"......... 675.00

Spode/Copeland

The following is a short chronological history of the Spode company:
1733: Josiah Spode I is born on March 23 at Lane Delph, Staffordshire.
1740: Spode is put to work in a pottery factory.

1754: Spode, now a fully proficient journeyman/potter, works for Turner and Banks in Stoke-on-Trent.

1755: Josiah Spode II is born.

1761: Spode I acquires a factory in Shelton where he makes cream-colored and blue-painted earthenware.

1770: This is the year adopted as the date Spode I founded the business.

1784: Spode I masters the art and techniques of transfer printing in blue under the glaze on earthenware.

1796: This marks the earliest known record of Spode selling porcelain dinnerware.

1800: Spode II produces the first bone china.

1806: Spode is appointed potter to the royal Family; this continues past 1983.

1813: Spode produces the first stone china.

1821: Spode introduces Feldspar Porcelain, a variety of bone china.

1833: William Taylor Copeland acquires the Spode factory from the Spode family and becomes partners with Garrett until 1847.

1870: System of impressing date marks on the backs of the dinnerware begins.

1925: Robert Copeland is born. (He presently resides in England.)

1976: The company merges with Worcester Royal Porcelain Company and forms Royal Worcester Spode Limited.

1986: The Spode Society is established.

1989: The holding company for Spode becomes the Porcelain and Fine China Companies Limited.

The price quotes listed in these three categories of Spode are for twentieth-century pre-1965 dinnerware in pristine condition — no cracks, chips, crazing, or stains. Minor knife cuts do not constitute damage unless extreme.

The patterns in the first group are the most common and popular earthenware lines. The second group contains the rarer and higher priced patterns; they are both earthenware and stoneware. Bone china patterns comprise the third group.

Our advisor for this category is Don Haase; he is listed in the Directory under Washington.

Tower Black, divided serving bowl, rare color (group values do not apply), 4x11", $325.00. (Photo courtesy Don Haase)

First Group: Earthenware/Imperialware

Ann Hathaway, Billingsley Rose, Buttercup, Byron, Camilla Pink, Chelsea Wicker, Chinese Rose, Christmas Tree (green), Cowslip, Fairy Dell, Fleur de Lis (blue/brown), Florence, Gadroon, Gainsborough, Hazel Dell, Indian Tree, Jewel, Moss Rose, Old Salem, Raeburn, Reynolds, Romney, Rosalie, Rose Briar, Valencia, Wickerdale, Wickerdell, Wickerlane.

Bowl, cereal; 6½"	25.00
Bowl, fruit; 5¼"	22.00
Coffeepot, 8-cup	195.00
Creamer, lg	55.00
Creamer, sm	45.00
Cup & saucer, demitasse	29.00
Cup & saucer, low/tall	29.00
Plate, bread & butter; 6¼"	16.00
Plate, butter pat	18.00
Plate, dinner	25.00
Plate, luncheon; rnd, 8-9"	22.00
Plate, salad; 7½"	20.00
Platter, oval, 13"	115.00
Platter, oval, 15"	135.00
Platter, oval, 17"	165.00
Sauceboat, w/liner	125.00
Soup, cream; w/liner	32.00
Soup, rim, 7½"	27.00
Soup, rim, 8½"	32.00
Sugar bowl, w/lid, lg	55.00
Sugar bowl, w/lid, sm	45.00
Teapot, 8-cup	195.00
Vegetable, oval, 9-10"	115.00
Vegetable, oval, 10-11"	135.00
Vegetable, sq, 8"	125.00
Vegetable, sq, 9"	145.00
Vegetable, w/lid	275.00
Waste bowl, 6"	29.00

Second Group: Earthenware/Imperialware

Aster, Butchart, Camilla Blue, Christmas Tree (magenta), Italian, Mayflower, Herring Hunt (green/magenta), Patricia, Tower Blue and Pink, Wildflower (blue/red), Fitzhugh (blue/red/green), Gloucester (blue/red), Rosebud Chintz, Tradewinds (blue/red).

Bowl, cereal; 6¼"	32.00
Bowl, fruit; 5½"	28.00
Coffeepot, 8-cup	345.00
Creamer, lg	75.00
Creamer, sm	65.00
Cup & saucer, demitasse	35.00
Cup & saucer, low/high	39.00
Plate, bread & butter; 6¼"	29.00
Plate, butter pat	27.00
Plate, chop; rnd, 13"	225.00
Plate, dinner; 10½"	55.00
Plate, luncheon; rnd, 8-9"	45.00
Plate, luncheon; sq, 8½"	47.00
Plate, salad; 7½"	35.00
Platter, oval, 13"	145.00
Platter, oval, 15"	165.00
Platter, oval, 17"	210.00
Sauceboat, w/liner	165.00
Soup, rim, 7½"	35.00
Soup, rim, 8½"	45.00
Sugar bowl, w/lid, lg	75.00
Sugar bowl, w/lid, sm	65.00
Teapot, 8-cup	315.00
Vegetable, oval, 9-10"	135.00
Vegetable, oval, 10-11"	155.00
Vegetable, sq, 8"	145.00
Vegetable, sq, 9"	165.00
Vegetable, w/lid	325.00
Waste bowl, 6"	33.00

Third Group: Bone China

Billingsley Rose Savoy, Bridal Rose, Carolyn, Chelsea Garden, Christine, Claudia, Colonel, Dimity, Dresden Rose Savoy, Fleur de Lis (gray/red/blue), Geisha (blue/pink/white), Irene, Maritime Rose, Primrose (pink), Shanghi, Savoy.

Bowl, cereal; 6¼"	42.00
Bowl, fruit; 5½"	37.00
Coffeepot, 8-cup	425.00
Creamer, lg	110.00
Creamer, sm	110.00
Cup & saucer, demitasse	55.00
Cup & saucer, low/tall	65.00
Plate, bread & butter; 6¼"	39.00
Plate, butter pat	35.00
Plate, chop; rnd, 13"	295.00
Plate, dessert; 8"	45.00
Plate, dinner; 10½"	59.00
Plate, luncheon; rnd, 9"	45.00
Plate, luncheon; sq, 8½"	55.00
Plate, salad; 7½"	49.00
Platter, oval, 13"	195.00
Platter, oval, 15"	225.00
Platter, oval, 17"	265.00
Sauceboat, w/liner	145.00
Soup, cream; w/liner	145.00
Soup, rim, 7½"	55.00
Soup, rim, 8½"	65.00
Sugar bowl, w/lid, lg	120.00
Sugar bowl, w/lid, sm	115.00
Teapot, 8-cup	425.00
Vegetable, oval, 9-10"	215.00
Vegetable, oval, 10-11"	235.00
Vegetable, sq, 8"	245.00
Vegetable, sq, 9"	265.00
Vegetable, w/lid	385.00
Waste bowl, 6"	47.00

Spongeware

Spongeware is a type of factory-made earthenware that was popular during the last quarter of the nineteenth century and into the first quarter of the twentieth century. It was decorated by dabbing color onto the drying ware with a sponge, leaving a splotched design at random or in simple patterns. Sometimes a solid band of color was added. The vessel was then covered with a clear glaze and fired at a high temperature. Blue on white is the most preferred combination, but green on ivory, orange on white, or those colors in combination may also occasionally be found. As with most pottery, rare forms and condition are major factors in establishing value. Spongeware is still being made today, so beware of newer examples. Our values are for undamaged examples, unless a specific condition code is given within the description.

Bank, gr/brn, pig figural, pierced eyes, 3½x6"	200.00
Bowl, bl/rust/wht, patterned sponging, paneled sides, 5x9"	100.00
Bowl, bl/wht, ribbed sides, 4⅜x11½", EX	150.00
Bowl, bl/wht, scalloped edge, 1½x9"	175.00
Bowl, mixing; bl/wht w/emb heart pattern, 5½x10", from $175 to	225.00
Butter crock, bl/wht, Jersey Cow on orange-peel texture, 4⅛x6"	350.00
Chamber pot, bl/wht, 5x8½"	200.00
Creamer, bl/wht, 3"	200.00
Crock, bl/wht, fine patterned sponging, loop hdl, no lid, 7x9"	75.00
Crock, bl/wht, patterned sponging, Butter, 5x6¼" dia	175.00
Crock, maroon/bl/brn, patterned sponging on yellow ware, 5x7", VG	150.00
Custard cup, gr/brn on yellow ware, 2x4½"	65.00
Inkwell, bl/wht, bl stencil: Empire, sq, 1⅜x1½x1½", NM	110.00

Jug, molasses; bl/wht, irregular patterned sponging, bail hdl, 8"	350.00
Pitcher, bl/wht, lg-patterned sponging, cylindrical, 10", EX	300.00
Pitcher, bl/wht, patterned sponging, bulge at base, angle hdl, 9"	400.00
Pitcher, bl/wht, patterned sponging, Cherry, tankard form, 7", EX	550.00
Pitcher, bl/wht, patterned sponging, Girl & Dog, 9"	515.00
Pitcher, bl/wht, patterned sponging, Wild Rose, 8¾", NM	275.00
Pitcher, bl/wht, patterned sponging, Wild Rose, 9½"	475.00
Pitcher, bl/wht, patterned sponging in arrowheads pattern, 8½"	165.00
Pitcher, bl/wht, patterned sponging in chicken-wire pattern, 9"	100.00
Pitcher, bl/wht, patterned sponging w/median bl stripe, 12", EX	300.00
Pitcher, bl/wht (band around ovoid body), Rhonesboro TX, 9½"	525.00
Pitcher, bl/wht (in vertical rows), Rhonesboro TX, ca 1900, 9½"	685.00
Pitcher, bl/wht w/2 brn bands, 13x9"	250.00
Pitcher, brn/bl on cream, patterned sponging, 11", EX	200.00

Pitcher, brown, green, and tan, 5½", $75.00.

Pitcher, gr/wht, patterned sponging, 5", VG	50.00
Pitcher, olive gr/wht w/bl edge band, 6½", EX	275.00
Shakers, bl/wht, patterned sponging, paneled sides, 4¼", pr	365.00
Spitton, bl/wht, patterned sponging, 2 bl stripes, 8" dia	200.00
Teapot, bl/wht, 8½", from $1,200 to	1,500.00
Washbowl & pitcher, bl/wht, allover sponging, 5x14", 10x7½"	750.00
Washbowl & pitcher, bl/wht, patterned sponging, bl stripe, 10", 14"	500.00
Waste pot, bl/wht, patterned sponging, bl lines, 4⅜x7½", EX	250.00

Spoons

Souvenir spoons have been popular remembrances since the 1890s. The early hand-wrought examples of the silversmith's art are especially sought and appreciated for their fine craftsmanship. Commemorative, personality-related, advertising, and those with Indian busts or floral designs are only a few of the many types of collectible spoons. In the following listings, spoons are sorted by city, character, or occasion.

Key:
B — bowl	gw — gold washed
emb — embossed	H — handle
eng — engraved	HR — handle reverse
ff — full figure	

Alamo/San Antonio TX enameling in B; Texas/star on H; Sterling	65.00
Alaska eng in B; miner ff H; Sterling, 5¼"	80.00
Avenue of Palms...Panama emb in B; train/ship/palms/tools on H; 5"	42.50
Baltimore eng in B; city seal/Poe's monument/banner on H; silver, 6"	55.00
Bartlesville OK & cowboy roping steer in B; Indian lady ff H; Sterling	55.00
Chisholm MN eng in gw B; miner ff H; Sterling, 5⅛"	55.00
Christmas tree/Santa/holly/bells form H; Merry Christmas/socks in B	75.00
Cincinnati OH/fountain emb in B; bridge/cityscape ff H: Paye & Baker	42.00
Crescent Hotel, Eureka Springs AR in gw B; floral H; Sterling, 5⅛"	75.00
Dome of Cologne HP in B; 2 coats of arms HP on H; gw coin silver, 5"	45.00
GN Depot Williston ND/scene in B; Nouveau floral H; Wallace, 5¼"	45.00

Golden Gate/Hotel St Francis B; San Francisco skyline H; Paye & Baker...65.00
Goldminer ff H; plain B; Sterling, ca 1915, 5⅝" 135.00
Indian chief ff H; plain B; silver, Shiebler & Co, ca 1880, 6⅛" 110.00
Joliet IL High School emb in B; IL scenes on H; Sterling, 6" 80.00
Key West FL & key on H: plain B; Wallace, Pat 1925, 5¾" 45.00
Kill Mts eng/2 cats emb in B; Indian chief/corn on H; Paye & Baker .. 70.00
Lawrence KS/First House emb in B; fruit on H: dtd '04 on H bk; hallmk .. 48.00
Mormon Temple emb in ruffled B; angel finial/Moroni on H; Sterling... 60.00
Mudlavia eng in B; squirrel w/nut finial H; Sterling, 4⅛" 100.00
New Bedford MA/Whaling Ship Niger eng in B; Watson, 5" 70.00
Niagara & falls scene emb in B; falls scene/Indian H; silver, pre-1921 ... 50.00
Nome ND eng in B; nude Nouveau lady emb on H; silver, unknown mk, 5" .. 60.00
NV & 3 scenes emb on H; Pride of Desert Goldfield/cactus emb in B.. 135.00
Owen Sound eng in B; Indian chief ff H; silver, 4⅛" 55.00
Petersburg AK eng in B; bear/walrus/dogsled team emb on H; Sterling.. 65.00
Poland Spring/Poland Water/Poland Mineral Spring Water on H; Durgin .95.00
Salem & witch emb on H; plain B; Durgin for Daniel Low, 1892 .. 60.00
Sarlington WI High School emb in B; Plymouth pattern H; Gorham ..55.00
Union soldier finial H; GAR symbols/Dayton in gw B; Sterling, 4¼"... 110.00
Waukesha WI eng in B; Indian chief ff H; Sterling, 5¼" 65.00
Yale pennant in bl enamel on B; Horace/Alma Mater on H; 5⅞" 8.00

Sporting Goods

Vintage ammunition boxes, duck and goose calls, knives, and fishing gear are just a few of the items that collectors of this type of memorabilia look for today. Also favored are posters, catalogs, and envelopes from well known companies such as Winchester, Remington, Peters, Ithaca, and Dupont. See also Fishing Collectibles.

Barrel, DuPont Smokeless...Powder, wood w/tin litho label, 1-lb, EX.. 90.00
Book, Custom Built Rifles, R Simmons, 1949 1st ed, EX............... 60.00
Book, Single Shot Rifles, Grand, hardbk, 1947 1st ed, VG+.......... 60.00
Booklet, Shooting Facts, Out Door Life, 1928, 84-pg, 6¾x5", EX.. 40.00
Box, cartridge; Peters, print on dvtl wood, 9x15x9½", EX............ 400.00
Box, cartridge; Record Loaded Paper Shells, 2-pc, 4½", EX 80.00
Box, cartridge; Western 22 Cal Rim Fire ..., rare, NM................. 315.00
Box, shot shell; Ideal Non-Rusting..., 2-pc, EX.......................... 235.00
Box, shot shell; Peters .410, bl-wing teal, 2-pc, EX...................... 365.00
Box, shot shell; Peters High Velocity 20 Ga, 2-pc, empty, G 125.00
Box, shot shell; Peters High Velocity 28 Ga, 1-pc, full, EX............ 95.00
Box, shot shell; UMC New Club 16 Ga, holds 100, full, G.......... 175.00
Box, shot shell; UMC Nitro Club Game Loads, 2-pc, 4x4¼x2½", EX... 210.00
Box, shot shell; Winchester 28 Ga Repeater, game bird, 1-pc, EX ..875.00
Brochure, Hercules Sporting Powders, man/dog cover, 1927, EX... 35.00
Brochure, Remington UMC Kleanbore Hi-Speed 22s, foldout, 10x3¼", NM... 70.00
Bullet mold, Whitworth Paperpatch, .438 caliber by L Kranen, M.. 355.00
Calendar, beagles hunting, Peters Cartridge Co, full pad, 1927, EX...3,000.00
Calendar, Treasure of the March, muskrats, Maas & Steffen, 1943, EX .450.00
Call, crow; Faulk's Model C-50, M... 32.50
Call, deer; Herter's, wood & blk Bakelite, 2 reeds, 1962, 5½", MIB .. 40.00
Call, goose; Black Duck, wood, 5⅛", EX 38.00
Call, turkey; Easy Squeeze-O-Matic, Smith's Game Calls, NM 30.00
Can, powder; Am Powder Mills, revolver on paper label, 5½", VG+ ... 875.00
Can, powder; Curtiss & Harvey No 6, rabbit/pheasant, 5⅛x4½", EX. 150.00
Can, powder; Dead Shot, game bird reserve on gr, 1-lb, 5x3¾", VG..220.00
Can, powder; Dead Shot, game bird reserve on red, 4x3½x1", EX+...220.00
Can, powder; DuPont Superfine FFF..., oval, brass-plated cap, EX. 50.00
Can, powder; Laflin & Rand, flag on orange, dtd 1900, 6x411", EX ..100.00
Catalog, Abercrombie & Fitch, man w/2 dogs on cover, 1930, VG60.00
Catalog, J Stevens #52, lt soiling/wear, VG 115.00
Catalog, Winchester #67, 1901, 164-pg, VG+............................. 275.00
Cover, DuPont Powders, shooting contest, ca 1914, 3½x6½", EX... 100.00
Cover, Marlin Firearms, lady w/shotgun, cancelled 1916, 3½x6", NM ... 1,000.00
Cover, Peters Cartridges, elk scene, cancelled 1903, 3½x6½", NM.. 1,650.00
Cover, Remington UMC, game bird & shells, 3½x6½", EX......... 170.00
Cover, Stevens Arms, men shooting, cancelled 1904, 3½x6½", EX. 1,400.00
Crate, Peters Victor 12 Ga, dvtl wood, red/bl print, VG 60.00
Crate, Small Arms Smokeless Powder, Sears Roebuck, nailed wood, EX.. 300.00
Crate, US Cartridge Co Ajax 12 Ga, dvtl wood, red/blk print, G....50.00
Envelope, DuPont Monora, hunting dog, ca 1910, NM 250.00
Envelope, Hunter Arms Co, dog w/game bird, unused, M........... 255.00
Felt, Dead Shot Smokeless, mallard duck, 10x11¾", VG+ 200.00
Felt, UMC Cartridges, fading/stain, 10⅞x12", G........................ 250.00
Paperweight, Bakelite duck head, Animal Trap Co, 5x3¾x3½", NM... 450.00
Patch, MI Successfull Deer Hunter, issued by DNR, 1972, M...... 485.00
Postcard, DuPont Powder Wagon, after H Pyle, ca 1860, G......... 115.00
Poster, Infallible, pr of mallards, DuPont, 26x20", EX 4,850.00
Poster, Smokeless Shotgun Powder, hunter, DuPont, 1910, 27x18", VG.. 4,000.00
Poster, When Food Is Scarce, PA Game Commission, 14x11", EX.. 275.00

Sports Collectibles

When sports cards became so widely collectible several years ago, other types of related memorabilia started to interest sports fans. Now they search for baseball uniforms, autographed baseballs, game-used bats and gloves, and all sorts of ephemera. Although baseball is America's all-time favorite, other sports have their own groups of interested collectors. Our advice for this category comes from Paul Longo Americana. Mr. Longo is listed in the Directory under Massachusetts. To learn more about old golf clubs, we recommend *The Vintage Era of Golf Club Collectibles* by Ronald O. John (Collector Books).

Baseball

Baseball, Official Am League, cork center, 1950s, M in VG box .. 135.00
Baseball, Rawlings Official Nat'l League, early 1980s, MIB............ 75.00
Bat, Case Hardened Spalding No 5, wrapped hdl, 34⅝", G............ 90.00
Bat, JC Higgins, Babe Ruth in block letters, 1930s-40s, 34½", EX.. 175.00
Cleats, Sears, Ted Williams, blk leather, 1960s, M w/hang tag..... 100.00
Glove, Draper Maynard, Hughie Critz, brn leather 'lefty,' ca 1930, EX.. 325.00
Glove, Rawlings Model MM9, Mickey Mantle, brn leather, 1950s, NM .. 95.00
Glove, Smith, buckle-bk, full web, gold patch, pre-1920, EX 275.00
Glove, Walter Johnson Hutch #31, brn leather, 1920s-30s, EX ... 400.00
Pennant, Brooklin Dodgers, wht on red felt, late 1940s, M.......... 175.00
Pennant, Philadelphia Phillies, yel on blk felt, 1940s-50s, M 80.00
Pennant, St Louis Browns, orange/wht on brn, 1940s, EX 250.00

Football

Charm, University of MI football, 10k gold, 1926........................ 110.00
Doll, Red Grange, pnt leather, orig uniform, 1920s, 18", EX........ 550.00
Football, Official, leather, watermelon type, ca 1890-1907, EX ... 135.00
Helmet, Davega, red/blk leather, fleece lined, chin strap, 1930s, EX... 140.00
Helmet, JC Higgins, front wing/3 stripes on leather, wool lining, EX ... 325.00
Helmet, MacGregor, leather high-crown type, 1940s-50s, EX 175.00
Helmet, Rawlings, leather, w/chin strap, 1920s, EX 175.00
Helmet, Rawlings, yel & blk leather turtle-shell style, 1940s, EX ... 165.00
Helmet, Thomas E Wilson, leather dog-ear style, 1920s-30s, EX.. 165.00
Pants, wood slats for padding in ea leg, laces, olive gr, 1920s, NM ... 115.00
Pennant, Baltimore Colts, horse on bl felt, 1950s, EX.................. 125.00
Pennant, Boston Patriots, red felt, 1960s, 30", M 100.00
Pennant, Boston Yankees, yel on gr felt, ca 1944-48, 29", EX...... 150.00
Pennant, Cleveland Browns, mc on bl felt, 1950s, 30", NM 135.00
Pennant, LSU Tigers, yel & wht on purple felt, 1959, EX............ 100.00
Pennant, NY Yankees/player on blk felt, 1950, 29", EX 125.00

Postcard, photo of University of MI team, 1909, EX 225.00
Program, Al-Am Conference, NY Yankees vs Cleveland Browns, 1947, EX...250.00
Program, Auburn vs Tulane, October 1950, EX 130.00
Program, Chicago Bears vs Detroit Lions, NFL, 1935, EX........... 300.00
Program, Cleveland Bulldogs at Frankford, 1925, EX 525.00
Program, Duke vs Georgia Tech, 1934, M............................... 100.00
Program, Harvard vs Dartmouth, Nov 16, 1912, EX 300.00
Program, Notre Dame, Knute Rockne on cover, 1929, VG......... 575.00
Ticket pass, MI Wolverines season ticket for 1901-02 season, EX...250.00

Tennis Rackets

Most collectible tennis rackets date between 1880 and 1950. The year 1880 is a somewhat arbitrary beginning of the 'modern' tennis era, since the first official Wimbledon tournament was held in 1877, and the US National Lawn Tennis Association was formed in 1881. Many types of tennis rackets were produced well before 1880, but generally these were designed for games far different than the lawn tennis we know today.

Rackets produced between the 1880s and 1950s were generally made of wood, although some like those made by the Dayton Steel Company (1920s) or the Birmingham Aluminum Company (1920s) were made of metal. The most common head shape is oval, but some were flat on top, some flat transitional, and some even lopsided. Handles were generally larger than those seen today, and most were unfinished wood with vertical ribs called 'combing,' rarer models featured cork handles or 'checkered' wood. The leather-wrapped handle common today was not introduced widely until the mid-1930s. Unusual enlargements to the butt end of the handle are generally desirable and might be called fishtail, fantail, bulbous, tall tail, or flared. The 'wedge,' a triangular section of wood located at the junction of the handle and the head, might be solid or laminated and can be a good indication of age, since most solid wedges date to before 1905. Like most collectibles, racket values depend on rarity, age, and condition. Prices for well preserved rackets in this period may range from $50.00 to well over $1,000.00. Tennis ball cans are also very collectible and may be worth hundreds of dollars for rare unopened examples. Our advisor for this category is Donald Jones; he is listed in the Directory under Georgia.

Key:
cx-lam — convex laminated   tran — transitional
cx-s — convex solid

AJ Reach, Driver, concave wedge, combed hdl, oval head, 1920.. 125.00
Dayton, steel w/wooden hdl, 1924 .... 250.00
E Kent, Duchess, concave wedge, bulbous hdl, oval head, 1930 ..200.00
Hazel's Streamline, branched wedge, leather hdl, oval head, 1935...1,000.00
Horsman, Elberton, concave wedge, smooth hdl, flat-top head, 1885 ..600.00
Iver Johnson, Special, cx-s wedge, bulbous hdl, tran head, 1900.....250.00
Magnon, Superior, concave wedge, combed hdl, oval head, 1928...100.00
Slazinger, Demon, cx-lam wedge, fishtail hdl, oval head, 1910 ....400.00
Spaulding, Park, cx-s wedge, combed hdl, flat-top head, 1895 .....800.00
Wright-Ditson, Hub, cx-s wedge, checkered hdl, oval head, 1890..175.00

Miscellaneous

Basketball, belt buckle, University of KY Champions, 1987-88, M ..35.00
Basketball, guide, LSU Tigers, 1969-70, NM 200.00
Basketball, pennant, Denver Rockets, mc on wht felt, 1960s 200.00
Basketball, program, Boston Celtics vs MN Lakers, Nov 9, 1950, EX ...35.00
Basketball, program, KY vs Wake Forest, Dec 14, 1953, 9x6", EX ...35.00
Basketball, ring, 10k gold ball image on top, dtd 1932, girl's......... 60.00
Boxing, cabinet card, John L Sullivan in boxing pose, blk/wht, EX...225.00
Boxing, postcard, Jack Johnson & Jim James Jeffries photo, 1910, EX....135.00
Golf, club, Bethlehem Steel Lukens, chrome plated, limited ed, M..75.00

Golf, club, J Harland, wood shaft, leather grips, ca 1930, rpr, 40".. 50.00
Golf, club, Kroydon Imperial #9, red line to base, EX 30.00
Racing, belt buckle, Harley-Davidson, silver w/crossed flags, M.. 1,350.00
Racing, Charlie Paddock sprinting, blk/wht, 1922, 8½x6½", VG .. 45.00
Racing, Nat'l Air Races, Cleveland OH, 1938, 65-pg, EX 55.00
Racing, poster, Monaco Grand Prix, Geo Ham, 1933, 38x26", NM .. 40.00

St. Clair

The St. Clair Glass Company began as a small family-oriented operation in Elwood, Indiana, in 1941. Most famous for their lamps, the family made numerous small items of carnival, pink and caramel slag, and custard glass as well. Later, paperweights became popular production pieces; many command relatively high prices on today's market. Weights are stamped and usually dated, while small production pieces are often unmarked. Sulfide paperweights are especially popular with collectors. Lamps are in big demand (prices depend on size and whether or not they are signed), as are items signed by Paul or Ed St. Clair, brothers who only made pieces on their breaks. For further information we recommend *St. Clair Glass Collector's Book, Vol. II*, by our advisor Ted Pruitt. He is listed in the Directory under Indiana.

Animal dish, dolphin, bl, Joe St Clair... 175.00
Ashtray, brns, bowl shape w/3 rests, from $85 to 95.00
Bell, fruit pattern, bl carnival, from $90 to 100.00
Bell, rose, from $1,000 to.. 1,200.00
Bottle, Grape & Cable, w/stopper, red carnival, w/stopper........... 150.00

Bottle, interior with white flower and bubbles, $95.00.

Bowl, fluted rim, from $225 to.. 250.00
Candleholder, sulfide, mc floral, ea from $75 to............................ 85.00
Cordial, any color, from $50 to... 65.00
Figurine, Southern Belle, bl carnival... 75.00
Goblet, Rose in Snow, from $40 to 50.00
Lamp, blown ball shape, unsgn, from $275 to............................... 300.00
Lamp, TV; unsgn, from $975 to.. 1,000.00
Marble, baseball player, Ed St Clair, from $125 to......................... 150.00
Mug, Holly Band, caramel slag, from $90 to 95.00
Paperweight, pear, bl carnival... 100.00
Paperweight, rose, pk petals/4 gr leaves, Joe St Clair, 3½".......... 720.00
Paperweight, rose, various colors, windowed, ea......................... 1,200.00
Paperweight, sulfide, cat, windowed & etched, from $225 to....... 250.00
Paperweight, sulfide, Harry S Truman, from $125 to 150.00
Paperweight, sulfide, Kennedy, windowed, Paul St Clair, mini..... 500.00
Paperweight, turtle, from $150 to.. 175.00
Plate, Mt St Helens, from $20 to.. 25.00
Plate, Reagan - Bush, from $25 to 30.00
Ring holder, teapot shape, crimped or flowered, from $75 to 85.00
Salt dip, swan, wht or red, ea from $100 to................................... 125.00

Sugar bowl, Holly Band, wht carnival or amber Tiffany, ea from $85 to .. 100.00
Toothpick holder, Fan & Feather, from $25 to 30.00
Toothpick holder, fez hat, from $135 to 150.00
Toothpick holder, Mrs Degenhart, from $45 to 50.00
Vase, blown, waisted, from $175 to 200.00
Vase, Butterfly, paperweight base, from $300 to 350.00
Wine, Pinwheel, from $35 to 45.00

Staffordshire

Scores of potteries sprang up in England's Staffordshire district in the early eighteenth century; several remain to the present time. (See also specific companies.) Figurines and groups were made in great numbers; dogs were favorite subjects. Often they were made in pairs, each a mirror image of the other. They varied in heights from 3" or 4" to the largest, measuring 16" to 18". From 1840 until about 1900, portrait figures were produced to represent specific characters, both real and fictional. As a rule these were never marked.

Historical transferware was made throughout the district; some collectors refer to it as Staffordshire Blue. It was produced as early as 1780, and because much was exported to America, it was very often decorated with transfers depicting scenic views of well-known American landmarks. Early examples were printed in a deep cobalt. By 1830 a softer blue was favored, and within the next decade black, brown, pink, red, and green prints were used. Although sometimes careless about adding their trademark, many companies used their own border designs that were as individual as their names. This ware should not be confused with the vast amounts of modern china (mostly plates) made from early in the century to the present. These souvenir or commemorative items are usually marketed through gift stores and the like. (See Rowland and Marsellus.) Our advisor for this category is Jeanne Dunay; she is listed in the Directory under South Carolina. See also specific manufacturers.

Key:
blk — black
gr — green
d/b — dark blue
l/b — light blue
m/b — medium blue
m-d/b — medium dark blue

Figures and Groups

Benjamin Franklin, cobalt jacket, holding tricorn hat, 1800s, 13" ... 1,000.00
Bird on branch, lead-glazed creamware, late 18th C, 5¼" 2,350.00
Charity allegorical, lady w/baby & child, ca 1800, 8½" 175.00
Cockatoo, wht w/yel combs, sgn JT Jones, 20th C, 13", pr 1,295.00
Couple sitting in arbor, HP details w/gold & lustre, 14x10", EX .. 150.00
Departure/Return, sailor & lady, 19th C, 8½", pr 1,120.00
Dog on pillow w/tassels, rust/yel/brn/gr (Pratt palette), 3½", pr... 2,350.00
Empress of France on galloping horse, 1850s, 9½" 235.00
Fortitude allegorical, lady holding column, mc, ca 1820, 22" 1,765.00
George Washington bust, HP w/bl sponged coat, marbleized base, 8" .. 375.00
Hound, wht w/brn spots, naturalistic base, 1820s, 6¾" L 1,410.00
Joan & Darby having evening drink, mc, 5⅝" 100.00
Lion, brn w/gilt & blk details, glass eyes, 1800s, 10x5x10", pr 470.00
Lion, free-standing legs, thin body/comic face, on base, sponging, 6". 8,400.00
Lion Slayer, Scotsman holds lion by its bk paw, 16" 400.00
Lion w/paw on globe on base, mc, att Wood, 11" L 3,175.00
Madonna & Child, seated/joyful pose, early 19th C, 13¼" 950.00
Male bust on circular socle, gr marbled glaze, 19th C, 20" 3,175.00
Man in striped pants holding calico cat, mc, 7¾" 235.00
Naughty barmaid w/wine bottle & no undergarments, sm rprs, 8⅛" .. 350.00
Prince & Princess (Wales) in pony cart, HP w/gold trim, 7¼" 200.00
Pug reclines on rectangular base, translucent brn, 1700s, 3½" L 1,500.00
Queen Victoria (& Prince Albert), mc/bl underglaze, 1880s, 8", pr ... 325.00
Ram w/lamb below, coleslaw vegetation, sgn Walton, 6¾" 430.00
Royal Coat of Arms, group, pearlware, Walton, 1920s, 6" 4,400.00
Samson & lion, upright/wrestling, rpr to his orange scarf, 12" 420.00
Spaniel seated, blk spots, yel eyes, red collar, 12", pr 175.00
Spaniel sitting up & wearing tricorner hat, pitcher, 20th C, 10" ... 110.00
Spaniel standing on free-form oval base, early 19th C, 5", pr 500.00
St George & Dragon, naturalistic base, ochre/gr details, 11", G .. 400.00
St George & slain dragon, lead-glazed gray, 11½" 1,525.00
Venus w/Cupid atop dolphin/shells, mc pearlware, ca 1835, 9¾" .. 1,765.00

Transferware

Basket, Boston State House, d/b, rtcl, Rogers, 3x9¼x5½"+tray. 2,750.00
Basket, fruit; Regent St London, d/b, rtcl, Adams, 4⅜x11¼" 600.00
Bowl, Capitol Washington, d/b, Stevenson, 11" 2,645.00
Bowl, Sheltered Pheasants, d/b, att Hall, 2¼x10½" 300.00
Bowl, vegetable; couple in boat/castle beyond, d/b, Adams, 2¼x12" .. 385.00
Bowl, vegetable; NC State of Arms, d/b, unmk, 2¾x12¾x9¾" .. 5,175.00
Cup plate, Select Views, d/b, R Hall, 4" 125.00
Cup plate, Staughton's Church misidentified, d/b, Stevenson, 4⅛" ... 2,185.00
Pitcher, Abbey Ruins, d/b, Mayer, 10x8½" 650.00
Pitcher, Eagle, Scroll in Beak; Adams, 5¾" 625.00
Pitcher, Welcome Lafayette...Glory, d/b, Clews, 5", NM 2,100.00
Plate, Baltimore & OH Railroad (level), d/b, Wood & Sons, 10" ... 900.00
Plate, Cadmus, d/b, shell border, Wood & Sons, 10⅛" 355.00
Plate, Christ Church Oxford, d/b, Ridgway, 9¾", NM 195.00
Plate, City of Albany...NY, d/b, shell border, Woods & Sons, 10" ... 300.00
Plate, Fair Mount Near Philadelphia, m/b, eagle border, Stubbs, 10" .. 300.00
Plate, Landing of Gen Lafayette at NY 1824, d/b, Clews, 10" 265.00
Plate, Musketeer, d/b, Rogers, 7¾" 200.00
Plate, roses, d/b, Wm Smith & Co, 1830s, 7" 125.00
Plate, Seal of US, mc w/bl feather scalloped edge, 19th C, 8" ... 1,995.00
Plate, Valentine From Wilkies Designs, m/b, 9", pr 345.00
Plate, Winter View of Pittsfield, d/b, Clews, 8⅝" 295.00
Plate, Winter View of Pittsfield, d/b, floral border, Clews, 10½" ... 350.00
Platter, Canova, brn, Mayer, 1834-48, 15¾x13½" 700.00
Platter, Persian, brn, Ridgway, 1830-34, 18¾x15", NM 600.00
Platter, Venus, gr/brn, Podmore Walker, 15¾x12½" 500.00
Platter, Vue de Chateau Ermenonville, d/b, Wood, 12⅝x10" 460.00
Soup, 3-story building/Justice/Liberty/Washington, d/b, Clews, 10" ... 300.00
Sugar bowl, Wadsworth Tower, d/b, w/lid, Wood & Sons, 6x7" ... 400.00
Tea bowl & saucer, Wadsworth Tower, d/b, Wood & Sons, 2⅜", 5¾" ... 235.00
Teapot, Castle Toward, d/b, fruit & floral borders, Hall, 6¼" 385.00
Teapot, MacDonnough's Victory, d/b, 1819-46, sm chip, 7½" ... 2,000.00
Tureen, Pastoral Courtship, Stevenson, 1920s, 10x13x9" 1,200.00
Waste bowl, Lafayette at Franklin's Tomb, d/b, 3x5½", EX 375.00

Miscellaneous

Fish service, transfers, molded gilt edges, 8 8" plates+20" platter .. 500.00
Mug, cream-colored dicing/bands on brn & yel, 1750s, 6" 3,000.00
Plaque, Toby Filpot/cherubs/taverners, mc/relief, 1820s, 8¾" 3,175.00
Plate, salt glazed, emb floral/vine border, 1765, 9½" 1,000.00
Platter, gadrooned/scalloped rim, brn mottle w/mc spots, 18th C, 15" 1,050.00
Punch pot, streaky gr & brn lead glaze, crabstock hdl/spout, 7" ... 1,000.00
Tankard, salt glazed, 'GR' (George III) medallion, bl stain, 1760, 6" .. 950.00
Teapot, lead-glazed creamware, HP Aurora/angels, ca 1775, 5" ... 2,115.00
Teapot, lead-glazed creamware, HP Bacchus scenes, rpr, 1775, 5⅜" ... 1,400.00
Teapot, lead-glazed creamware, HP fruits/basketweave, 1775, 5" .. 950.00
Teapot, salt glazed, grapevines/florals emb on cobalt, 18th C, 4". 1,000.00
Teapot, salt glazed, paneled nudes, lion finial, 8-sided, 18th C, 4" .. 1,400.00
Teapot, salt glazed, shell panels, arm w/serpent spout, 18th C, 6" ... 1,200.00
Wall pocket, lead glazed, satyr mask among foliage, mc, 18th C, 8". 265.00

Stained Glass

There are many factors to consider in evaluating a window or panel of stained glass art. Besides the obvious factor of condition, quality of leadwork, intricacy, jeweling, beveling, and the amount of selenium (red, orange, and yellow) present should all be taken into account. Remember, repair work is itself an art and can be very expensive. Our advisor for this category is Carl Heck; he is listed in the Directory under Colorado. See also Tiffany.

Ceiling Lights

20" geometric shade w/wreath border, gr/caramel/red, +chain & mts ... 470.00
22" geometric w/wide floral skirt, uneven edge 2,645.00
24" gr slag geometric w/wide band of red lyres, crescent band at rim .. 600.00

24", shell motif, $6,750.00. (Photo courtesy Fontaine's Auction Gallery)

26" ogee shade w/row of simple Arts & Crafts tulips, Williamson .. 1,200.00
29" 6-panel brickwork shade w/cast-metal floral o/l, apron w/6 panes .. 18,400.00

Lamps

17" open-top 6-panel scalloped-edge shade; w/std, Duffner/Kimberly, 25" 2,760.00
18" dogwood/leaf border, uneven edge; slim std, Bigelow/Kennard, 20" 10,000.00
18" geometric-panel shade w/wide floral skirt, uneven edge; simple std .. 1,035.00
18" lotus-border (wide) & brickwork shade; lotus-emb std, Suess, 24" 5,000.00
18" shade w/6 bent panels+jeweled apron; ribbed std, Duffner/Kimberly .. 5,000.00
19" Louis XV 4-lobe shade; Louis XV dore std, Duffner/Kimberly, 23" 43,700.00
20" swirling tulips/leaves dome shade; ornate Nouveau std, 30" .. 3,500.00
21" Louis XV shade w/heavy rtcl metal strips & cap, Duffner/Kimberly .. 27,600.00
24" rose-bush dome shade w/uneven edge; simple std, Bigelow/Kennard 13,000.00

Windows and Doors

Am Aesthetic Period, floral mosaic, poured lead, Belcher, 104x66" ... 42,000.00
Arched transom, flowers/leaves on clear to etched field, 21x52" .. 400.00
Arts & Crafts, arrows/sqs, gold leaf/gr on clear, A Huen, 62x22", pr .. 5,400.00
Center: ldgl/HP w/child & dog, jeweled border, on light box, 24x28" .. 3,200.00
Flower basket w/in arch, trailing ribbons on clear field, 46x80" fr .. 1,500.00
Flower vase w/in niche, yel & ruby ground, fruitwood stain, 37x23" .. 300.00
Geometric panel w/HP cameo of Renaissance man, 75x14"+fr, pr .. 1,900.00
Ribbon loops & foliage border w/jewels, caramel center, 35x15"+fr .. 3,000.00
Ribbon swags/chunk-glass roses/flaming torches/etc, 19th C, 142x63" .. 10,000.00
Window, Semper Fidelis/coat of arms, HP details, 33x28" fr 650.00

Stanford

The Stanford Pottery Co. was founded in 1945 in Sebring, Ohio. One of the founders was George Stanford, a former manager at Spaulding China (Royal Copley). They continued in operations until the factory was destroyed by a fire about 1961. They produced a Corn Line, similar to that of the Shawnee Company, that is today very collectible. Most examples are marked (either Stanford Sebring Ohio or with a paper label), so there should be no difficulty in distinguishing one line from the other. For information on the other items made by Stanford, see *Garage Sale and Flea Market Annual* (Collector Books). Our advisor for this category is Joe Devine; he is listed in the Directory under Iowa.

Corn Line, butter dish 45.00
Corn Line, casserole, 8" L 40.00
Corn Line, cookie jar 75.00
Corn Line, creamer & sugar bowl w/lid 45.00
Corn Line, cup 15.00
Corn Line, grease jar, 6½" 45.00
Corn Line, pitcher, 7½" 45.00
Corn Line, plate, 9" L 25.00
Corn Line, relish tray 35.00
Corn Line, shakers, sm, pr 20.00
Corn Line, shakers, 4", pr 25.00
Corn Line, snack set, cup & plate w/indent, #709 .... 65.00
Corn Line, spoon rest 25.00
Corn Line, teapot 60.00
Corn Line, tumbler 25.00
Wall pocket, cherry branch, red pie-crust edge, #299, mk, 6¼" 28.00

Stangl

Stangl Pottery was one of the longest-existing potteries in the United States, having as its beginning in 1814 the Sam Hill Pottery, becoming the Fulper Pottery which gained eminence in the field of art pottery (ca 1860), and then coming under the aegis of Johann Martin Stangl. The German-born Stangl joined Fulper in 1910 as chemical engineer, left for a brief stint at Haeger in Dundee, Illinois, and rejoined Fulper as general manager in 1920. He became president of the firm in 1928. Although Stangl's name was on much of the ware from the late '20s onward, the company's name was not changed officially until 1955. J. M. Stangl died in 1972; the pottery continued under the ownership of Wheaton Industries until 1978, then closed. Stangl is best known for its extensive Birds of American line, styled after Audubon; its brightly colored, hand-carved, hand-painted dinnerware; and its great variety of giftware, including its dry-brushed gold lines. For more information we recommend *Collector's Encyclopedia of Stangl Artware, Lamps, and Birds, Second Edition,* by Robert Runge Jr. (Collector Books). Another good reference is *Stangl Pottery* by Harvey Duke; for ordering information refer to the listing for Nancy and Robert Perzel, Popkorn Antiques (our advisors for this category), in the Directory under New Jersey.

Artware and Novelties

Ashtray, bird, Silver Green, #3210, 1938-42, 4", from $50 to 60.00
Ashtray, coaster; Pink Butterfly, #3802, 1948, from $40 to 60.00
Ashtray, elephant sitting, Silver Green, #1052, 1925-32, from $100 to . 125.00
Bank, pig, red bsk, #5188, 1967-69, 4" 100.00
Bowl, Tangerine & bl, cut-out ft, #1945, 1935-36, 11", from $100 to ... 125.00
Bowl, Tangerine w/gr lining, #1148S, 1927-29, 6", from $25 .... 30.00
Bowl, vegetable; Persian Yellow, w/lid, Anchor Pottery mold, $100 to ... 125.00
Box, cigarette; tropical flower, #3793, 1948, from $250 to 350.00
Candleholder, rnd, Silver Green, #1371, 1930-34, 3x4", pr from $40 to .. 50.00
Candy dish, Colonial Blue, bird finial, #1388, 1930s, 5x5", from $80 to . 100.00
Candy dish, The Garden Flower, w/hdl, #3714, 1942, 8", from $70 to .. 85.00
Candy jar, Early Pennsylvania Artware, bl, #3684, 4x7", $60 to 80.00
Jar, ring; gold crackle lustre, Fulper decor, #1165, 1927-29, $150 to ... 200.00
Jar, sand; Satin White, rope hdls, #1593, 1932-38, from $250 to .. 300.00
Pitcher & bowl, wht, rose, 1965-72, lg, from $200 to 250.00

Punch cup & saucer, wht, rose motif, from $15 to 20.00
Rose bowl, Sunburst, acanthus decor, #1548, 1931+, 5½", $75 to ...100.00
Sugar bowl, Colonial Blue, w/bird finial on lid, from $60 to 75.00
Table, Apple Green, antlered deer, #1594, 24", from $2,000 to . 2,500.00
Vase, Blue-of-the-Sky, shell leaves, #1912, 1935-36, 7", from $45 to. 55.00
Vase, brn, scallops on body, ftd, #3217, 7", from $25 to................. 35.00
Vase, bud; wht, #4050, 8", from $15 to 20.00
Vase, Colonial Blue, urn form w/hdls, #1758, 1933-39, 12", from $65 to... 75.00
Vase, Eggplant & Oyster White, scroll decor, #2024, 1935-36, $165 to.185.00
Vase, horse head, Antique Gold, #3611, 1959-62, 13", from $200 to ...250.00
Vase, Persian Yellow, medallion, hdls, #2039, 1936-37, 8", $60 to...75.00
Vase, pitcher; Green Matt, #1666, 1933-35, 9½", from $80 to..... 125.00
Vase, rust, ball form, #1907S, 5", from $45 to................................. 55.00
Vase, Satin Blue, scalloped rim, ftd, #3222, 1938-41, 5½", $20 to ...30.00
Vase, Satin White, urn form w/hdls, #1758, 1933-39, 16", from $85 to.. 95.00
Vase, Silver Green, rnd base/scroll hdls, #2043, 1936, 9", from $70 to ..85.00
Vase, Silver Green, w/hdls, #2016, from $25 to 35.00
Vase, Sunburst (blended mc), acanthus decor, #1541, 1931+, 9", $125 to.150.00
Vase, Twilight Blue, oval/scalloped, w/hdls, #3191, 1938+, 9", $40 to ...50.00

Dinnerware

Americana #2000, bowl, fruit; 6", from $8 to.............................. 10.00
Americana #2000, bowl, salad; 10", from $25 to 35.00
Americana #2000, coffeepot, 6-cup, from $95 to...................... 120.00
Americana #2000, plate, 6", from $3 to......................................5.00
Americana #2000, salt shakers, pr from $16 to 20.00
Blue Tulip #3637, bowl, cereal; from $20 to.............................. 25.00
Blue Tulip #3637, butter dish, from $40 to 50.00
Blue Tulip #3637, cookie jar, from $45 to 55.00
Blue Tulip #3637, pitcher, 2-qt, from $95 to............................. 110.00
Bluebell #3334, bowl, salad; 10", from $60 to 70.00
Bluebell #3334, plate, 10", from $25 to 35.00
Bluebell #3334, platter, 12" L, from $75 to 85.00
Bluebell #3334, salt shakers, pr from $16 to.............................. 20.00
Bonita #3363, coffee cup, from $10 to 15.00
Bonita #3363, plate, 10", from $30 to 40.00
Carnival #3900, bowl, fruit; from $6 to.......................................8.00
Carnival #3900, cup, from $6 to...8.00
Carnival #3900, plate, 10", from $12 to 15.00
Colonial #1388, bowl, vegetable; oval, 12", from $50 to 60.00
Colonial #1388, candlestick, triple; ea from $65 to 75.00
Colonial #1388, plate, 6", from $4 to...6.00
Cosmos #3339, bowl, oval, 10", from $40 to 50.00
Cosmos #3339, plate, 6", from $10 to 12.00
Cosmos #3339, teapot, from $90 to... 130.00
Daisy #1870, bowl, nut; 4½", from $15 to 20.00
Daisy #1870, bowl, oval, 10", from $45 to................................. 55.00
Daisy #1870, bowl, relish; 6½", from $20 to 25.00
Daisy #1870, cup, from $12 to 15.00
Daisy #1870, plate, 6", from $15 to 20.00
Daisy #1870, saucer, from $5 to...7.00
Daisy #1870, teapot, from $135 to... 160.00
Dogwood #3668, creamer, from $20 to...................................... 25.00
Dogwood #3668, plate, 6", from $10 to 15.00
Floral #3342, bowl, salad; low, 12", from $90 to........................... 110.00
Floral #3342, bowl, salad; 12", from $80 to 95.00
Floral #3342, plate, 10", from $30 to... 40.00
Fluted #3600, ashtray, 5", from $10 to....................................... 15.00
Fluted #3600, creamer, from $10 to 15.00
Fluted #3600, sugar bowl, from $15 to 20.00
Fruit & Flowers #4030, bowl, salad; 12", from $90 to 125.00
Fruit & Flowers #4030, butter dish, from $60 to 75.00
Fruit & Flowers #4030, cigarette box, from $125 to 150.00

Fruit #3697, bowl, cereal; from $20 to.................................... 25.00
Fruit #3697, bowl, lug soup; from $15 to 20.00
Fruit #3697, bowl, mixing; 9", from $75 to 100.00
Fruit #3697, bowl, vegetable; 8", from $35 to 45.00
Fruit #3697, cake stand, from $20 to...................................... 25.00
Fruit #3697, platter, 11½" L, from $110 to 140.00
Fruit #3697, relish dish, from $30 to 45.00
Harvest #3341, ashtray, from $25 to 30.00
Harvest #3341, candlestick, ea from $15 to 20.00
Harvest #3341, cup, from $12 to 15.00
Harvest #3341, plate, 8", from $20 to 25.00
Harvest #3341, saucer, from $5 to 7.00
Jonquil #3774, bowl, coupe; 10", from $65 to 75.00
Jonquil #3774, plate, 10", from $25 to 35.00
Newport #3333, bowl, salad; 10", from $70 to 80.00
Newport #3333, cup, from $15 to... 20.00
Newport #3333, plate, 8", from $30 to 35.00
Norma #3364, bowl, salad; 10", from $80 to 95.00
Norma #3364, plate, 10", from $35 to 40.00
Norma #3364, teapot, from $125 to 150.00
Ranger #3304, ashtray, from $140 to.................................... 160.00
Ranger #3304, bowl, fruit; from $110 to 145.00
Ranger #3304, bowl, oval, 10", from $450 to......................... 550.00
Ranger #3304, creamer, from $100 to 125.00
Ranger #3304, plate, 6", $75 to... 90.00
Ranger #3304, plate, 10", from $275 to................................ 325.00
Ranger #3304, shaker, plain, ea from $65 to 85.00
Ranger #3304, teapot, from $850 to.................................1,000.00
Sunflower #3340, bowl, fruit; from $10 to 15.00
Sunflower #3340, creamer, from $20 to................................. 25.00
Sunflower #3340, plate, 10", from $35 to 45.00
Sunflower #3340, teapot, from $125 to 150.00
Thistle #3847, ashtray, fluted, 7", from $30 to 40.00
Thistle #3847, bowl, vegetable; w/lid, 8", from $75 to............. 100.00
Thistle #3847, coffeepot, 8-cup, from $75 to 85.00
Tropic #3338, bowl, salad; 10", from $70 to 85.00
Tropic #3338, creamer, from $20 to....................................... 25.00
Tropic #3338, cup, from $10 to 15.00
Tropic #3338, plate, 10", from $30 to 35.00
Tropic #3338, sugar bowl, from $20 to 25.00
Valencia #3320, bowl, salad; 12", from $100 to 150.00
Valencia #3320, plate, 10", from $65 to 75.00
Valencia #3320, sugar bowl, from $30 to................................ 35.00
Venice #3332, bowl, oval, 10", from $40 to 50.00
Venice #3332, creamer, from $15 to 20.00
Venice #3332, plate, 9", from $30 to 35.00
Venice #3332, sugar bowl, from $25 to 30.00

Stangl Birds and Animals

The Stangl company introduced their line of ceramic birds in 1940, taking advantage of an import market crippled by the onset of WWII. The figures were an immediate success. Additional employees were hired, and eventually 60 decorators worked at the plant itself, with the overflow contracted out to individuals in private homes. After the war when import trade once again saturated the market, Stangl curtailed their own production but continued to make the birds and animals on a limited basis as late as 1978. Nearly all the birds were marked. A four-digit number was used to identify the species, and most pieces were signed by the decorator. An 'F' indicates a bird that was decorated at the Flemington plant. Our advisors for this category are Nancy and Robert Perzel, Popkorn Antiques. (See the Directory under New Jersey.) Recommended reference books are listed in the Stangl Category.

Animals

#1076, Piggy bank, sponged wht, not cvd, Early Am Tulip, from $60 to .. 75.00
#1076, Piggy bank, Terra Rose, cvd, Early Am Tulip, from $75 to ..100.00
#3178A, Elkhound, wht w/blk overglaze, 3½", from $40 to 65.00
#3178F, Percheron, wht w/blk overglaze, 3½", from $50 to 75.00
#3178H, Squirrel, wht w/blk overglaze, 3½", from $50 to 75.00
#3178J, Gazelle, wht w/blk overglaze, 3½", from $60 to 75.00
#3243, Wire-Haired Terrier, 3¼", from $200 to 250.00
#3244, Draft Horse, 3", from $100 to 125.00
#3245, Rabbit, 2", from $255 to 275.00
#3246, Buffalo, 2½", from $250 to... 275.00
#3247, Gazelle, 3¾", from $200 to 250.00
#3248, Giraffe, 2½", from $400 to 500.00
#3249, Elephant, 3", from $175 to... 225.00
#3277, Colt, 5", from $1,200 to... 1,500.00
#3278, Goat, 5", from $1,300 to... 1,500.00
#3280, Dog sitting, 5¼", from $200 to 300.00
#3430, Duck, 22", from $8,000 to.....................................10,000.00
Cat, Siamese, Seal Point sitting, decor, 8½", from $500 to........... 600.00
Cat sitting, Granada Gold, 8½", from $150 to............................ 200.00

Birds

**#3433, Large Rooster, 16",
minimum value $8,000.00.**

(Photo courtesy David Rago)

#3250A, Duck standing, 3¼".. 100.00
#3250B, Duck preening, 3¼" 75.00
#3250D, Duck grazing, 3¾".. 75.00
#3250F, Duck quacking, 3¼".. 75.00
#3273, Rooster, hollow, 5¾", from $400 to 500.00
#3274, Penguin, 6"... 450.00
#3276D, Bluebirds (pr), 8½"... 150.00
#3281, Duck, mother, 6", from $500 to..................................... 600.00
#3285, Rooster, early, 4½".. 100.00
#3400, Lovebird, old version, 4".. 100.00
#3401, Wren, dk brn, revised, 3½" 45.00
#3401D, Wrens (pr), old version.. 450.00
#3401D, Wrens (pr), revised version.. 90.00
#3402D, Orioles (pr), revised, w/leaves, 5½" 100.00
#3404D, Lovebirds (pr) kissing, old version, 4½"....................... 350.00
#3405D, Cockatoos (pr), revised, 9½"...................................... 100.00
#3406, Kingfisher, teal, 3½" 75.00
#3406D, Kingfishers (pr), bl, 5".. 125.00
#3407, Owl, 5½x2½".. 300.00
#3408, Bird of Paradise, 5½".. 80.00
#3431, Duck standing, grayish wht w/blk spots........................1,000.00
#3443, Duck flying, gray, 9"... 250.00
#3443, Duck flying, teal, 9½x12".. 225.00
#3444, Cardinal, female.. 175.00

#3444, Cardinal, glossy pk, revised, 7" 70.00
#3445, Rooster, gray, 10" 225.00
#3448, Blue-Headed Vireo, 4¼" 55.00
#3450, Passenger Pigeon, 9x18"...1,800.00
#3451, Willow Ptarmigan..3,000.00
#3452, Painted Bunting, 5".. 75.00
#3453, Mountain Bluebird, 6⅛"..2,000.00
#3454, Key West Quail Dove, single wing up, 10"...................... 225.00
#3454, Key West Quail Dove, wings up, natural colors 1,750.00
#3455, Shoveler Duck, 12¼x14"...1,500.00
#3457, Chinese Pheasant walking, 7¼x15".............................3,000.00
#3458, Quail, 7½" 1,800.00
#3459, Fish Hawk...8,000.00
#3490D, Redstarts (pr), 9" 125.00
#3492, Cock Pheasant 150.00
#3518D, White-Crowned Pigeons (pr), bl w/wht heads, 8x14" ... 800.00
#3580, Cockatoo, med, 8⅞"... 125.00
#3580, Cockatoo, wht matt, med 550.00
#3581, Chickadees, brn/wht, group of 3, 5½x8½" 150.00
#3582D, Parakeets (pr), gr, 7".. 175.00
#3583, Parula Warbler, 4¼" 45.00
#3584, Cockatoo, sgn Jacob, lg, 11⅜" 250.00
#3584, Cockatoo, wht matt, lg 1,000.00
#3585, Rufous Hummingbird, 3" 70.00
#3586, Pheasant (Della Ware), natural colors 2,000.00
#3586, Pheasant (Della Ware), Terra Rose, gr 500.00
#3589, Indigo Bunting, 3½"... 50.00
#3590, Carolina Wren, 4½".. 150.00
#3591, Brewer's Blackbird, 3½".. 165.00
#3592, Titmouse, 3" 45.00
#3593, Nuthatch, 2½" 50.00
#3594, Red-Faced Warbler, 3" 100.00
#3595, Bobolink, 4¾" 150.00
#3597, Wilson Warbler, yel & blk, 3" 40.00
#3598, Kentucky Warbler, 3"... 45.00
#3599D, Hummingbirds (pr) 250.00
#3626, Broadtail Hummingbird, bl flower................................. 150.00
#3628, Rieffer's Hummingbird... 125.00
#3629, Broadbill Hummingbird, 4½" 125.00
#3634, Allen Hummingbird, 3½" 100.00
#3635, Gold Finches (group)... 175.00
#3715, Blue Jay, w/peanut, Fulper blk/bl glaze 2,000.00
#3716, Blue Jay, w/leaf, 10¼" 500.00
#3717, Blue Jays (pr)..3,500.00
#3747, Canary (left), bl flower, 6¼" 200.00
#3750, Scarlet Tanager, 8½" 300.00
#3751, Red-Headed Woodpecker, glossy pk, 6¼" 250.00
#3752D, Red-Headed Woodpeckers (pr), glossy pk, 7¼".............. 350.00
#3754, White-Wing Crossbill (single) 4,000.00
#3755, Audubon Warbler, pk flower, 4¼" 300.00
#3757, Scissor-Tailed Flycatcher, 11" 650.00
#3758, Magpie-Jay, 10¾" 1,000.00
#3811, Chestnut Chickadee, 5"... 125.00
#3813, Crested Goldfinch, 5" 125.00
#3814, Townsend Warbler, 3".. 150.00
#3815, Western Bluebird, 7"... 350.00
#3851, Red-Breasted Nuthatch, 3¾"... 85.00
#3852, Cliff Swallow, 3½" 100.00
#3853, Golden-Crowned Kinglets (family), 5½x5" 500.00
#3922, European Goldfinch...1,200.00
#3923, Vermillion Fly-Catcher, 5¾"......................................2,000.00
#3924, Yellow Throat, 6"... 500.00
#3925, Magnolia Warbler 3,000.00
Stangl Bird dealer sign...1,200.00

Statue of Liberty

Long before she began greeting immigrants in 1886, the Statue of Liberty was being honored by craftsmen both here and abroad. Her likeness was etched on blades of the finest straight razors from England, captured in finely detailed busts sold as souvenirs to Paris fairgoers in 1878, and presented on colorfully lithographed trade cards, usually satirical, to American shoppers. Perhaps no other object has been represented in more forms or with such frequency as the universal symbol of America. Liberty's keepsakes are also universally accessible. Delightful souvenir models created in 1885 to raise funds for Liberty's pedestal are frequently found at flea markets, while earlier French bronze and terra cotta Liberties have been auctioned for over $100,000.00. Some collectors hunt for the countless forms of nineteenth-century Liberty memorabilia, while many collections were begun in anticipation of the 1986 Centennial with concentration on modern depictions.

Ashtray, statue on side of coppered-metal base, glass insert, 6", EX ..20.00
Bell, shown w/NY skyline & Twin Towers, Sallee, Fenton, 6¼".....95.00
Booklet, Rays From Liberty's Torch, 1890..30.00
Box, Liberty on lid, Limoges, star closure, 3x1½" 65.00
Charm, figural, 14k yel gold...75.00
Clock/lamp, figural, flame bulb, copper-tone pot metal, 1940s, 16"..165.00
Cup, sterling, Windsor Club, 1907, 2" 22.00
Lamp, figural, bronze-tone metal, electric, 11".............................130.00
Match safe, silver w/emb Liberty & scrolls, Fr, 2x1½" 350.00
Medal, Central Valley Nat'l Bank 18.00
Pennant, felt, 1930s..25.00
Pin, figural in rayed ring, Sterling, 1950s, 1¼" dia, EX 45.00
Plate, emb scene of statue & NY skyline & QE II, Bossons, 10" dia...325.00
Plates, various makers, 1980s, ea from $10 to 20.00
Pocket watch, 1986 commemorative limited edition, quartz..........50.00
Postcard, NY Harbor/Statue of Liberty, 1906, hold-to-light, #1512L, EX..45.00
Postcard, statue/eagle/flag, Sanders, ca 1906, EX 20.00
Postcard, Uncle Sam pulling bk US flag to see statue, ca 1907, EX ..17.50
Poster, DeLand, WWI..150.00
Radio speaker stand, wht metal casting, Palcone, 17" 175.00
Reverse painting on glass, in plaster fr w/orig pnt, 25x19", EX 75.00
Runner, damask, ca 1890 ....85.00
Sampler, Liberty & God Bless America, mc on wht linen, 25x18"+fr...75.00
Scarf, head of Liberty, red/wht/bl, Hermes, 35" sq, NM................150.00
Scissors, emb metal, Liberty 1 side/Woolworth building on reverse, 6"..55.00
Smoke stand, figure w/tray on stepped base, patinated metal, 28" ...250.00
Smoke stand/lamp, Liberty at base, torch lights up, 1940s, 27", EX ...150.00
Snow dome, figural, Atlas Crystal Works, 1920s.............................55.00
Statue, Am Committee, gaslight, 1885, extremely rare, 36" 8,000.00
Statue, bronzed metal, Liberty Enlightening, 1883, 7" 125.00
Statue, bronzed metal, 19", EX...30.00
Statue, bronzed spelter, 9½"..25.00
Statue, hand-cvd wood, Mexico, 15" 20.00
Statue, Triang, Minic Ships accessories, EX...................................55.00
Statue, Wenck perfume, 1908 ....325.00
Ticket, Manhattan Day, Columbian Exposition, 1893 ....15.00
Ticket, souvenir of Gauthier et Cie (Liberty foundry), 1883, lg...105.00
Trade card, satirical, A&C Hams, 1880s..70.00
Vase, frosted Liberty hand, Gillinder, 1876 Centennial 70.00

Steamship Collectibles

For centuries, ocean-going vessels with their venturesome officers and crews were the catalyst that changed the unknown aspects of our world to the known. Changing economic conditions, unfortunately, have now placed the North American shipping industry in the same jeopardy as the American passenger train. They are becoming a memory. The surge of interest in railroad collectibles and the railroad-related steamship lines has lead collectors to examine the whole spectrum of steamship collectibles.

Reproduction (sometimes called 'replica') and fantasy dinnerware has been creeping into the steamship dinnerware collecting field. Some of the 'replica' ware is quite well done so one should practice caution and... 'Know Thy Dealer.' Our advisor for this category is Lila Shrader; she is listed in the Directory under California. For further information we recommend *Restaurant China*, *Volumes 1* and *2*, by Barbara Conroy (Collector Books).

Key:
BS — back stamped   SP — silver plated
Int'l — International Silver   TL — top logo
NBS — no back stamp   TM — top mark
R&B — Reed & Barton   w/w — woven design on white
SL — side logo   damask
SM — side mark

Dining Salon

Bone dish, Red Star Line, Blue Onion-like decor, TL 165.00
Bowl, soup; Great Lakes Transportation Co, Glenbrae, SL, 5½"..295.00
Butter pat, Goodrich Steamship Lines, boxed TL, 3" 88.00
Butter pat, Leyland Line TM on ribbon, Doulton, 3¼" 110.00
Butter pat, United States Shipping Board, Granite State, TL, 3" ..45.00
Champagne, United States Lines SL, saucer style, 4¾x3½" 30.00
Coffeepot, CPSS Lines, Empress, Minton, BS, 7"........................270.00
Coffeepot, Matson SS, SP, hinged lid, SM & BM, Int'l, 4¾" 225.00
Compote, Dollar Lines SM, SP, ftd, sq, Int'l, 4x7x7"..................195.00
Creamer, Eastern Steamship Lines, SL, no hdl, Buffalo, ind, 2¼" ..75.00
Creamer, White Star Line (US), Tashmoo, SL, hdl, ind, 3".........195.00
Cup, Harriman Blue Morgan, SP, SL w/house flag.......................285.00
Cup & saucer, Cleveland Cliffs Iron Co, border leaf design+SL 50.00
Cup & saucer, demitasse; Matson, Mariposa, Syracuse, NBS.........90.00
Egg cup, Mallory Line, Texas, SM, 3½"..135.00
Food warmer, United Fruit Co, SP, recessed hdl on lid, Int'l, 6" 70.00
Hot food cover, American Mail Line, SL, Buffalo, 6½"................128.00
Icer bowl, Matson, SP, SL, Int'l, 5½x8½"....................................180.00
Mug, coffee; Texaco, Michigan pattern SL, Mayer, 2½" 118.00
Napkin, SS United States Lines eagle logo, w/w damask, 20x20"..12.00
Pitcher, Colonial Line house-flag SL, Warwick, 1936, 6¾" 66.00
Plate, Boston & Philadelphia SS Co, TL, Greenwood China, 9½"..160.00
Plate, CD & GB Transit Co, Georgian Bay Line, TL, Syracuse, 6¾"...55.00
Plate, Cunard, 1st class, Lusitania, Minton TM, BS, 9" 750.00
Plate, Mobil Oil Corp, Mobil Chicago w/Pegasus in red, TL, 8"..110.00
Plate, rimmed soup; ESSO house-flag TM, 9"................................72.50
Plate, rimmed soup; Matson Line, Matsonia, TM, 9" 90.00
Plate, rimmed soup; US Light House Service, USLHS SL, 8½"...200.00
Plate, side salad; Cunard Oceanic Steam Nav Co, Greek Key, Spode ..485.00
Plate, soup; Grace Lines, Santa Barbara, TL, 1⅜x9"........................60.00
Plate, White Star, bl Daisy Chain, TM OSNCo, BM White Star, 7¼"...245.00
Platter, American President Lines, President Wilson, TL/Syracuse, 10" ..54.00
Relish dish, Canadian Pacific BC Coastal SS, Empress, BS, 10x5"..32.00
Sauceboat, CS&GT SS Co, beautiful SL, Buffalo, 6¼"................215.00
Shaker/cruet set, glass shaker/cruet, SP fr w/hdl, BM, Int'l 230.00
SP flatware, pickle fork, Ward Line, TL, Reed & Barton, 5¾" 12.00
Syrup, Pacific Mail SS, SP, hinged lid w/tab, attached liner, R&B..60.00
Tablecloth, SS United States Lines eagle logo, w/w, 51x51" 26.00
Tea set, Cunard, Cubist shape, BM, 2 pots+cr+cube sugar bowl ..285.00
Tray, triple; Red Star Line, Brownfield, w/hdl, TL, 10½"..............350.00
Tumbler, United States Lines SL on glass, 4¾"..............................20.00

Miscellaneous

Advertising sign, tin, American Line/Red Star Line, EX graphics, 3x12" **155.00**
Ashtray, RMS Queen Mary maiden voyage, propeller-like decor, 1936. **145.00**
Ashtray, souvenir; Andrea Doria, chrome w/ship image under glass, 5" .**215.00**
Ashtray, United States Lines, SS America, chrome w/enamel logo, 3¾". **55.00**
Book, Great Lakes Red Book, lists over 1,200 vessels, 1930 .... **25.00**
Book, Lloyd's Register of Shipping, 2-vol, hardbk, 1949-50, 1,600-pg. **75.00**
Book, Sailor's Union...Pacific, constitution/by-laws/wages, 1903, 4x5" .. **100.00**
Booklet, The New SS United States, 22-pg, 8½x11" **40.00**
Brochure, United Fruit, Great White Fleet, deck plans+, 1920s, 15-pg ... **90.00**
Clothes hanger, White Star Lines across wood curved top bar, 4x16".. **65.00**
Deck plans, Canadian Pacific Line/Empress of Japan, 1930, open: 30x40".. **115.00**
Engineering Spec booklets, SS United States, w/11' blprints, 7 for.... **580.00**
Flag, White Star swallowtail burgee, cotton, rope hoists, 36x48".. **585.00**
Letter opener, Alaska SS, The Alaska Line w/house flag on hdl **38.00**
Luggage label, Canadian Pacific SS, unused glue bk, oval, 6½".........**8.00**
Luggage tag, United States Lines, celluloid w/strap, 1½x2½" **17.00**
Map, wall; Alaska SS, detailed, whimsical Alaska map, 1939, 22x39"... **165.00**
Menu, SS Normandy, fold-over, diner de gala, 8/26/1939 .... **255.00**
Paperweight, Pacific Coast SS Co, glass dome, 3" dia.................. **100.00**
Pass, annual; Peoples Line, New Jersey SS Co, revenue stamp, 1869.. **120.00**
Pass, 1 trip only, Los Angeles SS Co, cardstock, 1937, 4⅛x3½".........**7.00**
Passenger list, Nord Deutscher Lloyd Bremen Europa, 1933, 18-pg, 5x8".. **52.00**
Passenger list, White Star Queen Mary, 1938, 24-pg, 5x8".... **75.00**
Pin-bk, C&B Line, City of Erie Steamship, mc, celluloid, 1¾" **34.00**
Postcard, Ohio river steamboat Lorena loading cargo, real photo, 1909... **22.00**
Poster, Grace Lines, ship docked at Curacoa, KN5/8/61, 28x42" .. **330.00**
Print, United States Lines, USS Santa Rosa enters NY harbor, 21x27"... **100.00**
Souvenir spoon, Grosser Kurfurst, HP bowl, Bremen crest, 5½" .. **155.00**
Souvenir vase, City of Cleveland portside profile, mini, 2¼" **45.00**
Tray, tip; United Fruit Co Line/SS Admiral Dewey, enameled tin, 4¾".. **360.00**

Steins

Steins have been made from pottery, pewter, glass, stoneware, and porcelain, from very small up to the four-liter size. They may be decorated by etching, in-mold relief, decals, and occasionally they may be hand painted. Some porcelain steins have lithophane bases. Collectors often specialize in a particular type — faience, regimental, or figural, for example — while others limit themselves to the products of only one manufacturer. See also Mettlach.

Key:
L — liter   tl — thumb lift
lith — lithophane

Character, Barbell, pottery, inlaid lid (rpr), 4F, #1251, .5L........... **485.00**
Character, Barmaid, porc, full color, sm rpr, .5L **4,225.00**
Character, Black Cat, pottery, inlaid lid, Schierholz, .5L **415.00**
Character, Black Student, pottery, high glaze, inlaid lid, .5L, NM ... **275.00**
Character, Bustle Lady, stoneware, pewter lid, Heuber & Reuther, .5L. **850.00**
Character, Cat, stoneware, inlaid lid, .5L....................................... **365.00**
Character, Devil, pottery, inlaid lid, #1565, .5L, EX.................... **550.00**
Character, Dog, porc lid, rpr pipe, Schierholz, .5L..................... **1,085.00**
Character, Elephant, porc, porc lid, Schierholz, .5L **1,800.00**
Character, Fox, porc, porc lid, Shierholz, .5L............................. **2,895.00**
Character, Frog, porc, Schierholz, .5L.. **1,325.00**
Character, Gentleman, pottery, inlaid lid, Thewalt, .5L.............. **550.00**
Character, Happy Radish, porc, Schierholz, inlaid lid, .5L.......... **525.00**
Character, Mountain, pottery, rpl pottery lid, 1L........................ **285.00**
Character, Munich Child, pottery, inlaid lid, hairlines, 4½" **275.00**
Character, Nurnberg Tower/city scenes, pottery, 5½" **195.00**

Character, owl, music box in base, .5L, $965.00. (Photo courtesy Andre Ammelounx)

Character, Rabbit, porc, porc lid, Schierholz, .5L..................... **1,850.00**
Character, Skull, porc, E Bohne & Sohne, .5L, NM **285.00**
Character, Skull, pottery, inlaid lid, #852, .5L **500.00**
Character, Skull on Book, porc, inlaid lid, E Bohne & Sohne, .5L, NM... **525.00**
Character, Wilhelm I, porc, porc lid, Shierholz, .5L, NM **900.00**
Character, Wilhelm II, porc, porc lid, .5L, EX **725.00**
Faience, anchor w/initials/floral/seamen, mc, pewter lid, 1780s, .5L .. **1,450.00**
Faience, floral, mc, pewter ring/lid, ca 1780, strap rpr, 1L........... **500.00**
Faience, floral, pewter base ring/lid, Bayreuth, 1798, 1L **1,750.00**
Faience, HP deer scene on bl, pewter lid & base ring, 1793, 1L, G.. **400.00**
Glass, blown, amber, Munich Child pewter o/l, pewter lid, .5L ... **175.00**
Glass, blown, amber w/gr glass prunts, HP design, pewter lid, .5L... **195.00**
Glass, blown, amber w/ornate pewter o/l, pewter lid, lion tl, 1L .. **400.00**
Glass, blown, bl opaline, glass inlaid lid, closed hinge, 1850s, 4" .. **365.00**
Glass, blown, clear, eng scene from spa, clear lid, 3¼".................. **315.00**
Glass, blown, clear, Mary Gregory-style girl, bl inlaid lid, 4¼"..... **170.00**
Glass, blown, clear w/bl stain, eng floral, clear lid, 1850s, 3½"..... **150.00**
Glass, blown, clear w/gr o/l, cut design, clear lid w/bl o/l, .5L ... **1,450.00**
Glass, blown, clear w/HP, Germania Sei's Panier, pewter lid, 1909, .5L.. **845.00**
Glass, blown, clear w/red stain, inlaid lid, 1850s, 4" **170.00**
Glass, blown, clear w/wht & pk o/l, leaf eng, ca 1850, .4L **5,175.00**
Glass, blown, gr, ornate pewter o/l, pewter lid, 3¾" **160.00**
Glass, blown, lav w/ornate cuttings, clear inlaid lid, 1850s, .5L... **300.00**
Glass, blown, peach w/HP floral, clear inlaid lid, 1850s, 3½" **100.00**
Glass, blown, red, fluted w/gold HP designs, ca 1850, .25L, EX ... **365.00**
Occupational, carpenter, faience/pewter base ring/lid, 1780s, 1L, EX. **1,100.00**
Pewter, relief: hunter/animals, dog & fox pewter lid, boy tl, .5L .. **115.00**
Pewter, scroll-hdl mug type, 90 St George..., mk Quart, 7" **230.00**
Pewter, 8 relief lion masks+1 w/ring, Josef Msel 1690, 9½" **460.00**
Porc, HP: bl onion design, inlaid lid, lith, .3L, NM..................... **180.00**
Porc, HP: crocodile w/3 babies/3 eggs, pewter lid, .5L **600.00**
Porc, HP: Nymphenburg festival scene, brass tl, ca 1850, .5L... **1,450.00**
Porc, transfer/HP: Kulmbacher Export Bierbrauerei..., pewter lid, .5L.. **400.00**
Porc, transfer/HP: Munchen shooting festival 1881, pewter lid, .5L.. **485.00**
Pottery, etch: people drinking at table, pewter lid, #1152, .3L **365.00**
Pottery, relief: couple on bicycles, pewter lid, #1248, .5L.............. **360.00**
Pottery, relief: dwarfs, pewter lid, Diesinger #728, .5L **195.00**
Pottery, relief: Falstaff, pewter lid, Dumler & Breiden #571, 1L.... **240.00**
Pottery, relief: Order of Eagles, ornate, rpl pewter lid, .5L............ **140.00**
Pottery, transfer/HP: Gruss Aus Munchen, pewter lid w/Munich child, 3". **200.00**
Pottery, transfer/HP: Heidelberg, pewter lid, 2½" **60.00**
Pottery, transfer/HP: Seminar Zeit 1898-1901, roster, pewter lid, .5L ... **275.00**
Pottery, transfer: rabbits in leaves, pewter lid, 3¾" **80.00**
Regimental, porc, Kgl Sachs 3...1905-07, Saschen tl, roster, .5L, 12".. **1,380.00**
Regimental, porc, 2 Esk 1 Garde Dragon...1902-05, lion tl, .5L... **600.00**
Regimental, porc, 3 Battr 1 Bad...1902-04, eagle tl, lith, .5L **350.00**
Regimental, porc, 4 Battr...1912-14, eagle tl, jeweled lid, .5L **600.00**
Regimental, porc, 4 Cp Pionier Batl...1899-01, anchor tl, lith, .5L.. **285.00**
Regimental, porc, 6 Comp 1 Kurhess...1906-08, eagle tl, roster, .5L .. **315.00**

Regimental, porc, 67 Infantry...1912-14, lion tl w/stanhope, .5L . 465.00
Regimental, pottery, transfer/HP: KB I Schw...Munchen 1917, .5L ...175.00
Regimental, pottery, 2 Cp Hann...1904-06, metal lid w/stanhope, 9"...400.00
Socialist, porc, transfer/HP: blksmith/lady w/torch, 1908, .5L, EX 445.00
Stoneware, etch: cavalier, pewter lid, Marzi & Remi #1765, .5L . 325.00
Stoneware, etch: drinking scene, Hauber & Reuther #161, .5L...215.00
Stoneware, etched/beaded: men drinking/cat/Art Nouveau, #432/1, .5L...200.00
Stoneware, transfer/HP: man in yel jacket, Ringer, pewter lid, .5L ..275.00
Stoneware, transfer/HP: Munich Child, pewter lid, Ringer, 4½"... 215.00
Stoneware, transfer/HP: shooting festival, inscr 1934, 1L 300.00
Wood, oak w/pewter o/l hunt scene, pewter lid, 1850s, 8" 700.00
3rd Reich, porc, transfer: SA soldiers w/flag, pewter lid, .5L 725.00
3rd Reich, pottery, transfer/HP: worker, 1935-36, pewter lid, .5L...365.00
3rd Reich, stoneware, transfer/HP: eagle/swastika, pewter lid, .5L..485.00

Steuben

Carder Steuben glass was made by the Steuben Glass Works in Corning, New York, while under the direction of Frederick Carder from 1903 to 1932. Perhaps the most popular types of Carder Steuben glass are Gold Aurene which was introduced in 1904 and Blue Aurene, introduced in 1905. Gold and Blue Aurene objects shimmer with the lustrous beauty of their metallic iridescence. Carder also produced other types of 'Aurenes' including Red, Green, Yellow, Brown, and Decorated, all of which are very rare. Aurene also was cased with Calcite glass. Some pieces had paper labels. Other types of Carder Steuben include Cluthra, Cintra, Florentia, Rosaline, Ivory, Ivrene, Jades, Verre de Soie; there are many more.

Frederick Carder's leadership of Steuben ended in 1932, and the production of colored glassware soon ceased. Since 1932 the tradition of fine Steuben art glass has been continued in crystal. In the following listings, examples are signed unless noted otherwise. When no color is mentioned, assume the glass is clear.

Key: ACB — acid cut back

Atomizer, Gold Aurene, eng floral, tubular w/wide ft, DeVillbis, 9"...700.00
Basket, clear open lattice w/berry prunts, side hdls, #7717, 10" W...300.00
Bonbon, Gold Aurene, undulating scalloped rim, #138, 5¾" 360.00
Bottle, scent; Blue Aurene, melon ribbed w/3 scroll ft, #2701, 5" .. 2,250.00
Bottle, scent; Blue Aurene, teardrop stopper w/long dauber, #3174, 8"...2,000.00
Bottle, scent; Gold Aurene, slim/ftd, blk-topped dauber, #6136, 7" ...420.00
Bottle, scent; Verre de Soie w/Celeste Blue stopper, melon ribs, 5" 240.00
Bowl, Amber, Grotesque, handkerchief style, #7535, 7x12½"...... 180.00
Bowl, Calyx, crystal, widely flaring freeform rim, #8115, 9½" 285.00
Bowl, clear to amethyst at rim, Grotesque, ftd handkerchief style, 6"...240.00
Bowl, clear w/controlled ruby threading, wide flat rim, ped ft, 14"...180.00
Bowl, Gold Aurene, pulled 'pillars' around rim, #2275, 10" 715.00
Bowl, Gold Aurene/Calcite, cupped w/ring base, 8" 240.00
Bowl, Gold Aurene/Calcite, flared sides/ring base, #2851, 10".....350.00
Bowl, Gold Aurene/Calcite, ftd compote form, 12"...................... 480.00
Bowl, Gold Aurene/Calcite, wide stretched rim, 14½" 450.00
Bowl, Jade Plum, inverted rim, triple cased, #2687, 4½x8" 720.00
Bowl, Marina Blue, slight ribbing, appl dome ft, 14½" 175.00
Bowl, Rosa, controlled bubbles/threaded, shallow, #3234, 14" 240.00
Bowl, Topaz w/Celeste Blue ft & rim, dome lid of open rigaree, 10" dia..1,095.00
Candlestick, Amber/Celeste Blue, #2958, 15", ea 780.00
Candlestick, Gold Aurene/Calcite, mushroom-cap bobeche, 6", ea ..485.00
Candlesticks, Amethyst, stem w/dbl balls, 10", pr 800.00
Candlesticks, clear twist stem w/Gold Ruby cabochons & rims, 12", pr .1,000.00
Candlesticks, Gold Aurene, twist stem, #686, 8", pr 1,550.00
Candlesticks, Gold Ruby, #6270, 10", pr.. 950.00
Candy dish, crystal, ram's head finial, #7936, script mk, 6" 460.00
Compote, Amber, ribbed wide egg shape on Pomona Green ped w/swirls, 8"..525.00

Compote, Amber, 6-side swirl bowl w/gr ft, 7" dia, +4" candlesticks... 700.00
Compote, Gold Aurene, baluster stem, disk ft, #2260, 5½".......... 540.00
Compote, Jade Green w/Alabaster ft & stem, 3½x8" 210.00
Compote, Rosaline w/Alabaster knop & loose ring hdls, #2942, 9x10"...1,050.00
Compote, Selenium Red, wide flaring flat rim, 5¼"................... 690.00
Cornucopia, Ivory on Black Amethyst ft, ruffled top, 8" 460.00
Creamer, crystal, #7778, script mk, 6½" 200.00
Creamer, Rosaline, Alabaster hdl, ground pontil, 1¾" 260.00
Decanter, Gold Aurene, ftd bottle form, Haviland, 10" 1,400.00
Figurine, pigeon, leaded glass w/eng & cut details, #6824, 6"....1,500.00
Finger bowl, Gold Aurene, ruffled stretched rim, Haviland, 7", +plate ..325.00
Goblet, toasting; crystal, int twist in stem, 19", pr...................... 690.00
Lamp, ACB floral w/Gold Aurene finger-like drips, spherical; brass mts..3,900.00
Lamp, ACB Rosalie/Alabaster, Chinese pattern; C-arm shaft, 10" 780.00
Lamp, ACB wheat, lt turq on gr, shouldered, emb gr metal mts, 34".. 1,800.00
Lamp, floor; Brown Aurene 10" w/Intarsia border; Handel harp std ..5,880.00
Lamp, mantel; Gold Aurene trumpet shade; 6-panel ft w/rtcl cup, 8", pr.1,955.00
Lamp, Oriental Poppy, jade opal w/red threads at neck, leafy mts, 23". 2,000.00
Lamp, 5-lily; Verre de Soie ribbed shades; std w/leaves in relief, EX..4,025.00
Plate, crystal, lg coiled hdl, #8025, 8½".. 230.00
Plate, Jade Green, fleur-de-lis mk, 8½".. 80.00
Plate, Lime Green, F Carder, 8½".. 150.00
Plate, Oriental Poppy, pk/opal panels alternate, lightly scalloped, 8" .. 180.00
Shade, boudoir; Blue Aurene, gold heart/vines, lt scallops to rim, 5".... 1,700.00
Shade, feathers, gr/gold on lt gold, gold int, unmk, 4x5" 300.00
Sherbet, Gold Aurene on Calcite, 3¾", +5¾" underplate 165.00
Tazza, Rosaline plate & ft, baluster Alabaster stem, #6402, 8", pr .. 1,200.00
Torchiere, Gold Aurene upright trumpet shade in rtcl metal ft, 8", pr...720.00
Tray, Celeste Blue, acid-etched leaf-band borders, #6111, 14" 360.00
Tumbler, Selenium Red w/threading, fleur-de-lis mk, 6"............... 125.00
Vase, ACB floral, Rosaline on Alabaster, rose-bowl shape, 8x7"..850.00
Vase, ACB gazelles, Ivory, shouldered, 10½"...........................2,530.00
Vase, ACB lily of the valley on Jade Green, ftd cone form, 6½" ..350.00

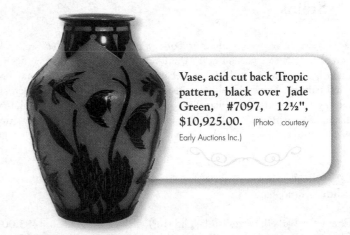

Vase, acid cut back Tropic pattern, black over Jade Green, #7097, 12½", $10,925.00. (Photo courtesy Early Auctions Inc.)

Vase, Amber w/etched line & flower head design, wide U-form w/ft, 11" ...360.00
Vase, Amber w/Pomona Green ft, fan form, #6287, 8" 180.00
Vase, Blue Aurene, cyindrical w/flared rim, short ft, label, 9¾"....920.00
Vase, Blue Aurene, hearts/vines at shoulder, #6299, bulbous, 6" ...7,015.00
Vase, Blue Aurene, shouldered, 8x7" 1,265.00
Vase, Blue Aurene, trumpet form w/flared & ruffled rim, #346, 8x6".. 1,265.00
Vase, Blue Aurene, tube w/disk ft, some inconsistencies in irid, 10" ...900.00
Vase, Blue Aurene, U-form w/disk ft, 9¾x8"...............................1,380.00
Vase, Blue Aurene, 3 ribbed shoulder applications, urn form, #6627, 6" ..1,100.00
Vase, Blue Aurene, 3-stump, plain disk ft, #2744, 6" 725.00
Vase, Blue Aurene w/gold & wht hearts & vines, #2587, 10½"... 3,220.00
Vase, bud; Blue Aurene, optic ribs, slim trumpet form w/knop stem, 12"..600.00
Vase, bud; Gold Aurene, tube shape on disk ft, 8"...................... 575.00
Vase, Calcite w/EX Blue Aurene int, ruffled trumpet form, unmk, 6". 1,380.00

Vase, Celeste Blue, ftd U-form, unmk, 11" 515.00
Vase, Cluthra, pk, shouldered w/flared rim, ground pontil, 6" ... 1,035.00
Vase, Cluthra, pk, squat w/flaring tooled ruffled rim, 4" 295.00
Vase, Cluthra, plum, U-form w/slightly flared rim, 10" 1,035.00
Vase, Cluthra, wht w/pk lip wrap, trumpet form, 17" 650.00
Vase, crystal & Gold Ruby, Grotesque, handkerchief style, 4x5½"... 240.00
Vase, crystal w/appl random threading, flared cylinder, #2364, 8" ...125.00
Vase, crystal w/red controlled threading, fan form, fleur-de-lis mk, 8". 200.00
Vase, deep gr, 3-stump, plain base, 6" 405.00
Vase, French Blue, ribbed optic swirl, #6325, 7½" 240.00
Vase, Gold Aurene, bulbous, #2683, 8½" 800.00
Vase, Gold Aurene, collar w/appl spikes, appl netting around body, 14" ..1,840.00
Vase, Gold Aurene, stretched border, #2712, 5" 720.00
Vase, Gold Aurene, trumpet form w/wide ruffled bl-edged rim, #723, 9"... 650.00
Vase, Grotesque, clear to gr, 11" 345.00
Vase, Ivory, Grotesque, flared sides, 4-'spout' rim, 6½x12" 345.00
Vase, Ivory, Grotesque, handkerchief type, #7091, 5½x8" 240.00
Vase, Ivory, shouldered, 8½" 345.00
Vase, Ivory, shouldered w/flaring rim, 10½" 450.00
Vase, Ivory, 3 bud-like prongs on knopped disk ft, #7321, 7½".. 1,600.00
Vase, Jade Green, Alabaster rim-to-shoulder hdls, spherical body, 12"....2,640.00
Vase, med gr, sq pillow form; in blk metal holder w/4 leaves, 11".. 400.00
Vase, millefiori, wht w/gr & brn leaves on platinum to bl, Aurene, 4" 4,050.00
Vase, millefiori, wht w/gr leafy vines on gold, Aurene, #611, 3".. 3,900.00
Vase, Mirror Black w/wht at rolled everted wide rim, ftd U-form, 6".. 180.00
Vase, Pomona Green, optic swirls, shouldered, #769, 8½"........... 210.00
Vase, Red Aurene, w/gold hearts & vines, classic form, #270, 9"... 33,350.00
Vase, Rosaline & Alabaster, 3-stump, #2744, 6½" 1,035.00
Vase, Rosaline on Alabaster disk ft, trumpet form, #2909, 6" 240.00
Vase, Selenium Red, diagonal optic ribs, #6030, 7" 395.00
Vase, Selenium Red, scalloped/flared rim, dbl-bulb body, #7447, 6"...360.00
Vase, Silverina, amethyst w/silver, ftd, wide rim, incurvate sides, 7" ..600.00
Vase, Silverina, clear w/mica flecks in dmn pattern, bulbous, 7".. 865.00
Vase, Tyrian, gold heart/vine on gr-bl to purple-gray, shouldered, 8"...17,250.00
Vase, Wisteria, Grotesque, handkerchief style, ftd, 9½" 1,500.00

Stevengraphs

A Stevengraph is a small picture made of woven silk resembling an elaborate ribbon, created by Thomas Stevens in England in the latter half of the 1800s. They were matted and framed by Stevens, usually with his name appearing on the mat or often with the trade announcement on the back of the mat. He also produced silk postcards and bookmarks, all of which have 'Stevens' woven in silk on one of the mitered corners. Anyone wishing to learn more about Stevengraphs is encouraged to contact the Stevengraph Collectors' Association, whose address can be found in the Directory under Clubs, Newsletters, and Catalogs. Unless noted otherwise, assume our values are for examples in very good original condition and the pictures matted and framed.

Baden Powell, portrait in tombstone-shape mat, G-.................... 110.00
Bookmark, Late Lamented President Lincoln, text, 2¼x12", NM ..420.00
Called To the Rescue, Heroism at Sea, 6x9", G........................... 325.00
Columbus Leaving Spain... 360.00
Crystal Palace (outside), 6x8¾"... 275.00
Death of Nelson, 7½x10½"... 240.00
Dick Turpin's Last Ride on His Black Bess............................ 275.00
Final Spurt, rarest of 2 in Crewing series, bk label, 6x9" 240.00
First Lap, bicycle race, bk label, 6x9", G.............................. 240.00
First Point, 6x9" 120.00
First Touch, bk label, 5½x8½", G 420.00
For Life or Death Heroism on Land, 2 horses, 5¼x8" 360.00
Full Cry, 6x9" 240.00

God Speed the Plough, 6x9" 120.00
God Speed the Plough (no birds in foreground), bk label, 8x11", EX.... 420.00
Good Old Days, coach & 4, 7½x10½", M............................... 195.00
Her Majesty Queen Alexandra, label, 8x6", G 75.00
His Majesty King Edward VII, 6x9", G-................................ 85.00
Home Stretch, 2nd jockey in ivory jersey, 6x10" 360.00
HRH Prince of Wales, 8x6"... 120.00
Iroquois & Fred Archer, Winner 1881 Derby, on brd, 4x8½"....2,240.00
Lady Godiva Procession, 6x9", EX 180.00
Last Lap, bicycle race, 6½x9¼", EX.................................... 840.00
Late Rt Hon WE Gladstone, 8x6"....................................... 75.00
Maj Gen JDP French, bk label, 8x6", G............................... 150.00
Marquis of Salisbury, KG; 9x6".. 90.00
Meet, rpl fr, NM... 250.00
Niagara Falls scene, 7x11", EX 575.00
Present From Edinburgh Internat'l Exhibition, 6 images, 10x12" ...180.00
Present Time, 60 Miles an Hour, 7¼x10"................................ 150.00
Slip, 6x9"... 145.00
Start, 6x9", G-... 120.00
Struggle, 4 horses, no bkground or other horses, unfr 250.00
Victoria, Queen of Empire on Which the Sun Never Sets, 6x9"... 195.00
Wellington & Blucher, 6¾x11", EX+.................................... 275.00
Ye Ladye Godiva, G.. 145.00

Miscellaneous

Bookmark, Happy May Thy Birthday Be, no tassel 60.00
Bookmark, Home Sweet Home, G...................................... 60.00
Bookmark, Little Busy Bee, 8x2"...................................... 165.00
Bookmark, To a Friend, poem by Eliza Cook, missing tassel......... 165.00
Inaugural, Tammany Hall/Cleveland - Stevenson, 1893, 2½x11" ...200.00
Merry Christmas, Happy New Year under 2nd red ribbon, open: 18x2" .. 65.00
Souvenir, Independence of America, Washington on horse/flags, 9".. 110.00
Souvenir, Pan American Expo w/Lincoln, orig tag, 12½" L, EX .. 180.00
Souvenir, Signing Declaration of Independence, Columbian World's Fair..180.00

Stevens and Williams

Stevens and Williams glass was produced at the Brierly Hill Glassworks in Stourbridge, England, for nearly a century, beginning in the 1830s. They were credited with being among the first to develop a method of manufacturing a more affordable type of cameo glass. Other lines were also made — silver deposit, alexandrite, and engraved rock crystal, to name but a few. Our advisor for this category is Don Williams; he is listed in the Directory under Missouri.

Cameo

Vase, floral/butterfly, wht on citron, neck ring, teardrop body, 5" 865.00
Vase, fruiting branches, wht on deep bl, 3 dbl camphor ft, 5½"... 4,000.00
Vase, intricate medallions, bl on wht w/gold line trim, att, 12", pr...2,185.00
Vase, raspberries, wht on Rose du Barry, bulbous bottle form, 9"...2,100.00
Vase, 4 Christmas roses, wht on red frost, elongated gourd form, 12".. 2,700.00

Miscellaneous

Bowl, Pompeian Swirl, rust/yel, bl int, incurvate/pleated rim, 7" .. 690.00
Bowl, ruffled amber top/rigaree, gr threaded bottom, in SP fr, 6" .. 175.00
Decanter, gr cut to clear w/flowers & leaves, cut hdl, att, 11" ...2,875.00
Ewer, Osiris, red/yel/maroon/wht pull-ups, pk int, clear hdl, 14".. 690.00
Finger bowl, Pompeian Swirl, caramel w/lt bl int, tightly crimped, 5".. 1,035.00
Lamp, Pompeian Swirl, gold/red/wht, bulb w/ruffled upright shade, 20"..920.00
Rose bowl, peachblow w/red cherries on amber stems (ft), tilted, 9"... 975.00

Rose bowl, Pompeian Swirl, bl, incurvate, 3" H 135.00
Rose bowl, Zipper, gr, #55693, 2½"... 90.00
Vase, Peachblow w/amber stems+4 opal & pk flowers, ruffled, 10"... 345.00
Vase, Pompeian Swirl, pk satin, ovoid, 4¼" 345.00
Vase, Pompeian Swirl, purple/bl, rnd w/long ogee neck, 8" 2,400.00
Vase, Pompeian Swirl, red/brn, bl int, stick neck, 8¾" 690.00
Vase, Pompeian Swirl, rose to chartreuse, shouldered cylinder, 14"..3,800.00

Vase, Silveria, amethyst, silver, and green with random green threading, signed, 6½", $4,885.00.

(Photo courtesy Early Auction Co.)

Stickley

Among the leading proponents of the Arts and Crafts Movement, the Stickley brothers — Gustav, Leopold, Charles, Albert, and John George — were at various times and locations separately involved in designing and producing furniture as well as decorative items for the home. (See Arts and Crafts for further information.) The oldest of the five Stickley brothers was Gustav; his work is the most highly regarded of all. He developed the style of furniture referred to as Mission. It was strongly influenced by the type of furnishings found in the Spanish missions of California — utilitarian, squarely built, and simple. It was made most often of oak, and decoration was very limited or non-existent. The work of his brothers display adaptations of many of Gustav's ideas and designs. His factory, the Craftsman Workshop, operated in Eastwood, New York, from the late 1890s until 1915, when he was forced out of business by larger companies who copied his work and sold it at much lower prices. Among his shop marks are the early red decal containing a joiner's compass and the words 'Als Ik Kan,' the branded mark with similar components, and paper labels.

The firm known as Stickley Brothers was located first in Binghamton, New York, and then Grand Rapids, Michigan. Albert and John George made the move to Michigan, leaving Charles in Binghamton (where he and an uncle continued the operation under a different name). After several years John George left the company to rejoin Leopold in New York. (These two later formed their own firm called L. & J. G. Stickley.) The Stickley Brothers Company's early work produced furniture featuring fine inlay work, decorative cutouts, and leaned strongly toward a style of Arts and Crafts with an English influence. It was tagged with a paper label 'Made by Stickley Brothers, Grand Rapids,' or with a brass plate or decal with the words 'Quaint Furniture,' an English term chosen to refer to their product. In addition to furniture, they made metal accessories as well.

The workshops of the L. & J. G. Stickley Company first operated under the name 'Onondaga Shops.' Located in Fayetteville, New York, their designs were often all but copies of Gustav's work. Their products were well made and marketed, and their business was very successful. Their decal labels contained all or a combination of the words 'Handcraft' or 'Onondaga Shops,' along with the brothers' initials and last name. The firm continues in business today. Our advisor for this category is Bruce Austin; he is listed in the Directory under New York.

Note: When only one dimension is given, it is length. Our values are from cataloged auctions and include the buyer's premium. Unless a condition code is present in the line, our values reflect the worth of items that are complete, in original condition, and retaining their original finishes. A rating of excellent (EX) may denote cleaning, small repairs, or touchups. Codes lower than that describe wear, losses, repairs, or damage in degrees relative to the condition given. Cleaning and/or refinishing can lower values as much as 15% to 30%. Replaced hardware or wood will also have a dramatic negative effect.

Key:
b — brand
d — red decal
h/cp — hammered copper
p — paper label
t — Quaint metal tag

Charles Stickley

Armchair, 3 bk slats, arched brd under wide arms, 38x35x30", VG ...3,900.00
Armchair, 4-slat bk, long corbels, loose cushion, b, 36x29x23", EX...840.00
Cabinet, paneled door, 2 drw w/in, h/cp hdw, att, 27x17x8" 1,800.00
Chair, side; 9-spindle bk, spring seat, 36x18x17" 600.00
Settee, vertical slats all around, drop arms, att, 58" L, EX 3,000.00

Gustav Stickley

Armchair, tall spindle bk/sides, new seat, 49x28x22" 3,360.00
Armchair, wide slat ea side/posts mortised through arms, 38x34x31", VG..3,120.00
Armchair, willow, open sqs in floor-length skirt, sm rstr, 33x33x25"..3,120.00
Armchair set, V-bk w/5 slats, tacked-on leather, VG, 4 for 3,000.00
Book rack, mahog, revolving, 4 parts, ea set at right angle, 10x13" sq.. 1,500.00
Bookcase, open, 3 fixed shelves per side, p/d, 57x42x13", EX ...1,560.00
Bookcase, 2 8-pane doors, keyed through-tenons, 56x52x13"...7,200.00
Bookcase, 2 8-pane doors, through-tenons, iron V pulls, p/d, 56x48"..6,600.00
Bookcase, 2-door, ea w/ldgl sqs & 2 lg rectangle panes, p, 57x54", VG...8,400.00
Box, shirtwaist; paneled top, 2 spindled sides, 16x30x16" 5,000.00
Cellarette, hinged top expands, sm drw/paneled door, d, 30x32x20"..22,800.00
Cellarette, pull-out copper tray, 1-drw, bottle rack w/in, 40x22", G ...2,640.00
Chair, billiards; V crestrail over 5 vertical slats, w/arms, 45x26"...10,000.00
Chair, lady's Morris; #367-368, 20-spindle sides, unmk, rpl/wear ..4,500.00
Chair, Morris; #332, 5-slat sides, new leather/color added, d, 39x32" ...10,200.00
Chair, Morris; 5-slat sides, drop-in seat/loose bk, recovered/rfn, 37"...5,400.00
Chair, Morris; 5-slat sides, 4-slat bk, no cushions, rfn/rpl, 39x38" ..4,500.00
Chair set, 3 horizonal bk slats, shaped crest rail, new seats, 8 for...5,400.00
Chest, #913, 6 sm drws over 3, arched front, p, 51x36x20" 7,500.00
Chest of drws, 2 sm drws over 4, strap/ring hdw, b, rfn, 48x36x21", EX. 12,000.00
China cabinet, overhang top, glazed door, 3-shelf, b/p, 60x36x15"..7,800.00
China cabinet, 2 8-pane doors/8-pane sides, arched aprons, 64x40", EX .5,100.00
Costumer, dbl, shoe ft, 6 iron hooks, 72x22x13", EX.................2,280.00
Desk, chalet; paneled drop-front, keyed through-tenons, 46x24x7", VG..2,520.00
Desk, drop front; 2 short over 2 long drw, plank sides, d, 44x32x15" ..2,500.00
Desk, drop front; 3-panel lid, plank sides, arched apron, 51x27", VG. 4,500.00
Desk, postcard; letter sorters at top, 2-drw, low shelf, d, 36x40", VG.. 1,500.00
Desk, writing; gallery top, 1 drw, wooden knobs, b, 33x32x20", VG.......840.00
Dresser, #905, sm sm drw over 3 long, w/mirror, p, 72x48x23"..6,000.00
Dresser, #911, 2 sm drw over 2 long, arched front, w/mirror, d, 66x48"..4,000.00
Footstool, horizontal slat ea side, tacked-on leather (torn), d, 21" L..600.00
Lamp, floor; sm silk-lined wicker shade, X-d base w/shoe ft, 58x14" ..4,500.00
Lamp, silk-lined 18" wicker shade; h/cp base, 22", EX..................660.00
Magazine stand, overhang top, 3-shelf, arched sides, b, 42x22", VG..1,800.00
Mirror, inverted V top w/iron hanging rings, d, 28x42"............2,160.00
Mirror, shaving; V-top mirror swivels in fr w/shoe ft, b, 22x23"... 2,000.00
Rocker, bk slats inlaid w/various metals, tall bk, rfn, 40x24x21", VG. 4,800.00
Rocker, 5-slat sides, drop-in spring seat/loose bk, rfn, 38x29x30" ...2,760.00
Rug, geometrics in bl/brn/tan, 139x111", VG............................1,800.00

Server, 3 sm drws over linen drw, p, 40x48x20", EX.................3,900.00
Settle, even arm; #208 variation, vertical slats, 29x66x32", VG ...4,800.00
Settle, even arm; 6-slat sides/12" horizontal bk splat, b, 36x84", VG..14,400.00
Sideboard, #814½, 2 doors/2 sm drw/linen drw/plate rail, 48x56", VG.....7,200.00
Sidebrd, linen drw+2 sm drw/doors, plate rail/open compartment, 46" L. 4,200.00
Table, dining; lg 4-leg ped, 6 leaves, rfn/rpr, 54" dia, VG 3,900.00
Table, dining; plank legs, octagonal apron, rfn, 59" dia, VG.....3,600.00
Table, dining; 5-leg w/str X-stretchers, keyed tenons, 30" dia ...7,200.00
Table, lamp; legs mortised through, X-stretchers, 26" dia........12,000.00
Table, library; copper/pewter/brass inlay, ship medallions, 30x30x18"..78,000.00
Table, library; overhang top/arched apron (no drw), H Ellis, 42" L, VG ..1,440.00
Table, library; 1-drw, overhang top, copper pull, d/p, 48" L, VG ...1,800.00
Table, library; 1-drw, overhang top, lower shelf, 29x36x24", VG ..1,320.00
Table, library; 12-spindle sides, wide shelf, p, 29x36x24", VG ..3,000.00
Table, library; 2 sm drw, overhang top, vnr lifting, 30x48x30"..1,920.00
Table, library; 2 sm drw/inverted V apron/shelf, 30x36x24"....10,200.00
Table, library; 3-drw, iron hdw, 54" L, VG 2,160.00
Table, library; 6-sided, trumpeted X-stretchers, p, 30x48", VG ..5,100.00
Table, Poppy, floriform top/shelf, cut-out legs, color added, 24x20" ..15,600.00
Table, trestle; shelf mortised through 2-plank sides, shoe ft, 48", VG.. 1,020.00
Table, 14" rnd top, shaped X-stretchers, b, 16", VG 960.00

L. & J. G. Stickley

Bookcase, #328½, 2 12-pane doors, through-tenons, wear/pnt residue.....3,900.00
Bookcase, #62203, 2 8-pane doors/side posts extend through top, 52x48"..2,520.00
Bookcase, 1 16-pane door, tenons keyed through sides, b, 55x32", EX ...4,500.00
Bookcase, 2 12-pane doors, faux keyed through-tenons, rfn/rstr, 55x45"..2,400.00
Bookcase, 2 12-pane doors, through-tenons, copper pulls, b, 55x49x12"..7,200.00
Chair, Morris; #830, 4 curved bk slats, flat arms/sq legs, 42x29" ..575.00
Chair, Morris; 6-slat sides, new leather, d, 39x32x35", EX 2,640.00
Chair set, #800, 3 bk slats/dbl side stretcher, later uphl, 36", 6 for....4,410.00
Clock, oak, blk #s on brass-wash face, att, 8x8x2½" 325.00
Dresser, mirror pivots, 2 sm over 2 long drw, d, rpl hdw, 70x48x22"...3,900.00
Drink stand, rnd top, sm rnd bottom shelf, X-stretcher, rfn, 29x18" ..1,140.00
Magazine stand, 3-slat sides, arched rails, 4-shelf, 42x21x2" 2,520.00
Rocker, 6-slat sides, recovered drop-in spring seat & loose bk, d, 37".. 3,360.00
Settee, drop arm; 13 bk slats, #225, new uphl, 52" L, VG 2,040.00
Settee, drop arm; 14 bk slats, 4 ea side, 76" L, VG 3,240.00
Settee, drop arm; 7 bk slats, 2 ea side, new cushion, rfn, 77" L, VG...3,900.00
Sideboard, bank of 3 sm drw ea side pr doors+linen drw, 36x54", VG....2,520.00
Table, cut-corner top w/sm sq lower shelf, d, 29x24", VG 1,080.00
Table, dining; trestle base w/extension arms+2 15" leaves, b, 62"..2,235.00
Table, octagonal top, shaped stretchers, 20x18" 1,200.00
Table, rectangular top/shelf, legs mortised through, d, 24x25x17"..2,160.00
Table, trestle; new leather top/stretcher mortisted through sides, 48" ... 1,440.00
Table, 8-sided top w/legs mortised through, d, rfn, 17x15", VG.....1,440.00

Stickley Bros.

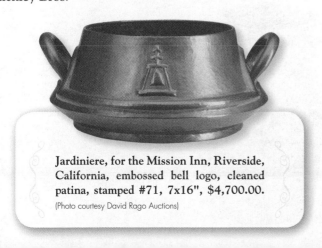

Jardiniere, for the Mission Inn, Riverside, California, embossed bell logo, cleaned patina, stamped #71, 7x16", $4,700.00.

(Photo courtesy David Rago Auctions)

Chair, desk; #604½, 1-slat bk w/2 cutouts, Macmurdo ft, 39", VG........450.00
Chair, desk; shaped/cut-out horizontal rails, 1 vertical rail, t, 38" ...900.00
Chair, Morris; #631½, bent-bk arms w/3 slats below, new seat, 39".......4,200.00
Chair set, 3-slat ladderbk, new leather, p/t, 37x19x17", 6 for....3,240.00
Chest, 2 half over 3 long drws, tilting mirror, ca 1912, 69x35x19"...1,650.00
China cabinet, like #8860, mirror bk w/caned sqs, rfn, 63x42", VG..1,440.00
Desk, like #2810, bookshelf below top (rfn)/ea side 1 drw, 40" 600.00
Magazine stand, 3-slat sides, 3-shelf, rfn, 32x18x12", VG 1,200.00
Mirror, dresser; 2 drws below swivel mirror, att, rfn, 22x31".........900.00
Plant stand, sq overhang rfn top, lower shelf, t, 32x18", EX.........900.00
Plant stand, tapering column on sq base & 4 ft, 34x12", EX 1,200.00
Rocker, shaped/cvd arm supports, wide str aprons, rfn, 39x30x38"...960.00
Server, 2 sm over 2 long drw/lower shelf, iron hdw, color added, 48" L...3,240.00
Table, child's; #658, 4-leg X-stretcher base, 18x24" dia................500.00
Table, dining; #2908, base w/cane panels, unmk, rfn, 44" dia, G ..575.00
Table, game; legs mortised through, X-stretcher, 40" dia, EX 900.00
Table, lamp; #2508, 4-post base w/rnd shelf, rfn, 30" dia..............700.00
Table, library; 2-drw, overhang top, long corbels, Quaint d, 48" L......1,200.00
Table, library; 2-drw, 2-brd shelf mortised through sides 54" L, VG ...1,440.00
Table, 3 sq spindles ea side, overhang top, shelf, unmk, 30x18x30"...1,200.00

Steigel

Baron Henry Stiegel produced glassware in Pennsylvania as early as 1760, very similar to glass being made concurrently in Germany and England. Without substantiating evidence, it is impossible to positively attribute a specific article to his manufacture. Although he made other types of glass, today the term Stiegel generally refers to any very early ware made in shapes and colors similar to those he is known to have produced — especially that with etched or enameled decoration. It is generally conceded, however, that most glass of this type is of European origin. Our advisor for this category is Mark Vuono; he is listed in the Directory under Connecticut. Unless a color is mentioned in the description, assume the glass to be clear.

Bottle, cobalt w/mc floral, half-post, no cap, 5½" 360.00
Bottle, scent; amethyst, dmn daisy motif above fluting, 1700s, 5½" ...2,820.00
Decanter, extensive florals around cobalt shield w/Zum Andenken, 11"... 1,645.00
Decanter, florals around wht shield w/Zum Andenker, 3 neck rings, 10" 415.00
Flask, bright amethyst, dmn daisy pattern, sheared mouth, 5¼".. 4,000.00
Sugar bowl, cobalt, 11-dmn, ftd, w/swirled rib final, 6½x4¼"....6,500.00

Stocks and Bonds

Scripophily (scrip-awfully), the collecting of 'worthless' old stocks and bonds, gained recognition as an area of serious interest around the mid-1970s. Collectors who come from numerous business fields mainly enjoy its hobby aspect, though there are those who consider scripophily an investment. Some collectors like the historical significance that certain certificates have. Others prefer the beauty of older stocks and bonds that were printed in various colors with fancy artwork and ornate engravings. Autograph collectors are found in this field, on the lookout for signed certificates; others collect specific industries.

Many factors help determine the collector value: autograph value, age of the certificate, the industry represented, whether it is issued or not, its attractiveness, condition, and collector demand. Certificates from the mining, energy, and railroad industries are the most popular with collectors. Other industries or special collecting fields include banking, automobiles, aircraft, and territorials. Serious collectors usually prefer only issued certificates that date from before 1930. Unissued certificates are usually worth one-fourth to one-tenth the value of one that has been issued. Inexpensive issued common stocks and bonds dated between the

1940s and 1990s usually retail between $1.00 to $10.00. Those dating between 1890 and 1930 usually sell for $10.00 to $50.00. Those over 100 years old retail between $25.00 and $100.00 or more, depending on the quantity found and the industry represented. Some stocks are one of a kind while others are found by the hundreds or even thousands, especially railroad certificates. Autographed stocks normally sell anywhere from $50.00 to $1,000.00 or more. A formal collecting organization for scripophilists is known as The Bond and Share Society with an American chapter located in New York City. As is true in any field, potential collectors should take the time to learn the hobby. Prices vary greatly at websites selling old stocks and bonds, sometimes by hundreds of dollars.

Collectors should avoid buying modern certificates being offered for sale at scripophily websites in the $20.00 to $60.00 range as they have little collector value despite the sales hype. One uncancelled share of some of the modern 'famous name' stocks of the Fortune 500 companies are being offered at two or four times what the stock is currently trading for. These should be avoided, and new collectors who want to buy certificates in modern companies will be better off buying 'one share' stocks in their own name and not someone else's. Take the time to study the market, ask questions, and be patient as a collector. Your collection will be better off. Generally, eBay serves as a good source for information regarding current values — search under 'Coins.' Our advisor for this category is Cheryl Anderson; she is listed in the Directory under Utah. In many of the following listings, two-letter state abbreviations precede the date. Unless noted otherwise, values are for examples in fine condition.

Key:
U — unissued   I/U — issued/uncancelled
I/C — issued/cancelled   vgn — vignette

Am Wire Cloth Co, ornate print, eagle vgn, NJ/1908, I/U 15.00
Barrel Cleansing Machine, eagle vgn, banner title, NY/1894, I/U...25.00
Central Pacific Railway, $1,000 Bond, title/vgn, CBNCo, UT/1944, I/C....20.00
Chino Copper, bold title/maiden vgn, gr print, ME/1917, I/C 18.00
Christmas Wonder Mining, Santa vgn, AZ named state error, NV/1907, I/C...165.00
Ft Schellbourne Mining & Milling, 3 vgns, gold border/seal, NV, I/U...20.00
Guardian Casualty & Guaranty, eagle vgn/art/gr seal, UT/1910, I/U....9.00
Haynes Copper Mining, uncommon print, brn border/seal, AZ/1910, I/C....12.00
Insull Utility Investments, man vgn, ABNCo, IL/1930, I/U 23.00
Little Miami RR, stock script, bl revenue tax stamp, OH/1870, I/C .. 18.00
Merchants & Miners Transportation, state seal vgn, MD/1918, IC ..9.00
Montgomery Shoshone...Mining, photo vgn, ABNCo, SD/1906, I/C ..25.00
Nat'l Coal Railway, capitol vgn w/title, brn print, UT/1926, I/C... 35.00
NW Kansas Consolidated Oil & Gas, eagle vgn, gold seal, WY/1909, I/U..23.00
PA Textile, fractional script, ABNCo, PA/1916, I/U 7.00
Park Cummings Mining, blk on wht w/brn border, vgn, UT/1928, I/U ... 18.00
Philadelphia/Baltimore/WA RR, $1,000 Gold Bond w/vgn, PA/1924, I/C...12.00
Pioche-Bristol Mining, miners vgn, gr border/seal, UT/1916, I/U....22.00
Pittsburg Silver Mining, globe vgn, 2-tone gr border, DE/1922, I/U .. 18.00
Pudge Bros Motor Co, blk on gr, ornate border/seal, CO/1938, I/U..18.00
Salina Coal Co, miners vgn, gr border/seal, UT/1926, I/U............. 17.00
Sumpter Valley Railway, $1,000 Gold Bond, ornate title/vgn, OR/1907, U....70.00
Triangle Mining &..., angel/blksmith/Liberty vgn, MT/1911, I/C.. 17.00
US Mining, bold title/2 vgns, bl print, ABNCo, ME/1903, I/C 22.00
UT Patent & Implement, eagle vgn, beige seal, UT/1917, I/U 11.00
W Frankfort Bank & Trust, Mercury vgn/artwork, gold seal, IL/1916, I/U...12.00
West Shore RR, $50,000 bond, bold title/vgn, ABNCo, NY/early 1900s, U.... 10.00

Stoneware

There are three broad periods of time that collectors of American pottery can look to in evaluating and dating the stoneware and earthenware in their collections. Among the first permanent settlers in America were English and German potters who found a great demand for their individually turned wares. The early pottery was produced from red and yellow clays scraped from the ground at surface levels. The earthenware made in these potteries was fragile and coated with lead glazes that periodically created health problems for the people who ate or drank from it. There was little stoneware available for sale until the early 1800s, because the clays used in its production were not readily available in many areas and transportation was prohibitively expensive. The opening of the Erie Canal and improved roads brought about a dramatic increase in the accessibility of stoneware clay, and many new potteries began to open in New York and New England.

Collectors have difficulty today locating earthenware and stoneware jugs produced prior to 1840, because few have survived intact. These ovoid or pear-shaped jugs were designed to be used on a daily basis. When cracked or severely chipped, they were quickly discarded. The value of handcrafted pottery is often determined by the cobalt decoration it carries. Pieces with elaborate scenes (a chicken pecking corn, a bluebird on a branch, a stag standing near a pine tree, a sailing ship, or people) may easily bring $1,000.00 to $12,000.00 at auction.

After the Civil War there was a need and a national demand for stoneware jugs, crocks, canning jars, churns, spittoons, and a wide variety of other pottery items. The competition among the many potteries reached the point where only the largest could survive. To cut costs, most potteries did away with all but the simplest kinds of decoration on their wares. Time-consuming brush-painted birds or flowers quickly gave way to more quickly executed swirls or numbers and stenciled designs. The coming of home refrigeration and Prohibition in 1919 effectively destroyed the American stoneware industry.

Investment possibilities: 1) Early nineteenth-century stoneware with elaborate decorations and a potter's mark is expensive and will continue to rise in price. 2) Late nineteenth-century hand-thrown stoneware with simple cobalt swirls or numbers is still reasonably priced and a good investment. 3) Mass-produced stoneware (ca. 1890 – 1920) is available in large quantities, inexpensive and slowly increases in price over the years. Generally speaking, prices will be stronger in the areas where the stoneware pottery originates. Skillfully repaired pieces often surface; their prices should reflect their condition. Look for a slight change in color and texture. The use of a black light is also useful in exposing some repairs. Buyer beware! Hint: Buy only from reputable dealers who will guarantee their merchandise. Assume that values are for examples in near mint condition with only minimal damage unless another condition code is given in the description. See also Bennington, Stoneware.

Batter pail, #1½/bird, unmk, make-do bail & tin lid, 1870s, 12" 575.00
Batter pail, #4/running bird, att Whites, Utica, bail hdl, 1870s, 10" ..525.00
Batter pail, accents, N White & Co, Binghamton, 1860s, chips, 8"...275.00
Bowl, accents/1832, Clark & Fox, Athens NY, ca 1832, chips, 6½" ..1,485.00
Churn, #3/triple flower, N Clark Jr, Athens NY, 1850s, 15" 575.00

Churn, #4/leaf, Frank B. Norton Worcester Mass, cobalt on salt glaze, Albany slip interior, 17", NM, $765.00. (Photo courtesy Skinner Inc. Auctioneers & Appraisers of Antiques & Fine Art)

Churn, #6/flower (lg), AO Whittemore, Havana NY, 1870s, rpr, 18" .. 800.00
Churn, #8/lg flower w/squiggle above, no name, wood lid, 20", EX.... 750.00
Cream pot, #1/bird, TF Reppert, Greensboro PA, 1880s, 8½" 440.00
Cream pot, #1/dotted bee, att N Clark, Athens NY, 1850s, ping, 7"... 210.00
Cream pot, #1/long-necked bird, NA White & Co, Binghamton, 1868, 9"... 385.00
Cream pot, #1/stylized fireworks, Wm E Warner, West Troy, 1850s, 9" .. 385.00
Cream pot, #2/brushed flower, N Clark Jr, Athens NY, 1850s, 8½" .. 275.00
Cream pot, #2/chicken pecking, Ottman Bros, Ft Edward NY, 1870s, 11".. 1,200.00
Cream pot, #2/grapes & flowered vine, unmk, ca 1860, stain, 11½" .. 465.00
Cream pot, #3/dotted hawk, Wm E Warner, West Troy, 1850s, 11½".. 2,200.00
Cream pot, #3/spitting flower, Savage & Rogers, Havana NY, 1850s, 12".. 1,595.00
Cream pot, #4/flower (dbl), Whites, Utica, ca 1865, hairline, 12" ... 275.00
Crock, #1½/accents, J Remmey NY, glued crack, 11" 1,925.00
Crock, #1½/bird, Ellenville, NY, 1870s, spider, 8" 275.00
Crock, #1½/flower & petal, J Remmey, Manhattan...NY, 1790s, 11"...... 5,060.00
Crock, #1½/vine, NA White & Sons, Utica NY, 1870s, 7½" 300.00
Crock, #1/bird, Binghamton NY, ca 1860, spiders/lines, 7" 415.00
Crock, #2/accents, Commeraw's, New York, rpl hdl, ca 1790, 11½" .. 1,150.00
Crock, #2/flowers/tree, unmk, 1850s, chips, 12" 385.00
Crock, #2/wreath, Burger & Co, Rochester NY, ca 1877, 9" 360.00
Crock, #3/acorns & leaf, J Burger Jr, Rochester NY, 1885, chips, 11" ... 300.00
Crock, #3/lyre, Whites, Utica, ca 1865, stains, 10½" 215.00
Crock, #4/chicken pecking corn, Adam Caire, Pookeepsie NY, 1880s, 12".... 850.00
Crock, #4/orchid, Whites, Utica, ca 1865, chips, 11" 185.00
Crock, #4/parrot on plume, FB Norton, Worcester MA, 1870s, lines, 11".. 550.00
Crock, #5/grapes, T Harrington, Lyons, 1850s, spider, 12" 1,435.00
Crock, #6/orchid (lg), Whites, Utica NY, tight line, ca 1865, 13" .. 450.00
Crock, #6/paddle-tail bird, NA White & Son, ca 1870, hairline, 14" .. 1,015.00
Crock, #6/wreath, Burger & Lang, Rochester NY, 1870s, spider, 15" .. 360.00
Crock, cake; #2/bird on branch, unmk NJ, 1870s, 7" 550.00
Crock, cake; #3/dbl flower, unmk NY state, 1850s, glued crack, 9" .. 220.00
Crock, cake; drooping flower, Cowden & Wilcox, Harrisburg, 1870s, 5".. 385.00
Crock, cake; SS Pierce...Grocers, cobalt on Bristol, #1 on lid, 1900s .. 635.00
Crock, foliage, 1858, imp: J Swank & Co Johnstown PA, rpl lid, 12", VG.. 2,300.00
Crock, 3-petal leaf, deep bl on lt brn, ovoid, 7x8" 215.00
Flowerpot, #3/stylized leaf, AK Ballard, Burlington VT, 1870s, 11"... 465.00
Jar, #1½/pear, WA Macquoid...NY, 1870s, stains, 10½" 1,550.00
Jar, accents, Clark & Co, Lyons NY, about 2-gal, 1850s, 12½"..... 600.00
Jar, canning; #½/pear, Palatine Pottery, Palatine WV, 1875, 8"..... 660.00
Jar, draped accents, att C Crolius NY, ca 1830, 13" 750.00
Jar, fruit; Bristol w/Heinz Apple Butter label, dtd 1906, 8½" 385.00
Jar, preserve; #½/ribbed vine, unmk, 1860s, 8½" 250.00
Jar, preserve; #2/brushed fan, Lyons, 1860s, ping/spider, 9" 215.00
Jar, preserve; #2/cabbage flower, J Burger...NY, 1865, drilled, 11" 300.00
Jar, preserve; #2/flower, unmk J Burger, Rochester NY, ca 1865, 11"..175.00
Jar, preserve; #2/leaf, AK Ballard, Burlington VT, 1870s, 11" 125.00
Jar, preserve; #2/leaves, Stetzenmeyer & Goetzman...NY, ca 1857, 11"..1,700.00
Jar, preserve; #2/pinwheel, Clark...Rochester NY, w/lid, 1850s, 11" ...1,375.00
Jar, preserve; #2/rooster crowing, CW Braun, 1860s, chips, 11".. 34,650.00
Jar, preserve; #2/snowflake, C Hart, Sherburne, ca 1858, chip, 11" .. 250.00
Jar, preserve; #3/dbl tulip, EA Montell, Olean NY, 1870s, lines, 12".. 165.00
Jar, preserve; ocher accents, Boston, ca 1805, chips, 9½" 190.00
Jar, sm cvd bl-filled flower, Jonathan Fenton, up-trn hdls, 1780s, 15"... 1,410.00
Jar, storage; mottled tan & brn, Paul Cushman, ca 1811, ½-gal, 9" .. 3,500.00
Jug, #1/accents, N Clark & Co, Mt Morris, ca 1835, 10½" 415.00
Jug, #1/bird, Whites, Utica, ca 1865, drilled, 10½" 175.00
Jug, #1/pine tree, NA White & Son, Utica NY, 1870s, stain, 11½" ... 200.00
Jug, #1/running bird, NA White & Son, Utica NY, ca 1870, chips, 11"..4,750.00
Jug, #2/accents, S Hart, Fulton NY, 1850s, tight spider, 13" 275.00
Jug, #2/bird on floral branch, Whites, Utica, ca 1865, 12½" 250.00
Jug, #2/bird on plume, FT Edward NY, 1870s, stain/bruise, 14" 415.00
Jug, #2/bird on twig, WA Lewis, Galesville NY, 1860s, stains, 13".... 600.00
Jug, #2/dbl flower, E Selby & Co, Hudson NY, 1850s, pings, 11½".... 275.00
Jug, #2/dotted flower, Harry F Miller...NY, 1850s, 14½" 525.00

Jug, #2/dotted leaf, J Fisher, Lyons NY, 1880s, chip, 14" 120.00
Jug, #2/flower, Stetzenmeyer & Goetsman, ca 1857, stains, 15" .. 2,525.00
Jug, #2/flower (lg), Penn Yan, 1860s, overglazed/chip, 10½" 330.00
Jug, #2/paddletail bird, att Whites, Utica, 1870s, drips/line, 14".. 600.00
Jug, #2/singing bird, Riedinger & Caire, Poughkeepsie NY, 1870s, 13"..575.00
Jug, #2/spitting flower, Whittemore, Havana NY, 1870s, 11½" 415.00
Jug, #3/dbl pheasant, strong cobalt, Whites, Utica, ca 1865, 16" ..6,325.00
Jug, #3/flower, Burger Bros & Co, Rochester NY, ca 1869, pings, 17"..220.00
Jug, #3/flower, J Burger Jr, Rochester NY, 1880s, burns, 15" 385.00
Jug, #3/potted flower/boar's head, att Purdy, OH, ca 1832, 14½"..550.00
Jug, #3/sunflower (lg), Clark & Co, Rochester NY, 1850s, flaws, 16".. 1,375.00
Jug, #4/peacock on stump, NY Stoneware, Ft Edward NY, 1880, 18".. 2,200.00
Jug, #5/orchid (lg), Whites, Utica NY, ca 1856, stack mks, 17"... 685.00
Jug, accents, emb G Benton L Stewart, Hartford, 1820s, 12" 385.00
Jug, batter; flower, AL Hissong Bloomsburg PA, tin lid, 9¼".....2,300.00
Jug, bird on flower, JA&CW Underwood Fort Edward NY, 14" ... 575.00
Jug, brushed accents, C Crolius, NY, ca 1835, about 1-gal, 10" .. 1,045.00
Jug, clamshell/accents, Commeraw's...NY, prof rstr, ca 1800, 13" ..2,300.00
Jug, Dan Deegan/846...NY, cobalt on Bristol, 1890s, ½-gal, 7" 110.00
Jug, dove w/incised outline & bl int, ovoid, some glaze loss, 11½" .. 1,150.00
Jug, flower (single), Whites, Utica, ca 1865, rstr chip, 11" 155.00
Jug, Geo A Dickel...Whiskey, cobalt/blk stencil on Bristol, 1900s, 9"..220.00
Jug, label: L&BC Chace & leaf, brushed, ovoid, strap hdl, 12", NM .. 375.00
Jug, MA Ingalls/Liquor...Little Falls, hdls, ca 1870, lg chip, 19"... 330.00
Jug, parrot/James A Bell advertising, ca 1865, 10" 900.00
Jug, Paul Cushman emb on brn, reeded spout, ca 1809, 8"........2,200.00
Jug, Potash Bros 14 Main St...NJ, cobalt on Bristol, 1880s, 14½"....220.00
Jug, S Amboy N Jersey/Warne Letts 1807/Liberty Forev (sic), rstr, 14"...9,900.00
Jug, syrup; #2/brushed leaf, Lyons, 1860s, chips, 14½" 220.00
Jug, syrup; #2/triple flower, Albany NY, ca 1865, prof rpr, 15" 300.00
Jug, 3 rosettes/circles/leaves/pineapple, unmk NY, ca 1795, 15½" .. 7,425.00
Meat tenderizer, orig hdl, emb Pat'd Dec 25, 1877, 10" 90.00
Pitcher, #½/butterfly, unmk, 1870s, chip/hairline, 8½" 300.00
Pitcher, #½/drooping flower, att NY state, 1870s, 9" 685.00
Pitcher, #1, dk brn Albany glaze, Lyons, 1850s, chips, 8" 495.00
Pitcher, #1/flowers, att Hermann, Baltimore MD, 1850s, flaw, 10"... 385.00
Pitcher, brn alkaline, unmk Paul Cushman form, ca 1809, 8"...6,000.00

Store

Perhaps more so than any other yesteryear establishment, the country store evokes feelings of nostalgia for folks old enough to remember its charms — barrels for coffee, crackers, and big green pickles; candy in a jar for the grocer to weigh on shiny brass scales; beheaded chickens in the meat case outwardly devoid of nothing but feathers. Today mementos from this segment of Americana are being collected by those who 'lived it' as well as those less fortunate! See also Advertising; Scales.

Bag rack, metal shelves, triangular, 30½x20x12" 300.00
Bean counter, wood w/paper label door fronts, 23 drws/bins, 144" L..2,500.00
Bin, coffee; Choice Roaster stencil on wood, 26x17x13", EX 150.00
Bin, coffee; lift lid, brass hdl/mts, 3-color pnt, 1880s, 8x20x23" .. 765.00
Bin, coffee; Parke's Dry Roast, pnt tin, late 1800s, 21", VG 990.00
Bin, walnut w/Fr ft, 2-part top (front part removes), rfn, 39x39x18" .. 350.00
Cabinet, Diamond Dyes, children w/balloon, 1908, 24x15", VG... 1,265.00
Cabinet, ribbon; Clark's, maple/walnut, mirror sides, 7-drw, 36x20", G... 345.00
Cabinet, seed; Rice Seeds, pnt wood, folds up, 22x45", VG 900.00
Cabinet, spool; Clark's ONT, cherry 6-drw w/foil fronts, 26x23x20", EX... 1,200.00
Cabinet, spool; Clark's ONT, tambour doors, 7 glass columns, 23x20"...2,000.00
Cabinet, spool; Clark's ONT, walnut w/gold foil drw fronts, 22x25", VG .575.00
Cabinet, spool; Hemingway, walnut w/red glass, 18" H, NM 3,575.00
Cabinet, spool; J&P Coats, oak w/7 open columns, 22½x16x16"....750.00
Cabinet, spool; Merrick's, oak, rnd w/curved tambour & glass, 1879..1,150.00

Candy jar, clear glass cylinder, ftd, ornate molded top, 18" 250.00
Candy jar, Pacific Globe, clear glass, 18", EX............................... 350.00
Candy rack, 11 glass jars on swivel base, 1 missing lid, 29" 15.00
Case, glass & oak w/rear sliding door, 1 shelf, 19x24x24"............. 225.00
Case, oak w/glass front, holds 14 collars (present), 25x13x7" 850.00
Cash register, NCR #35, NP, full rstr.. 600.00
Cash register, NCR #332, oak & NP, working, 21", EX................ 440.00
Cash register, WA Bevis, sm Barber type on lg base, EX............1,100.00
Display, bolt; pine w/porc knobs, 8-sided/80-drw, swivels, 34" 850.00
Display rack, Blu-J Brooms, tin litho/wood, 35x23x14", VG 350.00
Milliner's model, facial details/braids, 1800s, 15", VG.................. 290.00
Paper holder/dispenser, wooden fan form w/½" string holder, 1884..1,000.00
Sign, rvpt gilt on blk: Our Second Floor Devoted to..., 1900, 62x36"... 765.00

Spool cabinet, Merrick's, curved glass, $1,980.00.

(Photo courtesy Jackson's International Auctioneers & Appraisers of Fine Art & Antiques)

Stoves

Antique stoves' desirability is based on two criteria: their utility and their decorative merit. It's the latter that adds an 'antique' premium to the basic functional value that could be served just as well by a modern stove. Sheer age is usually irrelevant. Decorative features that enhance desirability include fancy, embossed ornamentation (especially with figures such as cherubs, Old Man Winter, gargoyles, etc.) rather than a solely vegetative motif, nickel plated trim, mica windows, ceramic tiles, and (in cooking stoves) water reservoirs and high warming closets rather than mere high shelves. The less sheet metal and the more cast iron, the better. Look for crisp, sharp designs in preference to those made from worn or damaged and repaired foundry patterns. Stoves with a pastel porcelain finish can be very attractive; blue is a favorite, white is least desirable. Chrome trim, rather than nickel, dates a stove to circa 1933 or later and is a good indicator of a post-antique stove. Though purists prefer the earlier models trimmed in nickel rather than chrome, there is now considerable public interest in these post-antique stoves as well, and some people are willing to pay a good price for these appliance-era 'classics.' (Note: Remember, not all bright metal trim is chrome; it is important to learn to distinguish chrome from the earlier, more desirable nickel plate.)

Among stove types, base burners (with self-feeding coal magazines) are the most desirable. Then come the upright, cylindrical 'oak' stoves, kitchen ranges, and wood parlors. Cannon stoves approach the margin of undesirability; laundries and gasoline stoves plunge through it.

There's a thin but continuing stream of desirable antique stoves going to the high-priced Pacific Coast market. Interest in antique stoves is least in the Deep South. Demand for wood/coal stoves is strongest in areas where firewood is affordable and storage of it is practical. Demand for antique gas ranges has become strong, especially in metropolitan markets, and interest in antique electric ranges is slowly dawning. The market for antique stoves is so limited and the variety

so bewildering that a consensus on a going price can hardly emerge. They are only worth something to the right individual, and prices realized depend very greatly on who happens to be in the auction crowd. Even an expert's appraisal will usually miss the realized price by a substantial percent.

In judging condition look out for deep rust pits, warped or burnt-out parts, unsound fire bricks, poorly fitting parts, poor repairs, and empty mounting holes indicating missing trim. Search meticulously for cracks in the cast iron. Our listings reflect auction prices of completely restored, safe, and functional stoves, unless indicated otherwise.

Note: Round Oak stoves carrying the words 'Estate of P.D. Beckwith' above the lower door were made prior to 1935. After that date, the company name was changed to Round Oak Company, and the Beckwith reference was no longer used. In our listings, the term 'tea shelf' has been used to describe both drop and swing shelves, as the function of both types was to accommodate teapots and coffeepots.

Key: func — functional

Base Burners

Art Garland #400, Michigan Stove, gargoyles/NP/mica, 1889, rstr ..10,750.00
Faultless, Redway & Burton, Cincinnati O, CI, 1873, 38x34x23"..475.00
Waverly #12, Thos Caffney, Boston MA, 40x20x22"................6,100.00

Franklin Stoves

Acme Orient #18, 6 tiles, mica windows, fancy, 1890.................. 315.00
Federal style, CI sunburst, ca 1810-20, 38x42" 500.00
Ideal #3, Magee, CI, 2 side trivets, 1892, 32x28"........................ 275.00
Iron Foundry...NH, ornate CI, grate missing, 1820s, 37x26x32"..250.00
Unmk, CI w/brass mts, 19th C, 40x49½" 150.00
Villa Franklin, Muzzy & Co, folding doors, 1830s, 30"+4" urn 200.00

Parlor Stoves

The term 'parlor stove' as we use it here is very general and encompasses at least six distinct types recognized by the stove industry: cottage parlor, double-cased airtight, circulator, cylinder, oak, and the fireplace heater.

#2, JH Shear, Albany NY, CI, column style, 56" 950.00
#20, Somersworth, tip-up dome top, 1850s, 39x30x29" 350.00
Barstow #137, Orient tile insets, CI, 1886, EX 900.00
Crown, Magee, ornate CI, cylindrical w/cabriole legs, urn finial, 63" ...400.00
Estate Triple Effect #5, gas heater, mica windows, NP, ornate, VG ..260.00
Grayville Active 1919, blk CI w/ornate urn & doors, 1903, 39" ...1,100.00
Hot Blast-Air Tight Florence #53, CI w/allover scrolls, 66x28x28" ...800.00
IA Sheppard & Co Excelsior, Fern 9, cylindrical, 34½" 250.00
Ideal Garland #200, wood/coal, no urn, ca 1898, rstr............... 1,300.00
Jewel #214, Detroit, ornate NP CI, urn finial, ca 1903, 54" 2,250.00
Modern Glenwood Wood Parlor, slide top, 1920s, 45x28x24½"..360.00
Moore's Heater, Joliet IL, ornate CI outer case, urn finial, 60x22x22"..600.00
Neoclassical CI, 4 fluted columns, paw ft, 2 urn sensors, 38x29x18"...600.00
Pearl, OH Stove, ornate CI/cabriole legs, scrollwork finial, 33x23x18"..500.00
Peerless, Pratt & Wentworth, tip-up dome, 1840s, 37x19x15" 150.00
Railway carriage, CI, 27½x24x18", EX... 150.00
Round Oak D-18, 1904, complete, unrstr 300.00
Sylvan Red Cross #31, Co-Op Foundry, tiles, gargoyle legs, Pat 1888-89..350.00
Union Airtight, Warnick & Leibrandt, ornate CI, 1851, 26" 350.00

Ranges (Gas)

Alcazar, Milwaukee, 4-burner/1-oven, 1928, G 50.00
Jewel, Detroit, 4-burner, blk/NP, glass oven door, 1918, VG........ 550.00

Magic Chef, wht, 6-burner/2-oven, high closet, 1938, rstr, up to .. 12,000.00
Magic Chef, 6-burner/2-oven, high closet, 1932, EX................2,750.00
MUCo, wht enamel, 3-burner, monogram on oven door, 32x26x17"..175.00
Quick Meal, 4-burner, bl, cabinet style, 1919, G.........................925.00
Quick Meal, 4-burner/1-oven, 1928, unrstr 300.00

Ranges (Wood and Coal)

Alpine Bride, CI, blk, ca 1920, rstr 300.00
Ideal Atlantic #8-20, Portland, ornate CI, bk shelf, 1890s........1,675.00
Kalamazoo Peerless, gray & wht, wood/coal/gas, 1920s, G 875.00
Kineo C, Noyes & Nutter, high warming closet, reservoir, 1920s . 715.00
Quick Meal, bl enamel, high warming closet, rnd shelf, 1920s 800.00
Walker & Pratt, Village Crawford Royal, tea shelves, 1920s........800.00
Wood/Bishop Popular Clarion, scrolling tea shelves, 1890s.........950.00

Stove Manufacturers' Toy Stoves

Buck's Jr #3, St Louis MO, new body/pnt/recast parts, 26" 850.00
Charter Oak #503, GF Filley, St Louis MO, 14x12x25", EX 2,050.00
Dainty, Reading Stove Works, PA, 7x13x8", VG 150.00
Jersey, Cook & Van Evera, Chicago, ca 1908, 28x15x12", EX ..6,400.00
Karr Qualified Range, aluminum/tin, dial on door, 21½x13", EX.775.00
Little Eva, T Southard, NYC, 8½x14x11", VG w/accessories 575.00
Royal American, Bridgeford, Louisville KY, 14x12x10", G..........950.00

Toy Manufacturers' Toy Stoves

Electric, Empire, Metal Ware, WI, functional burner+oven, '25, 15", VG ..50.00
Electric, Hotpoint, Arcade, pnt CI range, tan/gr, non-functional, VG...150.00
Wood/coal, Bing, bl steel cookstove, brass trim, Germany, 17", VG ...600.00
Wood/coal, Crescent, 4-hole, plated CI & steel, 11½", EX 230.00
Wood/coal, Eagle, Kenton, CI, heavily scrolled, 4-ft, 11½x10", G...125.00
Wood/coal, Little Giant, unmk/unidentified, 7½x8½x11", EX orig .675.00
Wood/coal, Pet, Adams, CI, cooking, ornate, 1857, 8½" W base. 300.00
Wood/coal, Royal, Kenton, 4-hole, CI & steel, ornate, 10", VG . 100.00
Wood/coal, Triumph, Kenton OH, 14x8½x19", G 195.00

Stretch Glass

Stretch glass, produced from circa 1916 through 1935, was made in an effort to emulate the fine art glass of Tiffany and Carder. The pressed or blown glassware was sprayed with a metallic salts mix while hot, then reshaped, causing a stretch effect in the iridescent finish. Pieces which were not reshaped had the iridized finish without the stretch, as seen on Fenton's #222 lemonade set and #401 guest set. Northwood, Imperial, Fenton, Diamond, Lancaster, Jeannette, Central, Vineland Flint, and the United States Glass Company were the manufacturers of this type of glass. See also specific companies.

Aquarium bowl, Celeste Blue w/blk base, Fenton, 6x9¾" 125.00
Bonbon, Velva Rose, rnd stem, Fenton, ½-lb, 6x5¼" 55.00
Bowl, Celeste Blue, cupped w/ribs, ftd, Fenton, 4¼x7⅝"................80.00
Bowl, Celeste Blue, flared, cupped, 27 rays, Fenton, 2x8" 35.00
Bowl, dk gr w/marigold irid, crimped rim, Diamond Glass, 3x7½"...........165.00
Bowl, lt cobalt bl, flared, crimped, Vineland, 3¼x8½" 75.00
Bowl, lt purple, 3-mold, flared, Diamond Glass, 2½x7½" 70.00
Bowl, Midnight Wisteria, cupped rim, Diamond Glass, 2x10¼" 200.00
Bowl, Ruby, crimped, 3-ftd, Fenton, 5¼x10⅜"............................650.00
Bowl, Ruby, crimped rim, Fenton, 6¼x11¼".............................400.00
Bowl, Russet, flared, ftd, Northwood, 5x11½".............................100.00
Bowl, Tangerine, wide flare, rolled rim, Fenton, 2x11½".................400.00
Bowl, Topaz, cupped, 27 optic rays, ftd, Northwood, 5¾x9¼" 130.00

Bowl, Topaz, Melon-Rib, cupped, Fenton, 3⅜x5¾" 60.00
Bowl, Wisteria, wide cupped tulip shape, Fenton, 2¾x8¾".............150.00
Cake plate, Rose Ice, ftd, Lancaster, 2¼x11" 90.00
Cake plate, Tangerine, Fenton, rare color, 2½x7¾" 90.00
Cake plate, Velva Rose, flared rolled rim, Fenton, 2½x8" 50.00
Candlesticks, gr, Central, 7x4", pr...70.00
Candlesticks, Green Ice, Imperial, 9", pr 150.00
Candlesticks, Topaz, Fenton, 10½", pr 120.00
Candlesticks, Wisteria, dolphin hdls, Fenton, 3½", pr...............225.00
Candlesticks, Wisteria, thick base, Vineland, 6¾" dia.................95.00
Candy jar, Iris Ice, optic rays, 3-ftd, Lancaster, 7⅛" dia 95.00
Candy jar, Persian Pearl, Fenton, 1-lb, 10x4¼"...........................50.00
Cheese & cracker, Topaz w/blk trim, US Glass, 2-pc....................60.00
Compote, bl, flared, hexagon ft, Diamond Glass, 6¾x9" 95.00
Compote, Celeste Blue, flared oval, Fenton, 3x4¾" 75.00
Compote, Celeste Blue, wide flare, high std, Fenton, 7x12" 200.00
Compote, Florentine Green, flared oval, Fenton, 3¾x6"................55.00
Compote, gr, Adams Rib, rolled rim, Diamond Glass, 4½x12"...........100.00
Compote, gr, flared, flattened, hexagon ft, Diamond Glass, 6x10"..........110.00
Compote, red, flared, rolled rim, 18 rays, Imperial, 3½x6" 130.00
Compote, Ruby, crimped, Fenton, rare, 5¼x6½" 350.00
Compote, Tangerine, flared, dolphin hdls, Fenton, 5x7" 125.00
Creamer & sugar bowl, tangerine, Fenton, 3½x3⅝" 120.00
Goblet, gr, Diamond Glass, 6½x3⅛" 45.00
Mug, Iris Ice, ftd, hdl, Imperial, Chesterfield, 5⅛x3½"..................75.00
Nut cup, bl, 8 panels, N mk, Northwood, scarce shape, 1⅝x3" 75.00
Plate, bl, 27 ribs, Northwood, 9½" 45.00
Plate, bread; Topaz w/blk rim, US Glass, 2x7x12".......................50.00
Plate, cake; pk w/gold floral & trim, hdls, Imperial, 10¼" 75.00
Plate, crystal w/gr trim, 12 optic panels, US Glass, 9⅛" 35.00
Plate, Egyptian Lustre, w/gold decor, Diamond Glass, 8⅜"..........125.00
Plate, gr, 2 sets of rings, Diamond Glass, 9" dia...........................60.00
Plate, Velva Rose, diamond optic, Fenton, scarce, 7¾" dia...............65.00
Server, Amber, star center, shovel hdl, Jeannette, 4½x10"............50.00
Server, Florentine Green, rnd, dolphin hdl, Fenton, 4½x10" 150.00
Sherbet, red, optic rays, Imperial, 3½x4"..................................75.00
Tumbler, Topaz, optic panels, Northwood, scarce shape, 4x2¾".............150.00
Vase, bl, flared, ftd, US Glass, 8¾x5" 80.00
Vase, Harding Blue, spittoon shape, Diamond Glass, 8½x6½" 125.00
Vase, Mandarin Yellow, waisted, US Glass, 8¼x4" 85.00
Vase, Persian Pearl, crimped, Fenton, 3¼x6" 40.00
Vase, Wisteria, flared, ftd, Vineland, 7x2⅛" 85.00

String Holders

Today, if you want to wrap and secure a package, you have a variety of products to choose from: cellophane tape, staples, etc. But in the 1800s and even well past the advent of Scotch tape in the early 1930s, string was often the only available binder; thus the string holder, either the hanging or counter type, was a common and practical item found in most homes and businesses. Chalkware and ceramic figurals from the 1930s, 1940s, and 1950s contrast with the cast and wrought-iron examples from the 1800s to make for an interesting collection. Our advisor for this category is Larry G. Pogue (L & J Antiques and Collectibles); he is listed in the Directory under Texas. See also Advertising.

Acorn w/gr leaves & short stem, pnt chalkware, 8½" 185.00
Apple w/4 gr leaves, pnt chalkware, 8" 65.00
Apples (2) w/gr leaves, pnt chalkware, 6¾" 165.00
Aunt Jemima, pnt chalkware, 1940s-50s, 7¾" 395.00
Betty Boop, face only, pnt chalkware, 1940s, 9x10" 750.00
Betty Boop w/shoulders, pnt chalkware, 1940s-50s, 7½" 550.00
Black boy & girl eating watermelon, pnt chalkware, c 1942, 7x8"..395.00

Black boy eating watermelon in tub, chalkware, ATCO, 1940s+, 7½" ..645.00
Black boy on chamber pot, pnt chalkware, c 1941, 9" 325.00
Black boy on whole watermelon, chalkware, c 1948, 7x6" 495.00
Black kids eating watermelon slice, pnt chalkware, c 1953 USA, 4¾"..295.00
Black porter, Fredericksburg Art Pottery USA, 6½" 425.00
Bonzo, bl dog w/wht & red belly, chalkware, 6½" 185.00
Bozo the Clown, pnt chalkware, 1950s, 7½" 285.00
Bride holding bouquet, bulbous bottom (skirt), ceramic, MIJ, 6¼" .. 130.00
Buddha seated, cream, pottery, Japan, 1940s, 5¾" 145.00
Campbell Soup Kid, pnt chalkware, c Campbell, 1950s, 6¼".......395.00
Carrots w/gr tops, pnt chalkware, 1950s, 10" 225.00
Cat, blk w/gr ball of twine, red bow, chalkware, 6½" 100.00
Cat, wht head, bow w/blk dots, holds scissors, ceramic, Japan, 5⅜"....145.00
Cat on ball of twine, ceramic, 5½" 95.00
Cat w/bow, orange & wht, ceramic, 5¾" 60.00
Chef, cold pnt, ceramic, Made in Japan, 6" 145.00
Chipmunk, blk & wht striped bow, ceramic, 5⅛" 135.00
Clown w/string tied to tooth, pnt chalkware, 5", 7" 250.00
Coca Cola Kid w/Coke lid cap, pnt chalkware, 1950s, 8".............650.00
Conovers Chef, wht chef's cap, chalkware, Conovers Orig 1945, 6x6"..245.00
Corn (single ear) w/gr leaves, pnt chalkware, 1950s, 9" 225.00
Corn (3 ears) w/gr leaves, pnt chalkware, 5½" 175.00
Dog w/collar, holds scissors, Arthur Wood, 4½" 155.00
Drunk man, pottery, mk Elsa, 5½" 210.00
Dutch boy w/match holder in cap, pnt chalkware, rare, 6½" 345.00
Elmer the Bull, employee's giveaway, chalkware, 7½" 425.00
Elsie the Cow, employee's premium, pnt chalkware, 8½" 475.00
Frito Kid w/bandana, pnt chalkware, 9", minimum value.............550.00
German girl, native bonnet, pnt chalkware, Germany, #054, 1950s, 8".195.00
Goldie the Goldfish, bl eyeshadow, pnt chalkware, 1950s, 6¾"....245.00
Heart, String Along w/Me, ceramic, 5½" 125.00
Howdy Doody, pnt chalkware, c 1950s, 6½" 495.00
Indian chief w/full headdress, chalkware, 1950s, 8¾" 275.00
Indian w/headband, pnt chalkware, 1950s, 10x7¼" 285.00
Jester w/match holder in top/cigar in mouth, chalk, rare, '50s, 7½"....275.00
Jiminy Cricket, gr w/bl hat, chalkware, WDP, 8" 395.00
Lady w/scarf at neck, pnt chalkware, 1940s-50s, 9½" 195.00
Lemon w/gr leaves & short stem, pnt chalkware, 1950s, 6¾" 165.00
Little Monk, pnt chalkware, Bello, c 1940, 9" 275.00
Little Red Riding Hood, pnt chalkware, Bello, 1941, 9½" 295.00
Mammy, blk face & hands, wht dress, ceramic, Japan, 6½" 295.00
Mammy, brn face, plaid dress, chalkware, 1930s, 6" 395.00
Mammy, half-doll type (no cloth skirt), pnt ceramic, 4½" 145.00
Mammy, place in bow for razor blade, pnt chalkware, 6½" 395.00
Mammy, scissors holder, rhinestone eyes, chalkware, 1940s, 6¾" .. 345.00
Mammy (big busted) w/apron, pnt chalkware, 1940s, 7¾" 395.00
Monkey on ball of twine, brn on bl, chalkware, 7½" 245.00
Monkey on bananas, pnt chalkware, 1950s, 8¼" 295.00
Morton Salt Girl, full figured, pnt chalkware, 9" 895.00
Mr Peanut, w/scissors holder, pnt chalkware, 1950s, 6" 450.00
Orange w/gr leaves & short stem, pnt chalkware, 1950s, 6¾" 165.00
Parrot, orange w/gr & yel, on branch w/flower, chalkware, 9¼" ...185.00
Pear w/gr leaves, pnt chalkware, 6¾" 125.00
Pear w/plums, pnt chalkware, 7¾" 85.00
Pineapple w/face, gr top, pnt chalkware, 1950s, 7" 175.00
Rooster head, pnt chalkware, #3021, 1950s, 9"...........................275.00
Rooster head, pnt chalkware, 8½" 225.00
Rose, red w/gr leaves, pnt chalkware, 8" 165.00
Sailor boy, chalkware, Bello, Chicago IL, 8" 225.00
Senor, sombrero tipped to side, chalkware, 8¼" 95.00
Senora w/comb in hair, flower at right ear, chalkware, 1940s, 8"...250.00
Shirley Temple, pnt chalkware, 1940s-50s, 6¾x6¼" 395.00
Smokey the Bear, pnt chalkware, c 1957 NM, 6½" 425.00
Strawberry w/blossoms, pnt chalkware, 1950s, 6½" 115.00

Strawberry w/gr top, pnt chalkware, 1950s, 6½" 175.00
Tomato face, pnt chalkware, 5½" 175.00
Westie dog, wht chalkware, 9"..195.00
Wonder Woman, pnt chalkware, DC Comics, 1950s, 8½" 325.00
Woody Woodpecker, pnt chalkware, Ellis Studios, 7½" 135.00
Yel squash, pnt chalkware, Ellis Studios, 7½" 135.00

Sugar Shakers

    Sugar shakers (or muffineers, as they were also called) were used during the Victorian era to sprinkle sugar and spice onto breakfast muffins, toast, etc. They were made of art glass, in pressed patterns, and in china. See also specific types and manufacturers (such as Northwood). Our co-advisors for this category are Jeff Bradfield and Dale MacAllister; they are listed in the Directory under Virginia.

Argus Swirl, milk glass w/HP decor, Consolidated, ca 1894-98, 3¼"..115.00
Beaded Twist, milk glass, 4x2⅞" 150.00
Challinor's Forget-Me-Not, bl opaque, late 1800s, 3¾" 250.00
Coin Spot, sapphire bl, 9-panel, Northwood, 5"...........................260.00
Coin Spot, wht opal, 9-panel, Northwood, 4½" 110.00
Coin Spot, Wide Waisted; ovoid, Northwood 4½" 110.00
Cone, bl opaque, Consolidated, late 1800s, 5"..............................150.00
Crysanthemum Base Swirl, cranberry, Buckeye, ca 1894-1917 ....425.00
Daisy & Fern, bl opal, Northwood, ca 1906-25 ....225.00
Daisy & Fern, cranberry opal, Northwood 425.00
Daisy & Fern, wht opal, Fenton 165.00

Diamond Quilted Mother-of-Pearl (English muffineer), butterscotch, 5¾", $450.00.

(Photo courtesy James D. Julia Inc.)

Guttage, pk cased, Consolidated 275.00
Henrietta (Big Block), US Glass, ca 1891 ....75.00
Invt T'print, sapphire bl w/HP floral, Hobbs, late 1800s, 5½" 325.00
Leaf Mold, pk & wht spatter, Northwood, ca 1889......................350.00
Melligo, bl opaque, Consolidated, ca 1895, 4½" 125.00
Melon shape, wht satin w/HP floral, Smith Bros, late 1800s, 2¾x4"..465.00
Mt Washington Egg, burmese color w/HP floral 275.00
Optic, rubena, Hobbs, 3½" 300.00
Quilted Phlox, amethyst, Northwood 350.00
Ribbed Lattice, wht opal, Hobbs, late 1800s, 4½" 145.00
Ribbed Pillar, cranberry spatter, Northwood, late 1800s, 4½" 275.00
Ring Neck Spatter, cranberry spatter, Hobbs, late 1800s, 4¾" 225.00
Snail, 5" 100.00
Spanish Lace, wht opal, Northwood, 4¾" 175.00
Stripe, bl opal, 4¾" 375.00
Swirl, gr opal 450.00
Windows Swirl, bl opal, Hobbs, late 1800s, 5"..............................500.00
Zipper, 4½" 40.00
9-Panel Invt T'print, cranberry, LG Wright, 1960s, 4½" 150.00

Sumida Ware

First made outside Kyoto, Japan, about 1870, Sumida Ware is a whimsical yet serious type of art pottery, easily recognized by its painted backgrounds and applied figures. Though most often painted red, examples with green or black backgrounds may be found as well. Vases and mugs are easier to find than other forms, and most are characterized by the human and animal figures that have been attached to their surfaces. Because these figures are in high relief, it is not unusual to find them chipped; it is important to seek a professional if restoration work is needed. It is not uncommon to find examples with the red background paint missing; collectors generally leave such pieces as they find them. Our advisor for this category is Jeffery Person; his is listed in the Directory under Florida.

Bowl, 12 figures perched on rim/peering inside, red/flambe, 2x5x7"...780.00
Box, boy finial, red/blk flambe, 3½x5" dia.. 65.00
Conch shell w/rabbit & boy, sgn, 5" L.. 300.00
Figurine, 2 Sumo wrestlers, sgn, ca 1920, 6¾x7", NM 1,440.00
Humidor, children at play appl on red, flambe top, child finial, 7x6"..240.00
Humidor, men appl on ridged red, wht flambe top, man on lid, 7", NM..480.00
Jardiniere, elephants in mtns, ivory/blk, flambe top, appl mk, 12x19"..1,560.00
Mug, elephant pr on cliffs appl on red, Koji/Koni cartouch, 5", NM..135.00
Mug, sage in bl/wht robe/foliage emb on red, bamboo hdl, 5" 120.00
Pitcher, 3 monkeys, lg 1 pouring water on 2nd, red/blk flambe, 13", EX..360.00
Pitcher, 3-D dragon hdl on blk/red flambe, 6¼"............................... 90.00
Teapot, 2 monkeys sharing peach on red, blk flambe top, rprs, 5", EX..400.00
Vase, children on branch appl on ridged red, flambe top, 12x6" ..390.00
Vase, dragon/cloud/Ishiguro Koko seal appl on red, flambe top, 15", EX..1,320.00
Vase, lady w/flute/2 servants, moon shape w/house in opening, 12x10"..990.00
Vase, man holding up incense burner on red/blk, drilled for lamp, 10"..90.00
Vase, wht irises on red, blk flambe basket hdl, 8x7"...................... 240.00
Wall pocket, crab figural, claws reach toward open mouth, tan, 9" W..180.00
Wall pocket, floral, wht/dk brn on red, elephant's trunk form, 10"...925.00

Sunderland Lustre

Sunderland lustre was made by various potters in the Sunderland district of England during the eighteenth an nineteenth centuries. It is often characterized by a splashed-on application of the pink lustre, which results in an effect sometimes referred to as the 'cloud' pattern. Some pieces are transfer printed with scenes, ships, florals, or portraits.

Bowl, Sailor's Farewell, verses & scenes, pk lustre border, 11"...... 720.00
Butter tub, View from CI Bridge.../sailors verse, 1820s, 4¾" H 200.00
Chamber pot, man/To the Wife/verse, ca 1840, hairline, 5¼" H...1,000.00
Jug, Mariner's arms/poems, 7"... 420.00
Jug, Masonic emblems, 11-line poem, rstr, 9", VG 450.00
Jug, Sailor's Farewell w/Ship/Farmer's Arms in blk-line reserve, 9" ..900.00
Jug, West View of Iron Bridge Near Sunderland/verse, 7" 420.00
Jug, West View of Iron Bridge Near Sunderland/verse, 9", EX 800.00
Jug, 3-masted ship/verse, pk lustre borders, 1820s, 6½" 400.00
Plaque, God Be Merciful to Me a Sinner, pk lustre border, 1830s, 8" W..300.00
Plaque, ship/Peace & Plenty verse, blk transfer, 8⅛x9" 800.00
Plaque, Thou God Sees't Me, eyeball above wreath surround, 8x9" ..230.00

Surveying Instruments

The practice of surveying offers a wide variety of precision instruments primarily for field use, most of which are associated with the recording of distance and angular measurements. These instruments were primarily made from brass; the larger examples were fitted with tripods and protective cases. These cases also held accessories for the instruments, and these can sometimes play a key part in their evaluation. Instruments in complete condition and showing little use will have much greater values than those that appear to have had moderate or heavy use. Instruments were never polished during use, and those that have been polished as decorator pieces are of little interest to most avid collectors.

Alidade, Dietzgen #14412, 12" telescope, 5" vial, EX, +mahog case..475.00
Alidade, W&LE Gurley #584, EXIB... 395.00
Clinometer, Reynolds, Birmingham England, 1767-81, VG 300.00
Compass, Abner Dod, brass, 5" silvered dial, 1800s, 14", +fitted case... 2,585.00
Compass, D Rittenhouse, 5¼" dial, brass, 8⅜x14½" 19,975.00
Compass, Eame's Improved, brass ring & 5½" 32-point card, 12" L ...1,175.00
Compass, J Hanks, 5¾" silvered dial/sights on wide shaped limb, 15"..2,235.00
Compass, T Greenough, eng 4½" HP card, eng 1737, 8"...........2,115.00
Compass, vernier; B Platt, 6" silvered dial, gimballed, 15" L.....6,465.00
Compass, vernier; BK Hagger & Son, brass w/5½" dial, 10x15"+case.. 1,525.00
Compass, whittled from 1 block of maple w/jackknife, brass hub, 9" .. 700.00
Compass, Ziba Blakslee, brass w/5½" silvered dial, 9x15"+case .. 5,875.00
Heliotrope, Steinheil; Bausch & Lomb, ca 1910, EX 1,500.00
Level, combination; AS Aloe, ca 1923, 12", EXIB...................... 450.00
Level, gunner's; KK Artill Arsenall #4302, brass, 6½" L, +case.... 150.00
Level, wye; Gurley, aluminum & brass, ca 1948, 18", EXIB 450.00
Level, wye; W&LE Gurley, brass, 20" telescope, 7" vials, EX+ case ...200.00
Leveling head, plane table; Buff & Buff, ca 1900, EX 400.00
Miner's dial/theodolite, brass, dial sgn Newton Late Wilton, 12½"..590.00
Octant, ebony w/bone scale, 10" radius, EXIB............................. 500.00
Protractor, charting; Lille & Son London, +leather-covered case. 150.00
Protractor, Thos Jones, brass, dbl-rotating index arm, 5¾" dia..... 295.00
Quadrant, J Bennett...MA, pewter scale, alidade w/trough, 8½"..585.00
Quadrant, TR Hoyt, 4½"-radius quarter-circle, 1876, 14" 940.00
Semi-circumferentor, J Hale, brass, 11" dia protractor, 14", +case...765.00
Sextant, Graham & Parkes, silvered scale, 2 sights, ca 1944, 9" .295.00
Sextant, vernier; 9" radius, brass lattice pattern, 4-tube, EXIB 550.00
Theodolite, att Benj Cole, 4" silvered dial, 9" telescope, EXIB....825.00
Theodolite, C Leach, trough compass/brass X-strut, 1792, 6" dia..2,470.00
Theodolite, E Draper, brass, 3½" dial, 2 verniers, darkened, 13"...2,350.00
Theodolite, homemade, wood w/silvered compass by E Kroedel 12" ..235.00
Theodolite, T Cooke & Sons, ca 1890, EXIB...........................2,000.00
Theodolite, W&S Jones, 3½" dial, 13" telescope (defective), 9"... 415.00
Transit, Gurley, Burts Pat Solar attachment, 4¾" dial, 15"+tripod ...7,650.00
Transit, Keuffel & Esser #5077, w/9" scope/compass & full circle, EX...875.00
Transit, mtn; W&LE Gurley #171074, 3¼" silvered dial, 11½", EXIB..500.00
Tripod, tapered post w/thimble, 1750s-1800s, EX......................... 500.00
Waywiser, B Martin, mahog w/brass dial, eng conversion, 32" wheel . 2,000.00

Syracuse

Syracuse was a line of fine dinnerware and casual ware which was made for nearly a century by the Onondaga Pottery Company of Syracuse, New York. Early patterns were marked O.P. Company. Collectors of American dinnerware are focusing their attention on reassembling some of their many lovely patterns. In 1966 the firm became officially known as the Syracuse China Company in order to better identify with the name of their popular chinaware. Many of the patterns were marked with the shape and color names (Old Ivory, Federal, etc.), not the pattern names. By 1971 dinnerware geared for use in the home was discontinued, and the company turned to the manufacture of hotel, restaurant, and other types of commercial tableware.

Bowl, oatmeal; Whitfield Gardenia, hard to find, 2x5½"............... 28.00
Bowl, Romance, short ft, 9".. 55.00
Bowl, soup; FanFare, ca 1960s, 8¾", 10 for 225.00

Bowl, soup; Longhorn, brn airbrushing on wht, rare, 8" 42.00
Bowl, soup; Selma, 4¾", +6½" underplate, set of 6 .... 120.00
Bowl, soup; Sherwood, Old Ivory, 8¾", 8 for 90.00
Bowl, vegetable; Corabel, w/lid, 5x10" L 45.00
Bowl, vegetable; Romance, w/lid, 9¾" L 90.00
Bread plate, FanFare, ca 1960, oval, 7" L 18.00
Bread tray, airbrushed palm tree/sailboat, gray on wht, 10" L 16.00
Coffeepot, Stansbury, Federal shape, ca 1949-70, 9" 120.00
Creamer, Ancient Membreno, Santa Fe RR, 1950s, w/hdl, 2¼" .. 325.00
Cup & saucer, airbrushed fish, bl/gr/pk on wht, Econo-rim 9-S mk..60.00
Cup & saucer, Apple Blossom, gold trim 25.00
Egg cup, Traveler, flying geese, pk on wht, 3" 65.00
Gravy boat, Mayview, Federal shape, w/attached underplate 35.00
Gravy boat, Sherwood, Old Ivory, w/attached underplate, 9" L 40.00
Plate, Apple Blossom, gold trim, 10" 18.00
Plate, Carolina Jessamine, American Song Birds, 10½" 35.00
Plate, dessert; Romance, sq, 8x8", 8 for 75.00
Plate, Dogwood, oval, 10" L 15.00
Plate, House of Blues, bl letters/bands on wht, 10½" 30.00
Plate, narrow red floral border, lg interwining 'PLE' in center, 9".. 150.00
Plate, Pocahontas, flower/corn-stalk border, ca 1906, 9¾" 65.00
Plate, sidewheeler w/Am flag, Robert Fulton Hotel, 10" 65.00
Plate, Suzanne, mc floral border, gold trim, 10½" 22.00
Plate, Traveler, flying geese, pk on wht, Milwaukee RR, 9½" 75.00
Plate, Victoria, Federal shape, 10½" 18.00
Plate, Western Ranch, American Scene collection by A Dehn, 1st ed, 10"..65.00
Platter, Apple Blossom, 10" L 55.00
Platter, Bracelet, gold rim, 14" 45.00
Platter, Minuet, silver trim, 14" 45.00
Platter, Romance, Virginia shape, 14" 50.00
Platter, Shalimar, 14" 38.00
Platter, yel gardenia in center on wht, yel tone at scalloped rim, 12" ...90.00
Saucer, Traveler, flying geese, pk on wht, Milwaukee RR, from $35 to... 45.00
Teapot, Sherwood, 7" 135.00

Syrups

Values are for old, original syrups. Beware of reproductions and watch handle area for cracks! See also various manufacturers (such as Northwood) and specific types of glass. Our coadvisors are Jeff Bradfield and Dale MacAllister; they are listed in the Directory under Virginia. See also Pattern Glass.

Amberina, Coin Spot, New England, silver flip lid, 5½", $1,725.00.
(Photo courtesy Early Auction Co.)

Argus Swirl, pigeon blood, clear hdl 425.00
Buckeye Lattice, cranberry opal 765.00
Bulbous Base Coin Spot, sapphire blue, Hobbs, 1890s 325.00
Challinor's Forget-Me-Not, pk 300.00
Coin Spot, wht opal, 9-panel, 7" 275.00
Coinspot & Swirl, bl opal, Hobbs, 1890s, 5¾" 250.00
Coinspot & Swirl, wht opal, Hobbs, 6" 225.00
Cone, pk cased, squatty 300.00
Daisy & Fern, cranberry opal, Northwood mold 650.00
Diamond Swirl (Zippered Swirl & Diamond), US Glass, ca 1895, 8¼". 100.00
Flat Flower, turq opaque, Northwood 400.00
Grape & Leaf, gr opaque, Dugan 285.00
Invt T'print, vaseline 400.00
Ivy in the Snow, ruby stained, 5½" 585.00
Leaf & Flower, amber stained, Hobbs, ca 1888 .... 265.00
Leaf Mold, cased cranberry spatter 600.00
Ribbed Lattice, bl opal, late 1800s, 7" 750.00
Spanish Lace, wht opal, Northwood, 6¼" 400.00
Venetian Diamond, cranberry 650.00
Wildflower, amber 250.00
9-Panel, sapphire bl, Northwood, late 1800s, 5½" 350.00

Target Balls and Related Memorabilia

Prior to 1880 when the clay pigeon was invented, blown glass target balls were used extensively for shotgun competitions. Approximately 2¾" in diameter, these balls were hand blown into a three-piece mold. All have a ragged hole where the blowpipe was twisted free. Target balls date from approximately 1840 (English) to World War I, although they were most widely used in the 1870 – 1880 period. Common examples are unmarked except for the blower's code — dots, crude numerals, etc. Some balls were embossed in a dot or diamond pattern so they were more likely to shatter when struck by shot, and some have names and/or patent dates. When evaluating condition, bubbles and other minor manufacturing imperfections are acceptable; cracks are not. The prices below are for mint condition examples. Our advisor for this category is C. D. Kilhoffer; he is listed in the Directory under Maryland.

Boers & CR Delft Flesschen Fabriek, lt gr, rare, 2⅝" 470.00
Bogardus' Glass Ball Pat'd April 10 1877, amber, hobnails, 2⅝".. 3,000.00
Bogardus' Glass Ball Pat'd April 10 1877, cobalt, 2¾", $700 to ... 800.00
Bogardus' Glass Ball Pat'd April 10 1877, gr, 4-dot variant, $1,200 to.. 1,475.00
C Newman, Dmn Quilt, amber, rare, 2⅝" 800.00
CTB Co, blk pitch, Pat dates on bottom, Am 150.00
Dmn Quilt w/plain center band, cobalt, 2⅝" 210.00
Dmn Quilt w/shooter emb in 2 panels, clear, English 300.00
Dmn Quilt w/shooter emb in 2 panels, cobalt, English 500.00
Dmn Quilt w/shooter emb in 2 panels, deep moss gr, English 500.00
Dmn Quilt w/shooter emb in 2 panels, med gr, English 375.00
Emb dmns, dk amber w/hint of red, 2⅝" 325.00
Emb dmns, dk cobalt, 2¾" 500.00
For Hockey's Pat Trap, gr aqua, 2⅜" 500.00
Glashuttenewotte Un Charlottenburg, clear, emb dmns, 2⅝" 600.00
Gurd & Son, London, Ontario, amber, Canadian 500.00
Hockey's Pat Trap, aqua, English, 2½" 700.00
Horizontal bands (7), tobacco amber, 2⅝" 250.00
Ilmenau (Thur) Sophiehutte, amber, Dmn Quilt, Germany 320.00
Man shooting, cobalt, emb dmns, 2⅝" 600.00
Mauritz Widfords, honey amber, 2⅝", EX 500.00
NB Glass Works Perth, pale gr, English 100.00
Plain, amber w/mold mks 65.00
Plain, cobalt w/mold mks 125.00
Plain, dk teal gr w/mold mks, 2¾" 250.00
Plain, pk amethyst w/mold mks, 2⅝" 250.00
PMP London, cobalt, chip, 2⅛" 175.00
T Jones, Gunmaker, Blackburn, cobalt, English, 2⅝" 400.00
T Jones, Gunmaker, Blackburn, pale bl, English 125.00
Van Cutsem A St Quentin, cobalt, 2¾" 150.00

Related Memorabilia

Ball thrower, dbl; old red pnt, ME Card, Pat...78, 79, VG	800.00
Clay birds, Winchester, Pat May 29 1917, 1 flight in box	100.00
Pitch bird, blk DUVROCK	1.00
Shell, dummy, w/single window, any brand	50.00
Shell set, dummy, Gamble Stores, 2 window shells, 3 cut out	125.00
Shell set, dummy, Winchester, 5 window shells	175.00
Shell set, dummy shotgun, Peters, 6 window shells+full box	175.00
Shot-shell loader, rosewood/brass, Parker Bros, Pat 1884	50.00
Target, Am, sheet metal, rod ends mk Pat Feb 8 '21, set	25.00
Target, BUST-O, blk or wht breakable wafer	20.00
Thrower, oak wood base, heavy steel spring, leather wrap, ca 1900, EX	1,200.00
Trap, Chamberlain Cartridge...Nov 7th 05...USA, CI, 21½" L, EX	1,300.00
Trap, DUVROCK, w/blk pitch birds	125.00

Taylor, Smith & Taylor

Producers of mainly dinnerware and kitchenware, this company operated in Chester, West Virginia, from about 1900 to 1982. Today collectors enjoy reassembling some of their lovely patterns. Some of their most collectible lines are Lu Ray and Vistosa (see also those categories), but many of their decorated lines are popular as well. Reville Rooster features a large colorful red and orange rooster on simple shapes; Pebble Ford is a plain-colored ware with specks of dark and light blue-green, yellow, gray, and tan sprinkled throughout. There are many others. They made advertising pieces and souvenir ware as well.

Autumn Leaves, bowl, rimmed soup; 8"	15.00
Autumn Leaves, cup & saucer	12.50
Autumn Leaves, plate, dinner; 10½"	10.00
Boutonniere, bowl, vegetable; 9"	15.00
Boutonniere, creamer, 8-oz	10.00
Boutonniere, plate, dinner; 10"	6.00
Boutonniere, relish, 2-part, 12"	12.50
Bride's Bouquet, creamer	20.00
Bride's Bouquet, cup & saucer, ftd	20.00
Bride's Bouquet, sugar bowl, w/lid	25.00
Greenbriar, cup & saucer, flat, 2¼"	10.00
Greenbriar, gravy boat, w/underplate	40.00
Greenbriar, sugar bowl, w/lid	17.50
Pebbleford, creamer, turq	8.00
Pebbleford, cup & saucer, Granite	8.00
Pebbleford, plate, serving; center hdl, mint gr	25.00
Pebbleford, platter, dk orange, oval, 11½"	27.50
Random Leaves, creamer	8.00
Random Leaves, cup & saucer	8.00
Random Leaves, plate, salad	7.00
Reveille Rooster, bowl, vegetable; oval, 9½" L	20.00
Reveille Rooster, bowl, vegetable; 9"	22.00
Reveille Rooster, butter dish	25.00
Reveille Rooster, cup & saucer, flat	7.50
Reveille Rooster, plate, bread & butter; 6½", from $3 to	5.00
Wheat, plate, dinner; 10"	6.00
Wheat, platter, oval, 11"	18.00

Tea Caddies

Because tea was once regarded as a precious commodity, special boxes called caddies were used to store the tea leaves. They were made from various materials: porcelain, carved and inlaid woods, and metals ranging from painted tin or tole to engraved silver.

Blk lacquer & gilt, fitted int, Chinese Export, 19th C, 6x5½x9"	1,175.00
Blk lacquer/gold figures on veranda/scrolls, paw ft, China, 8" L, VG	380.00
English burl & rosewood vnr w/brass shield escutcheon, rfn, 8x14x7"	575.00
Mahog Regency-style w/concave sides, lion mask hdls, 1880s, 7x13" L	350.00
Mahog w/check-banded borders, bracket ft, 3-compartment, 11" L	265.00
Mahog w/inlay Geo III, 8-sided, 2-compartment, 1800s, 5x6x4"	385.00
Oak w/specimen wood inlay, bombe form, ogee bracket ft, 1850s, 10"	295.00
Parquetry, Georgian style, 1 foil-lined well w/lid, 1880s, 4x5x5"	265.00
Pear form, MOP lozenge escutcheon, Georgian style, 5x4" dia	120.00
Pollard oak, pewter/MOP inlay, Wm IV, sarcophagus form, 12" L	735.00
Rosewood, Wm IV, 2 lidded comartments w/in, bun ft, 12" L	520.00
Rosewood w/MOP inlay, Wm IV, sarcophagus form, trn knobs/bun ft, 15" L	765.00
Satinwood/mahog Geo III, lead-lined int, oval, ca 1785, 5x7½x4"	880.00
Tortoiseshell vnr sarcophagus form, brass lion hdls/paw ft, 13"	4,995.00

Tea Leaf Ironstone

Tea Leaf Ironstone became popular in the 1880s when middle-class American housewives became bored with the plain white stone china that English potters had been exporting to this country for nearly a century. The original design has been credited to Anthony Shaw of Burslem, who decorated the plain ironstone with a hand-painted copper lustre design of bands and leaves. Originally known as Lustre Band and Sprig, the pattern has since come to be known as Tea Leaf Lustre. It was produced with minor variations by many different firms both in England and the United States. By the early 1900s, it had become so commonplace that it had lost much of its appeal. Items marked Red Cliff are reproductions made from 1950 until 1980 for this distributing and decorating company of Chicago, Illinois. Hall China provided many of the blanks. It is assumed that all pieces listed below are in good condition with excellent lustre. Our advice for this category comes from Anne Miller; her address is listed in the Directory under Illinois.

Bowl, oval, Shaw, 4½x6" L	35.00
Bowl, vegetable; Fish Hook, bracket ft, w/lid, Meakin, 11x7"	165.00
Bowl, vegetable; Lily of the Valley, w/lid, 11" L, NM	225.00
Bowl, vegetable; Sunburst, ftd, Shaw, w/lid, 11½x5½", EX	225.00
Brush box, Cable, Burgess	295.00
Butter pat, Anthony Shaw & Sons, VG	16.00
Butter pat, Meakin, 3¼", from $10 to	15.00
Cake plate, emb scrolls w/lustre trim, Meakin, 9¼"	70.00
Chamber pot, w/lid, Mellor Taylor, 7½x9½"	165.00
Coffeepot, Bordered Fuchsia, Anthony Shaw, 1860s	275.00
Coffeepot, Daisy 'n Chain, Wilkinson, 1890s, 8½"	165.00
Coffeepot, Grape Octagon, Livesley & Powell, 8¾"	115.00
Coffeepot, 6-sided w/low emb ribs, H Burgess, 8¼"	165.00
Compote, sq, ftd, Wedgwood, 5x8"	295.00
Cup & saucer, Lily of the Valley, Shaw	95.00
Cup & saucer, Meakin	30.00
Cup & saucer, Pomegranate	85.00
Cup plate, Wilkinson, 3¼"	60.00
Gravy boat, basketweave rim, Shaw, 3¾x8"	90.00
Gravy boat, ftd, T Furnival & Sons, 3¾x7¾"	60.00
Gravy boat, gold lustre, ftd, Mellor Taylor, 4½x7½"	75.00
Gravy boat, W&E Corn, 8½"	65.00
Mug, very simple, Shaw, sm rpr chip, 3½"	65.00
Mustache cup, no saucer	668.00
Pitcher, Meakin, 3-qt, 8¼"	180.00
Pitcher, Meakin, 7"	100.00
Pitcher, Shaw, ca 1860, 5½x4"	245.00
Plate, John Edwards, 9"	20.00
Plate, Morning Glory, 9¾"	45.00
Plate, Wedgwood, 8⅝"	20.00

Platter, oval, Wilkinson, 14x10" 25.00
Platter, rectangular, Meakin, 14x10" 25.00
Platter, rectangular, Meakin, 15¾x11¼" 35.00
Relish dish, DeSoto shape, Shaw, ca 1865 .... 95.00
Relish dish, oval, Alcock, 5x8½" 145.00
Sauce dish, rnd, Meakin, 4¾" 18.00
Shaving mug, Anthony Shaw, 3¼x3½" 95.00
Shaving mug, Meakin, 3¼x3½" 185.00
Soap dish, hdld lid, drip plate, Wedgwood, 3½x5¼x 4¼" 80.00
Sugar bowl, Fig (variant), pk lustre, rpr lid, Davenport, 4¼", EX-. 190.00
Sugar bowl, low emb ribs, w/lid, Burgess, 6½" 165.00
Sugar bowl, Morning Glory, Portland, w/lid, Elsmore & Forster, 7¾" ... 190.00
Teapot, Bamboo, Meakin, 8" 75.00
Teapot, Fish Hook, Meakin, 8½" 125.00
Teapot, 6 panels, ribbed, Adams & Sons, 44-oz, 7" 90.00
Toothbrush holder, Fish Hook, Meakin 130.00
Toothbrush holder, ftd cylinder, very simple, 5½", NM 125.00
Tureen, soup; Shaw, 6x14¼x8", NM, +lid, ladle & underplate 850.00
Washbowl & pitcher, very simple, Meakin, 12", 15" 225.00
Washbowl & pitcher, WH Grindley 200.00
Waste bowl, Burgess, 3x5⅜" 60.00
Waste bowl, very simple, ftd, unmk, 3x6" 45.00

Teco

Teco artware was made by the American Terra Cotta and Ceramic Company, located near Chicago, Illinois. The firm was established in 1886 and until 1901 produced only brick, sewer tile, and other redware. Their early glaze was inspired by the matt green made popular by Grueby. 'Teco Green,' a smooth microcrystalline glaze, often accented by charcoaling in creases, was made for nearly 10 years. The company was one of the first in the United States to perfect a true crystalline glaze. The only decoration used was through the modeling and glazing techniques; no hand painting was attempted. Favored motifs were naturalistic leaves and flowers. The company broadened their lines to include garden pottery and faience tiles and panels. New matt glazes (browns, yellows, blue, and rose) were added to the green in 1910, as was a bright multicolored crystalline glaze called Aventurine. By 1922 the artware lines were discontinued; the company was sold in 1930.

Values are dictated by size and shape, with architectural and organic forms being more desirable. Teco is almost always marked with a vertical stamp spelling 'Teco.' Our advisors for this category are Suzanne Perrault and David Rago; they are listed in the Directory under New Jersey.

Vase, green with reticulated blades of grass, 11½x4½", $9,600.00. (Photo courtesy David Rago Auctions)

Vase, aventurine, rstr chips, X, 15x6½" 3,900.00
Vase, brn, 4-hdl, glaze bubbles, #175, 14x10" 3,000.00
Vase, brn w/gr, 2 buttress hdls, 5½x8½" 2,160.00
Vase, gr, beaker shape, 7x6", pr 2,160.00
Vase, gr, cylinder w/collar neck, WD Gates, 8x4" 660.00
Vase, gr, flaring, 16¾x8½" 5,400.00
Vase, gr, gourd shape, rstr chips, #661, 10x7" 3,900.00
Vase, gr, long dimpled 4-sided neck, bun base, 16x8", NM ... 3,240.00
Vase, gr, organic shape, 14x6" 4,500.00
Vase, gr, 2 buttress hdls, 5½x3" 1,140.00
Vase, gr, 2 lg integral hdls, 5½x8½" 3,120.00
Vase, gr, 4-hdl, 7¾x6", EX 3,600.00
Vase, gr, 4-sided w/open loop base hdls, recessed sqs, Hals, rstr, 13" ..26,400.00
Vase, gr & bl, 4-ftd, ball top, drilled, 18½x7½" 7,800.00
Vase, gr w/charcoal, columbine flowers/leaves, 8⅜" ... 2,650.00
Vase, gr w/charcoal, organic tulip form, 4 buttressed leaves, 12x6"...5,400.00
Vase, gr w/charcoal, Prairie School relief, rstr hairlines, 17x7"...9,600.00
Vase, gr w/charcoal, 3 lobes, (rnd w/domed tops) form rim, #163, 18x6".10,200.00
Vase, gr w/charcoal, 4 buttresses as angle rim hdls & ft, Dunning, 11" . 7,500.00
Vase, gr/gunmetal, bullet-shape encased in 4 buttresses, rstr, 17x7"....9,600.00
Vase, pk, 4-hdl, 7x4¼", EX 1,560.00
Vase, yel, flared lip, ovoid body encased in 4 buttresses, Gates, 7".. 4,800.00
Vase, yel, widens toward bottom, F Albert, 12" 3,100.00
Wall pocket, gr, Asian pattern, 6½x5¼" 1,080.00
Wall pocket, gr w/charcoal, leaves/2 sm buttresses, lower 'shelf,' 17" .. 2,400.00

Teddy Bear Collectibles

The story of Teddy Roosevelt's encounter with the bear cub has been recounted with varying degrees of accuracy, so it will suffice to say that it was as a result of this incident in 1902 that the teddy bear got his name. These appealing little creatures are enjoying renewed popularity with collectors today. To one who has not yet succumbed to their obvious charms, one bear seems to look very much like another. How to tell the older ones? Look for long snouts, jointed limbs, large feet and felt paws, long curving arms, and glass or shoe-button eyes. Most old bears have a humped back and are made of mohair stuffed with straw or excelsior. Cute expressions, original clothes, a nice personality, and, of course, good condition add to their value. Early Steiff bears in mint condition may go for a minimum of $150.00 per inch for a small bear up to $300.00 to $350.00 (sometimes even more) per inch for one 20" high or larger. These are easily recognized by the trademark button within the ear. (Please see Toys, Steiff, for values of later and character bears.)

Key: jtd — jointed

Gund, Snuffles, mint gr, 12", EX 535.00
Gund, Snuffles, tan & wht mohair, marble-like eyes, 21", NM 365.00
Ideal, brn mohair, googly button eyes, hump, jtd, ca 1904, 13", VG ... 850.00
Merrythought, blond mohair, glass eyes, squeaker, 1920s, 14", EX ... 275.00
Merrythought, gold mohair w/velvet muzzle, jtd, 25", M 650.00
Schuco, acrobat, lt gr mohair, button eyes, silk suit, 1920s, 10", EX...1,299.99
Schuco, Yes-No, gold mohair, glass eyes, embr nose/mouth, 12", EX .. 285.00
Schuco, Yes-No Tricky, gray mohair, glass eyes, orig clothes, 6½", EX ..300.00
Steiff, beige mohair, button eyes, hump, jtd, early 1900s, no ID, 9", EX.825.00
Steiff, blond mohair, button eyes, embr nose, rpl pads, ca 1905, 17", EX..2,935.00
Steiff, blond mohair, embr claws w/felt pads, w/button, 10", G 600.00
Steiff, brn mohair, growler, jtd, 1927-30, w/button, sm rprs, 19", VG . 1,100.00
Steiff, caramel mohair, glass eyes, jtd, 1950s, w/button, 16", EX .. 495.00
Steiff, cinnamon mohair, straw stuffed, shoe button eyes, 24", VG ..4,485.00
Steiff, cinnamon mohair w/center seam, embr nose, ca 1905, 16", EX 3,525.00
Steiff, commemorative, w/tag & button in left ear, 1980s, limited ed, EX. 200.00
Steiff, honey gold mohair, glass eyes, 1940-50s, 26", EX............2,250.00

Steiff, lt brn mohair, button eyes, jtd, 1925-34, w/button, 16", EX...1,000.00
Steiff, Orig Teddy, brn mohair, glass eyes, squeaker, 20", NM 475.00

Telephones

Since Alexander Graham Bell's first successful telephone communication, the phone itself has undergone a complete evolution in style as well as efficiency. Early models, especially those wall types with ornately carved oak boxes, are of special interest to collectors. Also of value are the candlestick phones from the early part of the century and any related memorabilia. Unless otherwise noted, our values reflect the worth of examples that are working and in excellent original condition.

Automatic Electric, payphone, rotary dial, 1950s 225.00
Automatic Electric, payphone, 3-slot, touch-tone, 1960s 150.00
Automatic Electric #34, desk, rotary dial, brass trim, 1930s 175.00
Automatic Electric Starlite, desk, touch-tone, 1970, rstr 175.00
Automatic Electric Type 21, candlestick, w/ringer box, 1920s, rstr .. 600.00
Connecticut TP6-A, desk, chrome & plastic, rotary dial, 1940s, rstr.. 325.00
Ericsson PTT, desk, blk Bakelite, rotary dial, 1958, rstr 125.00
ITT 500, rotary dial, 1980s, M 20.00
Kellogg, ivory polymer table model, 2nd quarter 20th C, 4¼x9"... 200.00
Kellogg #100 Chrome Red Bar, desk, rotary dial, 1940s, working 200.00
Kellogg #900 Pyramid, desk, blk Bakelite, rotary dial, 1930s, rstr..... 135.00
Kellogg #1000 Masterphone, desk, brn Bakelite, 1940s, rstr 375.00
Kellogg #1000 Red Bar, wall, blk Bakelite, 1940s, rstr................. 275.00
Leich Electric, desk, blk Bakelite, rotary dial, 1930s, rstr 185.00
North Electric Gallion, desk, blk Bakelite, rotary dial, 1940s 150.00
Receiver, Ericsson, NP terminals/ebonite fittings, 6½" 120.00
Sterling Electric, magneto crank wall type, 2 bells, oak case, rfn . 235.00
Stromberg-Carlson, desk, blk Bakelite, rotary dial, 1930s, rstr..... 125.00
Stromberg-Carlson, wall, blk Bakelite, rotary dial, 1940s, rstr 135.00
Stromberg-Carlson, wall, crank hdl, phone-book shelf, rfn oak ... 275.00
Stromberg-Carlson, wall, 2-box, walnut case 385.00
Stromberg-Carlson #1212 Fat Boy, desk, rotary dial, 1940s, rstr .. 275.00
Western Electric, desk, brn faux reptile, touch-tone, 1970s 50.00
Western Electric #102, desk, rotary dial, 1920s........................... 225.00
Western Electric #202, desk, rotary dial, 1920s........................... 150.00
Western Electric #202, desk, rotary dial w/ringer box, 1930s 225.00
Western Electric #202 Extension w/F1 hand set, rstr, 1932 .... 200.00
Western Electric #293, wall, railroad type, 1940s 225.00
Western Electric #301 Fiddlebk, wall, walnut case, 1907, rstr, 30" 385.00
Western Electric #302 w/F1W hand set, blk plastic, rotary dial 75.00
Western Electric #500, blk & wht, rotary dial, 1956 .... 100.00
Western Electric #500, soft plastic, rotary dial, 1961.................... 25.00
Western Electric #554, wall, beige, 1965, w/cover plate................ 25.00
Western Electric #151AL, candlestick, rotary dial/scissor gate, 1920s .. 400.00
Western Electric #2500, desk, touch-tone, 1973, M rstr................. 20.00
Western Electric Princess #702, desk, rotary dial, 1950s 125.00

Large Original Blue Bell Paperweights

First issued in the early 1900s, bell-shaped glass paperweights were used as 'give-aways' and/or presented to telephone company executives as tokens of appreciation. The paperweights were used to prevent stacks of papers from blowing off the desks in the days of overhead fans. Over the years they have all but vanished — some taken by retiring employees, others accidentally broken. The weights came to be widely used for advertising by individual telephone companies; and as the smaller companies merged to form larger companies, more and more new paperweights were created. They were widely distributed with the opening of the first transcontinental telephone line in 1915. The bell-shaped paperweight embossed 'Opening of Trans-Pacific Service, Dec. 23, 1931,' in peacock

blue glass is very rare, and the price is negotiable. (Weights with 'open' in the price field are also rare and impossible to accurately evaluate.) In 1972 the first Pioneer bell paperweights were made to sell to raise funds for the charities the Pioneers support. This has continued to the present day. These bell paperweights have also become 'collectibles.' For further study we recommend *Blue Bell Paperweights, Telephone Pioneers of America Bells and Other Telephone Related Items, 2003 Revised Edition*, by Jacqueline Linscott Barnes; she is listed in the Directory under Florida.

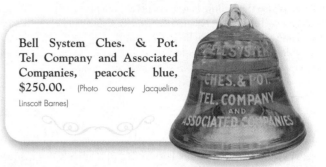

Bell System Ches. & Pot. Tel. Company and Associated Companies, peacock blue, $250.00. (Photo courtesy Jacqueline Linscott Barnes)

Bell Telephone Manufacturing Co Anvers-Belgique, cobalt 900.00
Bell Telephone Manufacturing Co Anvers-Belgique, peacock .. 1,000.00
Blue Telephone Company, cobalt 200.00
Missouri & Kansas Telephone Company, cobalt 100.00
Nebraska Telephone Company, peacock 350.00
Opening of Trans-Pacific Service Dec 23, 1931, peacock .... open
Pays 7% Mountain States Telephone, peacock 175.00
Time Is Money Don't Go - Don't Write But Telephone..., peacock... 1,200.00
Western Electric Company, cobalt (inkwell) 650.00

Large Telephone Pioneers of America (TPA) Commemoratives

Break-Up of the Bell System, opaline/bl swirl............................... 50.00
Laureldale Council 1959-1979, peacock 25.00
Lucent Technologies, ruby red w/gold emb 50.00
New York Telephone/Cornell University 1963, cobalt................. 150.00
Pacific Bell/Nevada Bell, blk 80.00
Region 10 Assembly, bl... 100.00
Southwestern Bell/Pacific Bell, cobalt w/wht slag swirls................ 45.00
Unembossed, blk... 75.00
West Virginia Centennial 1863-1963, cobalt 135.00

Novelty Telephones

Alvin (Alvin & the Chipmunks), 1984, MIB 50.00
Bart Simpson, Columbia Tel-Com, 1990s, MIB........................... 35.00
Beetle Bailey, MIB, from $125 to 135.00
Cabbage Patch Girl, 1980s, EX, from $65 to 75.00
Darth Vader, 1983, MIB 195.00
Ghostbusters, wht ghost in red circle, Remco, 1987, EX 20.00
Mickey Mouse, Western Electric, 1976, EX 175.00
Oscar Mayer Weiner, EX 65.00
Pillsbury's Poppin' Fresh, figure on bl base, 1980s, VG 100.00
Sly Dog, 1986, MIB, from $85 to.. 110.00
Star Trek Enterprise, 1993, NM 25.00
Strawberry Shortcake, M 55.00
Tetley Tea, man in wht boat on rnd bl base, 9", EX...................... 100.00
Ziggy, 1989, MIB... 75.00

Small Commemorative Bells

Bell System, peacock 60.00
Bell System The Chesapeake-Potomac...Associated Companies, ice bl .. 425.00

Bell System/Bell System, Bell South Volunteers in base, emerald gr.. 25.00
Bell System/Bell System, Bell South Volunteers in base, forest gr.. 25.00
Bell System/Bell System, Bell South Volunteers in base, lt bl 25.00
Bell System/Bell System, NC Volunteers in base, gold 25.00
Bell System/Bell System, Region 21 in base, lt bl 25.00
Bell System/Bell System, Region 21 in base, pk............................. 25.00
Bell System/Bell System, Region 21 in base, topaz 25.00
Bell System/Bell System, Region 21 in base, Wisteria 25.00
Bell System/Bell System, SC Volunteers in base, gold................... 25.00
It Pays To Use the Yellow Pages, cobalt 95.00
Save Time - Telephone, cobalt... 100.00
Save Time - Telephone, ice bl 75.00
The Ohio Bell Telephone Company, cobalt 145.00
Universal Service, ice bl.. 75.00

Telescopes

Antique telescopes were sold in large quantities to sailors, astronomers, voyeurs, and the military but survive in relatively few numbers because their glass lenses and brass tubes were easily damaged. Even scarcer are antique reflecting telescopes, which use a polished metal mirror to magnify the world. Telescopes used for astronomy give an inverted image, but most old telescopes were used for marine purposes and have more complicated optics that show the world right-side up. Spyglasses are smaller, hand-held telescopes that collapse into their tube and focus by drawing out the tube to the correct length. A more compact instrument, with three or four sections, is also more delicate, and sailors usually preferred a single-draw spyglass. They are almost always of brass, occasionally of nickel silver or silver plate, and usually covered with leather, or sometimes a beautiful rosewood veneer. Solid wood barrel spyglasses (with a brass draw tube) tend to be early and rare. Before the middle of the 1800s, makers put their names in elaborate script on the smallest draw tube, but as 1900 approached, most switched to plain block printing. British instruments from World War One made by a variety of makers are commonly found, sharing a format of a 2" objective, 30" long with three draws extended, a tapered main tube, and sometimes having low- and high-power oculars and beautiful leather cases. U.S. Navy WWII spyglasses are quite common but have outstanding optics and focus by twisting the eyepiece, which makes them weather-proof. The Quartermaster (Q.M.) 16x spyglass is 31" long, with a tapered barrel and a 2½" objective. The Officer of the Deck (O.D.D.) is a 23" cylinder with a 1½" objective. Very massive, short, brass telescopes are usually gun sights or ship equipment and have little interest to most collectors. World War II marked the first widespread use of coated optics, which can be recognized by a colored film on the objective lens. Collectible post-WWII telescopes include early refractors by Unitron or Fecker and reflectors by Cave or Questar. Modern spotting scopes often use a prism to erect the image and are of great interest if made by the best makers, including Nikon and Zeiss. Several modern makers still use lacquered brass, and many replica instruments have been produced.

A telescope with no maker's name is much less interesting than a signed instrument, and 'Made in France' is the most common mark on old spyglasses. Dollond of London made instruments for 200 years and this is probably the most common name on antiques; but because of their important technical innovations and very high quality, Dollond telescopes are always valuable. Bardou, Paris, telescopes are also of very high quality. Bardou is another relatively common name, since they were a prolific maker for many years, and their spyglasses were sold by Sears. Alvan Clark and Sons were the most prolific early American makers, in operation from the 1850s to the 1920s, and their astronomical telescopes are of great historical import.

Spyglasses are delicate instruments that were subject to severe use under all weather conditions. Cracked or deeply scratched optics are impossible to repair and lower the value considerably. Most lenses are doublets, two lenses glued together, and deteriorated cement is common. This looks like crazed glaze and is fairly difficult to repair. Dents in the tube and damaged or missing leather covering can usually be fixed. The best test of a telescope is to use it, and the image should be sharp and clear. Any accessories, eyepieces, erecting prisms, or quality cases can add significantly to value. The following prices assume that the telescope is in very good to fine condition and give the objective lens (obj.) diameter, which is the most important measurement of a telescope.

Accessories from vintage astronomical telescopes often have collectible value by themselves. Spectroscope and micrometer attachments for Ziess, Clark, Brashear, Fecker, and Mogey telescopes are rarely seen. Eyepieces alone from many famous makers also may be found. Our advisor for this category is Peter Bealo; he is listed in the Directory under New Hampshire.

Key: obj — objective lens   ODD — Officer of the Deck

Adams, George; 2" reflecting, brass cabriole tripod 3,500.00
Bardou & Son, Paris, 4-draw, 50mm obj, leather, 36"................. 250.00
Bausch & Lomb, 1-draw, 45mm obj, wrinkled pnt, 17"................. 90.00
Brashear, 3½" obj, brass, tripod, w/eyepcs.................................4,500.00
Cary, London (script), 2" obj, tripod, w/3 eyepcs......................3,000.00
Clark, Alvan; 4" obj, 48", iron mt on wooden legs...................9,000.00
Criterion RV-6 Dynascope, 6" reflector, 1960s............................. 500.00
Dallmeyer, London (script), 5-draw, 2½" obj, SP, 49".................. 800.00
Dollond, London (block), 2-draw, 2" obj, leather cover.............. 290.00
Dollond, London (script), brass, 3" obj, 40", on tripod.............2,900.00
Dollond, London (script), 2-draw, 2" obj, leather cover.............. 450.00
France or Made in France, 3-draw, 30mm obj, lens cap................. 80.00
McAlister (script), brass, 3½" obj, 45", tripod..........................3,000.00
Messer, London Day & Night, brass, mahog handgrip, 2-draw, 1860s, EX ..200.00
Mogey, brass, 3" obj, 40", on tripod, w/4 eyepcs.......................4,000.00
Negretti & Zambra, 2½" obj, equatorial mt, 36", tripod............2,500.00
Plossl, Wein, 2½" obj, Dialytic optics, 24", tabletop tripod.......4,000.00
Queen & Co (script), 6-draw, 70mm obj, wood vnr, 50"...........1,000.00
Questar, reflecting, on astro mt, 1950s, 3½" dia........................3,000.00
R&J Beck, 2" obj, 24", tabletop tripod w/cabriole legs..............2,500.00
Short, James; 3" dia reflecting, brass cabriole tripod..................4,000.00
Student's No 52, altazimuth to equatorial, 36" focal length, w/stand .. 125.00
TB Winter...Newcastle on Tyne, brass, 17" on tripod, 42" L, EX .. 650.00
Tel Sct Regt Mk 2 S (many maker's names), UK, WWI.............. 120.00
Unitron, 4" obj, wht, 60", on tripod, many accessories.............3,000.00
Unmk, brass, 2" obj, spyglass, leather cover, from $150 to.......... 300.00
Unmk, brass, 2" obj, stand w/cabriole legs................................1,200.00
Unmk floor-standing tripod type, brass, clear optics, EX.............. 525.00
US Military, brass, very heavy, from $100 to................................ 300.00
US Navy, QM Spyglass, 16X, MK II, in box................................ 220.00
Vion, Paris, 40mm obj, 3-draw, 40-power, leather, 21"............... 110.00
Voigtander & Sohn Wein, brass, 1-draw, tapered bbl, 31", EX..... 275.00
Wollensak Mirroscope, 1950s, 12x2" dia, leather case................. 300.00
Wood bbl, rnd taper, 1½" obj, sgn, 1800s.................................... 350.00
Wood bbl, 8-sided, 1½" obj, 1700s, 30"......................................1,500.00
Yeates & Son Dublin, brass, 2-draw, QA-style stand, 15x38".......575.00
Zeiss, brass, 60mm obj, w/eyepcs & porro prism, tripod.............1,700.00
Zeiss Asiola, 60mm obj, prism spotting scope, pre-WWII............650.00

Televisions

Many early TVs have escalated in value over the last few years. Pre-1943 sets (usually with only one to five channels) are often worth $500.00 to $5,000.00. Unusually styled small-screen wooden 1940s TVs are 'hot'; but most metal, Bakelite, and large-screen sets are still shunned by collectors. Color TVs from the 1950s with 16" or smaller tubes are valuable; larger color sets are not. One of our advisors for this category is Harry Poster, author of *Poster's Radio & Television Price Guide 1920 – 1990, 2nd Edition*; he is listed in the Directory under New Jersey.

Key: t/t — tabletop

Admiral #19A12, ebony Bakelite, t/t, 1948, 7"..............................150.00
Airline #94GSE-3015, includes Telephoto Control, t/t, 1948, 7" ...150.00
Arvin #4080T, metal w/mahog front, t/t, 1950, 8".......................150.00
CBS-Columbia #RX89, blond wood, color prototype, console, 1953, 15" ..3,000.00
Coronado #FA 43-8965, mahog wood, t/t, 1949, 7" 125.00
Crosley #9-419, mahog wood, DuMont Chassis, 1949, 12" 100.00

DuMont Club, wooden tabletop model made for use in bars, 15" black and white CRT, front metal door protects controls, scarce, 26x30x27", $550.00.
(Photo courtesy Harry Poster)

DuMont #RA 103D, wood, t/t, 1949, 12" 100.00
DuMont #RA 119, mahog, console, w/radio, Royal Sovereign, 1951, 30"..300.00
Garod #930TV, mahog wood, w/radio, console, 1948, 10" 175.00
GE #10T1, Bakelite, 1948, 10"...100.00
GE #806, wood, t/t, 1949, 10" 100.00
Hallicrafters #T-54, metal, t/t, 1948, 7".......................................175.00
Motorola #TS 902, color, console, 1954, 15" 300.00
Motorola #VT71, wood, t/t, 1947, 7"...175.00
Motorola #9T1, Bakelite, t/t, 1950, 8"..150.00
RCA #6TS30, wood, 1st postwar mass-production set, 1946, 10"...250.00
RCA #721, 1 channel, t/t, 1947, 10"..150.00
RCA #721 TCS, wood, console, 1947, 10".....................................200.00
Scott, #741 PCS, projection TV, 1947..425.00
Sentinel #405TV, wood, portable, 1949, 7" 150.00
Silvertone #9116, cloth covered, upright portable, 1950s, 7".......150.00
Zenith #24H21, wood cabinet, console, 1950, 19" 175.00
Zenith #27F20, wood, console, Broadmoor, 1948, 12" 200.00

Philco Predictas and Related Items

Made in the years between 1958 and 1960, Philco Predictas have become the most sought-after line of televisions in the postwar era. The Predicta line continues to be highly collectible, due mainly to its atom-age styling. Philco Predictas feature a swivel or separate enclosed picture tube and radial cabinet designs. The values given here are for as-found, average, clean, complete, unrestored sets, running or not, that have good picture tubes. Predictas that are missing parts or have damaged viewing screens will have lower values. Those that have the UHF optional tuner will have only slightly higher values. Predictas that have been fully restored in appearance and electronically can bring three or more times the stated values. Collectors should note that some Predictas will have missing parts (knobs, antennas, viewing screen, etc.). These sets and those that have been damaged in shipping will be very costly to restore. This is due to the fact that no new parts are being made and the availability of 'new' old stock is nonexistent. These facts have driven the cost of replacement parts sky high. Collectors will find it better to combine two sets, using the parts from one to complete the better set. Our advisor for Predicta televisions is David Weddington; he is listed in the Directory under Tennessee.

G4242 Holiday 21" t/t, wood cabinet, blond finish 475.00
G4654 Barber Pole 21" console, bommerang front leg, blond......725.00
G4710 Tandem 21" separate screen w/25' cable, mahog finish.....650.00
G4720 Stereo Tandem 21" separate screen, 4 brass legs, mahog ..900.00
G4720 Stereo Tandem 21" w/matching 1606S phonoamp, mahog...1,200.00
H3406 Motel 17" t/t, metal cabinet, cloth grille, no antenna 200.00
H3408 Debutante 17" t/t, cloth grille, w/antenna, charcoal.........375.00
H3410 Princess 17" t/t, metal grille, plastic tuner window...........400.00
H3410 Princess 17" t/t, orig metal stand, red finish 525.00
H3412 Siesta 17" t/t, w/clock-timer above tuner, gold finish 575.00
H4744 Town House 21" room-divider, walnut shelves, brass finish ...1,400.00
17DRP4 picture tube, MIB, replacement for all 17" t/t Predicas..275.00
21FDP4 picture tube, MIB, replacement for all 21" t/t Predicas...275.00

Terra Cotta

Terra cotta is a type of earthenware or clay used for statuary, architectural facings, or domestic articles. It is unglazed, baked to durable hardness, and characterized by the color of the body which may range from brick red to buff.

Pedestal, pharaohs/classical trophies, Retour de'Egypte, 30x12", pr ...550.00
Statue, lady in long gown, 1 breast exposed, doves at ft, 58".....5,600.00
Statue, nude female bather, pale brn finish, after Perron, 21" ...1,175.00
Statue, Virgin Mary w/crucifix & roses, mc pnt, 19th C, 73x21x14" .. 3,525.00
Urn, relief swags, wine/gr daubs, mk Terre d'Anduze, 22x18", pr ..1,800.00

Thermometers

Few objects man has invented have been so eloquently expressed both functionally and artistically as the ubiquitous thermometer. Developed initially by Galileo in 1593 as a scientific device, thermometers slowly evolved into decorative objets d'art, functional household utensils, and eye-catching advertising specialties. Most American thermometers manufactured early in the twentieth century were produced by Taylor (Tycos), and today their thermometers remain the most plentiful on the market. Decorative thermometers manufactured before 1800 are now ensconced in the permanent collections of approximately a dozen European museums. Because of their fragility, few devices of this era have survived in private collections. Nowadays most antique thermometers find their way to market through estate sales.

Advertising

Many companies have utilitzed thermometers as a means of promoting their products. From gasoline to soda pop, there are scores to choose from. Many were 'button' styles, approximately 12" in diameter with a protective, see-through dome-like cover and a sweep hand. Unless otherwise described, assume that the 12" round examples in our listing are of this design. Advertising thermometers were most often made of painted tin or metal; other materials will be noted in the description. Porcelain paint (abbreviated 'porc' in lines) is a glass material fused to metal by firing. Our advisor for this category is Richard T. Porter, who holds the Guinness Book of World Records certificate for his collection of over 5,000 thermometers; he is listed in the Directory under Massachusetts.

Ajax Antifreeze, Be Wise This Winter, owl on branch, 1940s, 36x24", EX..425.00
B-1 Lemon-Lime, More Zip in Every Sip, bl & wht stripes, 16x4", EX ..160.00
BP Energol Motor Oil, enameled porc, 1950s, 26x11", NM.........700.00
Calumet Baking Powder, store advertising on wood, 27x7", EX...800.00
Caterpillar, yel w/blk lettering, 1950s, 36x8", EX 240.00
Clicquot Club Ginger Ale, bottle image, 13½x5⅝", EX...............155.00

Dad's Root Beer, Tastes Like Root Beer Should, metal, 1950s, 27x7", EX....200.00
Double Cola, You'll Like It Better, gr bkground, 17x5", EX 190.00
Dr Pepper, When Hungry, Thirsty or Tired, 1940, 25x10", EX 350.00
Ed Pinaud's Hair Tonic, barber w/product, red/wht/bl, 26x9", VG...1,400.00
Fatima Cigarettes, yel w/red & wht, arched top, porc, 27", EX+..425.00
Frostie Root Beer, Frostie behind bottle cap, on wht, 1950s, 36x8", NM..200.00
Goodman Bros Royal Chinook Shoes, wooden fish shape, 16x5", VG+..425.00
Hills Bros Coffee, porc, 21x8¾", EX..480.00
Honest Scrap Tobacco, porc, prof rstr, 27¼x7", EX 350.00
Jaeger's Butternut Bread, Fresh Wisconsin Butter Added, 12" dia, EX..275.00
Keen Kutter Tools, logo center w/yel border, 12" dia, NM 180.00
Mail Pouch Tobacco, Treat Yourself to the Best, bl, porc, 40", EX..160.00
McKesson's Aspirin, Best for Pain, porc, 1920s-30s, 27x8", EX....200.00
Nesbitt's Orange Soda, A Soft Drink Made From Real Oranges, 22x6", EX...200.00
Old Dutch Beer, red/cream blk on wood, 15x4x½", EX................180.00
Orange Crush, bottle shape, 29", NM..260.00
Pepsi-Cola, Bigger Better, w/bottle, 1940s, 15x8", EX.................360.00
Pepsi-Cola, logo at bottom on wht, heavy glass face, 1963, 18" dia, EX..230.00
Pollack Wheeling Stogies, yel on bl, curved top/bottom, porc, 39", EX..400.00
Prestone Anti-Freeze, You're Set, Safe, Sure, porc, 1950s, 36x8", EX..195.00
Pure Oil, Be Sure W/Pure, bl on wht, glass face, 12" dia, EX 230.00
Rislone Oil Treatment, yel & red w/can, 25x10", EX 200.00
Royal Crown Cola, Drink RC, red/bl on wht, glass face, 1960s, 12", NM..230.00
Sanilac Cattle Spray, cattle scene, arched top, wood, 19x8½", EX...600.00
ShellZone Anti-Freeze, yel & wht on red, 17x3¼", EX 150.00
Squirt, Enjoy, bottle w/sm boy, 1960s, 13½x6", EX.....................275.00
Sunbeam Bread, Reach for Sunbeam Bread, Miss Sunbeam, 1957, 12", NM..875.00
Suncrest Orange Soda, Get Tingle-ated, w/bottle, '50s, 12" dia, EX..175.00
Tom Collins Jr, Tasty Lemon Drink, w/bottle, 25¾x10", EX 145.00
Tom Long Tobacco, Smoke Tom Long, Grand Old Rich Tobacco, 23x7", EX..325.00
Varsity Ginger Ale, blk & cream, pnt wood, 12x3", EX 90.00
Wool Toilet & Bath Soap, metal case, 1895, 1x6" dia, EX...........190.00

Ornamental

Decorative thermometers run the gamut from plain tin household varieties to the highly ornate creations of Tiffany and Bradley and Hubbard. They have been manufactured from nearly every conceivable material — oak, sterling, brass, and glass being the favorites — and have tested the artistry and technical skills of some of America's finest craftsmen. Ornamental models can be found in free-hanging, wall-mounted, or desk/mantel versions. American-made thermometers available today as collectors' items were made between 1875 and 1940. The golden age of decoratives ended in the early 1940s as modern manufacturing processes and materials robbed them of their natural distinctiveness. Prices are based on age, ornateness, and whether mercury or alcohol is used as the filler in the tube. A broken or missing tube will cut at least 40% off the value.

Key:
Cen — Centigrade   Rea — Reaumer
Fah — Fahrenheit   sc — scale
mrc — mercury in tube

Amadio, Fish, Corn Hill, ivory pillar/compass, mrc, 1890, 10" 850.00
Blk/Starr/Frost, desk, barometer, sterling, Fah/Cen, mrc, '10, 11"..2,200.00
Carpenter & Westley, desk, ivory w/glass dome, mrc, 1800, 6" 950.00
Cheshire Silversmiths, desk, bronze candelabra, mrc, 1875, 10" ...4,500.00
Clark, desk, ivory ped, crown, mrc, 1904, 7".................................400.00
Creswel, travel, ivory/case/mirror, removable mrc, 2½".............2,800.00
Desk, cvd walrus tusk, 2-tier disk base, inlay sc, 1860, 9" 430.00
Dixie, W (London), desk, gilt/bronze, Gothic, SP sc, mrc, 8" 790.00
Dollard London, hanging, mahog fr, sterling sc, mrc, 1810, 18"..4,600.00
England, wall, bronze game-bag fr, Fah sc, mrc, 1890, 9x5".......1,650.00
Farley, travel, walnut base mt, ivory Fah/Cen sc, mrc, 5" 900.00

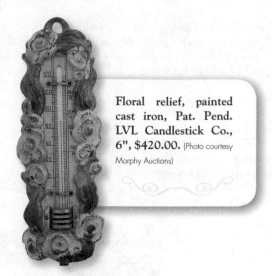

Floral relief, painted cast iron, Pat. Pend. LVL Candlestick Co., 6", $420.00. (Photo courtesy Morphy Auctions)

G Cooper, desk, bell shape w/cupola, sterling, dial, 2x3"..............400.00
J Waldstein, wall, bronze Rea sc on wood, mrc, 1990s, 10½" 920.00
Pig w/branch of tree, Pairpoint #5604, 5¼"................................375.00
Rowley & Sons, travel, ivory sc, mrc, 1894, 4", +case.................350.00
Tycos, max/minimum, japanned tin/bronze, mrc, T-5452, 8" 125.00
Unknown, desk, alabaster w/eagle, Rea/Cen sc, mrc, 8"..............875.00
West, desk, Gothic design, bronze, 1900, 12" 1,360.00
Whitehead & Hoag, Lambrecht's Polymeter, mrc, 9" 1,200.00

Thousand Faces

The name of this china arises from the claim that 1,000 faces can be seen on every dinner plate. Though the overall pattern is called Thousand Faces, there are several variations, including Men in Robes and Thousand Geishas. (The Immortals, a Satsuma style of china, is not considered to be Thousand Faces, although many people list it as such.) This china was made in the early part of the century and stayed popular through the 1930s, 1940s, and 1950s. Although few items are marked (many of them were brought into the country by servicemen), the ones that are carry a variety: Made in Japan, Made in Occupied Japan, Kutani, or other Japan marks. The tea/coffee sets are often found to serve four, five, or six people, many having dragon spouts on the teapot and creamer.

The two main colors are gold-face and black-face. As its name suggests, the gold-face pattern is primarily gold; it features rings of multiple colors with gold faces painted on them. This color has always been the most prevalent, and is today the easiest to find and the most popular. The black-face pattern has a background of white with rings of multiple colors; it has black faces painted on the rings. It's not as popular, and it's harder to find — even so, the two patterns command similar prices. Even though the gold-face is easier to find, many think it is the more striking of the two.

The blue and green patterns are rarely seen. In both types, the primary color has rings of the same color in varying shades with gold-painted faces and accents. As expected, these two colors command a higher price (for pieces in mint condition.) Complete sets are rarely if ever found, but the component pieces that turn up from time to time vouch for their existence. There are other variations in color, such as the black-face pattern with black or cobalt blue rims, but the more popular variations are Men in Robes and Thousand Geishas.

Men in Robes is a striking variation with bursts of colors coming from the robes instead of the rings of color. There are usually gold accents and a ring of color around the rim. Often the faces are concentrated in one area of the piece while the other section is filled with robes, giving the impression that the men are standing.

Thousand Geishas is a striking variation similar to Men in Robes. The colors come from the kimonos worn by the ladies, all of whom have black hair in the true geisha fashion. The Thousand Geishas pattern may be found in various colors, including lighter shades. EBay is a good source of information regarding Thousand Faces china and its variations. Our advisor for this category is Suzi Hibbard; she is listed in the Directory under California.

Key: MIJ — Made in Japan   MIOJ — Made in Occupied Japan

Bowl, serving; gold, Kutani, 2½x5", +plate & spoon, from $35 to ...50.00
Bowl, soup; Men in Robes, w/lid, Kutani, from $50 to 75.00
Cup & saucer, coffee; gr, MIJ, from $50 to...................................... 125.00
Cup & saucer, coffee; Thousand Geishas, unmk, from $40 to........ 60.00
Dresser set, blk, unmk, tray+hatpin holder+jar+hair receiver, $200 to. 300.00
Lamp, gold, unmk, 10½", from $100 to 150.00
Plate, blk, MIJ, 7¼", from $15 to.. 30.00
Plate, Men in Robes, Kutani, 7¼", from $30 to 40.00
Plate, Men in Robes, unmk, 9½", from $25 to 35.00
Tea set, demi; gold, unmk, pot+cr/sug+6 c/s+tray, 17-pc, from $125 to..200.00
Tea set, gold, MIJ, 17-pc, from $150 to 275.00
Tea set, gold, rattan hdl, mk, 20-pc, from $175 to 250.00
Tea set, Men in Robes, 24-pc, from $200 to.................................... 325.00
Teapot, Men in Robes, Shofu - MIJ, from $35 to............................. 50.00
Teapot, Thousand Geishas, mk, 6x7", from $45 to 85.00
Vase, gold, 5", from $45 to.. 70.00
Vase, Men in Robes, red/blk, mk, 2⅞", from $50 to....................... 125.00

Tiffany

Louis Comfort Tiffany was born in 1848 to Charles Lewis and Harriet Young Tiffany of New York. By the time he was 18, his father's small dry goods and stationery store had grown and developed into the world-renowned Tiffany and Company. Preferring the study of art to joining his father in the family business, Louis spent the next six years under the tutelage of noted artists. He returned to America in 1870 and until 1875 painted canvases that focused on European and North African scenes. Deciding the more lucrative approach was in the application of industrial arts and crafts, he opened a decorating studio called Louis C. Tiffany and Co., Associated Artists. He began seriously experimenting with glass, and eschewing traditionally painted-on details, he instead learned to produce glass with qualities that could suggest natural textures and effects. His experiments broadened, and he soon concentrated his efforts on vases, bowls, etc., that came to be considered the highest achievements of the art. Peacock feathers, leaves and vines, flowers, and abstracts were developed within the plane of the glass as it was blown. Opalescent and metallic lustres were combined with transparent color to produce stunning effects. Tiffany called his glass Favrile, meaning handmade.

In 1900 he established Tiffany Studios and turned his attention full time to producing art glass, leaded-glass lamp shades and windows, and household wares with metal components. He also designed a complete line of jewelry which was sold through his father's store. He became proficiently accomplished in silverwork and produced such articles as hand mirrors embellished with peacock feather designs set with gems and candlesticks with Favrile glass inserts. Tiffany's work exemplified the Art Nouveau style of design and decoration, and through his own flamboyant personality and business acumen he perpetrated his tastes onto the American market to the extent that his name became a household word. Tiffany Studios continued to prosper until the second decade of this century when due to changing tastes his influence began to diminish. By the early 1930s the company had closed.

Serial numbers were assigned to much of Tiffany's work, and letter prefixes indicated the year of manufacture: A – N for 1896 – 1900, P – Z for 1901 – 1905. After that, the letter followed the numbers with A – N in use from 1906 – 1912; P – Z from 1913 – 1920. O-marked pieces were made especially for friends and relatives; X indicated pieces not made for sale.

Our listings are primarily from the auction houses in the East where both Tiffany and Comany and Tiffany Studio items sell at a premium. All pieces are signed unless noted otherwise.

Basket, feathers, wht on bl pastel; bronze enameled fr #516, 7"... 3,000.00
Bottle, cologne; feathers on gold band over frost, bulbous body, 7" ..1,550.00
Bowl, bl, optic ribs, ovoid w/scalloped rim, 3½x9½" 900.00
Bowl, bl irid, wide-rib body, scalloped rim, 3½x10¼" 1,035.00
Bowl, dk bl irid, very shallow, ped ft, 2¾x11½"......................... 840.00
Bowl, gold, leaves etched w/in, scalloped/wide ribbed, 2½x6½" . 1,680.00
Bowl, gold, low ft, very simple, 2x3½"...................................... 375.00
Bowl, gold, wide cupped petal rim on onion body, ped ft, 6½x6½" ..1,080.00
Bowl, gold, 10", +2-tier flower frog #7997.................................. 1,600.00
Bowl, gold w/EX irid, pinched/petal rim, 5x5", +6" underplate.... 865.00
Bowl, opal shading to gr irid border, simple shape, 2¼x4½" 300.00
Bowl, peacock feathers in EX bl/purple irid, 9", +2-tier flower frog ..3,395.00
Candleholders, pastel gr bobeche, clear ped ft, 4", pr 1,095.00
Candleholders, pastel yel w/wht opal stripes, opal stem/ft, 4", pr. 1,668.00
Chalice, gold w/appl threading & pods, 4½"............................... 1,035.00
Compote, feathers, wht on lemon-yel, #1701, 4½" 1,200.00
Compote, floriform; gold, wide lobed/scalloped rim, 4¾" 1,080.00
Compote, gold w/intaglio band: leaves/grapes, 3½x4½" 960.00
Compote, gr irid stretch bowl on opal stem/ft, 4½" 600.00
Compote, raspberry/lav pastel w/wht rays, oblong w/clear stem, 7x7" . 1,495.00
Cordial, gold w/intaglio leaves & grape band, 4½" 420.00
Cordial, purple/bl irid, stem w/2 rings under cup, 6"................... 805.00
Decanter, gold, 4-pinch body/stopper, 10", +7 1¾" jiggers 3,795.00
Dish, pastel gr to wht opal w/radial stripes & irid, 2 uptrn sides, 6"..860.00
Finger bowl, gold, deeply scalloped rims, 5", 8 for...................... 1,665.00
Finger bowl, gold, ribbed/scalloped, 2¼x5" 210.00
Finger bowl, hearts & vines/wht millefiori on amber, +5½" plate....960.00
Flower frog, gold, 3 tiers of loops, #4230K, 6x4" 300.00
Goblet, apple gr w/intaglio leaves, tall 2-ball stem, 8", 4 for 920.00
Goblet, feathers, wht on gold, faceted stem, shaped cup, 5".......... 480.00
Goblet, leaves, opal on yel pastel, opic ribs, clear twist stem, 8" ..840.00
Paperweight, turtlebk tile in bronze mt #935, 5¾" L 1,955.00
Pitcher, gold, flared cylinder, 3¼" 540.00
Plate, pastel bl w/radiating wht panels, 10½" 920.00
Plate, pastel gr, scalloped opal rim, onion-skin border, 10½"........ 480.00
Salt cellar, gold, scalloped/lobed rim, 2½" dia............................ 205.00
Salt cellar, gold w/bl irid, ruffled/fluted top, lt ribbing, 2½" 260.00
Shade, candlestick; swirls/waves, grs/gold/platinum, ruffled, 7" W ..750.00
Shade, feathers, gr/gold on oyster, waisted, scalloped rim, 4¾".... 1,380.00
Shade, gold, wide ribs, tulip shape, 5", from $900 to 1,200.00
Sherbet, gold w/sm pulled random prunts, 3¼" 400.00
Tumblers, gold w/pastel irid & central threaded band, 3¾", 8 for ..2,300.00
Urn, bl irid, ovoid body, elongated pointed lid, 9½" 2,935.00
Vase, agate w/silver-gold irid, heavy Egyptian pulled chain decor, 9" .. 5,465.00
Vase, bl irid, lg raised Xs surround corset-shaped body, 5" 1,840.00
Vase, bl-purple irid, trumpet in dore fr (wear), 15" 3,735.00
Vase, bud; bl irid, tube neck, wide bun ft, 6"............................. 2,070.00
Vase, Cypriote, gold cased in wht, bottle form w/disk ft, 4¾"....3,000.00
Vase, damascene on bl irid, pinched sides, 1½"........................... 2,050.00
Vase, feather bands, gold on amber opal w/red tones, 9x6" 2,750.00
Vase, feathers, gold on apple gr irid, Q-5123/sticker, 5" 2,070.00
Vase, feathers, gold/gr on cream, gold int, trumpet in bronze ft #1048.. 1,600.00
Vase, feathers, gr irid on bright bl irid, slim w/bun base, 10" 9,040.00
Vase, feathers, gr on gold, elongated trumpet form, 20" 4,315.00
Vase, feathers, gr on gold, tubular, bronze ft w/appl scrolls, 14"..2,875.00
Vase, floriform; deep bl irid, stretched ruffled widely flared top, 5" ...2,990.00
Vase, floriform; feathers, gr on cream, flared gold stretch rim, 6x8"..3,750.00
Vase, floriform; feathers, gr on opal, in bronze stem holder, 17" .2,530.00
Vase, floriform; feathers, gr on opal, wide scalloped rim, 9½"....4,600.00
Vase, floriform; feathers, gr on oyster, upright elongated top, 13" ... 7,765.00

Vase, floriform; gold, upright lobed rim, swirled base, flaw, 10½" ...3,740.00
Vase, floriform; gold, upright w/stretched ruffled rim, 12" 4,800.00
Vase, gold, cylindrical neck w/ruffled rim, appl tadpoles, 8" 840.00
Vase, gold, flared/stretched/ruffled top on rnd body w/4 sm ft, 3", NM ... 575.00
Vase, gold, narrow neck on elongated ftd ovoid, 6" 450.00
Vase, gold, ribbed, pinched sides, scalloped apron under rim, 4".. 480.00
Vase, gold, wide ruffled cupped rim on sm 4-ftd pot, 3½" 1,080.00
Vase, gold trumpet form in dore metal artichoke ft, 15", NM .. 2,000.00
Vase, gold w/Egyptian chain under flaring rim, bun bottom, 3½x5"...2,300.00
Vase, gold w/intaglio gr leaves/vines, trumpet shape, 13" 3,740.00
Vase, gold w/internal tooling, widens at base, 11" 1,140.00
Vase, hearts/vines, gr on bl, elongated tulip form, 6½" 1,800.00
Vase, hearts/vines, gr on gold, shouldered, 4x3" 1,200.00
Vase, hearts/vines, mc on bl-gr irid, drilled & filled, 21" 5,175.00
Vase, irregular waves, bl/platinum on lt gr, flared/lobed shape, 5"...2,415.00
Vase, jack-in-pulpit; gold w/EX irid, slim stem/bun base, 16x9"....13,225.00
Vase, leaves/vines, deep bl on blk irid, ovoid, 5¾" 8,625.00
Vase, leaves/vines, gr/gold on med bl, bulbous, 2¾" 2,590.00
Vase, millefiori/lily pads on smoky turq bl 'water,' bulbous, 6" ..5,750.00

Vase, paperweight; aquamarine with three pond lilies and five lily pads, #8524K; provenance: 1946 Park-Bernet, Metropolitan Museum of Art, Shulman & McKean, and Riseman; sold with 1946 Parke-Bernet catalog, three in-making stress fractures, 15", $83,375.00.

(Photo courtesy James D. Julia Inc.)

Vase, pastel yel w/opal striations, trumpet form, 7"...................... 600.00
Vase, peacock feathers, mc irid on lt gr, 23" 8,625.00
Vase, pigeon blood red w/irid int, shouldered, w/label, 10" 4,370.00
Vase, platinum/purple irid on lt bl, classic shape, #2162, 3" 865.00
Vase, sapphire bl irid, 2 sm pulled hdls, 3" 865.00
Vase, wht opal irid to clear, 2 pulled-out hdls, bulbous, 2¾" 345.00
Wine, bl/purple irid, amber stem, #1167, 5½", set of 6 .... 1,495.00
Wine, gold, stem w/knob under cup, 6½" 865.00
Wine, gold, twisted stem, 7", 4 for... 2,300.00
Wine, gold w/wheel-cvd fleur-de-lis under rim, 5¾" 600.00

Lamps

Lamp prices seem to be getting stronger, especially for leaded lamps with brighter colors (red, blue, purple). Bases that are unusual or rare have brought good prices and added to the value of the more common shades that sold on them. Bases with enamel or glass inserts are very much in demand. Our advisor for Tiffany lamps is Carl Heck; he is listed in the Directory under Colorado.

Key: c-b — counterbalance

Base only, bridge lamp, 5 legs w/spade ft, harp top, 59", EX 1,750.00
Base only, octagonal urn w/fleur-de-lys at shoulder, #15047, 22" ...3,600.00
Boudoir, textured gold irid flaring shade; 3-strap conical std #426....1,500.00

Bridge, damascene 7" gr shade; harp std #419 w/ribbed ft, 13½"....6,000.00
Candle, feathered shade; 3-lobe stem w/3 root ft & blown-in glass, 22"..8,050.00
Candle, gold ruffled shade, feathered riser, gold twist base, 13" ..2,400.00
Candle, gold ruffled/stretch-rim shade, feather stem, twist base, 11"..1,800.00
Candle, gold Tel el Amarana shade; std #1201, 4-leg w/cat's paws, 17"..3,000.00
Candle, 4 feathered shades, cups w/blown-in glass, 18", pr......24,150.00
Chandelier, ldgl 18" swirling leaf-band shade; on 3 chains/cap, 35"....23,000.00
Desk, dbl turtle-bk tiles shade w/EX color; Zodiac harp std #541, 14" ..18,000.00
Desk, Grapevine 7" shade w/blown-in gr glass; harp std #424, 17"...3,960.00
Desk, King Tut 7" gr w/silver irid dome shade; c-b base #S207, 12" ..13,800.00
Desk, turtle-bk tiles (2) shade; harp std #268 w/glass 'jewels,' 15" 20,700.00
Floor, bronze shade w/rtcl frieze band, glass lined; 4-ftd std #502.... 6,600.00
Floor, damascene 10" gold to yel shade (EX); harp std w/pad ft, 55" .. 6,900.00
Floor, ldgl 14" acorn-band shade; harp std w/5 tall legs, 58", EX...16,800.00
Hanging, rtcl 11" shade w/blown-in glass, beaded fringe, metal mts ..6,900.00
Lily, 3-light, gold shades; #306 std w/ribbed ft, parcel gilt, 17" 7,500.00
Lily, 7-light, gold shades; bronze lily-pad base #29788, 20x10"...26,400.00
Lily, 12-light, gold shades (M-EX); dore hdw & std #332 w/lily pads ...27,600.00
Lily, 12-light, gold/ribbed sgn shades; lily-pad brn-patina base #382 ...34,500.00
Sconce, bronze/turtle-bk tile 4-sided shade, hinged bottom, 22", pr ...64,625.00
Table, feathered 11" gold shade w/gold prisms & matching base, 19" ... 7,820.00
Table, gold 6" optic-rib bell shade; adjustable arm on std, 21" ..1,200.00
Table, ldgl 14" dragonfly shade; simple std #26881, 19"...........43,700.00
Table, ldgl 16" acorn-band shade; unmk urn base in 4-leg support, 21"....12,075.00
Table, ldgl 16" daffodil shade; std #6842 w/fine patina, 22".....48,875.00
Table, ldgl 16" feathered jewel shade (VG); std #364, rfn, 21"..1,500.00
Table, ldgl 16" geometric #1900 shade; gilt std #522, 21"..........6,550.00
Table, ldgl 16" Greek key shade; simple std #534, 22".............21,275.00
Table, ldgl 16" pansies (yel on lapis bl) shade; #533 std, EX....84,000.00
Table, ldgl 16" poinsettia shade #1667; Grecian urn font #181, 20"..34,500.00
Table, ldgl 16" poppy tuck-under shade; simple Colonial-style std (EX)..66,125.00
Table, ldgl 16" shade w/band of glass balls; blown-in-metal std #338....89,125.00
Table, ldgl 16" shade w/4 rows of ovals, gold-gr; std #368, 25", EX.. 18,800.00
Table, ldgl 18" brickwork shade #444; urn-in-harp std #1013, 22" ..22,800.00
Table, ldgl 18" geometric rolled-under shade; std #533, 24" ..34,500.00
Table, ldgl 18" lemon-leaf band shade; ribbed std w/wide base & 4 ft....29,900.00
Table, ldgl 18" poinsettia shade #1558; leaf-emb #21363 base, 17" ...46,000.00
Table, ldgl 20" brickwork shade; simple std #531, 30" 23,000.00
Table, ldgl 20" vertical brickwork shade; #368 std w/long emb leaves ..27,600.00
Table, linen-fold 8" gr shade (EX); c-b #415 base, 16", pr 19,500.00
Table, linen-fold 19" amber 12-panel shade; rib-base dore std #370..22,000.00
Table, rtcl 13" bronze Adam shade; Adam dore base #539, 18", EX..12,075.00
Table, spiral-lined gr bell-shaped shade w/wht int; std #606, 15"...5,400.00

Metal Work

Grapevine and Pine Needle are the most sought-after lines — dependent, of course, on condition. In the following listings, items are bronze unless otherwise noted.

Blotter ends, Grapevine, #998, 12" L, pr..................................... 115.00
Blotter ends, Pine Needle, #998, minor wear, 12" L, pr................. 90.00
Box, Bookmark, dore, #1661, 2¼x4½" L...................................... 960.00
Box, stamp; Grapevine, caramel slag, monogram, #809, 2x7x4" .. 385.00
Candelabrum, central stem w/twisted tendrils, #1230, new patina, 9x7"... 3,240.00
Candelabrum, 2 cups in 3-finger supports, central stem/bud, dore, 9"... 4,300.00
Candelabrum, 4 cups in 3-finger supports, flat base w/6 'jewels,' 12"..4,300.00
Candelabrum, 6 cups, in 3-finger supports on wide branch, dore, #1290..4,500.00
Candlestick, cup w/cabochons on stem, 3 4-toed ft, #1200, 12", ea ...3,000.00
Candlestick, 6 fingers w/leaves support cup on stem, #1210, 10", ea..960.00
Candlesticks, upright cobra by cup in 3-finger support, dore, 8", pr..1,725.00
Candlesticks, Zodiac, 8-sided cups & base, 5¾", pr 1,440.00
Candlesticks, 3-leg, base emb: Jury...1905-06, reeded cups, 8x5", pr.1,560.00
Card tray, seminude lying on stone ledge, 5" L 920.00

Charger, abalone disks inlaid in rim, #1730, lt wear, 12" 520.00
Clock, desk, Greek Key, flaring trapezoid w/design in ea angle, 6x5" .5,400.00
Clock, desk; twisted filigree w/red enamel accents, dore, gabled, 8" ...6,900.00
Clock, mantel; octagonal w/chain around bezel, dore, #168070, 10x11" .4,600.00
Compote, emb knotched band at rim, monogram, 6½" dia, EX ... 175.00
Desk set, Abalone, postal scale/fr/calendar/letter holder+11 pcs ..12,000.00
Desk set, Adam, dore, blotter ends/rocker botter/pen tray+5 pcs ... 4,300.00
Desk set, Bookmark, cigar & stamp boxes/blotter ends/magnifying glass.3,480.00
Desk set, Greek Key, match holder/pen brush/note pad (7½" L) ..1,320.00
Desk set, Indian, paper holder/pen tray/ink stand/calendar+2 pcs. 3,000.00
Desk set, Venetian, letter holder/ink stand/clock/fr/blotter+3 sm pcs. 5,875.00
Desk set, Venetian, lg inkwell on 4x10" tray+blotter & ink pad, dore 3,000.00
Dish, banded Morrish design, dore, #707, 9" W 400.00
Frame, Adam, dore, #1016, 12x9", from $2,750 to 3,150.00
Frame, brass bands w/gold glass, oval opening, #56, 10½x7" 3,600.00
Frame, dk gr enamel w/relief flowers, rnded top corners, 9x7"...1,600.00
Frame, Grapevine, caramel glass, #947, 9x7½", EX 1,380.00
Frame, Pine Needle, gr glass, 8x9", EX............................1,035.00
Frame, Zodiac, dore, #923, 8x7" 1,300.00
Inkwell, Graduate, dore, sq, 3x3" 360.00
Inkwell, orb-like lid supported by 3 scarabs, gr patina, #2157, 3¾".. 10,350.00
Inkwell, Zodiac, dore, hexagonal, #1072, 6½" W 480.00
Inkwell, Zodiac, hexagonal, #842, 4" W, from $350 to 480.00
Letter holder, Pine Needle, 3-slot, dore fr w/beading, #1019, 6" L.975.00
Letter holder, Zodiac, 3-slot, dore, #1030, 8½x12" 660.00
Letter opener, Zodiac, #1095, 10½" 145.00
Matchbox cover, Zodiac, open ovals ea side, 2½x1⅝" 175.00
Note holder, Grapevine, #1019, 4¾" 690.00
Paperweight, recumbent bulldog, 2" L 430.00
Paperweight, recumbent lioness, acid-etched, #932 2x5" 1,320.00
Paperweight, recumbent lioness, dore, #832, 5" L 750.00
Pen holder, Grapevine, caramel slag glass, dore, #1103, 4½x5".... 960.00
Plate, geometric rim, dore, #1745, 12" 345.00
Smoker stand, Artichoke, brn patina w/gr highlights, #1651, 26".. 3,160.00
Tray, Abalone, dore, #1730, 12" dia, EX 400.00
Tray, Chinese, #1756, 3¾x12" 220.00

Pottery

Vase, emb poppies on ivory, #7, 9½x5".......................10,800.00
Vase, emb vines/fruit, gr/blk wash on ivory, pumpkin shape, 5x8"... 17,825.00
Vase, gr, basic Arts & Crafts style, hairline/rstr, 15" 1,600.00
Vase, spring gr matt on wht clay, 7¾"............................. 765.00

Silver

Key: t-oz — troy ounces

Bowl, center; appl vertical bands, #22888, ca 1940, 3½x9", 27-t-oz...1,460.00
Bowl, fruit; serpentine border, repousse foliage, 1875-91, 17" L... 3,815.00
Bowl, presentation; swan hdls, eng Cupid blacksmith, 7x9" 2,585.00
Cake plate, repousse flowers, pattern #17266, ftd, 1908, 12"........ 720.00
Candy dish, repousse band w/in, bellflower ring hdls, 1885, 8" L, pr..1,150.00
Child's bowl & plate, figures in relief, inscribed/dtd 1908, #5472..1,645.00
Dish, pansy shape, ca 1950s, ¾x3¼" 145.00
Fruit basket, scalloped sides w/rtcl ivy leaves, monogram, 11x14x9"..2,800.00
Ice cream slice, Olympia, 1891-02, 10⅞", 6-t-oz......................1,000.00
Ladle, tomato pattern on heavy curved hdl, swirled bowl, 10x3½" ..1,440.00
Salver, chased/emb flowers/leaves, 4 paw ft, monogram, 11", 30-t-oz. 1,525.00
Spoon, berry; lg bowl w/line decor, hdl terminal w/3 strawberries, 9".. 500.00
Spoon, Chrysanthemum, shell bowl, hdl w/emb leaves & flowers, 9", +bag.345.00
Spoon, sifting; Vine, floriform stem, monogram, 1875-91, 6⅜".... 380.00
Tazza, rtcl/cast raspberry clusters, monogram, 1891-02, 3½x7½"..825.00
Tray, plain surface w/foliate/gadroon rim, 1921-47, 22x16", 73-t-oz.2,400.00

Tiffin Glass

The Tiffin Glass Company was founded in 1889 in Tiffin, Ohio, one of the many factories composing the U.S. Glass Company. Its early wares consisted of tablewares and decorative items such as lamps and globes. Among the most popular of all Tiffin products was the stemware produced there during the 1920s. In 1959 U.S. Glass was sold, and in 1962 the factories closed. The plant was re-opened in 1963 as the Tiffin Art Glass Company. Products from this period were tableware, hand-blown stemware, and other decorative items. Those interested in learning more about Tiffin glass are encouraged to contact the Tiffin Glass Collectors' Club, whose address can be found in the Directory under Clubs, Newsletters, and Catalogs. See also Black Glass; Glass Animals.

Cadena, crystal, bowl, grapefruit; ftd, #251 .... 50.00
Cadena, crystal, candlestick, #5831, ea......................... 30.00
Cadena, crystal, creamer, #5831 .... 20.00
Cadena, crystal, parfait, 8-oz, 6¼" 35.00
Cadena, crystal, pitcher, ftd, #194............................225.00
Cadena, pk or yel, bowl, cream soup; #5831 .... 45.00
Cadena, pk or yel, bowl, pickle; #5831, 10" 45.00
Cadena, pk or yel, decanter, w/stopper.........................300.00
Cadena, pk or yel, mayonnaise, w/liner, ftd, #5831 .... 50.00
Cadena, pk or yel, plate, #5831, 7¾" 20.00
Cadena, pk or yel, plate, 9¼" 75.00
Cadena, pk or yel, vase, 9".....................................165.00
Cherokee Rose, crystal, bell, table; lg, #9742.................. 75.00
Cherokee Rose, crystal, bowl, fruit or nut; #5902, 6".......... 30.00
Cherokee Rose, crystal, cake plate, center hdl #5902, 12½" 55.00
Cherokee Rose, crystal, pitcher, sleek top dips to hdl, #5859....... 650.00
Cherokee Rose, crystal, plate, sandwich; #5902, 14" 55.00
Cherokee Rose, crystal, relish, 3-part, #5902, 12½" 60.00
Cherokee Rose, crystal, tumbler, juice; ftd, #17399, 5-oz 24.00
Cherokee Rose, crystal, vase, bud; #14185, 6" 25.00
Cherokee Rose, crystal, vase, teardrop, 8½"................... 85.00
Cherokee Rose, crystal, water, #17399, 9-oz 28.00
Classic, crystal, candy jar, ftd, w/lid, ½-lb.................150.00
Classic, crystal, creamer, ftd, #5931.......................... 35.00
Classic, crystal, tumbler, iced tea; flat, 12-oz............... 35.00
Classic, pk, finger bowl, ftd, #14185.......................... 50.00
Classic, pk, mayonnaise, ftd, w/ladle 75.00
Classic, pk, plate, #8833, 8".................................. 25.00
Flanders, crystal, ashtray, w/cigarette rest, 2¼x3¾"........... 55.00
Flanders, crystal, decanter...................................195.00
Flanders, pk, bowl, bouillon; hdls............................135.00
Flanders, pk, plate, 6".. 18.00
Flanders, yel, bowl, console; ftd, 11" 95.00
Flanders, yel, vase, ftd, #2, 8"..............................175.00
Fontaine, amber, gr or pk, creamer, stem ft, #4 .... 50.00
Fontaine, amber, gr or pk, sundae, #033 .... 25.00
Fontaine, Twilight, plate, #8818, 10".........................175.00
Fontaine, Twilight, vase, bowed top, #7, 9¼".................250.00
Fuchsia, crystal, bell, #15083, 5" 55.00
Fuchsia, crystal, bowl, salad; #5902, 7¼".................... 40.00
Fuchsia, crystal, pitcher, flat 395.00
Fuchsia, crystal, shakers, #2, pr.............................155.00
Fuchsia, crystal, sugar bowl, pearl edge...................... 50.00
Fuchsia, crystal, tumbler, water; #15083, 9-oz, 5¼".......... 25.00
Julia, amber, candy jar, ftd, w/lid, #9557 ....135.00
Julia, amber, cordial, #15011 .... 65.00
Julia, amber, jug, ftd, w/lid, #194...........................350.00
Julia, amber, plate, dinner; #8818............................ 14.00
Julia, amber, tumbler, seltzer; ftd, #14185................... 22.00

Julia, amber, wine, #15011... 38.00
June Night, crystal, bowl, salad; deep, 10" 70.00
June Night, crystal, plate, sandwich; 14".................................. 45.00
June Night, crystal, shakers, #2, pr 225.00
June Night, crystal, table bell, #9742 .... 85.00
June Night, crystal, tumbler, oyster cocktail; 4½-oz..................... 20.00
Jungle Assortment, colors, bottle, cologne; #5722....................... 125.00
Jungle Assortment, colors, bowl, centerpiece; #320 .... 55.00
Jungle Assortment, colors, candy box, flat, 5½" 55.00
Jungle Assortment, colors, lamp.. 110.00
Jungle Assortment, colors, tumbler, #444, 12-oz........................ 32.00
Jungle Assortment, colors, vase, sweet pea; #151, 7" 80.00
Lamp, parrot perched on log figural, orange/gr on blk 3-ftd base, 14" ...800.00
Luciana, crystal, claret, #016 .... 85.00
Luciana, crystal, creamer, #6.. 75.00
Luciana, crystal, plate, #8833, 6"....................................... 15.00
Luciana, crystal, water, #043.. 55.00
Psyche, crystal, finger bowl, ftd... 45.00
Psyche, crystal, pitcher 495.00
Psyche, crystal, saucer 20.00
Psyche, crystal, sherbet 30.00
Psyche, crystal, tumbler, juice.. 40.00

Miscellaneous

Ashtray, Ribbon Green Fantasy #5528, 4-lobed, 10 optic ribs, 8". 140.00
Candy jar, orange satin, conical ftd base, dome lid, 7½"................. 50.00
Compote, amberina satin w/gold twist stem, 10x7½" 60.00
Paperweight, deep bl w/clear casing & int bubbles, w/gold label, 6"..95.00
Pitcher, Columbine variant floral cutting, clear w/amber hdl/ft, 10"..145.00
Pitcher, optic Festoon, vaseline w/pk hdl, ftd, 7½"................... 150.00
Vase, amberina satin on separate blk ped base, 6½"..................... 60.00
Vase, bl satin w/Rockwell silver 0/l, trumpet top, open hdls, ftd, 7".80.00
Vase, Canary Yellow, trumpet shape, ftd, 7x4¾" 75.00
Vase, Cellini, crown finial on lid, 13½"................................ 175.00
Vase, coralene flowers, yel/orange/gr on blk, bulbous, 5" 160.00
Vase, Killarney Green, str sides, clear ftd base, 11x6½" 75.00
Vase, poppies relief, red on blk, shouldered, 9" 175.00
Vase, poppies relief on blk satin, bulbous, 5½", NM 65.00
Vase, poppies relief on turq satin, bulbous, 5½" 55.00
Vase, Twilight, blown cornucopia form w/2 legs, 7x14".................. 65.00
Wall pocket, bl, morning glory shape w/stem curling over top, 8", pr ..90.00
Wall pocket, blk, slim bell form, 9" L................................. 85.00

Tiles

Revival of the ancient art of tile-making dates to mid-nineteenth century England. Following the invention of the dust-pressing process for the manufacturing of buttons, potteries such as Minton and Wedgwood borrowed the technique for mass producing tiles. The Industrial Revolution market thus encouraged replacing the time-consuming medieval encaustic or inlay process for the foolproof press-molding method or the very decorative transferprint. English tiles adorned American buildings until a good native alternative became available following the Philadelphia Centennial Exposition of 1876. Shortly thereafter, important tile companies sprung up around Boston, Trenton, and East Liverpool, Ohio. By the turn of the century, Victorian aesthetics began to give way to the Arts and Crafts style that was being set forth by John Ruskin and Thomas Carlyle and practiced by William Morris and his Pre-Raphaelite Brotherhood. Tile bodies were once more pressed from wet or faience clay and decorated in bas-relief or in the ancient Spanish techniques of cuenca or cuerda seca. The glazes adorning them became matt and vegetal, reflecting the movement's fondness for medieval and Japanese aesthetics. During the 1920s designs became simpler and more commercialized, but some

important artists were still employed by the larger companies (for example, Louis Solon at AETCo), and the California tile industry continued to reflect the love of nature and Spanish Missions well into the 1930s.

Collecting tiles today means purchasing architectural salvage or new old stock. Arts and Crafts pottery and tiles are still extremely collectible. Important and large panels will fetch prices into the six figures. The prices for Victorian tiles have not increased over the last decade, but the value of California tiles, both matt and glossy, has gone through the roof. Catalina pottery and tile collectors are a particularly voracious lot. Larger pieces usually bring more, and condition is paramount. Look for damage and repair, as tiles often will chip or crack during the removal process. Our advisor for this category is Suzanne Perrault; she is listed in the Directory under New Jersey. See also California Faience; Grueby; Newcomb; Rookwood; other specific manufacturers.

AE Tile, bearded Middle Ages man, bl gloss, 6" 195.00
AE Tile, dedication: AE Tile..., classical maiden, bl gloss, 4⅛" 155.00
AE Tile, leaves & berries, dk gr gloss, flakes, 6" 30.00
AE Tile, stag, bl, minor flakes, 4" 80.00
California Art, house & palm trees, mc, 5¾"+Arts & Crafts fr.... 720.00
California Art, peacock on grapevine, matt pastels, 12x8".......... 600.00
California Art, Spanish mission scene, cvd/pnt, 7¾x4"+fr........... 480.00
California Art, thatch-roofed cottage scene, bl/buff, 4"+oak fr.... 435.00
Claycraft, animals/flowers, 63-tile panel, loose, 34½x26¾".......4,550.00
Claycraft, CA landscape w/mission at bk, 7¾x4"+Arts & Crafts fr..960.00
Claycraft, cottage & stone bridge, mc pastels, 5¾x11¾"+fr 725.00
Claycraft, flowers in bowl, mc on blk, flecks, 7¾" 725.00
Claycraft, hilly landscape w/tall conifer, amber/celadon, chips, 16x4".. 1,080.00
Claycraft, medieval village scene, 3-tile frieze, chips, 7¾x23½" .. 1,300.00
Claycraft, mission courtyard w/fountain, sm rstr, 8½x16½"+fr..1,550.00

Claycraft, pirates on the deck of a ship, in oak frame, 12x16", NM, $1,200.00.
(Photo courtesy David Rago Auctions)

Claycraft, Yosemite Falls, chip, 11¾x7¾"................................1,440.00
Columbia, Victorian lady in profile, brn gloss, 6" 180.00
De Porceleyne Fles, duck in flight, 4"+quartersawn oak fr............ 195.00
De Porceleyne Fles, Dutch village w/church/windmill, mc, 4½" .. 150.00
De Porceleyne Fles, flamingo facing right in cuenca, 12x4½" 540.00
De Porceleyne Fles, goose & marsh in cuenca, chips, 4¼x12½"... 540.00
De Porceleyne Fles, ibis at oasis before pyramid, 13½x5", pr........ 720.00
De Porceleyne Fles, leaping hare/branches w/fruit in cuenca, 4¾x9".. 840.00
De Porceleyne Fles, owls (2) by stone wall w/arch, 4¾x9" 720.00
De Porceleyne Fles, peacock, minute flecks, 4¾x17" 720.00
De Porceleyne Fles, peacock/brick wall w/ivy panel, mc, 12x4", pr..1,200.00
De Porceleyne Fles, rooster, wht on dk indigo, cuenca, 8¼x4¼".. 450.00
De Porceleyne Fles, sailboats in choppy sea, cuenca, chips, 4¾"+fr...85.00
De Porceleyne Fles, swan & 2 cygnets in cuenca, 13x4¾"+fr...1,140.00
De Porceleyne Fles, tall ships regatta, 4¼x8¼" 120.00
De Porceleyne Fles, windmill scene in cuenca, 8x5¾"+fr............. 120.00
Flint, Hereford Hazford Bocaldo 3d (bull), 5-color cuenca, 12", EX ..1,560.00
Franklin, boy fishing, dog at side, blk/mustard/gr, nicks, 9" 1,020.00
Franklin, daffodils in pk bowl in cuenca, 9"............................ 360.00

Franklin, lantern lighter, blk silhouette on mustard, 9", NM....... 720.00
Franklin, moose & geese, brn silhouette on yel, self-fr, 13½x8¾".. 5,100.00
Franklin, sailing ship, mc gloss & matt, 9"....... 600.00
Franklin, Viking ships, pastels, rstr chips, 9"....... 480.00
Grohn, Nouveau flower, red/amber/indigo, 6", pr....... 240.00
Grueby-Pardee, fountain in courtyard, cuerda seca, 4"+blk enamel fr.. 720.00
Grueby-Pardee, hilly landscape in cuenca, 4¼"+Arts & Crafts fr.. 1,900.00
Hamilton, dog's portrait, gr gloss, 5⅝"+fr....... 145.00
Harris Strong, children in park, 6-tile scene, 16x30"+fr....... 480.00
Harris Strong, colonial landscape, 5-tile panel, 10x33½", NM.... 120.00
Harris Strong, houses, 4-tile frieze, 24x6"+fr....... 240.00
Harris Strong, New England coastal scene, 6-tile frieze, 18x30"+fr.. 660.00
Harris Strong, pitcher & fruit, Picasso-like, 15x10⅝"....... 180.00
Harris Strong, sailboats on choppy water, 12-tile frieze, 12x35½" ... 360.00
Harris Strong, 4 musicians by bridge, 15-tile panel, fr: 36x24".. 1,020.00
Hartford, Eventide, lady's portrait, mc, 13x8"+Arts & Crafts fr.. 9,600.00
Kensington, War/Victoire (warriors), 2 3-tile friezes, ea: 18x12"... 960.00
Low, bearded gentleman, bl, 6x4⅜"....... 190.00
Low, geometric floral, amber crackle, 8"+14" Tiffany brass fr.... 1,200.00
Muller, female figures/winter Zodiac signs, sm chip, 18x17"....... 600.00
Providential, classical lady, brn/amber, 6"+9" fr....... 180.00
San Jose, ducks flying over marsh, cuerda seca, sm chips, 8"....... 530.00
San Jose, Indian working at loom, cuerda seca, 8"....... 840.00
San Jose, men in sombreros at cockfight, cuerda seca, 6"....... 480.00
San Jose, San Jose mission, bright mc, cuerda seca, 6"....... 575.00
Taylor, mission complex, 6-tile frieze, sm chips, 16x24"....... 2,400.00
TH Deck/E Carriere, 12-tile panel w/ducks & flowers, 40x30", EX.. 5,700.00
Trent, girl w/kerchief facing right, gr-gold, 1890, 2⅝" dia....... 70.00
Trenton, lady's portrait, brn tones, 6"+fr....... 120.00
Wedgwood, Raising of Priapus emb on turq, late 19th C, 9x9".... 440.00
Wm de Morgan, roses & thorny branches, 2-tile panel, 12x6".. 1,300.00

Tinware

In the American household of the seventeenth and eighteenth centuries, tinware items could be found in abundance, from food containers to foot warmers and mirror frames. Although the first settlers brought much of their tinware with them from Europe, by 1798 sheets of tin plate were being imported from England for use by the growing number of American tinsmiths. Tinwares were often decorated either by piercing or painted designs which were both freehand and stenciled. (See Toleware.) By the early 1900s, many homes had replaced their old tinware with the more attractive aluminum and graniteware. In the nineteenth century, tenth wedding anniversaries were traditionally celebrated by gifts of tin. Couples gave big parties, dressed in their wedding clothes, and reaffirmed their vows before their friends and families who arrived bearing (and often wearing) tin gifts, most of which were quite humorous. Anniversary tin items may include hats, cradles, slippers and shoes, rolling pins, etc. See also Primitives and Kitchen Collectibles.

Anniversary pc, top hat, lt rust, 8"....... 525.00
Bunt pan, swirled body, 3x6¾"....... 35.00
Candle box, cylindrical, brass fastener, hinged, 14x3½" dia....... 70.00
Coffeepot, flared cylinder, 10", +2 short & squat mugs....... 120.00
Coffeepot, patriotic wrigglework on tapered form, PA, 8¾", VG .. 3,150.00
Coffeepot, punched pots of tulips/intertwined lines, brass finial, 11" .. 230.00
Colander, conical, 2 ribbed hdls, dent at ft, 5¾x11"....... 150.00
Frying pan, Cold Handle L&G GMf'g Co 53, late 1800s, 9½" dia+hdl... 15.00
Infant feeder, conical, sm spout, strap hdl, w/cap, 4⅞"....... 285.00
Muffineer, 5-pointed star-punched top, ca 1900, 3x1¾"....... 20.00
Roaster oven, bk door, side spout for drips, wrought-iron spit, 8x10" .. 100.00
Sconce, oval dish-shaped reflector, crimped rim, 10⅛"....... 175.00
Scoop, primitive strap hdl, EX patina, 4x2⅛"....... 15.00
Steamer, ca 1900, 3-pc, 11x10½"....... 55.00
Strainer, cheese; 4x6⅞"+hdl....... 30.00
Strainer, removable screen, EX patina, 4½" dia, 8¼" w/hdl....... 18.00
Tinderbox, rnd w/finger loop & soldered candle socket on lid, 2¾" ... 495.00
Tinderbox, rnd w/hdl & candle socket on lid, lt rust, 3¾"....... 285.00

Tobacciana

Tobacciana is the generally accepted term used to cover a field of collecting that includes smoking pipes, cigar molds, cigarette lighters, humidors — in short, any article having to do with the practice of using tobacco in any form. Perhaps the most valuable variety of pipes is the meerschaum, hand carved from hydrous magnesium, an opaque white-gray or cream-colored mineral of the soapstone family. (Much of this is today mined in Turkey which has the largest meerschaum deposit in the world, though there are other deposits of lesser significance around the globe.) These figural bowls often portray an elaborately carved mythological character, an animal, or a historical scene. Amber is sometimes used for the stem. Other collectible pipes are corn cob (Missouri Meerschaum) and Indian peace pipes of clay or catlinite. (See American Indian Art.)

Chosen because it was the Indians who first introduced the white man to smoking, the cigar store Indian was a symbol used to identify tobacco stores in the nineteenth century. The majority of them were hand carved between 1830 and 1900 and are today recognized as some of the finest examples of early wood sculptures. When found they command very high prices. For further information on lighters, refer to *Collector's Guide to Cigarette Lighters* by James Flanagan. See also Advertising; Snuff Boxes.

Ashtray, smiling man's face, cast metal, unmk, 4x2¾x2", NM....... 50.00
Ashtray, sterling, 4 pie wedges fit together, Carier, 5" dia....... 375.00
Ashtray, 14k yel gold, rectangular w/shaped corners, Carier, 4" ... 570.00
Cigar box, Yellow Cab, paper litho on cardboard, 7" W, EX....... 75.00
Cigar cutter, alligator figural, brass, 5"....... 350.00
Cigar cutter, Artie Cigar, CI, figural Artie seated atop, 10x6x7", EX+ ... 2,700.00
Cigar cutter, brass key, push in tip & it cuts at keyhole, 4"....... 40.00
Cigar cutter, Country Gentleman, counter style, 1891....... 360.00
Cigar cutter, dachshund figural hdl, brass & steel, 5"....... 200.00
Cigar cutter, elephant figural, wht metal, 4½"....... 240.00
Cigar cutter, ferns emb, brass & steel, hammer on 1 end, 8½"....... 60.00
Cigar cutter, General Green, CI w/rnd portrait insert, 1890s, 8", EX+ ... 2,400.00
Cigar cutter, monkey sitting on tray, brass, 4½"....... 85.00
Cigar cutter, Old Crow, figural CI pig on tray, 6", EX....... 1,800.00
Cigar cutter, Optimo All Havana, emb CI w/rnd portrait, 7x9x6", EX... 2,400.00
Cigar cutter, parrot figural, 7"....... 420.00
Cigar cutter, shot-shell form, press top to cut, 4½"....... 150.00
Cigar cutter/ashtray, brass, lion's mouth opening, guillotine type, 6" ... 90.00
Cigar cutter/ashtray, SP w/emb flowers/feathers, #1502, 5x4"....... 50.00
Cigar holder, brass w/jewels, strike plate & tray, holds 8, 5x8" dia .. 175.00
Cigar lighter, Aladdin's lamp form, SP metal, dolphin-head hdl, 5"... 50.00
Cigar lighter, cherub w/globe, cast metal, 9½x3½x3", EX....... 275.00
Cigar lighter, eagle figural, brass, European, heavy, 8"....... 100.00
Cigar lighter, man in chair figural, CI, basket on bk, 6x3½x4", EX.. 180.00
Cigar lighter, man's head, kerosene flame from his cigar, bronze, 9" ... 2,000.00
Cigar lighter, pirate w/treasure chest, LD Bloch, electric, 1928, 11" ... 460.00
Cigar lighter, Punch figural, brass, w/gas line, 7x2¾", EX....... 100.00
Cigar lighter, Scottish man figural, flip-top head, metal, 9½"....... 125.00
Cigarette box, silver, 4-part wood int, Gorham #302, 6½" L....... 95.00
Cigarette case, early open auto enameled on sterling, 3½x2½".... 600.00
Cigarette case, horse & buggy enameled on sterling....... 660.00
Cigarette case, hunting dogs (2) enameled on .900 silver, 3½x3"..... 1,440.00
Cigarette case, nude scene in 1890s style, mc enamel, 3½x3"...... 840.00
Cigarette holder, 2 Deco ladies holding box, gr glass/blk metal, EX ... 500.00
Cigarette/match holder, Black porter nodder, musical, metal, 38", EX.... 2,520.00

Humidor, Ben Bay, It's a Pleasure, tin litho, 6x9x3", EX 90.00
Humidor, Black banjo player HP on porc, metal lid 360.00
Humidor, champagne bottle figural, cedar-lined SP, unmk, 9x2½"... 120.00
Humidor, mahog coffer w/scrolls & ornaments, glass-lined int, 8x16x9".. 695.00
Pipe, meerschaum, Black lady (detailed), no stem, 3½", NM in case.. 315.00
Pipe, meerschaum, tiger (3" figure), w/stem 120.00
Pipe, porc, goat/goatherd figural, goat's head w/brass lid, 10x3" ... 275.00
Pipe box, poplar w/red stain, cut-out sides, dvtl drw, 18x5" 1,850.00
Sign, EL McClain Horse Collars, paper, horse at desk, fr, 24", EX+ . 3,200.00
Smoking stand, CI butler holds tray, minor rpt, 35", EX 385.00
Store figure, Indian chief, pnt compo, unmk, sm rstr, 1930s, 18x4x4" .. 875.00
Store figure, well-dressed Black man, cvd wood w/mc pnt, rstr, 27", VG.. 2,650.00
Tobacco cutter, tombstone-shaped walnut brd w/iron blade, 1861, 17".. 350.00

Toby Jugs

The delightful jug known as the Toby dates back to the eighteenth century, when factories in England produced them for export to the American colonies. Named for the character Toby Philpots in the song *The Little Brown Jug,* the Toby was fashioned in the form of a jolly fellow, usually holding a jug of beer and a glass. The earlier examples were made with strict attention to detail such as fingernails and teeth. Originally representing only a non-entity, a trend developed to portray well-known individuals such as George II, Napoleon, and Ben Franklin. Among the most-valued Tobies are those produced by Ralph Wood I in the late 1700s. By the mid-1830s Tobies were being made in America. When no manufacturer is give, assume the Toby to have been made in Staffordshire, nineteenth century; unless otherwise described, because of space restrictions, assume the model is of a seated man. See also Occupied Japan; Royal Doulton.

Dr Johnson seated w/jug & cup, Staffordshire, 1800, 8" 1,295.00
Hearty Good Fellow standing, sponged base, Pratt-type, 1880, 6½" .. 4,110.00

Home Brewed Ale, man on barrel with inscription, 11", $365.00. (Photo courtesy Skinner Inc. Auctioneers & Appraisers of Antiques & Fine Art)

Martha Gunn seated, brn & bl, Staffordshire, late 1700s, 11"... 5,285.00
Seated, hands on knees, Delftware, Holland, 1770, 10" 880.00
Seated, hat in 1 hand/other: silver-lustre lantern, Staffordshire, 9".. 470.00
Seated, holds jug, gold/brn on stoneware, Derbyshire, 1800s, 8½" .. 560.00
Seated, holds jug, pipe at side, Staffordshire pearlware, 1780s, 10" .. 880.00
Seated, holds jug, pipe leaning by side, Pratt-type, 1780s, 8" 1,175.00
Seated, holds jug, spatter base/bk/hdl, Yorkshire-type pearlware, 7". 590.00
Seated, holds jug, sponged base/bk/hdl, Pratt-type, 1800, 7½" 880.00
Seated, holds jug, striped hose, Pratt-type, 1800, 9½" 1,175.00
Seated, holds redware jug, Staffordshire creamware, 1780s, 10" .. 1,525.00
Seated, jug in left hand/cup in other, R Wood, 1760, 6¾" 2,115.00
Seated, jug in 1 hand/cup in other, pearlware, 1700s, 6½" 1,175.00
Seated, jug in 1 hand/pipe in other, Pratt-type, 1800, 7" 700.00

Seated, mug in hand, semi-translucent, att Ralph wood, 1770s, 10", EX... 1,165.00
Seated, orange face, frothing jug, Pratt type, 1800, 10" 1,650.00
Seated, shield: It Is All Out..., R Wood-type pearlware, 1700s, 10" ... 880.00
Seated, sponged coat, w/jug, Staffordshire pearlware, 1780s, 9" .. 1,175.00
Seated, sponged hat/ft rim, caryatid hdl, Yorkshire pearlware, 10" . 1,295.00
Seated, w/jug, pipe aside, R Wood type, #51, 1700s, 9¾" 2,585.00
Seated, yel/gr glazes, brn hat, Staffordshire creamware, 1700s, 9¾".. 1,410.00
Seated lady holds bottle/cup, feathered hat, Staffordshire, 1780, 11".. 7,050.00
Seated on bbl, holds ale jug, brn stoneware, Doulton Lambeth, 10½".... 880.00
Seated on bbl, holds cup & wine sack, pewter lid, Sceaux Faience, 12" .. 1,000.00
Seated on bbl: Home Brewed Ale, w/jug & cup, Staffordshire, 1850s, 11"..365.00
Seated on sea chest, anchor at ft, Staffordshire pearlware, 1700s, 11"... 3,000.00
Standing, hair en queue, tree-trunk hdl, tin glazed, Holland, 1820, 11". 530.00

Toleware

The term 'toleware' originally came from a French term meaning 'sheet iron.' Today it is used to refer to paint-decorated tin items, most popular from 1800 to 1850s. The craft flourished in Pennsylvania, Connecticut, Maine, and New York state. Early toleware has a very distinctive look. The surface is dull and unvarnished; background colors range from black to cream. Geometrics are quite common, but florals and fruits were also favored. Items made after 1850 were often stenciled, and gold trim was sometimes added. American toleware is usually found in practical, everyday forms — trays, boxes, and coffeepots are most common — while French examples might include candlesticks, wine coolers, jardinieres, etc. Be sure to note color and design when determining date and value, but condition of the paint is the most important worth-assessing factor. Unless noted otherwise, values are for very good examples with average wear.

Box, deed; bird/pavilion, top w/foliate center, Am, 1840, 7x10x6" .. 465.00
Box, deed; floral, mc on blk japanning, sgn DC, 12x8¾x4¾".... 1,495.00
Box, deed; fruit & swags, mc on blk japanning, dome top, 5½x9x5"..750.00
Box, deed; swags/pinwheels, mc on dk japannings, 7x10x5" 925.00
Candlestick, foliage, mc on dk japanning, sq base w/pushup, 5", ea...800.00
Coffeepot, floral, mc on old red w/yel accents, cylindrical, 10" .. 2,300.00
Coffeepot, floral on gr reserve on dk japanning, domed lid, 10½" .. 3,100.00
Coffeepot, fruit/leaves, mc on blk japanning, brass finial, 10"...1,375.00
Coffeepot, fruit/leaves, 3-color on red, PA, lighthouse shape, 10".. 8,345.00
Coffeepot, leaves, yel on salmon red, lighthouse shape, sm dents, 10".. 3,100.00
Match safe, tulips/swags, mc on blk japanning, 7½" 575.00
Muffineer, tulips/foliage, mc on dk japanning, worn top, 4" 1,300.00
Mug, floral (bold), mc on dk japanning, att PA, 4¼".................2,400.00
Mug, foliate band w/squiggles, mc on dk japanning, flakes, 1⅞" .. 775.00
Mug, swags & flowers on dk japanning, 5⅞" 375.00
Plate warmer, florals, mc on bl, 2-shelf, domed lid, paw ft, 30x18"... 1,000.00
Tankard, floral on dk japanning, strap handle, 5¾" 700.00
Tea caddy, berries/foliage/swags on dk japanning, split seam, 5", EX..1,495.00
Tea caddy, berries/leaves/swags, mc on red, split seam, 4⅛", G..... 925.00
Tea caddy, roses/carnations, 3-color/japanned, yel shoulder swags, 8".. 585.00
Tray, apple; foliage, red & gr on japanning, crystallized int, 13x8".. 345.00
Tray, apple; foliate bands on bright red, 2⅝x12¾x7½" 2,875.00
Tray, cherries in band, crystallized center, 8-sided, 12½x8½" 1,500.00
Tray, floral, mc on dk red, ogee rim, early 20th C, 27⅝" dia 325.00
Tray, floral/fruit, (bold) 3-color on japanning, octagonal, 8x12", EX..5,750.00
Tray, floral/fruit on blk japanning, 8-sided, 12¼x8½" 5,750.00

Tools

Before the Civil War, tools for the most part were handmade. Some were primitive to the point of crudeness, while others reflected the skill of those who took pride in their trade. Increasing demand for quality tools and the dawning of the age of industrialization resulted in tools that were mass produced. Factors important in evaluating antique tools are scarcity, usefulness, and portability. Those with a manufacturer's mark are worth more than unmarked items. When no condition is indicated, the items listed here are assumed to be in excellent condition. Our advisor for this category is Jim Calison; he is listed in the Directory under New York. For more information, we recommend *Antique Tools* by Kathryn McNerney (Collector Books). See also Keen Kutter; Winchester.

Bit, screwdriver; Keen Kutter, 4½", EX 15.00
Broad axe, OR Bartchall (?), goose wing, 18" 50.00
Caliper, vernier; Brown & Sharpe #570, 15¼" L, EX (fitted box).. 55.00
Chisels, woodworking; Stanley #60 set, szs 1½-¼", EX 45.00
Drawknife, Jennings, Pat 2-20-08, EX 30.00
Gauge, angle; Stanley #25, rosewood w/brass, EX 20.00
Gauge, mortise & marking; Stanley #61, sq head, 8½", EX ... 20.00
Hammer, cutter; hand forged, 5-lb, 6½x1¾" head w/14½" hdl, EX ... 30.00
Level, J Rabone, England, brass & walnut, 1", EX 17.50
Plane, Craftsman #619-3741, 1950s, NMIB 40.00
Plane, dbl router; Stanley #71, Pat 3-4-84, VG+ 50.00
Plane, Defiance, Made in USA, 9½x2¼", VG+ 15.00
Plane, jointer; Stanley #7, lateral lever w/o disk, rare, EX 65.00
Plane, low angle block; Stanley #60, Pat 10-12-97, VG+ 55.00
Plane, low angle; Record #60½, NRFB 60.00
Plane, moulding; Record #044C, metal fr, EX 40.00
Plane, moulding; Sandusky #100, 9½", EX 20.00
Plane, scraper; Stanley #12, brass thumb screw mk Stanley Works, EX ... 125.00
Plane, Stanley #6, wood hdls, VG 25.00
Saw, crosscut; 2-man, Richardson Bros, ca 1869, 54", EX 50.00
Scissors, Winchester #9029, 10", EX 35.00
Socket set, Hinsdale #12, complete in metal box, EX 30.00
Spoke shave, Stanley #51, raised hdl, 10x2⅛", VG+ 35.00
Tap & die set, Little Giant Screw Plate, Greenfield #310, EX ... 150.00
Tape measure, Lufkin, woven tape, 50 ft, NMIB 35.00
Tile cutter, Crane Model A, VG 100.00
Trimmer, wall paper; Ridgeley's Model D, EXIB 40.00
Vise, bench; Abernathy Vise & Tool Co, 19" w/6¾" jaw, EX ... 70.00
Vise, bench; Pexto #12¼, screw-on clamp, 7" w/2¼" jaw, EX ... 60.00
Vise, drill press; Jacob #75, universal, 8½x4" w/3⅜" jaw, EX ... 70.00
Vise, pin adjustable, unknown maker, Pat Sept 22 1914, EX ... 165.00
Vise, saw; Disston #1, screw-on clamp, universal, EX 55.00
Wrench, combination; International Harvester/Chattanooga #CP4003, EX ... 22.50
Wrench, pipe; B&C, set of 3: 6", 10", & 12", EX 45.00
Wrench, pipe; Improved Stillson H9, 1930s, 14", EX 30.00

Toothbrush Holders

Most of the collectible toothbrush holders were made in prewar Japan and were modeled after popular comic strip, Disney, and nursery rhyme characters. Since many were made of bisque and decorated with unfired paint, it's not uncommon to find them in less-than-perfect paint, a factor you must consider when attempting to assess their values.

Boy & girl kissing, Poets Je Tanden on base, porc, 1920s, 5" 80.00
Boy w/accordion, red hat/pants, yel instrument, Japan, 3¼" 30.00
Child on sleigh, both arms raised, mc bsk, Japan, 4¾" 30.00
Count Chocula, 2-D plastic standup, in-pack premium ca 1970s .. 40.00
Donald between Mickey & Minnie, mk bsk, 1940s, Disney/Japan S1354, rpr...175.00
Donald Duck (2, 1 looks left, 2nd right), WD/Japan S1132, 4½", VG...420.00
Duck stands sideways by post, wht w/orange & gr details, Czech/8725... 50.00
Dutch boy & girl kissing/hugging, vivid mc, Goldcastle/Japan, 5½" 65.00
Equestrienne standing in red coat, blk boots/hat, Foreign/6677, 4"....150.00
Football player stands by bulldog, rooster weather vane Japan mk, 6"..45.00

Genie child, scarf-wrapped head, short red jacket, wall mt, Japan, 7" ..60.00
Girl w/lg rose as skirt holds rose, Germany/15496, 5½" 65.00
Keystone cop (comic/googly eyed), huge pocket ea side, Czech, 5" .50.00
Listerine boy stands, red shirt/blk shorts, tin litho, 6" 145.00
Mickey & Minnie seated on couch, mc bsk, Disney/Japan...........210.00
Mickey & Minnie stand arm-in-arm, mc bsk, Japan label, 4½"....275.00
Mickey holds handkerchief to Pluto's nose, Geo Borgfeldt, 4½" ..240.00
Mickey Mouse standing, string-jointed right arm, bsk, Disney/Japan, 5" ..325.00
Minnie Mouse standing, looking right, S Maw, Disney 789572, 4"..350.00
Miss Piggy stands in wht gown w/long pk gloves, Sigma 185.00
Pk elephant, upright, head trn right, trunk up, Japan, 5" 45.00
Pk flamingo preening, porc, Japan, 5x4x2½" 65.00
Pony (wht w/lt brn & bl plaid) atop red base w/3 slots, Japan, 4¾"...45.00
Red Riding hood stands w/basket under right arm, name on base.. 95.00
Sailor boy stands by sq post, wht w/minimal color, Germany, 3½" ...70.00
Sleepy/Dopey, posts of fence (behind) hold brushes, Disney c/'38, 3" ...210.00
Snow White stands, arms behind her bk, porc, Foreign, Disney, 6" ...125.00
Southern belle holds open basket at waist, Erphila/Czech, 8" 30.00
Three Little Pigs, bricklayer/2 musicians, Disney/Japan, 1930s, 4x4"...65.00
Three Little Pigs, Maw of London, 1930s, 4¼", set of 3 .... 180.00
Walking Ware, red polka-dotted ft under cup, Carlton, 4½" 65.00
Winnie Pooh, Piglet & Eeyore sit at base of tree stump, 4x4"........ 28.00

Toothpick Holders

Once common on every table, the toothpick holder was relegated to the china cabinet near the turn of the century. Fortunately, this contributed to their survival. As a result, many are available to collectors today. Because they are small and easily displayed, they are very popular collectibles. They come in a wide range of prices to fit every budget. Many have been reproduced and, unfortunately, are being offered for sale right along with the originals. These 'repros' should be priced in the $10.00 to $30.00 range. Unless you're sure of what you're buying, choose a reputable dealer. In addition to pattern glass, you'll find examples in china, bisque, art glass, and various metals. For further information we recommend *Glass Toothpick Holders* by Neila and Tom Bredehoft and Jo and Bob Sanford, and *China Toothpick Holder* by Judy Knauer and Sandra Raymond. Examples in the listings that follow are glass, unless noted otherwise, and clear unless a color is mentioned in the description. See also specific companies (such as Northwood) and types of glassware (such as Burmese, cranberry, etc.).

Glass

Alabama 65.00
Arched Fleur-de-Lis 65.00
Arched Fleur-de-Lis, amber stained, ca 1898, 1⅜" 110.00
Atlanta (Royal Crystal), ruby stained, Tarentum, ca 1894, 2½"...250.00
Atlas, ruby stain, US Glass 50.00
Beaumont's Columbia, vaseline 65.00
Beveled Windows, US Glass, ca 1909, 2⅜x2½" 48.00
Blocked Thumbprint Band, ruby stained 60.00
Broken Pillar & Reed, gr or bl 55.00
Buckeye Butterfly, Buckeye Glass Co, 1880s-90s, 2¾" 120.00
Burmese, hat form w/bl threading at collar, shiny, 2" 285.00
Carnation, #88, New Martinsville, ca 1906, 2⅝x1⅞" 68.00
Chrysanthemum Leaf 30.00
Co-op's Royal 30.00
Colonial, #400, Heisey, ca 1909, 2¾x2¼" 135.00
Cord Drapery, Indiana, 1898-1903 .... 160.00
Criss Cross, wht opal, Consolidated, ca 1894, 2⅜" 285.00
Daisy (Sunk Daisy), HP decor, Co-Operative Flint, ca 1897, 2⅜" ...50.00
Daisy & Button, amberina, 3-ftd, Hobbs Brockunier, 3" (+)....... 145.00
Daisy & Button, vaseline, from $45 to (+) 55.00

Daisy & Button w/V Ornament, amber 45.00
Deep File, National, ca 1902, 2⅜x1¾" 50.00
Estelle, Paden City, ca 1916, 1⅜x1½" 30.00
Esther, amber stained 120.00
Forget-Me-Not, rose blush, Challinor Taylor, 1⅞x2⅜" 90.00
Frisco, #1229, Fostoria, ca 1903, 2⅜x2⅛" 42.00
Horse w/Cart, #1396, Central Glass, mid-1880s, 2½x2" 42.00
Ivanhoe, #65D, Dalzel, Gilmore & Leighton, ca 1897, 2⅝" 135.00
Jefferson Optic, apple gr, Jefferson, ca 1910, 2¼x1¾" 52.00
Liberty Torch (Hand w/Torch), amber, ca 1888, 3¾" 75.00
Louis XV, ivory w/gold, Northwood, ca 1898, 2½" 700.00
Maine (Stippled Paneled Flower), emerald gr, US Glass, ca 1899, 2½" .. 500.00
Majestic, ruby stained, McKee, ca 1894, 2½x2" 115.00
Naomi (Rib & Bead), National, ca 1901, 2⅜x2¼" 38.00
Paddle Wheel, clear w/gold, Westmoreland Specialty, ca 1912, 2¾" .. 48.00
Paneled Sunflower, Kokomo, 2½x1¾" 52.00
Peachblow, hat form w/ribbed body, Libbey, 2" 575.00
Peerless, emerald gr, Model Flint, ca 1898, 2¼x1⅞" 80.00
Radium, #2635, Cambridge, ca 1906 .... 42.00
Ranson (Gold Band), Riverside, ca 1899, 2⅜x2" 32.00
Stippled Forget-Me-Not, Findlay Flint, ca 1890, 2⅜x1⅝" 135.00
Sunbeam, gr, McKee, ca 1900, 2½x2¼" 50.00
Sunset, #50, bl opaque, Dithridge & Co, ca 1894, 2¼x2⅛" 85.00
Sweet #61, clear w/silver o/l, Duncan & Miller, ca 1906, 2¾" 50.00
Swirl, #326, sapphire opal, Hobbs, Brockunier & Co, 2½x2" 385.00
Tennessee, US Glass, ca 1900, 2⅝x1⅞" 100.00
Venetian, clear w/vertical amber & wht lattice lines, 6 cabochons, 2" ... 200.00
Zippered Swirl & Diamond, US Glass, ca 1895, 2⅜x2½" 38.00

Silver Plate

Bear beside banded holder, Pairpoint #3705 .... 225.00
Bull stands w/head low, sword toothpicks inserted in shoulders, 3x4" .. 85.00

Dog by cup with ornate lattice top, #2692, $85.00. (Photo courtesy Jackson's International Auctioneers & Appraisers of Fine Art & Antiques)

Dog w/glass eyes, paw on bone, by basket holder, Tufts #2684 .... 85.00
Dogs (2) by holder w/ornate top, Tufts #2691, rstr SP 85.00
Hunting dog by holder w/ornate lattice top, Tufts #2792 .... 85.00
Lady in long dress by holder, Derby Silver #2303 .... 160.00
Man on high-wheel bicyle, holder on bk, #2649 .... 700.00
Moth crouching beside vase w/petal rim, Derby #2308 .... 210.00
Pigtailed girl holds toothpick holder w/rope, Meriden Britannia #44 .. 95.00
Pug dog w/blk glass bead eyes by basket, paw raised, Derby #2304 ... 85.00
Pug dog w/blk glass eyes by holder (paws down), Derby #2306 ...... 75.00
Squirrel eating nut beside holder on base, Rockford #48 .... 210.00

Torquay Pottery

Torquay is a unique type of pottery made in the South Devon area of England as early as 1869. At the height of productivity, at least a dozen companies flourished there, producing simple folk pottery from the area's natural red clay. The ware was both wheel-turned and molded and decorated under the glaze with heavy slip resulting in low-relief nature subjects or simple scrollwork. Three of the best-known of these potteries were Watcombe (1869 – 1962), Aller Vale (in operation from the mid-1800s, producing domestic ware and architectural products), and Longpark (1883 until 1957). Watcombe and Aller Vale merged in 1901 and operated until 1962 under the name of Royal Aller Vale and Watcombe Art Pottery.

A decline in the popularity of the early classical terra-cotta styles (urns, busts, figures, etc.) lead to the introduction of painted and glazed terra-cotta wares. During the late 1880s, white clay wares, both turned and molded, were decorated with colored glazes (Stapleton ware, grotesque molded figures, ornamental vases, large jardinieres, etc.). By the turn of the century, the market for art pottery was diminishing, so the potteries turned to wares decorated in colored slips (Barbotine, Persian, Scrolls, etc.).

Motto wares were introduced in the late nineteenth century by Aller Vale and taken up in the present century by the other Torquay potteries. This eventually became the 'bread and butter' product of the local industry. This was perhaps the most famous type of ware potted in this area because of the verses, proverbs, and quotations that decorated it. This was achieved by the sgraffito technique — scratching the letters through the slip to expose the red clay underneath. The most popular patterns were Cottage, Black Cockerel, Multi-Cockerel, and a scrollwork design called Scandy. Other popular decorations were Kerswell Daisy, ships, kingfishers, applied bird decorations, Art Deco styles, Egyptian ware, and many others. Aller Vale ware may sometimes be found marked 'H.H. and Company,' a firm who assumed ownership from 1897 to 1901. 'Watcombe Torquay' was an impressed mark used from 1884 to 1927. Our advisors for this category are Jerry and Gerry Kline; they are listed in the Directory under Ohio. If you're interested in joining a Torquay club, you'll find the address of The North American Torquay Society under Clubs, Newsletters, and Catalogs.

Art Pottery

Biscuit barrel, Apple Blossom, porc, unmk, 6½" 275.00
Biscuit barrel, parrots on branches on bl, wrapped hdl, 6" 125.00
Bottle, scent; Hill's English Lavender, pitcher shape, 2¾" 62.00
Bottle, scent; rose, pk on bl, att Watcombe, 3" 70.00
Bottle, scent; Scandy, Exeter Art Pottery, crown stopper, 3¼" 75.00
Candlesticks, Scroll, Aller Vale, ca 1900, 6", pr 100.00
Canoe, Kingfisher, Royal Torquay, 2x9" 88.00
Ewer, Apple Blossom, unmk, 6½" 110.00
Ginger jar, Apple Blossom, SP lid & hdl, Watcombe, 4" 150.00
Hatpin holder, geometric floral, Longpark, 1890s, 5x3½" 147.00
Jardiniere, Daffodil, Longpark, 1910, 5½x7¼" 325.00
Jardiniere, Scroll, Aller Vale, early 1900s, 3¾" 75.00
Jug, Persian, Aller Vale, wht clay, 4½" 85.00
Mug, Lindisfarne Castle Holy Island, Watcombe, 2½" 55.00
Tray, dresser; windmill, Aller Vale, no motto, 10½x7" 395.00
Vase, Alexandria Rose, twist hdls, 4½" 65.00
Vase, Kingfisher & Iris, Longpark, 3-hdl, 12" 160.00
Vase, windmill scene, Crown Dorset, motto, early 1900s, 4", pr .. 175.00
Wall pocket, flowers on horn shape, Exeter, 6½x4½" 175.00

Devon Motto Ware

Basket, Multi-Cockerel, Longpark, 2¾x5x3¼" 105.00
Biscuit jar, Cottage, Watcombe, 'May Your Joys Be...,' 5x6½" 275.00
Bowl, Cottage, Dartmouth, 'Waste Not Want Not,' 3¾" 37.00
Bowl, Cottage, Watcombe, 'Good Courage Breaks Ill Luck,' 1½x4½" ... 50.00
Bowl, junket; Scandy, 'Help Yourself...,' 3⅜x6⅞" 175.00
Chamberstick, Aller Vale, 'Last in Bed Blows Out...,' 1902-04 .... 125.00
Cheese dish, Cottage, unmk, 'Help Yourself Don't Be Shy,' 6½" .. 130.00

Coffeepot, Black Rooster, 'If You Can't Be Aisy...,' 6½" 175.00
Coffeepot, Cottage, side hdl, 'May You Find That...,' 8" 195.00
Couldron/pot, Longpark, 'The Diels Aye Kin Lae...,' 2¾x4" 45.00
Creamer, Black Cockerel, 'Elp Yersef Teu Cram,' 2½" 50.00
Creamer & sugar bowl, Shamrock, Watcombe, mini, 2", 1½" 60.00
Cup & saucer, 'Have Another Cup Full,' 3x3⅜", 5⅛" 68.00
Egg cup, Seagull, Dartmouth 35.00
Hatpin holder, Colored Cockerel, 'Keep Me on the Dressing...,' 4½" ... 175.00
Humidor, Black Cockerel, Longpark, w/motto, 5" 235.00
Inkwell, 'Absent Friends Are Glad of News,' ca 1900 .... 85.00
Inkwell & stand, Scandy, Watcombe, 'Send Us a Scrape...,' 2¾x5¼"... 175.00
Jardiniere, Cottage, Watcombe, 'Masters Two Will Never...,' 3x4¼" ...95.00
Jardiniere, Passion Flower, HM Exter, 'For Every Ill...,' 6¾" 275.00
Jug, Black Cat (unusual), Aller Vale, 'Oh Where Is My Boy...,' 5x4".. 195.00
Jug, Black Cockerel, 'Good Morning & Fresh...,' 4½" 80.00
Jug, Cottage, 'Kind Words Are Music...,' 5¾" 95.00
Jug, Cottage, Watcombe, 'Don't Worry It May Never...,' 5½" 90.00
Jug, Kerswell Daisy, Aller Vale, 'Earth I Am...,' 8¼x7" 225.00
Jug, puzzle; Colored Cockerel, 'This Yer Jug Was...,' 3½" 200.00
Jug, Scandy, 'Say Well Is Good...Better,' 4x4" 105.00
Jug, Scandy, Longpark, 'Drink Ye Old Heatherdale...,' 5", NM 125.00
Jug, Scandy, Longpark, 'Niver Zay Die...,' 3-hdl, 3¼" 85.00
Jug, Scroll, 'If Ye Can't Be Aisy...,' 5" 130.00
Jug, water; Cottage, Watcombe, Lynmouth souvenir................... 135.00
Match holder, Cottage, Watcombe, 'A Match for Any Man'....... 100.00
Match striker, Scandy, 2½" 85.00
Mug, Cottage, 'Enough's as Good as a Feast,' 3½x4" 80.00
Mug, Cottage, 'Up to the Lips Over the Gums...' 95.00
Mug, Parrots, 'Still Water Runs Deep,' bl background, 3½" 60.00
Mustard pot, 'Soft Words Win Hard Hearts,' 3" 62.00
Plate, Longpark, 'Always Help a Lame Dog...,' 3¾" 60.00
Plate, Scandy, unmk, 'Rolling Storie Gathers...,' 4"....................... 60.00
Salt cellar, Cottage, 'Elp Yerzel...,' 3¼" 65.00
Teapot, Black Cockerel, Longpart, 'Dauntee Be Fraid...,' 1-cup, 2½".. 175.00
Teapot, Colored Cockerel, Longpark, motto, 3½" 150.00
Teapot, Scandy, Longpark, 'Dauntee Be Fraid Aut...,' 3½" 145.00
Tray, Cottage, Watcombe, 'Do Not Stain Today's Blue Sky... ,' 11"..275.00
Vase, Cottage, Watcombe, no motto, ca 1910, 10x4½"............... 195.00
Vase, Ship, 'There Is No Wealth But Life,' conical, hdls, 3⅞" 55.00

Tortoiseshell

The outer shell of several species of land turtles, called tortoises, was once commonly used to make brooches, combs, small boxes, and novelty items. It was often used for inlay as well. The material is easily recognized by its mottled brown and yellow coloring. Because some of these turtles are now on the endangered list, such use is prohibited.

Box, marquetry inlay, separates into 3 trays, 1x3¾", EX 140.00
Box, silver string inlay, ivory bun ft, faceted lid, 6" L 1,500.00
Clock, Fr silver/wood w/tortoise front panel, 15-jewel, 4¼x3" 210.00
Lorgnette, gold w/tortoise hdl, retractable folding mechanism 90.00
Notebook cover, silver/MOP inlay, velvet int, ca 1900, 4x3", EX.. 65.00
Pocketknife, SP steel blade w/emb ferrule, dtd 1821, 5¼" 435.00
Ring, w/plastic & gilt heart-shaped photo compartment, 1930s 50.00
Tea caddy, bombe w/canted corners, stepped-bk dome lid, 1830, 6x6x4"..1,150.00

Toys

Toys can be classified into at least two categories: early collectible toys with an established history, and the newer toys. The antique toys are easier to evaluate. A great deal of research has been done on them, and much data is available. The newer toys are just beginning to be studied; relative information is only now being published, and the lack of production records makes it difficult to know how many may be available. Often warehouse finds of these newer toys can change the market. This has happened with battery-operated toys and to some extent with robots. Review past issues of this guide. You will see the changing trends for the newer toys. All toys become more important as collectibles when a fixed period of manufacture is known. When we know the numbers produced and documentation of the makers is established, the prices become more predictable.

The best way to learn about toys is to attend toy shows and auctions. This will give you the opportunity to compare prices and condition. The more collectors and dealers you meet, the more you will learn. There is no substitute for holding a toy in your hand and seeing for yourself what they are. If you are going to be a serious collector, buy all the books you can find. Read every article you see. Knowledge is vital to building a good collection. Study all books that are available. These are some of the most helpful: *Schroeder's Collectible Toys, Antique to Modern*; *Breyer Animal Collector's Guide*, by Felicia Browell; *Matchbox Toys, 1947 – 2003, The Other Matchbox Toys*, and *Toy Car Collector's Guide*, all by Dana Johnson; *Hot Wheels, The Ultimate Redline Guide, 1968 – 1977*, and *Hot Wheels, The Ultimate Red Line Companion*, both by Jack Clark and Robert P. Wicker; *Rubber Toy Vehicles* by Dave Leopard; and *Big Book of Toy Airplanes* by W. Tom Miller. All are published by Collector Books. Other informative books are *Collecting Toys, Collecting Toy Soldiers*, and *Collecting Toy Trains* by Richard O'Brien; and *Toys of the Sixties, A Pictorial Guide*, by Bill Bruegman. In the listings that follow, toys are listed by manufacturer's name if possible, otherwise by type. Measurements are given when appropriate and available; if only one dimension is noted, it is the greater one — height if the toy is vertical, length if it is horizontal. See also Children's Things; Personalities. For toy stoves, see Stoves.

Key:
b/o — battery operated r/c — remote control
cl — celluloid   w/up — windup

Toys by Various Manufacturers

Alps, Antique Gooney Car, litho tin w/vinyl-headed figure, 1960s, 9"..75.00
Alps, Chippy the Chipmunk, b/o, 1950s, 12", MIB..................... 125.00
Alps, Juggling Clown, w/up, twirls balls & plates on sticks , 6", EXIB... 300.00
Alps, Pontiac Firebird III, friction, litho tin, 1950s, 11", EX........ 300.00
Bandai, Musical Ice Cream Truck, 1960s, 11", NM 150.00
Bandai, Plane w/Tow Car, b/o, litho tin, 26", MIB 575.00
Buddy L, Dump Truck, curved cab, 1930s, 25", EX................... 1,045.00
Buddy L, Railway Express Van, screened sides, 1925, 24", EX...4,125.00
Champion, Midget Racer #63, w/driver, friction, tin, 7", NM 935.00
Chein, Popeye the Drummer, 7", NM....................................... 3,000.00
Chein, Tow Truck, Hercules series, 18", EX 600.00
Corgi, Beatle's Yellow Submarine, #803, MIB, from $700 to........ 750.00
Corgi, Crime Busters gift set, #3008, scarce, from $825 to 900.00
Corgi, Ford Thunderbird, w/motor, #214, MIB, from $300 to...... 325.00
Corgi, Heavy Equipment Transporter, #1135, MIB, from $450 to...500.00
Corgi, Land Rover, #438, Lepra, MIB, from $375 to 425.00
Corgi, London Transport Routemaster Bus, #468, MIB, from $1,000 to..1,250.00
Corgi, Magic Roundabout Playground, #853, MIB, from $1,000 to...1,750.00
Corgi, Mini Cooper Monte Carlo, #317, MIB, from $175 to 225.00
Corgi, Pop Art Morris Mini, #349, from $1,750 to.................... 2,250.00
Corgi, Stromberg Helicopter, #926, MIB, from $85 to 100.00
Corgi, Stunt Bike, #681, MIB, from $250 to............................... 275.00
Corgi, UNCLE car, #1005B, Junior on base, MIB, from $1,500 to...1,750.00
Corgi, US Army Rover, #500, MIB, from $450 to 500.00
Cragstan, Clown the Magician, b/o, #40244, cloth, 1950s, 11", EXIB.. 200.00
Cragstan, Teddy Bear, b/o, S&E, plush, tin desk, 1950s, 9", EXIB...275.00
Dinky, Bedford Comet Lorry w/Tailboard, MIB, from $275 to 300.00

Dinky, Big Bedford Van, Heinz Ketchup bottle, MIB, from $2,000 to 2,250.00
Dinky, Fire Station, #954, MIB, from $425 to 450.00
Dinky, Horse Box Express, #980, MIB, from $850 to................ 1,000.00
Dinky, TS Motorcycle Patrol, #271, MIB, from $275 to.............. 350.00
Ertl, Dodge Ram Truck, red or blk, 1995, 1:18 scale, MIB, from $30 to ... 35.00

Fisher-Price, Circus Wagon, #156, 1942, 13", NM, $400.00.

(Photo courtesy Morphy Auctions)

Hubley, Poultry Truck, diecast, w/accessories, 10", MIB, from $265 to ... 300.00
Hubley, Sports Car, yel w/blk convertible top, rare, 13", MIB, $850 to ...1,000.00
Johnny Lightning, Custom Eldorado, mirror finish, 1969, MIP.. 1,200.00
Johnny Lightning, Custom XKE, standard finish, 1969, MIP....... 750.00
Lehmann, Anxious Bride, w/up, NMIB 2,000.00
Lehmann, Berolina Convertible, w/up, NM 3,500.00
Lehmann, Going to the Fair, NM 3,000.00
Lehmann, Paddy & the Pig, w/up, EX 1,100.00
Linemar, Androcles Lion, w/up, plush, appearing to lick paw, 6", EXIB... 115.00
Linemar, Choo Choo Train, w/up, litho tin, 12", EXIB................ 115.00
Linemar, Dockyard Crane, w/up, tin, w/logs & pallet, 9", EXIB... 100.00
Linemar, Donald Duck Delivery Wagon, friction, tin w/plastic head, EX....355.00
Marusan, Ford Stake Truck, friction, tin, Ford hubcaps, 8", NMIB.. 150.00
Marusan, Grasshopper, w/up, mostly tin, walking motion, 7", MIB...250.00
Marx, Coast-to-Coast Double-Decker Bus, tin, 10", EX............... 525.00
Marx, Disney Parade Roadster, w/up, 11", NMIB 750.00
Marx, Flintstone Car, Wilma; friction, 4", NMIB...................... 525.00
Marx, Hootin' Hollow House, b/o, 11", EXIB............................ 875.00
Marx, Jetspeed Racer, b/o, tin w/vinyl driver, 17", NMIB 500.00
Marx, Twinkle Toes Ballet, friction, 5", EXIB.......................... 100.00
Marx, Whistling Spooky Kooky Tree, b/o, 14", EXIB................. 1,320.00
Matchbox, MGA Sports Car, #19, 1958, wht w/gold grille, MIP, $450 to...525.00
Matchbox, Standard Jeep CJ5, #72, 1966, wht int, MIP, $1,000 to.. 1,250.00
Matchbox, 1913 Cadillac, gold-plated, 1967, MIP, from $225 to.. 275.00
MT, Lucky Cement Mixer Truck, b/o, 1960s, 12", M 150.00
MT, Magic Snow Man, b/o, holding broom, 1950s, 11", EXIB..... 140.00
Nifty, Skidoodle, w/up, litho tin, 8", EX............................... 1,100.00
Nifty, Toonerville Trolley, w/up, litho tin, 7", EX 750.00
Remco, Batman Flying Batplane, b/o, plastic, r/c, 12", EXIB............125.00
S&E, Drinking Captain, b/o, cloth outfit, 12", MIB.................... 125.00
Sansco, Funland Cup Ride, b/o, 1960s, 7", NMIB..................... 350.00
Strauss, Emergency Tow Car, w/up, #54, EX 1,200.00
Strauss, Parcel Post Truck, w/up, NM.................................12,500.00
Strauss, Tip Top Dump Truck, w/up, NM............................... 1,000.00
Structo, Racer, w/up, 2-seater, Structo decal on radiator, 12½", EX ...550.00
TN, Farm Truck (John's Truck), b/o, 1950s, 9", MIB................. 350.00
Tootsietoy, Fleet Set, diecast, 12 navy ships, 6" ea, EXIB............. 440.00
Tootsietoy, Trailer Truck Set, diecast, cab w/2 trailers, 8", NMIB....600.00
Unique Art, GI Joe & His Jouncing Jeep, w/up, tin, 7", EXIB 275.00
Wyandotte, Hoky & Poky Handcar, w/up, tin, 6½", EXIB 300.00

Farm Toys

Combine, John Deere, w/driver, CI, Vindex, 1930s, 1/16 scale, EX .3,800.00
Combine, John Deere 45, 10 corn head, rnd bk, Ertl/Prestige, MIB.... 125.00
Combine, Massey Harris, Reuhl, rpt/rstr decals, 1950s, 1/20th scale... 650.00
Picker, Eska John Deere, 2-row/short nose, Ertl/'54, 1/16th scale, MIB..265.00
Picker, Oliver, 1-row, CI, Made in USA, 1/32 scale, M................ 160.00
Plow, International Harvester, 2-bottom, diecast, Ertl, 6" L, NM....250.00
Thrashing machine, McCormick Deering, CI, Arcade, 7x11½", EX. 375.00
Tractor, Allis-Chalmers, CI, orig pnt & decals, Arcade, 4½x7", EX.. 590.00
Tractor, Case SC, diecast, Franklin Precision, 1/12 scale, MIB.... 135.00
Tractor, Cockshutt, diecast, Advanced Products, 1946, 1/16 scale, VG...155.00
Tractor, John Deere 3020 wide front, Ertl, 1960s, 1/16th scale, NM... 165.00
Tractor, Massey Harris 44, diecast, 1950, 1/16 scale, M in VG box....235.00
Tractor, McCormick 450 w/front end loader, CI/steel rims, 13" L, VG..200.00
Tractor, McCormick Deering WD-40 Diesel, Wheatbelt, 1/16 scale, MIB..400.00
Truck, stake; Tonka Farms, pressed steel, Tonka, 1959, NM 225.00
Truck, Tonka Farms, bl w/red stock rack, w/6 animals, Tonka, 1950s, EX....415.00
Wagon, John Deere, blk rubber tires, hinged tongue, MIB........... 215.00
Wagon, silage; New Holland, diecast, Ertl, ca 1960s, 5x12", EX 100.00

Guns and Cap Bombs

In years past, virtually every child played with toy guns, and the survival rate of these toys is minimal, at best. The interest in these charming toy guns has recently increased considerably, especially those with western character examples, as collectors discover their scarcity, quality, and value. Toy gun collectibles encompass the early and the very ornate figural toy guns and bombs through the more realistic ones with recognizable character names, gleaming finishes, faux jewels, dummy bullets, engraving, and colorful grips. This section will cover some of the most popular cast-iron and diecast toy guns from the past 100 years. Recent market trends have witnessed a decline of interest in the earlier (1900 – 1940) single-shot cast-iron pistols. The higher collector interest is for known western characters and cap pistols from the 1960 – 1965 era. Generic toy guns such as, Deputy, Pony Boy, Marshal, Ranger, Sheriff, Pirate, Cowboy, Dick, Western, Army, etc., generate only minimal collector interest.

American Cap Pistol, Kilgore, eagle on grips, 1940s, 9", EX 325.00
Automic Ray Gun, MT, b/o, tin, 18½", EXIB 250.00
Buck'n Bronc Cap Guns w/Cowboy Double Holster Set, Russell, NMIB...350.00
Colt 45 Cap Pistol, Hubley, w/6 metal cartridges, 13½", NMIB... 250.00
Cowboy Repeating Cap Pistol, Hubley, wht grips, 1950s, 11½", NMIB...200.00
Derringer w/Dagger, Hubley, NP w/red plastic push-out dagger, 7", NM.. 90.00
Flashy Ray Gun, TN, b/o, 1950s, 18", NMIB.............................. 200.00
Hide-A-Mite Secret Holster & Nichols Cap Pistol, Carnell, MOC .. 45.00
Long Tom Cap Pistol, Kilgore, 2-pc revolving cylinder, wht grips, EXIB....500.00
Ric-O-Shay 45 Cap Pistol, Hubley, revolving cylinder, 1950s, 12", NM...125.00
Shootin' Shell Cap Pistol, Mattel, EXIB.................................... 300.00
Space Gun, Y, litho tin, 5", MIB 75.000

Model Kits

Adams, Around the World in 80 Days Balloon, 1960, MIB......... 325.00
Addar, Evil Knievel, 1974, MIB... 50.00
Airfix, Big Foot, 1978, MIB.. 75.00
AMT, Get Smart Sunbeam Car, 1967, MIB 75.00
AMT, Girl From UNCLE Car, 1974, MIB................................. 300.00
AMT, Sonny & Cher Mustang, 1960s, MIB.............................. 325.00
AMT, Star Trek, Klingon Cruiser, #S952-802, 1968, MIB 225.00
AMT/Ertl, Monkeemobile, 1990, MIB 100.00
Aurora, Addams Family Haunted House, 1964, MIB.................. 850.00
Aurora, Creature From the Black Lagoon, 1963, MIB................. 450.00
Aurora, Forgotten Prisoner, 1966, MIB 425.00
Aurora, Godzilla, 1964, MIB 550.00
Aurora, Lost in Space, Robot, 1968, MIB................................. 850.00
Hawk, Cobra II, 1950s, MIB... 75.00
Horizon, Bride of Frankenstein, 1990s, MIB.............................. 65.00

Horizon, Robocop, ED-209, 1989, MIB 70.00
Lindberg, SST Continental, 1958, MIB 175.00
Monogram, Snoopy & Motorcycle, snap-tite, 1971, MIB 100.00
Monogram, Voyage to the Bottom of the Sea, Flying Sub, 1979, MIB ... 175.00
MPC, Barnabas Vampire Van, Dark Shadows, 1969, MIB 250.00
MPC, Dukes of Hazzard, Sheriff Rosco's Police Car, 1982, NMIB ... 40.00
Pyro, Prehistoric Monsters Gift Set, 1950s, MIB 125.00
Remco, Flintstones, any kit, 1961, MIB 200.00
Revell, Apollo Astronaut on Moon, 1970, MIB 125.00
Revell, Disney's Love Bug Rides Again, 1974, MIB 100.00
Revell, Dune, Sand Worm, 1985, MIB 75.00
Revell, Moon Ship, 1957, MIB 225.00
Strombecker, Walt Disney's Spaceship, 1958, MIB 300.00
Superior, Beating Heart, 1959, MIB 35.00
Toy Biz, Storm, 1996, MIB 20.00
Tsukuda, Ghostbusters Terror Dog, MIB 125.00

Pedal Cars and Ride-On Toys

Airplane, Army Scout; Gendron, 1920s, 41", EX 2,000.00
Boat, wood w/metal seat, mk Moncano, 2 lg+2 sm wheels, 39", EX .. 2,090.00
Buick, Steelcraft, V-shaped windshield, dish wheels, rstr, 45", EX .. 1,320.00
Cadillac, Sidway Topliff, glass windshield, wood running brds, 36", EX .. 3,500.00
Chevrolet, NP mascot, windshield, curved seat, 1930, rstr, 36" ... 1,540.00
Chrysler Airflow, Steelcraft w/wood hood ornament, rstr, 46" .. 1,265.00
Deusenberg, chrome detail w/side pipes, wht spoked wheels, rstr, 69" .. 2,200.00
Early wooden car, tin hood lantern, England, 33", EX 825.00
Erskine, Toledo, 1927-1930, VG 3,500.00
Fire Ladder Truck, Murray, bell on hood, wood ladders, 1960s, 39", EX ... 990.00
Ford, Steelcraft, w/fenders, disk wheels w/cut-out detail, 33", EX ... 770.00
Murry Weston Coupe, Steelcraft, vinyl seat & top cover, rear spare, EX .. 1,980.00
Packard, Am National, 1920s, 45", EX 4,025.00
Racer #60, Garton, orig red w/wht 60 on sides & bk, 46", G 500.00
Station Wagon, Murray, w/rear rails, metal disk wheels, 42", EX .. 600.00

1937 Ford made by Garton, restored, M, from $1,500.00 to $1,800.00.

(Photo courtesy Nate Stoller)

Penny Toys

Airplane whistle toy, 4¼x3", VG 200.00
Bear w/penny whistle toy, bear holds pole, gold pnt, Germany, 4", VG .. 325.00
Boy seated on sled, Levy, VG 200.00
Delivery stake truck, open cab w/driver, Germany, 3½", EX 150.00
Dog (Spinning) whistle, France, 4", G 150.00
Double-decker bus, yel & orange, railed top, w/driver, 4½", EX ... 175.00
Girls spiral down pole, lever action, open seats, 8½", EX 300.00
Gnomes sawing wood, beveled oblong base, Meier, 4", VG 250.00
Goat on 4-wheeled platform, Meier, 3", EX 220.00
Horsedrawn wagon, open-slat wagon w/emb lanterns, Meier, 4½", EX .. 110.00

Locomotive (self moving), rubber band at axle, stamped tin, 3", VG . 225.00
Merry-go-round, Souvenir From Universal..., Chicago, 2½", EX .. 450.00
Monkey climbing pole, pull-string action, pole on fluted base, 7", VG . 110.00
Ox-drawn wagon, red rail-sided wagon w/gray canopy, Meier, 6", EX . 225.00
Stake truck, red & blk, open seat, flat roof, tapered nose, 4½", VG .. 125.00
Swing, gondola w/couple, A-frame on platform, Meier, 3⅛", EX . 325.00
Train on oval track w/signals/tunnel/bridge, Schuhlmann, 8½", NMIB ... 275.00
Vis-A-Vis, red & yel, w/driver, emb, spoke wheels, 3", VG 275.00

Pull and Push Toys

American Milk Co Milk Wagon, horse on 4-wheeled platform, 24", VG ... 770.00
Circus band wagon, tin w/circus band scene on sides, Converse, 18", VG .. 500.00
Dolls on wheeled musical box platform, 6 bsk-headed dolls, 9x13", EX .. 1,430.00
Elephants on wheeled platform bell toy, mother & baby, Fallows, 6", VG .. 660.00
Hillside farm wagon, 24", VG 330.00
Horse on wheeled platform, tin, wht w/red pnt blanket, Geo Brown, 9" . 245.00
Milk wagon, felt-covered horse on wheels, tin barrels, 7", VG 175.00
Plantation cart, w/driver & horse, Wilkens, 13", VG 385.00
Ringling Bros Circus wagon w/team of horses, wagon & animals, 37", VG .60.00
Sheep on platform, pnt tin, 11½", VG 385.00
Train locomotive, Union, pnt/stenciled tin, A Bergman, 1870s, 12", EX .. 2,475.00
US Mail Train, tin, Fallows, 1880s, 22", NM 3,000.00

Robots

Atom Robot, friction, tin, gray w/red, wht, bl & yel detail, 7", EXIB .. 485.00
Blink-A-Gear Robot, b/o, tin w/red arms, chest w/mc gears, Taiyo, NMIB ... 900.00
Chief Robotman, b/o, tin, KO, 12", NMIB 1,600.00
D Fighter Robot, w/up, mc tin body, plastic head w/horns, 9½", EX ... 190.00
Deep Sea Robot, w/up, scarce variation on Space Captain, tin, 8", EX .. 1,900.00
Gettsuko Kamen Robot, w/up, tin, Bullmark, 9", NMIB 550.00
High-Wheel Robot, w/up, tin w/mc gear box in chest, Yoshiya, 10", EXIB .. 412.00
Lantern Robot, r/c, Linemar, 8", VG 1,475.00
Mighty Robot, b/o, litho tin, Yoshiya, 12", EX 1,100.00
Mr Robot, w/up, ATC, 7", NMIB 575.00
Piston Action Robot, r/c, Robbie look-alike, TN, NMIB 1,550.00
Planet Robot, r/c, tin, KO, non-working, 9", EX 300.00
Radar Robot, r/c, tin, coil on head w/antenna, TN, 10", NMIB .. 1,600.00
Shoot Him Robot, b/o, tin, changes direction, Masudaya, 15", NMIB ... 8,500.00
Smoking Robot w/Lantern, r/c, silver w/red detail, Linemar, 8", EX .. 2,000.00
Video Robot, b/o, tin, mc lithoed controls, Japan, 9", EXIB 260.00
Winky Robot, w/up, tin w/rubber ears, chest meter, Y, 10", NMIB .. 2,800.00
Zero of Space Robot, b/o, plastic, Hong Kong, 1970s, NMIB 375.00

Schoenhut

Our advisor for Schoenhut toys is Keith Kaonis, who has collected these toys for 25 years. Because of his involvement with the publishing industry (currently *Antique DOLL Collector*, and during the '80s, *Collectors' SHOW-CASE*), he has visited collections across the United States, produced several articles on Schoenhut toys, and served a term as president of the Schoenhut Collectors' Club. Keith is listed in the Directory under New York.

The listings below are for Humpty Dumpty Circus pieces. All values are based on rating conditions of good to very good, i.e., very minor scratches and wear, good original finish, no splits or chips, no excessive paint wear or cracked eyes, and of course completeness and condition of clothes (if dressed figures). Clowns with two-part heads (a cast face applied to a wooden head) were made from 1903 to 1912 and are most desirable — condition always is important. There have been nine distinct styles in 14 different costumes recorded. Only eight costume styles apply to the two-part headed clowns. The later clowns had one-part heads whose features were pressed wood, and the costumes on the later ones, circa 1920+, were no longer tied at the wrists and ankles.

Humpty Dumpty Circus Clowns and Other Personel

Black Dude, 1-part head, purple coat, from $250 to	750.00
Black Dude, 2-part head, blk coat, from $400 to	1,000.00
Chinese Acrobat, 1-part head, from $200 to	900.00
Chinese Acrobat, 2-part head, rare, from $400 to	1,600.00
Clown, reduced sz, from $75 to	125.00
Hobo, reduced sz, from $200 to	400.00
Hobo, 1-part head, from $200 to	400.00
Hobo, 2-part head, curved-up toes, blk coat, from $500 to	1,200.00
Lady Acrobat, bsk head, from $300 to	800.00
Lady Acrobat, 1-part head, from $150 to	400.00
Lady Rider, bsk head, from $250 to	550.00
Lady Rider, 2-part head, very rare, from $500 to	1,000.00
Lion Tamer, 1-part head, from $150 to	700.00
Lion Tamer, 2-part head, early, very rare, from $700 to	1,600.00
Ringmaster, bsk, from $300 to	800.00
Ringmaster, 1-part head, from $200 to	450.00
Ringmaster, 2-part head, blk coat, very rare, from $800 to	1,800.00
Ringmaster, 2-part head, red coat, very rare, from $700 to	1,600.00

Humpty Dumpty Circus Animals

Humpty Dumpty Circus animals with glass eyes, ca. 1903 – 1914, are more desirable and can demand much higher prices than the later painted-eye versions. As a general rule, a glass-eye version is 30% to 40% more than a painted-eye version. (There are exceptions.) The following list suggests values for both GE (glass-eye) and PE (painted-eye) versions and reflects a **low PE price** to a **high GE price.**

There are other variations and nuances of certain figures: Bulldog — white with black spots or Brindle (brown); open- and closed-mouth zebras, camels, and giraffes; ball necks and hemispherical necks on some animals such as the pig, cat, and hippo, to name a few. These points can affect the price and should be judged individually. Condition and rarity affect the price most significantly and the presence of an original box virtually doubles the price.

Alligator, PE/GE, from $250 to	750.00
Arabian camel, 1 hump, PE/GE, from $250 to	750.00
Bactrain camel, 2 humps, PE/GE, from $200 to	1,200.00
Brown bear, PE/GE, from $200 to	800.00
Buffalo, cvd mane, PE/GE, from $200 to	1,200.00
Bulldog, PE/GE, from $400 to	1,500.00
Burro, farm set, PE/GE, no harness/no belly hole for chariot, $300 to	800.00
Burro, made to go w/chariot & clown, w/leather track, PE/GE, $200 to	800.00
Cat, PE/GE, rare, from $500 to	3,000.00
Cow, PE/GE, from $300 to	1,200.00
Deer, PE/GE, from $300 to	1,500.00
Donkey, PE/GE, from $75 to	300.00
Donkey w/blanket, PE/GE, from $100 to	600.00
Elephant, PE/GE, from $75 to	300.00
Gazelle, PE/GE, rare, from $500 to	3,000.00
Giraffe, PE/GE, from $200 to	900.00
Goose, PE only, from $200 to	750.00
Gorilla, PE only, from $1,500 to	4,000.00
Hippo, PE/GE, from $200 to	900.00
Horse, brn, saddle & stirrups, PE/GE, from $250 to	500.00
Horse, dapple pnt, platform, PE/GE, from $250 to	700.00
Hyena, PE/GE, very rare, from $1,000 to	6,000.00
Kangaroo, PE/GE, from $200 to	1,500.00
Lion, cvd mane, PE/GE, from $200 to	1,400.00
Monkey, 1-part head, PE only, from $200 to	600.00
Monkey, 2-part head, wht face, from $300 to	1,000.00
Ostrich, PE/GE, from $200 to	900.00

Pig, 5 versions, PE/GE, from $200 to	800.00
Polar bear, PE/GE, from $200 to	2,000.00
Poodle, PE/GE, from $100 to	300.00
Rabbit, PE/GE, very rare, from $500 to	3,500.00
Rhino, PE/GE, from $250 to	800.00
Sea lion, PE/GE, from $400 to	1,500.00
Sheep (lamb), w/bell, PE/GE, from $200 to	800.00
Tiger, PE/GE, from $250 to	1,200.00
Wolf, PE/GE, very rare, from $500 to	5,000.00
Zebra, PE/GE, rare, from $500 to	3,000.00

Humpty Dumpty Circus Accessories

There are many accessories: wagons, tents, ladders, chairs, pedestals, tightrope, weights, and more.

Managerie tent, early, ca 1904, from $1,500 to	3,000.00
Menagerie tent, later, 1914-20, from $1,200 to	2,000.00
Oval litho tent, 1926, from $4,000 to	10,000.00
Sideshow panels, 1926, pr from $2,000 to	5,000.000

Steiff

Margaret Steiff began making her stuffed felt toys in Germany in the late 1800s. The animals she made were tagged with an elephant in a circle. Her first teddy bear, made in 1903, became such a popular seller that she changed her tag to a bear. Felt stuffing was replaced with excelsior and wool; when it became available, foam was used. In addition to the tag, look for the 'Steiff' ribbon and the button inside the ear.

Early Steiff bears in mint condition may go for a minimum of $150.00 per inch for a small bear up to $300.00 to $350.00 (sometimes even more) per inch for one 20" high or larger. See also Teddy Bears.

Bear, Alfonzo, gold & wht tunic, w/button, 1990, 13", MIB	400.00
Bear, Alfonzo, red mohair, gold & wht jacket, 13", EX	400.00
Boy doll, stuffed felt body, pnt features, clothed w/hat, 16"	250.00
Cat seated, tan w/wht chest & brn stripes, gr button eyes, ID, 7", G	150.00
Charley Horse, rust/wht mohair, blk mohair mane/tail, 1904, 14", EX	1,175.00

Dog, mohair with excelsior-stuffed mohair, glass eyes, Steiff (underlined FF) button in ear, 8", EX, $500.00. (Photo courtesy McMasters Harris Auction Company)

Dog, Spotty, bell around neck, name tag, ear tag, 3½", VG	700.00
Golden Age of Circus Elephant Train, 5-pc set, ca 1986-90, EX	4,000.00
Kitten, gray striped, gr glass eyes, jtd, 1920s, 11", EX	350.00
Monkey on handcart, dk brn mohair w/lt tan felt accents, 10½x9", VG	150.00
Rabbit, glass eyes, embr mouth/nose, ear button, 1915, 6⅜", VG	515.00
Rabbit Skittles Game, 9 stuffed rabbits on bases w/ball, 9½", EX	8,000.00

Toy Soldiers and Accessories

Among the better-known manufacturers of 'Dimestore' soldiers are American Metal Toys, Barclay, and Manoil, all of whom made hollow cast-lead figures; Grey Iron, who used cast iron; and Auburn, who made figures of rubber. They measured about 3" to 3½" tall, and often accessories such as trucks, tents, tanks, and airplanes were designed to add to the enjoyment of staging mock battles, parades, encampments, and wars. Some figures are very rare and therefore expensive, but condition is just as important in making a value assessment. Percentages in the description lines refer to the amount of original paint remaining. our advisors for this category are Stan and Sally Alekna; they are listed in the Directory under Pennsylvania.

Am Metal Toys, soldier AA gunner, sliver, scarce, NM 65.00
Am Metal Toys, soldier grenade thrower, 97% 170.00
Am Metal Toys, soldier kneeling at searchlight, khaki, scarce, 99% .. 133.00
Am Metal Toys, soldier w/rifle leaning in wide stance, khaki, 97% 126.00
Auburn Rubber, soldier lying wounded, 97% 47.00
Auburn Rubber, White Guard officer, 92-94% 18.00
Barclay, AA gunner, red, pod ftd, scarce, 96% 120.00
Barclay, armored truck, khaki, wht rubber tires, 98% 27.00
Barclay, aviator, khaki, pod ft, 98% 24.00
Barclay, boy, 98% 16.00
Barclay, brakeman, 99% 10.00
Barclay, cavalryman, 1930s, 2¼", 98% 36.00
Barclay, couple in horsedrawn sleigh, 98% 102.00
Barclay, cowboy rider, masked, w/lasso, 97% 66.00
Barclay, cowboy rider w/gun drawn, 97% 60.00
Barclay, cowboy w/2 guns, 1 pointed outward, 97% 27.00
Barclay, cowboy w/2 guns, 1 raised, scarce, 97% 72.00
Barclay, dispatcher w/dog, 97% 90.00
Barclay, doctor, flat base, brn, 95% 26.00
Barclay, drummer, wht helmet, scarce, 97% 75.00
Barclay, elderly lady, pk, 97% 20.00
Barclay, field phone operator leaning out, gr cast helmet, rare, 98% .. 96.00
Barclay, fireman, NM 19.00
Barclay, fireman w/axe, 98% 42.00
Barclay, flagbearer, short stride, tin helmet, 97% 40.00
Barclay, girl, 99% 20.00
Barclay, girl on sled, NM 28.00
Barclay, girl skater, 99% 20.00
Barclay, HO man, 99% 10.00
Barclay, Indian Chief w/rifle, pod ft, scarce, 98% 40.00
Barclay, Indian w/bow & arrow, scarce, 93-95% 29.00
Barclay, Japanese soldier advancing w/rifle, scarce, 95% 45.00
Barclay, knight, blk, w/shield, 99% 42.00
Barclay, mailman, NM 22.00
Barclay, man putting skates on girl sitting on bench, scarce, 98% ... 190.00
Barclay, marine, bl, cast helmet, 85-88% 86.00
Barclay, minister walking, scarce, 99% 82.00
Barclay, nurse w/bowl & towel, red hair, pod ftd, scarce, 96% 40.00
Barclay, plane, single engine, red/wht/bl, rare, 99% 45.00
Barclay, sentry in overcoat, 95% 95.00
Barclay, soldier w/bazooka on bended knee, gr, scarce, M 135.00
Barclay, soldier w/pistol crawling, gr, pod ftd, 99% 40.00
Barclay, US Army truck, scarce, 98% 42.00
Barclay, workhorse, NM 20.00
Grey Iron, aviator, orange harness, very scarce, 96% 92.00
Grey Iron, doctor carring bag, wht suit, scarce, 96% 43.00
Grey Iron, Foreign Legion officer, 97% 62.00
Grey Iron, knight in armor, NM 45.00
Grey Iron, Legion color bearer, 95% 35.00
Grey Iron, Legion drum major, 98% 30.00

Grey Iron, soldier flagbearer, brn, pnt face, USD, very scarce, 94% .. 75.00
Grey Iron, soldier, wounded w/crutches, 96% 75.00
Grey Iron, US Marine, early, NM 33.00
Grey Iron, US Naval officer, wht, early, 93-95% 22.00
Jones, Waynes Legion soldier on guard w/bayonet, M 34.00
Lincoln Log, Indian brave standing, w/bow & arrow, 88-90% 29.00
Lincoln Log, officer, mounted, 1919 uniform, 97% 39.00
Lincoln Log, pioneer standing w/gun, 98% 19.00
Lincoln Log, sailor w/rifle at attention, scarce, 97% 30.00
Lincoln Log, train redcap, 98% 18.00
Manoil, aviator w/bomb standing, 98% 52.00
Manoil, blacksmith making horseshoes, Happy Farm set, 98% 29.00
Manoil, bomb thrower, 2 grenades, 99% 37.00
Manoil, carpenter carrying door, Happy Farm set, scarce, 98% 72.00
Manoil, cowboy w/gun raised, hollow base, 93-95% 49.00
Manoil, gun on wheels, 5-barrel, 97% 36.00
Manoil, hod carrier w/bricks, Happy Farm set, 98% 43.00
Manoil, hostess, wht, very scarce, 96% 300.00
Manoil, man carrying sack on bk, Happy Farm set, 98% 29.00
Manoil, man planting tree, Happy Farm set, scarce, M 68.00
Manoil, man w/barrel of apples, khaki, Happy Farm set, 98% 89.00
Manoil, soldier digging trench, scarce, 97% 69.00
Manoil, soldier sitting/eating, scarce, 98% 61.00
Manoil, soldier w/rifle charging, scarce, 98% 67.00
Manoil, soldier w/trench mortar, 98% 36.00
Manoil, woman sweeping w/broom, Happy Farm set, 99% 28.00
Marx, cowboy drawing pistol, tin, post WWII, scarce, NM 26.00
Marx, cowboy w/rifle, tin, oval base, post WWII, NM 26.00
Marx, Gordon Highlander, tin, NM 8.00
Marx, Indian brave w/hatchet, tin, post WWII, EX 20.00
Miller Plaster, soldier flagbearer planting flag, M 44.00
Miller Plaster, soldier stretcher bearer, 99% 30.00
Miller Plaster, soldier, wounded, w/stretcher, 99% 46.00

Trains

Electric trains were produced as early as the late nineteenth century. Names to look for are Lionel, Ives, and American Flyer. Identification numbers given in the listings below actually appear on the item.

Am Flyer, box car, #24409, Northern Pacific, EXIB 1,250.00
Am Flyer, caboose, #4011, yel & brn, EXIB 275.00
Am Flyer, church, #166, MIB 900.00
Am Flyer, flatcar, #24536, w/2 trailers, EX 1,300.00
Am Flyer, rocket sled car, #25515, NMIB 500.00
Am Flyer, set, Comet, loco & 3 cars, VG 450.00

American Flyer, Tank Car, AF Lines Air Service, MIB, $2,000.00; Tank Car, #4010, side ladders, MIB, $1,500.00. (Photo courtesy Stout Auctions)

Buddy L, outdoor pile driver on flatbed car, rstr, 27" 1,200.00
Buddy L, outdoor stock car, red opening side doors, 22", VG 1,200.00
Buddy L, outdoor tank car, yel, scarce version, 19" 1,650.00
Lionel, boxcar, Conrail, modern era, EXIB 25.00

Lionel, boxcar, State of Maine, #6464-275, variation 3, postwar, NMIB. 400.00
Lionel, boxcar, yel w/orange roof, #214, prewar, EXIB 525.00
Lionel, car, Christmas; #9400, modern era, 1985, MIB 850.00
Lionel, dispatch board, #334, postwar, EXIB............................40,000.00
Lionel, flat car, #9157, w/construction crane kit, modern era, NMIB .. 35.00
Lionel, horn shack, diesel, #2127, modern era, EX......................... 25.00
Lionel, locomotive, AEC switcher, #57, postwar, NM 1,700.00
Lionel, locomotive, Baltimore & OH F3 AB units, #2368, postwar, EX..3,100.00
Lionel, locomotove, Commodore Vanderbilt, #265, prewar, rstr .600.00
Lionel, set: locomotive, #402E, w/3 cars, prewar, rstr, EX............. 600.00
Lionel, telegraph set, #86, prewar, NMIB 1,300.00
Lionel, tender car, orange & maroon, #217, prewar, EXIB........... 900.00
Lionel, vat car, Lionel Railroader, #19940, modern era, MIB........ 25.00
Lionel, watchman's shanty w/bell, #76, prewar, G 100.00
Marklin, gondola, gr & orange, open, #2 gauge, VG 175.00
Marklin, locomotive 2-4-0 LMS, electric, rstr 385.00
Marklin, mail van, gr-pnt w/orange trim, blk roof, 6½", NM 1,200.00
Marx, set: NY Central Passenger, #35250, 5-pc, VGIB 200.00
Weeden, set: locomotive, tender & coach, live steam, VG 825.00

Trade Signs

Trade signs were popular during the 1800s. They were usually made in an easily recognizable shape that one could mentally associate with the particular type of business it was to represent, especially appropriate in the days when many customers could not read!

Carpenter wood block plane w/mc wood grain, brackets, 36x19", G.. 1,495.00
Farrier, wrought-iron horseshoe on iron bracket, 19th, 26x36".... 585.00
Fish & Oyster Co, cut-out salmon w/blk litho ad, 23" L.............. 460.00
Fishmonger, cvd catfish w/tin fins & whiskers, gray pnt, 20th C, 48" L..600.00
Fishmonger, fish form, cvd wood w/red/yel weathered pnt, 46" L.800.00
Grummet Shoeing Forge & General Smith, pnt wood, ca 1900, 18x30".. 3,000.00
Hotel Entrance, dk gr w/gilt relief-cvd lettering, 1900, 10x90".... 885.00
Jeweler/watchmaker, HP letters/watch/ring on wood, PA, 1890s, 18x41". 400.00
Octant, gr pnt, T-bar & fixed arm, 20th C, 31" radius.................. 235.00
Optometrist, rvpt glass lenses, gilt bronze nosepc & chain, 29" W..3,450.00
Optometrist, sheet copper/iron glasses over wood panel w/name, 37x38". 2,585.00
Optometrist, spectacles, pnt w/pine w/wrought-iron rod/chains, 25x58"... 2,350.00

Painter, painted pine panel with black lettering and molding, 19x78", $1,175.00. (Photo courtesy Skinner Inc. Auctioneers & Appraisers of Antiques & Fine Art)

Pocket watch, CI/pnt, Father Time/scythes ea side, 1880s, 30"....355.00
Shoe repair, plank stenciled w/'rip repaired free' on wht pnt, 7x49"...260.00
Tailor, man in fine clothes, CI, old blk finish, 44½"...................1,700.00
Tailor, wooden scissors, worn silver & blk pnt, NJ, 30¼" 400.00

Tramp Art

'Tramp' is considered a type of folk art. In America it was primarily made from the end of the Civil War through the 1930s, though it employs carving and decorating methods which are much older, originating mostly in Germany and Scandinavia. 'Trampen' probably refers to the itinerant stages of Middle Ages craft apprenticeship. The carving techniques were also used for practice. Tramp art was spread by soldiers in the Civil War and primarily practiced where there was a plentiful and free supply of materials such as cigar boxes and fruit crates. The belief that this work was done by tramps and hobos as payment for room or meals is generally incorrect. The larger pieces especially would have required a lengthy stay in one place.

There is a great variety of tramp art, from boxes and frames which are most common to large pieces of furniture and intricate objects. The most common method of decoration is chip carving with several layers built one on top of another. There are several variations of that form as well as others such as 'Crown of Thorns,' an interlocking method, which are completely different. The most common finishes were lacquer or stain, although paints were also used. The value of tramp art varies according to size, detail, surface, and complexity. The new collector should be aware that tramp art is being made today. While some sell it as new, others are offering it as old. In addition, many people mistakenly use the term as a catchall phrase to refer to other forms of construction — especially things they are uncertain about. This misuse of the term is growing, and makes a difference in the value of pieces. New collectors need to pay attention to how items are described. For further information we recommend *Tramp Art: A Folk Art Phenomenon* by Helaine Fendelmam, Jonathan Taylor (photographer), Stewart Tabori & Chang; *Hobo & Tramp Art Carving: An Authentic American Folk Tradition* by Adolph Vandertie, Patrick Spielman, Sterling Publications; and *Tramp Art, One Notch at a Time*, by Cornish and Wallach. Our advisors for this category are Matt Lippa and Elizabeth Schaff; they are listed in the Directory under Alabama.

Birdcage, pine, 3-turret, cvd/HP flowers, dtd 1909, 28x31x8" ...1,035.00
Box, chip-cvd, pincushion top, single drw, 5½x7x7" 175.00
Box, chip-cvd dmns/geometrics, paper-lined, compartments, 8x14x10"..480.00
Box, cutlery; chip-cvd, 3-compartment, center hdl, red pnt, 6x10x9"..180.00
Box, sq w/chip-cvd pyramidal lid/sides/base, ball finial, ftd, 18" .. 1,115.00
Cabinet, sewing; 2-tier spool rack/drw, made from cigar boxes, 10x9x5" .150.00
Chest, pine, peaked top, 13 drws/2 niches, cvd/HP rosettes, 39x26".11,785.00
Church, chip-cvd/pnt, wood/linoleum/mirrored glass/arched windows, 60".460.00
Frame, chip-cvd sawtooth borders & X forms, gold/silver pnt, 19x16" ...235.00
Frame, chip-cvd segments w/hearts/triangles/sqs/etc, 31x28" 2,700.00
Frame, chip-cvd shield shape w/bamboo stand, 13½x12" 120.00
Frame, graduating cut geometrics, lapped hearts, dk red pnt, 23x19".. 1,055.00
Frame, 8-point snowflakes & dmns w/chip-cvd edges, old pnt, 19x15"..135.00
Magazine rack, chip-cvd, orig varnish, center hdl, 16x11½" 315.00
Mirror, chip-cvd layers, sm mirrors inset in fr, dk stain, 15x16" ... 950.00
Mirror, chip-cvd stepped geometric fr, brn stain/orange pnt, 40x35" .. 530.00

Traps

Though of interest to collectors for many years, trap collecting has gained in popularity over the past 10 years in particular, causing prices to appreciate rapidly. Traps are usually marked on the pan as to manufacturer, and the condition of these trademarks is important when determining their value. Our advisor for this category is Boyd Nedry; he is listed in the Directory under Michigan. Our values are for traps in fine condition. Grading is as follows:

Good: one-half of pan legible.
Very Good: legible in entirety, but light.
Fine: legible in entirety, with strong lettering.
Mint: in like-new, shiny condition.

Alexander Clutch Trap, sz C 800.00
All-Steel #3, dbl long spring.. 135.00

Animal Trap Co #150, bear trap..395.00
Anti-Cat, metal mousetrap...285.00
Beaten Path, metal mousetrap..45.00
Bell #0, single long spring, Canada......................................95.00
Bergs Drowner, mousetrap...225.00
Blake-Lamb #44, dbl under spring w/teeth................................45.00
Briddell #1, under spring, 7-hole pan...................................45.00
Champion #0, single long spring..100.00
Chasse, killer, wood mousetrap...70.00
Cooks, gopher trap...80.00
Cooper #2, barrel trap..150.00
Cortland #1, single long spring...250.00
Cosey Killer...35.00
Cruso, wood snap rattrap...25.00
Dauffer, killer..65.00
Decoy, wood snap rattrap..140.00
Delusion, tin & wood self-setting mousetrap.............................135.00
Diamond #21½, single long spring...20.00
Diamond #51 Walloper, coil spring, stop loss.............................65.00
Eclipse #1, dbl under spring..190.00
Elenchik #1½, coil spring..40.00
Elgin, tin mousetrap...35.00
EPP, chain loop...1,500.00
Evans Eagle Claw, mouse sz..465.00
Fatal, drowner, tin & wood mousetrap....................................225.00
Flip Mouse Trap, Seattle Mfg Co, wood snap...............................35.00
Funsten Bros Fur Stretcher...30.00
Fut Set, metal rattrap...35.00
Gabriel, fish & game trap...580.00
Gibbs Hawk, dbl coil spring...165.00
Gibbs King Bee #0, single coil spring....................................50.00
Good Housekeepers, wood snap mousetrap...................................15.00
Half Moon, tin mousetrap, Canada..250.00
Hector #1, single long spring..25.00
Herters #41AY, bear trap w/clamps.......................................500.00
Hotchkiss, tin, rnd, 5-hole mousetrap....................................40.00
Hotchkiss & Sons #2, dbl long spring....................................325.00
Ideal, metal box mousetrap..250.00
Iron Cat, metal snap mousetrap...85.00
Jack Frost, body grip killer...20.00
Jillson, spear type, brass & iron mousetrap.............................685.00
Joker, wood snap mousetrap...40.00
Ketchum #3, tile trap...125.00
Klip Trap, mousetrap...10.00
Kompakt #0, single under spring..35.00
Kriket #1, single under spring...32.00
Last Word, wood snap mousetrap...45.00
Little Champ, plastic mousetrap..40.00
Lohmar #3, dbl coil spring...85.00
Mascot #1½, single under spring..30.00
McGill, wood snap mousetrap..20.00
Mousemobile, 3 wheels, tin mousetrap..................................1,500.00
New House #0, single long spring..125.00
New House #114, dbl long spring...150.00
Northwoods #4, dbl long spring, offset jaws..............................35.00
Nox, wood snap mousetrap...60.00
OK, wood snap rattrap..45.00
Oneida #13, single under spring, w/teeth.................................28.00
Pennsylvania, L-shape, wood rattrap......................................40.00
Pioneer #1½, coil spring...30.00
Prott #1, single long spring...40.00
PS&W/Good Luck, swastika cut in pan/#1...................................45.00
Rapid Transit, metal mousetrap..250.00
Runway, red tin mousetrap..40.00

Sabo, den trap w/cast jaws & setting tool...............................140.00
Sav-A-Leg #110...30.00
Security, metal, mousetrap...35.00
Snappy, rattrap..15.00
Sta-Kawt #1½, single long spring...22.00
Taylor Runway, pan type..65.00
Trailzend #2, dbl long spring...100.00
Triumph #3XK, easy set, dbl coil spring..................................45.00
Triumph 3-Jaw, single long spring.......................................129.00
Twister, fly trap on fruit jar...60.00
Up-To-Date, Morrison Specialty Co, mousetrap.............................65.00
Verbail #1, chain hold trap..90.00
Victor #40, 2 traps in 1..165.00
Victor Little Champ, mousetrap...55.00
Victoria #1, single long spring...175.00
X-Terminator, plastic live mousetrap.....................................20.00

Trenton

Trenton, New Jersey, was an area that supported several pottery companies from the mid-1800s until the late 1960s. A consolidation of several smaller companies that occurred in the 1890s was called Trenton Potteries Company. Each company produced their own types of wares independent of the others.

Tile, leaves/berries relief, brn wash on wht gloss, 6x6".................25.00
Vase, aqua, classic form, 9x8"..110.00
Vase, lt bl, 3 graduated disks w/common lower rim, mk TAC, 9"............70.00
Vase, med bl gloss, sphere w/3 lines at equator, 8x8"...................120.00
Vase, Persian Rose, floriform on oval base, 12"..........................60.00
Vase, rose gloss, flared/fluted toward top, mk Tepeco, 8x3"..............45.00
Vase, wht, Art Modern 'Futura' form, 4-sided cone on inverted base, 8"..120.00
Vase, yel gloss, rnd, in 4-finger cradle base, ca 1930s, 7".............145.00

Trivets

Although strictly a decorative item today, the original purpose of the trivet was much more practical. They were used to protect table tops from hot serving dishes, and irons heated on the kitchen range were placed on trivets during use to protect work surfaces. The first patent date was 1869; many of the earliest trivets bore portraits of famous people or patriotic designs. Florals, birds, animals, and fruit were other favored motifs. Watch for remakes of early original designs. Some of these are marked Wilton, Emig, Wright, Iron Art, and V.M. for Virginia Metalcrafters. However, many of these reproductions are becoming collectible. Expect to pay considerably less for these than for the originals, since they are abundant.

Brass

Britain's Might As Iron Stands, spade shaped, #352236, 1900, 7x3⅜"......70.00
Concentric hearts w/steel heart in center, English mk, 4x6½"...........175.00
Cup of Peace & Plenty That Cheers, rnd, mk Greenlees Glasgow, 1800s.....75.00
Forget Me Not, plaque, horseshoe shape w/2 angels, 1880s, 6x3⅜".........70.00
Fox on spade shape, hollow cast, mid to late 1800s, 8¾x4⅛"..............70.00
Home Sweet Home, plaque, horseshoe shape, 1880s, 6x3⅞"..................75.00
Iris on spade shape, Rd #129938, ca 1889, 6⅞x3⅛x1⅛".....................90.00
Lacy Round w/hdl, 3-ftd, ft screw into base, 1800s, 7¼x4x1".............70.00
Peacock on spade shape, heavy, Seeley, #11147D, 1880-1940, 8⅛x4".......50.00
Pixie w/in horseshoe emb Good Luck, ca 1900-30s, 6½x5"..................80.00
Prince of Wales on spade shape, mid to late 1800s, 7x4"................115.00
Spade shape, mk Rd #129937, 3-ftd, 1889, 8½x3⅝x1".......................80.00
Spade shape, 1880 on face, 3-ftd, British, 1880, 8⅞x4x1"................85.00

Cast Iron

Beaver, rough oval casting, 3-ftd, mid-1800s, 6½x3⅛" 125.00
Bonzo the Dog, splayed legs, 3-leg, unmk, 5¾" dia 70.00
Bug, Rochester Sadiron on face, 3-ftd, 1800s, 5¾x4½" 60.00
Carron, sadiron shape, mk CARRON #4, 3-ftd, 1859, 6⅝x 5¼" 100.00
Christmas tree, spade shape, 3-ftd, early 1900s, 7x3⅞" 45.00
Cleveland Star & Sunburst, sadiron shape, 3-leg, 1891, 6x4⅜" 25.00
Cupids, mk JHD, 4-ftd, 1850-1890s, 8½x5¼" 135.00
Danish Spade, 3-ftd, 1800-1850, 11¾x4" 115.00
Economy E, sadiron shape, late 1800s-1900, 6x4¾" 45.00
God Bless Our Home/Sailor's House Blessing, horseshoe shape..... 75.00
Kansas Sunflower State, flower center, heavy, pre-1940, 7⅞x4¾" .. 45.00
Leaf in circle, NPCI, 3-ftd, Ober, 1890s-1916, 5¼" dia 135.00
RNH on sadiron shape, unmk, late 1800s, 7¼x5¼" 85.00

Wrought Iron

Curliques (3) in center of circle, 3-leg, 7x9½" dia 72.50
Curliques along 7 bars, 4-ftd, lengthy hdl, 18th C, 32" overall 540.00
Heart shape w/leaf eng on surface, 3-ftd, 2x10" L 720.00
PA Dutch design on flatiron shape, 19th C, 2x9x4¼" 36.00
Scrolls/hearts/fleur-de-lis, revolves, 3 flared legs, 9x12½" dia 240.00

Tuthill

The Tuthill Glass Company operated in Middletown, New York, from 1902 to 1923. Collectors look for signed pieces and those in an identifiable pattern. Condition is of utmost importance, and examples with brilliant cutting and intaglio (natural flowers and fruits) combined fetch the highest prices. Unless noted otherwise, values are for signed items.

Bowl, cut hobstars & arches, serrated/scalloped rim, 8" 135.00
Bowl, Rex, brilliant cut, serrated/scalloped rim, 8", EX 1,440.00
Bowl, Rex, brilliant period, unmk, 8" 900.00
Bowl, wild rose, intaglio/cut, serrated rim, 8" 110.00
Cake plate, cut hobstars etc, serrated rim, 10" 450.00
Compote, poppy intaglio, ruffled rim, knop std, 8½x8½" 325.00
Compote, vines/berries intaglio, star-cut ft, 7x5½", pr................. 150.00
Decanter, wild rose, intaglio/cut, w/stopper, 12", +6 3½" tumblers...4,080.00
Pitcher, tankard; central hobstar/4 pinwheels/fan & dmn cuttings, 13" ...325.00
Pitcher, tankard; Thousand Eye/hobstars, brilliant cut, 9½" 300.00
Pitcher, tankard; Vintage intaglio, 10½" 600.00
Sugar shaker, floral intaglio panels, 6-sided, silver top, 5" 240.00
Tumbler, Primrose intaglio, 3¾", 6 for 600.00
Vase, cut fruit & leaves, petal rim, ftd flaring funnel shape, 10", EX ..120.00
Vase, cut hobstars, serrated/scalloped rim, trumpet shape, 14" 510.00
Vase, fine eng florals near top/on disk ft, stick form, 12" 325.00
Vase, floral intaglio to 4 sides, flared serrated rim, 12" 660.00
Vase, Vintage, cut/intaglio, sq w/flared rim, 10" 1,440.00

Twin Winton

Twin brothers Don and Ross Winton started this California-based company during the mid-1930s while still in high school. In the mid-1940s they shut it down while in the armed forces and started up again in the late 1940s, when older brother Bruce Winton joined them and bought them out in the early 1950s. The company became a major producer of cookie jars, kitchenware, and household items sold nationally until it closed its San Juan Capistrano location in 1977. They're also well known for their Hillbilly line — mugs, pitchers, bowls, lamps, ashtrays, decanters, and other novelty items, which evolved from the late 1940s through the

early 1970s with a variety of decorating methods still being discovered. Don Winton was the only designer for Twin Winton and created literally thousands of designs for them and hundreds of other companies. He is still sculpting in Corona del Mar, California, and collectors and dealers are continuing to find and document new pieces daily. To learn more about this subject, we recommend *Collector's Guide to Don Winton Designs* by our advisor, Mike Ellis; he is listed in the Directory under California.

Bank, Hotei, TW-411, 8".. 50.00
Bank, kitten, TW-415, 8"... 50.00
Bank, pig, TW-401, 8"... 50.00
Bank, poodle, TW-419, 8".. 65.00
Bookends, kitten, Expanimal, TW-126, 7½"................................... 125.00
Bowl, salad; Artist Palette Line, rare, 13" dia.................................. 250.00
Candleholder, El Greco, long, TW-500L, 5x9½", ea 15.00
Candleholder, Verdi, short, TW-501S, 4x6", ea............................... 12.00
Candy jar, Nut, w/2 squirrels, TW-353, 8x9" 75.00
Candy jar, Shack, TW-351, 6½x9½".. 65.00
Canister, House, Coffee; Canisterville, TW-103, 4x8" 75.00
Canister, House, Cookies; Canisterville, TW-40, 8x12".................. 175.00
Canister, House, Flour; Canisterville, TW-101, 7x11" 125.00
Cookie jar, Apple, TW-35, 8x11"... 180.00
Cookie jar, Baker, w/yel spatula & wht hat, TW-67, 7x11".......... 400.00
Cookie jar, Bear, no badge, TW-284, 7x12" 125.00
Cookie jar, Cookie Barn, TW-241, 8x12".. 175.00
Cookie jar, Cookie Cart, w/sitting donkey, TW-48, 7x12" 125.00
Cookie jar, Cookie Elf, TW-257, 8½x12".. 225.00
Cookie jar, Cop, TW-49, 7x12½"... 100.00
Cookie jar, Dog in Basket, TW-71, 8½x10" 85.00
Cookie jar, Duckling, TW-93, 8x11"... 250.00
Cookie jar, Dutch Girl, TW-247, 8½x12".. 225.00
Cookie jar, Grandma, TW-58, 7x10" 250.00
Cookie jar, Hobby Horse, TW-239, 8½x12" 300.00
Cookie jar, Hop-a-Long-Cassidy, w/gun, very rare, 15" 3,500.00

Cookie jar, Mopsy (Raggedy Ann), Collector's Series, San Juan Capistrano Calif., from $100.00 to $125.00. (Photo courtesy Fred and Joyce Roerig)

Cookie jar, Rooster, TW-268, 10x12" 125.00
Cookie jar, Sheriff, mouse in bl w/badge, TW-255, 8x11"............. 200.00
Creamer, Artist Palette Line, 4" dia 40.00
Cup, Artist Palette Line, 3" dia... 20.00
Decanter, Bowler, 300 Proof on base, #737, 11⅞".......................... 30.00
Decanter, Cowboy, Cactus Juice on base, #498, 12½" 75.00
Decanter, Pirate, Rum on base, #432, 11¾".................................... 50.00
Decanter, Santa Claus, Christmas Cheer on base, #510, 11" 40.00
Decanter, Scotsman, Scotch on base, #429, 11¾" 75.00
Figurine, Black boy holding teddy bear, T-13, 3½" 125.00
Figurine, cheerleader, red shirt & wht skirt, A-48, 5⅛" 15.00
Figurine, collie sitting, TW-602, 7½" 65.00
Figurine, girl playing in sand, T-12, 3½"...................................... 200.00

Figurine, Godey lady, layered pk gown, 2½" 60.00
Figurine, hunting dog, TW-601, 11" 85.00
Figurine, Mountain Man, w/hat, #760, 18½" 85.00
Figurine, Sam the Eagle, 12" 200.00
Figurine, Snow White holding flowers in apron, #603, 20¾" 50.00
Figurine, Standing Gnome, red hat, #545, 12½" 20.00
Figurine, Yogi Bear sitting on stump, 5" 150.00
Figurine, zebra, early, 5" 45.00
Flowerpot, girl w/red hat & flowers, A-44, 5¼" 12.00
Flowerpot, gnome w/watering can, A-36, 5⅛" 8.00
Ladies of the Mountain, stein, 8" 70.00
Lamp, Bambi, TW-254, 11" 175.00
Lamp, cat & fiddle, TW-252, 11" 175.00
Men of the Mountain, ice bucket, bathing, TW-31, 7½x16" 450.00
Men of the Mountain, ice bucket, suspenders, TW-30, 7½x14" ... 250.00
Men of the Mountain, punch bowl, 12", +8 cups 350.00
Men of the Mountain, stein, H-103, 8" 40.00
Miniature, cow, all brn, #450, 2" 11.00
Miniature, lazy burro, #311, 2" 8.00
Miniature, squirrel, sm & brn, #318, 1¾" 8.00
Mug, lamb, TW-502, 3¼" 85.00
Mug, owl, w/glasses, TW-501, 3¼" 85.00
Napkin holder, dog, TW-451, 6x4" 150.00
Napkin holder, owl, w/glasses, TW-472, 7x5" 65.00
Napkin holder, poodle, TW-474, 7x7" 75.00
Napkin holder, potbellied stove, TW-488, 7x5" 75.00
Napkin holder, rabbit, TW-452, 6x4" 150.00
Napkin holder, rooster, TW-483, 7x6" 75.00
Ornament, Christmas; flying angel w/trumpet, A-130, 3⅝" 4.00
Ornament, Christmas; girl elf holding doll, A-63, 3⅝" 8.00
Ornament, Christmas; Santa w/bag, A-53, 5⅝" 6.00
Planter, Bambi, TW-325, 8" 50.00
Planter, squirrel, TW-329, 8" 50.00
Shakers, butler, TW-160, pr 50.00
Shakers, cow, TW-169, pr 50.00
Shakers, foo dog, TW-151, pr 125.00
Shakers, friar, TW-185, pr 35.00
Shakers, frog, TW-175, pr 125.00
Shakers, Gunfighter Rabbit, TW-187, pr 45.00
Shakers, hillbilly couple, 4", pr 40.00
Shakers, lamb, TW-166, pr 30.00
Shakers, mouse, TW-181, pr 40.00
Shakers, Persian kitten, TW-144, pr 40.00
Shakers, Sailor Mouse, TW-163, pr 40.00
Spoon rest, elephant, w/hat, TW-13, 5x10" 40.00
Spoon rest, kitten TW-15, 5x10" 40.00
Wall pocket, puppy (head), TW-303 .... 100.00

Typewriters

The first commercially successful typewriter was the Sholes and Glidden, introduced in 1874. By 1882 other models appeared, and by the 1890s dozens were on the market. At the time of the First World War, the ranks of typewriter makers thinned, and by the 1920s only a few survived.

Collectors informally divide typewriter history into the pioneering period, up to about 1890; the classic period, from 1890 to 1920; and the modern period, since 1920. There are two broad classifications of early typewriters: (1) Keyboard machines, in which depression of a key prints a character and via a shift key prints up to three different characters per key; (2) Index machines, in which a chart of all the characters appears on the typewriter; the character is selected by a pointer or dial and is printed by operation of a lever or other device. Even though index type-writers were simpler and more primitive than keyboard machines, they were none-the-less a later development, designed to provide a cheaper alternative to the standard keyboard models that were selling for upwards of $100.00. Eventually second-hand keyboard typewriters supplied the low-price customer, and index typewriters vanished except as toys. Both classes of typewriters appeared in a great many designs.

It is difficult, if not impossible, to assign standard market prices to early typewriters. Over the past decade, competition from a handful of wealthy overseas collectors drastically affected the American market, but now Americans are among the top bidders. This surge in interest has resulted in much higher prices on the rarer models. Some auction-realized prices have been astronomical. We have updated values to reflect current market activity. Bear in mind that condition is a very important factor, and typewriters can vary infinitely in condition. Another factor to consider is that an early typewriter achieves its value mainly through the skill, effort, and patience of the collector who restores it to its original condition, in which case its purchase price is insignificant. Some unusual-looking early typewriters are not at all rare or valuable, while some very ordinary-looking ones are scarce and could be quite valuable. No general rules apply. See Clubs, Newsletters, and Catalogs in the Directory for information on the Early Typewriter Collectors Association. When no condition is indicated, the items listed below are assumed to be in excellent, unrestored condition.

Bennett (junior), 3-row, type wheel, ink roller 100.00
Blickensderfer #7, 3-row, type wheel 65.00
Burnett, 4-row, front-strike, 1908 .... 800.00
Century 10, 3-row, front-strike 50.00
Commercial Visible Fountain, 3-row, type wheel 500.00
Densmore #1b, 4-row, up-strike 200.00
Densmore #5, 4-row, up-strike 100.00
Famos, circular index 500.00
Fox Sterling, 3-row, front-strike 150.00
Franklin #7, curved 3-row keyboard, gilt transfers, 1891 .... 650.00
Franklin Type I, 3-row, curved keyboard, down-strike, decal on front ... 500.00
Hall #5767, Pat Mar 1881, mahog case, 15" L 350.00
Hammond Model I, curved w/ebony 'piano' keys, bentwood case, 1883 . 1,295.00
Hammond Multiplex Model 26, str 3-row keyboard, oak case, 14" . 120.00
Helios, 2-row, type wheel, 3rd shift key 300.00
Molle #3, blk, 3-row, front-strike 75.00
Monarch #2, 4-row, front-strike 30.00
Odell, rnd NP baseplate, sliding-type selector, 1890, 10" 325.00
Pittsburg Visible #10, 4-row, front-strike 200.00

Rem-Blick, in original wooden case, 12", EX, $165.00. (Photo courtesy Morphy Auctions)

Salter #6, 3-row, down-strike, 2 pillars on side of fr 350.00
Sampo, type-sleeve/linear index 700.00
Sampson Permograph, 4-row, type-wheel 250.00
Saturn, cable/key index, minimum value 1,000.00
Velograph, circular index, Swiss 1,000.00
World Type Write, Typewriter Improvement Co, Pat 1886, EX in case ... 380.00

Uhl Pottery

Founded in Evansville, Indiana, in 1849 by German immigrants, the Uhl Pottery was moved to Huntingburg, Indiana, in 1908 because of the more suitable clay available there. They produced stoneware — Acorn Ware jugs, crocks, and bowls — which were marked with the acorn logo and 'Uhl Pottery.' They also made mugs, pitchers, and vases in simple shapes and solid glazes marked with a circular ink stamp containing the name of the pottery and 'Huntingburg, Indiana.' The pottery closed in the mid-1940s. Those seeking additional information about Uhl pottery are encouraged to contact the Uhl Collectors' Society, whose address is listed in the Directory under Clubs, Newsletters, and Catalogs. For more information, we recommend *Uhl Pottery* by Anna Mary Feldmeyer and Kara Holtzman (Collector Books).

Animal, frog, open mouth, 6" 375.00
Animal, Scottie dog, solid blk, 6½" 450.00
Animal, turtle, pencil holder, 5½" 850.00
Ashtray, dog beside fire plug, brn, 4x5¼" 385.00
Bank, jug shaped, AG Abernathy...General Merchandise, 4½" ... 230.00
Basket, hanging; bl, basketweave decor, 5x4" 90.00
Bottle, elephant figural, bl, 3½" 100.00
Chicken feeder, UCO Feeder stamped in bl on wht stoneware 90.00
Churn, #6, stoneware, 18x10" 175.00
Cooler, Ice Tea, advertising, acorn mk, 3-gal 600.00
Crock, #3, 3-gal, 11" 50.00
Crock, #5, bl acorn on wht stoneware, 5-gal 90.00
Flower frog, bl-gr, 3½x2⅜" 110.00
Flowerpot, burgundy, 3 buttress ft, 3¾" 50.00
Jug, brn over wht, bl acorn, 6¾", NM 315.00
Jug, canteen; Army Air Corp insignia on wht, mini, 3½" 55.00
Jug, canteen; mustard yel, 7½x7½" 65.00
Jug, canteen; polar bear emb on pk, ca 1959, 8½x8", NM ... 100.00
Jug, Christmas, 1939 .... 260.00
Jug, speckled turq, ball form, #175, 1-pt 55.00
Novelty, football, dk brn, 3⅜" H 110.00
Pitcher, bl, #197, 7x8" 65.00
Pitcher, bl overflow on lt bl, wht int, mini, 2¼" 55.00
Pitcher, grapes emb on bl, #182, 7", from $65 to 95.00
Pitcher, Lincoln, portrait emb on bl, wht int, 1-qt, 6½", $140 to .. 165.00
Pitcher, Lincoln portrait emb on bl, 4½", from $95 to 125.00

Teapot, brown gloss, #143, eight-cup, 6", $125.00.

Vase, turq fan form, #157, 5" 75.00
Wren house, bl, att, 7x6" 110.00

Unger Brothers

Art Nouveau silver items of the highest quality were produced by Unger Brothers, who operated in Newark, New Jersey, from the early 1880s until 1919. In addition to tableware, they also made brushes, mirrors, powder boxes, and the like for milady's dressing table as well as jewelry and small personal accessories such as match safes and flasks. They often marked their products with a circle seal containing an intertwined 'UB' and '925 fine sterling.' Some Unger pieces contain a patent date near the mark. In addition to sterling, a very limited amount of gold was also used. Note: This company made no pewter items; Unger designs may occasionally be found in pewter, but these are copies. Items with English hallmarks or signed 'Birmingham' are English (not Unger).

Bowl, Nouveau foliage, scalloped rim, 1⅝x5¾" 110.00
Bowl, violet; Nouveau floral, 2½x9¼" 525.00
Brush, lint; repousse floral hdl, 5½x2⅝x¼" 225.00
Brush, vanity; Art Nouveau flowers/monogram, Pat Appl'd For, 4¼" .. 60.00
Button hook, lady w/flowing hair/floral repousse, 7¾" 195.00
Button hook, Love's Dream, 1904 .... 45.00
Ink eraser (desk pc), lady w/flowing hair, 6x1⅛" 125.00
Match safe, emb figures, ca 1900 .... 210.00
Match safe, Indian chief w/full headdress, ca 1905, 2¼x1⅞" 900.00
Napkin ring, 4-leaf clover, ca 1890-1900, 28 grams 355.00
Perfume, lay-down; clear glass w/ornate silver top, pre-1911, 3¾" .. 225.00
Spoon, preserves; Passaic, ca 1900, 7¼" 85.00
Sugar tongs, Narcissus, ca 1900 .... 65.00
Teaspoon, Cupid's Nosegay, 1904, 6" 35.00
Teaspoon, Narcissus, 1901, 6" 32.00
Thimble holder, silver repousse w/openwork, 1⅛x1" dia ... 225.00
Wallet, angels/cherubs silverwork on leather, 4½x3¼"(closed) 265.00

University City

Located in University City, Missouri, this pottery was open for only five years (1910 – 1915), but because of the outstanding potters associated with it, produced notable artware. The company's founder was Edward Gardner Lewis, and among the well-known artists he employed were Adelaide Robineau, Fredrick Rhead, Taxile Doat, and Julian Zsolnay.

Bowl, wide trees frieze, brn/gray on ivory, dtd 1911, 3½x8", VG . 3,100.00
Dish, sea life, bl/pk/wht crackle, emb shell, 3 ft w/jewels, TD, 3x5" ... 1,200.00
Jar, cafe-au-lait, ruffled uptrn lid collar, EG Lewis, 2¾x2", EX 480.00
Trivet, Atascadero Nymph of Springs (lady's head), lt bl, Doat, 5" dia ... 420.00
Vase, bl/olive gr flambe on porc, spherical, sm opening, M/EL, 5x5" . 4,440.00
Vase, celadon crystalline, spherical w/tiny neck, CU/1913, 5x5" .. 16,800.00
Vase, purple/gr/ivory drip glaze, shouldered, #1178, 5½" 1,200.00
Vase, stylized cvd blossoms/leaves, unglazed, cylindrical, 9x3" .. 1,020.00
Vase, stylized cvd trees, gray/dk gr mottled matt, att Rhead, 7", NM .. 4,800.00
Vase, wht/lt bl/gr full-blown crystals on yel, rstr, 7x4" 960.00

Val St. Lambert

Since its inception in Belgium at the turn of the nineteenth century, the Val St. Lambert Cristalleries has been involved in the production of high-quality glass, producing some cameo. The factory is still in production.

Cameo

Bowl, flowering vine, purple on frost, 5x5" 1,100.00
Vase, bud; bumblebees/pussy willows, red & amber to clear, 15" .. 3,650.00
Vase, floral, burgundy on pk frost, bulbous base, 11¾" 360.00
Vase, floral w/leaves, pk on frost, flared cylinder, 5¾" 135.00
Vase, leaves & berries, pk on frost, dbl gourd form, 10⅜" .. 1,500.00
Vase, orchid & foliage, coral pk on textured aqua, 8⅜" 425.00

Miscellaneous

Bowl, swirled triangle shape, low, 8" W 36.00
Candlesticks, triangular graduated design, 9½", pr 180.00
Figurine, dog seated, crystal, 6½" 48.00
Vase, cut crystal, 6-sided ft, 10¼" 120.00
Vase, cut crystal dmns, flared cylinder, 9" 75.00
Vase, cut crystal w/amethyst bands, 13½x9" 215.00

Valentines

If you are one of the many new collectors of valentine cards, welcome to the club. You can still have a wonderful time collecting valentines even on a tight budget, but as your collection expands, so must your budget. In a field so diverse, it is best to pick a category you might like and take it from there. But beware of restoration work! With the fabulous digital images available on the market today, you could possibly buy a card with a digitally reproduced image. Be cautious, but have fun. When you purchase a valentine, always keep these factors in mind: age, category, size, manufacturer, country of origin, artist signature, and condition. Our advisor for this category is Katherine Kreider. Books written by Kreider include *Valentines With Values*, *One Hundred Years of Valentines*, and *Valentines for the Eclectic Collector*. She is listed in the Directory under Pennsylvania. Values are for examples in excellent condition, showing no wear, fading, creases, or repair.

Key:
D — dimension   PIG — printed/published in Germany
dim — dimension/dimensional   HCPP — honeycomb paper puff

Dim, 1-D, dbl, swan sleigh, PIG, early 1900s, 8x6x3½" 150.00
Dim, 1-D, Love Boat, 1920s, 8½x11x2" 50.00
Dim, 1-D, swan carriage, comes in pk & bl, 1930s, 8½x10¾x3" 50.00
Dim, 3-D, butterfly w/fan, ca 1915, 5x3" 75.00
Dim, 4-D, cannon, early 1900s, PIG, 6x6½x3½" 150.00
Dim, 4-D, red Cinderella-type carriage, 1920s, 7¼x8x2¾" 75.00
Flat, African-Am children holding hands, Hallmark, 1940s, 4¼x4¼"...10.00
Flat, bear, honey, beehive, USA, 1940s, 3¾x2¾" 6.00
Flat, dog & cat, flocked, easel bk, Hallmark, 1940s, 8½x7" 10.00
Flat, Indians in canoe, 1940s, 4x5" 10.00
Flat, Rosie the Riveter, 1940s, 3½x3" 20.00
Flat, Uncle Sam, chromo litho, 1920s, 3½x3" 20.00
Flat w/dim, children w/flower basket, R Tuck, 1900s, PIG, 7½x8" ...75.00
Flat w/dim, Dutch girl, R Tuck & Sons, early 1900s, PIG, 9¼x5".. 75.00
Flat w/dim, vase die-cut w/emb HCPP flowers, 1900s, PIG, 22x18"... 95.00
Folded-flat, Asian children, USA, 4x3½x5" 15.00
Folded-flat, Little Red Riding Hood, 1940s, 4x5¼" 20.00
Folded-flat, Olive Oyl, USA, 1930s, 6½x6" 35.00
Folded-flat, roller coaster, USA, 1940s, 4x6" 15.00
Folded-flat, schnauzer, 6x5½" 15.00
Greeting card, Esther Howland, Worcester MA, 1840s, 7x4½" ... 350.00
Greeting card, Geo C Whitney, Worcester MA, 1870s, 3¾x3" 75.00
Greeting card, Kewpie, Rose O'Neill, Gibson, ca 1910-20, 6¼x4" ...95.00
Greeting card, Mary Had a Little Lamb, by Stanley, USA, 1950s, 6" ..10.00
Greeting card, St Valentine's Greeting, emb, early 1900s, 6x4½" .. 10.00
Greeting card, Thistle Scottie dog, 1940s, 4x3¾"......................8.00
HCPP, cherub flower basket, Beistle, 1920s, 10x7x3¾" 75.00
HCPP, flower basket w/dachshunds, PIG, 1920s, 12x8x3½" 75.00
HCPP, Gone w/the Wind lamp, PIG, early 1900s, 6½x2½x2½"... 125.00
HCPP, parasol, die-cut scrap accents, PIG, early 1900s, 14x8x6½" .. 150.00
HCPP, phonograph, PIG, early 1900s, 10½x8x4" 175.00
Mechanical-flat, ace of hearts, PIG, 1920s, 7x5¼", EX................. 35.00
Mechanical-flat, African-Am washwoman, easel bk, 1900s, 6¾x4¼"..75.00

Mechanical-flat, Blue Fairy, Disney, 1939, 5x4¾" 40.00
Mechanical-flat, Bohemian under palm tree, PIG, 1920s, 8½x4" .. 30.00
Mechanical-flat, Boston bull terrier, easel bk, 1930s, 9¾x4½" 50.00
Mechanical-flat, cowboy, USA, 1920s, 6½x4" 15.00
Mechanical-flat, dapper golfer, A-Tee, PIG, 1920s, 6½x4½" 35.00
Mechanical-flat, lady w/powder puff sits at vanity, USA, 1940s, 4x4" .20.00
Mechanical-flat, Wall St stockbroker, PIG, 1930s, 4½x3½" 25.00
Novelty, Love Boat, plastic w/orig lollipop, 5½x6x1¼" 50.00
Novelty, squeak toy, spaniel dog, PIG, early 1900s, 6½x5" 75.00
Novelty, Valentine book, Happy Times w/Jack & Jane, hardbk, 1934-39 . 75.00
Postcard, animals dressed, emb, PIG, mid-1900s 15.00
Postcard, cherub spinning web, Clapsaddle 15.00
Postcard, embr silk, From a Loving Heart, Fr, 1910-15 .... 15.00
Postcard, hold-to-light, cherub, emb, PIG, early 1900s 75.00
Postcard, mechanical, Forget-me-knot, Internat'l Publishing, mid-1900s.. 20.00

Vallerysthal

Fine glassware has been produced in Vallerysthal, France, since the middle of the nineteenth century.

Vase, cameo bees/hives/branches on gr textured cylinder, 8" 460.00
Vase, cameo daffodils, burgundy on lt bl, concave cylinder, 12".. 2,040.00
Vase, cameo irises/butterfly, bl/wine on gr texture w/gilt, 14"....2,650.00
Vase, cameo morning glories, dk amethyst on lt gr frost, 10" 2,040.00
Vase, cameo vines/dragonflies, appl serpent at long neck, 13"...1,250.00
Vase, floral, mc enamel on gr frost, cylindrical, 13" 2,760.00
Vase, Roman maid/warrier, gilt/acid-relief panels on pk, cone form, 6" ...2,160.00

Van Briggle

The Van Briggle Pottery of Colorado Springs, Colorado, was established in 1901 by Artus Van Briggle, whose early career had been shaped by such notables as Karl Langenbeck and Maria Nichols Storer. His quest for several years had been to perfect a completely flat matt glaze, and upon accomplishing his goal, he opened his pottery. His wife, Anne, worked with him, and they, along with George Young, were responsible for the modeling of the wares. Their work typified the flow and form of the Art Nouveau movement, and the shapes they designed played as important a part in their success as their glazes. Some of their most famous pieces were Despondency, Lorelei, and Toast Cup. Increasing demand for their work soon made it necessary to add to their quarters as well as their staff. Although much of the ware was eventually made from molds, each piece was carefully trimmed and refined before the glaze was sprayed on. Their most popular colors were Persian Rose, Ming Blue, and Mustard Yellow.

Van Briggle died in 1904, but the work was continued by his wife. New facilities were built; and by 1908, in addition to their artware, tiles, gardenware, and commercial lines were added. By the '20s the emphasis had shifted from art pottery to novelties and commercial wares. Reproductions of some of the early designs continue to be made. The double AA mark has always been in use, but after 1920 the dates and/or shape numbers were dropped. Mention should be made here as well that the Anna Van Briggle glaze is a later line which was made between 1956 and 1968. Our advisor for this category is Michelle Ross; she is listed in the Directory under Michigan. For more information, we recommend *The Collector's Encyclopedia of Van Briggle Art Pottery* by Richard Sasicki and Josie Fania (Collector Books).

Bowl, leaves, med/dk gr, 1916, 2½x10" 1,440.00
Bowl, tulips (4) form corners, gr, 3x8½x5" 125.00
Candleholders, dbl; Persian Rose, 4½", pr........................... 125.00
Candlesticks, tulip form, dk gray to red, pr 100.00

Covered dish, turtle figural, brn & gr gloss, Anna Van Briggle, 2x7" ...75.00
Paperweight, rabbit, gray to red, 1922-26, 2½" 300.00
Paperweight, rabbit, Ming Turquoise, 2⅞" 50.00
Pitcher, no emb, gr, bulbous, 4", from $80 to 110.00
Planter, conch shell, turq, 3⅝" 85.00
Sculpture, cat, blk gloss, Anna Van Briggle, 16" 150.00
Sculpture, Indian chief w/full headdress, turq, #186, 1979, 11½"..215.00
Sculpture, Indian maiden grinding corn, Ming Turquoise, 5⅜"....200.00
Shakers, flower emb, dusty rose, 2½", pr.................................100.00
Tile, trees/mtn range, 5-color cuenca, in Arts & Crafts fr, 6"....2,640.00
Vase, abstract floral, frothy bl, #654, 1908-11, 4x4" 840.00
Vase, bl-gray feathered brn, 1905, 8½x4" 1,440.00
Vase, bud; stemmed trefoils, purple/gr on celadon, #121, 1903, 7" ..3,900.00
Vase, calla lilies w/cutouts, sage gr, C Stevenson, #89, 12x5".......375.00
Vase, chartreuse, bottle shape, #39OE, 1902, 3x3" 1,560.00
Vase, dbl bud; mustard w/blk, wht at rim, Anna Van Briggle, 6½"...30.00
Vase, Despondency, nude atop, turq, D Ruff, no #, 1980s, 17x8" ..250.00
Vase, floral, maroon w/dk gr, Anna Van Briggle, 10" 650.00
Vase, flower buds/vines, celadon, shouldered, #88-15/70, 3x4" .2,350.00
Vase, frothy wht on blk gloss, Anna Van Briggle, 3⅝x6"...............48.00
Vase, gr (curdled), very bulbous w/rim hdls, 1903, 3" 12,000.00
Vase, leaves below rim, rose, 1920s, 5x10" 470.00
Vase, Lorelei, Ming Turquoise, 11¼" 300.00
Vase, Lorelei, Persian Rose, sgn BWL, no #, 11¼x4" 300.00
Vase, mistletoe, red/bl/gray flambe, strong detail, 1902, 6x3½" .3,480.00
Vase, morning glories, red/gr wash on gray, 1904, 11x5" 6,600.00
Vase, pansies, olive gr, globular, 3¾" 95.00
Vase, peacock feathers w/4 sm open hdls, Persian Rose, 1919, 14"...1,320.00
Vase, poppies, stems bent/leaves below, frothy purple/lt gr, 1903, 10"...5,700.00
Vase, poppy buds at rim, robin's egg bl, #21, 1906, 3½x4" 900.00
Vase, poppy stems on maroon & bl, post-1920, 8" 400.00
Vase, spade leaves in geometric panels, steel bl, 6½x6" 120.00
Vase, storks wrap shoulder, turq, Colo Spgs, no #, 18"..................345.00
Vase, stylized leaves, low hdls, burgundy to bl, 13¼" 150.00
Vase, triple bud; blk gloss, L Short, no #, 1980s, 7x4½"..................30.00
Vase, twisted form w/emb florals at top, purple to bl, 9" 220.00
Vase, woman cradles vase, wht, #85, 17x10"...............................450.00
Vase, 3 angels support globular form, turq, Stevenson, wood ped, 14x8" ...550.00

Van Erp, Dirk

Dirk van Erp was a Leeuwarden, Holland, coppersmith who emigrated to the United States in 1886 and began making decorative objects from artillery shell casings in the San Francisco shipyards. He opened a shop in 1908 in Oakland and in 1910 formed a brief one-year partnership with D'Arcy Gaw. Apprentices at the studio included his daughter Agatha and Harry Dixon, who was later to open his own shop in San Francisco. Gaw has been assigned design credit for many of the now famous hammered copper and mica lamp shade lamp forms. So popular were the lamps that other San Francisco craftspeople, Lillian Palmer, Fred Brosi, Hans Jauchen, and Old Mission Kopperkraft among them, began producing similar forms. In addition to lamps, he manufactured a broad range of objects including vases, bowls, desk sets, and smoking accessories. Van Erp's work is typically finely hammered with a deep red-brown patina and of good proportions. On rare occasions, van Erp created pieces in a 'warty' finish: an irregular, indeed lumpy, surface with a much redder appearance. Van Erp died in 1933. In 1929 the shop was taken over by his son, William, who produced hammered goods in both brass and copper. Many feature Art Deco-style designs and are of considerably lower value than his father's work. The van Erp mark is prominent and takes the form of a windmill above a rectangle that includes his name, sometimes D'Arcy Gaw's name, and sometimes San Francisco.

Please note: Cleaning or scrubbing original patinas diminishes the value of the object. Our prices are for examples with excellent original patina unless noted. Our advisor for this and related Arts and Crafts objects is Bruce Austin, he is listed in the Directory under New York.

Key: h/cp — hammered copper

Table lamp, mica shade, signed Dirk van Erp with a windmill, 18x17", EX, $18,400.00. (Photo courtesy James D. Julia Inc.)

Ash stand, h/cp, removable tray w/match holder, 31" 1,650.00
Bookends, h/cp, rectangle w/semicircle extension rtcl w/tree, 4x5" ...1,800.00
Bowl, center; SP h/cp w/curled hdls, ivory ball ft, 3½x19x12" 850.00
Bowl, h/cp, 7-lobed, ca 1915, 2⅝x9⅝" 500.00
Bowl, SP h/cp floriform, windmill mk, 1¾x14½" 1,200.00
Charger, h/cp, finger-shaped edge, 11½"..................................565.00
Fire screen, h/cp, 3-panel w/cut-out medallions, ball hinges 7,250.00
Jardiniere, h/cp w/warty finish, 6½x10½" 8,400.00
Lamp, boudoir; 12" h/cp & mica shade; h/cp bean pot base, 11"...7,750.00
Lamp, 17" 4-panel mica & h/cp flared shade w/rivets; pear-shape base..25,200.00
Lamp, 18" shade w/3 mica panels, h/cp tapered base, rfn, 20", NM..6,000.00
Vase, h/cp, bottle shape, lt cleaning, 6¾x3¼" 800.00
Vase, h/cp, bulbous, 4¼" 2,940.00
Vase, h/cp, warty w/wrinkled neck, scattered dk red blush, 9x7", M ...10,200.00
Vase, hp/c, sm shoulder, 8" 7,750.00
Wastebasket, woven willow, copper rivets, 13½x10½" dia.........2,500.00

Vance/Avon Faience

One of the many American potteries to evolve from a commercial ceramics plant, Vance Faience was organized in 1901 in Tiltonsville, Ohio, for the purpose of producing artistic and utilitarian wares. In 1902 the name was changed to The Avon Faience Company, with the talented William Jervis serving as manager and designer. His British colleague, Frederick Rhead, left England at his behest to join him there. Together they completely revamped the design direction of the company, transforming Victorian shapes and motifs into streamlined Arts & Crafts vases with squeeze-bag and sgraffito decoration.

In yet another reorganization, the company was incorporated at the end of 1902 with three potteries from nearby West Virginia as the Wheeling Potteries Company. This change of management encouraged the rapid manufacture of commercial wares, which hastened the departure of Jervis and Rhead. Artware production stopped altogether in 1905.

Marks include several versions of 'Vance' and 'Avon.' Our advisors for this category are Suzanne Perrault and David Rago; they are listed in the Directory under New Jersey.

Cookie jar, floral, HP/pks, MR Avon, 7x6½" 960.00
Jard & ped, abstract sgraffito/squeeze-bag devices, Rhead, 39", VG ...8,000.00
Jardiniere, stylized trees, 3 bar-like hdls, style of Rhead, 13", VG....600.00
Vase, allover mums, HP brn/gr on yel, M/FHR, bottle form, Avon, 9x6" ..1,200.00
Vase, broad leaves/flowers, gr/aqua on indigo, spherical, 4", NM ..660.00
Vase, chrysanthemum, yel/gr/brn, F Rhead, M/FHR, 8½x6" 1,200.00

Vase, floral (squeeze-bag), bl/ivory on tan, doughnut neck, 4½x6"..**330.00**
Vase, Nouveau floral, att FH Rhead, E125/1005, bulbous base, Avon, 6"..**825.00**
Vase, stylized landscape, dbl-bulb body widens at base, Rhead, 5"....**1,175.00**
Vase, tulip repeats, cvd/pnt, bl/gr, squat w/bulbous collar, Avon, 5" ...**420.00**
Vase, 4 mermaids/sea creatures emb on tan to brn, #118, 12x10"....**900.00**

Vaseline

Vaseline, a greenish-yellow colored glass produced by adding uranium oxide to the batch, was produced during the Victorian era. It was made in smaller quantities than other colors and lost much of its popularity with the advent of the electric light. It was used for pressed tablewares, vases, whimseys, souvenir items, oil lamps, perfume bottles, drawer pulls, and doorknobs. Pieces have been reproduced, and some factories still make it today in small batches. Vaseline glass will fluoresce under an ultraviolet light.

Bowl, centerpc; 3 lg scallops, sm ft, 4½x12" **40.00**
Bowl, flared rim, starburst center well, 1¾x7⅝" **50.00**
Butter dish, star pattern in base, gold trim, beaded rim, 5x7¾" dia ..**90.00**
Candleholders, trefoil shape, crackle finish, pr **35.00**
Candlesticks, barley-twist column, 6-petal bobeche, 9¼x4¼", pr .. **75.00**
Candy dish, HP floral, star-pattern base, 3-ftd, w/lid, 5x5½" **75.00**
Car vases, 6", pr.. **150.00**
Fishbowl, swirled body, rnded pillow form, 15½" **525.00**
Jar, brass filigree w/jewels, thistle finial, 5x4½" dia **360.00**
Pitcher, Finecut, Bryce Bros, 1870s, 8½" **145.00**
Plate, plain, flared rim, 7¼" **15.00**
Toothpick holder, Ranson w/gold band, Riverside, 2½" **30.00**

Verlys

Verlys art glass, produced in France after 1931 by the Holophane Company of Verlys, was made in crystal with acid-finished relief work in the Art Deco style. Colored and opalescent glass was also used. In 1935 an American branch was opened in Newark, Ohio, where very similar wares were produced until the factory ceased production in 1951. French Verlys was signed with one of three mold-impressed script signatures, all containing the company name and country of origin. The American-made glassware was signed 'Verlys' only, either scratched with a diamond-tipped pen or impressed in the mold. There is very little if any difference in value between items produced in France and America. Though some seem to feel that the French should be higher priced (assuming it to be scarce), many prefer the American-made product. In June of 1955, about 16 Verlys molds were leased to the A.H. Heisey Company. Heisey's versions were not signed with the Verlys name, so if an item is unsigned it is almost certainly a Heisey piece. The molds were returned to Verlys of America in July 1957. Fenton now owns all Verlys molds, but all issues are marked Fenton.

Bonbon, butterflies on lid, amber frost, 2½x6½" **150.00**
Bowl, centerpc; birds & bees, clear & frosted, 12" **125.00**
Bowl, poppies & leaves, clear & frosted, 2¾x13½" **275.00**
Bowl, radiating flower-like pattern, clear & frosted w/sepia, 12" ..**275.00**
Bowl, Water Lilies, clear & frosted, 13½" **240.00**
Charger, birds (3) soar above fish in sea, sapphire bl, 13½" **350.00**
Ice bucket, ladies pouring water/herons, clear & frosted, 8" **150.00**
Powder dish, floral bouquet on lid, clear & frosted, 7" dia, NM ... **125.00**
Vase, forest scene relief, amber, U-form, att, 10" **780.00**
Vase, Grasshopper (or moths), clear w/lt gray tint, 5x4½" **150.00**
Vase, Jem (floral blossoms), wht opal, 6¼" **200.00**
Vase, Lance, clear & frosted, 7¾" **265.00**
Vase, mermaids, wht opal, ca 1930, 10x9" **950.00**
Vase, Oriental man in garden w/flowers, clear & frosted, 9⅛" **165.00**

Vase, pineapples/leaves, opal, swollen cylinder, 10" **575.00**
Vase, wildflowers, fiery wht opal, 7½" **130.00**

Vernon Kilns

Vernon Potteries Ltd. was established by Faye G. Bennison in Vernon, California, in 1931. The name was later changed to Vernon Kilns; until it closed in 1958, dinnerware, specialty plates, artware, and figurines were their primary products. Among its wares most sought after by collectors today are items designed by such famous artists as Rockwell Kent, Walt Disney, Don Blanding, Jane Bennison, and May and Vieve Hamilton. Our advisor for this category is Ray Vlach; he is listed in the Directory under Illinois.

Chatelaine Shape

This designer pattern by Sharon Merrill was made in four color variations: Topaz, Bronze, decorated Platinum, and Jade.

Bowl, serving; Topaz or Bronze, 9", from $25 to.............................. **35.00**
Coffee cup, flat base, decor Platinum & Jade, from $15 to **20.00**
Plate, dinner; leaf 1 corner, Topaz & Bronze, 10½", from $15 to.... **17.00**
Plate, salad; Topaz & Bronze, 7½", from $12 to **15.00**
Sugar bowl, Topaz & Bronze, w/lid, from $20 to **30.00**
Teapot, decor Platinum & Jade, from $200 to.............................. **300.00**

Lotus and Pan American Lei Shape

Patterns on this shape include Lotus, Chinling, and Vintage. Pan American Lei was a variation with flatware from the San Marino line. To evaluate Lotus, use the low end of our range as the minimum value; the high end of values apply to Pan American Lei.

Ashtray, Pan American Lei only, 5½" **35.00**
Bowl, chowder; 6", from $10 to **18.00**
Butter tray, oblong, w/lid, from $35 to **60.00**
Coffee/teapot, 8-cup, from $35 to... **80.00**
Mug, 9-oz, from $15 to **35.00**
Plate, chop/coupe; Pan American Lei only, 13"............................. **50.00**
Plate, coupe; Pan American Lei only, 6" **12.00**
Tumbler, #5, 14-oz, from $18 to.. **35.00**

Melinda Shape

Patterns found on this shape are Arcadia, Beverly, Blossom Time, Chintz, Cosmos, Dolores, Fruitdale, Hawaii (Lei Lani on Melinda is two and a half times base value), May Flower, Monterey, Native California, and Philodendron. Two patterns, Rosedale and Wheat, were made for Sears, Roebuck & Co. and marked with Sears Harmony House backstamp. The more elaborate the pattern, the higher the value.

Bowl, lug chowder; 6", from $12 to **18.00**
Bowl, serving; rnd, 9", from $15 to **25.00**
Butter tray, oblong, w/lid, from $45 to **75.00**
Pitcher, 1½-pt, from $25 to... **45.00**
Plate, chop; 12", from $15 to **30.00**
Platter, 12", from $20 to.. **30.00**
Relish, single leaf shape, 12", from $20 to..................................... **25.00**
Shakers, pr from $15 to **25.00**

Monticeto Shape (and Coronado)

This was one of the company's most utilized shapes — well over

200 patterns have been documented. Among the most popular are the solid colors, plaids, the florals, westernware, and the Bird and Turnbull series. Bird, Turnbull, and Winchester 73 (Frontier Days) are two to four times base values. Disney hollow ware is seven to eight times base values. Plaids (except Tweed and Calico), solid colors, Brown-eyed Susan are represented by the lower range.

Ashtray, 5½" dia, from $15 to	20.00
Bowl, rim soup; 8½", from $12 to	15.00
Bowl, salad; rnd, 10½", from $40 to	50.00
Coaster, ridged, 3¾", from $18 to	22.00
Coaster/cup warmer, 4½", from $15 to	25.00
Jam jar, notched lid, 5", from $65 to	95.00
Muffin tray, tab hdls, dome lid, 9", from $50 to	75.00
Plate, grill; 11", from $25 to	30.00
Plate, salad; 7½", from $8 to	12.00
Spoon holder, from $45 to	75.00
Tumbler, #4, bulb bottom, 3¾", from $18 to	25.00

San Clemente (Anytime) Shape

Patterns you will find on this shape include Tickled Pink, Heavenly Days, Anytime, Imperial, Sherwood, Frolic, Young in Heart, Rose-A-Day, and Dis 'N Dot.

Bowl, chowder; 6", from $8 to	12.00
Bowl, fruit; 5½", from $5 to	8.00
Bowl, vegetable; 7½", from $10 to	12.00
Butter pat, 2½", from $30 to	40.00
Butter tray, w/lid, from $25 to	35.00
Cup & saucer, tea; from $8 to	12.00
Gravy boat, from $15 to	20.00
Plate, dinner; 10", from $8 to	12.00
Plate, salad; 7½", from $7 to	10.00
Platter, 11", from $14 to	20.00
Shakers, pr from $12 to	20.00
Syrup, drip-cut top, from $45 to	65.00
Sugar bowl, w/lid, from $15 to	25.00
Tumbler, 14-oz, from $12 to	25.00

San Fernando Shape

Known patterns for this shape are Desert Bloom, Early Days, Hibiscus, R.F.D., Vernon's 1860, and Vernon Rose.

Bowl, fruit; 5½", from $8 to	12.00
Bowl, mixing; RFD only, 5", from $15 to	19.00
Bowl, mixing; RFD only, 9", from $30 to	40.00
Bowl, serving; oval, 10", from $20 to	25.00
Coaster, RFD only, ridged, 3¾", from $18 to	22.00
Cup & saucer, AD; from $16 to	26.00
Platter, 14", from $35 to	50.00
Shakers, pr from $16 to	24.00
Tumbler, RFD only, style #5, 14-oz, from $20 to	25.00

San Marino Shape

Known patterns for this shape are Barkwood, Bel Air, California Originals, Casual California, Gayety, Hawaiian Coral, Heyday, Lei Lani (two and a half times base values), Mexicana, Pan American Lei (two and a half times base values), Raffia, Seven Seas, Shadow Leaf, Shantung, Sun Garden, and Trade Winds. The Mojave pattern was produced for Montgomery Ward, Wheat Rose for Belmar China Co.

Bowl, mixing; 5", from $15 to	18.00
Bowl, mixing; 6", from $15 to	22.00
Butter pat, ind; 2½", from $12 to	18.00
Casserole, w/lid, 8" dia, from $35 to	65.00
Creamer, regular, from $10 to	12.00

Trade Winds, cup, Colossal, from $95.00 to $150.00.

Cup, jumbo; from $20 to	30.00
Flowerpot, 3", from $20 to	25.00
Plate, salad; 7½", from $8 to	12.00
Platter, 9½", from $10 to	15.00

Transitional (Year 'Round) Shape

Patterns on this shape include Country Cousin, Lollipop Tree, Blueberry Hill, and Year 'Round.

Bowl, vegetable; 9", from $12 to	17.00
Butter tray, w/lid, from $25 to	35.00
Coffeepot, 6-cup, from from $25 to	45.00
Creamer, from $8 to	10.00
Gravy boat, from $18 to	25.00
Mug, 12-oz, from $12 to	20.00
Platter, 11", from $12 to	20.00
Shakers, pr from $12 to	15.00
Teacup & saucer, from $8 to	12.00
Teapot, from $25 to	50.00

Ultra Shape

More than 50 patterns were issued on this shape. Nearly all the artist-designed lines (Rockwell Kent, Don Blanding, and Disney) utilized Ultra. The shape was developed by Gale Turnbull, and many of the elaborate flower and fruit patterns can be credited to him as well; use the high end of our range as a minimum value for his work. For Frederick Lunning, use the mid range. For other artist patterns, use these formulae based on the high end: Blanding, 3x (Aquarium 5x); Disney, 5 – 7x; Kent — Moby Dick, 2 – 4x; Our America, 3 – 5x; Salamina, 5 – 7x.

Bowl, chowder; 6", from $12 to	20.00
Bowl, salad; 11", from $45 to	85.00
Casserole, w/lid, 8" inside, from $45 to	95.00
Creamer, ind; open, from $12 to	20.00
Muffin lid only (no tray), from $60 to	85.00
Mug, 8-oz, 3½", from $20 to	30.00
Plate, chop; 14", from $40 to	60.00
Plate, luncheon; 8½", from $15 to	20.00
Teapot, 6-cup, from $45 to	100.00

Fantasia and Disney Figures

Bowl, Winged Nymph, solid color, 2½x12"	300.00
Centaur, #31, from $1,000 to	1,200.00
Donkey Unicorn, #16, from $600 to	700.00

Elephant, #26, from $300 to 400.00
Ostrich, #28, #29 or #30, ea from $1,200 to 1,500.00
Pegasus, #21, from $200 to 300.00
Pegasus, Baby, blk, #19, from $250 to 300.00
Rearing Unicorn, #15, from $400 to 500.00
Unicorn sitting, #14, from $400 to 500.00
Vase, Winged Pegasus, w/decor, rare, 7½x12" 1,200.00

Specialty Ware

Ashtray, Detroit MI, red transfer of 7 structures, 5¾" 20.00
Figurine, Bette Davis, Janice Pettee, ca 1940, 10½" 1,200.00
Figurine, Paulette Goddard, Janice Pettee, #415, 1940, 10" 1,000.00
Figurine, Robert Preston as NW Mountie, Janice Pettee, 1940, 10" .. 1,000.00
Plate, Atlantic Charter, Roosevelt & Churchill portraits, 1942 .. 180.00
Plate, Austin TX, bl transfer, 10½" 50.00

Villeroy and Boch

The firm of Villeroy and Boch, located in Mettlach, Germany, was brought into being by the 1841 merger of three German factories — the Wallerfangen factory, founded by Nicholas Villeroy in 1787; and two potteries owned by Jean-Francois Boch, the earlier having been in operation there since 1748. Villeroy and Boch produced many varieties of wares, including earthenware with printed under-glaze designs which carried the well-known castle mark with the name 'Mettlach.' See also Mettlach.

Ash holder, hunter stands at edge, #2950, rpr, 7½x7" 300.00
Ashtray, monkey holding basket, glass eyes, brn tones, Dresden mk, 6" . 250.00
Bowl, monkey holding bowl, earth tones, 5x8" 150.00
Figurine, soldier w/snuff box, sm rpr, 7¼" 250.00
Paperweight, dwarf figural, majolica finish, 3¾x7", EX 250.00
Paperweight, dwarf on stomach, majolica, Dresden factory, 3x7x3", EX .. 245.00
Plate, Washington's Headquarters, Dresden, 6½x8½" 115.00
Punch bowl, pastoral scenes, floral band, ftd, 8½x17" 800.00
Tray, geometric in gr/bl/wht, rtcl metal border w/hdls, 1910, 20" L .. 325.00
Vase, stylized 3-color mushroom band, 4 dmn-emb buttresses, 21x11" .. 1,200.00

Vistosa

Vistosa was produced from about 1938 through the early 1940s. It was Taylor, Smith, and Taylor's answer to the very successful Fiesta line of their nearby competitor, Homer Laughlin. Vistosa was made in four solid colors: mango red, cobalt blue, light green, and deep yellow. 'Pie crust' edges and a dainty five-petal flower molded into handles and lid finials made for a very attractive yet nevertheless commercially unsuccessful product. Our advisor for this category is Ted Haun; he is listed in the Directory under Indiana.

Bowl, cereal; 6¾" 22.00
Bowl, cream soup; from $22 to 28.00
Bowl, fruit; 5¾", from $15 to 18.00
Bowl, salad; ftd, 12", from $200 to 225.00
Bowl, soup; lug hdl, from $30 to 35.00
Bowl, 3x9¼", from $35 to 40.00
Chop plate, 12", from $35 to 50.00
Chop plate, 15", from $40 to 55.00
Coffee cup, AD; from $40 to 50.00
Coffee saucer, AD; from $10 to 15.00
Creamer, from $20 to 25.00
Egg cup, ftd, from $50 to 70.00
Jug, water; 2-qt, from $120 to 150.00

Plate, 6", cobalt 25.00
Plate, 6", from $12 to 15.00
Plate, 7", from $14 to 18.00
Plate, 9", from $15 to 20.00
Plate, 10", from $35 to 45.00
Platter, 13", from $40 to 50.00
Sauceboat, from $175 to 200.00
Shakers, pr from $25 to 32.00
Sugar bowl, w/lid 25.00
Teacup & saucer, from $18 to 22.00
Teapot, 6-cup, from $190 to 225.00

Volkmar

Charles Volkmar established a workshop in Tremont, New York, in 1882. He produced artware decorated under the glaze in the manner of the early Barbotine work done at the Haviland factory in Limoges, France. He relocated in 1888 in Menlo Park, New Jersey, and together with J. T. Smith established the Menlo Park Ceramic Company for the production of art tile. The partnership was dissolved in 1893. From 1895 until 1902, Volkmar located in Corona, New York, first under the name Volkmar Ceramic Company, later as Volkmar and Cory, and for the final six years as Crown Point. During the latter period he made art tile, blue under-glaze Delft-type wares, colorful polychrome vases, etc. The Volkmar Kilns were established in 1903 in Metuchen, New Jersey, by Volkmar and his son, Leon. The production in the teens became more stylized, and bold shapes were covered in rich, crackled Persian glazes. The studio won prizes for a special line of enamel-decorated wares, in bright polychrome on Art Deco, Egyptian-Revival patterns. Difficult to find today, these command prices in the tens of thousands of dollars. Wares were marked with various devices consisting of the Volkmar name, initials, 'Durant Kilns,' or 'Crown Point Ware.' Our advisors for this category are Suzanne Perrault and David Rago; they are listed in the Directory under New Jersey.

Vase, horse carriage, Barbotine, CV, hairlines and chips, 12¾x8x3", $1,440.00. (Photo courtesy Rago Auctions)

Bottle, man in boat/bk: boats in Barbotine, hdls/stopper, EG/53, 14" . 1,450.00
Bowl, centerpc; gunmetal blk speckles on Persian Blue, 1916, 5x13½" 300.00
Bowl, floral band on crackled Persian Blue, oxblood int, 1918, 3x9" . 425.00
Candlestick, repeating incised decor on variegated brn, V mk, 6", ea. 175.00
Charger, cows/ducks pastoral scene in Barbotine, sgn, rstr, 10" 725.00
Charger, Indian chief in Barbotine, sgn, #14, 14" dia 1,000.00
Jardiniere, horses/hunters/foxes, Barbotine, sq w/4 legs, 8x15", EX .. 1,080.00
Oil on board, farming scene, sight: 7x12"+gilt metal fr 1,650.00
Pitcher, hunter scene, Barbotine, die-stamped, sm touchups, 12x9" .. 780.00
Tile, fisherman in landscape, Delft style, V mk, 8x8"+fr, NM 950.00
Vase, cattle scene in Barbotine, baluster, sgn, 14½x7½", NM .. 2,000.00
Vase, gr matt, onion base, 1911, 11x5½" 1,320.00
Watercolor on paper, landscape w/geese, Chas Volkmar, sight: 8x11½" .. 625.00

Volkstedt

Fine porcelain has been produced in the German state of Thuringia since 1760, when the first factory was established. Financed by the prince, the company produced not only dinnerware, but also the lovely figurines for which they are best known. They perfected the technique of using real lace dipped in soft paste porcelain which would burn away during the firing process, leaving a durable porcelain lace which they used extensively on their famous ballerina figurines.

By the 1830s, other small factories began to emerge in the area. One such company was begun by Anton Muller, who marked his wares with a crown over the letters MV (Muller, Volkstedt). Greiner and Holzappel (1804 – 1815) signed some of their pieces with an 'R' accompanied with a series of numbers. Several other marks were used on wares from this area, among them are the 'cross hair' mark with E, N, and S indicated within the pie sections, various marks with a crown over two opposing 'double fish hook' devices, partial crossed swords with a star, crossed forks (variations), a beehive, and a scrolled cartouche containing the crown and the Volkstedt designation. There were others. Later marks may be simply 'Volkstedt Germany.' Both the original Volkstedt factory and the Muller operation continue in production to this day.

Dish, female figure centering two leaf-form dishes, early twentieth century, 13", $960.00.

(Photo courtesy Skinner Inc. Auctioneers & Appraisers of Antiques & Fine Art)

Candlesticks, man (lady) as std, Delft style, late 1800s, 13", pr.... 275.00
Figurine, dancer, long ruffled tulle skirt w/appl floral, crown/MZ, 6"..210.00
Figurine, dancing pr on rococo base, mc/gilt, ca 1880, 12", pr 275.00
Figurine, hunter w/horn over shoulder, 2 dogs, 10x11x8", EX...... 360.00
Figurine, lady at vanity mirror, much tulle/lace, cat on pillow, 7x9"...360.00
Figurine, lady in much lace sits on divan w/dog at her ft, 9½", VG.. 180.00
Figurine, lady seated at table sculpting, Xd forks mk, 7".............. 200.00
Figurine, lady stands by sq marble plinth raising a chisel, 1900, 5"... 120.00
Figurine, man (lady) on horse, blanc de chine, 4½", pr............... 120.00
Figurine, owl, naturalistic, brn/gr feathers, ENS #7575, 10"......... 120.00
Figurine, parrot on leafy perch, mc, gr pnt: ENS mk, 11", pr........ 185.00
Group, courting pr seated, she w/flower basket, 1900s, rpr, 11x9"...360.00
Group, courting pr seated before bush, he w/shovel, E&E Triebner, 7".. 100.00
Group, Madonna sits w/Christ child/John Baptist, wht w/gilt, 7", EX.. 210.00
Group, pr horses/footman/couple greeting royal lady in carriage, 22" L..840.00
Group, 2 men (1 seated) & seated lady, rococo base, 1915-45, 11".. 720.00
Group, 3 playful cherubs on rnd ftd base, blanc de chine, 7½"..... 300.00
Group, 4 adults (1 seated) & child in parlor setting, 1900s, 22" L.. 2,160.00
Group, 6 musicians & dancing ladies, much lace, Muller, 20" L.. 480.00
Wall pocket, folded/ruffled form w/2 3-D cherubs & appl bow, 12"..240.00

Wade

The Wade Potteries was established in 1867 by George Wade and his partner, a man by the name of Myatt. It was located in Burslem, England, the center of that country's pottery industry. In 1882 George Wade bought out his partner, and the name of the pottery was changed to Wade and Sons. In 1919 the pottery underwent yet another name change and became known as George Wade & Son Ltd. The year 1891 saw the establishment of another Wade Pottery — J & W Wade & Co., which in turn changed its name to A. J. Wade & Co. in 1927. At this time (1927) Wade Heath & Co. Ltd. was also formed.

The three potteries plus a new Irish pottery named Wade (Ireland) Ltd. were incorporated into one company in 1958 and given the name The Wade Group of Potteries. In 1990 the group was taken over by Beauford PLC. and became Wade Ceramics Ltd. It sold again in early 1999 to Wade Management and is now a private company.

For those interested in learning more about Wade pottery, we recommend *The World of Wade*, *The World of Wade Book 2*, and *The World of Wade — Figurines and Miniatures*, all by Ian Warner and Mike Posgay; Mr. Warner is listed in the Directory under Canada.

Animal, Alsatian, glass eyes, 1936, 5¼x7½" 200.00
Animal, Cheeky Duckling, ca 1930, 7".. 350.00
Animal, Lion Cub, paw up, underglaze finish, 1935-39, 5¼x8"..... 550.00
Animal, Pluto's Pup No 1, ca 1937-38, 2½" 440.00
Animal, Single Budgerigar, w/o flower, 1940s-50s, 7½" 375.00
Bird, Goldfinch, wings open, underglaze finish, 1930s-mid 1950s, 4" ... 550.00
British character, Pearly Queen, ca 1959, 2⅞" 200.00
Disney, Merlin as Hare, 1965, 2¼x1⅜" 220.00
Disney, Mickey Mouse plate, 1934-late 1950s, 5¾" 50.00
Disney, Sammy the Seal, 6¼" 400.00
Disney, Sgt Tibbs, 1960-64, 2" 145.00
Disney, Tramp Blow-Up, 1961-65, 6" 490.00
Dog model, Dalmatian, cellulose finish, 1927-early 1930s, 7x8".. 400.00
Drum Box series, Clara or Jem, 1956-59, 2", ea 100.00
Flower, Pansy, 1930-39, 3¾" 50.00
Hanna-Barbera character, Huckleberry Hound, 1959-60, 2⅜"..... 145.00
Hanna-Barbera character, Yogi Bear, 1959-60, 2½" 150.00
Happy Families series, Pig Parent, 1978-86, 1½" 25.00
Happy Families series, Rabbit Baby, 1978-86, 1⅛" 18.00
Nursery Favourite, Boy Blue, 1972-81, 2⅞" 65.00
Nursery Rhyme character, Butcher, 1949-58, 3¼" 360.00
Nursery Rhyme character, Goldilocks, 1949-58, 4" 375.00
Nursery Rhyme character, Soldier, 1949-58, 3" 250.00
Red Rose Tea (Canada), Blue Bird, 1967-73 .... 10.00
Red Rose Tea (Canada), Butterfly, 1967-73, ½x1¾" 10.00
Red Rose Tea (USA), Koala bear, 1985, 1⅜"................................. 6.00
Van Hallen, Christina, cellulose-type finish, 11" 500.00
Van Hallen, Snow White, 1938, 6⅜" 500.00
Whimsey-on-Why Village Set, Butcher Shop, 1985, 1⅝" 35.00
Whimsey-on-Why Village Set, Morgan the Chemist, 1980, 1¾"... 24.00
Whimsies, Bison, 1979, 1⅜x1¾" 15.00
Whimsies, Hedgehog, 1974, ⅞".. 8.00
Whimsies, Polar Bear, 1953-59, 1¾" 50.00
Whimsies, Shetland Pony, 1955, 1⅜x2"...................................... 40.00
Whimsies, Shire Horse, brn glaze, 1953-59, 2x2⅛" 300.00
Whoppas, Brown Bear, 1976-81, 1½".. 30.00
Whoppas, Polar Bear, 1976-81, 1½"... 30.00
World of Dogs, West Highland Terrier, 1990-91, 1½" 12.00
World of Survival series, American Brown Bear, 1978-82, 4x5½"...425.00
World of Survival series, American Buffalo (Cape Buffalo) 475.00
World of Survival series, Harp Seal & Pup, 1978-82, 3¾x9"........ 500.00

Wallace China

Dinnerware with a Western theme was produced by the Wallace China Company, which operated in California from 1931 until 1964. Artist Till Goodan designed three lines, Rodeo, Pioneer Trails, and Boots and Saddle, which they marketed under the package name Westward Ho. When dinnerware with a western theme became so popular just a few years ago, Rodeo was reproduced, but the new trademark includes neither 'California' or 'Wallace China.'

This ware is very heavy and not prone to chips, but be sure to examine it under a strong light to look for knife scratches, which will lessen its value to a considerable extent when excessive.

Note: You'll find cups and saucers with only a border design, which is made up of the lariat and brands. This border was used not only on Rodeo but on Boots 'n Saddle and Little Buckaroo patterns as well. If you'd like to learn more about this company, we recommend *Collector's Encyclopedia of California Pottery* by Jack Chipman.

Boots & Saddle, bowl, cereal; 5¾"..	70.00
Boots & Saddle, bowl, fruit; 4⅞", from $50 to...............................	60.00
Boots & Saddle, bowl, oval, 9½" L, from $110 to.........................	120.00
Boots & Saddle, bowl, 10"...	250.00
Boots & Saddle, creamer & sugar bowl, 4¾x4⅝", from $210 to...	225.00
Boots & Saddle, cup & saucer, from $65 to...................................	75.00
Boots & Saddle, pitcher, disk type, 7½", from $225 to................	275.00
Boots & Saddle, plate, bread & butter; 7⅛"...................................	60.00
Boots & Saddle, plate, dinner; 10½", from $75 to.........................	100.00
Boots & Saddle, platter, oval, 15¼", from $200 to.......................	235.00
Chuck Wagon, bowl, fruit; 5", from $28 to...................................	35.00
Chuck Wagon, bowl, oval, 1½x8¼" L, from $65 to......................	85.00
Chuck Wagon, bowl, oval, 8x10", from $120 to............................	130.00
Chuck Wagon, creamer, 2-oz, 2½", from $65 to............................	80.00
Chuck Wagon, cup & saucer, demitasse..	110.00
Chuck Wagon, cup & saucer, 2½x3", 5½", from $55 to................	70.00
Chuck Wagon, platter, oval, 13x9", from $120 to........................	145.00
Chuck Wagon, sauceboat w/attached undertray, 9½" L..............	185.00
Dahlia, cup & saucer, from $35 to..	40.00
Dahlia, platter, oval, 11½"...	40.00
Dahlia, teapot..	100.00
El Rancho, bowl, soup; 6½"..	82.50
El Rancho, cup & saucer...	45.00
El Rancho, plate, dinner; 10¾", from $70 to..................................	90.00
El Rancho, plate, luncheon; 9½", from $50 to...............................	60.00
El Rancho, plate, salad; 8¼"..	45.00
El Rancho, platter, oval, 13½", from $120 to.................................	135.00
El Rancho, sugar bowl, w/lid, 4", from $50 to...............................	65.00
Longhorn, bowl, mixing; lg..	295.00
Longhorn, creamer, ftd, 3½x6¼", from $125 to............................	135.99
Longhorn, cup & saucer, from $150 to..	165.00
Longhorn, cup & saucer, jumbo; from $240 to.............................	270.00
Longhorn, plate, bread & butter; 7"...	75.00
Longhorn, shaker, 5", ea..	65.00
Longhorn, shot glass, glass w/fired-on longhorn.........................	75.00
Pioneer Trails, bowl, vegetable; 12", from $200 to......................	240.00
Pioneer Trails, cup & saucer, 3", 6"...	55.00
Pioneer Trails, plate, chop; 13½", from $250 to...........................	270.00
Pioneer Trails, plate, dinner; 10¾", from $85 to..........................	110.00
Pioneer Trails, plate, 7¼", from $50 to..	65.00
Rodeo, bowl, vegetable; oval, 11⅞", from $160 to........................	200.00
Rodeo, chop plate, 13", from $200 to..	230.00
Rodeo, creamer, 3½", from $50 to..	65.00
Rodeo, cup & saucer, from $50 to..	70.00
Rodeo, cup & saucer, jumbo; 3⅝", from $50 to.............................	70.00
Rodeo, pitcher, disk type, 7x7½", from $195 to............................	225.00
Rodeo, plate, bread & butter; w/center design, 7⅛", from $50 to...	60.00
Rodeo, plate, dinner; bronco rider, 10¾", from $85 to................	110.00
Rodeo, platter, oval, 15⅛", from $150 to.......................................	175.00
Rodeo, shakers, oversz, 4⅞", pr from $90 to.................................	120.00
Rodeo, sugar bowl, open, from $65 to..	75.00
Rodeo, sugar bowl, w/lid, 4½"..	125.00
Shadowleaf, plate, bread & butter; 7⅛"...	30.00

Shadowleaf, plate, 10½", from $65 to..	80.00
Southwest Desert, creamer...	65.00
Ye Olde Mill, plate, dinner; 10⅝"...	20.00
49ers, bowl, serving; 8" dia..	120.00

Walley

The Walley Pottery operated in West Sterling, Massachusetts, from 1898 to 1919. Never more than a one-man operation, William Walley himself handcrafted all his wares from local clay. The majority of his pottery was simple and unadorned and usually glazed in matt green. On occasion, however, you may find high- and semi-gloss green, as well as matt glazes in blue, cream, brown, and red. The rarest and most desirable examples of his work are those with applied or relief-carved decorations. Most pieces are marked 'WJW,' and some, made for the Worcester State Hospital, are stamped 'WSH.' Our advisors for this category are Suzanne Perrault and David Rago; they are listed in the Directory under New Jersey.

Bowl, gr (thick/dripping) on red clay, WJW, rim chip, 9"............	350.00
Flower holder, gr w/brick red streaks, recessed neck, 2¾x5".........	300.00
Jar, gr mottle, cylindrical, w/lid, WJW, 6¾", VG.........................	940.00
Pitcher, brn streams on cream, red clay, 3-D male at spout, 9½"..	2,115.00
Vase, gr drip, flared rim, 3 hdls, 8¾", NM...................................	1,115.00
Vase, gr matt (feathered), wide bottle form, 4¾x4"....................	1,080.00
Vase, gr streaming overglaze on caramel, Grecian hdls, rstr, 13"....	3,050.00
Vase, gr/brn flambe on brn matt, WJW, 10x4½"..........................	2,520.00
Vase, gr/brn matt, pear shape w/lobed rim, 7¼"..........................	1,200.00
Vase, leaves (full-height), gr w/exposed clay, WJW, 6½x4".......	2,640.00
Vase, red/ivory marbleized flambe, squat w/can neck, 4x4¾", EX..	2,520.00
Vase, 2 lizards, brn/gr, WJW, 3¼x4½"...	4,200.00

Walrath

Frederick E. Walrath learned his craft as a student of Charles Fergus Binns at Alfred University (1900 – 1904). Walrath worked first, and briefly, at Grueby Faience Company in Boston and then, from 1908 to 1918, as an instructor at the Mechanics Institute in Rochester, New York. He was chief ceramist at Newcomb Pottery (New Orleans) until his death in 1921. A studio potter, Walrath's work bears stylistic similarity to that of Marblehead Pottery, whose founder, Arthur Baggs, was also a student of Binns's. Vases featuring matt glazes of stylized natural motifs (especially florals) are most sought after; sculptural and figural forms (center bowls, flower frogs, various animals) are less desirable. Typically his work is signed with an incised circular signature: Walrath Pottery with conjoined M and I at the center. Our advisor for this and related Arts & Crafts objects is Bruce A. Austin; he is listed in the Directory under New York.

Bowl, flower; seated nude, cvd waves, gr/terra cotta, 8½x6½"......	900.00
Bowl, 3-D female sits on rnd ped in center, turq w/gr int, 9x8"....	400.00
Candlestick, putto atop column, 3 holders below, sm rpr, 12x5¾"..	625.00
Vase, floral, pk/orange on gr froth, 5½x3½", NM.......................	5,300.00
Vase, floral, yel & gr on dk gr, long slim neck, 10½x5¼"..........	9,000.00
Vase, geometric floral/foliage, pk/gr on gr mottle, 8¾x4½"........	9,800.00
Vase, irises, purple/lt gr on dk gr matt, EX color, 6½x6".........	10,800.00
Vase, trees, gr & brn on dk gr, sloped shoulder, 6¾x4½"............	5,500.00
Vase, water lilies & pads, orange/lt gr on gr, shouldered, 7¼", NM...	5,500.00

Walter, A.

Almaric Walter was employed from 1904 through 1914 at Verreries Artistiques des Freres Daum in Nancy, France. After 1919 he opened his own business where he continued to make the same type of quality objets d'art in pate-de-verre glass as he had earlier. His pieces are signed A. Walter, Nancy H. Berge Sc.

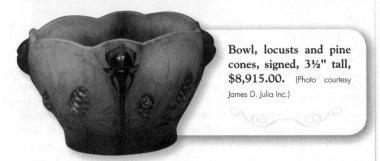

Bowl, locusts and pine cones, signed, 3½" tall, $8,915.00. (Photo courtesy James D. Julia Inc.)

Bowl, lg leaves, yel on shaded bl, chestnut on lid, 6" H............8,400.00
Box, cigarette; bl/dk bl w/floral cvg, sleigh form, yel florals on lid...9,660.00
Box, snail on lid, roses around circumfrence, bl ground, 4½" 4,200.00
Dish, 3 floral sprigs at 2/6/10 o'clock, rust on bl mottle, 7"........1,920.00
Figurine, sea lion on boulder, cadmium yel & brn, Mercier, 6⅝"...1,450.00
Inkwell, gr spotted lizard/bumblebee, grapes on lid, 3¾" 8,340.00
Paperweight, chameleon, gr/bl, 2½x3¼" dia 4,800.00
Paperweight, cicada on laurel branch, yel to gr, 1⅞x5" 1,325.00
Tray, fish to side, gr/yel 'waves,' 6" L, EX................................1,920.00
Tray, moth to 1 side, amber/shaded gr, rectangular, 4½" L.........1,920.00
Tray, pen; divider topped by lg brn beetle on gr, 9½" L...............2,300.00
Vase, snails/vegetation, gr/bl/yel, ftd U-shape, 8" 6,000.00

Warwick

The Warwick China Company operated in Wheeling, West Virginia, from 1887 until 1951. They produced both hand-painted and decaled plates, vases, teapots, coffeepots, pitchers, bowls, and jardinieres featuring lovely florals or portraits of beautiful ladies done in luscious colors. Backgrounds were usually blendings of brown and beige, but ivory was also used as well as greens and pinks. Various marks were employed, all of which incorporate the Warwick name. For a more thorough study of the subject, we recommend *Warwick, A to W,* a supplement to *Why Not Warwick* by our advisor, Donald C. Hoffmann, Sr.; his address can be found in the Directory under Illinois. In an effort to inform the collector/dealer, Mr. Hoffmann now has a video available that identifies the company's decals and their variations by number.

Bouquet #1, vase, brn, A-24, 11¾"..250.00
Bouquet #1, vase, brn, A-27, 11¾"..245.00
Bouquet #2, vase, brn, Anna Potacka, A-17, 10½".......................275.00
Bouquet #2, vase, brn, Gypsy w/bow, A-17, 10½"........................285.00
Bouquet #2, vase, floral, red overglaze, E-2, 10½".......................250.00
Bouquet #2, vase, Old Blonde, A-17, 10½"..................................250.00
Monroe, vase, floral, A-26, 10¼"...280.00
Monroe, vase, floral, A-27, 10¼"...280.00
Monroe, vase, nuts, tan on tan, M-2, 10¼"..................................300.00
Monroe, vase, portrait, A-17, 10¼"..290.00
Monroe, vase, portrait, tan on tan, M-1, 10¼".............................320.00
Narcis #1, vase, geese, wht, D-1, 8¼"...320.00
Narcis #1, vase, portrait, red overglaze, E-1, 8¼" 360.00
Narcis #1, vase, seagulls, wht, 8¼"...300.00
Narcis #2, vase, ducks, wht, D-1, 6¾" 280.00
Narcis #2, vase, portrait, red overglaze, E-1, 6¾" 330.00
Oriental, vase, floral on brn, A-27, 11"..350.00
Oriental, vase, peonies on brn, A-21, 11"....................................400.00
Pansy, vase, floral on brn, A-27, 4"... 90.00

Pansy, vase, floral on brn, A-6, 4"... 90.00
Pansy, vase, floral on red, E-2, 4"... 90.00
Penn, vase, floral on brn, A-16, 9½"...230.00
Penn, vase, gr matt, no decor, 9½"..375.00
Penn, vase, portrait on brn matt, M-1, 9½".................................225.00
Penn, vase, portrait on pk, H-1, 9½"...450.00
Poppy, vase, floral on brn, A-6, 10½"..290.00
Poppy, vase, floral on charcoal, C-4, 10½"..................................320.00
Poppy, vase, portrait on pk, H-1, 10½"..400.00
Regency, vase, floral on brn, A-16, 11½"......................................300.00
Regency, vase, floral on charcoal, C-6, 11½"................................350.00
Rose, vase, floral on brn, A-27, 8"...240.00
Rose, vase, floral on brn, A-6, 8"...200.00
Rose, vase, portrait on red overglaze, E-1, 8"..............................300.00
Royal #1, vase, floral on charcoal, C-5, 10"..................................300.00
Royal #1, vase, portrait on brn, A-17, 10"....................................300.00
Royal #1, vase, portrait on pk, H-1, 10".......................................350.00
Royal #2, vase, portrait on brn, A-17, 9"......................................350.00
Senator #1, vase, floral on brn, A-15, 11".....................................180.00
Senator #1, vase, floral on brn, A-27, 13".....................................180.00
Senator #2, vase, floral on brn, A-13, 13".....................................175.00
Senator #3, vase, floral on brn, A-23, 9¾"....................................215.00
Unnamed, ewer, floral on brn, A-27, 9¼".....................................300.00
Verbenia #1, vase, floral on brn, A-16, 9½"..................................195.00
Verbenia #1, vase, floral on brn, A-27, 9½"..................................195.00
Verbenia #2, vase, floral on brn, A-15, 7½"..................................275.00
Verbenia #2, vase, portrait on brn, A-17, 7½"..............................250.00
Verona, vase, floral on brn, A-16, 11¾"..280.00
Verona, vase, floral on brn, A-27, 11¾"..295.00
Verona, vase, portrait on gr, K-1, 11¾"..280.00
Verona, vase, rose on charcoal, C-5, 11¾"....................................400.00
Victoria, vase, floral on brn, A-16, 8¼"...375.00
Victoria, vase, portrait on yel to gr, K-1, 8¼"................................110.00
Violet, vase, floral on brn, A-22, 4".. 95.00
Violet, vase, floral on brn, A-6, 4".. 95.00
Violet, vase, floral on charcoal, C-5, 4"..115.00
Violet, vase, floral on charcoal, C-6, 4"..180.00
Virginia, vase, floral on brn, A-6, 10"...195.00
Virginia, vase, portrait on brn, A-17, 10".....................................310.00
Warwick, vase, floral on brn, A-40, 10"...320.00
Warwick, vase, portrait on pk, H-1, 10".......................................500.00

Watch Fobs

Watch fobs have been popular since the last quarter of the nineteenth century. They were often made by retail companies to feature their products. Souvenir, commemorative, and political fobs were also produced. Of special interest today are those with advertising, heavy equipment in particular. Some of the more pricey fobs are listed here, but most of those currently available were produced in such quantities that they are relatively common and should fall within a price range of $3.00 to $10.00. When no material is mentioned in the description, assume the fob is made of metal.

Arrowhead shape w/Indian headdress, silver, unmk 65.00
Avery Dog 80.00
Bloodstone in scrollwork, 14k gold fr, ⅞x1½" 160.00
Brotherhood of Locomtive, Fireman & Engineers, enameled 200.00
Buffalo Springfield Roller Co, roller shape.....................................65.00
Case Tractors, tractor in oval, advertising on bk, 1930s, EX 60.00
Dead Shot Smokeless Powder, game-bird celluloid insert, 1½" dia... 160.00
Dodge Bros Motor Vehicles, bl/wht/blk enamel.............................75.00
Doud Livestock Yard, Chicago, boy & girl in relief, EX 70.00

Ford car shape, cloisonne enameling in logo area, 1¼x1½" 150.00
Fordson Tractor 80.00
Golden Spike, KC Southern Lines, 50th Anniversary 150.00
Harley-Davidson Motorcycles, logo, sterling, EX 65.00
Hunter Trader Trapper, bear & guns, brass/bronze 110.00
Indian Motorcycles, Indian chief w/emb headband, sterling, 2½" 135.00
International Harvester, celluloid 150.00
Link Belt Speeder, Speeder Manufacturing Corp, Robbins, 1¼x1¾" ... 90.00
Live Stock Remedy Co, celluloid/metal oval, leather strap, EX ... 275.00
Locomotive & caboose, 1852, sterling silver 70.00
Monarch Tractors, Allis Chalmers Product, RR Johnstone MI on bk ... 70.00
NY to Paris, w/compass 95.00
Pueblo Saddle Co, RT Frazier, saddle form 90.00
Savage Arms Co, Indian head w/rifle, Panama Expo 1915, EX 155.00
Schlitz, keg shape, enamel, Judd's Bar on bk 50.00
Stanley Motor Carriage Co, Newton MA w/emb car, EX 80.00
Velvet Tobacco, pocket tin shape w/cloisonne on front, emb bk, 1⅞" ... 70.00
Winchester, man on horse, brass 90.00
369th Infantry, Harlem Hell Fighters, bronze, WWI era, 1½x1⅛" .. 165.00

Watch Stands

Watch stands were decorative articles designed with a hook from which to hang a watch. Some displayed the watch as the face of a grandfather clock or as part of an interior scene with figures in period costumes and contemporary furnishings. They were popular products of Staffordshire potters and silver companies as well.

Brass, rococo style, rstr gilt, 19th C, 12" 240.00
Faience obelisk, tapering column w/spherule surmount, Fr, 19th C, 14" .. 425.00
Gilt bronze, Louis XVI style, bowknot surmount, 19th C, 5¾x4½" ... 250.00
Majolica bear standing & holding tree, Royal Worcester, 3½" ... 1,875.00
Metal, crest/floral wreath/Father Time, late Victorian, 12x5" 600.00
Oak w/geometric inlay, brass finial, 2-compartment, 8¾" 600.00
Porc, mc flowers/serpent appl, rococo base w/Father Time, Meissen, 10" ... 3,000.00
Silver-tone muse (lady) on wooden stand, unmk, 7¼" 100.00
SP jockey on stool w/whip, Southington Quadruple Plate, 4" 225.00

Watches

First made in the 1500s in Germany, early watches were actually small clocks, suspended from the neck or belt. By 1700 they had become the approximate shape and size we know today. The first watches produced in America were made in 1810. The well-known Waltham Watch Company was established in 1850. Later, Waterbury produced inexpensive watches which they sold by the thousands.

Open-face and hunting-case watches of the 1890s were often solid gold or gold-filled and were often elaborately decorated in several colors of gold. Gold watches became a status symbol in this decade and were worn by both men and women on chains with fobs or jeweled slides. Ladies sometimes fastened them to their clothing with pins often set with jewels. The chatelaine watch was worn at the waist, only one of several items such as scissors, coin purses, or needle cases, each attached by small chains. Most turn-of-the-century watch cases were gold-filled; these are plentiful today. Sterling cases, though interest in them is on the increase, are not in great demand. For more information we recommend *Complete Price Guide to Watches* by Tom Engle, Richard E. Gilbert, and Cooksey Shugart. Our advice for this category comes from Maundy International Watches, Antiquarian Horologists, price consultants, and researchers for many watch reference guides and books on Horology. Their firm is a leading purveyor of antique watches of all kinds. They are listed in the Directory under Kansas. For character-related watches, see Personalities.

Key:
adj — adjusted
brg — bridge plate design
d/s — double sunk dial
fbd — finger bridge design
g/f — gold-filled
g/j/s — gold jewel setting
h/c — hunter case
HCI#P — heat, cold,
   isochronism & position
   adjusted
j — jewel
k — karat

k/s — key set
k/w — key wind
l/s — lever set
mvt — movement
o/f — open face
p/s — pendant set
r/g/p — rolled gold plate
s — size
s/s — single sunk dial
s/w — stem wind
w/g/f — white gold-filled
y/g/f — yellow gold-filled

Am Watch Co, 0s, 7j, #1891, 14k, h/c, Am Watch Co, M 550.00
Am Watch Co, 6s, 7j, #1873, y/g/f, h/c, Am Watch Co, M 250.00
Am Watch Co, 12s, 17j, #1894, 14k, o/f, Royal, M 475.00
Am Watch Co, 12s, 21j, #1894, 14k, h/c, M 900.00
Am Watch Co, 16s, 11j, #1872, p/s, silver h/c, Park Road, M 325.00
Am Watch Co, 16s, 15j, #1899, y/g/f, h/c, M 475.00
Am Watch Co, 16s, 16j, #1884, 5-min, 14k, Repeater, M 6,475.00
Am Watch Co, 16s, 17j, #1888, Railroader, M 1,750.00
Am Watch Co, 16s, 19j, #1872, 14k, h/c, Am Watch Woerd's Pat, M .8,500.00
Am Watch Co, 16s, 21j, #1888, h/c, 14k, Riverside Maximus, M.. 1,875.00
Am Watch Co, 16s, 21j, #1899, y/g/f, l/s, o/f, Crescent St, M 400.00
Am Watch Co, 16s, 21j, #1908, y/g/f, o/f, Grade #645, M 400.00
Am Watch Co, 16s, 23j, #1908, o/f, 18k, Premier Maximus, MIB.. 15,000.00
Am Watch Co, 16s, 23j, #1908, y/g/f, o/f, adj, RR, Vanguard, M .. 600.00
Am Watch Co, 16s, 23j, #1908, y/g/f, o/f, Vanguard Up/Down, EX .. 1,300.00
Am Watch Co, 18s, #1857, silver h/c, Samuel Curtiss k/w, M .. 4,200.00
Am Watch Co, 18s, 11j, #1857, k/w, 1st run, PS Barlett, M 8,650.00
Am Watch Co, 18s, 11j, #1857, silver h/c, k/w, DH&D, EX 2,600.00
Am Watch Co, 18s, 11j, #1857, silver h/c, k/w, s/s, Wm Ellery, EX ... 175.00
Am Watch Co, 18s, 15j, #1877, k/w, RE Robbins, M 475.00
Am Watch Co, 18s, 15j, #1883, y/g/f, 2-tone, Railroad King, EX ... 600.00
Am Watch Co, 18s, 17j, #1883, y/g/f, o/f, Crescent Street, M 325.00
Am Watch Co, 18s, 17j, #1892, HC, Canadian Pacific Railway, M .. 2,800.00
Am Watch Co, 18s, 17j, #1892, y/g/f, o/f, Sidereal, rare, M 4,200.00
Am Watch Co, 18s, 17j, 25-yr, y/g/f, o/f, s/s, PS Barlett, M 350.00
Am Watch Co, 18s, 21j, #1892, y/g/f, o/f, d/s, Crescent St, M 575.00
Am Watch Co, 18s, 21j, #1892, y/g/f, o/f, Grade #845, EX 325.00
Am Watch Co, 18s, 21j, #1892, y/g/f, o/f, Pennsylvania Special, M .. 6,000.00
Am Watch Co, 18s, 7j, #1857, silver case, k/w, CT Parker, M .. 3,850.00
Auburndale Watch Co, 18s, 7j, k/w, l/s, Lincoln, M 1,200.00
Aurora Watch Co, 18s, 11j, k/w, silver h/c, M 425.00
Aurora Watch Co, 18s, 15 ruby j, y/g/f, s/w, 5th pinion, M 1,600.00
Ball (Elgin), 18s, 17j, o/f, silver, Official RR Standard, M 975.00
Ball (Hamilton), 16s, 21j, #999, g/f, o/f, l/s, M 1,200.00
Ball (Hamilton), 16s, 23j, #998, y/g/f, o/f, Elinvar, M 3,850.00
Ball (Hamilton), 18s, 17j, #999, g/f, o/f, l/s, EX 550.00
Ball (Hampden), 18s, 17j, o/f, adj, RR, Superior Grade, M 2,100.00
Ball (Illinois), 12s, 19j, w/g/f, o/f, M 270.00
Ball (Waltham), 16s, 17j, y/g/f, o/f, RR, Commercial Std, M 475.00
Ball (Waltham), 16s, 21j, o/f, Official RR Standard, M 950.00
Columbus, 6s, 11j, y/g/f h/c, M 175.00
Columbus, 18s, 11-15j, k/w, k/s, M 400.00
Columbus, 18s, 15j, o/f, l/s, M 175.00
Columbus, 18s, 15j, y/g/f, o/f, Jay Gould on dial, M 2,500.00
Columbus, 18s, 21j, y/g/f, h/c, train on dial, Railway King, M .. 1,750.00
Columbus, 18s, 23j, y/g/f, h/c, Columbus King, M 2,500.00
Cornell, 18s, 15j, s/w, JC Adams, EX 450.00
Cornell, 18s, 15j, silver h/c, k/w, John Evans, EX 400.00
Dudley, 12s, #1, 14k, o/f, flip-bk case, Masonic, G 2,425.00
Elgin, 6s, 11j, 14k, h/c, M 450.00

Elgin, 6s, 15j, 20-yr, y/g/f, h/c, s/s, EX 80.00
Elgin, 10s, 18k, h/c, k/w, k/s, s/s, Gail Borden, M 675.00
Elgin, 12s, 15j, 14k, h/c, EX 400.00
Elgin, 12s, 17j, 14k, h/c, GM Wheeler, M 400.00
Elgin, 16s, 15j, doctor's, 4th model, 18k, 2nd sweep hand, h/c, M.. 1,650.00
Elgin, 16s, 15j, 14k, h/c, EX 650.00
Elgin, 16s, 21j, y/g/f, g/j/s, o/f, BW Raymond, EX 450.00
Elgin, 16s, 21j, y/g/f, g/j/s, 3 fbd, h/c, M 995.00
Elgin, 16s, 21j, y/g/f, o/f, l/s, RR, Father Time, M 575.00
Elgin, 16s, 21j, 14k, 3 fbd, grade #91, scarce, M 4,500.00
Elgin, 16s, 23j, up/down indicator, BW Raymond, EX 2,150.00
Elgin, 17s, 7j, k/w, orig silver case, Leader, M 175.00
Elgin, 18s, 11j, silver, h/c, k/w, gilded, MG Odgen, M 300.00
Elgin, 18s, 15j, o/f, d/s, k/w, silver, RR, BW Raymond 1st run, M.. 1,475.00
Elgin, 18s, 15j, silver, k/w, k/s, h/c, HL Culver, M 425.00
Elgin, 18s, 15j, silver h/c, Penn RR dial, BW Raymond k/w mvt, M.. 5,950.00
Elgin, 18s, 17j, silveroid h/c, BW Raymond, M 300.00
Elgin, 18s, 21j, y/g/f, o/f, Father Time, G 365.00
Elgin, 18s, 23j, y/g/f, o/f, 5-position, RR, Veritas, M 1,050.00
Fredonia, 18s, 11j, y/g/f, h/c, k/w, M 550.00
Hamilton, #910, 12s, 17j, 20-yr, y/g/f, o/f, s/s, EX 65.00
Hamilton, #912, 12s, 17j, y/g/f, o/f, adj, EX 65.00
Hamilton, #920, 12s, 23j, 14k, o/f, M 595.00
Hamilton, #922MP, 12s, 18k case, Masterpiece (sgn), M .. 1,450.00
Hamilton, #925, 18s, 17j, y/g/f, h/c, s/s, l/s, M 350.00
Hamilton, #928, 18s, 15j, y/g/f, o/f, s/s, EX 350.00
Hamilton, #933, 18s, 16j, h/c, nickel plate, low serial #, M 1,375.00
Hamilton, #938, 18s, 17j, y/g/f, adj, M 675.00
Hamilton, #940, 18s, 21j, nickel plate, coin silver, o/f, M .. 525.00
Hamilton, #946, 18s, 23j, y/g/f, o/f, g/j/s, M 1,575.00
Hamilton, #947 (mk), 18s, 23j, 14k, h/c, orig/sgn, EX 6,500.00
Hamilton, #950, 16s, 23j, y/g/f, o/f, l/s, sgn d/s, M 1,950.00
Hamilton, #965, 16s, 17j, 14k, p/s, h/c, brg, scarce, M 1,400.00
Hamilton, #972, 16s, 17j, y/g/f, g/j/s, o/f, d/s, l/s, adj, EX .. 155.00
Hamilton, #974, 16s, 17j, 20-yr, y/g/f, o/f, s/s, EX 95.00
Hamilton, #992, 16s, 21j, y/g/f, o/f, adj, d/s, dbl roller, M .. 495.00
Hamilton, #992B, 16s, 21j, y/g/f, o/f, l/s, Bar/Crown, M 800.00
Hamilton, #4992B, 16s, 22j, o/f, steel case, G 375.00
Hampden, 12s, 17j, w/g/f, o/f, thin model, Aviator, M 180.00
Hampden, 16s, 17j, o/f, adj, EX 45.00
Hampden, 16s, 17j, y/g/f, h/c, s/w, M 250.00
Hampden, 16s, 21j, g/j/s, y/g/f, NP, h/c, Dueber, ¾-mvt, M .. 295.00
Hampden, 16s, 23j, o/f, adj, dbl roller, Special Railway, M .. 675.00
Hampden, 16s, 7j, gilded, nickel plate, o/f, ¾-mvt, EX 40.00
Hampden, 18s, 15j, k/w, mk on mvt, Railway, M 1,450.00
Hampden, 18s, 15j, s/w, gilded, JC Perry, M 250.00
Hampden, 18s, 15j, silver, k/w, h/c, Hayward, M 250.00
Hampden, 18s, 15j, damascened, h/c, Dueber, M 175.00
Hampden, 18s, 21j, y/g/f, g/j/s, h/c, New Railway, M 600.00
Hampden, 18s, 21j, y/g/f, o/f, d/s, l/s, N Am Railway, M 525.00
Hampden, 18s, 23j, y/g/f, o/f, d/s, adj, New Railway, M 650.00
Hampden, 18s, 23j, 14k, h/c, Special Railway, M 1,250.00
Hampden, 18s, 7-11j, k/w, gilded, Springfield Mass, EX 145.00
Howard, E; 6s, 15j, s/w, 18k h/c, Series VIII, G sz, M 1,450.00
Howard, E; 16s, 15j, s/w, 14k h/c, L sz, M 2,000.00
Howard, E; 18s, 15j, h/c, silver case, k/w, Series I, N sz, M .. 4,200.00
Howard, E; 18s, 15j, 18k h/c, k/w, Series II, N sz, M 5,000.00
Howard, E; 18s, 17j, 25-yr, y/g/f, o/f, orig case, split plate, M .. 1,750.00
Howard (Keystone), 12s, 23j, 14k, h/c, brg, Series 8, M 500.00
Howard (Keystone), 16s, 17j, y/g/f, o/f, Series 9, M 250.00
Howard (Keystone), 16s, 21j, y/g/f, o/f, RR Chronometer II, M.. 900.00
Howard (Keystone), 16s, 23j, y/g/f, o/f, Series 0, jeweled bbl, M .. 1,450.00
Illinois, 0s, 7j, 14k, l/s, h/c, EX 375.00
Illinois, 8s, 13j, ¾-mvt, Rose LeLand, scarce, M 250.00

Illinois, 12s, 17j, y/g/f, o/f, d/s dial, EX 40.00
Illinois, 16s, 17j, y/g/f, o/f, d/s, Bunn, EX 265.00
Illinois, 16s, 21j, o/f, d/s, Santa Fe Special, M 975.00
Illinois, 16s, 21j, y/g/f, g/j/s, h/c, Burlington, M 295.00
Illinois, 16s, 21j, y/g/f, o/f, d/s, Bunn Special, M 625.00
Illinois, 16s, 23j, y/g/f, o/f, d/s, 60-hr, Sangamo Special, mk, M... 3,750.00
Illinois, 16s, 23j, y/g/f, stiff bow, o/f, Sangamo Special, EX .. 1,100.00
Illinois, 18s, 11j, #1, silver, k/w, Alleghany, EX 135.00
Illinois, 18s, 11j, #3, o/f, s/w, l/s, Comet, G 90.00
Illinois, 18s, 11j, Forest City, G 95.00
Illinois, 18s, 15j, #1, adj, y/g/f, k/w, h/c, gilt, Bunn, M 800.00
Illinois, 18s, 15j, #1, k/w, k/s, silver hunter, Stuart, M 875.00
Illinois, 18s, 15j, k/w, k/s, gilt, Railway Regulator, M 900.00
Illinois, 18s, 15j, s/w, silveroid, G 40.00
Illinois, 18s, 17j, g/j/s, adj, B&O RR Special (Hunter), h/c, M.. 2,950.00
Illinois, 18s, 17j, h/c, s/w, nickel plate, coin silver, Bunn, M .. 600.00
Illinois, 18s, 17j, o/f, d/s, adj, silveroid case, Lakeshore, G .. 75.00
Illinois, 18s, 17j, o/f, s/w, 5th pinion, Miller, EX 95.00
Illinois, 18s, 21j, g/j/s, g/f, o/f, A Lincoln, M 425.00
Illinois, 18s, 21j, g/j/s, o/f, adj, B&O RR Special, EX 2,150.00
Illinois, 18s, 21j, 14k, g/j/s, h/c, Bunn Special, M 1,800.00
Illinois, 18s, 23j, g/j/s, Bunn Special, EX 1,000.00
Illinois, 18s, 24j, g/j/s, adj, o/f, Chesapeake & Ohio, M .. 3,850.00
Illinois, 18s, 24j, g/j/s, o/f, Bunn Special, EX 1,200.00
Illinois, 18s, 26j, g/j/s, o/f, Ben Franklin USA, G 4,900.00
Illinois, 18s, 26j, 14k, Penn Special, M 8,500.00
Illinois, 18s, 7j, #3, o/f, Interior, G 50.00
Illinois, 18s, 7j, #3, silveroid, America, G 55.00
Illinois, 18s, 9-11j, o/f, k/w, s/s, silveroid case, Hoyt, M .. 250.00
Ingersoll, 16s, 7j, wht base metal, Reliance, G 20.00
Lancaster, 18s, 7j, o/f, k/w, k/s, eng silver case, EX 125.00
Marion US, 18s, h/c, k/w, k/s, ¾-plate, Asa Fuller, M 425.00
Marion US, 18s, 15j, nickel plate, h/c, s/w, Henry Randel, M .. 425.00
Melrose Watch Co, 18s, 7j, k/w, k/s, G 240.00
New York Watch Co, 18s, 7j, silver, h/c, k/w, Geo Sam Rice, EX .. 185.00
New York Watch Co, 19j, low sz #, wolf's teeth wind, M 1,650.00

Patek Philippe, Swiss, 18 jewel, 18k, adjusts to five positions; heat, cold, isochronism, and position adjusted; nickel movement SN 936491; mono-metallic balance with Breguet hairspring; whiplash micrometer regulation and shadow damascene; refinished dial; replacement crown; $4,450.00. (Photo courtesy R. O. Schmitt Fine Arts)

Patek Philippe, 12s, 18j, 18k, o/f, EX 2,550.00
Patek Philippe, 16s, 20j, 18k, h/c, M 3,600.00
Rockford, 16s, 17j, y/g/f, h/c, brg, dbl roller, EX 65.00
Rockford, 16s, 21j, #515, y/g/f, M 775.00
Rockford, 16s, 21j, g/j/s, o/f, grade #537, rare, M 1,900.00
Rockford, 16s, 23j, 14k, o/f, mk Doll on dial/mvt, M 3,600.00
Rockford, 18s, 15j, o/f, k/w, silver case, EX 175.00
Rockford, 18s, 17j, silveroid, 2-tone, M 275.00
Rockford, 18s, 17j, y/g/f, o/f, Winnebago, M 325.00
Rockford, 18s, 21j, o/f, King Edward, M 400.00
Seth Thomas, 18s, 17j, #2, g/j/s, adj, Henry Molineux, EX .. 595.00

Seth Thomas, 18s, 17j, Edgemere, G....35.00
Seth Thomas, 18s, 25j, g/j/s, g/f, Maiden Lane, EX....2,450.00
Seth Thomas, 18s, 7j, ¾-mvt, bk: eagle/Liberty model, M....250.00
South Bend, 12s, 21j, dbl roller, Grade #431, M....150.00
South Bend, 12s, 21j, orig o/f, d/s, Studebaker, M....450.00
South Bend, 18s, 21j, g/j/s, h/c, Studebaker, M....1,650.00
South Bend, 18s, 21j, 14k, h/c, M....1,300.00
Swiss, 18s, 18k, h/c, 1-min, Repeater, High Grade, M....5,000.00

Waterford

The Waterford Glass Company operated in Ireland from the late 1700s until 1851 when the factory closed. One hundred years later (in 1951) another Waterford glassworks was instituted that produced glass similar to the eighteenth-century wares — crystal, usually with cut decoration. Today Waterford is a generic term referring to the type of glass first produced there.

Bowl, Lismore, scalloped, 4x9"....140.00
Bowl, scalloped fan-cut rim over dmn cuttings, 4x8x11"....200.00
Candleholder, Linsmore, bulbous/ftd, 6½x4½"....90.00
Candy dish, Glandore, w/lid, 5x6" dia....90.00
Champagne flute, Klaemore, 8"....80.00
Christmas-tree topper, faceted spire over ball w/waffle cutting, 10"....145.00
Decanter, Alana, 11x3½"....125.00
Decanter, Glandore, 11"....115.00
Decanter, perfume; faceted stopper/neck, dmn-cut squat body, 8x4"..75.00
Decanter, ship's; Alana, 10x8"....165.00
Decanter, ship's; Colleen, faceted stopper, 10½x8"....175.00
Goblet, sherry; Colleen, short stem, 4¼", 4 for....115.00
Goblet, water; Tramore, 5½", 6 for....145.00
Goblet, wine; Colleen, short stem, 4¾", 4 for....140.00
Goblet, wine; Tramore, 5", 4 for....165.00
Holy water font, dmn cuttings, dmn-cut cross on bk, 8x3¾"....90.00
Lamp, hurricane; dmn-like cuttings, ball shade w/flared top, 14x7"...285.00
Paperweight, heart shape, vertical ribs on sides, waffle-cut top....50.00
Ring holder, tall spire centers rib-cut bowl, 3x3"....35.00
Shakers, ftd pear form w/dmn-cut lower half, 6", pr....125.00
Tumbler, dbl old-fashioned; Linsmore....60.00
Vase, fluted/scalloped waisted top, dmn-cut triangles in body, 9"..150.00
Vase, Georgian Strawberry, ftd, 7x3¾"....60.00
Vase, Glandore, 7x3¾"....45.00
Vase, Lismore, 7"....115.00

Watt Pottery

The Watt Pottery Company was established in Crooksville, Ohio, on July 5, 1922. From approximately 1922 until 1935, they manufactured hand-turned stone containers — jars, jugs, milk pans, preserve jars, and various sizes of mixing bowls, usually marked with a cobalt blue acorn stamp. In 1936 production of these items was discontinued, and the company began to produce kitchen utility ware and ovenware such as mixing bowls, spaghetti bowls and plates, canister sets, covered casseroles, salt and pepper shakers, cookie jars, ice buckets, pitchers, bean pots, and salad and dinnerware sets. Most Watt ware is individually hand painted with bold brush strokes of red, green, or blue contrasting with the natural buff color of the glazed body. Several patterns were produced: Apple, Autumn Foliage, Cherry, Dutch Tulip, Morning Glory, Rio Rose, Rooster, Tear Drop, Starflower, and Tulip, to name a few. Much of the ware was made for advertising premiums and is often found stamped with the name of the retail company.

Tragedy struck the Watt Pottery Company on October 4, 1965, when fire completely destroyed the factory and warehouse. Production never resumed, but the ware they made has withstood many years of service in American kitchens and is today highly regarded and prized by collectors. The vivid colors and folk art-like execution of each cheerful pattern create a homespun ambiance that will make Watt pottery a treasure for years to come.

Apple, bean pot, #76, w/lid & hdls, 6½x7½"....175.00
Apple, bowl, cereal; #94, 1¾x6"....50.00
Apple, bowl, mixing; #8, ribbed, 4½x8"....55.00
Apple, creamer, #62, 4½x4½"....90.00
Apple, mug, #121, 3¾x3"....185.00
Apple, pie plate, #33, 1½x9"....150.00
Apple, pitcher, #15, 5½x5¾"....75.00
Apple, platter, #31, 15" dia....350.00
Apple (Double), bowl, #73, 4x9"....125.00
Autumn Foliage, bowl, #106, 3½x10¾"....85.00
Autumn Foliage, dish, refrigerator; #02, 3x7½"....165.00
Autumn Foliage, shakers, hourglass shape, 4½x2½", pr....175.00
Cherry, bowl, mixing; #6, 3x6"....40.00
Cherry, pitcher, advertising, #15, 5½x5¾"....175.00
Cherry, shaker, bbl shape, 4x2½", ea....90.00
Eagle, bowl, mixing; #12, 6x12"....145.00
Eagle, pitcher, ice lip, 8x8½"....450.00
Kitch-N-Queen, bowl, #5, 2½x5"....45.00
Kitch-N-Queen, pitcher, ice lip, #17, 8x8½"....200.00
Morning Glory, cookie jar, #95, 10¾x7½"....400.00
Morning Glory, sugar bowl, #98, 4½x5"....250.00
Pansy (Cut Leaf), casserole, stick hdl, 3⅜x7½"....125.00
Pansy (Cut Leaf), creamer & sugar bowl, open....175.00
Pansy (Cut Leaf), pie plate, 1½x9"....150.00
Pansy (Cut Leaf), platter, 15" dia....110.00
Pansy (Cut Leaf) w/Bull's Eye, bowl, 2½x11"....90.00
Pansy (Old), casserole, w/lid, #3/19, 5x9"....75.00
Pansy (Old), platter, #49, 12"....85.00
Pansy (Raised), casserole, Fr hdl, ind, 3¾x7½"....90.00
Rooster, bowl, #5, 4x5"....190.00
Rooster, bowl, #58, 3¾x10½"....275.00
Rooster, ice bucket, unmk, 7¼x7½"....275.00
Starflower, bean pot, 2-hdl, #76, 6½x7½"....175.00
Starflower, bowl, berry; 1½x5¾"....35.00
Starflower, bowl, mixing; #5, 2½x5"....50.00
Starflower, grease jar, w/lid, #47, 5x4½"....250.00
Starflower, ice bucket, unmk, 7¼x7½"....185.00
Starflower, pie plate, #33, 1½x9"....200.00
Starflower, tumbler, #56, slanted sides, 4½x4"....325.00
Tear Drop, bowl, mixing; #63, 4½x6½"....45.00
Tear Drop, casserole, w/lid, sq, 6x8"....850.00
Tulip, bowl, nesting; #603, 2x5¾"....250.00
Tulip, cookie jar, #503, 8¼x8¼"....375.00
Tulip, pitcher, ice lip, #17, 8x8½"....300.00

Wave Crest

Wave Crest is a line of decorated opal ware (milk glass) patented in 1892 by the C. F. Monroe Co. of Meriden, Connecticut. They made a full line of items for every room of the house, but they are probably best known for their boxes and vases. Most items were hand painted with various levels of decoration, but more transfers were used in the later years prior to the company's demise in 1916. Floral themes are common; items with the scenics and portraits are rarer and more highly prized. Many pieces have ornately scrolled ormolu and brass handles, feet, and rims. Early pieces were unsigned (though they may have had paper labels); later, about 1898, a red banner mark was used. The black mark is probably from about 1902 – 1903. However, the glass is quite distinctive and has not been reproduced, so even unmarked items are easy to recognize. Our advisors for this category are Dolli and Wilfred Cohen; they are listed in the Directory under California. Note: There is no premium for signatures on Wave Crest. Values are given for hand-decorated pieces (unless noted 'transfer') that are *not* worn.

Ash receiver, roses on dk gr, 2½x6½" at hdls 250.00
Biscuit jar, Swirl, floral, pk on lt bl, SP lid & mt, 6½" 575.00
Biscuit jar, Swirl, floral at top, cylindrical, 10" 350.00
Bonbon, Swirl, asters on gr & wht panels, yel int, SP bail, 7x7" .. 650.00
Box, Baroque Shell, floral on wht, brass mts, unmk, 7¼" 450.00
Box, Cigars, pk w/gold floral on bl, 6¼" 900.00
Box, Egg Crate, amethyst reserve w/bl daisies on wht, 6½" L 325.00
Box, Egg Crate, floral reserve on cobalt, 4x6½x6½" 1,000.00
Box, Egg Crate, mc floral w/gold, 4 lion mask/scroll ft, 6x6½" 650.00
Box, Egg Crate, pointillism reserve on blk w/gold flecks, sq, ftd, 5"W .. 1,100.00
Box, glove; emb scrolls, flower garden on bl, ftd, 9½" 1,450.00
Box, Rococo, mill scene on lid, 4" dia 260.00
Box, Rococo, Venetian canal scene, no liner, 3½x4" dia 250.00
Box, Scroll, floral on wht, 6x7¼" dia 1,000.00
Box, Swirl, daisies/berries on wht, ormolu ft, 6x7" 1,100.00
Box, Swirl, lilacs on wht, orig ormolu mts, 4½x6" 600.00
Box, Swirl, orchid on yel to wht, 4¼x7" 750.00
Carafe, floral on wht, Swirl neck, 8", w/matching Swirl tumbler ... 1,200.00
Creamer & sugar bowl, daisies on wht, ormolu hdls & lid, 3", 4¼" .. 450.00
Ferner, floral, ormolu rim & hdls, insert, 3½x6" 600.00
Ice bucket, wild roses on bl, ornate lid & hdl, 6¼" dia 1,050.00
Letter holder, Egg Crate, floral, pk on lt bl, 4¼x5½" 200.00
Match holder, floral w/beading, 4 gold ft 375.00
Pin tray, floral, metal collar, 4" 75.00
Plaque, dancing maiden, gilt emb scrolling fr, ca 1890, 14½x11" .. 5,000.00
Plate, pond lily on lt bl, rtcl border, 7" 750.00
Shakers, cat & spider web decoration on flared shape, 3¾", pr 350.00
Shakers, lav/bl swirls w/wht & bl daisies, pr in Wilcox fr, 7x6" 275.00
Syrup pitcher, Swirl, floral, red on ivory, metal flip lid, 3½" 175.00
Toothpick holder, floral in wht opal reserve on lt bl, ormolu ped, 3" .. 130.00
Vase, floral, bottle form w/2-hdl ormolu neck mts & ped ft, 6", pr .. 325.00
Vase, floral, ovoid w/long neck, ormolu hdls & ft, 7½x2½" 550.00
Vase, irises, ornate ormolu hdls, dolphin ft, 23" 2,500.00

Weapons

Among the varied areas of specialization within the broad category of weapons, guns are by far the most popular. Muskets are among the earliest firearms; they were large-bore shoulder arms, usually firing black powder with separate loading of powder and shot. Some ignited the charge by flintlock or caplock, while later types used a firing pin with a metallic cartridge. Side arms, referred to as such because they were worn at the side, include pistols and revolvers. Pistols range from early single-shot and multiple barrels to modern types with cartridges held in the handle. Revolvers were supplied with a cylinder that turned to feed a fresh round in front of the barrel breech. Other firearms include shotguns, which fired round or conical bullets and had a smooth inner barrel surface, and rifles, so named because the interior of the barrel contained spiral grooves (rifling) which increased accuracy. For further study we recommend *Modern Guns* by Russell Quertermous and Steve Quertermous (Collector Books), available at your local bookstore. Our advisor for this category is Steve Howard; he is listed the Directory under California. Unless noted otherwise, our values are for examples in excellent condition. See also Militaria.

Key:
bbl — barrel							mod — modified

cal — caliber						oct — octagon
conv — conversion					O/U — over/under
cyl — cylinder						p/b — patch box
f/l — flintlock						perc — percussion
ga — gauge							/s — stock
hdw — hardware						Spec O — Special Order
mag — magazine

Carbines

Ball & Willams Ballard Civil War, 44 cal, 22" part oct bbl, dtd 1861 ... 4,850.00
Hall/North Fishtail, 54 cal, lever action, 21" rnd bbl, dtd 1840 .. 3,100.00
Krag 1899, 30-40 cal, 21½" rnd bbl, front/rear sights, walnut/s 750.00
Navy Arms Replica 1866, 38 cal, 19⅛" rnd bbl, NM 465.00
Peabody, 50 cal, 20" rnd bbl, std mks, saddle ring 3,450.00
Sharps New Model 1856, 52 cal, 22" rnd bbl, saddle ring, NM .. 8,500.00

Muskets

Colt Special 1861 Rifle, 58 cal, 40" rnd bbl, dtd 1863, VG 1,850.00
Harper's Ferry 1816, f/l, 69 cal, 41¾" rnd bbl, dtd 1810 .... 3,225.00
Harper's Ferry 1816, f/l, 69 cal, 42" rnd bbl, 1820 on lock plate .. 1,000.00
Leman, 67 cal, 33" part-oct bbl, rnd iron p/b, rpr, VG 2,100.00
Springfield 1855, 69 cal, 40" part-oct bbl, dtd 1858, w/bayonet, VG .. 2,100.00
Springfield 1863, 58 cal, 40" part-oct bbl, w/bayonnet & scabbard .. 2,875.00
Starr 1830, 69 cal, 42" rnd bbl, Drum conv dtd 1831, VG 950.00
Wheeler & Son Trade, 60 cal, 36¼" part-oct bbl, dtd 1822, rfn .. 3,750.00
Whitney 1855, 58 cal, 40" part oct bbl, dtd 1859, rpr/rfn/s 2,300.00

Pistols

Aston 1842 Martial, std mks, dtd 1848 on lock plate, VG 800.00
Colt #3 Derringer, 41RF cal, 2½" bbl, pearl grips 2,000.00
French 1777, f/l, 73 cal, 7⅜" rnd bbl, rpl ramrod, VG 1,200.00
Sharps Lg Fr Single Shot, 36 cal, 6⁷/₁₆" rnd bbl, Pat 1848-62 ..... 4,150.00
Tower, f/l, 66 cal, 8⅞" rnd bbl, dtd 1800 on /s, G 975.00

Revolvers

Colt Baby Dragoon, 31 cal, 5" oct bbl, 5-shot cyl w/eng scene .. 3,450.00
Colt 1849, 31 cal, 5-shot cyl, 4" oct bbl, 1-pc walnut grips, dtd 1861 ... 2,500.00
Colt 1862 Police, 36 cal, 6½" rnd bbl, rpl loading lever 1,150.00
Colt 1878 DA Frontier 6-Shooter, 44 WCF cal, 5½" bbl, compo grips .. 575.00
Freeman Army Civil War, 44 cal, 7" rnd bbl 3,100.00
Griswold New Orleans, perc, 34 cal, 3⅞" oct bbl, checkered grips ... 4,300.00
Pettingill Pocket Perk, 31 cal, 4" oct bbl, split loading lever 2,875.00
Prescott Belt, 38RF cal, 6" oct bbl, iron fr, Pat'd Oct 2 1860 .... 1,325.00
Rogers & Spencer Civil War Army, 44 cal, 7¼" oct bbl 2,875.00
Smith & Wesson #2, 32RF cal, 6" oct bbl, rfn 400.00
Smith & Wesson 1st Model 3rd Issue, 22 short cal, 3³/₁₆" keyhole bbl 400.00

Rifles

Dunmeyer KY, 32 cal, 36" oct bbl, brass mts, cvd maple/s 5,750.00
Evans Repeating Sporting Transitional, 44 cal, 24" oct bbl, 43" .. 300.00
Harper's Ferry, f/l, 64 cal, 36" part oct bbl, dtd 1818 on lock plate .. 1,500.00
Mannlicher Schoenauer 1903, 6.5X54MS cal, bolt action, 18" bbl, VG .. 700.00
Remington Zouave, 54 cal, 33" rnd bbl, dtd 1863, cartouches on /s, NM .. 5,175.00
Savage Model PE, 308 cal, lever action, eng 22" rnd bbl, eng scene, NM .. 2,300.00
Springfield 1898 Krag, 30-40 Krag cal, 30" bbl, full/s, VG 500.00
VA Mfg 1816, f/l, 69 cal, 42" rnd bbl, dtd 1818 .... 3,950.00
Winchester 64, 30WCF cal, 24" rnd bbl, lever action/⅔ mag, std grade 1,100.00
Winchester 70, 30-06 cal, bolt action, 24" rnd bbl, std grade 700.00
Winchester 1904, 22 cal boy's single shot, 21" rnd bbl, perch-belly/s .. 1,650.00

Shotguns

Am, 8 ga side-by-side 1-trigger perc dbl bbl, rfn 550.00
Ithaca 37 Featherweight, 12 ga, 28" mod bbl, late production, NM...300.00
Lefever A Grade, 12 ga dbl bbl, 25⅜" choked bbls, walnut/s........ 800.00
Libeau, f/l, 12 ga dbl bbl, 27⅜" Damascus bbls, platinum/gold, NM...7,500.00
Springfield Trapdoor Forager, 20 ga, 26" bbl w/brass head, dtd 1887, G ...975.00
Winchester Model 40 Semi-Auto, 12-ga, 23½" bbl, walnut/s, NM..635.00
Winchester Model 42, 410 cal, pump action, 26" plain bbl, walnut/s... 1,100.00
Winchester Super X 1, semi-auto, 12 ga, 30" vent rib bbl, NM ...475.00
Winchester 1897, 12 ga, 28" full-choke bbl, std grade pump, VG...400.00

Weather Vanes

The earliest weather vanes were of handmade wrought iron and were generally simple angular silhouettes with a small hole suggesting an eye. Later copper, zinc, and polychromed wood with features in relief were fashioned into more realistic forms. Ships, horses, fish, Indians, roosters, and angels were popular motifs. In the nineteenth century, silhouettes were often made from sheet metal. Wooden figures became highly carved and were painted in vivid colors. E. G. Washburne and Company in New York was one of the most prominent manufacturers of weather vanes during the last half of the century. Two-dimensional sheet metal weather vanes are increasing in value due to the already heady prices of the full-bodied variety. Originality, strength of line, and patina help to determine value. When no condition is indicated, the items listed below are assumed to be in excellent condition.

Key: f/fb — flattened full body

Horse, running (George Patchen, the 1863 world record holder), old verdigris with traces of yellow and gilt, attributed to J. W. Fiske, restorations, 39" long, $1,150.00. (Photo courtesy Garth's Auctions Inc.)

Arrow & banner, zinc/copper w/gilt traces/verdigris, ca 1900, 22x35".. 2,450.00
Banner, copper w/worn tan over verdigris, ball finials, 29x30"..1,150.00
Bull, fb copper w/appl ears/horns, verdigris/gilt, 13x25" 8,900.00
Centaur, fb copper & cast lead, att AL Jewell, verdigris, 32x39" ..51,700.00
Cod fish, wood body w/6 gilt metal fins & tail, 50%+ gilt, 49" L...7,425.00
Cow, fb tin w/worn gold pnt, on CI directional, cow: 9x15" 400.00
Cow, sheet-iron silhouette, drilled eye, blk pnt, 20" 315.00
Eagle, f/fb copper, old gilt, att LW Cushing & Sons, 30x30" 6,000.00
Eagle, sheet-iron silhouette, gr pnt, strap reinforcements, 25x39"...880.00
Eagle flying, fb copper w/gilt, balanced on ball w/arrow, Fiske, 31" W.. 3,165.00
Eagle w/spread wings, fb sheet copper, directionals, gold pnt, 48x30"... 1,765.00
Fisherman on rocky outcropping by pine tree, pnt sheet metal, 8x19".....400.00
Gamecock, f/fb sheet copper w/zinc head/ft, mc pnt, Harris, 29x26".... 8,800.00
Horse, f/fb copper w/cast-zinc head, streaky patina, 31x37"+post..5,980.00

Horse, sheet iron, leg raised, pnt traces/rust, 26x29" 495.00
Horse running, CI head w/molded sheet-copper body, verdigris, 22x30" .1,765.00
Horse running, cvd wooden panel w/copper ears, on iron shaft, 23x34"..1,115.00
Horse running, f/fb copper, Black Hawk, ca 1900, 17x23" 4,400.00
Horse running, f/fb copper w/verdigris, Harris, 19½x34"+rod ...2,800.00
Horse running, f/fb copper/cast zinc, Ethan Allen, ca 1900, 18x21".. 4,700.00
Horse running, molded sheet copper w/verdigris, 1800s, 20x31", G .. 5,875.00
Horse running (Patchen), f/fb copper w/zinc head, att Fiske, 21x39"..9,500.00
Horse w/jockey, f/fb copper w/zinc head, Fiske, EX verdigris, 33" L..... 7,765.00
Hunting dog, f/fb copper, att J Davis, 20th C, 18x28" 4,995.00
Quill pen, gilt molded sheet copper on copper rod, sphere atop, 23x35"..3,290.00
Rooster, CI w/emb details, rtcl sheet iron tail, mk/NH, 1800s, 33x35". 8,225.00
Rooster, f/fb copper, spurred legs w/traces of red on comb, 21"+stand... 4,485.00
Rooster, f/fb sheet copper, brn over gilt, Fiske, ca 1900, 24x21". 1,765.00
Rooster, f/fb sheet copper w/emb comb/wattle/tail, late 1800s, 39x33"..8,800.00
Rooster, fb copper w/cast ft, gr patina, bullet hole, 22x18"........1,495.00
Rooster, fb copper w/silhouette tail/comb/wattle, 24"+stand.....4,715.00
Rooster, pnt wood, cvt details, 1800s, mtd on wood base, 19x15".. 1,120.00
Rooster, sheet-iron silhouette, riveted battens, 25"+wood base.. 1,350.00
Rooster, sheet-metal silhouette, orig red pnt, 30" 375.00
Sea horse, sheet-metal silhouette, worn bl pnt, rprs, NE, 19x24"..3,565.00
St Julien w/Sulky, fb molded sheet copper, Fiske, 19th C, 23x40"...23,500.00
Stag leaping, fb copper w/verdigris, Washburne, 27x32".........11,750.00
Stag leaping, fb copper w/zinc head, brass antlers, 27x29",.......7,475.00
Trois Amis (schooner), pnt iron, in manner of F Adams, 20th C, 29x34"...415.00

Webb

Thomas Webb and Sons have been glassmakers in Stourbridge, England, since 1837. Besides their fine cameo glass, they have also made enameled ware and pieces heavily decorated with applied glass ornaments. The butterfly is a motif that has been so often featured that it tends to suggest Webb as the manufacturer. Our advisor for this category is Don Williams; he is listed in the Directory under Missouri. See also specific types of glass such as Alexandrite, Burmese, Mother of Pearl, and Peachblow.

Cameo

Bottle, scent; ginkgo/5 floral sprays, ovoid, silver mk lid (VG), 5" ...1,035.00
Bowl, floral vines, wht/lav on red, 5", +6" cupped saucer 4,300.00
Decanter, dogwood, wht/red on citron, bk: butterfly, flip lid, 9½"...3,900.00
Decanter, fuchsia, red/wht on citron, emb silver cap & collar, 9"...4,250.00
Decanter, morning glories allover, wht/red on wht, SP lid, 9½".. 8,575.00
Lamp, floral, wht on bl, ovoid base/shade, 2 camphor ft, 9" 7,200.00
Lamp, floral, wht/red on citron U-shape shade/squat 3-ftd body, 8"..10,950.00
Perfume, lay-down; duck's head, wht on cranberry, w/orig box, 9¼".13,225.00
Perfume, lay-down; floral/bk: fern, wht on red, Tiffany & Co, 7", NM..3,300.00
Perfume, lay-down; flowers, bk: butterfly, wht on bl, 4".............1,300.00
Perfume, lay-down; leaves, wht/red on citron, metal mk lid, 3½"..1,500.00
Perfume, lay-down; Peachblow w/gold ginkgo, silver mk lid, 4"... 750.00
Rose bowl, leaves/pods overall, 3-color, 3½" H.........................3,550.00
Rose bowl, morning glories, bk: branch, bl/wht on bl, 2¼" H 735.00
Vase, apple branches, rainbow cased on wht, elongated neck, 14"...9,600.00
Vase, brickwork/3 arched windows/floral branch, wht/gray on gr, 7x5"..28,750.00
Vase, daffodil, bk: butterfly, wht on citron, cylindrical, 5½".........500.00
Vase, floral, bk: floral, wht on citron, spherical w/short collar, 5".. 800.00
Vase, floral, red on wht, silver collar, conical, 2½".....................240.00
Vase, floral, wht on red, bulbous, 3" 650.00
Vase, floral, wht on red, ftd cylinder, 3" 650.00
Vase, floral (lg/detailed), red/wht on citron, bk: butterfly, 6x5"..2,400.00
Vase, floral w/butterfly & insect, wht on citron, 2¾" 690.00
Vase, Ivory, acanthus leaves, ruffled can neck, bulbous body, 6½"...540.00
Vase, Ivory, floral branch, squat ovoid w/short collar/ring ft, 3" ...520.00

Vase, morning glories, bk: butterfly, gray/pk on wht, bulbous, 9" ...3,750.00
Vase, Persian motif, wht on red on flint, bottle form, 10" 12,360.00
Vase, vines, bk: butterfly, wht on bl, 7½" 1,175.00
Vase, 4 arched floral neck panels, lg areas of gold, J Barbe, 8" ...9,775.00

Miscellaneous

Pitcher, teal satin shading to peach w/apple blossoms, ruffled, 8" 300.00
Vase, cased butterscotch w/gold & silver bird, bulbous, 7" 125.00
Vase, Dragon Blood w/gold & silver flowered scrolls, cased 11" ...225.00
Vase, gold/silver birds in garden on red cased in wht, stick neck, 10".. 300.00

Wedgwood

Josiah Wedgwood established his pottery in Burslem, England, in 1759. He produced only molded utilitarian earthenwares until 1770 when new facilities were opened at Etruria for the production of ornamental wares. It was there he introduced his famous Basalt and Jasperware. Jasperware, an unglazed fine stoneware decorated with classic figures in white relief, was usually produced in blues, but it was also made in ground colors of green, lilac, yellow, black, or white. Occasionally three or more colors were used in combination. It has been in continuous production to the present day and is the most easily recognized of all the Wedgwood lines. Jasper-dip is a ware with a solid-color body or a white body that has been dipped in an overlay color. It was introduced in the late 1700s and is the type most often encountered on today's market. (In our listings, all Jasper is of this type unless noted 'solid' color.)

Though Wedgwood's Jasperware was highly acclaimed, on a more practical basis his improved creamware was his greatest success, due to the ease with which it could be potted and because its lighter weight significantly reduced transportation expenses. Wedgwood was able to offer 'chinaware' at affordable prices. Queen Charlotte was so pleased with the ware that she allowed it to be called 'Queen's Ware.' Most creamware was marked simply 'WEDGWOOD.' ('Wedgwood & Co.' and 'Wedgewood' are marks of other potters.) From 1769 to 1780, Wedgwood was in partnership with Thomas Bentley; artwares of the highest quality may bear the 'Wedgwood & Bentley' mark indicating this partnership. Moonlight Lustre, an allover splashed-on effect of pink intermingling with gray, brown, or yellow, was made from 1805 to 1815. Porcelain was made, though not to any great extent, from 1812 to 1822. Bone china was produced before 1822 and after 1872. These types of wares were marked 'WEDGWOOD' (with a printed 'Portland Vase' mark after 1872). Stone china and Pearlware were made from about 1820 to 1875. Examples of either may be found with a printed or impressed mark to indicate their body type. During the late 1800s, Wedgwood produced some fine parian and majolica. Creamware, hand painted by Emile Lessore, was sold from about 1860 to 1875. From the twentieth century century, several lines of lustre wares — Butterfly, Dragon, and Fairyland (designed by Daisy Makeig-Jones) — have attracted the collector and, as their prices suggest, are highly sought after and admired. Nearly all of Wedgwood's wares are clearly marked. 'WEDGWOOD' was used before 1891, after which time 'ENGLAND' was added. Most examples marked 'MADE IN ENGLAND' were made after 1905. A detailed study of all marks is recommended for accurate dating. See also Majolica.

Key:
WW — WEDGWOOD   WWMIE — WEDGWOOD Made in England
WWE — WEDGWOOD England

Biscuit jar, Basalt, drapery swags, trn vertical lines, 6½" 700.00
Biscuit jar, Jasper, blk, Egyptian figures, ca 1900, 6¼" 600.00
Biscuit jar, Jasper, 3-color, classical figures, 1880s, 5¾" 1,080.00
Biscuit jar, Jasper, 3-color, Diceware, SP rim, 1870s, 5¾" 960.00
Biscuit jar, Jasper, 3-color, florets/trellis, ca 1882, 5¼" 360.00

Bottle, barber; Jasper, 3-color, medallions/Bacchus head hdls, 10" ... 1,800.00
Bottle, Jasper, gr, grapevine band/classic figures, hdls, 1900s, 7"... 880.00
Bottle, scent; Jasper, classical reliefs/arched panels, solid bl, 3".... 380.00
Bowl, Basalt, drapery swags, acanthus leaf ft, 19th C, 17" 5,285.00
Bowl, Daventry; Fairyland Lustre, Dana band, pagodas int, 1825, 10"... 17,625.00
Bowl, Dragon Lustre, gr mottle w/3 gold dragons, 8¾" 175.00
Bowl, Fairyland Lustre, Daventry, int: 4 bl lustre panels, 5x13"... 4,600.00
Bowl, Fairyland Lustre, elves leapfrogging, MOP int, ca 1925, 4½" ..4,700.00
Bowl, Fairyland Lustre, Garden of Paradise I, blk pillar on MOP, 11".. 4,600.00
Bowl, Fairyland Lustre, Lahore, int: 3 elephants, ftd, Z-5266, 6x11"..8,625.00
Bowl, Fairyland Lustre, Leaping Elves, int: Elves on Branch, 5".. 1,725.00
Bowl, Fairyland Lustre, Poplar Tree, int: Woodland Elves V/Bridge, 11"... 5,175.00
Bowl, Fairyland Lustre, Willow, coral/bronze; int: Willow on lt bl, 8" .. 3,450.00
Bowl, Fairyland Lustre, Woodland Elves V on flame lustre, Z-5360, 9"..7,475.00
Bowl, fruit; Basalt, floral festoons/scroll bands, ftd, 8¾" 1,400.00
Bowl, Jasper, bl, classical cameos, w/lid, ca 1800, 6" 1,125.00
Bowl, Jasper, gr, putti, lapidary polished int, 18th C, 6¼" 1,000.00
Bowl, Jasper, 3-color solid, flowers/acanthus leaves, late 19th C, 10".. 2,500.00
Bracelet & earrings, Jasper, classical reliefs on dk bl, 14k mts 940.00
Brooch, Jasper, lilac, classic relief, 1800s, 1½x2" 265.00
Bulb stand, Basalt, 2-tier, cherubs w/festoon, 1800s, 7" 3,800.00
Bust, Basalt, Aristotle, 19th C, 12" 1,175.00
Bust, Basalt, Duke of Edinburgh, ca 1953, 9" 355.00
Bust, Basalt, Horace, early 19th C, 14¾" 1,875.00
Bust, Basalt, Lord Palmerston, ca 1865, 10" 700.00
Bust, Basalt, Marcus Aurelius, WW & Bentley, ca 1775, 15"....4,400.00
Bust, Basalt, Seneca, ca 1877, 10⅛" 825.00
Bust, Basalt, Socrates, WW & Bentley, ca 1775, 19¾" 4,400.00
Bust, Basalt, Venus, waisted socle, 19th C, 9¼" 700.00
Bust, Basalt, Wesley, waisted socle, 1850s, 8" 650.00
Candlesticks, Basalt, classical figures, gilded/bronzed, 1880s, 7", pr..3,000.00
Candlesticks, Basalt, foliage, fluted, early 19th C, 12½", pr 650.00
Candlesticks, Basalt, mc floral, 6½", pr 1,115.00
Candlesticks, Jasper, dk bl, figures/floral ft band, 1850s, 8", pr 350.00
Candlesticks, Jasper, lt bl, classic figures/foliage, 7", pr 590.00
Centerpc, Jasper, 3-color Diceware, w/lid, 1972, ltd ed, 7¾" 1,000.00
Centerpc, Queen's Ware, 2 putti suport vase, gold trim, 1878, 11" .. 1,175.00
Cheese dish, Jasper, dk bl, figures/columns/foliage, 1878, 11" dia. 325.00
Cheese keeper, Jasper, dk bl, ferns/pine branches, 19th C, 11x12½" ..700.00
Coffee can, Jasper, 3-color Diceware, 1850s, +saucer, 5" 1,880.00
Custard cup, Jasper, wht solid, w/latticework lid, 18th C, 2½" ..1,175.00
Dish, Jasper, blk, floral swags w/ram's heads, 1850s, 10"............1,000.00
Dish, Jasper, lilac, Infant Academy cameo, leaf border, 18th C, 8"..1,300.00
Dog head, bone china, pug smoking pipe, gilt/pk collar, 1880, 3½"..9,400.00
Door plates, Jasper, bl, muse, laurel border, 19th C, 2⅝x8¼", pr .. 560.00
Egg basket & stand, Queen's Ware, bellflowers, 1800s, 11⅞" 885.00
Ewer, Jasper, Oenochoe, muses/female head hdl terminal, 1820s, 9"..1,400.00
Ewer, Rosso Antico, floral, satyr mask at hdl, 1800s, 17"...........2,115.00
Ewer, Rosso Antico, Oenochoe, leaf spout/satyr mask hdl, 1820s, 18"....3,500.00
Ewers: wine & water; Basalt, triton/sea monster/Bacchus, 15", pr .. 3,525.00
Figurine, Basalt, baby reclines/holds ball on sq base, 5½" L.......1,000.00
Figurine, Basalt, bear, E Light, 1913, 4¾" L 700.00
Figurine, Basalt, Cupid sits on rock atop raised base, late 19th C, 8" .. 500.00
Figurine, Basalt, Summer w/wreath in hand, late 19th C, 10⅛"... 500.00
Figurine, Basalt, Taurus the Bull, after Machin, 1966, 14½" L 265.00
Figurine, Basalt, Venus atop wave, ca 1900, 12¾" 1,295.00
Figurine, Basalt, Winter allegorical, ca 1900, 9½" 1,525.00
Foot bath, Queen's Ware, oval w/loop hdls, molded straps, 1800s, 17"...765.00
Hair receiver, Jasper, crimson, classic figures/acanthus, 1920, 4" dia..2,350.00
Hatpin, Jasper, bl, lozenge-shape w/leaf borders, 19th C, ⅞" dia ..415.00
Humidor, Queen's Ware, rider on elephant, gold/brn trim, SP lid, 1878..4,700.00
Incense burner, Basalt, dolphin, grid insert, flat lid, 19th C 825.00
Incense burner, Drabware, 3 dolphin ft, grid insert, w/lid, 1800s, 6" ..765.00
Inkstand, Moonlight Lustre, w/insert, 3 dolphin ft, 1810s, 5" ...1,650.00

Jar, canopic; Caneware, hieroglyphs & zodiac symbols, 1850s, 10" ..1,525.00
Jar, canopic; Jasper, lt bl, hieroglyphs & zodiac symbols, 1850s, 10" ...5,285.00
Jar, Jasper, lt bl solid, tree-fr panels/classical figures, 1800s, 8" ..1,400.00
Jardiniere, Jasper, olive gr, portrait medallions/acanthus, 1920, 7" H ..385.00
Jelly mold core, Pearlware, mc floral on cone shape, 1790s, 7¾" ...1,880.00
Jug, Etruscan; Jasper, crimson, figures/floret bands, pewter lid, 5" ..1,000.00
Jug, Etruscan; Jasper, yel w/blk figures/bands, 1930, 7½"...........1,500.00
Jug, Jasper, crimson, figures, tankard form, 1920s, 4¾" 530.00
Jug, Jasper, crimson, figures in foliate frs, ovoid, 1920, 4½" 1,175.00
Jug, Jasper, crimson, grapevines, rope-twist hdl, 1920s, 6¼" 2,000.00
Jug, Jasper, olive gr, WA/Franklin reserves, cylinder, 1920, w/lid, 8" ..295.00
Krater urn, Basalt, HP floral, rust bands, pierced grid, lg hds, 6".. 1,175.00
Lamp, Basalt, Aladdin form, lady w/jug on lid, ped on 8-side base, 9" .. 1,650.00
Lamp, oil; Jasper, bl, France & Minerva at altar of Faith, ca 1800, 6" ...950.00
Medallion, Jasper, bl solid, Francisco Albani, ca 1779, 2⅛x1¾"...325.00
Medallion, Jasper, bl solid, Lord Hood, late 18th C, 3¾x3" 2,350.00
Medallion, Jasper, bl solid, Queen Charlotte, WW & Bentley, 3¼+fr....1,400.00
Medallion, Jasper, bl solid, 2 classical heads, WW & Bentley, 2x2¾" . 825.00
Medallion, Jasper, dk bl, Frederick Augustus, late 18th C, 3¾x3" 1,000.00
Medallion, Jasper, 3-color, cherub/foliate border, 19th C, 2½" 475.00
Mug, Jasper, bl solid, classic figures/stippled ground, 1800, 4½" ... 560.00
Mustard pot, Jasper, 3-color, classical scene, SP trim, 19th C, 4" .. 765.00
Necklace, Jasper, bl, medallion/floret/swirled beads, 19th C, 11"...1,000.00
Pie dish, Cane Ware, simulated crust decor, leaf hdl, 1800s, w/lid, 8" ...600.00
Plaque, Basalt, classical female, gilded/bronzed, 1880s, 6⅜x4" ..1,000.00
Plaque, Fairyland Lustre, woodland w/elf smoking pipe, 8x11"... 19,550.00
Plaque, Jasper, blk, Dancing Hours, 19th C, 4x10"+mahog fr 600.00
Plaque, Jasper, gr, An Offering to Peace, 1850s, 6x12" 765.00

Plaque, Jasper, light blue, Apotheosis of Virgil, early nineteenth century, firing lines to the relief, 16", in modern frame, $3,875.00.

(Photo courtesy Skinner Inc. Auctioneers & Appraisers of Antiques & Fine Art)

Plaque, Jasper, lilac, Marriage of Cupid & Psyche, 19th C, 7x9¾" ...2,000.00
Plaque, Jasper, 3-color, children at play, 1820s, 6½x19"+fr 3,800.00
Plaque, Queen's Ware, Diana at Her Bath, Lessore, 1870, 16x12" ...3,825.00
Plaques, Jasper, lt bl solid, Muse in relief, 1850s, 4x6", pr............ 235.00
Plate, bone china, bl w/Greek key & leafy borders, 1900s, 10", 10 for ..235.00
Plate, dog transfer, brn on wht, after Kirmse, 10½", 8 for 1,050.00
Plate, gold geometrics/panels w/Orientals on med bl, octagonal, 11" ...80.00
Plate, Jasper, blk, figures/ram's heads/trophies, 1800s, 9" 940.00
Plate, Jasper, blk, floral border w/trophies & figures, 8¾" 1,175.00
Plate, Jasper, dk bl, classic relief, early 20th C, 10", 8 for 700.00
Plate, Jasper, lt bl solid, festoons/trophies/ etc, 1880s, 9" 560.00
Potpourri, Basalt, uptrn loop hdls, pierced lid, 19th C, 9" dia...... 950.00
Potpourri, Caneware, Famille Rose decor, loop hdls, 1820s, 12" ...1,400.00
Potpourri, Jasper, dk bl, figures/fruit bands, rtcl lid, 1900, 7" 295.00
Potpourri, Rosso Antico, appl Basalt florals, 3 dolphins on lid, 5".. 3,000.00
Potpourri, Smear Glaze, appl bellflowers, lav/gr on wht, rtcl lid, 5"....525.00
Sardine boat, Argenta majolica, titled Sardinia, fish/nets, 9½" L.. 585.00
Sugar bowl, Jasper, 3-color Diceware, cylindrical, 1800s, w/lid, 4"....2,000.00
Sugar bowl, Rosso Antico, mc florals, twig hdl & finial, 3¾" 440.00
Syrup jug, Jasper, 3-color, foliage/trellis, rope-twist hdl, 1882, 8" .. 650.00
Tea bowl & saucer, Jasper, gr, putti, late 18th C, 3", 5⅛"..........1,400.00
Tea set, Basalt, floral sprays, early 20th C, 5¼" pot+cr/sug 355.00
Tea tray, Jasper, bl solid, sunflower, leaf border, 18th C, 18"......1,525.00
Teakettle, Basalt, Dancing Hours, ca 1800, 8¼" 1,875.00
Teakettle, Basalt, Sybil finial, vertical engine-trn bands, 5" 585.00
Teapot, Jasper, crimson, classic relief/foliate borders, 1920, 4" ..1,000.00
Teapot, Jasper, crimson, figures/acanthus borders, bulbous, 1920, 5" ..1,645.00
Teapot, Jasper, lt bl solid, arabesque floral, 1800s, 3¾" 825.00
Teapot, Jasper, 3-color, Diceware, drum shape, 1850s, 4" 3,170.00
Tile, Midsummer Night's Dream, mc, ca 1878, 6", set of 12 in 2 fr...4,115.00
Tile, old man & young lady portraits, celadon, 12½x8"+fr, pr...... 585.00
Tile, Ruby Lustre, fish, Wm De Morgan (unsgn), ca 1885, 6"+fr...1,295.00
Tray, porc, shell form, shaded pk outlines, 1850s set of 4, 9½-11"..1,500.00
Urns, Basalt, children at play, gilded/bronzed, 1880s, 7", pr 6,450.00
Vase, Agate/Terra Cotta, coiled snakes at hdls, ca 1775, 15" 4,115.00
Vase, Basalt, Auro, gilt foliage/fruits, bottle shape, 1885, 9" 2,000.00
Vase, Basalt, band w/Muses, laurel border/trophy drops, hdls, 6", pr...350.00
Vase, Basalt, band w/scrolls & winged heads in gold/wht, 1 hdl, 12"..1,525.00
Vase, Basalt, bottle shape w/lion's head & mask hdls, ca 1868, 14"..1,300.00
Vase, Basalt, classical figures, gilded/bronzed, ca 1880, 11⅝".....6,450.00
Vase, Basalt, Dancing Hours band, Bacchus head hdls, 7", pr ...3,800.00
Vase, Basalt, mc floral, Portland shape, 2⅜"..............................1,295.00
Vase, Basalt, medallions/festoons, gilded/bronzed, w/lid, 1880s, 10"...5,000.00
Vase, Basalt, no decor, early 19th C, 13¼"................................1,645.00
Vase, Dragon Lustre on bl tones, rim int w/3 Oriental villages, 9x6" .. 460.00
Vase, Fairyland Lustre, Argus/Chinese pheasant, gold dragon rims, 12" ...6,325.00
Vase, Fairyland Lustre, Fairy Slide/Bird's Nest Robbers (daylight), 8"... 7,600.00
Vase, Fairyland Lustre, Flame, Willow, WWMIE, shouldered, 9".....5,750.00
Vase, Fairyland Lustre, front/bk: trees/city beyond, bl int, 8x5½" 3,450.00
Vase, Fairyland Lustre, Tree Serpent, flame lustre sky, Z-4968, 11" ..7,475.00
Vase, Fairyland Lustre, Tree Serpent, sgn SMJ, #3150, 12" 17,250.00
Vase, Fairyland Lustre, Willow on bl-gr, gnomes at base, Z-5228, 9"..6,900.00
Vase, hanging; Jasper, blk, Infant Academy, bottle form, 1820, 8" ...1,525.00
Vase, Ivory Vellum, mc/gilt emb floral, hdld bottle form, 1890, 15" ...700.00
Vase, Jasper, bl, Muses, satyr head hdls, rstr, 18th C, 11".............. 650.00
Vase, Jasper, dk bl, male figures/columns, Portland, 1850s, 10" ..3,050.00
Vase, Jasper, dk bl, uptrn hdls on low body width, ped ft, 1850s, 7"....700.00
Vase, Jasper, lt bl, classic figures/foliate borders, 1820s, 9", pr....1,115.00
Vase, Jasper, Portland, 1972 limited edition, 10" 2,700.00
Vase, Jasper, solid blk, Dancing Hours, Bacchus head hdls, 1900s, 9" ...880.00
Vase, Jasper, yel w/blk acanthus & festoons w/ram's heads, 1930, 8" ... 765.00
Vase, Jasper, 3-color, medallions/festoons, ormolu hdls/mts, 11", pr ...4,110.00
Vase, Jasper, 3-color, swags/columns/lion masks, 1820s, 5", pr...2,700.00
Vase, Jasper, 3-color Diceware, dk bl/gr/wht, 1790s, 7¼"...........3,525.00
Vase, Keith Murray, gr, ribbed w/wide mouth, 1930, 9" 295.00
Vase, Porphyry, cream classical figure/hdls, ca 1775, 14¼" 3,525.00
Vase, Queen's Ware, brn speckles, snake hdls, blk plinth, ca 1775, 15"...2,450.00
Vase, Stoneware, acanthus/bellflowers, bl on lilac, 1925, 5", pr ... 700.00
Vase, Victoria Ware, classical figures, red/gr/wht, 1870s, 11⅜"..... 325.00
Vase, Victoria Ware, trophies/festoons, gr/gilt/wht, 1870s, 9" 300.00
Wine cooler, Rosso Antico, bbl form, male mask head hdls, ca 1800, 9" .2,585.00

Weil Ware

Max Weil came to the United States in the 1940s, settling in California. There he began manufacturing dinnerware, figurines, cookie jars, and wall pockets. American clays were used, and the dinnerware was all hand decorated. Weil died in 1954; the company closed two years later. The last backstamp to be used was the outline of a burro with the words 'Weil Ware — Made in California.' Many unmarked pieces found today originally carried a silver foil label; but you'll often find a four-digit handwritten number series, especially on figurines. For further study we recommend *Collector's Encyclopedia of California Pottery,* by Jack Chipman (Collector Books).

Bowl, divided vegetable; Brentwood, 8x11½" 45.00
Bowl, lug soup; Yellow Rose, 5⅛x6", set of 6 .... 90.00
Bowl, Malay Bambu, tab hdls, 2x7" 15.00
Bowl, Maylay Blossom, sq w/tab hdls, 5x5¼" 16.00
Candlesticks, Malay Bambu, sq bottom, 2¼x4", pr 40.00
Canister, Ming Tree, sq, w/lid, 8x5½" 40.00
Cigarette set, Malay Bambu, 2x5x3" box w/2 leaf-shape ashtrays, 4" L..35.00
Coffeepot, Malay Bambu, pk, 8½" 45.00
Creamer, Malay Bambu, 3x5½" 10.00
Creamer & sugar bowl, Malay Bambu, w/lid, from $25 to 32.00
Cup & saucer, Malay Bambu, from $9 to 12.00
Cup & saucer, Malay Blossom, sq, from $8 to 12.00
Cup & saucer, Yellow Rose, sq... 10.00
Flower holder, blonde in wht dress w/bl floral trim, bl gloves, 7⅜"...25.00
Flower holder, boy in bl shorts/hat, pk shirt/socks w/sm bouquet, 11"..40.00
Flower holder, gr ext w/pk int, scalloped sides, #703, 5½" 25.00
Flower holder, lady in pk dress w/gr parasol, #4025, 10½" 40.00
Flower holder, lady stands w/heart vase behind, #4058, 9½" 65.00
Mustard jar, Mango, w/notched lid, sq, unmk, 3¾x3¼" 25.00
Planter, Ming Tree, 3x9" sq 25.00
Planter, Oriental lady kneeling between 2 bamboo pots, 10½" 45.00
Plate, Malay Bambu, 6¼", from $9 to 12.00
Plate, Malay Blossom, sq, 9¾", from $15 to 22.00
Teapot, Malay Blossom, 7" 40.00
Tidbit, Malay Bambu, 3-tiered, metal hdl 30.00
Tray, serving; Malay Blossom, 11½x6¼" 20.00
Trinket box, Ming Tree, 1½x5x4" 15.00
Tumbler, Malay Blossom, sq, 4¼" 22.50
Vase, Ming Tree, slanted top, 9½x3½", from $40 to 50.00

Weller

The Weller Pottery Company was established in Zanesville, Ohio, in 1882, the outgrowth of a small one-kiln log cabin works Sam Weller had operated in Fultonham. Through an association with Wm. Long, he entered the art pottery field in 1895, producing the Lonhuda Ware Long had perfected in Steubenville six years earlier. His famous Louwelsa line was merely a continuation of Lonhuda and was made in at least 500 different shapes. Many fine lines of artware followed under the direction of Charles Babcock Upjohn, art director from 1895 to 1904: Dickens Ware (First Line), under-glaze slip decorations on dark backgrounds; Turada, featuring applied ivory bands of delicate openwork on solid dark brown backgrounds; and Aurelian, similar to Louwelsa, but with a brushed-on rather than blended ground. One of their most famous lines was Second Line Dickens, introduced in 1900. Backgrounds, characteristically caramel shading to turquoise matt, were decorated by sgraffito with animals, golfers, monks, Indians, and scenes from Dickens novels. The work is often artist signed. Sicardo, 1902, was a metallic lustre line in tones of blue, green, or purple with flowing Art Nouveau patterns developed within the glaze.

Frederick Hurten Rhead, who worked for Weller from 1903 to mid-1904, created the prestigious Jap Birdimal line decorated with geisha girls, landscapes, storks, etc., accomplished through application of heavy slip forced through the tiny nozzle of a squeeze bag. Other lines to his credit are L'Art Nouveau, produced in both high-gloss brown and matt pastels, and Third Line Dickens, often decorated with Cruikshank's illustrations in relief. Other early artware lines were Eocean, Floretta, Hunter, Perfecto, Dresden, Etched Matt, and Etna.

In 1920 John Lessel was hired as art director, and under his supervision several new lines were created. LaSa, LaMar, Marengo, and Besline attest to his expertise with metallic lustres. The last of the artware lines and one of the most sought after by collectors today is Hudson, first made during the early 1920s. Hudson, a semimatt glazed ware, was beautifully artist decorated on shaded backgrounds with florals, animals, birds, and scenics. Notable artists often signed their work, among them Hester Pillsbury, Dorothy England Laughead, Ruth Axline, Claude Leffler, Sarah Reid McLaughlin, E. L. Pickens, and Mae Timberlake.

During the late 1920s Weller produced a line of gardenware and naturalistic life-sized and larger figures of frogs, dogs, cats, swans, ducks, geese, rabbits, squirrels, and playful gnomes, most of which were sold at the Weller store in Zanesville due to the fragile nature of their designs. The Depression brought a slow, steady decline in sales, and by 1948 the pottery was closed.

Note: Several factors come in to play when evaluating a piece of Hudson: subject matter, artist signature, and size are all important. Artist-signed florals from 5" to 7" range from $395.00 to $895.00; scenics and bud vases from 6" to 8" range from $2,500.00 to $5,000.00, with fine artwork from superior artists at the upper end. Pieces bearing the signatures of Mae Timberlake or Hester Pillsbury bring top prices. Our advisor for this category is Hardy Hudson; he is listed in the Directory under Florida.

Alvin, vase, dbl bud; 6" 95.00
Ardsley, console set, bowl w/iris frog 600.00
Ardsley, fan vase, 8" 200.00

Aurelian, umbrella stand, blackberries, unsigned, 24", $1,200.00. (Photo courtesy Treadway Gallery Inc.)

Baldin, bowl, apples, tan, 4" H 125.00
Barcelona, vase, hdls, 14½" 700.00
Blue Ware, jardiniere, 2 angels, 8½" H... 400.00
Bouquet, vase, 12" 400.00
Brighton, pheasant, 11½" L 800.00
Burntwood, vase, chickens, 9" 600.00
Claremont, candleholder, hdls, 8", ea 225.00
Claywood, bowl, flower; 2x3½" 65.00
Coppertone, trumpet vase, 4 frog heads at base, 12"..................3,500.00
Etched Matt, vase, roses on thorny stems, 4-sided, 10½"............. 450.00
Fairfield, vase, cherub band, fluted bottom, 8" 115.00
Flemish, tub, hdls, 4½"... 115.00
Glendale, vase, lovebirds on branch, 8½".....................................950.00
Glendale, wall pocket, cornucopia form, 12½" 450.00
Gloria, ewer, G-12, 9" 150.00
Hobart, bowl, 2½x9", +2-nudes flower frog, 7½".......................... 550.00
Jap Birdmal, vase, geisha girl, sgn VMH, 13" 3,500.00
Jewel, vase, slim, 9" 500.00
L'art Nouveau, vase, ear of corn, 4½" 300.00
Lamar, vase, no scratches, 8½" 450.00
Lorbeek, vase, 8" 200.00
Louella, basket, 6½", from $125 to 150.00
Mammy, cookie jar, 11", from $2,000 to 2,500.00
Manhattan, vase, 5½" 80.00

Marengo, vase, no mk, 8", from $300 to............................350.00
Mirror Black, vase, 12"...200.00
Muskota, nude on rock flower frog, 8"..........................700.00
Oak Leaf, vase, 8½", from $75 to...................................85.00
Paragon, vase, red, bulbous w/short collar neck, 7½".....450.00
Pearl, bowl, 3x6"..140.00
Pearl, vase, 7", from $125 to...150.00
Pop-Eye dog, 9½"..6,000.00
Pumila, vase, 9"...85.00
Roba, vase, rim-to-shoulder hdls, 12½"........................175.00
Roma, comport, 11"...150.00
Roma, jardiniere, flower basket, 10½" H......................325.00
Sabrinian, wall pocket, 8½"...700.00
Senic, vase, S-8, 9½"...150.00
Sicardo, vase, berries/leaves, cylindrical, 9¾x3½".......1,000.00
Sydonia, cornucopia, 8", from $70 to..............................80.00
Tutone, vase, 15"...300.00
Viole, fan vase, 8x9"..200.00
Warwick, planter, 3-ftd, branch hdls, 3½"......................120.00
Zona, mug, duck, 3"...95.00

Western Americana

The collecting of Western Americana encompasses a broad spectrum of memorabilia. Examples of various areas within the main stream would include the following fields: weapons, bottles, photographs, mining/railroad artifacts, cowboy paraphernalia, farm and ranch implements, maps, barbed wire, tokens, Indian relics, saloon/gambling items, and branding irons. Some of these areas have their own separate listings in this book. Western Americana is not only a collecting field but is also a collecting era with specific boundries. Depending upon which field the collector decides to specialize in, prices can start at a few dollars and run into the thousands.

Our advisor for this category is Bill Mackin, author of *Cowboy and Gunfighter Collectibles* (order from the author); he is listed in the Directory under Colorado. Values are for examples in excellent original condition, unless otherwise noted in the description.

Bookends, bronze steer heads mtd on wood, CM Russell, 1900s, pr...550.00
Boots, Newton Porter, mc flame stitch on brn leather, lady's, 1950s ..265.00
Branding iron, wrought-iron heart shape, 1900s, 23" 125.00
Chaps, brn leather w/German silver conchos & clips, 1920s, 38", VG ..275.00
Chaps, leather shotgun type w/nickel silver conchos, 1920s, 36", VG..450.00
Hat, Stetson, tan felt w/kettle curl brim, EXIB...........................360.00
Photograph, cattle at 1947 livestock show, blk/wht, 30x40" 90.00
Saddle, Al Nolte, San Francisco style w/tooling, trimmed fenders...600.00
Saddle, JC Higgins, brn leather, early 1900s, child sz 350.00
Saddle, Miles City Saddlery, rnd skirt, nickel horn, high bk cantle, G ...600.00
Spurs, Garcia, silver mts, basketweave design on straps, 1960s 225.00
Spurs, GS Garcia, Cat pattern #60, conchos/rowels/cvd leathers, 1920s..6,000.00
Spurs, GS Garcia, wrought steel w/silver insets, VG+...............1,800.00
Spurs, hand-wrought iron w/eng, 12-point star rowels, chains, 6"...270.00
Spurs, hand-wrought iron w/silver inlay, rowels, Mexican, 1920s, 7"..110.00
Stirrups, cvd wood, 1880s, 7½"...65.00
Stirrups, wrought iron w/conchos, silver inlay, 1920s, 6x4x5"......200.00
Trunk, chip-cvd floral all around, Mexico, 1940s, 10x23x13"......125.00

Western Pottery Manufacturing Company

This pottery was originally founded as the Denver China and Pottery Company; William Long was the owner. The company's assets were sold to a group who in 1905 formed the Western Pottery Manufacturing Company, located at 16th Street and Alcott in Denver, Colorado. By 1926, 186 different items were being produced, including crocks, flowerpots, kitchen items, and other stoneware. The company dissolved in 1936. Seven various marks were used during the years, and values may be higher for items that carry a rare mark. Numbers within the descriptions refer to specific marks, see the line drawings. Prices may vary depending on demand and locale. Our advisors for this category are Cathy Segelke and Pat James; they are listed in the Directory under Colorado.

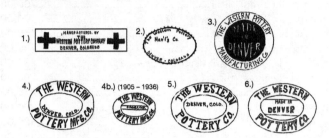

Churn, #2, hdl, 4-gal, M..75.00
Churn, #2, hdl, 5-gal, M..65.00
Churn, #2, no lid, 5-gal, G...80.00
Crock, #4, bail lip, 4-gal, G.......................................55.00
Crock, #4, hdl, no lid, 8-gal, M..................................90.00
Crock, #4, ice water; bl/wht sponge pnt, 3-gal, NM.....30.00
Crock, #4, 6-gal, EX..72.00
Crock, #4b, 15-gal, 22x17½", NM...........................150.00
Crock, #4b, 20-gal, M..200.00
Crock, #5, bail lip, 1½-gal, M....................................45.00
Crock, #5, no lid, 6-gal, M..70.00
Crock, #6, wire hdl, 10-gal, NM...............................100.00
Crock, #6, 3-gal, M..40.00
Crock, #6, 4-gal, M..50.00
Crock, #6, 5-gal, NM...60.00
Foot warmer, #6, M..60.00
Jug, #6, brn/wht, 1-gal, EX..25.00
Jug, #6, brn/wht, 5-gal, M..75.00
Rabbit feeder, #1, EX...25.00
Rabbit waterer, #1, M...25.00

Western Stoneware Co.

The Western Stoneware Co., Monmouth, Illinois, was formed in 1906 as a merger of seven potteries: Monmouth Pottery Co., Monmouth, IL; Weir Pottery Co., Monmouth, IL; Macomb Pottery Co. and Macomb Stoneware Co., Macomb, IL; D. Culbertson Stoneware Co., Whitehall, IL; Clinton Stoneware Co., Clinton, MO; and Fort Dodge Stoneware Co., Fort Dodge, IA. Western Stoneware Co. manufactured stoneware, gardenware, flowerpots, artware, and dinnerware. Some early crocks, jugs, and churns are found with a plant number in the Maple Leaf logo. Plants 1 through 7 turn up. In 1926 an artware line was introduced as the Monmouth Pottery Artware. One by one each branch of the operation closed; in April 2006, after 100 years of stoneware production, all operations ceased. Our advisor for this category is Jim Martin; he is listed in the Directory under Illinois. See also Old Sleepy Eye.

Ashtray, Cardinal Brand Flower Pots 500.00
Beehive jug, brn & wht, 1-gal 100.00
Birdbath, Burntwood 500.00
Book, Monmouth-Western Stoneware, Jim Martin & Bette Cooper, 1983..60.00
Bowl, bl banded, w/advertising.......................................85.00
Butter jar, #5, bl tint, w/lid & bail..................................150.00
Catalog, Maple Leaf Stoneware, 1939............................85.00

Chicken waterer, 1-gal 130.00
Churn, flowers on side, 3-gal 200.00
Churn, Maple Leaf mk, mini 1,000.00
Churn, Maple Leaf mk, 1-gal 1,200.00
Churn, Maple Leaf mk, 2-gal 150.00
Churn, Maple Leaf mk, 2-gal, oval 175.00
Churn, Maple Leaf mk, 6-gal, Plant 6 .... 250.00
Churn, Maple Leaf mk, 10-gal 300.00
Combinet, w/lid & hdl, mini 700.00
Crock, bl bands, 2-gal 200.00
Crock, cake; bl tint, no lid 2,300.00
Crock, Maple Leaf mk, mini 700.00
Crock, Maple Leaf mk, 2-gal, Plant 1, 3 or 4, ea 80.00
Crock, Maple Leaf mk, 5-gal 60.00
Crock, Maple Leaf mk, 20-gal 125.00
Crock, Maple Leaf mk, 50-gal 900.00
Crock, Maple Leaf mk, 60-gal 1,500.00
Custard cup, Colonial 350.00
Flowerpot, maple leaves, Burntwood, hanging, 10" 100.00
Flowerpot/ashtray, Cardinal, red flowerpot clay, no glaze 150.00
Hot-water bottle, pig, bl tint 225.00
Humidor, Duke of Monmouth, cobalt 300.00
Ice-water cooler, bl sponge, w/lid & spigot, 4-gal ...1,500.00
Jar, Maple Leaf & oval mk, 2-gal 50.00
Jardiniere, Egret, brushed gr 75.00
Jardiniere, Egyptian, brn-glazed int, 7" 75.00
Jug, mk Mercury, 5" 50.00
Jug, Monmouth advertising, 1-qt 125.00
Lard jar, w/lid, bl tint 200.00
Monkey jug, brn & wht, 1-gal 150.00
Mug, banded, bl tint 100.00
Mug, Cattail, bl tint 150.00
Paperweight, Maple Leaf, gr & brn 55.00
Pitcher, band & rivets, bl tint, ½-gal 200.00
Pitcher, band & rivets, side lip, bl tint, 1-pt 250.00
Pitcher, Cattail, bl & wht, 1-qt 150.00
Pitcher, General Pershing pattern, gray 150.00
Pitcher & bowl, Memphis, bl & wht 300.00
Rolling pin, bl & wht w/advertising 900.00
Rolling pin, Colonial 1,000.00
Ruler, wooden, 6" 50.00
Ruler, wooden, 12" 50.00
Shakers, 2nd Nat'l Bank, pr 30.00
Stock certificate, 1911 .... 90.00
Sugar jar, w/lid, bl tint 250.00
Sundial, Burntwood 500.00
Vase, cvd/pnt leaves, bl matt, 16", EX 150.00
Vase, Etruscan, gr & wht 45.00
Wall pocket, Egyptian, Burntwood, #312 .... 125.00
Water cooler, Cupid, bl & wht, 4-gal 1,000.00
Water cooler, Egyptian, 9¼x11" 450.00
Water cooler, emb maple leaves, bl & wht, w/lid & spigot, 4-gal ..2,000.00
Water cooler, Maple Leaf mk, no lid or spigot, 2-gal 400.00
Wren house, rnd, Burntwood 125.00

Westmoreland

Originally titled the Specialty Glass Company, Westmoreland began operations in East Liverpool, Ohio, producing utility items as well as tableware in milk glass and crystal. When the company moved to Grapeville, Pennsylvania, in 1890, lamps, vases, covered animal dishes, and decorative plates were introduced. Prior to 1920 Westmoreland was a major manufacturer of carnival glass and soon thereafter added a line of lovely reproduction art glass items. High-quality milk glass became their speciality, accounting for about 90% of their production. Black glass was introduced in the 1940s, and later in the decade ruby-stained pieces and items decorated in the Mary Gregory style became fashionable. By the 1960s colored glassware was being produced, examples of which are very popular with collectors today. Early pieces were marked with a paper label; by the 1960s the ware was embossed with a superimposed 'WG.' The last mark was a circle containing 'Westmoreland' around the perimeter and a large 'W' in the center. The company closed in 1985, and on February 28, 1996, the factory burned to the ground.

Note: Though you may find pieces very similar to Westmoreland's, their Della Robbia has no bananas among the fruits relief. In the descriptions that follow, items in this pattern described as 'crystal with trim' refers to those pieces with the colored lustre stains. For more information we recommend *Westmoreland Glass, The Popular Years*, by Lorraine Kovar (Collector Books). See *Garage Sale & Flea Market Annual* for a listing of many other items with current market values. Our advisor for this category is Philip Rosso, Jr. He is listed in the Directory under Pennsylvania. See also Animal Dishes with Covers; Carnival Glass; Glass Animals.

American Hobnail, ashtray, Olive Green, 4½" dia 7.50
American Hobnail, bowl, grapefruit; milk glass, 6½" 15.00
American Hobnail, compote, milk glass, flared, ftd, 4x8" 20.00

American Hobnail, compote, mint; blue opalescent; 7½", $40.00. (Photo courtesy Lorraine Kovar)

American Hobnail, cordial, crystal, 3⅜" 22.50
American Hobnail, decanter, crystal, w/stopper, 20-oz 125.00
American Hobnail, egg cup, dbl-ended, crystal 12.50
American Hobnail, tumbler, water; low ftd, crystal, 7½-oz, 4¾" 10.00
Ashburton, cake salver, any color, ftd 50.00
Ashburton, claret, any color, ftd, 5⅜" 12.50
Ashburton, tumbler, old-fashioned; any color, flat.................... 12.50
Beaded Edge, bowl, milk glass, oval, 9½x6½" 55.00
Beaded Edge, saucer, milk glass w/floral decor......................... 10.00
Beaded Edge, sherbet, milk glass w/fruit decor, low ft 30.00
Beaded Edge, sugar bowl, milk glass w/red trim, ftd 17.50
Beaded Grape, bowl, milk glass w/gold, flared, ftd, sq, 7" 45.00
Beaded Grape, parfait, milk glass, ftd 40.00
Beaded Grape, plate, bread & butter; milk glass, 6" 20.00
Beaded Grape, plate, luncheon; milk glass w/fruit decor, 8½" 48.50
Beaded Grape, vase, milk glass w/fruit decor, crimped, ftd, 9" 90.00
Cherry, cookie jar, milk glass, ftd, 12" 200.00
Cherry, creamer, milk glass, 3¼" 20.00
Colonial, ashtray, ruby, 7" dia.. 25.00
Colonial, tumbler, crystal, flat, 8-oz, 4" 12.50
Della Robbia, basket, crystal w/any stain, oval, 7½x9" 95.00
Della Robbia, compote, crystal, ruffled, stemmed ft, 5x5" 27.50
Della Robbia, creamer, Antique Blue, ftd, ind......................... 17.50
Della Robbia, plate, luncheon; gr w/frosted accents, 9" 35.00
Della Robbia, plate, torte; crystal w/any stain, 14" 85.00
Della Robbia, shakers, milk glass, ftd, pr............................... 40.00

Dolphin & Shell, candy dish, amber, 3-ftd, 6" 40.00
Dolphin & Shell, vase, Golden Sunset, 3-ftd, 8½" 45.00
English Hobnail, ashtray, crystal, 4½" dia 15.00
English Hobnail, bonbon, pastel pk, sq, flat, 6½" 15.00
English Hobnail, bowl, cream soup; crystal, hdls, 5" 12.50
English Hobnail, cigarette box, turq, 4½x3½" 35.00
English Hobnail, cruet, milk glass, 2-oz, 5" 22.00
English Hobnail, cup, milk glass 10.00
English Hobnail, decanter, crystal, 20-oz 130.00
English Hobnail, parfait, pk, rnd ft, 5½" 35.00
English Hobnail, pitcher, ruby, bulbous, 38-oz 250.00
English Hobnail, plate, pie; crystal, narrow rim, 7" 10.00
English Hobnail, puff box, cobalt, 5" 80.00
English Hobnail, rose bowl, crystal, 4x7" 45.00
English Hobnail, sherbet, gr, high w/rnd ft 20.00
English Hobnail, sugar bowl, Golden Sunset, hex ft, 4½" 17.50
English Hobnail, tumbler, gingerale; pk, flat, 5-oz, 3¾" 20.00
English Hobnail, tumbler, old-fashioned; crystal, flat, 3¼" ... 25.00
English Hobnail, tumbler, turq, rnd ft, 7-oz, 4¾" 18.50
English Hobnail, tumbler, water; Belgian Blue, flat, 8-oz, 4" ... 40.00
Lattice Edge, bowl, banana; milk glass, ftd, 8½x12" 55.00
Lattice Edge, cake salver, milk glass, ftd, 5x11" 55.00
Lotus, compote, Flame, pointed rim, 6" 35.00
Lotus, vase, milk glass, oval, ftd, hdls, 10½" 95.00
Maple Leaf, basket, Lilac Opal, oval, crimped, ftd, 14" 75.00
Maple Leaf, mayonnaise, gr, rolled edge, ftd, 7" 35.00
Old Quilt, ashtray, milk glass w/Forget-Me-Not, sq, 4½" 25.00
Old Quilt, bowl, fruit; milk glass, crimped, skirted ft, 9" 95.00
Old Quilt, cheese dish, Laurel Green 75.00
Old Quilt, creamer, crystal w/ruby stain, lg 30.00
Old Quilt, jardiniere, milk glass, str, ftd, 6½" 65.00
Old Quilt, pitcher, syrup; milk glass, 3-oz, 3½" 40.00
Old Quilt, plate, bread & butter; milk glass, 6" 25.00
Old Quilt, saucer, Purple Carnival 20.00
Old Quilt, tumbler, juice; Electric Blue Opal, flat, 5-oz 30.00
Old Quilt, vase, milk glass, str, flat 85.00
Paneled Grape, bowl, milk glass, shallow, 2x9" 45.00
Paneled Grape, butter dish, Crystal Velvet, ¼-lb 45.00
Paneled Grape, candleholder, milk glass, hdl, 5", ea 27.50
Paneled Grape, candy dish, Antique, Blue, 3-ftd, w/lid 5" 40.00
Paneled Grape, candy dish, any mist w/daisy, ftd, w/lid, 6½" ... 35.00
Paneled Grape, cocktail, milk glass, 3-oz, 4" 35.00
Paneled Grape, compote, milk glass, lipped, bell ft, 9" 55.00
Paneled Grape, creamer, Brandywine Blue, flat, ind 17.50
Paneled Grape, egg tray, crystal, center hdl, 10" 75.00
Paneled Grape, epergne, mint gr, flared, 3-pc, 14" 300.00
Paneled Grape, jardiniere, Antique Green, cupped, ftd, 4" ... 30.00
Paneled Grape, pickle dish, milk glass, oval 32.50
Paneled Grape, pitcher, Brandywine Blue, ftd, 1-qt 75.00
Paneled Grape, planter, any color mist, oblong, ftd, 5x9" 30.00
Paneled Grape, plate, salad; Laurel Green, 8½" 35.00
Paneled Grape, platter, milk glass, oval, 9" 65.00
Paneled Grape, puff box, blk, 4½" 25.00
Paneled Grape, vase, almond, ftd bell shape, 9" 40.00
Paneled Grape, vase, milk glass w/gold, str, ftd, 9½" 35.00
Princess Feather, bowl, Golden Sunset, flat, 12" 50.00
Princess Feather, cake salver, Golden Sunset, Doric ft, 10" ... 65.00
Princess Feather, plate, salad; Belgian Blue, 8" 27.50
Princess Feather, sherbet, Roselin, low ft 18.50
Princess Feather, vase, crystal, hand-blown, flat, 14" 75.00
Thousand Eye, bonbon, purple marble, flat 65.00
Thousand Eye, coaster, crystal 17.50
Thousand Eye, decanter, crystal w/stain 175.00
Thousand Eye, relish, crystal w/stain, 6-part, 10" 25.00

Waterford, finger bowl, crystal, flat, 2¼x4¾" 20.00
Waterford, sugar bowl, crystal, sq ft 15.00
Waterford, tumbler, iced tea; crystal w/ruby stain, ftd, 12½-oz ... 30.00

Wheatley, T. J.

In 1880 after a brief association with the Coultry Works, Thomas J. Wheatley opened his own studio in Cincinnati, Ohio, claiming to have been the first to discover the secret of under-glaze slip decoration on an unbaked clay vessel. He applied for and was granted a patent for his process. Demand for his ware increased to the point that several artists were hired to decorate the ware. The company incorporated in 1880 as the Cincinnati Art Pottery, but until 1882 it continued to operate under Wheatley's name. Ware from this period is marked 'T.J. Wheatley' or 'T.J.W. and Co.,' and it may be dated. The business was reorganized in 1903 as the Wheatley Pottery Company, and its production turned to Arts and Crafts vessels, particularly lamp bases, many of which were copies of Grueby shapes or those of other contemporaries. These were often covered in a thick curdled matt green glaze, although some are found in brown as well. Decorative and collectible, these have been referred to as the 'poor man's Grueby.' An incised or stamped mark reads 'WP' or 'WPCo' and might be hidden beneath glaze on the bottom.

Vase, ochre matt, drilled base, 20x6½", $2,100.00; Vase, green matt, #615, 14x9", $1,400.00. (Photo courtesy David Rago Auctions)

Vase, appl frog & cattails, gr on brn, #86, sm nick, 8½" 3,000.00
Vase, gr, bulbous, WP, 11½x9½" 840.00
Vase, gr (feathered), shouldered, 10x5" 1,440.00
Vase, leaves (Grueby-style), gr, 10x5" 1,320.00
Vase, leaves alternate w/4 tendrils, ochre, WP/#d, 12x6" 3,000.00
Vase, leaves/buds, gr, central ring/4 flared buttress ft, EC102, 10x8" .. 1,800.00
Vase, thistles, gr, unmk, 11½x10¼" 780.00

Whieldon

Thomas Whieldon was regarded as the finest of the Staffordshire potters of the mid-1700s. He produced marbled and black Egyptian wares as well as tortoise shell, a mottled brown-glazed earthenware accented with touches of blue and yellow. In 1754 he became a partner of Josiah Wedgwood. Other potters produced similar wares, and today the term Whieldon is used generically.

Biscuit barrel, tortoiseshell, tree stem, frog & fungus hdl, 6½" 450.00
Plate, tortoiseshell, tooled rim, 8-sided, 9½" 500.00
Plate, tortoiseshell w/acorn sprays/scrolls/diapering, 8" 525.00
Teapot, tortoiseshell, beaded border, lion finial, rprs, 6¾" 600.00
Teapot, tortoiseshell, emb vines, mask & paw ft, 1760-70, rprs, 9"..4,509.00
Vase, cornucopia; tortoiseshell w/emb foliage/fruited vine, rprs, 10"..200.00
Wall pocket, tortoiseshell shield w/satyr mask/gargoyle head, 8½" ...1,100.00

Wicker

Wicker is the basket-like material used in many types of furniture and accessories. It may be made from bamboo cane, rattan, reed, or artificial fibers. It is airy, lightweight, and very popular in hot regions. Imported from the Orient in the eighteenth century, it was first manufactured in the United States in about 1850. The elaborate, closely woven Victorian designs belong to the mid- to late 1800s, and the simple styles with coarse reedings usually indicate a post-1900 production. Art Deco styles followed in the '20s and '30s. The most important consideration in buying wicker is condition — it can be restored, but only by a professional. Age is an important factor, but be aware that 'Victorian-style' furniture is being manufactured today.

Key: H/W — Heywood Wakefield

Armchair, gentleman's; serpentine crest/rolled arms, Wakefield, 43" .. 415.00
Armoire, arched top, tight weave, gr pnt, 78x39x19" 155.00
Baby buggy, sleigh front, natural, H/W, 48x48x19", EX.............. 500.00
Baby carriage, tight weave, sleigh front, wooden wheels, 1900s, 59" L..500.00
Baby stroller, curved arms, bucket ftrest, bk adjusts, 35x51x23"... 200.00
Breakfast tray on bed stand, magazine rack ea side, wht pnt, 9x29x17".. 50.00
Chair, curlique bk & apron, continuous arms, wht pnt, 41", VG+.... 65.00
Chair, wingbk, cvd fr & fluted legs, uphl arms/bk/seat, 43", VG 65.00
Chaise lounge, continuous arms, wht pnt, uphl cushion, 67" L, VG..600.00
Cradle, flat woven edge, cvd wood rockers, C-shape support, 36" L..... 60.00
Dog carrier, tight weave, wirework door, breaks/grime, 21x17x24" 360.00
Hassock, tight weave w/scrolled arms, apron, wht pnt, 21x18x26" 100.00
Lamp, table; cone-shape 21" open-weave shade; trumpet base, 23" ...960.00

Loveseat, Haywood Bros., 32x48x24", EX, $2,600.00. (Photo courtesy Fontaine's Auction Gallery)

Loveseat, pnt wide & narrow horizontal striping, H/W, 57"......... 345.00
Planter, rectangular w/twisted ft, X-stretcher base, 30x31x13" 120.00
Rocker, child's; continuous flat arms, open X-weave bk/sides, 26" ...75.00
Rocker, continuous arms, open X-weave bk sides, spring seat, 32" ... 165.00
Rocker, ornate heart-shaped bk, curled arms, apron, wht pnt, 45" ... 100.00
Settee, scalloped bk, scroll/fan splats w/balls, H/W, 42x41", EX .. 700.00

Sofa, continuous arm, tight weave, uphl bk+3 seat cushions, 68" ...420.00
Suitcase, metal straps, orig closures, pnt wear, 22x32x10"........... 120.00
Table, breakfast; oak top w/2 drop leaves, pnt wicker base w/shelf, VG..200.00
Table, wood top, V-legs w/crisscross weave, 29x36x24"................ 175.00

Wiener Werkstatte

The Weiner Werkstatte was established in Austria in 1903. It was one of many workshops worldwide that ascribed to the new wave of design and style that was sweeping not only Austria but England and other European countries as well.

Its founders were Josef Hoffmann, Kolo Moser, and Fritz Warndorfer. Hoffmann had for some time been involved in a movement bent toward refining prevailing Art Nouveau trends. He was a primary initiator of the Viennese Secession, and in 1899 he worked as a professor at the Viennese School of Applied Arts. Through his work as an architect, he began to develop his own independent style, preferring and promoting clean rectangular shapes over the more accepted building concepts of the day. His progressive ideas resulted in contemporary designs, completely breaking away from past principles in all medias of art as well as architecture, completely redefining Arts and Crafts. At the Weiner Werkstatte, every object was crafted with exquisite attention to design, workmanship, and materials.

Basket, Gitterwerk, allover sm sqs, alpaca w/glass liner, Hoffmann, 11"..3,100.00
Basket, Gitterwerk, sm open sqs, pnt sheet iron, no liner, Hoffmann, 10".780.00
Basket, silver, low emb sides, arched 2-rod hdl, 4½x6½" 3,900.00
Bowl, amber glass, paneled, on inverted bowl ft, Hoffmann/Moser, 4x5" . 720.00
Bowl, ceramic, floral, rtcl rim, gr/pk/wht, D Kuttn, 2½x4¾" 480.00
Bowl, ruby crystal, sq-cut form, Hoffmann for Moser & Sohne, 3" H, EX ...235.00
Bowl, simple floral, rtcl rim, ftd, Dina Kuttn, 2⅝x4¾" 480.00
Box, paper, muted mc overlapping geometric forms, WW, 3¼x6x6".. 1,325.00
Brooch, blk glass sq w/appl silver frond, style of Peche, 1x1½" ...3,600.00
Bust (head & neck) lady w/flowers in hair, C Calm-Wierink, 9"...3,000.00
Candleabrum, ceramic, 2-light, floral on yel, Wieselthier, 8", NM...2,520.00
Cigarette tray/match holder, brass, beaded medallion, Hoffmann, 10" dia..540.00
Figural tray, ceramic, man sitting X-legged/smoking pipe, S Singer, 5"...540.00
Figurine, child stands w/lg grape cluster, blk/wht, Powolny, 15".. 6,000.00
Figurine, lady seated w/basket on head/1 on knee, Kopriva, 6" ..1,020.00
Figurine, maid standing/holding bird, S Singer, 13½", NM.......... 900.00
Figurine, rider on rearing horse, faience, M Flogl #252, rstr, 9" L...840.00
Figurine, 2 nude children, wht, blk/wht base, Powolny, 10"......1,200.00
Figurine, 2 nude ivory children on box w/blk geometrics, Powolny, 10"...1,175.00
Flower frog, 12" standing girl in 16" dia tray, Jugendstil 135.00
Handbag, striated leather, blk w/inlaid gold, strap hdl, 9x6x5¾"...2,400.00
Inkwell, on scalloped ftd tray, bronze, D Peche, 6x15½" 660.00
Jewel box, burlwood w/Nouveau bronze strapwork, 4x9x7" 720.00
Lamp, figural gray-stripe cat seated, glass eyes, Hoffmann, rpr, 14" .420.00
Mug, child emb on tan w/exposed red clay, Wieselthier, 5"............ 50.00
Pitcher, rooster's head spout, gr/yel over red clay, L Calm 1,140.00
Stein, clear glass w/appl red/bl prunts, threading & dots, waisted, 5" .. 300.00
Teapot, brass-washed copper, tin lining, rosewood hdl, Hoffmann, 6x10" ...6,600.00
Tray, ceramic, floral, leaf hdls, scalloped sides, Wieselthier, 8" L.. 600.00
Tray, SP, low swirl-rib curved hand-hammered sides, Hausler, 12" L..1,980.00
Vase, rtcl dmns/appl abstracts on red clay, Wieselthier, 8" 1,440.00
Vase, yel/rose flambe, ovoid w/2 pinched sides, 8x6x2½" 780.00
Wallet, gilt-tooled leather, moire silk lining, Hoffmann, 5" L...... 960.00

Will-George

After years of working in the family garage, William and George Climes founded the Will-George company in Los Angeles, California, in

1934. They manufactured high-quality artware, utilizing both porcelain and earthenware clays. Both brothers, motivated by their love of art pottery, had extensive education and training in manufacturing processes as well as decoration. In 1940 actor Edgar Bergen, a collector of pottery, developed a relationship with the brothers and invested in their business. With this new influx of funds, the company relocated to Pasadena. There they produced an extensive line of art pottery, but they excelled in their creation of bird and animal figurines. In addition, they molded a large line of human figurines similar to Royal Doulton. The brothers, now employing a staff of decorators, precisely molded their pieces with great care and strong emphasis on originality and detail, creating high-quality works of art that were only carried by exclusive gift stores.

In the late 1940s after a split with Bergen, the company moved to San Gabriel to a larger, more modern location and renamed themselves The Claysmiths. Their business flourished and they were able to successfully mass produce many items; but due to the abundance of cheap, postwar imports from Italy and Japan that were then flooding the market, they liquidated the business in 1956.

Bird figurine, eagle on rock, wht & brn, 10"	150.00
Bird figurine, flamingo, closed-S neck, wings closed, 11½", $125 to	145.00
Bird figurine, flamingo, head bk, wings closed, 10¼", $175 to	200.00
Bird figurine, flamingo, head down, wings closed, 7", from $65 to	85.00
Bird figurine, flamingo, head up, wings closed, 10½", from $150 to	165.00
Bird figurine, flamingo, head up, wings closed, 12"	235.00
Bird figurine, flamingo, head up, wings closed, 7½", from $60 to	85.00
Bird figurine, flamingo, head up, wings up, 8", from $225 to	250.00
Bowl, red onion, gr stem finial on lid, 4x4¾"	30.00
Candleholders, petal shape, gr w/pk int, 6½", pr	125.00
Figurine, lady in dress w/wht apron, flowered hat, #106, 1956, 5"	110.00
Figurine, monk, brn bsk, 4½"	50.00
Martini glass, rooster stem w/clear bowl, 5"	25.00
Planter, flamingo, 3¼x5¼"	325.00
Planter, Swiss hiker, flower in left hand, basket on bk, 16"	50.00
Plate, luncheon; red onion, 8½"	15.00
Platter, ½ red onion shape, 3x11x13"	45.00
Tray, flamingo pond, gr w/pk int, 8x12"	60.00
Tumbler, rooster, formed by tall tail feathers, 4½"	60.00
Tureen, soup; red onion shape, w/lid & ladle, 7½"	325.00

Willets

The Willets Manufacturing Company of Trenton, New Jersey, produced a type of belleek porcelain during the late 1880s and 1890s. Examples were often marked with a coiled snake that formed a 'W' with 'Willets' below and 'Belleek' above. Not all Willets is factory decorated. Items painted by amateurs outside the factory are worth considerably less. High prices usually equate with fine artwork. In the listings below, all items are Belleek unless noted otherwise. Our advisor for this category is Mary Frank Gaston; she is listed in the Directory under Texas.

Basket, wht wicker look w/appl floral rim, 7½" sq	925.00
Chalice, floral border on brn, waisted stem, ca 1900, 11¼"	180.00
Chalice, monk on brn, waisted stem, disk ft, 11¼"	125.00
Jug, concord & red grapes, ornate gold hdl/ft, cylindrical, 14"	900.00
Jug, ears of corn, brn/yel tones, ovoid, 7¼"	250.00
Jug, grapes, cylindrical, gold dragon hdl, 11¼"	175.00
Mug, photo portrait, mk Hinz Ceramic Photo Co..., ca 1900, 5½"	125.00
Tankard full-length nude, G Houghton, dragon hdl, 1906, 16x8"	2,400.00
Urn, figural medallions on pk lustre, gold rim, 14"	400.00
Urn, grapes, W Marsh, ornate gold scroll hdls, crimped rim, 11x13", pr	1,500.00
Vase, Arts & Crafts-style floral, G Packard, 1902, 13¾"	425.00
Vase, roses on cream & bl, folded/crimped, mk, 5½"	375.00

Vase, thistles on shaded gr, sgn Wirmey, ovoid, 16x8½"	425.00
Vase, whooping cranes by trees, cylindrical, #564, 16x5¼"	475.00

Winchester

The Winchester Repeating Arms Company lost their important government contract after WWI and of necessity turned to the manufacture of sporting goods, hardware items, tools, etc., to augment their gun production. Between 1920 and 1931, over 7,500 different items, each marked 'Winchester Trademark U.S.A.,' were offered for sale by thousands of Winchester Hardware stores throughout the country. After 1931 the firm became Winchester-Western. Collectors prefer the prewar items, and the majority of our listings are from this era.

Concerning current collecting trends: Oil cans that a short time ago could be purchased for $2.00 to $5.00 now often sell for $25.00, some over $50.00, and demand is high. Good examples of advertising posters and calendars seem to have no upper limits and are difficult to find. Winchester fishing lures are strong, and the presence of original boxes increases values by 25% to 40%. Another current trend concerns the price of 'diecuts' (cardboard stand-ups, signs, or hanging signs). These are out-pricing many other items. A short time ago the average value of a 'diecut' ranged from $25.00 to $45.00. Current values for most are in the $200.00 to $800.00 range, with some approaching $2,500.00. Our advisor for this category is James Anderson; he is listed in the Directory under Minnesota. See also Knives; Fishing Collectibles.

Auger bit, #3, solid core, 1920s-30s, 7¾", EX	40.00
Auger bit, #13, ¹³⁄₁₆", 9", EX	35.00
Auger bit, #18, 12", EX	40.00
Auger bit set, #WSB13, set of 13 bits, #4-#16, EX (VG wood case)	620.00
Axe, broad; #WBB2, 6x4½", w/wooden hdl, EX	100.00
Axe, broad; mk Winchester Ground Steel, 12x8¾" head, EX	85.00
Bat bag, #1932, G	750.00
Battery, No 6 Dry Cell General Purpose, 6x2½", VG+	50.00
Box, shot shell; Leader Staynless Lacquered 12 Ga, 2-pc, EX	60.00
Box, shot shell; New Rival 12 Ga, 2-pc, 4x4x2½", VG+	70.00
Brochure, Model 0042, M in 6½x4½" envelope, EX	50.00
Brochure, Model 0042 Shotgun, ca 1933, 3½x6¼" (folded), EX	40.00
Brochure, Model 1912 Hammerless Repeating Shotgun, 6½x9½", EX	70.00
Calendar, Bear Dogs, missing pages, 1925, 21x15", VG	875.00

Calender, Eugene Ward illustration, Atlantic Litho & Printing Co., 1934, 27", EX, $2,185.00. (Photo courtesy James D. Julia Inc.)

Chisel, cold; ¾x6¾", EX	30.00
Chisel, socket; #4987, beveled edge, 8⅛", EX	17.50
Chisel, wood; #4713, wooden hdl, 9", EX	35.00

Chisel, wood; #4989, 1¼x11¼", EX 20.00
Cover, rifles & cartridges, 2 men w/guns, ca 1914, 3½x6½", EX... 275.00
Display, cb die-cut, hunting scene/rifles, AD Fuller, 1932, 31x38", EX ...1,650.00
Drill, breast; #W33, G 265.00
Drill, breast; #8733, orig decal on gear, EX 100.00
Flashlight, #1511, red plastic top, 2 D-cell batteries, 7", EX.......... 20.00
Flashlight, #7022, copper, ca 1920s, 3", EX 100.00
Flashlight, holds 5 D-cell batteries, beveled glass lens, EX 35.00
Fly rod, G 210.00
Golf club (driver), G 145.00
Hatchet, camper's; #W20, 5x3" head, EX+ 45.00
Hatchet, framing; 3¼x6¼", 13" hdl, EX 70.00
Hatchet, hewing; beveled on 1 side only, 4½x6", EX 70.00
Hatchet, lathing; #WP420, 6" head, EX 50.00
Hatchet, rig builder's; #WRBG, Western-style w/octagonal neck, EX ...80.00
Hatchet, w/nail puller, 3¼x5¼", 14" hdl, EX 90.00
Hatchet, woodsman's; w/leather belt sheath, EX 135.00
Hay fork, G 225.00
Headlamp, miner's; elastic strap, EX 85.00
Knife, butter; #W8500, 9", NM, set of 4 .... 50.00
Knife, paper hanger's, VG... 110.00
Knife, putty; VG 135.00
Level, #WO, wood & brass, 30", EX 40.00
Level, #WO-26, wood & brass, 26", EX 125.00
Level, #9808, wood & brass, 18", EX 25.00
Level, #9811, wood & brass, 24", VG+ 25.00
Level, #9813, wood & brass, glass tubes, 26", VG+ 45.00
Lure, multi-wobbler, VG.. 425.00
Meat grinder, #W12, table mt, EX 45.00
Padlock, #W33, brass, w/key, EX 95.00
Padlock, mk Six Lever on front, w/key, EX 35.00
Plane, #5, wooden knob, EX.. 55.00
Plane, #102, 5½", NM 65.00
Plane, block; #W65, low angle, 7", VG+ 60.00
Plane, block; #3010, 14", EX 70.00
Plane, block; #3011, 15", EX 125.00
Plane, block; #3089, 7", EX 40.00
Plane, jointer; #3055, wood bottom, EX 85.00
Plane, rabbet; #3201, EX 110.00
Plane, smoothing; #3015, 18", EX 55.00
Pliers, side-cut; #2232, 4", EX 210.00
Pliers, snap-ring; #2186, 6", EX 175.00
Rake, garden; #WSB14.. 145.00
Razor, straight; #8625, wht celluloid hdl, EX 115.00
Razor, straight; detailed hdl, mk #8534 on blade, EX 220.00
Razor strop, G- 90.00
Reel, fishing; #4256, G 125.00
Ruler, folding; #9568, boxwood, 24", EX 85.00
Saw, hand; #10, wooden riveted hdl, Warranted Superior medallion, EX . 60.00
Saw, kitchen; #29, ca 1930s, 15", VG 35.00
Scale, mk This Scale Permitted for Household Use Only, 24-lb, 8", EX .. 120.00
Scissors, barber shop; 7½", NM 45.00
Scissors, fabric; 6", EX.. 40.00
Scooter, G- 525.00
Screwdriver, #7103, mk Pat Appl'd For, 4", VG+ 20.00
Screwdriver, #7113-4, brass ferrule, 8", EX 40.00
Shovel, dirt; G 170.00
Shuttle-cock, badminton; stamped inside w/rifle, 3½", NM 325.00
Sign, reel (model 1630), reverse: carving set, cb litho, 7x5", EX... 215.00
Tennis racket, #W4, G- 155.00
Wheelbarrow, all-purpose type, G 850.00
Wrench, adjustable; #1001, 6½", EX 65.00
Wrench, pipe; #WWP5, VG 160.00
Wrench, S-shape, ¼-⁵⁄₁₆", EX.. 35.00

Windmill Weights

Windmill weights made of cast iron were used to protect the windmill's plunger rod from damage during high winds by adding weight that slowed down the speed of the blades. Since they were constantly exposed to the elements, any painted surfaces would be seriously compromised. Our values are for 'as found' examples, as described.

Bull, Fairbury, flat body, red-brn & wht pnt, 24½" L................... 750.00
Bull, Simpson Wind Mill Co, 2-pc hollow body, blk/wht pnt, 14x14"....2,200.00
Crescent moon, no pnt, Eclipse/A13, 10" 45.00
Horse, bob-tailed; Demster, worn red rpt, 18½x17¾" 600.00
Horse, long-tail; Dempster, no pnt, 18½x19½" 900.00

Rooster, Elgin, 10 Ft #2, 16x16½", $1,450.00. (Photo courtesy Skinner Inc. Auctioneers & Appraisers of Antiques & Fine Art)

Rooster, Elgin (unmk), full body, rainbow tail, mc pnt, 18"+base .1,500.00
Rooster, Hummer, no pnt, short stem, ball-shaped base, 20".....1,265.00
Rooster, rainbow tail; old rpt, Elgin, 17¾" 1,495.00
Spear shape, CI, Challenge Co Batavia IL, 12x25½"+base 515.00
W, Althouse-Wheeler, 9x17" on modern metal base................... 525.00

Wire Ware

Very primitive wire was first made by cutting sheet metal into strips which were shaped with mallet and file. By the late thirteenth century, craftsmen in Europe had developed a method of pulling these strips through progressively smaller holes until the desired gauge was obtained. During the Industrial Revolution of the late 1800s, machinery was developed that could produce wire cheaply and easily; and it became a popular commercial commodity. It was used to produce large items such as garden benches and fencing as well as innumerable small pieces for use in the kitchen or on the farm. Beware of reproductions.

Basket, egg; holds 3, center hdl, ca 1900, EX patina.................... 135.00
Basket, fruit; 8 spines, 8 sm ft, 2 loop hdls, 5x11", EX 240.00
Basket, market; tight weave, thick gauged, 1900s, EX 175.00
Basket, potato; galvanized steel wire, 2 hdls, ca 1930, 17x18"...... 135.00
Bottle carrier, decorative zigzags throughout, slight rust, 9x14x11".. 150.00
Cradle, dmn weave, curlicues, 20x40" on stand w/brass castors ... 500.00
Egg tongs, 12"... 40.00
Letter holder, 3-tier, w/brass strips, ca 1900, 15x11½" 325.00
Loveseat, serpentine crest/scroll bk, 1880s, 44" L, +2 chairs 1,500.00
Planter, 2 graduated tiers w/curlique patterns, 59x14x24", EX..... 235.00
Soap dish, twisted loops, crimped wire, lt rust, 1900s, 6½x7x4" 85.00
Washer, vegetable; 2 shallow baskets w/D-form hdls, 4x7x10"....... 20.00

Wisecarver, Rick

Rick Wisecarver is a contemporary artist from Ohio who is well known not only for his renderings of Indian portraits, animals, cookie jars, and scenics on pottery that is reminiscent of that made by earlier Ohio companies, but for limited edition lithographs as well.

Bust, Indian in feathered/beaded headdress, sgn, 1996, 21x14".... 865.00
Coffee set, Indian portraits, mk Special 1 of a Kind set of 3, pot: 9"...400.00
Cookie jar, Geronimo, No 195-94 Chiricahua Wampam Old Age 1994, sgn ...265.00
Cookie jar, Mammy at cookstove, swan scene on apron, 1989..... 230.00
Cookie jar, Miss America (Black), No 51-92 RS, 13½"................. 200.00
Cookie jar, Wizard of Oz, Alice+3 other characters, ltd ed 485.00

Cookie jars: Mammy scrubbing boys, 11"; Mammy with hand on hips, 14½", $200.00 each.

Figurine, barefoot girl, Atlantic Mold, sgn, 1972, 15" 195.00
Mug, Indian on shaded brn, sgn/1895, 4½"................................... 50.00
Pin dish, flamingo figure w/lid on bk, pk/gr, sgn, 1971, 9", EX 40.00
Print, Forever Proud (Indian maiden), sgn, sight: 20x24", trimmed...185.00
Skull w/Indian portrait, sgn, 2001, 19x18"................................... 400.00
Slate painting, bust of Indian chief, sgn/97, 16x9½"................... 180.00
Tankard, rustic winter scenes, sgn FA, 10", +4 mugs 175.00
Vase, barn owl ready to take flight on brn, sgn/mk, 1980, 10x7".. 230.00
Vase, buck deer standing, sgn/mk, 5½".. 140.00
Vase, bull elk bugling, pillow form, sgn/mk, 9x7" 135.00
Vase, bust of lady in plumed hat, sgn/mk Shezane No 1, 13" 185.00
Vase, cowboy (waist up), bag over shoulder, sgn/RS, 1997, 15x11".. 285.00
Vase, floral stems (EX art), sgn/Shezane Florenz, 1983, rstr chip, 10".... 115.00
Vase, grizzly bear w/cub, sgn/RS, 1996, 10½x5¾" 345.00
Vase, horse (head/neck) on lt bl, sgn, pillow form, 1996, 8x8" ... 265.00
Vase, Indian, headdress/pipebone breast plate, sgn/mk Wihoa, '95, 21"..1,380.00
Vase, Indian brave, sgn/mk Wihoa's 1996 RS, 7½"...................... 375.00
Vase, Indian chief, full headdress, on lav, sgn/1984, 17x7"........... 250.00
Vase, Indian in headdress, sgn/#82 RS, pillow form, 5"............... 135.00
Vase, Indian portrait covers entire surface, sgn/1993/R sims, 16x12".. 1,380.00
Vase, Indian standing w/full-length headdress & bow, sgn/mk, 1991, 17"....750.00
Vase, lion's face on brn, sgn/Wild Life No 1, 1980, 15x7" 345.00
Vase, Loreli w/flowing hair, bl tones, rtcl shoulder, sgn/1984, 12x8" ..460.00
Vase, nude w/floating gauze (¾-figure) on brn, sgn/Shezane No 2, 17" 500.00
Vase, old farm bldgs/trees, #1 in Today series, 8x8" 165.00
Vase, period lady in mtns, bottle form, Gramma Miller line, '82, 19" ...230.00
Vase, winsome maid in sheer off-shoulder wrap, sgn/mk/1982, 11".. 335.00
Washbowl & pitcher, Indian chief, sgn/dtd 1933, 12", 9"............. 200.00

Wood, Beatrice

Born in San Francisco in 1893, the young Beatrice was educated in painting and theater in Paris. She worked as an actress in New York through the teens, where she befriended expatriate artists from the Dadist movement and furthered her explorations in fine arts. It was to follow the Theosophist Krishnamurti that Beatrice visited and then moved to California. She studied pottery with several California teachers, including Glen Lukens, Otto and Gertrud Natzler, and Vivika and Otto Heino.

Beatrice Wood taught ceramics and operated a studio in Ojai, becoming well known for her personal interpretation of ancient forms and glazes.

Besides throwing vases and plates, she built figural sculptures full of humor and eroticism. Her pieces, signed 'Beato,' are in collections and museums all over the world. She passed away in Ojai in 1998 at the ago of 105.

Centerbowl, fish shape, pc, Beato, 3x24x14" 6,000.00
Centerbowl, hen shape, pk glazes, Beato, 12x17x9" 3,360.00
Chalice, lime gr matt, Beato, 4½x6¾"......................................3,600.00
Plaque, Helen Freeman, nude, Beato, 17x13" 3,900.00
Plaque, Rock & Roll, dancers, pastels glazes, 17x13".................3,240.00
Sculpture, Good Morning America, figures in brothel, mc, Beato/Stephanie, 22x47x17" 22,800.00

Wood Carvings

Wood sculptures represent an important section of American folk art. Wood carvings were made not only by skilled woodworkers such as cabinetmakers, carpenters, etc., but by amateur 'whittlers' as well. They take the form of circus-wagon figures, carousel animals, decoys, busts, figurines, and cigar store Indians. Oriental artists show themselves to have been as proficient with the medium of wood as they were with ivory or hardstone. See also Carousel Animals; Decoys; Tobacciana.

Abraham Lincoln seated (as Lincoln Memorial), Pomerville, 10". 2,525.00
Alligator, EX detail & patina, rpr foreleg, 22¾" L 5,450.00
Beaver w/paw caught in split tree stump, ca 1900, 10x10½" 515.00
Bird, cvd wings/beak/eyes, wire legs, on wood block, early 20th C, 4" .. 110.00
Bird w/fruit (cherries?) in its beak, crazed pnt, att Bernier, 6" ...4,885.00
Boy w/pointed hat & watermelon slice, mc pnt, lawn ornament, 24"..85.00
Bulldog seated, red jewel eyes, EX features, opens to hold cigars, 10".. 175.00
Chicken, gesso covered, wht rpt w/gold showing, 10¼" 2,500.00
Chicken w/long neck, varnish/blk pnt, sgn V Robert, 22¾" 145.00
Civil War Union solider & sailor w/flag, mc pnt, on metal stand, 15"... 14,375.00
Cow, Holstein; cvd from joined pcs, real cvd horns, leather ears, 15"... 1,100.00
Dog, tan wash & blk stripe down bk, 11x21", EX......................... 800.00
Double eagle on wooden ball, sm shelf at back, gold leaf, rpr, 24x23".. 1,725.00
Dove, curly maple w/EX patina, simple form, 6¼"+wooden base .. 350.00
Dove, gray & yel pnt w/pk accents, glass eyes, 9¾x12"+base 145.00
Draft horses, wood w/old gesso & pnt, leather harness, 13x15", pr..4,150.00
Eagle, 34" wingspan, feather details, gilt/varnished, 20th C, 29"...1,400.00
Egret, inset glass eyes, wire legs, old pnt, on base, 1900s, 22" 1,765.00
Flag pole top, eagle w/31" wingspan on ball, EX detail, gilt, 22", EX..2,020.00
Hand, unclenched, natural finish, lt patina, 8½" 550.00
Horse, bay pnt, horsehair tail, lt wear, 12½" L 400.00
Horse w/trn head, cvd saddle & wire bit, crackled pnt, 1931, 9".. 550.00
Indian standing, relief cvd/pnt, 20th C, 75x19x12"...................2,350.00
Lion standing, mtd on wood plank, rpr, 1800s, 15" L 500.00
Man & lady in 18th-C dress, detailed pnt, rprs, ca 1800, 36", pr..2,300.00
Man in top hat & tails, pine w/thin red wash, on wooden base, 23"..2,750.00
Monk seated, blk robes, long wht beard, mc pnt, 29" 235.00
Moose & dog, stylized, mtd on burl, sgn L Johnson/1931, rpr, 7x7" ...350.00
Owl, glass eyes, stylized form w/old pnt, 10½".............................. 435.00
Owl perched on cvd branch, glass eyes, varnish, 14"+metal stand ...3,565.00
Parrot perched in ring, made from 1-pc, added wings/legs/metal ft, 23"..435.00
Ram, Black Forest, 1880s, 7½" 470.00
Santa, relief-cvd bands around coat & hat, natural finish, 20th C, 27" ...285.00
Sculpture of man's head (caricature) w/long beard & lg nose, 12x13" ..400.00
Snake, tan w/blk stripes, brn/yel details, 20th C, 61" 260.00
Union soldier at attention w/rifle, mc pnt, EX details, 12"........... 925.00

Woodenware

Woodenware (or treenware, as it is sometimes called) generally refers to those wooden items such as spoons, bowls, food molds, etc., that were used in the preparation of food. Common during the eighteenth and nineteenth centuries, these wares were designed from a strictly functional viewpoint and were used on a day-to-day basis. With the advent of the Industrial Revolution which brought with it new materials and products, much of the old woodenware was simply discarded. Today original handcrafted American woodenwares are extremely difficult to find. See also Primitives.

Basket, cvd burl (resembles bird's-eye maple), 1-pc, lg D hdl, 8x10x9"...690.00
Beaker, ash burl, gr pnt traces, old rfn, dtd 1714, 6¾" 1,035.00
Bowl, ash burl, EX patina, age splits at rim, 5½" 635.00
Bowl, ash burl, hewn, Am, 19th C, 6½x17½" 1,400.00

Bowl, ash burl, stylized horsehead carved on each end, incised details, signed AOSR/RG/8 Fer, refinished, 10x16", $1,725.00. (Photo courtesy Garth's Auctions Inc.)

Bowl, ash burl, thin red pnt near base, shallow, 2x14".................. 575.00
Bowl, ash burl, trn rim, lightly scrubbed w/med patina, splits, 5x13" .. 925.00
Bowl, ash burl w/EX figure, slight lip, age splits, 4x14¾" 700.00
Bowl, ash burl w/EX figure & color, raised band along rim, 9x24"..6,300.00
Bowl, ash burl w/old rfn nutty brn color, edge damage, 2x4½"..... 545.00
Bowl, ash burl w/tight figure, red traces, rfn/imperfection, 5x15".. 350.00
Bowl, ash burl w/tight figure, well-shaped sides, scrubbed, 6x18"..1,800.00
Bowl, dough; hewn birch w/red pnt, scrubbed int, oblong, 5x21x15"..650.00
Bowl, exterior w/allover geometric cvgs, red rpt, Quebec, 12" L, VG... 2,300.00
Bowl, incised band below rim, scrubbed int, old gr pnt, 3x15"..... 500.00
Bowl, maple w/gr pnt, warped, 1820s, 4x11x24" 355.00
Bowl, old bl pnt w/earlier gr under, scrubbed int, splits, 4x15"..... 300.00
Bowl, red pnt, 1800s, wear/cracks, 5x22" 765.00
Bowl, thin yel pnt, scrubbed int w/sm hole at rim to hang, 6x20"...400.00
Butter paddle, cvd horse-head finial, scrubbed, 9¼" 175.00
Butter paddle, red w/mustard stripe & HP cow scene, 10x6", EX..1,265.00
Canister, appl leather armorial, 1850s, 6¼x2⅞"............................. 65.00
Container, mustard pnt, rnd/ftd w/trn finial, 3¾" 575.00
Cup, ash burl w/make-do tin rpr at lip, sm hdl, scrubbed, 4x6" 575.00
Egg cup, strawberries on salmon, Lehnware, sm flakes, 2⅝" 950.00
Jar, camphor wood w/old red & yel wash, incised rings, w/lid, 10x6".. 525.00
Jar, Pease, squat, wear on finial, 6⅛" 600.00
Jar, red/wht roses on salmon w/strawberries on lid, Lehnware, 5x2⅝"..400.00
Jar, saffron; strawberries/tulips on salmon, Lehnware, 5"...........5,635.00
Scoop, natural patina, butter stamp of cow in hdl, 12x6¾" 575.00
Sugar bowl, gr pnt, lid trn in concentric circles, appl knob, 1820, 5".. 700.00
Sugar bowl, gr pnt, rnd trn bowl, w/lid, 1800s, minor rpr, 6x9".... 400.00
Trencher, hewn, good form on ends, worn bl pnt, 5¼x22x13" 460.00
Trencher, hewn birch w/worn red pnt, scrubbed int, 5x16x15"...515.00
Trencher, hewn butternut w/red wash, scrubbed int, oblong, 6x29x19"...800.00
Trencher, slate bl int, good form on ends, 2x5x12½", EX............. 460.00

Woodworking Machinery

Vintage cast-iron woodworking machines are monuments to the highly skilled engineers, foundrymen, and machinists who devised them,

thus making possible the mass production of items ranging from clothespins, boxes, and barrels to decorative moldings and furniture. Though attractive from a nostalgic viewpoint, many of these machines are bought by the hobbyist and professional alike, to be put into actual use — at far less cost than new equipment. Many worth-assessing factors must be considered; but as a general rule, a machine in good condition is worth about 65¢ a pound (excluding motors). A machine needing a lot of restoration is not worth more than 35¢ a pound, while one professionally rebuilt and with a warranty can be calculated at $1.10 a pound. Modern, new machinery averages over $3.00 a pound. Two of the best sources of information on purchasing or selling such machines are *Vintage Machines — Searching for the Cast Iron Classics*, by Tom Howell, and *Used Machines and Abused Buyers* by Chuck Seidel from *Fine Woodworking*, November/December 1984. Prices quoted are for machines in good condition, less motors and accessories. Our advisor for this category is Mr. Dana Martin Batory, author of *Vintage Woodworking Machinery, An Illustrated Guide to Four Manufacturers*, Volumes I and II, and *An Illustrated Guide to Four More Manufacturers*. See his listing in the Directory under Ohio for further information. No phone calls, please.

American Saw Mill Machinery Company, 1931

Band saw, Monarch Line, #X25, 30" w/built-in ball-bearing motor ...770.00
Jointer, Monarch Line, #XII, ball-bearing, 16" 1,200.00
Planer, Monarch Line, single surface, 30" 2,600.00
Sander, Monarch Line, #X8, ball-bearing drum & disk 560.00

American Wood Working Machinery Company, 1920

Band saw, 30" 750.00
Jointer, bench; 8" 100.00
Planer, #1, 16" 1,075.00
Shaper, #20-C, 2-spindle 1,700.00

Buss Machine Works, ca 1950

Planer, #4-L, 30" 3,120.00
Planer, #66, 30" 4,865.00
Planer, #208, 20" 1,460.00
Planer, #248, 24" 2,240.00

Delta Manufacturing Company, 1939

Band saw, #768, 10" 50.00
Disk sander, #1426, belt drive, 12" 35.00
Drill press, #1370-H, high speed, floor, 17" 200.00
Drill press, bench, 14" 50.00
Jointer, #654, ball-bearing, 6" 50.00
Lathe, #930, timken-bearing, 11" 45.00
Lathe, #955, timken-bearing, 9" 35.00
Shaper, #1180, ball-bearing, reversible...................................... 30.00
Table saw, #860, tilt top, 8" 35.00

Duro Metal Products Co., 1935

Band saw, #3020, 12" 55.00
Carver/router/shaper, #3100 .... 130.00
Drill press, bench; #3080 .... 50.00
Jigsaw, #3000, 12" 10.00
Jointer, #3000, 12" 10.00
Jointer, #3030, 4" 20.00
Lathe, #3053, 10" 30.00
Scroll saw, #3005, 24" 55.00
Tablesaw, #3010, 7" 15.00

F. H. Clement Co., 1896

Band saw, 28", Improved......................................1,040.00
Band saw, 34", Patent Improved........................635.00
Boring machine, #2, Post....................................325.00
Lathe, pattern maker's; iron bed, Improved, 20"..........815.00
Planer, #2½, dbl surface, 26"...........................3,000.00
Ripsaw, #2, iron fr, 16".......................................585.00
Sand belt machine, Improved..............................425.00
Sand-papering machine, #2, Universal.................585.00
Sander, #3, dbl spindle..585.00
Shaper, #1, reversible, Improved........................650.00
Splitting saw, #1, iron fr, wood top, 12".............325.00
Table saw, dbl arbor, Improved, 16"...................815.00

Hoyt & Brother Company, 1888

Band saw & resawing machine, #1194, 20".......1,700.00
Cut-off saw, overhung, traversing, 14"................650.00
Mortiser & borer, #2...780.00
Planing & matching machine, #7, 13"...............3,250.00
Scroll saw, #1...300.00
Table saw, #2, 14"...800.00
Tenoning machine, #2...650.00

J. A. Fay & Egan Company, 1900

Jointer, New #2, 16"...1,550.00
Jointer, New #2, 20"...1,625.00
Jointer, New #2, 30"...1,820.00
Jointer, New #4, extra heavy, 24".....................1,885.00
Jointer, New #4, extra heavy, 30".....................2,275.00
Molder, #1½, 4-sided, 4"..................................1,050.00
Molder, #2, 4-sided, 6"......................................1,500.00
Mortiser, #5, dbl hollow chisel, horizontal........1,100.00
Planer, #2½, dbl-belted surface, med sz, 26".....1,850.00
Ripsaw, #3, self feed, X-lg................................2,400.00

Northfield Foundry & Machine Co., 1950

Band saw, motor driven, 20"..............................585.00
Band saw, 27"...845.00
Jointer, heavy duty, 12".......................................975.00
Jointer, 12"...725.00
Planer, No 5, 24x6"..1,450.00
Table saw, No 2, 16"...450.00
Table saw, No 4, 20"...900.00

Powermatic, Inc., 1965

Band saw, #141, 14"..145.00
Jointer, #50, 6"...110.00
Planer, #100, 12"..200.00
Planer, #160, 16"..650.00
Planer, #221, 20"..725.00
Sander, #033, 6" belt...90.00
Scroll saw, #95, 24"...100.00
Table saw, #62, 10"...135.00
Table saw, #66, 10"...230.00

The Sidney Machine Tool Co., 1916 (Famous Woodworking Machinery)

Band saw, 20"...325.00

Band saw, 27"...535.00
Band saw, 32"...715.00
Jointer, 20"..1,220.00
Lathe, pattern-maker's, 20"................................325.00
Mortiser, hollow chisel, new model....................585.00
Mortiser & tenoner, combined...........................575.00
Planer, dbl-belted, 26x8"..................................1,755.00
Planer, 24"...975.00
Saw, combination; No 4, 16"..............................485.00
Saw, Variety, No 2, 20".......................................875.00
Saw, Variety, No 6, 16".......................................780.00
Saw, Variety, No 16, 20".....................................750.00
Woodworker, portable, hand...............................485.00
Woodworker, Universal, No 40.........................1,300.00

Sprunger Power Tools, 1950s

Band saw, 14"..60.00
Jigsaw, 20"..40.00
Lathe, gap bed, 10"..50.00
Table saw, tilt arbor, 10¼".....................................75.00

Worcester Porcelain Company

The Worcester Porcelain Company was deeded in 1751. During the first or Dr. Wall period (so called for one of its proprietors), porcelain with an Oriental influence was decorated in underglaze blue. Useful tablewares represented the largest portion of production, but figurines and decorative items were also made. Very little of the earliest wares were marked and can only be identified by a study of forms, glazes, and the porcelain body, which tends to transmit a greenish cast when held to light. Late in the fifties, a crescent mark was in general use, and rare examples bear a facsimile of the Meissen crossed swords. The first period ended in 1783, and the company went through several changes in ownership during the next 80 years. The years from 1783 to 1792 are referred to as the Flight period. Marks were a small crescent, a crown with 'Royal,' or an impressed 'Flight.' From 1792 to 1807 the company was known as Flight and Barr and used the trademark 'F&B' or 'B,' with or without a small cross. From 1807 to 1813 the company was under the Barr, Flight, and Barr management; this era is recognized as having produced porcelain with the highest quality of artistic decoration. Their mark was 'B.F.B.' From 1813 to 1840 many marks were used, but the most usual was 'F.B.B.' under a crown to indicate Flight, Barr, and Barr. In 1840 the firm merged with Chamberlain, and in 1852 they were succeeded by Kerr and Binns. The firm became known as Royal Worcester in 1862. The production was then marked with a circle with '51' within and a crown on top. The date of manufacture was incised into the bottom or stamped with a letter of the alphabet, just under the circle. In 1891 Royal Worcester England was added to the circle and crown. From that point on, each piece is dated with a code of dots or other symbols. After 1891 most wares had a blush-color ground. Prior to that date it was ivory. Most shapes were marked with a unique number.

During the early years they produced considerable ornamental wares with a Persian influence. This gave way to a Japanesque influence. James Hadley is most responsible for the Victorian look. He is considered the 'best ever' designer and modeller. He was joined by the finest porcelain painters. Together they produced pieces with very fine detail and exquisite painting and decoration. Figures, vases, and tableware were produced in great volume and are highly collectible. During the 1890s they allowed the artists to sign some of their work. Pieces signed on the face by the Stintons, Baldwyn, Davis, Raby, Powell, Sedgley, and Rushton (not a complete list) are in great demand. The company is still in production. There is an outstanding museum on the company grounds in Worcester, England.

Note: Most pieces had lids or tops (if there is a flat area on the top lip, chances are it had one), if missing deduct 30% to 40%.

Basket, fruit; rosettes/latticework, late 18th C, 8"..........................825.00
Bowl, bl chinoiserie scenes, trellis rim border, late 18th C, 3x8"... 295.00
Bowl, honeycomb w/medallions/gilt reserves/jewels, dbl walls, 4", pr.. 700.00
Bowl, Oriental flowers, mc/gold on wht, w/in bl-fr panels, 1770, 7"...350.00
Bowl, pheasant & floral panels, 3 ftd w/lion masks, 1870, 5x4" ...225.00
Bowl, wooded landscape, bl on wht, Dr Wall period, ca 1775, 6"..1,000.00
Bust, Alexandra, parian, ca 1864, 12½" 475.00
Cup & saucer, tea; Milkmaids, ca 1770s, 1¾x3", 5" 400.00
Ewer, floral on ivory w/gold trim, ca 1899, 13¼"...........................400.00
Ewer, floral on wht, gold coiled salamander hdl, TR, 11" 575.00
Figurine, Eastern water carrier w/jars, Hadley, ca 1891, 17", 18", pr ...885.00
Figurine, Greenaway-style child w/basket, stained ivory w/gold, 10"... 300.00
Figurine, lady dancing w/castanets in ea hand, 19th C, 13" 300.00
Figurine, Magnolia Bud, lady seated w/flower in hand, #3244, 1958, 5"...165.00
Figurine, maid draped in bl, urn on head, holds jug, 1894, 20", pr ..725.00
Figurine, male w/scythe, lady w/bbl, Hadley, ca 1888, 14" ...1,000.00
Figurine, Nautilus shell w/lizard on coral, ca 1880, 8⅞" 600.00
Figurine, The Grace, Age of Elegance series, 1978, #9/500, 11½"...275.00
Figurine, Yellow Straw, palomino horse, #RW3882, Doris Linder, 1971 ..1,000.00
Goblet, honeycomb rtcl w/medallions/jewels, dbl walls, 1875, 5⅜" ...1,525.00
Plate, marriage; bow & arrow w/floral decor, ca 1770, 8½"...........625.00
Potpourri, ferns, mc/gilt, rtcl lid, 1899 13".................................235.00
Salts, figural merman & mermaid w/clamshell, 1876, 3½", pr 275.00
Tazza, floral w/gold, leaf molded, ca 1887, 10⅛"...........................180.00
Tea set, honeycomb/jewels/gold, att G Owen, ca 1878, pot+jug+bowl+c/s..28,225.00
Thimble, HP birds on branches, gold rim, ½" dia 225.00
Trivet, pierced foliage/scrollwork, triangular, Grainger, ca 1885, 6"...215.00
Urn, cattle/stream, J Stinton, ornate gold hdls/trim, w/lid, 12", pr .2,760.00
Vase, Bamboo, red & gold enamel, 3-branch hdls, pierced neck, 1883, 7" ..500.00

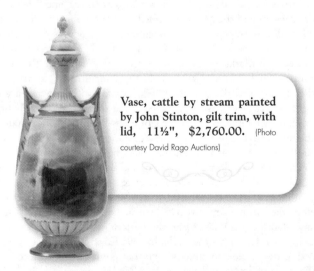

Vase, cattle by stream painted by John Stinton, gilt trim, with lid, 11½", $2,760.00. (Photo courtesy David Rago Auctions)

Vase, cornucopia w/goat head/jewels/foliage, #2092, ca 1900, 12¾" ..765.00
Vase, honeycomb rtcl w/serpent hdls, att G Owen, #871, ca 1900, 7" .31,725.00
Vase, honeycomb rtcl/medallions, att G Owen, #1552, ca 1894, 9" ...30,550.00
Vase, landscape cartouch w/cobalt/gold/jewels, w/lid, ca 1897, 7". 450.00
Vase, rtcl wht panels w/in red/gilt ribbing, ftd, dome lid, 1891, 11"..4,400.00
Vase, stork by river, angular hdls, Walter Powell, ca 1915, 10" 625.00
Vase, trumpet flower w/leaf base, #G467, 4½x4"...........................120.00

World's Fairs and Expos

Since 1851 and the Crystal Palace Exhibition in London, World's Fairs and Expositions have taken place at a steady pace. Many of them commemorate historical events. The 1904 Louisiana Purchase Exposition, commonly known as the St. Louis World's Fair, celebrated the 100th anniversary of the Louisiana Purchase agreement between Thomas Jefferson and Napoleon in 1803. The 1893 Columbian Exposition commemorated the 400th anniversary of the discovery of America by Columbus in 1492. (Both of these fairs were held one year later than originally scheduled.) The multitude of souvenirs from these and similar events have become a growing area of interest to collectors in recent years. Many items have a 'crossover' interest into other fields: i.e., collectors of postcards and souvenir spoons eagerly search for those from various fairs and expositions. Values have fallen somewhat due to eBay sales. Many of the so-called common items have come down in value. However 1939 World's Fair items are still hot. For additional information collectors may contact World's Fairs Collectors Society (WFCS), whose address is in the Directory under Clubs, Newsletters, and Catalogs, or our advisor, Herbert Rolfes. His address is listed in the Directory under Florida.

Key: T&P — Trylon & Perisphere   WF — World's Fair

1876 Centennial, Philadelphia

Banner, International Exhibition, silk, fr, EX 95.00
Booklet, Centennial Souvenir, map & photos of Expo, 3x4", VG+..10.00
Bookmark, Geo Washington w/verse, silk......................................100.00
Candy dish, EAPG, clear w/bear forearms as hdls, 5¼x9⅞" 60.00
Catalog, Official; Art Gallery & Annexes Dept IV, 6th revised ed, VG... 55.00
Lithograph, International Exhibition, king w/followers, 7x19¾", EX ..50.00
Medal, Fairmont Park w/Main Building on bk, wht metal, 2" dia..25.00
Photo, Statue of Liberty arm & torch w/info booth, 8x10" 15.00
Pin, gilted w/Art Gallery, ⅞" dia 35.00
Sample, silk cocoons, Corticelli Silk, graphics on box top, G (EX box)...35.00
Scale, souvenir; Fairbanks Scale, Centennial, 1776-86, 5x9½", EX ...315.00
Ticket, package; Admit the Bearer, Miss Columbia seated, 2¼x4", EX.. 20.00
Trade card, AW Crane Champion Sectional Boilers, 5 buildings... 25.00
Trade card, Howe Sewing Machine/Agricultural Hall, 3x4⅝" 50.00
Tumbler, 10-sided w/1876 in star, stemmed, 7x2½", EX+..............20.00

1893 Columbian, Chicago

Book, Columbia's Courtship, Prang lithos w/Crain verses, 13 pgs, VG+..75.00
Book, pop-up; Electrical Building+2 buildings, 10x12", EX, $150 to..200.00
Certificate, Award for Excellence, Krembs & Comp, 28x22"+fr..225.00
Clock, Chris Columbus on ship's deck, Jones Mfr, metal, windup, EX ...100.00
Directory, Official; maps, ads & fair scenes, 1,120 pgs, VG+........195.00
Dish, Goverment Building & Art Palace, scalloped edge, England, 10". 35.00
Elongated coin, 1893 Indian head cent, Type V 30.00
Fan, hand; Manufacturers/Liberal Arts Buildings, 13x25" (open), EX..100.00
Ginger jar, Satsuma, 2 buildings, gilted, lid w/mk, 5½x5", minimum..725.00
Guide, Official; 192 pgs, complete, EX...45.00
Hatchet, glass, Native American image, yel vaseline, 7¼" 100.00
Hatchet, glass, Washington portrait w/Father of This Country, 4x8".. 140.00
Medal, The Irish Villiage, w/One Thousand Dollars on bk, 1" dia...585.00
Paperweight, Agricultural Building, glass, Barnes & Abrams, 2x4"...75.00
Paperweight, Delaware State Building, glass, Libbey, 2¼x4" 75.00
Paperweight, Mines & Mining Building encased in glass, 2½x4"... 35.00
Pass, complimentary; Hon JP Root, 2½x4", EX 270.00
Pass, employee's; December, Forfeit If Transferred, 2⅜x3½", EX..255.00
Pitcher, Satsuma, Machinery Building & Japanese Building, 7¼", EX..100.00
Playing cards, Columbus' ships w/fair scenes on face, 52+joker, EX..75.00
Playing cards, Landing of Columbus on bk, fair scenes on faces, EXIB...120.00
Postcard set, Official; set of 10, EX (orig wrapper)......................200.00
Rose bowl, yel cased satin, WF 1893 in gold, 4½" 445.00
Spoon, Celtic harp on hdl w/Irish Villiage on bk of bowl, 4½" 100.00
Spoon, enameled sterling, Cascade Building in bowl, ornate hdl, 6" ..100.00

Tape measure, bbl shape, vegetable ivory, Fr, 1⅝", EX 125.00
Thimble holder, sailing ship, MOP, 3¼x3" 240.00
Ticket, Admit One, Java Theater Midway Plaisance, 1½x2½", EX .. 290.00
Ticket, Good Only on Day of Sale & on Special WF Trains..., EX ... 90.00
Ticket, Good Only on the John Bull Train, EX 115.00
Ticket, Ice Railway, 1x2", EX 270.00
Ticket, Natatorium/Gymnase Admission, 1x2¾", EX 400.00
Trade card set, Singer Mfg, Costumes of All Nations, 36 cards, EXIB ...75.00
Tumbler, girl in garden, Mary Gregory style, 3¾", EX 75.00
Vase, wht satin w/HP floral, 6x2¼" 325.00

1901 Pan American

Bell, made from brass from USS Maine, 3½" 125.00
Frying pan, Electric Tower, Pan-American 1901 on hdl 30.00
Letter opener, Pan-American on blade w/buffalo on hdl, aluminum, EX .. 25.00
Match safe, Souvenir Pan-American Exposition 1901, aluminum ... 60.00
Paperweight, Tower of Music encased in glass, 2½x4" 25.00
Pin-back, Indian w/flag feeding buffalo, Whitehead & Hoag, EX .. 85.00
Shot glass, frosted banner/buffalo/When You Drink Do of Me Think ... 45.00

1904 St. Louis

Bowl, Cascade Gardens, grape-leaf shape, yel w/bl border, 2x5" .. 145.00
Bowl, Palace of Liberal Arts, scalloped edge, gold trim, 1x6½" 150.00
Cigar holder, amber glass w/metal collar, red-lined case, 2½" 80.00
Cigar holder, mule beside lg bbl, St Louis 1904, brass plated, 4" .. 175.00
Cigar holder, Union Station, hinged lid, 2¾x5½" 35.00
Game, Down the Pike w/Mrs Wiggs..., Milton Bradley, complete, EXIB... 75.00
Handkerchief, T Roosevelt w/roses on border, cloth, 10½" sq, EX ... 125.00
Inkwell, crab shape, WF St Louis 1904, silver on blk 80.00
Letter opener, Louisiana Purchase on blade w/eagle hdl, brass, 7" 45.00
Lucky penny, 1904 Indian head cent mtd in horseshoe 30.00
Paperweight, mule w/pack standing on railroad tracks, metal, 3x3" ... 385.00
Plaque, City Hall in relief, wht w/gr bkground, bsk, 5½" dia 120.00
Plate, T Jefferson w/palaces, Louisiana Purchase Souvenir, 10" dia .. 125.00

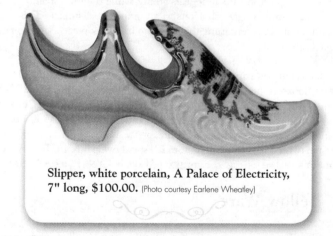

Slipper, white porcelain, A Palace of Electricity, 7" long, $100.00. (Photo courtesy Earlene Wheatley)

Souvenir, A Clam w/3 Feet emb w/Cascade Building on bk, 1¾", EX .. 180.00
Stein, Palace of Electricity, brass over metal, 6¼" 320.00
Tray, Indian maiden w/slain elk, mc litho, 13½x16½", EX 285.00
Tray, serving; Cascades under glass, metal fr w/cut-out stars, 4½" .. 50.00

1933 Chicago

Bank, book shape, leather cover w/T&P emb, VG 75.00
Book, Official Guide; EX 15.00
Booklet, Century of Progress, fair scenes, RH Donnelly, EX 20.00
Booklet, Official WF Weekly, Opening Week, 64 pgs, 11x8½", EX .. 20.00

Booklet, Report of the President to the Board of Trustees, 3/14/34, EX .. 12.00
Bracelet, logo w/6 buildings in vignettes 30.00
Corkscrew, WF Chicago 1934, emb metal, 2⅞" 15.00
Creamer, Railroad Building, Galatea pattern, 3" 35.00
Elongated cent, Train of Tomorrow 15.00
Letter opener, Hall of Religion, enameled brass, 4½", NM (EX card) .. 25.00
Lucky key, Keep Me for Luck, teeth cut as buildings, 2" 15.00
Medal, Research & Industry, bronze w/male in relief, 2¼" dia 35.00
Paperweight, Mickey Mouse on glass disk encased in glass, 3½" .. 180.00
Pitcher, cream; Administration Building, copper, 12-oz 15.00
Playing cards, Skyride, complete, EXIB 15.00
Playing cards, views of fair, 53 cards, complete, EXIB 15.00
Puzzle, jigsaw; Fort Dearborn, 225 pcs, EXIB 35.00
Shakers, T&P shape, ceramic, Japan, pr w/holder 80.00
Tape measure, General Exhibits Building, celluloid, 1½" dia, EX .. 75.00
Thermeter, key shape, brass, 8¾" 15.00
Thermometer, Havoline Tower shape, 4½" 30.00
Thermometer/picture, Hall of Science, 5x7" 15.00
Ticket, Teacher's Jubilee Day, 8/10/34, 2¼x5¾", EX 12.00
Token, Hoover Electric Cleaner, brass, 1¼" dia, VG+ 15.00

1939 New York

Ashtray, NY WF 1939 emb on edges, solid brass, 5 rests, 4½" 25.00
Banner, NYWF 1939, T&P on red, on dowel rod, 11x8", EX 30.00
Banner, Pillsbury Sno-Sheen Cake Flour 27¢, 18½x11", EX 60.00
Book, Souvenir View Book of NYWF, The World of Tomorrow, 50 pgs, EXIP ... 30.00
Booklet, World of Tomorrow, Indian Head Press, 24 pgs, EX 35.00
Bookmark, Scottie dog atop w/fair medallion, 3", EX 30.00
Bottle opener, T&P w/4 singers, Hail Hail the Gang's..., wood, EX .. 40.00
Brooch, ship's wheel w/T&P in center in red enamel, 1" 40.00
Butter pat, wht emb T&P on gr, Lenox 250.00
Cake plate w/serving knife, T&P, Cronin China, 10" 95.00
Camera, Bullet; New York World's Fair, Kodak, EX, minimum value ... 300.00
Cane/seat, Fair Seat, Transamerican Specialties, wood/metal, 33", EX .. 25.00
Cigarette pack case, plastic w/hinged lid, T&P on front, 3x2x1", EX .. 70.00
Coasters, T&P decor, papier-mache, set of 7, 4" dia, NMIB 50.00
Cup & saucer, T&P, HP ceramic, Japan, EX 60.00
Kan-O-Seat, Stanford Johnson Seating Corp, folds, 34½", EX 45.00
Map, Official WF Pictorial Map, Created by Tony Sarg, tri-fold, EX ... 35.00
Menu, Heineken's Restaurant, Holland water scene cover, 11x7½", EX .. 27.50
Paperweight, T&P, brass plated, 3½", EX 60.00
Pencil, mechanical; gold w/NYWF, screw-top action, 10½", EXIB ... 30.00
Pennant, NY WF, T&P, yel on bl, 13½", EX 35.00
Pennant, World of Tomorrow, fair scenes, gr & yel, 10x24", EX 40.00
Pin-back, T&P w/Dawn of a New Day, celluloid, 1¼" dia, EX 15.00
Plate, T&P & border in gr w/wht, Buffalo China, 10" dia 130.00
Plate, T&P w/scene border, Homer Laughlin, 10" 150.00
Poster, 100 Yrs of RR History Exhibit, 41x27", EX 400.00
Powder jar, bl w/wht T&P, w/lid, pottery, Japan, 1⅝x3⅛" 25.00
Press photo, aerial view, Underwood & Underwood, 8x10" 25.00
Press photo, Ford Auto Turntable, 10x8" 50.00
Press photo, Ford's Road of Tomorrow, 10x8" 45.00
Scarf, fair scenes on yel silk, 20x18", EX 45.00
Sheet music, Dawn of a New Day, Gershwin, 12½x9½", EX 25.00
Tire ashtray, Goodyear, rubber w/glass insert of T&P, 6", NMIB 90.00
Vase, bud; bl w/wht T&P, Japan, 3x2", pr 25.00
Wallet, T&P emb tanned leather, 4½x3½", NM 55.00

1939 San Francisco

Bank, Libby's 100 Famous Foods, slot on top, 3½x2⅛" dia 18.00
Brochure, SFWF, A Pageant of the Pacific, 8x10" (fold-out), EX .. 12.00
Lighter, Court of Pacifica, blk & silver, Match King 20.00

Pamphlet, Visit the SFWF...by Rail, Southern Pacific Lines, 9x4", EX .. 8.00
Ring, Bay Bridge w/GGIE, brass 12.00

1962 Seattle

Ashtray, floor; Space Needle shape, chrome-plated metal, 25", EX....450.00
Bank, Coliseum, bl & wht plastic, 8x8½", (VG box) 50.00
Bottle opener, fair scene w/jewels & ornate scrollwork, Vaughn.... 30.00
Lighter, table; Space Needle shape, chrome plated, 10½", EX 60.00
Model, Space Needle, brass, 6", MIB 17.50
Model, Space Needle, paper, 40", NMIB 35.00
Model, Space Needle, plastic, Stalco Products, 18", EXIB 30.00
Pill box, eng fair scene & logo, hinged lid, 1½x1½" 25.00
Pin-back, Don't Gouge Me I'm a Seattleite, EX, minimum value.. 10.00
Pin-back, I Rode the Alweg Monorail, 3⅜" dia, EX 10.00
Pin-back, Souvenir of...1962, Space Needle image, 3½", EX 20.00
Plate, over-view of fair w/Space Needle, Frederick & Nelson 12.00
Plate, wht w/bl fair scene & logo, 10½", set of 6 .... 30.00
Press kit, Gracie Hansen's Paradise Girlie Show, EX 22.50
Towel, Space Needle, terry cloth, Sayco Screen Prints, 29x19", EX .. 40.00
View-Master reel pak, 3 reels of fair scenes, MIP 40.00

1964 New York

Bank, Daily Dime Register; Unisphere, NMOC............................. 40.00
Brochure, Visit General Electric Progressland, Disney, 4¼x3", EX....20.00
Calendar, perpetual; Official, NM (EX box) 55.00
Cutting board, Heywood-Wakefield, solid wood, 10½x6¾", NM... 20.00
Dinosaurs, Sinclair Dinoland, plastic, set of 6, MIP 300.00
Egg timer, fair logo on top, 3x2" dia 20.00
License plate, yel on blk, w/holder, NM... 60.00
Medallion, Land of Lincoln Pavillion, Lincoln bust, brass, 1½", MIP..35.00
Paperweight, NY skyline w/logo above, chrome plated, 2¾x3x2" .. 20.00
Paperweight, Swedish Pavillion, horse inside Lucite, 1¾x2", EX.. 25.00
Placemats (8), birdcages pattern, from Denmark Pavillion, 12x16", MIP.. 40.00
Playing cards, fair scenes on face, MIP (sealed) 40.00
Press kit, IBM, photos, fact sheets, etc, 12x9", EX....................... 65.00
Puzzle, interlocking slide; Unisphere, MOC 40.00
Slide set, fair scenes, Photo Lab Inc, set of 90, EXIB 70.00
Ticket, opening day; April 22, 1964, EX.. 30.00

Wright, Frank Lloyd

Born in Richland Center, Wisconsin, in 1869, Wright became a pioneer in architectural expression, developing a style referred to as 'prairie.' From early in the century until he died in 1959, he designed houses with rooms that were open, rather than divided by walls in the traditional manner. They exhibited low, horizontal lines and strongly projecting eaves, and he filled them with furnishings whose radical aesthetics complemented the structures to perfection. Several of his homes have been preserved to the present day, and collectors who admire his ideas and the unique, striking look he achieved treasure the stained glass windows, furniture, chinaware, lamps, and other decorative accessories designed by Wright. Our advisor for this category and related Arts and Crafts subjects is Bruce Austin; he is listed in the Directory under New York.

Key: H — Heritage Henredon

Armchair, hexagonal bk/seat, aluminum fr w/red leather, 1956, 34" ..15,500.00
Armchair, wide slat bk, slat support ea side, sq form, uphl seat, 32" ...780.00
Chair, uphl bk/seat, oak trim, w/Niedecken for Irving House, 38", VG..3,200.00
Chair, wide plank extends from above bk rail to stretcher, armless ...37,500.00

Chair set, sq uphl bk/seat, H, Taliesin, rephl, 33", VG, 6 for........ 950.00
Check, FLW Foundation, lg-scale signature, dtd 1954 .... 1,400.00

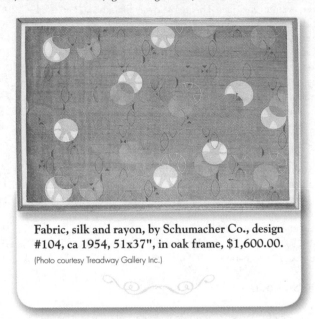

Fabric, silk and rayon, by Schumacher Co., design #104, ca 1954, 51x37", in oak frame, $1,600.00.

(Photo courtesy Treadway Gallery Inc.)

Lamp, cherry Taliesin II, sqs & boxes on post at varied angles, 30" ..1,140.00
Pitcher, water; silver, 4-sided cone w/long triangle spout, Tiffany Co.. 5,400.00
Print, int/ext+1 view of Larkin Co, German publisher, fr, 13x22" ..600.00
Shelf, H, designed for top of 2000 series sideboard, 18x86".......... 240.00
Sideboard, H, bank of drws on right, drw over 2 doors on left, 66" L.. 1,320.00
Table, dining; 48" dia top/X-stretcher base & 3 leaves+8 uphl chairs... 1,400.00

Wrought Iron

Until the middle of the nineteenth century, almost all the metal hand forged in America was made from a material called wrought iron. When wrought iron rusts it appears grainy, while the mild steel that was used later shows no grain but pits to an orange-peel surface. This is an important aid in determining the age of an ironwork piece. See also Fireplace Implements.

Broiler, rotates on tripod base, 3x25" 115.00
Game hooks, suspended from chains w/ring hanger, 12x11" dia .. 200.00
Hinges, circular ends, 30¼x14", pr.. 115.00
Kettle stand, tripod w/penny ft, heart & rope-twist detail, 14", VG...110.00
Planter, rococo scrollwork, 43x21" dia, pr..................................... 825.00
Toaster, twisted wire & wrought iron, 22" spiral swing hdl, 16" W... 100.00
Wine rack, arched top cage construction w/doors, holds 88, Fr, 69x30"...825.00

Yellow Ware

Ranging in color from buff to deep mustard, yellow ware which almost always has a clear glaze can be slip banded, plain, Rockingham decorated, flint enamel glazed, or mocha decorated. Black or red mocha decorated pieces are the most desirable. Although blue mocha decorated pieces are the most common, green decorated pieces command the lowest prices. Pieces having a combination of two colors are the rarest. The majority of pieces are plain and do not bear a manufacture's mark. Primarily produced in the United States, England, and Canada this utilitarian ware was popular from the mid-nineteenth century until the early twentieth century. Yellow ware was first produced in New York, Pennsylvania, and Vermont. However, the center for yellow ware production was East Liverpool, Ohio, a town which once supported more than 30 potters. Yellow ware is still being produced today in both the United States and England. Because of websites and Internet auctions, prices have tended to become uniform throughout the United States. The use of this pottery as accessories in decorating and its exposure in country magazines has caused prices to rise, especially for the more utilitarian forms such as plates and bowls. Note: Because this is a utilitarian ware, it is often found with damage and heavy wear. Damage does have a negative impact on price, especially for the common forms. For further information we recommend *Collector's Guide to Yellow Ware, Book I,* written by our advisor John Michel and Lisa McAllister, and *Collector's Guide to Yellow Ware, Books II* and *III,* by Lisa McAllister. Mr. Michel's address is in the Directory under New York. See also Rockingham.

Bowl, batter; emb ribs, spouring spout, 6½x14" 130.00
Bowl, bl & pk bands, 20th C, 5" 95.00
Bowl, bl & wht seaweed banding, 19th C, 4½x10" 450.00
Bowl, bl band & thin wht stripes, crazing, ca 1900, 12" 325.00
Bowl, milk; plain, flared sides, 19th C, 3x13½" 175.00
Bowl, mixing; cream band above 2 brn lines, 5¾x12¼" 195.00
Bowl, mixing; emb circles along rim, spout, 20th C, 5¼x9¼" 110.00
Bowl, vegetable; plain, oval, 9½" L, NM 120.00
Bowl, wide bl band amid narrow wht stripes, 6½x11¾" 225.00
Bowl, 2 brn & 2 cream stripes, 4½x9½" 125.00
Bowls, nesting; brn bands, 5", 7", 8", 9", set of 4, EX 200.00
Butter tub, brn & wht stripes, crazing, 5x7" 185.00
Canister, bl incised lines, flanged base, hdls, 7¾x8¼" 495.00
Chamber pot, wht band above 2 brn stripes, hdl, rstr rim, 5½x9" .. 75.00

Colander, brown (hard to find) and white bands, made by Jeffords and the Yellow Rock Company, 13", minimum value, $1,500.00.

Jug, wide bl band & 2 narrow bl lines, hairline/chip, 5" 250.00
Mold, ear of corn at top, scalloped sides, sm chips, 4x8½" 95.00
Mug, bl seaweed on wht band, 3⅝x4¼" 425.00
Mug, child's; A Trifle for Eliza (blk transfer), 2½x3" 295.00
Mug, cream & bl stripes, hairline/chip, 4½x5" 125.00
Pepper pot, bl stripes & wht bands, minor flake, 4¼" 1,250.00
Pie plate, plain, 11" 130.00
Pitcher, bl & wht seaweed bands, brn stripes, OH, 6⅜" 375.00
Pitcher, brn stripes/checkerboard brn bands, 1800s, 3½", VG 250.00
Potty, wht band w/2 brn stripes, 19th C, old rpr, 5x7½" 95.00
Rolling pin, wooden hdl through central bore, 15" overall 350.00
Salt cellar, wht band & pale bl stripes, ftd, flaw, 2x3" 150.00

Zanesville Art Pottery

Prior to 1900, this company was known as The Zanes Roofing Tile Company; then it was reorganized, and production shifted to the manufacture of art pottery. Their most familiar line, La Mora, was made in the standard brown glaze as well as in a matt version very similar to Owens' Matt Utopia.

Jardiniere, La Mora, tulips on brn, emb scrolls, nicks, 12x14½" ... 215.00
Jardiniere & ped, La Mora, tulips on brn, hairline, 27" 345.00
Pitcher, La Mora, red clover on brn, #806 5, sm chip, 6" 85.00
Vase, La Mora, wild roses on brn, sgn SO, 8¼x4" 180.00

Zanesville Glass

Glassware was produced in Zanesville, Ohio, from as early as 1815 until 1851. Two companies produced clear and colored hollow ware pieces in five characteristic patterns: 1) diamond faceted, 2) broken swirls, 3) vertical swirls, 4) perpendicular fluting, 5) plain, with scalloped or fluted rims and strap handles. The most readily identified product is perhaps the whiskey bottles made in the vertical swirl pattern, often called globular swirls because of their full, round bodies. Their necks vary in width; some have a ringed rim and some are collared. They were made in several colors; amber, light green, and light aquamarine are the most common. Our advisor for this category is Mark Vuono; he is listed in the Directory under Connecticut.

Bottle, amber, 24 swirled ribs, globular, blisters, 8½" 1,265.00
Bottle, aqua, 24 swirled ribs, globular, sm blisters, 7½" 400.00
Bottle, golden amber, globular, rolled mouth, 1820-40, 7¼" 900.00
Bottle, golden amber, 24 left-swirl ribs, globular, 1820-40, 8⅛" ... 550.00
Chestnut flask, sea gr w/appl rigaree on sides, 24 swirl ribs, 5½" .. 1,000.00
Chestnut flask, 10-Dmn, dk golden amber, pontil scar, 1820-40, 5½" .. 2,000.00
Creamer, golden amber, solid grooved-band hdl w/rigaree, 1820s, 4¼" ... 7,000.00
Tumbler, golden amber, 24-rib, sheared mouth, pontiled, 3⅞" .. 5,000.00

Zanesville Stoneware Company

Still in operation at its original location in Zanesville, Ohio, this company is the last surviving pottery dating from Zanesville's golden era of pottery production. They manufactured utilitarian stoneware, art ware vases, jardinieres and pedestals, dinnerware, and large hand-turned vases for use in outdoor gardens. Much of this ware has remained unidentified until today, since they often chose to mark their wares only with item numbers or the names of their various clients. Other items were marked with an impressed circular arrangement containing the company name and location or a three-line embossed device, the bottom line of which contained the letters ZSC.

Jardiniere, Matt Green, emb leaves, nicks, unmk, 9x11½" 120.00
Teapot, purple semi-matt, mk D24, sm, NM 48.00
Umbrella stand, Matt Green, emb foliate bands, 21" 360.00

Vase, embossed grapes and foliage, attributed, 16", $485.00 for the pair (one shown). (Photo courtesy Cincinnati Art Galleries)

Vase, Matt Green, emb geometrics, tapering cylinder, ftd, 9¼x4" ... 275.00
Vase, Matt Green, emb panels, #11, 7½" 55.00
Vase, Matt Green, shouldered, 12½" 120.00

Vase, Matt Green speckled, baluster, 12" 240.00
Vase, Neptune, bl & brn mottle, curled hdls, 18x13" 750.00

Zark

Established circa 1907 in St. Louis, Missouri, the Ozark Pottery made artware which it sold through an outlet called Zark Shops, hence the use of the Zark trademark. Most of their output was earthenware, but high-fired pottery has been reported as well. Some of the decoration was slip painted; other pieces were embossed. It operated for only a few years, perhaps closing as early as 1910. One of its founders and the primary designer was Robert Bringhurst, who was best known as a sculptor. Pieces are marked Zark, either incised or impressed. Our advisors for this category are Suzanne Perrault and David Rago; they are listed in the Directory under New Jersey.

Bowl, dk gr speckled, squat w/rim-to-width hdls, 3x7" 660.00
Bowl, Egyptian motif w/figural hdls & cvd bands, gr matt, 5x10", EX... 900.00
Bowl, motif on flat shoulder, lt/med bl matt, gr int, CCB, 3x9"... 1,200.00
Bust, Nouveau maid, dk bl-gr matt, ZARK/RPR, 2 hairlines, 9x12". 660.00

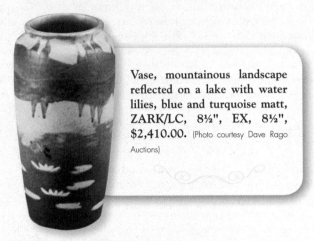

Vase, mountainous landscape reflected on a lake with water lilies, blue and turquoise matt, ZARK/LC, 8½", EX, 8½", $2,410.00. (Photo courtesy Dave Rago Auctions)

Vase, speckled turq/bl matt, 4 right-angle rim buttresses, JAC, 6x6"..1,920.00
Vase, stylized floral, blk on dk gr, JB, cylindrical, 10x4½"..........2,760.00

Zell

The Georg Schmider United Zell Ceramic Factories has a long and colorful history. Affectionately called 'Zell' by those who are attracted to this charming German-Dutch type tin-glazed earthenware, this type of ware came into production in the latter part of the last century. Zell has created some lovely majolica-like examples (which are beginning to attract their own following), but it is the German-Dutch scenes that are collected with such enthusiasm. Typical scenes are set against a lush green background with windmills on the distant horizon. Into the scenes appear typically garbed girls (long dresses with long white aprons and low-land bonnet head-gear) being teased or admired by little boys attired in pantaloon-type trousers and short rust-colored jackets, all wearing wooden shoes. There are variations on this theme, and occasionally a collector may find an animal theme or even a Kate Greenaway-like scene.

While Zell produced a wide range of wares and even quite recently (1970s) introduced an entirely hand-painted hen/rooster line, it is this early charming German-Dutch theme pottery that is coveted by increasing numbers of devoted collectors.

A similar ware in theme, technique, and quality but bearing the mark Haag or Made in Austria is included in this listing. Our advisor for this category is Lila Shrader; she is listed in the Directory under California.

Key:
BlkR — Black hen/rooster   KG — Kate Greenaway style
hdl/RA — handle at right   MIA — Made in Austria
     angle to spout

Bowl, Dutch boy w/toy boat, harbor scene, rtcl hdls, Baden, 10" ... 78.00
Bowl, rimmed soup; Dutch boy & girl in eerie woods, Baden, 7½" ..88.00
Bowl, water lilies on turq, majolica-like, rtcl hdls, Germany, 12" .. 40.00
Bread basket, 4x5" oval tile in base, 3½" H rtcl brass sides, Baden ... 290.00
Cake plate, costumed animals party in woods, rtcl hdls, Haag, 9½" . 130.00
Cake plate, Greenaway girls on bench, rtcl hdls/emb, Haag, 10½" .. 110.00
Candleholder, Dutch boys strolling, flared base, Baden, 7", ea..... 225.00
Canister, Dutch harbor scene, boats, bl/wht, Sucre, Haag, 6x4x4"....68.00
Child's feeding dish, Dutch boy & girl, MIA, 1½x7½" 65.00
Child's feeding dish, Dutch children in forest, Baden, 7½x1½" ... 135.00
Child's feeding dish, girl feeding lamb, KG, str sides, 7¾" 85.00
Creamer, Dutch boys strolling, harbor scene, KG, hdl/RA, 3½"............... 30.00
Creamer, Dutch children chatting/harbor scene, bl/wht, Haag, 4"...62.00
Creamer, Dutch girl shaking hands w/dog, Haag, MIA, 4½" 22.00
Creamer, geese chase Dutch boy w/golden goose, Haag, 4" 18.00
Cup & saucer, Dutch boy & girl strolling, Baden, from $12 to 45.00
Cup & saucer, various Dutch children scenes, Germany, from $12 to .30.00
Egg cup, Puss 'n Boots, MIA, 4½".. 75.00
Mug, Dutch girl w/stick & chicken, Germany, 3½" 27.00
Pitcher, Dutch boys stroll on path, hills beyond, Haag, MIA, 6" ... 48.00
Plaque, Dutch boy & girl embracing, rtcl brass fr, Haag, 12"........ 410.00
Plate, birds & grape on basketweave, majolica-like, Germany, 9".. 80.00
Plate, figs (dk) on basketweave, majolica-like, Germany, 8" 46.00
Plate, grandfather w/wheelbarrow & dogs, KG, Haag, 9" 100.00
Plate, grapes (purple) on basketweave, majolica-like, Germany, 7½"... 26.00
Plate, Nouveau water lilies in pool, majolica-like, Baden, 8" 65.00
Plate, Tom Thumb & pie, scalloped, MIA, 6½"............................. 58.00
Plates, lilies, cream on dk red, majolica-like, 9", set of 4 .... 48.00
Reamer, geese chase dog, MIA, 2-pc, 3½x5½" 385.00
Salt box, blk hen/rooster, open type, pierced for hanging, post 1970 ... 50.00
Shakers, Dutch boy & girl strolling, Baden, 3½", from $35 to 65.00
Sugar bowl, dish running away w/spoon, MIA, 3½" 38.00
Tankard, Dutch boys teasing girls, angular hdl, heavy base, 6½".... 62.00

Tankard, marked Baden, 11", $350.00. (Photo courtesy Lila Shrader)

Tile, Dutch girls whispering, octagonal, 4 sm ft, Baden, 5½" 90.00
Tile, sheep grazing, dog supervising, Haag, 6x6" 92.00
Vase, cat & fiddle, cylindrical, MIA, 5¾x2½".................................. 55.00

Zsolnay

Only until the past decade has the production of the Zsolnay factory become more correctly understood. In the beginning they produced only cement; industrial and kitchen ware manufacture began in the 1850s, and in the early 1870s a line of decorative architectural and art pottery was initiated which has continued to the present time.

The city of Pecs (pronounced Paach) is the major provincial city of southwest Hungary close to the Yugoslav border. The old German name for the city was Funfkirchen, meaning 'Five Churches.' (The 'five-steeple' mark became the factory's logo in 1878.)

Although most Americans only think of Zsolnay in terms of the bizarre, reticulated examples of the 1880s and 1890s and the small 'Eosine' green figures of animals and children that have been produced since the 1920s, the factory went through all the art trends of major international art potteries and produced various types of forms and decorations. The 'golden period,' circa 1895 – 1920, is when its Art Nouveau (Sezession in Austro-Hungarian terms) examples were unequaled. Vilmos Zsolnay was a Renaissance man devoted to innovation, and his children carried on the tradition after his death in 1900. Important sculptors and artists of the day were employed (usually anonymously) and married into the family, creating a dynasty.

Nearly all Zsolnay is marked, either impressed 'Zsolnay Pecs' or with the 'five steeple' stamp. Variations and form numbers can date a piece fairly accurately. For the most part, the earlier ethnic historical-revival pieces do not bring the prices that the later Sezession and second Sezession (Deco) examples do. Our advisors for this category are John Gacher and Federico Santi; they are listed in the Directory under Rhode Island.

Bowl, 3-D squirrel on oak branch on rim, brn/bl/gr lustre, 13" L, EX.... 2,040.00
Centerpc, 4 cherubs hold fruit-edged bowl aloft, metallic, 7½x13"..1,550.00
Figurine, bison, bl-gr Eosin, rectangular plinth, 6" 165.00
Figurine, fox w/tail curled around body, red flambe, Jubileum mk, 4".... 135.00
Figurine, frog, purple Eosin, Jubileum mk, 6" 225.00
Figurine, maid undressing by water urn, irid turq, cathedral mk, 11" .. 200.00

Figurine, nude boy gazes at open hand, gr Eosin, 1940s, 5¾" 215.00
Figurine, nymph kneels/hair covers face, gr/gold/red, #7981, 1900s, 5"...2,400.00

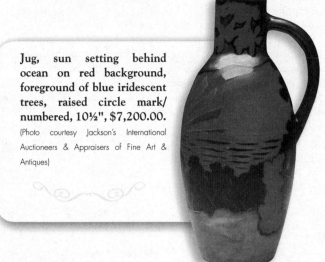

Jug, sun setting behind ocean on red background, foreground of blue iridescent trees, raised circle mark/ numbered, 10½", $7,200.00.

(Photo courtesy Jackson's International Auctioneers & Appraisers of Fine Art & Antiques)

Tray, appl lobster & snake, 1940s, 2½x10¾" 575.00
Vase, imp leafy stems, some w/flowerheads, turq Eosin, slim, 11".. 300.00
Vase, poppies, gold on bl & gr irid, cylindrical, ca 1900, 26x10"..10,000.00
Vase, random bl streaks on gold, fluted body w/ruffled rim, #5376, 8". 175.00
Vase, sailboats/birds, metallic gr on red, ovoid, #5330, 5¼" 1,080.00
Vase, stylized leaves/trees, gold & gr lustre, spherical, 1960, 3¾" .. 120.00
Vase, 3-D maid w/flowing hair by tree, gr/purple lustre, 18x9"..3,600.00
Vase, 4 raised floral bosses, metallic red/purple/gold, U-form, 7" ...2,520.00

Advisory Board

The editors and staff take this opportunity to express our sincere gratitude and appreciation to each person who has in any way contributed to the preparation of this guide. We believe the credibility of our book is greatly enhanced through their efforts. See each advisor's Directory listing for information concerning their specific areas of expertise.

You will notice that at the conclusion of some of the narratives the advisor's name is given. This is optional and up to the discretion of each individual. Simply because no name is mentioned does not indicate that we have no advisor for that subject. Our board grows with each issue and now numbers nearly 425; if you care to correspond with any of them or anyone listed in our Directory, you must send a SASE with your letter. If you are seeking an appraisal, first ask about their fee, since many of these people are professionals who must naturally charge for their services. Because of our huge circulation, every person who allows us to publish their name runs the risk of their privacy being invaded by too many phone calls and letters. We are indebted to every advisor and very much regret losing any one of them. By far, the majority of those we lose give that reason. Please help us retain them on our board by observing the simple rules of common courtesy. Take the differences in time zones into consideration; some of our advisors tell us they often get phone calls in the middle of the night. For suggestions that may help you evaluate your holdings, see the Introduction.

Barbara J. Aaronson Northridge, California	Scott Benjamin LaGrange, Ohio	Jim Calison Wallkill, New York	Rod Dockery Ft. Worth, Texas
Charles and Barbara Adams South Yarmouth, Massachusetts	Robert Bettinger Mt. Dora, Florida	Gene Cataldo Huntsville, Alabama	L.R. 'Les' Docks San Antonio, Texas
Ed & Sheri Alcorn Shady Hills, Florida	William M. Bilsland III Cedar Rapids, Iowa	Mike Carwile Lynchburg, VA	Rebecca Dodds-Metts Coral Springs, Florida
Beverly L. Ales Pleasanton, California	Brenda Blake York Harbor, Maine	Cerebro East Prospect, Pennsylvania	Darlene Dommel Minneapolis, Minnesota
Charles Alexander Indianapolis, Indiana	Robert and Stan Block Trumbull, Connecticut	Mick and Lorna Chase Cookeville, Tennessee	Robert A. Doyle, CAI, ISA, CAGA, CES Pleasant Valley, New York
Cheryl Anderson Cedar City, Utah	Clarence H. Bodine, Jr. New Hope, Pennsylvania	Victor J.W. Christie, Ed. D. Ephrata, Pennsylvania	Louise Dumont Leesburg, Florida
James Anderson New Brighton, Minnesota	Sandra V. Bondhus Farmington, Connecticut	Lanette Clarke Antioch, California	Jeanne Dunay Camden, South Carolina
Suzy McLennan Anderson Walterboro, South Carolina	Phyllis Bess Boone Tulsa, Oklahoma	John Cobabe Redondo Beach, California	Ken and Jackie Durham Washington, DC
Tim Anderson Provo, Utah	Clifford Boram Monticello, Indiana	Debbie and Randy Coe Hillsboro, Oregon	William Durham Belvidere, Illinois
Bruce A. Austin Pittsford, New York	Michael and Valarie Bozarth Williamsville, New York	Wilfred and Dolli Cohen Santa Ana, California	Rita and John Ebner Columbus, Ohio
Bobby Babcock Austin, Texas	Jeff Bradfield Dayton, Virginia	Ryan Cooper Yarmouthport, Massachusetts	Michael L. Ellis Costa Mesa, California
Veldon Badders Hamlin, New York	Shane A. Branchcomb Lovettsville, Virginia	J.W. Courter Kevil, Kentucky	Dr. Robert Elsner Boynton Beach, Florida
Rod Baer Vienna, Virginia	Harold Brandenburg Wichita, Kansas	John Danis Rockford, Illinois	Bryce Farnsworth Fargo, North Dakota
Wayne and Gale Bailey Dacula, Georgia	Jim Broom Effingham, Illinois	Patricia M. Davis Portland, Oregon	Arthur M. Feldman Tulsa, Oklahoma
Jacqueline Linscott Barnes Titusville, Florida	Dr. Kirby William Brown Paradise, California	Clive Devenish Orinda, California	Linda Fields Buchanan, Tennessee
Kit Barry Brattleboro, Vermont	Marcia Brown White City, Oregon	Joe Devine Council Bluffs, Iowa	Vicki Flanigan Winchester, Virginia
Dana Martin Batory Crestline, Ohio	Rick Brown Newspaper Collector's Society of America Lansing, Michigan	David Dilley Indianapolis, Indiana	Gene Florence Lexington, Kentucky
Peter Bealo Plaistow, New Hampshire	Donald A. Bull Wirtz, Virginia	Ginny Distel Tiffin, Ohio	Frank W. Ford Shrewsbury, Massachusetts

Auction Houses

We wish to thank the following auction houses whose catalogs have been used as sources for pricing information. Many have granted us permission to reproduce their photographs as well.

A-1 Auction Service
2042 N. Rio Grande Ave., Suite 'E,' Orlando, FL 32804; 407-839-0004. Specializing in American antique sales
a-1auction@cfl.rr.com
www.a-1auction.net

A&B Auctions Inc.
17 Sherman St., Marlboro, MA 01752-3314; 508-480-0006 or fax 508-460-6101. Specializing in English ceramics, flow blue, pottery and Mason's Ironstone; www.aandbauctions.com

Absolute Auction & Realty Inc./Absolute Auction Center
Robert Doyle
PO Box 1739, Pleasant Valley, NY 12569. Antique and estate auctions twice a month at Absolute Auction Center; Free calendar of auctions; Specializing in specialty collections.
www.AbsoluteAuctionRealty.com

Allard Auctions Inc.
Col. Doug Allard
PO Box 1030, 419 Flathead St., Ste. 4, Ignatius, MT 59865; 406-745-0500 Special-izing in American Indian collectibles.
info@allardauctions.com
www.allardauctions.com

America West Archives
Anderson, Cheryl
PO Box 100, Cedar City, UT 84721; 435-586-9497. Publishes 26-page illustrated catalog 5 times a year that includes auction section of scarce and historical early western documents, letters, autographs, stock certificates, and other important ephemera, Subscription: $13 per year.
info@americawestarchives.com
www.americawestarchives.com

American Bottle Auctions
1507 21st St., Ste. 203, Sacramento, CA 95814; 800-806-7722. Specializing in antique bottles.
info@americanbottle.com
www.americanbottle.com

Americana Auctions
c/o Glen Rairigh
12633 Sandborn, Sunfield, MI 48890. Specializing in Skookum dolls, art glass and art auctions.

Anderson Auctions/Heritage Antiques & Appraisal Services
Suzy McLennan Anderson
Batchelor Hill Antiques & Appraisal Services
246 E Washington St., Walterboro, SC 29488; 843-549-1300. Specializing in American furniture and decorative accessories; andersonauctions@aol.com
www.andersonauctions.net

Andre Ammelounx
The Stein Auction Company
PO Box 136, Palatine, IL 60078-0136; 847-991-5927 or fax 847-991-5947. Specializing in steins, catalogs available.
www.tsaco.com

Bertoia Auctions
2141 DeMarco Dr., Vineland, NJ 08360; 856-692-1881 or fax 856-692-8697. Specializing in toys, dolls, advertising, and related items. bertoiaauctions.com

Bider's
397 Methuen St., Lawrence, MA 01843; 978-688-0923 or 978-475-8336. Antiques appraised, purchased, and sold on consignment. bider@netway.com
www.biders-auction.com

Bonhams & Butterfields
220 San Bruno Ave., San Francisco, CA 94103; 415-861-7500 or fax 415-861-8951. Also located at: 7601 Sunset Blvd., Los Angeles, CA 90046; 323-850-7500 or fax 323-850-5843. Fine art Auctioneers and Appraisers since 1865.
info@butterfields.com
www.butterfields.com

Buffalo Bay Auction Co.
825 Fox Run Trail, Edmond, OK 73034; 405-285-8990. Specializing in advertising, tins and country store items.
buffalobayauction@hotmail.com
buffalobayauction.com

Cerebro
PO Box 327, E. Prospect, PA 17317-0327; 717-252-2400 or 800-69-LABEL. Specializing in antique advertising labels, especially cigar box labels, cigar bands, food labels, firecracker labels; Holds semiannual auction on tobacco ephemera, consignments accepted.

Cerebro@Cerebro.com
www.cerebro.com

Charles E. Kirtley
PO Box 2273, Elizabeth City, NC 27096-2273; 252-335-1262. Specializing in World's Fair, Civil War, political, advertising, and other American collectibles. cek@ckirtley.com
www.ckirtley.com

Cincinnati Art Galleries
225 E. Sixth, Cincinnati, OH 45202; 513-381-2128; fax: 513-381-7527. Specializing in American art pottery, American and European fine paintings, watercolors. www.cincinnatiartgalleries.com

Craftsman Auctions
1485 W Housatonic (Rt 20); Pittsfield, MA 01201; 413-448-8922. Specializing in Arts & Crafts furniture and accessories as well as American art pottery. Color catalogs available.
www.artsncrafts.com
www.ragoarts.com

Dargate Auction Galleries
214 N. Lexington, Pittsburgh, PA 15208; 412-362-3558. Specializing in estate auctions featuring fine art, antiques, and collectibles.
info@dargate.com
www.dargate.com

David Rago Auctions
333 N. Main, Lambertville, NJ 08530; 609-397-9374 or fax 609-397-9377. Specializing in American art pottery and Arts and Crafts.
info@ragoarts.com
www.ragoarts.com

Decoys Unlimited Inc.
West Barnstable, MA; 508-362-2766. Buy, sell, broker, appraise.
info@decoysunlimitedinc.net
www.decoysunlimitedinc.net

Du Mouchelles
409 E Jefferson Ave., Detroit, MI 48226-4300; 313-963-6255 or fax 313-963-8199. info@dumouchelle.com
dumouchelle.com

Dunbar's Gallery
Leila and Howard Dunbar
76 Haven St., Milford, MA 01757; 508-634-8697 or fax 508-634-8698.
dunbargallery@comcast.net
www.dunbarsgallery.com

Early American History Auctions
PO Box 3507, Rancho Santa Fe, CA 92067; 858-759-3290 or fax 858-759-1439. auctions@earlyamerican.com
www.earlyamerican.com

Early Auction Co.
123 Main St., Milford, OH 45150-1121; 513-831-4833 or fax 513-831-1441.

info@EarlyAuctionCo.com
EarlyAuctionCo.com

Flying Deuce Auctions & Antiques
14051 W. Chubbuck Rd., Chubbuck ID 83202 208-237-2002 or fax 208-237-4544. Specializing in vintage denim.
flying2@ida.net
www.flying2.com

Fontaine's Auction Gallery
1485 W. Housatonic St., Pittsfield, MA 01201; 413-448-8922 or fax 413-442-1550. Specializing in fine quality antiques; important 20th-century lighting, clocks, art glass. Color catalogs available. info@fontaineauction.com
www.fontaineauction.com

Frank's Antiques and Auctions
PO Box 516, 551625 U.S. Hwy 1, Hilliard, FL 32046; 1-800-481-6825. Specializing in antique advertising, country store items, rec room and restaurant decor; sporting goods; and nostalgia items.
franksauct@aol.com
franksauctions.com

Garth's Auctions Inc.
2690 Stratford Rd., Box 369, Delaware, OH 43015; 740-362-4771.
info@garths.com; www.garths.com

Glass-Works Auctions
102 Jefferson, East Greenville, PA 18041-11623; 215-679-5849 or fax 215-679-3068. America's leading auction company in early American bottles and glass and barber shop memorabilia.
glswrk@enter.net
www.glswrk-auction.com

Green Valley Auctions Inc.
2259 Green Valley Lane, Mt. Crawford, VA 22841; 540-434-4532. A leader in the field of Southern decorative and folk art, also pottery, furniture, carpets, fine art and sculpture, silver, jewelry, antique glass and ceramics, textiles, Civil War and militaria, toys and dolls, books, ephemera, advertising, Black Americana, toy trains, railroad material and much more.
info@greenvalleyauctions.com
www.greenvalleyauctions.com

Henry/Pierce Auctioneers
1456 Carson Court, Homewood, IL 60430-4013; 708-798-7508 or fax 708-799-3594. Specializing in bank auctions.

High Noon
9929 Venice Blvd., Los Angeles, CA 90034-5111; 310-202-9010 or fax 310-202-9011. Specializing in cowboy and western collectibles.
info@highnoon.com
www.highnoon.com

History Buff Auction
6031 Winterset, Lansing, MI 48911.

Specializing in paper collectibles spanning 5 centuries.
admin@historybuffauction.com
www.historybuffauction.com

Horst Auctioneers
Horst Auction Center
50 Durlach Rd. (corner of Rt. 322 & Durlach Rd., West of Ephrata), Ephrata, Lancaster County, PA 17522-9741; 717-738-3080. Voices of experience.
sale@horstauction.com
www.horstauction.com

Jackson's, International Auctioneers & Appraisers of Fine Art & Antiques
2229 Lincoln St., Cedar Falls, IA 50613; 319-277-2256 or fax 319-277-1252. Specializing in American and European art pottery and art glass, American and European paintings, Russian works of art, decorative arts, toys and jewelry.
www.jacksonsauction.com

James D. Julia Inc.
PO Box 830, Rt. 201, Skowhegan Rd., Fairfield, ME 04937-0830; 207-453-7125 or fax 207-453-2502.
jjulia@juliaauctions.com
www.juliaauctions.com

John Toomey Gallery
818 North Blvd., Oak Park, IL 60301-1302; 708-383-5234 or fax 708-383-4828. Specializing in furniture and decorative arts of the Arts & Crafts, Art Deco, and Modern Design movements; Modern Design Expert: Richard Wright.
info@johntoomeygallery.com
www.treadwaygallery.com

Joy Luke Fine Art Brokers & Auctioneers
The Gallery
300 East Grove St., Bloomington, IL 61701-5290; 309-828-5533 or fax 309-829-2266.
robert@joyluke.com
www.joyluke.com

Kit Barry Ephemera Auctions
74 Cotton Mill Hill #A252, VT 05301. Tradecard and ephemera auctions, fully illustrated catalogs with prices realized; Consignment inquiries welcome.
kbarry@surfglobal.net
www.tradecards.com/kb

L.R. 'Les' Docks
Box 691035, San Antonio, TX 78269-1035. Providing occasional mail-order record auctions, rarely consigned; The only consignments considered are exceptionally scarce and unusual records.
docks@texas.net
http://docks.home.texas.net

Lang's Sporting Collectables
633 Pleasant Valley Road; Waterville, NY 13480; 513-841-4623 or fax 315-841-8934. America's leading fishing tackle auctions.

LangsAuction@aol.com
www.langsauction.com

Leslie Hindman Auctioneers
122 N. Aberdeen St.
Chicago, IL 60607; 312-280-1212; Fax, 312-280-1211. www.lesliehindman.com

Lloyd Ralston Gallery Inc.
549 Howe Ave., Shelton, CT 06484; 203-924-5804 or fax 303-924-5834.
lrgallery@sbcglobal.net
www.lloydralstontoys.com

Lowe, James Lewis
PO Box 8, Norwood, PA 19074. Specializing in Kate Greenaway, postcards.
ClassicPostcards@juno.com

Majolica Auctions
Strawser Auction Group
200 North Main, PO Box 332, Wolcottville, IN 46795-0332; 260-854-2859. Issues colored catalog; Also specializing in Fiesta ware. info@strawserauctions.com
strawserauctions.com

Manion's International Auction House Inc.
PO Box 12214, Kansas City, KS 66112-0214; 913-299-6692 or fax 913-299-6792. Specializing in international militaria, particularly the US, Germany, and Japan. Extensive catalogs in antiques and collectibles, sports, transportation, political and advertising memorabilia and vintage clothing and denim. Publishes 9 catalogs for each of the 5 categories per year. Request a free sample of past auctions, 1 issue of current auction for $15.
collecting@manions.com
www.manions.com

Maritime Antiques & Auctions
935 US Rt. 1, PO Box 322, York, ME 03909-0322; 207-363-4247 or fax 353-1416. info@maritiques.com
www.maritiques.com

McMasters Harris Auction Company
PO Box 1755, 5855 Glenn Highway, Cambridge, OH 43725-8768; 800-842-3526. mark@mcmastersharris.com
www.mharrislive.com

Michael Ivankovich Antiques & Auction Company Inc.
PO Box 1536, Doylestown, PA, 18901; 215-345-6094. Specializing in early hand-colored photography and prints. Auction held 4 times each year, providing opportunity for collectors and dealers to compete for the largest variety of Wallace Nutting, Wallace Nutting-like pictures, Maxfield Parrish, Bessie Pease Gutmann, R. Atkinson Fox, Philip Boileau, Harrison Fisher, etc.
ivankovich@wnutting.com
www.wnutting.com

Michael John Verlangieri
PO Box 844, Cambria, CA 93428-0844;

805-927-4428. Specializing in fine California pottery; cataloged auctions (videos available). michael@calpots.com www.calpots.com

Monsen & Baer, Annual Perfume Bottle Auction
Monsen, Randall; and Baer, Rod
Box 529, Vienna, VA 22183; 703-938-2129 or fax 703-242-1357. Cataloged auctions of perfume bottles; Will purchase, sell, and accept consignments; Specializing in commercial, Czechoslovakian, Lalique, Baccarat, Victorian, crown top, factices, miniatures.

Morphy Auctions
2000 N. Reading Rd., Denver, PA 17517; 717-335-3435 or fax 717-336-7115. A division of Diamond International Galleries; with extensive worldwide media campaigns targeting the most influential antique publications and media venues; specializing in advertising, Americana, toys, trains, dolls and early holiday items. Hosts three to five consignment sales per year; based in Adamstown Antique Gallery.
www.morphyauctions.com

Neal Auction Company
Auctioneers & Appraisers of Antiques & Fine Art
4038 Magazine St., New Orleans, LA 70115; 504-899-5329 or 1-800-467-5329; fax 504-897-3803.
customerservice@nealauction.com
www.nealauction.com

New England Absentee Auctions
16 Sixth St., Stamford, CT 06905-4610; 203-975-9055. Specializing in Quimper pottery. neaauction@aol.com
www.neabsenteeauctions.com

New Orleans Auction Galleries Inc.
801 Magazine St., New Orleans, LA 70130; 800-501-0277, 504-566-1849. Specializing in American furniture and decorative arts, paintings, prints, and photography.
info@neworleansauction.com.
www.neworleansauction.com

Noel Barrett Antiques & Auctions
PO Box 300, 6183 Carversville Rd., Carversville, PA 18913; 215-297-5109.
toys@noelbarrett.com
www.noelbarrett.com

Norman C. Heckler & Company
79 Bradford Corner Rd., Woodstock Valley, CT 06282-2002; 860-974-1634 or fax 860-974-2003. Auctioneers and appraisers specializing in early glass and bottles. info@hecklerauction.com
www.hecklerauction.com

Past Tyme Pleasures
Steve & Donna Howard
PMB #204, 2491 San Ramon Blvd., #1, San Ramon, CA 94583; 925-484-4488.

Offers 2 absentee auction catalogs per year pertaining to old advertising items
pasttyme1@comcast.net
www.pasttyme1.com

Perrault-Rago Gallery
333 N. Main St., Lambertville, NJ 08530; 609-397-9374. Specializing in American Art Pottery, Tiles, Arts & Crafts, Moderns, and Bucks County Paintings. www.ragoarts.com

Pettigrew Auction Company
1645 S. Tegon Street, Colorado Springs, Colorado, 80903; 719-633-7963

Randy Inman Auctions Inc.
PO Box 726; Waterville, ME 04903; 027-872-6900 or fax 207-872-6966. Specializing in antique toys, advertising, general line.
www.inmanauctions.com

R.G. Munn Auction LLC
PO Box 705; Cloudcroft, NM 88317; 505-687-3676. Specializing in American Indian collectibles.
rgmunnauc@pvtnetworks.net

Richard Opfer Auctioneering Inc.
1919 Greenspring Dr., Timonium, MD 21093-4113; 410-252-5035; fax 410-252-5863. info@opferauction.com
www.opferauction.com

R.O. Schmitt Fine Arts
PO Box 162; Windham, NH 03087; 603-432-2237; 603-432-2271. Specializing in clocks, music boxes, and scientific instruments; holds catalog auctions.
www.roschmittfinearts.com

Roan Inc.
3530 Lycoming Creek Rd., Cogan Station, PA 17728; 570-494-0170
info@roaninc.com
www.roaninc.com

Sandy Rosnick Auctions
7 Big Rock Road, Manchester, MA 01944; 978-526-1093

Samuel T. Freeman & Co. Est. 1805
1808 Chestnut St., Philadelphia, PA 19103; 215-563-9275 or fax 215-563-8236. info@freemansauction.com
www.freemansauction.com

Schoolmaster Auctions and Real Estate
Kenn Norris
PO Box 4830; 513 N. 2nd St., Sanderson, TX 79848; 915-345-2640. Specializing in school-related items, barbed wire and related literature, and L'il Abner

Skinner Inc.
Auctioneers & Appraisers of Antiques and Fine Arts
The Heritage on the Garden, 63 Park Plaza, Boston, MA 02116-3925; 617-350-5400 or fax 617-350-5429. Second

address: 357 Main St., Bolton, MA 01740; 978-779-6241 or fax 978-779-5144. www.skinnerinc.com

SoldUSA.com
1418 Industrial Dr., Building 2, Box 11, Matthews, NC 28105; 704-815-1500. Specializing in fine sporting collectibles. support@soldusa.com
www.soldUSA.com

Sotheby's
1334 York Ave., New York, NY 10021; 212-606-7000
leiladunbar@sothebys.com
www.sothebys.com

Stanton's Auctioneers & Realtors
144 S. Main St., PO Box 146, Vermontville, MI 49096-0146; 517-726-018. Specializing in all types of property, at auction, anywhere.
stanton@voyager.net
www.stantons-auctions.com

Steffen's Historical Militaria
Major Auction Division
PO Box 280, Newport, KY 41072; 859-431-4499 or fax 859-431-3113. Specializing in quality militaria, military art, rare books, antique firearms

www.steffensmilitaria.com
Stout Auctions, Greg Stout
11 West Third Street; Williamsport, IN 47993-1119; 765-764-6901 or fax 765-764-1516. Specializing in Lionel, American Flyer, Ives, MTH, and other scale and toy trains.
stoutauctios@hotmail.com
www.stoutauctions.com

Superior Galleries
9478 West Olympic Boulevard, Beverly Hills, CA 90212-4246; 310-203-9855. Specializing in manuscripts, decorative and fine arts, Hollywood memorabilia, sports memorabilia, stamps and coins. info@sgbh.com. www.sgbh.com

Swann Galleries Inc.
104 E. 25th St., New York, NY 10010; 312-254-4710 or fax 212-979-1017. swann@swanngalleries.com
www.swanngalleries.com

Three Rivers Collectibles
Wendy and Leo Frese
PO Box 551542, Dallas, TX 75355; 214-341-5165. Annual Red Wing and Rum-Rill pottery and stoneware auctions.

Tom Harris Auctions
203 South 18th Avenue
Marshalltown, IA 50158
614-754-4890 or fax 641-753-0226. Specializing in clocks and watches, high quality antiques and collectibles; estate and lifetime collections, including eBay Live Auctions; Members of NAWCC, NAA, CAI. www.tomharrisauctions.com

Tradewinds Auctions
Henry Taron
PO Box 249, 24 Magnolia Ave., Manchester-By-The-Sea, MA 01944-0249; 978-526-4085. Specializing in antique canes. www.tradewindsantiques.com

Treadway Gallery Inc.
2029 Madison Rd., Cincinnati, OH 45208-3218; 513-321-6742 or fax 513-871-7722. Specializing in American Art Pottery; American and European art glass; European ceramics; Italian glass; fine American and European paintings and graphics; and furniture and decorative arts of the Arts & Crafts, Art Nouveau, Art Deco and Modern Design Movements. Modern Design expert: Thierry Lorthioir. Members: National Antique Dealers Association, American Art Pottery Association, International Society of Appraisers, American Ceramic Arts Society, Ohio Decorative Arts Society, Art Gallery Association of Cincinnati.
info@treadwaygallery.com
www.treadwaygallery.com

Vicki and Bruce Waasdorp Auctions
PO Box 434; 10931 Main St.; Clarence, NY 14031; 716-759-2361. Specializing in decorated stoneware.
waasdorp@antiques-stoneware.com
www.antiques-stoneware.com

VintagePostcards.Com
Antique Postcards for Collectors
312 Feather Tree Dr. Clearwater FL 33765; 727-467-0555.
quality@vintagepostcards.com
www.vintagepostcards.com

Weschler's
Adam A. Weschler & Son
905 E. St. N.W., Washington, DC 20004-2006; 202-628-1281.
www.weschlers.com

William Doyle Galleries
Auctioneers & Appraisers
175 East 87th St., New York, NY 10128; 212-427-2730.
info@DoyleNewYork.com
www.doylenewyork.com

Willis Henry Auctions
22 Main St., Marshfield, MA 02050-2808; 781-834-7774.
wha@willishenry.com
www.willishenry.com

Wm. Morford
Investment Grade Collectibles at Auction
RD #2, Cazenovia, NY 13035; 315-662-7625 or fax 315-662-3570. Specializing in antique advertising items and related collectibles; Maxfield Parrish items; rare and unique items at the upper end of the market with a heavy emphasis on quality, rarity and condition. Premier auctions held several times a year.
morf2bid@aol.com
www.morfauction.com

Directory of Contributors

When contacting any of the buyers/sellers listed in this part of the Directory by mail, you must include a SASE (stamped, self-addressed envelope) if you expect a reply. Many of these people are professional appraisers, and there may be a fee for their time and service. Find out up front. Include a clear photo if you want an item identified. Most items cannot be described clearly enough to make an identification without a photo.

If you call and get their answering machine, when you leave your number so that they can return your call, tell them to call back collect. And please take the differences in time zones into consideration. 7:00 AM in the midwest is only 4:00 AM in California! And if you're in California, remember that even 7:00 PM is too late to call the East Coast. Most people work and are gone during the daytime. Even some of our antique dealers say they prefer after-work phone calls. Don't assume that a person who deals in a particular field will be able to help you with related items. They may seem related to you when they are not.

Please, we need your help. This book sells in such great numbers that allowing their names to be published can create a potential nightmare for each advisor and contributor. Please do your part to help us minimize this, so that we can retain them on our board and in turn pass their experience and knowledge on to you through our book. Their only obligation is to advise us, not to evaluate your holdings.

Alabama

Cataldo, Gene
C.E. Cataldo
4726 Panorama Dr., S.E., Huntsville, 35801; 256-536-6893. Specializing in classic and used cameras
genecams@aol.com

Lippa, Matt; and Schaaf, Elizabeth
Artisans
PO Box 256, Mentone, 35984; 256-634-4037. Specializing in folk art, quilts, painted and folky furniture, tramp art, whirligigs, windmill weights
artisans@folkartisans.com;
www.folkartisans.com

Arizona

Jackson, Denis
Illustrator Collector's News
PO Box 6433, Kingman, 86401.
ticn@olypen.com

Arkansas

Freyaldenhoven, Tony
2200 Ada Ave., Ste. 304, 72034; 501-352-3559 or 501-932-0352. Specializing in Camark pottery
tonyfrey@conwaycorp.net

Roenigk, Martin
Mechantiques
Crescent Hotel & Spa
75 Prospect Ave., Eureka Springs, 72632; 800-671-6333. Specializing in mechanical musical instruments, music boxes, band organs, musical clocks and watches, coin pianos, orchestrions, monkey organs, automata, mechanical birds and dolls, etc. mroenigk@aol.com
www.mechantiques.com

Yohe, Darlene
Timberview Antiques
1303 S. Prairie St., Stuttgart, 72160-5132; 870-673-3437. Specializing in American pattern glass, historical glass, Victorian pattern glass, carnival glass, and custard glass

California

Aaronson, Barbara J.
The Victorian Lady
PO Box 7522, Northridge, 91327; 818-368-6052. Specializing in figural napkin rings, pickle castors, American Victorian silver plate
bjaaronson@aol.com
www.thevictorianlady.com

Ales, Beverly Schell
4046 Graham St., Pleasanton, 94566-5619; 925-846-5297.
Specializing in knife rests
Kniferests@sbcglobal.net

Babcock, Bobby
Jubilation Antiques
1034 Camino Pablo Drive, Pueblo West, 81007; 719-557-1252.
Specializing in Maxfield Parrish, Black Americana, and brown Roseville Pine Cone
jubantique@aol.com

Berg, Paul
PO Box 8895, Newport Beach, 92620. Author of *Nineteenth Century Photographica Cases and Wall Frames*

Brown, Dr. Kirby William
PO Box 1842, Paradise, 95967; 530-877-2159. Authoring book on history and products of California Faience, West Coast Porcelain, and Potlatch Pottery. Any contribution of information, new pieces, etc., is welcome.
kirbybrownbooks@sbcglobal.net

Clarke, Lanette
5021 Toyon Way, Antioch, 94532; 925-776-7784. Co-founder of *Haeger Pottery Collectors of America*; Specializing in Haeger and Royal Hickman
Lanette_Clarke@msn.com

Cobabe, John
800 So. Pacific Coast Hwy; Suite 8-301; Redondo Beach 90277; 310-544-8790. Specializing in Amphora, Zsolnay, and Massier
johncobabe@aol.com

Cohen, Wilfred and Dolli
Antiques & Art Glass
PO Box 27151, Santa Ana, 92799; 714-545-5673. Specializing in Wave Crest (C.F. Monroe); French cameo glass; Victorian-era art and pattern glass (salt shakers, toothpick holders, syrups, cruets, sugar shakers, tumblers, biscuit jars table and pitcher sets); art glass and cameo glass open salts; custard and ruby-stained glass; burmese, peachblow and amberina glass; pottery by Moorcroft (pre-1935 only); Buffalo (Deldare and Emerald ware); Polia Pillin; Shelley China; Chintz China; Clarice Cliff, and Moser Art Glass of Carlsbad Austria. Please include SASE for reply. A photo is very helpful for identification
antsandartglass@aol.com

Conroy, Barbara J.
PO Box 2369, Santa Clara, 95055-2369. Specializing in Commercial China; author and historian

Devenish, Clive
PO Box 708, Orinda, 94563; 925-254-8383. Specializing in still and mechanical banks; Buys and sells

Ellis, Michael L.
266 Rose Lane., Costa Mesa, 92627; 949-646-7112 or fax 949-645-4919. Author (Collector Books) of *Collector's Guide to Don Winton Designs, Identification & Values*; Specializing in Twin Winton

George, Tony
22431-B160 Antonio Parkway, #521, Rancho Santa Margarita, 92688; 949-589-6075. Specializing in watch fobs
Tony@strikezoneinc.com

Gibson, Pat
38280 Guava Dr., Newark, 94560; 510-792-0586. Specializing in R.A. Fox

Harrison, Gwynneth M.
11566 River Heights Dr., Riverside, 92505; 951-343-0414.
Specializing in Autumn Leaf (Jewel Tea)
morgan27@sbcglobal.com

Hibbard, Suzi
WanderWares
Specializing in Dragonware and 1000 Faces china, other Orientalia
Dragon_Ware@hotmail.com
www.Dragonware.com (related website)

Howard, Steve
Past Tyme Pleasures
PMB #204, 2491 San Ramon Valley Blvd., #1, San Ramon, 94583; 925-484-6442 or fax 925-484-6427. Specializing in Antique American firearms, bowie knives, Western Americana, old advertising, vintage gambling items, barber and saloon items
pasttyme1@sbcglobal.net
www.pasttyme1.com

Main Street Antique Mall
237 E Main St., El Cajon, 92020; 619-447-0800 or fax 619-447-0815.

Rutledge, Oveda L.
Oveda Rutledge Antiques
34 Greenfield Ave., San Anselmo, 94960; 415-454-6439. Specializing in 18th-century and early 19th-century American furniture, lighting, pewter, hearthware, glass, folk art, and paintings; Open by chance and appointment

The Meadows Collection
Mark and Adela Meadows
PO Box 819, Carnelian Bay, 96140; 530-546-5516. Specializing in Gouda and Quimper; lecturers, authors of *Quimper Pottery, A Guide to Origins, Styles, and Values*, serving on the Board of Directors of the Associated Antiques Dealers of America; Please include SASE for inquiries
meadows@meadowscollection.com
www.meadowscollection.com

Needham, Leonard
925-684-9674.
screensider@sbcglobal.net

Pardini, Dick
3107 N. El Dorado St., Dept. SAPG, Stockton, 95204-3412; 209-466-5550 (recorder may answer). Specializing

in California Perfume Company items dating from 1886 to 1928 and 'go-with' related companies: buyer and information center. Not interested in items that have Avon, Perfection, or Anniversary Keepsake markings. California Perfume Company offerings must be accompanied by a photo, photocopy, or sketching along with a condition report and, most importantly, price wanted. Inquiries require large SASE and must state what information you are seeking; not necessary if offering items for sale.

Sanford, Steve and Martha
230 Harrison Ave., Campbell, 95008; 408-978-8408. Authors of 2 books on Brush-McCoy and *Sanfords Guide to Mc-Coy Pottery* (available from the authors) www.sanfords.com

Shrader, Lila
Shrader Antiques
2025 Hwy. 199, Crescent City, 95531; 707-458-3525. Specializing in railroad, steamship, and other transportation memorabilia; Shelley China (and its predecessor, Wileman/Foley China); Buffalo China and Buffalo Pottery including Deldare; Niloak, and Zell (and Haag); Please include SASE for reply

Stillwell, Liz
Our Attic Antiques & Belleek
PO Box 1074, Pico Rivera, 90660; 323-257-3879. Specializing in Irish and American Belleek

Tanner, Joseph and Pamela
Tanner Treasures
5200 Littig Way, Elk Grove, 95757; 916-684-4006. Specializing in handcuffs, leg shackles, balls and chains, restraints and padlocks of all kinds (including railroad), locking and non-locking devices; Also Houdini memorabilia: autographs, photos, posters, books, letters, etc.

Thoerner, Sharon
15549 Ryon Ave., Bellflower, 90706; 562-866-1555. Specializing in covered animal dishes, powder jars with animal and human figures, slag glass

Thornton, Don
PO Box 57, Moss Beach, 94038; 650-563-9445. Specializing in egg beaters and apple parers; author of *The Eggbeater Chronicles, 2nd Edition* ($50.45 ppd.); and *Apple Parers* ($59 ppd.) dont@thorntonhouse.com

Vines, Linda
2390 Ocean Ave, #144, Torance, 90505-5856; 310-373-9293. Specializing in Snow Babies, Halloween, Steiff, and Santas (all German) lleigh2000@hotmail.com

Webb, Frances Finch
1589 Gretel Lane, Mountain View,

94040. Specializing in Kay Finch ceramics

Woodbury, Virginia; Past President of the American Hatpin Society
20 Montecillo Dr., Ro 310-326-2196. Quarterly meetings and newsletters; Membership: $30 per year; SASE required when requesting information HATPINGINIA@aol.com

---

Canada

Warner, Ian
PO Box 93022, 499 Main St. S., Brampton, Ontario, L6Y 4V8; 905-453-9074. Specializing in Wade porcelain, author of *The World of Wade, The World of Wade Book 2, Wade Price Trends, The World of Wade — Figurines and Miniatures,* and *The World of Wade Head Vase Planters;* Co-author: Mike Posgay idwarner@rogers.com

---

Colorado

Heck, Carl
Carl Heck Decorative Arts
Box 8416, Aspen, 81612; phone/fax: 970-925-8011. Specializing in Tiffany lamps, art glass, paintings, windows, and chandeliers; Also reverse-painted and leaded-glass table lamps, stained and beveled glass windows, bronzes, paintings, etc.; Buy and sell; Fee for written appraisals; Please include SASE for reply
carlheck5@aol.com
www.carlheck.com

Mackin, Bill
Author of *Cowboy and Gunfighter Collectibles,* available from author: 1137 Washington St., Craig, 81625; 970-824-6717, Paperback: $28 ppd. Other titles available. Specializing in old and fine spurs, guns, gun leather, cowboy gear, Western Americana (Collection in the Museum of Northwest Colorado, Craig)

Over, Naomi L.
8909 Sharon Lane, Arvada, 80002; 303-424-5922. Specializing in ruby glassware, author of *Ruby Glass of the 20th Century, Book I,* autographed copies available from author for $25 softbound or $32.50 hardbound, ppd.; Book II available (1999 values) for $32.50 softbound or $42.50 hardbound, ppd. Naomi will attempt to make photo identifications for all who include a SASE with correspondence.

Segelke, Cathy
970-522-5424. Specializing in crocks, Western Pottery Mfg. Co. (Denver, CO)

Stone, Steve
12795 W. Alameda Pkwy., Lakewood, 80225; 303-690-8649. Specializing in Blue & White stoneware

Toohey, Marlena
703 S. Pratt Pky., Longmont, 80501; 303-678-9726. Specializing in black amethyst and black opaque glass (buy, sell, or trade); Books available from author: Book 1 (over 600 colored pictures, descriptions, and price guide), $34 ppd. (nearly out of print); Book 2 (over 1,200 colored pictures, descriptions and price guide), $34 ppd. for softbound ($44 ppd. for hardbound)

White, John 'Grandpa'
Grandpa's Depot
6720 E. Mississippi Ave., Unit B, Denver, 80224; 303-758-8540 or fax 303-321-2889. Specializing in railroad-related items; Catalogs available; Author of *Fred Harvey: Behind the Scenes at Newton, Florence and Hutchinson,* available from author

---

Connecticut

Block, Robert and Stan
Block's Box
51 Johnson St., Trumbull, 06611; 203-926-8448. Specializing in marbles blockschip@aol.com

Bondhus, Sandra V.
16 Salisbury Way, Farmington, 06032; 860-678-1808. Author of *Quimper Pottery: A French Folk Art Faience;* Specializing in Quimper pottery

Lehrer, Gary
16 Mulberry Road, Woodbridge, 06525-1717. Specializing in pens and pencils; Catalog available
www.gopens.com

MacSorley, Earl
823 Indian Hill Rd., Orange, 06477; 203-387-1793 (after 7:00 p.m.). Specializing in nutcrackers, Bessie Pease Gutmann prints, figural lift-top spittoons

Postcards International
Martin J. Shapiro
2321 Whitney Ave., Suite 102, PO Box 185398, Hamden, 06518; 203-248-6621 or fax 203-248-6628. Specializing in vintage picture postcards
www.vintagepostcards.com

Van Deusen, Hobart D.
15 Belgo Road, Lakeville, 06039-1001; 860-435-0088. Specializing in Canton, SASE required when requesting information
rtn.hoby@snet.net

Vuono, Mark
16 6th St., Stamford, 06905; 203-357-

0892 (10 a.m. to 5:30 p.m. E.S.T.). Specializing in historical flasks, blown 3-mold glass, blown American glass

---

District of Columbia

Durham, Ken and Jackie (By appointment)
909 26 St. N.W., Suite 502, Washington, DC 20037. Specializing in slot machines, jukeboxes, arcade machines, trade stimulators, vending machines, scales, popcorn machines, and service manuals
www.GameRoomAntiques.com

Florida

Alcorn, Ed and Sheri
Animal Rescue of West Pasco
14945 Harmon Dr., Shady Hills, 34610; 727-856-6762. Specializing in Hagen-Renaker
horsenut@gate.net

Barnes, Jacqueline Linscott
Line Jewels
3557 Nicklaus Dr., Titusville, 32780; 321-267-9170. Specializing in glass insulators, bell paperweights and other telephone items. Author and distributor of 2003 edition of *Bluebell Paperweights, Telephone Pioneers of America Bells, and other Telephone Related Items;* LSASE required for information
bluebellwt@aol.com

Bettinger, Robert
PO Box 333, Mt. Dora, 32756; 352-735-3575. Specializing in American and European art pottery and glass, Arts & Crafts furniture and accessories, fountain pens, marbles, and general antiques
rgbett@aol.com

Dodds-Metts, Rebecca
Silver Flute
PO Box 670664, Coral Springs, 33067. Specializing in jewelry

Elsner, Dr. Robert
29 Clubhouse Lane, Boynton Beach, 33436; 561-736-1362. Specializing in antique barometers and nautical instruments

France, Madeleine
9 North Federal Highway, Dania Beach, 33004; 954-921-0022. Specializing in top-quality perfume bottles: Rene Lalique, Steuben, Czechoslovakian, DeVilbiss, Baccarat, Commercials; French dore bronze and decorative arts

Hirshman, Susan and Larry
Everyday Antiques
1624 Pine Valley Dr., Ft Myers, 33907. Specializing in china, glassware, kitchenware

Hudson, Hardy
1896 Wingfield Dr., Longwood, 32779; cell: 407-963-6093; shop: 407-657-2100. Specializing in majolica, American art pottery (buying one piece or entire collections); Also buying Weller (garden ornaments, birds, Hudson, Sicard, Sabrinian, Glendale, Knifewoood, or animal related), Roseville, Grueby, Newcomb, Overbeck, Pewabic, Ohr, Teco, Fulper, Clewell, Tiffany, etc., Also buying better art glass and paintings
todiefor@mindspring.com

Joyce, Harriet
415 Soft Shadow Lane, DeBary, 32713. Specializing in Cracker Jack and Checkers (a competitor) early prizes and Flossie Fisher items

Kuritzky, Louis
4510 NW 17th Place, Gainesville, 32605; 352-377-3193. Co-author (Collector Books) of *Encyclopedia of Bookends* (2005)
lkuritzky@aol.com

Person, Jeffrey M.
727-504-1139.
Specializing in Asian art including Cloisonnè, Sumida Ware, and fine carved furniture, Art Nouveau, and Jewelry; Has lectured, written articles, and been doing fine antique shows for 40 years
Person1@tampabay.rr.com

Posner, Judy
PO Box 2194 SC, Englewood, FL 34295, 941-475-1725. Specializing in Disneyana, Black memorabilia, salt and pepper shakers, souvenirs of the USA, character and advertising memorabilia, figural pottery; Buy, sell, collect
judyposner@yahoo.com

Rolfes, Herbert
Yesterday's World
PO Box 398, Mt. Dora, 32756; 352-735-3947. Specializing in World's Fairs and Expositions
NY1939@aol.com

Snyder-Haug, Diane
St. Petersburg, 33705. Specializing in women's clothing, 1850 – 1940

Supnick, Mark
2771 Oakbrook Manor, Ft. Lauderdale, 33332. Author of *Collecting Hull Pottery's Little Red Riding Hood* ($12.95 ppd.); Specializing in American pottery

Weisblut, Robert
International Ivory Society
5001 Old Ocean Blvd. #1, Ocean Ridge, 33435; 561-276-5657. Specializing in ivory carvings and utilitarian objects
rweisblut@yahoo.com

White, Douglass
A-1 Auction

2042 N. Rio Grande Ave., Suite E, Orlando, 32804; 407-839-0004. Specializing in Fulper, Arts & Crafts furniture (photos helpful)
a-1auction@cfl.rr.com

Georgia

Bailey, Wayne and Gale
3152 Fence Rd., Dacula, 30019; 770-963-5736. Specializing in Goebels (Friar Tuck)

Glenn, Walter
3420 Sonata Lane, Alpharetta, 30004-7492; 678-624-1298. Specializing in Frankart

Hoefs, Steven
PO Box 1024, Avalon, 90704; 310-510-2623. Specializing in Catalina Island Pottery; author of book, available from the author

Joiner, John R.
Aviation Collectors
130 Peninsula Circle, Newnan, 30263; 770-502-9565. Specializing in commercial aviation collectibles
propJJ@numail.org

Jones, Donald
107 Rivers Edge Dr., Savannah, 31406; 912-354-2133. Specializing in vintage tennis collectibles; SASE with inquiries please
Glassman912@comcast.net

Illinois

Broom, Jim
Box 65, Effingham, 62401. Specializing in opalescent pattern glassware

Danis, John
2929 Sunnyside Dr. #D362, Rockford, 61114; 815-978-0647. Specializing in R. Lalique and Norse pottery
danis6033@aol.com

Garmon, Lee
1529 Whittier St., Springfield, 62704; 217-789-9574. Specializing in Royal Haeger, Royal Hickman, glass animals

Hall, Doris and Burdell
210 W. Sassafras Dr., Morton, 61550-1254. Authors of *Morton's Potteries: 99 Years* (Vols. I and II); Specializing in Morton pottery, American dinnerware, early American pattern glass, historical items, elegant Depression-era glassware

Hamburg, Mary 'Tootsie'
Charlotte's, Queen Ann's, and Among Friends shops, all in Corner Victorian in Danville; 217-446-2323. Specializing in German Pink Pigs, Bakelite jewelry, general line

Hastings, Mary Jane
212 West Second South, Mt. Olive, 62069; 217-999-7519, cell: 618-910-1528. Specializing in Chintz dinnerware
sgh@chaliceantiques.com

Hoffmann, Pat and Don, Sr.
1291 N. Elmwood Dr., Aurora, 60506-1309; 630-859-3435. Authors of *Warwick, A to W*, a supplement to *Why Not Warwick?*; video regarding Warwick decals currently available
warwick@ntsource.com

Karman, Laurie and Richard; Editors of *The Fenton Flyer*
815 S. Douglas Ave., Springfield, 62704. Specializing in Fenton art glass

Martin, Jim
1095 215th Ave., Monmouth, 61462; 309-734-2703. Specializing in Old Sleepy Eye, Monmouth pottery, Western Stoneware

Miller, Anne
That's Interesting!
303 W. Erie St., Spring Valley, 61362; 815-664-2450. Specializing in white and tea leaf ironstone (no open shop); Shows and El Paso Antiques Mall in El Paso, Illinois

Miller, Larry
218 Devron Circle, E. Peoria, 61611-1605. Specializing in German and Czechoslovakian Erphila

Ochsner, Grace
Grace Ochsner Doll House
1636 E. County Rd. 2700, Niota, 62358; 217-755-4362. Specializing in piano babies, bisque German dolls and figurines

Rastello, Lisa
Milkweed Antiques
5N531 Ancient Oak Lane, St. Charles, 60175; 630-377-4612. Specializing in Depression-era collectibles

Rhoden, Joan and Charles
8693 N. 1950 East Rd., Georgetown, 61846-6264; 217-662-8046. Specializing in Heisey and other Elegant glassware, spice tins, lard tins, and Yard-Long prints; Co-authors of *Those Wonderful Yard-Long Prints and More*, and *More Wonderful Yard-Long Prints, Book II*, and *Yard-Long Prints, Book III*, illustrated value guides. rhoden@soltec.net

Schwab, Betty and Larry
The Paperweight Shoppe
2507 Newport Dr., Bloomington, 61704; 877-517-6518 and 309-662-1956. Specializing in glass paperweights; Now buying quality weights, one piece or a collection
thepaperweightshoppe@verizon.net
paperweightguy@yahoo.com

Spencer, Dick and Pat
Glass and More (Shows only)
1203 N. Yale, O'Fallon, 62269; 618-632-9067. Specializing in Cambridge, Fenton, Fostoria, Heisey, etc.

Spiess, Greg
230 E. Washington, Joliet, 60433; 815-722-5639. Specializing in Odd Fellows lodge items
spiessantq@aol.com

TV Guide Specialists
Box 20, Macomb 61455; 309-833-1809.

Vlach, Ray
Specializing in Homer Laughlin, Red Wing, Vernon Kilns, Russel Wright, Eva Zeisel, and childrens's ware china and pottery
rayvlach@hotmail.com

Waite, Jim
Main St., Farmer City, 61842; 800-842-2593. Specializing in Sebastians
bigjim@farmwagon.com

Yester-Daze Glass
c/o Illinois Antique Center
320 S.W. Commercial St., Peoria, 61604; 309-347-1679. Specializing in glass from the 1920s, 1930s, and 1940s; Fiesta; Hall; pie birds; sprinkler bottles; and Florence figurines

---

Indiana

Alexander, Charles
221 E. 34th St., Indianapolis, 46205; 317-924-9665. Specializing in Fiesta, Russel Wright, Eva Zeisel
chasalex1848@sbcglobal.net

Boram, Clifford
Antique Stove Information Clearinghouse
Monticello; Free consultation by phone only: 574-583-6465.

Dilley, David
6125 Knyghton Rd., Indianapolis, 46220; 317-251-0575. Specializing in Royal Haeger and Royal Hickman
glazebears@aol.com

Freese, Carol and Warner
House With the Lions Antiques
On the Square, Covington, 47932. General line

Garrett, Sandi
1807 W. Madison St., Kokomo, 46901. Specializing in Greentown glass, old postcards
sandpiper@iquest.net

Haun, Ted
2426 N. 700 East, Kokomo, 46901. Specializing in American pottery and china,

'50s items, Russel Wright designs
Sam17659@cs.com

Highfield, James
1601 Lincolnway East, South Bend, 46613-3418; 574-288-0300. Specializing in relief-style Capo-di-Monte-style porcelain (Doccia, Ginori and Royal Naples)

Hoover, Dave
1023 Skyview Dr., New Albany, 47150; 812-945-3614 (would rather receive calls than letters). Specializing in fishing collectibles; also miniature boats and motors
lurejockey@aol.com

Keagy, William
PO Box 106, Bloomfield, 47424; 812-384-3471. Co-author of *Those Wonderful Yard-Long Prints and More, More Wonderful Yard-Long Prints, Book II,* and *Yard-Long Prints, Book III,* illustrated value guides

McQuillen, Michael J. and Polly
Political Parade
PO Box 50022, Indianapolis, 46250-0022; 317-845-1721. Writer of column, *Political Parade,* which appears monthly in *AntiqueWeek* other newspapers; Specializing in political advertising, pinback buttons, and sports memorabilia; Buys and sells
michael@politicalparade.com
www.politicalparade.com

Miller, Robert
44 Hickory Lane North, Crawfordsville, 47833-7601. Specializing in Dryden pottery

Pruitt, Ted
3350 W. 700 N., Anderson, 46011. *St. Clair Glass Collector's Guide, Vol. 2,* available for $25 each from Ted at above address

Ricketts, Vicki
Covington Antiques Company
6431 W US Highway 136; Covington 47932. General line

Sanders, Lisa
8900 Old State Rd., Evansville, 47711. Specializing in MA Hadley
1dlk@insight.bb.com

Slater, Thomas D.
Slater's Americana
1325 W. 86th St., Indianapolis, 46260; 317-257-0863. Specializing in political and sports memorabilia

Taylor, Dr. E.E.
245 N. Oakland Ave., Indianapolis, 46201-3360; 317-638-1641. Specializing in radios; SASE required for replies to inquiries

Webb's Antique Mall
over 400 Quality Dealers
200 W. Union St., Centerville, 47330; 765-855-2489.
webbsin@antiquelandusa.com

Wright, Bill
325 Shady Dr., New Albany, 47150. Specializing in knives: Bowie, hunting, military, and pocketknives

---

Iowa

Bilsland, William M., III
PO Box 2671, Cedar Rapids, 52406-2671; 319-368-0658 (message) or cell 714-328-7219. Specializing in American art pottery

Devine, Joe
1411 S. 3rd St., Council Bluffs, 51503; 712-328-7305. Specializing in Royal Copley and other types of pottery (collector), author of *Collecting Royal Copley Plus Royal Windsor & Spaulding* (new in spring of 2006)

Jaarsma, Ralph
Red Ribbon Antiques
812 Washington St., c/o Red Ribbon Antique Mall, Pella, 50219. Specializing in Dutch antiques; SASE required when requesting information

Picek, Louis
Main Street Antiques
110 W. Main St., Box 340, West Branch, 52358; 319-643-2065. Specializing in folk art, country Americana, the unusual
msantiques@bigplanet.com

Kansas

Brandenburg, Harold
662 Chipper Lane, Wichita, 67212; 316-722-1200 (home). Specializing in Royal Bayreuth; Charter member of the Royal Bayreuth Collectors Club; Buys, sells, and collects

Maundy International
PO Box 13028-GG, Shawnee Mission, 66282; 1-800-235-2866. Specializing in watches — antique pocket and vintage wristwatches. mitime@hotmail.com

Old World Antiques
4436 State Line Rd., Kansas City, 66103; 913-677-4744. Specializing in 18th- and 19th-century furniture, paintings, accessories, clocks, chandeliers, sconces, and much more

Smies, David
Pops Collectibles
Box 522, 315 South 4th, Manhattan, 66502; 785-776-1433. Specializing in coins, stamps, cards, tokens, Masonic collectibles

Street, Patti
Currier & Ives (China) Quarterly newsletter
PO Box 504, Riverton, 66770; 316-848-3529. Subscription: $12 per year (includes 2 free ads)

Kentucky

Courter, J.W.
3935 Kelley Rd., Kevil, 42053; 270-488-2116. Specializing in Aladdin lamps; Author of *Aladdin — The Magic Name in Lamps, Revised Edition,* hardbound, 304 pages; *Aladdin Electric Lamps,* softbound, 229 pages; and *Angle Lamps Collectors Manual & Price Guide,* softbound, 48 pages

Florence, Gene and Cathy
Box 22186, Lexington, 40522. Author (Collector Books) on Depression glass, Occupied Japan; Elegant glass, Kitchen Glassware

Hornback, Betty
707 Sunrise Lane, Elizabethtown, 42701. Specializing in Kentucky Derby glasses, Detailed Derby, Preakness, Belmont, Breeder's Cup and others; Glass information and pictures available in a booklet for $15 ppd.

Ritchie, Roy B.
197 Royhill Rd., Hindman, 41822; 606-785-5796. Co-author of *Standard Knife Collector's Guide; Standard Guide to Razors; Cattaraugus Cutlery, Identification and Values;* and *The Big Knife Book;* Specializing in razors and knives, all types of cutlery

Stewart, Ron
PO Box 2421, Hazard, 41702; 606-436-5917. Co-author of *Standard Knife Collector's Guide; Standard Guide to Razors; Cattaraugus Cutlery, Identification and Values; The Big Book of Pocket Knives; and Remington Knives, Identification and Values.* Specializing in razors and knives, all types of cutlery

Willis, Roy M.
Heartland of Kentucky Decanters and Steins
PO Box 428, Lebanon Jct., 40150; heartlandky@ka.net Huge selection of limited edition decanters, beer steins and die-cast collectibles — open showroom; Include large self-addressed envelope (2 stamps) with correspondence; Fee for appraisals
www.decantersandsteins.com

Louisiana

Langford, Paris
Kollecting Kiddles
415 Dodge Ave., Jefferson, 70121; 504-733-0667. Specializing in all small vinyl dolls of the '60s and '70s; Author of *Liddle Kiddles Identification and Value Guide* (now out of print). Please include SASE when requesting information; Contact for information concerning Liddle Kiddle convention
bbean415@aol.com

Maine

Blake, Brenda
Box 555, York Harbor, 03911; 207-363-6566. Specializing in eggcups
Eggcentric@aol.com

Hathaway, John
Hathaway's Antiques
3 Mills Rd., Bryant Pond, 04219; 207-665-2214. Specializing in fruit jars; Mail order a specialty

Hillman, Alma
Antiques at the Hillman's
197 Coles Corner Rd. 04496; 207-223-5656. Co-author (Collector Books) of *Collector's Encyclopedia of Old Ivory China, The Mystery Explored, Identification & Values.* Specializing in Old Ivory China
oldivory@acadia.net

Rinaldi, John
Nautical Antiques and Related Items
Box 765, Dock Square, Kennebunkport, 04046; 207-967-3218. Specializing in nautical antiques, scrimshaw, naval items, marine paintings, naval items, etc.; Fully illustrated catalog: $5
jfrinaldi@adelphia.net

Simpson, Elizabeth
Elizabeth Simpson Antiques
PO Box 201, Freeport, 04032. Specializing in early glass and Sandwich glass

Zayic, Charles S.
Americana Advertising Art
PO Box 57, Ellsworth, 04605; 207-667-7342. Specializing in early magazines, early advertising art, illustrators

---

Maryland

Kilhoffer, C.D.
Churchville. Specializing in glass target balls

Meadows, John, Jean and Michael
Meadows House Antiques
919 Stiles St., Baltimore, 21202; 410-837-5427. Specializing in antique wicker furniture (rustic, twig, and old hickory), quilts, and tramp art

Screen, Harold and Joyce
2804 Munster Rd., Baltimore, 21234; 410-661-6765. Specializing in soda fountain 'tools of the trade' and paper: catalogs, 'Soda Fountain' magazines, etc.
hscreen@comcast.net

Welsh, Joan
7015 Partridge Pl., Hyattsville, 20782; 301-779-6181. Specializing in Chintz; Author of *Chintz Ceramics*

Massachusetts

Adams, Charles and Barbara
South Yarmouth, 02664; 508-760-3290 or business 508-587-5640. Specializing in Bennington (brown only)
adams_2340@msn.com

Cooper, Ryan
205 White Rock Rd., Yarmouthport, 02675; 508-362-1604. Specializing in flags of historical significance and exceptional design
rcmaritime@capecod.net

Dunbar's Gallery
Leila and Howard Dunbar
54 Haven St., Milford, 01757; 508-634-8697 (also fax). Specializing in advertising and toys
Dunbarsgallery@comcast.net
www.dunbarsgallery.com

Ford, Frank W.
Shrewsbury, 508-842-6459. Specializing in American iridescent art glass, ca 1900 – 1930

Frei, Peter
PO Box 500, Brimfield, 01010; 413-245-4660. Specializing in sewing machines (pre-1875, non-electric only), adding machines, typewriters, and hand-powered vacuum cleaners; SASE required with correspondence

Hess, John A.
Fine Photographic Americana
PO Box 3062, Andover, 01810. Specializing in 19th-century photography

Longo, Paul J.
Paul Longo Americana
Box 5510, Magnolia, 01930; 978-525-2290. Specializing in political pins, ribbons, banners, autographs, old stocks and bonds, baseball and sports memorabilia of all types

MacLean, Dale
183 Robert Rd., Dedham, 02026; 781-329-1303. Specializing in Dedham and Dorchester pottery
dedham-dorchester@comcast.net

Morin, Albert
668 Robbins Ave. #23, Dracut, 01826; 978-454-7907. Specializing in miscellaneous Akro Agate and Westite
akroal@comcast.net

Porter, Richard T., Curator
Porter Thermometer Museum
Box 944, Onset, 02558; 508-295-5504. Visits (always open) free, with 4,580 thermometers to see; Appraisals, repairs and traveling lecture (over 700 given, ages 8-98, all venues). Richard is also Vice President of the Thermometer Collectors Club of America
thermometerman@aol.com

Wellman, BA
PO Box 673, Westminster, 01473-0673 (willing to assist in identification through e-mail free of charge). Specializing in **all** areas of American ceramics, dinnerware, figurines, and art pottery
BA@dishinitout.com

Williams, Linda
1 School St. #305, Chester, 01011. Specializing in glass & china, general line antiques
e-mail sito1845@hotmail.com

Michigan

Brown, Rick
Newspaper Collector's Society of America
Lansing, 517-887-1255. Specializing in newspapers
help@historybuff.com
www.historybuff.com

Haas, Norman
252 Clizbe Rd., Quincy, 49802; 517-639-8537. Specializing in American art pottery

Hogan & Woodworth
Walter P. Hogan and Wendy L. Woodworth
520 N. State, Ann Arbor, 48104; 313-930-1913. Specializing in Kellogg Studio
http://people.emich.edu/whogan/kellogg/index.html

Iannotti, Dan
212 W. Hickory Grove Rd., Bloomfield Hills, 48302-1127S. 248-335-5042. Specializing in selling/buying: Reynolds, Sandman, John Wright, Capron, BOK, and other banks; Member of the Mechanical Bank Collectors of America
modernbanks@sbcglobal.net

Krupka, Rod
2641 Echo Lane, Ortonville, 48462; 248-627-6351. Specializing in lightning rod balls
krupka@qix.net

Marsh, Linda K.
1229 Gould Rd., Lansing, 48917. Specializing in Degenhart glass

Nedry, Boyd W.
728 Buth Dr., Comstock Park, 49321; 616-784-1513. Specializing in traps (including mice, rat, and fly traps) and trap-related items; Please send postage when requesting information

Nickel, Mike
A Nickel's Worth

PO Box 456, Portland, 48875; 517-647-7646. Specializing in American art pottery: Roseville, Van Briggle, Weller, Rookwood, Pillin, Newcomb, Kay Finch, Stangl, and Pennsbury Birds
mandc@voyager.net

Oates, Joan
1107 Deerfield Lane, Marshall, 49068; 269-781-9791. Specializing in Phoenix Bird chinaware
koates120@earthlink.net

Rairigh, Glen
Americana Auctions
12633 Sandborn, Sunfield, 48890. Specializing in Skookum dolls and antique auctions
www.AmericanAuctions.com

Ross, Michelle
PO Box 94, Berrien Center, 49102; 269-925-6382. Specializing in Van Briggle and American pottery
motherclay2@aol.com

Webster, Marty
6943 Suncrest Drive, Saline, 48176; 313-944-1188. Specializing in California porcelain and pottery, Orientalia

Minnesota

Anderson, James
Box 120704, New Brighton, 55112; 651-484-3198. Specializing in old fishing lures and reels, also tackle catalogs, posters, calendars, Winchester items

Dommel, Darlene
PO Box 22493, Minneapolis, 55422. Collector Books author of *Collector's Encyclopedia of Howard Pierce Porcelain*, *Collector's Encyclopedia of Dakota Potteries*, and *Collector's Encyclopedia of Rosemeade Pottery*; Specializing in Howard Pierce and Dakota potteries

Harrigan, John
1900 Hennepin, Minneapolis, 55403; 612-991-1271 or (in winter) 561-732-0525. Specializing in Battersea (English enamel) boxes, Moorcroft, Royal Doulton character jugs, and Toby jugs

Miller, Clark
4444 Garfield Ave., Minneapolis, 55419-1847; 612-827-6062. Specializing in Anton Lang pottery, American art pottery, Tibet postal history

Putratz, Barb
Spring Lake Park, 763-784-0422. Specializing in Norman Rockwell figurines and plates

Schoneck, Steve
HG Handicraft Guild, Minneapolis
PO Box 56, Newport, 55055; 651-459-2980. Specializing in American art

pottery, Arts & Crafts, HG Handicraft Guild Minneapolis

Missouri

Gillespie, Steve, Publisher
Goofus Glass Gazette
400 Martin Blvd, Village of the Oaks, 64118; 816-455-5558. Specializing in Goofus Glass, curator of 'Goofus Glass Museum,' had 4,000+ piece collection of Goofus Glass; Buy, sell and collect Goofus for 30+ years; Expert contributor to forums on Goofus Glass; Contributor to website for Goofus Glass
stegil@sbcglobal.net

Heuring, Jerry
28450 US Highway 61, Scott City, 63780; 573-264-3947. Specializing in Keen Kutter

Siegel, Brenda and Jerry
Tower Grove Antiques
3308 Meramec, St. Louis, 63118; 314-352-9020. Specializing in Ungemach pottery

Tarrant, Jenny
Holly Daze Antiques
4 Gardenview, St. Peters, 63376. Holiday for sale; Specializing in early holiday items, Halloween, Christmas, Easter, etc.; Always buying early holiday collectibles and German holiday candy containers
hollydaze@charter.net
www.hollydaze@charter.net

Wendel, David
F.E.I., Inc.
PO Box 1187, Poplar Bluff, 63902-1187; 573-686-1926. Specializing in Fraternal Elks collectibles

Wiesehan, Doug
D & R Farm Antiques
4535 Hwy. H, St. Charles, 63301. Specializing in salesman's samples and patent models, antique toys, farm toys, metal farm signs

Williams, Don
PO Box 147, Kirksville 63501; 660-627-8009 (between 8 a.m. and 6 p.m. only). Specializing in art glass; SASE required with all correspondence

Winslow, Ralph
PO Box 505, Carl Junction, 64834; 471-627-0258. Specializing in Dryden pottery
justsaya@sbcglobal.net

Nebraska

Johnson, Donald-Brian
3329 South 56th Street, #611; Omaha, NE 68106. Author of numerous Schiffer

Publishing Ltd. books on collectibles, including: *Ceramic Arts Studio, The Legacy of Betty Harrington* (in association with Timothy J. Holthaus and James E. Petzold); and with co-author Leslie Piña, *Higgins, Adventures in Glass; Higgins: Poetry in Glass; Moss Lamps: Lighting the '50s; Specs Appeal: Extravagant 1950s and 1960s Eyewear; Whiting & Davis Purses: The Perfect Mesh; Popular Purses: It's In the Bag!* and a four-volume series on the Chase Brass & Copper Co. Be sure to see Clubs, Newsletters, and Catalogs for information on the CAS Collectors club
donaldbrian@webtv.net

Nevada

Young, Willy
80 Promontory Pointe, Reno, 89509; 775-746-0922. Specializing in fire grenades

New Hampshire

Bealo, Peter
82 Sweet Hill Rd., Plaistow, 03865; 603-882-8023 or cell 978-204-9849. Please include SASE with mailed inquiries
pbealo@comcast.net

Holt, Jane
Jane's Collectibles
PO Box 115, Derry, 03038. Specializing in Annalee Mobilitee Dolls

Winston, Nancy
Willow Hollow Antiques
648 1st N.H. Turnpike, Northwood, 03261; 603-942-5739. Specializing in Shaker smalls, primitives, iron, copper, stoneware, and baskets

Doorstop Collectors of America
Doorstopper Newsletter
Jeanie Bertoia
2413 Madison Ave., Vineland, 08630; 609-692-4092. Membership: $20 per year, includes 2 newsletters and convention; Send 2-stamp SASE for sample

George, Dr. Joan M.
ABC Collector's Circle newsletter
67 Stevens Ave., Old Bridge, 08857. Specializing in educational china (particularly ABC plates and mugs)
drgeorge@nac.net

Harran, Jim and Susan
A Moment in Time
208 Hemlock Dr., Neptune, 07753. Specializing in English and Continental porcelains with emphasis on antique cups and saucers; Author of *Collectible Cups and Saucers, Identification and Values, Book I, II,* and *III; Dresden Porcelain Studios* and *Meissen Porcelain* (Collector Books) www.tias.com/stores/amit

Litts, Elyce
Happy Memories Antiques & Collectibles
PO Box 394, Morris Plains, 07950; 201-707-4241. Specializing in general line with special focus on Geisha Girl Porcelain, vintage compacts and Goebel figurines
happy-memories@worldnet.att.net
www.happy-memories.com

Meschi, Edward J.
129 Pinyard Rd., Monroeville, 08343; 856-358-7293. Specializing in Durand art glass, Icart etchings, Maxfield Parrish prints, Tiffany lamps, Rookwood pottery, occupational shaving mugs, American paintings, and other fine arts; Author of *Durand — The Man and His Glass*, (Antique Publications) available from author for $30 plus postage
ejmeschi@hotmail.com

Perrault, Suzanne
Perrault-Rago Gallery
333 N. Main St., Lambertville, 08530; 609-397-9374. Specializing in Arts and Crafts, art pottery, moderns, and tiles

Perzel, Robert and Nancy
Popkorn Antiques
505 Route 579, Ringoes, 08551; 908-782-9631. Specializing in Stangl dinnerware, birds, and artware; American pottery and dinnerware

Poster, Harry
Vintage TVs
Box 1883, S. Hackensack, 07606; 201-794-9606. Writes *Poster's Radio and Television Price Guide*; Specializes in vintage televisions, vintage radios, stereo cameras; Catalog available online
www.harryposter.com

Rago, David
333 N. Main St., Lambertville, 08530; 609-397-6780. Specializing in Arts & Crafts, art pottery
ragoarts@ragoarts.com
www.ragoarts.com

Rash, Jim
135 Alder Ave., Egg Harbor Township, 08234. Specializing in advertising dolls

Rosen, Barbara
6 Shoshone Trail, Wayne, 07470. Specializing in figural bottle openers and antique dollhouses

Visakay, Stephen
Vintage Cocktail Shakers (By appointment)
PO Box 1517, W. Caldwell, 07007-1517. Author of book and specializing in vintage cocktail shakers and bar ware
visakay@optonline.net

New Mexico

Hardisty, Don
Las Cruces; For information and questions: 505-522-3721 or cell 505-649-4191. Specializing in Bossons and Hummels. Don's Collectibles carries a full line of Bossons and Hummel figurines of all marks.
don@donsbossons.com
www.donsbossons.com

Manns, William
PO Box 6459, Santa Fe, 87502; 505-995-0102. Co-author of *Painted Ponies*, hardbound (226 pages), available from author for $47 ppd.; Specializing in carousel art and cowboy antiques
zon@nets.com

Nelson, Scott H.
PO Box 6081, Santa Fe, 87502-6081. Specializing in ethnographic art

New York

Austin, Bruce A.
1 Hardwood Hill Rd., Pittsford, 14534; 585-387-9820 (evenings); 585-475-2879 (week days); baagll@rit.edu. Specializing in clocks and Arts & Crafts furnishings and accessories including metalware, pottery, and lighting

Badders, Veldon
692 Martin Rd., Hamlin, 14464; 716-964-3360. Author (Collector Books) of *Collector's Guide to Inkwells, Identification & Values*; Specializing in inkwells

Bozarth, Michael and Valarie
Beaux Arts USA
Williamsville. Specializing in Cosmos, Audubon prints, and Currier & Ives prints
info@BeauxArtsUSA.com
www.BeauxArtsUSA.com

Calison, Jim
Tools of Distinction
PO Box 837, Wallkill, 12589; 845-895-8035. Specializing in antique and collectible tools, buying and selling

Doyle, Robert A., CAI, ISA, CAGA, CES
Absolute Auction & Realty, Inc./
Absolute Auction Center
PO Box 1739, Pleasant Valley, 12569; 845-635-3169. Antique and estate auctions twice a month at Absolute Auction Center; Free calendar of auctions available; Specializing in specialty collections
absoluteauction@hvc.rr.com
www.AbsoluteAuctionRealty.com

Gerson, Roselyn
PO Box 40, Lynbrook, 11563; 516-593-8746. Author/collector specializing in unusual, gadgetry, figural compacts, vanity bags and purses, solid perfumes and lipsticks

Handelsman, Burton
18 Hotel Dr., White Plains, 10605; 914-428-4480 (home) and 914-761-8880 (office). Specializing in occupational shaving mugs, accessories

Kaonis, Keith; Manager
Antique Doll Collector Magazine
6 Woodside Ave., Suite 300, Northport, 11768 or PO Box 344, Center Port, NY 11721-0344; 631-261-4100 or 631-361-0982 (evenings). Specializing in Schoenhut toys

Laun, H. Thomas and Patricia
Little Century
215 Paul Ave., Syracuse, 13206; December through March: 315-437-4156; April through December residence: 35109 Country Rte. 7, Cape Vincent, 13618; 315-654-3244. Specializing in firefighting collectibles; **All appraisals are free,** but we will respond only to those who are considerate enough to include a self-addressed stamped envelope (Photo is requested for accuracy); We will return phone calls as soon as possible

Malitz, Lucille
Lucid Antiques
Box KH, Scarsdale, 10583; 914-636-7825. Specializing in lithophanes, kaleidoscopes, stereoscopes, medical and dental antiques

Michel, John and Barbara
Iron Star Antiques
200 E. 78th St., 18E, New York City, 10021; 212-861-6094. Specializing in yellow ware, cast iron, tramp art, shooting gallery targets and blue feather-edge
jlm58@columbia.edu

Rifken, Blume J.
Author of *Silhouettes in America — 1790 – 1840 — A Collector's Guide*. Specializing in American antique silhouettes from 1790 to 1840

Russ, William A.
Russ Trading Post
23 William St., Addison 14801-1326. Animal lure manufacture; hunting and trapping supply; catalog $1

Safir, Charlotte F.
1349 Lexington Ave., 9-B, New York City, 10128-1513; 212-534-7933. Specializing in cookbooks, children's books (out-of-print only)

Schleifman, Roselle
Ed's Collectibles/The Rage
16 Vincent Road, Spring Valley, 10977; 845-356-2121. Specializing in Duncan & Miller, Elegant glass, Depression glass

Sherman, David
President of Phoenix & Consolidated Club

New York. Specializing in Phoenix and Consolidated glass

Smyth, Carole and Richard
Carole Smyth Antiques
PO Box 2068, Huntington, 11743. Authors of *Neptune's Treasures — A Study & Value Guide to Sea Shell Art; Pails by Comparison — A Study & Value guide to Sand Pails & Toys;* and *The Burning Passion — A Study & Value Guide to Antique and Collectible Pyrography;* All available from authors at the above address for $25 plus postage

Tuggle, Robert
105 W. St., New York City, 10023; 212-595-0514. Specializing in John Bennett, Anglo-Japanese china

Van Kuren, Jean and Dale
Ruth's Antiques, Inc.
PO Box 152, Clarence Center, 14032; 716-741-8001. Specializing chocolate molds, Buffalo pottery, Deldare ware
ruthsantq@aol.com

Van Patten, Joan F.
Box 102, Rexford, 12148. Author (Collector Books) of books on Nippon and Noritake

Weitman, Stan and Arlene
PO Box 1186; 101 Cypress St., N. Massapequa, 11758. Author of book on crackle glass (Collector Books)
scrackled@earthlink.net
www.crackleglass.com

North Carolina

Finegan, Mary J.
Marfine Antiques
PO Box 1105, Black Mountain, 2711.
marfine@earthlink.net
www.johnsonbrothersbook.com

Hussey, Billy Ray
Southern Folk Pottery Collector's Society
220 Washington Street, Bennett, 27208; 336-581-4246. Specializing in historical research and documentation, education, and promotion of the traditional folk potter (past and present) to a modern collecting audience
sfpcs@rtmc.net

Kirtley, Charles E.
PO Box 2273, Elizabeth City, 27096; 919-335-1262. Specializing in monthly auctions and bid sales dealing with World's Fair, Civil War, political, advertising, and other American collectibles

Newbound, Betty
2206 Nob Hill Dr., Sanford, 27330. Author (Collector Books) on Blue Ridge dinnerware, milk glass, wall pockets, figural planters and vases; Specializing in collectible china and glass

Savage, Jeff
Drexel Grapevine Antiques, 2784 US Highway 70 East, Valdese 28690; 828-437-5938. Specializing in pottery, china, antique fishing tackle, and much more
info@drexelantiques.com
www.drexelantiques.com

Sayers, R.J.
Southeastern Antiques & Appraisals
PO Box 629, Brevard, 28712. Specializing in Boy Scout collectibles, collectibles, Pisgah Forest pottery, primitive American furniture
rjsayers@citcom.net

North Dakota

Farnsworth, Bryce
1334 14½ St. South, Fargo, 58103; 701-237-3597. Specializing in Rosemeade pottery; If writing for information, please send a picture if possible, also phone number and best time to call

---

Ohio

Batory, Mr. Dana Martin
402 E. Bucyrus St., Crestline, 44827. Specializing in antique woodworking machinery, old and new woodworking machinery catalogs; Author of *Vintage Woodworking Machinery, an Illustrated Guide to Four Manufacturers* and *Vintage Woodworking Machinery, an Illustrated Guide to Four More Manufacturers,* currently available from Astragal Press, PO Box 239, Mendham, NJ 07945 for $25.95 and $33 ppd. or signed copies available from author for $30 and $35. In order to prepare a definitive history on American manufacturers of woodworking machinery, Dana is interested in acquiring (by loan, gift, or photocopy) catalogs, manuals photos, personal reminiscences, etc., pertaining to woodworking machinery and/or their manufacturers. Also available for $7.50 money order: 70+ page list of catalogs, owner's manuals, parts lists, company publications, etc. (updated quarterly). No phone calls please. A third volume devoted to Beach Mfg., C.B. Rogers & Co., DeWalt, Syncro, and H.B. Smith Co. is a work in progress.

Benjamin, Scott
PO Box 556, LaGrange, 44050-0556; 440-355-6608. Specializing in gas globes; Co-author of *Gas Pump Globes* and several other related books, listing nearly 4,000 gas globes with over 2,000 photos, prices, rarity guide, histories, and reproduction information (currently available from author); Also available: *Petroleum Collectibles Monthly* Magazine
www.oilcollectibles.com
www.gasglobes.com

China Specialties, Inc.
Box 471, Valley City, 44280. Specializing in high-quality reproductions of Homer Laughlin and Hall china, including Autumn Leaf

Distel, Ginny
Distel's Antiques
4041 S.C.R. 22, Tiffin, 44883; 419-447-5832. Specializing in Tiffin glass

Ebner, Rita and John
Columbus. Specializing in door knockers, cast-iron bottle openers, Griswold

Graff, Shirley
4515 Grafton Rd., Brunswick, 44212. Specializing in Pennsbury pottery

Guenin, Tom
Box 454, Chardon, 44024. Specializing in antique telephones and antique telephone restoration

Hall, Kathy
Monclova, 43542. Specializing in Labino art glass. kewpieluvin@msn.com

Hamlin, Jack and Treva Jo
145 Township Rd. 1088, Proctorville, 45669; 740-886-7644. Specializing in Currier and Ives by Royal China Co. and Homer Laughlin China (especially Virginia Rose, Priscilla and Dogwood dinnerware); Call — we carry a large inventory
jacktrevajo@zoominternet.net

Kao, Fern Larking
PO Box 312, Bowling Green, 43402; 419-352-5928. Specializing in jewelry, sewing implements, ladies' accessories

Kier, Anne and Don
202 Marengo St., Toledo, 43614-4213; 419-385-8211. Specializing in glass, china, autographs, Brownies, Royal Bayreuth, 19th-century antiques, general line
d.a.k.@worldnet.att.net

Kitchen, Lorrie
Toledo, 419-475-1759. Specializing in Depression-era glass, Hall china, Fiesta, Blue Ridge, Shawnee

Kline, Mr. and Mrs. Jerry and Gerry
Two of the founding members of the North American Torquay Society and members of Torquay Pottery Collectors' Society
604 Orchard View Dr., Maumee, 43537; 419-893-1226. Specializing in collecting Torquay pottery; please send SASE for info

Mangus, Bev and Jim
5147 Broadway NE, Louisville, 44641. Author (Collector Books) of *Shawnee Pottery, an Identification & Value Guide;* Specializing in Shawnee pottery

Mathes, Richard
PO Box 1408, Springfield, 45501-1408; 513-324-6917. Specializing in buttonhooks

Moore, Carolyn
Carolyn Moore Antiques
445 N. Prospect, Bowling Green, 43402-2002. Specializing in primitives, yellow ware, graniteware, collecting stoneware

Murphy, James L.
1023 Neil Ave., Columbus, 43201; 614-297-0746. Specializing in American Radford, Vance Avon
jlmurphy@columbus.rr.com

Otto, Susan
12204 Fox Run Trail, Chesterland, 44026; 440-729-2686. Specializing in nutcrackers, not toy soldier (Steinbach) type
nutsue@adelphia.net

Pierce, David
PO Box 205, Mt. Vernon, 43022. Specializing in Glidden pottery; Fee for appraisals

Roberts, Brenda
Specializing in Hull pottery and general line. Author of *Collector's Encyclopedia of Hull Pottery, Roberts' Ultimate Encyclopedia of Hull Pottery, The Companion Guide to Roberts' Ultimate Encyclopedia of Hull Pottery,* and *The Collector's Ultimate Encyclopedia of Hull Pottery,* all with accompanying price guides

Schumaker, Debbie Rees
Zanesville. Specializing in Watt, Roseville juvenile and other Roseville pottery, Zanesville area pottery, cookie jars, and Steiff

Shetlar, David
35 Vandeman Ave., Delaware, 43015; 740-369-1645. Specializing in Stretch glass and co-author of *American Iridescent Stretch Glass, Identification & Value Guide* (Collector Books)
stretchglasssociety@columbus.rr.com

Sublette, Tim
Partner, Seeker Antiques
PO Box 10083, Columbus, 43201-0583; 614-291-2203. Specializing in relief-molded jugs
seekersantiques@hotmail.com
www.seekersantiques.com

Trainer, Veronica
Bayhouse
Box 40443, Cleveland, 44140; 440-871-8584. Specializing in beaded and enameled mesh purses

Whitmyer, Margaret and Kenn
Box 30806, Gahanna, 43230. Authors (Collector Books) on children's dishes; Specializing in Depression-era collectibles

Young, Mary
Box 9244, Wright Brothers Branch, Dayton, 45409; 937-298-4838. Specializing in paper dolls; Author of several books

Oklahoma

Boone, Phyllis Bess
14535 E. 13th St., Tulsa, 74108; 918-437-7776. Author of *Frankoma Treasures*, and *Frankoma and Other Oklahoma Potteries*; Specializing in Frankoma and Oklahoma pottery

Feldman, Arthur M; Executive Director
The Sherwin Miller Museum of Jewish Art
2021 East 71st St., Tulsa, 74136-5408; 918-492-1818. Specializing in Judaica, fine art, and antiques
director@jewishmuseum.net
www.jewishmuseum.net

Moore, Art and Shirley
4423 E. 31st St., Tulsa, 74135; 918-747-4164 or 918-744-8020. Specializing in Lu Ray Pastels, Depression glass, Franciscan

Scott, Roger R.
4250 S. Oswego, Tulsa, 74135; 918-742-8710. Specializing in Victor and RCA Victor trademark items along with Nipper
Roger13@mindspring.com

Whysel, Steven
24240 S. Utica, Ave, Tulsa, 74114; 9;18-295-8666. Specializing in Art Nouveau, 19th- and 20th-century art and estate sales

Oregon

Brown, Marcia; author, appraiser, and lecturer
Sparkles
PO Box 2314, White City, 97503; 541-826-3039. Author of *Unsigned Beauties of Costume Jewelry*, *Signed Beauties of Costume Jewelry*, *Signed Beauties of Costume Jewelry, Volume II*, *Coro Jewelry, A Collector's Guide* and *Rhinestone Jewelry — Figurals, Animals, and Whimsicals* (all Collector Books), Co-author and host of 7 volumes: *Hidden Treasures* videos; Specializing in rhinestone jewelry; Please include SASE if requesting information

Coe, Debbie and Randy
Coe's Mercantile
PO Box 173, Hillsboro, 97123. Specializing in Elegant and Depression glass, Fenton glass, Liberty Blue, art pottery

Davis, Patricia Morrison
Antique and personal property appraisals
4326 N.W. Tam-O-Shanter Way, Portland, 97229-8738; 503-645-3084.
pam100davis@comcast.net

Foland, Doug
PO Box 66854, Portland, 97290; 503-772-0471. Author of *The Florence Collectibles, an Era of Elegance*, available at your local bookstore or from Schiffer publishers

Main Antique Mall
30 N. Riverside, Medford, 97501. Quality products and services for the serious collector, dealer, or those just browsing
http://mainantiquemall.com

Medford Antique Mall
Jim & Eileen Pearson, Owners
1 West 6th St., Medford 97501; 541-773-4983. medama11@mind.net

Miller, Don and Robbie
541-535-1231. Specializing in milk bottles, TV Siamese cat lamps, seltzer bottles, red cocktail shakers

Ringering, David and Angi
Kay Ring Antiques
1395 59th Ave., S.E., Salem, 97301; 503-364-0464 or cell 503-930-2247.Specializing in Rowland & Marsellus and other souvenir/historical china dating from the 1890s to the 1930s; Feel free to contact David if you have questions about Rowland and Marsellus or other souvenir china
AR1480@aol.com

Pennsylvania

Alekna, Stan and Sally
732 Aspen Lane, Lebanon, 17042-9073; 717-228-2361. Specializing in American dimestore toy soldiers; Send SASE for 3 to 4 mail-order lists per year; Always buying 1 or 100 top-quality figures
salekna@bellatlantic.net

Barrett, Noel
Noel Barrett Antiques & Auctions Ltd.
PO Box 300, Carversville, 18913; 215-297-5109. Specializing in toys; Appraiser on PBS Antiques Roadshow; Active in toy-related auctions
toys@noelbarrett.com
www.noelbarrett.com

Bodine, Clarence H., Jr., Proprietor
East/West Gallery
41B West Ferry St., New Hope, 18938. Specializing in antique Japanese woodblock prints, netsuke, inro, porcelains

Cerebro
PO Box 327, E. Prospect, 17317-0327; 717-252-2400 or 800-69-LABEL. Specializing in antique advertising labels, especially cigar box labels, cigar bands, food labels, firecracker labels
Cerebro@Cerebro.com
www.cerebro.com

Christie, Dr. Victor J.W.
Author/Appraiser/Broker

1050 West Main St., Ephrata, 17522; 717-738-4032. The family-designated biographer of Bessie Pease Gutmann. Specializing in Bessie Pease Gutmann and other Gutmann & Gutmann artists and author of 5 books on these artists, the latest in 2001: *The Gutmann & Gutmann Artists: A Published Works Catalog, Fourth Edition*; a signed copy is available from the author for $20 at the above address; Dr. Christie is an active member of the New England Appraisers Association, The Ephemera Society of America, and the American Revenue Association
thecheshirecat@dejazzd.com

Gottuso, Bob
Bojo
PO Box 1403, Cranberry Township, 16066-0403; Phone/fax: 724-776-0621. Specializing in Beatles, Elvis, KISS, Monkees, licensed Rock 'n Roll memorabilia
www.bojoonline.com

Hain, Henry F., III
Antiques & Collectibles
2623 N. Second St., Harrisburg, 17110; 717-238-0534. Lists available of items for sale

Hinton, Michael C.
246 W. Ashland St., Doylestown, 18901; 215-345-0892. Owns/operates Bucks County Art & Antiques Company and Chem-Clean Furniture Restoration Company; Specializing in quality restorations of art and antiques from colonial to contemporary; Also owns Trading Post Antiques, 532 Durham Rd., Wrightstown, PA, 18940-9615, a 60-dealer antiques co-op with 15,000 square feet — something for everyone in antiques and collectibles
iscsusn@comcast.net

Holland, William
1554 Paoli Pike, West Chester, 19380-6123; 610-344-9848. Specializing in Louis Icart etchings and oils; Tiffany studios lamps, glass, and desk accessories; Maxfield Parrish; Art Nouveau and Art Deco items; Author of *Louis Icart: The Complete Etchings*, *The Collectible Maxfield Parrish*, and *Louis Icart Erotica*
bill@hollandarts.com

Irons, Dave
Dave Irons Antiques
223 Covered Bridge Rd., Northampton, 18067; 610-262-9335. Author of *Irons By Irons*, *More Irons by Irons*, and *Even More Irons by Irons*, available from author (each with pictures of over 1,600 irons, current information and price ranges, collecting hints, news of trends, and information for proper care of irons); Specializing in pressing irons, country furniture, primitives, quilts, accessories
www.ironsantiques.com

Ivankovich, Michael
Michael Ivankovich Auctions, Inc.
PO Box 1536, Doylestown, 18901; 215-345-6094. Specializing in 20th-century hand-colored photography and prints; Author of *The Collector's Value Guide to Popular Early 20th Century American Prints*, 1998, $19.95; *The Collector's Guide to Wallace Nutting Pictures*, $18.95; *The Alphabetical and Numerical Index to Wallace Nutting Pictures*, $14.95; and *The Collector's Guide to Wallace Nutting Furniture*, $19.95. Also available: *Wallace Nutting General Catalog, Supreme Edition* (reprint), $13.95; *Wallace Nutting: A Great American Idea* (reprint), $13.95; and *Wallace Nutting's Windsor's: Correct Windsor Furniture* (reprint), $13.95 (all available at the above address); Shipping is $4.25 for the first item ordered and $1.50 for each additional item
ivankovich@wnutting.com
www.wnutting.com

Katz, Jerome R.
Downingtown, 19935; 610-269-7938. Specializing in technological artifacts

Knauer, Judy A.
National Toothpick Holder Collectors Society
1224 Spring Valley Lane, West Chester, 19380-5112; 610-431-4377. Specializing in toothpick holders and Victorian glass
winkj@comcast.net

Kreider, Katherine
PO Box 7957, Lancaster, 17604-7957; 717-892-3001. Author of *Valentines With Values*, available for $24.70 ppd. ($26.17 PA residents); *One Hundred Years of Valentines*, available for $29.70 ppd. ($31.20 PA residents); and *Valentines for the Eclectic Collector* ($29.70 ppd., $31.20 PA residents); Appraisal fee schedule upon request; Stop by Booth #315 in Stroud's Black Angus Mall in Adamstown, PA, Sundays only
katherinekreider@valentinesdirect.com
www.valentinesdirect.com

Lowe, James Lewis
Kate Greenaway Society
PO Box 8, Norwood, 19074.
Specializing in Kate Greenaway
PostcardClassics@juno.com

McManus, Joe
PO Box 153, Connellsville, 15425. Editor of *Purinton News & Views*, a newsletter for Purinton pottery enthusiasts; Subscription: $16 per year; Sample copies available with SASE; Specializing in Blair Ceramics and Purinton Pottery
jmcmanus@hhs.net

Reimert, Leon
121 Highland Dr., Coatesville, 19320; 610-383-9880. Specializing in Boehm porcelain

Rosso, Philip J. and Philip Jr.
Wholesale Glass Dealers
1815 Trimble Ave., Port Vue, 15133.
Specializing in Westmoreland glass

Scola, Anthony
215-484-8158
Specializing in Planters Peanuts
scolaville@aol.com

Weiser, Pastor Frederick S.
55 Kohler School Rd., New Oxford, 17350-9210; 717-624-4106. Specializing in frakturs and other Pennsylvania German documents; SASE required when requesting information; No telephone appraisals; Must see original or clear colored photocopies

---

Rhode Island

Gacher, John; and Santi, Federico
The Drawing Room of Newport
152 Spring St., Newport, 02840; 401-841-5060. Specializing in Zsolnay, Fischer, Amphora, and Austro-Hungarian art pottery
www.drawrm.com

The Occupied Japan Club
c/o Florence Archambault
29 Freeborn St., Newport, 02840-1821. Publishes bimonthly newsletter, *The Upside Down World of an O.J. Collector*; SASE required when requesting information
florence@aiconnect.com

South Carolina

Anderson, Suzy McLennan
246 E., Washington St., Walterboro, 29488; 843-549-1300. Specializing in American furniture and decorative accessories; Please include photo and SASE when requesting information; Appraisals and identification are impossible to do over the phone
andersonauctions@aol.com

Dunay, Jeanne
Bellflower Antiques
Camden. Specializing in historic and Romantic Staffordshire, 1790 – 1850

Greguire, Helen
Helen's Antiques
79 Lake Lyman Hgts., Lyman, 29365; 864-848-0408. Specializing in graniteware (any color), carnival glass lamps and shades, carnival glass lighting of all kinds; Author (Collector Books) of *The Collector's Encyclopedia of Graniteware, Colors, Shapes & Values, Bool 1* (out of print); Second book on graniteware now available (updated 2003, $33.70 ppd); Also available is *Carnival in Lights*, featuring carnival glass, lamps, shades, etc. ($13.45 ppd.); and *Collector's Guide*

to Toasters and Accessories, Identification & Values ($21.95 ppd.); Available from author; Please include SASE when requesting information; Looking for people interested in collecting toasters

Guthrie, John
1524 Plover Ave., Mount Pleasant, 29464; 843-884-1873. Specializing in Santa Barbara Ceramic Design

Roerig, Fred and Joyce
1501 Maple Ridge Rd., Walterboro, 29488; 843-538-2487. Specializing in cookie jars; Authors of *The Ultimate Collector's Encyclopedia of Cookie Jars*

Vogel, Janice and Richard
110 Sentry Lane, Anderson, 29621. Authors of *Victorian Trinket Boxes*and *Conta and Boehme Porcelain*. Specializing in Conta and Boehme German porcelain
vogels@contaandboehme.com
www.ContaAndBoehme.com

Sweden

Geary, William L.
Glass Appraiser (American and European Art Glass)
Gosta Bernards gata 1D, SE-593 30 Vastervik (0490) 36939. Specializing in Nordic art glass
margareta.geary@bredband.net

Tennessee

Chase, Mick and Lorna
Dishes Old and New
380 Hawkins Crawford Rd., Cookeville, 38501; 931-372-8333. Specializing in Fiesta, Harlequin, Riviera, Franciscan, Metlox, Lu Ray, Bauer, Vernon, other American dinnerware

Fields, Linda
230 Beech Lane, Buchanan, 38222; 731-644-2244 after 6:00 p.m. Specializing in pie birds
Fpiebird@compu.net

Grist, Everett
PO Box 91375, Chattanooga, 37412-3955; 423-510-8052. Specializing in covered animal dishes and marbles

Hudson, Murray
Murray Hudson Antiquarian Books, Maps, Prints & Globes
109 S. Church St., Box 163, Halls, 38040; 731-836-9057 or 800-748-9946. Specializing in antique maps, globes and books with maps, atlases, explorations, travel guides, geographies, surveys, and historical prints
mapman@ecsis.net
www.murrayhudson.com

Kline, Jerry
4546 Winslow Dr., Strawberry Plains, 37871; 865-932-0182. Specializing in Florence Ceramics of California, Rookwood pottery, English china, art glass, period furniture (small), tea caddies, brass and copper (early), and other quality items. artpotterynants@bellsouth.net

Weddington, David
Vintage Predicta Service
2702 Albany Ct., Murfreesboro, 37129; 615-890-7498. Specializing in vintage Philco Predicta TVs
service@50spredicta.com
www.50spredicta.com

Texas

Dockery, Rod
4600 Kemble St., Ft. Worth, 76103; 817-536-2168. Specializing in milk glass; SASE required with correspondence

Docks, L.R. 'Les'
Shellac Shack; Discollector
PO Box 780218, San Antonio, 78278-0218. Author of *American Premium Record Guide*; Specializing in vintage records
docks@texas.net
http://www.docks.home.texas.net

Frese, Leo and Wendy
Three Rivers Collectibles
Box 551542, Dallas, 75355; 214-341-5165. Specializing in RumRill, Red Wing pottery and stoneware

Gaston, Mary Frank
PO Box 342
Bryan, 77802. Author (Collector Books) on china and metals

Gibbs, Carl, Jr.
1716 Westheimer Rd., Houston, 77098. Author of *Collector's Encyclopedia of Metlox Potteries, Second Edition*, autographed copies available from author for $32.95 ppd.; Specializing in American ceramic dinnerware

Groves, Bonnie
402 North Ave. A, Elgin, 78621. Specializing in boudoir dolls
www.bonniescatsmeow.com

Koehn, Joanne M.
Temple's Antiques
7209 Seneca Falls Loop, Austin, 78739; 512-288-6086. Specializing in Victorian glass and china

Nelson, C.L.
4020 N. MacArthur Blvd., Suite 122-109, Irving, 75038. Specializing in English pottery and porcelain, among others: Gaudy Welsh, ABC plates, relief-molded jugs, Staffordshire transfer ware

Norris, Kenn
Schoolmaster Auctions and Real Estate
PO Box 4830, 513 N. 2nd St., Sanderson, 79848-4830; 915-345-2640. Specializing in school-related items, barbed wire, related literature, and L'il Abner (antique shop in downtown Sanderson)

Pogue, Larry G.
L&J Antiques & Collectibles
8142 Ivan Court, Terrell, 75161-6921; 972-551-0221. Specializing in string holders and head vases
landjantiques@direcway.com
www.landjantiques.com

Rosen, Kenna
9138 Loma Vista, Dallas, 75243; 972-503-1436. Specializing in Bluebird china
ke-rosen@swbell.net

Tucker, Richard and Valerie
Argyle Antiques
PO Box 262, Argyle, 76226; 940-464-3752. Specializing in windmill weights, shooting gallery targets, figural lawn sprinklers, cast-iron advertising paperweights and other unusual figural cast iron
lead1234@gte.net
rtucker@jw.com

Turner, Danny and Gretchen
Running Rabbit Video Auctions
PO Box 701, Waverly, 37185; 615-296-3600. Specializing in marbles

Waddell, John
2903 Stan Terrace, Mineral Wells, 76067. Specializing in buggy steps

Woodard, Dannie; Publisher
The Aluminist
PO Box 1346, Weatherford, 76086; 817-594-4680. Specializing in aluminum items, books and newsletters about aluminum

---

Utah

Anderson, Cheryl
America West Archives
PO Box 100, Cedar City, 84721; 435-586-9497. Specializing in old stock certificates and bonds, western documents and books, financial ephemera, autographs, maps, photos; Author of *Owning Western History*, with 75+ photos of old documents and recommended reference
info@americawestarchives.com

Anderson, Tim
Box 461, Provo, 84603. Specializing in autographs; Buys single items or collections — historical, movie stars, US Presidents, sports figures, and pre-1860 correspondence; Autograph questions? Please include photocopies of your autographs if possible and enclose a SASE for guaranteed reply
www.autographsofamerica.com

Spencer, Rick
Salt Lake City, 801-973-0805. Specializing in American silverplate and sterling flatware, hollowware, Shawnee, Van Tellingen, salt and pepper shakers; Appraisals available at reasonable cost

Whysel, Steve
24240 S. Utica Ave.
Tulsa, OK 74114; 918-295-8666.
Specializing in Art Nouveau, 19th- and 20th-century art and estate sales

Vermont

Barry, Kit
74 Cotton Mill Hill #A252, Brattleboro, 05301; 802-254-3634.
Author of Author of *Reflections 1* and *Reflections 2*, reference books on ephemera; Specializing in advertising trade cards and ephemera in general
kbarry@surfglobal.net

Virginia

Bradfield, Jeff
Jeff's Antiques
90 Main St., Dayton, 22821; 540-879-9961. Also located at Rolling Hills Antique Mall, Interstate 81, Exit 247B, Harrisonburg, VA. Specializing in candy containers, toys, postcards, sugar shakers, lamps, furniture, pottery, and advertising items

Branchcomb, Shane
12031 George Farm Dr., Lovettesville, 20180. Specializing in antique coffee mills, send SASE for reply
acmeman@erols.com

Bull, Donald A.
PO Box 596, Wirtz, 24184; 540-721-1128. Author of *The Ultimate Corkscrew Book, Boxes Full of Corkscrews, Bull's Pocket Guide to Corkscrews, Just for Openers* (with John Stanley); *Boxes of Corkscrews, Anri Woodcarvings* (with Philly Rains); *Corkscrew Stories, Vols. 1 and 2; Corkscrew Patents of Japan; Cork Ejectors;* and *Soda Advertising Openers.*
Specializing in corkscrews
corkscrew@bullworks.net
www.corkscrewmuseum.com

Carwile, Mike
180 Cheyenne Dr., Lynchburg, VA 24502; 804-237-4247. Author (Collec-

tor Books) on carnival glass
mcarwile@jeatbroadband.com

Flanigan, Vicki
Flanigan's Antiques
PO Box 1662, Winchester, 22604.
Member: Steiff Club, NADDA (National Antique Doll Dealers Assoc.); Specializing in antique dolls, hand fans, and teddy bears; SASE required with correspondence; Fee for appraisals, thank you

Haigh, Richard
PO Box 29562, Richmond 23242; 804-741-5770. Specializing in Locke Art, Steuben, Loetz, Fry, Italian; SASE required for reply

MacAllister, Dale
PO Box 46, Singers Glen, 22850. Specializing in sugar shakers and syrups

Monsen, Randall; and Baer, Rod
Monsen & Baer
Box 529, Vienna, 22183; 703-938-2129.
Specializing in perfume bottles, Roseville pottery, Art Deco

Washington

Frost, Donald M.
Country Estate Antiques (Appointment only)
14800 N.E. 8th St., Vancouver, 98684; 360-604-8434. Specializing in art glass and earlier 20th-century American glass

Haase, Don (Mr. Spode)
The Spode Shop at Star Center Mall
PO Box 818, Mukilteo, 98275. Specializing in Spode-Copeland China
mrspode@aol.com
www.mrspode.com

Jackson, Denis C., Editor
The Illustrator Collector's News
PO Box 1958, Sequim, 98382; 360-452-3810. Copy of recent sample: $3; Specializing in old magazines & illustrations such as Rose O'Neill, Maxfield Parrish, pinups, Marilyn Monroe, Norman Rockwell, etc.
ticn@olypen.com

Kelly, Jack
20909 NE 164th Circle, Brush Prairie, 98606; 360-882-8023. Please include SASE with mailed inquiries
binocs@msn.com

Payne, Sharon A.
Antiquities & Art
Specializing in Cordey
hotel_california94546@yahoo.com

Peterson, Gerald and Sharon
Sentimental Journeys
315 Deer Park Dr., Aberdeen, 98520; 360-532-4724. Specializing in Lotton glass, Flow Blue, Nippon, carnival glass
journeys@techline.com

Weldin, Bob
Miner's Quest
W. 3015 Weile, Spokane, WA 99208; 509-327-2897. Specializing in mining antiques and collectibles (mail-order business)

Whitaker, Jim and Kaye
Eclectic Antiques
PO Box 475 Dept. S, Lynnwood, 98046.
Specializing in Josef Originals and motion lamps; SASE required
www.eclecticantiques.com

Willis, Ron L.
PO Box 370, Ilwaco, 98624-0370. Specializing in military collectibles

Zeder, Audrey
1320 S.W. 10th Street #S, North Bend, 98045 (Appointment only). Specializing in British Royalty Commemorative souvenirs (mail-order catalog available); Author (Wallace Homestead) of *British Royalty Commemoratives*

West Virginia

Fostoria Glass Society of America, Inc.
Box 826, Moundsville, 26041. Specializing in Fostoria glass

Hardy, Roger and Claudia
West End Antiques
10 Bailey St., Clarksburg, 26301; 304-624-7600 (days) or 304-624-4523 (evenings). Authors of *The Complete Line of the Akro Agate Co.;* Specializing in Akro Agate

Wisconsin

Thomas, Darrell
Sweets & Antiques (mail order)
PO Box 418, New London, 54961. Specializing in art pottery, ceramics, Deco era, Goldscheider, Keramos, and eBay

auctions
wwodenclockworks@msn.com

Thorpe, Donna and John
204 North St., Sun Prairie, 53590; 608-837-7674. Specializing in Chase Brass and Copper Co.

Contributors by Internet address or eBay user name

www.dewittco.com specializing in vintage fabric, feed sacks, sewing patterns and transfers, ephemera and vintage paper of all kinds

www.gasolinealleyantiques.com (model kits, scale diecast cars, antique and collectible toys, sports memorabilia, yo-yos, comic character merchandise, boomerbalia)

www.lifeofrileycollectiques.com (American Art Pottery: Weller, Roseville, California, Stangl, Nicodemus, Rookwood, Sascha Brastoff, McCoy, Gort, Villeroy & Boch, and others)

www.retro-redheads.com (vintage and retro housewares: dinnerware; cocktail and beverage; holiday collectibles; kitchen towels, tablecloths, containers and miscellaneous items; aprons; and souvenir linens)

www.SweetlandForemost.com

www.timewasantiques.net (Shelley China, Cottage Ware, Wedgwood and Adams Jasperware, silver figural knife rests, sugar tongs, napkin rings, teacups, biscuit jars, transferware, Torquay Mottoware)

Randy Best (user name Antiquesrbest)

David Elyea (user name neatstuffdave)

Lori Kalal (user name: dlkunited, poodlegirl@hotmail.com)

Christine Padialla (user name frill_frippery_treasures)

Jerry Poarch (user name jerry9645)

Peter L. Smith (user name quarryman.2; quarryman2@ukonline.co.uk)

Sandy Truax (user name fastgril)

Clubs, Newsletters, and Catalogs

ABC Collectors' Circle (16-page news
letter, published 3 times a year)
Dr. Joan M. George
67 Stevens Ave., Old Bridge, NJ 08857.
Specializing in ABC plates and mugs
drjgeorge@nac.net or fax 732-679-
6102.

Abingdon Pottery Collectors Club
To become a mamber or for further
information, contact Nancy Legate at
mamaleg@abingdon.net or call 309-
462-2547. Dues $8 for single, $10 per
couple. Specializing in collecting and
preservation of Abingdon pottery

Akro Agate Collectors Club and *Clarksburg Crow* quarterly newsletter
Claudia and Roger Hardy
10 Bailey St., Clarksburg, WV 26301-
2524; 304-624-4523 (evenings) or
West End Antiques, 917 W. Pike St.,
Clarksburg, WV 26301; 304-624-7600
(Tuesday through Saturday). Annual
membership fee: $25

The Akro Arsenal, quarterly catalog
Larry D. Wells
5411 Joyce Ave., Ft. Wayne, IN 46818;
219-489-5842

The Aluminist
Dannie Woodard, Publisher
PO Box 1346, Weatherford, TX 76086.
Subscription: $20 (includes member-
ship)

America West Archives
Anderson, Cheryl
PO Box 100, Cedar City, UT 84721;
435-586-9497. Illustrated catalogs issued 6 times a year; Has both fixed-price
and auction sections offering early western documents, letters, stock certificates, autographs, and other important
ephemera; Subscription: $15 per year
info@americawestarchives.com

American Antique Deck Collectors
52 Plus Joker Club
Clear the Decks, quarterly publication
Clarence Peterson, Membership
12290 W. 18th Drive, Lakewood, CO,
80215. Membership: $20 (US and
Canada), $30 (foreign). Specializing in
antique playing cards
denverpete@comcast.net
www.52plusjoker.org

American Cut Glass Association
Kathy Emmerson, Executive Secretary
PO Box 482, Ramona, CA 92065-0482;
760-789-2715. Membership dues (includes subscription to newsletter, *The
Hobstar*: $45 (USA bulk mail) or $55
(first class and international)
acgakathy@aol.com
www.cutglass.org

American Hatpin Society
Jodi Lenocker, President
Virginia Woodbury Past President
20 Montecillo Dr., Rolling Hills Estates,
CA 90274; 310-326-2196. Newsletter
published quarterly; Meetings also quarterly; Membership: $40
HATPNGINIA@aol.com
www.americanhatpinsociety.com

American Historical Print Collectors
Society
PO Box 201, Fairfield, CT 06824. Regu-
lar one-year membership: $35

Antique & Collectors Reproduction News
Antiques Coast to Coast
Mark Chervenka, Editor
PO Box 12130, Des Moines, IA 50312-
9403; 515-274-5886 or (subscriptions
only) 800-227-5531. 12 monthly issues:
$32 (US); $41 (Canada); $59 (foreign)
acrn@repronews.com

Antique Advertising Association of
America (AAAA)
PO Box 1121, Morton Grove, IL 60053;
708-466-0904. Publishes *Past Times*
Newsletter; Subscription: $35 in US
AAAA@bblocksonline.com
www.pastimes.org

*Antique Amusements Slot Machine &
Jukebox Gazette*
Ken Durham, Editor
909 26 St., N.W., Suite 502, Washington, DC 20037. Eight-page newspaper
published once a year; Sample: $10
www.GameRoomAntiques.com

Antique Bottle & Glass Collector Magazine
Jim Hagenbuch, Publisher
102 Jefferson St., PO Box 180, East
Greenville, PA 18041; 215-679-5849.
Subscription (12 issues): $25 (US); $28
(Canada)
glswrk@enter.net

Antique Purses Catalog: $4
Bayhouse
PO Box 40443, Cleveland, OH 44140;
216-871-8584. Includes colored photos
of beaded and enameled mesh purses

Antique Radio Classified (ARC)
PO Box 2, Carlisle, MA 01741; 978-
371-0512. ARC@antiqueradio.com

Antique Souvenir Collectors' News News
Gary Leveille, Editor
PO Box 562, Great Barrington, MA 01230

Antique Stove Association
Norm Howe, Treasurer of Newsletter
204 Buckeye Lane, Brownsboro, AL
35741-9302

Antique Stove Exchange
c/o Caroline Royske
PO Box 2101, Waukesha, WI 53187-
2101; 262-542-9190 after 6 p.m.

Antique Telephone Collectors Association
PO Box 1252, McPherson, KS 67460;
620-245-9555. An international organization associated with the Museum of
Independent Telephony; Membership:
$35 (+$5 initiation fee for new membership
office@atcaonline.com
www.atcaonline.com

Antique Trader Weekly
Nancy Crowley, Editor
PO Box 1050, Dubuque, IA 52004-
1050. Featuring news about antiques
and collectibles, auctions and events;
Listing over 165,000 buyers and sellers in every edition; Subscription: $38
(US) for 52 issues per year; Toll free for
subscriptions only: 800-258-0929
collect@krause.com
www.collect.com

Antique Wireless Association
Ormiston Rd., Breesport, NY 14816

Appraisers National Association
25602 Alicia Parkway, PMB 245, Laguna Hills, CA 92653; 949-349-9179.
Founded in 1982, a nonprofit organization dedicated to the professionalism
and education of personal property appraiser. All members adhere to a code
of ethics and abide by professional
standards. ANA also works to develop
awareness of the professionalism of ap-
praising, and the service it provides to
the public. Free referrals to accredited
appraisers for antiques, collectibles, art,
jewelry, furniture and residential contents
info@ana-appraisers.org
www.ana-appraisers.org

Aspen Chamber Resort Assn.
970-925-1940.
www.aspenchamber.org

Association of Coffee Mill Enthusiasts
c/o Robert P. Palmer, Treasurer
PO Box 86, Olivet, MI 49076. Quarterly newsletter, annual convention; Dues
are $40 ($50 outside the continental
US and Canada), covers cost of quarterly newsletter and copy of membership roster

Auction Times for the West
Michael F. Shores, Publisher

Jeffrey Hill, Editor/General Manager
2329 Santa Clara Ave., Suite 207, Al-
amedo, CA 94501. 800-791-8592

Autograph Collector newsletter
Odyssey Publications
510-AS Corona Mall, Corona, CA
91719-1420; 909-371-7137.
DBTOG@aol.com

Autographs of America
Tim Anderson
PO Box 461, Provo, UT 84603; 801-
226-1787 (please call in the afternoon).
www.AutographsOfAmerica.com

Automatical Musical Instruments
Collector's Association
www.amica.org

Autumn Leaf
Glen Karlgaard Editor
13800 Fernando Ave., Apple Valley,
MN 55124; 952-431-1814

Avon Times (National Avon Collectors'
newsletter)
c/o Dwight or Vera Young
PO Box 9868, Dept. P., Kansas City,
MO 64134. Membership: $24 (US) or
$26 (Canada). SASE required when re-
questing information
AvonTimes@aol.com

Beatlefan
PO Box 33515, Decatur, GA 30033.
Subscription: $15 (US) for 6 issues or
$19 (Canada and Mexico)

Belleek Collectors International Society
PO Box 1498, Great Falls, VA 22066-
8498; 1-800-Belleek; 703-272-6270
(outside the US & Canada). Each new
member receives a certificate of membership, an new member/renewal gift,
a binder for the Belleek Collectors Society magazines, and the opportunity
to purchase exclusive limited edition
items; US membership: $43
info@belleek.com

Blue & White Pottery Club
224 12th St., NW, Cedar Rapids, IA
52405. Membership: $12 ($17 to include spouse)
www.blueandwhitepottery.org

Bojo
PO Box 1403, Cranberry Township, PA
16066-0403. Send $3 for 38 pages of
Beatles, toys, dolls, jewelry, autographs,
Yellow Submarine items, etc.
www.bojoonline.com

Bookend Collector Club
c/o Louis Kuritzky, M.D.
4510 NW 17th Place, Gainesville, FL
32650; 352-377-3193. Quarterly full-

color glossy newsletter, $25 per year; lkuritzky@aol.com

Bossons Briefs, quarterly newsletter
Requires membership in the International Bossons Collectors Society
John J. Cassidy, Executive Director
1317 N. San Fernando Blvd, Suite #325, Burbank, CA 91504.
bossonsman@aol.com

British Royal Commemorative
   Souvenirs Mail Order Catalog
Audrey Zeder
1320 SW 10th St. #S, North Bend, WA 98045. Catalog issued monthly, $5 each

Buckeye Marble Collectors Club
Brenda Longbrake, Secretary
PO Box 3051, Elida, OH 45807.
Membership: $10 (payable to club)
brenda@wcoil.com
www.buckeyemarble.com

Butter Pat Patter Association
The Patter newsletter
265 Eagle Bend Drive, Bigfork, MT 59911-6235. Subscription to newsletter: $22 (payable to Mary Dessoie at above address), includes a Royal Doulton butter pat; Sample copies also available by sending $4 and LLSASE (2 stamps)

The Buttonhook Society
BHS, PO Box 1089, Maidstone, Kent ME14 9BA, England or Box 287, White Marsh, MD 21162-0287. Publishes bimonthly newsletter *The Boutonneur*, which promotes collecting of buttonhooks and shares research and information contributed by members
buttonhooksociety@tiscali.co.uk
www.buttonhooksociety.com

Candy Container Collectors of America
c/o Jim Olean, 115 Mac Beth Dr., Lower Burrell, PA 15068-2628
or Contact: Jeff Bradfield
90 Main St., Dayton, VA 22821.
www.candycontainer.org

Cane Collectors Club
PO Box 1004, Englewood Cliff, NJ 07632; 201-886-8826.
liela@walkingstickworld.com

The Carnival Pump
International Carnival Glass Assoc., Inc.
Lee Markley
Box 306, Mentone, IN 46539; Dues: $25 per family per year in US and Canada or $25 overseas
www.internationalcarnivalglass.com

The Carousel News & Trader
87 Parke Ave. W., Suite 206, Mansfield, OH 44902. A monthly magazine for the carousel enthusiast. Subscription: $35 per year
www.carouseltrader.com

The Carousel Shopper Resource Catalog
Box 47, Dept. PC, Millwood, NY 10546.
Only $2 (+50¢ postage). A full-color catalog featuring dealers of antique carousel art offering single figures or complete carousels, museums, restoration services, organizations, full-size reproductions, books, cards, posters, auction services and other hard-to-find items for carousel enthusiasts

CAS Collectors
206 Grove St., Rockton, IL 61072.
Established in 1994 as the Ceramic Arts Studio Collectors Association, CAS Collectors welcomes all in with a common interest in the work of Ceramic Arts Studio of Madison, Wisconsin. The club publishes a quarterly newsletter and hosts an annual convention in Madison each August in conjunction with the Wisconsin Pottery Association Show & Sale. Family membership: $25 per year. Information about the club and its activities, as well as a complete illustrated CAS history, is included in the book *Ceramic Arts Studio: The Legacy of Betty Harrington* by Donald-Brian Johnson, Timothy J. Holthaus, and James E. Petzold (Schiffer Publishing, 2003).
www.cascollectors.com or for history www.ceramicartsstudio.org

A Catalog Collection
Kenneth E. Schneringer
271 Sabrina Ct., Woodstock, GA 30188-4228; 770-926-9383. Specializing in catalogs, promochures, view books, labels, trade cards, special paper needs
trademan68@aol.com
www.old-paper.com

Central Florida Insulator Collectors
Line Jewels, NIA #1380
3557 Nicklaus Dr., Titusville, FL 32780-5356. Dues: $10 per year for single or family membership (checks payable to Jacqueline Barnes); Dues covers the cost of *Newsnotes*, the club's monthly newsletter, which informs members of meetings and shows, articles of interest on insulators and other collectibles; For club information send SASE to above address.
bluebellwt@aol.com

China Specialties, Inc.
Fiesta Collector's Quarterly Newsletter
PO Box 361280, Strongsville, OH 44316-1280.
ewww.chinaspecialties.com

Chintz Connection Newsletter
PO Box 222, Riverdale, MD 20738.
Dedicated to helping collectors share information and find matchings; Subscription: 4 issues per year for $25

The Coca-Cola Collectors Club
PMB 609

4780 Ashford-Dunwoody Rd, Suite A Atlanta, GA 30338. Membership: $30 in US ($35, Canada)
www.cocacolaclub.org

Coin Operated Collectors Association
A club for those who collect antique coin-operated slot machines, trade stimulators, arcade machines, vending machines, and related collectibles. Call 202-338-2471 to join. Membership fee: $33 per year
www.CoinOpClub.org

The Cola Clan
Alice Fisher, Treasurer
2084 Continental Dr., N.E., Atlanta, GA 30345

Collector's Life
The World's Foremost Publication for Steiff Enthusiasts
Beth Savino
PO Box 798; Holland, OH 43528; 1-800-862-TOYS or fax 419-473-3947.
info@toystore.net
www.toystorenet.com
www.toystorenet.com

Collector Glass News
Promotional Glass Collectors Association
Box 308, Slippery Rock, PA 16057, 724-946-2838 or fax 724-946-9012.
An international publication providing current news to collectors of cartoon, fast-food, and promotional glassware; Subscription: $15 per household
cgn@glassnews.com
www.glassnews.com

Collectors of Findlay Glass
PO Box 256, Findlay, OH 45840. An organization dedicated to the study and recognition of Findlay glass; Newsletter *The Melting Pot*, published quarterly; Annual convention; Membership: $10 per year ($15 per couple)

Compact Collectors
Roselyn Gerson
PO Box 40, Lynbrook, NY 11563; 516-593-8746 or fax 516-593-0610.
Publishes *Powder Puff* Newsletter, which contains articles covering all aspects of powder and solid perfume compact collecting, restoration, vintage ads, patents, history, and articles by members and prominent guest writers; Seeker and sellers column offered free to members
compactldy@aol.com

Cookie Crumbs
Cookie Cutter Collectors Club
Ruth Capper, Secretary/Treasurer
PO Box 245, Cannon Falls, MN 55009.
Subscription $20 per year (4 issues, payable to CCCC)
www.cookiecollectorsclub.com

Cookies
Rosemary Henry

9610 Greenview Lane, Manassas, VA 20109-3320. Subscription: $15 per year (6 issues); Payable to Cookies

The Copley Courier
1639 N. Catalina St., Burbank, CA 91505

Cowan Pottery Museum Associates
CPMA, PO Box 16765, Rocky River, OH 44116 or contact Victoria Naumann Peltz, Curatorial Associate, Cowan Pottery Museum at Rocky River Public Library, 1600 Hampton Rd., Rocky River, OH 44116; 440-333-7610, ext. 214. Membership: $25 ($35 dual) includes subscription to biannual *Cowan Pottery Journal* Newsletter
www.cowanpottery.org

Cracker Jack® Collector's Assoc.
The Prize Insider Newsletter
Deb Gunnerson
3325 Edward St., NE, St. Anthony, MN 55418. Subscription/membership: $20 per year (single) or $24 (family)
raegun@comcast.net
www.collectoronline.com/CJCA/

Creamers, quarterly newsletter
Lloyd B. Bindscheattle
PO Box 11, Lake Villa, IL 60046-0011.
Subscription: $5 per year

(Currier & Ives) C&I Dinnerware
   Collector Club
Charles Burgess, Membership
308 Jodi Dr., Brownstown, IN 47220-1523; 812-358-4569. Membership: $15
annmah2@aol.com
www.currierandivesdinnerware.com

Custard Glass Collectors Society
Custard Connection quarterly newsletter
Sarah Coulon, Editor
591 SW Duxbury Ave., Port St. Lucie, FL 34983; 561-785-9446.
custardsociety@aol.com
www.custardsociety.com

Czechoslovakian Collectors Guild
   International
Alan Badia
15006 Meadowlake St., Odessa, FL 33556-3126. Annual membership: $65 in US
ab@czechartglass.com
www.czechartglass.com/ccgi

*The Dedham Pottery Collectors Society
   Newsletter*
Jim Kaufman, Publisher
248 Highland St., Dedham, MA 02026-5833; 800-283-8070. $5 per issue
DedhamPottery.com

Docks, L.R. 'Les'
Shellac Shack
Box 691035, San Antonio, TX 78269-1035. Send $2 for an illustrated booklet of 78s that Docks wants to buy, the prices

he will pay, and shipping instructions
docks@texas.net
http://docks.home.texas.net

Doorstop Collectors of America
Doorstopper Newsletter
Jeanie Bertoia
2413 Madison Ave., Vineland, NJ
08630; 609-692-4092. Membership:
$20 per year, includes 2 newsletters and
convention; Send 2-stamp SASE for
sample

Dragonware Club
c/o Suzi Hibbard
849 Vintage Ave., Fairfield, CA 94585.
Inquiries must be accompanied with
LSASE or they will not be responded
to; All contributions are welcome:
Dragonware related
Dragon_Ware@hotmail.com
www.Dragonware.com

Drawing Room of Newport
Gacher, John; and Santi, Federico
152 Spring St., Newport, RI 02840; 401-
841-5060. Book on Zsolnay available
www.drawrm.com

Early Typewriter Collectors Association
ETCetera newsletter
Chuck Dilts and Rich Cincotta, Co-
editors
PO Box 286; Southborough, MA 01772;
508-229-2064.   etcetera@writeme.com
www.typewriter.rydia.net/etcetera.htm
http://typewriter.rydia.net/etcetera.htm

Ed Taylor Radio Museum
245 N. Oakland Ave., Indianapolis, IN
46201-3360; 317-638-1641

Eggcup Collector's Corner
67 Stevens Ave., Old Bridge, NJ 08857.
Issued quarterly; Subscription: $20 per
year (payable to Joan George). Sample
copy: $5

The Elegance of Old Ivory Newsletter
Box 1004, Wilsonville, OR 97070

Fenton Art Glass Collectors of
    America, Inc.
Butterfly Net Newsletter
Kay Kenworthy, Editor
PO Box 384, 702 W. 5th St., Williamstown, WV 26187. Dues: $20 per year
(full membership +$5 for each associate
membership, children under 12 free)
faqcainc@wirefire.com
www.fagcainc.wirefire.com

The Fenton Flyer
Laurie & Rich Karman, Editors
815 S. Douglas, Springfield, IL 62704;
217-787-8166

Fiesta Collector's Quarterly Newsletter
PO Box 471, Valley City, OH 44280.
Subscription: $12 per year
www.chinaspecialties.com

Florence Ceramics Collectors Society
1971 Blue Fox Drive; Lansdale, PA
19446-5505. Newsletter and club membership: $35 per year (6 issues in color)
FlorenceCeramics@aol.com

Fostoria Glass Society of America, Inc.
PO Box 826, Moundsville, WV 26041.
Membership: $18
www.fostoriaglass.org

Frankoma Family Collectors Association
PO Box 32571, Oklahoma City, OK
73123-0771. Membership dues: $35
(includes newsletters); Annual convention
www.frankoma.org

Friends of Degenhart
c/o Degenhart Museum
PO Box 186, Cambridge, OH 43725;
740-432-2626. Membership: $5 ($10
for family) includes *Heartbeat* Newsletter (printed quarterly) and free admission to museum
www.degenhartmuseum.com

H.C. Fry Society
PO Box 41, Beaver, PA 15009. Founded
in 1983 for the sole purpose of learning
about Fry glass; Publishes *Shards,* quarterly newsletter

Goofus Glass Gazette
Steve Gillespie, Publisher
400 Martin Blvd., Village of the Oaks,
MO 64118; 888-455-5558.
stegil@sbcglobal.net
www.goofus.org

The Gonder Collector
917 Hurl Dr.
Pittsburgh, PA 15236

Grandpa's Depot
John 'Grandpa' White
6720 E. Mississippi Ave., Unit B, Denver, CO 80224; 303-758-8540 or fax
303-321-2889. Publishes catalogs on
railroad-related items

Haeger Pottery Collectors of America
Lanette Clarke
5021 Toyon Way, Antioch, CA 94509;
925-776-7784.
Newsletter published 6 times per year;
Dues: $20
Lanette-Clarke@msn.com

Hagen-Renaker Collector's Club
c/o Debra Kerr
2055 Hammock Moss Dr., Orlando, FL
32820. Subscription rate: $24 per year
wwww.hagenrenaker.com

Hall China Collector's Club Newsletter
Virginia Lee
PO Box 360488, Cleveland, OH 44136;
330-220-7456

Hammered Aluminum Collectors
    Association (HACA)
Dannie Woodard
PO Box 1346, Weatherford, TX 76086;
817-594-4680

Headhunters Newsletter
c/o Maddy Gordon
PO Box 83H, Scarsdale, NY 10583;
914-472-0227. Subscription: $26 yearly
(quarterly issues)

Homer Laughlin China Collectors
    Association (HLCCA)
The Dish magazine (a 16-page quarterly
included with membership; PO Box
721, North Platte, NE 69103-0721.
Membership: $25 (single), $40 (couple/
family)
info@hlcca.org
www.hlcca.org

The Illustrator Collector's News (TICN)
Denis C. Jackson, Editor
PO Box 6433, Kingman, AZ 86401. A
free use site ·on the Internet for paper
collectors of all kinds, listing paper and
magazine-related price guides available
for sale only at this site
www.olypen.com/ticn

Indiana Historical Radio Society
245 N. Oakland Ave., Indianapolis, IN
46201-3360; 317-638-1641. Membership: $15 (US), $19 (overseas) includes
IHRS Bulletin newsletter
home.att.net/~indianahistoricalradio

International Association of R.S.
    Prussia, Inc.
Linn or Leslie Schultz
PO Box 185, Lost Nation, IA 52254.
Membership: $30 per household; Yearly
convention
lschultz@netins.net
www.rsprussia.com

International Club for Collectors of
    Hatpins and Hatpin Holders (ICC
    of H&HH)
Audrae Heath, Managing Editor
PO Box 1009, Bonners Ferry, ID 83805-
1009. *Bimonthly Points* newsletter and
pictorial journal

International Ivory Society
Robert Weisblut, Co-Founder
5001 Old Ocean Blvd. #1, Ocean Ridge,
FL 33435; 561-276-5657. Free membership

International Map Collectors Society
Membership Secretary
104 Church Rd., Watford, WD17 4QB,
UK

International Antiquarian Mapsellers
    Association
www.antiquemapdealers.com

International Match Safe Association
Membership Chairman
PO Box 791, Malaga, NJ, 08328; 856-
694-4167. Membership: $50; Quarterly
newsletter and annual convention
IMSA@matchsafe.org
www.matchsafe.org

International Nippon Collectors Club
Dick Bettner
8 Geoley Ct., Thurmont, MD 21788.
Publishes newsletter 6 times a year;
Holds annual convention; Membership:
$30
www.nipponcollectorsclub.com

International Perfume and Scent Bottle
    Collectors Association
Randall Monsen
PO Box 529, Vienna, VA 22183
or Coleen Abbot
396 Croton Rd., Wayne, PA 19087-
2038. Membership: $45 (USA) or $55
(Foreign); Newsletter published quarterly
www.perfumebottles.org

International Rose O'Neill Club
Contact Irene Asher
103 W. Locust, Aurora, MO 65605-
1416. Publishes quarterly newsletter
Kewpiesta Kourier. Membership (includes newsletter): $20 (single) or $25
(family)

International Society of Antique Scale
    Collectors (ISASC)
Jan Macho, Executive Secretary
3616 Noakes St., Los Angeles, CA
90023; 323-263-6878. Publishes *Equi-
librium* Magazine; Quarterly newsletter;
Annual membership directory and out-
of-print scale catalogs; Annual convention; Please visit the ISASC website to
learn more: www.isasc.org; (This site
offers a research and reply service for a
fee.)

International Vintage Poster Dealers
    Association (IVPDA)
PO Box 501, Old Chelsea Station, New
York, NY 10113-0501. Specializing in
posters
info@ivpda.com
www.ivpda.com

John F. Rinaldi
Nautical Antiques and Related Items
(Appointment only)
Box 765, Dock Square, Kennebunkport,
ME 04046; 207-967-3218; fax 207-967-
2918. Illustrated catalog: $5
jfrinaldi@adelphia.net

Josef Originals Newsletter
Jim and Kaye Whitaker
PO Box 475, Dept. S, Lynnwood, WA
98046. Subscription (4 issues): $10 per
year

Kate Greenaway Society
James Lewis Lowe
PO Box 8, Norwood, 19074.
PostcardClassics@juno.com

Knife Rests of Yesterday and Today
Beverly L. Ales
4046 Graham St., Pleasanton, CA
94566-5619. Subscription: $20 per year
for 6 issues

The Laughlin Eagle
Joan Jasper, Publisher
Richard Racheter, Editor
1270 63rd Terrace S., St. Petersburg,
FL 33705; 813-867-3982. Subscription:
$18 (4 issues) per year; Sample: $4

Les Amis de Vieux Quimper (Friends of
    Old Quimper)
c/o Mark and Adela Meadows
PO Box 819, Carnelian Bay, CA 96140.
SASE required for written reply
meadows@oldquimper.com
www.oldquimper.com

Liddle Kiddle Konvention
Paris Langford
415 Dodge Ave. Jefferson, LA 70121.
Send SASE for information about up-
coming Liddle Kiddle Convention, also
send additional SASE for Liddle Kiddle
Newsletter information; Info and newsletter
bbean415@aol.com
liddlekiddlesnewsletter@yahoo.com

Central Florida Insulator Collectors
Line Jewels, NIA #1380
3557 Nicklaus Dr., Titusville, FL 32780

Majolica International Society
Michael Foley, Membership Chairman
77 Wright St., New Bedford, MA 02740.
Membership: $50 per year, includes an-
nual meeting and quarterly newsletter
Majolica Matters
www.majolicasociety.com

Marble Collectors' Society of America
51 Johnson St., Trumbull, CT 06611.
Publishes *Marble Mania*; Gathers and
disseminates information to further the
hobby of marbles and marble collecting;
$12 adds your name to the contributor
mailing list ($21 covers 2 years)
blockship@aol.com
www.blockglass.com

Marble Collectors Unlimited
PO Box 206, Northboro, MA 01532

Midwest Open Salt Society
c/o Ed Bowman
2411 W. 500 North, Hartford City, IN
47348. Dues: $10 ($6 for spouse)

Midwest Sad Iron Collector Club
Jerry Marcus, Secretary
67-10 161st St, Flushing, NY 11365-
3163; 718-591-0927. Membership $30

per year
reginabeau.aol.com

Moss Lamps, eBay group site: Moss
Lamps of California

Murray Hudson Antiquarian Books,
    Maps & Globes
109 S. Church St., Box 163, Halls, TN
38040; 800-748-9946 or 731-836-9057.
Buyer and seller specializing in antique
maps, globes, and books with maps:
atlases, explorations, travel guides, geographies, surveys, etc.; Largest ever
catalog of Civil War maps and graphics;
Largest selection of wall maps and world
globes
mapman@ecis.com
www.murrayhudson.com

The Museum of the American Cocktail
PO Box 38, Malverne, NY 11565.
svisakay@aol.com
www.MuseumOfTheAmericanCocktail.
org

Mystic Lights of the Aladdin Knights,
    bimonthly newsletter
c/o J.W. Courter
3935 Kelley Rd., Kevil, KY 40253-9532;
270-488-2116

National Association of Avon Collectors
c/o Connie Clark
PO Box 7006, Dept. P, Kansas City, MO
64113. Information requires LSASE

National Association of Breweriana
    Advertising (NABA)
Publishes *The Breweriana Collector*;
Collector; Holds annual convention;
Membership information and directory
available on
www.nababrew.org

National Association of Warwick China
    and Pottery Collectors
Betty June Wymer
28 Bachmann Drive, Wheeling, WV
26003; 304-232-3031. Annual dues $15
(single) or $20 (couple), checks pay-
able to NAWCPA; Publishes quarterly
newsletter; Holds annual convention in
Wheeling, West Virginia

National Autumn Leaf Collectors'
    Club
Bill Swanson, President
807 Roaring Springs Dr., Allen, TX
75002-2112; 972-727-5527 or fax 972-
727-2107. bescom@nalcc.org
or Gwynne Harrison
PO Box 1, Mira Loma, CA 91752-0001;
909-685-5434 or fax 909-681-1692;
Membership: $20, payable to NALCC,
c/o Dianna Kowales, PO Box 900968,
Palmdale, CA 93590-0968.
morgan99@pe.net
www.nalcc.org

National Blue Ridge Newsletter
Norma Lilly
144 Highland Dr., Blountville, TN
37617. Subscription: $15 per year (6
issues)

National Cambridge Collectors, Inc.
PO Box 416, Cambridge, OH 43725-
0416; 740-432-4245. Membership: $20
(Associate member: $3)
NCC-Crystal-Ball@compuserve.com
www.cambridgeglass.org

National Cuff Link Society
c/o Eugene R. Klompus
PO Box 5700, Vernon Hills, IL 60061;
phone/fax: 847-816-0035. $30 annual
dues includes subscription to *The Link*, a
quarterly magazine; write for free booklet *The Fun of Cuff Link Collecting*
genek@cufflink.com or ncls@bellsouth.net
www.cufflink.com

National Depression Glass Association
PO Box, 8264, Wichita, KS 67208-0264.
Publishes *News and Views*; Membership:
$20 (individual); $5 (associate)
www.ndga.net

National Fenton Glass Society
PO Box 4008, Marietta, OH 45750;
740-374-3345; fax: 740-376-9708.
Membership: $20, includes *The Fenton
Flyer* newsletter

National Graniteware Society
PO Box 9248, Cedar Rapids, IA 52409-
9248. Membership: $20
www.graniteware.org

National Greentown Glass Association
PO Box 107, Greentown, IN 46936-
0107. Membership: $20
www.greentownglass.org

National Imperial Glass Collectors'
    Society, Inc.
PO Box 534, Bellaire, OH 43906. Membership: $18 per year (+$3 for each associate member); Quarterly newsletter;
Convention every June
info@nigcs.org
www.imperialglass.org

National Insulator Association
1315 Old Mill Path, Broadview Heights,
OH 44147. Membership: $12
kwjacob@icsaero.com
www.nia.org

National Milk Glass Collectors' Society
    and *Opaque News*, quarterly newsletter
Membership: $18 (payable to club)
Barb Pinkston, Membership Chairman
1306 Stowe St., Inverfness, FL 34450-
6853. (Please include SASE)
membership@nmgsc.org
www.nmgcs.org

National Organization of Open Salt
    Collectors

C/o Ed Bowman
2411 W. 500 N, Hartford City, IN
47348

National Reamer Collectors Association
c/o Wayne Adickes
408 E. Reuss, Cuero, TX 77954. Membership: $27.50 per household
adickes@sbcglobal.net
www.reamers.org

National Shaving Mug Collectors
    Association
Dick Leidlein
3443 Boston Twp. Line Rd., Richmond,
IN, 47374. To stimulate the study, collection, and preservation of shaving mugs
and all related barbering items; Provides
quarterly newsletter, bibliography, and
directory; Holds 2 meetings per year
dleidlein@parallax.ws
www.nsmca.net

National Shelley China Club
Rochelle Hart, Secretary/Treasurer
591 West 67th Ave., Anchorage, AK
99518-1555; 907-562-2124.
Membership: $45 per year, 4 quarterly
newsletters plus many other benefits
and publications
imahart@alaska.net
www.nationalshelleychinaclub.com

National Toothpick Holder Collectors
    Society
Membership Chairperson
PO Box 852, Archer City, TX 76351.
Dues: $20 (single) or $25 (couple); Foreign dues: $23 (single) or $28 (couple)
in US dollars. Includes 10 *Toothpick
Bulletin* newsletters per year; Annual
convention held in August; Exclusive
toothpick holder annually
information@nthcs.org
www.nthcs.org

National Valentine Collectors Association
Nancy Rosin
PO Box 1404, Santa Ana, CA 92702;
714-547-1355; Membership: $16. Spe-
cializing in Valentines and love tokens

New England Society of Open Salt
    Collectors
Chuck Keys
21 Overbrook Lane, East Greenwich,
RI 02818. Dues: $7 per year

Newspaper Collector's Society of America
Rick Brown
Lansing, MI, 517-887-1255. An extensive, searchable, 300,000-word reference library of American history with
an emphasis on newspapers publishing
speeches; interactive crossword puzzles;
regular auctions of ephemera, historic
documents, and newspapers; a mall with
over 100 different online catalogs of paper collectibles; and much, much more
help@historybuff.com
www.historybuff.com

Night Light Club/Newsletter
Culver, Bob
3081 Sand Pebble Cove, Pinckney, MI 48169. Specializing in miniature oil lamps; Membership: $15 per year

NM (Nelson McCoy) Express
Carol Seman, Editor
8934 Brecksville Rd., Suite 406, Brecksville, OH 44141-2318; 440-526-2094 (voice & fax).
Membership: $26 per year (12 issues)
McCjs@aol.com
www.members.aol.com/nmXpress/
www.members.aol.com/nmXpress/

North American Torquay Society
Jerry and Gerry Kline, 2 of the Founding Members
604 Orchard View Dr., Maumee, OH 43537; 419-893-1226. Send SASE for information

North American Trap Collectors' Association
c/o Tom Parr
PO Box 94, Galloway, OH 43119-0094. Dues: $25 per year; Publishes bimonthly newsletter

North Dakota Pottery Collectors Society and Newsletter
c/o Sandy Short, Membership Chairman
Box 14, Beach, ND 58621. Membership: $15 (includes spouse); Annual convention in June; Quarterly newsletters
csshortnd@mcn.net
www.ndpcs.org

Novelty Salt & Pepper Shakers Club
Louise Davis
PO Box 416, Gladstone, OR 72037-0416. Publishes quarterly newsletter; Holds annual convention; Dues: $30 per year in US, Canada and Mexico ($5 extra for couple)
dmac925@yahoo.com

Nutcracker Collectors' Club and Newsletter
Susan Otto, Editor
12204 Fox Run Dr., Chesterland, OH 44026; 440-729-2686. Membership: $20 ($25 foreign) includes quarterly newsletters
nutsue@adelphia.net

The Occupied Japan Club
c/o Florence Archambault
29 Freeborn St., Newport, RI 02840-1821. Publishes *The Upside Down World of an O.J. Collector,* a bimonthly newsletter; Information requires SASE
florence@aiconnect.com
www.ojclub.com

Old Sleepy Eye Collectors Club of America, Inc.
PO Box 12, Monmouth, IL 61462. Membership: $10 per year with additional $1 for spouse (if joining)

oseclub@maplecity.com
www.maplecity.com/~MARKoseclub/

Old Stuff
Donna and Ron Miller, Publishers
PO Box 449, McMinnville, OR 97128. Published 6 times annually; Copies by mail: $3.50 each; Annual subscription: $20 ($30 in Canada)
millers@oldstuffnews.com
www.oldstuffnews.com

On the LIGHTER Side Newsletter (bi-monthly publication)
International Lighter Collectors
Judith Sanders, Editor
PO Box 1733, Quitman, TX 75783-1733; 903-763-2795 or fax 903-763-4953. Annual convention held in US; Subscription: $43 (overseas) $40 (US and Canada), $35 (Senior member); $25 (Junior member); Please include SASE when requesting information

Open Salt Collectors of the Atlantic Regions (O.S.C.A.R.)
Wilbur Rudisill, Treasurer
1844 York Rd., Gettysburg, PA 17325. Dues: $5 per year

Open Salt Seekers of the West, Northern California Chapter
Sara Conley
84 Margaret Dr., Walnut Creek, CA 94596. Dues: $7 per year

Open Salt Seekers of the West, Southern California Chapter
Janet Hudson
2525 E. Vassar Court, Visalia, CA 93277. Dues: $5 per year

Pacific Northwest Fenton Association
c/o Jackie Shirley
PO Box 881, Tillamook, OR 97141. Newsletter subscription: $25 per year (published quarterly, includes annual piece of glass made only for subscribers).
jshirley@oregoncoast.com
www.glasscastle.com/pnwfa.htm

Paden City Glass Collectors Guild
Paul Torsiello, Editor
42 Aldine Road, Parsippany, NJ, 07054. Publishes newsletter; for subscription information
pcguild1@yahoo.com

Paper & Advertising Collectors' Marketplace
PO Box 128, Scandinavia, WI 54977-0128; 715-467-2379 or fax 715-467-2243. Subscription: $19.95 in US (12 issues)
pacpcm@eagleonline.com
www.engleonline.com

Paperweight Collectors' Association, Inc.
PO Box 4153, Emerald Isle, NC 28594. Sustaining US membership $55 per year

(non-US: $35), includes quarterly *PCA Inc. Annual Bulletin* newsletter; Biannual convention
info@paperweight.org

Past Tyme Pleasures
Steve and Donna Howard
PMB #204, 2491 San Ramon Blvd., #1, San Ramon, 94583; 925-484-6442 or fax 925-484-6427.
Offers 2 absentee auction catalogs per year pertaining to old advertising
pasttyme@comcast.net
www.pasttyme1.com

Peanut Pals
Publishes *Peanut Papers;* Annual directory sent to members; Annual convention and regional conventions; Primary membership: $20 per year (associate memberships available); Sample newsletter: $2
www.peanutpals.org

Pen Collectors of America
Roger E. Wooden
PO Box 174, Garden Prairie, IL 61038-0174. Quarterly newsletter, *Pennant;* Annual membership: $40 in US and Canada (includes newsletter and access to reference library)
info@pencollectors.com
www.pencollectors.com

Pepsi-Cola Collectors Club Express
Bob Stoddard, Editor
PO Box 817; Claremont, CA 91711-0817

Perrault-Rago Gallery
333 N. Main St., Lambertville, NJ 08530; 609-397-9374. Specializing in 20th-century decorative arts, particularly art pottery and decorative tiles
e-mail:ragoarts@aol.com

Petroleum Collectibles Monthly
Scott Benjamin and Wayne Henderson, Publishers
PO Box 556, LaGrange, OH 44050-0556. 440-355-6608. Subscription: $35.95 per year (Canada, $44.50; International, $71.95; Samples $5) with over $2,000 subscribers; Scott advises Gasoline Globes and is devoted to gas and oil collectibles
www.pcmpublishing.com

Phoenix and Consolidated Glass Collectors' Club
Ruth Ann Davis, Treasurer
PO Box 387, Southington, CT 96489; 860-747-2275. Membership: $25 (single), $35 (family) per year; Please make checks payable to club
ruthan11@cox.net
http://home.earthlink.net/~jdwilson1/pgcc.htm

Phoenix Bird Collectors of America (PBCA)

1107 Deerfield Lane, Marshall, MI 49068; 269-781-9791. Membership: (payable to Joan Oates) $12 per year, includes *Phoenix Bird Discoveries,* published 2 times a year; Also available: 1996 updated value guide to be used in conjunction with Books 1 – IV; now $4.45 ppd; Newly cataloged Phoenix Bird since Book IV of 1989, Book V, published January, 2002, 96 pages (32 in color)
koates120@earthlink.net

Pickard Collectors Club, Ltd.
Membership office: 300 E. Grove St., Bloomington, IL 61701; 309-828-5533 or fax 309-829-2266. Membership (includes newsletter): $30 a year (single) or $40 (family)

Pie Birds Unlimited Club & Newsletter
Rita Reedy
1039 NW Hwy. 101, Lincoln City, OR 97367
ritazart@lycos.com

Political Collectors of Indiana Club
Michael McQuillen
PO Box 50022, Indianapolis, IN 46250-0022; 317-845-1721. Official APIC (American Political Items Collectors) Chapter comprised of over 300 collectors of presidential and local political items
michael@politicalparade.com
www.politicalparade.com

Porcelain Collector's Companion
c/o Dorothy Kamm
PO Box 7460, Port St. Lucie, FL 34985-4760; 561-464-4008

Posner, Judy and Jeff
Specializing in Disneyana, Black memorabilia, salt and pepper shakers, souvenirs of the USA, character and advertising memorabilia and figural pottery
www.judyposner.com

Powder Puff Compact Collectors' Chronicle
Roselyn Gerson
PO Box 40, Lynbrook, NY 11563; 516-593-8746 or fax 516-593-0610.
Author of six books related to figural compacts, vanity bags/purses, solid perfumes, lipsticks, and related gadgetry.
compactlady@aol.com

Purinton News & Views
Joe McManus, Editor
PO Box 153, Connellsville, PA 15425. Newsletter for Purinton pottery enthusiasts; Subscription: $16 per year

R.A. Fox Collector's Club
c/o Pat Gibson
38280 Guava Dr., Newark, CA, 94560; 510-792-0586

Ribbon Tin News Newsletter (quarterly publication)
Hobart D. Van Deusen, Editor
15 Belgo Rd, Lakeville, CT 06339; 860-435-0088. $30 per year for 24+ color plates; For collectors of typewriters, typewriter ribbon tins and go-withs; Indexed subscribers' list and participation in occasional mail/phone auctions
rtn.hoby@snet.net

Rosevilles of the Past Newsletter
Nancy Bomm, Editor
PO Box 656, Clarcona, FL 32710-0656; 407-294-3980 or fax 407-294-7836. $19.95 per year for 6 newsletters
rosepast@worldnet.att.net

Saint Patrick Notes Newsletter
Chuck Thompson, Editor
10802 Greencreek Dr., Suite 203, Houston, TX 77070-5365. For everyone interested in the legends, myths, and lore of this great missionary; This free publication is also of interest to collectors of St. Patrick cards and memorabilia; New issues every March; Requests filled all year; To receive a copy, send name and address with 2 postage stamps

Schoenhut Collectors Club
c/o Pat Girbach, Secretary
1003 W. Huron St., Ann Arbor, MI 48103-4217 for membership information

Shawnee Pottery Collectors' Club
PO Box 713, New Smyrna Beach, FL 32170-0713. Monthly nation-wide newsletter; SASE (c/o Pamela Curran) required when requesting information; $3 for sample of current newsletter

Shot Glass Exchange
PO Box 219, Western Springs, IL 60558; 708-246-1559. Primarily pre-prohibition glasses; Subscription (includes 2 semi-annual issues, available in US only): $13 per year, single copy $8

Society of Inkwell Collectors
PO Box 324, Missville, IL, 61552. Membership: $35 per year, includes subscription to *The Stained Finger*, a quarterly publication
membership@soic.com
www.soic.com

Society for Old Ivory and Ohme Porcelain
Pat Fitzwater Wimkin, Secretary/Treasurer
1650 S.E. River Ridge Dr., Milwaukie, OR 97222

Southern California Marble Club
18361-1 Strothern St., Reseda, CA 91335

Southern Folk Pottery Collectors Society quarterly newsletter
Society headquarters: 220 Washington St., Bennett, NC 27208; 336-581-4246 (Wednesday through Saturday, 10:00 to 5:00). Specializing in historical research and promotion of the traditional southern folk potter (past and present) to a modern collecting audience; Membership includes biannual absentee auction catalogs (at discounted prices), access to member pieces, opportunities to meet potters, participate in events, newsletter information, and more; The society auctions represent three centuries of productions from all of the southern states; The bi-annual absentee auctions are structured in a personalized format of sales that benefits both the seller and buyer; For more information contact the society
sfpcs@rtmc.net

Southern Oregon Antiques & Collectibles Club
PO Box 508, Talent, OR 97540; 541-535-1231 or fax 541-535-5109. Meets 1st Wednesday of the month; Promotes 2 shows a year in Medford, OR
contact@soacc.com
www.soacc.com

St. Patrick Notes Newsletter
Chuck Thompson, Editor
Room 24, 12400 Castlebridge Dr., Houston, TX 77065-5385

Stangl/Fulper Collectors Club
PO Box 538, Flemington, NJ 08822. Annual auction in June; American pottery and dinnerware show and sale in October
www.stanglfulper.com

Still Bank Collectors Club of America
Membership Chairman
440 Homestead Ave., Metairie, LA 70005. Membership: $35
contact@stillbankclub.com
www.stillbankclub.com

Stretch Glass Society Membership: $22 (US); $24 (International), International membership MUST be paid by money order; Quarterly newsletter with color photos; Annual convention
http://stretchglasssociety.org

Style: 1900 and *Modernism*
David Rago
333 N. Main St., Lambertville, 08530; 609-397-4104

The Tanner Restraints Collection
6442 Canyon Creek Way, Elk Grove, CA 95758-5431; 916-684-4006. 40-page catalog of magician/escape artist equipment from trick and regulation padlocks, handcuffs, leg shackles, and straight jackets to picks and pick sets; Books on all of the above and much more

Tarrant, Jenny
Holly Daze Antiques
4 Gardenview, St. Peters, MO 63376. Specializing in Halloween, Christmas, Easter, etc.; Buying & selling Halloween and holiday items; Antique holiday for sale
Jennyjol@aol.com www.holly-days.com

Tea Leaf Club International
Maxine Johnson, Membership Chairman
PO Box 377, Belton, MO 64012. Publishes *Tea Leaf Readings* Newsletter; Membership: $30 per household (up to 2 members)
www.tealeafclub.com

THCKK
The Hardware Companies Kollector's Klub
Jerry Heuring, 28450 US Highway 61, Scott City, MO 63780; 573-264-3947. Membership $20 per year
jheuring@charter.net
www.thckk.org

Thermometer Collectors' Club of America
Richard Porter, Vice President
PO Box 944, Onset, MA 02558; 508-295-4405. Visit the Porter Thermometer Museum (world's only, always open) free with 4,900+ thermometers to see. Appraisals, repairs and traveling lecture (600 given, ages 8 – 98, all venues)

Thimble Collectors International
Jina Samulka, Membership Chairperson; Membership: $25 (US), $30 (International)
membershopVP@thimblecollectors.com
www.thimblecollectors.com

Three Rivers Depression Era Glass Society
Meetings held 1st Monday of each month at 7:00 p.m. at Hoss's Restaurant, Canonsburg, PA
info@pghdepressionglass.org

Tiffin Glass Collectors
PO Box 554, Tiffin, OH 44883. Meetings at Seneca County Museum on 2nd Tuesday of each month; Tiffin Glass Museum, 25 S. Washington, Tiffin, OH, Wednesday – Sunday from 1:00 p.m. – 5:00 p.m.; Membership: $15
www.tiffinglass.org

Tins 'n Signs
Box 440101, Aurora, CO 80044. Subscription: $25 per year

Toaster Collectors Association
1615 Winding Trail, Springfield, OH 45503. Membership: $30 per year, holds convention, publishes quarterly newsletter
www.toastercollectors.org

Tops & Bottoms Club (Rene Lalique perfumes only)
c/o Madeleine France
9 N. Federal Highway, Dania Beach, FL 33004

Toy Shop
Mark Williams, Publisher
700 E. State St., Iola, WI 54990-0001; 715-445-2214 or fax 715-445-4087. Subscription $33.98 (26 issues) in US
www.toyshopmag.com

Trick or Treat Trader
577 Boggs Run Rd., Benwood, WV 26031; 304-233-1031.
Subscription: $15 (4 issues)
halloweenqueen@castlehalloween.com
www.castlehalloween.com

TW List (Typewriters)
Rich Cincotta
PO Box 286, Southboro, MA 01772; 508-229-2064.
typewriter@writeme.com
http://typewriter.rydia.net

Uhl Collectors' Society
Amy & Sam Busler, Secretary/Treasurer
398 S. Star Dr. Santa Claus, IN 47579; 812-544-2987. Membership: $15 per family
www.uhlcollectors.org

Vaseline Glass Collectors, Inc.
Squeaker Bootsma, Secretary
14560 Schleisman, Corona, CA 92880. An organization whose sole purpose is to unify vaseline glass collectors; newsletter *Glowing Report* published bimonthly; Convention held annually. Membership: $25
www.vaselineglass.org

Vetri: Italian Glass News
Howard Lockwood, Publisher
PO Box 191, Fort Lee, NJ 07024; 201-969-0373. Quarterly newsletter about 20th-century Italian glass

Vintage Fashion & Costume Jewelry Newsletter/Club
PO Box 265, Glen Oaks, NY 11004; 718-939-3095. Subscription (4 issues): $20 US, $25 Canada, $25 International. Back issues available at $5 each
vfck@aol.com
www.lizjewel.com/VF

Vintage TVs
Harry Poster
Box 1883, S. Hackensack, 07606; 201-794-9606. Specializes in vintage TVs, vintage radios, stereo cameras
www.harryposter.com

The Wallace Nutting Collector's Club
Pam & Bob Franscella, Membership
2944 Ivanhoe Glen, Madison, WI 53711; 608-274-4506. Membership: $20; Established in 1973, holds annual conventions; Generally recognized national center of Wallace Nutting-like

activity are Michael Ivankovich's Wallace Nutting & Wallace Nutting-Like Specialty Auctions, which provide the opportunity for collectors and dealers to compete for Wallace Nutting and Wallace or Wallace Nutting and Wallace Nutting-like pictures as well as giving sellers the opportunity to place items before the country's leading enthusiasts; When requesting information, a close-up photo which includes the picture's frame and a SASE are required
www.wallacenutting.com

Warwick China Collectors Club
Pat and Don Hoffmann, Sr.
1291 N. Elmwood Dr., Aurora, IL 60506-1309; 630-859-3435
warwick@ntsource.com

Watt Collectors' Association
Watt's News Newsletter, for Watt pottery enthusiasts
PO Box 253, Sussex, WI 53089-0253. Membership includes quarterly newslet-

ter) $20; annual convention

Wave Crest Collectors Club
c/o Whitney Newland
PO Box 2013, Santa Barbara, CA 93120. Membership dues: $25 (includes quarterly newsletter); Annual convention
whntique@gte.net

The Wedgwood Society of New York
5 Dogwood Court, Glen Head, NY 11545; 516-626-3427. Membership: $30 (single) or $35 (family). Publishes newsletter (6 times per year) and a scholarly magazine, *Ars Ceramica*, of original articles published by the Society; 6 meetings per year
www.wsny.org

Westmoreland Glass Collector's Newsletter
PO Box 143, North Liberty, IA 52317. Subscription: $16 per year; This publication is dedicated to the purpose of preserving Westmoreland glass and its history

Westmoreland Glass Society
Steve Jensen
PO Box PO Box 2883, Iowa City, IA 52240-2883. Membership: $15 (single) or $25 (household)
www.westmorelandglassclubs.org

The Whimsey Club
c/o Lon Knickerbocker
PO Box 312, Danville, NY, 14437. *Whimsical Notions*, quarterly newsletter with colored photos; Dues: $10 per year; Annual get together
mountainmonster@mountain.net

The White Ironstone China Association, Inc.
Diane Dorman, Membership Chairman
PO Box 855, Fairport, NY 14450-0855. Newsletter available for: $25 (single) or $30 (2 individuals at same address)
www.whiteironstonechina.com

Willow Review
PO Box 41312, Nashville, TN 37204.

Send SASE for information

World's Fair Collectors' Society, Inc.
Fair News Newsletter (bimonthly publication for members)
Michael R. Pender, Editor
PO Box 20806, Sarasota, FL 34276-3806; 941-923-2590. Dues: $20 (US), $25 (Canada), $30 (overseas)
wfcs@aol.com

The Zsolnay Store
152 Spring St., Newport, RI 02840; 401-841-5060. Zsolnay book available
www.drawrm.com

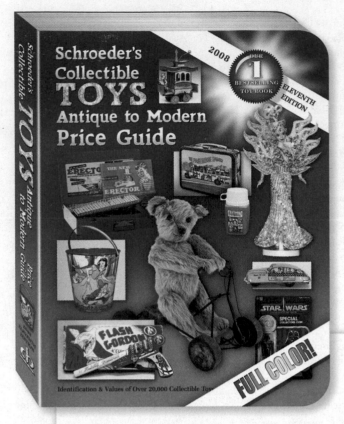
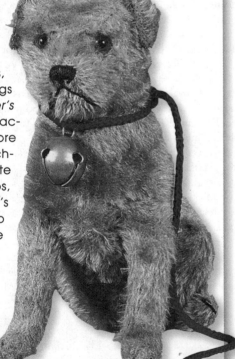